UNIVERSITY CASEBOOK SERIES®

FEDERAL INCOME TAXATION OF BUSINESS ORGANIZATIONS

SIXTH EDITION

MARTIN J. MCMAHON, JR.
Professor of Law Emeritus
University of Florida Levin College of Law

DANIEL L. SIMMONS
Professor of Law Emeritus
University of California at Davis

CHARLENE D. LUKE
Professor of Law
University of Florida Levin College of Law

BRET WELLS
Professor of Law
University of Houston Law Center

FOUNDATION
PRESS

University Casebook Series is a trademark registered in the U.S. Patent and Trademark Office.

© 1991, 1997, 1999, 2006 FOUNDATION PRESS
© 2014 LEG, Inc. d/b/a West Academic
© 2021 LEG, Inc. d/b/a West Academic
    444 Cedar Street, Suite 700
    St. Paul, MN 55101
    1-877-888-1330

Printed in the United States of America

ISBN: 978-1-64242-498-0

PREFACE

This book covers the federal income taxation of partnerships and corporations. It is for use in a course, or coordinated sequence of courses, covering C corporations, S corporations, and/or partnerships. Chapters 1–16 correspond to chapters 1–16 of the authors' *Federal Income Taxation of Corporations, 5th Ed.*, while chapters 17–25 correspond to chapters 1–9 of the authors' *Federal Income Taxation of Partnerships, 6th Ed.* (Chapter 10 of the standalone partnership book is about S corporations so is omitted from this book as it is redundant and less comprehensive than the S corporation chapter included here as Chapter 16.)

Depending on the level of detail covered, this book can be used in a variety of courses covering corporate and partnership taxation at either the J.D. or LL.M. level. It is impossible to cover the entire volume in any single course, but, depending on the level of detail covered, this volume can be used for as many as four or five separate courses at either the J.D. or LL.M. level. The arrangement in outline format of both the subdivisions within the chapters and the Detailed Analysis following the principal cases is intended to facilitate the assignment by the instructor of only selected portions of the material on any particular topic when the book is employed in a survey course on the taxation of business enterprises. At the same time, the text presents detailed discussion of complex issues in the proper statutory structural context for in-depth coverage in more advanced courses.

We recognize that teachers approach their courses with different objectives in mind and use different techniques for handling the materials. In selecting and organizing the materials, we have attempted to maximize the usefulness of these materials for whatever approach the teacher wishes to adopt—an intensive technical analysis, a problem oriented method, a consideration of the policies that underlie the technical tax structure, or a survey of the principal elements of the federal income taxation of corporations and partnerships. While the selection of authorities and the numerous examples discussed in the Detailed Analysis can, in effect, serve as problems for students and class discussion, many instructors choose to cover business entity taxation by using a series of detailed problems for class discussion. In this edition, we have now included Problem Sets keyed to the materials in this volume, and an accompanying teacher's manual is electronically available for download from the publisher. In general, the problems can be answered by reference to the materials in the section preceding the problem set, plus reference to relevant provisions of the Code and Regulations.

This book charts a course between those books that employ primarily textual explanation and those that rely for the most part on cases. Most chapters and sections of chapters are introduced by a textual discussion or outline of the basic issues and structure of the statute governing treatment of the particular item or transaction covered in the chapter or section. Principal cases have been included to illustrate key concepts not governed by a detailed statutory provision, as well as to illustrate how the courts have utilized the technical tools at their disposal. Numerous important changes in the statutory structure over the past few decades— the changing magnitude of the capital gain preference, the preferential rate for dividends, the 2017 reduction to the corporate tax rate, a maximum individual rate now substantially higher than the maximum corporate rate, and repeal of the *General Utilities* rule providing nonrecognition of gain upon the distribution of property by a corporation—have dramatically changed the important issues. Multiple statutory changes have made it impossible to include a judicial decision as a principal case to illustrate the application of a significant number of Code provisions. As a result, many cases long used in teaching materials are no longer helpful to students, even though they remain valid precedents. Accordingly, in many chapters the "principal case" is an excerpt from a congressional committee report or a Revenue Ruling, which helps the student understand the reasons underlying changes in the statute, as well as providing a road map to assist in mastering the detailed statutory provisions.

In the Detailed Analysis that follows the principal cases or textual introduction, we have attempted to provide sufficient discussion of rulings and cases to give an insight into the endless variety of factual situations to which the highly technical provisions of the Internal Revenue Code governing corporate and partnership taxation must be applied. The Detailed Analysis also provides important historical background and discussion of sequential amendments to particular sections of the Code and Regulations necessary to understand the significance of the current Code provisions. The breadth and detail of the Detailed Analysis is such that many instructors may wish to assign only portions of it depending on the scope of the particular course.

Of course, the Internal Revenue Code and Treasury Regulations are the centerpiece of any course in federal taxation. This text is intended to be used in conjunction with either a complete set of the Code and Regulations or one of the several available edited versions of the Code and Regulations. The statutory and regulatory references at the head of each topic are not intended to be exhaustive. Rather, they represent only the essential sections of the Code and Regulations that the student must understand to obtain the framework for the cases and materials under the particular topic. We have not undertaken completely to explain the operation of the Code and Regulations in the text. The student must work with the statute and regulatory material before undertaking the examination of its application in the materials in this volume, as well as before attempting to solve the problems in the Problem Sets.

This book is divided into eight Parts, each of which is which are further subdivided into chapters. Each Part, in general, represents a block of material as to which we think most instructors in a particular course will choose to cover all of the chapters, although the depth of the coverage within each chapter may differ with the overall scope of the course. Many instructors will cover more than one Part in a particular course. Alternatively, the entire volume could be used as a source book, without particular assignments, in an advanced, problem-oriented course in Business Planning.

Part I (Chapters 1–7) covers basic corporate taxation: the corporate income tax, classification, formation, capital structure, dividends, redemptions, and liquidations (except in connection with acquisitions). These materials could be combined with other Parts as one element in a broader course, although they may be used for a separate two or three hour course in basic corporate taxation.

Part II (Chapters 8–10) covers acquisition techniques. Chapter 8 discusses taxable acquisitions so that the student understands the framework for a taxable acquisition before considering the reorganization provisions. Chapter 9 covers bootstrap acquisitions. Chapter 10 covers tax-free mergers and acquisitions. Part III (Chapters 11–12) covers nonacquisitive corporate restructurings, with Chapter 11 dealing with single-entity reorganizations and Chapter 12 covering corporate divisions, such as spin-offs. Part IV (Chapter 13) is closely related to Parts II and III and covers carryover of corporate attributes in acquisitions and reorganizations. Parts II through IV could be taught as an advanced course on corporate taxation, whether in a J.D. or LL.M. program, or portions could be selected for use with a basic corporate tax course.

Part V (Chapter 14) covers corporate penalty taxes, which are still a feature of corporate taxation, but have become less relevant over time with changing rate structures.

Part VI (Chapter 15) covers affiliated corporations and consolidated returns. If the professor chooses to cover this material at the end of a course, then the impact on earlier topics such as acquisitive reorganizations or taxable dispositions will need to be revisited as the consolidated return regulations can significantly impact the general principles.

Part VII (Chapter 16) covers Subchapter S. This Part could be combined with Part I in a course in basic corporate taxation or with Part VIII in a course on pass-through taxation.

Part VIII (Chapters 17–25) provides complete coverage of partnership taxation, including the impact of rules extrinsic to Subchapter K such as the at-risk and passive activity loss rules. Throughout this part, the application of Subchapter K to limited liability companies is considered in contexts in which special problems arise. Part VIII may be utilized in either a two or three credit hour course covering partnership taxation. We expect, however, that some material (for example, the anti-abuse Regulations, "mixing bowl" transactions, tiered partnerships, and death of a partner) would have to be omitted in a two-hour course.

As to editorial matters, the statutory references throughout are to the 1986 Code, except where the text expressly indicates otherwise. References in the cases and other primary sources to the 1954 and 1939 Codes and prior statutes have been edited to conform them to the 1986 Code. Generally the practice is to omit the earlier citation and instead refer to the matter as "the former version," or "the predecessor," or to give the current relevant 1986 Code section if there has been no significant change in the statutory language. But if a significant change has occurred, that fact is noted and the prior language is given. Footnotes in cases and materials frequently have been omitted. Where retained the original numbering of the footnotes has been kept so that, in many instances, the footnote numbers are not consecutive. References to Tax Court Memorandum decisions are to the number assigned by the Tax Court and not to any particular commercial publication. In general, references to the Code, Regulations, cases and rulings are current as of April 30, 2019 as to the "C" and "S" corporation material and as of March 31, 2020, as to the partnership material.

MARTIN J. MCMAHON, JR.
DANIEL L. SIMMONS
CHARLENE D. LUKE
BRET WELLS

August 2020

SUMMARY OF CONTENTS

PART I. TAXATION OF CORPORATIONS AND SHAREHOLDERS

TABLE OF CONTENTS

PART I. TAXATION OF CORPORATIONS AND SHAREHOLDERS

PART II. CORPORATE ACQUISITION TECHNIQUES

PART VIII. TAXATION OF PARTNERS AND PARTNERSHIPS

TABLE OF CASES

The principal cases are in bold type.

TABLE OF INTERNAL REVENUE CODE SECTIONS

TABLE OF TREASURY REGULATIONS

TABLE OF PROPOSED TREASURY REGULATIONS

TABLE OF TEMPORARY TREASURY REGULATIONS

TABLE OF REVENUE RULINGS

The principal rulings are in bold type.

FEDERAL INCOME TAXATION OF BUSINESS ORGANIZATIONS

SIXTH EDITION

TAXATION OF CORPORATIONS AND SHAREHOLDERS

CHAPTER 1

TAXATION OF CORPORATE INCOME AND IDENTIFYING TAXABLE CORPORATE ENTITIES

SECTION 1. THE CORPORATE INCOME TAX

Corporations are taxpaying entities that are separate and distinct from their shareholders. Except in certain limited situations, a corporation must pay an income tax on its profits even if the corporation currently or subsequently distributes those profits to its shareholders as dividends taxable to them individually as a part of their taxable income. Thus, corporations differ from partnerships, which are not taxpaying entities, but which generally are treated as an aggregate of the partners who pay tax on their shares of partnership income.

The modern corporate income tax originated in 1909, four years before the adoption of the Sixteenth Amendment and the broad-based individual income tax, which it made possible. In Flint v. Stone Tracy Company, 220 U.S. 107 (1911), the Supreme Court upheld the 1909 corporate income tax against a constitutional challenge, which alleged that the corporate income tax was a direct tax that was not apportioned among the states according to population as required by Article I, Section 9, Clause 4 of the Constitution. Rather, the Court held that the corporate income tax was an excise tax on the privilege of doing business in the corporate form.

Ever since the enactment of the individual income tax in 1913, corporate income generally has been taxed twice, first when earned by the corporation and again when distributed to the shareholders as dividends or in liquidation. Historically, there have been some exceptions.[1] For taxable years after 2003, § 1(h)(11) generally taxes dividends paid to individuals at the same rate as long-term capital gains,

---

[1] Prior to 1936 there was a partial exclusion of dividends under the individual income tax, and during 1936 and 1937 corporations were allowed a deduction for the amount of dividends paid out to shareholders. From 1954 through 1986, individuals were permitted by former § 116 to exclude from income a relatively small portion of dividends received (the original exclusion was $50; this amount had increased to $100 per taxpayer immediately prior to repeal of the exclusion). In addition, from 1954 until 1963 shareholders were allowed a credit equal to 4% of dividends received (in excess of the exclusion). See Carl S. Shoup, The Dividend Exclusion and Credit in the Revenue Code of 1954, 8 Nat'l Tax J. 136 (1955).

3

with the applicable bracket—0%, 15%, or 20%—tied to the taxpayer's income level.[2]

Under current law the most significant exception to taxation of the corporation as a separate entity is the election under Subchapter S (§§ 1361–1379) to treat the corporation as a pass-through entity with gains and losses being reported on the shareholders' individual returns.[3] A number of restrictive conditions limit the availability of this election. Corporations that do not make an election under Subchapter S are called "C corporations"; corporations that make the election are called "S corporations." Approximately 60% of all corporations elect to be treated as S corporations. These corporations generally are very small, both in terms of assets and revenues, and usually have only a limited number of shareholders.

The policy decision to treat a corporation as a taxpaying entity separate and distinct from its shareholders entails certain structural requirements. A separate rate structure, currently specified in § 11, is applicable to corporations. The rate of tax on corporate income has varied over the years.[4] Legislation enacted in 2017 ("2017 Tax Act"), Pub. L. No. 115–97, § 11001, changed the corporate tax rate to a flat 21%, including for personal service corporations.

Taxable income of a corporation is basically determined by applying the same rules that govern the taxation of individuals. Thus, the gross income rules, the deduction rules, the accounting provisions, and the capital gain and loss provisions are all pertinent.[5] However, there are a number of important variations from these basic income tax provisions that are applicable only to corporations. For example, application of the deduction sections, such as § 162(a) and § 165(a), to corporations is generally guided by the premise that all corporations are engaged in

---

[2] For taxable years beginning after December 31, 2017, and before January 1, 2026, new legislation specifies that the rate depends on the taxpayer's filing status and taxable income. § 1(j)(5); Pub. L. No. 115–97, § 11001 (2017). For example, in the case of a joint return, the 0% rate applies if taxable income is below $77,200; the 15% rate applies if taxable income is below $479,000; and the 20% rate applies if taxable income is $479,000 or more. Under pre-2018 law (and post-2026 law if there is no new legislation), the capital gains rate was determined with reference to the taxable income rate brackets. The new breakpoints were, however, derived from the pre-2018 rate brackets, which means that the 2017 Tax Act largely preserves the pre-legislation capital gain rate structure.

[3] Subchapter S applies only to "small business corporations" having a limited number of shareholders. While Subchapter S is loosely referred to as permitting a corporation to elect to be taxed as a partnership, the operational effects under the Subchapter differ somewhat from partnership treatment. Subchapter S is discussed in Chapter 16.

[4] In 1909, when the corporate income tax was introduced, the rate was 1%. During World War I, it reached 12%; a 40% top rate was applicable during World War II; and a 52% rate was imposed during the Korean War. In 1964, the rate was reduced to 50% for that year and to 48% beginning in 1965. The rates and brackets were modified several times during the 1970's and 1980's. See J. Pechman, Federal Tax Policy, 135–37, 302–05, 321–22 (5th ed. 1987).

[5] Prior to the 2017 Tax Act, corporations were subject to the alternative minimum tax provided by § 55 through § 59 in any year in which the alternative minimum tax exceeded the regular tax. The alternative minimum tax rate for corporations was 20% and was imposed on "alternative minimum taxable income," a tax base that differed substantially from "taxable income."

trade or business. In addition, there are a number of special provisions that apply only to corporations, such as the dividends received deduction in § 243 for intercorporate dividends, which effectively excludes all or part of such dividends from a corporation's taxable income. The treatment of capital gains and losses recognized by corporations also differs. Corporations are ineligible for the preferential capital gains tax rates available to individuals. Under § 1212(a), capital losses are allowed only to the extent of capital gains, with a five-year carryover and a three-year carryback of any excess losses.

The passive activity loss rules of § 469 are not applicable to most corporations. Section 469 applies to a closely held C corporation, defined in § 469(j)(1) and § 465(a)(1)(B) as a C corporation more than 50% of the stock of which is held at some time during the last half of the taxable year by five or fewer persons, taking into account certain attribution rules. It also applies to "personal service corporations" defined in § 469(j)(2). Section 469 does not apply to S corporations, but it does apply to the shareholders in taking into account their shares of S corporation income or loss. Special rules govern the determination of whether a closely held C corporation or personal service corporation "materially participates" in an activity. See I.R.C. § 469(h)(4).

The rules governing choice of accounting methods and taxable years also differ for corporations. Most C corporations are required to use the accrual method of accounting. Exceptions are provided for personal service corporations and for corporations with average annual gross receipts of $25 million or less. See I.R.C. § 448(b)(3), (c). Although most C corporations are free to choose any taxable year, personal service corporations and S corporations generally are required to adopt a calendar year. See I.R.C. § 441(i), § 1378(b). A personal service corporation or S corporation may adopt a fiscal year, however, if the corporation can establish a business purpose for the fiscal year, or if it makes an election under § 444, which generally restricts deferral to no more than three months from the otherwise required year and requires that the corporation make an advance deposit of taxes. See I.R.C. § 7519.

Special problems also result from transactions unique to the corporate form, such as the tax consequences to a corporation of the issuance of its own stock or of dealings by it in its own stock. Section 1032 solves this problem by providing that a corporation does not realize income upon the sale or issuance of its own shares for money, property, or services. Further, securities issued by a corporation must be classified as either stock or debt because payment of interest on debt generates a deduction to the corporation under § 163 while the distribution of a dividend on stock does not. This classification issue, which is considered in Chapter 3, is a matter of considerable controversy.

Because the corporation is a separate tax entity, rules must be provided to specify the tax treatment for various events in the life of the corporation that involve the transfer of property or money to or from shareholders, e.g., upon the formation of the corporation. In general, if an individual, group of individuals, or partnership desires to incorporate a business and transfers the business's assets to a corporation formed for that purpose, no gain or loss will be recognized from the change in the form of the ownership of the assets. The transferor owns stock of a corporation holding the assets instead of holding the assets themselves, but the Code expressly provides that any gain or loss inherent in assets transferred to the corporation is not to be recognized when they are exchanged for only stock. The transferor's basis in the assets becomes the basis for the stock, and this asset basis likewise carries over to the corporation and becomes its basis for the assets. The rules governing formation of a corporation are discussed in Chapter 2.

Problems also arise as to the proper tax relationship between the ongoing corporation and its shareholders. The corporation may distribute cash, property, or its own stock. It is necessary to establish a standard for ascertaining the extent to which distributions represent corporate earnings (which should be taxed to the shareholders as dividends) or a return of capital (which should be applied against the basis of the shareholder's stock and taxed as gain if the distribution exceeds that basis). It also is necessary to decide whether the distribution of property by the corporation is an event that should result in the recognition of gain or loss to the corporation when the property has a value different from its basis. The rules governing the tax treatment of dividends are considered in Chapter 4. Special problems presented by dividends paid in the distributing corporation's own stock are discussed in Chapter 6.

Some or all of the shares of a shareholder or shareholders may be bought back—"redeemed"—by the corporation for cash or other property. In this case, it is necessary to determine whether the redemption should be taxed to the shareholder according to the form—that is, like a sale of the stock—or whether the transaction so essentially resembles a dividend that it should be taxed the same as a dividend. It is also necessary to determine whether it is appropriate for the corporation to recognize gain or loss if property, rather than cash, is distributed to the shareholder in the redemption. The rules required to determine the proper tax treatment of redemptions at the corporate and the shareholder level are considered in Chapter 5.

The shareholders later may decide to sell or liquidate the corporation. Again, it is necessary to provide rules for determining the gain or loss realized in such cases, and whether that gain or loss will be recognized at the corporate level, the shareholder level, or both. Special rules may be appropriate if shares in the liquidated corporation are owned mostly by one other corporation instead of by multiple shareholders or by an individual. In such a situation, nonrecognition of gain and loss to both corporations may be appropriate. Furthermore, consideration must be given to the treatment of sales and purchases of corporate assets in connection with a liquidation. The purchase of all of the stock of a corporation and the purchase of all of its assets as a going business may be alternatives from a non-tax perspective. Chapters 8 through 10 consider the extent to which the tax system treats these transactions identically and to what extent the form chosen by the parties governs the transaction.[6]

Since 2003, the double taxation of corporate profits has been partially mitigated. As noted above, for taxable years after 2003, § 1(h)(11) generally taxes dividends at the same rate as long-term capital gains. However, most of Subchapter C (as well as certain related penalty taxes found elsewhere in the Code) was developed in the context of, and frequently to deal with transactions designed to exploit, capital gains being taxed at rates substantially lower than the rate at which dividends were taxed. As you study the materials in the following chapters consider the extent to which the need for various provisions might have been obviated by equalizing the tax rates for dividends and long-term capital gains.

Another way of viewing the materials is from the standpoint of business planning requirements. What are the various routes to implement a given business decision when tax consequences are taken into consideration? Which are more or less expensive from a tax standpoint? In which situations do business needs appear to have shaped the tax rules, and conversely, in which situations has the development of the tax law determined the manner in which business transactions are carried out? The materials on the sale and purchase of the corporate business in Chapters 8 and 9, acquisitive tax-free reorganizations in Chapter 10, single corporation reorganizations in Chapter 11, and corporate divisions in Chapter 12 raise planning as well as structural questions.

The 2017 Tax Act complicates business planning. Prior to 2017, the double taxation of corporate earnings coupled with the near equivalency of the top corporate marginal tax rate of 35% and the top individual marginal income tax rate of 39.8% previously made it compelling in most situations for business owners to conduct business activities in pass-through entity structures. However, current law provides a substantially lower corporate tax of 21% and a top individual marginal tax rate (through the year 2025) of 37%. This tax rate differential creates a complex set of trade-offs that should be considered before deciding

---

[6] It would be possible to "integrate" the tax treatment of the corporation with the tax treatment of its shareholders. It is not essential to an income tax system that corporations be subject to a separate tax structure, in the sense that both the corporation and its shareholders bear tax on the same income. The tax systems of some countries have varying degrees of integration of the corporate and individual income taxes. A great deal has been written about the policy arguments for a separate corporate income tax versus integration of the taxation of corporations and their shareholders. See, e.g., Treas. Dep't, Integration of the Individual and Corporate Tax Systems: Taxing Business Income Once (1992); William Andrews, Am. Law Inst., Subchapter C: Reporter's Study on Corporate Distributions; Bret Wells, International Tax Reform by Means of Corporate Integration, 20 Fla. Tax Rev. 70 (2016); The limited integration offered by Subchapter S is considered in Chapter 16.

whether to conduct business activities in a pass-through entity or in a C corporation.[7] Section 199A (discussed in detail in Chapter 16) provides a potential 20% deduction for net qualified business income from pass-through entities (that is, partnerships and S corporations), which further complicates the analysis.

DETAILED ANALYSIS

If a C corporation earns income that is subject to corporate level taxation at a 21% rate, then the after-tax corporate earnings would be equal to 79% of the corporation's taxable income. This 79% after-tax corporate earnings could then be distributed to the shareholder as a qualified dividend. As discussed above, individual shareholders obtain concessionary capital gains rates under § 1(h) for qualified dividends, resulting in a maximum shareholder tax rate of 20%. High-earning individual shareholders would also be subject to a 3.8% surtax under § 1411(a) upon receipt of that dividend. As a result, the all-in corporate level tax cost would be 21%, and the maximum, all-in shareholder level tax cost of a qualified dividend would be 18.8%.[8]

The combination of the corporate level tax and shareholder level tax results in a combined tax cost of 39.8%. Thus, earning business income within a C corporation and distributing the after-tax corporate earnings as qualified dividends to top-bracket individual shareholders creates an overall tax cost that is slightly higher than the top individual marginal income tax rate of 37%. This straightforward comparison is, however, subject to several important caveats that further complicate the choice of business entity analysis.

For example, assume that the C corporation will delay distributing its corporate earnings for five years and assume that the business owner has a 10% cost of capital. The deferral benefit of delaying the shareholder level tax cost of 18.8% for five years causes the present value of this shareholder level tax cost to be only 11.67%.[9] Thus, in this scenario, the present-value cost of earning income in the C corporation is only 32.67% (i.e., 21% corporate tax plus 11.67%, which again represents the present-value cost of the 18.8% shareholder level tax that is deferred for five years). If the deferral period were twice as long, then the present-value cost of the 18.8% cost would be less than 7.25%.[10] Thus, in a situation where a business owner intends to reinvest earnings back into the business for a significant period of time and will thereby defer the shareholder level tax cost, the length of the deferral

---

[7]   See James R. Repetti, The Impact of the 2017 Act's Tax Rate Changes on Choice of Entity, 21 Fla. Tax Rev. 686 (2018).

[8]   The 18.8% is calculated by taking the after-corporate tax earnings of 79% (100% − 21% corporate tax) and multiplying that amount by the all-in 23.8% shareholder level tax arising from the 20% capital gains rate that applies on qualified dividends and the 3.8% surtax on net investment income under section 1411(a).

[9]   The 11.67% represents the present value of the 18.8% shareholder level tax if it is deferred for five years with a 10% cost of capital tax: $18.8\% \div (1 + 10\%)^5$.

[10]   For example, if one were to assume a ten-year deferral period of the 18.8% shareholder level tax, then the present value cost of the shareholder level tax would be approximately 7.25%.

with respect to the shareholder level tax can substantially reduce the present-value impact of that second level of taxation.

Moreover, if the individual shareholder does not distribute corporate earnings but instead disposes of the C corporate stock in a transaction that allows the individual shareholder to claim a § 1202 small business stock exemption for one-half of the capital gain, then the all-in tax cost would be limited to the corporate level tax cost of 21% plus half of the preferential capital gains rate for the shareholder. Alternatively, if the C corporation withheld distributions of corporate earnings until the shareholder's death, then § 1014 would provide a fair market value basis for the stock, with the consequence that the shareholder's estate or beneficiaries could then dispose of the stock without any shareholder level tax cost. In either of these two situations, the benefit of earning income in a C corporation and then avoiding the shareholder level tax (or deferring that shareholder level tax for a significant period of time) could result in a combined tax cost that is lower than earning that business income in a pass-through entity.

The analysis is, however, not complete. The benefits of earning income in a pass-through entity that is eligible for a 20% deduction under § 199A must be considered. Of course, § 199A has various limitations on its availability (see the discussion in Chapter 16), but consider the situation if business income were earned by a top-bracket individual who is eligible to claim the maximum § 199A deduction. Then, the individual taxpayer could achieve an effective tax rate on pass-through income of 29.6%.[11] This 29.6% rate is higher than the 21% tax rate applicable to C corporations, but it is lower than the combined tax rate for earning income in a C corporation and distributing dividends after a 5 year deferral period (i.e., 32.67% total tax rate). If, however, the assumptions change, then a different result could arise. For example, if the shareholder level tax were deferred for 10 years or could be minimized or avoided at the shareholder level by reason of § 1202 or § 1014, then the combined cost of earning income in a C corporation would be less than the tax cost of earning income in a pass-through entity structure.

These examples illustrate that the 2017 Tax Act added complex trade-offs to the choice of business entity decision. Yes, corporate earnings generally are subject to taxation at both the shareholder level and the corporate level, but the 21% corporate level tax rate is substantially lower than the individual tax rate for earning business income in pass-through entities, even with the benefit of utilizing a § 199A deduction. The shareholder level tax cost of 18.8% could cause the C corporate alternative to be less desirable, unless the shareholder level tax could be deferred for a significant period of time or could be avoided or minimized through other strategies. Thus, a careful discussion of the client's planning assumptions is needed.

Finally, the assumptions one makes about the sustainability of current law can also impact the business entity structure decision. In this regard,

---

[11] The 29.6% rate is computed by taking the 37% top individual marginal income tax rate and multiplying it by 80%, under the assumption that the individual shareholder was entitled to the maximum 20% deduction against taxable income under § 199A.

the 2017 Act was passed on a strictly party-line vote. So, one might question how long the corporate tax rate will remain at 21%. If one thought corporate tax rates might increase to 25% or higher before § 199A expires at the end of 2025, then the potential benefit of earning income in a C corporation would be substantially diminished versus earning income in a pass-through entity structure that entitles its owner to § 199A benefits. Thus, in this scenario, the added double taxation at the shareholder level may well cause C corporations to be less tax efficient than a pass-through entity structure.

SECTION 2. IDENTIFYING TAXABLE CORPORATE ENTITIES AND INTRODUCTION TO THE STEP TRANSACTION DOCTRINE

Prior to 1987, the maximum individual rate exceeded the maximum corporate rate by a substantial amount. In addition, although corporate earnings were taxed twice, if the distribution of earnings was delayed until liquidation of the corporation or of the shareholder's entire interest in the corporation, the shareholder level tax was incurred at preferential rates for long-term capital gains that were even more generous than the current preference. These factors, coupled with the pre-1987 statutory provisions that permitted corporations to distribute appreciated property to shareholders without recognizing a corporate level taxable gain on the appreciation, served as a strong tax inducement to incorporate a profitable business venture that was going to accumulate and reinvest earnings, even if no nontax factors indicated that incorporation was preferable to the partnership or sole proprietorship form. Conversely, if the venture was expected to produce a tax loss, for example a business experiencing tax losses in its early years attributable in part to tax preferences, it was advantageous to be taxed as a partnership or sole proprietorship, even though the use of the corporate form would have been desirable to accomplish some nontax objective.

As discussed in the preceding section, the 2017 Tax Act re-introduced a corporate rate that is considerably lower than the highest individual income tax rate. Corporate income is now taxed at a flat rate of 21%, while the maximum individual marginal tax rate is 37% (in the absence of new legislation, the maximum individual tax rate will revert to 39.6% in 2026). But in many other important respects, the landscape remains significantly different from pre-1987: qualified dividends and long-term capital gains are generally subject to the same rate, and corporations are no longer able to distribute appreciated property without gain recognition.

The pre-1987 incentive for individuals to shift income to a corporation (or obtain other tax benefits available only in corporate form) gave rise to controversies regarding whether income should be taxed to the corporation or directly to its owners. Whether the most recent legislation will trigger similar concerns remains to be seen. The materials in this section examine issues of corporate identity and income assignment in several contexts. This section also discusses the problem of determining whether the form of a particular transaction will actually control the tax consequences through an introduction to the step transaction doctrine.

A. WHAT IS A "CORPORATION" UNDER THE INCOME TAX?

INTERNAL REVENUE CODE: Sections 7701(a)(3); 7704.

REGULATIONS: Sections 301.7701–1(a) and (b), –2(a), (b)(1)–(7), –3(a), (b)(1), (c)(1)(i)–(iv), –4(a)–(c).

A business may be conducted by an entity that, under the law of the state (or foreign nation) in which the entity is organized, is a corporation, a partnership, a limited liability company (LLC), a business trust, or some other state law entity. For federal income tax purposes, however, Treasury Regulations—known as the "check-the-box" Regulations—specify three possibilities: corporation, partnership, and disregarded entity. Treas.Reg. § 301.7701–2 provides that a business entity with two or more members is classified as either a partnership or a corporation. For this purpose the term "business entity" is broad. See Treas.Reg. § 301.7701–1(a)(2). It includes not only corporations, partnerships (both limited and general), and limited liability companies formally organized as such under state law, but also less formally organized associations as well as business trusts. Under Treas.Reg. § 301.7701–2(b), any business organized as a "corporation" under relevant state or federal law automatically is classified as a corporation for federal income tax purposes, as are insurance companies and most banks. Treas.Reg. § 301.7701–2(b)(8) lists specified foreign entities that are *per se* corporations for federal income tax purposes.

A U.S. "business entity" that is not listed in Treas.Reg. § 301.7701–2(b) as a corporation is classified as a partnership if it has two or more members. Treas.Reg. § 301.7701–3(a) and (b). An entity that is classified as a partnership may elect to be taxed as a corporation, Treas.Reg. § 301.7701–3(a), but if no election is made, the entity is by default classified as a partnership. Treas.Reg. § 301.7701–3(b). Treas.Reg. § 301.7701–4 distinguishes businesses, financial operations, and ventures taxed as partnerships from trusts established for the protection and conservation of property (which may include a trade or business operated by the trust as a sole proprietor). A business entity with one member—for example, a single member LLC—that is not a corporation is disregarded for tax purposes. Treas.Reg. § 301.7701–2(c)(2), –3(b)(1)(ii). When an individual is the owner of a disregarded LLC, the individual will be treated as operating a sole proprietorship. If a corporation is the owner of a disregarded LLC, the LLC will generally be treated as a division of the corporation, and the LLC's tax items will be included on the corporation's tax return.

Rules and Regulations, Department of the Treasury, Internal Revenue Service, Simplification of Entity Classification Rules

T.D. 8697, 1997–1 C.B. 215.

Explanation of Provisions

Section 7701(a)(2) of the Code defines a partnership to include a syndicate, group, pool, joint venture, or other unincorporated organization, through or by means of which any business, financial operation, or venture is carried on, and that is not a trust or estate or a corporation. Section 7701(a)(3) defines a corporation to include associations, joint-stock companies, and insurance companies.

The existing regulations for classifying business organizations as associations (which are taxable as corporations under section 7701(a)(3)) or as partnerships under section 7701(a)(2) are based on the historical differences under local law between partnerships and corporations. Treasury and the IRS believe that those rules have become increasingly formalistic. This document replaces those rules with a much simpler approach that generally is elective.

As stated in the preamble to the proposed regulations, in light of the increased flexibility under an elective regime for the creation of organizations classified as partnerships, Treasury and the IRS will continue to monitor carefully the uses of partnerships in the international context and will take appropriate action when partnerships are used to achieve results that are inconsistent with the policies and rules of particular Code provisions or of U.S. tax treaties.

A.   Summary of the Regulations

Section 301.7701–1 provides an overview of the rules applicable in determining an organization's classification for federal tax purposes. The first step in the classification process is to determine whether there is a separate entity for federal tax purposes. The regulations explain that certain joint undertakings that are not entities under local law may nonetheless constitute separate entities for federal tax purposes; however, not all entities formed under local law are recognized as separate entities for federal tax purposes. Whether an organization is treated as an entity for federal tax purposes is a matter of federal tax law, and does not affect the rights and obligations of its owners under local law. For example, if a domestic limited liability company with a single individual owner is disregarded as an entity separate from its owner under § 301.7701–3, its individual owner is subject to federal income tax as if the company's business was operated as a sole proprietorship.

An organization that is recognized as a separate entity for federal tax purposes is either a trust or a business entity (unless a provision of the Code expressly provides for special treatment, such as the Qualified

Settlement Fund rules (§ 1.468B) or the Real Estate Mortgage Investment Conduit (REMIC) rules, see section 860A(a)). The regulations provide that trusts generally do not have associates or an objective to carry on business for profit. The distinctions between trusts and business entities, although restated, are not changed by these regulations.

Section 301.7701–2 clarifies that business entities that are classified as corporations for federal tax purposes include corporations denominated as such under applicable law, as well as associations, joint-stock companies, insurance companies, organizations that conduct certain banking activities, organizations wholly owned by a State, organizations that are taxable as corporations under a provision of the Code other than section 7701(a)(3), and certain organizations formed under the laws of a foreign jurisdiction (including a U.S. possession, territory, or commonwealth).

* * *

Any business entity that is not required to be treated as a corporation for federal tax purposes (referred to in the regulation as an eligible entity) may choose its classification under the rules of § 301.7701–3. Those rules provide that an eligible entity with at least two members can be classified as either a partnership or an association, and that an eligible entity with a single member can be classified as an association or can be disregarded as an entity separate from its owner.

* * *

In order to provide most eligible entities with the classification they would choose without requiring them to file an election, the regulations provide default classification rules that aim to match taxpayers' expectations (and thus reduce the number of elections that will be needed). The regulations adopt a passthrough default for domestic entities, under which a newly formed eligible entity will be classified as a partnership if it has at least two members, or will be disregarded as an entity separate from its owner if it has a single owner. The default for foreign entities is based on whether the members have limited liability. Thus a foreign eligible entity will be classified as an association if all members have limited liability. A foreign eligible entity will be classified as a partnership if it has two or more members and at least one member does not have limited liability; the entity will be disregarded as an entity separate from its owner if it has a single owner and that owner does not have limited liability. Finally, the default classification for an existing entity is the classification that the entity claimed immediately prior to the effective date of these regulations. An entity's default classification continues until the entity elects to change its classification by means of an affirmative election.

An eligible entity may affirmatively elect its classification on Form 8832, Entity Classification Election. The regulations require that the election be signed by each member of the entity or any officer, manager, or member of the entity who is authorized to make the election and who represents to having such authorization under penalties of perjury. An election will not be accepted unless it includes all of the required information * * *.

Taxpayers are reminded that a change in classification, no matter how achieved, will have certain tax consequences that must be reported. For example, if an organization classified as an association elects to be classified as a partnership, the organization and its owners must recognize gain, if any, under the rules applicable to liquidations of corporations.

B.   *Discussion of Comments on the General Approach and Scope of the Regulations*

Several comments requested clarification with regard to the rules for determining when an owner of an interest in an organization will be respected as a bona fide owner for federal tax purposes. Some commentators * * * relying on Rev.Rul. 93–4, 1993–1 C.B. 225, suggested that if two wholly-owned subsidiaries of a common parent were the owners of an organization, those owners would not be respected as bona fide owners and the organization would be treated as having only one owner (the common parent). Although the determination of whether an organization has more than one owner is based on all the facts and circumstances, the fact that some or all of the owners of an organization are under common control does not require the common parent to be treated as the sole owner. Consistent with this approach, Rev.Rul. 93–4 treated two wholly owned subsidiaries as associates and then classified the foreign entity based on the four corporate characteristics under section 7701. While these four factors will no longer apply with the adoption of the regulations, determining whether the subsidiaries are associates continues to be an issue.

* * *

C.   *Discussion of Comments Relating to the Elective Regime*

Most of the commentators agreed that the default rules included in the proposed regulations generally would match taxpayers' expectations. * * *

Some commentators requested that taxpayers be allowed to make classification elections with their first tax returns. The regulations retain the requirement that elections be made at the beginning of the taxable year. Treasury and the IRS continue to believe that it is appropriate to determine an entity's classification at the time that it begins its operations. Taxpayers can specify the date on which an election will be effective, provided that date is not more than 75 days prior to the date on which the election is filed (irrespective of when the interest was acquired) and not more than 12 months after the date the election was filed. * * *

The regulations limit the ability of an entity to make multiple classification elections by prohibiting more than one election to change an entity's classification during any sixty month period. * * * [T]he regulations permit the Commissioner to waive the application of the sixty month limitation by letter ruling. However, waivers will not be granted unless there has been more than a fifty percent ownership change. The sixty month limitation only applies to a change in classification by election; the limitation does not apply if the organization's business is actually transferred to another entity.

* * *

DETAILED ANALYSIS

1. LIMITED LIABILITY COMPANIES

A business may be conducted through a limited liability company (LLC) organized under state law, rather than through a partnership, corporation, or through direct ownership. Although state law recognizes an LLC as a distinct type of entity, as discussed in the preamble to the check-the-box entity classification Regulations, there is no single federal tax regime specifically dealing with LLCs. Rather, for federal tax purposes, an LLC can be treated as a corporation, a partnership, or be "disregarded" depending on the specific facts.

An LLC that has two or more members (owners) is an entity separate and distinct from its members and is treated either as a corporation or a partnership. Treas.Reg. § 301.7701–2(a). An LLC with two or more members that does not elect to be taxed as a corporation will be treated as a partnership for purposes of federal income taxation. Treas.Reg. § 301.7701–3(b)(1)(i). The LLC is taxed as a corporation only if it affirmatively elects to be so treated for federal tax purposes. Treas.Reg. § 301.7701–3(a). An LLC with a single owner (whether the owner is an individual, corporation, or partnership) may elect to be taxed as a corporation, but if it does not so elect, it will be disregarded as an entity separate and distinct from its owner. Treas.Reg. § 301.7701–3(b)(1)(ii). When an LLC is disregarded as an entity, its assets, liabilities, income items, and deduction items will be treated as owned, owed, received, and incurred directly by its owner. Thus, for example, if a corporation is the sole owner of a LLC that has not elected to be taxed as a corporation, the business conducted by the LLC will be treated as a division of the corporation, the income of which is reportable directly on the corporation's income tax return. In practice, LLCs rarely, if ever, elect to be taxed as corporations, unless they are also electing S corporation status, and virtually every LLC is either treated as a pass-through entity or is disregarded for federal tax purposes.

A single member LLC that is a disregarded entity provides a corporation with a vehicle to insulate other assets against the risks of the business in the LLC while allowing the corporation to offset losses from one line of business against profits from another line of business on its federal income tax return. A corporation that has a subsidiary cannot offset the losses from its subsidiaries' business against its profits in computing federal income taxes, unless the corporations file a consolidated return pursuant to the complex rules discussed in Chapter 15. Through the use of multiple LLCs that are disregarded entitles, an incorporated business can manage the risk of loss in its various lines of business without suffering adverse federal tax consequences. Thus, the practice is becoming increasingly common.

2.   PUBLICLY TRADED PARTNERSHIPS

2.1. *General*

Section 7704 generally treats as a corporation any partnership the interests in which are traded on an established securities market or are readily tradable on a secondary market or a substantial equivalent of a secondary market. The provision, in fact, only applies to limited partnerships and limited liability companies because under state law general partnership interests cannot be traded. The legislative history explains that a secondary market for partnership interests exists if prices are regularly quoted by brokers or dealers who are making a market for such interest. Occasional accommodation trades of partnership interests, a buy-sell agreement between the partners (without more), or the occasional repurchase or redemption by the partnership or acquisition by a general partner of partnership interests will not be treated as a secondary market or the equivalent thereof. However, if the partners have regular and ongoing opportunities to dispose of their interests, the interests are tradable on the equivalent of a secondary market. Meaningful restrictions imposed on the right to transfer partnership interests may preclude classification as a corporation, even if some interests are actually traded. See H.Rep. 100–495, 100th Cong., 1st Sess. 943–950 (1987).

2.2. *Meaning of "Publicly Traded"*

Treas.Reg. § 1.7704–1(b) and (c) provide definitions of the statutory terms "established securities market" and "readily tradable on a secondary market or the substantial equivalent of a secondary market." Established securities markets include not only exchanges, but also interdealer quotation systems. A secondary market or a substantial equivalent of a secondary market exists if the partners are readily able to buy, sell, or exchange their interests in a manner that is economically comparable to trading on an established securities market. Interests are readily tradable on a secondary market or its equivalent if (1) firm quote trading exists, even if only one person makes available bid or offer quotes; (2) the holder of an interest has a readily available, regular, and ongoing opportunity to sell or exchange such interest through a public means of obtaining or providing information of offers to buy, sell, or exchange interests; or (3) buyers and sellers have the opportunity to buy, sell, or exchange interests in a time frame and with the regularity and continuity that the existence of a market maker would provide. Interests are not readily tradable, however, unless the partnership participates in establishing the market or recognizes transfers by admission of purchasers to the partnership or recognizes their rights as transferees. Treas.Reg. § 1.7704–1(d). A redemption or repurchase plan can result in partnership interests being publicly traded.

The Regulations provide several "safe harbors." In determining whether there is public trading of the partnership interests, Treas.Reg. § 1.7704–1(e) disregards transfers in which the transferee has a transferred basis, transfers at death, transfers between family members, transfers pursuant to certain redemption agreements, and certain other transfers. The most broadly applicable safe harbor excludes from the definition of publicly traded partnership so-called "private placements"—that is, any partnership whose interests are not required to be registered under the Securities Act of 1933, but only if the partnership does not have more than 100 members. Treas.Reg. § 1.7704–1(h).

In addition, a partnership will not be considered to be traded on the substantial equivalent of a secondary market for any year in which no more than 2% of the total interests in partnership capital or profits is sold or disposed of in transactions other than private transfers, qualifying redemptions, and certain other safe harbors. Treas.Reg. § 1.7704–1(j). It is clear from § 7704(f), dealing with the effect of a partnership becoming a corporation, that § 7704 contemplates the possibility that a partnership which is initially taxed as a partnership might in a subsequent year become a corporation under § 7704. The "lack of actual trading" safe harbor, which applies on a year-by-year basis, suggests further that a partnership might be considered to be a corporation in one year and a partnership in the next, when it meets the safe harbor. This result could give rise to a constructive liquidation of the "corporation" with tax consequences to the entity and the investors or, conversely, the constructive formation of a new corporation.

2.3. *Exceptions*

A broad exception to § 7704 allows publicly traded limited partnerships more than 90% of whose gross income is from certain "passive sources" to continue to be treated as partnerships. Qualified income for this purpose, with some narrow exceptions, includes interest, dividends, real property rents, gain from the sale of real property, and income and gains from the exploration, development, extraction, processing, refining, etc., of oil and gas or any other natural resource. While the legislative history is silent as to the reason for this exception, it presumably is based on the historic use of limited partnerships in organizing such ventures and the availability of conduit taxation for other entity forms (e.g., real estate investment trusts) making investments of this type. See I.R.C. § 7704(c)–(d).

An additional exception permits publicly traded partnerships that were in existence on December 31, 1987 to continue to be treated as partnerships as long as they do not add a "substantial new line of business." See I.R.C. § 7704(g).

If a publicly traded partnership is not taxed as a corporation, the § 199A deduction is available with respect to the qualifying tax items allocated to its partners. I.R.C. § 199A(e)(4); see Chapter 16.

3. FOREIGN BUSINESS ENTITIES

Treas.Reg. § 301.7701–2(b)(8) lists certain foreign business entities (including entities organized in U.S. possessions, territories, and commonwealths) that are classified as *per se* corporations. The listed organizations are limited liability entities, such as the British Public Limited Company, the French Société Anonyme, the German Aktiengesellschaft, and the Sociedad Anónima in South American countries (Sociedade Anônima in Brazil). Other foreign entities can elect under Treas.Reg. § 301.7701–3(a) whether to be treated as a partnership or as a corporation. In contrast to the partnership default classification rules for domestic organizations, under Treas.Reg. § 301.7701–3(b)(2), the default rule for foreign entities is based on whether the members have limited liability. For a foreign entity that provides limited liability for its members and which is not a per se corporation (listed in Treas.Reg. § 301.7701–2(b)(8)(i)), the default rule is that the entity is a corporation unless it elects to be a partnership (if it has two or more members) or a disregarded entity (if it has only one member). A foreign entity is classified as a partnership if it has two or more members and at least one member does not have limited liability. If a foreign entity has only one owner, who does not have limited liability, the entity is disregarded unless it elects to be regarded as a corporation.

4. BUSINESS TRUSTS

Treas.Reg. § 301.7701–4(a) through (c) distinguish between "ordinary" trusts, the purpose of which are the protection or conservation of trust property, and trusts that are in effect a joint enterprise of the beneficiaries to conduct a business for profit and which will be classified as either a partnership or a corporation under Treas.Reg. § 301.7701–2 and –3. No cases have been decided or rulings issued under the current version of Treas.Reg. § 301.7701–4, but a number of cases were decided under the prior version of the classification regulations. In most of those cases, the question of whether the trust was an "ordinary trust" or a business association taxable as a corporation turned on whether the trust beneficiaries were in fact business associates. For example, in Outlaw v. United States, 494 F.2d 1376 (Ct.Cl.1974), a trust was formed to own and manage some 10,000 acres of farm land and employed 18 to 20 full-time and 60 to 70 temporary workers to engage in a full scale agricultural operation. The trust had 27 original investors, which increased over time to 41 investors; its objective was to carry on a business of owning, developing, and exploiting agricultural lands for income; its existence continued notwithstanding the withdrawal, death, bankruptcy, etc., of an investor; all decisions were made by an operating committee akin to a corporate board of directors; the investor-beneficiaries were liable only to the extent of their proportionate interests in the trust assets; and the investors could freely transfer their interests after giving notice to the trustee. Based on these facts, the trust was classified as a business entity taxable as a corporation. See also Rev.Rul. 80–75, 1980–1 C.B. 314 (trust established by promoter to conduct business activity and to which beneficiaries contributed cash in exchange for income interests and a remainder to person designated by the holder of income interest was classified as a business association).

In contrast, in Estate of Bedell v. Commissioner, 86 T.C. 1207 (1986), a testamentary trust that actively conducted a manufacturing business was held not to be an association because it lacked "associates": the beneficiaries had "not planned a common effort or entered into a combination for the conduct of a business enterprise," only a few of the beneficiaries participated in trust affairs, and their interests were not transferrable.

Under current Treas.Reg. § 301.7701–4, trusts such as those involved in *Outlaw* and *Estate of Bedell* would be classified as business entities rather than as ordinary trusts, and under Treas.Reg. § 301.7701–2 and –3 then would be classified as partnerships unless the trusts elected to be taxed as corporations.

Treas.Reg. § 301.7701–4(d) provides, however, a special rule for "liquidating" trusts; under this rule, as long as the primary purpose of the trust is the liquidation and distribution of the assets transferred to it, the trust will not be an association taxable as a corporation. See Rev.Rul. 75–379, 1975–2 C.B. 505, and Rev.Rul. 63–228, 1963–2 C.B. 229, finding certain trusts that engaged in business activities to fall within the "liquidation" exception; Rev.Proc. 82–58, 1982–2 C.B. 847, amplified by Rev.Proc. 91–15, 1991–1 C.B. 484 (guidelines for advance rulings on classification of liquidation trusts), modified and amplified by Rev. Proc. 94–45, 1994–2 C.B. 684 (income reporting requirements and checklist for ruling requests).

5. SPECIAL CLASSES OF CORPORATIONS

5.1. *Conduit Corporations Relieved of Federal Tax*

Regulated investment companies investing in securities (mutual funds, including exchange traded funds) are in effect relieved of corporate tax liability with respect to the dividends and capital gains from their stock investments if they currently distribute this income to their shareholders. A mutual fund to this extent is thus treated as a conduit rather than a taxable entity. See I.R.C. §§ 851–855.

In 1960 Congress extended conduit treatment to real estate investment trusts (REITs) otherwise taxable as corporations (see §§ 856–860); in 1986 conduit treatment was extended to real estate mortgage investment conduits (REMICs) (§§ 860A–860G).

5.2. *Other Special Corporate Treatment*

Certain classes of corporations are given special treatment as to the computation or treatment of taxable income, e.g., banks, insurance companies, and foreign corporations; some types of corporations receive exemption from tax, e.g., the various tax-exempt organizations (as to which, however, the corporate income tax is applicable to the extent of "unrelated business taxable income," §§ 511–514).

PROBLEM SET 1

1.   Anne and Bill plan to form a limited liability company to engage in the business of developing and marketing computer software. They have identified between 35 and 50 potential investors who will contribute varying amounts of cash for membership interests totaling approximately 75%–85% of profits and losses (after Anne and Bill receive handsome salaries). Under the governing state law, the LLC may be member-managed or manager-managed, membership interests may be freely transferable or nontransferable, and the LLC may or may not be dissolved by the death,

bankruptcy, retirement, or expulsion of a member, all as provided in the LLC agreement. Anne and Bill want the LLC to be managed by themselves, with the investors having only the minimal rights of members required by state law. Only Anne and Bill will have authority to act on behalf of the LLC. Because of the limited powers that the investor-members will be granted, Anne and Bill think it best that the investors be permitted to sell or assign their membership interests if they so desire, although Anne and Bill think that the actual opportunities for resale will be limited by market forces. Of course, Anne and Bill want the business of the LLC to be uninterrupted by the death, bankruptcy, etc., of an investor-member. Will the LLC be taxed as a corporation if organized in the manner contemplated by Anne and Bill?

2.   (a) Rabbit Battery Manufacturing Corp. formed two wholly owned limited liability companies: Cadmium Disposal LLC and Mercury Recycling LLC. What is the effect, if any, on Rabbit's taxable income if Cadmium Disposal has net losses of $2,000,000 this year and Mercury Recycling has net income of $3,000,000.

      (b) Rabbit Battery Manufacturing Corp. has a wholly owned subsidiary, Cadmium Disposal, Inc. Rabbit owns 8 of 10 membership units in Mercury Recycling LLC, a limited liability company, in which Cadmium Disposal owns the other 2 membership units. What is the effect, if any, on Rabbit's taxable income if Cadmium Disposal has net losses of $2,000,000 this year and Mercury Recycling has net income of $3,000,000?

B. REGARD AND DISREGARD OF THE CORPORATE ENTITY

Prior to the late 1980s, a combination of tax and nontax factors led many individuals to choose to operate businesses, whether closely held or publicly held, as C corporations subject to the double tax regime. More recently, the development of the limited liability company business form, coupled with the adoption of the check-the-box classification Regulations, and the pre-2018 rate structure have strongly influenced individuals to conduct closely held businesses in a form subject to the partnership taxation rules of Subchapter K, particularly if capital is a material income producing factor, or to the rules of Subchapter S, which eliminates the corporate level tax and results in the corporation's income being taxed directly to the shareholders. As discussed above, only time will tell whether the changes introduced by the 2017 Tax Act will cause individuals to again prefer business entities organized as C corporations.

In the case of pass-through entities, the question of whether business income or deductions are properly attributable to the entity or directly to the owners does not frequently arise. In the classic C corporation, however, the question of whether particular items of income or deduction are properly attributable to the corporation or directly to the shareholders is very important. Most of the case law regarding this issue developed in the context of closely held businesses in which capital was a material income producing factor.

Strong v. Commissioner*

United States Tax Court, 1976.
66 T.C. 12.

■ TANNENWALD, JUDGE: * * *

Petitioners formed a partnership for the purpose of constructing and operating an apartment complex on real estate contributed by several partners. In order to obtain financing for the project, it was necessary to transfer the property to a corporation wholly owned by the partnership so that mortgage loans could be made at an interest rate in excess of the limit imposed by State usury laws on loans to individuals. Construction and operation of the apartments generated net operating losses during the years in issue which were reported on the partnership's returns and as distributive shares on the individual returns of the petitioners. The respondent determined that the corporation, as owner of the property, was the proper party to report those losses. Petitioners allege that the corporation was a nominee whose ownership should be disregarded for tax purposes. The crux of petitioners' case is that the corporation was merely a sham or device used for the purpose of avoiding the New York usury statute, that it performed no acts other than those essential to that function, and that to treat it as the actual owner of the property would be to exalt form over substance.

The use of sham or dummy corporations to avoid application of the usury laws is a recognized practice in New York. Hoffman v. Lee Nashem Motors, Inc., 20 N.Y.2d 513, 231 N.E.2d 765, 285 N.Y.S.2d 68 (1967) * * *. There is no doubt that petitioners sought to do business in partnership form and that the corporation was, at least in their eyes, a mere tool or conduit. Their argument is not without some appeal, but we conclude that it should not be accepted.

The principal guidepost on the road to recognition of the corporate entity is Moline Properties v. Commissioner, 319 U.S. 436 (1943). In that case, a corporation was organized as part of a transaction which included the transfer of mortgaged property to it by the shareholder, the assumption by it of the outstanding mortgages, and the transfer of its stock to a voting trustee named by the mortgagee as security for additional advances. Later the indebtedness was repaid and the shareholder reacquired control of the corporation. Thereafter it mortgaged and sold some of the property it held, and leased another portion. The Court held that the corporation was a separate entity from its inception, and stated its rule of decision as follows:

> The doctrine of corporate entity fills a useful purpose in business life. Whether the purpose be to gain an advantage under the law of the state of incorporation or to avoid or to comply with the demands of creditors or to serve the creator's personal or undisclosed convenience, *so long as that purpose is*

---

*   [Ed.: The decision was affirmed by order, 553 F.2d 94 (2d Cir.1977).]

the equivalent of business activity or is followed by the carrying on of business by the corporation, the corporation remains a separate taxable entity. * * * In Burnet v. Commonwealth Improvement Co., 287 U.S. 415, this Court appraised the relation between a corporation and its sole stockholder and held taxable to the corporation a profit on a sale to its stockholder. This was because the taxpayer had adopted the corporate form for purposes of his own. The choice of the advantages of incorporation to do business, it was held, required the acceptance of the tax disadvantages. [319 U.S. at 438–439. Fn. refs. omitted; emphasis supplied.]

Cases following *Moline Properties* have generally held that the income from property must be taxed to the corporate owner and will not be attributed to the shareholders, unless the corporation is a *purely passive dummy* or is used for a tax-avoidance purpose. Harrison Property Management Co. v. United States, 475 F.2d 623 (Ct.Cl.1973); Taylor v. Commissioner, 445 F.2d 455 (1st Cir.1971); National Investors Corp. v. Hoey, 144 F.2d 466 (2d Cir.1944) * * *. This is particularly true where the demand that the corporate entity be ignored emanates from the shareholders of a closely held corporation. See Harrison Property Management Co. v. United States, supra at 626; David F. Bolger, 59 T.C. 760, 767 n. 4 (1973).[8] It has been suggested that the prevailing approach misses the point by focusing (as do the parties herein) on the viability of the corporate entity rather than the situs of real beneficial or economic ownership. Kurtz & Kopp, "Taxability of Straw Corporations in Real Estate Transactions," 22 Tax Lawyer 647 (1969). However, the thrust of the case law, as we read it, is to leave the door open to the argument that a corporation played a purely nominal or "straw" role in a transaction, while closing it firmly against any contention that a corporation may be disregarded simply because it is the creature of its shareholders. * * *

The Supreme Court has held that shareholder domination, even to the extent that a corporation could be said to lack beneficial ownership of its assets and income, is insufficient to permit taxpayers to ignore the corporation's existence. National Carbide Corp. v. Commissioner, 336 U.S. 422, 433–434 (1949); Moline Properties v. Commissioner, supra. The Court of Appeals for the Second Circuit, to which appeal will lie herein, has similarly refused to disregard the interposition of a corporate entity between shareholders and their property, except where the corporation has not purported to deal with the property in its own right. The focus is on business purpose or activity with respect to the particular property whose ownership is in question.

---

[8]   See also Higgins v. Smith, 308 U.S. 473 (1940). Cf. Colin v. Altman, 39 App.Div.2d 200, 333 N.Y.S.2d 432, 433–434 (1st Dept.1972): "the corporate veil is never pierced for the benefit of the corporation or its stockholders. * * * [The sole stockholder] is not the corporation either in law or fact and, having elected to take the advantages [of incorporation], it is not inequitable to subject him to the disabilities consequent upon his election."

In Paymer v. Commissioner, 150 F.2d 334 (2d Cir.1945), two brothers formed a pair of corporations (Raymep and Westrich) to which they transferred legal title to certain real estate. Their purpose was to deter execution against the property by their individual creditors. Neither corporation engaged in any business activity except that Raymep obtained a loan and as part security "assigned to the lender all the lessor's rights, profits and interest in two leases on the property and covenanted that they were in full force and effect and that it was the sole lessor." 150 F.2d at 336. Westrich was disregarded on the ground that it "was at all times but a passive dummy which did nothing but take and hold title to the real estate conveyed to it. It served no business purpose *in connection with the property*." 150 F.2d at 337. (Emphasis added.) Raymep, however, was not disregarded, because it did perform a business function as the owner of the property.

In Jackson v. Commissioner, 233 F.2d 289 (2d Cir.1956), affg. 24 T.C. 1 (1955), the Court of Appeals disregarded holding companies which lacked separate business purpose or activity, stating that the situation was encompassed within the foregoing language in its opinion in *Paymer* and further observing:

> A natural person may be used to receive income which in fact is another's. So, too, a corporation, although for other purposes a jural entity distinct from its stockholders, may be used as a mere dummy to receive income which in fact is the income of the stockholders or of someone else; in such circumstances, the company will be disregarded. [233 F.2d at 290 n. 2.]

Finally, in Commissioner v. State-Adams Corp., 283 F.2d 395 (2d Cir.1960), revg. 32 T.C. 365 (1959)(which involved a different factual situation), the court characterized its holding in *Paymer* as "nothing more than a restatement of the fundamental rule that income from real estate held in the name of a nominee will be taxed to the beneficial owner, not to the nominee." 283 F.2d at 398 (fn. ref. omitted). The mere fact that some of the documents herein speak in terms of a corporate nominee is not sufficient to bring petitioners within the exception to the general rule. Harrison Property Management Co. v. United States, supra.

In short, a corporate "straw" may be used to separate apparent from actual ownership of property, without incurring the tax consequences of an actual transfer; but to prevent evasion or abuse of the two-tiered tax structure, a taxpayer's claim that his controlled corporation should be disregarded will be closely scrutinized. If the corporation was intended to, or did in fact, act in its own name with respect to property, its ownership thereof will not be disregarded.

The degree of corporate purpose and activity requiring recognition of the corporation as a separate entity is extremely low. Thus, it has been stated that "a determination whether a corporation is to be considered as doing business is not necessarily dependent upon the quantum of business" and that the business activity may be "minimal." See Britt v. United States, 431 F.2d 227, 235, 237 (5th Cir.1970).

In this case, the corporation's purpose and activities were sufficient to require recognition of its separate ownership of the property in question and, a fortiori, of its existence as a taxable entity. The purpose to avoid State usury laws is a "business purpose" within the meaning of *Moline Properties.* Collins v. United States, supra; David F. Bolger, supra. The corporation had broad, unrestricted powers under its charter. Compare Collins v. United States, supra. Its activities were more extensive than those which required recognition of Raymep in Paymer v. Commissioner, supra. Like Raymep, it borrowed money on the security of rents; in addition, it mortgaged the property itself and it received and applied the loan proceeds. It engaged in the foregoing activities on more than one occasion and is more vulnerable than was the corporation in Collins v. United States, supra, which was also formed to avoid usury law restrictions and placed only a single mortgage. These activities, carried out in its own name, go beyond "transactions essential to the holding and transferring of title." See Taylor v. Commissioner, 445 F.2d at 457. The fact that the corporation in this case, unlike those in other cases, did not enter into any leases does not, in our opinion, constitute a sufficient basis for distinguishing their thrust.[10]

Furthermore, the corporation was otherwise treated by the partnership in a manner inconsistent with petitioners' contention that the two were the same entity. The partnership agreement required that deeds, loan agreements, and mortgages "executed by or on behalf of the partnership" be signed by both Jones and Strong; property standing in the corporate name was so dealt with on Jones' signature alone. Separation of title to the various parcels permitted the creation of mutual easements, an act which would have been prevented by the doctrine of merger had the properties been under common ownership. See Parsons v. Johnson, 68 N.Y. 62 (1877); Snyder v. Monroe County, 2 Misc.2d 946, 153 N.Y.S.2d 479, 486 (1956), affd. mem. 6 A.D.2d 854, 175 N.Y.S.2d 1008 (4th Dept.1958). The corporation applied for and received insurance on the property in its own name.

Finally, although not determinative, an element to be considered is the fact that the corporate vehicle in this case, whatever the parties' intentions, carried with it the usual baggage attending incorporation, including limitation of the shareholders' personal liability during construction. Jones alone was potentially responsible (as guarantor) for repayment of the construction loans.

---

[10] In Raymep Realty Corp., 7 T.C.M. 262 (1948), relied upon by petitioners we held the execution of a lease in the name of a corporate nominee titleholder did not require the corporation to be recognized as a taxable entity. We characterized that single act as "a purely nominal adjunct to the holding of title." Here, by contrast, the business activity was the raison d'être of the corporation.

In the final analysis, the corporation herein fits the mold articulated in Collins v. United States, supra:

> The fact remains, however, that the corporation did exist and did perform the function intended of it until the permanent loan was consummated. It was more than a business convenience, it was a business necessity to plaintiffs' enterprise. As such, it came into being. As such, it served the purpose of its creation. [386 F.Supp. at 21.]

The fact that the purpose and use of the corporation was limited in scope is beside the point. See Sam Siegel, 45 T.C. 566, 577 (1966).

The tide of judicial history is too strong to enable petitioners to prevail, albeit that the activities of the corporation were substantially less than those involved in most of the decided cases with the exception of Collins v. United States, supra.

Having set up a separate entity through which to conduct their affairs, petitioners must live with the tax consequences of that choice. Indeed, the very exigency which led to the use of the corporation serves to emphasize its separate existence. See Moline Properties v. Commissioner, 319 U.S. at 440; David F. Bolger, 59 T.C. at 766. Our conclusion is not based upon any failure of the petitioners to turn square corners with respondent; they consistently made clear their intention to prevent separate taxation of the corporation if legally possible. They took most precautions consistent with business exigency to achieve that end. We simply hold that their goal was not attainable in this case.

Reviewed by the Court.

Decisions will be entered for the respondent.

Commissioner v. Bollinger

Supreme Court of the United States, 1988.
485 U.S. 340.

■ JUSTICE SCALIA delivered the opinion of the Court.

Petitioner the Commissioner of Internal Revenue challenges a decision by the United States Court of Appeals for the Sixth Circuit holding that a corporation which held record title to real property as agent for the corporation's shareholders was not the owner of the property for purposes of federal income taxation. 807 F.2d 65 (1986). * * *

I

Respondent Jesse C. Bollinger, Jr., developed, either individually or in partnership with some or all of the other respondents, eight apartment complexes in Lexington, Kentucky. (For convenience we will refer to all the ventures as "partnerships.") Bollinger initiated development of the first apartment complex, Creekside North Apartments, in 1968. The Massachusetts Mutual Life Insurance Company agreed to provide permanent financing by lending $1,075,000 to "the corporate nominee of Jesse C. Bollinger, Jr." at an annual interest rate of eight percent, secured by a mortgage on the property and a personal guaranty from Bollinger. The loan commitment was structured in this fashion because Kentucky's usury law at the time limited the annual interest rate for noncorporate borrowers to seven percent. Ky.Rev.Stat. §§ 360.010, 360.025 (1972). Lenders willing to provide money only at higher rates required the nominal debtor and record title holder of mortgaged property to be a corporate nominee of the true owner and borrower. On October 14, 1968, Bollinger incorporated Creekside, Inc., under the laws of Kentucky; he was the only stockholder. The next day, Bollinger and Creekside, Inc., entered into a written agreement which provided that the corporation would hold title to the apartment complex as Bollinger's agent for the sole purpose of securing financing, and would convey, assign, or encumber the property and disburse the proceeds thereof only as directed by Bollinger; that Creekside, Inc., had no obligation to maintain the property or assume any liability by reason of the execution of promissory notes or otherwise; and that Bollinger would indemnify and hold the corporation harmless from any liability it might sustain as his agent and nominee.

Having secured the commitment for permanent financing, Bollinger, acting through Creekside, Inc., borrowed the construction funds for the apartment complex from Citizens Fidelity Bank and Trust Company. Creekside, Inc., executed all necessary loan documents including the promissory note and mortgage, and transferred all loan proceeds to Bollinger's individual construction account. Bollinger acted as general contractor for the construction, hired the necessary employees, and paid the expenses out of the construction account. When construction was completed, Bollinger obtained, again through Creekside, Inc., permanent financing from Massachusetts Mutual Life in accordance with the earlier loan commitment. These loan proceeds were used to pay off the Citizens Fidelity construction loan. Bollinger hired a resident manager to rent the apartments, execute leases with tenants, collect and deposit the rents, and maintain operating records. The manager deposited all rental receipts into, and paid all operating expenses from, an operating account, which was first opened in the name of Creekside, Inc., but was later changed to "Creekside Apartments, a partnership." The operation of Creekside North Apartments generated losses for the taxable years 1969, 1971, 1972, 1973, and 1974, and ordinary income for the years 1970, 1975, 1976, and 1977. Throughout, the income and losses were reported by Bollinger on his individual income tax returns.

Following a substantially identical pattern, seven other apartment complexes were developed by respondents through seven separate partnerships. For each venture, a partnership executed a nominee agreement with Creekside, Inc., to obtain financing. (For one of the ventures, a different Kentucky corporation, Cloisters, Inc., in which

Bollinger had a 50 percent interest, acted as the borrower and titleholder. For convenience, we will refer to both Creekside and Cloisters as "the corporation.") The corporation transferred the construction loan proceeds to the partnership's construction account, and the partnership hired a construction supervisor who oversaw construction. Upon completion of construction, each partnership actively managed its apartment complex, depositing all rental receipts into, and paying all expenses from, a separate partnership account for each apartment complex. The corporation had no assets, liabilities, employees, or bank accounts. In every case, the lenders regarded the partnership as the owner of the apartments and were aware that the corporation was acting as agent of the partnership in holding record title. The partnerships reported the income and losses generated by the apartment complexes on their partnership tax returns, and respondents reported their distributive share of the partnership income and losses on their individual tax returns.

The Commissioner of Internal Revenue disallowed the losses reported by respondents, on the ground that the standards set out in National Carbide Corp. v. Commissioner, 336 U.S. 422, 69 S.Ct. 726, 93 L.Ed. 779 (1949), were not met. The Commissioner contended that *National Carbide* required a corporation to have an arm's length relationship with its shareholders before it could be recognized as their agent. Although not all respondents were shareholders of the corporation, the Commissioner took the position that the funds the partnerships disbursed to pay expenses should be deemed contributions to the corporation's capital, thereby making all respondents constructive stockholders. Since, in the Commissioner's view, the corporation rather than its shareholders owned the real estate, any losses sustained by the ventures were attributable to the corporation and not respondents. Respondents sought a redetermination in the United States Tax Court. The Tax Court held that the corporations were the agents of the partnerships and should be disregarded for tax purposes. Bollinger v. Commissioner, 48 TCM 1443 (1984), ¶ 84,560 PBH Memo TC. On appeal, the United States Court of Appeals for the Sixth Circuit affirmed. 807 F.2d 65 (1986). We granted the Commissioner's petition for certiorari.

II

For federal income tax purposes, gain or loss from the sale or use of property is attributable to the owner of the property. See Helvering v. Horst, 311 U.S. 112, 116–117, 61 S.Ct. 144, 147 (1940); Blair v. Commissioner, 300 U.S. 5, 12, 57 S.Ct. 330 (1937) * * *. The problem we face here is that two different taxpayers can plausibly be regarded as the owner. Neither the Internal Revenue Code nor the regulations promulgated by the Secretary of the Treasury provide significant guidance as to which should be selected. It is common ground between the parties, however, that if a corporation holds title to property as agent for a partnership, then for tax purposes the partnership and not the corporation is the owner. Given agreement on that premise, one would suppose that there would be agreement upon the conclusion as well. For each of respondents' apartment complexes, an agency agreement expressly provided that the corporation would "hold such property as nominee and agent for" the partnership, App. to Pet. for Cert. 21a, n. 4, and that the partnership would have sole control of and responsibility for the apartment complex. The partnership in each instance was identified as the principal and owner of the property during financing, construction, and operation. The lenders, contractors, managers, employees, and tenants—all who had contact with the development—knew that the corporation was merely the agent of the partnership, if they knew of the existence of the corporation at all. In each instance the relationship between the corporation and the partnership was, in both form and substance, an agency with the partnership as principal.

The Commissioner contends, however, that the normal indicia of agency cannot suffice for tax purposes when, as here, the alleged principals are the controlling shareholders of the alleged agent corporation. That, it asserts, would undermine the principle of Moline Properties v. Commissioner, 319 U.S. 436, 63 S.Ct. 1132 (1943), which held that a corporation is a separate taxable entity even if it has only one shareholder who exercises total control over its affairs. Obviously, *Moline*'s separate-entity principle would be significantly compromised if shareholders of closely held corporations could, by clothing the corporation with some attributes of agency with respect to particular assets, leave themselves free at the end of the tax year to make a claim— perhaps even a good-faith claim—of either agent or owner status, depending upon which choice turns out to minimize their tax liability. The Commissioner does not have the resources to audit and litigate the many cases in which agency status could be thought debatable. Hence, the Commissioner argues, in this shareholder context he can reasonably demand that the taxpayer meet a prophylactically clear test of agency.

We agree with that principle, but the question remains whether the test the Commissioner proposes is appropriate. The parties have debated at length the significance of our opinion in *National Carbide Corp. v. Commissioner,* supra. In that case, three corporations that were wholly owned subsidiaries of another corporation agreed to operate their production plants as "agents" for the parent, transferring to it all profits except for a nominal sum. The subsidiaries reported as gross income only this sum, but the Commissioner concluded that they should be taxed on the entirety of the profits because they were not really agents. We agreed, reasoning first, that the mere fact of the parent's control over the subsidiaries did not establish the existence of an agency, since such control is typical of all shareholder-corporation relationships, id., 336 U.S. at 429–434, 69 S.Ct., at 730–732; and second, that the agreements to pay the parent all profits above a nominal amount were not determinative since income must be taxed to those who actually earn it without regard to anticipatory assignment, id., at 435–436, 69 S.Ct., at 733–734. We acknowledged, however, that there was such a thing as "a true corporate agent * * * of [an] owner-principal," id. at 437, 69 S.Ct., at 734, and proceeded to set forth four indicia and two requirements of such status, the sum of which has become known in the lore of federal income tax law as the "six *National Carbide* factors":

> "[1] Whether the corporation operates in the name and for the account of the principal, [2] binds the principal by its actions, [3] transmits money received to the principal, and [4] whether receipt of income is attributable to the services of employees of the principal and to assets belonging to the principal are some of the relevant considerations in determining whether a true agency exists. [5] If the corporation is a true agent, its relations with its principal must not be dependent upon the fact that it is owned by the principal, if such is the case. [6] Its business purpose must be the carrying on of the normal duties of an agent." Id., at 437, 69 S.Ct., at 734 (footnotes omitted).

We readily discerned that these factors led to a conclusion of nonagency in *National Carbide* itself. There each subsidiary had represented to its customers that it (not the parent) was the company manufacturing and selling its products; each had sought to shield the parent from service of legal process; and the operations had used thousands of the subsidiaries' employees and nearly $20 million worth of property and equipment listed as assets on the subsidiaries' books. * * *

The Commissioner contends that the last two *National Carbide* factors are not satisfied in the present case. To take the last first: The Commissioner argues that here the corporation's business purpose with respect to the property at issue was not "the carrying on of the normal duties of an agent," since it was acting not as the agent but rather as the owner of the property for purposes of Kentucky's usury laws. We do not agree. It assuredly was not acting as the owner in fact, since respondents represented themselves as the principals to all parties concerned with the loans. Indeed, it was the lenders themselves who required the use of a corporate nominee. Nor does it make any sense to adopt a contrary-to-fact legal presumption that the corporation was the principal, imposing a federal tax sanction for the apparent evasion of Kentucky's usury law. To begin with, the Commissioner has not established that these transactions were an evasion. Respondents assert without contradiction that use of agency arrangements in order to permit higher interest was common practice, and it is by no means clear that the practice violated the spirit of the Kentucky law, much less its letter. It might well be thought that the borrower does not generally require usury protection in a transaction sophisticated enough to employ a corporate agent— assuredly not the normal *modus operandi* of the loan shark. That the statute positively envisioned corporate nominees is suggested by a provision which forbids charging the higher corporate interest rates "to a corporation, the principal asset of which shall be the ownership of a one (1) or two (2) family dwelling," Ky.Rev.Stat. § 360.025(2)(1987)—which would seem to prevent use of the nominee device for ordinary home-mortgage loans. In any event, even if the transaction did run afoul of the usury law, Kentucky, like most States, regards only the lender as the usurer, and the borrower as the victim. See Ky.Rev.Stat. § 360.020 (1987) (lender liable to borrower for civil penalty), § 360.990 (lender guilty of misdemeanor). Since the Kentucky statute imposed no penalties upon the borrower for allowing himself to be victimized, nor treated him as *in pari delictu,* but to the contrary enabled him to pay back the principal without any interest, and to sue for double the amount of interest already paid (plus attorney's fees), see Ky.Rev.Stat. § 360.020 (1972), the United States would hardly be vindicating Kentucky law by depriving the usury victim of tax advantages he would otherwise enjoy. In sum, we see no basis in either fact or policy for holding that the corporation was the principal because of the nature of its participation in the loans.

Of more general importance is the Commissioner's contention that the arrangements here violate the fifth *National Carbide* factor—that the corporate agent's "relations with its principal must not be dependent upon the fact that it is owned by the principal." The Commissioner asserts that this cannot be satisfied unless the corporate agent and its shareholder principal have an "arm's-length relationship" that includes the payment of a fee for agency services. The meaning of *National Carbide's* fifth factor is, at the risk of understatement, not entirely clear. Ultimately, the relations between a corporate agent and its owner-principal are *always* dependent upon the fact of ownership, in that the owner can cause the relations to be altered or terminated at any time. Plainly that is not what was meant, since on that interpretation all subsidiary-parent agencies would be invalid for tax purposes, a position which the *National Carbide* opinion specifically disavowed. We think the fifth *National Carbide* factor—so much more abstract than the others—was no more and no less than a generalized statement of the concern, expressed earlier in our own discussion, that the separate-entity doctrine of *Moline* not be subverted.

In any case, we decline to parse the text of *National Carbide* as though that were itself the governing statute. As noted earlier, it is uncontested that the law attributes tax consequences of property held by a genuine agent to the principal; and we agree that it is reasonable for the Commissioner to demand unequivocal evidence of genuineness in the corporation-shareholder context, in order to prevent evasion of *Moline.* We see no basis, however, for holding that unequivocal evidence can only consist of the rigid requirements (arm's-length dealing plus agency fee) that the Commissioner suggests. Neither of those is demanded by the law of agency, which permits agents to be unpaid family members, friends, or associates. See Restatement (Second) of Agency §§ 16, 21, 22 (1958). It seems to us that the genuineness of the agency relationship is adequately assured, and tax-avoiding manipulation adequately avoided, when the fact that the corporation is acting as agent for its shareholders with respect to a particular asset is set forth in a written agreement at the time the asset is acquired, the corporation functions as agent and not principal with respect to the asset for all purposes, and the corporation is held out as the agent and not principal in all dealings with third parties relating to the asset. Since these requirements were met here, the judgment of the Court of Appeals is

Affirmed.

DETAILED ANALYSIS

1. APPLICATION OF THE BUSINESS ACTIVITY TEST

1.1. *General*

In cases involving the issue whether a corporation should be taxed as a separate entity, the taxpayer and the IRS may be on different sides, depending on the tax stakes involved. For example, a taxpayer whose personal tax bracket exceeds the corporate rate may urge that the corporation be recognized for tax purposes so as to postpone imposition of the taxpayer's higher individual rate on the income; the IRS may seek to disregard the corporate entity. Conversely, as in *Strong* and *Bollinger*, the taxpayer who seeks to deduct directly losses that result from activities of the "corporation" or who utilizes the corporate form only for nominal purposes, will urge that the formal existence of the corporation be ignored; the IRS will assert that the activities of the corporation warrant its recognition as a separate taxable entity. Historically, taxpayers generally had little success in attempts to assert that a corporation they created should be disregarded for tax purposes; the courts generally have upheld the IRS's position that the activities of the corporation were sufficient to warrant it being regarded as a separate entity for tax purposes. (Note that even in *Bollinger*, in which the taxpayer prevailed, the corporation was not ignored for tax purposes; it was treated as the shareholders' agent.) On the other hand, in certain cases the corporate entity should be disregarded to prevent tax avoidance. The following cases illustrate the results reached by the courts in this area.

1.2. *Insufficient Business Activity—Corporate Entity Disregarded*

In Greenberg v. Commissioner, 62 T.C. 331 (1974), aff'd per curiam, 526 F.2d 588 (4th Cir.1975), two individuals formed five corporations to develop large residential subdivisions. All the corporations performed identical functions. Following a disagreement between the two shareholders, four corporations were liquidated, and one of the shareholders was redeemed out of the remaining corporation. The taxpayer was left as the sole shareholder of the remaining corporation. The taxpayer reported capital gains on the amounts received in liquidation of the four corporations. The court held that the four liquidated corporations were merely shams; all the income earned by those corporations was the income of the continuing corporation; and the amounts distributed to the taxpayer were simply a dividend: "These [liquidated] corporations served no purpose except to obtain a tax benefit which is not 'business' sufficient to grant them recognition as separate 'taxworthy' entities for Federal tax purposes."

In Robucci v. Commissioner, T.C. Memo 2011–19, the Tax Court disregarded the entity status of two corporations formed by a practicing psychiatrist on the advice of an accountant in order to avoid federal employment taxes. The psychiatrist was the sole shareholder of both corporations. One corporation was formed as a professional services corporation and was a 5% limited partner in a limited liability company (LLC) in which 95% of the partnership interests were held by the psychiatrist and through which he conducted his practice. The corporation entered into a management agreement with the LLC, but it did not have any assets, employees, contracts, or customers other than the LLC, and it did not actually perform any services. The court concluded that the corporation "was not formed for a purpose that 'is the equivalent of a business activity' within the meaning of Moline Props., Inc. v. Commissioner, 319 U.S. at 429." The second corporation was formed purportedly to manage reimbursements of various expenses of the LLC, including a medical reimbursement plan, but while it maintained a bank account to which and from which some deposits and withdrawals were made, there was "scant evidence" of regular transfers of funds related to the purported activity of the corporation. The transfers of funds "to the extent they occurred, were the equivalent of taking money from one pocket and putting it into another. Such a procedure hardly qualifies as a 'business activity' within the contemplation of Moline Props., Inc." The court concluded that both corporations were hollow shells, neither of which carried on any business after incorporation. Thus, their income was the taxpayer's income. Because the professional services corporation was disregarded as an entity, the limited liability company was treated as a sole member disregarded entity, and all of its income was taxed directly to the taxpayer.

In Noonan v. Commissioner, 52 T.C. 907 (1969), aff'd per curiam, 451 F.2d 992 (9th Cir.1971), a corporation received income as a limited partner from a business enterprise in which the sole shareholder was a general partner. The Tax Court acknowledged that the corporation had been properly organized, but it refused to recognize the separate corporate entity where the record was devoid of evidence showing any active business purpose.

1.3. *Sufficient Business Activity—Corporate Entity Respected*

1.3.1. *General*

In situations similar to that in Strong v. Commissioner, the courts have rejected taxpayers' attempts to have a corporation holding title to real estate disregarded and treated as a "mere dummy" for tax purposes. In Bolger v. Commissioner, 59 T.C. 760 (1973), the taxpayer was engaged in real estate investment and finance. The taxpayer would locate a building that a business desired to lease. The following transactions would take place, often all on the same day: Taxpayer would organize a nominally capitalized corporation with the shareholders being himself and other individuals; the corporation would purchase the building and enter into a lease with the user;

and the corporation would then issue its notes, secured by a mortgage on the property and an assignment of the lease, to an institutional lender to obtain funds for the purchase. The term of the mortgage notes and the primary term of the lease were usually coextensive. The mortgage provided that the property could be transferred, with the transferees being obligated to fulfill the terms of the mortgage and the lease, except that the transferees would assume no personal financial obligation for the payment of principal and interest on the note. Such transferees were also obligated to keep the corporation in existence. Immediately after these transactions, the corporation would then convey the property to its shareholders subject to the lease and mortgage and without any cash payment to the corporation. The transferee shareholders would assume the corporation's obligation under the lease and mortgage, but they had no personal liability thereon except to the extent of the property they received. The taxpayers claimed that they were entitled to the depreciation deductions generated by the properties. The IRS asserted that only the corporation had a depreciable interest in the property. The court first held that both at the time the corporation was created and after the transfer of the property to the shareholders, the corporation was a viable business entity. Although at the latter point the corporation was stripped of its assets and, by virtue of its various agreements could not engage in any business activity, the court held it was sufficient that the corporation continued to be liable on its obligations to the lender and remained in existence with full powers to own property and transact business. The court went on to hold, however, that because of the transfer of the property to the shareholders, the individual taxpayers were entitled to the depreciation deductions. The case presaged the Tax Court's position in *Strong* that there is very little room for a taxpayer successfully to assert disregard of the corporate form adopted by the taxpayer.

Weekend Warrior Trailers, Inc. v. Commissioner, T.C. Memo. 2011–105, involved the formation of a corporation solely to engage in a series of transactions designed to reduce income taxes using a strategy to shift income to an employee stock ownership plan (ESOP), a scheme that no longer is possible because the relevant statutory rules that produced the results were amended after the years in question in the case. The sole shareholder of the taxpayer, Weekend Warrior Trailers, which manufactured travel trailers, established a sibling corporation, Leading Edge, to provide design and management services, to be performed by the taxpayer's shareholder as an employee of Leading Edge (while he also continued to serve as a managerial employee of the taxpayer), for the taxpayer's manufacturing operations. The taxpayer also transferred its employees to Leading Edge, which then leased the employees to the taxpayer. The taxpayer made substantial payments (millions of dollars) to Leading Edge for management services. The IRS disallowed a deduction for the taxpayer's management fee on the grounds that (1) Leading Edge " 'should be disregarded for Federal income tax purposes as Leading Edge Design, Inc. lacked both economic substance and economic purpose and was formed for the primary purpose of obtaining tax benefits', and (2) 'Transactions entered into between Leading Edge Design, Inc. and Weekend Warrior Trailers, Inc. should be disregarded for Federal Income tax' purposes because they lacked economic substance and economic purpose and were entered into for the primary purpose of obtaining tax benefits.' " Applying the *Moline Properties* doctrine, the Tax Court rejected the IRS's arguments, stating as follows:

> Even if a corporation was not formed for a valid business purpose, it nevertheless must be respected for tax purposes if it actually engaged in business activity. See Moline Props., Inc. v. Commissioner, 319 U.S. at 438–439; Bass v. Commissioner, [50 T.C. 595, 602 (1968)]. The prongs of the test under Moline Props. are alternative prongs. See Moline Props., Inc. v. Commissioner, supra at 438–439; Bass v. Commissioner, supra at 602; see also Rogers v. Commissioner, T.C. Memo. 1975–289 ("Moline establishes a two-pronged test, the first part of which is business purpose, and the second, business activity. * * * Business purpose or business activity are alternative requirements."). Accordingly, the issue turns on whether Leading Edge engaged in business activity. Whether a corporation is carrying on sufficient business activity to require its recognition as a separate entity is a question of fact. Bass v. Commissioner, supra at 602 (status of a corporation respected when testimony established that "the corporation was managed as a viable concern, and not as simply a lifeless facade.")

The court concluded that, on the record, Leading Edge was not a "lifeless facade." Nevertheless, the taxpayer's scheme failed because the court went on to hold that the evidence did not prove that the management fees paid by Weekend Warrior to Leading Edge were necessary or reasonable.

Recognition of the corporate entity because the corporation conducts sufficient business activity does not preclude a *Bollinger* type argument that the corporation nevertheless was acting merely as the agent of its shareholders.

1.3.2.   *Investment Activity*

Taxpayers have sometimes been successful in having their corporations recognized as separate entities under the *Moline Properties* concept of "business activity" even though the corporate function consisted only of a single investment asset rather than active business operations. In Siegel v. Commissioner, 45 T.C. 566 (1966) (acq.), the taxpayer, wishing to limit his potential liability, established a Panamanian corporation to invest in a farm joint venture in Cuba. The taxpayer had no immediate need for the profits and his plan at the time of the incorporation was ultimately "to obtain the fruits of the venture through liquidation of the corporation." Although the other members of the joint venture actively participated in the farming operation, the corporation's only activity was to receive money from the venture, deposit it in its account, and periodically invest and reinvest the funds in the Cuban farming venture. The Tax Court concluded that there was a sufficient amount of business activity: "Nor may it be said that [the corporation's] minimal activity did not constitute the conduct of business. The point is that [the corporation] was formed for only a limited purpose, namely, to invest in the joint venture * * *."[12] See also Bateman v. United States, 490 F.2d 549 (9th Cir.1973) (corporation that owned a limited partnership interest in a partnership in which its sole shareholder was active and that conducted no business activities other than holding passive investments was treated as a separate taxable entity based on the trial court's finding that the business purpose for the corporation was to build a cash reserve fund to buy out retiring or deceased partners' interests).

2. IRRELEVANCE OF ACTUAL DIRECTION OF CORPORATE ACTIVITIES

In attempting to have the corporation disregarded for tax purposes, the IRS has argued unsuccessfully that the corporation is not engaged in "business activity" in cases in which the shareholder-owner has completely dominated the corporate activities. For example, in Bass v. Commissioner, 50 T.C. 595 (1968), the taxpayer organized a Swiss corporation to which he transferred working interests in oil and gas leases. The IRS attempted to discount the business actions of the corporation on the theory that the taxpayer "actually made the business decisions for the corporation." The Tax Court concluded that the corporation was a viable business entity since it had "acted" like a genuine corporation in paying the expenses of the business and filing returns. The *Bass* opinion emphasized the Supreme Court's language in National Carbide Corp. v. Commissioner, 336 U.S. 422 (1949), that "the fact that the owner retains direction of its affairs down to the minutest detail * * * [makes] no difference tax-wise." A like result was reached in Ross Glove Co. v. Commissioner, 60 T.C. 569 (1973) (acq.).

After failing to prevent the classification of professional service corporations as corporations for tax purposes, see, e.g., Kurzner v. United States, 413 F.2d 97 (5th Cir. 1969), the IRS began to attack professional service corporations generally on the basis that such corporations were shams that did not actually earn their incomes. However, as long as corporate formalities were followed and the shareholder-employees respected the corporate form in conducting business, the IRS met with little success. Compare Achiro v. Commissioner, 77 T.C. 881 (1981) (corporate form of management services company respected at taxpayer's behest even though shareholders were sole employees and primary purpose of forming corporation was to reduce income taxes), with Jones v. Commissioner, 64 T.C. 1066 (1975) (court reporter who formed personal service corporation taxed individually because court rules required reporter to be an individual rather than a corporation).

3. APPLICATION OF THE AGENCY RATIONALE

The *Moline Properties* doctrine makes it difficult to disregard the corporate entity if the corporation conducts any business, particularly because the requisite activity threshold is low. Taxpayers have sought to achieve the same substantive result that is produced by disregarding corporate entity status by arguing that a principal-agent relationship exists between the shareholder and the corporation. If such arguments succeed, the

---

[12] Section 951, added in 1962, would now deal with the situation in *Siegel* to the extent that the utilization of a foreign rather than a domestic corporation was involved.

income (or deduction) involved is the shareholder's rather than the corporation's. As explained in the *Bollinger* opinion, this argument was based on language in National Carbide Corp. v. Commissioner, 336 U.S. 422, 437–39 (1949).

Prior to the *Bollinger* decision, most cases turned on application of the fifth *National Carbide* factor: whether the relations between the principal and the agent depended on the principal's ownership of the agent. For example, in Harrison Property Management Co., Inc. v. United States, 475 F.2d 623 (Ct.Cl.1973), three partners transferred title to oil-bearing property to the corporation, retaining all beneficial rights and interests in the property in themselves. The primary reason for the formation of the corporation was the orderly management of the property in the event of the death of one of the individuals. The corporation received the income from oil leases, paid expenses incident thereto, and filed a fiduciary income tax return showing all net income distributed to the three individuals. The individuals reported the amounts in their individual returns. The IRS contended that the corporation should be treated as a separate entity and was taxable on the income. The court first held that the corporation was a taxable entity under the *Moline Properties* test and then rejected the taxpayer's alternative contention that an agency relationship existed between the corporation and the three individuals:

> *National Carbide* makes it clear that the formal designation of "agency agreement" is not conclusive; the significant criteria, as we understand them, are whether the so-called "agent" would have made the agreement if the so-called "principals" were not its owners, and conversely whether the "principals" would have undertaken the arrangement if the "agent" were not their corporate creature. * * *

> [W]e do not doubt that the present plaintiffs fail the test. It is inconceivable that Harrison Property Management Co., Inc. would have made its alleged "agency" contract with property owners other than its own shareholders, the Harrisons, or that the latter would have agreed to such an arrangement with the corporation if they did not own and control it. Obviously the agreement was deliberately drawn, in conjunction with the special provisions of the corporate charter, so that the company would service its owners alone, and was made solely because they were its owners. The entire operating arrangement was custom-made for that very purpose. * * * In other words, all of the corporation's relations with the beneficial owners of the managed property were wholly dependent on the fact that they were the sole shareholders. * * *

The Courts of Appeals decisions preceding *Bollinger* viewed the six *National Carbide* factors as being of greater importance than did the Supreme Court in *Bollinger,* and also emphasized the fifth factor. Roccaforte v. Commissioner, 708 F.2d 986 (5th Cir.1983), rev'g, 77 T.C. 263 (1981), held that while the first four factors were relevant, in order to establish an agency relationship it was mandatory that the final two factors—relations between the principal and agent must be arms' length and the business purpose of the corporation must be to carry on the normal duties of an agent—be met. Because the Tax Court had found that the relations between the shareholders and the corporation were dependent on the fact that the "agent" was owned by the principals, the court held that a true agency had not been established. The facts upon which the non-arms' length relationship conclusion was based were that the corporation was owned by its shareholders in the same percentages that the shareholders held their interests in the partnership, which they claimed owned the property for tax purposes; the sole function of the "agent" was to borrow money in avoidance of state usury laws; and it was not compensated for its services. Similar results were reached in Frink v. Commissioner, 798 F.2d 106 (4th Cir.1986), vacated 485 U.S. 973 (1988); George v. Commissioner, 803 F.2d 144 (5th Cir.1986), vacated 485 U.S. 973 (1988); Vaughn v. United States, 740 F.2d 941 (Fed.Cir.1984). In all of these cases, the Courts of Appeals concluded that a corporation that is not compensated and that is owned by one or more of its principals could not be a true agent under the fifth *National Carbide* factor.

Several Courts of Appeals decisions, however, applied an agency rationale to avoid corporate taxation. In general, these decisions focused on the fact that the corporation was not owned proportionately by the principals. The Sixth Circuit in its opinion in *Bollinger* distinguished *Roccaforte* because in *Bollinger* the corporation's stock was not owned by the same individuals who claimed to be the principals. 807 F.2d 65 (6th Cir.1986). See also Moncrief v. United States, 730 F.2d 276 (5th Cir.1984) (corporation wholly owned by 25% partner was true agent of partnership; *Roccaforte* distinguished); Raphan v. United States, 759 F.2d 879 (Fed.Cir.1985) (principals owned no stock of agent corporation).

The above Courts of Appeals decisions might be of less relevance after *Bollinger*, if the *Bollinger* opinion signals that form will control. The Supreme Court's opinion stresses that a written agency agreement, the terms of which are respected, should be sufficient to establish the agency. Apparently these facts should suffice even in the case of an individual claiming that a wholly owned corporation is the shareholder's agent. If so, the analysis in *Harrison Property Management Co.*, discussed in *Strong* supra, is no longer valid. From the perspective of preventing tax avoidance through self-serving labeling of transactions, the *Harrison Property Management Co.* analysis is preferable to the *Bollinger* rule. On the other hand, the *Bollinger* rule appears to be more administrable than the *Harrison Property Management Co.* analysis. Some cases after *Bollinger* have confronted the situation where no written agreement exists, and the issue is whether the agency argument should be rejected on the ground that form has not been followed, or whether the court should engage in a facts-and-circumstances search for a "real" agency relationship. Heaton v. Commissioner, T.C. Memo. 1989–459, held that under *Bollinger* the absence of a written agency agreement was fatal to the taxpayer's agency claim, but the court also examined other factors to find that the taxpayer failed to satisfy every one of the *Bollinger* standards. The importance of form under the *Bollinger* standards also was emphasized in Greenberg v. Commissioner, T.C. Memo. 1989–12.

In re LeBlanc, 79 A.F.T.R.2d 97–754 (Bkrtcy.E.D.La.1997), held that *Bollinger* did not merely establish a safe harbor but established a definite standard, although less stringent than the *National Carbide* test, that must be met for a genuine agency relationship to exist. According to the *LeBlanc* court, the tripartite *Bollinger* test requires: "(1) 'the fact that the corporation is acting as agent for its shareholders with respect to a particular asset is set forth in a written agreement at the time the asset is acquired'; (2) 'the corporation functions as agent . . . with respect to the asset for all purposes'; and (3) 'the corporation is held out as the agent . . . in all dealings with third parties relating to the asset.' "

In First Chicago Corp. v. Commissioner, 96 T.C. 421 (1991), the Tax Court returned to the *National Carbide* factors to reject the taxpayer's argument that stock of a foreign corporation owned by various subsidiary members of an affiliated group of corporations was owned by the subsidiaries as agents for the parent corporation (which claimed a foreign tax credit under § 902 of the Code that is only available to a 10% stockholder of a foreign corporation). The Tax Court focused specifically on the last two *National Carbide* factors. In Bramblett v. Commissioner, 960 F.2d 526 (5th Cir.1992), a partnership sold land to a corporation owned by the partners. The corporation then developed and sold the land. The IRS denied the partnership capital gains treatment on the sale of the land, claiming that the corporation was acting as the partnership's agent in developing the land. In holding that the corporation was not the agent of the partnership, the Court of Appeals treated the *National Carbide* factors as the primary test for an agency relationship, and described *Bollinger* as a case involving additional factors that may indicate an agency relationship exists.

Apart from the broader issue of what factors generally establish a true agency relationship or, conversely, preclude a true agency relationship, the *Bollinger* opinion arguably is flawed on its particular facts in finding an agency relationship. The sole purpose and activity of the corporation was to obtain a loan at a rate that would have been usurious under state law if the loan had been made to an individual. According to the opinion in *Bollinger,* the individual rather than the corporation was taxed because the corporation was a genuine agent. If that is true, then the principal—an individual—was the true borrower, and the loan was usurious under state law. Thus the lender would have violated state law. In Commissioner v. First Security Bank of Utah, N.A., 405 U.S. 394 (1972), the Supreme Court refused to apply § 482, discussed below, to tax a bank on income received by a commonly controlled insurance company. A key element in the Court's reasoning was that it would have been illegal for the bank to have received the income. From this perspective, *Bollinger* is inconsistent with *First Security Bank of Utah.*

PROBLEM SET 2

Donald Dudley and Webster Dudley are local real estate developers, well known for developing Spindletop Industrial Park, Calumet Garden Apartments, the Moreford & McAdams Office Tower, and numerous other projects. The Dudleys generally conduct their business as a partnership under the name Dudley Brothers Construction Co. They have found in recent years that when they attempt to obtain options for, or title to, various parcels of real estate in order to put together a suitable tract for development, the owners, knowing the partnership's reputation, usually demand quite a high price for their real estate. The partners therefore propose in the future to organize a corporation for each new development, hoping thereby to disguise the identity of the partnership, and in that way obtain options or title to property at a lower price. Immediately after such a corporation, acting as a nominee for the Dudley brothers, has obtained all options or land necessary for development, the options or the land will be conveyed to the partnership for development.

The corporations will never issue any stock except for qualifying shares. The funds necessary to acquire the options or land will be contributed to the corporation by the partnership as a capital contribution as necessary. There will be only an initial meeting of each of the corporations. At that meeting the Dudleys will be elected directors and officers of the corporation and will then authorize and execute an agreement between the corporation and Dudley Brothers Construction Company providing that the corporation is only a nominee of the partnership, and that immediately upon obtaining all options or land necessary for the development title to such options or land will be conveyed to Dudley Brothers Construction Company.

The Dudley brothers have asked your advice whether the corporations will be taxed as separate corporations or whether they will be ignored for tax purposes and all of their activities attributed to Dudley Brothers Construction Company under the following fact patterns:

(a) A corporation might obtain the land and some period of time may elapse between the acquisition and the commencement of construction. To minimize carrying costs, after the acquisition but prior to transferring title of the land to Dudley Brothers Construction Company upon commencement of construction, the corporation will lease out the vacant land. For example, rural land may be rented out for farming and city land may be rented out to another company to run a parking lot. The nominee corporation would simply receive rents, deposit checks to a bank account, and immediately pay the rent over to Dudley Brothers Construction Company using its own checks.

(b) One or more of the corporations would acquire fee simple title and/or options on the land in its own name, and upon completing the acquisition would immediately transfer title to the land and/or the options to the partnership.

C. REALLOCATION OF INCOME

INTERNAL REVENUE CODE: Section 482.

Section 482 authorizes the IRS to reallocate items of income, deduction, or credit among two or more organizations, trades or businesses under common control when necessary to prevent evasion of taxes or clearly to reflect income. This provision may apply in a variety of contexts, but the common theme is that when related entities deal with one another at less than arm's length the IRS can adjust their taxable incomes to reflect the income that each would have earned had they dealt at arm's length. Thus, an increase in the income of one of the related parties, reflecting a payment that would have been made in an arm's length relationship but that was not made, must be accompanied by a correlative deduction or capitalized item for the other related party. Treas.Reg. § 1.482–1(g)(2).[13]

The extensive Regulations under § 482 are intended to ensure that taxpayers clearly reflect income attributable to controlled transactions by placing commonly controlled taxpayers on "a tax parity with an uncontrolled taxpayer by determining the true taxable income of the controlled taxpayer." Treas.Reg. § 1.482–1(a)(1). True taxable income resulting from a transaction is computed by applying an "arm's length" standard, which attempts to equate the result of a controlled transaction with the result that would have occurred if uncontrolled taxpayers had engaged in the same transaction under similar circumstances. Treas.Reg. § 1.482–1(b)(1). The Regulations provide various methods that, if followed, are deemed to result in an arm's length price. See Treas.Regs. § 1.482–2 (loans, services, and rents), § 1.482–3 (sales of tangible property), and § 1.482–4 (sales of intangible property). Although § 482 does not authorize taxpayers to invoke its terms to reallocate income or deductions, Treas.Reg. § 1.482–1(a)(3) permits a taxpayer to report income on a return using prices that vary from the prices actually charged in a controlled transaction in order to reflect an arm's length result. A § 482 reallocation makes sense only if the parties involved are subject to significantly different tax rates or regimes. Thus, § 482 is employed primarily in the international context. In some instances, however, the provision is invoked by the IRS in the purely domestic context, but there have been virtually no reported judicial decisions involving the application of § 482 in a domestic context in over 30 years. That fact could reflect that the IRS's application of § 482 domestically is moribund—but perhaps the rate changes introduced by the 2017 Tax Act could breathe new life into domestic use of § 482.

The interplay of § 482 in the context of a corporation controlled by an individual who also provides personal services on behalf of the

---

[13] Treas.Reg. § 1.482–1(g) permits taxpayers whose incomes have been adjusted under § 482 to make payments or setoffs reflecting the adjustments without further tax consequences. See Rev.Proc. 99–32, 1999–2 C.B. 296.

corporation creates difficult questions in terms of deciding what income belongs to the corporation and what income should have been earned by the individual on account of that individual's personal services, as the following case illustrates.

Victor Borge v. Commissioner
United States Court of Appeals, Second Circuit, 1968.
405 F.2d 673.

■ HAYS, CIRCUIT JUDGE:

Petitioners seek review of a decision of the Tax Court sustaining the Commissioner's determination of deficiencies in their income tax payments for the years 1958 through 1962, inclusive. The Tax Court upheld both the Commissioner's allocation to Borge under Section 482 of the Internal Revenue Code of 1954, 26 U.S.C. § 482 (1964), of a portion of the compensation received by Danica Enterprises, Inc., Borge's wholly owned corporation, for services performed by Borge as an entertainer. * * * We affirm.

From April 1952 through February 28, 1959, Borge conducted a poultry business on a 400-acre farm in Connecticut under the name of ViBo Farms. The farm business centered on and pioneered in the development and commercial sale of processed, quality chickens called rock cornish hens.

Borge incurred substantial losses in his poultry business. For each of the years 1954 through 1957 the poultry losses exceeded $50,000. In the first two months of 1958 the poultry losses amounted to $23,133, and market conditions were unfavorable. * * * Borge organized Danica, and, on March 1, 1958, transferred to the corporation, in exchange for all of its stock and a loan payable, the assets of the poultry business (except the farm real property).

Borge is a well-known professional entertainer. During the years preceding the organization of Danica he made large sums from television, stage and motion picture engagements.

Since Danica had no means of meeting the expected losses from the poultry business, Borge and Danica entered into a contract at the time of the organization of the corporation under which Borge agreed to perform entertainment and promotional services for the corporation for a 5-year period for compensation from Danica of $50,000 per year. Danica offset the poultry losses against the entertainment profits, which far exceeded the $50,000 per year it had contracted to pay Borge. Borge obviously would not have entered into such a contract with an unrelated party.

Danica did nothing to aid Borge in his entertainment business. Those who contracted with Danica for Borge's entertainment services required Borge personally to guarantee the contracts. Danica's entertainment earnings were attributable solely to the services of Borge, and Danica's only profits were from the entertainment business.

The only year during the period in dispute in which Danica actually paid Borge anything for his services was 1962, when Borge was paid the full $50,000.

The issues in controversy are (1) whether the Commissioner, acting under Section 482 of the Internal Revenue Code of 1954, 26 U.S.C. § 482 (1964), properly allocated to Borge from Danica $75,000 per year from 1958 through 1961 and $25,000 for 1962, and (2) whether the Commissioner, acting under Section 269 of the Internal Revenue Code of 1954, 26 U.S.C. § 269 (1964), properly disallowed Danica's loss deductions in excess of $50,000 per year for fiscal years 1959 through 1961 and its net loss carryovers for fiscal years 1960 through 1962.

* * *

When two or more organizations, trades or businesses, whether or not incorporated, are owned or controlled by the same interests, Section 482 of the Internal Revenue Code of 1954, 26 U.S.C. § 482 (1964), authorizes the Commissioner to apportion gross income between or among such organizations, trades or businesses if he deems that apportionment is necessary clearly to reflect income or to prevent evasion of tax. We conclude that the Commissioner could properly have found that for purposes of Section 482 Borge owned or controlled two businesses, an entertainment business and a poultry business, and that the allocation to Borge of part of the entertainment compensation paid to the corporation was not error.

We accept, as supported by the record, the Tax Court's finding: that Borge operated an entertainment business and merely assigned to Danica a portion of his income from that business; that Danica did nothing to earn or to assist in the earning of the entertainment income; that Borge would not have contracted for $50,000 per year with an unrelated party to perform the services referred to in his contract with Danica. Thus Borge was correctly held to be in the entertainment business.

At the same time Danica, Borge's wholly owned corporation, was in the poultry business.

Petitioners, relying primarily on Whipple v. Commissioner, 373 U.S. 193, 83 S.Ct. 1168, 10 L.Ed.2d 288 (1963), argue that Borge is not an "organization, trade or business" and that Section 482 is therefore inapposite.

In *Whipple* the Supreme Court held only that where one renders services to a corporation as an investment, he is not engaging in a trade or business:

"Devoting one's time and energies to the affairs of a corporation is not of itself, and without more, a trade or business of the person so engaged. Though such activities may produce income, profit or gain in the form of dividends or enhancement in the value of an investment, this return is distinctive to the process of investing and is generated by the successful operation of the corporation's business as distinguished from the trade or business of the taxpayer himself. When the only return is that of an investor, the taxpayer has not satisfied his burden of demonstrating that he is engaged in a trade or business since investing is not a trade or business and the return to the taxpayer, though substantially the product of his services, legally arises not from his own trade or business but from that of the corporation." 373 U.S. at 202, 83 S.Ct. at 1174.

Here, however, Borge was in the business of entertaining. He was not devoting his time and energies to the corporation; he was carrying on his career as an entertainer, and merely channeling a part of his entertainment income through the corporation.

Moreover, in *Whipple* petitioner was devoting his time and energies to a corporation in the hope of realizing capital gains treatment from the sale of appreciated stock. When the hoped-for appreciation did not materialize he attempted to deduct his losses as ordinary losses. The Court decided that where one stands to achieve capital gains through an investment, any losses incurred in connection with the investment are capital losses. Borge is clearly earning ordinary income; the only question is who should pay the taxes on it. Thus, *Whipple* is not apposite.

For somewhat similar reasons we find Commissioner v. Gross, 236 F.2d 612 (2d Cir. 1956), on which petitioner also seeks to rely, also inapposite.

Nor do we consider the other cases cited by petitioners persuasive. The Commissioner is not arguing here, as he did, for example, in Charles Laughton, 40 B.T.A. 101 (1939), remanded, 113 F.2d 103 (9th Cir. 1940), that the taxpayer should be taxed on the entire amount paid into the wholly owned corporation, i.e. that the corporation should be ignored. See also Pat O'Brien, 25 T.C. 376 (1955); Fontaine Fox, 37 B.T.A. 271 (1938). Instead he recognizes the existence of the corporation, but under Section 482 allocates a portion of its income to its sole shareholder who alone was responsible for the production of such income.

Petitioner contends that the Congress, in enacting the personal holding company and collapsible corporation provisions of the Code, precluded the Commissioner's action in this case under Section 482. We do not read those provisions, however, as the only available methods for dealing with the situations there involved. As the Third Circuit said in National Sec. Corp. v. Commissioner, 137 F.2d 600, 602 (3d Cir.), cert. denied, 320 U.S. 794, 64 S.Ct. 262, 88 L.Ed. 479 (1943),

"In every case in which (Section 482) is applied its application will necessarily result in an apparent conflict with the literal requirements of some other provision of the (Internal Revenue Code). If this were not so Section (482) would be wholly superfluous."

The fact that similar, but not identical, factual situations have been dealt with by legislation does not mean that this situation, because it was not also specifically dealt with by legislation, cannot be reached even by a general code provision.

We thus conclude that the Tax Court was correct in upholding the Commissioner's ruling that Borge controlled two separate businesses. See Pauline W. Ach, 42 T.C. 114 (1964), aff'd, 358 F.2d 342 (6th Cir.), cert. denied, 385 U.S. 899, 87 S.Ct. 205, 17 L.Ed.2d 131 (1966).

The Commissioner's action in allocating a part of Danica's income to Borge was based upon his conclusion that such allocation was necessary in order clearly to reflect the income of the two businesses under Borge's common control. The Commissioner's allocation has received the approval of the Tax Court. As this Court held in dealing with the predecessor of Section 482, "Whether the Tax Court was correct in allocating income to the petitioner under § 45 (of the Internal Revenue Code of 1939) is essentially one of fact and the decision below must be affirmed if supported by substantial evidence." Advance Mach. Exch. v. Commissioner, 196 F.2d 1006, 1007–08 (2d Cir.), cert. denied, 344 U.S. 835, 73 S.Ct. 45, 97 L.Ed. 650 (1952). See Int.Rev.Code of 1954, § 7482(a), 26 U.S.C. § 7482(a) (1964). Here the determination of the Commissioner and the decision of the Tax Court are supported by substantial evidence that the income of Borge's two businesses has been distorted through Borge's having arranged for Danica to receive a large part of his entertainment income although Danica did nothing to earn that income, and the sole purpose of the arrangement was to permit Danica to offset losses from the poultry business with income from the entertainment business. The amount allocated by the Commissioner ($75,000 per year) was entirely reasonable—indeed, generous—in view of the fact that Danica's annual net income from Borge's entertainment services averaged $166,465 during the years in question.

DETAILED ANALYSIS

1. APPLICATION TO TRANSACTIONS INVOLVING INDIVIDUAL SHAREHOLDERS AND THEIR CONTROLLED CORPORATIONS

In the context of transactions involving individual shareholders and their controlled corporations, § 482 has been applied to dealings such as inadequate or excessive rental agreements and to dealings between commonly controlled corporations at an inadequate or at an excessive price, such as the sale of goods or services from X Corporation to Y Corporation, both of which are owned by the same shareholders. See, e.g., Fegan v. Commissioner, 71 T.C. 791 (1979) (79% shareholder of a corporation leased a motel to the corporation for less than its fair rental value); Peck v.

Commissioner, 752 F.2d 469 (9th Cir.1985) (reallocation due to less than arm's length rental).

Virtually all of the case law involving the domestic application of § 482 arose prior to the dramatic changes in the rate structure in 1986. Accordingly, most of the cases involved an allocation of income from a corporation to individual shareholders. Under the rate structure of the late 1980s and early 1990s, in which corporate rates exceeded the maximum individual rate, the situations that were likely to raise § 482 issues were different. Between 1986 and 1993, the IRS had the incentive only to allocate income from the individual shareholders to the corporation. More recent changes to the rate structure, including a significant capital gains preference and the reduction of the corporate rate to 21% may, however, lead to a renewal of the historic pattern. The following cases (involving both income allocations to and from corporations) illustrate how the IRS and the courts have applied § 482 in the individual shareholder-corporation context.

In Cooper v. Commissioner, 64 T.C. 576 (1975), the taxpayer transferred a construction business to a corporation and retained the depreciable assets. The taxpayer did not charge the corporation with any rent. The court upheld the IRS's allocation of the fair rental value of the depreciable assets to the individual taxpayer under § 482; the taxpayer was still engaged in a trade or business by virtue of retention of assets essential to the conduct of the construction business. See also Powers v. Commissioner, 724 F.2d 64 (7th Cir.1983) (shareholder leased property from one corporation at greater than arm's length rental and subleased to another corporation at less than arm's length rental; reallocations from both corporations to shareholder upheld).

Section 482 can be applied to allocate gross income between related taxpayers regardless of whether one or both of them have taxable income or loss for the year. Treas.Reg. § 1.482–1(f)(1)(ii). In Procacci v. Commissioner, 94 T.C. 397 (1990), a partnership leased a golf course to a corporation controlled by the partners. Because the corporation's operating expenses to third parties exceeded its available funds, the corporation paid no rent to the partnership. The IRS invoked § 482 to allocate rental income to the partnership. The court rejected the taxpayer's argument that § 482 could not be applied to reallocate income from a taxpayer with net operating losses, but nevertheless held that the IRS's § 482 allocation was improper. At the time the partnership acquired the golf course, it had physically deteriorated. The partnership's goals were to improve the course to "championship status," to enhance the value of adjacent land that the partnership planned to develop, and to enable the partnership profitably to develop golf condominiums on the golf course property. Since, under the circumstances, operating expenses of the golf course were too high to permit its profitable operation, an unrelated lessee would have demanded a subsidy from the partnership. Accordingly, on the facts, the court found that a zero rental was an arm's length amount.

In some situations in which § 482 might be invoked, other principles are applied. These other rules do not necessarily require correlative adjustments such as those required under § 482. Thus, when an employee-shareholder is paid an excessive salary, the IRS often simply disallows a deduction to the corporation under § 162(a)(1) rather than invoking § 482. When a shareholder purchases or leases property from a corporation at a bargain price, the IRS asserts that the bargain element is a dividend to the shareholder. See Chapter 4. Finally, below market rate of interest loans are subject to the rules of § 7872, although § 482 also may be relevant. See Treas.Reg. § 1.482–2(a)(3).

2.   THE EXISTENCE OF "CONTROL"

The existence of control is a practical rather than formalistic question when § 482 is invoked. In Hall v. Commissioner, 32 T.C. 390 (1959) (acq.), aff'd, 294 F.2d 82 (5th Cir. 1961), a sole proprietor sold goods manufactured by him to a foreign corporation at a price considerably below his usual list price; the stock of the corporation, according to the taxpayer, was owned by his son and another. The Tax Court said that § 482 was applicable regardless of the legal ownership of the stock since the taxpayer in fact exercised control over the corporation and dominated it. The court therefore allocated a part of the corporation's income to the taxpayer by treating the sales as if made in accordance with the taxpayer's list prices. In Ach v. Commissioner, 358 F.2d 342 (6th Cir.1966), the proprietor of a profitable clothing business sold the assets of a dress business to a corporation with loss carryovers controlled by her son. The government argued that the sale should be ignored completely and the income from the dress business taxed directly to the proprietor. The Tax Court refused to take this approach ("The corporation was actually in existence, and there was a genuine transfer of assets to it that were actually used in the conduct of the dress business," 42 T.C. 114, 123 (1964)), but went on to allocate 70% of the profits of the dress business to the proprietor because of her continuing management activities. The Court of Appeals sustained the allocation.

In a case in which two unrelated taxpayers each owned 50% of the stock in a subsidiary corporation, the Tax Court originally held that the predecessor of § 482 was not applicable since the subsidiary was not "controlled" by the same interests despite the fact that the taxpayers were acting in furtherance of their common purposes. Lake Erie & Pittsburg Railway Co. v. Commissioner, 5 T.C. 558 (1945). The IRS initially acquiesced in this decision (1945 C.B. 5), but in 1965 reexamined its position and indicated that it would no longer follow the Lake Erie holding. Rev.Rul. 65–142, 1965–1 C.B. 223. Lake Erie was likewise rejected by B. Forman Co. v. Commissioner, 453 F.2d 1144 (2d Cir.1972). In that case, two unrelated corporations formed a subsidiary, in which they each owned 50% of the stock, to build and operate a shopping center next to their department stores. The court held § 482 allowed the IRS to allocate to the shareholders interest income on non-interest bearing loans made to the subsidiary: "Whether [the two shareholders] are regarded as a partnership or joint venture, de facto, in forming [the subsidiary], the conclusion is inescapable that they acted in concert in making loans without interest to a corporation, all of whose stock they owned and all of whose directors and officers were their alter egos. They were not competitors in their dealings with one another or with [the subsidiary]. Their interests in [the subsidiary] were identical. When the

Commissioner withdrew his acquiescence in *Lake Erie,* he gave reality of control as one of the reasons for doing so * * *. We agree."

3.   INADEQUATE SALARY PAID TO SHAREHOLDER-EMPLOYEES

3.1. *Background*

When individual rates substantially exceed corporate tax rates, as was the case prior to 1987 and is again the case after the 2017 Tax Act, a sole shareholder, who is also the principal officer of his corporation, might not take any salary from the corporation, planning instead to build up the value of the corporation and then sell the stock, paying tax at capital gain rates. This was the essential posture of the taxpayer in *Borge* that is introduced at the beginning of this section. In this context, the question is raised whether § 482 permits the IRS to allocate a fair salary to the shareholder (which the employee is then treated as having recontributed to the corporation) on which the shareholder-employee must pay tax. An important issue is whether the IRS can also apply the principles of § 61 and Lucas v. Earl, 281 U.S. 111 (1930), to tax the corporation's income to the shareholder-employee. Similar issues have arisen in situations in which the corporation is a personal services corporation through which the shareholder-employee renders services that he previously performed as a sole proprietor.

3.2. *Application of Section 482*

When the controlling shareholder's only relationship to the corporation is that of an investor, the IRS has not been successful in asserting § 482's application. The reason for not applying § 482 in that context is that § 482 requires two separate trades or businesses to exist, and the shareholder's status as an investor-shareholder is not a relationship that by itself rises to the level of a separate trade or business so as to implicate § 482. See Whipple v. Commissioner, 373 U.S. 193, 83 S.Ct. 1168, 10 L.Ed.2d 288 (1963). *Whipple* is cited for this proposition in *Borge* and is a leading case for this line of authority.

However, when the controlling shareholder's relationship to the corporation is more than simply that of a shareholder, then the IRS has been more successful in applying § 482 as the *Borge* decision so indicates. For example, when the controlling shareholder also serves as an employee of a controlled corporation (as was the case in *Borge*), the IRS has been able to argue that the shareholder's employment income must be reasonable in amount and satisfy the arm's length standard, and other cases are consistent with this line of reasoning. See, also, Rubin v. Commissioner, 429 F.2d 650 (2d Cir.1970), on remand, 56 T.C. 1155 (1971) (acq.), aff'd per curiam, 460 F.2d 1216 (2d Cir.1972). In *Borge*, the IRS was successful in allocating all of the entertainment income back to Victor Borge, but in other cases where § 482 applied, the application of § 482 has not resulted in an entire allocation of income. Compare Sargent v. Commissioner, 929 F.2d 1252 (8th Cir. 1991) (upholding income as earned by a personal service corporation ("Chiefy-Cat") of a hockey player for the North Stars; lower salary paid to the hockey player satisfied § 482's arm's length standard; Chiefy-Cat was formed for a bona fide business purpose; the taxpayer was a contractually bound employee of the corporation; and the corporation had a recognized contract of employment with the hockey team), with Allen Leavell v. Commissioner, 104 T.C. 140 (1995) (fees paid by the Houston Rockets to the personal service corporation of basketball player were reallocated in their entirety to the basketball player under § 482 in a decision where the Tax Court refused to follow the Eighth Circuit's decision in *Sargent* outside of the Eighth Circuit).

Even apart from the factual question of what amount of the total income received by the personal service corporation must be paid as reasonable compensation to the individual service provider in order to satisfy the arm's length standard imposed under § 482, one circuit entirely rejects the application of § 482 in the context of a personal service corporation where its controlling shareholder provides personal services exclusively to that corporation. In Foglesong v. Commissioner, T.C. Memo. 1976–294, the taxpayer was a sales representative for a pipe company. He formed a corporation that issued 98% of its common stock to him. The taxpayer's children were issued preferred stock with a stated value of $400. Thereafter, the corporation entered into an employment contract with the taxpayer and into contracts with the pipe manufacturers for whom the taxpayer sold pipe products; commissions earned on sales were paid by the manufacturers directly to the corporation, from which the taxpayer received a salary. The taxpayer's compensation over the next several years was less than two-thirds of the commissions paid to the corporation, which had no other employees or sources of income. During that period dividends of $32,000 were paid on the preferred stock; no dividends were paid on the common stock. The Tax Court weighed the legitimate business purposes for the arrangement against its tax avoidance potential and held that the taxpayer so controlled and directed the earning of the income of the corporation that he was personally taxable on 98% of such income under the principles of Lucas v. Earl.

On appeal, the Seventh Circuit Court of Appeals vacated and remanded the case. 621 F.2d 865 (7th Cir.1980). The Court of Appeals concluded that applying § 61 was imprecise and directed the Tax Court to reconsider the case based on the IRS's power to reallocate income under § 482. On remand, the Tax Court held that § 482 was properly applied to allocate 98% of the corporation's income to the taxpayer because his salary was unreasonably low. 77 T.C. 1102 (1981). The Tax Court applied its earlier decision in Keller v. Commissioner, 77 T.C. 1014 (1981), discussed further below, to hold that the requisite "two organizations" existed: Foglesong was in the trade or business of selling pipe as an employee of the corporation, and the corporation was in the trade or business of selling pipe (through the efforts of Foglesong). The taxpayer appealed again, and the Court of Appeals vacated and remanded the decision a second time. A different panel held that § 482 could not be invoked to allocate income from a personal service corporation to its shareholder-employee who performs services solely for the corporation. The Court of Appeals did not consider the "two organizations" requirement to have been met.

The IRS does not follow the Seventh Circuit Court of Appeals decision in *Foglesong*. Rev.Rul. 88–38, 1988–1 C.B. 246. Similarly, notwithstanding the reversal by the Seventh Circuit in *Foglesong*, the Tax Court continues to hold that § 482 can be applied to allocate income between a corporation and a shareholder-employee who performs services solely for a controlled corporation, at least where appeal does not lie to the Seventh Circuit. See Haag v. Commissioner, 88 T.C. 604 (1987) (income of professional service corporation reallocated to physician-sole shareholder who drew nominal salary).

In determining whether a reallocation of income is appropriate under § 482, the inquiry is whether the shareholder-employee's total compensation (including salary, bonuses, deferred compensation, and other fringe benefits) approximates the amount he would have received absent incorporation of the business. See Keller v. Commissioner, 77 T.C. 1014 (1981), aff'd, 723 F.2d 58 (10th Cir.1983) (§ 482 applicable, but on facts no reallocation was warranted because total compensation approximated preincorporation earnings).

3.3. *Applicability of Assignment of Income Principles*

Because the Tax Court relies on § 482 in cases of nominal compensation to controlling shareholder-employees, it applies § 61 and Lucas v. Earl only in cases in which the corporation does not control the income. In Johnson v. Commissioner, 78 T.C. 882 (1982), aff'd by order, 734 F.2d 20 (9th Cir.1984), the Tax Court promulgated a two part test for determining when the corporation controls the income: "First, the service-performer employee must be just that—an employee of the corporation whom the corporation has the right to direct or control in some meaningful sense. Second, there must exist between the corporation and the person or entity using the services a contract or other similar indicium recognizing the corporation's controlling position." In that case the individual taxpayer, a professional basketball player, was held to control the income because even though the team for which he played paid the salary directly to the corporation, the only contract was between the player and the team. In contrast, in *Haag*, supra, the corporation was treated as controlling the income, because the individual and corporation entered into an employment contract and the recipients of services treated the services as being rendered by the corporation.

3.4. *Section 269A—Reallocation of Personal Service Corporation Income*

Due to taxpayer successes in navigating § 482 in the personal service corporation context, Congress enacted another provision to address this factual context but through a different means. In Keller v. Commissioner, 77 T.C. 1014 (1981) aff'd 723 F.2d 58 (10th Cir. 1983), the physician shareholder of the professional service corporation involved in the case had been a partner in a medical partnership prior to formation of the corporation. Thereafter, Dr. Keller's professional service corporation was substituted for him as a partner. The purpose of this arrangement was to permit Dr. Keller to custom-tailor a deferred compensation and fringe benefit plan for himself, which could permit evasion of the nondiscrimination rules with respect to pension plans and statutory fringe benefits. The Tax Court refused to apply § 482 in this context because the total compensation (both current and deferred compensation arrangements) were arm's length in amount. Congress responded to the *Keller* decision with the enactment of § 269A. See H.R.Rep. No. 97–760, 97th Cong., 2d Sess. 633–34 (1982). This provision authorizes reallocation of income from a personal service corporation to the employee-owner if (1) the principal purpose of forming or using the corporation is the avoidance of federal income tax by reducing the income of any employee-owner; (2) the corporation performs substantially all of its services on behalf of one other corporation, person, or partnership; and (3) substantially all of the services provided by the corporation are performed by employees who own more than 10% of the stock. Thus, § 269A does not apply to personal services corporations with more than one customer, which is normally the case or, for example, if ten physicians form a corporation to provide emergency room services exclusively to one hospital and each physician owns 10% of the stock. For the mechanics of the reallocation under § 269A, see Prop.Reg. § 1.269A–1 (1983), 1983–1 C.B. 1052. As noted previously, the 1982 Act made several changes in the treatment of qualified deferred compensation plans that greatly reduced the tax benefits from personal service corporations. These changes have reduced the number of incorporations to which § 269A might be applied.

PROBLEM SET 3

Georgia, an individual, owns all of the stock of Malific Xenophobe Oil Distributing Corporation, which not only has not shown a profit, but has consistently lost money in every year since Georgia acquired the stock. Georgia also conducted an oil and gas equipment leasing business as a sole proprietor. Georgia's largest drilling rig normally leases for $1,000 a day. Recently Malific Xenophobe used Georgia's drilling rig for 60 days, and because Malific Xenophobe's reserves and credit were insufficient to permit it both to pay its workers and pay Georgia $60,000, Georgia rented the drilling rig to Malific Xenophobe for the 60 days for $5,000. What are the tax consequences to Georgia and Malific Xenophobe?

D. THE STEP TRANSACTION DOCTRINE

One of the key challenges for lawyers is to synthesize the highly technical provisions that apply to entities taxed under Subchapter C. Understanding the technical rules of Subchapter C and how they interact is, however, only part of the challenge. The preceding discussion illustrated situations when a corporation may be disregarded or treated as an agent as well as situations when the IRS may use other tools—such as § 482 or § 269A—to re-allocate tax items. These are but one subset of tools that may be relevant to the IRS and taxpayers in determining whether form or substance controls. For example, taxpayers (and their lawyers) must also determine whether formally separate steps should be substantively analyzed as a combined transaction or whether each individual step should be respected. The combining of steps and testing the several transaction steps as though they were one unified transaction implicates what has come to be called the step transaction doctrine.

The classic articulation of the step transaction doctrine is found in Minnesota Tea Co. v. Helvering, 302 U.S. 609, 613 (1938): "A given result at the end of a straight path is not made a different result because reached by following a devious path." When this judicial doctrine is applied, the tax treatment of several transactions is determined by examining their overall effect rather than giving effect to each of the several transactions in sequence. In some cases, however, the form of a transaction will be allowed to control.

In order to evaluate whether the step transaction doctrine will be applied, it is important to know the legally relevant standard that a court would apply to a particular transaction. A succinct analysis of the various formulations of the step transaction doctrine (the binding commitment test, the end result test, and the mutually interdependent test) is set forth in Penrod v. Commissioner, which is reproduced below. In *Penrod*, the Tax Court eventually concluded that the step transaction doctrine should not apply in that particular case regardless of its formulation. A more difficult factual situation is, however, presented where the facts might pose a step transaction concern under the broadest formulation of the step transaction doctrine but would not pose a step transaction concern under a narrower formulation. Thus, the particular formulation of the step transaction doctrine can make a substantive difference in the outcome. In the chapters to follow, you will come to understand that in some contexts the step transaction doctrine will not apply at all because the chosen form is a matter of taxpayer election blessed by Congress, the Treasury, and/or the IRS, while in other contexts only the narrowest formulation (the binding commitment test) will be used. In still other situations (such as in tax-free reorganizations), the step transaction doctrine's formulation may reach its broadest formulation (the end result test). In actual practice, a taxpayer (and the taxpayer's lawyer) confronted with a series of transaction steps must determine which formulation of the step transaction doctrine is likely to be applied and then determine whether the specific facts satisfy the criteria necessary for the step transaction doctrine to apply.

The result of applying the step transaction doctrine, as articulated in Minnesota Tea Co. v. Helvering, 302 U.S. 609, 613 (1938), is to combine steps so that the tax result is viewed in terms of the overall transaction. At times, however, the courts have been invited to utilize the step transaction doctrine not to integrate separate steps but rather to treat the steps as happening in a different order from how they actually occurred. Resequencing of transaction steps remains a very real possibility in the context of "bootstrap" acquisitions (discussed in Chapter 9), but, outside of the bootstrap acquisition context, a significant line of judicial authority is resistant to the idea that separate steps that have economic significance are subject to being resequenced. The decision in Esmark v. Commissioner, excerpted below, rejected the use of the step transaction doctrine as a justification for reordering transaction steps that have independent legal significance. The case suggests that the step transaction doctrine can and does combine multiple steps into a unified transaction, but the resequencing of steps is rarely appropriate.

Penrod v. Commissioner

Tax Court of the United States, 1987.
88 T.C 1415.

[Eds.: The taxpayers in this case argued that they were entitled to tax-free treatment for an exchange of stock in one corporation for stock in McDonald's under the § 368 reorganization provision. The government argued that the taxpayers' subsequent sale of the McDonald's stock caused the original transaction to be ineligible for § 368 reorganization treatment because, in effect, the transaction appeared to the IRS to have been an exchange of stock for the ultimate receipt of cash not eligible for nonrecognition treatment.]

* * *

The resolution of this issue turns on the application of the so-called step transaction doctrine. The step transaction doctrine is in effect another rule of substance over form; it treats a series of formally separate "steps" as a single transaction if such steps are in substance integrated, interdependent, and focused toward a particular result. * * * There is no universally accepted test as to when and how the step transaction doctrine should be applied to a given set of facts. Courts have applied three alternative tests in deciding whether to invoke the step transaction doctrine in a particular situation.

The narrowest alternative is the "binding commitment" test, under which a series of transactions are collapsed if, at the time the first step is entered into, there was a binding commitment to undertake the later step. * * * The binding commitment test has the advantage of promoting certainty in the tax planning of shareholders. Under such test, a court must make an objective determination as to whether the acquired shareholders were bound by an obligation to sell the shares received in an acquisition. Other factors, such as intent by such shareholders to sell their shares, are not considered. However, there have been objections to that test on the ground that the result is easily manipulable by taxpayers. As the court observed in King Enterprises, Inc. v. United States, 418 F.2d 511, 518 (Ct. Cl. 1969), "the step transaction doctrine would be a dead letter if restricted to situations where the parties were *bound* to take certain steps." (Emphasis in original).

At the other extreme, the most far-reaching alternative is the "end result" test. Under this test, the step transaction doctrine will be invoked if it appears that a series of formally separate steps are really pre-arranged parts of a single transaction intended from the outset to reach the ultimate result. The end result test is based upon the actual intent of the parties as of the time of the merger. It can be argued that any test which requires a court to make a factual determination as to a party's intent promotes uncertainty and therefore impedes effective tax planning. However, in contrast to the binding commitment test, the end result test is flexible and bases tax consequences on the real substance of the transactions, not on the formalisms chosen by the participants.

The third test is the "interdependence" test, which focuses on whether 'the steps are so interdependent that the legal relations created by one transaction would have been fruitless without a completion of the series. This test concentrates on the relationship between the steps, rather than on their 'end result.' * * * However, since the interdependence test requires a court to find whether the individual steps had independent significance or whether they had meaning only as part of the larger transaction, the court may be called upon to determine the result the participants hoped to achieve. Thus, the interdependence test is a variation of the end result test.

Courts have applied each of these three alternatives to a variety of transactions to determine whether the transactions should be "stepped." * * * [Eds.: The opinion then analyzed various decided cases that had applied differing formulations of the step transaction doctrine.] In the present case, there was no binding commitment by the Penrods at the time of the acquisition to sell their stock. However, we need not decide whether the absence of a binding commitment, standing alone, is sufficient to prevent the application of the step transaction doctrine; after carefully examining and evaluating all the circumstances surrounding the acquisition and subsequent sale of the McDonald's stock received by the Penrods, we have concluded that, at the time of the acquisition, the Penrods did not intend to sell their McDonald's stock and that therefore the step transaction doctrine is not applicable under either the interdependence test or the end result test.

Esmark v. Commissioner

Tax Court of the United States, 1988.
90 T.C. 171.

* * *

We recently described the step-transaction doctrine as another rule of substance over form that "treats a series of formally separate 'steps' as a single transaction if such steps are in substance integrated, interdependent, and focused toward a particular result." Penrod v. Commissioner, 88 T.C. 1415, 1428 (1987). Respondent contends that Mobil's acquisition and subsequent disposition of petitioner's shares were simply steps in an integrated transaction designed to result in Mobil's acquisition of Vickers and petitioner's redemption of its stock.

That Mobil's tender offer was but part of an overall plan is not in dispute. The existence of an overall plan does not alone, however, justify application of the step-transaction doctrine. Whether invoked as a result of the "binding commitment," "interdependence over" or "end result" tests, the doctrine combines a series of individually meaningless steps into a single transaction. In this case, respondent has pointed to no meaningless or unnecessary steps that should be ignored.

Petitioner had two objectives: a disposition of its energy business and a redemption of a substantial portion of its stock. Three direct routes to these objectives were available. * * * No route was more "direct" than the others. Each route required two steps, and each step involved two of three interested parties. Each route left petitioner, petitioner's shareholders, and the purchaser in the same relative positions. Faced with this choice, petitioner chose the path expected to result in the least tax.

Respondent proposes to recharacterize the tender offer/redemption as a sale of the Vickers shares to Mobil followed by a self-tender. This recharacterization does not simply combine steps; it invents new ones. Courts have refused to apply the step-transaction doctrine in this manner. * * * In this case, in contrast, there were no steps without independent function. Each of the steps—the purchase of petitioner's stock by Mobil and the redemption of that stock by petitioner—had permanent economic consequences. In an economic sense, there is no difference between the form chosen by petitioner and the "substance" alleged by respondent. * * * We believe that ad hoc extension of doctrine [to authorize resequencing of transaction steps in lieu of combining steps] to achieve a result on any of the difficult issues in this case is unwarranted and unwise.

CHAPTER 2

FORMATION OF THE CORPORATION

SECTION 1. RECEIPT OF STOCK FOR PROPERTY

A. BASIC PRINCIPLES

INTERNAL REVENUE CODE: Sections 351(a), (b), (d); 357; 358(a), (b)(1); 362(a); 362(e)(2); 1032; 1223(1), (2).

REGULATIONS: Sections 1.351–1(a); 1.358–2(b)(2); 1.1032–1(a), (d).

When its requirements are met, § 351 permits a taxpayer to exchange property for stock of a transferee corporation without the current recognition of gain. Under § 351, gain or loss is not recognized on the transfer of property to a corporation solely in exchange for stock[1] of the corporation if immediately after the transaction the transferor or transferors collectively "control" the corporation. "Control" requires that the transferor or transferors collectively own at least 80% of the voting stock and 80% of each class of nonvoting stock of the transferee corporation. Section 351 permits the incorporation of a proprietorship, a partnership (including a limited liability company), or a new business without the recognition of gain, and prevents the recognition of loss. The section also permits the tax-free creation of a subsidiary corporation by another corporation. In addition, § 351 applies to the transfer of property to an existing corporation in exchange for stock if after the exchange the transferor (or transferors) meet the stock ownership requirement.

When the nonrecognition rule of § 351 applies to the exchange of property for stock, § 358 provides that the basis of stock received in exchange for the property contributed to the corporation will be the same as the basis of property transferred to the corporation. Section 362(a) generally provides the corporation with a basis in the property equal to the transferor's basis, as long as the transferor's basis for the property does not exceed its fair market value. When the basis of the transferred property exceeds it fair market value, § 362(e)(2) limits the aggregate basis of all property transferred to the corporation by any particular transferor to the aggregate fair market value of the transferred property.

Section 351 overrides the rule of § 1001(c), which generally requires recognition of gain or loss on the exchange of one property for another property. Thus, unless the conditions of § 351 have been met, a person

---

[1] Prior to an amendment in 1989, § 351 nonrecognition treatment also applied if the corporation issued "securities," generally long-term debt, along with stock. As a result of the amendment, the transfer of appreciated property for anything other than stock is a recognition event.

who transfers property to a corporation in exchange for stock of the transferee corporation must recognize gain or loss. One court described the purpose of § 351 to defer recognition of gain or loss in "transactions where gain or loss may have accrued in a constitutional sense, but where in popular and economic sense there has been a mere change in the form of ownership and the taxpayer has not really 'cashed in' on the theoretical gain, or closed out a losing venture." Portland Oil Co. v. Commissioner, 109 F.2d 479, 488 (1st Cir.1940). This explanation is a bit of hyperbole, since § 351 permits taxpayers to significantly rearrange the benefits and burdens of the ownership of property in a way that permits them to realize real and not merely theoretical economic gain. While this judicial description of the impact of § 351 might have some grain of truth in the case of the incorporation of a sole proprietorship or the formation of a corporate subsidiary, it is wholly specious where a number of taxpayers transfer various different properties to a newly formed corporation and each of them receives a number of shares that taken alone constitute less than substantially all of the shares of stock of the corporation.

Section 351 applies regardless of the intent of the taxpayer if the conditions of the section are in fact satisfied. Gus Russell, Inc. v. Commissioner, 36 T.C. 965 (1961). In situations covered by § 351, if the taxpayer is seeking the advantage of nonrecognition of gain on the transfer, the conditions of the section represent requirements to be satisfied. On the other hand, if the assets to be transferred have decreased in value, so that a loss would be realized on their transfer, the transferor might desire a recognition transaction. But if § 351 applies, the loss will not be recognized. In such a case, the qualifying conditions of § 351 represent factors to be avoided if the loss is to be recognized. Similarly, since the corporation succeeds to the transferor's basis if § 351 applies, the taxpayer might in some limited cases be willing to recognize gain in order to obtain for the corporation a depreciable basis equal to the fair market value of the transferred assets instead of the lower basis that it would obtain if the gain were not recognized. In this case also, the conditions of the section must be avoided if such a stepped-up basis is to be obtained.

Although by its terms § 351(a) applies only if the transferor receives stock as the sole consideration for the transfer of property to a controlled corporation, § 351(b) allows for the receipt of cash or other property— "boot" in tax jargon. When boot is received in addition to stock, the transferor's realized gain is recognized to the extent of the money and the fair market value of other property, which includes cash and debt obligations of the transferee corporation, received as boot.[2] Loss, however, is never recognized even though boot may be present. I.R.C. § 351(b)(2). However, under § 358(a) the transferor's basis in stock received is adjusted to reflect the receipt and taxation of the boot. The

---

[2] In both respects, § 351 operates in much the same manner as § 1031 (like-kind exchanges).

corporation's basis in property received is increased by gain recognized to the transferor. I.R.C. § 362(a).

Generally, § 351 provides nonrecognition regardless of whether the transferor receives common stock, preferred stock, or a hybrid, such as participating preferred stock. However, under § 351(g) certain types of preferred stock that have characteristics that cause the stock more nearly to resemble a debt instrument are treated as boot. If a particular transferor receives only nonqualified preferred stock in exchange for property, § 351 does not apply to that transferor at all, and § 1001(c) applies.

The main requirement of § 351, apart from the question of boot, is acquisition of control by the transferors. As defined in § 368(c), control requires that the transferor, or in the case of multiple transferors in related transactions, the transferors collectively, own at least 80% of the stock of the transferee corporation immediately after the exchange. This requirement normally will be satisfied on an incorporation, with problems arising only if there is an immediate transfer of stock to a person not transferring property to the corporation. As a result, the control requirement is most significant with respect to transfers to an existing corporation.

Where incorporation of a proprietorship or partnership is contemplated, it is likely that the properties involved will be subject to liabilities. In taxable transactions, the assumption of a liability by the transferee or the taking of property subject to a liability is ordinarily regarded as additional consideration paid by the transferee to the transferor. The application of this rule to § 351 transactions would frequently produce boot in the amount of the liabilities, which would frustrate § 351's underlying policy of facilitating the transition from the unincorporated to the corporate form. Consequently, § 357 provides that the corporate assumption of a liability or the corporate acquisition of property subject to a liability does not constitute boot for the purpose of § 351, unless a tax avoidance scheme is involved or unless the liabilities assumed exceed the basis of the property transferred. While the liability is not considered boot for purposes of gain recognition, its assumption by the corporation provides an economic benefit equivalent to the transfer of money by the corporation to the shareholder since the shareholder will no longer be obligated to repay the debt. Accordingly, § 358(d) provides that solely for the purpose of computing the transferor's basis in the stock received in the exchange, liabilities of the transferor that are assumed by the corporation are treated as money received. This results in decreasing the transferor's basis for the stock received in the exchange.

If liabilities assumed by the corporation and/or liabilities encumbering transferred property exceed the transferor's basis in the transferred property, § 357(c) requires the transferor to recognize gain to the extent the liabilities exceed the total basis of transferred property. In such a case, appropriate adjustments to both the shareholder's basis in the stock received in the exchange and the corporation's basis in the assets received in the exchange are required by § 358(a) and § 361(a), respectively.

The corporate transferee also avoids recognition of gain or loss upon the issuance of its stock. Section 1032 provides nonrecognition treatment to a corporate transferee on the issuance of its stock in exchange for cash, property, or services, regardless of whether the person to whom the stock is issued is accorded nonrecognition under § 351. If the transferor of property to the corporation is accorded nonrecognition under § 351, under § 362(a)(1) the basis of transferred property in the hands of the transferee corporation is the same as the basis of the transferred property in the hands of the transferor, plus any gain recognized by the transferor on the exchange.

Suppose A transfers a building worth $100,000, with an adjusted basis of $10,000, to a newly created corporation in return for 100 shares of its stock, and, as part of the same planned transaction, B transfers land worth $50,000, with a basis of $40,000, to the corporation in exchange for 50 shares of its stock. Because A and B together control the corporation, neither A nor B recognizes any gain. Under § 358(a), A's basis for the 100 shares of stock is $10,000, and B's basis for the 50 shares of stock is $40,000. Under § 362(a)(1), the corporation's basis for the building is $10,000, and its basis in the land is $40,000.

If the corporation had been in existence and was owned by both A and B and it had issued to A both 70 shares of stock and $30,000 cash for the building, while issuing only an additional 50 shares of stock to B, A would have realized a gain of $90,000, but would have been required to recognize a gain of only $30,000 (the extent of the boot, assuming that the value of the stock was $70,000 and assuming that no dividend was involved); A's basis in the stock would be $10,000; the corporation would have a basis in the building of $40,000 ($10,000 basis in transferor A's hands, plus gain of $30,000 recognized by A). The consequences to B would be unchanged.

The corporation's basis in an asset under § 362(a) is thus dependent only on the transferor shareholder's basis in the transferred assets and the amount of gain, if any, that is recognized by the shareholder. It does not depend upon nor is it affected by any actual cost that the corporation may incur. Hence, in the example, where the corporation paid out $30,000 cash as well as stock, if the shareholder's basis for the building had been exactly equal to the value of the stock and the cash received, so that the shareholder realized and recognized neither gain nor loss, the corporation's basis for the building would still be the same as that of the shareholder. The corporation's basis for the building would not be increased by the $30,000 cash that it paid.

If § 351 is applicable, the combined effect of the two basis provisions, § 358(a) and § 362(a)(1), is to produce the possibility of two gains—the gain on the sale of the stock and the gain on the sale of the property transferred to the corporation—where only one existed before. However, a subsequent recognition of the shareholder's gain may be postponed if the stock is later transferred in a tax-free transaction, e.g., a reorganization. Furthermore, if the stock is held by an individual shareholder until death, one of the two gains or losses is eliminated by the rule of § 1014, which provides for a basis equal to the value of the stock at the date of death. Although at first blush, the combined effect of § 358(a) and § 362(a)(1) also appears to raise the possibility of two losses—the loss on the sale of the stock and the loss on the sale of the property transferred to the corporation—where only one existed before, § 362(e)(2), discussed below, generally prevents this from occurring.

Where the shareholder transfers a capital asset or a § 1231 asset in exchange for stock in a § 351 transaction, § 1223(1) provides that the shareholder's holding period for the stock includes the period for which the shareholder held the capital asset or § 1231 asset. Similarly, § 1223(2) provides that the corporation's holding period for any capital asset or § 1231 asset received in an exchange to which § 351 applies to the shareholder includes the period for which the transferor shareholder held the capital or § 1231 asset. If a mix of assets, only some of which qualify for a tacked holding period for the shareholder under § 1223(1), are transferred to the corporation, a proportionate number of shares (by value) should be assigned a tacked holding period and the remaining shares should take a holding period beginning with the exchange. See Runkle v. Commissioner, 39 B.T.A. 458 (1939).

If § 351 is not applicable—for example, if in the immediately preceding example A and B lacked control of the corporation immediately after the transfer because they had a pre-existing obligation to sell the stock received in the exchange to a third party—the shareholders' entire gain would be recognized under § 1001(c). A and B would take a cost basis in the stock under § 1012, and they would not be able to use § 1223(1) to obtain a tacked holding period. The corporation would, however, continue to rely on § 1032, and the basis of the building and land in the corporation's hands would be determined under § 1012 cost basis principles even though the corporation would not recognize gain on the transfer of its own stock. Treas.Reg. § 1.1032–1(d). Case law applying § 1012 to property exchanges outside of the § 1032 context generally provide that cost basis is determined with reference to the fair market value of the property received (e.g., Philadelphia Park Amusement Co. v. United States, 126 F. Supp. 184 (Ct. Cl. 1954)), but in the case of a corporation using its own stock, Rev.Rul. 56–100, 956–1 C.B. 624, specifies that, if it is available, the value of the stock transferred should be used to determine the corporation's cost basis in the received assets. The corporation would not have the benefit of § 1223(2).

DETAILED ANALYSIS

1. "PROPERTY": CASH AND PROMISSORY NOTES

For purposes of § 351, "property" includes cash. Rev.Rul. 69–357, 1969–1 C.B. 101. Since gain and loss can never be recognized on the purchase of stock for cash, the importance of Rev.Rul. 69–357 lies in the principle that a transferor of cash can be included in the control group along with transferors of appreciated or depreciated property.

A shareholder who issues the shareholder's own promissory note to the corporation in exchange for stock should be treated in the same manner as one who pays cash to the corporation for stock for purposes of determining the control group. Section 351 is not necessary to provide nonrecognition to the shareholder who gives the corporation the shareholder's own promissory note for the stock. Under general tax principles, the issuance of the shareholder's note to acquire the stock is not a realization event for the shareholder issuing the note. See Treas.Reg. § 1.61–12(c)(1). Further, there really has not been any "exchange" of "property" because the note does not exist as an item of property until ownership vests in the corporation. Thus, the transaction should be considered a stock purchase for purposes of determining the obligor-shareholder's tax consequences.

The term "property" also includes accounts receivable, regardless of whether the transferor used the cash or accrual method of accounting, Rev.Rul. 80–198, 1980–2 C.B. 113, as well as § 453 installment notes owned by the transferor that were received from another person in a prior transaction. Under Treas.Reg. § 1.453–9(c)(2), in general no gain or loss results from the transfer of installment obligations to a corporation in an exchange to which § 351 applies despite the fact that part of the tax on the installment gain may in effect be shifted to the other shareholders.[3]

Section 351 may apply to transfers to an existing corporation as well as to transfers to a newly organized corporation, provided the control requirement is met. Thus, the question can arise of whether a transfer of outstanding indebtedness of an existing corporation in exchange for stock of that corporation can qualify for nonrecognition under § 351. This will be particularly important if the transferor purchased the indebtedness at less than face value, and the value of the stock received in exchange for the debt instrument exceeds its basis to the shareholder. The question also arises of whether the corporation's obligation is a § 453 installment obligation in the hands of the shareholder. Sections 351(d)(2) and (3) provide that stock issued to satisfy an indebtedness of the issuing corporation not evidenced by a security, or to pay interest on indebtedness of the issuing corporation, is not considered as issued in return for property. Rev.Rul. 73–423, 1973–2 C.B. 161, held that where the obligor on the installment obligation is the corporation itself, then the § 351 transaction constitutes a "satisfaction" of the installment obligation under § 453B(a) and results in a tax to the

---

[3] Section 453B replaced former § 453(d), which is the provision under which Treas.Reg. § 1.453–9(c)(2) was promulgated. A Regulation project is underway to move the rule into a new § 453B Regulation. Prop.Reg. § 1.453B–1(c)(1) (2014).

transferor. When finalized, Prop.Reg. § 1.453B–1(c)(2) (2014), will formalize this holding.

Section 351(e)(2) provides that § 351 is not applicable if a corporation in a bankruptcy or insolvency proceeding transfers assets to another corporation and then distributes the stock received to its creditors. The transaction is treated as if the assets had first been distributed to the creditors and the creditors had then transferred the property to the new corporation. Furthermore, if the corporation is solvent and not in bankruptcy,[4] and the sum of the principal amount of the debt, whether or not represented by a security, plus accrued but unpaid interest, exceeds the fair market value of the stock issued in the transaction, then pursuant to § 108(e)(8), the corporation is treated as having satisfied the indebtedness with an amount of money equal to the fair market value of the stock. As a result, the transaction produces cancellation of debt income for the corporation under § 61(a)(12) to the extent the amount of the debt exceeds the value of the stock. Section 1032 does not apply to the cancellation of debt income.

2.   SHAREHOLDER'S STOCK BASIS

2.1. *Generally*

If the shareholder receives stock of different classes, e.g., some common stock and some preferred stock, the shareholder's aggregate basis in all of the stock must be allocated among the stock of different classes in proportion to the fair market values of the stock in each class. I.R.C. § 358(b)(1); Treas.Reg. § 1.358–2(b)(2). Thus, for example, if A transfers real property with a basis of $20 and fair market value of $100 to X, a controlled corporation, in a nonrecognition transaction under § 351, and A receives in exchange common stock with a value of $80 and preferred stock with a value of $20, A's substituted basis in the common stock is $16 ($20 × $80/$100) and A's substituted basis in the preferred stock is $4 ($20 × $20/100). The shareholder cannot allocate the basis of some transferred assets to one block of stock, for example, preferred stock, and the lower basis of other assets to another block of stock. See Rev.Rul. 85–164, 1985–2 C.B. 117.

Under general principles of taxation, stock in a corporation acquired in exchange for the shareholder's promissory note takes a § 1012 cost basis equal to the principal amount of the note (assuming the note bears adequate interest). See Treas.Reg. § 1.1012–1(g); Rev.Rul. 2004–37, 2004–1 C.B. 583.

2.2. *Special Rule for Stock Received in Exchange for Stock of Another Corporation*

Regulations proposed in 2009 would have adopted the tracing principles of Treas.Reg. § 1.358–2 applicable to stock-for-stock exchanges in corporate reorganizations, see Chapter 10. Under this approach, in the case of a § 351 exchange in which stock of another corporation is transferred to the corporation, and no liabilities are assumed, the basis of each share of stock received in the exchange will be the same as the basis of the share or shares

---

[4]   Any cancellation of debt income realized by an insolvent or bankrupt debtor is excluded from gross income to the extent provided by § 108(a)(1).

transferred in exchange. The 2009 Proposed Regulations contained rules for basis if different blocks were transferred or if more or fewer shares were received than were transferred. The Proposed Regulations were withdrawn in March 2019, with the Treasury explaining, "After thoroughly considering the comments received, the Treasury Department and the IRS have determined that it is unlikely that the approach of the 2009 Proposed Regulations can be implemented in comprehensive final regulations without significant modifications. . . . The Treasury Department and the IRS are continuing to study the issues addressed in the 2009 Proposed Regulations." 84 Fed. Reg. 11686 (Mar. 28, 2019).

3.   TAX CONSEQUENCES TO THE ISSUING CORPORATION

Section 1032, which applies both to newly issued stock and treasury stock, provides that the issuance of its own stock is not a taxable event for the corporation. Thus, whether or not the shareholders are eligible to use § 351, § 1032 provides nonrecognition of the "profit" realized by a corporation purchasing and reissuing its own shares.

If § 351 applies to the shareholders, § 362(a) governs the basis the corporation takes in the property received (discussed below). If the transaction does not fall under § 351, Treas.Reg. § 1.1032–1(d) provides that the basis of the property acquired by the corporation in exchange for its stock is a "cost" basis under § 1012. As noted briefly above, Rev.Rul. 56–100, 1956–1 C.B. 624, interprets this provision to require that the property received by the corporation in a taxable exchange not subject to § 351 be assigned a basis in the corporation's hands equal to the fair market value of the stock exchanged for the property, and not the fair market value of the property received, if those values differ. The ruling notes, "Evidence as to the fair market value of the assets received is admissible to show the fair market value of the stock used in making the acquisition, but is of less weight than available direct evidence of the fair market value of such stock." Case law also has consistently reached this result. See, e.g., FX Systems Corp. v. Commissioner, 79 T.C. 957 (1982); see also Pittsburgh Terminal Corp. v. Commissioner, 60 T.C. 80, aff'd by order, 500 F.2d 1400 (3d Cir. 1974) (addressing cost basis valuation when stock value is not available).

4.   THE CORPORATION'S ASSET BASIS

4.1. *Multiple Asset Transfers*

When a shareholder exchanges more than one item of property solely for stock in a § 351 transfer, the corporation's basis in each item of property is the same as it was in the hands of the shareholder. See I.R.C. § 362(a); P.A. Birren & Son v. Commissioner, 116 F.2d 718 (7th Cir.1940); Gunn v. Commissioner, 25 T.C. 424, 438 (1955), aff'd per curiam, 244 F.2d 408 (10th Cir.1957). Thus, for example, if the shareholder transfers Blackacre, with a basis of $100 and a fair market value of $300 and Whiteacre with a basis of $200 and a fair market value of $300, the basis of each property remains the same. The aggregate basis of $300 is not reallocated among the properties. The problems encountered in allocating a basis increase attributable to the transferor's recognized gain when multiple assets are involved are discussed later in this Chapter.

4.2. *Limitations on Built-In Losses*

4.2.1. *Anti-Loss Duplication Rules for Transferred Built-In Loss Property*

Section 362(e)(2) prevents taxpayers from transmuting a single economic loss into two (or more) tax losses by taking advantage of the dual application of the substituted basis rules in § 358 for stock received in a § 351 transaction and in § 362 for assets transferred to a corporation in a § 351 transaction. If the aggregate basis of the property transferred to a corporation by any one transferor in a § 351 transaction exceeds the aggregate fair market value, the aggregate basis of the property must be reduced to its fair market value. Thus, for example, if A transfers Blackacre, with a basis of $1,000 and a fair market value of $600 to newly formed X Corporation in exchange for all of the X Corporation stock, X Corporation's $1,000 basis in Blackacre, determined under § 362(a), will be reduced to $600 under § 362(e)(2). Alternatively, pursuant to § 362(e)(2)(C),[5] A and X Corporation may jointly elect to reduce A's basis in the X Corporation stock, which here is otherwise an exchanged basis of $1,000 pursuant to § 358, to its fair market value, here presumably $600, with the transferee, X Corporation, taking a normal transferred basis in Blackacre under § 362(a)—here $1,000.

The operation of § 362(e)(2) is more complex where multiple assets are involved. When a transferor transfers some appreciated property, § 362(e)(2) does not necessarily result in the basis of every item of loss property being reduced to its fair market value. Section 362(e)(2)(A) requires that the aggregate basis of the transferred property be reduced by the excess of the aggregate basis over the aggregate fair market value, and § 362(e)(2)(B) requires that the aggregate basis reduction be allocated among the transferred properties in proportion to the built-in losses in the properties before taking into account § 362(e)(2). Assume, for example, that B transferred three properties to newly formed Y Corporation in exchange for all of the stock: a copyright, fair market value $4,500, basis $3,000; land, fair market value $7,000, basis $9,000; and a machine, fair market value $4,000, basis $5,000. The aggregate fair market value of the three properties is $15,500 and their aggregate basis is $17,000, thus requiring a basis reduction of $1,500 ($17,000 − $15,500) with respect to the land and the machine, the two properties with a basis that exceeds fair market value. The land has a built-in loss of $2,000 and the machine has a built-in loss of $1,000. The $1,500 basis reduction is allocated 2/3 to the land ($2,000/($2,000 + $1,000)), and 1/3 to the machine ($1,000/($2,000 + $1,000)). Thus, the basis of the land is reduced by $1,000 (2/3 × $1,500), from $9,000 to $8,000, leaving an unrealized loss of $1,000 ($8,000 basis − $7,000 fair market value)

---

     [5]   Treas.Reg. § 1.362–4(d) provides details on how to make the § 362(h)(2)(C) election to reduce the transferor's stock basis in lieu of the corporation reducing asset basis. For an election to be effective: (1) prior to filing "a Section 362(e)(2)(C) Statement" the transferor and transferee must enter into a written, binding agreement to elect to apply § 362(e)(2)(C), and (2) detailed requirements for filing the "Section 362(e)(2)(C) Statement," which is required to contain extraordinarily detailed information about the transfer, must be followed. The transferor must include the "Section 362(e)(2)(C) Statement" on or with its timely filed (including extensions) original return for the taxable year in which the transfer occurred. A § 362(e)(2)(C) election is irrevocable. It may be made protectively and will have no effect to the extent it is determined that § 362(e)(2) does not apply.

inherent in the land, and the basis of the machine is reduced by $500 (1/3 × $1,500), from $5,000 to $4,500, leaving an unrealized loss of $500 ($4,500 basis − $4,000 fair market value) inherent in the machine.

Section 362(e)(2) applies transferor-by-transferor. Thus, if the copyright, land, and machine described above were transferred to the corporation by C, D, and E, respectively, the $2,000 built-in loss with respect to the land and the $1,000 built-in loss with respect to the machine would be taken into account separately, and would not be offset by the $1,500 built-in gain with respect to the copyright. As a result, the basis of the land would be reduced from $9,000 to $7,000, and the basis of the machine would be reduced from $5,000 to $4,000. Alternatively, D could elect (jointly with the corporation) to reduce the basis of the stock received in exchange for the land from $9,000 to $7,000, leaving the corporation with a $9,000 basis in the land; and E could separately elect (jointly with the corporation) to reduce the basis of the stock received in exchange for the machine from $5,000 to $4,000, leaving the corporation with a $5,000 basis in the machine.

When a § 362(e)(2)(C) election is made, the basis reduction is allocated among the shares of stock received by the transferor in proportion to the fair market value of each share. Treas.Reg. § 1.362–4(d)(2). This rule is of greatest significance when the transferor receives shares of more than one class, for example, both common and preferred.

4.2.2.   *Limitations on Importation of Built-In Losses*

Section 362(e)(1) applies property-by-property to reduce the corporation's basis of transferred property from the normal § 362(a) transferred basis to its fair market value, if (1) there is net built-in loss in the aggregate transferred properties and (2) gain or loss realized by the transferor with respect to the property was not subject to U.S. income tax immediately prior to the transfer. This provision applies principally to transfers by foreign shareholders to U.S. corporations and transfers by tax-exempt organizations to U.S. corporations.

5.   TRANSFER OF PROPERTY TO AN EXISTING CORPORATION WITHOUT ISSUANCE OF ADDITIONAL STOCK

5.1. *Transfer to a Controlled Corporation*

Section 351 also applies when a controlling shareholder transfers property to a controlled corporation without any additional stock being issued to the transferor. Lessinger v. Commissioner, 872 F.2d 519 (2d Cir. 1989); Rev.Rul. 64–155, 1964–1 C.B. 138. This most commonly occurs when property is transferred to a wholly owned corporation, since the issuance of additional stock would be a meaningless gesture. In such a case, the transferor adds the basis of the transferred property to the basis of stock already owned, and the corporation takes a transferred basis in the property under § 362(a), subject to the limitations in § 362(e).

5.2. *Contributions to Capital of a Corporation Not Controlled by the Transferor*

If a shareholder who does not control the corporation contributes additional capital to the corporation in the form of assets that have appreciated or depreciated in value without receiving additional shares of stock in return, presumably no gain or loss will be realized because nothing is received in return. The transferor simply adds the basis of the contributed property to the basis for his stock. Pursuant to § 362(a)(2) the corporation takes a transferred basis from the transferor, subject to § 362(e). Section 118(a) provides that a "contribution to capital" is excluded from a corporation's gross income, but, as amended in 2017, § 118(b) defines contribution to capital in such a way that a corporation must treat as gross income "any contribution in aid of construction or any other contribution as a customer or potential customer" as well as "any contribution by any governmental entity or civic group (other than a contribution made by a shareholder as such)."

6. BUSINESS PURPOSE REQUIREMENT

In circumstances that evidence overly aggressive tax planning, the courts sometimes impose a business purpose requirement as a prerequisite for obtaining nonrecognition under § 351. For example, in West Coast Marketing Corp. v. Commissioner, 46 T.C. 32 (1966), the corporation owned an interest in a tract of land, and its sole shareholder owned an interest in two adjacent tracts. At a time when a taxable exchange of the lands for stock in a publicly held corporation was imminent, West Coast Marketing and its shareholder organized another corporation, Manatee, and transferred their interests in the land to Manatee in exchange for stock of Manatee. Soon thereafter, all of the stock of Manatee was transferred to a publicly held corporation, Universal, in exchange for Universal stock in a transaction that in form was a tax-free, Type (B) reorganization under § 368(a)(1)(B), discussed in Chapter 10. Shortly thereafter Manatee was liquidated and its assets transferred to Universal in a formally tax-free transaction. The Tax Court held that Manatee was not organized or used for any bona fide business purpose, and that the substance of the transaction was a taxable exchange of an interest in land for stock of Universal. Rev.Rul. 70–140, 1970–1 C.B. 73, reached the same result on similar facts.

Estate of Kluener v. Commissioner, 154 F.3d 630 (6th Cir.1998), also imposed a business purpose requirement, which was not met. Kluener owned all of the stock of APECO, which had over $4 million of net operating loss carryovers and was in financial straits. Kluener also directly owned highly leveraged real estate and thoroughbred horses, both of which activities were losing substantial amounts of money. To help stem his losses, he decided to sell some horses. On the advice of his accountants, Kluener transferred the horses to APECO to shelter the gains (approximately $1.2 million) with APECO's net operating loss carryovers. Kluener hid the transfer from APECO's directors and did not use the $2.5 million sales proceeds to alleviate APECO's financial straits, but instead caused the corporation shortly after the sale to distribute most of the funds to himself for personal use—mostly repayment of personal debts. The Sixth Circuit affirmed the Tax Court's holding that the transfer to APECO lacked a business purpose. Accordingly, the transfer to APECO was not respected for tax purposes and the gain was taxed directly to Kluener because Kluener himself was the true seller of the horses.

Notwithstanding these cases, there are no authorities requiring that there be a business purpose for organizing a corporation to conduct a business, as opposed to using an unincorporated form to conduct a business, or for transferring to an existing corporation additional assets to be used in a trade or business conducted or to be conducted by the corporation.

7.   RECEIPT OF STOCK DISPROPORTIONATE TO PROPERTY TRANSFERRED

The 1939 Code predecessor of § 351 required that for the provision to be applicable the nonrecognition property received by each transferor had to be substantially in proportion to the transferor's interest in the transferred property prior to the exchange. The 1954 Code dropped the proportionate interest requirement as a factor in the nonrecognition of gain, but retained it as a factor indicating the possible existence of compensation or a gift. See the cross-references in § 351(h)(3)–(4). Treas.Reg. § 1.351–1(b)(1) states that "in appropriate cases" the stock will be treated as if first received in proportion to assets transferred, and then transferred to the ultimate recipients by way of gift or compensation if the facts so warrant. Rev.Rul. 76–454, 1976–2 C.B. 102, expanded the list of possible transfer types by finding a dividend in a situation in which a shareholder and his controlled corporation formed a new corporation with the shareholder receiving a disproportionately large amount of the stock of the newly formed corporation. The dividend was in the form of stock of the newly formed corporation constructively received by the original corporation in the § 351 transaction and constructively distributed to the shareholder.

8.   SECURITIES "SWAP FUNDS"

Section 351(e) provides that § 351 does not apply to transfers to investment companies, which are corporations holding a diverse investment portfolio that are operated to permit an exchange of a single investment for a diverse portfolio. Suppose that an individual owns a large amount of a particular stock that has greatly appreciated in value. The taxpayer would like to diversify that investment but feels that the tax on capital gains is too high a price to pay for diversification. There are many other individuals in a similar situation, but with different stocks. An investment house forms a regulated investment company (mutual fund)—which is a corporation for federal tax purposes—and invites an exchange of the stocks of the individuals in return for stock of the fund. This exchange would provide the individuals with the desired diversification, since they would now have, through their participation in the mutual fund, an interest in many different stocks, including their former shares. During the early 1960s, such swap funds flourished. In 1966, however, Congress enacted the statutory predecessor of § 351(e), which provides that § 351 does not apply to transfers to investment companies. As a result, gain or loss is recognized by the transferors in such transactions.[6]

Treas.Reg. § 1.351–1(c) provides that a transfer will be considered to be to an "investment company" if the transaction results, directly or indirectly,

---

[6] Section 683 provides similar rules for transfers to trusts used as swap funds, and § 721(b) deals with diversification through partnership formation.

in a diversification of the transferor's interest and the transferee is a regulated investment company, a real estate investment trust, or a corporation more than 80% of the value of the assets of which is held in readily marketable stocks or securities, or in regulated investment companies or real estate investment trusts. Under Treas.Reg. § 1.351–1(c)(5), a transaction ordinarily results in diversification "if two or more persons transfer nonidentical assets to a corporation in the exchange." The IRS has taken the position that the requirement that two or more persons transfer nonidentical assets to the corporation is satisfied if one group of transferors transfers the stock of a single corporation and another group transfers cash to a newly organized corporation that is a regulated investment company, i.e., a mutual fund. Rev.Rul. 87–9, 1987–1 C.B. 133.

In Rev.Rul. 88–32, 1988–1 C.B. 113, the IRS ruled that a transfer of stock does not result in diversification unless diversification is the result of a nonrecognition transaction. Thus, there is no proscribed diversification if the transferor transfers stock of a single corporation to a controlled investment company that sells the stock in a taxable transaction and reinvests the sales proceeds in a diverse portfolio of stock.

PROBLEM SET 1

1.   Amy and Ben plan to organize X Corporation to engage in the construction business. Amy will contribute a truck with a fair market value of $150,000 and a basis of $50,000 and a power shovel with a basis of $125,000 and a fair market value of $100,000 in exchange for 20 shares of voting common stock. Ben will contribute $100,000 in cash and undeveloped land, previously held as an investment, having a fair market value of $150,000 a basis of $20,000, in exchange for 100 shares of $1,000 par value nonvoting preferred stock with an 8% dividend preference and 12 shares of voting common stock. The fair market value of the preferred stock is $100,000. What are the tax consequences to Amy, Ben, and X Corporation as a result of the formation of the corporation? Specifically, how much, if any, gain must each recognize; what is the basis to each shareholder in the stock received; and what is the corporation's basis in the assets received by it?

2.   (a) Claire and Don formed Y Corporation to engage in the waste hauling and landfill business. Claire contributed a solid waste truck with a basis of $150,000 and a fair market value of $100,000 in exchange for 10 shares of voting common stock. Don contributed land with a basis of $30,000 and a fair market value of $100,000 in exchange for 10 shares of voting common stock. What are the tax consequences to Claire, Don, and Y Corporation as a result of the formation of the corporation?

(b) Suppose alternatively that Claire contributed a solid waste truck with a basis of $150,000 and a fair market value of $100,000 and a liquid waste truck with a basis of $60,000 and a fair market value of $100,000 in exchange for 20 shares of voting common stock. Don contributed land with a basis of $30,000 and a fair market value of $200,000 in exchange for 20 shares of voting common stock. What are the tax consequences to Claire, Don, and Y Corporation as a result of the formation of the corporation?

(c)   Suppose alternatively that Claire contributed a solid waste truck with a basis of $150,000 and a fair market value of $100,000, a liquid waste truck with a basis of $40,000 and a fair market value of $100,000, and a bulldozer with a basis of $75,000 and a fair market value of $50,000, in exchange for 25 shares of voting common stock. Don contributed land with a basis of $30,000 and a fair market value of $250,000 in exchange for 25 shares of voting common stock. What are the tax consequences to Claire, Don, and Y Corporation as a result of the formation of the corporation?

3.   Ed, Fran, and Georgie formed Z Corporation. Ed transferred 1,000 shares of stock of Specific Motors, Inc. with a basis of $150,000 and a fair market value of $100,000. Fran transferred 500 shares of stock of Worldwide Business Machines, Inc. with a fair market value of $100,000 and a basis of $20,000. Georgie transferred 2,000 shares of stock of Pear Computer Corporation with a fair market value of $100,000 and a basis of $5,000. Ed, Fran, and Georgie each received 10 shares of Z Corporation stock. Specific Motors, Worldwide Business Machines, and Pear Computer Corporation are all traded on the New York Stock Exchange. What are the tax consequences to Ed, Fran, Georgie, and Z Corporation as a result of the formation of the corporation?

B.   SCOPE OF SECTION 351 IN SUPPLANTING THE ASSIGNMENT OF INCOME DOCTRINE AND SIMILAR DOCTRINES

Hempt Bros., Inc. v United States
United States Court of Appeals, Third Circuit, 1974.
490 F.2d 1172.

■ ALDISERT, CIRCUIT JUDGE:

In this appeal by a corporate taxpayer from a grant of summary judgment in favor of the government in a claim for refund, we are called upon to decide the proper treatment of accounts receivable and of inventory transferred from a cash basis partnership to a corporation organized to continue the business under 26 U.S.C. 351(a). This appeal illustrates the conflict between the statutory purpose of Section 351, postponement of recognition of gain or loss, and the assignment of income and tax benefit doctrines. * * *

From 1942 until February 28, 1957, a partnership comprised of Loy T. Hempt, J. F. Hempt, Max C. Hempt, and the George L., Hempt Estate was engaged in the business of quarrying and selling stone, sand, gravel, and slag; manufacturing and selling ready-mix concrete and bituminous material; constructing roads, highways, and streets, primarily for the Pennsylvania Department of Highways and various political subdivisions of Pennsylvania, and constructing driveways, parking lots, street and water lines, and related accessories.

The partnership maintained its books and records, and filed its partnership income tax returns, on the basis of a calendar year and on the cash method of accounting, so that no income was reported until actually received in cash. Accordingly, in computing its income for federal income tax purposes, the partnership did not take uncollected receivables into income, and inventories were not used in the calculation of its taxable income, although both accounts receivable reflecting sales already made and physical inventories existed to a substantial extent at the end of each of the partnership's taxable years. Rather than using the inventory method of accounting, the partnership deducted the costs of its physical inventories of sand, gravel, and stone as incurred.

On March 1, 1957, the partnership business and most of its assets were transferred to the taxpayer solely in exchange for taxpayer's capital stock, the 12,000 shares of which were issued to the four members of the partnership. These shares constituted 100% of the issued and outstanding shares of the taxpayer. This transfer was made pursuant to Section 351(a) of the Internal Revenue Code of 1954; . . . . Thereafter, the taxpayer conducted the business formerly conducted by the partnership.

Among the assets transferred by the partnership to the taxpayer for taxpayer's shares of stock were accounts receivable in the amount of $662,824.40 arising from performance of construction projects, sales of stone, sand, gravel, etc., and rental of equipment prior to March 1, 1957. Also among the assets transferred were physical inventories of sand, gravel, and stone, with respect to which the partnership had deducted costs of $351,266.05 and the value of which was no less than $351,266.05.

* * *

Taxpayer argues here, as it did in the district court, that because the term "property" as used in Section 351 does not embrace accounts receivable, the Commissioner lacked statutory authority to apply principles associated with Section 351. The district court properly rejected the legal interpretation urged by the taxpayer.

The definition of Section 351 "property" has been extensively treated by the Court of Claims in E.I. Du Pont de Nemours and Co. v. United States, 471 F.2d 1211, 1218–1219 (Ct.Cl.1973), describing the transfer of a non-exclusive license to make, use and sell area herbicides under French patents:

> Unless there is some special reason intrinsic to . . . (Section 351) . . . the general word "property" has a broad reach in tax law . . . . For section 351, in particular, courts have advocated a generous definition of "property," . . . and it has been suggested in one capital gains case that nonexclusive licenses can be viewed as property though not as capital assets . . . .

We see no adequate reason for refusing to follow these leads.

We fail to perceive any special reason why a restrictive meaning should be applied to accounts receivables so as to exclude them from the general meaning of "property." Receivables possess the usual capabilities and attributes associated with jurisprudential concepts of property law. They may be identified, valued, and transferred. Moreover, their role in an ongoing business must be viewed in the context of Section 351 application. The presence of accounts receivable is a normal, rather than an exceptional accoutrement of the type of business included by Congress in the transfer to a corporate form. They are "commonly thought of in the commercial world as a positive business asset." Du Pont v. United States, supra, at 1218. As aptly put by the district court: "There is a compelling reason to construe 'property' to include . . . (accounts receivable): a new corporation needs working capital, and accounts receivable can be an important source of liquidity." Hempt Bros., Inc. v. United States, [354 F.Supp. 1172, 1176 (M.D. Pa. 1973)]. In any event, this court had no difficulty in characterizing a sale of receivables as "property" within the purview of the "no gain or loss" provision of Section 337 as a "qualified sale of property within a 12-month period." Citizens Acceptance Corp. v. United States, 462 F.2d 751, 756 (3d Cir. 1972).

The taxpayer next makes a strenuous argument that "the government is seeking to tax the wrong person." It contends that the assignment of income doctrine as developed by the Supreme Court applies to a Section 351 transfer of accounts receivable so that the transferor, not the transferee-corporation, bears the corresponding tax liability. It argues that the assignment of income doctrine dictates that where the right to receive income is transferred to another person in a transaction not giving rise to tax at the time of transfer, the transferor is taxed on the income when it is collected by the transferee; that the only requirement for its application is a transfer of a right to receive ordinary income; and that since the transferred accounts receivable are a present right to future income, the sole requirement for the application of the doctrine is squarely met. In essence, this is a contention that the nonrecognition provision of Section 351 is in conflict with the assignment of income doctrine and that Section 351 should be subordinated thereto. Taxpayer relies on the seminal case of Lucas v. Earl, 280 U.S. 538, 50 S.Ct. 16, 74 L.Ed. 600 (1929), and its progeny for support of its proposition that the application of the doctrine is mandated whenever one transfers a right to receive ordinary income.

On its part, the government concedes that a taxpayer may sell for value a claim to income otherwise his own and he will be taxable upon the proceeds of the sale. Such was the case in Commissioner v. P. G. Lake, Inc., 356 U.S. 260, 78 S.Ct. 691, 2 L.Ed.2d 743 (1958), in which the taxpayer-corporation assigned its oil payment right to its president in consideration for his cancellation of a $600,000 loan. Viewing the oil payment right as a right to receive future income, the Court applied the reasoning of the assignment of income doctrine, normally applicable to a gratuitous assignment, and held that the consideration received by the taxpayer-corporation was taxable as ordinary income since it essentially was a substitute for that which would otherwise be received at a future time as ordinary income.

Turning to the facts of this case, we note that here there was the transfer of accounts receivable form the partnership to the corporation pursuant to Section 351. We view these accounts receivable as a present right to receive future income. In consideration of the transfer of this right, the members of the partnership received stock—a valid consideration. The consideration, therefore, was essentially a substitute for that which would otherwise be received at a future time as ordinary income to the cash basis partnership. Consequently, the holding in *Lake* would normally apply, and income would ordinarily be realized, and thereby taxable, by the cash basis partnership-transferor at the time of receipt of the stock.

But the terms and purpose of Section 351 have to be reckoned with. By its explicit terms Section 351 expresses the Congressional intent that transfers of property for stock or securities will not result in recognition. It therefore becomes apparent that this case vividly illustrates how Section 351 sometimes comes into conflict with another provision of the Internal Revenue Code or a judicial doctrine, and requires a determination of which of two conflicting doctrines will control.

As we must, when we try to reconcile conflicting doctrines in the revenue law, we endeavor to ascertain a controlling Congressional mandate. Section 351 has been described as a deliberate attempt by Congress to facilitate the incorporation of ongoing businesses and to eliminate any technical constructions which are economically unsound.

Appellant-taxpayer seems to recognize this and argues that application of the Lake rationale when accounts receivable are transferred would not create any undue hardship to an incorporating taxpayer. "All a taxpayer (transferor) need do is withhold the earned income items and collect them, transferring the net proceeds to the Corporation. Indeed ... the transferor should retain both accounts receivable and accounts payable to avoid income recognition at the time of transfer and to have sufficient funds with which to pay accounts payable. Where the taxpayer [transferor] is on the cash method of accounting [as here], the deduction of the accounts payable would be applied against the income generated by the accounts receivable." (Appellant's Brief at 32.)

While we cannot fault the general principle "that income be taxed to him who earns it," to adopt taxpayer's argument would be to hamper the incorporation of ongoing businesses; additionally it would impose technical constructions which are economically and practically unsound. None of the cases cited by taxpayer, including *Lake* itself, persuades us otherwise. In *Lake* the Court was required to decide whether the proceeds from the assignment of the oil payment right were taxable as ordinary income or as long term capital gains. Observing that the provision for long term capital gains treatment "has always been narrowly construed so as to protect the revenue against artful devices," 356 U.S. at 265, 78 S.Ct. at 694, the Court predicated its holding upon an emphatic distinction between a conversion of a capital investment—"income-producing property"—and an assignment of income per se. "The substance of what was assigned was the right to receive future income. The substance of what was received was the present value of income which the recipient would otherwise obtain in the future." Ibid., at 266, 78 S.Ct. at 695. A Section 351 issue was not presented in *Lake*. Therefore the case does not control in weighing the conflict between the general rule of assignment of income and the Congressional purpose of nonrecognition upon the incorporation of an ongoing business

We are persuaded that, on balance, the teachings of *Lake* must give way in this case to the broad Congressional interest in facilitating the incorporation of ongoing businesses. As desirable as it is to afford symmetry in revenue law, we do not intend to promulgate a hard and fast rule. We believe that the problems posed by the clash of conflicting internal revenue doctrines are more properly determined by the circumstances of each case. Here we are influenced by the fact that the subject of the assignment was accounts receivable for partnership's goods and services sold in the regular course of business, that the change of business form from partnership to corporation had a basic business purpose and was not designed for the purpose of deliberate tax avoidance, and by the conviction that the totality of circumstances here presented fit the mold of the Congressional intent to give nonrecognition to a transfer of a total business from a non-corporate to a corporate form.

But this too must be said. Even though Section 351(a) immunizes the transferor from immediate tax consequences, Section 358 retains for the transferors a potential income tax liability to be realized and recognized upon a subsequent sale or exchange of the stock certificates received. As to the transferee-corporation, the tax basis of the receivables will be governed by Section 362. * * *

DETAILED ANALYSIS

1. ASSIGNMENT OF INCOME

Where a cash method taxpayer transfers all of the assets of a going business to a corporation in exchange for stock of the corporation, the assignment of income doctrine will not be invoked to tax the transferor on the income realized from collection of the receivables as Hempt Bros., Inc. v. United States, 490 F.2d 1172 (3d Cir.1974), so indicates. Applying the assignment of income doctrine in that context would frustrate the policy of § 351, which is to facilitate incorporation of a going business. Rev.Rul. 80–198, 1980–2 C.B. 113, adopts the holding of *Hempt Brothers* where all of the assets of a going business are transferred to a corporation for a valid business reason, but adds that assignment of income principles will apply to tax the transfer of cash method receivables if that is the only asset transferred to the corporation. However, notwithstanding the general rule that the assignment of income doctrine will not supplant the application of § 351 upon the incorporation of the entire business, the IRS has been more successful in applying the assignment of income doctrine in preference to § 351 in situations where the income-producing assets remain outside of the corporation and the incorporator attempts to simply assign the contractual rights to the income to the corporation. See Weinberg v. Commissioner, 44 T.C. 233 (1965), aff'd in part and rev'd in part sub nom. Commissioner v. Sugar Daddy, Inc., 386 F.2d 836 (9th Cir.1967).

2.　SECTION 482 ALLOCATIONS

Section 482 was introduced in Chapter 1. Treas.Reg. § 1.482–1(f)(1)(iii) now expressly provides that § 482 may be applied to override § 351. Provided that neither the assignment of income doctrine nor § 482 taxes the collected amounts to the transferor, pursuant to § 362(a), the corporation will have a zero basis in receivables transferred by a cash method transferor and will thus be required to recognize on collection the full amount as income.

3.　TAX BENEFIT RULE

In general, the tax benefit rule requires current inclusion in income of previously deducted items when a subsequent event is inconsistent with the prior deduction. Hillsboro National Bank v. Commissioner, 460 U.S. 370 (1983), held, however, that the tax benefit rule did not apply to the transferor of previously expensed property transferred to another party in a transaction in which the transferee took a transferred basis (a corporate liquidation governed by a now repealed provision). This result is appropriate in a § 351 transaction because the corporation takes a transferred basis under § 362(a). If, on the other hand, the transaction provides the transferee with a stepped-up basis, then application of the tax benefit rule to "recapture" the prior deduction is appropriate. See *United States v. Bliss Dairy, Inc.*, a case consolidated with *Hillsboro National Bank*.

PROBLEM SET 2

Alicia and Bart are the sole shareholders of X Corporation, which is engaged in a financial services business. Alicia and Bart each own 50 shares of common stock. Alicia contributed a § 453 installment note with a basis of $20,000 and a fair market value of $100,000 to X Corporation in exchange for 10 shares of stock worth $100,000. Alicia received the note earlier this year in exchange for land that she had held for investment for many years. Bart, who has a real estate license but does not actively conduct any real estate brokerage business, contributed a cash method account receivable in the amount of $15,000, which arose from brokering a commercial lease on behalf of a friend who owned an office building. Bart also contributed a parcel of land held for sale to customers in the ordinary course of his unincorporated real estate development business, which had a fair market value of $85,000 and a basis of $20,000, and which was subject to a binding executory purchase and sale contract. In exchange, Bart received 10 shares of stock worth $100,000. What are the tax consequences to Alicia, Bart, and X Corporation as a result of the formation of the corporation?

C. "SOLELY FOR STOCK"—THE RECEIPT OF OTHER PROPERTY

INTERNAL REVENUE CODE: Sections 351(b), (g); 358(a), (b); 362(a); 453(a)–(c), (f)(6), (g); 1239(a), (b)(1), (c)(1)(A).

REGULATIONS: Sections 1.301–1(a); 1.351–2.

PROPOSED REGULATIONS: Section 1.453–1(f)(1)(iii), (f)(3)(ii).

The nonrecognition rule of § 351(a) is limited to an exchange of property "solely for stock" of the controlled corporation. Section 351(b) permits the receipt of other property, but requires that the transferor recognize gain to the extent of the fair market value of other property plus the amount of money received. The basis rules of § 358 adjust the transferor's basis in the stock of the controlled corporation to account for boot by decreasing basis in an amount equal to the fair market value of property and the amount of money received, and increasing basis by the amount of any gain recognized. The transferee corporation's basis in transferred assets is also increased under § 362(a) by the amount of gain recognized by the transferor on the § 351 exchange.

In some circumstances, a taxpayer may desire to treat the transfer of property to a controlled corporation as a "sale" rather than as an exchange governed by § 351. If the taxpayer has property that has declined in value, a "sale" may be desirable to enable the transferor to recognize a loss on the depreciated assets. Sale treatment may be achieved only if the property is transferred in exchange for property other than stock or only for nonqualified preferred stock (as defined in § 351(g)). If the transaction qualifies as a § 351 transaction, even where boot is received, no loss can be recognized in the transaction.

Under certain circumstances, if there is a significant differential between the individual capital gains rate and the corporate tax rate, a transferor might be willing to pay a capital gain tax on the sale of appreciated assets to permit the corporation to obtain a step-up in basis for the assets, thereby providing the corporation higher depreciation or capital recovery deductions against ordinary income (but see § 1239). The receipt of "property" other than stock in a § 351 transaction also would provide the corporation a basis increase under § 362(a) to the extent of gain recognized by the shareholder under § 351(b).

Where property is transferred to a controlled corporation for stock and debt obligations, whether or not the debt is a security, no part of the transaction constitutes a sale with a resulting recognition of loss. The debt instrument constitutes "other property" (boot) and the tax consequences thus are governed by § 351(b). Under § 351(g), certain types of preferred stock that have characteristics that cause the stock more nearly to resemble debt are also treated as boot. When the shareholder receives boot in addition to stock, any gain realized on the exchange is recognized to the extent of the fair market value of other property, but no loss is recognized. The taxpayer cannot alter these tax consequences by attempting to denominate part of the transaction as a "sale" of some assets and the balance as a transfer under § 351. See, e.g., Nye v. Commissioner, 50 T.C. 203 (1968).

Where the transferor receives only cash or property, including debt securities (and no stock), the transaction is a sale or exchange and gain or loss will be recognized accordingly. Thus, the taxpayer can achieve sale treatment by transferring property for debt instruments ("securities") rather than stock. If, however, the transferor owns stock constituting control of the corporation, sale treatment will not be accorded the transaction if the purported debt instrument is in fact "equity" (see Chapter 3), thus bringing § 351 into play. In addition, a shareholder who transfers loss property to the corporation and who receives only nonqualified preferred stock (as defined in § 351(g)) may recognize the loss, notwithstanding that for some other purposes, the preferred stock might be "equity."

The method of computing gain upon the receipt of stock and boot in exchange for two or more different assets is explained in Rev.Rul. 68–55, which follows.

Revenue Ruling 68–55

1968–1 C.B. 140.

Advice has been requested as to the correct method of determining the amount and character of the gain to be recognized by Corporation X under section 351(b) of the Internal Revenue Code of 1954 under the circumstances described below.

Corporation Y was organized by X and A, an individual who owned no stock in X. A transferred $20x$ dollars to Y in exchange for stock of Y having a fair market value of $20x$ dollars and X transferred to Y three separate assets and received in exchange stock of Y having a fair market value of $100x$ dollars plus cash of $10x$ dollars.

In accordance with the facts set forth in the table below if X had sold at fair market value each of the three assets it transferred to Y, the result would have been as follows:

	Asset I	Asset II	Asset III
Character of asset......	Capital asset held more than 6 months.	Capital asset held not more than 6 months.	Section 1245 property.
Fair market value......	$22	$33x	$55x
Adjusted basis............	40x	20x	25x
Gain (loss)..........	($18x)	$13x	$30x
Character of gain or loss................	Long-term capital loss.	Short-term capital gain.	Ordinary income.

The facts in the instant case disclose that with respect to the section 1245 property the depreciation subject to recapture exceeds the amount of gain that would be recognized on a sale at fair market value. Therefore, all of such gain would be treated as ordinary income under section 1245(a)(1) of the Code.

Under section 351(a) of the Code, no gain or loss is recognized if property is transferred to a corporation solely in exchange for its stock and immediately after the exchange the transferor is in control of the corporation. If section 351(a) of the Code would apply to an exchange but for the fact that there is received, in addition to the property permitted to be received without recognition of gain, other property or money, then under section 351(b) of the Code gain (if any) to the recipient will be recognized, but in an amount not in excess of the sum of such money and the fair market value of such other property received, and no loss to the recipient will be recognized.

The first question presented is how to determine the amount of gain to be recognized under section 351(b) of the Code. The general rule is that each asset transferred must be considered to have been separately exchanged. See the authorities cited in Revenue Ruling 67–192, C.B. 1967–2, 140, and in Revenue Ruling 68–23, [1968–1 C.B. 144] * * *. Thus, for purposes of making computations under section 351(b) of the Code, it is not proper to total the bases of the various assets transferred and to subtract this total from the fair market value of the total consideration received in the exchange. Moreover, any treatment other than an asset-by-asset approach would have the effect of allowing losses that are specifically disallowed by section 351(b)(2) of the Code.

The second question presented is how, for purposes of making computations under section 351(b) of the Code, to allocate the cash and stock received to the amount realized as to each asset transferred in the exchange. The asset-by-asset approach for computing the amount of gain realized in the exchange requires that for this purpose the fair market value of each category of consideration received must be separately allocated to the transferred assets in proportion to the relative fair market values of the transferred assets. See section 1.1245–4(c)(1) of the Income Tax Regulations which, for the same reasons, requires that for purposes of computing the amount of gain to which section 1245 of the

Code applies each category of consideration received must be allocated to the properties transferred in proportion to their relative fair market values.

Accordingly, the amount and character of the gain recognized in the exchange should be computed as follows:

	Total	*Asset I*	*Asset II*	*Asset III*
Fair market value of asset transferred	$110x$	$22x$	$33x$	$55x$
Percent of total fair market value	—	20%	30%	50%
Fair market value of Y stock received in exchange.......................	$100x$	$20x$	$30x$	$50x$
Cash received in exchange...................	$10x$	$2x$	$3x$	$5x$
Amount realized........	$110x$	$22x$	$33x$	$55x$
Adjusted basis...................	—	$40x$	$20x$	$25x$
Gain (loss) realized ...	—	($18x$)	$13x$	$30x$

Under section 351(b)(2) of the Code the loss of 18x dollars realized on the exchange of Asset Number I is not recognized. Such loss may not be used to offset the gains realized on the exchanges of the other assets. Under section 351(b)(1) of the Code, the gain of 13x dollars realized on the exchange of Asset Number II will be recognized as short-term capital gain in the amount of 3x dollars, the amount of cash received. Under sections 351(b)(1) and 1245(b)(3) of the Code, the gain of 30x dollars realized on the exchange of Asset Number III will be recognized as ordinary income in the amount of 5x dollars, the amount of cash received.

DETAILED ANALYSIS

1. THE CORPORATION'S BASIS

If no gain is recognized, the corporation takes a transferred basis from the shareholder in each separate asset under § 362(a)(1). This transferred basis is increased by the transferor's recognized gain, which requires an allocation of the gain to different assets. Rev.Rul. 68–55 applies the principle of Williams v. McGowan, 152 F.2d 570 (2d Cir.1945), now codified in § 1060, requiring the seller of multiple assets to compute gain or loss on an asset-by-asset basis, to § 351 transactions involving boot. See also Treas.Reg. § 1.1245–4(c). Although the Regulations under § 362 are silent on the issue, and no Revenue Ruling directly addresses the point, this comminution rule also should apply to determine adjustments to the corporation's basis in the transferred assets. The amount of gain allocated to each asset for purposes of the basis adjustment required by § 362(a) should be the amount of gain recognized by the seller with respect to that asset under Rev.Rul. 68–55.

Thus the corporation's basis in each of the assets involved in Rev.Rul. 68–55 should be as follows:

	Asset I	Asset II	Asset III
Transferor's Basis	$40x	$20x	$25x
Transferor's Gain		$ 3x	$ 5x
Corporation's Basis	$40x	$23x	$30x

Note that there is no basis adjustment to Asset I because, with respect to that asset, the transferor realized an unrecognized loss.

2. EXCHANGE OF PROPERTY FOR CORPORATE DEBT

2.1. *Installment Sale Treatment*

The receipt of the transferee corporation's debt obligations as boot by the shareholder might result in installment sale treatment subject to deferred recognition of gain under the rules of § 453. An installment sale is defined as a disposition of property for payments that are received from the transferee of the property after the close of the taxable year in which disposition occurs. Installment reporting does not apply if the boot the shareholder receives is not a debt obligation issued by the transferee corporation but is instead that of a third party who owes the corporation.

Generally speaking, § 453 installment sale treatment is available only with respect to capital and § 1231 assets. Even as to § 1231 assets, § 453 installment sale treatment is not available with respect to the portion of the gain that is § 1245 recapture (or rarely occurring § 1250 recapture[7]), which is taxed as ordinary income. I.R.C. § 453(i). Thus, installment treatment frequently is not available for transfers of depreciable personal property, including intangibles that have been subject to amortization under § 197. This limitation, however, does not generally affect transfers of real property, because it does not apply to gain taxed as "unrecaptured § 1250 gain" under § 1(h), which is a subset of § 1231 gain that is treated as long-term capital gain. Section 453 installment reporting is not available for boot debt obligations allocable to transfers of inventory or property held primarily for sale to customers in the ordinary course of business. I.R.C. § 453(b)(2). Nor is § 453 installment sale reporting available if the corporation's debt obligations issued to the transferor shareholder are payable on demand or are readily tradable. I.R.C. § 453(f)(5).

If the transferor receives a debt obligation that is eligible for installment reporting, then under § 453(c) the gain recognized with respect to any payment in an installment sale is an amount that bears the same ratio to the payment as the gross profit on the installment sale bears to the total contract price. Section 453(f)(6) provides, with respect to a like-kind exchange under § 1031(b), that payments and total contract price do not include property that may be received without recognition of gain. Prop.Reg.

---

[7] Depreciation recapture under § 1250 occurs with respect to buildings placed in service after 1980 only if the building is sold within one year of being placed in service. I.R.C. § 1250(b)(1). Thus, it is infrequently encountered.

§ 1.453–1(f)(3)(ii) (1984) applies the rules of § 453(f)(6) to a § 351 exchange in which the transferor shareholder receives boot in the form of a debt obligation of the corporation. Prop.Reg. § 1.453–1(f)(1)(iii) (1984) allocates the transferor's basis in transferred property first to the stock received without recognition under § 351, to the extent of the fair market value of the stock. Any remaining basis is used to offset gain recognized on the installment sale. In effect, neither payments nor total contract price include stock permitted to be received under § 351 without recognition of gain.

Assume, for example, that A transfers property with an adjusted basis of $40 and a fair market value of $100 to a corporation controlled by A in exchange for stock worth $70 and a note for $30, payable in three annual installments, with adequate interest, beginning in the year following the transfer. Because under Treas.Reg. § 1.1001–1(g) the amount realized on account of the note is $30, § 351(b) requires that A recognize $30 of A's $60 realized gain. Under § 453, however, since "payments" do not include the stock received in the year of the exchange, no gain is recognized immediately. Under the Proposed Regulations, A's $40 basis is allocated to the stock, leaving no basis to reduce gain on the installment sale. Recognition is deferred until the receipt of each $10 payment, whereupon A recognizes the full $10 ($10 × $30/$30). Alternatively, if A's basis in the property transferred were $85 dollars, $70 of basis would be allocated to the stock, leaving $15 of basis to offset A's installment gain. A would recognize $15 of gain under § 351(b), but the recognition would be deferred under § 453. A would recognize $5 of gain on each $10 payment ($10 × $15/$30).

Prop.Reg. § 1.453–1(f)(3)(ii) (1984) provides that the transferor's basis in stock as determined under § 358 includes the deferred gain to be recognized under the installment method. Thus, in the first example above, A's basis in the stock is $40 consisting of A's basis in the property transferred increased by the gain recognized and decreased by the fair market value of the note. A's basis in the second example is $70. With respect to the transferee corporation's basis under § 362(a), however, Prop.Reg. § 1.453–1(f)(3)(ii) (1984) provides that the transferor's recognized gain under the installment method will not be included in the transferee's basis until the deferred gain is actually recognized by the transferor. Section 453(d) allows the transferor to elect out of installment sale treatment in which case the full fair market value of the note is recognized as gain in the year of the exchange. The election would permit the corporation immediately to step-up its basis in the transferred property under § 362(a).

Section 453(g) restricts use of the installment method in the case of a transfer of depreciable property to a corporation if the transferor owns more than 50% of the stock of the corporation, a transaction to which § 1239 applies. In Vest v. Commissioner, T.C. Memo. 2016–187, the Tax Court held that to avoid the application of § 453(g) a taxpayer can satisfy the burden of proof only by submitting evidence that clearly negates an income tax avoidance plan, with "more weight to objective facts than to the taxpayer's mere denial of tax motivation," and that the enhanced depreciation deductions available to the related buyer is relevant in deciding whether the seller had a principal purpose of avoiding tax.

2.2. *Sale for Debt Versus Exchange for Equity*

In Burr Oaks Corp. v. Commissioner, 365 F.2d 24 (7th Cir.1966), three individuals transferred land to a controlled corporation and received in exchange three two-year 6% notes each in the amount of $110,000 (although the land was found to be worth only one-half of the face value of the notes). The taxpayers asserted that the transaction was a sale, but the Tax Court found the transaction was an equity contribution to the corporation and the notes were treated as preferred stock rather than debt. The paid-in capital of the corporation was only $4,500 at a time when the corporation incurred "liabilities" of 80 times that amount. The Court of Appeals upheld the Tax Court: "When the payment to the transferors is dependent on the success of an untried undercapitalized business with uncertain prospects, a strong inference arises that the transfer is an equity contribution." The requirements of § 351 being otherwise met, the corporation received only a transferred basis in the land transferred to the corporation. The opposite result was reached in Gyro Engineering Corp. v. United States, 417 F.2d 437 (9th Cir.1969). The principal shareholders transferred three apartment buildings to a corporation for $30,000 cash and $2,343,000 in notes. The transaction was treated as a sale and not as a contribution to capital because the property was generating revenue sufficient to pay the notes.

Chapter 3 will discuss in greater detail the difficulties of distinguishing debt from equity. The subsequent enactment of § 351(g) provides, however, a further analytical hurdle to § 351's applicability that was not present at the time that these early cases were decided. In this regard, the debt instrument in *Burr Oaks Corp.* was held to be preferred stock, but if that preferred stock is described as "nonqualified preferred stock," then that form of equity will be treated as boot under § 351(b) with the consequence that the property's basis to the corporation will be transferred but increased by the amount of gain recognized by the transferor by reason of the received boot (in the form of nonqualified preferred stock). The next section discusses in greater detail § 351(g) nonqualified preferred stock.

3. "NONQUALIFIED PREFERRED STOCK"—PREFERRED STOCK AS BOOT

Section 351(g) treats certain "nonqualified preferred stock" as other property (boot), requiring recognition of gain under § 351(b) to the extent of the fair market value of the nonqualified preferred stock. A transferor who receives only nonqualified preferred stock in exchange for property (other than cash) recognizes either gain or loss because § 351 does not apply to the transferor. But a transferor who also receives some other stock, either common or preferred, in addition to nonqualified preferred stock is subject to the loss disallowance rule of § 351(b). Nonqualified preferred stock is preferred stock that has significant characteristics that cause it to resemble debt. Determining whether stock is "nonqualified preferred stock" is a two-step process.

First, the stock must be "preferred stock." For this purpose, preferred stock is stock that is limited and preferred as to dividends and that does not participate in corporate growth. I.R.C. § 351(g)(3)(A). Thus, participating preferred stock, because its rights are not limited and it participates in corporate growth, cannot be nonqualified preferred stock. The last sentence of § 351(g)(3)(A) provides: "Stock shall not be treated as participating in corporate growth to any significant extent unless there is a real and meaningful likelihood of the shareholder actually participating in the earnings and growth of the corporation." The purpose of this provision is to prevent taxpayers from avoiding nonqualified preferred stock treatment by creating illusory rights to share in earnings or growth of the corporation. For example, stock with a limited right on liquidation but rights to dividends identical to the rights accorded to common stock nevertheless would be nonqualified preferred stock if the corporation in fact did not pay dividends on either the common or the preferred stock.

Second, the preferred stock is "nonqualified" only if the issuer or a related person, within a 20-year period of issue, (1) may be required by the holder to redeem the stock, (2) is required to redeem the stock, or (3) has a right to redeem the stock, and it is more likely than not that the right to redeem will be exercised. Preferred stock also is nonqualified preferred stock if the dividend rate is determined in whole or in part by reference to interest rates, commodity prices, or similar indices. I.R.C. § 351(g)(2)(A).

Gerdau MacSteel, Inc. v. Commissioner, 139 T.C. 67 (2012), is the only case to have dealt with whether a particular class of preferred stock was nonqualified preferred stock. The issue arose when a corporation transferred high basis, low value property to its wholly owned subsidiary, with which it filed a consolidated return, solely in exchange for the preferred stock. When the corporation shortly thereafter sold the preferred stock received in the exchange, it claimed a § 358 exchanged basis in the stock rather than a low cost basis equal to the value of the stock. (The purpose of the transaction was to create a capital loss to shelter capital gains recognized on the sale of two other subsidiary corporations.) The stock in question was voting preferred stock with (a) "an assumed" $100 per share issue price, (b) cumulative dividends of 9.5%, payable quarterly, (c) which the parent had rights to call after five years and which the shareholders could put to the parent after seven years, and (d) providing for a liquidation value equal to the greater of (i) $125 or (ii) an amount equal to the lesser of (a) a percent of certain tax savings determined formulaically or (b) the subsidiary's book net equity. The Tax Court held that the preferred stock was nonqualified preferred stock and that pursuant to § 351(g)(1)(A), since the parent had received no other stock in the transaction, the transaction was not governed by § 351(a); the preferred stock thus took a cost basis. The court found the transactions were structured in such a way that it was highly likely when the preferred stock was issued that it would be redeemed within the five- and seven-year periods and that the redemption payment would be $125 per share. Although the stock had an assumed issue price of $100 per share and would be redeemed at $125 per share, because of the ceiling on the redemption price, the court concluded that the stock " 'does not participate in corporate growth to any significant extent' within the meaning of I.R.C. sec. 351(g)(3)(A)."

4.   THE RECEIPT OF STOCK OPTIONS AND OTHER CONTINGENT
      INTERESTS

Treas.Reg. § 1.351–1(a)(1) provides that stock rights or stock warrants
are not "stock" for § 351 purposes. This provision raises the issue of whether
stock options received along with stock in a § 351 transaction constitute boot
subject to § 351(b). In Hamrick v. Commissioner, 43 T.C. 21 (1964) (acq. in
result only, 1966–2 C.B. 5), the taxpayer transferred property to a controlled
corporation in exchange for stock plus a contingent right to additional stock
dependent upon the performance of the corporation. The Tax Court held that
the taxpayer's subsequent receipt of the contingent stock qualified for
nonrecognition treatment under § 351. The Tax Court followed the decision
in Carlberg v. United States, 281 F.2d 507 (8th Cir. 1960), holding that
transferable contingent rights to receive stock were stock for purposes of
§ 354 (nonrecognition treatment for an exchange of stock for stock in
corporate reorganizations). In both cases, the opinions concluded that the
contingent rights received by the taxpayers could represent either stock or
nothing at all. The IRS has indicated that it will follow the result of *Hamrick,*
but only because the rights received by the taxpayer were nonassignable and
nonmarketable and could only give rise to the receipt of additional stock by
one who was a party to the transfer. Rev.Rul. 66–112, 1966–1 C.B. 68, 70.

5.   TRANSFERS OF DEPRECIABLE PROPERTY: DEPRECIATION
      RECAPTURE AND SECTION 1239

Section 1245(b)(3) provides that there is no recapture of depreciation in
§ 351 transactions except to the extent of the gain required to be recognized
by § 351(b). Treas.Reg. § 1.1245–4(c)(1) provides that if a taxpayer transfers
both § 1245 property and other property to a corporation in a § 351
transaction and receives boot in addition to stock, the amount of the
recognized gain that is § 1245 depreciation recapture ordinary income is
determined under principles identical to those applied in Rev.Rul. 68–55.

If there is a significant differential between the individual capital gains
rate and the corporate tax rate, a taxpayer owning an asset with a low basis
but a high value, but with little or no recapture ordinary income potential,
might attempt to step-up the basis for depreciation by selling the asset to
another taxpayer under the taxpayer's control, with the larger depreciation
deductions offsetting the capital gain. When the sale is between a
corporation and a more than 50% shareholder (determined after application
of a constructive ownership rule), § 1239 meets this problem by providing
ordinary income treatment on the sale. If the ownership threshold is met,
section 1239 applies to the gain recognized under § 351(b) (boot) and thus
also to the gain required to be recognized under § 357(c) (liabilities in excess
of basis). Rev.Rul. 60–302, 1960–2 C.B. 223; Alderman v. Commissioner, 55
T.C. 662 (1971).

6.   TRANSFERS TO EXISTING CONTROLLED CORPORATIONS

6.1. *Dividend Distributions*

Since § 351 applies to transfers to an existing corporation, as well as to
transfers to form a new corporation, a taxpayer might be tempted to combine
a transfer of property with a distribution of cash. For example, a sole

shareholder transfers a capital asset worth $10,000 to a corporation for additional shares of stock plus $1,000 cash. Rather than being treated as boot in a § 351 transaction, resulting in capital gain, the $1,000 cash could be classified as a dividend, if the distribution otherwise fails to qualify for an exception (dividends and redemptions are discussed in Chapters 4 and 5, respectively). While § 351(h) does not include a cross-reference to the dividend sections, it would seem that dividend treatment is appropriate in such a case. See Treas.Reg. §§ 1.351–2(d) and 1.301–1(*l*).

If property worth $10,000 is sold by a sole shareholder to an existing corporation for $10,000 cash, the transaction presumably is a sale. If, however, the shareholder cannot establish a business purpose for the transfer, the shareholder might be regarded as making a contribution to capital of $10,000 and receiving a dividend of $10,000. But see Curry v. Commissioner, 43 T.C. 667 (1965) (nonacq.), where the court summarily disposed of the IRS's contention that there was no "business purpose" for a sale of real estate to a controlled corporation: "It would seem that the mere desire to sell, even if the sole purpose was to realize capital gains, should be a sufficient business purpose (assuming always that the substance complies with the form). . . . Indeed, it is difficult to imagine what added business purpose respondent would require for a sale of property."

6.2. *Treatment of Corporation Transferring Appreciated Property as Boot*

Section 351(f) provides that if in addition to its own stock a corporation transfers appreciated property to a shareholder as boot in a § 351 exchange, the corporation must recognize gain under § 311(b) with respect to the boot property it transfers to the shareholder. Section 311(b) requires recognition of gain as if the property transferred by the corporation had been sold for its fair market value. Thus, corporate level gain will be recognized on a transfer of appreciated property to a shareholder as boot in a § 351 exchange.

This provision is most likely to come into play when transfers are made to a preexisting corporation, but it could apply in a formation as well. Suppose A and B want to form a corporation that they will own equally to operate Blackacre, which is owned by A and has a fair market value of $1,000, and Whiteacre, which is owned by B and has a fair market value of $800. To incorporate with equal contributions, in addition to contributing Whiteacre, B also contributes marketable securities with a basis of $20 and a fair market value of $100, which the corporation distributes to A. (As a result of the contribution of the marketable securities by B and their distribution to A, each of A and B has contributed a net amount of $900.) In addition to A being required to account for $100 of boot under § 351(b), the corporation will recognize a gain of $80 under § 351(f).

PROBLEM SET 3

1.   Claire, Don, and Erin plan to organize a corporation to engage in the construction business. They will each make the following contributions in exchange for the specified interest in the corporation and cash (assume the corporation had the ability to borrow the necessary amounts). What are the tax consequences to each of the investors and to the corporation as a result

of the formation of the corporation? Specifically, how much, if any, gain must each recognize; what is the character of the gain; what is the basis to each shareholder in the stock received; and what is the corporation's basis in the assets received by it? (For a more challenging—and realistic—version of this problem, consider how your answer would change if instead of receiving $200,000 of cash, each shareholder received a promissory note from the corporation for $200,000 due in 10 years and bearing adequate stated interest.)

(a) Claire will contribute construction supplies previously held for sale to customers in the ordinary course of business, with a fair market value of $450,000 and a basis of $300,000, in exchange for 20 shares of common stock and $200,000 of cash.

(b) Don will contribute a bulldozer with a fair market value of $180,000 and an adjusted basis of $300,000 and a cement mixer truck with an adjusted basis of $150,000 and a fair market value of $270,000 in exchange for 20 shares of common stock and $200,000 of cash. All of the gain inherent in the cement mixer is subject to § 1245 recapture.

(c) Erin will contribute land and a building previously held as a rental property. The land has a basis of $60,000 and the building an adjusted basis of $210,000. Their combined fair market value is $450,000. The building is not subject to either § 1245 or § 1250 recapture. Erin will receive 20 shares of common stock and $200,000 of cash.

(1) Assume that the land has a fair market value of $90,000 and the building a fair market value of $360,000.

(2) Assume alternatively that the land has a fair market value of $180,000 and the building a fair market value of $270,000.

2. Fran, Glenn, and Helen formed Y Corporation by making the following transfers. Fran and Glenn each transferred $100,000 of cash and received 100 shares each of common stock. Helen transferred unimproved real estate with a basis of $25,000 and received 20 shares of common stock, worth $20,000, and Y Corporation's note for $80,000 payable in 21 years, with interest payable annually at 6% (which you should assume is adequate stated interest).

(a) What are the tax consequences to Helen? What is Helen's basis in the Y Corporation stock? What is Y Corporation's basis in the land?

(b) How would your answer change if Helen received 10 shares of common stock, having an aggregate fair market value of $20,000, and 80 shares of $1,000 par preferred stock, which paid a dividend of 6% annually and is redeemable in 21 years at the option of either Y Corporation or Helen? The preferred stock had an aggregate fair market value of $80,000.

(c) Would your answer change if the 80 shares of $1,000 par preferred stock Helen received was sinking fund preferred stock redeemable in 20 years at the option of either Y Corporation or Helen?

SECTION 2.   "SOLELY" FOR STOCK: ASSUMPTION OF LIABILITIES

INTERNAL REVENUE CODE: Sections 357; 358(d).

REGULATIONS: Sections 1.357–1, –2; 1.358–3.

A. BASIC PRINCIPLES

Under § 357(a), the assumption of a liability, or receipt of property subject to a liability, is not treated as the receipt of money or other property by the transferor. Section 357(a) is subject to two exceptions. Section 357(b), enacted in 1939 as part of the original provision, treats liabilities as boot if either (1) a tax avoidance purpose is present, or (2) there is no bona fide business purpose for transferring the liabilities. The structure of § 351(b) thus requires the transferor to demonstrate a business purpose for the assumption of the liabilities by the corporation. Second, under § 357(c) if the amount of liabilities assumed exceeds the basis of the property transferred, gain results to the extent of such excess, regardless of the purpose of the debt or the assumption. For purposes of determining the transferor's basis in nonrecognition property received in the exchange, § 358(d) treats the assumption of a liability of the transferor or a transfer of property subject to a liability as the receipt of cash by the transferor, without regard to how the debt is treated under § 357. The result is a reduction in the transferor's basis in the stock to the extent of the liability.

DETAILED ANALYSIS

1.   SECTION 357(b) SITUATIONS

Under § 357(b), the total amount of liabilities assumed or to which transferred property is subject is treated as money received unless the taxpayer can show that the principal purpose of the assumption or transfer subject to liabilities was not tax avoidance and was a bona fide business purpose. Section 357(b)(2) adds that the taxpayer must meet the burden of proof by "the clear preponderance of the evidence." Under the express terms of the statute, if any liability is found to have been assumed by the corporation for the forbidden tax avoidance purpose, or without a bona fide business purpose, all liabilities are treated as money. Treas.Reg. § 1.357–1(c). Because its application depends on the facts relating to "business purpose" and "tax avoidance purpose," however, the precise scope of the application § 357(b) is not always clear.

1.1. *Purchase Money Liabilities Relating to Transferred Assets*

An assumption of liabilities incurred initially to acquire the business assets transferred to the transferee should satisfy the bona fide business purpose requirement. See Jewell v. United States, 330 F.2d 761 (9th Cir.1964) (§ 357(b) was not triggered by corporation's assumption of transferor's debt incurred to acquire the assets that were later transferred to the corporation). In Rev.Rul. 79–258, 1979–2 C.B. 143, the IRS concluded that in a type (D) reorganization (discussed in Chapter 10), a nonrecognition transaction that is also subject to § 357(b), there was no tax avoidance motive where the transferor refinanced a portion of an existing long-term debt on the eve of assumption of the debt by the transferee corporation. The refinanced indebtedness was attributable to business assets received by the transferee.

1.2. *Liabilities Unrelated to Acquisition of Transferred Assets*

Section 357(b) has been applied to treat assumed debt as boot in cases involving the assumption of personal nonbusiness liabilities of the transferor. In Estate of Stoll v. Commissioner, 38 T.C. 223 (1962), the taxpayer transferred all the assets of a newspaper business to a corporation, which assumed $1,015,000 of the taxpayer's debts. To the extent of $600,000, the liability represented a refinancing of debt related to the newspaper business that took place just prior to the incorporation and was secured by property transferred to the corporation. The $415,000 balance of the liability was secured by life insurance policies on the taxpayer's life that were not transferred to the corporation. The Tax Court held that the 1939 Code predecessor of § 357(b) applied to treat the $415,000 of indebtedness as boot because there was no business purpose for the assumption of the liability by the corporation and the liability was not related to the transferred business. However, the predecessor of § 357(b) did not apply to treat as boot the $600,000 liability that related to the transferred business. Note that unlike its 1939 Code predecessor, § 357(b)(1) requires that the *total liability* be treated as boot if there is a tax avoidance purpose or if there is no bona fide business purpose for the assumption of any liability.

If a liability, such as a bank loan, is incurred just before a transfer of property to a controlled corporation so that the shareholder obtains the cash loan proceeds, the corporation assumes the debt, and subsequently pays the bank, the transaction viewed as a whole is the equivalent of a payment of cash by the corporation to the shareholder in exchange for the property. The assumption of the liability in such cases generally is found to fall under § 357(b), because of the presence of a tax avoidance purpose, whether or not the liability is secured by the transferred property. In Campbell v. Wheeler, 342 F.2d 837 (5th Cir.1965), the taxpayer transferred a partnership interest to a corporation subject to liabilities that had been incurred just prior to the transfer in order to pay the personal income tax liability of the taxpayer. The court held that the transaction was governed by § 357(b) and the amount of the liabilities assumed constituted boot. Similarly, in Thompson v. Campbell, 64–2 U.S.T.C. ¶ 9659 (N.D.Tex.1964), aff'd per curiam, 353 F.2d 787 (5th Cir.1965), the taxpayer borrowed money with the loan secured by corporate stock and other intangible assets that he already owned. The next day, he transferred the assets, but not the cash proceeds of the loan to a wholly owned corporation that assumed the debt. The transfer to the controlled corporation of assets subject to liabilities incurred the day before incorporation resulted in boot under § 357(b).

On the other hand, when a liability secured by the transferred property predates the inception of the plan to incorporate, the assumption by the corporation of the liability in connection with the transfer of assets generally has been found not to run afoul of § 357(b), regardless of the application of the loan proceeds, because there is a business purpose for the debt assumption, i.e., the debts follow the encumbered asset, and no tax avoidance plan. In Simpson v. Commissioner, 43 T.C. 900 (1965) (acq.), the taxpayer transferred the assets of two department stores, cash, and publicly traded securities to a corporation in a § 351 transaction. The corporation also assumed liabilities in an amount that was slightly less than the aggregate basis of the assets transferred. Most of the liabilities were liens against the publicly traded stock. An admitted purpose of transferring the stock to the corporation was to reduce the income taxes incurred with respect to the dividends received from the stock. In addition, however, ownership of its own marketable securities would make it easier for the corporation to obtain financing, income from the securities would enable the business to weather hard times, and the business would have adequate working capital for expansion and other purposes, all of which the court found to constitute a valid business reason to transfer the securities to the corporation. The IRS asserted that § 357(b) applied, but the court held that the arrangement for the assumption of liabilities was not subject to § 357(b) because the liabilities were secured by transferred property and the loans were not incurred in anticipation of the transfer. Furthermore, the fact that the transferred securities were selected with a view to avoid § 357(c)—the aggregate basis of the stock slightly exceeded the amount of the debt assumed—also was not a tax avoidance purpose.

In Drybrough v. Commissioner, 376 F.2d 350 (6th Cir.1967), the taxpayer in 1957 transferred real estate to four corporations, each assuming a portion of the mortgage debt on the property that had been incurred in 1953. Another property was transferred to a fifth corporation subject to a mortgage that had been placed on the property in 1957, just three months prior to the transfer. The proceeds of the 1957 mortgage had been invested in tax-exempt bonds. About one-half of the 1953 mortgage proceeds had been used to pay off a loan incurred in 1946 secured by the properties, and most of the balance was also invested in tax-exempt bonds. The court held that the assumption of the 1953 indebtedness was not governed by § 357(b); the use to which the proceeds of the mortgage were put was not relevant in determining whether there was a tax avoidance purpose for the exchange. There was a valid business purpose for placing the real estate subject to the mortgage in the corporation. On the other hand, the assumption of the 1957 indebtedness was governed by § 357(b); the creation of the debt was directly in anticipation of having the corporation assume the indebtedness and constituted a plan to avoid recognition of gain. (Note that the application of § 357(b) to the 1957 loan did not result in the application of § 357(b) to the 1953 loan in *Drybrough* because the 1957 loan was assumed by a different corporation from the one that assumed the 1953 loan.)

In rare cases a borrowing immediately before the transfer has been found not to run afoul of the business purpose requirement. In Easson v. Commissioner, 33 T.C. 963 (1960), rev'd on other grounds, 294 F.2d 653 (9th Cir.1961), the Tax Court construed the 1939 Code predecessor of § 357(b) not to apply on the facts of the case to a mortgage debt placed on the assets shortly before incorporation because the taxpayer had a valid business purpose for the corporate assumption of the mortgage (i.e., insulation of personal assets from potential liabilities and facilitation of management of the real estate and estate planning by obtaining liquidity), and the corporation was an active business entity. The *Easson* case appears, however, to be an aberration, and it is unlikely that it would be followed currently.

2.   TRANSFEROR DEBT OWED TO TRANSFEREE CORPORATION

In Kniffen v. Commissioner, 39 T.C. 553 (1962) (acq.), the taxpayer transferred assets and liabilities of a sole proprietorship to a pre-existing corporation. Among the liabilities assumed by the corporation was a debt the taxpayer owed to the corporation. The assumption eliminated the taxpayer's debt by operation of law. The IRS asserted that the taxpayer realized cancellation of debt income as boot under § 351(b) and that there was no assumption of debt to bring § 357 into play. The court held for the taxpayer; the debt was assumed and then discharged so that § 357 applied. Under the current statutory pattern, however, it appears that § 108(e)(4) would require the recognition of cancellation of indebtedness income (unless otherwise not recognized under § 108) if the transferor "controls" the transferee corporation (control for this purpose being defined in § 267(b), which provides a more than 50% of value test for control, after application of constructive ownership rules).

PROBLEM SET 4

1.   Frank and Jessie plan to organize a corporation to operate a college textbook store, which will be named Fleecem Folios, Ltd. They will each engage in the exchanges described below. What are the tax consequences to Frank, Jessie, and Fleecem Folios that result from the formation of the corporation? Specifically, how much, if any, gain must each recognize; what is the basis to each shareholder in the stock received; and what is the corporation's basis in the assets received by it?

(a)   Frank will contribute 10,000 law school text books, previously held for sale to customers in the ordinary course of business, with a fair market value of $450,000 and a basis of $300,000, in exchange for 10 shares of common stock, worth $250,000. In addition, the corporation will assume $200,000 of Frank's debts that are secured by a perfected purchase money security interest in the books.

(b)   Jessie will contribute land previously held as an investment on which the new corporation will build a store. The land has a fair market value of $350,000 and a basis of $260,000. Jessie will receive 10 shares of common stock and the corporation will assume a $100,000 debt Jessie owed to the First National Bank of Northfield.

(1)   Assume that Jessie's debt was incurred four years ago to pay gambling debts incurred in Atlantic City and is unsecured.

(2)   Assume alternatively that Jessie's debt to the First National Bank of Northfield was secured by a mortgage on the land.

    (3)   Assume alternatively that the land was used as a parking lot and Jessie's debt was unsecured but was incurred last year to fund deductible operating expenses of the now failed sole proprietorship parking lot business in connection with which Jessie previously had used the land.

2.   Al, Bev, and Carl each owned one third of the outstanding stock of X Corporation. Al, Bev, and Carl owned Blackacre as equal tenants in common. Blackacre had a fair market value of $450,000 and was subject to a nonrecourse purchase money mortgage of $450,000. Each of Al, Bev, and Carl had a basis in the respective undivided one-third interests of $170,000. Al, Bev and Carl contributed Blackacre to X Corporation. What are the tax consequences?

B. LIABILITIES IN EXCESS OF BASIS

(1) GENERAL RULES

INTERNAL REVENUE CODE: Sections 357(c); 358(d); 362(d)(1).

REGULATIONS: Sections 1.357–2; 1.358–3.

    Section 357(c)(1) requires the recognition of gain to a transferor if in connection with a transfer subject to § 351 the transferee corporation assumes liabilities of the transferor in excess of the adjusted basis of the property transferred to the corporation. Suppose that A owned an asset worth $100,000, which cost $10,000 and was subject to a mortgage of $50,000 to secure a bank loan of $50,000 obtained by A in a separate transaction. If A were permitted to transfer the asset to a controlled corporation subject to the liability without recognition of gain, A would avoid tax on $40,000, the difference between A's original investment of $10,000 and the $50,000 cash received by A from the borrowing. The problem is resolved by § 357(c)(1). The gain recognized under § 357(c)(1) is capital or ordinary according to the ratio of capital assets to ordinary assets transferred. Treas.Reg. § 1.357–2(b).

    In calculating the shareholder's basis in the stock received in the exchange, § 358(d)(1) requires that the full amount of the transferor's debts assumed by the corporation be treated as boot received by the transferor for purposes of applying § 358(a). Thus, in the above example, the shareholder's basis in the stock is $0: the $10,000 basis of transferred property, minus the $50,000 debt assumed by the corporation, plus the $40,000 gain recognized. Under § 362(a), the corporation's basis in the property is increased by the gain recognized to the transferor. Thus, in the above example, the corporation takes the property with a $50,000 basis ($10,000 plus $40,000).

    Section 357(c) applies with respect to the aggregate amount of the transferor's liabilities assumed by the corporation and the aggregate amount of the bases of the properties transferred to the corporation by a particular transferor. Treas.Reg. § 1.357–2(a). Thus, in the above situation, A could avoid recognition of gain under § 357(c) by transferring to the corporation along with the property, cash in the amount of $40,000 or other property with a basis of at least $40,000. The following case deals with the question of whether the same result is obtained when the transferor gives the corporation a promissory note rather than cash or additional property in which the transferor has a basis.

Peracchi v. Commissioner

United States Court of Appeals, Ninth Circuit, 1998.
143 F.3d 487.

■ KOZINSKI, CIRCUIT JUDGE:

We must unscramble a Rubik's Cube of corporate tax law to determine the basis of a note contributed by a taxpayer to his wholly-owned corporation.

The Transaction

The taxpayer, Donald Peracchi, needed to contribute additional capital to his closely-held corporation (NAC) to comply with Nevada's minimum premium-to-asset ratio for insurance companies. Peracchi contributed two parcels of real estate. The parcels were encumbered with liabilities which together exceeded Peracchi's total basis in the properties by more than half a million dollars. As we discuss in detail below, under section 357(c), contributing property with liabilities in excess of basis can trigger immediate recognition of gain in the amount of the excess. In an effort to avoid this, Peracchi also executed a promissory note, promising to pay NAC $1,060,000 over a term of ten years at 11% interest. Peracchi maintains that the note has a basis equal to its face amount, thereby making his total basis in the property contributed greater than the total liabilities. If this is so, he will have extracted himself from the quicksand of section 357(c) and owe no immediate tax on the transfer of property to NAC. The IRS, though, maintains that (1) the note is not genuine indebtedness and should be treated as an unenforceable gift; and (2) even if the note is genuine, it does not increase Peracchi's basis in the property contributed.

The parties are not splitting hairs: Peracchi claims the basis of the note is $1,060,000, its face value, while the IRS argues that the note has a basis of zero. If Peracchi is right, he pays no immediate tax on the half a million dollars by which the debts on the land he contributed exceed his basis in the land; if the IRS is right, the note becomes irrelevant for tax purposes and Peracchi must recognize an immediate gain on the half million. The fact that the IRS and Peracchi are so far apart suggests they are looking at the transaction through different colored lenses. To figure out whether Peracchi's lens is rose-tinted or clear, it is useful to take a guided tour of sections 351 and 357 and the tax law principles undergirding them.

Into the Lobster Pot: Section 351[2]

The Code tries to make organizing a corporation pain-free from a tax point of view. A capital contribution is, in tax lingo, a "nonrecognition" event: A shareholder can generally contribute capital without recognizing gain on the exchange. * * * See I.R.C. § 351. So long as the shareholders contributing the property remain in control of the corporation after the exchange, section 351 applies: It doesn't matter if the capital contribution occurs at the creation of the corporation or if—as here—the company is already up and running. * * *

Gain Deferral: Section 358(a)

* * * [W]hen a shareholder like Peracchi contributes property to a corporation in a nonrecognition transaction, * * * the shareholder must substitute the basis of that property for what would otherwise be the cost basis of the stock.[6] This preserves the gain for recognition at a later day: The gain is built into the shareholder's new basis in the stock, and he will recognize income when he disposes of the stock.

The fact that gain is deferred rather than extinguished doesn't diminish the importance of questions relating to basis and the timing of recognition. In tax, as in comedy, timing matters. Most taxpayers would much prefer to pay tax on contributed property years later-when they sell their stock-rather than when they contribute the property.[7] Thus what Peracchi is seeking here is gain deferral: He wants the gain to be recognized only when he disposes of some or all of his stock.

Continuity of Investment: Boot and section 351(b)

* * * [T]he central exception to nonrecognition for section 351 transactions comes into play when the taxpayer receives "boot"—money or property other than stock in the corporation—in exchange for the property contributed. See I.R.C. § 351(b). Boot is recognized as taxable income because it represents a partial cashing out. * * *

Peracchi did not receive boot in return for the property he contributed. But that doesn't end the inquiry: We must consider whether Peracchi has cashed out in some other way which would warrant treating part of the transaction as taxable boot.

Assumption of Liabilities: Section 357(a)

The property Peracchi contributed to NAC was encumbered by liabilities. Contribution of leveraged property makes things trickier from a tax perspective. When a shareholder contributes property encumbered

---

[2] "Decisions to embrace the corporate form of organization should be carefully considered, since a corporation is like a lobster pot: easy to enter, difficult to live in, and painful to get out of." Boris I. Bittker & James S. Eustice, Federal Income Taxation of Corporations and Shareholders ¶ 2.01[3] (6th ed.1997) (footnotes omitted) (hereinafter Bittker & Eustice).

[6] See I.R.C. § 358(a) * * *.

[7] Of course, should the taxpayers be lucky enough to die before disposing of the stock, their heirs would take a stepped-up basis in the stock equal to its fair market value as of the date of death. See I.R.C. § 1014.

by debt, the corporation usually assumes the debt. And the Code normally treats discharging a liability the same as receiving money: The taxpayer improves his economic position by the same amount either way. See I.R.C. § 61(a)(12). NAC's assumption of the liabilities attached to Peracchi's property therefore could theoretically be viewed as the receipt of money, which would be taxable boot. See United States v. Hendler, 303 U.S. 564 * * * (1938).

The Code takes a different tack. Requiring shareholders like Peracchi to recognize gain any time a corporation assumes a liability in connection with a capital contribution would greatly diminish the nonrecognition benefit section 351 is meant to confer. Section 357(a) thus takes a lenient view of the assumption of liability: A shareholder engaging in a section 351 transaction does not have to treat the assumption of liability as boot, even if the corporation assumes his obligation to pay. * * *

This nonrecognition does not mean that the potential gain disappears. Once again, the basis provisions kick in to reflect the transfer of gain from the shareholder to the corporation: The shareholder's substitute basis in the stock received is decreased by the amount of the liability assumed by the corporation. See I.R.C. § 358(d), (a). The adjustment preserves the gain for recognition when the shareholder sells his stock in the company, since his taxable gain will be the difference between the (new lower) basis and the sale price of the stock.

Sasquatch and The Negative Basis Problem: Section 357(c)

Highly leveraged property presents a peculiar problem in the section 351 context. Suppose a shareholder organizes a corporation and contributes as its only asset a building with a basis of $50, a fair market value of $100, and mortgage debt of $90. Section 351 says that the shareholder does not recognize any gain on the transaction. Under section 358, the shareholder takes a substitute basis of $50 in the stock, then adjusts it downward under section 357 by $90 to reflect the assumption of liability. This leaves him with a basis of minus $40. A negative basis properly preserves the gain built into the property: If the shareholder turns around and sells the stock the next day for $10 (the difference between the fair market value and the debt), he would face $50 in gain, the same amount as if he sold the property without first encasing it in a corporate shell.[8]

But skeptics say that negative basis, like Bigfoot, doesn't exist. Compare Easson v. Commissioner, 33 T.C. 963, 970 (1960) (there's no such thing as a negative basis) with Easson v. Commissioner, 294 F.2d 653, 657–58 (9th Cir.1961) (yes, Virginia, there is a negative basis). Basis

---

[8]   If the taxpayer sells the property outright, his amount realized includes the full amount of the mortgage debt * * * and the result is as follows: Amount realized ($10 cash + $90 debt) − $50 Basis = $50 gain.

normally operates as a cost recovery system: Depreciation deductions reduce basis, and when basis hits zero, the property cannot be depreciated farther. At a more basic level, it seems incongruous to attribute a negative value to a figure that normally represents one's investment in an asset. Some commentators nevertheless argue that when basis operates merely to measure potential gain (as it does here), allowing negative basis may be perfectly appropriate and consistent with the tax policy underlying nonrecognition transactions. See, e.g., J. Clifton Fleming, Jr., The Highly Avoidable Section 357(c): A Case Study in Traps for the Unwary and Some Positive Thoughts About Negative Basis, 16 J. Corp. L. 1, 27–30 (1990). Whatever the merits of this debate, it seems that section 357(c) was enacted to eliminate the possibility of negative basis. * * *

Section 357(c) prevents negative basis by forcing a shareholder to recognize gain to the extent liabilities exceed basis. Thus, if a shareholder contributes a building with a basis of $50 and liabilities of $90, he does not receive stock with a basis of minus $40. Instead, he takes a basis of zero and must recognize a $40 gain.

Peracchi sought to contribute two parcels of real property to NAC in a section 351 transaction. Standing alone the contribution would have run afoul of section 357(c): The property he wanted to contribute had liabilities in excess of basis, and Peracchi would have had to recognize gain to the extent of the excess, or $566,807:

	Liabilities	Basis
Property #1	1,386,655	349,774
Property #2	161,558	631,632
	1,548,213	981,406
Liabilities	1,548,213	
Basis	981,406	
Excess (357(c))	566,907	

The Grift: Boosting Basis with a Promissory Note

Peracchi tried to dig himself out of this tax hole by contributing a personal note with a face amount of $1,060,000 along with the real property. Peracchi maintains that the note has a basis in his hands equal to its face value. If he's right, we must add the basis of the note to the basis of the real property. Taken together, the aggregate basis in the property contributed would exceed the aggregate liabilities:

	Liabilities	Basis
Property #1	1,386,655	349,774
Property #2	161,558	631,632
Note	0	1,060,000
	1,548,213	2.041,406

Under Peracchi's theory, then, the aggregate liabilities no longer exceed the aggregate basis, and section 357(c) no longer triggers any gain. The government argues, however, that the note has a zero basis. If so, the note would not affect the tax consequences of the transaction, and Peracchi's $566,807 in gain would be taxable immediately.

Are Promises Truly Free?

Which brings us (phew!) to the issue before us: Does Peracchi's note have a basis in Peracchi's hands for purposes of section 357(c)?[12] The language of the Code gives us little to work with. The logical place to start is with the definition of basis. Section 1012 provides that "[t]he basis of property shall be the cost of such property. . . ." But "cost" is nowhere defined. What does it cost Peracchi to write the note and contribute it to his corporation? The IRS argues tersely that the "taxpayers in the instant case incurred no cost in issuing their own note to NAC, so their basis in the note was zero." Brief for Appellee at 41. See Alderman v. Commissioner, 55 T.C. 662, 665 (1971); Rev.Rul. 68–629, 1968–2 C.B. 154, 155.[13] Building on this premise, the IRS makes Peracchi out to be a grifter: He holds an unenforceable promise to pay himself money, since the corporation will not collect on it unless he says so.

It's true that all Peracchi did was make out a promise to pay on a piece of paper, mark it in the corporate minutes and enter it on the corporate books. It is also true that nothing will cause the corporation to enforce the note against Peracchi so long as Peracchi remains in control. But the IRS ignores the possibility that NAC may go bankrupt, an event that would suddenly make the note highly significant. Peracchi and NAC are separated by the corporate form, and this gossamer curtain makes a difference in the shell game of C Corp organization and reorganization. Contributing the note puts a million dollar nut within the corporate shell, exposing Peracchi to the cruel nutcracker of corporate creditors in the

---

[12] Peracchi owned all the voting stock of NAC both before and after the exchange, so the control requirement of section 351 is satisfied. * * * Peracchi did not receive any stock in return for the property contributed, so it could be argued that the exchange was not "solely in exchange for stock" as required by section 351. Courts have consistently recognized, however, that issuing stock in this situation would be a meaningless gesture: Because Peracchi is the sole shareholder of NAC, issuing additional stock would not affect his economic position relative to other shareholders. See, e.g., Jackson v. Commissioner, 708 F.2d 1402, 1405 (9th Cir.1983).

[13] We would face a different case had the Treasury promulgated a regulation interpreting section 357(c). A revenue ruling is entitled to some deference as the stated litigating position of the agency which enforces the tax code, but not nearly as much as a regulation. Ruling 68–629 offers no rationale, let alone a reasonable one, for its holding that it costs a taxpayer nothing to write a promissory note, and thus deserves little weight.

event NAC goes bankrupt. And it does so to the tune of $1,060,000, the full face amount of the note. Without the note, no matter how deeply the corporation went into debt, creditors could not reach Peracchi's personal assets. With the note on the books, however, creditors can reach into Peracchi's pocket by enforcing the note as an unliquidated asset of the corporation.

The key to solving this puzzle, then, is to ask whether bankruptcy is significant enough a contingency to confer substantial economic effect on this transaction. If the risk of bankruptcy is important enough to be recognized, Peracchi should get basis in the note: He will have increased his exposure to the risks of the business—and thus his economic investment in NAC—by $1,060,000. If bankruptcy is so remote that there is no realistic possibility it will ever occur, we can ignore the potential economic effect of the note as speculative and treat it as merely an unenforceable promise to contribute capital in the future.

When the question is posed this way, the answer is clear. Peracchi's obligation on the note was not conditioned on NAC's remaining solvent. It represents a new and substantial increase in Peracchi's investment in the corporation.[14] The Code seems to recognize that economic exposure of the shareholder is the ultimate measuring rod of a shareholder's investment. * * * Peracchi therefore is entitled to a step-up in basis to the extent he will be subjected to economic loss if the underlying investment turns unprofitable. * * *

The economics of the transaction also support Peracchi's view of the matter. The transaction here does not differ substantively from others that would certainly give Peracchi a boost in basis. For example, Peracchi could have borrowed $1 million from a bank and contributed the cash to NAC along with the properties. Because cash has a basis equal to face value, Peracchi would not have faced any section 357(c) gain. NAC could then have purchased the note from the bank for $1 million which, assuming the bank's original assessment of Peracchi's creditworthiness was accurate, would be the fair market value of the note. In the end the corporation would hold a million dollar note from Peracchi—just like it does now—and Peracchi would face no section 357(c) gain.[15] The only economic difference between the transaction just described and the transaction Peracchi actually engaged in is the additional costs that would accompany getting a loan from the bank. Peracchi incurs a "cost" of $1 million when he promises to pay the note to the bank; the cost is not diminished here by the fact that the transferor controls the initial

---

[14] We confine our holding to a case such as this where the note is contributed to an operating business which is subject to a non-trivial risk of bankruptcy or receivership. NAC is not, for example, a shell corporation or a passive investment company; Peracchi got into this mess in the first place because NAC was in financial trouble and needed more assets to meet Nevada's minimum premium-to-asset ratio for insurance companies.

[15] * * * We readily acknowledge that our assumptions fall apart if the shareholder isn't creditworthy. Here, the government has stipulated that Peracchi's net worth far exceeds the value of the note, so creditworthiness is not at issue. But we limit our holding to cases where the note is in fact worth approximately its face value.

transferee. The experts seem to agree: "Section 357(c) can be avoided by a transfer of enough cash to eliminate any excess of liabilities over basis; and since a note given by a solvent obligor in purchasing property is routinely treated as the equivalent of cash in determining the basis of the property, it seems reasonable to give it the same treatment in determining the basis of the property transferred in a § 351 exchange." Bittker & Eustice ¶ 3.06[4][b].

We are aware of the mischief that can result when taxpayers are permitted to calculate basis in excess of their true economic investment. * * * [W]e do not believe our holding will have such pernicious effects. First, and most significantly, by increasing the taxpayer's personal exposure, the contribution of a valid, unconditional promissory note has substantial economic effects which reflect his true economic investment in the enterprise. * * * Peracchi will have to pay the full amount of the note with after-tax dollars if NAC's economic situation heads south. Second, [i]t is the pass-through of losses that makes artificial increases in equity interests of particular concern. * * * We don't have to tread quite so lightly in the C Corp context, since a C Corp doesn't funnel losses to the shareholder.[16] * * *

We find further support for Peracchi's view by looking at the alternative: What would happen if the note had a zero basis? The IRS points out that the basis of the note in the hands of the corporation is the same as it was in the hands of the taxpayer. Accordingly, if the note has a zero basis for Peracchi, so too for NAC. See I.R.C. § 362(a).[17] But what happens if NAC—perhaps facing the threat of an involuntary petition for bankruptcy—turns around and sells Peracchi's note to a third party for its fair market value? According to the IRS's theory, NAC would take a carryover basis of zero in the note and would have to recognize $1,060,000 in phantom gain on the subsequent exchange, even though the note did not appreciate in value one bit. That can't be the right result.

Accordingly, we hold that Peracchi has a basis of $1,060,000 in the note he wrote to NAC. The aggregate basis exceeds the liabilities of the properties transferred to NAC under section 351, and Peracchi need not recognize any section 357(c) gain.

---

[16] Our holding therefore does not extend to the partnership or S Corp context.

[17] But see Lessinger v. Commissioner, 872 F.2d 519 (2d Cir.1989). In *Lessinger*, the Second Circuit analyzed a similar transaction. It agreed with the IRS's (faulty) premise that the note had a zero basis in the taxpayer's hands. But then, brushing aside the language of section 362(a), the court concluded that the note had a basis in the corporation's hands equal to its face value. The court held that this was enough to dispel any section 357(c) gain to the taxpayer, proving that two wrongs sometimes do add up to a right.

We agree with the IRS that *Lessinger's* approach is untenable. Section 357(c) contemplates measuring basis of the property contributed in the hands of the taxpayer, not the corporation. Section 357 appears in the midst of the Code sections dealing with the effect of capital contributions on the shareholder; sections 361 et seq., on the other hand, deal with the effect on a corporation, and section 362 defines the basis of property contributed in the hands of the corporation. Because we hold that the note has a face value basis to the shareholder for purposes of section 357(c), however, we reach the same result as *Lessinger*.

Genuine Indebtedness or Sham?

The Tax Court never reached the issue of Peracchi's basis in the note. Instead, it ruled for the Commissioner on the ground that the note is not genuine indebtedness. The court emphasized two facts which it believed supported the view that the note is a sham: (1) NAC's decision whether to collect on the note is wholly controlled by Peracchi and (2) Peracchi missed the first two years of payments, yet NAC did not accelerate the debt. These facts certainly do suggest that Peracchi paid imperfect attention to his obligations under the note, as frequently happens when debtor and creditor are under common control. But we believe the proper way to approach the genuine indebtedness question is to look at the face of the note and consider whether Peracchi's legal obligation is illusory. And it is not. First, the note's bona fides are adequate: The IRS has stipulated that Peracchi is creditworthy and likely to have the funds to pay the note; the note bears a market rate of interest commensurate with his creditworthiness; the note has a fixed term. Second, the IRS does not argue that the value of the note is anything other than its face value; nothing in the record suggests NAC couldn't borrow against the note to raise cash. Lastly, the note is fully transferable and enforceable by third parties, such as hostile creditors. On the basis of these facts we hold that the note is an ordinary, negotiable, recourse obligation which must be treated as genuine debt for tax purposes. * * *

The IRS argues that the note is nevertheless a sham because it was executed simply to avoid tax. Tax avoidance is a valid concern in this context; section 357(a) does provide the opportunity for a bailout transaction of sorts. For example, a taxpayer with an unencumbered building he wants to sell could take out a nonrecourse mortgage, pocket the proceeds, and contribute the property to a newly organized corporation. Although the gain would be preserved for later recognition, the taxpayer would have partially cashed out his economic investment in the property: By taking out a nonrecourse mortgage, the economic risk of loss would be transferred to the lender. Section 357(b) addresses this sort of bailout by requiring the recognition of gain if the transaction lacks a business purpose.

Peracchi's capital contribution is not a bailout. Peracchi contributed the buildings to NAC because the company needed additional capital, and the contribution of the note was part of that transaction. The IRS, in fact, stipulated that the contribution had a business purpose. Bailout potential exists regardless of whether the taxpayer contributes a note along with the property; section 357(b), not 357(c), is the sword the Service must use to attack bailout transactions.

* * *

The Aftermath

We take a final look at the result to make sure we have not placed our stamp of approval on some sort of exotic tax shelter. We hold that

Peracchi is entitled to a step up in basis for the face value of the note, just as if he contributed cash to the corporation. See I.R.C. § 358. If Peracchi does in fact keep his promise and pay off the note with after tax dollars, the tax result is perfectly appropriate: NAC receives cash, and the increase in basis Peracchi took for the original contribution is justified. Peracchi has less potential gain, but he paid for it in real dollars.

But what if, as the IRS fears, NAC never does enforce the note? If NAC goes bankrupt, the note will be an asset of the estate enforceable for the benefit of creditors, and Peracchi will eventually be forced to pay in after tax dollars. Peracchi will undoubtedly have worked the deferral mechanism of section 351 to his advantage, but this is not inappropriate where the taxpayer is on the hook in both form and substance for enough cash to offset the excess of liabilities over basis. By increasing his personal exposure to the creditors of NAC, Peracchi has increased his economic investment in the corporation, and a corresponding increase in basis is wholly justified.[20]

Conclusion

We hold that Peracchi has a basis of $1,060,000 in the note, its face value. As such, the aggregate liabilities of the property contributed to NAC do not exceed its basis, and Peracchi does not recognize any § 357(c) gain. The decision of the Tax Court is REVERSED. The case is remanded for entry of judgment in favor of Peracchi.

■ FERNANDEZ, CIRCUIT JUDGE, Dissenting:

Is there something that a taxpayer, who has borrowed hundreds of thousands of dollars more than his basis in his property, can do to avoid taxation when he transfers the property? Yes, says Peracchi, because by using a very clever argument he can avoid the strictures of 26 U.S.C. § 357(c). He need only make a promise to pay by giving a "good," though unsecured, promissory note to his corporation when he transfers the property to it. That is true even though the property remains subject to the encumbrances. How can that be? Well, by preparing a promissory note the taxpayer simply creates basis without cost to himself. But see 26 U.S.C. § 1012; Rev.Rul. 68–629, 1968–2 C.B. 154; Alderman v. Commissioner, 55 T.C. 662, 665 (1971). Thus he can extract a large part of the value of the property, pocket the funds, use them, divest himself of the property, and pay the tax another day, if ever at all.

But as with all magical solutions, the taxpayer must know the proper incantations and make the correct movements. He cannot just transfer

---

[20] What happens if NAC does not go bankrupt, but merely writes off the note instead? Peracchi would then face discharge of indebtedness income to the tune of $1,060,000. This would put Peracchi in a worse position than when he started, since discharge of indebtedness is normally treated as ordinary income. Peracchi, having increased his basis in the stock of the corporation by $1,060,000 would receive a capital loss (or less capital gain) to that extent. But the shift in character of the income will normally work to the disadvantage of a taxpayer in Peracchi's situation.

the property to the corporation and promise, or be obligated, to pay off the encumbrances. That would not change the fact that the property was still subject to those encumbrances. According to Peracchi, the thaumaturgy that will save him from taxes proceeds in two simple steps. He must first prepare a ritualistic writing—an unsecured promissory note in an amount equal to or more than the excess of the encumbrances over the basis. He must then give that writing to his corporation. That is all.[1] But is not that just a "promise to pay," which "does not represent the paying out or reduction of assets?" Don E. Williams Co. v. Commissioner, 429 U.S. 569, 583 * * * (1977). Never mind, he says. He has nonetheless increased the total basis of the property transferred and avoided the tax. I understand the temptation to embrace that argument, but I see no real support for it in the law.

Peracchi says a lot about economic realities. I see nothing real about that maneuver. I see, rather, a bit of sortilege that would have made Merlin envious. The taxpayer has created something—basis—out of nothing.

Thus, I respectfully dissent.

DETAILED ANALYSIS

1.   DETERMINATION OF AMOUNT OF LIABILITY ASSUMED

Section 357(d) provides statutory rules for determining the extent to which a debt of the transferor has been assumed by the transferee corporation for purposes of determining the transferor's gain under § 357(c) and the corporate transferee's step-up in basis under § 362(a) that results from the transferor's recognition of gain.[8] Recourse debt is treated as having been assumed only if, based on all the facts and circumstances, the transferee corporation has agreed to pay the debt and is expected to pay the debt, regardless of whether or not the transferor shareholder has been relieved of liability vis-à-vis the creditor. The transferee corporation is treated as assuming any nonrecourse debt encumbering property it receives, but the amount of the debt assumed is reduced by the lesser of: (1) the amount of the debt secured by assets not transferred to the corporation that another person or corporation has agreed (and is expected) to satisfy, or (2) the fair market value of the other assets secured by the debt.

Seggerman Farms v. Commissioner, 308 F.3d 803 (7th Cir. 2002), held that § 357(c) requires gain recognition when the liabilities assumed by the corporation exceed the transferor shareholder's basis in the property even if the transferor remains liable as a guarantor. The shareholders argued that

---

[1] What is even better, he need not even make payments on the note until after the IRS catches up with him. I, by the way, am dubious about the proposition that the Tax Court clearly erred when it held that the note was not even a genuine indebtedness.

[8] In REG–100818–01, Liabilities Assumed in Certain Transactions, 68 F.R. 23931 (May 6, 2003), the IRS and Treasury announced that they are concerned that § 357(d) and § 362(d) do not always produce appropriate results and that it might be desirable to modify certain rules by Regulation, as permitted by § 357(d)(3). The notice explains the issues and the rules the IRS and Treasury are considering proposing.

because they had personally guaranteed the debt, they were not relieved of their obligations on the transferred property, and, thus, no gain should be recognized on the transfer. The court rejected the taxpayers' argument that under "the emerging equitable interpretation of § 357(c)" their guarantees should be treated in the same manner as the shareholders' promissory notes to the corporations in *Peracchi* and *Lessinger*, reasoning that the guarantee, standing alone, does not constitute an "economic outlay." Although the case arose prior to the enactment of § 357(d), the court noted in its opinion that the result would not be different under the current statute.

On the other hand, § 357(d) has changed the results in Rosen v. Commissioner, 62 T.C. 11 (1974), aff'd by order, 515 F.2d 507 (3d Cir.1975), and Owen v. Commissioner, 881 F.2d 832 (9th Cir.1989), cited in footnote 10 of the *Peracchi* opinion. Both of those cases held that § 357(c) applied in situations in which the transferor remained personally liable on recourse debts secured by property transferred to a corporation where the corporation did not expressly assume the obligations but merely took the property subject to the encumbrances. Prior to the enactment of § 357(d), § 357(c) applied as long as the property received by the corporation was subject to the debt.

2.   CONTRIBUTION OF SHAREHOLDER'S PROMISSORY NOTE: DETERMINATION OF TRANSFEROR'S BASIS

Peracchi was not the first case to consider the question whether a transferor of encumbered property could eliminate recognized gain under § 357(c) by the transfer of the transferor's own promissory note. Several courts have confronted the issue, and each has analyzed it differently. In Rev.Rul. 68–629, 1968–2 C.B. 154, the IRS held that for purposes of applying § 357(c) a shareholder's note contributed to the corporation had a zero basis because the shareholder "incurred no cost in making the note." The Tax Court first faced the issue in Alderman v. Commissioner, 55 T.C. 662 (1971), where, as in *Peracchi*, the taxpayers transferred assets to their corporation, which assumed liabilities in excess of the transferors' basis for the assets. In order to increase the assets of the corporation and avoid gain under § 357(c), the taxpayers executed a note payable to the corporation in an amount slightly in excess of the amount by which the assumed liabilities exceeded the basis of the transferred assets. Following Rev.Rul. 68–629, the Tax Court held that because the taxpayers incurred no cost in making the note, their basis in the note was zero. Thus, gain resulted under § 357(c). Presumably, however, the note should give rise to an immediate adjustment to the obligor-shareholder's basis for the stock. If there is no immediate basis adjustment for the note, the shareholder should receive an increased basis for the stock for additional capital contributed to the corporation as the note is paid. Pursuant to § 1032, the corporation would not be required to recognize gain either when the note itself was received or when payment was received. (However, in dictum, the court gratuitously—erroneously in the opinion of the authors of this text—added that the corporation's basis in the note also was zero).

In Lessinger v. Commissioner, 872 F.2d 519 (2d Cir.1989), the Court of Appeals for the Second Circuit refused to follow *Alderman*. Lessinger transferred the assets of a sole proprietorship to his wholly owned corporation in a transaction to which § 351 applied. The proprietorship was insolvent in that its liabilities exceeded the value of the transferred assets. The liabilities assumed by the corporation also exceeded Lessinger's basis in the transferred assets. The transferee corporation created a "loan receivable" due from Lessinger on the corporate books in the amount that the liabilities of the proprietorship exceeded the value of the transferred assets. Reversing the Tax Court (85 T.C. 824 (1985)), the Court of Appeals held that Lessinger was not required by § 357(c) to recognize gain, but followed a different path of reasoning than the Ninth Circuit Court of Appeals did in *Peracchi*. The Second Circuit agreed with the *Alderman* holding that a taxpayer has no basis in the taxpayer's own promise to pay, but also concluded that the basis of Lessinger's obligation in the hands of the corporate transferee was equal to the face amount of the obligation. The court reasoned that the transferee corporation "incurred a cost in the transaction involving the transfer of the obligation by taking on the liabilities of the proprietorship that exceeded its assets." The court also pointed out that unless the corporation had a basis in Lessinger's obligation, it would have to recognize gain on payment of the debt. The court then held that "where the transferor undertakes genuine personal liability to the transferee, 'adjusted basis' in § 357(c) refers to the transferee's basis in the obligation which is its face amount." Finally, the court also noted that Lessinger did not avoid recognition of economic gain on the transaction because he undertook "genuine personal liability" to the corporation for the liabilities exceeding the basis of the assets.

The Second Circuit's reasoning in *Lessinger* is unsupportable. First, in total disregard of § 362(a), the court concluded that the corporation took a basis in the transferor's promissory note equal to its face amount. (That result might be true for other reasons, but it does not occur by reason of § 362(a).) Second, since the payments on the note should be treated as shareholder capital contributions, the corporation will not recognize any gain as it receives payments. Third, the court's reasoning that gain under § 357(c) is computed with reference to the transferee's basis in the transferred property rather than the transferor's basis is contrary to the otherwise universally accepted rule that gain is computed with reference to the transferor's basis.

The courts' reasoning in each of *Peracchi* and *Lessinger*, as well as the Tax Court's reasoning in *Alderman* and the IRS's reasoning in Rev.Rul. 68– 629, are misguided, but ultimately the court in *Peracchi* reaches the correct conclusion, at least where the debt obligation is genuine. All of these authorities focus on determining whether the transferor shareholder's basis in the shareholder's own note is zero or its principal (face) amount in applying § 357(c). All of the court decisions, including *Peracchi*, as well as the IRS, miss the point that the statutory rule in § 357(c) is inadequate to deal with the issue because the statute focuses on the transferor's basis in property "transferred." To transfer property the transferor must own the property prior to the transfer. However, the transferor never owned the transferor's own promissory note. It did not come into existence as "property" until it was owned by the corporation. The shareholder "issued" the note to the corporation; the shareholder did not "transfer" it; the note was created by its issuance. *Alderman* and the IRS attempt to follow the statutory pattern of Subchapter C quite literally, without resort to general principles of taxation. *Peracchi*, on the other hand, superimposes on Subchapter C the general principle that payment with a promissory note is treated the same as payment in cash. For basis purposes, the acquisition of property for a note is the same as the acquisition of property for cash. See Rev.Rul. 2004–37, 2004–1 C.B. 583, holding that under general principles of taxation, stock in a corporation acquired in exchange for the shareholder's promissory note takes a § 1012 cost basis equal to the principal amount of the note, just as it would if cash had been paid. From this perspective it should not matter whether a taxpayer, on the one hand, transfers property and cash to a corporation in exchange for stock or, on the other hand, transfers property and a promissory note in exchange for stock. If the exchange were a taxable transaction, the tax consequences to both the shareholder and corporation would be identical in each case. Thus, the issuance of shareholder's promissory note to the corporation in addition to the transfer of property in connection with which the corporation assumes debts of the shareholder should be treated in the same manner as a contribution of cash equal to the principal amount of the debt. Perhaps this is the reason that no case, Revenue Ruling, or any informal IRS guidance has applied or cited either *Alderman* or Rev.Rul. 68–629 since *Peracchi* was decided.

3.   THE CORPORATION'S BASIS

When a single asset is transferred in a situation to which § 357(c) applies, determination of the corporation's basis is not difficult. But where multiple assets are transferred—a common situation because the contribution of improved real estate involves two separate assets, the building and the land under it—determining the basis of each asset to the corporation under § 362(a) is difficult. If § 357(b) applies to treat liabilities as boot, the recognition of gain is no different than in the case of cash or other property. Thus, the basis increase for the corporation with respect to each asset equals the gain recognized to the transferor with respect to that asset. Allocation of gain recognized by the transferor under § 357(c), however, presents different issues.

The principle of Rev.Rul. 68–55, reproduced above, upon which the allocation of § 351(b) gain among assets for purposes of the basis adjustment in § 362(a)(1) is based, does not help because, unlike § 351(b) gain, § 357(c) gain is not computed asset-by-asset. Gain under § 357(c) results only when aggregate liabilities assumed by the corporation exceed the aggregate basis of all transferred assets. If a liability is secured by a particular asset, however, gain recognized by the transferor under § 357(c) with respect to the liability reasonably might be allocated solely to the encumbered asset. But in many cases this simplified allocation method will be unavailing. For example, assume that A transfers two assets to X, a controlled corporation. One asset is real property with a fair market value of $75 and a basis of $15, and the second asset is equipment with a value of $25 and a basis of $30. X assumes unsecured liabilities of $50, which requires that A recognize $5 of gain under § 357(c). Here the recognized gain occurs because in the aggregate the basis of transferred assets is less than the liabilities. Unlike the case in which boot is received, the recognized gain is not attributable to specific assets. Nonetheless, an allocation of A's $5 gain to the real property rather than an apportionment between the two assets has some appeal because the allocation will not result in increasing the difference between the fair market value and the adjusted basis of any asset.

This same logic would indicate that if a single transferor transfers two or more appreciated assets and recognizes gain under § 357(c), the basis adjustment should be made by apportioning the gain among the assets relative to the amount by which the fair market value of each asset exceeds its basis. The Regulations are silent regarding these questions, however, and the IRS has never issued a Revenue Ruling on point. Treas.Reg. § 1.357–2(b), which deals with determining the character of the transferor's gain, suggests that the basis increase should be allocated in proportion to the fair market values of the assets, but Treas.Reg. § 1.357–2(b) is deeply flawed from a theoretical perspective because it can cause allocation of gain to an asset that is not appreciated. Section 362(d)(1) provides that under § 362(a) the basis of any property transferred to the corporation cannot be increased to an amount above its fair market value by reason of any gain recognized to the transferor as a result of the assumption of a liability.

4. INTERACTION OF SECTIONS 351(b) AND 357

Rev.Rul. 60–302, 1960–2 C.B. 223, illustrates the simultaneous application of § 351(b) and § 357(c) to a transfer. In the ruling, A transferred property with a fair market value of $500 and a basis of $200 to a corporation in a transaction subject to § 351. In addition to issuing stock, the corporation assumed a $210 liability secured by the property and gave the transferor a note for $80. The ruling held that A recognized a $10 gain under § 357(c) and an $80 gain under § 351(b), for a total of $90.

The application of these principles is more complex where multiple assets are transferred. Suppose that B transfers two assets to X Corporation: (1) Blackacre, with a fair market value of $700 and a basis of $250, subject to a mortgage debt of $350, and (2) publicly traded stock with a fair market value of $300 and a basis of $300, subject to a lien debt of $150. In exchange, B receives all of the common stock of X Corporation (fair market value $300), a promissory note for $200, and X Corporation assumes the $500 of debt encumbering the transferred assets. Because the $500 of debt does not exceed the aggregate basis of Blackacre and the stock ($550), no gain is recognized under § 357(c). Applying the principles of Rev.Rul. 68–55, excerpted supra, under § 351(b), B recognizes a gain of $140 with respect to Blackacre, but does not recognize any gain or loss with respect to the stock.

	Blackacre	Stock
Fair market value	$700	$300
Percent of fair market value	70%	30%
Amount realized		
Fair market value of stock received in exchange ($300)	$210	$ 90
Promissory note ($200)	$140	$ 60
Debt assumption ($500)	$350	$150
	$700	$300
Basis	$250	$300
Gain (loss) realized	$450	$ 0
Gain (loss) recognized	$140	$ 0

B's basis in the stock of X Corporation, as determined under § 358 is negative $10, computed as follows:

Basis of transferred property		
Blackacre	$250	
Stock	$300	
		$550
Minus boot & debt		
Note	$200	
Debt assumed	$500	
		($700)
Plus gain recognized		$140
Basis of stock		($ 10)

Properly applying the Code to this fact pattern, there is no way around negative basis. Notwithstanding what Judge Kozinski might have said about it in *Peracchi*, negative basis, unlike Bigfoot, does exist. Rev.Rul. 68–55 leads inexorably to this result. Prop.Reg. § 1.351–2(b) (2009) would have incorporated the holding of Rev.Rul. 68–55 into Regulations. However, the 2009 Proposed Regulations were withdrawn in March 2019, with the Treasury explaining, "After thoroughly considering the comments received, the Treasury Department and the IRS have determined that it is unlikely that the approach of the 2009 Proposed Regulations can be implemented in comprehensive final regulations without significant modifications. * * * The Treasury Department and the IRS are continuing to study the issues addressed in the 2009 Proposed Regulations." 84 Fed. Reg. 11686 (Mar. 28, 2019). Yet, Rev.Rul. 68–55 has not been withdrawn.

PROBLEM SET 5

1.   (a) Bonnie and Clyde formed FastGetaway Corporation to engage in a limousine charter service business. Bonnie contributed $50,000 in cash. Clyde contributed a Mercedes-Benz limousine with a fair market value of $80,000 and a basis of $10,000, subject to a purchase money lien indebtedness of $30,000, which was assumed by the corporation. What are the tax consequences to Clyde and the corporation?

   (b) Assume alternatively that Bonnie contributed $100,000 in cash. Clyde contributed a Mercedes-Benz limousine with a fair market value of $80,000 and a basis of $12,000, subject to a purchase money lien indebtedness of $25,000, which was assumed by the corporation, and a Lincoln limousine with a fair market value of $60,000 and a basis of $48,000, subject to a purchase money lien indebtedness of $15,000, which was assumed by the corporation. What are the tax consequences to Clyde and the corporation?

2.   Oscar and Patty formed NHC Corporation. Oscar contributed $250,000 in cash in exchange for 10 shares of common stock. Patty contributed land and a warehouse building. The land has a basis of $10,000 and the building has an adjusted basis of $30,000. The fair market value of the land is $87,500. The fair market value of the building is $262,500. Patty received 10 shares of common stock and the corporation assumed a $100,000 purchase money mortgage secured by the land and building. What are the tax consequences to Patty and the corporation?

3.   (a) Evan and William formed Barleycorn Corporation to engage in the distilling business. Evan contributed $250,000 in cash and William contributed land and a warehouse building previously held out for rental. The land had a basis of $10,000, and the building had an adjusted basis of $30,000. The fair market value of land is $87,500, and the fair market value of the building is $262,500. William will receive 10 shares of common stock, and the corporation will take the property subject to $100,000 nonrecourse purchase money mortgage lien, but it will not expressly assume the mortgage indebtedness. What are the tax consequences to William and the corporation?

   (b) Would your answer differ if the mortgage was a recourse mortgage and the corporation did not expressly assume the mortgage?

   (c) How would your answer in part (a) differ if the fair market value of land was $10,000, and the fair market value of the building was $340,000?

4.   Edmund and Tenzig formed Sasquatch Corporation. Tenzig contributed $3,000,000 of cash in exchange for 75 shares of common stock. Edmund contributed land with a fair market value of $2,000,000 and a basis of $800,000, subject to a $1,500,000 nonrecourse mortgage debt, and Edmund's negotiable promissory note payable to the order of Sasquatch Corporation, in the amount of $500,000, in exchange for 25 shares of common stock. Edmund's note bore interest at the prime rate plus 2%, payable annually, with $100,000 of principal due on each of the first five anniversaries of the date of the note. What are the tax consequences to Edmund and to Sasquatch Corporation?

(2) ASSUMPTION OF DEBTS THAT WOULD BE DEDUCTIBLE WHEN PAID: SECTION 357(c)(3)

INTERNAL REVENUE CODE: Sections 357(c); 358(d), (h).

Revenue Ruling 95–74
1995–2 C.B. 36.

ISSUES

(1) Are the liabilities assumed by S in the § 351 exchange described below liabilities for purposes of §§ 357(c)(1) and 358(d)?

(2) Once assumed by S, how will the liabilities in the § 351 exchange described below be treated?

FACTS

Corporation P is an accrual basis, calendar-year corporation engaged in various ongoing businesses, one of which includes the operation of a manufacturing plant (the Manufacturing Business). The plant is located on land purchased by P many years before. The land was not contaminated by any hazardous waste when P purchased it. However, as a result of plant operations, certain environmental liabilities, such as potential soil and groundwater remediation, are now associated with the land.

In Year 1, for bona fide business purposes, P engages in an exchange to which § 351 of the Internal Revenue Code applies by transferring substantially all of the assets associated with the Manufacturing Business, including the manufacturing plant and the land on which the plant is located, to a newly formed corporation S, in exchange for all of the stock of S and for S's assumption of the liabilities associated with the Manufacturing Business, including the environmental liabilities associated with the land. P has no plan or intention to dispose of (or have S issue) any S stock. S is an accrual basis, calendar-year taxpayer.

P did not undertake any environmental remediation efforts in connection with the land transferred to S before the transfer and did not deduct or capitalize any amount with respect to the contingent environmental liabilities associated with the transferred land.

In Year 3, S undertakes soil and groundwater remediation efforts relating to the land transferred in the § 351 exchange and incurs costs (within the meaning of the economic performance rules of § 461(h)) as a result of those remediation efforts. Of the total amount of costs incurred, a portion would have constituted ordinary and necessary business expenses that are deductible under § 162 and the remaining portion would have constituted capital expenditures under § 263 if there had not been a § 351 exchange and the costs for remediation efforts had been incurred by P. See Rev.Rul. 94–38, 1994–1 C.B. 35 (discussing the treatment of certain environmental remediation costs).

LAW AND ANALYSIS

Issue 1: Section 351(a) provides that no gain or loss shall be recognized if property is transferred to a corporation solely in exchange for stock and immediately after the exchange the transferor is in control of the corporation.

Section 357(a) provides a general rule that a transferee corporation's assumption of a transferor's liability in a § 351 exchange will not be treated as money or other property received by the transferor. Section 357(b) provides an exception to the general rule of § 357(a) when it appears that the principal purpose of the transferor in having the liability assumed was avoidance of Federal income tax on the exchange or, if not such purpose, was not a bona fide business purpose.

Section 357(c)(1) provides a second exception to the general rule of § 357(a). Section 357(c)(1) provides that if the sum of the liabilities the transferee corporation assumes and takes property subject to exceeds the total of the adjusted basis of the property the transferor transfers to the corporation pursuant to the exchange, then the excess shall be considered as gain from the sale or exchange of the property.

For purposes of applying the exception in § 357(c)(1), § 357(c)(3)(A) provides that a liability the payment of which would give rise to a deduction (or would be described in § 736(a)) is excluded. This special rule does not apply, however, to any liability to the extent that the incurrence of the liability resulted in the creation of, or an increase in, the basis of any property. Section 357(c)(3)(B).

Section 358(a)(1) provides that in a § 351 exchange the basis of the property permitted to be received under § 351 without the recognition of gain or loss shall be the same as that of the property exchanged, decreased by (i) the fair market value of any other property (except money) received by the transferor, (ii) the amount of any money received by the transferor, and (iii) the amount of loss to the transferor which was recognized on such exchange, and increased by (i) the amount which was treated as a dividend and (ii) the amount of gain to the transferor which was recognized on such exchange (not including any portion of such gain which was treated as a dividend).

Section 358(d)(1) provides that where, as part of the consideration to the transferor, another party to the exchange assumed a liability of the transferor, such assumption (in the amount of the liability) shall, for purposes of § 358, be treated as money received by the transferor on the exchange. Section 358(d)(2) provides that § 358(d)(1) does not apply to any liability excluded under § 357(c)(3).

* * *

A number of cases concerning cash basis taxpayers were litigated in the 1970s with respect to the definition of "liabilities" for purposes of § 357(c)(1), with sometimes conflicting analyses and results. * * * In response to this litigation, Congress enacted § 357(c)(3) to address the concern that the inclusion in the § 357(c)(1) determination of certain deductible liabilities resulted in "unforeseen and unintended tax difficulties for certain cash basis taxpayers who incorporate a going business." S.Rep. No. 1263, 95th Cong., 2d Sess. 184–85 (1978), 1978–3 C.B. 482–83.

Congress concluded that including in the § 357(c)(1) determination liabilities that have not yet been taken into account by the transferor results in an overstatement of liabilities of, and potential inappropriate gain recognition to, the transferor because the transferor has not received the corresponding deduction or other corresponding tax benefit. *Id.* To prevent this result, Congress enacted § 357(c)(3)(A) to exclude certain deductible liabilities from the scope of § 357(c), as long as the liabilities had not resulted in the creation of, or an increase in, the basis of any property (as provided in § 357(c)(3)(B)). * * *

While § 357(c)(3) explicitly addresses liabilities that give rise to deductible items, the same principle applies to liabilities that give rise to capital expenditures as well. Including in the § 357(c)(1) determination those liabilities that have not yet given rise to capital expenditures (and thus have not yet created or increased basis) with respect to the property of the transferor prior to the transfer also would result in an overstatement of liabilities. Thus, such liabilities also appropriately are excluded in determining liabilities for purposes of § 357(c)(1). *Cf.* * * * Rev.Rul. 88–77, 1988–2 C.B. 129 (accrued but unpaid expenses and accounts payable are not liabilities of a cash basis partnership for purposes of computing the adjusted basis of a partner's interest for purposes of § 752).

In this case, the contingent environmental liabilities assumed by *S* had not yet been taken into account by *P* prior to the transfer (and therefore had neither given rise to deductions for *P* nor resulted in the creation of, or increase in, basis in any property of *P*). As a result, the contingent environmental liabilities are not included in determining whether the amount of the liabilities assumed by *S* exceeds the adjusted basis of the property transferred by *P* pursuant to § 357(c)(1).

Due to the parallel constructions and interrelated function and mechanics of §§ 357 and 358, liabilities that are not included in the determination under § 357(c)(1) also are not included in the § 358 determination of the transferor's basis in the stock received in the § 351 exchange. * * * Therefore, the contingent environmental liabilities assumed by S are not treated as money received by P under § 358 for purposes of determining P's basis in the stock of S received in the exchange.

Issue 2: In *Holdcroft Transp. Co. v. Commissioner*, 153 F.2d 323 (8th Cir.1946), the Court of Appeals for the Eighth Circuit held that, after a transfer pursuant to the predecessor to § 351, the payments by a transferee corporation were not deductible even though the transferor partnership would have been entitled to deductions for the payments had the partnership actually made the payments. The court stated generally that the expense of settling claims or liabilities of a predecessor entity did not arise as an operating expense or loss of the business of the transferee but was a part of the cost of acquiring the predecessor's property, and the fact that the claims were contingent and unliquidated at the time of the acquisition was not of controlling consequence.

In Rev.Rul. 80–198, 1980–2 C.B. 113, an individual transferred all of the assets and liabilities of a sole proprietorship, which included accounts payable and accounts receivable, to a new corporation in exchange for all of its stock. The revenue ruling holds, subject to certain limitations, that the transfer qualifies as an exchange within the meaning of § 351(a) and that the transferee corporation will report in its income the accounts receivable as collected and will be allowed deductions under § 162 for the payments it makes to satisfy the accounts payable. In reaching these holdings, the revenue ruling makes reference to the specific congressional intent of § 351(a) to facilitate the incorporation of an ongoing business by making the incorporation tax free. The ruling states that this intent would be equally frustrated if either the transferor were taxed on the transfer of the accounts receivable or the transferee were not allowed a deduction for payment of the accounts payable. * * *

The present case is analogous to the situation in Rev.Rul. 80–198. For business reasons, P transferred in a § 351 exchange substantially all of the assets and liabilities associated with the Manufacturing Business to S, in exchange for all of its stock, and P intends to remain in control of S. The costs S incurs to remediate the land would have been deductible in part and capitalized in part had P continued the Manufacturing Business and incurred those costs to remediate the land. The congressional intent to facilitate necessary business readjustments would be frustrated by not according to S the ability to deduct or capitalize the expenses of the ongoing business.

Therefore, on these facts, the Internal Revenue Service will not follow the decision in *Holdcroft Transp. Co. v. Commissioner*, 153 F.2d 323 (8th Cir.1946). Accordingly, the contingent environmental liabilities assumed from P are deductible as business expenses under § 162 or are capitalized under § 263, as appropriate, by S under S's method of accounting (determined as if S has owned the land for the period and in the same manner as it was owned by P).

HOLDINGS

(1) The liabilities assumed by S in the § 351 exchange described above are not liabilities for purposes of § 357(c)(1) and § 358(d) because the liabilities had not yet been taken into account by P prior to the transfer (and therefore had neither given rise to deductions for P nor resulted in the creation of, or increase in, basis in any property of P).

(2) The liabilities assumed by S in the § 351 exchange described above are deductible by S as business expenses under § 162 or are capital expenditures under § 263, as appropriate, under S's method of accounting (determined as if S has owned the land for the period and in the same manner as it was owned by P).

DETAILED ANALYSIS

1. CASH METHOD ACCOUNTS PAYABLE

As described in Rev.Rul. 95–74, prior to the Revenue Act of 1978 special problems were present when accounts receivable and accounts payable were transferred by a cash method taxpayer in a § 351 transaction. Since the accounts receivable would not have been included in the transferor's income by the time of the transfer, their tax basis in the hands of the transferor is zero. On the other hand, the accounts payable, by definition not yet paid or deducted by a cash method taxpayer, would, under the literal language of § 357(c), constitute "liabilities" assumed by the corporation in the incorporation transaction. As a result, a cash method taxpayer could realize income in a § 351 transaction if the accounts payable were transferred to a corporation in connection with accounts receivable or other assets with a low tax basis. The courts struggled with different approaches. Compare Raich v. Commissioner, 46 T.C. 604 (1966), with Focht v. Commissioner, 68 T.C. 223 (1977) (acq.) (the Tax Court abandoned its position in *Raich* and held that cash method payables are not liabilities under § 357(c) to the extent the payables would be deductible when paid). The Revenue Act of 1978 resolved many of the issues by adding § 357(c)(3), which provides that liabilities that would give rise to a deduction on payment are not considered for purposes of § 357(c)(1). The 1978 Act also enacted § 358(d)(2), which provides that such liabilities are not treated as money received for purposes of determining the transferor's basis in stock or securities received.

Accounts payable that are treated as not being liabilities by § 357(c)(3) typically include cash method trade accounts payable and other cash method liabilities, such as interest and taxes, that relate to the transferred trade or business. Whether a transferor is a cash method taxpayer is determined separately for each item. For example, a taxpayer using a hybrid method of accounting (e.g., utilizing inventories and the accrual method in computing income from purchases and sales while using the cash method in computing all other items of income and expenses) is considered a cash method taxpayer for purposes of applying § 357(c) to accounts payable for items computed on the cash method of accounting, but not with respect to liabilities relating to inventory. See Staff of the Joint Committee on Taxation, General Explanation of the Revenue Act of 1978, 218–20 (Comm.Print 1978).

Not all of the potential problems with payables are resolved by § 357(c)(3). In Orr v. Commissioner, 78 T.C. 1059 (1982), which arose before the effective date of § 357(c)(3), the taxpayer transferred to a newly formed corporation customers' cash deposits for travel received in the course of the taxpayer's business as a travel agent. The deposits were refundable and had not been taken into income by the taxpayer. The taxpayer's liability to refund

(c) To what extent may Payoff Peddlers deduct payment of the accounts payable?

2. Jeff and Louis started Border-on-the-Nile.com, Inc. to market and sell books over the internet. Each received 10 shares of common stock. Jeff contributed $200,000 in cash. Louis, who is an accrual method taxpayer, contributed an inventory of books worth $250,000, with a basis of $40,000. In addition, the corporation agreed to pay a $50,000 prize to whoever holds the winning lottery ticket from a contest run by Louis in his former bricks-and-mortar-based bookstore business. All of the tickets have been distributed, but the winner has not yet been drawn. Pursuant to § 461(h), and the Regulations thereunder, Louis's deduction for the $50,000 prize is not allowed until economic performance, which in this case is payment of the prize money to the winner. What are the tax consequences to Louis and Border-on-the-Nile.com?

3. Toxic Chemical Corp. formed a new wholly owned subsidiary, Chimera, Inc. by transferring Brownacre, land that is the site of an arsenic mine formerly operated by Toxic, with a gross fair market value of $500,000 and with a basis of $300,000, in exchange for common stock. Chimera agreed to be responsible for any and all future environmental remediation expenses with respect to the property that might be required by federal and state agencies. Toxic estimated that the future environmental remediation expenses would be approximately $400,000. Shortly thereafter, Toxic sold the Chimera stock for $100,000. What are the tax consequences to Toxic?

SECTION 3.   THE "CONTROL" REQUIREMENT

INTERNAL REVENUE CODE: Sections 351(a), (c)(1); 368(c).

REGULATIONS: Section 1.351–1(a), (b).

Section 351 provides nonrecognition of gain or loss only if *immediately after the transfer* the transferor or transferors of property are in "control" of the corporation as defined in § 368(c), which requires ownership of 80% of the combined voting power of all stock and 80% of all other classes of stock. Thus, for example, if individual A transfers property to a pre-existing corporation, in which A previously owned no stock, in exchange for 25% of the only class of voting common stock, § 351 does not apply to provide nonrecognition of gain or loss. This rule raises the question of the meaning of "immediately after" in situations in which at the time of the transfer it is contemplated that the transferor will dispose of the stock or that additional stock will be issued to a person who is not also a transferor of property. This question, in turn, requires analysis of when two putatively separate transactions will be viewed together as a single transaction under the "step transaction doctrine," introduced in Chapter 1.

Intermountain Lumber Company v. Commissioner

Tax Court of the United States, 1976.
65 T.C. 1025.

[Eds.: Dee Shook owned a sawmill that was damaged in a fire in March 1964. Shook was financially unable to rebuild the mill on his own and convinced Milo Wilson to guarantee a $200,000 loan to rebuild the mill. In return, Wilson insisted on becoming an equal shareholder with Shook. On May 28, 1964, Shook, Wilson, and two other individuals, all acting as incorporators, executed articles of incorporation for S & W Sawmill, Inc. (hereinafter S & W). Shook executed a bill of sale for his sawmill equipment and deeded his sawmill site to S & W on July 15 and 16, 1964, respectively. In exchange, Shook received 364 S & W shares on July 15, 1964. Shook and Wilson also received 1 share each as incorporators. The 364 shares and the 4 incorporation shares constituted all outstanding capital stock of S & W on July 15, 1964. Also on that date, minutes of a special meeting stated in part that Dee Shook and Milo Wilson had entered into an agreement whereby Mr. Wilson was to purchase 182 shares of Mr. Shook's stock for a promissory note. S & W rebuilt the sawmill with a loan that was guaranteed by Shook and Wilson. Before Wilson had paid Shook under the promissory note, S & W was sold by Shook and Wilson to Intermountain Lumber. After the acquisition, Intermountain Lumber caused S & W to file an amended return for its 1965 tax year, claiming that the mill's contribution provided a cost basis to S & W at the time of its formation. Intermountain Lumber and S & W had filed consolidated tax returns from 1967 through 1970, and Intermountain Lumber filed amended tax returns for its consolidated group for that period claiming that it had understated the depreciation related to the S & W sawmill. The Tax Court's opinion follows.]

■ WILES, JUDGE:

Section 351 provides, in part, that no gain shall be recognized if property is transferred to a corporation by one or more persons solely in exchange for stock or securities in such corporation and immediately after the exchange such person or persons are in control of the corporation. "Control" is defined for this purpose in section 368(c) as ownership of stock possessing at least 80 percent of the total combined voting power of all classes of stock entitled to vote and at least 80 percent of the total number of shares of all other classes of stock of the corporation.

In this case, respondent is in the unusual posture of arguing that a transfer to a corporation in return for stock was nontaxable under section 351, and Intermountain is in the equally unusual posture of arguing that the transfer was taxable because section 351 was inapplicable. The explanation is simply that Intermountain purchased all stock of the corporation, S & W, from its incorporators, and that Intermountain and S & W have filed consolidated income tax returns for years in issue.

Accordingly, if section 351 was applicable to the incorporators when S & W was formed, S & W and Intermountain must depreciate the assets of S & W on their consolidated returns on the incorporators' basis. Sec. 362(a). If section 351 was inapplicable, and the transfer of assets to S & W was accordingly to be treated as a sale, S & W and Intermountain could base depreciation on those returns on the fair market value of those assets at the time of incorporation, which was higher than the incorporators' cost and which would accordingly provide larger depreciation deductions. Secs. 167(g), 1011, and 1012.

Petitioner thus maintains that the transfer to S & W of all of S & W's property at the time of incorporation by the primary incorporator, one Dee Shook, was a taxable sale. It asserts that section 351 was inapplicable because an agreement for sale required Shook, as part of the incorporation transaction, to sell almost half of the S & W shares outstanding to one Milo Wilson over a period of time, thereby depriving Shook of the requisite percentage of stock necessary for "control" of S & W immediately after the exchange.

Respondent, on the other hand, maintains that the agreement between Shook and Wilson did not deprive Shook of ownership of the shares immediately after the exchange, as the stock purchase agreement merely gave Wilson an option to purchase the shares. Shook accordingly was in "control" of the corporation and the exchange was thus nontaxable under section 351.

Respondent has abandoned on brief his contention that Wilson was a transferor of property and therefore a person to also be counted for purposes of control under section 351. Respondent is correct in doing so, since Wilson did not transfer any property to S & W upon its initial formation in July of 1964. Wilson's agreement to transfer cash for corporate stock in March of 1965 cannot be considered part of the same transaction.

Since Wilson was not a transferor of property and therefore cannot be counted for control under section 351, *William A. James*, 53 T.C. 63, 69 (1969), we must determine if Shook alone owned the requisite percentage of shares for control. This determination depends upon whether, under all facts and circumstances surrounding the agreement for sale of 182 shares between Shook and Wilson, ownership of those shares was in Shook or Wilson.

A determination of "ownership," as that term is used in section 368(c) and for purposes of control under section 351, depends upon the obligations and freedom of action of the transferee with respect to the stock when he acquired it from the corporation. Such traditional ownership attributes as legal title, voting rights, and possession of stock certificates are not conclusive. If the transferee, as part of the transaction by which the shares were acquired, has irrevocably foregone or relinquished at that time the legal right to determine whether to keep the shares, ownership in such shares is lacking for purposes of section

351. By contrast, if there are no restrictions upon freedom of action at the time he acquired the shares, it is immaterial how soon thereafter the transferee elects to dispose of his stock or whether such disposition is in accord with a preconceived plan not amounting to a binding obligation. * * *

After considering the entire record, we have concluded that Shook and Wilson intended to consummate a sale of the S & W stock, that they never doubted that the sale would be completed, that the sale was an integral part of the incorporation transaction, and that they considered themselves to be coowners of S & W upon execution of the stock purchase agreement in 1964. These conclusions are supported by minutes of the first stockholders meeting on July 7, 1964, at which Shook characterized the agreement for sale as a "sale"; minutes of a special meeting on July 15, 1964, at which Shook stated Wilson was to "purchase" half of Shook's stock; the "Agreement for Sale and Purchase of Stock" itself, dated July 15, 1964, which is drawn as an installment sale and which provides for payment of interest on unpaid principal; Wilson's deduction of interest expenses in connection with the agreement for sale, which would be inconsistent with an option; the S & W loan agreement, in which Shook and Wilson held themselves out as the "principal stockholders" of S & W and in which S & W covenanted to equally insure Shook and Wilson for $100,000; the March 1965 stock purchase agreement with S & W, which indicated that Shook and Wilson *are* to remain *equal* "shareholders in S & W; the letter of May 1967 from Shook and Wilson to Intermountain, which indicated that Wilson owed Shook the principal balance due on the shares as an unpaid obligation; and all surrounding facts and circumstances leading to corporate formation and execution of the above documents. Inconsistent and self-serving testimony of Shook and Wilson regarding their intent and understanding of the documents in evidence is unpersuasive in view of the record as a whole to alter interpretation of the transaction as a sale of stock by Shook to Wilson.

We accordingly cannot accept respondent's contention that the substance varied from the form of this transaction, which was, of course, labeled a "sale." The parties executed an "option" agreement on the same day that the "agreement for sale" was executed, and we have no doubt that they could and indeed did correctly distinguish between a sale and an option.

The agreement for sale's forfeiture clause, which provided that Wilson forfeited the right to purchase a proportionate number of shares for which timely principal payments were not made, did not convert it into an option agreement. Furthermore, the agreement for sale made no provision for forgiving interest payments on the remaining principal due should principal payments not be made on earlier dates; indeed, it specifically provided that "Interest payment must always be kept current before any delivery of stock is to be made resulting from a payment of principal."

We thus believe that Shook, as part of the same transaction by which the shares were acquired (indeed, the agreement for sale was executed before the sawmill was deeded to S & W), had relinquished when he acquired those shares the legal right to determine whether to keep them. Shook was under an obligation, upon receipt of the shares, to transfer the stock as he received Wilson's principal payments. * * * We note also that the agreement for sale gave Wilson the right to prepay principal and receive all 182 shares at any time in advance. Shook therefore did not own, within the meaning of section 368(c), the requisite percentage of stock immediately after the exchange to control the corporation as required for nontaxable treatment under section 351.

We note also that the basic premise of section 351 is to avoid recognition of gain or loss resulting from transfer of property to a corporation which works a change of form only. * * * Accordingly, if the transferor sells his stock as part of the same transaction, the transaction is taxable because there has been more than a mere change in form. * * * In this case, the transferor agreed to sell and did sell 50 percent of the stock to be received, placed the certificates in the possession of an escrow agent, and granted a binding proxy to the purchaser to vote the stock being sold. Far more than a mere change in form was effected.

We accordingly hold for [Intermountain Lumber].

Revenue Ruling 2003–51
2003–1 C.B. 938.

ISSUE

Whether a transfer of assets to a corporation (the "first corporation") in exchange for an amount of stock in the first corporation constituting control satisfies the control requirement of § 351 of the Internal Revenue Code if, pursuant to a binding agreement entered into by the transferor with a third party prior to the exchange, the transferor transfers the stock of the first corporation to another corporation (the "second corporation") simultaneously with the transfer of assets by the third party to the second corporation, and immediately thereafter, the transferor and the third party are in control of the second corporation.

FACTS

Corporation W, a domestic corporation, engages in businesses A, B, and C. The fair market values of businesses A, B, and C are $40x, $30x, and $30x, respectively. X, a domestic corporation unrelated to W, also engages in business A through its wholly owned domestic subsidiary, Y. The fair market value of X's Y stock is $30x. W and X desire to consolidate their business A operations within a new corporation in a holding company structure. Pursuant to a prearranged binding agreement with X, W forms a domestic corporation, Z, by transferring all of its business A assets to Z in exchange for all of the stock of Z (the "first transfer").

Immediately thereafter, W contributes all of its Z stock to Y in exchange for stock of Y (the "second transfer"). Simultaneous with the second transfer, X contributes $30x to Y to meet the capital needs of business A after the restructuring in exchange for additional stock of Y (the "third transfer"). After the second and third transfers, Y transfers the $30x and its business A assets to Z (the "fourth transfer"). After the second and third transfers, W and X own 40 percent and 60 percent, respectively, of the outstanding stock of Y. Viewed separately, each of the first transfer, the combined second and third transfers, and fourth transfer qualifies as a transfer described in § 351.

LAW

Section 351(a) provides that no gain or loss shall be recognized if property is transferred to a corporation by one or more persons solely in exchange for stock in such corporation and immediately after the exchange such person or persons are in control (as defined in § 368(c)) of the corporation.

Section 368(c) defines control to mean the ownership of stock possessing at least 80 percent of the total combined voting power of all classes of stock entitled to vote and at least 80 percent of the total number of shares of all other classes of stock of the corporation.

Section 1.351–1(a)(1) of the Income Tax Regulations provides that the phrase "immediately after the exchange" does not necessarily require simultaneous exchanges by two or more persons, but comprehends a situation where the rights of the parties have been previously defined and the execution of the agreement proceeds with an expedition consistent with orderly procedure.

Courts have held that the control requirement of § 351 is not satisfied where, pursuant to a binding agreement entered into by the transferor prior to the transfer of property to the corporation in exchange for stock, the transferor loses control of the corporation by a taxable sale of all or part of that stock to a third party who does not also transfer property to the corporation in exchange for stock. See, e.g., *S. Klein on the Square, Inc. v. Commissioner*, 188 F.2d 127 (2d Cir.), cert. denied, 342 U.S. 824 (1951); *Hazeltine Corp. v. Commissioner*, 89 F.2d 513 (3d Cir. 1937); *Intermountain Lumber Co. v. Commissioner*, 65 T.C. 1025 (1976). The IRS has reached the same conclusion when addressing similar facts. See Rev.Rul. 79–194, 1979–1 C.B. 145; Rev.Rul. 79–70, 1979–1 C.B. 144; Rev.Rul. 70–522, 1970–2 C.B. 81.

In Rev.Rul. 70–140, 1970–1 C.B. 73, A, an individual, owns all of the stock of corporation X and operates a business similar to that of X through a sole proprietorship. Pursuant to an agreement between A and Y, an unrelated, widely held corporation, A transfers all of the assets of the sole proprietorship to X in exchange for additional shares of X stock. A then transfers all his X stock to Y solely in exchange for voting common stock of Y. The ruling reasons that because the two steps of the transaction are parts of a prearranged plan, they may not be considered independently of each other for Federal income tax purposes. The ruling concludes that A's receipt of the X stock in exchange for the sole proprietorship assets is transitory and without substance for tax purposes because it is apparent that the assets of the sole proprietorship are transferred to X to enable Y to acquire those assets without the recognition of gain to A. Accordingly, the ruling treats A as transferring its sole proprietorship assets directly to Y in a transfer to which § 351 does not apply, and Y as transferring these assets to X, independently of A's transfer of the X stock to Y in exchange for Y voting stock. The exchange by A of the stock of X solely for voting stock of Y constitutes an exchange to which § 354 applies. * * *

In Rev.Rul. 77–449, 1977–2 C.B. 110, *amplified by* Rev.Rul. 83–34, 1983–1 C.B. 79, and Rev.Rul. 83–156, 1983–2 C.B. 66, a corporation transfers assets to a wholly owned subsidiary, which in turn transfers, as part of the same plan, the same assets to its own wholly owned subsidiary. The ruling states that the transfers should be viewed separately for purposes of § 351. Because each transfer satisfies the requirements of § 351, no gain or loss is recognized by the transferor.

In Rev.Rul. 83–34, corporation P owns 80 percent of the stock of a subsidiary, S1. An unrelated corporation owns the remaining 20 percent. P transfers assets to S1 solely in exchange for additional shares of S1 stock. As part of the same plan, S1 transfers the same assets to S2, a newly formed corporation of which S1 will be an 80 percent shareholder. An unrelated corporation will own the remaining 20 percent of the S2 stock. Citing Rev.Rul. 77–449, the ruling concludes that the transfers should be viewed separately for purposes of § 351 and that each transfer satisfies the requirements of § 351.

In Rev.Rul. 84–111, 1984–2 C.B. 88, *Situation 1*, a partnership transfers all of its assets to a newly formed corporation in exchange for all the outstanding stock of the corporation and the assumption by the corporation of the partnership's liabilities. The partnership then terminates by distributing all the stock of the corporation to the partners in proportion to their partnership interests. The steps undertaken by the partnership were parts of a plan to transfer the partnership operations to a corporation organized for valid business reasons in exchange for its stock and were not devices to avoid or evade recognition of gain. The ruling concludes that, under § 351, the partnership recognizes no gain or loss on the transfer of its assets to the corporation in exchange for the corporation's stock and the corporation's assumption of the partnership's liabilities, notwithstanding the partnership's subsequent distribution of the corporation's stock to the partners and consequent loss of control within the meaning of § 368(c) of the corporation.

ANALYSIS

As described above, if the first transfer were viewed as separate from each of the other transfers, the first transfer would satisfy the technical requirements of a transfer under § 351 because W transfers property to Z in exchange for stock in Z and, immediately after the exchange, W is in control of Z. However, because the first and second transfers are undertaken pursuant to a prearranged binding agreement, it is necessary to determine whether the second transfer causes the first transfer to fail to satisfy the control requirement of § 351.

"Section 351 has been described as a deliberate attempt by Congress to facilitate the incorporation of ongoing businesses and to eliminate any technical constructions which are economically unsound." *Hempt Bros., Inc. v. United States*, 490 F.2d 1172, 1177 (3d Cir.), *cert. denied*, 419 U.S. 826 (1974). Section 351(a) is intended to apply to "certain transactions where gain or loss may have accrued in a constitutional sense, but where in a popular and economic sense there has been a mere change in the form of ownership and the taxpayer has not really 'cashed in' on the theoretical gain, or closed out a losing venture." *Portland Oil Co. v. Commissioner*, 109 F.2d 479, 488 (1st Cir.), *cert. denied*, 310 U.S. 650 (1940). See S. Rep. No. 67–275, at 12 (1921) (explaining that the predecessor to § 351 was enacted in 1921 to "permit business to go forward with the readjustments required by existing conditions"). A transaction described under § 351 "lacks a distinguishing characteristic of a sale, in that, instead of the transaction having the effect of terminating or extinguishing the beneficial interests of the transferors in the transferred property, . . . the transferors continue to be beneficially interested in the transferred property and have dominion over it by virtue of their control of the new corporate owner of it." *American Compress & Warehouse Co. v. Bender*, 70 F.2d 655, 657 (5th Cir.), *cert. denied*, 293 U.S. 607 (1934).

As described above, courts have held that the control requirement of § 351 is not satisfied where, pursuant to a binding agreement entered into by the transferor prior to the transfer of property to the corporation in exchange for stock, the transferor loses control of the corporation by a taxable sale of all or part of that stock to a third party that does not also transfer property to the corporation in exchange for stock. Treating a transfer of property that is followed by such a prearranged sale of the stock received as a transfer described in § 351 is not consistent with Congress' intent in enacting § 351 to facilitate the rearrangement of the transferor's interest in its property. Treating a transfer of property that is followed by a nontaxable disposition of the stock received as a transfer described in § 351 is not necessarily inconsistent with the purposes of § 351. Accordingly, the control requirement may be satisfied in such a case, even if the stock received is transferred pursuant to a binding commitment in place upon the transfer of the property in exchange for stock. For example, in Rev.Rul. 84–111, *Situation 1*, the partnership's transfer of property to the transferee corporation qualified as a transfer described in § 351, even though the partnership relinquished control of

Nevertheless, the decisions in both *Wilgard* and *Stanton* were clearly predicated on the power of the transferor to designate who will receive the stock rather than the precise moment that the power was exercised. These cases do not turn on whether the tune Dr. D'Angelo called was written in two/four time, but on his power to call the tune. And it is on this score that both Florida Machine & Foundry Co. and Mojonnier & Sons, Inc., are distinguishable from *Wilgard, Stanton,* and the facts before us.

2.2. *Transfer of Assets to Subsidiary in Exchange for Stock of Parent Corporation*

Rev.Rul. 84–44, 1984–1 C.B. 105, held that § 351 is not applicable to the transfer of property to a corporate subsidiary in exchange for stock of the transferee subsidiary's parent corporation, which is in turn controlled by the transferor. The same result can, however, be accomplished by restructuring the transaction first as a transfer of the property to the controlled parent corporation in exchange for its stock, followed by a transfer of the property by the parent corporation to its controlled subsidiary. Rev.Rul. 83–34, 1983–1 C.B. 79, holds that although these transfers may be undertaken pursuant to an integrated plan, each transfer is treated as a separate transaction that satisfies § 351. See also Rev.Rul. 83–156, 1983–2 C.B. 66 (holding that § 351 applies to a transfer of assets to a wholly owned subsidiary that then transfers the assets to a partnership). Although nonrecognition of gain or loss under § 351 is based in principle on the transferors' continued investment in the transferred property, and requires a continued proprietary interest in the transferee corporation through the receipt of stock representing control, there is no express requirement that the transferors maintain a continued interest in the transferred assets.

3. WHO ARE THE TRANSFERORS?

3.1. *General*

Section 351 applies when one or more persons who transfer property to the corporation are in control immediately after the transfer. The control requirement thus requires identification of the group of transferors who are to be counted.

In some cases taxpayers have attempted to count existing shareholders as members of the control group in order to classify an exchange of appreciated property for stock by non-controlling persons as a nonrecognition transaction under § 351. For example, in Estate of Kamborian v. Commissioner, 469 F.2d 219 (1st Cir.1972), taxpayers holding 76% of the stock of a corporation transferred appreciated property to the corporation in exchange for additional stock. A trust that held 13% of the stock of the transferee corporation purchased a small number of shares for cash in an attempt to qualify the transfer under § 351. The taxpayers claimed that the trust was a transferor so that together the combined holdings of transferors exceeded 80%. The court held that it is "permissible to consider transfers by other owners only if those transfers were, in economic terms, sufficiently related to * * * make all of the transfers parts of a single transaction." The court added that, "[t]he trustees' desire to help the [other] stockholders avoid taxes, warrantably found by the Tax Court to have been the primary motive for the trust's purchase cannot be used to make a single transaction out of otherwise unrelated transfers."

The issue in *Kamborian* is addressed in Treas.Reg. § 1.351–1(a)(1)(ii), which provides that, if the primary purpose of the transfer of property by an existing shareholder is to qualify for § 351 treatment a transfer of property to the corporation by another person, and if the stock newly received by the existing shareholder is of "relatively small value" in comparison to the value of that shareholder's stock owned before the transfer, then the newly received stock of the existing shareholder will not be counted in determining the control group. Rev.Proc. 77–37, § 3.07, 1977–2 C.B. 568, indicates that the property transferred will not be considered to be of "relatively small value" if it has a value equal to at least 10% of the value of the stock owned by the existing shareholder before the transfer.

Rev.Rul. 79–194, 1979–1 C.B. 145, held that a pre-arranged sale between two transferors of property for stock does not affect the control requirement. Z Corporation transferred property to Newco for 80% of Newco stock. A group of investors transferred property for 20% of Newco stock. Following the transfers to Newco, Z sold stock to the investors. At the end of the transaction, Z owned 49% of the Newco stock. The ruling held that because Z and the investors were transferors, the persons transferring property to Newco in exchange for Newco stock owned 100% of Newco stock immediately after the exchange. Where, however, the investor group transferred property in exchange for only 1% of the Newco stock, with Z receiving 99%, the investors' stock ownership was not sufficient to qualify them as transferors of property and thus the control requirement was not satisfied because of the subsequent sale of stock by Z to the investors.

In contrast to Rev.Rul. 79–194, Rev.Rul. 79–70, 1979–1 C.B. 144, held that the requirements of § 351 had not been met where the prearranged sale of stock was to a creditor of the corporation. In the ruling, X Corporation transferred property to newly organized Y Corporation and, pursuant to a prearranged binding contract, sold 40% of the Y stock to Z Corporation. Simultaneously, Z purchased securities for cash from Y. Rev.Rul. 79–194 held that Z Corporation was not a transferor of property because it received only debt securities from Y. Z's ownership of the Y stock acquired by purchase from X Corporation could not be counted in determining whether the control requirement of § 351 was satisfied. Because Z therefore received only securities for cash and was not a shareholder prior to the exchange, it was not a member of the control group for § 351 purposes. X was the only transferor of property, it received only 60% of the stock, and the transaction therefore did not qualify under § 351.

3.2. *Underwriting Situations*

Treas.Reg. § 1.351–1(a)(3) provides that if a person acquires stock from an underwriter in exchange for cash in a "qualified underwriting transaction," then, for purposes of § 351, the person who purchases the stock from the underwriter is treated as transferring the cash directly to the corporation in exchange for the stock and the underwriter's role in the transaction is disregarded. A "qualified underwriting transaction" is an underwriting in which a corporation issues stock for cash in which either the underwriter is an agent of the corporation or the underwriter's ownership of stock is transitory.

4.   CONTROL WHEN THERE ARE MULTIPLE CLASSES OF STOCK

Section 351(a) specifies that control is "as defined in section 368(c)." There is little available guidance regarding the meaning § 368(c)'s phrase, "total combined voting power of all classes of stock entitled to vote." The existence of multiple classes of voting stock requires a determination regarding the relative voting power of each class in order to determine whether the transferors of property are in control. In Rev.Rul. 63–234, 1963–2 C.B. 148, the IRS ruled under § 368(c) (in a type (B) reorganization) that preferred stock that entitled its holders to elect two of twelve directors was voting stock in that "it conferred upon the holders of such stock the right to significant participation in the management of the affairs of the corporation." The IRS relied on its earlier ruling in I.T. 3896, 1948–1 C.B. 72 (declared obsolete in Rev.Rul. 68–100, 1968–1 C.B. 572), which considered voting control for purposes of membership in an affiliated group, holding that the voting power of preferred stock was in proportion to the number of directors elected by the preferred shareholders. Thus preferred stock with the right to elect two of twelve directors possessed 2/12, or 16.7% of voting control. See also Rev.Rul. 69–126, 1969–1 C.B. 218, applying the same analysis for purposes of defining voting control under § 1504. Under this standard, a shareholder who receives common stock for services might receive more than 20% of the common stock by value without defeating § 351 nonrecognition treatment for transferors of property if the common stock transferred to the service shareholder represents a separate class of stock with limited voting rights.

Section 368(c) also states control requires ownership of "at least 80 percent of the total number of shares of all other classes of stock of the corporation." The IRS has ruled in Rev.Rul. 59–259, 1959–2 C.B. 115, that this phrase requires that, in addition to 80% of the combined voting power of all classes of voting stock, the transferor shareholders must also own 80% of the number of shares of *each* class of nonvoting stock. Ownership of 80% of the total number of shares outstanding is not sufficient.

Nonqualified preferred stock, as defined in § 351(g), is treated as property other than stock for purposes of determining whether the transferor who receives such stock in exchange for property recognizes gain or loss in a § 351 transaction. Nevertheless, except to the extent otherwise provided by Regulations, nonqualified preferred stock is treated as stock for purposes of determining whether the control requirement has been met and the transaction as a whole qualifies under § 351(a). See S.Rep. No. 174, 105th Cong., 2d Sess. 177 (1998).

PROBLEM SET 7

1.   Bill owned a copyright on a computer software program, with a fair market value of $10,000,000 and a basis of $1,000. Bill transferred the

copyright on the program to newly formed Doors Corporation in exchange for all 30,000 shares of voting common stock. Doors was unable to further develop and market the software without the investment of significant additional capital. To this end, pursuant to a prearranged plan, three months later Merrill-Goldman, an investment banking house, sold $40,000,000 par value nonvoting preferred stock of Doors Corporation to public investors on behalf of Doors. As agreed upon in the contract between Doors and Merrill-Goldman, upon completion of the public offering, Doors issued 10,000 shares of common stock to Merrill-Goldman. What are the tax consequences to Bill and to Doors?

2.   (a)   Maria owned a hotel property consisting of land and a building. The fair market value of the land was $1,000,000 and the basis of the land was $100,000; the fair market value of the building was $19,000,000, its adjusted basis was $8,000,0000 and it original cost (unadjusted basis before depreciation) was $22,000,000. In January, the Tripletree Hotel Corporation, offered to purchase Maria's hotel for $20,000,000. The offer was open until April 15. On February 15th, pursuant to advice from her C.P.A., Ernie Whinney, Maria transferred the land and building to newly formed Reality TV Corp. in exchange for all 100 shares of its stock. On March 1st, Maria counter-offered to Tripletree's offer, stating that she would accept $19,500,000 in exchange for all of the stock of Reality TV Corp. This offer was accepted by Tripletree and the deal was closed on April 1st. Ernie Whinney has advised Maria that the incorporation of Reality TV Corp. was tax-free under § 351. Is he correct?

       (b)   Suppose alternatively, that after transferring the hotel to Reality TV Corp. in exchange for all of its stock, pursuant to a pre-arranged plan, Maria transferred all of the stock of Reality TV to Las Margaritas, Inc., in exchange for 100 shares of stock. Simultaneously, José, who theretofore had owned all 200 shares of the stock of Las Margaritas, transferred to Las Margaritas a restaurant building with a fair market value of $4,000,000 and a basis of $500,000, in exchange for 20 additional shares of stock. What are the tax consequences to Maria?

3.   Paducah Oil Company has recently acquired a chain of gas stations previously operated by Leviathan Oil Corp. in Kentucky, following Leviathan's decision to cease its marketing operations there. In addition to the 75 company owned gas stations acquired from Leviathan by Paducah, Leviathan had an additional 100 or so independent retailers that owned their own gas stations and purchased gasoline from Leviathan Oil.

       Paducah plans to convert all 75 gas stations that it acquired from Leviathan to convenience store/gas stations that it will operate under the trade name BlueCat, but which will sell gasoline refined by Paducah. The management of Paducah believes that outlet name recognition would be enhanced, and hence average profits per store would be enhanced, if substantially more than 75 BlueCat stores were operated in Kentucky. Additionally, it is looking for additional outlets for its refined products.

       To accomplish these goals the management of Paducah plans to form a subsidiary, BlueCat Stores, Inc., to which it will contribute all 75 gas stations that it purchased from Leviathan, some cash, and a quantity of refined petroleum products. In exchange, Paducah will receive 100% of the voting common stock of BlueCat. Immediately thereafter, Paducah will offer to exchange with the 100 independent dealers previously selling Leviathan gasoline in Kentucky a number of its shares of BlueCat equal to the fair market value of each of their respective businesses, in consideration of the transfer directly to BlueCat of all of their business assets, including their gasoline stations, inventory, customer accounts, etc. It is anticipated that if all of the independent owners accept the offer, in the aggregate the previously independent owners will hold a 50% interest in BlueCat. No individual owner, however, will hold more than 2 or 3% of the BlueCat stock. The owners will continue to operate their stations as managers of the convenience stores and will receive salaries, bonuses and fringe benefits from BlueCat.

The management of Paducah is concerned whether this transaction will be a tax-free incorporation. Although Paducah's cost basis for the 75 gas stations is not substantially less than fair market value, BlueCat will be a going concern, and its stock, therefore, may have a value in excess of the fair market value of the underlying assets. Additionally, the refined gasoline to be contributed has a value substantially in excess of its basis. More importantly, however, Paducah wants to be able to assure the independent retailers that they will not owe any income taxes as a result of the exchange of their business assets for BlueCat stock. If the exchanges are taxable, Paducah is concerned that the station owners may prefer to sell for cash or debt instruments and the Paducah management would prefer not to use a cash or debt acquisition route.

Will § 351 apply to the incorporation of BlueCat Stores, Inc.?

SECTION 4.   RECEIPT OF STOCK FOR SERVICES

INTERNAL REVENUE CODE: Section 83(a)–(c)(2), (h); 351(d)(1).

REGULATIONS: Sections 1.83–1(a)(1), –6(a)(1); 1.351–1(a)(1), (2), Exs. (2) and (3).

Section § 351 applies only to the transfer of "property" in exchange for stock. Section 351(d)(1) specifically provides that stock issued for services is not issued for property. Section 83 applies to stock issued for services. Thus, the shareholder who receives stock for services realizes ordinary income equal to the fair market value of the stock. If the stock is subject to a substantial risk of forfeiture or other restrictions that prevent it from being fully vested, § 83 provides rules for determining the year in which the value of the stock interest must be included in income. Pursuant to § 83(h), the corporation will be able to deduct the fair market value of the stock (with the timing of the deduction tied to when the service provider has income), if the services provided by the transferee were not capital in nature. See also Treas.Reg. § 1.83–6. Otherwise the corporation must capitalize the value of the stock.

If a single transferor transfers both property and services for stock, the transaction must be bifurcated and treated as the receipt of stock for property of equivalent value and the receipt of stock for services. Thus, the transferor may be accorded nonrecognition under § 351 with respect to the stock received for property even though the receipt of the remainder of the stock is taxable under § 61 and § 83.

If a person who only provides services to the corporation and does not transfer any property to a newly formed corporation receives more than 20% of the voting stock or more than 20% of any particular class of nonvoting stock upon the formation of a new corporation, the transferors of property will not be in "control" of the corporation immediately after the transfer. In such a case, the issuance of stock for services will preclude § 351 nonrecognition treatment for the transferors of property. See Mojonnier & Sons, Inc. v. Commissioner, 12 T.C. 837 (1949) (nonacq.) (§ 351 did not apply to the transferor of property where upon incorporation of a sole proprietorship former employees received more than 20% of stock in consideration for past services).

A transferor of services who receives more than 20% of the stock for his services and who also transfers some property to the corporation for stock can, however, qualify as a "transferor of property," so that both the stock received for services and the stock received for property will be counted in determining whether the control test is met. However, Treas.Reg. § 1.351–1(a)(1)(ii) warns that if the primary purpose of the property transfer is to qualify the stock received for services and the property transferred constitutes only a "relatively small value" in comparison to the value of the services stock, the stock received for services will not be counted in determining the control group. Rev.Proc. 77–37, § 3.07, 1977–2 C.B. 568, indicates that the property transferred will not be considered to be of "relatively small value" if it has a value equal to at least 10% of the value of the stock received for services by the person providing services (i.e., the value of the property is at least 9.09% of the total value of the stock received by the person who provided both property and services).

DETAILED ANALYSIS

1. "PROPERTY" DISTINGUISHED FROM SERVICES AND SERVICE FLAVORED ASSETS

"Property" for § 351 purposes does not include all interests that may be considered property interests for other purposes. The question of whether assets that have been produced as the result of the taxpayer's personal efforts constitute "property" for purposes of § 351 is identical to that encountered in exchanges of property for a partnership interest accorded nonrecognition treatment under § 721, and is similar, but not identical, to that encountered in connection with whether an asset constitutes "property" for purposes of determining capital asset status under § 1221. Thus, the term "property" includes secret processes and formulae, whether patentable or not. Under Rev.Rul. 64–56, 1964–1 C.B. 133, if the transferred information qualifies as property, then § 351 applies even though services are to be performed in connection with the transfer; the services, however, must be ancillary and subsidiary to the property transfer. Continuing technical assistance, employee training, and construction assistance will ordinarily be considered services for purposes of § 351 transfers. Rev.Rul. 71–564, 1971–2 C.B. 179, holds that trade secrets are property for purposes of § 351 transfers as long as the transferee corporation receives an exclusive right to the trade secret until it becomes public knowledge and is no longer protectable under applicable law. E.I. Du Pont de Nemours & Co. v. United States, 471 F.2d 1211 (Ct.Cl.1973), held, however, that the transfer of a royalty-free, nonexclusive license qualified as a transfer of "property" in a § 351 exchange. The fact that a taxable transfer of the nonexclusive license would not have qualified for capital gain treatment did not prevent § 351 from applying.

Rev.Rul. 70–45, 1970–1 C.B. 17, provides that business goodwill is property. In Rev.Rul. 79–288, 1979–2 C.B. 139, the IRS ruled further that a corporate name registered in a foreign country and protected under the laws of the foreign country is property for § 351 purposes, but that an unregistered, unprotected name with no goodwill value is not property.

In United States v. Frazell, 335 F.2d 487 (5th Cir.1964), a geologist entered into an agreement under which he was to identify potentially productive oil and gas properties, using several oil maps that he owned. Frazell was paid for his services and was to receive a specified interest in the properties after the other venturers had recovered certain costs. Eventually, instead of an interest in the properties, he received stock in a corporation to which the properties had been transferred. One of the court's alternative holdings was that Frazell realized ordinary income under § 351 on the theory that, if the stock were a substitution for the partnership interest originally contemplated, it would be compensation for services (and not received in exchange for "property"), and hence taxable under § 351. To the extent that the geological maps constituted "property," the taxpayer was entitled to § 351 nonrecognition treatment as to these items.

In James v. Commissioner, 53 T.C. 63 (1969), the taxpayer and Talbot entered into an agreement to develop a real estate project. Talbot was to contribute land, and the taxpayer was to promote the project and obtain the necessary FHA commitment and financing for the project. The taxpayer obtained the commitments in the name of the corporation, and the taxpayer and Talbot then transferred the land and financing commitments to a corporation. The stock of the corporation was issued 50–50 to the taxpayer and Talbot. The taxpayer argued that he had transferred contract rights (analogous to patents or secret processes) to the corporation and therefore § 351 controlled. Following *Frazell,* the court held that the stock was received for services and was therefore ordinary income to the taxpayer. Furthermore, the only transferor of "property" was Talbot, who owned only 50% of the stock after the transaction. Thus, § 351 did not apply to Talbot's transfer because the 80% control test was not met and taxable gain resulted.

James was distinguished in United States v. Stafford, 727 F.2d 1043 (11th Cir.1984), which held that an unenforceable letter of intent to provide financing was property under § 721, which provides for nonrecognition of gain or loss on the contribution of property to a partnership. The court indicated that it would reach the same result under § 351. The court pointed out that Stafford had developed the letter of intent for his own account and owned the letter of intent individually. The financing commitment in *James* was in the name of the corporation.

2.   TREATMENT OF THE CORPORATION

Whether a corporation issues stock in exchange for services in a § 351 transaction upon its formation or after the corporation is formed, the corporation recognizes no gain under § 1032 and is entitled either to a deduction under § 162 or to capitalize the value of the stock, depending on the nature of the services. Rulings clearly state that the nonrecognition provisions of § 1032 have no effect on business expense deductions otherwise allowable under § 162. Rev.Rul. 62–217, 1962–2 C.B. 59; Rev.Rul. 69–75, 1969–1 C.B. 52. Justification for the corporation claiming a deduction or acquiring basis while not recognizing any income is not self-evident.

PROBLEM SET 8

1.   (a) Alberto, Beryl, and Chris have been operating a fashion design business (as a partnership) under the name Ritzy Rags for the past several years. Because they are planning to expand to manufacturing, Alberto, Beryl, and Chris are planning to incorporate the business. Debby, an employee who is one of the nation's hottest fashion designers, has been an important factor in the success of the business. Recently Debby received an offer from another apparel company that included stock and stock options in a compensation package. To induce Debby to remain with Ritzy Rags, Alberto, Beryl, and Chris have offered her 25% of the common stock of the new Ritzy Rags Corporation, to which the business will be transferred. Advise the parties regarding the tax consequences of the incorporation transaction.

(b) What if Debby's stock must be sold back to Ritzy Rags for $10 per share if her employment terminates any time in the next four years?

(c) What if Debby doesn't receive any stock in Ritzy Rags immediately upon its incorporation, but she receives an option to purchase from the corporation at any time in the next five years an amount of stock equal to the number of shares originally received by each of Alberto, Beryl, and Chris (i.e., if Alberto, Beryl, and Chris each received 100 shares, Debby would have an option for 100 shares) at the same price paid by Alberto, Beryl, and Chris?

2.   (a) Fran, Les, Pat, and Sean plan to organize a corporation to engage in the construction business. Fran will contribute $400,000 in cash for 40 shares of common stock. Les will contribute equipment with a fair market value of $200,000 and a basis of $90,000 for 20 shares of common stock. Pat will contribute building materials with a fair market value of $200,000 and a basis of $210,000 for 20 shares of common stock. Sean will contribute a contract with Falls City University for the construction by Sean or Sean's assignee of a new Dental School building, a letter of intent from the University of the Bluegrass to enter into a contract with Sean or Sean's

assignee for construction of a new Engineering School building, and Sean's services in organizing the corporation and supervising the construction of the two buildings. Sean will receive 20 shares of common stock.

What are the tax consequences to each of the shareholders and to the corporation of the formation of the corporation?

(b) How might your answer to (a) differ if Fran were to receive participating preferred stock instead of common stock? Does it matter whether the participating preferred stock has voting rights to elect directors?

3. Ellen, Fred, Ginny, and Hank plan to form X Corporation. Ellen, Fred, and Ginny are contributing appreciated property. Hank is contributing only services. Under which of the following alternative capital structures will the incorporation qualify under § 351.

(a) (1) Ellen, Fred, and Ginny collectively receive 80 shares of Class A $1,000 par value, 7%, voting participating preferred stock, and Hank receives 20 shares of Class B voting common stock. The Class A participating preferred stock is entitled to a cumulative 7% preferred dividend and a $1,000 per share liquidation preference. After the Class A preference has been satisfied, both Class A and Class B stock share equally, share-by-share, in all current and liquidating distributions.

(2) What if, in the alternative, Hank's Class B common stock was nonvoting?

(3) What if, in the alternative, Ellen, Fred, and Ginny's Class A stock was voting common stock and Hank's 20 shares of Class B stock was $1,000 par value, 7%, nonvoting limited and preferred stock?

(4) What if, in the alternative, Ellen, Fred, and Ginny collectively received 80 shares of voting common stock and Hank received a $20,000 bond (promissory note), convertible at any time in the next four years into 40 shares of voting common stock?

(b) Ellen, Fred, and Ginny collectively receive 80 shares of Class A voting common stock and 80 shares of Class B nonvoting common stock. Hank receives 20 shares of Class A voting common stock and 20 shares of Class C nonvoting preferred stock.

(c) Ellen, Fred, and Ginny collectively receive 75 shares of Class A voting common stock, and Hank receives 25 shares of Class B voting common stock. The only difference between the shares is that the Class A stock elects four directors and the Class B stock elects one director.

CHAPTER 3

THE CAPITAL STRUCTURE OF THE CORPORATION

SECTION 1. DEBT VERSUS EQUITY

The tax treatment of the various forms that an investment in a corporation can take is a central issue in the pattern of corporate taxation. Unlike in the partnership situation, the return on capital invested in ownership interests in the corporation, i.e., corporate stock, is subject to two levels of tax, once in the hands of the corporation and again when dividends are distributed to individual shareholders. On the other hand, the return on an investment in a corporation as a creditor, i.e., the interest paid by the corporation for the funds advanced, is only subject to a single level of tax since the interest payment, unlike a dividend, is deductible by the corporation (subject to limitations with unlimited carryforward) and thus avoids the corporate level tax. Moreover, if the investor is a tax-exempt entity, such as a pension fund, debt classification generally eliminates the yield from the corporate tax base entirely. The tax "bias" in favor of investment as a creditor has been a source of great strain on the tax system. Taxpayers and their advisors have attempted to structure obligations that qualify as debt for tax purposes, with the attendant single level of tax on the return, while at the same time giving the investor an opportunity to participate in the growth of the business enterprise—a typical aspect of an ownership or equity investment.

Whether an investment is treated as equity or debt also affects the tax consequence of recognition of loss on disposition of the investment. Gain or loss recognized by a corporate or individual stockholder on the sale, exchange, or retirement of stock will be capital gain or loss. Loss incurred on worthless stock is also a capital loss. However, § 1244 allows individuals an ordinary loss deduction on stock in certain small business companies, and a corporation is allowed an ordinary loss deduction on the worthless stock of a controlled subsidiary (§ 165(g)(3)).

Gain or loss recognized on the sale, exchange, or retirement of a debt obligation is also capital to a corporate or individual holder (unless there is an element of original issue or market discount involved). I.R.C. § 1271. Loss on a worthless debt obligation that is classified as a "security" is treated as a capital loss to both the corporate and individual holder, except that an ordinary loss may be available to a corporation for the securities of its controlled subsidiary. I.R.C. § 165(g). A debt obligation is a "security" if it is in registered form or has coupons attached. No loss is allowed in the case of a worthless debt that is a "registration required debt" but that has not been registered. I.R.C. § 165(j). An individual's loss on a debt obligation that is not a security is a short-term capital loss, unless the debt arose in the individual's trade or business, in which case the loss is ordinary. Loss incurred by a corporate holder on a nonsecurity debt obligation is ordinary. See I.R.C. §§ 165(g), 166(a), (d).

The debt/equity equation is further complicated by the preferential tax rate accorded to most dividends on stock. Since 2003, § 1(h)(11) generally taxes dividends received by individuals at the same preferential rates enjoyed by long-term capital gains (see Chapter 1). As a result, the tax bias in favor of debt financing is ameliorated to some extent. While interest remains deductible to the corporation, the lender is taxed on interest received at the lender's normal marginal rate—up to 37% for individuals. Dividends, on the other hand, while not deductible to the corporation are taxed to the investor at a substantially lower rate. Thus, an individual investor who is concerned only with the investor's own tax situation will prefer to receive dividends on a stock investment rather than interest on a loan, if the before-tax yields are similar. But if the investor is wearing the hats of both a lender and a shareholder and is concerned with the corporation's overall tax picture, the financial interests of the investor and the corporation may be intertwined, thus shifting the balance somewhat in the direction of debt rather than equity financing. The 2017 Act has complicated the analysis by adding some limitations on the ability of corporations to take immediate deductions for interest paid (§ 163(j)) and by reducing the overall corporate tax rate to 21%.

If differing tax rates are taken out of consideration, an investor generally is indifferent to the formal classification of the investment instrument. From the investment perspective, the question is the yield on the investment in relation to the level of risk involved, and the formal classification of the return as "interest" or "dividend" is not a matter of concern (except, of course, from a tax point of view). As a general matter, the higher the level of legal and economic protection provided in the instrument, the lower the investment return. Historically, an equity investment was considered to be riskier than debt, with its promised return of principal plus interest, and thus an investor in equity expected a higher rate of return. Given the imagination of the marketers of financial products, the possible combinations of ownership and creditor interests in a particular financial instrument are, however, almost infinite.

The development of tax principles in this area has lagged far behind the development of investment products. This lag may be traceable to two causes. In the first place, the legal rules for the classification of investment instruments as debt or equity have developed primarily in the context of small, closely held corporations in cases in which the investors were both shareholders and "lenders." The method of analysis developed by the courts in that context has been largely inadequate to deal with situations such as large venture capital firms investing in an emerging business or the issuance of highly complex and sophisticated financial instruments by publicly traded companies. Secondly, and closely related, is the fact that, in developing the debt-equity rules, the courts generally have applied an "all or nothing" approach. That is, a particular instrument is either a debt instrument in its entirety for tax purposes or an equity instrument in its entirety. This approach is totally at odds with the various combinations of debt and equity features that can be employed in a particular financial instrument. Nonetheless, except when Congress has been willing to provide a legislative alternative (which in a few situations it has been forced to do), the all-or-nothing approach continues to prevail. This approach has made it relatively easy for sophisticated investors and their equally sophisticated tax advisors to craft instruments that combine the desirable legal features of ownership and creditor status with the most advantageous tax treatment.

The material in this Chapter first considers the "traditional" debt-equity classification issues primarily as they have developed in the context of closely held corporations, including recent efforts to add regulations regarding this classification. The material then deals with the classification issues that are raised by more complex financial instruments and the more specific congressional responses to those issues.

The present distinction between debt and equity capital presents the corporation and its investors with different tax issues and planning possibilities. As respects the corporation issuing the obligation,[1] if the obligation is debt, interest is deductible, retirement at a discount may result in cancellation of indebtedness income, or retirement at a premium may provide an additional interest deduction. If the obligation is stock, dividends are not deductible and generally the corporation does not recognize income or loss on retirement. Retention of earnings to retire debt generally will not run afoul of the § 531 penalty tax on improperly accumulated earnings, see Chapter 14, but such retention might result in that tax in the case of stock. Also, the availability of the deduction for original issue discount requires that the obligation be classified as debt; no such deduction is allowed for the issuance of stock.

Payments on an obligation will also produce different tax results for the holder depending on the character of the obligation. If the payment constitutes interest it will be includible in the recipient's income whether or not the corporation has earnings and profits, whereas inclusion as a dividend depends on the presence of earnings and profits. If a corporation holds the obligation, the intercorporate dividends received deduction under § 243 (see Chapter 4) depends on the presence of a "dividend,"

---

[1] The term "obligation" is used in the following materials to include stock, debt, and instruments with attributes of both stock and debt whose proper classification is in doubt.

which requires that the obligation be treated as stock. If the advances to the corporation are regarded as contributions to capital, i.e., additional stock investment, repayment usually will be a dividend to the stockholder, but if regarded as loans, the repayment will not be taxable. Where the obligation is retired, if it is stock, the retirement under some circumstances will be a dividend under § 301; if a debt, retirement will produce capital gain or loss (in the absence of original issue discount or premium).

The preceding discussion is not exhaustive, and there are other facets to the problem. For example, the classification of the obligation as stock or debt is important under the reorganization provisions to both the investor and the corporation. Also, classification of the obligation as stock or debt is important in determining the applicability of the personal holding company tax. See Chapter 14.

A. CLASSIFICATION AS DEBT OR EQUITY

INTERNAL REVENUE CODE: Section 385.

REGULATIONS: Sections 1.385–1(a)–(c), –2(a)–(d), (f), –3(a), (b)(1)–(b)(4), (c)(4).

Indmar Products Co., Inc. v. Commissioner
United States Court of Appeals, Sixth Circuit, 2006.
444 F.3d 771.

■ McKEAGUE, CIRCUIT JUDGE.

Indmar Products Co., Inc. ("Indmar") appeals the decision of the Tax Court to disallow interest deductions the company claimed for tax years 1998–2000, and to assess accuracy-related tax penalties for those years. The interest deductions relate to a number of advances made to Indmar by its majority stockholders over several years. Indmar argued at trial that the advances were legitimate loans made to the company, and thus it could properly deduct the interest payments made on these advances under 26 U.S.C. § 163(a). The Tax Court, following the position taken by the Commissioner of Internal Revenue (the "Commissioner"), disagreed, concluding that the advances were equity contributions and therefore the company could not deduct any purported interest payments on these advances. The court imposed penalties on Indmar based on the deductions. *Indmar Prods. Co., Inc. v. Comm'r*, T.C.M.2005–32.

Upon review of the record, we conclude that the Tax Court clearly erred in finding the advances were equity. The Tax Court failed to consider several factors used by this court for determining whether advances are debt or equity, ignored relevant evidence, and drew several unsupported inferences from its factual findings. We reverse and find that the stockholder advances were bona fide debt.

I.   BACKGROUND

A.   Stockholder Advances to Indmar

Indmar, a Tennessee corporation, is a marine engine manufacturer. In 1973, Richard Rowe, Sr., and Marty Hoffman owned equal shares of Indmar. In 1987, after Hoffman passed away, Richard and his wife, Donna Rowe, together owned 74.44% of Indmar, with their children and children's spouses owning the rest. By all accounts, Indmar has been a successful company. From 1986 to 2000, Indmar's sales and costs-of-goods sold increased from $5m and $3.9m to $45m and $37.7m, respectively. In addition, Indmar's working capital (current assets minus current liabilities) increased from $471,386 to $3.8m. During this period, Indmar did not declare or pay formal dividends.

Since the 1970s, Indmar's stockholders have advanced funds to it, receiving a 10% annual return in exchange. Hoffman started the practice in the 1970s. Beginning in 1987, the Rowes (as well as their children) began to make advancements on a periodic basis. Indmar treated all of the advances as loans from stockholders in the corporate books and records, and made monthly payments calculated at 10% of the advanced funds. Indmar reported the payments as interest expense deductions on its federal income tax returns. Consistent with Indmar's reporting, the Rowes reported the payments as interest income on their individual income tax returns.

The parties did not initially document the advances with notes or other instruments. Beginning in 1993, the parties executed notes covering all of the advances at issue. Specifically, Indmar executed a promissory note in 1993 with Donna Rowe for $201,400 (i.e., her outstanding balance). The note was payable on demand and freely transferable, had no maturity date or monthly payment schedule, and had a fixed interest rate of 10%. In 1995, Indmar executed a similar promissory note with Richard Rowe for $605,681 (i.e., his outstanding balance). In 1998, when the outstanding transfers totaled $1,222,133, Indmar executed two line of credit agreements with the Rowes for $1m and $750,000. The line of credit agreements provided that the balances were payable on demand and the notes were freely transferable. In addition, the agreements provided a stated interest rate of 10% and had no maturity date or monthly payment schedule. None of the advances were secured.

Repayments of the advances were paid on demand, based on the needs of the stockholders, and not subject to set or predetermined due dates. The record indicates that between 1987 and 2000, the total advance balances ranged from $634,000 to $1.7m, and Indmar made purported interest payments between $45,000 and $174,000 each year.

The parties structured the advances as demand loans to give the Rowes flexibility as creditors. Moreover, as demand loans, the advances were treated by the Rowes as short-term debt under Tennessee law, thereby excepting interest payments from a 6% state tax on dividends and interest on long-term debts. Tenn.Code Ann. §§ 67–2–101(1)(B)(i), 67–2–102 (2005). Indmar, however, reported the advances as long-term liabilities on its financial statements to avoid violating loan agreements with First Tennessee Bank ("FTB"), its primary creditor, who required a minimum ratio of current assets to current liabilities.

In order to reconcile the treatment and execution of the advances as demand loans versus listing them as long-term debt in its financial reports, Indmar received waivers from the Rowes agreeing to forego repayment on the notes for at least 12 months. From 1989 to 2000, the notes to Indmar's financial statements disclosed that "The stockholders have agreed not to demand payment within the next year," and in 1992 and 1993, the Rowes signed written agreements stating that they would not demand repayment of the advances. Indmar did all of this under the direction of its accountant.

Despite the annual waivers, the Rowes demanded and received numerous partial repayments of the advances. Specifically, in 1994 and 1995, Richard Rowe demanded repayment of $15,000 and $650,000, respectively, to pay his taxes and purchase a new home. He also demanded repayment of $84,948, $80,000, $25,000, and $70,221 from 1997–2000 to pay litigation expenses, boat repairs, and tax expenses. Donna Rowe demanded repayment of $180,000 in 1998 for boat repairs. The Rowes made additional advances in 1997 and 1998 of $500,000 and $300,000, respectively. The balance of notes payable to stockholders on December 31, 2000, totaled $1,166,912.

As Indmar was a successful, profitable company, numerous banks sought to lend money to it. FTB worked hard to retain Indmar's business, made funds immediately available upon request, and was willing to lend Indmar 100% of the stockholder advances.

In its loan agreements with Indmar, FTB required the company to subordinate all transfers, including stockholder advances, to FTB's loans. FTB did not strictly enforce the subordination provision, however, as Indmar repaid—with FTB's knowledge—some of the stockholder advancements at the same time FTB loans remained outstanding. As an example, when Richard demanded repayment of $650,000 to purchase a new home, Indmar borrowed the entire amount from FTB at 7.5% (the prime lending rate was 8.75%). Indmar secured the loan with inventory, accounts and general intangibles, equipment, and the personal guarantee of the Rowes. Richard Moody, the FTB lending officer who worked with Indmar on the loan, testified that he knew Indmar used the proceeds to repay Richard. Indmar had loans outstanding with FTB at the time.

As stipulated by the parties, the prime lending rate ranged from a low of 6% to a high of 10.5% between 1987–1998. In 1997, Indmar and FTB executed a promissory note for $1m that was modified in 1998. The interest rate on the note (7.85%) was below the prime lending rate.

Indmar also had a collateralized line of credit with FTB. Similar to the stockholder advances, the bank line of credit was used for short-term working capital. * * *

B. Claimed Deductions at Issue

On its tax returns for 1998–2000, Indmar claimed deductions for the purported interest payments paid on the stockholder advances. The Commissioner issued a notice of deficiency. Indmar filed a petition in the Tax Court challenging the Commissioner's decision. After trial, the Tax Court concluded that the advances did not constitute genuine indebtedness and thus the payments to the stockholders were not deductible. The Tax Court calculated a total tax deficiency of $123,735 and assessed $24,747 in penalties. Indmar timely appealed.

II. LEGAL ANALYSIS

A. Determining Whether Advance Is Debt or Equity

As a general matter, the Commissioner's determination of a deficiency is entitled to a presumption of correctness. It is the taxpayer's burden to prove the determination to be incorrect or arbitrary. *Ekman v. Comm'r*, 184 F.3d 522, 524 (6th Cir.1999).

The basic question before us is whether the advances made to the company by the stockholders were loans or equity contributions. Under 26 U.S.C. § 163(a), a taxpayer may take a tax deduction for "all interest paid or accrued . . . on indebtedness." There is no similar deduction for dividends paid on equity investments. Thus, if the advances were loans, the 10% payments made by Indmar to the Rowes were "interest" payments, and Indmar could deduct these payments. If, on the other hand, the advances were equity contributions, the 10% payments were constructive dividends, and thus were not deductible.

Over the years, courts have grappled with this seemingly simple question in a wide array of legal and factual contexts. The distinction between debt and equity arises in other areas of federal tax law, *see, e.g., Roth Steel Tube Co. v. Comm'r*, 800 F.2d 625, 629–30 (6th Cir.1986) (addressing the issue in the context of the deductibility of advances as bad debt under 26 U.S.C. § 166(a)(1)), as well as bankruptcy law, *see, e.g.,* In re *AutoStyle Plastics, Inc.*, 269 F.3d 726, 750 (6th Cir.2001). The Second Circuit set out the "classic" definition of debt in *Gilbert v. Commissioner*: "an unqualified obligation to pay a sum certain at a reasonably close fixed maturity date along with a fixed percentage in interest payable regardless of the debtor's income or lack thereof." 248 F.2d 399, 402 (2d Cir.1957). "While some variation from this formula is not fatal to the taxpayer's effort to have the advance treated as a debt for tax purposes, . . . too great a variation will of course preclude such treatment." *Id.* at 402–03. The question becomes, then, what is "too great a variation"?

To determine whether an advance to a company is debt or equity, courts consider "whether the objective facts establish an intention to create an unconditional obligation to repay the advances." *Roth Steel*, 800 F.2d at 630 (citing *Raymond v. United States*, 511 F.2d 185, 190 (6th Cir.1975)). In doing so, courts look not only to the form of the transaction, but, more importantly, to its economic substance. *See, e.g., Fin Hay Realty Co. v. United States*, 398 F.2d 694, 697 (3d Cir.1968) ("The various factors . . . are only aids in answering the ultimate question whether the investment, analyzed in terms of its economic reality, constitutes risk capital entirely subject to the fortunes of the corporate venture or represents a strict debtor-creditor relationship."); *Byerlite Corp. v. Williams*, 286 F.2d 285, 291 (6th Cir.1960) ("In all cases, the prevailing consideration is that artifice must not be exalted over reality, whether to the advantage of the taxpayer, or to the government.").

The circuit courts have not settled on a single approach to the debt/equity question. We elucidated our approach in *Roth Steel*, setting out eleven non-exclusive factors for courts to consider:

> (1) the names given to the instruments, if any, evidencing the indebtedness; (2) the presence or absence of a fixed maturity date and schedule of payments; (3) the presence or absence of a fixed rate of interest and interest payments; (4) the source of repayments; (5) the adequacy or inadequacy of capitalization; (6) the identity of interest between the creditor and the stockholder; (7) the security, if any, for the advances; (8) the corporation's ability to obtain financing from outside lending institutions; (9) the extent to which the advances were subordinated to the claims of outside creditors; (10) the extent to which the advances were used to acquire capital assets; and (11) the presence or absence of a sinking fund to provide repayments. 800 F.2d at 630. No single factor is controlling; the weight to be given a factor (if any) necessarily depends on the particular circumstances of each case. *Id.; see also Universal Castings Corp.*, 37 T.C. 107, 114 (1961) ("It is not enough when examining such a precedential checklist to test each item for its presence or absence, but it is necessary also to weigh each item."), *aff'd*, 303 F.2d 620 (7th Cir.1962). In essence, the more a stockholder advance resembles an arm's-length transaction, the more likely it is to be treated as debt. *AutoStyle Plastics*, 269 F.3d at 750.

800 F.2d at 630. No single factor is controlling; the weight to be given a factor (if any) necessarily depends on the particular circumstances of each case. *Id.; see also Universal Castings Corp.*, 37 T.C. 107, 114 (1961) ("It is not enough when examining such a precedential checklist to test each item for its presence or absence, but it is necessary also to weigh each item."), *aff'd*, 303 F.2d 620 (7th Cir.1962). In essence, the more a stockholder advance resembles an arm's-length transaction, the more likely it is to be treated as debt. *AutoStyle Plastics,* 269 F.3d at 750.

* * *

C. Roth Steel Factors

After discussing some, but not all, of the *Roth Steel* factors, the Tax Court concluded that the Rowes' advances were equity contributions. Specifically, it found the following factors weighed in favor of equity: (i) Indmar did not pay any formal dividends (although this is not one of the *Roth Steel* factors); (ii) there was no fixed maturity date or obligation to repay; (iii) repayment came from corporate profits and would not be paid if there were not sufficient profits; (iv) advances were unsecured; (v) there was no sinking fund; and (vi) at the time advances were made, there was no unconditional and legal obligation to repay. The court found that several factors weighed in favor of debt: (i) Indmar reported the advances on its federal income tax returns as interest expenses; (ii) external financing was available; (iii) Indmar was adequately capitalized; (iv) the advances were not subordinated to all creditors; and (v) the Rowes did not make the advances in proportion to their respective equity holdings. The court concluded that the factors favoring equity "certainly outweigh" those favoring debt. . . .

As explained below, we find that the Tax Court clearly erred in concluding that the advances were equity contributions rather than bona fide debt. The Tax Court failed to consider several *Roth Steel* factors. It also did not address in its analysis certain uncontroverted testimony and evidence upon which the parties stipulated. Consideration of all of the record evidence in this case leaves us "with the definite and firm conviction that a mistake has been committed." *Holmes*, 184 F.3d at 543.

1. Fixed Rate of Interest and Interest Payments

The first factor to which we look is whether or not a fixed rate of interest and fixed interest payments accompanied the advances. *Roth Steel*, 800 F.2d at 631. The absence of a fixed interest rate and regular payments indicates equity; conversely, the presence of both evidences debt. *Id.;* 7 Mertens Law of Fed. Income Tax'n § 26:28 ("A fixed interest rate is indicative of a deductible interest payment.") (collecting cases). In its findings of fact, the Tax Court determined that the advances were made with a 10% annual return rate. The court also found that Indmar made regular monthly interest payments on all of the advances.

The fixed rate of interest and regular interest payments indicate that the advances were bona fide debt. In its analysis, however, the Tax Court took a different view. Rather than analyzing these facts within the *Roth Steel* framework (i.e., as objective indicia of debt or equity), the Tax Court focused instead on why the Rowes made the advancements: it concluded that the Rowes "characterized the cash transfers as debt because they wanted to receive a 10-percent return on their investment and minimize estate taxes." *Indmar*, 2005 T.C.M. LEXIS 31, at *11. Yet, neither of these intentions is inconsistent with characterizing the advances as loans.

For tax purposes, it is generally more important to focus on "what was done," than "why it was done." *United States v. Hertwig*, 398 F.2d 452, 455 (5th Cir.1968). "In applying the law to the facts of this case, . . . it is "clear that the objective factors . . . are decisive in cases of this type." " *Raymond*, 511 F.2d at 191 (quoting *Austin Village*, 432 F.2d at 745). It is largely unremarkable that the Rowes wanted to receive a return from their advances. Most, if not all, creditors (as well as equity investors) intend to profit from their investments. *Bordo Prods. Co. v. United States*, 476 F.2d 1312, 1322 (Ct.Cl.1973). As long as the interest rate is in line with the risks involved, a healthy return on investment can evidence debt.

Of course, "[e]xcessively high rates would . . . raise the possibility that a distribution of corporate profits was being disguised as debt. Were such the purpose of an exorbitant interest rate, the instrument involved would probably not qualify as debt in form." *Scriptomatic, Inc. v. United States*, 555 F.2d 364, 370 n.7 (3d Cir.1977) (citing William T. Plumb, Jr., *The Fed. Income Tax Significance of Corporate Debt: A Critical Analysis & A Proposal*, 26 Tax L.Rev. 369, 439–40 (1971)). The Tax Court found that the 10% rate exceeded the federal prime interest rate during most of the period at issue, as well as the rate charged by FTB on several of its loans to Indmar.

The record indicates that the 10% rate was not an "exorbitant interest rate" under the circumstances. Indmar had a collateralized line of credit with FTB, which, similar to the stockholder advances, was available for short-term working capital. The rate charged by FTB for the line of credit ranged between 8%–9.5%, a rate not much below the fixed rate of 10% charged by the Rowes. The rate differential makes financial sense when considering the differences in security—the FTB line of credit was secured while the Rowes' advances were not.[2]

As for the Rowes' desire to minimize their estate taxes, this also offers little to the analysis. "Tax avoidance is entirely legal and legitimate. Any taxpayer 'may so arrange his affairs that his taxes shall be as low as possible; he is not bound to choose that pattern which will best pay the Treasury; there is not even a patriotic duty to increase one's taxes.' " *Estate of Kluener v. Comm'r*, 154 F.3d 630, 634 (6th Cir.1998) (quoting *Helvering v. Gregory*, 69 F.2d 809, 810 (2d Cir.1934) (L.Hand, J.)). The desire to avoid or minimize taxes is not itself directly relevant to the question whether a purported loan is instead an equity investment. Rather, such a desire is only tangentially relevant, by acting as a flag to the Commissioner and courts to look closely at the transaction for any objective indicia of debt.

---

[2]   The government took pains during trial to show that Indmar could have received a lower interest rate from FTB than its stockholders. Had the 10% rate been exorbitant, this would have been a useful line of inquiry. Under the circumstances here, the rate was not exorbitant, and whether Indmar could have received a better rate through FTB is of no import. To show bona fide debt, a taxpayer does not need to prove that it received the financially optimal rate, just a commercially reasonable one.

Far from proving the Commissioner's position, the existence and consistent payment of a fixed, reasonable interest rate strongly supports the inference that the advances were bona fide loans.

2. *Written Instruments of the Indebtedness*

"The absence of notes or other instruments of indebtedness is a strong indication that the advances were capital contributions and not loans." *Roth Steel*, 800 F.2d at 631. In its analysis, the Tax Court found that Indmar "failed to establish that, at the time the transfers were made, it had the requisite unconditional and legal obligation to repay the Rowes (e.g., the transfers were *not documented*)." *Indmar*, 2005 T.C.M. LEXIS 31, at *15 (emphasis added).[3]

The Tax Court focused on only half the story. For years 1987–1992, the Rowes did make advancements without executing any notes or other instruments. Beginning in 1993, and for all the tax years at issue in this case, the parties executed notes of loans and lines of credit covering all of the advances at issue, as the Tax Court noted in its findings of fact. Yet, in its analysis of the *Roth Steel* factors, the Tax Court was silent as to the subsequent execution of notes. After-the-fact consolidation of prior advances into a single note can indicate that the advances were debt rather than equity contributions. *See, e.g., Dev. Corp. of Am. v. Comm'r*, T.C.M.1988–127. The Tax Court erred by focusing on the initial lack of documentation without addressing the subsequent history of executed notes.[4]

3. *Fixed Maturity Date and Schedule of Payments*

"The absence of a fixed maturity date and a fixed obligation to repay indicates that the advances were capital contributions and not loans." *Roth Steel*, 800 F.2d at 631. Based on the Rowes' waivers, the Tax Court concluded that there was no fixed maturity date or fixed obligation to repay. While correct, we find that this factor carries little weight in the final analysis. The parties structured the advances as demand loans, which had *ascertainable* (although not fixed) maturity dates, controlled by the Rowes. *Piedmont Minerals*, 429 F.2d at 563 n. 5 ("The absence of a fixed maturity date is a relevant consideration, but it is far from controlling. The maturity of a demand note is always determinable by its holder."). Furthermore, the temporary waiver of payment does not convert debt into equity "since [the stockholders] still expected to be repaid." *AutoStyle Plastics*, 269 F.3d at 751.

---

[3] The Tax Court did count in favor of debt the fact that Indmar consistently reported the payments as interest expense on its federal taxes.

[4] The Tax Court was troubled by the treatment of the advances in the company's records as both demand debt and long-term debt. While we share the Tax Court's concerns, this was not the issue before the Tax Court or us on appeal. Importantly, regardless of whether it classified the payments as demand debt or long-term debt, the company *at all times* identified the advances as some form of debt. We leave it to the Tennessee authorities to determine whether Indmar owes any state taxes or penalties as a result of its reporting and accounting practices.

Where advances are documented by demand notes with a fixed rate of interest and regular interest payments, the lack of a maturity date and schedule of payments does not strongly favor equity. To give any significant weight to this factor would create a virtual *per se* rule against the use of demand notes by stockholders, even though "[m]uch commercial debt is evidenced by demand notes." *Piedmont Minerals*, 429 F.2d at 563 n. 5; *see also AutoStyle Plastics*, 269 F.3d at 750 (cautioning against a "rigid" rule that the factor always indicates equity).

4.   *The Source of Repayments*

"An expectation of repayment *solely* from corporate earnings is not indicative of bona fide debt regardless of its reasonableness." *Roth Steel*, 800 F.2d at 631 (emphasis added). Repayment can generally come from "only four possible sources . . . : (1) liquidation of assets, (2) profits from the business, (3) cash flow, and (4) refinancing with another lender." *Bordo Prods.*, 476 F.2d at 1326 (quoting Plumb, supra, at 526).

The Tax Court found that the "source of repayments" factor favored equity. It relied upon Richard Rowe's testimony that Indmar was expected to make a profit and that repayment "has to come from corporate profits or else the company couldn't pay for it." *Indmar*, 2005 T.C.M. LEXIS 31, at *14. The full colloquy from the testimony, however, is more equivocal:

> Q.   . . . At the time that you made these advances, were you anticipating that the repayment was going to come from corporate profits?
>
> A.   Yes, sir. It has to come from corporate profits or else the company couldn't pay for it. Unless it made profit—and I have always believed from the first day we started, that we were going to be profitable.
>
> Q.   Was it your understanding and intent, at the time you made these advances, that if the company was not, in fact, profitable, you would not be repaid?
>
> A.   I had no intentions of not being repaid, sir.
>
> Q.   Why is that?
>
> A.   I believe it's me. It's my personality.
>
> Q.   Is that because you intended to make a profit?
>
> A.   Yes, sir.

There are at least two plausible ways to read this testimony. One can read it the way the Tax Court apparently did—Rowe's testimony was, at best, contradictory: repayment must come from profits, but he had no intention of not being repaid, regardless of the company's fortunes. Given the apparent contradiction, one should focus on the statement against Indmar's interest: Rowe admitted that repayment of the advances "has to come from corporate profits or else the company couldn't pay for it." If repayment "has" to come from profits, then this would imply that repayment was tied to the company's fortunes, suggesting the advances were equity contributions.

Another way to read the testimony, however, is that Rowe, as a small businessman and unsecured creditor, believed that full repayment of all of Indmar's debt required a thriving, successful business, which, ultimately, required profits. In other words, struggling companies near or at bankruptcy do not repay their debts, at least not dollar for dollar. Under this reading, his testimony is consistent with debt. In fact, we sounded a similar note in an earlier decision addressing the debt/equity issue: "One who makes a loan to a corporation also takes a risk, and while he may receive evidence of an obligation, payable in any event, often such obligation is never paid. . . . 'All unsecured loans involve more or less risk.' " *Byerlite*, 286 F.2d at 292 (quoting *Earle v. W.J. Jones & Son, Inc.*, 200 F.2d 846, 851 (9th Cir.1952)).

If there was no other evidence to support one view or the other, we could not say that the Tax Court's reading was clearly erroneous. Credibility determinations are left to the fact finder, and our review on appeal is strictly limited. The "Tax Court 'is not bound to accept testimony at face value even when it is uncontroverted if it is improbable, unreasonable or questionable.' " *Lovell & Hart, Inc. v. Comm'r*, 456 F.2d 145, 148 (6th Cir.1972) (quoting *Comm'r v. Smith*, 285 F.2d 91, 96 (5th Cir.1960)). On the other hand, the Tax Court cannot ignore relevant evidence in making its factual findings and any inferences from those findings.

Here, there is undisputed testimony by Rowe and the FTB lending officer, corroborated by stipulated evidence in the record, that clearly weighs in favor of debt on this factor. Indmar repaid a significant portion of the unpaid advances—$650,000—not from profits but by taking on additional debt from FTB. While the interest rate on the FTB loan was lower than 10%, Indmar had to secure the bank loan with inventory, accounts and general intangibles, equipment, and personal guarantees. Thus, Indmar repaid a significant portion of the unsecured stockholder advancements by taking on secured debt from a bank, rather than by taking the funds directly from earnings. This is important evidence that the parties had no expectation that Indmar would repay the advances "solely" from earnings. The Tax Court did not discuss or even cite this evidence in its *Roth Steel* analysis.

5. *The Extent to Which the Advances Were Used to Acquire Capital Assets*

Nor did the Tax Court address whether Indmar used the advances for working capital or capital expenditures. "Use of advances to meet the daily operating needs of the corporation, rather than to purchase capital assets, is indicative of bona fide indebtedness." *Roth Steel*, 800 F.2d at 632. Richard Rowe testified that Indmar always went to a bank for funds to buy capital equipment. He also testified that all of the advances he made to Indmar were used for working capital, as opposed to capital equipment. This is uncontroverted testimony. The government points, however, to Rowe's testimony that he advanced funds even when Indmar did not "need" the funds, and argues that this somehow cuts against his testimony that the advances were used as working capital.

The government's argument is unpersuasive. We do not find that Rowe's testimony on this subject was "improbable, unreasonable or questionable," especially in the absence of the Tax Court addressing this factor in its analysis.[5] A review of Indmar's financial statements shows that it used all of the funds it received in various ways, including working capital and capital equipment expenditures. Thus, Indmar used the advances it received from the Rowes, even if not immediately upon receipt—i.e., Indmar identified a "need" for the advances at some point. There is nothing specific in the record, including Indmar's financial statements, that suggests the advances went to purchase capital equipment as opposed to being used for working capital. Accordingly, the government's supposition does not counter Rowe's testimony, and this factor squarely supports a finding of debt.

6. Sinking Fund

"The failure to establish a sinking fund for repayment is evidence that the advances were capital contributions rather than loans." *Id.* The Tax Court was correct to point out that the lack of a sinking fund favors equity. This factor does not, however, deserve significant weight under the circumstances. First, a sinking fund (as a type of reserve) is a form of security for debt, and the Tax Court also counted the general absence of security for the stockholder advances as favoring equity. Second, the presence or absence of a sinking fund is an important consideration when looking at advances made to highly leveraged firms. In that case, the risk of repayment will likely be high on any unsecured loans, so any commercially reasonable lender would require a sinking fund or some other form of security for repayment. Where a company has sound capitalization with outside creditors ready to loan it money (as here), there is less need for a sinking fund. *See Bordo Prods.*, 476 F.2d at 1326.

7. The Remaining Roth Steel Factors

On the remaining *Roth Steel* factors, the Tax Court determined that one favored equity (lack of security for the advances) and four favored debt (the company had sufficient external financing available to it; the company was adequately capitalized; the advances were not subordinated to all creditors; and the Rowes did not make the advances

---

[5]   As the Tax Court did not address this factor, it made no credibility determinations with respect to Richard Rowe's testimony relating to the use of the advancements. At one point in its decision the Tax Court did find that Rowe's testimony was "contradictory, inconsistent, and unconvincing" and that the parties "manipulated facts," but this was in specific reference to its discussion about the inconsistent treatment of the advances as demand debt and long-term debt. *See Indmar*, 2005 T.C.M. LEXIS 31, at *12–13; *see also* supra note 4.

in proportion to their respective equity holdings). These findings are well-supported in the record.

8. *Failure to Pay Dividends*

The Tax Court included in its discussion of *Roth Steel* a factor not actually cited in that case—Indmar's failure to pay dividends. In support, the Tax Court cited our decision in *Jaques v. Commissioner.*

The relevance of *Jaques* to this case is questionable. That case involved the withdrawal of funds by a controlling stockholder from his closely-held corporation. The stockholder argued that the withdrawal itself was a loan. We rejected the argument, relying in part on the fact that the corporation had never issued a formal dividend, and thus the withdrawal could have been a disguised dividend. *Jaques*, 935 F.2d at 107–08. The situation here is the exact opposite—the stockholders were advancing money to the corporation (not from), and it is the nature of those advances that we must determine.

Had the Rowes charged Indmar an exorbitant interest rate, the lack of any formal dividends might have been relevant to showing that the payments were not interest payments, but disguised dividends. As this was not the case, *see* supra Section II.C.1, we do not address further the relevance, if any, of the lack of dividend payments to the debt/equity question presented here.

D. *The Tax Court Committed Clear Error*

To summarize, eight of the eleven *Roth Steel* factors favor debt. The three remaining factors suggest the advances were equity, but, as we explained above, two of the factors—the absence of a fixed maturity date and schedule of payments and the absence of a sinking fund—deserve little weight under the facts of this case. Moreover, the non-*Roth Steel* factor relied upon by the Tax Court—Indmar's failure to pay dividends—has questionable relevance to our inquiry. The only factor weighing in favor of equity with any real significance—the lack of security—does not outweigh all of the other factors in favor of debt.[6]

Accordingly, the trial evidence, when reviewed as a whole, conclusively shows that the Rowes' advances to Indmar were bona fide loans. The Tax Court committed clear error in finding otherwise.

---

[6] Judge Moore in her dissent suggests that we give "minimal deference" to the conclusions of the Tax Court. We respectfully disagree. Much of our analysis is expressly predicated on the Tax Court's findings of fact. *See, e.g.,* supra §§ II.C.1 & 2 (relying on the Tax Court's findings of a fixed 10% interest rate and regular interest payments, and documentation of advances from 1993–2000); 3 & 6 (accepting the Tax Court's findings of no fixed maturity date or schedule of payments, and no sinking fund, but concluding that these factors do not deserve significant weight under the circumstances); and 7 (accepting in full the Tax Court's findings on five of the *Roth Steel* factors). On the remaining two *Roth Steel* factors, we point to clear, uncontroverted evidence in the record favoring debt, evidence that the Tax Court unfortunately did not discuss in its *Roth Steel* analysis. On the issue of witness credibility, it is apparent from our analysis that we take issue not with any credibility determinations the Tax Court may have made as to Rowe's testimony on certain topics, but with the its failure to address evidence.

III. CONCLUSION

For the foregoing reasons, we reverse the Tax Court's determination that the stockholders' advances were equity contributions. We find that the advances exhibited clear, objective indicia of bona fide debt. Accordingly, we also reverse the Tax Court's assessment of accuracy-related penalties.

■ ROGERS, CIRCUIT JUDGE, concurring.

I concur fully in the majority opinion. I write separately to explain why the legal, non-factual components of the tax court's analysis are properly examined on appeal without deference to the tax court, notwithstanding the overall "clearly erroneous" standard that our court has stated to be applicable to the determination of whether a particular transaction is debt or equity.

Whether an issue to be determined by the courts is one of fact or law is sometimes pretty simple. But often, especially when the issue can be stated in the form of "Does the item before us fit within the legal definition of *x*?", the factual-versus-legal nature of the issue can be perplexing. This is because the seemingly single question really has two different components: "What is the nature of this item?" and "What is the legal meaning of *x*?" In a case where there is total agreement between the parties as to the nature of the item, the question whether the item is an *x* is a legal one. In a case where there is total agreement between the parties as to the meaning of *x*, but a dispute as to the nature of the item, the issue of whether the item is an *x* is totally factual. Where there is some dispute on each of the two issues, the issue of whether the item is an *x* is a mixed question of law and fact.

* * *

Thus, in cases like the present one where the objective characteristics of a transaction have significant importance, our treatment of those objective characteristics does not require deference to the lower court. As we said in *Holmes v. Commissioner*, 184 F.3d 536, 543 (6th Cir. 1999) (emphasis added):

> On review, the Tax Court's *factual findings, and inferences drawn from the facts*, especially witness credibility determinations, are entitled to deference by the appellate court. . . . By contrast, the Tax Court's *application of legal standards*, and its legal conclusions, are reviewed *de novo*.

In my view, these cases are perfectly consistent with *not* deferring to the legal aspects of the lower court's reasoning, and avoidance of the fallacy described above requires us not to defer to such legal determinations. *See Livernois Trust*, 433 F.2d at 883 (McCree, J., concurring). Thus, while the majority opinion in this case cannot be faulted for stating that the overall scope of review in this case is "clear error," that conclusion must be interpreted to incorporate de novo review of legal questions necessary to our determination. Viewed in this way, the majority opinion's analysis is compelling.

In the instant case there is, to be sure, a limited factual aspect. One of the relevant *Roth* factors (the fourth) is whether repayment was intended to depend on company profit. 800 F.2d at 630. The tax court found that Indmar always intended to repay Mr. Rowe solely from profits because Mr. Rowe so testified. Clearly erroneous review requires substantial deference to this conclusion, but even applying such deference it is necessary to reject the factual conclusion: the undisputed facts show that it is not what happened. Indmar repaid advances on two occasions by tapping its line of credit (i.e., when there was not sufficient profits to cover the demand amount).

More importantly, however, the facts relevant to all the remaining factors are simply not in dispute. Even assuming that the payments were intended to be paid solely from profits, these other factors as a matter of law require the legal conclusion that the transactions represent debt rather than equity. There is no dispute as to the content of the transactions, form of the obligation, perfect repayment history, Indmar's solid creditworthiness, Indmar's equity-heavy capitalization, respective ownership interest of the parties, subordination of the notes, and applicable market interest rates. These undisputed facts make the tax court's legal conclusion that Indmar's obligation was equity erroneous. In other words, the extensive legal aspects of the question of whether these transactions amounted to debt are subject to our independent review, notwithstanding the applicability of a general "clearly erroneous" rubric to the overall question. Or stated differently, because the issue in dispute in this case is predominantly legal, cases requiring "clearly erroneous" review are pro tanto distinguishable. Either way, in a case like this one where a case that is largely factually indistinguishable could easily arise before a different lower court in the future, we must-to the extent that the facts are indeed objectively undisputed-rule in a way that insures consistent results. Applying "clearly erroneous" deference to lower court legal determinations, no matter how hidden or embedded such determinations are in overall determinations that are partly or even largely factual, is fundamentally at odds with the rule of law.

■ KAREN NELSON MOORE, CIRCUIT JUDGE, dissenting.

I respectfully dissent because I believe that the Tax Court's conclusion that the shareholder advances to taxpayer were equity contributions rather than genuine debt is not clearly erroneous. Far from being left "with the definite and firm conviction that a mistake has been committed," *Holmes v. Comm'r*, 184 F.3d 536, 543 (6th Cir. 1999) (internal quotation marks omitted), I believe that the record provides significant support for the Tax Court's conclusion, and I would affirm.

The majority is of course correct when it states that in reviewing Tax Court decisions, we review factual findings for clear error and conduct a more searching de novo inquiry into legal conclusions of the lower court. . . . Similarly, I share the concern expressed by Judge Rogers that we must take care to avoid being unduly deferential to trial court determinations of law, particularly when we are considering questions like this "where factual issues predominate, [and thus] the predominant scope of review is 'clearly erroneous.'" Concurrence at 14. However, we must not be so concerned about avoiding being overly deferential that we fail to afford due deference to a lower court's determinations when our standard of review so requires. While other courts have concluded that the ultimate issue of whether a shareholder advance constitutes equity or debt is a question of law or a mixed question of law and fact that is reviewed de novo, we have repeatedly held that this specific question is a question of fact reviewed for clear error, and we remain bound by this precedent. * * * I am therefore troubled by the robustness of the majority opinion's clear error review of several of the factual aspects of this case as well as the ultimate question of whether the payments were debt or equity, and I believe that the majority has "misapprehended and misapplied the clearly-erroneous standard." * * *

Here the shareholder advances to Indmar are subject to "particular scrutiny" because, like advances between a controlling corporation and its subsidiary, "the control element suggests the opportunity to contrive a fictional debt." *Roth Steel*, 800 F.2d at 630 (internal quotation marks omitted). The taxpayer bears "the burden of establishing that the advances were loans rather than capital contributions." *Id.* (citing *Smith*, 370 F.2d at 180). The Tax Court's conclusion that Indmar failed to meet this burden was not clearly erroneous. While several of the *Roth Steel* factors support Indmar's claim that the shareholder advances were bona fide debt, several others instead favor equity. The unsecured nature of the shareholder advances "is a strong indication that the advances were capital contributions rather than loans." *Id.* at 631. Indmar's failure to establish a sinking fund is further "evidence that the advances were capital contributions rather than loans." *Id.* at 632. While the majority appears to view the absence of a sinking fund as redundant with the consideration that the transfers were unsecured, *Roth Steel* considers both as factors, and here both factors indicate equity. In addition, Indmar did not have any fixed maturity date or fixed obligation to repay the Rowes. This "indicates that the advances were capital contributions and not loans." *Id.* at 631. Nor did the Tax Court err in viewing Mr. Rowe's statement that repayment would have to come from corporate profits as a strong indicator of equity, because "an expectation of repayment solely from corporate earnings is not indicative of bona fide debt regardless of its reasonableness." *Id.*

* * *

In the particular circumstances of this case, which include the "contradictory, inconsistent, and unconvincing" testimony of the majority shareholder, I cannot conclude that it was clearly erroneous for the Tax Court to decide that the factors that favored equity were deserving of more weight than those that favored debt. Because I believe the record supports two permissible views of the evidence, I cannot join the majority's conclusion that the Tax Court's determination was clearly erroneous. *Anderson*, 470 U.S. at 574. I would affirm the decision of the Tax Court.

DETAILED ANALYSIS

1.　THE NATURE OF THE INQUIRY

1.1.　*Generally*

Indmar Products is illustrative of a multitude of opinions involving classification of obligations issued by closely held corporations as debt or equity based on a list of factors developed by the courts to make the distinction. In Gilbert v. Commissioner, 248 F.2d 399 (2d Cir.1957), the court identified debt as an "unqualified obligation to pay a sum certain at a reasonably close fixed maturity date along with a fixed percentage in interest payable regardless of the debtor's income or lack thereof." *Gilbert* was one of the first cases to apply a multi-factor approach to separate a fixed obligation to pay from a payment that was dependent upon the fortunes of a corporate business. The courts, following the *Gilbert* analysis, began to search for factors that would help to distinguish the unqualified obligation to repay from an equity investment. As a result the courts began to develop formidable lists of factors, such as the *Roth* factors described in *Indmar Products,* against which obligations could be measured to determine if they more resembled debt or equity.

In Estate of Mixon v. United States, 464 F.2d 394, 402 (5th Cir.1972), the court enumerated a list of thirteen factors as follows:

(1) the names given to the certificates evidencing the indebtedness;

(2) the presence or absence of a fixed maturity date;

(3) the source of payments;

(4) the right to enforce payment of principal and interest;

(5) participation in management flowing as a result;

(6) the status of the contribution in relation to regular corporate creditors;

(7) the intent of the parties;

(8) "thin" or adequate capitalization;

(9) identity of interest between creditor and stockholder;

(10) source of interest payments;

(11) the ability of the corporation to obtain loans from outside lending institutions;

(12) the extent to which the advance was used to acquire capital assets; and

(13) the failure of the debtor to repay on the due date or to seek a postponement.

At one point, the "factor check-off list" approach threatened to become as mechanical as the earlier obsession with debt-equity ratios.

Congress joined in the list making process with the Tax Reform Act of 1969. Section 385(a) directs the Secretary of the Treasury to promulgate regulatory guidelines to distinguish debt from equity. The legislative history contains the following non-exclusive list of factors to be included in the guidelines:

(1) Whether there is a written unconditional promise to pay on demand or on a specified date a sum certain in money in return for an adequate consideration in money or money's worth, and to pay a fixed rate of interest;

(2) Whether there is subordination to, or preference over, any indebtedness of the corporation;

(3) The ratio of debt to equity of the corporation;

(4) Whether there is convertibility into the stock of the corporation; and

(5) The relationship between holdings of stock in the corporation and holdings of the interest in question.

General Explanation of the Tax Reform Act of 1969, Staff of the Joint Committee on Internal Revenue Taxation, 123–24 (1970). The first set of final § 385 regulations were issued in December 1980, applicable to instruments issued after April 30, 1981. T.D. 7747, 1981–1 C.B. 141. The effective date was extended several times, and the regulations were withdrawn on August 5, 1983. T.D. 7920, 1983–2 C.B. 69. Although elegant in structure and theoretical underpinning, the regulations were difficult to apply in the myriad of situations that they were required to cover. In 2016, the Treasury issued new final § 385 regulations. These are discussed in greater detail below. In general, the new § 385 regulations focus on implementing documentation requirements and on characterizing arrangements between certain related entities. They have been subject to significant criticism, and the effective date of the documentation requirements has been delayed. Notice 2017–36, 2017–33 I.R.B. 208 (Aug. 14, 2017). Even if the new regulations are not altered or withdrawn, judicial authority will continue to govern in areas not controlled by the regulations (such as closely held businesses), and in many instances the new regulations require taxpayers to look to existing judicial authority. See Treas.Reg. § 1.385–1(b).

Courts now generally avoid the "factor check-off list" approach, as a mechanical solution to the debt/equity conundrum. As the court noted in Slappey Drive Industrial Park v. United States, 561 F.2d 572 (5th Cir. 1977), "We have always recognized . . . that the various factors are not equally significant. 'The object of the inquiry is not to count factors, but to evaluate them.' Tyler v. Tomlinson, 414 F.2d 844, 848 (5th Cir.1969). Each case turns on its own facts; differing circumstances may bring different factors to the fore." Under this view, the trier of fact must weigh the various factors in the light of the entire evidence presented and not give undue weight to any one factor. Nonetheless, the courts' refusal to sanction a relatively mechanical test such as the debt-equity ratio, has resulted in a great deal of uncertainty for tax advisors and the government, with the inevitable consequence that a substantial amount of litigation has been generated in the debt-equity area.

Consistent with the view that the inquiry is inherently factual, the IRS will not "ordinarily" rule on whether advances to a corporation constitute debt or equity. See, e.g., Rev.Proc. 2019–3, § 4.02(1), 2019–1 I.R.B. 130.

1.2. *The Relevance of Evidentiary "Factors"*

The temptation to create legal shopping lists of factors should be resisted. It is the factors *in relationship* that appear to determine the results in debt-equity cases, even in those cases in which the court may emphasize particular factors. For instance, if a court considers subordination significant, it is generally subordination in relation to the absence of other factors that would demonstrate debt which is determinative, not subordination as such. Each of the factors considered by the courts contributes in varying degree to the resolution of the classification issue. For example, in Fin Hay Realty Co. v. United States, 398 F.2d 694 (3d Cir.1968), the court listed sixteen factors to be considered in distinguishing debt from equity, but described the factors as "only aids in answering the ultimate question whether the investment, analyzed in terms of its economic reality, constitutes risk capital entirely subject to the fortunes of the corporate venture or represents a strict debtor-creditor relationship. Since there is often an element of risk in a loan, just as there is an element of risk in an equity investment, the conflicting elements do not end at a clear line in all cases * * *."

The factors listed in the cases can best be understood in the context of the *Gilbert* language describing debt as an obligation to pay a fixed sum at a reasonably certain maturity date with fixed interest payments. Contrast a fixed obligation to repay debt with a discretionary corporate distribution of dividends at the behest of corporate management when the entity has sufficient earnings to permit a distribution to shareholders that is, therefore, dependent upon the success of the corporate enterprise. Thus, in Lane v. United States, 742 F.2d 1311 (11th Cir.1984), the court stated: "In order for an advance of funds to be considered a debt rather than equity, the courts have stressed that a reasonable expectation of repayment must exist which does not depend solely on the success of the borrower's business." The taxpayer who advanced funds to three failing corporations for demand notes testified in the trial court that he expected repayment when the corporations were in a position to retransfer the funds without damage to their ongoing businesses. The court concluded from the taxpayer's testimony that repayment was dependent upon the success of the business. As a consequence the advances constituted equity rather than debt. Compare Hardman v. United States, 827 F.2d 1409 (9th Cir.1987), which held that a note received on sale of property to a controlled corporation was debt, not equity, because payment of the note was not dependent on the fortunes of the business nor did the note lack a fixed maturity date since repayment was tied to "a fairly certain event—sale of the property."

1.3. *The Role of Risk*

In Slappey Drive Industrial Park v. United States, 561 F.2d 572 (5th Cir. 1977), the court distinguished debt and equity on the basis of the risk assumed by the holder of an obligation as follows:

> Articulating the essential difference between the two types of arrangement that Congress treated so differently is no easy task. Generally, shareholders place their money "at the risk of the business" while lenders seek a more reliable return. * * * That statement of course glosses over a good many considerations with which even the most inexperienced investor is abundantly familiar. A purchaser of General Motors stock may bear much less risk than a bona fide lender to a small corporation. * * *

> Nevertheless, the "risk of the business" formulation has provided a shorthand description that courts have repeatedly invoked. Contributors of capital undertake the risk because of the potential return, in the form of profits and enhanced value, on their underlying investment. Lenders, on the other hand, undertake a degree of risk because of the expectancy of timely repayment with interest. Because a lender unrelated to the corporation stands to earn only a fixed amount of interest, he usually is unwilling to bear a substantial risk of corporate failure or to commit his funds for a prolonged period. A person ordinarily would not advance funds likely to be repaid only if the venture is successful without demanding the potential enhanced return associated with an equity investment. * * *

The court added that the risk analysis has little to contribute in a case where a shareholder makes a loan to the shareholder's own corporation.

1.4. *Standard of Review*

The different views of the three opinions in *Indmar Products* illustrate the difficulty in identifying the degree to which the debt/equity analysis is a question of fact, a question of law, or a mixed question of law and fact. While the inherent factual nature of the inquiry leads to variable judicial decisions that turn on the court's assessment of facts through the lens of the various factors developed by the courts, an appellate court's assessment of the factual versus legal nature of the inquiry affects that deference that the appellate court will provide to the findings of the trial court. As do most Courts of Appeals, the court in *Indmar Products* treated the trial court's conclusion as a finding of fact, which under Fed.R.Civ.P. 52(a) can be set aside only if it is clearly erroneous. See also Hardman v. United States, 827 F.2d 1409 (9th Cir.1987). The three judges in *Indmar Products* disagreed as to what was clearly erroneous. In the Fifth and Eleventh Circuits, however, the ultimate inference from the facts as to whether an obligation constitutes debt or equity is a matter of law, not of fact. See Alterman Foods, Inc. v. United States, 505 F.2d 873 (5th Cir.1974); Lane v. United States, 742 F.2d 1311 (11th Cir.1984). In the Eighth Circuit, the issue is considered to be one of mixed law and fact. J.S. Biritz Construction Co. v. Commissioner, 387 F.2d 451 (8th Cir.1967).

2. ANALYSIS OF PARTICULAR FACTORS

Each of the multiple factors used by the courts to distinguish debt from equity can be assessed in terms of whether the presence or absence of the factor identifies the likelihood of a fixed obligation to pay principal and interest regardless of the fortunes of the business. The presence of a fixed obligation to pay principal and interest indicates a lower risk attached to the return of invested capital plus the promised return on the investment. The absence of a fixed obligation under all of the facts and circumstances indicates that the investment is more dependent upon the business fortunes of the issuer.

2.1. *Proportion of Debt to Stockholdings*

When debt and equity obligations are held in the same proportion, individual stockholders are, apart from tax considerations, indifferent with respect to whether distributions from the corporation are made in the form of interest or dividends. In the event of cash flow problems that make the payment of the fixed obligations of debt instruments difficult for the corporation, controlling stockholders who hold debt obligations in the same proportion as equity may forego repayment rather than threaten the continued value of their equity investment. In all cases, therefore, it can be said that payment of proportionately held debt is subject to the fortunes of the business. But the pro rata holding of debt and equity is not an absolute barrier to recognition of debt status, even when a sole stockholder is present. Whether proportionately held debt obligations will be paid in a timely fashion depends on other factors such as the existence of adequate equity capital to insure debt repayment or an income stream sufficient to meet payments of interest and principal. In some cases, the absence of proportional holdings of stock and debt has been considered as a factor favoring debt status. See Adelson v. United States, 737 F.2d 1569 (Fed.Cir.1984) (taxpayer advances to clients in which the taxpayer held only a minor equity interest treated as debt; taxpayer was dealing with client companies as an outsider whose dominant motive was not to further an equity interest in the companies).

Tomlinson v. 1661 Corp., 377 F.2d 291 (5th Cir.1967), held that proportionate shareholder advances constituted debt. The shareholders advanced funds to their corporation on a pro-rata basis, with a resulting debt-equity ratio of approximately 4:1. The evidence indicated that the corporation could have borrowed from outside sources but would have had to pay a higher rate of interest to do so. The shareholder notes were subordinated only to secured mortgage debt. The interest was accrued but unpaid; all interest had, however, to be paid before dividends could be paid. The proportionality of debt and equity was not conclusive because the debt was freely transferable whereas the stock was not because of shareholder agreements; thus, the proportionality could have been destroyed at any time. Even including third-party mortgage debt, the debt-equity ratio was only

14.6:1. The court declined to speculate on the business reasons for the nonpayment of interest.

2.2. *Thin Capitalization*

A high proportion of debt relative to shareholder equity is an indication that the corporation lacks reserves to pay interest and principal on debt when corporate income is insufficient to meet current payments. In such a case, the debt holders' potential recovery is subject to entrepreneurial risk because repayment is dependent on the success of the venture. Thus, a high ratio of debt to equity is a factor favoring equity classification. See John Kelley Co. v. Commissioner, 326 U.S. 521 (1946) (subordinated convertible debentures were true debt because the corporation was not "thinly capitalized").

While generally the decisions mention the debt-equity ratio, they offer little discussion of the rules governing its determination. In Slappey Drive Industrial Park v. United States, 561 F.2d 572 (5th Cir. 1977), the court looked at the relation of the debt both to the book value of the corporation's assets and to their fair market value. In Bauer v. Commissioner, 748 F.2d 1365 (9th Cir.1984), the court held that the debt to equity ratio compares total liabilities to the stockholders' equity that includes initial paid-in capital plus accumulated earnings. The court reversed the Tax Court's holding that shareholder loans were contributions to capital. The Tax Court had based its holding, in part, on a stipulation by the parties that the corporate debt/equity ratio was 92 to 1, the ratio of liabilities to the shareholders' initial capital contributions. Comparing liabilities with total shareholder equity, determined by including both paid-in capital and accumulated earnings, produced debt to equity ratios ranging from 2 to 1 to 8 to 1.

In determining the ratio of debt to equity, courts may consider all of the outstanding indebtedness of the corporation even though it is typically shareholder debt that is being tested for equity equivalence. Thus, an outstanding bank loan can have an influence on the "thinness" of the corporation's capital structure. See, e.g., Berkowitz v. United States, 411 F.2d 818 (5th Cir.1969).

A high ratio of debt to equity is not automatically fatal to debt status. In Bradshaw v. United States, 683 F.2d 365 (Ct.Cl.1982), notwithstanding a very high ratio of debt to equity (the corporation's capital consisted of an automobile valued at $4,500), the court classified as debt five notes, each in the face amount of $50,000, given to a sole shareholder of the debtor corporation in exchange for real property transferred to the corporation by the shareholder. The court emphasized the fact that the corporation's cash flow was sufficient to meet its obligations under the notes to pay interest and principal on fixed dates and that the corporation paid principal and interest on the notes when due. See also Delta Plastics, Inc. v. Commissioner, T.C. Memo. 2003–54 (pro-rata shareholder loans to a start-up corporation were respected as such and an interest deduction allowed, even though the corporation's debt-equity ratio was 26:1, where the corporation made all scheduled payments when due).

2.3. *Subordination to Other Creditors*

In P.M. Finance Corp. v. Commissioner, 302 F.2d 786 (3d Cir.1962), the court held that shareholder "loans" were equity by placing heavy reliance on the fact that the loans were subordinated to all "present and future bank loans." Complete subordination, the court noted, "tends to wipe out a most significant characteristic of the creditor-debtor relationship, the right to share with general creditors in the assets in the event of dissolution or liquidation, * * * but it also destroys another basic attribute of creditor status: i.e., the power to demand payment at a fixed maturity date." Subordination, however, is not invariably fatal to debt classification. See Jones v. United States, 659 F.2d 618 (5th Cir.1981) (debt status upheld despite state regulations requiring subordination to insurance corporation's policy holders); Federal Express Corp. v. United States, 645 F.Supp. 1281 (W.D.Tenn.1986) (debt status sustained for obligations subordinate only to senior debt; the challenged obligations were negotiated at arm's length by sophisticated institutional investors and were in parity with trade debt).

2.4. *Intent, Business Purpose, and Tax Avoidance*

Although courts frequently list the taxpayer's "intent" as a factor in determining whether an obligation constitutes debt or equity, most cases recognize that "intent" is simply a way of stating the conclusion and instead examine more objective factors to determine the debt-equity status of the particular obligation. In general, earlier cases in which taxpayer "intent" or "business purpose" appeared to take on an independent status have not been followed. See, e.g., Gooding Amusement Co. v. Commissioner, 236 F.2d 159 (6th Cir.1956); Tomlinson v. 1661 Corp., 377 F.2d 291 (5th Cir.1967). In Estate of Mixon v. United States, 464 F.2d 394 (5th Cir.1972), however, the court sustained the taxpayer's treatment of an interest-free shareholder advance to a bank, as required by bank examiners, as debt under its 13-factor analysis; the court indicated that where the objective signs point in all directions, the trial court was correct in looking to the subjective intent of the parties to decide which direction to follow.

2.5. *Absence of New Investment*

If a corporation has been in existence for some time, and then issues a dividend in the form of a debt obligation or, by recapitalization, issues a debt obligation in exchange for previously outstanding stock, the IRS has attempted to treat the new obligation as stock on the ground that there is no new investment to permit the obligation to be considered as debt. Compare Sayles Finishing Plants, Inc. v. United States, 399 F.2d 214 (Ct.Cl.1968) (notes issued for stock in a reorganization constituted equity because no new funds were added to the corporation by issuing the debt and the only benefit to the business was the obtaining of the interest deduction), with Monon Railroad v. Commissioner, 55 T.C. 345 (1970) (acq.) (debentures issued to acquire outstanding shares of stock were valid debt; it was not necessary that new funds be received by the corporation in exchange for the debt where other factors pointed to debt classification).

2.6. *Fixed Payments*

The court in *Indmar Products Co.*, excerpted supra, stated that, "The first factor to which we look is whether or not a fixed rate of interest and fixed interest payments accompanied the advances. . . . The absence of a fixed interest rate and regular payments indicates equity; conversely, the presence of both evidences debt." The court thus held that demand notes to corporate shareholders with a fixed rate of interest and regular payments were debt.

Payment of interest was of paramount significance to the D.C. Circuit in Cerand & Co. v. Commissioner, 254 F.3d 258 (D.C. Cir. 2001). The corporate taxpayer transferred funds to its three sister corporations through an "open accounts receivable" for each borrower without any formal documents describing the nature of the transfers. The taxpayer claimed bad debt deductions for the advances when the three "borrower" corporations went out of business. The Tax Court, T.C. Memo. 1998–423, originally held that the advances were contributions to capital, not loans, citing the absence of an agreement to memorialize the debt, the absence of a fixed maturity date or repayment schedule, the absence of a stated interest rate, and the Tax Court's ultimate conclusion that the repayment was inconsistent and appeared dependent on financial success. The Tax Court's conclusion also was based on the sister corporations' thin capitalization and lack of historical success, further indicating that the likelihood of repayment was low. In remanding the case back to the Tax Court, the D.C. Circuit held that the Tax Court "abused its discretion in assessing the evidence. The critical flaw in the tax court's analysis is its failure, despite the taxpayer having pressed the point, to consider Cerand's contemporaneous treatment of sums received from its sister corporations as in part the payment of 'interest,' taxable as income to Cerand." The Court of Appeals did not address the other factors considered by the Tax Court. On remand the Tax Court again denied the bad debt deduction, affirming its original holding that the advances were not debt. T.C. Memo. 2001–271. As a factual matter the Tax Court found that the purported interest payments were sporadic and varied as a percentage of the amount advanced. The Tax Court reiterated its reasoning that classification as debt or equity depends on an analysis of multiple factors and repeated its holding, "In the overall setting of this case, however, the repayments and interest accruals are insufficient to overcome the weight of the evidence reflecting that, in form and substance, neither petitioner nor its sister corporations intended the advances to be loans, nor did they treat them as loans."

3.   SHAREHOLDER-GUARANTEED LOANS

Some arrangements have been structured to escape the debt-equity imbroglio by having the corporation, instead of borrowing from a shareholder, borrow from a commercial lending institution, which agrees to make the loan only upon the condition that the shareholder personally guarantees the corporate obligation. In Plantation Patterns, Inc. v. Commissioner, 462 F.2d 712 (5th Cir.1972), Mrs. Jemison owned all the shares of stock of the taxpayer corporation, which had been capitalized at $5,000. Exercise of the elements of ownership of the shares, however, was dominated by Mr. Jemison, her husband. The taxpayer corporation acquired the business of another corporation and issued notes to the shareholders of the acquired corporation in a transaction that called for a purchase price of almost $650,000 in excess of the book net worth of the acquired corporation. All but $100,000 of the notes were subordinated to the corporate debt of the taxpayer, but the notes were personally guaranteed by Mr. Jemison. The debt-equity ratio of the taxpayer corporation was 100.5:1. The court held that the notes were in fact those of the guarantor, Mr. Jemison, which he contributed as capital to the corporation; therefore, the interest deduction was disallowed to the taxpayer corporation. Mrs. Jemison, the shareholder, correspondingly, received dividends on the note payments. The court based its decision on the facts that the notes were used to purchase capital assets of the taxpayer corporation; the guarantee by Mr. Jemison was essential to the transaction; subordination was present; there was complete identity of interest between the shareholder and the guarantor, with Mr. Jemison being regarded as the "constructive owner" of his wife's shares; and no value was given to the intangible financial skills of Mr. Jemison in determining the debt-equity ratio. On the last point the court stated: "[W]e conclude that intangible assets such as those claimed for Mr. Jemison have no place in assessing debt-equity ratio unless it can be shown by convincing evidence that the intangible asset has a direct and primary relationship to the well-being of the corporation. Additionally, it is clear to us that the assets sought to be valued must be something more than management skills and normal business contacts. These are expected of management in the direction of any corporation."

A contrary result was reached in Murphy Logging Co. v. United States, 378 F.2d 222 (9th Cir.1967), in which two partners formed a corporation that purchased logging equipment from the partnership. The corporation borrowed money from a bank to make the acquisition and the shareholders guaranteed the bank note. The IRS treated the transaction as if the bank loan had gone directly from the bank to the shareholders, who had then made a contribution to the capital of the corporation in a § 351 transaction. Payments by the corporation on the bank loan then were treated as constructive dividends to the shareholders (who presumably would also be treated as having made the bank payments, with possible corresponding interest deductions to the shareholders individually). The District Court upheld the IRS's treatment of the transaction, 239 F.Supp. 794 (D.Or.1965). The Court of Appeals, however, reversed and held that the debt ran from the bank to the corporation and allowed the corporate interest deduction. Although the shareholders had placed only $1,500 in the corporation and had sold the equipment to the corporation for $238,150, the court included the integrity and reputation of the shareholders as intangible assets to be considered in valuing the equity capital of the corporation. With this factor added, the court concluded that there was no thin capitalization. In addition, the transaction by which the corporation acquired the logging equipment was treated as a sale rather than a § 351 transaction, which permitted the corporation to use a cost basis for the equipment. See also Smyers v. Commissioner, 57 T.C. 189 (1971) (in the absence of thin capitalization, the shareholder guarantee did not convert a loan to equity even though it was "reasonable to assume that these unsecured loans would not have been made without petitioners' guarantee").

Comparison of the results in various cases reveals that the existence of a shareholder guarantee generally does not result in treating a bank loan to a corporation as a disguised equity contribution by the shareholder-guarantor whenever it can be established that the bank was looking primarily to the corporation for repayment, and the guarantee was only additional security for the bank or part of the bank's general policy of requiring shareholder guarantees on loans to closely held corporations.

4.   LOANS BETWEEN RELATED CORPORATIONS

Transactions between related corporations also give rise to debt-equity problems. New regulations under § 385 will recharacterize "covered debt instruments" between specified related entities as equity under certain conditions. Treas.Reg. §§ 1.385–3, –3T. The new regulations are discussed later in this Chapter. To the extent the new regulations do not require that related-party debt be treated as equity, judicial decisions regarding the treatment of related entities remain relevant. That is, even if the new regulations do not require recharacterization of debt as equity, the purported debt remains subject to being scrutinized under existing case law.

In Jack Daniel Distillery v. United States, 379 F.2d 569 (Ct.Cl.1967), the taxpayer, a subsidiary, issued its $3.5 million note to its parent corporation to reflect an advance of that amount by the parent corporation. The parent corporation also contributed another $2 million in cash to the capital of the subsidiary. The court held that the subsidiary's note was a valid debt obligation because it was an unconditional obligation to pay regardless of earnings; interest was accrued for both book and tax purposes; the note was subordinated only to specific debts and not to creditors generally; the subsidiary had the ability to, and did in fact, borrow from unrelated banks (the parent having borrowed the $3.5 million contributed to the subsidiary with knowledge on the part of the lenders that the funds were going to be utilized by the subsidiary); further advances to the subsidiary were not necessary and the loan was repaid in full; despite the fact that the note was unsecured, there was a reasonable expectation that the amounts would be repaid; and substantial equity contributions had been made by the parent.

But in National Farmers Union Service Corp. v. United States, 400 F.2d 483 (10th Cir.1968), a parent's advance to a subsidiary was treated as an equity contribution where there was no acceleration clause, the note was unsecured, the funds were used to supply capital, some notes were canceled prior to maturity, the likelihood of repayment was remote, no sinking fund had been established, and a third party would not have made the loan. Although the parent had borrowed the money that was transferred to the subsidiary, the lenders did not know that the funds were going to be placed in the subsidiary, thus distinguishing the case from *Jack Daniel Distillery*, supra. On similar grounds, the court in Roth Steel Tube Co. v. Commissioner, 800 F.2d 625 (6th Cir.1986), upheld the Tax Court's ruling that advances to a 62% subsidiary, acquired by the taxpayer following a bankruptcy

the issuer or a related entity, or in equity held by the issuer (or any related party) in any other entity. Interest or principal payable, at the option of the holder, in equity interests in the issuing corporation or a related party will be subject to § 163(l) if there is a "substantial certainty" that the option will be exercised. The basis of any such equity is increased by the amount of any disallowed interest. Dealers in securities are in general exempt from the disallowance rule of § 163(l). Rev.Rul. 2003–97, 2003–2 C.B. 380, approved a device adopted to avoid the limitation of § 163(l). The IRS ruled that interest was deductible on a five-year corporate note issued as part of a package—dubbed by the investment banking community as "Feline Pride"—that included a forward contract obligating the note holder to acquire stock of the issuer on a settlement date that was three years from the date of issue. The amount of the holder's obligation to purchase stock was the same as the principal amount of the note. The holder's obligation to purchase the stock was secured by the note. The ruling was based on the IRS's finding that the note and the futures contract constituted separate properties.

7.2. *Bifurcation of Debt and Equity Features*

In two cases, the courts bifurcated the debt and equity components of a single financial instrument. In Helvering v. Richmond, F. & P. R.R. Co., 90 F.2d 971 (4th Cir.1937), the corporation was allowed an interest deduction for guaranteed 7% dividends paid on preferred stock, but payments in excess of the guarantee were treated as dividends, a return on equity. The preferred stock provided for participation in corporate earnings above the 7% guaranteed dividends and possessed full voting rights. The guaranteed dividends were a first lien on corporate assets and took precedence over all creditors, including general creditors.

In Farley Realty Corp. v. Commissioner, 279 F.2d 701 (2d Cir.1960), the corporation borrowed money from a nonshareholder to acquire a building. The obligation required fixed payments of interest and had a fixed maturity date. In addition, the obligation holder was entitled to 50% of the appreciation on sale of the building, whether this event occurred before or after the maturity date. The IRS allowed the corporation to deduct fixed interest payments on the loan but disallowed any deduction for payment in settlement of the creditor's interest in appreciation.

In contrast, in Rev.Rul. 83–51, 1983–1 C.B. 48, the IRS held that contingent interest in the form of shared appreciation paid by the borrower to the mortgagee on a home residence loan was deductible interest. The loans provided for a fixed interest rate plus 40% of the appreciation on the sale of the residence or at the end of the 10 year term of the loan. The Ruling described the interest as ascertainable because it was dependent on fixed events. The Ruling expressly provides that it is not applicable in a commercial context.

Section 385(a) authorizes regulations classifying obligations as debt in part and equity in part. The legislative history indicates that "such treatment may be appropriate in circumstances where a debt instrument provides for payments that are dependent to a significant extent (whether in whole or in part) on corporate performance, whether through equity kickers, contingent interest, significant deferral of payment, subordination, or an interest rate sufficiently high to suggest a significant risk of default." H.Rep. No. 101–247, 101st Cong., 1st Sess. 1235–1236 (1989). Recent regulations (discussed in greater detail in the next section) do not contain rules for bifurcation but do reserve the issue. Treas.Reg. § 1.385–1(e).

8.   SECTION 385 REGULATIONS

Regulations promulgated in 2016 narrowly focus the regulatory debt versus equity characterization regime only on instruments issued between related corporations. T.D. 9790, Treatment of Certain Interests in Corporations as Stock or Indebtedness, 81 F.R. 72858 (October 21, 2016). For this purpose, the regulations adopt a definition of related party that includes an expanded group of corporations identified under § 1504(a), discussed in Chapter 15, to include corporations, other than S corporations, related through ownership of stock representing 80% of voting power and value, expanded to apply to corporations related by ownership of 80% of vote *or* value, and including exempt entities, foreign corporations, and certain controlled partnerships. Treas.Reg. § 1.385–1(c)(4). Although foreign corporations may be part of the "expanded group," a key term, "covered member," includes only domestic corporations and reserves application to other corporations. Treas.Reg. § 1.385–1(c)(2). Thus, as a result, the rules currently reach debt instruments issued by certain U.S. corporations. Further, none of the rules in the regulations apply to indebtedness between members of a consolidated group (discussed in Chapter 15) during the period the corporations are members of the consolidated group, unless the debt instrument is transferred outside the consolidated group. Temp.Reg. § 1.385–4T; Treas.Reg. § 1.385–2(d)(2)(ii)(A).

Treas.Reg. § 1.385–2 provides detailed requirements for documentation and financial analysis of instruments issued as indebtedness between related parties, similar to what generally would be expected on issuance of debt instruments between unrelated parties. For an instrument to be treated as debt, documentation and information must be developed at the time an instrument is issued to demonstrate (1) an unconditional binding obligation to repay, (2) that the creditor has the typical legal rights of a creditor to enforce the terms of the instrument, including rights to trigger a default and accelerate payments, (3) evidence of a reasonable expectation of repayment, including cash flow projections, financial statements, business forecasts, asset appraisals, determination of debt-to-equity and other relevant financial ratios of the issuer (compared to industry averages), and (4) timely evidence of an ongoing debtor-creditor relationship. The documentation rules only apply if (1) the instrument is issued by a "covered member" (i.e., a U.S. corporation) or a disregarded entity owned by a covered member; and (2) threshold limitations are reached. The threshold limitations limit the rules to "large taxpayer groups," meaning the stock of any member of the expanded group is publicly traded, all or any portion of the expanded group's financial results are reported on financial statements with total assets exceeding $100 million, or the expanded group's financial results are reported on financial statements that reflect annual total revenue that exceeds $50 million.

As a general rule, Treas.Reg. § 1.385–3 treats an expanded group debt instrument as per se stock to the extent it is issued by a corporation to a member of the corporation's expanded group (1) in a distribution (including a redemption distribution), (2) in exchange for expanded group stock (subject to certain exceptions), or (3) as boot in an asset reorganization described in § 368(a)(1)(A), (C), (D), (F), or (G) (discussed in Chapter 10). All or a portion of an issuance of a debt instrument may be described in more than one prong of the general rule without changing the result that follows from being described in a single prong.

Treas.Reg. § 1.385–3(b)(3), the "funding rule," extends the per se stock rule to treat as stock an expanded group debt instrument to the extent that it is issued for property, including cash, when the debt instrument is issued to an affiliate with a principal purpose of funding (1) a distribution of cash or other property to a related corporate shareholder, (2) an acquisition of affiliate stock from an affiliate, or (3) certain acquisitions of property from an affiliate pursuant to an internal asset reorganization. A per se rule automatically recharacterizes as equity any related party debt issued in the 36-month period before or after a distribution or acquisition described in the general rule. (However, certain short-term debt and loans in the ordinary course of business are excluded from this recharacterization rule. See Temp.Reg. § 1.385–3T(b)(3)(vii)). As a back-up, Treas.Reg. § 1.385–3(b)(4) provides an anti-abuse rule specifying that a debt instrument is treated as stock if it is issued with a principal purpose of avoiding the application of the proposed regulations.

The per se stock rules of Treas.Reg. § 1.385–3 apply only when the debt that would be converted to equity exceeds $50 million. Exceeding the $50 million threshold would have a cliff effect; if the threshold is exceeded, all of the debt, and not merely the excess over $50 million would be treated as equity.

The new administration has signaled that it may revisit the § 385 regulations, and it delayed the documentation rules. The Treasury's Second Report to the President on Identifying and Reducing Tax Regulatory Burdens, 82 F.R. 48,013, 48,016–17 (Oct. 16, 2017), explains:

> Treasury and the IRS do not believe that taxpayers should have to expend time and resources designing and building systems to comply with rules that may be modified to alleviate undue burdens of compliance. Accordingly * * * Treasury and the IRS announced in Notice 2017–36 that application of the documentation rules would be delayed until 2019.

> After further study of the documentation regulations, Treasury and the IRS are considering a proposal to revoke the documentation regulations as issued. Treasury and the IRS are actively considering the development of revised documentation rules that would be substantially simplified and streamlined in a manner that will lessen their burden on U.S. corporations, while requiring sufficient legal documentation and other information for tax administration purposes. In place of any revoked regulations,

Treasury and the IRS would develop and propose streamlined documentation rules, with a prospective effective date that would allow time for comments and compliance. Consideration is being given, in particular, to modifying significantly the requirement, contained in the documentation regulations, of a reasonable expectation of ability to pay indebtedness. This aspect of the documentation regulations proved particularly problematic. The treatment of ordinary trade payables under the documentation regulations is also being reexamined.

* * *

[A]fter careful consideration, Treasury believes that proposing to revoke the existing distribution regulations before the enactment of fundamental tax reform, could make existing problems worse. If legislation does not entirely eliminate the need for the distribution regulations, Treasury will reassess the distribution rules and Treasury and the IRS may then propose more streamlined and targeted regulations.

9.   LIMITATION ON BUSINESS INTEREST DEDUCTION

Legislation enacted in 2017 imposes a new limitation on the deductibility of interest expense. Under § 163(j), the deduction for business interest shall not exceed the sum of the taxpayer's business interest income plus 30% of the taxpayer's adjusted taxable income, plus the taxpayer's "floor plan financing interest," if any.

Business interest means any interest paid or accrued on indebtedness properly allocable to a trade or business. Business interest income means the amount of interest includible in the gross income of the taxpayer for the taxable year that is properly allocable to a trade or business. Notice 2018–28 states that for a C corporation, all interest paid or accrued by the corporation will be business interest, and all interest on indebtedness held by a C corporation that is includible in its gross income will constitute business interest income; proposed regulations require this approach See Preamble to Proposed § 163(j) Regulations (Nov. 2018); Prop.Reg. § 1.163(j)–6(j). Floor plan financing interest is defined as interest paid to finance motor vehicles that are held for sale or lease.

Adjusted taxable income is defined in § 163(j)(8) as the taxpayer's taxable income computed without regard to nonbusiness deductions, any business interest income, any net operating loss deduction, the deduction allowed under § 199A, and any deduction allowable for depreciation. For tax years beginning on or after January 1, 2022, however, depreciation deductions may not be added back.

In scope, § 163(j)'s restriction on the deductibility of interest expense applies across-the-board regardless of the form of business entity utilized to conduct the business. However, § 163(j)(3) provides an exception for small businesses, which § 163(j)(3) defines by cross-reference to § 448(c) as a business with average annual gross receipts (computed over 3 years) of $25 million or less. For passthrough entities, the restriction on the interest expense deduction is computed at the passthrough entity level but the restriction is placed on the partner or shareholder (see Chapter 16 for a more detailed discussion regarding § 163(j)'s application to S corporations). Furthermore, § 163(j)(7) provides further exceptions to § 163(j) because that section narrows § 163(j)'s application to trades or businesses other than the following: (i) a trade or business of performing services as an employee; (ii) any *electing* real property trade or business (cross-referenced to the definition in § 469(c)(7)(C)); (iii) any electing farming business (cross-referenced to § 263A(e)(4) or for cooperatives to § 199A(g)(2)); or (iv) for certain utility trades or businesses (e.g., electrical energy, water, or sewage disposal services).

If a real estate business elects to be exempt from § 163(j), then § 168(i)(8) requires that real estate business to utilize the alternative depreciation system for its real property, thus causing it to have a longer recovery period. Because real estate businesses making the election allowed by § 163(j)(7)(B) must use the alternative depreciation system for so-called qualified improvement property (among other categories), electing out of the § 163(j)'s interest expense limitation makes these electing real estate businesses ineligible to claim bonus depreciation with respect to any qualified improvement property even if it might otherwise have been entitled to do so.

Any disallowed interest expense is allowed to be carried forward indefinitely under § 163(j)(2) and utilized in a subsequent year to the extent that the taxpayer has excess limitation when the limitation calculation is made for that later year.

10. PLANNING CONSIDERATIONS

In view of the number of factors considered by the courts in resolving debt-equity cases and the unpredictable weight given to any particular factor, the tax advisor faces a difficult problem in advising clients as to the proper mix of debt and equity in determining the capital structure of a corporation. In some cases, the client simply may wish to avoid any problem and take his entire investment in the corporation in the form of equity interests. Where other corporate planning considerations—or the more adventurous nature of the client—indicate the use of debt, the tax planning problems are more difficult.

Some of the various factors in the debt-equity equation are clearly within the control of the taxpayer. Thus, proper attention to the form of the debt obligation can help to avoid problems. But how, for example, can the tax advisor establish that outside lenders would have made a loan, a factor that many of the cases consider significant? Here it would be important at the outset to determine through an analysis of the corporation's projected cash flow and operating capital requirements that a bank would have considered a loan under these circumstances and perhaps some documentation from a bank that it would have made such a loan. Other factors may be more difficult to control. For example, where shareholder debt is to be combined with some outside financing, a bank may insist on subordination of the shareholder debt and this factor cannot be "planned around."

Once the formalities indicating a debtor-creditor relationship between the corporation and its shareholders are established, it is important that the formalities be followed. For example, interest and principal should in fact be paid according to the terms of the instrument. But here the planning considerations become more complicated. While payment of principal may be helpful in establishing the debt character of the obligation, it also exposes the shareholder to the risk of dividend taxation should the tax advisor have "guessed wrong" on the debt-equity question. Would it be better to provide in the original instrument that no principal payments will be made for a period of time, with larger payments to be made later in the term of the note? If such a course is taken, however, the taxpayer loses the argument that principal payments were in fact made, a factor sometimes stressed by the courts. On the other hand, even if principal payments are postponed, complete assurance is still not possible. Even though the corporation has been audited and the loans accepted as debt for purposes of the interest deduction, the IRS could still challenge the status of the obligation in subsequent years when principal payments are made. In the end, there is no sure escape from the difficult decisions that the current status of the tax law on debt and equity require.

B. DEDUCTIONS FOR LOSS OF INVESTMENT IN A CORPORATION

INTERNAL REVENUE CODE: Sections 165(g); 166(a), (b), (d), (e); 1244; 1271(a)(1).

REGULATIONS: Sections 1.165–5; 1.1244(a)–1(a)–(b); 1.1244(b)–1(a)–(b); 1.1244(c)–1(a), (c)–(d); 1.1244(c)–2(a)(1)–(3).

The capital versus ordinary distinction is important to both individual and corporate taxpayers who suffer losses as well as to individuals who realize gains. Deduction of corporate capital losses is limited to the corporation's capital gains. I.R.C. § 1211(a). Capital loss deductions of a noncorporate taxpayer are limited to the taxpayer's capital gains plus $3,000 annually. I.R.C. § 1211(b).

Section 165(g) in general treats a loss on worthless *"securities"* as a capital loss. In contrast, § 166(a) allows ordinary loss treatment on debts not represented by securities. Section 166(d), however, requires short-term capital loss treatment for *nonbusiness bad debt* held by a noncorporate taxpayer. For purposes of § 165(g), "securities" is defined to include stock, rights to acquire stock, and any bond, debenture, note, or other evidence of indebtedness issued by a corporation (or a governmental entity) that is in registered form or has interest coupons attached. § 165(g)(2). An obligation is in registered form if the rights to principal and stated interest are transferable through a book entry system maintained by the issuer. See, e.g., Treas.Reg. § 5f.103–1(c). Section 163(f) disallows an interest deduction with respect to obligations issued by a person other than an individual which are offered to the public unless the obligation is in registered form.[2] If a "registration required obligation" is not issued in registered form, § 165(j) further disallows a deduction for any loss sustained by the holder.

Section 1244 allows an individual stockholder to treat a loss on certain small business stock, called § 1244 stock, as an ordinary loss rather than a capital loss, whether the loss is attributable to worthlessness or realized upon a sale of the stock. This ordinary loss treatment is limited to $50,000 per year, or $100,000 on a joint return. The ordinary loss treatment is available only to the individual (or individuals who are members of a partnership) to whom the stock was issued.

Under § 165(g)(3), the corporate holder of a worthless security of an "affiliated corporation" is entitled to ordinary loss treatment. Whether a corporation is an affiliated corporation for this purpose is determined under § 1504, which, generally speaking, requires that the parent corporation directly or indirectly own at least 80% of the aggregate voting power and 80% of the aggregate value of the subsidiary, excluding nonvoting stock that is limited and preferred as to dividends and liquidating distributions. In addition, the affiliated corporation must have derived 90% of its aggregate gross receipts for all taxable years from sources other than passive investments such as rents, royalties, dividends, and interest. Treas.Reg. § 1.165–5(d)(2)(iii) provides that the term gross receipts includes all corporate receipts without reduction for the cost of goods sold, except that gross receipts from the sale or exchange of stock or securities are taken into account only to the extent of the gains from such sales.

Section 1271(a)(1) provides that amounts received on the retirement of any debt instrument issued by a corporation are considered to have been received in an exchange, thus providing the exchange element prerequisite for capital gain or loss treatment. The provision does not independently characterize gain or loss. Under § 1271(a), gain or loss on retirement of a debt instrument that is a capital asset in the hands of the debt-holder will be treated as gain or loss on the exchange of the capital asset resulting in capital gain or loss treatment; gain or loss on retirement of a debt obligation that is not a capital asset is ordinary. A debt is "retired" for this purpose even if the debt is settled for less than its full amount. McClain v. Commissioner, 311 U.S. 527 (1941). Section 1272, however, requires current inclusion as ordinary income of original discount attributable to the bond; and § 1276 requires ordinary income treatment of any market discount realized upon retirement of a corporate bond. See Section 2 of this Chapter.

---

[2]   There is an exception for obligations that are not held by a U.S. person on which interest is payable only outside of the United States. I.R.C. § 163(f)(2)(B).

As a result of these provisions, the following is the general pattern of loss treatment for *individuals* on the worthlessness of their investments in corporations:

1.   Stocks, bonds, and other securities generally result in capital losses, allowable in full but only against capital gains plus $3,000 of ordinary income, with an unlimited carryover of excess losses.

2.   Nonbusiness bad debts not represented by "securities," i.e., advances and notes not qualifying under § 165(g)(2)(C), result in short-term capital losses, also allowable in full but only against capital gains (and offset first against short-term gains) and $3,000 of ordinary income with an unlimited carryover of excess losses.

3.   Business bad debts not represented by "securities" (as defined in § 165(g)(2)(C)), i.e., advances related to a trade or business of the investor, result in ordinary losses under § 166(a), allowable in full against ordinary income or capital gain and are included in the net operating loss deduction.

4.   Section 1244 small business stock losses and § 1242 small business investment company stock losses result in ordinary losses, allowable in full against ordinary income or capital gain and are included in the net operating loss deduction.

The following is the general pattern of loss treatment for *corporations* when their investments in other corporations become worthless:

1.   Stocks, bonds, and other securities (except those in certain subsidiaries) result in long-term capital losses, allowable in full but only against capital gains with a three year carryback and a five year carryforward.

2.   Bad debts not represented by "securities," i.e., advances and notes not described in § 165(g)(2)(C), result in ordinary losses, allowable in full against ordinary income or capital gain and includable in the net operating loss deduction.

3.   Stocks or securities in affiliated (80% owned) operating subsidiaries result in ordinary losses (under § 165(g)(3)), allowable in full against ordinary income or capital gain and includable in the net operating loss deduction. (If the stock is not worthless, then on liquidation of the subsidiary no loss is allowed on the stock under § 332, but the subsidiary's asset bases and its net operating losses are carried over to the parent.)

4.   Certain corporations, such as small business investment companies and banks, have special rules providing ordinary losses in some situations.

Thus, classification of a loss as a bad debt for a corporation, or a business bad debt for an individual, remains important to obtain ordinary loss treatment. Deduction of a capital loss on an equity investment or a loss on a nonbusiness bad debt is limited by § 1211.

DETAILED ANALYSIS

1. DEBT-EQUITY ASPECTS

The initial question in considering the loss character of shareholder advances to a corporation not represented by a security is whether the corporate obligation involved is classified as debt or equity. The rules of § 166 are applicable only if a true debt is created. If the advances are found to constitute a contribution to capital, the capital loss limitations of § 165(g) are generally applicable, and the issue of business versus nonbusiness bad debt is not reached. As was the case in Gilbert v. Commissioner, 248 F.2d 399 (2d Cir.1957), the characterization of an advance as debt or equity for purposes of § 166 requires the same analysis used to determine whether payments with respect to an obligation are dividends or deductible interest, discussed earlier in this Chapter.

2. BUSINESS VERSUS NONBUSINESS BAD DEBT

Loss incurred by a noncorporate creditor-investor on an advance that qualifies as a debt, and hence is not a contribution to capital, that is not evidenced by a security, is deductible as an ordinary loss only if the advance qualifies as a business bad debt. A bad debt is a business bad debt only if the creditor-investor is engaged in a trade or business and has established the necessary degree of connection between the debt and the business to qualify the debt as a business bad debt. If these two tests are met, the loss falls under § 166(a) and (b) as a business bad debt and avoids the limitation of § 166(d).

2.1. *Protection of Employment Versus Protection of Investment*

Most frequently, the question of whether a debt is a business bad debt or a nonbusiness bad debt arises when a shareholder-employee makes a loan to the corporation. Employment by the corporation clearly constitutes a trade or business, so the crucial inquiry is whether the loan was "proximate" to the taxpayer's activity as an employee or the taxpayer's activity as a shareholder. See Treas.Reg. § 1.166–5. The seminal case on this issue is United States v. Generes, 405 U.S. 93 (1972). The Supreme Court held that a debt qualifies as a business bad debt only if the taxpayer's "dominant" motivation was preservation of the taxpayer's business, i.e., employment, rather than preservation of the value of the taxpayer's equity investment in the corporation. A "significant" business motivation, if not dominant, is not sufficient. The taxpayer in *Generes* lent several hundred thousand dollars to a corporation in which he owned 44% of the stock and from which he earned an annual salary of approximately $12,000 as a part-time employee. (He was a full time employee of a bank at a salary of $19,000.) He had invested approximately $39,000 in stock of the corporation. The Supreme Court held that it was unreasonable to think that the taxpayer's dominant motive was preservation of his salary, rather than his investment.

As one factor in the determination, the *Generes* opinion stressed the relation between the taxpayer's after-tax salary—$7,000 in that case—and the amount of his investment. In Adelson v. United States, 737 F.2d 1569 (Fed.Cir.1984), the court concluded that the dominant motive test of *Generes* required the trial court to compare the potential risk and reward of the taxpayer's equity interest in client companies to which the taxpayer advanced funds with the taxpayer's interest in his salary as a financial consultant. On remand, the Claims Court found that the taxpayer's dominant motive was business, but the Court of Appeals again remanded the case to the Claims Court for specific findings comparing the potential profits that might have inured to the taxpayer's business interest with the potential profits from the taxpayer's equity interests. The court stressed, however, that determination of dominant motive does not necessarily depend upon a mathematical analysis of relative benefits. Adelson v. United States, 782 F.2d 1010 (Fed.Cir.1986). On remand, after reevaluating the record, the Claims Court determined that the taxpayer established that advances to three corporations were business debts, but did not prove that loans to three other corporations had a dominant business motive. Adelson v. United States, 12 Cl.Ct. 231 (1987). The Claims Court based its determinations on a specific comparison of the taxpayer's potential fee income with the potential return on the taxpayer's equity investment in each corporation.

Litigated cases generally turn on the court's view of the taxpayer's dominant motive. See e.g., Tennessee Securities, Inc. v. Commissioner, 674 F.2d 570 (6th Cir.1982) (payments by taxpayers' stock brokerage corporation on taxpayers' guarantees of loans of a third-party lender to an unrelated corporation that the taxpayers hoped would undertake a public stock offering utilizing the taxpayer's brokerage corporation as the underwriter were treated as dividends to the taxpayers, and the payments on the guarantees were treated as a nonbusiness bad debt deductible by the taxpayers); Bowers v. Commissioner, 716 F.2d 1047 (4th Cir.1983) (business bad debt deduction allowed for advances to a major client real estate brokerage firm to protect the income of taxpayer's controlled corporation and thereby the taxpayer's own enhanced employment income); Estate of Mann, 731 F.2d 267 (5th Cir.1984) (business bad debt deduction allowed for advances to the taxpayer's brother's corporation in which the taxpayer had only a negligible stock interest and from which the taxpayer had earned substantial commissions as a broker in several corporate acquisitions); Litwin v. United States, 983 F.2d 997 (10th Cir.1993) (allowed bad debt deductions for advances and payments on guarantees with respect to the taxpayer's closely held corporation on the court's conclusion that taxpayer principally formed the corporation to earn a salary, be employed, and remain useful to society even though salary payments to the taxpayer had been deferred for the full three year existence of the corporation).

2.2. *Is the Taxpayer Engaged in a "Trade or Business"—the Promoter Cases*

In Whipple v. Commissioner, 373 U.S. 193 (1963), the Supreme Court considered whether an investor was engaged in a trade or business. The court denied a business bad debt deduction for advances made by the taxpayer to a company that he had formed and to which he had leased property he owned:

> Devoting one's time and energies to the affairs of a corporation is not of itself, and without more, a trade or business of the person so engaged. Though such activities may produce income, profit or gain in the form of dividends or enhancement in the value of an investment, this return is distinctive to the process of investing and is generated by the successful operation of the corporation's business as distinguished from the trade or business of the taxpayer himself. When the only return is that of an investor, the taxpayer has not satisfied his burden of demonstrating that he is engaged in a trade or business since investing is not a trade or business and the return to the taxpayer, though substantially the product of his services, legally arises not from his own trade or business but from that of the corporation. Even if the taxpayer demonstrates an independent trade or business of his own, care must be taken to distinguish bad debt losses arising from his own business and those actually arising from activities peculiar to an investor concerned with, and participating in, the conduct of the corporate business.

> If full-time service to one corporation does not alone amount to a trade or business, which it does not, it is difficult to understand how the same service to many corporations would suffice. To be sure, the presence of more than one corporation might lend support to a finding that the taxpayer was engaged in a regular course of promoting corporations for a fee or commission * * * or for a profit on their sale * * *, but in such cases there is compensation other than the normal investor's return, income received directly for his own services rather than indirectly through the corporate enterprise * * *. On the other hand, since the Tax Court found, and the petitioner does not dispute, that there was no intention here of developing the corporations as going businesses for sale to customers in the ordinary course, the case before us inexorably rests upon the claim that one who actively engages in serving his own corporations for the purpose of creating future income though those enterprises is in a trade or business. That argument is untenable * * *.

In many cases taxpayers have seized upon the suggestion in *Whipple* that promotional services provided to a number of corporations might constitute a trade or business. Although, as was observed by the court in Bell v. Commissioner, 200 F.3d 545 (8th Cir. 2000), "[t]axpayers have been litigating this theory for decades," taxpayer victories in these contests are few and far between. In *Bell,* the taxpayer failed to establish that he was engaged in the trade or business of "buying, rehabilitating, and reselling corporations" because he did not provide any services to the distressed companies that might result in a return exceeding a typical investor's return and there was no pattern of sales indicating that profits on resale were attributable to taxpayer's work to rehabilitate corporations. There is something of a "Catch-22" in the taxpayer's situation in these cases, in that the courts are prone to state that to prove that the taxpayer was in the trade or business of "buying, rehabilitating, and reselling corporations" the taxpayer must introduce evidence that the sales of the corporations occurred "in a manner that confirms that the taxpayer's profits were * * * 'received directly for his own service'" or of "'an early and profitable sale' of the corporation." *Id.* Of course, the fact that a loan to the corporation has turned into a bad debt generally is factually inconsistent with either of these possibilities, unless the loan has continued to be outstanding for long after the sale. See also Townshend v. United States, 384 F.2d 1008 (Ct.Cl.1967) (over a 20-year period the taxpayer had investigated a number of business opportunities and had organized five corporations; although he was considered a "promoter" for securities law purposes, the court refused to allow a business bad debt deduction for advances made by the taxpayer; there was no showing that fees or commissions from promotional activities were received, and the taxpayer realized no profits from a quick turnover of the investments).

2.3. *Shareholder Guarantee of Corporate Debts*

In Putnam v. Commissioner, 352 U.S. 82 (1956), the Supreme Court held that payments by a guarantor because of the default of the primary obligor are subject to the limitations of § 166 and are thus deductible only as capital losses unless the obligation can qualify as a business bad debt: "The familiar rule is that, *instanter* upon the payment by the guarantor of the debt, the debtor's obligation to the creditor becomes an obligation to the guarantor, not a new debt, but by subrogation, the result of the shift of the original debt from the creditor to the guarantor who steps into the creditor's shoes. Thus, the loss sustained by the guarantor unable to recover from the debtor is by its very nature a loss from the worthlessness of a debt."

Legislative history clarifies that one of the purposes of an amendment to § 166 in 1976 is to apply § 166 whether or not the guarantor has a right of subrogation. Thus, Treas.Reg. § 1.166–9 draws no such distinction. The only effect of a right of subrogation is to affect the timing of the guarantor's deduction. See Staff of the Joint Committee on Taxation, General Explanation of the Tax Reform Act of 1976, at 156–157 (Comm. Print 1976). See also Black Gold Energy Corporation v. Commissioner, 99 T.C. 482 (1992), aff'd by order, 33 F.3d 62 (10th Cir. 1994), in which the Tax Court held that only an actual payment made pursuant to a guarantee can give rise to a deduction under § 166; the accrual method taxpayer was not allowed a bad debt deduction in the year all events fixed the amount of the liability, nor was the taxpayer allowed to claim a bad debt deduction for the amount of a note given to the creditor as a result of the guarantee.

Because the guarantor's deduction is a bad debt deduction, it may be claimed only upon the worthlessness of the guarantor's right of subrogation against the primary obligor. Thus, in Intergraph Corp. v. Commissioner, 106 T.C. 312 (1996), aff'd by order, 121 F.3d 723 (11th Cir.1997), the taxpayer's deduction for paying a guarantee of its Japanese subsidiary's debt was denied because the subrogation right was not worthless. Even though the corporate primary obligor was insolvent at the time the guarantee was satisfied, the subsidiary continued to conduct business as a going concern.

The *Putnam* decision does not itself insure that payments made by a stockholder in satisfaction of a guarantee of corporate debt will be deductible as a nonbusiness bad debt under § 166. If a stockholder's guarantee of a loan from an outside lender is found to be a substitute for the infusion of additional equity capital, the stockholder's payment under the guarantee will be treated as a capital contribution. Treas.Reg. § 1.166–9(c). See Lane v. United States, 742 F.2d 1311 (11th Cir.1984) (applying the 13-factor test of *Slappey Drive Industrial Park* to distinguish debt from equity, the court concluded that the stockholder's intent at the time the guarantees were extended was to use the guarantees as short-term substitutes for more capital stock; the stockholder's payment was treated as a contribution to capital); Casco Bank & Trust Co. v. United States, 544 F.2d 528 (1st Cir.1976) (stockholder advances to corporation in order to avoid default on bonds guaranteed by the stockholder were held to be equity contributions; the stockholder's deduction of a nonbusiness bad debt was not allowed because at the time of the stockholder advances, there was little reasonable expectation that the stockholder would be repaid). In such a case the shareholder is allowed a bad debt deduction only when the shareholder's stock becomes worthless, not at the time the loan guarantee is satisfied. The amount of the § 165 loss deduction for worthless stock is augmented by the amount of the payment, which is added to the basis of the stock at the time the guarantee is satisfied.

Treas.Reg. § 1.166–9(a) and (b) expressly provide that § 166 and not § 163 applies to all payments made with respect to guarantees, including interest.

3.   ORDINARY LOSS ON STOCK

3.1. *Section 1244 Stock*

Section 1244 allows a stockholder to treat a loss recognized from the sale or worthlessness of stock in certain small corporations, called § 1244 stock, as an ordinary loss rather than a capital loss. The loss is also available in computing the stockholder's net operating loss deduction. This ordinary loss treatment is limited to $50,000 per year, or $100,000 on a joint return. Ordinary loss treatment under § 1244 is available only to the individual (not including a trust) or partnership to whom the stock was issued, and in the case of a partnership the loss may be passed through to the individual partners with the dollar limitations applying at the partner level.

Section 1244 stock is defined essentially as stock of a "small business corporation." The stock must be issued for money or other property, other than stocks or securities and, under Treas.Reg. § 1.1244(c)–1(d), other than for services. It is important that stock actually be issued in exchange for each separate contribution to the corporation. See Pierce v. Commissioner, T.C. Memo. 1989–647 (§ 1244 does not apply to the portion of basis of § 1244 stock attributable to additional capital contributions to corporation made after issuance of stock, even though § 1244 would have applied if additional shares had been issued in exchange for the additional contributions). In Adams v.

Commissioner, 74 T.C. 4 (1980), § 1244 stock issued to a third party was reacquired by the corporation and then reissued to the taxpayer. Ordinary loss treatment was not allowed to the taxpayer when the stock became worthless. The taxpayer failed to demonstrate that the stock purchase price paid by the taxpayer was anything more than a substitution for capital paid out by the corporation on reacquisition of stock from the first holder. There was no net flow of funds into the corporation.

A corporation is a "small business corporation" if, at the time of the issuance of the stock for which an ordinary loss is claimed, the aggregate amount of equity capital received by the corporation does not exceed $1 million. If a qualified corporation issues common stock in excess of $1 million, Treas.Reg. § 1.1244(c)–2(b)(2) provides for designation of shares which were issued before the limit was exceeded as "§ 1244 stock."

If a corporation is a small business corporation when the stock was issued, it may lose that status thereafter without disqualifying the stock previously issued. The number of shareholders or the existence of several classes of stock is not material. In addition to being a small business corporation, however, the corporation also must have derived more than 50% of its gross receipts from operating income for a period up to five years prior to the loss on the stock, unless its deductions exceed its gross income. I.R.C. § 1244(c)(1)(C), (2)(C). Treas.Reg. § 1.1244(c)–1(e)(2) provides that, even if deductions exceed gross income, ordinary loss treatment will be denied if the corporation is not "largely an operating company." The validity of the regulations was upheld and ordinary loss treatment denied in Davenport v. Commissioner, 70 T.C. 922 (1978), in which the corporation derived more than 50% of its aggregate gross receipts from interest during the five years preceding the loss, but during those years its deductions exceeded gross income; seven dissenters would have held for the taxpayer on the basis that the corporation was a small loan company and hence was an "operating company" even though its income was interest income. Special provisions regarding § 1244 stock cover stock dividends, recapitalizations, and reorganizations and disallow any loss attributable to property with a basis in excess of the value of property contributed to the corporation in exchange for § 1244 stock.

Since the benefits of § 1244 do not extend to debt, the provision creates an advantage for equity capital, which must be weighed against the tax advantages accorded to debt obligations.

Taxpayer attempts to avoid the limitations of § 166 by having their insolvent corporate debtors issue § 1244 stock on which an ordinary loss was then claimed have been unsuccessful. See, e.g., Hollenbeck v. Commissioner, 50 T.C. 740 (1968), aff'd, 422 F.2d 2 (9th Cir.1970) (stock received in exchange for release of purported debt obligation did not qualify because the "debt" was found to be equity). In addition, notes issued in exchange for § 1244 stock do not receive ordinary loss treatment. Benak v. Commissioner, 77 T.C. 1213 (1981) (worthless note issued on redemption of § 1244 stock resulted in non-business bad debt treatment).

3.2. *Small Business Investment Company Stock*

The Small Business Investment Act of 1958 authorized the formation of small business investment companies organized to provide equity capital to small businesses through the purchase of their convertible debentures. These small business investment companies are private corporations with a paid-in capital and surplus of at least $300,000. The Small Business Administration is authorized to lend such a company up to $150,000 through the purchase of the latter's subordinated debentures. Under § 1242, if a stockholder investing in the stock of a small business investment company suffers a loss on the stock, the loss is treated as an ordinary loss and may be utilized in a net operating loss deduction. Also, under § 1243, if the small business investment company itself suffers a loss on stock acquired by it pursuant to the conversion privilege on convertible debentures, the loss is treated as ordinary.

4.   LOSS ON SURRENDER OF STOCK VERSUS CONTRIBUTION TO CAPITAL

In Commissioner v. Fink, 483 U.S. 89 (1987), the Supreme Court held that controlling stockholders cannot recognize a loss on the surrender of a portion of their stock to the corporation. The taxpayers, husband and wife, owned 72.5% of the common stock of the corporation. They surrendered some of their shares, reducing their ownership interest to 68.5% in order to make the corporation's capital structure more attractive to outside investors. The taxpayers claimed an ordinary loss under § 165 to the extent of the basis in their surrendered shares. The Sixth Circuit allowed the taxpayers' loss deduction by treating each share of stock as a separate investment, adopting a "fragmented" view of stock ownership under which gain or loss is recognized separately on the sale or other disposition of each share of stock. Fink v. Commissioner, 789 F.2d 427 (6th Cir.1986). The Supreme Court, however, treated the controlling stockholders' stock as a unitary investment:

> A shareholder who surrenders a portion of his shares to the corporation has parted with an asset, but that alone does not entitle him to an immediate deduction. Indeed, if the shareholder owns less than 100 percent of the corporation's shares, any non-pro rata contribution to the corporation's capital will reduce the net worth of the contributing shareholder. A shareholder who surrenders stock thus is similar to one who forgives or surrenders a debt owed to him by the corporation; the latter gives up interest, principal, and also potential voting power in the event of insolvency or bankruptcy. But * * * such forgiveness of corporate debt is treated as a contribution to capital rather than a current deduction. * * * The Finks' voluntary surrender of shares, like a shareholder's voluntary forgiveness of debt owed by the corporation, closely resembles an investment or contribution to capital * * *.

PROBLEM SET 1

1.   Howard Cunningham and John Walton have decided to combine their respective sole proprietorships, Cunningham's Hardware Store and Walton's

Lumber Mill, into a corporation to be named Milwaukee Mountain Lumber & Hardware Supply, Inc. (MML&HS). Each will contribute the land, buildings, inventory, and accounts receivable of their respective businesses. MML&HS will assume all outstanding mortgages and accounts payable of both businesses, which total $2,500,000. The net assets of each business are worth $400,000. Additional capital to expand the business will be provided by Joan B. Tipton, who will contribute $400,000 cash. Cunningham, Walton, and Tipton each will receive 100 shares of MML&HS common stock. The corporation will immediately borrow $2,000,000 from the Usury Bank & Trust Co. and will refinance the preexisting $2,500,000 debt into a $4,500,000 note. The note will bear interest at prime rate plus 2%, adjusted quarterly, with the principal due in 10 years, and the note will be secured by a mortgage on the property of the corporation.

After the contribution and the new borrowing, the gross assets of the corporation will be $5,700,000; the net assets of the corporation will be $1,200,000; and the corporation's basis in its assets (other than cash) will be $2,500,000.

MML&HS will require an additional $4,500,000 to expand its operations. Barbara Beancounter, CPA, who has been advising Cunningham, Walton, and Tipton regarding the formation of MML&HS, has presented a number of alternative proposals for raising the additional $4,500,000. She has advised the incorporators that any of these plans will secure an interest deduction for the corporation, as well as avoid dividend treatment to Cunningham, Walton, and Tipton with respect to any distributions that they receive. Evaluate each of the following alternative proposals to determine if the instruments will be accorded debt treatment by the IRS and the Courts.

(a) Cunningham, Walton, and Tipton will each loan MML&HS $1,500,000 and receive a five-year note, with interest at 1% below prime, adjusted and payable annually.

(b) Cunningham, Walton, and Tipton will each loan MML&HS $1,500,000 and receive a 20-year subordinated income note with interest at 10% payable annually only out of net profits of the corporation.

(c) Usury Bank & Trust will loan MML&HS an additional $4,500,000, but will require the personal guarantee of the shareholders who will be jointly and severally liable. Does it matter whether the loan is adequately secured by corporate assets? What if the loan is unsecured with respect to the corporation, but secured by personal assets of the shareholders?

(d) Tipton will loan the corporation $4,500,000 and receive a five-year note, with interest at 1% below prime, adjusted and payable annually. What will happen if two years later MML&HS experiences cash flow problems and stops paying interest on the note?

(e) The spouse of each shareholder will loan the corporation $1,500,000 and receive a five-year note, with interest at 1% below prime, adjusted and payable annually.

2. After several years of operation, MML&HS (from problem 1) is a highly successful enterprise, with average annual gross receipts exceeding

$30,000,000. At the beginning of the year, MML&HS purchases a new state-of-the-art factory for $10,000,000, and borrows all $10,000,000 of the purchase price. Assume that annual interest is a flat 10% rate and that the principal is due in a single, balloon payment in 10 years. How much of the year's $1,000,000 interest will MML&HS be able to deduct currently given the following alternatives?

(a)   MML&HS has $3,000,000 of taxable income, of which $100,000 is interest income and no depreciation deductions as the plant was not finished (placed in service) during the year.

(b)   MML&HS has $1,500,000 of taxable income, of which $100,000 is interest income and no depreciation deductions as the plant was not finished (placed in service) during the year.

3.   Macrosoft Corp. is a small computer software development business established a few years ago by Bernie and Mike, who contributed a total of $400,000 cash to capitalize Macrosoft. As a result of subsequent stock issues to Bernie (for an additional $200,000) and to employees of the corporation (in lieu of cash bonuses when the corporation was nearly bankrupt a few years ago), Bernie now owns 45% of the stock, Mike owns 20%, and 35% is owned by 60 different employees, none of whom holds more than 1% of the stock. The aggregate value of the stock of Macrosoft, which is not publicly traded, is about $5,000,000, but if Macrosoft does not keep pace with the development of new software, it could be bankrupt within a year. The corporation requires approximately $1,000,000 to fund new research and has devised the following plan:

(a)   Bernie will lend the corporation $200,000. The loan will be represented by a promissory note due in 10 years, and will bear interest at the prime rate, plus 3%, compounded and due semi-annually.

(b)   Mike will lend the corporation $100,000 for one year, at the prime rate, and purchase 100 shares of $300 dollar par value preferred stock for $300,000.

(c)   Ivan Milkem, a venture capitalist, will purchase $400,000 worth of common stock.

SECTION 2.   BOND DISCOUNT AND PREMIUM

A. ORIGINAL ISSUE DISCOUNT

INTERNAL REVENUE CODE: Sections 163(e); 483; 1272(a); 1273; 1274(a)–(d); 1274A; 1275(a)(1), (a)(2), (b), (c).

Tax Reform Act of 1984 General Explanation of the Revenue Provisions

Staff of the Joint Committee on Taxation 108 (1984).
[Pre-1984] Law.

Timing of inclusion and deduction of interest: The OID rules

If, in a lending transaction, the borrower receives less than the amount to be repaid at the loan's maturity, the difference represents "discount." Discount performs the same function as stated interest; that is, it compensates the lender for the use of its money. Sections 1232A and 163(e) of [pre-1984] law (the "OID rules") generally required the holder of a discount debt obligation to include in income annually a portion of the original issue discount on the obligation, and allowed the issuer to deduct a corresponding amount, irrespective of whether the cash method or the accrual method of accounting was used.[7]

Original issue discount was defined as the excess of an obligation's stated redemption price at maturity over its issue price. This amount was allocated over the life of the obligation through a series of adjustments to the issue price for each "bond period" (generally, each one-year period beginning on the issue date of the bond and each anniversary). The adjustment to the issue price for each bond period was determined by multiplying the "adjusted issue price" (the issue price increased by adjustments prior to the beginning of the bond period) by the obligation's yield to maturity, and then subtracting the interest payable during the bond period. The adjustment to the issue price for any bond period was the amount of OID allocated to that bond period.

The OID rules did not apply to obligations issued by individuals,[8] obligations with a maturity of one year or less, or obligations issued in

---

[7]   The premise of the OID rules was that an OID obligation should be treated in the same manner as a nondiscount obligation requiring current payments of interest for tax purposes. To accomplish this result, the rules in essence treated the borrower as having paid the lender the annual unpaid interest accruing on the outstanding principal balance of the loan, which amount the borrower was allowed to deduct as interest expense and the lender was required to include in income. The lender was then deemed to have lent this amount back to the borrower, who in subsequent periods was deemed to pay interest on this amount as well as on the principal balance. This concept of accruing interest on unpaid interest is commonly referred to as the "economic accrual" of interest, or interest "compounding."

[8]   Prior to 1982, the OID provisions applied only to corporate and taxable government obligations. The Tax Equity and Fiscal Responsibility Act of 1982 (TEFRA) extended these provisions to noncorporate obligations other than those of individuals.

exchange for property where neither the obligation nor the property received for it was traded on an established securities exchange.

Measurement of interest in deferred-payment transactions involving property: the imputed interest rules

A deferred-payment sale of property exempt from the OID rules was generally subject to the unstated interest rules of § 483. If the parties to the transaction failed to state a minimum "safe-harbor" rate of interest to be paid on the loan by the purchaser-borrower, § 483 recharacterized a portion of the principal amount as unstated interest. This "imputation" of interest was performed by assuming that interest accrued at a rate higher than the safe-harbor rate.

The safe-harbor rate was a simple interest rate; the imputation rate was a compound rate. The safe-harbor and imputation rates were 9 percent and 10 percent, respectively, when the Act became law. The safe-harbor interest rate applicable to certain transfers of land between members of the same family was 6 percent.

* * *

If interest was imputed under § 483, a portion of each deferred payment was treated as unstated interest. The allocation between unstated interest and principal was made on the basis of the size of the deferred payment in relation to the total deferred payments. Amounts characterized as unstated interest were included in the income of the lender in the year the deferred payment was received (in the case of a cash method taxpayer) or due (in the case of an accrual method taxpayer). The borrower correspondingly deducted the imputed interest in the year the payment was made or due.

Reasons for Change

Mismatching and noneconomic accrual of interest

Enacted in 1969, the OID rules were designed to eliminate the distortions caused by the mismatching of income and deductions by lenders and borrowers in discount lending transactions. Prior to that time, an accrual method borrower could deduct deferred interest payable to a cash method lender prior to the period in which the lender included the interest in income. Although the OID rules prevented mismatching in many situations, the potential for distortion continued to exist where the obligation was excepted from the OID rules. Some taxpayers attempted to exploit these exceptions, particularly the exception relating to nontraded obligations issued for nontraded property, to achieve deferral of tax on interest income and accelerated deductions of interest expense.

For example, in a typical transaction, real estate, machinery, or other depreciable property was purchased for a promissory note providing that interest accrued annually but was not payable until the note matured. The issuer, who used the accrual method of accounting, would claim annual interest deductions for accrued but unpaid interest. The holder, a cash method taxpayer, would defer interest income until it was actually received.

Such a mismatching of income and deductions had serious revenue consequences, since the present value of the income included by the lender in the later period was less than the present value of the deductions claimed by the borrower. The greater the length of time between the borrower's deduction and the lender's inclusion, the greater the loss of tax revenues.

This revenue loss was magnified if the accrual-method purchaser computed its interest deduction using a noneconomic formula such as straight-line amortization, simple interest, or the "Rule of 78's". In Rev.Rul. 83–84, 1983–1 C.B. 9, the Internal Revenue Service stated that interest may be deducted only to the extent it has accrued economically, using a constant yield-to-maturity formula. Some taxpayers, however, took the position that the ruling incorrectly interpreted existing law. Other taxpayers construed the ruling narrowly, as applying only to the precise facts set forth in the ruling.

In light of the significant distortions occurring under prior law, both in the form of mismatching of interest income and deductions and in the form of noneconomic accruals of interest, Congress believed it appropriate to extend the periodic inclusion and deduction rules of sections 1232A and 163(e) of prior law to nontraded debt instruments issued for nontraded property. The same policy objectives that led to the application of these rules to interest on traded debt instruments or instruments issued for cash—namely, better compliance by holders and clearer reflection of income—were believed to apply equally in the case of nontraded instruments issued for nontraded property.

The principal obstacle to applying the OID rules to a transaction in which neither side is traded is the difficulty of determining the issue price of the debt instrument directly. Both the issue price and the redemption price of an instrument must be known to compute the amount of OID. In a transaction involving the issuance of an note for cash, the issue price is simply the amount of cash received. Where the issuer receives nontraded property, however, the fair market value of the property determines the obligation's issue price.[14] Using a "facts and circumstances," case-by-case analysis to determine fair market value in these situations was considered impracticable. Congress believed that the valuation problem could best be resolved by incorporating into the OID rules a mechanism for testing the adequacy of interest in a sale of property already present in the Code—the unstated interest rules of section 483—with certain modifications. An approximation of the maximum fair market value of property (and hence the issue price of the obligation issued in exchange

---

[14] The issue price of the obligation in such a transaction is the value of the property received by the issuer, less any cash down payment made to the holder.

for it) could be arrived at by assuming a minimum rate of interest which parties dealing at arm's-length and without tax motivations could be expected to agree upon.

* * *

Finally, Congress believed there was no justification for continuing the exemption from the OID rules for holders of obligations not constituting capital assets in the holder's hands. Sales of ordinary income assets may involve deferred interest to the same degree as sales of capital assets, and the timing of income in such sales is as important as its character.

While acknowledging the complexity of the OID rules, Congress believed that the rules could be extended to a broader range of transactions without disrupting the routine, legitimate transactions of individuals or small businesses, which might have difficulty applying the rules. The Act exempts many such routine transactions.

Mismeasurement of interest in transactions involving nontraded property

Congress recognized that, under prior law, it was possible for taxpayers in a sale of nontraded property for nontraded debt to achieve unwarranted tax benefits not only by mismatching interest income and deductions, but by manipulating the principal amount of the debt. This could be accomplished by artificially fixing interest at a below-market rate. Although economically the parties were in the same position as if interest had been accurately stated, significant tax advantages often resulted from characterizing the transaction as involving a lower rate of interest and a larger loan principal amount. If recognized for tax purposes, this mischaracterization of interest as principal resulted in an overstatement of the sales price and tax basis of the property. In cases where the property was a capital asset in the hands of the seller, the seller was able to convert interest income, which should have been taxable as ordinary income in the year it accrued, into capital gain taxable at lower rates (and, under the installment method provided in sec. 453, generally only as installment payments were made). If the property was depreciable in the hands of the purchaser, the inflated basis enabled the purchaser to claim excessive cost recovery (ACRS) deductions * * *.

These same tax advantages accrued to taxpayers who engaged in low-interest transactions entirely for nontax reasons.

Explanation of Provisions

a.   Extension of OID rules

Overview

The Act extends the rules for periodic inclusion and deduction of original issue discount by lenders and borrowers to debt instruments that are issued for property that is not publicly traded, and that are themselves not publicly traded. The Act also repeals * * * the exemption from the income accrual requirement for cash-method holders of obligations not constituting capital assets in the holder's hands. Exceptions from the rules are provided to ensure that they will not apply to * * * *de minimis* transactions * * *.

If either the debt instrument or the property for which it is exchanged is publicly traded, the amount of OID is determined as under [pre-1984] law. The market value of the traded side determines the issue price of the obligation, and the excess of the redemption price over the issue price is original issue discount. Where neither side is traded, the transaction is tested for the adequacy of stated interest in a manner similar to that prescribed in section 483 of [pre-1984] law.

If the stated rate of interest is not equal to or greater than a safe-harbor rate, the issue price is determined by imputing interest to the transaction at a higher rate. The safe-harbor rate and the imputation rate are equal to * * * [the "applicable federal rate,"] a rate based on the yields of marketable securities of the United States government. [Eds.: The original 1984 legislation imputed interest of 120 percent of the applicable federal rate if the parties failed to specify interest of at least 110 percent of the applicable federal rate. The 1988 Act adopted the applicable federal rate as both the safe-harbor and imputed interest rate.]

* * *

Regulatory authority

The Act authorizes the Treasury Department to issue regulations dealing with the treatment of transactions involving varying interest rates, put or call options, indefinite maturities, contingent payments, assumptions of debt instruments, or other circumstances.

* * *

DETAILED ANALYSIS

1.   ECONOMIC ACCRUAL OF INTEREST

Section 1272 requires that original issue discount be accounted for by both the issuer and holder of the bond as the interest reflected by the discount economically accrues, i.e., on a compounding, or constant interest, basis. Ratable deduction and inclusion of original issue discount, which was the rule prior to 1984, did not accurately reflect the economic accrual of interest over the life of the bond. For example, a three-year bond with a face amount of $1,265.32 issued for $1,000 reflects an interest rate of 8%, compounded semiannually (or an effective annual rate of 8.16%). Accounting for the $265.32 of original issue discount ratably over the three years would result in a deduction of $88.44 each year for three years. However, in economic terms, the original issue discount transaction is the same as if the borrower had borrowed additional money each year to pay interest. Interest in each period is computed on the original principal plus the borrowed interest. Using a constant interest rate, the amount of the interest should be lower in the early years and then grow as the outstanding "principal" of the loan increases due to the interest which has been "borrowed" back.[3] This calculation allows the interest expense to be "compounded," i.e., interest is charged on the interest that is borrowed back. The following table illustrates the difference between ratable treatment and economic accrual treatment.

	Ratable Interest	Economic Interest	"Principal" Outstanding
Year 1	$88.44	$81.60	$1,081.60
Year 2	$88.44	$88.26	$1,169.86
Year 3	$88.44	$95.46	$1,265.32

Under § 1272(a)(3) and (5), original issue discount is calculated by determining the "yield to maturity" based on semiannual compounding (8% in the above example). Under Treas.Reg. § 1.1272–1(b)(1)(i), the original issue discount for any accrual period is calculated first by determining the yield to maturity of the debt instrument, that is, "the discount rate that, when used in computing the present value of all principal and interest payments to be made under the debt instrument produces an amount equal to the issue price of the debt instrument." Then, under Treas.Reg. § 1.1272–1(b)(1)(ii), an accrual period must be determined, which can be any interval not exceeding one year. The regulations point out that the computation of yield is simplified if the accrual periods correspond to the intervals between payment dates provided by the terms of the debt instrument. The original issue discount allocable to each accrual period is the adjusted issue price of the instrument multiplied by the yield to maturity of the debt instrument, reduced by the amount of qualified stated interest allocable to the accrual period. Treas.Reg. § 1.1272–1(b)(1)(iii). "Adjusted issue price" is the original issue price increased by accrued but unpaid original issue discount and decreased by payments. Treas.Reg. § 1.1275–1(b). "Qualified stated interest" is interest that is unconditionally payable at a fixed rate at least annually. Treas.Reg. § 1.1273–1(c). See Rev.Rul. 95–70, 1995–2 C.B. 124 (scheduled interest payments are not "unconditionally payable," as required to qualify as "qualified stated interest," merely because failure to pay the interest when due results in either (1) the corporate issuer being required to forgo dividend payments or (2) past due payments accruing interest at a rate two points higher than the stated yield).

The holder of an original issue discount bond is required to include the daily portions of original issue discount for each day the bond is held. I.R.C. § 1272(a)(1). The daily portion is determined by ratably allocating to each day in a semiannual accrual period the interest increment occurring during that period. I.R.C. § 1272(a)(3). The issuer deducts original issue discount in the same manner. I.R.C. § 163(e).

---

[3]   This would be the result when a three-year note required annual interest payments but provided that in any year in which interest was not paid, the unpaid interest would be added to principal and would bear interest at the rate stated in the note.

The bondholder's basis in the original issue discount obligation is increased to reflect the amount included in income by the holder. I.R.C. § 1272(d)(2). If the holder of the obligation disposes of it before maturity, the purchaser steps into the original bondholder's shoes with respect to the remaining original issue discount attributable to the bond. The original bondholder treats any amount received in excess of the adjusted basis as gain on disposition; the second owner is entitled to deduct any such excess over the remaining life of the bond from the amount of original issue discount otherwise required to be included in income. I.R.C. § 1272(a)(7).

Under these principles, assuming that the bond in the above example was issued on December 31st of Year 0 and the issuer chose to apply semi-annual compounding, at the beginning of Year 3 the adjusted issue price is $1,169.86, reflecting the original issue price of $1,000 and the accrued interest for Years 1 and 2. The amount of original issue discount deducted by the borrower and included by the lender for year 3 is $95.46.

2. ORIGINAL ISSUE DISCOUNT OBLIGATIONS ISSUED FOR PROPERTY

2.1. *Introduction*

When A sells property to B in a transaction in which some of the payments for the property are deferred, two separate economic transactions are involved. A is both selling the property to B and loaning B the amount of the unpaid purchase price, while B is correspondingly purchasing the property and simultaneously borrowing the unpaid purchase price from A. Original issue discount is present if the stated principal amount of B's obligation is greater than the fair market value of the transferred property.

2.2. *Publicly Traded Bonds or Property*

Section 1273(b)(3) provides that original issue discount arises in the case of bonds issued for property when either the bonds or the property (in the form of stock or securities) are traded on an established securities market and the face amount of the bonds issued exceeds the fair market value of the property received. If the bond is publicly traded or is issued for stock or securities that are publicly traded (whether or not the bond is publicly traded), the issue price of the bond is the trading price of the publicly traded stock or securities. Treas.Reg. § 1.1273–2(b) and (c). If publicly traded bonds are issued for other property (such as real estate or stock of a closely held corporation), however, the issue price of the bond is the fair market value of the bonds. Treas.Reg. § 1.1273–2(b). If neither of these established market conditions of § 1273(b) is satisfied, the bond's issue price generally must be computed under § 1274. Treas.Reg. § 1.1273–2(f) provides that property is traded on an established market if it is traded on a recognized exchange, or if the property appears on a system of general circulation that provides a reasonable basis to determine fair market value through dissemination of either price quotations or reports of recent sales.

2.3. *Obligations Issued for Other Property*

Determination of the issue price of an obligation is more difficult where neither side of a deferred payment sale involves publicly traded property. Section 1274 applies the original issue discount rules to sales of property on a deferred basis if the stated interest rate on deferred payments is less than the "applicable federal rate"—the rate paid on federal obligations with a similar maturity[4]—the original issue discount rules apply. For purposes of determining the issue price of the original issue discount obligation, the present value of all payments to be made under the instrument is calculated on the basis of the applicable federal rate. The resulting difference between the hypothetical issue price and the actual payments to be made under the instrument is original issue discount which must be currently included by the seller and deducted by the buyer using a constant interest rate.

The following example illustrates the application of § 1274. Suppose that A agrees to sell property to X Corp. for $1,000,000 on the following terms. Payment for the property will be due three years from the date of the sale and will bear simple interest at 8% with all interest to be paid at the end of the third year. Assume that the applicable federal rate is 9%. The first question is whether the obligation bears "adequate stated interest." It does not since (1) the stated rate is only 8%, (2) the interest is not compounded, and (3) the interest is only payable at the maturity of the obligation. By using a below-market interest rate, A and B have attempted to convert a portion of the financing transaction into a sales transaction. Thus, under § 1274(a)(2), the "imputed principal amount" is treated as the issue price for purposes of determining the original issue discount. The imputed principal amount is defined in § 1274(b) as the present value of all payments due on the debt instrument, using as a discount rate the applicable federal rate. On this basis, the present value of the $1,240,000 payment to be made in year 3 is $952,191. This amount is then treated as the issue price of the obligation for purposes of determining the original issue discount on the financing portion of the transaction and as the sales price for the sales portion of the transaction.

Section 1274 thus isolates the unstated interest element in the transaction, using the applicable federal rate as the applicable norm. The resulting computation indicates that economically A sold the property to B for $952,191 and loaned B that amount in return for a promise to pay $1,240,000 in three years reflecting a 9% interest rate, compounded semiannually. B has a basis of $952,191 in the property for purposes of depreciation and sale. On the financing side of the transaction, A is required to include currently the appropriate amount of original issue discount income and B is treated as paying interest for a corresponding amount, thus matching interest income and interest expense. Deduction of the interest expense is subject to rules regarding deduction of interest.

If the rate of interest charged and payable at least annually under the contract had been equal to the applicable federal rate (or 9% in the case of a qualified instrument to which § 1274A(a) applies) compounded semi-annually, the original issue discount rules would not have applied to

---

[4] The applicable federal rate is determined on a monthly basis. The rate used is the lowest federal rate for similar obligations in effect in the 3 months prior to the date of the contract of sale. I.R.C. § 1274(d)(2).

recalculate the sales price.[5] The agreed price for the property would determine A's gain on the sale portion of the transaction and B's basis for the property. The interest expense and interest income would likewise be matched because the interest payments must be made currently to prevent the application of the original issue discount rules, thus requiring current inclusion by the cash method seller.

By using the applicable federal rate to identify the interest element of the transaction, § 1274 avoids the necessity of directly valuing nontraded property for purposes of calculating the original issue discount. In effect, it requires the buyer and seller to use at least the appropriate federal rate on the financing portion of the transaction. The remainder of the payments is then considered to be the price paid for the underlying property. The section thus works backward from a given interest rate to calculate the current value of the property.

2.4. *Exceptions to Section 1274 and the Application of Section 483*

Enacted in an era of higher interest rates than currently prevail, § 1274A(a) and (b) provides that the discount rate for purposes of § 1274 is not to exceed 9%, compounded semiannually, if the stated principal of the obligation is not in excess of $2.8 million, as adjusted for inflation since 1989,[6] and the obligation is not issued as consideration for the sale or exchange of certain tangible personal property used in a trade or business. Property for which this exception is not applicable is "§ 38 property" within the meaning of § 48(b), which, in general, includes depreciable machinery and equipment and certain limited classes of improvements to real property. Section 1274A(a) and (b) do apply to sales of buildings generally.

Some deferred payment sales are not subject to § 1274: the sale of a farm by an individual or small business for less than $1 million; the sale of a principal residence; any sale or exchange of property if the total amount receivable under the obligation does not exceed $250,000; and certain sales of patents to the extent the sale price is contingent on income from the patent. Transactions not covered by § 1274 are subject to the imputed interest rules of § 483.

With some exceptions, the amount of imputed interest is calculated for purposes of § 483 in the same manner as under § 1274. Imputed interest under § 483 is the difference between issue price and the present value of the payments required by the obligation using the applicable federal rate, compounded semiannually, as the discount rate. I.R.C. § 483(b). Unlike original issue discount under § 1274, however, imputed interest under § 483 is taken into account by a cash method taxpayer only when payment is received or paid, and by an accrual method taxpayer when payment is due.

---

[5]   Under § 1274(d)(1)(D), regulations may be promulgated to permit the taxpayer to use a rate lower than the applicable federal rate if it can be established that it would have been possible for the taxpayer to borrow in an arm's length transaction at such lower rate.

[6]   The 2017 legislation amended § 1274A(d)(2) to specify that the inflation adjustment calculation is made with reference to § 1(f)(3), except that "calendar year 1988" is substituted for "calendar year 2016" in § 1(f)(3)(A)(ii).

B. BOND PREMIUM

INTERNAL REVENUE CODE: Sections 171(a), (b); 249.

REGULATIONS: Sections 1.61–12(c); 1.163–13(a), (c), (d).

DETAILED ANALYSIS

1. PREMIUM AT ORIGINAL ISSUE

The issuer of a bond with a stated interest rate in excess of prevailing market rates may be in a position to demand a premium for the bond, i.e., consideration in excess of the stated principal amount of the bond. This premium is not treated as income to the issuer at the time of receipt. Treas.Reg. § 1.61–12(c)(1). Instead, Treas. Regs. § 1.61–12(c)(2) and 1.163–13 generally require the issuer to include bond premium over the term of the bond, using the constant interest method, by reducing the issuer's interest deductions.

For the bondholder, § 171 provides an election to amortize premium over the term of the obligation using the constant interest method of § 1272(a). See Treas.Reg. § 1.1272–2. The premium reduces the interest income, although the creditor may also treat the premium as a deduction. I.R.C. § 171(e). The election is irrevocable without the consent of the Commissioner and applies to all bonds held by the taxpayer. See I.R.C. § 171(c). If the bondholder does not make the election with respect to fully taxable bonds, the premium paid is recovered as a loss on redemption of the bond for an amount less than its basis. Section 171(b) requires the creditor to amortize the bond premium over the full term to maturity, even though the bond may be callable at an earlier date.

Bond premium may also arise as the creditor pays an additional consideration for the privilege of converting the obligation into stock. Section 171(b)(1) excludes from bond premium "any amount attributable to the conversion features."

2. PREMIUM PAID BY THE ISSUER ON REDEMPTION

Bond premium paid by the issuer on redemption of an obligation is deductible by the issuer as additional interest on the obligation. In the case of convertible obligations, however, § 249 limits the deduction for redemption premium to an amount representing a "normal call premium" on obligations that are not convertible. The balance is a capital transaction. Thus, in the case of bond premium paid to redeem convertible bonds, the creditor is not allowed to amortize any portion of the premium attributable to the conversion feature, nor is the issuer allowed an interest deduction for that portion of a premium paid upon redemption of its bonds that is attributable to the conversion feature. This result presumably corresponds to the parallel treatment of original issue discount between issuer and holder. The treatment of the convertibility feature is, however, different as between original issue discount and bond premium in the case of convertible bonds. The regulations adopt the view that in the case of convertible bonds, the conversion feature is not separable from the debt for purposes of determining original issue discount, hence preventing a larger original issue discount from resulting; on the other hand, in the case of bond premium the conversion feature is deemed under the Code to be a feature separable from the debt portion of the obligation and hence the amount, if any, attributable to the conversion element is not deductible as interest.

In Tandy Corp. v. United States, 626 F.2d 1186 (5th Cir.1980), the court denied a deduction under § 163 for premium on conversion of debt into stock. The taxpayer claimed that the excess of the fair market value of the stock issued over the face of the bonds was deductible as interest. The court concluded that, under the terms of the indenture, conversion extinguished the obligation to pay accrued interest or bond premium. Thus, no accrued interest or bond premium was involved. The court did not consider the application of § 249.

In National Can Corp. v. United States, 687 F.2d 1107 (7th Cir.1982), an overseas finance subsidiary issued debentures convertible into the stock of its parent corporation. The parent redeemed its subsidiary's debentures with its own stock, the fair market value of which exceeded the issue price of the debentures. The parent claimed a deduction for the difference as premium under § 171 and § 162. The parent corporation argued that the limitation of § 171(b)(1) applied only to obligations convertible into the stock of the issuing corporation, and not to obligations convertible into the stock of another. The court broadly interpreted § 171(b)(1) to limit deduction of premium attributable to any conversion feature. The court concluded that the premium was due to the unexercised conversion feature of the bonds so that amortization of premium was barred by § 171(b)(1) and Treas.Reg. § 1.171–2(c). The court also disallowed the taxpayer's claimed deduction under § 162, holding that under § 1032 the corporation recognizes no gain or loss when it issues stock in satisfaction of a conversion obligation of the bonds of a subsidiary. In the District Court the taxpayer also asserted that the value of the conversion feature at the time the bonds were issued reduced the issue price of the bonds thereby creating amortizable original issue discount in an amount equal to the value of the conversion rights. The District Court refused to treat the conversion rights as a separate asset capable of valuation apart from the debt component of the bonds. National Can Corp. v. United States, 520 F.Supp. 567 (N.D.Ill.1981). The taxpayer abandoned this claim on appeal.

PROBLEM SET 2

1.   X Corp. is planning to issue bonds to raise cash to expand its business operations. Consider the following transactions.

(a)   On June 30th of the current year, X Corp. issues $100,000 face value bonds due in 10 years, which pay zero stated interest, for an issue price of $37,688.95. How much interest may X Corp. deduct during the current year and the next year?

(b)   On June 30th, X Corp. issues for cash $100,000, 10-year bonds that bear interest at the prime rate plus 1%, which you may assume for all relevant periods computes to 6%. Interest is payable semiannually. The applicable federal rate for the current year is 7%. How much interest may X Corp. deduct in the current year?

(c) On June 30th, X Corp. issues $100,000 10-year bonds bearing interest at 10%, payable semi-annually, but no interest is due and payable until the second anniversary of the bond issue. The applicable federal rate is 7%. How do you determine whether the bonds are OID instruments?

(d) X Corp. issues $100,000 10-year convertible bonds. Each bond is convertible into X Corp. common stock at any time prior to redemption at an exchange ratio of one share of stock for $10. When the bonds were issued, X Corp. stock was trading on the stock exchange at 9-7/8 per share. The bonds pay interest annually at 7%. The applicable federal rate was 7% when the bonds were issued. Are the bonds OID bonds?

2. Empire Realty Development Corp. purchased the Palace Hotel from Don. In exchange for the Palace, Don received an Empire bond in the face amount of $5,000,000 due in ten years. No express interest is due on the bond. At the time of the sale the applicable federal rate was 7%.

(a) What is Empire's basis for the Palace? If the deal closed on June 30th, how much interest may Empire deduct in the year of the sale?

(b) Suppose that the stated principal amount of the bond was $5,000,000 and interest accrued at 7% compounded semi-annually, but no interest was payable until the bond was due in 10 years. At that time, Don was to receive the $5,000,000 principal and $4,948,944 of interest, for a total amount due of $9,948,944. How much interest must Don include and how much interest may Empire deduct for the year of sale?

(c) Suppose that the stated principal amount of the bond was $2,342,112 and interest accrued at 15% compounded semi-annually, but no interest was payable until the bond was due in 10 years. At that time, Don was to receive the $2,342,112 principal and $7,606,831 of interest, for a total amount due of $9,948,944. How much interest must Don include and how much interest may Empire deduct for the year of sale? Do you need to know whether Empire uses the cash method or the accrual method in order to answer the question?

3. On July 1, Year 1, Adam purchased a newly issued $100,000 debt instrument issued by the Pari-Mutuel Insurance Company, Inc. The stated terms of the bond provided for annual interest at 10%, payable semiannually with the principal due on June 30, Year 10. Because interest rates had fallen between the time the bonds and the prospectus were printed, to adjust for the higher than market stated interest rate, the bonds were sold for $102,500. What are the tax consequences to Adam when he receives $5,000 of interest in Year 1? When he receives $10,000 of interest in Year 2? When he receives the $100,000 principal payment in Year 10?

CHAPTER 4

DIVIDEND DISTRIBUTIONS

SECTION 1.   INTRODUCTION

The income tax treatment of corporate distributions to shareholders is a complex matter and the rules must be traced through many sections. The starting point is § 301(a), which generally covers all distributions of money or property by a corporation to its shareholders in their capacity as shareholders. As the general rule, § 301(a) is applicable to a broader range of distributions than just dividends in the corporate law sense. Section 301(a) provides that, unless some other Code section provides a different treatment, the distribution will be governed by § 301(c). Section 301(c), in turn, classifies distributions within the ambit of § 301 between dividends for tax purposes, which are included directly in gross income (§ 61(a)(7), § 301(c)(1)), and distributions that are not dividends for tax purposes. Non-dividend distributions are treated first as a return of capital that reduces stock basis, but not below zero (§ 301(c)(2)); any excess is treated as gain from the sale or exchange of property (§ 301(c)(3)), thus bringing the capital gain provisions into play.

Before 2003, dividends were taxed at ordinary income rates, which were significantly higher than capital gains rates.[1] This historic pattern of taxation of dividends was changed in 2003, and dividends received by taxpayers other than corporations generally are taxed at the same preferential rates as long-term capital gains (see the discussion in Chapter 1).

Dividends received by a corporation are not accorded a special statutory rate. Instead, § 243(a)(1) provides a corporation that is a shareholder in another corporation with a deduction equal to 50% of intercorporate dividends received; § 243(c) increases the deduction to 65% if the shareholder corporation owns at least 20% of the stock of the payor corporation; and § 243(a)(3) extends this deduction to 100% for affiliated corporations that so elect. There are numerous limitations on the intercorporate dividends received deduction, which is discussed in Section 5 of this chapter.

As already noted, not all distributions by corporations are dividends. Section 316(a) defines dividends for purposes of § 301(c)(1) with reference to the "earnings and profits" of the corporation. The statutory dividend test is two-fold: any distribution to a shareholder is a dividend if it is out of either (1) earnings and profits accumulated after February 28, 1913, or (2) earnings and profits of the current year regardless of a lack of, or deficit in, accumulated earnings and profits. Earnings and profits differ

---

[1]   Dividends were taxed at the same rate as capital gains from 1987 to 1991 because there was no preferential rate for long-term capital gains in those years.

substantially from taxable income, being more akin to net income in a financial accounting sense, but, because some significant adjustments to earned surplus in the corporate sense are not taken into account in computing earnings and profits, it is inaccurate to say that the taxability of the shareholder depends essentially on the earned surplus account of the corporation. To the extent a distribution exceeds current and accumulated earnings and profits, the distribution is not a dividend for tax purposes and will instead reduce the shareholder's stock basis (but not below zero), with the excess taxed as gain on the sale of the stock. I.R.C. § 301(c)(2)–(3).

Section 316(a) eliminates most tracing requirements by specifying in the second sentence that if any earnings and profits exist, the distribution is deemed to be out of such earnings and profits rather than from any other source, and first from the most recently accumulated earnings and profits. But while tracing difficulties are largely avoided, the problem of ascertaining the amount of a corporation's earnings and profits remains. If the earnings and profits of the current year exceed the distribution, the amount of the accumulated earnings and profits is irrelevant. If accumulated earnings and profits are present, the precise determination of the earnings and profits of the current year is likewise unnecessary. But in some situations the precise dollar amount of either current or accumulated earnings and profits may be crucial, and it is here that the exact scope of the statutory phrase "earnings and profits" must be determined. As will be seen, the phrase is only partially defined in § 312, thus requiring extensive judicial and administrative interpretation.

Section 301(b) determines the amount of the distribution in situations in which property or liabilities are involved, and § 301(d) establishes the basis of the distributed property in the shareholder's hands.

The scope of § 301(a) is qualified by various other sections dealing with corporate distributions, as the cross-references in § 301(f) indicate. Section 302 provides sale or exchange treatment for specified distributions *in redemption of stock*. If § 302 applies, capital gain or loss normally is recognized. Section 331 provides sale or exchange treatment for distributions in complete liquidation of the corporation; and § 302(b)(4) does the same for distributions to noncorporate shareholders in partial liquidation of the corporation. The definitions of complete and partial liquidations are tax words of art that are somewhat confusing. Certain distributions in corporate reorganizations also are specially treated (§ 354 et seq.), as are certain distributions in redemption of stock to pay estate and inheritance taxes (§ 303) and distributions involving related corporations (§ 304).

Sections 305, 306, and 307 relate to the distribution of a "stock dividend." In general, these sections treat the distribution as a nontaxable event for the shareholder. However, there are many exceptions that can cause the receipt of the stock dividend to be taxable. In addition, some stock dividends, though they possess a nontaxable character on receipt, may on disposition generate ordinary income, although taxed at the same rate as dividends, to the extent of the amount realized rather than capital gain.

This statutory pattern provides opportunities for controversies to flourish. Even though dividends received by individuals are taxed at capital gains rates, they remain ordinary income and cannot be offset by capital losses. Similarly, the shareholder's basis in the stock cannot be offset against dividend distributions. Liquidations, whether partial or complete, and certain stock redemptions achieve sale or exchange treatment in which the shareholder may apply the basis of the redeemed stock against the amount realized. Any gain is capital gain, against which capital losses may be deducted, and which may be taxed at a preferential rate if capital gains exceed capital losses for the year. But since a transaction cast in the form of a partial liquidation or other stock redemption may realistically amount to no more than the distribution of a dividend, the line is not crystal clear. Historically, because dividends generally have been subject to higher tax rates than capital gains, the differing treatment of dividends, on the one hand, and liquidations, partial liquidations, and redemptions, on the other hand, has been of great significance. The stakes of characterization of a transaction as either a dividend or as a redemption or liquidating distribution, have been significantly reduced by the enactment of § 1(h)(11) in 2003. When dividends and capital gains are taxed at the same rate, the benefit to a noncorporate shareholder of characterization of a distribution as a redemption or liquidating distribution is limited to allowing recovery of basis under § 1001 and Treas.Reg. § 1.61–6(a)—which may result in offsetting a different amount of basis against the distribution than does § 301(c)(2)—and the ability to claim capital losses against capital gains. Furthermore, but now of importance primarily as a timing matter, the statutory exemption from taxation as current ordinary income of the receipt of many stock dividends historically provided the shareholder with the opportunity to create capital gain situations through the later sale of the dividend stock unless effective safeguards to prevent this tactic were placed in the statute.

Corporate level recognition of gain on distributions is another facet of the taxation of corporate distributions that has shaped the historical development of Subchapter C. The Tax Reform Act of 1986 amended § 311 and § 336 to require that gain be recognized by the corporation on the distribution of property, other than in liquidation of the corporation, and that both gain and loss be recognized on liquidating distributions. Before 1986, the predecessors of § 311 and § 336 provided nonrecognition treatment to the corporation with respect to gain or loss inherent in distributed assets, whether by dividend, redemption, or liquidation. Where the corporate profits had not been realized but were represented by appreciation in value of corporate assets, distribution of appreciated assets in-kind permitted avoidance of corporate level tax on built-in gain. Over the years, numerous limitations were imposed on nonrecognition of gain with respect to distributed property, culminating in the current recognition rules of § 311 and § 336. Much of the logic behind the shape of the current provisions, and some of the historical cases to be encountered in the following chapters can be understood only if the former nonrecognition rules are kept in mind. As § 311 was tightened to limit nonrecognition on distributions of appreciated property, corporate taxpayers attempted to devise increasingly complex schemes to come within the remaining nonrecognition rules, and the courts and Congress were forced to respond. Since 1986, corporate taxpayers have continued to seek gaps in the recognition rule of § 311 to try to avoid the tax on appreciation at the corporate level.

The background of controversial areas involves two other statutory provisions, relating to the corporation rather than to the shareholder, which appear in the Code outside of Subchapter C. If shareholders are taxed on distributions of corporate earnings, retention of corporate earnings and consequent postponement of the shareholder tax are the inevitable results of the treatment of the corporation as a taxpaying entity. As a force in the other direction, the Code contains in §§ 531–537 a special tax (at the maximum tax rate imposed on dividends) on a corporation that accumulates its earnings for the purpose of avoiding the imposition of the individual tax on its shareholders. Such a special tax presents its own problems of application. By its presence it also precipitates some of the controversial transactions mentioned above when the accumulation of earnings approaches the danger zone created by the § 531 accumulated earnings tax, since the shareholders will then usually act to draw some of the earnings out of the corporation. If the accumulation of earnings largely reflects passive investments of a closely held corporation, such as the holding of stocks and other securities, even if the special § 531 tax can be avoided, another special 20% tax (the "personal holding company tax") may be imposed on the undistributed income if the passive income receipts meet the objective standards of §§ 541–547.

These penalty taxes were enacted at a time when the maximum rate of tax on individual income substantially exceeded the maximum rate of tax on corporate income, thereby giving rise to an incentive to earn income through a corporation that retained that income. When, however, the maximum individual rate is below or only slightly higher than the maximum corporate rate, there generally is little incentive to cause earnings that might otherwise be realized directly by an individual to be realized and accumulated by a corporation. Thus, beginning from the early 1980s, the penalty taxes were of much less relevance. With the introduction in 2017 of a maximum individual rate (37%) that again

("Earnings and Profits"[5]). Specifically, § 1.312–6 provides in relevant part:

> In determining the amount of earnings and profits * * * due consideration must be given to the facts, and, while mere bookkeeping entries increasing or decreasing surplus will not be conclusive, the amount of the earnings and profits in any case will be dependent upon the method of accounting properly employed in computing taxable income * * *. *For instance, a corporation keeping its books and filing its income tax returns * * * on the cash receipts and disbursement basis may not use the accrual basis in determining its earnings and profits. * * *

Id. (emphasis added). As the Commissioner points out, we owe substantial deference to regulations issued by the agency Congress entrusted to administer the statute. * * *

We note in this regard that the Supreme Court approved a precursor to § 1.312–6(a) in Commissioner v. South Tex. Lumber Co., 333 U.S. 496 (1948), reh'g denied, 334 U.S. 813 (1948). Although that case arose under the excess profits tax, that tax used the same "accumulated earnings and profits" language which is contained in the current § 316. * * * In upholding a Treasury Regulation in pertinent respects remarkably similar to the one at issue here,[6] the Court rejected an attempt by a corporation which kept the relevant portion of its books using the installment method to use the accrual method in computing its earnings and profits[.] * * *

We owe the regulation heightened deference on account of its protracted history. * * * The Commissioner adhered to the IRS' longstanding practice when he first promulgated the regulation at issue here in 1955. See T.D. 6152, 1955–2 C.B. 61, 104–05 (promulgating the regulation);[7] T.D. 5059, 1941–2 C.B. 125, 125–26 (Treasury decision

---

[5] The term "earnings and profits" is used in various sections of the Code (its predominant use is in the treatment of dividend distributions by corporations), but is not defined therein. The Commissioner, however, has issued various regulations and revenue rulings in an effort to define it. * * * Briefly, earnings and profits are calculated by first adding to taxable income: "all income exempted by statute, income not taxable by the Federal Government under the Constitution [and] items includable in gross income under [the Code]," Treas.Reg. § 1.312–6(b); certain items which a corporation may deduct in computing taxable income (such as percentage depletion and dividends received); and deductions based on artificial timing (such as accelerated depreciation and deferred income). Then, earnings and profits are reduced by items like expenses and losses which a corporation may not deduct from its taxable income (for instance, federal income taxes and, notably, capital losses in past years disallowed as deductions from taxable income under Subchapter P of the Code, see Treas.Reg. § 1.312–7(b)(1)). Finally, various unusual financial transactions (for example, corporate distributions or changes in capital structure) may affect earnings and profits. * * *

[6] Compare § 29.115–3 of Regulations 111 ("In determining the amount of earnings or profits * * * due consideration must be given to the facts, and, while mere bookkeeping entries increasing or decreasing surplus will not be conclusive, the amount of the earnings or profits in any case will be dependent upon the method of accounting properly employed in computing net income."), reprinted in South Tex. Lumber, 333 U.S. at 500 n. 6, 68 S.Ct. at 698 n. 6 with Treas.Reg. § 1.312–6(a).

[7] Treasury Regulation § 1.312–6 (1955) is, in all pertinent respects, identical to the current version.

issued to tax collectors containing virtually the identical language later incorporated into § 1.312–6(a)) * * *.

The tax court has also long adhered to the view that a cash basis taxpayer cannot deduct accrued but unpaid taxes from earnings and profits. * * *

Nonetheless, several old court of appeals opinions have come out otherwise, holding that a cash-basis corporation may deduct accrued but unpaid taxes from its earnings and profits. See Demmon v. United States, 321 F.2d 203, 204–06 (7th Cir.1963); Drybrough v. Commissioner, 238 F.2d 735, 738–40 (6th Cir.1956) * * *. The Commissioner's brief and the tax court, see, e.g., Webb v. Commissioner, 67 T.C. 1008, 1018 (1977), with whom we side, both provide incisive criticisms of the reasoning those appellate decisions utilized and advance cogent arguments why the applicable Treasury regulation is a reasonable construction of the Code which should govern the resolution of this question.[8]

B.

Drybrough primarily relied on cases which had allowed accrual method corporations to reduce earnings and profits by the amount of disputed federal taxes despite the fact that an accrual corporation generally cannot deduct disputed taxes from its income. Building on the reasoning those cases employed, the court in *Drybrough* engrafted a more discernible distortion onto the Code when it concluded that cash method corporations should also be permitted to reduce earnings and profits by the amount of accrued taxes. * * * We decline to brandish those ancient cases to fashion a similar rule * * *. The Commissioner forcefully argues, and we agree, that one objectionable departure from normal tax accounting practices does not justify another.[10]

We also take issue with the rationale expressed in *Drybrough* that general corporate law and accounting concepts of dividends and impairment of capital control the computation of earnings and profits for purposes of federal taxation. * * * As the tax court observed in *Webb*, *Drybrough* evidently "assumes that there must be some correlation between general corporate law concepts of capital and earning surplus and the Federal income tax concepts of capital and earnings and profits, an assumption which is not correct." *Webb*, 67 T.C. at 1020–21. * * *

---

[8]   None of these appellate decisions considered the Treasury regulation which controls the outcome of this case, even though it was in effect when the later two decisions (*Demmon* and *Drybrough*) were handed down.

[10]   Moreover, like the tax court, we discern no basis for differentiating between accrued taxes and other accrued liabilities when it comes to computing earnings and profits. See *Webb*, 67 T.C. at 1019. Besides our aforementioned deference to § 1.312–6, which contains no exception for tax liabilities, we believe that granting tax (as opposed to other) liabilities special treatment would institute inconsistent accounting methods (the cash method for most items but the accrual method for tax liabilities) for items taken into account in computing earnings and profits. Such special treatment would unnecessarily add complexity to the Code, undesirably distort earnings and profits, and unjustifiably engraft an unprincipled exception onto the Code.

Given the disparate purposes behind the federal tax code and the corporate law impairment of capital doctrine, we agree.

* * *

The Seventh Circuit Court of Appeals in *Demmon*, supra, relied upon *Drybrough* * * * in resolving that "both reason and authority" support the argument that a cash basis corporation may deduct its accrued and unpaid taxes in computing earnings and profits. * * * [I]nsofar as we believe *Drybrough* to be flawed, we think so is *Demmon*.

* * *

C.

Finally, we consider Mazzocchi's assertion that "[c]ourts which have reduced earnings and profits by accrued but unpaid income tax liability have done so with the understanding that earnings and profits are intended to provide a measure of the ability of the Corporation to make distributions which are not out of its capital." That much is certainly true, but even if a Treasury regulation did not tie our hands, it is far from clear that the cash method does not accomplish that goal equally well. Earnings and profits ideally represent what the corporation has earned, whether during that fiscal year or since its inception, in excess of capital invested in it. But we think that in many cases, contrary to the suggestion of Mazzocchi, the cash method accurately reflects that amount, for it treats as earnings and profits the difference between the amount of cash received or gained and the amount of cash spent, depleted, or lost that year.

The cash basis method is not always meticulously accurate, as is illustrated by the case sub judice: a corporation may be deemed to have earnings and profits in one year although in a later year it has to pay taxes (or judgments, liabilities, or other losses) attributable to income earned in the earlier year, which exaggerates in the earlier year (but, by the same token, understates in the later year) the corporation's ability to distribute dividends. But the accrual system also has its drawbacks from an economic perspective. To take but one example, since the corporation has not yet collected the receipts it has accrued, it cannot distribute them (unless it takes out a loan with the accrued income as security, but economically that would be equivalent to selling the accrued income for present cash, rendering the modified accrual method akin to the cash method), and thus the accrual system may also overstate in the current year (and conversely understate in a later year) the corporation's ability to distribute dividends. In short, neither the cash nor the accrual method of accounting may accurately represent in an economic sense the amount of net assets that a corporation has available to distribute as dividends to its shareholders during any given year. Some inaccuracies inhere in the administrative necessity artificially to divide time into discrete years for tax purposes.

We find several significant drawbacks to Mazzocchi's suggested approach allowing a corporate taxpayer the freedom to choose which accounting system to use for calculating earnings and profits irrespective of the accounting method it uses to calculate its taxable income. First, it would tend to skew substantially the payment of taxes in favor of the taxpayer's shareholders, as the taxpayer will choose whichever method minimizes its shareholders' tax liability. * * * Second, to allow the choice would impose upon the Commissioner the burden of maintaining—and auditing—two sets of books for each taxpayer electing inconsistent accounting methods for income and earnings and profits purposes.

* * *

D.

In conclusion, we hold that the tax court correctly rejected Mazzocchi's argument that the earnings and profits of MBC, a cash basis corporation, should be reduced by the amount of accrued but unpaid taxes, penalties, and interest attributable to its income tax deficiencies for the years in issue. To preclude the distortion of tax liability and to spare the Commissioner the concomitant onerous bookkeeping tasks which would follow from a corporation's using one accounting method to compute income while using a different accounting method to calculate earnings and profits, § 1.312–6(a) of the Treasury regulations has long provided that a corporation must use the same accounting method in calculating earnings and profits as it uses in determining its taxable income. * * *

DETAILED ANALYSIS

1. DISTRIBUTIONS OUT OF EARNINGS AND PROFITS

1.1. *General*

Treas.Reg. § 1.316–2 provides rules for ascertaining the source of a distribution. Dividends are deemed to have been distributed first out of current earnings and profits for the year, to the extent thereof, without diminution by reason of the distributions during the year. It makes no difference that some of the earnings and profits accrued after the date of a distribution. Current earnings and profits are prorated among all distributions during the year. Suppose that as of January 1, Y Corporation had no accumulated earnings and profits. From January 1 through June 30 it had operating profits (for earnings and profits purposes) of $50,000, and on July 1 it distributed $40,000 in cash to its shareholders. As of December 31, Y Corporation had only $30,000 of current earnings and profits for the year. Only $30,000 of the July 1 distribution is taxable as a dividend because current earnings and profits always are determined at the end of the year without regard to distributions during the year, not at the time of the distribution. Accumulated earnings and profits are significant only if the earnings and profits of the current year do not cover the total distributions for the year. See Treas.Reg. § 1.316–1(a)(1). In the latter event, the current earnings and profits are prorated among all of the year's distributions and the remaining amount of the distributions is charged against accumulated earnings and profits as of the beginning of the year in the order in which the distributions were made. See G.C.M. 36,138 (Jan. 15, 1975) (interpreting Treas.Reg. § 1.316–2 as being applicable to cash and property distributions).

If the net operating result for the entire current year is a loss, the result is negative earnings and profits for the year. A distribution will, however, constitute a dividend to the extent of positive accumulated earnings and profits computed to the date of the distribution. If the actual current earnings and profits deficit to the date of the distribution cannot be shown, then the current deficit is prorated and applied as of the date of the distribution to reduce the accumulated earnings and profits. The distribution will be a dividend to the extent of any remaining accumulated earnings and profits. Treas.Reg. § 1.316–2(b); Rev.Rul. 74–164, 1974–1 C.B. 74. See also FSA 200225014 (allowing corporation to choose proration even when actual information was available).

For example, suppose that as of January 1, X Corporation had $50,000 of accumulated earnings and profits. For the current year X Corporation had an operating loss of $80,000. On April 1, it distributed $40,000 in cash to its shareholders. Prorating X Corporation's $80,000 loss for the year (using a 30-day month convention for simplicity) results in treating $20,000 of the loss ($80,000 × 3/12) as occurring from January 1 through March 31. That leaves X Corporation with only $30,000 of accumulated earnings and profits on April 1 ($50,000–$20,000). Thus, only $30,000 of the $40,000 distribution on April 1 constituted a dividend. Pursuant to § 312(a), the dividend distribution reduced X Corporation's earnings and profits to $0 as of April 1. At the end of the year, the $60,000 of X Corporation's $80,000 loss for the year that was prorated to the period April 1 to December 31 reduces X Corporation's accumulated earnings and profits to negative $60,000.

If there is no overall current earnings and profits deficit for the year, no proration is made. Suppose that on January 1, X Corporation had accumulated earnings and profits of $40,000. For the period January 1 through June 30, it had an operating loss (for earnings and profits purposes) of $50,000, but during the last portion of the year, the corporation had an operating increase that caused the current earnings and profits for the year to be a positive $10,000. On July 1, X Corporation distributed $50,000 of cash to its shareholders. Even though as of July 1, the operating loss incurred during the first half of the year would have eliminated the accumulated earnings and profits if the corporate books had been closed at that time, the entire distribution is a dividend, $10,000 out of current earnings and profits and $40,000 out of accumulated earnings. Because the corporation did not in fact incur a deficit for the year but rather earned $10,000, the deficit accrued as of July 1 did not reduce accumulated earnings and profits, which as of July 1 remained $40,000.

Allocation of earnings and profits among distributions with respect to different classes of stock presents more difficult problems where one class of stock has dividend priorities established by the corporate charter. Rev.Rul. 69–440, 1969–2 C.B. 46, involved a corporation that had three classes of stock, the first two of which had priority with respect to dividend payments.

The corporation distributed amounts to the first two classes of stock in excess of earnings and profits. The ruling held that if the preferred stock, the first priority stock, had dividend priority under the corporate charter, then earnings and profits were first to be allocated to all of the dividends paid on the preferred stock. If this treatment exhausted earnings and profits and distributions were made with respect to other classes of stock, then those distributions simply reduced the basis of that stock.

1.2. *Timing of Dividend Inclusion*

A dividend is included in the shareholder's gross income when "received," regardless of whether the shareholder uses the cash receipts or accrual method. See Commissioner v. American Light & Traction Co., 156 F.2d 398 (7th Cir.1946), relying on the rule in Treas.Reg. § 1.301–1(b), and rejecting the other possible dates such as declaration or record; Rev.Rul. 64–290, 1964–2 C.B. 465. Similarly, the date of payment (and not the date of declaration) is the date of distribution from the standpoint of the corporation and, accordingly, dividends are taken into account to reduce earnings and profits in the year of payment. Rev.Rul. 62–131, 1962–2 C.B. 94; Bush Bros. & Co. v. Commissioner, 73 T.C. 424 (1979), aff'd, 668 F.2d 252 (6th Cir.1982). Dividend checks payable and mailed on December 31 affect earnings and profits for the corporation in that year, even though the shareholder does not include the dividend in income until the following year. Rev.Rul. 65–23, 1965–1 C.B. 520.

2.   DISTRIBUTIONS NOT OUT OF EARNINGS AND PROFITS

To the extent a distribution not "out of earnings and profits" (because there are insufficient current and accumulated earnings and profits), it is applied first to reduce the shareholder's basis for the stock to zero under § 301(c)(2), and any excess results in capital gain under § 301(c)(3).[3]

A taxpayer who purchased shares at different dates will need to determine how to allocate the § 301(c)(2) basis reduction. Johnson v. United States, 435 F.2d 1257 (4th Cir.1971), held that a taxpayer who had several blocks of stock with different bases was required to treat a distribution on the stock not out of earnings and profits as made pro rata among the blocks of stock in order to determine the gain realized by the taxpayer on the distribution; the taxpayer was not allowed to aggregate the total basis in the stock and offset that total against the amount of the distribution. Prop.Reg. § 1.301–2 (2009), withdrawn in March 2019, expressly adopted the rule of *Johnson* to provide that the portion of a distribution that is not a dividend will be applied to reduce the basis of each share within the class of stock on which the distribution is made pro rata on a share-by-share basis. As a consequence, the distribution may require recognition of gain under § 301(c)(3) with respect to some shares while the distributee shareholder retains basis in other shares. In withdrawing the Proposed Regulations, the Treasury cited *Johnson* with approval and noted, "The Treasury Department

---

[3]   Distributions traceable to pre-March 1, 1913 profits are treated entirely as a return of capital. Since § 316(a) provides that for tax purposes all of the earnings and profits accumulated after February 28, 1913 must be distributed before a distribution may be regarded as out of the pre-March 1, 1913 profits, the latter type of distributions are unlikely to occur in the case of profitable corporations.

and the IRS continue to believe that under current law, the results of a section 301 distribution should derive from the consideration received by a shareholder in respect of each share of stock, notwithstanding designations otherwise." 84 Fed. Reg. 11687 (Mar. 28, 2019).

3. DETERMINATION OF EARNINGS AND PROFITS

3.1. *General*

The earnings and profits of a year are not synonymous with either taxable income or book net income. Accumulated earnings and profits is not earned surplus in the corporate sense, but the aggregate of annual earnings and profits, as adjusted for distributions and certain other transactions involving shareholders. Although the Code does not comprehensively define the term "earnings and profits," numerous statutory rules governing the determination of earnings and profits move the concept closer to economic income than to either taxable or book income. Nevertheless, the starting point for computing earnings and profits is taxable income, which must then be adjusted to take into account income items excluded from taxable income, expenses (not chargeable to a capital account) that are disallowed as deductions, and myriad differences regarding the timing of income and deductions. Taxable income is used as a starting point, in part, because it is an amount that must be computed in any event based on an ascertainable standard. However, taxable income must be adjusted to account for items of economic income and expenditure not reflected in the income tax base.

3.2. *Treatment of Special Income Items*

Most items of wholly or partially exempt income, such as tax-exempt interest, life insurance proceeds, and intercorporate dividends, are included in earnings and profits. Treas.Reg. § 1.312–6(b). But some items excluded from gross income also are excluded in the computation of earnings and profits. For example, nontaxable contributions to capital under § 118 do not enter into earnings and profits. Rev.Rul. 66–353, 1966–2 C.B. 111. If receipts are treated as nontaxable contributions to capital rather than as taxable income for services, and thus have no effect on earnings and profits, no depreciation deduction is allowed with respect to the property under Rev.Rul. 66–353, and hence earnings and profits in subsequent years would be increased correspondingly. Although there is no express authority on point, § 312(f)(1) (flush language) should exclude from earnings and profits the value of property and cash received in exchange for the corporation's tax-free issuance of its own stock or stock options under § 1032, such as occurs in transfers governed by § 351. See Treas.Reg. § 1.312–7(b).

A bad debt previously deducted without an income tax benefit, but which nevertheless reduced earnings and profits, increases earnings and profits on its recovery. Rev.Rul. 58–546, 1958–2 C.B. 143.

Cancellation of an indebtedness of the corporation increases earnings and profits if the cancellation results in taxable income. Schweppe v. Commissioner, 168 F.2d 284 (9th Cir.1948), aff'g 8 T.C. 1224 (1947). But if the cancellation is excluded from income under § 108 and there is a corresponding basis adjustment under § 1017, then no current increase in earnings and profits results from the cancellation. § 312(*l*); see also Rev.Rul.

58–546, supra. To the extent that there is no basis reduction, however, earnings and profits must be increased, even though other tax attributes are reduced under § 108(b).

3.3. *Treatment of Deduction Items*

Most expense items that are disallowed as deductions in computing taxable income are nonetheless subtracted in determining earnings and profits. Such items include federal income taxes, unreasonable compensation (to the extent not recharacterized as a dividend), excess charitable contributions, disallowed capital losses, and deductions disallowed on grounds of public policy under § 162(c), (e), (f), and (g). See Rev.Rul. 77–442, 1977–2 C.B. 264 (payments covered by § 162(c) reduce earnings and profits).

A net operating loss carryover deduction does not reduce current earnings and profits because the adjustment to earnings and profits was made in the year the loss was incurred. The same is true with respect to capital loss carryovers under § 1212.

Some deductions permitted in computing taxable income are eliminated in computing earnings and profits. Treas.Reg. § 1.312–6(c) provides that a percentage depletion deduction allowed in computing taxable income must be adjusted to the cost depletion method for the computation of earnings and profits. Similarly, the intercorporate dividends received deduction under § 243 is disallowed. Although a charitable contribution deduction equal to the fair market value of property donated to charity may be allowable under § 170, Rev.Rul. 78–123, 1978–1 C.B. 87, held that a corporation's earnings and profits are reduced only by the adjusted basis of the property since the appreciation element had never entered into earnings and profits. Kaplan v. Commissioner, 43 T.C. 580 (1965) (nonacq.), is to the contrary and in our view is incorrect.

3.4. *Treatment of Matters of Timing*

As discussed in *Mazzocchi Bus Co.*, except where the Code otherwise specifically so provides, the timing of earnings and profits adjustments is determined by the accounting method used by the corporation in computing taxable income. Treas.Reg. § 1.312–6(a). Thus, for example, a reserve for estimated future expenses, while proper under accounting principles, would not reduce earnings and profits if not deductible for tax purposes. See also Rev.Rul. 66–35, 1966–1 C.B. 63 (amortizable bond premium and bond discount on taxable bonds are reflected in earnings and profits in the same year in which includible or deductible in computing taxable income); Rev.Rul. 60–123, 1960–1 C.B. 145 (corporation deducted interest and taxes for tax purposes, but capitalized such items on its books for regulatory purposes; held, such items are deductible in computing earnings and profits in the same manner and year as allowed for purposes of computing taxable income).

Section 312(f)(1) directs that realized gains and losses be taken into account in computing earnings and profits in the year that they are recognized. Thus, for example, gain deferred on a like-kind exchange under § 1031 does not increase earnings and profits. On the other hand, when gain realized on the sale of property is reported on the installment basis under

§ 453, § 312(n)(5) directs that the entire gain is added to earnings and profits in the year of the sale, rather than as each installment is received. If it later is determined that the taxpayer realized an overall loss on the transaction, earnings and profits are decreased in the subsequent year. Luckman v. Commissioner, 56 T.C. 1216 (1971).

In computing taxable income, accelerated depreciation deductions are allowed under § 168, and § 179, § 179A, and § 179B permit a limited amount of certain capital expenses to be deducted currently. In computing earnings and profits, however, § 312(k)(3) provides that: (1) amounts expensed under § 179, § 179A, and § 179B must be deducted ratably over a five-year period; and (2) depreciation deductions for tangible property to which § 168 applies must be computed under the less rapid alternative depreciation system of § 168(g)(2). Section 312(k) is designed to prevent the distribution of nontaxable dividends attributable to the excess of accelerated depreciation over the lesser amount of depreciation considered more accurately to reflect economic decline in value. See S.Rep. No. 91–552, 91st Cong., 1st Sess. 176 (1969). Under Treas.Reg. § 1.312–15(a), § 312(k) also applies to amortization under § 169, § 184, § 187, § 188, or "any similar provision."

Because depreciation is allowed at a different rate for earnings and profits purposes, depreciable property has a different basis for this purpose. Accordingly, the gain or loss on the sale of depreciable property for earnings and profits purposes will differ from the taxable gain or loss. I.R.C. § 312(f), flush language. Also, because depreciation on manufacturing plant and equipment must be treated as an inventory cost under § 263A, inventories will differ for earnings and profits purposes from those used in computing taxable income.

Section 312(n) requires a number of other adjustments to earnings and profits to reflect more accurately a corporation's economic gain or loss. Among the most significant are that: (1) earnings and profits be increased annually by the "LIFO recapture amount," which generally speaking is tantamount to requiring that earnings and profits be computed using only the first in-first out (FIFO) inventory method; and (2) deductible intangible drilling and development costs and solid mineral exploration and development costs be capitalized and amortized in future years.

3.5. *Effect of Stock Option Transactions*

In Luckman v. Commissioner, 418 F.2d 381 (7th Cir.1969), a shareholder received from a corporation a cash distribution that he treated as a nontaxable return of capital. In prior years, the corporation had sold stock to its employees under "restricted stock options" at a purchase price that was about $3.4 million less than the fair market value of the stock at the time of sale. Under a now repealed provision, the employees were not taxed on the discount. The taxpayer nevertheless argued that the difference between the option price and the fair market value reduced the earnings and profits of the corporation, creating a deficit in the corporation's earnings and profits account, and thus rendered the distributions received by the taxpayer nontaxable. The Tax Court held that earnings and profits were not reduced as the result of the exercise of the stock options (50 T.C. 619 (1968)), but the Court of Appeals reversed:

> As used in federal taxation, [the earnings and profits] concept represents an attempt to separate those corporate distributions with respect to stock which represent returns of capital contributed by the stockholders from those distributions which represent gain derived from the initial investment by virtue of the conduct of business. The crucial issue is whether a given transaction has a real effect upon the portion of corporate net worth which is not representative of distributed capital and which results from its conduct of business. In order to make this determination it is necessary to scrutinize the economic effects of the particular transaction as well as its character and relation to the corporate business. * * *

> Had the compensation been paid in cash and then used to purchase stock, there could be no question that the corporation had incurred a true economic expense which reduced earnings and profits. The amount of corporate assets available for distribution to those who owned the stock at the time of the transaction is reduced to the same extent in either case. The economic effect of the two transactions is identical.

418 F.2d at 383–83. Accord Divine v. Commissioner, 500 F.2d 1041 (2d Cir.1974), rev'g 59 T.C. 152 (1972).

Stock options that are governed by § 422 or by § 83 should produce the same result as in *Luckman*. Rev.Rul. 2001–1, 2001–1 C.B. 726, confirmed that earnings and profits are reduced to reflect the corporation's deduction under § 83(h) and § 162 when an employee receives stock upon the exercise of a nonstatutory stock option.

3.6. *Federal Income Tax Costs*

An accrual method corporation takes federal income taxes into account in determining earnings and profits in the year to which the taxes relate, even in the case of a deficiency that is not discovered and paid until a later year. Treas.Reg. § 1.312–6(a) (first sentence provides for computation of earnings and profits using the taxpayer's method of accounting). Deutsch v. Commissioner, 38 T.C. 118 (1962).

As discussed in *Mazzocchi Bus Co.*, however, the treatment of federal income taxes for cash method corporations has proved troublesome. *Mazzocchi Bus Co.* followed Helvering v. Alworth Trust, 136 F.2d 812 (8th Cir.1943), Webb v. Commissioner, 67 T.C. 1008 (1977), aff'd per curiam, 572 F.2d 135 (5th Cir.1978), and Rev.Rul. 70–609, 1970–2 C.B. 78, in holding that a cash method corporation could not subtract the federal income taxes until the year paid, and refused to follow Drybrough v. Commissioner, 238 F.2d 735 (6th Cir.1956), and Demmon v. United States, 321 F.2d 203 (7th Cir.1963), which permitted subtraction in the year to which the taxes related. Since Congress has narrowed the types of C corporations that can use the cash method of accounting, the problem now is of diminished importance. But for those C corporations that can use the cash method of accounting, the *Mazzocchi Bus Co.* approach produces a result more consistent with the purposes of the earnings and profits concept.

3.7. *Effect of Distributions*

Accumulated earnings and profits represents a running account, which is based upon the algebraic sum of the yearly earnings and profits or loss figures from the commencement of the corporate life, reduced by distributions chargeable to earnings and profits. Thus, distributions reduce earnings and profits by the amount of the distribution but only "to the extent" of earnings and profits. I.R.C. § 312(a). Thus, distributions do not cause or increase a deficit in earnings and profits. Deficits in the accumulated earnings and profits resulting from operating losses must be made up by subsequent earnings and profits before the account will be on the plus side. But an impairment of capital resulting from capital distributions need not be restored. Hence a distribution that does not constitute a dividend for tax purposes (even if business law would label it a dividend) does not produce a deficit in the earnings and profits account and does not prevent subsequent earnings from producing positive accumulated earnings and profits. See Estate of Uris v. Commissioner, 605 F.2d 1258 (2d Cir.1979) (deficit in earnings and profits can be created only by operating losses).

The cancellation by a corporation of a shareholder's debt to the corporation is a distribution of property to the shareholder that reduces earnings and profits. Shephard v. Commissioner, 340 F.2d 27 (6th Cir.1965). In Maher v. Commissioner, 55 T.C. 441 (1970) (nonacq.), the Tax Court held that the assumption of a shareholder's liability on a note constituted a distribution that was the equivalent of money and was therefore a taxable dividend in the year of the assumption to the extent of earnings and profits, which were reduced accordingly. The Court of Appeals reversed, holding that a dividend resulted, not in the year the liability was assumed, but in the year payments were actually made by the corporation on the principal obligation; the taxpayer had remained secondarily liable on the note assumed by the corporation and hence the dividend arose only at the time of payment. 469 F.2d 225 (8th Cir.1972). The IRS announced in Rev.Rul. 77–360, 1977–2 C.B. 86, that it would follow the Court of Appeals decision in *Maher* in cases involving similar facts. Notwithstanding the IRS's concession, the Tax Court's approach is the theoretically correct one; once the corporation incurred the debt, a claim on the corporation's earnings was created and its capacity to distribute dividends was reduced at that time.

4.   PARENT AND SUBSIDIARY EARNINGS AND PROFITS

The earnings and profits of parent and subsidiary corporations that do not file consolidated returns are generally not aggregated for purposes of determining whether distributions by the parent corporation to its shareholders are out of earnings and profits and hence taxable as dividends. (As will be discussed in Chapter 15, members of an affiliated group of corporations filing consolidated returns do combine the earnings and profits of the group.) As a result, in the non-consolidated return context, it is possible for the parent corporation to make distributions to its shareholders that will not be treated as dividends despite the existence of earnings and profits in the subsidiary corporation.

Suppose that X Corporation, which has earnings and profits, wishes to make cash available to a shareholder but the shareholder does not want the distribution treated as a dividend. The shareholder transfers the stock of X Corporation to Y Corporation, a newly formed holding company, in a § 351 exchange. Y Corporation then obtains a loan from a bank, secured by the X Corporation stock, and distributes the loan proceeds to the shareholder. Dividends are then paid by X Corporation to Y Corporation, which it uses to pay off the bank loan. Assuming that the distribution by Y Corporation to the shareholders is made in a taxable year that ends before dividends are paid to it by X Corporation, and if the form of the transaction is respected, the taxpayer would have achieved return of basis treatment (§ 301(c)(2)) for what is in effect a distribution of the subsidiary's profits. However, Rev.Rul. 80–239, 1980–2 C.B. 103, held that the distribution from Y Corporation was in fact a disguised dividend paid by X Corporation. Section 304, discussed in Chapter 5, was amended in 1982 specifically to govern such transactions, and reaches substantially the same result as the ruling through different mechanics.

PROBLEM SET 1

1. Bugs-Я-Us Corporation is an accrual method taxpayer engaged in a local pest control business. Last year it had the following receipts and expenses. Compute its earnings and profits.

Receipts

Gross receipts from exterminating services	$106,000
Dividend income	$ 10,000
Interest on municipal bonds	$ 5,000
Capital gain	$ 4,000
Additional capital contribution by shareholders	$ 2,000
	$127,000

Expenses

Wages, rent & supplies	$ 33,000
Fines payable for violation of state law	$ 4,000
Depreciation on equipment	$ 6,000
(would have been only $3,000 under § 168(g))	
Section 179 deduction for machinery purchase	$ 10,000
Interest on loan to buy municipal bonds	$ 3,000
Capital losses	$ 5,000
	$ 61,000

What are Bugs-Я-Us Corporation's earnings and profits for the taxable year?

2.   Determine the amount of the dividend received by the shareholders of Benny's Bait Shop & Sushi Bar, Inc. in each of the following situations and the consequences of any distributions that are not dividends.

(a)   Ben owns all of the stock of Benny's Bait Shop & Sushi Bar, Inc. His basis in the stock is $24,000. In its first year of existence, Benny's Bait Shop & Sushi Bar, Inc. earned $30,000 of earnings and profits. One-half of this sum was earned in the period January to June; the other half was earned in July through December. On July 1, Benny's Bait Shop & Sushi Bar borrowed $50,000 from the Usury National Bank and distributed $40,000 to Ben.

(b)   Assume that in its first year of business Benny's Bait Shop & Sushi Bar lost $20,000, measured by earnings and profits. In its second year of existence, Benny's Bait Shop & Sushi Bar earned $24,000 of earnings and profits and distributed $15,000 to Ben.

(c)   Assume that after several years of operation Benny's Bait Shop & Sushi Bar had $36,000 of accumulated earnings and profits. During the current year, Benny's Bait Shop & Sushi Bar earned an additional $24,000 of earnings and profits. On April 1, Benny's Bait Shop & Sushi Bar distributed $40,000 to Ben. On July 1, Ben sold half of his Benny's Bait Shop & Sushi Bar stock to Molly for $50,000. On December 31, Benny's Bait Shop & Sushi Bar distributed $20,000 to each of Ben and Molly.

(d)   (1)   Assume (as in problem (c)) that after several years of operation Benny's Bait Shop & Sushi Bar had $36,000 of accumulated earnings and profits. During the current year Benny's Bait Shop & Sushi Bar has a $32,000 loss (as measured by current earnings and profits) from ordinary business operations. On April 1, Benny's Bait Shop & Sushi Bar distributed $40,000 to Ben. On July 1, Ben sold half of his Benny's Bait Shop & Sushi Bar stock to Molly for $50,000. On December 31, Benny's Bait Shop & Sushi Bar distributed $20,000 to each of Ben and Molly. What are the consequences to Ben and Molly. What are the corporation's accumulated earnings and profits at the beginning of the next year?

(2)   Assume alternatively that Benny's Bait Shop & Sushi Bar's $32,000 loss this year was entirely attributable to the sale of a single § 1231 asset on February 1 and that ordinary business operations for the year were exactly breakeven. Does your answer change?

3.   Glowing Waters Nuclear Electric Power Corp. has 100,000 shares of $1,000 par value, 7% dividend, preferred stock and 100,000 shares of common stock outstanding. Glowing Waters has no accumulated earnings and profits and this year had current earnings and profits of $850,000. It distributed $700,000 on the preferred stock and $250,000 on the common stock. How much of each distribution should be treated as a dividend?

4.   Alice owns 900 shares of common stock of E-Machines Computer Corp. She purchased 300 shares six years ago for $9,000 and the other 600 shares 15 years ago for $2,000. The corporation, which is publicly traded, made a

distribution, which was a dividend under state law, of $11 on each share. Alice received $9,900. Because E-Machines Computer Corp. made aggregate distributions to its shareholders in excess of its combined current and accumulated earnings and profits, it properly sent Alice a Form 1099 stating that the amount of the dividends received was only $3,300. How should Alice treat the other $6,600 that she received?

5.   Standard Oil of Alaska, Inc. has a wholly owned subsidiary, Fish Oil Corp. During the current year Standard Oil had accumulated and current earnings and profits totaling $100,000, and Fish Oil had accumulated and current earnings and profits totaling $300,000. Standard Oil distributed $250,000 to its shareholders this year. What portion of the $250,000 distribution constitutes a dividend?

SECTION 3.   DISTRIBUTION OF A DIVIDEND IN KIND

INTERNAL REVENUE CODE: Sections 301(a), (b), (c), (d); 311; 312(a)(3), (b), (c); 336(b).

REGULATIONS: Sections 1.301–1(g); 1.312–3, –4.

Section 311(a) contains a general rule of nonrecognition at the corporate level for distributions by a corporation "with respect to its stock" of its stock (or rights to acquire its stock) and "property." However, § 311(b) overwhelms this rule with respect to distributions of appreciated property that are subject to § 301 or § 302. Under § 311(b) a distribution of property where the fair market value of the distributed property exceeds its basis is treated as a sale of the property by the distributing corporation for fair market value. Thus, the distributing corporation is required to recognize gain on the distribution. By reference to § 336(b), § 311(b)(2) provides that where distributed property is subject to a liability in excess of the fair market value of the property, the fair market value of the property will be treated as not less than the amount of the liability, and thus the sale price will be the amount of the liability. Section 311(a) continues to prevent the recognition of a loss.

Section 336, discussed in Chapter 7, provides for recognition of corporate gains and losses on distribution of property in a corporate liquidation.

DETAILED ANALYSIS

1.   HISTORIC DEVELOPMENT

1.1. *The General Utilities Doctrine*

In General Utilities & Operating Co. v. Helvering, 296 U.S. 200 (1935), the taxpayer corporation distributed to its three shareholders 19,090 shares of stock in another corporation, Islands Edison Co., which had a basis to the distributing corporation of $1,900 but which was worth approximately $1,071,426. The dividend was declared as payable in the stock of the Islands Edison Co., and the distribution was made after the corporation became aware that another corporation wished to purchase its Islands Edison stock.

The distributing corporation's purpose was to avoid paying a corporate tax on the gain on the sale of the stock. The IRS sought to tax General Utilities & Operating Co. on the appreciation inherent in the stock at the time of the distribution on a number of different theories, including that the dividend was in effect a cash dividend that created a debt that was discharged by the transfer of appreciated property. The Supreme Court upheld the decisions of the lower courts that the taxpayer corporation did not realize any gain because there was no sale; the dividend was payable directly in stock, not in cash, and thus no debt ever arose.

Notwithstanding that the actual issue on appeal in *General Utilities* was narrower,[4] the case generally came to be regarded as standing for the proposition that no gain or loss ever was realized by a corporation that distributed property as a dividend. The IRS steadily attacked this rule, but its arguments were consistently rejected by the courts. See, e.g., Transport, Trading & Terminal Corp. v. Commissioner, 9 T.C. 247 (1947) (nonacq.), rev'd on other issues, 176 F.2d 570 (2d Cir.1949).

In the 1954 revision of the Internal Revenue Code, Congress codified the *General Utilities* approach in former versions of § 311, governing distributions not in liquidation, and § 336, governing distributions in liquidation of the corporation. These sections provided for nonrecognition of both gain and loss at the corporate level on the distribution of property by a corporation. Over the next thirty years, however, Congress slowly but steadily added exceptions to the nonrecognition of gain rule in § 311 (and to a lesser extent § 336), while leaving nonrecognition of losses wholly intact. By 1984, the exceptions had nearly swallowed the general rule as recognition of gain was extended to almost all dividend and redemption distributions of appreciated property. Nonrecognition generally was limited to partial liquidation distributions received by certain individuals and dividend or redemption distributions of capital (or § 1231) assets if specific restrictive conditions had been met. Nonrecognition to the corporation on liquidating distributions as provided under § 336, however, continued unchanged. The reason given for the 1984 amendments to § 311, in Staff of the Joint Committee on Taxation, General Explanation of the Tax Reform Act of 1984, 98th Cong., 2d Sess., 148–149 (1984), was straightforward:

> Under a double tax system, corporate income generally is taxed twice. Such income is taxed first to the corporation that earns it. It is taxed a second time to the ultimate shareholders of such corporation when it is distributed to them. Any failure to treat distributions of appreciated property as taxable events to the distributing corporation, however, provided opportunities for deferring, or even avoiding, corporate level tax. The Congress believed that such a result was inappropriate under a double-tax system.

4　The Supreme Court declined to consider the Commissioner's argument that the taxpayer in effect sold the Island Edison Co. stock to the buyer, followed by a distribution of the proceeds to the shareholders, because the argument was not raised before the trial court.

The 1984 Act only partially repealed the *General Utilities* doctrine by leaving intact nonrecognition of gain and loss on liquidation distributions. This inconsistency prompted taxpayers to resort to complete liquidation transactions in order to avoid the corporate level recognition of gain mandated by § 311. In the Tax Reform Act of 1986, Congress responded to this inconsistency by replacing the *General Utilities* rule with one of gain recognition on any distribution of appreciated property by a corporation. The legislative history indicates that, "the *General Utilities* rule may be responsible, at least in part, for the dramatic increase in corporate mergers and acquisitions in recent years. The committee believes that the Code should not artificially encourage corporate liquidations and acquisitions, and believes that repeal of the *General Utilities* rule is a major step towards that goal." House Ways and Means Committee Report, Tax Reform Act of 1986, H.Rep. No. 99–426, 99th Cong., 1st Sess., 281–82 (1985). As a second reason for complete repeal of the *General Utilities* doctrine, the committee report adds:

> [T]he *General Utilities* rule tends to undermine the corporate income tax. Under normally applicable tax principles, nonrecognition of gain is available only if the transferee takes a carryover basis in the transferred property, thus assuring that a tax will eventually be collected on the appreciation. Where the *General Utilities* rule applies, assets generally are permitted to leave corporate solution and to take a stepped-up basis in the hands of the transferee without the imposition of a corporate-level tax. Thus, the effect of the rule is to grant a permanent exemption from the corporate income tax.

2.   SCOPE OF RECOGNITION AT THE CORPORATE LEVEL

2.1. *General*

Section 311(b)(1) requires recognition of gain by the corporation "as if such property were sold to the distributee at its fair market value." In Pope & Talbot, Inc. v. Commissioner, 104 T.C. 574 (1995), the taxpayer transferred property to a newly formed limited partnership in which its shareholders were the limited partners. The taxpayer argued that the gain recognized under § 311 should be computed with reference to the fair market value of the property received by the shareholders, i.e., the aggregate fair market value of the partnership interests, rather than by the fair market value of the distributed property if sold as an entirety. The court rejected this argument, finding that it would undermine the purposes of § 311. On further proceedings in *Pope & Talbot*, the Tax Court held that the trading value of the distributed limited partnership interests was relevant, but not determinative, in valuing the land. Because the aggregate trading value of the limited partnership units was less than the value of the land, the court found that the land should be valued at the lower end of the possible range of values for the land itself. T.C. Memo. 1997–116. The Tax Court's decision was affirmed, 162 F.3d 1236 (9th Cir. 1999).

2.2. *Character of Gain*

Section 311(b) specifies that gain should be recognized as if the corporation had sold the distributed property. This rule should control characterization of the gain as ordinary or capital, as well as its amount. Thus, gain recognized by the corporation on the distribution of appreciated capital assets can be offset by recognized capital losses. See § 1211. Gain on the distribution of § 1231 assets may be capital or ordinary, subject to the § 1231 computation and the applicability of the various recapture rules (primarily § 1245). Section 1239 may recharacterize gain as ordinary when the property is distributed to a more than 50% shareholder (taking into account attribution) in whose hands the property is depreciable.

2.3. *Losses*

The 1986 Act did not eliminate all of the anomalies in the treatment of property distributions by corporations. Section 336 allows the recognition of loss at the corporate level, subject to certain exceptions, on liquidating distributions. But under § 311(a), no loss is allowed when depreciated property is distributed. Suppose that X Corporation purchased two parcels of land: Tract 1 for $5,000 in Year 8, and Tract 2 for $7,000 in Year 9. In Year 13, when each parcel had a fair market value of $6,000, X Corporation distributed both parcels as a dividend. X Corporation cannot offset the loss on Tract 2 against the gain on Tract 1.

Since X Corp. cannot offset the loss against the gain, can the nonrecognition of the loss on Tract 2 be sidestepped by selling it to the shareholders? A sale might be accomplished in either of two ways. First, the shareholders could pay the corporation cash for the property. Alternatively, the corporation could declare a $6,000 cash dividend, thereby creating a debt to the shareholders, and then distribute the property in satisfaction of the debt. If the debt is bona fide and the subsequent transfer of property in satisfaction of the debt is an independent transaction, a loss should be allowed on the disposition of the property. But if the two distributions are related and the step transaction doctrine is applied to integrate the transactions, the loss would be disallowed by § 311(a).

If a sale is to a more than 50% shareholder, § 267(a)(1) disallows any loss at the corporate level. But if the shareholder later sells the property at a gain, pursuant to § 267(d) the gain will not be recognized to the extent of the previously disallowed loss. Section 311 does not permit the transferee in effect to use the disallowed loss in this fashion. If § 311 were amended to provide for recognition of loss to the distributing corporation, § 267 could still apply to disallow the loss in proper circumstances.

Congress did not explain why the 1986 revisions retained the *General Utilities* rule as to current distributions of loss property. Is there any sound policy reason for denying the loss deduction? Since under § 301(d) the shareholder's basis for distributed property is its fair market value at the time of distribution, the loss is eliminated forever. The disallowance of the loss may be avoided by selling the property to a third party and distributing the proceeds to the shareholders or, assuming § 267 does not apply, by selling the property to the shareholders. In the first case, however, the shareholders may desire the actual property, not its equivalent value. In the second case, the transaction is economically different. Perhaps the unarticulated reason for disallowing the recognition of losses is congressional concern with tax avoidance transactions in closely held corporations. If the tax avoidance potential of allowing corporations a loss on distributions of property to majority shareholders is the concern, it would appear that the problem could have been addressed by subjecting losses at the corporate level resulting from distributions to shareholders to the same rules that govern losses realized on sales to shareholders.

2.4. *Distributions of Encumbered Property*

The distribution of property subject to a lien, whether or not the shareholder expressly assumes the corporation's liability, results in realization of the same amount of gain as would have been realized if the property had been sold by the corporation. To deal with situations in which the amount of the lien exceeds the fair market value of the property, § 311(b)(2), through a cross reference to § 336(b), provides that for this purpose the fair market value of the property will be treated as not less than the amount of the liability. If the corporate debt secured by the property is nonrecourse, this rule is merely duplicative of § 7701(g).

3. TREATMENT OF SHAREHOLDERS

Section 301(b)(1) provides that in the case of both corporate and individual shareholders the amount of any distribution is the fair market value of the distributed property. However, where the property is subject to a lien or the shareholder assumes a corporate indebtedness in connection with the distribution, § 301(b)(2) directs that the amount of the distribution be reduced by the amount of the debt. In all cases, nevertheless, the shareholder's basis in the distributed property is its fair market value. § 301(d). But see Tabbi v. Commissioner, T.C. Memo. 1995–463 (daughter of shareholder took a zero basis in property received from controlled corporation, as an indirect gift from father, because father did not report transfer as a constructive dividend to him). Suppose that a corporation with sufficient earnings and profits to support dividend treatment of the entire distribution distributes property having a fair market value of $100, subject to a mortgage of $60. The shareholder has a dividend of $40, but takes a basis in the distributed property of $100. If the shareholder then sells the property for $40 cash, with the purchaser assuming the $60 mortgage, the shareholder realizes no gain. This is the correct theoretical result because it treats the shareholder who receives a distribution of encumbered property in the same manner as a taxpayer who receives encumbered property in a fully taxable exchange of property, e.g., the receipt of land in exchange for publicly traded stock.

Treas.Reg. § 1.301–1(g)(1) provides that the amount of indebtedness encumbering distributed property will reduce the amount of the distribution under § 301(b) only to the extent that the shareholder assumes the debt within the meaning of § 357(d), discussed in Chapter 2. Suppose a corporation distributes to a shareholder a parcel of land with a fair market value of $100, which is subject to a recourse mortgage lien of $35, and the

(c)   What if the $140,000 mortgage was a recourse mortgage and Ricardo took the property subject to the mortgage but did not expressly assume the mortgage?

3.   (a)   At a time when Bassamatic Corp. had accumulated earnings and profits of $140,000 and during a year in which it had no current earnings and profits from operations, Bassamatic Corp. distributed to Yima, its sole shareholder, land having a fair market value of $100,000 and a basis of $130,000.

> (1)   How much loss may Bassamatic Corp. recognize?

> (2)   What is the amount of the dividend to Yima? What is Yima's basis in the land? How much gain must Yima recognize if Yima later sells the land for $180,000?

(b)   What would be the consequences if in (a) Bassamatic sold the land to Yima for $100,000 and Yima later sold the land for $180,000? See § 267. What policy reason might there be for the answer being different than in (a)?

4.   (a)   Omaha Wizard Corp. distributed to Warren, its sole shareholder, 200 shares of stock of Exxon-Mobil Corp., which it purchased on the New York Stock Exchange to hold as an investment. The fair market value of the stock was $100 per share. One hundred of the shares were purchased at $75 per share; the other 100 shares were purchased at $125 per share. Assume that Omaha Wizard Corp.'s accumulated earnings and profits exceed $1,000,000. What are the tax results to Omaha Wizard Corp. and to Warren?

(b)   Insider Corp. distributed to Martha, its sole shareholder, a parcel of real estate consisting of two acres of land and a potpourri factory building. The basis of the land was $400,000 and its fair market value was $2,000,000. The adjusted basis of the building was $3,000,000 and its fair market value was $1,400,000. The property has been held for many years for use in the corporation's business. Insider Corp.'s accumulated earnings and profits are $10,000,000, and it has no current earnings and profits from operations. What are the tax results to Insider Corp. and to Martha?

5.   Ophelia owns 25 shares and Hamlet owns 50 shares of common stock of Elsinore Corp., which has 75 shares outstanding. Elsinore Corp. has $115,000 of accumulated earnings and profits and no current earnings and profits from operations. On April 15th, Elsinore Corp. distributed $70,000 of cash to Ophelia. On September 15th Elsinore Corp. distributed to Hamlet land with a basis of $50,000 and a fair market value of $140,000. What is the amount of the dividend received by each of Hamlet and Ophelia? Assume Elsinore Corp. reports on the cash method.

6.   (a)   Graceland Corp. has $100,000 of accumulated earnings and profits. The corporation distributes to Elvis, its sole shareholder, a promissory note having a face value of $50,000, due in 20 years, with no stated interest. Assume that $20,000 is the "issue price" of the note under § 1273(b). In general, what are the consequences of the issuance and payment of the note? (Do not bother to make any year-by-year OID computations.)

(b)   What statutory provisions apply to determine the "issue price" of a promissory note issued by a corporation as a dividend? What is the method for determining the "issue price"?

SECTION 4.   DISGUISED DIVIDENDS

INTERNAL REVENUE CODE: Sections 61(a)(7); 301(a), (b); 316(a); 317(a).
REGULATIONS: Sections 1.162–7, –8; 1.301–1(c), (j), (m).

Ireland v. United States
United States Court of Appeals, Fifth Circuit, 1980.
621 F.2d 731.

■ AINSWORTH, CIRCUIT JUDGE:

Appellant Charles W. Ireland ("Ireland") used aircraft provided by his company to travel between his home and the firm's headquarters. The Internal Revenue Service ("IRS") assessed additional income to Ireland in the amount of the alleged value of the plane rides. After paying the resulting deficiency, Ireland brought suit in district court seeking a refund. The district court upheld the assessment and denied the refund. Ireland therefore appeals. We affirm the district court's holding that the value of the plane trips is taxable income to Ireland, but disagree, however, with the method used by the IRS and adopted by the district court in calculating the value. Accordingly, we remand for further proceedings in that regard.

Ireland was employed by Birmingham Slag Company in 1939. Virtually all of the stock in the company was owned by members of appellant's family. Working his way through the corporate ladder, appellant became the president of the firm in 1951. In 1956, Birmingham Slag merged with Vulcan Detinning Company to form Vulcan Material Company ("Vulcan"), with Ireland as its president. Since the merger, Vulcan has been a publicly held corporation with its principal office in Birmingham, Alabama.

* * *

[Eventually, Ireland became Chairman of the Board of Directors of Vulcan and Bernard Monaghan became President of Vulcan. Ireland and Monaghan differed in their views of corporate policy. Lower management personnel bypassed the corporate chain of command and brought problems directly to Ireland. The resulting conflict interfered with the efficient operation of the company. To resolve the deleterious effect of the conflict between Monaghan and Ireland, Monaghan was given sole control over the company's daily operations while Ireland concentrated on the development of long-range policies. To make Ireland less accessible to Vulcan's management personnel, thereby forcing them to deal directly with Monaghan, Ireland left Vulcan's Birmingham office.]

Ireland moved from Birmingham to Lynn Haven, Florida, in 1965, to a home owned by his wife. After the move, Vulcan paid for his long-distance calls to the Birmingham office as well as the cost of office supplies used in conjunction with a business office maintained in appellant's Lynn Haven home.

While in Lynn Haven, Ireland had frequent occasion to travel to Birmingham in order to attend meetings of the executive committee or the Board of Directors. Ireland also traveled to various other locations in conjunction with certain business deals * * *. Whenever Ireland desired, the company would arrange for one of its airplanes to fly to Panama City, the nearest airport to Lynn Haven, to pick up Ireland. The cost of these flights was borne by Vulcan. On occasion, Ireland's family or friends would travel with him on the flights on a space-available basis.

* * *

Ireland raises two issues on appeal. First, he challenges the district court's finding that the value of the airplane flights provided by Vulcan constituted income to him. Ireland contends that the flights were not regular commuting expenses because he was forced to move to Lynn Haven in order to solve the management crisis resulting from his personal conflict with Monaghan. Assuming the district court was correct on the first issue, Ireland also argues that the method of determining the value of the flights was improper. We address these issues in order.

THE VALUE OF THE FLIGHTS AS INCOME

* * * Under section 61(a)(7), gross income includes the receipt of any dividend. A dividend under the Code is "any distribution of property made by a corporation to its shareholders." 26 U.S.C. § 316(a). There is no requirement that the dividend be formally declared or even intended by the corporation. Loftin and Woodard, Inc. v. United States, 577 F.2d 1206, 1214 (5th Cir.1978) * * *. Accordingly, an expenditure made by a corporation for the personal benefit of a stockholder, or the use by the shareholder of corporate-owned facilities for his personal benefit, may result in the taxpayer being found to have received a constructive dividend. See, e. g., Commissioner v. Riss, 374 F.2d 161, 170 (8th Cir.1967) (taxpayer's use of company-owned automobile); Nicholls, North, Buse Co. v. Commissioner, 56 T.C. 1225 (1971) (use of boat purchased by company and used by taxpayer's son for predominantly personal purposes); International Artists, Ltd. v. Commissioner, 55 T.C. 94, 105–08 (1970) (use of residence provided by corporation). * * *

In determining whether a constructive dividend has been made, "(t)he crucial concept * * * is that the corporation conferred an economic benefit on the stockholder without expectation of repayment." United States v. Smith, 418 F.2d 589, 593 (5th Cir.1969). * * * Of course, economic benefit per se is not the only factor determining taxability. In order for a company-provided benefit to be treated as income, the item must primarily benefit taxpayer's personal interests as opposed to the business interests of the corporation. * * * The district court found that the airplane flights between Panama City and Birmingham were in the nature of commuting expenses and therefore the flights primarily served Ireland's personal interests.

* * *

Our consideration of the nature of the traveling expenses incurred in the present case is aided by the Supreme Court's landmark decision in Commissioner v. Flowers, 326 U.S. 465, 66 S.Ct. 250 * * * (1946). In *Flowers*, the taxpayer was an attorney practicing in Jackson, Mississippi. He received an offer of employment from a railroad company located in Mobile, Alabama. He accepted the position with an understanding that he would continue to reside in Jackson where he had an established home and community of friends. Thereafter, Flowers lived in Jackson, but traveled to Mobile frequently. He sought to deduct the costs of commuting between Jackson and Mobile. The Supreme Court denied the deduction. Focusing on the business purpose for his living arrangement, the Court noted that Flowers' decision to reside in Jackson served no interest of the railroad company, but reflected only his personal preferences. * * * Since the costs occasioned by Flowers' lengthy commute did not aid the corporation, the expense was personal and not deductible.

The threshold question presented in this case is somewhat different from that posed in *Flowers*. Here, we first must determine whether the value of flights provided by a company can be included in income under section 61, whereas in *Flowers*, the Court considered the deductibility of traveling expenses incurred by the taxpayer. Despite the different focus, both questions turn on the nature of the traveling expense. The Court in *Flowers* held that if traveling expenses were personal, no deduction was permitted. Similarly, if a company provides facilities that allow a taxpayer to avoid incurring an otherwise personal expense, then the value of the services rendered must be included in income in the absence of an overriding business purpose. *Flowers* necessarily determined that traveling expenses such as those encountered in that case are personal. As items of personal expense, *Flowers* implicitly holds that they cannot be provided directly by a company, in the absence of a business purpose, without the taxpayer including in income the value received.

Appellant does not disagree with the principle that a taxpayer's use of company-provided facilities for personal commuting should be included in income. Rather, Ireland seeks to distinguish *Flowers* by arguing that his decision to reside in Lynn Haven was based on business reasons. Specifically, Ireland contends that he moved * * * in order to serve Vulcan's interests in having him physically separated from Monaghan. The district court acknowledged the relevancy of Vulcan's interest in the separation, but rejected it as the basis of appellant's move. * * * [T]he district court found that Vulcan's corporate interest could have been equally well served by Ireland "establishing an office in his home in Birmingham and instructing subordinate officials to communicate with Monaghan and not with [Ireland.]" Under this view, Ireland's move to Lynn Haven was based on personal concerns so that the increase in traveling costs was also personal, as in *Flowers*.

* * * On the basis of the evidence presented, it cannot be said that Ireland was directed by Vulcan to leave Birmingham. Any conclusion of business purpose in this regard is pure surmise. Accordingly, the record adequately supports the district court's finding that the move, while indirectly benefitting Vulcan, was primarily personal in nature so that the transportation expenses between Lynn Haven and Birmingham were personal, as was the case in *Flowers*. Therefore, the value of the company-provided flights was properly included in Ireland's income for the 1970 tax year.

VALUING THE FLIGHTS

Having resolved the threshold question, we now must consider whether the district court properly determined the value of the flights. As an initial matter, we note that the parties agree on the basic principle controlling the determination of value. As the Government states in its brief, "the amount of income attributable to taxpayer by reason of his personal use of the corporate aircraft is measured by the fair market value of obtaining similar services or facilities in an arms-length transaction in the open market." (Appellee's brief, p. 20) In light of the acknowledged standard, it is surprising that the IRS chose to base its measure not on the fair market value of some comparable service, but on an allocable portion of the total cost of operating Vulcan's air fleet. Specifically, the IRS first determined the total cost of operating Vulcan's entire fleet, including charges for depreciation, during 1970. That figure was divided by the total number of miles flown by Vulcan's planes to arrive at a cost per mile figure. The IRS calculated its assessment of value by multiplying the number of miles Ireland flew for personal trips by the cost per mile figure.

The Government's position is that the total cost method based on the corporation's costs of operating its airplanes is an adequate measure of value, and that Ireland did not introduce sufficient evidence of superior alternative methods of valuation to overcome the presumptive correctness of the IRS method. It is clear, however, that the total cost approach is not the preferred approach. Fair market value of the services received is the overriding concept in the measurement of a constructive dividend and "(t)he equation of value with costs, is therefore, not the norm but the exception." Loftin and Woodard, supra, 577 F.2d at 1223.

Despite the preference for a fair market value approach, the taxpayer has the burden of proving that the assessment was incorrect. * * * At trial, Ireland introduced competent evidence demonstrating the cost of charter air service. Specifically, appellant introduced an exhibit showing charter rates from six different companies including mileage rates, hourly charges, deadhead charges, overnight rates, as well as discounts available for volume customers. * * *

The Government contends that charter air service is not comparable to the company-provided flights. The Government presents a number of factors showing the differences between the two. First, the company planes were "on-call" and could be obtained by Ireland with little prior notice. Second, the charter service did not have the same "aura of distinction" that one could achieve by traveling on company planes. Third, the planes available for charter were not necessarily of the same quality as Vulcan's planes especially since the company occasionally provided Ireland with the use of its Lear jet. Finally, Vulcan's planes, in accordance with company policy, had two pilots to minimize the risk of accidents, whereas charter planes would have been piloted by a single person. The Government contends that these points when considered together create a sufficient distinction to require a finding that charter flights were not comparable to the company-provided trips.

We believe that the Government's argument too narrowly construes the concept of comparability. * * * The general nature of the service was air transportation in a private airplane at a time and place determined by Ireland. Certainly, the type of transportation afforded Ireland differs qualitatively from commercial passenger flights where service is limited to a few predetermined flights. Yet, charter service adequately falls within the guidelines mentioned above. * * *

Our analysis is underscored by a brief consideration of the inequities in the Government's model. By basing its calculation on Vulcan's total cost of operating the airplanes, the model ties the determination of value to an arbitrary figure. Much of the total cost figure is a charge for certain fixed costs such as depreciation. The fixed costs allocable to Ireland's personal trips would depend on the total use of Vulcan's planes in any given year. Thus, in a year with heavy business travel, Ireland's share of the fixed costs would be lower than in a year with less business travel. This variation has no basis in any commercial reality or actual value to Ireland. While such an inequity might be acceptable in circumstances with no readily acceptable comparable service, this is not the situation in this case. * * *

The IRS' mandate in this case is only to assess a reasonable amount of taxes based on the approximate value of the services rendered to Ireland by Vulcan. Determination of that value is not capable of mathematical exactitude, and reasonableness should play a prominent role. We hold that Ireland presented sufficient evidence demonstrating the inherent comparability of charter air flights to the services provided by Vulcan. Value of the flights should properly have been based on a comparison with existing charter rates in the year in question. We remand the determination of value so that the district court can assess the evidence and arrive at a proper figure for the value.

DETAILED ANALYSIS

1.   CONSTRUCTIVE DIVIDENDS IN GENERAL

1.1. *Generally*

As long as sufficient earnings and profits exist for a distribution to be characterized as a dividend under § 316(a), any distribution to a shareholder in the capacity of a shareholder that is not excluded from dividend treatment under § 301(f) will be taxed as a dividend, even if not distributed in proportion to stock ownership. See Treas.Reg. § 1.301–1(c). If there is a direct benefit to an individual shareholder as a result of the corporate payment, the benefit is a dividend for tax purposes—a so-called "constructive" or "disguised" dividend, although it may not be a formal dividend as far as state corporation law is concerned. In Paramount-Richards Theatres v. Commissioner, 153 F.2d 602 (5th Cir.1946), the court described this doctrine as follows:

> Corporate earnings may constitute a dividend notwithstanding that the formalities of a dividend declaration are not observed; that the distribution is not recorded on the corporate books as such; that it is not in proportion to stockholdings, or even that some of the stockholders do not participate in its benefits. Nothing in the statute or decisions warrants the view that a dividend distribution loses its character as such and becomes a deductible business expense merely because stockholders do not benefit equally from the distribution.

In many cases, as in *Ireland*, a disguised dividend is in the form of a benefit obtained by the shareholder as a result of corporate action not involving an actual monetary distribution to the shareholder, such as permitting the shareholder to use an automobile or personal residence owned by the corporation. In many of these cases, the corporation nevertheless claims a deduction as an ordinary and necessary business expense for its costs incurred in providing the benefit to the shareholder. At the same time, the shareholder often does not report any income.

In some situations, there may be a payment to the shareholder that nominally is termed interest, rent, compensation, or something else, but which is recharacterized as a dividend based on the true substance of the transaction. In these cases, for the most part, the principal issue is deductibility to the corporation of the payment. Interest, compensation and rent are deductible by the corporation, but dividends are not deductible. The shareholder would be taxed on the payment as ordinary income regardless of the characterization.

In other situations the corporation may make a clearly nondeductible distribution to the shareholder that the shareholder claims is nevertheless a nontaxable receipt, such as loan proceeds or a return of capital. Hutchins Standard Service, Inc. v. Commissioner, T.C. Memo. 1981–33, held that repayment by the corporation of a "loan" that had been recharacterized as an equity contribution from the shareholder to the corporation was a dividend.

While in some cases nonreporting by the shareholder may be based on a good faith belief that the distribution was a loan or that nothing of value was received from the corporation, many cases involve tax avoidance or even fraud. There is an increasing tendency for the courts to impose negligence and civil fraud penalties in cases in which the corporation distributes cash to the shareholder or pays expenditures providing a clear economic benefit to the shareholder and the shareholder fails to include the value of the benefit in income. See, e.g., Hagaman v. Commissioner, 958 F.2d 684 (6th Cir.1992) (fraud penalty imposed because shareholder diverted cash receipts of corporation for payment of personal expenses and did not report distribution as income).

As discussed in *Ireland*, if an expenditure serves a corporate purpose, even though a shareholder is benefited, the payment of an expense by the corporation may not be a constructive dividend. In Magnon v. Commissioner, 73 T.C. 980 (1980) (acq.), the Tax Court explained the test as follows:

> Where a corporation confers an economic benefit on a shareholder without the expectation of repayment, that benefit becomes a constructive dividend, taxable to the shareholder, even though neither the corporation nor the shareholder intended a dividend. However, "not every corporate expenditure which incidentally confers economic benefit on a shareholder is a constructive dividend." The crucial test of the existence of a constructive dividend is whether the "distribution was primarily for the benefit of the shareholder."

Applying this standard, the court found that corporate payments for construction work on the shareholder's residence were constructive dividends but that payments to another corporation owned by the shareholder, which were made to further the payor corporation's business, were not.[6]

Hood v. Commissioner, 115 T.C. 172 (2000), involved the question of whether corporate payments of a shareholder's legal fees primarily benefited the corporation or the shareholder. From 1978 through 1988 Hood had operated a sole proprietorship that was incorporated as HIF in 1988. There was no express agreement by HIF to assume the proprietorship's debts,[7] but HIF paid the accounts payable in the ordinary course of business. Hood was the sole shareholder and president, and was described as "indispensable" to the corporation. After HIF was incorporated, Hood was indicted and tried, but acquitted, for criminal tax evasion arising from his alleged failure to report income from the sole proprietorship. HIF paid Hood's legal fees in connection with the criminal charges and claimed a deduction. The Tax Court held that the payment of legal fees was a nondeductible constructive dividend because the payment primarily benefited Hood as the sole shareholder. The legal fees were Hood's obligation and since the corporation had not been indicted it was not protecting its own interests. Even though Hood was indispensable to the corporation's business, the payment of his

---

[6] Compare Stinnett's Pontiac Service, Inc. v. Commissioner, 730 F.2d 634 (11th Cir.1984).

[7] *Hood* arose in a year prior to enactment of § 357(d).

legal fees was not necessary to protect the business because he had adequate personal assets from which to pay the fees. The court followed the Fifth Circuit's decision in Jack's Maintenance Contractors, Inc. v. Commissioner, 703 F.2d 154 (5th Cir. 1983), rev'g. per curiam T.C. Memo. 1981–349, and to the extent its own prior opinion was inconsistent, overruled it. In *Jack's Maintenance Contractors, Inc.*, the Tax Court had found the legal fees to be deductible because the criminal charge had its origin in a business (rather than personal) situation.[8] Therefore, the Tax Court had permitted the legal fees to be deducted by the corporation because the shareholder was "essential" to the corporation's operation. In *Hood*, however, the Tax Court found that the payment was made primarily for the benefit of the shareholder, and the Court held that, in light of the reversal by the Fifth Circuit, the Tax Court's decision in *Jack's Maintenance Contractors, Inc.* should not be followed because it did not sufficiently consider the possibility of a constructive dividend.

Pittman v. Commissioner, 100 F.3d 1308 (7th Cir.1996), held that if funds have been diverted from the corporation to a shareholder, a deficiency based on a constructive dividend must be upheld unless the shareholder proves that he received no personal benefit. The absence of a corporate business purpose for an expenditure made at the direction of a sole shareholder alone may be sufficient to establish that the expenditure is a constructive dividend to the shareholder, without any separate demonstration of an actual benefit to the shareholder. See United States v. Mews, 923 F.2d 67 (7th Cir.1991) (upholding shareholder's conviction for criminal tax fraud for failure to report constructive dividends). In King's Court Mobile Home Park, Inc. v. Commissioner, 98 T.C. 511 (1992), a controlling shareholder-officer of the taxpayer diverted rental income from the corporation to himself. The corporation, on an amended return, included the amount of the diverted funds in income and claimed an offsetting deduction for wages. The court denied the deduction and treated the amount as a dividend because the taxpayers failed to establish the corporation's intent to compensate its shareholder-officer.

In Zhadanov v. Commissioner, T.C. Memo. 2002–104, the taxpayer's wholly owned corporation fraudulently under-reported approximately $750,000 of income from its business of manufacturing plastic bottles for sale to crack cocaine dealers. The cash receipts were not deposited in the corporation's bank account, but were diverted to a safe in the sole shareholder's home. The court held that the diversion and possession of the cash by the sole shareholder was not a constructive dividend because, although he had physical control of the cash, he never used any of it for personal purposes, and it was still in the safe when it was seized by DEA agents. That none of the diverted cash was used for personal purposes was

---

[8] The proposition that tax evasion by a sole proprietor is business-related is highly questionable, but in Midwest Stainless, Inc. v. Commissioner, T.C. Memo. 2000–314, a case in which the legal issues were substantially similar to those in *Hood*, the IRS conceded that a sole proprietor may deduct legal fees incurred in defenses of criminal tax fraud charges arising from failure to report income from the sole proprietorship.

supported by the taxpayer's cash receipts journal—a second set of books—that accounted for the cash.

1.2. *Significance of Earnings and Profits*

As with the case of formally declared dividends, a constructive distribution is a dividend for tax purposes only to the extent that the corporation has either accumulated or current earnings and profits. In Truesdell v. Commissioner, 89 T.C. 1280 (1987) (acq.), the Tax Court rejected the IRS's argument that corporate income diverted to a sole shareholder's personal account was taxable in full without regard to the corporation's earnings and profits, and instead applied constructive dividend analysis. In so doing the Tax Court followed the approach adopted by the Ninth Circuit in Simon v. Commissioner, 248 F.2d 869 (8th Cir.1957). In *Simon*, black market profits not reported by the corporation and diverted to the shareholders were taxable to the latter only to the extent of corporate earnings and profits. But if a shareholder's diversion of corporate income is more in the nature of embezzlement or diversion of funds to defraud other shareholders or corporate creditors, some cases treat the diverted funds as fully taxable rather than as corporate distributions. If the IRS asserts that a constructive distribution is taxable in full as a dividend, the taxpayer bears the burden of establishing that the corporation had insufficient earnings and profits to support treatment of the entire distribution as a dividend. DiZenzo v. Commissioner, 348 F.2d 122 (2d Cir.1965).

2. COMPENSATION TO SHAREHOLDERS

2.1. *Salary and Bonuses*

Disguised dividends frequently take the form of excessive salary and bonus payments made to shareholder-employees. Recharacterization of excessive salaries and compensation to shareholder-employees is facilitated by § 162(a)(1), allowing a deduction for "a reasonable allowance for salaries or other compensation for personal services actually rendered." Treas.Reg. § 1.162–7(b)(1) re-enforces this message by specifically providing that "[a]n ostensible salary paid by a corporation may be a dividend on its stock." Recharacterization of purported compensation as dividends of necessity turn on the particular facts of each case. Although there are many formulations of the relevant factors, the following are among those most frequently enumerated: (1) the extent and importance of the shareholder-employee's role in corporate management and activities; (2) the comparability of the purported compensation with that paid to employees performing similar services for other employers; (3) the size, complexity, and economic condition (profitability) of the corporate business; (4) the relationship of the purported compensation to shareholdings (e.g., proportionality); and (5) the corporation's dividend policy. See Elliotts, Inc. v. Commissioner, 716 F.2d 1241 (9th Cir.1983), in which the court also considered whether the corporate profits remaining after paying the purported compensation would provide an acceptable rate of return to a hypothetical investment in the corporation's stock by an outside investor.

A portion of the compensation paid to shareholder-employees will not be recharacterized as a dividend merely because the corporation has a history of paying little or no dividends, if the amount of the compensation itself is found to be reasonable. See, e.g., Laure v. Commissioner, 70 T.C. 1087 (1978) (acq.), aff'd, 653 F.2d 253 (6th Cir.1981); Charles Schneider & Co. v. Commissioner, 500 F.2d 148 (8th Cir.1974); and Edwin's, Inc. v. United States, 501 F.2d 675 (7th Cir.1974). In Rev.Rul. 79–8, 1979–1 C.B. 92, the IRS announced that it too would eschew an "automatic dividend" rule, concluding that although "the failure of a closely held corporation to pay more than an insubstantial portion of its earnings as dividends on its stock is a very important consideration," deductions for compensation to shareholder-employees found to be otherwise reasonable in amount will not be denied solely on that ground.

Contingent compensation to shareholder-employees based on corporate profitability, particularly when combined with infrequent dividend payments or compensation in proportion to shareholdings, often results in recharacterization of the contingent compensation as dividends. See, e.g., Charles Schneider & Co., Inc., supra; Paul E. Kummer Realty Co. v. Commissioner, 511 F.2d 313 (8th Cir.1975). Contingent compensation arrangements are accorded some protection by Treas.Reg. § 1.162–7(b)(2), which provides that a deduction will be allowed for otherwise excessive compensation paid under an arm's length contingent compensation agreement, the terms of which are reasonable at the time it is entered into. See Kennedy v. Commissioner, 671 F.2d 167 (6th Cir.1982) (contingent compensation reasonable where not in proportion to shareholdings); *Elliotts, Inc.*, supra. The underlying rationale for recognizing contingent compensation contracts in the case of shareholder-employees is not as strong as in cases involving nonshareholder employees. A principal shareholder needs no additional incentive to give his best efforts in managing his business. This fact was noted in University Chevrolet Co. v. Commissioner, 16 T.C. 1452, 1455 (1951), aff'd 199 F.2d 629 (5th Cir.1952), as follows: "For the sole owner to pay himself a bonus to do his best in managing his own business is nonsense." However, although contingent compensation contracts between a corporation and its sole shareholder may be suspect, under the *Moline Properties* doctrine, discussed in Chapter 1, which treats a corporation and its shareholders as separate entities, such contracts cannot be subjected to an automatic dividend rule. See Comtec Systems, Inc. v. Commissioner, T.C. Memo. 1995–4 (allowing a deduction for "catch-up" compensation paid to president-sole shareholder of corporation to compensate him for inadequate compensation in prior years).

For payments to be deductible to the corporation as compensation, however, Treas.Reg. § 1.162–7(a) requires not only that they be "reasonable" in amount, but that they are "in fact payment purely for services." In Pediatric Surgical Associates, P.C. v. Commissioner, T.C. Memo. 2001–81, the Tax Court disallowed deductions for payments to shareholder-employees without regard to their "reasonableness" because the court found that the payments were not solely for services. The corporation, a medical professional corporation, had four shareholder-employees and 16 other employees, including two physicians who were not shareholders. Because the shareholder-physicians were not the only physicians, a portion of the shareholder-employee's bonuses represented the portion of the corporation's net profits (before the bonuses) attributable to the services of the nonshareholder-physicians. Accordingly, that portion of the bonuses was not paid to the shareholder-employee's as compensation for their services, but rather by virtue of their status as shareholders, and was not deductible.

Mulcahy, Pauritsch, Salvador & Co. v. Commissioner, 680 F.3d 867 (7th Cir. 2012), held that purported consulting fee payments to the three entities owned by three shareholders of a professional services corporation did not constitute deductible compensation but, instead, constituted disguised dividends. Unlike a small professional services corporation in which the shareholders are the only professional employees and which is therefore "a pane of glass" between the billings of and the salaries of its professionals, the corporation in this case had 40 employees in multiple branches and the amount of invested capital was relatively large. The court noted that treating the consulting fees as salary expenses reduced the firm's return to equity to zero even though the firm was "doing fine."

The incentive to pay compensation to the point at which the corporation has no taxable income, which existed under prior law and undergirds many of the historic excessive compensation classes, no longer is a significant incentive under current law. It is true that a corporation that pays compensation to its shareholders in their capacity as employees is generally entitled to claim a corporate level deduction for reasonable compensation whereas dividends paid to shareholders are not deductible at the corporate level. In addition, a qualified dividend is taxable to individual shareholders at a preferential tax rate. But, even though corporate earnings distributed to shareholders are technically subject to double taxation, current law has largely equated the tax consequences of dividends with compensation paid to shareholders. In this regard, if a corporation makes payments to shareholders as compensation, the corporation obtains a deduction, but the shareholder is taxable at regular individual tax rates of up to 37%, and this compensation may also be subject to additional FICA taxes and would be subject to Medicare taxes. Said differently, even if the shareholder's compensation exceeds the maximum FICA cap for the year, the shareholder would be subject to a 37% regular shareholder level taxes plus the incremental Medicare taxes of up to 2.35%[9] for a total of 39.35%.

Now, contrast the above 39.35% tax result with a situation where the corporation is taxable on the business earnings and distributes those earnings as a qualified dividend to its shareholder. In this situation, because dividends are not deductible at the corporate level, the C corporation is subject to corporate level taxation at a 21% tax rate on the business income. The after-tax corporate earnings of 79% could then be distributed to the shareholder as a qualified dividend. Under current law, individual shareholders are entitled to obtain concessionary capital gains rates under section 1(h) for qualified dividends, resulting in a maximum shareholder tax rate of 20%. High-income individual shareholders would also be subject to a 3.8% surtax under § 1411(a) upon receipt of that dividend. Thus, the all-in

---

[9] See § 3101(b).

corporate tax cost would be 21%, and the all-in shareholder level tax cost on the shareholder's receipt of the qualified dividend distribution of the 79% after-tax earnings amount would be 18.8%.[10] In combination, the corporate level tax and shareholder level tax results create a combined tax cost of 39.8%.

Thus, unlike for much of U.S. tax history, the combination of the substantially lower corporate tax rate versus the individual rate, plus the concessionary tax rate at the shareholder level for qualified dividends, has combined to largely eliminate the double tax disparity of earning business income in a corporation and distributing the after-tax income as a dividend versus the alternative of paying those amounts out to the shareholder as compensation payments.

2.2. *Fees for Services*

Tulia Feedlot, Inc. v. United States, 513 F.2d 800 (5th Cir.1975), aff'g 3 Cl.Ct. 364 (1973), held that payments by a corporation to shareholders in consideration of guaranteeing corporate debts were constructive dividends because the fees had no reasonable connection with the amount of loans guaranteed. For a subsequent year, however, the taxpayer prevailed in a different forum because it established that the guarantees were necessary to obtain the loans, the guarantees would not have been given without the payment of fees to the guarantor shareholders, and the fees were paid in proportion to the amount of debt guaranteed rather than in proportion to shareholdings. See also Olton Feed Yard, Inc. v. United States, 592 F.2d 272 (5th Cir.1979) (loan guarantee fees paid to shareholders were constructive dividends because payments were proportionate to stock ownership in a profitable corporation that never paid any dividends).

3. CORPORATE PAYMENTS RESULTING IN ECONOMIC BENEFIT TO SHAREHOLDERS

3.1. *General*

Corporate payments ostensibly incurred in furtherance of the business enterprise have been found to be nondeductible constructive dividends because of the personal benefits derived therefrom by the shareholders in a variety of circumstances. Constructive dividends often take the form of the rent-free use of corporate property by shareholders for personal purposes. See, e.g., Dean v. Commissioner, 187 F.2d 1019 (3d Cir.1951) (rent-free use of residence owned by corporation). In Melvin v. Commissioner, 88 T.C. 63 (1987), aff'd on other grounds, 894 F.2d 1072 (9th Cir.1990), shareholders obtained the use of corporate vehicles for personal purposes by reimbursing the corporation for its costs incurred with respect to the automobiles. The shareholders were found to have a dividend equal to the amount by which the fair rental values of the automobiles exceeded the reimbursements paid to the corporation.

---

[10] The 18.8% is calculated by taking the after-corporate tax earnings of 79% (100% − 21% corporate tax) and multiplying that amount by the all-in 23.8% shareholder level tax arising from the 20% capital gains rate that applies on qualified dividends and the 3.8% surtax on net investment income under § 1411(a).

Payments for goods and services delivered to shareholders, for which there is no expectation of payment in return, is another frequently encountered example of constructive dividends. See, e.g., Gibbs v. Tomlinson, 362 F.2d 394 (5th Cir.1966) (improvements to a shareholder's land). The same principle applies to payments of a shareholder's personal living expenses. See, e.g., Meridian Wood Products Co., Inc. v. United States, 725 F.2d 1183 (9th Cir.1984) (shareholder's personal travel and entertainment expenses).

DKD Enterprises, Inc. v. Commissioner, 685 F.3d 730 (8th Cir. 2012), held that expenses incurred by a corporation to "breed, show, and sell" cats, the deductions for which were disallowed because the cattery was not operated with a genuine profit-seeking motive, constituted constructive dividends to the corporation's sole shareholder because the corporation operated the cattery "for the personal pleasure of . . . its sole stockholder, and that during each of those years that activity was incident to [her] personal hobby." Because the corporation did not have "a legitimate business purpose to operate the cattery," the expenditures to operate it constituted a constructive dividend "even though this activity conferred no tangible economic benefit on [the shareholder]."

Not all corporate expenditures that benefit shareholders are found to be constructive dividends. See, e.g., Ghosn v. Commissioner, T.C. Memo. 1995–192 (corporate payments of sole shareholder/employee's personal expenses constituted additional compensation, not a dividend, because stated salary was extraordinarily low). In Welle v. Commissioner, 140 T.C. 420 (2013), the absence of cost or lost opportunity to the corporation allowed the corporation's sole shareholder to avoid constructive dividend treatment. The taxpayer utilized his wholly owned construction company to order and bill for building supplies used in the construction of a personal residence. Otherwise the taxpayer acted as his own contractor, hiring subcontractors and ordering building supplies through the corporation. The court rejected the IRS's assertion that the taxpayer received a constructive dividend in the amount of lost profits the corporation otherwise would have derived on the resale of building materials. The court held that constructive dividend treatment is appropriate only where corporate assets are diverted for the benefit of a shareholder, which did not occur in this case. The court concluded that, at the most, the corporation was used as a conduit for paying subcontractors and vendors and also observed that the taxpayer reimbursed the corporation for all costs.

3.2. *Valuation of Constructive Distributions Attributable to Use of Corporate Assets*

As demonstrated in *Ireland*, the fair rental value is the generally preferred measure of the amount of a dividend if the shareholder receives the rent-free use of corporate property for personal purposes. In the absence of reliable evidence of this value, or as a starting point, however, the IRS and the courts frequently use the costs incurred by the corporation to provide such property as a surrogate for the fair rental value. In contrast to the *Ireland* decision, Cirelli v. Commissioner, 82 T.C. 335 (1984), held that the amount of a constructive dividend equaled the expenses of maintaining a yacht that were disallowed as corporate deductions. The court acknowledged that the proper measure of the dividend was fair rental value of the property, but it did not apply that measure because the taxpayer failed to prove that the fair rental value was less than the disallowed expenses.

3.3. *Payment of Shareholder's Debts*

Payment by a corporation of a shareholder's debt generally constitutes a constructive dividend. See Sachs v. Commissioner, 277 F.2d 879 (8th Cir.1960) (corporate payment of fine imposed on stockholder-president for filing a false corporate tax return, where he and his brothers owned almost all of the stock). If there is a corporate purpose for the payment, however, it might not be a dividend even though the shareholder also benefits. In Dolese v. United States, 605 F.2d 1146 (10th Cir.1979), the payment by four corporations of legal fees incurred by their shareholder with respect to his divorce were held to be constructive dividends. But the portion of those legal fees that related to clarification of an injunction, issued in the course of the divorce proceedings, restraining the corporations from engaging in any transactions outside the ordinary course of business was not a constructive dividend because those costs were incurred to resist actions that were detrimental to the corporation.

Nominal corporate liability on the obligation does not preclude treatment of payment as a constructive dividend. In Yelencsics v. Commissioner, 74 T.C. 1513 (1980), a corporation cosigned a note with its shareholder without receiving any consideration and without any corporate business purpose. When the corporation paid the note, the shareholder received a constructive dividend. Constructive dividends likewise may result if corporate funds are used to discharge an obligation that the shareholder had personally guaranteed. See Wortham Machinery Co. v. United States, 521 F.2d 160 (10th Cir.1975).

3.4. *Insurance on Shareholders' Lives*

If the shareholder, or the beneficiaries designated by the shareholder, have irrevocable rights in a life insurance policy, payment of premiums by the corporation constitutes a dividend. See, e.g., Genshaft v. Commissioner, 64 T.C. 282 (1975). On the other hand, if the corporation is the owner and beneficiary, no dividend results from premium payments. In Casale v. Commissioner, 247 F.2d 440 (2d Cir.1957), a corporation obtained an insurance policy on its principal shareholder, who was also president of the corporation, to fund its liability under a deferred compensation contract with the shareholder. The corporation was the beneficiary of the policy, and the shareholder-president had only a right to future payments under the deferred compensation contract. Thus, there was no dividend to the shareholder. Rev.Rul. 59–184, 1959–1 C.B. 65, follows *Casale*.

4. LOANS TO SHAREHOLDERS

4.1. *Loan Versus Distribution*

Shareholder withdrawals from a corporation may constitute loans or dividends. The ultimate factual inquiry is whether there is a reasonable expectation of repayment and an intent to enforce the repayment of the disbursed funds. Compare Pierce v. Commissioner, 61 T.C. 424 (1974) (acq.)

(advances to shareholders were loans because an intent to repay was found and substantial repayments were in fact made), with Electric & Neon, Inc. v. Commissioner, 56 T.C. 1324 (1971) (acq.), aff'd by order, 496 F.2d 876 (5th Cir. 1974) (advances were dividends rather than loans because there was no express obligation evidencing the indebtedness and it was unrealistic to expect that the corporation would demand payment from its 97% shareholder). To ascertain these subjective facts, the courts examine numerous subsidiary "objective" facts and circumstances. Among the most important "objective" facts are the following: (1) the extent of shareholder control over the corporation; (2) limitations on the amount that could be disbursed to the shareholder, (3) the retained earnings and dividend history of the corporation; (4) the size of the withdrawals; (5) the presence or absence of conventional indicia of debt, such as promissory notes with a determinable maturity date, collateral, and provision for interest; (6) the treatment of the advances in the corporate records; (7) the history of payment of interest and principal; (8) the shareholder's ability to repay the funds: (9) whether the corporation sought to enforce the debt: and (10) the shareholder's use of the funds. These factors are highly similar to those used to distinguish debt from equity in the case of shareholder contributions, discussed in Chapter 3, and, as is the case there, no one factor is determinative. See, e.g., Turner v. Commissioner, T.C. Memo. 1985–159, aff'd 812 F.2d 650 (11th Cir.1987); Teymourian v. Commissioner, T.C. Memo. 2005–232 (using seven factors to hold that an advance from a corporation to a shareholder should be characterized as loan or a dividend).

4.2. *Below Market Rate of Interest Loans*

Section 7872 requires the imputation of a dividend if a corporation makes a below-market or interest-free loan to a shareholder. The shareholder may then be entitled to an offsetting interest deduction under § 163. The deductibility of such imputed interest by the shareholder, however, is subject to all of the limitations that generally apply to the deductibility of the interest depending on the use to which the loan proceeds are applied by the shareholder. See, e.g., I.R.C. § 163(d) (limiting deductions for investment interest); I.R.C. § 163(h) (disallowing deductions for personal interest); I.R.C. § 163(j) (limitation on deductibility of business interest); I.R.C. § 263A(f) (requiring capitalization of certain production period interest); I.R.C. § 265 (disallowing deduction of interest incurred with respect to tax-exempt bonds); I.R.C. § 469 (restrictions on deductions of passive losses). The corporation recognizes interest income but, of course, obtains no offsetting deductions for the imputed dividend. When the loan is payable on demand, both payments are deemed to have been made on December 31st of each year the loan is outstanding, and the amount of the dividend and the deemed interest payment equals the forgone interest for the year. § 7872(a). But if the loan is for a specified term, § 7872(b) provides that the dividend distribution is made on the date the loan is made, and its amount is determined by subtracting the net present value, using a specified discount rate, of the payment due to the corporation from the amount of the loan; the imputed interest payments are treated as occurring over the term of the loan by applying OID principles, discussed in Chapter 3, Section 2.

In KTA-Tator, Inc. v. Commissioner, 108 T.C. 100 (1997), a corporation made advances to its shareholders to finance the construction of real estate projects owned by the shareholders. No interest was charged during the construction period, and the amounts were recorded on corporate books as "advances." Upon completion of the construction period, the advances were converted to interest bearing loans with a specific amortization schedule. Under § 7872, the advances were treated as interest free demand shareholder loans during the construction period, resulting in the realization of interest income by the corporation without any deduction for the deemed dividend distributions to the shareholders.

In Rountree Cotton Co. v. Commissioner, 113 T.C. 422 (1999), aff'd by order, 12 Fed. Appx. 641 (10th Cir. 2001), the taxpayer corporation had four related shareholders, none of whom owned more than approximately one-third of its stock. The corporation made interest-free loans to another corporation and to four partnerships in which one or more of its shareholders and their relatives owned stock or partnership interests in varying amounts. The court held that § 7872 applies to indirect corporation-to-shareholder loans effected by loans from a corporation to other corporations or partnerships in which its shareholders own stock or partnership interests. The facts that no one shareholder of the lender corporation held a majority interest in the lender and also held an interest in the borrower, or that other related individuals owned interests, even a majority interest, in two of the partnerships, did not affect the applicability of § 7872.

5. BARGAIN TRANSACTIONS

A sale of property to a shareholder at a price below fair market value results in the "bargain" element being taxed as a dividend. In Honigman v. Commissioner, 466 F.2d 69 (6th Cir.1972), the shareholder purchased a hotel from the corporation for $661,000. The IRS on audit took the position that the hotel was worth $1,300,000 and asserted the tax on the excess of that amount over the actual purchase price as a dividend. Appraisal evidence submitted at the trial showed a range of values between $625,000 and $1,300,000. The Tax Court, in a portion of its opinion affirmed by the Court of Appeals, found the fair market value of the property was $830,000 and accordingly taxed $169,000 as a dividend. The Court of Appeals rejected the taxpayer's argument that in a bargain purchase situation there must be an intent to distribute a dividend before dividend characterization of the bargain element is possible.

Leases of corporate property to shareholders at less than fair rental value similarly result in constructive dividends. A lease by a corporation to a stockholder of a theater at a rental price obviously too low in view of the profits from the property was held to result in the profits being taxed to the corporation and then to the shareholder as a dividend. 58th Street Plaza Theatre, Inc. v. Commissioner, 195 F.2d 724 (2d Cir.1952).

A lease of the shareholder's property to the corporation for a rental in excess of fair rental value also gives rise to a constructive dividend. For example, in Lucas v. Commissioner, 71 T.C. 838 (1979), aff'd 657 F.2d 841 (6th Cir.1981), the shareholders leased a coal deposit from a third party for a royalty of 25 cents per ton and subleased the coal to another party who agreed to pay royalties of 50 cents per ton on coal sold to the lessors' wholly owned corporation and 25 cents per ton on coal sold to unrelated parties. The additional 25 cents per ton royalty on coal sold to the corporation was held to be a dividend from the corporation.

Cox Enterprises Inc. v. Commissioner, T.C. Memo. 2009–134, demonstrates that not all transactions that result in a diminution of corporate assets necessarily result in constructive dividend treatment, but the case is unusual and probably does not provide support for avoiding constructive dividend treatment except on substantially similar facts. In that case, a corporation that was a member of the Cox Enterprises affiliated group of corporations transferred the assets of a television station to a partnership in exchange for a majority interest in the partnership in a transaction that normally would be tax-free under § 721. Two family partnerships, the partners of which were beneficiaries of three trusts that together held a 98% majority interest in the Cox Enterprises parent corporation, contributed cash to the partnership and received minority interests. The IRS asserted that under § 311(b), the Cox Enterprises corporate group recognized gain on the transfer to the trusts of a portion of the partnership interest it received in exchange for the assets because the partnership interest received by the Cox Enterprises group member that transferred the assets was worth $60.5 million less than the value of the transferred assets. The IRS's theory was that to the extent of the excess value of the contributed assets, the Cox Enterprises group had made a constructive distributed distribution "for the benefit of" the shareholder trusts. On the taxpayer's motion for summary judgment, for purposes of the motion, the $60.5 million disparity between the value of the assets and the value of the partnership interest it received in return was admitted. The Tax Court found that the undisputed facts established that Cox Enterprises' primary purpose was not to provide an economic benefit to the family partnerships and, derivatively, to the shareholder trusts. In summarizing the applicable case law, the court quoted Gilbert v. Commissioner, 74 T.C. 60, 64 (1980): " '[T]ransfers between related corporations can result in constructive dividends to their common shareholder if they were made primarily for his benefit and if he received a direct or tangible benefit.' If the benefit to the shareholder is 'indirect or derivative in nature, there is no constructive dividend.' " Applying this legal standard to the factual conclusion, there was not a constructive dividend to the shareholder trusts, even though an economic benefit was conferred on the beneficiaries of the shareholder trusts. Accordingly, no gain was recognized under § 311(b). The court rejected the IRS's argument that to find a constructive dividend "it is only necessary to establish that appreciated assets left the corporate solution . . . , for the benefit of its Shareholder Trusts, to establish that there has been a distribution with respect to [the] Shareholder Trusts' stock to which section 311 applies."

6. INDIRECT BENEFITS TO SHAREHOLDERS: PAYMENTS TO SHAREHOLDERS' RELATIVES

6.1. *General*

A distribution of money or property to a relative of a shareholder that serves a personal purpose of the shareholder rather than a corporate business purpose can be a constructive dividend to the shareholder, even though the shareholder personally did not receive anything. See, e.g., Snyder v. Commissioner, T.C. Memo. 1983–692 (shareholder received constructive dividends as a result of use of corporation's automobiles by shareholder's daughters for nonbusiness purpose, payment by corporation to shareholder's son of salary in excess of the amount deductible under § 162(a)(1) as reasonable compensation, payment by corporation of credit card charges incurred by shareholder's son to pay living expenses while at college, and payment of alimony to shareholder's ex-wife). Constructive dividends of this nature arise most commonly when a corporation pays excessive compensation to a relative of a shareholder and the corporation's deduction is disallowed under § 162(a)(1). The distributee relative is then treated as having received a tax free gift, and the shareholder may be liable for a gift tax as well. See Caledonian Record Publishing Co., Inc. v. United States, 579 F.Supp. 449 (D.Vt.1983) (excessive compensation paid to the controlling shareholder's son was a gift to the son; the IRS did not assert deficiency against father based on constructive dividend theory). But see Smith v. Manning, 189 F.2d 345 (3d Cir.1951) (excessive salaries paid by father to daughters taxed to daughters as compensation and not as a gift, notwithstanding disallowance of father's deduction).

In Speer v. Commissioner, T.C. Memo. 1996–323, the Home Shopping Network entered into a contract for data processing services with a corporation wholly owned by the son of the HSN's majority shareholder. The contract provided for fees to the son's corporation equal to 1% of HSN's gross profits. Because the son actually designed data processing software; the contract was on arm's-length terms; important unrelated minority HSN shareholders did not object, believing it to be fair; and the contract served a valid business purpose, the court rejected the IRS's argument that a constructive dividend to the HSN majority shareholder resulted from the contract. In Lanier v. Commissioner, T.C. Memo 1998–7, the court held that there was no constructive dividend from a contribution to a political campaign committee supporting the shareholders' son. The campaign committee was a separate legal entity. As a result, the contribution did not satisfy any direct obligations of the shareholders' son, and the economic benefit of the contribution accrued to a legal entity distinct from the shareholders or their family.

A bargain sale of property to a relative of a shareholder will be a constructive dividend to the shareholder if the transaction occurred by virtue of the shareholder's position as a shareholder and was personally motivated, as opposed to being an arm's length bargain between the corporation and the shareholder's relative. In Baumer v. United States, 580 F.2d 863 (5th Cir.1978), a corporation granted to the sole shareholder's son an option to purchase an undivided one-half interest in a tract of land for an amount equal to approximately one-half of the corporation's cost. At that time the possibility of developing the tract was ripe. The consideration for the option was substantially below its fair market value. The transaction was motivated by the sole shareholder's desire to make recompense for having advised his son not to purchase the property at a time prior to its purchase by the corporation. The court held that the dividend occurred at the time the option was granted, but because the value of the option was unascertainable at that time, the open transaction doctrine should be applied. Thus, the option was valued with reference to the amount received by the son on the sale of the property immediately after the exercise of the option in a later year. The amount of the distribution was the price paid by the ultimate buyer, minus the sum of the amount paid by the son to acquire the option, plus the amount paid by the son to purchase the property upon exercise of the option. The distribution was taxable to the father in the later year.

7.   TRANSACTIONS BETWEEN RELATED CORPORATIONS

Transactions between commonly controlled corporations, for example, the lease or sale of property or the provision of services for inadequate consideration, the making of a loan, etc., may involve constructive dividend issues. Most cases involve loans between related corporations in which the IRS attempts to treat the entire loan as a constructive distribution by the "lender" to the controlling shareholder coupled with a capital contribution by the shareholder to the "borrower." Not all loans between related corporations are susceptible to such recharacterization. The "loan" first must be found not to constitute bona fide indebtedness. Even then, a constructive dividend to the shareholder will be found only if the shareholder receives a direct benefit, distinct from an indirect benefit as a shareholder, from the making of the loan.

Transfers that discharge an obligation of the shareholder generally are found to serve a shareholder purpose. See, e.g., Gilbert v. Commissioner, 74 T.C. 60 (1980) (purported loan the proceeds of which were used to redeem stock of other 50% shareholder was constructive dividend to continuing shareholder); Stinnett's Pontiac Service, Inc. v. Commissioner, 730 F.2d 634 (11th Cir.1984) (loan to related corporation satisfying common shareholder's obligation to make additional capital contributions to "borrower" corporation was a constructive dividend). Transfers to a related corporation that serve a corporate business purpose generally escape constructive dividend treatment. In Davis v. Commissioner, T.C. Memo. 1995–283, the court articulated a four factor test to determine whether a purported loan from one corporation to another commonly controlled corporation is a constructive dividend to the common shareholder: (1) Was the common shareholder able to use the transferor as a source of risk capital for the transferee without using his or her personal resources? (2) Could the common shareholder carry on a business with extremely thin capitalization without having his or her personal funds subordinated to the transferee's indebtedness? (3) Was the value of the common shareholder's equity interest in the transferee enhanced by the transfer? And (4) was the common shareholder relieved of potential liability on personal guarantees or loans made to the transferee that were repaid with the transferred funds?

In Key Carpets, Inc. v. Commissioner, T.C. Memo. 2016–30, a single shareholder owned all the stock of two corporations. One corporation, Key Carpets, Inc., sold carpets to businesses. The other corporation, Clean Hands Co., Inc., was attempting to develop a voice-activated hand washing monitoring system based on a patent owned by the shareholder. Clean Hands employed a computer technician who developed the voice-activated hand washing monitoring system. In addition to assisting with the development of the hand washing monitoring system, the Clean Hands computer technician provided information technology services to Key Carpets. Clean Hands paid the computer technician a salary of $100,000. The computer technician spent 85% to 95% of his time working on the Clean Hands hand washing monitoring system. Key Carpets paid Clean Hands $130,000 purportedly for "computer service and consulting." The IRS asserted deficiencies against both Key Carpets and the shareholder on the grounds that the payments by Key Carpets to Clean Hands were not ordinary and necessary business expenses but were constructive dividends. The Tax Court upheld the deficiencies with respect to 85% of the amounts of the payments; only 15% of the amounts paid to Clean Hands by Key Carpets were actually paid for information technology services provided to Key Carpets by Clean Hands' computer technician. Because Key Carpets had no actual ownership interest in the hand washing monitoring system, Key Carpets' transfer of funds to Clean Hands provided significant economic benefit to the shareholder and Clean Hands. Thus, following Stinnett's Pontiac Serv., Inc. v. Commissioner, T.C. Memo. 1982–314, aff'd, 730 F.2d 634 (11th Cir. 1984), the payments were for the personal benefit of the common shareholder and thus a constructive dividend to that shareholder. Section 6662 accuracy related penalties were upheld.

A sale of property from one commonly controlled corporation to another at less than an arm's-length price may be treated as if the selling corporation had made a distribution in an amount equal to the bargain element to its shareholders, who in turn contributed that amount to the capital of the buying corporation. Rev.Rul. 69–630, 1969–2 C.B. 112, held that this result automatically followed if as a result of a tax avoidance transaction, § 482 was applied to reallocate income between the related corporations to reflect an arm's-length price. The case law usually has applied this approach when there has been an intentional diversion of funds from one corporation to the other. See Arnold v. Commissioner, T.C. Memo. 1994–97 (constructive dividend to the owner of commonly controlled corporations resulted from a sale and leaseback between corporations at a bargain price because the transaction was structured to benefit the shareholder). But consider Rev.Rul. 78–83, 1978–1 C.B. 79, involving the diversion of funds from one sister corporation to another to avoid foreign exchange control restrictions, which indicated that the "constructive distribution-contribution to capital" analysis applies even though there was no motive to allocate income or deductions improperly.

Section 482, discussed in Chapter 1 and Chapter 15, may also have application. See White Tool and Machine Co. v. Commissioner, T.C. Memo. 1980–443, aff'd 677 F.2d 528 (6th Cir.1982) (no constructive dividend to common shareholder although corporation paid excessive rent to related corporation; reallocation of income under § 482 was adequate remedy).

PROBLEM SET 3

1. Do any of the following situations give rise to disguised dividends? If so, how do you determine the amount of the dividend?

(a) Wolf and Stein are the shareholders of Mortal Doom Video Games Corp. Wolf owns 60% of the stock and Stein owns 40% of the stock. Mortal Doom is engaged in the design, manufacture, and sale of computer video game software. The corporation has over $20,000,000 of net assets and has 30 employees in addition to Wolf and Stein. Wolf is the vice-president and his salary is $1,200,000 per year. Stein is the president and his salary is $800,000 per year. The corporation had $3,000,000 of profits after payment of Wolf and Stein's salaries.

(b) Wolf, the 60% shareholder, is the president and his salary is $1,200,000 per year. Stein, the 40% shareholder, is the vice-president and his salary is $800,000 per year. The corporation had $3,000,000 of profits after payment of Wolf's and Stein's salaries.

(c) (1) Wolf, the 60% shareholder, is the president and his salary is $1,000,000 per year. Stein, the 40% shareholder, is the vice-president and his salary is $800,000 per year. The corporation had $30,000 of profits after payment of Wolf and Stein's salaries.

(2) This year Wolf received a bonus of $1,000,000 and Stein received a bonus of $800,000. The corporation had $4,000,000 of undistributed profits after payment of Wolf's and Stein's salaries and bonuses.

(3) This year Wolf received a bonus of $1,800,000 and Stein received a bonus of $1,200,000. The corporation had $1,000,000 of undistributed profits after payment of Wolf and Stein's salaries and bonuses.

(4) This year Wolf received a bonus of $1,200,000 and Stein received a bonus of $600,000. The corporation had $1,200,000 of undistributed profits after payment of Wolf's and Stein's salaries and bonuses.

(d) Would your answers be affected if Mortal Doom Video Games Corp. stock is widely held and traded on the New York Stock Exchange?

2. Ponzi & Company, Inc., an investment banking firm in New York, owns a working horse farm in Lexington, Kentucky. Carla Ponzi, who owns 80% of the stock, and her family have the exclusive use of a mansion located on the horse farm when they visit Lexington during racing season, which is all of April and October. Last year the corporation deducted $48,000 depreciation on the mansion, paid real estate taxes of $12,000 (attributable to the mansion apart from the working farm), and paid utilities and repair bills for the mansion of $24,000. Carla works full-time in the corporation's investment banking business but performs no services with respect to the

horse farm business of the corporation, which is left entirely to a professional manager.

3.   Augie owned 100% of the stock of Dog's Breath Saloon & Brew Pub Corp., which has more than $200,000 in earnings and profits. Dog's Breath made a $100,000 interest-free loan to Augie. The loan was represented by a promissory note and was for a 10 year term, but was unsecured. The applicable federal rate on the date the loan was made was 5%. Assume that the net present value of the $100,000 obligation, discounted at the AFR, was $61,000.

4.   Kenny owns 100% of the stock of Outron Energy Corporation. Outron has millions of dollars of earnings and profits. Last year Outron sold Kenny an oil well for $1,000,000. Within days Kenny sold the oil well to a major oil company for $3,000,000. Has Outron made a dividend distribution to Kenny? What is the amount, if any, of the dividend?

5.   (a)   Laura owns 60% of the stock of the Prairie Star Pharmaceutical & Brewing Corp.; the other 40% is owned by Antonia, who is unrelated. In Year 1, when it had accumulated earnings and profits of $1,000,000, Prairie granted to Laura's daughter, Rose, who owned no stock, an option to purchase one of its breweries for $750,000. Rose paid $10 for the option. At that time the fair market value of the brewery was $750,000. The option was exercisable any time during the next three years. In Year 3, Rose exercised the option at a time when the value of the brewery was $1,300,000. At that time the corporation had $500,000 of earnings and profits.

      (b)   What if the corporation had only 200,000 of total earnings and profits in Year 3?

6.   Jeff owns 100% of the stock of Jeff's Reliable Used Car Corp. and Jeff's Friendly Finance, Inc. Jeff's Reliable Used Car Corp. was caught rolling back odometers and was fined $10,000 as a result of prosecution by the State. Because Jeff's Reliable Used Car Corp was short of cash, the fine was paid with a check drawn on Friendly Finance, Inc. Might there be a constructive dividend to Jeff? What additional evidence must be developed in order to be certain?

SECTION 5.   INTERCORPORATE DIVIDENDS

INTERNAL REVENUE CODE: Sections 243(a), (b)(1) and (2), (c); 246(c); 246A; 301(e); 1059.

Corporate shareholders of domestic corporations may in effect exclude all or a portion of dividend income they receive. Prior to 1936 all intercorporate dividends were excluded in full. Taxation of a portion of intercorporate dividends was introduced in that year, reflecting a general policy in the early 1930s of discouraging complicated corporate structures. Under current law, however, the tax on intercorporate dividends affects primarily investments in public corporations by other corporations. These investments generally have little to do with corporate operating structures.

Without some exclusion, successive taxation of a dividend as it passed from corporation to corporation in a chain of corporations would result in multiple taxation of the dividend and leave little for the ultimate individual shareholder. However, if the corporate shareholder has an insubstantial degree of ownership or control of the distributing corporation, the argument in favor of relief from corporate taxation of dividend income is not as strong. For example, if a corporation has excess cash to invest on a short-term basis, it can be argued that the tax treatment of the corporation's investment return should not depend on whether the short-term investment is in portfolio stock or certificates of deposit. On the other hand, interest is deductible by the payor and dividends are not, so that if one believes that there should be only one tax imposed as long as earnings remain in corporate solution, the dividends received deduction is appropriate even in short-term investment situations.

If one corporation owns 80% or more of the voting stock and 80% or more in value of the stock of another corporation (excluding certain nonvoting, limited and preferred stock), these affiliated corporations may file a consolidated return, which eliminates dividends paid by the subsidiary to the parent in computing their consolidated taxable income. See §§ 1501–1505. See Chapter 15. If affiliated corporations choose not to file consolidated returns, the parent nevertheless may deduct an amount equal to all dividends received from the subsidiary, subject to the conditions and limitations of § 243(b). See I.R.C. § 243(a)(2); Treas.Reg. § 1.243–4.

For many years prior to the 1986 Act, § 243(a) granted a deduction equal to 85% of intercorporate dividends received by any corporation that did not elect to file a consolidated return or qualify for the 100% deduction under § 243(b). The 1986 Act reduced this intercorporate dividend received deduction to 80%. The 1987 Act further amended § 243(a) and added § 243(c), thereby reducing the intercorporate dividend deduction to 70% for corporations that do not own 20% or more (in value and voting power) of the distributing corporation's stock. In 2017, Congress reduced the intercorporate dividend deduction to 50% for intercorporate dividends paid to corporate shareholders that do not own more than 20% of the distributing corporation, and Congress modified § 243(c) to reduce the intercorporate dividend deduction to 65% for corporate shareholders that own 20% or more but less than 80% (in value and voting power) of the distributing corporation's stock. Thus, a higher rate of tax is imposed on dividends received on what might be broadly viewed as "portfolio" investments.

The availability of the intercorporate dividend deduction creates a variety of tax arbitrage opportunities for corporations. Statutory provisions designed to limit the tax arbitrage benefits of transactions structured to take advantage of the dividends received deduction are explored in the following material.

DETAILED ANALYSIS

1. DEBT FINANCED PORTFOLIO STOCK

One tax arbitrage situation involves debt-financed acquisitions of dividend-paying stock. For example, X Corporation borrows $1,000,000, agreeing to pay 10% interest, and purchases, at par, $1,000,000 of preferred stock paying annual dividends of 10%. X Corporation will realize no pretax gain or loss because the interest expense equals the dividend income. However, if the interest paid to finance the acquisition and 50% of the dividends received from the debt-financed portfolio stock are both deductible, then the corporation will have an after-tax profit, even if the stock does not increase in value, because it will recognize income of $100,000, but claim $150,000 of deductions. For example, at the current 21% corporate tax rate, the excess deductions would yield tax savings of $10,500 (21% of $50,000).

Section 246A reduces the intercorporate dividend received deduction by the percentage of the corporation's portfolio stock that was debt financed during the applicable measuring period.[11] Thus, for example, if the acquisition is three-quarters debt financed, the dividends received deduction is reduced by 75%. The dividends received deduction is never reduced, however, by an amount in excess of the interest deduction attributable to the debt that financed the portfolio stock. Section 246A(c)(2) defines "portfolio stock" in such a way that the provision generally does not apply to dividends received by a corporation that owns stock representing at least 50% of the total value and the total voting power of the outstanding stock of the distributing corporation. Section 246A also does not apply to dividends paid by certain closely held corporations.

In OBH, Inc. v. United States, 397 F.Supp.2d 1148 (D. Neb. 2005), the court refused to apply § 246A to reduce OBH's (a subsidiary of Berkshire Hathaway) § 243 dividend received deduction with respect to dividends received on its portfolio stock investments, because the court found that OBH's indebtedness was not directly traceable to its acquisition of dividend-paying stock. Although an IRS agent testified that he was able to trace loan proceeds to stock purchases, the court concluded that there was no direct or immediate connection between the funds that OBH borrowed and the stock it purchased, and that the agent's findings were based on arbitrary allocations of funds among numerous transactions over a period of several months. The court's conclusion was reinforced by its acceptance as credible of Warren Buffett's uncontradicted testimony that the dominant purpose in incurring the indebtedness was to increase and fortify the corporation's capital base, and that at the time the taxpayer engaged in the borrowing transactions, Buffett, who personally made the investment decisions, did not know how the debt proceeds would be invested.

---

[11] H Enterprises International, Inc. v. Commissioner, T.C. Memo. 1998–97, held that § 246A may be applied in cases in which one member of an affiliated group of corporations incurs the borrowing and another member of the group purchases the portfolio stock. In that case a subsidiary corporation borrowed funds that it then distributed to its parent corporation, which in turn used the distributed loan proceeds to purchase the portfolio stock.

Is the problem addressed by § 246A created by the dividends received deduction or by the interest deduction? Compare the approach adopted in § 279, discussed in Chapter 8, which disallows the interest deduction for certain acquisition indebtedness.

2.   DIVIDEND-RELATED LOSSES: MINIMUM HOLDING PERIOD

A corporation's basis in stock generally is unaffected by the receipt of an intercorporate dividend. Section 301(c)(2) requires a reduction in basis for the portion of a distribution that is not a dividend and, therefore, is treated as a return of capital. However, § 301(c)(2) does not apply to the untaxed portion of intercorporate dividends. The intercorporate dividend deduction is intended to prevent double taxation at the corporate level, and reducing basis by the amount of the deduction would only postpone the exaction of such double tax.

Arguably, however, the intercorporate dividend deduction coupled with short-term holding of stock purchased in anticipation of receiving a dividend creates inappropriate tax arbitrage benefits. For individual shareholders, the qualified dividend rate presents a similar tax arbitrage opportunity; individual shareholders are subject to a holding period requirement. A similar framework applies to corporate shareholders.

To see how the arbitrage possibility works for a corporate shareholder, suppose X Corporation realized a $500,000 capital gain and no offsetting capital loss during its current tax year. Shortly before the end of its taxable year, X Corporation purchases 10,000 shares of Z Corporation stock for $1,000,000. Before the close of its taxable year, X Corporation (1) receives a $200,000 dividend on its Z Corporation shares, and (2) sells its Z Corporation shares for $800,000 (the value of the shares having declined as a result of the dividend). X Corporation realizes a $200,000 loss on disposition of the Z Corporation shares because its basis in the stock was not reduced by the intercorporate dividend received. This transaction is uneconomic because the dividend income is offset by the resulting capital loss. However, X Corporation pays tax at an effective rate of 10.5% (50% of the 21% corporate tax rate) on the $200,000 intercorporate dividend received (resulting in a tax of $21,000), while using the loss to offset a $200,000 capital gain that otherwise would have been taxed at the rate of 21% (saving $42,000 of tax). Thus, the transaction produces an after-tax benefit of $21,000.

Section 246(c) is aimed at such transactions and provides that the dividends received deduction is not allowed with respect to any dividends on any share of stock that is held for less than 46 days during the 91 day period beginning on the date that is 45 days before the date on which the stock becomes ex-dividend. (Under stock exchange rules, stock generally becomes ex-dividend one business day before the "record date" for paying dividends.) For preferred stock, if the dividends received are attributable to a period in excess of 366 days, the minimum holding period is extended to 91 days during the 181 day period beginning on the date that is 90 days before the date on which the stock becomes ex-dividend.

Section 246(c)(4) tolls the taxpayer's holding period of stock for any period in which its risk of loss is diminished through a put option, contract to sell, or short position. See Treas.Reg. § 1.246–5. In Progressive Corp. v. United States, 970 F.2d 188 (6th Cir.1992), the taxpayer acquired stock in anticipation of dividend distributions, and simultaneously held both put and call options on the stock at the same strike price. The taxpayer also acquired stock ex-dividend and simultaneously held in-the-money call options on the stock. The Sixth Circuit held that the taxpayer's holding period was tolled under § 246(c)(3) during the period it held the options. The District Court had misapplied Treas.Reg. § 1.246–3(d)(2) by concluding that the holding period is tolled only when the taxpayer is in a true "short position," i.e., had borrowed and sold the stock and did not own any similar shares with which to satisfy its outstanding obligation to return a like number of shares.

Debt-equity classification issues can be important under § 246(c). Rev.Rul. 94–28, 1994–1 C.B. 86, involved an instrument that was classified as debt for state corporate law purposes but as stock for federal income tax purposes. The instrument provided for a payment of a fixed amount on a stated date. Accordingly, the corporate purchaser of this instrument had an "option to sell" or was under a "contractual obligation to sell" within the meaning of § 246(c)(4)(A). Thus, the 45-day holding period of § 246A(c)(1)(A) was stayed.

Would it be preferable to approach the basic problem addressed by § 243(c) by denying the loss deduction if the purchase and sale are closely related in time to a dividend payment?

3. BASIS REDUCTION FOR EXTRAORDINARY DIVIDENDS

3.1. *General*

Congress considered § 246(c) to be inadequate to deal with the tax avoidance possibilities created by the availability of the dividends received deduction for extraordinarily large dividends. If an extraordinary dividend was expected to be paid on stock of another corporation, the corporation owning the stock would be willing to hold the stock for the period required to avoid the limitation in § 246(c). In response, Congress enacted § 1059, briefly discussed in the context of individual shareholders earlier in this Chapter. Congress justified its enactment as follows:

> When a stock pays an extraordinary dividend, the acquisition of the stock often may be viewed as the acquisition of two assets: the right to the distributions to be made with respect to the stock and the underlying stock itself. In instances in which the acquisition of stock is the acquisition of two assets, the committee concludes that it is appropriate to reduce the basis of the underlying stock to reflect the value of the distribution not taxed to the corporate distributee. In the committee's view, the failure of [prior] law to apply a two-asset analysis in cases of extraordinary distributions when the taxpayer's holding period in the stock is short, leads to tax arbitrage opportunities * * *.

H.Rep. No. 98–342, 98th Cong., 2d Sess. 1186 (1984).

Section 1059 requires that a corporate shareholder that receives an "extraordinary dividend" on stock that it has not held for more than two years before the dividend announcement date must reduce the basis of the stock (but not below zero) by the amount of the untaxed portion of the dividend. This basis reduction is treated as occurring at the beginning of the ex-dividend date of the extraordinary dividend. I.R.C. § 1059(d)(1). To the extent that the untaxed portion of any extraordinary dividend exceeds the shareholder's basis for the stock, the excess is taxed as gain on the sale of the stock in the taxable year in which the extraordinary dividend is received (in addition to gain otherwise recognized). I.R.C. § 1059(a)(2). The amount by which the basis of the stock is reduced is intended to represent the portion of the cost of the "two assets" allocated to the extraordinary dividend. The "basis" of the extraordinary dividend is never recovered because the dividends received deduction is allowed in its place. Because there is no untaxed portion of the dividend if § 246(c) applies, § 1059 operates only if the holding period requirement for avoiding § 246(c) has been met.

Section 1059(c) defines an extraordinary dividend in terms of the size of the dividend in relation to the shareholder's adjusted basis in its stock (after taking into account any prior basis reductions under § 1059), subject to an alternative test using fair market value instead of basis at the taxpayer's election. (For the application of the alternative test, see Rev.Rul. 88–49, 1988–1 C.B. 297.) A dividend is extraordinary if aggregate dividends received in any 85 day period exceed 10% of the basis of common stock, or 5% of the basis of preferred stock, with respect to which the dividends were paid. Furthermore, if aggregate dividends paid with respect to stock in any one year period exceed 20% of the corporate shareholder's basis for the stock, then all such dividends are aggregated and considered to be an extraordinary dividend.

Section 1059(e)(1) treats certain distributions as *per se* extraordinary dividends. This rule applies to any distribution (without regard to the holding period for the stock or the relative magnitude of the distribution) to a corporate shareholder in partial liquidation of the distributing corporation (as defined in § 302(e), discussed in Chapter 5). Any redemption of stock that is non-pro rata (irrespective of the holding period of the stock or the relative size of the distribution) is treated as an extraordinary dividend.[12] Finally, § 1059(f) treats as extraordinary all dividends on preferred stock if according to the terms of the stock the dividend rate declines over time or the issue price exceeds the liquidation or redemption value.

3.2. *Exceptions*

There are a number of exceptions to § 1059. Section 1059(d)(6) generally exempts from the rules of § 1059 distributions to a corporate shareholder that has held the stock of the distributing corporation for the entire period the distributing corporation (and any predecessor corporation) has been in existence. Section 1059(e)(2) provides that the basis reduction rules do not apply to distributions between members of an affiliated group filing

---

[12] Stock redemptions that are treated as dividends as a result of option attribution under § 318(a)(4), see Chapter 5, also are *per se* extraordinary dividends, as are distributions in corporate reorganizations that are treated as dividends due to option attribution. The purpose of these two rules is to prevent the use of options to cause a distribution to a corporate shareholder that would otherwise result in sale or exchange treatment to benefit from the dividends received deduction.

consolidated returns or to distributions that constitute qualifying dividends within the meaning of § 243(b)(1), except to the extent the dividends are attributable to pre-affiliation earnings or appreciation of the payor corporation. The § 1059(d)(6) and (e)(2) exceptions do not apply, however, to distributions in partial liquidations or non-pro rata redemptions treated as extraordinary dividends under § 1059(e)(1). Treas.Reg. § 1.1059(e)–1.

3.3. *Special Rules for Preferred Stock*

Under the general rule, preferred stock that pays a dividend of 5% or more within any period of 85 days or less is paying an extraordinary dividend. Thus, a 5% preferred stock dividend that is paid once annually would be extraordinary. On the other hand, preferred stock that paid four quarterly 4.9% dividends, which on an annual basis is a substantially higher percentage, would not be subject to a basis adjustment under the general rule. To provide relief for preferred stock like the 5% preferred stock in the above example, § 1059(e)(3) applies a special rule to preferred stock that pays dividends at a fixed rate not less often than annually, provided the stock was not purchased when dividends were in arrears. If the taxpayer holds the stock for more than 5 years, no dividends received by the shareholder will be treated as extraordinary dividends, and therefore no basis reduction will be required, if during the period the shareholder held the stock the dividend rate did not exceed an annualized rate of 15% of the lower of (a) the taxpayer's adjusted basis or (b) the liquidation preference of the stock. If, however, the actual rate of return from dividends on qualifying preferred stock during this period exceeds 15%, no relief is available and all of the dividends are extraordinary dividends.

If the corporate taxpayer does not hold the preferred stock for 5 years, dividends announced during the two year period after the purchase (but not thereafter) are extraordinary to the extent they exceed the dividends "earned" by the taxpayer. I.R.C. § 1059(e)(3)(A)(ii). To determine whether the taxpayer's dividends received exceed the dividends it earned, the taxpayer's actual rate of return is computed. The actual rate of return is the average annual amount of dividends received (or deemed received under § 305 or any other provision) during the period the taxpayer owned the stock, computed as a return on the taxpayer's adjusted basis or, if less, the stock's liquidation preference. This is then compared to the stock's stated rate of return, which is the return represented by the annual fixed preferred dividends payable on the stock. If the actual rate of return exceeds the stated rate of return, a portion of each dividend received or deemed received will be an extraordinary dividend, and basis will be reduced by the untaxed portion of such dividend. The Conference Committee Report, Tax Reform Act of 1986, H.Rep. No. 99–841, 99th Cong., 2d Sess., Vol. II, 165 (1986) provides the following example of this determination:

> [A]ssume that on January 1, 1987, a corporation purchases for $1,000 ten shares of preferred stock having a liquidation preference of $100 per share and paying fixed preferred dividends of $6 per share to shareholders of record on March 31 and September 30 of each year. If the taxpayer does not elect to have the special rule apply, the basic rule would generally require the taxpayer to reduce

the basis in the stock by the untaxed portion of each dividend received prior to the expiration of the two-year holding period. This is because a dividend exceeding 5% of adjusted basis (or fair market value, if shown to the satisfaction of the Secretary) paid semi-annually is an extraordinary dividend under the general rule. However, [the] special rule will apply to the preferred stock. Under this provision, the taxpayer's stated dividend rate is 12% ($12/$100). If the taxpayer sells the stock on October 1, 1988, (after holding the stock for 1.75 years) and no dividends in excess of the fixed preferred dividends have been paid, its actual dividend rate will be 13.7% ($240/$1,000 divided by 1.75). This 13.7% exceeds the 12% stated dividend rate by 1.7%. This excess, as a fraction of the actual dividend rate, is 12.4% (1.7 divided by 13.7). Accordingly, each of the dividends will be treated as an extraordinary dividend described in § 1059(a) to the extent of 0.74 per share ($6 × 12.4%). However, if the corporation does not sell the stock until January 1, 1989, and no dividends in excess of the fixed preferred dividends have been paid, its "actual dividend rate" will be 12% ($240/$1000 divided by 2.0). This does not exceed the stated dividend rate; accordingly, no portion of any dividend will be treated as an extraordinary dividend.

Notwithstanding the preceding, dividends on "disqualified preferred stock" will be extraordinary without regard to the taxpayer's holding period. I.R.C. § 1059(f). Preferred stock will be disqualified if according to the terms of the stock the dividend rate declines (or can reasonably be expected to decline) over time, the issue price exceeds the liquidation or redemption value, or the stock is structured "to avoid the other provisions" of § 1059 and "to enable corporate shareholders to reduce tax through a combination of dividend received deductions and loss on the disposition of the stock."

4.   EARNINGS AND PROFITS RECALCULATION FOR
      DISTRIBUTIONS TO TWENTY PERCENT CORPORATE
      SHAREHOLDER

Section 301(e) provides a special rule for determining the portion of any distribution that is not a dividend to a corporate shareholder holding at least 20%, by either voting power or value, of the stock of the distributing corporation. When § 301(e) applies, earnings and profits of the distributing corporation are computed without regard to § 312(k) or (n), except the adjustments described in § 312(n)(7), relating to redemptions of corporate stock are taken into account. Section 312(k) and (n), in general, changes the timing of certain depreciation and income items, the net effect of which is that earnings and profits will be reduced. Thus, § 301(e) converts a distribution that otherwise might have been wholly a dividend, subject to the intercorporate dividends received deduction, into a return of capital under § 301(c)(2), reducing the distributee's basis in its stock of the distributing corporation, or giving rise to a gain under § 301(c)(3). This narrow provision is aimed at certain manipulative devices involving the distribution of an extraordinary dividend followed by the sale of subsidiary stock after the subsidiary has realized an economic gain but before the subsidiary's corresponding taxable gain has been recognized, such as in the case of an installment sale under § 453. See H.Rep. No. 98–861, 98th Cong., 1st Sess. 842 (1984).

5.   DIVIDENDS DISTRIBUTED IN CONNECTION WITH THE SALE OF A CORPORATE BUSINESS

When a subsidiary corporation pays a dividend to its parent shortly before the sale of the stock of the subsidiary by the parent, the issue arises whether the distribution is a dividend eligible for the dividends received deduction under § 243 or is to be treated as a portion of the amount realized on the sale of the stock, and, therefore, ineligible for the deduction. The result can differ depending on the facts and circumstances surrounding the distribution. This matter is discussed in detail in Chapter 9.

PROBLEM SET 4

1.   Domestic Business Machines, Inc. purchased 1,000 shares of Abacus Computer Corp. in a transaction on the NASDAQ. The stock cost $50,000, and the purchase was financed by borrowing $50,000 from the Improvident Bank & Trust Co. The loan was secured by the stock.

(a)   What are the tax consequences for the current year in which Domestic Business Machines receives $4,000 of dividends on the Abacus Computer stock and pays $4,500 interest on the loan?

(b)   What if Domestic Business Machines received $10,000 of dividends?

(c)   What if Domestic Business Machines had borrowed only $30,000 of the $50,000 to purchase the stock and paid only $1,500 of interest?

(1)   Assume Domestic Business Machines received $4,000 of dividends.

(2)   Assume Domestic Business Machines received $10,000 of dividends.

(d)   What if Domestic Business Machines had borrowed $50,000,000 and purchased 80% of the stock of Abacus Computer? DBM received $6,000,000 of dividends and paid $5,000,000 of interest.

2.   On March 15, Monolith Corporation declared a dividend of $2 per share, payable on April 1 to shareholders of record as of March 20. Close Corp. thereupon purchased 1,000 shares of Monolith common stock, which was trading on the New York Stock Exchange, for $30,000. On April 1, Close Corp. received a dividend of $2,000, and on April 5, Close Corp. sold the Monolith Corp. stock for $28,000.

(a)   What are the tax consequences to Close Corp.?

(b)   How would your answer differ if Close Corp. sold the stock on December 1, instead of April 5?

(c)   What is your answer if, in addition to the $2,000 dividend received on April 1, Close Corp. received another $2,000 dividend on June 1 and sold the stock on December 1?

CHAPTER 5

STOCK REDEMPTIONS

SECTION 1.   INTRODUCTION

INTERNAL REVENUE CODE: Sections 302(a), (b)(1)–(4), (c)(1), (d), (e); 311; 317; 318.

REGULATIONS: Sections 1.302–1(a), –2.

When a shareholder sells stock back to the issuing corporation, it is necessary to determine whether the transaction more nearly resembles a sale of stock or a dividend distribution. If the transaction is thought to resemble a sale, the shareholder should be entitled to a recovery of basis with respect to the surrendered shares and capital gain or loss treatment. Since liquidating distributions generally are entitled to capital gain treatment under § 331, similar treatment is appropriate if all of a shareholder's shares are sold back to the issuing corporation. Such treatment likewise appears to be appropriate if the shareholder's voting power and right to earnings are substantially reduced. But if there is no significant change in the voting rights or the share of earnings of the corporation to which a shareholder is entitled, the distribution is more like a normal dividend distribution and ordinary income treatment for the entire amount received, with no return of capital aspect, is appropriate.

Section 302(a) provides the rule for distinguishing sales of stock back to the issuing corporation that are entitled to sale or exchange treatment from those that more nearly resemble dividends. Section 302(a) provides that a redemption distribution to a shareholder is a "payment in exchange for the stock" if the transaction meets one of the tests of § 302(b). If the transaction does not meet one of those tests, then the amounts distributed by the corporation in redemption of the stock are treated by § 302(d) as distributions of property under § 301, and, if earnings and profits are present, constitute dividend distributions.

Historically, the stakes turning on the classification of a redemption under these rules were high as far as individual shareholders were concerned. Dividend treatment used to sweep the entire distribution under the rates applicable to ordinary income. Redemption treatment resulted in no income to the extent of the shareholder's basis in the redeemed shares and taxation of the excess as capital gain, which could be offset by capital losses and which could be subject to a lower preferential rate.

Under current law, dividends received by noncorporate shareholders are taxed at the same rates as those that apply to long-term capital gains. As a result, the significance of characterizing a distribution as a dividend or as a redemption is greatly reduced. For a noncorporate shareholder receiving the distribution, the only important differences are that (1) all of a dividend distribution is includable in gross income, while only the amount by which a redemption distribution exceeds the redeemed stock's basis is includable, and (2) gains on redemption distributions can be offset by capital losses, while dividend income cannot be offset by capital losses, although § 1211(b) provides individuals with a deduction of up to $3,000 of capital loss deductions in excess of capital gains.

If the redeemed shareholder is a corporation, the consequences of the characterization under § 302 can be important because dividend characterization qualifies the distribution for the intercorporate dividends received deduction under § 243 (see Chapter 4), but the gain on a redemption (which is the distribution reduced by the basis of the redeemed stock) is taxed in full, albeit now at a flat rate of 21%. If the redeemed corporate shareholder's basis for the redeemed stock is less than the dividend received deduction, dividend characterization results in less current tax liability than § 302 redemption characterization. Assume, for example, that X corporation owns less than 20% of the stock of Y Corporation (and thus is eligible for the 50% dividends received deduction under § 243); 10 shares of Y Corporation owned by X Corporation, having a basis of $40, are redeemed for $100. If § 302(a) applies, X Corporation recognizes a $60 gain, taxed at normal corporate tax rates (currently, 21%). But if § 302(a) does not apply, and the $100 distribution is taxed as a dividend, after the resulting $50 dividend received deduction, only $50 is taxed at normal corporate tax rates. Thus, X Corporation would prefer the distribution to be characterized as a dividend. However, a disproportionate redemption that does not qualify for sale or exchange treatment under § 302(b), and which therefore is eligible for the § 243 dividends received deduction, is an extraordinary dividend with respect to which the basis of any remaining stock must be reduced under § 1059.

Subsections (b)(2) and (3) of § 301 furnish two reasonably specific rules for identifying a redemption eligible for sale or exchange treatment: the § 302(b)(2) test of a substantially disproportionate redemption, applicable if the particular shareholder retains some stock after the redemption, with the degree of disproportion specified in mathematical terms; and the § 302(b)(3) termination test, applicable if all of the stock of the particular shareholder is redeemed. If these tests are not met, resort must be made to the vague, and possibly subjective, test of § 302(b)(1)—a redemption is treated as a capital transaction if it is "not essentially equivalent to a dividend." In applying all three of these tests, shareholders are treated as owning not only those shares of stock actually owned by them, but also any shares in the corporation owned by certain family members and related entities. See I.R.C. §§ 302(c)(1), 318; Treas.Reg. § 1.302–1(a).

In addition, § 302(b)(4) provides that a redemption of stock held by an individual shareholder in partial liquidation of the corporation will be entitled to exchange treatment. Unlike § 302(b)(1) through (b)(3), which are applied by examining the effect of the distribution at the shareholder level, § 302(b)(4) examines the distribution from the perspective of the distributing corporation to determine whether a reduction in the size of the corporation justifies exchange treatment for the shareholders.

Section 304 specifies that a sale of stock by the shareholder of one controlled corporation to another controlled corporation is tested as a redemption distribution; the provision is intended to prevent a shareholder from escaping dividend treatment on a transaction that has clear similarities to a redemption. Section 304 is complex but involves two basic factual patterns: sales between brother-sister corporations and sales involving parent-subsidiary corporations.

Finally, § 303, which is intended to relieve the perceived hardship of treating redemptions to pay estate taxes as a dividend, permits exchange treatment with respect to redemptions of certain stock held by a deceased shareholder's estate even though § 302(b) is inapplicable.

DETAILED ANALYSIS

1. EFFECT ON EARNINGS AND PROFITS

The impact on earnings and profits of a redemption distribution subject to § 302 is important because any reduction in earnings and profits caused by the distribution will reduce the potential "pool" of earnings and profits available for subsequent distributions taxable as dividends under § 301 and § 316. If a redemption fails to qualify under § 302(a) and is treated as a § 301 distribution, earnings and profits are reduced under § 312(a) by the amount of the distribution. Calculating the reduction in earnings and profits is more complicated if the redemption qualifies for exchange treatment under § 302(a) or § 303.

Section 312(n)(7) provides that if a distribution qualifies as a redemption under § 302(a) the amount by which earnings and profits is reduced for the distribution "shall be an amount which is not in excess of the ratable share of the earnings and profits of such corporation * * * attributable to the stock so redeemed." Assume, for example, that a corporation with $100,000 of earnings and profits redeemed 10% of its stock for $15,000. The maximum charge to earnings and profits is $10,000—10% of the total earnings and profits. The remaining $5,000 of the redemption proceeds represented payment for unrealized appreciation in the corporation's assets. That $5,000 should not reduce earnings and profits because the economic gains that it represented had not previously been taken into earnings and profits.

The legislative history of § 312(n)(7) provides some guidelines for dealing with certain situations where the application of the statute is unclear. First, no amount of earnings and profits generally should be attributable to nonconvertible preferred stock, unless the distribution includes dividend arrearages. H.Rep. No. 98–861, 98th Cong., 2d Sess. 840 (1984). Presumably, however, the amount of any redemption premium might reduce earnings and profits. Second, as was also true for non-redemption distributions, earnings and profits are not reduced by more than the amount distributed. S.Rep. No. 98–169, 98th Cong., 2d Sess. 202 (1984). Thus, for example, if a corporation with $100,000 of accumulated earnings and profits redeemed 10% of its stock for $9,500, the *maximum* charge to earnings and profits would be $9,500. However, if the stock were redeemed in exchange for property having a basis of $12,000 and a fair market value of $9,500, § 312 appears to permit earnings and profits to be reduced by $10,000. Section 312(a)(3) specifies that the distribution amount is the adjusted basis if the fair market value is lower than the basis, while § 312(n)(7) limits the reduction to the ratable share. Reading the two provisions together suggests that distribution amount is determined under § 312(a) and (b), with § 312(n)(7) then imposing an additional limitation on the earnings and profits reduction.

If current earnings and profits are not sufficient to cover both ordinary dividend distributions and redemptions made in the same year, the ordinary dividend distributions are treated as the first distributions out of earnings and profits. Baker v. United States, 460 F.2d 827 (8th Cir.1972); Rev.Rul. 74–339, 1974–2 C.B. 103. Assume, for example, that as of January 1 of the current year, Y Corporation had 30 shares outstanding, which were held equally by shareholders, A, B, and C. Y Corporation had no accumulated earnings and profits. For the current year, Y Corporation had current earnings and profits of $90. On July 1, Y Corporation redeemed all 10 of A's shares for $60. On December 31, Y Corporation distributed $45 to each of B and C. The entire distribution to each of B and C is treated as out of earnings and profits, and thus as a dividend. No portion of the current earnings and profits is attributed to the redemption. If, however, Y Corporation had $120 of current earnings and profits, a portion of the $30 of current earnings and profits in excess of the $90 applied to B's and C's dividend distributions would be attributed to A's redemption distribution. After current earnings and profits are applied to § 301 distributions, the excess is added to accumulated earnings and profits and attributed among the shares on a per share/per day basis. Thus, as of July 1 (assuming for simplicity this is exactly one-half way through the year), $5 of earnings and profits accumulated during the current year were attributable to A's 10 shares ((1/2 x $30 remaining current earnings and profits) x 1/3). Accordingly, earnings and profits would be reduced by $5, and Y Corporation would have $25 of accumulated earnings and profits as of January 1 of the following year.

2. REDEMPTION WITH PROPERTY

A distribution of appreciated property by a corporation to a shareholder results in gain recognition at the corporate level, regardless of whether the distribution is treated as a redemption or as a distribution to which § 301 applies. I.R.C. § 311(b). If stock is redeemed in exchange for loss property, however, § 311(a) disallows recognition of any realized loss.

3. REDEMPTION OF SECURITIES OTHER THAN STOCK

Section 301(a) refers to a distribution to a shareholder with "respect to its stock." Treas.Reg. § 1.301–1(c) states that § 301 is not applicable unless the distribution is to the shareholder in his or her capacity as a shareholder. Hence the redemption of a debt instrument from a stockholder is not governed by either § 301 or § 302, but instead falls under the general rules governing the disposition of debt instruments. As a consequence, the rules relating to the classification of corporate obligations as stock or debt (discussed in Chapter 3) are important here.

4. SECTION 305 ASPECTS OF STOCK REDEMPTIONS

A stock redemption can bring § 305 into play since it involves an increase in the proportionate interest in the corporation for those shareholders whose stock is not redeemed. See Chapter 6.

5. "GREENMAIL"

Section 162(k) was enacted due to Congressional concern that corporations might deduct expenses incurred to redeem stock in order to fight hostile takeover attempts. See S.Rep. No. 99–426, 99th Cong., 2d Sess. 248–49 (1987); H.Rep. No. 99–841, 99th Cong., 2d Sess. II–168–69 (1987). Currently, § 162(k) applies to "any amount paid or incurred by a corporation in connection with the reacquisition of its stock or the stock of any related person." Thus, 162(k) denies any deduction for all expenses incurred with respect to any reacquisition and is not limited to redemptions or to reacquisitions made in the course of fighting a hostile takeover. Further, related person is defined with reference to the relatedness test used by § 465(b)(3)(C), which applies a low threshold tied to ownership of more than 10%. On the other hand, § 162(k) does not apply to disallow interest deductions on debt incurred to finance the repurchase or deductions for amortizable fees, such as investment banking fees, incurred in connection with such a loan.

To further discourage greenmail payments, § 5881 imposes a 50% excise tax on realized gain (whether or not recognized) on the recipient of greenmail payments under certain conditions.

PROBLEM SET 1

1. (a) (1) As of January 1, Year 1, Julia, Charlene, Mary Jo, and Suzanne each owned 25 of the 100 outstanding shares of voting common stock of Sugarbaker's Design Corp. Suzanne's basis for her 25 shares, which she had acquired directly from the corporation for cash over 10 years ago, was $80,000. Sugarbaker's had $120,000 of accumulated earnings and profits as of January 1, Year 1. During Year 1, Sugarbaker's had no current earnings and profits from operations. On July 1, Year 1, Sugarbaker's distributed a parcel of land to Suzanne in consideration of Suzanne surrendering her 25 shares of common stock. The land had an adjusted basis to the corporation of $90,000 and a fair market value of $150,000. What are the tax consequences to Suzanne and Sugarbaker's? What are Sugarbaker's accumulated earnings and profits as of January 1, Year 2?

(2) What if Suzanne had paid the corporation $160,000 to acquire the stock from it?

(b)   Assume all of the basic facts in part (a)(1). In addition to redeeming Suzanne's 25 shares of stock, on December 31, Year 1, Sugarbaker's made § 301 cash distributions of $35,000 to each of Julia, Charlene, and Mary Jo. What are the tax consequences to Julia, Charlene, Mary Jo, and Suzanne and Sugarbaker's. What are Sugarbaker's accumulated earnings and profits as of January 1, Year 2?

SECTION 2.   SUBSTANTIALLY DISPROPORTIONATE REDEMPTIONS

INTERNAL REVENUE CODE: Sections 302(a), (b)(2), (c)(1); 318.

REGULATIONS: Section 1.302–3.

Section 302(b)(2) provides a mathematical test for disproportionate redemptions to qualify for sale or exchange treatment under § 302(a). The test involves two aspects: first, after the redemption the shareholder must own less than 50% of the voting stock of the corporation, and second, the shareholder's percentage ownership of voting stock after the redemption must be less than 80% of the shareholder's percentage ownership before the redemption (and also a like reduction in ownership of common stock if some of the common stock is non-voting). Wholly apart from the less than 50% requirement, the reduction in size of the shareholding in the corporation required under the 80% rule can be quite large. In applying the 80% test, the shareholder's percentage ownership after the redemption is determined by taking into account the reduced number of shares outstanding after the redemption. Because the 80% test is based on comparing the percentage of outstanding shares of the corporation owned by the shareholder after the redemption to the percentage of outstanding shares of the corporation owned by the shareholder before the redemption, a redemption of merely a fraction of a percent more than 20% of the shareholder's stock does not qualify. For example, a shareholder owning 60 shares of stock of a corporation having 100 shares outstanding must have at least 24 shares redeemed to meet the 80% test—a 40% reduction in the number of shares held by the redeemed shareholder. In order to qualify under § 302(b)(2), the shareholder's percentage ownership after the redemption must have been reduced to below 48% (80% of 60%), taking into account the reduced number of shares outstanding as a result of the redemption.

Revenue Ruling 87–88
1987–2 C.B. 81.

ISSUE

If shares of both voting and nonvoting common stock are redeemed from a shareholder in one transaction, are the two classes aggregated for purposes of applying the substantially disproportionate requirement in section 302(b)(2)(C) of the Internal Revenue Code?

FACTS

X Corporation had outstanding 10 shares of voting common stock and 30 shares of nonvoting common stock. The fair market values of a share of voting common stock and a share of nonvoting common stock are approximately equal. A owned 6 shares of X voting common stock and all the nonvoting common stock. The remaining 4 shares of the X voting common stock were held by persons unrelated to A within the meaning of section 318(a) of the Code.

X redeemed 3 shares of voting common stock and 27 shares of nonvoting common stock from A in a single transaction. Thereafter, A owned 3 shares of X voting common stock and 3 shares of nonvoting common stock. The ownership of the remaining 4 shares of X voting common stock was unchanged.

LAW AND ANALYSIS

If a distribution in redemption of stock qualifies under section 302(b)(2) of the Code as substantially disproportionate, the distribution is treated under section 302(a) as a payment in exchange for the stock redeemed.

Under section 302(b)(2)(B) and (C) of the Code, a distribution is substantially disproportionate if (i) the shareholder owns less than 50 percent of the total combined voting power of the corporation immediately after the redemption, (ii) immediately after the redemption the ratio of voting stock owned by the shareholder to all the voting stock of the corporation is less than 80 percent of the same ratio immediately before the redemption, and (iii) immediately after the redemption the ratio of common stock owned by the shareholder to all of the common stock of the corporation (whether voting or nonvoting) is less than 80 percent of the same ratio immediately before the redemption.

Under section 302(b)(2)(C) of the Code, if more than one class of common stock is outstanding, the determination in (iii) above is made by reference to fair market value. Section 302(b)(2) applies to a redemption of both voting stock and other stock (although not to the redemption solely of nonvoting stock). Section 1.302–3(a) of the Income Tax Regulations.

With regard to requirements (i) and (ii) described above, after the redemption, A owned less than 50 percent of the voting power of X (43 percent), and A's voting power was reduced to less than 80 percent of the percentage of voting power in X that A owned before the redemption (from 60 percent to 43 percent for a reduction to 72 percent of the preredemption level).

With regard to requirement (iii) above, section 302(b)(2)(C) of the Code provides that, if there is more than one class of common stock outstanding, the fair market value of all of the common stock (voting and nonvoting) will govern the determination of whether there has been the requisite reduction in common stock ownership. The fact that this test is based on fair market value and is applied by reference to all of the common stock of the corporation suggests that the requirement concerning reduction in common stock ownership is to be applied on an aggregate basis rather than on a class-by-class basis. Thus, the fact that A has no reduction in interest with regard to the nonvoting common stock and continues to own 100 percent of this stock does not prevent the redemption of this class of stock from qualifying under section 302(b)(2) when the whole transaction meets section 302(b)(2) requirements. To conclude otherwise would require that, notwithstanding a redemption of one class of common stock in an amount sufficient to reduce the shareholder's aggregate common stock ownership by more than 20 percent in value, every other class of common stock owned by the shareholder must be subject to a redemption.

Prior to the redemption, A owned 90 percent of the total fair market value of all the outstanding X common stock (36 out of the 40 shares of voting and nonvoting common stock). After the redemption, A owned 60 percent of the total fair market value of all the X common stock (6 out of 10 shares). The reduction in ownership (from 90 percent to 60 percent) was a reduction to less than 80 percent of the fraction that A previously owned of the total fair market value of all the X common stock.

HOLDING

If more than one class of common stock is outstanding, the provisions of section 302(b)(2)(C) of the Code are applied in an aggregate and not a class-by-class manner. Accordingly, the redemption by X of 3 shares of voting common stock and 27 shares of nonvoting common stock qualifies as substantially disproportionate within the meaning of section 302(b)(2), even though A continues to own 100 percent of the outstanding nonvoting common stock.

Revenue Ruling 85–14
1985–1 C.B. 92.

ISSUE

Should qualification under section 302(b)(2) of the Internal Revenue Code of a redemption of one shareholder be measured immediately after that redemption, or after a second redemption of another shareholder that followed soon after the first redemption, under the following [f]acts?

FACTS

X, a corporation founded by A, is engaged in an ongoing business. As of January 1, 1983, X's sole class of stock, voting common stock, was held by A, B, C, and D, who are unrelated to each other. A owned 1,466 shares, B owned 210 shares, C owned 200 shares, and D owned 155 shares of X stock. A was president and B was vice-president of X.

X has a repurchase agreement with all X shareholders, except A. This agreement provides that if any such shareholder ceases to be actively connected with the business operations of X, such shareholder must promptly tender to X the then-held X shares for an amount equal to the book value of such stock. X has a reciprocal obligation to purchase such shares at book value within 6 months of such shareholder's ceasing to be actively connected with X's business operations.

On January 1, 1983, B informed A of B's intention to resign as of March 22, 1983. Based on this information, A caused X to adopt a plan of redemption and to redeem 902 shares of A's X stock, on March 15, 1983, for which A received 700x dollars. Thus, A then held 564 shares of the 1129 shares (49.96 percent) of the X stock still outstanding, temporarily yielding majority control over the affairs of X until B ceased to be a shareholder. On March 22, 1983, B resigned from X and, in accordance with the X stock purchase agreement, X redeemed for cash all of B's shares within the next 6 months, thus leaving 919 shares of X stock outstanding, restoring majority control to A.

LAW AND ANALYSIS

Section 302(a) of the Code provides that if a corporation redeems its stock and if one of the paragraphs of subsection (b) applies, then such redemption will be treated as a distribution in part or full payment in exchange for the stock.

Section 302(b)(2) of the Code provides that a redemption will be treated as an exchange pursuant to section 302(a) if the redemption is substantially disproportionate with respect to the shareholder, but that this paragraph will not apply unless immediately after the redemption the shareholder owns less than 50 percent of the total combined voting power of all classes of stock entitled to vote.

Under section 302(b)(2)(C) of the Code, one of the requirements for the distribution to be substantially disproportionate is that the ratio that the voting stock of the corporation owned by the shareholder immediately after the redemption bears to all the voting stock of the corporation at such time, is less than 80 percent of the ratio that the voting stock of the corporation owned by the shareholder immediately before the redemption bears to all the voting stock of the corporation at such time.

Section 302(b)(2)(D) of the Code, in dealing with a series of redemptions, provides that section 302(b)(2) is not applicable to any redemption made pursuant to a plan the purpose or effect of which is a series of redemptions resulting in a distribution which (in the aggregate) is not substantially disproportionate with respect to the shareholder.

The percentage provisions contained in sections 302(b)(2)(B) and 302(b)(2)(C) of the Code provide "safe harbor" exchange treatment. Examined separately, the transaction that occurred on March 15, 1983, would qualify as a substantially disproportionate redemption because (i) A's ownership of X's voting stock immediately after the redemption was less than 50 percent of the total combined voting power of all the X stock and (ii) A's ownership of X's voting stock was reduced from 72.18 percent to 49.96 percent, which meets the 80 percent requirement of section 302(b)(2)(C). However, if A's redemption is considered to be part of a section 302(b)(2)(D) series of redemptions which included X's redemption of B's shares, then A's redemption would not constitute a substantially disproportionate redemption because (i) A's ownership of X's voting stock after the redemptions exceeded 50 percent of the total combined voting power of X and (ii) A's ownership of X's voting stock after the redemptions was reduced from 72.18 percent to 61.37 percent, which does not meet the 80 percent requirement of section 302(b)(2)(C).

Section 1.302–3(a) of the Income Tax Regulations states that whether or not a plan described in section 302(b)(2)(D) of the Code exists will be determined from all the facts and circumstances.

In the present situation, although A and B had no joint plan, arrangement, or agreement for a series of redemptions, the redemption of A's shares was causally related to the redemption of B's shares in that A saw an apparent opportunity to secure exchange treatment under section 302(b)(2) of the Code by temporarily yielding majority control over the affairs of X.

Nothing in section 302(b)(2)(D) of the Code or in the legislative history of this section (S. Rep. 1622, 83d Cong., 2d Sess. 234–235 (1954)) indicates that the existence of a plan depends upon an agreement between two or more shareholders. Thus, a "plan" for purposes of section 302(b)(2)(D) need be nothing more than a design by a single redeemed shareholder to arrange a redemption as part of a sequence of events that ultimately restores to such shareholder the control that was apparently reduced in the redemption.

Under the facts and circumstances here, section 302(b)(2)(D) of the Code requires that the redemptions of A and B be considered in the aggregate. Accordingly, A's redemption meets neither the 50 percent limitation of section 302(b)(2)(B) nor the 80 percent test of section 302(b)(2)(C). Thus, the redemption of A's shares was not substantially disproportionate within the meaning of section 302(b)(2).

HOLDING

Under the facts of this ruling, qualification under section 302(b)(2) of the Code of A's redemption should not be measured immediately after that redemption, but, instead, should be measured after B's redemption that followed soon after A's redemption.

DETAILED ANALYSIS

1. REDEMPTION OF STOCK OTHER THAN VOTING COMMON STOCK

Under Treas.Reg. § 1.302–3, a redemption of either common or preferred non-voting stock may qualify under § 302(b)(2) only if there is a simultaneous redemption of voting stock. A redemption of non-voting stock (preferred or common) alone, however, may not qualify under § 302(b)(2); such a transaction is governed by § 302(b)(1) and § 302(b)(3).

The next to last sentence of § 302(b)(2)(C) does not require that common stock be redeemed in all cases. Rev.Rul. 81–41, 1981–1 C.B. 121, held that § 302(b)(2) could apply to a redemption solely of voting preferred stock if the shareholder did not own any common stock before or after the redemption. If the shareholder owns common stock, however, even if nonvoting, sufficient common stock to meet the 80% test must be redeemed along with sufficient voting stock, whether common or preferred, to meet the 50% test. There is no requirement that after the redemption the shareholder hold less than 50% of the *value* of the common stock.

2. CONSTRUCTIVE STOCK OWNERSHIP

Under § 302(c)(1), the attribution of stock ownership rules of § 318(a) respecting closely related family members and entities are applicable in determining whether the § 302(b)(2) tests have been met; the proportionate or disproportionate character of the distribution is tested by reference to the entire group of related parties. The network of attributed ownership can be quite wide under § 318(a). The attribution rules primarily deal with four situations:

(1) Section 318(a)(1) attributes stock ownership between *family members* standing in the specified familial relationships;

(2) Section 318(a)(2) attributes the ownership of stock held by partnerships, estates, trusts, and corporations to, as applicable, the partners, beneficiaries, and any shareholders owning 50% or more of the stock of a corporation;

(3) Section 318(a)(3) attributes stock owned by a partner, beneficiary, and any shareholder owning 50% or more of the stock of a corporation to, as applicable, the partnership, estate, trust, and corporation, if the stipulated relationships are present;

(4) Section 318(a)(4) treats a taxpayer as owning any stock that the taxpayer has an option to purchase.

In applying these rules, § 318(a)(5)(A) treats stock that is *constructively* owned by virtue of the application of the attribution rules as if it were *actually owned* for the purpose of reattribution. Thus, for example, if A is the beneficiary of a trust, stock owned by the trust would be attributed to A under § 318(a)(2)(B). Under § 318(a)(5)(A) that stock would then be considered as actually owned by A for "reattributing" the stock to A's parents under § 318(a)(1).

There are, however, some limits to the reattribution of constructively owned stock. Section 318(a)(5)(B) provides that the stock constructively owned by virtue of the application of the family attribution rules will not be considered as actually owned for purposes of its reattribution under those rules. Thus, pursuant to § 318(a)(5)(C), stock owned by A that is attributed to A's parents under § 318(a)(1) will not be reattributed through A's parents to A's brother or sister (there is no direct attribution between siblings). Similarly, if stock is attributed to a partnership, estate, etc., under

§ 318(a)(3), it will not then be reattributed to another partner, beneficiary, etc., under § 318(a)(2). These limitations on reattribution eliminate so-called "sideways" attribution.

Application of the attribution rules sometimes may help a taxpayer. Suppose that the husband owns voting common stock and the wife owns non-voting preferred stock. Some of the wife's preferred stock is redeemed in connection with a transaction in which part of the husband's common stock is redeemed, and the husband's redemption meets the requirements of § 302(b)(2). Section 302(b)(2) applies to qualify the wife's redemption under Treas.Reg. § 1.302–3. Rev.Rul. 77–237, 1977–2 C.B. 88. On the other hand, if the attribution rules make another the constructive owner of stock actually held by the taxpayer, the attribution does not reduce the taxpayer's "real" ownership for purposes of testing the disproportionality of the distribution. Northwestern Steel and Supply Co. v. Commissioner, 60 T.C. 356 (1973). For example if A, who owns 50 shares of stock, and B, who owns 40 shares of stock, are parent and child, A is deemed to own B's 40 shares in addition to A's own 50 shares; correspondingly B is deemed to own A's 50 shares. Thus, in testing a redemption of shares from either or both of A and B under § 302(b)(2), both A and B are deemed to own 90 shares before the transaction.

Treas.Reg. § 1.302–3(a) provides that the § 302(b)(2) is "applied to each shareholder separately and shall be applied only with respect to stock which is issued and outstanding in the hands of the shareholders." Rev.Rul. 68–601, 1968–2 C.B. 124, explains, "No mention is made as to what shares, if any, that may be acquired through the exercise of options are to be considered as issued and outstanding stock for this purpose." The ruling goes on to treat warrants and convertible debentures as options and also provides, "there should be considered as issued and outstanding, on a shareholder by shareholder basis without regard to the rights of unrelated shareholders to acquire unissued stock, those shares which a given shareholder may acquire by exercising his warrants and converting his debentures and those shares which that shareholder would constructively own by reason of other shareholders exercising their warrants and converting their debentures." Henry T. Patterson Trust v. United States, 729 F.2d 1089 (6th Cir.1984), is to the contrary. In that case, an individual shareholder had options to purchase shares; a trust shareholder had a portion of its stock redeemed. The individual shareholder and the trust shareholder were unrelated under § 318. The trust shareholder sought to include the shares represented by the option in the denominator for purposes of testing the redemption; the Sixth Circuit agreed, with the result that the redemption qualified for sale treatment (via the "not essentially equivalent to a dividend" test). See also Sorem v. Commissioner, 334 F.2d 275 (10th Cir.1964) (employees holding stock options on unissued stock treated as owning stock). Rev.Rul. 89–64, 1989–1 C.B. 91, held that the holder of an option to purchase shares from the corporation was deemed to hold the option shares even though the option was by its terms not exercisable until a future date.

3. SERIES OF DISTRIBUTIONS

3.1. *Generally*

Congress statutorily prescribed in § 302(b)(2)(D) that a series of redemptions should be analyzed according to their end result if those redemptions occur pursuant to a plan the purpose or effect of which is that the series of redemptions are not substantially disproportionate with respect to the shareholder. Thus, in the context of analyzing § 302(b)(2), Congress has statutorily prescribed a step transaction doctrine analysis in applying § 302(b)(2). In Rev.Rul. 85–14, reproduced above, the IRS addressed the legal standard for determining a "plan" for purposes of § 302(b)(2)(D) and the sufficiency of facts that are needed to find such a plan.

3.2. *Time Frame*

What time frame may a "plan" span? In Blount v. Commissioner, 425 F.2d 921 (2d Cir.1969), the IRS successfully integrated redemptions where the shareholders entered into an agreement whereby the corporation would redeem up to 20 shares in the two years following the shareholders' retirement and up to 15 shares each year thereafter; the court agreed to view "all the redemptions contemplated by the retirement agreement as part of a single plan." But, in Glacier State Electric Supply Co. v. Commissioner, 80 T.C. 1047 (1983), the Tax Court held that a possible future redemption upon the subsequent death of a shareholder pursuant to an executory buy-sell agreement should not be considered as part of a "plan" in testing whether a current redemption met the test of § 302(b)(2).

3.3. *Corporate Shareholders*

Because of the availability of the § 243 intercorporate dividend received deduction, a corporate shareholder frequently prefers to characterize a distribution as a dividend rather than as a § 302 redemption. In Bleily & Collishaw, Inc. v. Commissioner, 72 T.C. 751 (1979), aff'd by order, 647 F.2d 169 (9th Cir.1981), all of the shares of stock of another corporation held by a corporate shareholder were redeemed in seven installments over a six month period. Each of the first six installments left the shareholder with slightly more than 80% of the percentage ownership of stock that it held before that redemption. The shareholder claimed that each of the six distributions was a distribution under § 301 rather than § 302(a). Finding that there was a firm and fixed plan to eliminate the shareholder from the corporation, the Tax Court treated all of the installments as part of a single distribution in redemption of all of the taxpayer's shares under § 302(b)(3).

4. BASIS CONSIDERATIONS

4.1. *Generally*

If a redemption fails to qualify for exchange treatment under § 302(a) and the distribution is a dividend, the basis of the redeemed stock is not relevant in computing the shareholder's income. Under Treas.Reg. § 1.302–2(c), the basis of the redeemed stock is added to the basis of the other stock held by the taxpayer. If the taxpayer does not actually own any stock after the transaction, but is attributed stock in the corporation by, for example, family attribution rules under § 318, then Treas.Reg. § 1.302–2(c), Ex. (2)

suggests that the taxpayer's unrecovered basis in the stock shifts to the family member who actually owns the stock. Regulations proposed in 2009, discussed in the next section, would have altered this result, but they were withdrawn in 2019, albeit with the Treasury cautioning in the withdrawal notice against inappropriate basis shifts.

Redemption distributions to a corporate shareholder that are treated as dividends because of option attribution under § 318(a)(4) are extraordinary dividends under § 1059(e)(1)(A)(iii)(I). The corporate recipient is required to reduce the basis of its remaining stock to the extent that the dividend was not taxed by virtue of the § 243 dividends received deduction.

In H.J. Heinz Co. v. United States, 76 Fed. Cl. 570 (2007), the taxpayer attempted to take advantage of the shift in basis of redeemed stock to other stock in order to generate a capital loss. Heinz Credit Company (HCC, a Delaware lending subsidiary formed to minimize state taxes on intercompany loans) purchased on the open market 3,500,000 shares of its parent's (H.J. Heinz) stock with cash acquired from commercial lenders. H.J. Heinz redeemed 3,325,000 of these shares, giving HHC a subordinated zero coupon convertible note. H.J. Heinz and HHC treated the transaction as a dividend from H.J. Heinz to HCC under § 301 and § 302(d). HCC thus asserted that its basis in the full 3,500,000 shares shifted to its remaining 175,000 H.J. Heinz shares. Thereafter, HHC sold the 175,000 shares to an unrelated party claiming a $124 million capital loss, which was reported on the H.J. Heinz consolidated return. See Chapter 15. At the end of three years, HHC converted the note into H.J. Heinz stock. The court found that HCC possessed the benefits and burdens of ownership of the H.J. Heinz stock and that its transfer of the stock to H.J. Heinz met the definition of a redemption under § 317(b). Nonetheless, the court concluded that the transaction was a sham because the only purpose of the transaction was to produce a capital loss to offset capital gains realized on another transaction, and the transaction had no business purpose. The court also applied the step transaction doctrine to disregard the HCC purchase and redemption of shares.

4.2. *2009 Proposed Regulations*

In 2009, the Treasury Department proposed replacing the basis adjustment rules in Treas.Reg. § 1.302–2(c), which apply when a redemption is treated as a § 301 distribution, with an entirely different regime. These Regulations were withdrawn in March 2019, but the withdrawal notice indicated Treasury would continue to study the issue. See 84 Fed. Reg. 11687 (Mar. 28, 2019). Thus, although withdrawn, the 2009 Proposed Regulations provide an indication of possible future approaches.

Prop.Reg. § 1.302–5 (2009) provided that the portion of a redemption distribution subject to § 301 but that is not treated as a dividend under § 301(c)(1), and thus results in a basis reduction under § 301(c)(2), would be applied to reduce the basis of each share of stock held by the redeemed shareholder in the same class of stock that is redeemed. Prop.Reg. § 1.302–5(a)(1) (2009). The basis reduction would be applied pro rata on a share-by-share basis. As a consequence of this share-by-share approach, gain may be recognized under § 301(c)(3) with respect to some shares while the distributee shareholder holds other shares with unrecovered basis. Prop.Reg. § 1.302–5(a)(2) (2009) provided that after a reduction in basis under § 301(c)(2), the redeemed shareholder would be treated as exchanging all of the shareholder's shares (including the redeemed shares) in a nonrecognition corporate recapitalization under § 368(a)(1)(E), discussed in Chapter 11, for the number of shares retained after the redemption in which the basis of each share of stock received retains the same basis as the original shares deemed transferred. See Prop.Reg. § 1.358–2(b) (2009). This tracing rule would preserve the basis of different blocks of shares in the shares remaining after redemption.

In the case of redemption of all of the shares of the redeemed shareholder that is treated as a dividend distribution, Prop.Reg. § 1.302–5(a)(3) (2009) provided that the shareholder's unrecovered basis in the redeemed shares is treated as a loss on the date of the redemption, but recognition of the loss is deferred to a subsequent "inclusion date." In withdrawing the 2009 Proposed Regulations, the Treasury stated, "any unrecovered basis in the redeemed stock of a shareholder may be shifted to other stock only if such an adjustment is a proper adjustment within the meaning of § 1.302–2(c). Not all shifts of a redeemed shareholder's unrecovered basis result in proper adjustments, and certain basis adjustments can lead to inappropriate results." 84 Fed. Reg. 11687 (Mar. 28, 2019).

PROBLEM SET 2

1. Champion Breakfast Drink Corp. has 100 shares of common stock and 200 shares of nonvoting preferred stock outstanding. Dwayne owns 70 shares of common stock, and Kilgore owns 30 shares of common stock. Kilgore also owns 100 shares of nonvoting preferred stock. Which, if any, of the following alternative redemption transactions qualify under § 302(b)(2), and what are the tax consequences of each transaction:

(a) Champion Breakfast Drink Corp. redeems 5 shares of common stock from Kilgore for $5,000. Kilgore's basis in his 30 shares was $900 per share ($27,000 total).

(b) (1) Champion Breakfast Drink Corp. redeems 10 shares of common stock from Kilgore for $10,000. Kilgore's basis in his 30 shares of common stock was $900 per share ($27,000 total).

    (2) What if Kilgore's basis in his 30 shares of common stock was $1,200 per share ($36,000 total)?

(c) Champion Breakfast Drink Corp. redeems 35 shares of common stock from Dwayne for $35,000. Dwayne's basis in his stock is $900 per share ($31,500).

(d) Champion Breakfast Drink Corp. redeems 40 shares of common stock from Dwayne for $40,000. Dwayne's basis in his stock is $900 per share ($36,000).

(e)   Champion Breakfast Drink Corp. redeems 50 shares of preferred stock from Kilgore.

(f)   Champion Breakfast Drink Corp. redeems 15 shares of common stock and 50 shares of preferred stock from Kilgore.

(g)   Champion Breakfast Drink Corp. redeems 15 shares of common stock and 90 shares of preferred stock from Kilgore.

2.   Titan Siren Corp. has 100 shares of voting common stock outstanding. Malachi owns 60 shares and Winston owns 40 shares. They have both worked full time for the corporation. On February 1, Malachi went into semi-retirement, leaving most management to Winston, and Titan Siren Corp. redeemed 30 of Malachi's shares. On August 1st, Winston died and Malachi went back to work; in December, the corporation redeemed all of Winston's shares from his estate. Does Malachi's redemption qualify under § 302(b)(2)?

3.   Four years ago, Hoover's Pontiac Dealer, Inc. owned 40 shares of stock of voting common stock of Pilgrim Slaughterhouse Corp., which had 100 shares of voting common stock outstanding. Hoover's basis for the Pilgrim Slaughterhouse stock was $600 per share. Billy Pilgrim owned the other 60 shares of voting common stock. Three years ago, Pilgrim Slaughterhouse redeemed 10 shares of stock from Hoover's for $1,000 per share; two years ago Pilgrim Slaughterhouse redeemed 8 shares of stock from Hoover's for $1,000 per share; last year Pilgrim Slaughterhouse redeemed 5 shares of stock from Hoover's for $1,000 per share; this year Pilgrim Slaughterhouse redeemed 3 shares of stock from Hoover's for $1,000 per share. What are the tax consequences to Hoover's Pontiac Dealer, Inc.?

4.   Micando Corp. has 100 shares of voting common stock and 400 shares of nonvoting common stock outstanding. Each share of Micando Corp. voting common stock has a fair market value of $100. Each share of nonvoting common stock has a fair market value of $50. José owns 60 shares of Micando Corp. voting common stock and 200 shares of Micando Corp. nonvoting common stock. The remaining shares are owned by a number of unrelated individuals.

(a)   If Micando Corp. redeems 30 of José's voting common shares, will the redemption qualify for exchange treatment under § 302(b)(2)?

(b)   If Micando Corp. redeems 30 of José's voting common shares, how many of José's nonvoting common shares must be redeemed to qualify the transaction under § 302(b)(2)?

5.   Rosewater Corporation has 100 shares of voting common stock and 300 shares of voting preferred stock outstanding. Elliot owns 40 shares of voting common stock and 100 shares of voting preferred stock.

(a)   If Rosewater Corporation redeems all 40 of Elliot's shares of common stock, will the redemption transaction qualify under § 302(b)(2)?

(b)   If Rosewater Corporation redeems all 100 of Elliot's shares of preferred stock, will the redemption transaction qualify under § 302(b)(2)?

6.   X Corporation has 100 shares of stock outstanding, all of which are owned by six related individuals, as follows:

Shareholder	Relationship	Number of Shares
Amy		25
Ben	Amy's son	15
Cindy	Ben's wife	15
David	Ben & Cindy's son	15
Evan	Amy's son	15
Fran	Evan's daughter	15

(a) Determine how much stock is owned by each shareholder after taking into account the § 318 attribution rules.

(b) Would a redemption of 14 shares from Ben qualify under § 302(b)(2)?

(c) Would a redemption of 14 shares from Cindy qualify under § 302(b)(2)?

(d) Would a redemption of 10 shares from Fran qualify under § 302(b)(2)?

7.   Y Corp. has 100 shares of common stock outstanding. Fifteen shares are owned by A. Forty shares are owned by Z Corp., and A owns 60 of the 100 outstanding shares of stock of Z Corp. The remaining 45 shares of stock of Y Corp. are owned by the ABC Partnership, in which A is a one-third partner. Would a redemption of 10 of A's Y Corp. shares qualify under § 302(b)(2)?

8.   D owns 50% of the stock of each of V Corporation and W Corporation. The other 50% of the stock of each corporation is owned by various unrelated persons. V Corporation and W Corporation each own 40 shares of common stock of Q Corporation, which has 100 shares outstanding. The other 20 shares of the stock of Q Corporation are owned by various unrelated persons. Q Corporation redeemed 21 shares of its stock (with a basis of $40,000) from W Corporation for $100,000. What are the tax consequences to W Corporation?

SECTION 3.   TERMINATION OF A SHAREHOLDER'S INTEREST

INTERNAL REVENUE CODE: Sections 302(b)(3), (c); 318.

REGULATIONS: Section 1.302–4.

Since the termination of a shareholder's interest is an example of a substantially disproportionate distribution, § 302(b)(3), treating a redemption in complete termination of a shareholder's interest as an exchange, initially appears to add little to the operation of § 302(b). It does, however, serve two major functions. First, it permits the redemption of non-voting stock to qualify for capital gain treatment without resort to the vague "not essentially equivalent to a dividend" test of § 302(b)(1). Second, if all of the stock actually owned by a shareholder is redeemed, § 302(c) permits the family attribution rules of § 318(a)(1) to be disregarded in determining if the shareholder's interest has been completely terminated. This waiver of the family attribution rules is not available under § 302(b)(2). No other attribution rules can be waived. All of the other attribution rules continue to apply when all of the stock actually owned by a shareholder has been redeemed, and the application of those attribution rules can defeat the applicability of § 302(b)(3).

DETAILED ANALYSIS

1. SERIAL REDEMPTIONS

A frequent issue under § 302(b)(3) is the treatment of redemptions of less than all of a shareholder's stock in each of a series of redemptions where the ultimate result is the complete termination of the shareholder's interest. If there is a firm and fixed plan to eliminate the shareholder from the corporation, the component redemptions will be treated as a single redemption of the shareholder's entire interest. The plan does not need to be enforceable or in writing, but it must be more than a handshake. "Generally, a gentleman's agreement lacking written embodiment, communication, and contractual obligations will not suffice to show a fixed and firm plan. * * * On the other hand, a plan need not be in writing, absolutely binding, or communicated to others to be fixed and firm although these factors all tend to indicate that such is the case." Bleily & Collishaw, Inc. v. Commissioner, 72 T.C. 751 (1979), aff'd by order, 647 F.2d 169 (9th Cir.1981). If the time frame for the redemption is vague and the redeemed shareholder retains control over corporate affairs in the interim, however, the individual transactions will not be aggregated; the preliminary redemptions will be treated as § 301 distributions. Benjamin v. Commissioner, 592 F.2d 1259 (5th Cir.1979). In Johnston v. Commissioner, 77 T.C. 679 (1981), a shareholder and a closely held family corporation agreed to the annual redemption of 40 shares. In each of the years 1976, 1977, and 1978, the corporation redeemed 40 shares, but no redemptions occurred in 1974, 1975, and 1979. The shareholder did not attempt to enforce the corporation's redemption obligation in the years when it failed to redeem her shares. The court held that the 1976 redemption was not an integrated step in a firm and fixed plan to redeem the taxpayer's shares, and thus the distribution was essentially equivalent to a dividend.

Merrill Lynch & Co., Inc. v. Commissioner, 386 F.3d 464 (2d Cir. 2004), aff'g 120 T.C. 12 (2003), is the most recent case to examine whether all of the individual transactions in a series of redemptions should be viewed together as a complete termination for purposes of § 302(b)(3) or whether the preliminary transactions must be tested only under other subsections for qualification under § 302. Because the taxpayer-shareholder in that case was a corporation, it was to the taxpayer's advantage to classify the transactions as dividends rather than as redemptions. The IRS argued that § 302(b)(3) applied and that the distributions were not dividends. The Second Circuit affirmed the Tax Court's holding that the series of transactions should be viewed as a single complete redemption because they were effected pursuant to a "firm and fixed plan." Both the taxpayer and IRS argued that the "firm and fixed plan" test was the proper test, but they disagreed on how the test

there was no relationship between the obligations of the parties and the financial performance of HMI. The transactional documents admitted into evidence do not indicate otherwise. There is simply no evidence that the payment terms in the lease between the Hursts and HMI vary from those that would be reasonable if negotiated between unrelated parties. And the Hursts point out that the IRS itself has ruled that an arm's-length lease allowing a redeeming corporation to use property owned by a former owner does not preclude characterization as a redemption.

Furthermore, the court did not find that Hurst's rights under the lease were in fact a retained interest, even though, subsequent to the redemption, the parties modified both the lease and the note in a transaction in which the corporation surrendered an option to purchase the leased property in exchange for a reduction in the interest rate on the note issued for the stock.

The court then considered Mrs. Hurst's employment contract:

Mrs. Hurst did not own any HMI stock. Thus, she is not a "distributee" unable to have an "interest in the corporation (including an interest as officer, director, or employee), other than an interest as a creditor." * * * The Commissioner is thus forced to argue that her employment was a "prohibited interest" for Mr. Hurst. And he does, contending that through her employment Mr. Hurst kept an ongoing influence in HMI's corporate affairs. He also argues that an employee unrelated to the former owner of the business would not continue to be paid were she to work Mrs. Hurst's admittedly minimal schedule. And he asserts that her employment was a mere ruse to provide Mr. Hurst with his company car and health benefits, bolstering this argument with proof that the truck used by Mrs. Hurst was the same one that her husband had been using when he ran HMI. None of this, though, changes the fact that her compensation and fringe benefits were fixed, and again—like the notes and lease—not subordinated to HMI's general creditors, and not subject to any fluctuation related to HMI's financial performance. Her duties, moreover, were various administrative and clerical tasks—some of the same chores she had been doing at HMI on a regular basis for many years. And there was no evidence whatsoever that Mr. Hurst used his wife in any way as a surrogate for continuing to manage (or even advise) HMI's new owners.

Somewhat surprisingly, the court concluded that the fact that a default by the corporation on its obligations to Mrs. Hurst under the employment contract, as well as a default under the lease, also constituted a default on the promissory note to Mr. Hurst, thereby triggering his right to reacquire the stock did not, under all of the facts and circumstances, constitute a prohibited retained interest. The IRS argued that "intertwin[ing] substantial corporate obligations with the employment contract of only one of 45 employees * * * [was] proof that the parties to this redemption contemplated a continuing involvement greater than that of a mere creditor." The court responded:

> [T]he proof at trial [demonstrated] that there was a legitimate creditor's interest in the Hursts' demanding [the cross collateralization provisions] * * * They were, after all, parting with a substantial asset (the corporations), in return for what was in essence an IOU from some business associates. Their ability to enjoy retirement in financial security was fully contingent upon their receiving payment on the notes, lease, and employment contract. * * * The value of that security, however, depended upon the financial health of the company. Repossessing worthless shares as security on defaulted notes would have done little to ensure the Hursts' retirement. The cross-default provisions were their canary in the coal mine. If at any point the company failed to meet any financial obligation to the Hursts, Mr. Hurst would have the option to retrieve his shares immediately, thus protecting the value of his security interest instead of worrying about whether this was the beginning of a downward spiral. This is perfectly consistent with a creditor's interest, and there was credible trial testimony that multiple default triggers are common in commercial lending.

Accordingly, the court held that:

> [T]he cross-default provisions protected the Hursts' financial interest as creditors of HMI, for a debt on which they had received practically no downpayment, and the collection of which (though not 'dependent upon the earnings of the corporation' as that phrase is used in section 1.302–4(d), Income Tax Regs.) was realistically contingent upon HMI's continued financial health. * * * The number of legal connections between Mr. Hurst and the buyers that continued after the deal was signed did not change their character as permissible security interests. Even looked at all together, they were in no way contingent upon the financial performance of the company except in the obvious sense that all creditors have in their debtors' solvency.

2.3.5.   *Stock Ownership in Fiduciary Capacity*

Whether a redeemed shareholder who retains or reacquires voting power in a fiduciary capacity has a prohibited interest depends on the nature of the fiduciary position. Rev.Rul. 81–233, 1981–2 C.B. 83, held that a redeemed shareholder, who within 10 years became a custodian under the Uniform Gift to Minors Act with respect to stock given to his children by the shareholder's parents, had acquired a prohibited interest because he had the power to vote the stock. See also Rev.Rul. 71–426, 1971–2 C.B. 173 (stock of the corporation was owned by a mother and her four children, with the children's stock held by a voting trust; retention by the mother of the position as voting trustee was a prohibited interest). If the fiduciary position is as an executor or testamentary trustee, however, the IRS has ruled that the exception for interests acquired by bequest or inheritance applies. Rev.Rul. 79–334, 1979–2 C.B. 127 (testamentary trustee); Rev.Rul. 72–380, 1972–2 C.B. 201 (executor of estate).

2.4. *Stock Acquired from a Related Party*

Under § 302(c)(2)(B), the waiver of family attribution rules might not be available if the redeemed stock was acquired by the distributee within the preceding 10-year period from a related person (a person whose stock would be attributable to the distributee). Thus, a complete termination under § 302(b)(3) is not available to a husband-distributee who received the redeemed stock from his wife within the 10-year period. Waiver of family attribution also is unavailable if within the 10-year period the distributee gave stock to a related person (e.g., the wife above is the distributee).

However, the limitation of § 302(c)(2)(B), does not apply unless one of the principal purposes of the acquisition or disposition was tax avoidance. See § 302(c)(2)(B), flush language, and Treas.Reg. § 1.302–4(g), last sentence. The IRS has issued a number of rulings dealing with the question of whether transfers of stock between related parties within 10 years of the redemption were tax avoidance transactions. Rev.Rul. 77–293, 1977–2 C.B. 91, held that tax avoidance was not present in a case in which a father made a gift of a part of his stock to his son concurrently with a redemption of the remainder of the stock from the father. The purpose of the gift was to give the son control of the corporation in connection with the transfer to him of management responsibility. In Rev.Rul. 85–19, 1985–1 C.B. 94, a minority shareholder first sold to his father, the controlling shareholder, a number of shares received from the father by gift two years earlier, and the corporation then immediately redeemed the son's remaining shares, which he had acquired by bequest. The ruling held that there was no tax avoidance motive present and suggests that tax avoidance exists only if the transferor seeks to retain indirect control, such as by transferring stock to a spouse prior to a redemption of all of the shares actually owned, or if the transfer is in contemplation of a redemption of the shares from the transferee. See also Rev.Rul. 79–67, 1979–1 C.B. 128 (distribution of stock from estate to beneficiary to qualify redemption from beneficiary under § 302(b)(3) is not tax avoidance); Rev.Rul. 82–129, 1982–2 C.B. 76 (partition of stock held as community property is not a transfer).

2.5. *Waiver of Family Attribution by Entities*

Section 302(c)(2)(C) permits waiver of the family attribution rules by an entity to avoid attribution from a third party through the owner of an interest in the entity where the owner of the beneficial interest owns no stock directly. The attribution rules may be waived if after the redemption neither the entity (trust, estate, partnership, or corporation) nor the beneficiaries, partners, or shareholders hold an interest in the redeeming corporation and if both agree not to acquire such an interest in the stipulated 10 year period. Under § 302(c)(2)(C), only the *family* attribution rules may be waived; the attribution rules between entity and beneficiary may not be waived. For example, suppose A owns 50% of the stock of X Corporation and Trust T, created by a deceased aunt for the benefit of A's children, owns 50%. Under § 318, A's children are deemed to own A's stock and the trust is deemed to own the stock of the children. If all of the stock actually owned by the trust is redeemed, the trust can take advantage of the waiver of the family attribution rules provided in § 302(c)(2) and treat the redemption as a complete termination under § 302(b)(3).

3. BASIS OF STOCK REDEEMED IN NONQUALIFYING TRANSACTION

If a redemption is treated as a § 301 distribution under § 302(d), the basis of the redeemed shares is allocated to the shareholder's remaining shares. If the shareholder's actual interest is completely terminated but, due to the family attribution rules, the shareholder's entire interest has not been terminated, the basis of the redeemed shares should be added to the basis of the related person whose shares were attributed to the redeemed shareholder. Treas.Reg. § 1.302–2(c); see also Levin v. Commissioner, 385 F.2d 521 (2d Cir.1967) (basis of parent's redeemed shares added to basis of son's shares).

Prop.Reg. § 1.302–5 (2009), would have replaced the basis adjustment rules in Treas.Reg. § 1.302–2(c). Under the 2009 Proposed Regulations, the redeemed shareholder's basis in the redeemed stock would not shift to the related person whose stock ownership precluded § 302(b)(3) from applying, but would be retained by the redeemed shareholder. That basis would then generate a loss deduction at some future date, for example, upon the sale by the related shareholder of that shareholder's stock in the corporation. Although the 2009 Proposed Regulations were withdrawn, the Treasury warned in the withdrawal notice: "any unrecovered basis in the redeemed stock of a shareholder may be shifted to other stock only if such an adjustment is a proper adjustment within the meaning of § 1.302–2(c). Not all shifts of a redeemed shareholder's unrecovered basis result in proper adjustments, and certain basis adjustments can lead to inappropriate results." 84 Fed. Reg. 11687 (Mar. 28, 2019).

PROBLEM SET 3

1. Tony and Cora each owned 50 shares of stock in Tocoa Corporation. Tocoa redeemed all 50 shares of Cora's stock for $1,000,000 in cash. Cora continued to work full-time for Tocoa as public relations manager. Tony is Cora's nephew. Does the redemption distribution qualify under § 302(b)(3)?

2. Paradise Scenic Railway Corp. has 100 shares of voting common stock outstanding. Seventy shares are owned by Henry, and 30 shares are owned by his granddaughter, Jean. Which, if any, of the following redemption transactions qualify under § 302(b)(3)?

(a) Paradise redeems all of Henry's shares for a lump sum cash payment.

(b) (1) Paradise redeems all of Henry's shares for a promissory note, payable in ten equal annual principal installments (including interest at the prime rate plus 3%), and the note is secured by a mortgage lien on all of the corporation's assets.

(2) Same as in (b)(1), but Paradise agrees that during the term of the note it will not pay any dividends, incur any indebtedness outside the ordinary course of business, or acquire

any new business, be acquired, or liquidate, without Henry's consent.

    (3)   Same as in (b)(1) but Henry agrees to subordinate his note to any third party lender to the corporation upon request.

    (4)   Paradise redeems all of Henry's shares for a promissory note, the principal of which is payable in a lump sum in 10 years, with annual interest payable at the prime rate plus 3%, but if the corporation would have to borrow from a third party lender to make an interest payment the interest payment can be deferred until the due date of the principal.

3.   Bassbuster Boat Corp. has 100 shares of common stock outstanding. Roland owns 60 shares, and his son Orlando owns 40 shares. Roland plans to retire this year and turn complete management of the company over to Orlando. Because the corporation has inadequate retained earnings to redeem all of Roland's stock at one time and cannot borrow sufficient money to do so without incurring unreasonable business risks, the corporation will redeem 15 of Roland's shares this year and 15 shares in each of the next three years. Assuming that Roland files the § 302(c)(2) agreement, can the redemptions this year and in each of the next two years, as well as the final redemption, all qualify under § 302(b)(3)?

4.   Advanced Motor Car Concepts, Inc. has two shareholders, Tucker, who owns 60 shares, and his son, Edsel, who owns 40 shares. If the corporation redeems all of Tuckers's shares and Tucker files the § 302(c)(2) agreement, will the redemption qualify under § 302(b)(3) in the following alternative circumstances.

    (a)   Tucker remains as an unpaid director of the corporation.

    (b)   The corporation promises to pay Tucker a "pension" of $20,000 for each of the next 10 years. Tucker agrees not to establish any competing business and to render such consulting services as the corporation may from time to time request.

    (c)   Tucker is a lawyer, and four years later Tucker represented the corporation in a product liability litigation matter for a contingent fee.

    (d)   Tucker is an engineer, and five years later Tucker is hired as a consultant to help eliminate problems with the design of the company's revolutionary new engine that runs on poultry waste. Tucker's compensation was a fixed fee plus a percentage of gross sales from the first five years of sales of vehicles using the new engine.

    (e)   (1)   Tucker owns the building in which the corporation's factory and offices are located, and Tucker had leased the building to the corporation. The lease, which has ten more years to go, calls for rent of $5,000 per month.

    (2)   Same as (e)(1), but contemporaneously with the redemption, the lease is renegotiated to provide for rent equal to 1% of the corporation's net profits (before taking the rent into account) or $5,000, whichever is greater.

5.   John owned 70 out of 100 shares of the common stock of Walton's Lumber Mill Corp. John's son, Benjamin, owned the other 30 shares. Determine whether the following redemption transactions qualify under § 302(b)(3).

(a)   John gave 20 shares to his grandson, Jim-Bob, and four months later Walton's Lumber Mill redeemed John's remaining 50 shares.

(b)   John gave 40 shares to his wife, Olivia, and three months later Walton's Lumber Mill redeemed John's remaining 30 shares.

(c)   John gave 20 shares to his grandson, Jim-Bob, and six months later Walton's Lumber Mill redeemed Jim-Bob's 20 shares.

6.   Sacramento Delta Yacht Basin, Inc. has 100 shares of common stock outstanding, all of which are owned by the Connor family. Alice owns 25 shares; her son Bob owns 25 shares; Alice's daughter Cybill owns 25 shares; and Bob's son Don owns 25 shares. Which, if any, of the following redemption transactions qualify under § 302(b)(3)?

(a)   The corporation redeems all of Alice's shares and Alice files the § 302(c)(2) agreement. Six years later Cybill dies and bequeaths her shares to Alice.

(b)   The corporation redeems all of Bob's shares and Bob files the § 302(c)(2) agreement.

(1)   Seven years later, Alice dies and bequeaths all of her shares in trust for Don, naming Bob as the trustee.

(2)   Instead of bequeathing her shares to the trust for Don, Alice established an *inter vivos* trust shortly before she died and transferred her shares to the trust with Bob as the trustee.

7.   E-Z Rider Motorcycle Manufacturing Corp. has 100 shares of common stock outstanding. Peter owns 25 shares and Jane, Peter's sister, owns 25 shares. The other 50 shares are owned by the estate of Henry. Henry was the father of Peter and Jane. Can a redemption of the 50 shares owned by Henry's estate qualify under § 302(b)(3) by virtue of the waiver of attribution rules under the following alternative circumstances?

(a)   Frances, who is Peter's and Jane's mother, is the sole beneficiary of the estate.

(b)   Frances is the residuary beneficiary of the estate; Peter and Jane each received specific cash bequests.

(c)   Peter and Jane are the residuary beneficiaries of the estate.

SECTION 4. DISTRIBUTIONS NOT "ESSENTIALLY EQUIVALENT TO A DIVIDEND"

INTERNAL REVENUE CODE: Sections 302(b)(1), (c)(1); 318.

REGULATIONS: Section 1.302–2.

United States v. Davis

Supreme Court of the United States, 1970.
397 U.S. 301.

■ MR. JUSTICE MARSHALL delivered the opinion of the Court.

In 1945, taxpayer and E.B. Bradley organized a corporation. In exchange for property transferred to the new company, Bradley received 500 shares of common stock, and taxpayer and his wife similarly each received 250 such shares. Shortly thereafter, taxpayer made an additional contribution to the corporation, purchasing 1,000 shares of preferred stock at a par value of $25 per share.

The purpose of this latter transaction was to increase the company's working capital and thereby to qualify for a loan previously negotiated through the Reconstruction Finance Corporation. It was understood that the corporation would redeem the preferred stock when the RFC loan had been repaid. Although in the interim taxpayer bought Bradley's 500 shares and divided them between his son and daughter, the total capitalization of the company remained the same until 1963. That year, after the loan was fully repaid and in accordance with the original understanding, the company redeemed taxpayer's preferred stock.

In his 1963 personal income tax return taxpayer did not report the $25,000 received by him upon the redemption of his preferred stock as income. Rather, taxpayer considered the redemption as a sale of his preferred stock to the company—a capital gains transaction under § 302 of the Internal Revenue Code of 1954 resulting in no tax since taxpayer's basis in the stock equaled the amount he received for it. The Commissioner of Internal Revenue, however, did not approve this tax treatment. According to the Commissioner, the redemption of taxpayer's stock was essentially equivalent to a dividend and was thus taxable as ordinary income under §§ 301 and 316 of the Code. Taxpayer paid the resulting deficiency and brought this suit for a refund. The District Court ruled in his favor, 274 F.Supp. 466 (M.D.Tenn.1967), and on appeal the Court of Appeals affirmed. 408 F.2d 1139 (6th Cir.1969).

The Court of Appeals held that the $25,000 received by taxpayer was "not essentially equivalent to a dividend" within the meaning of that phrase in § 302(b)(1) of the Code because the redemption was the final step in a course of action that had a legitimate business (as opposed to a tax avoidance) purpose. That holding represents only one of a variety of treatments accorded similar transactions under § 302(b)(1) in the circuit courts of appeals.[2] We granted certiorari * * * in order to resolve this recurring tax question involving stock redemptions by closely held corporations. We reverse.

The Internal Revenue Code of 1954 provides generally in §§ 301 and 316 for the tax treatment of distributions by a corporation to its shareholders; under those provisions, a distribution is includable in a taxpayer's gross income as a dividend out of earnings and profits to the extent such earnings exist. There are exceptions to the application of these general provisions, however, and among them are those found in § 302 involving certain distributions for redeemed stock. The basic question in this case is whether the $25,000 distribution by the corporation to taxpayer falls under that section—more specifically, whether its legitimate business motivation qualifies the distribution under § 302(b)(1) of the Code. Preliminarily, however, we must consider the relationship between § 302(b)(1) and the rules regarding the attribution of stock ownership found in § 318(a) of the Code.

Under subsection (a) of § 302, a distribution is treated as "payment in exchange for the stock," thus qualifying for capital gains rather than ordinary income treatment, if the conditions contained in any one of the four paragraphs of subsection (b) are met. In addition to paragraph (1)'s "not essentially equivalent to a dividend" test, capital gains treatment is available where (2) the taxpayer's voting strength is substantially diminished, (3) his interest in the company is completely terminated, or (4) certain railroad stock is redeemed. Paragraph (4) is not involved here, and taxpayer admits that paragraphs (2) and (3) do not apply. Moreover, taxpayer agrees that for the purposes of §§ 302(b)(2) and (3) the attribution rules of § 318(a) apply and he is considered to own the 750 outstanding shares of common stock held by his wife and children in addition to the 250 shares in his own name.

Taxpayer, however, argues that the attribution rules do not apply in considering whether a distribution is essentially equivalent to a dividend under § 302(b)(1). According to taxpayer, he should thus be considered to own only 25 percent of the corporation's common stock, and the distribution would then qualify under § 302(b)(1) since it was not pro rata or proportionate to his stock interest, the fundamental test of dividend equivalency. See Treas.Reg. 1.302–2(b). However, the plain language of the statute compels rejection of the argument. In subsection (c) of § 302, the attribution rules are made specifically applicable "in determining the ownership of stock for purposes of this section." Applying this language,

---

[2]   Only the Second Circuit has unequivocally adopted the Commissioner's view and held irrelevant the motivation of the redemption. See Levin v. Commissioner, 385 F.2d 521 (1967). * * *

The other courts of appeals that have passed on the question are apparently willing to give at least some weight under § 302(b)(1) to the business motivation of a distribution and redemption. See, e.g., Commissioner v. Berenbaum, 369 F.2d 337 (C.A.10th Cir.1966); Kerr v. Commissioner, 326 F.2d 225 (9th Cir.1964). * * * Even among those courts that consider business purpose, however, it is generally required that the business purpose be related, not to the issuance of the stock, but to the redemption of it. * * *

both courts below held that § 318(a) applies to all of § 302, including § 302(b)(1)—a view in accord with the decisions of the other courts of appeals, a longstanding treasury regulation,[6] and the opinion of the leading commentators.[7]

Against this weight of authority, taxpayer argues that the result under paragraph (1) should be different because there is no explicit reference to stock ownership as there is in paragraphs (2) and (3). Neither that fact, however, nor the purpose and history of § 302(b)(1) support taxpayer's argument. The attribution rules—designed to provide a clear answer to what would otherwise be a difficult tax question—formed part of the tax bill that was subsequently enacted as the 1954 Code. As is discussed further, infra, the bill as passed by the House of Representatives contained no provision comparable to § 302(b)(1). When that provision was added in the Senate, no purpose was evidenced to restrict the applicability of § 318(a). Rather, the attribution rules continued to be made specifically applicable to the entire section, and we believe that Congress intended that they be taken into account wherever ownership of stock was relevant.

Indeed, it was necessary that the attribution rules apply to § 302(b)(1) unless they were to be effectively eliminated from consideration with regard to §§ 302(b)(2) and (3) also. For if a transaction failed to qualify under one of those sections solely because of the attribution rules, it would according to taxpayer's argument nonetheless qualify under § 302(b)(1). We cannot agree that Congress intended so to nullify its explicit directive. We conclude, therefore, that the attribution rules of § 318(a) do apply; and, for the purposes of deciding whether a distribution is "not essentially equivalent to a dividend" under § 302(b)(1), taxpayer must be deemed the owner of all 1,000 shares of the company's common stock.

II

After application of the stock ownership attribution rules, this case viewed most simply involves a sole stockholder who causes part of his shares to be redeemed by the corporation. We conclude that such a redemption is always "essentially equivalent to a dividend" within the meaning of that phrase in § 302(b)(1)[8] and therefore do not reach the Government's alternative argument that in any event the distribution should not on the facts of this case qualify for capital gains treatment.[9]

---

[6] See Treas.Reg. 1.302–2(b).

[7] See B. Bittker & J. Eustice, Federal Income Taxation of Corporations and Shareholders 292 n. 32 (2d ed. 1966).

[8] Of course, this just means that a distribution in redemption to a sole shareholder will be treated under the general provisions of § 301, and it will only be taxed as a dividend under § 316 to the extent that there are earnings and profits.

[9] The Government argues that even if business purpose were relevant under § 302(b)(1), the business purpose present here related only to the original investment and not at all to the necessity for redemption. See cases cited, n. 2, supra. Under either view, taxpayer does not lose

The predecessor of § 302(b)(1) came into the tax law as § 201(d) of the Revenue Act of 1921, 42 Stat. 228 * * *.

By the time of the general revision resulting in the Internal Revenue Code of 1954, the draftsmen were faced with what has aptly been described as "the morass created by the decisions." Ballenger v. United States, 301 F.2d 192, 196 (4th Cir.1962). In an effort to eliminate "the considerable confusion which exists in this area" and thereby to facilitate tax planning, H.R.Rep. No. 1337, 83d Cong., 2d Sess., 35, the authors of the new Code sought to provide objective tests to govern the tax consequences of stock redemptions. Thus, the tax bill passed by the House of Representatives contained no "essentially equivalent" language. Rather, it provided for "safe harbors" where capital gains treatment would be accorded to corporate redemptions that met the conditions now found in §§ 302(b)(2) and (3) of the Code.

It was in the Senate Finance Committee's consideration of the tax bill that § 302(b)(1) was added, and Congress thereby provided that capital gains treatment should be available "if the redemption is not essentially equivalent to a dividend." Taxpayer argues that the purpose was to continue "existing law," and there is support in the legislative history that § 302(b)(1) reverted "in part" or "in general" to the "essentially equivalent" provision of § 115(g)(1) of the 1939 Code. According to the Government, even under the old law it would have been improper for the Court of Appeals to rely on "a business purpose for the redemption" and "an absence of the proscribed tax avoidance purpose to bail out dividends at favorable tax rates." See Northup v. United States, 240 F.2d 304, 307 (2d Cir.1957); Smith v. United States, 121 F.2d 692, 695 (3d Cir.1941) * * *. However, we need not decide that question, for we find from the history of the 1954 revisions and the purpose of § 302(b)(1) that Congress intended more than merely to re-enact the prior law.

In explaining the reason for adding the "essentially equivalent" test, the Senate Committee stated that the House provisions "appeared unnecessarily restrictive, particularly, in the case of redemptions of preferred stock which might be called by the corporation without the shareholder having any control over when the redemption may take place." S.Rep. No. 1622, 83d Cong., 2d Sess., 44. This explanation gives no indication that the purpose behind the redemption should affect the result.[10] Rather, in its more detailed technical evaluation of § 302(b)(1), the Senate Committee reported as follows:

"The test intended to be incorporated in the interpretation of paragraph (1) is in general that currently employed under section

---

his basis in the preferred stock. Under Treas.Reg. 1.302–2(c) that basis is applied to taxpayer's common stock.

[10] See Bittker & Eustice, supra, n. 7 at 291: "It is not easy to give § 302(b)(1) an expansive construction in view of this indication that its major function was the narrow one of immunizing redemptions of minority holdings of preferred stock."

115(g)(1) of the 1939 Code. Your committee further intends that in applying this test for the future * * * the inquiry will be devoted solely to the question of whether or not the transaction by its nature may properly be characterized as a sale of stock by the redeeming shareholder to the corporation. For this purpose the presence or absence of earnings and profits of the corporation is not material. Example: X, the sole shareholder of a corporation having no earnings or profits causes the corporation to redeem half of its stock. Paragraph (1) does not apply to such redemption notwithstanding the absence of earnings and profits." S.Rep. No. 1622, supra, at 234.

The intended scope of § 302(b)(1) as revealed by this legislative history is certainly not free from doubt. However, we agree with the Government that by making the sole inquiry relevant for the future the narrow one whether the redemption could be characterized as a sale, Congress was apparently rejecting past court decisions that had also considered factors indicating the presence or absence of a tax-avoidance motive.[11] At least that is the implication of the example given. Congress clearly mandated that pro rata distributions be treated under the general rules laid down in §§ 301 and 316 rather than under § 302, and nothing suggests that there should be a different result if there were a "business purpose" for the redemption. Indeed, just the opposite inference must be drawn since there would not likely be a tax-avoidance purpose in a situation where there were no earnings or profits. We conclude that the Court of Appeals was therefore wrong in looking for a business purpose and considering it in deciding whether the redemption was equivalent to a dividend. Rather, we agree with the Court of Appeals for the Second Circuit that "the business purpose of a transaction is irrelevant in determining dividend equivalence" under § 302(b)(1). Hasbrook v. United States, 343 F.2d 811, 814 (1965).

Taxpayer strongly argues that to treat the redemption involved here as essentially equivalent to a dividend is to elevate form over substance. Thus, taxpayer argues, had he not bought Bradley's shares or had he made a subordinated loan to the company instead of buying preferred stock, he could have gotten back his $25,000 with favorable tax treatment. However, the difference between form and substance in the tax law is largely problematical, and taxpayer's complaints have little to

---

[11] This rejection is confirmed by the Committee's acceptance of the House treatment of distributions involving corporate contractions—a factor present in many of the earlier "business purpose" redemptions. In describing its action, the Committee stated as follows:

"Your committee, as did the House bill, separates into their significant elements the kind of transactions now incoherently aggregated in the definition of a partial liquidation. Those distributions which may have capital-gain characteristics *because they are not made pro rata* among the various shareholders, would be subjected, at the shareholder level, to the separate tests described in [§ 301 to § 318]. On the other hand, those distributions characterized by what happens solely at the corporate level by reason of the assets distributed would be included as within the concept of a partial liquidation."

S.Rep. No. 1622, supra, at 49. (Emphasis added.)

do with whether a business purpose is relevant under § 302(b)(1). It was clearly proper for Congress to treat distributions generally as taxable dividends when made out of earnings and profits and then to prevent avoidance of that result without regard to motivation where the distribution is in exchange for redeemed stock.

We conclude that that is what Congress did when enacting § 302(b)(1). If a corporation distributes property as a simple dividend, the effect is to transfer the property from the company to its shareholders without a change in the relative economic interests or rights of the stockholders. Where a redemption has that same effect, it cannot be said to have satisfied the "not essentially equivalent to a dividend" requirement of § 302(b)(1). Rather, to qualify for preferred treatment under that section, a redemption must result in a meaningful reduction of the shareholder's proportionate interest in the corporation. Clearly, taxpayer here, who (after application of the attribution rules) was the sole shareholder of the corporation both before and after the redemption, did not qualify under this test. The decision of the Court of Appeals must therefore be reversed and the case remanded to the District Court for dismissal of the complaint.

It is so ordered.

DETAILED ANALYSIS

1.   GENERAL

If a shareholder is unable to meet the "safe haven" requirements of § 302(b)(2) or § 302(b)(3), the shareholder still may fall back on the general language of § 302(b)(1), allowing capital gain treatment to distributions found to be not essentially equivalent to a dividend. But the *Davis* case makes the task of the shareholder attempting to fit the transaction under § 302(b)(1) very difficult.

First, the Court's holding that the attribution rules of § 318 apply to § 302(b)(1) situations means that, in a family-held corporation context, the shareholder almost invariably will be deemed to own a higher percentage of stock than is actually owned, and hence the distribution to the shareholder will more likely have or approach the pro rata character of a dividend distribution. For examples where the shareholder was deemed to own 100% of the stock of the corporation and hence the distribution was treated as a dividend, see Title Insurance and Trust Co. v. United States, 484 F.2d 462 (9th Cir.1973); Johnson v. United States, 434 F.2d 340 (8th Cir.1970); and Rev.Rul. 71–261, 1971–1 C.B. 108. Indeed, in some cases the interaction of the attribution rules and the redemption can actually *increase* the redeemed shareholder's interest after the redemption. See, e.g., Sawelson v. Commissioner, 61 T.C. 109 (1973).

Second, the Court's elimination of the "business purpose" factor in determining dividend equivalence under § 302(b)(1) removes from consideration any argument based on the reasons for the redemption (presumably including "shareholder" purposes, see Nicholson v.

Commissioner, 17 T.C. 1399 (1952)), and focuses attention solely on the "effect" of the distribution. The factors discussed below, some of which were developed in prior case law dealing with dividend equivalence, remain relevant after *Davis,* with the exception of those cases whose result turned on a finding of "business purpose" for the redemption.

Could the taxpayer in *Davis* have avoided the dividend result if, instead of receiving the preferred stock, he had made a subordinated loan to the corporation of $25,000?

2. "MEANINGFUL REDUCTION" IN THE SHAREHOLDER'S INTEREST

2.1. *Voting Stock*

2.1.1. *Effect on Control*

In attempting to give some content to the "meaningful reduction" standard set forth by the Supreme Court in *Davis,* subsequent cases and Revenue Rulings have focused principally on the effect that the redemption has on the shareholder's voting control of the corporation. Thus, in Rev.Rul. 75–502, 1975–2 C.B. 111, a redemption that reduced the shareholder's voting stock interest in the corporation from 57% to 50%, the other 50% being held by a single unrelated shareholder, qualified as a meaningful reduction. Rev.Rul. 75–502 indicated that if the redemption had not reduced the shareholder's interest in the voting stock to 50% or less, then § 302(b)(1) would not have been applicable. Compare Rev.Rul. 77–218, 1977–1 C.B. 81 (8% reduction in actual and constructive ownership that left the shareholder with more than 50% of the voting stock because of the attribution rules was not a meaningful reduction even though all of the shares actually owned by the taxpayer were redeemed). Benjamin v. Commissioner, 66 T.C. 1084 (1976), aff'd, 592 F.2d 1259 (5th Cir.1979), involving a redemption of voting preferred stock, found that the redemption did not qualify under § 302(b)(1) because of the shareholder's continuing voting control over the corporation after the redemption. The facts that the shareholder's interest in the net worth of the corporation and the right to participate in its earnings were reduced were not sufficient since "the retention of absolute voting control in the present case outweighs any other considerations."

Roebling v. Commissioner, 77 T.C. 30 (1981), involved the redemption of voting preferred stock pursuant to a plan of the corporation to redeem all of its outstanding preferred stock over a number of years. Before the series of redemptions commenced, the shareholder held 91.94% of the preferred stock and 39.6% of the common stock, which gave her 57.12% of the total voting shares. If the plan had been carried out in full, the shareholder would have been left with less than 40% of the voting stock of the corporation, which had approximately 500 shareholders. For the years in question, however, the shareholder's voting power was only reduced to 43.28%. Because the shareholder's voting power was reduced from majority control to less than 50%, the court concluded that the reduction was meaningful. This conclusion was reinforced by the reduction in the percentage of total dividend distributions that would be receivable by the taxpayer as a result of the redemption.

Rickey v. United States, 427 F.Supp. 484 (W.D.La.1976), aff'd on other grounds, 592 F.2d 1251 (5th Cir.1979), held that a reduction in voting stock from 72% to 58% was a qualifying redemption because the shareholder lost the ability to control the two-thirds vote necessary for certain corporate actions—e.g., amending the Articles of Incorporation, merger or consolidation, the voluntary sale, lease, exchange or disposition of all or substantially all of the assets of the corporation, or liquidation and dissolution—under the state corporation law. Henry T. Patterson Trust v. United States, 729 F.2d 1089 (6th Cir.1984), reached the same result in a case in which the shareholder's interest was reduced from 80% to 60%. This analysis was rejected by the IRS in Rev.Rul. 78–401, 1978–2 C.B. 127, which held that a reduction from 90% to 60% did not qualify under § 302(b)(1); the shareholder still had the right to control the day-to-day operations of the corporation, and the fact that he gave up the right to control actions requiring a two-thirds vote under state corporation law was not sufficient.

Situations involving redemptions of voting stock held by minority shareholders are analyzed similarly. In Rev.Rul. 76–364, 1976–2 C.B. 91, the shareholder held 27% of the voting stock of the corporation, and three other unrelated shareholders each had a 24.3% interest. A redemption that reduced the shareholder's 27% interest to 22.27% was held to be a meaningful reduction since through the redemption the shareholder lost the ability to control the corporation by acting in conjunction with only one of the other shareholders. See also Rev.Rul. 75–512, 1975–2 C.B. 112 (a reduction from 30% actual and constructive ownership to 24.3% constructive ownership qualified under § 302(b)(1) because all of the shares actually owned were redeemed). However, a small reduction in the interest of a minority shareholder who retains a large interest does not qualify. Rodgers P. Johnson Trust v. Commissioner, 71 T.C. 941 (1979) (acq.), held that a reduction from 43.6% to 40.8% of the voting stock of the corporation was not meaningful. Furthermore, in Conopco, Inc. v. United States, 100 A.F.T.R.2d 2007–5296 (D. N.J. 2007), the court held that periodic redemptions of stock from an Employee Stock Ownership Plan (ESOP) trust, the largest of which reduced the trust's interest from 2.7884% to 2.7809%, which was a reduction of only 7.5 thousandths of 1% (0.0075%), qualified as a dividend (which permitted a corporate deduction for the distribution to the ESOP under § 404(k)(1)).[1] The court concluded that none of the redemption distributions meaningfully reduced the trust's interest in the corporation.

Redemptions from shareholders of publicly traded corporations usually qualify under § 301(b)(1), but do not automatically do so. Rev.Rul. 76–385, 1976–2 C.B. 92, held that § 302(b)(1) applied to a redemption resulting in a 3.3% reduction in share ownership of a shareholder who had a .0001118% interest in a publicly held corporation. Because the shareholder effectively had no control at all with respect to the operation of the corporation, a 3.3% reduction in share ownership was meaningful. However, Rev.Rul. 81–289,

---

[1] The court also held that the dividend was not a deductible distribution to the ESOP under § 162(k), which bars a deduction for any expense incurred by a corporation in reacquisition of its stock. Accord, Ralston Purina Co. v. Commissioner, 131 T.C. 29 (2008), and General Mills v. United States, 103 A.F.T.R.2d 2009–589 (8th Cir. 2009).

1981–2 C.B. 82, held that a redemption of 2% of the stock of a shareholder holding less than 1% of a publicly traded corporation's outstanding stock was essentially equivalent to a dividend because simultaneous redemptions from other shareholders resulted in a total redemption of 2% of the corporation's outstanding stock. Thus, the shareholder's proportionate interest was unchanged.

2.1.2. *Effect of "Family Hostility" on Application of Constructive Stock Ownership Rules*

If, after the redemption, the shareholder's directly owned stock is insufficient to provide control but the shareholder is deemed to own over 50% of the voting stock because of the attribution rules, the shareholder is still treated as the controlling shareholder for purposes of testing the meaningful reduction in the shareholder's interest. See, e.g., Fehrs Finance Co. v. Commissioner, 487 F.2d 184 (8th Cir.1973); Rev.Rul. 77–218, supra. While *Davis* indicates that the attribution rules apply in such a situation, *Davis* could be viewed as permitting this shareholder to argue that where the related parties in fact were in disagreement, the attribution rules should not be applied in testing control. Several pre-*Davis* cases had adopted this approach. See, e.g., Estate of Squier v. Commissioner, 35 T.C. 950 (1961) (nonacq.). In the first case to raise the issue following *Davis*, however, the Tax Court held that the *Davis* view of the attribution rules precluded applying a "family fight" exception. Robin Haft Trust v. Commissioner, 61 T.C. 398 (1973). The Court of Appeals, 510 F.2d 43 (1st Cir.1975), reversed and remanded the case for consideration of whether "the existence of family discord [tended] to negate the presumption that taxpayers would exert continuing control over the corporation despite the redemption." In Rev.Rul. 80–26, 1980–1 C.B. 66, the IRS announced that it would not follow the Court of Appeals decision in *Robin Haft Trust* on the theory that a "family hostility" exception to the attribution rules is inconsistent with both *Davis* and the legislative history of § 302(b)(1). Likewise, the Fifth Circuit, in David Metzger Trust v. Commissioner, 693 F.2d 459 (5th Cir.1982), held that there is no family hostility exception to the attribution rules.

The Tax Court rejected any possibility of a family hostility or "bad blood" exception to the application of the § 318 attribution rules in Niedermeyer v. Commissioner, 62 T.C. 280 (1974), aff'd per curiam 535 F.2d 500 (9th Cir.1976). Subsequently, however, in Cerone v. Commissioner, 87 T.C. 1, 22 (1986), the Tax Court described the relevance of family hostility as follows:

> First, the attribution rules are plainly and straightforwardly applied. Second, a determination is made whether there has been a reduction in the stockholder's proportionate interest in the corporation. If not, the inquiry ends because, if there is no change in the stockholder's interest, dividend equivalency results. If there has been a reduction, then all of the facts and circumstances must be examined to see if the reduction was meaningful under *United States v. Davis,* supra. It is at this point, *and only then,* that family hostility becomes an appropriate factor for consideration.

Since the shareholder's interest in *Cerone* was not reduced, this version of the family hostility doctrine was, on the facts, inapplicable.

The circumscribed family hostility doctrine of *Cerone* could lead to unusual results. Suppose the stock of X Corp. is held as follows: A, 41 shares; B, 34 shares; C, 17 shares; and D, 8 shares. A and B are parent and child, but the shareholders are otherwise unrelated. If there was "bad blood" between A and B, a redemption of as few as one of B's shares might qualify under § 302(b)(1). But if ten shares were redeemed from each of B and C, the redemption never could qualify because, taking into account the attribution rules, B's ownership increased from 75% to 81.25%, even though actual ownership was reduced from 34% to 24% and A alone now holds actual voting control of the corporation. See Henry T. Patterson Trust v. United States, 729 F.2d 1089 (6th Cir.1984), in which all of the stock actually owned by the taxpayer was redeemed; in an alternative holding the court concluded that due to family hostility there was a meaningful reduction even though after applying the attribution rules, the taxpayer's interest was reduced only from 97% to 93%.

2.2. *Non-Voting Stock*

If a redemption of non-voting stock is involved, the "meaningful reduction" is tested in terms of the change in the shareholder's rights with respect to the corporation's earnings and profits and assets on liquidation. See Himmel v. Commissioner, 338 F.2d 815 (2d Cir.1964), analyzing the "complex of shareholder rights" in a situation involving a multi-class capitalization. Rev.Rul. 75–502, 1975–2 C.B. 111, describes "a shareholder's interest to include (1) the right to vote and thereby exercise control: (2) the right to participate in current earnings and accumulated surplus; and (3) the right to share in net assets on liquidation." Rev.Rul. 77–426, 1977–2 C.B. 87, held that any redemption of non-voting preferred stock constituted a meaningful reduction for purposes of § 302(b)(1) in a situation in which the stockholder did not hold directly or indirectly any voting common stock. The rights given up in the redemption were permanently lost and not retained through continuing common stock ownership.

On the other hand, if a preferred shareholder continues to own common stock, achieving a meaningful reduction with respect to a redemption of nonvoting preferred stock is much more difficult. For example in Hays v. Commissioner, T.C. Memo. 1971–95, the taxpayer owned 80% of the common stock of the corporation and all of the preferred stock. A redemption of 10% of the preferred stock was found to result in a dividend to the shareholder: "The redemption of 300 out of 3,000 shares of preferred stock held by Hays could not be termed 'meaningful.' Also, whatever significance the reduction might have standing alone, its importance is diminished upon consideration of the fact that Hays remained owner of 80 percent of the common stock in [the corporation]. Thus while his right to earnings and profits via the preferred stock was reduced * * *, he continued to have access to 80 percent of that amount via his common stock. Since Hays owned the overwhelming majority of the common, the only voting stock, his ability to declare dividends was assured." Rev.Rul. 85–106, 1985–2 C.B. 116, involved a redemption of two-thirds of a shareholder's non-voting preferred stock. Prior to the redemption, the shareholder, which was a trust, directly held approximately 18% of each of the nonvoting preferred stock and nonvoting common stock and, by attribution from its sole beneficiary, approximately 18% of the voting common stock. The ruling held that the redemption was essentially equivalent to a dividend because, after taking into account attribution, the redeemed shareholder's potential for participating in a control group by aligning itself with two other stockholders, who together held 38% of the voting common stock, was not reduced.

2.3. *Comparative Dividend Analysis*

Another approach to the problem of dividend equivalence is to compare the distribution on redemption with the distribution of a similar amount as a hypothetical dividend. This approach was applied in Himmel v. Commissioner, 338 F.2d 815 (2d Cir.1964), to hold that a redemption of preferred stock was not essentially equivalent to a dividend because the taxpayer received a substantially larger distribution in the redemption than would have been received as a dividend on the common stock. In contrast, Levin v. Commissioner, 385 F.2d 521 (2d Cir 1967), found that a redemption was essentially equivalent to a dividend where the redemption resulted in the shareholder receiving a distribution that was substantially less than would have been received had the distribution been a dividend on the common stock.

While the *Davis* opinion does not discuss this so-called "comparative dividend" method, it is not necessarily inconsistent with the Court's focus on the effect rather than the purpose of the distribution. In Grabowski Trust v. Commissioner, 58 T.C. 650 (1972), the Tax Court applied comparative dividend analysis, finding it consistent with *Davis*.

> In testing for dividend equivalency under this subsection, the Supreme Court in United States v. Davis, 397 U.S. 301 (1970), has now approved application of the "strict net effect" test * * *. This test considers whether the shareholders would have received the identical payments had the redemption been a dividend. In essence, the test measures whether the distribution has altered the shareholder's control over the corporation or the shareholder's rights to future earnings.

In that case the court held the redemption to be essentially equivalent to a dividend because (1) the redemption caused no reduction in the taxpayer's proportionate interest in the corporation, (2) had the distribution instead been a dividend, the taxpayer would have received more than it did in the actual redemption; and (3) the redemption caused an increase in the taxpayer's interest in the corporation's net worth.

Other cases decided after *Davis*, however, have rejected comparative dividend analysis. Brown v. United States, 477 F.2d 599 (6th Cir.1973), held the approach is inconsistent with *Davis*. Similarly, in Rev.Rul. 85–106, 1985–2 C.B. 116, the IRS rejected the use of comparative dividend analysis, stating that "*Himmel* fails to reflect developments in the law represented by *Davis*." In that ruling, the nonvoting common stock of an 18% shareholder capable of forming a majority control block (56%) with two other 19%

shareholders (the other 44% of the stock being widely held) was redeemed. The IRS ruled that § 302(b)(1) did not apply; because the shareholder's opportunity to act in concert with two other shareholders to form a control group was undiminished, there was no meaningful reduction of the shareholder's interest under *Davis*, notwithstanding the reduction in the shareholder's economic interest.

Do these developments since *Davis* indicate that in the redemption area Congress should rely exclusively on mechanical tests such as that in § 302(b)(2)?

3. INSUFFICIENT EARNINGS AND PROFITS

Suppose a distribution in redemption of stock is made under circumstances that would make it essentially equivalent to a dividend, but there are no current or accumulated earnings and profits. Treas.Reg. § 1.302–2(a) states that, despite the verbal difficulty of calling the distribution "essentially equivalent to a dividend," it should nevertheless be governed by § 302(d) and § 301(c) rather than § 302(a). The distribution would thus be applied against the basis of *all* of the distributee's stock, rather than only the redeemed stock, and taxable gain results only if the distributee's entire basis is exceeded.

PROBLEM SET 4

1.   Blueberry E-Mail Systems, Inc. has 100 shares of common stock outstanding, which are owned as follows:

Amanda	Bill	Clarissa	Derek
28	25	24	23

In each of the following alternative situations, determine whether the redemption qualifies as not essentially equivalent to a dividend under § 302(b)(1).

(a) (1) Blueberry redeems 5 shares from Bill, who is Amanda's son. The shareholders are otherwise unrelated.

(2) Blueberry redeems 5 shares from Amanda, who is Bill's mother. Amanda, who is a graduate of Enormous State University, and Bill have not been on speaking terms since Bill refused to attend ESU and instead enrolled at Athletic State A & M University, ESU's biggest sports rival.

(b) Blueberry redeems 5 shares from Clarissa, who is Amanda's daughter. The shareholders are otherwise unrelated.

(c) Blueberry redeems 4 shares from Clarissa, who is Amanda's daughter. The shareholders are otherwise unrelated.

(d) Blueberry redeems 7 shares from Amanda. The shareholders are unrelated.

(e) Blueberry redeems 5 shares from Derek, who is Clarissa's brother. The shareholders are otherwise unrelated.

2.   Organic Dairies, Inc. has 100 shares of common stock and 100 shares of nonvoting preferred stock outstanding. The preferred stock is not convertible into common stock and is not § 306 stock. Y Corp. is owned by the following unrelated shareholders.

Shareholder	Common	Preferred
Alonzo	60	10
Berta	25	55
Colin	15	15
Donna	0	20

(a)   If Organic Dairies, Inc. redeems 5 preferred shares from Donna, will the redemption qualify under § 302(b)?

(b)   If Organic Dairies, Inc. redeems all of its outstanding preferred stock, with respect to which shareholders will the redemption qualify under § 302(b)?

SECTION 5.   PARTIAL LIQUIDATIONS

INTERNAL REVENUE CODE: Section 302(b)(4), (e).

REGULATIONS: Sections 1.346–1, –2, –3.

Section 302(b)(4) extends sale or exchange treatment to redemptions of stock from *individual* shareholders in "partial liquidation" of the distributing corporation. The term "partial liquidation" is defined in § 302(e), and that definition makes clear that unlike the redemptions described in § 302(b)(1) through (b)(3), which focus upon the effect of the distribution to the shareholder, whether a distribution qualifies as a partial liquidation is determined with reference to its effect on the corporation. Although the statutory language of § 302(e)(1) refers to a distribution "not essentially equivalent to a dividend (determined at the corporate level rather than at the shareholder level)," § 302(e) is concerned with the concept of a distribution in connection with a "corporate contraction." The lineage of § 302(e) can be traced through former § 346(a)(2) of the 1954 Code back to provisions of the 1939 Code. The provision was described in the Conference Committee Report accompanying its enactment as "continuing" the law under former § 346(a)(2). See S.Rep. No. 83–1622, 83rd Cong., 2d Sess. 49, 261–2 (1954). The case law under the 1939 Code had focused on corporate contraction as the test for a partial liquidation. See, e.g., Blaschka v. United States, 393 F.2d 983 (Ct.Cl.1968) (distribution was essentially equivalent to a dividend "in that there was no contraction of [the corporation's] business"); see also Treas.Reg. § 1.346–1(a) ("genuine contraction of the corporate business"). While there is relatively little recent case law with respect to the "contraction" doctrine, the IRS has issued a number of rulings that provide guidelines in the area, and the case law under the 1939 Code and former § 346(a)(2) of the 1954 Code continues to be relevant under § 302(e)(1). See H.Rep. No. 97–760, 97th Cong.2d Sess. 530 (1982).

Section 302(e)(2) provides a mechanical safe harbor rule that satisfies the not essentially equivalent to a dividend requirement under § 302(e)(1) if it is met. If the distribution consists of *all* of the assets, or the proceeds from the sale, of an *active* trade or business conducted for at least five years (which was not acquired by the corporation within the five year period in a taxable transaction), *and* after the distribution the corporation continues to conduct an *active* trade or business with a similar five year history, the distribution is not essentially equivalent to a dividend.

Whether the distribution is pro rata or not is immaterial for purposes of § 302(e)(2). I.R.C. § 302(e)(4). Thus, although technically the attribution of ownership rules apply, as a practical matter they are not a factor under § 302(e).

As in the other redemption situations, classification of a transaction as a partial liquidation is important to the shareholders to permit a recovery of basis, absorb otherwise realized capital losses, and take advantage of the preferential rates accorded long-term capital gains.

Estate of Chandler v. Commissioner[*]
Tax Court of the United States, 1954.
22 T.C. 1158.

[All of the petitioners were stockholders of Chandler-Singleton Company (hereinafter referred to as the Company), a Tennessee corporation organized on May 9, 1923. The capital stock of the Company consisted of 500 shares of common stock of $100 par value, all of which was outstanding until November 7, 1946. The stock was essentially all held by the Chandler family group. From its organization until February 28, 1946, the Company was engaged in the operation of a general department store in Maryville, Tennessee. It had a ladies' ready-to-wear department, men's department, children's department, piece goods department, and a bargain basement.

Chandler was the president and manager of the Company. At the beginning of 1944 he was in very poor health. John W. Bush was the secretary of the Company, but until 1944 he had not been particularly active in its affairs. On January 1, 1944, he became assistant manager of the Company. By profession he was a civil engineer, but at that time he was unemployed due to a change in the administration of the City of Knoxville, Tennessee. During 1944 and 1945 Chandler was sick most of the time. In his absence John W. Bush managed the department store.

---

[*] [Eds.: The Tax Court's decision was affirmed, 228 F.2d 909 (6th Cir.1955), with the court stating that the finding as to dividend equivalence was a finding of fact sustained by the evidence. Some courts, however, would call this a conclusion of law.]

John W. Bush did not like being a merchant and decided to return to engineering. In November 1945 he informed Chandler that he was resigning as manager at the end of the year. Chandler, feeling unable to manage the department store himself, decided to sell.

At a stockholders' meeting held on February 20, 1946, it was unanimously agreed that the Company should accept an offer to purchase its merchandise, furniture and fixtures, and lease. The sale was consummated and the Company ceased operating the department store on February 28, 1946. The purchaser, Arthur's Incorporated, moved in that night and began operating the store the following day.

Chandler had worked hard in the department store and had no outside interest. He wanted something to do and did not want to get out of business entirely. It was planned that a ladies' ready-to-wear store would be opened by the Company to be managed by Clara T. McConnell (now Clara M. Register) who had managed the ladies' ready-to-wear department of the department store. Thirty shares of stock in the Company owned by Chandler's wife were cancelled on April 5, 1946. Ten of these shares were issued to Clara McConnell on April 13, 1946, in order that she might have an interest in the Company whose store she was going to manage. A men's store, to be eventually taken over by the eldest son of John and Margaret Bush, was also contemplated. It was thought that approximately half of the assets of the Company would be needed for each of the two stores.

About the first of June, 1946, the Company obtained space for the ladies' ready-to-wear store about one-half block from the old department store and the store was opened on September 23, 1946.

The ladies' ready-to-wear store was about the same size as that department in the former department store. The department store had occupied 8,000 to 9,000 square feet of floor space, had employed 10 to 20 persons, and had carried fire insurance in the amount of $65,000 on its stock and fixtures. The new store had approximately 1,800 square feet of floor space, employed four to six persons, and carried fire insurance in the amount of $10,000.

A special meeting of the stockholders was held on September 28, 1946, the minutes of which read in part as follows:

"The Chairman explained that the purpose of the meeting was to authorize partial liquidation for the following reasons:

"The old business was sold and plans were developed to go back into business, operating two stores, a ladies' ready-to-wear business and a men's store. The ladies' ready-to-wear store has been opened and is now operating. Up to now, we have been unable to negotiate a lease for a suitable location, and, after considerable thought, it has been decided to abandon the idea of operating an exclusive men's shop and operate only the one store at the present time. It appears that requirements of the one store will be approximately one-half the capital now invested in Chandler's, Inc.

"Upon motion of Margaret Chandler Bush, seconded by J.W. Bush, and unanimously carried, the officials were authorized and instructed to redeem from each shareholder one-half of his stock, paying therefor the book value, which is approximately $269.00 per share."

On November 7, 1946, each stockholder turned in one-half of his stock in return for cash, the total distributed being $67,250.

The amount of cash and United States Bonds possessed by the Company at the beginning of 1946 exceeded the amount required for the current operation of the business by approximately $45,000. Between January 1 and February 28, 1946, the Company's earned surplus increased by $39,460.44 out of which the Company paid dividends in the amount of $12,500. To the extent of at least $58,027.91, the excess cash possessed by the Company prior to the November 7 distribution was not created by a reduction in the amount of capital needed to operate the Company's business.

Petitioners reported the excess of the payments received over the cost of the stock in their individual income tax returns as capital gain. Respondent treated the payments, to the extent of the earned surplus of $58,027.91, as dividends and taxed them to the petitioners as ordinary income.

The acquisition and cancellation of one-half the Company's stock in 1946 was done at such a time and in such a manner as to make the distribution and cancellation essentially equivalent to the distribution of a taxable dividend to the extent of $58,027.91.]

OPINION

■ BRUCE, JUDGE: Respondent contends that the Company's pro rata distribution in redemption of half its capital stock at book value was made at such a time and in such a manner as to make the distribution essentially equivalent to the distribution of a taxable dividend to the extent of earnings and profits. If respondent's contention is correct the distribution to the extent of earnings and profits loses [its capital gain status and is treated as a taxable dividend].

A cancellation or redemption by a corporation of all of the stock of a particular shareholder has been held not to be essentially equivalent to the distribution of a taxable dividend. Cf. Carter Tiffany, 16 T.C. 1443; Zenz v. Quinlivan, (C.A.6), 213 F.2d 914 * * *. However, "A cancellation or redemption by a corporation of its stock pro rata among all the shareholders will generally be considered as effecting a distribution essentially equivalent to a dividend distribution to the extent of the earnings and profits accumulated after February 28, 1913." Regs. 111, sec. 29.115–9. * * * But, as pointed out by the regulations, a pro rata distribution is not always "essentially equivalent to the distribution of a taxable dividend" and each case depends upon its own particular circumstances. Commissioner v. Sullivan, (C.A.5), 210 F.2d 607, affirming John L. Sullivan, 17 T.C. 1420. The circumstances in the instant case, however, do not warrant a finding that to the extent of earnings and profits the pro rata distribution was not essentially equivalent to a taxable dividend.

Being a question of fact, the decided cases are not controlling. However, in Joseph W. Imler, 11 T.C. 836, 840, we listed some of the factors which have been considered important, viz., "the presence or absence of a real business purpose, the motives of the corporation at the time of the distribution, the size of the corporate surplus, the past dividend policy, and the presence of any special circumstances relating to the distribution." * * *

An examination of the facts reveals that the Company had a large earned surplus and an unnecessary accumulation of cash from the standpoint of business requirement, both of which could have been reduced to the extent of earnings and profits by the declaration of a true dividend. The only suggested benefit accruing to the business by the distribution in cancellation of half the stock was the elimination of a substantial amount of this excess cash. Ordinarily such cash would be disposed of by the payment of a dividend. Coupled with the fact that the stockholders' proportionate interests in the enterprise remained unchanged, these factors indicate that [§ 115(a) of the 1939 Code respecting distributions essentially equivalent to a dividend, the predecessor of § 302 and § 346] is applicable.

Petitioners seek to avoid application of [that section] by contending that the cash distribution and redemption of stock did not represent an artifice to disguise the payment of a dividend but was occasioned by a bona fide contraction of business with a resulting decrease in the need for capital. While important, the absence of a plan to avoid taxation is not controlling. A distribution in redemption of stock may be essentially equivalent to a taxable dividend although it does not represent an attempt to camouflage such a dividend. * * * Whether a cancellation or redemption of stock is "essentially equivalent" to a taxable dividend depends primarily upon the net effect of the distribution rather than the motives and plans of the shareholders or the corporation. * * * Moreover, we cannot find from the present record that the reduction of taxes was not the motivating factor causing the stockholders to make a distribution in redemption of stock rather than to declare a dividend to the extent of earnings and profits.

Petitioners' primary contention is that the sale of the department store and the opening of the smaller ladies' ready-to-wear store resulted in a contraction of corporate business. This is a vital factor to be considered, but a contraction of business per se does not render [the section in question] inapplicable. L.M. Lockhart, 8 T.C. 436. Furthermore, even though it is clear that there was a diminution in the size of the Company's business, there was no contraction such as was present in Commissioner v. Sullivan, Joseph W. Imler, and L.M. Lockhart, all supra. In those cases there was a contraction of business with a corresponding reduction in the amount of capital used. Here, although the business was smaller, the amount of capital actually committed to the corporate business was not reduced accordingly. On December 31, 1945, before the sale of the department store to McArthur's Incorporated, the Company had $32,736.53 tied up in fixed assets and inventories. On December 31, 1946, after the ladies' ready-to-wear store was opened, it had $31,504.67 invested in those items. Undoubtedly the department store required larger reserves than the ladies' ready-to-wear store for purchasing inventories and carrying accounts receivable. But to the extent of earnings and profits the excess cash distributed was not created by a reduction in the amount of capital required for the operation of the business. Most of the excess cash had existed since prior to the sale of the department store and did not arise from fortuitous circumstances, as petitioners contend, but from an accumulation of earnings beyond the needs of the business. This excess could have been eliminated by the payment of a taxable dividend, and its distribution in redemption of stock was essentially equivalent to a taxable dividend.

It is true that the entire $67,250 distribution could not have been made in the form of an ordinary dividend and to some extent a redemption of stock was required. But [the section] applies if the distribution is only "in part" essentially equivalent to a taxable dividend, and here the distribution was essentially equivalent to a taxable dividend to the extent of earnings and profits.

Decisions will be entered for the respondent.

DETAILED ANALYSIS

1. FIVE-YEAR SEPARATE BUSINESS SAFE HARBOR

Section 302(e)(2) deems a distribution consisting of *all* of the assets, or the proceeds from the sale, of an *active* trade or business conducted for at least five years and that was not acquired by the corporation within the five year period in a taxable transaction to be not essentially equivalent to a dividend if, after the distribution, the corporation continues to conduct an *active* trade or business with a similar five year history. Although the statute itself does not on its face require the distribution of all of the assets of the terminated business or all of the proceeds from the sale of the business, it has been interpreted by the IRS and the courts to so provide. See, e.g., Kenton Meadows, Inc. v. Commissioner, 766 F.2d 142 (4th Cir.1985); Rev.Rul. 79–275, 1979–2 C.B. 137. Furthermore, only the assets of the terminated trade or business, or the proceeds from the sale of such assets, or a combination thereof, can be distributed in a distribution qualifying as a partial liquidation. See Rev.Rul. 79–275, supra (distribution of unrelated assets rather than promissory notes received on sale of terminated business did not qualify).

Satisfaction of the mechanical test of § 302(e)(2) relates only to the "not essentially equivalent to a dividend" test of § 302(e)(1). It does not *per se* qualify the transaction under § 302(e)(1); the plan and timing tests of § 302(e)(1)(B) must be met even after satisfaction of § 302(e)(2). Rev.Rul. 77–468, 1977–2 C.B. 109.

The concept of an active business separately conducted for five years is also utilized with respect to corporate divisions under § 355 and is discussed more fully in relation to that section (see Chapter 12). The Regulations under § 355 provide detailed examples of what constitutes the active conduct of a trade or business that are relevant for purposes of § 302(e). See Treas.Reg. §§ 1.346–1(c)(2); 1.355–3(c). There is, however, a significant difference between the test under § 355 and the test under § 302(e)(2). While the division of a single business may be accomplished under § 355, § 302(e)(2) requires the existence of two distinct, separate trades or businesses prior to the partial liquidation. Kenton Meadows, Inc. v. Commissioner, 766 F.2d 142 (4th Cir.1985); Krauskopf v. Commissioner, T.C. Memo. 1984–386. In Bilar Tool & Die Corp. v. Commissioner, 530 F.2d 708 (6th Cir.1976), the court held that the division of a single business because of shareholder disputes, carried out by the transfer of one-half the assets and liabilities of the business to a newly created corporation for its stock followed by the redemption of one of the shareholders' stock in the old corporation in exchange for stock of the new subsidiary, did not constitute a partial liquidation. (Such a transaction is a type (D) reorganization coupled with a split-off, discussed in Chapter 12.) In determining whether the terminated activity constituted a separate trade or business, the inquiry focuses on (1) whether the activity produced a substantial part of the combined corporate income, and (2) whether there was separate supervision and control. Blaschka v. United States, 393 F.2d 983 (Ct.Cl.1968); Mains v. United States, 508 F.2d 1251 (6th Cir.1975).

The distributing corporation is not required to have conducted the terminated business throughout the five year predistribution period, as long as someone conducted the business and it was not acquired in a taxable transaction. I.R.C. § 302(e)(3). Basically, this rule disqualifies acquisitions by purchase within the five year period but permits termination of a trade or business acquired in a tax free reorganization to qualify as a partial liquidation. The provision is designed to prevent the distributing corporation from temporarily "parking" excess funds in a trade or business for a short period prior to "termination" of the newly acquired business. Since tax free reorganizations entail acquisitions in exchange for stock of the acquiring corporation rather than cash, the same considerations do not apply.

2.   CONTRACTION OF THE CORPORATE BUSINESS

As noted above, contraction of the corporate enterprise as the standard for testing nondividend equivalence originated under the 1939 Code, and that test has been carried forward through successive statutory revisions. It is available with respect to transactions that fail to come within the safe harbor of § 302(e)(2). See S. Rept. No. 1622, 83d Cong., 2d Sess. 49 (1954); Treas.Reg. § 1.346–1(a).

Imler v. Commissioner, 11 T.C. 836 (1948) (acq.) is the leading case finding sufficient corporate contraction to constitute a partial liquidation. A corporation, whose stock was held by three stockholders, owned a seven-story building and several smaller buildings and was engaged in retinning and soldering metals. It also rented out its excess space. A fire destroyed the two upper floors of the seven-story building in 1941. Because of the shortage of building materials, the corporation did not rebuild the two floors but reduced the building to a five-story building. Finding its facilities inadequate to store materials for the retinning and soldering activities and also that a scarcity of materials made those operations unprofitable, it discontinued those operations. The corporation distributed $15,000 pro rata in redemption of part of its stock, the cash in part representing the excess of insurance proceeds over repair costs. The redemption was held not to be a dividend, the court stressing the bona fide contraction of business operations, the consequent reduction in capital needed, and the fact that except for the fire no distribution would have been made.

In Lockhart v. Commissioner, 8 T.C. 436 (1947), the sole stockholder of a corporation in the business of oil production, drilling, and operation of a recycling plant desired to operate the business as an individual. He could not completely liquidate as some of the shares were pledged to secure an obligation; in addition, he desired to retain the corporate name and to obtain limited liability with respect to the drilling business. The stockholder also needed about $220,000 to pay pending income tax liabilities. Accordingly, net assets of about one million dollars, including about $250,000 in cash, were transferred to him in exchange for 16,245 out of his 17,000 shares, so that the corporation retained only the drilling assets, worth about $34,000. The court held that the reasons for and the results of the redemption did not render it essentially equivalent to a dividend.

In a case in which a corporation did not want to incur the risks of developing certain oil leases, a pro rata distribution of the leases in cancellation of some of its stock was held not to be a dividend. Commissioner v. Sullivan, 210 F.2d 607 (5th Cir.1954). A dissent stressed the pro rata aspect as being almost conclusive and that there was no business purpose for the redemption of the stock instead of a mere distribution.

The IRS has carried the principles of the above cases forward in Revenue Rulings issued after the 1954 Code revision. Rev.Rul. 74–296, 1974–1 C.B. 80, held that there was a genuine corporate contraction where a corporation changed from operating a large department store to a small discount clothing store. In contrast, Rev.Rul. 57–333, 1957–2 C.B. 239, involved a corporation that distributed only a small parcel of land adjacent to its place of business, which it had acquired in contemplation of expansion and leased out in the interim. There was not a contraction where the rentals represented only 2% of the corporation's gross receipts. Similarly, a corporation in the quarrying business distributed a portion of a condemnation award received with respect to a taking of a portion of its mineral reserves; there was no contraction because the current operations of the corporation were unaffected. Rev.Rul. 67–16, 1967–1 C.B. 77.

The contraction must be represented by the disposition of all or part of the property used by the corporation in a trade or business. Rev.Rul. 56–512, 1956–2 C.B. 173 (distribution by corporation engaged in paper business of mineral land leased for royalties did not qualify because the corporation was not engaged in a trade or business with respect to the distributed property); Rev.Rul. 76–526, 1976–2 C.B. 101 (same as to distribution of parcel of land subject to net lease).

In Viereck v. United States, 3 Cl.Ct. 745 (1983), a corporation distributed to its sole shareholder real estate used in its flower business. Although the real estate constituted 80% of the net worth of the corporation before the distribution, the court found no partial liquidation because the corporation continued to conduct its flower business on the same scale as it had done previously. See also Rev.Proc. 2014–3, 2014–1 I.R.B. 111 (IRS will not issue ruling that redemption is a partial liquidation unless corporation reduces net fair market value of assets, gross revenues, and number of employees by 20%).

If the contraction of corporate business test is met, the partial liquidation distribution may include the working capital attributable to the discontinued activity. Rev.Rul. 60–232, 1960–2 C.B. 115. But funds transferred from another business into the terminated business shortly before the distribution may not constitute part of the working capital of the terminated business. Rev.Rul. 76–289, 1976–2 C.B. 100. Similarly, a distribution of cash reserves for future acquisitions of equipment that are no longer needed because of a change of business operations does not qualify as a contraction. Rev.Rul. 78–55, 1978–1 C.B. 88. In determining the amount of the distribution that will be considered attributable to a contraction, the proceeds from the sale of assets and the working capital must be reduced by corporate liabilities attributable to the discontinued activity (including taxes on the sale of the assets). Rev.Rul. 77–166, 1977–1 C.B. 90.

Rev.Proc. 81–42, 1981–2 C.B. 611, provides a checklist of information required by the IRS to obtain an advance ruling as to the qualification of a transaction as a partial liquidation.

3.   REQUIREMENTS OF "PLAN" AND "REDEMPTION"

3.1. *"Plan"*

Section 302(e)(1)(B) limits partial liquidation treatment to redemption distributions that (1) are "pursuant to a plan," and (2) occur within the taxable year in which the plan is adopted or in the succeeding taxable year. A formal plan is not required, Fowler Hosiery Co. v. Commissioner, 301 F.2d 394 (7th Cir.1962), Rev.Rul. 79–257, 1979–2 C.B. 136. But Blaschka v. United States, 393 F.2d 983 (Ct.Cl.1968), found that the total absence of a plan precluded partial liquidation treatment where the intention to redeem some of the shareholder's stock did not arise until after the sale of the corporation's business. Adherence to the time limitations for distributions, however, is crucial.

The strict enforcement of the two-year window for distributions can be turned to the taxpayer's advantage if partial liquidation treatment is not desired. Section 302(e) is elective in the sense that its consequences may be avoided by failing to comply with the time requirements in § 302(e)(1)(B). See Rev.Rul. 77–468, 1977–2 C.B. 109. In some cases it may be important to determine precisely when the "plan" was adopted, a determination that may be difficult when the plan was not formally adopted. A number of cases and Revenue Rulings involving complete liquidations dealt with determining the date of adoption of an informal plan. See, e.g., Mountain Water Co. v. Commissioner, 35 T.C. 418 (1960) (acq.); Rev.Rul. 65–235, 1965–2 C.B. 88.

To qualify a distribution as a partial liquidation under § 302(e), the proceeds from the sale of the assets meeting either the safe harbor of § 302(e)(2) or the general "contraction" test must be distributed as soon as possible within the permissible time window. See Treas.Reg. § 1.346–1(c)(2). The distribution need not be immediate; the proceeds may be invested in portfolio securities pending distribution, but investment profits are not treated as distributions in partial liquidation. Rev.Rul. 76–279, 1976–2 C.B. 99; Rev.Rul. 71–250, 1971–1 C.B. 112. Investment of the proceeds in additional assets for use in the corporation's remaining business, however, precludes a subsequent distribution of an amount equal to the proceeds from qualifying as a partial liquidation. Rev.Rul. 67–299, 1967–2 C.B. 138. See also Rev.Rul. 58–565, 1958–2 C.B. 140 (use of proceeds to pay debts precludes treatment of subsequent distribution of equivalent amount as partial liquidation).

3.2. *Redemption of Shares*

An actual surrender of the shares is not required in the case of a pro rata distribution. Rev.Rul. 90–13, 1990–1 C.B. 65; *Fowler Hosiery Co.,* supra. If there is a genuine contraction of a corporate business in partial liquidation, a surrender of shares would be meaningless; thus, the shareholders are deemed to have surrendered a number of shares with a total fair market value equal to the amount of the distribution. If the corporation is not publicly traded, the number of shares deemed surrendered is considered to be the same ratio of total shares as the amount of the distribution bears to the value of all corporate assets prior to the distribution, regardless of actual shares surrendered. Rev.Rul. 56–513, 1956–2 C.B. 191. If the corporation is publicly traded, the number of shares deemed surrendered is considered to be the same ratio of total shares as the amount of the distribution bears to the fair market value of all of the outstanding stock immediately before the distribution. Rev.Rul. 77–245, 1977–2 C.B. 105. However, if the partial liquidation distribution was not pro rata, cases decided under the predecessor of § 302(e) have disqualified transactions if there was no actual redemption of the shares. E.g., Gordon v. Commissioner, 424 F.2d 378 (2d Cir.1970); Honigman v. Commissioner, 55 T.C. 1067 (1971), aff'd on this issue, 466 F.2d 69 (6th Cir.1972).

4.   EFFECT OF OPERATION THROUGH A SUBSIDIARY

If a parent corporation operating a business also owns the stock of a subsidiary operating a five-year active business, a sale of the stock and distribution of the proceeds does not satisfy § 302(e). Rev.Rul. 79–184, 1979–1 C.B. 143. Nor would a direct distribution of the stock of the subsidiary qualify under § 302(e), because § 355 is the controlling section in these situations. On the other hand, the parent could liquidate the subsidiary, sell its assets, and then make a qualifying distribution of the proceeds under § 302(e). Alternatively, the subsidiary could sell the assets prior to its liquidation with the parent in turn distributing the proceeds under § 302(e). Rev.Rul. 75–223, 1975–1 C.B. 109; Rev.Rul. 77–376, 1977–2 C.B. 107.

If a parent corporation does not operate any active business itself but is a holding company, the holding of the stock of two operating subsidiaries presumably would not satisfy the "trade or business" requirement of § 302(e)(2). See Blaschka v. United States, 393 F.2d 983 (Ct.Cl.1968) (management of a subsidiary did not establish a separate viable business for purposes of the two-business rule); Morgenstern v. Commissioner, 56 T.C. 44 (1971) (majority control of a corporation engaged in a business does not qualify the holder as engaged in that business for purposes of the two-active-businesses rule). The parent, however, could liquidate its operating subsidiaries and retain the assets of one while distributing the assets of the other to provide qualification under § 302(e)(2).

5. DISTRIBUTIONS TO CORPORATIONS

A partial liquidation distribution described in § 302(e) does not qualify as a redemption under § 302(b)(4) if received by a corporate shareholder. Thus, unless the redemption also is described in any of § 302(b)(1) through (3) with respect to the corporate shareholder, the redemption will be treated as a § 301 distribution. In determining whether the distributee is a corporation or an individual, § 302(e)(5) requires that stock owned by a trust or a partnership be treated as owned proportionately by the beneficiaries or partners.

Because a corporate distributee will be entitled to a § 243 dividends received deduction with respect to the distribution, denying partial liquidation treatment is not necessarily disadvantageous. The benefit of the dividends received deduction will be "recaptured," however, when the corporate shareholder later sells the stock with respect to which the partial liquidation distribution was received.

Section 1059(e)(1)(A) provides that a partial liquidation distribution is an "extraordinary dividend" regardless of the period for which the stock was held. Thus, under § 1059(a) the corporate shareholder must reduce the basis of the stock by an amount equal to the dividends received deduction claimed with respect to the partial liquidation distribution. As a result, the gain on a taxable disposition will increase or the loss will be reduced. If the basis would have been reduced below zero if the full amount of the dividends received deduction had been subtracted from basis, the excess deduction, which did not reduce basis, is recaptured upon disposition of the stock. Thus, the § 243 deduction operates only to defer taxes when it is claimed with respect to partial liquidation distributions.

6. EFFECT ON DISTRIBUTING CORPORATION

If the corporation distributes appreciated property in a partial liquidation, gain is recognized under § 311(b). No loss may be recognized on the distribution of depreciated property. § 311(a). This result is in contrast to the treatment of distributions in complete liquidation, discussed in Chapter 7, in which losses are generally allowed by § 336.

Section 312(n)(7) governs the effect on earnings and profits of any redemption subject to § 302(a), including partial liquidations. These rules were discussed earlier in this Chapter.

7.   OTHER ASPECTS OF PARTIAL LIQUIDATIONS

7.1.   *Qualification Under Section 302(b)(4) or Sections 302(b)(1)–(3)*

Treas.Reg. § 1.302–1(a) indicates that partial liquidation treatment controls if a distribution could be treated either as a partial liquidation or as a different redemption under § 302(b). If a distribution fails to qualify as a redemption under § 302(b)(4), it still may qualify under one of § 302(b)(1) through (3) and vice versa. Rev.Rul. 82–187, 1982–2 C.B. 80, held that a non-pro rata partial liquidation resulted in sale or exchange treatment, even though the redemption could not have qualified under any of § 301(b)(1) through (b)(3). See also Treas.Reg. § 1.346–2. Also, if a distribution may be either a complete termination under § 302(b)(3) only by virtue of the waiver of family attribution or a partial liquidation, § 302(b)(5) provides that the prohibition on the acquisition of a prohibited interest within 10 years under § 302(c)(2)(A) does not apply.

7.2.   *Partial Liquidation Under Section 302(e) Versus Serial Installment in Complete Liquidation*

Distributions that are one of a series leading to complete liquidation are treated as distributions in complete liquidation under § 331, rather than as distributions in partial liquidation. See Chapter 7. Characterization of a distribution in this regard may be important as respects the shareholder for two reasons. First, a loss may be realized and recognized (subject to the limitations in § 267) on a distribution in partial liquidation. See Rev.Rul. 56–513, 1956–2 C.B. 191. But in a complete liquidation, no loss may be claimed until the series of distributions is completed. Second, corporate distributees never qualify for exchange treatment under § 302(b)(4) but always will be accorded exchange treatment if the distribution is pursuant to a plan of complete liquidation. From the perspective of the distributing corporation, the difference is significant because the corporation under § 311 recognizes only gains (with realized losses being disallowed) on the distribution of property in a partial liquidation, but recognizes both gains and losses on the distribution of property in complete liquidation under § 336, subject to loss limitations under § 336(d) and § 267.

7.3.   *Other Recharacterizations*

If the shareholder, following the receipt of assets in a partial liquidation, transfers the assets to a new corporation, the liquidation-reincorporation issue, discussed in Chapter 10, may be encountered. See, e.g., Rev.Rul. 76–429, 1976–2 C.B. 97 (subsidiary sold assets of one of two businesses and liquidated; parent placed assets of the other business in a newly created subsidiary; the liquidation and reincorporation were ignored and the transaction was treated as a partial liquidation). The characterization of the transaction is important with respect to whether the distributing corporation recognizes gain or loss on the distribution of the assets and to whether the shareholders currently recognize gain or loss with respect to the stock.

PROBLEM SET 5

1. Griswold Corporation has one class of common stock outstanding, which is owned equally by Clark and Eddie. Each shareholder owns 1000 shares. Clark's basis is $900,000, Eddie's basis is $12,000,000. The fair market value of each share of Griswold is $10,000. The aggregate value of the shares is $20,000,000. Griswold directly operates two distinct businesses, "Wings," an air charter business with three airplanes, and "Wally World," an amusement park. Griswold also owns all of the stock of Caddy Shack Golf Club Manufacturing, Inc., which it has held for seven years.

What are the tax consequences of the following alternative transactions?

(a) (1) Griswold sells Wally World for $4,000,000 and distributes the cash proceeds pro rata to its shareholders. Each shareholder receives $2,000,000 and surrenders 200 shares of stock. Griswold has operated Wings and Wally World for more than five years.

(2) What if each shareholder surrenders 400 shares of stock?

(3) What if neither shareholder surrenders any stock?

(b) Would your answer to the question in part (a)(1) differ if Griswold distributed only $3,000,000 to its shareholders and used the other $1,000,000 to expand the Wings business?

(c) (1) What would be the result in (a)(1) if Griswold had started the Wings business three years ago out of retained earnings?

(2) Would the answer differ if Griswold also owned 5,000 acres of undeveloped land that it purchased nine years ago as an investment, but grazing rights on the undeveloped land have been leased to a rancher for more than five years?

(3) Would the result in (a)(1) differ if Wings had been established six years ago by Joe and was purchased for cash by Griswold three years ago?

(4) Would the result in (1)(a) differ if Wings had been established six years ago by Joe and was acquired in a tax free merger of Wings into Griswold three years ago?

(d) (1) All of Griswold's businesses have been owned and operated for more than five years. The largest of Wing's several airplanes was destroyed in a hurricane and Griswold received $5,000,000 of insurance proceeds. Griswold used $2,000,000 of the insurance to buy a replacement airplane that was much smaller and carried many fewer passengers, and it distributed the remaining $3,000,000 equally among its shareholders in redemption of 150 shares of stock (worth $1,500,0000) from each.

(2) Would the answer differ if Griswold distributed $4,000,000 of insurance proceeds and used the other $1,000,000 to expand the Wally World business?

(3) Would the answer in part (d)(2) differ if Griswold also owned 5,000 acres of undeveloped land that it purchased nine years ago as an investment?

(e) Griswold distributed pro rata 5,000 acres of undeveloped land that it purchased nine years ago as an investment, but grazing rights on the undeveloped land have been leased to a rancher for more than five years?

(f) (1) Griswold sells all of its Caddy Shack stock for $2,000,000 and distributes $1,000,000 to each shareholder in redemption of 10 shares from each.

    (2) Griswold liquidates Caddy Shack, acquiring all of its assets as the sole shareholder, sells the assets for $2,000,000, and distributes $1,000,000 to each shareholder in redemption of 20 shares from each.

2. Ward owned 30 shares of Cleaver Cutlery Manufacturing Corporation, Ward's wife, June, owned 30 shares, and their son, Theodore, owned the other 40 shares. Cleaver Cutlery Manufacturing Corporation had two divisions, the kitchen cutlery division and the tableware division. Cleaver Cutlery Manufacturing Corporation sold its tableware division and distributed the proceeds to Ward in redemption of all of his stock. June continued to hold her stock in Cleaver Cutlery Manufacturing Corporation, and Ward and June continued to serve on the board of directors. What are the tax consequences of the redemption of Ward's stock?

3. Ahab Corporation has 200 shares of common stock outstanding, which are owned equally by Jonah and Leviathan Corporation. Jonah's basis for his stock is $2,000,000; Leviathan's basis for its stock is $4,000,000. Ahab has operated two distinct businesses, a wholesale fish bait business and chain of fast-food sushi bars, for over 10 years. The sushi bar business is worth $6,000,000; the wholesale fish bait business is worth $14,000,000. What are the tax consequences of the following alternative transactions?

(a) Pursuant to a plan of partial liquidation, Ahab distributes the assets of the sushi bar business to its shareholders pro rata in redemption of 30 shares from each of them.

(b) Pursuant to a plan of partial liquidation, Ahab distributes the assets of the sushi bar business to Leviathan Corporation in redemption of 60 of its shares.

SECTION 6.   REDEMPTIONS THROUGH THE USE OF RELATED CORPORATIONS

INTERNAL REVENUE CODE: Sections 304 (omitting sections 304(b)(3)(C) and (D), (b)(4)–(b)(6)); 318.

REGULATIONS: Sections 1.304–2, –3, –5.

Section 304 provides that a sale of stock by the shareholder of one controlled corporation to another controlled corporation is to be treated as a redemption distribution. Section 304 is designed to prevent a shareholder from escaping dividend treatment on a transaction formally structured as a sale that has obvious similarities to a redemption. Because of the controlled nature of the corporations involved, there might not be a significant economic change in the shareholder's overall position. Section 304 requires that the sales proceeds received in such a transaction be treated as a corporate distribution that must meet the test of either § 302 or § 303 to qualify for sale or exchange treatment.[2] Section 304 deals with two basic factual patterns: sales between brother-sister corporations and sales involving parent-subsidiary corporations.

(1)   Brother-Sister Corporations

Suppose that the shareholder owns all the stock of X Corporation and all of the stock of Y Corporation. If the shareholder sells some of the X Corporation stock to Y Corporation, § 304 restructures the transaction as a redemption distribution by Y Corporation. Dividend equivalence under § 302, however, is tested in terms of the shareholder's change in ownership in the corporation whose stock is sold, i.e., X Corporation. I.R.C. § 304(b)(1). The amount actually taxed as a dividend, however, is a function of the earnings and profits of *both* corporations, although § 304(b)(2) specifies that the earnings and profits of the purchasing corporation, i.e., Y Corporation, are attributed to the distribution before the earnings and profits of the corporation whose stock is sold, i.e., X Corporation. The X Corporation stock that was actually transferred to Y Corporation is treated as having been contributed to the corporation in a § 351 transaction by the shareholder who received the distribution.

Although § 304(b)(1) directs that the determination of whether the transaction is entitled to redemption treatment is made with respect to the stock of the issuing corporation, i.e., the corporation the stock of which was sold, the treatment of the transaction by § 304(a)(1) as a redemption by the *purchasing* corporation is important. If the combined earnings and profits of the issuing and purchasing corporations are not sufficient to support dividend treatment of the entire distribution, the excess distribution is applied against the basis of the purchasing corporation stock and, when that basis has been reduced to zero, the balance is taxable gain. The basis of the selling shareholder in any remaining shares of the issuer may not be applied against the distribution to avoid gain recognition.

(2)   Parent-Subsidiary Situations

The second situation with which § 304 is concerned involves the purchase by a subsidiary of its parent's stock from the shareholders of its parent corporation (subsidiary being defined in terms of 50% or greater stock ownership). Under § 304(a)(2) the shareholders are treated as if the parent redeemed its stock from them. In testing for dividend equivalence under § 302, stock of the parent owned by the subsidiary after the

---

[2]   For qualification for sale or exchange treatment under § 303 of a sale of stock subject to § 304, see Webb v. Commissioner, 67 T.C. 293 (1976), aff'd per curiam, 572 F.2d 135 (5th Cir.1978). Section 303 is discussed later in this Chapter.

transaction is attributed under § 318(a)(2)(C) first to the parent corporation and then again under § 318(a)(2)(C) to the shareholders of the parent. Assume, for example, that A owns 80% (80 out of 100 shares) of the stock of P Corporation, which in turn owns 70% (70 out of 100 shares) of S Corporation. If A sells 40 shares of P Corporation stock to S Corporation, A now actually owns only 40 of 100 shares, or 40% of P Corporation. But 70% of the 40 shares of P Corporation owned by S (28 shares) are attributed to P Corporation under § 318(a)(2)(C) and 40% of the 28 P Corporation shares thus constructively owned by P are attributed to A under § 318(a)(2)(C), with the result that A constructively owns 11.2 shares of P Corporation. A's total ownership of P has therefore been reduced only from 80% to 51.2%, and dividend treatment is likely. Because § 304(b)(2) permits the earnings and profits of both the issuer and the acquiring corporation to support dividend treatment, a dividend may result even though the parent corporation has no earnings and profits.

Because dividends currently are taxed at the same rate as long-term capital gains, the incentive for noncorporate shareholder-taxpayers to attempt to disguise dividends as stock sales—the avoidance transaction at which § 304 is directed—is greatly reduced. For a noncorporate shareholder, the only important differences between a dividend and a stock sale are that (1) all of a dividend distribution is includable in gross income, while only the amount by which sales proceeds exceed the basis of the stock is includable, and (2) gains on stock sales can be offset by capital losses, while dividend income cannot be offset by capital losses, although § 1211(b) does provide a small, $3,000 deduction to individuals for excess capital losses.

Fehrs Finance Co. v. Commissioner*
Tax Court of the United States, 1972.
58 T.C. 174.

■ SIMPSON, JUDGE. [Mr. and Mrs. Fehrs owned all of the stock of Fehrs Rental Corporation (Rental). In December, 1964, Mr. Fehrs made gifts of the Rental stock to members of his family, and after the gifts Mr. Fehrs owned 982 shares, Mrs. Fehrs owned 177 shares, and 221 shares were owned by his son-in-law, his daughters and his grandchildren. Approximately two months later, Fehrs Finance Company (Finance) was incorporated with two of the Fehrs daughters as its sole shareholders. Immediately thereafter Mr. and Mrs. Fehrs transferred all of the remaining Rental stock which they held to Finance in return for Finance's promise to pay them annuities totaling $70,000 per year for the rest of their lives. Finance immediately resold the Rental stock to Rental in exchange for $100,000 cash and an unsecured promissory note of

---

* [Eds.: The decision of the Tax Court was affirmed in an opinion that essentially followed the reasoning of the Tax Court, 487 F.2d 184 (8th Cir.1973).]

$625,000. The Commissioner asserted a deficiency against Finance based on the gain it allegedly recognized on the disposition of the Rental stock.]

The issue ultimately to be decided in this case appears to be simple: Did the petitioner realize a capital gain on the sale of the Rental stock in 1965? However, to reach that ultimate issue, we must work our way through an amazing maze of preliminary issues. At no time has the respondent taken the position that Rental's acquisition of its stock constituted a redemption under section 302 and that the payments received by the petitioner should be treated as dividends; at all times, he has treated such payments as a capital gain. The controversy revolves about the petitioner's basis in the stock. The respondent contends that section 304 is applicable to the petitioner's acquisition of stock from Mr. and Mrs. Fehrs and that its basis in such stock is therefore determined under sections 304 and 362(a). He concedes that if section 304 is applicable to the petitioner's acquisition of such stock, the gain which it realized on the transfer of such stock to Rental is taxable as a long-term capital gain. Thus, the initial issue for us to consider is whether section 304 is applicable to the petitioner's acquisition of the stock.

Section 304(a)(1) provides in relevant part that, if one or more persons are in "control" of each of two corporations, and if one of those corporations acquires stock in the other corporation from the person or persons in control, then the transaction shall be treated as a redemption under section 302. The stock shall be treated by the acquiring corporation as having been received as a contribution to its capital. The term "control" is defined in section 304(c)(1) as "the ownership of stock possessing at least 50 percent of the total combined voting power of all classes of stock entitled to vote, or at least 50 percent of the total value of shares of all classes of stock." Furthermore, section 304(c)(2) states that the rules contained in section 318(a) with respect to the constructive ownership of stock shall apply for the purpose of determining "control," except that the 50-percent limitations of sections 318(a)(2)(C) and 318(a)(3)(C) shall be disregarded for such purpose. Section 318(a) provides that an individual shall be considered as actually owning the stock which is owned by his spouse, his children, and his grandchildren.

Section 304(a)(1) applies to what is commonly referred to as a "redemption by related or brother-sister corporations." It is clear that by its terms, such section applies to the factual situation in this case. Immediately prior to the transactions here in issue, Mr. and Mrs. Fehrs actually owned 1,159 of the 1,380 outstanding shares of Rental and their daughters and grandchildren owned 196 shares; thus, a total of 1,355 shares, or 98.2 percent of the outstanding stock, was actually or constructively owned by either Mr. Fehrs or Mrs. Fehrs. Only the 25 shares owned by Mr. Vlcek were not attributed to either of the Fehrses under section 318(a). All of the outstanding shares of the petitioner were owned by the daughters of the Fehrses, and were, therefore, similarly attributable to Mr. Fehrs or Mrs. Fehrs. Thus, either Mr. Fehrs or Mrs.

Fehrs, or both, were regarded as the person or persons in control of both the petitioner and Rental prior to the transactions in issue. The transaction in which the petitioner acquired stock in Rental from Mr. and Mrs. Fehrs in return for the annuities must be treated as a redemption, and the stock of Rental so acquired must be treated as having been transferred by Mr. and Mrs. Fehrs to the petitioner as a contribution to its capital, under the express mandate of section 304(a)(1). See Rose Ann Coates Trust, 55 T.C. 501 (1970), [aff'd, 480 F.2d 468 (9th Cir. 1973).].
* * *

[W]e now reach the question as to what was the petitioner's basis for the Rental stock under section 304. The petitioner must treat the stock as if it received the stock from the Fehrses as a contribution to its capital; therefore, the petitioner's basis equals the basis of the transferred stock in the hands of Mr. and Mrs. Fehrs plus the amount of gain, if any, which was recognized by Mr. and Mrs. Fehrs upon the transfer. [Secs. 304(a)(1) and 362(a).] It has been stipulated that the basis of the transferred stock in the hands of the Fehrses was zero, so the only remaining question in computing the petitioner's basis in such stock is with respect to the amount of the gain, if any, which Mr. and Mrs. Fehrs recognized upon the transfer. According to the income tax regulations, there is no step-up in the petitioner's basis if the redemption is treated as essentially equivalent to a dividend under section 302 and if the payments to Mr. and Mrs. Fehrs are taxable as a dividend under sections 302(d) and 301, but if the redemption qualifies as an exchange under section 302(b), the petitioner's basis is increased by the gain recognized by Mr. and Mrs. Fehrs. Sec. 1.304–2(c), examples (1) and (3), Income Tax Regs. The validity of such rules has not been challenged. Thus, to determine whether there is any step-up in the petitioner's basis in the stock, it becomes necessary to determine first whether the redemption is essentially equivalent to a dividend under section 302 or whether it qualifies as an exchange under such section.

Section 302 sets forth in subsection (b) the conditions under which a redemption of stock shall be treated as an exchange, and provides in subsection (d) that if those conditions are not met, then the distribution is one to which section 301 applies. If the redemption meets any one of the four tests set forth in section 302(b), it is treated as an exchange, and the amount of the distribution is treated as payment for the stock. Neither party argues the applicability of section 302(b)(2) or 302(b)(4) in this case, but the petitioner argues that the redemption should be treated as an exchange because it meets the test of either section 302(b)(1) or 302(b)(3). We shall consider each such test.

Section 302(b)(1) states, in effect, that the redemption shall be treated as an exchange if it "is not essentially equivalent to a dividend." To meet this test, a redemption must result in a meaningful reduction of the shareholder's proportionate interest in the corporation, after applying the attribution rules of section 318(a) to the stock ownership

interests as they existed both before and after the redemption. Secs.
1.302–1(a), 1.302–2(b), Income Tax Regs.; United States v. Davis, 397
U.S. 301, 90 S.Ct. 1041 (1970). * * *

After applying the attribution rules, Mr. and Mrs. Fehrs are
considered as owning 98.2 percent of the outstanding shares of Rental—
1,355 out of 1,380—both immediately before and immediately after the
redemption by the petitioner. We discussed previously the method of
computing the preredemption figure; the postredemption figure is
reached by attributing to the Fehrses the shares owned by the petitioner
as well as those owned by their descendants. The latter result obtains
from attributing the petitioner's 1,159 shares to Mmes. Vlcek and May
by virtue of section 318(a)(2)(C), the 50-percent requirement of which is
not applicable here by reason of section 304(b)(1), and then attributing
those shares in turn to the Fehrses under section 318(a)(1)(A)(ii).

The respondent contends that the correct comparison of the Fehrses'
stock ownership before and after the redemption is to measure the
percentage of the shares owned by them *immediately* before and
immediately after the redemption; if such contention is accurate, it is
clear that the Fehrses' stock ownership (as viewed through the prism of
the attribution rules) was not changed at all by the redemption, and thus
the redemption clearly fails to meet the test of section 302(b)(1) as
articulated by the Supreme Court in United States v. Davis, supra, and
as followed by this Court in the decisions previously cited.

* * *

The petitioner also argues that the attribution rules should be
considered only for the purpose of "determining the ownership of stock,"
as prescribed by section 302(c)(1), but not for the purpose of determining
control as part of a dividend equivalency test under section 302(b)(1);
thus, the petitioner argues, we should take cognizance of the alleged fact
that the redemption "eliminated the actual control of Edward J. Fehrs
over the affairs of Fehrs Rental Co." However, in section 304, Congress
expressly indicated that the attribution rules are to be applied in
determining control. Section 304(a)(1) applies when one or more persons
"control" each of two corporations; section 304(c)(1) defines control by
stating that "control means the ownership" of stock possessing a specified
percentage of voting rights or value; and section 304(c)(2) expressly
provides, with one exception not here relevant, "Section 318(a)(relating
to the constructive ownership of stock) shall apply for purposes of
determining control under paragraph (1) [of section 304(c)]." The
application of the attribution rules of section 318 to a redemption under
section 304(a) can operate in such a way as to cause a person who actually
owns no shares in a corporation to be treated as having 100-percent
control of it. Coyle v. United States, 415 F.2d 488, 490 (C.A.4, 1968),
reversing 268 F.Supp. 233 (S.D.W.Va.1967). In *Coyle,* there is no
indication that the taxpayer exercised actual control over the affairs of
such corporation; the Fourth Circuit regarded the attribution rules alone

as sufficient to impute complete control to him. This Court, too, has applied the attribution rules to determine who controlled a corporation involved in a redemption under section 304. Ralph L. Humphrey, supra at 205.

* * * We hold that the redemption cannot be treated as an exchange under section 302(b)(1).

The next question is whether section 302(b)(3) is applicable. Such section provides that the redemption is to be treated as an exchange "if the redemption is in complete redemption of all of the stock of the corporation owned by the shareholder." However, under section 302(c)(1), the attribution rules of section 318 are applicable in determining whether a redemption has resulted in the complete termination of a shareholder's interest under section 302(b)(3), but section 302(c)(2) sets forth certain conditions under which the attribution rules are not applicable for such purposes. Obviously, Mr. and Mrs. Fehrs did actually transfer all of their stock in Rental, but whether the redemption can qualify under section 302(b)(3) depends upon whether the conditions of section 302(c)(2) have been met so that the attribution rules are not applicable.

[The court then held that section 302(b)(3) did not apply because the Fehrs had failed to file the agreements required by section 302(c)(2).]

For the foregoing reasons, the redemption in which the petitioner acquired the Rental stock from Mr. and Mrs. Fehrs does not qualify for treatment as an exchange under any of the provisions of section 302(b), and therefore, under section 302(d), the redemption shall be treated as a distribution of property governed by section 301.

Section 301(c)(1) provides in effect that, to the extent that it is made out of the corporation's earnings and profits, the distribution is treated as a dividend and is taxed as ordinary income to the recipient. Section 301(c)(2) goes on to provide that, to the extent that the distribution is not a dividend, it is first applied against the recipient's adjusted basis in the stock, and then, according to section 301(c)(3), the amount which exceeds such adjusted basis is treated as gain from the sale or exchange of property. The petitioner argues that, because it had no earnings and profits during its 1965 taxable year, the tax consequences to Mr. and Mrs. Fehrs of the annuity payments are governed by section 301(c)(2) and (3) and that the petitioner's basis in the stock acquired in the redemption should include, for purposes of computing its gain on the sale of the stock in 1965, the gains to be recognized in subsequent years by Mr. and Mrs. Fehrs as a result of the receipt of the annuity payments.

Initially, the respondent contends that there should be no increase in the petitioner's basis by reason of any gain recognized by the Fehrses under section 301. The respondent argues that section 362(a) provides for an increase in basis by reason of a gain recognized on the transfer and that such language does not apply to gains recognized under section 301(c)(3). There is nothing in the statute or the legislative history to support such contention. The words of section 362(a) are clearly broad enough to apply to a gain recognized under section 301(c)(3), and accordingly, we reject such contention of the respondent.

The petitioner's argument that the annuity payments to Mr. and Mrs. Fehrs will be taxable, after recovery of basis, as a gain under section 301(c)(3) rests on the propositions that it had no earnings and profits in its 1965 taxable year and that the tax treatment of the payments that Mr. and Mrs. Fehrs will receive in later years is determined by its earnings and profits, or lack thereof, in 1965. * * * Thus, we must first decide what constituted the property distributed to the Fehrses, when the distribution or distributions occurred, and for what year or years the earnings and profits of the petitioner are determinative of the tax treatment of such property.

The petitioner argues that the making of the annuity contracts in 1965 constituted distributions of property under section 301, but we do not agree. * * * Whatever the Fehrses may have considered the agreements to be worth to them, the agreements were in no way the equivalent of cash. Unlike the recipient of an ordinary promise to make a payment at a certain time in the future, the Fehrses did not receive anything in 1965 which they could have disposed of even at a substantial discount.

* * *

Since no annuity payments were made to Mr. and Mrs. Fehrs in 1965, and since we have concluded that the making of the annuity contracts did not constitute a distribution of property to them in that year, no amount of gain was recognized by them in 1965 as a result of the transfer of their stock to the petitioner. The petitioner argues that its basis should include the amount of gains to be recognized by Mr. and Mrs. Fehrs in subsequent years. Although there may be circumstances in which the acquiring corporation's basis in property should take into consideration the gains to be recognized by the transferors in later years—a question which we need not and do not decide—it seems clear that such a prediction of future gains could be appropriate only when there is a reasonably reliable method for ascertaining the amount of such gains. Here, it is utterly impossible to anticipate the amount of gains to be recognized in the future. * * * [I]t is impossible to forecast whether such payments will be treated as dividends under section 301(c)(1) or as gains under section 301(c)(3). * * * Thus, we conclude that the petitioner's basis in 1965 must be limited to any gain recognized by the transferors in that year; that is, zero. * * * Accordingly, we hold that in 1965, the petitioner's basis for the purpose of computing its gain on the sale of the Rental stock must be zero, and it must recognize as a gain the entire payment which it received in that year. * * *

Decision will be entered under Rule [155].

DETAILED ANALYSIS

1. BROTHER-SISTER TRANSACTIONS

1.1. *"Control"*

Section 304(a)(1) applies to sales of stock in the brother-sister context only if "one or more persons are in control" of each corporation. "Control" for this purpose is defined in § 304(c)(1) as ownership of 50% or more of *either* combined voting power or value of all classes of stock. See Rev.Rul. 89–57, 1989–1 C.B. 90 (an individual who owned less than 50% of the voting stock, but more than 50% of the total value of the outstanding stock of a corporation, controlled the corporation). Control of the corporation the stock of which is sold (the issuer) is measured before the sale, while control of the corporation to which the stock is sold (the purchaser) is measured after the sale (to take account of the possibility that some of the consideration paid for the issuer's stock might be stock of the purchaser). I.R.C. § 304(c)(2); Treas.Reg. § 1.304–5(b). In measuring 50% ownership for testing control, the attribution rules of § 318 apply, but § 318(a)(2)(C) and (a)(3)(C)—dealing with attribution from and to corporations—are applied by substituting a greater than 5% threshold of ownership for the normal greater than 50% threshold. I.R.C. § 304(c)(3)(B). Moreover, there is no minimum ownership threshold for attribution to or from corporations when testing for dividend equivalency under § 302(b). I.R.C. § 304(b)(1). For example, if A owns 30% of X Corporation directly and A also owns 30% of Y Corporation, which owns the other 70% of X Corporation, A owns an additional 21% of X Corporation through Y Corporation (70% x 30%). Thus, A owns 51% of X Corporation solely for purposes of applying the control test. If A sold one-half of A's X Corporation stock to Z Corporation, of which A owned one-half of the stock and thus also controlled, after the sale A continues to own 21% of X corporation through Y corporation and 15% directly. A also now owns 7.5% of X corporation through Z corporation, for a total ownership of 43.5% of X corporation. Thus, A's ownership of X Corporation was reduced from 51% to 43.5%—15% directly, 21% through Y Corporation, and 7.5% through Z Corporation. The reduction in ownership of X Corporation fails the test of § 302(b)(2) but might meet the test of § 302(b)(1).

Related sales transactions involving a number of shareholders can be subject to § 304 using a control group concept. See Treas.Reg. § 1.304–2(b). In Bhada v. Commissioner, 89 T.C. 959 (1987), aff'd, 892 F.2d 39 (6th Cir.1989) and sub nom. Caamano v. Commissioner, 879 F.2d 156 (5th Cir.1989), an exchange of shares of a publicly traded corporation was, in part, subject to § 304. In determining whether the 50% threshold has been met, the attribution rules of § 318 apply, with certain modifications. Thus, as was the case in *Fehrs Finance Co.*, if A owns all of the stock of X Corporation, and A sells that stock to Y corporation, all of the stock of which is owned by A's child, B, § 304 applies to the transaction. However, if the selling shareholder's entire *actual* interest in the corporation has been terminated, waiver of family attribution under § 302(c) may be available to avoid dividend treatment. In Fehrs v. United States, 556 F.2d 1019 (Ct.Cl.1977), the individual shareholders, who were not parties to the Tax Court litigation, and thus not collaterally estopped, argued in the Court of Claims that the § 302(c)(2) agreement was timely filed, thus qualifying the § 304(a)(1) constructive redemption for capital gain treatment under § 302(b)(3). The Court of Claims, refusing to follow the case involving the corporate taxpayer, found the filing of the agreements in "substantial compliance" with § 302(c)(2). It left open, however, the question whether a tax avoidance motive was present in the gifts of the stock by Fehrs to his family members which, if present, would prevent qualification under § 302(b)(3).

In Niedermeyer v. Commissioner, 62 T.C. 280 (1974), aff'd per curiam 535 F.2d 500 (9th Cir.1976), the taxpayers sold all of their common stock in a corporation controlled by two of their sons to another corporation, in which they actually owned no stock, controlled by three other sons. Although the selling shareholders filed a § 302(c) waiver agreement, the court held it invalid because they retained some preferred stock in the first corporation. In requiring dividend treatment, the Tax Court rejected the taxpayer's argument that due to hostility between the brothers controlling the two different corporations the attribution rules should not have been applied to determine control.

Suppose that A owned 50% of the stock of X Corporation and A's child, B, owned the other 50%, and all of A's stock in X Corporation was redeemed in a transaction that qualified under § 302(b)(3) by virtue of a waiver of family attribution under § 302(c)(3). Subsequently, A sold all of the stock of Y Corporation to X Corporation. Section 304(a) applies to treat A's sale of the Y Corporation stock to X Corporation as an acquisition of X Corporation stock in exchange for stock of Y Corporation followed by an immediate redemption of the newly issued X Corporation stock for cash. Rev.Rul. 88–55, 1988–2 C.B. 45, held that the prior waiver of attribution for purposes of § 302(b)(3) did not affect application of the attribution rules in determining ownership of the Y stock held by X Corporation when applying § 304 to the sale of stock by A. Thus, since A continued to own by attribution 100% of Y Corporation after the sale, the transaction was treated as a redemption by X Corporation that was substantially equivalent to a dividend. The Ruling also held, however, that treatment of A as receiving a distribution with respect to X Corporation stock was not a prohibited interest in X Corporation in violation of the waiver of family attribution rules.

1.2. Treatment of Distributions

Section 304(a)(1) provides that if one or more persons are in control of each of two corporations, and one of the corporations acquires stock of the other from controlling shareholders, then the transaction is treated as a redemption of stock by the acquiring corporation. However, whether the redemption qualifies for sale or exchange treatment, rather than treatment as a § 301 distribution, is tested by applying § 302(b) with reference to the change in the selling shareholder's ownership in the stock of the corporation that issued the stock that was sold. I.R.C. § 304(b)(1). But if after the application of § 302(b) the transaction is characterized as a § 301 distribution, dividend status is determined with reference to the combined earnings and profits of both corporations, looking first to the earnings and profits of the acquiring corporation and then to the earnings and profits of the corporation that issued the stock that was sold. I.R.C. § 304(b)(2). Furthermore, if the transaction is treated as a § 301 distribution, for purposes of determining the transferor's basis in the stock of the acquiring corporation, as well as for purposes of determining the portion of the distribution, if any, that is a return of capital under § 301(c)(2) if the distribution is not wholly a dividend, the transferor is deemed to have contributed the exchanged stock to the acquiring corporation in exchange for stock of the acquiring corporation in a § 351 transaction, following which that stock is promptly redeemed. The shareholder's basis of the issuing corporation stock deemed to have been contributed to the acquiring corporation in the § 351 transaction is transferred to the shares of stock of the acquiring corporation deemed to have been issued (§ 358) and promptly redeemed. If the combined earnings and profits of the corporations are insufficient to support dividend treatment for the entire amount received by the shareholder, the basis of all of the stockholder's shares of the acquiring corporation, and not merely the redeemed shares, is taken into account in determining the portion of the distribution that is a return of capital under § 301(c)(2). See Prop.Reg. § 1.304–2(a)(4), (c), Ex.(2) (2009) (withdrawn, 84 Fed. Reg. 11687 (Mar. 28, 2019)). If the amount of the distribution exceeds the combined earnings and profits of the corporations, but is less than the sum of the combined earnings and profits of the corporations and the basis transferred from the issuing corporation stock to the acquiring corporation stock that is deemed to have been issued and redeemed, the excess transferred basis is added to the basis of the shareholder's remaining stock in the acquiring corporation. See Treas.Reg. §§ 1.302–2(c); 1.304–2(a).

The following examples illustrate the application of § 304(a)(1).

(1) Assume that A owned 80 of the 100 shares of stock of X Corporation and 50 of the 100 shares of stock of Y Corporation. Each share of X Corporation stock had a basis of $1 and each share of Y Corporation stock had a basis of $2. X Corporation had earnings and profits of $90, and Y Corporation had earnings and profits of $40. A sold 40 shares of X Corporation stock to Y Corporation for $300. After the sale, A owns 40 shares of X Corporation directly, and pursuant to § 318(a)(2)(C), A owns 20 shares of X Corporation through A's 50% ownership of Y Corporation. Thus, A's ownership interest in X Corporation was reduced from 80% to 60% (60/100) shares. (Note that unlike in the case of an actual redemption, in which the number of outstanding shares is reduced by the redemption, in the case of a transaction subject to § 304, the number of outstanding shares of the issuing corporation with respect to which § 302 is applied to test for sale or exchange treatment remains unchanged.) This reduction in ownership of X Corporation stock does not satisfy the requirements of § 302(b). Accordingly, the $300 is treated as a § 301 distribution by Y Corporation, but both Y Corporation's earnings and profits of $40 and X Corporation's earnings and profits of $90 support dividend treatment under § 301(c)(1) for $130 of the distribution. To determine the portion of the remaining $170 that is a return of capital, A is treated as having contributed the 40 shares of X Corporation stock with an aggregate basis of $40 (40 shares × $1) to Y Corporation in a § 351 transaction, thereby increasing A's basis in A's Y Corporation stock

from $100 (50 shares × $2) to $140. Thus, $140 of the $170 of the distribution that exceeds the $130 dividend is a return of capital pursuant to § 301(c)(2) and $30 of capital gain is recognized under § 301(c)(3). A's basis in the Y Corporation stock is reduced to zero.

(2)   Assume all of the same facts as in Example (1), except that A's basis in the X Corporation stock is $5 per share, for an aggregate basis of $200 in the 40 shares of X Corporation stock sold to Y Corporation. Again, the $300 is treated as a § 301 distribution by Y Corporation, of which $130 is a dividend. In this case, however, all of the remaining $170 of the distribution is a return of capital. A is treated as having contributed the 40 shares of X Corporation stock with an aggregate basis of $200 to Y Corporation in a § 351 transaction, thereby increasing A's basis in A's Y Corporation stock from $100 to $300. Those 40 shares are then treated as being redeemed (in a transaction subject to § 301 by virtue of § 302(d)) and under § 301(c)(2) the $170 is treated as a return of capital. The remaining $30 of the basis of the Y Corporation shares deemed to have been issued in exchange for the X Corporation shares and to have been redeemed is transferred to A's 50 Y Corporation shares pursuant to Treas.Reg. § 1.302–2(c), which now have a basis of $130.

(3)   Assume all of the same facts as in Example (1), except that A owned only 60 of the 100 shares of stock of X Corporation and A sold 30 shares of X Corporation stock to Y Corporation for $300. After the sale, A owns 30 shares of X Corporation directly, and pursuant to § 318(a)(2)(C), A owns 15 shares of X Corporation through A's 50% ownership of Y Corporation. Thus, A's ownership interest in X Corporation was reduced from 60% to 45% (45/100) shares. This reduction in ownership of X Corporation stock satisfies the requirements of § 302(b)(2) (45% < (60% × 80%)). Accordingly, the sale of the X Corporation stock by A to Y Corporation is treated as a sale or exchange, and A recognizes a $270 capital gain ($300 − $30). See Treas.Reg. § 1.304–2(a). The basis of A's 50 shares of Y Corporation stock is unaffected by the transaction. Id.

1.3.   *Shareholder Basis Issues*

What happens if the selling shareholder does not actually own any stock of the purchasing corporation after the transaction but, due to attribution rules, constructively controls the purchasing corporation, for example, because the selling shareholder's child controls the purchasing corporation? Rev.Rul. 71–563, 1971–2 C.B. 175, held that the basis of the sold stock should be added to the selling shareholder's basis for any remaining stock of the issuer.

What is the effect on basis if, as in *Fehrs Finance Co.,* the selling shareholder actually owns no stock of either the issuer or the purchaser after the transaction? Coyle v. United States, 415 F.2d 488 (4th Cir.1968), suggests that in such a case the basis of the selling shareholder's stock could be added to the basis of the stock in the purchasing corporation held by the related person actually owning stock of the purchasing corporation. But Rev.Rul. 70–496, 1970–2 C.B. 74, held that the basis of the stock simply disappears. In that ruling, Y Corporation sold its wholly owned subsidiary,

S Corporation, to Z Corporation. Both Y Corporation and Z Corporation were controlled by X Corporation. Due to the § 318 attribution rules, Y Corporation continued to own 100% of S Corporation after the sale and § 304(a)(1) recharacterized the transaction as a dividend. Because Y Corporation had no actual interest in Z Corporation, it had no basis to adjust, and X Corporation was denied a basis adjustment with respect to either Y Corporation or Z Corporation.

Regulations proposed in 2009 treated a deemed redemption that is subject to § 301 as a distribution subject to § 302(d) for all purposes of the tax law. To the extent that the deemed § 301 distribution exceeded earnings and profits, the basis of the common stock deemed issued in a § 351 exchange was reduced on a share-by-share basis under the rules of Prop.Reg. § 1.302–5(a) (2009). Under that provision, any unrecovered basis would result in a loss that could not be recognized until the occurrence of an inclusion event, which was an event that would qualify the deemed redemption as an exchange transaction under § 302(a) or the stock of the redeeming corporation became worthless. The 2009 Proposed Regulations were, however, withdrawn in March 2019. See 84 Fed. Reg. 11687 (Mar. 28, 2019) ("The Treasury Department and the IRS are continuing to study the issues addressed in the 2009 Proposed Regulations, with a particular focus on issues surrounding . . . [§] 304 . . . .").

1.4. *Purchasing Corporation's Basis in Stock*

Section 304(a)(1) provides that if a transaction tested under § 304 is treated as a § 301 distribution, the transferor is deemed to have contributed the exchanged stock to the acquiring corporation in exchange for stock of the acquiring corporation in a § 351 transaction. As a result, the acquiring corporation's basis in the stock is determined under § 362(a). Thus, the acquiring corporation's basis in the stock of the issuing corporation received in the transaction will be the same as the transferor's basis in the stock, increased by any gain recognized on the transfer. Prior to 1997, when *Fehrs Finance Co.* was decided and Treas.Reg. § 1.304–2(c), Ex. (3), was promulgated, the last sentence of § 304(a)(1) provided as follows: "To the extent that such distribution is treated as a distribution to which section 301 applies, the stock so acquired shall be treated as having been transferred by the person from whom acquired, and as having been received by the corporation acquiring it, as a contribution to the capital of such corporation." *Fehrs Finance Co.* interpreted the interaction of this statutory rule and § 362(a) as resulting in the acquiring corporation receiving a step-up in basis as a result of any § 301(c)(3) gain recognized by the redeemed shareholder on the overall transaction. In 1997, the last sentence of § 304(a)(1) was amended to read as it now does. If the last sentence of current § 304(a)(1) is read literally, it is difficult to discern how the shareholder can recognize any gain on the "transfer" of the issuing corporation's stock to the acquiring corporation—the gain is realized on the constructive redemption of the acquiring corporation's stock—and thus it is difficult to see how the acquiring corporation can obtain any step-up in the basis of the issuing corporation's stock. On the other hand, the same interpretative difficulties existed under the prior statutory language, which was interpreted to provide the basis step up, and that result appears to be theoretically correct.

If the transaction sufficiently reduces the selling shareholder's stock interest in the issuing corporation that the requirements of § 302(b) are met, the transaction is accorded sale or exchange treatment, and the purchasing corporation takes a § 1012 cost basis in the purchased stock. See Prop.Reg. § 1.304–2(a)(5) (2009) (withdrawn, 84 Fed. Reg. 11687 (Mar. 28, 2019)). Although Treas.Reg. § 1.304–2(c), Ex. (3) indicates that in such a case the acquiring corporation's basis is the transferor's basis increased by the transferor's recognized gain, the Regulation clearly misinterprets the statute, even though on its assumptions, the example inadvertently reaches the correct answer. In reality, the answer in the Regulations virtually always will be incorrect, because the shareholder's amount realized (basis + gain) will not equal the corporation's cost basis—the shareholder's amount realized would be decreased by the shareholder's transaction costs, and the corporation's cost basis would be increased by its transaction costs.

1.5. *Effect of Sale of Stock for Promissory Notes*

Fehrs Finance Co. concluded that no gain was recognized under § 301(c)(3) in the year the annuity contracts were received because they could not be valued. That is not the result if the sale is for a promissory note. A promissory note will be taken into account at its stated principal amount provided it bears interest at the applicable federal rate; if the obligation does not bear interest at the applicable federal rate, its principal amount will be determined under the OID rules discussed in Chapter 3. Suppose that A controls both X Corporation and Y Corporation and sells all of the stock of X Corporation to Y Corporation for a $100,000 promissory note, bearing adequate interest, due in 10 years. Suppose further, that the corporations' combined earnings and profits are only $20,000 and A's basis in the Y Corporation stock is zero. A recognizes an $80,000 gain under § 301(c)(3). Even though A received a promissory note, Cox v. Commissioner, 78 T.C. 1021 (1982), held that § 453 installment reporting of gains is not available for § 301(c)(3) gain because no "sale" occurs as a result of the distribution.

1.6. *Interaction with Section 351*

Section 304(b)(3) requires bifurcation of a transaction in which § 304 and § 351 overlap, with § 304 controlling the distribution of property and § 351 controlling the distribution of the acquiring corporation's stock. Suppose, for example, A owns more than 50% of the stock of X Corporation and transfers the X Corporation stock to Y Corporation, in which A owns 80% of the stock, in exchange for additional Y Corporation stock and cash. The transaction would fall within the literal language of § 351. Under this approach, the cash received would be boot entitled to capital gain treatment. Section 304, however, treats the cash distribution as a § 301 distribution unless the change in A's ownership of X Corporation stock meets one of the tests of § 302(b).

If a shareholder transfers stock in a controlled corporation subject to a liability to a second controlled corporation, § 304(b)(3)(A) overrides § 357 and treats the assumption of the liability by the transferee corporation as a distribution of property. However, § 304(b)(3)(B) provides an exception for certain debt incurred to acquire the stock of a corporation that is assumed by a controlled corporation acquiring the stock; assumption of such debt is an alternative to a debt-financed direct acquisition by the acquiring company. In applying these rules, indebtedness includes debt to which the stock is subject as well as debt assumed by the acquiring company.

2.   PARENT-SUBSIDIARY SITUATIONS

2.1. *Control*

If a shareholder sells stock to a subsidiary of the issuer that is controlled by the issuer under the 50% test in § 304(c), § 304(a)(2) treats the transaction as a redemption of the issuer parent's own stock. Dividend equivalence under § 302 is tested by reference to the change in ownership of the parent's stock. In applying the tests of § 302(b), stock of the parent owned by the subsidiary is attributed under § 318(a)(3)(C) first to the parent corporation and then, under § 318(a)(2)(C), to the shareholders of the parent. Moreover, pursuant to § 304(b)(1), there is no minimum ownership threshold for applying § 318(a)(2)(C) attribution from a corporation in applying the § 302(b) tests.

Section 304(a)(2) is not limited to situations in which the selling shareholder controls the parent corporation. Assume that individual A owns 40% of the stock of P Corporation (40/100 shares), which in turn owns 80% of the stock of S Corporation. A sells 10 shares of P Corporation stock to S Corporation. After the transfer, A directly owns 30% of the outstanding shares of P Corporation. In addition, 80% of the 10 shares of P Corporation owned by S (8 shares) are attributed to P Corporation under § 318(a)(2)(C) and 30% of the 8 P Corporation shares thus constructively owned by P are attributed to A, with the result that A constructively owns 2.4 shares of P Corporation. A's total ownership of P Corporation thus is 32.4%. Because A's ownership of P has been reduced only from 40% to 32.4%, § 302(b)(2) does not apply, and unless the distribution is not essentially equivalent to a dividend under § 301(b)(1)—which depends on the distribution of ownership of the remaining 60 shares of P Corporation stock—dividend treatment is likely.

2.2. *Special Problems in Applying the Attribution Rules*

The attribution rules raise special problems under § 304(a) since two corporations, which, absent these rules, are in a brother-sister relationship, can be viewed by virtue of the attribution rules as being in a parent-subsidiary relationship. Similarly, in the converse situation, a real parent-subsidiary relationship can constructively become a brother-sister arrangement. Treas.Reg. § 1.304–2(c), without discussion, appears to take the position that "real" brother-sister corporations will not be characterized as parent-subsidiary for purposes of § 304. Broadview Lumber Co. v. United States, 561 F.2d 698 (7th Cir.1977), held in the converse situation that two corporations in a "real" parent-subsidiary relationship would not be recharacterized for purposes of § 304 as brother-sister corporations.

The application of the attribution rules in the § 304 context can create some unusual results. In Continental Bankers Life Insurance Co. v. Commissioner, 93 T.C. 52 (1989), P Corporation owned 100% of the stock of

X Corporation and Y Corporation. P Corporation owned 56% of Z Corporation, and Y Corporation owned 20% of the stock of Z Corporation. X Corporation purchased all of the stock of Z Corporation held by Y. Although Y Corporation held no X Corporation stock directly, by attribution through P Corporation, Y Corporation controlled both X Corporation and Z Corporation. Thus, the acquisition was a redemption of X Corporation stock pursuant to § 304(a)(1).

See also Rev.Rul. 74–605, 1974–2 C.B. 97, holding that the attribution rules did not cause § 304 to apply to situations involving a purchase by the parent of stock of a second tier subsidiary.

2.3. *Meaning of "Property" in Section 304(a)(2)*

Suppose that A controls P Corporation, which in turn owns all of the stock of S Corporation. To reverse the parent subsidiary relationship, A transfers to S Corporation more than 50% of the stock of P Corporation in exchange for newly issued shares constituting more than 50% (but less than 80%) of the stock of S Corporation. Does § 304(a)(2) apply to the transaction? Section 317(a) defines property so as to include all corporate stock other than "stock in the corporation making the distribution." Section 304(a)(2) recharacterizes transfers of stock to a subsidiary as a redemption by the issuer, i.e., the issuer is the distributing corporation. In the example, since P Corporation is the issuing corporation, which is deemed to make the distribution, and S Corporation stock was distributed, it is arguable that the S Corporation stock would be "property" as defined in § 317(a). However, Bhada v. Commissioner, 89 T.C. 959 (1987), aff'd, 892 F.2d 39 (6th Cir.1989) and sub nom. Caamano v. Commissioner, 879 F.2d 156 (5th Cir.1989), held that the "distribution" in § 304(a) is not the deemed redemption, *but the actual transaction.* Thus, in the example, the distribution by S Corporation to A is a distribution of its own stock, which under § 317(a) is not property. The court reinforced its conclusion that the exchange was not subject to § 304 by noting that in receiving stock of the subsidiary, the shareholders of the parent did not withdraw assets from either the parent or the subsidiary. Rather, "[t]he transaction resulted in a change in the ownership structure of the two corporations. Congress did not intend to prevent such a change in corporate ownership by enacting section 304."

2.4. *Acquiring Corporation's Basis in Parent Corporation's Stock*

Regardless of whether the transaction is treated as a dividend or as a sale or exchange for the selling shareholder, the acquiring subsidiary takes a § 1012 cost basis in the parent corporation's stock purchased in the transaction. Rev.Rul. 80–189, 1989–2 C.B. 106. Furthermore, the purchase by the subsidiary is not treated as a constructive distribution to the parent. Id. Thus, there is no possibility of an adjustment to the parent's basis in the subsidiary stock.

3. RELATIONSHIP OF SECTION 304 TO PARTIAL LIQUIDATION RULES

Based upon a technical analysis of the language of a prior version of § 304 and the statutory predecessor of § 302(e), Blaschka v. United States, 393 F.2d 983 (Ct.Cl.1968), concluded that when § 304 overlaps with the partial liquidation rules of § 302(b)(4), qualification for sale and exchange treatment under § 304 is determined by applying the test for a partial liquidation with reference to the acquiring corporation, rather than with reference to the issuing corporation. Assume, for example, that A owns all of the stock of X Corporation, which in turn owns all of the stock of Y Corporation, and A transfers a portion of his shares in X Corporation to Y Corporation in exchange for the proceeds from the sale of all of the assets of one of Y Corporation's two operating divisions. This transaction is described by § 304 and is a partial liquidation of Y Corporation under § 302(b)(4). The partial liquidation of Y Corporation avoids the application of § 304. The court in *Blaschka* explained its reasoning as follows:

> The function of § 304, then is to complement § 302. To that end, § 304(b)(1) provides that such a sale is defined as a redemption of the stock of the acquiring corporation, and that for purposes of § 302(b), whether such stock acquisition is to be treated as a distribution in exchange for the stock is determined by reference to the stock of the issuing corporation. * * * The essential question is whether the distribution has affected the stockholder's proportionate interest and control in the issuing corporation, and for that reason the special rule of § 304(b)(1) points to the issuing corporation to apply § 304(a) to § 302. * * * [N]o mention is made of * * * any provision in § 304 or elsewhere in the 1954 Code, as to which corporation is to be tested to determine whether there has been a partial liquidation in a stock redemption through use of related corporations. * * * [H]owever, * * * the considerations underlying the tax treatment of partial liquidations requires that a § 304 stock redemption, involving the question of a partial liquidation under [§ 302(b)(4) and § 302(e)], be tested on the level of the acquiring corporation. * * * The very nature of a partial liquidation, at least as purportedly involved in this case, is a curtailment or contraction of the activities of the acquiring corporation, and the distribution to a stockholder of unneeded funds in exchange for stock in a related corporation. It is concluded that the purported partial liquidation is not to be measured by § 302[(b)(1)–(3)], but that a general rule of § 304(a)—that the stock sale is to be treated as a redemption by the acquiring corporation—applies subject, however, to the statutory definition as to what constitutes a partial liquidation under [§ 302(b)(4)] and [§ 302(e)] * * *, applied to the acquiring corporation.

4.   EXTRAORDINARY DIVIDENDS

Under § 1059(e)(1)(A)(iii)(II), distributions to a corporate shareholder that are treated as § 301 distributions by virtue of § 304(a)(1), and thus are eligible for the dividends received deduction under § 243, are classified as extraordinary dividends. As a consequence, the corporate shareholder is required to reduce its basis in the stock of the acquiring corporation by the amount of the dividend that is not included in income. I.R.C. § 1059(a). Amounts in excess of basis are treated as exchange gain.

PROBLEM SET 6

1. Alicia owned all 100 outstanding shares of X Corp., with a basis of $60 per share. Alicia sells 60 shares of X Corp. stock to Y Corp. for $18,000 ($300 per share). Prior to the sale, X Corp. had accumulated earnings and profits of $8,000; Y Corp. had accumulated earnings and profits of $2,000 and current earnings and profits of $1,000. What are the tax consequences of the sale in the following alternative situations?

    (a) Alicia is the sole shareholder of Y Corp. Alicia's basis in the Y Corp. stock is $2,000.

    (b) Alicia is the sole shareholder of Y Corp. but Y Corp. has no current earnings and profits and a $9,000 deficit in accumulated earnings and profits.

    (c) Alicia owns 40% of the stock of Y Corp. The remaining Y Corp. stock is owned by unrelated parties.

    (d) Alicia owns no stock of Y Corp., but her daughter is the sole shareholder of Y Corp.

2. Becky owns 60 of 100 outstanding common shares of W Corp. and 50 out of 100 common shares of Z Corp. Becky sells 30 shares of W Corp., having a basis of $10,000, to Z Corp. for $50,000. W Corp. and Z Corp. each have accumulated earnings and profits of more than $50,000. What are the tax consequences to Becky?

3. Carmela owns 80 shares of the common stock of X Corp., which has 100 shares of common stock outstanding. X Corp. owns 65 shares of common stock of Y Corp., which has 100 shares outstanding. Carmela sells 35 shares of X Corp. stock to Y Corp. for $100 per share. Assume that Carmela has a basis of $25 per share in the X Corp. stock, and that X Corp. has $4,000 and Y Corp. has $6,000 of accumulated earnings and profits. What are the tax consequences to Carmela?

4. Gabrielle owned 70 out of 100 shares of common stock of Q Corporation and 30 out of 80 shares of stock of V Corporation. Gabrielle transferred 30 shares of Q Corporation stock, with a basis of $40,000, to V Corporation in exchange for 20 shares of V Corporation stock worth $50,000 and $50,000 in cash. V Corporation had over $100,000 of earnings and profits. What are the tax consequences to Gabrielle?

5. Felicity owned all of the stock of Transamerica, Inc. and Desperate Soap Corporation. Felicity's basis in the Transamerica stock was $999,999. For many years, Desperate Soap had operated separately an advertising business and a chain of day care centers. This year, Desperate Soap sold the day care center business for $1,000,000 and used the proceeds to purchase all of Felicity's Transamerica stock. Desperate Soap had over $1,000,000 of earnings and profits. What are the tax consequences to Felicity?

SECTION 7.   STOCK REDEMPTION DISTRIBUTIONS TO PAY ESTATE AND INHERITANCE TAXES

INTERNAL REVENUE CODE: Section 303(a)–(c).

Revenue Ruling 87–132

1987–2 C.B. 82.

ISSUE

Whether the application of section 303 of the Internal Revenue Code to a stock redemption is precluded when the stock redeemed was newly distributed as part of the same transaction.

FACTS

X corporation had outstanding 300 shares of voting common stock that were owned equally by an estate and by *A*, an individual, who had no interest in the estate under section 318 of the Code. The value of the *X* stock held by the estate exceeded the amount specified in section 303(b)(2)(A). The estate wanted to effect a redemption pursuant to section 303 to pay death taxes.

In order to maintain relative voting power and to preserve continuity of management, *X* undertook the following two steps. First, *X* issued 10 shares of a new class of nonvoting common stock on each share of common stock outstanding. Thus, the estate and *A* each received 1,500 shares of this stock. Immediately thereafter, 1,000 shares of the non-voting common stock were redeemed by *X* from the estate in exchange for cash. The overall result of these two steps was that the estate obtained the cash it needed while giving up only nonvoting stock.

The redemption of the *X* nonvoting common stock occurred within the time limits prescribed by section 303(b)(1)(A) of the Code and did not exceed the amount permitted by section 303(a).

LAW AND ANALYSIS

Section 303(a) of the Code provides that a distribution of property to a shareholder by a corporation in redemption of stock of the corporation, which (for federal estate tax purposes) is included in determining the gross estate of a decedent, is treated as a distribution in full payment in exchange for the stock redeemed to the extent of the sum of certain taxes and expenses. These taxes and expenses are the estate, inheritance, legacy and succession taxes plus the amount of funeral and administrative expenses allowable as deductions for federal estate tax purposes.

Section 303(c) of the Code provides that if a shareholder owns stock of a corporation (new stock) the basis of which is determined by reference to the basis of stock of a corporation (old stock) that was included in determining the gross estate of a decedent, and section 303(a) would apply to a distribution in redemption of the old stock, then section 303(a) applies to a distribution in redemption of the new stock. Section 1.303–2(d) of the Income Tax Regulations specifically provides that section 303 applies to a distribution in redemption of stock received by an estate in a distribution to which section 305(a) applies.

Section 305(a) of the Code provides that, generally, gross income does not include the amount of any distribution of the stock of a corporation made by the corporation to its shareholders with respect to its stock. Section 305(b)(1), however, provides that if the distribution is, at the election of any of the shareholders (whether exercised before or after the declaration of the distribution), payable either in its stock or in property, then the distribution of stock is treated as a distribution to which section 301 applies. Section 305(b)(2) provides that if the distribution has the result of the receipt of property by some shareholders and an increase in the proportionate interest of other shareholders in the assets or earnings and profits of the corporation, then the distribution of stock is treated as a distribution to which section 301 applies.

Section 307(a) of the Code provides that if a shareholder already owning stock in a corporation ("old stock") receives additional stock ("new stock") in a distribution to which section 305(a) applies, then the basis of the old stock prior to the distribution is allocated between the old stock and new stock subsequent to the distribution.

Here, 3,000 shares of nonvoting common stock were distributed and 1,000 shares were subsequently redeemed by X as part of a plan designed to allow the estate to avail itself of the benefits of section 303 of the Code. The intent of Congress in enacting the statutory predecessor of section 303 was to provide an effective means whereby the estate of a decedent owning an interest in a family enterprise could finance the estate tax without being required to dispose of its entire interest in the family business in order to avoid the imposition of an ordinary dividend tax. H.R.Rep. No. 2319, 81st Cong., 2d Sess. 63–64 (1950). Given this intent, it follows that the estate should be able to obtain the benefits of section 303 without a substantially adverse effect on the estate's ownership of the family business.

Moreover, section 303(c) of the Code is a remedial provision that was added to expand the application of section 303 to the redemption of stock which, despite a technical change in the form of ownership, represents the same stock as that owned at death. S.Rep. No. 1622, 83rd Cong., 2nd Sess. 239 (1954). The sole requirement for application of section 303 to the redemption, under section 303(c), is that the basis of the stock redeemed ("new stock") be determined by reference to the basis of the "old stock" included in the estate. Section 1.303–2(d) of the regulations provides that stock received by an estate in a section 305(a) distribution is entitled to section 303 treatment. Rev.Rul. 83–68, 1983–1 C.B. 75, holds that a distribution of stock that is immediately redeemable at the option of a shareholder gives the shareholder an election to receive either stock or property within the meaning of section 305(b)(1) and, therefore, is a distribution to which section 301 applies. See also Rev.Rul. 76–258, 1976–2 C.B. 95.

The nature of section 303 of the Code and the limited time period for redemption provided in section 303(b)(1) are generally indicative of a Congressional intent that section 303 be applicable to stock issued as part of the same plan as the redemption. Consequently, for purposes of section 303 only, section 305 should be applied prior to, and without reference to, the subsequent redemption.

HOLDING

The exclusion from gross income provision of section 305(a) of the Code, and the carryover of basis provisions of section 307(a), apply to X's distribution of its new nonvoting common stock to A and the estate. Section 303(a) applies to X's distribution of cash to the estate in redemption of the 1,000 shares of its new nonvoting common stock. For the tax consequences to A (the nonredeeming shareholder) as a result of this transaction, see section 305.

* * *

DETAILED ANALYSIS

1.   GENERAL

Section 303, whose provisions were first adopted in 1951, has a significant effect upon estate planning since it permits certain redemptions for the purpose of paying estate taxes to qualify for sale or exchange treatment, even though the redemption does not meet any of the tests of § 302. In order to qualify under § 303 the stock must (1) have been included in the decedent's gross estate for federal estate tax purposes; (2) have comprised the specified percentage of the gross estate (less certain expenses); (3) be redeemed from a person who bears the burden of the estate tax; and (4) be redeemed within a specified period of time after the decedent's death. A redemption that qualifies under § 303 generally produces limited tax consequences to the distributee as regards gain recognition because § 1014 provides the deceased shareholder's successor in interest with a basis in the stock equal to its value on the decedent's date of death. On the other hand, if § 303 is not satisfied, dividend treatment, which would generally be the case, would not allow tax-free basis recovery so the section in this regard gives the taxpayer a substantial advantage. As such, § 303(a) represents another means (outside of § 302(b)) to avoid dividend treatment for payments made by a corporation to its shareholder. Because § 1014 gives a fair market value basis in the stock owned by a decedent as of the date of death, § 303(a)'s redemption treatment ensures that the only gain realized with respect to the redeemed stock is limited to the gain arising from the change in the value of the stock between the date of the decedent's death and the date of the § 303(a) redemption transaction, if any. In addition, the corporation's earnings and profits attributable to the shares redeemed in the § 303(a) redemption are eliminated, thus ensuring that the underlying corporate earnings attributable to the redeemed shares will never be taxed as a dividend to any shareholder.

Scholars have roundly criticized the basis step-up at time of death that is afforded under § 1014 as inappropriate. But, the addition of § 303(a), in combination with § 1014, compounds the § 1014 error because § 303(a) recasts a corporation's cash payment that would otherwise have been treated as a cash dividend instead as the receipt of sales proceeds derived from a transaction in which no gain or loss is realized. This sale or exchange characterization frustrates the "classic view" of treating corporations and shareholders as separate and distinct taxpayers because § 303(a), in combination with § 1014, allows a corporation's cash payment to its shareholder not to create any realized income at the shareholder level even though the shareholder may not have meaningfully reduced its interest in the corporation. Moreover, because the underlying corporate earnings and profits associated with the stock redeemed in the § 303(a) redemption are eliminated, the further consequence of § 303(a)'s application is that the underlying corporate earnings and profits will never be treated as a dividend at the shareholder level at any time thereafter.

2.   POLICY BASIS FOR SECTION 303

By making the treasury of a closely held corporation available as a source of funds at the death of a principal shareholder, the problem of meeting estate taxes may be substantially eased. The enactment of this provision was justified as follows:

> It has been brought to the attention of your committee that the problem of financing the estate tax is acute in the case of estates consisting largely of shares in a family corporation. The market for such shares is usually very limited, and it is frequently difficult, if not impossible, to dispose of a minority interest. If, therefore, the estate tax cannot be financed through the sale of the other assets in the estate, the executors will be forced to dispose of the family business. In many cases the result will be the absorption of a family enterprise by larger competitors, thus tending to accentuate the degree of concentration of industry in this country.

S.Rep. No. 81–2375, 81st Cong., 2d Sess. 54 (1951). But even though this hardship case was the stated reason for adopting § 303's predecessor, it was recognized even at the time of its adoption that the relief afforded by § 303(a) was not confined to situations of actual illiquidity or hardship.[3]

---

[3]   This criticism of § 303's predecessor has been levied since the original enactment of this provision:

> Some hardship cases may occur where the bulk of an individual's estate is tied up in his corporation. Of course if the corporation had obeyed the law and distributed unneeded earnings and profits, the stockholder could have usually accumulate sufficient funds outside his corporation to provide for the inevitable estate tax. But the proposal here permits the few hardship cases to serve as a front for brazen tax avoiders. The House version of this proposal at least had the virtue of relieving only the hardship cases. But even this limitation has disappeared from the bill before us now.

Statement of Senator Humphrey, 96 Cong. Rec. 13,983 (Aug. 29, 1950).

Since the enactment of § 303, the Code has been amended by the addition of § 6166, which provides an extension of time for payment of the estate tax if the estate consists largely of an interest in a closely held business. It would seem that the availability of relief under this provision should be sufficient to mitigate any hardship in paying estate taxes attributable to stock in closely held corporations and § 303 is, in fact, largely unnecessary. Thus, it is surprising that § 303 has remained in the tax laws even though Congress has substantially eliminated the hardship case that galvanized support for section 303(a)'s enactment in the first place. In this regard, the estate tax exemption amount has been increased to $10 million and is indexed for inflation. I.R.C. § 2010(c). Secondarily, qualified dividends are entitled to concessionary capital gains rates that in most cases are capped at 20%. Thus, whatever illiquidity or hardship concerns might have justified Congress's decision to allow a corporation to make exempt dividend payments to its shareholder's estate, that hardship rationale has been radically curtailed now that the estate tax exemption amount is significantly higher and the shareholder's income tax burden with respect to the receipt of taxable dividends is substantially reduced.[4]

3. TECHNICAL ASPECTS OF SECTION 303

Suppose the stock redeemed to pay estate and inheritance taxes is § 306 preferred stock (discussed in Chapter 6). Since the § 306 stock was included in the decedent's estate and its basis was determined under § 1014, it would lose its § 306 "taint" and can be redeemed under § 303 so as to receive exchange treatment at the shareholder level. See I.R.C. § 306(c)(1)(C).

Section 2035(c)(1)(A) includes in a decedent's gross estate for purposes of computing the § 303(b)(2) percentages (but not for purposes of computing federal estate taxes) the value of any stock transferred by the decedent for less than adequate consideration within three years prior to death. Such transferred shares, however, may not be redeemed under § 303. Rev.Rul. 84–76, 1984–1 C.B. 91.

Moreover, § 303(a) does not require that the proceeds of the § 303(a) redemption transaction be applied to the payment of estate taxes or must actually be used to pay the administrative expenses of the estate. Instead, § 303(a) simply requires that an otherwise qualifying § 303(a) redemption transaction must occur within a statutorily prescribed time period, which § 303(b)(1) defines as follows: (i) within 90 days after the assessment period for the federal estate tax,[5] (iii) within the 60th day after a Tax Court's decision has become final, or (iii) the last day of an installment payment plan as defined by § 6166.

---

[4]   For a further analysis of the technical aspects of § 303 and a more expansive argument for its outright repeal, see Bret Wells, Reform of Corporate Distributions in Subchapter C, 37 Va. Tax Rev. 365 (2018).

[5]   In Rev.Rul. 69–47, 1969–1 C.B. 94, the IRS ruled that the time period for a corporate distribution under § 303 is not shortened when the decedent's estate tax return is filed early because, for purposes of computing the period of limitations under § 6501(b)(1) and § 303(b)(1)(A), the return is deemed filed on the last permissible day. However, in Rev. Rul. 73–204, 1973–1 C.B. 170, the IRS ruled that "if the estate tax return is filed late then a redemption under section 303 may be made within three years and ninety days of the late return's filing."

An otherwise qualifying § 303 redemption transaction can be accomplished in a series of redemptions.[6] Moreover, in Rev.Rul. 67–425, 1967–2 C.B. 134, the IRS ruled that a redemption transaction satisfied the § 303(b)(1) time period requirements and thus qualified for sale or exchange treatment under § 303(a) even though the corporation distributed a promissory note in exchange for the redeemed stock and even though the note was not retired until after the time periods prescribed by § 303(b)(1). The effect of Rev.Rul. 67–425's holding is that § 303(a) treatment can apply to a transaction that provides no actual cash liquidity to pay the estate taxes or to pay the estate's administrative expenses. Thus, the holding of Rev.Rul. 67–425 expands the application of § 303(a) so that it provides tax relief in situations that are outside the stated policy goals expressed at the time of the original enactment of § 303's predecessor (namely, to provide tax relief to estates that needed to redeem closely held stock in order to pay estate taxes or administrative expenses of the estate).

If § 303 provides sale or exchange treatment to the redeeming shareholder, then the nonredeeming shareholders will not be considered to have received a constructive stock dividend under § 305 (discussed in the next Chapter) even though the nonredeeming shareholders experienced an increase in their proportionate interest in the corporation in a transaction where the redeeming shareholder has received what would have been considered a cash dividend apart from the application of § 303(a). Thus, § 303 provides a corollary tax benefit to nonredeeming shareholders as it allows the nonredeeming shareholder to avoid any realized income for the increase in their proportionate stock interest in the corporation in a transaction that, apart from § 303(a)'s application, would have been viewed as a cash dividend received by the redeeming shareholders and the receipt of a taxable stock dividend by the nonredeeming shareholders "but for" the application of § 303(a).

For example, in Rev.Rul. 87–132, reproduced supra, an estate and an unrelated party each owned 50% of the stock of a corporation. As part of an integrated plan, nonvoting common stock was issued to each party, and, as part of that same plan, a portion of the nonvoting common stock issued to the estate was redeemed by the corporation. The IRS stated that, as a general rule, § 305(b)(2) provides that if a stock distribution has the result of allowing some shareholders to obtain the receipt of property and results in other shareholders experiencing an increase in their proportionate interest in the assets or earnings and profits of the corporation, then the distribution of stock to the nonredeeming shareholder generally would be treated as a distribution to which § 301 applies by reason of § 305(b)(2). However, the IRS then stated that, because the estate's redemption transaction qualified for sale or exchange treatment by reason of § 303(a), the proportionate increase in stock interest experienced by the nonredeeming shareholders was nontaxable under § 305(b) because their proportionate interest in corporate

---

[6] See Treas.Reg. § 1.303–2(g); Rev.Rul. 86–54, 1986–1 C.B. 356. The ordering rules for applying § 303(a) in the context of redemptions that exceed the maximum amount allowable under § 303(a) is beyond the scope of this Chapter but is adequately addressed elsewhere. See e.g., Marc P. Blum & Dana L. Trier, Planning for Maximum Benefits of 303 Redemptions with Estate Tax Deferral, 53 J. Tax'n 236 (1980).

stock increased as a part of a transaction where the redeeming shareholder was afforded sale or exchange treatment. Treas.Reg. § 1.305–3(a). Thus, Rev.Rul. 87–132 stands for the proposition that § 303(a)'s application supplants the stock dividend result otherwise required under § 305 for the nonredeeming shareholder who experiences a proportionate increase in interest.

CHAPTER 6

STOCK DIVIDENDS

SECTION 1.   TAXABLE VERSUS NONTAXABLE STOCK
   DIVIDENDS

A. JUDICIAL BACKGROUND

Eisner v. Macomber

Supreme Court of the United States, 1920.
252 U.S. 189.

[The taxpayer was the owner of 2,200 shares of common stock in the Standard Oil Company of California. The corporation declared a 50% stock dividend, and the taxpayer received 1,100 additional shares of which 198.77 shares represented surplus of the corporation earned between March 1, 1913, and January 1, 1916, the latter date being the date of the stock dividend. The shares representing the post-March 1, 1913 surplus had a par value of $19,877, and the Commissioner treated the stock dividend as taxable income to the extent of the par value of such shares. Cash dividends in such an amount would have constituted taxable income. The applicable statute expressly included stock dividends in income. The taxpayer asserted that the stock dividend was not income within the meaning of the Sixteenth Amendment. The District Court rendered judgment against the Government.]

■ MR. JUSTICE PITNEY delivered the opinion of the Court. * * *

In Towne v. Eisner, [245 U.S. 418], the question was whether a stock dividend made in 1914 against surplus earned prior to January 1, 1913, was taxable against the stockholder under the Act of October 3, 1913, which provided that net income should include "dividends," and also "gains or profits and income derived from any source whatever." * * * When the case came here, after overruling a motion to dismiss made by the government upon the ground that the only question involved was the construction of the statute and not its constitutionality, we dealt upon the merits with the question of construction only, but disposed of it upon consideration of the essential nature of a stock dividend disregarding the fact that the one in question was based upon surplus earnings that accrued before the Sixteenth Amendment took effect. Not only so, but we rejected the reasoning of the District Court, saying (245 U.S. 366):

"Notwithstanding the thoughtful discussion that the case received below we cannot doubt that the dividend was capital as well for the purposes of the Income Tax Law as for distribution between tenant for life and remainderman. What was said by this court upon the latter question is equally true for the former. 'A stock dividend really takes nothing from the property of the corporation, and adds nothing to the interests of the shareholders. Its property is not diminished, and their interests are not increased. * * * The proportional interest of each shareholder remains the same. The only change is in the evidence which represents that interest, the new shares and the original shares together representing the same proportional interest that the original shares represented before the issue of the new ones.' Gibbons v. Mahon, 136 U.S. 549, 559, 560. In short, the corporation is no poorer and the stockholder is no richer than they were before. 255, 261 * * * If the plaintiff gained any small advantage by the change, it certainly was not an advantage of $417,450, the sum upon which he was taxed. * * * What has happened is that the plaintiff's old certificates have been split up in effect and have diminished in value to the extent of the value of the new."

This language aptly answered not only the reasoning of the District Court but the argument of the Solicitor General in this court, which discussed the essential nature of a stock dividend. And if, for the reasons thus expressed, such a dividend is not to be regarded as "income" or "dividends" within the meaning of the act of 1913, we are unable to see how it can be brought within the meaning of "incomes" in the Sixteenth Amendment; it being very clear that Congress intended in that act to exert its power to the extent permitted by the amendment. In Towne v. Eisner it was not contended that any construction of the statute could make it narrower than the constitutional grant; rather the contrary. * * * We adhere to the view then expressed, and might rest the present case there, not because that case in terms decided the constitutional question, for it did not, but because the conclusion there reached as to the essential nature of a stock dividend necessarily prevents its being regarded as income in any true sense.

Nevertheless, in view of the importance of the matter, and the fact that Congress in the Revenue Act of 1916 declared that a "stock dividend shall be considered income, to the amount of its cash value," we will deal at length with the constitutional question, incidentally testing the soundness of our previous conclusion.

* * *

[I]t becomes essential to distinguish between what is and what is not "income," as the term is there used, and to apply the distinction, as cases arise, according to truth and substance, without regard to form. Congress cannot by any definition it may adopt conclude the matter, since it cannot by legislation alter the Constitution, from which alone it derives its power to legislate, and within whose limitations alone that power can be lawfully exercised.

The fundamental relation of "capital" to "income" has been much discussed by economists, the former being likened to the tree or the land, the latter to the fruit or the crop; the former depicted as a reservoir supplied from springs, the latter as the outlet stream, to be measured by its flow during a period of time. For the present purpose we require only a clear definition of the term "income," as used in common speech, in order to determine its meaning in the amendment, and having formed also a correct judgment as to the nature of a stock dividend, we shall find it easy to decide the matter at issue.

After examining dictionaries in common use (Bouv.L.D.; Standard Dict.; Webster's Internat. Dict.; Century Dict.), we find little to add to the succinct definition adopted in two cases arising under the Corporation Tax Act of 1909 (Stratton's Independence v. Howbert, 231 U.S. 399, 415; Doyle v. Mitchell Bros. Co., 247 U.S. 179)—"Income may be defined as the gain derived from capital, from labor, or from both combined," provided it be understood to include profit gained through a sale or conversion of capital assets, to which it was applied in the Doyle Case, 247 U.S. 179, 185.

Brief as it is, it indicates the characteristic and distinguishing attribute of income essential for a correct solution of the present controversy. The government, although basing its argument upon the definition as quoted, placed chief emphasis upon the word "gain," which was extended to include a variety of meanings; while the significance of the next three words was either overlooked or misconceived. "*Derived— from—capital*"; "the *gain—derived—from—capital*," etc. Here we have the essential matter: *not* a gain *accruing to* capital; not a *growth* or *increment* of value *in* the investment; but a gain, a profit, something of exchangeable value, *proceeding from* the property, *severed from* the capital, however invested or employed, and *coming in*, being "*derived*"— that is, *received* or *drawn by* the recipient (the taxpayer) for his *separate* use, benefit and disposal—*that* is income derived from property. Nothing else answers the description.

The same fundamental conception is clearly set forth in the Sixteenth Amendment—"incomes, *from* whatever *source derived*"—the essential thought being expressed with a conciseness and lucidity entirely in harmony with the form and style of the Constitution.

Can a stock dividend, considering its essential character, be brought within the definition? To answer this, regard must be had to the nature of a corporation and the stockholder's relation to it. * * *

In the present case, the corporation had surplus and undivided profits invested in plant, property, and business, and required for the purposes of the corporation, amounting to about $45,000,000, in addition to outstanding capital stock of $50,000,000. In this the case is not extraordinary. The profits of a corporation, as they appear upon the balance sheet at the end of the year, need not be in the form of money on hand in excess of what is required to meet current liabilities and finance current operations of the company. Often, especially in a growing business, only a part, sometimes a small part, of the year's profits is in property capable of division; the remainder having been absorbed in the acquisition of increased plant, equipment, stock in trade, or accounts receivable, or in decrease of outstanding liabilities. When only a part is available for dividends, the balance of the year's profits is carried to the credit of undivided profits, or surplus, or some other account having like significance. If thereafter the company finds itself in funds beyond current needs it may declare dividends out of such surplus or undivided profits; otherwise it may go on for years conducting a successful business, but requiring more and more working capital because of the extension of its operations, and therefore unable to declare dividends approximating the amount of its profits. Thus the surplus may increase until it equals or even exceeds the par value of the outstanding capital stock. This may be adjusted upon the books in the mode adopted in the case at bar—by declaring a "stock dividend." This, however, is no more than a book adjustment, in essence not a dividend but rather the opposite; no part of the assets of the company is separated from the common fund, nothing distributed except paper certificates that evidence an antecedent increase in the value of the stockholder's capital interest resulting from an accumulation of profits by the company, but profits so far absorbed in the business as to render it impracticable to separate them for withdrawal and distribution. In order to make the adjustment, a charge is made against surplus account with corresponding credit to capital stock account, equal to the proposed "dividend"; the new stock is issued against this and the certificates delivered to the existing stockholders in proportion to their previous holdings. This, however, is merely bookkeeping that does not affect the aggregate assets of the corporation or its outstanding liabilities; it affects only the form, not the essence, of the "liability" acknowledged by the corporation to its own shareholders, and this through a readjustment of accounts on one side of the balance sheet only, increasing "capital stock" at the expense of "surplus"; it does not alter the preexisting proportionate interest of any stockholder or increase the intrinsic value of his holding or of the aggregate holdings of the other stockholders as they stood before. The new certificates simply increase the number of the shares, with consequent dilution of the value of each share.

A "stock dividend" shows that the company's accumulated profits have been capitalized, instead of distributed to the stockholders or retained as surplus available for distribution in money or in kind should opportunity offer. Far from being a realization of profits of the stockholder, it tends rather to postpone such realization, in that the fund represented by the new stock has been transferred from surplus to capital, and no longer is available for actual distribution.

The essential and controlling fact is that the stockholder has received nothing out of the company's assets for his separate use and benefit; on the contrary, every dollar of his original investment, together with whatever accretions and accumulations have resulted from employment of his money and that of the other stockholders in the business of the company, still remains the property of the company, and subject to business risks which may result in wiping out the entire investment. Having regard to the very truth of the matter, to substance and not to form, he has received nothing that answers the definition of income within the meaning of the Sixteenth Amendment. * * *

We are clear that not only does a stock dividend really take nothing from the property of the corporation and add nothing to that of the shareholder, but that the antecedent accumulation of profits evidenced thereby, while indicating that the shareholder is the richer because of an increase of his capital, at the same time shows he has not realized or received any income in the transaction.

It is said that a stockholder may sell the new shares acquired in the stock dividend; and so he may, if he can find a buyer. It is equally true that if he does sell, and in doing so realizes a profit, such profit, like any other, is income, and so far as it may have arisen since the Sixteenth Amendment is taxable by Congress without apportionment. The same would be true were he to sell some of his original shares at a profit. But if a shareholder sells dividend stock he necessarily disposes of a part of his capital interest, just as if he should sell a part of his old stock, either before or after the dividend. What he retains no longer entitles him to the same proportion of future dividends as before the sale. His part in the control of the company likewise is diminished. Thus, if one holding $60,000 out of a total $100,000 of the capital stock of a corporation should receive in common with other stockholders a 50 per cent. stock dividend, and should sell his part, he thereby would be reduced from a majority to a minority stockholder, having six-fifteenths instead of six-tenths of the total stock outstanding. A corresponding and proportionate decrease in capital interest and in voting power would befall a minority holder should he sell dividend stock; it being in the nature of things impossible for one to dispose of any part of such an issue without a proportionate disturbance of the distribution of the entire capital stock, and a like diminution of the seller's comparative voting power—that "right preservative of rights" in the control of a corporation. Yet, without selling, the shareholder, unless possessed of other resources, has not the wherewithal to pay an income tax upon the dividend stock. Nothing could more clearly show that to tax a stock dividend is to tax a capital increase, and not income, than this demonstration that in the nature of things it requires conversion of capital in order to pay the tax.

* * *

Conceding that the mere issue of a stock dividend makes the recipient no richer than before, the government nevertheless contends that the new certificates measure the extent to which the gains accumulated by the corporation have made him the richer. There are two insuperable difficulties with this: In the first place, it would depend upon how long he had held the stock whether the stock dividend indicated the extent to which he had been enriched by the operations of the company; unless he had held it throughout such operations the measure would not hold true. Secondly, and more important for present purposes, enrichment through increase in value of capital investment is not income in any proper meaning of the term. * * *

It is said there is no difference in principle between a simple stock dividend and a case where stockholders use money received as cash dividends to purchase additional stock contemporaneously issued by the corporation. But an actual cash dividend, with a real option to the stockholder either to keep the money for his own or to reinvest it in new shares, would be as far removed as possible from a true stock dividend, such as the one we have under consideration, where nothing of value is taken from the company's assets and transferred to the individual ownership of the several stockholders and thereby subjected to their disposal.

* * *

Thus, from every point of view we are brought irresistibly to the conclusion that neither under the Sixteenth Amendment nor otherwise has Congress power to tax without apportionment a true stock dividend made lawfully and in good faith, or the accumulated profits behind it, as income of the stockholder. The Revenue Act of 1916, in so far as it imposes a tax upon the stockholder because of such dividend, contravenes the provisions of article 1, § 2, cl. 3, and article 1, § 9, cl. 4, of the Constitution, and to this extent is invalid, notwithstanding the Sixteenth Amendment.

Judgment affirmed.

* * *

B. THE STATUTORY STRUCTURE

INTERNAL REVENUE CODE: Sections 305(a)–(d); 307(a).

REGULATIONS: Sections 1.305–1(a), (b); 1.305–2; 1.305–3(a)–(c), (e) Exs. 1–6; 1.305–5(a), (b)(1)–(3), (d), Exs. 4, 5; 1.305–6; 1.305–7; 1.307–1, –2.

Senate Finance Committee Report, Tax Reform Act of 1969

S.Rep. No. 91–552, 91st Cong., 1st Sess. 150–53 (1969).

[*Pre-1969*] *law.*—In its simplest form, a stock dividend is commonly thought of as a mere readjustment of the stockholder's interest, and not as income. For example, if a corporation with only common stock outstanding issues more common stock as a dividend, no basic change is made in the position of the corporation and its stockholders. No corporate assets are paid out, and the distribution merely gives each stockholder more pieces of paper to represent the same interest in the corporation.

On the other hand, stock dividends may also be used in a way that alters the interests of the stockholders. For example, if a corporation, with only common stock outstanding declares a dividend payable at the election of each stockholder, either in additional common stock or in cash, the stockholder, who receives a stock dividend is in the same position as if he received a taxable cash dividend and purchased additional stock with the proceeds. His interest in the corporation is increased relative to the interests of stockholders who took dividends in cash.

[Pre-1969] law (sec. 305(a)) provides that if a corporation pays a dividend to its shareholders in its own stock (or in rights to acquire its stock), the shareholders are not required to include the value of the dividend in income. There are two exceptions to this general rule. First, stock dividends paid in discharge of preference dividends for the current or immediately preceding taxable year are taxable. Second, a stock dividend is taxable if any shareholder may elect to receive his dividend in cash or other property instead of stock.

These provisions were enacted as part of the Internal Revenue Code of 1954. Before 1954 the taxability of stock dividends was determined under the "proportionate interest test," which developed out of a series of Supreme Court cases, beginning with Eisner v. Macomber, 252 U.S. 189 (1920). In these cases the Court held, in general, that a stock dividend was taxable if it increased any shareholder's proportionate interest in the corporation. The lower courts often had difficulty in applying the test as formulated in these cases, particularly where unusual corporate capital structures were involved.

Soon after the proportionate interest test was eliminated in the 1954 Code, corporations began to develop methods by which shareholders could, in effect, be given a choice between receiving cash dividends or increasing their proportionate interests in the corporation in much the same way as if they had received cash dividends and reinvested them in the corporation. The earliest of these methods involves dividing the common stock of the corporation into two classes, A and B. The two classes share equally in earnings and profits and in assets on liquidation. The only difference is that the class A stock pays only stock dividends and class B stock pays only cash dividends. The market value of the stock dividends paid on the class A stock is equated annually to the cash dividends paid on the class B stock. Class A stock may be converted into class B stock at any time. The stockholders can choose, either when the classes are established, when they purchase new stock, or through the convertibility option whether to own class A stock or class B stock.

In 1956, the Treasury Department issued proposed regulations which treated such arrangements as taxable (under sec. 305(b)(2)) as distributions subject to an election by the stockholder to receive cash instead of stock. In recent years, however, increasingly complex and sophisticated variations of this basic arrangement have been created. In some of these arrangements, the proportionate interest of one class of shareholders is increased even though no actual distribution of stock is made. This effect may be achieved, for example, by paying cash dividends on common stock and increasing by a corresponding amount the ratio at which convertible preferred stock or convertible debentures may be converted into common stock. Another method of achieving this result is a systematic periodic redemption plan, under which a small percentage, such as 5 percent, of each shareholder's stock may be redeemed annually at his election. Shareholders who do not choose to have their stock redeemed automatically increase their proportionate interest in the corporation.

On January 10, 1969, the Internal Revenue Service issued final regulations (T.D. 6990) under which a number of methods of achieving the effect of a cash dividend to some shareholders and a corresponding increase in the proportionate interest of other shareholders are brought under the exceptions in section 305(b), with the result that shareholders who receive increases in proportionate interest are treated as receiving taxable distributions.

General reasons for change.—The final regulations issued on January 10, 1969, do not cover all of the arrangements by which cash dividends can be paid to some shareholders and other shareholders can be given corresponding increases in proportionate interest. For example, the periodic redemption plan described above is not covered by the regulations, and the committee believes it is not covered by the present statutory language (of sec. 305(b)(2)).

Methods have also been devised to give preferred stockholders the equivalent of dividends on preferred stock which are not taxable as such under present law. For example, a corporation may issue preferred stock for $100 per share which pays no dividends, but which may be redeemed in 20 years for $200. The effect is the same as if the corporation distributed preferred stock equal to 5 percent of the original stock each year during the 20-year period in lieu of cash dividends. The committee believes that dividends paid on preferred stock should be taxed whether they are received in cash or in another form, such as stock, rights to receive stock, or rights to receive an increased amount on redemption. Moreover, the committee believes that dividends on preferred stock should be taxed to the recipients whether they are attributable to the current or immediately preceding taxable year or to earlier taxable years.

Explanation of [section 305].—The bill continues (in sec. 305(b)(1)) the provision of present law that a stock dividend is taxable if it is payable at the election of any shareholder in property instead of stock.

The bill provides (in sec. 305(b)(2)) that if there is a distribution or series of distributions of stock which has the result of the receipt of cash or other property by some shareholders and an increase in the proportionate interests of other shareholders in the assets or earnings and profits of the corporation, the shareholders receiving stock are to be taxable (under sec. 301).

For example, if a corporation has two classes of common stock, one paying regular cash dividends and the other paying corresponding stock dividends (whether in common or preferred stock), the stock dividends are to be taxable.

On the other hand, if a corporation has a single class of common stock and a class of preferred stock which pays cash dividends and is not convertible, and it distributes a pro rata common stock dividend with respect to its common stock, the stock distribution is not taxable because the distribution does not have the result of increasing the proportionate interests of any of the stockholders.

In determining whether there is a disproportionate distribution, any security convertible into stock or any right to acquire stock is to be treated as outstanding stock. For example, if a corporation has common stock and convertible debentures outstanding, and it pays interest on the convertible debentures and stock dividends on the common stock, there is a disproportionate distribution, and the stock dividends are to be taxable (under section 301). In addition, in determining whether there is a disproportionate distribution with respect to a shareholder, each class of stock is to be considered separately.

The committee has added two provisions to the House bill (secs. 305(b)(3) and (4)) which carry out more explicitly the intention of the House with regard to distributions of common and preferred stock on common stock, and stock distributions on preferred stock. The first of these provides that if a distribution or series of distributions has the result of the receipt of preferred stock by some common shareholders and the receipt of common stock by other common shareholders, all of the shareholders are taxable (under sec. 301) on the receipt of the stock.

The second of the provisions added by the committee (sec. 305(b)(4)) provides that distributions of stock with respect to preferred stock are taxable (under sec. 301). This provision applies to all distributions on preferred stock except increases in the conversion ratio of convertible preferred stock made solely to take account of stock dividends or stock splits with respect to the stock into which the convertible stock is convertible. * * *

The bill provides (in sec. 305(c)) that under regulations prescribed by the Secretary or his delegate, a change in conversion ratio, a change in redemption price, a difference between redemption price and issue price, a redemption treated as a section 301 distribution, or any transaction (including a recapitalization) having a similar effect on the interest of any shareholder is to be treated as a distribution with respect to each shareholder whose proportionate interest is thereby increased. The purpose of this provision is to give the Secretary authority to deal with transactions that have the effect of distributions, but in which stock is not actually distributed.

The proportionate interest of a shareholder can be increased not only by the payment of a stock dividend not paid to other shareholders, but by such methods as increasing the ratio at which his stock, convertible securities, or rights to stock may be converted into other stock, by decreasing the ratio at which other stock, convertible securities, or rights to stock can be converted into stock of the class he owns, or by the periodic redemption of stock owned by other shareholders. It is not clear under present law to what extent increases of this kind would be considered distributions of stock or rights to stock. In order to eliminate uncertainty, the committee has authorized the Secretary or his delegate to prescribe regulations governing the extent to which such transactions shall be treated as taxable distributions. * * *

DETAILED ANALYSIS

1. SCOPE OF SECTION 305

1.1. *General*

The blanket exclusion afforded stock dividends by § 305 prior to 1969 led to some difficulties as taxpayers probed for favorable tax techniques based on that exclusion. A variety of sophisticated schemes arose that in effect allowed shareholders to choose, sometimes on a year-to-year basis, whether to receive cash dividends or instead to obtain an increase in their equity participation in the corporation. These plans had the effect of allowing shareholders who chose the second course to substitute potential capital gain income for current ordinary income cash dividends, which historically were subject to higher tax rates. The IRS attempted to reach some of these arrangements under Regulations, but as the Senate Finance Committee Report indicates, the then existing statutory structure was not sufficiently broad to cover all of the situations. As a result, the 1969 legislation made some fundamental changes to the theory on which the taxation of stock dividends is based. Several related policies seem to lie behind the 1969 changes. The dominant themes were to limit the possibility of converting ordinary income into capital gain and to limit the ability of taxpayers to defer income inclusion despite having received the economic equivalent of a dividend. With the current taxation of qualified dividends and net capital gain at the same rate for individuals, the first theme now has limited relevance.

1.2. *Stock in Lieu of Cash*

From the beginning, Congress wished to prevent a shareholder from having an obvious choice on a year-by-year basis whether to receive cash dividends or an increase in the shareholder's proportionate interest in the corporation. Thus, § 305(b)(1) provides that where the shareholder has an explicit election to receive stock or cash (or other property) the stock distribution will be taxable. This is in effect a specific application of the general principle of constructive receipt, i.e., the shareholder cannot avoid taxation by simply ignoring a possible cash dividend and taking a stock dividend instead.

1.3. *Disproportionate Distributions*

Even if the shareholders do not have an obvious choice to receive stock or cash, a stock distribution will be taxable under § 305(b)(2) if it has the result of (1) an increase in the proportionate interest of some shareholders coupled with (2) a receipt of property (including cash) by other shareholders in a distribution subject to § 301 or § 356(a)(2). See Treas.Reg. § 1.305–3(b)(3). For example, suppose a corporation has two classes of common stock, one class paying quarterly cash dividends and the other class paying quarterly stock dividends, with the amount of the stock dividend adjusted to correspond to the amount of the cash dividend distribution. Under § 305(b)(2), the stock dividend would be treated as a taxable dividend, since some shareholders receive cash distributions (which are subject to § 301) while others receive an increase in their proportionate interest in the corporation's earnings and assets by virtue of the stock dividends. See Treas.Reg. § 1.305–3(b)(2).

Section 305(b)(3), which taxes stock distributions when some shareholders receive common stock while others receive preferred, is in effect a variation on the disproportionate distributions treated by § 305(b)(2). Under § 305(b)(3), the shareholders receiving common stock are increasing their equity interests while other shareholders receive preferred stock, which is analogous to the receipt of cash or other property in the § 305(b)(2) situation. Paragraph (b)(3) is necessary to cover the situation described because § 317 excludes the distributed stock described in paragraph (b)(3) from "property," and hence it is not "other property" under paragraph (b)(2).

Section 305(b)(5), dealing with distributions of convertible preferred stock, is likewise related to the problem of disproportionate distributions and amplifies § 305(b)(2). Suppose a corporation makes a pro rata distribution on its common stock of preferred stock convertible into common stock. If all of the convertible preferred stock is converted into common, the effect of the distribution will be the same as a distribution of common on common, which would not affect the shareholder's proportionate interest in the corporation. On the other hand, if some of the recipients of the convertible exercise the conversion privilege while others do not exercise but sell the preferred, the net effect will be an increase in the proportionate interest in the corporation by the converting shareholders and a corresponding receipt of cash by the selling shareholders, thus having the result that § 305(b)(2) was intended to prevent. Accordingly, § 305(b)(5) makes the distribution of convertible preferred taxable, unless the distribution is not likely to result in an increase in the proportionate interest for some shareholders. See Treas.Reg. § 1.305–6(a); compare Treas.Reg. § 1.305–4(b), Ex. (2), and § 1.305–6(b), Ex. (2).

Section 305(b)(2), as reinforced by § 305(b)(3) and § 305(b)(5), thus appears to express a congressional judgment that the same corporation should not be allowed to arrange its dividend policies to attract simultaneously both the investor who desires current cash distributions and the investor who seeks an increase in the value of the stock investment through corporate growth (and thus future capital gain rather than currently taxable cash distributions). This policy thus goes beyond the problems with which § 305(b)(1) is concerned (i.e., the year-to-year option to receive stock dividends rather than cash) and seems to express a general view that the investor must choose at the time of making a particular investment whether the investor wished to stress capital appreciation or current cash dividends; the same corporation cannot simultaneously offer both alternatives to the investing community. To reach this result, the statute in some way returns to the judicially developed proportionate interest test of the pre-1954 law by making increases in proportionate interests an element in the tax pattern imposed on stock dividends. In keeping, however, with the policy discussed above, the increases in the proportionate interests of some of the shareholders must be accompanied by a property distribution to other shareholders. Hence, § 305 does not fully mirror the pre-1954 case law, and its basic policy stands on a somewhat different footing.

1.4. *Distributions on Preferred Stock*

Section 305(b)(4) responds to a different problem than those considered above. While the 1954 version of § 305 dealt to a limited extent with stock dividends on preferred stock issued in lieu of cash distributions, it was generally possible under the 1954 provision to give preferred stockholders "the equivalent of dividends" through devices that allowed them to obtain capital gain treatment. For example, convertible preferred stock might pay no cash dividends but the ratio at which it was converted into common might increase annually by a specified percentage. On conversion, the shareholder would sell the shares that, in effect, were issued in lieu of cash dividend distributions at capital gain rates. Section 305(b)(4) prevents this result by currently taxing all stock dividends, either actual or constructive, received by holders of preferred stock.

1.5. *Constructive Distributions*

Under § 305(c), the Treasury is given broad discretionary authority to issue Regulations dealing with situations that result in an increase in a shareholder's proportionate interest in the corporation. This authority was intended to forestall taxpayer attempts to probe the limits of nontaxability under the § 305 stock distribution rules and to prevent disputes as to the authority of the Treasury to deal with the ingenious arrangements that would and do inevitably develop. Under § 305(c), a number of devices such as a change in conversion ratio or redemption price, certain redemptions of preferred stock for an amount substantially in excess of its issue price, a recapitalization, etc., that have the effect of an increase in a shareholder's proportionate interest are treated as falling under § 305(b), thus making the constructive stock distribution potentially taxable. For example, the increase in proportionate interest of some shareholders caused by the redemption of the shares of other shareholders can, in the appropriate circumstances, be treated as a constructive distribution under § 305(c).

2. TECHNICAL AND INTERPRETIVE PROBLEMS UNDER SECTION 305

2.1. *General*

In the years since the enactment of § 305, only a few stock dividend cases governed by its provisions have been decided, and two of those cases involved the same very narrow issue. The IRS, however, has issued a number

stock dividend in shares of preferred stock, the distribution is tax free under § 305(a) (although the preferred stock would be § 306 stock, discussed later in this Chapter). If, however, at a time when preferred stock was outstanding, a stock dividend in preferred shares was issued to the holders of the common stock, § 305(b)(2) could be applicable since the class of common shareholders would increase its proportionate interest in the distributing corporation's earnings and assets by virtue of the common shareholders' receipt of additional preferred stock while the preferred shareholders, on the subsequent payment of dividends, would receive the necessary cash distribution. But, a distribution of new junior preferred stock on common stock, coupled with payment of cash dividends on the senior preferred, does not invoke § 305(b)(2) since the subordination of the junior preferred prevents the required increase in proportionate interest. On the other hand, a distribution of new preferred stock on one class of common, coupled with a cash dividend on a different class of common stock, is subject to § 305(b)(2). If a corporation has outstanding both common stock and preferred stock convertible into common stock, a distribution of a common stock dividend on the common stock with no change in the conversion ratio of the convertible preferred, would, if coupled with a cash payment on the convertible preferred, make the common stock dividend taxable. See Treas.Reg. § 1.305–3(e), Ex. 4.

2.8. *Fractional Shares*

The Senate version of the 1969 bill contained a de minimis provision but it was eliminated by the Conference Committee. As a consequence, it was feared for a time that the distribution of cash in lieu of fractional shares in a stock dividend distribution might trigger the application of § 305(b)(2) since the literal terms of the statute would apply; some shareholders would receive a dividend solely in stock, increasing their proportionate interest in the corporation, while other shareholders would receive cash in lieu of their fractional shares, thus providing the necessary property distribution for purposes of § 305(b)(2). But Treas.Reg. § 1.305–3(c) takes the position that § 305(b)(2) will not apply in such situations if "[t]he purpose of the distribution of cash is to save the corporation the trouble, expense, and inconvenience of issuing and transferring fractional shares . . . and not to give any particular group of shareholders an increased interest in the assets or earnings and profits of the corporation."

2.9. *Distributions on Preferred Stock*

Preferred stock does not normally pay stock dividends except in the event of default in the payment of cash dividends or to prevent dilution. Rev.Rul. 84–141, 1984–2 C.B. 80, involved cumulative preferred stock that gave the holders the option to elect to receive an amount of common stock equal in value to accrued past due dividends, increased by an interest factor, whenever dividends were past due for two or more successive quarters. The Ruling held that the preferred shareholders constructively received a stock dividend taxable under § 305(b)(4) upon the passage of two successive quarters without the payment of cash dividends. The common stock attributable to the interest factor was treated as a distribution, not as interest.

Treas.Reg. § 1.305–3(d) elaborates on the statutory exception for distributions in the form of an increase in the conversion ratio of convertible preferred stock to take into account a stock dividend or a split in the common stock into which the preferred is convertible. Rev.Rul. 83–42, 1983–1 C.B. 76, held that an actual distribution of common stock to holders of convertible preferred stock to compensate for dilution as a result of a split of the common stock was taxable. The exception in § 305(b)(4) is limited to changes in the conversion ratio and does not encompass actual distributions of stock even if the purpose is anti-dilution.

Treas.Reg. § 1.305–5(a) defines preferred stock for purposes of § 305(b)(4): "The term 'preferred stock' generally refers to stock which, in relation to other classes of stock outstanding, enjoys certain limited rights and privileges (generally associated with specified dividend and liquidation priorities) but does not participate in corporate growth to any significant extent. The distinguishing feature of 'preferred stock' for the purposes of section 305(b)(4) is not its privileged position as such, but that such privileged position is limited, and that such stock does not participate in corporate growth to any significant extent. However, a right to participate that lacks substance will not prevent a class of stock from being treated as preferred stock."

2.10. *Constructive Distributions Under Section 305(c)*

2.10.1. *Redemptions in General*

Because of the operation of § 305(c), a stock redemption can bring § 305(b)(2) into play if the redemption involves an increase in the proportionate interest in the corporation for those shareholders whose stock is not redeemed, and the redeemed shareholders receive cash in the redemption, so that the "receipt of property" required by § 305(b)(2) is present. A redemption transaction will not generate a taxable deemed distribution to the remaining shareholders under § 305(c) if the redemption qualifies for § 302 exchange treatment. See Treas.Reg. § 1.305–7(a). If, however, the redemption distribution is treated as a dividend under § 302(d) and § 301, the increase in proportionate interest on the part of the other shareholders can be taxable under § 305(b)(2) and § 305(c). Rev.Rul. 78–60, 1978–1 C.B. 81, involved a corporation that adopted a plan whereby each shareholder was entitled to have the corporation redeem two-thirds of 1% of the shareholder's stock annually. Pursuant to the plan, in a particular year the corporation redeemed shares from 8 of the 24 shareholders. All of the redemption distributions were treated as distributions subject to § 301. The Ruling held that the shareholders whose shares were not redeemed received a taxable stock dividend, the amount of which was to be computed under Treas.Reg. § 1.305–3(e).

Treas.Reg. § 1.305–3(b)(3) provides an exception for "isolated" redemptions: "[A] distribution of property incident to an isolated redemption of stock (for example, pursuant to a tender offer) will not cause section 305(b)(2) to apply even though the redemption distribution is treated as a distribution of property to which section 301 . . . applies." Although the exact scope of "isolated" is unclear, Regulation examples indicate "isolated" requires the redemption be "not part of a periodic redemption plan." Treas.Reg. § 1.305–3(e), Exs. 10–11; see Rev.Rul. 77–19, 1977–1 C.B. 83 (§ 305(c) did not apply where over a three-year period a publicly held corporation redeemed shares from 20 different retiring or deceased shareholders; the redemptions fell under the "isolated" redemption exception).

Where a publicly held corporation purchases its own shares in the market, viewed as redemptions, the purchases could result in constructive stock dividends to the other shareholders of the corporation. However, Treas.Reg. § 1.305–3(e), Ex. 13, exempts such transactions from the application of § 305(b)(2) if the shares are purchased for use in connection with employee stock investment plans, for future acquisitions, etc., and there is no plan to increase the proportionate interests of some shareholders and distribute property to other shareholders.

2.10.2. *Redemptions of Callable Preferred Stock*

Section 305(c) also provides that a difference between the redemption price of stock and its issue price can be treated as a constructive stock distribution to the shareholder. The provision is aimed at a technique by which the corporation issues preferred stock with an excessive redemption price on which it pays no dividends and which it subsequently redeems in a transaction qualifying for capital gain treatment under § 302(b). The transaction in effect converts what otherwise would have been current dividend income into deferred capital gain. Section 305(c) prevents this result by treating the excess redemption premium as a constructive distribution on the preferred stock, taxable under § 305(b)(4).

Section 305(c) directs the Treasury to promulgate Regulations treating an unreasonable call premium on preferred stock that the issuer is required to redeem at a certain time, or the holder has an option to put to the corporation, as a distribution to be taken into account by the holder under the economic accrual rules of § 1272 (see Chapter 3). In addition, the Treasury is granted authority in § 305(c) to extend these principles to callable preferred stock bearing a redemption premium. Under this provision, "unreasonable" call premium must be recognized as income by the stockholder as if it were original issue discount. Unreasonable call premium is any call premium in excess of one-quarter of 1% of the stated redemption price of the stock multiplied by the number of years until the stock is redeemable. Technically, § 305(c)(1) limits the application of § 305(c) to a call premium that exceeds the amount ignored for OID purposes under § 1273(a)(3); this amount is 1/4 of 1% of the redemption price at maturity, multiplied by the number of years until maturity.

Treas.Reg. § 1.305–5(b) implements the application of § 305(c) to redemptions of preferred stock. The Regulations apply the OID principles to preferred stock if the issuer is required to redeem the stock at a specified time or the holder has the option (whether or not currently exercisable) to require the issuer to redeem the stock. Treas.Reg. § 1.305–5(b)(2). OID principles also apply if the issuer has a right (but not an obligation) to redeem at a premium if "based on all the facts and circumstances as of the issue date, redemption pursuant to that right is more likely than not to occur." See Treas.Reg. § 1.305–5(b)(3)(i). Either the fact that the preferred stock will obtain voting control if not redeemed by a particular date or that the yield to the preferred stock can be minimized (thereby reducing the issuer's cost of capital) by calling it at a certain time indicates that it more likely than not will be redeemed. See Treas.Reg. § 1.305–5(d), Exs. 5 and 7. The constructive distribution rules do not apply, however, if the redemption premium "is solely in the nature of a penalty for premature redemption." Treas.Reg. § 1.305–5(b)(3)(i). This exception can apply only if the premium is paid as a result of changes in market conditions over which neither the issuer nor the holder has control. The Regulations do not provide an example of such a situation. Finally, a safe harbor treats a redemption as not being "more likely than not to occur," thereby excepting callable preferred stock from the constructive distribution rule, if (1) the issuer and the holder are not related, (2) there are no arrangements effectively requiring a redemption, and (3) exercise of the issuer's redemption right would not reduce the yield of the stock. Treas.Reg. § 1.305–5(b)(3)(ii). Treas.Reg. § 1.305–5(d), Ex. 4 applies this safe harbor rule to callable convertible preferred stock that is redeemable at a very substantial premium. Because of the tight restrictions on situations not within the safe harbor, the safe harbor "exception" is very broad.

Section 305(c) can also be relevant in situations in which the redemption provisions are being used to effect a sale of the corporate business, see Chapters 5 and 9, or in the case of a corporate recapitalization, see Chapter 11.

2.10.3.   *Proposed Regulations Regarding Adjustments to Conversion Rights*

Proposed amendments to Regs. §§ 1.305–1, 1.305–3, and 1.305–7 deal with distributions of warrants, subscription rights, options, convertible instruments that give the holder a right to convert the instruments into shares of stock in the issuing corporation, and similar instruments. These Proposed Regulations also deal with adjustments to a convertible instrument that increase the number of shares of stock a holder would receive upon conversion that correspond to distributions of stock, cash, or other property made to actual shareholders, as well as with rights to acquire stock that prevent actual shareholders' interests from being diluted as a result of distributions of stock, cash, or other property to deemed shareholders (i.e., holders of rights to acquire stock). REG–133673–15, 81 Fed. Reg. 21795 (April 4, 2016).

The 2016 Proposed Regulations provide an answer to an ambiguity with respect to valuation if an adjustment results in a § 301 deemed distribution through operation of § 305(b)–(c). As the preamble explains, "The current regulations may reasonably be interpreted as providing either that such a deemed distribution is treated as a distribution of a right to acquire stock (the amount of which is the fair market value of the right), or that such a distribution is treated as a distribution of the actual stock to which the right relates (the amount of which is the fair market value of the stock)." The 2016 Proposed Regulations resolve the ambiguity by providing that a deemed distribution of a right to acquire stock will be treated as a distribution of additional rights to acquire stock, the amount of which is the fair market value of the right.

The Proposed Regulations also provide guidance with respect to timing. If an adjustment is or results in a deemed distribution under Prop.Reg. § 1.305–7(c)(1) or (2) (2016), the deemed distribution occurs at the time the adjustment occurs (pursuant to the terms of the relevant instruments), but in no event later than the date of the distribution of cash or property that results in the deemed distribution. For rights with respect to publicly traded stock, if the relevant instrument does not provide when the adjustment occurs, the deemed distribution would occur immediately prior to the opening of business on the ex-dividend date for the distribution of cash or property that results in the deemed distribution.

2.11. *Situations to Which Section 305 Does Not Apply*

Though § 305 has a wide scope, the Regulations explicitly exempt some transactions that otherwise might fall within the terms of the section. Thus, a change in conversion ratio or redemption price of stock that is in effect an adjustment in the purchase price of assets acquired in exchange for the stock will not fall within § 305. Treas.Reg. § 1.305–1(c). Similarly, if stock is issued in what is in effect a security arrangement and it is anticipated that the bulk of the corporation's earnings will be used to redeem the stock, the redemptions will not be treated as subject to § 305(b)(2). Treas.Reg. § 1.305–3(e), Ex. 14; Rev.Rul. 78–115, 1978–1 C.B. 85.

3.   STOCK OPTIONS

The general rules respecting stock options or stock rights issued on outstanding stock follow those for stock dividends. There is no income inclusion on issuance of the options, except for the cases in § 305(b). See Rev.Rul. 90–11, 1990–1 C.B. 10 (adoption by the corporation of a "poison pill" plan, which provides for the issuance of a separately tradable right to purchase a fractional share of preferred stock for every share of common stock in the event of an unfriendly takeover attempt, is not a distribution of "property" to shareholders). On a sale of the options, the proceeds would be capital gain, with the holding period of the rights being that of the stock (§ 1223(4)), unless the stock rights were classified as § 306 stock in which event ordinary income could result. If the value is 15% or more of the value of the old stock *and* the rights are either sold or exercised, the basis of the rights is an allocable portion of the basis of the old stock. I.R.C. § 307(a); Treas.Reg. § 1.307–1. If the value of the rights is less than 15% of the value of the old stock, the basis of the rights is zero unless an election is made under § 307(b) to allocate the stock basis between the rights and the stock. Treas.Reg. § 1.307–2. If the rights are allowed to lapse, no loss arises (regardless of the value of the rights) since for this purpose no part of the basis of the old stock is allocated to them, and the basis of the old stock is not reduced.

If the stock rights involve the option to purchase stock of another corporation, the distribution cannot be subject to § 305(a). The shareholders receive a distribution subject to § 301, and the distributing corporation may be required to recognize gain under § 311.

PROBLEM SET 1

1.   (a) X Corp. has a single class of voting common stock with 10,000 shares outstanding. The fair market value of each share is $300. If the corporation declares a dividend of one share of nonconvertible $200 par value preferred stock on each share of common stock, will the stock dividend be taxable or tax-free under § 305?

    (b) Arnie, one of the shareholders of X Corp., owns 200 shares of common stock (purchased in a single block) with a basis of $6,000 and fair market value of $300 per share before the issuance of preferred stock. Assuming that the fair market value of the preferred stock after issuance is $100 per share and the fair market value of the common stock drops to $200 per share after the issuance of the preferred stock, what are the bases of Arnie's 200 shares of common and 200 shares of preferred, respectively?

2.   Y Corporation has a single class of voting common stock outstanding. Y Corporation maintains a "dividend reinvestment program" by which any shareholder may elect to receive additional shares of common stock in lieu of cash dividends. If a shareholder elects to receive stock instead of cash, the stock dividend will consist of a number of whole or fractional shares having a fair market value equal to 110% of the dollar value of the declared cash dividend. Thus, for example, if the declared cash dividend is $1 per share at a time when shares are trading at $10 per share, a holder of 500 shares who elected to receive stock would receive 55 shares instead of a cash dividend of $500.

    (a) Are the stock dividends taxable? If so, what is the amount of the distribution?

    (b) Would the stock dividends be taxable if every shareholder elected to receive additional stock and none received cash?

3.   Z Corporation has two classes of common stock, Class A and Class B. The two classes are alike in all respects except that only the Class A shares vote. Al, Beth, Chuck, and Debbie each own 200 shares of Class A voting common. Earl, Fran, George, and Helen each own 200 shares of nonvoting class B common stock. Z Corporation declared a one-on-one dividend of newly issued Class B nonvoting common stock on all common stock. Simultaneously, Z Corporation offered to redeem up to one-half of the newly issued shares received by any Class A shareholder for $100 per share. None of the class A shareholders tendered any stock for redemption. To what extent, if any, is the stock dividend taxable?

4.   X Corporation has two classes of stock outstanding, Class A voting common and Class B nonvoting $100 par value 6% preferred. X Corp. also has authorized but unissued shares of Class C nonvoting $100 par value 7% preferred.

    (a) (1) X Corporation distributes a stock dividend of newly issued Class B preferred to the Class A shareholders. Is the distribution taxable? Does it matter whether or not X Corporation regularly paid the Class B dividend?

(2)   Would your answer change if, prior to the distribution, all of both classes of stock were held by a single shareholder?

(b)   X Corporation distributes a stock dividend of newly issued Class C preferred to the Class A shareholders. The Class C preferred is junior to the Class B preferred. Is the distribution taxable?

5.   Y Corporation has only a single class of voting common stock outstanding. Y Corporation also has issued a series of $1,000, 6% debt instruments convertible into common stock at the rate of ten shares of common stock for each $1,000 debt instrument. Y Corporation declared a two-for-one stock split, distributing to each shareholder newly issued shares equal in number to the shares previously held. Must the conversion ratio on the debt instruments be increased to avoid a taxable stock dividend?

6.   Z Corporation has outstanding Class A voting common stock and Class B participating preferred stock. Class B is entitled to a noncumulative preferred dividend of $1 per share if cash dividends are declared, and a liquidation preference of $100 per share. After the preference is satisfied, Class A and Class B share dividends and liquidation proceeds in a 60% to 40% ratio. Z Corporation declared a stock dividend of one share of Class A stock on each share of Class A stock and one share of Class B stock on each share of Class B stock. Is the distribution taxable?

7.   X Corporation has outstanding Class A voting common stock and Class B nonvoting convertible preferred stock. The Class B stock is convertible into Class A at the ratio of 10 shares of Class A for each share of Class B. X Corporation pays regular dividends on the Class B preferred stock.

(a)   X Corporation declares a one-for-one stock dividend on the Class A common stock and the conversion ratio for the Class B stock is increased to 20 to 1. Is there a taxable stock dividend?

(b)   Would there be a taxable stock dividend if the ratio at which Class B was convertible into Class A stock were adjusted to 21 to 1?

(c)   Would there be a taxable stock dividend if the ratio at which Class B was convertible into Class A stock were adjusted to 19 to 1?

8.   Y Corporation has outstanding a single class of voting common stock. The corporation declared a dividend on the common stock of newly issued convertible preferred stock. The preferred stock is convertible into common stock at any time in the next 20 years at a price equal to 110% of the common stock's market price on the date of the distribution of the convertible preferred. Is the stock dividend taxable?

9.   W Corporation, the common stock of which is publicly traded, proposes to distribute as a pro rata stock dividend on its common stock newly issued $100 par value, 10% Class B nonvoting convertible preferred stock. The preferred stock will be callable by W Corporation after 10 years at $120, and, if it is not called, it becomes convertible into W Corporation common stock at a price equal to 50% of the then current trading price of the common stock. How will the preferred stock be treated if it is issued?

10.   Z Corporation's stock is publicly traded. If Z Corporation purchases 10% of its outstanding common stock on the open market, for the purpose of

enhancing the value of the shares remaining outstanding, have the holders of the remaining stock received a taxable stock dividend?

11. X Corporation has one class of outstanding common stock, which is held by unrelated individuals D (500 shares), E (300 shares) and F (200 shares). Will § 305(c) create a constructive stock dividend if X Corporation agrees to redeem annually 50 shares of stock at the election of each shareholder, and D makes such an election for two consecutive years?

SECTION 2.   THE PREFERRED STOCK BAILOUT

A. THE SOURCE OF THE PROBLEM

Suppose that Z Corporation has outstanding only common stock, which is held equally by individuals A and B. At a time when Z Corporation has accumulated earnings and profits in excess of $100,000, the corporation declares a dividend payable in 100 shares of $1,000 par value 9% cumulative preferred stock that is subject to mandatory redemption in 5 years. A and B each receive 50 shares of preferred stock, having an aggregate par value of $50,000 and a fair market value that would in all likelihood be close to par value. This stock dividend would be tax free under § 305(a). Suppose further that before the distribution A and B each had a basis in their common stock of $60,000 and that, after the distribution, the fair market value of the common stock held by each shareholder was $25,000. Under § 307, A and B would each allocate a basis of $40,000 to their preferred stock. Suppose now that A and B each sell their preferred stock to X Corporation for $50,000. If the transaction is treated as an ordinary sale of stock, A and B each would recognize a capital gain of $10,000. X Corporation will have a basis in the preferred stock of $100,000, and when the stock is redeemed in 5 years, it will recognize neither gain nor loss. In its brief in *Helvering v. Sprouse*[1], which involved a pro rata distribution of preferred stock to common shareholders in a manner that did not alter the common shareholder's proportionate interest in the corporation, the government argued that a preferred stock distribution represented an alteration in the common shareholder's interest that should constitute a taxable stock dividend. The distribution of a preferred stock dividend to common shareholders constitutes a readjustment of the corporate ownership that facilitates a cashing-out transaction via the sale of the preferred stock at a later date. The preferred stock does not alter the common shareholder's control over the enterprise. Moreover, the preferred stock represents a corporate ownership interest that is different in kind from what the common shareholder owned beforehand. Finally, a cash dividend does not alter the stockholder's proportionate interest in the corporation's earnings and profits, and yet it is indisputably taxable as income; the result should not be different with the distribution of preferred stock that is limited and

---

[1]   See Petitioner's Brief in Helvering v. Sprouse at 5–6 (Oct. 19, 1942), 1942 WL 53893 (318 U.S. 604 (1943)).

preferred as to dividends as it is a close proxy for cash. Nonetheless, the Supreme Court rejected the government's argument and held that a distribution of preferred stock must bring about a change in the proportional interest of the common stockholder in the corporation before the preferred stock distribution would be taxable as a stock dividend. 318 U.S. 604 (1943). Thus, even though Z Corporation effectively has distributed $100,000 of its earnings and profits to A and B, without diminishing their voting rights or percentage ownership in the assets or residual profits of the corporation (except as necessary to pay dividends on and redeem the preferred stock), they would not be required to recognize that amount as ordinary income.

The bailout potential inherent in a preferred stock issuance is clearly seen in Chamberlin v. Commissioner, 207 F.2d 462 (6th Cir.1953). The taxpayers in that case asserted that the stock dividend, which was distributed in 1946, was a nontaxable distribution under the principles that governed stock dividends under the 1939 Code. The IRS argued that under the circumstances there was not a true stock dividend—that in effect the taxpayers had received a cash distribution even though the corporation had not distributed the cash in 1946. The court held that the distribution was a stock dividend in substance as well as form, even though the taxpayer conceded that the form of the transaction was motivated by tax avoidance. Because the insurance company that purchased the stock acquired a bona fide investment in the corporation and the redemption features of the stock were not unreasonable, the court refused to treat the otherwise nontaxable stock dividend as taxable solely because the stock was sold soon after its receipt. Thus, the shareholders in *Chamberlin* were able not only to treat a portion of the sales proceeds as a recovery of basis but also were able to report the gain as taxable at the preferential rate that applied to long-term capital gains. If the principle of the *Chamberlin* case prevailed, closely held corporations in effect could have avoided ever paying taxable cash dividends.

Expressly responding to the *Chamberlin* decision, Congress foreclosed this tax avoidance route with the enactment of § 306 in the 1954 Code. Rather than adopting the Commissioner's position in *Chamberlin* that the stock distribution itself was taxable, however, Congress chose to "taint" with ordinary income treatment any future disposition of the stock as explained in the following excerpt from the Senate Finance Committee Report, S.Rep. No. 83–1622, 83d Cong., 2d Sess. 46 (1954):

> Your committee has * * * acted to close a possible loophole of existing law known as the "preferred stock bail-out." * * * Your committee's approach to this problem imposes a tax on the recipient of the dividend stock at the time of its sale. This dividend stock would be called "section 306 stock" and any stock received as a dividend would be section 306 stock to the extent

of its allocable share of corporate earnings at the time of issuance, except common stock issued with respect to common stock.

The tax imposed at the time of the sale of the stock is at ordinary income rates to the extent of its allocable share of earnings and profits of the corporation at the time the stock dividend was declared. Any amount received for the section 306 stock which exceeds the earnings and profits attributable to it will be taxed as capital gain. If, instead of selling the section 306 stock, the shareholder redeems it, the proceeds received will be taxed as a dividend to the extent of corporate earnings at the time of redemption. * * * [C]ertain exceptions to this basic rule of ordinary income treatment with respect to dispositions of section 306 stock are provided.

Before § 306's enactment the House Ways and Means Committee had formulated its own set of alternative solutions to the preferred stock bailout concern, and the minority report that accompanied the House Ways and Means committee report criticized alternatives that abandoned "the current Government position of asserting tax liability at ordinary rates at the time of issuance of the preferred stock," and in fact that minority report argued that the government's current litigating position "could be retained."[2] Said differently, the minority report suggested that Congress should have legislatively overturned the decision in *Sprouse*, and if it had done so then the added complexity of § 306 would not have been needed. Treating the issuance of preferred stock to the common shareholders as an outright taxable event was the original litigating position of the government in *Sprouse*, and it was the natural solution to the core problem posed by the preferred stock bailout transaction evidenced in *Chamberlin* without the need to rely on the added complexity of § 306.

As a result of the equalization of tax rates on dividends and long-term capital gains, the incentive for noncorporate shareholder-taxpayers to attempt preferred stock bailouts—the avoidance transaction at which § 306 is directed—has been reduced. For a noncorporate shareholder, the only important differences between a dividend and a stock sale are that (1) all of a dividend distribution is includable in gross income, while only the amount by which sales proceeds exceed the basis of the stock is includable, and (2) gains on stock sales can be offset by capital losses, while dividend income can be offset by capital losses only to a very limited extent under § 1211. Thus, after the 2003 Act, one aspect of the potential tax avoidance at which § 306 is directed was eliminated. Nevertheless, § 306 continues to serve a function. When preferred stock is received as a tax-free stock dividend, a portion of the basis of the stock on which the dividend was issued is allocated to the preferred stock pursuant to § 307.

---

[2]   See H.R. Rep. No. 1337, 83rd Cong. 2d Sess. at B20-1 (March 9, 1954) (minority report).

In the case of a sale or redemption of the preferred stock, § 306 requires a portion of the amount received to be treated as income before any basis recovery is allowed. There is no rate arbitrage involved because § 306(a)(1)(D) provides that ordinary income recognized by virtue of § 306 nevertheless is taxed at the same rate as qualified dividends and long-term capital gains. However, if § 306 were repealed, it would be preferable to treat the preferred stock distribution as a taxable event at the time of the preferred stock's issuance to common shareholders, thus adopting the government's litigating position in *Sprouse* and the alternative proposal set forth in the minority report in 1954.[3]

B. OPERATION OF SECTION 306

INTERNAL REVENUE CODE: Section 306(a)–(d).

REGULATIONS: Section 1.306–1; –2; –3(a)–(c), (e).

Pescosolido v. Commissioner[*]
Tax Court of the United States, 1988.
91 T.C. 52.

■ COHEN, JUDGE:

* * *

The sole issue for decision is whether petitioners' deductions for charitable contributions of section 306 stock are allowable at fair market value or limited to cost basis in the stock.

* * *

Petitioner graduated from Deerfield Academy and, in 1934, from Harvard College. He went to work for an oil company because other jobs were not available. In 1949, petitioner invested his savings in the formation of Valley Oil Co. Through this closely held corporation, petitioner distributed fuel oil and gasoline. As petitioner's business grew, petitioner bought out several other small oil companies. Petitioner also established corporations in Maine and other parts of Massachusetts to carry out various aspects of his business.

The growth of petitioner's business was haphazard and unplanned. In 1976, petitioner decided to consolidate his enterprise into one efficient and cost-effective organization. He also planned to effect a "freeze" of the value of his stock for estate tax purposes. In a tax-free reorganization, petitioner merged his six controlled corporations into the Lido Corp. of New England, Inc. (Lido). Through counsel, petitioner obtained a ruling letter from the Internal Revenue Service with respect to the reorganization. The application for a ruling represented, among other

---

[3] For a further analysis of this proposal, see Bret Wells, Reform of Corporate Distributions in Subchapter C, 37 Virginia Tax Rev. 365 (2018).

[*] The Tax Court decision was affirmed, 883 F.2d 187 (1st Cir.1989).

things, that nonvoting preferred stock to be issued by Lido would not be redeemed for 5 years. Among other things, the ruling stated: "The Corp. A Preferred to be received by [petitioner] and [William Pescosolido] will constitute 'section 306 stock' within the meaning of section 306(c)."

Immediately after the reorganization, petitioner held all of the 2,500 shares of Lido class A voting stock and 11,708 shares of nonvoting preferred stock. Petitioner's sons, daughter, and brother received nonvoting common stock. The cost basis of petitioner's preferred stock was $16.32 per share.

By receiving all of the Lido voting stock, petitioner retained control over Lido's growth and development. Petitioner's children, who were employed by the company, were given an interest in Lido's welfare through their nonvoting shares. Petitioner's preferred stock also advanced the interests of petitioner's family by serving petitioner's estate planning needs. Petitioner did not plan at that time to sell or otherwise dispose of the preferred stock.

Petitioner had long been an ardent supporter of Deerfield Academy and Harvard College. As petitioner built his business, he contributed small amounts of cash and donated his time to the Harvard College Schools Committee.

* * *

As the energy crises of the early 1970's came to an end, petitioner's fortunes markedly improved. Petitioner felt that he was now in a position to make more substantial donations to Deerfield and Harvard. In 1978 and 1979, petitioner made the following donations of Lido preferred stock:

Years	Number of preferred shares	Fair market value dollar amount	Recipient
1978	500	$50,000	Harvard University
1979	500	50,000	Harvard University
1979	500	50,000	Deerfield Academy

Deerfield and Harvard were at all material times educational institutions described in section 501(c)(3). In each of the years in issue, the donees of the shares received 7-percent dividends.

At the time of the gifts, petitioner did not seek professional advice concerning the tax consequences of his gifts of preferred stock.

* * *

On their tax returns, petitioners deducted the contributions to Harvard and Deerfield calculated at $100 per share as follows:

Tax year	Contributions deduction dollar amount
1978	$50,000
1979	78,601
1980	21,399

* * *

In a notice of deficiency, respondent disallowed petitioners' charitable contribution deductions in their entirety. Respondent now concedes that petitioners are entitled to deduct their cost basis of $16.32 per share.

OPINION

Section 170(a) allows a deduction for any charitable contribution. Section 1.170–1(c), Income Tax Regs., provides that if the charitable contribution is made in property other than money, the amount of the deduction allowed under section 170(b) is the fair market value of the property on the date of the contribution. In such a case, section 170(e) imposes a significant limitation on the amount of an otherwise allowable deduction. That section provides, in pertinent part, as follows:

SEC. 170(e). CERTAIN CONTRIBUTIONS OF ORDINARY INCOME AND CAPITAL GAIN PROPERTY.—

(1) GENERAL RULE.—The amount of any charitable contribution of property otherwise taken into account under this section shall be reduced by the sum of—

(A) the amount of gain which would not have been long-term capital gain if the property contributed had been sold by the taxpayer at its fair market value (determined at the time of such contribution) * * *.

The property to which section 170(e)(1)(A) applies includes stock described in section 306(a). Sec. 1.170A–4(b)(1), Income Tax Regs.

Section 306 is designed to prevent "preferred stock bailouts," in which shareholders extract corporate earnings and profits as capital gain, rather than ordinary income, while retaining ownership of a corporation. Fireoved v. United States, 462 F.2d 1281, 1284–1286 (3d Cir.1972); Bialo v. Commissioner, 88 T.C. 1132, 1138–1139 (1987). Section 306(a) generally provides that if a shareholder sells or otherwise disposes of "section 306 stock," the amount realized on the disposition of the stock will be treated as ordinary income. The parties agree that the stock given by petitioner to Deerfield and Harvard was "section 306 stock." Petitioner argues, however, that his "tainted" stock was "purged" by section 306(b)(4), which provides, in pertinent part, as follows:

SEC. 306(b). EXCEPTIONS.—subsection (a) shall not apply—

* * *

(4) TRANSACTIONS NOT IN AVOIDANCE.—If it is established to the satisfaction of the Secretary—

(A) that the distribution, and the disposition or redemption
* * *

* * *

was not in pursuance of a plan having as one of its principal purposes the avoidance of Federal income tax.

Petitioner has the burden of proving that neither the distribution nor the disposition of section 306 stock was part of a plan of tax avoidance; that burden is a heavy one. Bialo v. Commissioner, 88 T.C. at 1138; Roebling v. Commissioner, 77 T.C. 30, 59 (1981).[2]

Petitioner testified, without contradiction, that he received Lido preferred stock in an attempt to "freeze" the value of his equity in the company for estate planning purposes. See Northern Trust Co., Transferee v. Commissioner, 87 T.C. 349 (1986), affd. sub nom. Citizens Bank & Trust Co. v. Commissioner, 839 F.2d 1249 (7th Cir.1988). There is no evidence that petitioner planned at the time of the distribution to sell or otherwise dispose of the preferred stock. Petitioner further testified that he was an ardent supporter of Deerfield Academy and Harvard College, institutions that he believes changed his life. Petitioner struggled for many years to build a prosperous family business. After years of effort he found himself in a position to repay his alma maters. Petitioner argues that he has thus negated a tax avoidance purpose for disposition of the stock and brought himself within the exception of section 306(b)(4)(A).

According to respondent, section 306(b)(4)(A) will generally apply *only* to minority shareholders who are not in control of the distributing corporation. Thus, he argues, petitioner cannot bring himself within this exception.

Respondent's argument is based on the following language in section 1.306–2(b)(3), Income Tax Regs.:

(b) Section 306(a) does not apply to—

* * *

---

[2] Respondent does not argue that the language in sec. 306(b)(4), "If it is established to the satisfaction of the Secretary," creates a special standard of review. See Fireoved v. United States, 318 F.Supp. 133 (E.D.Pa.1970), affd. in part and revd. in part 462 F.2d 1281, 1287 n. 10 (3d Cir.1972); 3B J. Mertens, Law of Federal Income Taxation, sec. 22:90 (1980): "it is questionable whether this [language] confers any greater prerogative or discretion on the Commissioner than normally resides in him with respect to the usual kind of determination which first is made on the administrative level and which receives a presumption of correctness." See also sec. 3B J. Mertens, supra at 38D.35 n. 20.

(3) A disposition or redemption, if it is established to the satisfaction of the Commissioner that the distribution, and the disposition or redemption, was not in pursuance of a plan having as one of its principal purposes the avoidance of Federal income tax. * * * For example, in the absence of such a plan and of any other facts the first sentence of this subparagraph would be applicable to the case of dividends and isolated dispositions of section 306 stock by minority shareholders. * * *

The regulatory language pertaining to minority shareholders is prefaced by the words "For example." Thus, an isolated disposition of section 306 stock by a minority shareholder is but one instance in which disposition of "tainted" stock is not part of a tax-avoidance plan. The regulation does not purport to set forth an exhaustive list of all situations that fall within section 306(b)(4). Certainly the statute contains no reference to the taxpayer's percentage of ownership or degree of control of the corporation. Respondent's argument, therefore, is overstated.

Respondent also cites the report of the Senate Finance Committee, S.Rept. 1622, 83d Cong., 2d Sess. 243–244 (1954), which states:

Paragraph (4) of subsection (b) excepts from the general rule of subsection (a) those transactions not in avoidance of this section where it is established to the satisfaction of the Secretary that the transaction was not in pursuance of a plan having as one of its principal purposes the avoidance of Federal income tax. Subparagraph (A) of this paragraph applies to cases where the distribution itself, coupled with the disposition or redemption was not in pursuance of such a plan. This subparagraph is intended to apply to the case of dividends and isolated dispositions of section 306 stock by minority shareholders who do not in the aggregate have control of the distributing corporation. In such a case it would seem to your committee to be inappropriate to impute to such shareholders an intention to remove corporate earnings at the tax rates applicable only to capital gains.

This legislative history was given persuasive effect in Fireoved v. United States, supra, and Bialo v. Commissioner, supra, the cases relied on by respondent. In Fireoved, the taxpayer contended that distribution and disposition of certain stock received by him as a stock dividend and later redeemed by the corporation fell within the exception of section 306(b)(4)(A). The taxpayer argued that the purpose of the stock dividend was business related, to wit, to obtain additional capital for the corporation from third parties. The Court of Appeals stated that the existence of a business purpose was not inconsistent with a conclusion in the statutory language that "one of [the] principal purposes" of the stock dividend was "the avoidance of Federal income tax." The Court of Appeals stated:

In a situation such as the one presented in this case, where the facts necessary to determine the motives for the issuance of a stock dividend are peculiarly within the control of the taxpayer, it is reasonable to require the taxpayer to come forward with the facts that would relieve him of his liability. Here the stipulation was equivocal in determining the purpose of the dividend and is quite compatible with the thought that "one of the principal purposes" was motivated by "tax avoidance." We hold then that the district court did not err in refusing to apply the exception created by section 306(b)(4)(A). [462 F.2d at 1287; fn. ref. omitted.]

With respect to the redemption of the corporate stock by the corporation, the taxpayer argued that he had sold 24 percent of his underlying common stock in the corporation in order to give greater control to another investor and that the subsequent redemption of a part of his section 306 stock related to that business purpose. The Court of Appeals concluded:

More important, however, is that an examination of the relevant legislative history indicates that Congress did not intend to give capital gains treatment to a portion of the preferred stock redeemed on the facts presented here. [462 F.2d at 1288.]

After quoting S.Rept. 1622, supra, the Court of Appeals continued:

Thus, it is reasonable to assume that Congress realized the general lack of a tax avoidance purpose when a person sells *all* of his control in a corporation and then either simultaneously or subsequently disposes of his section 306 stock. However, when *only a portion* of the underlying common stock is sold, and the taxpayer retains essentially all the control he had previously, it would be unrealistic to conclude that Congress meant to give that taxpayer the advantage of section 306(b)(4)(B) when he ultimately sells his section 306 stock. Cf. United States v. Davis, 397 U.S. 301, 90 S.Ct. 1041, 25 L.Ed.2d 323 (1970).

* * * although Mr. Fireoved did sell a portion of his voting stock prior to his disposition of the section 306 stock, he retained as much control in the corporation following the sale of his common stock as he had prior to the sale. Under these circumstances it is not consonant with the history of the legislation to conclude that Congress intended such a sale of underlying common stock to exempt the proceeds of the disposition of section 306 stock from treatment as ordinary income. Accordingly, the district court erred when it held that any of the preferred shares Mr. Fireoved redeemed were not subject to section 306(a) by virtue of section 306(b)(4)(B). [462 F.2d at 1289–1290; fn. refs. omitted; emphasis in original.]

Bialo v. Commissioner, supra, presented an easier case than Fireoved v. United States, supra, or the instant case. In Bialo, the taxpayers' closely held corporation issued a pro rata dividend of preferred stock on common stock. The preferred stock was contributed to a charitable trust and then redeemed by the corporation. The evidence did not establish the business purpose of the donation argued by the taxpayers on brief, and:

> The only document admitted into evidence, however, which was prepared prior to the distribution of stock and subsequent contribution to the Trust discusses only the tax advantages of the transaction. * * * The memorandum also notes that a contribution of stock in a privately held corporation is likely to result in quick redemption by the charitable organization. The majority shareholder who contributed such stock would thereby be restored to the status of a 100-percent shareholder. [88 T.C. at 1141.]

Thus we held that the amount of the charitable contribution deduction must be reduced under section 170(e)(1)(A).

In this case, there is evidence of the taxpayer's bona fide charitable intent in the disposition of the stock. Evidence of tax motivation is not as clear as it was in *Bialo*. The reasoning of *Fireoved*, however, is persuasive and applies to the facts of this case. Here, as in other areas of the law, the ultimate purpose of a transaction must be inferred from the objective facts rather than from the taxpayer's mere denial of tax motivation. Petitioner was a sophisticated businessman, making deliberate decisions and advised of the nature of section 306 stock at the time that he received it. We must assume that the potential tax consequences of future disposition of the section 306 stock were explained to petitioner by counsel who requested and received the ruling from the Internal Revenue Service in relation to the reorganization. That ruling specifically stated that the stock would be section 306 stock. See Roebling v. Commissioner, 77 T.C. at 60.

On his 1978 tax return, petitioner claimed a deduction for the fair market value of the stock as if he had made a $50,000 cash contribution. We are not persuaded that he was unaware that the consequence of such a deduction would be the avoidance of ordinary income tax on the bailout of corporate earnings. His testimony that he did not have tax advice at the time of the gifts does not mean that he was ignorant of the tax benefits that he was claiming.

Petitioners have presented a credible purpose other than income tax avoidance for both the distribution and the disposition of Lido stock. The statutory language and purpose and petitioner's control of the corporation, however, require that the evidence clearly negate an income-tax-avoidance plan to satisfy petitioner's burden. His control of the corporation permits an inference of unity of purpose and plan between the corporate issuer and the shareholder, and the substantial tax savings that would result from the bailout and contribution of appreciated stock permit an inference of income-tax-avoidance purpose. Unlike those of a minority shareholder, petitioner's circumstances do not require an exception to section 306 to avoid the trap for the unwary in section 306 or invoke the relief anticipated by Congress in limited circumstances. * * *

Petitioners' deduction for contributions of section 306 stock to Harvard and Deerfield are therefore limited to his cost basis in the stock, pursuant to section 170(e)(1)(A).

DETAILED ANALYSIS

1.   DEFINITION OF SECTION 306 STOCK

1.1. *Stock Other than Common Stock Received as a Tax Free Stock Dividend*

Section 306(c) defines § 306 stock with reference to the potential for "bailing out" earnings and profits inherent in stock received in a tax free distribution. The basic rule, in § 306(c)(1)(A), defines § 306 stock to include any stock *other than common stock* received as a tax free stock dividend under § 305(a) by the shareholder disposing of the stock. This basic rule is limited by § 306(c)(2), which provides that stock that would otherwise have been § 306 stock will not be treated as such if the corporation had no current or accumulated earnings and profits at the time the stock dividend was issued.

1.2. *Definition of "Common Stock"*

Neither the Code nor the Regulations provide much assistance in defining the term "common stock" beyond the rule of § 306(e)(2) that common stock that is convertible into something other than common stock is not "common stock." See Treas.Reg. § 1.306–3. The scope of the term "common stock" has been clarified by a series of Revenue Rulings that illustrate that not all preferred stock is § 306 stock and that stock that is not traditional preferred stock may be § 306 stock.

In Rev.Rul. 76–387, 1976–2 C.B. 96, the IRS held that if the stock in question was nonvoting and limited in either the right to dividends or the right to assets upon liquidation, it was considered to be "other than common stock" and was § 306 stock. See also Rev.Rul. 76–386, 1976–2 C.B. 95 (the fact that voting common stock is subject to a right of first refusal by the corporation in the case of sale does not prevent it from being classified as "common stock"); Rev.Rul. 57–132, 1957–1 C.B. 115 (common stock redeemable at the option of the corporation at a price in excess of its book value is not "common stock"). Subsequently, Rev.Rul. 79–163, 1979–1 C.B. 131, expanded the definition of other than common stock to include any stock with restricted rights to dividends or rights to assets upon liquidation, even if the stock in question is the only stock outstanding entitled to vote.

Rev.Rul. 81–91, 1981–1 C.B. 123, involved "Class B" voting stock entitled to a preferential liquidation distribution equal to par value and an annual dividend equal to 6% of par value prior to dividends being paid on the Class A stock. After satisfaction of the Class B preference, the Class A and

Class B stock shared equally in liquidation and dividend rights. In holding that the Class B stock was "common stock" and therefore not § 306 stock, the Ruling stated: "[S]tock is other than 'common stock' for purposes of section 306 not because of its preferred position as such, but because the preferred position is limited and the stock does not participate in corporate growth to any significant extent." Rev.Rul. 82–191, 1982–2 C.B. 78, expanded on this explanation as follows: "[T]he factors used to determine whether the stock in question was other than common stock were whether it could be disposed of without a loss in voting control and without a loss in an interest in the unrestricted equitable growth of the corporation. In other words, if a stock in question is nonvoting and is limited in either the right to dividends or the right to assets upon liquidation then it is considered to be other than common stock * * *." Rev.Rul. 82–191 held that *voting* preferred stock was section 306 stock because it was limited as to dividends and had a fixed liquidation preference. On the other hand, non-voting common stock presumably is still "common stock."

1.3. *Stock Received in Section 351 Transactions and Corporate Reorganizations*

Section 306(c)(3) provides that any stock other than common stock issued in a § 351 transaction will be § 306 stock if it is issued in exchange for stock of another controlled corporation that has earnings and profits. This provision prevents the possibility that a taxpayer could create a holding company and, in a § 351 transaction, transfer to it stock of a controlled operating corporation that had earnings and profits in exchange for holding company common and preferred stock. Absent § 306(c)(3), the preferred stock would not constitute § 306 stock, due to the absence of earnings and profits in the newly formed holding company, and gain on the sale of the preferred stock would thus be capital gain. The technical rules for determining the available earnings and profits are discussed in connection with § 304 (see Chapter 5).

Section 306(c)(1)(B) extends the § 306 taint to stock other than common stock received in a corporate reorganization (as defined in § 368) or a corporate division (as defined in § 355) if either (a) the effect of the transaction was substantially the same as the receipt of a stock dividend, or (b) the stock was received in exchange for § 306 stock. This provision is discussed in Chapter 10.

1.4. *Miscellaneous Definitional Issues*

1.4.1. *Stock Having Transferred or Substituted Basis*

Section 306(c)(1)(C) brings within the meaning of § 306 stock any stock having a transferred or substituted basis determined with reference to the basis of § 306 stock. One of the principal effects of this rule is that the taint of § 306 stock carries over from a donor to a donee of such stock. If, however, § 306 stock receives a fair market value basis under § 1014 when it is transferred at death, the § 306 "taint" is purged and the stock can be disposed of without ordinary income consequences. See Treas.Reg. § 1.306–3(e).

1.4.2. *Stock Rights and Convertible Stock*

Section 306(d) applies the § 306 taint to stock rights to purchase stock that would have been § 306 stock if the stock had been issued directly as a stock dividend. Stock purchased pursuant to such rights is also tainted. See Treas.Reg. § 1.306–3(b).

Section 306(e) provides that if § 306 stock is converted into common stock, either through a conversion privilege or otherwise, the § 306 taint is purged. This rule will apply even though the common stock has an exchanged basis. Section 306(e) also provides that common stock convertible into stock other than common stock is not treated as common stock. Thus, such stock may be § 306 stock. Does such stock present the bailout potential at which § 306 is directed?

2.   TAXATION OF DISPOSITIONS OF SECTION 306 STOCK

2.1. *Sales*

Section 306(a)(1) treats the entire amount realized on the sale of § 306 stock as ordinary income to the extent of the stock's ratable share of earnings and profits of the issuing corporation at the time of the distribution of the stock, i.e., the amount that would have been a taxable dividend if the original stock distribution had been a taxable distribution of money rather than a tax free stock dividend under § 305. The excess of any amount realized over the dividend amount is treated first as a return of capital that reduces the basis of the stock, and after the basis of the stock has been reduced to zero, any further excess is treated as capital gain on the sale of the stock. These rules are illustrated in the following example.

Suppose that X Corporation has outstanding 100 shares of common stock having a basis of $6 per share and a fair market value of $30 per share. Assume further that the X Corporation common stock is held in equal shares by A and B. At a time when X Corporation has no accumulated earnings and profits and $500 of current earnings and profits, it distributes a stock dividend of 50 shares of $10 par value preferred stock (which is § 306 stock) to each shareholder. The dividend is tax free under § 305. Assuming that after the distribution the fair market value of the common stock is $20 per share and the fair market value of the preferred stock is $10 per share, under § 307 the basis of the preferred stock is $2 per share. After five years, A sells for $500 the 50 shares of preferred stock received in the distribution. Absent § 306, A would recognize a $400 capital gain. Under § 306(a)(1), however, A realizes ordinary income of $250 (50% of the $500 earnings and profits at the time the stock was issued), receives a return of capital of $100, and recognizes a capital gain of $150. The amount that "would have been a dividend at the time of distribution" of the stock is a ceiling on the amount of ordinary income realized on the sale. See Treas.Reg. § 1.306–1(b)(2), Ex. (1).

While the *sale* of § 306 stock may result in ordinary income, the income is not dividend income under § 301(c)(1) and § 316. Thus, the amount of the corporation's current and accumulated earnings and profits in the year of the sale is irrelevant; and the earnings and profits of the issuing corporation are not reduced by the amount taxed to the shareholder as ordinary income.

Treas.Reg. § 1.306–1(b)(1). In the same vein, a corporate shareholder may not claim the § 243 deduction with respect to ordinary income realized on the sale of § 306 stock. However, pursuant to § 306(a)(1)(D), for individuals the ordinary income resulting from the sale of § 306 stock is taxed at the same rate that applies to dividends under § 1(h)(11).

No loss is allowed on the sale of § 306 stock. I.R.C. § 306(a)(1)(C). Thus, in the above example, if A sold the 50 shares of preferred stock for only $310, A would realize $250 of ordinary income and recover $60 of basis. The remaining $40 of the basis of the preferred stock is reallocated to common stock on which the § 306 stock originally was issued. See Treas.Reg. § 1.306–1(b)(2), Ex. (2).

2.2. Redemptions

When § 306 stock is redeemed by the issuing corporation, the amount realized is treated by § 306(a)(2) as a distribution subject to § 301. The corporation's current and accumulated earnings and profits for the year of the redemption determine the portion of the distribution that will be taxed as ordinary income, albeit at the same rate as long-term capital gains. Thus, even though the corporation may have had sufficient earnings and profits at the time of the distribution of the stock to support dividend treatment of a cash distribution of equal value, if the corporation has no earnings and profits at the time of the redemption, no part of the distribution is ordinary income. If the corporation has earnings and profits at the time of the redemption, however, the "ratable share" of earnings and profits rule of § 306(a)(1)(A)(ii), which applies to limit ordinary income treatment in the case of sales, does not apply to redemptions of § 306 stock (although the proration of current earnings and profits rules of Treas.Reg. § 1.316–2(b) may apply). But, if at the time of the stock distribution the corporation had no earnings and profits, no part of the amount distributed in redemption of the stock will be subject to § 306. See I.R.C. § 306(c)(2).

Application of these rules is illustrated in the following example. Suppose that Y Corporation has outstanding 100 shares of common stock that have a fair market value of $45 per share. Assume further that the Y Corporation common stock is held in equal shares by C and D, who each have a basis of $9 per share. At a time when Y Corporation has no accumulated earnings and profits and $600 of current earnings and profits, it distributes a stock dividend of 50 shares of $15 par value preferred stock (which is § 306 stock) to each shareholder. Assuming that after the distribution the fair market value of the common stock is $30 per share and the fair market value of the preferred stock is $15 per share, the basis of the preferred stock is $3 per share. After five years, Y Corporation has $700 of accumulated earnings and profits and no current earnings and profits. Y Corporation then distributes $750 to C in redemption of all 50 of C's shares of preferred stock; none of D's shares are redeemed. C is treated as receiving a $700 dividend and a $50 return of capital. The remaining $100 of C's basis for the preferred stock is reallocated to C's common stock. Y Corporation reduces its accumulated earnings and profits by $700. If D's 50 shares were redeemed the following year, and if Y Corporation had no current earnings and profits, no portion of the distribution would be ordinary income.

Section 306 operates independently and overrides the rules of § 302(a) and (b), discussed in Chapter 5, under which redemption distributions may be accorded capital gain treatment.

2.3. *Other Dispositions*

Note that § 306(a) applies if a shareholder "sells or otherwise *disposes*" of § 306 stock. Treas.Reg. § 1.306–1(b)(1) indicates that other dispositions may include a pledge of the stock if the lender can look only to the stock to satisfy the loan (i.e., a nonrecourse loan secured by § 306 stock). Such a transaction, however, usually is not viewed as a recognition event. As is implicit in the *Pescosolido* case, a transfer by gift to a noncharitable donee of § 306 stock is not a realization event and thus is not a disposition that results in recognition of ordinary income to the donor. In such a case, however, pursuant to § 306(c)(1)(C), the stock retains its § 306 "taint" in the hands of the donee. See Treas.Reg. § 1.306–3(e). Hence § 306 income can be shifted from one member of the family group to another by means of a donative transfer.

At one time, the tax disadvantages inherent in § 306 preferred stock could be avoided by a contribution of the stock to a charitable organization. The shareholder would escape tax with respect to the § 306 stock, there being no sale, and could also treat its fair market value as a charitable contribution. See Rev.Rul. 57–328, 1957–2 C.B. 229. The Tax Reform Act of 1969 eliminated this tax advantage by adding § 170(e)(1)(A), which was applied in *Pescosolido,* requiring the charitable deduction to be reduced by the amount of potential ordinary income gain in the property. See also Bialo v. Commissioner, 88 T.C. 1132 (1987). For an example of the computations involved when § 306 stock is donated to a charity, see Rev.Rul. 76–396, 1976–2 C.B. 55.

3. EXCEPTIONS TO ORDINARY INCOME TREATMENT

Section 306(b) provides a number of exceptions to the ordinary income treatment generally accorded to § 306 stock. Two of the exceptions are straightforward in their application. Section 306(b)(2) exempts redemptions in complete liquidation of the corporation; § 306(b)(3) provides that the various nonrecognition provisions of the Code take precedence over the recognition rules of § 306. In the latter case, however, § 306(c)(1)(B) and (c)(1)(C) assure that the § 306 taint will attach to any stock of a corporation acquired in such a transaction, even though that stock would not otherwise be § 306 stock. See Treas.Reg. § 1.306–3(e).

Section 306(b)(1) provides an exception when the shareholder disposes (other than by redemption) of the shareholder's entire interest in the corporation (taking into account the § 318 attribution rules) to a person not related to the shareholder within the § 318 attribution rules. (Section 318 is discussed in Chapter 5.) A redemption in complete termination of the shareholder's interest in the corporation under § 302(b)(3) or in partial liquidation under § 302(b)(4) is excepted by § 306(b)(2).

Section 306(b)(4) provides two additional exceptions. Applicability of the exception in § 306(b)(4)(A) was at issue in the *Pescosolido* case. The exception in § 306(b)(4)(B) is explained in the following excerpt from the 1954 Senate Finance Committee Report:

> Subparagraph (B) of subsection (b)(4) applies to a case where the shareholder has made a prior or simultaneous disposition (or redemption) of the underlying stock with respect to which the section 306 stock was issued. Thus if a shareholder received a distribution of 100 shares of section 306 stock on his holdings of 100 shares of voting common stock in a corporation and sells his voting common stock before he disposes of his section 306 stock, the subsequent disposition of his section 306 stock ordinarily would not be considered a tax avoidance disposition since the shareholder has previously parted with the stock that allows him to participate in the ownership of the business. However, variations of the above example may give rise to tax avoidance possibilities that are not within the exception of subparagraph (B). Thus if a corporation has only one class of common stock outstanding and it issues stock under circumstances that characterize it as section 306 stock, a subsequent issue of a different class of common having greater voting rights than the original common will not permit a simultaneous disposition of the section 306 stock together with the original common to escape the rules of subsection (a) of section 306.

S.Rep. No. 83–1622, 83d Cong., 2d Sess. 244 (1954).

In practice, the exception in § 306(b)(4)(B) has very limited application. Rev.Rul. 75–247, 1975–1 C.B. 104, discussed in *Pescolido*, held that a disposition of both a portion of the shareholder's common stock and a corresponding portion of § 306 stock that had been issued with respect to the common stock did not of itself establish the non-tax avoidance purpose required by § 306(b)(4). See also Fireoved v. United States, 462 F.2d 1281 (3d Cir.1972), in which the taxpayer failed to qualify for § 306(b)(4) relief, even though he sold a portion of his common stock prior to a redemption of § 306 stock, because he retained sufficient common stock to avoid any effective diminution in voting power and failed to prove that one of the principal purposes of the stock dividend was not tax avoidance.

Treas.Reg. § 1.306–2(b)(3) gives illustrations of non-tax avoidance transactions falling outside § 306 by reason of § 306(b)(4). In Rev.Rul. 81–81, 1981–1 C.B. 122, the IRS held that the exception in § 306(b)(4)(A) applied to cash received by minority shareholders in lieu of fractional shares in connection with a distribution of a dividend payable in preferred stock. Rev.Rul. 89–63, 1989–1 C.B. 90, held that the fact that § 306 stock was issued by a corporation whose stock is widely held is not sufficient grounds, standing alone, to apply the § 306(b)(4)(A) exception to a sale of the stock. See also Rev.Rul. 77–455, 1977–2 C.B. 93 (§ 306(b)(4)(B) exception available because the shareholder's entire *actual* interest was terminated; attributed ownership under § 318 was not fatal because the § 302(c)(2) waiver was effective); Rev.Rul. 80–33, 1980–1 C.B. 69 (reaching same result as in *Pescosolido*).

Previously the IRS would issue letter rulings to the taxpayer on the § 306(b)(4) issue. Somewhat surprisingly, given the inherently factual nature of the issue, rulings were issued with some frequency. Currently, however, the IRS will not ordinarily rule in advance on § 306(b)(4) issues. Rev.Proc. 2019–3, 2019–1 I.R.B. 130, § 4.01(26).

PROBLEM SET 2

1.   Tacoma Grace Urgent Treatment Centers, Inc. is owned by 5 shareholders who each own 1,000 shares of the common stock. Until Year 11, Tacoma Grace had only one class of stock outstanding. In Year 11, Tacoma Grace declared a dividend of 1 share of $1,000 par value 7% voting preferred stock for every 10 shares of common then held by its shareholders. Each shareholder received 100 shares of preferred stock. Immediately after the distribution, the fair market value of each share of preferred stock was $1,000 and the fair market value of each share of common stock was $50. Tacoma Grace had no current earnings and profits in Year 11, but it had accumulated earnings and profits of $295,000. Tacoma Grace made no other distributions in Year 11.

(a)   (1)   In Year 14, when Tacoma Grace had current earnings and profits of $200,000 and accumulated earnings and profits from prior years of $300,000, one shareholder, Dr. Burke, who originally had an adjusted basis of $45,000 in his Tacoma Grace common stock, sold his 100 shares of preferred stock to another shareholder for $100,000 ($1,000 per share). What are the tax consequences of the sale?

(2)   Would your answer change if, in Year 14, Tacoma Grace had no current earnings and profits and only $10,000 of accumulated earnings and profits?

(3)   Would your answer differ if in Year 11, when the stock dividend was distributed, Tacoma Grace had $1,000,000 of accumulated earnings and profits?

(4)   What if Dr. Burke sold 500 shares of his common stock and 50 shares of his preferred stock to Dr. Grey, who previously owned no shares in Tacoma Grace?

(5)   Would your answer to (a)(1) differ if the preferred stock were participating preferred stock, which after its preference shared dividend and liquidation rights with the common stock in a 9-to-1 ratio?

(6)   What if Dr. Burke gave his preferred stock to his niece, who then sold the stock to the Rock of Ages Insurance Co.?

(7)   What if Dr. Burke died and bequeathed all of his common and preferred stock to his niece, who kept the common stock but sold the preferred stock to the Rock of Ages Insurance Co.?

(b)   (1)   In Year 14, when Tacoma Grace had current earnings and profits of $200,000 and accumulated earnings and profits from prior years of $300,000, Tacoma Grace redeemed from Dr. Webber, another Tacoma Grace shareholder, all 100 of her preferred shares for $100,000. Dr. Webber originally had an adjusted basis of $90,000 in her Tacoma Grace common stock.

    (2) Would your answer change if in Year 14 Tacoma Grace had no current earnings and profits and only $10,000 of accumulated earnings and profits at the time of the redemption?

    (3) What if Dr. Webber retired and Tacoma Grace redeemed all of her common and preferred stock at the same time?

CHAPTER 7

CORPORATE LIQUIDATIONS

SECTION 1. INTRODUCTION

The termination of a corporation's existence through liquidation—the distribution of all of its assets to its shareholders—is treated as an exchange of stock by the shareholder for the amount of the liquidation distribution from the corporation. I.R.C. § 331. This treatment resolves a number of important structural issues for the income tax. A corporate liquidating distribution is not treated as analogous to a dividend distribution and thus the earnings and profits of the distributing corporation are not taxable as a dividend in the hands of the shareholder. Because the corporation is disappearing, the shareholder is allowed a tax-free recovery of basis either through an offset against gain realized to the extent that the distribution exceeds basis or a loss deduction to the extent the amount received in the liquidation is less than the basis of the stock, and capital gain, even though dividend treatment might be considered to be more appropriate to the extent of a pro rata share of the corporation's earnings and profits. The sale or exchange treatment provided for liquidation distributions is similar to exchange treatment for redemption distributions that sufficiently reduce the interest of the distributee shareholder (discussed in Chapter 5), although the corporation's earnings and profits do not completely disappear in a redemption transaction.

As an alternative, the liquidation of a corporation might be likened to the tax-free incorporation transaction under § 351. However, unlike Subchapter K, which accords nonrecognition to the liquidation of a partnership, Subchapter C long has treated a corporate liquidation as a recognition event from the shareholders' perspective. If the nonrecognition analogy were followed, a mechanism for providing the shareholders with an exchanged or transferred basis in the distributed property would be necessary. In addition, if this model were applied, rules for dealing with cash distributions, which cannot be accorded nonrecognition if the distribution exceeds the shareholder's stock basis, would be necessary. From the corporation's perspective, the primary issue is whether gains and losses should be recognized with respect to the distribution to the shareholders of built-in gain and loss assets.

As for characterization of the income, the sale of stock model generally has been accepted, and shareholders are taxed on capital gains to the extent that the distribution exceeds the basis for their stock; if the amount of the distribution is less than the basis of a shareholder's stock, a capital loss is recognized. See I.R.C. § 331. This characterization historically was of great importance because, unlike in the redemption situation, the corporate accumulated earnings and profits disappear at the termination of the corporation's existence. Thus, as a result of the liquidation, the accumulated earnings and profits could permanently escape treatment as ordinary income to the shareholders.

With the taxation of dividends and long-term capital gains at the same rates for individuals, the significance of characterizing a distribution as a dividend or as a liquidating distribution has, however, been reduced. For a noncorporate shareholder receiving the distribution, the only important differences are that (1) all of a dividend distribution is includable in gross income, while only the amount by which a liquidating distribution exceeds the basis of the stock with respect to which the distribution has been made is includable, and (2) gains on liquidating distributions can be offset by capital losses, while dividend income cannot be offset by capital losses, except that § 1211(b) allows individuals to deduct up to $3,000 of capital losses in excess of capital gains.

From the corporation's perspective, the primary issue is whether gains and losses should be recognized with respect to the distribution to the shareholders of built-in gain and loss assets. The Tax Reform Act of 1986 included provisions to ensure two levels of taxation of the corporation's economic profits by requiring the corporation to recognize built-in gain and loss upon the distribution of property in liquidation. Prior to 1986, the general rule was that neither gain nor loss was recognized as a result of liquidating distributions of appreciated or depreciated property. This treatment was a facet of the *General Utilities* rule, discussed in Chapter 4, which accorded nonrecognition to the corporation on all distributions of property. This gap in the two-level taxation system was filled by the repeal of the *General Utilities* doctrine in 1986, and under § 336 the liquidating corporation now must recognize gains and losses on distributed assets (although loss limitation rules apply).

The distribution of appreciated property may result in a tax to both the corporation and the shareholder. Because, however, there is generally no relationship between the basis of a corporation's assets and the basis of a shareholder's stock, the corporation may recognize gain while the shareholder recognizes a loss, or vice versa. For example, assume that a corporation, with a single asset having a basis of $100 and a fair market value of $400, distributes the asset in a liquidating distribution to its shareholder, who has a $500 basis for the stock. The corporation recognizes a gain of $300 while the shareholder recognizes a loss of $100 (§ 267(a)(1) does not apply to liquidating distributions). Given the potential for two taxes on liquidating distributions, including a corporate tax on gain that accrued prior to the formation of the corporation, taxpayers must be very sure that the corporate form is, and for the foreseeable future will be, the form in which they wish to carry on business. Undoing a decision to operate in corporate form can be expensive.

Liquidation of the corporation may occur in a number of contexts. In some cases, the shareholders may use the distributed assets to continue the corporation's trade or business or another trade or business, either separately or as partners. Even though in this case some plausible policy arguments may be made for nonrecognition based on continuity of the business enterprise, gain and loss nevertheless always have been recognized by the shareholders. In other cases, the sale of the business may be the objective. Under one selling method, the corporation sells its assets and distributes the cash proceeds to the shareholders as a liquidating distribution. As a policy matter, in a system that adopts two-level taxation of corporate profits, recognition of gain and loss at both the corporate and shareholder level is appropriate. On the other hand, a sale of stock results in only a single level tax to the selling shareholder.[1]

The nature of the shareholder also may affect issues involved in corporate liquidation. Thus, suppose the shareholder is another corporation rather than an individual. Should there be any analogy drawn to the exclusion of intercorporate dividends allowed under § 243, discussed in Chapter 4? If so, it could be argued that a corporation that receives a liquidating distribution should be able to exclude a portion of the distribution attributable to the liquidating corporation's earnings and profits (with an appropriate basis adjustment). Nevertheless, except in the case of liquidations of controlled (80% or more) subsidiary corporations, the rules governing corporate liquidations generally are applied in the same manner to both individual and corporate shareholders. In the case of liquidations of controlled subsidiaries, § 332 and § 337 generally provide for nonrecognition of gains and losses to both the liquidating corporation and the distributing corporation. As is usual in nonrecognition transactions, the transferee must take an exchanged or transferred basis. In this case, § 334(b) requires that the parent corporation take the subsidiary's basis as its basis for the assets received in the liquidating distribution.

The materials in this Chapter are concerned both with the rules that govern corporate liquidations in general and with the special rules governing subsidiary liquidations. Chapter 8 contrasts the problems encountered when a liquidation occurs in the context of a sale of the assets of the corporation with those encountered when the shareholders choose to dispose of the corporate business by selling the stock of the corporation. In these cases the tax treatment accorded to the purchaser may influence the form of the transaction. Chapter 10 examines the treatment of those "tax free" reorganizations that involve the disposition of either corporate stock or corporate assets in exchange for stock of another corporation.

---

[1] From a tax perspective, however, the buyer of a going business may prefer to purchase the assets rather than the stock. The tension between the seller's desire to sell the stock and avoid the double tax and the buyer's preference to purchase assets is discussed in Chapter 8.

Detailed Analysis

1.   EXISTENCE OF A "LIQUIDATION"

1.1. *Generally*

Section 346(a) purports to define "complete liquidation" by providing as follows: "For purposes of this subchapter, a distribution shall be treated as in complete liquidation of a corporation if the distribution is one of a series of distributions in redemption of all of the stock of the corporation pursuant to a plan." This definition is tautological and consequently is of virtually no help in identifying when the process of liquidating a corporation commences. It merely informs that a complete liquidation can occur in a series of distributions and does not require that there be only a single distribution to each shareholder. Section 346(a) does not provide any assistance in determining whether a particular distribution is the first of a series of distributions in the process of liquidation, and thus governed by § 336 at the corporate level and § 331 at the shareholder level, or a pre-liquidation dividend distribution, governed by § 311 at the corporate level and § 301 and/or § 302 at the shareholder level.

Nor do the Regulations under § 331, § 336, and § 346 define a "liquidation," and thus whether a particular distribution is in "liquidation" of the corporation may be an issue. Treas.Reg. § 1.332–2(c), which defines the term "liquidation" in the context of liquidation of a corporate subsidiary, does, however, provide some guidance: "A status of liquidation exists when the corporation ceases to be a going concern and its activities are merely for the purpose of winding up its affairs, paying its debts, and distributing any remaining balance to its shareholders."

In Estate of Maguire v. Commissioner, 50 T.C. 130 (1968), the court formulated the test for determining whether a liquidation has in fact occurred as follows: "[T]here are three basic tests: (1) There must be a manifest intention to liquidate; (2) there must be a continuing purpose to terminate corporate affairs; and (3) the corporation's activities must be directed to such termination." Under these tests, distributions received in 1960 were held to be dividends and not liquidating distributions; although a plan of liquidation had been adopted in 1944, the corporation after the 1960 distributions still had assets of over $48 million and annual income of over $1.5 million, and liquidation had not been completed by 1964.

The factual nature of this inquiry is illustrated by contrasting *Estate of Maguire* with Olmsted v. Commissioner, T.C. Memo. 1984–381. During 1969 and 1970, the shareholders entered into contractual agreements to wind up the corporation's affairs and liquidate it. The board of directors began selling properties in 1970, but shareholders did not approve a plan of liquidation until December 1973. Due to difficulties in selling mineral and timber properties, the corporation leased the properties to others and received almost $1,200,000 of income from mineral royalties, timber sales, and rents during the period 1973 through 1981. It distributed over $1,900,000 to shareholders over the same period. The Tax Court held that a status of liquidation existed during 1974 and 1975. Because the corporation would have had difficulty selling its properties, the leasing and royalty arrangements were substitutes for sales and were not inconsistent with the status of liquidation; the fact that the corporation ceased exploration and development of new mineral properties evidenced an intent to wind up business.

Formal action by the directors or shareholders is not necessarily required to effect a complete liquidation for tax purposes. Distributions may be treated as having been received in a *de facto* liquidation if the facts and circumstances indicate that notwithstanding a failure to comply with the formalities of corporate law, the corporation actually has ceased to be a going business. For example, in Rendina v. Commissioner, T.C. Memo. 1996–392, a corporation distributed all of its business assets to its sole shareholder, who in connection with the distribution assumed all of the corporation's liabilities. The corporation, however, did not formally dissolve. Relying on the tests for liquidation status in Treas.Reg. § 1.332–2(c), *Estate of Maquire*, and *Olmsted*, the court found that a *de facto* liquidation had occurred and declined to uphold the Commissioner's deficiency based on treatment of the distribution as a dividend.

1.2. *"Unchecking-the-Box" by Limited Liability Companies*

Treas.Reg. § 301.7701–3(g)(1) deals with situations in which an unincorporated entity, e.g., a limited liability company (LLC), that previously had elected to be taxed as a corporation under Treas.Reg. § 301.7701–3(c), discussed in Chapter 1, revokes the election. In such a case, the entity is treated as if it had distributed all of its assets to its shareholders in a taxable liquidation. Section 336 applies to the entity taxed as a liquidating corporation and § 331 applies to the shareholders. If the entity has only one owner, the entity becomes a disregarded entity for tax purposes, and it is deemed simply to have distributed its assets to its owner. If the entity has two or more owners, the liquidation is treated as if the owners immediately contributed all the assets to a newly formed partnership.

SECTION 2.   TREATMENT OF THE CORPORATION

INTERNAL REVENUE CODE: Sections 336(a)–(c), (d)(1)–(2); 6043.

Section 336(a) requires recognition to the corporation of gain or loss as if the property distributed in liquidation had been sold to the distributee for its fair market value. Gain and loss are computed separately on each asset. Generally the gain will be characterized with reference to the purpose for which the corporation held the property. Thus, ordinary income will be recognized if inventory is distributed; capital gain will be recognized with respect to capital assets; § 1231 gain will be recognized with respect to depreciable property and land used in the corporation's business; and recapture income will be recognized where appropriate. As a result, in some cases the liquidating corporation may find itself with both ordinary income and capital losses that may not be deducted against that income. See I.R.C. § 1211(a).

The treatment of liquidating distributions differs from current distributions in kind, which under § 311 result in recognition of gain but not of loss (see Chapter 4). The legislative history of § 311 and § 336 does not explain the reason for this differing treatment. Perhaps the answer is that Congress was concerned that allowing losses to be recognized on current distributions would have presented too much opportunity for manipulation, for example, by distributing an asset, such as portfolio securities, that had temporarily fallen in value but that was expected to regain its value. On the other hand, a liquidation terminates the corporate existence, and even though loss assets may regain value after the liquidation, the liquidating distribution is not a selective distribution and is less subject to manipulation. Thus, it is appropriate to permit the corporation to recognize losses on liquidating distributions. To this end, § 267(a), which generally disallows deductions for losses incurred on sales and exchanges between certain related taxpayers, by its terms does not apply to losses recognized under § 336 (or under § 331 for the shareholders). Congress, however, has provided for disallowance of losses that it considered to be artificial or duplicative of shareholder losses; § 336(d) imposes a complex web of limitations on losses that may be recognized by the corporation with respect to certain distributions to majority shareholders and distributions of property that has been recently contributed to the corporation.

DETAILED ANALYSIS

1. ISSUES WITH RESPECT TO GAIN RECOGNITION UNDER SECTION 336

1.1. *Distributions of Encumbered Property*

Generally, distributions of encumbered property present no special problems under § 336(a). If a liquidating corporation distributes property having a basis of $200 and a fair market value of $1,000, subject to a $600 mortgage, the amount of the mortgage is irrelevant to the computation. The corporation recognizes a gain of $800. If the mortgage encumbering the distributed property exceeds the fair market value of the property, § 336(b) deems the value of the property to be not less than the amount of the liability. Thus, if the mortgage on the property in the immediately preceding example were $1,150, the corporation would recognize a $950 gain. Section 336(b) should apply on an asset-by-asset basis. Where a liability does not specifically encumber a particular property but a shareholder assumes the liability in connection with the distribution, the liability should be allocated among the distributed properties relative to their respective fair market values. See Rev.Rul. 80–283, 1980–2 C.B. 108 (applying now repealed version of former § 311(c), which was analogous to present § 336(b)).

1.2. *Distributions of Depreciable Property to Majority Shareholders*

Section 336(a) provides that gain is recognized "as if such property were sold to the distributee." Thus, in most cases the purpose for which the corporation held the property determines the character of the gain. Section 1239, however, treats as ordinary income any gain recognized with respect to any property distributed to a shareholder who owns more than 50% of the value of the stock (taking into account attribution under § 267(c), excluding § 267(c)(3)) if the *shareholder* holds the property as depreciable property. Thus, for example, if a corporation distributes to its sole shareholder a building, having an adjusted basis of $100,000 and a fair market value of $1,000,000, the entire $900,000 gain is ordinary income to the corporation, without regard to any applicable depreciation recapture, if the shareholder holds the building for use in a trade or business. The purpose for which the corporation held the building is not relevant under § 1239. Since corporate capital gains are not subject to preferential rates, this issue is important only if the distributing corporation has capital losses, which are deductible by a corporation under § 1211(a) only to the extent of its capital gains.

2.   LIMITATIONS ON LOSS RECOGNITION UNDER SECTION 336

2.1. *Distributions to Related Persons*

2.1.1.   *Non-Pro Rata Distributions to Related Shareholders*

If a specific item of loss property is distributed among the shareholders other than in undivided interests proportionate to their shareholdings, any loss attributable to the portion of the property distributed to a related person is disallowed. I.R.C. § 336(d)(1)(A)(i). This loss disallowance rule applies only with respect to property distributed to a shareholder who is "related" within the meaning of § 267, generally, a more than 50% shareholder. Assume, for example, that 60% of the stock of Y Corporation is held by B and 40% is held by C, who is unrelated to B. The corporation makes a liquidating distribution as follows: B receives Blackacre, having a fair market value of $60 and a basis of $70; C receives Whiteacre, having a fair market value of $40 and a basis of $50. Y Corporation may recognize the loss on the distribution of Whiteacre to C because C is not a related person. But because B is a related person and B received 100% of the asset, none of the loss on Blackacre may be recognized. However, if Y Corporation had distributed an undivided 60% of each asset to B and an undivided 40% of each asset to C, it would have been allowed to recognize the loss with respect to both assets. Like the rule disallowing losses on distributions to related persons of property contributed within five years of the distribution (discussed below), this rule applies without regard to whether there was a valid business purpose for distributing the property non-pro rata. Furthermore, the disallowance rule applies regardless of how the corporation acquired the property.

The purpose of § 336(d)(1)(A)(i) is puzzling. If Y Corporation distributed Blackacre and Whiteacre to B and C pro rata, under § 334(a), B and C each would have a basis in their respective interests in the property equal to fair market value. Thus, immediately after the distribution they could exchange undivided interests of equal value received in the liquidating distribution without realization of gain or loss. To continue the immediately preceding example, C's 40% interest in Blackacre is of equal value ($24) to B's 60% interest in Whiteacre ($24). B and C could exchange these interests without gain or loss, and, assuming the exchange is respected, B would end up with all of Blackacre, C would receive all of Whiteacre, and the corporation would recognize its losses. The IRS might successfully apply the "step transaction" doctrine to treat the distribution as being made by the corporation non-pro rata, but that is perhaps less likely if it makes good business sense for B to own all of Blackacre and C to own all of Whiteacre.

2.1.2. *Distributions to a Related Shareholder of Recently Contributed Property*

Section 336(d)(1)(A)(ii) disallows any loss deduction to the corporation with respect to a distribution to a related shareholder if the property was acquired in a § 351 transaction or as a contribution to capital within the five year period ending on the date of the distribution. This rule was enacted in 1986, long before the enactment of § 362(e), discussed in Chapter 2, to prevent "stuffing" property with built-in losses into the corporation in anticipation of the liquidation. At that time, in the absence of the rule in § 336(d)(1)(A)(ii), the corporation could recognize losses to offset gains on property held by the corporation; the shareholder also would recognize an additional loss on the liquidation because the basis of the stock would be increased under § 358 by the basis of the appreciated asset. At the same time, only the fair market value of the asset would be taken into account as an amount realized in computing gain or loss on the liquidation. This "double loss" situation was a corollary of the double taxation of gains. Congress has limited the availability of these double losses because of the tax avoidance potential. See H.Rep. No. 99–841, 99th Cong., 2d Sess. II–200 (1986). The importance of § 336(d)(1)(A)(ii) is reduced, but not completely eliminated by, the enactment in 2004 of § 362(e)(2), requiring that the corporation reduce the aggregate basis of the property transferred to a corporation in a § 351 transaction to its fair market value if the aggregate basis of the property in the hands of the transferor exceeds its aggregate fair market value. Because, however, § 362(e)(2) compares the aggregate basis of contributed property with its aggregate fair market value, if both built-in gain property and built-in loss property are contributed to a corporation, the corporation's basis in a particular contributed asset can exceed the asset's fair market value thereby triggering application of § 336(d)(1)(A)(ii).

Suppose, for example, that A and B formed X Corporation, to which A contributed cash of $60 in exchange for 60 shares of common stock, and B contributed both Whiteacre, with a fair market value of $25 and a basis of $10, and Blackacre with a fair market value of $15 and a basis of $30, in exchange for 40 shares of stock. Section 362(e)(2) does not operate to reduce the basis of Blackacre to less than $30 because the aggregate basis of Blackacre and Whiteacre ($40) does not exceed their aggregate fair market value ($40). Four years later (when the bases and values of the properties are unchanged), X Corporation is liquidated. Blackacre, Whiteacre, and cash are distributed to A; other property and cash are distributed to B. Although § 336(a) requires X Corporation to recognize the $15 gain with respect to Whiteacre, § 336(d)(1)(A)(ii) disallows recognition of the $15 loss with respect to Blackacre.

Furthermore, in operation, § 336(d)(1)(A)(ii) is mechanical and applies without regard to whether the property had a built-in gain or built-in loss at the time it was contributed to the corporation. Suppose, for example, that for a valid business purpose C contributes two items of property to Y Corporation in exchange for all of its stock. The first asset has a basis of $500 and a fair market value of $1,000; the second has a basis of $1,000 and a fair market value of $1,600. Four years later, Y Corporation is liquidated and both properties are distributed to C. At the time of the liquidation, the first property has appreciated in value to $2,000 and its basis remains $500; the second property has declined in value to $600 and its basis remains $1,000. Y Corporation must recognize the $1,500 gain on the first property but may not recognize the $400 loss on the second property.

2.2. *Distributions and Sales of Recently Contributed Built-In Loss Property*

In cases where § 336(d)(1) is not applicable, § 336(d)(2), which applies without regard to the amount of stock of the corporation owned by a distributee shareholder, might disallow losses at the corporate level with respect to property distributed or *sold* to any person in the process of liquidation. Section 336(d)(2) applies to property acquired by the corporation in a § 351 transaction or as a contribution to capital if "the acquisition of such property by the liquidating corporation was part of a plan a principal purpose of which was to recognize loss by the liquidating corporation with respect to such property in connection with the liquidation." I.R.C. § 336(d)(2)(B)(i)(II). Section 336(d)(2), which also is intended to disallow built-in double losses, is more accurately targeted than § 336(d)(1)(A)(ii). Section 336(d)(2) disallows only that portion of the loss that is attributable to the excess of the adjusted basis of the property immediately after the acquisition over the fair market value of the property at that time. In other words, only the built-in loss is disallowed; any loss accruing while the property was owned by the corporation is allowed. Mechanically, this result is accomplished by reducing the basis of the contributed property in an amount equal to the built-in loss.

As is the case with respect to § 336(d)(1)(A)(ii), the subsequent enactment of § 362(e)(2) has reduced, but not eliminated, the importance of § 336(d)(2). Suppose, for example, that D and E formed Z Corporation, to which D contributed cash of $40 in exchange for 40 shares of common stock, and E contributed $20 of cash, Whiteacre, with a fair market value of $25 and a basis of $10, and Blackacre with a fair market value of $15 and a basis of $30, in exchange for 60 shares of stock. Section 362(e)(2) does not operate to reduce the basis of Blackacre to less than $30 because the aggregate basis of Blackacre and Whiteacre ($40) does not exceed their aggregate fair market value ($40). One year later (when the bases and values of the properties are unchanged) Z Corporation is liquidated. Blackacre and Whiteacre are distributed to D; cash is distributed to E. Section 336(d)(2) reduces the basis of Blackacre by $15, the amount of the built-in loss at the time of the contribution, from $30 to $15 before applying § 336(a). While § 336(a) requires Z Corporation to recognize the $15 gain with respect to Whiteacre, no gain or loss is realized with respect to Blackacre.

The basis reduction under § 336(d)(2) applies only for purposes of computing losses. For example, if an asset was contributed to the corporation at a time when its basis was $500 and its fair market value was $400 and the asset was distributed when its adjusted basis, without regard to § 336(d)(2), was $450 and its fair market value was $150, the adjusted basis would be reduced to $350, reflecting the $100 built-in loss, and only a $200 loss would be allowed, assuming that § 336(d)(1) does not also apply. Because, however, the basis reduction rule does not apply when computing gain, if the property had a fair market value of at least $350 but not more than $450 at the time it was distributed, the corporation would recognize neither a gain nor a loss.

Although the general applicability of the loss disallowance rule of § 336(d)(2) is based on intent, a timing element is introduced by § 336(d)(2)(B)(ii), which conclusively deems property contributed to the corporation within two years prior to adoption of the plan of liquidation to have been contributed as part of the proscribed plan, except as otherwise provided in Regulations. The Conference Committee Report indicates, however, that the Regulations should provide that the presumption "will be disregarded *unless* there is no clear and substantial relationship between the contributed property and the conduct of the corporation's current or future business enterprises." H.Rep. No. 99–841, 99th Cong., 2d Sess. II–201 (1986). Stated affirmatively, the Committee Report suggests that the presumption should not apply to assets used in the corporation's trade or business, and the question reverts to one of intent. Thus, for example, contributions of portfolio securities would be presumed to have been made for the prohibited purpose. Furthermore, the Conference Report indicates that the loss disallowance rule should not apply at all if a plan of liquidation is adopted within two years of formation of the corporation. Id. However, the statute on its face does not appear to be self-executing, and the rules for disregarding the presumption explained in the Committee Report thus are not in force until Regulations are promulgated.

Technically, the loss disallowance rule of § 336(d)(2) applies to property transferred to the corporation more than two years prior to adoption of the plan of liquidation if the acquisition by the corporation was pursuant to a plan having the prohibited purpose. The Conference Committee Report indicates, however, that § 336(d)(2) should be applied to property contributed more than two years prior to adoption of the plan of liquidation "only in the most rare and unusual cases." Id. at II–200.

The flush material of § 336(d)(2)(B)(i) indicates that property subject to the basis adjustment includes any property the basis of which is determined with reference to property contributed pursuant to the proscribed plan. Thus, if contributed property is subject to a basis adjustment under § 336(d)(2), the taint cannot be purged by exchanging the property for other property that takes an exchanged basis (such as in a § 351 transaction or a § 1031 like-kind exchange).

3.   EXCEPTIONS TO SECTION 336

Section 336 does not apply to distributions that are part of a corporate reorganization. I.R.C. § 336(c). However, § 361(c) may require recognition of gain, but not loss, with respect to property other than stock or securities of the acquiring corporation distributed in liquidations pursuant to a corporate reorganization. Corporate reorganizations are discussed in Chapter 10.

Section 337 displaces § 336 and provides nonrecognition in the case of liquidating distributions by an 80% controlled corporate subsidiary.

4. TRANSFERS TO TAX-EXEMPT ORGANIZATIONS

Pursuant to broad regulatory authority contained in § 337(d), Treas.Reg. § 1.337(d)–4(a)(1) requires recognition of built-in gain or loss by a taxable corporation on the transfer of substantially all of its assets to a tax-exempt entity. Recognition of loss is limited by Treas.Reg. § 1.337(d)–4(d) with respect to assets acquired in a § 351 exchange or as a contribution to capital and assets distributed to a shareholder or member of the taxable corporation's affiliated group if the transaction is part of a plan the principal purpose of which is to recognize a loss. Conversion of a taxable corporation into a tax-exempt entity is treated as a transfer of substantially all of its assets, thereby triggering recognition of gain or loss. Treas.Reg. § 1.337(d)–4(a)(2). Exceptions to the recognition rules are available for taxable corporations that were previously tax-exempt and which return to tax-exempt status within three years, and new corporations that acquire a tax exemption within three years of formation. Treas.Reg. § 1.337(d)–4(a)(3). In addition, assets transferred to a tax-exempt entity that are used in an activity subject to the tax on unrelated business taxable income of § 511(a) are excepted from the recognition rule until sold by the tax-exempt entity. Treas.Reg. § 1.337(d)–4(b).

SECTION 3. TREATMENT OF SHAREHOLDERS

INTERNAL REVENUE CODE: Sections 331; 334(a); 346(a); 453(h)(1)(A)–(C), (2).

REGULATIONS: Section 1.331–1.

Section 331 treats a distribution in complete liquidation as being received in exchange for the stock of the liquidating corporation, resulting in recognition of capital gain or loss to the shareholder. The shareholder takes a basis in any property received in the liquidation equal to its fair market value. I.R.C. § 334(a). While these basic rules generally are not difficult to apply, certain situations may cause problems. Only distributions in *complete* liquidation are accorded sale or exchange treatment under § 331. Where a liquidation is accomplished through a series of distributions, § 346(a) provides that all distributions in the series pursuant to a plan to liquidate the corporation will be treated as liquidating distributions. Generally, a distribution other than one in liquidation will be subject to § 301 and will be taxed as ordinary income to its full extent if the corporation has sufficient earnings and profits. Section 346(a) eliminates the necessity to distinguish between dividend distributions and liquidating distributions once the liquidation process begins, but determining when the liquidation process begins sometimes presents difficult factual questions. The status of liquidation is important to the tax treatment of the shareholder, since capital gain and recovery of basis with respect to the liquidating distribution result only if a "liquidation" exists; otherwise, the shareholder will generally be treated as having received an ordinary dividend.

Where property is distributed in liquidation and the shareholder assumes liabilities of the corporation in connection therewith, the shareholder's gain is computed by subtracting the shareholder's stock basis from the fair market value of the property received reduced by any liabilities assumed by the shareholder.[2] See Rev.Rul. 59–228, 1959–2 C.B. 59. For purposes of computing gain on a subsequent sale, the shareholder's basis for the property under § 334(a) is the fair market value of the property at the time of distribution without any adjustment to reflect the assumed liabilities. Ford v. United States, 311 F.2d 951 (Ct.Cl.1963). This failure to take liabilities directly into account in computing basis is appropriate because the liabilities were subtracted from the fair market value of the distributed property in computing the shareholder's amount realized on the liquidation. Because the shareholder must pay the liabilities, they are a cost of acquiring the property and properly should be reflected in basis. Since only the net fair market value of the property was taken into account in computing the shareholder's gain realized in the liquidation, providing the property with a basis equal to its fair market value undiminished by liabilities indirectly includes the liabilities in its basis. For this reason, it likewise is proper not to increase basis by the amount of the assumed liabilities; to do so would take them into account twice.

Section 331 provides that a liquidating distribution is received in *exchange* for the stock, thereby providing the vital link to § 1222 that produces capital gain or loss treatment. Suppose the stock of the corporation has become worthless prior to the liquidation and the shareholder receives nothing in the liquidation. Because there has been no liquidating distribution, there is no sale or exchange of the stock, and, in the absence of an exception, the loss would be an ordinary rather than capital loss. See Aldrich v. Commissioner, 1 T.C. 602 (1943). Section 165(g) operates, however, to prevent an ordinary loss by requiring capital loss treatment upon the worthlessness of corporate stock and securities. However, § 1244, discussed in Chapter 3, provides for ordinary loss treatment on the sale or exchange or worthlessness of certain stock in a "small business corporation," which is a narrowly defined term.

Section 267(a)(1) generally disallows loss deductions on the sale or exchange of property between a shareholder and a corporation of which the shareholder directly or through attribution owns more than 50% of the stock. Losses incurred on the complete liquidation of a corporation, however, are exempted from disallowance under § 267 by the express terms of that provision.

---

[2]   If the amount of a liability is contingent at the time of the distribution and the shareholder later repays an amount in excess of the liability taken into account in computing his gain or loss on the distribution, the repayment will give rise to a capital loss, not an ordinary deduction. See Arrowsmith v. Commissioner, 344 U.S. 6 (1952).

DETAILED ANALYSIS

1. ALLOCATION OF LIQUIDATING DISTRIBUTIONS AMONG SHARES

1.1. *Single Liquidating Distribution*

Where the shareholder of a liquidating corporation owns a single block of stock acquired at the same time and at the same cost, and receives a single liquidating distribution, the distribution is applied first to the basis of the stock. Gain is recognized to the extent the fair market value of the assets received exceeds the basis of the stock. Where, however, a series of liquidating distributions are received, or where the shareholder owns different blocks of stock acquired at different times and at different costs, each distribution must be allocated to each block of stock, and gain or loss is computed separately for each block of stock. Treas.Reg. § 1.331–1(e). Rev.Rul. 68–348, 1968–2 C.B. 141, amplified in Rev.Rul. 85–48, 1985–1 C.B. 126, provides examples of how to make the required allocations.

Assume that C purchased 200 shares of stock of X Corporation for $11,000 five years ago and also purchased 100 shares of stock of X Corporation for $1,000 three months ago. X Corporation liquidates and C receives $30 per share for a total of $9,000. C received a distribution of $6,000 with respect to the 200 shares purchased five years ago for $11,000 and recognizes a $5,000 long-term capital loss with respect to those shares. C received a distribution of $3,000 with respect to the 100 shares purchased three months ago for $1,000, and recognizes a $2,000 short-term capital gain with respect to those shares. These gains and losses are not directly netted but are taken into account separately in calculating C's net long-term capital gain and net short-term capital loss for the year pursuant to § 1222.

Computation of gain and loss on a block-by-block basis when the shareholder receives a single liquidating distribution generally is relevant either if long-term capital gains are taxed differently than short-term capital gains or if liquidating distributions are made over the course of two or more years. Thus, block-by-block computations often are unnecessary. A block-by-block computation may have an impact, however, where the taxpayer holds a block of stock as a capital asset that has declined in value and holds an appreciated block as an ordinary income asset, as may be the case with a dealer in securities.

1.2. *Serial Liquidating Distributions*

Where the shareholder receives a series of distributions with respect to two or more blocks of stock, significant timing differences may occur as a result of the block-by-block computation. After each distribution has been allocated among the blocks of stock, gain is recognized with respect to a block of stock after its basis has been recovered. This treatment, ratified by Rev.Rul. 85–48, supra, reflects the "open transaction" doctrine of Burnet v. Logan, 283 U.S. 404 (1931), even though such treatment generally is not available for installment sales. See Treas.Reg. § 15a.453–1(c). However, no loss is recognized in a § 331 liquidation until after the corporation has made its final distribution. Rev.Rul. 68–348, 1968–2 C.B. 141; Schmidt v. Commissioner, 55 T.C. 335 (1970). Thus, gain may be recognized on a particular block before basis has been completely recovered on another block. Furthermore, where the series of distributions spans two or more years, it is possible for a shareholder with no overall gain to recognize capital gain in one year and a capital loss in a subsequent year, without being able to offset the two.

Assume that B holds 300 shares of common stock of X Corporation. B's basis for 100 shares (Block 1) is $500; B's basis for the other 200 shares (Block 2) is $2,000. In Year 1, X Corporation adopts a plan of liquidation pursuant to which it distributes $1,800 to B in Year 1 and $900 in Year 2. One-third of the $1,800 received in Year 1, $600, is allocated to Block 1, and B recognizes a $100 gain with respect to Block 1. The remaining $1,200 received in Year 1 is allocated to Block 2 and is applied against basis to reduce the basis of Block 2 from $2,000 to $800. When the $900 is received in Year 2, $300 is allocated to Block 1, and B recognizes a $300 gain with respect to Block 1; $600 is allocated to Block 2, and B recognizes a $200 loss with respect to Block 2. Overall, B recognizes total net gain of $200, of which $100 is recognized in each of Year 1 and Year 2. Had B been permitted to aggregate the basis of both blocks and apply distributions against the aggregate basis before recognizing any gain, no gain would have been recognized in Year 1; the entire $200 would have been recognized in Year 2.

2. DISTRIBUTION OF INSTALLMENT NOTES

2.1. *Generally*

Where the corporation distributes in liquidation a § 453 installment note previously received from another person on the sale of property by the corporation, § 453B requires the corporation to include any remaining deferred gain in income. The shareholders generally are not entitled to use the installment method under § 453 with respect to the note. Instead, the shareholders must treat the fair market value of the note as an amount received from the corporation in a liquidating distribution. Any gain recognized is capital gain, and the note takes a basis in the hands of the shareholders equal to its fair market value at the time of the distribution. Rev.Rul. 66–280, 1966–2 C.B. 304. If the principal amount of the note exceeds its fair market value on the date of the distribution, the excess, when collected, is ordinary income, either pursuant to the market discount rules of § 1276 or judicial interpretation of the sale or exchange requirement of § 1222.

2.2. *Section 453(h)*

Section 453(h) provides a limited exception to the shareholder recognition rule (but not to the rules requiring recognition by the corporation upon distribution of the note) when the shareholders receive installment obligations arising from a sale or exchange of corporate assets occurring after the adoption of a plan of complete liquidation that is completed within twelve months after it was adopted,[3] and it applies whether the installment sale is

---

[3]   Section 453(k)(2), denying installment sale treatment for sales of marketable stock and securities, might render § 453(h) unavailable in the liquidation of a publicly traded corporation, but it is highly unlikely that a publicly traded corporation ever would liquidate in a manner to which § 453(h) could apply.

pursuant to a complete acquisition of the seller's business or a dispersal sale. This provision applies only if the liquidation is completed within twelve months following adoption of the plan.[4] If this requirement is met, shareholders recognize gain on the liquidation with respect to the notes under the installment method of § 453 as they receive payments on the obligations. If an installment obligation arises from the sale of inventory, however, deferred recognition is available only if substantially all of the inventory attributable to a particular trade or business of the corporation was sold in bulk to a single purchaser.

Assume, for example, that C is the sole shareholder of Y Corporation. C's basis for the stock is $1,000. Y Corporation owns a factory and inventory. If Y Corporation sells the factory and inventory for a $10,000 promissory note, payable in five equal principal installments (with interest), and then distributes the note to C in complete liquidation, C recognizes no gain at the time of the liquidation but instead recognizes $1,800 of gain under § 331 as each $2,000 installment is received (C also recognizes interest income). If the factory were sold for $6,000 cash and the inventory were sold in bulk for a $4,000 note, due in four equal principal installments (with interest), and Y Corporation liquidated, C would allocate a pro rata portion of the $1,000 basis in the stock, $600 ($1,000 × $6,000/($6,000 + $4,000)) to the cash distribution, and C would recognize a $5,400 gain upon receipt of the cash distribution; C would allocate $100 of basis to each $1,000 payment received on the note and recognize $900 of gain as each payment is received.

Section 453(h) has some limitations. If the property sold for an installment obligation is depreciable property and the purchaser is related to the shareholder (i.e., the shareholder's spouse, a trust of which the shareholder or the shareholder's spouse is a beneficiary, or a corporation or partnership more than 50% controlled by the shareholder of the selling corporation), installment reporting is not available to the shareholder. Where a corporation distributes cash or property (other than qualifying installment obligations) in one tax year and then in a subsequent tax year (but within 12 months) distributes installment obligations qualifying under § 453(h), the gain included in the first year must be recomputed—usually on an amended return—to reflect treatment of the earlier cash distribution as an installment payment. In turn, a portion of the basis for the stock originally used to offset the cash distribution must be allocated to the installment obligation, thereby increasing the gain recognized in the first year. Treas.Reg. § 1.453–11 provides detailed rules regarding the application of § 453(h).

3. DISTRIBUTIONS OF GOODWILL

Where goodwill is distributed in a liquidation, the value of the goodwill is includible for purposes of determining shareholder gain. See Carty v. Commissioner, 38 T.C. 46 (1962) (acq.). As will be discussed in greater detail

---

[4]   Section 453(h) is a vestige of the pre-1987 rules under which a corporation did not recognize gain or loss on the sale or exchange of certain assets if the assets were sold after the adoption of a plan of liquidation and the liquidation was completed within twelve months. Although those rules were repealed by the Tax Reform Act of 1986, installment reporting of shareholder gain was continued.

in Chapter 8, § 1060 requires that in any "applicable asset acquisition," the value of acquired goodwill be determined by the "residual" method, which values goodwill as the excess of the purchase price over the fair market value of all other assets, including both tangible and intangible assets (other than going concern value and goodwill). See Treas.Reg. § 1.1060–1. The definition of "applicable asset acquisition" in § 1060(c), if read literally, might include corporate liquidations in which the shareholders acquire the assets of a trade or business of the corporation. In the context of liquidations of closely held corporations, application of the "residual" method to distributed goodwill is problematic because that valuation method contemplates that the consideration for the transferred assets is susceptible to valuation without reference to the assets themselves. In the case of a closely held corporation, the stock usually is valued with reference to the value of the assets, including the value of goodwill determined under a capitalization of earnings method. But see Treas.Reg. § 1.1060–1(b)(3), Ex. 3, requiring the application of § 1060 when assets are acquired from the corporation in a stock redemption transaction.

In some cases, a closely held corporation might not own goodwill apart from that of its shareholder employees. In Norwalk v. Commissioner, T.C. Memo 1998–279, an accounting services professional corporation dissolved and distributed its assets to its two CPA shareholders, who in turn contributed the assets to a partnership that they joined in the same year. The IRS asserted that in addition to its tangible assets, the corporation distributed to its shareholders customer-based intangible assets, including the corporation's client base, client records, goodwill, and going concern value, which resulted in an additional gain to the corporation under § 336 and also increased the amount realized and thus the capital gain recognized by the shareholders on the liquidation. The court, however, upheld the taxpayer's argument that because any clients would have followed the individual CPAs, the corporation's earnings were entirely attributable to the CPA-shareholders. Thus, it owned no goodwill or customer-based intangibles that could be separately sold. Because clients sought the personal ability, personality, and reputation of the individual CPAs, these assets did not belong to the corporation. The corporation's name had no goodwill value. Martin Ice Cream Co. v. Commissioner, 110 T.C. 189 (1998), also suggests that business goodwill based on an individual shareholder's personal relationship with a supplier—specifically in that case, an importer's relationship with the management of Häagen-Dazs—remains property owned by the shareholder individually, even though the corporation avails itself of the goodwill to conduct business. Similarly, in H & M, Inc. v. Commissioner, T.C. Memo. 2012–290, the court rejected the IRS's assertion that a compensation agreement with the selling shareholder of an insurance agency that was dependent on customer relations with the shareholder represented goodwill of the corporation. Thus, the court held that the corporation did not recognize additional gain on the sale under § 336 on distribution of appreciated goodwill.[5]

---

[5]   But see Howard v. United States, 106 A.F.T.R.2d 2010–5533 (E. D. Wa. 2010), aff'd, 448 Fed. Appx. 752 (9th Cir. 2011), holding that compensation for a noncompetition clause signed

In *Bross Trucking, Inc. v. Commissioner*, T.C. Memo. 2014–107, for many years Bross had owned and operated Bross Trucking, Inc., using leased vehicles. Bross Trucking's principal customers were three businesses owned by other Bross family members. Bross Trucking did not have any formal written service agreements with its customers, relying instead on Bross's close personal relationships with the owners of the customer businesses. Due to violations of state regulatory law, Bross Trucking was in danger of losing its hauling authority. As a result, Bross's sons—who were owners of Bross Trucking's customers—formed a new company, LWK Trucking, 98.2% of which was owned by Bross's sons and the remainder of which was owned by an unrelated third party. Bross was not involved in managing LWK Trucking. LWK Trucking hired several Bross Trucking employees and leased trucks that formerly had been leased to Bross Trucking. The IRS asserted that Bross Trucking had distributed "its operations," including "(1) goodwill; (2) established revenue stream; (3) developed customer base; (4) transparency of the continuing operations between the entities; (5) established workforce including independent contractors; and (6) continuing supplier relationships," all of which the court collectively described as "goodwill" to Bross, triggering gain to Bross Trucking under § 311(b) (rather than § 336(a) because liquidation did not occur until several years later) and that Bross in turn had made a gift of that goodwill to his sons. The Tax Court, after reviewing the facts and results in *Martin Ice Cream Co.* and Solomon v. Commissioner, T.C. Memo. 2008–102, concluded that, except for workforce in place, Bross Trucking had no goodwill at the time of the "alleged transfer." Although it "might have had elements of corporate goodwill at some point . . . through various regulatory infractions Bross Trucking lost any corporate goodwill because of an impending suspension and the negative attention brought by the Bross Trucking name." Judge Paris went on to find that "The remaining attributes assigned to Bross Trucking's goodwill all stem from Mr. Bross's personal relationships. Bross Trucking's established revenue stream, its developed customer base, and the transparency of the continuing operations were all spawned from Mr. Bross's work in the road construction industry." Furthermore, "Mr. Bross did not transfer any goodwill to Bross Trucking through an employment contract or a noncompete agreement." No other Bross Trucking intangible assets were transferred because Bross Trucking's prior customers became LWK's customers and no longer wanted to deal with Bross Trucking due to its regulatory problems, and "LWK Trucking did not benefit from any of Bross Trucking's assets or relationships."[6]

---

by a selling shareholder on sale of his dental practice was ordinary income rather than capital gain on the sale of personal goodwill. The court held that because the taxpayer was the corporation's employee with a covenant not to compete with it, any goodwill generated during that time period was the corporation's goodwill. The court also rested its holding that the goodwill was a corporate asset on its conclusion that the income associated with the practice was earned by the corporation and the covenant not to compete, which extended for three years after the taxpayer no longer owned stock in the corporation rendered any personal goodwill "likely [of] little value."

[6] For an analysis by one of the co-authors that disagrees and argues that goodwill created through payments that are deductible under § 162 by the corporation and create a goodwill intangible belong to the party that funded those payments under established § 482 principles, see Bret Wells and Craig Bergez, *Disposable Personal Goodwill, Frosty the Snowman, and*

4. DISTRIBUTIONS OF ASSETS WITH UNASCERTAINABLE VALUE

Suppose that a corporation liquidates and distributes to the shareholders a contractual right to receive royalties with respect to sales by a licensee of a product to which the corporation holds the patent. At the time of liquidation, there is no reasonable basis for estimating future sales. May the shareholders treat the liquidation as an open transaction, applying distributions and royalty payments against the basis of the stock and reporting gain only when the basis of the stock has been recovered fully? A number of cases allowed open transaction treatment for liquidating distributions of rights with a speculative or unascertainable value that occurred in years prior to the enactment of § 453(j)(2), which limited the use of the open transaction approach generally. See, e.g., Likins-Foster Honolulu Corp. v. Commissioner, 840 F.2d 642 (9th Cir.1988) (open transaction doctrine applied at Commissioner's behest to claims for condemnation of liquidated subsidiary's property); Cloward Instrument Corp. v. Commissioner, T.C. Memo. 1986–345, aff'd by order, 842 F.2d 1294 (9th Cir. 1988) (royalty contract). In other cases, income-producing intangibles were valued and the liquidation was taxed as a closed transaction. See, e.g., Waring v. Commissioner, 412 F.2d 800 (3d Cir.1969) (patent royalty contract).

Whether § 453(j)(2) applies to liquidating distributions is unclear; literally a liquidation may fall within the definition of "installment" sale in § 453(b)(1). If § 453(j)(2) is applicable, open transaction reporting of a liquidating distribution generally will be foreclosed, and the shareholder will recover the basis of the stock ratably over fifteen years, unless a different basis recovery period can be established. See Temp.Reg. § 15a.453–1(c)(4).

5. DISTRIBUTIONS IN PAYMENT OF SHAREHOLDER HELD DEBT

Payments of debts owed by the corporation to its shareholders are not treated as liquidating distributions. See, e.g., Braddock Land Co., Inc. v. Commissioner, 75 T.C. 324 (1980). Thus, a cash method shareholder generally will recognize ordinary income when in the course of liquidation, the corporation pays an account payable due to the shareholder. In *Braddock Land Co., Inc.*, the shareholder's forgiveness of a corporate indebtedness for accrued compensation and interest after the corporation had adopted a plan of liquidation was ignored because the court determined that there was no "business purpose" for the forgiveness. Payment of the indebtedness was not part of a liquidation distribution and was treated as ordinary income to the shareholder. See also Dwyer v. United States, 622 F.2d 460 (9th Cir.1980) (shareholder who purportedly forgave accrued interest on debt owed to him by corporation realized ordinary income equal to "forgiven" interest upon liquidation). Furthermore, if a shareholder contributes to the corporation a corporate debt owed to the shareholder, § 108(e)(6) might require the corporation to recognize income. The result may not be so clear where a cash

---

Martin Ice Cream All Melt Away in the Bright Sunlight of Analysis, 91 Neb. L. Rev. 170 (2012). The Tax Court's failure to consider § 482 principles in the related party shareholder-corporation context or the equitable "duty of consistency doctrine" calls into question the correctness of these holdings.

method shareholder forgives a corporate indebtedness prior to adoption of a plan of liquidation but shortly before the corporation liquidates.

6. "RECEIPT" OF DISTRIBUTION

A liquidation distribution need not actually be received for a shareholder to be taxed on the realized gain. Rev.Rul. 80–177, 1980–2 C.B. 109, held that a cash method shareholder had constructively received a liquidating distribution on the date announced by the corporation as the date on which it would make a liquidating distribution to any shareholder presenting a stock certificate for surrender. If a shareholder makes a gift of stock in a liquidating corporation after a plan of liquidation has been adopted but prior to receiving the liquidating distribution, the gain generally will be taxed to the donor, even though the distribution is received by the donee. See Kinsey v. Commissioner, 477 F.2d 1058 (2d Cir.1973) (charitable contribution of stock following adoption of plan of liquidation); Dayton Hydraulic Co. v. United States, 592 F.2d 937 (6th Cir.1979) (corporation taxed on gain of stock of another corporation distributed to shareholder).

Typically, distributions in complete liquidation of a corporation are pro rata in amount to the shareholders. If, however, a non-pro rata distribution occurs in a § 331 liquidation, a shareholder who receives less than a pro rata share of the value of the liquidating distribution is treated as having received a pro rata share and then, in a separate transaction, having conveyed a portion of the liquidating distribution (equal to the difference between a pro rata share and the share actually received) to the other shareholders as compensation, gifts, in satisfaction of obligations, or the like, as the facts indicate. Rev.Rul. 79–10, 1979–1 C.B. 140.

In some cases a liquidating distribution may be made to a trust for the benefit of the shareholders rather than directly to the shareholders. A liquidation often is structured in this manner to facilitate a post-liquidation sale of assets that are not readily divisible where there are numerous shareholders. Generally, the shareholders will be treated as receiving a liquidating distribution when the assets are transferred to the trust. See Rev.Rul. 72–137, 1972–1 C.B. 101. The trust is then treated as a grantor trust for income tax purposes. I.R.C. §§ 671–679. If, however, a liquidation involving a liquidating trust is unreasonably prolonged, or the business activities of the trust are significant enough to obscure its stated purpose of facilitating an orderly liquidation, the trust may be reclassified as an association taxable as a corporation or as a partnership. Treas.Reg. § 301.7701–4(d). See also Rev.Proc. 82–58, 1982–2 C.B. 847, amplified, Rev.Proc. 91–15, 1991–1 C.B. 484, modified and amplified, Rev.Proc. 94–45, 1994–2 C.B. 685 (requirements for advance ruling on classification of liquidating trust).

PROBLEM SET 1

1. Wilbur owns 600 of 1,000 outstanding shares of Dayton Airplane and Bicycle Corporation (Dayton). Wilbur acquired 400 shares for $50,000 approximately 20 years ago and 200 shares late last year for $1,900,000.

What are the tax consequences to Wilbur on the liquidation of Dayton in the following alternative situations?

(a)   Dayton sells its assets for cash, after which it has aggregate current and accumulated earnings and profits of $7,400,000. After paying all its debts, Dayton distributes $6,000,000 to Wilbur in complete liquidation.

(b)   Dayton sells its assets for cash, after which it has a deficit in earnings and profits. Dayton distributes $300,000 to Wilbur in complete liquidation.

(c)   Dayton was unable to find a single purchaser for all of its assets. It sold some of its assets last year and distributed $3,000,000 to Wilbur last year. This year, after selling its remaining assets and paying its debts, it distributes $1,500,000 to Wilbur. Is the date of adoption of a formal plan of liquidation crucial? Does the nature of the assets sold last year have any bearing on whether the adoption of a formal plan of liquidation is important?

(d)   Assume that Wilbur acquired all 600 shares at the same time for $2,000,000. Dayton sells it assets and distributes to Wilbur in complete liquidation $4,500,000 of cash and a promissory note from Armstrong Corp., which purchased some of the Dayton assets, with a principal amount of $1,500,000, due in five years, with interest payable semi-annually at the prime rate plus 3%.

(1)   What if the promissory note was received by Dayton two years ago in exchange for a bicycle factory building, which had an adjusted basis of $300,000?

(2)   What if the promissory note was received by Dayton eleven months ago, after Dayton had adopted a resolution to liquidate, in exchange for a bicycle factory, which had an adjusted basis of $300,000?

(3)   What if the promissory note was received by Dayton eleven months ago, after Dayton had adopted a resolution to liquidate, in exchange for all its inventory, which had an adjusted basis of $300,000?

(4)   What if the promissory note was received by Dayton eleven months ago, after Dayton had adopted a resolution to liquidate, in exchange for its bicycle inventory, which had an adjusted basis of $300,000, and Dayton's remaining inventory was sold to other purchasers?

2.   Steve owned 500 shares of stock of Florida Gator Farms, Inc. His basis for the stock was $1,000,000. Florida Gator Farms, Inc. liquidated, and in the process, after the corporation paid all of its debts (other than mortgages encumbering distributed real estate), reserving enough cash to pay its tax liability for the year, it distributed to Steve $2,000,000 of cash and Swampacre, a parcel of real estate previously used in its trade or business. Florida Gator's adjusted basis for Swampacre was $3,000,000. Its fair market value was $10,000,000.

(a)   How much gain or loss must be recognized by Florida Gator Farms and by Steve?

(b)   How much gain or loss must be recognized by Florida Gator Farms and by Steve if Swampacre is subject to a mortgage of $4,000,000 that Steve assumes? What is the character of the corporation's gain? What is Steve's basis in the property after it is distributed?

(c)   Would your answer differ if the mortgage was a nonrecourse mortgage and Steve merely took the property subject to the mortgage rather than assuming the mortgage?

(d)   How would your answers in parts (a) and (b) differ if the amount of the mortgage were $11,000,000?

3.   Fern is the sole shareholder of Radiant Organix Corp. Her basis for the stock is $200,000. The sole asset of Radiant Organix is a parcel of farm land.

(a)   The corporation's adjusted basis for the land is $300,000. The fair market value of the land is $300,000. How much gain or loss must be recognized by Radiant Organix and by Fern if the corporation distributes the property to Fern subject to a mortgage of $300,000? What is Fern's basis in the property after it is distributed?

(b)   How would your answer differ if the corporation's adjusted basis for the land was $320,000 and the amount of the mortgage was $315,000?

(c)   How would your answer differ if the corporation's adjusted basis for the land was $200,000 and the amount of the mortgage was $300,000?

4.   The outstanding stock of the Balsamic Corporation is owned by Julia, who owns 60 shares, and Mario, who owns 40 shares. Balsamic's assets available for distribution after paying all of its debts, including taxes for the year of the liquidation, are as follows:

Asset	Adj. Basis	FMV
Factory	$100,000	$300,000
Equipment	$300,000	$200,000
Inventory	$100,000	$200,000
Cash	$300,000	$300,000

On January 1 of the current year, Balsamic adopted a plan of complete liquidation. What are the tax consequences to Balsamic of each of the following alternative distributions?

(a)   (1)   Balsamic distributes its assets pro rata to Julia and Mario, who will thereafter operate the business as 60/40 partners.

(2)   Balsamic transfers all of the assets to the newly formed Pasta Magic LLC in exchange for all 10 membership units of the LLC, immediately after which Balsamic liquidates by distributing 6 Pasta Magic LLC units to Julia and 4 Pasta Magic LLC units to Mario.

(b)   Balsamic distributes the Factory, Inventory, and $100,000 of cash to Julia, and the Equipment and $200,000 of Cash to Mario.

(c)   Balsamic distributes the Factory, Equipment, and $100,000 of cash to Julia, and the Inventory and $200,000 of cash to Mario.

5.   Shrub Game Farm and Real Estate Development Corp. has 100 shares of common stock outstanding. Selina owns 80 shares and Gary owns 20 shares. Shrub owns two parcels of land, Carlsbad and Teton, and has $200,000 in cash. Both properties have been operated as game farm hunting reserves, where well-heeled lawyers and lobbyists could entertain politicians (for a price, of course). The basis and fair market values of the properties are as follows:

Asset	Adj. Basis	FMV
Carlsbad	$400,000	$600,000
Teton	$500,000	$200,000

What are the tax consequences to the corporation of the following alternative liquidating distributions?

(a)   Shrub distributes its assets to Selina and Gary as tenants in common, Selina taking an undivided 4/5ths in each parcel of real estate (and $160,000 in cash) and Gary taking an undivided 1/5th in each parcel of land (and $40,000 in cash). Teton was acquired four years ago, when its fair market value and basis were both $500,000, as a contribution by Selina in a § 351 transaction in exchange for enough stock to increase her stock ownership from 40% to 80%.

(b)   (1)   Shrub sells Carlsbad for $600,000 and Teton for $200,000 and distributes $800,000 in cash to Selina and $200,000 in cash to Gary. Carlsbad had been held for six years, but Teton, and another property, Old Faithful (which was sold last year), were contributed by Selina eighteen months ago in exchange for stock in a § 351 transaction. Teton's fair market fair market value at that time was $380,000, and its adjusted basis was $500,000. Old Faithful's fair market fair market value at that time was $200,000, and its adjusted basis was $80,000. Both Carlsbad and Teton were operated as hunting reserves and the primary customers were well-heeled lawyers and lobbyists who paid the corporation to use the facilities to entertain politicians.

(2)   What if Teton was land held for speculative investment and no business was conducted on the property?

(3)   What if Teton was held for speculative investment and Shrub had no plans to develop it, and it was contributed two and one-half years ago?

6.   Jordan and Garret each own 50 shares of stock of Cavanaugh & Macy, P.S.C., which operates a pathology laboratory. Each of them has a basis of $20,000 in their stock. The corporation has over 20 employees. The corporation's tangible assets consist of equipment with a fair market value of $50,000 and a basis of $15,000. It operates its business in leased premises. Because of the good reputation of the business and its large customer base, a much larger medical laboratory corporation, Frankenstein, Inc. recently

offered to purchase the business for $1,000,000. Jordan and Garret declined the offer. Jordan and Garret are now considering liquidating the corporation and continuing the business as a partnership. What are the tax consequences?

7.   Walter is the sole shareholder of Blue Sky Corporation. Blue Sky's sole asset is a patent on a pharmaceutical product that has been licensed to Madrigal Drugs, Inc. for manufacturing and marketing. The terms of the license call for Madrigal to pay Blue Sky 5% of gross sales from the drug. Blue Sky has not yet started marketing the drug, but plans to do so starting next year. Sales are estimated to be anywhere between $6,000,000 and $100,000,000 a year for at least six to ten years. As a result, over that period royalties might total as little as $300,000 or as much as $5,000,000. What are the tax consequences of liquidating Blue Sky Corporation?

SECTION 4.   LIQUIDATION OF SUBSIDIARY CORPORATIONS—SECTION 332

INTERNAL REVENUE CODE: Sections 332; 334(b); 337(a), (b)(1), (c), (d); 381(a), (c)(1)(A), (c)(2)–(c)(7); 453B(d).

REGULATIONS: Sections 1.332–2, –5, –7.

Pursuant to § 332, where a parent corporation completely liquidates a subsidiary corporation, no gain or loss is recognized to the parent if the parent owns a requisite amount of stock of the subsidiary. This provision also applies if a controlled subsidiary merges into its parent corporation. Treas.Reg. § 1.332–2(d). Under § 334(b), the basis of the assets in the parent corporation's hands remains the same as the basis of the assets to the subsidiary corporation.

Section 332(b)(1), through a cross reference to § 1504(a)(2), limits nonrecognition to situations in which the parent corporation's stock ownership of the subsidiary constitutes both (1) 80% or more of the voting power of the subsidiary's stock, and (2) 80% or more of the total value of all stock of the subsidiary corporation, except that pursuant to § 1504(a)(4), nonparticipating, nonconvertible, nonvoting preferred stock is not counted in determining control. When the nonrecognition rule of § 332 applies, the parent's basis in the stock of the subsidiary is irrelevant, and any potential gain or loss inherent in the stock disappears.[7] This treatment differs from the exchanged basis rule that is more commonly encountered in tax free transactions and is the same as the transferred basis rule generally applied to the transferee corporation in a § 351 exchange or a corporate reorganization. Elimination of the potential gain inherent in the subsidiary's stock prevents two levels of taxation of corporate profits that have not been distributed out of corporate solution. In this regard, § 332 serves a purpose analogous to the dividends received deduction under § 243 (see Chapter 4). The theory

---

[7]   Additional considerations come to bear when the parent and subsidiary have been filing a consolidated return.

behind § 332 is also reflected in the consolidated return provisions of § 1501 through § 1504, discussed in Chapter 15, which permit affiliated corporations (defined with reference to the 80% control test) to file a single income tax return reflecting their combined incomes. Although § 332 governs the liquidation in both cases, the results of liquidating a subsidiary with which the parent did not file a consolidated return, however, are not always the same as the results of a liquidation of a subsidiary in a group filing a consolidated return.

Under § 332, the term "property" includes money. Rev.Rul. 69–379, 1969–2 C.B. 48. Thus, the parent corporation recognizes neither gain nor loss even though only cash is received on the liquidation. International Investment Corp. v. Commissioner, 11 T.C. 678 (1948), aff'd per curiam, 175 F.2d 772 (3d Cir.1949). Taxable gain or loss would have been recognized previously by the subsidiary on the conversion of its assets to cash.

When § 332 applies to the parent of a liquidating corporation, § 337 provides a general exception to the basic rule of § 336 that a liquidating corporation recognizes gain or loss on liquidating distributions.[8] Under § 337(a), no gain or loss is recognized on a distribution to an "80 percent distributee," defined in § 337(c) as a corporation that meets the stock ownership requirements of § 332(b). The final sentence of § 337(c), referring to the consolidated return Regulations, requires that a single corporation meet the 80% requirement; it is not sufficient for two or more affiliated corporations to have aggregate holdings meeting the 80% test. In concert, § 332 and § 337 provide for complete nonrecognition of gain or loss at the corporate level on the liquidation of a wholly owned subsidiary.

As a corollary to the nonrecognition treatment accorded to both the liquidating subsidiary and the distributee parent corporation, § 381(a), discussed in Chapter 13, provides that the tax attributes of the subsidiary carry over to the parent. The most notable of these attributes are net operating loss carryovers, capital loss carryovers, and the earnings and profits accumulations or deficits. If the parent corporation receives less than 100% of the subsidiary's assets, then the parent succeeds only to the portion of the subsidiary's earnings and profits not allocable to distributions to minority shareholders. Treas.Reg. § 1.381(c)(2)–1(c)(2). If either the parent or the subsidiary has a deficit in its earnings and profits accounts, after a § 332 liquidation the parent must maintain separate earnings and profits accounts; the deficit of one corporation cannot be used to offset any surplus existing at the liquidation date in the earnings and profits account of the other. I.R.C. § 381(c)(2); Luckman v. Commissioner, 56 T.C. 1216 (1971). Earnings

---

[8]   To prevent the complete avoidance of tax on appreciation in the subsidiary's assets, subject to certain exceptions, § 337 does not apply to a liquidation of a subsidiary of a tax-exempt organization. I.R.C. § 337(b)(2). This provision is necessary because notwithstanding a carryover basis under § 334(b), a subsequent sale of the former subsidiary's assets generally would not be taxable.

and profits accumulated by the parent after the liquidation are used to exhaust the deficit account before the accumulated earnings and profits account of the parent is increased. Treas.Reg. § 1.312–11(b)(2), (c).

Granite Trust Co. v. United States
United States Court of Appeals, First Circuit, 1956.
238 F.2d 670.

[Eds.: The parent corporation made sales and charitable gifts of stock to cause the parent's ownership of the subsidiary to drop below 80%. This was done on December 13, 1943, on advice of counsel so that § 332's predecessor would not apply. On December 30, 1943, the directors formally distributed the liquidating proceeds. The Fifth Circuit's opinion follows.]

The taxpayer concedes that it would not have made the sales described above had it not been for § 112(b)(6) of the Internal Revenue Code of 1939. While the taxpayer maintains that the gift to the United War Fund was but part of the total gift to that organization for the year 1943, it seems clear, because this was the only case where shares of stock rather than cash were distributed to the charity, that at least the specific object given at this time was dictated by § 112(b)(6).

The precise issue before us is whether or not to give effect for tax purposes to the aforesaid sales and gift by the taxpayer. If the answer is in the affirmative, there is no doubt that the liquidation distribution of the property of the Building Corporation was not in "complete liquidation" within the very special meaning of that phrase in § 112(b)(6) of the 1939 Code, and, accordingly, the taxpayer may recognize the loss on its investment.

Although there is no dispute that the transactions in form at least purport to be sales and a gift, the Commissioner nevertheless maintains that we should not accord them that significance. The Commissioner's argument is in two parts: The first proposition derives from the basic finding of the district court that the taxpayer effected the liquidation "in such manner as to achieve a tax reduction' and that this was 'without legal or moral justification." The Commissioner attempts to bolster this argument by his traditional corporation reorganization analysis to the effect that, so long as the "end-result" of the transactions involved complies with the "criteria of the statute," intermediary steps (in this case the sales and gift) should be ignored as if they were nonexistent. His reasoning is that, if the final outcome is complete liquidation of a subsidiary corporation which at the outset was wholly owned by the taxpayer, the entire procedure comes within the intendment of the statute and "[c]ircuitous steps to avoid Section § 112(b)(6)" occurring prior to the ultimate liquidation should be disregarded.

The Commissioner's second proposition is that there were *in fact* no valid sales or gift of stock made by the taxpayer. This argument rests on the taxpayer's admission that the transfers were motivated solely by tax considerations and were made in a friendly atmosphere to friendly people who knew of the decision to liquidate the corporation before the end of the year. As the Commissioner points out, the liquidation took place shortly after the transfers, and the transferees then received back the money they had paid in, plus a small profit. Therefore, the Commissioner argues, relying heavily on Gregory v. Helvering, 1935, 293 U.S. 465, 55 S.Ct. 266, 79 L.Ed. 596, that "the stock transfers in question had no independent purpose or meaning—either for the transferor or the transferees—but constituted merely a transitory and circuitous routing of legal title for the purpose of avoiding taxes, within the meaning of Gregory v. Helvering, supra. It was not expected or intended by any of the parties that the transferees should become true stockholders. Legal title passed; but beneficial ownership surely never passed. The transferees who paid money for their stock knew that the subsidiary would be liquidated in a few days and that they would get their money back—as in fact they did, with additional amounts to pay them for their cooperation in serving as conduits of title." The gift of stock to the United War Fund is dismissed as "nothing more than a gift of the cash."

The Commissioner also makes reference to carefully selected language from Griffiths v. Helvering, 1939, 308 U.S. 355, 357, 358, 60 S.Ct. 277, 84 L.Ed. 319, and Commissioner of Internal Revenue v. Court Holding Co., 1945, 324 U.S. 331, 334, 65 S.Ct. 707, 89 L.Ed. 981, but these cases are factually remote from the one at bar.

Our conclusion is that the Commissioner's arguments must be rejected, and that the taxpayer should be permitted to "recognize" the loss on its investment, which it undoubtedly realized upon the liquidation of the Building Corporation.

Initially we may note, without ruling upon it, one legal argument made by the Commissioner having to do with the efficacy of the purported sale of 1,025 shares of stock to Howard D. Johnson Company on December 6, 1943. The Commissioner contends that, to satisfy the first condition of nonrecognition prescribed in § 112(b)(6), it is not necessary to have a formal plan of liquidation, evidenced by a corporate resolution, but it is sufficient if there is a "definitive determination" to achieve dissolution. It is claimed by the Commissioner that such a definitive determination existed here by November 10, 1943, and, therefore, that the sale of stock to Howard D. Johnson Company which took place on December 6, 1943 (before the formal adoption of the plan of liquidation) occurred *after* the "adoption of the plan of liquidation" within the meaning of § 112(b)(6). In this view the taxpayer owned 100 per cent of the subsidiary's stock on the date the plan of liquidation was adopted, from which it would follow, on the basis of the first condition of § 112(b)(6), that the loss should not be "recognized."

We need not consider the foregoing legal argument on its merits, because the subsequent actions by the taxpayer—the sales to Johnson individually and to Richmond on December 13, 1943, and the gift of stock on the same day to the United War Fund—of themselves, if valid, successfully accomplished the taxpayer's purpose of avoiding the nonrecognition provisions of § 112(b)(6) under the second condition contained in that subsection. This second condition prescribes, in a sort of backhanded way, that gain or loss shall be recognized if, at any time on or after the date of the adoption of the plan of liquidation and prior to the date of the receipt of the property distributed in final liquidation, the receiving corporation is the owner of a greater percentage of any class of stock of the corporation being liquidated than the percentage of such stock owned by it at the time of the receipt of the property—which means that this condition precedent to the nonrecognition of a realized gain or loss is not satisfied if, in the described period, the receiving corporation has made an effective disposition of any of the shares of stock held in the subsidiary corporation, without making any countervailing acquisitions of such stock.

Turning then to the basic contentions of the Commissioner, not much need be said with reference to the proposition that the tax motive for the sales and gift rendered the transactions "immoral" and thus vitiated them. Again and again the courts have pointed out that a "purpose to minimize or avoid taxation is not an illicit motive." Sawtell v. Commissioner, 1 Cir., 1936, 82 F.2d 221, 222. The Gregory case itself makes this clear, Gregory v. Helvering, supra, 293 U.S. at page 469 * * *, 55 S.Ct. at page 267. To the same effect see Jones v. Grinnell, 10 Cir., 1950, 179 F.2d 873, 874.

As for the Commissioner's "end-result" argument, the very terms of § 112(b)(6) make it evident that it is not an "end-result" provision, but rather one which prescribes specific conditions for the nonrecognition of realized gains or losses, conditions which, if not strictly met, make the section inapplicable. In fact, the Commissioner's own regulations (Reg. 111, § 29.112(b)(6)) emphasize the rigid requirements of the section and make no allowance for the type of "step transaction" theory advanced in this case.

The legislative history of § 112(b)(6) likewise tends to support the position of the taxpayer. That history indicates that Congress was primarily concerned with providing a means of facilitating the simplification of corporate structures pursuant to the general policy enunciated in the Public Utility Holding Company Act of 1935, 49 Stat. 803, 15 U.S.C.A. § 79 et seq. See Seidman's Legislative History of Federal Income Tax Laws 240–43 (1938); Helvering v. Credit Alliance Corp., 1942, 316 U.S. 107, 112, 62 S.Ct. 989, 86 L.Ed. 1307. This fact, while perhaps not conclusive as to the proper interpretation of § 112(b)(6), nevertheless does lend a favorable background to the taxpayer's contention that the subsection, as a relief measure, was "not designed as a strait jacket into which corporations should be forced at the penalty of forfeiture of losses on liquidation of subsidiaries."

The more specific and more important bit of legislative history is found in the Report of the Senate Finance Committee at the time that § 112(b)(6) was reenacted, with amendments, as § 332 of the Internal Revenue Code of 1954. At this time, when Congress was engaged in a comprehensive reexamination of the Internal Revenue Code, the well-known case of Commissioner of Internal Revenue v. Day & Zimmermann, Inc., 3 Cir., 1945, 151 F.2d 517, had been decided in favor of the taxpayer, and it reasonably could be supposed that Congress, had it disapproved of the decision in that case, would have overturned its conclusion by making over § 112(b)(6) into an "end-result" provision. In the Day & Zimmermann case, the taxpayer, admittedly in order to avoid the nonrecognition provisions of § 112(b)(6), had sold at public auction a sufficient number of shares of a wholly owned subsidiary corporation to reduce its holdings below 80 per cent. These shares were bought, after general bidding, by the treasurer of the taxpayer, who, after receiving cash dividends in the subsequent liquidation of the companies, reported his gain and paid income tax thereon. The Third Circuit held that § 112(b)(6) did not apply to the liquidation, emphasizing that the treasurer had paid a fair price for the shares, had used his own money, had not been directed by anyone to bid, and that there had been no showing of any understanding existing between him and the corporation by which the latter was to retain any sort of interest in the securities or in the proceeds therefrom. See Avco Mfg. Co. v. Commissioner, 1956, 25 T.C. 975, to the same effect. Commissioner of Internal Revenue v. Day & Zimmermann, Inc., is not to be distinguished, as the Commissioner suggests, on the ground that the sale of stock was at public auction, without specific negotiation between the treasurer and the taxpayer. The significant thing in the case is its ultimate rationale that the purported sales of stock to the treasurer were in fact sales, notwithstanding the tax motive which prompted the corporation to enter into the transaction; from which it would seem to be irrelevant how the transfer was arranged, or whether or not it occurred at a public auction or exchange, so long as the beneficial as well as legal title was intended to pass and did pass.

Now, what did the Congress do in 1954 in view of Commissioner of Internal Revenue v. Day & Zimmermann, Inc., holding that a parent corporation contemplating the liquidation of a wholly owned subsidiary might elect, by making a transfer of an appropriate portion of the stock in the subsidiary, to avoid the conditions precedent to the nonrecognition of gain or loss prescribed in § 112(b)(6)? In reenacting that section in 1954, the Congress struck out the second condition, but left in the first condition which the taxpayer had successfully utilized in the Day & Zimmermann case in order to avoid a nonrecognition of a realized loss. This is what the Report of the Senate Finance Committee said at the time:

"Section 332. Complete Liquidations of Subsidiaries.

"Except for subsection (c) section 332 corresponds to and in general restates section 112(b)(6) of the 1939 Code and provides for the liquidation of a subsidiary corporation by its parent without the recognition of gain or loss to the parent corporation. Your committee has, however, deleted a provision which now appears in section 112(b)(6)(A) which removes a liquidation from the application of that section if the parent corporation at some time on or after the time of the adoption of the plan of liquidation and until the receipt of the property owns more stock than that owned at the time of the receipt of the property. Your committee has removed this provision with the view to limiting the elective features of the section." (Sen. Finance Committee Report, H.R. 8300, 83d Cong., 2d Sess. 255 (1954).)

The above reference to the "elective features" of the subsection seems inescapably to reflect a legislative understanding (admittedly not contemporaneous with enactment, however) that taxpayers can, by taking appropriate steps, render the subsection applicable or inapplicable as they choose, rather than be at the mercy of the Commissioner on an "end-result" theory. Nowhere in the subsection is there any express reference to an "election" or an "option," and the use of the word "elective" in the committee report therefore strongly indicates, as the taxpayer argues, that the committee believed that corporations could avoid the nonrecognition provisions by transfers designed to eliminate the specific conditions contained in the subsection.

We come then to the Commissioner's second major contention, resting on Gregory v. Helvering, supra, that the sales of stock by the corporation should be ignored on the ground that they were not bona fide, and that the taxpayer therefore retained "beneficial ownership". The Commissioner characterizes the transfers as artificial, unessential, transitory phases of a completed tax avoidance scheme which should be disregarded.

In answer to this contention, it is first necessary to determine precisely what the Gregory case held. Judge Learned Hand, in Chisholm v. Commissioner, 2 Cir., 1935, 79 F.2d 14, 15, 101 A.L.R. 200, certiorari denied 1935, 296 U.S. 641, 56 S.Ct. 174, 80 L.Ed. 456, analyzed the case as follows:

"The question always is whether the transaction under scrutiny is in fact what it appears to be in form; a marriage may be a joke; a contract may be intended only to deceive others; an agreement may have a collateral defeasance. In such cases the transaction as whole is different from its appearance. * * * In Gregory v. Helvering, supra, 293 U.S. 465, 55 S.Ct. 266 * * * the incorporators adopted the usual form for creating business corporations; but their intent, or purpose, was merely to draught the papers, in fact not to create corporations as the

court understood that word. That was the purpose which defeated their exemption, not the accompanying purpose to escape taxation; that purpose was legally neutral. Had they really meant to conduct a business by means of the two reorganized companies, they would have escaped whatever other aim they might have had, whether to avoid taxes, or to regenerate the world." [Italics added by court.]

In the present case the question is whether or not there actually were sales. Why the parties may wish to enter into a sale is one thing, but that is irrelevant under the Gregory case so long as the consummated agreement was no different from what it purported to be.

Even the Commissioner concedes that "[l]egal title" passed to the several transferees on December 13, 1943, but he asserts that "beneficial ownership" never passed. We find no basis on which to vitiate the purported sales, for the record is absolutely devoid of any evidence indicating an understanding by the parties to the transfers that any interest in the stock transferred was to be retained by the taxpayer. If Johnson or Richmond had gone bankrupt, or the assets of both had been attached by creditors, on the day after the sales to them, we do not see how the conclusion could be escaped that their Building Corporation stock would have been included in their respective assets; and if Johnson or Richmond had died, surely the holdings of stock of each would have passed to his executors of administrators, or legatees.

In addition to what we have said, there are persuasive reasons of a general nature which lend weight to the taxpayer's position. To strike down these sales on the alleged defect that they took place between friends and for tax motives would only tend to promote duplicity and result in extensive litigation as taxpayers led courts into hairsplitting investigations to decide when a sale was not a sale. It is no answer to argue that, under Gregory v. Helvering, there is an inescapable judicial duty to examine into the actuality of purported corporate reorganizations, for that was a special sort of transaction, whose bona fides could readily be ascertained by inquiring whether the ephemeral new corporation was in fact transacting business, or whether there was in fact a continuance of the proprietary interests under an altered corporate form. See Lewis v. Commissioner, 1 Cir., 1949, 176 F.2d 646.

What we have said so far is related chiefly to the validity of the sales. When we turn to the gift on December 13, 1943, to the United War Fund, the taxpayer is on even firmer ground. The Commissioner says that the gift was nothing more than a gift of cash, that the charity "was, at most, a passive transferee, without independent purpose, which held legal title to two shares for four days." This assertion rests, when examined closely, on the simple fact that the purpose for the gift was a tax avoidance one. But this does not disqualify it as an effective gift, transferring title. A gift certainly may have a tax motive. See Commissioner of Internal Revenue v. Newman, 2 Cir., 1947, 159 F.2d 848; Sawtell v. Commissioner, supra,

4. DISTRIBUTION MADE ON "ALL ITS STOCK"

4.1. *Generally*

For § 332 to apply there must be some distribution applicable to the common stock, so as to supply the "cancellation or redemption of *all* [the] stock" required by § 332(b)(2). Thus, if the assets of the subsidiary are insufficient to pay its debts or do not exceed the amount necessary to both pay its debts and satisfy the liquidation preference of its preferred shares, including those held by the parent, the common stock simply becomes worthless rather than being cancelled or redeemed, and § 332 is therefore inapplicable. In such a case, the tax consequences of the liquidation depend on whether the subsidiary is insolvent, and thus makes no distributions with respect to any class of its stock, or, while solvent, has net assets sufficient only to make a distribution on its preferred stock.

4.2. *Distribution Only on Preferred Stock*

In H.K. Porter Co. v. Commissioner, 87 T.C. 689 (1986), the parent corporation owned all the outstanding common and preferred stock of its Australian subsidiary. The subsidiary sold all its assets and distributed the cash to the taxpayer in liquidation. The amount received by the parent was less than the liquidation preference in the preferred stock; no distribution therefore was made on the common stock. The taxpayer claimed a § 165 loss deduction. The court rejected the Commissioner's argument that § 332 applied to the transaction and allowed the taxpayer's loss. The court concluded that the phrase "all its stock" did not include "nonvoting stock which is limited and preferred as to dividends." The court further noted:

> The statute is specific in that there must be a "distribution" in liquidation and the distribution must be "in complete cancellation or redemption of *all its [parent's] stock*." What does the phrase "all its stock" mean? Clearly it means at least 80 per cent of the common or voting stock. Does it also mean to include nonvoting stock which is limited and preferred as to dividends? We think not. The statute specifically excepts such preferred stock from the classes of stock which the parent should own—it could be owned by the parent or outsiders. * * * This means the payment in liquidation, in satisfaction of the preferred stock claim, whether to the parent or outsiders, will be immaterial. * * * Here there was no payment or distribution to the parent after the payment of the preferred stock claim in liquidation. The preferred stock claim captured all of the assets. There was nothing left to distribute to the parent as a common stockholder in the subsidiary. We hold the parent received no distribution in liquidation on its common stock within the intendment of the statute. Petitioner merely received in liquidation, payment of a part of its preferred stock claim—a fact which the statute, in effect, states will be immaterial.

The same result was reached in Spaulding Bakeries Inc. v. Commissioner, 27 T.C. 684 (1957), aff'd 252 F.2d 693 (2d Cir. 1958).

Even though a liquidation of a subsidiary might not qualify under § 332, the transaction nevertheless might qualify as a tax-free reorganization under § 368, discussed in Chapter 10. See Treas.Reg. § 1.368–2(d)(4)(i). The tax-free reorganization that occurs in this situation would be what is commonly termed "an upstream § 368(a)(1)(C) reorganization," which is described in Treas.Reg. § 1.368–2(d)(4)(i). See Notice of Proposed Rulemaking and Notice of Public Hearing, The Solely for Voting Stock Requirement in Certain Corporate Reorganizations, REG–115086–98, 64 Fed. Reg. 31770 (June 14, 1999); see also Treas.Reg. § 1.368–1(e)(1), (e)(8), Ex. 7.

Treas.Reg. § 1.368–2(d)(4)(ii), Ex. 1 illustrates a tax-free upstream § 368(a)(1)(C) reorganization in a slightly different, but analogous context.

> Corporation P (P) holds 60 percent of the Corporation T (T) stock that P purchased several years ago in an unrelated transaction. T has 100 shares of stock outstanding. The other 40 percent of the T stock is owned by Corporation X (X), an unrelated corporation. T has properties with a fair market value of $110 and liabilities of $10. T transfers all of its properties to P. In exchange, P assumes the $10 of liabilities, and transfers to T $30 of P voting stock and $10 of cash. T distributes the P voting stock and $10 of cash to X and liquidates.

The example concludes that the transactions constitute a tax-free reorganization under § 368(a)(1)(C). Because the transaction is a tax-free reorganization, under § 361, Target-Subsidiary does not recognize gain or loss, and, under § 354, Parent does not recognize gain or loss. Furthermore, Parent takes a transferred basis in the Target-Subsidiary's assets pursuant to § 362(b) and succeeds to the Target-Subsidiary's tax attributes under § 381. In the context of a liquidation that fails to qualify under § 332 because there was no distribution with respect to the Parent's common stock, but which is a tax-free upstream (C) reorganization, the Parent will not recognize any gain or loss with respect to the preferred stock, but will recognize a loss with respect to the common stock.

4.3. *Insolvent Subsidiary*

Section 332 does not apply to the liquidation of an insolvent subsidiary. For purposes of § 332, insolvency exists when the fair market value of the subsidiary's assets is less than the sum of its debts. In such a case the parent corporation can recognize a worthless stock deduction under § 165(g) with respect to all of its stock in the subsidiary. In most cases, § 165(g)(3) treats the loss as an ordinary loss rather than as a capital loss if the conditions of that provisions have been met. Northern Coal & Dock Co. v. Commissioner, 12 T.C. 42 (1949) (acq.). Furthermore, since nonrecognition of gain or loss to the subsidiary under § 337 is conditioned on the liquidation qualifying under § 332, gain or loss will be recognized by the subsidiary with respect to transfers of property to the parent, and the parent takes a cost basis in those assets. In such cases, there is no carryover of the tax attributes of the subsidiary under § 381. Rev.Rul. 68–359, 1968–2 C.B. 161; Rev.Rul. 59–296, 1959–2 C.B. 87.

Difficult valuation problems may exist where the subsidiary is potentially insolvent, especially where intangible assets, such as patents, copyrights, and goodwill, are involved. See, e.g., Swiss Colony, Inc. v. Commissioner, 52 T.C. 25 (1969) (judicial determination of fair market value of patents), aff'd on other issues, 428 F.2d 49 (7th Cir.1970); Continental Grain Co. v. Commissioner, T.C. Memo. 1989–155 (in determining that subsidiary was insolvent, court took into account imputed interest on book account debt to parent). In addition, problems arise in determining whether advances to the subsidiary by the parent in fact constituted equity. Inductotherm Industries, Inc. v. Commissioner, T.C. Memo. 1984–281, aff'd by order, 770 F.2d 1071 (3d Cir. 1985), reclassified as equity a subsidiary's purported indebtedness to the parent, thereby eliminating an insolvency situation and bringing the liquidation within the nonrecognition rule of § 332.

If a subsidiary is insolvent due to indebtedness owed to the parent, cancellation of the debt by the parent to make the subsidiary solvent followed by liquidation of the subsidiary might enable the liquidation to qualify under § 332, and hence, for example, make available to the parent a net operating loss carryover of the subsidiary; but such a cancellation of indebtedness will be ignored if it was an integral part of the liquidation. Rev.Rul. 68–602, 1968–2 C.B. 135. Often, however, this will not be a desirable planning technique because under § 108(e)(6), the subsidiary will recognize income as a result of the cancellation of indebtedness, even if the cancellation is classified as a contribution to capital.

5. RELEVANCE OF ULTIMATE DISPOSITION OF SUBSIDIARY'S ASSETS

The liquidation of a subsidiary clearly qualifies under § 332 where the parent uses the assets to continue to conduct the same business as a division following the liquidation, Rev.Rul. 70–105, 1970–1 C.B. 70, or if the parent uses the assets of the subsidiary in the parent's business even though the business of the subsidiary is discontinued, Rev.Rul. 70–357, 1970–2 C.B. 79. In addition, it is generally understood that § 332 applies if a subsidiary liquidates and the parent thereafter also liquidates. Kamis Engineering Co. v. Commissioner, 60 T.C. 763 (1973) (nonacq.), and Rev.Rul. 69–172, 1969–1 C.B. 99, obsoleted by Rev.Rul. 95–71, 1995–2 C.B. 323, although not expressly dealing with the issue, reach holdings that assume that § 332 applies in situations where the parent liquidates following the liquidation of the subsidiary. See also Private Letter Rulings 8331017, 8336056, and 8413045; Action on Decision, 1974 AOD LEXIS 268 (Jan. 7 1974) (nonacquiescence in *Kamis*, stating "it is the position of the Service that Code § 332 . . . will apply in simultaneous parent-subsidiary liquidations . . .."). If, however, the order of the liquidations is reversed, i.e., the parent liquidates and distributes the subsidiary stock to its shareholders, and the subsidiary then liquidates by distributing its assets to the former parent's shareholders, § 331 and § 336 control both liquidations. See *Kamis Engineering Co.*, supra.

6. TRANSFERS INVOLVING INTERCORPORATE INDEBTEDNESS

6.1. *Subsidiary Indebted to Parent*

If the subsidiary is indebted to the parent corporation and, pursuant to a plan of liquidation to which § 332 applies, the subsidiary distributes property in satisfaction of the debt, § 332 does not apply to provide nonrecognition if the parent's basis for the debt differs from the amount received in payment. See Treas.Reg. § 1.332–7. As long as the subsidiary is solvent, however, the parent will not realize any gain or loss upon payment of the subsidiary's obligations unless the parent purchased them from a third party to whom they were issued.[9] Under § 337(b)(1), the distributing subsidiary corporation recognizes no gain or loss, and the parenthetical clause in § 334(b)(1) provides the parent corporation with a transferred basis in the assets used to satisfy the debt. Thus, insofar as concerns liquidation of a solvent subsidiary, in most cases no distinction is made between distributions to satisfy an indebtedness to the parent and distributions in exchange for surrender of the parent's stock in the subsidiary. This treatment prevents any attempt selectively to recognize losses by satisfying indebtedness with loss property while distributing gain property in a nonrecognition distribution.

6.2. *Parent Indebted to Subsidiary*

In Rev.Rul. 74–54, 1974–1 C.B. 76, a note of the parent corporation held by the subsidiary was cancelled in a § 332 liquidation; the note was held to constitute property received by the parent corporation in the liquidation, and it therefore did not realize cancellation of indebtedness income under either § 61(a)(12) or Treas.Reg. § 1.301–1(m). Subsequent amendments to § 108 and the original issue discount rules cast doubt on the continuing vitality of this ruling, and the preamble to the former Proposed Regulations under § 108(e)(4) dealing with the acquisition of debt by persons related to the issuer indicated that the Treasury intended to promulgate Regulations under which the parent would recognize cancellation of indebtedness income to the extent that redemption price of the parent's note exceeded its basis in the subsidiary's hands at the time of the liquidation. See Notice of Proposed Rulemaking, Income From Discharge of Indebtedness—Acquisition of Indebtedness by Person Related to the Debtor, CO–90–90, 1991–1 C.B. 774, 777. No such Regulations have yet been promulgated.

7.   SUBSIDIARY LIMITED LIABILITY COMPANIES

Suppose a corporation owns a limited liability company (LLC) that previously had elected to be taxed as a corporation under Treas.Reg. § 301.7701–3(c), discussed in Chapter 1, and the LLC revokes the election. As a result the LLC becomes a disregarded entity under Treas.Reg. § 301.7701–3(b)(1)(ii), and all of its assets and liabilities are treated as assets and liabilities of its owner. Consequently, the LLC is treated as a subsidiary corporation that has distributed its assets to its parent corporation in complete liquidation. See Treas.Reg. § 301.7701–3(g)(1)(iii). To facilitate compliance with the "plan of liquidation" requirement in § 332, since the LLC does not in fact liquidate, Treas.Reg. § 301.7701–3(g)(2)(ii) provides that a

---

[9]   Note that if the parent purchased the subsidiary's indebtedness at a discount from a third party holder to whom it was originally issued, under § 108(e)(4) the subsidiary would have been required to recognize cancellation of indebtedness income equal to the discount at that time. The debt is treated as a new debt issued for the parent's purchase price, and the excess of the amount due at maturity over the purchase price is treated as original issue discount. See Treas.Reg. § 1.108–2(a), (g)(4), Ex. 1.

plan of liquidation is deemed to have been adopted immediately before the deemed liquidation resulting from the election to change entity classification, unless a formal plan of liquidation that contemplates the filing of the elective change was adopted at an earlier date.

Rev.Rul. 2003–125, 2003–2 C.B. 1243, dealt with an election to change the classification of a wholly-owned subsidiary LLC that previously had elected to be taxed as a corporation to a disregarded entity. The fair market value of the LLC's assets (including goodwill and going concern value) did not exceed the LLC's liabilities. Thus, in the deemed liquidation of the LLC, the controlling corporation did not receive any distribution on its stock. Accordingly, the controlling corporation was allowed an ordinary loss deduction for worthless stock under § 165(g)(3).

8. LIQUIDATION OF A FOREIGN SUBSIDIARY

Section 332 generally applies to the liquidation of a controlled subsidiary whether the subsidiary is a U.S. corporation or a foreign corporation. (An exception to non-recognition with respect to certain foreign holding companies is provided in § 332(d)). If the controlled subsidiary is a foreign corporation, however, § 334(b)(1)(B) limits the parent's basis in properties received in the liquidation to the properties' fair market values if the subsidiary's aggregate basis in the transferred properties exceed their aggregate fair market value. The rule thus prevents the importation of assets with built-in losses into the U.S. tax system. Furthermore, under § 367(b) and Treas.Reg. § 1.367(b)–3, generally speaking, the parent corporation will be required to recognize gain to the extent of the earnings and profits of the foreign subsidiary accrued during the period the parent owned the subsidiary.

PROBLEM SET 2

1. Global Automotive Corp. owns 80 shares of the 100 outstanding shares of common stock of Specific Motors Corp. The remaining 20 shares of the Specific Motors stock are owned by Tucker Vehicles, Inc. Global's basis for its shares is $8,000,000; Tucker's basis is $2,000,000. Specific Motor's assets consist of an automobile factory, with a fair market value of $20,000,000 and a basis of $9,000,000 and 100 shares of stock in Adobe Motors Corp., with a fair market value of $5,000,000 and a basis of $4,000,000. Both assets have been held for more than 5 years.

(a) If Specific Motors liquidates and distributes the factory to Global and the Adobe Motors stock to Tucker, what are the tax consequences to Specific Motors, Global, and Tucker?

(b) How would your answer to (a) differ if Global's basis for the Specific Motors stock was $30,000,000?

(c) How would your answer to (a) differ if Specific Motor's basis for the factory was $30,000,000 and its basis for the Adobe stock was $6,000,000?

(d) (1) How would your answer to (a) differ if Global's 80 shares of common stock was 100% of the common stock and Tucker's 20 shares was preferred stock?

(2)   What if Tucker's 20 shares of Global was participating preferred stock?

2.   Diamond Airlines Corp. owns all 100 outstanding shares of common stock of Southland Commuter AirLink, Inc. Its basis in the 100 shares of common stock is $6,000,000 and the fair market value of the common stock is $5,000,000. Southland's assets consist of four airplanes, each with an adjusted basis of $600,000 and a fair market value of $700,000, and terminal facilities at several airports with an aggregate basis of $800,000 and a fair market value of $1,000,000, and licenses and landing rights with a basis of $2,000,000 and a fair market value of $1,200,000.

(a)   Could Diamond and Southland recognize their loss if Diamond sold 21 shares of its common stock in Southland to National Airlines prior to voting on a plan of liquidation?

(b)   Could Diamond and Southland recognize their loss if Diamond sold 21 shares of its common stock in Southland to National Airlines after voting on a plan of liquidation?

(c)   Could Diamond recognize its loss if Southland issued 1,000 shares of $1,000 par value voting preferred stock to an investment banking firm for cash before voting on a plan of liquidation?

(d)   Could Diamond recognize its loss if Southland adopted a liquidation resolution and then distributed one airplane this year, and another airplane on December 31st of each of the next three years, and the terminal facilities and landing rights on January 1st following the distribution of the last airplane?

3.   Sunny Entertainment Corporation owns 75% of the stock of Rock-Around-the-Clock Digital Media Company. Motown Recording Company owns the other 25% of the Rock-Around-the-Clock stock. The assets of Rock-Around-the-Clock are worth $20,000,000. Sunny's basis in the stock of Rock-Around-the-Clock is $6,000,000 and the fair market value of the stock is $15,000,000. Sunny plans to liquidate Rock-Around-the-Clock and has asked your opinion regarding whether either or both of the following plans would permit Sunny to avoid recognizing its gain with respect to its stock in Rock-Around-the-Clock.

(a)   Prior to holding a vote to liquidate Rock-Around-the-Clock, Sunny would purchase all of the stock owned by Motown for $5,000,000 (thereby receiving $20,000,000 in the liquidating distribution as a result of owning all the stock).

(b)   Prior to holding a vote to liquidate Rock-Around-the-Clock, Sunny would cause Rock-Around-the-Clock to redeem all of the stock owned by Motown for $5,000,000 (thereby resulting in Sunny receiving $15,000,000 in the liquidation).

4.   Salad Chopper, Inc. owns all of the stock of Bassamatic Corporation. Bassamatic is capitalized with (1) 200 shares of common stock, (2) 2,000 shares of $1,000 par value preferred stock, with an aggregate liquidation preference of $2,000,000, and (3) a $3,000,000 promissory note held by Salad Chopper. Salad Chopper's basis in the common stock of Bassamatic is

$4,000,000, its basis in the preferred stock is $2,000,000, and its basis in the debt is $3,000,000. What are the tax consequences to Salad Chopper of the liquidation of Bassamatic if Bassamatic's assets have the following alternative fair market values and bases?

(a) Fair market value of $5,100,000 and a basis of $8,000,000.

(b) Fair market value of $4,900,000 and a basis of $8,000,000.

(c) Fair market value of $4,900,000 and a basis of $1,000,000.

(d) Fair market value of $3,000,000 and a basis of $1,000,000.

5.   VideoGiant Corporation owns all of the common stock of Diode Corporation. VideoGiant's basis in the stock is $10,000,000. Diode owes VideoGiant $1,000,000 on a five year, 10% promissory note issued in connection with an infusion of working capital to Diode two years ago. Diode's assets consist of a factory with a fair market value of $10,000,000 and a basis of $6,000,000 and a patent with a fair market value of $1,000,000 and a basis of $4,000,000. What are the tax consequences if Diode liquidates by transferring the patent to VideoGiant in payment of the promissory note and transferring the factory in cancellation of the stock?

PART II

CORPORATE ACQUISITION TECHNIQUES

CHAPTER 8

TAXABLE ACQUISITIONS: THE PURCHASE AND SALE OF A CORPORATE BUSINESS

The material considered up to this point has focused on the provisions of Subchapter C from the perspective of their function in the statutory structure provided for the taxation of corporations and shareholders. The material in this Part changes from this structural focus to concentrate on the application of the corporate rules to a specific transaction, the purchase and sale of a corporate business. This Chapter and Chapter 9 deal with the tax aspects of a taxable purchase and sale of the corporate business.[1] The various forms of tax-free acquisitions are considered in Chapter 10.

A taxable purchase and sale of a business involves the application of the general principles of taxation of sales and exchanges of property, supplemented by a limited number of special rules. The exact application of the principles depends on the form of the transaction. There are basically three approaches to the sale of a corporate business: A corporation may sell its assets and distribute the proceeds to its shareholders in liquidation; the corporation may distribute its assets to its shareholders in liquidation, following which the shareholders sell the assets; or the shareholders may simply sell the stock of the corporation, which continues in existence.

Suppose that A owns all of the stock of X Corporation, which operates a business consisting of two assets, Asset #1, having a fair market value of $500 and a basis of $50, and Asset #2, having a fair market value of $200 and a basis of $250. Also assume that the basis of A's stock is $200. If Y Corporation desires to acquire the business of X Corporation, it might purchase the assets of X Corporation for $700. X Corporation would realize a net gain of $450 on the sale of Asset #1 and a loss of $50 on Asset #2. Assuming that the gain and loss could be offset (which would be true unless Asset #2 was a capital asset and Asset #1 was not), X Corporation's net gain on the sale of its assets would be $400. If this gain were taxed at the maximum tax rate of 21%, X Corporation would pay taxes of $84 and make a $616 liquidating distribution to A, who would recognize a capital gain of $416. A would pay a tax, at the preferential capital gains rate of 20% (assuming that A would be required to pay at this highest net capital gain rate), of $83.20 and would receive net after-tax proceeds of $532.80. Y Corporation would take a basis of $500 for

---

[1]   Chapter 9 examines the problems that arise when corporate distributions are made in connection with the sale of a corporate business.

Asset #1 and $200 for Asset #2. On a subsequent sale of the assets, assuming that their fair market values remain unchanged, Y Corporation would realize neither gain nor loss. In some situations, however, issues peculiar to the sale of a corporate business have arisen and rules have been fashioned, either by Congress or by the courts, to deal with these issues. Section 1 of this Chapter deals with the sale of a business that takes the form of a sale of corporate assets and explores the problems that this transaction form historically has generated and the currently applicable rules.

Rather than purchasing X Corporation's assets, Y Corporation might purchase the stock of X Corporation from A. If Y Corporation paid $700 for the stock, A would recognize a gain of $500. The basis of the assets in X Corporation's hands would be unaffected by the sale of the stock, and on a subsequent sale of the assets, X Corporation would recognize a net gain of $400 and, with a tax rate of 21%, a tax of $84. Because the economic burden of the tax on this gain would be borne by Y Corporation, presumably it would offer A less than $700 for the stock of X Corporation to reflect this inherent tax burden. If the net gain were to be realized and taxed contemporaneously with the purchase, it could be expected that Y Corporation would offer A only $616 for the stock, the same amount that A would receive in a liquidating distribution following a taxable sale by X corporation of its assets. But if the net gain were not expected to be realized until sometime in the future, Y Corporation may be willing to pay somewhat more for the stock.

Section 2 of this Chapter focuses on this second basic alternative form for the sale of a corporate business, the sale of the shares of stock of the corporation and again focuses on the corporate tax rules designed for this form of transaction.

The manner in which the parties have structured transactions involving the sale of a corporate business is influenced by two significant federal income tax factors: (1) the seller's desire to maximize the portion of the gain that would be taxed as capital gain rather than as ordinary income; and (2) the buyer's desire to obtain as high a basis as possible for the corporation's assets, particularly inventory and depreciable property.[2] In addition, asset sales and stock sales often have significantly different consequences under state tax law.

Tax results are not the only factors that influence the form of a sale and purchase of a corporate business. Indeed, tax results in many cases

---

[2] Before 1987 the sale of a corporate business was structured around the ability to avoid recognition of gain at the corporate level under either the *General Utilities* doctrine or the pre-1987 version of § 337. The elimination of this last factor by the 1986 Tax Reform Act significantly altered the stakes in many transactions, but important issues remain. The general rule of former § 337, as in effect from 1954–1987, was that a corporation recognized neither gain nor loss on the sale or exchange of assets after the adoption of a plan of liquidation if all of the assets (including proceeds from the sale of assets) were distributed in liquidation within 12 months of adoption of the plan. Elimination of the corporate tax through nonrecognition of gain depended, however, on following mechanical formulae involving time intervals, bulk inventory sales of a certain nature, and the like.

are of lesser importance than nontax factors. In many cases, a single purchaser for all of the corporation's business activities cannot be located, and one line of business is sold to one purchaser while another line of business is sold to a second purchaser. In other cases, a purchaser might be unwilling to acquire the stock of a corporation because of concerns regarding contingent or unascertained liabilities. On the other hand, an asset purchase might be ruled out if the acquired business owns contract rights that are not assignable; in such a case the acquisition must be structured as a sale and purchase of stock. In addition, the impact of various potential liabilities, including contingent liabilities such as environmental remediation obligations and product liability claims, influences the form of the transaction. Other important factors to be considered include state law rights of dissenting shareholders, federal and state securities laws, and the authority of state and federal regulatory agencies to approve or disapprove a transaction.

PROBLEM SET 1

1. Seamus owns all of the stock of QBox, Inc. His basis for the stock is $1,000,000. QBox, Inc. has only one asset, a patent on a video game device and the integrated software. The patent has a basis of $3,000,000. Redmond Corp. desires to acquire the QBox patent.

(a) What are the tax consequences for QBox, Seamus, and Redmond if Redmond pays QBox $23,000,000 for the patent and QBox uses the net proceeds of the sale to enter the pharmaceutical business?

(b) What are the tax consequences for QBox, Seamus, and Redmond if Redmond pays QBox $23,000,000 for the patent and QBox liquidates?

(c) (1) What are the tax consequences for QBox, Seamus, and Redmond if Redmond pays Seamus $23,000,000 for all of the stock of QBox?

(2) What are the tax consequences for QBox, Seamus, and Redmond if Redmond pays Seamus $18,800,000 for all of the stock of QBox?

(3) Why is it unlikely that Redmond would be willing to pay the same price for stock of QBox as it would be willing to pay for the assets of QBox, and why is it likely that Seamus will be willing to accept less?

SECTION 1. ASSETS SALES AND ACQUISITIONS

INTERNAL REVENUE CODE: Sections 197(a)–(e), (f)(1), (3), (7); 453(h)(1)(A)–(C), (2); 1060.

REGULATIONS: Sections 1.1001–1(g); 1.1001–2; 1.1060–1(a)(1), (b)(1)–(3), (6), (7), (c)–(e); 1.338–6(b).

If a corporation sells its business by selling its assets to the purchaser, it recognizes gain or loss with respect to each separate asset, as would a partnership or sole proprietorship selling its business. On liquidation the shareholders recognize capital gain or loss under the rules governing complete liquidations, discussed in Chapter 7, subject to the exception under § 332 for liquidations of controlled subsidiaries. Thus, gain or loss generally results to both the corporation and the shareholders. The same tax results follow if the corporation liquidates first, recognizing gain or loss under § 336, with the shareholders again taxable under § 331. In this case the shareholders take a fair market value basis in the corporation's assets pursuant to § 334(a), and they realize no gain or loss upon the immediate sale of the assets.

In an asset sale, both buyer and seller must allocate the purchase price to the various assets transferred—the seller in order to determine the amount of gain or loss on each asset, and the buyer to establish the tax basis for each of the newly acquired assets. These allocations generally present no problem if the parties have bargained on an asset-by-asset basis, but that is rarely the case. More commonly, the parties bargain for the sale and purchase based on a lump sum price. After the total purchase price has been determined, the parties often then bargain as to the allocation of the price among all of the assets. The parties' objectives in this ex post allocation are to a large extent determined by tax considerations. Generally, allocations of the purchase price agreed upon by the parties have been respected by the IRS and the courts on the theory that the parties had adverse tax interests and that a bargained-for allocation is therefore presumptively correct.

Historically, however, there was the danger that the Treasury could be "whipsawed" by inconsistent allocations in which each party allocated the purchase price in the manner most advantageous to that party and differently from the other party. This was a particularly serious problem prior to the 1993 enactment of § 197, which allows 15-year amortization of almost all purchased intangible assets. Prior to § 197's enactment, cost recovery was not available for goodwill and going concern value. Thus, purchasers preferred to minimize the amount allocated to those assets and maximize the amount allocated to depreciable assets and to inventory. From the seller's perspective, however, it was more desirable to allocate purchase price to goodwill and going concern value, because the gain on those assets was capital gain, rather than to inventory and depreciable equipment subject to § 1245 recapture, which resulted in ordinary income. In addition, purchasers attempted to allocate all or part of a "premium" payment in excess of the value of the assets among all of the assets, rather than allocating the premium solely to goodwill or going concern value. Congress responded to these problems with the 1986 enactment of § 1060, requiring the use of the "residual method" of valuing goodwill or going concern by both the buyer and the seller on the sale of a trade or business. This provision was intended not only to prevent the allocation of any purchase price premium to depreciable assets but also to help ensure that the seller and purchaser allocate the price consistently.

With the enactment of § 197, providing for uniform amortization of purchased intangible assets over 15 years, however, the former function of § 1060 has diminished in importance and the latter function has become more significant. Pursuant to its statutory authority, the Treasury Department has promulgated Regulations requiring both parties to file information returns with respect to the purchase price allocation, thus allowing the IRS to identify situations in which allocations have been made on an inconsistent basis. See Treas.Reg. § 1.1060–1(e).

DETAILED ANALYSIS

1. ALLOCATION OF PURCHASE PRICE

1.1. *General*

Section 1060 refers to preexisting Regulations under § 338(b)(5), which contain a detailed set of rules for the allocation of the purchase price among acquired assets. Treas.Reg. § 1.1060–1(a)(1) adopts the allocation rules of Treas.Reg. § 1.338–6, which divide all assets into seven classes. Class I includes cash and general deposit accounts, not including certificates of deposit; Class II includes actively traded personal property, such as marketable stocks and securities, and certificates of deposit and foreign currency (but stock of target corporation affiliates is excluded); Class III assets are (1) assets that the taxpayer marks-to-market annually for tax purposes, and (2) debt instruments, including accounts receivable, mortgages, and credit card receivables that arise in the ordinary course of a business; Class IV includes stock in trade, inventory, and property held for sale to customers in the ordinary course of a trade or business; Class V includes all assets not specifically assigned to the other classes (including stock of target affiliates); Class VI includes all § 197 intangibles except for goodwill and going concern value; and Class VII includes goodwill and going concern value, whether or not amortizable under § 197. The term "§ 197 intangibles" is intended to be broader than the term "amortizable § 197 intangibles" and includes, for example, § 197 intangibles that are amortizable by the buyer but not by the seller. See T.D. 8711, 1997–1 C.B. 85, 86. Class V contains most tangible assets, including depreciable buildings and equipment, as well as land (which is not depreciable) and some depreciable intangible assets, such as computer software, while Class VI typically contains intangible assets, such as patents, copyrights, trademarks, tradenames, franchises, customer lists, and covenants not to compete. Class VI assets are amortizable over 15 years under § 197.

The purchase price is allocated first to Class I assets based on their aggregate fair market value, then to Class II assets, and so on through Class VI. Within each class, the price is allocated among assets relative to their respective fair market values. Since each asset in Classes I–VI should be allocated a portion of the purchase price equal to its fair market value, any amount designated as paid for goodwill or going concern value, as well as the entire premium, if any, is allocated to Class VII. Conversely, if a going business is purchased for less than its liquidation value, the Class VI assets, and the Class V assets if the Class VI assets are insufficient enough or the discount is deep enough, are allocated an amount less than their individual fair market values.

Nevertheless, even after the enactment of § 197, under Treas.Reg. § 1.338–6, some conflict of interest between buyer and seller remains.

Class V contains both depreciable and nondepreciable assets, such as land. Purchasers will want to establish as high a fair market value as is possible for depreciable assets, but for the seller such an allocation may give rise to ordinary § 1245 recapture income instead of capital gain.

The interests of buyer and seller may vary with respect to allocations to Class V versus Class VI because Class V contains many assets for which cost recovery under § 168 is more rapid than is cost recovery under § 197 for Class VI and Class VII assets. Section 179 may be available to further accelerate cost recovery, and legislation enacted in 2017 (temporarily) allows § 168(k) bonus depreciation with respect to used property, unless certain situations apply. At the same time, Class V also contains important assets, e.g., real property, for which cost recovery under § 168 is not as rapid as cost recovery for intangibles under § 197. Generalizations as to which of the seller or purchaser is benefitted by an allocation to Class V versus Class VI are impossible because the analysis is fact specific.

Because all amortizable § 197 intangibles are amortized over 15 years, the division of § 197 intangibles between two classes—Class VI and Class VII—for purposes of determining basis is significant only if some, but not all, of the amortizable intangibles acquired in a single transaction are subsequently sold at a gain, necessitating calculation of individual bases of the intangibles that were sold. From the seller's side, however, it is more likely that § 1245 recapture will apply with respect to Class VI assets than with respect to Class VII assets, since Class VI may contain amortizable self-created intangibles, but Class VII goodwill and going concern are amortizable, and thus subject to § 1245 on sale, only if purchased.

1.1.1.   *Covenants Not to Compete*

The purchase and sale of a corporate business often is accompanied by the shareholders' agreement not to compete with the buyer in the field of business involved. Like goodwill, the cost of a covenant not to compete must be capitalized and amortized by the buyer. See I.R.C. § 197(f)(3). Section 1060 did not completely address the problem of artificial allocations between goodwill and covenants not to compete. A covenant not to compete, even though created in the sale transaction, is a Class VI asset. Treas.Reg. § 1.1060–1(b)(7), (d), Ex. 2. Goodwill, however, is a Class VII asset. Because a covenant not to compete is as difficult to value as goodwill itself, the tension has continued after the enactment of § 197. Both a covenant not to compete and purchased goodwill must be amortized over 15 years under § 197, regardless of the term of the covenant or the payment schedule, and no loss deduction is allowed for the basis allocated to one as long as the other is retained. I.R.C. § 197(f)(1). The buyer is thus indifferent as to the allocation between the two. As to the seller, however, payments received for a covenant not to compete are ordinary income (Hamlin's Trust v. Commissioner, 209

F.2d 761 (10th Cir.1954); Rev.Rul. 69–643, 1969–2 C.B. 10), while amounts received for self-created goodwill produce capital gain and amounts received for purchased goodwill produce § 1231 gain (subject to § 1245 recapture for prior amortization; see § 197(f)(7)), which might result in capital gain treatment. Thus, if the seller is an individual (or a partnership of individuals) who, unlike a corporation, enjoys a preferential rate for capital gains, the seller will want as much as possible of the purchase price that exceeds the fair market value of other assets allocated to goodwill rather than to a covenant not to compete. If, however, the covenant not to compete involves the shareholders of the corporation whose assets are acquired, they might prefer an allocation to a covenant not to compete because, although the payments are taxed as ordinary income rather than capital gain, they will not be subject to the double tax regime as they would be if the payments were allocated to goodwill of the corporate business. Bemidji Distributing Company v. Commissioner, T.C. Memo. 2001–260, aff'd sub nom. Langdon v. Commissioner, 59 Fed.Appx. 168 (8th Cir. 2003), involved a taxable year before enactment of § 197, where the parties allocated $1,000,000 to the individual shareholder's covenant not to compete, and nothing to corporate level goodwill. Based on all the facts and circumstances, e.g., the seller's ability to compete and expert witnesses' valuation testimony, the Tax Court found that the value of the covenant was only $334,000 and that the $666,000 allocated to the covenant by the taxpayer was really the price of goodwill. The reallocation resulted in corporate level recognition of gain on the sale of goodwill. In addition, $666,000 of the amount paid to the shareholder for the covenant was treated as a constructive dividend to the shareholder.

In many cases the buyer's business need for an enforceable covenant not to compete will prevent the parties from omitting a covenant not to compete from the transaction entirely. See Beaver Bolt, Inc. v. Commissioner, T.C. Memo. 1995–549 (buyer's allocation of $383,000 of price to seller's covenant not to compete was reduced to $324,000; a substantial allocation was proper, even though the parties had no adverse tax interests, because seller had the ability to compete and realistically might have competed in the absence of the covenant). Nevertheless, artificial allocations might continue to be a problem.

1.1.2. *Shareholder Owned Goodwill*

In the overwhelming number of transactions, there is no doubt that business goodwill is owned by the corporation and not by the shareholders. A few cases, however, suggest that occasionally, in transactions involving the sale of the assets of a closely held corporation in which the shareholders are also the primary entrepreneurs and key employees, some or all of the business goodwill might be owned by shareholder/employees individually. In Martin Ice Cream Co. v. Commissioner, 110 T.C. 189 (1998), Häagen-Dazs repurchased the rights to distribute Häagen-Dazs ice cream in the United States from the business that had been distributing Häagen-Dazs under an oral agreement between Häagen-Dazs and the majority shareholder. The IRS treated the amounts received in consideration of the distributorship rights as an amount realized by the corporation, but the corporation and its majority shareholder argued that the amounts were received directly by the shareholder. The Tax Court agreed with the taxpayer, holding that the shareholder, rather than the corporation, owned the distribution rights and sold them back to Häagen-Dazs, reasoning that the rights were based on personal relationships with supermarket chains and the shareholder's personal oral agreement with the founder of Häagen-Dazs, which had never become corporate property. The court emphasized that ownership of the distribution rights could not be attributed to the corporation because the shareholder, who owned the rights before he began conducting the business through the corporation, never entered into a covenant not to compete with the corporation or any other agreement—not even an employment contract— by which any of the shareholder's distribution agreements with Häagen-Dazs, the shareholder's relationships with supermarkets, or his ice cream distribution expertise became the property of the corporation. " '[P]ersonal relationships' of a shareholder-employee are not corporate assets when the employee has no employment contract with the corporation. Those personal assets are entirely distinct from the intangible corporate asset of corporate goodwill."

A similar result was reached in Norwalk v. Commissioner, T.C. Memo 1998–279, which involved a CPA professional services corporation that dissolved and distributed its assets to its two CPA shareholders, who in turn contributed the assets to a partnership that they joined in that year. The IRS asserted that, in addition to the tangible assets expressly distributed, the corporation distributed various customer-based intangible assets, including goodwill, which resulted in a gain to the corporation under § 336 and also increased the capital gain realized by the shareholders on the liquidation. The Tax Court upheld the taxpayer's contention that the corporation's earning were entirely attributable to the CPA-shareholders—any clients would have followed the individual CPAs—and that it owned no goodwill that could be separately sold. The court reasoned that, on the facts, clients sought the personal ability, personality, and reputation of the individual CPAs, and these assets did not belong to the corporation; the corporation's name and its business location did not contribute to goodwill.

In H&M, Inc. v. Commissioner, T.C. Memo. 2012–290, the Tax Court rejected the IRS's assertion that a portion of amounts paid to the selling sole shareholder of an incorporated insurance business represented an amount realized by the corporation for corporate goodwill. A bank purchased H&M's insurance business for $20,000 and entered into an employment agreement with the corporation's sole shareholder pursuant to which he was paid total compensation of over $600,000 over a six-year period for continuing to run the insurance business on behalf of the bank. The IRS asserted a deficiency against H&M, Inc. based on the "substance over form" theory that a significant portion of the compensation paid to the shareholder by the bank under the employment agreement actually was a payment to H&M, Inc. for the sale of the insurance business, and that H&M, Inc. thus realized significant capital gains and interest income over the period the compensation was paid to the shareholder. Applying the holding of *Martin Ice Cream Co.*, the court stated that payments by a purchaser of a corporate business to a controlling shareholder for that shareholder's customer relationships were not taxable to the corporation "where the business of a corporation depends on the personal relationships of a key individual [i.e., the controlling shareholder], unless he transfers his goodwill to the corporation by entering into a covenant not to compete or other agreement so that his relationships become property of the corporation." The court concluded that the insurance business was " 'extremely personal,' and the development of [the] business before the sale was due to the shareholder's ability to form relationships with customers and keep big insurance companies interested in a small insurance market." Furthermore, the compensation paid to the shareholder was reasonable, and there were no other intangibles to be accounted for in the purchase price.

Some recent cases reflect hesitation on the part of courts to liberally apply the holding of *Martin Ice Cream*. In Solomon v. Commissioner, T.C. Memo. 2008–102, the taxpayers argued that the principles of *Martin Ice Cream Co.* and *Norwalk* should apply, but the Tax Court found those cases to be distinguishable on the facts. In *Solomon*, the corporation (Solomon Colors), of which the taxpayers (father and son) were dominant, but not sole, shareholders and key employees, sold one of its several lines of business. In connection with the sale, the taxpayers entered into covenants not to compete. Provisions in the contracts described payments received by the taxpayers as consideration for their entering into covenants not to compete, but other documents allocating the purchase price and payments among assets described those payments as consideration for the shareholders' ownership interests in the customer list for the line of business that was sold. The court rejected the taxpayers' argument that, as in *Martin Ice Cream Co.*, the payments were consideration for the sale of goodwill owned by the shareholders. The *Solomon* court found that the value of the Solomon Colors' business was not attributable to the quality of service and customer relationships developed by the shareholders, which distinguished the facts from *Martin Ice Cream Co.* Because the Solomon Colors' business involved processing, manufacturing, and sale of a product, rather than the provision of services, the corporation's success did not depend entirely on the personal goodwill of its shareholder/employees. Furthermore, the fact that the purchaser did not require the shareholders to enter into employment or consulting agreements made it unlikely that it was purchasing their personal goodwill. Accordingly, the payments were entirely consideration for the shareholders' covenants not to compete and thus were ordinary income, not capital gain.

In Howard v. United States, 448 Fed. Appx. 752 (9th Cir. 2011), aff'g 106 A.F.T.R.2d 2010–5533 (E.D. Wash. 2010), the taxpayer was a dentist who practiced through a solely owned (before taking into account community property law) professional corporation until the practice was sold to a third party. He had an employment agreement with the corporation that included a noncompetition clause that survived for three years after the termination of his stock ownership. The purchase and sale agreement allocated approximately $550,000 of the total $600,000 price to the taxpayer-shareholder's personal goodwill. The IRS recharacterized the goodwill as a corporate asset and treated the amount received by the taxpayer from the sale to the third party as a dividend from the taxpayer's professional service corporation (which had not been liquidated in the year of the sale). The government argued that (1) the goodwill was a corporate asset, because the taxpayer was a corporate employee with a covenant not to compete for three years after he no longer owned any stock, (2) the corporation earned the income, and correspondingly earned the goodwill, and (3) attributing the goodwill to the taxpayer-shareholder did not comport with the economic reality of his relationship with the corporation. After reviewing the principles of *Norwalk* and *Martin Ice Cream Co.*, the District Court held that because the taxpayer was the corporation's employee with a covenant not to compete with it, any goodwill generated during that time period was the corporation's goodwill. The court also reasoned that the goodwill was a corporate asset based on its conclusions that the income associated with the practice was earned by the corporation, and the covenant not to compete, which extended for three years after the taxpayer no longer owned stock in the corporation, rendered any personal goodwill "likely [of] little value." In affirming the District Court, the Ninth Circuit concisely summarized the current state of the law:

> Goodwill "is the sum total of those imponderable qualities which attract the custom of a business,—what brings patronage to the business." *Grace Brothers v. Comm'r*, 173 F.2d 170, 175–76 (9th Cir. 1949). For purposes of federal income taxation, the goodwill of a professional practice may attach to both the professional as well as the practice. * * * Where the success of the venture depends entirely upon the personal relationships of the practitioner, the practice does not generally accumulate goodwill. See *Martin Ice Cream Co. v. Comm'r*, 110 T.C. 189 at 207–08 (1998). The professional may, however, transfer his or her goodwill to the practice by entering into an employment contract or covenant not to compete with the business. See, e.g., *Norwalk v. Comm'r*, 76 T.C.M. (CCH) 208, (1998) (finding that there is no corporate goodwill where "the business of a corporation is dependent upon its key employees, unless they enter into a covenant not to compete with the corporation or other agreement whereby their personal relationships with clients become property of the corporation") (emphasis added); *Martin Ice Cream Co.*, 110 T.C. at 207–08 (finding that "personal relationships . . . are not corporate assets when the employee has no employment contract [or covenant not to compete] with the corporation") (emphasis added); *Macdonald v. Comm'r*, 3 T.C. 720, 727 (1944) (finding "no authority which holds that an individual's personal ability is part of the assets of a corporation . . . where . . . the corporation does not have a right by contract or otherwise to the future services of that individual") (emphasis added). In determining whether goodwill has been transferred to a professional practice, we are especially mindful that "each case depends upon particular facts. And in arriving at a particular conclusion . . . we . . . take into consideration all the circumstances . . . [of] the case and draw from them such legitimate

inferences as the occasion warrants." *Grace Brothers v. Comm'r*,
173 F.2d 170, 176 (9th Cir. 1949).

Looking at the facts as found by the District Court, the Ninth Circuit
concluded that "while the relationships that Dr. Howard developed with his
patients may be accurately described as personal, the economic value of
those relationships did not belong to him, because he had conveyed control
of them to the Howard Corporation." This conclusion regarding "personal
relationships" of shareholder-employees is markedly different than the
conclusion in *Martin Ice Cream Co.*

1.1.3.   *Effect of Parties' Agreement on Price Allocation*

Section 1060(a) binds both the transferor and transferee to any written
agreement between them with respect to the allocation of the purchase price
or the fair market value of the assets, unless the IRS determines that the
allocation is not appropriate. Treas.Reg. § 1.1060–1(c)(4) provides that the
agreement will be binding on both parties unless a party is able to refute the
allocation under the standards of Commissioner v. Danielson, 378 F.2d 771
(3d Cir. 1967). See also H.Rep. 101–964, 101st Cong., 2d Sess. 95 (1990).
Danielson allows a party to refute an agreement only on proof admissible in
an action to show unenforceability because of mistake, undue influence,
fraud, or duress.

In Peco Foods, Inc. v. Commissioner, T.C. Memo. 2012–18, aff'd, 522
Fed. Appx. 840 (11th Cir. 2013), the taxpayer entered into an agreement with
the sellers of two poultry processing plants that allocated a large portion of
the purchase price to processing plants on which the taxpayer claimed
depreciation deductions as nonresidential real property with a § 168
recovery period of 39 years. The agreements separately listed agreed-upon
prices for land, buildings, and machinery and equipment. Subsequently,
after a cost segregation study, the taxpayer attempted to change its method
of accounting to separate out components of the buildings as equipment and
machinery and claim accelerated depreciation on the basis of shorter § 168
recovery periods. The Tax Court held that under § 1060 and Commissioner
v. Danielson, 378 F.2d 771 (3d Cir. 1967), the taxpayer was bound by the
purchase price allocation agreement unless it could show fraud, undue
influence, duress, or similar. The court rejected the taxpayer's argument that
nothing in § 1060 precluded the taxpayer from segregating components of
assets broadly described as a production plant into components consisting of
the real property and related equipment and machinery. The court also
refused to accept the taxpayer's assertion that the agreements with the
sellers should be disregarded because the use of the terms "Processing Plant
Building" and "Real Property: Improvements" were ambiguous. Finally, the
court agreed with the IRS that the IRS did not abuse its discretion in
prohibiting the taxpayer from adopting depreciation schedules that were
inconsistent with the terms of the purchase agreements. The Court of
Appeals affirmed the Tax Court's decision.

The IRS, in contrast, is not restricted from challenging the taxpayers'
allocations. Treas.Reg. § 1.1060–1(c)(4); see also S.Rep. No. 99–313, 99th
Cong., 2d Sess. 255 (1986). Both the buyer and seller are required to file

information returns reporting the amount of consideration in the transaction and its allocation among the assets transferred. Treas.Reg. § 1.1060–1(e). In general, there is no requirement in § 1060 or in the Regulations that the parties agree on an allocation or that they file consistent information returns. As a practical matter, however, the purchaser often requires a contractual provision that consistent information returns be filed.

1.2. *Applicable Asset Acquisition*

The legislative history indicates that § 1060 applies to any sale and purchase of assets that constitute an active trade or business under § 355, discussed in Chapter 12, or to which "goodwill or going concern value could under any circumstances attach." S.Rep. No. 99–313, 99th Cong., 2d Sess. 255 (1986). Treas.Reg. § 1.1060–1(b)(2) and (3), Exs. 1–4 indicate that the term "applicable asset acquisition" is to be broadly construed. Thus, if a liquidating corporation sells a portion of its assets to each of several purchasers, several applicable asset acquisitions may have occurred. Conversely, if a purchasing corporation acquires assets of a seller that constitute a trade or business of the seller, an applicable asset acquisition has occurred even though the purchaser discontinues the seller's trade or business and uses the assets in a different trade or business conducted by it. Section 1060 does not apply to a stock purchase treated as an asset purchase under § 338, discussed in Section 2 of this Chapter. See H.Rep. 101–882, 101st Cong., 2d Sess. 102 (1990). A transfer of assets from seller to buyer in a series of related transactions also will be treated as an applicable asset acquisition. Treas.Reg. § 1.1060–1(b)(5). Assets acquired in an acquisition that includes more than one trade or business are treated as a single trade or business in order to avoid allocations of purchase price among two or more trades or businesses. Treas.Reg. § 1.1060–1(b)(6).

2.   LIABILITIES

Assumption by the buyer of the seller's liabilities is generally treated as a payment received by the seller. Treas.Reg. § 1.1001–2. This is true even in cases in which those liabilities would have given rise to a deduction when paid. For the buyer, the assumption of liabilities increases basis. In Commercial Security Bank v. Commissioner, 77 T.C. 145 (1981) (acq.), the purchaser of all of the business assets of a cash method corporation assumed the seller's accounts payable as part of the consideration paid. The court held that the selling corporation must include the payables in the amount realized on the sale but is entitled to an offsetting deduction because the seller in effect paid the liabilities at the time of the sale through the receipt of less cash on the sale to account for the liabilities. The court stated that the purchaser was required to capitalize the assumed liabilities into the basis of acquired assets and could not deduct them when paid.[3] See also Pacific

---

[3]   A different approach was taken in Focht v. Commissioner, 68 T.C. 223 (1977) (acq.), with respect to liabilities under § 357(c) before adoption of § 357(c)(3) treating assumed payables of a cash method taxpayer as not constituting liabilities. The court determined that since the liabilities would be deductible when paid, the assumption of liabilities could be treated as a receipt of payment followed by the deduction. The court in Crane v. Commissioner, 331 U.S. 1, 13 n. 34 (1947), similarly held that liabilities for accrued but unpaid interest deductible by the seller were not included in the amount realized on the sale of assets This view reflects the current policy of the IRS in § 351 transactions. See Rev.Rul. 95–74, 1995–2 C.B. 36. There are

Transport Co. v. Commissioner, 483 F.2d 209 (9th Cir.1973) (requiring capitalization by the purchaser of payments that would have been deductible by the seller); Holdcroft Transportation Co. v. Commissioner, 153 F.2d 323 (8th Cir. 1946) (where the taxpayer acquired the business and assets of a partnership in a taxable transaction in exchange for the taxpayer's common stock and the assumption of the partnership's liabilities that would have been deductible by the partnership if paid, the payment of the liabilities by the taxpayer was capitalized).

Corporate acquisitions may involve the assumption of contingent liabilities, such as environmental damage, products liability, pension plan, and other employment related claims. Such contingent liabilities also raise tax issues. For example, in Illinois Tool Works Inc. v. Commissioner, 355 F.3d 997 (7th Cir. 2004), aff'g 117 T.C. 39 (2001), the taxpayer acquired the assets of another corporation (for approximately $126 million) in a taxable transaction in which the taxpayer assumed the target's liabilities, including a contingent liability for a patent infringement claim (Lemelson v. Champion Spark Plug Co., 975 F.2d 869 (1992)), for which it established a reserve of $350,000. Subsequently, the taxpayer, as the target's successor, was held liable for damages, interest, and court costs (totaling over $17 million), which it paid. The court upheld the IRS's treatment requiring capitalization of the payments by the purchaser as a cost of acquiring the assets rather than a deductible expense, even though the parties had not adjusted the purchase price to reflect the contingent liability. The liability was known, was considered in setting the price, and was expressly assumed. The fact that the taxpayer considered it highly unlikely that it would be called upon to pay was not relevant. *Holdcroft Transportation Co.*, supra, reached the same result with respect to contingent liabilities for tort claims.

When a contingent obligation related to the acquisition of property is satisfied, the amount of the satisfied obligation is added to the purchaser's basis in the acquired assets of the target. This is analogous to the treatment of costs paid to remedy pre-acquisition issues with respect to property. See Treas.Reg. § 1.263(a)–3(j)(1) (capitalized betterment if payment "[a]meliorates a material condition or defect that either existed prior to the taxpayer's acquisition of the unit of property or arose during the production of the unit of property, whether or not the taxpayer was aware of the condition or defect at the time of acquisition or production").

In Albany Car Wheel Co. v. Commissioner, 40 T.C. 831 (1963), aff'd per curiam, 333 F.2d 653 (2d Cir.1964), the purchaser of a business assumed the seller's contingent liability for severance pay under a union contract if the purchased factory was closed. Because the obligation was "speculative," the court held that it could not be taken into account in determining the basis of the purchased assets until the liability was paid. If the property is depreciable (or amortizable), the taxpayer may depreciate (or amortize) the increased basis over the property's remaining cost recovery period; a new cost recovery period is not commenced. See Meredith Corp. v. Commissioner,

---

fundamental differences between a nonrecognition transaction in which a transferee can be viewed as "stepping into the transferor's shoes" and a taxable transaction to which such a perspective is not logically applicable.

102 T.C. 406, 462–463 (1994). If the property's cost recovery period has expired prior to the contingent obligation having been satisfied, however, an ordinary loss deduction is allowable. See Meredith Corp. v. Commissioner, 108 T.C. 89 (1997).

In many cases, noncontingent consideration paid by the purchaser exceeds the value of all of the assets in Classes I–VI and the amount of the contingent obligation that is capitalized when it is paid is added to the basis of the Class VII assets—goodwill and going concern, which are amortizable over fifteen years under § 197. See Treas.Reg. § 1.338–7 (rules for redetermining allocation of consideration if "required under general principles of tax"; applicable through cross-reference in Treas.Reg. § 1.1060–1(a)(1)).

3. TAXABLE "CASH" MERGERS

The use of a statutory merger under state law allows an acquisition to take place on a tax-free basis if the various requirements of § 368, discussed in Chapter 10, are met. The statutory merger technique sometimes is used instead of a direct asset sale to carry out a taxable acquisition in which the acquiring corporation pays the shareholders of the target corporation cash, corporate bonds (installment obligations), or a combination of cash and installment obligations in connection with the merger. One of the reasons for using a "cash" merger is to effect a transfer of the properties of the acquired corporation directly to the acquiring corporation as a matter of state law, avoiding the need to document separately each transfer. In addition, a merger forces out any minority shareholders in the acquired corporation who dissented from the merger. Furthermore, if the acquisition takes the form of a "reverse" merger in which the acquired corporation is the surviving corporation, problems can be avoided with regard to assets that cannot be assigned or transferred, for example, assets subject to a restriction on transferability in connection with a loan agreement.

To take the simplest case, suppose T Corporation is merged into A Corporation in a transaction in which the T Corporation shareholders all receive cash or debt instruments of A Corporation. For tax purposes, the transaction is treated as a sale of assets followed by the liquidation of T Corporation. See West Shore Fuel, Inc. v. United States, 598 F.2d 1236 (2d Cir.1979) (all-debt merger treated as corporate assets sale); Rev.Rul. 69–6, 1969–1 C.B. 104 (merger of mutual savings banks). Thus, both the acquired corporation and its shareholders recognize gain or loss on the transaction. This double tax treatment of cash mergers may be avoided through the use of a "reverse" triangular merger, the merger of a subsidiary of the acquiring corporation into the target corporation, with the shareholders of the target receiving cash from the parent. Rev.Rul. 90–95, 1990–2 C.B. 67, and Rev.Rul. 79–273, 1979–2 C.B. 125, indicate that this transaction will be treated as a sale and purchase of shares of the target corporation.

4. SALE OF WHOLLY OWNED LIMITED LIABILITY COMPANY

There has been an increasing trend to operate different divisions of a corporation's business through a number of separately organized limited liability companies (LLCs). Under the so-called "check-the-box" Regulations, unless an LLC with a single owner elects to be taxed as a corporation, Treas.Reg. § 301.7701–3(a), it will be disregarded as an entity separate from its owner. Treas.Reg. § 301.7701–3(b)(1)(ii). When an LLC is a disregarded entity, its assets, liabilities, income items, and deduction items are treated as owned, owed, received, and incurred directly by its owner. Thus, if a corporation sells the membership units of a wholly owned LLC that is a disregarded entity—as virtually all wholly owned LLCs are—the transaction will be treated as an asset sale and purchase.

In Dover Corp. v. Commissioner, 122 T.C. 324 (2004), the taxpayer corporation had complete ownership of a business entity organized under the laws of a foreign jurisdiction. Under Treas.Reg. § 301.7701–3, the entity was taxable as a corporation unless it elected to be a disregarded entity.[4] The taxpayer sold the subsidiary entity to another party and, solely for the purpose of reducing the taxes on the sale, elected effective immediately before the sale to treat the subsidiary entity as a disregarded entity. As a result, the subsidiary corporation was treated as having been liquidated in a transaction to which § 332, discussed in Chapter 7, applied to provide nonrecognition. The transaction was thus transmuted from a stock sale and purchase to an asset sale and purchase. The Tax Court upheld the taxpayer's treatment of the sale as an asset sale rather than a stock sale. The proposition that a non-tax business purpose is not a prerequisite for a check-the-box election was implicit in the Tax Court's holding.

Applying *Dover* in the domestic context, the owner of an LLC that is a disregarded entity has the last minute option of structuring the sale of the entity's business as either an asset sale and purchase, by simply selling the membership units of the LLC, or as a stock sale and purchase by first electing to treat the LLC as a corporation, which would be an incorporation governed by § 351, discussed in Chapter 2, and then selling the membership units of the LLC, which as a result of the election are treated as stock.

5. INSTALLMENT REPORTING BY ACQUIRED CORPORATION'S SHAREHOLDERS

5.1. *Generally*

If the consideration in an asset sale consists in whole or in part of the acquiring corporation's bonds or other debt instruments, the installment method of § 453 may apply in some circumstances. In situations in which the selling corporation liquidates, the possibilities for installment reporting are limited. Installment reporting of gains from inventory and depreciation recapture is not permitted in any event. See I.R.C. § 453(b)(2), (i)(2). In addition, as a result of distribution of installment obligations in liquidation, under § 453B the corporation must recognize all of its gain on any installment notes for which § 453 installment sale accounting otherwise would have been available. Then the question is whether the shareholders may report their gain on the installment method when they receive the purchaser's debt obligations in the liquidating distribution. If the seller

---

[4] For certain foreign entities with limited liability that are not per se corporations, the default rule is that the entity is a corporation unless it elects to be a disregarded entity—the opposite of the rule for domestic entities. Treas.Reg. § 301.7701–3(b)(2).

receives purchaser's bonds that are readily tradable, § 453(f)(4) precludes installment sale reporting. Furthermore, if the stock of the selling liquidating corporation was publicly traded, § 453(k)(2) might deny installment sale treatment. If disqualifying facts are not involved and if the conditions of § 453(h) are satisfied, the shareholders of the selling corporation may be eligible to report gain using the installment method in either an asset sale followed by a liquidation or a taxable merger.

Suppose that under the terms of the merger agreement, the shareholders of T Corporation may elect to receive either cash or installment obligations of A Corporation. Will those shareholders electing to receive the installment obligations nonetheless be found to be in constructive receipt of cash and thus currently taxable? Rev.Rul. 73–396, 1973–2 C.B. 160, held that the constructive receipt doctrine did not apply in a situation in which the purchaser was willing to pay cash but the seller insisted on deferred payments.

5.2. *Section 453(h)*

Section 453(h) provides a limited exception to the shareholder recognition rule (but not to the § 453B rules requiring recognition by the corporation upon distribution of the note) when the shareholders receive installment obligations arising from a sale or exchange of corporate assets occurring after the adoption of a plan of complete liquidation that is completed within 12 months after it was adopted,[5] and it applies whether the installment sale is pursuant to a complete acquisition of the seller's business or a dispersal sale. This provision applies only if the liquidation is completed within 12 months following adoption of the plan.[6] If this requirement is met, shareholders recognize gain on the liquidation with respect to the notes under the installment method of § 453 as they receive payments on the obligations. If an installment obligation arises from the sale of inventory, however, deferred recognition is available only if substantially all of the inventory attributable to a particular trade or business of the corporation was sold in bulk to a single purchaser. Section 453(h) was discussed in further detail in Chapter 7.

6.   USE OF PARENT CORPORATION'S STOCK AS PAYMENT MEDIUM

Treas.Reg. § 1.1032–3 deals with the treatment of a subsidiary that uses the stock of its parent corporation as the medium of payment in a taxable transaction. If a subsidiary receives its parent's stock as a contribution to capital or in a § 351 transaction (i.e., a transaction in which the subsidiary's basis in acquired property otherwise is determined under § 362(a)), and immediately transfers the stock for money, other property, or services in a purchase-type transaction, then the transaction is treated as if the acquiring

---

[5]   Section 453(k)(2), denying installment sale treatment for sales of marketable stock and securities, might render § 453(h) unavailable in the liquidation of a publicly traded corporation, but it is highly unlikely that a publicly traded corporation ever would liquidate in a manner to which § 453(h) could apply.

[6]   Section 453(h) is a vestige of the pre-1987 rules under which a corporation did not recognize gain or loss on the sale or exchange of certain assets if the assets were sold after the adoption of a plan of liquidation and the liquidation was completed within 12 months. Although those rules were repealed by the Tax Reform Act of 1986, installment reporting of shareholder gain was continued.

years, the basis of the assets acquired in the liquidation would be determined by the purchase price of the stock, i.e., in the same manner as if the assets had been purchased directly. Although nominally not elective, former § 334(b)(2) in fact provided significant flexibility to the purchasing corporation to obtain a purchase price basis for only selected assets, particularly where the acquired corporation was the parent of an affiliated group. In addition, the computations of asset basis if the liquidation was delayed raised problems of their own. For these reasons, former § 334(b)(2) was repealed and replaced by § 338 in 1982.

Section 338 permits an election by a corporate purchaser following a "qualified stock purchase" of another corporation to treat the acquired subsidiary as if it sold all its assets pursuant to a plan of complete liquidation at the close of the stock acquisition date. That deemed asset sale results in the recognition of gain (or loss) with respect to all of the acquired corporation's assets. The acquired corporation is then deemed to re-acquire its assets on the next day, thereby providing a basis for the acquired assets determined with reference to the stock purchase price, which is intended to approximate the fair market value of the assets. A qualified stock purchase is defined, through a cross reference to § 1504(a) as the acquisition within a 12-month period of stock representing 80% of voting power and 80% of the value of all stock, excluding nonvoting stock that is limited and preferred as to dividends and does not participate in corporate growth to any significant extent, of the acquired corporation. Because of the required recognition of gain on the deemed asset sale, § 338 elections are rarely beneficial except in some special circumstances.

Revenue Ruling 90–95
1990–2 C.B. 67.

ISSUES

(1) If a corporation organizes a subsidiary solely for the purpose of acquiring the stock of a target corporation in a reverse subsidiary cash merger, is the corporation treated on the occurrence of a merger as having acquired the stock of the target in a qualified stock purchase under section 338 of the Internal Revenue Code?

(2) If the corporation makes a qualified stock purchase of the target stock and immediately liquidates the target as part of a plan to acquire the assets of the target, is the corporation treated as having made an asset acquisition pursuant to the *Kimbell-Diamond* doctrine or a section 338 qualified stock purchase followed by a liquidation of the target?

FACTS

Situation 1. P, a domestic corporation, formed a wholly owned domestic subsidiary corporation, S, for the sole purpose of acquiring all of the stock of an unrelated domestic target corporation, T, by means of a reverse subsidiary cash merger. Prior to the merger, *S* conducted no activities other than those required for the merger.

Pursuant to plan of merger, *S* merged into *T* with *T* surviving. The shareholders of *T* exchanged all of their *T* stock for cash from *S*. Part of the cash used to carry out the acquisition was received by *S* from *P*; the remaining cash was borrowed by *S*. Following the merger, *P* owned all of the outstanding *T* stock.

Situation 2. The facts are the same as in *Situation 1*, except that *P* planned to acquire *T*'s assets through a prompt liquidation of *T*. State law prohibited *P* from owning the stock of *T*. Pursuant to the plan, *T* merged into *P* immediately following the merger of *S* into *T*. The merger of *T* into *P* satisfied the requirements for a tax-free liquidation under section 332 of the Code. The liquidation was not motivated by the evasion of avoidance of federal income tax.

LAW AND ANALYSIS

In *Kimbell-Diamond Milling Co. v. Commissioner*, 14 T.C. 74 (1950), *aff'd per curiam*, 187 F.2d 718 (5th Cir. 1951), *cert. denied*, 342 U.S. 827 (1951), the court held that the purchase of the stock of a target corporation for the purpose of obtaining its assets through a prompt liquidation should be treated by the purchaser as one transaction, namely, a purchase of the target's assets with the purchaser receiving a cost basis in the assets. Old section 334(b)(2) of the Code was added in 1954 to codify the principles of *Kimbell-Diamond*. See S. Rep. No. 1622, 83d Cong. 2d Sess. 257 (1954).

In 1982, Congress repealed old section 334(b)(2) of the Code and enacted section 338. Section 338 was "intended to replace any nonstatutory treatment of a stock purchase as an asset purchase under the *Kimbell-Diamond* doctrine." H.R. Conf. Rep. No. 760, 97th Cong, 2d Sess. 536 (1982), 1982–2 C.B. 600, 632. Under section 338, in the case of any qualified stock purchase, rules are provided governing whether the transaction gives rise to purchase of target stock treatment or purchase of target asset treatment. Under these rules, stock purchase or asset purchase treatment generally results whether or not the target is liquidated, merged into another corporation, or otherwise disposed of by the purchasing corporation. *See* Section 1.338–4T(d) *Question and Answer 1*, temporary Income Tax Regulations.

A qualified stock purchase is generally the purchase by a corporation of at least 80 percent of a target's stock, by vote and value, within a 12-month period. Section 338(d)(3). The requirements for a qualified stock purchase may be satisfied through a combination of purchases of target stock by purchasing corporation and redemptions by the target. Section 1.338–4T(c)(4) of the temporary regulations.

Stock purchase or asset purchase treatment generally turns on whether the purchasing corporation makes or is deemed to make a section 338 election. If the election is made or deemed made, asset purchase treatment results and section 338 of the Code generally treats all of the assets of the target as having been sold by the target at fair market value on the date of the qualified stock purchase and then repurchased by the target on the following day. The basis of the target's asset is adjusted to reflect the stock purchase price and other relevant items. If an election is not made or deemed made, the stock purchase treatment generally results. In such a case, the basis of the target's assets is not adjusted to reflect the stock purchase price and other relevant items. * * *

In *Situations 1 and 2*, the step-transaction doctrine is properly applied to disregard the existence of *S* for federal income tax purposes. *S* had no significance apart from *P*'s acquisition of the *T* stock. *S* was formed for the sole purpose of enabling *P* to acquire the *T* stock, and *S* did not conduct any activities that were not related to that acquisition. Accordingly, the transaction is treated as a qualified stock purchase of *T* stock by *P*.

In *Situation 2*, the step-transaction doctrine does not apply to treat the stock acquisition and liquidation as an asset purchase. Section 338 of the Code replaced the *Kimbell-Diamond* doctrine and governs whether a corporation's acquisition of stock is treated as an asset purchase. Under section 338, asset purchase treatment turns on whether a section 338 election is made (or is deemed made) following a qualified stock purchase of target stock and not on whether the target's stock is acquired to obtain the assets through a prompt liquidation of the target. The acquiring corporation may receive stock purchase treatment or asset purchase treatment whether or not the target is subsequently liquidated. A qualified stock purchase of target stock is accorded independent significance from a subsequent liquidation of the target regardless of whether a section 338 election is made or deemed made. This treatment results even if the liquidation occurs to comply with state law. Accordingly, in *Situation 2*, the acquisition is treated as a qualified stock purchase by *P* of *T* stock followed by a tax-free liquidation of *T* into *P*.

HOLDINGS

(1) In *Situations 1 and 2*, *P* is treated as having acquired stock of *T* in a qualified stock purchase under section 338 of the Code.

(2) In *Situation 2*, *P* is treated as having acquired stock of *T* in a qualified stock purchase under section 338, followed by a liquidation of *T* into *P*, rather than having made an acquisition of assets pursuant to the *Kimbell-Diamond* doctrine.

DETAILED ANALYSIS

1. SECTION 338 TURNS OFF THE STEP TRANSACTION DOCTRINE IN THE TAXABLE STOCK ACQUISITION CONTEXT

In many important respects, § 338 eliminated or resolved the problems and discontinuities that arose under former § 334(b)(2). An acquiring corporation may obtain a step-up in basis without liquidating a newly acquired subsidiary that for independent business reasons the acquiring corporation wishes to continue to operate as a subsidiary. Conversely, a newly acquired subsidiary may be liquidated for independent business reasons, either with or without a step-up (or step-down) in the basis of its assets. Inevitably, § 338 has given rise to its own complexity: new interpretive issues have been raised and different avenues for manipulation of the rules governing taxable acquisitions have been created.

One by-product of § 338 has been to create a form of corporate acquisition that was not previously possible—the purchase of the stock in the target corporation followed by the immediate liquidation of the target with preservation of all the target's tax attributes. Under the mechanical rules of former § 334(b)(2), the transaction resulted in a step-up in basis of the acquired assets but elimination of all the tax attributes of the target corporation. If no § 338 election is made with respect to the acquisition, the liquidation of the target will be governed by § 332; the acquired corporation's basis in the assets will be carried over under § 334(b); and all corporate attributes such as earnings and profits, net operating loss carryovers, etc., will be preserved under § 381(a). Such a procedure might be preferable to the § 338 route where, for example, the target corporation's basis in its assets is high relative to the stock purchase price and the target has net operating loss carryovers that could be utilized by the acquiring corporation. (See Chapter 13 for limitations that are applicable to the use of such carryover items following a corporate acquisition.)

The above elective results apply regardless of whether the step transaction doctrine would have integrated the transaction steps under judicially created principles. In this regard, when Congress enacted § 338, it supplanted any application of the step transaction doctrine or the asset acquisition doctrine espoused in *Kimbell-Diamond* in the taxable asset acquisition context. Instead of applying those judicial doctrines, a taxable purchase of stock followed by a liquidation of the target corporation will be governed by § 338's prescriptive standards. Rev.Rul. 90–95, *supra*, explains how one should rationalize the supplanting of the step transaction doctrine due to the enactment of § 338.

In Chapter 10, we will return to the interplay of § 338 and the step transaction doctrine in the context of nontaxable acquisitive reorganizations. In that context, the enactment of § 338 does not supplant the application of the step transaction doctrine unless the taxpayer elects to treat the transaction as a taxable acquisition by making an affirmative § 338 election.

2.   IMPACT OF *GENERAL UTILITIES* REPEAL

2.1. *General*

When § 338 originally was enacted, the pre-1987 version of § 337 provided nonrecognition to the target corporation on the deemed sale of its assets under § 338(a) when a § 338 election was made. Thus, except to the extent that one of the exceptions to former § 337 required that gain be recognized on the sale of a liquidating corporation's assets, the effect of a § 338 election was to secure a step-up in basis without an attendant gain.

Because of this highly advantageous treatment, § 338 elections frequently were made when the qualifying conditions were satisfied. Section 338 was amended by the 1986 Act to conform it with the repeal of the *General Utilities* doctrine. Since then, § 338 elections (other than § 338(h)(10) elections, discussed infra) have been rare.

Section 338(a)(1) provides that if an election is made under § 338(g), the target corporation will be treated as having sold all of its assets in a transaction in which gain or loss is fully recognized. This corresponds to the treatment that the target corporation would have received if it had distributed all of its assets in liquidation or had made a direct sale of the assets. Thus, in all circumstances in which the purchaser obtains, directly or indirectly, a step-up in basis for the target corporation's assets, the target corporation will be required to recognize gain currently. This change substantially reduces the advantage of a § 338 election. The tax benefit of increased future depreciation or amortization deductions generated by the step-up in basis must be "purchased" at the price of a present tax liability with respect to any appreciation in the acquired corporation's assets. With the current corporate tax rate currently at a flat 21% and the possibility of accelerated cost recovery, there may be circumstances where this election would make economic sense to the parties—for example, where the target corporation has a net operating loss that would shield the gain required to be recognized under § 338 or where the purchaser has the ability to obtain substantial first-year expensing. See I.R.C. § 382(h)(1)(C) (permitting the net operating loss of an acquired corporation to be used to offset recognized built-in gain without regard to the limitations otherwise imposed by § 382, discussed in Chapter 13). The 2017 Tax Act (temporarily) expanded bonus depreciation under § 168(k), including allowing used property, such as equipment, to be eligible for bonus depreciation under certain conditions.

2.2. *Example*

Generally, as long as the parties take into account tax burdens in negotiating the price, and the seller does not have otherwise unusable capital loss deductions, from a tax perspective it makes no difference to either the seller or the buyer whether a purchase and sale is structured as an asset sale or as a stock sale followed by a § 338 election and a § 332 liquidation.

Suppose that individual B owns all of the stock of T Corporation. B's basis for the stock is $2,000. T Corporation's sole asset has a basis of $1,000 and a fair market value of $4,000. If T Corporation sold the asset to P Corporation for $4,000, it would owe taxes of $630 on its $3,000 gain (assuming a flat corporate tax of 21%) and would distribute $3,370 to B in a liquidating distribution. B would pay taxes of $274 (assuming a 20% rate) on B's $1,370 gain, leaving B with $3,096 of net proceeds.

Alternatively, P Corporation could pay B $3,370 in cash for the stock, again leaving B with $3,096 after taxes. P Corporation could make a § 338 election, which would give rise to a $630 tax liability on the deemed sale of T Corporation's asset. The asset would acquire a $4,000 basis, which under § 334(b) would carry over to P corporation if it liquidated T

Corporation pursuant to § 332. Again, P Corporation has paid a total of $4,000 to acquire T Corporation's asset with a basis of $4,000.

In actual practice, however, things will work somewhat differently. Although the two levels of tax theoretically cannot be avoided, the corporate level tax can be deferred through a sale and purchase of stock without a § 338 election. Alternatively, one level of tax can be deferred through an installment purchase of assets coupled either with continuation of the selling corporation or the use of § 453(h). If the acquiring corporation is willing to buy stock, it will not likely be willing to make the § 338 election; hence, it will not pay the shareholders of the target corporation the full net asset value (including goodwill and going concern value) of the target corporation, but will discount the offset for the corporate level tax to reflect the deferral of that tax. Thus, in the preceding example, P Corporation likely would pay B more than $3,370 but less than $4,000 for the stock of T Corporation. Thus, § 338 is something of an anachronism after 1986, providing a complex solution to a situation that seldom arises.

2.3. *Policy Issues*

The broad purpose of § 338 is to equalize the treatment of stock and asset acquisitions by providing a stepped-up basis in either case, albeit at the price of an immediate corporate level tax on asset appreciation. The treatment of the two transactions is not always equalized, however, because of the elective aspects of the transaction. This situation raises the question whether the tax treatment of stock and asset acquisitions should be fully equalized by amending the Code to apply § 338 to every "qualified stock purchase" on a mandatory basis.

3. QUALIFYING CONDITIONS

3.1. *General*

An election under § 338 is available only to a corporation that makes a "qualified stock purchase" of stock of another corporation. A "qualified stock purchase" is defined in § 338(d)(3), through a cross reference to § 1504(a)(2), as the acquisition by purchase within a 12-month period of 80% or more of the voting stock and 80% or more of the total value of all stock of the corporation, excluding nonvoting stock that is limited and preferred as to dividends and does not participate in corporate growth to any significant extent. Stock of the target corporation already owned by the acquiring corporation is not counted toward the 80% requirement. Thus, for example, if P Corporation has owned 21% of the stock of T Corporation for one year or more, P Corporation cannot thereafter complete a "qualified stock purchase." Note that § 338(h)(8) provides that all acquisitions by corporations that are part of an affiliated group are treated as made by one corporation. Thus, if P Corporation purchases 40% of the stock of T Corporation and P Corporation's controlled subsidiary, S Corporation, purchases an additional 40% of the T Corporation stock, a qualified stock purchase has been made, presumably by P Corporation.

3.2. *The "Purchase" Requirement*

A "purchase" under § 338(h)(3) includes any "acquisition" that is not specifically excluded. Section 338(h)(3)(A) provides three specific exclusions:

(1) stock the basis of which is determined in whole or in part with reference to the transferor's basis, i.e., transferred basis stock, and stock acquired from a decedent; (2) stock acquired in certain nonrecognition transactions, including § 351 transactions and corporate reorganizations; and (3) stock acquired from a person from whom it would be attributed to the purchaser under § 318.[8] Thus, for example, stock of a subsidiary acquired by another corporate subsidiary from its parent is not "purchased" at the time of the transfer. See In re Chrome Plate, Inc., 614 F.2d 990 (5th Cir.1980).

The stock of a subsidiary of the target is deemed to have been purchased if the new target corporation owns 80% of the voting power and value of the subsidiary's stock within the meaning of § 1504(a)(2). Treas.Reg. § 1.338–3(b)(2). The purchase requirement is satisfied even if no part of the buyer's purchase price is allocated to the subsidiary's stock under the residual allocation rules of Treas.Reg. § 1.338–6(b). Stock acquired in a § 301 distribution is "purchased" (unless received from a corporation of which the shareholder owns 50% or more of the stock), since it is "acquired" in a transaction that is not excluded. See Rev.Rul. 74–211, 1974–1 C.B. 76 (applying statutory predecessor of § 337), obsoleted by Rev.Rul. 2003–99, 2003–2 C.B. 388.

In Rev.Rul. 90–95, reprinted supra, P Corporation formed a subsidiary, S Corporation, for the purpose of merging S Corporation into T Corporation. The T Corporation shareholders received cash in exchange for their T Corporation stock and T Corporation became a subsidiary of P Corporation in a reverse cash merger. The Ruling held that the existence of S Corporation should be disregarded and P Corporation was treated as acquiring the T Corporation stock in a qualified stock purchase under § 338. If as part of a plan, T Corporation were liquidated, the transaction would be treated as a qualified stock purchase under § 338 followed by a liquidation of T Corporation into S Corporation under § 332.

The purchase requirement in § 338 is derived from former § 334(b)(2), and cases decided under that provision remain relevant. In Madison Square Garden Corp. v. Commissioner, 500 F.2d 611 (2d Cir.1974), the taxpayer purchased 52% of the stock of another corporation. The acquired corporation then redeemed some of its stock. Following the redemption, the taxpayer owned approximately 79% of the stock of the acquired corporation, and the taxpayer then acquired by purchase additional stock sufficient to give it 80.22% ownership. The acquired corporation was then merged into the taxpayer. Under Treas.Reg. § 1.332–2(d) and (e), the merger was treated as a liquidation for tax purposes, and the taxpayer argued that former § 334(b)(2) was applicable. The IRS asserted that the 80% requirement applied to the shares of stock outstanding at the time the purchase of the stock began, and thus former § 334(b)(2) was not satisfied. The Court of Appeals, affirming the Tax Court, held that the taxpayer had acquired the requisite 80% by "purchase." See also Yoc Heating Corp. v. Commissioner, 61 T.C. 168 (1973). The issue posed by *Madison Square Garden* is relevant

---

[8] Under Treas.Reg. § 1.338–3(b)(3)(ii), the purchase is treated as being from a related person if the relationship specified in § 318 exists immediately after the purchase of the target stock.

in determining whether a redemption reduces a target's outstanding stock for purposes of meeting the percentage thresholds required for a § 338 "qualified stock purchase." Treas.Reg. § 1.338–3(b)(5) follows the result in *Madison Square Garden Corp.* and provides that redemptions from unrelated shareholders are taken into account in determining whether the target stock purchased within the 12-month acquisition period satisfies the 80% ownership requirement.

3.3. *The Timetable*

The statutory 12-month period within which a "qualified stock purchase" must be made begins to run on the date of the first "purchase" of stock by the acquiring corporation, § 338(h)(1), but each purchase starts a new 12-month period running. For example, if P Corporation purchases 10% of the stock of T Corporation on January 1, Year 1, and another 10% on February 1, Year 1, the purchase of an additional 70% of the stock of T Corporation any time before February 2, Year 2, will constitute a "qualified stock purchase." Section 338(g) gives the acquiring corporation 8 1/2 months after the end of the month in which a qualified stock purchase is completed to make the election. See also Treas.Reg. § 1.338–2(d). For example, if P Corporation acquires 70% of the stock of T Corporation on March 1, Year 1, 10% on May 1, Year 1, and 20% on June 1, Year 1, the period for making the election begins to run on May 1, Year 1, and the election must be made by January 15, Year 2. The deadline will not be extended by P Corporation's purchase of additional T Corporation stock on June 1, Year 1.

4.   DEEMED SALES PRICE

4.1. *General*

Section 338(a)(1) provides that as a result of a § 338 election the target corporation is treated as having sold all of its assets at "fair market value." In general, this definition should obviate the need separately to account for the target corporation's liabilities in computing its gain. However, since § 338 applies to stock sales and purchases, not asset transactions, there is no market valuation of the corporation's assets to which to look for the relevant valuation. Thus, Treas.Reg. § 1.338–4 provides mechanical rules for determining the "aggregate deemed sale price" (ADSP) of the target's assets. Under this formula, the ADSP is the sum of the "grossed-up amount realized" on the sale of the purchasing corporation's "recently purchased stock" of the target, liabilities of the target (including tax liabilities arising from the § 338 election), and other relevant items. Recently purchased stock is stock acquired in the "qualified stock purchase." The grossed-up amount realized of the recently purchased stock for purposes of computing the ADSP is the amount realized by the seller of that stock divided by the percentage of target corporation stock by value that is recently purchased stock. Treas.Reg. § 1.338–4(c). Thus, the value of stock of the target that has not been purchased and that remains outstanding (for example, nonvoting limited preferred stock that is not counted in determining whether a qualified stock purchase has occurred) reduces the denominator of the fraction, thereby increasing the grossed-up amount realized to a value greater than the amount paid for the stock. The purpose of the "grossed-up amount realized" concept is to approximate the fair market value of 100% of the stock of the target in cases where the acquiring corporation purchases less than 100% of the target stock within the 12-month acquisition period.

Liabilities taken into account in calculating ADSP are those liabilities of the target corporation that properly would be taken into account as amount realized on a disposition by the target of its assets to an unrelated purchaser who assumed the liabilities or acquired the assets subject to the target's liabilities, including the liability for the income tax on the gain recognized as a result of the deemed sale. Treas.Reg. § 1.338–4(d)(1). This rule is intended to require inclusion in amount realized of contingent liabilities to the same extent that such liabilities are included in amount realized under Treas. Regs. § 15a.453–1T(d)(2)(iii) and Treas. Reg. § 1.1001–1(g)(2) in a sales transaction. The rule thereby largely precludes open transaction treatment with respect to a § 338 election. See Reg–107069–97, 1999–2 C.B. 346, 352–353. The Regulations provide that ADSP may be re-determined under general principles of tax law if liabilities not originally included in amount realized are subsequently taken into account. Treas.Reg. § 1.338–4(b)(2)(ii). An increase or decrease in amount realized may also affect the target corporation's tax liability, which would in turn require further adjustment to ADSP. See Treas.Reg. § 1.338–7 (specifying method for adjustments to ADSP).

4.2. *Acquisition of Target with Subsidiaries*

If the target corporation owns stock in a subsidiary corporation and the acquiring corporation makes a § 338 election, the acquisition by the "new" target corporation of the subsidiary corporation's stock in the § 338 deemed sale will itself qualify as a "purchase" for purposes of § 338. I.R.C. § 338(h)(3)(B). The acquiring corporation may make a § 338 election with respect to only the target corporation or both of the target and its subsidiary corporations. See Treas.Reg. § 1.338–3(b)(2), (4).

Application of the statutory rules of § 338 presents a special problem where a target corporation has subsidiary corporations and the acquiring corporation makes a § 338 election with respect to both the target and its subsidiaries. Assume that P Corporation purchases 100% of the stock of T Corporation, which owns 100% of the stock of S Corporation, and P Corporation makes a § 338 election with respect to both. (Under § 338(h)(3)(B) the deemed sale and repurchase of the stock of S Corporation by T Corporation constitutes a "purchase" of that stock for purposes of § 338, thus enabling T Corporation to make the election with respect to S Corporation.) There could be a double tax at the corporate level if T Corporation is taxed on the deemed sale of the S Corporation stock and S Corporation is taxed on the deemed sale of its assets. The IRS has concluded that Congress did not intend for the repeal of the *General Utilities* rule to lead to such double taxation. Accordingly, Treas.Reg. § 1.338–4(h)(2) provides that T Corporation does not recognize any gain on the deemed sale of the S Corporation stock; the deemed gain on the sale by S Corporation of its assets is recognized.

5. DETERMINATION OF ASSET BASIS

5.1. *General*

In general, § 338 is intended to produce the same tax consequences as a direct asset acquisition. However, § 338 does not directly assign to each asset of the target corporation a fair market value basis. Instead, under § 338(b) the aggregate basis of the assets, termed "adjusted grossed-up basis" (AGUB) by Treas.Reg. § 1.338–5, is first determined according to a formula based on the acquiring corporation's basis for all of the stock of the target corporation which it owns, adjusted for liabilities assumed (including tax liabilities arising from the § 338 election), and the aggregate basis then is allocated among the assets as provided in Treas.Reg. § 1.338–6. The basis allocation rules are substantially the same as the allocation rules under § 1060 and many of the same valuation issues arise.

5.2. *Adjusted Grossed-Up Basis*

Section 338(b)(1) provides that the starting point for determining the AGUB, the deemed purchase price of the target corporation's assets, is the sum of (1) the "grossed-up basis" of the "recently purchased stock" of the target and (2) the basis of the "nonrecently purchased stock." Treas.Reg. § 1.338–5 provides detailed rules for computing the AGUB. Recently purchased stock generally is defined as stock acquired in the "qualified stock purchase." Nonrecently purchased stock is stock owned by the acquiring corporation prior to commencement of the acquisition period, which is not counted toward the "qualified stock purchase." I.R.C. § 338(b)(6). The grossed-up basis of the recently purchased stock is the basis of that stock multiplied by a fraction, the numerator of which is 100 minus the percentage of target corporation stock by value owned by the acquiring corporation that is not recently purchased stock and the denominator of which is the percentage of stock by value of the target that is recently purchased stock. I.R.C. § 338(b)(4); Treas.Reg. § 1.338–5(c). Note that the value of stock of the target that has not been purchased and that remains outstanding (for example, nonvoting limited preferred stock that is not counted in determining whether a qualified stock purchase has occurred) reduces the denominator of the fraction, thereby increasing the grossed-up basis to a value greater than the amount paid for the stock. The grossed-up basis is then increased by the acquisition costs of the recently purchased stock, which are not themselves grossed-up. Treas.Reg. § 1.338–5(c)(3). "Grossed-up basis" for purposes of determining AGUB under Treas.Reg. § 1.338–5 differs from the definition of "grossed-up amount realized" for computing ADSP under Treas.Reg. § 1.338–4 in that the former includes the old basis of nonrecently purchased stock whereas grossed-up amount realized is adjusted to reflect the fair market value of all of the target stock. Section 338(b)(3) permits the acquiring corporation to elect to recognize gain attributable to any nonrecently purchased stock and add that amount to its deemed purchase price. In such a case, the basis of nonrecently purchased stock is adjusted to reflect the recognized gain. Treas.Reg. § 1.338–5(d)(3).

The purpose of the "grossed-up basis" concept is to assign to the target's assets a basis equal to the aggregate fair market value of the target corporation's stock where the acquiring corporation purchases more than 80% but less than all of the target corporation's stock. For example, assume that P Corporation, which previously owned none of the stock of T Corporation, purchases 85% of the T Corporation stock for $850. The grossed-up basis of the stock is $1,000, computed as follows: $850 × (100−0)/85.

Section 338(b)(2) provides for an adjustment to the deemed purchase price in computing AGUB to reflect the acquired corporation's liabilities that would have been included in the purchaser's basis if the transaction had been an asset purchase. Treas.Reg. § 1.338–5(b)(1)(iii). Target liabilities that increase basis are those liabilities that would be included in the basis of the target's assets under general principles of tax law if the target had acquired its assets from an unrelated person for consideration that would have included the assumption of or taking property subject to the liabilities. Treas.Reg. § 1.338–5(e). These liabilities include the target corporation's tax liability arising from the deemed sale of its assets under § 338(a)(1). Treas.Reg. § 1.338–5(g), Ex. 1.

The Regulations provide that AGUB is re-determined if, under general principles of tax law, liabilities not originally included in AGUB are subsequently taken into account. Treas.Reg. § 1.338–5(b)(2)(ii). An increase or decrease in amount realized may also affect the target corporation's tax liability, which would in turn require further adjustment to AGUB. See Treas.Reg. § 1.338–7 (specifying method for adjustments to AGUB).

6. COMPUTATION AND ALLOCATION OF TAX LIABILITY

A § 338 election results in closing the taxable year of the target. As long as the target corporation was not purchased from a parent that was a member of an affiliated group filing a consolidated return, the old target's final return includes the deemed sale. Treas.Reg. § 1.338–10(a)(1). As a general rule, if the target corporation otherwise would have been included in a consolidated return, it is "disaffiliated" from the consolidated group immediately before the deemed asset sale and is required to file a special "deemed sale return" reporting the items from the § 338 sale. Treas.Reg. § 1.338–10(a)(2). See Chapter 15 for discussion of consolidated groups. Section 338(h)(9) requires that, except as provided in § 338(h)(10), a target corporation is not treated as a member of any affiliated group with respect to the deemed sale of its assets; this precludes the use of net operating losses or capital losses of the purchaser (or its consolidated group) to offset the gain recognized on the deemed sale. However, if the acquiring corporation on the same acquisition date made qualified stock purchases with respect to two or more corporations that were members of the same consolidated group prior to the purchases, a consolidated deemed sale return covering all of such corporations may be filed. I.R.C. § 338(h)(15); Treas.Reg. § 1.338–10(a)(4).

While the target corporation nominally bears the liability for any taxes generated by the § 338 deemed sale, economically the burden is borne by the purchasing corporation, except to the extent that the purchase price is reduced to reflect the tax burden.

7.   SECTION 338(h)(10) ELECTION ON ACQUISITION OF A
     SUBSIDIARY FROM AFFILIATED GROUP

7.1. *Section 338(h)(10): Purchase of Stock of Subsidiary from Consolidated
     or Affiliated Group*

A special rule is available when a corporation makes a qualified stock purchase of the stock of a controlled subsidiary of another corporation and the target corporation and the selling parent corporation were members of an affiliated group (defined with reference to § 1504(a)(2)), or filed a consolidated return. Treas.Reg. § 1.338(h)(10)–1(b)(3). Section 338(h)(10) allows a joint election by the acquiring corporation and the former affiliated or consolidated group of the target corporation pursuant to which the gain or loss on the sale of the stock will not be recognized by the selling parent, but the selling group or parent will include on its tax return the gain and loss recognized under § 338(a)(1) by virtue of the § 338 election. See Treas.Reg. § 1.338(h)(10)–1(c)   (extending   § 338(h)(10)   elective   treatment   to nonconsolidated, affiliated group).

In essence, this election permits the selling corporation to treat the sale as if its subsidiary first had made a taxable sale of its assets that, in most cases, was followed by a § 332 liquidation. Treas.Reg. § 1.338(h)(10)–1(d)(3), (4). The Regulations treat both the parent and the subsidiary corporations as if the subsidiary actually had been liquidated, Treas.Reg. § 1.338(h)(10)–1(d)(4)(i), which, as long as the subsidiary is solvent, will be governed by § 332 and § 337, discussed in Chapter 7. As a result, the affiliated group of the selling shareholder corporation bears the tax liability for any gain recognized with respect to the § 338 election. Thus, in the case of a § 338(h)(10) election, neither the ADSP nor the AGUB reflects the tax liability resulting from the deemed sale of the target S corporation's assets. See Treas.Reg. § 1.338(h)(10)–1(e), Ex. 5.

If the § 338(h)(10) route is followed, the tax attributes of the target corporation are inherited by the selling parent corporation. Treas.Reg. § 1.338(h)(10)–1(d)(4)(i). The election results in both corporations being treated as if the subsidiary actually had been liquidated. As long as the subsidiary is solvent, the liquidation will be governed by § 332 with the result that the subsidiary's earnings and profits and NOLs will carry over to the parent under § 381.

The existence of § 338(h)(10) allows the parties to keep the form of the transaction as a sale of stock but have the tax results of an asset sale. Since this situation does not involve a double tax on the sale of the stock and the deemed liquidating sale of assets, a § 338 election remains a viable tax planning technique when § 338(h)(10) is available, despite the repeal of the *General Utilities* doctrine. It is a particularly attractive planning device when the selling group has losses from other activities that will offset the gains on the consolidated return, since § 338(h)(9) does not apply where a § 338(h)(10) election has been made.

7.2. *Consistency Requirements*

Section 338 imposes two statutory consistency requirements. Section 338(f) requires that the acquiring corporation make consistent elections with respect to all "qualified stock purchases" of target corporations that are members of the same affiliated group if the purchases are made within the consistency period defined in § 338(h)(4). Generally, the consistency period begins one year before the first stock purchase of a series that culminates in a qualified stock acquisition and extends until one year after the stock acquisition transaction by which control has been obtained, i.e., a "qualified stock acquisition" has been completed. Section § 338(h)(4)(B) extends the consistency period in limited circumstances.

The second consistency rule is in § 338(e), which provides for a deemed § 338 election if the acquiring corporation or any of its affiliates purchase any assets (other than in the ordinary course of business) from the target corporation or any of its affiliates during the period beginning one year before the first stock acquisition that is part of a qualified stock purchase and ending one year after the date of the transaction by which the acquiring corporation acquired 80% control of the target corporation.

Both of these consistency rules are vestigial provisions of the era when, due to the *General Utilities* rule, a § 338 election resulted in a tax free step-up in basis. The consistency rules were designed to minimize the possibilities for an acquiring corporation to structure an acquisition to obtain a tax free step-up in basis for gain assets while avoiding a step-down in the basis of loss assets, for which no loss deduction was allowed. Generally, after 1986 this problem no longer exists because the step-up in basis under § 338 is coupled with recognition of gain and loss. Thus, Treas.Reg. § 1.338–4(a) provides that neither the asset consistency rules of § 338(e) nor the stock consistency rules of § 338(f) will be applied except in narrow circumstances.

Under the Regulations, the asset consistency rules will be applied to situations in which an asset is acquired from a target corporation and the target corporation is a member of an affiliated group filing a consolidated return (see Chapter 15). This rule is necessary because the asset purchase would result in an investment adjustment increasing the parent's basis in its stock in the target corporation, thereby reducing the gain realized on the sale of the target corporation stock. The asset consistency rules also apply in situations in which a nonconsolidated target corporation pays a dividend to its selling parent prior to the sale of the target stock and the dividend is subject to the 100% dividends paid deduction under § 243. This rule is required because the transaction might have a result similar to that in the investment adjustment accounts in consolidated returns; the tax free dividend reduces the gain realized on the sale even though the overall before-tax proceeds realized by the selling corporation, including the dividend, equal the amount that would have been realized on a sale of the subsidiary's stock without the prior payment of the dividend. Finally, the asset consistency rules apply in the case of assets acquired from affiliates of the target if an arrangement to avoid the consistency requirement exists. See Treas.Reg. § 1.338–8(a)(3), (f), (j).

When these limited asset consistency rules apply, rather than imposing a deemed § 338 election when none has been made (as provided in § 338(e)), Treas.Reg. § 1.338–8(a)(2) requires that the purchasing corporation take a carryover basis for all assets acquired from the target corporation during the consistency period if the target corporation is a subsidiary in a consolidated group. Thus, for example, if S Corporation and its controlled subsidiary T Corporation are members of a consolidated group, the consistency rules apply if P Corporation on July 1, Year 4, purchases an asset from T and then any time before July 2, Year 5, makes a qualified stock purchase of the stock of T Corporation from S Corporation. The asset purchased from T Corporation on July 1, Year 4, will have a carryover basis in P Corporation's hands unless a § 338 election is made with respect to the qualified stock purchase. Treas.Reg. § 1.338–8(e)(2), Ex. 1. If P Corporation makes a § 338 election, the asset consistency rules are not applicable. As a result, the purchasing corporation is given the choice of having all of the assets of the target corporation acquired during the consistency period take either a transferred basis or a stepped-up basis by making or not making a § 338 election.

Treas.Reg. § 1.338–8(a)(6) provides that the stock consistency rules of § 338(f) normally will not be applied. Thus, for example, if P Corporation purchases all of the stock of T Corporation, which owns controlled subsidiary S Corporation, P Corporation may make a § 338 election with respect to T Corporation without making an election with respect to S Corporation. See Treas.Reg. § 1.338–8(e)(2), Ex. 6. Similarly, if P Corporation purchases at least 80% of the stock of S Corporation from T Corporation and then also purchases at least 80% of the stock of R Corporation from T Corporation within the consistency period, the stock consistency rules normally should not apply. The stock consistency rules will be applied only if necessary to prevent avoidance of the asset consistency rules.

8.   SECTION 336(e) ELECTIONS: STOCK TRANSFER TREATED AS ASSETS TRANSFER

8.1. *Generally*

Section 336(e), enacted as part of the Tax Reform Act of 1986 in conjunction with the repeal of the *General Utilities* doctrine, authorizes Regulations allowing a corporation that sells, exchanges, or distributes stock in another corporation (target) meeting the requirements of § 1504(a)(2) to elect to treat the disposition as a sale of all of the target's underlying assets in lieu of treating it as sale, exchange, or distribution of stock. See Treas.Reg. § 1.336–2(a). The purpose of a § 336(e) election is to prevent creation of a triple layer of taxation—one at the controlled corporation level, one at the transferor corporation level, and, ultimately, one at the shareholder level. Assume, for example, that individual A owns all of the stock of P Corporation, which in turn owns all of the stock of T Corporation, and B, an individual, purchases all of the T Corporation stock from P Corporation. In some cases this transaction produces "triple" taxation as a result of the repeal of *General Utilities*. P Corporation recognizes a taxable gain on the sale of the stock of T Corporation; if A were to liquidate P Corporation to acquire the proceeds from the sale of T Corporation, A would recognize a taxable gain on the liquidation (assuming that P Corporation's sole asset was the cash proceeds from the sale of T Corporation, P Corporation would recognize no gain on the liquidation). Because B is an individual, T Corporation would recognize gain under § 336 if B liquidated T Corporation to acquire its assets (assuming that the purchase price equaled the value of the assets, B would not realize any gain on the liquidation). Thus, a triple tax would have resulted from the removal of both the assets and the sale proceeds from corporate solution.

Treas. Regs. §§ 1.336–0 through 1.336–5 provide the requirements, mechanics for, and consequences of treating as an asset sale a stock sale, exchange, or distribution that is not eligible for a § 338 election. Under the Regulations, the results of a § 336(e) election generally are the same (with certain exceptions) as those of a § 338(h)(10) election. The structure of the Regulations resembles the § 338(h)(10) Regulations regarding the allocation of consideration, application of the asset and stock consistency rules, treatment of minority shareholders, and the availability of the § 453 installment method, although certain definitions and concepts differ to reflect differences between § 336 and § 338(h)(10). A transaction that meets the definition of both a qualified stock disposition and a qualified stock purchase under § 338(d)(3) generally will be treated only as a qualified stock purchase and does not qualify for a § 336(e) election. Treas.Reg. § 1.336–1(b)(6)(ii).

A qualified stock disposition for which a § 336(e) election may be made is any transaction or series of transactions in which stock meeting the requirements of § 1504(a)(2) (80% of voting power and value) of a domestic corporation is either sold, exchanged, or distributed, or any combination thereof, by another domestic corporation or the shareholders of an S corporation in a disposition (as defined in Treas.Reg. § 1.336–1(b)(5)), during the 12-month disposition period (as defined in Treas.Reg. § 1.336–1(b)(7)). (For this purpose, all members of a consolidated group are treated as a single transferor. Treas.Reg. § 1.336–2(g)(2)). Stock transferred to a related party (determined after the transfer) is not considered in determining whether there has been a qualified stock disposition. Treas. Regs. §§ 1.336–1(b)(5)(i)(C) and 1.336–1(b)(6)(i). A § 336(e) election is available for qualifying dispositions of target stock to non-corporate transferees, as well as to corporate transferees. Treas.Reg. § 1.336–1(b)(2).

Because the Regulations require only that stock meeting the requirements of § 1504(a)(2) be transferred, the transferor (or a member of its consolidated group) may retain a portion of the stock of the target. Treas. Regs. §§ 1.336–2(b)(1)(v) and 1.336–2(b)(2)(iv). Furthermore, the Regulations allow amounts of target stock transferred to different transferees in different types of transactions to be aggregated in determining whether there has been a qualified stock disposition. For example, the sale of 50% of the target's stock to an unrelated person and a distribution of another 30% to its unrelated shareholders (who might or might not be the purchasers of the 50% that was sold) within a 12-month period would constitute a qualified stock disposition. Treas.Reg. § 1.336–1(b)(5).

8.2. *Election Procedures*

Under Treas.Reg. § 1.336–2(h) the election is made by the transferor and the target by entering into a binding written agreement before the due date of the tax return for the year of the stock disposition and filing a required statement of election with the tax return for the appropriate year.

The consent of both transferor and the target (effectively on behalf of the buyer(s)) are required to avoid surprises to the transferee.[9] The target must retain a copy of the written agreement. If the seller and target are members of a consolidated group, the seller and target must enter into a binding written agreement, retained by the parent of the consolidated group, and the common parent of the group must attach an election statement to the consolidated return for the year of the disposition.

A holder of nonrecently disposed stock may irrevocably elect (similar to the election under § 338) to treat the nonrecently disposed stock as being sold on the disposition date. Treas.Reg. § 1.336–4(c). The gain recognition election is mandatory if a purchaser owns (after applying § 318(a), other than § 318(a)(4)) 80% or more of the voting power or value of target stock. Treas. Regs. §§ 1.336–1(b)(15) and 1.336–4(c).

A taxpayer is allowed to make a protective § 336(e) election if it is unsure whether a transaction constitutes a qualified stock disposition, e.g., the disposition date is the first day of the 12-month disposition period that may span two taxable years. A protective election will have no effect if the transaction does not constitute a qualified stock disposition, but it will otherwise be binding and irrevocable. Treas.Reg. § 1.336–2(j).

8.3. *Sales or Exchanges of Target Stock*

In general, if a corporation sells or exchanges target stock in a qualified stock disposition, the treatment of old target, seller, and purchaser are similar to the treatment of target (old target), the selling corporation, and the purchasing corporation under § 338(h)(10). If a § 336(e) election is made, Treas.Reg. § 1.336–2(b)(1)(i)(A) provides that the sale or exchange of target stock is disregarded. Instead, target (old target) is treated as selling all of its assets to an unrelated corporation in a single transaction at the close of the disposition date (the deemed asset disposition). Old target recognizes the deemed disposition tax consequences from the deemed asset disposition on the disposition date while it is a subsidiary of seller. Treas.Reg. § 1.336– 2(b)(1)(i)(A). Old target is then treated as liquidating into seller, which, if the seller is a corporation, in most cases will be treated as a § 332 liquidation to which § 337 applies. Treas.Reg. § 1.336–2(b)(1)(iii).

The target is treated as having purchased all of its assets from an unrelated party. Treas.Reg. § 1.336–2(b)(1)(ii). If the target was an S corporation and still qualifies for an S election, a new election is required to maintain S corporation status. Treas.Reg. § 1.336–2(b)(1)(ii). Additionally, the deemed purchase of the assets of old target by new target constitutes a deemed purchase of any subsidiary stock owned by target, and a § 336(e) election may be made for the deemed purchase of the stock of a target subsidiary if it constitutes a qualified stock disposition. A § 336(e) election generally does not affect the tax consequences (e.g., stock basis) to a purchaser of target stock.

---

[9]   An election for an S corporation target requires a binding written agreement between the target S corporation and all of the S corporation shareholders, including shareholders who do not sell stock, before the due date of the tax return for the year of the stock disposition and an election statement attached to the return for the year of the disposition.

8.4. *Distributions of Target Stock Not Subject to § 355*

A § 336(e) election can be made for a taxable distribution of target stock (e.g., dividend, redemption, liquidation), but the election does not affect the tax treatment of the shareholders. Special rules assure that the tax consequences to a distributee are the same as if no § 336(e) election was made. Treas.Reg. § 1.336–1(b)(5). If a distribution is a qualified stock disposition, the distributing corporation is treated as purchasing from new target (immediately after the deemed liquidation of old target) the amount of stock distributed and to have distributed the new target stock to its shareholders. Treas.Reg. § 1.336–2(b)(1)(i)(A). The distributing corporation recognizes no gain or loss on the distribution (old target having recognized gain on the deemed asset sale). Treas.Reg. § 1.336–2(b)(1)(i)(A). If the distribution is a § 301 distribution, the portion that is a dividend may be affected by the difference between (1) the § 311 gain, and thus earnings and profits, that would have been recognized on a stock distribution and (2) the gain, and thus earnings and profits, that results from the deemed asset disposition and liquidation of target. See Treas.Reg. § 1.336–2(c). Realized losses on the deemed asset disposition are allowed to offset realized gains, Treas.Reg. § 1.336–2(b)(1)(i)(B)(2)(i). The Regulations, however, disallow a net loss recognized on the deemed asset disposition in proportion to the amount of stock disposed of by the seller in one or more distributions during the 12-month disposition period. Treas.Reg. § 1.336–2(b)(1)(i)(B)(2)(ii), (iii).

8.5. *Aggregate Deemed Asset Disposition Price (ADADP) and Adjusted Grossed-Up Basis (AGUB)*

To calculate old target's gain under a § 336(e) election, the Regulations define a new term, "aggregate deemed asset disposition price" (ADADP). New target's asset basis is determined with reference to adjusted grossed-up basis (AGUB), as used in § 338 and Treas.Reg. § 1.338–5. Under Treas.Reg. §§ 1.336–3 and 1.336–4, ADADP and AGUB are determined similarly to the way ADSP and AGUB are determined under the § 338 Regulations. The Regulations account for the lack of an actual amount realized on a stock distribution by treating the grossed-up amount realized as including the fair market value of distributed target stock on the date of distribution. Treas.Reg. § 1.336–3(c)(1)(i)(B). In addition, because in the case of a § 336(e) election (unlike in the case of a § 338 election, where there is only one purchasing corporation and it is relatively easy to determine the purchaser's basis in nonrecently purchased stock in order to determine AGUB), there can be multiple purchasers or distributees who acquired target stock prior to the 12-month disposition period, the Regulations provide that "nonrecently disposed stock," which has a similar meaning to the term "nonrecently purchased stock" in § 338(b)(6)(B), includes only stock in a target corporation held by a purchaser (or a related person) who owns (with § 318(a) attribution, except § 318(a)(4)), at least 10% of the total voting power or value of the stock of target that is not recently disposed stock. Treas.Reg. § 1.336–1(b)(18).

New target is treated as acquiring all of its assets from an unrelated person in a single transaction at the close of the disposition date, but before the deemed liquidation (or, in the case of a § 355 distribution, before the distribution) in exchange for an amount equal to the AGUB. With certain modifications, Treas.Reg. § 1.336–4 generally resembles Treas.Reg. § 1.338–5 to determine target's AGUB for target. New target allocates AGUB among its assets in the same manner as in Treas. Regs. §§ 1.338–6 and 1.338–7. Treas.Regs. § 1.336–2(b)(1)(ii) and (b)(2)(ii).

Any stock retained by a seller (or a member of its consolidated group) is treated as acquired by the seller on the day after the disposition date at its fair market value, which is a proportionate amount of the grossed-up amount realized on the transfer under the § 336(e) election. Treas.Regs. § 1.336–2(b)(1)(v) and (b)(2)(iv). A continuing minority shareholder is generally unaffected by the § 336(e) election. Treas.Reg. § 1.336–2(d).

9. SPECIAL PROBLEMS OF SUBORDINATED CONVERTIBLE DEBENTURES: SECTION 279

Suppose the purchaser does not have sufficient cash or borrowing power to finance the purchase of either the stock or assets of the target corporation. In this case, the purchasing corporation may try to bootstrap the transaction by utilizing the future earnings of the acquired corporation and, optimally, to pay out those earnings in a deductible manner, i.e., as interest on debt incurred to finance the acquisition. In the late 1960s, Congress became concerned over acquisition activities that involved as the payment vehicle the use of various kinds of debt instruments, frequently convertible into the common stock of the acquiring corporation. This use of convertible debt had several advantages in the acquisition. Because interest on the debentures was deductible the corporation was willing to pay a much higher price for the acquired corporation; if the selling shareholders could report the gain under the installment method of § 453, taxation of the gain realized on the transaction could be deferred for many years; and the convertibility feature gave to the shareholders of the acquired corporation the opportunity to secure an equity interest in the acquiring corporation at a future date.

In the Tax Reform Act of 1969, Congress took several steps to restrict the use of convertible debentures by corporations engaged in aggressive acquisition programs. Installment payment treatment under § 453 was denied to selling shareholders who received readily marketable debentures.[10] See I.R.C. § 453(f)(4). The original issue discount rules, discussed in Chapter 3, required the debenture holders to include the discount in income over the life of the debentures. Finally, Congress added § 279, which disallows the interest deduction to the acquiring corporation on certain "corporate acquisition indebtedness."

In brief, § 279 disallows a deduction for interest on debt obligations issued by a corporation to acquire the stock or assets of another corporation (in the case of asset acquisitions only if such assets constitute at least two-thirds of the value of all of the assets used in the trades or businesses carried on by the acquired corporation) if all of the following conditions are met:

(1) The obligation is subordinated to the claims of trade creditors generally or expressly subordinated to any substantial amount of unsecured

---

[10] Section 453 has since been amended also to preclude installment reporting of gains from the sale of publicly traded stock.

indebtedness, whether presently outstanding or subsequently issued, of the issuing corporation;

(2) The obligation is convertible into the stock of the issuing corporation or is part of an investment unit that includes an option to acquire stock in the issuing corporation (through warrants, rights, etc.); and

(3) Either the ratio of debt to equity of the issuing corporation after the issuance of the obligation exceeds 2:1, or the "projected earnings" of the issuing corporation (or of the combined corporations, if "control" has been acquired), do not exceed three times the annual interest to be paid or incurred with respect to the obligation.

In order to avoid the disallowance of the interest deduction under § 279, a corporation need only avoid any one of the conditions. Thus, for example, a corporation's obligations will not be affected by § 279 if not subordinated to trade creditors generally, even though the obligations may be subordinated to a very substantial amount of secured debt. In addition, as another hurdle to the application of § 279, interest on "acquisition indebtedness" must exceed $5 million annually in order for the provision to apply. And then, only the acquisition indebtedness interest in excess of the $5 million safe harbor threshold is disallowed. For a corporation that pays 8% interest, this means that it can have outstanding $62.5 million dollars of debt without running afoul of § 279. There is also a de minimis rule that provides § 279 will not apply if the issuing corporation after the transaction owns less than 5% of the voting stock of the corporation whose stock has been acquired with the debt. Finally, the provisions in § 279(d)(3) and (4) offer means for removing the § 279 "taint" once acquired.

The debt-equity principles discussed in Chapter 3, take precedence over § 279, so that it would be possible for an obligation to fall outside the conditions of § 279 but for a deduction for the interest on the obligation still to be disallowed on the grounds that the instrument constituted an equity instrument. See Treas.Reg. § 1.279–1, –7. In addition, new § 163(j), added to the Code in 2017 and discussed in Chapter 3, imposes limitations applicable to business interest deductions more generally.

PROBLEM SET 3

1.   George owned all of the stock of Arpix, Inc., which produces software for 3D computer animation for the film industry. George's basis in the stock was $1,000,000. George sold all of the stock to Steve for $10,000,000 in cash. At that time Arpix owed $1,000,000 to the Millennium National Bank. Arpix asset's consisted of a copyright with a basis of $500,000 and computer equipment with a basis of $50,000.

(a)   What is the total amount realized by George?

(b)   What is Steve's basis in the Arpix stock?

(c)   How much gain or loss does Arpix recognize?

(d)   What is Arpix's basis in its assets?

2.   West Electric Corporation produces and sells cellular telephones. Mabel owned all of the stock of West Electric. Mabel's basis for the stock was

$2,000,000. West's assets on the balance sheet (and estimates of the current fair market value of each asset) are as follows:

Asset	Basis	FMV
Marketable securities	$ 500,000	$ 600,000
Accounts receivable	$1,000,000	$ 900,000
Inventory	$1,000,000	$6,000,000
Land	$1,000,000	$2,500,000
Factory	$1,500,000	$4,000,000
Franchise agreements with cellular service providers	$ 0	$1,000,000
Patents	$ 0	$5,000,000

West Electric owed $5,000,000 to the Monopolistic National Bank. Centel Corp. purchased all of Mabel's stock of West Electric for cash.

(a) (1) What are the tax consequences to all parties if the cash purchase price was $19,750,000 and Centel does not make a § 338 election?

(2) What are the tax consequences to all parties if the cash purchase price was $19,750,000 and Centel makes a § 338 election?

(3) What are the tax consequences to all parties if the cash purchase price was $10,270,000 and Centel makes a § 338 election?

3. (a) Great Wall Automotive Corp. began purchasing stock of Studebaker Car Corporation on the New York Stock exchange on January 2 of last year. By April 15 of last year, Great Wall had acquired 21% of the stock of Studebaker. Between April 16 of last year and January 2 of this year. Great Wall acquired an additional 58% of Studebaker, for a total of 79%. On April 17 of this year Great Wall acquired the remaining 21% of Studebaker from a single institutional investor. May Great Wall make a § 338 election with respect to Studebaker?

(b) Suppose that during a single calendar year Great Wall Automotive Corp. purchased exactly 80% of the stock of Studebaker Car Corporation in stock exchange transactions for an aggregate purchase price of $15,800,000. Studebaker's basis in its assets was $5,000,000 and it had no outstanding debts. If Great Wall makes a § 338 election with respect to Studebaker, what is the resulting aggregate basis in Studebaker's assets?

4. Earleton Boatworks, Inc. manufactures and sells bass-fishing boats. All of the stock of Earleton Boatworks is owned by Richard's & Son's Pecan Farm & Real Estate Development Corp. Earleton Boatworks, Inc.'s assets on the balance sheet (and estimates of the current fair market value of each asset) are as follows:

Asset	Basis	FMV
Marketable securities	$ 500,000	$ 600,000
Accounts receivable	$1,000,000	$ 900,000
Inventory	$5,000,000	$6,000,000
Land	$1,000,000	$2,500,000
Factory	$1,500,000	$4,000,000
Franchise agreements with boat dealers	$ 0	$1,000,000
Patents	$ 0	$5,000,000
Goodwill	$ 0	$5,000,000

Earleton Boatworks owed $5,000,000 to the Gator National Bank. If Bassamatic Corp. purchased all of the stock of Earleton Boatworks for $20,000,000 in cash, should Richard's & Son's and Bassamatic make a § 338(h)(10) election?

(a) Assume Richard's & Son's basis for its Earleton Boatworks stock was $3,000,000.

(b) Assume Richard's & Son's basis for its Earleton Boatworks stock was $7,000,000.

5.   Assume that individual A owns all of the stock of P Corp., which in turn owns all of the stock of T Corp. A's basis for the stock of P is $100, and the fair market value of the stock is $500. P Corp.'s only asset is the T Corp. stock, with a basis of $100 and a fair market value of $500. T Corp. has assets with a basis of $100 and a fair market value of $500. (Note that T Corp.'s assets are the only tangible property involved in the problem.)

(a) If P liquidates T and sells the T assets to individual B for $500, after which P liquidates and distributes the cash to A, what are the tax consequences?

(b) If P sells the stock of T to B for $500, after which B liquidates T and A liquidates P, what are the tax consequences?

(c) How do you explain any difference in your answers to questions (a) and (b) in light of the fact that the end results are the same? Are P and T able to make a § 336(e) election? Should they do so? What are the tax consequences if they do?

CHAPTER 9

DISTRIBUTIONS MADE IN CONNECTION WITH THE SALE OF A CORPORATE BUSINESS: "BOOTSTRAP" ACQUISITIONS

The sale of a corporate business may be accompanied by a reduction in the size of the corporation prior to the sale. There can be a variety of motivations for structuring the transaction in this manner. The corporation may have assets that the purchaser does not wish to acquire. Alternatively, the purchaser may not be able to afford the "full" corporation and may wish to have it reduced in size prior to the acquisition, thus acquiring a smaller corporation for a correspondingly smaller purchase price. Finally, tax planning to maximize the after-tax proceeds to the seller sometimes may be a principal purpose for the structure of the sale and purchase.

The reduction in size of the corporation can take place either through a redemption of some of the shares of an existing shareholder or through a dividend distribution to the shareholder. Which technique is preferable may depend in part on the status of the shareholder. When dividends were taxed at ordinary tax rates, as they generally were prior to 2004, a redemption distribution taxed as a capital gain under § 302 was more advantageous to an individual shareholder than the ordinary income treatment that a normal dividend distribution would receive. For years after 2003, however, with dividends taxed to individuals at the same rate as long-term capital gains, there is much less at stake for a selling individual shareholder. For an individual shareholder receiving the distribution, the only important differences are that (1) all of a dividend distribution is includable in gross income, while only the amount by which a redemption distribution exceeds the basis of the stock with respect to which the distribution has been made is includable, and (2) gains on redemption distributions can be offset by capital losses, while dividend income cannot be offset by capital losses, except that § 1211(b) allows individuals to deduct up to $3,000 of capital losses in excess of capital gains. Unless the shareholder has otherwise unusable capital losses, tax liability will be unaffected in cases in which the shareholder receiving the distribution disposes of all of the shareholder's stock as part of the series of transactions, because full basis recovery will be allowed. If, however, the shareholder receiving the distribution retains some stock in the corporation, then the issue of the proper amount of basis that may offset the distribution remains.

If the shareholder is a corporation, dividend treatment, with a corresponding intercorporate dividend deduction under § 243, may be preferable to recognizing capital gain on the sale of the stock, depending on the basis of the stock. In addition, the timing of the distribution is important because the redemption or dividend distribution may be deemed to have taken place after the actual ownership of the stock has been transferred to the purchaser by the seller. In some cases whether the distribution is characterized as a redemption or as a dividend turns on when the distribution is considered to have been made. The materials that follow are concerned with various aspects of the issues created by distributions to individual shareholders and corporate shareholders, respectively, in connection with the sale of corporate stock.

SECTION 1.   BOOTSTRAP TRANSACTIONS INVOLVING INDIVIDUALS: CAPITAL GAIN VERSUS ORDINARY INCOME

Holsey v. Commissioner

United States Court of Appeals, Third Circuit, 1958.
258 F.2d 865.

■ MARIS, CIRCUIT JUDGE. This is a petition to review a decision of the Tax Court. * * * The facts as found by the Tax Court, some of which were stipulated, may be summarized as follows:

J.R. Holsey Sales Company, a New Jersey corporation, was organized on April 28, 1936, as an Oldsmobile dealership. Taxpayer has been president and a director of the company since its organization. Only 20 shares were issued out of the 2,500 shares of no par value stock authorized; these 20 shares were issued to Greenville Auto Sales Company, a Chevrolet dealership, in exchange for all of the latter's right, title, and interest to the Oldsmobile franchise and other assets with respect to the franchise which had been owned and operated by the Greenville Company. The 20 shares issued were assigned a value of $11,000. Taxpayer's father, Charles V. Holsey, in 1936, owned more than two-thirds of the outstanding stock of the Greenville Company, and taxpayer was vice-president and a director of that corporation.

On April 30, 1936, taxpayer acquired from the Greenville Company an option to purchase 50% of the outstanding shares of the Holsey Company for $11,000, and a further option to purchase, within ten years after the exercise of the first option, all the remaining shares for a sum to be agreed upon. The Greenville Company owned all of the outstanding stock of the Holsey Company from its organization in 1936 until November, 1939, when taxpayer exercised his first option and purchased 50% of the outstanding stock of the Holsey Company for $11,000.

On June 28, 1946, the further option in favor of taxpayer was revised. Under the terms of the revised option, taxpayer was granted the right to purchase the remaining outstanding shares of the Holsey Company at any time up to and including June 28, 1951, for $80,000. The revised option was in favor of taxpayer individually and was not assignable by him to anyone other than a corporation in which he owned not less than 50% of the voting stock. On the date of the revision of this option, taxpayer's father owned 76% of the stock of the Greenville Company and taxpayer was a vice-president and director of that corporation. On April 28, 1948, the Holsey Company declared a 3-for-1 stock dividend and the common stock was allocated a value of $750 per share. This stock dividend increased the outstanding stock to 80 shares which was held in equal amounts by taxpayer and the Greenville Company.

On January 19, 1951, taxpayer assigned his revised option to the Holsey Company; on the same date the Holsey Company exercised the option and paid the Greenville Company $80,000 for the stock held by it. This transaction resulted in taxpayer becoming the owner of 100% of the outstanding stock of the Holsey Company. In his income tax return for the year 1951, taxpayer gave no effect to this transaction.

The principal officers and only directors of the Holsey Company from April 28, 1936, to December 31, 1951, were taxpayer, his brother, Charles D. Holsey, and their father, Charles V. Holsey. On January 19, 1951, when the revised option was exercised, the earned surplus of the Holsey Company was in excess of $300,000.

The Oldsmobile franchise, under which the Holsey Company operated, was a yearly contract entered into by the Corporation and the manufacturer in reliance upon the personal qualifications and representations of taxpayer as an individual. It was the manufacturer's policy to have its dealers own all of the stock in dealership organizations.

The Commissioner determined that the effect of the transaction of January 19, 1951, wherein the Holsey Company paid $80,000 to the Greenville Company for 50% of the outstanding stock of the Holsey Company, constituted a dividend to taxpayer, the remaining stockholder. The Commissioner therefore asserted a deficiency against taxpayer in the sum of $41,385.34. The Tax Court sustained the Commissioner. 28 T.C. 962.

The question presented for decision in this case is whether the Tax Court erred in holding that the payment by the Holsey Company of $80,000 to the Greenville Company for the purchase from that company of its stock in the Holsey Company was essentially equivalent to the distribution of a taxable dividend to the taxpayer, the remaining stockholder of the Holsey Company. To determine that question we must begin with the applicable statute [reference is made to the predecessors of § 316(a) and § 302].

It will be observed that [§ 316(a)] defines a dividend as a distribution made by a corporation "to its shareholders". Accordingly unless a distribution which is sought to be taxed to a stockholder as a dividend is made to him or for his benefit it may not be regarded as either a dividend or the legal equivalent of a dividend. Here the distribution was made to the Greenville Company, not to the taxpayer. This the Government, of course, concedes but urges that it was made for the benefit of the taxpayer. It is true that it has been held that a distribution by a corporation in redemption of stock which the taxpayer stockholder has a contractual obligation to purchase is essentially the equivalent of a dividend to him since it operates to discharge his obligation. Wall v. United States, 4 Cir., 1947, 164 F.2d 462; Ferro v. Commissioner of Internal Revenue, 3 Cir., 1957, 242 F.2d 838; Zipp v. Commissioner of Internal Revenue, 6 Cir., 1958, 259 F.2d 119. But where, as here, the taxpayer was never under any legal obligation to purchase the stock held by the other stockholder, the Greenville Company, having merely an option to purchase which he did not exercise but instead assigned to the Holsey Company, the distribution did not discharge any obligation of his and did not benefit him in any direct sense.

It is, of course, true that the taxpayer was benefited indirectly by the distribution. The value of his own stock was increased, since the redemption was for less than book value, and he became sole stockholder. But these benefits operated only to increase the value of the taxpayer's stock holdings; they could not give rise to taxable income within the meaning of the Sixteenth Amendment until the corporation makes a distribution to the taxpayer or his stock is sold. Eisner v. Macomber, 1920, 252 U.S. 189 * * *; Schmitt v. Commissioner of Internal Revenue, 3 Cir., 1954, 208 F.2d 819. * * * We think that the principle thus stated is equally applicable here. Indeed the Tax Court itself has so held in essentially similar cases. S.K. Ames, Inc. v. Commissioner, 1942, 46 B.T.A. 1020; Fred F. Fischer v. Commissioner, 1947, 6 T.C.M. 520.

The question whether payments made by a corporation in the acquisition and redemption of its stock are essentially equivalent to the distribution of a taxable dividend has been often before the courts and certain criteria have been enunciated. The most significant of these is said to be whether the distribution leaves the proportionate interests of the stockholders unchanged as occurs when a true dividend is paid. Ferro v. Commissioner of Internal Revenue, 3 Cir., 1957, 242 F.2d 838, 841. The application of that criterion to the facts of this case compels the conclusion that in the absence of a direct pecuniary benefit to the taxpayer the Tax Court erred in holding the distribution in question taxable to him. For in his case prior to the distribution the taxpayer and the Greenville Company each had a 50% interest in the Holsey Company whereas after it was over the taxpayer had 100% of the outstanding stock and the Greenville Company none.

The Government urges the lack of a corporate purpose for the distribution and the taxpayer seeks to establish one. But we do not consider this point for, as we have recently held, "It is the effect of the redemption, rather than the purpose which actuated it, which controls the determination of dividend equivalence." Kessner v. Commissioner of Internal Revenue, 3 Cir., 1957, 248 F.2d 943, 944. Nor need we discuss the present position of the Government that the transaction must be treated as a sham and the purchase of the stock as having been made by the taxpayer through his alter ego, the Holsey Company. For the Tax Court made no such finding, doubtless in view of the fact that at the time the taxpayer owned only 50% of the stock and was in a minority on the board of directors. On the contrary that court based its decision on the benefit which the distribution by the corporation to the Greenville Company conferred upon the taxpayer, which it thought gave rise to taxable income in his hands.

For the reasons stated we think that the Tax Court erred in its decision. The decision will accordingly be reversed and the cause remanded for further proceedings not inconsistent with this opinion.

■ McLAUGHLIN, CIRCUIT JUDGE (dissenting). I think that the net effect of the facile operation disclosed in this case amounts to the distribution of a taxable dividend to the taxpayer. I do not think that the Schmitt decision controls here. Quite the contrary to the Schmitt facts, this taxpayer himself acquired a valuable option to buy the shares and solely on the theory of a gift of the option rights would make the corporation the true purchaser. I agree with the Tax Court that "The assignment of the option contract to J.R. Holsey Sales Co. was clearly for the purpose of having that company pay the $80,000 in exercise of the option that was executed for petitioner's personal benefit. The payment was intended to secure and did secure for petitioner exactly what it was always intended he should get if he made the payment personally, namely, all of the stock in J.R. Holsey Sales Co."

I would affirm the Tax Court decision.

Zenz v. Quinlivan

United States Court of Appeals, Sixth Circuit, 1954.
213 F.2d 914.

■ GOURLEY, DISTRICT JUDGE.

The appeal relates to the interpretation of [§ 302] of the Internal Revenue Code and poses the question—

Is a distribution of substantially all of the accumulated earnings and surplus of a corporation, which are not necessary to the conduct of the business of the corporation, in redemption of all outstanding shares of stock of said corporation owned by one person *essentially equivalent to the distribution of a taxable dividend under the Internal Revenue Code?*

* * *

Appellant is the widow of the person who was the motivating spirit behind the closed corporation which engaged in the business of excavating and laying of sewers. Through death of her husband she became the owner of all shares of stock issued by the corporation. She operated the business until remarriage, when her second husband assumed the management. As a result of a marital rift, separation, and final divorce, taxpayer sought to dispose of her company to a competitor who was anxious to eliminate competition.

Prospective buyer did not want to assume the tax liabilities which it was believed were inherent in the accumulated earnings and profits of the corporation. To avoid said profits and earnings as a source of future taxable dividends, buyer purchased part of taxpayer's stock for cash. Three weeks later, after corporate reorganization and corporate action, the corporation redeemed the balance of taxpayer's stock, purchasing the same as treasury stock which absorbed substantially all of the accumulated earnings and surplus of the corporation.

Taxpayer, in her tax return, invoked [the predecessor of § 302(b)] as constituting a cancellation or redemption by a corporation of all the stock of a particular shareholder, and therefore was not subject to being treated as a distribution of a taxable dividend.

The District Court sustained the deficiency assessment of the Commissioner that the amount received from accumulated earnings and profits was ordinary income since the stock redeemed by the corporation was "at such time and in such manner as to make the redemption thereof essentially equivalent to the distribution of a taxable dividend" * * *.

The District Court's findings were premised upon the view that taxpayer employed a circuitous approach in an attempt to avoid the tax consequences which would have attended the outright distribution of the surplus to the taxpayer by the declaration of a taxable dividend.

The rationale of the District Court is dedicated to piercing the external manifestations of the taxpayer's transactions in order to establish a subterfuge or sham.

Nevertheless, the general principle is well settled that a taxpayer has the legal right to decrease the amount of what otherwise would be his taxes or altogether avoid them, by means which the law permits. Gregory v. Helvering, 293 U.S. 465, 469, 55 S.Ct. 266 * * *. The taxpayer's motive to avoid taxation will not establish liability if the transaction does not do so without it. Chamberlain v. Commissioner of Internal Revenue, 6 Cir., 207 F.2d 462 * * *.

The question accordingly presented is not whether the overall transaction, admittedly carried out for the purpose of avoiding taxes, actually avoided taxes which would have been incurred if the transaction had taken a different form, but whether the sale constituted a taxable dividend or the sale of a capital asset. * * *

It is a salutary fact that [§ 302(b)] is an exception to [§ 301 and § 316] that all distributions of earning and profits are taxable as a dividend.

The basic precept underlying the capital gains theory of taxation as distinguished from ordinary income tax is the concept that a person who has developed an enterprise in which earnings have been accumulated over a period of years should not be required to expend the ordinary income tax rate in the one year when he withdraws from his enterprise and realizes his gain.

* * *

We cannot concur with the legal proposition enunciated by the District Court that a corporate distribution can be essentially equivalent to a taxable dividend even though that distribution extinguishes the shareholder's interest in the corporation. To the contrary, we are satisfied that where the taxpayer effects a redemption which completely extinguishes the taxpayer's interest in the corporation, and does not retain any beneficial interest whatever, that such transaction is not the equivalent of the distribution of a taxable dividend as to him. Tiffany v. Commissioner of Internal Revenue, 16 T.C. 1443.

The statutory concept of dividend is a distribution out of earnings and profits, and normally it is proportionate to shares and leaves the shareholder holding his shares as his capital investment. Flinn v. Commissioner of Internal Revenue, 37 B.T.A. 1085.

Complete and partial liquidations are treated for the purpose of the statute, as sales with a consequent measure of gain or loss, even though the proceeds may to some extent be derived from earnings. Hellmich v. Hellman, 276 U.S. 233 * * *.

The use of corporate earnings or profits to purchase and make payment for all the shares of a taxpayer's holdings in a corporation is not controlling, and the question as to whether the distribution in connection with the cancellation or the redemption of said stock is essentially equivalent to the distribution of a taxable dividend under the Internal Revenue Code and Treasury Regulation must depend upon the circumstances of each case.

Since the intent of the taxpayer was to bring about a complete liquidation of her holdings and to become separated from all interest in the corporation, the conclusion is inevitable that the distribution of the earnings and profits by the corporation in payment for said stock was not made at such time and in such manner as to make the distribution and cancellation or redemption thereof essentially equivalent to the distribution of a taxable dividend.

* * *

We do not feel that a taxpayer should be penalized for exercising legal means to secure a tax advantage. The conduct of this taxpayer does not appear to contravene the purport or congressional intent of the provisions of the Internal Revenue Act which taxpayer invoked.

We conclude that under the facts and circumstances of the present case the District Court was in error, and the taxpayer is not liable as a distributee of a taxable dividend * * *.

DETAILED ANALYSIS

1.   *HOLSEY* SITUATION IN GENERAL

Suppose A and B each own 50% of the stock of a corporation. A desires to end A's participation and B buys A's stock for its fair market value, $150,000. In effect, B has decided to invest $150,000 more in the corporation, and now owns 100% of a $300,000 corporation. Alternatively, suppose that B did not have sufficient funds or never contemplated buying A's stock. Instead of the above arrangement, therefore, the corporation redeems A's stock for $150,000. B now owns 100% of a corporation worth $150,000. Was the Tax Court, which was reversed by the Court of Appeals in the *Holsey* opinion, supra, saying that in this latter case B has a dividend of $150,000? How has B benefitted? While B is now the sole owner, B is the sole owner of a corporation half as large. Another possible view of the Tax Court decision, which does not rest on a dividend distribution, is that the redemption and consequent change in the interests of the shareholders may be treated as an appropriate occasion to tax any increase in the value of the shares of the remaining shareholders over the tax basis for their shares. But to treat this event as a realization of that gain would be a departure from existing rules. These questions are related to the problem of the proper treatment of the increase in the shareholder's proportionate interest in the corporation caused by a stock dividend, either actual or constructive, see Chapter 6.

Going back to the first situation, suppose that B first had agreed to buy A's stock and then, after B had received the stock and undertaken this obligation, the obligation was assumed by the corporation and it paid A. Here, in form and legal effect, an obligation of B has been discharged by the corporation and B should have dividend income. The relief from a $150,000 debt is the receipt of income. This was the situation in *Zipp*, referred to in the *Holsey* opinion. Suppose then, as the next case, A and B are about to conclude a contract for the purchase by B, and B's lawyer, thinking of taxes, suddenly says the corporation should buy A's stock. The contract is hastily redrawn and the corporation acquires A's stock. Is the case to fall on the dividend side or on the nondividend side? The question here is whether the parties proceeded so far along the "purchase" by B that the taking over of B's obligation by the corporation came too late.

Where does the *Holsey* case itself fall? Certainly the parties were moving along the "purchase by B" route and then changed. Also, the option was a favorable one, since $80,000 was less than the value of 50% of the stock. Let us assume that value was $200,000. To gain this $120,000 benefit, the taxpayer B had to have $80,000. By taking over this option and providing the $80,000, the corporation produced a benefit for the taxpayer B. Is this what the Tax Court had in mind? If so, is the dividend $80,000 or $120,000?

Rev.Rul. 58–614, 1958–2 C.B. 920, states that the IRS will follow the *Holsey* case where the stock was not in reality purchased by the continuing shareholder.

2. TREATMENT OF THE CONTINUING SHAREHOLDER

2.1. *Was the Corporation or the Continuing Shareholder the Purchaser of the Stock?*

2.1.1. *Conditional Versus Unconditional Obligation to Purchase Shares*

The primary issue is whether the continuing shareholder has a "personal, unconditional, primary obligation" to purchase the stock such that the continuing shareholder receives a taxable benefit from the corporation's purchase of stock from the selling shareholder. In Sullivan v. United States, 363 F.2d 724 (8th Cir.1966), the majority shareholder in a corporation was obligated personally to purchase stock from a minority shareholder on the latter's leaving the employ of the corporation. When the minority shareholder left the employ of the corporation, however, instead of purchasing it himself, the majority shareholder caused the corporation to redeem the minority shareholder's stock. The redemption of the employee's shares in lieu of purchase by the majority shareholder under the agreement resulted in a dividend.

In general, however, both the cases and the rulings in this area have been quite favorable to taxpayers. Thus, for example, in Priester v. Commissioner, 38 T.C. 316 (1962), a minority shareholder agreed to purchase the majority interest in a corporation but was financially unable to meet his commitment under the agreement. He then assigned the contract of sale to a third party with an understanding that the shares to be purchased by the third party would be redeemed by the corporation within a short period of time. Seven months following the purchase the shares were redeemed. The court found no dividend to the continuing shareholder since his obligation to the original owner of the stock was extinguished by the third party's purchase of the shares and not by the corporate distribution; the court refused to view the third party as a "straw man" through whom the taxpayer indirectly received the benefit of the corporate distribution. In addition, the Tax Court indicated that it would follow the Court of Appeals holding in *Holsey* that the benefit derived by the shareholder in becoming the sole shareholder of the corporation as a result of the redemption was not a taxable event.

Rev.Rul. 69–608, 1969–2 C.B. 42, discussed a number of commonly recurring situations in which the redemption of stock from retiring shareholders will not result in a constructive dividend to the continuing shareholder. In general, the Ruling allows the continuing shareholder to avoid dividend consequences as long as at the time of the redemption there is no existing primary and unconditional obligation on the continuing shareholder's part to purchase the redeemed shares. Thus, in one situation, A and B owned all of the outstanding stock of a corporation and had an agreement that, on the death of either, the survivor would purchase the decedent's shares from his estate. The cancellation of the agreement prior to the death of either shareholder, in favor of a new contract under which the corporation would redeem the shares of the decedent, was held not to result in a constructive dividend since at the time of the revision of the agreement there was no unconditional obligation to purchase the shares. In another situation dealt with by the ruling, an individual entered into a contract for the purchase of the stock of a corporation. The contract provided that it could be assigned to another corporation, thereby releasing the purchaser from the purchaser's obligations under the contract. The individual organized a corporation and assigned the stock purchase contract to it, the corporation borrowing funds to consummate the transaction. The purchasing corporation was subsequently merged into the acquired corporation, which then satisfied the loan liabilities. The ruling, following Kobacker v. Commissioner, 37 T.C. 882 (1962) (acq.), found no dividend on the repayment of the loan since the shareholder was not unconditionally obligated to purchase the stock. See also Smith v. Commissioner, 70 T.C. 651 (1978) (taxpayer was found to be unconditionally obligated to purchase stock under a stock purchase agreement with one shareholder but not so obligated with respect to another shareholder who only had an option to sell the stock to the taxpayer; consequently only redemptions in connection with the binding stock purchase agreement constituted dividends to the taxpayer).

On the other hand, Rev.Rul. 69–608 makes clear that where the continuing shareholder has become unconditionally bound to purchase the retiring or deceased shareholder's stock, a redemption by the corporation will give rise to a constructive dividend to the continuing shareholder. Thus, a constructive dividend was found where A and B agreed that upon the death of either the survivor would purchase the decedent's stock, and after the death of B, A caused the corporation to redeem the stock from B's estate. But, if the obligation is not unconditional, constructive dividend treatment may be avoided. Thus, the ruling holds that no constructive dividend occurred where A and B and the corporation agreed that upon the death of either A or B, the corporation would redeem the decedent's shares and, to the extent that the corporation did not so redeem the shares, the survivor would purchase them. The same result follows where A agreed that if B desired to sell his shares, A would purchase the shares or cause another person to purchase the shares, and A caused the corporation to purchase the shares.

The results in individual cases turn on whether under state contract law the continuing shareholder has a contractual obligation. For example, in Apschnikat v. United States, 421 F.2d 910 (6th Cir.1970), the court found that the negotiations and correspondence between the purchaser and the sellers resulted in a binding obligation on the purchaser to purchase the stock and were not simply pre-contract dealings. Accordingly, payments for the stock by a corporation to which the purchaser had transferred the sales contract resulted in dividends to him.

If a shareholder of X Corporation is obligated to purchase stock of Y Corporation and, rather than purchasing the Y Corporation stock directly, the shareholder assigns the contractual obligation to X Corporation, which purchases the stock, there is no dividend to the shareholder. In this case X Corporation has not redeemed its own stock. Rather it has received fair value for the amount paid, and thus it is not a distribution. See Citizens Bank & Trust Co. v. United States, 580 F.2d 442 (Ct.Cl.1978).

2.1.2. *Continuing Shareholder as Agent of Corporation*

In situations in which the shares first pass through the continuing shareholder, the courts sometimes may regard the continuing shareholder as an agent acquiring the stock on behalf of the corporation, which was the real purchaser, so that no dividend results. In Bennett v. Commissioner, 58 T.C. 381 (1972) (acq.), the majority shareholder in the corporation wished to terminate his interest. The taxpayer, a minority shareholder, suggested that the corporation redeem the shares but the retiring shareholder (in order not to incur a possible liability to creditors of the corporation because of a depletion of corporate assets) insisted that the taxpayer appear as the purchaser of the shares. It was agreed that the corporation would borrow money to advance to the taxpayer, the latter would then purchase the shares from the retiring shareholder, and the corporation would immediately redeem. The transaction was consummated in this manner and the Tax Court found no dividend, distinguishing the *Wall* case, relied on by the IRS, as follows:

> In *Wall,* the taxpayer in one transaction acquired stock, paid an amount of cash, and obligated himself personally to pay additional amounts; in a subsequent, separate transaction the corporation paid the notes. In contrast, [the taxpayer here] never intended to acquire personal ownership of the Jones stock and never incurred any personal obligation to do so; at all times, he was serving as a conduit or agent for the Corporation in a single, integrated transaction in which it acquired the stock.

A similar result was reached in Ciaio v. Commissioner, 47 T.C. 447 (1967) (acq.), where, as a result of disagreements, two shareholders agreed to sell their stock to the corporation, leaving the taxpayer as the sole shareholder. To finance the transaction, the corporation obtained a bank loan. The bank, as a condition of the loan (imposed under banking law), required that the stock be deposited with it as security and that the documents reflect the continuing shareholder and not the corporation as the buyer of the stock. The continuing shareholder was also required to guarantee the bank loan. The loan proceeds were used to redeem the shares of the two retiring shareholders. The court found no dividend to the continuing shareholder on account of the redemption since he was at all times acting as an agent for the corporation. Compare Deutsch v. Commissioner, 38 T.C. 118 (1962), rejecting the agency argument where the contract for the purchase of the stock was at all times between the individual taxpayer and the seller, and Glacier State Electric Supply Co. v. Commissioner, 80 T.C. 1047 (1983), holding that a parent corporation was the true owner of redeemed stock of its wholly owned subsidiary, rather than an agent of the parent corporation's shareholders who were asserted to be the beneficial owners of the stock of the subsidiary.

In Schroeder v. Commissioner, 831 F.2d 856 (9th Cir.1987), the selling shareholder, after initially agreeing to cause the corporation to redeem 90%

of her stock and to sell 10% of her stock to the purchaser, on the advice of counsel changed her mind and insisted on selling all of the stock to the purchaser. The bank which was financing the acquisition, however, required that the permanent loan be made to the corporation as primary obligor and be guaranteed by the purchaser. In order to effect the acquisition of all of the stock directly by the purchaser, a "bridge" loan was made directly to the purchaser, subject to an agreement between the purchaser and the bank that immediately after the acquisition, the corporation would assume primary responsibility for the loan in consideration of a redemption of a proportionate amount of its stock. In fact, the corporation assumed approximately two-thirds of the loan two months after the acquisition, and it redeemed a proportionate amount of stock. The taxpayer argued that the purchase and the redemption were part of a single transaction that should have been treated as a redemption from the seller. The court rejected this argument as follows:

> The Tax Court found that "there was no common or mutually agreed plan of action between the estate of Fred Collins [the seller], Schroeder [the buyer], and Skyline [the corporation] whose object was the ultimate redemption by Skyline of a part of its stock." * * * We agree with the Tax Court. The record confirms Schroeder's stated intentions, but also shows that this intention was particular to him. Donna Collins, as the personal representative of her husband's estate and as the seller of Skyline's stock, made it clear to Schroeder by April 13, 1976, that she would not agree to Skyline redeeming its stock as part of a bootstrap acquisition of Skyline proposed by Schroeder. Instead, she insisted that Schroeder buy the stock personally, which Schroeder undertook to do. In addition, Skyline cannot have had any intention different from Donna's, since she controlled 100 percent of Skyline's stock.

> Schroeder, because of Donna's insistence, could not undertake a bootstrap acquisition and had to buy the Skyline stock himself. He had business reasons for choosing the form of the transaction that he did. He cannot now argue that he is immunized from tax because the transaction was really something that never occurred. * * *

> Schroeder's contention that he acted as an agent or conduit of the corporation pursuant to a prearranged plan is without merit. First, as noted above, there was no mutually agreed plan between Collins and Schroeder or between Schroeder and Skyline. The intention to have the corporation redeem its own stock was Schroeder's intention alone. Second, when he acquired the stock on April 30, 1976, "Schroeder was neither an officer, director nor a shareholder of Skyline, and he had no apparent authority to bind or commit Skyline to acquire its own stock or to borrow $600,000 from the bank in Skyline's name." * * * It was not until he acquired sole ownership of the Skyline stock, on July 1, 1976, when the debt to State Bank was restructured, and on August 1, 1976, when Skyline redeemed his stock, that Schroeder caused his intention to

become Skyline's as well. Schroeder was not Skyline's agent or conduit on April 30, 1976.

Can *Schroeder* be distinguished from *Bennett* and *Ciaio*?

2.1.3.   *Post-Acquisition Redemption from Purchaser*

As long as dividends and capital gains are taxed at the same rate, the issue in *Zenz* is of limited importance—it arises only with respect to the ability to offset basis against a distribution by the corporation where the selling shareholder does not completely terminate the shareholder's interest in the corporation and is seeking redemption treatment under § 302(b)(1) or (2) rather than under § 302(b)(3). With respect to post-acquisition redemptions from the purchaser, however, even with the tax rates on dividends and long-term capital gains equalized, the issue remains important. First, if a redemption occurs within a year after the stock purchase and § 302(a) applies, there will be basis recovery, but any resulting short-term capital gain will be taxed at the same rates as ordinary income, whereas if the redemption is treated as a dividend under § 302(d) the entire distribution will be taxed, albeit at a preferential rate. Second, if a redemption occurs more than a year after the stock purchase, basis recovery will be allowed if § 302(a) applies, but not if the redemption is treated as a dividend under § 302(d).

While a well-tailored plan for the purchase of a corporate business can use part of the corporation's assets to finance the transaction, the formalities generally must be observed. If an agency argument fails, a distribution to the purchaser following the acquisition of all of the stock, for the purpose of reducing the net out-of-pocket purchase price paid for the corporate business, will be a dividend to the purchaser. In Television Industries, Inc. v. Commissioner, 284 F.2d 322 (2d Cir.1960), the purchasing shareholder borrowed money to complete the purchase of all the shares then had some of the shares redeemed to obtain funds to repay the loan; a dividend resulted. Even though in economic effect and intent this transaction may not differ from a pre-acquisition redemption from the seller, the form of the transaction will control for tax purposes. See Jacobs v. Commissioner, T.C. Memo. 1981–81, aff'd, 698 F.2d 850 (6th Cir.1983), in which upon finding that the corporation acted as the continuing shareholders' agent in acquiring the seller's shares, the Tax Court observed as follows: "Petitioners could very easily have avoided dividend treatment of this transaction had they obtained tax advice from the start. * * * Unfortunately, this is another area of the law in which 'the formalities of handling a particular transaction assume a disproportionate importance and * * * a premium is placed upon consulting one's lawyer early enough in the game.' * * * Petitioners have chosen the wrong form and consequently must suffer the consequences." Is the agency theory employed in *Bennett* and *Ciaio* inconsistent with the "form controls" theory of *Jacobs*?

2.2. *Section 305 Aspects*

While the case law after *Holsey* was unanimous in rejecting the government's argument that the continuing shareholder's increase in proportionate interest in the corporation as a result of the redemption of other shareholders constituted a taxable dividend to the shareholder, increase in proportionate interest again became relevant with the amendments to § 305 in 1969 (see discussion in Chapter 6). Under § 305(b)(2) the increase in the proportionate interests of some shareholders in the earnings or assets of the corporation caused by a stock dividend, when coupled with the receipt of property by other shareholders, can result in a taxable distribution to the former group. Under § 305(c), the increase in proportionate interest caused by a redemption can be treated as a constructive stock dividend for purposes of § 305(b)(2). The Regulations, however, provide that in a situation like *Holsey,* where the redemption distribution is entitled to capital gains treatment under § 302(b), no constructive dividend will result to the continuing shareholders. Treas.Reg. § 1.305–3(b)(3). In addition, an isolated redemption will not trigger a constructive stock dividend under § 305(c). Treas.Reg. § 1.305–7(a). See Treas.Reg. § 1.305–3(b)(3), (e), Ex. 10 (no constructive dividend as a result of isolated redemption even though redemption was treated as a § 301 distribution). For an example of a redemption situation in which § 305(b)(2) was applicable by virtue of § 305(c), see Rev.Rul. 78–60, 1978–1 C.B. 81.

3.   TREATMENT OF THE REDEEMED SHAREHOLDER

Where a prospective purchaser of the stock is unwilling to pay for all the stock at its present value and the parties arrange for the corporation to redeem some of the shares of the existing shareholders contemporaneously with the sale of the balance of their stock to the purchaser, who thus is required to pay a lesser figure (but who also receives a corporation with fewer assets), the courts generally have followed the approach of *Zenz.* See, e.g., In re Estate of Lukens, 246 F.2d 403 (3d Cir.1957) (father had part of his stock redeemed at book value and gave the balance to his adult children, who also were shareholders and who managed the corporation).

The IRS has ruled that it will follow *Zenz,* Rev.Rul. 55–745, 1955–2 C.B. 223, and that the actual sequence of the redemption and the sale will be ignored in a *Zenz*-type corporate sale as long as the two steps are both part of an integrated plan to reduce the outgoing shareholders' interest. Thus, the fact that the redemption precedes the sale of the shares will not cause the outgoing shareholder to receive dividend treatment; the formal order of the steps in the transaction is not crucial. See Rev.Rul. 77–226, 1977–2 C.B. 90 (corporate shareholder tendered part of its shares for redemption and sold the remaining shares of stock on the market; it treated the redemption as a § 301 distribution under § 302(d) qualifying for the intercorporate dividends deduction and claimed a capital loss on the disposition of the remaining shares which were attributed the basis of the shares which were redeemed; held, the entire transaction resulted in a termination of the corporate shareholder's interest and hence a taxable capital gain).

It is not necessary for the selling shareholder's interest to be completely terminated in order for the *Zenz* principle to apply. Rev.Rul. 75–447, 1975–2 C.B. 113, held that the reduction in interest effected through a combined sale and redemption should be aggregated to determine whether the redemption qualified for sale or exchange treatment under § 302(b)(2).

Furthermore, in private letter rulings the IRS has applied *Zenz* to qualify a redemption under § 302(b)(1). See Ltr.Rul. 8540074 (Jul. 10, 1985).

A variation on *Zenz* was involved in McDonald v. Commissioner, 52 T.C. 82 (1969). There the shareholder, who owned all of the preferred stock and most of the common stock in a corporation, had the preferred stock redeemed and, as part of a prior arrangement, exchanged his common stock for the common stock of a public corporation in a tax-free exchange. The IRS argued that the preferred stock redemption constituted a dividend, distinguishing *Zenz,* because in this situation the shareholder retained a continuing interest in the assets of the old corporation by virtue of his stock ownership in the acquiring corporation. The court found the redemption and subsequent reorganization effected a "substantial change" in the shareholder's interest and refused to treat the redemption as a dividend.

An interesting twist on the *Zenz* principle is found in Estate of Durkin v. Commissioner, 99 T.C. 561 (1992). The taxpayer purchased a corporate asset for a price substantially below fair market value. At the same time, the taxpayer's stock was redeemed by the corporation for a price equal to its basis, with the taxpayer reporting no gain or loss on the redemption. The IRS asserted that the bargain sale of corporate assets was a constructive dividend to the taxpayer. The taxpayer argued that the substance of the transaction was a redemption qualified under § 302(b)(3) under *Zenz*. The Tax Court sustained the IRS's assertion of dividend treatment with respect to the bargain purchase holding that the taxpayer was to be held to the form of the transaction that he chose, which was selected in an attempt to avoid recognition of gain on the redemption.

4. DIVIDENDS DISTRIBUTED IN CONNECTION WITH THE SALE OF A CORPORATE BUSINESS

While the treatment of redemptions made as part of the sale of a corporate business is fairly well established since the initial decisions in *Holsey* and *Zenz,* the appropriate treatment of dividend distributions in similar situations raises a different question. Some question remains whether a dividend distribution to a selling shareholder that is made as an integral part of the sale and purchase of stock is to be recharacterized as a dividend distribution to the purchaser, and taxed to the purchaser, with the same amount being, in turn, treated as having been paid by the purchaser to the selling shareholder as part of the purchase price.

In Casner v. Commissioner, 450 F.2d 379 (5th Cir.1971), substantial shareholders in the corporation wished to withdraw by selling their stock to the remaining shareholders. The buyers did not have enough cash to finance the transaction. It was agreed that a distribution of some of the cash of the corporation would be made pro rata to all the shareholders, thus reducing the value of the corporation and giving the continuing shareholders some cash to pay a portion of the purchase price. Accordingly, the corporation made a cash distribution and contemporaneously the retiring shareholders sold their shares. The selling shareholders treated all the payments, including the distributions, as sales proceeds; the buying shareholders regarded themselves as conduits for the distributions to the selling shareholders. The Tax Court treated the corporate distributions to both the selling and buying shareholders as dividends. T.C. Memo. 1969–98. The Court of Appeals reversed, finding that the distributions to the *selling* shareholders were in fact part of the payment of the purchase price and as such resulted in constructive dividends to the *buying* shareholders (in addition to the latter's own direct dividends). The court found alternatively that the buying stockholders were the beneficial owners of the stock at the time of the dividend distribution.[1]

The *Casner* treatment of the distributions to the selling shareholders as dividends to the buying shareholders followed by a payment of the purchase price to the sellers is inconsistent with the obligation-to-purchase standard of the *Wall and Sullivan* line of cases dealing with a similar factual pattern. The IRS will not apply *Casner* to tax the buyer where the payment of the dividend to the selling shareholder does not reduce the buyer's obligation to pay an agreed upon purchase price, Rev.Rul. 75–493, 1975–2 C.B. 108. This position is consistent with the redemption cases, which likewise focus on the question of whether the distribution by the corporation discharges the buying shareholder's personal obligation. It similarly places a premium on the careful timing of the transactions since very different tax consequences result depending on whether the distribution is made before or after entering into a binding purchase agreement.

Even where the dividend does not reduce the buying shareholder's obligation under the purchase agreement, a dividend to the buyer may still be found on the theory that the buyer had become the beneficial owner of the stock at the time the dividend was declared. See Steel Improvement & Forge Co. v. Commissioner, 314 F.2d 96 (6th Cir.1963); Walker v. Commissioner, 544 F.2d 419 (9th Cir.1976).

5.   REDEMPTIONS IN CONNECTION WITH SHAREHOLDERS' DIVORCE

Often in a divorce, corporate assets are used to acquire the stock of a closely held corporation held by one spouse while the other spouse continues to own the remaining stock of the corporation. The use of corporate assets to acquire the stock of one spouse may result in a constructive dividend to the continuing shareholder who is treated as transferring property to the selling spouse in a tax-free settlement under § 1041, or the transaction may be treated as a taxable redemption of the selling spouse. Under Treas.Reg. § 1.1041–2(a), promulgated in 2003 to resolve conflicting case law, the determination of whether there is a constructive dividend to the continuing shareholder is based on "applicable tax law," meaning the unconditional obligation test of *Wall* and *Sullivan*. Treas.Reg. § 1.1041–2(a)(2) provides that, if under the *Wall* and *Sullivan* principles, the redemption of stock from one spouse (the transferor spouse whose stock is redeemed) is treated as a constructive dividend to the other spouse (the non-transferor spouse, who continues as a shareholder), the transferor spouse is treated as transferring the stock to the non-transferor, spouse in exchange for the redemption

---

[1]   The *Casner* result is advantageous where the seller and purchaser are corporations that can take advantage of the dividends received deduction of § 243 as discussed in Section 2.

proceeds in a nonrecognition exchange under § 1041. The transferor spouse does not recognize gain or loss. The non-transferor spouse is treated as receiving a distribution subject to § 302, which generally results in a dividend under § 301, and then transferring the distributed money or property to the transferor spouse. Treas.Reg. § 1.1041–2(b)(2). Thus, for example, if A and B are married to each other and own all of the stock of X Corporation, and pursuant to a decree of divorce A is obligated to acquire B's X Corporation stock and causes the corporation to redeem the stock, A is treated as receiving a constructive § 302 distribution, which will most likely be treated as a dividend under § 301. B is treated as transferring the X corporation stock to A in a nontaxable transfer under § 1041.

If the non-transferor spouse is not obligated to acquire the stock of the transferor spouse so that the redemption is not treated as a constructive dividend to the non-transferor spouse under the principles of *Wall* and *Sullivan*, then the transaction will be taxed in accordance with its form; the transferor spouse will be treated as receiving a taxable distribution under § 302. Treas.Reg. § 1.1041–2(a)(1) and (b)(1). Thus, in the above example, if A is not obligated to acquire B's X Corporation stock under the standards of *Wall* and *Sullivan*, the transaction is treated as a redemption distribution to B, who recognizes the gain or loss on disposition of the stock, and A is not treated as receiving a taxable distribution.

The Regulations permit the spouses to designate the tax treatment of the redemption by agreeing to treat the redemption inconsistently with the generally applicable tax law regarding constructive dividends. Treas.Reg. § 1.1041–2(c)(1) provides that even though the redemption results in a constructive dividend distribution to the non-transferor spouse under applicable tax law, if the spouses agree in the divorce or separation instrument (or other valid written agreement) that the redemption will be treated as a redemption distribution to the transferor spouse, then the redemption will be treated as a redemption taxable to the transferor spouse notwithstanding that the redemption otherwise would result in a constructive dividend distribution to the non-transferor spouse. Conversely, Treas.Reg. § 1.1041–2(c)(2) provides that even though the redemption does not result in a constructive dividend distribution to the non-transferor spouse under applicable tax law, if the spouses agree in the divorce or separation instrument (or other valid written agreement) that the redemption will be treated as a dividend distribution to the non-transferor spouse, then the redemption will be treated as a transfer by the transferor spouse of the redeemed stock to the non-transferor spouse in exchange for the redemption proceeds, and the receipt of the redemption proceeds by the non-transferor spouse as a distribution from the corporation. Thus, the spouses can agree to nonrecognition treatment for the transferor spouse who is redeemed, coupled with constructive dividend treatment for the non-transferor spouse who continues as a shareholder.

PROBLEM SET 1

1. Al, Georgiana, and Pete each owned one third of the outstanding common stock of the Pocatello Raiders Football Club, Inc. The three

shareholders signed a contract under which on the death of any shareholder the remaining shareholders would purchase the stock of the deceased shareholder from his or her estate at a price set by a formula in the contract. The Pocatello Raiders insured the lives of all three shareholders with Pari-Mutuel Insurance Co. This year Al died, and Pocatello Raiders received life insurance proceeds that it used to redeem Al's stock.

(a) What are the tax consequences?

(b) If the shareholders had come to you for advice last year, how would you have suggested that they amend their contract?

2. Alina owned 40 shares of stock of X Corp. common stock, and Bryce owned the other 60 shares. Consider the following alternative transactions.

(a) Pursuant to a prearranged plan, X Corp. redeemed 5 shares from Alina on April 15th, and on July 1st, Alina sold 10 shares to Cedric. Does Alina's redemption on April 15th qualify under § 302(a)?

(b) Pursuant to a prearranged plan, X Corp. redeemed 18 shares from Bryce on April 15th, and on July 1st, Bryce sold 1 share to Alina. Does Bryce's redemption on April 15th qualify under § 302(a)?

3. Catherine and Henry own as joint tenants all of the stock of Aragon Advocacy, Inc., which is engaged in the business of managing political campaigns. The shares of the corporation are Catherine and Henry's principal asset. Catherine and Henry's combined basis in the stock is $80,000. The fair market value of the stock is $200,000. Henry has filed for divorce. Catherine will continue to own the corporation. Henry will be paid for his interest in cash. The only cash available is in the corporation, which also can borrow to pay off Henry. Catherine and Henry agree in the divorce settlement that one-half of the corporate shares will be deemed to belong to Henry and that Catherine will cause the corporation to redeem Henry's shares for cash. What are the tax consequences of the redemption distribution to Catherine and Henry?

SECTION 2. BOOTSTRAP TRANSACTIONS INVOLVING CORPORATIONS

Different problems arise where a dividend in connection with a sale is paid to a selling shareholder that is itself a corporation and thus able to take advantage of the reduction or elimination of tax on intercorporate dividends under § 243. Suppose that X Corporation owns 100% of the stock of Y Corporation, which has a basis of $200 and a fair market value of $500. (Also assume that X Corporation and Y Corporation do not file a consolidated return.) If X Corporation sold the stock of Y Corporation to Z Corporation for $500, after paying taxes (at 21%) on its $300 gain, X Corporation would have net after-tax proceeds of $437. Now suppose that prior to the sale Y Corporation declared a dividend of $200, which was eligible for 100% exclusion under § 243(a)(3), following which X Corporation sold the stock of Y Corporation for $300. In this case, X Corporation would pay taxes on only a $100 gain, and after taxes it would receive $479.

The IRS generally argues that such a dividend payment is in fact additional purchase price, and therefore constitutes capital gain that is not eligible for the § 243 deduction. See Rev.Rul. 75–493, 1975–2 C.B. 108, characterizing such a transaction as a "sham designed to disguise the true substance of the transaction." The IRS has had mixed success with this argument in the courts.

Litton Industries, Inc. v. Commissioner

Tax Court of the United States, 1987.
89 T.C. 1086.

[The taxpayer's board of directors began to consider a sale of its subsidiary, Stouffer, in July of 1972. In late August, Stouffer declared a $30 million dividend, which was paid in the form of a negotiable promissory note for $30 million; and on September 7, Litton announced that it was interested in selling Stouffer. After considering a public offering of the Stouffer stock in late 1972, on March 1, 1973, Litton sold its Stouffer stock to Nestle for $75 million; simultaneously, it sold the promissory note to Nestle for $30 million. The IRS contended that the $30 million "dividend" was in fact part of the purchase price and disallowed Litton's dividends received deduction.]

OPINION

* * *

The instant case is substantially governed by Waterman Steamship Corp. v. Commissioner, 50 T.C. 650 (1968), revd. 430 F.2d 1185 (5th Cir.1970), cert. denied 401 U.S. 939 (1971). [The Commissioner] urges us to follow the opinion of the Fifth Circuit * * *. [Taxpayer] contends that the reasoning of the Fifth Circuit in *Waterman Steamship* should not apply since the facts here are more favorable to petitioner. Additionally, petitioner points out that several business purposes were served by the distribution here which provide additional support for recognition of the distribution as a dividend. For the reasons set forth below, we conclude that the $30 million distribution constituted a dividend which should be recognized as such for tax purposes. * * *

In many respects, the facts of this case and those of *Waterman Steamship* are parallel. The principal difference, and the one which we find to be most significant, is the timing of the dividend action. In *Waterman Steamship*, the taxpayer corporation received an offer to purchase the stock of two of its wholly owned subsidiary corporations, Pan-Atlantic and Gulf Florida, for $3,500,000. The board of directors of Waterman Steamship rejected that offer but countered with an offer to sell the two subsidiaries for $700,000 after the subsidiaries declared and arranged for payments of dividends to Waterman Steamship amounting in the aggregate to $2,800,000. Negotiations between the parties ensued, and the agreements which resulted therefrom included, in specific detail, provisions for the declaration of a dividend by Pan-Atlantic to Waterman

Steamship prior to the signing of the sales agreement and the closing of that transaction. Furthermore, the agreements called for the purchaser to loan or otherwise advance funds to Pan-Atlantic promptly in order to pay off the promissory note by which the dividend had been paid. Once the agreement was reached, the entire transaction was carried out by a series of meetings commencing at 12 noon on January 21, 1955, and ending at 1:30 p.m. the same day. * * *

As the Fifth Circuit pointed out, "By the end of the day and within a ninety minute period, the financial cycle had been completed. Waterman had $3,500,000, hopefully tax-free, all of which came from Securities and McLean, the buyers of the stock." 430 F.2d at 1190. This Court concluded that the distribution from Pan-Atlantic to Waterman was a dividend. The Fifth Circuit reversed, concluding that the dividend and sale were one transaction. 430 F.2d at 1192.

The timing in the instant case was markedly different. The dividend was declared by Stouffer on August 23, 1972, at which time the promissory note in payment of the dividend was issued to Litton. There had been some general preliminary discussions about the sale of Stouffer, and it was expected that Stouffer would be a very marketable company which would sell quickly. However, at the time the dividend was declared, no formal action had been taken to initiate the sale of Stouffer. It was not until 2 weeks later that Litton publicly announced that Stouffer was for sale. There ensued over the next 6 months many discussions with various corporations, investment banking houses, business brokers, and underwriters regarding Litton's disposition of Stouffer through sale of all or part of the business to a particular buyer, or through full or partial public offerings of the Stouffer stock. All of this culminated on March 1, 1973, over 6 months after the dividend was declared, with the purchase by Nestle of all of Stouffer's stock. * * *

In the instant case, the declaration of the dividend and the sale of the stock were substantially separated in time in contrast to *Waterman Steamship* where the different transactions occurred essentially simultaneously. In *Waterman Steamship,* it seems quite clear that no dividend would have been declared if all of the remaining steps in the transaction had not been lined up in order on the closing table and did not in fact take place. Here, however, Stouffer declared the dividend, issued the promissory note, and definitely committed itself to the dividend before even making a public announcement that Stouffer was for sale. Respondent argues that the only way petitioner could ever receive the dividend was by raising revenue through a sale of Stouffer. Therefore, respondent asserts the two events (the declaration of the dividend and then the sale of the company) were inextricably tied together and should be treated as one transaction for tax purposes. In our view, respondent ignores the fact that Stouffer could have raised sufficient revenue for the dividend from other avenues, such as a partial public offering or borrowing. Admittedly, there had been discussions at

Litton about the sale of Stouffer which was considered to be a very salable company. However, there are many slips between the cup and the lip, and it does not take much of a stretch of the imagination to picture a variety of circumstances under which Stouffer might have been taken off the market and no sale consummated. Under these circumstances, it is unlikely that respondent would have considered the dividend to be a nullity. On the contrary, it would seem quite clear that petitioner would be charged with a dividend on which it would have to pay a substantial tax. Petitioner committed itself to the dividend and, thereby, accepted the consequences regardless of the outcome of the proposed sale of Stouffer stock. See Crellin v. Commissioner, 17 T.C. 781, 785 (1951), affd. 203 F.2d 812 (9th Cir.1953), cert. denied 346 U.S. 873 * * * (1953).

Since the facts here are distinguishable in important respects and are so much stronger in petitioner's favor, we do not consider it necessary to consider further the opinion of the Fifth Circuit in *Waterman Steamship*.

* * * [T]he $30 million distribution by Stouffer would clearly constitute a dividend if the sale of Stouffer had not occurred. We are not persuaded that the subsequent sale of Stouffer to Nestle changes that result merely because it was more advantageous to Litton from a tax perspective.

It is well established that a taxpayer is entitled to structure his affairs and transactions in order to minimize his taxes. This proposition does not give a taxpayer carte blanche to set up a transaction in any form which will avoid tax consequences, regardless of whether the transaction has substance. Gregory v. Helvering, 293 U.S. 465, 55 S.Ct. 266 (1935). A variety of factors present here preclude a finding of sham or subterfuge. Although the record in this case clearly shows that Litton intended at the time the dividend was declared to sell Stouffer, no formal action had been taken and no announcement had been made. There was no definite purchaser waiting in the wings with the terms and conditions of sale already agreed upon. At that time, Litton had not even decided upon the form of sale of Stouffer. Nothing in the record here suggests that there was any prearranged sale agreement, formal or informal, at the time the dividend was declared.

Petitioner further supports its argument that the transaction was not a sham by pointing out Litton's legitimate business purposes in declaring the dividend. Although the Code and case law do not require a dividend to have a business purpose, it is a factor to be considered in determining whether the overall transaction was a sham. T.S.N. Liquidating Corp. v. United States, 624 F.2d 1328 (5th Cir.1980). Petitioner argues that * * * since Litton was considering disposing of all or part of Stouffer through a public or private offering, the payment of a dividend by a promissory note prior to any sale had two advantages. First, Litton hoped to avoid materially diminishing the market value of the Stouffer stock. At that time, one of the factors considered in valuing a stock, and in determining the market value of a stock was the "multiple of earnings" criterion. Payment of the dividend by issuance of a promissory note would not substantially alter Stouffer's earnings. Since many investors were relatively unsophisticated, Litton may have been quite right that it could increase its investment in Stouffer by at least some portion of the $30 million dividend. Second, by declaring a dividend and paying it by a promissory note prior to an anticipated public offering, Litton could avoid sharing the earnings with future additional shareholders while not diminishing to the full extent of the pro rata dividend, the amount received for the stock. Whether Litton could have come out ahead after Stouffer paid the promissory note is at this point merely speculation about a public offering which never occurred. The point, however, is that Litton hoped to achieve some business purpose, and not just tax benefits, in structuring the transaction as it did.

Under these facts, where the dividend was declared 6 months prior to the sale of Stouffer, where the sale was not pre-arranged, and since Stouffer had earnings and profits exceeding $30 million at the time the dividend was declared, we cannot conclude that the distribution was merely a device designed to give the appearance of a dividend to a part of the sales proceeds. In this case, the form and substance of the transaction coincide; it was not a transaction entered into solely for tax reasons, and it should be recognized as structured by petitioner.

DETAILED ANALYSIS

1.   OTHER JUDICIAL DECISIONS

As in *Waterman Steamship,* discussed in the excerpt from *Litton Industries,* the IRS met with success in the District Court in TSN Liquidating Corp. v. United States, 77–2 U.S.T.C. ¶ 9741 (N.D.Tex.1977), but on appeal the decision was reversed, 624 F.2d 1328 (5th Cir.1980). In that case, Union Mutual agreed to purchase from TSN the stock of TSN's subsidiary, CLIC, but Union Mutual insisted that prior to the acquisition CLIC distribute to TSN certain securities, primarily stock of closely held corporations, constituting some 78% of CLIC's total assets. Although Union Mutual did not desire CLIC to hold the particular securities distributed pursuant to the agreement, neither did it desire to own a "smaller" corporation. To the contrary, for reasons having to do with state law it desired to maintain the net assets of CLIC, and shortly after the closing, Union Mutual contributed to CLIC cash and marketable securities slightly in excess of the amount distributed to TSN.

Emphasizing that the distribution of investment assets immediately prior to the sale of the stock was matched by a post-acquisition infusion of investment assets, the IRS argued that the conduit rationale of *Waterman Steamship* applied. Although it agreed with the District Court that "the substance of the transaction controls over the form," the Court of Appeals found *Waterman Steamship,* upon which the District Court had relied, to be distinguishable. The earlier case involved a "sham transaction," which even the IRS did not argue was the case in *TSN Liquidating.* Instead, the IRS argued, successfully in the District Court, that from CLIC's perspective there was no business purpose for the distribution, which could not have occurred other than in the context of the sale. The Court of Appeals, however, concluded as follows:

> We agree that the transaction must be viewed as a whole and we accept the district court's finding of fact that the dividend of the unwanted assets was "part and parcel of the purchase arrangement with Union Mutual," motivated specifically by Union Mutual's unwillingness to take and pay for such assets. That being the case, we decline to focus on the business purpose of one participant in the transaction—a corporation controlled by the taxpayer—and instead find that the business purpose for the transaction as a whole, viewed from the standpoint of the taxpayer, controls. The facts found by the district court clearly demonstrate a business purpose for the presale dividend of the unwanted assets which fully explains that dividend. We note that there is no suggestion in the district court's opinion of any tax avoidance motivation on the part of the taxpayer TSN. The fact that the dividend may have had incidental tax benefit to the taxpayer, without more, does not necessitate the disallowance of dividend treatment.

In Basic Inc. v. United States, 549 F.2d 740 (Ct.Cl.1977), the court refused to respect the taxpayers' structure of the transaction even though payment of an intercorporate dividend was not in effect a conduit device to transfer funds from the purchaser to the seller. Basic owned all the shares of Falls, which in turn owned all the shares of Carbon. A corporate purchaser was interested in buying the shares of Falls and Carbon, but, in order to take advantage of a now repealed provision governing a subsequent liquidation of the subsidiaries, it desired to purchase the stock of both Falls and Carbon directly rather than simply purchasing the Falls stock and obtaining the Carbon stock on a liquidation of Falls. After an irrevocable offer by the purchaser to purchase the Falls and Carbon stock, Falls distributed the Carbon stock to Basic as a dividend. The dividend of the stock was entitled to the dividends received deduction under § 243(a)(1) but because under § 301(d) the basis of the Carbon stock was not reduced to reflect the dividends received deduction, Basic acquired an essentially "cost free" basis in the Carbon stock against which to offset the sales price to be paid for the stock of the two corporations. The Court of Claims held that the transfer of the Carbon stock to Basic did not qualify as a dividend. The court rested its decision on general notions of tax avoidance, citing Gregory v. Helvering, 293 U.S. 465 (1935), and took the position that for a corporate distribution to qualify as a dividend it must have an independent "business purpose":

> These facts leave no room for a conclusion that a business interest was served by the claimed dividend. From all that appears, the case is plain that Falls, through its controlling parent, was caused to transfer the property whose sale the parent had decided upon for its own separate purposes. Nothing therefore remains save the obvious: the transaction reduced the tax that Basic would

otherwise have incurred in the sale of its own property, i.e., the shares of Falls. * * *

Under the facts and circumstances presented here, plaintiff has not shown that there was a reason for the transfer of the Carbon stock from Falls to Basic aside from the tax consequences attributable to that move. Accordingly, for purposes of taxation, the transfer was not a dividend within the meaning of § 316(a)(1). Instead, it should be regarded as a transfer that avoided part of the gain to be expected from the sale of the business to Carborundum, and should, therefore, be now taxed accordingly. Such a treatment is in keeping with the results reached in like situations. Waterman Steamship Corp. v. Commissioner, supra; Steel Improvement & Forge Co. v. Commissioner, 314 F.2d 96, 98 (6th Cir.1963) * * *.

The *Basic, Inc.* opinion cannot be reconciled with *Litton Industries* and *TSN Liquidating. Basic, Inc.* appears to require that the payor have a business purpose for paying the dividend totally apart from the business purpose of the parent. It will be difficult, if not impossible, ever to establish an independent business purpose for the payment of an extraordinary dividend by a controlled subsidiary.

The cases involving intercorporate dividends associated with a bootstrap acquisition requiring that a dividend distribution must have a "business purpose" are in marked contrast to the cases in the redemption area in which the form which the taxpayer has selected for the extraction of corporate assets prior to a sale of the corporation is in general respected without regard to any inquiry into purposes. Does the fact that intercorporate dividends are in general either tax free or subject to reduced taxation mean that special safeguards are required with respect to such distributions in the context of corporate acquisitions? If so, is the introduction of a "business purpose" doctrine an appropriate response?[2]

2.   SECTION 1059

Section 1059 requires that a corporate shareholder that receives an "extraordinary dividend" under certain circumstances must, in computing the gain or loss realized upon the sale of the stock, reduce the basis of the stock by the amount of the untaxed portion of the dividend. As long as the stock has been held for more than two years prior to the dividend announcement date, however, only a distribution in partial liquidation of the corporation (as defined in § 302(e)) or a non-pro rata redemption distribution generally will be treated as an extraordinary distribution.

Section 1059 generally does not apply to "qualifying dividends" (as defined in § 243(b)) received by a corporation from an 80% controlled subsidiary, except to the extent that the dividends were attributable to pre-affiliation earnings and profits. I.R.C. § 1059(e)(2). Section 1059 also applies

---

[2]   Compare the treatment given intercorporate dividends in the consolidated return situation, where the parent corporation upon receipt of an excluded intercorporate dividend must reduce its basis in the stock of the subsidiary by an amount equal to the dividend. Thus, in a consolidated return context, the intercorporate dividend prior to the sale does not produce a tax advantage to the seller.

to qualifying dividends that are the proceeds of a partial liquidation as defined in § 302(e). Treas.Reg. § 1.1059(e)–1(a) provides that the exception for qualifying dividends in § 1059(e)(2) does not apply to § 1059(e)(1), which treats a dividend distribution to a corporation in partial liquidation of its interest in another corporation as an extraordinary dividend. Nevertheless, § 1059 would not apply, for example, to a transaction identical to that in *Litton*, because the distribution was not a partial liquidation.

Section 1059 was not enacted for the purpose of dealing with *Litton* type transactions, but the mechanical approach of § 1059 could be extended to apply to such transactions if Congress considered bootstrap acquisitions involving intercorporate dividends to involve inappropriate tax avoidance.

PROBLEM SET 2

1. (a) Cumberland Consolidated Corporation (CCC) is the sole shareholder of Natural Bridge Mining Corp. CCC and Natural Bridge do not file a consolidated return, and CCC has held its Natural Bridge stock for more than two years. CCC has a $150,000 basis in its Natural Bridge stock. Lake Island Coal Corporation is a prospective buyer and is willing to purchase all of the Natural Bridge stock, but it is unable to pay the $500,000 price demanded by CCC even though it believes the price is fair. Natural Bridge has $100,000 of cash on hand and $170,000 of accumulated earnings and profits. To solve these problems, the parties have agreed on the following plan. CCC will cause Natural Bridge to distribute $100,000 to it as a dividend. Promptly thereafter, CCC will sell its Natural Bridge stock to Lake Island Coal Corp. for $400,000. What are the tax consequences of this plan?

(b) Assume that CCC held only 75% of the stock of Natural Bridge and that the remaining 25% was held by Gregory Macomber (an individual). What would Macomber think of this plan? How might he want to change the plan? Does Macomber's basis for his stock affect how he views the plan?

SECTION 3. BOOTSTRAP SALE TO CHARITABLE ORGANIZATION

The bail-out of earnings and profits without creating a shareholder level tax consequence has also arisen in the context of charitable contributions. A donor could be paid a dividend from the donor's controlled corporation and then make a charitable contribution, with the result that the donor would have dividend income and then a charitable contribution deduction. In contrast, the donor could gift the shares to a qualifying charity and claim a charitable contribution deduction equal to the fair market value of the shares under § 170(e). The charitable organization could then have its shares redeemed by the controlled corporation. If the form were respected under this latter alternative, then the donor obtains a charitable contribution deduction equal to the fair market value of the donated shares without receiving a dividend as the funds from the controlled subsidiary are used to redeem the charity.

Grove v. Commissioner

United States Court of Appeals, Second Circuit, 1973.
490 F.2d 241.

■ KAUFMAN, CHIEF JUDGE:

We are called upon, once again, to wrestle with the tangled web that is the Internal Revenue Code and decipher the often intricate and ingenious strategies devised by taxpayers to minimize their tax burdens. We undertake this effort mindful that taxpayer ingenuity, although channelled into an effort to reduce or eliminate the incidence of taxation, is ground for neither legal nor moral opprobrium. As Learned Hand so eloquently stated, "any one may so arrange his affairs that his taxes shall be as low as possible; he is not bound to choose that pattern which will best pay the Treasury; there is not even a patriotic duty to increase one's taxes . . . ." Helvering v. Gregory, 69 F.2d 809, 810 (2d Cir. 1934), aff'd, 293 U.S. 465, 55 S.Ct. 266, 79 L.Ed. 596 (1935).

The case before us involves charitable contributions to an educational institution. * * *

* * *

In 1954, Dr. Livingston Houston, RPI's president, suggested to Grove that he make a gift under the "life income funds" plan. Grove explained that his only significant holdings were shares of his own corporation, but expressed a willingness to donate some of these shares under the plan, with certain qualifications. The Corporation, he stated, could not agree to any obligation or understanding to redeem shares held by RPI. This condition, of course, stemmed from a fear that RPI might seek redemption at a time when the Corporation was hard pressed for cash, which, as we have noted, was an asset crucial to a company in the heavy construction business. Moreover, since Grove at that time was unsure of RPI's money-management qualifications, he further conditioned his gift on a requirement that if RPI disposed of the shares, any proceeds would be invested and managed by an established professional firm.

RPI found these terms acceptable and on December 30, 1954, Grove made an initial gift of 200 shares, valued at $25,560. A letter accompanying the donation set forth the conditions we have recited. Moreover, in addition to retaining an interest in the income from the gift for his life, Grove specified that in the event he should predecease his wife Harriet, she would receive the income until her death.

On the same day, the Corporation and RPI signed a minority shareholder agreement. RPI agreed not to "sell, transfer, give, pledge or hypothecate, or in any way dispose of the whole or any part of the common stock of the Corporation now or hereafter owned . . . until (RPI) shall have first offered the Corporation the opportunity to purchase said shares upon the terms and conditions hereinafter provided." The redemption price was established at book value of the shares as noted on the Corporation's most recent certified financial statement prior to the offer. Pursuant to the contract, the Corporation was "entitled (but not obligated) to purchase all or any part of the shares of stock so offered." If the Corporation did not exercise its option to purchase within sixty days, RPI could transfer the shares to any other party and the Corporation's right of first refusal would not subsequently attach to such transferred shares.

The 1954 gift was the first in a series of annual contributions to RPI by Grove. From 1954 to 1968, Grove donated to RPI between 165 and 250 shares of the Corporation each year, reaching a cumulative total of 2,652 shares, subject to terms substantially similar to those noted earlier.

Generally, RPI offered donated shares to the Corporation for redemption, between one and two years after they were donated by Grove. The transactions followed a similar pattern. On each occasion, the Finance Committee of RPI's Board of Trustees first authorized the sale of specific shares of the Corporation. RPI's treasurer or controller would then write to Sidney Houck, the Corporation's treasurer, informing him of RPI's desire to dispose of the shares. Upon receipt of this letter, Houck would call a special meeting of the Corporation's board of directors to consider whether or not to exercise the Corporation's right of first refusal. The Board would adopt a resolution authorizing redemption and Houck would so inform RPI's financial officer, enclosing a company check for the amount due. By return mail, RPI would forward the appropriate stock certificate to the Corporation for cancellation.

At the time of the first redemption, in December, 1955, RPI opened an investment account at the Albany, New York, office of Merrill Lynch, Pierce, Fenner & Beane ("Merrill Lynch"). The account was captioned "Rensselaer Polytechnic Institute (Philip H. Grove Fund) Account." In accordance with Grove's wishes concerning the management of disposition proceeds, RPI authorized Merrill Lynch to act directly upon investment recommendations made by Scudder, Stevens, & Clark, Grove's personal investment adviser. RPI deposited the proceeds of each redemption transaction into this account which, pursuant to Scudder, Stevens & Clark's instructions, were generally invested in securities of large corporations whose shares traded on organized stock exchanges. Merrill Lynch paid the income from these investments to RPI on a monthly basis. RPI, in turn, made quarterly remittances to Grove, accompanied by an analysis of all account transactions.

On his personal income tax return for 1963, Grove reported as taxable income dividends of $4,939.28 and interest of $2,535.73 paid to him by RPI from the Merrill Lynch account. For 1964, Grove reported $6,096.05 in dividends and $3,540.81 in interest. The Commissioner, however, assessed deficiencies in Grove's taxable income for these years, asserting that Grove "realized additional dividends in the amounts of $29,000 and $25,800 in 1963 and 1964, respectively, as the result of the

redemption of stock by Grove Shepherd Wilson & Kruge, Inc."
Accordingly, the Commissioner increased Grove's taxable income by
these amounts and demanded payment of additional taxes—in excess of
$13,000—for each year. Grove refused to pay and petitioned the Tax
Court for a redetermination of his tax liability. The Court, concluding
that Grove had made a bona fide gift to RPI, ruled in favor of the taxpayer
and the Commissioner appealed.

* * *

The Commissioner's view of this case is relatively simple. In essence,
we are urged to disregard the actual form of the Grove-RPI-Corporation
donations and redemptions and to rewrite the actual events so that
Grove's tax liability is seen in a wholly different light. Support for this
position, it is argued, flows from the Supreme Court's decision in
Commissioner of Internal Revenue v. Court Holding Co., 324 U.S. 331,
65 S.Ct. 707, 89 L.Ed. 981 (1945), which, in language familiar to law
students, cautions that "the incidence of taxation depends upon the
substance of a transaction . . . . To permit the true nature of a transaction
to be disguised by mere formalisms, which exist solely to alter tax
liabilities, would seriously impair the effective administration of the tax
policies of Congress." Id. at 334, 65 S.Ct. at 708. In an effort to bring the
instant case within this language, the Commissioner insists that
whatever the appearance of the transactions here under consideration,
their "true nature" is quite different. He maintains that Grove, with the
cooperation of RPI, withdrew substantial funds from the Corporation and
manipulated them in a manner designed to produce income for his
benefit. In the Commissioner's view, the transaction is properly
characterized as a redemption by the Corporation of Grove's, not RIP's
shares, followed by a cash gift to RPI by Grove. This result, it is said,
more accurately reflects "economic reality."

The Commissioner's motives for insisting upon this formulation are
easily understood once its tax consequences are examined. Although
Grove reported taxable dividends and interest received from the Merrill
Lynch account on his 1963 and 1964 tax returns, amounts paid by the
Corporation to redeem the donated shares from RPI were not taxed upon
distribution. If, however, the transactions are viewed in the manner
suggested by the Commissioner, the redemption proceeds would be
taxable as income to Grove. Moreover, because the redemptions did not
in substance alter Grove's relationship to the Corporation—he continued
throughout to control a majority of the outstanding shares—the entire
proceeds would be taxed as a dividend payment at high, progressive
ordinary-income rates, rather than as a sale of shares, at the fixed, and
relatively low, capital gains rate. See, 26 U.S.C. § 302; United States v.
Davis, 397 U.S. 301, 90 S.Ct. 1041, 25 L.Ed.2d 323 (1970).

Clearly, then, the stakes involved are high. We do not quarrel with
the maxim that substance must prevail over form, but this proposition
marks the beginning, not the end, of our inquiry. The court in Sheppard

v. United States, 361 F.2d 972, 176 Ct.Cl. 244 (1966) perceptively remarked that "all such 'maxims' should rather be called 'minims' since they convey a minimum of information with a maximum of pretense." Id. at 977 n.9. Each case requires detailed consideration of its unique facts. Here, our aim is to determine whether Grove's gifts of the Corporation's shares to RPI prior to redemption should be given independent significance or whether they should be regarded as meaningless intervening steps in a single, integrated transaction designed to avoid tax liability by the use of mere formalisms.

The guideposts for our analysis are well marked by earlier judicial encounters with this problem. "The law with respect to gifts of appreciated property is well established. A gift of appreciated property does not result in income to the donor so long as he gives the property away absolutely and parts with title thereto before the property gives rise to income by way of sale." Carrington v. Commissioner of Internal Revenue, 476 F.2d 704, 708 (5th Cir. 1973), quoting Humacid Co., 42 T.C. 894, 913 (1964). As noted below by the Tax Court, the Commissioner here "does not contend that the gifts of stock by (Grove) to RPI in 1961 and 1962 were sham transactions, or that they were not completed gifts when made." If Grove made a valid, binding, and irrevocable gift of the Corporation's shares to RPI, it would be the purest fiction to treat the redemption proceeds as having actually been received by Grove. The Tax Court concluded that the gift was complete and irrevocable when made. The Commissioner conceded as much and we so find.

It is argued, however, that notwithstanding the conceded validity of the gifts, other circumstances establish that Grove employed RPI merely as a convenient conduit for withdrawing funds from the Corporation for his personal use without incurring tax liability. The Commissioner would have us infer from the systematic nature of the gift-redemption cycle that Grove and RPI reached a mutually beneficial understanding: RPI would permit Grove to use its tax-exempt status to drain funds from the Corporation in return for a donation of a future interest in such funds.

We are not persuaded by this argument and the totality of the facts and circumstances lead us to a contrary conclusion. Grove testified before the Tax Court concerning the circumstances of these gifts. The court, based on the evidence and the witnesses' credibility, specifically found that "there was no informal agreement between (Grove) and RPI that RPI would offer the stock in question to the corporation for redemption or that, if offered, the corporation would redeem it." Findings of fact by the Tax Court, like those of the district court, are binding upon us unless they are clearly erroneous, 26 U.S.C. § 7482(a); Rule 52, F.R.Civ.P., and "the rule . . . applies also to factual inferences (drawn) from undisputed basic facts." Commissioner of Internal Revenue v. Duberstein, 363 U.S. 278, 291, 80 S.Ct. 1190, 1200, 4 L.Ed.2d 1218 (1960). It cannot seriously be contended that the Tax Court's findings here are "clearly erroneous" and no tax liability can be predicated upon a nonexistent agreement between Grove and RPI or by a fictional one created by the Commissioner.

Grove, of course, owned a substantial majority of the Corporation's shares. His vote alone was sufficient to insure redemption of any shares offered by RPI. But such considerations, without more, are insufficient to permit the Commissioner to ride roughshod over the actual understanding found by the Tax Court to exist between the donor and the donee. Behrend v. United States (4th Cir. 1972), 73–1 USTC P9123, is particularly instructive. There, two brothers donated preferred shares of a corporation jointly controlled by them to a charitable foundation over which they also exercised control. The preferred shares were subsequently redeemed from the foundation by the corporation and the Commissioner sought to tax the redemption as a corporate dividend payment to the brothers. The court, in denying liability, concluded that although "it was understood that the corporation would at intervals take up the preferred according to its financial ability . . ., this factor did not convert into a constructive dividend the proceeds of the redemption . . . [because] the gifts were absolutely perfected before the corporation redeemed the stock." Id.

Nothing in the December, 1954, minority shareholder agreement between the Corporation and RPI serves as a basis for disturbing the conclusion of the Tax Court. Although the Corporation desired a right of first refusal on minority shares—understandably so, in order to reduce the possibility of unrelated, outside ownership interests—it assumed no obligation to redeem any shares so offered. In the absence of such an obligation, the Commissioner's contention that Grove's initial donation was only the first step in a prearranged series of transactions is little more than wishful thinking grounded in a shaky foundation. * * *

We are not so naive as to believe that tax considerations played no role in Grove's planning. But foresight and planning do not transform a non-taxable event into one that is taxable. Were we to adopt the Commissioner's view, we would be required to recast two actual transactions—a gift by Grove to RPI and a redemption from RPI by the Corporation—into two completely fictional transactions—a redemption from Grove by the Corporation and a gift by Grove to RPI. Based upon the facts as found by the Tax Court, we can discover no basis for elevating the Commissioner's "form" over that employed by the taxpayer in good faith. "Useful as the step transaction doctrine may be in the interpretation of equivocal contracts and ambiguous events, it cannot generate events which never took place just so an additional tax liability might be asserted." Sheppard v. United States, supra, at 978. In the absence of any supporting facts in the record we are unable to adopt the Commissioner's view; to do so would be to engage in a process of decision that is arbitrary, capricious and ultimately destructive of traditional notions of judicial review. We decline to embark on such a course.

Accordingly, the judgment of the Tax Court is affirmed.

■ OAKES, CIRCUIT JUDGE (dissenting):

Review of the tax consequences of a business transaction requires consideration of the economic realities of the entire transaction. * * * Whether a transaction should be viewed as two or more steps or as one integrated transaction may result in entirely different tax consequences. * * *

Here, as I see it, the form of the transaction was two-step: a gift of stock followed by a redemption of the stock by the donor controlled corporation. The substance of the transaction, however, was a payment out of corporate earnings and profits to a charity designated by the donor who retained a life interest in the gift.

The factors which distinguish the RPI-Grove transactions from other charitable donations of securities and which persuade me to treat this as an integrated transaction are two: first, the gifts made by the Groves were of stock in a closed corporation that was inevitably redeemed annually; second, by virtue of retaining a life income from the reinvested proceeds and by retaining a measure of control over how those proceeds should be reinvested (by designating the investment adviser who was also the Groves' personal adviser), the Groves were able to achieve a bail-out from their non-dividend-paying closed corporation.

Viewing the economic realities of the situation, the pattern of redemption always following upon the gifts makes it clear that by the tax years here in issue Grove could confidently expect that RPI would quickly redeem and reinvest the Grove stock in safe income bearing securities. From the time Grove first began giving RPI shares in 1955, until 1964 when Grove was assessed with the taxes here in dispute, RPI consistently and without exception offered for redemption the Grove shares approximately one year after they were received. Not only was the practice consistent, thus indicating that at least as of 1963 the Groves could count on annual redemption offers, but it was the only practice which a university treasurer could correctly take and still meet his own statutory obligations as a fiduciary to RPI. See N.Y. Estates, Powers and Trust Law § 11–2.1 & .2 (McKinney 1967 & Supp. 1972). As pointed out in the majority opinion, construction company stock may be quite risky. Given the relatively conservative nature of university investments, it would have been obvious to Grove from the beginning that RPI's treasurer (pursuant to direction from the finance committee of the RPI board of trustees) would redeem the Grove shares quite soon after their receipt. RPI was required as a condition to the gifts to offer any Grove shares to the Grove corporation for redemption prior to resale elsewhere. Grove as majority shareholder had control over whether the shares would be redeemed by the corporation. Thus it is entirely unimportant that there was no written agreement requiring that RPI offer its Grove stock for redemption. Judge Learned Hand observed in Commissioner of Internal Revenue v. Transport Trading & Terminal Corp., 176 F.2d 570, 572 (2d Cir. 1949) (dictum), cert. denied, 338 U.S. 955, 70 S.Ct. 493, 94

L.Ed. 589 (1950), that the "sure expectation of a later transaction might be sufficient to bring a transaction within the principle enunciated in Gregory v. Helvering, supra. There surely was a "sure expectation" of redemption here. It did not become any the less sure when Grove became a term trustee of RPI in 1957, and subsequently a life, and then an honorary trustee.

Moreover, the reinvestment which took place gave the Groves a life interest in an entirely different sort of security than they had had as owners of the shares of Grove Shepherd Wilson & Kruge, Inc.—thus accomplishing a financially desirable diversification and creating a dependable interest and dividend flow. Their closed corporation paid no dividends during the period here in question, although it could have done so. * * * The fact that Grove could depend on RPI's investment of the Grove shares in stocks and bonds paying substantial dividends and interest is clear. Indeed, he selected the investment firm advising RPI on such reinvestment. This firm also personally advised him, and RPI acknowledged in writing as early as 1955 that it was pleased to conform to Grove's wishes, to have the investment of the redemption proceeds coordinated with Grove's personal investment program. The investment firm could be expected to act, and did in fact act as far as the record indicates, to make investments which provided good yearly income to Grove as well as a safe capital base for RPI.

If Grove had given RPI listed "safe" securities equivalent to those invested in by Scudder, Stevens & Clark to RPI rather than the risky construction company stock he would have received no benefit from these transactions (other than the gift tax deduction). But in this case his gifts acted as a sort of low risk pension fund for himself and his wife in case of failure of the construction business, without his having to pay a tax on any dividends that might be declared by his corporation. The Groves were in the very same financial position after the gift-redemption-reinvestment transaction as if the corporation had paid them a cash dividend in the amount of the gift, a dividend which they had then given to RPI to be reinvested safely. The Groves maintained their position as controlling shareholders. Cf. United States v. Davis, 397 U.S. 301, 313, 90 S.Ct. 1041, 25 L.Ed.2d 323 (1970). Finally, the corporation was also in the same financial position as if it had declared and paid a cash dividend since it redeemed the shares of stock for cash (except that on redemption it was better off in that it rather than the Groves owned its shares redeemed). But a tax on the amount of the dividend, had one been declared, had—hopefully for corporation and shareholder alike—been avoided and under the majority decision was in fact avoided.

The majority opinion relies heavily on two cases which I believe are readily distinguishable from the situation here. One is Carrington v. Commissioner of Internal Revenue, 476 F.2d 704 (5th Cir. 1973), relied on for the proposition that "a gift of appreciated property does not result in income to the donor so long as he gives the property away absolutely and parts with title before the property gives rise to income by way of sale." Here the Groves did not part with all interest in the construction company stock. The reservation of a life interest in the stock (or its reinvested proceeds), when coupled with taxpayer's right, however indirect, to direct the manner in which proceeds would be invested, gave the Groves a very great continuing interest and control, a fact of not inconsiderable tax significance. Cf. Corliss v. Bowers, 281 U.S. 376, 378, 50 S.Ct. 336, 74 L.Ed. 916 (1930) (Holmes, J.) ("taxation is not so much concerned with the refinements of title as it is with actual command over the property taxed . . . ."). More importantly, Carrington involved only one contribution of stock and one redemption; there was no pattern of redemption of stock as was clearly established here at least by the time of the tax years in question.

In Behrend v. United States, CCH 1973 Stand.Fed.Tax Rep. P9123 (4th Cir. 1972), also relied upon by the majority, the proceeds of the redemption were used wholly for the benefit of the charitable foundation which was the recipient of the stock; there was no life estate reserved for the personal benefit of the donors. See 1973 Stand.Fed.Tax Rep. P9123 at 80,067 ("Predominant force" in Behrend decision is "indisputable fact" that the taxpayers therein 'did not participate whatsoever in the beneficence of the foundation').

Thus, I believe that when, as here, the nature and conditions of the charitable gift and the pattern of donor-charity behavior are such as to make it for all practical purposes inevitable that the stock given will be offered for redemption and accepted by the closely held corporation, resulting in providing the equivalent of a safe pension fund for the donor stockholders, then the transaction must be treated as a distribution of dividends under 301(a), 301(c) and 316(a) of the Internal Revenue Code of 1954. The majority opinion refers to an "absence of any supporting facts in the record" for the Commissioner's position, but omits to rely upon the one most important fact on which the case should turn: the pattern of redemption over years of giving. I accordingly dissent.

DETAILED ANALYSIS

1. STEP TRANSACTION DOCTRINE

The disagreement between the majority opinion and the dissent can be framed in terms of which formulation of the step transaction doctrine should apply in the charitable transfer bootstrap context. The majority opinion refused to apply the step transaction doctrine unless the binding commitment test was met. The dissent would have applied the step transaction doctrine if the mutually interdependent test had been met. After its defeat in Grove and a similar defeat in Palmer v. Commissioner, 523 F.2d 1308 (8th Cir. 1975), the IRS issued Rev.Rul. 78–197, 1978–1 C.B. 83, which stated that the IRS would follow Palmer and Grove under facts similar to those cases and would not assert that a prearranged charitable contribution of shares followed by a redemption of the gifted shares constituted a redemption from the donor as long as the charitable organization was not bound to go through with the redemption. Said differently, the IRS agrees that prospectively it would apply the step transaction principles only in situations where the "binding commitment" for their redemption or resale existed at the time of the charity's receipt of those shares. Thus, the charitable transfer bootstrap context provides an explicit statement that the step transaction doctrine may apply under the narrowest formulation of that doctrine, namely the binding commitment test.

2. MEANING OF LEGAL OBLIGATION

In Blake v. Commissioner, 697 F.2d 473 (2d Cir. 1982), the Second Circuit dealt with a similar charitable contribution of stock followed by a redemption of the contributed stock. In that case, there was no written binding obligation for the corporation to redeem the donated stock. However, the Second Circuit believed that an "informal understanding" existed between the charity and the taxpayer and, given that understanding, that the charity had an enforceable cause of action to have the stock redeemed under state law.

3. CHARITABLE CONTRIBUTION OF 306 STOCK

The ability to obtain a charitable contribution deduction for gifted stock is curtailed in the context of § 306 stock. In this regard, § 170(e) reduces the amount of the donor's charitable contribution deduction by the amount of the noncapital gain portion of the stock. See Rev.Rul. 80–33, 1980–1 C.B. 69.

CHAPTER 10

TAX-FREE ACQUISITIVE REORGANIZATIONS

SECTION 1.   ACQUISITIVE REORGANIZATION TYPES

A.   EARLY JUDICIAL BACKGROUND

Marr v. United States

Supreme Court of the United States, 1925.
268 U.S. 536.

■ MR. JUSTICE BRANDEIS delivered the opinion of the Court.

Prior to March 1, 1913, Marr and wife purchased 339 shares of the preferred and 425 shares of the common stock of the General Motors Company of New Jersey for $76,400. In 1916, they received in exchange for this stock 451 shares of the preferred and 2,125 shares of the common stock of the General Motors Corporation of Delaware which (including a small cash payment) had the aggregate market value of $400,866.57. The difference between the cost of their stock in the New Jersey corporation and the value of the stock in the Delaware corporation was $324,466.57. The Treasury Department ruled that this difference was gain or income * * *.

The exchange of securities was effected in this way. The New Jersey corporation had outstanding $15,000,000 of 7 per cent. preferred stock and $15,000,000 of the common stock; all shares being of the par value of $100. It had accumulated from profits a large surplus. The actual value of the common stock was then $842.50 a share. Its officers caused to be organized the Delaware corporation with an authorized capital of $20,000,000 in 6 percent nonvoting preferred stock and $82,600,000 in common stock; all shares being of the par value of $100. The Delaware corporation made to stockholders in the New Jersey corporation the following offer for exchange of securities: For every share of common stock of the New Jersey corporation, five shares of common stock of the Delaware corporation. For every share of the preferred stock of the New Jersey corporation, one and one-third shares of preferred stock of the Delaware corporation. In lieu of a certificate for fractional shares of stock in the Delaware corporation, payment was to be made in cash at the rate of $100 a share for its preferred and at the rate of $150 a share for its common stock. On this basis all the common stock of the New Jersey corporation was exchanged and all the preferred stock except a few shares. These few were redeemed in cash. For acquiring the stock of the New Jersey corporation only $75,000,000 of the common stock of the

Delaware corporation was needed. The remaining $7,600,000 of the authorized common stock was either sold or held for sale as additional capital should be desired. The Delaware corporation, having thus become the owner of all the outstanding stock of the New Jersey corporation, took a transfer of its assets and assumed its liabilities. The latter was then dissolved.

It is clear that all new securities issued in excess of an amount equal to the capitalization of the New Jersey corporation represented income earned by it; that the new securities received by the Marrs in excess of the cost of the securities of the New Jersey corporation theretofore held were financially the equivalent of $324,466.51 in cash; and that Congress intended to tax as income of stockholders such gains when so distributed. The serious question for decision is whether it had power to do so. Marr contends that, since the new corporation was organized to take over the assets and continue the business of the old, and his capital remained invested in the same business enterprise, the additional securities distributed were in legal effect a stock dividend; and that under the rule of Eisner v. Macomber, 252 U.S. 189, 40 S.Ct. 189, applied in Weiss v. Stearn, 265 U.S. 242, 44 S.Ct. 490, he was not taxable thereon as income, because he still held the whole investment. The government insists that identity of the business enterprise is not conclusive; that gain in value resulting from profits is taxable as income, not only when it is represented by an interest in a different business enterprise or property, but also when it is represented by an essentially different interest in the same business enterprise or property; that, in the case at bar, the gain actually made is represented by securities with essentially different characteristics in an essentially different corporation; and that, consequently, the additional value of the new securities, although they are still held by the Marrs, is income under the rule applied in United States v. Phellis, 257 U.S. 156, 42 S.Ct. 63; Rockefeller v. United States, 257 U.S. 176, 42 S.Ct. 68; and Cullinan v. Walker, 262 U.S. 134, 43 S.Ct. 495. In our opinion the government is right.

In each of the five cases named, as in the case at bar, the business enterprise actually conducted remained exactly the same. In United States v. Phellis, in Rockefeller v. United States, and in Cullinan v. Walker, where the additional value in new securities distributed was held to be taxable as income, there had been changes of corporate identity. That is, the corporate property, or a part thereof, was no longer held and operated by the same corporation; and, after the distribution, the stockholders no longer owned merely the same proportional interest of the same character in the same corporation. In Eisner v. Macomber and in Weiss v. Stearn, where the additional value in new securities was held not to be taxable, the identity was deemed to have been preserved. In Eisner v. Macomber the identity was literally maintained. There was no new corporate entity. The same interest in the same corporation was represented after the distribution by more shares of precisely the same character. It was as if the par value of the stock had been reduced, and three shares of reduced par value stock had been issued in place of every two old shares. That is, there was an exchange of certificates but not of interests. In Weiss v. Stearn a new corporation had, in fact, been organized to take over the assets and business of the old. Technically there was a new entity; but the corporate identity was deemed to have been substantially maintained because the new corporation was organized under the laws of the same state, with presumably the same powers as the old. There was also no change in the character of securities issued. By reason of these facts, the proportional interest of the stockholder after the distribution of the new securities was deemed to be exactly the same as if the par value of the stock in the old corporation had been reduced, and five shares of reduced par value stock had been issued in place of every two shares of the old stock. Thus, in Weiss v. Stearn, as in Eisner v. Macomber, the transaction was considered, in essence, an exchange of certificates representing the same interest, not an exchange of interests.

In the case at bar, the new corporation is essentially different from the old. A corporation organized under the laws of Delaware does not have the same rights and powers as one organized under the laws of New Jersey. Because of these inherent differences in rights and powers, both the preferred and the common stock of the old corporation is an essentially different thing from stock of the same general kind in the new. But there are also adventitious differences, substantial in character. A 6 per cent. nonvoting preferred stock is an essentially different thing from a 7 per cent. voting preferred stock. A common stock subject to the priority of $20,000,000 preferred and a $1,200,000 annual dividend charge is an essentially different thing from a common stock subject only to $15,000,000 preferred and a $1,050,000 annual dividend charge. The case at bar is not one in which after the distribution the stockholders have the same proportional interest of the same kind in essentially the same corporation.

Affirmed.

■ The separate opinion of MR. JUSTICE VAN DEVANTER, MR. JUSTICE MCREYNOLDS, MR. JUSTICE SUTHERLAND, and MR. JUSTICE BUTLER.

We think this cause falls within the doctrine of Weiss v. Stearn, 265 U.S. 242, 44 S.Ct. 490, and that the judgment below should be reversed. The practical result of the things done was but the reorganization of a going concern. The business and assets were not materially changed, and the stockholder received nothing actually severed from his original capital interest—nothing differing in substance from what he already had.

Weiss v. Stearn did not turn upon the relatively unimportant circumstance that the new and old corporations were organized under the laws of the same state, but upon the approved definition of income from capital as something severed therefrom and received by the taxpayer for his separate use and benefit. Here stockholders got nothing from the old business or assets except new statements of their undivided interests, and this, as we carefully pointed out, is not enough to create taxable income.

DETAILED ANALYSIS

1. STATUTORY NONRECOGNITION

By the time *Marr* was decided the Internal Revenue Code already contained rudimentary provisions for nonrecognition in certain corporate reorganizations. The first such provisions were enacted in 1918 (and thus did not apply to the transaction in *Marr,* which occurred in 1916), and these early statutes were exceedingly simplistic. For example, both the 1924 and 1928 Acts defined a tax-free reorganization as follows:

> [A] merger or consolidation (including the acquisition by one corporation of at least a majority of the voting stock and at least a majority of the total number of shares of all other classes of stock of another corporation, or substantially all the properties of another corporation).

The statutory definition of reorganization was expanded and refined through the 1930s. Most of the basic principles regarding nonrecognition, however, were in place by 1928. Further changes were made when the 1954 Code was adopted, and a number of refinements have been enacted since that time.

B. THE TYPES OF REORGANIZATIONS

INTERNAL REVENUE CODE: Sections 368 (omitting (a)(2)(F) and (a)(3)); see also 336(c).

REGULATIONS: Section 1.368–1(a)–(c), –2(a), (b), (f), (g).

The corporate reorganization sections cover a variety of corporate transformations. In general, these sections are designed to permit business transactions involving certain corporate acquisitions and readjustments to be carried out without a tax being incurred by the participating corporations or their shareholders at the time of the transaction. The policy rationale for according nonrecognition to these transactions, however over-inclusive and unrealistic that rationale might be, is that although such acquisitions and readjustments change the form of a business enterprise, these changes do not alter the nature or character of the relationship of the enterprise's owners to the enterprise sufficiently to warrant taxation of gain (generally capital gain) or allowance of loss. Because these sections, like the other nonrecognition provisions, permit nonrecognition and hence postponement of gain and loss, special provisions are needed to reflect such nonrecognition in the basis of the corporate assets and stock involved.

This Chapter deals with the application of the provisions permitting deferral of gain recognition upon the sale and purchase of a corporate business. Such transactions are usually referred to as "tax-free" reorganizations. The transactions covered are the same in form as those considered in Chapter 8, i.e., the sale may be completed by the transfer of stock or assets of the target corporation. But in the case of "tax-free" reorganizations, the consideration for the purchase medium is different. In general, the acquiring corporation uses its own stock (or in some cases the stock of its parent corporation), rather than cash or notes, to make the acquisition. As a policy matter, consider whether this difference justifies such a radical difference in tax treatment, particularly where publicly traded corporations are involved. Further, within the tax-free reorganization provisions themselves, small differences in form can produce significantly different tax results. Consider whether these differences are either justified or necessary. Perhaps in no other area of corporate taxation is the late Professor James Eustice's dictum more apt: "In subchapter C, form *is* the substance."

In addition to "acquisitive" reorganizations, there are a number of other corporate readjustments that are governed by the reorganization provisions. Although the acquisition of one corporation by another may be furthered by one of these types of reorganization, more frequently they involve a realignment of the ownership of a single corporation. Such nonacquisitive reorganizations are considered in subsequent chapters.

The term "reorganization" is narrowly defined in § 368(a), which states that the term "reorganization" "*means*" the specifically described transactions rather than "*includes*" those transactions, thus precluding other transactions from qualifying under the statute. The reorganizations considered in this Chapter are as follows:

Type (A) Reorganization: Statutory Merger. Section 368(a)(1)(A) describes a merger or consolidation in compliance with the substantive state corporation law statutes permitting such transactions—such as where the target corporation merges into the acquiring corporation or two corporations consolidate into a newly formed corporation. Treas.Reg. § 1.368–2(b)(1)(ii). Regulatory and judicial authority impose requirements relating to continuity of interest, continuity of business enterprise, and business purpose; these apply to all acquisitive reorganizations, but continuity of interest and continuity of business enterprise tend to be most important in the case of type (A) reorganizations. Where the acquiring corporation acquires the assets of the target corporation in a statutory merger, the acquiring corporation may then transfer part or all of the assets to its controlled subsidiary without disqualifying the (A) reorganization. See I.R.C. § 368(a)(2)(C).

Type (B) Reorganization: Stock-for-Stock Exchange. Section 368(a)(1)(B) defines as a tax-free reorganization the acquisition of stock of the target corporation solely in exchange for the stock of the acquiring corporation if, following the exchange, the acquiring corporation is in control of the target corporation. The shareholders of the target corporation become shareholders in the acquiring corporation. They may be minority or majority shareholders, depending on the amount of stock issued by the acquiring corporation, which depends on the relative size of the target and acquiring corporations. If the target corporation is liquidated (which may be accomplished under § 332 without recognition of gain or loss), the end result is the same as either a statutory merger under (A), above, or a stock-for-assets acquisition under (C), below.

In order to qualify as a (B) reorganization, after the stock-for-stock exchange, the acquiring corporation must have *control* of the target corporation, which is defined in § 368(c) as ownership of 80% of the total combined voting power of all classes of stock entitled to vote and 80% of the total number of shares of all other classes of stock. Rev.Rul. 59–259, 1959–2 C.B. 115, interpreted the statute to require ownership of 80% of each class of nonvoting stock. In addition, to qualify as a reorganization the acquisition of stock of the target corporation must be *solely* in return for *voting stock* of the acquiring corporation. No other consideration is permissible.

There is no requirement that 80% or more of the stock of the target corporation be acquired in one transaction. Thus, any particular acquisition is a reorganization if after that acquisition the acquiring corporation has "control" of the target corporation. Hence, while a previous acquisition of some shares of the target corporation for cash or non-voting stock, or for voting stock but without "control," would not constitute a reorganization, the earlier acquisition would not prevent a later separate acquisition for voting stock from being a reorganization if after the latter acquisition the requisite 80% of the shares of the target corporation are held by the acquiring corporation as a result of the several acquisitions. This acquisition of control over a period of time is called a "creeping acquisition." Even though this rule has been in the statute for nearly 50 years, its application is uncertain, in that an acquisition for cash related in time or by plan to an acquisition for stock may be treated as one transaction and prevent a reorganization, since the "acquisition" would not be solely for voting stock. Treas.Reg. § 1.368–2(c).

A controlled subsidiary corporation may acquire the stock of the target corporation solely in return for the *voting* stock of its parent corporation. In addition, a transaction is not disqualified as a (B) reorganization if, after the transaction, the acquiring corporation in turn transfers the stock of the target corporation to its subsidiary. I.R.C. § 368(a)(2)(C).

Type (C) Reorganization: Stock-for-Assets Exchange. The acquisition by one corporation of "substantially all" the assets of another corporation—as where the acquiring corporation acquires the assets of the target corporation rather than its stock (as in (B) above)—may qualify as a reorganization under § 368(a)(1)(C). Subject to a limited exception, the acquisition must be *solely* by means of the *voting* stock of the acquiring corporation. This asset acquisition is sometimes referred to as a "practical merger." Because of this analogy to a merger, the acquiring corporation must obtain all or substantially all of the target corporation's assets. The IRS considers a transfer of 90% of the net assets and 70% of the gross assets as clearly qualified under the "substantially all the assets" requirement. Rev.Proc. 77–37, 1977–2 C.B. 568. Depending on the circumstances, however, lower percentages may qualify, particularly if the retained assets are used to pay creditors. In addition (and analogous to the end result of a statutory merger), as part of the overall transaction the target corporation must be liquidated, distributing the acquiring corporation stock it receives, as well as any other assets it has retained, to the target corporation's shareholders. I.R.C. § 368(a)(2)(G).

While the acquisition in general must be solely for the voting stock of the acquiring corporation, several exceptions allow the use of other consideration. First, the assumption by the acquiring corporation of the liabilities of the target corporation does not prevent the acquisition from being regarded as solely for voting stock. I.R.C. § 368(a)(1)(C); see also I.R.C. § 357(d)(1) (defining liability assumption). Second, cash or other property may be used if at least 80% of *all* of the assets of the target corporation are acquired for voting stock. Any additional assets may be acquired for cash, other property, or other stock. However, in applying the 20% limitation, liabilities of the target corporation assumed by the acquiring corporation are treated as cash. I.R.C. § 368(a)(2)(B).

Section 368(a)(1)(C) also permits the assets of the target corporation to be acquired by a controlled subsidiary corporation in exchange for the voting stock of its parent. Whether the acquisition was made directly by the acquiring corporation or by a controlled subsidiary corporation in exchange for voting stock of its controlling parent corporation, the corporation that initially acquired the assets may then transfer the assets to a controlled subsidiary corporation without destroying the reorganization treatment. See I.R.C. § 368(a)(2)(C).

Forward Triangular Merger. Section § 368(a)(2)(D) permits a subsidiary corporation, which may either be an existing or a newly created subsidiary, to acquire the assets of the target corporation in a statutory merger between the subsidiary corporation and target corporation in which the shareholders of the target corporation receive the stock of the acquiring subsidiary's parent corporation, for "substantially all" of the properties of the target corporation if (1) the transaction would have qualified as an (A) reorganization if the merger had been directly into the parent corporation,[1] and (2) no stock of the acquiring subsidiary corporation is used in the transaction. If these conditions are met, the transaction will be treated as a type (A)

---

[1] The restriction that the transaction "would have qualified" as an (A) reorganization if it had involved the acquiring corporation directly does not require that the hypothetical merger would have been permissible under state merger statutes; it has reference to qualification under judicially developed restrictions on tax-free reorganizations such as "business purpose," "continuity of interest," etc., discussed below; see Treas.Reg. § 1.368–2(b)(2).

reorganization. The § 368(a)(2)(D) transaction frequently is referred to as a "forward" triangular reorganization.

Reverse Triangular Merger. Section 368(a)(2)(E) permits a "reverse" triangular merger to qualify under certain specified conditions. Here, rather than a merger of the target corporation into the acquiring subsidiary corporation (using the stock of the parent corporation), the acquiring subsidiary corporation is merged into the target corporation (which survives the transaction), with the shareholders of the target corporation receiving stock of the acquiring subsidiary's parent corporation. This transaction qualifies if (1) after the transaction the surviving target corporation holds substantially all of its properties and the properties of the acquiring subsidiary corporation (other than stock of the parent corporation that may have been issued to the subsidiary corporation to be distributed in the transaction to the shareholders of the target corporation), and (2) in the transaction the former shareholders of the target corporation exchange for *voting* stock of the acquiring subsidiary's parent corporation an amount of stock in the target corporation that constitutes *control* of the target corporation. If these conditions are met, the transaction will qualify as an (A) reorganization.

Under § 368(a)(2)(E), the target corporation ends up as a subsidiary of the acquiring parent corporation, replacing the original subsidiary corporation. In contrast, in a § 368(a)(2)(D) forward triangular transaction, the target corporation ceases to exist and its assets end up as a part of the acquiring subsidiary corporation. In both cases, however, the shareholders of the target corporation become shareholders of the acquiring parent corporation. The "forward triangular merger" leaves the shareholders of the target corporation in the same position as if the target corporation had merged into the acquiring parent corporation in an (A) reorganization followed by a § 368(a)(2)(C) drop down of the target's assets into a subsidiary of the acquiring corporation. The end result of a "reverse triangular merger" is like a (B) stock-for-stock reorganization by the acquiring parent corporation of the target stock, followed by the merger of a controlled subsidiary into the target. The target corporation ends up as a controlled subsidiary of the acquiring corporation. In effect, the rules are designed to qualify as tax-free the differing merger mechanics utilized to obtain the same end result.

The statutory development has not, however, been an orderly one, and there are different technical requirements to be satisfied depending on the route chosen to reach the end result. It is useful to think of § 368(a)(2)(D) and (E) transactions as representing two separate and independent forms of corporate reorganization. The technical differences are significant—for example, § 368(a)(2)(E) requires that the acquiring corporation use its voting stock as consideration in contrast to the allowance of the use of nonvoting stock in a § 368(a)(2)(D) transaction.

Type (D) Reorganization: Transfer of Assets for Stock. The transfer of some or all of a corporation's assets to a newly created or existing corporation followed by the distribution of the stock of the transferee corporation to the shareholders of the transferor corporation is a type (D) reorganization if, the stock distribution meets the requirements of § 354, § 355, or § 356. Thus, for example, if X corporation transfers some or all of its assets to a new or existing Y corporation followed by a distribution of a controlling amount of the Y corporation stock to the X corporation shareholders in a distribution that qualifies under § 354 or § 355 (with § 356 potentially applicable to each type, depending on the presence of boot), the asset transfer is a type (D) reorganization. The requirements for a type (D) reorganization differ significantly depending on whether the distribution is nondivisive (§ 354) or divisive (§ 355). The current chapter focuses on nondivisive type (D) reorganizations, while Chapter 12 discusses divisive type (D) transactions.

For a nondivisive type (D), the transferor corporation must transfer "substantially all" of its assets to the transferee corporation and liquidate. I.R.C. § 354(b)(1). The transferor or its shareholders must "control" the transferee corporation immediately after the asset transfer, but the control requirement will be met through ownership of either at least 50% of the combined voting power or 50% of the total value of shares of stock, determined after taking into account (with some small adjustments) § 318 constructive ownership rules. I.R.C. § 368(a)(2)(H) (via a cross reference to § 304(c)). In a nondivisive type (D) via § 354, the liquidating distribution by the transferor corporation of transferee stock to the transferor corporation shareholders need not constitute a controlling amount of transferee corporation stock. Because of the lower control threshold, nondivisive type (D) reorganizations include a range of transactions.

For example, if X Corporation, the stock of which was owned equally by A and B, transferred all of its assets to Y Corporation, in which A, B, and C each owned 10 shares, in exchange for 30 shares of voting stock, which X Corporation distributed equally between A and B in a liquidating distribution qualifying under § 354, the transaction is a type (D) reorganization. In this, case, after the reorganization, Y Corporation's shares are owned as follows: A owns 25, B owns 25, and C owns 10. As a second example, if X Corporation, the stock of which was owned equally by A and B, transferred all of its assets to Y Corporation, all 50 of the shares of which were owned by C, in exchange for 50 shares of newly issued Y voting stock, which X Corporation distributed to A and B in a liquidating distribution qualifying under § 354, the transaction also is a type (D) reorganization. In this case, after the reorganization, Y Corporation's shares are owned as follows: A, 25, B, 25, and C 50. In both instances the reorganization is a type of acquisitive reorganization.

A type (D) reorganization also can take place through transactions in which there is little or no change in beneficial ownership. For example, if A and B equally own all of each of V Corporation and W Corporation, and V Corporation transfers all of its assets to W Corporation, following which V Corporation liquidates, the transaction is a type (D) reorganization.

Type (G) Reorganization: Bankruptcy Reorganization. A transfer of the assets of a corporation involved in a bankruptcy reorganization, or a receivership, foreclosure, or similar judicial proceeding in a federal or state court is a tax-free reorganization under § 368(a)(1)(G) if the stock or securities received from the insolvent corporation are distributed pursuant to a plan of reorganization in a transaction that qualifies under § 354, § 355 or § 356. Section 368(a)(1)(G) applies only to judicially supervised insolvency proceedings. Thus, a nonjudicial reorganization of an insolvent corporation must qualify under one of the other provisions of § 368 in order to achieve reorganization status. But, where a transaction qualifies both as a type (G) and, as a result of its form, as another type of reorganization, for example a type (C), it will be treated as a type (G). I.R.C. § 368(a)(3)(C).

The reorganization provisions in subparagraphs (A), (B), (C), (D), and (G) of § 368(a)(1), together with subparagraphs (D) and (E) of § 368(a)(2), cover methods by which several corporations may be combined into one ownership. The types (A), (C), (D), and (G) reorganizations, and the forward triangular merger under § 368(a)(2)(D) are analogous to asset acquisitions; the type (B) reorganization and the reverse triangular merger under § 368(a)(2)(E) are analogous to stock acquisitions. While the various statutorily defined reorganizations overlap to a considerable extent, there are differences among them that can influence the choice of the particular reorganization route to be utilized and that may present traps to disqualify a reorganization that fails the proper form.

Section 368 does not govern the tax consequences of a reorganization; it merely defines a reorganization. The operative provisions providing nonrecognition and the attendant basis consequences appear elsewhere in the Code, and are discussed in detail in subsequent sections of this Chapter.

PROBLEM SET 1

Which of the following transactions are eligible to qualify as a reorganization as defined in § 368. If the transaction qualifies, which subsection of § 368 applies?

1.   (a) Pursuant to a state law statute governing mergers, T Corp. is merged into P Corp. The T Corp. shareholders surrender their stock, which is cancelled, in exchange for P Corp. voting common stock.

    (b) Pursuant to state law statute governing mergers, T Corp. is merged into P Corp. The T Corp. shareholders surrender their stock, which is cancelled, in exchange for P Corp. nonvoting preferred stock.

(c)   Pursuant to state law statute governing mergers, T Corp. is merged into P Corp. The T Corp. shareholders surrender their stock, which is cancelled, in exchange for P Corp. 25-year sinking fund 6% debentures.

(d)   Pursuant to state law statute governing mergers, T Corp. is merged into P Corp. The T Corp. shareholders surrender their stock, which is cancelled, in exchange for P Corp. voting common stock. Immediately after the merger of T Corp. into P. Corp., P Corp. transfers all of the T Corp. assets to its newly formed wholly owned subsidiary, S Corp.

(e)   Pursuant to state law statute governing mergers, T Corp. is merged into PS LLC, a limited liability company wholly owned by P Corp. The T Corp. shareholders surrender their stock, which is cancelled, in exchange for P Corp. voting common stock.

2.   (a)   P Corp. makes a tender offer directly to the shareholders of T Corp. to acquire the T Corp. stock in an exchange for one share of P Corp. voting common stock for each share of T Corp. stock.

(1)   Shareholders owning 80% of the shares of T Corp. accept the tender offer.

(2)   Shareholders owning 79% of the shares of T Corp. accept the tender offer.

(b)   P Corp. makes a tender offer to the shareholders of T Corp. to acquire the T Corp. stock in an exchange of one share of P Corp. nonvoting common stock for each share of T Corp. stock, and all of the shareholders of T Corp. accept the offer.

(c)   P Corp. makes a tender offer to the shareholders of T Corp. to acquire the T Corp. stock in an exchange of one share of P Corp. voting common stock, worth $95 and $5 of cash, for each share of T Corp. stock, and all of the shareholders of T Corp. accept the offer.

(d)   S Corp., a wholly owned subsidiary of P Corp. makes a tender offer to the shareholders of T Corp. of one share of P Corp. voting preferred stock for each share of T Corp. stock. 80% of the shareholders of T Corp. accept the tender offer.

(e)   P Corp. makes a tender offer to the shareholders of T Corp. to acquire the T Corp. stock in an exchange of one share of P Corp. voting common stock for each share of T Corp. stock, and all of the shareholders of T Corp. accept the offer. Immediately after the acquisition of the T Corp. stock, P Corp. transfers all of the T Corp. stock to its newly formed wholly owned subsidiary, S Corp.

3.   (a)   (1)   Pursuant to a purchase and sale agreement, T Corp. transfers all of its assets to P Corp., which assumes all of T Corp.'s liabilities ($200,000), for 1000 shares of voting common stock of P Corp., worth $1,000,000. T Corp. liquidates and distributes the stock to its shareholders.

(2)   What if T Corp. does not liquidate?

(b)   Pursuant to a purchase and sale agreement, T Corp. transfers all of its assets to P Corp., which assumes all of T Corp.'s liabilities ($200,000), for 900 shares of voting common stock of P Corp., worth $ 900,000 and

$100,000 of cash. T Corp. liquidates and distributes the stock to its shareholders.

(c) Pursuant to a purchase and sale agreement, T Corp. transfers all of its assets to S Corp., 80% of the stock of which is owned by P Corp., for 1000 shares of voting preferred stock of P Corp., worth $1,000,000. T Corp. liquidates and distributes the P Corp. stock to its shareholders.

(d) Pursuant to a purchase and sale agreement, T Corp. transfers all of its assets to P Corp. in exchange for 1000 shares of voting common stock of P Corp. T Corp. liquidates and distributes the stock to its shareholders. Immediately after the merger of T Corp. into P. Corp., P Corp. transfers all of the T Corp. assets to its newly formed wholly owned subsidiary, S Corp.

4.   Pursuant to state law statute governing mergers, T Corp. is merged into S Corp., a wholly owned subsidiary of P Corp.

(a) The T Corp. shareholders surrender their stock, which is cancelled, for P Corp. voting common stock.

(b) The T Corp. shareholders surrender their stock, which is cancelled, for P Corp. nonvoting common stock.

5.   Pursuant to state law statute governing mergers, S Corp., a wholly owned subsidiary of P Corp. is merged into T Corp.

(a) The T Corp. shareholders surrender their stock, which is cancelled, in exchange for P Corp. voting stock. P Corp. exchanges its S Corp. stock, which is cancelled, for newly issued T Corp. stock, which then constitutes 100% of the T Corp. outstanding stock.

(b) The T Corp. shareholders surrender their stock, which is cancelled, for P Corp. nonvoting preferred stock. P Corp. exchanges its S Corp. stock, which is cancelled, for newly issued T Corp. stock, which then constitutes 100 % of the T Corp. outstanding stock.

6.   (a)   T Corp., which is equally owned by A, B, and C, sold all of its assets to P Corp., the voting common stock of which was equally owned by C and D, for 600 shares of P Corp nonvoting preferred stock. T Corp. liquidated and distributed the P Corp nonvoting preferred stock equally among A, B, and C.

(b) T Corp., which is equally owned by A and B sold all of its assets to P Corp., in which B, C and D each originally owned 100 shares of voting common stock, for 150 shares of P Corp voting common stock. T Corp. liquidated and distributed the P Corp stock equally between A and B.

SECTION 2.   REORGANIZATION FUNDAMENTALS AND TYPE (A) REORGANIZATIONS

A. OVERVIEW

The principal requirements for a Type (A) are not found in the statute, which specifies only "a statutory merger or consolidation." Instead, the requirements have their roots in numerous judicial decisions and have been formalized through Regulations. These include the requirements that there be "continuity of interest," "continuity of business enterprise," and business purpose. These requirements apply generally to all the reorganizations discussed in this Chapter, but in the case of continuity of interest and continuity of business enterprise, greater statutory specificity may reduce the need to refer to judicial and regulatory authorities. This Section explains the continuity of interest and continuity of business enterprise requirements; it also discusses in detail the tax consequences of a qualifying Type (A) reorganization. Discussion of business purpose, and other substance-over-form principles, is deferred to the end of the Chapter after the reader has gained greater familiarity with the formal rules governing reorganizations.

DETAILED ANALYSIS

1. THE DEFINITION OF "STATUTORY MERGER"

1.1. *Mergers Involving a Disregarded Entity*

Treas.Reg. § 1.368–2(b)(1) provides that a statutory merger or consolidation under § 368(a)(1)(A) is limited to transactions pursuant to a statute (whether domestic or foreign) that effects the merger or consolidation and that results in one corporation and all of its related disregarded entities[2] (defined as a "combining unit") acquiring the assets and liabilities of each member of another combining unit. Subject to very limited exceptions, each member of the acquired combining unit must simultaneously cease its separate legal existence for all purposes.[3] The Regulations describe the acquiring and target corporations as "combining units" in order to provide that a merger of a target corporation into a disregarded entity that is owned by a corporation will be treated as a statutory merger of the target corporation into the corporation owning the acquiring disregarded entity.

The preamble to the Proposed Regulations indicated that this result is consistent with the theory that all of the assets of a disregarded entity are treated as directly owned by the corporate owner of the disregarded entity. See Reg.–126485–01, Statutory Mergers and Consolidations, 66 F.R. 57400 (Nov. 15, 2001). Otherwise, as provided by Treas.Reg. § 1.368–2(b)(1)(iii), a state law merger involving an entity that is disregarded for federal tax purposes under Treas.Reg. § 301.7701–3(b)(1)(ii), such as a single member LLC that has not elected to be taxed as a corporation, cannot qualify as a merger under § 368(a)(1)(A).

Mergers involving disregarded entities that do not qualify as a type (A) reorganization under Treas.Reg. § 1.368–2(b)(1) might qualify as a reorganization under another subsection of § 368, such as § 368(a)(1)(C), dealing with voting-stock-for-asset reorganizations, if all the applicable requirements are met. Likewise, a merger of a disregarded entity into an acquiring corporation might qualify as a reorganization under § 368(a)(1)(D),

---

[2] Disregarded entities are generally ignored as entities separate from their owners and their assets are treated as held directly by their owners.

[3] The requirements that all of the assets and liabilities of the target entity be acquired and that the acquired entity cease to exist prevent divisive transactions, which are governed by § 355, discussed in Chapter 12, from qualifying for nonrecognition as a statutory merger.

if all relevant requirements are met. (The merger of a disregarded entity owned by one corporation into another corporation, or into a disregarded entity owned by another corporation, may also be tested under § 355, discussed in Chapter 12, under which it rarely will qualify for nonrecognition.)

1.2. *Merger of Controlled Subsidiary into Parent*

If an 80% controlled subsidiary is merged into its parent, Treas.Reg. § 1.332–2(d) and (e) provide that the transaction will be taxed as if the subsidiary had been liquidated. H.K. Porter Co. v. Commissioner, 87 T.C. 689 (1986), and Spaulding Bakeries Inc. v. Commissioner, 27 T.C. 684 (1957), aff'd 252 F.2d 693 (2d Cir. 1958), provide that § 332 applies only to those cases in which the recipient corporation receives at least partial payment for each class of stock that it owns in the liquidating corporation. If the liquidation of a subsidiary fails to qualify under § 332, the transaction nevertheless might qualify as a tax-free reorganization under § 368. The tax-free reorganization that occurs in this liquidation scenario would be what is commonly termed "an upstream § 368(a)(1)(C) reorganization," described in Treas.Reg. § 1.368–2(d)(4)(i); see also Treas.Reg. § 1.368–1(e)(1), (e)(8), Ex. 7; Treas.Reg. § 1.368–2(d)(4)(ii), Ex. 1; Notice of Proposed Rulemaking and Notice of Public Hearing, The Solely for Voting Stock Requirement in Certain Corporate Reorganizations, REG–115086–98, 64 Fed. Reg. 31770 (June 14, 1999).

In Rev.Rul. 69–617, 1969–2 C.B. 57, a parent corporation owned more than 80% of the stock of its subsidiary. In order to operate its subsidiary as a wholly-owned subsidiary, it merged the subsidiary into itself and the minority shareholders of the subsidiary received the parent's stock. The parent then transferred all of the assets acquired from the subsidiary to a newly created wholly-owned subsidiary. The ruling held that the transaction constituted an (A) reorganization; § 332 was not applicable because the immediate transfer of the subsidiary's assets to the newly created subsidiary meant that there was not a complete liquidation of the former subsidiary. Thus, the minority shareholders of the former subsidiary received tax-free reorganization treatment, whereas under liquidation treatment, gain would have resulted to them.

In Kass v. Commissioner, 60 T.C. 218 (1973), aff'd by order, 491 F.2d 749 (3d Cir.1974), the IRS conceded that "theoretically" it would be possible for the same transaction to be treated as a liquidation under § 332 and § 334(b) at the corporate level and as a reorganization from the point of view of minority shareholders. While no case has expressly so held, such treatment was implicit in King Enterprises, Inc. v. United States, 418 F.2d 511 (Ct.Cl.1969). Treas.Reg. § 1.332–2(d) also strongly implies that a statutory merger treated as a liquidation under § 332 as to the parent and subsidiary corporations can be a reorganization under § 368 as far as minority shareholders are concerned. In certain cases, however, *Kass* will require that minority shareholders of the subsidiary who receive parent corporation stock in the merger recognize gain or loss on the exchange of their shares.

B. THE CONTINUITY OF SHAREHOLDER INTEREST REQUIREMENT

(1) QUALITATIVE AND QUANTITATIVE ASPECTS

REGULATIONS: Sections 1.368–1(a), (b), (e) (excluding (e)(2)(iv), Exs. 4–6, 8–12), –2(a).

Le Tulle v. Scofield

Supreme Court of the United States, 1940.
308 U.S. 415.

■ MR. JUSTICE ROBERTS delivered the opinion of the court.

* * *

The Gulf Coast Irrigation Company was the owner of irrigation properties. Petitioner was its sole stockholder. He personally owned certain lands and other irrigation properties. November 4, 1931, the Irrigation Company, the Gulf Coast Water Company, and the petitioner, entered into an agreement which recited that the petitioner owned all of the stock of the Irrigation Company; described the company's properties, and stated that, prior to conveyance to be made pursuant to the contract, the Irrigation Company would be the owner of certain other lands and irrigation properties. These other lands and properties were those which the petitioner individually owned. The contract called for a conveyance of all the properties owned, and to be owned, by the Irrigation Company for $50,000 in cash and $750,000 in bonds of the Water Company, payable serially over the period January 1, 1933, to January 1, 1944. The petitioner joined in this agreement as a guarantor of the title of the Irrigation Company and for the purpose of covenanting that he would not personally enter into the irrigation business within a fixed area during a specified period after the execution of the contract. Three days later, at a special meeting of stockholders of the Irrigation Company, the proposed reorganization was approved, the minutes stating that the taxpayer, "desiring also to reorganize his interest in the properties," had consented to be a party to the reorganization. The capital stock of the Irrigation Company was increased and thereupon the taxpayer subscribed for the new stock and paid for it by conveyance of his individual properties.

The contract between the two corporations was carried out November 18, with the result that the Water Company became owner of all the properties then owned by the Irrigation Company including the property theretofore owned by the petitioner individually. Subsequently all of its assets, including the bonds received from the Water Company, were distributed to the petitioner. The company was then dissolved. The petitioner and his wife filed a tax return * * * in which they reported no gain as a result of the receipt of the liquidating dividend from the Irrigation Company. The latter reported no gain for the taxable year in virtue of its receipt of bonds and cash from the Water Company. The Commissioner of Internal Revenue assessed additional taxes against the * * * taxpayers, by reason of the receipt of the liquidating dividend, and against the petitioner as transferee of the Irrigation Company's assets in virtue of the gain realized by the company on the sale of its property. The tax was paid and claims for refund were filed. * * * [The taxpayer] alleged that the transaction constituted a tax-exempt reorganization as defined by the Revenue Act. The * * * causes were * * * tried by the District Court without a jury. The respondent's contention that the transaction amounted merely to a sale of assets by the petitioner and the Irrigation Company and did not fall within the statutory definition of a tax-free reorganization was overruled by the District Court and judgment was entered for the petitioner.

* * *

The Circuit Court of Appeals concluded that, as the Water Company acquired substantially all the properties of the Irrigation Company, there was a merger of the latter within the literal language of the statute, but held that, in the light of the construction this Court has put upon the statute, the transaction would not be a reorganization unless the transferor retained a definite and substantial interest in the affairs of the transferee. It thought this requirement was satisfied by the taking of the bonds of the Water Company, and, therefore, agreed with the District Court that a reorganization had been consummated. * * *

[Ed.: The Circuit Court then reversed the District Court as to part of the petitioner's tax liability on grounds that had not been raised by the parties. The Circuit Court concluded that the petitioner was taxable on the gain attributable to the transfer of his individually owned assets to the Irrigation Company for transfer to the Water Company. The petitioner sought to overturn the Circuit Court decision on this ground. The Commissioner, having won in the Circuit Court, did not seek certiorari.]

We find it unnecessary to consider petitioner's contention that the Circuit Court of Appeals erred in deciding the case on a ground not raised by the pleadings, not before the trial court, not suggested or argued in the Circuit Court of Appeals, and one as to which the petitioner had never had the opportunity to present his evidence, since we are of opinion that the transaction did not amount to a reorganization and that, therefore, the petitioner cannot complain, as the judgment must be affirmed on the ground that no tax-free reorganization was effected within the meaning of the statute.

Section 112(i) provides, so far as material: "(1) The term 'reorganization' means (A) a merger or consolidation (including the acquisition by one corporation of at least a majority of the voting stock and at least a majority of the total number of shares of all other classes of stock of another corporation, or substantially all the properties of another corporation) * * * "

As the court below properly stated, the section is not to be read literally, as denominating the transfer of all the assets of one company for what amounts to a cash consideration given by the other a reorganization. We have held that where the consideration consists of cash and short term notes the transfer does not amount to a reorganization within the true meaning of the statute, but is a sale upon which gain or loss must be reckoned.[3] We have said that the statute was not satisfied unless the transferor retained a substantial stake in the enterprise and such a stake was thought to be retained where a large proportion of the consideration was in common stock of the transferee,[4] or where the transferor took cash and the entire issue of preferred stock of the transferee corporation.[5] And, where the consideration is represented by a substantial proportion of stock, and the balance in bonds, the total consideration received is exempt from tax under § 112(b)(4) and 112(g).[6]

In applying our decision in the Pinellas case the courts have generally held that receipt of long term bonds as distinguished from short term notes constitutes the retention of an interest in the purchasing corporation. There has naturally been some difficulty in classifying the securities involved in various cases.[7]

We are of opinion that the term of the obligations is not material. Where the consideration is wholly in the transferee's bonds, or part cash and part such bonds, we think it cannot be said that the transferor retains any proprietary interest in the enterprise. On the contrary, he becomes a creditor of the transferee; and we do not think that the fact referred to by the Circuit Court of Appeals, that the bonds were secured solely by the assets transferred and that, upon default, the bondholder would retake only the property sold, changes his status from that of a creditor to one having a proprietary stake, within the purview of the statute.

We conclude that the Circuit Court of Appeals was in error in holding that, as respects any of the property transferred to the Water Company, the transaction was other than a sale or exchange upon which gain or loss must be reckoned in accordance with the provisions of the revenue act dealing with the recognition of gain or loss upon a sale or exchange.

Had the respondent sought and been granted certiorari the petitioner's tax liability would, in the view we have expressed, be

---

[3]   Pinellas Ice & Cold Storage Co. v. Commissioner, 287 U.S. 462.

[4]   Helvering v. Minnesota Tea Co., 296 U.S. 378.

[5]   Nelson Co. v. Helvering, 296 U.S. 374.

[6]   45 Stat. 816, 818. See Helvering v. Watts, 296 U.S. 387.

[7]   Worcester Salt Co. v. Commissioner, 75 F.2d 251; Lilienthal v. Commissioner, 80 F.2d 411, 413; Burnham v. Commissioner, 86 F.2d 776; Commissioner v. Kitselman, 89 F.2d 458; Commissioner v. Freund, 98 F.2d 201; * * * L. & E. Stirn, Inc. v. Commissioner, 107 F.2d 390.

substantially increased over the amount found due by the Circuit Court of Appeals. Since the respondent has not drawn into question so much of the judgment as exempts from taxation gain to the irrigation Company arising from transfer of its assets owned by it on and prior to November 4, 1931, and the part of the liquidating dividend attributable thereto, we cannot afford him relief from that portion of the judgment which was adverse to him.

* * *

The judgment of the Circuit Court of Appeals is affirmed * * *.

John A. Nelson Co. v. Helvering

Supreme Court of the United States, 1935.
296 U.S. 374.

■ Mr. Justice McReynolds delivered the opinion of the Court.

The petitioner contests a deficiency income assessment made on account of alleged gains during 1926. It claims that the transaction out of which the assessment arose was reorganization within the statute. Section 203, Revenue Act, 1926 * * * is relied upon.

In 1926, under an agreement with petitioner, the Elliott-Fisher Corporation organized a new corporation with 12,500 shares non-voting preferred stock and 30,000 shares of common stock. It purchased the latter for $2,000,000 cash. This new corporation then acquired substantially all of petitioner's property, except $100,000, in return for $2,000,000 cash and the entire issue of preferred stock. Part of this cash was used to retire petitioner's own preferred shares, and the remainder and the preferred stock of the new company went to its stockholders. It retained its franchise and $100,000, and continued to be liable for certain obligations. The preferred stock so distributed, except in case of default, had no voice in the control of the issuing corporation.

The Commissioner, Board of Tax Appeals, and the court all concluded there was no reorganization. This, we think, was error.

The court below thought the facts showed "that the transaction essentially constituted a sale of the greater part of petitioner's assets for cash and the preferred stock in the new corporation, leaving the Elliott-Fisher Company in entire control of the new corporation by virtue of its ownership of the common stock."

"The controlling facts leading to this conclusion are that petitioner continued its corporate existence and its franchise and retained a portion of its assets; that it acquired no controlling interest in the corporation to which it delivered the greater portion of its assets; that there was no continuity of interest from the old corporation to the new; that the control of the property conveyed passed to a stranger, in the management of which petitioner retained no voice.

The case law never clearly established a specific minimum percentage of the total consideration that must be received in the form of stock of the acquiring corporation. Note, however, that although the issue before the Supreme Court in John A. Nelson Co. v. Helvering, 296 U.S. 374 (1935), supra § 1.1 Detailed Analysis, was whether preferred stock, as opposed to common stock, provided adequate *qualitative* continuity of interest, which the Supreme Court answered affirmatively, finding the continuity of interest requirement to have been satisfied, on the facts only 38.46% of the consideration received by the former shareholders of the target corporation was stock of the acquiring corporation. Although the IRS did not argue that the quantitative aspect of the continuity of interest requirement was not met in *John A. Nelson Co.*, the case came to be cited by taxpayers for the proposition that 38.46% was adequate quantitative continuity of interest.

In 2005, the Treasury Department promulgated Regulations that include an example that sets the administratively sanctioned threshold for adequate quantitative continuity of interest at 40% stock consideration. Treas.Reg. § 1.368–1(e)(2)(v), Ex. 1. Conversely, Treas.Reg. § 1.368–1(e)(2)(v), Ex. 2, indicates that stock consideration of 25% is insufficient. See also Kass v. Commissioner, 60 T.C. 218 (1973), aff'd by order, 491 F.2d 749 (3d Cir.1974) (16% insufficient); Yoc Heating Corp. v. Commissioner, 61 T.C. 168 (1973) (15% insufficient). Note, however, that because of the existence of statutory quantitative continuity of interest requirements for type (B), type (C), and § 368(a)(2)(E) reverse triangular mergers, this 40% continuity of interest safe harbor generally applies only to type (A) and § 368(a)(2)(D) forward triangular merger reorganizations. Type (D) reorganizations have unique continuity of interest requirements.

Rev.Rul. 66–224, 1966–2 C.B. 114, held that the continuity of interest requirement is to be applied with reference to the aggregate consideration received by the entire group of the shareholders of the acquired corporation. Thus, for example, if A, B, C, D, and E each owns 20% of the stock of the target corporation, and the target corporation is merged into the acquiring corporation in consideration of $80,000 worth of the acquiring corporation stock and $120,000 of cash, the transaction will qualify as a type (A) reorganization regardless of how the consideration is distributed among A, B, C, D, and E. Thus, A and B could receive only stock while C, D, and E received only cash. The gain attributable to the cash boot that must be recognized by each shareholder, however, will be determined individually. In this regard, note, however, that if a particular shareholder receives only cash (or debt instruments) in exchange for the shareholder's stock, § 356 does not apply to that particular shareholder; rather, § 1001 applies to that shareholder.

2.2. *Date of Valuation*

Treas.Reg. § 1.368–1(e)(2) provides that if the consideration to be provided to the target corporation shareholders is fixed in the binding contract and includes only stock of the issuing corporation and money, the determination of whether the continuity of interest requirement is satisfied is based on the value of the consideration to be exchanged for the proprietary interests in the target corporation as of the end of the last business day before the first date there is a binding contract to effect the potential reorganization. The number of shares of stock of the acquiring corporation that will be exchanged for stock of the target corporation generally is fixed by agreement at a time significantly in advance of the actual closing of the transaction. The Regulation is intended to eliminate uncertainty where the target corporation shareholders receive cash (or debt instruments) in addition to acquiring corporation stock and, at the time the transaction is agreed upon, the amount of the boot equals the value of the agreed upon number of shares of the acquiring corporation stock to be received. Otherwise, the transaction might fail to satisfy the continuity of interest requirement if the value of the acquiring corporation's stock declined between the date the parties agreed to the terms of the transaction (the signing date) and the date the transaction closed if the quantitative aspect of the continuity of interest requirement were tested on the closing date rather than the signing date.

Under Treas.Reg. § 1.368–1(e)(2)(iii)(A), a contract provides for fixed consideration if it specifies the number of shares of the acquiring corporation, the amount of money, and the other property (identified by value or by description) that is to be exchanged for the stock of the target corporation. With an Orwellian flourish, Treas.Reg. § 1.368–1(e)(2)(iii)(C)(1) states that "a contract that provides for contingent consideration will be treated as providing for fixed consideration if it would satisfy the requirements of paragraph (e)(2)(iii)(A) of this section without the contingent adjustment provision." Treas.Reg. § 1.368–1(e)(2)(iii)(C)(2) adds that contingent consideration will not be fixed consideration if the adjustments prevent the target shareholders from being subject to the economic benefits and burdens of ownership of the acquiring corporation stock as of the last business day before a binding contract. Thus, adjustments that reflect changes in the value of the stock or assets of the acquiring corporation at a later date will prevent the contract from being treated as providing for fixed consideration. The preamble to the almost identical Temporary Regulations that preceded the current Regulations suggests that adjustments to the consideration are permitted if they do not

> decrease the ratio of the value of the shares of issuing corporation stock to the value of the money or other property (determined as of the last business day before the first date there is a binding contract) to be delivered to the target corporation shareholders relative to the ratio of the value of the shares of the issuing corporation stock to the value of the money or other property (determined as of the last business day before the first date there is a binding contract) to be delivered to the target corporation shareholders if none of the contingent consideration were delivered to the target corporation shareholders.

T.D. 9316, 2007–1 C.B. 962 (2007).

Under Treas.Reg. § 1.368–1(e)(2)(iii)(B), if the target corporation's shareholders may elect to receive either stock or money, the contract provides for fixed consideration if the determination of the number of shares of issuing corporation stock to be provided to the target corporation shareholder is based on the value of the issuing corporation stock on the last business day before the first date there is a binding contract (known as the "signing date"). The preamble to the identical Temporary Regulations indicated that the IRS and Treasury believe that if shareholders have an election to receive stock of the acquiring corporation at an exchange rate based on the value of the acquiring corporation stock on the signing date, the target shareholders are at risk for the economic benefits and burdens of ownership of the acquiring corporation stock as of the signing date. T.D. 9316. Thus, the preamble concluded that it is appropriate to value the stock of the acquiring corporation as of the signing date for purposes of testing continuity of interest. Treas.Reg. § 1.368–1(e)(2)(v), Ex. 9, provides an example of the application of the shareholder election:

> On January 3 of year 1, P and T sign a binding contract pursuant to which T will be merged with and into P on June 1 of year 1. On January 2 of year 1, the value of the P stock and the T stock is $1 per share. Pursuant to the contract, at the shareholders' election, each share of T's 100 shares will be exchanged for cash of $1, or alternatively, P stock. The contract provides that the determination of the number of shares of P stock to be exchanged for a share of T stock is made using the value of the P stock on the last business day before the first date there is a binding contract (that is, $1 per share). The contract further provides that, in the aggregate, 40 shares of P stock and $60 will be delivered, and contains a proration mechanism in the event that either item of consideration is oversubscribed. On the closing date, the value of the P stock is $.20 per share, and all target shareholders elect to receive cash. Pursuant to the proration provision, each target share is exchanged for $.60 of cash and $.08 of P stock. Pursuant to paragraph (e)(2)(iii)(A) of this section, the contract provides for fixed consideration because it provides for the number of shares of P stock and the amount of money to be exchanged for all the proprietary interests in the target corporation. Furthermore, pursuant to paragraph (e)(2)(iii)(B) of this section, the contract provides for fixed consideration because the number of shares of issuing corporation stock to be provided to the target corporation shareholders is determined using the pre-signing date value of P stock. Accordingly, whether the transaction satisfies the continuity of interest requirement is determined by reference to the value of the P stock on January 2 of year 1. Because, for continuity purposes, the T stock is exchanged for $40 of P stock and $60 of cash, the transaction preserves a substantial part of the value of the proprietary interest in T. Therefore, the transaction satisfies the continuity of interest requirement.

Treas.Reg. § 1.368–1(e)(2)(ii)(A) provides that a binding contract is an instrument enforceable under applicable law. However, the presence of a condition outside of the control of the parties, such as a requirement for regulatory approval, will not prevent an instrument from being treated as a binding contract. Treas.Reg. § 1.368–1(e)(2)(ii)(B)(1). If in a transaction that provides for adequate continuity of interest, the contract is modified to increase the amount of stock of the acquiring corporation to be delivered to the target shareholders, or to decrease the amount of cash or value of other property, then the modification will not be treated as a modification of the binding contract. Treas.Reg. § 1.368–1(e)(2)(ii)(B)(2). Similarly, in a transaction that does not qualify as a reorganization for failure to meet the continuity of interest requirement, a modification that reduces the number of shares of stock to be received by the target shareholders, or increases the amount of money or value of property, will not be treated as a modification of the binding contract so that the consideration will continue to be valued as of the signing date. Treas.Reg. § 1.368–1(e)(2)(ii)(B)(3).

Treas.Reg. § 1.368–1(e)(2)(ii)(C) provides rules pursuant to which a tender offer can be considered to be a binding contract, even though it is not enforceable against the offerees, if certain conditions are met. The Regulations on tender offers also provide for modifications of a binding contract; if the contract is modified to change the amount or type of consideration that the target shareholders would receive, the date of the modification becomes a new signing date for purposes of testing for continuity of interest.

Treas.Reg. § 1.368–1(e)(2)(iii)(D) provides that stock that is escrowed to secure customary pre-closing covenants and representations and warranties is not treated as contingent consideration, which would render the safe harbor unavailable. However, escrowed consideration that is forfeited is not taken into account in determining whether the continuity of interest requirement has been met. Treas.Reg. § 1.368–1(e)(2)(v), Ex. 2.

On the same day that the above described rules in Treas.Reg. § 1.368–1(e) were promulgated, the Treasury Department published Prop.Reg. § 1.368–1(e)(2)(vi), 76 Fed. Reg. 78591 (Dec. 19, 2011), under which application of the signing date principles for determining whether continuity of interest is satisfied would be expanded. The Proposed Regulations would also permit the use of an average value for issuing corporation stock, in lieu of the value of issuing corporation stock on the closing date, in certain circumstances. Further guidance is provided by Rev.Proc. 2018–12, which implements valuation methods and explains as follows:

> The Treasury Department and the IRS received comments on the 2011 Proposed Regulations to the effect that parties to potential reorganizations frequently use average trading price methods to value Issuing Corporation stock in determining the amount and/or the mix of consideration to be exchanged for Target stock. The IRS agrees that such methods often produce a more reliable estimate of the fair market value of Issuing Corporation stock than its trading price on a single date. Accordingly, the IRS has concluded that, in certain circumstances, taxpayers should be able to rely on such methods for purposes of determining whether the COI requirement is satisfied. The IRS also agrees with commenters that taxpayers should be able to rely on such methods regardless of whether the Signing Date Rule or the Closing Date Rule applies to a particular transaction.

The Revenue Procedure then goes on to provide "certain Safe Harbor Valuation Methods and Measuring Periods."

2.3. *Insolvent Target*

In Helvering v. Alabama Asphaltic Limestone Co., 315 U.S. 179 (1942), the Supreme Court held that a transfer of assets pursuant to which creditors of a bankrupt concern became the controlling stockholders of a new corporation provided the requisite continuity of interest. Although the old continuity of proprietary interest was broken when the creditors took steps to enforce their demands against the insolvent concern, by such action they stepped into the shoes of the stockholders and hence continuity was present on the subsequent exchange. Similarly, in Norman Scott, Inc. v. Commissioner, 48 T.C. 598 (1967), the court held that a statutory merger between the surviving corporation and its insolvent sister corporation qualified as an (A) reorganization; the continuity of interest test was satisfied since the principal shareholder-creditors of the insolvent corporation received stock in the surviving corporation.

Treas.Reg. § 1.368–1(e)(6), promulgated in 2009, deals with the issues raised in cases such as *Alabama Asphaltic Limestone* and *Norman Scott, Inc.* and describes the circumstances in which a corporation's creditors will be treated as holding a proprietary interest in a target corporation immediately before a potential reorganization. A creditor has a proprietary interest only if the target corporation's liabilities exceed the fair market value of its assets immediately prior to the potential reorganization (or the target corporation is in a title 11 or similar case, as defined in § 368(a)(3)). If any creditor receives a proprietary interest in the acquiring corporation, every claim of that class of creditors and every claim of all equal and junior classes of creditors (in addition to the claims of shareholders) is a proprietary interest in the target corporation immediately prior to the potential reorganization. Generally, in applying continuity of interest principles, the value of a creditor's proprietary interest is the fair market value of the creditor's claim. A special rule applies to the most senior class of creditors receiving stock of the acquirer (and claims of any equal class of creditors). The value of those most senior creditors' proprietary interests in the target is determined by multiplying the fair market value of the claim by a fraction, the numerator of which is the aggregate fair market value of the acquirer's stock received in exchange for claims of those classes of creditors and the denominator of which is the total amount of money and the fair market value of all other consideration (including acquirer stock) received in exchange for such claims.

The special aspects of reorganizations involving insolvent corporations are considered in Section 7 of this Chapter.

PROBLEM SET 2

1. P Corporation acquires T pursuant to a state law statutory merger. Assume that apart from the continuity of interest requirement, all other requirements for a tax-free reorganization under § 368(a)(1)(A), are satisfied. Given the following *alternative* additional facts, consider whether or not a tax-free reorganization has occurred.

(a) P acquires T solely for P's voting common stock and the former T shareholders become shareholders of P. After the merger, each of the five former shareholders of T own approximately 1% in value of the outstanding common stock of P.

(b) Would your answer change if the former T shareholders received nonvoting common stock of P?

(c) Would your answer change if the former T shareholders received P Corp. nonvoting preferred stock with a par value and fair market value of $20,000,000?

(d) Would your answer change if instead of issuing stock, P acquired T by issuing to the former T shareholders 11% bonds due in the year 2075 with an aggregate face value of $10,000,000, which are securities for purposes of § 354?

2. T Corporation is owned equally by Franklin, Gert, Harvey, Irene, and José. P Corporation acquires T pursuant to a statutory merger. Assume that all requirements for a tax-free reorganization under I.R.C. § 368(a)(1)(A), apart from continuity of interest, are satisfied. Given the following *alternative* additional facts, consider whether or not a tax-free reorganization has occurred.

(a) P Corp. acquires T Corp. for 100,000 shares of P Corp. voting common stock, worth $10,000,000 and $10,000,000 cash. Franklin, Gert, Harvey, Irene, and José each receive 20,000 shares of P Corp. stock (FMV $2,000,000) and $2,000,000 cash.

(b) Would your answer differ if P Corp. acquires T Corp. for 80,000 shares of P Corp. voting common stock, worth $8,000,000 and $12,000,000 cash? Franklin, Gert, Harvey, Irene, and José each receive 16,000 shares of P Corp. stock (FMV $1,600,000) and $2,400,000 cash.

(c) Would your answer differ if P Corp. acquires T Corp. for 60,000 shares of P Corp. voting common stock, worth $6,000,000 and $14,000,000 cash? Franklin, Gert, Harvey, Irene, and José each receive 12,000 shares of P Corp. stock (FMV $1,200,000) and $2,800,000 cash.

(d) Would your answer differ if Franklin, Gert, Harvey, Irene, and José received the following consideration ($ are in $1,000s):

Shareholder	Cash (FMV)	P Shares
Franklin	$ 4,000	$ 0
Gert	$ 4,000	$ 0
Harvey	$ 3,500	$ 500
Irene	$ 500	$3,500
José	$ 0	$4,000
	$12,000	$8,000

Is this a reorganization? Which shareholders are affected by whether it is a reorganization? Which shareholders are not affected by whether it is a reorganization?

3.   P Corporation acquires T pursuant to a state law statutory merger. The consideration issued to the T shareholders by P consists of (1) $2,500,000 worth of P Corp. voting common stock, (2) bonds, which are securities for purposes of § 354, with a $4,000,000 principal amount, and (3) $3,500,000 cash. Has a tax-free reorganization occurred?

4.   P Corp and T Corp are publicly traded. P Corp and T Corp entered into a merger agreement that provided for the merger of T into P. The agreed upon exchange was that each share of T would be surrendered in exchange for one share of P common stock and $55 cash. The merger agreement had no provision to adjust the exchange ratio to reflect stock price fluctuations between the date of the merger agreement and the effective date of the merger (the closing). On the day before the merger agreement, P stock was trading at $45 per share. On the date of the merger (the closing), P stock was trading at $25 per share. Has a tax-free reorganization occurred?

5.   P Corp and T Corp are publicly traded. P Corp and T Corp entered into a merger agreement that provided for the merger of T into P. The merger agreement provided that each share of T would be surrendered in exchange for (1) two shares of P common stock, and (2) at the election of each T shareholder, either two additional shares of P Common stock or $80 cash. The merger agreement had no provision to adjust the exchange ratio to reflect stock price fluctuations between the date of the merger agreement and the effective date of the merger (the closing). On the day before the merger agreement, P stock was trading at $40 per share. On the date of the merger (the closing), P stock was trading at $20 per share. All of the former T shareholders elected to receive only $80 of cash. Has a tax-free reorganization occurred?

6.   P Corp. owned 80% of the voting common stock of S Corp. Fiona owned the other 20% of the voting common stock of S Corp. Pursuant to state law governing mergers, S Corp. merged into P Corp. The S Corp. stock owned by P Corp. was cancelled, and Fiona received P. Corp. nonvoting preferred stock. How is the transaction characterized for each of P Corp., S Corp., and Fiona?

(2) "REMOTE CONTINUITY OF INTEREST" AND "PARTY TO A REORGANIZATION"

REGULATIONS: Section 1.368–2(k).

Section 368(a)(2)(C) permits the acquiring corporation to drop assets or stock of the target corporation down to a controlled subsidiary following the initial acquisition. In addition, § 368(a)(2)(D) includes within the definition of a reorganization a "triangular merger," which is a merger in which the shareholders of the acquired corporation receive stock of the acquiring corporation's parent (and in which they receive no stock of the acquiring subsidiary), and § 368(a)(2)(E) permits "reverse triangular mergers" subject to several restrictive conditions.

These statutory provisions are in response to cases that restricted the ability to bring triangular acquisitions within the definition of a "reorganization." In Groman v. Commissioner, 302 U.S. 82 (1937), P Corporation desired to acquire T Corporation. Accordingly, P Corporation organized S Corporation and held all of its common stock. The shareholders of T Corporation transferred their T stock to S Corporation in return for preferred stock of S Corporation, preferred stock of P Corporation, and cash. S Corporation then liquidated T Corporation. In effect, the assets of T Corporation went to a newly formed subsidiary of P Corporation. The Court held that the preferred stock of P Corporation was not stock in a "party to a reorganization" and hence was boot received by the T Corporation shareholders. The Court relied on the continuity of interest doctrine and stated that since P Corporation had not received the T Corporation assets, the possession of the P stock by the T shareholders did not represent a continuing interest in those assets. *Groman* was followed in Helvering v. Bashford, 302 U.S. 454 (1938), where P Corporation's receipt of the T Corporation stock was followed immediately by the planned transfer by P Corporation of the stock to its subsidiary S Corporation. The T Corporation shareholders received some common stock of S Corporation and some preferred and common stock of P Corporation. Because the ownership of the T stock by P Corporation was only transitory and the transfer to S Corporation was part of a plan, the transitory ownership did not serve to distinguish the *Groman* case.

In the *Groman* and *Bashford* cases the former stockholders had divided their ownership—they owned some stock in the subsidiary corporation to which the assets had been transferred and also some stock in the parent corporation. They were thus free to dispose of one interest without the other. Suppose, however, that the assets had gone to a wholly-owned subsidiary of the parent and the former owners had received only stock in the parent? The courts still held that the results were the same. This was also the result under some decisions where the assets were first transferred to the parent and then transferred by it to the subsidiary, if the latter step was contemplated as part of the plan of reorganization. See Anheuser-Busch, Inc. v. Helvering, 115 F.2d 662 (8th Cir.1940); Hedden v. Commissioner, 105 F.2d 311 (3d Cir.1939); Campbell v. Commissioner, 15 T.C. 312 (1950) (acq.).

Sections 368(a)(2)(C), (D) and (E) changed the results in these cases, although § 368(a)(2)(D), but not § 368(a)(2)(C) and (E), prohibits the splitting of interests, as was present in the *Groman* and *Bashford* cases. The statutory provisions do not, however, expressly deal with a variety of situations that can give rise to "remote continuity of interest" issues. For a number of years the IRS dealt with these situations on an *ad hoc* basis through revenue rulings, prior to the promulgation of Treas.Reg. § 1.368–2(k), which provides a more comprehensive, but still incomplete set of rules for dealing with situations not addressed by the statute.

Rev.Rul. 2002–85, which follows, is an example of the IRS's reasoning in such situations.

Revenue Ruling 2002–85
2002–2 C.B. 986.

ISSUE

Whether an acquiring corporation's transfer of a target corporation's assets to a subsidiary controlled by the acquiring corporation as part of a plan of reorganization will prevent a transaction that otherwise qualifies as a reorganization under § 368(a)(1)(D) of the Internal Revenue Code from so qualifying.

FACTS

A, an individual, owns 100 percent of T, a state X corporation. A also owns 100 percent of P, a state Y corporation. For valid business reasons and pursuant to a plan of reorganization, (i) T transfers all of its assets to P in exchange for consideration consisting of 70 percent P voting stock and 30 percent cash, (ii) T then liquidates, distributing the P voting stock and cash to A, and (iii) P subsequently transfers all of the T assets to S, a preexisting, wholly owned state X subsidiary of P, in exchange for stock of S. S will continue T's historic business after the transfer and P will retain the S stock. Without regard to P's transfer of all the T assets to S, the transaction qualifies as a reorganization under § 368(a)(1)(D).

LAW

Section 368(a)(1)(D) provides that the term reorganization means a transfer by a corporation of all or a part of its assets to another corporation if immediately after the transfer the transferor, or one or more of its shareholders (including persons who were shareholders immediately before the transfer), or any combination thereof, is in control of the corporation to which the assets are transferred; but only if, in pursuance of the plan, stock or securities of the corporation to which the assets are transferred are distributed in a transaction which qualifies under § 354, 355, or 356.

Section 354(a) provides that, in general, no gain or loss shall be recognized if stock or securities in a corporation a party to a reorganization are, in pursuance of the plan of reorganization, exchanged solely for stock or securities in such corporation or in another corporation a party to the reorganization. Section 354(b)(1) provides that § 354(a) shall not apply to an exchange in pursuance of a plan of reorganization within the meaning of subparagraph (D) or (G) of § 368(a)(1) unless (A) the corporation to which the assets are transferred acquires substantially all of the assets of the transferor of such assets; and (B) the stock, securities, and other properties received by such transferor, as well as the other properties of such transferor, are distributed in pursuance of the plan of reorganization.

Section 368(a)(2)(A) provides that if a transaction is described in both §§ 368(a)(1)(C) and 368(a)(1)(D), then, for purposes of subchapter C (other than for purposes of § 368(a)(2)(C)), such transaction shall be treated as described only in § 368(a)(1)(D).

Section 368(a)(2)(C) provides that a transaction otherwise qualifying under § 368(a)(1)(A), (B), (C), or (G) shall not be disqualified by reason of the fact that part or all of the assets or stock which were acquired in the transaction are transferred to a corporation controlled (as defined in § 368(c)) by the corporation acquiring such assets or stock.

Section 368(b) provides that the term "a party to a reorganization" includes a corporation resulting from a reorganization, and both corporations in the case of a reorganization resulting from the acquisition by one corporation of the properties of another.

Congress enacted § 368(a)(2)(C) in response to the Supreme Court decisions in Groman v. Commissioner, 302 U.S. 82 (1937), and Helvering v. Bashford, 302 U.S. 454 (1938). In *Groman*, the shareholders of one corporation (Target) entered into an agreement with another corporation (Parent) pursuant to which Target would merge into Parent's newly formed subsidiary (Sub). In the transaction, the Target shareholders transferred their Target shares to Sub in exchange for shares of Parent, shares of Sub, and cash, and Target liquidated. The Court concluded that, even though the statutory definition of "party to a reorganization" was not exclusive, Parent was not a party to the reorganization because it received nothing in the exchange. The Court then stated that an exchange that is pursuant to a plan of reorganization is not taxable to the extent the interest of the stockholders of a corporation continue to be definitely represented in substantial measure in a new or different corporation. The stock of Parent, however, did not represent a continued substantial interest in the assets conveyed to Sub. Because Parent was not a party to the reorganization, the Court held that the receipt of the stock of Parent was taxable.

In *Bashford*, a corporation (Parent) wished to acquire three competitors (Targets). Pursuant to a plan, Parent formed a new corporation (Sub) and acquired all the preferred shares and a majority of the common shares of Sub. Sub became the owner of the stock and assets of the Targets. The former stockholders of the Targets exchanged their shares in the Targets for shares of Sub, shares of Parent, and cash. Because any direct ownership by Parent of the Targets was transitory and without real substance, the Court saw no significant distinction between this transaction and the transaction in *Groman*. Therefore, the Court concluded that Parent was not a party to the reorganization. Hence, the Parent stock received by the shareholders of the Targets did not confer the requisite continuity of interest.

In 1954, Congress enacted § 368(a)(2)(C) in response to *Groman* and *Bashford*. See S. Rep. No. 1622, 83d Cong., 2d Sess. 52, 273, 275 (1954). As originally enacted, § 368(a)(2)(C) applied only to reorganizations under §§ 368(a)(1)(A) and 368(a)(1)(C), but Congress has since amended the statute to apply to other reorganizations. Specifically, Congress amended § 368(a)(2)(C) in 1964 to apply to reorganizations under § 368(a)(1)(B), and, in 1980, to reorganizations under § 368(a)(1)(G).

Section 1.368–2(k)(1) of the Income Tax Regulations restates the general rule of § 368(a)(2)(C) but permits the assets or stock acquired in certain types of reorganizations to be successively transferred to one or more corporations controlled (as defined in § 368(c)) in each transfer by the transferor corporation without disqualifying the reorganization.

Section 1.368–2(f) provides that, if a transaction otherwise qualifies as a reorganization, a corporation remains a party to the reorganization even though the stock or assets acquired in the reorganization are transferred in a transaction described in § 1.368–2(k).

To qualify as a reorganization under § 368, a transaction must satisfy the continuity of business enterprise (COBE) requirement. The COBE requirement is intended to ensure that reorganizations are limited to readjustments of continuing interests in property under modified corporate form. Section 1.368–1(d)(1). Section 1.368–1(d)(1) provides that COBE requires the issuing corporation (generally the acquiring corporation) in a potential reorganization to either continue the target corporation's historic business or use a significant portion of the target's historic business assets in a business. Pursuant to § 1.368–1(d)(4)(i), the issuing corporation is treated as holding all of the businesses and assets of all members of its qualified group. Section 1.368–1(d)(4)(ii) defines a qualified group as one or more chains of corporations connected through stock ownership with the issuing corporation, but only if the issuing corporation owns directly stock meeting the requirements of § 368(c) in at least one other corporation, and stock meeting the requirements of § 368(c) in each of the corporations (except the issuing corporation) is owned directly by one of the other corporations.

In Rev.Rul. 88–48, 1988–1 C.B. 117, in a taxable transaction, corporation X sold 50 percent of its historic business assets to unrelated purchasers for cash. Immediately afterwards, pursuant to an overall plan, X transferred to corporation Y, a corporation unrelated to X and the purchasers, all of its assets, including the cash from the sale. The ruling holds that X's transfer of assets to Y satisfied the substantially all requirement of § 368(a)(1)(C).

In Rev.Rul. 2001–25, 2001–1 C.B. 1291, pursuant to a plan, corporation S, a wholly owned subsidiary of corporation P, merged with and into corporation T in a state law merger. Immediately after the merger and as part of a plan that included the merger, T sold 50 percent of its operating assets for cash to an unrelated corporation. After the sale of the assets to corporation X, T retained the sales proceeds. Without regard to the requirement that T hold substantially all of the assets of T and S immediately after the merger, the merger satisfied all the other requirements applicable to reorganizations under §§ 368(a)(1)(A) and 368(a)(2)(E). The IRS ruled that even though T's post-merger sale of 50 percent of its operating assets prevented T from holding substantially all of its historic business assets immediately after the merger, because the sales proceeds continued to be held by T, the merger did not violate the requirement of § 368(a)(2)(E) that the surviving corporation hold substantially all of its properties after the transaction.

In Rev.Rul. 2001–24, 2001–1 C.B. 1290, corporation X merged with and into corporation S, a newly organized, wholly owned subsidiary of corporation P, in a transaction intended to qualify as a reorganization under §§ 368(a)(1)(A) and 368(a)(2)(D). S continued the historic business of X following the merger. Following the merger and as part of the plan of reorganization, P transferred the S stock to corporation S1, a preexisting, wholly owned subsidiary of P. The IRS ruled that the transaction satisfied the continuity of business enterprise requirement of § 1.368–1(d). Analyzing whether P's transfer of the S stock to S1 caused P to fail to control S for purposes of § 368(a)(2)(D) and caused P to fail to be a party to the reorganization, the IRS noted that the legislative history of § 368(a)(2)(E) suggests that forward and reverse triangular mergers should be treated similarly. Section 1.368–2(k)(2) permits the transfer of stock or assets to a controlled corporation following a reverse triangular merger under §§ 368(a)(1)(A) and 368(a)(2)(E), which supports permitting P to transfer the S stock to S1 without causing the transaction to fail to qualify as a reorganization under §§ 368(a)(1)(A) and 368(a)(2)(D). Furthermore, although §§ 368(a)(2)(C) and 1.368–2(k) do not specifically address P's transfer of S stock to S1 following a reorganization under §§ 368(a)(1)(A) and 368(a)(2)(D), § 368(a)(2)(C) is permissive rather than exclusive or restrictive. Accordingly, the IRS concluded that the transfer of the S stock to S1 would not cause P to be treated as not in control of S for purposes of § 368(a)(2)(D) and would not cause P to fail to be treated as a party to the reorganization.

ANALYSIS

Neither § 368(a)(2)(C) nor § 368(a)(2)(A) indicates that an acquiring corporation's transfer of assets to a controlled subsidiary necessarily prevents a transaction that otherwise qualifies as a reorganization under § 368(a)(1)(D) from so qualifying. Because § 368(a)(2)(C) is permissive and not exclusive or restrictive, the absence of § 368(a)(1)(D) from § 368(a)(2)(C) does not indicate that such a transfer following a transaction that otherwise qualifies as a reorganization under § 368(a)(1)(D) will prevent the transaction from qualifying as such. Furthermore, although § 368(a)(2)(A) contains the parenthetical exception "other than for purposes of [§ 368(a)(2)(C)]," that exception appears to have been provided in the same spirit as § 368(a)(2)(C), i.e., to resolve doubts about the qualification of transactions as reorganizations, and does not indicate that the transfer of assets to a controlled subsidiary necessarily prevents a transaction from qualifying as a reorganization under § 368(a)(1)(D). See S. Rep. No. 313, 99th Cong., 2d Sess. 914 (1986).

Accordingly, an acquiring corporation's transfer of assets to a controlled subsidiary following a transaction that otherwise qualifies as a reorganization under § 368(a)(1)(D) will not cause a transaction to fail to qualify as such, provided that the original transferee is treated as acquiring substantially all of the assets of the target corporation, the transaction satisfies the COBE requirement and does not fail under the remote continuity principle of *Groman* and *Bashford*, and the transfer of assets to a controlled corporation does not prevent the original transferee from being a "party to the reorganization."

Section 354(b)(1)(A) requires that, in a reorganization under § 368(a)(1)(D), the corporation to which the assets are transferred acquire substantially all of the assets of the transferor of such assets. In this case, the requirement that P acquire substantially all of T's assets is satisfied because P retains the stock of S. See Rev.Rul. 2001–24; Rev.Rul. 88–48.

To qualify as a reorganization under § 368(a)(1)(D), a transaction must satisfy the COBE requirement of § 1.368–1(d). In the present transaction, P and S constitute a qualified group, and S will continue T's historic business after the transfer. Therefore, the transaction satisfies the COBE requirement.

As described above, Congress enacted § 368(a)(2)(C) in response to the Supreme Court's holdings in *Groman* and *Bashford*. After the enactment of § 368(a)(2)(C), however, the IRS continued to apply the principles of *Groman* and *Bashford* to transactions that otherwise qualified as reorganizations under § 368(a)(1)(B). See Rev.Rul. 63–234, 1963–2 C.B. 148. In response to this position, Congress expanded the scope of § 368(a)(2)(C) to include reorganizations under § 368(a)(1)(B). Congress' response to the application of the principles of *Groman* and *Bashford* has been to limit the application of those principles. Implicit in Congress' enactment and expansion of § 368(a)(2)(C) is a rejection of the principle that the transfer of acquired stock or assets to a controlled subsidiary of the acquiring corporation creates a remote continuity problem that causes a transaction that otherwise qualifies as a reorganization to fail to so qualify. See H.R. Rep. No. 1337, 83d Cong., 2d Sess. A134 (1954) (stating, after citing *Groman* and *Bashford* in reference to proposed legislation that ultimately became § 368(a)(2)(C), "a corporation may not acquire assets with the intention of transferring them to a stranger").

Under the COBE regulations, stock or assets acquired in transactions that satisfy certain provisions of § 368(a)(1) may be transferred without limitation to successive lower-tier controlled subsidiaries within a qualified group. The Preamble to the final COBE regulations states that "the IRS and Treasury believe the COBE requirements adequately address the issues raised in *Groman* and

Bashford and their progeny. Thus, [the final COBE regulations] do not separately articulate rules addressing remote continuity of interest." T.D. 8760, 1998–1 C.B. 803, Supplementary Information (Explanation of Provisions). Accordingly, a transfer of acquired stock or assets will not cause a transaction to fail for remote continuity if it satisfies the COBE requirement.

Under the facts described above, P's transfer of the T assets to S pursuant to the plan of reorganization satisfies the COBE requirement. Therefore, the transaction does not fail for remote continuity.

Section 368(b) provides that the term "a party to a reorganization" includes a corporation resulting from a reorganization, and both corporations in the case of a reorganization resulting from the acquisition by one corporation of the properties of another. The use of the word "includes" in § 368(b) indicates that the definition of "party to a reorganization" is not exclusive. See § 7701(c); *Groman*, supra, at 86 (stating that "when an exclusive definition is intended the word 'means' is employed * * * whereas [in the definition of 'party to a reorganization'] the word used is 'includes' "). Furthermore, § 1.368–2(f), which interprets § 368(b), provides that, if a transaction otherwise qualifies as a reorganization, a corporation remains a party to a reorganization even though the stock or assets acquired in the reorganization are transferred in a transaction described in § 1.368–2(k). Section 1.368–2(k) does not reference § 368(a)(1)(D). Nonetheless, because § 1.368–2(k) restates and interprets § 368(a)(2)(C), which is a permissive and not an exclusive or restrictive provision, § 1.368–2(k) also should be viewed as permissive and not exclusive or restrictive. Therefore, because §§ 368(b), 1.368–2(f), and 1.368–2(k) are not exclusive or restrictive provisions, the absence of § 368(a)(1)(D) from § 1.368–2(k) does not prevent a corporation from remaining a party to a reorganization even if the acquired stock or assets are transferred to a controlled subsidiary.

Reorganizations under § 368(a)(1)(D), like reorganizations under §§ 368(a)(1)(A) and 368(a)(1)(C), are asset reorganizations. In reorganizations under §§ 368(a)(1)(A) and 368(a)(1)(C), the original transferee is treated as a party to a reorganization, even if the acquired assets are transferred to a controlled subsidiary of the original transferee. The differences between reorganizations under § 368(a)(1)(D) on the one hand and reorganizations under §§ 368(a)(1)(A) and 368(a)(1)(C) on the other hand do not warrant treating the original transferee in a transaction that otherwise satisfies the requirements of a reorganization under § 368(a)(1)(D) differently from the original transferee in a reorganization under § 368(a)(1)(A) or 368(a)(1)(C) for purposes of § 368(b). Therefore, the original transferee in a transaction that otherwise satisfies the requirements of a reorganization under § 368(a)(1)(D) is treated as a party to the reorganization, notwithstanding the original transferee's transfer of acquired assets to a controlled subsidiary of the original transferee.

For the reasons set forth above, P's transfer of the T assets to S will not prevent P's acquisition of those assets from T in exchange for P voting stock and cash from qualifying as a reorganization under § 368(a)(1)(D).

HOLDING

An acquiring corporation's transfer of the target corporation's assets to a subsidiary controlled by the acquiring corporation as part of a plan of reorganization will not prevent a transaction that otherwise qualifies as a reorganization under § 368(a)(1)(D) from so qualifying.

* * *

DETAILED ANALYSIS

1.   DROP-DOWNS AND PUSH-UPS FOLLOWING ACQUISITIONS

Treas.Reg. § 1.368–2(k) provides that a transaction otherwise qualifying as a reorganization under § 368(a) will not be disqualified as a result of the transfer or successive transfers ("drop-downs") to one or more corporations controlled in each transfer by the transferor corporation of part or all of either (1) the assets of any party to the reorganization, or (2) the stock of any party to the reorganization (other than the acquiring corporation whose stock is issued). Consonantly, Treas.Reg. § 1.368–2(f), dealing with the definition of a "party to a reorganization" requirement, and Treas.Reg. § 1.368–1(d)(4)(i)(A) and (B), dealing with the continuity of business enterprise requirement, provide that a post-acquisition distribution ("push-up") by an acquisition subsidiary that is a member of the acquiring corporation's group to a corporation that controls the acquiring corporation of either (1) the target corporation's stock (following a § 368(a)(1)(B) or § 368(a)(2)(E) reorganization) or (2) the target corporation's assets (following a § 368(a)(1)(A), § 368(a)(1)(C), or § 368(a)(2)(E) reorganization) does not disqualify the acquisition from reorganization treatment, even though there is no statutory provision expressly providing that such transfers do not affect the validity of reorganization treatment. The combined effect of these provisions is to permit the acquiring corporation to rearrange ownership of the target corporation's assets or stock, as the case may be, in almost any manner it desires among all of the members of its qualified group (based on § 368(c) control) without disqualifying the reorganization.

(3) TEMPORAL ASPECTS

REGULATIONS: Sections 1.368–1(a), (b), (e)(1), (3)–(7), –2(a). See also section 1.338–2(c)(3).

Rules and Regulations, Department of the Treasury, Internal Revenue Service, Continuity of Interest and Continuity of Business Enterprise
T.D. 8760, 1998–1 C.B. 803.

Explanation of Provisions

The Internal Revenue Code of 1986 provides general nonrecognition treatment for reorganizations specifically described in section 368. In addition to complying with the statutory requirements and certain other requirements, a transaction generally must satisfy the continuity of interest requirement and the continuity of business enterprise requirement.

A. *Continuity of Interest*

The purpose of the continuity of interest requirement is to prevent transactions that resemble sales from qualifying for nonrecognition of gain or loss available to corporate reorganizations. The final regulations provide that the COI requirement is satisfied if in substance a substantial part of the value of the proprietary interest in the target corporation (T) is preserved in the reorganization. A proprietary interest in T is preserved if, in a potential reorganization, it is exchanged for a proprietary interest in the issuing corporation (P), it is exchanged by the acquiring corporation for a direct interest in the T enterprise, or it otherwise continues as a proprietary interest in T. The issuing corporation means the acquiring corporation (as the term is used in section 368(a)), except that, in determining whether a reorganization qualifies as a triangular reorganization (as defined in § 1.358–6(b)(2)), the issuing corporation means the corporation in control of the acquiring corporation. However, a proprietary interest in T is not preserved if, in connection with the potential reorganization, it is acquired by P for consideration other than P stock, or P stock furnished in exchange for a proprietary interest in T if the potential reorganization is redeemed. All facts and circumstances must be considered in determining whether, in substance, a proprietary interest in T is preserved.

Rationale for the COI Regulations

The * * * regulations permit former T shareholders to sell P stock received in a potential reorganization to third parties without causing the reorganization to fail to satisfy the COI requirement. Some commentators have questioned whether the regulations are consistent with existing authorities.

The COI requirement was applied first to reorganization provisions that did not specify that P exchange a proprietary interest in P for a proprietary interest in T. Supreme Court cases imposed the COI requirement to further Congressional intent that tax-free status be accorded only to transactions where P exchanges a substantial proprietary interest in P for a proprietary interest in T held by the T shareholders rather than to transactions resembling sales. See LeTulle v. Scofield, 308 U.S. 415 (1940); Helvering v. Minnesota Tea Co., 296 U.S. 378 (1935); Pinellas Ice & Cold Storage Co. v. Commissioner, 287 U.S. 462 (1933). * * *

None of the Supreme Court cases establishing the COI requirement addressed the issue of whether sales by former T shareholders of P stock received in exchange for T stock in the potential reorganization cause the COI requirement to fail to be satisfied. Since then, however, some courts have premised decisions on the assumption that sales of P stock received in exchange for T stock in the potential reorganization may cause the COI requirement to fail to be satisfied. McDonald's Restaurants of Illinois, Inc. v. Commissioner, 688 F.2d 520 (7th Cir.1982); Penrod v. Commissioner, 88 T.C. 1415 (1987); Heintz v. Commissioner, 25 T.C. 132 (1955), nonacq., 1958–2 C.B. 9 * * *. The apparent focus of these cases is on whether the T shareholders intended on the date of the potential reorganization to sell their P stock and the degree, if any, to which P facilitates the sale. Based on an intensive inquiry into nearly identical facts, some of these cases held that as a result of the subsequent sale the potential reorganization did not satisfy the COI requirement; others held that satisfaction of the COI requirement was not adversely affected by the subsequent sale. The IRS and Treasury Department have concluded that the law as reflected in these cases does not further the principles of reorganization treatment and is difficult for both taxpayers and the IRS to apply consistently.

Therefore, consistent with Congressional intent and the Supreme Court precedent which distinguishes between sales and reorganizations, the final regulations focus the COI requirement generally on exchanges between the T shareholders and P. Under this approach, sales of P stock by former T shareholders generally are disregarded.

The final regulations will greatly enhance administrability in this area by both taxpayers and the government. The regulations will prevent "whipsaw" of the government, such as where the former T shareholders treat the transaction as a tax-free reorganization, and P later disavows reorganization treatment to step up its basis in the T assets based on the position that sales of P stock by the former T shareholders did not satisfy the COI requirement. See, e.g., *McDonald's Restaurants*, supra. In addition, this approach will prevent unilateral sales of P stock by former majority T shareholders from adversely affecting the section 354 nonrecognition treatment expected by former minority T shareholders.

Dispositions of T Stock

* * * The IRS and Treasury Department believe that issues concerning the COI requirement raised by dispositions of T stock before a potential reorganization correspond to those raised by subsequent dispositions of P stock furnished in exchange for T stock in the potential reorganization. * * * [T]he final regulations apply the rationale of the proposed COI regulations to transactions occurring both prior to and after a potential reorganization. Cf. J.E. Seagram Corp. v. Commissioner, 104 T.C. 75 (1995) (sales of T stock prior to a potential reorganization do not affect COI if not part of the plan of reorganization). The final regulations provide that, for COI purposes, a mere disposition of T stock prior to a potential reorganization to persons not related to P is disregarded and a mere disposition of P stock received in a potential reorganization to persons not related to P is disregarded. * * *

In soliciting comments on the effect upon COI of dispositions of T stock prior to a potential reorganization, the preamble to the proposed COI regulations specifically requests comments on King Enterprises, Inc. v. United States, 418 F.2d 511 (Ct.Cl.1969) (COI requirement satisfied where, pursuant to a plan, P acquires the T stock for 51 percent P stock and 49 percent debt and cash, and T merges upstream into P), and Yoc Heating Corp. v. Commissioner, 61 T.C. 168 (1973) (COI requirement not satisfied where, pursuant to a plan, P acquires 85 percent of the T stock for cash and notes, and T merges into P's newly formed subsidiary with minority shareholders receiving cash). Consistent with these cases, where the step transaction doctrine applies to link T stock purchases with later acquisitions of T, the final regulations provide that a proprietary interest in T is not preserved if, in connection with the potential reorganization, it is acquired by P for consideration other than P stock. Whether a stock acquisition is made in connection with a potential reorganization will be determined based on the facts and circumstances of each case. See generally § 1.368–1(a). This regulation does not address the effect, if any, of section 338 on corporate transactions * * *. See generally § 1.338–[3(d)] (certain tax effects of a qualified stock purchase without a section 338 election on the post-acquisition elimination of T).

Related Person Rule

* * * The final regulations provide * * * that a proprietary interest in T is not preserved if, in connection with a potential reorganization, a person related (as defined below) to P acquires, with consideration other than a proprietary interest in P, T stock or P stock furnished in exchange for a proprietary interest in T in the potential reorganization. The IRS and Treasury Department believe, however, that certain related party acquisitions preserve a proprietary interest in T and therefore, the rule includes an exception to the related party rule. Under this exception, a proprietary interest in T is preserved to the extent those persons who were the direct or indirect owners of T prior to the potential reorganization maintain a direct or indirect proprietary interest in P. See, e.g., Rev.Rul. 84–30 (1984–1 C.B. 114).

* * * [The] regulations adopt a * * * related person definition which has two components in order to address two separate concerns.

First, the IRS and Treasury Department were concerned that acquisitions of T or P stock by a member of P's affiliated group were no different in substance from an acquisition or redemption by P, because of the existence of various provisions in the Code that permit members to transfer funds to other members without significant tax consequences. Accordingly, § [1.368–1(e)(4)(i)(A)] includes as related persons corporations that are members of the same affiliated group under section 1504, without regard to the exceptions in section 1504(b).

Second, because the final regulations take into account whether, in substance, P has redeemed the stock it exchanged for T stock in the potential reorganization, the final regulations treat two corporations as related persons if a purchase of the stock of one corporation by another corporation would be treated as a distribution in redemption of the stock of the first corporation under section 304(a)(2) (determined without regard to § 1.1502–80(b)).

Because the final regulations focus generally on the consideration P exchanges, related persons do not include individual or other noncorporate shareholders. * * *

T Stock Not Acquired in Connection With a Potential Reorganization

* * * The final regulations provide that a proprietary interest in T is preserved if it is exchanged by the acquiring corporation (which may or may not also be P) for a direct interest in the T enterprise, or otherwise continues as a proprietary interest in T.

* * *

Transactions Following a Qualified Stock Purchase

As stated above, these final regulations focus the COI requirement generally on exchanges between the T shareholders and P. Accordingly, the language of § 1.338–[3(d)] is conformed to these final COI regulations to treat the stock of T acquired by the purchasing corporation in the qualified stock purchase as though it was not acquired in connection with the transfer of the T assets.

* * *

DETAILED ANALYSIS

1.   CONTINUITY OF INTEREST AND HISTORIC SHAREHOLDERS

1.1. *Generally*

As discussed in T.D. 8760, prior to 1998, usually at the IRS's behest, a number of decisions imposed the requirement that continuity of interest be tested with respect to the "historic" shareholders of the acquired corporation, not those persons who owned the stock of the acquired corporation immediately before the merger. In Superior Coach of Florida, Inc. v. Commissioner, 80 T.C. 895 (1983), the court held that for shareholders to be considered historic shareholders the acquired corporation's shares must be "old and cold" in the hands of the shareholders participating in the reorganization. A contrary result was reached in J.E. Seagram Corp. v. Commissioner, 104 T.C. 75 (1995), in which the Tax Court held that the pre-reorganization sales and purchases of a publicly held target corporation's stock did not vitiate the continuity of interest requirement, thereby largely abandoning any "historic shareholder" continuity of interest requirement. In adopting current Treas.Reg. § 1.368–1(e), the Treasury rejected the *Superior Coach* approach in favor of the *J.E. Seagram* approach. But if the acquiring corporation (or a related corporation) itself purchases stock of the target corporation prior to the reorganization, as noted in T.D. 8760, vestiges of the historic shareholder continuity of interest requirement come into play.

Rev.Rul. 99–58, 1999–2 C.B. 701, held that the open market purchase of its shares by a publicly traded corporation following a tax-free reorganization in which the shareholders of the target corporation received 50% cash and 50% stock did not violate the continuity of interest requirement under Treas.Reg. § 1.368–1(e), even though the acquiring corporation's intent to repurchase shares (to prevent dilution) had been announced prior to the reorganization, because the repurchase was not negotiated with the target or its shareholders and there was no "understanding" between the acquiring corporation and the target shareholders that their ownership would be transitory.

1.2. *Reorganizations Immediately Following Stock Purchases*

In Kass v. Commissioner, 60 T.C. 218 (1973), aff'd by order, 491 F.2d 749 (3d Cir.1974), A and B, two familial groups of individuals owning target shares, desired to obtain control of the target corporation. To accomplish this goal, A and B organized the acquiring corporation and contributed their target corporation stock to the acquiring corporation. As a result, the acquiring corporation held 10.23% of the stock of the target corporation. Shortly thereafter, the acquiring corporation purchased for cash an additional 83.95% of the stock of the target corporation. Finally, the target corporation was merged into the acquiring corporation, with the remaining shareholders of the target corporation stock, who held 5.82% of the target corporation stock, receiving the acquiring corporation stock. The taxpayer, who was one of the minority shareholders who received the acquiring corporation stock in the merger, claimed that the transaction was a type (A) reorganization. The court agreed with the IRS's argument that as far as the taxpayer was concerned, the transaction was a taxable sale because more than 80% of the shares of the target corporation prior to the commencement of the series of transactions culminating in the merger of the target corporation had been sold for cash. Thus the continuity of interest requirement was not satisfied. A similar result was reached on similar facts in Yoc Heating Corp. v. Commissioner, 61 T.C. 168 (1973), which involved the tax treatment of the target corporation.

As noted in T.D. 8760, under Treas.Reg. § 1.368–1(e), the shareholders in cases such as *Kass* and *Yoc Heating* generally will not be considered to have participated in a reorganization if the cash purchases by the acquiring corporation are of such a magnitude relative to the stock consideration that the continuity of interest requirement has not been met. See Treas.Reg. § 1.368–1(e)(1) and (e)(8), Ex. 2. As far as the corporations themselves are concerned, however, Treas.Reg. § 1.338–3(d) might produce a different result. Suppose P Corporation makes a qualified stock purchase of T Corporation, i.e., it purchases at least 80% (by vote and value) of the stock of T, but does not make a § 338 election (see Chapter 8). P then causes the assets of T to be transferred to P (or another member of P's affiliated group, such as another subsidiary) in a reorganization defined in § 368. The Regulation states that P will be treated as the relevant owner, i.e., "historic owner" of the T stock for purposes of testing continuity of interest under Treas.Reg. § 1.368–1(b) and (e). Any minority shareholders of T, however, will continue to be tested under generally applicable principles. As a result of the treatment under the Regulations, the reorganization may qualify as a tax-free reorganization under § 368 for the acquiring corporation's controlled group; it will not be a "taxable merger." T will not recognize gain or loss on the transfer of its assets, and P (or a related corporation that acquires T's assets in the reorganization) will not obtain a step-up in basis for the T assets. Thus, the result in *Yoc Heating* has been changed by the Regulations, but the result in *Kass* has not been affected. The position of the Regulations that a reorganization can exist with respect to some shareholders but not with respect to other shareholders is difficult to justify.

2. EFFECT OF PRE-ACQUISITION DISTRIBUTIONS BY TARGET CORPORATION

Treas.Reg. § 1.368–1(e)(1)(ii) deals with the effect on the continuity of interest requirement of pre-acquisition redemptions of one or more of the target corporation's shareholders. The Regulation in effect provides that stock of the target corporation's shareholders that is redeemed prior to the acquisition will not be taken into account in determining whether continuity of interest has been preserved to the extent that the consideration received by those shareholders prior to the potential reorganization is not treated as boot received from the acquirer (or from a related party) in exchange for target stock for purposes of § 356 (or would have been so treated if the target shareholder also had received acquirer stock in exchange for target stock owned by the shareholder, thus dealing with pre-acquisition complete redemptions of one or more target shareholders). Treas.Reg. § 1.368–1(e)(1)(ii) also provides that extraordinary pre-acquisition distributions to the shareholders of the target—which have the economic effect of reducing the amount of acquirer stock necessary to effect the acquisition—likewise will not be taken into account in determining the percentage of the target corporation's stock that has been surrendered in the acquisition unless the amount received in the distribution is treated as boot received from the acquirer. The only example of the application of these rules, which is in Treas.Reg. § 1.368–1(e)(8), Ex. 9, is not particularly illuminating, because it provides no guidance regarding how to determine whether the pre-acquisition consideration provided to target shareholders is treated as boot received from the acquirer.

PROBLEM SET 3

1. Gordon and Helene each owned 50% of the outstanding stock of T Corporation. P Corporation, which is not publicly traded, offered to acquire T Corporation in a statutory merger in which 100% of the consideration would be P Corporation voting common stock. Gordon and Helene wanted cash rather than P Corporation stock, but P Corporation refused to pay cash. Thereupon, Gordon and Helene sold their T Corporation stock for cash to Isaac, who was unrelated to Gordon, Helene, or P Corporation, but whose participation in the transaction was suggested by P Corporation. Following the sale, Isaac, acting on behalf of T Corporation, accepted the P Corporation proposal and voted to merge T Corporation into P Corporation in a statutory merger in which 100% of the consideration was P Corporation stock. Does the merger qualify as a tax-free reorganization? Why does it matter?

2. (a) Jerry and Karen each owned 50% of the outstanding stock of T Corporation. P Corporation, which is not publicly traded, offered to acquire T Corporation in a statutory merger in which 100% of the consideration would be P Corporation voting common stock. Jerry and Karen wanted cash rather than stock in P Corporation, but P Corporation refused to pay cash. P Corporation informed Jerry and Karen that within a year P Corporation was going to make an initial public offering, and once the P Corporation stock was publicly traded, P Corporation would facilitate the sale of its stock received by Jerry and Karen in the merger through stock exchange transactions. After a contract to this effect was executed, Jerry and Karen thereupon voted to merge T Corporation into P Corporation. Jerry and Karen received P Corporation stock in the merger and seven months later, after P Corporation went public, Jerry and Karen sold in a New York Stock Exchange transaction all of the P Corporation stock received in the merger. Does the merger qualify as a tax-free reorganization?

(b) Suppose that the contract between Jerry and Karen and P Corporation also provided that if P Corporation was not taken public within a year of the merger that P Corporation would secure a purchaser for the P Corporation stock received in the merger by Jerry and Karen. If P Corporation did not go public and P Corporation arranged a purchase of the P Corporation stock received by Jerry and Karen, does the merger qualify as a tax-free reorganization under the following circumstances:

(1) P Corporation redeemed the stock.

(2) P Corporation caused its wholly owned subsidiary, S Corporation, to purchase the stock.

(3) Lorenzo, the president of P Corporation, purchased the stock with Lorenzo's own funds.

(4) P Corporation arranged with Goldman-Lynch Investment Bankers that Goldman-Lynch would purchase the stock.

3.   Pablo, Rebekah, and Sebastian each owned one-third of the outstanding common stock of T Corp. P Corp., which is not publicly traded, offered to acquire T Corp. in a statutory merger in which 100% of the consideration would be P Corp. voting common stock. Pablo was willing to accept the offer, but Rebekah and Sebastian wanted cash rather than stock in P Corp. and P Corp. refused to pay cash. To effectuate the merger, with P Corp.'s consent, T Corp. sold obsolete assets that were no longer useful in its business for cash and used the cash to redeem Rebekah's and Sebastian's stock. Thereafter, T merged into P Corp., which thereby obtained T's modern business assets which it put to immediate use. In the merger, Pablo received P voting common stock in exchange for his T stock, which was cancelled. Is the merger a tax-free statutory merger under § 368(a)(1)(A)?

4.   Melissa, Noel, and Olga each owned one-third of the outstanding common stock of T Corp. Melissa and Noel sold their stock (in the aggregate representing two-thirds of the outstanding stock) to P Corp. for cash. Olga refused to sell. Immediately after obtaining two-thirds voting control, P Corp. voted its shares in favor of merging T Corp. into S Corp., a wholly owned subsidiary of P Corp. Pursuant to the merger, Olga received voting common stock of P Corp., and P Corp.'s stock in T Corp. was cancelled.

(a)   Is continuity of interest present? (Assume the other requirements of a forward triangular merger under § 368(a)(2)(D) have been met.) If not, what is it?

(b)   Assume alternatively that Melissa and Noel each owned 40% of the stock of T Corp. and received all cash for their shares. In the subsequent merger of T Corp. into S Corp., Olga received P Corp. stock for her 20% of the T Stock. Is this transaction a tax-free merger? How will the two corporations treat the transaction? How will Olga treat the transaction?

C.   THE CONTINUITY OF BUSINESS ENTERPRISE REQUIREMENT

REGULATIONS: Sections 1.368–1(d), –2(k)(1).

Honbarrier v. Commissioner
United States Tax Court, 2000.
115 T.C. 300.

■ RUWE, JUDGE:

* * *

The sole issue for decision is whether the merger of Colonial into Central Transport, Inc. (Central), on December 31, 1993, qualifies as a tax-free reorganization within the meaning of section 368(a)(1)(A).

FINDINGS OF FACT

* * *

Colonial was a trucking company that operated as a common carrier of packaged freight. * * * When the trucking industry was deregulated at the Federal level in the 1980's, Colonial was subjected to competition from small individual truckers, with low overhead costs. As a result, Colonial's ICC operating authority became worthless, and the company experienced significant business reversals. * * * In 1988, as a result of its financial losses, Colonial stopped hauling freight and began selling its operating assets. By December 31, 1990, Colonial had sold all of its operating assets, except for the ICC and North Carolina operating authorities, for cash and cash equivalents. On August 21, 1992, Colonial sold its North Carolina authority for $5,000 but retained its ICC authority.

Colonial invested the proceeds from the sale of its operating assets almost exclusively in tax-exempt bonds and a municipal bond fund. Colonial held 18 tax-exempt bonds, 16 of which were purchased in 1990 and 1991, and 2 of which were purchased in 1992. One bond was redeemed in 1991, and three bonds were redeemed in 1992 and 1993. Colonial continued to hold the remaining 14 bonds as of the end of 1993.

As of October 31, 1993, 2 months prior to the merger, Colonial held approximately $7.35 million in tax-exempt bonds and a municipal bond fund and approximately $1,500 in cash. On December 31, 1993, Colonial liquidated one of its tax-exempt bonds and its municipal bond fund. The proceeds of this liquidation together totaled more than $2,550,000. * * *

From 1985 to December 31, 1993, Mr. Honbarrier owned 100 percent of Colonial's issued and outstanding shares. * * *

From 1951 through 1997, Central was a trucking company that operated as a bulk carrier of liquid and dry chemicals. Some of the chemicals that Central hauled were toxic. Central transported bulk chemicals in tanker trailers pulled by tractors. * * * Central was an S corporation. Central was highly successful in its bulk chemical hauling business * * *. [At the end of 1993, the balance in Central's accumulated adjustments account exceeded $10,000,000.]

Unlike Colonial, Central did not invest in tax-exempt bonds. Central held passive investments in the form of short-term liquid investments, such as certificates of deposit, because it needed cash and cash equivalents to operate its business. * * *

From 1982 through 1997, all of Central's stock was owned by Mr. and Mrs. Honbarrier and their children * * *.

On December 31, 1993, Colonial merged into Central in accordance with the laws of North Carolina. Central was the surviving corporation. * * * Pursuant to the merger, Mr. Honbarrier's 245 shares of Colonial stock were exchanged for 17,840 shares of Central stock.

On December 22, 1993, the board of directors of Central also declared a $7 million distribution payable to its shareholders on December 31, 1993. The shareholder distribution was allocated on a pro rata basis among the shareholders based on their stock ownership in Central on December 22, 1993. * * * With the exception of the amount allocable to

Mr. Honbarrier, all of the declared distributions were paid by check on December 31, 1993. Central made the $5,042,772 distribution to Mr. Honbarrier in two parts. The first part was paid via a $493,626 check drawn on Central's account on December 31, 1993. * * * The second part of the distribution to Mr. Honbarrier was made on January 3, 1994, and consisted of $4,549,146 in tax-exempt bonds. The tax-exempt bonds distributed to Mr. Honbarrier on January 3, 1994, were the same bonds acquired by Central from Colonial in the merger.

For Federal income tax purposes, petitioners treated the merger as a tax-free reorganization within the meaning of section 368(a)(1)(A) and treated the $7 million distribution as a payment of previously taxed income reflected in Central's accumulated adjustments account.

OPINION

* * *

Section 368(a)(1)(A) defines a reorganization as "a statutory merger or consolidation". A statutory merger or consolidation is one effected pursuant to the corporate laws of the United States, a State, a territory, or the District of Columbia. See sec. 1.368–2(b)(1), Income Tax Regs. The merger of Colonial into Central meets this literal requirement. Petitioners argue that they are entitled to tax-free treatment under the Code because the merger was a complete and valid transaction for State law purposes.

It has long been held that qualification as a merger under State law is not, by itself, sufficient to qualify as a reorganization under section 368(a)(1)(A). Courts have interpreted section 368 as imposing three additional requirements for a merger to be treated as a reorganization under section 368(a)(1)(A). These are: (1) Business purpose; (2) continuity of business enterprise; and (3) continuity of interest. * * * Following judicial precedent, the regulations also require that there be a business purpose for the transaction, continuity of business enterprise, and continuity of interest, in order for a merger to qualify as a reorganization under section 368(a)(1)(A). See sec. 1.368–1(b), Income Tax Regs.; T.D. 7745, 1981–1 C.B. 134. Failure to comply with any one of these requirements will preclude treatment as a tax-free reorganization within the meaning of section 368(a)(1)(A).

Respondent argues that the merger failed to meet the continuity of business enterprise requirement necessary to qualify the merger as a tax-free reorganization within the meaning of section 368(a)(1)(A). The continuity of business enterprise requirement was first expressed in Cortland Specialty Co. v. Commissioner, supra. * * * This requirement is now embodied in section 1.368–1(b), Income Tax Regs., and described in paragraph (d) of the same section. These regulations are based on an interpretation of judicial precedents which articulate the continuity of business enterprise doctrine. See T.D. 7745, 1981–1 C.B. 134. The basic concept behind the continuity of business enterprise requirement is that the receipt of a new ownership interest in an entity that retains none of the business attributes of the shareholder's former corporation is more closely akin to a sale or liquidation than to a mere adjustment in the form of ownership. * * *

Under the income tax regulations, a transaction constitutes a tax-free reorganization only if there is "a continuity of the business enterprise under the modified corporate form". Sec. 1.368–1(b), Income Tax Regs. Continuity of business enterprise requires that the acquiring corporation either continue the acquired corporation's historic business or use a significant portion of the acquired corporation's historic business assets in a business. See sec. 1.368–1(d)(2), Income Tax Regs. In essence, the acquiring corporation must retain a link to the business enterprise of the acquired corporation by continuing the acquired corporation's business or by using the acquired corporation's business assets in a business. See Berry Petroleum Co. v. Commissioner, 104 T.C. 584, 635–636 (1995), affd. 142 F.3d 442 (9th Cir. 1998). In this case, as explained below, we find that Central neither continued Colonial's historic business nor used a significant portion of Colonial's historic business assets in Central's business operations.

1. *Continuation of Acquired Corporation's Historic Business*

In general, a corporation's historic business is the business it has conducted most recently. See sec. 1.368–1(d)(3)(iii), Income Tax Regs. Petitioners contend that there is a continuity of Colonial's trucking business because Central is also in the trucking business. We disagree.

Colonial terminated its business of hauling packaged freight in 1988. It then began selling its operating assets. From 1988 forward, Colonial had no customers. By the end of 1990, Colonial had essentially disposed of its trucking operation assets for cash and cash equivalents. * * *

Colonial stopped hauling freight approximately 5 years prior to the merger, had essentially sold all of its operating assets 3 years prior to the merger, and for 3 years prior to the merger kept most of its assets in tax-exempt bonds and a municipal bond fund. We conclude that Colonial had abandoned its trucking business well before the merger.[13] Colonial's most recent business type activity was acquiring and holding tax-exempt bonds and a municipal bond fund. This was Colonial's historic business at the time of the merger for purposes of determining whether there was a continuity of business enterprise. See, e.g., Abegg v. Commissioner, 50 T.C. 145 (1968), affd. 429 F.2d 1209 (2d Cir. 1970).[14]

---

[13] We also note: (1) The type of trucking business conducted by Central involving hauling solid and liquid (and sometimes toxic) chemicals in expensive tanker trailers was different from the operations previously conducted by Colonial; (2) Central never operated as a packaged-freight carrier; and (3) Central never used the ICC operating authority acquired from Colonial in the merger.

[14] We recognize that investment activity is not a trade or business for some purposes. See Commissioner v. Groetzinger, 480 U.S. 23 * * * (1987). However, investment activity has been recognized as a historic business for purposes of the continuity of business enterprise doctrine. See Abegg v. Commissioner, 50 T.C. 145 (1968), affd. 429 F.2d 1209 (2d Cir. 1970); see also T.D.

As of October 31, 1993, 2 months prior to the merger, Colonial held approximately $7.35 million in tax-exempt bonds and a municipal bond fund and approximately $1,500 in cash. On December 31, 1993, Colonial liquidated one of those bonds and its municipal bond fund for more than $2,550,000. As a result, Colonial's cash position increased significantly.

The fair market value of the tax-exempt bonds held directly by Colonial totaled $4,549,146 just before the merger on December 31, 1993. Three days after the merger, Central distributed these same tax-exempt bonds to Mr. Honbarrier. This distribution occurred on January 3, 1994. The last tax-exempt bond acquired by Central in the merger was worth $300,000 and held in the Alex Brown and Sons account. This bond was liquidated by Central 4 months after the merger. Unlike Colonial, Central did not invest in tax-exempt bonds. Central placed its money in short-term liquid investments, such as certificates of deposit because it needed cash and cash equivalents to operate its business. Thus, we conclude that Central did not continue Colonial's business of holding tax-exempt bonds and municipal bond funds.

2.   *Significant Use of Acquired Corporation's Business Assets*

Continuity of business enterprise can also be satisfied if the acquiring corporation uses a significant portion of the acquired corporation's historic business assets in a business. See sec. 1.368–1(d)(4)(i), Income Tax Regs. A corporation's historic business assets are the assets used in its historic business. See sec. 1.368–1(d)(4)(ii), Income Tax Regs. Business assets may include stock and securities. See id. In general, the determination of the portion of the corporation's assets considered "significant" is based on the relative importance of the assets to the operation of the business. See sec. 1.368–1(d)(4)(iii), Income Tax Regs. However, all other facts and circumstances, such as the net fair market value of those assets, will be considered. See id.

Colonial's historic business assets were its tax-exempt bonds and municipal bond fund. It was never intended that Colonial's tax-exempt bonds and municipal bond fund be held by Central and, after the merger, Central did not use those assets in its business. On the day of the merger, Colonial liquidated a tax-exempt bond and its municipal bond fund for more than $2.5 million in cash. On the same day, Central made a cash distribution to Central's shareholders in the total amount of $2,450,854. Three days after the merger, tax-exempt bonds totaling $4,549,146 that had been held by Colonial were distributed to Mr. Honbarrier. The remaining tax-exempt bond, valued at $300,000 * * * was liquidated 4 months later.

As a result of the transactions surrounding the merger, all of Colonial's investments in tax-exempt bonds and the municipal bond fund were disposed of and Colonial ceased to exist. We find that Central did

---

7745, 1981–1 C.B. 134, 139 (Investment operations may constitute a historic business if the investment assets were not acquired as part of a plan of reorganization).

not use a significant portion of Colonial's historic business assets in a business.

3. *Conclusion*

Central did not continue either Colonial's historic business or use a significant portion of Colonial's historic business assets in a business. As a result, Central did not satisfy the continuity of business enterprise requirement. See sec. 1.368–1(b), Income Tax Regs.

We hold that the merger of Colonial into Central was not a tax-free reorganization within the meaning of section 368(a)(1)(A). Because this merger did not qualify as a reorganization under section 368(a)(1)(A), Mr. Honbarrier's exchange of Colonial stock for valuable consideration was a taxable event. * * *

In the notice of deficiency to Colonial, respondent determined that Colonial had a gain on the sale or exchange of its assets in the merger transaction. However, respondent now agrees that Colonial did not realize any gain because the fair market value of its assets equaled its tax basis in those assets. * * *

DETAILED ANALYSIS

1. PRE-1981 CASE LAW

Treas.Reg. § 1.368–1(b) states that one prerequisite to a "reorganization" is "a continuity of the business enterprise under the modified corporate form." Prior to 1981, establishing the scope of this requirement was left to case law and revenue rulings. In general, the requirement was not particularly difficult to satisfy; as long as the acquiring corporation used the assets of the acquired corporation in some business, even though different than the historic business of the acquired corporation, the continuity of business enterprise test was met. See, e.g., Bentsen v. Phinney, 199 F.Supp. 363 (S.D.Tex.1961) (merger of land development business into insurance company, which thereafter conducted only an insurance business); Atlas Tool Co. v. Commissioner, 614 F.2d 860 (3d Cir.1980) (continuity of business enterprise existed where acquired corporation's business was discontinued and its assets were held in reserve for future use in acquiring corporation's business; assets were restored to use within three months following acquisition). Wortham Machinery Co. v. United States, 521 F.2d 160 (10th Cir.1975), found no continuity of business enterprise where the transferor corporation in a purported (C) reorganization was engaged in no business activity at the time of the transfer and the acquiring corporation merely tried to dispose of the acquired assets; there was more than a "temporary suspension" of business activities. Consequently there was no reorganization: "Liquidation of assets is not continuation of a business enterprise."

2. POST-1981 REGULATION ANALYSIS

2.1. *Generally*

Treas.Reg. § 1.368–1(d), issued in 1981, expanded substantially the continuity of business enterprise requirement applicable to post-1981 acquisitions. The Regulation requires that the acquiring corporation either (1) continue at least one of the acquired corporation's historic businesses or (2) use a significant portion of the acquired corporation's historic assets in a business. Thus, as under prior law, the historic business of either corporation may be discontinued as long as some business is conducted after the acquisition. Examples in the Regulations indicate that continuity of business enterprise does not exist where the historic assets of the acquired corporation are sold either before the acquisition (thereby rendering it an investment company) or shortly after the acquisition.

Rev.Rul. 81–92, 1981–1 C.B. 133, held that the continuity of business enterprise requirement under Treas.Reg. § 1.368–1(d) was not met where, in a transaction that was in form a reorganization described in § 368(a)(1)(B), the acquired corporation's assets consisted solely of cash that it realized from the sale of assets it previously used in its manufacturing business.

Laure v. Commissioner, 653 F.2d 253 (6th Cir.1981), involved the merger of a corporation that was conducting a failing air charter business into a manufacturing corporation owned by the same shareholders. Prior to the merger the acquired corporation had operated its air charter service, using leased aircraft. The acquiring corporation frequently used the services of the target corporation. After the merger, all of the target's air charter business assets, other than land and an airport hangar on the land, were sold. The hangar was leased to the purchaser of the bulk of the assets, who in turn provided contract air charter services to the acquiring corporation. The Tax Court found that there was no continuity of business enterprise because there was no evidence that the acquiring corporation either continued any of the target corporation's business activities or used any of the target corporation's assets in the conduct of its own business. The Tax Court was not persuaded that continuing to own the land and hangar was sufficient to support reorganization treatment where the acquirer did not use the property in its business or, since it received no rent even though it assumed liabilities in the merger, did not receive any financial benefit from the property. The Court of Appeals reversed, holding that the Tax Court's finding of a lack of continuity of business enterprise was clearly erroneous. Because the acquiring corporation hired the air charter service operated by the purchaser of the target's assets, the retained land and hanger were "substantial both in relation to the other assets transferred and in importance to the acquiring corporation," even though only 27% of the acquired corporation's operating assets were retained. Although the case involved a tax year prior to the 1981 Regulations, the Sixth Circuit noted that it believed that the Regulations supported its conclusion that the continuity of business requirement was satisfied. In so doing, it focused not on the percentage of the assets by value that were retained but on what it described as "the extreme importance of the assets retained" to the acquiring corporation's business. Since there is no indication that the 1981 Regulations were intended to ease the pre-Regulations standards for meeting the continuity of business enterprise requirements, it appears to be unlikely that the Tax Court would follow the Sixth Circuit's decision in *Laure*, except in a case appealable to the Sixth Circuit.

Payne v. Commissioner, T.C. Memo. 2003–90, held that the transfer of substantially all the assets of one corporation (2618 Inc.) to another corporation (JKP) that was wholly owned by the same shareholder, in a transaction that otherwise met all of the statutory requirements of § 368(a)(1)(D), was a tax-free reorganization, even though at the time of the transfer the shareholder contemplated selling the business and three months later the transferee corporation did sell all of its assets. The continuity of business enterprise requirement of Treas.Reg. § 1.368–1(d) was met. The court stated:

> [T]here is no direct evidence that JKP's actual sale of its assets was part of an overall plan existing at the time of the transfer of the club's operation from 2618 [Inc.] to JKP; and we do not infer the existence of such a plan by reason of the proximity in time of the two transactions. The mere fact that petitioner may have contemplated selling the club at the time of its transfer from 2618 to JKP does not require a finding that such transfer lacked COBE. * * *.

We hold that * * * the transfer of the club from 2618 to JKP possessed COBE.

2.2. *Holding Company Situations*

Treas.Reg. § 1.368–1(d)(1) provides that the general COBE rule's application to "certain transactions, such as mergers of holding companies, will depend on all facts and circumstances." Where the target corporation is a holding company, the continuity of business requirement is satisfied as long as a significant business of one of the target holding company's subsidiary corporations is conducted directly or indirectly by the acquiring corporation, for example by a second tier subsidiary of the acquiring corporation. Rev.Rul. 85–198, 1985–2 C.B. 120. Where a holding company is merged into its operating subsidiary, the continuity of business interest requirement is satisfied by looking through the holding company to treat the operating subsidiary's business as the business of the holding company. Rev.Rul. 85–197, 1985–2 C.B. 120.

2.3. *Acquirer's Historic Business*

The Regulations are silent with regard to whether the acquiring corporation also must meet the continuity of interest requirement. Prior to the promulgation of the Regulations, the IRS had ruled that the continuity of business enterprise doctrine was satisfied where the acquiring corporation discontinued its own historic business and continued the business of the acquired corporation. Rev.Rul. 63–29, 1963–1 C.B. 77 (acquirer discontinued its toy business and continued acquired target's steel distribution business). After the Regulations were promulgated, the IRS obsoleted Rev.Rul. 63–29 in Rev.Rul. 81–25, 1981–1 C.B. 132, which states: "The holding of Rev.Rul. 63–29 is now reflected in the recent amendment to section 1.368–1 (1.368–

1(d)) of the regulations, which looks only to the transferor's historic business or historic business assets for determining if the continuity of business enterprise requirement is satisfied. * * * In a section 368(a)(1) reorganization the continuity of business enterprise requirement does not apply to the business or business assets of the transferee corporation prior to the reorganization."

3. REMOTE CONTINUITY OF BUSINESS ENTERPRISE

3.1. *Generally*

Treas.Reg. § 1.368–1(d) provides that certain post-reorganization transfers by the acquiring corporation of (1) the target corporation's assets or (2) the stock of the acquired corporation, depending on the form of the reorganization, to partnerships do not cause the transaction to fail to satisfy the continuity of business enterprise requirement. These rules dovetail with Treas.Reg. § 1.368–2(k), which provides specific guidance regarding drop-downs permitted under § 368(a)(2)(C). The purpose of these provisions is to reflect that "a valid reorganization may qualify as tax-free even if the acquiring corporation does not directly carry on the historic T business or use the historic T assets in a business." T.D. 8760, Rules and Regulations, Department of the Treasury, Internal Revenue Service, Continuity of Interest and Continuity of Business Enterprise, 1998–1 C.B. 803, 805. Thus, for example, a merger followed by a drop-down of the acquired corporation's assets to a third tier subsidiary would qualify under § 368. See Treas.Reg. §§ 1.368–1(d)(5), Ex. 6; see also Treas.Reg. § 1.368–2(k). The Regulations, however, do not expand the scope of triangular reorganizations to permit an acquisition using stock of a grandparent or higher tier corporation to qualify. Rev.Rul. 74–565, 1974–2 C.B. 125, disqualifies such transactions.

3.2. *Transfers to Related Corporations*

Under Treas.Reg. § 1.368–1(d)(4), the assets of the acquired corporation (or the stock of the acquired corporation if the reorganization is in the form of a stock acquisition) can be transferred among the members of the acquiring corporation's "qualified group" without violating the continuity of business enterprise requirements. The qualified group consists of one or more chains of controlled corporations, within the meaning of § 368(c) or, in the case of any triangular reorganization, the parent of the acquiring corporation. Treas.Reg. § 1.368–1(d)(4)(i), (ii). The Regulations do not address the issue of whether the "solely for voting stock" requirement of a § 368(a)(1)(C) reorganization is satisfied when a member of the "qualified group" other than the acquiring corporation assumes the acquired corporation's liabilities in connection with the transfer, but Rev.Rul. 70–224, 1970–1 C.B. 79, should permit such an indirect assumption of liabilities.

Consistent with Treas.Reg. § 1.368–1(d)(4), Treas.Regs. §§ 1.368–2(f), dealing with the definition of "party to a reorganization," and 1.368–2(k), dealing with post-acquisition asset and stock transfers generally, facilitate post-acquisition restructurings of a controlled group of corporations involving the target corporation after an otherwise qualifying reorganization. In addition to post-acquisition drops of assets to lower-tier subsidiaries, post-acquisition cross-chain transfers and distributions by an acquisition subsidiary that is a member of the acquiring corporation's group to a corporation that controls the acquiring corporation of either the target corporation's stock (following a § 368(a)(1)(B) or § 368(a)(2)(E) reorganization) or assets (following a § 368(a)(1)(A), § 368(a)(1)(C), or § 368(a)(2)(D) reorganization) subsequent to the acquisition, do not disqualify the acquisition from reorganization treatment, even though there is no statutory provision expressly providing that such distributions do not affect the validity of reorganization treatment, provided that the distribution would not result in the distributing corporation being treated as liquidated for income tax purposes. The Regulations thus permit the acquiring corporation to significantly rearrange ownership of the target corporation's assets or stock, as the case may be, among all of the members of its qualified group (based on § 368(c) control) without disqualifying the reorganization. Furthermore, the Regulations permit qualified group members to aggregate their direct stock ownership of a corporation, in a manner similar to aggregation under § 1504(a), in determining whether they have the requisite § 368(c) control of such corporation (provided that the issuing corporation has § 368(c) control in at least one other corporation).

3.3. *Transfer of Acquired Corporation's Assets to a Partnership*

If after the potential reorganization the acquiring corporation transfers assets of the target corporation to a partnership of which it (or one or more members of its qualified group) is a member, Treas.Reg. § 1.368–1(d)(4)(iii) governs whether the continuity of business enterprise requirement has been satisfied. The Regulations specify that a corporation will be treated as conducting a business of a partnership if either (1) members of the qualified group own a significant interest in the partnership business, measured in the aggregate, or (2) "one or more members of the qualified group have active and substantial management functions as a partner with respect to that partnership business." The Regulations then provide that, if a significant historic target business is conducted in a partnership, the fact that the acquiring corporation (or one or more members of the controlled group) is treated as conducting the business "tends to establish the requisite continuity, but is not alone sufficient." Treas.Reg. § 1.368–1(d)(4)(iii)(C). See also Treas.Reg. § 1.368–1(d)(5), Exs. 8–13.

PROBLEM SET 4

1.   P Corporation acquires T Corporation pursuant to a statutory merger. Assume that all statutory requirements for a tax-free reorganization are satisfied, apart from the continuity of business enterprise requirement. Given the following alternative additional facts, consider whether or not a tax-free reorganization has occurred:

(a)   P issues common stock for all of the assets of T. T's assets consist solely of stock and short-term securities. T obtained these assets by using cash obtained from a recent sale of T's operating assets formerly used in its gizmo business. P Corp. is engaged in manufacturing widgets and it plans to sell the stock and short-term securities obtained from T Corp. to raise cash to construct a new widget factory.

(b) Would your answer differ if P used T's stock and short-term securities to construct a new gizmo factory?

2.   Assume that T Corp. did not sell its gizmo business prior to the merger and it was engaged in manufacturing gizmos. P was engaged in manufacturing widgets. T merged into P and P continued T's gizmo operation. Three weeks after the merger, P sold its widgets operation to an unrelated party.

3.   Assume that up until three years prior to the merger, T historically engaged in manufacturing gizmos and that P engages in manufacturing widgets. Approximately three years prior to the merger T sold its assets for cash and invested in short-term securities. One year prior to the merger T invested substantially all its funds in an apartment project. Subsequent to the merger P continued to own and operate the apartment project and to manufacture widgets.

4.   (a) Assume that T manufactured gizmos, gadgets and bassamatics. Immediately after the merger P sold T's gizmo and gadget businesses and used the cash to expand the bassamatic business.

     (b)   What if P used the cash to expand its widget business?

     (c)   What if P used the cash to expand its widget business, discontinued the bassamatic business, but converted the bassamatic assets to manufacturing widgets?

5.   (a) P and T were competitors in the same product line. P acquired all of the assets of T in a statutory merger, and after the merger P retired all of T's assets except a customer list, which it used to sell products made using P's preexisting plant.

     (b)   P and T were competitors in the same product line. P acquired all of the assets of T in a statutory merger, and after the merger P retired all of T's assets, but it held T's former factory in reserve (and maintained it) in case P's assets broke down.

6.   T Corp. was engaged in manufacturing fishing equipment. P was engaged in manufacturing hunting equipment. P acquired T in a transaction in which T merged into P's wholly owned subsidiary, S, in a forward triangular merger described in § 368(a)(2)(D). The day after the merger, X Corp. made an offer to P to purchase all of the stock of S Corp. for cash, which included all of the T assets. P agreed to sell S Corp. and as expeditiously as possible the transaction closed.

7.   (a) T Corp. was engaged in manufacturing gizmos. P was engaged in manufacturing widgets. T merged into P, and P promptly transferred T's gizmo operation to S Corporation, its wholly owned subsidiary.

     (b)   T manufactured gizmos, gadgets, bassamatics, and whirligigs. T merged into P, and P transferred the gizmo business to W Corp., the gadget business to X Corp. the bassamatic business to Y Corp., and the Whirligig business to Z Corp. Z Corp, is an 80% controlled subsidiary of Y Corp., which is an 80% controlled subsidiary of X Corp., which is an 80% controlled subsidiary of W Corp., which is an 80% controlled subsidiary of S Corp., which is an 80% controlled subsidiary of P Corp.

8.   P owns no assets other than the stock of R Corp. and S Corp., both of which manufacture and sell widgets. T owns no assets other than the stock of U Corp. and W Corp., both of which manufacture and sell gizmos. P acquires all of the assets of T in a statutory merger.

9.   T and P are both controlled by Oscar, Patty, and Rafael. P was organized 20 years ago as a franchised wholesaler of widgets. T was formed three years ago to independently engage in the manufacture of widgets. T has never been successful and for the last six months its activities have been largely suspended. Manufacturing activities never reached beyond the preliminary stage. P acquires all of the assets of T in a statutory merger. Immediately prior to the merger T had net operating loss carry forwards of $150,000, which P hopes to use as a successor pursuant to § 381 (see Chapter 13).

D. TAX RESULTS TO THE PARTIES TO A TYPE (A) REORGANIZATION

The consequences to the parties to a reorganization generally do not vary significantly among the several different types of § 368 reorganizations. The type (A) reorganization represents the simplest type of acquisitive reorganization. Section 368(a)(1)(A) defines an (A) reorganization as a "statutory merger or consolidation." See Treas.Reg. § 1.368–2(b)(1)(ii). Thus, generally speaking, any type of amalgamation or consolidation of corporate entities under state or federal merger statutes meets the statutory definition. The assets and liabilities of the target corporation are transferred to the acquiring corporation by operation of state law; the shareholders of the target corporation receive the consideration agreed upon in the merger agreement in exchange for their stock. The consideration may include property other than stock or securities. There are no statutory requirements regarding the proportion of the consideration that must include stock; instead, the judicially developed continuity of interest requirement, now incorporated in the Regulations, is determinative in a type (A) reorganization.

The type (C) reorganization is similar to a statutory merger, and the forward triangular merger (§ 368(a)(2)(D)) and reverse triangular merger (§ 368(a)(2)(E)) reorganizations are merely variations of the type (A) reorganization as far as treatment of the parties to the reorganization is concerned. The type (B) reorganization, however, is the only form of tax-free reorganization that involves a direct transaction between the acquiring corporation and the shareholders of the target corporation. In addition, it is the only reorganization that does not involve at least one corporation that disappears in the transaction. As a result, it can produce somewhat different tax results to the parties to the reorganization.

This section examines the overarching principles involving taxation of the parties to a reorganization and deals comprehensively with the tax treatment of parties to a type (A) reorganization. Special aspects of the treatment of parties to other forms of reorganizations are discussed in succeeding sections, along with the detailed rules for qualifying as a tax-free reorganization under those subsections of § 368.

(1) TARGET SHAREHOLDERS AND SECURITY HOLDERS

INTERNAL REVENUE CODE: Sections 354(a); 356(a), (c), (d), (e); 358(a), (b), (d), (f); 368(b).

REGULATIONS: Sections 1.354–1(a), (b), (e); 1.356–1, –3, –4; 1.358–1, –2(a)(1), (2)(i)–(ii), (vii), (b), (c), Exs. 1–7; 1.368–2(f), (g).

Sections 354 and 356 control taxation of the shareholders in acquisitive reorganization transactions. Section 354(a) applies only to an exchange *solely* for stock or securities, so that the presence of boot prevents its application. Section 356(a)(1) operates to provide partial nonrecognition; any realized gain is recognized but only to the extent of the boot. If a loss has been realized, it may not be recognized even though boot has been received. I.R.C. § 356(c). Section 358(a) prescribes exchanged basis rules for the shareholders in § 354 and § 356 exchanges.

For example, in a type (A) merger, individual J, a shareholder of the target corporation, surrendered shares of stock of the target corporation having a basis to J of $100 in exchange for $40 of cash and shares of the acquiring corporation having a fair market value of $110. J realizes a gain of $50, but only $40, an amount equal to the cash boot, must be recognized. Under § 358(a), J's basis in the acquiring corporation stock would be $100 ($100 original basis + $40 of recognized gain − $40 of cash boot), thus accounting for the $10 of realized but unrecognized gain. If J's basis for the target corporation stock were instead $120, then J would realize a gain of only $30, all of which would be recognized. The receipt of the other $10 of cash "tax-free" would be taken into account by reducing the basis of the acquiring corporation stock received in the exchange from $120 to $110 pursuant to § 358(a)(1)(A).

The character of any gain recognized must also be determined. Section 356(a)(2) provides generally that if the distribution of boot pursuant to the plan of reorganization has the *effect of the distribution of a dividend*, the amount of the gain is taxed as a dividend and not as part of the exchange transaction. This provision is necessary as a safeguard to insure that distributions that in substance are dividends rather than additional consideration for the exchange of stock will be appropriately taxed. The resemblance to § 302 is apparent, but there are some differences.

As long as dividends and capital gains are taxed at the same rate, the question of whether boot is characterized as a dividend under § 356(a)(2) is of limited importance to individual shareholders of the target corporation. It matters primarily because capital gains can be offset by unrelated capital losses, but dividends cannot be offset by capital losses in computing taxable income. For corporate shareholders of the target corporation, however, the issue remains critical.

Characterization of boot as a dividend, rather than a capital gain, is advantageous to the corporate shareholder because of the consequent availability of the § 243 dividends received deduction.

Boot does not include only cash. An exchange of securities other than stock gives rise to boot under § 354(a)(2) if the corporation distributes securities with a principal amount in excess of the securities received in return. In such a case the amount of the boot as determined under § 356(d) is the fair market value of the excess principal amount, which, due to the operation of the original issue discount rules, in most cases equals the excess principal amount.[5] Section 357(a) does not apply to § 356(a), so that if any liabilities of the shareholders of the target corporation are assumed by the acquiring corporation, the liabilities are boot.

If § 354 and § 356 do not apply, then the distributions are considered under § 301, § 302, or § 331, depending on the form of the transaction. Sections 354 and 356 thus operate as exceptions to these other provisions respecting corporate distributions and exchanges, though the other sections do not contain any explicit references to the reorganization exceptions.

DETAILED ANALYSIS

1. RECOGNITION OF GAIN

If a shareholder exchanges more than one block of stock in exchange for stock and boot with respect to each block of stock, the gain must be computed separately on each block. Gain may be recognized on one block of stock while an unrecognized loss is realized on the other. Treas.Reg. § 1.356–1(b); Rev.Rul. 68–23, 1968–1 C.B. 144. If a loss has been realized with respect to a particular block of stock, it may not be recognized even though boot has been received. I.R.C. § 356(c).

Treas.Reg. § 1.356–1(b) provides that if a shareholder exchanges stock of more than one class for stock and boot, for purposes of computing gain recognized on an exchange, the terms of the plan of reorganization will determine the extent to which the other property or money has been received in exchange for a particular share of stock or security, provided that such terms are economically reasonable. See Treas.Reg. § 1.356–1(d), Ex. 4. If the plan of reorganization does not specify the stock and boot received in exchange for a particular share of stock or security surrendered, a pro rata portion of the other property and money received is treated as received in exchange for each share of stock and security surrendered, based on the fair market value of such surrendered share of stock or security. Treas.Reg. § 1.356–1(b), (d), Ex. 3.

Proposed Regulations, since withdrawn, would have clarified that, if the terms of the agreement specified the terms of the exchange in an economically reasonable way, then if no stock were received with respect to

---

[5]   Note that application of the original issue discount rules can produce a principal amount that differs from the face amount of the bond.

a particular class of stock and only cash (or debt instruments) were received with respect to that class of stock, gain *or loss* would be recognized as to that class. Prop.Reg. § 1.354–1(d)(1), (d)(2), and (e) Ex. 5 (2009); 84 Fed. Reg. 11687 (Mar. 28, 2019) (withdrawal notice). It is unclear the effect the withdrawal of the 2009 Proposed Regulations has on this planning technique.

For the nonrecognition protection of § 354 to apply, the stock must be received as part of the reorganization exchange. Thus, in Rev.Rul. 73–233, 1973–1 C.B. 179, where minority shareholders in a merger refused to vote in favor of the merger unless they received a disproportionate amount of stock in the acquiring corporation, the amount of stock received in excess of their proportionate interest was taxable under § 61. A contribution to capital by the majority shareholder was disregarded and the transaction was treated as if all of the parties had received their proportionate shares of stock in the acquiring corporation with the majority shareholder then transferring to the minority shareholders additional shares of stock as consideration for their voting in favor of the merger.

2. CHARACTERIZATION OF GAIN

2.1. *Dividend Versus Capital Gain*

Section 356(a)(2) treats recognized gain on the distribution of boot as a dividend if the exchange "has the effect of the distribution of a dividend." The characterization of recognized gain as a dividend was important when dividends were subject to a significantly higher tax rate than were capital gains. However, under current law, which taxes qualified dividends at the same rate as long-term capital gains, characterizing boot as a dividend under § 356(a)(2) or as capital gain has no significance in many instances. Because the amount of the dividend under § 356(a)(2) is limited to the lesser of the amount of the boot or the gain realized, a basis offset automatically occurs in either case. Thus, for a noncorporate shareholder receiving boot, the only important difference is that gain recognized with respect to boot received in a reorganization can be offset by capital losses, while § 356(a)(2) dividend income cannot be offset by capital losses, although individuals are able to deduct up to $3,000 of capital losses in excess of capital gains under § 1211(b). For a corporation that is a shareholder of the target corporation, however, characterization of boot as a dividend, rather than a capital gain, remains important. In this case characterization as a dividend is advantageous because of the consequent availability of the § 243 dividends received deduction.

In Commissioner v. Clark, 489 U.S. 726 (1989), the Supreme Court settled a long-standing dispute regarding the manner in which dividend equivalency under § 356(a)(2) is to be tested. In *Clark*, the sole shareholder of the target corporation in a triangular merger, in which the target was merged into a subsidiary of the acquiring corporation, received 300,000 shares of the acquiring corporation's stock plus $3,250,000 of cash. The IRS asserted that the gain from the boot was a dividend to the extent of the target corporation's earnings and profits at the time of the merger. The Supreme Court addressed a conflict among the Circuit Courts of Appeal regarding whether the tests for redemption under § 302 (discussed in Chapter 5) should be applied by treating the boot as received in exchange for a redemption of stock of the target corporation prior to the reorganization, or by treating the distribution of boot as a redemption of the stock of the surviving corporation after the reorganization. In Shimberg v. United States, 577 F.2d 283 (5th Cir. 1978), adopting the position of the IRS, the court held that the distribution of boot is treated as though it were made in a hypothetical redemption by the acquired corporation immediately prior to the reorganization. Under this approach, any pro rata distribution (including a distribution to a sole shareholder) would fail the disproportionate distribution tests of § 302(b) and result in dividend treatment. On the other hand, the Fourth Circuit in *Clark*, following Wright v. United States, 482 F.2d 600 (8th Cir. 1973), held that the distribution should be tested for redemption status under § 302 as if the acquiring corporation issued and then redeemed a number of shares equivalent in value to the boot. Under this approach, redemption status is tested by the reduction in ownership of the acquiring corporation represented by the hypothetical issue and redemption of shares represented by the boot. The Supreme Court adopted the approach of the Fourth and Eighth Circuits in *Clark* and *Wright*. The Court indicated that the post-redemption approach more accurately reflected congressional intent to treat a reorganization as an integrated transaction, rather than analyzing the payment of boot as an isolated distribution by the target corporation prior to the reorganization. Thus, under the Court's analysis, the shareholder in *Clark* was treated as if he had received an additional 125,000 shares of the acquiring corporation stock, the number of shares foregone in favor of the boot, which the acquiring corporation redeemed for the $3,250,000 cash payment. The hypothetical redemption of 125,000 shares reduced the shareholder's interest in the acquiring corporation from 1.3% of the outstanding stock to 0.9%. As a result, the taxpayer held less than 80% of his previous interest in the acquiring corporation and less than 50% of voting stock, thereby satisfying the disproportionate distribution test of § 302(b)(2), and resulting in capital gain treatment.

The pre-reorganization redemption analysis urged by the IRS, which was rejected by the Court in *Clark,* would lead to a dividend in all cases in which the boot is paid pro rata to the shareholders of the acquired corporation. The dissent in *Clark* described the distribution of boot as a pro rata redemption of stock to the shareholder of the target corporation that should be taxed as a dividend under United States v. Davis, 397 U.S. 306 (1970), excerpted and discussed in Chapter 5 (redemptions). Justice White observed in the *Clark* dissent: "Transporting § 302 from its purpose to frustrate shareholder sales of equity back to their own corporation, to § 356(a)(2)'s reorganization context, however, is problematic. Neither the majority nor the Court of Appeals explains why § 302 should obscure the core attribute of a dividend as a pro rata distribution to a corporation's shareholders; nor offers insight into the mechanics of valuing hypothetical stock transfers and equity reductions; nor answers the Commissioner's observations that the sole shareholder of an acquired corporation will always have a smaller interest in the continuing enterprise when cash payments combine with a stock exchange." (footnotes omitted).

Contrary to the protestations of the dissent, however, the post-reorganization constructive redemption analysis adopted in *Clark* does not eliminate dividend treatment in all cases. Under the analysis adopted in *Clark*, proportionately larger cash distributions to the shareholders of the target corporation are more likely to receive capital gains treatment than relatively smaller amounts of boot, which remain susceptible to dividend characterization. Suppose that A and B each own 200 shares of common stock of T Corporation, which has outstanding 400 shares. Each of their blocks of stock has a basis of $50,000 and a fair market value of $200,000. In a valid type (A) reorganization, T Corporation is merged into P Corporation. Prior to the merger, P Corporation had outstanding 800 shares of common stock, which had an aggregate fair market value of $400,000. Each corporation has retained earnings and profits in excess of $200,000. Pursuant to the merger, A and B each receive in exchange for their T stock 240 newly issued shares of P Corporation common stock having a fair market value of $120,000 plus $80,000 of cash. Under the analysis of *Clark*, if A and B had received stock instead of cash, they each would have received 400 shares of P stock. Each would have held 25% of the outstanding P stock (400/1600 shares). After the $80,000 cash redemption, A and B each would have had 18.75% of the outstanding P stock (240/1280 shares). The boot thus qualifies for capital gain treatment as a redemption under § 302(b)(2) (18.75% is less than 80% of 25%). If A and B each were to receive $25,000 of cash and 350 shares of P stock, the boot is more likely to be treated as a dividend. A and B each would own 23.33% of the outstanding P stock (350 of 1500 outstanding shares). Under the analysis of *Clark*, the reduction in their interest from the 25% interest they would have held if they had received all stock to 23.33% is not enough to qualify the distribution as a redemption under § 302(b)(2). However, the boot might qualify as not essentially equivalent to a dividend under § 302(b)(1), although that result is anything but clear. See Rev.Rul. 76–364, 1976–2 C.B. 91, and Rev.Rul. 75–512, 1975–2 C.B. 112, both of which involved additional circumstances.

Proposed Regulations, since withdrawn, would have clarified that whether the receipt of boot has the effect of a dividend is to be determined by taking into account the overall exchange of all stock. Prop.Reg. § 1.354–1(d)(1) (2009); 84 Fed. Reg. 11687 (Mar. 28, 2019) (withdrawal notice).

2.2. *Earnings and Profits*

If the position of the IRS argued in *Clark* had been upheld, the logical implication would have been that only the earnings and profits of the acquired corporation would have been relevant in determining dividend equivalency under § 356(a)(2). Although there have been no cases or rulings involving the computation of earnings and profits in mergers for purposes of applying § 356(a)(2), prior to *Clark*, in cases involving type (D) reorganizations, the courts reached conflicting decisions. In Davant v. Commissioner, 366 F.2d 874 (5th Cir.1966), the Fifth Circuit looked to the earnings and profits of both corporations where there was identity of ownership. In Atlas Tool Co. v. Commissioner, 70 T.C. 86 (1978), aff'd, 614

F.2d 860 (3d Cir. 1980), however, the Tax Court and the Third Circuit both held that dividend status was measured by the earnings and profits of the target (transferor) corporation, rejecting the IRS's argument that dividend status should be determined from the combined earnings and profits of the acquiring and target corporations. The *Davant* approach was specifically rejected. In American Manufacturing Co. v. Commissioner, 55 T.C. 204 (1970), which reached a result similar to that in *Atlas Tool*, the Tax Court reasoned that "[t]he legislative history of the section leads to the conclusion that Congress was concerned with a bailout of the earnings and profits of the transferor corporation, and Congress did not seem to consider that there could be, under certain circumstances, a bailout of those of the transferee as well."

Following the post-acquisition redemption analysis of *Clark*, which views the exchange as an integrated whole, the distribution that is treated as a post-acquisition distribution by the acquiring corporation logically should be treated as coming from the earnings and profits of the acquiring corporation, as enhanced by the earnings and profits of the target corporation pursuant to § 381. Under § 381(a) and (c)(2), discussed in Chapter 13, the acquiring corporation in a type (A) or type (C) reorganization inherits the earnings and profits of the target corporation. The earlier authorities may be distinguished as predating *Clark* and by differences between type (A) and type (D) reorganizations, particularly in the context of the liquidation/reincorporation transactions at issue. The opinion in *Clark* does not, however, directly address which corporation's earnings and profits are to be used to determine whether a distribution of boot is a dividend under § 316.

What if neither the target corporation nor the acquiring corporation has accumulated earnings and profits as of the date of a reorganization, but the acquiring corporation has current earnings and profits for the taxable year in which it distributes boot that is taxable as a dividend under § 356(a)(2)? The reference of § 356(a)(2) to the distributee's "ratable share of earnings and profits accumulated after February 28, 1913," suggests that dividend status is dependent upon earnings and profits accumulated to the date of the distribution. See also Treas.Reg. § 1.356–1(b)(1).

3.   BASIS CONSIDERATIONS

The basis for the stock of the acquiring corporation received by the shareholders of the target corporation without recognition of gain under § 354 is determined under § 358(a). That section provides that the basis of the stock is the same as the stock in the target corporation that was surrendered in the reorganization transaction. If, in addition to stock or securities of the acquiring corporation, nonqualifying "boot" is received, the basis of the stock received is the same as the basis of the stock surrendered, decreased by the amount of money and the fair market value of property treated as boot that is received and increased by the amount of gain recognized including the amount of gain treated as a dividend. I.R.C. § 358(a)(1). Property received as boot is assigned a basis equal to its fair market value. I.R.C. § 358(a)(1).

The basis of stock and securities received without recognition of gain is allocated among the qualified stock and securities, as provided in Treas.Reg. § 1.358–2. In general, Treas.Reg. § 1.358–2 requires that the basis be allocated among the stock or securities received in proportion to their fair market values. Where a single class of stock or securities has been surrendered, the Regulations permit the aggregate basis of the stock or securities to be used as the starting point in a single computation. Treas.Reg. § 1.358–2(a)(2) and (3), (c), Ex. 2. But where multiple classes or blocks of stock, or both stock and securities, have been exchanged, the basis for each class of stock or securities surrendered must be assigned to the particular stock and securities received in exchange therefor. Treas.Reg. § 1.358–2(a)(2)(i).

In a reorganization, shareholders often exchange blocks of the same class of stock in the target corporation that were acquired at different times for different prices for shares of the acquiring corporation. Treas.Reg. § 1.358–2 provides that the basis of each share of stock (or each security) received in a reorganization will be the same as the basis of the share or shares of stock (or security or securities) surrendered. Thus, under the Regulation, a particular share or block of shares of the acquiring corporation received in the exchange is traced to a particular share or block of shares of the target corporation surrendered in the reorganization exchange. The Regulations thus prevent a reorganization from triggering averaging of the bases of the exchanged blocks of stock. According to the preamble to the Proposed Regulations that preceded the final Regulations, the IRS was "concerned that averaging the bases of the exchanged blocks of stock may inappropriately limit the ability of taxpayers to arrange their affairs or may afford opportunities for the avoidance of certain provisions of the Code."

If more than one share of stock or more than one security (or a combination of shares of stock and securities) is received in exchange for one share of stock or one security, the basis of the share of stock or security surrendered is allocated to the shares and/or securities received based on the fair market value of the shares and/or securities received. In addition, if one share of stock or security is received in respect of more than one share of stock or security or a fraction of a share of stock or security is received, the basis of the shares of stock or securities surrendered must be allocated to the shares of stock or securities received in a manner that, to the greatest extent possible, reflects that a share of stock or security received is received in respect of shares of stock or securities acquired on the same date and at the same price. Treas.Reg. § 1.358–2(a)(2)(i). Suppose, for example, that B acquired 100 shares of stock of T Corporation in Year 1 for $4,000 and 200 shares of stock of the target corporation in Year 2 for $6,000 and, pursuant to a reorganization in a subsequent year, the shareholder exchanges those shares for 150 shares of P Corporation. Under the Regulations, 50 shares of P Corporation are treated as acquired for the 100 shares of T Corporation the shareholder acquired in Year 1, and 100 shares of P Corporation are treated as acquired for the 200 shares of T Corporation acquired in Year 2. Accordingly, 50 shares will have a basis of $4,000, and the other 100 shares will have a basis of $6,000. This rule minimizes the chances of creating shares or securities with split holding periods.

If a shareholder cannot identify the specific shares (i.e., block of stock) of the target corporation involved in an exchange for specific shares of the acquiring corporation, the shareholder may designate the particular share or shares surrendered in exchange for the new share or shares (or securities for securities). Treas.Reg. § 1.358–2(a)(2)(vii). The designation must, however, be consistent with the terms of the exchange or distribution and must be made on or before the first date on which the basis of a share or security received is relevant. In instances where a shareholder holds two or more blocks of a single class of stock of the target that are exchanged for stock of the acquiring corporation, this will almost always be the case.

If the terms of the plan of reorganization specify which shares of stock or securities are received in exchange for a particular share of stock or security or a particular class of stock or securities, the terms of the plan will control for purposes of determining the basis of the stock or securities received, provided that such terms are economically reasonable. Treas.Reg. § 1.358–2(a)(2)(ii). This rule is important primarily in reorganizations pursuant to which a shareholder or security holder surrenders shares of stock of one or more classes (or a security) and receives shares of stock (or securities) of more than one class, or receives "other property" or money in addition to shares of stock or securities. If the terms of the plan do not specify which shares of stock or securities are received in exchange for a particular share of stock or security or a particular class of stock or securities, a pro rata portion of the shares of stock and securities of each class received is treated as received in exchange for each share of stock and security surrendered, based on the fair market value of the surrendered stock and securities. Treas.Reg. § 1.358–2(a)(2)(i) and (ii).

4. RECEIPT OF SECURITIES

4.1. *Amount of Boot*

Section 354(a) extends nonrecognition treatment to an exchange of "stock or securities * * * for stock or securities."[6] Thus, where the target corporation's securities become securities of the acquiring corporation under state law in a statutory merger, no gain or loss is recognized. Section 354(a)(2) and § 356(d), however, treat the target shareholders as receiving boot if the principal amount of securities received is greater than the principal amount of any securities surrendered. The fair market value of the excess principal amount of securities received is treated as "other property." Where securities are received in exchange for only stock, the entire fair market value of the securities is treated as boot. Treas.Reg. § 1.356–3(c), Ex. 1. Where securities are received in exchange for other securities, only the fair

---

[6]   Generally, under state law in a statutory merger, outstanding securities of the target corporation become liabilities of the acquiring corporation. Without intervention of a nonrecognition provision the exchange of securities may be a taxable transaction. Treas.Reg. § 1.1001–3(e)(4)(i)(B) provides, however, that a change in the obligor of a debt instrument in a transaction to which § 381 applies, which includes reorganizations qualified under § 368(a)(1)(A), is not a significant modification of the debt resulting in a taxable exchange.

market value of the excess principal amount constitutes boot. The value of the excess principal amount is determined by the following formula:

$$\text{Fair Market Value of Securities Received} \times \frac{\text{Principal Amount of Securities Received} \quad \text{Minus} \quad \text{Principal Amount of Securities Surrendered}}{\text{Principal Amount of Securities Received}}$$

In determining the "principal amount" of securities exchanged in the reorganization, the original issue discount (OID) rules of § 1272 and § 1274, discussed in Chapter 3, must be taken into account. If the OID rules do not apply, generally speaking, the amount of any excess face value of a security received over the face value of securities surrendered also will be the value of the excess. If, however, the OID rules apply, the principal amount of the securities exchanged must be reduced as required by those rules to an amount less than their face value when computing gain under § 356. Thus, receipt of a security having a *face* value in excess of the principal amount of the security surrendered will not give rise to boot under § 356 if under the OID rules the imputed principal amount of the security received does not exceed the principal amount of the security surrendered. Section 1273(b) applies to the determination of the amount of OID if either the securities surrendered or the securities received are publicly traded. If the securities received are publicly traded, their "issue price," and thus "principal amount," is their fair market value, i.e., trading price, on the day they are issued. Treas.Reg. § 1.1273–2(b)(1). Thus, if new publicly traded bonds are issued for outstanding publicly traded bonds, the principal amount of the new bonds is their trading price, not the trading price of the old bonds. But if securities that are not publicly traded are issued for publicly traded securities, the issue price, and thus principal amount, of the new securities is the trading price of the old securities. Treas.Reg. § 1.1273–2(c)(1). Section 1274 controls if the securities involved in the exchange are not publicly traded. See also Treas.Reg. § 1.356–3(c), Exs. 2–6.

Not all debt instruments qualify as "securities" for purposes of § 354. In Neville Coke & Chemical Co. v. Commissioner, 148 F.2d 599 (3d Cir.1945), the taxpayer held stock, bonds, three-, four-, and five-year notes, and accounts receivable of an insolvent corporation. In a reorganization involving the debtor corporation, the taxpayer received new common stock for its stock, new debentures for its bonds, and new debentures and common stock for its notes and accounts receivable. The IRS asserted that the taxpayer recognized a gain on the exchange of the notes and accounts receivable for debentures and common stock. The taxpayer asserted that the notes and accounts receivable were "securities" within the meaning of the predecessor of § 354(a)(1) and that it had exchanged "securities" for "stock and securities," thereby entitling it to nonrecognition on the exchange. In holding for the IRS, the court held that "securities" has the same meaning in the context of the interest surrendered as it does in the context of the interest received, that a "security" entails having a "proprietary" interest in the corporation, and that the rights of the taxpayer as a note holder were merely those of a creditor.

Conventional wisdom is that debt instruments with a term of more than five years generally qualify as "securities." Camp Wolters Enterprises v. Commissioner, 230 F.2d 555 (5th Cir. 1956), held that a series of notes issued by a corporation that were payable between the fifth and ninth year after issuance constituted "securities." Nevertheless, quoting the Tax Court opinion that it affirmed, the court noted as follows:

> The test as to whether notes are securities is not a mechanical determination of the time period of the note. Though time is an important factor, the controlling consideration is an overall evaluation of the nature of the debt, degree of participation and continuing interest in the business, the extent of proprietary interest compared with the similarity of the note to a cash payment, the purpose of the advances, etc.

See also Rev.Rul. 59–98, 1959–1 C.B. 76 (first mortgage bonds with a term of six and one-half years were securities).

Rev.Rul. 2004–78, 2004–2 C.B. 108, however, held that debt instruments with a term of two years received in a merger qualified as securities under the particular circumstances in which they were received. That ruling involved a merger that qualified as a reorganization under § 368(a)(1)(A) in which the holders of the target corporation's long-term securities that had only two years remaining before maturity received in exchange for those securities debt instruments of the acquirer that matured in two years and which, except for the interest rate, bore identical rights to the surrendered securities. Nevertheless, the ruling described the case law as concluding that an instrument with a term of less than five years generally is not a security.

4.2. *Installment Reporting*

Gain recognized on the receipt of securities in a reorganization may be reported using the installment method under § 453 unless either the stock or securities surrendered were readily tradable on an established securities market (§ 453(h)(1)) or the securities received are readily tradable (§ 453(f)(4)). See Prop.Reg. § 1.453–1(f)(2) (1984). In the case of gain reported under the installment method, the basis of the stock received in the reorganization is computed under Prop.Reg. § 1.453–1(f)(2) (1984) in the same manner that the basis of stock received in a § 351 transaction is computed if an installment note is received as boot.

5.   STOCK RIGHTS AND WARRANTS

Treas. Regs. §§ 1.354–1(e) and 1.356–3(b) treat rights to acquire stock (options and warrants) of a corporation that is a party to a reorganization as securities of the corporation having no principal amount. The term "rights to acquire stock" of an issuing corporation has the same meaning as for purposes of §§ 305(d)(1) and 317(a). Thus, an exchange of options to purchase stock of the target corporation for options to purchase stock of the acquiring corporation is accorded nonrecognition, as is an exchange of target corporation bonds for acquiring corporation options. Likewise, an exchange of stock for stock and an option, or an exchange of an option for stock and an option, is not taxable. See Treas.Reg. § 1.356–3(b) and (c), Exs. 7 and 8. If, however, warrants are exchanged for debt securities, gain must be recognized. Treas.Reg. § 1.356–3(c), Ex. 9. Arguably, however, because the receipt solely of warrants in exchange for stock is not covered by § 354, see Treas.Reg. § 1.354–1(d), Ex. 4, and § 356 technically applies only if some permissible consideration under § 354 is received in the exchange, an exchange of target stock solely for options to purchase stock of the acquiring corporation is not entitled to nonrecognition. The Regulations do not address this point and it is not clear whether or not the ambiguity was intended. (In any event, a purported reorganization involving the exchange of target stock for only options to purchase stock of the acquiring corporation would fail the continuity of interest requirement.)

Rights exercisable against persons other than the issuer of the stock are not covered by Treas.Reg. § 1.354–1(e). Rev.Rul. 69–265, 1969–1 C.B. 109, held that a conversion privilege contained in a stock or debt instrument generally is not considered to be a separate property right received in the reorganization, and the Regulations do not change that result. Treas. Regs. §§ 1.354–1(e) and 1.356–3(b) apply only in determining the amount of gain recognized in an otherwise qualifying reorganization. Thus, the Regulations do not affect pre-existing law under which stock rights are not taken into account in determining whether the continuity of shareholder interest test has been satisfied. See Notice of Proposed Rulemaking and Notice of Public Hearings, Reorganizations, Receipt of Securities, REG–249819–96, 1997–1 C.B. 793, 794.

6. PREFERRED STOCK

6.1. *Nonqualified Preferred Stock*

Sections 354(a)(2)(C) and 356(e) require that "nonqualified preferred stock" be treated as boot for purposes of §§ 354 and 356. Nonqualified preferred stock is defined in § 351(g)(2). Preferred stock is stock that is limited and preferred as to dividends and which does not participate in corporate growth. I.R.C. § 351(g)(3)(A). Preferred stock is "nonqualified" only if within 20 years after issue, the issuer or a related person (1) may be required by the holder to redeem the stock, (2) is required to redeem the stock, or (3) has a right to redeem the stock and it is more likely than not that the right to redeem will be exercised. I.R.C. § 351(g)(2). Preferred stock is also nonqualified preferred stock if the dividend rate is determined in whole or in part by reference to interest rates, commodity prices, or similar indices.

Because nonqualified preferred stock received in an exchange will not be treated as stock or securities but, instead, will be treated as boot, the receipt of nonqualified preferred stock will result in recognition of gain under § 356 unless a specified exception applies. Sections 354(a)(2)(C) and 356(e)(2) provide that nonqualified preferred stock is treated as stock rather than as other property in cases where the nonqualified preferred stock is received in exchange for other nonqualified preferred stock. In these cases, the receipt of nonqualified preferred stock will not result in recognition of gain under

§ 356. Treas. Regs. §§ 1.354–1(f) and 1.356–7(b) provide additional rules to deal with various aspects of exchanges of nonqualified preferred stock in reorganizations. Under the general rule in the Regulations, the nonrecognition rules apply only if nonqualified preferred stock is received with respect to "substantially identical" nonqualified preferred stock. Stock is considered to be substantially identical if two conditions are met: First, the stock received does not contain any terms which, in relation to the terms of the stock previously held, decrease the period in which a redemption or purchase right will be exercised, increase the likelihood that such a right will be exercised, or accelerate the timing of the returns from the stock instrument (including the receipt of dividends or other distributions). Second, as a result of the receipt of the stock, the exercise of the right or obligation does not become more likely than not to occur within a 20-year period beginning on the issue date of the stock previously held.

6.2. *Section 306 Aspects*

If pursuant to the reorganization the shareholders of the acquired corporation surrender common stock and receive both common stock and preferred stock, the preferred stock will be characterized as § 306 stock pursuant to § 306(c)(1)(B) if "the effect of the transaction was substantially the same as the receipt of a stock dividend." See Treas.Reg. § 1.306–3(d). (Section 306 is discussed in Chapter 6.) The Regulations indicate that unless a cash distribution in lieu of the preferred stock would have been a dividend under § 356(a)(2), the stock will not be § 306 stock. As a result of the decision in Commissioner v. Clark, discussed above, classification of preferred stock received in an acquisitive reorganization as § 306 stock depends on the ratio of common stock to preferred stock received by the shareholder in the reorganization. Generally speaking, the higher the ratio of common to preferred, the more likely the preferred stock will be characterized as § 306 stock, and the lower the ratio the more likely the preferred stock will not be so characterized.

Rev.Rul. 89–63, 1989–1 C.B. 90, held that where both common and preferred stock of a publicly held acquiring corporation were issued to the former holders of the common stock of a publicly held target corporation in a type (A) statutory merger, the preferred stock was § 306 stock. The ruling did not provide any rationale for its conclusion that the stock was § 306 stock, and if cash had been distributed in lieu of the preferred stock, under *Clark* the cash would not have been substantially equivalent to a dividend. The fact that the corporations were publicly held, standing alone, was not sufficient to bring the preferred stock within the § 306(b)(4) exception for transactions not involving tax avoidance.

Preferred stock received for preferred stock in acquisitive reorganizations will not be § 306 stock if it is of equal value to the preferred stock surrendered, the terms of the new preferred stock are not substantially different from the terms of the old preferred stock, and the preferred stock surrendered in the exchange was not itself § 306 stock. Rev.Rul. 88–100, 1988–2 C.B. 46 (holding that Treas.Reg. § 1.306–3(d), Ex. (2), applies to acquisitive reorganizations); Rev.Rul. 82–118, 1982–1 C.B. 56. The rulings emphasize that in such cases the new preferred stock is merely a substitute for the old preferred stock, and the distribution therefore does not have the effect of a distribution of earnings and profits. However, if the surrendered preferred stock was § 306 stock, then any preferred stock (or common stock) received in exchange for the tainted preferred stock will be § 306 stock. I.R.C. § 306(c)(1)(C).

7. CONTINGENT STOCK PAYOUTS

The shareholders of the target corporation may receive the right to obtain additional voting shares in the future if specified conditions are met, e.g., the earnings of the target corporation reach a certain level. Generally, such contingent stock payout agreements are utilized in situations in which the parties to the reorganization are unable to agree on the fair market value of the target corporation's stock. The right to receive voting shares in the future is not the same as the present receipt of voting shares as such and arguably could violate the solely for voting stock restriction.

Carlberg v. United States, 281 F.2d 507 (8th Cir.1960), held that certificates representing a contingent interest in shares in the acquiring corporation should be treated as "stock" for purposes of nonrecognition under § 354 (a result disputed by the IRS because the certificates in question were negotiable). In Hamrick v. Commissioner, 43 T.C. 21 (1964), the court treated a nonnegotiable contingent right to receive additional shares of stock as the equivalent of stock for purposes of § 351. Neither case had to decide whether the contingent interest represented "voting stock," a somewhat more difficult question. Subsequently, Rev.Rul. 66–112, 1966–1 C.B. 68, held that the receipt of a contingent contractual right to additional voting shares that was not assignable and could only ripen into additional voting shares did not violate the solely for voting stock requirement in a type (B) reorganization. The holding in Rev.Rul. 66–112 also is relevant in the context of type (C) reorganization and with respect to reverse triangular mergers under § 368(a)(2)(E).

Rev.Proc. 77–37, § 3.03, 1977–2 C.B. 568, amplified by Rev.Proc. 84–42, 1984–1 C.B. 521, set forth nine conditions under which a favorable ruling would be issued on the solely for voting stock question in a contingent stock payout situation. The principal requirements are that all the additional stock must be issued within five years from the date of the original reorganization transaction, there must be a valid business reason for not issuing all the stock immediately, such as the difficulty of valuing the stock of one or both of the corporations, the maximum number of shares that may be issued is stated, and at least one-half of the total number of shares to be issued must be issued in the initial distribution.

The OID Regulations under § 1272 through § 1275 (governing the imputation of interest) do not deal with contingent stock payout situations because the OID rules apply only to "debt instruments," and a contingent stock right is not a debt instrument. Section 483, however, applies to impute interest on "contingent payments," and Treas.Reg. § 1.483–4(b), Ex. 2 applies § 483 to a contingent stock payout. As a result, upon receipt of the contingent stock, a portion of the stock will be characterized as interest taxable as ordinary income and not entitled to nonrecognition under § 354.

Rev.Rul. 75–94, 1975–1 C.B. 111, dealt with a variation on a contingent stock payout situation. In 1973, a type (B) reorganization took place. In the following year it was discovered that the acquiring corporation had misrepresented its earnings because of an improper accounting practice. Upon correction of the improper practice, the earnings were reduced and the target corporation's stockholders asserted that they were entitled to additional stock of the acquiring corporation to satisfy the negotiated acquisition price. After discussions between the parties, the acquiring corporation did issue additional stock. The ruling concluded that the additional shares received were part of the original "plan of reorganization" and hence qualified as part of the (B) reorganization.

The "escrowed stock" arrangement is another technique that is employed where the parties cannot agree upon the value of the corporations. Under such an arrangement, the acquiring corporation issues its stock to the shareholders of the target corporation, but part of the stock is placed in escrow to be returned to the acquiring corporation upon the occurrence of a specified event, for example, the failure of the target corporation to reach a specified earnings level. If the earnings level is reached, the stock is transferred out of escrow to the former shareholders of the target corporation. Since the stock is actually issued, subject to subsequent forfeiture, some problems of contingent stock payouts are avoided. For example, interest will not be imputed under § 483 if the transaction is properly structured. Rev.Rul. 70–120, 1970–1 C.B. 124 (shareholders entitled to unrestricted voting rights and received dividends on stock); Feifer v. United States, 500 F.Supp. 102 (N.D.Ga.1980) (same even though voting rights were restricted).

Rev.Rul. 76–42, 1976–1 C.B. 102, held that no gain or loss is recognized by the shareholders of the target corporation if the escrowed stock is returned to the acquiring corporation where the number of shares to be returned was based on their initially negotiated value. The adjusted basis of the returned shares is added to the basis of those received by the shareholders of the target corporation. Compare Rev.Rul. 78–376, 1978–2 C.B. 149 (because the number of shares to be returned from the escrow to discharge an indemnity obligation was based on the value of the shares on the date of the return from escrow and not on the initially negotiated price, the taxpayer was required to realize gain since he received a benefit from the appreciation in value that was used to discharge his obligations).

Rev.Proc. 77–37, § 3.06, 1977–2 C.B. 568, amplified by Rev.Proc. 84–42, 1984–1 C.B. 521, sets forth nine conditions under which a favorable ruling would be issued in escrowed stock transactions. The principal requirements are that there must be a valid reason for establishing the arrangement, the stock subject to the escrow agreement must be treated as issued and outstanding stock of the acquiring corporation for all purposes, voting rights must be exercisable by the shareholders or their agent, all shares must be released from the escrow within five years, and not more than 50% of the total number of shares to be issued may be subject to the escrow.

Contingent stock and escrowed stock arrangements are not unique to any particular type of reorganization. They may be used in connection with any type of acquisition, but different problems may arise with respect to qualifying the transaction under different provisions of § 368. For example, Rev.Rul. 76–334, 1976–2 C.B. 108, involved the use of an escrow arrangement in a type (C) reorganization in which the transferor corporation liquidated and distributed all rights in the escrowed stock to its shareholders. The purpose of the escrow was to protect the acquiring corporation from a breach of representations and warranties made by the target corporation as a part of the reorganization transaction. The acquiring corporation asserted a breach, and the escrow agent returned part of the escrowed stock to the acquiring corporation, with the balance being distributed to the target corporation's shareholders. Those shareholders, however, disputed the validity of the acquiring corporation's claim to a return of part of the escrowed stock. Negotiations between the parties resulted in a settlement pursuant to which the acquiring corporation paid cash equal to one-half the value of the escrowed shares distributed to the shareholders and the shareholders returned the balance of the escrowed shares to the acquiring corporation. The ruling held that the cash payment was separate from, and did not violate the solely for voting stock requirement of, the (C) reorganization. There was a redemption of one-half the escrowed stock under § 302 and the other one-half was simply returned pursuant to the escrow arrangement with no gain or loss being recognized by the target corporation's shareholders under the principles of Rev.Rul. 76–42.

PROBLEM SET 5

1.   Assume that all of the following *alternative* transactions occurred pursuant to a valid type (A) reorganization. A is a shareholder of T Corp., the acquired corporation, which is publicly traded. P Corp. is the acquiring corporation and also is publicly traded. In each case, what are the tax consequences to A? What is the amount of gain, if any, that A must recognize? What is A's basis in the stock or securities received?

   (a)   A exchanged 300 shares of T stock, with a basis of $30 per share ($9,000 total) and fair market value of $15,000, for 150 shares of P common stock, having an aggregate fair market value of $15,000.

   (b)   A exchanged 100 shares of T stock, with a basis of $45 per share ($4,500 total) and fair market value of $5,000, and 200 shares of T stock, with a basis of $22.50 per share ($4,500 total) and fair market value of $10,000, for 150 shares of P common stock, having an aggregate fair market value of $15,000.

   (c)   A exchanged 300 shares of T stock, with a basis of $30 per share ($9,000 total) and fair market value of $12,000, for 60 shares of P common stock, having a fair market value of $8,000, and 20 shares P nonvoting preferred stock, having a fair market value of $4,000.

   (d)   A exchanged 300 shares of T stock, with a basis of $30 per share ($9,000 total) and fair market value of $12,000, for 100 shares of P common stock, having an aggregate fair market value of $10,000, and $2,000 of cash.

(e)   A exchanged 300 shares of T stock, with a basis of $30 per share ($9,000 total) and fair market value of $12,000, for 80 shares of P common stock, having an aggregate fair market value of $8,000 and $4,000 of cash.

(f)   (1)   A exchanged 100 shares of T stock, with a basis of $80 per share ($8,000 total) and fair market value of $4,000, and 200 shares of T stock, with a basis of $5 per share ($1,000 total) and fair market value of $8,000, for 150 shares of P common stock, having an aggregate fair market value of $9,000, and $3,000 of cash.

(2)   A exchanged 100 shares of T preferred stock, with a basis of $80 per share ($8,000 total) and fair market value of $4,000, and 200 shares of T common stock, with a basis of $5 per share ($1,000 total) and fair market value of $8,000, for 133 shares of P common stock, having an aggregate fair market value of $8,000, and $4,000 of cash. The merger agreement provided that the holders of T common stock would receive P common stock and that the holders of T preferred stock would receive cash.

(g)   (1)   A exchanged 300 shares of T stock, with a basis of $30 per share ($9,000 total) and fair market value of $10,000, for 100 shares of P common stock, having an aggregate fair market value of $9,000, and options to purchase an additional 500 shares of P common stock at $92 per share. The 500 options have a fair market value of $1,000.

(2)   What is A's tax treatment if the P warrants lapse before exercise?

(h)   (1)   A exchanged 300 shares of T stock, with a basis of $30 per share ($9,000 total) and fair market value of $12,000, for 60 shares of P common stock, having a fair market value of $8,000, and a P Corp. 20 year debt instrument, with a principal amount of $4,000 and a fair market value of $4,000.

(2)   A exchanged 300 shares of T stock, with a basis of $30 per share ($9,000 total) and fair market value of $12,000, and a 20 year T debt instrument having a redemption value and fair market value of $6,000, but which had a basis of only $5,400 because it was purchased at a market discount (not OID), for 50 shares of P common stock, having a fair market value of $9,000 and three P Corp. 20 year debt instruments, each of which had both a redemption value and fair market value of $3,000.

(3)   A exchanged 300 shares of T stock, with a basis of $30 per share ($9,000 total) and fair market value of $12,000, for 60 shares of P common stock, having a fair market value of $8,000, and a P Corp. 20 year debt instrument, with a redemption value of $5,000, but which under the OID rules has a principal amount of only $4,000 because the stated interest rate is below the prevailing rate. How and when will A be taxed on any difference between the basis of the debt instrument and its redemption value?

2.   B and C each own 200 shares of common stock of T Corporation. (T has a total of 400 outstanding shares.) Each of their blocks of stock has an aggregate basis of $50,000 and a fair market value of $200,000. In a valid

type (A) reorganization, T Corporation was merged into P Corporation. Prior to the merger, P Corporation had outstanding 400 shares of common stock, which had an aggregate fair market value of $400,000. Each corporation had retained earnings and profits in excess of $300,000. Pursuant to the merger each of B and C received 120 shares of newly issued P common stock, having a fair market value of $120,000, and $80,000 in cash in exchange for their T stock.

    (a)   (1)   What is the character of the gain recognized by B and C? Does it matter which corporation's cash reserves were used to pay B and C?

        (2)   Would your answer to question (a)(1) be different if B and C each received 150 shares of P stock, having an aggregate fair market value of $150,000, and $50,000 of cash?

        (3)   Would your answer to question (a)(2) differ if P Corp. had $40,000 of accumulated earnings and profits and T Corp. had $30,000 of accumulated earnings and profits?

    (b)   What would be the consequences if B and C each received 150 shares of P common stock, having an aggregate fair market value of $150,000, and 50 shares of $1,000 par value nonvoting preferred stock, with limited rights to dividends and liquidation distributions?

3.   F holds a publicly traded T Corporation 20 year debt instrument, which pays interest of 10% per annum, compounded semi-annually, was issued for $100,000 in cash, and has a redemption value of $100,000. Pursuant to a valid type (A) reorganization in which T Corp. is merged into P Corp., F exchanges the T Corp. debt instrument for a publicly traded P Corp. debt instrument. What are the tax consequences to F and to P Corp. under the following alternative situations?

    (a)   The prevailing interest rate is 8% and the fair market value of F's T Corp. debt instrument is $125,000. F receives a P Corp. 20 year 8% P Corp. debt instrument having a redemption value of $125,000.

    (b)   The prevailing interest rate is 12.5% and the fair market value of F's T Corp. debt instrument is $80,000. F receives a P Corp. 12.5% debt instrument having a redemption value of $80,000.

    (c)   The prevailing interest rate is 10% and the fair market value of the T Corp. debt instrument, which has 20 years remaining until maturity, is $100,000. F receives a 20 year P Corp. debt instrument that pays no interest and has a redemption value of $704,000. The fair market value of the P debt instrument is $100,000. (The net present value of $704,000 due in 20 years, discounted at 10% per annum, compounded semi-annually, is $100,000.)

4.   T Corp. is a closely held corporation that designs computer software. It has 1000 shares issued and outstanding. P Corp., which is publicly traded, proposes to acquire T Corp. by merger in a transaction where the T shareholders would exchange all of their T stock solely for P stock, but the parties cannot agree on an exchange ratio. P Corp. has been trading on the NASDAQ system at between $18 and $22 a share during the last year. The parties agree that the T Corp. stock is worth between $1,000 and $2,000 per share, depending on the performance of a new data base management

program introduced by T Corp. last week. The profitability of the new product should be clear in three or four years at the outside. How can the acquisition be structured to take into account the uncertain value of T Corporation? What are the relative tax and non-tax advantages and disadvantages of using a contingent stock arrangement versus an escrowed stock arrangement?

(2) TREATMENT OF THE CORPORATIONS PARTICIPATING IN A TYPE (A) REORGANIZATION

INTERNAL REVENUE CODE: Sections 357(a), (b); 358(a), (b)(1), (e), (f); 361; 362(b); 368(b).

DETAILED ANALYSIS

1. TARGET CORPORATION

Section 361 protects the target corporation from gain recognition in a type (A) reorganization regardless of the nature of the consideration received from the acquiring corporation. If only stock or securities of the acquiring corporation are received in the reorganization, § 361(a) provides nonrecognition upon receipt of the stock or securities. (Section 361(b)(2) bars the recognition of any loss.) In addition, no gain or loss is recognized by the target corporation on the distribution of the acquiring corporation's stock or securities. I.R.C. § 361(c)(1), (2)(B). If boot is received by the target, § 361(b)(1) requires that the target corporation recognize gain upon receipt only if that boot is not distributed to either its shareholders or creditors pursuant to the plan of reorganization. See also § 361(c). Since in an (A) reorganization the target corporation disappears by operation of law, all of the boot must be distributed and no gain will be recognized under § 361(b).

Section 361(c)(2) provides for recognition of gain to the target corporation upon the distribution of appreciated boot. However, because § 358(a)(2) provides the target corporation with a fair market value basis in any boot received in the reorganization transaction and in a Type (A) merger there will not be time for the boot to change in value before it is distributed, no gain will be realized.

2. ACQUIRING CORPORATION

2.1. *Nonrecognition of Gain*

The acquiring corporation in an (A) reorganization is protected from gain recognition on the issue of its stock by § 1032. However, if the acquiring corporation also transfers non-qualifying "boot" (other than its own securities) that has appreciated in value, neither § 1032 nor any of the reorganization nonrecognition provisions apply to the acquiring corporation with respect to the boot, and gain must be recognized on the transfer. Rev.Rul. 72–327, 1972–2 C.B. 197. Loss is similarly recognized if the basis of the boot property is less than its fair market value.

2.2. *Basis of Acquired Assets*

Under § 362(b), the acquiring corporation takes as its basis in the acquired assets the basis that the assets had in the hands of the transferor corporation. The statute provides that the basis of the assets in the hands of the acquiring corporation is increased by any gain recognized by the target-transferor corporation in the reorganization transaction, but since gain is only recognized if the property received is not distributed, and in a type (A) reorganization it will be distributed, the acquiring corporation always takes a transferred basis in the assets without any increase for gain recognized to the transferor.

2.3. *Carry Over of Corporate Attributes*

Under § 381, the tax attributes of the target corporation, e.g., net operating loss carryovers, earnings and profits accounts, etc., carry over to the acquiring corporation. However, § 382 limits the post-acquisition use of any net operating loss carryovers of the target corporation. See Chapter 13.

PROBLEM SET 6

1. P Corp. acquired T Corp. in a statutory merger in which the shareholders of T Corp. received P Corp. stock with a fair market value of $2,100,000 and $900,000 cash. T Corp.'s assets were as follows:

Asset	Adj. Basis	FMV
Factory	$100,000	$600,000
Equipment	$300,000	$700,000
Inventory	$100,000	$800,000
Patent	$ 0	$900,000

How much gain must T Corp. recognize? What is P Corp.'s basis in the assets after the merger?

2. (a) In a statutory merger, P Corp. acquired real estate from T Corp. The real estate had a gross fair market value of $400, was subject to a mortgage of $100 and had a basis of $125. The sole shareholder of T Corp. had a $190 basis in her T Corp. stock and received 150 shares of P Corp. (fair market value of $300) in the merger. What are the tax consequences to the corporations?

(b) Suppose the mortgage was $160. What are the tax consequences to the corporations?

SECTION 3.   STOCK FOR STOCK ACQUISITIONS: TYPE (B) REORGANIZATIONS

INTERNAL REVENUE CODE: Sections 354; 362(b); 368(a)(1)(B), (a)(2)(C), (c).

REGULATIONS: Section 1.368–2(c).

Chapman v. Commissioner
United States Court of Appeals, First Circuit, 1980.
618 F.2d 856.

■ LEVIN H. CAMPBELL, CIRCUIT JUDGE.

* * * We must decide whether the requirement of Section 368(a)(1)(B) that the acquisition of stock in one corporation by another be solely in exchange for voting stock of the acquiring corporation is met where, in related transactions, the acquiring corporation first acquires 8 percent of the acquiree's stock for cash and then acquires more than 80 percent of the acquiree in an exchange for voting stock. The Tax Court agreed with the taxpayers that the latter exchange constituted a valid tax-free reorganization. Reeves v. Commissioner, 71 T.C. 727 (1979).

THE FACTS

Appellees were among the more than 17,000 shareholders of the Hartford Fire Insurance Company who exchanged their Hartford stock for shares of the voting stock of International Telephone and Telegraph Corporation pursuant to a formal exchange offer from ITT dated May 26, 1970. On their 1970 tax returns, appellees did not report any gain or loss from these exchanges. * * *

* * * In October 1968, ITT executives approached Hartford about the possibility of merging the two corporations. This proposal was spurned by Hartford, which at the time was considering acquisitions of its own. In November 1968, ITT learned that approximately 1.3 million shares of Hartford, representing some 6 percent of Hartford's voting stock, were available for purchase from a mutual fund. After assuring Hartford's directors that ITT would not attempt to acquire Hartford against its will, ITT consummated the $63.7 million purchase from the mutual fund with Hartford's blessing. From November 13, 1968 to January 10, 1969, ITT also made a series of purchases on the open market totaling 458,000 shares which it acquired for approximately $24.4 million. A further purchase of 400 shares from an ITT subsidiary in March 1969 brought ITT's holdings to about 8 percent of Hartford's outstanding stock, all of which had been bought for cash.

In the midst of this flurry of stock-buying, ITT submitted a written proposal to the Hartford Board of Directors for the merger of Hartford into an ITT subsidiary, based on an exchange of Hartford stock for ITT's $2 cumulative convertible voting preferred stock. * * * [O]n April 9, 1969 a provisional plan and agreement of merger was executed by the two corporations. * * *

* * * By private letter ruling, the Service notified the parties on October 13, 1969 that the proposed merger would constitute a nontaxable reorganization, provided ITT unconditionally sold its 8 percent interest in Hartford to a third party before Hartford's shareholders voted to approve or disapprove the proposal. On October 21, the Service ruled that a proposed sale of the stock to Mediobanca, an Italian bank, would satisfy this condition, and such a sale was made on November 9.

On November 10, 1969, the shareholders of Hartford approved the merger, which had already won the support of ITT's shareholders in June. On December 13, 1969, however, the merger plan ground to a halt, as the Connecticut Insurance Commissioner refused to endorse the arrangement. ITT then proposed to proceed with a voluntary exchange offer to the shareholders of Hartford on essentially the same terms they would have obtained under the merger plan. * * * More than 95 percent of Hartford's outstanding stock was exchanged for shares of ITT's $2.25 cumulative convertible voting preferred stock. The Italian bank to which ITT had conveyed its original 8 percent interest was among those tendering shares, as were the taxpayers in this case.

In March 1974, the Internal Revenue Service retroactively revoked its ruling approving the sale of Hartford stock to Mediobanca, on the ground that the request on which the ruling was based had misrepresented the nature of the proposed sale. Concluding that the entire transaction no longer constituted a nontaxable reorganization, the Service assessed tax deficiencies against a number of former Hartford shareholders who had accepted the exchange offer. Appellees, along with other taxpayers, contested this action in the Tax Court, where the case was decided on appellees' motion for summary judgment. For purposes of this motion, the taxpayers conceded that questions of the merits of the revocation of the IRS rulings were not to be considered; the facts were to be viewed as though ITT had not sold the shares previously acquired for cash to Mediobanca. The taxpayers also conceded, solely for purposes of their motion for summary judgment, that the initial cash purchases of Hartford stock had been made for the purpose of furthering ITT's efforts to acquire Hartford.

THE ISSUE

Taxpayers advanced two arguments in support of their motion for summary judgment. Their first argument related to the severability of the cash purchases from the 1970 exchange offer. Because 14 months had elapsed between the last of the cash purchases and the effective date of the exchange offer, and because the cash purchases were not part of the formal plan of reorganization entered into by ITT and Hartford, the taxpayers argued that the 1970 exchange offer should be examined in isolation to determine whether it satisfied the terms of Section 368(a)(1)(B) of the 1954 Code. The Service countered that the two sets of transactions—the cash purchases and the exchange offer—were linked by a common acquisitive purpose, and that they should be considered together for the purpose of determining whether the arrangement met the statutory requirement that the stock of the acquired corporation be exchanged "solely for * * * voting stock" of the acquiring corporation. The Tax Court did not reach this argument; in granting summary judgment it relied entirely on the taxpayers' second argument.

For purposes of the second argument, the taxpayers conceded arguendo that the 1968 and 1969 cash purchases should be considered "parts of the 1970 exchange offer reorganization." Even so, they insisted upon a right to judgment on the basis that the 1970 exchange of stock for stock satisfied the statutory requirements for a reorganization without regard to the presence of related cash purchases. The Tax Court agreed with the taxpayers, holding that the 1970 exchange in which ITT acquired more than 80 percent of Hartford's single class of stock for ITT voting stock satisfied the requirements of Section 368(a)(1)(B), so that no gain or loss need be recognized on the exchange under section 354(a)(1). The sole issue on appeal is whether the Tax Court was correct in so holding.

I.

* * *

The single issue raised on this appeal is whether "the acquisition" in this case complied with the requirement that it be "solely for * * * voting stock." It is well settled that the "solely" requirement is mandatory; if any part of "the acquisition" includes a form of consideration other than voting stock, the transaction will not qualify as a (B) reorganization. See Helvering v. Southwest Consolidated Corp., 315 U.S. 194, 198, 62 S.Ct. 546, 550 (1942) (" 'Solely' leaves no leeway. Voting stock plus some other consideration does not meet the statutory requirement"). The precise issue before us is thus how broadly to read the term "acquisition." The Internal Revenue Service argues that "the acquisition * * * of stock of another corporation" must be understood to encompass the 1968–69 cash purchases as well as the 1970 exchange offer. If the IRS is correct, "the acquisition" here fails as a (B) reorganization. The taxpayers, on the other hand, would limit "the acquisition" to the part of a sequential transaction of this nature which meets the requirements of subsection (B). They argue that the 1970 exchange of stock for stock was itself an "acquisition" by ITT of stock in Hartford solely in exchange for ITT's voting stock, such that after the exchange took place ITT controlled Hartford. Taxpayers contend that the earlier cash purchases of 8 percent, even if conceded to be part of the same acquisitive plan, are essentially irrelevant to the tax-free reorganization otherwise effected.

The Tax Court accepted the taxpayers' reading of the statute, effectively overruling its own prior decision in Howard v. Commissioner,

24 T.C. 792 (1955), rev'd on other grounds, 238 F.2d 943 (7th Cir.1956). The plurality opinion stated its "narrow" holding as follows:

> "We hold that where, as is the case herein, 80 percent or more of the stock of a corporation is acquired in one transaction,[18] in exchange for which only voting stock is furnished as consideration, the 'solely for voting stock' requirement of section 368(a)(1)(B) is satisfied."

71 T.C. at 741. The plurality treated as "irrelevant" the 8 percent of Hartford's stock purchased for cash, although the opinion left somewhat ambiguous the question whether the 8 percent was irrelevant because of the 14-month time interval separating the transactions or because the statute was not concerned with transactions over and above those mathematically necessary to the acquiring corporation's attainment of control.[15]

II.

For reasons set forth extensively in section III of this opinion, we do not accept the position adopted by the Tax Court. Instead we side with the Commissioner on the narrow issue presented in this appeal, that is, the correctness of taxpayers' so-called "second" argument premised on an assumed relationship between the cash and stock transactions. As explained below, we find a strong implication in the language of the statute, in the legislative history, in the regulations, and in the decisions of other courts that cash purchases which are concededly "parts of" a stock-for-stock exchange must be considered constituent elements of the "acquisition" for purposes of applying the "solely for * * * voting stock" requirement of Section 368(a)(1)(B). We believe the presence of non-stock consideration in such an acquisition, regardless of whether such consideration is necessary to the gaining of control, is inconsistent with treatment of the acquisition as a nontaxable reorganization. It follows for purposes of taxpayers' second argument—which was premised on the assumption that the cash transactions were part of the 1970 exchange offer reorganization—that the stock transfers in question would not qualify for nonrecognition of gain or loss.

Our decision will not, unfortunately, end this case. The Tax Court has yet to rule on taxpayers' "first" argument. * * * The question of what factors should determine, for purposes of Section 368(a)(1)(B), whether a

---

[18] In determining what constitutes 'one transaction,' we include all the acquisitions from shareholders which were clearly part of the same transaction."

[15] If the holding rested on the former basis, it would be difficult to credit the Tax Court's repeated assertions that it was not reaching or deciding the severability issue. As the taxpayers conceded their cash purchases were "parts of the 1970 exchange offer reorganization," the Tax Court had no reason to consider the actual lapse of time which occurred as a factor in treating the cash purchases as legally irrelevant. We assume, therefore, that any indications in the Tax Court's opinion that the separation in time was necessary to its holding were inadvertent, and that the holding actually rests on the Tax Court's reading of the statute. If the Tax Court wishes explicitly to articulate a rule regarding the time period which will suffice to separate two transactions for purposes of Section 368(a)(1)(B), we think it will have an adequate opportunity to do so in considering on remand the issue of severability raised by taxpayers' first argument.

given cash purchase is truly "related" to a later exchange of stock requires further consideration by the Tax Court, as does the question of the application of those factors in the present case. We therefore will remand this case to the Tax Court for further proceedings on the question raised by the taxpayers' first argument in support of their motion for summary judgment.

We view the Tax Court's options on remand as threefold. It can hold that the cash and stock transactions here in question are related as a matter of law—the position urged by the Commissioner—in which case, under our present holding, there would not be a valid (B) reorganization. On the other hand, the Tax Court may find that the transactions are as a matter of law unrelated, so that the 1970 exchange offer was simply the final, nontaxable step in a permissible creeping acquisition. Finally, the court may decide that, under the legal standard it adopts, material factual issues remain to be decided, so that a grant of summary judgment would be inappropriate at this time.[17]

III.

A.

* * * We begin with the words of the statute itself. The reorganization definitions contained in Section 368(a)(1) are precise, technical, and comprehensive. They were intended to define the exclusive means by which nontaxable corporate reorganizations could be effected. See Treas.Reg. § 1.368–1 (1960) * * *. In examining the language of the

---

[17] We do not intend to dictate to the Tax Court what legal standard it should apply in determining whether these transactions are related. We would suggest, however, that the possibilities should include at least the following; perhaps others may be developed by counsel or by the Tax Court itself.

One possibility—advanced by the taxpayers—is that the only transactions which should be considered related, and so parts of "the acquisition," are those which are included in the formal plan of reorganization adopted by the two corporations. The virtues of this approach—simplicity and clarity—may be outweighed by the considerable scope it would grant the parties to a reorganization to control the tax treatment of their formal plan of reorganization by arbitrarily including or excluding certain transactions. A second possibility—urged by the Commissioner—is that all transactions sharing a single acquisitive purpose should be considered related for purposes of Section 368(a)(1)(B). Relying on an example given in the legislative history, see S.Rep. No. 1622, 83d Cong., 2d Sess. 273, reprinted in [1954] U.S. Code Cong. & Admin.News, pp. 4621, 4911 [hereinafter cited as 1954 Senate Report], the Commissioner would require a complete and thoroughgoing separation, both in time and purpose, between cash and stock acquisitions before the latter would qualify for reorganization treatment under subsection (B).

A third possible approach, lying somewhere between the other two, would be to focus on the mutual knowledge and intent of the corporate parties, so that one party could not suffer adverse tax consequences from unilateral activities of the other of which the former had no notice. Cf. Manning, "In Pursuance of the Plan of Reorganization": The Scope of the Reorganization Provisions of the Internal Revenue Code, 72 Harv.L.Rev. 881, 912–13 (1959). Such a rule would prevent, for example, the situation where the acquiree's shareholders expect to receive favorable tax treatment on an exchange offer, only to learn later that an apparently valid (B) reorganization has been nullified by anonymous cash purchases on the part of the acquiring corporation. See Bruce v. Helvering, 64 App.D.C. 192, 76 F.2d 442 (D.C.Cir.1935), rev'g 30 B.T.A. 80 (1934).

Difficulties suggest themselves with each of these rules, and without benefit of thorough briefing and argument, as well as an informed decision by the lower court, we are reluctant to proceed further in exploring this issue. We leave to the Tax Court the task of breaking ground here.

(B) provision, we discern two possible meanings. On the one hand, the statute could be read to say that a successful reorganization occurs whenever Corporation X exchanges its own voting stock for stock in Corporation Y, and, immediately after the transaction, Corporation X controls more than 80 percent of Y's stock. On this reading, purchases of shares for which any part of the consideration takes the form of "boot" should be ignored, since the definition is only concerned with transactions which meet the statutory requirements as to consideration and control. To take an example, if Corporation X bought 50 percent of the shares of Y, and then almost immediately exchanged part of its voting stock for the remaining 50 percent of Y's stock, the question would arise whether the second transaction was a (B) reorganization. Arguably, the statute can be read to support such a finding. In the second transaction, X exchanged only stock for stock (meeting the "solely" requirement), and after the transaction was completed X owned Y (meeting the "control" requirement).

The alternative reading of the statute—the one which we are persuaded to adopt—treat the (B) definition as prescriptive, rather than merely descriptive. We read the statute to mean that the entire transaction which constitutes "the acquisition" must not contain any nonstock consideration if the transaction is to qualify as a (B) reorganization. In the example given above, where X acquired 100 percent of Y's stock, half for cash and half for voting stock, we would interpret "the acquisition" as referring to the entire transaction, so that the "solely for * * * voting stock" requirement would not be met. We believe if Congress had intended the statute to be read as merely descriptive, this intent would have been more clearly spelled out in the statutory language.[18]

The Tax Court's interpretation of the statute suffers from a * * * fundamental defect * * *. In order to justify the limitation of its holding to transactions involving 80 percent or more of the acquiree's stock, the Tax Court focused on the *passage* of control as the primary requirement of the (B) provision. This focus is misplaced. Under the present version of the statute, the *passage* of control is entirely irrelevant; the only material requirement is that the acquiring corporation *have* control immediately after the acquisition. As the statute explicitly states, it does not matter if the acquiring corporation already has control before the transaction begins, so long as such control exists at the completion of the reorganization. * * * In our view, the statute should be read to mean that the related transactions that constitute "the acquisition," whatever percentage of stock they may represent, must meet both the "solely for voting stock" and the "control immediately after" requirements of Section

---

[18] For example, Congress could have used the word "any" rather than the word "the" before "acquisition" in the first line of the (B) definition. This would have tended to negate the implication that this definition prescribes the conditions a transaction *must* meet to qualify, rather than simply describing that part of a transaction which is entitled to the statutory tax deferral.

368(a)(1)(B). Neither the reading given the statute by the Tax Court, nor that proposed as the first alternative above, adequately corresponds to the careful language Congress employed in this section of the Code.

* * *

IV.

* * *

Finally, we see no merit at all in the suggestion that we should permit "boot" in a (B) reorganization simply because "boot" is permitted in some instances in (A) and (C) reorganizations. Congress has never indicated that these three distinct categories of transactions are to be interpreted *in pari materia*. In fact, striking differences in the treatment of the three subsections have been evident in the history of the reorganization statutes. We see no reason to believe a difference in the treatment of "boot" in these transactions is impermissible or irrational.

Accordingly, we vacate the judgment of the Tax Court insofar as it rests on a holding that taxpayers were entitled to summary judgment irrespective of whether the cash purchases in this case were related by purpose or timing to the stock exchange offer of 1970. The case will be remanded to the Tax Court for further proceedings consistent with this opinion.

Vacated and remanded.

DETAILED ANALYSIS

1.   PERSPECTIVES ON *CHAPMAN*

Heverly v. Commissioner, 621 F.2d 1227 (3d Cir.1980), reached the same result as *Chapman* in a case involving other taxpayers involved in the Hartford-ITT acquisition.

The taxpayers in *Chapman* and *Heverly* petitioned for a writ of certiorari but the petitions were dismissed pursuant to agreement of the parties. 451 U.S. 1012 (1981). Under the agreement, ITT paid $18.5 million in taxes and the IRS agreed not to contest the tax-free treatment of the former Hartford shareholders on the exchange for ITT stock so long as the shareholders did not attempt to claim a stepped-up basis in the ITT shares. IR 81–53 (1981). If the case had not been settled, on remand the Tax Court would have had to decide whether the two acquisition transactions constituted a single transaction and, if so, whether the "sale" of the stock acquired for cash to the Italian bank in fact transferred the burdens and benefits of ownership so that the subsequent stock exchange could qualify as a (B) reorganization.

Prior to the decision of the Tax Court in Reeves v. Commissioner, 71 T.C. 727 (1979), the decision that was reversed in *Chapman,* it was generally accepted that the presence of nonqualifying consideration would defeat a (B) reorganization even though the requisite 80% control had been acquired solely for voting stock. See, e.g., Rev.Rul. 75–123, 1975–1 C.B. 115. Most of the prior case law and rulings in situations similar to *Chapman* were concerned with the taxpayer's alternative argument in *Chapman* that the nonqualifying consideration was not part of the "plan of reorganization" and therefore should not be taken into account in determining if the solely for voting stock requirement was met. After *Chapman,* the focus of attention in the (B) reorganization area will continue to be on whether any nonqualifying consideration was received pursuant to the plan of reorganization.

Notice how the solely for voting stock requirement obviates the need to undertake a separate continuity of interest examination.

2.   THE SOLELY FOR VOTING STOCK REQUIREMENT

2.1. *"Voting" Stock*

In Rev.Rul. 72–72, 1972–1 C.B. 104, a corporation acquired all the outstanding shares of a second corporation in exchange for its voting stock. The shareholders of the target corporation agreed that the former sole shareholder of the acquiring corporation would have the irrevocable right to vote the new shares received by the target shareholders for five years, after which time the target shareholders would receive their right to vote the stock of the acquiring corporation without restriction. The ruling held that the transaction did not qualify as a (B) reorganization; it was in effect an acquisition for non-voting common stock that would be converted to voting common stock in five years, and thus did not meet the voting stock test.

Rev.Rul. 63–234, 1963–2 C.B. 148, held that preferred stock entitled to elect two of the members of the Board of Directors of the issuing corporation qualified as "voting stock" in a (B) reorganization. The ruling indicates that to qualify as "voting stock" the shares must confer "upon the holders . . . the right to significant participation in the management of the affairs of the corporation."

2.2. *Cash Payments*

Rev.Rul. 85–139, 1985–2 C.B. 123, held that the "solely for voting stock" requirement had been violated where the acquiring corporation acquired 90% of the stock of the target corporation for the acquiring corporation's voting stock and, pursuant to the overall plan, the acquiring corporation caused its wholly owned subsidiary to purchase the remaining 10% of the target corporation stock for cash.

The IRS originally took the position that cash issued in lieu of fractional shares violated the solely for voting stock requirement, but this position was rejected in Mills v. Commissioner, 331 F.2d 321 (5th Cir.1964). The IRS subsequently indicated that it would follow *Mills* unless the cash received for the fractional shares was "separately bargained-for consideration." Rev.Rul. 66–365, 1966–2 C.B. 116. The cash received is not treated as "boot" but as a payment in redemption of the taxpayer's stock, the transaction thus being viewed as in effect the transfer of voting stock to the shareholder followed by a redemption. *Id.*

Payment by the acquiring corporation of the transferor shareholders' expenses incurred in connection with the (B) reorganization is not disqualifying consideration if the expenses were "solely and directly related to the reorganization." Rev.Rul. 73–54, 1973–1 C.B. 187. But the ruling cautions that payment of shareholders' expenses "for legal, accounting or investment advice or counsel pertaining to participation in, or action with respect to, the reorganization" will result in disqualification. Payment of shareholders' transfer taxes similarly results in disqualification. However, Rev.Rul. 67–275, 1967–2 C.B. 142, held that the acquiring corporation may pay the costs necessary to register the voting shares used in the acquisition with the Securities and Exchange Commission without violating the "solely for voting stock" requirement, on the theory that such costs are properly costs of the acquiring corporation and not of the transferor shareholders.

If the payment of cash or other property is made by the target corporation rather than the acquiring corporation, the solely for voting stock requirement is not violated.[7] Thus, the target corporation can make cash payments to shareholders who dissent without endangering the reorganization as long as the funds for the payment do not come from the acquiring corporation. See Rev.Rul. 68–285, 1968–1 C.B. 147 (funds were held in escrow). But if the redemption and stock exchange are steps in a single transaction and the stock of the target corporation that was redeemed prior to the exchange was redeemed for funds provided indirectly by the acquiring corporation, the solely for voting stock rule is violated. Rev.Rul. 75–360, 1975–2 C.B. 110.

If the cash transaction is separate from the stock transaction the solely for voting stock requirement is not violated. See Rev.Rul. 69–91, 1969–1 C.B. 106 (separate purchase for cash of convertible debentures); Rev.Rul. 68–562, 1968–2 C.B. 157 (unrelated purchase of shares by majority shareholder of acquiring corporation); Rev.Rul. 72–522, 1972–2 C.B. 215 (cash paid by the acquiring corporation to the target corporation in a (B) reorganization to provide it with working capital did not affect the solely for voting stock exchange at the shareholder level); Rev.Rul. 75–33, 1975–1 C.B. 115 (provision for payment of additional dividend on convertible preferred stock of acquiring corporation to insure that the shareholders of the target corporation would receive as large a dividend as they would have received had they accepted a competing offer from another corporation did not constitute "other property;" the right to the additional dividend was inherent in the stock itself, since the right was lost if the conversion privilege was exercised, and purchasers of the preferred stock also obtained the right to the extra dividend).

2.3. *Non-Cash Consideration*

Rev.Rul. 70–108, 1970–1 C.B. 78, involved an exchange in which the shareholders of the acquired corporation received voting convertible preferred stock under the terms of which the shareholder had an option upon

---

[7]   See, e.g., Rev.Rul. 68–435, 1968–2 C.B. 155 (dividend paid by the target corporation based on the dividend its shareholders would have received from the acquiring corporation had the final transaction been consummated as originally planned held not to violate the solely for voting stock requirement); Rev.Rul. 75–421, 1975–2 C.B. 108 ((B) reorganization upheld where the target corporation paid the fees of a financial consultant and accountant employed by its sole shareholder to determine the value of the acquiring company's stock; the fees were paid before the reorganization was consummated and constituted a dividend to the shareholder).

conversion to purchase an additional share of stock at a stipulated price. The IRS ruled that the solely for voting stock requirement was violated because the right to purchase the additional stock constituted property other than voting stock.

An exchange will fail to qualify as a (B) reorganization if shareholders of the target corporation who are also debenture holders exchange their shares and debentures for voting stock and new debentures of the acquiring corporation and some of the new debentures are determined to be part of the consideration attributable to the shares transferred. In Rev.Rul. 98–10, 1998–1 C.B. 643, the acquiring corporation acquired all of the stock of the target corporation from its shareholders solely in exchange for the acquiring corporation's voting stock. In addition, outstanding debentures of the target corporation were exchanged for an equivalent amount of debentures of the acquiring corporation. Some of the debentures were held by the target corporation's shareholders, but a substantial portion were held by persons who owned no target corporation stock. The IRS ruled that the transaction qualified as a (B) reorganization, specifically noting that all of the stock of the target corporation was exchanged for stock of the acquiring corporation. Although the exchange of debentures was part of the overall reorganization transaction, the IRS ruled that the exchange of debentures of the acquiring corporation did not constitute additional consideration for the stock of the target corporation.

Rev.Rul. 70–269, 1970–1 C.B. 82, and Rev.Rul. 78–408, 1978–2 C.B. 203, ruled that the acquiring corporation could substitute its stock options for options of the target corporation without affecting qualification as a (B) reorganization; the acquiring corporation's options were not given in consideration for stock of the target corporation. Treas. Regs. §§ 1.354–1(e) and 1.356–3(b) treat stock options of a corporation that is a party to a reorganization as securities of the corporation having no principal amount. Accordingly, a holder of options of the target corporation who, pursuant to the plan of reorganization, exchanges them for options of the acquiring corporation is entitled to nonrecognition under § 354(a) and § 356(d)(2).

In most stock-for-stock acquisitions, the liabilities of the target corporation simply stay with the corporation. However, an assumption of indebtedness of the shareholders of the target corporation in connection with the acquisition of their stock can prevent the qualification of the transaction as a (B) reorganization. In Rev.Rul. 70–65, 1970–1 C.B. 77, 60% of the stock of the target corporation was owned by Z Corporation and the balance by unrelated parties. The acquiring corporation obtained Z's stock of the target corporation, along with the remaining Z assets, in exchange for the acquiring corporation's voting stock and the assumption of Z's liabilities. The acquiring corporation then exchanged its voting stock for the remaining 40% of the shares of the target corporation. The acquisition of the target corporation's stock from Z (along with the remaining Z assets) qualified as a (C) reorganization, but neither of the acquisitions of the target corporation stock qualified as a (B) reorganization because of the assumption of Z's liabilities, the two transactions being treated as one for purposes of testing the transaction as a (B) reorganization.

Dealings between the acquiring corporation and the target corporation's creditors that are separate from the "plan of reorganization" do not disqualify an otherwise valid (B) reorganization. See Rev.Rul. 79–89, 1979–1 C.B. 152 (contribution of cash to the target corporation used to pay debt of the corporation guaranteed by a shareholder was not disqualifying additional consideration where the payment of the debt was not a condition of the exchange of stock). In Rev.Rul. 79–4, 1979–1 C.B. 150, however, the target corporation was thinly capitalized and a shareholder-guaranteed loan was treated as a direct loan by the shareholder. The acquiring corporation's assumption of the obligation as a condition of the reorganization exchange was treated as disqualifying consideration.

2.4. *Contingent Stock Payouts*

Contingent stock arrangements, discussed above in the context of Type (A) reorganizations, are permissible in type (B) reorganizations. Rev.Rul. 66–112, 1966–1 C.B. 68, held that the receipt of a contingent contractual right to additional voting shares that was not assignable and could only ripen into additional voting shares did not violate the solely for voting stock requirement in a (B) reorganization. Subsequently, the IRS ruled that the solely for voting stock requirement was not violated in the following rulings: Rev.Rul. 73–205, 1973–1 C.B. 188 (the conversion ratio of convertible preferred stock received in a (B) reorganization was subject to upward adjustment after five years based on the target corporation's earnings performance; the right to additional shares, if any, was forfeited by those shareholders who converted within the 5-year period); Rev.Rul. 75–456, 1975–2 C.B. 128 (subsequent to a (B) reorganization in which a contingent stock payout provision was employed, the acquiring corporation changed its place of incorporation by means of an (F) reorganization in which a new corporation was formed in another state and the acquiring corporation merged into it; the fact that the new corporation assumed the acquiring corporation's contingent stock payout obligation and agreed to issue its own additional shares of stock in lieu of the acquiring corporation's stock did not affect the status of the prior (B) reorganization); Rev.Rul. 75–237, 1975–1 C.B. 116 (acceleration of contingent stock payout agreement by acquiring corporation in a (B) reorganization prior to the transfer of all of its assets to a third corporation in a (C) reorganization did not affect the validity of the earlier (B) reorganization; same result if the earlier reorganization had itself been a (C) reorganization).

2.5. *Compensation Arrangements*

The shareholders of the target corporation may enter into employment contracts in connection with the reorganization. In Rev.Rul. 77–271, 1977–2 C.B. 116, the president of the target corporation as part of the plan of reorganization entered into a new employment contract with the target corporation and received additional stock of the acquiring corporation as consideration for entering into the contract. The IRS treated the employment arrangement as a transaction separate from the otherwise valid (B) reorganization; the additional stock received by the president constituted ordinary income to him. If, however, part of the alleged compensation for services is in fact paid for stock of the target corporation, the solely for voting stock requirement would not be met.

3. THE "CONTROL" REQUIREMENT

Rev.Rul. 59–259, 1959–2 C.B. 115, holds that "control" as defined by § 368(c) requires ownership of stock possessing at least 80% of the total combined voting power of all classes of voting stock and the ownership of at least 80% of the total number of shares of *each* class of outstanding non-voting stock. In Rev.Rul. 76–223, 1976–1 C.B. 103, the target corporation had outstanding 81 shares of voting common stock and 19 shares of non-voting preferred stock. The acquiring corporation wished to obtain all of the common, but none of the preferred stock in exchange for its voting stock. This transaction, however, would not have qualified as a (B) reorganization, since the "control" test requires ownership of 80% of each class of non-voting stock in addition to 80% of the voting stock. Accordingly, prior to the reorganization, the target corporation amended its charter to grant voting rights to the preferred stock. Voting stock of the acquiring corporation was then exchanged for the common stock of the target corporation. The ruling held that the control requirement was met since the acquiring corporation received over 80% of all the classes of stock entitled to vote at the time of the acquisition, there being no non-voting classes of stock outstanding in the target corporation at that time.

4. MULTI-STEP ACQUISITIONS

The taxpayer's alternative argument in *Chapman* was that the cash purchases of the stock and the exchange of stock for voting stock were separate transactions. If the cash acquisitions were separated from the stock exchange, the exchange by itself would have qualified as a (B) reorganization. The Tax Court did not face the factual issue of whether the stock purchases were "old and cold" and thus did not taint the share exchange because of its holding that a (B) reorganization occurred in any event. The Court of Appeals remanded for consideration of the factual question whether the cash purchase and the exchange were connected. However, the case was settled prior to consideration of this issue by the Tax Court. There is sparse authority regarding the extent to which prior or subsequent acquisitions for nonqualifying consideration will defeat a (B) reorganization. Treas.Reg. § 1.368–2(c) gives as an example of a qualifying reorganization a situation in which the acquiring corporation purchased 30% of the stock for cash and then 16 years later acquired an additional 60% in exchange for its voting stock. Whether the various steps in the acquisition will be considered together or separately depends in part on the time interval between the steps and in part on other circumstances that indicate that the various steps in the acquisition are part of the "same transaction". See Rev.Rul. 75–123, 1975–1 C.B. 115 (cash acquisition and stock exchange pursuant to the "same plan" resulted in a taxable exchange and not a (B) reorganization). The step transaction doctrine, discussed at the end of this Chapter, is relevant in this determination. See also Rev.Rul. 69–585, 1969–2 C.B. 56 (subsidiary distributed its previously acquired 25% of the stock of the target corporation to its parent as a dividend and the parent then acquired the remaining 75% of the stock of the target corporation from the latter's shareholders; parent's acquisitions held to constitute a valid (B) reorganization); Rev.Rul. 69–294, 1969–1 C.B. 110 (parent liquidated subsidiary to obtain 80% stock interest in target corporation that was held by the liquidated subsidiary, and then acquired the balance of the target stock in a stock-for-stock exchange; parent's acquisition held not to constitute a valid (B) reorganization since part of the acquired corporation's stock was obtained in the liquidation in exchange for the subsidiary's stock).

A similar question is involved when the acquisition is made solely in exchange for voting stock but the stock of the acquired company is obtained in a series of transactions. For exchanges occurring prior to the specific exchange in which control is acquired to be included within the B reorganization, Treas.Reg. § 1.368–2(c) seems to require that the requisite 80% control be acquired within a 12-month period. If this time limitation is satisfied, the series of acquisitions is in effect treated as a single transaction and all shares acquired in the 12-month period ending with the acquisition of control, as well as all exchanges occurring thereafter, will qualify for tax-free treatment. If, however, the 12-month time limitation in the Regulations is exceeded, then possibly only those shares acquired for stock that provide or exceed the 80% control requirement qualify for (B) reorganization treatment, and the exchanges that occurred prior to the exchange that resulted in the acquisition of control would be treated as taxable transactions. In American Potash & Chemical Corp. v. United States, 402 F.2d 1000 (Ct.Cl.1968), however, the government took the position that a transaction qualified as a (B) reorganization even though the series of acquisitions to obtain control of the target corporation occurred over a 14-month period, asserting that the 12-month rule in Treas.Reg. § 1.368–2(c) "is merely a guideline to determine which exchanges of a series of exchanges of stock for stock qualify as tax-free under the B reorganization provisions." In *American Potash,* the Government unsuccessfully sought reorganization treatment to prevent a step-up in basis on the subsequent liquidation of the acquired corporation; whether the IRS would accept a similar argument by a taxpayer seeking to qualify for reorganization treatment is unclear.

5.   PARTIES TO THE REORGANIZATION

Section 368(a)(2)(C) provides that the acquiring corporation in a (B) reorganization may transfer the stock of the target corporation to a subsidiary without disqualifying the reorganization. The target corporation, as a result, becomes a second tier subsidiary of the acquiring corporation. Moreover, by virtue of the first parenthetical provision in § 368(a)(1)(B) itself, a valid (B) reorganization can occur if an 80% controlled subsidiary is the acquiring corporation, using the stock of its parent in the reorganization. Again, as a result, the target corporation becomes a second tier subsidiary in the corporate group.

Treas.Reg. § 1.368–2(k), discussed earlier, allows post-reorganization transfers by the acquiring corporation of the target corporation's stock to related corporations without violating the continuity of interest requirement, even though the continuity is more remote than specifically permitted in §§ 368(a)(1)(B) and (a)(2)(C). For example, a stock-for-stock acquisition followed by a drop of the acquired corporation's stock to a third tier controlled subsidiary is permitted.

6. RELATIONSHIP OF (B) AND (C) REORGANIZATIONS

A valid (B) reorganization followed by the immediate liquidation of the acquired corporation may be treated by the IRS as a (C) reorganization. See Rev.Rul. 67–274, 1967–2 C.B. 141.

7. TAX RESULTS TO THE PARTIES TO A TYPE (B) REORGANIZATION

7.1. *Shareholders of Target Corporation*

In a type (B) reorganization the shareholders of the target corporation do not recognize any gain or loss. I.R.C. § 354(a). Section 356 does not come into play since receipt of "other property" disqualifies the transaction as a "reorganization" under § 368(a)(1)(B). The shareholders of the target corporation take as their basis in the acquiring corporation's shares received the basis of their stock in the target corporation. I.R.C. § 358(a).

7.2. *Bondholders of the Target Corporation*

In Rev.Rul. 98–10, 1998–1 C.B. 643, X Corporation acquired all of the outstanding stock of Y Corporation in exchange for its voting stock. Also pursuant to the plan of reorganization, X Corporation acquired the outstanding debentures of Y Corporation in exchange for its own debentures of an equal principal amount. Some debenture holders held Y Corporation stock but a substantial portion of the debentures were held by persons who owned no Y Corporation stock. The ruling held that the stock-for-stock exchange qualified as a (B) reorganization. The separate debenture for debenture exchange was pursuant to the plan of reorganization, and thus, under § 354, no gain or loss was recognized by the debenture holders.

7.3. *Acquiring Corporation*

No gain or loss is recognized by the acquiring corporation in a valid (B) reorganization. I.R.C. § 1032. If the acquiring corporation uses stock of its parent as is permitted by the parenthetical in § 368(a)(1)(B), § 1032 does not apply on its face, but Treas.Reg. § 1.1032–2 provides nonrecognition.

The acquiring corporation's basis in the stock of the target corporation is the aggregate of the bases of the transferring shareholders. I.R.C. § 362(b). This basis rule also applies to determine the basis that a subsidiary of the issuing corporation takes in the acquired target in a "triangular" type (B) reorganization in which the acquiring corporation uses voting stock of a corporation in "control" of the acquirer as the consideration paid to the target shareholders. In the case of such a triangular type (B) reorganization, the parent of the acquiring corporation, i.e., the corporation the stock of which is used as consideration for the acquisition, generally increases its basis in the stock of its subsidiary acquiring corporation by an amount equal to the subsidiary's § 362(b) basis in the stock of the target corporation. See Treas.Reg. § 1.358–6(c)(3).

Rev.Proc. 81–70, 1981–2 C.B. 729, amplified and modified by Rev.Proc. 2011–35, 2011–25 I.R.B. 890, amplified and modified by Rev.Proc. 2011–42, 2011–37 I.R.B. 318, provides guidelines for estimating the transferor shareholders' bases, including, where appropriate, the use of standard statistical methods using a probability sample. The guidelines reflect the fact that shares are often held by nominees under confidentiality agreements not to disclose true ownership. The revenue procedure provides safe harbors to determine the basis of shares acquired from various categories of transferring shareholders, including reporting shareholders, registered non-reporting shareholders, and nominees. The revenue procedure describes methodologies for determining the basis of acquired shares: the acquiring corporation may follow procedures for surveying all surrendering target shareholders, use a statistical sampling when a full survey is not feasible, or use one of two statistical sampling techniques when specified criteria are met. An acquiring corporation may use a different methodology as agreed between the IRS and the acquiring corporation. If, however, the acquiring corporation has actual knowledge of a surrendering shareholder's basis in acquired stock, that basis must be used for the acquired shares.

7.4. *Acquired Corporation*

The target corporation itself is unaffected by the reorganization exchange. The bases of the target corporation's assets are therefore unchanged and it retains its tax attributes.

PROBLEM SET 7

1.   In each of the following alternative transactions, P Corporation, the acquiring corporation, has exchanged its stock for stock of T Corporation, the acquired corporation. In each case determine whether, after taking into account the additional facts, a valid type (B) reorganization has occurred.

(a)   T Corp. had 1,000 shares of common stock outstanding. Prior to the transaction, P Corp. held no stock of T Corp.

(1)   P Corp. acquired 800 shares of T stock in exchange for 500 shares of P voting common stock.

(2)   P Corp. acquired 800 shares of T stock in exchange for 500 shares of P nonvoting common stock.

(3)   P Corp. acquired 800 shares of T stock in exchange for 500 shares of P voting preferred stock.

(4)   P Corp. acquired 800 shares of T stock in exchange for 500 shares of P preferred stock, which had no voting rights unless its cumulative, mandatory if earned, dividend had been missed for eight consecutive quarters; if the dividends were missed, the preferred stock had a right to elect a majority of the board of directors until the missed cumulative dividends had been paid.

(b)   T Corp. had 100,000 shares of common stock and 1,000 shares of nonvoting preferred stock outstanding. The common stock had an aggregate value of $9,000,000; the preferred stock had a value of $1,000,000. Prior to the transaction, P Corp. held no stock of T Corp.

(1)   P Corp. acquired all of the outstanding T Corp. common stock in exchange for its own voting common stock, but acquired none of the T Corp. preferred stock.

(2) P Corp. acquired 80,000 shares of T common stock for its voting common stock and all of the T nonvoting preferred stock in exchange for its own nonvoting preferred stock.

(3) P Corp. acquired 80,000 shares of T common stock for its voting common stock and 800 shares of the T nonvoting preferred stock in exchange for its own voting preferred stock.

(c) T Corp. has 1,000 shares of voting class A common stock, 3000 shares of class B nonvoting common stock, and 1,000 shares of nonvoting preferred stock outstanding. The class A common stock has an aggregate value of $900,000; the Class B common stock has an aggregate value of $2,000,000; and the preferred stock has an aggregate value of $3,000,000. P Corp. holds no stock of T Corp. but plans to acquire control. P Corp. will acquire all of the T Corp. class A common stock for its own voting common. It plans to issue additional voting common stock to acquire the minimum amount of the other two classes of stock required in order to qualify the transaction as a type (B) reorganization. How much of the T Corp. class B common and preferred stock must P Corp. acquire?

(d) T Corp. has 1000 shares of common stock outstanding. The value of a share of T common is $109. The value of a share of P common is $108. P acquires all of the T stock by offering one of its own shares of voting common stock, plus $1, for each share of T. Pursuant to the exchange offer, P issues 1000 shares of voting stock and pays the former T shareholders $1,000.

(e) T Corp. has 1000 shares of common stock outstanding. The value of a share of T common is $100. The value of a share of P common is $109. P acquires all of the T stock by offering 0.91743 of its own shares of voting common stock for each share of T, but fractional shares will not be issued. Cash will be paid in lieu of fractional shares. Pursuant to the exchange offer P gave each of the ten equal shareholders of T Corp. 91 shares of its voting stock and $81 cash in lieu of a 0.743 fractional share.

(f) T Corp. has 100,000 shares of voting common stock outstanding. The fair market value of a share of T is $100. P Corp. exchanges ten of its own shares, worth $10 each, plus options to purchase one of its shares for $9 anytime within the next year, worth $1, in exchange for each share of T. The purpose of the options was to make the exchange offer more attractive by offering a premium.

(g) Lee owns an option to purchase 1000 shares of T Corp. stock at $8. Lee's basis in this option is $2,000, and the fair market value of the option is $5,000. In exchange for the option, P Corporation gives Lee an option to purchase 1000 shares of P Corp. stock at $14 per share. The fair market value of this option is $5,000. Does this affect the status of the reorganization?

(h) Franklin, Gert, Harvey, Irene, and José are equal shareholders of T Corp. Each owns 20 shares. P Corp. acquires T Corp. by exchanging its voting stock for the T Corp. stock. Franklin, Gert, Harvey and Irene were willing to take P Corp. stock. José demanded and received cash.

(1)   T corporation redeems all of José's stock immediately before the exchange. The exchange was conditional on redemption of José's stock in T.

(i)   Does it matter if T Corp. borrows the money from P Corp. to pay José?

(ii)   What if T Corp. borrowed the money to pay José from the Last National Bank and the loan was repaid by a capital contribution from P Corp. two years later.

(2)   S Corp., an 80% controlled subsidiary of P Corp., purchases José's stock with funds obtained from operating revenues.

(3)   Katia, an individual who owns 27% of the stock of P, purchases José's stock for cash obtained by selling portfolio securities.

2.   Alex, Bonnie, Colin, and Danielle each own 19 shares of T Corp.; Earl owns the remaining 24 shares of T Corp. S Corp., a wholly owned subsidiary of P Corp., acquires T Corp. by exchanging P Corp. voting stock (which P Corp. contributed to S Corp. for this purpose) for the T Corp. stock.

(a)   All of the T Corp. shareholders agree to take P Corp. stock.

(b)   Alex, Bonnie, Colin, and Danielle are willing to take P Corp. stock. Earl demands cash. Z Corp., another wholly owned subsidiary of P Corp. buys Earl's stock.

3.   (a)   P Corp. owns all of the stock of X Corp., which in turn owns all of the stock of S Corp., i.e., S Corp is a second tier subsidiary of P Corp. S Corp. acquires T Corp. by exchanging P Corp. voting stock (which P Corp. contributed to X Corp., which in turn contributed the P stock to S Corp. for this purpose) for the T Corp. stock.

(b)   P Corp. acquired all of the stock of T Corp. in exchange for P Corp. voting stock. Immediately following the acquisition, P Corp. transferred all of the T stock to its wholly owned subsidiary, X Corp., as a contribution to capital and immediately after that transfer, X Corp. transferred all of the T stock to its own wholly owned subsidiary, S Corp.

(c)   The P Corp. affiliated group, which consists of P Corp. and its wholly owned subsidiaries, X Corp. and Y Corp., acquires the T Corp. stock in a transaction in which X Corp. acquires 60% of the outstanding T stock in exchange for P Corp. voting stock, which P Corp. contributed to X Corp. for this purpose, and Y Corp. acquires 40% of the outstanding T stock in exchange for P Corp. voting stock, which P Corp. contributed to Y Corp. for this purpose.

4.   Twenty years ago P Corp. acquired 30 of the 100 authorized and outstanding shares of voting common stock of T Corp. T Corp. currently has outstanding 100 shares of voting common stock, including the 30 held by P Corp. P Corp. proposes to acquire additional shares of T Corp. in exchange for its own voting stock.

(a) How many shares of T Corp. common must it obtain in order for the acquisition to be a valid type (B) reorganization?'

(b) Suppose that the 70 shares of T Corp. not owned by P are held by ten different individuals, each of whom owns 7 shares. P Corp. individually negotiates with each shareholder and makes the following acquisitions of all of each shareholder's T Corp. shares for P Corp. voting stock.

Shareholder	*Date*
Arthur	1/05/Year 16
Bertha	2/06/Year 16
Cristobal	4/15/Year 16
Dolly	5/01/Year 16
Edouard	1/08/Year 17
Fay	3/17/Year 17
Gustav	4/01/Year 17
Hanna	4/14/Year 17
Ike	4/15/Year 18
Josephine	4/15/Year 20

Which of these acquisitions are part of a type (B) reorganization?

5. On April 15 of this year, Leviathan Corp. made a cash purchase of 1,000,000 shares of common stock of Bullseye, Inc. from the Stallmuckers Union Pension Trust Fund. Bullseye, Inc. is publicly traded, but the acquisition was privately negotiated. If Leviathan Corp. desires to acquire control of Bullseye in a stock-for-stock acquisition, how long must it wait before making a public exchange offer in order for the acquisition to qualify as a (B) reorganization? When the exchange is made, how much of the Bullseye common stock must Leviathan obtain in the stock-for-stock exchange in order to qualify the transaction as a type (B) reorganization?

6. Suppose that G.M. acquired Ford in a type (B) reorganization, and five years later, G.M. decided to sell all of its Ford stock to Toyota. How would G.M. determine its basis in the Ford stock in computing gain or loss on the sale? (Assume that no events in the five years between the acquisition and the sale affected the basis of the Ford stock in G.M.'s hands.

SECTION 4.   STOCK FOR ASSETS ACQUISITIONS: TYPE (C) REORGANIZATIONS

INTERNAL REVENUE CODE: Sections 354; 356(a), (c); 357(a), (b); 358(a); 361; 362(b); 368(a)(1)(C), (a)(2)(B), (C), and (G).

REGULATIONS: Section 1.368–2(d).

The type (C) reorganization resembles an (A) reorganization in that the assets of the target corporation are transferred to the acquiring corporation in exchange for stock of the acquiring corporation. Indeed, the (C) reorganization is often referred to as a "practical merger." Nevertheless, the transaction is structurally different than a merger under state law; a transaction that might qualify as a type (C) reorganization generally is structured under state law as an asset sale and purchase transaction. Furthermore, to qualify as a type (C) reorganization the statute imposes several requirements that are not prerequisite to qualifying a state law merger as a type (A) reorganization.

For an acquisition to qualify as a reorganization under § 368(a)(1)(C), "substantially all" the assets of the target corporation must be exchanged in the transaction, and, since the target corporation in a (C) reorganization does not automatically disappear under state law, as it does in a merger that qualifies as an (A) reorganization, § 368(a)(2)(G) requires the target corporation to liquidate. Moreover, the (C) reorganization has elements in common with a (B) reorganization that are not present in an (A) reorganization, notably the requirement that the consideration for the target assets be "solely" voting stock of the acquiring corporation. But, in turn, the solely for voting stock requirement is less mitigated in the (C) reorganization, which allows up to 20% of the consideration (including debt assumption) to be other than voting stock. Thus, a number of the issues considered in connection with (A) and (B) reorganizations are also present in (C) reorganizations.

Revenue Ruling 57–518
1957–2 C.B. 253.

Advice has been requested as to the Federal income tax consequences of a reorganization between two corporations under the circumstances described below.

The M and N corporations were engaged in the fabrication and sale of various items of steel products. For sound and legitimate business reasons, N corporation acquired most of M corporation's business and operating assets. Under a plan of reorganization, M corporation transferred to N corporation (1) all of its fixed assets (plant and equipment) at net book values, (2) 97 percent of all its inventories at book values, and (3) insurance policies and other properties pertaining to the business. In exchange therefor, N corporation issued shares of its voting common stock to M corporation.

The properties retained by M corporation include cash, accounts receivable, notes, and three percent of its total inventory. The fair market value of the assets retained by M was roughly equivalent to the amount of its liabilities. M corporation proceeded to liquidate its retained properties as expeditiously as possible and applied the proceeds to its outstanding debts. The property remaining after the discharge of all its liabilities was turned over to N corporation, and M corporation was liquidated.

Section 368 of the Internal Revenue Code of 1954, in defining corporate reorganizations, provides in part:

(a) REORGANIZATION.—

(1) IN GENERAL.—* * * the term 'reorganization' means—* * *

(C) The acquisition by one corporation, in exchange solely for all or a part of its voting stock (or in exchange solely for all or a part of the voting stock of a corporation which is in control of the acquiring corporation), of substantially all of the properties of another corporation, * * *.

The specific question presented is what constitutes "substantially all of the properties" as defined in the above section of the Code. The answer will depend upon the facts and circumstances in each case rather than upon any particular percentage. Among the elements of importance that are to be considered in arriving at the conclusion are the nature of the properties retained by the transferor, the purpose of the retention, and the amount thereof. In Milton Smith, et al. v. Commissioner, 34 B.T.A. 702, acquiescence [1957–2 C.B. 3], a corporation transferred 71 percent of its gross assets. It retained assets having a value of $52,000, the major portion of which was in cash and accounts receivable. It was stated that the assets were retained in order to liquidate liabilities of approximately $46,000. Thus, after discharging its liabilities, the outside figure of assets remaining with the petitioner would have been $6,000, which the court stated was not an excessive margin to allow for the collection of re-receivables with which to meet its liabilities. No assets were retained for the purpose of engaging in any business or for distribution to stockholders. In those circumstances, the court held that there had been a transfer of "substantially all of the assets" of the corporation. The court very definitely indicated that a different conclusion would probably have been reached if the amount retained was clearly in excess of a reasonable amount necessary to liquidate liabilities. Furthermore, the court intimated that transfer of all of the net assets of a corporation would not qualify if the percentage of gross assets transferred was too low. Thus, it stated that, if a corporation having gross assets of $1,000,000 and liabilities of $900,000 transferred only the net assets of $100,000, the result would probably not come within the intent of Congress in its use of the words "substantially all."

The instant case, of the assets not transferred to the corporation, no portion was retained by *M* corporation for its own continued use inasmuch as the plan of reorganization contemplated *M's* liquidation. Furthermore, the assets retained were for the purpose of meeting liabilities, and these assets at fair market values, approximately equaled the amount of such liabilities. Thus, the facts in this case meet the requirements established in the case of *Milton Smith, supra.*

The instant case is not in conflict with I.T. 2373, C.B. VI–2 19 (1927), which holds that, where one corporation transferred approximately three-fourths of its properties to another corporation for a consideration of bonds and cash, it did not dispose of "substantially all the properties" owned by it at the time and, therefore, no corporate reorganization took place, so that the transaction constituted an exchange of property resulting in a gain or loss to the transferor for income tax purposes. I.T. 2372, *supra*, is obsolete to the extent that it implies that a corporate reorganization could have occurred where there was no continuity of interest. However, that ruling is still valid with regard to its discussion of the question of what constitutes "substantially all of the properties." From the facts as stated in that case, it appears that a major part of the 25 percent of the assets retained were operating assets, and it does not appear that they were retained for the purpose of liquidating the liabilities of the corporation. On the contrary, it seems likely that the corporation may have contemplated continuation of its business or the sale of the remainder of its operating assets to another purchaser. As a result, I.T. 2373, *supra*, is clearly distinguishable from the instant case.

Accordingly, since the assets transferred by M to N constitute "substantially all" of the assets of the transferor corporation within the meaning of that statutory phrase, the acquisition by N corporation, in exchange solely for part of its voting common stock, of the properties of M corporation pursuant to the plan will constitute a reorganization within the purview of section 368(a)(1)(C) of the Code. No gain or loss is recognized to the transferor as a result of the exchange of its property for common stock of the transferee under section 361 of the Code; and no gain or loss is recognized to the shareholders of M corporation, under section 354(a)(1) of such Code, as the result of their receipt of N common stock.

Revenue Ruling 67–274
1967–2 C.B. 141.

Corporation Y, pursuant to a plan of reorganization, acquired all of the outstanding stock of corporation X from the shareholders of X in exchange for some of the voting stock of Y and thereafter as part of the same plan Y completely liquidated X. *Held*, the transaction is a reorganization described in section 368(a)(1)(C) of the Internal Revenue Code of 1954.

Advice has been requested whether the transaction described below qualifies as a reorganization within the meaning of section 368(a)(1)(B) of the Internal Revenue Code of 1954.

Pursuant to a plan of reorganization, corporation Y acquired all of the outstanding stock of corporation X from the X shareholders in exchange solely for voting stock of Y. Thereafter X was completely liquidated as part of the same plan and all of its assets were transferred to Y which assumed all of the liabilities of X. Y continued to conduct the business previously conducted by x. The former shareholders of X continued to hold 16 percent of the fair market value of all the outstanding stock of Y.

Section 368(a)(1)(B) of the Code provides in part that a reorganization is the acquisition by one corporation, in exchange solely for all or a part of its voting stock, of stock of another corporation if, immediately after the acquisition, the acquiring corporation has control (as defined in section 368(c) of the Code) of such other corporation. Section 368(a)(1)(C) of the Code provides in part that a reorganization is the acquisition by one corporation, in exchange solely for all or a part of its voting stock, of substantially all of the properties of another corporation, but in determining whether the exchange is solely for stock the assumption by the acquiring corporation of a liability of the other, or the fact that property acquired is subject to a liability, is disregarded.

Under the circumstances of this case the acquisition of X stock by Y and the liquidation of X by Y are part of the overall plan of reorganization and the two steps may not be considered independently of each other for Federal income tax purposes. See Revenue Ruling 54–96, C.B. 1954–1, 111, as modified by Revenue Ruling 56–100, C.B. 1956–1, 624. The substance of the transaction is an acquisition of assets to which section 368(a)(1)(B) of the Code does not apply.

Accordingly, the acquisition by Y of the outstanding stock of X will not constitute a reorganization within the meaning of section 368(a)(1)(B) of the Code but will be considered an acquisition of the assets of X which is this case is a reorganization described in section 368(a)(1)(C) of the Code. * * * *

DETAILED ANALYSIS

1.　SOLELY FOR VOTING STOCK REQUIREMENT

1.1. *General*

As in the case of a (B) reorganization, § 368(a)(1)(C) imposes the requirement that the acquisition be "solely for voting stock." This phrase has the same meaning as in the context of a (B) reorganization and the materials discussed in the preceding section are equally applicable in interpreting the requirement in a (C) reorganization. The rigors of the solely for voting stock requirement are, however, relaxed to some extent where a (C) reorganization is involved. Section 368(a)(2)(B) allows the use of consideration other than voting stock if at least 80% of the value of *all* of the target corporation's assets is acquired for voting stock. This 20% leeway for boot in (C) reorganizations is, however, of limited scope. If any consideration other than voting stock is used in the acquisition, liabilities of the target that are assumed or to which its property are subject are also applied against the permissible 20% consideration that may be in a form other than voting stock. Moreover, the 80% voting stock consideration is tested by reference to "all" and not "substantially all" of the target's assets and thus presents significant valuation problems if some of the target's assets are not transferred but are instead distributed to the target's shareholders in the liquidation of the target.

1.2. *Assumption of Liabilities*

If assets are acquired for voting stock in a (C) reorganization, the assumption of the target corporation's debt by the acquiring corporation does not prevent qualification as a reorganization (except as provided by the operation of § 368(a)(2)(B)). Consequently, in a (C) reorganization, the acquiring corporation may, in addition to issuing voting stock, issue debt securities to the creditors of the target to replace the target's debt. Southland Ice Co. v. Commissioner, 5 T.C. 842, 850 (1945) (acq.). But if any portion of the consideration is boot, as permitted by § 368(a)(2)(B), then the total amount of boot plus the liabilities assumed may not exceed 20% of the value of *all* of the target corporation's assets. This requirement effectively eliminates the possibility of using any boot in a (C) reorganization whenever the target corporation's net assets are not more than 80% of its gross assets. See Rev.Rul. 85–138, 1985–2 C.B. 122.

If all of the consideration consists of voting stock and assumption of liabilities, there is no specific limitation on the portion of the consideration that may be in the form of assumption of liabilities. If, however, too high a percentage of the total consideration is debt assumption, there is some possibility that the "substantially all the assets" requirement might be violated.

Although most debt assumptions are permitted, some debt assumptions are treated as boot, which might result in disqualification. For example, in Helvering v. Southwest Consolidated Corp., 315 U.S. 194 (1942), the acquiring corporation had assumed a bank loan entered into by the bondholders' committee to obtain cash to pay nonparticipating security holders. The Court held that the bank loan did not fall within the assumption of liabilities clause, because the requirement to pay cash arose out of the reorganization plan itself and could not therefore be regarded as an obligation of the "other corporation." Subsequent cases, however, have limited the scope of *Southwest Consolidated*. See Claridge Apartments Co. v. Commissioner, 1 T.C. 163 (1942) (assumption of expenses of bankruptcy reorganization did not disqualify transaction); Alcazar Hotel, Inc. v. Commissioner, 1 T.C. 872 (1943) (same); Roosevelt Hotel Co. v. Commissioner, 13 T.C. 399 (1949) (loans used to pay preexisting liabilities did not disqualify transaction).

In Rev.Rul. 73–54, 1973–1 C.B. 187, the IRS declined to apply the holding of *Southwest Consolidated* to the fullest extent possible by ruling that the payment by the acquiring corporation of valid reorganization expenses of the target corporation does not violate the solely for voting stock requirement. On the other hand, in Rev.Rul. 73–102, 1973–1 C.B. 186, where the acquiring corporation assumed the obligation of the target corporation to pay the claims of dissenting shareholders, the assumption was treated as in substance a payment of cash (and thus not within the exception of § 368(a)(1)(C) for liability assumptions) and also did not fall within the exception for reorganization expenses set out in Rev.Rul. 73–54. Reorganization treatment was still possible, however, because the cash payment (plus other debts assumed) fell within the leeway allowed under § 368(a)(2)(B).

In Rev.Rul. 76–365, 1976–2 C.B. 110, prior to a (C) reorganization, the target corporation had employed an accountant and a financial consultant to value the stock of each of six prospective acquiring corporations, including the stock of the corporation with which the transaction was ultimately consummated. As part of the reorganization, the acquiring corporation paid the fees of the consultants. The ruling held that the expenses of valuing the stock of the acquiring corporation itself were covered by Rev.Rul. 73–54 and did not violate the solely for voting stock requirement. The expenses of evaluating the other five potential acquiring corporations were treated as liabilities of the target corporation assumed by the acquiring corporation. Hence, such assumption of liabilities fell within the exception in § 368(a)(1)(C) and the solely for voting stock requirement was satisfied.

Not all substitutions of the acquiring corporation's obligations for the acquired corporation's obligations on indebtedness constitute the mere "assumption" of indebtedness. In Stoddard v. Commissioner, 141 F.2d 76 (2d Cir.1944), the issuance of mortgage bonds to replace unsecured indebtedness of the target corporation was held to go beyond assumption of the target corporation's debts and to constitute additional impermissible consideration. But where new bonds issued by the acquiring corporation to replace outstanding bonds of the target vary only somewhat from the terms of the old bonds the courts have tended to treat the replacement as an assumption. See, e.g., Southland Ice Co. v. Commissioner, *supra*. The IRS likewise allows some leeway here. Rev.Rul. 79–155, 1979–1 C.B. 153, held that replacement of 8% nonconvertible bonds due in 1995 with 9% convertible bonds due in 1990 was treated as an "assumption."

The relaxation of the solely for voting stock requirement in § 368(a)(1)(C) applies only to the assumption of liabilities by "the acquiring corporation." Thus, the IRS has ruled that where the target corporation's assets are acquired using the acquiring corporation's parent's stock, as is permitted under § 368(a)(1)(C), the assumption by the parent of the target's liabilities violated the solely for voting stock requirement because the subsidiary is technically the acquiring corporation. Rev.Rul. 70–107, 1970–1 C.B. 78. Treas.Reg. §§ 1.368–2(k) and 1.368–1(d)(4), discussed in preceding sections, which were promulgated after the ruling, allow certain post-reorganization transfers by the acquiring corporation of the target corporation's assets to related corporations without disqualifying the reorganization, but the Regulations do not affect the result in Rev.Rul. 70–107. If, however, the parent retains the right to direct the transfer of the assets to the subsidiary, the parent is then considered the acquiring corporation and its assumption of liabilities falls within the exception. Rev.Rul. 70–224, 1970–1 C.B. 79. Note that the combined effect of Rev.Rul. 70–107 and Rev.Rul. 70–224 is to make § 368(a)(1)(C) elective depending on the form employed to reach identical end results.

Section 357(b), discussed in Chapter 2, treats all of the target corporation's debts assumed by the acquiring corporation as boot if a tax avoidance motive is present with respect to any of the assumed indebtedness. See Rev.Rul. 79–258, 1979–2 C.B. 143 (on the facts declining to apply § 357(b) to assumption of liabilities in a type (D) reorganization).

2. THE "SUBSTANTIALLY ALL OF THE PROPERTIES" REQUIREMENT

The "substantially all of the properties" requirement in § 368(a)(1)(C) appears to reflect the view that reorganization treatment should be allowed only if there is a continuation of the business enterprise. Perhaps too, the requirement may reflect elements of the continuity of interest requirement, i.e., that the shareholders of the target corporation retain a continuing interest in the assets which had comprised their pre-transfer investment.

As described in Rev.Rul. 57–518, supra, in Smith v. Commissioner, 34 B.T.A. 702 (1936) (acq.), the Board of Tax Appeals permitted 71% of the gross assets to qualify where the balance was retained for the sole purpose of liquidating liabilities. The Board, in distinguishing other cases, stressed the purpose of the retention and emphasized it was not to engage in business or to distribute assets to shareholders. Referring to this decision, the Tax Court in Southland Ice Company v. Commissioner, 5 T.C. 842 (1945), said, "Even this [the 'substantially all'] provision has been subjected to a construction which in effect applies a continuity test rather than mere blind percentages." Rev.Rul. 57–518 reflects similar reasoning. In National Bank of Commerce of Norfolk v. United States, 158 F.Supp. 887 (E.D.Va.1958), a transfer of 81% of the assets was held not to be "substantially all" where the remaining assets were retained not to meet liabilities but were to be distributed to shareholders.

In Rev.Proc. 77–37, § 3.01, 1977–2 C.B. 568, the IRS stated that it would issue advance rulings on the "substantially all" issue only where the transferred assets represent at least 90% of the fair market value of the net assets and at least 70% of the fair market value of the gross assets of the corporation immediately prior to the transfer. This test is only a guideline for advance rulings, and does not "define, as a matter of law, the lower limits of 'continuity of interest' or 'substantially all of the properties'." Rev.Proc. 77–37 also stated that payments to dissenters and pre-acquisition redemptions and extraordinary dividends that are part of the plan of reorganization are considered assets held immediately prior to the transfer for purposes of determining whether substantially all the assets are transferred to the acquiring corporation. See also Rev.Rul. 74–457, 1974–2 C.B. 122 (cash used in payment of regular cash dividend prior to the reorganization by the target corporation is not taken into account in applying the "substantially all" test; if, however, the payment occurred after the reorganization, the cash required to pay the dividend and the liability for payment of the dividend are taken into account).

Rev.Rul. 88–48, 1988–1 C.B. 117, found the "substantially all" requirement to have been met where the target corporation sold for cash one of its two historic businesses, which represented 50% of its historic business assets, and then transferred the cash and all its remaining assets to the acquiring corporation for the acquiring corporation's voting stock and assumption of the target corporation's liabilities. The sale of the assets was pursuant to the overall plan because the acquiring corporation did not wish to acquire the business that was sold. The ruling stressed that the IRS views the purpose of the "substantially all" requirement as preventing the use of § 368(a)(1)(C) to effect a divisive reorganization. Since the sale was to unrelated persons and no part of the proceeds was directly or indirectly retained by the shareholders of the target corporation, the test was met.

In Helvering v. Elkhorn Coal Co., 95 F.2d 732 (4th Cir.1937), the Elkhorn Coal and Coke Co. desired to transfer a part of its mining property to Mill Creek Company for stock. To qualify as a reorganization, since Mill Creek would not obtain control of Elkhorn Coal Co., Elkhorn would have had to transfer substantially all its assets. To accomplish this, Elkhorn first formed a new company, transferred the other Elkhorn properties to it for its stock, and distributed such stock to its shareholders, this distribution being nontaxable under the predecessors of §§ 368(a)(1)(D) and 355. It then transferred the mining properties, now "all its properties," to Mill Creek for stock, technically a reorganization. The new company then acquired the Elkhorn stock for its stock and dissolved Elkhorn so that the old Elkhorn stockholders ended up as the shareholders of a corporation that owned the remaining Elkhorn properties and stock of Mill Creek. The transaction predated the enactment of the liquidation requirement in § 368(a)(2)(G). Applying substance-over-form principles, the court disregarded the distribution of the stock of the new company and held that Elkhorn had not transferred substantially all of its assets to Mill Creek. Hence, no reorganization had occurred and the transaction was taxable. Compare Rev.Rul. 70–434, 1970–2 C.B. 83 (preacquisition spin-off of assets does not preclude type (B) reorganization treatment).

Rev.Rul. 2003–79, 2003–2 C.B. 80, found a valid type (C) reorganization in a transaction that reached substantially the same end result as *Elkhorn Coal* but that was structured slightly differently. In this ruling, X Corporation transferred a business consisting of one-half of its assets to newly formed subsidiary Y Corporation, following which X Corporation distributed all of the stock of Y Corporation to its shareholders in a transaction governed by § 355 (Chapter 12). After the distribution, P, an unrelated acquiring corporation, acquired all of the assets of Y in a stock-for-assets reorganization. The ruling held that the acquisition was a valid type (C) reorganization, even though an acquisition of the same properties from the X Corporation would have failed the substantially all the properties requirement if those properties had not been transferred to Y Corporation.

3.　LIQUIDATION REQUIREMENT

Section 368(a)(2)(G) requires that the target corporation liquidate and distribute the stock and securities it receives in the reorganization as well as its other properties to its shareholders in pursuance of the plan of reorganization. This requirement was added in 1984 to forestall tax avoidance effected by keeping the target corporation in existence as an investment company following the acquisition. The tax avoidance potential arose because under § 381 all of the target corporation's tax attributes are transferred to the acquiring corporation as a result of the reorganization. See Chapter 13. Thus, if not required to liquidate, the target corporation would have substantial assets, against which it might borrow to make distributions, but would have no earnings and profits to support dividend treatment. See H.Rep. No. 98–861, 98th Cong., 2d Sess. 205 (1984).

The distribution requirement may be waived by the IRS in circumstances in which an actual distribution would result in substantial hardship. However, the waiver will be granted only on the condition that the target corporation and its shareholders are treated as if the retained assets were distributed and then recontributed to a new corporation. See H.Rep. No. 98–861, 98th Cong., 2d Sess. 845–46 (1984). This constructive liquidation and contribution will trigger recognition of gain and loss to the target corporation under § 361(c)(2)(A) as well as recognition of gain to the shareholders of the target corporation under § 356(a).

As a further safeguard, § 312(h)(2) authorizes the Treasury to promulgate Regulations requiring that the earnings and profits of the target corporation be allocated between the acquiring and the target corporations.

4.   MULTI-STEP ACQUISITIONS

4.1. *Treated as Separate Transactions*

The problems of "creeping acquisitions," as in the case of a (B) reorganization, discussed above, might also arise in the (C) reorganization context. Treas.Reg. § 1.368–2(d)(4) provides that preexisting ownership of a portion of a target corporation's stock by an acquiring corporation generally does not negate satisfaction of the solely for voting stock requirement in a (C) reorganization. Thus, for example, if P Corporation acquires the assets of S Corporation, in which P corporation already owns 60% of the stock, in exchange for sufficient P Corporation stock to make a liquidating distribution to the 40% minority shareholders of S Corporation (with P corporation receiving nothing in the liquidation of S Corporation), the transaction can qualify as a type (C) reorganization. If, however, in connection with a potential (C) reorganization the acquiring corporation acquires any of the target corporation's stock for consideration other than its own voting stock (or its parent's voting stock if the parent's stock is used in an attempted triangular (C) reorganization), whether from a shareholder of the target corporation or from the target corporation itself, such consideration will be treated as money or other property exchanged by the acquiring corporation for the target corporation's assets for purposes of applying the boot limitation in § 368(a)(2)(B). Whether there has been an acquisition in connection with a potential (C) reorganization of a target corporation's stock for consideration other than voting stock will be made on the basis of all of the facts and circumstances.

Treas.Reg. § 1.368–2(d)(4) should provide tax-free treatment to minority shareholders who receive P stock in a type C reorganization in which a subsidiary is acquired by its parent. Compare Kass v. Commissioner, 60 T.C. 218 (1973), aff'd by order, 491 F.2d 749 (3d Cir.1974), in which the minority shareholders in an upstream type (A) reorganization closely following a cash purchase of over 80% of the stock of T were required to recognize gain.

Treas.Reg. § 1.368–2(d)(4) also provides nonrecognition treatment for liquidations of corporate subsidiaries that do not qualify for nonrecognition under § 332 and 337. Such transactions are commonly termed "an upstream § 368(a)(1)(C) reorganization." See Notice of Proposed Rulemaking and Notice of Public Hearing, The Solely for Voting Stock Requirement in Certain Corporate Reorganizations, REG–115086–98, 64 Fed. Reg. 31770 (June 14, 2001); see also Treas.Reg. § 1.368–2(e)(1); Treas.Reg. § 1.368–2(e)(6), Ex. 7.

Treas.Reg. § 1.368–2(d)(4)(i), Ex. 1, illustrates a tax-free upstream § 368(a)(1)(C) reorganization.

> Corporation P (P) holds 60 percent of the Corporation T (T) stock that P purchased several years ago in an unrelated transaction. T has 100 shares of stock outstanding. The other 40 percent of the T stock is owned by Corporation X (X), an unrelated corporation. T has properties with a fair market value of $110 and liabilities of $10. T transfers all of its properties to P. In exchange, P assumes the $10 of liabilities, and transfers to T $30 of P voting stock and $10 of cash. T distributes the P voting stock and $10 of cash to X and liquidates.

While this example does not deal with a "liquidation" under corporate law, it is sufficiently analogous to support treatment as a type (C) reorganization of a liquidation of a corporate subsidiary that does not qualify for nonrecognition under § 332 and 337.

4.2. *Treated as a Single Transaction*

The IRS may regard a stock-for-stock type (B) acquisition followed by the liquidation of the target corporation as a type (C) reorganization. See Resorts International, Inc. v. Commissioner, 60 T.C. 778 (1973), aff'd on this issue, 511 F.2d 107 (5th Cir.1975) (no intention to operate target corporations as subsidiaries; the liquidations were part of a series of continuing transactions that constituted a (C) reorganization); American Potash & Chemical Corp. v. United States, 399 F.2d 194 (Ct.Cl.1968). Rev.Rul. 67–274, reproduced above, sets forth a succinct summary of the IRS's position; compare its conclusion with the material discussed in Chapter 8 regarding taxable stock purchases, § 338, and *Kimbell-Diamond*.

The IRS's recharacterization of a (B) reorganization-liquidation as a (C) reorganization is grounded on the theory that under Kimbell-Diamond Milling Co. v. Commissioner, 14 T.C. 74 (1950), aff'd per curiam 187 F.2d 718 (5th Cir.1951), the transaction is actually an asset acquisition (see Chapter 8). See Rev.Rul. 74–35, 1974–1 C.B. 85 (holding that *Kimbell-Diamond* reasoning and Rev.Rul. 67–274 do not apply to recast a (B) reorganization where the target corporation does not transfer substantially all its assets to the acquiring corporation); Rev.Rul. 72–405, 1972–2 C.B. 217 ((C) reorganization upheld where a newly-created subsidiary acquired the assets of another corporation in a merger utilizing the parent corporation's stock, followed by a liquidation of the subsidiary).

Where one of the steps in a multi-step acquisition is a cash purchase of stock of the target corporation, which is followed by an asset acquisition using voting stock, the transaction may fail to qualify as a (C) reorganization because the "solely for voting stock" requirement has been violated. In Rev.Rul. 85–138, 1985–2 C.B. 122, P Corporation owned all of the stock of S1 and S2. Pursuant to a plan by which S1 would acquire substantially all the properties of the target corporation in consideration of P voting stock and the assumption by S1 of the target corporation's liabilities, S2 purchased some of the outstanding stock of the target corporation for cash in order to eliminate any possible adverse minority interest in the target corporation. The liabilities of the target corporation assumed by S1 exceeded 20% of the value of the target corporation's assets. Because the cash purchases of stock by S2 were part of a prearranged plan, the cash was treated as additional consideration provided by S1 and, since the cash and liabilities together exceeded the 20% limit in § 368(a)(2)(B), the acquisition did not qualify as a (C) reorganization.

5. PARTIES TO THE REORGANIZATION

Section 368(a)(2)(C) allows the acquiring corporation in a (C) reorganization to transfer the target's assets to a controlled subsidiary. Treas.Reg. § 1.368–2(k), also discussed in earlier sections, provides detailed rule regarding permissible drop downs of assets to lower tier subsidiaries in chains of subsidiaries meeting the 80% control test of § 368(c). See also Rev.Rul. 68–261, 1968–1 C.B. 147 (where the target corporation operated through six divisions and merged into the acquiring corporation, which then transferred each division to six wholly-owned subsidiaries, § 368(a)(2)(C) applied). The Regulations also permit assets acquired in a reorganization to be transferred to certain partnerships of which the acquiring corporation is a partner. Treas.Reg. § 1.368–1(d)(4).

In addition, by virtue of the parenthetical clause in § 368(a)(1)(C), a triangular type (C) is permitted—that is, a subsidiary can be utilized as the acquiring corporation, exchanging voting stock of its parent for substantially all the assets of the target corporation.

6. RELATIONSHIP OF TYPE (C) REORGANIZATIONS TO OTHER PROVISIONS

Section 368(a)(2)(A) provides that if a (C) reorganization also constitutes a (D) reorganization it will be treated only as a (D) reorganization, thus insuring that the (C) reorganization provisions cannot be used to accomplish a disguised tax-free division of a corporation that does not comply with the requirements of § 355. See Chapter 12.

Rev.Rul. 2007–8, 2007–1 C.B. 469, provides that § 357(c)(1), discussed in Chapter 2, will not apply to an acquisitive reorganization notwithstanding the fact that the transaction might also qualify as a § 351 transaction. Rev.Rul. 2007–8 declares obsolete Rev.Rul. 76–188, 1976–1 C.B. 99, which involved a transaction in which a parent corporation transferred all its assets to its wholly-owned subsidiary and the subsidiary assumed all of the parent corporation's liabilities. The liabilities assumed exceeded the basis of the assets transferred to the subsidiary. Section 357(c) was held to be applicable, since the transaction was one "described in" § 351 (a provision to which § 357(c) applies). The prior ruling concluded that the fact that it also constituted a (C) reorganization did not prevent the application of § 357(c), and the parent corporation accordingly recognized a gain on the transaction. Rev.Rul. 2007–8 concludes that since the transferor corporation ceases to exist, it cannot be enriched by the assumption of liabilities.

If brother-sister corporations are involved, it is possible for a (C) reorganization to overlap with § 304, discussed in Chapter 5. It is not clear which provision will control.

7. TAX RESULTS TO THE PARTIES TO A TYPE (C) REORGANIZATION

7.1. *Target Corporation and Shareholders*

Section 361(a) provides that the target corporation does not recognize gain or loss with respect to the assets it transfers in asset-acquisition reorganizations, such as type (C) reorganizations. Section 361(a) is, however, applicable only if the asset exchange is solely for stock or securities of another corporation that qualifies as a party to the reorganization. If money, property, or obligations not qualifying as stock or securities—that is, "boot"— is received by the target corporation, § 361(a) does not apply and instead § 361(b) and (c) determine the consequences to the target corporation.[8] Under § 361(b), no gain is recognized by the target corporation as a result of the receipt of the boot if the boot is transferred to its shareholders or creditors pursuant to the plan of reorganization. In a type (C) reorganization, the requirement in § 368(a)(2)(G) that the target corporation be liquidated generally will insure the required distribution. If, however, boot is received and expended, for example to pay ongoing expenses, so that it is not distributed, then gain will be recognized.

Section 358 prescribes the basis that the target corporation takes in the stock, securities, and boot received in the exchange. Section 358(a)(1) determines the target's basis in the property allowed to be received without recognition of gain or loss (i.e., the basis of the qualifying stock and securities, § 358(f)). Under § 358(a)(2), the basis to the target of boot it receives is the fair market value of the boot, even though the target recognizes no gain on receipt of the boot if it distributes the boot to its shareholders and creditors in the reorganization. Because the target corporation must be liquidated in a type (C) reorganization, these basis rules for the target are of limited consequence.

As for the liquidating distributions, no gain or loss is recognized by the target corporation on the distribution of qualified stock or securities. I.R.C. § 361(c)(1), (2)(B). Distribution of appreciated boot in the liquidation results in recognition of gain (but not loss) under § 361(c)(2), but because § 358(a)(2) provides the target corporation with a fair market value basis in any boot received in the reorganization transaction, no gain will be realized unless there is a change in value between the receipt and the liquidating

---

[8]   Technically speaking, § 361(c)(2) permits the distribution of stock, rights to acquire stock, or "obligations" of "another corporation which is a party to the reorganization." The scope of the term "obligations" presumably is broader than the term "securities."

distribution. If any property was retained by the target corporation instead of being transferred to the acquiring corporation, gain may be recognized by the target corporation as a result of distributing such property in the liquidation.

The operative rules of § 361 leave little room for the target corporation to recognize gain in a (C) reorganization. Although § 361(c)(3) accords tax-free treatment to the receipt and distribution of stock in satisfaction of creditors' claims, if, however, stock of the acquiring corporation received in the reorganization is *sold* by the target corporation and the proceeds used to pay creditors' claims, the target corporation must recognize gain on the sale; the receipt of the stock remains nontaxable.

For the shareholders of the target corporation, the tax results are similar to those in an (A) reorganization. No gain or loss is recognized if they receive solely the stock of the acquiring corporation in exchange for their stock in the target corporation. I.R.C. § 354(a). If the permissible amount of "boot" is involved and it is distributed to the shareholders, they may recognize gain under § 356, either as capital gain or as a dividend, depending on the circumstances, as discussed earlier. Section 358 then provides an exchanged basis for the acquiring corporation's stock. If any boot is received, however, the basis is determined by first increasing the basis by the amount of any gain recognized by the shareholders as the result of the receipt of boot, and then decreasing it by the amount of cash or the fair market value of any other property received.

7.2. *Acquiring Corporation*

Pursuant to § 1032, the acquiring corporation recognizes no gain or loss on the transfer of its shares in a (C) reorganization. If, however, the acquiring corporation transfers any boot other than cash or its own stock or securities, it must recognize gain or loss with respect to the boot transferred.

Under § 362(b) the acquiring corporation's basis in the acquired assets is equal to the target corporation's basis in those assets. Although § 362(b) provides that the acquiring corporation's basis in the assets is to be increased by any gain recognized under § 361(b) by the target corporation on the transfer of its assets to the acquiring corporation, as previously discussed, it is not likely that the target corporation will recognize gain as a result of the transfer of its assets to the acquiring corporation because the target liquidates and distributes all of its property to shareholders.

Under § 381, the tax attributes of the target corporation, e.g., net operating loss carryovers, earnings and profits accounts, etc., carry over to the acquiring corporation. However, § 382 limits the post-acquisition use of any net operating loss carryovers of the target corporation. See Chapter 13.

PROBLEM SET 8

1. In each of the following alternative transactions, T Corporation transfers assets to P Corporation in exchange for P Corporation stock (or other consideration stated in the question). In each case determine whether the transaction qualifies as a reorganization after taking into account the additional facts. If the transaction is not a reorganization, how is it treated?

(a) T transfers all of its assets for P voting preferred stock, which T distributes to its shareholders in liquidation.

(b) T transfers all of its assets for P nonvoting common stock, which T distributes to its shareholders in liquidation.

(c) T transfers all of its assets for P voting common stock, which T continues to hold.

2. Andrea, Barry, and Chantal own all of the common stock of T Corporation. Dean, Erin, and Felix collectively own T Corporation bonds due in 2075 in the principal amount of $5,000,000. The fair market value of all of the T Corporation assets is $3,000,000. Pursuant to a purchase and sale agreement, T Corporation transferred all of its assets to P Corp. in exchange for 3,000 shares of 6%, $1,000 par value voting preferred stock. T Corporation dissolved and distributed the 3,000 shares of the P Corp. preferred stock to Dean, Erin, and Felix. In the dissolution of T Corp., Andrea, Barry, and Chantal received nothing in exchange for their T Corp. stock, which was cancelled. Has a tax-free reorganization has occurred?

3. Evaluate each of the following alternative structures, including a discussion of the tax consequences to the parties.

(a) T transfers all of its assets, having a fair market value of $1,000,000 and a basis of $800,000, for $700,000 of P voting common stock. P assumes $300,000 of T's debts secured by the assets. T liquidates.

(b) T transfers all of its assets, having a fair market value of $1,000,000 and a basis of $200,000, for $700,000 of P voting common stock. P assumes $300,000 of T's debts secured by the assets. T liquidates.

(c) T transfers all of its assets, having a fair market value of $1,000,000 and a basis of $200,000, for $100,000 of P voting common stock. P assumes $900,000 of T's debts secured by the assets. T liquidates.

4. Evaluate each of the following alternative structures, including a discussion of the tax consequences to the parties.

(a) T transfers all of its assets, having a fair market value of $1,000,000, for $800,000 of P voting common stock and $200,000 of cash. T has no debts. T liquidates.

(b) T transfers all of its assets, having a fair market value of $1,000,000 for $700,000 of P voting common stock and $100,000 of cash. P assumes $200,000 of T's debts secured by the assets. T liquidates.

(c) T transfers 90% of its assets, having a fair market value of $900,000 for $750,000 of P voting common stock and $150,000 of cash. T has no debts. T liquidates.

5. Evaluate each of the following alternative structures, including a discussion of the tax consequences to the parties.

(a) T's assets consist of a factory, having a value of $700,000, subject to a mortgage of $200,000 and a warehouse, having a value of $300,000, also subject to a mortgage of $200,000. The factory is transferred to P for $500,000 of P stock and P takes the factory subject to the mortgage. T retains the warehouse, which it distributes to its shareholders in liquidation along with the P stock.

(b) T's assets consist of a factory, having a value of $600,000, which is unencumbered and a warehouse, having a value of $400,000, subject to a mortgage of $390,000. The factory is transferred to P for $600,000 of P stock. T retains the warehouse, which it distributes to its shareholders in liquidation along with the P stock.

(c) T's assets consist of a factory, having a value of $650,000 and undeveloped land held as an investment, having a value of $350,000. The factory is transferred to P for $650,000 of P stock. T retains the undeveloped land, which it distributes to its shareholders in liquidation along with the P stock.

6. P Corp. owns 70 of 100 shares of the stock of T; Omar owns the other 30 shares of T stock. T transfers all of its assets to P in exchange for 1000 shares of P stock, following which T liquidates, distributing 300 shares of P stock to Omar and 700 shares of P stock to P. The 700 shares of P stock transferred to T that were distributed to P in the liquidation are cancelled.

7. Marco owns 65 shares of T stock. Nana owns 35 shares of T stock. T's assets consist of a battery factory, having a value of $650,000, and a toxic waste dump site, having a value of $350,000. P wants to acquire T, including the factory, but not the toxic waste dump site. Marco is willing to accept P shares as consideration, but Nana is not. Pursuant to a prearranged plan, the toxic waste dump site is distributed to Nana in redemption of Nana's 35 shares. Immediately thereafter, Marco exchanges the 65 remaining T shares for P voting stock. Within weeks, P liquidates T. Has a valid reorganization occurred?

8. (a) T transfers all of its assets, which had an aggregate basis of $600,000, to P for 10,000 shares of P stock, having a fair market value of $1,000,000. Pursuant to the plan of reorganization, P does not assume any debts of T. Instead, T distributes $100,000 worth of P stock to T's creditors in full satisfaction of all of its debts as part of T's liquidation. What are the tax consequences to T?

(b) T transfers all of its assets, which had an aggregate basis of $600,000, to P for $1,000,000 of P voting stock. Pursuant to the plan of reorganization, P does not assume any debts of T. Instead, T sells 1,000 shares of P stock, worth $100,000, and pays the cash proceeds to its creditors in full satisfaction of all of its debts as part of T's liquidation. What are the tax consequences to T?

(c) How do you explain the difference in results in (a) and (b)?

SECTION 5.　TRIANGULAR REORGANIZATIONS

INTERNAL REVENUE CODE: Sections 368(a)(2)(D), (E); 368(c).

REGULATIONS: Sections 1.358–6; 1.368–2(b)(2), (j), (k); 1.1032–2. See also 1.1032–3.

The early reorganization statutes did not permit tax-free triangular mergers, as was explained in the discussion of Groman v. Commissioner, 302 U.S. 82 (1937), and Helvering v. Bashford, 302 U.S. 454 (1938), above. There is no policy reason, however, not to allow acquisitions by a subsidiary using the stock of a parent corporation to qualify for tax-free reorganization treatment. As discussed in the preceding materials, a series of amendments to the reorganization definitions made it possible to transfer assets or stock acquired in a reorganization transaction to a controlled subsidiary (§ 368(a)(2)(C)) or to employ the subsidiary itself as the acquiring vehicle in a type (B) or type (C) reorganization, using stock of the parent company as consideration for the acquisition. However, these amendments did not cover two situations that were important in practice. In the first place, a direct acquisition by the subsidiary of the target company's assets in an (A) reorganization in exchange for the parent stock was not possible since the parent was not considered to be a party to the reorganization under § 368(b). In addition, though the subsidiary could acquire assets in a (C) reorganization for the parent stock, the parent could not assume liabilities of the target corporation directly since § 368(a)(1)(C) applies only to liabilities assumed by the "acquiring" corporation, in this case the subsidiary. The desired results could have been obtained through other somewhat complicated means, such as the acquisition by the parent of the assets in a (C) reorganization and the subsequent transfer of the target assets to a newly formed subsidiary under § 368(a)(2)(C), with the parent assuming the liabilities of the target corporation.

In successive amendments to § 368 in 1968 and 1971, described in the following Senate Finance Committee Report, Congress made such arrangements unnecessary. In 1968 Congress added § 368(a)(2)(D), which, together with a corresponding amendment to the § 368(b) definition of "party to a reorganization," permits the direct use of the parent's stock by the subsidiary as consideration for assets acquired in an (A) reorganization. See Treas.Reg. § 1.368–2(b)(2).

Section § 368(a)(2)(E), added in 1971, covers the so-called "reverse triangular merger" situation by allowing the subsidiary to be merged into the target corporation using stock of the parent in an (A) reorganization. Thus, the target corporation becomes a subsidiary of the acquiring parent corporation. The stockholders of the target corporation exchange their target corporation stock for the stock of the acquiring parent corporation.

Senate Finance Committee Report, Public Law 91–693

S.Rep. No. 91–1533, 91st Cong., 2d Sess. 622–23 (1971).

[H.R. 19562] amends the tax law to permit a tax-free statutory merger when stock of a parent corporation is used in a merger between a controlled subsidiary of the parent and another corporation, and the other corporation survives—here called a "reverse merger."

In 1968 Congress added a provision to the tax laws permitting statutory mergers where the stock of the parent of the corporation making the acquisition was used in the acquisition (sec. 368(a)(2)(D)). At the time that statute was enacted, the use of stock of a parent corporation was permitted in the type of reorganization involving the acquisition of stock (subparagraph (B)) and in the type of reorganization involving the acquisition of assets (subparagraph (C)) but was not permitted in the case of a statutory merger of a subsidiary. After noting this fact, the House committee report went on to explain the reasons for the amendment as follows:

> Apparently the use of a parent's stock in statutory mergers was not initially provided for because there was no special concern with the problem at the time of the adoption of the 1954 code. However, this is no longer true. A case has been called to the attention of your committee in which it is desired to have an operating company merged into an operating subsidiary in exchange for the stock of the parent holding company. Your committee sees no reason why tax-free treatment should be denied in cases of this type where for any reason the parent cannot or, for business or legal reasons, does not want to acquire the assets (even temporarily) through a merger.

> For the reasons set forth above your committee concluded that it was desirable to permit the use of the stock of the parent corporation in a statutory merger in acquiring a corporation in essentially the same manner as presently is available in the case of other tax-free acquisitions. (House report on H.R. 18942 (90th Cong.))

Thus, under existing law, corporation X (an unrelated corporation) may be merged into corporation S (a subsidiary) in exchange for the stock in corporation P (the parent of S) in a tax-free statutory merger. However, if for business and legal reasons (wholly unrelated to Federal income taxation) it is considered more desirable to merge S into X (rather than merging X into S), so that X is the surviving corporation—a "reverse merger"—the transaction is not a tax-free statutory merger.

Although the reverse merger does not qualify as a tax-free statutory merger, it may, in appropriate circumstances, be treated as tax-free as a stock-for-stock reorganization (subparagraph (B)). However, in order to qualify as a tax-free stock-for-stock reorganization it is necessary that the acquisition be *solely* for voting stock and that no stock be target for cash or other consideration. Thus, if a small amount of the stock of X (the unrelated corporation) is acquired for cash before the merger of S into X, there often may be doubt as to whether or not the transaction will meet the statutory requirements of a stock-for-stock reorganization.

The committee agrees with the House, that there is no reason why a merger in one direction (S into X in the above example) should be taxable, when the merger in the other direction (X into S), under identical circumstances, is tax-free. Moreover, it sees no reason why in cases of this type the acquisition needs to be made solely for stock. For these reasons the amendment makes statutory mergers tax-free in the circumstances described above.

In discussions on this bill, the Treasury Department has expressed concern that the corporate reorganization provisions need review and modification. The committee in agreeing to this amendment does not intend to foreclose consideration of any substantive changes which the Treasury may propose in the corporate reorganization provisions in any future presentations.

Revenue Ruling 2001–26
2001–1 C.B. 1297.

ISSUE

On the facts described below, is the control-for-voting-stock requirement of section 368(a)(2)(E) of the Internal Revenue Code satisfied, so that a series of integrated steps constitutes a tax-free reorganization under sections 368(a)(1)(A) and 368(a)(2)(E) and section 354 or section 356 applies to each exchanging shareholder?

FACTS

Situation 1. Corporation P and Corporation T are widely held, manufacturing corporations organized under the laws of state A. T has only voting common stock outstanding, none of which is owned by P. P seeks to acquire all of the outstanding stock of T. For valid business reasons, the acquisition will be effected by a tender offer for at least 51 percent of the stock of T, to be acquired solely for P voting stock, followed by a merger of a subsidiary of P into T. P initiates a tender offer for T stock conditioned on the tender of at least 51 percent of the T shares. Pursuant to the tender offer, P acquires 51 percent of the T stock from T's shareholders for P voting stock. P forms S and S merges into T under the merger laws of state A. In the statutory merger, P's S stock is converted into T stock and each of the T shareholders holding the remaining 49 percent of the outstanding T stock exchanges its shares of T stock for a combination of consideration, two-thirds of which is P voting stock and one-third of which is cash. Assume that under general principles of tax law, including the step transaction doctrine, the tender offer and the statutory merger are treated as an integrated acquisition by P of all of the T stock. Also assume that all nonstatutory requirements for a reorganization under sections 368(a)(1)(A) and 368(a)(2)(E) and all statutory requirements of section 368(a)(2)(E), other than the requirement under section 368(a)(2)(E)(ii) that P acquire control of T in exchange for its voting stock in the transaction, are satisfied.

Situation 2. The facts are the same as in Situation 1, except that S initiates the tender offer for T stock and, in the tender offer, acquires 51 percent of the T stock for P stock provided by P.

LAW AND ANALYSIS

Section 368(a)(1)(A) states that the term "reorganization" means a statutory merger or consolidation. Section 368(a)(2)(E) provides that a transaction otherwise qualifying under section 368(a)(1)(A) will not be disqualified by reason of the fact that stock of a corporation (the "controlling corporation") that before the merger was in control of the merged corporation is used in the transaction, if (1) after the transaction, the corporation surviving the merger holds substantially all of its properties and of the properties of the merged corporation (other than stock of the controlling corporation distributed in the transaction), and (2) in the transaction, former shareholders of the surviving corporation exchanged, for an amount of voting stock of the controlling corporation, an amount of stock in the surviving corporation that constitutes control of such corporation (the "control-for-voting-stock requirement"). For this purpose, control is defined in section 368(c).

In King Enterprises, Inc. v. United States, 418 F.2d 511 (Ct. Cl. 1969), as part of an integrated plan, a corporation acquired all of the stock of a target corporation from the target corporation's shareholders for consideration, in excess of 50 percent of which was acquiring corporation stock, and subsequently merged the target corporation into the acquiring corporation. The court held that, because the merger was the intended result of the stock acquisition, the acquiring corporation's acquisition of the target corporation qualified as a reorganization under section 368(a)(1)(A).

* * *

Section 1.368–1(c) of the Income Tax Regulations provides that a plan of reorganization must contemplate the bona fide execution of one of the transactions specifically described as a reorganization in section 368(a) and the bona fide consummation of each of the requisite acts under which nonrecognition of gain is claimed. Section 1.368–2(g) provides that the term plan of reorganization is not to be construed as broadening the definition of reorganization as set forth in section 368(a), but is to be taken as limiting the nonrecognition of gain or loss to such exchanges or distributions as are directly a part of the transaction specifically described as a reorganization in section 368(a).

As assumed in the facts, under general principles of tax law, including the step transaction doctrine, the tender offer and the statutory merger in both Situations 1 and 2 are treated as an integrated acquisition by P of all of the T stock. The principles of King Enterprises support the conclusion that, because the tender offer is integrated with the statutory merger in both Situations 1 and 2, the tender offer exchange is treated as part of the statutory merger (hereinafter the "Transaction") for purposes of the reorganization provisions. Cf. J.E. Seagram Corp. v. Commissioner, 104 T.C. 75 (1995) (treating a tender offer that was an integrated step in a plan that included a forward triangular merger as part of the merger transaction). Consequently, the integrated steps, which result in P acquiring all of the stock of T, must be examined together to determine whether the requirements of section 368(a)(2)(E) are satisfied. Cf. section 1.368–2(j)(3)(i); section 1.368–2(j)(6), Ex. 3 (suggesting that, absent a special exception, steps that are prior to the merger, but are part of the transaction intended to qualify as a reorganization under sections 368(a)(1)(A) and 368(a)(2)(E), should be considered for purposes of determining whether the control-for-voting-stock requirement is satisfied).

In both situations, in the Transaction, the shareholders of T exchange, for P voting stock, an amount of T stock constituting in excess of 80 percent of the voting stock of T. Therefore, the control-for-voting-stock requirement is satisfied. Accordingly, in both Situations 1 and 2, the Transaction qualifies as a reorganization under sections 368(a)(1)(A) and 368(a)(2)(E).

Under sections 1.368–1(c) and 1.368–2(g), all of the T shareholders that exchange their T stock for P stock in the Transaction will be treated as exchanging their T stock for P stock in pursuance of a plan of reorganization. Therefore, T shareholders that exchange their T stock only for P stock in the Transaction will recognize no gain or loss under section 354. T shareholders that exchange their T stock for P stock and cash in the Transaction will recognize gain to the extent provided in section 356. In both Situations 1 and 2, none of P, S, or T will recognize any gain or loss in the Transaction, and P's basis in the T stock will be determined under section 1.358–6(c)(2) by treating P as acquiring all of the T stock in the Transaction and not acquiring any of the T stock before the Transaction.

* * *

DETAILED ANALYSIS

1. GENERAL

The Senate Finance Committee report suggests that a merger in one direction, the target corporation into the acquiring subsidiary, should not be treated differently than the reverse, the acquiring subsidiary into the target corporation. Note however, that in the case of a reverse triangular merger,

§ 368(a)(2)(E)(ii) requires that the original shareholders of the surviving corporation must receive voting stock of the acquiring parent corporation in exchange for stock representing control, as defined in § 368(c), of the surviving corporation. There is no such limitation applicable to a forward triangular merger under § 368(a)(2)(D). The reason for this requirement in § 368(a)(2)(E) is not grounded in a policy distinction between the two forms but rather on the difference in structures used by the taxpayers who sought the remedial legislation to effect these transactions before the remedial legislation was enacted. As noted in the Senate Finance Committee Report, a reverse triangular merger is functionally equivalent to a stock-for-stock exchange under § 368(a)(1)(B), but the reverse triangular merger allows somewhat more latitude with respect to non-stock consideration. The relationship of § 368(a)(2)(E) to § 368(a)(1)(B) is highlighted by Rev.Rul. 67–448, 1967–2 C.B. 144, which, prior to the enactment of § 368(a)(2)(E), held that a reverse triangular merger into corporate shell subsidiary in consideration solely for the parent's voting stock was a type (B) reorganization. There really is no continuing justification for the stricter statutory continuity of interest requirements of § 368(a)(2)(E).

On the other hand, the prohibition against a splitting of interests, reflected in the *Groman* and *Bashford* decisions, discussed above, is present in the requirement in § 368(a)(2)(D) that no stock of the subsidiary corporation be used in the transaction. In contrast, § 368(a)(2)(E) contains no such express prohibition, although the stricter continuity of interest requirement leaves little room for shareholders of the target corporation to continue to hold a minority interest in it after the acquisition.

2.   FORWARD TRIANGULAR MERGERS

2.1. *Permissible Consideration*

Since § 368(a)(2)(D) is grafted onto the basic type (A) reorganization definition, there is no restriction on the consideration that may be used by the subsidiary in the acquisition other than the general continuity of interest limitation in an (A) reorganization and the express statutory restriction that no stock of the subsidiary be used. Thus, as long as 40% of the consideration paid to the target corporation's shareholders is stock of the acquiring subsidiary's parent corporation, which may be of any class and either voting or nonvoting, the remainder of the consideration for the acquisition may be cash or debt obligations of either the acquiring subsidiary or its parent. Treas.Reg. § 1.368–2(b)(2). Under the principles of Rev.Rul. 66–224, 1966–2 C.B. 114, discussed above in the context of type (A) reorganizations, the continuity of interest requirement is to be applied with reference to the aggregate consideration received by the entire group of the shareholders of the acquired corporation.

The assumption of liabilities of the target corporation by the parent will not prevent the transaction from qualifying as a reorganization, nor will the assumption be treated as "boot" under § 361(b). In Rev.Rul. 79–155, 1979–1 C.B. 153, the holders of convertible securities of the target corporation in a forward triangular merger received securities on which the parent and the subsidiary were jointly and severally liable and which were convertible into stock of the parent, unless the parent sold the subsidiary, in which case the securities were convertible into stock of the subsidiary. The ruling held that the exchange of securities, which had identical principal amounts, was tax-free under § 354; in addition, conversion of the securities into stock of the parent was not a realization event. It is likely that the result in the ruling would have differed if the securities had been convertible into stock of the subsidiary from the outset.

2.2. *Substantially All of the Properties*

In a § 368(a)(2)(D) acquisition, the acquiring subsidiary must *acquire* substantially all of the properties of the target corporation. Treas.Reg. § 1.368–2(b)(2) indicates that the "substantially all" criteria developed in the context of (C) reorganizations are to be applied.

2.3. *Hypothetical Merger Requirement*

The requirement in § 368(a)(2)(D) that the merger "would have qualified" as an (A) reorganization if the transaction had taken place between the target corporation and the parent is not interpreted literally. It need not be established that the merger actually could have taken place under state or federal law; it is sufficient that the "general requirements of a reorganization (such as a business purpose, continuity of business enterprise and continuity of interest)" are met. Treas.Reg. § 1.368–2(b)(2). Section 368(a)(2)(D) applies only to a merger; a consolidation of the target corporation with the acquiring subsidiary in a new corporation is not covered. See, e.g., Rev.Rul. 84–104, 1984–2 C.B. 94 (§ 368(a)(2)(E) applies only to state law mergers, not to "consolidations" involving a subsidiary, but consolidation under federal banking law where the target corporation survived was treated as a merger).

3. REVERSE TRIANGULAR MERGERS

3.1. *Permissible Consideration*

The requirement of § 368(a)(2)(E)(ii) that former shareholders of the surviving corporation exchange a controlling interest in the target corporation for voting stock of the acquiring parent corporation assures that the continuity of interest test will be satisfied. While this requirement is reminiscent of the (B) reorganization, which is the antecedent to the reverse triangular merger, it also has aspects of a (C) reorganization in that a 20% leeway for other consideration is permissible. Within this exception there are no limits on the character of the boot that may be exchanged; theoretically stock of the surviving subsidiary, i.e., new stock of the target, is permissible. See also Treas.Reg. § 1.368–2(j)(4), permitting the acquiring parent to assume the target corporation's liabilities.

State law requirements that shareholders exercising statutory dissenters rights be redeemed for cash can present problems with respect to the 80% requirement of § 368(a)(2)(E)(ii). Treas.Reg. § 1.368–2(j)(3)(i) provides that stock of the target corporation that is redeemed for cash or property of the target corporation (in contrast to cash or property provided by the acquiring parent or its subsidiary) is not counted as outstanding immediately prior to the reorganization. Thus, for example, if the holders of 100 out of 1000 shares of the target corporation dissent from the merger, the target corporation may redeem those shares, and to qualify under § 368(a)(2)(E) the acquiring parent's stock need be exchanged only for 80% of the remaining 900 shares, or 720 shares; the remaining 180 shares may be acquired for cash. But if the funds to redeem the stock are provided by the acquiring parent or subsidiary, then all 1000 shares are taken into account and 800 shares must be acquired for the parent's voting stock. Not only does a redemption of stock by the target corporation not prevent compliance with the continuity of interest requirement, but the Regulations indicate that the redeemed stock is disregarded for purposes of determining continuity of interest even if the pre-reorganization redemption is of an extraordinary amount of target corporation stock. See Treas.Reg. § 1.368–1(e)(1)(ii), (e)(8), Ex. 9.

Cash and property of the target corporation used to redeem the stock of its own dissenting shareholders are, however, taken into account in determining whether the "substantially all the properties" test has been met. Treas.Reg. § 1.368–2(j)(6), Ex. 3. If the cash or property distributed in redemption of the dissenting stockholders' shares constitutes too high a percentage of the target corporation's assets, the transaction may fail to meet the "substantially all of the properties" test.

3.2. *Substantially All of the Properties*

In the case of a § 368(a)(2)(E) acquisition, the surviving corporation must *hold* substantially all of its properties *and* the properties of the merged subsidiary corporation (other than the stock of the parent distributed in the acquisition). Treas.Reg. § 1.368–2(j)(3)(iii) indicates that the "substantially all" criteria developed in the context of (C) reorganizations are to be applied, but assets transferred from the controlling corporation to the merged corporation pursuant to the plan of reorganization are not taken into account. Thus, for example, cash transferred from the controlling corporation to the merged corporation to pay dissenting shareholders of the surviving corporation pursuant to state law or to pay reorganization expenses would not be considered in determining whether the resulting corporation held "substantially all" the assets of the two corporations involved in the acquisition transaction.

Rev.Rul. 2001–25, 2001–1 C.B. 1291, addressed the application of the substantially all the properties requirement in § 368(a)(2)(E). That revenue ruling deals with whether a reverse triangular merger that otherwise qualified under § 368(a)(2)(E) was disqualified because immediately after the merger and as part of a plan that included the merger, T sold 50% of its operating assets to an unrelated corporation for cash. The IRS applied Rev.Rul. 88–48, 1988–1 C.B. 117, to conclude that the "substantially all of the properties requirement had been met." The reasoning of Rev.Rul. 2001–25 was as follows.

Section 368(a)(2)(E) uses the term "holds" rather than the term "acquisition" as do §§ 368(a)(1)(C) and 368(a)(2)(D) because it would be inapposite to require the surviving corporation to "acquire" its own properties. The "holds" requirement of § 368(a)(2)(E) does not impose requirements on the surviving corporation before and after the merger that would not have applied had such corporation transferred its properties to another corporation in a reorganization under § 368(a)(1)(C) or a reorganization under §§ 368(a)(1)(A) and 368(a)(2)(D).

In this case, T's post-merger sale of 50 percent of its operating assets for cash to X prevents T from holding substantially all of its historic business assets immediately after the merger. As in Rev.Rul. 88–48, however, the sales proceeds continue to be held by T. Therefore, the post-acquisition sale of 50 percent of T's operating assets where T holds the proceeds of such sale along with its other operating assets does not cause the merger to violate the requirement of § 368(a)(2)(E) that the surviving corporation hold substantially all of its properties after the transaction. Accordingly, the merger qualifies as a reorganization under §§ 368(a)(1)(A) and 368(a)(2)(E), notwithstanding the sale by T of a portion of its assets to X immediately after the merger and as part of a plan that includes the merger.

Rev.Rul. 2008–25, 2008–2 C.B. 986, dealt with the application of the step transaction doctrine where the target corporation was liquidated after a reverse triangular merger that otherwise would have qualified as a tax-free reorganization. In the ruling, all of the stock of T Corporation was owned by individual A. T had $150x of assets and $50x dollars of liabilities. P Corporation was unrelated to A or T Corporation, and was worth over four times the value of T Corporation. P Corporation formed a controlled subsidiary solely to effect the acquisition, and the subsidiary merged into T Corporation. As a result of the merger, P Corporation became the owner of all of the stock of T Corporation (which was newly issued by T in exchange for P's stock in the subsidiary), and A exchanged the T Corporation stock (which was cancelled) for P Corporation voting stock worth $90x and $10x in cash. As part of an integrated plan, following the merger, T Corporation was completely liquidated by P Corporation; T Corporation transferred all of its assets to P Corporation, which assumed all of T Corporation's liabilities. P Corporation continued to conduct the business previously conducted by T Corporation. Apart from the liquidation, the reverse triangular merger otherwise would have qualified as a tax-free reorganization under § 368(a)(2)(E). Because of the presence of the cash boot, the merger transaction, standing alone, could not have qualified as a tax-free reorganization under § 368(a)(1)(B), or (after taking into account T Corporation's debt) under § 368(a)(1)(C), or under § 368(a)(1)(D) because A did not own sufficient stock of P Corporation after the merger. The ruling reached two conclusions. First, because both the reverse triangular merger and liquidation occurred pursuant to an "integrated plan," the step transaction doctrine applied and the safe harbor in Treas.Reg. § 1.368–2(k) did not apply—the safe harbor in Treas.Reg. § 1.368–2(k) applies only if the target corporation, in this case T Corporation is not liquidated—and the reverse triangular merger did not qualify as a § 368(a)(2)(E) tax-free reorganization, because after the acquisition and liquidation, T Corporation, which no longer existed, did not hold substantially all of its properties.

Rev.Rul. 2008–25 then held, in a feat of Orwellian doublespeak, that in characterizing the transactions as other than a reorganization, the step transaction doctrine would not apply. Thus, the first step—the reverse triangular merger—was treated as a § 338(d)(3) qualified stock purchase under Treas.Reg. § 1.338–3(d) and Rev.Rul. 90–95, 1990–2 C.B. 67. The liquidation was a § 332 liquidation, with P Corporation taking a transferred basis under § 334(b) in T Corporation's assets, and T Corporation not recognizing gain or loss pursuant to § 337. In this regard, the ruling reasoned "integrating the acquisition of T stock with the liquidation of T would result in treating the acquisition of T stock as a taxable purchase of T's assets. Such treatment would violate the policy underlying § 338 that a cost basis in acquired assets should not be obtained through the purchase of stock where no § 338 election is made. Accordingly, consistent with the analysis set forth in Rev.Rul. 90–95, the acquisition of the stock of T is treated as a qualified stock purchase by P followed by the liquidation of T into P under § 332." It is interesting that disqualifying the initial transaction from reorganization status and recharacterizing it as a qualified stock purchase followed by a § 332 liquidation did not affect the ultimate tax treatment of either T Corporation or P Corporation. Only individual A, the shareholder of T Corporation, was affected because A was required to recognize all of the gain or loss. This was so even though apart from tax results, individual A has no interest in or reason to be concerned with whether P Corporation continued to operate T Corporation's business in a continuing T Corporation or as a division of P Corporation, and furthermore, individual A had little or no power over whether or not P Corporation liquidated T Corporation. Note that while the ruling describes the events as occurring pursuant to an "integrated plan," the ruling is silent regarding whether individual A had any knowledge or control over the plan, and it also fails to specify which version of the step transaction doctrine it applied.

3.3. *"Creeping" Acquisitions*

There is no such thing as a "creeping" reverse triangular merger under § 368(a)(2)(E). If the parent corporation already owns over 20% of the stock of the target corporation, a § 368(a)(2)(E) reorganization is not possible because of the statutory requirement that an amount of stock constituting "control" in the target corporation be exchanged in the reorganization transaction for voting stock of the acquiring parent corporation. Rev.Rul. 74–564, 1974–2 C.B. 124. A failed § 368(a)(2)(E) reverse triangular merger may, however, be recharacterized as a (B) reorganization under the principles of Rev.Rul. 67–448, 1967–2 C.B. 144, if the requirements for a (B) reorganization have been met. See Treas.Reg. § 1.368–2(j)(6), Exs. 4 and 5. This recharacterization will save the reorganization only if the sole consideration used is voting stock of the parent.

These problems are not presented in a § 368(a)(2)(D) forward triangular merger situation. Indeed, a forward triangular merger often is used as the second step in a "two-step acquisition" in which the acquiring corporation first purchases a majority of the stock of the target corporation and then causes the target to be merged into another subsidiary with the minority shareholders of the target receiving stock of the acquiring parent corporation. See, e.g., J.E. Seagram Corp. v. Commissioner, 104 T.C. 75 (1995).

4. "REMOTE" "CONTINUITY"

4.1. *Use of "Grandparent" Stock Prohibited*

While various subsections of § 368 permit the use by a first tier subsidiary of its parent's stock in a reorganization acquisition, the problem of "remote" continuity of interest still exists where stock of a corporation further removed in the chain of ownership is used in the acquisition transaction. Thus, Rev.Rul. 74–565, 1974–2 C.B. 125, held that an acquisition made by a second tier subsidiary using the stock of its "grandparent" did not qualify under § 368(a)(2)(E). Because, however, the second tier subsidiary that formally made the acquisition was formed solely for the purpose of the acquisition and disappeared as a result of the "reverse" merger, its existence was ignored; because the sole consideration was then the parent's voting stock, the transaction was viewed as an acquisition by the now first tier subsidiary of the stock of the target company in exchange for its parent's stock that qualified as a (B) reorganization under the principles of Rev.Rul. 67–448, 1967–2 C.B. 144.

4.2. *Drop-Downs Following Acquisitions*

Treas.Reg. §§ 1.368–1(d)(4) and 1.368–2(k), also discussed in preceding sections, permit certain post-reorganization transfers by the acquiring corporation of the target corporation's assets or stock to controlled corporations or to partnerships without violating the continuity of interest or continuity of business enterprise requirements. One of the purposes of these Regulations is to reflect the relaxation by Congress, in § 368(a)(2)(D) and (E), among other provisions, of the judicially developed doctrine that remote continuity of interest did not suffice to support reorganization treatment. See Notice of Proposed Rulemaking and Notice of Public Hearing, Continuity of Interest and Continuity of Business Enterprise, REG–252233–96, 1997–1 C.B. 802. Thus, for example, a forward triangular merger followed by a transfer of the acquired corporation's assets to a sister corporation can qualify under § 368. The Regulations do not, however, permit an acquisition using stock of a grandparent or higher tier corporation to qualify. Rev.Rul. 74–565, supra, continues to disqualify such transactions.

5. TAX RESULTS TO THE PARTIES TO A TRIANGULAR REORGANIZATION

5.1. *Section 368(a)(2)(D) Forward Triangular Merger*

5.1.1. *Target Corporation and Shareholders*

No gain or loss is recognized by the target corporation on the exchange with the acquiring corporation regardless of the nature of the property received from the acquiring corporation. Because the target corporation disappears by operation of state law, any nonqualifying boot not directly distributed to its shareholders or creditors is deemed to have been distributed to its shareholders or creditors, and thus no gain can be recognized under § 361(b).

As to the shareholders of the target corporation, no gain or loss will be recognized if they receive solely the stock of the acquiring parent corporation in exchange for their stock in the target corporation. I.R.C. § 354(a). If "boot" is involved, the shareholders may recognize gain under § 356, either as capital gain or as a dividend, depending on the circumstances. Section 358 provides an exchanged basis for the acquiring parent corporation's stock. If any boot is received, however, the basis is determined by first increasing the basis by the amount of any gain recognized by the shareholders as the result of the receipt of boot, and then decreasing it by the amount of cash and the fair market value of any other property received.

5.1.2.   *Acquiring Corporation*

Neither the acquiring subsidiary nor its parent generally recognizes any gain or loss on the transfer of the parent's shares in a forward triangular merger. Treas.Reg. § 1.1032–2 prevents gain recognition to the acquiring subsidiary corporation so long as the parent corporation stock was received by the subsidiary pursuant to the plan or reorganization. The acquiring subsidiary would be required to recognize gain, however, if it acquired some of its parent corporation's stock in a prior unrelated transaction and used that stock in the reorganization. If the acquiring subsidiary or its parent transfers any boot other than cash or its own securities, gain or loss must be recognized with respect to the boot transferred. Under § 362(b) the acquiring corporation's basis in the assets is equal to the target corporation's basis in those assets. The acquiring parent corporation's basis in its subsidiary's stock is determined under Treas.Reg. § 1.358–6, which is discussed in item 6, below.

Under § 381, the tax attributes of the target corporation, e.g., net operating loss carryovers, earnings and profits accounts, etc., carryover to the acquiring subsidiary corporation. Section 382 limits the post-acquisition use of any net operating loss carryovers of the target corporation. See Chapter 13.

5.2. *Section 368(a)(2)(E) Reverse Triangular Merger*

5.2.1.   *Target Corporation and Shareholders*

No gain or loss can be realized by the surviving target corporation as a result of the merger because it has not disposed of any of its assets. No statutory provision is necessary to shield it from recognition of gain or loss. The bases of all of its assets remain unchanged; the assets retain their historic bases.

The shareholders of the target corporation recognize no gain or loss if they receive solely the stock of the parent of the acquiring corporation in exchange for their stock in the target corporation. I.R.C. § 354(a). If "boot" is involved, the shareholders may recognize gain under § 356, as in the case for a forward triangular merger. Section 358 provides the stock received in the reorganization with an exchanged basis determined with reference to the basis of the target shares surrendered, subject to the same adjustments as are made in a forward triangular merger if boot is involved.

5.2.2. *Acquiring Corporation*

Neither the acquiring subsidiary corporation nor its parent generally recognizes any gain or loss on the transfer of the parent's shares in a § 368(a)(2)(E) reorganization. Although § 1032 on its face applies only to provide nonrecognition to the issuing parent corporation in a triangular merger, § 361 provides nonrecognition to the merged subsidiary of the parent in a § 368(a)(2)(E) reverse triangular merger. If the acquiring corporation or its parent transfers any boot other than cash or its own securities, gain or loss must be recognized with respect to the boot transferred. Because the target corporation remains in existence, its basis for its assets is unchanged. The acquiring parent corporation's basis in the stock of the surviving subsidiary is generally determined in the same manner as in a forward triangular merger.

Under § 381, the target corporation retains its tax attributes, but the § 382 limitations are applicable. See Chapter 13.

6. THE PARENT CORPORATION'S BASIS FOR THE STOCK OF THE SUBSIDIARY

There is no statutory provision to adjust the basis of the acquiring parent corporation in the stock of its subsidiary to reflect the subsidiary's basis in property acquired in a reorganization described in § 368(a)(2)(D) or (E). The statutory lacuna in the triangular reorganization area arose because of the grafting of §§ 368(a)(2)(D) and (E) onto the preexisting reorganization structure without adequate analysis of the implications of the change in structure. The issues are addressed in Treas.Reg. §§ 1.358–6 and 1.1032–2, which apply a common set of rules to forward and reverse triangular mergers, as well as to triangular (B) reorganizations and triangular (C) reorganizations. In general, the Regulations adopt an "over-the-top" model, i.e., the basis and gain results parallel those that occur if the parent corporation were to acquire the stock or assets of the target corporation and transfer them to its controlled subsidiary.

In a forward triangular merger and a triangular (C) reorganization, the acquiring parent corporation's basis in its subsidiary's stock after the transaction is adjusted as if the parent corporation had acquired the target corporation's assets in a transaction in which the parent corporation's basis in the assets was determined under § 362(b) and the parent corporation then transferred those assets to its subsidiary in a transaction in which the parent corporation's basis in the subsidiary corporation's stock was determined under § 358. As provided in § 358(d), the target corporation's liabilities must be taken into account in calculating the parent's basis in the acquiring subsidiary, but § 357(c) does not apply for these purposes. Treas.Reg. § 1.358–6(c). Thus, assuming that the subsidiary was a shell formed for purposes of the merger and the parent had a zero basis in the subsidiary immediately before the forward triangular merger, after the reorganization, the parent's basis in the subsidiary will be an amount equal to the subsidiary's basis for its assets acquired from the target minus the subsidiary's liabilities acquired from the target. See Treas.Reg. § 1.358–6(c)(1)(i), (c)(4), Ex. 1(e). Because § 357(c) does not apply, however, if the target's liabilities exceed its basis in the acquired assets, the parent's adjustment to the basis of its stock in the subsidiary equals zero, but the parent recognizes no gain. See Treas.Reg. § 1.358–6(c)(1)(ii), (c)(4), Ex. 1(f).[9]

Similar rules apply to a triangular (B) reorganization. The parent corporation is treated as having acquired the target corporation's stock directly and as having dropped the stock down to its subsidiary. Treas.Reg. § 1.358–6(c)(3).

The acquiring parent corporation's basis in the surviving subsidiary in a reverse triangular merger is also determined as if the target corporation's assets were acquired directly by the parent corporation and transferred to a subsidiary in a forward triangular merger. Treas.Reg. § 1.358–6(c)(2)(i)(A). If the acquiring parent corporation acquires less than all of the target corporation's stock in a reverse triangular merger, the parent corporation's basis in the surviving subsidiary is adjusted to reflect an allocable portion of the target corporation's basis in its assets. Treas.Reg. § 1.358–6(c)(2)(i)(B). A special rule applies if a reverse triangular merger is effected using a shell subsidiary corporation, organized for purposes of the merger, and the parent's voting stock is the only consideration. Because under Rev.Rul. 67–448, 1967–2 C.B. 144, such a transaction qualifies as a type (B) reorganization, the parent corporation may elect to take a basis in the target corporation's stock computed with reference to the aggregate basis of the former target corporation's shareholders. Treas.Reg. § 1.358–6(c)(2)(ii).

PROBLEM SET 9

1.   Ana, Bill, Claudette, Danny, and Erika each own 20 of the 100 issued and outstanding shares of voting common stock of T Corporation. T has no other stock outstanding. The fair market value of all 100 shares of T is $1,000,000. Each shareholder has a basis of $45,000. T Corporation is engaged in three businesses: it manufactures and sells the Bassamatic line of food processors; it packages and distributes frozen fish bait; and it operates a chain of fried squid fast food restaurants. P Corporation proposes to acquire T Corporation for stock and debt instruments, but for various non-tax reasons has decided that a direct asset acquisition is not desirable.

Which of the following alternative transactions will qualify as a tax-free reorganization? If the acquisition qualifies, is any boot involved? If there is boot, what is the amount of gain recognized by each shareholder of T?

(a)   T will merge into S Corporation, a newly formed subsidiary of P Corp. that has been capitalized with the consideration that will be transferred to the T shareholders. Each of the shareholders of T will receive the following consideration:

---

[9]   The Regulations for triangular reorganizations also apply in the consolidated return context. Treas.Reg. § 1.1502–30. In the consolidated return context, however, liabilities are taken into account in determining the parent corporation's basis in the stock of the acquiring subsidiary. As a result, the parent corporation will have an excess loss account to the extent liabilities exceed basis. This adjustment is possible in the consolidated return context because the excess loss account rules in effect permit the use of negative basis. Outside of consolidated returns, negative basis is not permitted.

(1) 800 shares of voting common stock of P having a fair market value of $160,000, plus a 20-year P debt instrument having an issue price and fair market value of $40,000.

(2) 400 shares of voting common stock of P having a fair market value of $80,000, plus a 20-year P debt instrument having an issue price and fair market value of $120,000.

(3) 300 shares of voting common stock of P having a fair market value of $60,000, plus a 20-year P debt instrument having an issue price and fair market value of $140,000.

(4) 800 shares of nonvoting preferred stock of P having a fair market value of $160,000, plus a 20-year P debt instrument having an issue price and fair market value of $40,000.

(5) 800 shares of voting common stock of P having a fair market value of $160,000, plus 200 shares of nonvoting preferred stock of S having a fair market value of $40,000.

(6) 800 shares of voting common stock of P having a fair market value of $160,000, plus a 20-year S debt instrument having an issue price and fair market value of $40,000.

(7) Ana and Bill each will receive 1,000 shares of voting common stock of P, worth $200 per share, while Claudette, Danny, and Erika each will receive $200,000 of cash.

(b) (1) T will sell the frozen fish bait business for $200,000 and will use the proceeds to redeem all of Erika's stock. Following the redemption, T will merge into S. Ana, Bill, Claudette, and Danny each will receive 400 shares of P stock having a value of $80,000 and $120,000 of P debt instruments. (Aggregate consideration paid to Ana, Bill, Claudette, and Danny is $320,000 in stock and $480,000 in debt instruments.)

(2) T will sell publicly traded portfolio stock investments that it accumulated in excess of working capital needs for $100,000 and will use the proceeds to redeem one-half of Erika's stock. Following the redemption, T will merge into S. Ana, Bill, Claudette, and Danny each will receive 400 shares of P stock having a value of $80,000 and $120,000 of P debt instruments. Erika will receive 200 shares of P stock having a value of $40,000 and $60,000 of P debt instruments. (Aggregate consideration paid to Ana, Bill, Claudette, Danny and Erika in the merger is $360,000 in stock and $540,000 in debt instruments.)

(c) (1) Assume the same basic facts as in (a), but last year, Ana, Bill, and Claudette each sold their shares of T to S Corp. for $200,000 cash. In the current year, T Corp. merged into S Corp. with Danny and Erika each receiving only stock of P Corp. worth $200,000.

(2) What if last year, Ana, Bill, Claudette, Danny, and Erika each sold 14 of their 20 shares of T to S Corp. for $140,000 cash. In the current year, T Corp. merged into S Corp. and Ana, Bill, Claudette, Danny, and Erika each received only stock of P Corp. worth $60,000 for their remaining 6 shares of T.

(d) Assume the same basic facts as in (a), but that T Corp. had outstanding options held by Fred, who does not otherwise hold an interest in T Corp., to purchase T stock. Fred's options entitled Fred to purchase 20 shares of T stock for $200,000.

(1) What are the consequences of Fred being issued an option to purchase 200 shares of P stock for $200,000 in consideration of cancellation of Fred's options to purchase T Corp. stock?

(2) What are the consequences Fred being paid cash to surrender the options on T stock?

(e) (1) Assume the same facts as in (a)(1), except that P Corp owns 300 shares of S Corp. voting common stock (all of the S Corp. voting stock), and S Corp. also has outstanding 100 shares of preferred stock. The preferred stock is nonvoting and all 100 shares of S Corp. nonvoting preferred stock are held by the Buggy Whip Manufacturer's Union Pension Trust Fund.

(2) The preferred stock is voting stock and only 75 shares of the S Corp. voting preferred stock held are by the Buggy Whip Manufacturer's Union Pension Trust Fund; P Corp. holds 25 shares of the S Corp. voting preferred stock.

(f) (1) Assume the same facts as in (a)(1). P Corp. owns 100% of the stock of X Corp., which in turn owns 100% of the stock of S Corp. T Corp. is merged into S Corp. and the shareholders of T receive voting common stock of P Corp.

(2) P Corp. owns 100% of the stock of both X Corp. and S Corp. T Corp. is merged into S Corp. and the shareholders of T receive voting common stock of P Corp. Following the merger P Corp, transfers the stock of S Corp. to X Corp.

(3) P Corp. owns 100% of the stock of X Corp., which in turn owns 100% of the membership units in S LLC. T Corp. is merged into S LLC and the shareholders of T receive voting common stock of P Corp.

2.   The stock of T Corporation is publicly traded and widely held. T has only voting common stock outstanding. P Corporation acquired T Corporation in the following transactions, the plan for which was announced in advance. P Corporation acquired 51% of the outstanding T stock pursuant to a tender offer in which it paid cash. Immediately thereafter, P formed a new wholly owned subsidiary, S Corporation, which it capitalized with P nonvoting preferred stock, followed by a merger of T Corporation into S Corporation. As a result of the merger of T Corporation into S Corporation, the T Corporation minority shareholders (who owned the 49% of T Corporation not acquired by P Corporation in the tender offer) surrendered all of their T stock and received P nonvoting preferred stock in exchange for their T Corporation stock. Do these transactions result in a tax-free forward triangular merger?

3.   T Corp. merged into S Corp., a newly formed subsidiary of P Corp. that had been capitalized with $1,000 plus 5,000 shares of P Corp. common stock having an aggregate fair market value of $1,000,000. T Corp.'s assets had a fair market value of $1,300,000 and a basis of $400,000. Pursuant to the

merger, S Corp. assumed $300,000 of T Corp.'s debts secured by the assets. Each of the shareholders of T received 1,000 of the P Corp. shares held by S Corp. immediately before the merger.

(a) What is P's basis for its S stock immediately after the merger?

(b) What if T Corp.'s debts were $500,000?

4. Ana, Bill, Claudette, Danny, and Erika each own 20 of the 100 issued and outstanding shares of voting common stock of T Corporation. T has no other stock outstanding. The fair market value of all 100 shares of T is $1,000,000. Each shareholder has a basis of $45,000. T Corporation is engaged in three businesses: it manufactures and sells the Bassamatic line of food processors; it packages and distributes frozen fish bait; and it operates a chain of fried squid fast food restaurants. P Corporation proposes to acquire T Corporation for stock and debt instruments, but for various non-tax reasons has decided that a direct asset acquisition is not desirable. (These are the same basic facts as in the introductory paragraphs to question 1.)

(a) P Corp. will form a new wholly owned subsidiary, S Corp., which will merge into T Corp. Under the terms of the merger, P's stock in S will be exchanged for T stock, and each of the shareholders of T will receive the following alternative consideration in exchange for their T stock:

(1) 800 shares of voting common stock of P having a fair market value of $160,000 plus a 20-year P debt instrument having an issue price and fair market value of $40,000.

(2) 750 shares of voting common stock of P having a fair market value of $150,000 plus a 20-year P debt instrument having an issue price and fair market value of $50,000.

(3) 1000 shares of nonvoting common stock of P having a fair market value of $200,000.

(4) 800 shares of voting preferred stock of P having a fair market value of $160,000 plus a 20-year P debt instrument having an issue price and fair market value of $40,000.

(5) 800 shares of voting common stock of P having a fair market value of $160,000 plus 200 shares of nonvoting preferred stock of T having a fair market value of $40,000.

(b) Assume the same facts as in question 4(a)(1) except that T Corporation also has outstanding 100 shares of nonvoting preferred stock, which are held by the State of Utopia Public Employees' Retirement Pension Trust Fund. Must the nonvoting preferred stock of T (which is the surviving corporation) be surrendered in exchange for P stock in order to qualify as a reorganization?

(c) Assume the basic facts as in question 4(a)(1), but Erika votes against the merger (which is adopted by a 80–20 vote of T's shares). Erika exercises state law dissenters' rights to be paid in cash. S is merged into T and Ana, Bill, Claudette, and Danny each receive 999 shares of voting stock of P, worth $199,800, and $200 cash. (Aggregate consideration paid to Ana, Bill, Claudette, and Danny is $799,200 in stock and $800 in cash.)

    (1)   Erika is paid out of T's cash balances existing before the merger.

    (2)   Erika is paid by T after the merger, with cash contributed by P.

5.   Assume the same basic facts as in the introductory paragraphs to question 4. S Corp. is an existing wholly owned subsidiary of P Corporation. S was organized 15 years ago and is engaged in the manufacture of fishing lures. S will be merged into T and each of the shareholders of T will receive 1,000 shares of voting stock of P, having a fair market value of $200,000. Are the following alternative transactions tax-free?

    (a)   Following the merger, T will sell the fishing lure business to Y Corp. for $1,000,000 and the proceeds will be used to expand the Bassamatic business.

    (b)   Following the merger, T will sell the frozen fish bait business and the fried squid business for $600,000 and use the proceeds to expand the fishing lure business.

    (c)   Following the merger, T will sell the frozen fish bait business and the fried squid business for $600,000 and use the proceeds to expand the Bassamatic business.

6.   (a)   Assume the same basic facts as in the introductory paragraphs to question 4. Three years ago, P purchased the 40 shares of T stock owned by Ana and Bill for $400,000, thus holding 40% of the outstanding T stock. Last year, S Corp., a newly formed subsidiary of P, was merged into T Corp. As a result of the merger, P's stock of S Corp. was canceled and Claudette, Danny, and Erika each received voting common stock of P Corp. worth $200,000 ($600,000 in the aggregate). P's 40 shares of T Corp. thereby became 100% of the outstanding stock of T What are the tax results to the parties?

    (b)   Three years ago, P purchased the 20 shares of T stock owned by Ana for $200,000, thus holding 20% of the outstanding T stock. Last year, S Corp., a newly formed subsidiary of P, was merged into T Corp. As a result of the merger, P's stock of S Corp. was canceled and Bill, Claudette, Danny, and Erika each received voting common stock of P Corp. worth $200,000 ($800,000 in the aggregate). P's 20 shares of T thereby became 100% of the outstanding stock of T. What are the tax results to the parties?

7.   (a)   P Corp. owns 100% of the stock of X Corp., which in turn owns 100% of the stock of S Corp. S Corp. is merged into T Corp. and the shareholders of T receive voting common stock of P Corp. What are the tax results to the parties?

    (b)   P Corp. owns 100% of the stock of both X Corp. and S Corp. S Corp. is merged into T Corp. and the shareholders of T receive voting common stock of P Corp. Following the merger P Corp, transfers the stock of T Corp. to X Corp.

    (c)   P Corp. owns 100% of the stock of X Corp., which in turn owns 100% of S LLC, a special purpose vehicle organized solely for the purpose of the acquisition and which was capitalized only with the consideration to be received by the T shareholders in the merger. S LLC is merged into T Corp. and the shareholders of T receive voting common stock of P Corp.

8.   P Corp. formed a wholly owned subsidiary, S Corp., for the purpose of acquiring T Corp. in a reverse triangular merger. P Corp. capitalized S Corp. with 100 shares of voting common stock of P Corp. that would be the consideration provided to the sole shareholder of T Corp. in the merger, and P Corp. received one share of S Corp. stock. T Corp.'s sole asset was a parcel of land with a basis of $100,000, subject to mortgage of $95,000. T Corp.'s sole shareholder, Franklin, had a basis of $70,000 in the T Corp. stock. In the merger of S Corp. into T Corp., Franklin received the 100 shares of P Corp. voting common stock P held by S Corp., and P Corp.'s one share of S Corp. was converted into the only outstanding share of T Corp. What is P Corp.'s basis in its T Corp. stock after the reverse triangular merger?

SECTION 6.   ACQUISITIVE TYPE (D) REORGANIZATIONS

INTERNAL REVENUE CODE: Sections 354(b); 357(a); 368(a)(1)(D), (a)(2)(A), (a)(2)(H), (c); 312(h)(2).

REGULATIONS: Section 1.368–2(k)(2), Ex. 6, –2(*l*).

A type (D) reorganization occurs upon the transfer of some or all of a corporation's assets to a newly created or existing corporation, for example, where X Corporation transfers some of its assets to new or existing Y Corporation, if, following the transfer, the transferor corporation (X Corporation) distributes the stock of the transferee corporation (Y Corporation) to its shareholders in a distribution that meets the requirements of § 354 or § 355, with § 356 potentially applicable to each type, depending on the presence of boot. The requirements for a type (D) reorganization differ significantly, however, depending on whether the distribution to the shareholders of the transferor corporation qualifies for nonrecognition under § 354/§ 356, on the one hand, or § 355/§ 356, on the other hand. As a result, there are many different types of transactions, some of which are quite dissimilar, that qualify as type (D) reorganizations. A type (D) reorganization that results by virtue of a distribution of stock that qualifies under § 354 is commonly termed a "nondivisive" or "acquisitive" type (D) "reorganization," while a type (D) reorganization that results by virtue of a distribution of stock that qualifies under § 355 is commonly termed a "divisive" type (D) reorganization. This Chapter focuses on nondivisive type (D) reorganizations under § 354. (Divisive reorganizations qualifying under § 355 are discussed in Chapter 12.)

For the distribution to the shareholders to qualify under § 354, the transferor corporation (X) must transfer "*substantially all*" of its assets to the transferee (Y) and liquidate (I.R.C. § 354(b)(1)). Neither of these requirements is prerequisite for the stock distribution to the shareholders to qualify under § 355. The asset distribution and liquidation requirements of § 354(b) are designed to prevent a corporate division that does not qualify for nonrecognition under § 355 from qualifying as a reorganization under § 368.

In addition, one or more of the transferor corporation's shareholder's must "control" the transferee corporation after the transaction. In an acquisitive type (D) reorganization "*control*" of the transferee corporation (Y), which after the transaction must be held by the transferor corporation's (X's) shareholders, is defined by § 368(a)(2)(H), through a cross reference to § 304(c), as *at least 50%* of combined voting power *or* at least 50% of total value of shares of all classes of stock, rather than by § 368(c). But in a divisive type (D) reorganization, whether or not the transferor corporation (X) liquidates, for the distribution to the shareholders to qualify under § 355, and thus for the asset transfer to constitute a type (D) reorganization, control is defined by the normal rule in § 368(c), requiring 80% of combined voting power and 80% of each other class of stock.

A variety of transactions fall under the rubric of "nondivisive" type (D) reorganizations. These transactions can be quite dissimilar. A nondivisive type (D) reorganization often involves little or no change in beneficial ownership. For example, if A and B equally own all of each of X Corporation and Y Corporation, and X Corporation transfers all of its assets to Y Corporation, following which X Corporation liquidates, the transaction is a type (D) reorganization. Other type (D) reorganizations, however, can effect a substantial change in beneficial ownership.

(1) If W Corporation, the stock of which was owned equally by E and F, transferred all of its assets to Z Corporation, in which E, F, and G each owned 10 shares, in exchange for 30 shares of Z corporation voting stock, which W Corporation distributed to E and F in a liquidation distribution qualifying under § 354, the transaction is a type (D) reorganization. In this, case, after the reorganization Z Corporation's shares are owned as follows: E owns 25, F owns 25, and G owns 10. E and F have substantially increased their ownership of Z Corporation.

(2) If T Corporation, the stock of which was owned equally by E and F, transferred all of its assets to Q Corporation, all 50 of the shares of which were owned by G in exchange for 50 shares of Q corporation voting stock, which T Corporation distributed to E and F in a liquidation distribution qualifying under § 354, the transaction also is a type (D) reorganization. In this, case, after the reorganization Q Corporation's shares are owned as follows: E owns 25, F owns 25, and G owns 50. G has acquired a substantial interest in T Corporation.

The asset transfer in both acquisitive and divisive type (D) reorganizations can overlap with a § 351 incorporation transfer, which, like a reorganization, is a nonrecognition event. There is not an overlap, however, in the case of acquisitive type (D) reorganizations that depend on the 50% control test rather than the 80% control test of § 351 (through cross-reference to § 368(c)). The liquidation of the transferor corporation, the second step in an acquisitive type (D) reorganization, overlaps with the liquidation provisions, which, when they apply, require corporate and shareholder gain or loss recognition. However, when the liquidation is pursuant to a plan of reorganization, § 354 provides nonrecognition to the shareholders, except to the extent of boot, which is governed by § 356. Section 361 displaces § 336 to provide nonrecognition to the liquidating corporation. Section 361(c) requires, however, that the liquidating corporation recognize gain (but not loss) with respect to all other property distributed in the liquidation.

Atlas Tool Co., Inc. v. Commissioner

United States Court of Appeals, Third Circuit, 1980.
614 F.2d 860.

■ GIBBONS, CIRCUIT JUDGE.

* * * Stephan Schaffan is the sole stockholder of Atlas, a New Jersey corporation still in existence, and of Fletcher, also a New Jersey corporation, which was dissolved in 1970. The deficiency assessed against the Schaffans involves the tax treatment of over $400,000 in cash distributed to Schaffan upon the dissolution of Fletcher. The Schaffans reported this distribution as a long-term capital gain but the Commissioner of Internal Revenue and the Tax Court treated it as a dividend, taxable as ordinary income. The individual taxpayers contend that the distribution from Fletcher qualified for capital gains treatment, while the Commissioner urges that the Tax Court erred in calculating the amount of the dividend, and that a higher tax is due. * * * We affirm the Tax Court in all respects.

I.   The Schaffan's Individual Tax Liability

In October 1970, Schaffan owned all the stock of Atlas and of Fletcher. Atlas was then engaged in the business of designing and selling products for the hobby industry, principally model railroads. Prior to 1960, Atlas also manufactured such products. In 1960, Fletcher was incorporated, acquired Atlas' plastic molding machines, and thereafter, conducted the manufacturing operations previously conducted by Atlas. * * * Atlas was virtually the only customer of Fletcher.

During the 1960's, Atlas continually increased its purchase of foreign manufactured components, which were cheaper than those domestically manufactured. Eventually, Schaffan decided that the manufacturing operations being performed by Fletcher were no longer essential since the same quality components could be acquired at a lower cost from foreign sources. Accordingly, in October 1970, at the directors' and stockholders' meetings, it was voted that Fletcher liquidate * * *.

On November 5, 1970, Fletcher transferred to Atlas all its machinery and equipment for an appraised price of $100,250, and all its inventory for its $14,600 cost. * * * On November 19, 1970, Schaffan received from Fletcher a cash distribution of $482,246.82 which represented all of its remaining assets. * * *

The machinery and equipment transferred to Atlas remained in place in the building otherwise occupied by Atlas. Fletcher's former employees were employed by Atlas, initially in its packing and shipping departments. The machinery and equipment, left in place, was idle for a time. However, by December 1970, Atlas began experiencing delivery and quality difficulties with its foreign suppliers, and to keep its inventory adequate, it soon started operating some of the Fletcher machines. By the end of 1971, all the machinery and equipment acquired from Fletcher were in operation.

On the Schaffan's 1970 federal income tax return they reported $400,000 as a distribution from Fletcher in complete liquidation under section 331 * * *. They claimed an adjusted basis of $10,000 for the Fletcher stock, and paid tax on a long-term capital gain of $390,000. In the notice of deficiency, the Commissioner asserted that the amount distributed to Schaffan was actually $482,246.82 (an amount not contested by the taxpayer) and that the transaction was not a section 331–337 liquidation, but a reorganization within the meaning of 26 U.S.C. § 368(a)(1)(D). * * * [I]f the transaction was a reorganization, the distribution by Fletcher to Schaffan would be covered by the "boot" provision of section 356, and thus be treated as ordinary income rather than as a capital gain pursuant to section 331.

Section 356(a)(2) provides that money distributed to stockholders in a reorganization shall, to the extent of the stockholders' gain, be treated as a dividend out of earnings and profits of "the corporation." The Commissioner contends that when, as here, there is complete identity of shareholders in the two corporate parties to a D reorganization, the earnings and profits of both corporations should be taken into account to determine how much of the cash distributed by either is the equivalent of a dividend. The combined earnings and profits of Fletcher and Atlas exceeded $5 million, and thus the Commissioner proposes to treat the entire $482,246.82, less Schaffan's $10,000 basis for his Fletcher stock, as a section 356(a)(2) dividend.

The Tax Court held that the transaction was a D reorganization, and therefore section 356(a)(2) applied, but that the dividend treatment was authorized only to the extent of earnings and profits of Fletcher. It computed those earnings and profits as $440,342.56, and determined that the difference between that sum and $472,246.82 was taxable as a long-term capital gain. The Schaffans contend that the entire $472,262.82 was a long-term capital gain. The Commissioner contends it was all a section 356(a)(2) dividend.

We turn first to the Schaffan's contention. They point to the adoption by appropriate corporate resolution of a plan of complete liquidation of Fletcher * * *, to the accomplishment of both the disposition and distribution of Fletcher's assets * * *, and to Fletcher's dissolution. * * * [T]hey argue that the distribution is "in complete liquidation" of Fletcher and should, therefore, "be treated as in full payment in exchange for (Fletcher) stock" pursuant to section 331. Taxpayers contend that in the absence of any proof of an intent to avoid taxes, it was error for the Tax Court to characterize the transaction as a D reorganization instead of a complete liquidation.

Our starting point is the text of section 368(a)(1)(D) * * *. Clearly there was, as that section requires, a transfer by Fletcher of all or part of its assets in this case all its machinery, equipment and inventory were transferred to another corporation, Atlas. In addition, Schaffan, the sole stockholder of Fletcher, was in control of Atlas "immediately after" the transfer. No stock or securities of Atlas were distributed to Schaffan. But despite the language in section 368(a)(1)(D) to that effect, it has been held that a distribution is not necessary where the ownership of the transferor and transferee is identical because such a distribution would be a mere formality.[3]

A distribution pursuant to section 368(a)(1)(D) must also qualify under section 354 or section 355 in order for section 356 to be applicable. Section 355, which concerns the distribution of stock and securities of a controlled corporation, does not come into play in the Fletcher-Atlas transaction. Section 354, however, is applicable to the facts in this case. It provides for the nonrecognition of gain or loss on an exchange of stock or securities solely for stock or securities. Where there is complete identity of ownership, section 354, like section 368(a)(1)(D), has been construed not to require the meaningless formality of such an exchange.[4] However, section 354(a):

> shall not apply to an exchange in pursuance of a plan of reorganization within the meaning of section 368(a)(1)(D), unless—
>
> (A) the corporation to (Atlas) which the (Fletcher) assets are transferred acquires substantially all of the assets of the transferor of such assets. . . .

26 U.S.C. § 354(b)(1)(A). The "substantially all" requirement is chiefly determined by focusing on the transfer of the operating assets by the transferor, and not on the unneeded liquid assets such as cash and

---

[3]   See Davant v. Commissioner, 366 F.2d 874, 886–87 (5th Cir. 1966) cert. denied, 386 U.S. 1022 * * * (1967); James Armour, Inc. v. Commissioner, 43 T.C. 295, 307 (1964); Commissioner v. Morgan, 288 F.2d 676, 680 (3d Cir. 1961) * * *.

[4]   Wilson v. Commissioner, 46 T.C. 334, 344 (1966); James Armour, Inc. v. Commissioner, 43 T.C. at 307; cf. Commissioner v. Morgan, 288 F.2d at 680.

accounts receivable.[5] In light of the facts that all of Fletcher's assets except cash and accounts receivable went to Atlas, that Atlas had hired all of Fletcher's employees, that the operating assets never changed location, and were utilized within four months to manufacture the same products, we conclude that the "substantially all" assets requirement of section 354(b)(1)(A) was satisfied.

Section 354(b)(1)(B) requires, as well, that the distribution of securities in a D reorganization be "in pursuance of a plan of reorganization." The transfer was certainly a part of an overall plan. The controlling shareholder chose to call the transaction a plan of liquidation. If what resulted was a plan of reorganization, the chosen label is not dispositive.

We conclude, as did the Tax Court, that the transaction which resulted in Fletcher's distribution of $482,246.82 to Schaffan met all the statutory requisites of a D reorganization. The Schaffans urge, however, that two nonstatutory requirements must be satisfied before a transaction, characterized by a taxpayer as a liquidation, may be treated as a reorganization: tax avoidance motive and a continuity of business enterprise.

The Tax Court, while expressing some skepticism about the absence of a tax avoidance motive in structuring the transaction, held that a finding of such a motive was not required. The Schaffans, in advancing their tax avoidance motive argument, rely on cases such as Gregory v. Helvering, 293 U.S. 465 * * * (1935), which held that taxpayers cannot take advantage of the tax-free reorganization provisions of the Code in the absence of a business purpose for the transaction other than a purpose to avoid taxes. That requirement was imposed to prevent the resort to liquidation and reincorporation as a way of bailing out earnings and profits without appropriate payment of taxes.

There is no disagreement among the parties that a business purpose is required for a reorganization. The Schaffans contend that there was a business purpose for liquidation as opposed to reincorporation, and that from this business purpose for liquidation one can infer a non-tax avoidance motive for the overall transaction. However, the liquidation-reincorporation doctrine is aimed at recharacterizing liquidations in light of the entire transaction, notwithstanding liquidation motives. Thus the liquidation purpose alone, and therefore the inference of a non-tax avoidance motive from it, cannot by definition be dispositive, and

---

[5] See American Mfg. Co. v. Commissioner, 55 T.C. 204, 221–22 (1970) (transfer of operating assets sufficient; receivables and cash not necessary to conduct business); Reef Corp. v. Commissioner, 368 F.2d 125, 131 (5th Cir. 1966) * * * (transfer of operating assets without liquid cash assets qualified as substantially all); Moffat v. Commissioner, 363 F.2d 262, 268 (9th Cir. 1966) * * * (transfer of key personnel and operating assets qualified as substantially all); James Armour, Inc. v. Commissioner, 43 T.C. at 309 (transfer of cash and receivables not necessary to qualify as substantially all); cf. DeGroff v. Commissioner, 444 F.2d 1385, 1386 (10th Cir. 1971) (substantially all requirement met without actual transfer where taxpayer owned and controlled both corporations). * * *

certainly does not prevent the characterization of the transaction as a D reorganization.

The Treasury Regulations state the essence of the requirement as:

> [t]he readjustments involved in the exchanges or distributions effected in the consummation (of a plan of reorganization) must be undertaken for reasons germane to the continuance of the business of a corporation a party to the reorganization.

26 C.F.R. § 1.368–2(g) (1979). The focus of the nonstatutory test is not, therefore, whether there were tax avoidance motives, but whether, objectively, there was continuity of business rather than termination of business. It is not significant that one party to the transaction was liquidated since that is a fairly common feature of a reorganization. What is critical is whether the new corporation carries forward the business enterprise of the old. The continuity of interest concept is "at the heart of the nonrecognition provisions."[12]

Sometimes, a taxpayer will seek to establish that the reorganization took place, thus postponing payment of any tax. In other cases, especially where, as here, there is a distribution of liquid assets, the taxpayer will prefer to have the liquidation aspect separated from the rest of the transaction so as to qualify for capital gains treatment. In response, the Commissioner will seek to treat all the events as one transaction and thus characterize it as a reorganization in order to tax the distribution under section 356(a) at ordinary income rates. The subjective motivation of neither the taxpayer nor the Commissioner is relevant. The test must be whether, objectively, the transferee corporation, if it otherwise qualifies for reorganization treatment, has a continuity of business enterprise with the transferor corporation. Thus we agree with the Tax Court that there was no requirement that it find a tax avoidance motive in order to classify the transaction as a D reorganization.

While the Schaffans urge that there was no continuity of business enterprise, the record establishes otherwise. * * * Within four months, the machinery and equipment was placed in operation and within a year all of it was utilized to make the same products as formerly. Atlas retained all of Fletcher's employees. The business enterprise which Atlas conducted was substantially the same as that formerly conducted by Fletcher. Complete identity of business operations is not required.* * * The Tax Court did not err in holding that the Fletcher-Atlas transaction provided the continuity of business enterprise referred to in the Treasury Regulations. Since both the statutory requirements for a D reorganization and the nonstatutory continuity of business enterprise test are on this record satisfied, we must affirm the Tax Court's determination that there was a reorganization and that section 356(a) applies to the distribution of cash from Fletcher to Schaffan.

---

[12] B. Bittker & J. Eustice, Federal Income Taxation of Corporations and Shareholders, P 14.01 at 14–3 (abridged ed. 1971).

DETAILED ANALYSIS

1.   CONSEQUENCES OF (D) REORGANIZATION CLASSIFICATION

As in *Atlas Tool Co.*, a type (D) reorganization frequently is found where the form of the transaction under state law is something else, such as an asset sale and purchase. Because there are no statutory restrictions on boot, and pursuant to judicial doctrine and the Regulations, it is not necessary actually to issue any stock where the ownership of the transferor and transferee corporations are perfectly congruent; asset sales from one corporation to another corporation with identical stock ownership followed by a cash distribution in liquidation of the transferor corporation are particularly susceptible to recharacterization as a (D) reorganization.

Whether the characterization of a transaction as a type (D) reorganization is disadvantageous or advantageous to the taxpayers depends on a variety of facts and circumstances, including the amount of gain or loss realized by the transferor corporation, which will be recognized if the transaction is treated as a sale but will not be recognized if the transaction is treated as a type (D) reorganization. At the shareholder level, if the shareholders are individuals, liquidation treatment results in recovery of basis of the stock and capital gains treatment of the excess of the amount realized over basis, while (D) reorganization treatment results in possible dividend treatment under § 356(a)(2). As long as long-term capital gains and dividends are both taxed at the same rate, however, this differing consequence is of little import unless the shareholder has otherwise unusable capital losses. If, however, the shareholder is a corporation, reorganization treatment is more advantageous because corporations do not enjoy any capital gain preference, but are entitled to a § 243 dividends received deduction with respect to amounts characterized as a dividend under § 356(a).

2.   DEFINITIONAL PROBLEMS

2.1. *Reorganization Versus Asset Sale and Purchase*

In Warsaw Photographic Associates, Inc. v. Commissioner, 84 T.C. 21 (1985), the taxpayer sought type (D) reorganization status, but the Tax Court held that a reorganization had not occurred. Warsaw Studios, Inc. (Studios) conducted a photography business. Warsaw & Co., Inc. owned all the preferred stock and 7,549 shares of common stock of Studios. Approximately 2,000 shares of Studio's common stock were owned by ten employees of Studios. The ten employee-shareholders of Studios formed Warsaw Photographic Studios, Inc. (Photographic), which issued 100 shares of common stock to each of the ten shareholders. At the same time, Studios transferred its operating assets to Photographic for $21,000, and the employee-shareholders surrendered their stock in Studios. No Photographic stock was transferred to Studios or to Warsaw & Co, but Photographic issued 10 additional shares to each of its ten shareholders. Photographic took the position that the transaction constituted a (D) reorganization, claiming depreciation deductions on the operating assets based on a transferred basis from Studios and utilizing Studios' net operating loss carryover deductions. The court held that the absence of a transfer of stock from Photographic to

Studios and a subsequent distribution of that Photographic stock to the shareholders of Studios was fatal to the claimed reorganization. It distinguished *Atlas Tool Co.* and similar cases finding a reorganization without the requisite stock-for-assets transfer and stock distribution on the ground that in all of those cases the stock ownership of the transferor and transferee was identical and that therefore the actual distribution of stock "would be a mere formality." The additional 100 shares of Photographic stock issued to its existing shareholders did not meet the statutory requirement because they were issued to the acquiring corporation's shareholders in proportion to their pre-existing ownership of the acquiring corporation rather than to the shareholders of the acquired corporation (Studios) in proportion to their ownership in that corporation. The transaction had been carefully structured to avoid the transfer of any Photographic stock to Studios at any time, and Warsaw & Co., Inc., the dominant shareholder of Studios, received no stock of Photographic. The transaction was held to be a sale and purchase of assets.

2.2. *"All Cash" Type (D) Reorganizations*

Treas.Reg. § 1.368–2(*l*) adopts the long-standing judicial and administrative position reflected in *Atlas Tool* that a stock distribution is meaningless when the ownership of the target and acquiring corporations is identical. Treas.Reg. § 1.368–2(*l*)(2)(i) provides that the distribution requirement under §§ 368(a)(1)(D) and 354(b)(1)(B) is deemed to have been satisfied despite the fact that no stock and/or securities are actually issued in a transaction otherwise described in § 368(a)(1)(D) if the same person or persons own, directly or indirectly, all of the stock of the transferor and transferee corporations in identical proportions.[10] For purposes of determining identity of ownership, an individual, all members of the individual's family, as described in § 318(a)(2)(C), will be treated as one individual. In addition, the attribution from entity rules of § 318(a)(2) are applied without regard to the 50% ownership limitation for attribution from corporations. Treas.Reg. § 1.368–(*l*)(2)(ii). Complete identity of ownership is not required. The Regulations disregard a de minimis variation in ownership. Treas.Reg. § 1.368–2(*l*)(3), Ex. 4, illustrates a de minimis variation with a situation in which A, B, and C each own, respectively, 34%, 33%, and 33% of the transferor's stock and A, B, C, and D each own, respectively, 33%, 33%, 33% and 1% of the transferee's stock. In addition, preferred stock described in § 1504(a)(4) (generally non-voting preferred stock with limited participation in growth) is not taken into account in determining ownership. Treas.Reg. § 1.368–2(*l*)(2)(ii).

The Regulations provide that if no consideration is received, or the value of the consideration received in the transaction is less than the fair market value of the transferor corporation's assets, the transferee corporation is treated as issuing stock with a value equal to the excess of the fair market value of the transferor corporation's assets over the value of the consideration actually received in the transaction. If the value of the

---

[10] An exception provides that the no-distribution-is-necessary rule will not apply to cause a related party triangular reorganization that is a type (A), (C), or (G) reorganization to be treated as a type (D) reorganization. Treas.Reg. § 1.368–2(*l*)(2)(iv).

consideration received in the transaction is equal to the fair market value of the transferor corporation's assets, the transferee corporation will be deemed to issue a nominal share of stock to the transferor corporation in addition to the actual consideration exchanged for the transferor corporation's assets. The deemed stock is then deemed to be distributed to the shareholders of the transferor corporation and transferred through chains of ownership to the extent necessary to reflect the actual ownership of the transferee and transferor corporations. Treas.Reg. § 1.368–2(*l*)(2)(i)

2.2.1.   *Allocation of Basis in All Cash D Reorganizations*

Treas.Reg. § 1.358–2 deals with stock basis in an all cash type D reorganization. If an actual shareholder of the acquiring corporation is deemed to receive a nominal share of stock of the issuing corporation described in Treas.Reg. § 1.368–2(*l*), that shareholder must, after allocating and adjusting the basis of the nominal share in accordance with the rules of Treas.Reg. § 1.358–1, and after adjusting the basis in the nominal share for any transfers described in Treas.Reg. § 1.358–1, designate the share of stock of the acquiring corporation to which the basis, if any, of the nominal share will attach. Under these rules, the ability to designate the share of stock of the acquiring corporation to which the basis of the surrendered stock or securities of the target will attach applies only to a shareholder that actually owns shares in the issuing corporation. Thus, for example, if in an all cash type-D reorganization, Y Corporation, a first tier subsidiary of P Corporation, acquires the assets of T Corporation, a second tier subsidiary of P Corporation, owned by X Corporation, a first tier subsidiary of P Corporation, X Corporation cannot designate any share of Y Corporation stock to which the basis, if any, of the nominal share of Y Corporation stock will attach; and P Corporation cannot designate a share of Y Corporation stock to which basis will attach because P Corporation's basis in the nominal share of Y Corporation stock (deemed to have been distributed to it by X Corporation) is zero (its fair market value).

2.3. *Reorganization Versus Stock Sale and Purchase*

A type (D) reorganization sometimes can be found in purported "cross-chain" sales of corporate subsidiaries. In Rev.Rul. 2004–83, 2004–2 C.B. 157, a parent corporation (P) sold the stock of a wholly owned subsidiary (T) for cash to another wholly owned subsidiary (S), following which the acquired subsidiary (T) was completely liquidated into the acquiring subsidiary (S). The ruling held that if the events occurred pursuant to an integrated plan, the transaction would be treated as a type (D) reorganization. As a consequence, § 338 could not apply to step-up the basis in the T assets because there was no stock purchase within the meaning of § 338(h)(3)(A). Note that if P, S, and T are not members of a consolidated group and the step transaction doctrine does not apply to step together the stock sale and liquidation, the stock sale would be treated as a distribution in redemption of the S stock under § 304(a)(1) and the liquidation of T into S would qualify as a liquidation under § 332. In this regard, the ruling concluded: "There is no policy that requires § 304 to be applied when § 368(a)(1)(D) would otherwise apply. See J. Comm. on Tax'n., 98th Cong. 2nd Sess., General Explanation of the Revenue Provisions of the Deficit Reduction Act of 1984

192 (Comm. Print 1984). Moreover, the legislative history to the Deficit Reduction Act of 1984, P.L. 98–369, 1984–3 (Vol. 1) C.B. 1, indicates that § 304 was not intended to override reorganization treatment."

2.4. *Section 351 Transaction Versus Reorganization*

Rev. Rul. 2015–10, 2015–21 I.R.B. 973, dealt with the characterization of a transaction in which pursuant to a plan (1) a parent corporation transferred all of the interests in its wholly-owned limited liability company that was taxable as a corporation to its subsidiary (first subsidiary) in exchange for additional stock; (2) the first subsidiary transferred all of the interests in the limited liability company to its subsidiary (second subsidiary) in exchange for additional stock; (3) the second subsidiary transferred all of the interests in the limited liability company to its subsidiary (third subsidiary) in exchange for additional stock; and (4) the limited liability company elected to be disregarded as an entity separate from its owner for federal income tax purposes effective after it was owned by the third subsidiary. The ruling concluded that the series of events was properly treated as two transfers of stock in exchanges governed by § 351, followed by a § 368(a)(1)(D) reorganization. Even though the parent's transfer was part of a series of transactions undertaken as part of a prearranged, integrated plan involving successive transfers of the LLC interests, the transfer satisfied the formal requirements of § 351, including the requirement that the transferor control the subsidiary immediately after the exchange. Viewing the transaction as a whole did not dictate that the parent's transfer be treated other than in accordance with its form. Section 351 similarly, applied to the first subsidiary's transfer of the LLC interests to its subsidiary. But the transfer by the second subsidiary to the third subsidiary, coupled with the LLC's election to become a disregarded entity was characterized as a § 368(a)(1)(D) reorganization. If an acquiring corporation acquires all of the stock of a target corporation from a person controlling the acquiring corporation (within the meaning of § 304(c), via § 368(a)(2)(H)(i)) in an exchange otherwise qualifying as a § 351 exchange, and as part of a prearranged, integrated plan, the target corporation thereafter transfers its assets to the acquiring corporation in liquidation, the transaction is more properly characterized as a reorganization under § 368(a)(1)(D), to the extent it so qualifies. See Rev.Rul. 67–274, 1967–2 C.B.141.

3. LIQUIDATION-REINCORPORATION TRANSACTIONS AND THE TYPE (D) REORGANIZATION PROVISIONS

3.1. *Background*

Historically, the nondivisive (D) reorganization provision was used principally by the IRS as a weapon to attack liquidation-reincorporation transactions, in connection with (F) reorganizations (discussed in Chapter 11). Indeed, the definition of "control" for purposes of (D) reorganizations subject to § 354 is reduced from the 80% benchmark in § 368(c) to 50% (§ 368(a)(2)(H)), making it easier to fit liquidation-reincorporation transactions under the (D) reorganization definition when there is a change in the shareholder ownership between the "new" and "old" corporations. See S.Rep. No. 98–169, 98th Cong., 2d Sess. 207–209 (1984).

In general, the courts were liberal in interpreting the (D) reorganization requirements in order to find a reorganization with an accompanying dividend in order to block the tax avoidance possibilities in the liquidation-reincorporation situations. In testing whether "substantially all" the assets have been transferred, as is required by § 354(b)(1)(A), the focus has been on the operating assets of the corporation. See, e.g., Smothers v. United States, 642 F.2d 894 (5th Cir.1981):

> To maintain the integrity of the dividend provisions of the Code, "substantially all assets" in this context must be interpreted as an inartistic way of expressing the concept of "transfer of a continuing business." * * * Properly interpreted, therefore, the assets looked to when making the "substantially all assets" determination should be all the assets, and only the assets, necessary to operate the corporate business—whether or not those assets would appear on a corporate balance sheet. * * * Inclusion of assets unnecessary to the operation of the business in the "substantially all assets" assessment would open the way for the shareholders of any enterprise to turn dividends into capital gains at will. * * * [E]xclusion of assets not shown on a balance sheet * * * would offer an unjustified windfall to owners of service businesses conducted in the corporate form. The most important assets of such a business may be its reputation and the availability of skilled management and trained employees * * *. [F]or example a sole legal practitioner who owns nothing but a desk and chair could incorporate himself, accumulate earnings, and then set up a new corporation and liquidate the old at capital gain rates—as long as he is careful to buy a new desk and chair for the new corporation, rather than transferring the old.

3.2. *Control and Continuity of Interest*

The requirement that the transferor corporation or its shareholders be in control of the transferee corporation after the transfer has been strictly construed. For example, in Breech v. United States, 439 F.2d 409 (9th Cir.1971), a corporation sold all of its assets to a second corporation, the stock of which was owned 20% by one of its shareholders and 80% by a third corporation in which its shareholders had a 75% interest. The court refused to ignore the separate existence of the third corporation or to apply the attribution rules in § 318 (which by their terms did not then apply) to find control of the transferee in the shareholders of the transferor. Hence a (D) reorganization was not present. A similar result was reached in Commissioner v. Berghash, 361 F.2d 257 (2d Cir.1966). Section 368(a)(2)(H) now incorporates the attribution rules of § 318 for purposes of determining controlling stock ownership.

The IRS attempted to fit liquidation-reorganization transactions into the (D) reorganization definition by considering pieces of the transaction that might defeat reorganization treatment as "functionally unrelated" to the reorganization. Reef Corporation v. Commissioner, 368 F.2d 125 (5th Cir.1966), upheld the IRS in finding a (D) reorganization (as well as an (F) reorganization) coupled with a redemption in a series of transactions having substantially the same result as described above, where the continuing shareholders held 52% of the old corporation's stock at a time when the control test for type (D) reorganizations was 80%, not 50% as it now is. Other cases hesitated to separate related transactions in order to find a reorganization. Thus, in *Commissioner v. Berghash*, supra, the sole shareholder of a corporation agreed to transfer to a corporate employee a 50% ownership interest in the business, which the employee demanded as a condition of his continued employment. The employee was willing to invest $25,000 in the business but, because of the size of the business, this would not have entitled him to a 50% interest. Accordingly, the corporation was liquidated and its operating assets transferred to a new corporation in exchange for notes and 50% of the stock. The additional 50% of the stock was issued to the employee for cash. The old shareholder treated the transaction as a liquidation entitled to capital gain treatment under § 331. The IRS argued that the sale of stock to the employee should be disregarded as an "unrelated step," and thus the transaction would fit the pattern of a (D) or an (F) reorganization and an accompanying boot distribution under § 356. The Tax Court, however, finding the sale a "critical fact" in evaluating the transaction, refused to find a reorganization and a boot distribution, and the Court of Appeals affirmed.

4. OVERLAP OF TYPE (D) AND OTHER REORGANIZATIONS

A transaction meeting the definition of a type (D) reorganization also might meet the definition of a type (C) reorganization. Suppose that X Corporation owns all of the stock of both Y Corporation and Z Corporation. If Z Corporation transfers all of its assets to Y Corporation for Y stock and then liquidates, the transaction meets the definitions of both a (C) and a (D) reorganization. In such a case, § 368(a)(2)(A) requires that the transaction be treated as a type (D) reorganization. As discussed in *Atlas Tool*, the asset transfer from Z to Y would be classified as a (D) reorganization even if no additional Y Corporation stock were issued since X would own 100% of Y in any event. Likewise, a merger of a corporation into another corporation controlled by the same shareholders (defined by § 368(a)(2)(H)) as at least 50% of vote or at least 50% of value) that qualifies under § 368(a)(1)(A) also will be treated as a reorganization under § 368(a)(1)(D). See Rev.Rul. 75–161, 1975–1 C.B. 114, obsoleted by Rev.Rul. 2007–8, 2007–1 C.B. 469; P.L.R.200442008 (Oct. 15, 2004). The consequences of the reorganization, however, are the same regardless of its classification.

On the other hand, an overlap between a type (D) and type (F) reorganization, discussed in the next Chapter, results in classification as a type (F). Rev.Rul. 57–276, 1957–1 C.B. 126; Rev.Rul. 87–27, 1987–1 C.B. 134 (reincorporation of domestic corporation in foreign country which is both a type (F) and type (D) reorganization is treated as type (F)); Rev.Rul. 87–66, 1987–2 C.B. 168 (reincorporation of foreign corporation in U.S. which is both a type (D) and a type (F) reorganization treated as a type (F)). In tax years when net operating carrybacks are statutorily available, this classification is significant, because carrybacks of net operating losses are allowed following an (F) reorganization, but they are not allowed following a (D) reorganization. (Legislation in 2017 generally repealed net operating carrybacks.)

PROBLEM SET 10

1.   Alberto, Beryl, Chris, and Debby each owned 25 of the 100 outstanding shares of common stock of Cyclone Fence Corp. Cyclone Fence Corp. sold all of its assets to Tropical Landscapers, Inc. in exchange for 200 shares of voting common stock of Tropical Landscapers, worth $800,000 and $800,000 in cash. After the asset sale, Cyclone Fence Corp. liquidated, distributing the Tropical Landscapers stock and cash pro rata to Alberto, Beryl, Chris, and Debby. Is the acquisition of Cyclone Fence Corp. by Tropical Landscapers a reorganization under the following alternative fact patterns?

(a)   Before the acquisition, Tropical Landscapers, Inc. had 200 shares of voting common stock outstanding, which was owned equally by Earl and Fiona (100 shares each).

(b)   Before the acquisition, Tropical Landscapers, Inc. had 210 shares of voting common stock outstanding, which was owned equally by Earl, Fiona, and Gaston (70 shares each).

(c)   Before the acquisition, Tropical Landscapers, Inc. had 210 shares of voting common stock outstanding, which was owned equally by Debby, Earl, and Fiona (70 shares each).

(d)   Before the acquisition, Tropical Landscapers, Inc. had had 200 shares of voting common stock outstanding, which was owned equally by Earl and Fiona (100 shares each), and Hermine held all 100 shares of issued and outstanding nonvoting limited and preferred stock of Tropical Landscapers, Inc., which had a par value and fair market value of $2,000,000.

2.   (a)   X Corp. owned all the stock of both Y Corp. and Z Corp. Y Corp. owned Blackacre and Whiteacre. Blackacre had a fair market value of $2,000,000 and a basis of $500,000. Whiteacre had a fair market value of $2,000,000 and a basis of $3,500,000. Y Corp. sold Blackacre and Whiteacre to Z Corp. for $4,000,000 in cash and liquidated. What is the basis of each of Blackacre and Whiteacre to Z Corp?

(b)   Would your answer differ if immediately after the sale acquisition of Blackacre and Whiteacre by Z Corp., Z Corp. transferred the properties to its wholly owned subsidiary, S Corp., as a contribution to capital?

3.   Ida and Joaquin are equal shareholders of Windward Properties, Inc. Each of them has a $100,000 basis in the stock of Windward Properties. Windward Properties' assets consist of a parcel of land with a fair market value of $10,000 and a basis of $70,000 and cash of $30,000. Ida and Joaquin have a plan to liquidate Windward Properties, then contribute the land to a newly formed corporation, Leeward Properties, owned equally by them and sell the stock of Leeward Properties to Kate. What are the tax consequences of this transaction?

SECTION 7.   BANKRUPTCY REORGANIZATIONS: TYPE G REORGANIZATIONS

INTERNAL REVENUE CODE: Section 368(a)(1)(G), (a)(3).

Senate Finance Committee Report, Bankruptcy Tax Act of 1980

S.Rep. No. 96–1035, 96th Cong., 2d Sess. 8 (1980).

* * *

C.   Corporate Reorganization Provisions

[Pre-1981] Law

Definition of reorganization.—A transfer of all or part of a corporation's assets, pursuant to a court order in a proceeding under chapter X of the Bankruptcy Act (or in a receivership, foreclosure, or similar proceeding), to another corporation organized or utilized to effectuate a court-approved plan may qualify for tax-free reorganization treatment under special rules relating to "insolvency reorganizations" (secs. 371–374 of the Internal Revenue Code).

These special rules for insolvency reorganizations generally allow less flexibility in structuring tax-free transactions than the rules applicable to corporate reorganizations as defined in section 368 of the Code. Also, the special rules for insolvency reorganizations do not permit carryover of tax attributes to the transferee corporation, and otherwise differ in important respects from the general reorganization rules.[1] While some reorganizations under chapter X of the Bankruptcy Act may be able to qualify for nonrecognition treatment under Code section 368, other chapter X reorganizations may be able to qualify only under the special rules of sections 371–374 and not under the general reorganization rules of section 368.

* * *

Reasons for Change.—The committee believes that the provisions of existing Federal income tax law which are generally applicable to tax-free corporate reorganizations should also apply to reorganizations of corporations in bankruptcy or similar proceedings, in order to facilitate the rehabilitation of financially troubled businesses.

---

[1]   Under [pre-1981] law, it is not clear to what extent creditors of an insolvent corporation who receive stock in exchange for their claims may be considered to have "stepped into the shoes" of former shareholders for purposes of satisfying the nonstatutory "continuity of interest" rule, under which the owners of the acquired corporation must continue to have a proprietary interest in the acquiring corporation. Generally, the courts have found the "continuity of interest" test satisfied if the creditors' interests were transformed into proprietary interests prior to the reorganization (e.g., Helvering v. Alabama Asphaltic Limestone Co., 315 U.S. 179 (1942); Treas.Reg. § 1.371–1(a)(4)). It is unclear whether affirmative steps by the creditors are required or whether mere receipt of stock is sufficient.

Also, the committee believes that a creditor who exchanges securities in a corporate reorganization (including an insolvency reorganization) should be treated as receiving interest income on the exchange to the extent the creditor receives new securities, stock, or any other property for accrued but unpaid interest on the securities surrendered.

Explanation of Provisions.—[The Act] generally conforms the tax rules governing insolvency reorganizations with the existing rules applicable to other corporate reorganizations. * * *

Definition of reorganization.—*In general.*—The bill adds a new category—"G" reorganizations—to the general Code definition of tax-free reorganizations (sec. 368(a)(1)). The new category includes certain transfers of assets pursuant to a court-approved reorganization plan in a bankruptcy case under new title 11 of the U.S. Code, or in a receivership, foreclosure, or similar proceeding in a Federal or State court.

* * *

In order to facilitate the rehabilitation of corporate debtors in bankruptcy, etc., these provisions are designed to eliminate many requirements which have effectively precluded financially troubled companies from utilizing the generally applicable tax-free reorganization provisions of present law. To achieve this purpose, the new "G" reorganization provision does not require compliance with State merger laws (as in category "A" reorganizations), does not require that the financially distressed corporation receive solely stock of the acquiring corporation in exchange for its assets (category "C"), and does not require that the former shareholders of the financially distressed corporation control the corporation which receives the assets (category "D").

The "G" reorganization provision added by the bill requires the transfer of assets by a corporation in a bankruptcy or similar case, and the distribution (in pursuance of the court-approved reorganization plan) of stock or securities of the acquiring corporation in a transaction which qualifies under sections 354, 355, or 356 of the Code. This distribution requirement is designed to assure that either substantially all of the assets of the financially troubled corporation, or assets which consist of an active business under the tests of section 355, are transferred to the acquiring corporation.

"Substantially all" test.—The "substantially all" test in the "G" reorganization provision is to be interpreted in light of the underlying intent in adding the new "G" category, namely, to facilitate the reorganization of companies in bankruptcy or similar cases for rehabilitative purposes. Accordingly, it is intended that facts and circumstances relevant to this intent, such as the insolvent corporation's need to pay off creditors or to sell assets or divisions to raise cash, are to be taken into account in determining whether a transaction qualifies as a "G" reorganization. For example, a transaction is not precluded from

satisfying the "substantially all" test for purposes of the new "G" category merely because, prior to a transfer to the acquiring corporation, payments to creditors and asset sales were made in order to leave the debtor with more manageable operating assets to continue in business.[5]

Relation to other provisions.—A transaction which qualifies as a "G" reorganization is not to be treated as also qualifying as a liquidation under section 332, an incorporation under section 351, or a reorganization under another category of section 368(a)(1) of the Code.

A transaction in a bankruptcy or similar case which does not satisfy the requirements of new category "G" is not thereby precluded from qualifying as a tax-free reorganization under one of the other categories of section 368(a)(1). For example, an acquisition of the stock of a company in bankruptcy, or a recapitalization of such a company, which transactions are not covered by the new "G" category, can qualify for nonrecognition treatment under sections 368(a)(1)(B) or (E), respectively.

Continuity of interest rules.—The "continuity of interest" requirement which the courts and the Treasury have long imposed as a prerequisite for nonrecognition treatment for a corporate reorganization must be met in order to satisfy the requirements of new category "G". Only reorganizations—as distinguished from liquidations in bankruptcy and sales of property to either new or old interests supplying new capital and discharging the obligations of the debtor corporation—can qualify for tax-free treatment.

It is expected that * * * shareholders or junior creditors, who might previously have been excluded, may now retain an interest in the reorganized corporation.

For example, if an insolvent corporation's assets are transferred to a second corporation in a bankruptcy case, the most senior class of creditor to receive stock, together with all equal and junior classes (including shareholders who receive any consideration for their stock), should generally be considered the proprietors of the insolvent corporation for "continuity" purposes. However, if the shareholders receive consideration other than stock of the acquiring corporation, the transaction should be examined to determine if it represents a purchase rather than a reorganization.

Thus, short-term creditors who receive stock for their claims may be counted toward satisfying the continuity of interest rule, although any gain or loss realized by such creditors will be recognized for income tax purposes.

---

[5] Because the stated intent for adding the new "G" category is not relevant to interpreting the "substantially all" test in the case of other reorganization categories, the comments in the text as to the appropriate interpretation of the "substantially all" test in the context of a "G" reorganization are not intended to apply to, or in any way to affect interpretations under present law of, the "substantially all" test for other reorganization categories.

Triangular reorganizations.—[Section 368(a)(1)(G)] permits a corporation to acquire a debtor corporation in a "G" reorganization in exchange for stock of the parent of the acquiring corporation rather than for its own stock.

In addition, [section 368(a)(1)(G) and (a)(3)(E)] permits an acquisition in the form of a "reverse merger" of an insolvent corporation (i.e., where no former shareholder of the surviving corporation receives any consideration for his stock) in a bankruptcy or similar case if the former creditors of the surviving corporation exchange their claims for voting stock of the controlling corporation which has a value equal to at least 80 percent of the value of the debt of the surviving corporation.

Transfer to controlled subsidiary.—[Section 368(a)(1)(G)] permits a corporation which acquires substantially all the assets of a debtor corporation in a "G" reorganization to transfer the acquired assets to a controlled subsidiary without endangering the tax-free status of the reorganization. This provision places "G" reorganizations on a similar footing with other categories of reorganizations.

* * *

"Principal amount" rule; "boot" test.—* * * "G" reorganizations are subject to the rules governing the tax treatment of exchanging shareholders and security holders which apply to other corporate reorganizations.

Accordingly, an exchanging shareholder or security holder of the debtor company who receives securities with a principal amount exceeding the principal amount of securities surrendered is taxable on the excess, and an exchanging shareholder or security holder who surrenders no securities is taxed on the principal amount of any securities received. Also, any "boot" received is subject to the general dividend-equivalence test of Code section 356.

Treatment of accrued interest.—[Section 354(b)(2)(B) provides that] a creditor exchanging securities in any corporate reorganization described in section 368 of the Code (including a "G" reorganization) is treated as receiving interest income on the exchange to the extent the security holder receives new securities, stock, or any other property attributable to accrued but unpaid interest (including accrued original issue discount) on the securities surrendered. This provision, which reverses the so-called *Carman* rule, applies whether or not the exchanging security holder realizes gain on the exchange overall. Under this provision, a security holder which had previously accrued the interest (including original issue discount) as income recognizes a loss to the extent the interest is not paid in the exchange.

Example.—The reorganization provisions of the bill are illustrated in part by the following example.

Assume that Corporation A is in a bankruptcy case commenced after December 31, 1980. Immediately prior to a transfer under a plan of reorganization, A's assets have an adjusted basis of $75,000 and a fair market value of $100,000. A has a net operating loss carryover of $200,000. A has outstanding bonds of $100,000 (on which there is no accrued but unpaid interest) and trade debts of $100,000.

Under the plan of reorganization, A is to transfer all its assets to Corporation B in exchange for $100,000 of B stock. Corporation A will distribute the stock, in exchange for their claims against A, one-half to the security holders and one-half to the trade creditors. A's shareholders will receive nothing.

The transaction qualifies as a reorganization under new section 368(a)(1)(G) of the Code, since all the creditors are here treated as proprietors for continuity of interest purposes. Thus, A recognizes no gain or loss on the transfer of its assets to B (Code sec. 361). B's basis in the assets is: $75,000 (sec. 362), and B succeeds to A's net operating loss carryover (sec. 381).

* * * [T]he pro-rata distribution of B stock to A's creditors does not result in income from discharge of indebtedness or require attribute reduction.

Assume the same facts as above except that B also transfers $10,000 in cash, which is distributed by A to its creditors. Although A would otherwise recognize gain on the receipt of boot in an exchange involving appreciated property, the distribution by A of the $10,000 cash to those creditors having a proprietary interest in the corporation's assets for continuity of interest purposes prevents A from recognizing any gain (Code sec. 361(b)).

DETAILED ANALYSIS

1. GENERALLY

Inside or outside of a formal bankruptcy proceeding, a financially troubled corporation generally has three options available to it. It can try to work with its creditors to reduce or restructure existing debt. It can issue stock for debt, thus replacing debt with equity on its balance sheet. Or it can seek to be acquired by another corporation. The first two transactions, each of which envisions a recapitalization of the corporation within the confines of a single entity, are discussed in greater detail in Chapter 11. The transfer of assets by an insolvent corporation in exchange for the stock of the acquiring corporation may be accomplished as a nonrecognition transaction under § 368(a)(1)(A), (C) or (G).

In any of these transactions, the insolvent corporation may realize discharge of indebtedness income. In general, however, a corporation involved in a bankruptcy proceeding or an insolvent corporation will avoid recognition of discharge of indebtedness income under § 108(a)(1)(A) or (B).

This issue is discussed in the context of debt for debt exchanges and stock for debt exchanges.

2.   ACQUISITION REORGANIZATIONS IN BANKRUPTCY

A transfer by the target corporation of all or part of its assets to the acquiring corporation in a bankruptcy reorganization or a receivership, foreclosure, or similar judicial proceeding in a federal or state court is a tax-free reorganization under § 368(a)(1)(G) if the stock or securities received from the acquiring corporation are distributed pursuant to the plan of reorganization in a transaction that qualifies under § 354, § 355, or § 356. The target corporation recognizes no gain or loss if any boot that it receives is distributed. I.R.C. § 361(b).

Section 368(a)(1)(G) applies only to judicially supervised insolvency proceedings. Thus a nonjudicial reorganization of an insolvent corporation must qualify under one of the other provisions of § 368 in order to achieve reorganization status, assuming the continuity of interest test can be met. But, if a transaction qualifies both as a type (G) and, as a result of its form, as another type of reorganization, for example a type (C), it will be classified solely as a type (G). I.R.C. § 368(a)(3)(C).

When an insolvency reorganization qualifies as a type (G) reorganization, §§ 354 and 356 continue to control taxation of the shareholders and creditors. Thus, for example, short-term creditors who do not hold "securities" will have a taxable exchange; shareholders and other securities holders will be subject to the usual pattern of reorganization taxation.

3.   CONTINUITY OF INTEREST IN A BANKRUPTCY REORGANIZATION

In Helvering v. Alabama Asphaltic Limestone Co., 315 U.S. 179 (1942), a creditors' committee formed a new corporation to acquire the assets of an insolvent corporation. An involuntary bankruptcy proceeding was instituted in which the creditors' claims were satisfied by the transfer of assets to the new corporation pursuant to a judicial sale. Ninety-five percent of the stock of the new corporation was issued to note holders, and the balance was issued to unsecured creditors of the insolvent corporation. The new corporation claimed depreciation based on a transferred basis from the old corporation, arguing that a reorganization had taken place. The IRS contended that the assets were acquired by purchase because the continuity of shareholder interest requirement had not been satisfied. Citing LeTulle v. Scofield, 308 U.S. 415 (1940), the IRS argued that for a transaction to qualify as a reorganization, a substantial ownership interest in the transferee company must be retained by the holders of the ownership interest in the transferor. In holding that the assets had been acquired in a tax-free reorganization, the Supreme Court explained the application of the continuity of interest rules to insolvent acquired corporations as follows:

> We conclude, however, that it is immaterial that the transfer shifted the ownership of the equity in the property from the stockholders to the creditors of the old corporation. Plainly, the old continuity of interest was broken. Technically, that did not occur in

this proceeding until the judicial sale took place. For practical purposes, however, it took place not later than the time when the creditors took steps to enforce their demands against the insolvent debtor. In this case, that was the date of the institution of the bankruptcy proceedings. From that time on, they had effective command over the disposition of the property. The full priority rule * * * in bankruptcy * * * gives creditors, whether secured or unsecured, the right to exclude the stockholders entirely from the reorganization plan when the debtor is insolvent. When the equity owners are excluded and the old creditors become the stockholders of the new corporation, it conforms to realities to date their equity ownership from the time when they invoked the process of the law to enforce their rights to full priority. At the time they stepped into the shoes of the old stockholders. * * *

That conclusion involves no conflict with the principals of the *Le Tulle* case. A bondholder interest in a solvent corporation plainly is not the equivalent of a proprietary interest * * *.

This approach continues under the (G) reorganization provisions. In testing for continuity, all classes of creditors who receive stock in the reorganized corporation are considered to be the historic shareholders of the corporation. In addition, if the shareholders receive anything for their shares, they too will be taken into account in the continuity test. Thus, for example, if all the stock in the reorganized company is received by junior creditors, with the secured creditors receiving cash and the shareholders receiving nothing, continuity of interest would be present. On the other hand, if the secured creditors also receive stock, they too would be counted in testing for continuity, which might be lacking if the amount of the cash payment is too large in relation to the stock. If shareholders receive cash, the Committee Report indicates that the transaction may be considered a purchase rather than a reorganization.

Treas.Reg. § 1.368–1(e)(6) describes the circumstances in which a corporation's creditors will be treated as holding a proprietary interest in a target corporation immediately before a potential reorganization. A creditor has a proprietary interest only if the target corporation's liabilities exceed the fair market value of its assets immediately prior to the potential reorganization (or the target corporation is in a title 11 or similar case, as defined in § 368(a)(3)). If any creditor receives a proprietary interest in the acquiring corporation, every claim of that class of creditors and every claim of all equal and junior classes of creditors (in addition to the claims of shareholders) is a proprietary interest in the target corporation immediately prior to the potential reorganization. Generally, in applying continuity of interest principles, the value of a creditor's proprietary interest is the fair market value of the creditor's claim. A special rule applies to the most senior class of creditors receiving stock of the acquirer (and claims of any equal class of creditors). The value of those creditors' proprietary interests in the target is determined by multiplying the fair market value of the claim by a fraction, the numerator of which is the aggregate fair market value of the acquirer's stock received in exchange for claims of those classes of creditors and the denominator of which is the total amount of money and the fair market value of all other consideration (including acquirer stock) received in exchange for such claims.

4. SECURITIES

Neither § 354 nor the Regulations under § 354 define the term "securities." In Neville Coke & Chemical Co. v. Commissioner, 148 F.2d 599 (3d Cir.1945), the taxpayer held stock, bonds, three-, four-, and five-year notes, and accounts receivable of an insolvent corporation. Pursuant to a bankruptcy proceeding, the debtor corporation was recapitalized and the taxpayer received new common stock for its stock, new debentures for its bonds, and new debentures and common stock for its notes and accounts receivable. The IRS asserted that the taxpayer recognized a gain on the exchange of the notes and accounts receivable for debentures and common stock. The taxpayer asserted that the notes and accounts receivable were "securities" within the meaning of the predecessor of § 354(a)(1) and that it had exchanged "securities" for "stock and securities," thereby entitling it to nonrecognition on the exchange. In holding for the IRS, the court held that "securities" has the same meaning in the context of the interest surrendered as it does in the context of the interest received, that a "security" entails having a "proprietary" interest in the corporation, and that the rights of the taxpayer as a note holder were merely those of a creditor.

Rev.Rul. 2004–78, 2004–2 C.B. 108, supra, described the case law as concluding that an instrument with a term of less than five years generally is not a security, although on the particular facts of that ruling, it concluded that two year instruments were securities.

Under § 368(a)(1)(G), while short-term creditors who receive stock in the reorganization will be counted for continuity purposes, the exchange of their debt claims for stock presumably will be a taxable transaction, because the "securities" test has not been met.

5. TAX RESULTS TO THE PARTIES TO A TYPE (G) REORGANIZATION

5.1. *Target Corporation and Shareholders*

Normally no gain or loss is recognized by the target corporation on the exchange with the acquiring corporation regardless of the nature of the property received from the acquiring corporation. If only stock or securities of the acquiring corporation are received in the reorganization, § 361(a) provides nonrecognition. If nonqualifying boot is received, § 361(b) requires that the target corporation recognize gain upon receipt only if the boot is not distributed to either its shareholders or creditors pursuant to the plan of reorganization.

The target corporation may realize discharge of indebtedness income, but because a type (G) reorganization is limited to a corporation involved in a bankruptcy proceeding, discharge of indebtedness income is excluded under § 108(a)(1)(A).

As for the liquidating distributions, no gain or loss is recognized by the target corporation on the distribution of qualified stock or securities. I.R.C.

§ 361(c)(1), (2)(B). Distribution of appreciated boot in the liquidation results in recognition of gain (but not loss) under § 361(c)(2), but because § 358(a)(2) provides the target corporation with a fair market value basis in any boot received in the reorganization, no gain will be realized unless there is a change in value between the receipt and the liquidating distribution. If any property was retained by the target corporation, gain may be recognized by the corporation as a result of distributing such property in the liquidation.

For the shareholders of the target corporation, the tax results are similar to those in an (A) reorganization. No gain or loss will be recognized if they receive solely the stock of the acquiring corporation in exchange for their stock in the target corporation. I.R.C. § 354(a). If the permissible amount of "boot" is involved and it is distributed to the shareholders, they may recognize gain under § 356, either as capital gain or as a dividend, depending on the circumstances. Section 358 then provides an exchanged basis for the acquiring corporation's stock. If any boot is received, however, the basis is determined by first increasing the basis by the amount of any gain recognized by the shareholders as the result of the receipt of boot, and then decreasing it by the amount of cash or the fair market value of any other property received. If, as may be the case, the shareholders of the target corporation receive nothing in the reorganization, they may recognize losses under § 165(g).

5.2. Acquiring Corporation

Pursuant to § 1032, the acquiring corporation recognizes no gain or loss on the transfer of its shares in a (G) reorganization. If, however, the acquiring corporation transfers any boot other than cash or its own stock or securities, it must recognize gain or loss with respect to the boot transferred.

Under § 362(b) the acquiring corporation's basis in the assets is equal to the target corporation's basis in those assets. Although § 362(b) provides that the acquiring corporation's basis in the assets is to be increased by any gain recognized under § 361(b) by the target corporation on the transfer of its assets to the acquiring corporation, the target corporation will not recognize gain as a result of the transfer of its assets if the target corporation distributes all of its property to shareholders.

In Washington Mutual Inc. v. United States, 636 F.3d 1207 (9th Cir. 2011), the Court of Appeals appears to have disregarded the transferred basis rule of § 362(b) to allow a cost basis for certain rights acquired in a § 368(a)(1)(G) reorganization. The taxpayer, as the successor corporation to Home Savings of America, filed a refund action claiming amortization deductions for certain rights and loss deductions for abandonment of branching rights, created in a § 368(a)(1)(G) reorganization by the Federal Savings and Loan Insurance Corporation (FSLIC) in which Home Savings acquired three failed savings and loan associations. The District Court granted summary judgment for the government, concluding that Home Savings had no basis in the rights. The Ninth Circuit reversed and remanded, disagreeing with the District Court's conclusion regarding basis. As part of the acquisition of the three failed thrifts in a supervisory merger transaction structured as a type G reorganization, FSLIC entered into an

"Assistance Agreement" with Home Savings that included, among other things, approval for Home Savings to establish branches in Florida and Missouri as if Home Savings maintained its home office in those states, and approval of the purchase method of accounting under which Home Savings was permitted to apply a percentage of acquired intangible assets in its deposit base and for amortization of the remainder over 40 years. The Ninth Circuit concluded that the excess of liabilities of the acquired thrifts over the value of assets represented a cost that was consideration for the rights created in the assistance agreement in the integrated transaction, and that allowing the taxpayer a cost basis was not inconsistent with characterizing the transaction as a § 368(a)(1)(G) reorganization, notwithstanding the transferred basis rule of § 362(b). The Ninth Circuit rejected the government's assertion that "recognizing Home Savings a cost basis in the Rights based on the assumption of FSLIC's liabilities requires characterizing some of the acquired thrifts' liabilities as FSLIC's liabilities, because Home Savings did not pay FSLIC or the Bank Board separate consideration for the Rights." The District Court had concurred with the government's position holding that the excess liabilities of the acquired thrifts were the same as FSLIC's insurance liabilities that remained liabilities of FSLIC. The Ninth Circuit reasoned that Home Savings received a generous incentive package, the cost of which was the excess of the failing thrifts liabilities over the value of their assets. A concurring opinion argued that the acquired rights had a fair market value basis as acquired directly from FSLIC in exchange for taking over the liabilities of the failed thrifts. The Ninth Circuit remanded the case to the District Court to determine the proper amortization amounts for the intangibles and the amount of abandonment loss for the branch rights.

Under § 381, the tax attributes of the target corporation, most significantly net operating loss carryovers, which may be an important asset of the target corporation, carry over to the acquiring corporation. The limitations of § 382(b) are, however, applicable. Under § 382, a corporation's net operating loss carryover is limited if there has been a greater than 50% change in ownership over a three year testing period (an "ownership change"). See Chapter 13. In the case of a bankruptcy or insolvency proceeding, however, the § 382 limitation is not applied if, following an ownership change, the creditors and former stockholders of the loss corporation own at least 50% of the loss corporation stock. I.R.C. § 382(*l*)(5)(A).

SECTION 8.   SECTION 351 OVERLAP WITH THE REORGANIZATION PROVISIONS

The issue of how to treat a larger acquisitive transaction that could also qualify for § 351 presents unique tax planning opportunities. In the diagram below, T-1 is involved in a reverse subsidiary merger where subsidiary S-1 is merged into T-1, with the T-1 shareholders exchanging their stock in T-1 for new P stock. Pursuant to the same overall plan, a separate reverse subsidiary merger occurs where subsidiary S-2 is merged into T-2, with the T-2 shareholders exchanging their T-2 stock for a combination of cash and new P stock.

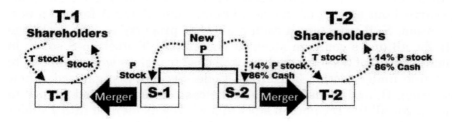

As to the transaction with the T-1 Shareholders, the issuance of the new P stock for the T-1 stock could qualify for nonrecognition treatment under § 368(a)(1)(B) if the exchange of new P voting stock for T-1 stock were solely a stock-for-stock exchange. The exchange of new P voting stock for T-1 stock could also qualify for nonrecognition treatment under § 368(a)(2)(E) if it occurs as part of a reorganization where S-1 merges into T-1. Finally, if the T-2 shareholders are joint transferors with the T-2 shareholders, then the transaction could also qualify for nonrecognition treatment under § 351 because the joint contributors are in control of new P immediately after the exchange.

However, the transaction with the T-2 shareholders diverges. That exchange could not possibly qualify for nonrecognition treatment under § 368(a)(1)(B) because the T-2 stock was not exchanged solely for new P voting stock. Furthermore, the transaction could not qualify for nonrecognition treatment under § 368(a)(2)(E) because control of T-2 was not acquired solely with new P voting stock. But, if the T-2 shareholders are joint transferors with the T-1 shareholders, that is, where T-1 and T-2 shares are transferred to new P in exchange for new P stock, then the transaction could qualify for § 351 treatment.

In Rev.Rul. 84–71, the IRS addressed the right side of the above diagram and ruled that § 351 treatment could apply even if the transaction would have failed the most basic continuity of interest standards for a reorganization.

Revenue Ruling 84–71
1984–1 C.B. 106.

* * *

In Rev. Rul. 80–284, 1980–2 C.B. 117, fourteen percent of T corporation's stock was held by A, president and chairman of the board, and eighty-six percent by the public. P, an unrelated, publicly held corporation wished to purchase the stock of T. All the T stockholders except A were willing to sell the T stock for cash. A wished to avoid recognition of gain.

In order to accommodate these wishes, the following transactions were carried out as part of an overall plan. First, P and A formed a new corporation, S. P transferred cash and other property to S in exchange solely for all of S's common stock; A transferred T stock to S solely in exchange for all of S's preferred stock. These transfers were intended to be tax-free under section 351 of the Code. Second, S organized a new corporation, D, and transferred to D the cash it had received from P in exchange for all the D common stock. Third, D was merged into T under state law. As a result of the merger, each share of T stock, except those shares held by S, were surrendered for cash equal to the stock's fair market value and each share of D stock was converted into T stock.

Rev. Rul. 80–284, 1980–2 C.B. 117, concluded that if a purported section 351 exchange is an integral part of a larger transaction that fits a pattern common to acquisitive reorganizations, and if the continuity of shareholder interest requirement of section 1.368–1(b) of the Income Tax Regulations is not satisfied with respect to the larger transaction, then the transaction as a whole resembles a sale and the exchange cannot qualify under section 351 because that section is not intended to apply to sales. Rev. Rul. 80–285, 1980–2 C.B. 119, reached a similar conclusion with respect to an asset, rather than stock, acquisition in which a purported section 351 exchange was also part of a larger acquisitive transaction.

Upon reconsideration, the Service has concluded that the fact that "larger acquisitive transactions," such as those described in Rev. Rul, 80–284 and Rev. Rul. 80–285, 1980–2 C.B. 119, fail to meet the requirements for tax-free treatment under the reorganization provisions of the Code does not preclude the applicability of section 351(a) to transfers that may be described as part of such larger transactions, but also, either alone or in conjunction with other transfers, me[et] the requirements of section 351(a).

DETAILED ANALYSIS

Rev.Rul. 84–71 is a powerful mechanism in the acquisitive context to side-step the continuity of interest requirement that is required of all tax-free reorganizations under § 368(a). If the acquiring corporation is willing to itself be acquired by a new entity that simultaneously acquires both the target company and the acquiring company as depicted in the above diagram, then the transaction can qualify for § 351 treatment as both public shareholder groups will be joint transferors who are collectively in control of new P immediately after the exchange. The transaction structured in that manner would qualify for § 351 treatment notwithstanding the fact that only 14% shareholder continuity of interest was preserved. The transaction set forth in the above diagram has been used repeatedly since 1984 in high profile public transactions.

SECTION 9.   JUDICIAL DOCTRINES AND LIMITATIONS

REGULATIONS: Section 1.368–1(a)–(c).

In an early edition of this book, Professor Stanley S. Surrey wrote:

"The reorganization sections are written against a background of many varied business transactions. They are stated in terms of specific rules which chart a tax-free corridor through which may flow the corporate transactions intended to be so favored. But the very breadth of the transactions to which the rules could extend and the mechanical terms in which they are written combine to make that corridor a tempting avenue of tax avoidance to persons who were not intended to be the recipients of such a safe-conduct pass. This is especially true in the case of closely-held family corporations where the corporation may be readily maneuvered by the shareholders. From the very beginning the courts, prompted by the Commissioner, have undertaken the task of policing this tax-free corridor. Their guarding has been vigorous and diligent, and many a corporation or shareholder who presented a pass carefully prepared to match the literal language of the sections has nevertheless been denied entrance. As a consequence, the literal language of the sections cannot be relied upon,[11] and safe passage depends upon knowledge of the rules of the judicial gendarmerie. An attorney who reads section 368(a)(1)(A) and believes that a statutory merger always constitutes a reorganization may be sadly mistaken—his particular statutory merger may be on the judicial proscribed list if it fails to possess the necessary continuity of interest. Some of these judicial rules have been incorporated in the statute; part of their flavor is in the Regulations.[12] But most of them still remain as they originated—judicial safeguards devised to protect the underlying statutory policy. Nor is the role of the judiciary confined to enforcing rules previously announced. Anyone applying for passage through the corridor runs the risk of the judicial policeman inventing a new rule on the spot if he thinks such action is demanded. And the Internal Revenue Service, in administering the statutory provisions, is alert to bring these situations before the courts. It must be remembered that most of the taxpayers who thus prompt administrative and judicial ingenuity have no real business in the corridor. But when such trespassers are in the throng, the barriers designed to separate them may catch an innocent, or may force the innocent to take added precautions to identify himself. The rules may also produce some uncertainty and confusion where the innocent too

---

[11] E.g., Helvering v. Alabama Asphaltic Limestone Co., 315 U.S. 179 (1942): "It has been recognized that a transaction may not qualify as a 'reorganization' under the various revenue acts though the literal language of the section is satisfied."

[12] See, e.g., Regulations, sections 1.368–1(b); 1.368–1(c), referring to "plan of reorganization"; 1.368–2(a); 1.368–2(g); 1.1002–1(b), (c).

closely resembles a trespasser. Some have criticized the judicial vigilance on this score. Others believe that any effort to prescribe statutory rules covering all of the everyday transactions of the business world is bound to fail unless courts and administrators are able to cope with transactions that would otherwise involve a distorted application of those rules."

Professor Surrey's words apply with equal force today.

A. BUSINESS PURPOSE

Gregory v. Helvering
Supreme Court of the United States, 1935.
293 U.S. 465.

[*The Facts.* Mrs. Gregory in 1928 owned all of the stock of United Mortgage Corporation. That corporation held among its assets 1,000 shares of Monitor Securities Corporation. The value of the Monitor shares exceeded their basis. Mrs. Gregory's problem was to have the Monitor shares sold and to obtain in her hands the cash received on such sale. One method would be to have the Monitor shares distributed as a dividend and then sold by her. But this would result in a tax on the value of the shares as ordinary income, which she wished to avoid. She was willing to pay some capital gains tax. The key to Mrs. Gregory's maneuvers to achieve her goals was § 112(g) of the 1928 Act. That section provided for no gain to the shareholder on the distribution by a corporation, a party to a reorganization, of stock or securities of another corporation, also a party to the reorganization, even though the shareholder did not surrender any shares, so that it in effect exempted a dividend distribution of such stock or securities. Section 112(g) was thus similar to present § 355 (applicable to corporate divisions, such as spin-offs), but without the latter's conditions.

Mrs. Gregory proceeded to follow the statute in literal fashion. To that end, she caused the Averill Corporation to be organized under the laws of Delaware on September 18, 1928. Three days later, the United Mortgage Corporation transferred to the Averill Corporation the 1,000 shares of Monitor stock, for which all the shares of the Averill Corporation were issued to Mrs. Gregory. This was a short-cutting step, whose effect was the same as the issuance of the Averill shares to United and their distribution by United to Mrs. Gregory. On September 24, the Averill Corporation was dissolved, and liquidated by distributing all its assets, namely the Monitor shares, to its sole shareholder, Mrs. Gregory. No other business was ever transacted, or intended to be transacted, by Averill. She immediately sold the Monitor shares for $133,333.33. She then contended that the transfer to Averill was a reorganization as United controlled Averill; the distribution to her of Averill shares was tax free under the old § 112(g); the Averill shares took part ($57,325.45) of the basis of her United shares (originally $350,000) on an allocation of her United basis based on the market values of the United and Averill shares; the liquidation of Averill and her acquisition thereby of the Monitor shares worth $133,333.33 produced a capital gain (of $76,007.88) taxable at capital gain rates; the sale of the Monitor shares resulted in no gain since the taxable liquidation resulted in a basis in her hands equal to their market value.

The Commissioner argued that the creation of the Averill Corporation was without substance and had to be disregarded, with the result that the entire transaction would be taxed as a dividend distribution of the Monitor shares, producing ordinary income of $133,333.33, the value of such shares. The sale of the Monitor shares had no tax effect under his theory, since, once taxed as a dividend, they had a basis equal to their value.

The Decision of the Board of Tax Appeals, 27 B.T.A. 223 (1932). The Board held for Mrs. Gregory:

> A statute so meticulously drafted must be interpreted as a literal expression of the taxing policy, and leaves only the small interstices for judicial consideration. The general legislative plan apparently was to recognize the corporate entity and, in view of such recognition, to specify when the gains or losses would be recognized and upon what basis they should be measured. We may not destroy the effectiveness of this statutory plan by denying recognition to the corporation and thus preventing consideration of its transactions.

The Decision of the Second Circuit Court of Appeals, 69 F.2d 809 (1934). The Circuit Court held for the Commissioner, in an opinion by Judge Learned Hand:

> We agree with the Board and the taxpayer that a transaction, otherwise within an exception of the tax law, does not lose its immunity, because it is actuated by a desire to avoid, or, if one choose, to evade, taxation. Any one may so arrange his affairs that his taxes shall be as low as possible; he is not bound to choose that pattern which will best pay the Treasury; there is not even a patriotic duty to increase one's taxes. * * * Therefore, if what was done here, was what was intended by [the section corresponding to present § 368(a)(1)(D), but without the present requirement of a distribution of the stock], it is of no consequence that it was all an elaborate scheme to get rid of income taxes, as it certainly was. Nevertheless, it does not follow that Congress meant to cover such a transaction, not even though the facts answer the dictionary definitions of each term used in the statutory definition. It is quite true, as the Board has very well said, that as the articulation of a statute increases, the room for interpretation must contract; but the meaning of a sentence may be more than that of the separate words, as a melody is more than the notes, and no degree of particularity can ever obviate recourse to the setting in which all appear, and

which all collectively create. The purpose of the section is plain enough; men engaged in enterprises—industrial, commercial, financial, or any other—might wish to consolidate, or divide, to add to, or subtract from, their holdings. Such transactions were not to be considered as "realizing" any profit, because the collective interests still remained in solution. But the underlying presupposition is plain that the readjustment shall be undertaken for reasons germane to the conduct of the venture in hand, not as an ephemeral incident, egregious to its prosecution. To dodge the shareholders' taxes is not one of the transactions contemplated as corporate "reorganizations."

We do not indeed agree fully with the way in which the Commissioner treated the transaction; we cannot treat as inoperative the transfer of the Monitor shares by the United Mortgage Corporation, the issue by the Averill Corporation of its own shares to the taxpayer, and her acquisition of the Monitor shares by winding up that company. The Averill Corporation had a juristic personality, whatever the purpose of its organization; the transfer passed title to the Monitor shares and the taxpayer became a shareholder in the transferee. All these steps were real, and their only defect was that they were not what the statute means by a "reorganization," because the transactions were no part of the conduct of the business of either or both companies; so viewed they were a sham, though all the proceedings had their usual effect. But the result is the same whether the tax be calculated as the Commissioner calculated it, or upon the value of the Averill shares as a dividend . . . .

On this theory the value of the Averill shares, and hence the amount taxed as a dividend, would be $133,333.33, the value of the underlying Monitor shares. The later liquidation of Averill and sale of the Monitor shares would have no tax effect since the Averill shares, taxed as a dividend, thereby obtained a basis equal to the value of the Monitor shares.]

■ MR. JUSTICE SUTHERLAND delivered the opinion of the Court. * * *

It is earnestly contended on behalf of the taxpayer that since every element required by [the section of the 1928 Act corresponding to present § 368(a)(1)(D), but without the present requirement of a distribution of the stock] is to be found in what was done, a statutory reorganization was effected; and that the motive of the taxpayer thereby to escape payment of a tax will not alter the result or make unlawful what the statute allows. It is quite true that if a reorganization in reality was effected within the meaning of [that provision], the ulterior purpose mentioned will be disregarded. The legal right of a taxpayer to decrease the amount of what otherwise would be his taxes, or altogether avoid them, by means which the law permits, cannot be doubted. United States v. Isham, 17 Wall. 496, 506; Superior Oil Co. v. Mississippi, 280 U.S. 390, 395, 396, 50 S.Ct. 169;

Jones v. Helvering, * * * 71 F.2d 214, 217. But the question for determination is whether what was done, apart from the tax motive, was the thing which the statute intended. The reasoning of the court below in justification of a negative answer leaves little to be said.

When [the statutory provision] speaks of a transfer of assets by one corporation to another, it means a transfer made "in pursuance of a plan of reorganization" * * * of corporate business; and not a transfer of assets by one corporation to another in pursuance of a plan having no relation to the business of either, as plainly is the case here. Putting aside, then, the question of motive in respect of taxation altogether, and fixing the character of the proceeding by what actually occurred, what do we find? Simply an operation having no business or corporate purpose—a mere device which put on the form of a corporate reorganization as a disguise for concealing its real character, and the sole object and accomplishment of which was the consummation of a preconceived plan, not to reorganize a business or any part of a business, but to transfer a parcel of corporate shares to the petitioner. No doubt, a new and valid corporation was created. But that corporation was nothing more than a contrivance to the end last described. It was brought into existence for no other purpose; it performed, as it was intended from the beginning it should perform, no other function. When that limited function had been exercised, it immediately was put to death.

In these circumstances, the facts speak for themselves and are susceptible of but one interpretation. The whole undertaking, though conducted according to the terms of [the statutory provision], was in fact an elaborate and devious form of conveyance masquerading as a corporate reorganization, and nothing else. The rule which excludes from consideration the motive of tax avoidance is not pertinent to the situation, because the transaction upon its face lies outside the plain intent of the statute. To hold otherwise would be to exalt artifice above reality and to deprive the statutory provision in question of all serious purpose.

Judgment affirmed.

DETAILED ANALYSIS

1. **REPEAL AND RESTORATION OF FORMER SECTION 112(g).**

The tax avoidance potential of former § 112(g) had led to its elimination in 1934, prior to the Supreme Court's decision in *Gregory*. But in 1951 the provision was revived in altered form as the predecessor of current § 355, discussed in Chapter 12.

2. **JUDGE HAND ON THE GREGORY DECISION**

A year after *Gregory* was decided, in Chisholm v. Commissioner, 79 F.2d 14 (2d Cir.1935), Judge Learned Hand described the *Gregory* case as follows:

It is important to observe just what the Supreme Court held in that case. It was solicitous to reaffirm the doctrine that a man's motive to avoid taxation will not establish his liability if the transaction does not do so without it. The question always is whether the transaction under scrutiny is in fact what it appears to be in form; a marriage may be a joke; a contract may be intended only to deceive others; an agreement may have a collateral defeasance. In such cases the transaction as a whole is different from its appearance. True, it is always the intent that controls; and we need not for this occasion press the difference between intent and purpose. We may assume that purpose may be the touchstone, but the purpose which counts is one which defeats or contradicts the apparent transaction, not the purpose to escape taxation which the apparent, but not the whole, transaction would realize. In Gregory v. Helvering, supra, 293 U.S. 465, 55 S.Ct. 266, the incorporators adopted the usual form for creating business corporations; but their intent, or purpose, was merely to draught the papers, in fact not to create corporations as the court understood that word. That was the purpose which defeated their exemption, not the accompanying purpose to escape taxation; that purpose was legally neutral. Had they really meant to conduct a business by means of the two reorganized companies, they would have escaped whatever other aim they might have had, whether to avoid taxes, or to regenerate the world.

And in 1948, Judge Hand said in Commissioner v. National Carbide Corporation, 167 F.2d 304 (2d Cir.1948), aff'd, 336 U.S. 422 (1949):

In Gregory v. Helvering the taxpayer had organized a corporation only to serve as a means of transfer; it was used once and only for that purpose, and was dissolved as soon as it had done so. The Court held that it was not a "corporation" within the meaning of that term, as Congress must be understood to have used it, because in common speech, it means a jural person created to conduct industry, commerce, charity or some other commonly practiced activity, and not to serve merely as an escape from taxation. Such a corporation might be in some contexts a "corporation"; but words are chameleons, which reflect the color of their environment, and in a tax statute "corporation" could not have been so intended.

This decision has at times been thought to trench upon the doctrine—which courts are never tired of repeating—that the rights resulting from a legal transaction otherwise valid, are not different, vis-a-vis taxation, because it has been undertaken to escape taxation. That is a doctrine essential to industry and commerce in a society like our own, in which, so far as possible, business is always shaped to the form best suited to keep down taxes. Gregory v. Helvering, supra, was no exception, in spite of the fact that it was the purpose for which the taxpayer created the corporation that determined the event; for it is not the presence of an accompanying motive to escape taxation that is ever decisive, but the absence of any motive which brings the corporation within the group of those enterprises which the word ordinarily includes. Indeed, a corporation may be a "sham" and "unreal," when the only reason for its creation was "to deter the creditors of one of the partners," who organized it, for that is not an activity commonly understood to be corporate.

3.   OTHER ASPECTS OF *GREGORY*

As Randolph Paul stated: "Few cases have been the subject of such violent disagreement and confusion as the *Gregory* case. The case is all things to all men."[13] The disagreement is between those who follow the philosophy of the Board of Tax Appeals in that case and those who follow the view of Judge Hand and the Supreme Court. But while the dispute may be heated, every wise tax advisor realizes that the attitude of the *Gregory* decision is still alive today in the tax world. Tax avoidance schemes must reckon with that attitude and with judicial and administrative ingenuity in applying it. The principle of the decision is not limited to the reorganization provisions, but pervades the entire Code. The *Gregory* decision is expressed in many ways and words, all of which come to the pointed warning, "Beware—Proceed with Caution," that faces tax reduction plans having any element of artificiality or non-conformance with normal business or family conduct.

There are, as the quotations above from Judge Hand's opinions indicate, many facets to the *Gregory* "business purpose" doctrine. While the facets often overlap, there are some recognizable patterns. For example:

1.   *Sham Situations.* The business purpose test is applied to disregard the existence of a particular entity or the effect of a particular status where its existence serves no function apart from its tax-saving function. This is the *Gregory* case itself.

2.   *Transactions Lacking Economic Reality.* Suppose that a transaction is entered into that involves binding legal obligations not of a transitory character, so it is not a "sham," and that its arrangements and end result comply as a technical matter with the statutory requirements, so that it is not affected by the step transaction doctrine. The transaction, however, lacks economic or business reality in the sense that it would not be entered into except for the benefit that results solely from the expected tax consequences. Here courts sometimes will apply the "business purpose" doctrine to defeat such plans on the ground that they represent a distortion of the function of the particular statutory provisions in question or will require that the transaction involve some "purposive" activity apart from the tax benefits to be derived. For example, Wortham Machinery Co. v. United States, 521 F.2d 160 (10th Cir.1975), denied a net operating loss carryover (otherwise available under § 381 and § 382, discussed in Chapter 13) to the acquiring corporation in a transaction that literally complied with the statutory requirements for a type (C) reorganization. In the transaction a corporation transferred its assets, which consisted primarily of a net operating loss carryover, to its sister corporation in exchange for that corporation's stock. The stock was distributed to the controlling shareholders

---

[13]   Paul, Studies in Federal Taxation, Third Series (1940) 125 and references cited.

of both corporations in a liquidating distribution. The court held that while the "questioned transaction was within the 'inert language' of section 368(a)(1)(C) the only attraction shown by the record for the acquisition of [the assets of the transferor] was the net operating loss carryover which [the acquiring corporation] used in its tax return to reduce its tax liability." Hence, there was no business purpose for the transaction.

In 2010, Congress added § 7701(o) to the Code. It addressed a judicial doctrine that explored both taxpayer motivation and economic reality. In terms of taxpayer motive, the statute asks whether "the taxpayer has a substantial purpose (apart from federal income tax effects) for entering into such transaction" and, in terms of economic reality, whether "the transaction changes in a meaningful way (apart from federal income tax effects) the taxpayer's economic position." Section 7701(o) did not so much codify the economic substance doctrine as settle some disagreements among the jurisdictions regarding the elements of the test. In particular, the statute clarified that a transaction could be disregarded for lack of economic substance if a taxpayer failed to satisfy either inquiry.[14] Congress also added substantial, strict liability penalties. See I.R.C. §§ 6662(b)(6), 6664(c)(2), (d)(2); see also I.R.C. § 6676.

3. *Step Transactions.* The business purpose test may be applied to disregard the separate existence of several steps and instead to judge the transaction by its end result with the intervening steps omitted. The Step Transaction Doctrine is discussed in greater detail below.

One or more of these doctrines often are loosely applied by a court invoking the principles of "substance over form." As far as corporate reorganizations are concerned, the business purpose doctrine has been incorporated into Treas.Reg. § 1.368–1(c) and –2(g), but the *Gregory* decision and the ramifications of the business purpose doctrine stand as judicial warnings that *some* provisions are off limits in *some* situations. This combination of the existence of a rule permitting transactions to be disregarded but uncertainty as to when the rule will be applied has an *in terrorem* effect that dampens the enthusiasm of some would-be tax manipulators but prompts others to take a chance where little is at risk if the scheme fails. But it is difficult to see how the Internal Revenue Code could be applied successfully without the safeguards afforded by the *Gregory* doctrine and its various facets. It is a technique of statutory interpretation difficult to apply but essential to our tax system as it now operates.

B. STEP TRANSACTION DOCTRINE

The step transaction doctrine, introduced in Chapter 1, is especially important in the area of corporate reorganizations. The classic articulation of the step transaction doctrine is found in Minnesota Tea Co. v. Helvering, 302 U.S. 609, 613 (1938): "A given result at the end of a straight path is not made a different result because reached by following

---

[14] See Charlene D. Luke, The Relevance Games: Congress's Choices for Economic Substance Gamemakers, 66 Tax Lawyer 551 (2013) (describing codification process and continued role of courts in determining the relevance of the doctrine).

a devious path."[15] When this judicial doctrine is applied, the tax treatment of several transactions is determined by examining their overall effect rather than giving effect to each of the several transactions in sequence. In some cases, however, the form of a transaction will be allowed to control. Predicting when the step transaction doctrine will be applied is difficult.

King Enterprises, Inc. v. United States

United States Court of Claims, 1969.
418 F.2d 511.

■ PER CURIAM:

* * *

This is an action to recover Federal income taxes paid by petitioner for the fiscal year ended June 30, 1960. The issues involve the proper characterization for tax purposes of the transaction in question, and the tax treatment of the resulting gain. * * *

Petitioner, King Enterprises, Inc., * * * was one of 11 shareholders in Tenco, Inc. * * * Tenco was financially successful over the years, and by 1959 had become the second largest producer of soluble coffee in the United States. Despite its financial success there was stockholder discontent.

Minute Maid Corporation had become by 1958 one of the nation's principal producers of frozen concentrated citrus juices. * * * Between January and July 29, 1959, Minute Maid submitted and the Tenco directors rejected three separate proposals for acquisition of Tenco stock. A fourth proposal was approved by the respective boards on August 25, 1959, and on September 3, 1959, petitioner and other Tenco shareholders signed an agreement with Minute Maid entitled "Purchase and Sale Agreement".

Pursuant to the Agreement providing for the sale of their Tenco stock to Minute Maid, the Tenco shareholders received a total consideration consisting of $3,000,000 in cash, $2,550,000 in promissory notes, and 311,996 shares of Minute Maid stock valued at $5,771,926. Petitioner's share of the total consideration consisted of $281,564.25 in cash, $239,329.40 in promissory notes, and 29,282 shares of Minute Maid stock valued at $541,717. The Minute Maid stock received by Tenco stockholders represented 15.62 percent of the total outstanding Minute Maid shares, and constituted in excess of 50 percent of the total consideration received.

---

[15] See also Del Commercial Properties, Inc. v. Commissioner, 251 F.3d 210 ("a particular step in a transaction is disregarded for tax purposes if the taxpayer could have achieved its objective more directly, but instead included the step for no other purpose than to avoid U.S. taxes").

On December 10, 1959, the Minute Maid directors approved the November 24th recommendation of its general counsel to merge the company's four subsidiaries, including Tenco, into the parent company, and authorized that the merger be submitted to its stockholders for approval at a meeting scheduled for February 1960. Minute Maid's annual report to stockholders announced the merger plan about December 3, 1959. On January 5, 1960, Minute Maid requested a ruling from the Commissioner of Internal Revenue whether in the event of the proposed Tenco merger the basis of Tenco assets in Minute Maid's hands would be determined under [former] section 334(b)(2) of the Internal Revenue Code of 1954. This was approved by the Commissioner by ruling of February 25, 1960 that "Under the provisions of section 334(b)(2) that basis of the property received by Minute Maid upon the complete liquidation of Tenco will be determined by reference to the adjusted basis of the Tenco stock in the hands of Minute Maid." On April 30 and May 2, 1960, in accordance with the applicable state laws, Tenco and certain other subsidiaries were merged into Minute Maid.

On its income tax return for the fiscal year ended June 30, 1960, * * * [t]he value of the Minute Maid stock received by petitioner was not reported, it being petitioner's position that such stock was received in connection with a nontaxable corporate reorganization. The District Director of Internal Revenue assessed a deficiency on the ground that the gain portion of the total consideration received (cash, notes, and Minute Maid stock) constituted taxable capital gain from the sale of a capital asset.

* * *

Petitioner contends that the transfer by the Tenco stockholders of their Tenco stock to Minute Maid in exchange for Minute Maid stock, cash and notes, followed by the merger of Tenco into Minute Maid, were steps in a unified transaction qualifying as a reorganization under section 368(a)(1)(A) of the 1954 Code. * * * The Government asserts that the transfer of Tenco stock to Minute Maid was an independent sales transaction; therefore, the entire gain realized by petitioner on the payment to it of cash, notes and Minute Maid stock is taxable as gain from the sale of a capital asset.

I

The Reorganization Issue

The threshold issue is whether the transfer of Tenco stock to Minute Maid is to be treated for tax purposes as an independent transaction of sale, or as a transitory step in a transaction qualifying as a corporate reorganization. Significant tax consequences turn on which characterization is determined to be proper.

The general rule is that when property is sold or otherwise disposed of, any gain realized must also be recognized, absent an appropriate nonrecognition provision in the Internal Revenue Code. One such nonrecognition provision, section 354(a)(1), provides in pertinent part:

> No gain or loss shall be recognized if stock or securities in a corporation a party to a reorganization are, in pursuance of the plan of reorganization, exchanged solely for stock or securities in such corporation or in another corporation a party to the reorganization.

By its terms, this exception to the general rule of taxation depends for its operation on the existence of a corporate reorganization. The term "reorganization", moreover, is a word of art in tax law and is specifically defined in section 368(a)(1) as comprising six types of transactions, exclusively.

* * *

It is not disputed that there was a Type A reorganization in April 1960 when Tenco and Minute Maid were merged in accordance with state law. Nor does the Government dispute that Minute Maid continued the business of Tenco following the merger, or that the former Tenco shareholders had a continuity of interest in the enterprise by virtue of their ownership of stock in Minute Maid received in the exchange. The disagreement centers on whether the initial exchange of stock was a step in a unified transaction pursuant to a "plan of reorganization".

The underlying theory of the petitioner's claim is that the tax consequences of business transactions are properly determined by their substance and not by the form in which they are cast. Thus petitioner views the substance of the transaction under review to be an acquisition by Minute Maid of Tenco's assets in exchange for transferring Minute Maid stock, cash and notes to Tenco's stockholders. * * * The value of the Minute Maid stock received, which exceeded 50 percent of the total consideration, constituted a sufficient continuity of interest to support a Type A reorganization.[5] Petitioner concludes, therefore, that the net result of the entire transaction is a reorganization, not to be altered by splitting the entire transaction into its component transitory steps. * * * Petitioner's conclusion is justified in fact and in law.

The problem of deciding whether to accord the separate steps of a complex transaction independent significance, or to treat them as related steps in a unified transaction, is a recurring problem in the field of tax law.[6] The principle that even extended business transactions have

---

[5] In Rev.Rul. 66–224, 1966–2 C.B. 114, the IRS ruled that the continuity of interest requirement of section 1.368–1(b) is satisfied when, pursuant to a statutory merger, 50% of the consideration received by stockholders of the dissolved corporation is comprised of stock of the surviving corporation.

[6] In coping with this and related problems, courts have enunciated a variety of doctrines, such as step transaction, business purpose, and substance over form. Although the various doctrines overlap and it is not always clear in a particular case which one is most appropriate, their common premise is that the substantive realities of a transaction determine its tax consequences.

determinate limits for tax purposes is based on a strong preference for "closed transactions" upon which to impose tax consequences. This preference is tempered, however, with respect for the integrity of an entire transaction. Accordingly, the essence of the step transaction doctrine is that an "integrated transaction must not be broken into independent steps or, conversely, that the separate steps must be taken together in attaching tax consequences". Bittker and Eustice, Federal Income Taxation of Corporations and Shareholders, p. 18 (1966) * * *. The mere recitation of the doctrine, however, does not clarify the necessary relationship between the steps requisite to characterization as an integrated transaction.

Analysis of the reported cases and the diverse business transactions they encompass reveals that there is no universal test applicable to step transaction situations. See * * * American Bantam Car Co. v. Commissioner of Internal Revenue, 11 T.C. 397 (1948), aff'd, 177 F.2d 513 (3d Cir.1949); * * * Commissioner of Internal Revenue v. Gordon, 391 U.S. 83 * * * (1968). It has been persuasively suggested that "the aphorisms about 'closely related steps' and 'integrated transactions' may have different meanings in different contexts, and that there may be not one rule, but several, depending on the substantive provision of the Code to which they are being applied". Mintz and Plumb, Step Transactions, pp. 247, 252–253 (1954).

In their attempt to define the criteria upon which application of step transaction principles depend, the courts have enunciated two basic tests. The "interdependence test" requires an inquiry as to "whether on a reasonable interpretation of objective facts the steps were so interdependent that the legal relations created by one transaction would have been fruitless without a completion of the series". Paul and Zimet, Step Transactions, Selected Studies in Federal Taxation (2d Series, 1938), pp. 200, 254. * * * The "end result" test, on the other hand, establishes a standard whereby:

> * * * purportedly separate transactions will be amalgamated into a single transaction when it appears that they were really component parts of a single transaction intended from the outset to be taken for the purpose of reaching the ultimate result.[7]

Despite the real differences between the tests, each is faithful to the central purpose of the step transaction doctrine; that is, to assure that tax consequences turn on the substance of a transaction rather than on its form.

In support of its position that the step transaction doctrine is inapplicable to the facts of this case the Government correctly points out that there was no binding commitment for the merger of Tenco to follow the acquisition of its stock. Defendant erroneously concludes, however,

---

[7]   Herwitz, Business Planning, p. 804 (1966). * * *

that the absence of such a commitment here renders the step transaction doctrine inapplicable. The binding commitment requirement relied upon by the Government, was enunciated by the Supreme Court in Commissioner of Internal Revenue v. Gordon, supra, * * * wherein the Court said "if one transaction is to be characterized as a 'first step' there must be a binding commitment to take the later steps". Analysis of the statement in its proper context, however, dispels its application to the case before us. In Gordon, Pacific transferred certain of its assets to a new company, Northwest, in exchange for all of the latter's common stock, and debt paper. In 1961 Pacific distributed to its shareholders rights to purchase about 57 percent of Northwest's common stock at $16 per share, a price below its market value. Pacific notified its stockholders that "[i]t is expected that within about three years * * * the Company by one or more offerings will offer for sale the balance of such stock * * *." 391 U.S., at 97, 88 S.Ct., at 1525. In 1963 the remaining Northwest stock was offered to Pacific stockholders through distributed rights. Taxpayers were minority stockholders of Pacific who received rights in the 1961 distribution. Taxpayers sold four rights and exercised the balance, but they reported no income for the year 1961 from these transactions.

The primary issue in Gordon was whether the 1961 distribution was part of a Type D reorganization. To qualify as a D reorganization, Pacific must have distributed all or an amount constituting control (80 percent) of the Northwest stock. Sec. 355(a)(1)(D). In disposing of taxpayers' contention that the 1963 distribution (43 percent), taken in conjunction with the 1961 distribution (57 percent), satisfied the statutory requirement, the Supreme Court said at pp. 96–97 * * *:

> * * * The Code requires that "the distribution" divest the controlling corporation of all of, or 80% control of, the controlled corporation. Clearly, if an initial transfer of less than a controlling interest in the controlled corporation is to be treated for tax purposes as a mere first step in the divestiture of control, it must at least be identifiable as such at the time it is made. Absent other specific directions from Congress, Code provisions must be interpreted so as to conform to the basic premise of annual tax accounting. It would be wholly inconsistent with this premise to hold that the essential character of a transaction, and its tax impact, should remain not only undeterminable but unfixed for an indefinite and unlimited period in the future, awaiting events that might or might not happen. This requirement that the character of a transaction be determinable does not mean that the entire divestiture must necessarily occur within a single tax year. It does, however, mean that if one transaction is to be characterized as a "first step" there must be a binding commitment to take the later steps.

Here, it was little more than a fortuity that, by the time suit was brought alleging a deficiency in taxpayers' 1961 returns, Pacific had distributed the remainder of the stock. * * *.

The opinion in Gordon contains not the slightest indication that the Supreme Court intended the binding commitment requirement as the touchstone of the step transaction doctrine in tax law. Nor is there any indication that the Court intended to overrule any prior decisions applying the step transaction doctrine to other types of transactions where there were no binding commitments. On the contrary, the opinion addressed a narrow situation (a D reorganization) involving a specific statutory requirement (divestiture of control), and limited the potential for dilution and circumvention of that requirement by prohibiting the indefinite extension of divestiture distributions. Its interpretation should be so limited.[8] Clearly, the step transaction doctrine would be a dead letter if restricted to situations where the parties were bound to take certain steps.

The doctrine derives vitality, rather, from its application where the form of a transaction does not require a particular further step be taken; but, once taken, the substance of the transaction reveals that the ultimate result was intended from the outset. * * * In the majority of cases, it is the Government that relies on the step transaction doctrine for tax characterization. General application of the binding commitment requirement would effectively insure taxpayers of virtual exemption from the doctrine merely by refraining from such commitments. Such an untoward result cannot be intended by the Gordon opinion; indeed, defendant acknowledges as much in its brief by stating "the Supreme Court seems to have restricted the step transaction doctrine at least in one type of transaction, a corporate distribution of stock in a controlled corporation". The present case involves no such transaction.

In the alternative, the Government asserts that the step transaction doctrine has no application to this case because the merger of Tenco into Minute Maid was not the intended end result from the outset. Although the appropriate standard is invoked, defendant's assertion is inconsistent with the inferences to be drawn from the record.

The operative facts emerging from the record in this case suggest that Minute Maid, desirous of diversifying its operations in order to stabilize its income, was presented with the opportunity to acquire the entire stock of Tenco for a bargain "price". Tenco's record of financial success and its asking price for Tenco stock of seven or eight times its earnings (while other companies were asking 20 times their earnings),

---

[8] See Mintz v. Plumb, supra, at 285, where in regard to the similarly restrictive interdependence test it is concluded:

[The interdependence test] applies * * * in cases * * * where the concept of a "plan or reorganization" is not pertinent. In reorganization cases, except possibly in applying the "control" requirement * * * the determinative test seems to be whether the step was intended, or even contemplated as an alternative possibility, under the plan or reorganization, and the test of "interdependence" has not been applied.

without more, constituted an attractive investment. After the stock acquisition, moreover, Minute Maid was at liberty to operate Tenco as a wholly owned subsidiary, if it so desired. There is no persuasive evidence, however, that Minute Maid's appetite was limited to these goals, though worthy, when there was more in sight. On the contrary, the record reveals that, prior to the acquisition of Tenco stock, the officers of Minute Maid considered merging its existing subsidiaries into the parent in order to eliminate some of the general ledgers and extra taxes, and to bring about other savings. In fact, the merger of subsidiaries as a money-saving device was Mr. Speeler's (Minute Maid's vice president and general counsel) pet idea, which he discussed with Minute Maid's President Fox before the initial agreement with Tenco.

Shortly after the stock acquisition, Minute Maid instituted steps to consummate the merger of Tenco into Minute Maid. The proposed merger was motivated by a desire to avoid additional income tax on intercorporate dividends, to eliminate duplicate costs in the approximate amount of $50,000, and to obtain a stepped-up basis for stock in foreign corporations and other assets owned by Tenco. The potential step-up in basis for the foreign stock was estimated at $750,000 and the step-up for Tenco's other assets, although unable to be precisely ascertained, was considerable and probably sufficient as a justification for the merger independent of the other assigned reasons.[10]

Minute Maid applied for on January 5, 1960, and received on February 25, 1960, a ruling by the Internal Revenue Service that Minute Maid's basis in property received upon the complete liquidation of Tenco would be determined under section 334(b)(2) by reference to the adjusted basis of Tenco stock in Minute Maid's hands. Subsequently, on April 30 and May 2, 1960, in accordance with applicable state laws, Tenco and certain other subsidiaries were merged into Minute Maid.

No express intention on the part of Minute Maid to effect a merger of Tenco surfaces in the record until after the initial agreement to exchange stock. It strains credulity, however, to believe other than that the plan to merge was something more than inchoate, if something less than announced, at the time of such exchange. One gains the impression that the record of intentions is edited, so in reconstruction we must lean heavily on the logic of tell-tale facts and lightly on chameleon words. It is difficult to believe that sophisticated businessmen arranging a multimillion dollar transaction fraught with tax potentials were so innocent of knowledge of the tax consequences as the testimony purports. Perhaps testimony from private tax authorities serving the parties would have yielded more explicit knowledge of the questions asked and the advice given, but a trial record is rarely perfect in retrospect and a

---

[10] Petitioner asserts that the potential step-up in basis of Tenco assets is approximately $5,525,000. There is also evidence that Minute Maid believed such step-up to be approximately $5,950,000. The actual step-up, though undisclosed by the available facts, is probably at least several million dollars.

decision must be reached on an objective appraisal of the facts, including the inferences to be squeezed from them.

The operative facts in this case clearly justify the inference that the merger of Tenco into Minute Maid was the intended result of the transaction in question from the outset, the initial exchange of stock constituting a mere transitory step. Accordingly, it is concluded that the initial exchange and subsequent merger were steps in a unified transaction qualifying as a Type A reorganization, and that petitioner received its Minute Maid stock pursuant to the plan of reorganization shown by the facts and circumstances above to have existed.[11]

* * *

Bruce v. Helvering
Court of Appeals for the District of Columbia, 1935.
76 F.2d 442.

■ GRONER, ASSOCIATE JUSTICE.

In January, 1928, E. E. Bruce & Co. was a Nebraska corporation conducting business in Omaha in that state. Its capital structure consisted of 2,380 shares of common stock. Petitioner owned 700 shares, her sister owned 700 shares, and the remaining 980 shares were owned by employees and former employees of the corporation. The Board found as a fact that petitioner and her sister, as of the time mentioned, desired to sell a part of their Bruce stock, in order to reduce their investment in that company and bring it more in line, as to amount, with their other investments.

On January 27, 1928, Churchill Drug Company, also a Nebraska corporation, determined, if possible, to acquire the entire capital stock of Bruce Company, and to that end authorized its president and secretary to purchase the stock on such terms and conditions as they thought advisable.

On January 28, the president and secretary of Churchill Company offered to purchase from petitioner and her sister 400 shares of the capital stock of Bruce Company for $96,000 cash. Each sister accepted the offer for 200 shares. Immediately after the sale had been agreed to, the president of Churchill Company stated to the two sisters that his company desired and intended to obtain all the outstanding stock of Bruce Company in order to merge the two corporations, and then offered on behalf of Churchill Company to exchange 2,400 shares of its preferred stock for the remaining 1,000 shares of Bruce stock then owned by the two sisters. The sisters had never before received such an offer, nor were they previously aware of Churchill Company's purpose, but after considering the offer for a part of that day, they accepted it. Within a few

---

[11] A formal plan or reorganization is not necessary if the facts of the case show a plan to have existed. See William H. Redfield, 34 B.T.A. 967 (1936).

days thereafter the exchange of stocks was consummated, and at the same time the payment of the purchase money on account of the 400 shares was duly made.

On or before April 18 following, Churchill Company had acquired all the outstanding shares of Bruce Company, and on that day the board of directors of Bruce Company authorized the transfer to Churchill Company of all its assets; and thereupon Bruce Company was dissolved. The Commissioner treated the sale of the 200 shares and the exchange of the 500 shares of Bruce stock belonging to petitioner as a single transaction and determined gain from the transaction to the extent of the $48,000 of cash which petitioner received. Petitioner, in her tax return for 1928, treated the two transactions as separate, and reported the $48,000 cash received by her for 200 shares of Bruce stock and paid the tax on the basis of the difference in its cost price and sale price. She treated the exchange of the 500 shares of Bruce stock for 1,200 shares of Churchill stock as a tax exempt exchange under [the predecessor of § 354]. The result of the Commissioner's action was to increase the tax liability some $4,000. The Board sustained the Commissioner's determination, and this appeal resulted. * * *

The Board, after finding the facts to be as we have stated them, was of opinion that despite the fact petitioner had entered into a binding agreement for the sale of 200 shares of her Bruce stock before she had heard of the plan of reorganization, and therefore before she negotiated for the exchange of her remaining shares, "still both transactions were made pursuant to the same plan of reorganization," and the Board apparently thought this was conclusive even though, as it suggests, the plan of reorganization was not her plan, and even though, likewise, she had not heard of it when she sold her 200 shares of stock for money.

The Board says: "Here the petitioner, pursuant to the plan of reorganization, gave up her rights to 700 shares of the stock of E. E. Bruce & Co. and received not only stock of the Churchill Drug Co., but also cash. Thus [the predecessor of § 354] does not apply, but the exchange which she made of the 700 shares would have been within the provisions of [the predecessor of § 354] if it were not for the fact that the property received in the exchange consisted not only of property permitted by such paragraph to be received without the recognition of gain, but also of money."

Our criticism of this statement is that its foundation is without factual support. Petitioner did not give up her rights to 700 shares of Bruce Company stock for stock in Churchill Company and cash. On the contrary, she sold 200 shares of stock for money. When that was done, she had but 500 shares remaining, and only these she exchanged for Churchill stock. Unless, therefore, the Commissioner is right in treating the two separate transactions as one, it follows necessarily the Board's conclusion is wrong.

The Commissioner gives no reason for his holding, nor does the Board, and we ourselves are unable to supply one. If petitioner, after making a binding contract for the sale of 200 shares of stock, had declined the subsequent offer of exchange, it is perfectly obvious the transaction would have been just an ordinary sale of stock for money with no relation to the reorganization plan. On the other hand, if the sale of her 200 shares of stock for money had been conditioned on the exchange of her 500 shares of stock for stock in the other company, the transaction would have been one directly under the provisions of [the predecessor of § 356]. And so also it would have been if the separation of the transactions were a fraud or a trick; but neither of these conditions is even contended for. Petitioner, as all agree, determined, entirely for investment purposes, to sell part of her share holdings in Bruce Company. With that purpose in view, she bargained with the president of Churchill Company for the sale of a limited number of shares at so much per share in money. She committed herself and was bound. The transaction was a completed one; the minds of the parties met and carried with it unconditional liability each to the other. It was a closed sale, and beneficial ownership passed. Not until then was petitioner informed by the purchaser he intended, on behalf of his company, to buy all other shares of Bruce stock outstanding, except those belonging to petitioner and her sister; and that for these he was willing to deliver, in exchange, 2,400 shares of the preferred stock of his company. That this proposal was accepted later in the same day is neither significant nor, as we think, important. There being no challenge to the good faith of petitioner or to the verity of the facts on which she relies, the result would be the same if the two transactions had been thirty or sixty days apart, and we think it certainly would not be contended in the latter case there was but a single transaction involving, as to all 700 shares, an exchange of stock in one corporation for stock and money in another.

The case we have would be wholly different if it appeared the plan was one designed to defeat the payment of taxes. In such a case it would be just as subject to condemnation as was the fictitious transfer of assets by one corporation to another, and thence to the sole stockholder, which, though accomplished in strict conformity with the statute, the Supreme Court denounced in Gregory v. Helvering, [293 U.S. 465 (1935)].

But here there is not a suspicious circumstance suggesting that what was done was a sham. The sale on the one hand, and the exchange on the other, stand on the admitted facts separate and apart; and as the Supreme Court has said, and as we also have said time and again, in such circumstances the correct rule is to give effect to what actually was done, for that, after all, is the test.

DETAILED ANALYSIS

1.   VARIATIONS OF THE STEP TRANSACTION DOCTRINE

As should be evident from the opinion in *King Enterprises, Inc.*, the difficulty in predicting when the step transaction doctrine will be applied is compounded by the fact that there are several different variations of the step transaction doctrine. It is likewise difficult to predict which variation of the doctrine will be applied. In Penrod v. Commissioner, 88 T.C. 1415 (1987), which was reproduced in Chapter 1 but whose succinct summary regarding these variations bears repeating, the Tax Court explained:

> * * * There is no universally accepted test as to when and how the step transaction doctrine should be applied to a given set of facts. Courts have applied three alternative tests in deciding whether to invoke the step transaction doctrine in a particular situation.
>
> The narrowest alternative is the "binding commitment" test, under which a series of transactions are collapsed if, at the time the first step is entered into, there was a binding commitment to undertake the later step. See Commissioner v. Gordon, 391 U.S. 83, 96 (1968) * * *. The binding commitment test has the advantage of promoting certainty in the tax planning of shareholders. Under such test, a court must make an objective determination as to whether the acquired shareholders were bound by an obligation to sell the shares received in an acquisition. Other factors, such as intent by such shareholders to sell their shares, are not considered. However, there have been objections to that test on the ground that the result is easily manipulable by taxpayers. * * *
>
> At the other extreme, the most far-reaching alternative is the "end result" test. Under this test, the step transaction doctrine will be invoked if it appears that a series of formally separate steps are really prearranged parts of a single transaction intended from the outset to reach the ultimate result. See King Enterprises, Inc. v. United States, 418 F.2d at 516 * * *. The end result test is based upon the actual intent of the parties as of the time of the merger. It can be argued that any test which requires a court to make a factual determination as to a party's intent promotes uncertainty and therefore impedes effective tax planning. However, in contrast to the binding commitment test, the end result test is flexible and bases tax consequences on the real substance of the transactions, not on the formalisms chosen by the participants.
>
> The third test is the "interdependence" test, which focuses on whether "the steps are so interdependent that the legal relations created by one transaction would have been fruitless without a completion of the series." Redding v. Commissioner, 630 F.2d at 1177 * * * American Bantam Car Co. v. Commissioner, 11 T.C. 397 (1948), affd. 177 F.2d 513 (3d Cir.1949). This test concentrates on the relationship between the steps, rather than on their "end result." * * * However, since the interdependence test requires a court to find whether the individual steps had independent

significance or whether they had meaning only as part of the larger transaction, the court may be called upon to determine the result the participants hoped to achieve. Thus, the interdependence test is a variation of the end result test.

Courts have applied each of these three alternatives to a variety of transactions to determine whether the transactions should be "stepped." * * *

The impact of the variation of the step transaction doctrine that the court chooses to apply can be significant. For example, if the court in *King Enterprises, Inc.* had determined that the mutual interdependence test or the binding commitment test ought to have been applied, rather than the end result test, Tenco and its shareholder, King Enterprises, Inc., would not have been involved in a reorganization.

2. OTHER EXAMPLES OF APPLICATION OF THE STEP TRANSACTION DOCTRINE

As in *King Enterprises, Inc.*, in some cases the step transaction doctrine is applied to find a reorganization where none would have existed if each step of the overall transaction were viewed independently. Unlike in the *King Enterprises* case, however, in most of these cases, the step transaction doctrine is applied at the IRS's behest to produce a tax-free reorganization, thereby denying a loss deduction, where following the form of the several steps would have produced a taxable transaction. For example, in Heller v. Commissioner, 2 T.C. 371 (1943), aff'd, 147 F.2d 376 (9th Cir.1945), the shareholders of a Delaware corporation organized a California corporation, contributing borrowed cash for the stock of the California corporation. The California corporation then borrowed additional cash and purchased the assets of the Delaware corporation, which paid its existing indebtedness and distributed the balance of the cash to its shareholders in liquidation. The taxpayer claimed a deductible loss on the liquidation of the Delaware corporation because his basis for his stock in that corporation exceeded the amount of the liquidating distribution. The IRS disallowed the loss, asserting that the series of steps was in fact a single transaction that was a reorganization under the predecessors of § 368(a)(1)(D) or § 368(a)(1)(F) and that, accordingly, pursuant to the predecessor of § 354(a)(1), no loss was recognizable. In response, the taxpayer argued that even if the transaction had the same result as a reorganization, no exchange of stock for stock as required by the predecessor of § 354(a)(1), had occurred.

The Tax Court held for the IRS, reasoning as follows:

In determining the substance of a transaction it is proper to consider the situation as it existed at the beginning and end of the series of steps as well as the object sought to be accomplished, the means employed, and the relation between the various steps. * * *

Petitioner and two others, the stockholders and directors of the Delaware corporation, decided to have the business, assets, and liabilities of that company taken over by a new California corporation. The desired end was accomplished by a series of steps, all of which were planned in advance. * * * The net result was that petitioner and the other two stockholders had substituted their interest in the Delaware corporation for substantially the same interest in the California corporation. The nonrecognition of gain or loss provisions of the statute are "intended to apply to cases where a corporation in form transfers its property, but in substance it or its stockholders retain the same or practically the same interest after the transfer." * * *

The result achieved under the plan could have been accomplished by having the California corporation acquire the assets of the Delaware corporation for its stock, and by having the latter distribute the stock to its stockholders in complete liquidation. Petitioner and his associates apparently chose the longer route, hoping that they might thereby become entitled to a loss deduction. However, as the Supreme Court pointed out in Minnesota Tea Co. v. Helvering, 302 U.S. 609, 613, "a given result at the end of a straight path is not made a different result because reached by following a devious path." The effect of all the steps taken was that petitioner made an exchange of stock of one corporation for stock of another pursuant to a plan of reorganization."

In Rev.Rul. 67–448, 1967–2 C.B. 144, P Corporation formed a subsidiary, S Corporation, and contributed P's stock to the subsidiary. S Corporation was then merged into unrelated corporation Y with shareholders of Y receiving P Corporation stock in the merger. The ruling treated the series of transactions as the direct acquisition by P of the Y stock in exchange for its own shares, thereby qualifying the transaction as a type (B) reorganization. "It is evident that the shortest route to the end result described above would have been achieved by a transfer of P voting stock directly to the shareholders of Y in exchange for their stock. This result is not negated because the transaction was cast in the form of a series of interrelated steps. The transitory existence of the new subsidiary, S, will be disregarded. The effect of all the steps taken in the series is that Y became a wholly owned subsidiary of P, and P transferred solely its voting stock to the former shareholders of Y." The ruling dealt with a situation arising before the enactment of § 368(a)(2)(E).

In some cases, a reorganization undoubtedly has occurred, but the question is the scope of the reorganization and the identification of the transactions that will be accorded nonrecognition as occurring "pursuant to the plan of reorganization." This type of issue was the question addressed in *King Enterprises, Inc.* Another case raising a similar issue was *J.E. Seagram Corp. v. Commissioner*, 104 T.C. 75 (1995). This case involved a battle of corporate giants for control of Conoco. J.E. Seagram Corp. approached Conoco to negotiate a friendly takeover. After negotiations broke down, Seagram made a public tender offer to acquire for cash at least 33% of the Conoco shares. In the meantime, Conoco entered into an agreement with DuPont pursuant to which DuPont agreed to acquire at least 51% of Conoco's shares for either stock or cash, provided a minimum number of shares had been acquired for stock. Pursuant to the agreement, after the requisite number of shares had been acquired, Conoco would then be merged into a subsidiary of DuPont, and Conoco shareholders would receive DuPont stock. Mobil Oil then entered the fray and an escalating round of purchase price increases ensued. Seagram acquired 32% of the Conoco stock for cash. Mobil dropped out. DuPont's tender offer was successful, and it acquired 51% of the Conoco shares for either stock or cash, including approximately 16 million newly issued Conoco shares acquired pursuant to an option granted by Conoco to DuPont. At this point, Seagram decided to accept DuPont stock, which constituted a little over 20% of the outstanding stock of DuPont, in exchange for its Conoco stock, and this exchange was completed pursuant to the tender offer. DuPont then completed its agreement with Conoco by merging Conoco into a DuPont subsidiary. Seagram claimed a loss on the exchange, on the theory that because approximately 78% of the original Conoco shareholders had sold their stock for cash, the transaction lacked the requisite continuity of interest to qualify as a reorganization, even though approximately 54% of the Conoco shares were acquired by DuPont in exchange for its own shares. The IRS denied the loss, claiming that there was an integrated plan of reorganization and § 354 was thus applicable.

The first issue in *J.E. Seagram Corp.* was whether the exchange of Conoco stock held by J.E. Seagram for DuPont stock was "in pursuance of the plan of reorganization," as required by § 354 as a condition for nonrecognition. J.E. Seagram argued that the exchange of its Conoco common stock for DuPont common stock was not done in pursuance of a plan of reorganization, as required by § 354, and that therefore it could recognize a loss on the exchange. It claimed that DuPont's tender offer and the subsequent merger were separate independent transactions.

The Tax Court rejected J.E. Seagram's argument:

> The concept of "plan of reorganization" * * *is one of substantial elasticity. * * * One commentator has stated that

>> The courts, and the Service where it has served its purposes, have adopted a functional approach to the problem that is undoubtedly consistent with congressional intent. They have held that a plan of reorganization is a series of transactions intended to accomplish a transaction described as a reorganization in section 368, regardless of how and in what form the plan is expressed and whether the parties intended tax free treatment. * * * [Faber, "The Use and Misuse of the Plan of Reorganization Concept," 38 Tax L. Rev. 515, 523 (1982–1983).]

> The DuPont/Conoco Agreement was the definitive vehicle spelling out the interrelated steps by which DuPont would acquire 100 percent of Conoco's stock. To explain the mechanics of the type of procedure utilized by DuPont and Conoco, respondent submitted an Expert Affidavit of Bernard S. Black. Black is a Professor of Law at the Columbia University School of Law, where he teaches courses in Corporate Finance, Securities and Capital Markets Regulations, and Corporate Acquisitions. * * *

that even though "the step-transaction doctrine is properly applied to disregard the existence of the [merged subsidiary]," so that the first step is treated as a stock purchase, the acquisition of the target corporation's stock is accorded independent significance from the subsequent liquidation of the target corporation and, therefore, is treated as a qualified stock purchase regardless of whether a § 338 election is made.

Section 1.338–3(d) of the Income Tax Regulations incorporates the approach of Rev.Rul. 90–95 into the regulations by requiring the purchasing corporation (or a member of its affiliated group) to treat certain asset transfers following a qualified stock purchase (where no § 338 election is made) independently of the qualified stock purchase. In the example in § 1.338–3(d)(5), the purchase for cash of 85 percent of the stock of a target corporation, followed by the merger of the target corporation into a wholly owned subsidiary of the purchasing corporation, is treated (other than by certain minority shareholders) as a qualified stock purchase of the stock of the target corporation followed by a § 368 reorganization of the target corporation into the subsidiary. As a result, the subsidiary's basis in the target corporation's assets is the same as the basis of the assets in the target corporation's hands.

Section 368(a)(1)(A) defines the term "reorganization" as a statutory merger or consolidation. Section 368(a)(2)(E) provides that a transaction otherwise qualifying under § 368(a)(1)(A) shall not be disqualified by reason of the fact that stock of a corporation (controlling corporation), which before the merger was in control of the merged corporation, is used in the transaction if (i) after the transaction, the corporation surviving the merger holds substantially all of its properties and the properties of the merged corporation, and (ii) in the transaction, former shareholders of the surviving corporation exchange, for an amount of voting stock of the controlling corporation, an amount of stock in the surviving corporation which constitutes control of such corporation.

In Rev.Rul. 67–274 (1967–2 C.B. 141), Corporation Y acquires all of the stock of Corporation X in exchange for some of the voting stock of Y and, thereafter, X completely liquidates into Y. The ruling holds that because the two steps are parts of a plan of reorganization, they cannot be considered independently of each other. Thus, the steps do not qualify as a reorganization under § 368(a)(1)(B) followed by a liquidation under § 332, but instead qualify as an acquisition of X's assets in a reorganization under § 368(a)(1)(C).

ANALYSIS

Situation (1)

Because of the amount of cash consideration paid to the T shareholders, the Acquisition Merger could not qualify as a reorganization under § 368(a)(1)(A) and § 368(a)(2)(E). If the Acquisition Merger and the Upstream Merger in Situation (1) were treated as separate from each other, as were the steps in Situation (2) of Rev.Rul.

90–95, the Acquisition Merger would be treated as a stock acquisition that is a qualified stock purchase, because the stock is not acquired in a § 354 or § 356 exchange. The Upstream Merger would qualify as a liquidation under § 332. However, if the approach reflected in Rev.Rul. 67–274 were applied to Situation (1), the transaction would be treated as an integrated acquisition of T's assets by X in a single statutory merger (without a preliminary stock acquisition). Accordingly, unless the policies underlying § 338 dictate otherwise, the integrated asset acquisition in Situation (1) is properly treated as a statutory merger of T into X that qualifies as a reorganization under § 368(a)(1)(A). *See King Enterprises, Inc. v. United States*, 418 F.2d 511 (Ct. Cl. 1969) (in a case that predated § 338, the court applied the step transaction doctrine to treat the acquisition of the stock of a target corporation followed by the merger of the target corporation into the acquiring corporation as a reorganization under § 368(a)(1)(A)); *J.E. Seagram Corp. v. Commissioner*, 104 T.C. 75 (1995) (same). Therefore, it is necessary to determine whether the approach reflected in Rev.Rul. 90–95 applies where the step transaction doctrine would otherwise apply to treat the transaction as an asset acquisition that qualifies as a reorganization under § 368(a).

Rev.Rul. 90–95 and § 1.338–3(d) reject the approach reflected in Rev.Rul. 67–274 where the application of that approach would treat the purchase of a target corporation's stock without a § 338 election followed by the liquidation or merger of the target corporation as the purchase of the target corporation's assets resulting in a cost basis in the assets under § 1012. The rejection of step integration in Rev.Rul. 90–95 and § 1.338–3(d) is based on Congressional intent that § 338 "replace any nonstatutory treatment of a stock purchase as an asset purchase under the *Kimbell-Diamond* doctrine." H.R. Rep. No. 760, 97th Cong., 2d Sess. 536 (1982), 1982–2 C.B. 600, 632. (In *Kimbell-Diamond Milling Co. v. Commissioner*, 14 T.C. 74, *aff'd per curiam*, 187 F.2d 718 (1951), *cert. denied*, 342 U.S. 827 (1951), the court held that the purchase of the stock of a target corporation for the purpose of obtaining its assets through a prompt liquidation should be treated by the purchaser as a purchase of the target corporation's assets with the purchaser receiving a cost basis in the assets.) Rev.Rul. 90–95 and § 1.338–3(d) treat the acquisition of the stock of the target corporation as a qualified stock purchase followed by a separate carryover basis transaction in order to preclude any nonstatutory treatment of the steps as an integrated asset purchase.

The policy underlying § 338 is not violated by treating Situation (1) as a single statutory merger of T into X because such treatment results in a transaction that qualifies as a reorganization under § 368(a) (1)(A) in which X acquires the assets of T with a carryover basis under § 362, and does not result in a cost basis for those assets under § 1012. Thus, in Situation (1), the step transaction doctrine applies to treat the Acquisition Merger and the Upstream Merger not as a stock acquisition that is a qualified stock purchase followed by a § 332 liquidation, but instead as an acquisition of T's assets through a single statutory merger of T into X that qualifies as a reorganization under § 368(a)(1)(A). Accordingly, a § 338 election may not be made in such a situation. * * *

HOLDING

Under the facts presented, if, pursuant to an integrated plan, a newly formed wholly owned subsidiary of an acquiring corporation merges into a target corporation, followed by the merger of the target corporation into the acquiring corporation, the transaction is treated as a single statutory merger of the target corporation into the acquiring corporation that qualifies as a reorganization under § 368(a)(1)(A).* * *

Revenue Ruling 2008–25
2008–1 C.B. 986.

What is the proper Federal income tax treatment of the transaction described below?

FACTS

T is a corporation all of the stock of which is owned by individual A. T has 150x dollars worth of assets and 50x dollars of liabilities. P is a corporation that is unrelated to A and T. The value of P's assets, net of liabilities, is 410x dollars. P forms corporation X, a wholly owned subsidiary, for the sole purpose of acquiring all of the stock of T by causing X to merge into T in a statutory merger (the "Acquisition Merger"). In the Acquisition Merger, P acquires all of the stock of T, and A exchanges the T stock for 10x dollars in cash and P voting stock worth 90x dollars. Following the Acquisition Merger and as part of an integrated plan that included the Acquisition Merger, T completely liquidates into P (the "Liquidation"). In the Liquidation, T transfers all of its assets to P and P assumes all of T's liabilities. The Liquidation is not accomplished through a statutory merger. After the Liquidation, P continues to conduct the business previously conducted by T.

LAW

Section 368(a)(1)(A) of the Internal Revenue Code provides that the term "reorganization" means a statutory merger or consolidation. Section 368(a)(2)(E) provides that a transaction otherwise qualifying under § 368(a)(1)(A) shall not be disqualified by reason of the fact that stock of a corporation in control of the merged corporation is used in the transaction, if (i) after the transaction, the corporation surviving the merger holds substantially all of its properties and of the properties of the merged corporation (other than stock of the controlling corporation distributed in the transaction), and (ii) in the transaction, former shareholders of the surviving corporation exchanged, for an amount of voting stock of the controlling corporation, an amount of stock in the surviving corporation which constitutes control of the surviving corporation. Further, § 1.368–2(j)(3)(iii) of the Income Tax Regulations provides that "[i]n applying the 'substantially all' test to the merged corporation, assets transferred from the controlling corporation to the merged corporation in pursuance of the plan of reorganization are not taken into account."

Section 368(a)(1)(C) provides in part that a reorganization is the acquisition by one corporation, in exchange solely for all or part of its voting stock, of substantially all of the properties of another corporation, but in determining whether the exchange is solely for stock, the assumption by the acquiring corporation of a liability of the other shall be disregarded. Section 368(a)(2)(B) provides that if one corporation acquires substantially all of the properties of another corporation, the acquisition would qualify under § 368(a)(1)(C) but for the fact that the acquiring corporation exchanges money or other property in addition to voting stock, and the acquiring corporation acquires, solely for voting stock described in § 368(a)(1)(C), property of the other corporation having a fair market value which is at least 80 percent of the fair market value of all of the property of the other corporation, then such acquisition shall (subject to § 368(a)(2)(A)) be treated as qualifying under § 368(a)(1)(C). Section 368(a)(2)(B) further provides that solely for purposes of determining whether its requirements are satisfied, the amount of any liabilities assumed by the acquiring corporation shall be treated as money paid for the property.

Section 1.368–1(a) generally provides that in determining whether a transaction qualifies as a reorganization under § 368(a), the transaction must be evaluated under relevant provisions of law, including the step transaction doctrine.

Section 1.368–2(k) provides, in part, that a transaction otherwise qualifying as a reorganization under § 368(a) shall not be disqualified or recharacterized as a result of one or more distributions to shareholders (including distribution(s) that involve the assumption of liabilities) if the requirements of § 1.368–1(d) are satisfied, the property distributed consists of assets of the surviving corporation, and the aggregate of such distributions does not consist of an amount of assets of the surviving corporation (disregarding assets of the merged corporation) that would result in a liquidation of such corporation for Federal income tax purposes.

Rev.Rul. 67–274, 1967–2 C.B. 141, holds that an acquiring corporation's acquisition of all of the stock of a target corporation solely in exchange for voting stock of the acquiring corporation, followed by the liquidation of the target corporation as part of the same plan, will be treated as an acquisition by the acquiring corporation of substantially all of the target corporation's assets in a reorganization described in § 368(a)(1)(C). The ruling explains that, under these circumstances, the stock acquisition and the liquidation are part of the overall plan of reorganization and the two steps may not be considered independently of each other for Federal income tax purposes. See also, Rev.Rul. 72–405, 1972–2 C.B. 217.

Rev.Rul. 2001–46, 2001–2 C.B. 321, holds that, where a newly formed wholly owned subsidiary of an acquiring corporation merged into a target corporation, followed by the merger of the target corporation into the acquiring corporation, the step transaction doctrine is applied to integrate the steps and treat the transaction as a single statutory merger of the target corporation into the acquiring corporation. Noting that the rejection of step integration in Rev.Rul. 90–95, 1990–2 C.B. 67, and § 1.338–3(d) is based on Congressional intent that § 338 replace any nonstatutory treatment of a stock purchase as an asset purchase under the Kimbell-Diamond doctrine, the Service found that the policy underlying § 338 is not violated by treating the steps as a single statutory merger of the target into the acquiring corporation because such treatment results in a transaction that qualifies as a reorganization in which the acquiring corporation acquires the assets of the target corporation with a carryover basis under § 362, rather than receiving a cost basis in those assets under § 1012. (In *Kimbell-Diamond Milling Co. v. Commissioner*, 14 T.C. 74, *aff'd per curiam*, 187 F.2d 718 (1951), *cert. denied*, 342 U.S. 827 (1951), the court held that the purchase of the stock of a target corporation for the purpose of obtaining its assets through a prompt liquidation should be treated by the purchaser as a purchase of the target corporation's assets with the purchaser receiving a cost basis in the assets.)

Section 338(a) provides that if a corporation makes a qualified stock purchase and makes an election under that section, then the target corporation (i) shall be treated as having sold all of its assets at the close of the acquisition date at fair market value and (ii) shall be treated as a new corporation which purchased all of its assets as of the beginning of the day after the acquisition date. Section 338(d)(3) defines a qualified stock purchase as any transaction or series of transactions in which stock (meeting the requirements of § 1504(a)(2)) of one corporation is acquired by another corporation by purchase during a 12-month acquisition period. Section 338(h)(3) defines a purchase generally as any acquisition of stock, but excludes acquisitions of stock in exchanges to which § 351, § 354, § 355, or § 356 applies.

Section 338 was enacted in 1982 and was "intended to replace any nonstatutory treatment of a stock purchase as an asset purchase under the Kimbell-Diamond doctrine." H.R. Conf. Rep. No. 760, 97th Cong, 2d Sess. 536 (1982), 1982–2 C.B. 600, 632. Stock purchase or asset purchase treatment generally turns on whether the purchasing corporation makes or is deemed to make a § 338 election. If the election is made or deemed made, asset purchase treatment results and the basis of the target assets is adjusted to reflect the stock purchase price and other relevant items. If an election is not made or deemed made, the stock purchase treatment generally results. In such a case, the basis of the target assets is not adjusted to reflect the stock purchase price and other relevant items.

Rev.Rul. 90–95 (Situation 2), holds that the merger of a newly formed wholly owned domestic subsidiary into a target corporation with the target corporation shareholders receiving solely cash in exchange for their stock, immediately followed by the merger of the target corporation into the domestic parent of the merged subsidiary, will be treated as a qualified stock purchase of the target corporation followed by a § 332 liquidation of the target corporation. As a result, the parent's basis in the target corporation's assets will be the same as the basis of the assets in the target corporation's hands. The ruling explains that even though "the step-transaction doctrine is properly applied to disregard the existence of the [merged subsidiary]," so that the first step is treated as a stock purchase, the acquisition of the target corporation's stock is accorded independent significance from the subsequent liquidation of the target corporation and, therefore, is treated as a qualified stock purchase regardless of whether a § 338 election is made. Thus, in that case, the step transaction doctrine was not applied to treat the transaction as a direct acquisition by the domestic parent of the assets of the target corporation because such an application would have resulted in treating a stock purchase as an asset purchase, which would be inconsistent with the repeal of the Kimbell-Diamond doctrine and § 338.

Section 1.338–3(d) incorporates the approach of Rev.Rul. 90–95 into the regulations by requiring the purchasing corporation (or a member of its affiliated group) to treat certain asset transfers following a qualified stock purchase (where no § 338 election is made) independently of the qualified stock purchase. In the example in § 1.338–3(d)(5), the purchase for cash of 85 percent of the stock of a target corporation, followed by the merger of the target corporation into a wholly owned subsidiary of the purchasing corporation, is treated (other than by certain minority shareholders) as a qualified stock purchase of the stock of the target corporation followed by a § 368 reorganization of the target corporation into the subsidiary. As a result, the subsidiary's basis in the target corporation's assets is the same as the basis of the assets in the target corporation's hands.

ANALYSIS

If the Acquisition Merger and the Liquidation were treated as separate from each other, the Acquisition Merger would be treated as a stock acquisition that qualifies as a reorganization under § 368(a)(1)(A) by reason of § 368(a)(2)(E), and the Liquidation would qualify under § 332. However, as provided in § 1.368–1(a), in determining whether a transaction qualifies as a reorganization under § 368(a), the transaction must be evaluated under relevant provisions of law, including the step transaction doctrine. In this case, because T was completely liquidated, the § 1.368–2(k) safe harbor exception from the application of the step transaction doctrine does not apply. Accordingly, the Acquisition Merger and the Liquidation may not be considered independently of each other for purposes of determining whether the transaction satisfies the statutory requirements of a reorganization described in § 368(a)(1)(A) by reason of § 368(a)(2)(E). As such, this transaction does not qualify as a reorganization described in § 368(a)(1)(A) by reason of § 368(a)(2)(E) because, after the transaction, T does not hold substantially all of its properties and the properties of the merged corporation.

In determining whether the transaction is a reorganization, the approach reflected in Rev.Rul. 67–274 and Rev.Rul. 2001–46 is applied to ignore P's acquisition of the T stock in the Acquisition Merger and to treat the transaction as a direct acquisition by P of T's assets in exchange for 10x dollars in cash, 90x dollars worth of P voting stock, and the assumption of T's liabilities.

However, unlike the transactions considered in Revenue Rulings 67–274, 72–405 and 2001–46, a direct acquisition by P of T's assets in this case does not qualify as a reorganization under § 368(a). P's acquisition of T's assets is not a reorganization described in § 368(a)(1)(C) because the consideration exchanged is not solely P voting stock and the requirements of § 368(a)(2)(B) are not satisfied. Section 368(a)(2)(B) would treat P as acquiring 40 percent of T's assets for consideration other than P voting stock (liabilities assumed of 50x dollars, plus 10x dollars cash). See Rev.Rul. 73–102, 1973–1 C.B. 186 (analyzing the application of § 368(a)(2)(B)). P's acquisition of T's assets is not a reorganization described in § 368(a)(1)(D) because neither T nor A (nor a combination thereof) was in control of P (within the meaning of § 368(a)(2)(H)(i)) immediately after the transfer. Additionally, the transaction is not a reorganization under § 368(a)(1)(A) because T did not merge into P. Accordingly, the overall transaction is not a reorganization under § 368(a).

Additionally, P's acquisition of the T stock in the Acquisition Merger is not a transaction to which § 351 applies because A does not control P (within the meaning of § 368(c)) immediately after the exchange.

Rev.Rul. 90–95 and § 1.338–3(d) reject the step integration approach reflected in Rev.Rul. 67–274 where the application of that approach would treat the purchase of a target corporation's stock without a § 338 election followed by the liquidation or merger of the target corporation as the purchase of the target corporation's assets resulting in a cost basis in the assets under § 1012. Rev.Rul. 90–95 and § 1.338–3(d) treat the acquisition of the stock of the target corporation as a qualified stock purchase followed by a separate carryover basis transaction in order to preclude any nonstatutory treatment of the steps as an integrated asset purchase.

In this case, further application of the approach reflected in Rev.Rul. 67–274, integrating the acquisition of T stock with the liquidation of T, would result in treating the acquisition of T stock as a taxable purchase of T's assets. Such treatment would violate the policy underlying § 338 that a cost basis in acquired assets should not be obtained through the purchase of stock where no § 338 election is made. Accordingly, consistent with the analysis set forth in Rev.Rul. 90–95, the acquisition of the stock of T is treated as a qualified stock purchase by P followed by the liquidation of T into P under § 332.

HOLDING

The transaction is not a reorganization under § 368(a). The Acquisition Merger is a qualified stock purchase by P of the stock of T under § 338(d)(3). The Liquidation is a complete liquidation of a controlled subsidiary under § 332.

DETAILED ANALYSIS

1.   REVENUE RULING 2001–46 AND REVENUE RULING 2008–25

Note that the IRS utilized the step transaction doctrine to determine whether the transaction qualified as a tax-free reorganization. If the first step had been separately tested without integration with the second step, then the first step would not have qualified as a triangular reorganization under § 368(a)(2)(E). But, when the second step merger of the target corporation is integrated, then the transaction is tested on an overall basis as a § 368(a)(1)(A) reorganization and it satisfies that requirement.

Consider the similarity in the step transaction doctrine's application in Rev.Rul. 2001–46 (where two steps were integrated to find a § 368(a)(1)(A) reorganization) and Rev.Rul. 67–274 (where two steps were integrated to find a § 368(a)(1)(C) reorganization). The difference in outcome is attributable to whether or not the target corporation disappeared by reason of merger (implicating a § 368(a)(1)(A) reorganization) or whether it disappeared by reason of a liquidation (implicating § 368(a)(1)(C) reorganization).

Finally, compare the results in Rev.Rul. 2001–46 with situation 2 in Rev.Rul. 90–5, which was discussed in Chapter 8. In both rulings, the transaction could qualify as a tax-free reorganization by reason of the step transaction doctrine. However, in Rev.Rul. 90–5, the facts posit that the taxpayer made an affirmative election to apply § 338. Having done so, the transaction is then treated as a taxable acquisition subject to § 338, and the separate steps are given independent significance in accordance with the prescriptive rules set forth under § 338. Thus, the step transaction doctrine is supplanted once the taxpayer elects to apply § 338.

In Rev.Rul. 2008–25, the step transaction doctrine analysis was again utilized to determine whether the transaction could qualify under one of the reorganization provisions of § 368(a). The IRS concluded that it could not. After determining that the transaction could not qualify as a tax-free reorganization even with the aid of the step transaction doctrine, the IRS then concluded that the transaction represented a taxable acquisition. Once a transaction is determined to be a taxable acquisition, then the step transaction doctrine is not applicable to the taxable stock acquisition and solely § 338 is applicable.

PROBLEM SET 11

1.   Calvin owned all of the stock of True Believer Publishers, Inc. Calvin's basis for the stock was $4,000,000. Gimmie Shelter, Inc., offered to acquire all of the stock of True Believer in exchange for 60,000 shares of Gimmie Shelter, worth $3,000,000 (trading at $50 per share on the NYSE). Calvin counter-offered for 59,000 shares, worth $2,950,000 and $25,000 in cash. Gimmie Shelter accepted the counter-offer and acquired all of the stock of True Believer for 59,000 shares of Gimmie Shelter, worth $2,950,000, and $25,000 in cash. Calvin claimed a $1,025,000 capital loss on his tax return. Calvin has been audited and the IRS asserts that there was no business purpose for the injection of cash into the deal and that Calvin's loss should be disallowed. Assess Calvin's chances of prevailing in litigation of the issue.

2.   Paul owned a large parcel of land with a basis of $100,000. In January, BigBox Store Corp. asked Paul if he was interested in selling the land to BigBox for $10,000,000 in cash, or BigBox stock worth $10,000,000, or a combination of both. The offer was open until April 15. On February 1st, pursuant to advice from his C.P.A., Ernie Whinney, Paul transferred the land to newly formed Holding Corp. in a § 351 transfer. Paul owned all of the outstanding stock of Holding Corp. On March 1st, Paul counter-offered to BigBox's offer, stating that he would accept $10,000,000 of BigBox voting common stock (publicly traded on the NASDAQ system) in exchange for all of the stock of Holding Corp. This offer was accepted by BigBox and the deal was closed on April 1st. Shortly thereafter, Holding Corp. was dissolved and the land was distributed to BigBox in a § 332 liquidation. Ernie Whinney has advised Paul that the transaction with BigBox was a valid tax-free reorganization. Is he correct?

3.   Debby owned all of the stock of Cleveland Rock & Opera Recording Corp. Debby's basis for the Cleveland Rock stock was $5,000,000. P Corp., which is publicly traded, offered to purchase all of the Cleveland Rock. stock from Debby for $3,000,000. The purchase price was to be paid in the form of 12,000 shares of P Corp. worth $1,200,000 and $1,800,000 in cash. Debby's tax advisor, GMPK, CPA, LLC, advised Debby that a straightforward sale of the Cleveland Rock stock for $1,200,000 of P Stock and $1,800,000 of cash would not qualify as a reorganization under § 368 and that Debby could recognize a $2,000,000 loss of the sale of the Cleveland Rock stock. Debby never inquired about P Corp.'s plans for dealing with Cleveland Rock or Cleveland Rock's assets after the stock purchase and sale. Unbeknownst to Debby, P Corp intended to merge Cleveland Rock into P Corp.'s preexisting wholly owned subsidiary, S Corp., which it did promptly after the acquisition. Upon audit of Debby's tax return the IRS asserted that Debby disposed of the Cleveland Rock stock in a forward triangular merger pursuant to § 368(a)(1)(A) and (a)(2)(D), and that Debby could not recognize the loss. Assess Debby's chances of prevailing in litigation on the issue.

4.   The stock of T Corporation is publicly traded and widely held. T has only voting common stock outstanding. P Corporation acquired T Corporation in the following transactions, the plan for which was announced in advance. P Corporation made a tender offer in which it offered to pay two shares of P

corporation voting common stock for each share of T stock, pursuant to which it acquired 60% of the outstanding T stock. Immediately thereafter, P formed a new wholly owned subsidiary, S Corporation, which it capitalized with cash and P voting common stock in equal amounts, followed by a merger of S Corporation into T Corporation. As a result of the merger of S Corporation into T Corporation, the T Corporation minority shareholders (who owned the 40% of T Corporation not acquired by P Corporation in the tender offer) surrendered all of their T stock and received one share of P voting common stock, plus an amount of cash of equal value to one share of P voting common stock, for each share of T Corporation stock surrendered. After the merger, P Corporation owned 100% of T Corporation. Do these transactions result in a tax-free reorganization? If so, what type?

PART III

NONACQUISITIVE REORGANIZATIONS

CHAPTER 11

SINGLE-CORPORATION REORGANIZATIONS

SECTION 1. STATUTORY STRUCTURE

While the reorganization provisions are most important in the context of acquisition transactions, some forms of reorganizations allow exchanges of stock or securities to modify aspects of the corporate capital structure of a single corporation without requiring the current recognition of gain (or allowing the recognition of loss). The present statutory structure provides for reorganization treatment in two situations. Section 368(a)(1)(E) deals with corporate "recapitalizations," i.e., adjustments to the corporation's capital structure, as when a bondholder exchanges bonds for stock in the corporation or a shareholder exchanges stock of one class for stock of another class in the same corporation. Section 368(a)(1)(F) deals with a change in corporate structure involving a change in the place of incorporation or form of organization, such as when a California corporation reincorporates in Delaware.

The controversies involving these nonacquisitive reorganizations have primarily involved attempts by taxpayers to avoid dividend treatment on cash or other property extracted from the corporation. When dividends were taxed at ordinary rates rather than the preferential rates imposed on capital gains, as was the case in years prior to 2004, generally the issue was whether the reorganization rules themselves, as properly applied, should result in the receipt of a dividend when a shareholder received property (often debt instruments issued by the corporation) in the context of an admitted reorganization. With a preferential rate for dividends that mirrors the preferential rate for capital gains, generally a maximum rate of 20%, the stakes in this regard are greatly reduced. In other cases, the question is whether the transaction is in fact a reorganization at all, or whether it is more appropriately characterized as some form of sale or liquidation transaction, which qualifies for capital gain treatment at the shareholder level and results in recognition of gain or loss by the corporation. In these latter cases, it often has been the IRS that was arguing for characterization as a reorganization in order to apply the reorganization rules requiring dividend treatment.

The requirements of § 311 and § 336 that the corporation recognize gain on the distribution of appreciated property have curtailed taxpayer attempts to convert potential dividend income into capital gain by distributing property from the corporation. There remains, however, the fundamental question of whether an otherwise taxable transaction should be given nonrecognition treatment when it takes place in the context of a corporate adjustment or restructuring.

Section 368 provides the following definitions of the reorganizations considered in this Chapter:

Type (E) Recapitalizations. Section 368(a)(1)(E) covers the recapitalization of an existing corporation, such as, for example, the exchange of one type of stock for another, of new stock for old bonds, or of new bonds for old bonds. Here, only one corporation and its shareholders (or bondholders) are involved. These same transactions, however, can be implemented under § 368(a)(1)(A) or (C), for example, by a corporation that creates a new subsidiary corporation and has the new corporation issue to the parent, in return for the parent's assets, stock and securities of the nature desired, which the parent will then distribute to its shareholders on its liquidation.

Type (F) Change of Identity, Form, or Place of Organization. A mere change in identity, form, or place of organization of one corporation, however effected, is governed by § 368(a)(1)(F). For example, X Corporation may change its state of incorporation from New Jersey to Delaware by forming Y Corporation, a Delaware subsidiary into which X Corporation merges with the shareholders (and bondholders) of X Corporation receiving identical securities of Y Corporation in exchange for their interests in X Corporation. But if X Corporation simultaneously effects a recapitalization, for example, by exchanging both common and preferred shares of Y Corporation for X Corporation common stock (as was the case in Marr v. United States, 268 U.S. 536 (1925) (reprinted in Chapter 10)), then the transaction might not be an (F) reorganization. Such a transaction is not easily characterized as an (E) reorganization either. In this case, unless the single transaction can be bifurcated into simultaneous but separate (E) and (F) reorganizations, the transaction will be a reorganization only if it fits within the definition of one of the other subparagraphs, such as type (A).

SECTION 2.   RECAPITALIZATIONS: TYPE (E) REORGANIZATIONS

INTERNAL REVENUE CODE: Sections 108(e)(8), (10); 368(a)(1)(E); 354(a); 356(a), (c)–(f); 306(c)(1)(B), (C).

REGULATIONS: Sections 1.354–1(d), (e); 1.356–1, –3, –4, –5; 1.368–1(b); 1.368–2(e); 1.306–3(d), (e); 1.301–1(*l*).

Bazley v. Commissioner*

Supreme Court of the United States, 1947.
331 U.S. 737.

■ MR. JUSTICE FRANKFURTER delivered the opinion of the Court.

The proper construction of provisions of the Internal Revenue Code relating to corporate reorganizations is involved in both these cases. Their importance to the Treasury as well as to corporate enterprise led us to grant certiorari, 329 U.S. 695, 67 S.Ct. 62; 329 U.S. 701, 67 S.Ct. 77. While there are differences in detail to which we shall refer, the two cases may be disposed of in one opinion.

In the Bazley case, No. 287, the Commissioner of Internal Revenue assessed an income tax deficiency against the taxpayer for the year 1939. Its validity depends on the legal significance of the recapitalization in that year of a family corporation in which the taxpayer and his wife owned all but one of the Company's one thousand shares. These had a par value of $100. Under the plan of reorganization the taxpayer, his wife, and the holder of the additional share were to turn in their old shares and receive in exchange for each old share five new shares of no par value, but of a stated value of $60, and new debenture bonds, having a total face value of $400,000, payable in ten years but callable at any time. Accordingly, the taxpayer received 3,990 shares of the new stock for the 798 shares of his old holding and debentures in the amount of $319,200. At the time of these transactions the earned surplus of the corporation was $855,783.82.

The Commissioner charged to the taxpayer as income the full value of the debentures. The Tax Court affirmed the Commissioner's determination, against the taxpayer's contention that as a "recapitalization" the transaction was a tax-free "reorganization" and that the debentures were "securities in a corporation a party to a reorganization," "exchanged solely for stock or securities in such corporation" "in pursuance of a plan of reorganization," and as such no gain is recognized for income tax purposes. [The Court cites the predecessors of § 368(a)(1)(E) and § 354(a)(1)**.] The Tax Court found

---

*   Together with No. 209, Adams v. Commissioner of Internal Revenue.

**   [Eds.: The case arose under the 1939 Code which did not contain provisions corresponding to § 354(a)(2) and § 356(d), which treat the excess principal amount of securities received in a reorganization as boot.]

that the recapitalization had "no legitimate corporate business purpose" and was therefore not a "reorganization" within the statute. The distribution of debentures, it concluded, was a disguised dividend, taxable as earned income under [the predecessors of §§ 61(a), 301, 302 and 318(a)]. 4 T.C. 897. The Circuit Court of Appeals for the Third Circuit, sitting en banc, affirmed, two judges dissenting. 155 F.2d 237.

Unless a transaction is a reorganization contemplated by [the predecessor of § 368(a)(1)], any exchange of "stock or securities" in connection with such transaction, cannot be "in pursuance of the plan of reorganization" under [the predecessor of § 354(a)(1)]. While [§ 368(a)(1)] informs us that "reorganization" means, among other things, "a recapitalization," it does not inform us what "recapitalization" means. "Recapitalization" in connection with the income tax has been part of the revenue laws since 1921. Congress has never defined it and the Treasury Regulations shed only limited light. [Citing the predecessor of Treas.Reg. § 1.368–2(e).] One thing is certain. Congress did not incorporate some technical concept, whether that of accountants or of other specialists, into [§ 368(a)(1)], assuming that there is agreement among specialists as to the meaning of recapitalization. And so, recapitalization as used in [§ 368(a)(1)] must draw its meaning from its function in that section. It is one of the forms of reorganization which obtains the privileges afforded by [§ 368(a)(1)]. Therefore, "recapitalization" must be construed with reference to the presuppositions and purpose of [§ 368(a)(1)]. It was not the purpose of the reorganization provision to exempt from payment of a tax what as a practical matter is realized gain. Normally, a distribution by a corporation, whatever form it takes, is a definite and rather unambiguous event. It furnishes the proper occasion for the determination and taxation of gain. But there are circumstances where a formal distribution, directly or through exchange of securities, represents merely a new form of the previous participation in an enterprise, involving no change of substance in the rights and relations of the interested parties one to another or to the corporate assets. As to these, Congress has said that they are not to be deemed significant occasions for determining taxable gain.

These considerations underlie [§ 368(a)(1)] and they should dominate the scope to be given to the various sections, all of which converge toward a common purpose. Application of the language of such a revenue provision is not an exercise in framing abstract definitions. In a series of cases this Court has withheld the benefits of the reorganization provision in situations which might have satisfied provisions of the section treated as inert language, because they were not reorganizations of the kind with which [§ 368] in its purpose and particulars, concerns itself. See Pinellas Ice & Cold Storage Co. v. Commissioner, 287 U.S. 462, 53 S.Ct. 257; Gregory v. Helvering, 293 U.S. 465, 55 S.Ct. 266; Le Tulle v. Scofield, 308 U.S. 415, 60 S.Ct. 313.

Congress has not attempted a definition of what is recapitalization and we shall follow its example. The search for relevant meaning is often satisfied not by a futile attempt at abstract definition but by pricking a line through concrete applications. Meaning frequently is built up by assured recognition of what does not come within a concept the content of which is in controversy. Since a recapitalization within the scope of [§ 368(a)(1)] is an aspect of reorganization nothing can be a recapitalization for this purpose unless it partakes of those characteristics of a reorganization which underlie the purpose of Congress in postponing the tax liability.

No doubt there was a recapitalization of the Bazley corporation in the sense that the symbols that represented its capital were changed, so that the fiscal basis of its operations would appear very differently on its books. But the form of a transaction as reflected by correct corporate accounting opens questions as to the proper application of a taxing statute; it does not close them. Corporate accounting may represent that correspondence between change in the form of capital structure and essential identity in fact which is of the essence of a transaction relieved from taxation as a reorganization. What is controlling is that a new arrangement intrinsically partake of the elements of reorganization which underlie the Congressional exemption and not merely give the appearance of it to accomplish a distribution of earnings. In the case of a corporation which has undistributed earnings, the creation of new corporate obligations which are transferred to stockholders in relation to their former holdings, so as to produce, for all practical purposes, the same result as a distribution of cash earnings of equivalent value, cannot obtain tax immunity because cast in the form of a recapitalization-reorganization. The governing legal rule can hardly be stated more narrowly. To attempt to do so would only challenge astuteness in evading it. And so it is hard to escape the conclusion that whether in a particular case a paper recapitalization is no more than an admissible attempt to avoid the consequences of an outright distribution of earnings turns on details of corporate affairs, judgment on which must be left to the Tax Court. See Dobson v. Commissioner, 320 U.S. 489, 64 S.Ct. 239.

What have we here? No doubt, if the Bazley corporation had issued the debentures to Bazley and his wife without any recapitalization, it would have made a taxable distribution. Instead, these debentures were issued as part of a family arrangement, the only additional ingredient being an unrelated modification of the capital account. The debentures were found to be worth at least their principal amount, and they were virtually cash because they were callable at the will of the corporation which in this case was the will of the taxpayer. One does not have to pursue the motives behind actions, even in the more ascertainable forms of purpose, to find, as did the Tax Court, that the whole arrangement took this form instead of an outright distribution of cash or debentures, because the latter would undoubtedly have been taxable income whereas what was done could, with a show of reason, claim the shelter of the immunity of a recapitalization-reorganization.

The Commissioner, the Tax Court and the Circuit Court of Appeals agree that nothing was accomplished that would not have been accomplished by an outright debenture dividend. And since we find no misconception of law on the part of the Tax Court and the Circuit Court of Appeals, whatever may have been their choice of phrasing, their application of the law to the facts of this case must stand. A "reorganization" which is merely a vehicle, however elaborate or elegant, for conveying earnings from accumulations to the stockholders is not a reorganization under [§ 368(a)(1)]. This disposes of the case as a matter of law, since the facts as found by the Tax Court bring them within it. And even if this transaction were deemed a reorganization, the facts would equally sustain the imposition of the tax on the debentures under [the predecessors of § 356(a)(1) and (2)]. Commissioner v. Estate of Bedford, 325 U.S. 283, 65 S.Ct. 1157.

In the Adams case, No. 209, the taxpayer owned all but a few of the 5914 shares of stock outstanding out of an authorized 6000, par value $100. By a plan of reorganization, the authorized capital was reduced by half, to $295,700, divided into 5914 shares of no par value but having a stated value of $50 per share. The 5914 old shares were cancelled and the corporation issued in exchange therefor 5914 shares of the new no-par common stock and 6 per cent 20 year debenture bonds in the principal amount of $295,700. The exchange was made on the basis of one new share of stock and one $50 bond for each old share. The old capital account was debited in the sum of $591,400, a new no-par capital account was credited with $295,700, and the balance of $295,700 was credited to a "Debenture Payable" account. The corporation at this time had accumulated earnings available for distribution in a sum not less than $164,514.82, and this account was left unchanged. At the time of the exchange, the debentures had a value not less than $164,208.82.

The Commissioner determined an income tax deficiency by treating the debenture bonds as a distribution of the corporation's accumulated earnings. The Tax Court sustained the Commissioner's determination, 5 T.C. 351, and the Circuit Court of Appeals affirmed. 155 F.2d 246. The case is governed by our treatment of the Bazley case. The finding by the Tax Court that the reorganization had no purpose other than to achieve the distribution of the earnings, is unaffected by the bookkeeping detail of leaving the surplus account unaffected. See [the predecessor to § 316(a), second sentence], and Commissioner v. Wheeler, 324 U.S. 542, 546, 65 S.Ct. 799.

* * *

Judgments affirmed.

Revenue Ruling 84–114

1984–2 C.B. 90.

ISSUE

When nonvoting preferred stock and cash are received in an integrated transaction by a shareholder in exchange for voting common stock in a recapitalization described in section 368(a)(1)(E) of the Internal Revenue Code, does the receipt of cash have the effect of the distribution of a dividend within the meaning of section 356(a)(2)?

FACTS

Corporation X had outstanding 420 shares of voting common stock of which A owned 120 shares and B, C and D each owned 100 shares. A, B, C and D were not related within the meaning of section 318(a) of the Code. X adopted a plan of recapitalization that permitted a shareholder to exchange each of 30 shares of voting common stock for either one share of nonvoting preferred stock or cash. Pursuant to the plan, A first exchanged 15 shares of voting common stock for cash and then exchanged 15 shares of voting common stock for 15 shares of nonvoting preferred stock. The facts and circumstances surrounding these exchanges were such that the exchanges constituted two steps in a single integrated transaction for purposes of sections 368(a)(1)(E) and 356(a)(2). The nonvoting preferred stock had no conversion features. In addition, the dividend and liquidation rights payable to A on 15 shares of nonvoting preferred stock were substantially less than the dividend and liquidation rights payable to A on 30 shares of voting common stock. B, C, and D did not participate in the exchange and will retain all their voting common stock in X. X had a substantial amount of post-1913 earnings and profits.

The exchange by A of voting common stock for nonvoting preferred stock and cash qualified as a recapitalization within the meaning of section 368(a)(1)(E) of the Code.

LAW AND ANALYSIS

Section 354(a)(1) of the Code provides that no gain or loss will be recognized if stock or securities in a corporation a party to a reorganization are, in pursuance of the plan of reorganization, exchanged solely for stock or securities in such corporation or in another corporation a party to the reorganization.

Section 356(a)(1) of the Code provides that if section 354 would apply to an exchange but for the fact that the property received in the exchange consists not only of property permitted by section 354 to be received without the recognition of gain but also of other property or money, then the gain, if any, will be recognized, but in an amount not in excess of the sum of the money and fair market value of the other property. Section 356(a)(2) provides that if such exchange has the effect of the distribution of a dividend (determined with the application of section 318(a)), then there will be treated as a dividend to each distributee such an amount of the gain recognized under section 356(a)(1) as is not in excess of each distributee's ratable share of the undistributed earnings and profits of the corporation accumulated after February 28, 1913.

Under section 302(b)(1) and section 302(a) of the Code a redemption will be treated as a distribution in part or full payment in exchange for stock if it is not essentially equivalent to a dividend to the shareholder.

Rev.Rul. 74–515, 1974–2 C.B. 118, and Rev.Rul. 74–516, 1974–2 C.B. 121, state that whether a reorganization distribution to which section 356 of the Code applies has the effect of a dividend must be determined by examining the facts and circumstances surrounding the distribution and looking to the principles for determining dividend equivalency developed under section 356(a)(2) and other provisions of the Code. * * * Rev.Rul. 74–516 indicates that in making a dividend equivalency determination under section 356(a)(2), it is proper to analogize to section 302 in appropriate cases. * * *

In *United States v. Davis*, 397 U.S. 301 (1970), *rehearing denied*, 397 U.S. 1071 (1970), 1970–1 C.B. 62, the Supreme Court of the United States held that a redemption must result in a meaningful reduction of the shareholder's proportionate interest in the corporation in order not to be essentially equivalent to a dividend under section 302(b)(1) of the Code.

Rev.Rul. 75–502, 1975–2 C.B. 111, sets forth factors to be considered in determining whether a reduction in a shareholder's proportionate interest in a corporation is meaningful within the meaning of *Davis*. The factors considered are a shareholder's right to vote and exercise control, to participate in current earnings and accumulated surplus, and to share in net assets on liquidation. The reduction in the right to vote is of particular significance when a redemption causes a redeemed shareholder to lose the potential for controlling the redeeming corporation by acting in concert with only one other shareholder. *See* Rev.Rul. 76–364, 1976–2 C.B. 91.

The specific issue is whether, in determining dividend equivalency under section 356(a)(2) of the Code, it is proper to look solely at the change in *A*'s proportionate interest in *X* that resulted from *A*'s exchange of voting common stock for cash, or instead, whether consideration should be given to the total change in *A*'s proportionate interest in *X* that resulted from the exchange of voting common stock for both cash and nonvoting preferred stock.

In Rev.Rul. 55–745, 1955–2 C.B. 223, the Internal Revenue Service announced that for purposes of section 302(b)(3) of the Code, it would follow the decision in *Zenz v. Quinlivan*, 213 F.2d 914 (6th Cir.1954), that a complete termination of shareholder interest may be achieved when a shareholder's entire stock interest in a corporation is disposed of partly through redemption and partly through sale. *See also* Rev.Rul. 75–447,

1975–2 C.B. 113, in which the *Zenz* rationale was applied to section 302(b)(2).

Since the exchange of voting common stock for cash and the exchange of voting common stock for nonvoting preferred stock constitute an integrated transaction, in this situation involving a single corporation it is proper to apply the *Zenz* rationale so that both exchanges are taken into consideration in determining whether there has been a meaningful reduction of A's proportionate interest in X within the meaning of *Davis*.
* * *

If the exchange of voting common stock for preferred stock and cash in this situation had been tested under section 302 of the Code as a redemption, it would not have qualified under section 302(b)(2) or (3) because there was neither an adequate reduction in *A*'s voting stock interest nor a complete termination of that interest. In determining whether this situation is analogous to a redemption meeting the requirements of section 302(b)(1), it is significant that *A*'s interest in the voting common stock of *X* was reduced from 28.57 percent (120/420) to 23.08 percent (90/390) so that *A* went from a position of holding a number of shares of voting common stock that afforded *A* control of *X* if *A* acted in concert with only one other shareholder, to a position where such action was not possible. Moreover, it is significant that *A* no longer holds the largest voting stock interest in *X*. In addition, although *A* received dividend and liquidation rights from the 15 shares of nonvoting preferred stock, these were substantially less than the dividend and liquidation rights of the 30 shares of voting common stock *A* surrendered. Accordingly, the requirements of section 302(b)(1) would have been met if the transaction had been tested under section 302, and, therefore, the cash received by *A* did not have the effect of the distribution of a dividend within the meaning of section 356(a)(2).

HOLDING

When *A* received cash and nonvoting preferred stock of *X* in an integrated transaction in exchange for voting common stock of *X* in a recapitalization described in section 368(a)(1)(E) of the Code, the receipt of cash did not have the effect of the distribution of a dividend within the meaning of section 356(a)(2).

DETAILED ANALYSIS

1.   DEFINITION OF "RECAPITALIZATION" IN GENERAL

Section 368(a)(1)(E) includes within the definition of a reorganization a "recapitalization." The term "recapitalization" is not defined in either the Code or regulations, however, and its scope and contours have been left to judicial development. In general, a recapitalization involves a "reshuffling of a capital structure within the framework of an existing corporation," Helvering v. Southwest Consolidated Corporation, 315 U.S. 194, 202 (1942), and encompasses transactions involving exchanges of one class of stock or securities in a corporation for another class issued by the same corporation. Treas.Reg. § 1.368–2(e) provides examples of five different recapitalization exchanges, but those examples are not exhaustive.

The Courts of Appeals and the Tax Court held in the *Bazley* and *Adams* cases that no corporate business purpose existed and that the business purpose test must be viewed in terms of the corporation qua corporation and apart from the shareholders. Dissenting opinions in both courts contended that the shareholders had persuasive business reasons for the transaction (obtaining a more marketable security and one that could be sold without reducing stock control of the corporation, an equal footing with creditors to the extent of the debentures, and a more permanent dedication of the accumulated profits to the business). They rejected the view that shareholder business purposes do not supply the necessary corporate business purpose, stating that such a distinction between "corporate" and "shareholder" purposes lacked substance since a corporation did not have purposes apart from its shareholders. The government's brief stressed the argument that the transaction was not actuated by a purpose germane to the corporation's business, relied strongly on the *Gregory* case, and stated in effect that the stockholders' purposes were not relevant. In the light of this background, note the Supreme Court's avoidance of direct "business purpose" terminology. For a similar issue in the context of divisive reorganizations, see Chapter 12.

Rev.Rul. 77–238, 1977–2 C.B. 115, found an (E) reorganization existed where the certificate of incorporation required retiring employees owning common stock to exchange that stock for preferred. The purpose of the provision was to eliminate common stockholdings by employees no longer with the corporation, thus supplying the business purpose necessary to support the reorganization.

Treas.Reg. § 1.368–1(b) provides that neither the continuity of shareholder interest doctrine nor the continuity of business enterprise doctrine embodied in Treas.Reg. § 1.368–1(d) apply to a recapitalization. Thus, for example, a recapitalization might convert all of the shareholders to creditors and some or all of the corporation's creditors to shareholders; although § 356 would require gain recognition by the shareholders who became creditors, § 354 would accord nonrecognition of gain or loss to security holders who became shareholders. Likewise, incident to a recapitalization a corporation may sell all of its assets and purchase new assets to engage in a different line of business. Presumably, the corporation also could sell its assets and acquire investment assets, thereby becoming a holding company.

2. EXCHANGE OF OUTSTANDING STOCK FOR NEW STOCK OR NEW BONDS

2.1. *General*

The exchange of outstanding preferred stock for new preferred stock or of outstanding common stock for new common stock constitutes a recapitalization.[1] The exchange of outstanding preferred stock for common stock is likewise a recapitalization as is an exchange of common stock for common and preferred stock. Treas.Reg. § 1.368–2(e). In the latter situation, however, special rules apply to limit the "bailout" potential of the transaction.

It is not necessary that all shareholders in a recapitalization exchange their stock. Thus, a valid (E) reorganization results where only one of three shareholders exchanges common stock for preferred stock and the fair market value of the preferred equals the fair market value of the common stock exchanged. If there is a difference in value between the common and the preferred stock, the difference may constitute a gift, compensation, or "whatever purpose the facts indicate." Rev.Rul. 74–269, 1974–1 C.B. 87. See also Rev.Rul. 89–3, 1989–1 C.B. 278 (recapitalization whereby shareholder who had acquired shares by gift from controlling shareholder exchanged common stock for new voting common, and donor shareholder exchanged common stock for new common stock with restricted voting rights resulted in a taxable gift).

2.2. *Basis Aspects*

If a taxpayer acquires a corporation's stock at different times and at different prices and exchanges the acquired stock in a recapitalization, the bases of the acquired stock are not blended or averaged in computing the basis of the stock received in the recapitalization. Under Treas.Reg. § 1.358–1(a) and § 1.358–2(a)(2), the basis of each share of stock (or each security) received in a reorganization is the same as the basis of the share or shares of stock (or security or securities) surrendered. Assume, for example, that a shareholder purchased 200 shares of X corporation common stock for $1,000 and at another time purchased 100 shares of X Corporation common stock for $3,000. If in a recapitalization the shareholder exchanges the 300 shares of X Corporation common stock for 60 shares of preferred stock, 20 shares of the preferred stock will have a basis of $1,000 and 40 shares will have a basis of $3,000.

Special rules in Treas.Reg. § 1.358–2(a)(2) deal with more complex exchanges. If more than one share of stock or security is received in exchange for one share of stock or security, the basis of the share of stock (or security) surrendered is allocated among the shares of stock (or securities) received in the exchange in proportion to the fair market value of the shares of stock (or securities) received. If one share of stock or security is received in respect of more than one share of stock or security or a fraction of a share of stock or security is received, the basis of each share of stock or security surrendered must be allocated to the shares of stock or securities received in a manner that reflects, to the greatest extent possible, that a share of stock or security received is received in respect of shares of stock or securities acquired on the same date and at the same price. The regulations also provide rules for

---

[1]   Where the exchange is of stock for stock, there is an overlap of § 368(a)(1)(E) and § 1036. That section applies both to an exchange between shareholders and one between the shareholder and the issuing corporation. See Treas.Reg. § 1.1036–1(a). Both sections, however, produce the same result, at least where no boot is involved. Rev.Rul. 72–57, 1972–1 C.B. 103, held that where boot is involved, only the reorganization provisions apply.

situations in which a share of stock is received in exchange for more than one share of stock (or a fraction of a share of stock is received).

2.3. *Stock Surrendered in Exchange for Securities*

2.3.1. *General—Continuity of Interest*

In Hickok v. Commissioner, 32 T.C. 80 (1959) (nonacq. withdrawn, 1977–2 C.B. 3), the Tax Court held that the continuity of interest doctrine, discussed in Chapter 10, does not apply to recapitalizations. The IRS followed this principle in Rev.Rul. 77–415, 1977–2 C.B. 311, obsoleted by T.D. 8182, 2005–11 I.R.B. 713. Finally, in 2005, Treas.Reg. § 1.368–1(b) was amended to expressly provide that the continuity of interest doctrine does not apply to recapitalizations. Thus, for example, if A, B, C, and D each held 25% of the stock of X Corporation, a transaction in which A exchanged common stock for new common stock and new preferred stock, while B, C, and D exchanged their stock for debentures, would qualify as a recapitalization. B, C, and D would recognize gain, but A would be entitled to nonrecognition. Likewise, a pre-arranged sale of newly issued stock received in an (E) reorganization does not impair the validity of the reorganization. See Rev.Rul. 77–479, 1977–2 C.B. 119.[2]

2.3.2. *Security Bailouts*

Sections 354(a)(2) and 356(d) extend the rationale of the *Bazley* case to all recapitalization and other reorganization exchanges since the value of the excess in principal amount of securities received by the shareholder over the principal amount of securities given up is considered "other property" or "boot." Hence, if a shareholder exchanges stock, whether common or preferred, for new stock, whether common or preferred, and debt securities, the securities will be boot and governed by § 356(a). If stock is exchanged for securities alone, § 354(a)(2) renders § 354(a)(1) inapplicable entirely, § 356(a)(1)(B) does not come into play, and the treatment of the exchange is determined under § 301, § 302, and § 331. Treas.Reg. § 1.354–1(d), Ex. 3.

Thus, although lack of continuity of equity interest does not destroy the validity of a type (E) reorganization, § 354(a)(2) in effect applies a continuity of interest concept on a shareholder by shareholder basis. Where the recapitalization exchange "has the effect" of a dividend distribution, dividend income is recognized to the extent of the gain realized on the exchange. I.R.C. § 356(a)(2).[3] See Commissioner v. Estate of Bedford, 325 U.S. 283 (1945). As discussed in Rev.Rul. 84–114, reprinted above, dividend equivalency of boot

---

[2]   Rev.Rul. 77–479 was obsoleted by T.D. 8182, 2005–11 I.R.B. 713, because the primary holding in the ruling, which dealt with continuity of interest issues, has been superseded by regulations.

[3]   The effect of § 1036 must also be considered. On the face of the statute, there is an overlap of § 368(a)(1)(E) and § 1036 in these various situations. Where boot is involved in a § 1036 exchange, § 1031(b), which applies to § 1036 transactions, controls taxation of the boot. But in cases of an overlap between § 1036 and § 368(a)(1)(E), Treas.Reg. § 1.1031(b)–1(a)(3) defers to the reorganization provisions, See Rev.Rul. 72–57, 1972–1 C.B. 103 (exchange of outstanding stock for stock and cash as part of a transaction to eliminate minority shareholders was a recapitalization and therefore, under Treas.Reg. § 1.1031(b)–1(a)(3), was not a § 1036 exchange coupled with the receipt of nonqualifying property by the majority shareholder under § 1031(b)); Rev.Rul. 78–351, 1978–2 C.B. 148, modifying Rev.Rul. 72–57, held the cash was a § 356(a)(2) dividend to the majority shareholder.

distributions made in connection with a recapitalization is determined by applying the principles of § 302, which governs redemptions. See also Johnson v. Commissioner, 78 T.C. 564 (1982) ($850 per share boot in recapitalization which converted nonvoting common stock into voting common stock was a dividend because it was pro rata and compensated nonvoting shareholders for dividends previously withheld). The reasoning in Commissioner v. Clark, 489 U.S. 726 (1989) (discussed in Chapter 10), which significantly limits the application of § 356(a)(2) in the case of acquisitive reorganizations, should not affect the application of that section to recapitalizations because only a single corporation is involved. The IRS has so ruled in the context of a divisive reorganization of a single corporation under § 355. See Rev.Rul. 93–62, 1993–2 C.B. 118. In addition, in the appropriate circumstances, the IRS might argue that under the approach of *Bazley,* the full amount of the boot was a dividend. Treas.Reg. § 1.301–1(*l*) preserves this contention.

2.4. *Preferred Stock Bailouts—Exchange of Outstanding Common Stock for New Preferred Stock*

In a recapitalization variant of the preferred stock dividend bailout, dealt with by § 306, holders of common stock may exchange some common stock for new preferred, or exchange all of their common stock for new common stock and new preferred, so that after the exchange they own both common stock and preferred stock. Section 306(c)(1)(B) extends the § 306 solution to the recapitalization exchange if "the effect of the transaction was substantially the same as the receipt of a stock dividend." Treas.Reg. § 1.306–3(d) refers to § 356(a)(2) and states that if any cash received in lieu of the stock would have been a dividend under § 356(a)(2), then the stock is § 306 stock. If a cash distribution would not have been taxable under § 356(a)(2) because of the "dividend within the gain" limitation, then the stock apparently is not § 306 stock.

Rev.Rul. 81–186, 1981–2 C.B. 85, suggests that the § 318 attribution of ownership rules do not apply in determining whether preferred stock received in a recapitalization is § 306 stock. For example, if a husband retains his common stock but his wife receives preferred stock in a recapitalization, the preferred stock is not § 306 stock. That ruling held that where a sole shareholder exchanged some of his common stock for preferred stock in a recapitalization and gave his remaining common stock to his children, the preferred stock was not § 306 stock; if the shareholder had received cash it would not have been a dividend because he would have terminated his entire interest in the corporation. See Zenz v. Quinlivan, 213 F.2d 914 (6th Cir.1954) (excerpted in Chapter 9).

Where, in a reorganization, boot is distributed in exchange for § 306 stock, § 356(f) applies to treat the boot under § 301. In Rev.Rul. 76–14, 1976–1 C.B. 97, the majority shareholder desired to transfer control of the business to an employee-minority shareholder. Under a recapitalization plan, the majority shareholder turned in his common stock for cash and his preferred stock (which was § 306 stock) for a new class of nonvoting common stock. The ruling held § 356(f) applied; thus the cash received was applied first to the § 306 stock, with a resulting dividend. But if cash is distributed to minority shareholders in lieu of fractional shares, the exception in § 306(b)(4)(A) applies, and the cash will be treated as received in a redemption subject to § 302. Rev.Rul. 81–81, 1981–1 C.B. 122. If in the reorganization, stock that is other than common stock is issued for § 306 stock under § 306(c)(1)(B), the new stock is § 306 stock.

A recapitalization exchange can occur without a direct exchange of stock. Thus, in Rev.Rul. 56–654, 1956–2 C.B. 216, a corporation with outstanding common and preferred stock amended its charter to increase the liquidation value of the preferred stock. The ruling states that this represented an exchange of all preferred stock and a portion of the common stock for new preferred stock; presumably the increase in value of the preferred stock is § 306 stock. Rev.Rul. 66–332, 1966–2 C.B. 108, modified by Rev.Rul. 81–91, 1981–1 C.B. 123, held that a "reclassification" of outstanding common stock together with the issuance of additional classes of stock could result in the reclassified stock being treated as § 306 stock if, as a result of the change in its rights under the reclassification, it ceased to be common stock.

2.5. *Relation of Security Bailout to Preferred Stock Bailout*

The IRS's view of *Bazley* type recapitalizations prior to the 1954 Code was that the vice lay in splitting a common stockholder's interest into common stock (which could be retained) and another interest, preferred stock, or debt (which could be sold), thereby obtaining capital gain treatment for a part of the accumulated earnings without reducing the shareholder's common stock interest. The current Code embodies the view that an exchange of outstanding stock for debt must meet the tests of the dividend sections. It is akin to the policy of § 306 respecting preferred stock bailouts in that it seeks to block the efforts to convert situations having potential dividend taxation into situations involving capital gain potential only. The solution for the "security bailout," however, is that of an immediate tax, while under § 306 the solution for the "preferred stock bailout" is that of "tainting"—that is, giving the preferred stock an ordinary income status on future disposition.

3.   EXCHANGE OF DEBT SECURITIES FOR DEBT SECURITIES

3.1. *Qualification as a Recapitalization*

The regulations under § 368(a)(1)(E) and its predecessors never have expressly provided that an exchange of only debt securities qualifies as a recapitalization. See Treas.Reg. § 1.368–2(e). Treatment of the exchange of outstanding debentures for new corporate debentures as a recapitalization was first established judicially.

Commissioner v. Neustadt's Trust, 131 F.2d 528 (2d Cir.1942), involved the exchange of outstanding 20 year, 6% debentures for a like face amount of 10 year, 3¼% convertible debentures of the corporation. The IRS contended that a taxable gain resulted, but the court disagreed and applied the reorganization provisions:

> The first question is whether the debentures are "securities" within the meaning of [the predecessor of § 354(a)(1)]. The word is used in contrast to "stock"; it necessarily refers to bonds of some

issued in the transaction. I.R.C. § 108(e)(8). To the extent of the fair market value of the stock, § 1032 provides nonrecognition to the corporation.

If the holder of a security that is an OID instrument receives stock in exchange for the instrument in a recapitalization, the balance of the OID will not be included in the income of the exchanging bondholder. See Rev.Rul. 75–39, 1975–1 C.B. 272. The stock will take a basis under § 358 equal to the basis of the debt instrument, which includes all previously accrued OID.

On a related point, the exercise of a conversion privilege of a bond convertible into stock of the same corporation is not an "exchange" and hence the recapitalization provision and § 354 are not involved, Rev.Rul. 72–265, 1972–1 C.B. 222. See also Rev.Rul. 79–155, 1979–1 C.B. 153 (parent of subsidiary that issued debt obligations convertible into stock of parent was treated as a joint obligor on debt, thereby resulting in conversion not being a taxable event).

5. SECTION 305 ASPECTS

A recapitalization, which would be tax-free under the reorganization provisions, is one of the transactions that can result in a constructive stock dividend under § 305(c). See Chapter 6. For example, in a recapitalization in which a shareholder exchanges preferred stock with dividend arrearages for new common and preferred stock, the exchange would be a tax-free recapitalization under § 368. See e.g., Kaufman v. Commissioner, 55 T.C. 1046 (1971) (acq.). When viewed from the perspective of § 305, however, the recapitalization has the effect of a distribution of additional shares of stock to the preferred stockholder, which would result in a taxable dividend under § 305(c) and 305(b)(4). Treas.Reg. § 1.305–5(d), Ex. 1 (taxable stock dividend if arrearages are eliminated). See Treas.Reg. § 1.305–3(e), Ex. 12, however, illustrating that § 305 is inapplicable to a "single and isolated" recapitalization transaction.

PROBLEM SET 1

1.   Louisville Coal and Oil Co., Inc. (LCO), which is publicly traded, has 1,000,000 shares of no par common stock outstanding. LCO also has outstanding 10,000 shares of $100 par, 5% preferred stock. LCO's indebtedness consists of: (1) $10,000,000 principal amount 6% debt instruments due in 2020, which were issued for their face amount; and (2) $8,000,000 in bank loans. To what extent do any of the following proposed transactions qualify as a recapitalization? Do any shareholders or creditors of LCO, or LCO itself, nevertheless recognize any gain or loss even though the transaction may qualify as a recapitalization?

(a)   Common shareholders could exchange existing voting common stock for newly created Class B common stock at the ratio of 12 shares of new class B nonvoting common stock for every ten shares of voting common stock surrendered. With the exception of voting privileges, the class B common stock would be identical to the class A common stock.

(b)   (1)   Common shareholders could exchange up to one-half of their existing common stock for authorized but unissued nonvoting preferred stock at the exchange rate of five shares of common for one share of nonvoting preferred stock.

(2) Would your answer differ if the preferred stock were sinking fund preferred stock redeemable 25 years after issuance?

(c) All common shares would be converted into newly created Class A common stock and newly created Class B preferred stock at the exchange rate of one share of old common in exchange for one share of newly issued voting common and one share of newly issued nonvoting preferred stock.

(d) Common shareholders could elect to surrender up to 10% of their shares of LCO voting common stock in exchange for subordinated debt instruments of LCO bearing interest at two percentage points over the prime rate, which would be due in 2050.

(e) Preferred shareholders could elect to convert their preferred stock into common stock at the ratio of six shares of common for every share of preferred.

(1) Does the trading price of the common matter? Assume alternatively that the common is trading for $18 per share, $20 per share, and $22 per share.

(2) Would your answer differ if the preferred stock had $10 of dividends in arrears?

(f) The outstanding $1,000 debt instruments are currently trading for $680. LCO's debt instrument holders could exchange their debt instruments on the following alternative terms:

(1) Ten old debt instruments for seven new $1,000 debt instruments bearing interest two percentage points over the prime rate at the time of issuance. LCO expects the new debt instruments would trade for their face amount.

(2) Debt instrument holders could exchange a $1,000 debt instrument for 36 shares of LCO common stock, which is expected to be trading at $20 per share on the exchange date. Thus, each bondholder would receive stock worth $720 for each $1,000 bond worth $680.

(3) Would your answers be affected if the recapitalization were pursuant to Chapter 11 of the Bankruptcy Act?

(g) The Last National Bank, which holds a $2,000,000 demand note, with $500,000 of interest in arrears, would exchange the note for 90,000 shares of LCO common stock, which is currently trading at $20 per share.

SECTION 3.   CHANGES IN IDENTITY, FORM, OR PLACE OF ORGANIZATION: TYPE (F) REORGANIZATIONS

INTERNAL REVENUE CODE: Section 368(a)(1)(F).

REGULATIONS: Section 1.368–2(m).

Section 368(a)(1)(F) treats as a reorganization a change in "identity, form or place of organization of one corporation." The definition of a type

(F) reorganization focuses on purpose and effect, not the form of the transaction. Thus, the type (F) reorganization definition overlaps with other forms of reorganizations. For example, in order to change its state of incorporation, X Corporation might form a new Y Corporation in another jurisdiction and then merge into it. The transaction is both a type (A) and a type (F) reorganization, but the IRS has indicated that in these circumstances the transaction will be characterized as a type (F) reorganization. Rev.Rul. 57–276, 1957–C.B. 126.[5] The phrase "of one corporation" in § 368(a)(1)(F) precludes treating a merger of two or more pre-existing operating companies as a type (F) reorganization.[6]

If a transaction is a type (F) reorganization, the old corporation's taxable year does not end.[7] (Before the 2017 Tax Act repealed the § 172 net operating loss carryback provision, the new corporation was entitled to carry back to taxable years of the old corporation post-type (F) reorganization net operating losses. See I.R.C. § 381(b).) This result reflects the fact that the reorganized corporation is "really" unchanged by the reorganizing transaction. In other respects, the new (or acquiring) corporation succeeds to the old (or acquired) corporation's tax attributes under § 381, discussed in Chapter 13, in the same manner as in any other reorganization.

In 2015, the Treasury Department finalized Treas.Reg. § 1.368–2(m), dealing with the definition of a reorganization under § 368(a)(1)(F). The preamble to the final regulations, which follows, describes the scope of (F) reorganizations.

---

[5] See also Rev.Rul. 88–25, 1988–1 C.B. 116 (conversion of foreign corporation to domestic corporation by filing domestication certificate under state law); Rev.Rul. 87–27, 1987–1 C.B. 134 (reincorporation of domestic corporation in foreign country is a type (F) reorganization); Rev.Rul. 87–66, 1987–2 C.B. 168 (reincorporation of foreign corporation in U.S. is a type (F) reorganization); Rev.Rul. 80–105, 1980–1 C.B. 78 (conversion of federal mutual savings and loan association to state stock savings and loan association was a type (F) reorganization).

[6] Section 368(a)(1)(F) was amended in 1982 to add the phrase "of one corporation" to make it clear that the provision does not apply to the merger of pre-existing operating companies. See H.Rep. No. 97–760, 97th Cong., 2d Sess. 540–541 (1982). Prior to the amendment, some courts had permitted (F) reorganization treatment in such circumstances. See, e.g., Home Construction Corp. v. United States, 439 F.2d 1165 (5th Cir.1971).

[7] In cases where the type (F) and type (D) reorganization overlap, classification as a type (F) has an additional effect. Type (F) reorganizations differ from Type (D) reorganizations in that § 357(c) applies to type (D) reorganizations but not to type (F) reorganizations. Rev.Rul. 79–289, 1979–2 C.B. 145 (§ 357(c) does not apply to reorganization meeting requirements for both (D) and (F)). For example, if X Corporation, whose sole asset is land and a building, which has a basis of $50,000 and is subject to a $70,000 mortgage, reincorporates in a different state by merging into Y Corporation, a wholly owned subsidiary formed solely for the reincorporation transaction, no gain is recognized to X Corporation, and Y Corporation takes a $50,000 basis in the land and building.

Reorganizations Under Section 368(a)(1)(F); Section 367(a) and Certain Reorganizations Under Section 368(a)(1)

Treasury Decision 9739.
80 F.R. 56904 (Sept. 21, 2015).

SUMMARY: This document contains final regulations that provide guidance regarding the qualification of a transaction as a corporate reorganization under section 368(a)(1)(F) by virtue of being a mere change of identity, form, or place of organization of one corporation (F reorganization).

* * *

Background

1. Introduction

* * *

Section 368(a)(1) describes several types of transactions that constitute reorganizations. One of these, described in section 368(a)(1)(F), is "a mere change in identity, form, or place of organization of one corporation, however effected" (a Mere Change). One court has described the F reorganization as follows:

> [The F reorganization] encompass[es] only the simplest and least significant of corporate changes. The (F)-type reorganization presumes that the surviving corporation is the same corporation as the predecessor in every respect, except for minor or technical differences. For instance, the (F) reorganization typically has been understood to comprehend only such insignificant modifications as the reincorporation of the same corporate business with the same assets and the same stockholders surviving under a new charter either in the same or in a different State, the renewal of a corporate charter having a limited life, or the conversion of a U.S.-chartered savings and loan association to a State-chartered institution.

Berghash v. *Commissioner,* 43 T.C. 743, 752 (1965) (citation and footnotes omitted), *aff'd,* 361 F.2d 257 (2d Cir. 1966).

Although the statutory description of an F reorganization is short, and courts have described F reorganizations as simple, questions have arisen regarding the requirements of F reorganizations. In particular, when a corporation changes its identity, form, or place of incorporation, questions have arisen as to what other changes (if any) may occur, either before, during, or after the Mere Change, without affecting the status of the Mere Change (that is, what other changes are compatible with the Mere Change). These questions can become more pronounced if the transaction intended to qualify as an F reorganization is composed of a series of steps occurring over a period of days or weeks. Moreover, changes in identity, form, or place of organization are often undertaken to facilitate other changes that are difficult to effect in the corporation's current form or place of organization.

* * *

Explanation of Revisions

   1. Overview

* * *

* * * The Final Regulations provide that a transaction that involves an actual or deemed transfer of property by a Transferor Corporation to a Resulting Corporation is a Mere Change that qualifies as an F reorganization if six requirements are satisfied (with certain exceptions). The Final Regulations provide that a transaction or a series of related transactions to be tested against the six requirements (a Potential F Reorganization) begins when the Transferor Corporation begins transferring (or is deemed to begin transferring) its assets to the Resulting Corporation, and ends when the Transferor Corporation has distributed (or is deemed to have distributed) the consideration it receives from the Resulting Corporation to its shareholders and has completely liquidated for federal income tax purposes. The concept of a Potential F Reorganization was added to the Final Regulations to aid in determining which steps in a multi-step transaction should be considered when applying the six requirements to a potential mere change (that is, which steps are "in the bubble").

In the context of determining whether a Potential F Reorganization qualifies as a Mere Change, deemed asset transfers include, but are not limited to, those transfers treated as occurring as a result of an entity classification election under paragraph § 301.7701–3(c)(1)(i), as well as transfers resulting from the application of step transaction principles. One example of such a transfer would be the deemed asset transfer by the Transferor Corporation to the Resulting Corporation resulting from a so-called "liquidation-reincorporation" transaction. *See, for example, Davant* v. *Commissioner*, 366 F.2d 874 (5th Cir. 1966); § 1.331–1(c) (liquidation-reincorporation may be a tax-free reorganization). Another example of such a deemed asset transfer would include the deemed transfer of the Transferor Corporation's assets to the Resulting Corporation in a so-called "drop-and-check" transaction in which a newly formed Resulting Corporation acquires the stock of a Transferor Corporation from its shareholders and, as part of the plan, the Transferor Corporation liquidates into the Resulting Corporation. *See, for example,* steps (d) and (c) of Rev.Rul. 2015–10, 2015–21 IRB 973; Rev.Rul. 2004–83, 2004–2 CB 157; Rev.Rul. 67–274, 1967–2 CB 141.

* * * Viewed together, [the] six requirements ensure that an F reorganization involves only one continuing corporation and is neither an acquisitive transaction nor a divisive transaction. Thus, an F reorganization does not include a transaction that involves a shift in ownership of the enterprise, an introduction of assets in exchange for equity (other than that raised by the Transferor Corporation prior to the F reorganization), or a division of assets or tax attributes of a Transferor Corporation between or among the Resulting Corporation and other acquiring corporations. An F reorganization also does not include a transaction that leads to multiple potential acquiring corporations having competing claims to the Transferor Corporation's tax attributes under section 381.

Certain exceptions, * * * apply to these six requirements. Three of these exceptions allow de minimis departures from the six requirements for purposes unrelated to federal income taxation.

2.   F Reorganization Requirements and Certain Exceptions

A.   Resulting Corporation Stock Issuances and Identity of Stock Ownership

* * * [T]he first and the second requirements of the Final Regulations reflect the Supreme Court's holding in *Helvering* v. *Southwest Consolidated Corp, supra,* that a transaction that shifts the ownership of the proprietary interests in a corporation cannot qualify as a Mere Change. Thus, the Final Regulations provide that a transaction that involves the introduction of a new shareholder or new equity capital into the corporation "in the bubble" does not qualify as an F reorganization.

* * * [T]he first requirement in the Final Regulations is that immediately after the Potential F Reorganization, all the stock of the Resulting Corporation must have been distributed (or deemed distributed) in exchange for stock of the Transferor Corporation in the Potential F Reorganization. * * * The Treasury and the IRS believe * * * that a focus on the distribution of the stock of the Resulting Corporation better matches the transactions that occur (or are deemed to occur) in reorganizations.

* * * [T]he second requirement is that, subject to certain exceptions, the same person or persons own all the stock of the Transferor Corporation at the beginning of the Potential F Reorganization and all of the stock of the Resulting Corporation at the end of the Potential F Reorganization, in identical proportions.

Notwithstanding these requirements * * * the Final Regulations allow the Resulting Corporation to issue a de minimis amount of stock not in respect of stock of the Transferor Corporation, to facilitate the organization or maintenance of the Resulting Corporation. This rule is designed to allow, for example, reincorporation in a jurisdiction that requires minimum capitalization, two or more shareholders, or ownership of shares by directors. It is also intended to allow a transfer of assets to certain pre-existing entities, for reasons explained further in section 2.B. of this Explanation of Revisions.

In addition, the Final Regulations allow changes of ownership that result from either (i) a holder of stock in the Transferor Corporation exchanging that stock for stock of equivalent value in the Resulting Corporation having terms different from those of the stock in the Transferor Corporation or (ii) receiving a distribution of money or other property from either the Transferor Corporation or the Resulting Corporation, whether or not in redemption of stock of the Transferor Corporation or the Resulting Corporation. In other words, the corporation involved in a Mere Change may also recapitalize, redeem its stock, or make distributions to its shareholders, without causing the Potential F Reorganization to fail to qualify as an F reorganization. These exceptions reflect the determination of the Treasury Department and the IRS that allowing certain transactions to occur contemporaneously with an F reorganization is appropriate so long as one corporation could effect the transaction without undergoing an F reorganization. These exceptions also reflect the case law * * * holding that certain transactions qualify as F reorganizations even if some shares are redeemed in the transaction, and rulings by the IRS that a recapitalization may happen at the same time as an F reorganization. See, for example, Rev.Rul. 2003–19, 2003–1 CB 468, and Rev.Rul. 2003–48, 2003–1 CB 863 (both providing that certain demutualization transactions may involve both E reorganizations and F reorganizations).

B.   Resulting Corporation's Assets or Attributes and Liquidation of Transferor Corporation

* * * [T]he third requirement (limiting the assets and attributes of the Resulting Corporation immediately before the transaction) and the fourth requirement (requiring the liquidation of the Transferor Corporation) under the Final Regulations reflect the statutory mandate that an F reorganization involve only one corporation. Although the Final Regulations generally require the Resulting Corporation not to hold any property or have any tax attributes immediately before the Potential F Reorganization, * * * the Resulting Corporation is allowed to hold a de minimis amount of assets to facilitate its organization or preserve its existence (and to have tax attributes related to these assets), and the Resulting Corporation is allowed to hold proceeds of borrowings undertaken in connection with the Potential F Reorganization.

A commenter * * * stated that the Final Regulations should allow the Resulting Corporation to hold, in addition to the proceeds of borrowings, cash proceeds of stock issuances before the Mere Change. The Treasury Department and the IRS do not believe that the Resulting Corporation should be allowed to issue more than a de minimis amount of stock before a transaction constituting a Mere Change because that would allow a substantial investment of new capital and/or new shareholders, or an acquisition of assets from more than one corporation. This rule does not, however, preclude the Transferor Corporation from issuing new stock before a Potential F Reorganization constituting an F reorganization. Nor does it preclude the Resulting Corporation from issuing new stock after the Potential F Reorganization.

Under the fourth requirement in the Final Regulations, the Transferor Corporation must completely liquidate in the Potential F Reorganization for federal income tax purposes. Nevertheless, . . . the Transferor Corporation is not required to legally dissolve and is allowed to retain a de minimis amount of assets for the sole purpose of preserving its legal existence.

C.   One Section 381(a) Acquiring Corporation, One Section 381(a) Transferor Corporation

The fifth requirement under the Final Regulations is that immediately after the Potential F Reorganization, no corporation other than the Resulting Corporation may hold property that was held by the Transferor Corporation immediately before the Potential F Reorganization, if such other corporation would, as a result, succeed to and take into account the items of the transferor corporation described in section 381(c). Thus, a transaction that divides the property or tax attributes of a Transferor Corporation between or among acquiring corporations, or that leads to potential competing claims to such tax attributes, will not qualify as a Mere Change.

The sixth requirement under the Final Regulations is that immediately after the Potential F Reorganization, the Resulting Corporation may not hold property acquired from a corporation other than the Transferor Corporation if the Resulting Corporation would, as a result, succeed to and take into account the items of such other corporation described in section 381(c). Thus, a transaction that involves simultaneous acquisitions of property and tax attributes from multiple transferor corporations (such as the transaction described in Rev.Rul. 58–422, 1958–2 CB 145) will not qualify as a Mere Change.

* * *

* * * [N]otwithstanding the overall flexibility provided with respect to transactions occurring contemporaneously with a Mere Change, the Final Regulations provide that a Mere Change cannot accommodate transactions that occur at the same time as the Potential F Reorganization if those other transactions could result in a corporation other than the Resulting Corporation acquiring the tax attributes of the Transferor Corporation.

* * * Consistent with the statutory language of section 368(a)(1)(F), the Treasury Department and the IRS believe that a Mere Change involves only one Transferor Corporation and one Resulting Corporation. Thus, the Final Regulations provide that only one Transferor Corporation can transfer property to the Resulting Corporation in the Potential F Reorganization. If more than one corporation transfers assets to the Resulting Corporation in a Potential F Reorganization, none of the transfers would constitute an F reorganization.

3. Series of Transactions

In some cases, business or legal considerations may require extra steps to complete a transaction that is intended to qualify as a Mere Change. * * * [T]he Treasury Department and the IRS concluded that the words "however effected" in the statutory definition of F reorganization reflect a Congressional intent to treat a series of transactions that together result in a Mere Change as an F reorganization, even if the transfer (or deemed transfer) of property from the Transferor Corporation to the Resulting Corporation occurs indirectly. The Final Regulations confirm this conclusion by providing that a Potential F Reorganization consisting of a series of related transactions that together result in a Mere Change may qualify as an F reorganization, whether or not certain steps in the series, viewed in isolation, might, for example, be treated as a redemption under section 304(a), as a complete liquidation under section 331 or section 332, or as a transfer of property under section 351. For example, the first step in an F reorganization of a corporation owned by individual shareholders could be a dissolution of the Transferor Corporation, so long as this step is followed by a transfer of all the assets of the Transferor Corporation to a Resulting Corporation. However, *see* § 1.368–2(k) for completed reorganizations that will not be recharacterized as a Mere Change as a result of one or more subsequent transfers of assets or stock, such as where a Transferor Corporation transfers all of its assets to its parent corporation in liquidation, followed by the parent corporation's retransfer of those assets to a new corporation. *See also* Rev.Rul. 69–617, 1969–2 CB 57 (an upstream merger followed by a contribution of all the target assets to a new subsidiary corporation is a reorganization under sections 368(a)(1)(A) and 368(a)(2)(C)).

4. Mere Change Within Larger Transaction

* * * [T]he Treasury Department and the IRS recognized that an F reorganization may be a step, or a series of steps, before, within, or after other transactions that effect more than a Mere Change, even if the Resulting Corporation has only a transitory existence following the Mere Change. In some cases an F reorganization sets the stage for later transactions by alleviating non-tax impediments to a transfer of assets. In other cases, prior transactions may tailor the assets and shareholders of the Transferor Corporation before the commencement of the F reorganization. Although an F reorganization may facilitate another transaction that is part of the same plan, the Treasury Department and the IRS have concluded that step transaction principles generally should not recharacterize F reorganizations because F reorganizations involve only one corporation and do not resemble sales of assets. From a federal income tax perspective, F reorganizations are generally neutral, involving no change in ownership or assets, no end to the taxable year, and inheritance of the tax attributes described in section 381(c) without

a limitation on the carryback of losses. *See, for example,* Rev.Rul. 96–29 * * *.

The Final Regulations adopt the Related Events Rule * * *, which provided that related events preceding or following the Potential F Reorganization that constitutes a Mere Change generally would not cause that Potential F Reorganization to fail to qualify as an F reorganization. Notwithstanding the Related Events Rule, in the cross-border context, related events preceding or following an F reorganization may be relevant to the tax consequences under certain international provisions that apply to F reorganizations . . . .

The Final Regulations also * * * [provide] that the qualification of a Potential F Reorganization as an F reorganization would not alter the treatment of other related transactions. For example, if an F reorganization is part of a plan that includes a subsequent merger involving the Resulting Corporation, the qualification of a Potential F Reorganization as an F reorganization will not alter the tax consequences of the subsequent merger.

5.   Transactions Qualifying Under Other Provisions of Section 368(a)(1)

A comment * * * stated that, in some cases, an asset transfer that would constitute a step in an F reorganization is also a necessary step for characterizing a larger transaction as a nonrecognition transaction that would not constitute an F reorganization. For example, assume that corporation P acquires all of the stock of unrelated corporation T in exchange for consideration consisting of $50 cash and P voting stock with $50 value (without making an election under section 338), and, immediately thereafter and as part of the same plan, T is merged into corporation S, a newly-formed corporation wholly owned by P. Viewed in isolation, the merger of T into S appears to constitute a Mere Change. Provided the requirements for Asset Reorganization treatment are otherwise satisfied, however, the step transaction doctrine is applied to integrate the steps and treat the transaction as a statutory merger of T into S in which S acquires T's assets in exchange for $50 cash, $50 of P voting stock and assumption of T's liabilities, and T distributes the cash and P stock to its shareholders. This merger qualifies as a reorganization under section 368(a)(1)(A) by reason of section 368(a)(2)(D), and P's momentary ownership of T stock is disregarded. *See* Situation 2 of Rev.Rul. 2001–46, 2001–2 CB 321 (same). The stock of S is not treated as issued for the assets of T; the historic shareholders of T are replaced by P as the shareholder of the resulting corporation (S); and the transaction is not a Mere Change.

To clarify this and similar situations, the Treasury Department and the IRS have determined that, if the Potential F Reorganization or a step thereof involving a transfer of property from the Transferor Corporation to the Resulting Corporation is also a reorganization or part of a reorganization in which a corporation in control (within the meaning of section 368(c)) of the Resulting Corporation is a party to the reorganization (within the meaning of section 368(b)), the Potential F Reorganization is not a Mere Change and does not qualify as an F reorganization. This rule will apply to transactions qualifying as reorganizations (i) under section 368(a)(1)(C) by reason of the parenthetical language therein, (ii) under section 368(a)(1)(A) by reason of, and section 368(a)(2)(D), and (iii) under sections 368(a)(1)(A) or (C) by reason of section 368(a)(2)(C).

The IRS has long taken the position that, if a Transferor Corporation's transfer of property qualifies as a step in both an F reorganization and another type of reorganization in which the Resulting Corporation is the acquiring corporation, the transaction qualifies for the benefits accorded to an F reorganization. *See, for example,* Rev.Rul. 57–276, 1957–1 CB 126 (section 381(b) applies such that the parts of the Transferor Corporation's taxable year before and after an F reorganization constitute a single taxable year of the Acquiring Corporation, notwithstanding that the transaction also qualifies as another type of reorganization under section 368(a)(1)); Rev.Rul. 79–289, 1979–2 CB 145 (section 357(c) does not apply to an F reorganization even if the transaction also qualifies as another type of reorganization to which section 357(c) applies); § 1.381(b)–1(a)(2) (providing for rules applicable to F reorganizations, regardless of whether such reorganizations also qualify as another type of reorganization).

To avoid confusion in the application of the reorganization provisions, the Treasury Department and the IRS have decided that, except as provided earlier in this section 5. of the Explanation of Revisions, if a Potential F Reorganization qualifies as a reorganization under section 368(a)(1)(F) and would also qualify as a reorganization under section 368(a)(1)(A), 368(a)(1)(C), or 368(a)(1)(D), then for all federal income tax purposes the Potential F Reorganization qualifies only as a reorganization under section 368(a)(1)(F). This rule does not apply to a reorganization within the meaning of sections 368(a)(1)(E) (*see* Rev.Rul. 2003–19, 2003–1 CB 468, and Rev.Rul. 2003–48, 2003–1 CB 863 (providing that certain demutualization transactions may involve both E Reorganizations and F reorganizations)) or 368(a)(1)(G) (*see* section 368(a)(3)(C)).

6. Distributions

* * *

Although the Treasury Department and the IRS considered whether a distribution occurring during a Potential F Reorganization should prevent it from qualifying as an F reorganization, the Treasury Department and the IRS determined to allow flexibility for such distributions. Nevertheless, unlike other types of reorganizations, which generally involve substantial changes in economic position, F reorganizations are mere changes in form. Accordingly, the Treasury

Department and the IRS have concluded that any concurrent distribution should be treated as a transaction separate from the F reorganization. *See* § 1.301–1(*l*); *see also Bazley* v. *Commissioner,* 331 U.S. 737 (1947) (distribution in the context of a purported E reorganization treated as a dividend).

An F reorganization is a Mere Change involving only one continuing corporation and is neither an acquisitive transaction nor a divisive transaction. From a federal income tax perspective, F reorganizations generally are neutral, involving no change in ownership or assets, no end to the taxable year, and inheritance of the tax attributes described in section 381(c). A distribution that occurs at the same time as a Mere Change is, in substance, a distribution from one continuing corporation and is functionally separate from the Mere Change. The Treasury Department and the IRS believe that a distribution from one continuing corporation should not be treated the same as an exchange of money or other property for stock of a target corporation in an acquisitive reorganization. Instead, the distribution should be treated as a separate transaction occurring at the same time. * * * [T]he Treasury Department and the IRS believe it is sufficient to treat the distribution as a separate transaction that occurs at the same time as the F reorganization.

7. *Entities Treated as Corporations for Federal Tax Purposes*

As explained in this preamble, the first requirement of the Final Regulations is that all of the stock of the Resulting Corporation be distributed in exchange for stock of the Transferor Corporation. Certain entities may be treated as corporations for federal tax purposes even though they do not have owners that could be treated as shareholders for federal tax purposes to whom the profits of the corporation would inure (for example, some charitable organizations described in section 501(c)(3)). Nevertheless, these entities may be able to engage in corporate reorganizations. Thus, no inference should be drawn from the use of the terms "stock" or "shareholders" in these Final Regulations with respect to the ability of such entities to engage in reorganizations under section 368(a)(1)(F).

* * *

PROBLEM SET 2

1.   Pig Pit Barbecue Corp., a Kentucky corporation, originally operated a small barbecue restaurant in Owensboro, Kentucky. Due to the phenomenal success of its sauce recipe, Pig Pit has come to enjoy a national reputation, and its founder, Barbecue Bob, wants to take the corporation public. In preparation for an initial public offering, corporate counsel has advised Bob to "reincorporate" in Delaware.

(a)   How should the "reincorporation" be structured to assure the reincorporation is a type (F) reorganization?

(b)   Can the reincorporation be a type (F) reorganization if Pig Pit currently also has outstanding a class of preferred stock, held by Bob's cousin Geri, who provided financing to expand the kitchen a few years ago, and in connection with moving the state of incorporation from Kentucky to Delaware, Bob and Geri have agreed that Geri's preferred stock would be converted into common stock?

(c)   Can the reincorporation be a type (F) reorganization if Bob owned 60% of the common stock of Pig Pit and Bob's cousin Geri owned 40% of the common stock, and in connection with moving the state of incorporation from Kentucky to Delaware, Bob and Geri have agreed that Geri's common stock would be redeemed?

2.   Earlier this year, P Corp. acquired 100% of the stock of S Corp. in a reverse triangular merger. Because S Corp. is engaged in the same line of business as X Corp., another wholly owned subsidiary of P Corp., P Corp. wants to merge S Corp. into X Corp.

(a)   Will the merger be tax free? Will it be a Type (F) reorganization?

(b)   Would the merger be tax free if X Corp. were a shell and the purpose of the merger was to change the state of incorporation of the S Corp. business? Would it be a Type (F) reorganization?

CHAPTER 12

CORPORATE DIVISIONS: SPIN-OFFS, SPLIT-OFFS, AND SPLIT-UPS

SECTION 1.   CORPORATE DIVISIONS: GENERAL RULES

INTERNAL REVENUE CODE: Sections 355(a)(1), (2); 368(a)(1)(D), (2)(A), (2)(H)(ii); 354(b); 356(a) and (b); 358(a)–(c).

REGULATIONS: Sections 1.355–1(b), –2(a), (b)(1)–(3), –3(a), –4.

In contrast to provisions for acquisitive reorganizations, which allow the merger or consolidation of separate corporate entities, § 355 provides nonrecognition treatment for the division of a corporation's existing business into separate corporate entities owned by the shareholders. A divisive transaction under § 355 may take one of three basic forms.

1.   *Spin-Off.* A spin-off occurs when a corporation distributes the stock of an existing subsidiary to its stockholders pro rata or transfers assets to a controlled subsidiary in a type (D) reorganization and distributes the stock of the subsidiary pro rata to its stockholders. For example, X Corporation, which conducts business A and owns all of the stock of Y Corporation, which conducts business B, may spin-off Y Corporation by distributing the Y corporation stock to X Corporation's stockholders. Alternatively, X Corporation, conducting businesses A and B, may divide by transferring business B to a newly formed subsidiary, Y Corporation, and then distributing the stock of Y Corporation pro rata to the stockholders of X Corporation. A division may also be undertaken by a corporation operating a single business that is capable of division into two separate, independently functioning trades or businesses. X Corporation divides its single business into two parts by transferring some of its assets to Y Corporation which, following the transaction, is also actively engaged in the conduct of a trade or business. X Corporation then distributes all of the stock of Y Corporation to the X Corporation stockholders. In each of these transactions, the shareholders of the distributing corporation, which formerly owned multiple businesses (or a single business capable of division), own the same businesses, but the businesses are now in separate corporations.

2.   *Split-Off.* In a split-off, the distributing corporation distributes the stock of a new or existing subsidiary to its

stockholders in exchange for a portion of the outstanding stock of the distributing corporation. For example, X Corporation, which conducts business A and owns all of the stock of Y Corporation, which conducts business B, distributes the stock of Y Corporation to some or all of the stockholders of X Corporation in exchange for some or all of the shareholders' X Corporation stock. While this transaction does not involve a reorganization of either X Corporation or Y Corporation, the ownership of each corporation is changed as a result of the exchange. Alternatively, X Corporation, which conducts both business A and business B, might transfer business B to newly formed Y Corporation in a type (D) reorganization and then distribute the Y Corporation stock to its stockholders in exchange for a portion of its own outstanding stock. A split-off distribution that results in a pro rata exchange of stock among the stockholders of the distributing corporation is functionally equivalent to a "spin-off." A non-pro rata split-off, however, results in a change in proportionate ownership of both businesses. In these transactions, some or all of the shareholders of the distributing corporation own fewer shares of the distributing corporation in exchange for ownership of a corporation conducting a business previously conducted by the distributing corporation.

3.   *Split-Up.* In a split-up, the original corporation transfers a separate trade or business to each of two or more subsidiaries in a type (D) reorganization. The distributing corporation then transfers the stock of the subsidiaries to its stockholders and liquidates. Each separate trade or business, still in corporate solution, may be distributed to different stockholders. Thus, X Corporation, which owns businesses A and B, transfers business A to a new Y Corporation and business B to a new Z Corporation. X Corporation then liquidates, distributing the stock of Y to one group of X stockholders and the stock of Z to the other group of X stockholders. Alternatively, a holding company that conducts all of its businesses through subsidiaries might liquidate, distributing the stock of its subsidiaries to its former shareholders in a liquidation. Thus, in these transactions, the shareholders of the distributing corporation divide the distributing corporation's businesses among corporations now owned by different groups of the distributing corporation's former shareholders.

As noted above, each of these divisive transactions may involve as the initial step a transfer of a business to a new subsidiary followed by a distribution of the subsidiary's stock to stockholders. A divisive transaction that involves the reorganization of the corporate structure is a type (D) reorganization, defined as the transfer of assets to another corporation if immediately after the transfer the transferor or one or more of its shareholders is in control of the corporation to which the assets are transferred. In the context of corporate divisions, to qualify as a reorganization under § 368(a)(1)(D), the distribution to stockholders must comply with § 355, the pivotal section in the tax treatment of transactions seeking to accomplish a corporate division. Regardless of whether the distribution is preceded by the transfer of assets by the distributing corporation to either a new or pre-existing subsidiary, if the qualifying conditions have been met, § 355(a) provides nonrecognition to the shareholders upon receipt of the stock of the controlled corporation.

Subject to a number of special exceptions, the distributing corporation also is entitled to nonrecognition of gain on the distribution of the stock of the controlled subsidiary, with the result that § 311(b) (and § 336 in the case of a split-up) are displaced by one of two operative nonrecognition provisions. If the controlled corporation that is distributed is a pre-existing subsidiary to which assets were not transferred in a § 368(a)(1)(D) reorganization prior to the distribution, § 355(c) provides nonrecognition to the distributing corporation with respect to the stock of the controlled corporation. If the distribution is preceded by a transfer of assets from the distributing corporation to the controlled corporation in a § 368(a)(1)(D) reorganization, then § 361(c) generally provides nonrecognition for the distributing corporation. If, however, the controlled corporation assumes liabilities of the distributing corporation or takes property subject to liabilities in excess of the basis of property transferred to the controlled corporation in a divisive type (D) reorganization subject to nonrecognition under § 355, § 357(c) applies to require recognition of gain by the distributing corporation to the extent of the excess of the liabilities over the basis of assets transferred to the controlled corporation, even though the transfer might be classified as a § 368(a)(1)(D) reorganization rather than as a § 351 transfer.[1]

The essence of a § 355 division is the separate ownership at the stockholder level of the corporate businesses. In many cases, the businesses are already divided or separated prior to the distribution to the stockholders. In the spin-off paragraph above, A and B in the first example could have been conducted as separate branches or divisions of X Corporation; in the third example, they were conducted separately through a parent-subsidiary operation. X Corporation, in the first example, could separate the businesses simply by placing business B in new Y Corporation under § 351 and operating it as a subsidiary. If the desired separation is a degree of insulation of one business from the other, that goal is readily accomplished through a parent-subsidiary operation. Section 355 applies to a different type of separation, that of separate ownership at the stockholder level.

---

[1]   Note that § 357(c) does not apply to an asset transfer accompanied by an assumption of liabilities in excess of basis in a nondivisive § 368(a)(1)(D) reorganization that qualifies by virtue of a distribution by the transferor corporation of transferee corporation stock that meets the requirements of § 354(b), discussed in Chapter 10.

The separate ownership at the stockholder level following a distribution of the controlled corporation's stock may be pro rata or non-pro rata to the ownership of the distributing corporation's stock, depending on the specific facts of the transaction. Thus, § 355 potentially applies to very different divisions of corporate ownership. Suppose X Corporation is owned by individuals C and D. If X Corporation distributes the stock of its subsidiary Y Corporation pro rata in a spin-off, each individual stockholder now owns what the stockholder owned before—a one-half interest in each business—but the stockholders have separated the form of ownership. X and Y Corporations have been transmuted from parent-subsidiary corporations to brother-sister corporations. If the distribution of the Y Corporation stock is completely non-pro rata, as where stockholder D surrenders his stock in X Corporation for all the stock of Y Corporation in a split-off, then a complete division of ownership has been accomplished at the stockholder level in addition to the division at the corporate level. The corporations are no longer related in any way, assuming there is no family or other special relationship between stockholders C and D.

Prior to 1987, and between 1992 and 2003, when dividends for individuals were taxed at higher rates than capital gains, the pro rata corporate division into brother-sister corporations presented the potential for a bail-out of corporate profits taxable to individual stockholders at capital gains rates. Thus, in the examples above, if the stockholders of X and Y Corporations sell the stock of Y Corporation, they end up with stock of X Corporation and cash taxed at capital gain rates. This situation, it will be recalled, is also the end result of a "preferred stock bail-out" or a "security bail-out." Section 355 imposes limitations intended to ensure that the tax-free corporate division privilege is not abused. Currently, with individual dividend rates the same as individual long-term capital gain rates, the incentive to "bail-out" earnings and profits by means of a corporate division is significantly reduced. In this situation, the tax stakes for the individual distributee shareholders in a corporate division are whether they receive a current taxable dividend equal to the fair market value of the stock received or a distribution of stock on which tax is deferred until a subsequent sale. Even though the tax rate may be the same in both cases, deferral of tax can be a great financial benefit. In addition, the gain realized on the sale would be reduced by some portion of original basis in the stock of the distributing corporation.

The limitations of § 355 also play a key role in ensuring that a corporate division is not used to avoid corporate level tax on appreciated assets, the gain on which otherwise would be recognized under § 311(b) or § 336. Over the past several decades, Congress has enacted detailed amendments to § 355 that are intended to limit corporate tax planning to avoid § 311(b) and § 336 by channeling transactions through § 355. These statutory provisions are implemented through some of the more complex and detailed Regulations promulgated under the Code. Whether those limitations are necessary to achieve that objective is a matter that warrants further attention by tax policymakers.

Because the basic framework for nonrecognition divisions evolved when dividends were taxed to individuals at rates greater than those for long-term capital gains, most of the statutory pattern in § 355 and § 368(a)(1)(D) can be understood in terms of its attempt to prevent the bail-out of corporate earnings at preferential capital gains rates.

With respect to § 355:

1.   The transaction must not be used principally as a *device* for the distribution of the earnings and profits of either of the corporations. I.R.C. § 355(a)(1)(B).

2.   To prevent the isolation of cash or passive investments into a separate corporation, with its potential for ready sale at capital gains rates, each corporation after the division must operate an active trade or business. In addition, to prevent either the distributing corporation or the controlled corporation from utilizing accumulated earnings to acquire the active business, the active businesses must have been operated for five years preceding the distribution and must not have been acquired in a taxable transaction within the five-year period. I.R.C. § 355(a)(1)(C), (b).

3.   All of the stock and securities that the distributing parent owns in the controlled corporation being separated must be distributed to the stockholders (or at least 80% of the stock of the controlled corporation if retention of the balance of stock and securities can be justified). I.R.C. § 355(a)(1)(D). This requirement was originally designed to differentiate between genuine separations and incidental distributions of a controlled corporation's stock that took the place of current cash dividends. If, in addition, boot is distributed, pursuant to either § 356(a)(2) or § 356(b), the distribution may be taxed as a dividend to the extent of the boot. The distributing corporation also must recognize gain with respect to appreciated property distributed as boot. I.R.C. §§ 355(c); 361(c). Further, the distributing corporation is required to recognize gain on the distribution of stock of the controlled corporation to a person who, by virtue of an acquisition by purchase of the stock of either the distributing or the controlled corporation within the five-year period ending on the date of the distribution, holds a 50% or greater interest in either the distributing corporation or the controlled corporation. I.R.C. § 355(d). This requirement is aimed at preventing a transfer of ownership of the distributed corporation that avoids corporate level recognition of gain on the disposition.

4.   A "security bail-out" is not permitted as part of a corporate division, and rules similar to § 354(a)(2) are utilized to treat the excess principal amount of securities received over the principal amount of

securities surrendered as boot. I.R.C. §§ 355(a)(3), (a)(4)(A); 356(b), (d)(2)(C).

With respect to § 368(a)(1)(D) reorganizations:

Due to the statutory requirements of the various specific forms of corporate reorganizations, only the § 368(a)(1)(D) reorganization has the potential for a corporate division. For a transaction to constitute a reorganization under § 368(a)(1)(D), it must either (1) comply with the requirement of § 354(b)(1)(A) that substantially all of the assets of the distributing corporation be transferred to the controlled corporation so as to eliminate the effect of a division, or (2) constitute a step in a series of transactions culminating in a distribution qualifying under § 355. This pattern is found in the addition of the last clause in § 368(a)(1)(D), which requires that a corporation forming a controlled subsidiary must, to qualify as a reorganization, distribute the stock of the subsidiary to its stockholders in a transaction qualifying under § 354 (and § 356) or § 355 (and § 356). The reference to § 355 thus brings into play the tests for qualifying corporate divisions. The reference to § 354 brings into play § 354(b), which makes § 354 inapplicable unless substantially all the assets are transferred and the transferor liquidates. As a result, a transfer that divides assets of the distributing corporation cannot qualify under § 354. (Acquisitive type (D) reorganizations are discussed in Chapter 10.) If the requirements of § 354(b) are not met, as where only some of the assets are transferred or where the transferor does not liquidate, then a corporate division is present because the stockholders will now own stock in the old and the new corporations. Section 354(a) is not applicable, and the exchange with the stockholders will qualify for nonrecognition only if the transaction meets the corporate division tests of § 355.[2] Section 368(a)(2)(H)(ii) provides, however, that in determining whether a transfer of assets to a subsidiary prior to a distribution of stock qualifying under § 355 meets the requirements of § 368(a)(1)(D), the fact that the shareholders of the distributing corporation dispose of all or part of the stock of either the distributing corporation or the controlled corporation, or whether the controlled corporation issues additional stock, shall not be taken into account.[3]

---

[2]   Section 368(a)(2)(A) is intended to prevent a transaction that otherwise would fit the definition of both a type (C) and a type (D) reorganization, as in the case of the transfer of substantially all the assets to a controlled subsidiary, from escaping the requirements regarding corporate divisions by being treated as a type (C) reorganization. Although the subsequent enactment of § 368(a)(2)(G), requiring complete liquidation of the target corporation in a type (C) reorganization, precludes the use of a type (C) reorganization as a divisive transaction, any overlap possibility is intended to be eliminated by exclusively regarding the transaction as a type (D) reorganization, so that the mechanisms described above to channel the reorganization into § 355 are operative. If a corporation desires to transfer some of its assets in a tax-free transaction to a controlled subsidiary and retain the stock of the latter, it therefore cannot proceed under the reorganization provisions, but it can proceed under § 351, which does not require distribution of the transferee's stock to the stockholders of the transferor.

[3]   The purpose of § 368(a)(2)(H)(ii) is to assure that assets transferred to a subsidiary prior to the distribution of the stock of the subsidiary to the transferor corporation's shareholders retain transferred basis under § 362 and do not take fair market value basis. This result is

Although analysis of a transaction under § 355 may not always start with an exploration of the device requirement, each of the substantive requirements of § 355 traces its origin in part to the same purpose— identifying a distribution that is a step in a "bail-out" of earnings and profits.[4] The requirement of § 355(b) that following a distribution each of the resulting corporations be engaged in the active conduct of a trade or business prevents the distribution of stock of a subsidiary that can easily be sold because it possesses only passive assets unnecessary to the conduct of the business of the distributing corporation. The five-year history required by § 355(b)(2) prevents the distributing corporation from converting cash or passive assets into a going trade or business to be distributed under § 355. The presence of a business purpose obviates the use of the transaction as a "device."

In a tax system in which dividends and capital gains are taxed at the same rates, the potential for an earnings bail-out is generally minimized, apart from recovery of basis issues, and the device restriction focused on this problem seems unnecessary. A corporate division permits, however, the transfer of stock to the distributee stockholders without recognition of gain by either the distributing corporation or the stockholders. Thus, the limitations of § 355 also have a role in ensuring that a corporate division is not used to avoid corporate level tax on appreciated assets that otherwise would be recognized under § 311 or § 336. The business purpose test inherent in the "device" clause may serve to identify corporate reorganizations that are appropriate transactions for this nonrecognition treatment. In this connection, compare the direct distribution of a corporate trade or business in partial liquidation under § 302(b)(4) and (e), discussed in Chapter 5. A partial liquidation transaction results in recognition of gain by the corporation on distribution of appreciated assets under § 311 and a second level recognition by the distributee stockholders of capital gain on the distribution. A somewhat economically similar transaction that meets the requirements of § 355 can, however, be completed on a tax-free basis. As is the case with acquisitive reorganizations, nonrecognition and carryover basis are justified, if at all, by the stockholders' continued ownership of assets in corporate solution in transactions covered by § 355 in contrast to the extraction of the assets from corporate solution in partial liquidation transactions.

---

reinforced by § 351(c), which has the same effect as § 368(a)(2)(H)(ii), regardless of whether the subsequent stock distribution qualifies under § 355 or is controlled by another section.

[4] The term "bail-out" is something of a misnomer because the combined earnings and profits of the distributing and distributed corporations are the same as they were before the transaction. It would be more appropriate to refer to the problem as a "conversion" issue, i.e., converting cash received by the recipient shareholders on a subsequent sale of the distributed stock into capital gain from ordinary income if cash had been paid as a dividend by the distributing corporation. Nonetheless, the term "bail-out" is so deeply entrenched in the tax jargon that the term is used here.

DETAILED ANALYSIS

1. SCOPE OF SECTION 355

Section 355 does not apply to transactions that are in effect exchanges of interests between stockholders of brother-sister corporations. Treas.Reg. § 1.355–4. Thus, assume that A and B each own 50% of the stock of X and Y Corporations. A and B transfer their stock to a newly created Z Corporation in a transaction to which § 351 applies. In a split-up, Z Corporation then distributes the stock of X Corporation to A and the stock of Y Corporation to B. As a result, A owns all the stock of X Corporation, and B owns all the stock of Y Corporation. In effect, A and B have made a taxable exchange of their 50% interests in X and Y Corporations and the transaction will not qualify under § 355.

In Portland Mfg. Co. v. Commissioner, 56 T.C. 58 (1971) (acq.), aff'd by order, 75–1 U.S.T.C. ¶ 9449 (9th Cir.1975), two corporations each owned 50% of a third corporation and 50% of a joint venture. Because of disagreements between the two corporations, the mechanics of a tax-free split-off under § 355 were implemented at the conclusion of which one corporation owned all the stock of the third corporation. The court upheld the Commissioner's treatment of the transaction as a taxable exchange. A similar result was reached in Atlee v. Commissioner, 67 T.C. 395 (1976) (acq.), where the taxpayers sought to avoid having the transaction characterized as a taxable exchange by making pre-spin-off contributions to capital.

2. THE "CONTROL" REQUIREMENT OF § 355(a)(1)(A)

Two different "control" tests are relevant in determining the status of divisive transactions. First, immediately prior to the distribution, the distributing corporation must have "control," as defined in § 368(c), of the corporation whose stock is being distributed. I.R.C. § 355(a)(1)(A). Control thus requires ownership of 80% of combined voting power and 80% of the total number of shares of each other class of stock. Secondly, as discussed later in this Chapter, § 355(a)(1)(D) requires that the distributing corporation distribute to its shareholders no less than a controlling interest, as defined in § 368(c), in the subsidiary. There does not, however, appear to be any requirement that the shareholders of the distributing corporation maintain control of the subsidiary following the distribution. Although § 355 itself is silent with respect to this issue, § 368(a)(2)(H)(ii) provides that in determining whether a transfer of assets to a subsidiary prior to a distribution of stock qualifying under § 355 meets the requirements of § 368(a)(1)(D), the fact that the shareholders of the distributing corporation dispose of all or part of the stock of either distributing corporation or the controlled corporation, or whether the controlled corporation issues additional stock, shall not be taken into account. Since a § 368(a)(1)(D) reorganization cannot occur without a subsequent distribution that qualifies under either § 354, which cannot occur in a divisive (D) reorganization, or § 355, the inference is that there is no requirement that the shareholders of the distributing corporation maintain control of the subsidiary following the distribution. Nevertheless, Treas.Reg. § 1.355–2(c), which was promulgated prior to the enactment of current § 368(a)(2)(H)(ii), appears to require that the shareholders of the distributing corporation maintain post-distribution continuity of interest in both the distributing corporation and the distributed subsidiary.

Pre-distribution transfers to the distributing corporation solely for the purpose of giving it the requisite 80% stock ownership of the distributed corporation under § 368(c) may be disregarded. In Rev.Rul. 63–260, 1963–2 C.B. 147, the sole stockholder of a corporation that owned 70% of the stock of a subsidiary transferred an additional 10% of the subsidiary stock to the parent corporation that then spun off the subsidiary shares to the sole stockholder. The ruling held that § 355 was inapplicable because the distributing corporation did not have "control" except in a "transitory and illusory sense." But if there is greater economic reality to the transaction in which the distributing corporation obtains control, then § 355 treatment is allowed. Rev.Rul. 69–407, 1969–2 C.B. 50, involved a situation in which X Corporation owned 70% of the stock of Y Corporation and A and B, two individuals, owned the remaining 30%. In a type (E) recapitalization, two classes of voting stock were created; A and B received shares of one class, and X Corporation received the other class. The relative values of the interests of X Corporation, A, and B did not change, but after the recapitalization, X Corporation held over 80% of the total voting power. X Corporation then distributed the Y Corporation stock to its stockholders. The ruling held that the transaction constituted a valid (E) recapitalization followed by a § 355 distribution; the recapitalization resulted in a permanent realignment of voting control, and hence Rev.Rul. 63–260 was distinguishable. See also Rev.Rul. 71–593, 1971–2 C.B. 181 (a transfer of additional assets to a 75% owned subsidiary in exchange for sufficient stock to give the parent 90% control, followed by a split-off of the subsidiary's stock, was held to constitute a "meaningful exchange" and § 355 was applicable). In Rev.Rul. 70–18, 1970–1 C.B. 74, A, an individual, owned 100% of the stock of X and Y Corporations. In turn, Y Corporation owned 60% of Z Corporation and X Corporation owned 40% of Z Corporation. X Corporation was required by a regulatory agency to divest itself of its Z stock. Y Corporation merged into X Corporation, and X Corporation then distributed all of the Z stock to A. The ruling held that there were substantial business reasons for the merger other than giving X Corporation control of Z Corporation for the purposes of a spin-off, and the transaction qualified under § 355.

In Rev.Rul. 77–11, 1977–1 C.B. 93, A and B each owned 50% of the stock of X and Y Corporations, each of which was engaged in the construction business. The parties desired B to be the sole owner of a corporation engaged in the construction business. X and Y Corporations each contributed one-half of their assets to Z Corporation in exchange for Z stock, with X receiving 84% of the Z stock and Y 16%. X then distributed all the Z stock to B for B's X stock, and Y distributed all its Z stock to B for B's Y stock. As a result, A owned all the stock of X and Y, and B owned all the stock of Z. The ruling held: (1) The transfers by X and Y to Z followed by the distribution of the Z stock constituted a valid § 351 transaction and a good (D) reorganization; (2) the distribution of Z stock by X to B qualified under § 355 because before the distribution X had the requisite control over Z (the predecessor to Treas.Reg.

§ 1.355–4, did not require treatment of the transaction as a taxable exchange because Z received operating assets and A remained as a stockholder in X and Y); and (3) the distribution of Z stock by Y to B did not qualify under § 355 because Y owned less than 80% of the Z stock before the distribution; this aspect of the transaction was treated as a redemption under § 302 that qualified for capital gain treatment under § 302(b)(3).

PROBLEM SET 1

1.   (a)   D Corp. was engaged in the production and sale of both computer hardware and computer software. D Corp. transferred all of the assets of its computer software business to a newly formed wholly owned subsidiary, C Corp., and immediately thereafter, pursuant to a prearranged plan, distributed all of the stock of C Corp. pro rata to the D Corp. shareholders. Is it possible for these transactions to qualify for nonrecognition treatment, or must D Corp. recognize gain and its shareholders recognize dividend income?

    (b)   D Corp. was engaged in the production and sale of computer hardware. D Corp.'s wholly owned subsidiary, C Corp., was engaged in the production and sale of computer software. The stock of D Corp. was owned equally by Alma, Boris, and Christina. D Corp. distributed the stock of C Corp. to Alma in redemption of all of Alma's stock in D Corp. Is it possible for the distribution to qualify for nonrecognition treatment, or must either or both of D Corp. and Alma recognize gain?

    (c)   D Corp. was engaged in the construction business. The stock of D Corp. was owned equally by Dolores and Enrique. D Corp transferred one-half of the assets of its construction business to a newly formed wholly owned subsidiary, C Corp., and immediately thereafter, pursuant to a prearranged plan, distributed all of the stock of C Corp. to Dolores, in complete redemption of all of her stock of D Corp. Is it possible for these transactions to qualify for nonrecognition treatment, or must either or both of D Corp. and Dolores recognize gain?

    (d)   D Corp. was engaged in the manufacture and sale of cellphones. D Corp.'s wholly owned subsidiary, C Corp. was engaged in the manufacture and sale of radios. The 90 shares of stock of D Corp. were owned equally by Felicia, Guillermo, and Hilda (30 shares each). D Corp distributed all of the stock of C Corp. to Felicia in redemption of one-tenth of her stock of her stock of D Corp., i.e., 3 shares. Is it possible for the distribution to qualify for nonrecognition treatment, or must either or both of D Corp. and Felicia recognize gain?

2.   (a)   Aletta and Bud each own 50 shares of stock of X Corp., which is a holding company that does not directly engage in any business. X Corp. owns all of the stock of both Y Corp. and Z Corp. Y Corp. manufactures gizmos and Z Corp. manufactures gadgets. X Corp. liquidates and distributes all of the stock of Y Corp. to Aletta and all of the stock of Z Corp. to Bud. Is it possible for the distribution to qualify for nonrecognition treatment, or must X Corp., Aletta, and Bud recognize gain?

(b)   (1)   Suppose instead that Aletta and Bud each owned 50 shares of stock of both Y Corp. and Z Corp. (and X Corp. did not initially exist). Aletta and Bud formed X Corp. by contributing their stock of both Y Corp. and Z Corp. to X Corp. solely in exchange for X Corp. stock. Six months later, pursuant to a prearranged plan, X Corp. liquidated and distributed all of the stock of Y Corp. to Aletta and all of the stock of Z Corp. to Bud. Is it possible for the transactions to qualify for nonrecognition treatment, or must X Corp., Aletta, and Bud recognize gain?

(2)   Would your answer change if there were no prearranged plan to liquidate X Corp. but the decision to liquidate X Corp. was reached 3 years later when Aletta and Bud had a falling-out over how best to conduct the businesses?

3.   Carlotta owned 70 out of the 90 shares of X Corp.; Daniel owned the other 20 shares of X Corp. X Corp. owned 75 out of 100 shares of Y Corp. Carlotta owned the other 25 shares of Y Corp. Carlotta transferred her 25 shares of Y Corp. to X Corp. in exchange for 10 additional shares of X Corp. (Assume that the 25 shares of Y Corp. are equal in value to the to 10 additional shares of X Corp.) Thereafter, X Corp. distributed all of the stock of Y Corp. to Carlotta and Daniel pro rata. Is it possible for these transactions to qualify for nonrecognition treatment, or must X Corp. recognize gain and Carlotta and Daniel recognize dividend income?

SECTION 2.   "ACTIVE CONDUCT OF A TRADE OR BUSINESS," "DEVICE," AND OTHER LIMITATIONS

A.   GENERALLY

INTERNAL REVENUE CODE: Section 355(a)(1)(B)–(C), (b).

Rafferty v. Commissioner

United States Court of Appeals, First Circuit, 1971.
452 F.2d 767.

■ MCENTEE, CIRCUIT JUDGE. Taxpayers, Joseph V. Rafferty and wife, appeal from a decision of the Tax Court, 55 T.C. 490, which held that a distribution to them of all the outstanding stock of a real estate holding corporation did not meet the requirements of § 355 of the Internal Revenue Code of 1954 and therefore was taxable as a dividend. Our opinion requires a construction of § 355 and the regulations thereunder.

The facts, some of which have been stipulated, are relatively simple. The taxpayers own all the outstanding shares of Rafferty Brown Steel Co., Inc. (hereinafter RBS), a Massachusetts corporation engaged in the processing and distribution of cold rolled sheet and strip steel in Longmeadow, Massachusetts. In May 1960, at the suggestion of his accountant, Rafferty organized Teragram Realty Co., Inc., also a Massachusetts corporation. In June of that year RBS transferred its Longmeadow real estate to Teragram in exchange for all of the latter's outstanding stock. Thereupon Teragram leased back this real estate to RBS for ten years at an annual rent of $42,000. In 1962 the taxpayers also organized Rafferty Brown Steel Co., Inc., of Connecticut (RBS Conn.), which corporation acquired the assets of Hawkridge Brothers, a general steel products warehouse in Waterbury, Connecticut. Since its inception the taxpayers have owned all of the outstanding stock in RBS Conn. From 1962 to 1965 Hawkridge leased its real estate in Waterbury to RBS Conn. In 1965 Teragram purchased some unimproved real estate in Waterbury and built a plant there.[2] In the same year it leased this plant to RBS Conn. for a term of fourteen years. Teragram has continued to own and lease the Waterbury real estate to RBS Conn. and the Longmeadow realty to RBS, which companies have continued up to the present time to operate their businesses at these locations.[3]

During the period from 1960 through 1965 Teragram derived all of its income from rent paid by RBS and RBS Conn. Its earned surplus increased from $4,119.05 as of March 31, 1961, to $46,743.35 as of March 31, 1965. The earned surplus of RBS increased from $331,117.97 as of June 30, 1959, to $535,395.77 as of June 30, 1965. In August 1965, RBS distributed its Teragram stock to the taxpayers. Other than this distribution, neither RBS nor Teragram has paid any dividends.

Joseph V. Rafferty has been the guiding force behind all three corporations, RBS, RBS Conn., and Teragram. He is the president and treasurer of Teragram which, while it has no office or employees, keeps separate books and records and filed separate tax returns for the years in question.

On various occasions Rafferty consulted his accountant about estate planning, particularly about the orderly disposition of RBS.[5] While he anticipated that his sons would join him at RBS, he wanted to exclude his daughters (and/or his future sons-in-law) from the active management of the steel business. He wished, however, to provide them with property which would produce a steady income. The accountant recommended the formation of Teragram, the distribution of its stock, and the eventual use of this stock as future gifts to the Rafferty daughters. The taxpayers acted on this advice and also on the accountant's opinion that the distribution of Teragram stock would meet the requirements of § 355.

In their 1965 return the taxpayers treated the distribution of Teragram stock as a nontaxable transaction under § 355. The Commissioner viewed it, however, as a taxable dividend and assessed a deficiency. He claimed (a) that the distribution was used primarily as a device for the distribution of the earnings and profits of RBS or Teragram

---

[2] Teragram contracted for the construction of the plant, arranged mortgage financing by using the Longmeadow and Waterbury properties as security, and became solely obligated on the mortgage.

[3] Both properties are also suitable for use by other companies in other types of business.

[5] Rafferty's concern is understandable in view of the fact that he had nine children.

or both, and (b) that Teragram did not meet the active business requirements of § 355.

We turn first, to the Tax Court's finding that there was no device because there was an adequate business purpose for the separation and distribution of Teragram stock. In examining this finding we are guided by the rule that the taxpayer has the burden of proving that the transaction was not used principally as a device. Wilson v. Commissioner of Internal Revenue, 42 T.C. 914, 922 (1964), rev'd on other grounds, 353 F.2d 184 (9th Cir.1965). Initially, we are disturbed by the somewhat uncritical nature of the Tax Court's finding of a business purpose. Viewing the transaction from the standpoint of RBS, RBS Conn., or Teragram, no immediate business reason existed for the distribution of Teragram's stock to the taxpayers. Over the years the businesses had been profitable, as witnessed by the substantial increase of the earned surplus of every component, yet none had paid dividends. The primary purpose for the distribution found by the Tax Court was to facilitate Rafferty's desire to make bequests to his children in accordance with an estate plan.[6] This was a personal motive. Taxpayers seek to put it in terms relevant to the corporation by speaking of avoidance of possible interference with the operation of the steel business by future sons-in-law, pointing to Coady v. Commissioner of Internal Revenue, 33 T.C. 771 (1960), aff'd per curiam 289 F.2d 490 (6th Cir.1961).

In *Coady,* however, the separation was in response to a seemingly irreconcilable falling-out between the owners of a business. This falling-out had already occurred and, manifestly, the separation was designed to save the business from a substantial, present problem. See also Olson v. Commissioner of Internal Revenue, 48 T.C. 855, 867 modified, 49 T.C. 84 (1967). In the case at bar there was, at best, only an envisaged possibility of future debilitating nepotism. If avoidance of this danger could be thought a viable business purpose at all, it was so remote and so completely under the taxpayers' control that if, in other respects the transaction was a "device," that purpose could not satisfy the taxpayers' burden of proving that it was not being used "principally as a device" within the meaning of the statute.

Our question, therefore, must be whether taxpayers' desire to put their stockholdings into such form as would facilitate their estate planning, viewed in the circumstances of the case, was a sufficient personal business purpose to prevent the transaction at bar from being a device for the distribution of earnings and profits. While we remain of the view, which we first expressed in Lewis v. Commissioner of Internal Revenue, 176 F.2d 646 (1st Cir.1949), that a purpose of a stockholder, qua stockholder, may in some cases save a transaction from condemnation as a device, we do not agree with the putative suggestion

---

[6] This plan incorporated two objectives: (1) the exclusion of daughters and sons-in-law from active management of the steel business and (2) providing his daughters with investment assets, safe and independent from the fluctuations of the steel business.

in Estate of Parshelsky v. Commissioner of Internal Revenue, 303 F.2d 14, 19 (2d Cir.1962), that any investment purpose of the stockholders is sufficient. Indeed, in *Lewis,* although we deprecated the distinction between stockholder and corporate purpose, we were careful to limit that observation to the facts of that case, and to caution that the business purpose formula "must not become a substitute for independent analysis." 176 F.2d at 650. For that reason we based our decision on the Tax Court's finding that the transaction was "undertaken for reasons germane to the continuance of the corporate business." Id. at 647.

This is not to say that a taxpayer's personal motives cannot be considered, but only that a distribution which has considerable potential for use as a device for distributing earnings and profits should not qualify for tax-free treatment on the basis of personal motives unless those motives are germane to the continuance of the corporate business. * * * We prefer this approach over reliance upon formulations such as "business purpose," and "active business." * * * The facts of the instant case illustrate the reason for considering substance. Dividends are normally taxable to stockholders upon receipt. Had the taxpayers received cash dividends and made investments to provide for their female descendants, an income tax would, of course, have resulted. Accordingly, once the stock was distributed, if it could potentially be converted into cash without thereby impairing taxpayers' equity interest in RBS, the transaction could easily be used to avoid taxes. The business purpose here alleged, which could be fully satisfied by a bail-out of dividends, is not sufficient to prove that the transaction was not being principally so used.

Given such a purpose, the only question remaining is whether the substance of the transaction is such as to leave the taxpayer in a position to distribute the earnings and profits of the corporation away from, or out of the business. The first factor to be considered is how easily the taxpayer would be able, were he so to choose, to liquidate or sell the spun-off corporation. Even if both corporations are actively engaged in their respective trades, if one of them is a business based principally on highly liquid investment-type, passive assets, the potential for a bail-out is real. The question here is whether the property transferred to the newly organized corporation had a readily realizable value, so that the distributee-shareholders could, if they ever wished, "obtain such cash or property or the cash equivalent thereof, either by selling the distributed stock or liquidating the corporation, thereby converting what would otherwise be dividends taxable as ordinary income into capital gain. * * *" Wilson v. Commissioner, supra, 42 T.C. at 923. In this connection we note that the Tax Court found that a sale of Teragram's real estate properties could be "easily arranged." 55 T.C. at 353. Indeed, taxpayers themselves stressed the fact that the buildings were capable of multiple use.

There must, however, be a further question. If the taxpayers could not effect a bail-out without thereby impairing their control over the on-going business, the fact that a bail-out is theoretically possible should not be enough to demonstrate a device because the likelihood of it ever being so used is slight. "[A] bail-out ordinarily means that earnings and profits have been drawn off without impairing the shareholder's residual equity interest in the corporation's earning power, growth potential, or voting control." B. Bittker & J. Eustice, Federal Income Taxation of Corporations and Shareholders (3d ed. 1971) § 13.06. If sale would adversely affect the shareholders of the on-going company, the assets cannot be said to be sufficiently separated from the corporate solution and the gain sufficiently crystallized as to be taxable. See Lewis v. Commissioner of Internal Revenue, supra, 176 F.2d at 650. In this case, there was no evidence that the land and buildings at which RBS carried on its steel operations were so distinctive that the sale of Teragram stock would impair the continued operation of RBS, or that the sale of those buildings would in any other way impair Rafferty's control and other equity interests in RBS.[7]

In the absence of any direct benefit to the business of the original company, and on a showing that the spin-off put saleable assets in the hands of the taxpayers, the continued retention of which was not needed to continue the business enterprise, or to accomplish taxpayers' purposes, we find no sufficient factor to overcome the Commissioner's determination that the distribution was principally a device to distribute earnings and profits.

The taxpayers fail for a further reason. * * *

It is our view that in order to be an active trade or business under § 355 a corporation must engage in entrepreneurial endeavors of such a nature and to such an extent as to qualitatively distinguish its operations from mere investments. Moreover, there should be objective indicia of such corporate operations. Prior to 1965 Teragram's sole venture was the leasing back to its parent of its only asset for a fixed return, an activity, in economic terms, almost indistinguishable from an investment in securities. Standing by itself this activity is the type of "passive investment" which Congress intended to exclude from § 355 treatment. Furthermore, there are hardly any indicia of corporate operations. Prior to 1965 Teragram paid neither salaries nor rent. It did not employ independent contractors, and its only activity appears to have been collecting rent, paying taxes, and keeping separate books. Prior to 1965 it failed to meet either set of criteria for an active trade or business. We need not reach the more difficult question of whether its activities in 1965 constituted an active trade or business.

Affirmed.

---

[7]   Our conclusion is reinforced by the fact that RBS and RBS Conn. were guaranteed occupancy of Teragram property under long term leases at fixed rents.

DETAILED ANALYSIS

1.   POST-*RAFFERTY* REGULATIONS

As the discussion in *Rafferty* indicates, the scope and interpretation of the tests specified in § 355 have been the object of considerable dispute and continued development. Much of the uncertainty is created by the statutory structure itself, which raises a number of questions. What is the role of the "active trade or business" requirement? What is the nature and degree of activity required before an "active" trade or business is present? What is the relationship of the active business requirement to the "device" prohibition? How do the business purpose and continuity of interest requirements of the Regulations relate to those issues?

Prior to 1973, the IRS relied primarily on the "active trade or business" requirement to police divisive reorganizations. The IRS seemed to exclude absolutely from the active trade or business category investment activities and transactions involving owner-occupied real estate. Moreover, it was the IRS's position that two separate pre-division businesses were required before § 355 could be employed by a taxpayer. The *Coady* case, discussed in *Rafferty,* rejected the second position and the *Rafferty* court articulated an entirely different standard to test for "active" business operations.

Beginning in 1973, the IRS appeared to shift its position to conform more closely to the approach adopted in *Rafferty.* Thus, in its published rulings, the IRS seemed to rely to a greater extent upon the "device" limitation and adopted a view of the active trade or business requirement patterned on the *Rafferty* test. Regulations proposed in 1977 and finally adopted in 1989, confirmed these developments.[5] The Regulations place significant emphasis on the "device" limitation as a measure to ensure that spin-off transactions do not involve bail-outs of earnings and profits. The Regulations provide significant details regarding the active trade or business requirement and clarified its close interaction with the device requirement. In addition, the Regulations relax the prior requirements concerning the types of business activities that may be split up. The Regulations also elevate the business purpose requirement discussed in *Rafferty* to the level of an independent test and add a specific continuity of interest requirement which theretofore had played only a subsidiary role. These latter two requirements are important with respect to a divisive transaction designed to avoid double tax on appreciated corporate assets but that may not involve any attempt to bail out accumulated earnings.

2.   IMPACT OF REPEAL OF *GENERAL UTILITIES* DOCTRINE AND TAX RATE CHANGES

The equalization of the income tax rates on dividends and long-term capital gains in the 2003 Act eliminated for the most part the need for avoidance measures to prevent conversion of ordinary income into capital gains. With dividends and long-term capital gains taxed at the same rates,

---

[5]   The ability of taxpayers to obtain an advance ruling under § 355 has narrowed over time. See Rev.Proc. 96–30, 1996–1 C.B. 696 (checklist of information required), modified and amplified by Rev.Proc. 2003–48, 2003–2 C.B. 86, obsoleted in part and superseded in part by Rev.Proc. 2013–32, 2013–28 I.R.B. 55.

rate-arbitrage based bailout *per se* is no longer a relevant concern. Thus, the role of the "device" restriction in § 355 is substantially diminished. Nevertheless, bailout issues remain. First, basis recovery upon the sale of the stock of either the distributing or controlled corporation after the distribution effects a bailout. Second, because § 311(b) and § 336, enacted in 1986 to repeal the *General Utilities* doctrine, impose tax at the corporate level on asset appreciation in corporate redemptions and liquidations, § 355 remains important because it draws the line between distributions that trigger corporate level recognition and distributions that are permitted to enjoy corporate level tax deferral. Thus, § 355 has a role in plugging the dike of double taxation in place since 1986. From this perspective, the active trade or business requirement now assumes a greater role. Furthermore, the business purpose and continuity of interest requirements, which were originally derived in part from the device restriction, continue to limit nonrecognition treatment in divisive transactions.

B. ACTIVE CONDUCT OF A TRADE OR BUSINESS

INTERNAL REVENUE CODE: Section 355(a)(1)(C) and (b).

REGULATIONS: Section 1.355–3.

The technical rules of § 355(a)(1)(C) and (b) require each of the surviving corporations following a division to be actively engaged in the conduct of a trade or business. In addition, the business in each corporation must have been actively conducted for the five-year period preceding the distribution to stockholders. These rules require not only the classification of assets in each of the corporations surviving a divisive reorganization as an active trade or business but also identification of the scope of the trade or business conducted during the five-year qualifying period.

The "active business" requirements of § 355(a)(1)(C) and (b) are directed at several different, though related, aspects of divisive transactions and raise a number of interpretive problems. At the first level, the provisions are designed to prevent the tax-free separation of liquid assets from operating assets because of the substantial bail-out potential involved in such transactions. The principal interpretive problems concern the classification of owner-occupied real estate (and real estate leased by a subsidiary to its parent) as an active trade or business or as property that constitutes an investment asset. The question is whether the nature and extent of the taxpayer's activities are sufficient to qualify as an "active business."

A second set of issues arises when the plan is to divide a single business, to divide a business along geographical lines, to separate different lines of business (e.g., wholesale from retail), or to separate a particular function (e.g., research). Here, the issues are whether there are separate businesses following division, each of which consists of an individual profit-making enterprise, and whether each of the separated businesses may inherit the five-year operating history of the original business.

The purpose of the five-year rule is to prevent the use of corporate earnings generated by one business—and otherwise available for dividend distributions to its stockholders—to establish or acquire another business that could be spun-off and sold, creating capital gains. The difficult questions in this area involve a determination of the point at which simple expansion of an existing business becomes the acquisition of a new business that must then establish its own five-year history. As a backstop to the basic five-year rule, § 355(b)(2)(C) and (D) preclude tax-free distribution of a business acquired in a taxable transaction during the five years preceding the spin-off.

McLaulin v. Commissioner*

United States Tax Court, 2000.
115 T.C. 255.

■ HALPERN, JUDGE.

* * *

After concessions, the only issue for decision is whether the January 15, 1993, distribution by Ridge Pallets, Inc., a Florida corporation (Ridge), of all of the outstanding stock of Sunbelt Forest Products, Inc., also a Florida corporation (Sunbelt), qualifies as a tax-free "spinoff" of Sunbelt to petitioners, the sole shareholders of Ridge, pursuant to section 355. We hold that it does not. Our reasons follow.

FINDINGS OF FACT

Introduction * *

Ridge and Sunbelt

Ridge was incorporated in 1959 by Richard B. Craney (Craney). From 1977 until July 25, 1993, the sole, equal shareholders of Ridge were McLaulin, King (Craney's stepson), and Holland. Ridge was engaged in the forest products business. Ridge was profitable, with more than $13 million in retained earnings as of July 25, 1993.

On December 31, 1986, Ridge elected to become an S corporation as that term is defined by section 1361(a)(1) (S corporation), effective for its taxable year ended July 25, 1988. Ridge qualified as an S corporation for each taxable year thereafter, through and including its taxable year ended July 25, 1994.

Sunbelt was incorporated in 1981. Initially, its sole, equal shareholders were Craney, Ridge, and an otherwise unrelated individual, John L. Hutto (Hutto). In 1986, Craney's shares of stock were redeemed

---

* The Court of Appeals affirmed the Tax Court's decision with minimal discussion: "The tax court found that the facts of Rev.Rul. 57–144 were not distinguishable from the present case in any significant way. We agree." 276 F.3d 1269 (11th Cir. 2001).

by Sunbelt, and, from then until January 15, 1993, Ridge and Hutto were the sole, equal shareholders of Sunbelt. Hutto was president of Sunbelt and chairman of its board of directors. He was responsible for all executive functions of Sunbelt. Sunbelt produced and sold pressure-treated lumber. That business was profitable. In February 1989, based on Hutto's experience in the millwork business (manufacturing doors and window frames), Sunbelt entered the millwork business (the millwork division). The millwork division lost money from its inception to its shutdown in mid-1990. Because of Sunbelt's management's focus on the millwork division, Sunbelt's core business (pressure-treating lumber) also suffered. Nonetheless, Sunbelt had over $1.8 million in retained earnings as of the close of its fiscal taxable year ended June 26, 1993.

Events Leading to Ridge's Distribution of the Sunbelt Stock to Ridge's Shareholders

In 1982, Sunbelt began to borrow money from Citrus and Chemical Bank, in Bartow, Florida (the Bank), pursuant to a series of renewable notes (the notes). Beginning in 1984, and until 1989, Ridge stood as a guarantor of the notes. Borrowings pursuant to the notes reached $2 million by 1989. On February 26, 1990, the board of directors of Ridge (the Ridge board) authorized the withdrawal of Ridge's guaranty of Sunbelt's debt to the bank (the Ridge guaranty) if there was not "a prompt cessation and controlled liquidation of the millwork division." Ridge could not force a shutdown of the millwork division because it was unable to outvote Hutto, who, like Ridge, was a 50-percent shareholder in Sunbelt. The Ridge board reasoned that, without the Ridge guaranty, Sunbelt would be unable to obtain new funds to cover future losses, and, as a result, Hutto would be forced to shut down the millwork division.

On May 18, 1990, Ridge withdrew the Ridge guaranty and, shortly thereafter, the millwork division was liquidated. On September 17, 1990, Ridge purchased Sunbelt's 1989 note (the 1989 note) from the Bank for $630,000, the balance due. Thereafter, Ridge financed Sunbelt directly by extending and modifying the 1989 note on numerous occasions. In that way, Ridge was able to exercise control over the management of Sunbelt.

In mid-1992, Hutto decided to sell his shares in Sunbelt and leave the company. Hutto's decision culminated several months of negotiations between Ridge and Hutto, in which Ridge sought either to purchase Hutto's interest in Sunbelt or sell its interest to Hutto. Ridge instigated those negotiations because of its dissatisfaction with Hutto's management of Sunbelt. Earlier in 1992, Ridge and Hutto had tentatively agreed to a price of $825,000 for a 50-percent stock interest in Sunbelt, applicable whether Hutto was the buyer or the seller. Ridge and Hutto finally agreed that Ridge and Hutto would cause Sunbelt to redeem Hutto's shares in Sunbelt (the redemption) in exchange for $828,943.75 in cash and real estate valued at $101,000. The redemption was accomplished on January 15, 1993. Immediately thereafter, Ridge owned the only outstanding shares of Sunbelt.

Also on January 15, 1993, subsequent to the redemption, Ridge made a distribution with respect to its stock of all of its shares in Sunbelt (the distribution and the Sunbelt shares, respectively). The distribution was to petitioners, the sole shareholders of Ridge, pro rata. * * *

Funding the Redemption

Sunbelt needed cash in the amount of $828,243.74 to fund the redemption. Although Sunbelt had assets and accumulated earnings in excess of that amount, it did not have the necessary cash. On January 14, 1993, the amount available to Sunbelt pursuant to the 1989 note was increased from $2 million to $3 million, and, on that same date, Sunbelt took advantage of its increased borrowing power under the 1989 note and borrowed $900,000 from Ridge, which, in part, it used to make the redemption.

OPINION

I.   *Introduction*

The fundamental question we must answer is whether gain is to be recognized to Ridge on account of the distribution. If so, then, since, for Ridge's taxable year ending July 25, 1993, it was an S corporation, petitioners must take into account their pro rata shares of such gain. See sec. 1366(a). No gain will be recognized to Ridge on account of the distribution if that transaction qualifies for nonrecognition treatment pursuant to section 355. * * * If the distribution does not qualify for section 355 nonrecognition treatment, then gain will be recognized to Ridge pursuant to section 311(b). * * * Respondent argues that the distribution does not qualify for section 355 nonrecognition treatment on two separate and independent grounds:

(1) The contemporaneous redemption and distribution fail to satisfy the requirements of section 355(b) as to active trade or business. Specifically, respondent argues that, although Sunbelt had been engaged in an active trade or business for more than 5 years on the date of the distribution, control of Sunbelt was acquired by the distributing corporation (Ridge), within such 5-year period, in a transaction (the redemption) in which gain was recognized, thereby violating the requirements of section 355(b)(2)(D)(ii).

(2) Petitioners have failed to prove that the distribution was designed to achieve a corporate business purpose, as required by section 1.355–2(b), Income Tax Regs.

Because we agree with respondent's first ground, we do not address respondent's second ground.

II.   *Active Business Requirement*

A.   *Pertinent Provisions of the Internal Revenue Code*

One of the specific requirements for section 355 nonrecognition treatment on the pro rata distribution of the shares of a controlled corporation (a so-called spinoff) is that "the requirements of subsection

(b) [of section 355] (relating to active businesses) are satisfied". Sec. 355(a)(1)(C). Section 355(b)(1)(A) provides that both the distributing and the controlled corporation must be "engaged immediately after the distribution in the active conduct of a trade or business". Section 355(b)(2) defines the circumstances under which "a corporation shall be treated as engaged in the active conduct of a trade or business". Section 355(b)(2)(B) provides that the trade or business must have been "actively conducted throughout the 5-year period ending on the date of the distribution" (the 5-year period). Section 355(b)(2)(D) provides, in pertinent part, that control of the corporation engaged in the active conduct of a trade or business on the date of acquisition of control must not have been acquired within the 5-year period or, if acquired within such period, it must have been acquired "only by reason of transactions in which gain or loss was not recognized in whole or in part, or only by reason of such transactions combined with acquisitions before the beginning of such period." Sec. 355(b)(2)(D)(ii).

B.   *Arguments of the Parties*

Respondent does not dispute that both Ridge and Sunbelt were engaged in the active conduct of a trade or business immediately after the distribution. Nor does he dispute that both businesses had been actively conducted throughout the 5-year period. Respondent argues, however, that Ridge violated the conditions of section 355(b)(2)(D)(ii) because it acquired control of Sunbelt within the 5-year period in a transaction (the redemption) in which gain or loss was recognized. In reaching that conclusion, respondent relies upon the statutory language and upon Rev. Rul. 57–144, 1957–1 C.B. 123, in which respondent determined that a personal holding company's distribution to its shareholders of the stock of one of its two controlled operating subsidiaries does not qualify as a tax-free spinoff where control of the parent's other operating subsidiary (which was merged into the parent after the distribution) was obtained during the 5-year period as a result of that subsidiary's redemption of a portion of a more than 20-percent minority interest.

Petitioners respond that this case simply does not involve tax avoidance of a kind that the active business requirement of section 355(b) and, in particular, section 355(b)(2)(D) is designed to combat. In that regard, petitioners argue that (1) Ridge's accumulated adjustment account under section 1368(e)(1) (in this case, Ridge's undistributed, previously taxed earnings) exceeded the value of the distributed Sunbelt stock so that the distribution could not have constituted a taxable dividend to petitioners even if it had taken the form of a cash distribution (see sec. 1368(c)(1)), and 2) the redemption was not an acquisition of control by Ridge for purposes of section 355(b)(2)(D). Alternatively, petitioners argue that, even if the combined redemption-distribution is deemed to have violated the literal terms of the statute (since gain was, in fact, recognized to Hutto), respondent has allowed tax-free treatment for other transactions that failed to meet the literal statutory requirements for nonrecognition of gain. Petitioners claim that nonrecognition of gain is equally justified in this case. Petitioners also argue that the facts of Rev. Rul. 57–144, supra, are distinguishable from the facts of this case, and, therefore, it is not germane.

C. *Discussion*

1. *Acquisition of Control*

We generally treat a revenue ruling as merely the Commissioner's litigating position not entitled to any judicial deference or precedential weight. See, e.g., Norfolk S.S. Corp. v. Commissioner, 104 T.C. 13, 45–46 (1995), supplemented by 104 T.C. 417 (1995), affd. 140 F.3d 240 (4th Cir. 1998) * * *. We may, however, take a revenue ruling into account where we judge the underlying rationale to be sound. See Spiegelman v. Commissioner, 102 T.C. 394, 405 (1994) * * *. The degree to which we must respect the Respondent's longstanding position in Rev. Rul. 57–144, supra, is of no concern, however, because, in the circumstances of this case, we reach the same result.

First of all, we do not agree with petitioners that the facts in Rev. Rul. 57–144, supra, are distinguishable from the facts in this case in any significant way. While it is true that the ruling involves (1) a parent holding company and two operating subsidiaries rather than, as in this case, a parent operating company and a single operating subsidiary, and (2) a taxable stock redemption by the retained rather than by the distributed subsidiary, those are distinctions of no legal significance. The key determination by respondent in Rev. Rul. 57–144, supra, which is relevant to this case, is the determination that a parent corporation is considered to acquire control of its subsidiary by virtue of the subsidiary's redemption of the stock of another shareholder whose interest in the subsidiary before the redemption exceeded 20 percent.

In opposition to that determination by respondent, petitioners argue that, where control of the subsidiary is the result of the subsidiary's redemption of its own stock, there is no "acquisition" of control by the parent distributing corporation as contemplated by section 355(b)(2)(D). Again, we disagree with that blanket assertion. As one commentator has noted:

> The literal statutory language supports the redemption rule of Rev. Rul. 57–144, since P acquired control of S as a result of a taxable transaction. Although the purpose of section 355(b)(2)(D) to prevent Distributing from using its liquid assets to buy a corporation conducting an active business would not at first blush seem to be violated by a redemption of S stock before a spin-off (because P is not using any of its own assets in a way contrary to the purpose of section 355(b)(2)(D)), the *fungibility of cash makes such a redemption problematic*. It may be difficult to determine whether, in true economic effect, the cash used in

the redemption could be attributed to P—as, for instance, if S used all of its cash normally used for its working capital requirements for the redemption, which P made up to S after the redemption. * * *

Ridgway, 776–2d Tax Mgmt. (BNA), Corporate Separations at A–42, A–43 (2000) (fn. refs. & citations omitted; emphasis added).

In this case, all of the cash needed to accomplish the redemption came directly from Ridge, the parent distributing corporation. On January 14, 1993, Sunbelt borrowed $900,000 from Ridge. On the following day, Sunbelt redeemed all of Hutto's stock for $828,943.75, in cash, plus real estate with a value of $101,000. Petitioners specifically acknowledge that Sunbelt lacked sufficient liquidity to fund the redemption and, therefore, needed to borrow the necessary funds. Although, as petitioners point out, Sunbelt might have borrowed the funds from a third-party lender, it did not. Moreover, the negotiations between Hutto and Ridge prior to the redemption, whereby the two parties sought to terminate their joint ownership of Sunbelt by having one buy the stock of the other, clearly indicate that Ridge was the motivating force for the buyout of Hutto's interest in Sunbelt and that Sunbelt was, in effect, serving Ridge's purpose in accomplishing this goal. Any distinction between that series of transactions and an outright purchase of the stock by Ridge, the distributing corporation, is illusory for purposes of section 355(b)(2)(D)(ii).[8]

Under Rev. Rul. 57–144, 1957–1 C.B. 123, section 355(b)(2)(D) applies to any taxable redemption during the 5-year period that results in control of the subsidiary by the distributing corporation. We need not and do not decide whether we would reach the same result as Rev. Rul. 57–144, supra, in all such cases. We decide only that we reach the same result under the circumstances of this case.

2. *Additional Arguments*

In reaching our decision, we find none of petitioners' additional arguments persuasive.

a. *Active Business Test*

Petitioners argue that the fundamental goal of the active business test is to prevent shareholder withdrawal of accumulated earnings at capital gain rates, and that, because Ridge's accumulated adjustment account under section 1368(e)(1) exceeded the value of the distributed Sunbelt stock, an otherwise taxable distribution (including a cash dividend) would not have been taxable to petitioners. Therefore, petitioners continue, there could not have been any conversion of

---

[8] See Waterman S.S. Corp. v. Commissioner, 430 F.2d 1185 (5th Cir. 1970), revg. 50 T.C. 650 (1968), in which the court held that, where a subsidiary-payor distributed a promissory note to its shareholder-payee in the form of an intercompany dividend, the payor's discharge of the note with funds borrowed from the purchaser of the payor's stock from the payee was, in substance, the purchaser's payment of additional purchase price for the stock.

ordinary income into capital gain. Additionally, petitioners argue that the issue in this case, the taxation of corporate level gain, is not addressed by section 355(b)(2)(D).

Petitioners' first argument ignores the fact that, pursuant to sections 1367(a)(2)(A) and 1368(e)(1)(A), the accumulated adjustment account is reduced by the amount of the distribution (the value of the distributed Sunbelt stock) thereby reducing the interval before additional distributions by Ridge would become taxable to petitioners. Moreover, petitioners' argument proves too much, as it would also apply to Ridge's purchase of Hutto's Sunbelt stock directly from Hutto during the 5-year period.

Petitioners' additional argument (section 355(b)(2)(D) does not deal with corporate level gain) ignores the post-1986 evolution of section 355 (including amendments to section 355(b)(2)(D)) into a weapon against avoidance of the repeal of the *General Utilities*[9] doctrine, which, prior to its repeal by the Tax Reform Act of 1986, Pub. L. 99–514, sec. 631(c), 100 Stat. 2085, 2272, generally provided for the nonrecognition of gain realized by a corporation on the distribution of appreciated property to its shareholders. As noted by one commentator:

> It should not be surprising that more attention has been directed toward Section 355 today than was ever the case in the past. From a tax perspective, its attraction is grounded on the fact that it is one of the few (some might say the only) viable opportunity to escape the repeal of the *General Utilities* doctrine. * * *

Gould, "Spinoffs: Divesting in a Post-General Utilities World, with Emphasis on Practical Problems", 69 TAXES 889 (Dec. 1991); (fn. refs. omitted). Indeed, petitioners themselves place obvious reliance upon section 355 to avoid taxation pursuant to section 311(b).

B. *Literal Compliance with Section 355 Not Always Required*

Petitioners also argue that nonrecognition treatment is justified herein on the basis of case law and respondent's pronouncements in which nonrecognition of gain was afforded to a transaction despite a failure to satisfy the literal terms of the governing statute. * * *

The other authorities relied upon by petitioners are also distinguishable because, in each, either the taxable acquisition (or incorporation) of the subsidiary to be spun off within the 5-year period or the spinoff itself less than 5 years after a taxable purchase of the subsidiary occurred within the context of an affiliated group of corporations. Thus, Commissioner v. Gordon, supra, involves a subsidiary spun off within 5 years of its incorporation in a transaction involving the receipt of "boot" (a demand note) taxable to the transferor parent. The Court of Appeals for the Second Circuit held that the section

---

[9]   See General Utils. & Operating Co. v. Helvering, 296 U.S. 200, * * * 56 S. Ct. 185 (1935).

355(b)(2)(C) and (D) prohibition against acquiring a business or a corporation in a taxable transaction within the 5-year period must be restricted to acquisitions from outside the affiliated group in order to carry out the legislative intent of section 355(b), which, it concluded, was to prevent "the temporary investment of liquid assets in a new business in preparation for a 355(a) division." Id. at 506 (emphasis added).[10] Respondent adopted that reasoning in Rev. Rul. 78–442, supra, and Counsel did so in G.C.M. 35633, supra, both of which involve the incorporation of an operating division preparatory to a spinoff of the newly formed subsidiary in a transaction intended to qualify as a tax-free reorganization under section 368(a)(1)(D). In both pronouncements, the incorporation of the more-than-5-year-old division involves the assumption of liabilities in excess of the transferor's basis, resulting in gain recognized to the transferor under section 357(c). Respondent and Counsel, like the Court of Appeals for the Second Circuit in Commissioner v. Gordon, supra, determined that section 355(b)(2)(C) is intended to prevent the acquisition of a new business from outside the affiliated group within the 5-year period. Therefore, they found no violation of that provision by virtue of the section 357(c) gain on the distributing corporation's incorporation of an existing business.[11]

In Rev. Rul. 69–461, supra, respondent determined that a distribution by a subsidiary to its parent of the stock of the former's subsidiary, within 5 years of the first-tier subsidiary's purchase of such stock, does not violate section 355(b)(2)(D). Respondent reasoned that section 355(b)(2)(D) is not intended to apply to a distribution "that merely has the effect of converting indirect control into direct control", but, rather, "applies to a transaction in which stock is acquired from outside a direct chain of ownership." Rev. Rul. 69–461, 1969–2 C.B. at 53. * * *

In this case, the redemption accomplished more than merely the conversion of indirect to direct control of Sunbelt. It accomplished the acquisition of control where none had existed previously. For that reason, it represents, in the language of the Court of Appeals for the Second Circuit in Commissioner v. Gordon, 382 F.2d at 506, "the temporary investment of liquid assets in a new business in preparation for * * * [a spinoff]". We hold that, in contrast to the circumstances involved in the pronouncements cited by petitioners, the distribution within 5 years of the redemption is precisely the type of transaction section 355(b)(2)(D) is

---

[10] In Baan v. Commissioner, 45 T.C. 71 (1965), revd. and remanded 382 F.2d 485 (9th Cir. 1967), we reached the same result as the Court of Appeals for the Second Circuit, but on the ground (rejected by the Court of Appeals) that the incorporation of the subsidiary was, in fact, a nonrecognition transaction because the gain attributable to the receipt of boot was eliminated in consolidation.

[11] Sec. 1.355–3(b)(4)(iii), Income Tax Regs., applicable to acquisitions prior to the Revenue Act of 1987, Pub. L. 100–203, 101 Stat. 1330, and the Technical and Miscellaneous Revenue Act of 1988, Pub. L. 100–647, 102 Stat. 3342, also provides that sec. 355(b)(2)(C) and (D) does not apply to an acquisition of assets or stock by one member of an affiliated group from another member of the same group, even if the acquisition is taxable.

designed to eliminate from nonrecognition treatment under section 355(a).

III. *Conclusion*

Respondent's deficiencies against petitioners are sustained.

DETAILED ANALYSIS

1.   ACTIVE TRADE OR BUSINESS

1.1. *What Is a Trade or Business?*

For purposes of § 355, Treas.Reg. § 1.355–3(b)(2)(ii) defines a "business" as a specific group of activities consisting of the operations necessary to the process of earning income or profit. Activities that merely contributed to the process of earning income before the distribution may themselves constitute a business. Treas.Reg. § 1.355–3(c), Ex. (9), provides that a research department of a manufacturing activity may be spun-off as a separate business. The example states that the status of the research department as a separate business is independent of whether it furnishes services solely to the distributing corporation or undertakes to contract with others. The example cautions, however, that if the research department continues to function as a secondary business providing service solely to the distributing corporation, that fact is evidence of a "device" under Treas.Reg. § 1.355–2(d)(2)(iv). See also Treas.Reg. § 1.355–3(c), Ex. (10) (sales function separated from processing function), and Ex. (11) (captive coal mine separated from steel products manufacturing). Treas.Reg. § 1.355–2(d)(2)(iv)(C) indicates that the functional relationship between the active trade or businesses of the distributing and controlled corporations may be evidence of a "device."

1.2. *Rental Real Estate and Other Activities as an "Active" Trade or Business?*

The operation and maintenance of owner-occupied rental real estate, as well as other rental property, may be classified as the operation of a trade or business depending upon whether the nature of the relationship of the distributing corporation to the rental activity is the *active* conduct of that business. The pre-1989 Regulations refused to find an active trade or business if owner-occupied real estate was involved unless the rental activities with respect to, and the rental income from, third parties were substantial. Some cases used a similar approach; see, e.g., Bonsall v. Commissioner, 317 F.2d 61 (2d Cir.1963) (lease of small part of owner-occupied building as an accommodation to a supplier and rental of another building was not a trade or business where rental income small); Appleby v. Commissioner, 35 T.C. 755 (1961), aff'd per curiam, 296 F.2d 925 (3d Cir.1962) (rental of less than 50% of space in building occupied by insurance agency where rentals were small part of total income did not constitute an active trade or business).

Furthermore, the IRS held the view that if "investment" property was involved, no amount of activity with respect to the investment would constitute an active trade or business. See Rev.Rul. 66–204, 1966–2 C.B. 113

(substantial activity in managing an investment portfolio of a broker-dealer not an active trade or business).

But *Rafferty* signaled a new approach to the treatment of investment property and property used in the trade or business of the owner under the active trade or business test of § 355. Under *Rafferty,* the satisfaction of the active trade or business test turns on the question whether the corporation engaged "in entrepreneurial endeavors of such a nature and to such an extent as to qualitatively distinguish its operations from mere investments." Under the *Rafferty* approach, it is possible for the operation of owner-occupied real estate to constitute an active trade or business under § 355, even though no renting of the property to third parties is present. In *Rafferty* the real property was owned and operated in a subsidiary. The IRS appears to regard the parent-subsidiary rental situation as a variation on the owner-occupied real estate situation and uses the same tests in each to determine whether the requisite level of business activity is present. Thus, the analysis should not be altered by the form in which property is held. The result in *Rafferty* would be the same if the property had been owned directly by the parent and managed and operated as a real estate division, with the real estate division "charging" rent to the operating division for internal accounting purposes.

King v. Commissioner, 458 F.2d 245 (6th Cir.1972), applied the *Rafferty* approach in a transaction in which a transportation company owned three subsidiaries formed earlier to acquire real estate, erect terminals, and lease the terminals on a net lease basis to the parent company. To facilitate a merger with another operating company, the transportation company decided to put all of the transportation operations in one corporate group and the nonoperating corporations in a separate corporate group. The stock of the real estate subsidiaries was distributed to the stockholders of the transportation company who then transferred the stock to a sister corporation and the business activities were operated as before. In reversing the Tax Court, the Court of Appeals concluded that the financing and construction activities of the real estate group constituted an active trade or business, even though performed by the identical persons who were employees of the operational group and no third party leasing was involved.

Rev.Rul. 73–234, 1973–1 C.B. 180, reflected a shift in the IRS's interpretation of the active conduct of a trade or business requirement. The ruling stated that an actively conducted business denoted "substantial management and operational activities directly carried on by the corporation itself." A corporation that engaged in farming through tenant farmers, who were independent contractors, was held to be engaged in an active trade or business because it performed substantial management activities with respect to the farm business. But see Rev.Rul. 86–126, 1986–2 C.B. 58 (leasing to tenant farmers did not constitute active conduct where the corporation engaged in only "some managerial and operational activity but not enough to 'qualitatively distinguish its operations from mere investments' ").

Rev.Rul. 89–27, 1989–1 C.B. 106, discussed the role of services performed by outside contractors:

> [I]n order for a trade or business to be actively conducted, substantial management and operational activities generally must be directly carried on by the corporation itself and such activities generally do not include the activities of others outside the corporation, including independent contractors. However, the fact that a portion of a corporation's business activities is performed by others will not preclude the corporation from being engaged in the active conduct of a trade or business if the corporation itself directly performs active and substantial management and operational functions.

The ruling held that the owner of a working interest in an oil lease was actively engaged in the conduct of a business despite outside work by independent contractors. See also Rev.Rul. 73–237, 1973–1 C.B. 184 (construction corporation acting as a general contractor was in an active trade or business even though it utilized independent subcontractors for actual construction work; the general contractor's activities were substantial). In Rev.Rul. 86–125, 1986–2 C.B. 57, the IRS held, however, that a subsidiary's ownership of an office building that was operated and managed by an independent real estate management company was not the active conduct of a business. The subsidiary's limited managerial and operational activities were compared to those of a prudent investor.

Treas.Reg. § 1.355–3(b)(2)(iii) incorporates a requirement that to satisfy the "active conduct" test the corporation must "perform active and substantial management and operational functions." The current Regulations modify the strict rule of the prior Regulations by stating that the holding of real or personal property used in a trade or business can satisfy the active conduct test if the owner performs significant services with respect to the operation and management of the property. Treas.Reg. § 1.355–3(b)(2)(iv)(B). See also Rev.Rul. 92–17, 1992–1 C.B. 142 (a corporation that was a general partner of a real estate limited partnership, and whose officers performed active and substantial management functions for the partnership, was engaged in an active trade or business), amplified by Rev.Rul. 2002–49, 2002–2 C.B. 288 (dealing with a similar situation involving a corporation that was a managing member of an LLC taxed as a partnership).

In Rev.Rul. 2007–42, 2007–2 C.B. 44, which further modified Rev.Rul. 92–17, the IRS held that a distributing corporation that owned a one-third interest in an LLC that was engaged in the active conduct of a trade or business was itself engaged in the active conduct of a trade or business. The ruling reasons that ownership of a one-third interest in the LLC was significant and that the LLC itself performed the requisite management functions constituting an active trade or business. The ruling also held, however, that ownership of a 20% interest in an LLC is not sufficient to constitute engagement in an active trade or business by the distributing corporation.

Despite the modification in principle of the IRS's prior strict rule regarding investment property (other than stocks, securities and similar portfolio type investments) and owner-occupied real estate, however, Exs.

(1)–(3), (12), and (13) in Treas.Reg. § 1.355–3(c) indicate that the IRS will continue to closely scrutinize divisive transactions involving investment assets and owner-occupied real estate. Indeed, only one of the examples, Example (12), concludes that an active trade or business is involved. In that example, the owner of a building occupied only one of eleven floors and the spun-off corporation continued the prior practice of renting the other 10 floors to unrelated tenants. Example (13) indicates that if the controlled corporation leases the property it owns back to the distributing corporation, it will be difficult to establish that an active trade or business is present.

As a related matter, § 355(h), enacted in 2015, provides that § 355 does not apply if either the distributing corporation or the controlled corporation is a Real Estate Investment Trust (REIT). The distribution may, however, still qualify under § 355 if both the distributing corporation and the controlled corporation are REITs immediately after the distribution or if, during the three year period ending on the date of the distribution, the controlled corporation was a REIT subsidiary of the distributing corporation at all times and the distributing corporation controlled the controlled corporation at all times.

1.3. *Vertical Division of a Single Business Activity*

As noted by the court in *Rafferty,* the IRS position for many years was that § 355 could not be applied to divide a single business, which did have the requisite five-year active trade or business history, into two separate corporations. The IRS position was rejected in Coady v. Commissioner, 33 T.C. 771 (1960) (acq.), aff'd per curiam, 289 F.2d 490 (6th Cir.1961), holding invalid Regulations providing that § 355 did not apply to the separation of a single business. Accord, United States v. Marett, 325 F.2d 28 (5th Cir.1963). In Rev.Rul. 64–147, 1964–1 C.B. 136, the IRS announced that it would follow *Coady* and *Marett.* Treas.Reg. § 1.355–3(c), Ex. (4) and (5), now specifically sanction the use of § 355 to divide a single business with the requisite five-year pre-distribution history. See also Treas.Reg. § 1.355–1(b) and –3(c), Exs. (6) and (7); Rev.Rul. 2003–99, 2003–2 C.B. 388 (obsoleting Rev.Rul. 64–147).

1.4. *Single Business Versus Two Separate Businesses*

As a result of the *Coady* and *Marett* cases, the IRS and taxpayers tended to shift sides in the single business versus separate businesses controversy. The IRS contended that an activity involved two separate businesses, and one of the two did not satisfy the five-year rule; the taxpayer argued that the activities constituted a single business, which could be divided under *Coady.* The question of whether an activity constitutes a single business or two separate businesses may arise in several different contexts.

1.4.1. *Geographical Division*

The creation of branches in each of its market areas by a multi-state business may be treated as an expansion of a single business with a continuing history. In Burke v. Commissioner, 42 T.C. 1021 (1964), the IRS asserted that establishing a second retail store in another town constituted the creation of a separate trade or business as to which the five-year rule was not satisfied. The court upheld the taxpayer's assertion that under the *Coady* rule the second store constituted a branch of a single retail business that satisfied the five-year rule. In Lockwood's Estate v. Commissioner, 350 F.2d 712 (8th Cir.1965), a corporation operated in the Midwest through branches that were ultimately separately incorporated and spun-off. In 1949 it began to make sales in New England and in 1954 established a branch office in Maine. In 1956, the branch was incorporated separately and the stock distributed. No sales activity was present in Maine from 1951 to 1953, and the IRS asserted that the business had not been actively conducted in the Maine location for the five years preceding the division in 1956. The court rejected the IRS's reliance on its "geographical area" test:

> Nothing in the language of § 355 suggests that prior business activity is only to be measured by looking at the business performed in a geographical area where the controlled corporation is eventually formed. In this case, when the entire Lockwood market is viewed, it can be seen that Lockwood was engaged in active business as required by § 355 for the five years prior to the incorporation of Maine, Inc. Since its incorporation Maine, Inc. has carried on the same kind of manufacturing and selling business previously and concurrently performed by Lockwood. Thus all § 355 prerequisites are met. * * *

> Since there is no Congressional intent evidenced to the contrary, the test, restated, is not whether active business had been carried out in the geographic area later served by the controlled corporation. But, simply, whether the distributing corporation, for five years prior to distribution, had been actively conducting the type of business now performed by the controlled corporation without reference to the geographic area.

Treas.Reg. § 1.355–3(c), Ex. (7), now follows the *Burke* and *Estate of Lockwood* cases. Example (6) likewise approves the separation of the downtown and suburban branches of a retail clothing store. See also Treas.Reg. § 1.355–3(c), Ex. (8).

1.4.2.   *Separate Lines of Business*

In Lester v. Commissioner, 40 T.C. 947 (1963) (acq.), a corporation was both a warehouse distributor (in which capacity it sold to "jobbers") and a "jobber" (in which capacity it sold to retailers). Jobber customers objected to purchasing from a corporation that was also a competitor, and the warehouse activity was spun-off. The court reaffirmed *Coady,* but in any event found that the activities constituted two separate businesses, each with its own five-year history. See also Wilson v. Commissioner, 42 T.C. 914 (1964), rev'd on other grounds, 353 F.2d 184 (9th Cir.1965) (furniture business and its financing activities were two separate businesses). In Rev.Rul. 56–451, 1956–2 C.B. 208 (obsoleted by Rev.Rul. 2003–99, 2003–2 C.B. 388), the IRS ruled that the publication of a trade magazine for one industry was a business separate from the publication of three magazines for another industry, and the former could be spun-off since the requirements of § 355 were met.

The problems in this area are closely related to the "functional division" situations discussed above, and the position in the Regulations that there can be a valid functional division of a single business under § 355 will presumably have an impact in the single business vs. two separate businesses context as well. As discussed below, Treas.Reg. § 1.355–2(d)(2)(iv)(C), focuses on the device test in this context.

2. FIVE-YEAR HISTORY

2.1. *Acquisitions of a Going Business Within the Five-Year Period*

The active trades or businesses of the distributing corporation must be the historic trades or businesses of the distributing corporation or its subsidiary. Section 355(b)(2)(C) and (D) stand as barriers to bailing out corporate earnings and profits through the acquisition of a new business shortly before it is distributed. Section 355(b)(2)(C) disqualifies an active trade or business that was acquired in a taxable transaction within the five-year period ending on the date of the distribution. Section 355(b)(2)(D) disqualifies a trade or business in a controlled corporation that was acquired by the distributing corporation or any distributee corporation in a taxable transaction within the five-year period.

In Rev.Rul. 78–442, 1978–2 C.B. 143, a corporation transferred assets and liabilities of one of its businesses to a newly formed corporation, which assumed the liabilities associated with the transferred business, and then distributed the stock. The parent corporation recognized gain on the transfer of the assets to the subsidiary under § 357(c) because the liabilities assumed exceeded the bases of the assets transferred. The ruling held that despite the fact that gain was recognized on the transfer of the business to the subsidiary, § 355(b)(2)(C) did not disqualify the distribution from qualifying under § 355, because § 355(b)(2)(C) was not intended to apply to an acquisition of a trade or business by a controlled corporation from the distributing corporation.

Rev.Rul. 2002–49, 2002–2 C.B. 288, dealt with whether the five-year active conduct of a trade or business requirement of § 355(b) was satisfied when, during the five-year period prior to a transaction that otherwise met the requirements of § 355, a corporation holding a membership interest in a member-managed limited liability company (LLC), which was taxed as a partnership, purchased the remaining interests in the LLC, contributed a portion of the LLC's business to a newly formed controlled subsidiary, and then distributed the stock of the controlled subsidiary to its shareholders. In *Situation 1*, originally D Corporation's sole asset was 20% of the LLC, which operated numerous rental properties. D's officers actively participated in the management of the LLC, along with the officers of another 20% owner; none of the other owners participated in management. (As a result, under Rev.Rul. 92–17, noted above, D was engaged in the active conduct of the leasing business for the first two years.) After two years, D purchased the other 80% of the interests, and the LLC became a disregarded entity. On the first day of Year 6, the LLC distributed 40% of the rental properties to D, which contributed the properties to C, in exchange for all of C's stock, following which C was spun-off to D's shareholders. Notwithstanding Rev.Rul. 99–6, 1999–1 C.B. 432 (holding that the sale and purchase of all of the remaining interests in an LLC is treated as the distribution of assets to the selling members and the purchase of assets by the continuing members), the purchase of the 80% interest in the LLC within five years did not violate § 355(b)(2)(C), even though gain or loss was recognized in the transaction, because the transaction was not the acquisition of a new or different business under Treas.Reg. § 1.355–3(b)(3)(ii). *Situation 2* was the same as *Situation 1*, except that D obtained the 20% interest in the LLC on the first day of Year 2, in exchange for appreciated securities in a § 721 transaction, before the spin-off in Year 6. That situation did not qualify, however, because D was treated as having acquired the LLC's business in a transaction in which gain or loss was recognized within the five-year pre-distribution period proscribed by § 355(b)(2)(C). Although pursuant to § 721 no gain or loss was recognized on D's acquisition of the LLC interest in year 2, if D had directly acquired the LLC's business in exchange for the property D contributed to the LLC, the exchange would have been a transaction in which gain or loss was recognized. For purposes of § 355(b), therefore, D was treated as acquiring the LLC's business in Year 2 in a transaction in which gain or loss was recognized. The analysis in this revenue ruling reflects a remarkable interpretation of the term "a transaction in which gain or loss was recognized."

Rev.Rul. 2017–9, 2017–21 I.R.B. 1244, dealt with whether the step transaction doctrine applied if a parent corporation (P) transferred property constituting an active trade or business to its controlled subsidiary (D) for the purpose of assuring that D met the requirements of § 355(b)(1)(A), and pursuant to the same overall plan, the transfer was followed by a distribution by D of the stock of its controlled subsidiary (C) to P. In the ruling, P had been engaged in an active business A for more than 5 years, and C had been engaged in an active business B for more than 5 years. Both businesses met the active conduct of a trade or business test of § 355(b). D, however, was not engaged in the active conduct of a trade or business, directly or through any member of its separate affiliated group (within the meaning of § 355(b)(3)) other than C. The ruling held that the two transactions are not stepped together. Each is independently respected. The first transaction was treated as an exchange under § 351, and the second transaction qualified as a distribution governed by § 355. If the transactions had been stepped together into a single exchange, P would have been treated as transferring the business property to D in exchange for a portion of the C stock in an exchange to which § 1001 applied. Gain or loss would have been recognized to P on the transfer of the property to D; gain or loss would have been recognized to D, under § 1001(a), upon its transfer of the C stock to P in exchange for the property transferred to it. In addition, because the value of the business transferred from P to D equaled 25% of the value of C, § 355 would not have applied to any part of the distribution of C stock because D would not have distributed stock constituting § 368(c) control of C. Gain would have been recognized to D, under § 311(b) upon the distribution of the remaining 75% of the C stock with respect to P's stock in D to which § 301 would have applied. The ruling reasoned as follows:

> The transfer of property permitted to be received by D in a nonrecognition transaction has independent significance when

undertaken in contemplation of a distribution by D of stock and securities described in § 355(a)(1)(A). The transfer thus is respected as a separate transaction, regardless of whether the purpose of the transfer is to qualify the distribution under § 355(b). See, e.g., Rev. Rul. 78–330; § 1.355–6(d)(3)(v)(B), Example 1; and Athanasios v. Comm'r, T.C. Memo 1995–72. Back-to-back nonrecognition transfers are generally respected when consistent with the underlying intent of the applicable Code provisions and there is no compelling alternative policy. See, e.g., Rev.Rul. 2015–9, 2015–21 I.R.B. 972, and Rev.Rul. 2015–10, 2015–21 I.R.B. 973.

P's transfer on Date 1 is the type of transaction to which § 351 is intended to apply. Analysis of the transaction as a whole does not indicate that P's transfer should be properly treated other than in accordance with its form. Each step provides for continued ownership in modified corporate form. Additionally, the steps do not resemble a sale, and none of the interests are liquidated or otherwise redeemed. On these facts, nonrecognition treatment under §§ 351 and 355 is not inconsistent with the congressional intent of these Code provisions. The effect of the steps in Situation 1 is consistent with the policies underlying §§ 351 and 355. Accordingly, the Date 1 and Date 2 transfers described in Situation 1 will be respected as separate transactions for federal income tax purposes. Therefore, § 351 applies to P's transfer on Date 1 and § 355 applies to D's transfer on Date 2.

In contrast, the ruling held that, where a dividend was paid by C to D pursuant to a plan that included a transfer by D of appreciated assets to C and a distribution by D of the C stock that qualified under § 368(a)(1)(D) and § 355, the step transaction applied to integrate all three transactions. Because D retained the money and property distributed pursuant to the dividend declaration, that money and property was taxable boot received by D in the § 368(a)(1)(D) reorganization.

2.2. *Diversification and Expansion of an Existing Business with a Five-Year History*

The active trades or businesses in the distributing and controlled corporations must be the same as those conducted earlier. Thus, if the distributing corporation or the distributed controlled corporation contains only a new business started within the preceding five years, the active trade or business test is not satisfied. What about changes in product, location, or methods? What about growth itself? Is a small rental business started in 2012 the same business as a large rental activity with many more properties in 2022? Is the operation of a single retail store in 2012 the same business as the operation in 2022 of a chain of 50 stores?

The IRS has addressed the business expansion issue in revenue rulings. In Rev.Rul. 2003–18, 2003–1 C.B. 467, a corporation that had a five-year history of being a dealer of brand X automobiles acquired a franchise to sell and service brand Y automobiles, and the assets to operate that franchise, in a taxable transaction within five years before transferring the brand X automobile franchise assets to C, its wholly-controlled subsidiary, and spinning-off C pro rata. The IRS held that the acquisition of the brand Y franchise and assets was merely an expansion of the brand X business under Treas.Reg. § 1.355–3(b)(3)(ii), rather than the acquisition of a new or different business. The facts of the ruling state that the brand X and brand Y dealership businesses were conducted on adjacent leaseholds, but the analysis does not incorporate this fact. Conversely, the facts are silent regarding the relative quality and customer market for brand X and brand Y automobiles. The analysis succinctly states:

> [B]ecause (i) the product of the brand X automobile dealership is similar to the product of the brand Y automobile dealership, (ii) the business activities associated with the operation of the brand X automobile dealership (i.e., sales and service) are the same as the business activities associated with the operation of the brand Y automobile dealership, and (iii) the operation of the brand Y automobile dealership involves the use of the experience and know-how that D developed in the operation of the brand X automobile dealership, the brand Y automobile dealership is in the same line of business as the brand X dealership and its acquisition does not constitute the acquisition of a new or different business * * *.

Rev.Rul. 2003–38, 2003–1 C.B. 811, dealt with an expansion of a retail business from bricks to clicks. For more than five years, D corporation operated a retail shoe store business in shopping malls and other locations, under the name "D." D's business enjoyed favorable name recognition, customer loyalty, and goodwill in the retail shoe market. D created a website and began selling shoes at retail through the internet. To take advantage of D's name recognition, customer loyalty, and established goodwill, and to enhance the website's chances for success, the website was named "D.com." To a significant extent, the operation of the website drew upon D's experience and know-how. Two years later, D transferred the website-based business's assets and liabilities to C, a newly formed controlled subsidiary, and spun-off C pro rata. The IRS ruled that under Treas.Reg. § 1.355–3(b)(3)(ii), the internet sales operation was an expansion of the retail store business, not a new business. Thus, each of D and C was engaged in the active conduct of a five-year trade or business. The model used by the revenue ruling to determine that the clicks business was an expansion of the bricks business was based on analyzing the facts that the two shared (1) subject matter; (2) operational activities; and (3) knowledge and experience. The first two characteristics were shared, but the third was not. The products and the principal business activities of the retail shoe store business and the internet-based business were the same. Although selling shoes on the internet required some know-how different from operating a retail store (different marketing approaches, distribution chains, and technical operations issues), the website's operation drew significantly on D's existing experience and know-how, and its success would depend largely on D's pre-existing goodwill. The failure of the two businesses to share the third common characteristic was cured by the overlapping goodwill.

2.3. *Conduct of the Business for the Five-Year Period*

Occasionally a question arises as to whether the business has been conducted for the requisite five-year period. An unusual case is W.E. Gabriel Fabrication Co. v. Commissioner, 42 T.C. 545 (1964) (acq.). Two brothers, who owned a corporation that was actively engaged in three businesses, decided to divide up the corporation because of disputes between them. The taxpayer-brother was to receive two of the businesses. Pursuant to an agreement entered into in 1955, the corporation loaned the assets of the two businesses to the taxpayer who operated the businesses as a sole proprietor for about 14 months. In 1956, a new corporation was formed to which the assets of the businesses were formally transferred, and this corporation was spun-off to the taxpayer. The taxpayer then transferred his sole proprietorship interest (in which the "loaned" assets had been used) to the new corporation. Under the facts, the distributing corporation had ceased to engage in the spun-off businesses for the 14-month period prior to the distribution, and the new corporation itself had not engaged in the business until after the distribution. The court upheld the taxpayer's argument that § 355 nonetheless applied since it concluded that there was no requirement that the business in the five-year period preceding the distribution be conducted by either the distributing corporation or the distributee corporation. It was sufficient that the business itself was conducted during the five-year period, and the taxpayer was permitted to add on the 14-month operation as a sole proprietorship to the time when the businesses had been conducted by the distributing corporation for the purpose of satisfying the five-year requirement.

In Rev.Rul. 82–219, 1982–2 C.B. 82, a subsidiary corporation that manufactured pollution control equipment for a single unrelated automobile manufacturer was required to cease its production activities for a year when the automobile manufacturer unexpectedly filed for bankruptcy. During the year in which it was shut down, the subsidiary pursued new customers for its products. The subsidiary was spun-off by its parent corporation for valid business reasons. The fact that the subsidiary had income in only four of the five years preceding the distribution of its stock to its parent's stockholders did not defeat the five-year active conduct of business requirement.

2.4. *Proposed Minimum Size for Five Year Business*

Prop.Reg. § 1.355–9, 81 Fed. Reg. 46004, 46018 (Jul. 15, 2016), would provide a new minimum size requirement for an active business to qualify under § 355. The requirements of § 355(a)(1)(C) and (b) would be satisfied with respect to a distribution only if the five-year-active-business asset percentage (as defined in the Regulations) of each of Distributing and Controlled is at least 5%. These Proposed Regulations are discussed below in greater detail in *C. The "Device" Limitation*, Detailed Analysis 4.

3.   SALE OF ASSETS FOLLOWING DISTRIBUTION

Suppose that shortly after the distribution, the distributed corporation sells all of its operating assets and winds up its business. Martin Ice Cream Co. v. Commissioner, 110 T.C. 189 (1998), held that a post-distribution sale of all of the assets of the distributed controlled corporation six weeks after a split-off, but pursuant to a pre-arranged plan, resulted in the distribution failing to qualify under § 355 because the active business requirement of § 355(a)(1)(A) had not been met after the distribution. The same result should occur if the distributing corporation sells all of its assets and liquidates immediately after the distribution.

4.   HOLDING COMPANIES

Section 355(b)(1)(B) provides that if the distributing corporation has "no assets other than stock or securities in the controlled corporations," then to qualify, "each of the controlled corporations is engaged immediately after the distribution in the active conduct of a trade or business." Regulations allow for a de minimis amount of assets to be held by the distributing corporation. Treas.Reg. § 1.355–3(a)(1)(ii). Before it was amended in 2007, § 355(b)(2)(A) provided that a holding company would be engaged in the active conduct of a trade or business if "substantially all" of its assets consists of stock or securities of controlled corporations that are each actively engaged in the conduct of a business.

5.   ACTIVE TRADE OR BUSINESS OF AFFILIATED CORPORATIONS

For purposes of determining whether the active business requirement of § 355(b)(1) has been met, § 355(b)(3) provides that all members of a corporation's separate affiliated group (SAG) will be treated as a single corporation. A corporation's SAG is the affiliated group that would be determined under § 1504(a) if the corporation were the common parent (and § 1504(b) did not apply). Prop.Reg. § 1.355–3(b), 72 Fed. Reg. 26012, 26026 (May 8, 2007), would treat all of the subsidiaries of the common parent of a SAG as divisions of the common parent for purposes of determining whether either the distributing or controlled SAG is engaged in a qualified trade or business. The separate affiliated group of the distributing corporation (DSAG) is the affiliated group consisting of the distributing corporation and all of its affiliated corporations. The separate affiliated group of a controlled corporation (CSAG) is determined in a similar manner, but by treating the controlled corporation as the common parent. Accordingly, prior to a distribution, the DSAG includes CSAG members if the ownership requirements are met. Prop.Reg. § 1.355–3(b)(1)(iii) (2007).

The SAG rule is applied for purposes of determining whether a corporation has conducted a trade or business throughout the requisite five-year period preceding the distribution and whether the distributing and controlled corporations are actively conducting a trade or business following distribution. These Proposed Regulations will affect the application of the active business requirement in a number of respects.

First, if ownership requirements are met, members of the distributing corporation DSAG and the controlled corporation SAG will be treated as belonging to a single SAG during the pre-distribution period, which facilitates identifying the appropriate trades or businesses regardless of how the assets are distributed among the SAG members. See Prop.Reg. § 1.355–3(b)(3)(i) (2007).

Second, the SAG rule applies for purposes of determining whether there has been a taxable acquisition of the trade or business within the five years preceding the distribution under § 355(b)(2)(C) or (D). Because the subsidiaries of the common parent of a SAG are treated as divisions of the common parent, a stock acquisition of a corporation that becomes a member of a SAG is treated as an asset acquisition (which affects the application of § 355(b)(2)(D) regarding acquisition of control of a corporation conducting an active business). Prop.Reg. § 1.355–3(b)(1)(ii) (2007).

Third, Prop.Reg. § 1.355–3(b)(4)(iii) (2007) permits certain taxable acquisitions of the assets of a trade or business by the distributing corporation from affiliated corporations without violating the restrictions of § 355(b)(2)(C) and (D), which are interpreted as preventing the use of the assets of the distributing corporation to acquire a trade or business in lieu of dividend distributions. The Proposed Regulations disregard a taxable acquisition by the controlled SAG from the distributing SAG, disregard the use of cash to pay off fractional shares, and to a limited extent, disregard taxable acquisitions from members of the same SAG. However, the Proposed Regulations do not disregard the recognition of gain or loss in transactions between affiliated corporations unless the affiliates are members of the same SAG. (Analogous to current Regulations, taxable acquisitions to expand an existing business within a SAG are disregarded. Prop.Reg. § 1.355–3(b)(3)(ii) (2007).)

Fourth, the application of § 355(b)(2)(D)(i) (control acquired by any distributee corporation) is limited to situations designed to avoid the impact of the repeal of the *General Utilities* doctrine. Thus, the Proposed Regulations allow a taxable acquisition by a distributee corporation of control of the distributing corporation in a transaction where the basis of the acquired distributing stock is determined in whole or by reference to the transferor's basis. Prop.Reg. § 1.355–3(b)(4)(iii)(C) (2007).

Fifth, the Proposed Regulations interpret § 355(b)(2)(C) and (D) to have the common purpose of preventing the direct or indirect acquisition of the trade or business by a corporation in exchange for assets other than its stock. Thus, if (1) a DSAG member or controlled corporation acquires the trade or business solely for the distributing corporation's stock, (2) the distributing corporation acquires control of the controlled corporation solely for the distributing corporation's stock, or (3) the controlled corporation acquires the trade or business from the distributing corporation solely in exchange for stock of the controlled corporation, in a transaction in which no gain or loss was recognized, § 355(b)(2)(C) and (D) are satisfied. If, however, the trade or business is acquired in exchange for assets of the distributing corporation (other than stock of a corporation in control of the distributing corporation used in a reorganization) § 355(b)(2)(C) and (D) are not satisfied. Under this rule, for example, an acquisition by a controlled corporation (while controlled by the distributing corporation) from an unrelated party in exchange for the controlled corporation stock has the effect of an indirect acquisition by the distributing corporation in exchange for its assets. Such an acquisition violates the purpose of § 355(b)(2)(C) and will be treated as one in which gain or loss is recognized. Prop.Reg. § 1.355–3(b)(4)(ii) (2007).

6. ACQUISITION OF CONTROL OF THE DISTRIBUTING CORPORATION BY A DISTRIBUTEE CORPORATION

Section 355(b)(2)(D) was amended in 1987 to apply the five-year rule to the acquisition of control by the distributee corporation of a corporation conducting a trade or business. Following repeal of the *General Utilities* doctrine by the 1986 Act, there was concern that a § 355 division could be used to thwart recognition of corporate level gain in a corporate acquisition followed by a disposition of unwanted assets. For example, T Corporation operates two separate businesses. X Corporation wishes to acquire business A, but not business B. T is not willing to dispose of the businesses separately. To accomplish the transaction, T transfers each business into separate subsidiaries, S1 and S2, in a nontaxable transaction under § 351. X acquires the T stock from the T stockholders. X causes T to distribute the stock of S1, the wanted subsidiary, to it in a § 355 distribution. Subsequently, X sells the T stock thereby disposing of the unwanted assets of business B (held in S2) without corporate level recognition of unrealized gain in the assets of business B.[6] In the example, because X, the distributee of the S1 stock, indirectly acquired control of S1 and S2 within the five-year period preceding the distribution, under § 355(b)(2)(D), § 355 would not apply to the distribution of S1 stock to X. T will be required to recognize gain on the distribution of S1 stock to X under § 311.

In Rev.Rul. 74–5, 1974–1 C.B. 82 (obsoleted by Rev.Rul. 89–37, 1989–1 C.B. 107), the IRS ruled that an acquiring corporation that had purchased stock in a distributing corporation two years prior to the spin-off of a controlled subsidiary's stock could constitute a historic shareholder and thus could qualify for § 355 treatment even though the shareholder had not owned stock in the distributing corporation for five years. This ruling provided a pathway for a corporate purchaser to acquire stock in a target corporation and then break-up and sell the target corporation's ownership structure without incurring corporate level taxation. (The acquiring corporation would be able to allocate its cost basis in the target corporation's stock to the stock in the controlled subsidiary and the retained stock in the target corporation based on their relative fair market value per § 358.)

The "bust-up" transaction made possible by Rev.Rul. 74–5 is not objectionable under a "weak form" of *General Utilities* repeal as the assets held in corporate solution retain a carryover basis. This transaction is, however, objectionable under a "strong form" of *General Utilities* repeal because historic assets are being transferred outside the economic group to new shareholders without incurring corporate level taxation. Thus, after the final repeal of the *General Utilities* doctrine in 1986, this transaction created

---

[6]   This transaction was thought to have been approved by Rev.Rul. 74–5, 1974–1 C.B. 82, obsoleted by Rev.Rul. 89–37, 1989–1 C.B. 107, in which P Corporation in 1969 acquired all of the stock of X Corporation for cash. X Corporation in turn owned all of the stock of Y Corporation that it had acquired in 1965. In 1971, X distributed the Y stock to P, and in 1972 P distributed the Y stock to its stockholders. The Ruling held that the 1971 distribution satisfied § 355(b)(2)(D), since P was neither the distributing nor the controlled corporation but simply the stockholder of the distributing corporation. On the other hand, the 1972 distribution did not satisfy § 355(b)(2)(D), since the business of controlled Corporation Y was acquired indirectly by P through another Corporation (X) in a transaction within five years in which gain or loss had been recognized.

an early test for determining the correct form (a "weak form" or "strong form") of *General Utilities* repeal that Congress intended. Congress quickly responded by asserting that § 355's usage in this context was inconsistent with the intended scope of its repeal of the *General Utilities* doctrine as it inappropriately allowed a new shareholder (an acquiring corporation) to obtain ownership of a historic business without the corporation incurring corporate level taxation on the disposition. Specifically, in 1987, Congress amended § 355(b)(2)(D) to disqualify from § 355 a distribution of stock in a controlled subsidiary to a shareholder who had acquired control of the distributing corporation within five years of the spin-off. In the legislative history, Congress clarified that the tax-free spin-off of a controlled subsidiary to a new acquiring shareholder was akin to a sale of the controlled subsidiary as the following legislative history makes plain:

> The committee believes that the requirements of section 355 of the Code should generally prevent the use of that section to accomplish a sale of recently distributed subsidiary (or its recently acquired parent) without corporate level tax, or effectively to accomplish a sale of a subsidiary to any significant shareholder by a distribution with respect to recently purchased stock.

H.R. Rep. No. 100–391, at 1083 (1987), as reprinted in 1987 U.S.C.C.A.N. 2313–378, 2313–697. Thus, the normative policy concern that motivated Congress to amend § 355 in 1987 was a situation where a historic active business was being transferred to a non-historic shareholder. Section 355's application in this context was seen as inconsistent with the repeal of the *General Utilities* doctrine as it allowed a disposition of a historic business to a new shareholder without incurring corporate level tax on the disposition.

A second key aspect of § 355(b)(2)(D)'s enactment was Congress's desire to have an objective pre-transaction continuity of interest period. In this regard, in the context of a transaction that was akin to a disposition, Congress explicitly provided in § 355(b)(2)(D) that the shareholder who obtained control must be a shareholder for five years prior to the § 355 transaction in order to be considered a historic shareholder. Thus, Congress decided to clarify the testing period by setting forth a predetermined and objective five-year time period in lieu of relying on the subjective "old and cold" analysis[7] that had been employed.

The statutory amendment enacted in 1987 was narrowly tailored and thus does not comprehensively effectuate its stated "strong form" policy goals. Congress's amendment to § 355(b)(2)(D) did not provide for any post-transaction continuity requirement. Moreover, although Congress's 1987 amendment to § 355(b)(2)(D) did apply a five-year testing period, that five-year testing period only applied to a purchasing shareholder—like the one posited in Rev.Rul. 74–5—that obtained control, as defined in § 368(c),

---

[7]   Prior to this date, the continuity of interest standard was expressed as a subjective standard. See Treas.Reg. § 1.355–3(c) (2002). And the IRS had held that two years was sufficient for purposes of meeting this test. See Rev.Rul. 74–5, 1974–C.B. 82. With the enactment of § 355(b)(2)(D), transactions that had been described as a disposition now required the corporate purchaser to be a five-year historic shareholder to avail itself of § 355. See Rev.Rul. 89–37, 1989–1 C.B. 107.

through a taxable purchase of the distributing corporation's stock. See Rev.Rul. 89–37, 1989–1 C.B. 107 (discussing rationale for the 1987 amendments and that the amendment of § 355(b)(2)(D) was explicitly designed to reverse the holding of Rev.Rul. 74–5). In other words, the amendments to § 355(b)(2)(D) did not prevent § 355 from applying to a purchasing corporation that acquired less than 80% of the stock of a target corporation and then subsequently exchanged the target stock for stock in a controlled subsidiary two years later in a § 355 distribution.[8] Thus, the amendment to § 355(b)(2)(D) sought to restrict the tax-free spin-off of a controlled subsidiary to a non-historic shareholder, but § 355(b)(2)(D), as drafted, was underinclusive in terms of meeting that policy goal. The obvious planning technique, therefore, was for the acquiring corporation to acquire a less than 80% interest in the target corporation and then split-off a controlled subsidiary to the new shareholder thereafter.

Congress subsequently has recognized that its amendment to § 355(b)(2)(D) in 1987 was underinclusive in terms of fully achieving a "strong form" version of *General Utilities* repeal,[9] and the further legislative amendments to § 355 since 1987 that attempt to better harmonize § 355's continued existence with Congress's repeal of the *General Utilities* doctrine is discussed below in Section 4, Detailed Analysis 4.3–4.6.

PROBLEM SET 2

1.   Mullet Corp. is engaged in the processing and sale of frozen seafood products. Its packing plant is owned by its wholly owned subsidiary, Seashell Corp. Mullet proposes to distribute all the stock of Seashell Corp. to its shareholders, pro rata. Consider whether the corporate division would meet the "active business" test of § 355 given the following alternative additional facts.

(a)   Seashell Corp. operates the packing plant using its employees and sells the packaged seafood to Mullet, which markets it.

(b)   Seashell Corp. leases the packing plant to Mullet, which operates it with Mullet employees. Seashell has no assets other than the packing plant and a bank account.

(c)   (1)   Seashell's real estate holdings include not only the packing plant, which it leases to Mullet, but a restaurant that it leases to Tuna Corp., which is unrelated to Seashell, Mullet, or Mullet's shareholders.

(2)   Seashell's real estate holdings include not only the packing plant and restaurant, but a large marina that it leases to Poseidon Corp., which is unrelated to Seashell, Mullet, or Mullet's shareholders.

---

[8]   See Alan S. Kaden & Richard A. Wolfe, Spin-Offs, Split-Offs, and Split-Ups: A Detailed Analysis of Section 355, 44 Tax Notes 565, 575 (1989); Michael L. Schler, Avoiding the Technical Requirements of New Section 355, 38 Tax Notes 417, 417–18 (1988).

[9]   See H.R. Rep. No. 101–881, at 340–41 (1990). For a more complete discussion of the efforts to right-size § 355 with the intended scope of Congress' intended repeal of the *General Utilities* doctrine and the remaining discontinuities that need to be addressed, see Bret Wells, Reform of Section 355, 68 Am. U. L. Rev. 447 (2018).

(d) Seashell's assets include the packing plant, which it leases to Mullet, and a sushi bar restaurant that it operates.

2. SweatSox Corp., which is equally owned by Calvin and Dora, sells athletic wear at retail. Until four years ago, its operations were confined to the Eastern Seaboard, where it had over 100 stores from Maine to Florida. Four years ago, SweatSox began retail sales on the West Coast, and in the past four years it has opened 50 stores from Southern California to Seattle. Consider whether the corporate division would meet the "active business" test of § 355 given the following alternative additional facts.

(a) SweatSox proposes to transfer the California and Florida stores to a new subsidiary, SunshineSports Corp., and then to distribute all of the SunshineSports Corp. stock to Calvin in complete redemption of his stock in SweatSox.

(b) SweatSox Corp. proposes to transfer the West Coast stores to a new subsidiary, LeftCoast, Inc., and then to distribute all of the LeftCoast, Inc., stock to Dora in complete redemption of her stock in SweatSox.

3. Mako Corp. is engaged in the business of manufacturing scuba diving equipment. Frostbite Corp., a wholly owned subsidiary of Mako, is engaged in the business of manufacturing snowmobiles. Except as provided in the individual questions, each business has been conducted for six years. Mako distributes the stock of Frostbite pro rata to its shareholders. Does the distribution qualify under the active business test, if:

(a) Frostbite purchased the snowmobile business from an unrelated seller four years ago?

(b) Frostbite purchased the snowmobile business from an unrelated seller six years ago?

(c) Frostbite purchased the snowmobile business from Icicle Corp., another wholly owned subsidiary of Mako, four years ago?

(d) Frostbite Corp. itself was acquired by Mako 3 years ago in a reverse triangular merger (which qualified under § 368(a)(2)(E)) in which no boot was distributed?

(e) Frostbite was acquired 3 years ago in a reverse triangular merger (which qualified under § 368(a)(2)(E)) in which 10% of the consideration was cash?

(f) Frostbite was formed four years ago (in a § 351 transaction) by Mako, which contributed the snowmobile business, which Mako previously had operated as a division for three years? In the transaction to form Frostbite, Mako transferred assets with a fair market value of $5,000,000 and a basis of $1,000,000, subject to $1,500,000 of liabilities that were assumed by Frostbite.

(g) Frostbite was formed 10 years ago with Stinkpot Corp, a manufacturer of power boats. Mako and Stinkpot each owned 50% of the stock until three years ago. Three years ago, Frostbite redeemed all of Stinkpots's stock, leaving Mako as the sole shareholder.

4.   Blueberry Corp. is engaged in the business of wireless handheld e-mail devices. Tunes Corp., a wholly owned subsidiary of Blueberry, is engaged in the business of manufacturing portable media players. Both businesses have been conducted for 6 years. One-half the stock of Blueberry is owned by Peaches Corp. and the other one-half is owned by MacroSoft, Inc. Peaches and Macrosoft are wholly owned subsidiaries of Dredmon Corp. Peaches and Macrosoft purchased their stock of Blueberry three years ago. Blueberry distributes the stock of Tunes pro rata to Peaches and Macrosoft. Does the distribution qualify under the active business test?

5.   Point-N-Click Corp. is engaged in the retail camera sales business. Until three years ago, Point-N-Click's business was confined to consumer-grade digital cameras sold through an internet website. Three years ago, Point-N-Click opened several retail stores catering to professional photographers, in which it sold high-end digital cameras and film cameras. The management of Point-N-Click believes that the retail stores catering to professional photographers would perform better if ownership were separated from the internet based business catering to consumers. The plan is to transfer the retail stores to a newly formed subsidiary, Daguerreotype, and then to spin-off Daguerreotype to the Point-N-Click shareholders. Does the distribution qualify under the active business test?

C. THE "DEVICE" LIMITATION

INTERNAL REVENUE CODE: Section 355(a)(1)(B).

REGULATIONS: Section 1.355–2(d).

The "device" language of § 355(a)(1)(B) permits nonrecognition in a divisive transaction only if the transaction is not used principally as a "device" for the distribution of earnings and profits of either the distributing or controlled corporations, or both. The restriction is aimed at preventing a division from being merely a step in a bail-out of earnings and profits through the sale of the stock or liquidation of one of the corporations. The division of a part of one corporation into distributed stock of another corporation provides an opportunity to dispose of the distributed assets in a stock sale that produces capital gains and basis recovery deferred to the date of sale, in contrast to immediate recognition of ordinary income in the amount of the full fair market value of the distributed property in the form of a dividend. Thus, as previously noted, the reason for the presence of the "device" restriction in § 355 has been diminished by the equalization of the income tax rates on dividends and capital gains in years after the 2003 Act because with dividends and long-term capital gains taxed at the same rates, rate-arbitrage based bailout *per se* is no longer a relevant concern. Nevertheless, bailout issues remain. First, basis recovery upon the sale of the stock of either the distributing or controlled corporation after the distribution effects a bailout. Second, because § 311(b) and § 336, enacted in 1986 to repeal the *General Utilities* doctrine, impose tax at the corporate level on asset appreciation in corporate redemptions and liquidations, § 355 remains important because it draws the line between distributions that trigger corporate level recognition and those distributions that are permitted to enjoy corporate level tax deferral.

What constitutes a "device" is far from clear. The requirement may be important to identifying a distribution that is essentially equivalent to a dividend, or it may apply to identify tax avoidance of the *Gregory* type. Treas.Reg. § 1.355–2(d)(1) states: "Section 355 recognizes that a tax-free distribution of the stock of a controlled corporation presents a potential for tax avoidance by facilitating the avoidance of the dividend provisions of the Code through the subsequent sale or exchange of stock of one corporation and the retention of the stock of another corporation." The presence of the "device" test in § 355 focuses the inquiry on the circumstances under which the corporate division has taken place. The problem is how to identify those situations in which dividend treatment is nonetheless proper because every corporate division carries with it the potential for extracting earnings from the corporation with no dividend consequences. Compare, however, the treatment of partial liquidations under § 302(b)(4) and (e)(2), discussed in Chapter 5, in which a corporate "division" is involved, but no "device" limitation is imposed.

South Tulsa Pathology Laboratory, Inc. v. Commissioner

United States Tax Court, 2002.
118 T.C. 84.

■ MARVEL, JUDGE.

[Eds. The taxpayer corporation provided pathology related medical services including anatomic pathology and clinical pathology. In 1993 the taxpayer's shareholders agreed to sell the clinical pathology business to National Health Laboratories, Inc. (NHL). The assets of the clinical pathology business were transferred to a newly formed corporation, Clinpath, in exchange for the Clinpath stock. The Clinpath stock was then distributed to taxpayer's shareholders. As part of a plan the shareholders sold the Clinpath stock to NHL. The transaction predated § 355(e). The distributing corporation had accumulated earnings and profits of at least $236,347 as of its taxable year beginning July 1, 1993. There was no proof that either the taxpayer or the controlled corporation had current earnings and profits as of October 30, 1993.]

OPINION

I.   *The Statutory Framework*

Section 361(a) provides that "No gain or loss shall be recognized to a corporation if such corporation is a party to a reorganization and exchanges property, in pursuance of the plan of reorganization, solely for stock or securities in another corporation a party to the reorganization." Section 368(a)(1) defines reorganization for purposes of section 361 to include:

(D) a transfer by a corporation of all or a part of its assets to another corporation if immediately after the transfer the transferor, or one or more of its shareholders (including persons who were shareholders immediately before the transfer), or any combination thereof, is in control of the corporation to which the assets are transferred; but only if, in pursuance of the plan, stock or securities of the corporation to which the assets are transferred are distributed in a transaction which qualifies under section 354, 355, or 356; * * *

The above-described transaction, commonly referred to as a "D" reorganization, is sometimes used to divide an existing corporation on a tax-deferred basis into more than one corporation for corporate business purposes. In order for a divisive D reorganization to qualify for tax-deferred treatment at the corporate level under section 361, however, there must be a qualifying distribution of stock under section 355.

In this case, petitioner divided its existing business into two parts by way of a spinoff. It transferred its clinical business to a newly formed subsidiary, Clinpath, in exchange for 100 percent of Clinpath's stock. Petitioner then immediately distributed the Clinpath stock to its shareholders in a transaction petitioner claims met the requirements of section 355.

If a spinoff does not qualify under section 355, it could result in a taxable dividend to the distributing corporation's shareholders under section 301 to the extent of corporate earnings and profits and in tax to the distributing corporation computed in accordance with sections 311(b)(1) and 312. Secs. 355(c), 361(c). Section 311(b)(1) provides that, if a corporation distributes property to a shareholder in a transaction governed by sections 301 through 307 and the fair market value of such property exceeds its adjusted basis in the hands of the distributing corporation, then gain shall be recognized to the distributing corporation as if such property were sold to the distributee at its fair market value. Section 312(b) provides that, on a distribution of appreciated property by a corporation with respect to its stock, earnings and profits of the corporation are increased by the excess of the fair market value of the property over its basis.

II. *The Parties' Arguments*

The primary issue in this case is whether petitioner's spinoff of Clinpath qualified as a valid reorganization under section 368(a)(1)(D). Respondent claims it did not so qualify because the distribution of Clinpath's stock to petitioner's shareholders did not qualify as a nontaxable distribution under section 355. Respondent asserts that the spinoff of Clinpath and the subsequent sale of Clinpath stock to NHL were, in reality, a prearranged sale by petitioner of its clinical business which failed to qualify as a reorganization under section 368 and a nontaxable distribution of stock to petitioner's shareholders under section 355. Consequently, respondent contends petitioner realized and must recognize gain on the distribution of Clinpath stock. Sec. 311(b)(1). Petitioner disagrees, urging us to conclude that it structured the spinoff of its clinical business and the subsequent sale of Clinpath's stock for legitimate corporate business purposes and that the spinoff satisfied the requirements of sections 368(a)(1)(D) and 355. Therefore, petitioner contends, it is not required to recognize gain on the distribution of Clinpath stock to its shareholders.

* * *

In order to resolve these disputes, we must first decide whether the distribution of Clinpath stock to petitioner's shareholders met the section 355 requirements. We conclude that it did not for the reasons set forth below.

III. *Section 355 Distribution*

Section 355(a)(1) permits a nontaxable distribution by a corporation to its shareholders of stock in a controlled corporation if the distribution meets four statutory requirements: (1) Solely stock of a controlled corporation is distributed to shareholders with respect to their stock in the distributing corporation; (2) the distribution is not used principally as a device for the distribution of earnings and profits of the distributing corporation or the controlled corporation or both; (3) the requirements of section 355(b) (relating to active businesses) are satisfied; and (4) all of the controlled corporation's stock held by the distributing corporation, or an amount constituting control, is distributed. Sec. 355(a)(1). In addition to these statutory requirements, the regulations under section 355 require that the distribution have an independent corporate business purpose and that there be continuity of proprietary interest after the distribution. Sec. 1.355–2(b) and (c), Income Tax Regs.

* * *

A. *Nondevice Requirement of Section 355(a)(1)(B)*

A transaction fails to qualify under section 355 if that transaction is used principally as a device for the distribution of the earnings and profits of the distributing corporation, the controlled corporation, or both. Sec. 355(a)(1)(B); see also Sec. 1.355–2(d)(1), Income Tax Regs. We analyze whether a transaction was used principally as a device for distributing earnings and profits by examining all the facts and circumstances, including, but not limited to, the presence of the device factors listed in section 1.355–2(d)(2), Income Tax Regs., and the presence of the nondevice factors listed in section 1.355–2(d)(3), Income Tax Regs.

Petitioner essentially concedes that there is evidence of device as described in section 1.355–2(d)(2), Income Tax Regs.; however, it argues that a lack of substantial earnings and profits, Sec. 1.355–2(d)(5), Income Tax Regs., and a corporate business purpose, Sec. 1.355–2(d)(3), Income Tax Regs., outweigh any evidence of device.

1.   *Device Factors*

Section 1.355–2(d)(2), Income Tax Regs., identifies the following factors as evidence that a transaction was a device for the distribution of a corporation's earnings and profits: (1) Pro rata distribution among the shareholders of the distributing corporation and (2) subsequent sale or exchange of stock of the distributing or the controlled corporation. Our analysis of these factors is set forth below.

A distribution that is pro rata or substantially pro rata among shareholders of the distributing corporation is more likely to be used principally as a device and is evidence of device. Sec. 1.355–2(d)(2)(ii), Income Tax Regs. Petitioner does not dispute that the Clinpath stock was distributed pro rata to petitioner's shareholders. The parties stipulated that pursuant to the reorganization agreement, petitioner would and did distribute all the Clinpath stock to its shareholders in proportion to their stock ownership in petitioner. This factor is evidence of device.

A sale or exchange of the distributing or controlled corporation's stock after a distribution is also evidence of device. Sec. 1.355–2(d)(2)(iii)(A), Income Tax Regs. Generally, the greater the percentage of stock sold and the shorter the period of time between the distribution and the sale or exchange, the stronger the evidence of device. Id. On brief, petitioner concedes "100% of Clinpath's stock was sold to NHL, and the distribution and the subsequent sale of stock occurred on" October 30, 1993.

In addition, a sale or exchange negotiated or agreed upon before the distribution is substantial evidence of device. Sec. 1.355–2(d)(2)(iii)(B), Income Tax Regs. On brief, petitioner concedes that "there is no question that the sale of the Clinpath stock to NHL was prearranged prior to the spin-off transaction in which the clinical laboratory assets of Petitioner were transferred to Clinpath." Indeed, the sale of Clinpath stock to NHL was discussed, negotiated, and agreed upon by NHL and petitioner and was anticipated by both parties well before the distribution. Sec. 1.355–2(d)(2)(iii)(D), Income Tax Regs. This factor is substantial evidence of device.

We conclude, based on a review of the applicable factors, that the facts and circumstances of this case present substantial evidence of device within the meaning of section 355(a)(1)(B).

2.   *Nondevice Factors and Absence of Earnings and Profits*

In order to overcome the substantial evidence of device, petitioner argues that: (1) Although both petitioner and Clinpath had some accumulated earnings and profits during the periods in question, these amounts were not significant enough to warrant the conclusion that the spinoff of Clinpath was a device in contravention of section 355(a)(1)(B), and (2) several compelling corporate business purposes drove the entire transaction.

a. *Earnings and Profits*

Section 1.355–2(d)(5), Income Tax Regs., specifies three types of distributions that ordinarily do not present the potential for tax avoidance and will not be considered to have been used principally as a device for the distribution of earnings and profits even if there is other evidence of device. A distribution that takes place at a time when neither the distributing nor the controlled corporation has earnings or profits is one of the distributions described in section 1.355–2(d)(5), Income Tax Regs., and is the only type of distribution thus described that petitioner argues applies in this case.

A distribution ordinarily is considered not to have been used principally as a device if: (1) The distributing and controlled corporations have no accumulated earnings and profits at the beginning of their respective taxable years; (2) the distributing and controlled corporations have no current earnings and profits as of the date of the distribution; and (3) no distribution of property by the distributing corporation immediately before the separation would require recognition of gain resulting in current earnings and profits for the taxable year of the distribution. Sec. 1.355–2(d)(5)(ii), Income Tax Regs. Petitioner claims that the distribution at issue here satisfies these requirements.

In its opening brief, petitioner concedes, "that the balance sheet for * * * [petitioner] as of June 30, 1993, reflected current and accumulated earnings and profits of $252,928.64, for both the anatomic and clinical pathology portions of * * * [petitioner's] business." Petitioner argues, however, that:

> While petitioner concedes that it and Clinpath had some earnings and profits during the periods in question, these amounts were not meaningful and certainly do not provide a basis for a "bailout" of these earnings and profits amounts in order to avoid dividend treatment to Petitioner's shareholders.

Respondent disagrees, contending that the presence of any earnings and profits precludes petitioner from utilizing section 1.355–2(d)(5)(ii), Income Tax Regs., and that there is no credible evidence that petitioner lacked accumulated or current earnings and profits on the distribution date.

We agree with respondent for several reasons. First, petitioner reported it had over $230,000 of accumulated earnings and profits as of July 1, 1993, and petitioner did not introduce any evidence to prove that it had no current earnings and profits as of October 30, 1993. Section 1.355–2(d)(5)(ii)(A) and (B), Income Tax Regs., emphasizes that a distribution ordinarily will not be considered to have been used principally as a device if the distributing and controlled corporations have "no accumulated earnings and profits at the beginning of their respective taxable years" and "no current earnings and profits as of the date of the distribution". (Emphasis added.) Section 1.355–2(d)(5)(ii),

Income Tax Regs., does not provide a safe harbor for corporations with "insignificant" or "minimal" earnings and profits, as petitioner contends.

Second, petitioner ignores the fact that the spinoff enabled it to claim that the substantial gain on the distribution of Clinpath stock to its shareholders, which ordinarily would have increased its current and accumulated earnings and profits, need not be recognized for corporate income tax purposes or reflected in the calculation of its earnings and profits as of October 30, 1993 and at year end. * * *

Neither party disputes that, if the spinoff of Clinpath does not qualify as a tax-free transaction under sections 368 and 355, petitioner must realize and recognize substantial gain as of the date of distribution, Sec. 311(b)(1), which will substantially increase petitioner's earnings and profits, Sec. 312(b). Nevertheless, petitioner dismisses the prospect that it would have substantial current earnings and profits as a result of the spinoff and overlooks what respondent describes as "the conspicuous fact that the corporate profits petitioner's shareholders clearly intended to bail out were the anticipated profits of the prearranged sale." Despite petitioner's efforts to suggest otherwise, we simply are not convinced that the decision to structure this transaction as a spinoff and subsequent stock sale was prompted by NHL; NHL usually structured its acquisitions as asset sales to minimize its exposure to liabilities that can arise from the purchase of an active business. Petitioner's protestations notwithstanding, the spinoff of Clinpath followed immediately by a prearranged sale of the Clinpath stock on the same day appears to have been designed to eliminate the corporate-level tax that would have been due had petitioner sold its clinical business to NHL directly or distributed its clinical business to its shareholders prior to any sale.

For the reasons set forth above, petitioner has failed to prove that it did not have accumulated or current earnings and profits as of the date of the distribution within the meaning of section 1.355–2(d)(5)(ii), Income Tax Regs.

b.   *Corporate Business Purpose*

The presence of a valid corporate business purpose may trump a conclusion that the transaction was used principally as a device for the distribution of earnings and profits. Sec. 1.355–2(b)(4), (d)(3)(ii), Income Tax Regs. Section 1.355–2(b)(2), Income Tax Regs., defines "corporate business purpose" as a "real and substantial non-Federal tax purpose germane to the business of the distributing corporation, the controlled corporation, or the affiliated group * * * to which the distributing corporation belongs."

The stronger the evidence of device, such as the presence of the device factors specified in section 1.355–2(d)(2), Income Tax Regs., the stronger the corporate business purpose required to prevent the conclusion that the transaction was used principally as a device. Sec. 1.355–2(d)(3), Income Tax Regs. The assessment of the strength of the business purpose must be made based upon all the facts and circumstances, including, but not limited to: (1) The importance of achieving the purpose to the success of the business; (2) the extent to which the transaction is prompted by a person not having a proprietary interest in either corporation, or by other outside factors beyond the control of the distributing corporation; and (3) the immediacy of the conditions prompting the transaction. Sec. 1.355–2(d)(3)(i) and (ii), Income Tax Regs.

Petitioner identifies three purported corporate business purposes for the disputed distribution: (1) Increased competition caused by a changing economic environment that favored the larger, national laboratories; (2) Oklahoma State law restricting the ownership of petitioner to licensed physicians or physician-owned entities licensed to practice medicine within Oklahoma; and (3) NHL's requirement that each of petitioner's physician-shareholders sign binding and enforceable covenants not to compete in the clinical laboratory business. Respondent contends there was no valid corporate business purpose for the distribution. We consider each of the purported corporate business purposes below.

i. *Increased Competition*

The first purported corporate business purpose asserted by petitioner is that the changing economic environment in the clinical laboratory market in 1993 favored the large, national laboratories over the smaller clinical laboratories, such as petitioner's. * * * We do not question, and respondent does not dispute, that the economic factors cited by petitioner may have forced it out of the clinical business within a few years. Although these factors may have been the impetus behind the decision to sell the clinical business in the first instance, such factors do not demonstrate a corporate business purpose for petitioner's decision to distribute the Clinpath stock to its shareholders before selling the stock to NHL. A transfer of the clinical laboratory assets directly to Clinpath would have sufficed to achieve petitioner's desired result; i.e., to create a new company containing solely the assets of the clinical business in order to sell the clinical business with minimum liability to the buyer. Minimizing the effect of the economic factors cited by petitioner, however, did not require the nearly simultaneous distribution of Clinpath stock to its shareholders. The purpose of separating the clinical laboratory assets in preparation for the sale to NHL and shielding NHL from liability was achieved as soon as the clinical business was contributed to Clinpath by petitioner in exchange for Clinpath stock. See generally Sec. 1.355–2(b)(5), *Example (3)*, Income Tax Regs.

* * *

ii. *Petitioner's Status as a Professional Corporation*

The second purported corporate business purpose arises from petitioner's claim that Oklahoma State law mandated the final structure of the spinoff transaction. Petitioner essentially argues that it was constrained from selling, and NHL was prevented from purchasing, petitioner's stock because petitioner's status as a professional corporation prevented NHL from owning any interest in it. * * *

Even if petitioner were precluded from selling its stock to nonphysicians as petitioner contends, such a bar would justify only petitioner's decision to transfer its clinical business to a separate general business corporation, i.e., Clinpath; it would not lend support to petitioner's decision to distribute Clinpath stock to petitioner's shareholders. * * *

iii.   *Covenants Not To Compete*

The third purported corporate business purpose cited by petitioner is NHL's requirement that each of Clinpath's physician-shareholders sign a binding and enforceable covenant not to compete. * * * [P]etitioner contends that representatives for both petitioner and NHL believed that a covenant not to compete would be enforced under Oklahoma State law only if it were entered into in connection with the sale of goodwill or the dissolution of a partnership. Petitioner contends that the final structure of the transaction as a sale of Clinpath stock by Clinpath's shareholders, and not by petitioner, was mandated by NHL's desire to obtain from the shareholders valid and enforceable covenants not to compete. Therefore, a corporate business purpose existed for the distribution of Clinpath stock to the shareholders.

We do not agree. Even if we were to conclude that NHL's desire to obtain enforceable covenants not to compete qualified as a corporate business purpose of either petitioner or Clinpath, as section 1.355–2(b)(2), Income Tax Regs., requires, we would still reject petitioner's argument. Okla. Stat. Ann. tit. 15, Sec. 217 (West 1986 and Supp. 2000), provides that "Every contract by which any one is restrained from exercising a lawful profession, trade or business of any kind, otherwise than as provided by Sections 218 and 219 of this title, is to that extent void." Oklahoma State courts interpret Okla. Stat. Ann. tit. 15, Sec. 217, to prohibit only unreasonable restraints on the exercise of a lawful profession, trade, or business. * * * Even unreasonable contracts in restraint of trade, which are normally void and unenforceable under Oklahoma State law, are enforceable if they fall within one of the two statutorily created exceptions to the general rule—covenants given in connection with the sale of goodwill or covenants given in connection with the dissolution of a partnership. Okla. Stat. Ann. tit. 15, Secs. 218 and 219 (West 1986 and Supp. 2000) * * *. Assuming the covenants in this case were reasonable and/or were given in connection with the sale of goodwill, it was unnecessary to first distribute the Clinpath stock to petitioner's shareholders. Petitioner has failed to demonstrate either that the covenants in question were unreasonable or that they were not adequately tied to the sale of goodwill under Oklahoma State law.

We conclude, therefore, that NHL's demand for binding and enforceable covenants not to compete does not constitute a corporate business purpose within the meaning of section 1.355–2(d)(3)(ii), Income Tax Regs., and, therefore, is insufficient to overcome the substantial evidence of device in this case.

3. *Conclusion*

There is substantial evidence of device in this case, which is not overcome by substantial evidence of nondevice or by proof that petitioner and Clinpath lacked current or accumulated earnings and profits. We hold, therefore, that the distribution of Clinpath stock failed to satisfy the requirements of section 355(a)(1).

* * *

DETAILED ANALYSIS

1.   NON-PRO RATA DISTRIBUTIONS

Pro rata divisions represent a clear situation in which there is a bail-out potential in a divisive distribution. Thus, Treas.Reg. § 1.355–2(d)(2)(ii) treats the fact that a distribution is pro rata, or substantially pro rata, as evidence that the transaction is used as a device to effect a distribution of earnings and profits. At the other extreme, however, Treas.Reg. § 1.355–2(d)(5) provides that a non-pro rata distribution that qualifies as a redemption under § 302(a) ordinarily will not be considered to be a device. There is no "bail-out" potential in a transaction that would produce capital gains in any event. See also Rev.Rul. 71–383, 1971–2 C.B. 180 (a distribution that was substantially disproportionate under § 302(b)(2) did not constitute a "device" since under that section the taxpayer was entitled to capital gain treatment); Rev.Rul. 64–102, 1964–1 C.B. 136 (transfer to a previously existing subsidiary of assets representing more than 50% of the value of the subsidiary to equalize the value of the subsidiary stock with the value of the parent company stock owned by a minority stockholder, followed by a distribution of the subsidiary stock in exchange for the minority stockholder's parent stock, did not amount to a "device" since the transaction as to the minority stockholder would have entitled him to capital gain treatment under § 302(b)(3)). For the same reason, Treas.Reg. § 1.355–2(d)(5)(ii) provides that there is ordinarily no device present if neither the distributing nor controlled corporations have earnings and profits (including built-in gain property that would create earnings if distributed) that would cause taxable dividend treatment on a distribution to stockholders. In these situations, however, the "business purpose" and "continuity of interest" requirements of the Regulations still must be met.

2.   POST-DISTRIBUTION SALE OR EXCHANGE

Treas.Reg. § 1.355–2(d)(2)(iii)(A) provides that a sale or exchange of the stock of either the distributing or the spun-off corporation following a division is evidence that the transaction was used principally as a device for distribution of the earnings and profits of either or both of the corporations. The percentage of stock sold and the period of time before the stock sale affect the strength of this evidence of a "device." If the stock sale is negotiated or agreed upon before the § 355 division occurs, the evidence of a "device" is elevated by the Regulations to the level of "substantial evidence," while a sale or exchange arranged only after the division is merely "evidence" of a "device." Treas.Reg. § 1.355–2(d)(2)(iii)(B) and (C).

Treas.Reg. § 1.355–2(d)(2)(iii)(E) also provides that a post-distribution exchange of stock of either the distributing or the controlled corporation in a reorganization in which no more than an insubstantial amount of gain is recognized will not be treated as a subsequent sale or exchange constituting evidence of a "device." This portion of the Regulations adopts the holding of Commissioner v. Morris Trust, 367 F.2d 794 (4th Cir.1966). In *Morris Trust,* a state bank desired to merge into a national bank. The state bank, however, operated an insurance department, an operation that could not be continued by the national bank. To avoid a violation of the national banking laws, the state bank organized a new corporation to which it transferred the insurance business assets and then distributed the stock in the insurance corporation to its stockholders. Following the distribution, the state bank was merged into the national bank. The IRS argued in part that there was "an inherent incompatibility in substantially simultaneous divisive and amalgamating reorganizations." The court rejected the IRS's argument, holding that there was no "discontinuance of the [distributing corporation's] banking business" even though conducted in a different corporate form, and that the stockholders of the distributing corporation retained the requisite continuity of interest through their majority stock interest in the resulting national bank.[10] See also Rev.Rul. 70–434, 1970–2 C.B. 83, in which the stockholders of the distributing corporation, after receiving the stock of the spun-off corporation, then exchanged their stock in the distributing corporation in a (B) reorganization. Helvering v. Elkhorn Coal Company, 95 F.2d 732 (4th Cir.1937), indicates, however, that a (C) reorganization is not available following a spin-off because of the requirement that the acquired corporation transfer "substantially all" its assets in the (C) reorganization.

In Rev.Rul. 77–377, 1977–2 C.B. 111, an estate owned 80% of the stock of X Corporation. In a split-up transaction, X transferred its assets to new Y and Z Corporations, and then liquidated. Prior to the split-up, the estate had contemplated a § 303 redemption of a part of its X stock to pay estate taxes. The § 303 redemption could not be completed before the split-up. Therefore, after the split-up, new Y and Z Corporations redeemed part of the estate's stock in each under § 303. The ruling held that no "device" was involved since the dividend provisions of the Code had not been avoided. See Treas.Reg.

---

[10] Curtis v. United States, 336 F.2d 714 (6th Cir.1964), was to the contrary, holding that § 355 did not apply where following the distribution of the stock of the corporation holding the unwanted assets, the distributing corporation merged into another corporation. It construed § 355 to require the distributing corporation to stay in existence.

The IRS also argued in *Morris Trust* that the active business requirements of § 355(b)(1)(A) were not met since the state bank's business was not continued in unaltered corporate form. The court found no specific limitation in § 355 preventing continuation of the active conduct of the business of the distributing corporation in altered corporate form and concluded that permitting nonrecognition under § 355 did not violate the principles underlying the provision.

In Rev.Rul. 68–603, 1968–2 C.B. 148, the IRS announced that it would follow the *Morris Trust* decision to the extent that it held (1) the active trade or business requirement is met even though the distributing corporation merges following the distribution; (2) the control requirement of a (D) reorganization implies no limits on the reorganization of the distributing corporation after the spin-off; and (3) there is a business purpose for the spin-off and the merger.

§ 1.355–2(d)(5)(iii) (a transaction is generally not considered to be a device if the distribution would have been treated as a redemption under § 303).

Finally, the 1997 Act added § 355(e) and (f), which are colloquially referred to as "the anti-*Morris Trust* rules," even though they would not actually apply to the specific transaction in that case if it were to occur today. If pursuant to a plan or arrangement in connection with a corporate division there is a change of ownership of 50% or more of either the distributing corporation or the controlled corporation, under § 355(e) the distributing corporation generally must recognize gain as if the stock of the controlled corporation had been sold for fair market value on the date of distribution. The distributee shareholders, however, continue to receive nonrecognition treatment if § 355 otherwise applies. Acquisitions occurring within two years before or after the date of the distribution are presumed to have occurred pursuant to a plan or arrangement. Special rules under § 355(f) apply to divisive distributions of stock from one member of an affiliated group of corporations (as defined in § 1504(a)) to another member of the group followed by a sale outside the group. These provisions, which are discussed in greater detail in Section 5, are primarily designed to prevent selective disposition of corporate assets without recognizing gain under § 311 or § 336.

3.   NATURE AND USE OF ASSETS

Treas.Reg. § 1.355–2(d)(2)(iv)(A) provides that in determining whether a transaction is principally a device for the distribution of earnings and profits, consideration will be given to the "nature, kind, amount, and use" of the assets of both corporations immediately after the transaction. There are two aspects to this consideration.

A proposed amendment to the nature and use of assets device factor in Treas.Reg. § 1.355–2(d)(2)(iv) would focus on assets used in a business (as defined in Prop.Reg. § 1.355–2(d)(2)(iv)(B) (2016)) rather than only assets used in an active business meeting the five-year history requirement of § 355(b). The preamble to the Proposed Regulations states that the Treasury and IRS have concluded that the presence of business assets, whether or not held for five years, generally does not raise any more device concerns than the presence of assets used in a five-year active business. REG–134016–15, Guidance Under Section 355 Concerning Device and Active Trade or Business, 81 F.R. 46004 (July 15, 2016).

3.1. *Nonbusiness Assets*

The presence of assets not related to the trade or business of one of the corporations, such as cash and other liquid assets, is evidence of a device. Treas.Reg. § 1.355–2(d)(2)(iv)(B). The presence of unrelated assets is particularly damaging if the amount of unrelated assets transferred to or retained by one corporation is disproportionate to the relative value of the business assets in that corporation. See Treas.Reg. § 1.355–2(d)(4), Ex. (3). In Rev.Rul. 86–4, 1986–1 C.B. 174, the IRS held that the transfer of investment assets to the controlled corporation in a spin-off is a factor to be considered in determining whether the transaction is a device regardless of the percentage of the investment assets relative to the total amount of assets transferred to the controlled corporation. In 2016 Proposed Regulations, discussed in greater detail below, the Treasury and IRS concluded that device potential exists if either (1) distributing or controlled owns a large percentage of assets not used in business operations compared to total assets or (2) distributing's and controlled's percentages of these assets differs substantially. REG–134016–15, Guidance under Section 355 Concerning Device and Active Trade or Business, 81 F.R. 46004 (July 15, 2016).

In Rev.Rul. 73–44, 1973–1 C.B. 182, clarified by Rev.Rul. 76–54, 1976–1 C.B. 96, the distributing corporation conducted three businesses: (1) a manufacturing and distribution business that it had conducted for more than five years and that constituted over one-half the value of the corporation's total business assets; (2) a newspaper business, acquired in a taxable transaction within the preceding five years, which had been transferred to a newly created subsidiary in a nontaxable transaction; and (3) a separate manufacturing business conducted for more than five years. The distributing corporation transferred business (3) to the newspaper subsidiary and then distributed all the stock of the subsidiary to its shareholders. Business (3) represented a "substantial portion" of the value of the spun-off corporation, but less than one-half. The ruling held that a "device" was not present since the newspaper business acquired in the taxable transaction represented "operating businesses and not assets that would be used" as a device.

A contribution to the capital of the controlled corporation preceding a spin-off of the subsidiary's stock also may provide an opportunity for the distribution of earnings to stockholders. In Rev.Rul. 83–114, 1983–2 C.B. 66, the IRS held that a predistribution capital contribution to the controlled corporation was not per se a device. P was required by an antitrust decree to divest itself of its subsidiary S. In order to improve S's capital and expand S's business opportunities, P discharged S's indebtedness to it. The debt discharge increased S's net worth by more than 100%. P distributed S stock to P stockholders. The ruling concluded that there was no device since both the distribution of S stock and the discharge of S's indebtedness were undertaken for valid business reasons.

3.2. Related Business Activities

The second part of the inquiry into the nature of transferred assets concerns the relationship of the businesses of the two corporations. Although the Regulations recognize that § 355 can be employed to divide a single business or to effect a functional division of the business, there is evidence of a device if the businesses of the distributing and controlled corporations are functionally related in the sense that one of the businesses is a secondary business of the other, and the secondary business can be sold without adversely affecting the other. Treas.Reg. § 1.355–2(d)(2)(iv)(C). Example (10) of Treas.Reg. § 1.355–3(c), illustrates this concept. A corporation engaged in the manufacture of steel products spins off a subsidiary that owns a coal mine supplying the steel plant. Evidence of a device exists if the principal function of the coal mine is to satisfy the requirements of the steel business for coal and the stock of the coal mine could be sold without adversely affecting the steel business by depriving it of the supply of coal from the mine.

(b)   Carboniferous sells its coal to various customers and for the past few years has been selling approximately 25% of its output to Suphuric Electric Power. Carboniferous is expected to continue to operate in the same manner after the distribution.

3.   National Telephone & Telegraph Co. (NT&T), the stock of which is publicly traded, is engaged in three lines of business: (1) it provides cellphone service in portions of 46 states; (2) it provides land-line long distance telephone service nationwide; and (3) it manufactures personal computers. NT&T proposes to spin-off its personal computer business by forming a new subsidiary, Citrus Computer Corp., which will be distributed to NT&T's shareholders. Citrus Computer Corp. will start public trading on NASDAQ immediately after the spin-off. Will this transaction be a device?

4.   Worldwide Waste Management Corp. has approached the board of directors of Bay State By-Products Corp. with an offer to acquire Bay State, but Worldwide does not want to acquire Bay State's controlled subsidiary, Toxic Trucking, Inc. Worldwide and Bay State have devised the following plan. Bay State will distribute Toxic to its shareholders pro rata. Following the distribution, Bay State will be merged into Worldwide in a merger in which the Bay State shareholders will receive only Worldwide common stock (with cash for fractional shares). Is the transaction a "device?" Might it fail to qualify under § 355 for some other reason?

5.   Colonel King owns and operates a fast food restaurant and also owns all of the stock of a controlled subsidiary, Minnie D, which in turn owns and operates another fast food restaurant. The value of the business assets of Colonel King's and Minnie D's fast food restaurants are $100 and $105, respectively. Colonel King also has $195 cash, which it holds as a nonbusiness asset. Colonel King and Minnie D operate under franchise agreements, but the two franchisors are competitors. The franchisor of Minnie D has recently changed its franchise policy and will no longer renew its franchise because its stock is owned by a corporation operating through a competing franchise. Thus, Minnie D will lose its franchise if it remains a subsidiary of Colonel King. The franchise is about to expire.

Colonel King's restaurant building lease will expire in 24 months, and the business will be forced to relocate. Colonel King is weighing whether to purchase a building for the relocation. Evaluate the following alternatives.

(a)   Colonel King contributes $45 to Minnie D, which Minnie D will retain; Colonel King distributes the Minnie D stock pro rata among Colonel King's shareholders.

(b)   The facts are the same as above except that Colonel King contributes $95 cash to Minnie D.

(c)   The facts are the same as (a) except that the lease for Colonel King's location will expire in six months instead of 24 months, and Colonel King will use $80 of the $150 cash it retains to purchase a nearby building for the relocation of its own franchise.

D. THE "BUSINESS PURPOSE" REQUIREMENT

REGULATIONS: Sections 1.355–2(b) and (d)(3)(ii).

The role of "business purpose" in the § 355 framework is important and has several aspects. Under Treas.Reg. § 1.355–2(d)(3)(ii) the presence of a corporate business purpose for the transaction is evidence that a "device" is not present. The stronger the device factors, the stronger the evidence of business purpose necessary to overcome the presence of a device. In addition, Treas.Reg. § 1.355–2(b) independently requires a corporate business purpose for nonrecognition treatment in order to limit nonrecognition to "distributions that are incident to readjustments of corporate structures required by business exigencies and that effect only readjustments of continuing interests in property under modified corporate forms." This business purpose test is independent of the "device" language, so that even upon a finding of no "device," the transaction nonetheless may fail to qualify for want of a "business purpose." The Regulations are consistent with the decision in Commissioner v. Wilson, 353 F.2d 184 (9th Cir.1965), holding that § 355 was inapplicable where, although the transaction was not a "device" because there was no tax avoidance motive, no affirmative business purpose was demonstrated for the transaction, and that under the *Gregory* doctrine (excerpted in Chapter 10) "business purpose," is an essential ingredient of the law. *Rafferty* (see section 2 above), on the other hand, appears to deal with "business purpose" only as a factor under the "device" prohibition.

Revenue Ruling 2003–52

2003–1 C.B. 960.

ISSUE

Whether, in the situation described below, the distribution of the stock of a controlled corporation satisfies the business purpose requirement of § 1.355–2(b) of the Income Tax Regulations.

FACTS

Corporation X is a domestic corporation that has been engaged in the farming business for more than five years. The stock of X is owned 25 percent each by Father, age 68, Mother, age 67, Son, and Daughter. Although Father and Mother participate in some major management decisions, most of the management and all of the operational activities are performed by Son, Daughter, and several farmhands. The farm operation consists of breeding and raising livestock and growing grain.

Son and Daughter disagree over the appropriate future direction of X's farming business. Son wishes to expand the livestock business, but Daughter is opposed because this would require substantial borrowing by X. Daughter would prefer to sell the livestock business and concentrate on the grain business. Despite the disagreement, the two siblings have cooperated on the operation of the farm in its historical manner without disruption. Nevertheless, it has prevented each sibling from developing, as he or she sees fit, the business in which he or she is most interested.

Having transferred most of the responsibility for running the farm to the children, Father and Mother remain neutral on the disagreement between their children. However, because of the disagreement, Father and Mother would prefer to bequeath separate interests in the farm business to their children.

For reasons unrelated to X's farm business, Son and Daughter's husband dislike each other. Although this has not impaired the farm's operation to date, Father and Mother believe that requiring Son and Daughter to run a single business together is likely to cause family discord over the long run.

To enable Son and Daughter each to devote his or her undivided attention to, and apply a consistent business strategy to, the farming business in which he or she is most interested, to further the estate planning goals of Father and Mother, and to promote family harmony, X transfers the livestock business to newly formed, wholly owned domestic corporation Y and distributes 50 percent of the Y stock to Son in exchange for all of his stock in X. X distributes the remaining Y stock equally to Father and Mother in exchange for half of their X stock. Going forward, Daughter will manage and operate X and have no stock interest in Y, and Son will manage and operate Y and have no stock interest in X. Father and Mother will also amend their wills to provide that Son and Daughter will inherit stock only in Y and X, respectively. After the distribution, Father and Mother will still each own 25 percent of the outstanding stock of X and Y and will continue to participate in some major management decisions related to the business of each corporation.

Apart from the issue of whether the business purpose requirement of § 1.355–2(b) is satisfied, the distribution meets all of the requirements of §§ 368(a)(1)(D) and 355 of the Internal Revenue Code.

LAW

Section 355 provides that if certain requirements are met, a corporation may distribute stock and securities in a controlled corporation to its shareholders and security holders without causing the distributing corporation or the distributees to recognize gain or loss.

To qualify as a distribution described in § 355, a distribution must, in addition to satisfying the statutory requirements of § 355, satisfy certain requirements in the regulations, including the business purpose requirement. Section 1.355–2(b)(1) provides that a distribution must be motivated, in whole or substantial part, by one or more corporate business purposes. A corporate business purpose is a real and substantial non-Federal tax purpose germane to the business of the distributing corporation, the controlled corporation, or the affiliated group to which the distributing corporation belongs. Section 1.355–2(b)(2). A shareholder purpose (for example, the personal planning purposes of a shareholder) is not a corporate business purpose. *Id.* Depending upon the facts of a particular case, however, a shareholder purpose for a transaction may be so nearly coextensive with a corporate business purpose as to preclude any distinction between them. *Id.* In such a case, the transaction is carried out for one or more corporate business purposes. *Id.* A transaction motivated in substantial part by a corporate business purpose does not fail the business purpose requirement merely because it is motivated in part by non-Federal tax shareholder purposes. Preamble to the § 355 regulations, T.D. 8238, 1989–1 C.B. 92, 94.

In Example (2) of § 1.355–2(b)(5), Corporation X is engaged in two businesses: the manufacture and sale of furniture and the sale of jewelry. The businesses are of equal value. The outstanding stock of X is owned equally by unrelated individuals A and B. A is more interested in the furniture business, while B is more interested in the jewelry business. A and B decide to split up the businesses and go their separate ways. A and B expect that the operations of each business will be enhanced by the separation because each shareholder will be able to devote his undivided attention to the business in which he is more interested and more proficient. Accordingly, X transfers the jewelry business to new corporation Y and distributes the stock of Y to B in exchange for all of B's stock in X. The example concludes that the distribution is carried out for a corporate business purpose, notwithstanding that it is also carried out in part for shareholder purposes.

ANALYSIS

The disagreement of Son and Daughter over the farm's future direction has prevented each sibling from developing, as he or she sees fit, the business in which he or she is most interested. The distribution will eliminate this disagreement and allow each sibling to devote his or her undivided attention to, and apply a consistent business strategy to, the farming business in which he or she is most interested, with the expectation that each business will benefit. Therefore, although the distribution is intended, in part, to further the personal estate planning of Father and Mother and to promote family harmony, it is motivated in substantial part by a real and substantial non-Federal tax purpose that is germane to the business of X. Hence, the business purpose requirement of § 1.355–2(b) is satisfied.

HOLDING

In the situation described above, the distribution of the stock of a controlled corporation satisfies the business purpose requirement of § 1.355–2(b).

Revenue Ruling 2003–55

2003–1 C.B. 961.

ISSUE

Is the business purpose requirement of § 1.355–2(b) of the Income Tax Regulations satisfied if the distribution of the stock of a controlled corporation is, at the time of the distribution, motivated, in whole or substantial part, by a corporate business purpose, but that purpose cannot be achieved as the result of an unexpected change in circumstances following the distribution?

FACTS

D is a publicly traded corporation that conducts Business A and Business B directly and Business C through its wholly owned subsidiary C. Business C needs to raise a substantial amount of capital in the near future to invest in plant and equipment and to make acquisitions. D has been advised by its investment banker that the best way to raise this capital is through an initial public offering of C stock after C has been separated from D. The investment banker believes, based on its analysis of comparable situations, and taking into account the current market climate, that such an offering would be more efficient than a stock offering by C or D without first separating from the other because it would raise the needed capital with significantly less dilution of the existing shareholders' interests in the combined enterprises.

In reliance on the investment banker's opinion, D distributes the stock of C to its shareholders, and C prepares to offer its stock to the public as soon as practicable but with a target date approximately six months after the distribution. Following the distribution and before the offering can be undertaken, market conditions unexpectedly deteriorate to such an extent that, in the judgment of C and its advisors, the offering should be postponed. One year after the distribution, conditions have not improved sufficiently to permit the offering to go forward and C funds its capital needs through the sale of debentures.

Apart from the issue of whether the business purpose requirement of § 1.355–2(b) is satisfied, the distribution meets all of the requirements of § 355 of the Internal Revenue Code.

LAW

Section 355 provides that if certain requirements are met, a corporation may distribute stock and securities in a controlled corporation to its shareholders and security holders without causing the distributing corporation or the distributees to recognize gain or loss.

To qualify as a distribution described in § 355, a distribution must, in addition to satisfying the statutory requirements of § 355, satisfy certain requirements in the regulations, including the business purpose requirement. Section 1.355–2(b)(1) provides that a distribution must be motivated, in whole or substantial part, by one or more corporate business purposes. A corporate business purpose is a real and substantial non-Federal tax purpose germane to the business of the distributing corporation, the controlled corporation, or the affiliated group to which the distributing corporation belongs. Section 1.355–2(b)(2). The principal reason for the business purpose requirement is to provide nonrecognition treatment only to distributions that are incident to readjustments of corporate structures required by business exigencies and that effect only readjustments of continuing interests in property under modified corporate forms. Section 1.355–2(b)(1).

ANALYSIS

To satisfy the business purpose requirement of § 1.355–2(b)(1), a distribution of controlled corporation stock must be motivated, in whole or substantial part, by a corporate business purpose. A corporate business purpose is a real and substantial non-Federal tax purpose germane to the business of the distributing corporation, the controlled corporation, or the affiliated group to which the distributing corporation belongs. The regulations do not require that the corporation in fact succeed in meeting its corporate business purpose, as long as, at the time of the distribution, such a purpose exists and motivates, in whole or substantial part, the distribution. An unexpected change in market or business conditions following a distribution that prevents achievement of the business purpose will not prevent satisfaction of the business purpose requirement. Hence, notwithstanding the fact that, as a result of the unexpected deterioration in market conditions, C does not complete the stock offering that motivated its separation from D, the business purpose requirement of § 1.355–2(b)(1) is satisfied.

HOLDING

The business purpose requirement of § 1.355–2(b) is satisfied if the distribution of the stock of a controlled corporation is, at the time of the distribution, motivated, in whole or substantial part, by a corporate business purpose, but that purpose cannot be achieved as the result of an unexpected change in circumstances following the distribution.

DETAILED ANALYSIS

1. BUSINESS PURPOSE FOR THE DISTRIBUTION OF STOCK

Treas.Reg. § 1.355–2(b)(3) indicates that the "business purpose" must relate not only to the need for separate operations in corporate form of the two businesses, but that the corporate business purpose must extend also to the distribution of the stock to the stockholders. There might be business reasons for separate corporate operations, but these frequently can be satisfied by a parent-subsidiary operation. Thus, a distribution will not qualify for nonrecognition treatment under § 355 if the corporate business purpose can be achieved through a nontaxable separation of the businesses into two corporations without a distribution to stockholders. To illustrate, in Treas.Reg. § 1.355–2(b)(5), Ex. (3), X Corporation is engaged in the manufacture and sale of toys and candy. The stockholders of X wish to protect the candy business from the risks of the toy business. To achieve this business purpose, X transfers the assets of the toy business to a new corporation Y and distributes the Y stock to X stockholders. The Regulations conclude that since the purpose of protecting the candy business from the risks of the toy business is accomplished at the moment the separate businesses are divided into separate corporations, the distribution of Y stock to X's stockholders is not carried out for a corporate business purpose.

The requisite business purpose must be a nontax business purpose of one or both of the corporations involved in a division. Treas.Reg. § 1.355–2(b)(2). The Regulations expressly provide that a shareholder purpose such as personal planning is not a corporate business purpose. The Regulations recognize, however, that a stockholder purpose may be "so nearly coextensive" with the corporation's business purpose as to preclude any distinction between them. Compare the decision in *Rafferty,* which employed the business purpose test as one factor relevant to a determination of the "device" issue, with the taxpayer having the burden of proving that no device was involved. The court stated that if the only purpose for the distribution is a "stockholder" purpose, the bail-out potential of the transaction is to be closely scrutinized.

Rev.Rul. 75–337, 1975–2 C.B. 124, concluded that a stockholder's purpose could supply the requisite "business purpose" if the estate planning problem faced by the stockholder was immediate and was directly related to the ability of the corporation to carry on its business without interruption or loss. X Corporation held an automobile sales franchise and its subsidiary Y was in the automobile rental business. Fifty-three percent of the X Corporation stock was held by A and the remainder was held by A's five daughters. Three of the daughters were active in X's automobile sales business. To facilitate A's estate planning, Y Corporation stock was distributed pro-rata to the X Corporation stockholders. The spin-off was justified by the fact that the franchise policy of the automobile manufacturer required that the stockholders of a corporation owning a franchise be actively involved in the business. On A's death, the inactive stockholders would receive their inheritance in Y stock and assets, and no interest in X. The ruling distinguished *Rafferty* on the basis that the stockholder problem involved there had only a "remote and conjectural" impact on the business.

2. NONTAX BUSINESS PURPOSE

Treas.Reg. § 1.355–2(b)(2) stresses that the requisite business purpose must be a purpose unrelated to federal taxes and germane to the business of the corporations involved. A corporate separation to save state taxes satisfies the business purpose requirement only if there is no corresponding federal income tax savings that is greater than or substantially co-extensive with the state tax savings. Under this provision, a parent corporation cannot justify distribution of the stock of a subsidiary with a claim that the distribution is necessary to qualify for elective status under a state pass-through taxation provision similar to Subchapter S, if the distribution also would allow qualification for federal Subchapter S status. See Treas.Reg. § 1.355–2(b)(5), Ex. (7). See also Rev.Rul. 89–101, 1989–2 C.B. 67

(distribution to domestic parent corporation by foreign first tier subsidiary of all of the stock of second tier foreign subsidiary for purposes of reducing foreign taxes satisfied business purpose requirement); Rev.Rul. 76–187, 1976–1 C.B. 97 (valid business purpose to distribute stock of subsidiary to reduce state and local taxes on the capital value of the subsidiary).

3. EXAMPLES

The adequacy of business purpose for nonrecognition under § 355 is generally a question that depends upon the facts and circumstances of particular cases. Treas.Reg. § 1.355–2(b)(1) provides that the potential for tax avoidance is relevant in determining the extent to which the distribution is motivated by a bona fide corporate business purpose. There are numerous authorities identifying valid business purposes for a distribution under § 355. The following authorities illustrate the wide range of reasons for distributing the stock of a subsidiary that qualify as a business purpose.

In Pulliam v. Commissioner, T.C. Memo. 1997–274 (nonacq.), the court found a valid business purpose for a spin-off of a corporation holding one of two funeral homes originally operated directly by the distributing corporation where 49% of the stock of the spun-off corporation was sold to a valued employee, who operated the spun-off funeral home after the spin-off. The purpose for the distribution was that state law required funeral home corporations to be PSCs in which a majority interest was owned directly by licensed funeral directors, so the original corporation could not hold a majority interest in a subsidiary in which the employee licensed funeral director owned the other 49%. On a related point, Rev.Rul. 69–460, 1969–2 C.B. 51, found a valid business purpose for a pro rata spin-off of a subsidiary corporation effected to permit key employees to buy stock of the parent corporation at a price that they could afford. However, the ruling also concluded that if the key employees desired to buy into the subsidiary corporation, there was no business purpose for distribution of the subsidiary. The difference is that the spin-off reduced the value of the shares of the parent corporation, but did not substantially affect the value of the shares of the subsidiary.

Rev.Rul. 2003–110, 2003–2 C.B.1083, held that a spin-off to deal with "public perception problems" that arose from conducting two seemingly inconsistent businesses had a business purpose notwithstanding that the transaction was structured specifically to avoid recognition of § 311 gain. In the ruling, a publicly traded corporation that conducted a pesticide business spun-off its controlled subsidiary that conducted a baby food business because "public perception problems" caused potential baby food buyers to avoid dealing with the subsidiary as long as it was affiliated with a pesticide producer. Similarly, Lester v. Commissioner, 40 T.C. 947 (1963) (acq.), held that a business purpose for a pro rata spin-off existed where a corporation that was both warehouse distributor and jobber of auto parts separated the two businesses because the warehouse business sold to other jobbers who objected to doing business with a company that was a competitor insofar as its jobber business was concerned. Olson v. Commissioner, 48 T.C. 855 (1967) (acq.), held that management's desire to confine union difficulties to one corporation and to avoid to the extent possible a spread of union organizing attempts to other corporations, which management believed would be facilitated by separating ownership of the lines of business, was a valid business purpose for a spin-off.

Rev.Rul. 2003–74, 2003–2 C.B. 77, held that the separation of corporations to facilitate management focus was a valid business purpose. The distributing corporation was a publicly traded corporation that conducted a software technology business, and the controlled corporation conducted a paper products business. The managers of each corporation preferred to concentrate their efforts solely on the business conducted by that corporation, but, according to the stated facts, the ownership of the subsidiary prevented the parent corporation's management from concentrating solely on the software business.

A valid business purpose often is found in cases where the distribution facilitates raising and applying capital for the different businesses. Rev.Rul. 2004–23, 2004–1 C.B. 585, held that a spin-off by a *publicly held* corporation that was expected to cause the aggregate value of the stock of the two corporations to exceed their aggregate pre-distribution value satisfied the corporate business purpose requirement where the increased value was expected to serve a corporate business purpose of either or both corporations, e.g., to increase the amount that might be raised by a subsequent stock offering, even though the increased value benefitted the shareholders as well. Rev.Rul. 85–122, 1985–2 C.B. 118, found a valid business purpose for the separation of an unprofitable ski resort from profitable golf and tennis resort because a securities underwriter recommended that the separation would facilitate marketing debentures to raise additional capital for the golf and tennis resort. Rev.Rul. 2003–75, 2003–2 C.B. 79, found a business purpose for a distribution by a publicly held corporation of the stock of a subsidiary where the businesses of the parent (pharmaceuticals) and subsidiary (cosmetics) were competing for capital from borrowing and internal cash flows. The distribution resolved a capital allocation problem between the two corporations. See also Rev.Rul. 82–130, 1982–2 C.B. 83 (valid business purpose to distribute stock of real estate subsidiary with long-term indebtedness to facilitate financing by parent in high-technology business; underwriters stated that subsidiary's long-term debt would make it difficult for the parent to raise equity in a public offering and that significant commitment to subsidiary's real estate activities made the parent corporation less attractive to investors; also notes that a holding company with parent and subsidiary as subsidiaries would raise the same problems); Rev.Rul. 77–22, 1977–1 C.B. 91 (valid business purpose to distribute stock of subsidiary to enable each corporation to obtain separate borrowing limits from a bank, the aggregate borrowing limits of the two separate corporations being greater than that of the parent-subsidiary).

Where one line of business is subject to special governmental regulation but another line of business is not regulated, a spin-off to improve profitability by eliminating the regulator's authority with respect to one of the lines of business serves a valid business purpose. See Rev.Rul. 88–33, 1988–1 C.B. 115 (valid business purpose to distribute stock of subsidiary to allow parent to escape burdensome administrative compliance costs imposed on it because of subsidiary's business; subsidiary was subject to state regulatory scheme that also required burdensome registration and compliance by the parent; stock of the subsidiary spun-off pro rata to the parent's stockholders in order to free the parent of the registration requirement); Rev.Rul. 82–131, 1982–2 C.B. 83 (valid business purpose to distribute stock of unregulated subsidiary by regulated parent to justify parent's rate increase for its regulated business; regulatory agency included subsidiary's earnings in rate base to deny rate increase to parent).

Finally, a business purpose has been found for distributions that facilitate acquisitions that otherwise could not be easily completed or to comply with local law regarding stock ownership. Rev.Rul. 83–23, 1983–1 C.B. 82 (valid business purpose for spin-off to satisfy foreign decree requiring 60% direct ownership of local business by nationals); Rev.Rul. 76–527, 1976–2 C.B. 103 (valid business purpose to distribute stock of subsidiary to enable subsidiary to acquire an unrelated corporation, because the acquired corporation would not accept the subsidiary stock if it were controlled by the distributing corporation); Rev.Rul. 72–530, 1972–2 C.B. 212 (valid business purpose to distribute stock of subsidiary to facilitate a merger involving the parent corporation, because state law restrictions imposed serious disadvantages on handling transaction through creation of a new corporation).

PROBLEM SET 4

1.   Julio and Karina own 50% of Grouper Corp. Grouper Corp. is engaged in the frozen fish bait business and the operation of a sushi bar restaurant. Each business has been conducted for 6 years. Consider whether each of the following corporate divisions would meet the "business purpose" test of § 355.

(a)   Julio is more interested in operating a sushi bar, and Karina is more interested in operating a fish bait business. To this end, Grouper transfers the sushi bar business to a new wholly owned subsidiary, Sake Corp., and Grouper distributes all of the Sake stock to Julio in exchange for his Grouper stock.

(b)   Julio and Karina have decided that it would be prudent to separate the fish bait business from the risks of the sushi bar business. To this end, Grouper transfers the sushi bar business to a new wholly owned subsidiary, Sake Corp., and Grouper distributes all of the Sake stock pro rata to Julio and Karina.

2.   Carlo, a licensed civil engineer, owns 100% of the stock of Goethals Corporation, which conducts two related but separate businesses, a civil engineering consulting business and a construction business. Dalila is a brilliant and valued employee in the construction business. Dalila has received an offer from another company that includes an equity interest. To induce Dalila to stay, Carlo proposes to cause Goethals Corporation to drop the construction business into a newly formed subsidiary, Bricks & Mortar, Inc., which will be spun-off to Carlo, following which Dalila will receive a bonus from Bricks & Mortar in the form of stock that will total 25% of the then outstanding stock and an option to purchase enough additional shares

from Bricks & Mortar to give Dalila a 50% interest. The reason for the transaction is to provide Dalila an equity interest in the Bricks & Mortar division, in which she is employed, but not in the civil engineering business (Dalila is not a licensed civil engineer). Does this transaction satisfy the business purpose requirement? Does it matter whether or not applicable state law allows individuals who are not licensed as civil engineers to own stock in a corporation that performs civil engineering consulting services?

3.   (a)   Kenneth owns 100% of the stock of Barleycorn Corp., which is engaged in whiskey distilling and natural whole grain bread baking businesses. Each business has been conducted for over 20 years. Kenneth is 60 years old and as part of his estate planning wants to transfer his business to his children, Linda and Max. Linda wants to operate the bread baking business, and Max wants to operate the whiskey distilling business. To this end, Barleycorn Corp. plans to transfer the bread baking business to a new wholly owned subsidiary, Wheatberry Corp., all of the stock of which will be distributed to Kenneth. As soon as possible thereafter, Kenneth will transfer the Wheatberry stock to Linda and the Barleycorn stock to Max. Does this transaction meet the device and business purpose tests of § 355?

(b)   Suppose that after the distribution of Wheatberry to Kenneth but before he could transfer the stock of Wheatberry and Barleycorn and to Linda and Max, both Linda and Max unexpectedly died in an accident. As a result, Kenneth was left owning and operating both Wheatberry and Barleycorn. Is your answer affected?

SECTION 3.   DISTRIBUTION OF "CONTROL" AND CONTINUITY OF INTEREST REQUIREMENTS

INTERNAL REVENUE CODE: Section 355(a)(1)(A), and (D); 368(a)(2)(H)(ii).

REGULATIONS: Section 1.355–2(a), –2(c).

The nonrecognition principles of § 355 apply to the distribution of stock of a corporation that is "controlled" by the distributing corporation immediately before the distribution. Control is defined in § 368(c) as ownership of 80% of voting power and 80% of each other class of stock of a corporation. In addition, § 355(a)(1)(D) requires the distributing corporation to distribute all of the stock or securities of the controlled corporation held by it immediately before the distribution, or, with the permission of the IRS, at least a controlling amount of the stock of the controlled corporation. This distribution requirement results, at least initially, in continued ownership of the business of the controlled corporation by the shareholders of the distributing corporation. This rule is bolstered by a requirement in Treas.Reg. § 1.355–2(c) that the shareholders of the distributing corporation maintain a continuing interest in the business of both the distributing and controlled corporations. Section 368(a)(2)(H)(ii), however, provides that in determining whether a transfer of assets to a subsidiary prior to a distribution of stock qualifying under § 355 meets the requirements of § 368(a)(1)(D), the fact that the shareholders of the distributing corporation dispose of all or part of the stock of the distributed corporation, or whether the distributed corporation issues additional stock, shall not be taken into account.[12] Since a § 368(a)(1)(D) reorganization cannot occur without a subsequent distribution that qualifies under either § 354, which cannot occur in a divisive (D) reorganization, or § 355, the inference is that there is no requirement that the shareholders of the distributing corporation maintain any interest in the distributed corporation following the distribution.

The Supreme Court addressed the control requirement in Commissioner v. Gordon, 391 U.S. 83 (1968). The taxpayers were minority shareholders in the Pacific Telephone and Telegraph Company (Pacific). Ninety percent of the Pacific stock was owned by AT&T. In 1961, AT&T. decided to split Pacific into two separate corporations, Pacific and Pacific Northwest Bell. Pacific transferred all of the assets and liabilities related to its business in Oregon, Washington, and Idaho to Northwest Bell in exchange for all of the Northwest Bell stock and some debt instruments. Pacific retained assets related to its business in California. Also in 1961, Pacific distributed warrants entitling Pacific stockholders to purchase Pacific Northwest Bell stock representing 57% of the outstanding stock at a price substantially below the market price at which the stock traded on a public exchange. In 1963, Pacific distributed additional warrants to its stockholders entitling the Pacific stockholders to purchase the remaining 43% of Pacific Northwest Bell. The IRS argued that the transaction failed the requirements of § 355 because Pacific did not distribute enough stock of Pacific Northwestern Bell in 1961 to constitute control. The IRS thus asserted that the taxpayers realized ordinary income in an amount equal to the difference between the value of the Pacific Northwest Bell stock and the purchase price paid on exercise of the warrants. The Supreme Court agreed with the IRS, rejecting the taxpayers' argument that in combination the 1961 and 1963 distributions satisfied the requirements of § 355(a)(1)(D).[13]

* * * The Code requires that "the distribution" divest the controlling corporation of all of, or 80% control of, the controlled corporation. Clearly, if an initial transfer of less than a controlling interest in the controlled corporation is to be treated for tax purposes as a mere first step in the divestiture of control, it must at least be identifiable as such at the time it is made. Absent other specific directions from Congress, Code provisions

---

[12] The purpose of § 368(a)(2)(H)(ii) is to assure that assets transferred to a subsidiary prior the distribution of the stock of the subsidiary to the transferor corporation's shareholders retain a transferred basis under § 362 and do not take a fair market value basis. This result is reinforced by § 351(c), which has the same effect as § 368(a)(2)(H)(ii), regardless of whether the subsequent stock distribution qualifies under § 355 or is controlled by another section.

[13] The IRS also argued that the transaction failed under § 355 because the Pacific Northwestern Bell stock received by the taxpayers was not distributed to them by Pacific but was instead sold to the taxpayers for cash under the terms of the warrants. The Court declined to address this argument. One of the taxpayers sold some warrants for cash. The taxpayer was required to treat the sales proceeds as ordinary income.

must be interpreted so as to conform to the basic premise of annual tax accounting. It would be wholly inconsistent with this premise to hold that the essential character of a transaction, and its tax impact, should remain not only undeterminable but unfixed for an indefinite and unlimited period in the future, awaiting events that might or might not happen. This requirement that the character of a transaction be determinable does not mean that the entire divestiture must necessarily occur within a single tax year. It does, however, mean that if one transaction is to be characterized as a "first step" there must be a binding commitment to take the later steps.

The continuity of interest requirement of Treas.Reg. § 1.355–2(c) is closely related to the "device" provision in terms of preventing post-distribution sales. See Rev.Rul. 59–197, 1959–1 C.B. 77 (treating a pre-distribution sale of a minority interest in the stock of the distributing corporation as in effect a binding contract to sell stock in the newly-created corporation after the distribution, but the transaction did not constitute a "device" in view of the valid business purpose for the spin-off, i.e., to permit a key employee to obtain a proprietary interest in the spun-off business). Nonetheless, under the Regulations, continuity of interest is an independent requirement aimed at limiting nonrecognition in corporate separations to transactions in which shareholders of the original corporation maintain a continuing interest in each of the corporations surviving a division.

As noted above, 1998 amendments to § 368(a)(2)(H)(ii), indicate, however, that post-distribution sales of stock of the controlled corporation by shareholders of the distributing corporation, which may terminate the interest of the former shareholders in the controlled corporation, should not be taken into account in determining whether the requirements of § 355 are met. This provision may have eliminated shareholder continuity of interest, at least with respect to the business transferred to the controlled corporation.

The continuity of interest requirement of Treas.Reg. § 1.355–2(c) is satisfied in a divisive reorganization as long as one or more of the stockholders of the original corporation retain sufficient continuing interest in each of the divided corporations, but not necessarily in both. Thus, the Regulations indicate that the continuity of interest requirement is satisfied in the following example: A and B own all of the stock of X Corporation. X in turn owns the stock of S Corporation. C acquires 49% of A's stock in X. Immediately thereafter, and as part of a prearranged plan, X distributes its S stock to B in exchange for B's stock in X. There is sufficient continuity of interest for nonrecognition treatment under § 355 since the former stockholders of X have a continuing interest in one of the businesses formerly undertaken by X. A has a 51% continuing interest in X; B has 100% continuing interest in S. Treas.Reg. § 1.355–2(c)(2), Ex. (2).[14]

Treas.Reg. § 1.355–2(c)(2), Exs. (3) and (4), further indicate that if C purchased all of A's X stock, or purchased 80% of A's X stock, before the division, continuity would not exist because the original stockholders of X would have an insufficient continuing interest in one of the two corporations following division. This result is, however, also indirectly precluded by § 355(d), which was enacted after the examples in Treas.Reg. § 1.355–2(c)(2) were promulgated. Section 355(d) would require recognition of gain by the distributing corporation, X, on the distribution of S stock to B, because C acquired by purchase within the five-year period ending on the date of distribution stock representing a 50% interest in the distributing corporation immediately after the distribution. Section 355(d) thus indirectly creates a limited continuity of interest requirement with respect to corporate nonrecognition in certain circumstances.

DETAILED ANALYSIS

1. THE DISTRIBUTION REQUIREMENT

1.1. *General*

In Redding v. Commissioner, 630 F.2d 1169 (7th Cir.1980), rev'g. 71 T.C. 597 (1979), the court was presented with a transaction similar to that before the Supreme Court in *Gordon.* In *Redding,* the parent corporation distributed transferable rights to its stockholders that enabled the stockholders to subscribe to shares of stock of the parent corporation's wholly owned subsidiary. The rights could be exercised only for a two-week period. A stockholder could receive one share of the subsidiary's stock for two rights plus $5. During the two-week period the fair market value of the subsidiary's stock ranged from $5.70 per share to $7 per share. An over-the-counter market for the warrants developed during this subscription period. After the two-week period, the warrants became worthless. The IRS and the taxpayers stipulated that, as the result of the exercise of the stock rights, more than 80% of the subsidiary's stock was distributed in the offering. The parties stipulated further that there was a good business purpose for the distribution of the subsidiary stock, the distribution was not a device for the distribution of earnings and profits, and the 20% of the subsidiary's stock retained by the parent corporation was not held for tax avoidance purposes under § 355(a)(1)(D)(ii).

The IRS asserted that the rights distribution constituted a taxable dividend under § 301, relying on Rev.Rul. 70–521, 1970–2 C.B. 72, to that effect. The taxpayers, on the other hand, asserted that the transaction was an integrated transaction and qualified under § 355. The Tax Court held that the requirements of § 355(a)(1)(A) and (D) were met. The issuance of the

---

[14]   The example in the Regulations provides that B acquires 50% of A's stock. In that case, however, § 355(d)(3) would require recognition of gain by the distributing corporation, X, on distribution of stock to B.

rights by the distributing corporation "was merely a procedural device to give [the distributing corporation] stockholders the opportunity to be included or excluded from the [subsidiary] stock distribution." Having found that the distribution of the stock rights was "merely a brief transitory phase of the corporate separation," the Tax Court concluded that the requirements of § 355(a)(1)(A) and (D) were met. The requisite 80% of the subsidiary stock was in fact distributed and after the transaction the stockholders held only stock of the subsidiary.

The Court of Appeals disagreed with the Tax Court's finding that the issuance of the warrants was only a procedural step and concluded that the warrants had independent economic significance in light of their readily ascertainable market value and transferability on an open market. The issuance of the warrants could not, therefore, be disregarded as a mere transitory step in the distribution of the stock of the subsidiary to stockholders of the distributing corporation. The Court of Appeals concluded further that the distribution of the stock of the subsidiary failed the requirement of § 355(a)(1)(A) that the stock of the controlled corporation be distributed with respect to the stock of the distributing corporation. Since the warrants had independent significance, the distribution of the subsidiary's stock was made with respect to the warrants rather than the stock of the distributing corporation. The court held that the distribution of warrants was a dividend to the stockholders. (Receipt of the warrants was not sheltered from dividend treatment under § 305 because the warrants did not represent rights to acquire the stock of the distributing corporation.)

Although it felt bound by the parties' stipulation that 80% control of the subsidiary was distributed to the stockholders of the distributing corporation, the Court of Appeals in *Redding* questioned whether the control requirement of § 355(a)(1)(D) was in fact satisfied. For valid business reasons, the distributing corporation retained 1 share less than 20% of the subsidiary's stock. Fifty thousand shares of the subsidiary's stock were distributed to underwriters. The remaining shares distributed with respect to exercised warrants represented approximately 76% of the subsidiary's stock. The Court of Appeals read § 355(a)(1)(D) in conjunction with § 355(a)(1)(A) to require the distribution of control to persons who were the stockholders of the distributing corporation before the division. That requirement was not satisfied in *Redding* because of the distribution of stock to the underwriters.

The IRS has indicated that it will use the step transaction doctrine to find a qualifying distribution in a § 355 transaction in appropriate cases. In Rev.Rul. 83–142, 1983–2 C.B. 68, a foreign subsidiary of a U.S. parent corporation distributed assets to a new subsidiary, the controlled corporation, in exchange for stock. To satisfy a requirement of the foreign country in which it was incorporated, the subsidiary sold the stock of the controlled corporation to its parent for cash. The subsidiary thereupon redistributed the cash to its parent as a dividend. The IRS held that the transfer of stock of the controlled corporation to the parent was a § 355 distribution by the subsidiary. The subsidiary's sale of stock and subsequent return of cash as a dividend were disregarded for Federal tax purposes as transitory steps taken for the purpose of complying with local law.

1.2. *Retention of Stock or Securities*

Section 355(a)(1)(D) permits the distributing corporation to retain some of the stock of the distributed corporation if it is established that the retention of the stock was not motivated by tax avoidance purposes. Treas.Reg. § 1.355–2(e)(2) warns, however, that ordinarily the corporate business purpose for a divisive reorganization will require the distribution of all the stock and securities of the controlled corporation. The IRS, in addition to examining whether there is a good business purpose for retention of any stock or securities, also looks to whether the retained stock gives the distributing corporation "practical control" over the spun-off corporation. See Rev.Rul. 75–321, 1975–2 C.B. 123 (pursuant to federal banking laws, distributing corporation was required to divest itself of at least 95% of the stock of a bank subsidiary; retention of a percent of the bank stock to use as collateral for short-term financing for the distributing corporation's remaining business enterprises was for a valid business purpose and the retained interest did not give the distributing corporation practical control).

2.   CONTROL AND CONTINUITY OF INTEREST

Treas.Reg. § 1.355–2(c) requires as an independent qualification for nonrecognition under § 355 "that one or more persons who, directly or indirectly, were the owners of the enterprise prior to the distribution or exchange own, in the aggregate, an amount of stock establishing a continuity of interest in each of the modified corporate forms in which the enterprise is conducted after the separation." Two statutory provisions impact application of the continuity of interest rules.

First, § 368(a)(2)(H)(ii), enacted in 1998, provides that in determining whether a transfer of assets to a subsidiary prior to a distribution of stock qualifying under § 355 meets the requirements of § 368(a)(1)(D), the fact that the shareholders of the distributing corporation dispose of all or part of the stock of either the controlled corporation or the distributing corporation, or whether the controlled corporation issues additional stock, shall not be taken into account. This implies that a post-distribution sale or exchange of the stock of either corporation will not defeat either the control requirement or the continuity of interest requirement for purposes of shielding the shareholders from recognition of gain under § 355(a).[15] Since a § 368(a)(1)(D) reorganization cannot occur without a subsequent distribution that qualifies under either § 354, which cannot occur in a divisive (D) reorganization, or § 355, the inference is that there is no requirement that the shareholders of the distributing corporation maintain any interest in the distributed corporation following the distribution.

The enactment of § 355(d), (e) and (f) after promulgation of Treas.Reg. § 1.355–2(c) adds an additional complication. Sections 355(d), (e), and (f), discussed in greater detail below, require recognition of gain by the

---

[15] This result is reinforced by § 351(c), which has the same effect as § 368(a)(2)(H)(ii), regardless of whether the subsequent stock distribution qualifies under § 355 or is controlled by another section.

distributing corporation in the case of pre- and post-distribution acquisitions of a 50% or greater interest in one of the corporations. Although these provisions do not directly affect recognition of gain or loss by the shareholders under § 355(a), the imposition of a recognition requirement on the distributing corporation in the case of a 50% ownership change by historic shareholders is in effect a statutory continuity of interest requirement for completely tax-free divisive restructuring.

The legislative history accompanying § 355(e) states as follows:

> The House bill does not change the present law requirement under section 355 that the distributing corporation must distribute 80 percent of the voting power and 80 percent of each other class of stock of the controlled corporation. It is expected that this requirement will be applied by the Internal Revenue Service taking account of the provisions of the proposal regarding plans that permit certain types of planned restructuring of the distributing corporation following the distribution, and to treat similar restructurings of the controlled corporation in a similar manner. Thus, the 80-percent control requirement is expected to be administered in a manner that would prevent the tax-free spin-off of a less-than-80-percent controlled subsidiary, but would not generally impose additional restrictions on post-distribution restructurings of the controlled corporation if such restrictions would not apply to the distributing corporation.

H.R.Rep. No. 105–220, at 529–30 (1997). In Rev.Rul. 98–27, 1998–1 C.B. 1159, the IRS interpreted this language as follows:

> [T]he Service will not apply *Court Holding* [324 U.S. 331 (1945)] (or any formulation of the step transaction doctrine) to determine whether the distributed corporation was a controlled corporation immediately before the distribution under § 355(a) solely because of any post distribution acquisition or restructuring of the distributed corporation, whether prearranged or not. In otherwise applying the step transaction doctrine, the Service will continue to consider all facts and circumstances. See, e.g., Rev.Rul. 63–260, 1963–2 C.B. 147. An independent shareholder vote is only one relevant factor to be considered.

It is unclear whether this statement means that the IRS believes that there no longer is any post-distribution continuity of interest requirement, apart from the "device" and business purpose tests, that must be satisfied in order to qualify for § 355 treatment. But at first blush, it appears to be difficult to understand how the enactment of § 355(e), which affects only the treatment of the distributing corporation under § 355(a) and (c), could be interpreted to eliminate a requirement for qualifying the shareholders for nonrecognition under § 355(a).

The legislative history of the 1998 amendments to § 351(c)(2) and § 368(a)(2)(H)(ii), which are related to the enactment of § 355(e) the prior year, also, however, implies that there no longer should be any shareholder continuity of interest requirement imposed with respect to § 355 transactions. S.Rep. No. 105–174, 105th Cong., 2d Sess. (1998) describes the 1998 amendments as follows:

> [I]n the case of certain divisive transactions in which a corporation contributes assets to a controlled corporation and then distributes the stock of the controlled corporation in a transaction that meets the requirements of section 355 (or so much of section 356 as relates to section 355), solely for purposes of determining the tax treatment of the transfers of property to the controlled corporation by the distributing corporation, the fact that the shareholders of the distributing corporation dispose of part or all of the distributed stock shall not be taken into account for purposes of the control immediately after requirement of section 351(a) or 368(a)(1)(D). For purposes of determining the tax treatment of transfers of property to the controlled corporation by parties other than the distributing corporation, the disposition of part or all of the distributed stock continues to be taken into account, as under prior law, in determining whether the control immediately after requirement is satisfied.

> *Example 1*: Distributing corporation D transfers appreciated business X to subsidiary C in exchange for 100 percent of C stock. D distributes its stock of C to D shareholders. As part of a plan or series of related transactions, C merges into unrelated acquiring corporation A, and the C shareholders receive 25 percent of the vote or value of A stock. If the requirements of section 355 are met with respect to the distribution, then the control immediately after requirement will be satisfied solely for purposes of determining the tax treatment of the transfers of property by D to C. Accordingly, the business X assets transferred to C and held by A after the merger will have a carryover basis from D. Section 355(e) will require D to recognize gain as if the C stock had been sold at fair market value.

> *Example 2*: Distributing corporation D transfers appreciated business X to subsidiary C in exchange for 85 percent of C stock. Unrelated persons transfer appreciated assets to C in exchange for the remaining 15 percent of C stock. D distributes all its stock of C to D shareholders. As part of a plan or series of related transactions, C merges into acquiring corporation A; and the interests attributable to the D shareholders' receipt of C stock with respect to their D stock in the distribution represent 25 percent of the vote and value of A stock. If the requirements of section 355 are met with respect to the distribution, then the control immediately after requirement will be satisfied solely for purposes of determining the tax treatment of the transfers of property by D to C. Section 355(e) will require recognition of gain as if the C stock had been sold for fair market value. The business X assets transferred to C and held by A after the merger will have a carryover basis from D. The persons other than D who transferred assets to C for 15 percent of C stock will recognize gain on the

appreciation in their assets transferred to C if the control immediately after requirement is not satisfied after taking into account any post spin-off dispositions that would have been taken into account under prior law.

Example 3: The facts are the same as in example 2, except that the interests attributable to the D shareholders' receipt of C stock with respect to their D stock in the distribution represent 55 percent of the vote and value of A stock in the merger. If the requirements of section 355 are met with respect to the distribution, then the control immediately after requirement will be satisfied solely for purposes of determining the tax treatment of the transfers by D to C. The business X assets in C (and in A after the merger) will therefore have a carryover basis from D. Because the D shareholders retain more than 50 percent of the stock of A, section 355(e) will not apply. The persons other than D who transferred property for the 15 percent of C stock will recognize gain on the appreciation in their assets transferred to C if the control immediately after requirement is not satisfied after taking into account any post-spin-off dispositions that would have been taken into account under prior law.

Although the introductory paragraph of the legislative history quoted above refers only to the impact of the amendments with respect to the treatment of the transfer of assets to the controlled subsidiary, the examples presume that a post-distribution disposition of the stock received in the spin-off does not necessarily destroy the § 355 treatment of the distribution by the shareholders even though the shareholders who received the distribution do not indirectly retain a majority interest in the distributed corporation. If this is so, the continuity of interest requirement in Treas.Reg. § 1.355–2(c) has been *sub silentio* repealed with respect to the controlled corporation.

To treat Treas.Reg. § 1.368–2(c) as having been effectively repealed by events subsequent to its promulgation is also consistent with the 1998 revisions to the continuity of interest requirement in Treas.Reg. § 1.368–1(e)(1) applicable to acquisitive reorganizations, discussed in Chapter 10. Treas.Reg. § 1.368–1(e)(1) provides that "a mere disposition of stock of the target corporation prior to a potential reorganization . . . and a mere disposition of stock of the issuing corporation received in a potential reorganization . . . is disregarded" (although the disposition cannot be to a person related to the acquirer or the issuer). If "continuity of interest" has the same meaning under Treas.Reg. § 1.368–2(c) as it does under Treas.Reg. § 1.368–1(e)(1), neither a pre-distribution nor a post-distribution sale or exchange of the stock of either the distributing corporation or the controlled corporation should affect the application of § 355(a) to the shareholders if all of the other conditions of § 355 have been met. Nevertheless, such transactions could result in recognition to the distributing corporation under § 355(d) or (e).

There are no authorities directly applying the Treas.Reg. § 1.355–2(c) continuity of interest provision since its promulgation. Some rulings issued before the current Regulations were promulgated illustrate the historic application of the continuity of interest requirement under § 355. These authorities have current relevance only if the Treas.Reg. § 1.355–2(c) continuity of interest requirement has survived the enactment of § 355(e) and § 368(a)(2)(H)(ii) and the 1998 revisions to the continuity of interest requirement in Treas.Reg. § 1.368–1(e)(1) applicable to acquisitive reorganizations.

A number of authorities pre-dating the 1997 and 1998 statutory revisions addressed continuity of interest in the context of post-distribution dispositions of stock of the distributing or controlled corporations. Commissioner v. Morris Trust, 367 F.2d 794 (4th Cir.1966), discussed above, held that a post-distribution tax-free reorganization of the distributing corporation in which its shareholders received a majority of the stock of the surviving corporation did not invalidate a § 355 transaction. On the other hand, in Rev.Rul. 79–273, 1979–2 C.B. 125, continuity of interest was found lacking where P Corporation distributed the stock of its subsidiary to P stockholders as part of a reverse cash merger in which P was acquired by an unrelated corporation. Since the former P stockholders had no continuing interest in P, the distribution of S stock to the P stockholders did not qualify for nonrecognition treatment under § 355.

A result similar to that in Rev.Rul. 79–273 was reached on different reasoning in Rev.Rul. 70–225, 1970–1 C.B. 80, obsoleted by Rev.Rul. 98–44, 1998–2 C.B. 315. In Rev.Rul. 70–225, the IRS held that an attempted post-distribution (B) reorganization involving the stock of the controlled subsidiary defeated nonrecognition treatment because of the control requirement of § 368(a)(1)(D). T Corporation desired to acquire one of two businesses of R Corporation. Pursuant to a prearranged plan, R Corporation transferred the assets of the desired business to a newly created subsidiary and then distributed the stock of the subsidiary to its sole stockholder. The stockholder then immediately exchanged the stock of the subsidiary for stock of T Corporation in an attempted (B) reorganization. The spin-off failed because the stockholder did not acquire control of the distributed corporation. The transaction was treated in effect as a transfer by R Corporation of part of its assets in exchange for stock of T Corporation, followed by a distribution of the T Corporation stock as a dividend to the sole stockholder of R Corporation. The result in Rev.Rul. 70–225 appears to have been reversed by the 1998 amendment to § 368(a)(2)(H)(ii), which led the IRS to declare Rev.Rul. 70–225 obsolete. Rev.Rul. 98–44, 1998–2 C.B. 315.

3. COMPARISON WITH PARTIAL LIQUIDATIONS

Apart from the principal focus of § 355 as preventing a corporate bail-out of earnings and profits, § 355 is significant with respect to the question of recognition of corporate level gain on appreciated assets when there is a change of ownership. A comparison of the tax treatment of the spin-off or split-off of a trade or business under § 355 with the tax consequence of the distribution of a trade or business to stockholders in a partial liquidation under § 302(b)(4), discussed in Chapter 5, is illustrative. Both transactions involve the distribution of a trade or business with a five-year history. If appreciated property is distributed to stockholders in a partial liquidation, gain is recognized at both the corporate and stockholder levels. Under § 355, if, however, the distributed trade or business is housed in a corporation, no gain or loss is recognized at either level. This different treatment is justified in a § 355 transaction by the stockholders' continued interest in business assets that remain in corporate solution. The double tax regime is protected because gain or loss will ultimately be recognized at the stockholder and corporate levels on disposition of the stock and assets, respectively. A distribution in partial liquidation removes the business assets from corporate solution, thus eliminating the opportunity for future taxation of corporate level appreciation. See Simon and Simmons, The Future of Section 355, 40 Tax Notes 291, 296–7 (1988).

PROBLEM SET 5

1.   Y Corporation, which is publicly traded, owned all of the stock of X Corporation. To increase stock values, Y Corporation plans to spin-off X Corporation, which would also become publicly traded. Simultaneously, Y desires to raise some additional cash. To this end, Y Corporation proposes to distribute 80% of the stock of X Corporation to the Y Corporation shareholders pro rata, and simultaneously to distribute pro rata to its shareholders options to purchase the remaining 20% of the stock of X Corporation at fair market value. Will the distribution qualify under § 355?

2.   Cayo Hueso Corp. has approached the board of directors of Margaritaville Corp. with an offer to acquire Margaritaville, except it does not want to acquire Margaritaville's controlled subsidiary, Conch Corp. Cayo Hueso and Margaritaville have devised the following plan. Margaritaville will distribute Conch to its shareholders pro rata. (Assume that this distribution could have qualified under § 355 if nothing further transpired.) Following the distribution, Margaritaville will be merged into a subsidiary of Cayo Hueso in a forward triangular merger in which the Margaritaville shareholders will receive Cayo Hueso common stock. Does the subsequent merger affect the validity of treating the distribution as a § 355 transaction? Does your answer depend on whether or not after the post-distribution merger the former Margaritaville Corp. shareholders own at least 50% of the outstanding Cayo Hueso Corp. stock?

3.   Cayo Hueso Corp. has approached the board of directors of Margaritaville Corp. with an offer to acquire Margaritaville's controlled subsidiary, Conch Corp. Cayo Hueso and Margaritaville have devised the following plan. Margaritaville will distribute Conch to its shareholders pro rata. (Assume that this distribution could have qualified under § 355 if nothing further transpired.) Following the distribution, Conch will be merged into a subsidiary of Cayo Hueso in a forward triangular merger in which the Conch shareholders will receive Cayo Hueso common stock. Does the subsequent merger affect the validity of treating the distribution as a § 355 transaction? Does your answer depend on whether or not after the post-distribution merger the former Conch Corp. shareholders own at least 50% of the outstanding Cayo Hueso Corp. stock?

SECTION 4.   CONSEQUENCES TO PARTIES TO A CORPORATE DIVISION

INTERNAL REVENUE CODE: Sections 355(a)(1), (2), (c); 361(c); 368(a)(1)(D), (2)(A), (2)(H)(ii); 354(b); 356(a) and (b); 358(a)–(c); 312(h).

REGULATIONS: Sections 1.356–1, –2; 1.358–1(a), –2(a), (c), Ex. 13.

As noted previously, if the conditions of § 355 have been met, § 355(a) provides nonrecognition to the shareholders upon receipt of the stock of the controlled corporation. Pursuant to § 358, the shareholders take a transferred basis in the stock of the distributed corporation. If the shareholder continues to hold stock of the distributing corporation, as well as holding stock of the controlled corporation after the distribution, the shareholder's basis in the stock of the distributing corporation immediately prior to the distribution (as adjusted for gain recognition and the receipt of boot) is apportioned between the basis of the stock in the distributing and controlled corporation held immediately after the distribution in proportion to fair market value.

Subject to a number of special exceptions, the distributing corporation also is entitled to nonrecognition of gain on the distribution of the stock of the controlled subsidiary, § 311(b) (and § 336) being displaced by one of two operative nonrecognition provisions. Section 355(c) provides nonrecognition to the distributing corporation with respect to the stock of the controlled corporation if the controlled corporation that is distributed is a pre-existing subsidiary to which assets were not transferred in a § 368(a)(1)(D) reorganization prior to the distribution. If the distribution is preceded by a transfer of assets from the distributing corporation to the controlled corporation in a § 368(a)(1)(D) reorganization, then § 361(c) generally provides nonrecognition for the distributing corporation. If, however, prior to a distribution otherwise qualifying under § 355, the distributing corporation transfers property to the controlled corporation and the controlled corporation assumes liabilities of the distributing corporation in excess of the basis of the transferred assets, § 357(c) applies to require recognition of gain to the distributing corporation on the asset transfer, even though the transfer might be classified as a § 368(a)(1)(D) reorganization rather than as a § 351 transfer.[16]

---

[16]   Note that § 357(c) does not apply to an asset transfer accompanied by an assumption of liabilities in excess of basis in a § 368(a)(1)(D) reorganization that qualifies by virtue of a distribution by the transferor corporation of transferee corporation stock that meets the requirements of § 354.

DETAILED ANALYSIS

1.   BOOT IN A SECTION 355 TRANSACTION

1.1. *Distributions of Cash or Other Property*

The shareholder nonrecognition rule of § 355(a) is limited to the distribution of stock or securities of the controlled corporation, or to the exchange of stock or securities solely for stock or securities of the controlled corporation. Section 356 allows for the receipt of cash or other property (including the receipt of securities in excess of the securities transferred) with the recognition of gain to the extent of the boot. The form of the division will, however, affect the tax treatment of the boot. In the case of a non-pro rata split-off, which involves an exchange by the shareholder of the distributing corporation's shares for the controlled corporation's shares, § 356(a)(2) provides for ordinary income treatment of recognized gain to the extent of the distributee's pro rata share of earnings and profits if the distribution is essentially equivalent to a dividend. Rev.Rul. 93–62, 1993–2 C.B. 118, requires that the distribution of boot be tested for dividend equivalency under § 302 as if the boot were distributed prior to the divisive transaction in redemption of an amount of stock of the distributing corporation equal to the value of the boot. If, however, the distribution does not involve an exchange, as would be the case in a pro rata spin-off, § 356(b) provides that any boot will be treated as a distribution under § 301. Thus, in the case of a spin-off, since there has been no exchange, the amount of the dividend is not limited to gain realized on the exchange of stock of the distributing corporation for stock of the controlled corporation.

1.2. *Stock of the Controlled Corporation as Boot*

Section 355(a)(3)(B), known as the "hot stock" rule, provides that stock of the controlled corporation that has been acquired by the distributing corporation in a taxable transaction within the five-year period preceding distribution to stockholders will be treated as other property taxable to the stockholders as boot. As amended in 2011, Treas.Reg. § 1.355–2(g), conforms § 355(a)(3)(B) to the 2005 amendments of § 355(b)(3) that treat a "separate affiliated group" (SAG) as a single corporation for purposes of determining whether the active trade or business requirements of § 355 have been met. The Regulations provide that the general hot stock rule applies to the acquisition of stock of the controlled corporation by a member of the separate affiliated group of the distributing corporation (DSAG). If, however, the controlled corporation becomes a DSAG member at any time after the acquisition (but prior to the distribution of controlled), then the Regulations provide for an exception. (Because DSAG membership relies on § 1504 affiliation tests while § 355 relies on § 368(c) control, it is possible to have a controlled corporation that is not a DSAG member.) Taxable transfers of controlled corporation stock owned by DSAG members immediately before and immediately after the transfer are disregarded and are not treated as acquisitions for purposes of the hot stock rule. The Regulations also provide that the hot stock rule does not apply to acquisitions of controlled corporation stock by the distributing corporation from a member of the affiliated group (as defined in Treas.Reg. § 1.355–3(b)(4)(iii)) of which the distributing corporation was a member.

Trust of E.L. Dunn v. Commissioner, 86 T.C. 745 (1986) (acq. in result), narrowly interpreted the meaning of "acquired" in a taxable transaction. In a taxable reverse triangular merger consummated on May 12, 1982, AT&T acquired all of the stock of Pacific Telephone and Telegraph with the exception of nonvoting preferred stock held by institutional investors. Following this transaction, AT&T owned the only share of Pacific common stock outstanding. The reverse triangular merger was a taxable transaction because, by virtue of the outstanding nonvoting preferred stock, AT&T did not meet the control requirement of § 368(c). On August 24, 1982, a long standing antitrust action between AT&T and the U.S. government was settled with a judicially approved agreement that AT&T would divest itself of each of its regional telephone operating companies, including Pacific. At that time, AT&T was the common parent of a group of corporations known as the Bell System. The divestiture plan required AT&T to group its 22 operating companies into seven regional holding companies. The stock of the regional holding companies was distributed to AT&T stockholders pro rata. As part of this plan, Pacific was reorganized under § 368(a)(1)(E) to convert the single share of Pacific stock held by AT&T into 224,504,982 shares of voting common stock (the number of shares outstanding before AT&T's taxable reorganization of Pacific) and to convert the nonvoting preferred stock into voting preferred stock. By virtue of this transaction the holding company to which Pacific was transferred, the PacTel Group, would acquire control of Pacific within the meaning of § 368(c). AT&T transferred its Pacific stock along with other assets to the PacTel Group in exchange for all of the stock of the PacTel Group, which was then distributed to AT&T stockholders in the divestiture.

The IRS asserted that the receipt of PacTel Group stock was taxable in part to the AT&T stockholders as a dividend under § 355(a)(3)(B) because a portion of the value of the PacTel Group stock represented the stock of Pacific that was acquired by AT&T in a taxable merger within five years of the distribution. The Tax Court rejected the IRS's argument and held that the distribution was completely tax-free to the AT&T stockholders. The court read § 355(a)(3)(B) literally, concluding that the provision applied only to the stock of the controlled corporation that is distributed to the stockholders of the distributing corporation. The controlled corporation is the corporation that the distributing corporation controls immediately before the distribution. The Tax Court refused to look through the controlled corporation, in this case the PacTel Group, to examine the stock of its subsidiaries for purposes of applying the boot rule of § 355(a)(3)(B). The court reasoned in part that since Congress carefully provided a look-through rule for purposes of identifying under § 355(b)(2)(D) whether a trade or business had been acquired "directly (or through 1 or more corporations)" in a taxable transaction by the controlled corporation, Congress would have specifically provided a similar look-through rule in subdivision (a)(3)(B) if it had intended such a rule to be applied.

2.   SHAREHOLDER BASIS ISSUES

Pursuant to § 358(b)(2) and Treas.Reg. § 1.358–1(a) and –2(a)(2)(iv), in a spin-off in which shareholders of the distributing corporation receive a distribution of stock in the controlled corporation without surrendering any stock of the distributing corporation, each shareholder allocates the original basis of the shareholder's stock of the distributing corporation between the stock of the controlled corporation received in the distribution and the retained stock of the distributing corporation in proportion to the respective fair market values of the stockholdings *after* the distribution. Suppose, for example, that A owned 100 shares of X Corporation, with a basis of $1,000 and a fair market value of $5,000. A received 50 shares of Y Corporation in a spin-off. After the distribution, A's 100 shares of X Corporation had a fair market value of $2,000 and A's 50 shares of Y Corporation had a fair market value of $3,000. A's basis in the 100 shares of X Corporation is $400 ($1,000 × $2,000/($3,000 + $2,000)); A's basis in the 50 shares of Y Corporation is $600 ($1,000 × $3,000/($3,000 + $2,000)).

If the shareholder holds two or more blocks of stock acquired at different times or for different prices, then the basis of each share of stock of the distributing corporation will be allocated between the share of stock of the distributing corporation and the share of stock received with respect to that share of stock of the distributing corporation in proportion to their fair market values. For an example of the application of this rule, see Treas.Reg. § 1.358–2(c), Ex. 13. If one share of stock is received in respect of more than one share of stock or a fraction of a share of stock is received, the basis of each share of stock or security of the distributing corporation must be allocated to the shares of stock or securities received in a manner that reflects, to the greatest extent possible, that a share of stock or security received is received in respect of shares of stock or securities acquired on the same date and at the same price.

In a non-pro rata split-off subject to § 355 involving a complete redemption of a shareholder's interest in the distributing corporation, § 358(a) provides the shareholder an exchanged basis (increased by any gain or dividends recognized pursuant to § 356 and reduced by the amount of any boot received) in the shares of the controlled corporation received in the exchange. Suppose, for example, B owned 100 shares of Z Corporation, with a basis of $5,000, and B received 400 shares of W Corporation in a complete redemption of B's Z Corporation stock pursuant to a split-off governed by § 355. B's basis in the 400 shares of W Corporation is $5,000. Treas.Reg. § 1.358–2(a)(2)(i) provides that the basis of each share of stock received in the exchange is the same as the basis of the share or shares of stock (or allocable portions thereof) exchanged, as adjusted for gain under Treas.Reg. § 1.358–1. If more than one share of stock is received in exchange for one share of stock, the basis of the share of stock surrendered is allocated among the shares of stock received in the exchange in proportion to the fair market value of the shares of stock received. If one share of stock or security is received in respect of more than one share of stock or security or a fraction of a share of stock or security is received, the basis of each share of stock or security of the distributing corporation must be allocated to the shares of stock or securities received in a manner that reflects, to the greatest extent possible, that a share of stock or security received is received in respect of shares of stock or securities acquired on the same date and at the same price. The Regulations provide more detailed rules for situations in which a share of stock is received in exchange for more than one share of stock (or a fraction of a share of stock is received).

The same principles control in a non-pro rata split-off subject to § 355 that involves less than a complete redemption of a shareholder's interest in the distributing corporation. Section § 358(a) provides the shareholder an exchanged basis (increased by any gain or dividends recognized pursuant to § 356 and reduced by the amount of any boot received) in the shares of the controlled corporation received in the exchange. Suppose, for example, C owned 200 shares of Q Corporation, with a basis of $6,000, and C received 300 shares of V Corporation in redemption of 150 of C's 200 shares of Q Corporation stock pursuant to a split-off governed by § 355. C's basis in the 300 shares of V Corporation should be $4,500 ($6,000 × 150/200); C's basis in the remaining 50 shares of Q Corporation should be $1,500 ($6,000 × 50/200).

If in a split-off a shareholder surrenders a share of stock in the distributing corporation in exchange for stock of more than one class of the distributing corporation, or receives money or other boot in addition to stock, then, to the extent the plan specifies that shares of stock of a particular class or boot is received in exchange for a particular share of stock, the terms of the plan control, provided the terms are economically reasonable. If the plan does not specify the exchange, a pro rata portion of the shares of each class of controlled corporation stock received and a pro rata portion of the boot shall be treated as received in exchange for each share of stock surrendered, based on the fair market value of the stock surrendered. Treas.Reg. § 1.358–2(a)(2)(v).

3. EXCHANGES OF OPTIONS TO PURCHASE STOCK OF DISTRIBUTING AND CONTROLLED CORPORATION

Treas. Regs. §§ 1.355–1(c) and 1.356–3(b) treat rights to acquire stock of a corporation (options and warrants) issued by either the distributing corporation or the controlled corporation as securities of the respective corporations having no principal amount. The term "rights to acquire stock" of an issuing corporation has the same meaning for purposes of § 355 and § 356 as for purposes of § 305(d)(1) and § 317(a). Accordingly, as long as the other requirements of § 355, particularly the "distribution" of stock constituting "control" of the distributed corporation, have been met, the recipient of stock rights in either corporation is not required to recognize gain under § 356(d)(2)(B). Thus, for example, a shareholder of the distributing corporation who surrenders stock in the distributing corporation for stock of the controlled corporation in a split-off and also exchanges options to purchase stock of the distributing corporation in exchange for options to purchase stock of the controlled corporation does not recognize any gain or loss on the exchange of options. Likewise, nonrecognition is available in the case of a split-up of a corporation having outstanding options, which must be replaced by options to purchase stock of the distributed corporations. Rights exercisable against persons other than the issuer of the stock are not covered by Treas.Reg. § 1.355–1(c).

4.   RECOGNITION OF GAIN BY THE DISTRIBUTING CORPORATION

4.1. *Distributions of Property*

Generally, under § 361(b) the distributing corporation can avoid recognition of gain with respect to money or other property received from the controlled corporation in a § 368(a)(1)(D) reorganization that precedes a § 355 divisive transaction as long as the money or other property is distributed pursuant to the plan of reorganization. Section 361(b)(3) also permits a corporation that is a party to a reorganization to avoid recognition on the receipt of boot if the money or other property is transferred to the creditors of the distributing corporation. However, the last sentence of § 361(b)(3) requires recognition of gain on the transfer of money or other property to creditors by the distributing corporation to the extent that the amount of money and the fair market value of the distributed property exceeds the basis of assets transferred to the controlled corporation.

The recognition rule applicable to distributions to creditors is necessary to prevent avoidance of the otherwise required gain recognition under § 357(c) applicable to a § 368(a)(1)(D) reorganization qualified for nonrecognition under § 355. For example, assume that D transfers assets with a basis of $100 and subject to a liability of $150 to C in a transaction meeting the requirements of § 368(a)(1)(D), and D distributes the C stock to D's shareholders in a transaction that meets the requirements of § 355. Section 357(c) would require D to recognize $50 of gain. Instead of transferring the assets subject to the liability, D causes C to borrow $150 which C distributes to D along with C stock. D distributes the $150 to creditors to pay the liability. Thus, C does not assume any liabilities subject to § 357(c). Under § 361(b)(3), D is, however, required to recognize the $50 gain triggered by the receipt of boot in excess of the basis of the transferred assets.

Rev.Rul. 2017–9, 2017–21 I.R.B. 1244, dealt with whether the step transaction doctrine applied to integrate a dividend from a controlled corporation to a distributing corporation with a § 368(a)(1)(D) reorganization related to a § 355 distribution. On Date 1, C transferred $15X of money and property having a fair market value of $10X to D, pursuant to a dividend declaration, and D retained the money and property. On Date 2, D transferred to C property having a basis of $20X and a fair market value of $100X, and D distributed all the C stock to P in a transaction qualifying as a reorganization under § 368(a)(1)(D) and § 355. C and D planned and executed the Date 1 transfer in pursuance of the plan of reorganization. The ruling held that because the distribution was made pursuant to the plan of reorganization, the step transaction doctrine applied to integrate the Date 1 and Date 2 transactions. The "tax treatment of the transaction will follow its substance." Thus, the distribution of money and other property was treated as boot received by D in the § 368(a)(1)(D) reorganization that was subject to recognition of gain under § 361(b). The ruling reasoned as follows:

[I]n Estates of Bell v. Comm'r[, T.C.M. 1971–285], the Tax Court explained that the boot rules are "the exclusive measure of dividend income provided by Congress where cash is distributed to shareholders as an incident of a reorganization." See also American Manufacturing. Co. v. Comm'r, 55 T.C. 204 (1970). Section 361 broadly looks to whether transfers of money or other property occur "in pursuance of the plan of reorganization" or "in connection with the reorganization."

In Situation 2, the distribution is made in pursuance of the plan of reorganization. A distribution of money and other property in pursuance of the plan of reorganization will be treated as boot subject to recognition of gain, consistent with the congressional intent underlying § 361.

Therefore, the federal income tax treatment of the transaction will follow its substance, and the distribution of money and property by C to D will constitute a distribution of boot under § 361(b).

In contrast, the ruling held that the step transaction doctrine did not apply where a parent corporation (P) transferred property constituting an active trade or business to its controlled subsidiary (D) for the purpose of assuring that D met the requirements of § 355(b)(1)(A), and pursuant to the same overall plan, the transfer was followed by a distribution by D of the stock of its controlled subsidiary (C) to P.

4.2. *Distributions of Appreciated Property as Boot*

Under either § 355(c) or § 361(c), whichever may be applicable, the distributing corporation must recognize gain on the distribution of appreciated property as boot. The statute requires recognition of gain with respect to the distribution of any property with a fair market value in excess of basis that is not "qualified property." Qualified property is limited to stock or securities of the controlled corporation. I.R.C. § 355(c)(2)(B). Gain is recognized as if the nonqualified property were sold to the distributee for its fair market value. If the distributed property is subject to liabilities (or liabilities are assumed by the distributee), the fair market value of distributed property is deemed to be at least the amount of the liabilities. I.R.C. § 355(c)(2)(C).

4.3. *Shareholder's Disqualified Stock*

Section 355(d) requires recognition of gain by the distributing corporation (but not the shareholder) on all of the stock of the controlled corporation distributed in a transaction that otherwise qualifies under § 355 if *any* shareholder holds "disqualified stock." See Treas.Reg. § 1.355–6(b)(4)(ii), Ex. The shareholders receiving the distribution, including the shareholder holding the disqualified stock, nevertheless are entitled to nonrecognition under § 355(a). A shareholder holds disqualified stock if immediately after the distribution the shareholder holds stock that constitutes either (1) a 50% or greater interest in the distributing corporation acquired by purchase within the five-year period ending on the date of the distribution, or (2) a 50% or greater interest in the controlled corporation that was received as a distribution on stock of the distributing corporation that was purchased within the five-year period. I.R.C. § 355(d)(3). An acquisition by purchase is generally defined as any acquisition in which the basis of the stock in the hands of the acquiring shareholder is not determined by reference to its basis in the hands of the transferor. I.R.C. § 355(d)(5)(A). Acquisition by purchase includes, however, the acquisition of stock in a § 351 exchange to the extent that the stock is acquired in exchange for cash, marketable securities, or debt of the transferor. In the case of a transferred basis acquisition from a person who acquired the stock by purchase, the five-year period begins with the date of purchase by the person transferring the stock to the shareholder. The five-year period is suspended during any period in which the holder's risk of loss is substantially diminished by an arrangement such as an option, short sale, a special class of stock, or any other such device or transaction. I.R.C. § 355(c)(6).

The contours of § 355(d) and the tax treatment of a shareholder's disposition of "disqualified stock" is best understood in the context of the congressional amendments to § 355 that have occurred in the post-*General Utilities* era.[17] Congress's initial effort in 1987 to right-size § 355's scope with the intended scope of its *General Utilities* repeal was expressed with the enactment of § 355(b)(2)(D), but, as discussed in Section 2 above, that provision left significant opportunities for new purchasers to acquire an interest in a target corporation and then divvy up that corporation via a distribution of a controlled subsidiary in transactions that resembled a tax-free disposition of corporate assets to new owners while avoiding corporate level taxation on the disposition. The legislative history that accompanied the enactment of § 355(d) is remarkably similar to the 1987 legislative history that had accompanied § 355(b)(2)(D)'s amendment in that both endorse a "strong form" version of its *General Utilities* repeal as the following excerpt indicates:

> The Committee is concerned that some corporate taxpayers may attempt, under present-law rules governing divisive transactions, to dispose of subsidiaries in transactions that resemble sales .... The avoidance of corporate level tax is inconsistent with the repeal of the *General Utilities* doctrine .... The provisions for tax-free divisive transactions under section 355 were a limited exception to the repeal of the *General Utilities* doctrine, intended to permit historic shareholders to continue to carry on their historic corporate businesses in separate corporations .... The present-law provisions granting tax-free treatment at the corporate level are particularly troublesome because they may offer taxpayers an opportunity to avoid the general rule that corporate-level gain is recognized when an asset (including stock of a subsidiary) is disposed of.

The excerpt clarifies that Congress was comfortable with affording nonrecognition treatment under § 355 for a corporate separation of historic

---

[17] For an in-depth analysis of § 355(d) and Congress' repeated efforts to reform § 355 so that it is harmonized with Congress' repeal of the *General Utilities* doctrine, see Bret Wells, *Reform of Section 355*, 68 Am. U. L. Rev. 447 (2018). The views set forth in the text were adapted in part from views expressed in this article.

businesses between historic shareholders, but Congress did not want to extend the nonrecognition treatment to transactions that resemble a disposition of a historic business to new shareholders outside the historic economic group. Moreover, Congress also reiterated its desire to utilize a five-year pre-§ 355 transaction testing period for situations that resembled a disposition.

Just as it had done in 1987, Congress, however, adopted an amendment to § 355 that yet again was too narrow to achieve its explicitly stated "strong form" policy goal. Under a "weak form" of *General Utilities* repeal, section 355(d) would not have been necessary as assets remain in corporate solution with a carryover basis. But, under a "strong form" of *General Utilities* repeal, section 355(d) is justifiable exactly because historic business assets are being transferred to new shareholders outside of the historic economic group in a transaction that avoids corporate level taxation with respect to the disposition.

The policy implications of § 355(d)'s adoption cannot be more clear: Congress wanted to effectuate a "strong form" of *General Utilities* repeal such that historic assets that are disposed to new shareholders would not avoid corporate level taxation. However, § 355(d) does not rely solely on whether a spin-off occurred as part of a 50% or more ownership change to a new shareholder. Of course, section 355(d) looks to whether there has been a 50% or greater ownership change within five years prior to the § 355 transaction, but then it limits § 355(d)'s applicability to only those ownership changes that occur "by purchase" within that five-year period. In other words, § 355(d)(3)–(5) does not restrict corporate level nonrecognition treatment for a new shareholder who acquires stock in a tax-free manner. Section 355(d)(3) provides its own list of new shareholder stock acquisitions that are not treated as having arisen "by purchase" and also gives the Treasury authority to provide further exceptions to the "by purchase" designation. I.R.C. § 355(d)(9)(B). See Treas.Reg. § 1.355–6 (for myriad complex details regarding application of § 355(d)).

The Regulations indicate that a distribution will not be treated as a disqualified distribution under § 355(d)(2) if the distribution and any related transactions do not violate the purpose of § 355(d). Distributions that do not violate that purpose are described as distributions that neither increase direct or indirect ownership in the distributing corporation or any controlled corporation by a disqualified person, nor provide a disqualified person with a cost basis in the stock of any controlled corporation. Treas.Reg. § 1.355–6(b)(3)(i). For an example of a distribution and related transactions that do not violate the purpose of § 355(d), see Treas.Reg. § 1.355–6(b)(3)(vi), Ex. 1.[18]

4.4. *Cash-Rich Distributee Corporations*

In 2005, Congress became concerned about so-called "cash rich" split-offs that occur as part of a 50% or greater ownership change. When either

---

[18] For a further discussion for how to right-size § 355(e) and the other post-1986 amendments to § 355 so that § 355 does not provide a means to circumvent the intended scope of Congress' repeal of the *General Utilities* doctrine, see Bret Wells, Reform of Section 355, 68 Am. U. L. Rev. 101 (2018).

the distributing corporation or the controlled subsidiary has more than two-thirds of its value attributable to investment assets, and when a shareholder obtains a 50% or greater interest in a disqualified investment corporation as a result of the corporate separation, then the corporate separation is denied nonrecognition treatment under § 355(g). Thus, if a substantial majority of the value of a corporation after a corporate separation relates to non-historic business assets, then the principle reason for the spin-off is attributable to factors other than separating the historic business between historic shareholders. Section 355(g) is consistent with Congress's goal of not allowing § 355 to represent a device for circumventing the repeal of the *General Utilities* doctrine. However, § 355(g) has several deficiencies. First, § 355(g) does not apply if the transaction represents a spin-off where no shareholder group increases its proportionate interest in the disqualified investment by 50% or more. Second, the tainted investment asset threshold is set at a high threshold so that only super cash-rich split-offs are subject to this provision.

4.5. *Section 355(h) and the Spin-REIT Transaction*

In 2015, Congress became concerned about § 355 when a controlled subsidiary is distributed in a § 355 transaction and either the distributing corporation or the controlled subsidiary subsequently elect real estate investment trust (REIT) status. The combination of a tax-free corporate separation under § 355 coupled with a REIT election with respect to one of the corporations involved in the § 355 transaction allowed assets to permanently leave corporate solution after the subsequent REIT election without incurring corporate level tax. Initially, the IRS issued favorable § 355 rulings for the "spin-REIT" transaction, finding that a controlled subsidiary's real estate activities could satisfy the active trade or business standard of § 355 through its real estate management activities and once distributed could elect REIT status. See, e.g., I.R.S. Priv. Ltr. Rul. 12–73–348 (Sept. 13, 2013) (describing the process a company took to meet REIT status). In 2015, the Treasury Department reversed course and expressed concerns about a § 355 spin-off that is followed by either the distributing corporation or the controlled subsidiary making a REIT election after the spin-off. Notice 2015–59, 2015–40 C.B. 459. Shortly thereafter, on December 18, 2015, Congress enacted § 355(h) and § 856(c)(8).

Under § 355(h), a REIT generally will be ineligible to participate in a tax-free spin-off as either the distributing corporation or controlled corporation unless those corporations were already REITs or the corporate separation would be subjected to corporate level taxation. In addition, if a corporation is a party to a § 355 transaction, then that corporation is not eligible to make a REIT election for 10 years from the date of the § 355 transaction. Even with the passage of § 355(h), the Treasury Department was concerned that this statutory provision, by itself, did not fully protect against the ability of taxpayers to combine a § 355 transaction with a subsequent REIT or RIC election. Thus, in order to protect against an inappropriate circumvention of Congress's repeal of the *General Utilities* doctrine, the Treasury Department issued Temporary Regulations on June 7, 2016, that would cause a corporation that merged into a REIT within 10 years of its participation in a § 355 transaction must recognize all of the corporate-level built-in gain at the time of its REIT conversion. Treas.Reg. § 1.337(d)–7T(f).

5. TREATMENT OF CORPORATE ATTRIBUTES

5.1. *Earnings and Profits*

Section 381, which provides for the carryover of corporate attributes (including earnings and profits) in certain reorganizations and liquidations, discussed in Chapter 13, is not applicable to a corporate division under § 355. However, § 312(h) specifies that the earnings and profits of the two corporations must be allocated as provided in Regulations. In the case of a § 355 transaction that is a § 368(a)(1)(D) reorganization with a newly created controlled corporation, earnings and profits are allocated between the distributing corporation and the controlled corporation in proportion to the fair market value of assets transferred to the controlled corporation. In the case of a divisive type (D) reorganization involving the transfer of trade or business assets to an existing controlled corporation, earnings and profits may be allocated with respect to the relative net bases of assets transferred to the controlled corporation and assets retained by the distributing corporation, or by some other appropriate method. Treas.Reg. § 1.312–10(a).

In a § 355 division that involves an existing controlled corporation and thus is not a type (D) reorganization, the earnings and profits of the distributing corporation are decreased by the lesser of the amount by which earnings and profits would be decreased by allocating earnings and profits to the controlled corporation in proportion to the value of the stock of the controlled corporation as if the stock were a newly created corporation under the rules of Treas.Reg. § 1.312–10(a), or in an amount equal to the net worth of the controlled corporation. If the earnings and profits of the controlled corporation immediately before the transaction are less than the decrease of earnings and profits of the distributing corporation, the earnings and profits of the controlled corporation after the transaction will be the same as the amount of the decrease of earnings and profits to the distributing corporation. If the earnings and profits of the controlled corporation are greater than the amount of the decrease, the earnings and profits of the controlled corporation are not changed. Treas.Reg. § 1.312–10(b).

5.2. *Net Operating Losses*

The treatment of net operating loss carryovers in a § 355 transaction is discussed in Rev.Rul. 77–133, 1977–1 C.B. 96. In a split-off under § 355, M Corporation transferred assets constituting a business to S, a newly formed corporation, and distributed all of the S stock to one of M's two stockholders in exchange for all of stockholder's M stock. The IRS held that no part of M's net operating loss carryover was transferred to S in the split-off but that M could continue to use its loss carryover. Where, however, the transaction is a split-up under § 355 in which the loss corporation transfers separate businesses to each of two new corporations and distributes the stock of each corporation to different stockholders in complete liquidation, Rev.Rul. 56–373, 1956–2 C.B. 217, held that neither of the successor corporations can take advantage of the distributing corporation's unused net operating loss carryover. The ruling concluded that because all of the assets of the distributing corporation were transferred to two corporations, the type (D) reorganization is not a transaction described by § 354(b)(1) and therefore was not subject to attribute carryover under § 381(a)(2). Thus, the survival of net operating loss carryovers in a divisive type (D) reorganization depends upon whether the transaction is structured as a split-off or a split-up, even though the economic results of the two transactions may be identical.

The limitations on net operating loss carryovers of § 382, discussed in Chapter 13, will apply to unused net operating loss carryovers that survive a split-off as described in Rev.Rul. 77–133 if the continuing stockholders of the loss corporation increase their ownership interest by more than 50 percentage points.

PROBLEM SET 6

1.   The stock of Rock of Ages Corp. is owned 60% by Elvis, whose basis for his stock is $1,000,000; 22% by Bey, whose basis for her stock is $750,000; and 18% by Zee, whose basis for his stock is $450,000. Rock of Ages has two independent divisions: Classic Rock Division and the Hip Hop Division. The Classic Rock Division has assets with a basis of $1,000,000 and a fair market value of $1,800,000. The Hip Hop Division has assets with a basis of $1,000,000 and a fair market value of $1,200,000. (Neither division has any liabilities.) Rock of Ages has $2,000,000 of accumulated earnings and profits ($1,200,000 attributable to the Classic Rock business and $800,000 attributable to the Hip Hop business) and a $500,000 net operating loss attributable to its Hip Hop business.

(a)   Rock of Ages transfers the Hip Hop business assets to a new subsidiary, Beatbox Corp., the stock of which it then distributes to its shareholders pro rata.

(1)   Assuming that the transaction qualifies under § 355, what are the tax consequences to the corporations and to the shareholders?

(2)   Assuming that the transaction did not qualify under § 355, what are the tax consequences to the corporations and to the shareholders?

(b)   Rock of Ages transfers the Hip Hop business assets to a new subsidiary, Beatbox Corp., the stock of which it then distributes to Bey and Zee in exchange for all of their shares of Rock of Ages. Bey receives 55% of the Beatbox stock and Zee receives 45% of the Beatbox stock.

(1)   Assuming that the transaction qualifies under § 355, what are the tax consequences to the corporations and to the shareholders?

(2)   Assuming that the transaction did not qualify under § 355, what are the tax consequences to the corporations and to the shareholders?

2.   San Francisco Dungeness Crab Corp. (SFDC) owned 60% of the stock of Cedar Key Clam Farms, Inc. (CKCF); SFDC's basis in the CKCF stock was

$300,000. The remaining 40% of the stock of CKCF was held by Diane. In January Year 11, SFDC purchased Diane's CKCF stock for $1,000,000 in cash. In December Year 14, after a dispute among the shareholders, SFDC distributed all of the stock of CKCF to Earl, one of SFDC's shareholders, in complete redemption of Earl's shares of SFDC to settle the dispute.

   (a)   (1)   What are the tax consequences to Earl and to SFDC?

         (2)   Would your answer change if SFDC had acquired Diane's CKCF stock in November Year 9?

         (3)   Would your answer change if SFDC had acquired Diane's CKCF stock in January Year 11 in exchange for SFDC voting common stock? (Assume that Diane's basis for the CKCF stock was $100,000.)

   (b)   Suppose that San Francisco Dungeness Crab Corp. (SFDC) had owned 80% of the stock of CKCF for more than five years, but purchased the remaining 20% from Diane last year for $1,000,000 in cash. This year SFDC distributed CKCF to Earl in redemption of all of his stock. What are the tax consequences to Earl and to SFDC?

3.   (a)   (1)   Prior to January, Year 10, all of the stock of Aloha Corp. was owned by Akoni, Ema, and Hana. In January, Year 10, Iolana purchased 30% of the stock of Aloha Corp. In December of Year 14, Aloha distributed 60% of the stock of its previously controlled subsidiary, Waikiki Corp., to Iolana in exchange for all of Iolana's stock of Aloha. The remaining 40% of the Waikiki stock was distributed to Hana in redemption of all of Hana's Aloha stock. Assuming that the transaction qualifies under § 355, what are the tax consequences under § 355(d)?

         (2)   How would your answer differ if Iolana had acquired the Aloha stock in a type B reorganization?

         (3)   How would your answer differ if Iolana had acquired the Aloha stock in November, Year 9?

   (b)   Instead of distributing the Waikiki stock to Iolana and Hana, in December of Year 14, Aloha distributed all of the stock of Waikiki Corp. to Akoni and Ema in exchange for all of their stock of Aloha. Iolana continued as a shareholder of Aloha owning 30 shares, and Hana continued as a shareholder of Aloha owning 20 shares. Assuming that the transaction qualifies under § 355, what are the tax consequences under § 355(d)?

SECTION 5.   DIVISIVE DISTRIBUTIONS IN CONNECTION WITH ACQUISITIONS

INTERNAL REVENUE CODE: Sections 351(c)(2); 355(e), (f); 368(a)(2)(H)(ii).

REGULATIONS: Section 1.355–7.

   As is evident from the preceding material, a source of continuing tension has been whether, and the extent to which, tax-free treatment under § 355 is warranted in the case of a divisive transaction prior to and in contemplation of a subsequent acquisition (whether by taxable purchase or tax-free reorganization) of either the distributing or distributed corporation. In general, a prearranged spin-off of the corporation to be acquired was denied § 355 nonrecognition. On the other hand, as illustrated by *Commissioner v. Morris Trust*, a spin-off followed by a merger in which the distributing corporation's shareholders retained more than 50% of the merged entity could be tax-free under § 355. The controversial issue was whether a corporation that was the target of an acquisition could be "customized" by spinning-off to its pre-acquisition shareholders the stock of a subsidiary that the acquiring corporation did not want to acquire.

Revenue Ruling 2005–65

2005–2 C.B. 684.

ISSUE

Under the facts described below, is a distribution of a controlled corporation by a distributing corporation part of a plan pursuant to which one or more persons acquire stock in the distributing corporation under § 355(e) of the Internal Revenue Code and § 1.355–7 of the Income Tax Regulations?

FACTS

Distributing is a publicly traded corporation that conducts a pharmaceuticals business. Controlled, a wholly owned subsidiary of Distributing, conducts a cosmetics business. Distributing does all of the borrowing for both Distributing and Controlled and makes all decisions regarding the allocation of capital spending between the pharmaceuticals and cosmetics businesses. Because Distributing's capital spending in recent years for both the pharmaceuticals and cosmetics businesses has outpaced internally generated cash flow from the businesses, it has had to limit total expenditures to maintain its credit ratings. Although the decisions reached by Distributing's senior management regarding the allocation of capital spending usually favor the pharmaceuticals business due to its higher rate of growth and profit margin, the competition for capital prevents both businesses from consistently pursuing development strategies that the management of each business believes are appropriate.

To eliminate this competition for capital, and in light of the unavailability of nontaxable alternatives, Distributing decides and publicly announces that it intends to distribute all the stock of Controlled pro rata to Distributing's shareholders. It is expected that both businesses will benefit in a real and substantial way from the distribution. This business purpose is a corporate business purpose (within the meaning of § 1.355–2(b)). The distribution is substantially motivated by this business purpose, and not by a business purpose to facilitate an acquisition.

After the announcement but before the distribution, X, a widely held corporation that is engaged in the pharmaceuticals business, and Distributing begin discussions regarding an acquisition. There were no discussions between Distributing or Controlled and X or its shareholders regarding an acquisition or a distribution before the announcement. In addition, Distributing would have been able to continue the successful operation of its pharmaceuticals business without combining with X. During its negotiations with Distributing, X indicates that it favors the distribution. X merges into Distributing before the distribution but nothing in the merger agreement requires the distribution.

As a result of the merger, X's former shareholders receive 55 percent of Distributing's stock. In addition, X's chairman of the board and chief executive officer become the chairman of the board and chief executive officer, respectively, of Distributing. Six months after the merger, Distributing distributes the stock of Controlled *pro rata* in a distribution to which § 355 applies and to which § 355(d) does not apply. At the time of the distribution, the distribution continues to be substantially motivated by the business purpose of eliminating the competition for capital between the pharmaceuticals and cosmetics businesses.

LAW

Section 355(c) generally provides that no gain or loss is recognized to the distributing corporation on a distribution of stock in a controlled corporation to which § 355 (or so much of § 356 as relates to § 355) applies and which is not in pursuance of a plan of reorganization. Section 355(e) generally denies nonrecognition treatment under § 355(c) if the distribution is part of a plan (or series of related transactions) (a plan) pursuant to which one or more persons acquire directly or indirectly stock representing a 50-percent or greater interest in the distributing corporation or any controlled corporation.

Section 1.355–7(b)(1) provides that whether a distribution and an acquisition are part of a plan is determined based on all the facts and circumstances, including those set forth in § 1.355–7(b)(3) (plan factors) and (4) (non-plan factors). The weight to be given each of the facts and circumstances depends on the particular case. The determination does not depend on the relative number of plan factors compared to the number of non-plan factors that are present.

Section 1.355–7(b)(3)(iii) provides that, in the case of an acquisition (other than involving a public offering) before a distribution, if at some time during the two-year period ending on the date of the acquisition there were discussions by Distributing or Controlled with the acquirer regarding a distribution, such discussions tend to show that the distribution and the acquisition are part of a plan. The weight to be accorded this fact depends on the nature, extent, and timing of the discussions. In addition, the fact that the acquirer intends to cause a distribution and, immediately after the acquisition, can meaningfully participate in the decision regarding whether to make a distribution, tends to show that the distribution and the acquisition are part of a plan.

Section 1.355–7(b)(4)(iii) provides that, in the case of an acquisition (other than involving a public offering) before a distribution, the absence of discussions by Distributing or Controlled with the acquirer regarding a distribution during the two-year period ending on the date of the earlier to occur of the acquisition or the first public announcement regarding the distribution tends to show that the distribution and the acquisition are not part of a plan. However, this factor does not apply to an acquisition where the acquirer intends to cause a distribution and, immediately after the acquisition, can meaningfully participate in the decision regarding whether to make a distribution.

Section 1.355–7(b)(4)(v) provides that the fact that the distribution was motivated in whole or substantial part by a corporate business purpose (within the meaning of § 1.355–2(b)) other than a business purpose to facilitate the acquisition or a similar acquisition tends to show that the distribution and the acquisition are not part of a plan.

Section 1.355–7(b)(4)(vi) provides that the fact that the distribution would have occurred at approximately the same time and in similar form regardless of the acquisition or a similar acquisition tends to show that the distribution and the acquisition are not part of a plan.

Section 1.355–7(h)(6) provides that discussions with the acquirer generally include discussions with persons with the implicit permission of the acquirer.

Section 1.355–7(h)(9) provides that a corporation is treated as having the implicit permission of its shareholders when it engages in discussions.

ANALYSIS

Whether the X shareholders' acquisition of Distributing stock and Distributing's distribution of Controlled are part of a plan depends on all the facts and circumstances, including those described in § 1.355–7(b). The fact that Distributing discussed the distribution with X during the two-year period ending on the date of the acquisition tends to show that the distribution and the acquisition are part of a plan. *See* § 1.355–7(b)(3)(iii). In addition, X's shareholders may constitute acquirers who intend to cause a distribution and who, immediately after the acquisition, can meaningfully participate (through X's chairman of the board and chief executive officer who become D's chairman of the board and chief executive officer) in the decision regarding whether to distribute Controlled. *See id.* However, the fact that Distributing publicly announced the distribution before discussions with X regarding both an acquisition and a distribution began suggests that the plan factor in § 1.355–7(b)(3)(iii) should be accorded less weight than it would have been accorded had there been such discussions before the public announcement.

With respect to those factors that tend to show that the distribution and the acquisition are not part of a plan, the absence of discussions by Distributing or Controlled with X or its shareholders during the two-year period ending on the date of the public announcement regarding the distribution would tend to show that the distribution and the acquisition are not part of a plan only if X's shareholders are not acquirers who intend to cause a distribution and who, immediately after the acquisition, can meaningfully participate in the decision regarding whether to distribute Controlled. *See* § 1.355–7(b)(4)(iii). Because X's chairman of the board and chief executive officer become the chairman and chief executive officer, respectively, of Distributing, X's shareholders may have the ability to meaningfully participate in the decision whether to distribute Controlled. Therefore, the absence of discussions by Distributing or Controlled with X or its shareholders during the two-year period ending on the date of the public announcement regarding the distribution may not tend to show that the distribution and the acquisition are not part of a plan.

Nonetheless, the fact that the distribution was substantially motivated by a corporate business purpose (within the meaning of § 1.355–2(b)) other than a business purpose to facilitate the acquisition or a similar acquisition, and the fact that the distribution would have occurred at approximately the same time and in similar form regardless of the acquisition or a similar acquisition, tend to show that the distribution and the acquisition are not part of a plan. *See* § 1.355–7(b)(4)(v), (vi). The fact that the public announcement of the distribution preceded discussions by Distributing or Controlled with X or its shareholders, and the fact that Distributing's business would have continued to operate successfully even if the merger had not occurred, evidence that the distribution originally was not substantially motivated by a business purpose to facilitate the acquisition or a similar acquisition. Moreover, after the merger, Distributing continued to be substantially motivated by the same corporate business purpose (within the meaning of § 1.355–2(b)) other than a business purpose to facilitate the acquisition or a similar acquisition (§ 1.355–7(b)(4)(v)). In addition, the fact that Distributing decided to distribute Controlled and announced that decision before it began discussions with X regarding the combination suggests that the distribution would have occurred at approximately the same time and in similar form regardless of Distributing's combination with X and the corresponding acquisition of Distributing stock by the X shareholders.

Considering all the facts and circumstances, particularly the fact that the distribution was motivated by a corporate business purpose (within the meaning of § 1.355–2(b)) other than a business purpose to facilitate the acquisition or a similar acquisition, and the fact that the distribution would have occurred at approximately the same time and in similar form regardless of the acquisition or a similar acquisition, the acquisition and distribution are not part of a plan under § 355(e) and § 1.355–7(b).

HOLDING

Under the facts described above, the acquisition and the distribution are not part of a plan under § 355(e) and § 1.355–7(b).

DETAILED ANALYSIS

1.   ASPECTS OF SECTION 355(e)

1.1. *Background and Relationship of Sections 355(d) and 355(e)*

Section 355(e) was enacted to buttress the perceived deficiencies of § 355(d) in terms of limiting § 355 so that it would not provide an inappropriate means to circumvent the intended scope of Congress' repeal of the *General Utilities* doctrine.[19] But, to understand its intended scope, it is helpful to review the shortcomings of § 355(d) in order to understand the intended scope of § 355(e).

After § 355(d)'s enactment, a distributing corporation could still spin-off a subsidiary that contained an "unwanted business" to its historic shareholders and then the historic shareholders could exchange their stock in the distributing corporation for stock in an acquiring corporation in a qualifying tax-free reorganization. In this situation, the pre-merger spin-off transaction could sidestep the amendments to § 355(d) if the acquiring corporation acquired stock in either the distributing corporation or in the controlled subsidiary by a means other than "by purchase." This could be accomplished via an acquisitive tax-free reorganization as that form of acquisition was not "by purchase" within the meaning of § 355(d).[20] Thus, a corporate separation could qualify for nonrecognition treatment at the corporate level by reason of § 355 even though that corporate separation is coupled with an acquisitive reorganization where a historic business is transferred to a new shareholder group. This technique of engaging in a pre-merger spin-off of a subsidiary followed by a subsequent acquisitive reorganization of the distributing corporation by the unrelated acquiring corporation is commonly referred to as a "*Morris Trust*" transaction. The transaction takes its name from the transaction that was blessed in Commissioner v. Mary Archer W. Morris Trust, 367 F.2d 794 (4th Cir. 1966). IRS pronouncements have addressed the *Morris Trust* technique and defined what constitutes an adequate business purpose for engaging in a pre-merger spin-off. See, e.g., Rev.Proc. 96–30, 1996–1 C.B. 696; Rev.Rul. 78–251, 1978–1 C.B. 89.

Moreover, a reverse-*Morris Trust* transaction was also authorized under the pre-1997 law, as long as the controlled subsidiary's post spin-off merger

---

[19] For an in-depth analysis of § 355(e) and Congress's repeated efforts to reform § 355 so that it is harmonized with Congress' repeal of the *General Utilities* doctrine, see Bret Wells, Reform of Section 355, 68 Am. U. L. Rev. 447 (2018). The views set forth in the text were adapted in part from views expressed in this article.

[20] For an in-depth analysis of section 355(d)'s scope, see Mark J. Silverman, et al., The Proposed Section 355(d) Regulations: Narrowing the Scope of an Overly Broad Statute, 26 J. Corp. Tax'n 269 (2000).

was approved in a subsequent vote of the controlled subsidiary that was not contingent as to its acceptance or occurrence at the time of the spin-off. See Rev.Rul. 98–27, 1998–1 C.B. 1159 (stating that the IRS would not apply a *Court Holdings* or step transaction doctrine to determine continuity if the outcome of public shareholder vote was uncertain at the time of the spin-off of the controlled subsidiary); Rev.Rul. 98–44, 1988–2 C.B. 315 (obsoleting earlier rulings that would have resequenced the steps to disqualify § 355 from applying in a reverse-*Morris Trust* fact pattern where the controlled subsidiary was first the subject of a spin-off followed by a subsequent merger of the controlled subsidiary for purposes of disqualifying the spin-off from receiving § 355 treatment).

In response to § 355(d)'s perceived deficiencies, Congress chose to enact § 355(e) and (f), which require corporate level gain recognition with respect to the stock of the controlled distributee corporation if, pursuant to a plan or arrangement in connection with a corporate division, there is a change of ownership of a 50% or greater interest of either the distributing corporation or the controlled corporation. In such cases, the distributing corporation generally must recognize gain as if the stock of the controlled corporation had been sold for fair market value on the date of distribution. If the distributee corporation was formed in a § 368(a)(1)(D) reorganization in contemplation of the distribution, § 368(a)(2)(H)(ii) preserves the tax-free status of that transaction for the asset transfer from D to C, thus assuring that the assets retain a transferred basis, even if the controlling corporation's shareholders dispose of the stock of the distributed corporation in a transaction subject to § 355(e). Acquisitions occurring within two years before or after the date of the distribution are presumed to have occurred pursuant to a plan or arrangement. If, however, a divisive distribution of stock is from one member of an affiliated group of corporations (as defined in § 1504(a)) to another member of the group, e.g., S1 distributes the stock of its subsidiary, S2 to S1's parent, P, § 355(f) provides that § 355 does not apply at all if the distribution is part of a plan or series of related transactions pursuant to which a 50% or greater interest in the distributing corporation or controlled corporation will be transferred to new owners.

Nevertheless, notwithstanding these bright-line standards, § 355(e) has unique deficiencies. First, § 355(e) uses a different time period for purposes of determining a historic shareholder than does § 355(b)(2)(D) and (d): namely a period that commences two years before and ends two years after the § 355 spin-off. Second, § 355(e) only targets a corporate separation that effectuates an ownership change of either the distributing corporation or the controlled corporation as part of a "plan or series of related transactions." As will be discussed in the next section, identifying when a multi-step transaction constitutes a "plan or series of transactions" that runs afoul of this restriction has become an area where upfront tax planning can significantly impact the ultimate determination.

1.2. *Plan or Series of Related Transactions*

The recognition rule of § 355(e) applies to a divisive distribution that is part of a plan or a series of related transactions in which one or more persons acquire stock representing a 50% or greater interest in either the distributing or any controlled corporation. I.R.C. § 355(e)(2)(A)(ii). Section 355(e)(2)(B) provides that if one or more persons acquires a 50% or greater interest in the distributing or any controlled corporation within a four-year period beginning two-years before the date of the distribution and ending two-years after the date of the distribution "such acquisition *shall* be treated as pursuant to a plan * * * unless it is established that the distribution and the acquisition are not pursuant to a plan or series of related transactions." As the legislative history indicates, "taxpayers can avoid gain recognition by showing that an acquisition occurring during this four-year period was unrelated to the distribution."

A perceived need for certainty has spawned complicated Regulations providing guidance for identifying the presence of the prohibited plan. After promulgating a series of ever changing Temporary Regulations over the course of the years since the enactment of § 355(e), in 2005 the Treasury Department promulgated final Regulations. The Regulations disregard the presumption of § 355(e)(2)(B) and provide that "whether a distribution and an acquisition are part of a plan is determined based on all the facts and circumstances." Treas.Reg. § 1.355–7(b)(1). In the case of an acquisition not involving a public offering that occurs within two-years following the date of a distribution, the distribution and acquisition "will be treated as part of a plan *only* if there was an agreement, understanding, arrangement, or substantial negotiations regarding the acquisition or a similar acquisition at some time during the two-year period ending on the date of the distribution." Treas.Reg. § 1.355–7(b)(2) (italics added). The "super safe harbor" implicit in this rule trumps all other facts and circumstances. The Regulations add that the existence of an agreement, understanding, arrangement, or substantial negotiations during the two-year period preceding the distribution tends to show that the distribution and acquisition are part of a plan, and further describe such an understanding etc., as merely a factor among the facts and circumstances to be evaluated. See Treas.Reg. § 1.355–7(b)(3)(i). If the acquisition involves a public offering after the distribution, the presence of discussions during the two-year period preceding the distribution with an investment banker regarding a distribution is a factor indicating the existence of a plan. Treas.Reg. § 1.355–7(b)(3)(ii). The Regulations add that in the case of an acquisition involving a public offering after the distribution, the absence of discussions with an investment banker within the two-year period ending on the date of the distribution is a factor indicating the absence of a plan. Treas.Reg. § 1.355–7(b)(4)(i).

Whether there is an agreement, understanding, or arrangement is a question of facts and circumstances. Treas.Reg. § 1.355–7(h)(1)(iii). A binding agreement is not required, but an agreement, understanding, or arrangement "clearly exists if a binding contract to acquire stock exists." Also, an agreement may exist even though the parties have not reached agreement on all significant economic terms. "Substantial negotiations" are said to "require discussions of significant economic terms . . . by one or more officers or directors acting on behalf of [the corporations], . . . controlling shareholders" or "another person or persons with the implicit or explicit permission of one or more of such officers, directors, or controlling shareholders." Treas.Reg. § 1.355–7(h)(1)(iv). A "controlling shareholder" with respect to a publicly traded corporation is a 5% shareholder who actively participates in the management or operation of the corporation. Treas.Reg. § 1.355–7(h)(3)(i). With respect to a corporation the stock of which is not publicly traded, a controlling shareholder is any person that owns stock possessing voting power representing a meaningful voice in the governance of the corporation. Treas.Reg. § 1.355–7(h)(3)(ii). In the case of an acquisition involving a public offering, the existence of an agreement, etc., depends on discussions with investment bankers by one or more officers, directors, or controlling shareholders of either the distributing or controlled corporations. Treas.Reg. § 1.355–7(h)(1)(vi).

Under Treas.Reg. § 1.355–7(e) the acquisition of stock pursuant to an option will result in the option agreement being treated as an agreement to acquire the stock as of the date the option was written, transferred, or modified if the option is more likely than not to be exercised as of such date.

In the case of an acquisition that precedes the distribution, the existence of a plan is indicated by discussions within the two-year period preceding the acquisition by either the controlled or distributing corporation with the acquirer regarding a distribution. Treas.Reg. § 1.355–7(b)(3)(iii). The absence of discussions regarding a distribution during the two-year period ending on the earlier to occur of (a) the acquisition, or (b) the first public announcement regarding the distribution, is a factor indicating that the acquisition and distribution were not part of a plan. Treas.Reg. § 1.355–7(b)(4)(iii). If the acquisition involves a public offering before the distribution, the presence of discussions during the two-year period preceding the acquisition with an investment banker regarding a distribution is a factor indicating the existence of a plan. Treas.Reg. § 1.355–7(b)(3)(iv). A change in the market or business conditions after the acquisition that results in a distribution that was otherwise unexpected is a factor that indicates that the acquisition and distribution are not part of a plan. Treas.Reg. § 1.355–7(b)(4)(iv).

In the case of a distribution either before or after the acquisition, the Regulations provide that the existence of a corporate business purpose, as defined in Treas.Reg. § 1.355–2(b), other than a business purpose to facilitate the acquisition, is a factor indicating the absence of a plan. Treas.Reg. § 1.355–7(b)(4)(v). Discussions by either the distributing or controlled corporation with outside advisors, as well as internal discussions of either corporation provide an indication of a business purpose for the distribution. Treas.Reg. § 1.355–7(c)(1). Similarly, the absence of a plan is indicated if the distribution would have occurred at approximately the same time and in similar form regardless of the acquisition. Treas.Reg. § 1.355–7(b)(4)(vi). Treas.Reg. § 1.355–7(c)(2) provides that discussions with the acquirer regarding a distribution to decrease the likelihood of an acquisition of either the distributing or controlled corporation by separating it from the corporation that is likely to be acquired will be treated as having a business purpose to facilitate acquisition of the corporation that is likely to be acquired. Nonetheless, a distribution that facilitated trading in the stock of the distributing or controlled corporation will not be taken into account in determining whether a distribution and acquisition are part of a plan. Treas.Reg. § 1.355–7(c)(3).

Treas.Reg. § 1.355–7(d) provides nine safe harbors from the stormy seas of prohibited plans. A distribution and an acquisition are not part of a plan if they are described in one of the following safe harbors:

1.   An acquisition occurs more than six months after a distribution, there was no agreement, understanding, arrangement, or substantial negotiations concerning the acquisition during a period from one year before the distribution to six months following the distribution, and the distribution was motivated in whole or substantial part by a corporate business purpose other than a business purpose to facilitate an acquisition.

2.   An acquisition occurs more than six months after a distribution for which there was no agreement, understanding, arrangement, or substantial negotiations concerning the acquisition during a period from one year before the distribution to six months following the distribution. This safe harbor applies where the distribution was not motivated by a business purpose to facilitate an acquisition of either the distributing or controlled corporations, and no more than 25% of the stock of the corporation whose stock was acquired in the acquisition was either acquired or the subject of an agreement, understanding, arrangement, or substantial negotiations during a period from one year before the distribution to six months following the distribution.

3.   An acquisition occurs after the distribution and there was no agreement, understanding, arrangement, or substantial negotiations concerning the acquisition at the time of the distribution or within one-year thereafter. This provision disregards the two-year post-distribution presumption of the statute and replaces it with a one-year safe harbor. Rev.Rul. 2005–65, 2005–2 C.B. 684, reproduced above, demonstrates the planning techniques afforded by this regulatory exception. In Rev.Rul. 2005–65, the IRS considered a situation where a controlled subsidiary's spin-off was publicly announced for valid business reasons prior to the commencement of discussions with an acquiring corporation. After the spin-off had been announced but before it had been consummated, the distributing corporation began negotiations and agreed to be acquired by an acquiring corporation in an acquisitive reorganization where the acquirer's shareholders would obtain 55% of the stock in the resulting combined company. Thus, Rev.Rul. 2005–65 posits a situation where new shareholders receive a historic business within two years of a § 355 transaction. Moreover, the acquisitive reorganization that involved the distributing corporation was agreed to prior to the spin-off of the controlled subsidiary. Thus, a historic business was transferred in a manner akin to a disposition. Yet, the IRS ruled that the spin-off, which facilitated the ultimate disposition of the distributing corporation, was entitled to § 355 nonrecognition treatment because the § 355

transaction was publicly announced *prior* to any actual negotiations with the acquiring corporation with the consequence that no prohibited "plan (or series of transactions)" existed at the time of the initial section 355 transaction's announcement. The ruling provides a roadmap for how one can transfer a historic business to new shareholders in a transaction that resembles a disposition but avoids running afoul of § 355(e).[21]

4. An acquisition occurs before a distribution but before the first "disclosure event" regarding the distribution. A "disclosure event" is any communication to the acquirer or any other third person by an officer, director, controlling shareholder, or employee of any of the distributing corporation, the controlled corporation, or a corporation related to either of them, or an outside advisor to any of those corporations regarding the distribution, or the possibility thereof. To assure that this safe harbor is not available for acquisitions by a person who could participate in the decision to effect a distribution, it does not apply to acquisitions by a person that was a controlling shareholder or a 10% shareholder of the acquired corporation at any time during the period beginning immediately after the acquisition and ending on the date of the distribution. The safe harbor is also unavailable if the acquisition occurs in connection with a transaction in which the aggregate acquisitions represent 20% or more (by vote or value) of the stock of the acquired corporation.

5. An acquisition of the distributing corporation (not involving a public offering) that occurs prior to a pro rata distribution, if the acquisition occurs after the date of a public announcement regarding the distribution, but there were no discussions by the distributing corporation or the controlled corporation with the acquirer regarding a distribution on or before the date of the first public announcement regarding the distribution. To assure that this safe harbor is not available for acquisitions by a person who could participate in the decision to effect a distribution, it does not apply to acquisitions by a person that was a controlling shareholder or a 10% shareholder of the acquired corporation at any time during the period beginning immediately after the acquisition and ending on the date of the distribution. The safe harbor is also unavailable if the acquisition occurs in connection with a transaction in which the aggregate acquisitions represent 20% or more (by vote or value) of the stock of the acquired distributing corporation.

6. A distribution and an acquisition involving a public offering occurring before the distribution if: (1) in the case of an acquisition of stock that is not listed on an established market, the acquisition occurs before the first disclosure event regarding the distribution, or (2) in the case of an acquisition of stock that is listed on an

---

[21] For a further analysis of the efforts to right-size § 355 with the intended scope of Congress' intended repeal of the *General Utilities* doctrine and the remaining discontinuities that need to be addressed, see Bret Wells, Reform of Section 355, 68 Am. U. L. Rev. 101 (2018).

established market, the acquisition occurs before the date of the first public announcement regarding the distribution. This safe harbor is based on the view that a public offering and a distribution are not likely to be part of a plan if the acquirers in the offering are unaware that a distribution will occur.

7.   An acquisition (other than through a public offering) of stock of the distributing or controlled corporation that is listed on an established market that occurs because of transfers involving shareholders of distributing or controlled who are not controlling shareholders (5% shareholders who participate in management) or 10% shareholders. This safe harbor is not available if the transferor or transferee of the stock is a corporation that is controlled by the acquired corporation, is a member of a controlled group that includes the acquired corporation, or is an underwriter with respect to the acquisition.

8.   An acquisition of stock by an employee, director, or independent contractor in connection with the performance of services. The safe harbor does not apply to acquisitions by controlling shareholders or 10% shareholders.

9.   Certain acquisitions by qualified pension or retirement plans.

Section 355(e) may well be considered the wrong solution to a problem that does not exist. Nonetheless, the presumption that an acquisition and distribution within two-years of each other are part of a plan is contained in statutory language. Consider whether it is appropriate for the Treasury Department to write the presumption out of the statute by Regulations where Treasury thinks the provision does not represent good policy.

1.3. *Corporate Level Issues*

Even though § 355(e) requires corporate level recognition of gain with respect to stock in transactions that otherwise qualify for nonrecognition under § 355, nonrecognition at the shareholder level is still the order of the day. What is the precise tax policy justification for § 355(e)? Section 355(e) can, and often will, apply even though neither the distributing corporation nor the distributed corporation has itself received any consideration, let alone any cash consideration, and the only consideration that the shareholders have received is stock in one or more corporations. Furthermore, none of the assets held in corporate solution has received a step-up in basis. Given these parameters, why should the distributing corporation recognize gain with respect to the stock of the distributed corporation?

Nevertheless, customizing spin-offs do have the potential for abuse. Assume, for example, that T manufactures toys and airplanes. P wants to acquire the airplane business, but not the toy business, and is willing to pay in stock and deferred cash. To effectuate the transaction, T borrows an amount equal to one-half of the negotiated purchase price. T then contributes the cash and the toy business to S, which is spun-off to the T shareholders. Thereafter, T, which retained the liability for the borrowed money that has been transferred to S, is merged into P, and the T shareholders (who also are the S shareholders) receive P stock. Since S holds cash equal to one half of the total consideration effectively provided by P, the transaction has significant overtones of a sale of the airplane division at the corporate level. If this perceived abuse is the real problem with which Congress was concerned, could it have drafted a more narrowly targeted remedy?

Another strange aspect of § 355(e) is the measure of gain. Regardless of whether the distributing corporation or the controlled corporation is the corporation that is subsequently acquired, the recognized gain is measured with reference to the stock of the controlled corporation.[22] This might be a reasonable measure of the gain to be recognized in cases where the controlled corporation is the subsequently acquired corporation. If, however, the distributing corporation is the corporation that is acquired, as in the above example, it is difficult to understand why Congress considered the proper measure of gain to be the appreciation in the stock of the controlled corporation, which is retained by the shareholders of the acquired target corporation.

1.3.1.   *Section 336(e) Election*

A distribution subject to either § 355(d) (50% shareholder with disqualified stock), or § 355(e) carries the potential for gain recognition at three levels: gain recognized by the distributing corporation on distribution of the stock of the controlled corporation, gain recognized by the controlled corporation on disposition of appreciated assets, and gain recognized by the shareholders of the controlled corporation. Section 336(e) provides in the case of a sale or distribution of stock representing control under § 1504(a)(2) (80% of voting stock and value), the selling or distributing corporation may elect to treat the sale or distribution as a sale of the assets of the distributed corporation rather than as a stock sale. Section 336(e) is discussed in Chapter 8. Treas.Reg. § 1.336–2(b)(2) provides rules for a § 336(e) election when the distributing corporation distributes stock of the controlled corporation representing control under § 1504(a)(2) (a "qualified stock disposition") and is required to recognize its realized gain under § 355(d) or (e). If a § 336(e) election is made by the distributing corporation, the controlled corporation is deemed to have sold its assets in a taxable transaction to an unrelated person for an aggregate deemed asset disposition price (Treas.Reg. § 1.336–3), which, in general, reflects the net fair market value of the assets plus liabilities grossed-up to reflect non-recently disposed-of stock. The gain or loss is recognized while the controlled corporation is controlled by the distributing corporation.

Net losses from the deemed asset sale are recognized only in relation to the amount of stock sold or exchanged in the qualified stock disposition during the 12-month disposition period. Treas.Reg. § 1.336–2(b)(2)(i)(B)(2)(iii). However, if the controlled corporation has any subsidiaries for which a § 336(e) election is made, the general deemed asset disposition methodology shall apply. This prevents taxpayers from

---

[22] If the controlled corporation was formed in a § 368(a)(1)(D) reorganization in contemplation of the distribution, § 368(a)(2)(H)(ii) preserves the tax-free status of that transaction even if the distributing corporation's shareholders dispose of the stock of the controlled corporation in a transaction subject to § 355(e).

effectively electing whether the attributes of the lower tier subsidiary become those of target, by doing an actual sale of target subsidiary's assets followed by a liquidation of target subsidiary, or remain with target subsidiary, by making a § 336(e) election for target subsidiary.

The controlled corporation is deemed to have repurchased its assets for an amount equal to the adjusted grossed basis, determined under the rules of Treas.Reg. § 1.338–5. Treas.Reg. § 1.336–2(b)(2)(ii). The controlled corporation is not deemed to liquidate into the distributing corporation but is treated as acquiring all of its assets from an unrelated person, and the distributing corporation is treated as distributing the stock of the controlled corporation to its shareholders. Treas.Reg. § 1.336–2(b)(2)(i)(A). Because the controlled corporation is not treated as liquidating, it retains its tax attributes despite the § 336(e) election. Furthermore, the controlled corporation will take into account the effects of the deemed asset disposition to adjust its earnings and profits immediately before allocating earnings and profits pursuant to Treas.Reg. § 1.312–10. Treas.Reg. § 1.336–2(b)(2)(vi).

The distributing corporation does not recognize gain or loss on the qualified stock disposition of the stock of the controlled corporation. Treas.Reg. § 1.336–2(b)(2)(iii). The deemed sale and repurchase of assets by the controlled corporation does not cause the distribution to fail the requirements of § 355. Treas.Reg. § 1.336–2(b)(2)(v).

1.4. *Shareholder Level Issues*

In Rev.Rul. 96–30, 1996–1 C.B. 36, obsoleted by Rev.Rul. 98–27, 1998–1 C.B. 1159, D Corporation distributed the stock of a controlled subsidiary, C Corporation, to its shareholders. Soon after the distribution, Y Corporation proposed to acquire C Corporation, and subsequently C Corporation was merged into Y Corporation in a tax-free merger in which the former C Corporation shareholders received 25% of the stock of Y Corporation. No negotiations had occurred between D Corporation and Y Corporation, and the C Corporation shareholders were free to vote their stock as they saw fit. The IRS ruled that the step transaction doctrine must be applied to determine whether the substance of the transaction was the same as its form or whether in substance C Corporation had been merged into Y Corporation prior to the distribution by D Corporation, followed by a constructive distribution by D Corporation to its shareholders of the Y Corporation stock received in the merger. In the latter case, the transaction would not have qualified under § 355. Based on the facts and circumstances, particularly the fact that there had been no pre-distribution negotiations regarding the acquisition of C Corporation by Y Corporation, the IRS ruled that the form of the transaction would be respected and § 355 thus applied.

Following the enactment of § 355(e), in Rev.Rul. 98–27, 1998–1 C.B. 1159, the IRS obsoleted Rev.Rul. 96–30. Rev.Rul. 98–27 states that the IRS will no longer apply *Court Holding Company* principles (or any other variant of the step transaction doctrine) to determine whether for purposes of § 355(a) the distributed corporation qualifies as a controlled corporation solely because of any post-distribution acquisition or restructuring of the distributed corporation, whether prearranged or not. According to the ruling, any implication that § 355(a) restricts post-distribution acquisitions or restructurings of a controlled corporation is inconsistent with § 355(e) and its legislative history (citing H.R.Rep. No. 105–220, at 529–30). In applying the step transaction doctrine to divisive transactions for other purposes, however, the IRS will continue to consider all facts and circumstances.

2.   ASPECTS OF SECTION 355(f)

2.1. *Background*

The effect of § 355(e), which triggers gain to the distributing corporation if it applies, is rather straightforward. The effect of § 335(f), which removes the transaction from the ambit of § 355 entirely, however, is not so clear. Section 355(f) provides that a transaction is not subject to § 355 when the distributee shareholders are one or more corporations that are members of the same affiliated group of corporations as the distributing and controlled corporations and the transaction is part of a plan to transfer ownership as described in § 355(e)(2). Special rules control the taxation of the distribution even though § 355 does not apply. The precise treatment of the transaction depends on whether or not the corporations involved in the transaction file consolidated returns, which are discussed in Chapter 15.

2.2. *Effect of Section 355(f)*

If the corporations involved in the transaction do not file consolidated returns, the distributing corporation generally must recognize gain (but not loss) under § 311 with respect to the distributed stock of the controlled corporation. (If, however, the distributing corporation liquidates as part of the transaction, § 337 may provide nonrecognition of gain or loss with respect to the stock of the controlled corporation.) The distributee corporation recognizes dividend income equal to the fair market value of the stock, but the income item is entirely offset by a 100% dividends received deduction under § 243. Nevertheless, pursuant to § 301(d), the distributee corporation takes a fair market value basis in the stock of the controlled corporation. The distributee corporation's basis in the distributing corporation stock that it continues to hold is not affected. See I.R.C. § 1059(e)(2). Thus, whether the distributing corporation or the controlled corporation is acquired after the spin-off, the tax consequence of the spin-off is limited to recognition of gain by the distributing corporation with respect to the controlled corporation's stock.

PROBLEM SET 7

1.   Reconsider problem 2 from Problem Set 5 in Section 3. Even if the distribution qualifies under § 355(a), is any aspect of it nevertheless taxable?

2.   Reconsider problem 3 from Problem Set 5 in Section 3. Even if the distribution qualifies under § 355(a), is any aspect of it nevertheless taxable?

3.   In October of last year, the management of D Corp., which is publicly traded, decided to spin-off C Corp., one of D Corp.'s many operating subsidiaries. C Corp.'s manufacturing operations produced toxic waste, and an investment banker had advised D Corp. that divesting itself of C Corp. would enhance the long-run value of D Corp. and provide it with better access

to public capital markets. D Corp. completed the spin-off of C Corp. in March. In which, if any of the following circumstances, must D Corp. recognize gain with respect to the C Corp. stock?

(a) (1) In February of this year, P Corp. approached the D Corp. management with a proposal to acquire D Corp., conditional on the spin-off of C Corp., which was scheduled to occur the following month. D Corp.'s management agreed to consider the offer. In May, D Corp.'s management made a counter proposal to P Corp. regarding the terms of the proposed acquisition, and P Corp.'s management agreed to the counter-offer. Following shareholder approval, D Corp. was acquired by P Corp. in August of this year in a reverse triangular merger pursuant to which the D Corp. shareholders received P Corp. stock that constituted 45% of the outstanding stock of P Corp.

(2) Would your answer change if D Corp. shareholders received P Corp. stock that constituted 52% of the outstanding stock of P Corp?

(b) In January of last year, P Corp. approached the D Corp. management with a proposal to acquire D Corp. In February of last year, D Corp.'s management made a counter proposal to P Corp. regarding the terms of the proposed acquisition, which P Corp. rejected. D Corp. completed the spin-off of C Corp. in March of this year. In October of this year, P Corp. approached the D Corp. management with a new proposal to acquire D Corp., at a higher price than in the proposal made last year, and D Corp.'s management agreed to the offer. Following shareholder approval, D Corp. was acquired by P Corp. in December of this year in a reverse triangular merger pursuant to which the D Corp. shareholders received P Corp. stock that constituted 45% of the outstanding stock of P Corp.

(c) In November of last year, P Corp. approached the D Corp. management with a proposal to acquire D Corp. D Corp.'s management agreed to the offer. Following shareholder approval, D Corp. was acquired by P Corp. in January of this year in a reverse triangular merger pursuant to which the D Corp. shareholders received P Corp. stock that constituted 45% of the outstanding stock of P Corp.

PART IV

CORPORATE ATTRIBUTES IN REORGANIZATIONS AND OTHER TRANSACTIONS

CHAPTER 13

CARRY OVER AND LIMITATION OF CORPORATE TAX ATTRIBUTES

SECTION 1.   CARRY OVER OF TAX ATTRIBUTES

INTERNAL REVENUE CODE: Section 381.
REGULATIONS: Section 1.381(a)–1(a), (b)(1) and (2).

Commissioner v. Sansome
United States Court of Appeals, Second Circuit, 1932.
60 F.2d 931.

[In 1921 Corporation X transferred all its assets to newly formed Corporation Y in return for all of the latter's stock, which went to the Corporation X shareholders. Corporation X had a large amount of earnings and profits. Corporation Y did not earn profits after its formation but instead suffered some losses. Corporation Y then made cash distributions in 1923 which under the applicable statute, § 201 of the 1921 Act, were taxable if those distributions were out of "its earnings and profits." If the earnings and profits of Corporation X were taken into account, then the distributions would be taxable. The 1921 transaction was a reorganization under the applicable statute, § 202(c)(2) of the 1921 Act.]

■ L. HAND, CIRCUIT JUDGE. * * * It seems to us that [§ 202(c)(2) of the 1921 Act] should be read as a gloss upon [§ 201 of the 1921 Act]. That section provides for cases of corporate "reorganization" which shall not result in any "gain or loss" to the shareholder participating in them, and it defines them with some particularity. He must wait until he has disposed of the new shares, and use his original cost as the "base" to subtract from what he gets upon the sale. Such a change in the form of the shares is "an exchange of property," not a "sale or other disposition" of them * * *. It appears to us extremely unlikely that what was not "recognized" as a sale or disposition for the purpose of fixing gain or loss, should be "recognized" as changing accumulated profits into capital in a section which so far overlapped the latter. That in substance declared that some corporate transactions should not break the continuity of the corporate life, a troublesome question that the courts had beclouded by recourse to such vague alternatives as "form" and "substance," anodynes for the pains of reasoning. The effort was at least to narrow the limits of judicial inspiration, and we cannot think that the same issue was left at large in the earlier section. Hence we hold that a corporate reorganization which results in no "gain or loss" under [§ 202(c)(2) of the 1921 Act], does not toll the company's life as a continued venture under [§ 201 of the 1921 Act], and that what were "earnings or profits" of the original * * * company remain, for purposes of distribution, "earnings and profits" of the successor * * *.

Order reversed; cause remanded for further proceedings in accord with the foregoing.

DETAILED ANALYSIS

1. GENERAL

The *Sansome* doctrine respecting earnings and profits is but one facet of the larger problem of the extent to which the acquiring corporation is to be regarded as succeeding to the tax characteristics, benefits, and obligations possessed by the transferor corporation, where both are parties to a tax-free reorganization. Prior to 1954, the rules regarding carry over of corporate attributes were found mainly in court decisions.

Section 381, enacted in 1954, contains detailed but non-exclusive statutory rules regarding the carry over of items in corporate liquidations and reorganizations in which the acquiring corporation steps into the shoes of the transferor or distributing corporation. Under § 381(a), corporate attributes carry over on the liquidation of a controlled subsidiary in which the parent takes the basis of the subsidiary's assets pursuant to § 332 and § 334(b), discussed in Chapter 7, and in type (A), (C), and (F) reorganizations and nondivisive type (D) and (G) reorganizations, discussed in Chapter 10. In general, § 381 applies to transactions in which the transferor corporation is absorbed by the acquiring corporation in a tax free transaction, such as a reorganization. Section 381 does not apply to taxable acquisitions, for example, a "cash merger."

Under Treas.Reg. § 1.381(a)–1(b)(2), the acquiring corporation that succeeds to tax attributes of the transferor is the corporation that acquires directly or indirectly all of the assets transferred by the transferor. Under the regulations, there may be only one acquiring corporation. Thus, if X Corporation acquires all of the assets of T in a type (C) reorganization and thereafter transfers one-half of the assets to its wholly owned subsidiary, S1 and the remaining one-half of the T assets to a wholly owned subsidiary S2, X, as the corporation that first acquired all of T's assets, is treated as the acquiring corporation so that neither S1 nor S2 succeeds to T's corporate attributes. See Treas.Reg. § 1.381(a)–1(b)(2)(ii), Ex. (4).

2. CARRY OVER OF EARNINGS AND PROFITS

Sections 381(a) and 381(c)(2) provide in general that, for the transactions covered under § 381(a), the earnings and profits, or deficit in earnings and profits, of the transferor or distributing corporation carry over to the acquiring corporation, but that any deficit in earnings and profits of the corporations involved shall be used only to offset earnings and profits accumulated after the date of transfer or distribution. Treas.Reg.

§ 1.381(c)(2)–1(a)(5). Thus, a deficit earnings account of one corporation cannot be used to offset pre-transfer accumulated earnings of the other. Treas.Reg. § 1.381(c)(2)–1(a)(2). If both corporations either have accumulated earnings, or a deficit in accumulated earnings, the earnings and profits accounts are consolidated into a single account in the surviving corporation. Treas.Reg. § 1.381(c)(2)–1(a)(4). Treas.Reg. § 1.381(c)(2)–1(a)(2) also provides that earnings and profits inherited by the acquiring corporation become part of its accumulated earnings and profits, but not part of current earnings and profits for purposes of § 316(a)(2).

The rule that a deficit in accumulated earnings can offset only profits accumulated after the date of transfer requires identification of the transfer date. Treas.Reg. § 1.381(b)–1(b)(1) provides that the relevant date is the date on which the transfer is finally completed. Treas.Reg. § 1.381(b)–1(b)(2) and (3) also allow the taxpayer to specify a transfer date by filing a statement indicating the date on which substantially all of the assets of the transferor are transferred and the transferor has ceased business operations.

Treas.Reg. § 1.381(a)–1(b)(2) provides that for purposes of determining the corporation that succeeds to the target corporation's tax attributes, including earnings and profits, in a tax-free reorganization, the acquiring corporation is the corporation that, pursuant to the plan of reorganization, directly acquires the assets transferred by the transferor corporation, even if that corporation ultimately retains none of the assets so transferred. According to the preamble to the Proposed Regulations (which were largely unchanged when finalized in 2014):

> The [prior] regulations under section 381 yield an identical result, except when a single controlled subsidiary of the direct transferee corporation acquires all of the assets transferred by the transferor corporation pursuant to a plan of reorganization. In that case, the [prior] regulations treat the subsidiary as the acquiring corporation, a result that effectively permits a taxpayer to choose the location of a transferor corporation's attributes by causing the direct transferee corporation either to retain or not to retain a single asset. The IRS and the Treasury Department believe the [amended provision] produces more appropriate results because it . . . eliminate[s] this electivity.

Acquiring Corporation for Purposes of Section 381, 79 F.R. 26190 (May 7, 2014).

Treas.Reg. § 1.381(c)(2)–1(c) requires an adjustment to the earnings and profits of the transferor corporation to reflect distributions. In the case of a reorganization in which the transferor distributes other property along with stock or securities allowed to be received under § 354 without recognition of gain, the earnings and profits of the transferor corporation as of the transfer date are reduced by the amount attributable to the distribution. In the case of a liquidation of the transferor corporation under § 332, the earnings and profits of the transferor must be adjusted to account for distributions of property to minority stockholders. In both cases, the adjustments are required whether the distributions are made before or after the transfer date.

3. CARRY OVER OF NET OPERATING LOSSES

3.1. *General*

Net operating losses are probably the most significant corporate tax attribute affected by § 381. Section 172(a) now provides that a net operating loss carryforward is allowed to create a deduction in the carryforward year in an amount equal to the lesser of the aggregate of the net operating loss carryovers or 80% of taxable income in the carryforward year. Thus, a limitation is imposed within § 172(a) on the amount of a net operating loss carryforward that can be used to only 80% of the corporation's taxable income before the allowance of the net operating loss carryforward. Section 382 also imposes a limitation on the use of tax attributes after an ownership change. Although an explicit ordering rule is not provided, it would seem that the taxpayer should subject its net operating losses to the limits afforded under Section 172(a) first and then should apply the further limitation on the usage of a net operating loss under § 382 thereafter. In addition, § 172(b)(1) provides that the net operating loss carryforward can be carried forward indefinitely, but in a change from prior law the net operating can generally no longer be carried back. The inability to carry back a net operating loss curtails the ameliorative effects of the net operating loss provisions in a fact pattern where a corporation has income and then sustains losses during a trough in its business cycle.

Section 381(c)(1) allows the transfer of an acquired corporation's net operating loss carryover to the acquiring corporation in a transaction covered by § 381(a), but limits the carryover to taxable income of the acquiring corporation attributable to the period following the transfer date. If the transfer date is any day other than the last day of the acquiring corporation's taxable year, the taxable year of the acquiring corporation is divided into two periods, and taxable income is allocated to each period on a daily basis. An inherited loss carryover may be deducted by the acquiring corporation in the year of the transfer only against income allocated to the period subsequent to the transfer date. This rule results in the creation of two separate years for carryover purposes; one carryover year for the transferor corporation ending on the transfer date, and a second period ending on the last day of the acquiring corporation's taxable year.

If the acquiring corporation acquires several loss corporations during a taxable year, the taxable year of the acquiring corporation will be divided into several short periods, one for the transfer date of each acquisition. Treas.Reg. § 1.381(c)(1)–2(b)(2). If the transfer occurs on the last day of the acquiring corporation's taxable year, the inherited loss carryover may be used only in subsequent taxable years.

Even though § 381 provides for the carryover of net operating losses to the acquiring corporation, § 382, discussed in Section 2, restricts the rate at which those losses may be claimed against post-acquisition income, including income that is derived from the business of the acquired corporation.

The taxable year of the transferor corporation ends on the transfer date. I.R.C. § 381(b)(1). The 2017 Tax Act repealed the net operating loss carryback (with narrow exceptions for farming losses and certain insurance companies). Even should it be reinstated, under § 381(b)(3), net operating losses of the acquiring corporation may not be carried back to taxable years of the transferor corporation preceding the transfer date, except in an (F) reorganization.

3.2. *Liquidation of a Worthless Subsidiary*

In the case of a parent-subsidiary relationship, there is an interplay between § 381 and § 165(g)(3). If § 332 applies to the liquidation of a controlled subsidiary, § 381 provides that the subsidiary's tax attributes are carried over to the parent. However, § 332 does not apply to the liquidation of an 80% controlled subsidiary unless some assets of the liquidating subsidiary are allocable to the common stock after payment of all creditors and preferred stockholders including the parent. If the common stock of the subsidiary is worthless, then § 332 is not applicable and § 381(a) does not permit a carry over of net operating losses. See Rev.Rul. 68–359, 1968–2 C.B. 161; Rev.Rul. 68–602, 1968–2 C.B. 135. However, if the subsidiary was operating a business, § 165 applies to give the parent an ordinary loss on its stock and security investment in the subsidiary where the parent directly or indirectly owns at least 80% of the aggregate voting power and 80% of the aggregate value of the subsidiary, excluding nonvoting stock that is limited and preferred as to dividends and liquidating distributions. In this context, the term "securities" means any debt obligation that is in registered form or with interest coupons.[1] If the debt obligation is not a security, an ordinary loss still results under § 166. These ordinary losses in turn can create loss carryovers for the parent under § 172. If § 165(g)(3) does not apply, the parent's worthless stock and security losses are capital losses.

In Marwais Steel Co. v. Commissioner, 354 F.2d 997 (9th Cir.1965), a subsidiary corporation borrowed operating capital from its parent and incurred net operating losses. The parent claimed bad debt deductions with respect to loans made to the subsidiary. The subsidiary was subsequently liquidated and the parent attempted to use the subsidiary's net operating losses under § 381. Despite the literal satisfaction of § 381, the court denied the carryover since the net operating losses had formed the rationale for the previous bad debt deductions, and a double deduction was not permitted. But in Textron, Inc. v. United States, 561 F.2d 1023 (1st Cir.1977), a parent corporation was allowed to claim a deduction for the worthless stock of its subsidiary despite the fact that the subsidiary was subsequently able to acquire a new profitable business and use its net operating loss carryovers to offset the income from the new business. Section 382(g)(4)(D) now limits the use of net operating losses in a *Textron*-type situation.

4.   CAPITAL LOSS CARRYOVERS

Under § 381(c)(3), the transferor's excess capital losses carry over to the acquiring corporation on much the same terms as net operating losses. The inherited capital loss carryover becomes a capital loss carryover of the

---

[1]   Securities rarely are issued in bearer form with interest coupons. See Chapter 3.

acquiring corporation for purposes of § 1212, the capital loss carryover provision. The transferor's capital losses are available to the acquiring corporation in the acquiring corporation's first taxable year ending after the transfer date. I.R.C. § 381(c)(3)(A). The amount of the transferor's capital loss that can be utilized by the acquiring corporation in the year of the transfer is limited to the proportion of the acquiring corporation's capital gain net income that is allocable on a daily basis to the portion of the acquiring corporation's taxable year remaining after the transfer date. I.R.C. § 381(c)(3)(B). In addition, under § 381(b)(3), any net capital loss of the acquiring corporation incurred after the transfer date cannot be carried back to offset capital gain net income of the transferor derived in a taxable year ending on or prior to the transfer date.

5.   CARRY OVER OF OTHER ATTRIBUTES

In addition to earnings and profits and loss carryovers, § 381(c) lists a number of separate corporate attributes that carry over in a transaction described by § 381(a). Several of these provisions deal with accounting issues. In general, § 381(c)(4) provides for continuation of the transferor's method of accounting, but authorizes Regulations to prescribe the method to be used if the parties to the transfer use different methods. Under Treas.Reg. § 1.381(c)(4)–1(b)(2), if the acquiring corporation maintains the assets of the transferor as a separate and distinct trade or business, the acquiring corporation must continue to use the accounting method of the transferor with respect to that trade or business. If the transferor's assets are integrated into a trade or business of the acquiring corporation, the acquiring corporation must adopt whichever accounting method is determined to be the "principal method of accounting" based on a comparison of the relative asset bases and gross receipts of the component businesses immediately preceding the transfer date. Treas.Reg. § 1.381(c)(4)–1(b)(2), (c). In any event, the method adopted must clearly reflect income of the acquiring corporation, and the acquiring corporation may apply for permission from the IRS to adopt a different method of accounting. Any change in a method of accounting under these provisions may require adjustments under § 481, which is intended to avoid double counting of income and deduction items. A method of accounting for purposes of § 381(c)(4) includes, under § 446, the accounting treatment of any material item of income or deduction in addition to the taxpayer's overall method of accounting. Treas.Reg. § 1.381(c)(4)–1(b)(1); § 1.446–1(e)(2)(ii)(*a*). Thus, § 381(c)(4) applies broadly to numerous items not specifically enumerated in § 381(c).

Several accounting matters are specifically described in § 381(c): inventory accounting carries over under rules similar to accounting methods, § 381(c)(5); the acquiring corporation inherits the transferor's depreciation and capital recovery elections and methods, § 381(c)(6); the transferor's installment sales reporting continues without change, § 381(c)(8); amortization of premium and discount on the transferor's bonds for which the acquiring corporation becomes liable are reported by the acquiring corporation as they would have been by the transferor, § 381(c)(9); and the acquiring corporation is entitled to the benefits of § 111 with respect to the recovery of items previously deducted by the transferor, § 381(c)(12).

The acquiring corporation steps directly into the shoes of the transferor with respect to some deduction and credit items: the acquiring corporation may deduct contributions to employee benefit plans under § 404, § 381(c)(11); the acquiring corporation inherits an obligation to replace property involuntarily converted if nonrecognition treatment was claimed by the transferor under § 1033, § 381(c)(13); the acquiring corporation becomes entitled to general business credit carryovers and is potentially liable for credit recapture, § 381(c)(24); and the acquiring corporation becomes entitled to the transferor's § 53 credit for prior year alternative minimum tax liability, § 381(c)(25).

Section 381(c)(16) allows the acquiring corporation to deduct payments of liabilities that result from obligations of the transferor that are assumed by the acquiring corporation if the liability would have been deductible by the transferor if paid by it. This provision permits the acquiring corporation to avoid capitalization of such liabilities as part of the cost of the acquired assets. However, § 381(c)(16) provides that deductibility is available only if the assumed obligation is not reflected in the amount of stock or securities transferred by the acquiring corporation for the assets of the transferor. Treas.Reg. § 1.381(c)(16)–1(a)(5) provides that if the liability is known at the time of transfer, and the amount of consideration transferred by the acquiring corporation is reduced to account for the liability, the liability will be treated as reflected in the stock transfer. Otherwise, it is presumed that a liability is not reflected in the consideration transferred. Treas.Reg. § 1.381(c)(16)–1(a)(1) provides that a liability not subject to § 381(c)(16) is subject to the general accounting provision of § 381(c)(4). Although this reference may be read to require that a liability assumed as part of the consideration for the acquisition must be capitalized, that is not necessarily the case. In Rev.Rul. 83–73, 1983–1 C.B. 84, the taxpayer acquired the assets of Y Corporation in a type (A) reorganization. The assets were subject to an outstanding contingent claim against Y which the taxpayer settled for $700x. Pursuant to an agreement entered into at the time of the reorganization, the former stockholders of Y reimbursed the taxpayer for $500x. The $500x reimbursement was based on the taxpayer's cost of settling the claim, taking into account the taxpayer's § 162 deduction for the payment. The IRS held that, because of the former stockholders' indemnity agreement, the contingent liability was reflected in the consideration given for the transfer of the assets. Thus, payment of the liability was not covered by § 381(c)(16). The ruling further held, however, that the $500x reimbursement from Y's former stockholders was to be deemed a nontaxable contribution by them to Y's capital, and that the taxpayer's satisfaction of the claim was deductible under Y's accounting method which carried over to the taxpayer under § 381(c)(4) and Treas.Reg. § 1.381(c)(4)–1(a)(1).

PROBLEM SET 1

1.   X Corp. acquired Y Corp. in a type (A) merger. Immediately before the merger, X Corp. had accumulated earning and profits of $1,000,000, and Y Corp. had a negative accumulated earnings and profits account of $1,100,000. During the year of the merger, neither X Corp. nor Y Corp. had

any current earnings and profits. If X Corp. distributes $200,000 to its shareholders after the merger, how much of the distribution is a dividend? Does it matter whether a shareholder always held X Corp. stock or whether the shareholder is a former Y Corp. shareholder who acquired the X Corp. stock in the merger?

2.   (a)   The year after X Corp. acquired Y Corp. (in problem 1), X Corp. had current earnings and profits of $600,000; it made no distributions. What is its accumulated earnings and profits account at the end of the first year after the merger?

(b)   Alternatively, the year after X Corp. acquired Y Corp. (in problem 1), X Corp. lost $600,000. What is its accumulated earnings and profits account at the end of the first year after the merger?

SECTION 2.   LIMITATIONS ON NET OPERATING LOSS CARRYOVERS FOLLOWING A CHANGE IN CORPORATE OWNERSHIP

INTERNAL REVENUE CODE: Sections 382; 383; 384; 269.

REGULATIONS: Section 1.382–2T(a)(1) and (a)(2)(i).

General Explanation of the Tax Reform Act of 1986
Staff of the Joint Committee on Taxation 288–299 (1987).

Overview

In general, a corporate taxpayer is allowed to carry a net operating loss ("NOL(s)") forward for deduction in a future taxable year, as long as the corporation's legal identity is maintained. After certain nontaxable asset acquisitions in which the acquired corporation goes out of existence, the acquired corporation's NOL carryforwards are inherited by the acquiring corporation. Similar rules apply to tax attributes other than NOLs, such as net capital losses and unused tax credits. Historically, the use of NOL and other carryforwards has been subject to special limitations after specified transactions involving the corporation in which the carryforwards arose (referred to as the "loss corporation"). [Pre-1986] law also provided other rules that were intended to limit tax-motivated acquisitions of loss corporations.

The operation of the special limitations on the use of carryforwards turned on whether the transaction that caused the limitations to apply took the form of a taxable sale or exchange of stock in the loss corporation or one of certain specified tax-free reorganizations in which the loss corporation's tax attributes carried over to a corporate successor. After a purchase (or other taxable acquisition) of a controlling stock interest in a loss corporation, NOL and other carryforwards were disallowed unless the loss corporation continued to conduct its historical trade or business. In the case of a tax-free reorganization, NOL and other carryforwards were generally allowed in full if the loss corporation's shareholders received stock representing at least 20 percent of the value of the acquiring corporation.

NOL and other carryforwards

Although the Federal income tax system generally requires an annual accounting, a corporate taxpayer was allowed to carry NOLs back to the three taxable years preceding the loss and then forward to each of the 15 taxable years following the loss year (sec. 172). [Eds.: The 2017 Tax Act repealed the NOL carryback and added an indefinite carryforward. Narrow exceptions apply in the case of farming losses and for certain insurance companies.] The rationale for allowing the deduction of NOL carryforwards (and carrybacks) was that a taxpayer should be able to average income and losses over a period of years to reduce the disparity between the taxation of businesses that have stable income and businesses that experience fluctuations in income.

In addition to NOLs, other tax attributes eligible to be carried back or forward include unused investment tax credits (secs. 30 and 39), excess foreign tax credits (sec. 904(c)), and net capital losses (sec. 1212). Like NOLs, unused investment tax credits were allowed a three-year carryback and a 15-year carryforward. Subject to an overall limitation based on a taxpayer's U.S. tax attributable to foreign-source income, excess foreign tax credits were allowed a two-year carryback and a five-year carryforward. For net capital losses, generally, corporations had a three-year carryback (but only to the extent the carrybacks did not increase or create a NOL) and a five-year carryforward.

NOL and other carryforwards that were not used before the end of a carryforward period expired.

Carryovers to corporate successors

In general, a corporation's tax history (e.g., carryforwards and asset basis) was preserved as long as the corporation's legal identity was continued. Thus, under the general rules of [pre-1986] law, changes in the stock ownership of a corporation did not affect the corporation's tax attributes. Following are examples of transactions that effected ownership changes without altering the legal identity of a corporation:

(1) A taxable purchase of a corporation's stock from its shareholders (a "purchase"),

(2) A type "B" reorganization, in which stock representing control of the acquired corporation is acquired solely in exchange for voting stock of the acquiring corporation (or a corporation in control of the acquiring corporation) (sec. 368(a)(1)(B)),

(3) A transfer of property to a corporation after which the transferors own 80 percent or more of the corporation's stock (a "section 351 exchange"),

(4) A contribution to the capital of a corporation, in exchange for the issuance of stock, and

(5) A type "E" reorganization, in which interests of investors (shareholders and bondholders) are restructured (sec. 368(a)(1)(E)).

Statutory rules also provided for the carry over of tax attributes (including NOL and other carryforwards) from one corporation to another in certain tax-free acquisitions in which the acquired corporation went out of existence (sec. 381). These rules applied if a corporation's assets were acquired by another corporation in one of the following transactions:

(1) The liquidation of an 80-percent owned subsidiary (sec. 332),

(2) A statutory merger or consolidation, or type "A" reorganization (sec. 368(a)(1)(A)),

(3) A type "C" reorganization, in which substantially all of the assets of one corporation is transferred to another corporation in exchange for voting stock, and the transferor completely liquidates (sec. 368(a)(1)(C)),

(4) A "nondivisive D reorganization," in which substantially all of a corporation's assets are transferred to a controlled corporation, and the transferor completely liquidates (secs. 368(a)(1)(D) and 354(b)(1)),

(5) A mere change in identity, form, or place of organization of a single corporation, or type "F" reorganization (sec. 368(a)(1)(F)), and

(6) A type "G" reorganization, in which substantially all of a corporation's assets are transferred to another corporation pursuant to a court approved insolvency or bankruptcy reorganization plan, and stock or securities of the transferee are distributed pursuant to the plan (sec. 368(a)(1)(G)).

In general, to qualify an acquisitive transaction (including a B reorganization) as a tax-free reorganization, the shareholders of the acquired corporation had to retain "continuity of interest." Thus, a principal part of the consideration used by the acquiring corporation had to consist of stock, and the holdings of all shareholders had to be traced. Further, a tax-free reorganization was required to satisfy a "continuity of business enterprise" test. Generally, continuity of business enterprise requires that a significant portion of an acquired corporation's assets be used in a business activity (see Treas.Reg. sec. 1.368–1(d)).

Acquisitions to evade or avoid income tax

The Secretary of the Treasury was authorized to disallow deductions, credits, or other allowances following an acquisition of control of a corporation or a tax-free acquisition of a corporation's assets if the principal purpose of the acquisition was tax avoidance (sec. 269). This provision applied in the following cases:

(1) where any person or persons acquired (by purchase or in a tax-free transaction) at least 50 percent of a corporation's voting stock, or stock representing 50 percent of the value of the corporation's outstanding stock;

(2) where a corporation acquired property from a previously unrelated corporation and the acquiring corporation's basis for the property was determined by reference to the transferor's basis; and

(3) where a corporation purchased the stock of another corporation in a transaction that qualified for elective treatment as a direct asset purchase (sec. 338), a section 338 election was not made, and the acquired corporation was liquidated into the acquiring corporation (under sec. 332).

Treasury regulations under section 269 provided that the acquisition of assets with an aggregate basis that is materially greater than their value (i.e., assets with built-in losses), coupled with the utilization of the basis to create tax-reducing losses, is indicative of a tax-avoidance motive (Treas.Reg. § 1.269–3(c)(1)).

* * *

1954 Code special limitations

The application of the special limitations on NOL carryforwards was triggered under the 1954 Code by specified changes in stock ownership of the loss corporation (sec. 382). In measuring changes in stock ownership, section 382(c) specifically excluded "nonvoting stock which is limited and preferred as to dividends." Different rules were provided for the application of special limitations on the use of carryovers after a purchase and after a tax-free reorganization. Section 382 did not address the treatment of built-in losses.

If the principal purpose of the acquisition of a loss corporation was tax avoidance, section 269 would apply to disallow NOL carryforwards even if section 382 was inapplicable.

* * *

Special limitations on other tax attributes

Section 383 incorporated by reference the same limitations contained in section 382 for carryforwards of investment credits, foreign tax credits, and capital losses.

* * *

Reasons for Change

* * *

Preservation of the averaging function of carryovers

The primary purpose of the special limitations is the preservation of the integrity of the carryover provisions. The carryover provisions perform a needed averaging function by reducing the distortions caused by the annual accounting system. If, on the other hand, carryovers can be transferred in a way that permits a loss to offset unrelated income, no legitimate averaging function is performed. With completely free transferability of tax losses, the carryover provisions become a mechanism for partial recoupment of losses through the tax system. Under such a system, the Federal Government would effectively be required to reimburse a portion of all corporate tax losses. Regardless of the merits of such a reimbursement program, the carryover rules appear to be an inappropriate and inefficient mechanism for delivery of the reimbursement.

Appropriate matching of loss to income

[Amendments to § 382 enacted in 1976 which never became effective] reflect the view that the relationship of one year's loss to another year's income should be largely a function of whether and how much the stock ownership changed in the interim, while the *Libson Shops* business continuation rule[*] measures the relationship according to whether the loss and the income were generated by the same business. The Act acknowledges the merit in both approaches, while seeking to avoid the economic distortions and administrative problems that a strict application of either approach would entail.

A limitation based strictly on ownership would create a tax bias against sales of corporate businesses, and could prevent sales that would increase economic efficiency. For example, if a prospective buyer could increase the income from a corporate business to a moderate extent, but not enough to overcome the loss of all carryovers, no sale would take place because the business would be worth more to the less-efficient current owner than the prospective buyer would reasonably pay. A strict ownership limitation also would distort the measurement of taxable income generated by capital assets purchased before the corporation was acquired, if the tax deductions for capital costs economically allocable to post-acquisition years were accelerated into pre-acquisition years, creating carryovers that would be lost as a result of the acquisition.

Strict application of a business continuation rule would also be undesirable, because it would discourage efforts to rehabilitate troubled businesses. Such a rule would create an incentive to maintain obsolete and inefficient business practices if the needed changes would create the

---

. * [Eds.: In Libson Shops, Inc. v. Koehler, 353 U.S. 382 (1957), the Court held that following a merger of seventeen separate entities (all of which were engaged in the same line of business and owned by the same stockholders) into a single corporation, the loss carryovers of three of the merged entities could not be deducted from the income of the combined enterprise. The Court held that the prior year's loss could be offset against the current year's income only to the extent that income was derived from the operation of substantially the same business that produced the loss. The Court stated that it could find no indication in the legislative history to the predecessor of § 172 that it was intended "to permit the averaging of the pre-merger losses of one business with the post-merger income of some other business which had been operated and taxed separately before the merger."

Maxwell Hardware Company v. Commissioner, 343 F.2d 713 (9th Cir.1965), held that enactment of the predecessor to § 382 in the 1954 Code destroyed the precedential value of *Libson Shops. Maxwell Hardware* was followed in Frederick Steel Co. v. Commissioner, 375 F.2d 351 (6th Cir.1967); Euclid-Tennessee, Inc. v. Commissioner, 352 F.2d 991 (6th Cir.1965); United States v. Adkins-Phelps, Inc., 400 F.2d 737 (8th Cir.1968). However, the IRS announced that it would continue to apply the *Libson Shops* doctrine to any loss carryover case under the 1954 Code where there has been both a 50 percent or more shift in beneficial interests in a loss carryover and a change of business. T.I.R. No. 773, 657 CCH 6751 (1965).]

risk of discontinuing the old business for tax purposes, thus losing the benefit of the carryovers.

Permitting the carry over of all losses following an acquisition, as is permitted under the 1954 Code if the loss business is continued following a purchase, provides an improper matching of income and loss. Income generated under different corporate owners, from capital over and above the capital used in the loss business, is related to a pre-acquisition loss only in the formal sense that it is housed in the same corporate entity. Furthermore, the ability to use acquired losses against such unrelated income creates a tax bias in favor of acquisitions. For example, a prospective buyer of a loss corporation might be a less efficient operator of the business than the current owner, but the ability to use acquired losses could make the loss corporation more valuable to the less efficient user and thereby encourage a sale.

Reflecting the policies described above, the Act addresses three general concerns: (1) the approach of prior law (viz., the disallowance or reduction of NOL and other carryforwards), which is criticized as being too harsh where there are continuing loss-corporation shareholders, and ineffective to the extent that NOL carryforwards may be available for use without limitation after substantial ownership changes, (2) the discontinuities in the prior law treatment of taxable purchases and tax-free reorganizations, and (3) defects in the prior law rules that presented opportunities for tax avoidance.

General approach

After reviewing various options for identifying events that present the opportunity for a tax benefit transfer (e.g., changes in a loss corporation's business), it was concluded that changes in a loss corporation's stock ownership continue to be the best indicator of a potentially abusive transaction. Under the Act, the special limitations generally apply when shareholders who bore the economic burden of a corporation's NOLs no longer hold a controlling interest in the corporation. In such a case, the possibility arises that new shareholders will contribute income-producing assets (or divert income opportunities) to the loss corporation, and the corporation will obtain greater utilization of carryforwards than it could have had there been no change in ownership.

To address the concerns described above, the Act adopts the following approach: After a substantial ownership change, rather than reducing the NOL carryforward itself, the earnings against which an NOL carryforward can be deducted are limited. This general approach has received wide acceptance among tax scholars and practitioners. This "limitation on earnings" approach is intended to permit the survival of NOL carryforwards after an acquisition, while limiting the ability to utilize the carryforwards against unrelated income.

The limitation on earnings approach is intended to approximate the results that would occur if a loss corporation's assets were combined with those of a profitable corporation in a partnership. This treatment can be justified on the ground that the option of contributing assets to a partnership is available to a loss corporation. In such a case, only the loss corporation's share of the partnership's income could be offset by the corporation's NOL carryforward. Presumably, except in the case of tax-motivated partnership agreements, the loss corporation's share of the partnership's income would be limited to earnings generated by the assets contributed by the loss corporation.

For purposes of determining the income attributable to a loss corporation's assets, the Act prescribes an objective rate of return on the value of the corporation's equity. Consideration was given to the arguments made in favor of computing the prescribed rate of return by reference to the gross value of a loss corporation's assets, without regard to outstanding debt. It was concluded that it would be inappropriate to permit the use of NOL carryforwards to shelter earnings that are used (or would be used in the absence of an acquisition) to service a loss corporation's debt. The effect of taking a loss corporation's gross value into account would be to accelerate the rate at which NOL carryforwards would be used had there been no change in ownership, because interest paid on indebtedness is deductible in its own right (thereby deferring the use of a corresponding amount of NOLs). There is a fundamental difference between debt capitalization and equity capitalization: true debt represents a claim against a loss corporation's assets.

Annual limitation

The annual limitation on the use of pre-acquisition NOL carryforwards is the product of the prescribed rate and the value of the loss corporation's equity immediately before a proscribed ownership change. The average yield for long-term marketable obligations of the U.S. government was selected as the measure of a loss corporation's expected return on its assets.

The rate prescribed by the Act is higher than the average rate at which loss corporations actually absorb NOL carryforwards. Indeed, many loss corporations continue to experience NOLs, thereby increasing-rather than absorbing-NOL carryforwards. On the other hand, the adoption of the average absorption rate may be too restrictive for loss corporations that out-perform the average. Therefore, it would be inappropriate to set a rate at the lowest rate that is theoretically justified. The use of the long-term rate for Federal obligations was justified as a reasonable risk-free rate of return a loss corporation could obtain in the absence of a change in ownership.

Anti-abuse rules

The mechanical rules described above could present unintended tax-planning opportunities and might foster certain transactions that many would perceive to be violative of the legislative intent. Therefore, the Act includes several rules that are designed to prevent taxpayers from circumventing the special limitations or otherwise appearing to traffic in loss corporations by (1) reducing a loss corporation's assets to cash or other passive assets and then selling off a corporate shell consisting primarily of NOLs and cash or other passive assets, or (2) making pre-acquisition infusions of assets to inflate artificially a loss corporation's value (and thereby accelerate the use of NOL carryforwards). In addition, the Act retains the prior law principles that are intended to limit tax-motivated acquisitions of loss corporations (e.g., section 269), relating to acquisitions to evade or avoid taxes * * *.

* * *

Continuity-of-business enterprise

The requirement under the 1954 Code rules that a loss corporation continue substantially the same business after a purchase presented potentially difficult definitional issues. Specifically, taxpayers and the courts were required to determine at what point a change in merchandise, location, size, or the use of assets should be treated as a change in the loss corporation's business. It was also difficult to identify a particular business where assets and activities were constantly combined, separated, or rearranged. Further, there was a concern that the prior law requirement induced taxpayers to continue uneconomic businesses.

The Act eliminates the business-continuation rule. The continuity-of-business-enterprise rule generally applicable to tax-free reorganizations also applies to taxable transactions.

* * *

Built-in gains and losses

Built-in losses should be subject to special limitations because they are economically equivalent to pre-acquisition NOL carryforwards. If built-in losses were not subject to limitations, taxpayers could reduce or eliminate the impact of the general rules by causing a loss corporation (following an ownership change) to recognize its built-in losses free of the special limitations (and then invest the proceeds in assets similar to the assets sold).

The Act also provides relief for loss corporations with built-in gain assets. Built-in gains are often the product of special tax provisions that accelerate deductions or defer income (e.g., accelerated depreciation or installment sales reporting). Absent a special rule, the use of NOL carryforwards to offset built-in gains recognized after an acquisition would be limited, even though the carryforwards would have been fully available to offset such gains had the gains been recognized before the change in ownership occurred. (Similarly, a partnership is required to allocate built-in gain or loss to the contributing partner.)

Although the special treatment of built-in gains and losses may require valuations of a loss corporation's assets, the Act limits the circumstances in which valuations will be required by providing a generous de minimis rule.

* * *

Explanation of Provisions

Overview

The Act alters the character of the special limitations on the use of NOL carryforwards. After an ownership change, as described below, the taxable income of a loss corporation available for offset by pre-acquisition NOL carryforwards is limited annually to a prescribed rate times the value of the loss corporation's stock immediately before the ownership change. In addition, NOL carryforwards are disallowed entirely unless the loss corporation satisfies continuity-of-business enterprise requirements for the two-year period following any ownership change. The Act also expands the scope of the special limitations to include built-in losses and allows loss corporations to take into account built-in gains. The Act includes numerous technical changes and several anti-avoidance rules. Finally, the Act applies similar rules to carryforwards other than NOLs, such as net capital losses and excess foreign tax credits.

Ownership change

The special limitations apply after any ownership change. An ownership change occurs, in general, if the percentage of stock of the new loss corporation owned by any one or more 5-percent shareholders (described below) has increased by more than 50 percentage points relative to the lowest percentage of stock of the old loss corporation owned by those 5-percent shareholders at any time during the testing period (generally a three-year period) (new sec. 382(g)(1)).[27] The determination of whether an ownership change has occurred is made by aggregating the increases in percentage ownership for each 5-percent shareholder whose percentage ownership has increased during the testing period. For this purpose, all stock owned by persons who own less than five percent of a corporation's stock generally is treated as stock owned by a single 5-percent shareholder (new sec. 382(g)(4)(A)). The determination of whether an ownership change has occurred is made after any owner shift involving a 5-percent shareholder or any equity structure shift.

Determinations of the percentage of stock in a loss corporation owned by any person are made on the basis of value. Except as provided in regulations to be prescribed by the Secretary, changes in proportionate ownership attributable solely to fluctuations in the relative fair market values of different classes of stock are not taken into account (new sec. 382(*l*)(3)(D)).

---

[27] Unless specifically identified as a taxable year, all references to any period constituting a year (or multiple thereof) means a 365-day period (or multiple thereof).

limitation is increased by built-in gain recognized by virtue of a section 338 election (to the extent such gain is not otherwise taken into account as a built-in gain). Finally, if the section 382 limitation for a taxable year exceeds the taxable income for the year, the section 382 limitation for the next taxable year is increased by such excess.

If two or more loss corporations are merged or otherwise reorganized into a single entity, separate section 382 limitations are determined and applied to each loss corporation that experiences an ownership change.

* * *

Special rule for post-change year that includes the change date.—In general, the section 382 limitation with respect to an ownership change that occurs during a taxable year does not apply to the utilization of losses against the portion of the loss corporation's taxable income, if any, allocable to the period before the change. For this purpose, except as provided in regulations, taxable income (not including built-in gains or losses, if there is a net unrealized built-in gain or loss) realized during the change year is allocated ratably to each day in the year. The regulations may provide that income realized before the change date from discrete sales of assets would be excluded from the ratable allocation and could be offset without limit by pre-change losses. Moreover, these regulations may provide a loss corporation with an option to determine the taxable income allocable to the period before the change by closing its books on the change date and thus forgoing the ratable allocation.

Value of loss corporation

The value of a loss corporation is generally the fair market value of the corporation's stock (including preferred stock described in section 1504(a)(4)) immediately before the ownership change (new sec. 382(e)(1)). If a redemption occurs in connection with an ownership change—either before or after the change—the value of the loss corporation is determined after taking the redemption into account (new sec. 382(e)(2)). The Treasury Department is given regulatory authority to treat other corporate contractions in the same manner as redemptions for purposes of determining the loss corporation's value. The Treasury Department also is required to prescribe such regulations as are necessary to treat warrants, options, contracts to acquire stock, convertible debt, and similar interests as stock for purposes of determining the value of the loss corporation (new sec. 382(k)(6)(B)(i)).

In determining value, the price at which loss corporation stock changes hands in an arms-length transaction would be evidence, but not conclusive evidence, of the value of the stock. Assume, for example, that an acquiring corporation purchased 40 percent of loss corporation stock over a 12-month period. Six months following this 40 percent acquisition, the acquiring corporation purchased an additional 20 percent of loss corporation stock at a price that reflected a premium over the stock's proportionate amount of the value of all the loss corporation stock; the premium is paid because the 20-percent block carries with it effective control of the loss corporation. Based on these facts, it would be inappropriate to simply gross-up the amount paid for the 20-percent interest to determine the value of the corporation's stock. Under regulations, it is anticipated that the Treasury Department will permit the loss corporation to be valued based upon a formula that grosses up the purchase price of all of the acquired loss corporation stock if a control block of such stock is acquired within a 12-month period.

* * *

Long-term tax-exempt rate

The long-term tax-exempt rate is defined as the highest of the Federal long-term rates determined under section 1274(d), as adjusted to reflect differences between rates on long-term taxable and tax-exempt obligations, in effect for the month in which the change date occurs or the two prior months (new sec. 382(f)). The Treasury Department will publish the long-term tax-exempt rate by revenue ruling within 30 days after the date of enactment and monthly thereafter. The long-term tax-exempt rate will be computed as the yield on a diversified pool of prime, general obligation tax-exempt bonds with remaining periods to maturity of more than nine years.

The use of a rate lower than the long-term Federal rate is necessary to ensure that the value of NOL carryforwards to the buying corporation is not more than their value to the loss corporation. Otherwise there would be a tax incentive to acquire loss corporations. If the loss corporation were to sell its assets and invest in long-term Treasury obligations, it could absorb its NOL carryforwards at a rate equal to the yield on long-term government obligations. Since the price paid by the buyer is larger than the value of the loss company's assets (because the value of NOL carryforwards are taken into account), applying the long-term Treasury rate to the purchase price would result in faster utilization of NOL carryforwards by the buying corporation. The long-term tax-exempt rate normally will fall between 66 (1 minus the maximum corporate tax rate of 34 percent) and 100 percent of the long-term Federal rate.

* * *

Continuity of business enterprise requirements

Following an ownership change, a loss corporation's NOL carryforwards (including any recognized built-in losses, described below) are subject to complete disallowance (except to the extent of any recognized built-in gains or section 338 gain, described below), unless the loss corporation's business enterprise is continued at all times during the two-year period following the ownership change. If a loss corporation fails to satisfy the continuity of business enterprise requirements, no NOL carryforwards would be allowed to the new loss corporation for any post-change year. This continuity of business enterprise requirement is the same requirement that must be satisfied to qualify a transaction as a tax-free reorganization under section 368. (See Treasury regulation section 1.368–1(d)). Under these continuity of business enterprise requirements, a loss corporation (or a successor corporation) must either continue the old loss corporation's historic business or use a significant portion of the old loss corporation's assets in a business. Thus, the requirements may be satisfied even though the old loss corporation discontinues more than a minor portion of its historic business. Changes in the location of a loss corporation's business or the loss corporation's key employees, in contrast to the results under the business-continuation rule in the 1954 Code version of section 382(a), will not constitute a failure to satisfy the continuity of business enterprise requirements under the conference agreement.

Reduction in loss corporation's value for certain capital contributions

Any capital contribution (including a section 351 transfer) that is made to a loss corporation as part of a plan a principal purpose of which is to avoid any of the special limitations under section 382 shall not be taken into account for any purpose under section 382. For purposes of this rule, except as provided in regulations, a capital contribution made during the two-year period ending on the change date is irrebuttably presumed to be part of a plan to avoid the limitations. The application of this rule will result in a reduction of a loss corporation's value for purposes of determining the section 382 limitation. The term "capital contribution" is to be interpreted broadly to encompass any direct or indirect infusion of capital into a loss corporation (e.g., the merger of one corporation into a commonly owned loss corporation). Regulations generally will except (i) capital contributions received on the formation of a loss corporation (not accompanied by the incorporation of assets with a net unrealized built-in loss) where an ownership change occurs within two years of incorporation, (ii) capital contributions received before the first year from which there is an NOL or excess credit carryforward (or in which a net unrealized built-in loss arose), and (iii) capital contributions made to continue basic operations of the corporation's business (e.g., to meet the monthly payroll or fund other operating expenses of the loss corporation). The regulations also may take into account, under appropriate circumstances, the existence of substantial nonbusiness assets on the change date (as described below) and distributions made to shareholders subsequent to capital contributions, as offsets to such contributions.

* * *

Losses subject to limitation

The term "pre-change loss" includes (i) for the taxable year in which an ownership change occurs, the portion of the loss corporation's NOL that is allocable (determined on a daily pro rata basis, without regard to recognized built-in gains or losses, as described below) to the period in such year before the change date, (ii) NOL carryforwards that arose in a taxable year preceding the taxable year of the ownership change and (iii) certain recognized built-in losses and deductions (described below).

For any taxable year in which a corporation has income that, under section 172, may be offset by both a pre-change loss (i.e., an NOL subject to limitation) and an NOL that is not subject to limitation, taxable income is treated as having been first offset by the pre-change loss (new sec. 382(*l*)(2)(B)). This rule minimizes the NOLs that are subject to the special limitations. For purposes of determining the amount of a pre-change loss that may be carried to a taxable year (under section 172(b)), taxable income for a taxable year is treated as not greater than the section 382 limitation for such year reduced by the unused pre-change losses for prior taxable years. (New sec. 382(*l*)(2)(A)).

Built-in losses

If a loss corporation has a net unrealized built-in loss, the recognized built-in loss for any taxable year ending within the five-year period ending at the close of the fifth post-change year (the "recognition period") is treated as a pre-change loss (new sec. 382(h)(1)(B)).

Net unrealized built-in losses.—The term "net unrealized built-in loss" is defined as the amount by which the fair market value of the loss corporation's assets immediately before the ownership change is less than the aggregate adjusted bases of a corporation's assets at that time. Under a de minimis exception, the special rule for built-in losses is not applied if the amount of a net unrealized built-in loss does not exceed [15] percent of the value of the corporation's assets immediately before the ownership change. For purposes of the de minimis exception, the value of a corporation's assets is determined by excluding any (1) cash, (2) cash items (as determined for purposes of section 368(a)(2)(F)(iv)), or (3) marketable securities that have a value that does not substantially differ from adjusted basis.

* * *

Recognized built-in losses.—The term "recognized built-in loss" is defined as any loss that is recognized on the disposition of an asset during the recognition period, except to the extent that the new loss corporation establishes that (1) the asset was not held by the loss corporation immediately before the change date, or (2) the loss (or a portion of such loss) is greater than the excess of the adjusted basis of the asset on the change date over the asset's fair market value on that date. The recognized built-in loss for a taxable year cannot exceed the net unrealized built-in loss reduced by recognized built-in losses for prior taxable years ending in the recognition period.

The amount of any recognized built-in loss that exceeds the section 382 limitation for any post-change year must be carried forward (not carried back) under rules similar to the rules applicable to net operating loss carryforwards and will be subject to the special limitations in the same manner as a pre-change loss.

* * *

Built-in gains

If a loss corporation has a net unrealized built-in gain, the section 382 limitation for any taxable year ending within the five-year recognition period is increased by the recognized built-in gain for the taxable year (new sec. 382(h)(1)(A)).

Net unrealized built-in gains.—The term "net unrealized built-in gain" is defined as the amount by which the value of a corporation's assets exceeds the aggregate bases of such assets immediately before the ownership change. Under the de minimis exception described above, the special rule for built-in gains is not applied if the amount of a net unrealized built-in gain does not exceed [15] percent of the value of a loss corporation's assets.

Recognized built-in gains.—The term "recognized built-in gain" is defined as any gain recognized on the disposition of an asset during the recognition period, if the taxpayer establishes that the asset was held by the loss corporation immediately before the change date, to the extent the gain does not exceed the excess of the fair market value of such asset on the change date over the adjusted basis of the asset on that date. The recognized built-in gain for a taxable year cannot exceed the net unrealized built-in gain reduced by the recognized built-in gains for prior years in the recognition period.

* * *

Carryforwards other than NOLs

The Act also amends section 383, relating to special limitations on unused business credits and research credits, excess foreign tax credits, and capital loss carryforwards. Under regulations to be prescribed by the Secretary, capital loss carryforwards will be limited to an amount determined on the basis of the tax liability that is attributable to so much of the taxable income as does not exceed the section 382 limitation for the taxable year, with the same ordering rules that apply under present law. Thus, any capital loss carryforward used in a post-change year will reduce the section 382 limitation that is applied to pre-change losses. In addition, the amount of any excess credit that may be used following an ownership change will be limited, under regulations, on the basis of the tax liability attributable to an amount of taxable income that does not exceed the applicable section 382 limitation, after any NOL carryforwards, capital loss carryforwards, or foreign tax credits are taken into account. The Act also expands the scope of section 383 to include passive activity losses and credits and minimum tax credits.

* * *

Notice 2003–65

2003–2 C.B. 747.

Purpose

The Internal Revenue Service (IRS) is studying the circumstances under which items of income, gain, deduction, and loss that a loss corporation recognizes after an ownership change should be treated as recognized built-in gain (RBIG) and recognized built-in loss (RBIL) under section 382(h) of the Internal Revenue Code. This notice provides guidance regarding the identification of built-in items and requests comments on this subject. As described below under the heading Reliance on Notice, taxpayers may rely upon this guidance until the IRS and Treasury Department issue temporary or final regulations under section 382(h). This notice discusses two alternative approaches for the identification of built-in items for purposes of section 382(h): the 1374 approach and the 338 approach. [Eds.: Under the § 1374 approach, net unrealized built-in gain or loss is determined under rules derived from § 1374, which is applicable to determining built-in gain or loss of a Subchapter S corporation. See Chapter 16.]

Background

Section 382 provides that, after an ownership change, the amount of a loss corporation's taxable income for any post-change year that may be offset by pre-change losses shall not exceed the section 382 limitation for that year. The section 382 limitation generally equals the fair market value of the old loss corporation multiplied by the long-term tax-exempt rate. A loss corporation is any corporation that has a net operating loss, a net operating loss carryforward, or a net unrealized built-in loss for the taxable year in which the ownership change occurs. An ownership change is a greater than 50-percentage-point increase in ownership by 5-percent shareholders during the testing period, which is generally three years. Congress intended the section 382 limitation to apply when shareholders that did not bear the economic burden of the losses acquire a controlling interest in the loss corporation. *See* H.R. Rep. No. 99–426, 1986–3 C.B. (Vol. 2) 256; S. Rep. No. 99–313, 1986–3 C.B. (Vol. 3) 232.

Section 382(h) provides rules for the treatment of built-in gain or loss recognized with respect to assets owned by the loss corporation at the time of its ownership change. Section 382(h), as described below, reflects that, as a general matter, losses that offset built-in gain should not be subject to the section 382 limitation merely because the gain is recognized after an ownership change because if the gain had been recognized before the ownership change, it would have been offset without limitation by the loss corporation's net operating losses. Similarly, built-in loss should not escape the section 382 limitation merely because it is recognized after an ownership change because if the loss had been recognized before the ownership change, it would have been subject to the section 382 limitation.

The question of whether RBIG increases the section 382 limitation or whether RBIL is subject to the section 382 limitation begins with a determination of whether the loss corporation has a net unrealized built-in gain (NUBIG) or a net unrealized built-in loss (NUBIL). Pursuant to section 382(h)(3), a loss corporation's NUBIG equals the excess, if any, of the aggregate fair market value of its assets immediately before an ownership change over the assets' aggregate adjusted basis at that time, adjusted by the amount of certain items of income or deduction described in section 382(h)(6)(C) (described below). In addition, a loss corporation's NUBIL equals the excess, if any, of the aggregate adjusted basis of its assets immediately before an ownership change over the assets' aggregate fair market value at that time, adjusted by the amount of certain items of income or deduction described in section 382(h)(6)(C). Under section 382(h)(3)(B), if a loss corporation's NUBIG or NUBIL does not exceed a threshold amount (the lesser of $10,000,000 or 15% of the fair market value of its assets immediately before the ownership change), the loss corporation's NUBIG or NUBIL is zero. Thus, a loss corporation cannot have both a NUBIG and a NUBIL, but it can have neither.

If a loss corporation has a NUBIG, pursuant to section 382(h)(1)(A), any RBIG for any taxable year within the 5-year recognition period following the ownership change increases the section 382 limitation for that year. Similarly, if a loss corporation has a NUBIL, pursuant to section 382(h)(1)(B), any RBIL for any taxable year within the 5-year recognition period following the ownership change is treated as a pre-change loss subject to the section 382 limitation. Thus, only a loss corporation with a NUBIG can increase the section 382 limitation by RBIG, and only a loss corporation with a NUBIL can have RBIL that is treated as a pre-change loss.

In the case of dispositions of assets during the recognition period, section 382(h)(2) places the burden on the loss corporation to establish that any gain recognized is RBIG, and, conversely, that any loss recognized is not RBIL. Section 382(h)(2)(A) defines RBIG as any gain recognized during the 5-year recognition period on the disposition of any asset to the extent the new loss corporation establishes that (i) it held the asset on the change date and (ii) such gain does not exceed the asset's built-in gain on the change date. Furthermore, section 382(h)(2)(B) defines RBIL as any loss recognized during the 5-year recognition period on the disposition of any asset except to the extent the new loss corporation establishes that (i) it did not hold the asset on the change date or (ii) such loss exceeds the asset's built-in loss on the change date.

Section 382(h)(6) and the second sentence of section 382(h)(2)(B) provide rules treating certain items of income or deduction as RBIG or RBIL. Specifically, section 382(h)(6)(A) provides that any item of income "properly taken into account during the recognition period" is treated as RBIG if the item is "attributable to periods before the change date." Section 382(h)(6)(B) provides that any item of deduction "allowable as a deduction during the recognition period" is treated as RBIL if the item is "attributable to periods before the change date." In addition, the second sentence of section 382(h)(2)(B) provides that allowable depreciation, amortization, or depletion deductions are treated as RBIL except to the extent the loss corporation establishes that the amount of the deduction is not attributable to the asset's built-in loss on the change date. Finally, section 382(h)(6)(C) provides that NUBIG or NUBIL shall be properly adjusted for items of income and deduction that would be treated as RBIG or RBIL under section 382(h)(6) if they were properly taken into account or allowable as a deduction during the recognition period.

The IRS has issued two notices concerning guidance under section 382(h). In Notice 87–79, 1987–1 C.B. 388, the IRS announced that it anticipated that regulations under section 382 would permit income from a discharge of indebtedness that is integrally related to a transaction resulting in an ownership change to be allocated to the pre-change period. In Notice 90–27, 1990–1 C.B. 336, the IRS announced that it would promulgate regulations providing that, if a taxpayer that sells a built-in gain asset either prior to or during the recognition period reports the gain using the installment method under section 453, the provisions of section 382(h) will continue to apply to RBIG from the installment sale after the recognition period (including any gain recognized from the disposition of the installment obligation).

* * *

The 338 Approach

The 338 approach identifies items of RBIG and RBIL generally by comparing the loss corporation's actual items of income, gain, deduction, and loss with those that would have resulted if a section 338 election had been made with respect to a hypothetical purchase of all of the outstanding stock of the loss corporation on the change date (the "hypothetical purchase"). As a result, * * * under the 338 approach, built-in gain assets may be treated as generating RBIG even if they are not disposed of at a gain during the recognition period, and deductions for liabilities, in particular contingent liabilities, that exist on the change date may be treated as RBIL.

A. *Calculation of NUBIG and NUBIL*

Under the 338 approach, NUBIG or NUBIL is calculated in the same manner as it is under the 1374 approach. Accordingly, unlike the case in which a section 338 election is actually made, contingent consideration (including a contingent liability) is taken into account in the initial calculation of NUBIG or NUBIL, and no further adjustments are made to reflect subsequent changes in deemed consideration.

Example 10. Immediately before an ownership change, LossCo has one asset with a fair market value of $100 and a basis of $10 and a deductible contingent liability estimated at $40. Disregarding the threshold requirement of section 382(h)(3)(B), LossCo has a NUBIG of

who have not borne the burden of pre-acquisition losses. The existence of a net operating loss carryover that is transferable to new owners, however, allows the previous owners to recoup a portion of their loss from the new owners who are willing to pay for the future tax savings available from an acquired net operating carryover. The *General Explanation* indicates that eliminating net operating loss carryovers completely following a substantial ownership change would discourage the sale of a loss corporation and hence the partial recoupment of the losses by the historic shareholders who have borne the losses. Thus, Congress adopted the "limitation of earnings" approach that focuses on the market value of the loss to the loss corporation.

In general terms, the market value of a net operating loss carryover to a loss corporation (and indirectly to its existing shareholders) is the present value of its anticipated tax savings on future earnings. The present value of a loss carryover is dependent on the net return the loss corporation can expect to derive from its invested capital. Likewise the value of a loss carryover to a purchaser is the present value of anticipated tax savings on the future earnings that will be offset by acquired losses. Since a profitable enterprise may be expected to achieve a higher rate of return on its investment than a loss corporation (whose rate of return may be negative), an unlimited loss carryover will be more valuable to a profitable purchaser than to the loss corporation. The difference in value may result in a sale of loss carryovers for a price substantially less than the value of the carryover to the purchaser or, in any event, at a price somewhere between the value to the purchaser and the value to the loss corporation. Thus, an unlimited loss carryover not only provides a form of recoupment of prior losses for the seller of a loss corporation, but also provides a windfall profit for the purchaser financed by the Treasury. Section 382 is intended to eliminate this windfall potential by limiting the value of a loss carryover following a substantial ownership change to an approximation of the value of the carryover to the loss corporation. So limited, the carryover has the same value to both seller and purchaser. The cost of this limitation falls, in part, on the loss corporation, which is limited in the amount it can receive for the transfer of loss carryovers.

Theoretically, because the loss carryover has the same value to each, the seller and the purchaser should be neutral with respect to the presence of a loss carryover as part of an asset transfer. This "neutrality" principle works only if the limitation on the use of acquired loss carryovers does not reduce the value of loss carryovers to an amount less than the present value of the losses to the loss corporation. An overly restrictive limitation will inhibit the transfer of assets to more efficient operators. A limitation that is too generous, however, will provide a windfall profit to one of the parties. Section 382 attempts to strike a balance by limiting the annual recovery of a net operating loss carryover following an ownership change to the fair market value of the equity interests in the loss corporation multiplied by a federal tax-exempt rate. This formula is based on the theory that a loss corporation could dispose of its assets and invest the proceeds in risk-free taxable government bonds thereby earning an annual rate of return at least equal to the rate on long-term federal instruments. Senate Finance

Committee, Final Report on Subchapter C, The Subchapter C Revision Act of 1985 (Staff Report), S. Prt. 99–47, 99th Cong., 1st Sess. 71 (1985). The Conference Report on the 1986 Act indicates that the rate is reduced to a tax-exempt rate, in part, because Congress believed that the fair market value of the loss corporation includes the value of the loss carryover itself. The loss carryover is an asset that could not be individually sold and the proceeds reinvested. See H. Rep. No. 99–841, 99th Cong., 2d Sess. II–188 (1986). In addition, congressional studies have indicated that loss corporations typically have absorbed net operating losses at the rate of 4.4% of book net worth. (This rate will itself overstate the true rate of recovery on the fair market value of assets if book values are less than fair market value.) Senate Finance Committee, Final Report on Subchapter C, The Subchapter C Revision Act of 1985 (Staff Report), S. Prt. 99–47, 99th Cong., 1st Sess. 71 (1985). The federal tax-exempt rate, which has varied between approximately 8% and 2.5% since § 382 was enacted, is generous when compared with actual experience. (The federal tax-exempt rate is determined monthly by the IRS and announced in Revenue Rulings.) Some commentators have argued, however, that the limitation based on the federal exempt rate is too low thereby undervaluing the loss corporation's loss carryovers. See, e.g., N.Y. State Bar Ass'n Tax Section, Comm. on Net Operating Losses, The Net Operating Loss and Excess Credit Carryforwards Under H.R. 3838, 31 Tax Notes 725, 729 (1986).

2.   OWNERSHIP CHANGE

2.1. *In General*

The limitation on loss carryovers in § 382 is triggered by an "ownership change," which in general is a greater than 50 percentage point increase in the ownership of the stock of a loss corporation by one or more 5% stockholders over a three-year testing period. I.R.C. § 382(g)(1). Disposition of a corporate business by a majority of the investors who suffered the burden of losses terminates the averaging function of loss carryovers as to those investors and thus eliminates this particular justification for further loss carryovers. The only remaining justification for allowing loss carryovers to the new owners of a loss corporation is to provide the former investors with some recovery of a portion of their loss in the form of consideration paid for the carryover. Thus, a more than 50 percentage point change of ownership of the loss corporation is deemed an appropriate trigger for imposing limitations on loss carryovers.

Under the statutory language, an ownership change may result from an "owner shift," defined as any change in ownership of a loss corporation's stock involving a 5% stockholder, or an "equity structure shift," which is a reorganization of a loss corporation (with the exception of divisive (D), divisive (G) reorganizations, and (F) reorganizations). Under the statutory definitions, an equity structure shift that results in an ownership change also will qualify as an owner shift. This is true even for a publicly held corporation with no single 5% stockholder because of rules that aggregate the stock ownership of non-5% stockholders. I.R.C. § 382(g)(4)(B)–(C). The preamble to the § 382 Temporary Regulations states that there are no substantive differences (except for some transitional rule purposes) between classifying a transaction as an owner shift or an equity structure shift. T.D. 8149, 52 Fed. Reg. 29,668, 29,670 (1987); see also Temp.Reg. § 1.382–2T(e)(2)(iii) (an equity structure shift that affects the stock ownership of a 5% stockholder is also an owner shift). There is no apparent reason for the distinction, which appears to be attributable to an early version of the statute that was changed during the drafting process.

The recipient of stock by reason of death, as a gift, or in a transfer from a spouse by reason of divorce or separation, is treated as the owner of the stock for the period the stock was held by the transferor. I.R.C. § 382(l)(3)(B). These transfers, therefore, are not counted in testing for an ownership change.

Technically, the § 382 limitation applies to losses carried over to any "post change year" of a "new loss corporation." I.R.C. § 382(a). A new loss corporation is defined as a corporation entitled to a net operating loss carryover following an ownership change. I.R.C. § 382(k)(1), (3). A "post change year" is any taxable year ending after the date of an ownership change. I.R.C. § 382(d)(2). A loss corporation to which the limitation applies following an ownership change is any corporation entitled to a net operating loss carryover or which incurred a net operating loss in the year of an ownership change. I.R.C. § 382(k)(1). The term "loss corporation" also includes a corporation with built-in losses, which are also subject to the § 382 limitation. A corporation that is a loss corporation before the date of an ownership change is referred to as an "old loss corporation." I.R.C. § 382(k)(2).

2.2. Counting Owner Shifts During the Testing Period

An ownership change occurs if the percentage stock ownership of 5% stockholders on the date of any owner shift or equity structure shift (the "testing date") has increased by more than 50 percentage points over the lowest percentage of stock ownership of 5% stockholders at any time within the three-year period preceding the testing date. I.R.C. § 382(g)(1). An ownership change may result from the sum of unrelated stock transfers by 5% stockholders and transfers from less than 5% stockholders to persons who become 5% stockholders. A loss corporation is thus required during a rolling three-year period to keep track of all stock transfers from or to persons who are or who become 5% stockholders.

A full three-year lookback is not necessary in all cases. The testing period does not begin until the first day of a taxable year in which a loss corporation incurs a net operating loss that is carried over into a taxable year ending after the testing date. I.R.C. § 382(i)(3). Thus, stock transfers occurring in a year in which a corporation has neither a net operating loss nor loss carryover do not count towards an ownership change. In addition, a new testing period begins following an ownership change. I.R.C. § 382(i)(2). Stock transfers predating an ownership change will not be counted again towards a subsequent ownership change.

The basic operation of these rules is illustrated by the following example. As of January 1, Year 10, A, B, C, D, and E each owned 20 of the 100 outstanding shares of L Corporation. L Corporation had no net operating loss carryovers as of that date and did not incur a net operating loss in Year 10. On July 1, Year 10, A sold A's 20 shares of L Corporation stock to P Corporation, which previously owned no L Corporation stock. In Year 11, L Corporation incurred a net operating loss, which is carried forward. On January 1, Year 11, B sold B's 20 shares to P Corporation, and on June 30, Year 13, C sold C's 20 shares to P Corporation. Although P has increased its stock ownership of L from 0% to 60% during the three-year period ending on June 30, Year 13, because L Corporation did not have any net operating loss carryovers from Year 10 or earlier years, the owner shift effected by the July 1, Year 10, purchase from A is not counted in determining whether there has been an ownership change. On December 31, Year 13, D sold D's 20 shares to P Corporation. Looking backwards from December 31, Year 13, P has increased its stock ownership by 60 percentage points, from 20% to 80%. Because L had a net operating loss in Year 11 that was carried forward to subsequent years, the purchases from B, C, and D are taken into account and an ownership change has occurred. Because the ownership change starts a new testing period, if E were to sell E's stock to F on June 1, Year 16, there would be no ownership change, even though in the three-year period ending June 1, Year 16, P Corporation would have increased its stock ownership by 40 percentage points (from 40% to 80%) and F would have increased F's stock ownership by 20 percentage points, for a total shift of 60 percentage points.

In some circumstances, the requirement of § 382(g)(1)(B) that an ownership change be tested with respect to the lowest percentage of stock owned by a 5% stockholder during the testing period can have a surprising result. For example, L Corporation has 200 shares of stock outstanding, of which A owns 100 shares, and B and C each own 50 shares. On January 2, Year 13, A sells 60 shares of L stock to B. B's ownership interest increases by 30 percentage points, from 25% of L stock to 55%. A's interest drops to 20%. On January 1, Year 14, A acquires all of C's L stock. A and B have in the aggregate increased their percentage ownership of L by only 25 percentage points during the testing period; B's interest has increased by 30 percentage points, and A's percentage interest has declined by five percentage points. Nonetheless, Temp.Reg. § 1.382–2T(c)(4)(i) treats A's acquisition of C's stock as an ownership change. The temporary regulation concludes that, as a result of A's purchase of C's stock, A's percentage interest increased from a low of 20%, the lowest percentage of A's ownership interest during the testing period, to 45%. A's 25 percentage points increase plus B's 30 percentage points increase within the testing period are sufficient to trigger an ownership change despite the fact that their aggregate overall increase in stock ownership during the testing period is only 25 percentage points. The temporary regulation reaches this result even if A's sale to B and purchase from C are part of an integrated plan. Temp.Reg. § 1.382–2T(c)(3).

Arguably, the temporary regulation misreads § 382(g)(1) and reaches an unduly harsh result. Section 382(g)(1) can be interpreted as requiring that the increased interests of A and B be aggregated for purposes of both subsections (A) and (B). To paraphrase the statutory language, A and B's stock ownership of L has increased by only 25 percentage points over the lowest percentage of stock owned by A and B together ("such shareholders") at any time during the testing period (from a low of 75% [20% plus 55%] to 100%). Given the Treasury's broad regulatory authority under § 382(m) to interpret § 382, however, it is not likely that its interpretation of § 382(g)(1) could be challenged successfully.

2.3. *Stock Ownership and Five Percent Stockholders*

2.3.1. *Identifying Five Percent Stockholders*

The § 382 trigger focuses on stock transfers to or by persons who own 5% or more of the loss corporation stock. Proportionate stock ownership is determined by the value of stock held by the stockholder. I.R.C. § 382(k)(6)(C). A person is treated as a 5% stockholder if the person was a 5% stockholder at any time during the testing period, even though the person may not own 5% of the loss corporation stock on the testing date. Temp.Reg. § 1.382–2T(g)(1)(iv). The 5% figure was chosen to relieve companies from the burden of keeping track of trades among stockholders with a minor interest. H.Rep. No. 99–841, 99th Cong., 2d Sess. II–176 (1986).[2] Thus, stock transfers between less than 5% stockholders are not counted in testing for an ownership change. Temp.Reg. § 1.382–2T(e)(1)(ii). The less than 5% stockholders as a group, however, are treated as a single 5% stockholder regardless of the percentage interest held by such persons. I.R.C. § 382(g)(4)(A). Temp.Reg. § 1.382–2T(f)(13) refers to the group of less than 5% stockholders as a "public group." As a single 5% stockholder, transfers to or by a public group can trigger an ownership change. Thus, for example, a public issue of more than 50% of the stock of a closely held loss corporation to less than 5% stockholders will trigger an ownership change because the public group of new stockholders increases its ownership interest from zero preceding the public offering to more than 50% following the public offering. See Temp.Reg. § 1.382–2T(e)(1)(iii), Ex. (5). Various groups of less than 5% stockholders separately may represent 5% stockholders and transfers between those groups can be an ownership change.

Notice 2010–50, 2010–27 I.R.B. 12, provides guidance for measuring owner shifts of loss corporations that have more than one class of stock outstanding when the value of one class of stock fluctuates relative to another class of stock. The IRS will accept use of the "full value methodology," under which all shares are "marked to market" on each testing date. Under this method, the percentage of stock owned by any person is determined with reference to "the relative fair market value of the stock owned by such person to the total fair market value of the outstanding stock of the corporation. . . . [C]hanges in percentage ownership as a result of fluctuations in value are taken into account if a testing date occurs, regardless of whether a particular shareholder actively participates or is otherwise party to the transaction that causes the testing date to occur. . . ." The IRS also will accept use of the "hold-constant principle." Under this methodology, "the value of a share, relative to the value of all other stock of the corporation, is established on the date that share is acquired by a particular shareholder. On subsequent testing dates, the percentage interest

---

[2]   In general, any person who owns 5% or more of the stock of a publicly traded corporation is required to file reports with the Securities and Exchange Commission.

represented by that share (the "tested share") is then determined by factoring out fluctuations in the relative values of the loss corporation's share classes that have occurred since the acquisition date of the tested share. Thus, as applied, the hold constant principle is individualized for each acquisition of stock by each shareholder." The "hold-constant principle" has several variations that the notice identifies as acceptable. An acquisition is not an event upon which the acquiring shareholder marks to fair market value other shares that it holds under any hold-constant principle variation. To be acceptable, whichever methodology is selected must measure the increased percentage ownership represented by a stock acquisition by dividing the fair market value of that stock on the acquisition date by the fair market value of all of the outstanding stock of the loss corporation on that date. Any alternative treatment of an acquisition is inconsistent with § 382(*l*)(3)(C) and is not acceptable. Any method selected, whether the "full value methodology" or a particular variation of the "hold-constant principle" must be applied consistently to all testing dates in a "consistency period." With respect to any testing date, the consistency period includes all prior testing dates, beginning with the latest of: (1) the first date on which the taxpayer had more than one class of stock; (2) the first day following an ownership change; or (3) the date six years before that testing date.

2.3.2. *Attribution Rules*

With certain modifications, the attribution rules of § 318 apply to identify proportionate stock ownership. I.R.C. § 382(*l*)(3). In general, the modifications to § 318 have two effects. First, members of a family who are subject to stock attribution under § 318(a)(1) are treated as a single individual. Thus, stock transfers among family members to whom stock is attributable will not trigger an ownership change.[3] If an individual is a member of more than one family group under the attribution rules, that individual will be treated as a member of the family that results in the smallest increase in stock held by 5% stockholders on a testing date. Temp.Reg. § 1.382–2T(h)(6)(iv). The Regulations also provide that an individual who is not otherwise a 5% stockholder will not be treated as a 5% stockholder as a result of family attribution. Second, stock of a loss corporation owned by any entity (corporation, partnership, or trust) that has a 5% or greater interest is attributed up the ownership chain to the last person from whom no further attribution is possible. I.R.C. § 382(*l*)(3)(A)(ii)(II); Temp.Reg. § 1.382–2T(g)(2), (h)(2)(i). Intermediate entities are disregarded. Temp.Reg. § 1.382–2T(h)(2)(i)(A). Treas.Reg.

---

[3] Garber Industries Holding Co., Inc. v. Commissioner, 124 T.C. 1 (2005), aff'd, 435 F.3d 555 (5th Cir. 2006), held that the family aggregation rule of § 382(*l*)(3)(A)(i) applies solely from the perspective of individuals who are shareholders (as determined under the attribution rules of § 382(*l*)(3)(A)) of the loss corporation. Thus, the sale of stock from one sibling to another that resulted in a more than 50% increase in stock ownership by the purchasing sibling triggered the application of § 382. The fact that each sibling and either of their parents would be viewed as a single shareholder did not result in the siblings being treated as a single shareholder where neither of their parents was a shareholder. The court recognized the possibility that the rule it announced might result in arbitrary distinctions between cases in which a parent of the siblings also was a shareholder and cases in which the parent was not a shareholder, but concluded that the announced rule was the one most compatible with the statutory language and legislative history.

§ 1.382–3(a)(1)(i) includes as an entity for this purpose any group of less than 5% shareholders who act pursuant to a plan to acquire 5% of the stock of a loss corporation.

Temp.Reg. § 1.382–2T(g)(4), Ex. (1), illustrates application of these attribution rules as follows. The stock of L, a loss corporation is owned 20% by A, 10% by corporation P1, and 20% by E, a joint venture. The remaining 50% of L stock is publicly held ("Public Group L"). B owns 15% of the stock of P1 Corporation. The remaining 85% of the shares of P1 are publicly held ("Public Group P1"). E, the joint venture, is owned 30% by corporation P2 and 70% by corporation P3. Both P2 and P3 are publicly held ("Public Group P2" and "Public Group P3"). L's ownership structure is illustrated as follows:

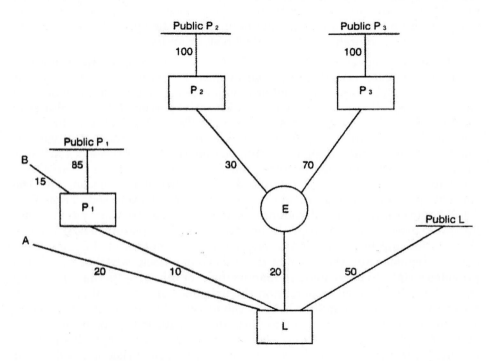

A is a 5% stockholder of L because of A's direct ownership of 20% of L stock. Public Group L is a single 5% stockholder by virtue of its collective 50% interest in L.

B is not a 5% stockholder. Although B is a 5% stockholder of P1, and thereby indirectly owns the L stock owned by P1, Temp.Reg. § 1.382–2T(g)(2), B's ownership interest in L is only 1.5% (15% of P1's 10%). Because B is not a 5% stockholder of L, B is treated as a member of the Public Group P1. See Temp.Reg. § 1.382–2T(j)(1)(iv). P1 is not a 5% stockholder because its interest is attributable to its stockholders. P1's public stockholders, Public P1, are treated as a single 5% stockholder of L owning 10% of the L stock, 8.5% plus B's 1.5%.

Public Group P2 is also a 5% stockholder. P2 has a 6% interest attributed from P2's 30% interest in E, which in turn owns 20% of L (30% ×

20% = 6%). P2's 6% interest is attributed to the P2 public group which owns 100% of P2. Public Group P3 is also a 5% stockholder with a 14% interest attributed to it (20% × 70%=14%).

2.3.3. *Option Attribution*

Even in the absence of a direct stock transfer, outstanding options and other rights to acquire stock (including convertible debt) may create an owner shift that must be taken into account in determining whether there is an ownership change during a testing period. Section 382(*l*)(3)(A)(iv) provides that, except to the extent provided in the Regulations, an option or other right to acquire stock will be treated as exercised if the deemed exercise results in an ownership change. However, Treas.Reg. § 1.382–4(d)(2) provides that an option will be treated as exercised on the date of its issue, transfer, or on a subsequent testing date, only if the option satisfies one of three tests, an ownership test, a control test, or an income test.

Under the *ownership* test of Treas.Reg. § 1.382–4(d)(3), an option will be treated as exercised if a principal purpose of the issuance, transfer, or structure of the option is to avoid or ameliorate the impact of an ownership change by providing its holder with a substantial portion of the attributes of ownership of the underlying stock. Under Treas.Reg. § 1.382–4(d)(6)(i), factors that indicate the presence or absence of a purpose to avoid or ameliorate the impact of an ownership change (under all three of the tests) include whether there are business purposes for the issuance, transfer or structure of the option, the likelihood of exercise of the option, and the consequences of treating the option as having been exercised. Treas.Reg. § 1.382–4(d)(6)(ii) specifically identifies additional factors that indicate that an option provides its holder with the attributes of ownership. These include the relationship between the exercise price of the option at the time of its issue or transfer and the value of the underlying stock, whether the option provides a right to participate in management or other rights that ordinarily would be held by stock owners, and the existence of reciprocal options (e.g. offsetting put and call options held by the prospective seller and purchaser). The ability of the option holder to participate in future appreciation in the value of the underlying stock may be considered, but is not of itself sufficient to satisfy the ownership test. Conversely, the absence of risk of loss does not preclude treating an option as exercised.

An option will be treated as exercised under the control test of Treas.Reg. § 1.382–4(d)(4) if a principal purpose of the issuance, transfer, or structure of the option is to avoid or ameliorate the impact of an ownership change and the option holder (or a related person) directly or indirectly has a more than 50% interest in the loss corporation determined by including the ownership interest that would result from exercise of the option. Treas.Reg. § 1.382–4(d)(6)(iii) indicates that economic interests in the loss corporation and influence over management of the loss corporation held by the holder and related persons will be taken into account in applying the control test.

The *income* test of Treas.Reg. § 1.382–4(d)(5) treats an option as exercised if a principal purpose of the issuance, transfer, or structure of the option is to avoid or ameliorate the impact of an ownership change of the loss corporation by facilitating the creation of income or value in the loss corporation prior to the exercise of the option. Under this test, an option will be treated as exercised if in connection with the issuance or transfer of an option the loss corporation engages in transactions that accelerate income thereby utilizing loss carryovers prior to an ownership change, or the option holder or related person purchases stock or makes a capital contribution that increases the value of the loss corporation. Treas.Reg. § 1.382–4(d)(6)(iv).

Treas.Reg. § 1.382–4(d)(7) contains a list of safe harbors that exclude some options from the deemed exercise rules. Commercially reasonable contracts to acquire stock when obligations to complete the transaction are subject only to reasonable closing conditions, and which close on a change date within one year after the contract is entered into, will not be treated as exercised under the ownership test or the control test. These contracts will be subject to the income test. In addition, the safe harbors shelter options that are part of a security agreement in a lending transaction, options issued as compensation for performance of services, options exercisable only on death, disability or retirement, and a "bona fide" right of first refusal with "customary terms." The deemed exercise rules are not applicable to transfers of options if neither party to the transfer is a 5% shareholder, the transfer is between members of separate public groups, or the transfer occurs by reason of death, gift, divorce, or separation. Treas.Reg. § 1.382–4(d)(11).

2.3.4.   *The Definition of Stock*

By reference to § 1504(a)(4), § 382(k)(6)(A) defines stock for § 382 purposes as excluding nonvoting, nonconvertible stock interests that are limited as to dividends and that do not participate in corporate growth "to any significant extent." This provision prevents a loss corporation from increasing the amount of its outstanding stock with equity interests that are insignificant in order to avoid an ownership change. In addition, § 382(k)(6)(B) directs the Treasury to promulgate Regulations treating certain stock that is stock under § 1504(a)(4) (such as voting stock with no significant participation in growth) as nonstock for § 382 purposes. Temp.Reg. § 1.382–2T(f)(18)(ii) contains a three part test for the identification of such "nonstock stock": (A) the likely participation of the interest of a 5% stockholder at the time of the stock's issue is disproportionately small compared to the fair market value of outstanding stock of the corporation, (B) treating the interest as nonstock would result in an ownership change, and (C) net operating losses and built-in losses are at least twice the annual limitation (two times the value of the loss corporation times the tax-exempt rate).

To cover the field completely, under the authority of § 382(k)(6)(B)(ii), Temp.Reg. § 1.382–2T(f)(18)(iii) treats certain interests that are not normally classified as stock (potential equity disguised as debt) as constituting stock for § 382 purposes if (A) at the time of issue, a nonstock interest issued to a 5% stockholder offers the potential for significant participation in corporate growth, (B) treating the interest as stock would result in an ownership change, and (C) the loss corporation's net operating losses and built-in losses are at least twice the annual limitation. This provision is designed to prevent avoidance of the ownership change rules by the issue of equity-flavored instruments that are not equity in form. This provision does not apply to treat an option (such as a convertible instrument), whether or not deemed to be exercised, as stock. Treas.Reg. § 1.382–4(d)(12). The rules treating nonstock interests as stock are thus independently applicable to only a narrow range of nonconvertible nonstock instruments such as a debt instrument with a contingent payout large enough to constitute a significant participation in future growth. Such an instrument likely would be classified as stock under debt-equity rules, but the drafters of the Regulations were not willing to leave the question open to the vagaries of litigation. Identifying instruments that provide a significant participation in future growth may prove, however, to be no less difficult.

Under Treas.Reg. § 1.382–2(a)(3)(ii), convertible stock is treated as stock. Thus, preferred stock that is classified as nonstock under the § 1504(a)(4) rules, but that is convertible into stock, is treated as stock. Convertible stock is also treated as an option if the terms of the conversion feature permit or require consideration other than the stock being converted. Treas.Reg. § 1.382–4(d)(9)(ii). As a consequence, the presence of convertible stock may trigger an ownership change if the conversion is deemed exercised under the tests of Treas.Reg. § 1.382–4(d)(2).

2.3.5.   *Aggregation and Segregation of Less than Five Percent Stockholders*

All stockholders of a corporation who individually own less than 5% of the stock are aggregated into a group (a "public group") and treated as a single 5% stockholder regardless of the percentage of stock held by less than 5% stockholders either individually or as a group. I.R.C. § 382(g)(4)(A). Section 382(g)(4)(B) and (C) provide for the segregation of identifiable groups of less than 5% stockholders for purposes of determining whether an ownership change has occurred with respect to 5% stockholders following either an equity structure shift or an owner shift. In certain transactions, particularly equity structure shifts, it is possible to trace the changes in ownership of separate identifiable public groups. For example, in the merger of a publicly held loss corporation into another publicly held corporation, there are two identifiable groups of less than 5% stockholders: the public group of the loss corporation and the public group of the acquiring corporation. The transfer of ownership of the loss corporation from its pre-merger public stockholders to the public stockholders of the acquiring corporation may be treated as a stock transfer from the loss corporation public group to the pre-merger public group of the acquiring corporation. Similar transfers by or to a public group can be identified with respect to other reorganizations (whether taxable or nonrecognition transactions), a public offering (the new stockholders are a separate 5% stockholder), or a redemption (stockholders whose interests are increased are a separate 5% stockholder).

Temp.Reg. § 1.382–2T(j)(1) first aggregates groups of less than 5% stockholders of a loss corporation into different public groups depending upon direct and indirect ownership of stock in a loss corporation. For example, all individuals who directly own less than 5% of the stock of the loss corporation are treated as a single 5% stockholder. Temp.Reg. § 1.382–2T(j)(2) then segregates into two or more public groups any public group of less than 5% stockholders that can be separately identified as having acquired their stock in a particular transaction, such as a prior reorganization or a stock issue covered by § 1032 (e.g., a public issue of stock). Similar principles apply if some individuals in the public group increase their interest in the corporation through a redemption of shares; the public group is divided into the group whose shares were not redeemed and the group whose shares were redeemed. The same aggregation and segregation rules apply to stockholders who are less than 5% stockholders of a loss corporation by attribution from an entity that directly or indirectly owns 5% or more of the loss corporation stock. Temp.Reg. § 1.382–2T(j)(3). However, 2013 amendments to Treas.Reg. § 1.382–3 reduce the complexity of applying § 382 in tracking transactions involving small amounts of stock of a loss corporation. Treas.Reg. § 1.382–3(j)(13) provides that transfer of a direct ownership in the loss corporation by a first-tier 5% entity, or a transfer by a 5% shareholder, to public shareholders will not create a new segregated public group. Instead, existing public groups will be treated as acquiring the transferred interest. In addition, Treas.Reg. § 1.382–3(j)(14) provides a special exception under which a loss corporation may annually redeem 10% of the value of its stock, or 10% of the shares of a particular class of stock, without triggering the segregation rules and the creation of new 5% groups. Under the Regulations, transactions that result in the creation of a new public group, and thus a possible owner shift, simply will be folded into the existing public groups, thereby reducing the chance of an ownership change.

Once an ownership change has occurred following a transaction that requires segregation of different groups of less than 5% stockholders, the groups are no longer treated as separate 5% stockholders. Temp.Reg. § 1.382–2T(j)(2)(iii)(B)(2), Ex. (3)(iv).

Treas.Reg. § 1.382–3(j) exempts certain small stock issues from the segregation requirement so that the loss corporation is not required to treat recipients of a small stock issue as a separate group of less than 5% stockholders. A stock issue is subject to the exception if the value of all stock issued during the taxable year does not exceed 10% of the total value of outstanding stock at the beginning of the year, or if, on a class-by-class basis, the total number of shares of any class of stock issued during the taxable year does not exceed 10% of the number of shares of stock of that class outstanding at the beginning of the taxable year. Treas.Reg. § 1.382–3(j)(2).

In addition, Treas.Reg. § 1.382–3(j)(3) exempts from the segregation rules stock issued for cash if the total amount of the newly issued stock does not exceed one-half of the stock ownership of direct public groups immediately preceding the stock issue. Stock exempted from the segregation rules under these provisions is treated as acquired by existing direct public groups in proportion to the existing public groups' pre-issuance ownership interests. Treas.Reg. § 1.382–3(j)(5). If, however, the loss corporation has actual knowledge that a particular direct public group acquired a greater percentage of newly issued stock than its proportionate share, the loss corporation may treat that public group as receiving the higher percentage. Treas.Reg. § 1.382–3(j)(5)(ii).

The small issue and cash issue exemptions from the segregation rules also apply to stock issues of first tier and higher tier entities. Treas.Reg. § 1.382–3(j)(11).

The operation of the aggregation and segregation rules is illustrated by the following example:

L, a loss corporation, P1, and P2 each have 1000 shares of stock outstanding. The stock of L is owned 600 shares by P1, 200 shares by P2, and 170 shares by a public group, none of whom owns more than 5% of the L stock, and A who owns 30 shares. A owns 50 shares of the P1 stock. The remaining 950 shares of P1 stock are owned by public stockholders none of whom owns more than 5% of P1 stock. A owns 100 shares of P2 stock. The remaining 900 shares of P2 stock are held by public stockholders none of whom owns more than 5% of P2 stock. The ownership structure of L is as follows:

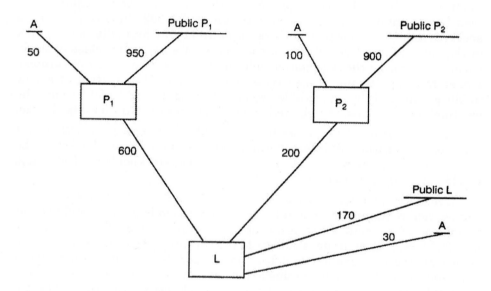

L's stock is held by three separate public groups, each of which is treated as a single 5% stockholder: the public group that directly holds L stock; the public group of P1 stockholders, which by attribution holds 60% of L stock; and the public group of P2 stockholders, which by attribution holds 20% of L stock.

Although A directly and indirectly owns more than 5% of L stock, A is not a 5% stockholder of L. A owns 3% of L directly. As a 5% owner of P1, A is attributed a proportionate share of P1's L stock, an interest of 3% (5% × 60%). Since A's interest is less than 5%, A is treated as a member of the P1 public group. Temp.Reg. § 1.382–2T(j)(1)(iv)(A). As a 10% owner of P2, A indirectly owns an additional 2% of L, but again A's stock interest is included as part of the interest of the P2 public group. Temp.Reg. § 1.382–2T(j)(1)(iii) contains a presumption that stockholders, including 5% owners of a higher tier entity that owns stock in a loss corporation, who are not 5% stockholders of a loss corporation are not members of more than one public group. Thus, A's 3% direct interest, A's 3% interest through P1, and A's 2% interest through P2 are not accumulated to make A a 5% stockholder of L. Because L is required to keep track of only 5% stockholders who can be traced through a chain of at least 5% ownership interests, L is presumed not to have knowledge of A's existence as a 5% stockholder. A will, however, be treated as a 5% stockholder if L has actual knowledge of A's ownership interests. Temp.Reg. § 1.382–2T(j)(1)(iii), (k)(2). As the example demonstrates, this distinction can be significant.

On April 1, Year 11, L issues 111 shares of new stock to the public. The stock is not purchased by any person who owns 5% of L stock. The issue of L stock to less than 5% stockholders creates a new public group, which is treated as a 5% stockholder.[4] This new group ("New Public L") increased its interest in L during the testing period from 0% before the stock offering to 10% (111/1111) afterwards. Temp.Reg. § 1.382–2T(j)(1)(iii) presumes that there is no cross-ownership between the old public stockholders of L and the new public stockholders. Thus, absent actual knowledge by L, any acquisition of the newly issued L stock by existing stockholders will be ignored. The stock issue is, therefore, a 10% owner shift.

On April 1, Year 12, all of the assets of P1, including the L stock, are acquired by P2 in a statutory merger. The P1 stockholders receive one share of P2 stock for every four shares of P1 stock. A receives 12.5 shares of P2 stock in exchange for A's 50 P1 shares; the remaining P1 stockholders receive 237.5 shares of P2 stock in exchange for their 950 P1 shares. P2 now owns 72% (800/1111 shares) of L. The transaction is tested for an ownership change by segregating the post-merger stockholders of P2 into two public groups, the original P2 stockholders, who now own 72% of P2 ("Old Public P2"), and the pre-merger P1 stockholders ("New Public P2"). (As will be discussed below, A has become a 5% stockholder of L and is therefore no longer included in a P2 public group.) Before the reorganization, the original P2 public group, including A, owned 18% of L by attribution from P2 (200/1111). After the reorganization, the original P2 public group owns 51.8% of L ([800/1111] × [900/1250]). Thus, Old Public P2 has increased its ownership interest in L by 33.8%.

---

[4]   Treas.Reg. § 1.382–3(j) does not prevent segregation of the new public group because the stock issue exceeds 10% of the outstanding stock and is more than one-half of the stock held by direct public groups immediately preceding the stock issue.

Following the merger, the ownership structure of L is as follows:

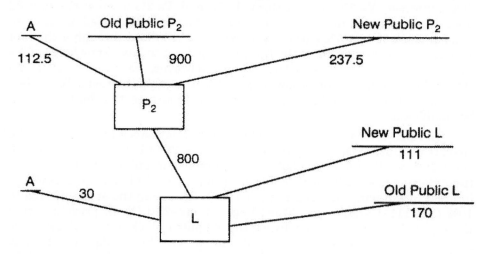

Within the testing period, the 33.8% owner shift in L from New Public P2 to Old Public P2, plus the 10% owner shift from Old Public L to New Public L, are not sufficient to trigger an ownership change of L. However, A's interest in the transaction causes an ownership change to be triggered. Before the merger of P1 into P2, A's cross-ownership was disregarded under the presumption of Temp.Reg. § 1.382–2T(j)(1)(iii), and A was treated as a less than 5% stockholder whose stock interests are part of public groups. In contrast to A's pre-merger ownership interests, after the merger A has an identifiable interest greater than 5% that is traceable through a connection of 5% ownership interests. A thus becomes a distinct 5% stockholder who must be counted. After the merger, A owns 112.5 shares of P2 stock, 9% of P2. A is, therefore, deemed to own 6.5% of L by attribution from P2 (9% × 72%). Even though A is now identified as a 5% stockholder, A's ownership interest is presumed to include only A's 6.5% interest through P2. A's 2.7% direct interest in L is still treated as part of the Old Public L group. Temp.Reg. § 1.382–2T(j)(1)(vi), Ex. (5). As a result, A's interest as an identified 5% stockholder increased from zero before the transaction to 6.5% after the merger. A's 6.5% owner shift, when added to the increased interests of Old Public P2 and New Public L, result in an increased interest by 5% stockholders of 50.3%, sufficient to trigger an ownership change.

If L has actual knowledge of A's pre-merger stock ownership interest, L may overcome the presumption of Temp.Reg. § 1.382–2T(j)(1)(iii), and avoid the ownership change. See Temp.Reg. § 1.382–2T(k)(2). After L's public offering, but before the merger of P1 and P2, A's lowest actual percentage interest during the testing period was 7.2%, 2.7% direct interest in L stock, 2.7% attributed through P1, and 1.8% attributed through P2. A's percentage interest in L after the merger is 9.2%, of which 6.5% is attributed from P2 and 2.7% is direct. Based on actual knowledge, the owner shift attributable to A is only 2%. In addition, without A as a member, Public P2's ownership interest goes from 16.2% (200/1111 × 90%) to 51.8%, an ownership change of

35.6%. That is not sufficient to trigger an ownership change on the merger of P1 into P2 (35.6% + 10% + 2% = 47.6%).

2.3.6.   *Reporting Requirements*

Temp.Reg. § 1.382–2T(a)(2)(iii) and Treas.Reg. § 1.382–11 impose extensive information reporting and record keeping requirements that require the corporation to monitor its status under § 382 even if there is only a remote possibility of an ownership change. In any taxable year in which a corporation is a loss corporation (see § 382(k)(1)), the corporation must file a statement with its tax return indicating whether there has been a testing date during the year, identifying any testing dates on which an ownership change occurred, identifying testing dates that occurred closest to the end of each calendar quarter of the taxable year, and indicating the percentage stock ownership of each 5% stockholder on each testing date reported and the percentage increase of each 5% stockholder during the testing period. Temp.Reg. § 1.382–2T(k)(1) allows a publicly held loss corporation to rely on filings with the Securities and Exchange Commission to disclose the existence of 5% stockholders. A loss corporation is also allowed to rely on statements by responsible persons (such as officers, trustees, partners, etc.), signed under penalties of perjury, which disclose the ownership interests and changes in interest of the owners of an upper-tier entity that owns an interest in the loss corporation. The Temporary Regulations also require a loss corporation to maintain records adequate to identify 5% stockholders and ascertain whether an ownership change has occurred. In many cases, it is possible that the cost of providing information returns will outweigh the value of loss carryovers.

3.   COMPUTING THE SECTION 382 LIMITATION

3.1. *Valuing the Loss Corporation*

The annual limitation on income of a loss corporation that can be offset by net operating loss carryovers following an ownership change is computed by multiplying the value of the loss corporation by the federal long-term tax-exempt rate. I.R.C. § 382(b)(1). Value is based on the value of the stock of the loss corporation on the date immediately preceding an ownership change. I.R.C. § 382(e)(1). As noted in the *General Explanation*, the value of a loss corporation includes the value of interests that are not treated as stock under § 1504(a)(4). The value of the loss corporation also includes nonstock that is treated as stock under Temp.Reg. § 1.382–2T(f)(18)(iii).

To prevent a loss corporation from artificially enhancing its value on the eve of an ownership change, § 382(*l*) provides that any capital contributed to the loss corporation as part of a plan to increase the limitation shall not be taken into account in determining value. Section 382(*l*)(2) provides that, except as otherwise provided in Regulations, any capital contribution within 2 years of the date of an ownership change shall be treated as part of a forbidden plan.

Additional anti-abuse rules are found in § 382(*l*)(4), which reduces the value of a loss corporation that has substantial nonbusiness assets. The value of the loss corporation is reduced by the fair market value of nonbusiness assets, less liabilities attributable to such assets. A loss corporation has substantial nonbusiness assets if more than one-third of the total value of the loss corporation consists of investment assets. This limitation is intended to prevent the sale of carryovers by a loss corporation which has disposed of its operating assets. Given the severity of the limitation imposed by § 382, a market for shell corporations with loss carryovers is, however, not likely to exist in any event. The provision ultimately works only to reduce the sales price of a loss corporation with substantial investment assets.

Under § 382(e)(2), if an ownership change occurs in connection with a redemption or other corporate contraction, the value of the loss corporation immediately before the ownership change must be adjusted to account for assets distributed in the redemption.

3.2. *Valuing Members of Controlled Groups of Corporations*

Treas.Reg. § 1.382–8 contains rules for the valuation of a loss corporation that is a member of a controlled group of corporations (as defined in § 1563(a)). These rules are designed to avoid duplication of the value of assets of one member of a controlled group by including in the value of the stock of an upper-tier corporation the value of stock of a subsidiary member of the controlled group held directly by the upper-tier corporation. Thus, in general, for purposes of determining the § 382 limitation with respect to a loss of a controlled group, the value of the stock of each component member of the controlled group (as defined in § 1563(b)) is reduced by the value of the stock of any other member of the controlled group held directly by the component member of the controlled group. Treas.Reg. § 1.382–8(c)(1).

3.3. *Built-In Gains and Losses*

Section 382 also deals with unrealized losses of a loss corporation that could be utilized to offset future income following an ownership change in the same manner as a net operating loss carryforward. Without application of the limitation, the loss corporation could realize the losses after an ownership change to offset post-change income. Net unrealized losses existing at the time of an ownership change are subject to the annual § 382 limitation in the taxable year the losses are recognized. I.R.C. § 382(h)(1)(B). Recognized built-in losses that are not deductible in the taxable year because of the § 382 limitation are carried forward into subsequent taxable years (subject to the limitation in future years) in the same manner as a net operating loss that arose in the year of recognition. I.R.C. § 382(h)(4).

With respect to built-in gains, § 382 takes into account the fact that a loss corporation could at any time absorb its loss carryovers by disposing of assets with unrealized appreciation. Section 382(h)(1)(A) thus allows a loss corporation to increase its annual limitation following an ownership change by built-in gain recognized during the taxable year.

The built-in gain or loss rules of § 382(h) apply only to unrealized gains or losses recognized by the loss corporation within five years of an ownership change, and only if the corporation has net unrealized gain or loss on the date of an ownership change. Net unrealized built-in gains and losses are based on the difference between the fair market value and adjusted bases of the assets of a loss corporation immediately before an ownership change.

I.R.C. § 382(h)(3)(A). Net unrealized loss also includes any depreciation or other capital recovery deductions attributable to the excess of the adjusted basis of an asset over its fair market value on the date of an ownership change. I.R.C. § 382(h)(2)(B). Thus, a valuation of the corporation's assets is required as of the date of an ownership change. Net unrealized built-in gain or loss is ignored, however, if the amount of unrealized gain or loss is not greater than the lesser of $10,000,000 or 15% of the fair market value of the loss corporation's assets (computed without regard to cash or marketable securities the value of which approximates cost) immediately prior to the date of an ownership change. I.R.C. § 382(h)(3)(B). In the case of a corporation with respect to which a § 338 election (discussed in Chapter 8) is in effect following an ownership change, the § 382 limitation is increased by the lesser of gain recognized by reason of the § 338 election, or built-in gain determined without regard to the limitation of § 382(h)(3)(B). I.R.C. § 382(h)(1)(C).

One might imagine that a taxpayer must recognize a built-in gain in order to have a recognized built-in gain under § 382. But this is not the case. Pending the issuance of Regulations, Notice 2003–65, 2003–2 C.B. 747, reprinted above, provides two optional methods for calculating net unrealized built-in gains and losses and recognized built-in gains and losses under the rules of § 382(h). The most attractive method is the § 338 method. Under this method, the taxpayer determines how much "hypothetical" additional depreciation would have occurred if the taxpayer had recognized all built-in gains at the time of an ownership change and then would have been able to claim additional depreciation over the five year period specified in § 382(h). The IRS then states that the taxpayer is entitled to claim an increase in its § 382 limitation by the amount of this foregone hypothetical additional depreciation deduction. Under the 2017 Tax Act, taxpayers are generally allowed immediately to claim a deduction for the acquisition of property that has a life of 20 years or less. The effect of providing an immediate increase in the § 382 limitation by the full amount of this hypothetical bonus depreciation for property was found objectionable and inconsistent with the purposes of § 382. So, in Notice 2018–30, 2018–21 I.R.B. 610, the Treasury Department indicated that the hypothetical cost recovery deductions used by the § 338 methodology of Notice 2003–65 are to be determined under § 168 but under the assumption that § 168(k) bonus depreciation is not in effect. Moreover, the 2017 Tax Act also provided for an indefinite carryforward of net operating losses, but for purposes of § 382(h) one looks to the hypothetical depreciation that occurs only during the five-year recognition period specified in § 382(h)(7). Thus, these two changes brought about by the 2017 Tax Act do not provide any significant adjustment to the general § 382(b) limitations that might otherwise be calculated under the law that existed prior to the 2017 Tax Act.

Section 382(h)(6) provides that income earned prior to the date of an ownership change, but which has not been taken into account by the loss corporation, will be treated as built-in gain recognized in the year the item is properly taken into account. Thus, earned but unreported income items increase the annual limitation in the year the item is properly accounted for by the loss corporation. Treas.Reg. § 1.382–7 provides, however, that for the purposes of computing the § 382 limitation, income received before a change date that is attributable to services to be performed after the change date is not treated as recognized built-in gain. This includes income that is received prior to the change date where recognition is deferred under Treas.Reg. § 1.451–5 (advance payments for goods or long-term contracts), or Rev.Proc. 2004–4, 2004–1 C.B. 991 (certain advance payments that are deferred on financial statements). Conversely, deduction items attributable to periods predating the date of an ownership change, but which have not been deducted by the loss corporation, are treated as recognized built-in losses in the year the item is deducted. These items are thus subject to the § 382 limitation in the year deducted. Whether items of income or deduction are attributable to a period prior to the change date is determined as an economic matter, not by the taxpayer's method of accounting.

Temp.Reg. § 1.382–2T(d)(3)(ii) provides a special rule for commencement of the three year testing period in the case of a corporation with built-in losses. The testing period generally begins on the earlier of the first day of a taxable year from which there is a loss or excess tax credit carryforward, or the first day of a taxable year in which a testing date occurs. In the case of a corporation with a net unrealized built-in loss, the testing date extends back a full three years from the date of an owner shift or equity structure shift that requires testing for an ownership change. The testing period may be shortened, however, if the corporation can show that unrealized built-in losses accrued at a later date, in which case the testing period will begin on the first day of the taxable year in which the losses accrued, from which there is a loss carryover, or the year the transaction being tested occurs, whichever is earlier.

3.4. *Worthless Stock Deduction by a Fifty Percent Stockholder*

In Textron, Inc. v. United States, 561 F.2d 1023 (1st Cir.1977), a parent corporation claimed a worthless stock deduction for the stock of its controlled subsidiary. The court held that the net operating loss carryover of the subsidiary was unaffected by the parent's worthless stock deduction and thus the subsidiary was permitted to claim its loss carryover as a deduction against future income. In effect, *Textron, Inc.* allowed the same loss to be counted twice, once at the corporation level and once at the stockholder level. Section 382(g)(4)(D) was enacted in 1987 to overrule this result.

Section 382(g)(4)(D) treats a worthless stock deduction by a greater than 50% stockholder, who continues to own the stock at the close of the taxable year, as an owner shift. The stockholder is treated as acquiring the stock on the first day of the taxable year following the year in which the stock is claimed to have become worthless, and as not having any stock ownership preceding that date. The consequence is an owner shift from 0% to an ownership interest of more than 50%. This owner shift triggers an ownership change thereby subjecting the corporation's loss carryovers to the § 382 limitation. The value of the loss corporation subject to a worthless stock deduction will be zero. See I.R.C. §§ 165(a) and (g)(1), 382(e)(1). As a result, the annual limitation on carryovers of the loss corporation will be zero and the loss carryovers will not be available to offset the corporation's post change income. H.R.Rep. No. 100–495 (Conf.Rep.), 100th Cong., 1st Sess. A–40 (1987).

4.   CONTINUITY OF BUSINESS ENTERPRISE

Prior to the 1986 revision of § 382, loss carryovers survived a change in ownership of the loss corporation in a purchase transaction if the corporation continued to conduct business substantially the same as before the ownership change. Section 382(c) retains a vestige of the business continuity requirements by disallowing loss carryovers following an ownership change if the corporation "does not continue the business enterprise" of the loss corporation for a period of at least 2 years. The legislative history indicates that § 382(c) is intended to adopt the continuity of business requirement applied to reorganizations by Treas.Reg. § 1.368–1(d). See Chapter 10. Thus, the continuity requirement is satisfied if the new loss corporation either continues the trade or business that existed before an ownership change or uses a significant portion of the business assets of the old loss corporation in a business. The Conference Report makes it clear that loss carryovers survive an ownership change even if the new loss corporation discontinues more than a minor portion of the historic business of the old loss corporation. H.Rep. No. 99–841, 99th Cong., 2d Sess. II–189 (1986).

The insistence on continuity of business is to some extent inconsistent with the basic theory behind the limitation of § 382, which is based, in part, on the assumption that the loss corporation could dispose of its assets, invest the proceeds in income generating securities, and absorb its loss carryover with interest income. There is no continuity of business restriction preventing use of loss carryovers following such a transaction. Why is it necessary to encourage continued investment in a loss operation following an ownership change? Perhaps the answer is that the continuity of business requirement is necessary to prevent the acquisition of a corporation to acquire only loss carryovers. The § 382 limitation itself is, however, sufficiently restrictive to eliminate transactions motivated by only tax reduction. To the extent the continuity requirement inhibits the purchaser, it restrains the sale of the loss corporation, encourages continuation of an unprofitable business, and thereby violates the neutrality principle on which § 382 is based.

5.   LIMITATIONS ON CARRYOVERS UNDER SECTION 383

Section 383 applies the limitation of § 382 following an ownership change to capital loss carryovers, general business credits, minimum tax credits under the alternative minimum tax, and foreign tax credits. Section 383(b) states that Regulations are to be issued to provide that capital losses carried forward from a year pre-dating an ownership change are limited under § 382 principles and shall reduce the § 382 limitation on net operating losses. Section 383(a) and (c) provide for Regulations to limit the use of tax credit carryforwards to tax liability computed on income up to the § 382 limitation. Tax credits are thereby converted into their taxable income equivalents for limitation purposes. See Treas.Reg. § 1.383–1.

6.   APPLICATION OF SECTION 382 IN BANKRUPTCY AND INSOLVENCY PROCEEDINGS

6.1. *Stock for Debt Exchange*

In the case of a loss corporation involved in a Title 11 bankruptcy or similar proceeding, the § 382 limitation is not applied if, following an ownership change, the creditors and former stockholders of the loss corporation own at least 50% of the loss corporation stock. I.R.C. § 382(*l*)(5)(A). In effect, the creditors of the financially distressed corporation are treated as stockholders for purposes of testing for an ownership change. Under this provision, an exchange of debt for stock by creditors does not trigger the § 382 limitation. The relief of § 382(*l*)(5)(A) is available only with respect to an exchange of stock for indebtedness that has been held by the creditor for at least 18 months preceding the date of filing of the bankruptcy or insolvency proceeding, or with respect to indebtedness incurred in the ordinary course of business of the old loss corporation that at all times has been held by the same person. I.R.C. § 382(*l*)(5)(E).

There is a substantial cost imposed for avoiding the general § 382 limitation under the exception provided by § 382(*l*)(5)(A). Section 382(*l*)(5)(B) requires that loss carryovers be reduced by the amount of interest on indebtedness converted into stock that has been paid or accrued during the taxable year of the ownership change and the three year period preceding the taxable year of the ownership change. Theoretically, debt of the bankrupt corporation has had the characteristics of equity during this period so that the interest deduction should not be available to increase loss carryovers.

Under § 382(*l*)(5)(C), cancelled indebtedness for interest that is taken into account to reduce net operating loss carryovers does not create cancellation of indebtedness income under § 108(e)(8). Cancellation of indebtedness income is created under § 108(e)(8) in the amount by which the fair market value of stock issued in exchange for debt is less than the amount of the debt.

If there is a second ownership change within two years with respect to a corporation that avoided the § 382 limitation under § 382(*l*)(5)(A), the § 382 limitation following the second ownership change will be zero. I.R.C. § 382(*l*)(5)(D).

6.2. *Qualified Debt Holders*

Relief from an ownership change under § 382(*l*)(5) is available only with respect to debt held by the creditor for 18 months preceding the ownership change, or trade or business debt held at all times by the same person. Under Treas.Reg. § 1.382–9(d)(3), debt held by a person who is a less than 5% shareholder after the ownership change will be treated as owned by the same creditor for the 18-month period preceding the filing of a bankruptcy or insolvency petition. Thus, qualification under § 385(*l*)(5) does not require tracing of ownership during this "continuity period" of widely held debt that is converted into equity. This provision does not apply to an entity through which a 5% shareholder owns an indirect ownership interest in the loss corporation. In addition, if the loss corporation has knowledge of the acquisition of its debt by a group of persons with the principal purpose of exchanging the debt for stock, the indebtedness and stock will be treated as owned by an entity. Treas.Reg. § 1.382–9(d)(3)(ii)(A). Treas.Reg. § 1.382–9(d)(4) also provides that indebtedness held by a beneficial owner that is a 5% shareholder after the ownership change of the loss corporation and that is a corporation (or other entity) that has itself experienced an ownership change, will not be treated as indebtedness qualified for § 385(*l*)(5) treatment if the indebtedness represents more than 25% of the beneficial owner's gross assets on the beneficial owner's ownership change date.

For purposes of determining whether the 18-month holding period is met, Treas.Reg. § 1.382–9(d)(5) provides that the transferee of indebtedness in certain transactions is treated as holding the indebtedness during the transferor's holding period. Transfers subject to this "tacking rule" include (1) transfers between related parties, (2) transfers pursuant to customary loan syndications, (3) transfers by an underwriter in the course of an underwriting, (4) transfers in which the transferee's basis is determined under § 1014 (death-time transfers), § 1015 (gifts), or with reference to the transferor's basis (nonrecognition transactions in general), (5) transfers in satisfaction of a pecuniary bequest, (6) transfers pursuant to a divorce or separation agreement, and (7) transfers by reason of subrogation. The tacking rule does not apply, however, if the transfer is for the principal purpose of taking advantage of the losses of the loss corporation. In addition, Treas.Reg. § 1.382–9(d)(5)(iv) provides for tacking of the holding period and character of indebtedness incurred in the course of a trade or business in the case of indebtedness received from the loss corporation in exchange for old indebtedness. This tacking rule also applies to a change in the terms of an indebtedness that constitutes an exchange under § 1001.

6.3. *Election out*

A loss corporation may elect under § 382(*l*)(5)(G) not to have § 382(*l*)(5) apply to it. Treas.Reg. § 1.383–9(i) provides that the election is irrevocable and specifies the language that must be filed with the electing corporation's tax return by the due date (including extensions) for the loss corporation's return for the taxable year that includes the change date.

If an ownership change in a Title 11 bankruptcy reorganization or similar case does not qualify for the benefits of § 382(*l*)(5), or the loss corporation has elected out of the provision, under § 382(*l*)(6) the value of the loss corporation will reflect any increase in value that results from the surrender of debt in the transaction. Although § 382(*l*)(1) provides that capital contributions intended to increase the value of the loss corporation shall not be taken into account, Treas.Reg. § 1.382–9(j) recognizes that economically the direct conversion of debt into stock, or a stock issuance for cash that is used to satisfy creditors, have the same effect on the corporation. See CO–88–90, 1992–2 C.B. 616. Subject to a number of anti-abuse rules (see Treas.Reg. § 1.382–9(k)), Treas.Reg. § 1.382–9(j)(1) and (2) basically provide that the value of a loss corporation to which § 382(*l*)(6) applies is the lesser of the value of the stock of the loss corporation immediately after the ownership change or the value of the loss corporation's pre-change assets. Limiting the value of the loss corporation to the value of pre-change assets, if less than stock value, in effect removes from the valuation the benefit of contributions to capital that are not used to satisfy creditors and that would otherwise be reflected in stock value.

6.4. *Continuity of Business Requirement*

Treas.Reg. § 1.382–9(m)(1) provides that the continuity of business requirement for utilizing net operating loss carryovers imposed by § 382(c) does not apply to a loss corporation that is not subject to the § 382 limitation by virtue of § 382(*l*)(5). As a corollary, Treas.Reg. § 1.269–3(d)(1), indicates that a change of control in an ownership change covered by § 382(*l*)(5) will be considered under § 269 to be made for the principal purpose of tax avoidance unless the corporation carries on more than an insignificant amount of an active trade or business during and subsequent to the Title 11 or similar case.

7.   ACQUISITION OF BUILT-IN GAIN PROPERTY BY A LOSS CORPORATION: SECTION 384

The § 382 limitation does not apply to restrict loss carryovers if, instead of being acquired by new owners, the loss corporation directly or indirectly acquires appreciated assets of a profitable enterprise in a carryover basis transaction and uses its loss carryover to avoid tax on gain recognized on disposition of the acquired assets. Section 384 was enacted in 1987 to deal with this situation. The legislative history explains the provision as follows:

> [Section 384] provides that loss corporations will be precluded from using their losses to shelter built-in gains of an acquired company recognized within five years of the acquisition. Built-in gains for this purpose includes any item of income which is attributable to periods before the acquisition date. For example, built-in gains for this purpose include so-called "phantom" gains on property on which depreciation had been taken prior to the acquisition. It is likewise expected that built-in gains for this purpose will also include any income recognized after an acquisition in which the fair market value of the property acquired is less than the present value of the taxes that would be due on the income associated with the property (for example, in the case of a "burnt-out" leasing subsidiary with built-in income transferred to a loss corporation). No inference is intended that such situations are not subject to § 269 of present law.

H.Rep. No. 100–391, 100th Cong., 1st Sess. 1093–1094 (1987).

Section 384 applies to built-in gain recognized during the five-year period following the corporate acquisition of control of another corporation, or the acquisition of corporate assets in an (A), (C) or (D) reorganization, when either the acquiring corporation or the acquired corporation has a "net unrealized built-in gain" at the time of acquisition. By reference to § 382(h), net unrealized built-in gain exists if the aggregate value of transferred assets at the time of acquisition exceeds the aggregate adjusted bases of such assets. I.R.C. § 384(c)(1) and (8). Section 384 prohibits the use of pre-acquisition losses (including recognized built-in losses) of one corporation to offset recognized built-in gain of the gain corporation. It does not prevent a loss corporation from acquiring an ongoing profitable enterprise for the purpose of using its loss carryovers to offset future income (other than recognized built-in gain) of the acquired business. However, such an acquisition may be subject to § 269.

8.   SECTION 269 AND LOSS CARRYOVERS

Section 269 allows the IRS to deny the benefit of deductions made possible by an acquisition of control of another corporation or assets with a carryover basis when the principal purpose of the acquisition is tax avoidance. The legislative history of the 1986 Act indicates that § 382 does not alter the application of § 269 to acquisitions made to evade or avoid taxes. H.Rep. No. 99–841, 99th Cong., 2d Sess. II–194. Before 1986, § 269 was a moderately important weapon for the IRS to prevent abusive acquisitions of shell corporations with loss carryovers. See, e.g., Scroll, Inc. v. Commissioner, 447 F.2d 612 (5th Cir.1971). After 1986, however, § 382 so severely discounts net operating loss carryforwards following an ownership change that there is no longer a significant tax avoidance potential in a transaction subject to the limitation. Thus, Treas.Reg. § 1.269–7 provides that § 269 may be applied following an ownership change subject to § 382, but the reduced value of net operating loss carryforwards under the § 382 limitation will be taken into account in determining whether the change of control was undertaken with the prohibited tax avoidance motive. Nonetheless, because the more than 50% ownership change rules of § 382 and the acquisition of control provisions of § 269 are not identical, there is a possibility that an acquisition will fall within § 269 without triggering an ownership change under § 382. For example, P, which owns 49% of L, a loss corporation, acquires an additional 31% of the loss corporation stock. P then liquidates L under § 332 thereby inheriting L's loss carryover under § 381. If there have been no other owner shifts with respect to the L stock during the three year testing period, P has acquired control of L for § 269 purposes without triggering the § 382 limitation on L's loss carryovers. If P's acquisition of L, or its assets, is undertaken with the requisite tax avoidance purpose, § 269 may be invoked to deny P the benefit of L's loss carryforward even though the transaction escapes the reach of § 382.

The § 382 limitation is applicable only to an ownership change of the loss corporation itself. Although § 384 restricts the acquisition of assets with built-in gain by a loss corporation, there is nothing in the statutory scheme to prevent a loss corporation from acquiring a profitable business in a taxable or nontaxable transaction to generate income to absorb the corporation's loss carryforward. In Rev.Rul. 63–40, 1963–1 C.B. 46, the IRS indicated that it would not contend that an acquisition is undertaken for tax avoidance purposes under § 269 if a loss corporation acquires the stock of a profitable corporation, liquidates the profitable business, and discontinues the loss business. The ruling does not apply, however, if the purchase price for the profitable business is paid over a long period of time or exceeds the fair market value of the acquired business. Could the IRS ever successfully overcome a loss corporation's assertion that its acquisition of a profitable enterprise was undertaken for valid business purposes? Indeed, would imposition of § 269 restrictions on this transaction achieve a desirable policy goal? If the stockholders who suffered the losses are still in the picture, there is not the windfall that is present in the case in which newcomers acquire a loss corporation, the typical "trafficking in loss corporation" case.

PROBLEM SET 2

1.   Five individuals, A, B, C, D, and E, each owned 20% of the stock of L Corp. At the end of last year L Corp. had a net operating loss carryover (NOL) of $5,000,000. On January 1st of this year, P Corp. bought all of the stock of L Corp. for $10,000,000 in cash. This year, L Corp. made $4,000,000 before taking any NOL into account. On January 1st, the "long term tax exempt federal rate" was 1%.

(a)   What is L Corp.'s taxable income after taking its NOL into account?

(b)   Would your answer differ if instead of P Corp. buying the stock of L Corp. from A, B, C, D, and E, the purchaser had been F, another individual?

(c)   Would your answer differ if instead of P Corp. buying the stock of L, P Corp. had acquired L Corp. in a type B reorganization, giving each of A, B, C, D, and E, $2,000,000 worth of P Corp. common stock?

2.   Five individuals, A, B, C, D, and E, each owned 20% of the stock of L Corp. Prior to Year 10, L Corp. had no NOLs. In Year 10, L Corp. incurred an NOL of $10,000,000. Over the past few years, P Corp. has made the following purchases of L Corp. stock.

Selling Shareholder		Purchase Date
A	20%	June 1, Year 9
B	20%	Jan. 1, Year 10
C	20%	June 30, Year 12
D	20%	Dec. 31, Year 12
E	20%	June 30, Year 13

As of what date does § 382 apply to limit the use of any of L Corp.'s Year 10 NOL that is then unused?

3.   X Corp. is a closely held start up high technology company. A and B each own 1,000,000 shares. It has an unexpired NOL due to significant R&D deductions under § 174. X Corp. makes an initial public offering of 3,000,000 shares at $15 per share. Does § 382 apply to X Corp. as a result of the IPO?

4.   P Corp. owns 80% of the stock of L Corp. C, an individual, owns the remaining 20% of the stock of L Corp. L Corp. has an unexpired NOL.

(a)   Z Corp. purchased 70% of the stock of P Corp. Assuming that C owns no stock of either P Corp. or L. Corp., does § 382 apply to L Corp.?

(b)   Z Corp. purchased 40% of the stock of P Corp. Assuming that C owns no stock of either P Corp. or Z Corp., does § 382 apply to L Corp.?

(c)   Z Corp. purchased 70% of the stock of P Corp. Assuming that C owns no stock of P Corp. but C does own 20% of the stock of Z Corp., does § 382 apply to L Corp.?

5.   Y Corp. owns 51% of the stock of L Corp. D, an individual owns 49% of the stock of L Corp. D owns 4% of the stock of Y Corp. Does § 382 apply to L Corp. if D purchases all of the L stock owned by Y Corp.?

6.   Loss Corp. experienced an ownership change after the close of business on December 31, Year 10 and has a $50 million net operating loss as of the close of business on December 31, Year 10 that is able to be carried over to subsequent years indefinitely. At the time of its ownership change, the fair market value of the Loss Corp. stock was $100 million. The long-term tax exempt rate per § 382(f) that applied during the month of the ownership change was 2%. Loss Corp. has land that is subject to significant environmental contamination and thus has a significant built-in loss. But, Loss Corp. possesses other assets that have significant built-in gains. In total, Loss Corp. had the following assets and liabilities:

Assets	Basis	FMV
Receivables and Cash	$15,000,000	$ 15,000,000
Plant and Equipment	$ 0	$ 10,000,000
Land	$40,000,000	$ 30,000,000
Intangible Assets	$ 0	$ 15,000,000
Goodwill	$ 0	$ 45,000,000
Liabilities		
Accounts Payable	($ 5,000,000)	($ 5,000,000)
Debt	($10,000,000)	($ 10,000,000)
Net Assets		$100,000,000

(a)   What is the amount of the annual limitation under § 382 before considering any application of the adjustments made by § 382(h)? Would it make any difference in your answer if $10 million was contributed to Loss Corp. earlier in Year 9?

(b)   Assume the same basic facts as in Problem 6(a) except that there have been no shareholder contributions. In addition, assume that Loss Corp. has $1.5 million of taxable income in Year 11 and $5 million of taxable income in Year 12. What are the relevant limitations for Year 11 and Year 12. In your answer, do not consider the impact of § 382(h).

(c)   Assume the same facts as in Problem 6(b) but now assume that the taxpayer elects to apply the hypothetical § 338 method that is allowed under Notice 2003–65 as modified by Notice 2018–30. Please assume that Loss Corp. had taxable income before any utilization of its NOLs in Years 11 through 15 as follows: $1.5 million in Year 11; $5 million in Year 12; $10 million in Year 13; $15 million in Year 14; $20 million in Year 15. What are the § 382 limitations as adjusted by § 382(h) for each of Year 11 through Year 15?

PART V

SPECIAL RULES TO PREVENT AVOIDANCE OF SHAREHOLDER LEVEL TAX

CHAPTER 14

PENALTY TAXES

The Code contains two sets of provisions to prevent the use of a corporation to accumulate income in avoidance of progressive individual tax rates on dividend distributions and to convert ordinary income at the corporate level into stockholder capital gain. First, the accumulated earnings tax of §§ 531–537 imposes a penalty tax on corporate earnings that are accumulated beyond the reasonable needs of the business. Second, the personal holding company tax of §§ 541–547 imposes a penalty tax on undistributed passive investment income of closely held holding companies.

The incentive to accumulate corporate income will vary depending on the applicable rates. Until the 1980s, the higher individual marginal rates were substantially higher than the top rate on corporate income and dividends were taxed at higher rates than capital gains, thereby creating an incentive for accumulating earnings at the corporate level. From 2003 through 2012, the highest rate—35%—was the same for individuals and corporations. Since 2003 dividends have been taxed at the same rates as long-term capital gains, with the highest rate now 20%. From 2013 through 2017, the highest individual income tax rate was 39.6%; the 2017 tax legislation reduced the corporate rate to 21% and decreased the highest income tax rate to 35%. Currently, even though there is now a considerable difference between the top corporate and top individual rate, the incentive to accumulate likely remains fairly insignificant because of the low dividend and capital-gain rates. It should, however, be noted that the basis step-up afforded by § 1014 may prompt closely held businesses to accumulate rather than to distribute because, for example, stock inherited from a decedent stockholder could be sold without gain recognition, thereby yielding a single layer of tax.

SECTION 1. THE ACCUMULATED EARNINGS TAX

INTERNAL REVENUE CODE: Sections 531–537.

REGULATIONS: Sections 1.532–1(a); 1.533–1(a); 1.537–1(a), (b), –2, –3.

Sections 531 and 532 impose a tax of 20% on the "accumulated taxable income" of a corporation that has been formed or availed of for the purpose of avoiding the imposition of income tax on its shareholders, or the shareholders of another corporation, by permitting earnings and profits to accumulate instead of being distributed. In Ivan Allen Company v. United States, 422 U.S. 617 (1975), at a time when the top individual rate was significantly higher than the top corporate rate, the Court described the purpose and function of the accumulated earnings tax as follows:

Under our system of income taxation, corporate earnings are subject to tax at two levels. First, there is the tax imposed upon the income of the corporation. Second, when the corporation, by way of a dividend, distributes its earnings to its shareholders, the distribution is subject to the tax imposed upon the income of the shareholders. Because of the disparity between the corporate tax rates and the higher gradations of the rates on individuals, a corporation may be utilized to reduce significantly its shareholders' overall tax liability by accumulating earnings beyond the reasonable needs of the business. Without some method to force the distribution of unneeded corporate earnings, a controlling shareholder would be able to postpone the full impact of income taxes on his share of the corporation's earnings in excess of its needs. * * *

In order to foreclose this possibility of using the corporation as a means of avoiding the income tax on dividends to the shareholders, every revenue act since the adoption of the Sixteenth Amendment in 1913 has imposed a tax upon unnecessary accumulations of corporate earnings effected for the purpose of insulating shareholders.

The Court has acknowledged the obvious purpose of the accumulation provisions of the successive acts:

> As the theory of the revenue acts has been to tax corporate profits to the corporation, and their receipt only when distributed to the stockholders, the purpose of the legislation is to compel the company to distribute any profits not needed for the conduct of its business so that, when so distributed, individual stockholders will become liable not only for normal but for surtax on the dividends received. Helvering v. Chicago Stock Yards Co., 318 U.S. 693, 699, * * * (1943).

This was reaffirmed in United States v. Donruss Co., 393 U.S. 297 * * * (1969).

It is to be noted that the focus and impositions of the accumulated earnings tax is upon "accumulated taxable income," § 531. This is defined in § 535(a) to mean the corporation's "taxable income," as adjusted. The adjustments consist of the various items described in § 535(b), including federal income tax, the deduction for dividends paid defined in § 561, and the accumulated earnings credit defined in § 535(c). The adjustments prescribed by § 535(a) and (b) are designed generally to assure that a corporation's "accumulated taxable income" reflects more accurately than "taxable income" the amount actually available to the corporation for business purposes. This explains the deductions for dividends paid and for federal income taxes; neither of these enters into the computation of taxable income. Obviously, dividends paid and federal income taxes deplete corporate resources and must be recognized if the corporation's economic condition is to be properly perceived. Conversely, § 535(b)(3) disallows, for example, the deduction, available to a corporation for income tax purposes under § 243, on account of dividends received; dividends received are freely available for use in the corporation's business.

The purport of the accumulated earnings tax structure established by §§ 531–537, therefore, is to determine the corporation's true economic condition before its liability for tax upon "accumulated taxable income" is determined. The tax, although a penalty and therefore to be strictly construed, Commissioner v. Acker, 361 U.S. 87, 91, * * * (1959), is directed at economic reality.

* * *

Accumulation beyond the reasonable needs of the business, by the language of § 533(a), is "determinative of the purpose" to avoid tax with respect to shareholders unless the corporation proves the contrary by a preponderance of the evidence. The burden of proof, thus, is on the taxpayer. A rebuttable presumption is statutorily imposed. To be sure, we deal here, in a sense, with a state of mind. But it has been said that the statute, without the support of the presumption, would "be practically unenforceable without it." United Business Corp. v. Commissioner, 62 F.2d 754, 755 (CA2), cert. denied, 290 U.S. 635 * * * (1933). What is required, then, is a comparison of accumulated earnings and profits with "the reasonable needs of the business." Business needs are critical. And need, plainly, to use mathematical terminology, is a function of a corporation's liquidity, that is, the amount of idle current assets at its disposal. The question, therefore, is not how much capital of all sorts, but how much in the way of quick or liquid assets, it is reasonable to keep on hand for the business.

Generally, the IRS has attempted to apply the accumulated earnings tax only to closely held corporations. The requirement that the corporation be formed or availed of to avoid shareholder tax is less likely to exist in the case of publicly owned companies. In some instances, the tax has been applied to widely held companies that were controlled by a small group of stockholders;[1] and since 1984, § 532(c) has provided that

---

[1] See Trico Products Corp. v. Commissioner, 137 F.2d 424 (2d Cir.1943) and Trico Products v. McGowan, 169 F.2d 343 (2d Cir.1948) (corporation owned by 2,000 stockholders but 74% of the stock was held by six stockholders). But in Golconda Mining Corp. v. Commissioner, 507 F.2d 594 (9th Cir.1974), the appellate court reversed the Tax Court's holding that the accumulated earnings tax was applicable to a corporation whose management group owned from 12% to 17% of the stock. The court held that the accumulated earnings tax could apply only if a

the accumulated earnings tax is to be applied without regard to the number of stockholders.

DETAILED ANALYSIS

1. THE RELATIONSHIP BETWEEN THE PROSCRIBED ACCUMULATION "PURPOSE" AND THE REASONABLE NEEDS OF THE BUSINESS

In United States v. Donruss Co., 393 U.S. 297 (1969), the Court resolved a conflict as to whether, as urged by the government, a taxpayer to rebut the presumption contained in § 533(a) must establish that tax avoidance with respect to the shareholders was not "one" of the purposes for the accumulation or whether, as some Courts of Appeals had held, the presumption could be rebutted by demonstrating that tax avoidance was not the "dominant, controlling, or impelling" purpose for the accumulation. The Court sustained the Government's position.

To understand the impact of the holding in *Donruss*, consider the situation of the taxpayer in that case on remand. Since the jury that decided the case below had already found that the accumulation was beyond the reasonable needs of the business, the presumption in § 533(a) that the purpose was to avoid income taxes with respect to the shareholders had been brought into play. It would thus now be up to the taxpayer to prove by a preponderance of the evidence the negative proposition that not one of the purposes of the accumulation was tax avoidance, an almost impossible task. Though the statute makes a finding of the proscribed purpose the crucial event for the imposition of the tax, the *Donruss* holding made the finding as to the reasonableness of the accumulation the determinative factor in the vast majority of cases. See, e.g., Bahan Textile Machinery Co., Inc. v. United States, 453 F.2d 1100 (4th Cir.1972) (after an accumulation beyond the reasonable needs of the business was established, the taxpayer unsuccessfully tried to overcome the presumption as to purpose by showing that the controlling shareholder was "an overly cautious man, fearful of long-term debt and conservative in financial outlook"). Compare Bremerton Sun Publishing Co. v. Commissioner, 44 T.C. 566 (1965) ("Although we feel that the total accumulation was somewhat beyond the reasonable foreseeable business needs of petitioner, we are convinced that the only reason for the excessive retention of earnings was the conservative policies of the directors and not their concern for the surtax liability of [the shareholders]."); Starman Investment, Inc. v. United States, 534 F.2d 834 (9th Cir.1976) (even if accumulation beyond reasonable needs, lack of tax avoidance motive precludes imposition of tax).

---

relatively small group of stockholders exercised control, a situation that could exist only if a small group of stockholders owned more than 50% of the stock of the corporation.

In Technalysis Corp. v. Commissioner, 101 T.C. 397 (1993), the court held that the accumulated earnings tax is applicable to a publicly held corporation without regard to whether control was exercised by a relatively small group of shareholders. The court, however, concluded that, although the corporation's accumulations were beyond the reasonable needs of the business, the corporation was not formed or availed of to avoid income tax with respect to its shareholders.

In Magic Mart, Inc. v. Commissioner, 51 T.C. 775 (1969), the court concluded that since accumulations beyond the reasonable needs of the business were not present, a finding as to the purpose of the accumulations was unnecessary in light of the credit in § 535(c) for reasonable accumulation, and the *Donruss* issue was not reached. In contrast to Magic Mart, some courts have apparently been of the view that, to escape tax, the accumulations, in addition to being reasonable in an objective sense, must have been motivated by business needs and not tax avoidance purposes. Apollo Industries, Inc. v. Commissioner, 358 F.2d 867 (1st Cir.1966), remanded the case to the Tax Court for an answer to the following question: "[E]ven if accumulated earnings did not exceed reasonably anticipated business needs in one or both years, was avoidance of taxes on shareholders nevertheless a dominant purpose?" The Court of Appeals in *Donruss* apparently was of the same view (384 F.2d 292, 294 (6th Cir.1967)), though the cases it cited for this proposition were decided prior to the enactment of § 535(c). The Tax Court uniformly has taken the view that if the accumulations do not exceed the reasonable needs of the business so that a sufficient credit would be present quite apart from any issue as to the purpose for the accumulation, the issue as to the purpose of the accumulations is irrelevant. Dielectric Materials Co. v. Commissioner, 57 T.C. 587 (1972) (acq.); John P. Scripps Newspapers v. Commissioner, 44 T.C. 453 (1965).

2.   FACTORS BEARING ON REASONABLE BUSINESS NEEDS

2.1. *General*

Determining the "reasonable business needs" involves a complex factual inquiry into all aspects of the corporation's business. Courts generally start with the statement that they are reluctant to substitute their judgment for the business judgment of the management as to the need for the accumulations (see, e.g., Dielectric Materials Co. v. Commissioner, 57 T.C. 587 (1972)), and then proceed with an exhaustive analysis of the corporation's financial and business history. While the cases are not easily classified, each turning on its own facts, they typically involve the factors discussed below.

2.2. *Accumulations for Expansion or Diversification*

The expansion or replacement of existing business facilities often is given as a justification for accumulations. Treas.Reg. § 1.537–1(b)(1) requires that the corporation "must have specific, definite, and feasible plans for the use of such accumulations." The courts have applied this requirement with varying degrees of strictness. See, e.g., Faber Cement Block Co., Inc. v. Commissioner, 50 T.C. 317 (1968) (acq.) (taxpayer's operations on its property constituted a nonconforming use under the local zoning ordinances and any expansion would have required an additional variance; accumulations over a long period of time for a proposed expansion were justified).

In addition to expansion of facilities, accumulations often are justified on the ground that they are needed to diversify the existing business. Treas.Reg. § 1.537–3(a) defines the "business" of a corporation broadly as "not merely that which it has previously carried on but includ[ing], in general, any line of business which it may undertake." On the other hand, investments that are "unrelated" to the activities of the business of the taxpayer are an indication of unreasonable accumulations, Treas.Reg. § 1.537–2(c)(4); the line between an "unrelated investment" and the beginning of a new "business" is not a clear one. See, e.g., Electric Regulator Corp. v. Commissioner, 336 F.2d 339 (2d Cir.1964) (taxpayer produced a small patented voltage regulator that was successful commercially, resulting in large accumulated profits; taxpayer's justification for the accumulation based on the desire to develop new products was sustained); Hughes Inc. v. Commissioner, 90 T.C. 1 (1988) (purchase of an orange grove and interests in partnerships holding real estate were justified as part of efforts to diversify the business of owning and leasing improved real and tangible personal properties); J. Gordon Turnbull, Inc. v. Commissioner, 41 T.C. 358 (1963) (fact that an architectural and engineering firm invested large sums in real estate was found indicative of an accumulation beyond the reasonable needs of its business); Cataphote Corp. v. United States, 535 F.2d 1225 (Ct.Cl.1976) (acquisition of 26 fractional working interests in oil and gas ventures by a corporation in the truck leasing business did not mean that the corporation was also in the oil and gas business for accumulated earnings tax purposes; the corporation did not have the necessary business responsibilities, and the interests constituted mere investments unrelated to the active business of the corporation).

2.3. *Working Capital Needs*

Treas.Reg. § 1.537–2(b)(4) recognizes the need to accumulate earnings "to provide necessary working capital for the business." The courts have struggled to develop standards for the determination of a reasonable allowance for working capital. Earlier cases allowed an accumulation of working capital to cover some arbitrary period of time, such as one year, or stressed the relationship between current liabilities and current assets in assessing working capital needs. More recent cases, following the approach taken initially in Bardahl Mfg. Corp. v. Commissioner, T.C. Memo. 1965–200, attempt to relate the corporation's need for working capital to its "operating cycle." In J.H. Rutter Rex Mfg. Co. v. Commissioner, 853 F.2d 1275 (5th Cir.1988), the court described the operating cycle approach as follows:

> An operating cycle for a manufacturing business like Rutter Rex is the period of time needed to convert cash into raw materials, raw materials into inventory, inventory into accounts receivable, and accounts receivable into cash. In other words, an operating cycle is the time a corporation's working capital is tied up in producing and selling its product. * * *

The "operating cycle" as originally formulated in *Bardahl Manufacturing* is broken down into two sub-cycles: an inventory cycle and an accounts receivable cycle. These cycles are measured in terms of days. An inventory cycle is the time necessary to convert raw materials into finished goods and to sell those goods. An accounts receivable cycle is the time necessary to convert the accounts receivable created by the sale of finished goods into cash. These two cycles are added together to determine the total number of days in the operating cycle. The number of days in the operating cycle is then divided by 365; the resulting fraction is multiplied by the amount of the corporation's operating expenses for one year, including costs of goods sold, selling expenses, general and administrative expenses, and estimated federal and state income tax payments (but excluding depreciation). The resulting figure is the amount of liquid assets necessary to meet the ordinary operating expenses for the complete operating cycle.

The *Bardahl* formula is also applied by taking account of a credit cycle. The credit cycle is based on the amount of time between the corporation's receipt of raw materials, supplies, labor, and other inputs, and the corporation's payment for these items. The deferral of payment reduces the corporation's need for capital, and thus the credit cycle is subtracted from the operating cycle determined from inventory and receivables cycles. See C.E. Hooper, Inc. v. United States, 539 F.2d 1276 (Ct.Cl.1976). In *J.H. Rutter Rex Mfg. Co.*, supra, the taxpayer convinced the appellate court that application of a credit cycle to reduce its working capital needs was inappropriate because of the lack of evidence that the corporation utilized an extension of credit from its major suppliers to any significant degree.

Despite the seeming exactness of the operating cycle formula, its limitations must be recognized. See Ready Paving & Construction Co. v. Commissioner, 61 T.C. 826 (1974) ("special investment warrants" received as payment for contracting work done for municipal governments constituted assets available for use as working capital under the *Bardahl* formula; correspondingly, the warrants did not constitute accounts receivable for determining the amount of accumulated earnings needed for working capital; consistent treatment of the items was required in both aspects of the *Bardahl* formula); Dielectric Materials Co. v. Commissioner, 57 T.C. 587 (1972) (*Bardahl* not strictly applied because the formula was not sufficiently "flexible" to take into account the fact that taxpayer had additional working capital needs in the light of a threatened labor dispute).

2.4. *Provision for Contingencies*

Fears, both real and imagined, of contingent liabilities also have been used to justify accumulations of earnings. In Halby Chemical Co., Inc. v. United States, 180 Ct.Cl. 584 (1967), the court allowed accumulations for self-insurance against the "enduring possibility of a disastrous fire or explosion" which could not adequately be covered by insurance because of the risk of taxpayer's operations. In Hughes Inc. v. Commissioner, 90 T.C. 1 (1988), a closely held corporation that rented warehouses to a publicly held corporation used accumulated earnings to purchase stock of the public corporation in order to prevent a hostile takeover of its lessee. The court said that investments in marketable securities that bear some relationship to a corporation's business are considered a proper business application of funds and may be accumulated with impunity. On the other hand, in Oyster Shell Products Corp. v. Commissioner, 313 F.2d 449 (2d Cir.1963), the taxpayer unsuccessfully attempted to justify accumulations on the ground that possible flooding of the river on which its operations were located could result in large expenses; the court rejected the argument as "conjured up" after the accumulated earnings tax issue was first raised by the Government.

In Otto Candies, LLC v. United States, 288 F. Supp. 2d 730 (E.D. La. 2003), an accumulation of between $15 and $21 million during the years in question by a closely held corporation (an LLC that elected to be taxed as a corporation) was found to meet the reasonable needs of the business. The taxpayer, a family corporation with three shareholders, was "one of the leading providers of marine transportation in the Gulf of Mexico." The corporation was found to be engaged in a volatile business and the dominant shareholder was conservative and avoided debt. The accumulations were required to fund necessary periodic fleet replacement, including newer vessels with modern technology meeting customer demands, new ventures into related businesses, and to internally fund future redemptions under a shareholder buy/sell agreement upon the death of a shareholder.

Section 537(b)(4) specifically provides for the accumulation of a reserve for reasonably anticipated product liability losses.

2.5. *Accumulations to Fund Stock Redemptions*

If a redemption is treated as a dividend under § 301, no accumulated earnings tax issue arises because the distribution is fully taxed at the shareholder level. But redemptions qualifying under § 302(b) or § 303 are not treated as dividends and thus raise an accumulated earnings tax issue. Pelton Steel Casting Co. v. Commissioner, 251 F.2d 278 (7th Cir.1958), held that the accumulated earnings tax applied in a case in which the corporation accumulated income to redeem the stock of two of its three shareholders rather than paying its earnings out as dividends to all of the shareholders and, presumably, then redeeming the stock at a lower price. The purpose of the redemption was to prevent the redeemed shareholders from selling their stock to outsiders, which was found not to be a corporate business purpose.

Mountain State Steel Foundries, Inc. v. Commissioner, 284 F.2d 737 (4th Cir.1960), held that the accumulated earnings tax did not apply to earnings in 1951 through 1954 used to pay a promissory note issued by the corporation in redemption of 50% of its shares in 1950. The Court emphasized that there was a business purpose for the redemption because the redeemed shareholders, who were inactive, had conflicting interests regarding corporate management with the continuing shareholders, who were active.

Is a business purpose such as was found in *Mountain State Steel Foundries* sufficient to justify a pre-redemption accumulation, as occurred in *Pelton Steel Casting Co.*? The lower courts have found a proper "corporate purpose" sufficient to avoid the accumulated earnings tax in a number of situations involving minority shareholders or retiring employee-shareholders. See Farmers & Merchants Investment Co. v. Commissioner, T.C.Memo. 1970–161 ("promotion of harmony in the conduct of the business"); Ted Bates & Co., Inc. v. Commissioner, T.C.Memo. 1965–251 (redemption made in order to assure "continuity of [taxpayer's] management"). In contrast, accumulations to redeem uncontentious large shareholders have been held subject to the tax. See John B. Lambert & Associates v. United States, 212 Ct.Cl. 71 (Ct.Cl.1976); Lamark Shipping Agency, Inc. v. Commissioner, T.C.Memo. 1981–284.

Section 537(a)(2) specifically provides that accumulations to fund redemptions that qualify under § 303 are to meet the reasonable need of the business. Section 537(b)(1), however, limits qualification under this rule to accumulations in the year the shareholder dies and subsequent years. Accumulations in years prior to the year of death cannot be justified by subsequent use for a § 303 redemption. See S.Rep. No. 91–522, 91st Cong., 1st Sess. 291 (1969).

2.6. *Shareholder Loans, Dividend Record, and Shareholder Tax Bracket*

While the fact that the corporation has paid no dividends is, of course, not conclusive on the issue of the proscribed purpose, it is a factor. Failure to pay dividends, together with loans to shareholders by the corporation, indicates an availability of funds to make dividend distributions. See, e.g., Bahan Textile Machinery Co. v. United States, 453 F.2d 1100 (4th Cir.1972) (loans to shareholders and relatives "show not only that the company was dissipating funds which it claimed were needed for the business, but also indicated a purpose to distribute corporate profits indirectly rather than as dividends that would be taxable to the recipients").

In GPD, Inc. v. Commissioner, 60 T.C. 480 (1973), rev'd, 508 F.2d 1076 (6th Cir.1974), the Tax Court held that the corporation was subject to the accumulated earnings tax for a year in which there had been a decrease in the corporation's earnings and profits. The Tax Court took the position that since there was no accumulation of earnings and profits, the accumulated earnings tax could not apply, even though in that year, the corporation did have accumulated taxable income under § 535.[2] The Court of Appeals reversed the Tax Court, holding that the legislative history of the accumulated earnings tax did not show any intent to require the accumulations of earnings and profits in the current year as a condition precedent to the imposition of the tax. The Court of Appeals observed that if the Tax Court position were adopted, and a corporation distributed the exact amount of its earnings and profits for a year, no accumulated earnings tax could be imposed on accumulated taxable income of the corporation in that year; on the other hand, one cent of undistributed earnings and profits for the year would subject the entire accumulated taxable income to the tax. Moreover, the Court of Appeals observed that the Tax Court rule in effect gave a corporation a double accumulated earnings tax credit, since a corporation would be protected both in the year of accumulation and also in the year in which the actual redemption reduced earnings and profits.

Atlantic Properties, Inc. v. Commissioner, 519 F.2d 1233 (1st Cir.1975), involved a corporation owned by four equal shareholders but whose corporate charter required an 80% vote of the shareholders for any corporate action. Three of the shareholders desired to have the corporation adopt a policy of

---

[2] Accumulated taxable income was present despite a reduction in earnings and profits because stock redemptions, not being dividends, had no effect on the determination of accumulated taxable income.

dividend distributions; one shareholder did not, in part because of the adverse tax consequences of the dividend distribution to him. The court held that the accumulated earnings tax applied since the corporation was availed of for a proscribed purpose, even though a majority of the shareholders did not agree with that purpose.

2.7. *Accumulations by and for Subsidiaries*

Treas.Reg. § 1.537–3(b) provides that under certain circumstances the accumulated earnings of a parent corporation may be justified by the reasonably anticipated business needs of its subsidiary. In the converse situation, the Court of Appeals in Inland Terminals, Inc. v. United States, 477 F.2d 836 (4th Cir.1973), held that it was also possible to justify a controlled subsidiary's accumulated earnings with reference to the parent corporation's reasonably anticipated business needs that the parent corporation itself could not satisfy. On remand, the District Court held that the parent corporation's alternative diversification or relocation plans were such as would take all or substantially all of its own earnings and those of the subsidiary; thus, the combined earnings of the two corporations did not exceed the reasonable needs of the parent's business. 73–2 U.S.T.C. ¶ 9724 (D.Md.1973).

In Chaney & Hope, Inc. v. Commissioner, 80 T.C. 263 (1983) (acq.), the court held that accumulations for the business needs of a brother or sister corporation cannot generally be considered as accumulations to meet reasonable business needs because the business of the sister corporation is not the business of the brother corporation. The court also held, however, that the taxpayer could accumulate its earnings to meet the reasonably anticipated future needs of an expanded business to be conducted by its successor corporation, a sister corporation into which the taxpayer would be merged. Permissible accumulations were limited to earnings accumulated after the time plans for the merger became definite.

In Advanced Delivery and Chemical Systems of Nevada, Inc. v. Commissioner, T.C. Memo 2003–250, a holding company was found not to be liable for accumulated earnings tax where the business activities of its subsidiaries and partnerships in which it was a partner were attributed to it under Treas.Reg. § 1.537–3(b). Because of the rapid growth of the affiliates' businesses, the accumulations did not exceed the holding company's reasonable needs for expansion of the affiliates. Furthermore, on the particular facts, even if the accumulations did exceed the taxpayers' reasonable needs, there was not a tax avoidance purpose.

2.8. *Valuation Aspects*

In Ivan Allen v. United States, 422 U.S. 617 (1975), the issue was whether, in determining the reasonable needs of the business, marketable securities owned by the corporation should be counted at cost, as the taxpayer asserted, or their net liquidation value, as claimed by the IRS. The Court pointed out that the accumulated earnings tax itself is imposed only on accumulated taxable income, which includes only realized gains. The Court held, however, that in determining whether accumulations exceed the reasonable needs of the business the full value of readily available liquid assets should be taken into account.

The decision of the Supreme Court in *Ivan Allen* was correct from the standpoint of the policy behind the accumulated earnings tax. The actual value that the corporation could realize from its investments and distribute to its shareholders is the best measure of the amount and reasonableness of its total accumulation; the cost basis of the investments is not relevant to that determination. Nevertheless, there are some difficulties in implementing the Court's decision. The majority in *Ivan Allen* assumed that the proper time for valuation of the securities was the end of the taxable year of the corporation. In some instances, other dates, for example, the date on which the Board of Directors makes its dividend decision for the year, might be more appropriate. There are also some technical problems. In other areas of the tax law, valuation of securities is made by taking a "blockage" factor into account, i.e., the size of the block of stock held by a particular shareholder can reduce the total value below a fair market value based on the quoted per share value because a single sale of the entire block would depress the market. Valuation of closely held stock will present similar difficulties.

The majority in *Ivan Allen* went to some length to emphasize that its opinion was directed toward "readily marketable portfolio securities." But, as the dissenters pointed out, the majority's "rationale is not so easily contained." If a corporation holds securities that are not readily marketable but are still unrelated to its business, the majority's reasoning appears equally applicable; the lack of marketability or difficulties in disposition would be relevant to the valuation issue but do not lead to the conclusion that cost basis should be employed. Likewise, a finding that investments in real estate, timber land, and other such assets are unrelated to the business of the corporation should call into play the fair market value approach adopted by the majority.

In footnote 9 of the opinion, the majority stated that it was expressing no view with respect to the valuation of items such as inventory or accounts receivable. Motor Fuel Carriers, Inc. v. Commissioner, 559 F.2d 1348 (5th Cir.1977), held that accounts receivable should be treated as liquid assets for accumulated earnings tax purposes and valued at fair market value.

3. PROCEDURAL ASPECTS

In addition to the presumptions in § 533, discussed above, § 534 sets forth a complicated allocation of the burden of proof on certain issues in Tax Court proceedings. The provision is intended to ease the burden on the taxpayer in an accumulated earnings tax case. See Senate Finance Committee Report, S.Rep. No. 83–1622, 83rd Cong., 2d Sess. 70–71 (1954). The provision, however, has not been of much help to taxpayers because the Tax Court has been quite strict regarding the required content of the taxpayer's statement under § 534(c). It must contain adequate factual material and not simply "conclusory" statements. Consider J.H. Rutter Rex Mfg. Co. v. Commissioner, 853 F.2d 1275, 1283 (5th Cir.1988), in which the taxpayer's statement was found wanting because of its failure to quantify working capital needs and provide financial information supporting its claim: "Obviously the statute does not contemplate shifting the burden of proof when a taxpayer merely tells the Commissioner it is going to challenge the imposition of the accumulated earnings tax. There must be notice of the specific grounds and contentions." See Hughes Inc. v. Commissioner, 90 T.C. 1 (1988) (taxpayer provided sufficient detail which, if proven, would support the alleged business needs for the accumulation with respect to some but not all of the grounds asserted). The significance of the shift in the burden of proof provided by § 534 is reduced by § 7491, enacted in 1998, which shifts the burden of proof to the IRS after the taxpayer has produced credible evidence in support of the taxpayer's position, but only if the taxpayer has cooperated with the IRS.

Sections 561–563 provide a deduction for dividends paid within two and one-half months of the close of the taxable year, which dividends reduce the taxpayer's accumulated earnings and profits for the prior year for purposes of the accumulated earnings tax.

SECTION 2.   THE PERSONAL HOLDING COMPANY TAX

INTERNAL REVENUE CODE: Sections 541–547; 6501(f).

Section 541 imposes a special tax on the undistributed personal holding company income of a corporation that qualifies as a personal holding company. For most of its history, the personal holding company tax was imposed on corporate income at the highest individual tax rate. Under current law, a 20% tax—the same rate as the maximum rate that applies to dividends—is imposed by § 541 on the undistributed personal holding company income of a personal holding company. A corporation is classified as a personal holding company under § 542(a) if at least 60% of its adjusted ordinary gross income is personal holding company income and more than 50% in value of its stock is directly or indirectly owned by five or fewer individuals.[3]

The tax operates as an automatic obstacle to corporate accumulations intended to avoid the individual tax on the shareholders, since it does not turn on the need, reasonableness, or purpose of an accumulation but instead is applied if its objective conditions are met.

Even an apparent operating company unexpectedly may find itself with a sufficiently high proportion of personal holding company income to trigger the tax. See Eller v. Commissioner, 77 T.C. 934 (1981) (acq.). Similarly, an active corporation that is in the process of liquidating and

---

[3]   Rev.Rul. 89–20, 1989–1 C.B. 170, holds that for purposes of determining whether five or fewer persons own 50% or more of the stock of a corporation, stock held directly or indirectly by a shareholder will only be counted once. Thus, stock that is attributed from one person to another under the family and partnership attribution rules of § 544(a)(2) is not taken into account a second time, either as stock of the person who owns it directly or as stock of a third person to whom it is also attributable. If stock owned directly by one person is attributed to another and counted as the stock of that second person, the first person may nevertheless be counted among the five largest shareholders by virtue of attribution to that person of stock that is directly owned by others and that has not otherwise been taken into account for purposes of § 542(a)(2).

selling its assets can become a personal holding company by virtue of the passive investment income that is generated by investments of the sales proceeds prior to distribution in liquidation. See Lachinski v. Commissioner, T.C. Memo. 1986–334 (interest on installment sale of active business received pending liquidation triggered personal holding company tax; the court rejected the taxpayer's argument that personal holding company income is limited to passive rather than active income).

DETAILED ANALYSIS

1. PERSONAL HOLDING COMPANY INCOME

1.1. *Incorporated Passive Investments*

A personal holding company has been called an "incorporated pocketbook," a corporation used by the taxpayer to derive investment income at lower corporate rates. Personal holding company income includes passive rents,[4] dividends, interest,[5] non-mineral royalties, produced film rents, amounts under certain personal service contracts, and mineral royalties.[6] Personal holding company income excludes "active rental income" (rental income earned by a corporation if such income is more than 50% of adjusted ordinary gross income) but only if undistributed personal holding company income (not including rents) does not exceed 10% of the corporation's ordinary gross income. The 10% rule, in effect, requires $900 of adjusted income from rents to shield $100 of dividend income from the personal holding company tax. Similar limitations apply with respect to oil, gas, and mineral royalties, and copyright royalties. I.R.C. § 543(a)(3) and (4). Section 543(a)(1)(C) excludes royalties received from computer software from the definition of personal holding company income.

1.2. *Incorporated Personal Services*

The personal holding company provisions are also aimed at an "incorporated talent," a corporation formed to shelter the personal service income of a particular individual from individual income tax rates and to provide fringe benefits such as an employer provided health plan or retirement plan. Under § 543(a)(7) personal holding company income includes amounts received under personal service contracts if someone other than the corporation has the right to designate the person who is to perform the services and that designated person owns more than 25% of the outstanding stock of the corporation. For example, in Kenyatta Corp. v. Commissioner, 86 T.C. 171 (1986), aff'd, 812 F.2d 577 (9th Cir. 1987), former pro-basketball star Bill Russell formed a corporation to contract for his promotional services. The corporation entered into contracts with different media outlets and the Seattle SuperSonics (who separately employed Russell

---

[4]   As to whether receipts constitute rents, see, e.g., Hilldun Corp. v. Commissioner, 408 F.2d 1117 (2d Cir.1969); Rev.Rul. 70–153, 1970–1 C.B. 139.

[5]   Personal holding company interest includes interest imputed to the taxpayer from interest free loans to related persons. See Likins-Foster Honolulu Corp. v. Commissioner, 840 F.2d 642 (9th Cir.1988); Krueger Co. v. Commissioner, 79 T.C. 65 (1982).

[6]   As to whether receipts constitute mineral royalties, see Bayou Verret Land Co., Inc. v. Commissioner, 450 F.2d 850 (5th Cir.1971); Rev.Rul. 72–148, 1972–1 C.B. 170.

as a coach) for promotional appearances and a newspaper column. On examination of the taxpayer's contracts, the Tax Court found that the contracting party was contracting specifically for Russell's services.

In general, however, the IRS has been surprisingly liberal in its interpretation of the "right to designate" requirement of § 543(a)(7). For example, Rev.Rul. 75–67, 1975–1 C.B. 169, held that no personal services income resulted from a contract to render medical services between a patient and a professional corporation even though the principal shareholder-doctor was the only medical doctor employed by the corporation. Since the contract between the patient and the corporation did not explicitly state that the doctor would personally perform the services, no "designation" was present despite the fact that it was clear that both parties anticipated that the doctor would perform the services. See also Rev.Rul. 75–249, 1975–1 C.B. 171 (the fact that a client may solicit and expect the services of a professional entertainer is not a designation as long as there is no personal obligation to perform). Thus, as long as the person contracting for the services of a professional is willing to run the slight, but real, risk that the professional in theory has the right to substitute the performance of another, the personal holding company provisions can be avoided. In RAS of Sand River, Inc. v. Commissioner, T.C. Memo. 1990–322, aff'd by order, 935 F.2d 270 (6th Cir.1991), the taxpayer's sole shareholder incorporated the taxpayer to provide engineering services. Although the written contract between the corporation and its customer did not designate a particular person to perform the work or give the customer the right to designate the person to perform the work, the court found that an oral agreement with the customer required the work to be performed by the taxpayer's sole shareholder. The court reached this result even though the shareholder's services were not so valuable or unique as to be irreplaceable.

1.3. *Incorporated Personal Use Assets*

The third device targeted by the personal holding company provisions is incorporation of personal use property such as a yacht or vacation home. Individuals would put personal use property in a corporation along with passive investments producing sufficient income to maintain the personal use property. The more aggressive taxpayer would then attempt to deduct the cost of maintaining the personal use property from income produced by the passive investment, thereby maintaining the personal use property with tax-free income. In a modified form, the taxpayer might rent the personal use property from the corporation for an arm's-length rental which was less than the cost of maintenance, and fund the difference with income from passive assets. To combat these attempts, § 543(a)(6) includes as personal holding company income amounts received as compensation for the use of tangible property of the corporation if a 25% or greater shareholder is entitled to personal use of the property. In addition, § 545(b)(6) provides that in computing taxable income subject to the personal holding company tax, no deduction for depreciation and maintenance expense shall be allowed against rental income from property held by a personal holding company unless the corporation can establish (A) that the rent received was the highest rent attainable, (B) that the property is held in the course of a business carried on for bona fide profit, and (C) that there is either an expectation that operation of the property would produce a profit or that the property is necessary for the conduct of the business. Section 545(b)(6) is intended to insure that deductions attributable to property used by a shareholder do not reduce other personal holding company income.

2. COMPUTING THE PERSONAL HOLDING COMPANY TAX BASE

Section 541 imposes the personal holding company tax on the corporation's "undistributed personal holding company income." Section 545 defines this undistributed taxable income as the current year's taxable income less deductions for other taxes,[7] dividends[8] (including consent dividends not involving actual distributions), and other disbursements. In addition, § 547 allows a deficiency dividend deduction under which a deficiency in personal holding company tax may be avoided by a dividend distribution to shareholders after a determination of the deficiency. This device is helpful, for example, if the corporation does not realize it is a personal holding company or if, even though it realizes it is a personal holding company, believes that it has distributed all of its income only to find that undistributed income exists either because the IRS has found additional income items or has disallowed deductions. This device is not available, however, if fraud is present or there was a willful failure to file an income tax return.

3. ADDITIONAL ASPECTS OF THE PERSONAL HOLDING COMPANY PROVISIONS

There are several facets of the relationship between the accumulated earnings tax and the personal holding company tax. A corporation may escape the accumulated earnings tax, which is based upon the accumulation of earnings and profits, but still be subject to the personal holding company tax, because the latter tax depends upon the existence of undistributed personal holding company income, a concept entirely distinct from earnings and profits. Also, the concept of "accumulation" is essentially absent from the personal holding company tax. On the other hand, if the corporation is a personal holding company, the accumulated earnings tax does not apply. I.R.C. § 532(b)(1). But a corporation that avoids personal holding company status must still face the possibility that its accumulations will be reached under the accumulated earnings tax.

---

[7] The deduction for taxes paid is limited to taxes accrued during the taxable year. Contested tax liabilities are not properly accrued and therefore not allowed as a deduction in computing income subject to the personal holding company tax. Kluger Associates, Inc. v. Commissioner, 617 F.2d 323 (2d Cir.1980); LX Cattle Company v. United States, 629 F.2d 1096 (5th Cir.1980).

[8] Treas.Reg. § 1.562–1(a) provides that the reduction in income for dividends if appreciated property is distributed as a dividend in kind is limited to the adjusted basis of the property. The Supreme Court in Fulman v. United States, 434 U.S. 528 (1978), resolving a conflict in the Circuits, upheld the regulation as it applies to distributions of appreciated property. The Court, after describing a rather confusing legislative history, found a "reasonable basis" for the regulation limiting the corporate deduction to the basis of the property despite the fact that the full fair market value of the property is included in the income of the shareholder as a dividend. The limitation to adjusted basis no longer may be appropriate as the distributing corporation is required to recognize gain on the distribution of appreciated property.

An active manufacturing company with some investment income may fall accidentally into personal holding company status. For manufacturing companies, "gross income" is not "gross receipts" but instead constitutes gross receipts less cost of goods sold. Thus, in a bad year in which the cost of goods sold exceeded gross receipts, the corporation might find itself with less than 40% of its adjusted ordinary gross income from non-personal holding income sources.

The at-risk provisions of § 465, limiting the taxpayer's ability to take deductions in connection with nonrecourse financing, apply to "closely held" corporations that meet the stock ownership requirements of § 542(a)(2). This limitation in turn can have an impact on the calculation of adjusted ordinary gross income and thus on the status of the corporation as a personal holding company.

PART VI

AFFILIATED CORPORATIONS

CHAPTER 15

AFFILIATED CORPORATIONS

Business activities linked by common ownership may be conducted as separate divisions in a single corporation or divided into separate corporate entities. Related corporate entities may share common ownership through identity of stockholders, i.e., each corporation is owned pro rata by the same group of stockholders (brother-sister corporations), or may be linked through a chain of parent subsidiary corporations in which the ultimate stockholders own the stock of the common parent corporation.

The corporate tax system must identify whether and under what circumstances separate incorporation of activities under common control will be recognized for tax purposes. If separate business activities are conducted within a single corporation, the income and operating losses of each activity are netted to produce a single taxable income or loss for the combined operation within the corporation. Earnings and profits, net operating losses, and many corporate elections, such as the taxable year, are combined and shared by each of the separate activities. On the other hand, separation of business activities related by common ownership and control into different corporations may result in very different tax consequences. The operating losses of one activity will be separated from the taxable income of another. Thus, one activity may be subject to tax on its income while the other has unused net operating losses that will be carried forward to other taxable years of that corporation. Elections, taxable years, accounting methods, all may vary among the entities. The conduct of business activities through different entities also makes it possible to attempt to affect the profitability of each activity by manipulating the price of goods and services in transactions between jointly owned corporations. Thus, X Corporation could reduce its taxable income by selling goods to related Y Corporation at a price less than its cost of manufacturing the goods and thereby increase the taxable income of Y Corporation, which could sell the goods outside of the related group at a higher price.[1]

The Code contains two different regimes for dealing with some of the issues raised by related corporations. Rules prevent creation of losses between related entities, I.R.C. § 267, and the use of intercompany pricing among controlled corporations to avoid tax, I.R.C. § 482, which is significant mostly with respect to non-U.S. operations. The second regime, the consolidated return provisions of § 1501 through § 1504, accommodates affiliated groups of parent-subsidiary corporations that

---

[1] Although the international tax regime is beyond the scope of this text, this technique becomes particularly significant in the international context when related corporations are formed in different countries with different tax rates and structural rules.

want to combine the incomes and losses of separately incorporated activities into a single consolidated income for the entire group.

SECTION 1.   REALLOCATION OF INCOME UNDER SECTION 482

INTERNAL REVENUE CODE: Section 482.

The cases arising under § 482 discussed in Chapter 1 involved attempts by taxpayers to channel income between the corporation and its stockholder so as to take advantage of the differences between individual and corporate tax rates. The issues under § 482 as it applies to related corporations involve the same strategic goal of reduced taxation, though the situations are somewhat different. With a uniform 21% corporate tax rate, there is not much in the way of tax savings to be obtained by strategic arrangements of transactions among domestic corporations. Nonetheless, special situations still exist that prompt such arrangements and in turn prompt the IRS to apply § 482. For example, a tax advantage can be obtained by the artificial shifting of income from a profitable corporation to a related corporation with a net operating loss that it would not otherwise be able to use. See, e.g., Ballentine Motor Co. v. Commissioner, 321 F.2d 796 (4th Cir.1963) (appreciated inventory was transferred by a parent to a subsidiary with a loss carryover, with the subsidiary subsequently realizing the income; held, IRS properly allocated the income on the sale to the parent under § 482); Likins-Foster Honolulu Corp. v. Commissioner, 417 F.2d 285 (10th Cir.1969) (§ 482 allocation prevented use of losses in a consolidated return). For other cases applying § 482 in a domestic context, see Engineering Sales, Inc. v. United States, 510 F.2d 565 (5th Cir.1975); Liberty Loan Corp. v. United States, 498 F.2d 225 (8th Cir.1974).

Section 482 is of greatest importance in the international area. Here, the significance of transactions between related corporations arises because of the deferral of U.S. tax on the profits of foreign subsidiaries controlled by U.S. parent corporations that operate in countries with tax rates lower than the United States. If, for example, a U.S. parent corporation sells its products to its controlled foreign subsidiary at an artificially low price and the subsidiary then sells the products in the foreign market, there would be an understatement of the parent's portion of the profits on the transactions, and an overstatement of the subsidiary's portion. In addition, even if the foreign related corporation is taxed at rates comparable to U.S. rates, so that no overall tax saving is involved, § 482 is necessary to ensure that the U.S. obtains its appropriate share of revenues from international transactions. For representative cases see Bausch & Lomb v. Commissioner, 933 F.2d 1084 (2d Cir.1991) (IRS's increase of sales price of soft contact lenses from Irish manufacturing subsidiary to domestic parent corporation was an abuse of discretion, but 5% royalty for use of intangibles paid to parent was too low; the court rejected the IRS's assertion that a royalty in the range of

27% to 33% was proper and adopted a royalty of 20%); Eli Lilly & Co. v. Commissioner, 856 F.2d 855 (7th Cir.1988); G.D. Searle & Co. v. Commissioner, 88 T.C. 252 (1987) (§ 482 applied to reallocate income from the manufacture of pharmaceuticals in Puerto Rico based on patents and research developed by the United States parent corporation); Seagate Technology, Inc. v. Commissioner, 102 T.C. 149 (1994) (acq. in result) (IRS's reallocation of income from a Singapore manufacturing subsidiary to its U.S. parent for sales of component parts and completed disk drives was arbitrary and capricious; the subsidiary's 1% royalty rate to its parent on direct sales was increased to 3%; compensation for procurement services rendered to the subsidiary was adequate; and research and development expenses were reallocated between the parent and subsidiary).

Congress has steadily tightened the application of § 482 in the international context, particularly as it applies to intangibles. See § 367 and § 482 (last two sentences). The Treasury Department has promulgated a complex set of Regulations under § 482 to ensure that taxpayers clearly reflect income attributable to controlled transactions by placing commonly controlled taxpayers on "a tax parity with an uncontrolled taxpayer by determining the true taxable income of the controlled taxpayer." Treas.Reg. § 1.482–1(a)(1). True taxable income results from a transaction under an "arm's length" standard, which attempts to equate a controlled transaction with the result that would have occurred if the uncontrolled taxpayers had engaged in the same transaction under similar circumstances. Treas.Reg. § 1.482–1(b)(1). The Regulations contain detailed methodologies for determining arm's length pricing in a variety of transactions. See Treas.Regs. §§ 1.482–2 through –6. Treas.Reg. § 1.482–1(a)(2) authorizes the IRS to reallocate items affecting taxable income among members of a controlled group. Although § 482 does not authorize taxpayers to invoke its terms to reallocate income or deductions, Treas.Reg. § 1.482–1(a)(3) permits a taxpayer to report income on a return using prices that vary from the prices actually charged in a controlled transaction in order to reflect an arm's length result.

The treatment of intercompany transactions under § 482 should be compared with the approach in the consolidated return context where a deferred accounting technique is used to postpone the recognition of gain or loss on intercompany sales until the property is sold outside the group.

SECTION 2.   CONSOLIDATED RETURNS

INTERNAL REVENUE CODE: Sections 1501; 1503(b); 1504(a)–(b).

REGULATIONS: Sections 1.1502–1(f), (g), –2, –11(a), –12, –13(a), (b), (c)(7)(ii), Exs. 1–4, (d), –19(a)–(g), –21(a), (b)(1), –22(a)–(b), –32(a) and (b), –33(a), (b), (c), (d)(1), (e)(1), –34.

Virtually all publicly owned corporations that have subsidiaries, as well as the handful of large privately owned corporations that have subsidiaries and cannot (or chose not to) make an election under Subchapter S, as well as the domestic subsidiary groups of foreign corporations, elect to report their income for federal tax purposes as part of a consolidated group rather than as separate entities. In one form or another, the consolidated return regime dates back to 1917, although the current regime is far more sophisticated than its early forerunners. The modern consolidated return regime is highly complex and articulated by voluminous Regulations. Nevertheless, judging by the paucity of litigation in the area, one must conclude that the regime works surprisingly well.

Election to File a Consolidated Return—Section 1501 provides that all members of an affiliated group of corporations may elect to file a consolidated income tax return. A consolidated return permits the includible corporations (as defined in § 1504(b)) that are members of an affiliated group of corporations to combine their incomes, net operating losses, credits, and other items into a single return. Section 1502 authorizes the Treasury to promulgate Regulations as necessary in order "that the tax liability of any affiliated group of corporations making a consolidated return and of each corporation in the group * * * may be returned, determined, computed, assessed, collected, and adjusted, in such manner as clearly to reflect the income tax liability and the various factors necessary for the determination of such liability, and in order to prevent avoidance of such tax liability." Section 1502 specifically provides that the consolidated return Regulations may contain "rules that are different from the provisions . . . that would apply if such corporations filed separate returns." Broadly speaking, the Regulations reflect a "single entity" approach to dealings within the group that attempts to treat the several members of a consolidated group in the same manner as divisions of a single corporation. In certain instances, a separate-corporation approach applies, however, to coordinate separate-return and consolidated-return years and to properly associate certain tax attributes with particular members of the group.

The members of an affiliated group includible in a consolidated return are identified under § 1504(a) as the common parent corporation and one or more corporations affiliated through a chain (or chains) of corporations connected by ownership of stock representing 80% of the voting power and value of each affiliated member. (The value determination is made without regard to certain non-voting, nonconvertible preferred stock. I.R.C. § 1504(a)(4).) Unless otherwise excluded by statutory provision, any corporation that is connected to the common parent or another member of an affiliated group by meeting this ownership requirement is treated as an "includible corporation" and must be included on the consolidated return. I.R.C. § 1501. Foreign subsidiaries are specifically excluded from the definition of "includible corporation" and thus are almost never included in a consolidated return. I.R.C. § 1504(b)(3).

Advantages of Filing a Consolidated Return: Net Operating Losses— The principal advantage of filing consolidated returns is the ability to combine the income and loss of each member of an affiliated group into a single taxable income. Treas.Reg. § 1.1502–11(a). Thus, net operating losses of one member of the group can be used to offset the taxable income of another member. This ability to offset losses of one member of the group against income of another member of the group does not extend to affiliated corporations that do not file a consolidated return.

In addition, net operating losses of a member of the group incurred during consolidated return years of the group in which the group as a whole operates at a loss contribute to the overall net operating loss of the group, which may be carried forward to other consolidated return years, offsetting income of any member of the group. There are, however, limitations on carryovers of losses incurred by a corporation in separate return years before the corporation became a member of the affiliated group. Treas.Reg. § 1.1502–21(c). Filing a consolidated return also permits the members of the affiliated group to exclude intercompany dividends from gross income in computing taxable income and to defer recognition of gain or loss on intercompany transactions. The basis of stock of one member of a consolidated group held by another member is adjusted to reflect taxable income, loss, and the other items of the lower-tier member. Intercompany distributions and contributions also affect the basis of stock of a member of an affiliated group that is held by the common parent or other members, thereby increasing or decreasing gain or loss on disposition of the stock. In addition, deferred intercompany gains and losses may be taken into account in the event that a member leaves the consolidated group, even if the transaction otherwise would be accorded nonrecognition treatment as a tax-free reorganization. Filing consolidated returns requires that all members of the consolidated group use the taxable year of the common parent, but, subject to an anti-abuse rule, the individual members may use different accounting methods. Treas.Regs. § 1.1502–76(a), –17.

Advantages of Filing a Consolidated Return: Intercompany Transactions—The treatment of intercompany transactions within members of a consolidated group offers significant advantages in many instances. In general, the tax consequences of intercompany transactions between members of the same consolidated group are accounted for in consolidated taxable income as transactions between divisions of a single corporation. Treas.Reg. § 1.1502–13(a)(2). In the case of payment for services or a sale or exchange of property, gain or loss that is recognized by the selling member under its method of accounting is deferred until the item can be matched with the buying member's accounting of its corresponding item in the form of a deduction or a recovery of basis when the expenditure is capitalized. Treas.Reg. § 1.1502–13(c)(2). Thus, in the case of an intercompany sale of property, the selling member defers accounting for its recognized gain or loss until the date on which the buying member sells the property outside of the consolidated group or an analogous event requiring acceleration occurs. In this manner, the gain or loss is deferred until the property is disposed of outside of the consolidated group, as would be the case with respect to an exchange of property between divisions of a single corporation. The character of the selling member's deferred gain and the buying member's recognized gain on sale outside of the group also will be determined by single entity principles. The activities of each, therefore, may affect the character of the other's gain. Treas.Reg. § 1.1502–13(c)(1)(i). For example, assume that S Corporation and B Corporation are members of an affiliated group filing a consolidated return. S Corporation sells appreciated investment real estate to B Corporation. Subsequently, B Corporation develops the land as residential real estate for sale to customers in the ordinary course of B Corporation's trade or business. When B Corporation disposes of the land, S Corporation must recognize its deferred gain. Even though S Corporation held the land for investment at the time of its sale to B Corporation, both S Corporation and B Corporation's gain will be treated as ordinary income. Treas.Reg. § 1.1502–13(c)(7)(ii), Ex. 2.

In the case of a sale of depreciable property, the selling member will defer its gain or loss to the time when the buying member claims increased capital cost recovery deductions. Treas.Reg. § 1.1502–13(c)(7)(ii), Ex. 4. For example, under the single entity approach of the Regulations, if the selling member sells depreciable property at a gain, the increased capital recovery deductions that result from the buying member's cost basis will be offset by the corresponding gain taken into account by the selling member. In this fashion, these transactions have no net effect on the overall taxable income of the group, which is the same result that would have occurred if the selling and buying members had been divisions of a single corporation, rather than separate corporations filing a consolidated return. Any increased deduction or basis recovery by the buying member will be offset on the consolidated return by an equivalent recognition of deferred gain by the selling member.

Deferred gain or loss from intercompany transactions is accelerated into a year in which it becomes no longer possible to match the buying member's corresponding item with the selling member's deferred gain or loss. Treas.Reg. § 1.1502–13(d). Thus, gain or loss deferred by the selling member will be accounted for if either the buying member or the selling member ceases to be a member of the consolidated group before the buying member accounts for its matching item corresponding to the selling member's deferred gain or loss.

Distributions—Distributions from one member of an affiliated group to another are also treated under the single entity principle. Distributions are not included in the income of the recipient, Treas.Reg. § 1.1502–13(f)(2)(ii), but only so long as there is a matching reduction in the basis of the stock of the distributing member held by the recipient member under the investment adjustment rules of Treas.Reg. § 1.1502–32. Gain recognized by the distributing member under § 311(b) is deferred under the matching principle until the property is sold outside the group, the property is depreciated by the distributee member, or either the distributing or distributee corporation leaves the group. Treas.Reg. § 1.1502–13(f)(2)(iii).

Aggregate Versus Entity Theory—Even though the federal tax liability of an affiliated group filing a consolidated return is based on the combined taxable incomes of the members of the affiliated group, the separate tax identity of each member of the group is respected through maintenance of individual earnings and profits accounts and basis adjustments with respect to the stock of each member. Treas.Regs. §§ 1.1502–19, –31, –32, and –33. Accounting for the separate tax identity of each member is required to determine tax consequences in the event that an includible corporation enters or leaves the affiliated group. As a result, while accounting for certain intercompany transactions is deferred for purposes of computing taxable income of the group under the consolidated return rules, those transactions will affect the earnings and profits and stock basis of the component members.

Investment Adjustment Accounts—The Regulations require a series of "investment adjustments" to the basis of stock of subsidiaries held by other members of an affiliated group. Treas.Reg. § 1.1502–32. These adjustments are intended to eliminate potential double tax consequences as the separate taxable income or loss of each member of the consolidated group is reflected on the consolidated return. Treas.Reg. § 1.1502–32(a)(1). Investment adjustments begin with the stock of the lowest-tier subsidiary in a chain and work their way up to stock of includible corporations held by the common parent. Treas.Reg. § 1.1502–32(a)(3)(iii). Positive adjustments increase the basis of the stock of a subsidiary member of the group held by another member, and negative adjustments decrease basis. Treas.Reg. § 1.1502–32(b)(2). Adjustments are made for the net amount of the subsidiary's taxable income or loss, expired loss carryover, tax-exempt income, non-deductible non-capital expenses (e.g., fines and disallowed losses), and distributions with respect to the stock of the subsidiary. Losses of a subsidiary and/or distributions may exceed the upper-tier corporation's basis in the stock of the subsidiary. In that case, Treas.Reg. § 1.1502–32(a)(3)(ii) provides for the creation of an "excess loss account," which is the equivalent of a negative basis in the subsidiary's stock.[2] The amount of an excess loss account attributable to the stock of an includible subsidiary is recognized as income (1) on a sale of the stock, (2) whenever either the subsidiary or the includible corporation holding the stock ceases to be a member of the consolidated group, or (3) if the subsidiary's stock becomes worthless (as defined in the Regulations). Treas.Reg. § 1.1502–19(a)(1), (b). The gain is generally treated as gain from the disposition of stock and is thus capital gain. To the extent that the subsidiary is, however, insolvent (or deemed to be insolvent), gain is ordinary, except to the extent that the excess loss account is attributable to distributions. Treas.Reg. § 1.1502–19(b)(4).

Elections—In the first year that a group files a consolidated return, each member of the affiliated group for any part of that year must consent to filing the return; generally, that consent must be demonstrated by the member filing a Form 1122 with the first return. Treas.Reg. § 1.1502–75(a)(1), (b)(2). The common parent consents to the return by filing the return. After the first year, each member is deemed to consent to the return, even if it joins the group after that first year. Treas.Reg. § 1.1502–75(a)(2).

An election to file a consolidated return may not be revoked without the consent of the IRS. Permission to discontinue filing a consolidated return will be granted only on a showing of good cause. Treas.Reg. § 1.1502–75(c). Treas.Reg. § 1.1502–75(c)(1)(ii) describes "good cause" as including a change in the Code, Regulations, or other law which has a "substantial adverse effect" on the tax liability of an affiliated group relative to the aggregate tax liability of the members of the group filing separate returns. The IRS has additional authority to grant blanket permission to discontinue filing consolidated returns to all groups, or to a class of groups, in the event of a change in the law of the type that will have a "substantial adverse effect on the filing of consolidated returns." Treas.Reg. § 1.1502–75(c)(2). The election to file a consolidated return will, therefore, affect the tax liability of an affiliated group for the current and future tax years, and a proposal to file a consolidated return must be carefully analyzed.

DETAILED ANALYSIS

1. ELIGIBILITY AND INCLUDIBLE CORPORATIONS

1.1. *Stock Ownership*

An affiliated group consists of the common parent and one or more chains of corporations connected through stock ownership with the common parent. I.R.C. § 1504(a)(1). The common parent must own stock of at least one other corporation that represents at least 80% of the total voting power of the stock of that corporation and has value equal to at least 80% of the total value of the stock of that corporation. I.R.C. § 1504(a)(1), (2). In

---

[2]   Reg. § 1.1502–19(a)(2)(ii) refers to the amount of an excess loss account as "basis that is negative in amount."

addition, each includible corporation must be connected to the common parent or to one or more corporations owned by the common parent with the requisite 80% of voting power and value. Thus, a single chain of connected corporations or parallel brother-sister corporations connected to a common parent corporation can qualify as an affiliated group. All shares of stock within a class are treated as having the same value. Control premiums, minority discounts, and blockage discounts are not taken into account. Treas.Reg. § 1.1504–4(b)(2)(iv).

Generally, voting power relates to the right to elect members of the board of directors, although other factors may be considered for complicated voting arrangements. In Alumax Inc. v. Commissioner, 109 T.C. 133 (1997), aff'd, 165 F.3d 822 (11th Cir. 1999), the court was required to interpret the 80% voting power requirement of § 1502(a)(2) in the face of a complicated voting arrangement. Alumax had two classes of stock outstanding. The class C stock, which was owned by an affiliated group claiming control, was entitled to elect four of six voting members of the Alumax Board. The class B stock was entitled to elect two of six voting members. The class B and class C directors, in the aggregate and not voting by class, elected one of two special non-voting directors. By agreement between the two classes of stockholders, the class B directors were permitted to name this special director. The other special non-voting director was the CEO of Alumax. Each of the two class B directors had one vote. Each of the four class C directors had two votes. However, a majority of the directors of each of the two classes was required to approve certain corporate actions. Likewise, with respect to shareholder votes, each share of class C stock had four votes while each share of class B stock had one vote. A majority vote of each class of stock was required with respect to a number of restricted stockholder matters. The court rejected the taxpayer's assertion that a mechanical application of these voting formulae represented 80% voting control. The court held that the impact of various restrictions on the actions of elected directors must be taken into account in assessing the existence of voting power under § 1502(a)(2). Accordingly, the control test was not met and Alumax was not part of the affiliated group.

Certain stock that possesses more "debt-like" features than equity features is not included for purposes of determining whether the voting power and value tests of § 1504(a)(2) are satisfied. Section 1504(a)(4) provides that "stock" does not include non-voting stock that is limited and preferred as to dividends and does not participate in corporate growth to any significant extent, if its liquidation and redemption rights do not exceed its issue price (except for a reasonable liquidation or redemption premium), and it is not convertible into another class of stock. In addition, § 1504(a)(5) authorizes Regulations that treat certain convertible instruments as not constituting stock.

The Regulations provide in general that options will not be treated as stock or as deemed to have been exercised unless it can be reasonably anticipated that the issue or transfer of the underlying stock will result in a substantial federal income tax saving and it is reasonably certain that the option will be exercised. Treas.Reg. § 1.1504–4(b)(1), (2)(i). The Regulations broadly define options as including any instrument that provides for the transfer of stock. Treas.Reg. § 1.1504–4(d)(1). This definition, therefore, includes convertible stock. The inquiry is undertaken at the time of issue or transfer of an option, the "measurement date," with some exceptions.[3] If an option is treated as exercised, it will be taken into account in determining the percentage of the value of stock held by the option holder relative to other parties, but not for purposes of determining the option holder's voting power. Treas.Reg. § 1.1504–4(c)(4).

1.2. *Includible Corporations*

An includible corporation is any domestic corporation that is a member of the affiliated group at any time during the taxable year under the stock ownership tests of § 1504(a) that is not excluded under § 1504(b). Includible corporations do not include, among others, tax-exempt corporations, insurance companies,[4] regulated investment companies (mutual funds), and real estate investment trusts. An includible corporation must be included in the consolidated return of an affiliated group for the part of any year during which the includible corporation meets the stock ownership tests. I.R.C. § 1501. If a corporation ceases to be a member of an affiliated group, absent the consent of the IRS, the corporation may not again be included within the consolidated return of the affiliated group for five years after the close of the taxable year in which the corporation ceased to be a member of the group. I.R.C. § 1504(a)(3). See also Rev.Proc. 2002–32, 2002–1 C.B. 959 (permitting certain qualifying corporations to obtain a waiver of the § 1504(a)(3) bar).

In Elko Realty Co. v. Commissioner, 29 T.C. 1012 (1958), aff'd per curiam, 260 F.2d 949 (3d Cir.1958), the court held that two subsidiaries acquired for the purpose of using losses to offset income of the profitable acquiring corporation were not includible on a consolidated return. The court indicated that if ownership of a subsidiary's stock serves no business purpose other than a tax reduction purpose, the subsidiary is not an affiliate for purposes of the consolidated return provisions. The court also disallowed loss deductions under the predecessor to § 269.

2.   CONSOLIDATED TAXABLE INCOME

The consolidated group computes its regular federal income tax liability on the basis of its consolidated taxable income, which combines the income and loss of each member of the consolidated group into a single taxable income. The computation of consolidated taxable income begins with the determination of the separate taxable incomes of each member of the consolidated group. Treas.Reg. § 1.1502–11(a)(1). In general, each member of the consolidated group computes its separate taxable income as a separate corporation. Treas.Reg. § 1.1502–12.

---

[3] A "measurement date" does not include a transfer between spouses that is covered by § 1041 or a transfer between persons none of whom is a member (or related to a member) of an affiliated group that includes the issuing corporation. Treas.Reg. § 1.1504–4(c)(4)(ii).

[4] Section 1504(c) permits insurance companies to form a consolidated group that includes only affiliated insurance companies. In addition, the common parent of an affiliated group can elect to include an insurance company on the consolidated return of the group after the insurance company has been a member of the affiliated group for five consecutive years.

In determining separate taxable income, with limited exceptions, all of the generally applicable rules of the Code apply, except as modified by the consolidated return Regulations themselves. Treas.Reg. § 1.1502–80. Separate taxable income excludes, however, distributions with respect to the stock of other members of the group, deferred gains and losses from intercompany transactions, capital gains and losses, § 1231 gains and losses, and charitable contributions. Items excluded from the taxable income of members are separately consolidated and accounted for in consolidated taxable income as provided in specific Regulations. Treas.Reg. § 1.1502–11(a)(2)–(8). Tax liability for the consolidated group is determined by applying the § 11 tax rate, and other relevant provisions of the Code, to the consolidated taxable income of the group. Treas.Reg. § 1.1502–2. Tax liability is reduced by consolidated credits attributable to members of the group. See Treas.Reg. § 1.1502–3. The members of the group typically provide for each member to contribute to the payment of the consolidated tax liability, which is remitted by the parent. Nevertheless, vis-à-vis the IRS, each member of a consolidated group is severally liable for the tax on consolidated taxable income. Treas.Reg. § 1.1502–6(a).

3. CONSOLIDATED NET OPERATING LOSSES

3.1. *Generally*

In some instances, it may be important whether the consolidated group computes its income with respect to certain items on a "single entity" basis in which all such items are consolidated, or whether the different impact of an item on the taxable income of separate entities is taken into account. Thus, it may be necessary to determine whether a particular item is characterized separately by a member corporation, whose net taxable income or loss is then separately calculated based on that characterization and aggregated with the net taxable income or loss of other member corporations, or whether the item must be characterized with reference to the overall income and expense items of the consolidated group viewed as a single entity without regard to how it would separately be taken into account by a member in computing the member's separately taxable income.

In United Dominion Industries, Inc. v. United States, 532 U.S. 822 (2001), the Supreme Court adopted the single entity approach regarding consolidated net operating losses, making it clear that there is only a consolidated net operating loss, not a collection of the separate members' losses, although separate member losses must be identified when members enter and leave a group. United Dominion Industries was the parent of an affiliated group that reported a consolidated net operating loss in each of three years. The consolidated net operating losses included losses attributable to so-called product liability expenses that gave rise to product liability losses. Before legislation enacted in 2017, product liability losses could be carried back for 10 years. Five of the corporate members of the affiliated group, which collectively generated $3.1 million of product liability expenses over three years, had sufficient income to offset their product liability expenses, thereby producing positive separate taxable income in each entity. The government argued that the consolidated group could not carry back product liability expenses incurred by a profitable member because the product liability expenses that were offset with positive income did not enter into the consolidated net operating loss of the group. The Supreme Court reasoned that there is only a single definition of consolidated net operating loss in Treas.Reg. § 1.1502–21(f) and no definition in the Regulations of a separate NOL for a single member of the consolidated group. The subsidiary's specified liability loss deduction items reduced the subsidiary's separate taxable income dollar-for-dollar and thereby contributed to the overall consolidated net operating loss of the affiliated group. A product liability loss subject to the prior law 10-year carryback was the lesser of product liability expenses or the taxpayer's NOL for the taxable year. Identifying the product liability loss first required calculation of the consolidated group's consolidated net operating loss, the only NOL available under the consolidated return Regulations, then determining product liability loss from all of the product liability expenses within the consolidated group. Thus, a portion of the consolidated NOL could be carried back 10 years.

The consolidated net operating loss of a consolidated group generally includes the consolidated net operating loss carryovers of the consolidated group. Treas.Reg. § 1.1502–21(a). (Legislation enacted in 2017 removed the ability to carry back NOLs, with very narrow exceptions.) Furthermore, Treas.Reg. § 1.1502–21(b) allows the net operating losses of a member of an affiliated group to be carried over from a pre-consolidation return period against the consolidated income of the group. This general rule is, however, subject to two mutually exclusive limitations. If after a change of ownership, the corporation is a member of a controlled group of corporations filing a consolidated return and § 382 is applicable, then the carryovers are limited accordingly. See Treas.Reg. § 1.1502–91. Alternatively, if there was no change of control within the meaning of § 382, but the loss year was a "separate return limitation year" (SRLY), then the loss may be carried over only against the income of the member of the group that generated the loss. Treas.Reg. § 1.1502–21(c) (NOLs) and –22(c) (capital loss carryovers). The SRLY restriction of Treas.Reg. § 1.1502–21(c) allows the use of losses from a separate return year of a member of the group only to the extent of income produced by that member. Under Treas.Reg. § 1.1502–21(g), the SRLY rule does not apply if a corporation becomes a member of a consolidated group within six months of the change date of an ownership change. Thus, in cases of overlap, only the § 382 limitation is applicable. Section 382 is discussed in Chapter 13.

3.2. *Application of Section 382 to Consolidated Groups*

Treas.Regs. §§ 1.1502–90 through 1.1502–99 provide detailed rules applying the § 382 limitation in the consolidated return context. The Regulations generally treat the members of a consolidated group as a single entity for purposes of determining whether an ownership change has occurred with respect to a loss corporation and ascertaining the value of the loss corporation stock. Before an ownership change, a consolidated group of corporations is able to absorb net operating losses of some members against the income of other members as a single entity. Following an ownership change, the consolidated taxable income of a group that may be offset by pre-ownership change losses and built-in losses of the group is limited by the § 382 consolidated limitation applied to the group as a whole. Treas.Reg. § 1.1502–91(a)(1). Under Treas.Reg. § 1.1502–92(b)(1), a consolidated loss group has an ownership change for purposes of § 382 and Temp.Reg. § 1.382–2T if there has been an ownership change of the common parent. In determining whether an ownership change has occurred, losses of the group are treated as the losses of the common parent, and the testing period is measured by losses of members of the loss group. Treas.Reg. § 1.1502–92(b)(1)(A) and (B).

Treas.Reg. § 1.1502–91(d) provides for the identification of loss subgroups within a consolidated group for the purpose of applying the § 382 limitation on the basis of a loss subgroup. There is an ownership change with respect to a loss subgroup if there is an ownership change of the common parent of the loss subgroup. Treas.Reg. § 1.1502–92(b)(1)(B)(ii). The Regulations also treat brother-sister corporations as a loss subgroup if two or more corporations that become members of a consolidated group at the same time were affiliated with each other immediately before becoming members of the new group and the common parent of the acquiring group elects to treat the new members as a loss subgroup. Treas.Reg. § 1.1502–91(d)(4).

The § 382 limitation, which under § 382(b)(1) is based on the value of the stock of the loss corporation multiplied by the applicable long-term tax-exempt rate, is determined from the value of the stock of the consolidated loss group or subgroup as a single entity. Treas.Reg. § 1.1502–93(a). The value of the consolidated loss group immediately before an ownership change is the value of the stock of each member of the group, other than the value of stock of a member of the group that is held directly by another member of the group. Treas.Reg. § 1.1502–93(b)(1).

In some circumstances, a subsidiary will be required to recognize an ownership change on a separate corporation basis with respect to its portion of the consolidated return net operating loss of the group. See Treas.Reg. § 1.1502–96(b)(1).

Treas.Reg. § 1.1502–94 contains a separate set of rules applying § 382 to carryover losses of a new member of a consolidated group that were incurred by the new member in a separate return limitation year with respect to the current consolidated group. In general, a new loss member of a consolidated group is treated as a separate entity for purposes of applying the § 382 limitation. Thus, the amount of consolidated taxable income of the group that may be offset with losses of the new member is limited by a § 382 limitation that is computed with respect to the value of the new member corporation's stock at the time of its ownership change. Treas.Reg. § 1.1502–94(b)(1). If the § 382 limitation does not apply, under the SRLY limitation, the amount of the new member's losses that may be absorbed by the consolidated group is also limited to the new member's aggregate contribution to the consolidated taxable income of the group. Treas.Regs. §§ 1.1502–21(c), 1.1502–94(b)(4), Ex. 1.

As noted, a consolidated loss group subject to the § 382 limitation is treated as a single entity subject to the limitation on the basis of the stock value of the entire group. If a loss corporation leaves a consolidated loss group or subgroup that has had an ownership change while the departing corporation was a member of the group, losses apportioned to the departing loss corporation under Treas.Reg. § 1.1502–21(b), remain subject to the § 382 limitation. Under Treas.Reg. § 1.1502–95, the § 382 limitation applicable to the departing loss corporation will be zero unless the common parent (not a loss subgroup parent) elects to apportion part of the § 382 limitation of the consolidated loss group to the departing loss corporation. Treas.Reg. § 1.1502–95(c)(2). The § 382 limitation apportioned to the departing member will reduce the § 382 limitation of the remaining consolidated loss group. Treas.Reg. § 1.1502–95(c)(3). The Regulations also permit an election to apportion part of the net unrealized built-in gain of the loss group, which increases the § 382 limitation, to the departing member. Treas.Reg. § 1.1502–95(c)(2)(ii). Treas.Reg. § 1.1502–95(e) requires an allocation to a departing member of a pro-rata portion of the group's net unrealized built-in loss.

3.3. *Separate Return Limitation Year*

3.3.1.   *Generally*

Treas.Reg. § 1.1502–1(f) provides the definition for "separate return limitation year." In general it is a year in which any member of the consolidated group filed a separate return. But there are exceptions. Treas.Reg. § 1.1502–1(f)(2)(i) excepts the parent from the general rule. This exception permits a loss corporation to acquire a profitable subsidiary and apply its own loss carryovers against the profits of the newly acquired subsidiary. Acquisition of a corporation with built-in gain, however, is subject to the limitations of § 384, discussed in Chapter 13, which restricts the use of preacquisition losses against recognized built-in gain of either the acquired or acquiring corporation. In addition, a SRLY does not include a separate return year for a subsidiary that was a member of the affiliated group at the time the loss was incurred but that was not included in a consolidated return for that year. See Treas.Reg. § 1.1502–1(f)(2)(ii).

Wolter Construction Co., Inc. v. Commissioner, 634 F.2d 1029 (6th Cir.1980), upheld the validity of the SRLY Regulations. In that case, losses incurred by a subsidiary in separate return years could not be used by the consolidated group even though the corporations in their separate return years were commonly controlled by individual stockholders as brother-sister corporations. Since the stockholders were individuals and not corporations, the group did not fall within the "common parent" exception in Treas.Reg. § 1.1502–1(f)(2)(i). The court in *Wolter Construction Co.* described the operation of the SRLY rule as follows:

> Reg. 1.1502–21(b)(1) is concerned with the use of net operating losses on a consolidated return. That regulation permits an affiliated group to use net operating losses sustained by any members of the group in "separate return years" if the losses could be carried over pursuant to the general principles of § 172 of the

Code. A "separate return year" is defined as any year in which a company filed a separate return or in which it joined in the filing of a consolidated return by another group. Reg. 1.1502–1(e).

As a general rule, then, net operating losses reported on a separate return can be carried over to and used on a consolidated return. An important exception to this rule is found in Reg. 1.1502–21(c). That section provides that the net operating loss of a member of an affiliated group arising in a "separate return limitation year" which may be included in the consolidated net operating loss deduction of the group shall not exceed the amount of consolidated taxable income contributed by the loss-sustaining member for the taxable year at issue. The term "separate return limitation year" is defined in Reg. 1.1502–1(f), in essence, as a separate return year in which the member of the group (except, with qualifications, the common parent) was either: 1) not a member of the group for its entire taxable year; or 2) a member of the group for its entire taxable year, that enjoyed the benefit of multiple surtax exemptions. In summary, losses incurred by a brother-sister corporation or by a corporation which is unrelated at the time of its losses to its subsequent affiliates, before it becomes a member of an affiliated group filing a consolidated return, can only be carried forward and used on the consolidated return to the extent that the corporation that incurred the losses has current income reflected on the consolidated return.

In *Wolter Construction Co.*, the fact that the Regulations provided a greater limitation on net operating loss carryovers in the context of the consolidated return than is contained in § 381 and § 382 did not invalidate the Regulations.

Under Treas.Reg. § 1.1502–21(c)(1), deduction of a SRLY loss by the consolidated group in any taxable year is limited to the taxable income contributed to the group by the member with the SRLY loss. The member's contribution to consolidated taxable income is measured on a cumulative basis over the entire period during which the SRLY corporation is a member of the group. Thus, a member's SRLY losses may be absorbed in any consolidated return year to the extent of the member's cumulative net contribution to consolidated taxable income in prior consolidated return years of the group, even though the member may not have consolidated taxable income in the year the loss is absorbed.

Treas.Reg. § 1.1502–21(c)(2) applies similar rules on the basis of a SRLY subgroup, rather than fragmenting the limitation on a corporation-by-corporation basis. A SRLY subgroup consists of corporations affiliated with the loss corporation continuously from the year in which the loss was incurred to the year into which the loss is carried.

3.3.2. *Reverse Acquisition*

Since the SRLY limitation does not apply in the case of a change of ownership of the common parent, there remains a possibility that the assets of a profitable corporation may be merged into the common parent in exchange for more than 50% of the stock of the common parent of the loss group. For example, assume that a profitable P Corporation merges into L Corporation, which is the common parent of a consolidated group of corporations, and as a result of the merger the persons who were shareholders of former P Corporation immediately before the merger end up owning more than 50% of the stock of L Corporation. The SRLY rule does not limit the losses of the L Corporation consolidated group that were not incurred in a separate return limitation year (remember, the § 382 limitation applies where there is a more than 50% change in ownership of the loss corporation). Treas.Reg. § 1.1502–1(f)(3), however, treats this transaction as a "reverse acquisition" to deny the net operating loss carryover against the profits of the "acquired corporation."

In *Wolter Construction Co., supra*, the taxpayer argued that the common parent exception to the SRLY limitation and the reverse acquisition exception to the exception were intended to insure that loss carryovers were available only to the stockholders who owned the corporation when the losses were incurred, and that this policy should be applied to allow use of losses by the common parent affiliated with its former sister corporation. The court rejected the argument and described the reverse acquisition rule as follows:

> In a typical reverse acquisition in the loss carryover context, substantially all the assets or stock of a profit corporation are nominally acquired by a loss corporation in exchange for more than 50 percent of the latter's stock, so that control of the loss corporation has shifted to the stockholders of the profit corporation as they existed prior to the acquisition. The Regulations essentially treat the loss corporation as having been acquired, and under Section 1.1502–1(f)(3) of the Treasury Regulations, all taxable years of the loss corporation prior to the reverse acquisition are treated as separate return limitation years, notwithstanding its status as the common parent corporation of the new affiliated group consisting of it and the profit corporation. Conversely, the separate return years of the profit corporation prior to the acquisition are not treated, in general, as the separate return limitation years. Accordingly, the net operating losses sustained by the loss corporation, but not the profit corporation, in its separate return years are subject to the carryover limitation contained in Section 1.1502–21(c). The purpose and effect of the reverse acquisition rules is to prevent trafficking in loss corporations. This is accomplished by redirecting the SRLY limitation to the ostensibly acquiring corporation. This "simple technical rule thwarts the attempts of those who would seek to present that the ailing David is trying to improve its financial strength by drawing on the earning power of Goliath." Gans [A Practical Guide to Consolidated Returns (1976)], at 828.2.

3.3.3.   *Built-In Deductions*

Under Treas.Reg. § 1.1502–15, if losses are economically incurred in a prior separate return year but recognized for tax purposes in a consolidated year, the losses are treated as arising in a separate return limitation year

(SRLY) and thus may not be applied against consolidated income but may be used only to offset the income of the corporation that realized the loss. Net unrealized built-in losses are thus subject to the SRLY limitations of Treas.Regs. §§ 1.1502–21(c) and –22(c). The Regulations adopt the definition of built-in loss contained in § 382(h)(3), discussed in Chapter 13, which refers to the excess of adjusted basis of assets over their fair market value.[5] Under Treas.Reg. § 1.1502–15, the SRLY limitation applies to the recognition of "net unrealized built-in losses" of a new member of a consolidated group (as determined under § 382(h)(3)) but only during a five year recognition period after the new member joins the group. However, Treas.Reg. § 1.1502–15(g), provides that the SRLY limitation on built-in-loss does not apply if the losses are also subject to the built-in-loss limitation of § 382.

3.3.4. *Post-Acquisition Losses of an Acquired Member*

Treas.Reg. § 1.1502–21(b)(1) provides for the carryover of the consolidated net operating loss of the group under the principles of § 172(b). The consolidated net operating loss does not, however, include losses apportioned under Treas.Reg. § 1.1502–21(b)(2) to a separate return year of a member of the consolidated group. In Amorient, Inc. v. Commissioner, 103 T.C. 161 (1994), the taxpayer incurred a consolidated net operating loss that was allocable in part to separate return years of a corporation that had been a Subchapter S corporation prior to acquisition by the consolidated group. The Tax Court held that the portion of the taxpayer's consolidated net operating loss allocable to separate return years of the former S corporation was to be carried back to the S corporation's separate return year even though deduction of net operating losses by an S corporation is barred by § 1373(d). The Tax Court justified its result in part on its conclusion that losses that are not deductible in carryback separate return years of the S corporation are to be carried forward to a year when either the former S corporation or the consolidated group can utilize the loss. Treas.Reg. § 1.1502–21(b)(2)(i) partially addresses the issues raised in *Amorient* by providing that the portion of a consolidated net operating loss that is apportioned to a member and carried back to a separate return year of the member may not be carried back to an equivalent or earlier year of the consolidated group. Legislation enacted in 2017 eliminated NOL carrybacks except in narrow situations, but the regulation remains relevant because, likewise, if a consolidated net operating loss is carried forward to a separate return year of a member of the group, that carryforward loss may not be used in an equivalent or later consolidated return year of the group.

4. INVESTMENT ADJUSTMENTS

4.1. *Stock Basis: Investment Adjustment Rules*

4.1.1. *Generally*

Treas.Reg. § 1.1502–32 requires each member of the group owning stock in another member of the group to adjust its basis for that stock to account for income, losses, and other items attributable to the subsidiary that are reflected in consolidated taxable income. The purpose of the investment

---

[5]   Built-in loss under § 382(h) includes deduction items that are attributable to a SRLY but that are accounted for in a consolidated return year. See I.R.C. § 382(h)(6)(B).

adjustment rule is to prevent gain or loss that has been recognized by the subsidiary from being recognized a second time as investment gain or loss by the parent upon disposition of the subsidiary's stock. These rules treat the consolidated group as a single entity by accounting for gains and losses within the consolidated group only once.

A parent corporation's basis in the stock of its consolidated subsidiary is increased or decreased annually by the net amount of the subsidiary's taxable income or loss, tax exempt income, nondeductible noncapital expenses, and distributions to the parent corporation. Treas.Reg. § 1.1502–32(a)–(b). This rule applies with respect to both the common parent and subsidiaries that are in turn parents of lower-tier subsidiaries. A positive adjustment increases basis, while a negative adjustment decreases basis. These items cause an adjustment to the parent's basis in subsidiary stock in the taxable year in which the item is taken into account in determining consolidated taxable income. Thus, items of income and loss, and distributions, will result in adjustments to the parent's basis in the stock of a consolidated subsidiary. Adjustments to the basis of a member's stock are taken into account in determining the basis adjustments of higher-tier members; the adjustments are applied in the order of the tiers, from lowest to highest. If a parent corporation does not own all of the common stock of a subsidiary, only a proportionate part of the subsidiary's income or loss is taken into account in making investment adjustments. For example, if P Corporation owns 90% of the stock of S Corporation and S Corporation has $100 of taxable income included on the consolidated return, P Corporation increases its basis in the S Corporation stock by only $90. See Treas.Reg. § 1.1502–32(c)(5), Ex. 1. The basis adjustment is made at the end of the year unless an interim basis adjustment is necessary to determine a tax liability, for example, as a result of the sale of some of the stock. Treas.Reg. § 1.1504–32(b)(1).

Negative adjustments are allocated only to common stock and then among the shares to reflect the manner in which the shares suffer the economic loss. Positive adjustments are allocated first to preferred stock to reflect distributions and dividend arrearages accrued during the period the subsidiary was a member of the group, Treas.Reg. § 1.1504–32(c)(1)(iii), (c)(3), and then to the common stock. Treas.Reg. § 1.1504–32(c)(2). Adjustments to the common stock generally are made equally to each share, but if any shares have an excess loss account, the adjustments are first allocated among the shares with an excess loss account to equalize and then to eliminate the excess loss accounts. Treas.Reg. § 1.1504–32(c)(2). Basis adjustments attributable to distributions are allocated to the shares on which the distribution was made. Treas.Reg. § 1.1504–32(c)(1)(i).

For purposes of the investment adjustment rules, a member's taxable income or loss includes items of income or loss attributable to the member that are included in the consolidated taxable income of the group. Treas.Reg. § 1.1502–32(b)(3)(i). Operating losses are included in the investment adjustment in the year the loss is absorbed into consolidated taxable income. Thus, a net operating loss carryforward is reflected in a basis adjustment for the year to which the loss is carried. Treas.Reg. § 1.1502–32(b)(3)(i)(A) and (B).

4.1.2. *Adjustment for Tax Liabilities*

A lower-tier member's federal taxes are nondeductible noncapital expenditures that result in a negative basis adjustment for the stock of the lower-tier member held by a higher-tier member. Treas.Reg. § 1.1502–32(b)(3)(iii)(A). In general, the Regulations require a negative adjustment to the basis of the stock of each group member to reflect its tax liability under the method applied to determine earnings and profits under § 1552, discussed in paragraph 5. Treas.Reg. § 1.1502–32(b)(3)(iv)(D). The basic rule apportions the tax liability of the consolidated group among the members in proportion to each member's contribution to consolidated taxable income, as a percentage of the total tax attributable to the member if the tax of each member were computed on a separate return basis, on the basis of each member's actual contribution to consolidated taxable income including reductions in income. The group may, however, select another method. Many consolidated groups enter into what are called "tax sharing agreements," which are contracts that specifically provide for payments by members with a positive separate tax liability to members with net operating losses and to the member—generally the common parent—that remits the group's taxes to the IRS. Regardless of whether the group has a tax sharing agreement, when one member owes a payment to a second member (as determined under the Regulations or pursuant to a tax sharing agreement), the first member is treated as indebted to the second member. The right to receive a payment is treated as a positive adjustment, and the obligation to make a payment is treated as a negative adjustment under paragraph (b)(3)(iii) of this section. If the obligation is not paid, the amount not paid generally is treated as a distribution, contribution, or both, depending on the relationship between the members. Thus, stock basis is determined by the actual payment or receipt of cash by one member from another member. If no amount is actually paid, no stock basis adjustment is made. See Treas.Reg. § 1.1502–32(c)(5), Ex. 1(a), (b), (d).

4.2. *Excess Loss Accounts*

Under Treas.Reg. § 1.1502–11, the utilization by the consolidated group of the operating losses of a subsidiary is not limited by the group's current investment in the subsidiary. When the losses are utilized, however, the parent's investment adjustments under Treas.Reg. § 1.1502–32 may reduce the basis in the subsidiary stock below zero. This negative basis creates an "excess loss account" with respect to the subsidiary's stock. Treas.Reg. § 1.1502–32(a)(3)(ii). The purpose of the excess loss account is to allow losses in excess of basis and to ensure the subsequent recapture in consolidated taxable income of negative adjustments to the stock of a subsidiary upon the occurrence of specified events. Treas.Reg. § 1.1502–19(a)(1). The excess loss account is treated as a "negative basis" reflecting the fact that the group has been able to utilize current deductions in excess of the investment in the subsidiary. The negative basis reflected in an excess loss account is used as adjusted basis to determine the tax consequence of transactions involving the stock. Treas.Reg. § 1.1502–19(a)(2)(ii).

The existence of an excess loss account has an important impact on a number of corporate transactions involving the stock of the subsidiary. For example, if the stock of the subsidiary is sold to a third party outside the group, under Treas.Reg. § 1.1502–19 the amount of gain realized by the parent on the transaction includes not only the sales proceeds received but also the amount of the parent's excess loss account for the subsidiary. Treas.Reg. § 1.1502–19(b)(1).

The amount of gain on the sale resulting from the excess loss account is treated as capital gain. Arguably, the gain attributable to the excess loss account should be treated as ordinary income when it represents deductions previously taken against ordinary income. The Regulations allow, however, capital gain treatment, apparently on the theory that, had the subsidiary realized the appreciation in its assets prior to the disposition, the earnings and profits so generated would have eliminated the excess loss account and this is in effect what is happening when the parent sells the stock at a gain. If the subsidiary is insolvent at the time of the disposition, however, then ordinary income results from the transaction to the extent of the insolvency. Treas.Reg. § 1.1502–19(b)(4)(i).[6] The amount treated as ordinary income is limited to the amount of the excess loss account redetermined to exclude distributions to the parent. Treas.Reg. § 1.1502–19(b)(4)(ii).

The existence of an excess loss account also can affect transactions that otherwise would be tax-free. For example, the disposition of stock in a reorganization involving an unrelated corporation will trigger recognition of gain if the subsidiary involved had generated an excess loss account. Treas.Reg. § 1.1502–19(b)(2)(ii) and (c)(1)(ii). On the other hand, tax-free reorganizations within the group generally do not require the inclusion of the excess loss account in income; instead the excess loss account is applied to the stock received without recognition of gain or loss under § 354, either reducing the basis of the stock received or adding to the excess loss account of that stock. Treas.Reg. § 1.1502–19(b)(2)(i). (Tax-free reorganizations are discussed in Chapter 10.) A liquidation to which § 332 and § 334(b) (discussed in Chapter 7) apply eliminates the excess loss account. The transaction is in effect treated as if the parent had owned the subsidiary's assets directly from the beginning; triggering the excess loss account in this situation could lead to duplication of gain. See Treas.Reg. § 1.1502–19(b)(2)(i).

Other events, such as the deconsolidation of a subsidiary (e.g., by virtue of a stock issuance or sale that results in failure to meet the stock ownership requirements), the discontinuation of filing consolidated returns, or the worthlessness of the stock of the subsidiary, also require the inclusion in income of the amount of the excess loss account. Treas.Reg. § 1.1502–19(c)(1)(iii) and (2). Recognition of gain attributable to an excess loss account of a worthless subsidiary is deferred from the date the stock becomes

---

[6] Covil Insulation Co. v. Commissioner, 65 T.C. 364 (1975), upheld the validity of Treas.Reg. § 1.1502–19, and required the parent corporation to include as ordinary income the excess loss account with respect to a subsidiary whose stock had become worthless. Both the treatment of the stock's worthlessness as an income generating event with respect to the excess loss account and characterization of the gain as ordinary were "permissible exercise[s] of the rulemaking power granted by section 1502."

worthless under the normal facts and circumstances test of § 165(g) to the date on which substantially all of the subsidiary's assets are disposed of or abandoned or the date on which the subsidiary realizes cancellation of indebtedness income that is accorded nonrecognition under § 108(a) by virtue of insolvency or in a bankruptcy proceeding. Treas.Reg. § 1.1502–19(c)(1)(iii).

In *Garvey, Inc. v. United States*, 726 F.2d 1569 (Fed. Cir. 1984), the parent corporation acquired stock of a subsidiary in a tax-free type (B) reorganization (an exchange of stock for stock under § 368(a)(1)(B) pursuant to which under § 354 no gain or loss is recognized) that resulted in a $250,000 basis in the subsidiary stock for the common parent under § 358. Subsequent to acquisition, the subsidiary distributed $4.9 million in dividends out of pre-affiliation earnings and profits. Under the predecessor of Treas.Regs. §§ 1.1502–32(b)(2)(iv) and 1.1502–19(a)(2), the dividend distribution created an excess loss account of $4.65 million, which was required to be recognized as income when the group disaffiliated. The court rejected the taxpayer's argument that application of the Regulations unfairly created phantom income that would not have existed had the group filed separate tax returns. The court pointed out that in electing consolidated treatment the taxpayer "must now take the bitter with the sweet."

4.3. *Section 357(c) Situations*

In the consolidated return context, Treas.Reg. § 1.1502–80(d) provides that § 357(c) does not apply to an intercompany transaction. Instead, § 358 applies, sometimes resulting in a negative basis (i.e., excess loss account), due to investment adjustments. Suppose that P Corporation, the parent of a consolidated group, forms S Corporation, which immediately becomes a member of the P Corporation consolidated group. In exchange for all of the stock of S Corporation, P contributes to S an asset with a basis of $100, subject to a liability of $130, which S corporation assumes. Apart from the consolidated return rules, § 357(c) would require P to recognize gain of $30—an amount equal to the excess of the liabilities assumed over the basis of the property transferred. But P Corporation takes a basis of negative $30 in the stock of S Corporation, and S Corporation's basis in the asset remains $100.

4.4. *Triangular Reorganizations*

Treas.Reg. §§ 1.358–6 and 1.1032–2, which provide rules for determining a parent corporation's basis in a subsidiary in forward and reverse triangular mergers (as well as triangular (B) reorganizations and triangular (C) reorganizations), discussed in Chapter 10, also apply in the consolidated return context. Treas.Reg. § 1.1502–30. However, in the consolidated return context, liabilities are taken into account in determining the parent corporation's basis in the stock of the acquiring subsidiary. As a result, the parent corporation will have an excess loss account to the extent liabilities exceed the basis of the subsidiary's assets.

5. EARNINGS AND PROFITS

Earnings and profits are tracked on a separate member basis because it is necessary to know when each member pays a dividend. In a consolidated group, special adjustments are, however, required in the earnings and profits accounts of the parent corporation to reflect the consolidated situation. If the parent of the group was not required to include in its earnings and profits the earnings and profits of subsidiaries in the group, under § 301 a parent corporation with profitable subsidiaries and no earnings and profits of its own could make tax-free distributions to its stockholders despite the group as a whole having current or accumulated earnings. The earnings and profits of a consolidated subsidiary are determined under the applicable provisions of the Code and passed up through higher-tier entities to be consolidated in the earnings and profits of the common parent. Treas.Reg. § 1.1502–33(a) and (b). If the common parent, or any other member of the group, owns less than all of the common stock of a lower-tier member of the group, only a proportional amount of the earnings and profits is tiered-up. Treas.Reg. § 1.1502–33(b)(3)(ii), Ex. 3.

A separate determination of the parent's basis in the stock of a consolidated subsidiary is required for purposes of determining the increase or decrease in earnings and profits resulting from the sale of the subsidiary's stock. Treas.Reg. § 1.1502–33(c). Gain or loss on the disposition of the stock of a member of the consolidated group is determined from the basis of the stock as adjusted by the investment adjustment rules of Treas.Reg. § 1.1502–32, which are based on the subsidiary's contribution to taxable income. There are differences in the computation of earnings and profits and taxable income, however, primarily because § 312(k) and (n) require adjustments to earnings and profits for a number of items including depreciation, inventory amounts, and installment sales, which differ from the amounts taken into account in computing taxable income or loss. To account for these differences in determining the effect on the parent's earnings and profits of the sale of stock in a subsidiary, the basis of a subsidiary's stock must be determined using earnings and profits as the basis for investment adjustments. Thus, the basis of stock of a subsidiary for earnings and profits purposes is increased by the earnings and profits of the subsidiary and decreased by a deficit in earnings and profits. Treas.Reg. § 1.1502–33(c)(1).

Under § 1552, tax liability of the consolidated group is apportioned against the earnings and profits of each of the members in proportion to the member's contribution to consolidated taxable income, as a percentage of the total tax attributable to the member if the tax of each member were computed on a separate return basis, on the basis of each member's actual contribution to consolidated taxable income including reductions in income, or by any other method selected by the group and approved by the IRS. Section 1552 does not provide a device to account for the effect of the absorption of one member's tax attributes by another member, e.g., one member's income may be absorbed by another member's losses. The Regulations provide rules to account for the impact of the absorption of tax attributes, which are intended to reflect in earnings and profits the reduction of one member's tax liability by attributes of another that would have reduced the latter member's earnings and profits in a different year if not used by the first member. Treas.Reg. § 1.1502–33(d).

Finally, to the extent a lower-tier member of the group's earnings and profits were taken into account by a higher-tier member of the group under the tiering-up rules, upon deconsolidation the lower-tier member's earnings and profits are eliminated. Treas.Reg. § 1.1502–33(e).

6. INTERCOMPANY TRANSACTIONS

6.1. *Transactions Between Members of a Consolidated Group*

6.1.1. *Generally*

Treas.Reg. § 1.1502–13 provides rules for transactions between members of the same consolidated group involving the sale or exchange of property, the provision of services by one member of the group to another, the licensing or rental of tangible and intangible property, and the lending of money. The regulation also controls the treatment of intercompany distributions with respect to the stock of a member. Treas.Reg. § 1.1502–13(f). The intercompany transaction rules are treated as a method of accounting that is applied in addition to the member's other methods of accounting. Treas.Reg. § 1.1502–13(a)(3). The timing rules of the intercompany transaction Regulations control over other accounting methods, however. See also Treas.Reg. § 1.446–1(c)(2)(iii), which provides that the consolidated return rules are a method of accounting under § 446(e).

The Regulations treat members engaging in an intercompany transaction in some ways like separate corporations and in other ways like divisions of a single corporation. In determining the amount and location of items related to those transactions, the members are treated as separate corporations. For example, if one member sells an asset to another member, the seller recognizes gain or loss under § 1001, while the buyer takes a cost basis in the asset under § 1012. To determine the timing, character, and other attributes of the transaction, the members are, however, treated as divisions of a single corporation. Thus, in the example above, the seller does not take its gain or loss on asset sale into account until the buyer takes its basis into account, and the character of the seller's gain or loss may depend on the buyer's and seller's collective activity. The Regulations accomplish these results with two rules, the matching rule and the acceleration rule.

6.1.2. *Matching Intercompany Items Related to Deferred Gains and Losses*

Under Treas.Reg. § 1.1502–13(c)(2), gain or loss recognized by the selling member in an intercompany transaction is accounted for by the selling member under its method of accounting, but is not accounted for in consolidated taxable income until the "corresponding item" (see Treas.Reg. § 1.1502–13(b)(3)) resulting from the transaction is taken into account by the buying member under its method of accounting. For example, on a sale of property, the selling member's gain or loss is not accounted for in consolidated taxable income until the buying member disposes of the property outside of the consolidated group, or otherwise recovers its corresponding basis in the acquired property. In this fashion, items resulting from an intercompany transaction are taken into account in a manner that produces the same net result in terms of consolidated taxable income as if the transaction occurred between divisions of a single entity. If a member sells an asset at a gain to another member and the purchasing member later sells that asset outside the consolidated group, the purchasing member's reduced gain or increased loss attributable to the purchase price paid to the selling member is offset in consolidated taxable income by the selling member's deferred gain. Under this single entity principle, the character, source, and other attributes of intercompany transactions are determined with reference to the activities of both the selling and buying members of the consolidated group. Treas.Reg. § 1.1502–13(c)(1). For purposes of identifying the amount and location of specific items, each party to an intercompany transaction is, however, treated as a separate entity. Treas.Reg. § 1.1502–13(a)(2).

The Regulations illustrate the single entity approach with the following example. Treas.Reg. § 1.1502–13(c)(7)(ii), Ex. 1(f). In Year 1, S Corporation sells property for $100 that it has held for investment with a basis of $70 to B Corporation, which is a member of the consolidated group that includes S Corporation. The accounting in consolidated taxable income for S Corporation's recognized gain on the sale is deferred. As a separate entity, B Corporation holds the property with an adjusted basis of $100, and S Corporation will be required to recognize its deferred gain when B Corporation takes advantage of the $30 basis increase. Treas.Reg. § 1.1502–13(a)(2). In Year 3, B Corporation resells the property for $90 to a customer in the ordinary course of B Corporation's business. If S Corporation and B Corporation were divisions of a single entity, B Corporation would succeed to S Corporation's $70 basis in the land and realize $20 of gain. Under the matching principle of Treas.Reg. § 1.1502–13(c), in the year of B Corporation's sale, S Corporation must take into income an amount that reflects the difference for the year between the "corresponding item," which is the amount actually taken into account by B Corporation as a separate entity, a $10 loss ($90 − $100), Treas.Reg. § 1.1502–13(b)(3), and the "recomputed corresponding item," a $20 gain ($90 − $70), which is the amount that B Corporation would take into account if S Corporation and B Corporation were divisions of a single entity. Treas.Reg. § 1.1502–13(b)(4); see Treas.Reg. § 1.1502–13(c)(7)(ii), Ex. 1(d). Thus, in Year 3, S Corporation is required to recognize $30 ($20 − negative $10 = $30). Treas.Reg. § 1.1502–13(c)(2)(ii). B Corporation recognizes its $10 loss in Year 3. Treas.Reg. § 1.1502–13(c)(2)(i). The net effect on consolidated taxable income is $20 gain. The character of S Corporation's and B Corporation's gain (or loss) is also determined as if S Corporation and B Corporation were divisions of a single entity. Thus, if B Corporation's activities with respect to the property convert the property from investment property into property described in § 1221(a)(1), both S Corporation's and B Corporation's gain or loss will be ordinary. Treas.Reg. § 1.1502–13(c)(1) and (7)(ii), Ex. 2. The gain and loss taken into account by S Corporation and B Corporation will be preserved on a separate entity basis for purposes of stock basis and earnings and profits adjustments as required by Treas.Regs. §§ 1.1502–32 and –33. See Treas.Reg. § 1.1502–13(a)(2).

The matching principle of the Regulations also requires an accounting for the selling member's deferred gain as the buying member claims capital recovery deductions on its purchase price basis of depreciable property in an intercompany transaction. Assume for example, that S Corporation and B Corporation are members of the same consolidated group. In Year 8, S

Corporation acquires depreciable five year property for $150 and properly claims capital recovery deductions of $30 in Year 8 and $48 in Year 9. On the first day of its Year 10 taxable year, S Corporation sells the property to B Corporation for $110. At the time of sale, S Corporation's basis in the property is $72 ($150 − [$30 + 48]). S Corporation recognizes $38 of gain, which is deferred. Under § 168(i)(7), B Corporation must use the same depreciation rate as S Corporation with respect to so much of the adjusted basis of the property in B Corporation's hands as does not exceed S Corporation's adjusted basis at the time of the transfer. Thus, in taxable Year 10, B Corporation deducts $28.80, which is the depreciation deduction that would have been available to S Corporation under § 168. In addition, B Corporation is permitted to recover its remaining basis as if the property were new five-year property. Thus, in Year 10, B Corporation claims an additional $7.60 depreciation deduction (20% of adjusted basis of $38, applying the half-year convention as if the property were new five-year property). The additional depreciation deduction claimed by B Corporation requires that S Corporation take into account $7.60 of its deferred intercompany gain in Year 10. In Year 11, B Corporation deducts $17.28 of depreciation with respect to the basis that would have been its basis had it taken a transferred basis from S Corporation, plus $12.16 of depreciation based on its $28 basis increase from the intercompany transaction. S Corporation is required to take into account $12.16 of its deferred intercompany gain in Year 11. Treas.Reg. § 1.1502–13(c)(7)(ii), Ex. 4. Under the single entity principle, which treats S Corporation and B Corporation as divisions of a single corporation, the character of S Corporation's recognized gain will reflect the tax consequence of B Corporation's depreciation. Treas.Reg. § 1.1502–13(c)(1)(i) and (c)(4). Thus, because S Corporation's deferred gain offsets B Corporation's increased depreciation, S Corporation's gain is treated as ordinary income. Treas.Reg. § 1.1502–13(c)(7)(ii), Ex. 4(d). In this fashion, the Regulations recognize separate entity aspects of the transaction as reflected in B Corporation's increased basis and depreciation but treat the overall consequence to consolidated taxable income as though the property were transferred between divisions of a single entity through the matching of B Corporation's increased depreciation deductions with restoration of S Corporation's deferred intercompany gain.

If, on the first day of its Year 12 taxable year, B Corporation sells the property to X Corporation, which is not a member of the S-B consolidated group, for $120 payable in two annual installments with adequate interest, both B Corporation and S Corporation must account for recognized gain. B Corporation recognizes gain of $75.84 ($120 − $44.16; B Corporation's adjusted basis is its $110 purchase price minus $65.84 of depreciation for Year 10 and Year 11). As a consequence of B Corporation's sale, S Corporation must also recognize recapture gain. If S and B Corporations were divisions of a single entity, on its Year 12 sale of the property, the Corporation would have realized $94.08 of gain, determined by subtracting from the $120 amount realized an adjusted basis of $25.92 computed without regard to B Corporation's purchase from S Corporation ($150 original cost less four years' capital recovery deductions totaling $94.08). The difference between the gain recognized on a single entity basis and the gain recognized by B Corporation as a separate entity, $18.24 ($94.08 − $75.84), is B Corporation's "recomputed corresponding item," which must be accounted for by S Corporation at the time of B Corporation's disposition.[7] As a consequence, the consolidated taxable income of the group reflects the tax consequence of the sale of the property on a single entity basis; S Corporation's gain of $18.24 plus B Corporation's gain of $75.84 is the equivalent of the gain that would have been recognized on the sale of the property outside of the group without the intervention of the intercompany sale from S Corporation to B Corporation. Continuing with the single entity model, because all of the gain recognized on disposition of the property would have been recaptured as ordinary income under § 1245, the gain recognized by both S Corporation and B Corporation is treated as ordinary gain. Treas.Reg. § 1.1502–13(c)(1)(i). Under § 453(i) none of the gain is eligible for installment reporting. If B Corporation had sold the property to X for $160, an amount that would have produced $10 of § 1231 gain in addition to depreciation recapture, B Corporation would have been eligible to report $5 of its gain under the § 453 installment method in each of the two years payments are received from X. S Corporation's deferred gain accounted for in the year of sale would not have been eligible for installment reporting, however, because all of S Corporation's deferred gain on its intercompany sale to B Corporation is § 1245 ordinary income recapture gain. Treas.Reg. § 1.1502–13(c)(7)(ii), Ex. 5(f).[8]

6.1.3. *Acceleration of Deferred Gains and Losses*

Under the acceleration rule, the presence of deferred intercompany gain or loss within the consolidated group will also affect transactions involving the stock of subsidiaries. The Regulations address stock transactions by requiring "acceleration" of deferred intercompany items in the case of an event that prevents accounting for an item under the matching rules. Treas.Reg. § 1.1502–13(d)(1). For example, if either the selling or buying member leaves the consolidated group, it is no longer possible to match the selling member's deferred gain or loss with the buying member's subsequent accounting for its corresponding item. Thus, if either member ceases to be a member of the consolidated group, the selling member generally is required to account for its deferred gain or loss.[9] In the first example above, where S Corporation sold investment property with a $70 basis to B Corporation for $100, if B Corporation should cease being a member of the consolidated group in Year 2 before selling the property, S Corporation would be required to account for its deferred $30 gain in that year. See Treas.Reg. § 1.1502–13(d)(3), Ex. 1. As a separate entity, or as a member of a different

---

[7] The recomputed corresponding item is equivalent to S's deferred gain of $38 less gain recognized by S Corporation in Year 10 and Year 11 as B Corporation claimed increased capital recovery deductions.

[8] In the case of an installment sale reported under § 453, the regulation also provides that B and S must account for the interest charge of § 453A on gains deferred under the installment method if the aggregate tax installment obligations of the group outstanding at the end of the taxable year exceed $5 million. Treas.Reg. § 1.1502–13(c)(7)(ii), Ex. 5(b).

[9] The deferred gain or loss is not accelerated when the group is acquired in a reverse acquisition defined in § 368(a)(2)(E) (see Chapter 10), another group acquires the common parent's stock, or another group acquires the common parent's assets in a § 381(a)(2) transaction. Treas.Reg. § 1.1502–13(j)(5).

consolidated group, B Corporation would continue to hold the property with a $100 basis. The character of S Corporation's gain would be determined under the matching principles of Treas.Reg. § 1.1502–13(c) as if S Corporation and B Corporation were divisions of the same entity. Treas.Reg. § 1.1502–13(d)(1)(ii). Thus B Corporation's activities with respect to the property could convert S Corporation's deferred investment gain into ordinary gain.

The common parent of a consolidated group may request that the IRS consent to the group accounting for intercompany transactions on a separate entity basis. Treas.Reg. § 1.1502–13(e)(3). This consent may be granted for all items or a class of items of the consolidated group.

6.2. *Distributions with Respect to the Stock of a Member*

6.2.1. *Section 301 Distributions*

The single entity approach to intercompany transactions involving the stock of the members of a consolidated group applies to distributions on the stock of one group member made to another group member. Treas.Reg. § 1.1502–13(f). Intercompany distributions with respect to the stock of a member of the consolidated group that are subject to § 301 are excluded from the gross income of the distributee member, but only to the extent that the distributee reflects a corresponding negative adjustment to the basis of the stock of the distributing member. Treas.Reg. § 1.1502–13(f)(2)(ii). Thus, an intercompany distribution will increase recognized gain, or decrease loss, on a disposition of the stock of the distributing member. Under the investment adjustment rules of Treas.Reg. § 1.1502–32, if the distribution exceeds the recipient member's basis in the stock of the distributing member, the recipient's negative basis creates an excess loss account. The existence of an excess loss account will trigger recognition of gain if either the distributing or recipient member ceases to be a member of the consolidated group. Treas.Reg. § 1.1502–19.

6.2.2. *Intercompany Distributions of Appreciated and Depreciated Property*

Both gain and loss on intercompany distributions of appreciated or depreciated property with respect to the stock of the distributing member are recognized under the principles of § 311(b) but are accounted for as deferred intercompany gain or loss under the matching rule if the property is sold to a non-member. Treas.Reg. § 1.1502–13(f)(2)(iii). While deferred § 311(b) gain always is included in consolidated taxable income, loss is, however, allowed only if the property subsequently is sold to a nonmember; the deferred loss in excess of the transferee's gain is permanently disallowed if the property is distributed to a nonmember shareholder. If either member leaves the consolidated group, it will no longer be possible to match accounting for the distributing corporation's deferred item with the recipient's corresponding item, and the acceleration rule of Treas.Reg. § 1.1502–13(d)(1) will require the distributing corporation to account for deferred gain or loss recognized on the distribution. Treas.Reg. § 1.1502–13(c)(6) and (f)(7), Ex. 4(d).

The application of these rules in the context of a transaction that creates an excess loss account is illustrated by Treas.Reg. § 1.1502–13(f)(7), Ex. 2.

(a)   Facts. S owns all of T's only class of stock with a $10 basis and $100 value. S has substantial earnings and profits, and T has $10 of earnings and profits. On January 1 of Year 1, S declares and distributes a dividend of all of the T stock to P. Under section 311(b), S has a $90 gain. Under section 301(d), P's basis in the T stock is $100. During Year 3, T borrows $90 and declares and makes a $90 distribution to P to which section 301 applies, and P's basis in the T stock is reduced under § 1.1502–32 from $100 to $10. During Year 6, T has $5 of earnings that increase P's basis in the T stock under § 1.1502–32 from $10 to $15. On December 1 of Year 9, T issues additional stock to X and, as a result, T becomes a nonmember.

(b)   Dividend exclusion. Under [Treas.Reg. § 1.1502–13(f)(2)(ii)], P's $100 of dividend income from S's distribution of the T stock, and its $10 of dividend income from T's $90 distribution, are not included in gross income.

(c)   Matching and acceleration rules. Under § 1.1502–19(b)(1), when T becomes a nonmember P must include in income the amount of its excess loss account (if any) in T stock. P has no excess loss account in the T stock. Therefore P's corresponding item from the deconsolidation of T is $0. Treating S and P as divisions of a single corporation, the T stock would continue to have a $10 basis after the distribution, and the adjustments under § 1.1502–32 for T's $90 distribution [which decrease basis] and $5 of earnings [which increase basis] would result in a $75 excess loss account [$10 − $90 + $5]. Thus, the recomputed corresponding item from the deconsolidation is $75. Under the matching rule, S takes $75 of its $90 gain into account in Year 9 as a result of T becoming a nonmember, to reflect the difference between P's $0 gain taken into account and the $75 recomputed gain. S's remaining $15 of gain is taken into account under the matching and acceleration rules based on subsequent events (for example, under the matching rule if P subsequently sells its T stock, or under the acceleration rule if S becomes a nonmember).

In the example, if the basis of the T stock had not been adjusted as a result of S's distribution of the T stock to P, the $90 distribution to P would have resulted in an excess loss account with respect to the T stock. On a single entity basis, the excess loss account would have been $75, the original $10 of basis, increased by $5 of earnings and profits and decreased by the $90 distribution. Accordingly, S is required to take into account $75 of deferred gain when T ceases to be a member of the consolidated group. The remaining $15 of S's deferred gain remains a deferred item for S, which can be matched with P's disposition of its remaining T stock, or accelerated if either S or P ceases to be members of the same consolidated group. Treas.Reg. § 1.1502–19.

6.2.3.   *Liquidation of a Subsidiary*

Section 332, which provides nonrecognition to a parent corporation upon the complete liquidation of a subsidiary, operates within the consolidated return regime as well as outside the consolidated return regime.[10] The stock ownership test to qualify for nonrecognition under § 332 and § 337 is, through a cross reference in § 332(b)(1), to § 1504(a)(2), the ownership stock test required to be eligible to file consolidated returns. When § 332 applies to the liquidation, under § 334(b) the parent corporation receiving the distribution takes a transferred basis in the subsidiary's assets.

When § 332 applies to the parent of a liquidating corporation, § 337 provides a general exception to the basic rule of § 336 that a liquidating corporation recognizes gain or loss on liquidating distributions. Under § 337(a), no gain or loss is recognized on a distribution to an "80 percent distributee," defined in § 337(c) as a corporation that meets the stock ownership requirements of § 332(b).

In determining whether a member of the group holds sufficient stock to qualify for nonrecognition under § 332, stock owned by other members of the group is taken into account. Treas.Reg. § 1.1502–34. Assume, for example, that Y Corporation and Z Corporation, which are members of the same consolidated group, owned 60% and 40%, respectively, of the stock of S Corporation, and S Corporation liquidates by distributing 60% of its assets to Y Corporation and 40% of its assets to Z. Section 332 accords nonrecognition to each of Y Corporation and Z Corporation. Section 337(c) provides, however, that the determination of whether a corporation receiving a liquidating distribution is an "80-percent distributee," distributions to which do not result in recognition by the liquidating corporation under § 337(a), is to be made without regard to any consolidated return regulation. Thus, for purposes of § 337, neither Y Corporation nor Z Corporation meets the 80% stock ownership requirement of § 332(b), and S Corporation must recognize gain but not loss. I.R.C. § 336(d)(3). The gain is, however, deferred, and Y and Z succeed to S's deferred gain. Treas.Reg. § 1.1502–13(j)(2)(ii) and (j)(9), Ex. 7. But the manner in which that deferred gain is allocated between the distributee corporations is unclear.

An intercompany sale of the stock of a member of the consolidated group, followed by a liquidation of the subsidiary creates an interesting problem under the single entity approach. The intercompany sale of the stock of the member gives rise to deferred gain. Although there are some exceptions to the matching principle that will result in certain intercompany items being redetermined to be treated as excluded or as a nondeductible, noncapital amount, see Treas.Reg. § 1.1502–13(c)(6), this rule does not apply to gain on the sale of stock to another group member, followed by a § 332 liquidation in which the purchaser does not recognize gain. Treas.Reg. §§ 1.1502–13(c)(6)(ii), 1.1502–13(f)(5). The problem is illustrated by the following example based on Treas.Reg. § 1.1502–13(f)(7), Ex. 6(c). B Corporation, S Corporation, and T Corporation are members of the same

---

[10] Section 332 also applies if a controlled subsidiary merges into its parent corporation. Treas.Reg. § 1.332–2(d).

consolidated group. S Corporation owns all of the T Corporation stock, which has a fair market value of $100. S Corporation's basis in the T Corporation stock is $70. The fair market value of T Corporation's assets is $100 and the assets have a basis of $10. On July 1 of Year 1, B Corporation purchases the T Corporation stock from S Corporation for $100. S Corporation's $30 gain on the intercompany sale to B Corporation in Year 1 is deferred in determining consolidated taxable income in that Year. On July 1 of Year 3, when T Corporation's assets are still worth $100, T Corporation distributes all of its assets to B Corporation in a complete liquidation governed by § 332. B Corporation's basis in the T Corporation stock is $100. On liquidation of T Corporation, B Corporation receives a $100 distribution and thus has zero realized gain. In addition, B Corporation recognizes no gain or loss on the liquidation under § 332. If the transfer of T Corporation stock from S Corporation to B Corporation had been between divisions of a single entity, B Corporation's realized gain on liquidation of T Corporation would have been $30, but the gain would not have been recognized under § 332. Thus, B Corporation's recomputed corresponding item is $30 of unrecognized gain, which must be taken into account by S Corporation in Year 3. Although the attributes of S Corporation and B Corporation's gain, including its status as a nonrecognition item, are determined as if S Corporation and B Corporation were divisions of a single entity, Treas.Reg. § 1.1502–13(c)(1)(i), gain subject to a nonrecognition provision that is not permanently and explicitly disallowed is not treated as having the attribute of an item excluded from income. Treas.Reg. § 1.1502–13(c)(6)(ii). Thus, S Corporation's $30 of deferred gain is taken into account as capital gain in Year 3. This result seems to be necessary because B Corporation inherits T Corporation's asset basis and the T Corporation stock is no longer available as a corresponding item to match S Corporation's deferred gain from the sale of the T Corporation stock to B Corporation. The Regulations allow, however, elective relief from S Corporation's accounting for its deferred gain. Treas.Reg. § 1.1502–13(f)(5)(ii) and (f)(7), Ex. 6(b).

Deferred loss on an intercompany sale of stock of a subsidiary followed by a § 332 liquidation of the subsidiary is treated as a nondeductible, noncapital item, Treas.Reg. § 1.1502–13(f)(7), Ex. 6(c), and thus is not taken into account by the selling member. However, the Regulations allow elective relief from S Corporation's treating its deferred loss as a nondeductible, noncapital item. Treas.Reg. § 1.1502–13(f)(5)(ii) and (f)(7), Ex. 6(c).

6.2.4.   *Transactions in Which a Member Acquires Stock of Another Member*

If one affiliated corporation purchases the stock of another affiliated corporation, § 304 does not apply in the consolidated return context and the transaction is respected as a stock sale and purchase. Treas.Reg. § 1.1502–80(b). The selling member of the group has a deferred intercompany transaction subject to the rules of Treas.Reg. § 1.1502–13. See Treas.Reg. § 1.1502–13(f)(7), Ex. 6. The purchasing member of the group takes a § 1012 cost basis in the stock. Special rules apply to transactions involving the intra-group sale of stock of the common parent. Treas.Reg. § 1.1502–13(f)(6). Outside of the consolidated return context, § 304 would apply to determine whether the transaction would, generally speaking, be respected as a sale and purchase or would instead be recharacterized as a dividend distribution from the purchaser to its controlling shareholder.

6.2.5. *Transactions in Which a Member Acquires Its Own Stock*

When a corporation acquires its own stock, as a consequence of the nonrecognition rules of § 1032, there will be no subsequent transaction in which the basis of the acquired stock is accounted for. To deal with this situation, the Regulations provide, in effect, that if a member of a consolidated group acquires its own stock in an intercompany transaction, gain or loss recognized by the selling member must be accounted for at the time of the transaction under the acceleration rule. Treas.Reg. § 1.1502–13(f)(4). The gain or loss is accelerated to the date of the intercompany transaction under the acceleration rule because there is no corresponding item with which to match deferred gain. See Treas.Reg. § 1.1502–13(f)(7), Ex. 4. If a corporation acquires its own stock in a redemption subject to § 302(a), the selling member must account for its gain. If a corporation acquires its own stock in a § 301 distribution from another member, the distributing member must account for gain recognized under § 311(b). Treas.Reg. § 1.1502–13(f)(7), Ex. 5(c). If the selling or distributing corporation realizes a loss on the transaction, the loss is accounted for as a noncapital, nondeductible amount. Treas.Reg. § 1.1502–13(c)(6) and (f)(7), Ex. 5(d).

6.2.6. *Transactions in Which a Member Acquires Debt of Another Member*

Treas.Reg. § 1.1502–13(g) addresses the treatment of debt obligations between members of the same consolidated group, an "intercompany obligation." The rules apply to three types of transactions: (1) transactions in which an obligation between a group member and a nonmember becomes an intercompany obligation, for example, the purchase by a consolidated group member of another member's debt from a nonmember creditor or the acquisition by a consolidated group member of stock of a nonmember creditor or debtor (inbound transactions); (2) transactions in which an intercompany obligation ceases to be an intercompany obligation, for example, the sale by a creditor member of another member's debt to a nonmember or the deconsolidation of either the debtor or creditor member (outbound transactions); and (3) transactions in which an intercompany obligation is assigned or extinguished within the consolidated group (intragroup transactions). Treas.Reg. § 1.1502–13(g)(3)(i)(B). In each of these circumstances the following sequence of events is deemed to occur immediately before, and independently of, the actual transaction: (1) the debtor is deemed to satisfy the obligation for a cash amount equal to the obligation's fair market value, and (2) the debtor is deemed to immediately reissue the obligation to the original creditor for that same cash amount. The parties are then treated as engaging in the actual transaction but with the new obligation. Treas.Reg. § 1.1502–13(g)(3)(ii). As a result, in the year of the purchase, the debtor recognizes cancellation of debt income under § 61(a)(11) unless one of the exceptions in § 108 applies, and the deemed reissuance of the obligation for an amount equal to its fair market value causes it to be an original issue discount (OID) obligation. Under the OID rules,[11] over the life of the obligation, the purchasing member (the creditor) recognizes interest income and the debtor member recognizes interest deductions.

The Regulations contain a number of exceptions to the application of the deemed-satisfaction-reissuance model where it is determined that application of the model is not necessary to achieve its purposes or that burdens associated with valuing the obligation or applying the mechanics of the deemed satisfaction-reissuance model outweigh the benefits achieved by its application.

To avoid misuse of the exceptions to the satisfaction-reissuance model, the Regulations provide two anti-abuse rules. The material tax benefit rule applies to an intragroup assignment or extinguishment of an obligation if the transaction is undertaken with a view to shifting built-in items among members to achieve a material tax benefit. Treas.Reg. § 1.1502–13(g)(3)(i)(C). The off-market issuance rule applies if an intercompany obligation is issued at a materially off-market interest rate with a view to shifting of built-in items from the obligation to secure a material tax benefit. In such cases, the intercompany obligation will be treated as originally issued for its fair market value, and any difference between the amount loaned and the fair market value of the obligation will be treated as transferred between the creditor member and the debtor member, as appropriate (for example, as a distribution or a contribution to capital). Treas.Reg. § 1.1502–13(g)(3)(i)(C).

6.2.7.   *Anti-Abuse Rules*

In language designed to force tax practitioners to bang their heads against a brick wall for pleasure, Treas.Reg. § 1.1502–13(h)(1) provides, "If a transaction is structured with a principal purpose to avoid the purposes of this section (including, for example, by avoiding treatment as an intercompany transaction), adjustments must be made to carry out the purposes of this section." Specific examples of abusive transactions described in the Regulation include the transfer of property to a partnership to avoid the SRLY limitation, the use of corporations formed under § 351 or partnerships to mix assets for the purpose of avoiding gain on disposition of appreciated property, and the use of a sale-leaseback transaction to create gain for the purpose of absorbing losses subject to the SRLY limitation. Treas.Reg. § 1.1502–13(h)(2). Similar anti-abuse language is attached to other consolidated return Regulations. See, e.g., Regs. §§ 1.1502–19(e), –32(e), and –33(g).

7.   DIVISIVE REORGANIZATIONS IN THE CONSOLIDATED RETURN CONTEXT

7.1. *Section 355(f)*

Section 355(f) provides that a transaction is not subject to § 355 when the distributee shareholders are one or more corporations that are members of the same affiliated group of corporations as the distributing and controlled corporations and the transaction is part of a plan to transfer ownership as

---

[11]   I.R.C. §§ 1272–1274, and the regulations thereunder, discussed in Chapter 3.

described in § 355(e)(2). Special rules control the taxation of the distribution even though § 355 does not apply. The precise treatment of the transaction depends on whether or not the corporations involved in the transaction file consolidated returns

As discussed in Chapter 12, if the corporations involved in the transaction do not file consolidated returns, the distributing corporation generally must recognize gain (but not loss) under § 311 with respect to the distributed stock of the controlled corporation. (If, however, the distributing corporation liquidates as part of the transaction, § 337 may provide nonrecognition of gain or loss with respect to the stock of the controlled corporation.) The distributee corporation recognizes dividend income equal to the fair market value of the stock, but the income item is entirely offset by a 100% dividends received deduction under § 243.

The effect of § 355(f) is different if the distributing and distributee shareholder corporation file consolidated returns. First, although the distributing corporation recognizes gain on the distribution of the controlled corporation under § 311(b), the dividend distribution is a deferred intercompany transaction, and pursuant to Treas.Reg. § 1.1502–13(f)(2)(iii), the gain is not immediately recognized. The distributee corporation excludes the dividend from gross income, Treas.Reg. § 1.1502–13(f)(2)(iii), but must reduce its basis in the stock of the distributing corporation by the amount of the excluded dividend, i.e., the fair market value of the stock of the controlled corporation received in the distribution. Treas.Reg. § 1.1502–32. If the distributee corporation subsequently disposes of the controlled corporation received in the spin-off, the distributing corporation must recognize its deferred gain without regard to whether the disposition is a sale or a tax-free reorganization. Treas.Reg. § 1.1502–13. The same result occurs if the distributee corporation disposes of the stock of the distributing corporation.

It is possible for both § 355(e) and § 355(f) to apply to a series of transactions involving an intragroup spin-off followed by a spin-off out of the group as part of a plan by which a majority interest in either of the distributing corporations or the distributed controlled corporation subsequently is acquired by new owners. Assume that X Corporation is publicly held and owns all of the stock of Y Corporation, which in turn owns all of the stock of Z Corporation. The corporations file a consolidated return. To facilitate the acquisition of X Corporation by P Corporation, Y Corporation distributes all of the stock of Z Corporation to X Corporation, which in turn distributes the Z Corporation stock to its public shareholders. Thereafter, X Corporation is merged into P Corporation. After the merger the former shareholders of X Corporation hold less than 50% of the P Corporation stock. Pursuant to § 355(f), § 355 does not apply to the distribution of Z Corporation stock to X Corporation by Y Corporation. The distribution is a taxable distribution, but Y Corporation can defer its intercompany gain and X Corporation can eliminate the dividend from gross income. X Corporation takes a fair market value basis in the Z Corporation stock, but must reduce its basis in its Y Corporation stock by a like amount. Section 355(e) applies to the distribution by X Corporation to its shareholders of the Z Corporation stock, but because X Corporation's basis in the Z Corporation stock equals its fair market value on the day it was received, if the distribution follows promptly, it is likely that little, if any, gain will be realized. As a result of the spin-off of Z Corporation by X Corporation, Y Corporation recognizes its deferred intercompany gain, and X Corporation increases its basis in Y Corporation by the amount of gain recognized. The same consequences would follow if P acquired Z Corporation.

7.2. *Special Basis Problems in Intragroup Spin-Offs*

In the case of an intragroup spin-off, i.e., a divisive distribution of stock from one member of an affiliated group of corporations (as defined in § 1504(a)) to another member of the group, the issues involving the appropriate effects on basis are essentially the same whether or not the spin-off is part of an acquisition. Spin-offs in the consolidated return context present special problems even if an acquisition is not in the wind. In this case, the basis of the distributed corporation is generally determined with reference to the basis of the distributing corporation. The basis allocation rules generally eliminate any excess loss account in the stock of a controlled corporation that is distributed within the group. See I.R.C. §§ 355(c), 358; Treas.Reg. § 1.1502–19(b)(2)(i). Congress also was concerned that a § 355 distribution within an affiliated group that does not file a consolidated return also could result in similar basis results, which it considered inappropriate. Congress addressed these issues by giving the Treasury Department broad regulatory authority in § 358(g), which is discussed in the following excerpt from Staff of the Joint Committee on Taxation, General Explanation of Tax Legislation Enacted in 1997, 203–204 (1997).

[Section 358(g)] provides that in the case of any distribution of stock of one member of an affiliated group of corporations to another member under section 355 ("intragroup spin-off"), the Secretary of the Treasury is authorized under section 358(g) to provide adjustments to the basis of any stock in a corporation which is a member of such group, to reflect appropriately the proper treatment of such distribution. It is understood that the approach of any such regulations applied to intragroup spinoffs that do not involve an acquisition may also be applied under the Treasury regulatory authority to modify the rule of section 355(f) as may be appropriate.

Congress believed that the concerns relating to basis adjustments in the case of intragroup spin-offs are essentially similar, whether or not an acquisition is currently intended as part of a plan or series of related transactions. The concerns include the following. First, under present law consolidated return regulations, it is possible that an excess loss account of a lower tier subsidiary may be eliminated. This creates the potential for the subsidiary to leave the group without recapture of the excess loss account, even though the group has benefitted from the losses or distributions in excess of basis that led to the existence of the excess loss account.

Second, under present law, a shareholder's stock basis in its stock of the distributing corporation is allocated after a spin-off between the stock of the distributing and controlled corporations, in proportion to the relative fair market values of the stock of those companies. If a disproportionate amount of asset basis (as compared to value) is in one of the companies (including but not limited to a shift of value and basis through a borrowing by one company and contribution of the borrowed cash to the other), present law rules under section 358(c) can produce an increase in stock basis relative to asset basis in one corporation, and a corresponding decrease in stock basis relative to asset basis in the other company. Because the spin-off has occurred within the corporate group, the group can continue to benefit from high inside asset basis either for purposes of sale or depreciation, while also choosing to benefit from the disproportionately high stock basis in the other corporation. If, for example, both corporations were sold at a later date, a prior distribution can result in a significant decrease in the amount of gain recognized than would have occurred if the two corporations had been sold together without a prior spin off (or separately, without a prior spin-off).

Example 6: P owns all the stock of S1 and S1 owns all the stock of S2. P's basis in the stock of S1 is 50; the inside asset basis of S1's assets is 50; and the total value of S1's stock and assets (including the value of S2) is 150. S1's basis in the stock of S2 is 0; the inside basis of S2's assets is 0; and the value of S2's stock and assets is 100. If S1 were sold, holding S2, the total gain would be 100. S1 distributes S2 to P in a section 355 transaction. After this spin-off, under present law, P's basis in the stock of S1 is approximately 17 (50/150 times the total 50 stock basis in S1 prior to the spin-off) and the inside asset basis of S1 is 50. P's basis in the stock of S2 is 33 (100/150 times the total 50 stock basis in S1 prior to the spin-off) and the inside asset basis of S2 is 0. After a period of time, S2 can be sold for its value of 100, with a gain of 67 rather than 100. Also, since S1 remains in the corporate group, the full 50 inside asset basis can continue to be used. S1's assets could be sold for 50 with no gain or loss. Thus, S1 and S2 can be sold later at a total gain of 67, rather than the total gain of 100 that would have occurred had they been sold without the spin-off.

As one variation on the foregoing concern, taxpayers have attempted to utilize spin-offs to extract significant amounts of asset value and basis, (including but not limited to transactions in which one corporation decreases its value by incurring debt, and increases the asset basis and value of the other corporation by contributing the proceeds of the debt to the other corporation) without creation of an excess loss account or triggering of gain, even when the extraction is in excess of the basis in the distributing corporation's stock.

The Treasury Department may promulgate any regulations necessary to address these concerns and other collateral issues. As one example, the Treasury Department may consider providing rules that require a carryover basis within the group (or stock basis conforming to asset basis as appropriate) for the distributed corporation (including a carryover of an excess loss account, if any, in a consolidated return). Similarly, the Treasury Department may provide a reduction in the basis of the stock of the distributing corporation to reflect the change in the value and basis of the distributing corporation's assets. The Treasury Department may determine that the aggregate stock basis of distributing and controlled after the distribution may be adjusted to an amount that is less than the aggregate basis of the stock of the distributing corporation before the distribution, to prevent inappropriate potential for artificial losses or diminishment of gain on disposition of any of the corporations involved in the spin-off. The Treasury Department may provide separate regulations for corporations in affiliated groups filing a consolidated return and for affiliated groups not filing a consolidated return, as appropriate to each situation.

8. SALES OF SUBSIDIARY STOCK: THE UNIFIED LOSS RULES

8.1. *Generally*

In some cases, application of the investment adjustment rules conflicts with the principles of § 311 and § 336, which require recognition of gain on the distribution by a corporation of appreciated property, and permit the recognition of loss on the distribution of depreciated property by a liquidating corporation, because it permits assets that are sold out of the consolidated group to obtain a step up in basis without the payment of a current corporate level tax. Suppose, for example, that S Corporation holds a single asset with a basis of $100 and a fair market value of $300. P Corporation purchases all of the stock of S Corporation for $300, P and S do not make a § 338 election, and P and S Corporations elect to file a consolidated return. S Corporation then sells the asset for $300. S Corporation recognizes a $200 gain, and P Corporation increases its basis in the S Corporation stock from $300 to $500. P Corporation then sells the stock of S Corporation for $300, realizing a $200 loss, which offsets the $200 gain. Absent a limitation on the recognition of this loss, tax on the gain realized from the sale of the assets effectively would be eliminated by P Corporation's loss on the sale of the stock of S. P Corporation's tax loss is artificial; it does not reflect an economic loss. The same problem arises if the asset is a depreciable asset that is consumed in the course of S Corporation's business.

To deal with this issue, Treas.Reg. § 1.1502–36 provides unified rules for loss on subsidiary stock transferred by a member of an affiliated group filing a consolidated return. A transfer of a loss share of stock (defined as a share of stock of an affiliate having a basis in excess of fair market value) includes any event in which (1) gain or loss would be recognized (apart from the rules in the Regulations), (2) the holder of a share and the subsidiary cease to be members of the same group, (3) a nonmember acquires an outstanding share from a member, or (4) the share is treated as worthless. The purpose of these rules is twofold, to prevent the consolidated return provisions from creating noneconomic losses on the sale of subsidiary stock and to prevent members of the affiliated group filing the consolidated return from claiming more than one tax benefit from a single economic loss. Under the Regulations, any transfer of a loss share requires the application in sequence of three basis rules.

First, under Treas.Reg. § 1.1502–36(b), a basis redetermination rule is applied to deal with tax losses attributable to investment adjustment account allocations among different shares of stock that result in disproportionate reflection of gain or loss in the shares' basis. Second, if any share is a loss share after application of the basis redetermination rule, a basis reduction rule is applied under Treas.Reg. § 1.1502–36(c) to deal with artificial loss attributable to investment adjustment account adjustments, but this reduction does not exceed the share's "disconformity amount." Third, if any duplicated losses remain after application of the basis reduction rule, under Treas.Reg. § 1.1502–36(d), an attribute reduction rule is applied to the corporation the stock of which was sold to prevent the duplication of a loss recognized on the transfer or preserved in the basis of the stock. If a chain of subsidiaries is transferred (rather than a single subsidiary), the order in which the rules are applied is modified. In this case, the basis redetermination rule and the basis reduction rule are applied sequentially, working down the chain, and the attribute reduction rule is then applied working up the chain, starting with the lowest tier subsidiary.

8.2. *The Basis Redetermination Rule*

The basis redetermination rule in Treas.Reg. § 1.1502–36(b) does not apply when all of the stock of the subsidiary has been transferred in a taxable transaction; thus, often it is not applicable. When the basis redetermination rule does apply, investment adjustments (exclusive of distributions) that were previously applied to members' bases in subsidiary stock are reallocated in a manner that, to the greatest extent possible, first eliminates loss on preferred shares and then eliminates basis disparity on all shares. This rule affects both positive and negative adjustments, and thus addresses both noneconomic and duplicated losses. First, the basis of any transferred loss share is reduced by any positive investment adjustments, but the basis will not be reduced to less than the value of the loss share. Second, to the extent of any remaining loss on the transferred shares, negative investment adjustments are removed from shares that are not transferred loss shares and are applied to reduce the loss on transferred loss shares. Third, the positive adjustments removed from the transferred loss shares are allocated to increase basis of other shares only after the negative adjustments have been reallocated. This rule does not affect the aggregate basis of the shares and, thus, does not apply if all of the shares of a subsidiary are sold or become worthless; it is important only when some, but not all, shares are sold. A number of special limitations on basis reallocation also must be considered in various specific circumstances.

8.3. *The Basis Reduction Rule*

If, after applying the basis redetermination rule in step one, any transferred share is a loss share (even if the share only became a loss share as a result of the application of the basis redetermination rule), the basis of that share is subject to reduction. The basis reduction rule in Treas.Reg. § 1.1502–36(c) eliminates noneconomic losses that arise from the operation of the investment adjustment account rules. Under this rule, the basis of each transferred loss share is reduced (but not below its value) by the lesser of (1) the share's disconformity amount, or (2) the share's net positive adjustment.

The "disconformity amount" with respect to a subsidiary's share is the excess of its basis over the share's allocable portion of the subsidiary's inside tax attributes (determined at the time of the transfer). Every share within a single class of stock has an identical allocable portion. Between shares of different classes of stock, allocable portions are determined by taking into account the economic arrangements represented by the terms of the stock. "Net inside attributes" is the sum of the subsidiary's loss carryovers, deferred deductions, cash, and asset bases, minus the subsidiary's liabilities. The disconformity amount identifies the net amount of unrealized appreciation reflected in the basis of the share.

A share's net positive adjustment is computed as the greater of (1) zero, or (2) the sum of all investment adjustments (excluding distributions) applied to the basis of the transferred loss share, including investment adjustments attributable to prior basis reallocations under the basis reallocation rule. The net positive adjustment identifies the extent to which a share's basis has been increased by the investment adjustment provisions for items of income, gain, deduction, and loss (whether taxable or not) that have been taken into account by the group. Special rules apply when the subsidiary the stock of which is transferred itself holds stock of a lower-tier subsidiary.

The application of the basis reduction rule is illustrated by the following example. Assume that P purchased all the stock of S for $500 at a time when S had a single capital asset with a basis of $400. During the period P owned S, S earned $50 (after taxes) and purchased a second capital asset. P sells all of the stock of S for $380, when P's basis in the S stock is $550, thereby realizing a $170 loss. At that time, the fair market value of S's assets is $380, and the basis of S's assets is $450. The disconformity amount is $100, the excess of P's $550 basis in the S stock over S's $450 basis in its assets, and the net positive basis adjustment is $50. The lesser of the two is $50. Thus, P's $550 basis in the S stock is reduced by $50 to $500 and only $120 of the loss is allowed.

8.4. *The Attribute Reduction Rule*

If any transferred share remains a loss share after application of the basis reallocation and basis reduction rules, any loss recognized with respect to the transferred share is allowed. In this instance, the subsidiary's tax attributes (including the consolidated attributes, e.g., loss carryovers, attributable to the subsidiary) are, however, reduced pursuant to Treas.Reg. § 1.1502–36(d). The attribute reduction rule addresses the duplication of loss by members of consolidated groups and is designed to prevent the group from recognizing more than one tax loss with respect to a single economic loss, regardless of whether the group disposes of the subsidiary stock before or after the subsidiary recognizes the loss with respect to its assets or operations. Under a type of *de minimis* rule, unless the group so elects, the attribute reduction rule does not, however, apply if the aggregate attribute reduction amount in the transaction is less than 5% of the total value of the shares transferred by members in the transaction. Treas.Reg. § 1.1502–36(d)(2)(ii).

Under the attribute reduction rule, the subsidiary's attributes are reduced by the "attribute reduction amount," which equals the lesser of (1) the net stock loss, or (2) the aggregate inside loss. The "attribute reduction amount" reflects the total amount of unrecognized loss that is reflected in both the basis of the subsidiary stock and the subsidiary's attributes. "Net stock loss" is the amount by which the sum of the bases (after application of the basis reduction rule) of all of the shares in the subsidiary transferred by members of the group in the same transaction exceeds the aggregate value of those shares. Treas.Reg. § 1.1502–36(d)(3)(ii). The subsidiary's "aggregate inside loss" is the excess of its net inside attributes over the aggregate value of all of the shares in the subsidiary. Treas.Reg. § 1.1502–36(d)(3)(iii). (Net inside attributes generally has the same meaning as in the basis reduction rule, subject to special rules for lower-tier subsidiaries.)

The attribute reduction amount is first applied to reduce or eliminate items that represent actual realized losses, such as operating loss carryovers (Category A), capital loss carryovers (Category B), and deferred deductions (Category C)—in that order unless the taxpayer elects to make a different allocation. If the subsidiary does not hold stock of any lower-tier subsidiaries, any excess attribute reduction amount is then applied to reduce the basis of assets (Category D) in the asset classes specified in Treas.Reg. § 1.338–6(b) other than Class I (cash and general deposit accounts, other than certificates of deposit held in depository institutions), but in the reverse order from the order specified in that section. Thus, the basis in any purchased goodwill is the first item reduced. If the subsidiary holds stock of one or more lower-tier subsidiaries, the Category D attribute reduction is first allocated between the subsidiary's basis in any stock of lower-tier subsidiaries and the subsidiary's other assets (treating the non-stock Category D assets as one asset) in proportion to the subsidiary's basis in the stock of each lower-tier subsidiary and its basis in the Category D assets other than subsidiary stock. Only the portion of the attribute reduction amount not allocated to lower-tier subsidiary stock is applied under the reverse residual method. (Additional special rules apply to prevent excessive reduction of attributes when the subsidiary itself holds stock of a lower-tier subsidiary. Treas.Reg. § 1.1502–36(d)(4)(ii).) If the attribute reduction amount exceeds all of the attributes available for reduction, that excess amount generally has no effect. If, however, cash or other liquid assets are held to fund payment of a liability that has not yet been deducted but will be deductible in the future (e.g., a liability the deduction for which is subject to the economic performance rules of § 461(h)), loss could be duplicated later, when the liability is taken into account. To prevent such loss duplication, the excess attribute reduction amount will be held in suspense and applied to prevent the deduction or capitalization of later payments with respect to the liability. Treas.Reg.

§ 1.1502–36(d)(4)(ii)(C). Additional special rules apply to prevent excessive reduction of attributes when the subsidiary itself holds stock of a lower-tier subsidiary.

The application of the attribute reduction rule is illustrated by continuing the preceding example. The "net stock loss" when P sold the stock of S was $120. The "aggregate inside loss"—the excess of the basis of S's assets ($450) over the value of the S stock ($380) is $70. The lesser of the two is $70. Thus, the basis of S's assets is reduced by $70, from $450 to $380. No gain or loss would be realized on the sale of S's assets for $380.

In cases where as a result of the stock transfer the subsidiary ceases to be a member of the group, an election may be made to reattribute attributes (other than asset basis) and/or to reduce stock basis (and thereby reduce stock loss) in order to avoid attribute reduction. Treas.Reg. § 1.1502–36(d)(4). If an election is made and it is ultimately determined that the subsidiary has no attribute reduction amount, the election will have no effect (or, if the election is made for an amount that exceeds the finally determined attribute reduction amount, the election will have no effect to the extent of that excess). In addition, taxpayers may elect to reduce (or not reduce) stock basis, or to reattribute (or not reattribute) attributes, or some combination thereof, in any amount that does not exceed the subsidiary's attribute reduction amount.[12]

Finally, if the subsidiary ceases to be a member of the consolidated group as a result of the transfer, the common parent of the group can elect to reduce stock basis (thereby reducing an otherwise allowable loss on the sale of the stock), reattribute attributes, or apply some combination of basis reduction and attribute reattribution after the otherwise required attribute reduction.

8.5. *Worthlessness*

If a member treats stock of the subsidiary as worthless under § 165(g) and the subsidiary continues as a member, or if a member recognizes a loss on subsidiary stock and on the following day the subsidiary is not a member and does not have a separate return year following the recognition of the loss, all Category A, Category B, and Category C attributes (i.e., capital loss carryovers, net operating loss carryovers, and deferred deductions) that have not otherwise been eliminated or reattributed, as well as any credit carryovers, are eliminated. Treas.Reg. § 1.1502–36(d)(7). A worthlessness determination must take into account the rules in Treas.Reg. § 1.1502–80(c), as well as under § 165.

PROBLEM SET

1.   T Corp. has two classes of stock outstanding. Class A is voting common stock and Class B is preferred stock. The management of P Corp. is considering the acquisition of some, but not all, of the outstanding stock of T Corp.

---

[12] The reattribution election may be made only if the subsidiary ceases to be a group member.

(a) Will P Corp. and T Corp. be eligible to file consolidated returns in the following alternative situations?

(1) The class B preferred is limited as to dividends and liquidation rights and is nonvoting except as required by state law. Each class of stock has 100 shares outstanding. P Corp. acquires 80% of the common stock and 10% of the preferred stock.

(2) The class B preferred stock is limited as to dividends and liquidation rights but is entitled to vote on a par with the Class A voting stock. Each class has 100 shares outstanding. P Corp. acquires 90% of the common stock and 75% of the preferred stock.

(i) Assume the Class A stock is worth $50 per share and the class B stock is worth $100 per share.

(ii) Assume the Class A stock is worth $49 per share and the class B stock is worth $100 per share.

(3) The class B preferred stock is nonvoting, but after satisfaction of its preference participates with common as to dividends and liquidation rights. There are 800 shares of class A common outstanding and 200 shares of class B shares outstanding. P Corp. acquires 79% of the common stock and 100% of the preferred stock.

(4) The class A stock is voting common stock. There are 9,000 shares of class A stock, worth $9,000,000. The class B stock is voting participating preferred stock. There are 1,000 shares of class B stock, worth $1,000,000. The voting rights of the Class A and Class B stock are identical, one vote per share, except that the board of directors is classified. The class A stock collectively and solely elects seven directors, and the class B stock collectively and solely elects three directors. P Corp. acquires all of the Class A stock and none of the class B stock.

(b) Why should the P Corp. management be concerned about the ability to file consolidated returns?

2. (a) P Corporation owns 80% of X Corp., and X Corp. owns 80% of Y Corp. May all three corporations join in a consolidated return?

(b) P Corporation owns 100% of Maple Leaf, Inc. a Canadian corporation, and Maple Leaf owns 100% of Glacier, Inc., a Montana corporation, which in turn owns 90% of Black Hill Corp., a South Dakota corporation. Which of the corporations are eligible to join in a consolidated return?

(c) P Corp. owns 80% of X Corp. and Y Corp. X Corp. and Y Corp. each own 50% of Z Corp. May Z Corp. be included in a consolidated return with the other corporations?

3. On January 1, Year 4, Empire Holding Corp., a publicly held corporation, purchased all of the outstanding stock of the Bluegrass Bourbon Distillery, Inc. for $3,000,000. For all relevant years Empire Holding Corp. and Bluegrass Bourbon Distillery filed consolidated returns.

(a) For Years 4 through 14, Bluegrass Bourbon Distillery had an aggregate operating loss of $4,000,000. On January 1, Year 15, Empire Holding Corp. sold all of the outstanding stock of Bluegrass Bourbon Distillery to Kentucky Industrial Hemp Corp. for $100,000. How much gain or loss does Empire recognize?

(b) For the Years 4 through 14, Bluegrass Bourbon Distillery had an aggregate operating loss of $4,000,000. The Distillery ceased operations on January 1, Year 15, and all of its assets, which you may assume for simplicity had a zero basis, were abandoned as worthless. How much gain or loss does Empire recognize?

4. Several years ago P Corp. formed S Corp. by contributing assets of an operating division with a combined basis of $1,000,000, subject to liabilities of $3,000,000, which S Corp. assumed, in exchange for 10 shares of stock. P and S filed consolidated returns. Over the period S has been a member of the consolidated group, its income has exactly equaled its losses. This year, P Corp. sold 5 shares of S Corp. to X Corp. for $10,000,000. What are the tax consequences to P Corp. from the sale of the 5 shares of S Corp. stock?

5. X Corp. owns all of the stock of Y Corp., which in turn owns all of the stock of Z Corp. X Corp., Y Corp., and Z Corp. file consolidated returns. None of the corporations have any accumulated earnings and profits. This year X Corp. had $100,000 of earnings and profits, Y Corp. lost $400,000 (as measured for earnings and profits), and Z Corp. had earnings and profits of $1,000,000.

(a) If X Corp. distributes $300,000 to its shareholders this year, what portion of the $300,000 is a dividend?

(b) If none of the corporations has any profit or loss next year and X Corporation distributes $200,000 to its shareholders, what portion of the $200,000 is a dividend?

(c) None of the corporations have any accumulated earnings and profits before last year. Last year X Corp. had $100,000 of earnings and profits, Y Corp. lost $400,000 (as measured for earnings and profits), and Z Corp. had earnings and profits of $1,000,000. On the first day of this year, X Corp, sold Y Corp. and realized neither gain nor loss. Later this year, Z Corp. distributed $300,000 to its new shareholders, even though Z Corp. had no current earnings and profits. What portion of the $300,000 is a dividend?

6. Petro, Inc. owns all of the stock of Leviathan Energy Corp. and Georges Bank Oil Drilling Corp. The three corporations file a consolidated return. In Year 6, Leviathan sold a mineral lease to Georges Bank for $5,000,000. Leviathan had a basis in the lease of $1,000,000.

(a) What are the tax consequences to Leviathan and Georges Bank if in Year 7, Georges Bank sells the lease to an unrelated party for $6,000,000?

(b) What are the tax consequences to Leviathan and Georges Bank if in Year 7, Georges Bank sells the lease to an unrelated party for $3,000,000?

(c) What are the tax consequences to Leviathan if in Year 7 Georges Bank extracts oil from the purchased deposit, and on the basis that 10% of the deposit was extracted, Georges Bank claims a cost depletion allowance under § 611 (analogous to depreciation) of $500,000, i.e., 10% of its cost basis for the oil lease?

(d)   What are the tax consequences to Leviathan and Petro if in Year 7 Petro sells all of the stock of Georges Bank to an unrelated party for an amount equal to its adjusted basis in the Georges Bank stock?

7.   (a)   P Corp. owns all of the stock of S Corp. Both corporations have over $1,000,000 of earnings and profits. Last year, S distributed an asset with a basis of $60,000 and fair market value of $100,000 to P. This year, P sold the asset to an unrelated party for $120,000. What are the tax consequences to S and to P?

(b)   (1)   How does the answer change if S's basis in the asset was $160,000?

(2)   How does the answer change if S's basis in the asset was $160,000 and when the asset was worth $120,000, P distributed the asset to a P shareholder as a dividend distribution?

8.   P Corp. owns all of the stock of X Corp. and Y Corp. X Corp owned 60% of the voting common stock of Z Corp. Its basis for the stock was $350. Y Corp. owned 40% of the voting common stock of Z Corp. Its basis for the stock was $250. Z Corp. liquidated and distributed Blackacre, with a basis of $ 200 and a fair market value of $600 to X Corp and distributed Whiteacre with a basis of $100 and a fair market value of $400 to Z Corp. What are the tax consequences?

9.   Recall that in Problem 3 Empire Holding Corp. purchased all of the outstanding stock of the Bluegrass Bourbon Distillery, Inc. for $3,000,000 in Year 9. For Years 9 through 19, Bluegrass Bourbon Distillery broke-even from operations. In December Year 19, Bluegrass Bourbon Distillery realized a gain of $2,000,000 on the sale of a nondepreciable asset that it had purchased in Year 6 for $100,000, and which was worth $1,000,000 on January 1, Year 1. On January 1, Year 20, Empire sold all of the outstanding stock of Bluegrass Bourbon Distillery to Kentucky Industrial Hemp Corp. for $3,500,000. At that time the aggregate basis of Bluegrass Bourbon Distillery's assets was 4,000,000. How much gain or loss does Empire recognize?

PART VII

ELECTIVE PASSTHROUGH TAX TREATMENT

CHAPTER 16

S CORPORATIONS

SECTION 1. INTRODUCTION

Overview. Subchapter S was enacted in 1958 to make it possible for "businesses to select the form of business organization desired, without the necessity of taking into account major differences in tax consequence." S.Rep. No. 85–1983, 85th Cong., 2d Sess. 87 (1958). As originally enacted, Subchapter S status was available only for corporations that had no more than 10 individual shareholders. Although shareholders were taxed on undistributed corporate profits in addition to actual dividend distributions, except for capital gains, the character of items did not pass through to the shareholders as in the case of partnerships. If the corporation had a net operating loss, it also passed through to stockholders. A stockholder's stock basis was increased by undistributed taxable income and decreased by pass-through net operating losses. An electing corporation was not subject to tax unless it realized extraordinary capital gains.[1]

In 1969 the Treasury Department, in conjunction with the Tax Section of the American Bar Association, proposed revising Subchapter S to conform more closely to the complete pass-through model of the partnership rules.[2] To alleviate problems caused by the hybrid nature of the S corporation under then current law, "not quite a corporation and not quite a partnership," the Treasury study recommended adoption of complete pass-through taxation of the entity's tax-significant items under the partnership rules, plus a number of other changes to simplify Subchapter S. The 1969 proposal was adopted in 1982, generally intact. Thus, while the detailed rules of Subchapter S have metamorphosed over the years, and will undoubtedly continue to evolve, the fundamental purpose of Subchapter S—to eliminate the corporation as a taxable entity and provide a system under which the operating profits of qualifying corporations are taxed directly to the shareholders—remains unchanged.

Prior to the mid-1980s, only a relatively small number of corporations elected Subchapter S status. One reason was that prior to 1982, Subchapter S status could not be maintained if more than 20% of the corporation's gross receipts were derived from passive investments such as interest, dividends, rents, and royalties. In many other cases, closely held corporations simply did not show a profit after paying shareholder-employees' salaries. The election was mostly valuable

---

[1] The corporate level tax was designed to discourage a "one-shot" election by a corporation anticipating gain on the disposition of capital (or § 1231) assets.

[2] U.S. Treasury Dept. Tax Reform Studies and Proposals, House Ways and Means Committee and Senate Finance Committee, 91st Cong., 1st Sess. (1969).

during the early years of a venture when the corporation produced losses that could be passed through to the stockholders.

After 1986, however, Subchapter S elections by eligible corporations became vastly more popular. This occurred because the maximum effective rate of taxation of distributed C corporation income subject to double taxation in 1987 was significantly higher than the maximum effective rate of taxation on S corporation income. But subsequent changes in the tax rate schedules, the reemergence of a significant capital gains preference, and the widespread enactment by states of limited liability company (LLC) statutes altered the attractiveness of S corporations.[3] In the 1990s, virtually every state enacted a limited liability company statute. Generally, LLCs are formed to be taxed as partnerships under Subchapter K, even though they confer limited liability on every member. From both the tax and nontax points of view, the LLC is a more flexible form of business organization than a corporation that makes a Subchapter S election. Nevertheless, whether Subchapter K or Subchapter S is the more desirable pass-through form depends on analysis of a broad range of factors—an analysis that has been further complicated by the 2017 tax legislation, with its substantially reduced tax rate for C corporations and its § 199A deduction for eligible income of pass-through entities and sole proprietorships.[4] Section 199A is discussed in the final section of this Chapter.

The Basic Framework of Subchapter S. To be eligible to make a Subchapter S election, a corporation must meet a number of requirements, including limitations on the number and identity of its shareholders. First, an electing corporation, referred to as an "S corporation," may have no more than 100 shareholders. I.R.C. § 1361(b)(1)(A). The 100 shareholder limit is somewhat illusory, however, because § 1361(c)(1) treats as a single shareholder all of the members of a family traced to a common ancestor no more than six generations removed from the youngest family member who is a shareholder. Qualifying shareholders include only individuals, grantor trusts, voting trusts, "qualified Subchapter S trusts" (QSSTs), "electing small business trusts," tax-exempt charitable organizations, and certain retirement pension trusts. It cannot have a shareholder who is a "nonresident alien," a corporation (other than a tax-exempt charitable organization), partnership, or LLC, and it may issue only one class of stock (although there is an exception for stock that varies in voting rights). I.R.C. § 1361(b)–(c). An S corporation may hold stock in a controlled subsidiary corporation but may not be a subsidiary of another corporation. A

---

[3]   See Erik Röder, Combining Limited Liability and Transparent Taxation: Lessons from the Convergent Evolution of GMBH & Co. KGS, S Corporations, LLCs, and Other Functionally Equivalent Entities, 21 Fla. Tax Rev. 762 (2018) (providing brief history regarding S corporations and LLCs).

[4]   See James R. Repetti, The Impact of the 2017 Act's Tax Rate Changes on Choice of Entity, 21 Fla. Tax Rev. 686 (2018).

corporation that is 100% owned by a parent S corporation may, however, at the parent S corporation's election be treated as a disregarded entity— in effect, as an operating division of its parent rather than a separate corporation. I.R.C. § 1361(b)(3).

S corporation status may be elected only with the consent of all shareholders at the time the election is filed. An election is effective on the first day of the taxable year following the filing of the election, except that an election filed within the first two and one-half months of the taxable year may be retroactive to the first day of the taxable year. In the latter case, the corporation must have satisfied all of the requirements for S corporation status beginning on the first day of the taxable year. I.R.C. § 1362(b). Once made, an election continues in effect until it is revoked by a majority of the shareholders, the corporation ceases to meet the qualifications as an S corporation, or the corporation has accumulated earnings and profits[5] and earns passive investment income in excess of 25% of gross receipts for three consecutive taxable years. I.R.C. § 1362(d).

Generally an S corporation is not subject to corporate tax. I.R.C. § 1363(a). There are two exceptions. Under § 1374, S corporations are taxable on certain gain recognized on disposition of appreciated assets or income items generated while the corporation was a C corporation or acquired from a C corporation in a nonrecognition transaction. In addition, under § 1375, an S corporation with accumulated earnings and profits is taxable at regular corporate rates to the extent that passive investment income exceeds 25% of its gross receipts.

S corporation items of income, loss, or deduction are passed through the entity to the shareholders and retain their character in the shareholder's hands, in the same manner that partnership items are passed through to partners under Subchapter K. I.R.C. § 1366. Thus, each item of income or deduction that may affect shareholders differently must be separately stated and reported to the shareholders. For example, tax-exempt interest income retains its exemption under § 103, and interest expense must be categorized under the complex interest allocation rules to determine its deductibility by the individual shareholders. Each shareholder reports the item on the shareholder's return as if the item were derived by the shareholder directly. The character of items, such as capital gain, is based on the character of income at the corporate level. The shareholder's basis in S corporation stock is increased for income items and decreased for deduction or loss items passed through to the shareholder from the corporation. I.R.C. § 1367. As under the partnership model, the shareholder's deductible loss is limited to the shareholder's basis in stock, but S corporation shareholders who lend money directly to the corporation may also deduct

---

[5]   A corporation will accumulate earnings and profits only in years it is a C corporation. Thus, this restriction does not apply to a corporation that has no tax history as a C corporation.

losses up to their basis in that loan to the S corporation. I.R.C. § 1366(d)(1).

Since S corporation income is taxed to the shareholders when realized by the corporation, subsequent distributions of the previously taxed income are received by shareholders without additional tax. I.R.C. § 1368. Distributions reduce the shareholder's basis in stock of the corporation. Distributions in excess of basis result in recognition of capital gain.

A second tier of distribution rules applies to an S corporation that has accumulated earnings and profits from taxable years in which it was a C corporation in order to preserve the "double" tax pattern for earnings originally generated in a C corporation. The corporation must maintain an "accumulated adjustments account" that reflects net corporate income items that have been passed through to shareholders. Distributions to the extent of this accumulated adjustments account are received by the shareholders without tax. I.R.C. § 1368(c). To the extent that distributions exceed the accumulated adjustments account, the distributions are treated as distributions of earnings and profits, to the extent thereof, and are taxed to the shareholders as dividends. Any further distributions are received by the shareholders as a reduction of basis, then as capital gain to the extent that a distribution exceeds the recipient shareholder's basis.

Comparison of S Corporations and Partnerships (Including LLCs). Although Subchapter S in general adopts the partnership model for passing through S corporation income, there are significant differences between the taxation of S corporations and partnerships that affect a taxpayer's choice between the two entities. (Since a multi-member LLC usually will be taxed as a partnership, the following considerations are generally applicable to LLCs as well.) As discussed previously, beneficial ownership of an S corporation nominally is limited to 100 shareholders, while there is no limit on the number of persons who may be partners in a partnership. Nor is there any restriction upon the types of entities or individuals that may be partners. The partnership form provides a significant advantage in the case of leveraged investments if losses are anticipated. Partners are allowed to include their shares of partnership debt in the bases of their partnership interests, which in turn allows partners to deduct partnership losses attributable to partnership level debt. In contrast, the shareholder's basis in Subchapter S stock or debt is limited to the shareholder's actual investment in the corporation. This limitation also means that while untaxed entity level cash, e.g., from a refinancing, can be distributed by a partnership free of tax, the same distribution by an S corporation may trigger gain recognition. For these reasons, S corporations generally have not been used for leveraged investments, such as real estate.

Subchapter S also differs from Subchapter K in its treatment of distributions of appreciated property. An S corporation is required by

§ 311(b) and § 336 to recognize gain on a distribution of appreciated property to shareholders. The recognized gain is passed through to the shareholders, who increase the basis of their stock accordingly. The distributee shareholder obtains a fair market value basis in the distributed property and decreases the basis of the S corporation stock by the same amount. Subject to some exceptions, distributions of appreciated property by a partnership generally do not trigger recognition of gain. Instead, generally the distributee partner takes the partnership's basis in the property, and recognition of gain is deferred until the distributee disposes of the property. As a corporation, an S corporation can terminate its election and offer shares to the public without tax consequence. In addition, an S corporation can avail itself of the corporate reorganization provisions of Subchapter C. The Code is thus not neutral as to the choice between a Subchapter S corporation and a partnership.

As the following material indicates, the tax treatment of S corporations that have always been S corporations is relatively straightforward. Technical complexities, of course, are encountered. But for such corporations, the governing provisions are not particularly difficult either in concept or in practice. While a corporation that has a C corporation history can elect S corporation status, the rules governing such corporations are much more complex than those applicable to S corporations with no C corporation history.

SECTION 2.   ELIGIBILITY, ELECTION, AND TERMINATION

A. SHAREHOLDER RULES

INTERNAL REVENUE CODE: Section 1361(b)(1), (c)(1)–(3), (d), (e).

REGULATIONS: Section 1.1361–1(e), (f).

Section 1361(b)(1) requires that the electing corporation have no more than 100 shareholders (with § 1361(c)(1) treating as a single shareholder all of the members of a family traced to a common ancestor no more than six generations removed from the youngest family member who is a shareholder) and that it have no shareholder who is not an individual, an estate, a grantor trust, a "qualified Subchapter S trust" (QSST), an "electing small business trust," a tax-exempt charitable organization, or a qualified retirement pension trust. When stock is held by a nominee, guardian, or custodian, the beneficial owner is treated as the shareholder. Treas.Reg. § 1.1361–1(e)(1). A corporation, partnership, or LLC (other than a single member LLC that is disregarded) may not be a shareholder in an S corporation other than as a nominee for the beneficial owner. See Treas.Reg. § 1.1361–1(e)(1).

Section 1361(c)(2) permits five types of domestic trusts as shareholders of an S corporation: (i) trusts treated as owned by a United

States citizen or resident (grantor trusts), (ii) grantor trusts that survive the death of the grantor (but only for a limited period), (iii) testamentary trusts (again only for a limited period), (iv) voting trusts, and (v) "electing small business trusts" (as defined in § 1361(e)). Section 1361(d) further provides that a "qualified Subchapter S trust" (QSST), a trust with a single income beneficiary who has elected to be treated as the owner of S corporation stock held by the trust, is a qualified shareholder; S corporation items of income and loss pass through the trust to the beneficiary. With the exception of these permitted trusts, trusts are ineligible shareholders.

Originally, an S corporation could have no more than 10 shareholders. The purpose of the number of shareholders requirement was to restrict S corporation status to corporations with a limited number of shareholders so as to obtain administrative simplicity in the administration of the corporation's tax affairs. That ceiling later was increased to 35 shareholders and then to 75 shareholders. Finally, in 2004, § 1361 was amended to increase the limit to 100 shareholders and to treat as one shareholder for purposes of the 100 shareholder limit all of the members of a family traced to a common ancestor no more than six generations removed from the youngest family member who is a shareholder. As a result of this last change there is no significant policy goal served by limiting the number of shareholders permitted in an S corporation.

The lack of any rational policy basis for the limitation on the number of shareholders is underscored by Rev.Rul. 94–43, 1994–2 C.B. 198, which allows two or more corporations, each with no more than 100 shareholders, to make S elections and form a partnership to conduct a business. Thus, for example, 100 S corporations, each with 100 shareholders, could form an LLC to operate a business. In this scenario, the business would, in substance, have 10,000 owners. The ruling reasoned that administrative simplicity is not affected by the corporation's participation in a partnership with other S corporation partners; nor should a shareholder of one S corporation be considered a shareholder of another S corporation because the S corporations are partners in a partnership. Thus, the ruling takes the position that having several S corporations as partners in a single partnership does not increase the administrative complexity at the S corporation level.

DETAILED ANALYSIS

1.   FAMILY MEMBERS AS SHAREHOLDERS

1.1. *Spouses as Shareholders*

In counting the number of shareholders, a married couple (and their respective estates) is treated as a single shareholder regardless of the form of ownership in which the stock is held. I.R.C. § 1361(c)(1)(A)(i). Under § 1361(b)(1)(C), an S corporation may not have a "nonresident alien" shareholder. In Ward v. United States, 661 F.2d 226 (Ct.Cl.1981), a corporation's Subchapter S election was held invalid because the taxpayer's nonresident alien wife was the beneficial owner of the corporation's stock under community property laws.

1.2. *Family Members*

Prior to 2004, each family member, other than spouses, counted as a separate shareholder. In 2004, § 1361(c)(1) was amended to provide that all of the members of a family traced to a common ancestor no more than six generations removed from the youngest family member who is a shareholder will be treated as a single shareholder. See I.R.C. § 1361(c)(1)(B). As a result of this rule, hundreds of members of a family might count as a single shareholder, and thousands of individuals who are members of up to 100 families might own an S corporation

The test to identify a common ancestor is applied as of the latest of (1) the date the S corporation election is made, (2) the earliest date a family member acquires stock in the S corporation, or (3) October 22, 2004. I.R.C. § 1361(c)(1)(B)(iii). Treas.Reg. § 1.1361–1(e)(3) provides that the test is applied only on the date specified. Thus, a later acquisition of S corporation stock by a lineal descendant (and spouse) more than six generations removed from the common ancestor will not affect S corporation status.

2.   ESTATES AND TRUSTS AS ELIGIBLE SHAREHOLDERS

2.1. *General*

Section 1361 permits the estate of a deceased shareholder, the estate of an individual in bankruptcy, and certain trusts, including "grantor trusts" if the grantor is a U.S. citizen or resident, voting trusts, and, for a time-limited period, testamentary trusts to be S corporation shareholders. In the case of a grantor trust, the grantor is treated as the shareholder; in the case of voting trusts, each beneficiary of the trust is treated as a shareholder. Treas.Reg. § 1.1361–1(h)(1)(i), (v). Rev.Rul. 92–73, 1992–2 C.B. 224, held that a trust qualified as an individual retirement account is not a permitted Subchapter S corporation shareholder because its income is not currently taxed to the beneficiary. Mourad v. Commissioner, 387 F.3d 27 (1st Cir. 2004), held that the filing of a bankruptcy petition by an S corporation for a Chapter 11 plan of reorganization neither terminates an S election nor creates a separate taxable entity. Accordingly, even though an independent trustee was appointed, the shareholder remained liable for the taxes on the sale of the S corporation's principal assets by the trustee.

A testamentary trust to which stock of an S corporation has been transferred is an eligible S corporation shareholder for only two years following the day on which the stock is transferred. I.R.C. § 1361(c)(2)(A)(iii). Similarly, under § 1361(c)(2)(A), a grantor trust may continue as an S corporation shareholder for two years from the date of the death of the grantor. Treas.Reg. § 1.1361–1(h)(1)(ii). In a community property state, the grantor trust of a decedent is treated as the S corporation shareholder only for that portion of the trust that is included in the decedent's gross estate. The surviving spouse is treated as the shareholder of the remaining portion of the S corporation stock. Treas.Reg. § 1.1361–1(h)(3)(i)(B). If grantor trust status terminates for some reason other than the death of the grantor—for example, if the grantor relinquishes the powers that make the trust a grantor trust—the trust becomes an ineligible shareholder, and the corporation's S corporation status is terminated immediately.

There is no statutory limit on the length of time that an estate may remain a qualified shareholder. However, Old Virginia Brick Co. v. Commissioner, 367 F.2d 276 (4th Cir.1966), held that an estate that was one of the shareholders of an S corporation and that was kept open substantially beyond the period necessary for the performance of administrative duties became, in effect, an ineligible testamentary trust; accordingly, the corporation was disqualified from S corporation status. See also Treas.Reg. § 1.641(b)–3(a) (an estate is deemed terminated for federal tax purposes after the expiration of a reasonable period for the performance by the executor of the duties of administration). But Rev.Rul. 76–23, 1976–1 C.B. 264, allowed retention of S corporation stock by an estate for purposes of the 10 year installment payment of estate taxes in § 6166.

2.2. *Qualified Subchapter S Trusts*

Section 1361(d) permits a "qualified Subchapter S trust" (QSST) to be an S corporation shareholder. A QSST is a trust that, by its terms, has only one current income beneficiary who will be the sole income beneficiary during the beneficiary's life or for the term of the trust.[6] I.R.C. § 1361(d)(3). See Rev.Rul. 93–31, 1993–1 C.B. 186 (separate and independent share of a trust within the meaning of § 663(c) cannot be a QSST if there is any possibility, however remote, that during the income beneficiary's lifetime the corpus will be distributed to someone other than the income beneficiary). To avoid any possibility of splitting S corporation income and deductions between the trust and the beneficiary, a QSST is an eligible shareholder only if the beneficiary elects in effect to treat the trust as a grantor trust with respect to the S corporation stock. Thus, the income beneficiary is treated as the owner of the portion of the trust that consists of S corporation stock. The beneficiary is taxed on the income and receives the deductions allocable to the S corporation stock without regard to the normal rules of trust taxation. I.R.C. § 1361(d)(1)(B). See generally Treas.Reg. § 1.1361–1(j). Gain from the sale of stock by a QSST trust is, however, not taxable to the beneficiary of the trust; instead, the trust itself is taxed on any such gain. Treas.Reg. § 1.1361–1(j)(8).

The strict requirements of § 1361(d) apparently were designed to prevent the use of trusts to avoid the 35 shareholder limitation that was in force prior to 1996, while facilitating pass-through taxation of the trust

---

[6]   In Rev. Rul. 92–64, 1992–2 C.B. 214, the QSST provided for distributions of trust income in December and June of each year. The income beneficiary died on May 1. The ruling allowed distributions of trust income accumulated between the last distribution and the date of the beneficiary's death to be made to either the deceased beneficiary's estate under state law or the successor beneficiary under a provision of the trust. The Ruling concluded that after the date of death, the successor income beneficiary is the only income beneficiary of the trust, even though the estate may become entitled to a distribution.

In Rev. Rul. 92–48, 1992–1 C.B. 301, the IRS ruled that a charitable remainder trust, qualified under § 664, cannot be qualified as a QSST. The ruling concluded that the scheme for the taxation of charitable remainder trusts is incompatible with the requirements of the QSST rules.

beneficiary as the ultimate recipient of the S corporation income. In light of subsequent amendments (1) increasing the number of permitted shareholders to 100 and (2) counting as a single shareholder all of the members of a family traced to a common ancestor no more than six generations removed from the youngest family member who is a shareholder, any valid policy-based purpose for the limitations in § 1361(d) is difficult to discern. The single beneficiary rule does, however, provide some simplification in identifying the individual taxable on S corporation income.

A trust is a QSST only if a timely election is filed with the IRS by the beneficiary (or the beneficiary's legal representative or parent if there is no legal representative appointed). A separate election is required with respect to the stock of each S corporation owned by a QSST. Failure to file the election for a trust that becomes an S corporation shareholder will result in revocation of the corporation's status as an S corporation. See Rev.Rul. 93–79, 1993–2 C.B. 269 (retroactive state court reformation of trust to conform to requirements for a QSST was not effective to validate S corporation election prior to reformation at a time when the trust did not qualify).

Section 1361(d)(2)(D) provides that an election to be a QSST is retroactively effective for the 2-month and 15-day period preceding the filing of the election. See Treas.Reg. § 1.1361–1(j)(6) for the detailed procedural rules respecting the election.

If it meets the requirements, a testamentary trust or a grantor trust can continue as an eligible S corporation shareholder by electing to be a QSST. See Treas.Reg. § 1.1361–1(h)(3)(i)(B). Treas.Reg. § 1.1361–1(j)(6)(iii)(C) provides that an estate or grantor trust can elect to become a QSST at any time during the two year period of eligibility as an S corporation shareholder provided by § 1361(c)(2)(A)(ii) and (iii), but no later than the 2-month and 16-day period following the date on which the testamentary or grantor trust ceases to qualify as an eligible shareholder. Treas.Reg. § 1.1361–1(j)(6)(iii)(D) provides a similar rule with respect to testamentary trusts. As of the effective date of the election, the beneficiary of the QSST becomes the eligible shareholder instead of the trust or estate. Treas.Reg. § 1.1361–1(h)(3)(i)(B) & (D).

2.3. *Electing Small Business Trusts*

Under § 1361(e), a trust may elect to be a "small business trust" (ESBT) if the only current beneficiaries of the trust are individuals, estates eligible to own S corporation stock, and tax-exempt charitable organizations, and none of the beneficiaries has purchased the interest in the trust.

The election is made by the trustee of the trust. Treas.Reg. § 1.1361–1(m)(2). If an election is made, the portion of the trust consisting of the S corporation stock is treated as a separate trust, and trust income attributable to the S corporation stock, including gain on the sale of the stock, is taxed to the trust at the highest individual rate, whether or not the income is distributed.[7] The beneficiaries, in turn, are not taxed on any trust

---

[7] Section 641(c)(2) allows an electing small business trust to deduct interest paid on debt incurred to purchase the S corporation stock against the trust's share of S corporation income, thereby offsetting income that is taxed at the highest individual rate.

distributions attributable to the stock. See I.R.C. § 641(c). This provision is designed to permit discretionary, or "spray" trusts to be S corporation shareholders, which may be desired by shareholders for estate planning purposes. Because under § 1361(c)(2)(B)(v) each potential current beneficiary of the trust is counted against the shareholder limit, the use of this provision may conceivably result in termination of S corporation status if several trusts with a large number of beneficiaries who are not members of the same family make an election. Section 1361(c)(2)(B)(v) states that each potential current beneficiary of an electing small business trust shall be treated as a shareholder of the S corporation. See Treas.Reg. § 1.1361–1(m)(4)(i) (treating each potential income current beneficiary of an ESBT as a shareholder of the corporation). Starting in 2018, this provision does not, however, apply in the case of a nonresident alien who is a potential current beneficiary.

Treas.Reg. § 1.1361–1(m) contains specific rules regarding the identification of the beneficiaries of an ESBT. A person whose entitlement to a distribution is contingent on a specified event or a specified time is not treated as a current beneficiary until occurrence of the event or passage of the time. Treas.Reg. § 1.1361–1(m)(4)(v). A person in whose favor a power of appointment may be exercised is not counted as a current beneficiary until the power is exercised. Treas.Reg. § 1.1361–1(m)(1)(ii)(C). A trust that is a beneficiary of an ESBT is not itself treated as a beneficiary of the ESBT.[8] Instead, the current income beneficiaries of the beneficiary trust are treated as beneficiaries of the ESBT. Treas.Reg. § 1.1361–1(m)(1)(ii)(B). A distributee trust that is entitled to a distribution of income or principal from an ESBT must, however, itself be qualified to be a shareholder of an S corporation or the Subchapter S election will terminate. Treas.Reg. § 1.1361–1(m)(4)(iv)(B).

If a potential income beneficiary of an ESBT becomes disqualified as an S corporation shareholder, the S corporation election will not be terminated if the trust disposes of all of its S corporation stock within one year of the disqualification. I.R.C. § 1361(e)(2); Treas.Reg. § 1.1361–1(m)(4)(iii).

Treas.Reg. § 1.1361–1(m)(2)(iv) provides that a grantor trust may elect to be an ESBT, if it qualifies, after the death of the person treated as the owner of the trust. Treas.Reg. § 1.1361–1(j)(12) provides that a QSST may convert to an ESBT. Treas.Reg. § 1.1361–1(m)(7) provides that an ESBT may convert to a QSST. Thus, a trust with a single current beneficiary that becomes a spray trust for multiple beneficiaries upon the death of the first beneficiary can successively be a QSST and then an ESBT.

2.4. *Individual Retirement Accounts*

Rev.Rul. 92–73, 1992–2 C.B. 224, held that a trust qualified as an individual retirement account is not a permitted Subchapter S corporation

---

[8]   A trust that is the beneficiary of an ESBT that is a charitable organization qualified to be an S Corporation shareholder is treated as a beneficiary of the ESBT. Treas.Reg. § 1.1361–1(m)(1)(ii)(B). Treas.Reg. § 1.1361–1(m)(4)(vi)(B) provides that if a trustee has a discretionary power to make distributions to one or more charitable organizations as a class, the organizations will be counted as only one potential income beneficiary. Organizations actually receiving a distribution will also be counted as a potential income beneficiary.

shareholder because its income is not currently taxed to the beneficiary. Taproot Administrative Services, Inc. v. Commissioner, 133 T.C. 202 (2003), aff'd, 679 F.3d 1109 (9th Cir. 2012), held that a custodial Roth IRA is not an eligible shareholder. The court agreed with the IRS's rationale in Rev.Rul. 92–73 that IRAs are not eligible S corporation shareholders because the beneficiary of the IRA is not taxed currently on the trust's share of corporate income, unlike the beneficiary of a custodial account or the grantor of a grantor trust who is subject to tax on the pass-through corporate income. If a Roth IRA were permitted as a shareholder of an S corporation, the income of the corporation owned by a Roth IRA would never be subject to tax.

3. POLICY ASPECTS OF THE 100 SHAREHOLDER LIMITATION

The legislative history of the Subchapter S Revision Act of 1982, which increased the number of permitted shareholders from 10 to 35, indicated that the 35 shareholder limit was intended to correspond to the private placement exemption of federal securities law. S.Rep. No. 97–640, 97th Cong. 2d Sess. 7 (1982). When the ceiling on the number of shareholders was increased from 35 to 75 in 1996, the reason given was to "facilitate corporate ownership by additional family members, employees and capital investors." H.R. Rep. No. 104–586, 104th Cong., 2d Sess. 82 (1996). When in 2004 the ceiling was increased to 100 shareholders, treating as a single shareholder all of the members of a family traced to a common ancestor no more than six generations removed from the youngest family member who is a shareholder, the stated reason was to "modernize the S corporation rules and eliminate undue restrictions on S corporations in order to expand the application of the S corporation provisions so that more corporations and their shareholders will be able to enjoy the benefits of subchapter S status." H.R. Rep. No. 108–548, 108th Cong, 2d Sess. 128 (2004). There is, however, no inherent tax policy rationale for limiting pass-through tax treatment to any particular number of shareholders, as long as the corporation is not publicly traded.[9] If there are too many shareholders, however, administrative problems may arise because audits are conducted and tax deficiencies are assessed and collected at the shareholder level. Although limiting the number of shareholders allowed in an S corporation reduces the complexity of accounting for allocations of corporate items to the shareholders, experience with Subchapter K demonstrates that pass-through accounting on a large scale is possible.

4. TAX-EXEMPT ENTITIES AS ELIGIBLE SHAREHOLDERS

Section 1361(c)(6) permits tax-exempt charities under § 501(c)(3) and tax-exempt employee benefit trusts under § 401(a) as shareholders of an S corporation. This provision allows an Employee Stock Ownership Plan (ESOP) to hold the stock of an S corporation. An ESOP is designed to invest primarily in securities of the employer of the beneficiaries of the plan. See I.R.C. § 409. As a consequence, S corporation income that is passed-through to the ESOP is not subject to tax until the income is withdrawn from the

---

[9]   Section 7704, which treats any partnership that is publicly traded as an association, subject to the corporate income tax, evidences a congressional intent that pass-through taxation is not appropriate for publicly traded businesses regardless of the form of organization.

ESOP by employees on retirement. An ESOP as the holder of S corporation stock (which may constitute 100% of the stock) allows deferral of unlimited amounts of income on behalf of the employees of an S corporation.[10]

Section 409(p) limits the use of an ESOP to defer S corporation income to an ESOP that provides broad coverage to employees. Qualification as an ESOP for a plan that holds S corporation stock requires that benefits do not accrue to a "disqualified person," defined as a person who is entitled to the benefit of 10% or more of the shares of the S corporation (or 20% of the shares of such person and members of the person's family) where disqualified persons own 50% or more of the total shares of the stock of the S corporation (including portions of stock attributed to disqualified persons from the ESOP). I.R.C. § 409(p)(3)–(4). In order to avoid an end-run around these limitations with devices to provide additional compensation to highly compensated employees and managers, § 409(p)(5) provides that a person's shares in an S corporation include "synthetic equity," which is a right to receive stock of the S corporation in the future, or a right to compensation based on the value of S corporation stock. Treas.Reg. § 1.409(p)–1T(f) expands the definition of synthetic equity to include nonqualified deferred compensation plans and rights to acquire stock in related entities.

PROBLEM SET 1

1. Would X Corp., a domestic corporation, qualify to make a valid Subchapter S election under the following alternative situations?

(a) X Corp. has 101 individual shareholders all of whom are unrelated except that two of them are married to each other.

(b) X Corp. has 101 individual shareholders, all of whom are unrelated, except for Alberto and Beryl, who are parent and child.

(c) (1) X Corp. has 101 unrelated individual shareholders except that two of whom are remote cousins whose grandmothers were sisters.

(2) X Corp. has 150,000 shareholders, each one of which belongs to one of 99 different families, within which each family member/shareholder can trace ancestry to a single great-great-great-great grandparent.

(3) X Corp. has 101 shareholders, all of whom are related only through a single common great-great-great-great-great grandparent.

(d) (1) X Corp. has one shareholder of record, Debby, a U.S. citizen, who is married to Ernesto, a Mexican citizen, and the stock was issued while they were married. Debby and Ernesto live in Santa Fe, New Mexico.

(2) What if Debby and Ernesto live in Mexico City, Mexico?

(3) What if Debby is married to Eddie, a Canadian citizen, and they live in Vancouver, Canada?

---

[10] See Daniel L. Simmons & Joseph G. De Angelis, ESOP-Owned Subchapter S Corporations: A Mistake in Need of a Fix, 82 Tax Notes 1325 (Mar. 1, 1999).

(e)   X Corp. has 10 equal shareholders. Nine of the shareholders are individual U.S. citizens. The tenth shareholder is a general partnership, the partners of which are two individual U.S. citizens.

2.   Y Corp. has five shareholders, A, B, C, D, and E. It made a valid Subchapter S election effective for a prior year. Would it be eligible to keep its election in effect under the following alternative circumstances?

(a)   Three years ago, A died and his estate held the shares for two years. This year, the estate terminated and distributed A's shares to a trust. Under the terms of the trust, A's surviving spouse, G, is entitled to the trust income for life, and upon G's death the corpus of the trust is to be distributed to A's descendants per capita.

(b)   This year, B transferred her shares to a revocable trust with income to be distributed in the trustee's discretion among B's three children until the death of the last child, when the remainder will be distributed to B's descendants per capita.

(c)   This year, C transferred his shares to an irrevocable inter vivos trust, under the terms of which C's child, H, is entitled to the trust income for life, and upon H's death, the income is to be distributed in the trustee's discretion between H's children, I and J for their lives, and, upon the death of the last of them to die, the corpus of the trust is to be distributed to C's descendants per capita.

(d)   This year, D and E transferred their shares to a voting trust, naming L as the trustee. L has the power to vote the shares, receive distributions, and remit the distributions to D and E.

B.   CORPORATE ELIGIBILITY

INTERNAL REVENUE CODE: Section 1361(a), (b)(1)(D), (b)(2)–(3), (c)(4).

REGULATIONS: Section 1.1361–1(b), (*l*).

Only a domestic corporation may elect to be an S corporation. A controlled subsidiary of an S corporation cannot itself make an S election because its parent, as a corporation, is an ineligible shareholder. Thus, the subsidiary is a C corporation. If, however, the subsidiary is wholly owned by the parent S corporation and the subsidiary would be eligible to be an S corporation if the stock of the corporation were held directly by the shareholders of its parent S corporation, § 1361(b)(3) allows the parent S corporation to elect to ignore the separate existence of its subsidiary for tax purposes and to treat its subsidiary's assets, liabilities, income, and deduction items as its own.

Certain corporations are ineligible for S corporation status. These include small (but not large) banks, insurance companies, and certain other corporations subject to a special tax regime. I.R.C. § 1361(b)(2).

Under § 1361(b)(1)(D), an S corporation is allowed to have only one class of stock. The purpose of this requirement is to avoid accounting difficulties that would arise if the corporation were permitted to create different interests in income and loss in different classes of stock. Thus, unlike partnerships, S corporations are not allowed to make special allocations of income and loss among S corporation shareholders.

Section 1361(c)(4) allows differences in voting rights without violating the one-class-of-stock rule so long as the outstanding shares are identical with respect to the rights of the holders in the profits and in the assets of the corporation. The existence of debt of an S corporation that might be classified as equity creates a risk that the re-classified equity interests will be treated as a prohibited second class of stock. To reduce this risk, § 1361(c)(5) provides a safe harbor in which certain "straight debt" will not be considered a second class of stock.

DETAILED ANALYSIS

1.   ONE CLASS OF STOCK

1.1. *General*

Treas.Reg. § 1.1361–1(*l*)(1) provides that a corporation has one class of stock if all of the outstanding shares of stock of the corporation confer identical rights to current distributions and liquidation proceeds. Differences in voting rights are disregarded. The determination of whether stock possesses identical distribution and liquidation rights is made under the formal governing provisions applicable to the corporation, including state law, the corporate charter, articles of incorporation, bylaws, and binding agreements relating to distributions and liquidation proceeds. Treas.Reg. § 1.1361–1(*l*)(2)(i). Contractual arrangements, such as a lease or a loan, will not be treated as a binding agreement regarding distributions or liquidation proceeds, and thus not a governing instrument, unless the principal purpose of the agreement is to circumvent the one class of stock requirement. Treas.Reg. § 1.1361–1(*l*)(2)(i) provides that "distributions . . . that differ in timing or amount are to be given appropriate tax effect in accordance with the facts and circumstances." Treas.Reg. § 1.1361–1(*l*)(2)(vi), Exs. 3–5, indicates that an agreement (which is not included in the corporate governing provisions) that pays non-deductible excessive compensation to shareholder-employees, makes fringe benefits available to employee-shareholders, or provides below market-rate loans to shareholders will not be treated as creating a second class of stock if the arrangement is not entered into to circumvent the one class of stock requirement.

Historically, the single class of stock limitation has been interpreted strictly. In Paige v. United States, 580 F.2d 960 (9th Cir.1978), a second class of stock was created as a result of conditions imposed by the California Department of Corporations on stock held by shareholders transferring property to the corporation. Similar conditions were not imposed on shareholders who had transferred cash to the corporation. Among the conditions were restrictions preventing dividend or liquidation distributions to the property shareholders until the cash shareholders received cumulative dividends equal to 5% of the purchase price. The result in *Paige* has been incorporated in Treas.Reg. § 1.1361–1(*l*)(2)(vi), Ex. 1.

Treas.Reg. § 1.1361–1(l)(2)(i) refers to "outstanding shares of stock" for purposes of the one-class of stock rules, and Treas.Reg. § 1.1361–1(l)(3) provides that except as otherwise provided (for restricted stock, deferred compensation plans, and "straight-debt") all "outstanding" stock is taken into account in determining whether the single class of stock requirement has been met. This implies that unissued or treasury stock of a different class than the outstanding stock should not create a second class of stock. In addition, Treas.Reg. § 1.1361–1(b)(3) provides that stock that has not been included in income by the holder under § 83 because it is substantially nonvested will not be treated as outstanding stock. Restricted stock for which an election has been made under § 83(b) is, however, taken into account in determining whether there is a second class of stock, but the stock will not be treated as a second class if rights to distributions and liquidation proceeds are identical to unrestricted stock. Treas.Reg. § 1.1361–1(l)(3). Instruments held as part of a deferred compensation plan that are not required to be taken into income by beneficiaries of the plan (e.g., stock appreciation rights) are not treated as a second class of stock. Treas.Reg. § 1.1361–1(b)(4).

1.2. *Voting Rights*

Section 1361(c)(4) allows variations in voting rights among the shares of common stock, including the issuance of nonvoting common stock, without creating a second class of stock. This provision settled an issue that gave rise to litigation under pre-1983 Subchapter S provisions. See, e.g., Parker Oil Co. v. Commissioner, 58 T.C. 985 (1972) (acq.).

1.3. *Options*

Call options, warrants and similar instruments will be treated as a second class of stock if, under the facts and circumstances, (1) the option is substantially certain to be exercised and (2) has an exercise price substantially below the fair market value of the underlying stock on the date the option is (a) issued (unless fair market value at exercise is used), (b) transferred by a person who is an eligible shareholder to a person who is not an eligible shareholder, or (c) materially modified. Treas.Reg. § 1.1361–1(l)(4)(iii)(A). A safe harbor exception applies if the exercise price is at least 90% of the fair market value of the underlying stock on the date the option is issued, transferred to an ineligible shareholder, or modified. Treas.Reg. § 1.1361–1(l)(4)(iii)(C). The regulation provides that a good faith determination of fair market value by the corporation will be respected unless it is shown to be substantially in error and not performed with reasonable diligence. Additional exceptions are provided for call options issued in connection with a loan to the corporation by a person regularly engaged in the business of lending or issued to an employee or independent contractor in connection with the performance of services, if the call option is nontransferable and does not have a readily ascertainable fair market value at the time the option is issued. Treas.Reg. § 1.1361–1(l)(4)(iii)(B).

1.4. *Debt Reclassified as Equity*

The one class of stock requirement was the subject of considerable litigation for years prior to 1983, but the straight debt safe harbor of

§ 1361(c)(5), enacted in 1982, has reduced the tension in this area. The Senate Finance Committee Report explained the provision as follows:

> In order to insure that the corporation's election will not terminate in certain situations where the existence of a purported debt instrument (that otherwise would be classified as stock) may not lead to tax avoidance and does not cause undue complexity, the bill provides that an instrument which is straight debt will not be treated as a second class of stock (within the meaning of sec. 1361(b)(1)(D)), and therefore cannot disqualify a Subchapter S election. For this purpose, a straight debt instrument means a written unconditional promise to pay on demand or on a specified date a sum certain in money so long as the interest rate, and payment date are fixed. For this purpose these factors are fixed if they are not contingent on the profits of the corporation, the discretion of the corporation, or other similar factors. However, the fact that the interest rate is dependent upon the prime rate or a similar factor not related to the debtor corporation will not disqualify the instrument from being treated under the safe harbor. In order for the "safe harbor" to apply, the instrument must not be convertible into stock, and must be held by a person eligible to hold Subchapter S stock.

S.Rep. No. 97–640, 97th Cong., 2d Sess. 8 (1982).

Section 1361(c)(5) was amended in 1996 to add to the list of straight debt a loan by a creditor "which is actively and regularly engaged in the business of lending money." This amendment was intended to extend the straight debt safe harbor to loans from financial institutions, even though most financial institutions are not eligible to be shareholders. The rationale for this provision is that it generally is unlikely that a loan from a financial institution in the business of lending money is a disguised equity interest.

Treas.Reg. § 1.1361–1(l)(5)(i) provides that for debt to qualify for the straight debt safe harbor it must be: (1) an unconditional written obligation to pay a sum certain on demand or on a specified date, that is not convertible into an equity interest; (2) held by a person or trust eligible to be an S corporation shareholder (a limitation that must be qualified by the subsequent amendment to § 1361(c)(5) permitting financial institutions to hold straight debt); and (3) neither the timing nor amount of payments of interest and principal can be contingent on the corporation's profits. Subordination of the debt to other corporate debt does not prevent its treatment as straight debt. Treas.Reg. § 1.1361–1(l)(5)(ii). Treas.Reg. § 1.1361–1(l)(5)(iv) provides that the payment of an unreasonably high rate of interest may be classified as a payment that is not interest. The Regulations add, however, that the payment will not be treated as creating a second class of stock.

Treas.Reg. § 1.1361–1(l)(4)(ii)(B)(2) provides that proportionately held debt reclassified as equity will not constitute a second class of stock. In a somewhat similar vein, Treas.Reg. § 1.1361–1(l)(4)(ii)(A) provides that debt reclassified as equity will not be treated as a second class of stock unless a principal purpose of issuing the instrument was to circumvent the rights to distribution or liquidation proceeds conferred by the outstanding shares of stock or to circumvent the limitations on eligible shareholders. Furthermore, unwritten advances from a shareholder that are reclassified as equity and that do not exceed $10,000 in the aggregate, are treated by the parties as debt, and are expected to be repaid within a reasonable period of time, will not be treated as a second class of stock. Treas.Reg. § 1.1361–1(l)(4)(ii)(B)(1). Failure of an unwritten advance to comply with the safe harbor will not create a second class unless the advance is reclassified as equity *and* a principal purpose of making the advance was to circumvent the rights to distribution or liquidation proceeds conferred by the outstanding shares of stock or to circumvent the limitations on eligible shareholders.

The potential classification of purported debt instruments as a second class of stock remains a problem if debt is convertible, held by a corporation related to a shareholder, or otherwise falls outside of the safe harbors. Treas.Reg. § 1.1361–1(l)(4)(iv) provides that debt convertible into equity will be treated as a second class of stock if the debt is reclassified as equity and a principal purpose of issuing the instrument was to circumvent the rights to distributions or liquidation proceeds conferred by the outstanding shares of stock or to circumvent the limitations on eligible shareholders. Convertible debt will also be classified as a second class of stock if it embodies rights equivalent to a call option that is substantially certain to be exercised and that has a conversion price substantially below the fair market value of the underlying stock on the date of issuance, on the date of transfer to a person who is not an eligible shareholder, or on the date of a material modification.

PROBLEM SET 2

1.   A, B, and C, all of whom are resident individuals, are planning to form Z Corp. Assuming that Z Corp. otherwise will qualify to make an S election, will the following alternative capital structures affect Z Corp.'s eligibility?

     (a)   A and B each will receive 100 shares of voting common stock. C will receive 100 shares of nonvoting preferred stock.

     (b)   A and B each will receive 100 shares of voting common stock. C will receive 100 shares of nonvoting common stock.

     (c)   A and B each will receive 100 shares of voting common stock. C will receive 100 shares of voting preferred stock.

     (d)   A, B, and C each will receive 100 shares of voting common stock. C, who will receive the stock for services (unlike A and B, who are contributing cash), has signed a shareholders' agreement providing that she may not transfer her shares without the consent of A and B, but if they do not consent they must purchase C's shares at book value. A and B are not subject to any restrictions on transfer.

     (e)   A, B, and C each will receive 100 shares of voting common stock. To attract D, who will be a key employee, Z Corp. will issue to D an option to acquire 100 shares at 80% of the then current fair market value.

2.   E, F, and G, all of whom are resident individuals, are planning to form Q Corp. E, F, and G each will receive 100 shares of voting common stock. Assuming that Q Corp. otherwise will qualify to make an S election, will the following alternative capital structures affect Q Corp.'s eligibility?

(a)   (1)   E will lend Q Corp. $600,000 and receive a promissory note due in 30 years, with interest payable annually at the prime rate plus 4%.

(2)   What if E's note is subordinated to all third party creditors, including trade creditors?

(3)   What if the promissory note E receives is convertible into Q Corp. common stock based on a price estimated to be 110% of the fair market value of the Q Corp. common stock on the date the note was issued?

(b)   E, F, and G each will lend Q Corp. $200,000 and receive a convertible promissory note due in 30 years, with interest payable annually at the prime rate plus 3%. The notes are convertible into Q Corp. common stock based on a price estimated to be 90% of the fair market value of the Q Corp. common stock on the date the note was issued.

(c)   (1)   The Stallmuckers Federal Credit Union will lend Q Corp. $600,000 and receive a promissory note due in 30 years, with interest payable annually at the prime rate plus 5 percentage points.

(2)   The Stallmuckers Federal Credit Union will lend Q Corp. $600,000 and receive a promissory note due in 30 years, with interest payable annually at the prime rate plus 5% of Q Corp.'s net profits.

C. S CORPORATION ELECTION PROCEDURES

INTERNAL REVENUE CODE: Section 1362(a), (b), (c), and (f).

REGULATIONS: Sections 1.1362–1, –6.

A Subchapter S election is made by the corporation, but the election is valid only if all of the shareholders file consents to this election. I.R.C. § 1362(a). After an election has been made, new shareholders are not required to consent. A shareholder individually cannot directly revoke or terminate an election, but undertaking a transaction that causes the corporation no longer to qualify for S corporation status may have that effect.

An election made any time during the taxable year will be effective for the corporation's next succeeding taxable year. I.R.C. § 1362(b)(1)(A). Section 1362(b)(1)(B) provides for an election retroactive to the first day of the taxable year if the election is made on or before the fifteenth day of the third month of the taxable year. A retroactive election is, however, effective for the taxable year in which made only if the corporation meets all of the requirements for S corporation status during the portion of the taxable year preceding the filing of the election and all of the shareholders consent to the election, including shareholders who were shareholders before the election was filed but who are no longer shareholders at the time of the election. I.R.C. § 1362(b)(2); Treas.Reg. § 1.1362–6(a)(2)(ii)(B). This requirement is intended to avoid an allocation of income and loss to pre-election shareholders who were either ineligible to hold S corporation stock or who did not consent to the election. S.Rep. No. 97–640, 97th Cong., 2d Sess. 11 (1982). If the corporation and its shareholders were not qualified to elect S corporation status during each day of the portion of the taxable year preceding a retroactive election, the election will be effective on the first day of the next taxable year. I.R.C. § 1362(b)(2).

DETAILED ANALYSIS

1.   SHAREHOLDER CONSENTS

Section 1362(a)(2) requires the consent of all shareholders of the corporation as of the day of the election. See Kean v. Commissioner, 469 F.2d 1183 (9th Cir.1972) (consent was required from the beneficial owner of stock of an electing corporation even though the person was not included on the corporate books as a shareholder of record); Cabintaxi Corp. v. Commissioner, T.C. Memo. 1994–316, aff'd in part, 63 F.3d 614 (7th Cir.1995) (election must be joined in by all persons who have contributed equity capital, not merely those to whom stock certificates have been issued; whether a person is a shareholder for this purpose depends on whether the person would have been required to report income from the S corporation if it were profitable and a valid election had been made). See Treas.Reg. § 1.1362–6 for procedural aspects of shareholder consents and extensions of time for filing consents.

Although spouses are treated as a single shareholder, Treas.Reg. § 1.1362–6(b)(2)(i) requires that both consent to the election if they own the stock as community property, tenants in common, joint tenants, or as tenants by the entirety. In Wilson v. Commissioner, 560 F.2d 687 (5th Cir.1977), the record owner of a single share of stock who lived in a community property state, held the stock as an accommodation to other shareholders. He filed a consent to the corporation's S election, but his wife did not. The court held that the husband had no beneficial interest in the stock and was therefore not required to consent to the corporation's S election. Thus, his wife's consent also was unnecessary.

Section 1362(f) authorizes the IRS to waive a defect rendering an election ineffective because all of the required shareholder consents (including QSST elections) were not obtained in a timely manner if (1) the defect was inadvertent, (2) within a reasonable period of time the corporation obtains the shareholder consents, and (3) the corporation and the shareholders all agree to report as if the S corporation had been effective originally. See also Treas.Reg. § 1.1362–6(b)(3)(iii) (providing for a waiver of the timely shareholder consent requirement in certain circumstances for years prior to the amendment of § 1362(f) to deal with this problem).

2.   CORPORATE ELECTION

It is necessary to identify the date on which the taxable year of a newly formed corporation begins in order to determine whether an election has been filed on or before the fifteenth day of the third month of the taxable year. Treas.Reg. § 1.1362–6(a)(2)(ii)(C) provides that the taxable year of a new corporation begins on the date the corporation has shareholders, acquires assets, or begins doing business, whichever is the first to occur. See Bone v. Commissioner, 52 T.C. 913 (1969) (first taxable year had begun when the corporation acquired assets and engaged in business even though no stock had been issued to shareholders; under state law the issuance of stock was not a prerequisite to corporate existence).

Treas.Reg. § 1.1362–6(a)(2)(ii)(C) provides that a month is measured from the first day of the corporation's taxable year to the day preceding the same numerical date of the following month, or the last day of the month if there is no corresponding date in the succeeding month. Treas.Reg. § 1.1362–6(a)(2)(iii), Ex. 1, promulgated before the 1996 amendments to § 1362(f), indicates that an election filed before the corporation begins its first taxable year will not be valid. Presumably, § 1362(f) now permits the IRS to treat such a premature election as an effective election.

Section 1362(b)(5) permits the IRS to waive a late election for "reasonable cause." Rev.Proc. 2013–30, 2013–36 I.R.B. 173, "provides the exclusive simplified methods for taxpayers to request relief for late S corporation elections, ESBT elections, QSST elections, QSub elections, and late corporate classification elections." The Rev.Proc. specifies general requirements for relief as well as additional specific requirements depending on the type of election. The general requirements for relief include that the entity "intended" to be classified as an S corporation, ESBT, QSST, or QSub as of the effective date; relief is requested within 3 years and 75 days after the effective date; the failure to qualify as an S corporation, EBST, QSST, or QSub was solely due to the failure to file a timely election; and the entity had "reasonable cause" and "acted diligently to correct the mistake upon its discovery." The more specific requirements vary depending on the relief requested. For example, in the case of a late S corporation filing, the entity must file a completed Form 2553 (the corporate election itself) as well as supplemental materials, including "statements from all shareholders during the period between the date the S corporation election was to have become effective and the date the completed Election Form is filed that they have reported their income on all affected returns consistent with the S corporation election for the year the election should have been filed and for all subsequent years." Multiple other conditions are specified. If the entity is unable to meet the requirements of Rev.Proc. 2013–30, a private letter ruling request may be submitted.

PROBLEM SET 3

1.   (a) X Corp. was formed on March 1 of the current year by A, B, and C, all of whom are resident individuals.

(1)   By what date must X Corp. make an election if it wants to be an S Corporation?

(2)   How is the election made? What if A, B, and C are married individuals, and A lives in California, which is a community property state, but B and C live in Florida, which is a common law property state?

(3)   If a valid election was made on March 5th of the current year, what would be the effect of C selling her shares to D on May 15th.

(b)   Y Corp. has been in existence for several years. Its stock has been owned by D and E, resident individuals, and F a nonresident alien. On February 1, of this year, D and E each purchased one-half of F's stock. Can Y Corp. elect to be an S corporation for this year? By when must it make an election if it wants to be an S corporation for next year?

D.   REVOCATION OR TERMINATION OF S CORPORATION STATUS

INTERNAL REVENUE CODE: Section 1362(d), (e), (f) and (g).

REGULATIONS: Sections 1.1362–2(a) and (b), –3(a), –4, –5.

An S corporation election is effective for the taxable year to which it first applies and all succeeding taxable years until revoked or terminated. S corporation status may be ended in three ways: voluntary revocation by shareholders holding a majority of the S corporation stock, failure to comply with the requirements for S corporation status, or receipt of passive investment income in excess of 25% of gross income for three consecutive years if the corporation has Subchapter C previously accumulated and undistributed earnings and profits in those years.[11] Section 1362(d)(1) provides that a voluntary revocation of S corporation status by shareholders can be effective on the date specified by the revocation. Termination of S corporation status because the corporation or its shareholders subsequently fail to meet the initial requirements for eligibility is effective on the date the corporation ceases to qualify as an S corporation. I.R.C. § 1362(d)(2). The S corporation's taxable year ends on the day preceding the effective date of a revocation or termination, and a new taxable year begins for the corporation as a C corporation on the following day. I.R.C. § 1362(e). Items of income and deduction must be allocated between the corporation's short Subchapter S and Subchapter C taxable years.

---

[11]   The rules governing an S corporation with a prior history as a C corporation are discussed in a later section of this Chapter.

DETAILED ANALYSIS

1.   TERMINATION BY VOLUNTARY REVOCATION

Section 1362(d)(1) allows revocation of an S election by shareholders owning a majority of outstanding stock. A revocation made on or before the fifteenth day of the third month of the taxable year will be retroactively effective as of the first day of the taxable year. Otherwise, a revocation is effective on the first day of the next taxable year. Alternatively, the revocation may specify an effective date as long as the date specified is on or after the date of the revocation. Treas.Reg. § 1.1362–2(a)(2)(ii) requires that the date be specified in terms of a day, month, and year, rather than in terms of a particular event. Treas.Reg. § 1.1362–2(a)(4) also allows rescission of a voluntary prospective revocation at any time before the revocation becomes effective. Rescission requires the consent of any person who consented to the revocation and any person who became a shareholder of the corporation after the revocation was filed.

2.   INADVERTENT TERMINATION

A corporation's S election terminates immediately upon an event that disqualifies the corporation or one of its shareholders under the initial requirements for S corporation status. I.R.C. § 1361(d)(2). The savings clause of § 1362(f) allows the IRS to overlook an inadvertent termination if (1) the IRS determines that disqualification was inadvertent, (2) the corporation and/or its shareholders take steps to remedy the disqualifying event within a reasonable period after discovery, and (3) the corporation and each shareholder agree to such adjustments as the IRS may prescribe. The Senate Finance Committee indicated that it "intends that the Internal Revenue Service be reasonable in granting waivers, so that corporations whose Subchapter S eligibility requirements have been inadvertently violated do not suffer the tax consequences of a termination if no tax avoidance would result from the continued Subchapter S treatment." S.Rep. No. 97–640, 97th Cong., 2d Sess. 10 (1982).

Treas.Reg. § 1.1362–4(b) provides that the burden is on the corporation to establish that termination is inadvertent under the facts and circumstances. The Regulations add: "The fact that the terminating event or invalidity of the election was not reasonably within the control of the corporation and, in the case of a termination, was not part of a plan to terminate the election, or the fact that the terminating event or circumstance took place without the knowledge of the corporation, notwithstanding its due diligence to safeguard itself against such an event or circumstance, tends to establish that the termination or invalidity of the election was inadvertent." See Rev.Proc. 2013–30, 2013–36 I.R.B. 173 (specifying procedures for obtaining relief under § 1362(f)). Rev.Rul. 86–110, 1986–2 C.B. 150, granted inadvertent termination relief to an S corporation that lost its eligibility because the majority shareholder transferred stock to trusts for the shareholder's children. The shareholder acted on the advice of counsel that the transfer would not disqualify the corporation's S election and would not have made the transfer but for the advice of counsel. Private letter rulings issued by the IRS indicate that it is fairly lenient in applying the authority granted under § 1362(f).

3. TRANSFER TO INELIGIBLE OWNER BY MINORITY SHAREHOLDER

A minority shareholder may intentionally and unilaterally, to the detriment of other shareholders, terminate an S election by transferring stock to a disqualified person or by otherwise taking action to fail the requirements for S corporation status. In T.J. Henry Associates, Inc. v. Commissioner, 80 T.C. 886 (1983) (acq.), the controlling shareholder of a Subchapter S corporation transferred a single share of stock to himself as custodian for his children under a Uniform Gifts to Minors statute. The transfer was intended to terminate the corporation's S election.[12] The Tax Court rejected the IRS's assertion that the transfer was not a bona fide transfer of beneficial ownership of the stock and that the shareholder acted as a custodian for his children merely as an accommodation. The Tax Court further held that, so long as there is a bona fide transfer of beneficial ownership, a transfer deliberately made to disqualify an S election should be recognized. The IRS has acquiesced in this result. 1984–2 C.B. 1.

Provisions in corporate documents and shareholder agreements often seek to limit the shareholder's ability to make a stock transfer that would terminate the corporation's S election. While not always effective to prevent termination, such provisions might give rise to civil liability for shareholders undertaking disqualifying events.

4. ELECTION FOLLOWING REVOCATION OR TERMINATION OF S CORPORATION STATUS

Under § 1362(g), if an S corporation election is revoked or terminated the corporation or its successor is not eligible to make a new election for five years unless the IRS consents to an earlier election. Treas.Reg. § 1.1362–5(a) provides that consent ordinarily will be denied unless it can be shown that the event causing termination was not reasonably within the control of the corporation or shareholders having a substantial interest in the corporation and was not part of a plan to terminate the election. The Regulations also provide that consent should be granted if more than 50% of the corporation's stock is owned by persons who were not shareholders at the time the election was terminated. Private letter rulings reflect a rather relaxed approach on the part of the IRS in granting the requisite consent.

PROBLEM SET 4

1.   Z Corp. has had a valid S election in effect for several years. G owns 40% of the stock; each of H, I, J, and K own 15%.

    (a) How can Z Corp. revoke its S election for the current year?

    (b) How can Z Corp. revoke its S election for the subsequent year?

---

[12] With respect to the taxable year involved, § 1372(e)(1) required an affirmative consent to the election by a new shareholder in order to maintain S corporation status. The shareholder in *T.J. Henry Assoc., Inc.* did not file the requisite consent.

(c)   If Z Corp. revokes its election for the current year, when can Z Corp. make a new effective Subchapter S election?

(d)   Suppose that in (b), the revocation was filed on July 1 of this year, to be effective as of January 1 of next year, but that on September 3 of this year, G, H, I, and J decide they want to revoke the termination election. K does not want to revoke the termination election. Can the termination election be revoked?

2.   H transferred her shares to a spray trust for her minor children. The financial planner and accountant who advised H assured her that the trust was an eligible shareholder, but in fact it is not. Is there any way that Z Corp.'s S election can be preserved without interruption?

3.   J wants to revoke the election, but none of the other shareholders want to revoke the election. With the intention of terminating Z Corp.'s S status, J transfers one of his shares to Inc. Corp., his wholly owned corporation. Has J succeeded in terminating the election?

E.   COORDINATION WITH SUBCHAPTER C

INTERNAL REVENUE CODE: Section 1371.

Section 1371(a) provides that, except when specifically displaced, the normal Subchapter C rules, including the rules governing corporate distributions, are applicable to Subchapter S corporations. This is in contrast to § 1361(b), which provides that subject to certain exceptions, the taxable income of an S corporation is computed in the same manner as an individual's taxable income. Trugman v. Commissioner, 138 T.C. 390 (2012), held that the first time homebuyer's credit under now-expired § 36, which was available to an "individual" who had no present ownership interest in a principal residence during the three-year period ending on the date of the purchase, was not allowable to an S corporation that purchased a home for its shareholders, notwithstanding that the § 36 credit was not one of the listed exceptions in § 1363(b). The court held that a corporation could not be an "individual" for purposes of § 36, and election of Subchapter S status did not change that characterization. The court reasoned that only individuals can have a principal residence—a corporation has a principal place of business. Thus, before concluding that a provisions that applies to individuals also applies to S corporations, the statutory provision in question must be carefully examined.

Section 1371 also contains rules coordinating the treatment of items that affect both Subchapter S and Subchapter C years when a former C corporation elects S corporation status or an S corporation revokes or terminates its Subchapter S election.

There are no carrybacks or carryovers of loss or other items from Subchapter C years to Subchapter S years and vice versa. I.R.C. § 1371(b). Thus, a carryover of net operating losses incurred in a Subchapter C year will not be available to reduce S corporation income

(1) One year after the effective date of the termination, or the due date for the last subchapter S return, whichever is later; or

(2) 120 days after a determination that the corporation's subchapter S election had terminated for a previous year. (A determination will be defined as a court decision which becomes final, a closing agreement, or an agreement between the corporation and the Internal Revenue Service that the corporation failed to qualify.)

3. Basis adjustment (sec. 1367)

Under [section 1367(a)], both taxable and nontaxable income and deductible and nondeductible expenses will serve, respectively, to increase and decrease a subchapter S shareholder's basis in the stock of the corporation. These rules generally will be analogous to those provided for partnerships under section 705. [Section 1368(d) requires that adjustments to basis as a result of distributions be taken into account under section 1367(a) prior to applying the rule of section 1366(d) limiting shareholder loss deductions to basis.*] Unlike the partnership rules, however, to the extent property distributions are treated as a return of basis, basis will be reduced by the fair market value of these properties * * *. Any passthrough of income for a particular year (allocated according to the proportion of stock held in the corporation) will first increase the shareholder's basis in loans to the corporation to the extent the basis was previously reduced by the passthrough of losses.

DETAILED ANALYSIS

1. DETERMINATION OF CHARACTER OF INCOME AND LOSS

Although the individual shareholders report the items of gain or loss on their own returns, the character of items is determined at the corporate level and passed through to the shareholders pursuant to § 1366(b), a provision analogous to § 702(b), which requires that partnership items be characterized at the partnership level. In Rath v. Commissioner, 101 T.C. 196 (1993), the Tax Court held that § 1244, discussed in Chapter 3, cannot apply to allow an ordinary loss to be recognized on the sale of stock in another corporation held by an S corporation. Even though the loss ultimately will be reported by individuals, under § 1366(b) the character of the loss is determined at the corporate level. An S corporation shareholder does not "step into the shoes of the corporation for purposes of determining the character of a loss." Since Treas.Reg. § 1.1244(a)–1(b) provides that a corporation cannot claim an ordinary loss for § 1244 stock, the loss passes through to the shareholders as a capital loss. On the other hand, Rev.Rul. 2000–43, 2000–2 C.B. 333, held that an accrual-method S corporation could not elect under § 170(a)(2) to treat a charitable contribution as paid in the year that it was authorized by its board of directors when the contribution

---

* [Eds.: The material in brackets reflects amendments to § 1366 and § 1368 made in the Small Business Job Protection Act of 1996.]

was paid by the S corporation after the close of the taxable year. This result was required because § 1363(b) generally requires S corporations to compute their taxable income in the same manner as individuals, subject to certain specified exceptions.

After the character of an item is determined at the corporate level, whether it must be separately stated depends on whether the characterization may affect the computation of tax at the shareholder level. Thus, Rev.Rul. 93–36, 1993–1 C.B. 187, held that a nonbusiness bad debt must be separately stated as a short term capital loss under § 166(d) and passed through to its shareholders as such. Because § 166 is not an enumerated exception to § 1363(b), § 166 applies in the same manner as it does for an individual in computing the taxable income of an S corporation.

Treas.Reg. § 1.1366–1(b)(2) and (3) contain exceptions to the general rule that gains and losses are characterized at the corporate level in cases where the corporation is formed or availed of by any shareholder, or group of shareholders, for the purpose of converting ordinary gain at the shareholder level on property contributed to the corporation, which holds the property as a capital asset, or, conversely, converting a capital loss at the shareholder level on contributed property to an ordinary loss on sale of the property by the corporation.

2. PERMITTED TAXABLE YEAR

Under § 1366(a), shareholders account for their share of an S corporation's items in the taxable year of the shareholder in which the taxable year of the S corporation ends. Section 1378(b)(1) generally requires an S corporation to report on the calendar year. In the absence of § 1378, calendar year shareholders of a profitable S corporation generally would prefer a taxable year for the corporation ending on January 31 in order to defer income for up to eleven months. If, on the other hand, the S corporation was passing through losses to the shareholders, the shareholders would prefer a calendar year so as to avoid any deferral of deductions. Although § 1378(b) allows an S corporation to adopt a different taxable year with the permission of the IRS if the corporation can establish a business purpose for the fiscal year, the last sentence of § 1378(b) prohibits shareholder tax deferral from being treated as a business purpose for adopting a fiscal year.

Rev.Proc. 2002–39, 2002–22 I.R.B. 1046, provides that a taxpayer "may establish a business purpose for the requested taxable year based on all the relevant facts and circumstances," but "administrative and convenience business reasons . . . will not be sufficient." A taxpayer able to demonstrate a "natural business year" and requesting a change to that year will generally be deemed to have satisfied business purpose. Three tests are provided for determining the natural business year. For example, an S corporation's natural business year may be established using the 25% gross receipts test, which looks to whether the corporation realizes 25% of its gross receipts (under the method of accounting used to prepare its tax returns) during the last two months of any 12-month period for three consecutive years. If the corporation has more than one natural business year, it may only adopt the one in which the highest percentage of gross receipts are received in the last two months.

The rigid rules of § 1378, limiting flexibility in choosing the S corporation's taxable year, are somewhat ameliorated by § 444. This provision allows an election, even if there is no business purpose, to a year where the "deferral period" is not longer than the shorter of 3 months or the "deferral period of the taxable year which is being changed." I.R.C. § 444(b)(2). Thus, for example, if a newly formed corporation elects S corporation status and otherwise is required to use the calendar year, it nevertheless may elect to adopt a fiscal year ending as early as September 30. The § 444 election available to an existing corporation, whether an S corporation or a C corporation electing S status, will depend on the length of its current deferral period; if it is shorter than 3 months, the S corporation will be limited to that period and will not be able to increase its deferral period to 3 months. If an election is made under § 444, the corporation must make a payment computed under § 7519 to compensate the Treasury for the deferral of taxes. This is a nondeductible entity level payment that is not credited against the shareholders' individual tax liabilities. This payment in effect converts the interest-free loan generated by any tax deferral resulting from the use of a fiscal year into an interest-bearing loan. If a § 444 election is terminated, no subsequent § 444 election may be made the S corporation. I.R.C. § 444(d)(2)(B).

3. SHAREHOLDER'S BASIS

3.1. *General*

The shareholder's basis in S corporation stock initially is determined in the same manner as the basis of any other stock. Thereafter, in general, the shareholder's basis is increased by items included in the shareholder's income (and the shareholder's share of the corporation's tax-exempt income) and reduced by deductions allocated and distributions made to the shareholder. I.R.C. § 1367. Treas. Regs. § 1.1367–1(b)(2) and (c)(3) provide that increases and decreases to the basis of Subchapter S stock are determined on a per share, per day basis. In the case of a charitable contribution of property by an S corporation, under § 1367(a)(2), a shareholder's basis is decreased by the shareholder's proportionate share of the adjusted basis of the contributed property.

Basis adjustments generally are made at the close of the taxable year, but if a shareholder sells stock during the year, the adjustment to the basis of the stock sold is effective immediately prior to the disposition. Treas.Reg. § 1.1367–1(d)(1). Adjustments to the basis of the stock are made in the following order: (1) increases for income items; (2) decreases for distributions; (3) decreases for noncapital nondeductible expenses; and (4) decreases for losses or deductions. Treas.Reg. § 1.1367–1(f). Treas.Reg. § 1.1366–2(a)(6)(ii) requires that losses incurred during the year of a transfer between spouses or former spouses be prorated on the basis of stock ownership at the beginning of the following taxable year.

Section 1367(a)(2)(D) requires a reduction in basis for expenses that are neither deductible nor chargeable to capital account. Treas.Reg. § 1.1367–

1(c)(2) clarifies this language as applying only to expenses for which no loss or deduction is allowable, and as not applying to deductions that are deferred to a later taxable year. The Regulations describe expenses to which § 1367(a)(2)(D) apply as including such things as fines, penalties, illegal bribes and kickbacks and other items disallowed under § 162(c) and (f); expenses incurred to earn tax-exempt income disallowed under § 265; losses disallowed under § 267 relating to related party transactions; and nondeductible entertainment expenses under § 274. This adjustment is necessary to prevent the shareholder from in effect recognizing the disallowed deduction by realizing less gain or greater loss on the subsequent sale of the stock.

3.2. *Effect of Corporate Level Cancellation of Indebtedness Income*

Sections 1366(a)(1) and 1367(a)(1) provide for an increase in a shareholder's basis with respect to the shareholder's separately stated and non-separately stated income items, including "tax-exempt" income. The committee reports accompanying the enactment of these rules give as an example of tax-exempt income interest excluded under § 103. See S. Rep. No. 97–640, excerpted above. Neither the Code nor the Regulations, however, clearly define "tax-exempt" income for this purpose, and the question arises regarding what is "tax-exempt income," which results in a current basis adjustment, versus what is "tax-deferred income," which does not result in a current basis increase. However, a 2002 Act amendment to § 108(d)(7) specifically provides that cancellation of indebtedness income excluded under § 108(a) will not be taken into account as tax-exempt income under § 1366(a).[14]

The 2002 amendment to § 108(d)(7) was enacted to reverse the result in Gitlitz v. Commissioner, 531 U.S. 206 (2001). The taxpayer in *Gitlitz* was the sole shareholder of an S corporation that realized cancellation of indebtedness (COD) income while it was insolvent. The corporation properly excluded the COD income under § 108(a). Upon the subsequent disposition of the stock (in the same year), the taxpayer shareholder claimed an increase in the basis of his stock in the corporation pursuant to § 1366(a)(1)(A) and § 1367(a)(1)(A) on the theory that the COD income was passed-through "exempt" income, and reported a long-term capital loss. The IRS disallowed the portion of the loss attributable to the untaxed COD income. The Tax Court, 110 T.C. 114 (1998), and the Court of Appeals, 182 F.3d 1143 (10th Cir. 1999), upheld the IRS's position and denied the basis increase. The Supreme Court reversed on the basis of its reading of the "plain meaning" of the statutory scheme. First, the Court concluded that COD was "income" within the meaning of § 1366(a)(1)(A), which increases shareholder basis under § 1367(a)(1)(A). The fact that COD may be "tax-deferred" because of the insolvency exclusion of § 108(a)(1)(B) does not take the income out of the definition of income under § 1366(a)(1)(A). In addition, although

---

[14] See also, Treas.Reg. § 1.1366–1(a)(2)(viii), promulgated in 1999 before *Gitlitz* was decided by the Supreme Court, providing that cancellation of indebtedness income excluded at the corporate level under § 108(d)(7)(A) is not "tax-exempt" income for purposes of § 1366 and § 1367. Although the validity of the regulation was questionable after *Gitlitz*, the regulation is consistent with the 2002 statutory change.

§ 108(d)(7)(A), as in effect for the year in question, provided that the exclusions of § 108(a) and the attribute reductions required by § 108(b) were to be applied to an S corporation at the corporate level, the Court concluded that § 108(b)(4)(A), which provides that attribute reduction under § 108(b)(2) takes place "after the determination of the tax imposed by this chapter," expressly requires that the S corporation's shareholder's pass-through of income and basis adjustment must be taken into account before the COD income is reduced by corporate level net operating losses. As a result of this reasoning, the S corporation shareholder in *Gitlitz* received a tax-free step-up in basis, which he was able to convert into a deductible capital loss. The Court addressed this concern by stating:

> [C]ourts have discussed the policy concern that, if shareholders were permitted to pass through the discharge of indebtedness before reducing any tax attributes, the shareholders would wrongly experience a "double windfall": They would be exempted from paying taxes on the full amount of the discharge of indebtedness, and they would be able to increase basis and deduct their previously suspended losses. See, e.g., 182 F.3d at 1147–1148. Because the Code's plain text permits the taxpayers here to receive these benefits, we need not address this policy concern.

4. LIMITATION OF LOSS DEDUCTIONS TO BASIS

4.1. *General*

When net losses have reduced a shareholder's basis to zero, additional allocations of deduction and loss items reduce the basis of any indebtedness of the S corporation held by the shareholder. I.R.C. § 1367(b)(2)(A). See also Treas.Reg. § 1.1366–2. (If an S corporation has a qualified S corporation subsidiary, any indebtedness of the subsidiary to a shareholder of the parent is treated as indebtedness of the parent S corporation to the shareholder for this purpose. I.R.C. § 1361(b)(3)(A)(ii); H.R. Rep. No. 104–586, 104th Cong., 2d Sess. 89 (1996).) When the basis of both the shareholder's stock and corporate indebtedness have been reduced to zero, passed through losses no longer can be deducted by the shareholder. The losses are suspended and may be deducted in a later year in which the shareholder acquires basis. I.R.C. § 1366(d). Treas.Reg. § 1.1367–2(b)(3) provides that if the shareholder holds multiple debts of the S Corporation, the reduction in basis is applied to each debt in proportion to the relative bases of the indebtedness. The legislative history of the Small Business Job Protection Act directs the IRS to promulgate Regulations governing the order in which the basis of indebtedness is reduced if a shareholder holds indebtedness of both an S corporation and the corporation's qualified Subchapter S subsidiary. H.R. Rep. No. 104–586, 104th Cong., 2d Sess. 89 (1996).

The reduction in basis occurs notwithstanding the taxpayer's inability to use the losses on the taxpayer's own tax return. In Hudspeth v. Commissioner, 914 F.2d 1207 (9th Cir.1990), the shareholders were required to reduce the basis of bonds because of the corporation's net operating losses. However, because the shareholders' shares of losses exceeded their incomes in the taxable year of the losses and in subsequent years, they received no tax benefit with respect to the losses. The court rejected the shareholders' assertion that under the tax benefit rule the basis of the bonds should not be reduced to the extent that the corporation's losses did not produce a tax benefit. The court indicated that to so hold would nullify the limited carryback and carryforward provisions of § 172 that were in place at the time of the decision.

For purposes of the loss limitation of § 1366(d), the basis of stock received as a gift is limited under the transferred basis rules of § 1015(a) for determining loss. Treas.Reg. § 1.1366–2(a)(7). Thus, the transferee's basis for purposes of § 1366(d) is the lesser of the fair market value or adjusted basis of the stock at the time of the gift.

4.2. *Shareholder Basis in S Corporation Indebtedness*

As amended in 2014, Treas.Reg. § 1.1366–2 provides that the basis of any indebtedness of the S corporation to the shareholder means the shareholder's adjusted basis (as defined in Reg. § 1.1011–1 and as provided in § 1367(b)(2)) in any "bona fide indebtedness of the S corporation that runs directly to the shareholder." Whether indebtedness is "bona fide indebtedness" to a shareholder is determined under general tax principles and depends on "all of the facts and circumstances." Treas.Reg. § 1.1366–2(a)(2)(i).

The Regulations do not attempt to clarify the meaning of "bona fide indebtedness," or provide any examples of relevant facts and circumstances, but rely on "general Federal tax principles." Earlier cases required an "actual economic outlay." For example, Maloof v. Commissioner, 456 F.3d 645 (6th Cir. 2006), denied any basis for a shareholder's guarantee of a bank loan to the corporation. With respect to another loan to the corporation that the shareholder cosigned, and that he thus "could one day be asked to pay," the court likewise denied any basis "because until that contingency transpired, the S corporation remained indebted to the bank, not to [the taxpayer]." See also Hitchins v. Commissioner, 103 T.C. 711 (1994); and Perry v. Commissioner, 54 T.C. 1293 (1970).

In the preamble to the final Regulations, the Treasury Department expressly declined to accept a commentator's suggestion that the final "regulations provid[e] that actual economic outlay is no longer the standard used to determine whether a shareholder obtains basis of indebtedness," but "[w]ith respect to guarantees, however, the final regulations retain the economic outlay standard." In Meruelo v. Commissioner, T.C. Memo. 2018–16, Judge Lauber weighed in:

> [T]he controlling test under prior case law, as under the new regulation, dictates that basis in an S corporation's debt requires proof of "bona fide indebtedness of the S corporation that runs directly to the shareholder." . . . Requiring that the shareholder have made an "actual economic outlay" is a general tax principle that may be employed under the new regulation, as it was applied under prior case law, to determine whether this test has been met.

Treas.Reg. § 1.1366–2(a)(2)(iii), Ex. 2, blesses a basis increase resulting from a back-to-back loan in which one S corporation lends money to a shareholder, who in turn lends the loan proceeds to a second S corporation, if the loan to the second S corporation "constitutes bona fide indebtedness" from the borrower S corporation to the shareholder. Treas.Reg. § 1.1366–2(a)(2)(iii), Ex. 3, blesses a basis increase resulting from a distribution to a shareholder by one S corporation (S1) of a note evidencing the indebtedness of a second S corporation (S2) if, after the distribution, S2 is indebted to the shareholder and "the note constitutes bona fide indebtedness" from S2 to the shareholder. Under local law, the distribution relieved S2 of its obligation to S1, and S2 was liable only to the shareholder; whether S2 is indebted to the shareholder rather than S1 is, however, determined under general federal tax principles and depends upon all of the facts and circumstances. Treas.Reg. § 1.1366–2(a)(2)(iii), Ex. 1, provides that a bona fide indebtedness from an S corporation to a disregarded entity (LLC) owned by the shareholder results in an increase in basis of indebtedness for the shareholder.

Finally, Treas.Reg. § 1.1366–2(a)(2)(ii) expressly provides that:

> A shareholder does not obtain basis of indebtedness in the S corporation merely by guaranteeing a loan or acting as a surety, accommodation party, or in any similar capacity relating to a loan. When a shareholder makes a payment on bona fide indebtedness of the S corporation for which the shareholder has acted as guarantor or in a similar capacity, then the shareholder may increase its basis of indebtedness to the extent of that payment.

Treas.Reg. § 1.1366–2(a)(2)(iii), Ex. 4, illustrates that the basis increase from satisfaction of a guarantee occurs pro tanto as serial payments on the guarantee are made.

4.3. *Restoration of Basis*

If a shareholder has reduced the basis in S corporation stock to zero and also has reduced the basis of corporate indebtedness by any amount, any "net increase in basis" attributable to passed-through income in a subsequent year (i.e., basis increase minus distributions for the year) will be applied to restore the basis of indebtedness before there is any increase in the basis of the stock. I.R.C. § 1367(b)(2)(B); Treas.Reg. § 1.1367–2(c). Assume for example, that A is the sole shareholder of X Corp., which has an S election in effect. The basis of A's stock in X Corp. is $10,000, and A holds a $5,000 promissory note from X Corp. In Year 10, X Corp. passes a $14,000 loss through to A, and A reduces the basis of the X Corp. stock to zero and the basis of the promissory note to $1,000. In Year 11, X Corp. has $6,500 of income and distributes $3,000 to A. To the extent of the $3,000 distribution, the passed through income is allocated to increase the basis of A's stock, and because the positive and negative adjustments to the stock basis offset, its basis remains zero. The remaining $3,500 of passed-through income increases the basis of the debt to $4,500. See Treas.Reg. § 1.1367–2(e), Ex. 2.

Nevertheless, § 1367(b)(2)(B) can produce an unexpected consequence to the shareholder. To the extent that corporate earnings passed through to the shareholder under § 1366 are allocated to increase the basis of shareholder debt, the shareholder's stock basis will not be adjusted to reflect income previously taxed to the shareholder. Distributions of these earnings in a subsequent year might be taxed to the shareholder to the extent distributions exceed the shareholder's stock basis even though the shareholder has basis in the debt. Thus, if in the immediately preceding example, in Year 12, X Corp. realized neither income nor loss and distributed $2,000 to A, A would recognize a $2,000 gain under § 1368. (But if X Corp. had distributed $5,000 to A in Year 11, A would have recognized no gain under § 1368, and the basis of the debt would have been increased to only $2,500.) As a consequence, the shareholder appears to be taxed twice on the same income; once as the shareholder is allocated a proportionate share of the income under § 1366, and a second time to the extent the distribution of that income exceeds the shareholder's stock basis. The "second" tax, however, can be viewed as a consequence of the pass through of losses in excess of stock basis, which has reduced the basis in the debt; the statute in effect requires those losses to be "recaptured" when distributions are made on the stock before the full basis of the debt has been accounted for.

Treas.Reg. § 1.1367–2(d) provides that adjustments to debt obligations held by shareholders are generally determined at the close of the taxable year, but if the debt is repaid during the year, its basis is adjusted immediately before the repayment. Suppose, for example, that in Year 10 a shareholder-creditor is allocated a loss that exceeds the basis of the shareholder's stock by $600, and as a result reduces the basis of a $1,000 corporate debt obligation to $400. In July, Year 11, the corporation repays the debt, and for Year 11, the shareholder's share of the S corporation's income is $700. If the debt had not been repaid until January 1, Year 12, its basis would have been increased from $400 to $1,000 as a result of the Year 11 income, and no gain would have been recognized upon repayment. Under Treas.Reg. § 1.1367–2(d), the shareholder's basis in the debt obligation is adjusted immediately before repayment to reflect the shareholder's share of the corporation's Year 11 income. As a result, the shareholder realizes no gain in Year 11.

4.4. *Carryover of Disallowed Losses*

The loss limitation of § 1366(d)(1) prevents a shareholder from claiming losses in excess of the shareholder's investment in the S corporation. Losses disallowed by § 1366(d)(1) may be carried over indefinitely to future years and deducted whenever the shareholder has sufficient basis to support the deduction. I.R.C. § 1366(d)(2). The loss carryover is personal to each individual shareholder and is not a loss carryover to the corporation. I.R.C. § 1366(d)(2); Treas.Reg. § 1.1366–2(a)(5). Thus, disposition of S corporation stock by the shareholder, including a disposition by gift that has a transferred basis to the donee under § 1015, generally terminates the loss carryforward attributable to that stock. However, § 1366(d)(2)(B) provides that if stock of an S corporation with respect to which there is a suspended loss is transferred between spouses or pursuant to a divorce, the suspended loss follows the stock and is available to the transferee spouse.

If pursuant to § 108(a)(1)(A), (B), or (C) cancellation of debt income realized by the S corporation was not recognized, Treas.Reg. § 1.108–7(d) treats any shareholder losses from the current year and prior years that have been suspended under the limitation-on-losses rule of § 1366(d) as net operating losses that are subject to attribute reduction under § 108(b). If the S corporation has more than one shareholder during the taxable year of the debt cancellation, each shareholder's disallowed losses or deductions is a pro rata share of the total losses and deductions allocated to the shareholder under § 1366(a) during the corporation's taxable year. The deemed NOL allocated to a shareholder consists of a proportionate amount of each item of the shareholder's loss or deduction that was disallowed under § 1366(d)(1) in the year of the debt cancellation.

A shareholder may have losses carried into the last taxable year of the S corporation. In such a case, the loss is treated as a loss incurred by the shareholder on the last day of a "post-termination transition period." The post-termination transition period is defined in § 1377(b) as the period beginning on the last day of the corporation's taxable year as an S corporation and ending on the later of (1) one year after the last day of the S corporation taxable year, (2) the due date for the tax return for the last taxable year as an S corporation (including extensions), (3) 120 days after any determination pursuant to a post-termination audit of a shareholder that adjusts any item of S corporation income, loss, or deduction for the period the corporation was an S corporation, or (4) if there is a judicial determination or administrative agreement that the corporation's S election terminated in an earlier taxable year, 120 days after the date of the determination. See also Treas.Reg. § 1.1377–2.

4.5. *Additional Shareholder Contributions to Capital*

Cash or property contributions to capital will increase the shareholder's stock basis, thereby allowing the shareholder to deduct losses otherwise in excess of basis. In Rev.Rul. 81–187, 1981–2 C.B. 167, the shareholder of an S corporation attempted to increase basis for purposes of deducting a net operating loss by transferring the shareholder's own promissory note to the corporation. The IRS ruled that the note did not increase the shareholder's basis because the shareholder incurred no cost in executing the note; the shareholder's basis in the note was zero. But see Peracchi v. Commissioner, 143 F.3d 487 (9th Cir.1998); Lessinger v. Commissioner, 872 F.2d 519 (2d Cir.1989); both cases are discussed in Chapter 2.

A contribution of additional assets will not necessarily increase basis, however, if the assets are encumbered or the corporation assumes liabilities of the shareholder in connection with the transfer. In Wiebusch v. Commissioner, 59 T.C. 777 (1973), aff'd per curiam, 487 F.2d 515 (8th Cir.1973), the taxpayer transferred the assets of a sole proprietorship to an existing S corporation that also assumed certain of the transferor's liabilities. The liabilities exceeded the taxpayer's basis for the assets, which resulted in gain to the taxpayer under § 357(c) (discussed in Chapter 2) and, as a result of § 358(d)(1), the taxpayer's basis in the stock was reduced to zero. Accordingly, the corporation's current losses could not be deducted by the taxpayer. As a result of the contribution, the taxpayer recognized gain and lost the benefit of a current loss deduction, neither of which would have occurred had the business continued to be operated as a sole proprietorship.

A shareholder contribution to capital excluded from the corporation's gross income under § 118 is not tax-exempt income for purposes of § 1366(a)(1)(A) and § 1367. In Nathel v. Commissioner, 131 T.C. 262 (2008), aff'd, 615 F.3d 83 (2d Cir. 2010), the taxpayer received loan repayments from an S corporation in excess of his basis in the debt. In an attempt to avoid gain recognition, the taxpayer argued that under Gitlitz v. Commissioner, discussed above, capital contributions are permanently excludable from income and thereby constitute tax-exempt income under Treas.Reg. § 1.1366–1(a)(2)(viii), which would first restore basis to the taxpayer's outstanding loans to the corporation under § 1367(b)(2)(B) before increasing basis of the taxpayer's stock. The court concluded that, under long standing principles, shareholder contributions to capital are added to the shareholder's basis in stock (Treas.Reg. § 1.118–1), that equity contributions and debt are treated differently, and that in any event, contributions to capital are not "income" treated as tax-exempt.

4.6. *Shareholder Advances*

As discussed in paragraph 4.1 of this Detailed Analysis, after stock basis is reduced to zero, an S corporation shareholder may claim losses against the basis of any indebtedness of the S corporation held by the shareholder. Repayment of a corporate indebtedness before the basis is restored will result in gain recognition. Open account advances and payments are, however, netted at the close of the taxable year so that only net repayment of open account advances during the year (where basis has not been restored) will result in recognized gain. Treas.Reg. § 1.1367–2(a)(2) limits open account debt for this purpose to advances not represented by a written instrument that do not exceed $25,000. Any advance not evidenced by a written instrument that results in the total running net open account advances exceeding $25,000, as well as each subsequent advance not evidenced by a written instrument, is treated as a separate indebtedness evidenced by a written instrument, subject to the rules of Treas.Reg. § 1.1367–2(d), rather than as open account indebtedness. In making this determination, Treas.Reg. § 1.1367–2(d)(2) requires that advances and payments on open account debt be netted continually as they occur. Under the Regulations, a shareholder may not offset the repayment of one shareholder advance with the basis of another shareholder advance. Treas.Reg. § 1.1367–2(c)(2). Treas.Reg. § 1.1367–2(c)(2) provides that any net increase in basis is applied first to restore the basis of any indebtedness (including open account indebtedness not exceeding $25,000) repaid during the taxable year to the extent necessary to offset any gain that would be realized on the repayment, then to restore the basis of each outstanding indebtedness in proportion to the amount that the basis of each indebtedness had been reduced by losses allowed under § 1367(b)(2)(A). Treas.Reg. § 1.1367–2(d)(1) provides that adjustments to basis of indebtedness are determined and effective as of the close of the taxable year (except as provided in Treas.Reg. § 1.1367–2(d)(2) for the purpose of determining if advances not evidenced by a written instrument exceed $25,000). Thus, the effect of the net advances and repayments is determined at the close of the year, or earlier if the taxpayer has disposed of the open account debt or the debt is repaid.

5.   LIMITATION ON BUSINESS INTEREST

Legislation enacted in 2017 added a limitation on the deductibility of interest properly allocable to a trade or business. I.R.C. § 163(j). The generally applicable aspects of § 163(j) were discussed in Chapter 3. Under § 163(j), the deduction for business interest shall not exceed the sum of the taxpayer's business interest income plus 30% of the taxpayer's adjusted taxable income, plus the taxpayer's "floor plan financing interest," if any. Section 163(j)(3) provides an exception for small businesses, which § 163(j)(3) defines by cross-reference to § 448(c) as a business with average annual gross receipts (computed over 3 years) of $25 million or less. Regulations proposed in December 2018 would require that an S corporation exempt from § 163(j) still provide its shareholders with the information needed to allow each S corporation shareholder to compute the shareholder's share of business interest expense, business interest income, and items of adjusted taxable income required for individual application of § 163(j).

Section 163(j) also contains special rules for pass-through entities. The limitation is applied at the S corporation level, and "any deduction for business interest shall be taken into account in determining the non-separately stated taxable income or loss of the [S corporation]." I.R.C. § 163(j)(4)(A). Although an entity-level approach can lead to administrative simplification, in this case, the approach requires an additional set of complex rules. First, an S corporation shareholder may have other businesses; as a result, a rule is required to prevent a shareholder from using the taxable income share from one S corporation to increase the shareholder's adjusted taxable income for purposes of applying the 30% limitation rule to business interest paid by the shareholder's other businesses. Otherwise, the shareholder will be able to use the S corporation's taxable income twice—once when the S corporation determines the limitation for its business and once when the shareholder determines the limitation as to other businesses. Second, the S corporation may have business interest income that is less than the maximum amount allowed (i.e., the business interest income is less than 30% of the S corporation's adjusted taxable income). In such a situation, a shareholder should be allowed to use the shareholder's share of the S corporation's excess taxable income for purposes of applying the 30% limitation to the business interest paid by through other businesses.

Section 163(j) resolves these two issues by requiring a shareholder to determine "adjusted taxable income" for purposes of applying the 30% limitation to any other businesses by disregarding *all* of the shareholder's S corporation tax items and then adding back in the shareholder's share, if any, of the "[S corporation's] excess taxable income." I.R.C. § 163(j)(4)(A)(ii). A shareholder's share of the excess taxable income is to be determined in the same manner as the shareholder's share of the nonseparately stated taxable income or loss of the S corporation. "Excess taxable income" is determined through a formula. The S corporation must create a fraction, the numerator of which is 30% of the S corporation's adjusted taxable income minus the amount of business interest it paid that exceeds its business interest income. The denominator is 30% of the S corporation's adjusted taxable income. The fraction is then applied to the S corporation's adjusted taxable income to obtain the "excess taxable income." For example, if an S corporation had $100,000 of adjusted taxable income, $20,000 of business interest paid, and $10,000 of business interest income, the excess taxable income would be $66,667—that is, 2/3 of $100,000 (the numerator would be $20,000, computed as $30,000 (30% of $100,000) minus $10,000 ($20,000 interest paid − $10,000 interest received); the denominator would be $30,000 (30% of $100,000). A shareholder with a one-third interest in the S corporation would increase taxable income for purposes of applying the 30% rule to the shareholder's other businesses by $22,222 (and change).

The statute is silent with respect to another potential problem: a shareholder's use of the shareholder's pro rata share of S corporation business interest income to offset business interest paid through other businesses or of the shareholder's pro rata share of the S corporation's "floor plan financing" to increase the shareholder's deduction. The statutory rules described in the preceding paragraphs regarding taxable income are insufficient to address these issues. Notice 2018–28 provides:

> The Treasury Department and the IRS intend to issue regulations providing that, for purposes of calculating a partner's annual deduction for business interest under section 163(j)(1), a partner cannot include the partner's share of the partnership's business interest income for the taxable year except to the extent of the partner's share of the excess of (i) the partnership's business interest income over (ii) the partnership's business interest expense (not including floor plan financing). Additionally, the Treasury Department and the IRS intend to issue regulations providing that a partner cannot include such partner's share of the partnership's floor plan financing interest in determining the partner's annual business interest expense deduction limitation under section 163(j). Such regulations are intended to prevent the double counting of business interest income and floor plan financing interest for purposes of the deduction afforded by section 163(j) and are consistent with general principles of Chapter 1 of the Code. Similar rules will apply to any S corporation and its shareholders.

Proposed Regulations issued in November 2018 incorporate these limitations (REG–106089–18).

If the deduction of business interest is limited by § 163(j), the disallowed business interest is carried forward. I.R.C. § 163(j)(2), (4). Section 163(j)(4)(B) contains special carryover rules for partnerships, but this subsection is not listed in the provision stating that similar rules will apply to S corporations. I.R.C. § 163(j)(4)(D) (listing only (j)(4)(A) and (C) as applying to S corporations and their shareholders). The preamble to the 2018 Proposed Regulations states that legislative history suggests that Congress did intend a different rule for S corporations. The Proposed Regulations would apply to S corporations the same carryover rules applicable to C corporations but requested comments regarding providing for an alternative option that would allow for S corporations to use rules similar to those for partnerships.

6. ALLOCATIONS IF STOCK OWNERSHIP CHANGES DURING THE YEAR

6.1. *In General*

Section 1377(a) provides that each shareholder's pro rata share of an S corporation's items passed through under § 1366 is determined on a day-by-day, share-by-share method if the ownership of shares changes during the year. See Treas.Reg. § 1.1377–1(a), (c), Ex. 1. This rule is similar to the proration method available to partnerships under § 706(d), except that in the case of an S corporation, the proration method is the default rule. Pursuant to authority granted in § 1377(a)(2), Treas.Reg. § 1.1377–1(b) allows an S corporation to close its year for purposes of allocating income among shareholders if a shareholder completely terminates the shareholder's interest and the corporation and all of the shareholders who are affected consent. If stock is sold, the affected shareholders are the seller and the purchaser(s); if stock is redeemed by the corporation, however, all shareholders are affected and must consent. I.R.C. § 1377(a)(2)(B); Treas.Reg. § 1.1377–1(b)(2). Treas.Reg. § 1.1368–1(g) provides a similar election if any shareholder disposes of 20% or more of the outstanding stock of the corporation during any 30-day period during the taxable year but has not disposed of all of the shareholder's stock. Treas.Reg. § 1.1368–1(g) requires consent of all shareholders, not just the "affected shareholders." The Treasury has not amended Treas.Reg. § 1.1368–1(g) to conform to the consent requirements in § 1377(a)(2), apparently because it was not promulgated under authority of that Code section, although the policy considerations are identical. The proration method is not applicable, however, and allocations based on the closing corporate books method are required if there is a sale or exchange of more than 50% of the corporation's stock during a year in which the corporation's S election terminates. I.R.C. § 1362(e)(6)(D).

If items are allocated by closing the corporation's books, the corporation prorates its income within each segment of the year among the shareholders in proportion to their ownership during that segment of the year and then adds together the share of items for each shareholder for all of the segments of the year. See Treas.Reg. § 1.1377–1(b), (c) Ex. 2 (method of making the election to allocate items under this method; illustrating method of making computations). On the day of the sale, the selling shareholder rather than the purchaser is counted as the shareholder. Treas.Reg. § 1.1377–1(a)(2)(ii). If two or more qualifying dispositions occur during the year, apparently it would be possible for the corporation to terminate its year with respect to one but to pro rate income with respect to the other.

These principles are illustrated by the following example. Assume that A, B, C, D, and E each owned 100 shares of stock of X Corp., which is an S corporation. X Corp.'s income for the year was $182,500, but by quarters it was as follows: 1st quarter, ($90,000); 2nd quarter, $90,000; 3rd quarter,

$229,000; 4th quarter, ($46,500). On March 31st of a non-leap year, A sold all of A's stock to F, and on September 30, B sold all of B's stock to G.

Under the normal method in § 1377(a), $500 of the corporation's $182,500 of income would be allocated to each day, and then $1 would be allocated to each share. The shareholders' income would be as follows:

Shareholder	Days	Shares	Income/Share/Day	Total
A	90	100	$1	$ 9,000
B	273	100	$1	$27,300
C	365	100	$1	$36,500
D	365	100	$1	$36,500
E	365	100	$1	$36,500
F	275	100	$1	$27,500
G	92	100	$1	$ 9,200

If, however, all affected shareholders consented to closing the books as of March 31, $18,000 of the corporation's $90,000 loss for the first quarter would be allocated to A, and $54,450 of the corporation's $272,500 income for the last three quarters (rounded off to $2.00 per share-per day) would be allocated to F. Section 1377(a)(2)(B) and Treas.Reg. § 1.1377–1(b)(2) define affected shareholders as including only the seller and purchaser. Thus, A and F are the only affected shareholders with respect to the March 31 sale, and only A and F need consent to closing the books on March 31. The overall annual $1 per share per day profit would be allocated among B, C, D, E, and G without regard to the closing of the books with respect to A and F. The results are as follows:

Shareholder	Days	Shares	Income/Share/Day	Total
A	90	100	($2)	($18,000)
B	273	100	$1	$27,300
C	365	100	$1	$36,500
D	365	100	$1	$36,500
E	365	100	$1	$36,500
F	275	100	$2	$54,500
G	92	100	$1	$ 9,200

Since F realizes significantly greater income by closing the books at the end of the first quarter than under the proration method, F is not likely to consent unless F is compensated in some manner. B's and G's shares are computed without reference to the March 31 closing of the books, which applies only to A and F. B and G could, however, make their own election to close the books with respect to their shares on September 30.

6.2. *Bankruptcy Situations*

In Williams v. Commissioner, 123 T.C. 144 (2004), the taxpayer owned all of the stock of two S corporations that incurred losses for the year. He filed a personal bankruptcy petition at the beginning of December and reported a pro rata share of the losses on his personal return. The court disallowed the passed-through losses on the grounds that § 1377(a) did not apply and that § 1398 allocated all of the losses to the bankruptcy estate. It reasoned that under § 1398(f)(1) "a transfer of an asset from the debtor to the bankruptcy estate when the debtor files for bankruptcy is not a disposition triggering tax consequences, and the estate is treated as the debtor would be treated with respect to that asset." Thus, the bankruptcy estate was treated as if it had owned all of the shares of the S corporations for the entire year and was entitled to all of the passed-through losses.

In contrast, Mourad v. Commissioner, 387 F.3d 27 (1st Cir. 2004), aff'g 121 T.C. 1 (2003), held that when an individual's wholly-owned S corporation filed for a bankruptcy Chapter 11 plan of reorganization and an independent trustee was appointed by the Bankruptcy Court, the individual remained liable for the tax on any income or gain recognized by the S corporation.

7.   ALLOCATIONS AMONG FAMILY GROUPS

The IRS is given authority to allocate items described in § 1366 among those shareholders who are members of the shareholder's family (spouse, ancestors, and lineal descendants) if the IRS determines that reallocation is necessary to reflect the value of services rendered by any of those persons. I.R.C. § 1366(e). See also Treas.Reg. § 1.1366–3. Thus, if a parent works for a low salary in an effort to shift income to the parent's shareholder-children, the IRS may allocate additional income to the parent or reduce the deduction for salary allocable to the parent. Unlike § 704(e), which reallocates partnership income in the case of an interest purchased from a related person, § 1366(e) permits reallocation of S corporation income among family members who purchased their stock from the corporation or from an outsider in an arm's length transaction. On the other hand, the authority provided to the IRS under § 1366(e) is more restrictive than § 704(e)(1) and (2) (which provide for reallocation of partnership income in the case of transfers by gift) in the sense that it permits reallocation only among family members.

In Davis v. Commissioner, 64 T.C. 1034 (1975), the Tax Court held that the IRS abused its discretion under the predecessor to § 1366(e) by allocating 100% of the income of two S corporations to the taxpayer. The taxpayer was an orthopedic surgeon who organized two corporations to perform X-ray and physical therapy services related to his medical practice. Ninety percent of the stock of each corporation was owned by the taxpayer's three minor children. The Tax Court indicated that the value of the taxpayer's services depended upon factors such as the nature of the services, the responsibilities involved, the time spent, the size and complexity of the business, economic conditions, compensation paid by others for comparable services, and salary paid to company officers in prior years. The court held that the 20 or so hours per year that the taxpayer spent directly performing services for the corporations was minimal and rejected the IRS's argument that the taxpayer's referral of patients to the corporations was personal service rendered by him to the corporations. Thus, the fees earned by the corporations were the result of the use of equipment owned by the corporations and the services of corporate employees, and not the result of services rendered by the taxpayer. The Tax Court also rejected the IRS's claim that income was allocable to the taxpayer under § 482 and assignment of income principles.

8.   ADDITIONAL LOSS LIMITATION RULES

The at-risk rules of § 465 apply to the shareholders of an S corporation. As a result, a loss that is passed through to a shareholder may be deducted only to the extent that the shareholder is at risk with respect to the activities that generated the loss. Under the aggregation rules of § 465(c)(3)(B), an S corporation may be treated as engaged in a single activity if its activities constitute a trade or business and 65% or more of the losses are allocable to persons who actively participate in the management of the trade or business. If passed through losses have been suspended by the at-risk rules and they have not been used by the shareholder prior to the termination of the corporation's S election, the suspended losses may be carried forward to the post-termination transition period (as defined in § 1377(b)) and can be deducted in the year or years within the post-termination transition period to the extent the taxpayer's at-risk amount is increased.

In Van Wyk v. Commissioner, 113 T.C. 440 (1999), the taxpayer and another person each owned 50% of the stock of an S corporation engaged in the farming business. The taxpayer and his wife borrowed funds from the other shareholder and his wife and re-lent them to the corporation, after which the taxpayer attempted to claim passed-through losses against the debt basis under § 1366(d)(1)(B). The court held that pursuant to § 465(b)(3), the taxpayer shareholder was not at risk for amounts lent to the corporation because he borrowed the funds from another shareholder (and that shareholder's spouse, from whom borrowing is treated in the same manner as borrowing from the shareholder under § 465(b)(3)(C)) to re-lend them to the corporation. The taxpayer was thus denied a current deduction for losses passed through under § 1366. Money that is borrowed from a third party by the taxpayer on the taxpayer's own credit and then invested or contributed by the taxpayer to an activity is not governed by § 465(b)(1)(A), but rather is treated as borrowing with respect to the activity and will be considered to be at risk only if the borrowing transaction passes muster under the several other subsections of § 465 dealing with the treatment of borrowed funds. Treas. Regs. §§ 1.465–8 and 1.465–20, promulgated in 2004, extend to all activities the rule that amounts borrowed from another party with an interest in the activity (other than a creditor) are not at risk, even if the borrowing is with full recourse. This rule does not apply, however, to amounts that are qualified nonrecourse borrowing under § 465(b)(6), or that would have been qualified nonrecourse borrowing if the debt had been nonrecourse.

The passive activity loss limitations of § 469 apply to losses passed through to S corporation shareholders in the same manner as they apply to partners. Thus, net losses of an activity operated by an S corporation in which the shareholder does not materially participate are deductible by the shareholder only to the extent of the shareholder's passive activity income. Disallowed losses are carried forward and treated as passive activity deductions in the next succeeding year until offset by the taxpayer's passive activity income. Complete disposition of the activity of the S corporation allows the taxpayer to deduct the unused loss attributable to the specific activity.

St. Charles Investment Co. v. Commissioner, 110 T.C. 46 (1998), rev'd 232 F.3d 773 (10th Cir. 2000), involved an S corporation that prior to making its S election had been subject to § 469 as a closely held C corporation. The corporation had unused passive activity loss carryovers from the period that it had been a C corporation. The Tax Court held that under § 1371(b)(1), the passive activity loss carryovers from C corporation years could not be claimed against passive activity income recognized in S corporation years. The Court of Appeals reversed and allowed the suspended losses to be carried over and applied to reduce the passive activity income passed through to the shareholders in years for which the S election was in effect.

For taxable years beginning after December 31, 2017, and before January 1, 2026, new § 461(*l*) adds a limitation on the deduction of business losses for noncorporate taxpayers, including individual partners and S corporation shareholders. Section 461(*l*) disallows the deduction of a taxpayer's "excess business loss." This is defined in § 461(*l*)(3) to mean the taxpayer's aggregate deductions for the year that are "attributable to trades or business of such taxpayer" over the sum of (1) the taxpayer's aggregate gross income or gain for the year attributable to the taxpayer's trades and (2) $250,000 (or $500,000 for joint filers), adjusted for inflation after 2018. Section 461(*l*) specifies that it applies after § 469.

Section 461(*l*) applies at the shareholder level for S corporations and provides:

> [E]ach partner's or shareholder's allocable share of the items of income, gain, deduction, or loss of the partnership or S corporation for any taxable year from trades or businesses attributable to the partnership or S corporation shall be taken into account by the partner or shareholder in applying [§ 461(*l*)] to the taxable year of such partner or shareholder with or within which the taxable year of the partnership or S corporation ends.

The statute explains that for S corporation shareholders, "allocable share" means their "pro rata share" of an item. § 461(*l*)(4).

If a taxpayer's deductions are disallowed, the disallowed amount is treated as a § 172 net operating loss in the subsequent year. § 462(*l*)(2). The 2017 Tax Act also changed the carryback and carryforward rules of § 172. For all taxpayers (other than certain insurance companies and farming businesses), the ability to carry back NOLs is eliminated and the carryover is limited to 80% of the taxpayer's taxable income. § 172(a)(2), (b)(1).

9. SHORT SUBCHAPTER S AND SUBCHAPTER C TAXABLE YEARS ON TERMINATION

Section 1362(e) requires that in any taxable year in which the S corporation election terminates effective on a date other than the first day of the taxable year, income and deduction items must be allocated between the portion of the year the corporation is qualified as an S corporation and the portion of the year the corporation is treated as a C corporation.[15] The Senate Finance Committee Report explained the allocation rule as follows:

> The day before the day on which the terminating event occurs will be treated as the last day of a short Subchapter S taxable year, and the day on which the terminating event occurs will be treated as the first day of a short regular (i.e., Subchapter C) taxable year. There will be no requirement that the books of a corporation be closed as of the termination date. Instead the corporation will allocate the income or loss for the entire year (i.e., both short years) on a proration basis.

S.Rep. No. 97–640, 97th Cong., 2d Sess. 11 (1982).

Each separately stated item of the corporation's income and loss during the short Subchapter S year must be allocated to each day of the short taxable year and taken into account by the shareholders. I.R.C. § 1362(e)(2). The remaining taxable income for the taxable year is allocated to the short C corporation year. Because of the flat 21% corporate tax rate added in the 2017 Tax Act, the procedures for annualizing the tax provided for in § 1362(e)(5) will not be necessary. If, however, the corporate tax rate is again made progressive, then this provision will need to be followed. Under § 1362(e)(5), first, the corporation's tax for the short Subchapter C year is determined as if it had earned a proportionate amount of taxable income for a full taxable year; then the corporation pays only the proportionate amount of the tax that corresponds to the portion of a full taxable year that it is deemed a C corporation. See Treas.Reg. § 1.1362–3(a) and (c)(2).

In lieu of a pro rata allocation of income between the short Subchapter S and C years, the corporation may elect, with the consent of *all* shareholders at any time during the S year and all shareholders on the first day of the C year, to report income and deductions on the basis of actual amounts shown on the corporate books. I.R.C. § 1362(e)(3). Allocation of amounts based on the corporate books is required if the corporation's stock is acquired by a corporation, thereby terminating the S election, if the acquiring corporation elects to treat the acquisition as an asset purchase under § 338 (see Chapter 8). I.R.C. § 1362(e)(6)(C). The "closing of the books" method may be desirable in situations in which the parties do not want events occurring after termination to affect income determination for the S corporation portion of the year. Note, however, that a single shareholder, who may be adversely affected, can prevent the use of the closing of the books method.

---

[15] Section 1362(e)(6)(A) provides that the short taxable years required by § 1362(e) will be treated as only one year for purposes of the carryback and carryforward of corporate items such as net operating losses.

10.   TAXABLE ACQUISITIONS INVOLVING S CORPORATIONS

10.1.   *Section 338(h)(10) Election*

The § 338(h)(10) election is available with respect to the purchase and sale of the stock of an S corporation by another corporation, including the purchase of the stock of one S corporation by another S corporation. Treas.Reg. § 1.338(h)(10)–1(c)(1). Because S corporation shareholders will include the corporate gains or losses on their individual returns, all of the shareholders of the S corporation, including any of them who have not sold their stock, must consent to the election. Treas.Reg. § 1.338(h)(10)–1(c)(2). Under the election, the shareholders of a Subchapter S corporation treat the stock sale as a sale of assets by the corporation. The S corporation recognizes gain and loss on the deemed sale of its assets based on the aggregate deemed sales price (ADSP) as determined under Treas.Reg. § 1.338–4 (see Chapter 8). The recognized gains and losses are passed through to the S corporation's shareholders under § 1366. This deemed passed-through gain or loss is then taken into account by the shareholders as a basis adjustment to their stock under § 1367, following which the S corporation is deemed to have been liquidated in a transaction in which the S corporation shareholders recognize gain or loss under § 331. In many cases the shareholders' basis in their stock will closely approximate the amount of the deemed liquidation distribution because of the basis adjustment resulting from the pass-through of the gain or loss on the deemed asset sale. See Treas.Reg. § 1.338(h)(10)–1(d)(4) & (5). But the deemed liquidation does not per se result in no recognition of gain or loss. No additional gain or loss will, however, be recognized on the stock sale. See Treas.Reg. § 1.338(h)(10)–1(d)(5)(i). Because the gain recognized by the target S corporation on the deemed sale of its assets is passed through to the corporation's shareholders who pay the resulting taxes, neither the ADSP nor the AGUB reflects the tax liability resulting from the deemed sale of the target S corporation's assets. See Treas.Reg. § 1.338(h)(10)–1(e), Ex. 10.

Treas.Reg. § 1.338(h)(10)–1(d)(8) enables shareholders of an S corporation who have sold their stock for § 453 installment notes and made a § 338(h)(10) election to report their gain on the installment method.

10.2.   *QSub Election by Acquiring S Corporations*

If an S corporation acquires all of the stock of another corporation, it may make a QSub election with respect to the newly acquired subsidiary regardless of whether the subsidiary previously was a QSub of another S corporation, a Subchapter S corporation itself, or a C corporation. H.R. Rep. No. 104–586, 104th Cong., 2d Sess. 88–89 (1996). As a result of the election, the subsidiary is deemed to have liquidated under § 332 and § 337 immediately before the election is effective. If the subsidiary previously was a C corporation, the § 1374 built-in gains tax and § 1363(d) LIFO recapture might apply, discussed later in this Chapter.

If the stock of the subsidiary was acquired by the S corporation in a qualified stock purchase, a § 338 election may be made with respect to the subsidiary. See H.R. Rep. No. 104–586, 104th Cong., 2d Sess. 88–89 (1996). If both a § 338 election and a QSub election are made, then the QSub election is not effective until after the consequences of the § 338 election are taken into account. The subsidiary must file a final return for the § 338 election as a C corporation. Treas.Reg. § 1.1361–4(b)(4).

10.3.   *Acquisitions of Qualified Subchapter S Subsidiaries*

If a QSub is acquired, the original QSub election is terminated. If the new owners of the stock are all eligible to be shareholders of an S corporation, an immediately effective S election can be made notwithstanding the provisions of § 1361(b)(3)(D), as long as there is no intervening day on which the corporation was a C corporation. If the purchaser of the QSub stock is another S corporation, the new 100% parent likewise may make an immediately effective QSub election with respect to the newly acquired subsidiary. See Treas.Reg. § 1.1361–5(c)(2).

10.4.   *Section 336(e)*

A § 336(e) election (discussed in Chapter 8) for an S corporation target requires a binding written agreement between the target S corporation and all of the S corporation shareholders, including shareholders who do not sell stock, before the due date of the tax return for the year of the stock disposition and an election statement attached to the return for the year of the disposition. The target must retain a copy of the written agreement.

In general, if a corporation sells or exchanges target stock in a qualified stock disposition, the treatment of old target, seller, and purchaser are similar to the treatment of old target, the selling corporation, and the purchasing corporation under § 338(h)(10). If a § 336(e) election is made, Treas.Reg. § 1.336–2(b)(1)(i)(A) provides that the sale or exchange of target stock is disregarded. Instead, target (old target) is treated as selling all of its assets to an unrelated corporation in a single transaction at the close of the disposition date (the deemed asset disposition). Old target recognizes the deemed disposition tax consequences from the deemed asset disposition on the disposition date while it is a subsidiary of seller. Treas.Reg. § 1.336–2(b)(1)(i)(A). In the case of a deemed asset sale by a Subchapter S corporation, the tax consequences of the deemed asset sale pass through to the S corporation shareholders. Old target is then treated as liquidating into seller, which, if the seller is a corporation, in most cases will be treated as a § 332 liquidation to which § 337 applies. Treas.Reg. § 1.336–2(b)(1)(iii). If the sellers are the shareholders of an S corporation, § 331 and § 336 will apply.

The target is treated as having purchased all of its assets from an unrelated party. Treas.Reg. § 1.336–2(b)(1)(ii). If the target was an S corporation and still qualifies for an S election, a new election is required to maintain S corporation status. Treas.Reg. § 1.336–2(b)(1)(ii). Any stock of the S corporation target retained by an S corporation shareholder is treated as acquired by the shareholder on the day after the disposition date at its fair market value, which is a proportionate amount of the grossed-up amount realized on the transfer under the § 336(e) election. Treas.Regs. § 1.336–2(b)(1)(v).

PROBLEM SET 5

1.   Cyclone Fashion Corp. elected S corporation status for its first year of operation. Cyclone Fashion Corp.'s common stock is owned by Andrea (100

shares with a $20,000 basis) and Barry (50 shares with a $22,000 basis). Cyclone Fashion Corp.'s operating income is derived primarily from the rental of high-fashion clothing and accessories. During the current year, Cyclone Fashion Corp. had the following income and expense items:

Income

Rental receipts	$198,000
Tax-exempt interest	$ 6,000
Gain from building sale (§ 1231 gain)	$ 36,000
STCG from sale of publicly traded stock	$ 30,000

Expenditures and Losses

Salaries	$ 62,000
Equipment expenses deducted under § 179	$ 15,000
Depreciation	$ 9,000
Rent	$ 40,000
Interest expense (on loan to purchase clothing)	$ 12,000
LTCL from the sale of investment real estate	$ 18,000
Lobbying expenses re: anti-sweatshop legislation	$ 12,000

(a) How should Cyclone Fashion Corp., Andrea, and Barry report these items?

(b) What will be Andrea's and Barry's bases in their Cyclone Fashion Corp. stock at the end of the current year?

2. The stock of Hurricane Hardware & Lumber Co., Inc., which has had a valid S election in effect at all times, is owned equally by Chantal and Dean, each of whom had a $6,000 basis in the stock as of January 1 of last year. On July 1 of last year, Chantal lent $7,000 to Hurricane Hardware & Lumber Co. and received a 6% demand note from the corporation.

(a) (1) What are the consequences to Chantal and Dean if Hurricane Hardware & Lumber Co. has a $20,000 loss from business operations last year?

(2) Would your answer differ if on December 30 of last year, Hurricane Hardware & Lumber Co. repaid Chantal $4,000 of the $7,000 owed on the promissory note?

(b) (1) If after losing $20,000 last year, Hurricane Hardware & Lumber Co. realizes $12,000 of net income from business operations in this year, what are the consequences to Chantal and Dean? Assume that the $7,000 debt from the corporation to Chantal remains outstanding.

(2) Would your answer differ if during this year Hurricane Hardware & Lumber Co. distributed $6,000 to each shareholder?

(c) What would be the result in (a)(1) if Hurricane Hardware & Lumber's S corporation status terminated as of January 1 of this year.

3.   As of January 1 of the current year, Erin and Felix each owned one-half of the 100 outstanding shares of Tropical Wave Rider Mfg. Corp., which has had a valid S election in effect since its incorporation. During the current year, Tropical Wave had $360,000 of net income from business operations. Net operating income of $90,000 was realized in January through June, and net operating income of $270,000 was realized in July through December. In addition, in March, Tropical Wave sold an item of § 1231 property and recognized a $120,000 loss. Tropical Wave made no distributions during the current year. At the beginning of the current year, Erin's basis in her stock was $140,000. On June 30, Erin sold 25 of her 50 shares to Gabrielle for $180,000.

(a)   What are the consequences to Erin and Gabrielle if no election is made to "close the books" under Treas.Reg. § 1.1368–1(g)?

(b)   What are the consequences to Erin and Gabrielle if an election is made to "close the books" under Treas.Reg. § 1.1368–1(g)?

4.   Helene and Isaac each owned one-half of the 100 outstanding shares of Miami Windmill Mfg. Corp., which had a valid S election in effect since from the time of its incorporation until July of the current year. As of July 1, Miami Windmill's S election was terminated. From January through June, Miami Windmill had earned $500,000 in income and had $200,000 of deductions. As of December 31, Miami Windmill had $2,000,000 of income and $600,000 of deductions for the year. How must the parties account for the income and deductions?

5.   The stock of Gale Force Wind Anemometer and Barometer Mfg. Corp., which has had a valid S election in effect at all times, is owned equally by Jackson and Lorelei, each of whom had $20,000 basis in the stock as of January 1 of the current year. For the current year, Gale Force realized a $70,000 operating loss and had no other relevant tax items. To what extent may each of Jackson and Lorelei deduct their $35,000 share of the loss under the following circumstances?

(a)   On December 31, the Last National Bank of Key West lent Gale Force $60,000 and both Jackson and Lorelei guaranteed repayment of the full amount of the loan if Gale Force defaulted. Jackson and Lorelei each gave the bank a mortgage on their personal residences to secure the guarantee.

(b)   (1)   On December 31, the Last National Bank of Key West lent each of Jackson and Lorelei $30,000, at the prime rate, due in two years. Jackson and Lorelei in turn each lent the $30,000 to Gale Force at the prime rate, due in two years.

(2)   Would your answer be affected if Gale Force guaranteed repayment of the full amount of the loans by the bank to Jackson and Lorelei if they defaulted and Gale Force gave the bank a mortgage on its factory to secure the guarantee?

6.   Maria and Nick each own 50 of the 100 outstanding shares of common stock of Opticon Corporation, which has a valid Subchapter S election in effect. Maria's basis in the Opticon stock is $6,000,000; Nick's basis in the

Opticon stock is $4,000,000. Opticon manufactures VR equipment. The assets recorded on its balance sheet consist of the following:

Asset	Basis	FMV
Inventory	$ 1,000,000	$ 9,000,000
Factory Land	$ 5,000,000	$ 6,000,000
Factory Building	$ 5,000,000	$ 5,000,000
Equipment	$ 3,000,000	$ 2,000,000
Patent	$ 4,000,000	$ 8,000,000
Total	$18,000,000	$30,000,000

Opticon has one liability; it owes the Last National Bank $5,000,000. Hubble Opticals, Inc. has proposed to purchase all of the Opticon stock either (1) for $26,000,000 in cash ($13,000,000 each) if Maria and Nick agree to make a § 338(h)(10) election, or (2) $24,000,000 in cash ($12,000,000 each) if there is no § 338(h)(10) election. Maria and Nick want to sell. Which offer should they accept? Why?

B. DISTRIBUTIONS

INTERNAL REVENUE CODE: Sections 1368; 1371(c) and (e); 453B(h).

REGULATIONS: Sections 1.1367–1(d)(1), (f), (h), Ex. 2; 1.1368–1(a)–(c), (e)(2), –3, Ex. 2.

Senate Finance Committee Report, Subchapter S Revision Act of 1982

S.Rep. No. 97–640, 97th Cong., 2d Sess. 20 (1982).

Explanation of Provisions

1.   Taxation of shareholders (secs. 1368 and 1371(c))

Under [section 1368(a)], the amount of any distribution to a shareholder will equal the amount of cash distributed plus the fair market value of any property distributed * * *.

The amount of a distribution by a corporation without accumulated earnings and profits will be tax-free to the extent of the shareholder's basis in the stock. The distribution will be applied to reduce the shareholder's basis in his stock. To the extent the amount of the distribution exceeds basis, capital gains generally will result.

No post-1982 earnings of a subchapter S corporation will be considered earnings and profits for this purpose. Thus, under [section 1371(c)(1)], a corporation will not have earnings and profits attributable to any taxable year beginning after 1982 if a subchapter S election was in effect for that year.

* * *

2. Treatment of corporation [sec. 311]

Gain will be recognized by a subchapter S corporation on a distribution of appreciated property, other than distributions [of property permitted to be received without recognition of gain under sections 354, 355 or 356], in the same manner as if the property had been sold to the shareholder at its fair market value. Like other corporate gain, it will pass-thru to the shareholders.

Without this rule, assets could be distributed tax-free (except for recapture in certain instances) and subsequently sold without income recognition to the selling shareholder because of the stepped-up fair market value basis.

DETAILED ANALYSIS

1. DISTRIBUTIONS OF APPRECIATED PROPERTY

1.1. *Generally*

Section 311(b) requires recognition of gain at the corporate level on the distribution of appreciated property to shareholders, which is a significant departure from the partnership provisions on which treatment of S corporation distributions is generally based. (In the corresponding partnership situation, gain recognition is postponed through the rules on basis adjustments.[16] Presumably, Congress believed that the partnership approach would have been too complex to apply in a corporate context.) Technically, this result is reached under § 1371(a), which provides that, except when specifically displaced, the normal Subchapter C rules, including the rules governing corporate distributions, are applicable to Subchapter S corporations. Thus, § 311(b) requires recognition of corporate level gain on the distribution of appreciated property as if the property were sold for its fair market value. H.Rep.No. 100–795, 100th Cong., 2d Sess. 64 (1988). The recognized gain is passed through to shareholders who report the gain as income under § 1366. Under § 1368, the distribution of the property itself is tax-free to the shareholder to the extent of the shareholder's basis in the stock. The shareholder's basis in the property received is its fair market value, I.R.C. § 301(d), and the shareholder reduces by a like amount the basis of the stock with respect to which the distribution was made. Thus, in comparison to the treatment accorded distributions by a partnership, the distribution of appreciated property by an S corporation accelerates the payment of tax, although there is still only one level of tax.

1.2. *Liquidating Distributions*

Liquidating distributions by an S corporation are also subject to the liquidation rules of Subchapter C. Section 336 (see Chapter 7) requires recognition of gain or loss at the corporate level as if the property were sold for its fair market value. The gain or loss is passed through to shareholders under § 1366 and the shareholders' bases in their stock are adjusted

---

[16] Except to the extent required by § 751, no gain is recognized by a partnership on a distribution of appreciated property. The partnership basis carries over to the distributee partner to the extent of the partner's basis in the partner's partnership interest.

accordingly pursuant to § 1367. Under § 331, liquidating distributions are treated as received by the shareholders in exchange for their stock; gain is recognized to the extent the distribution exceeds basis, or loss is recognized if the distribution is less than the shareholder's basis. Gain or loss is recognized in situations where the shareholder's stock basis is not the same as the shareholder's ratable share of the corporation's asset bases, e.g., where the shareholder acquired the stock by purchase or bequest.

Distribution of a § 453 installment obligation generally results in immediate recognition of gain to the corporation under either or both of § 311 and § 453B, and the gain will be passed through to the shareholders. Section 453B(h) provides, however, a very narrow exception for the distribution of an installment obligation acquired by an S corporation on the sale of its assets within 12 months preceding complete liquidation of the corporation. Treas.Reg. § 1.453–11(c). Corporate level gain is not triggered by the distribution in liquidation of the installment obligation,[17] and the shareholder does not treat receipt of the installment obligation itself as a payment in exchange for the shareholder's stock in the liquidation. I.R.C. § 453(h). Instead, the receipt of each installment payment by the shareholder is a taxable event. Thus, S corporation shareholders are permitted to defer recognition of liquidation gain in the same manner that § 453(h) permits deferral of recognition by C corporation shareholders. But § 453B(h) requires that the character of the shareholder's gain be determined as if the corporation had recognized the gain and the gain had passed through to the shareholders under § 1366.

2. TIMING OF BASIS ADJUSTMENTS FOR GAIN AND LOSS AND DISTRIBUTIONS

Section 1368(d) requires that positive adjustments to a shareholder's stock basis under § 1367(a)(1) reflecting the shareholder's share of corporate income, be taken into account before applying the distribution rules of § 1368(b). On the other hand, § 1368(d) requires distributions to be taken into account before negative adjustments to a shareholder's stock basis reflecting the shareholder's share of corporate loss are made under § 1367(a)(2). See also Treas.Reg. § 1.1367–1(f), (h), Ex. 2; see also Staff of the Joint Committee on Taxation, General Explanation of Tax Legislation Enacted in the 104th Congress 122–124 (Comm. Prt. 1996). This asymmetrical rule works to the shareholder's advantage by preventing interim distributions of profits during the year from being treated as distributions in excess of basis, thereby triggering gain under § 1368(b)(2). Conversely, if the corporation loses money, distributions will not be taxed to the extent they did not exceed the shareholder's basis at the beginning of the year (subject to adjustment for items other than passed-through corporate losses).

Suppose that A is a 50% shareholder of X Corp., an S Corporation. A's adjusted basis in the X Corp. stock on January 1, Year 6, was $1,000. During

---

[17] Section 453B(h) does not apply for purposes of determining the corporation's tax liability under Subchapter S. Thus, the corporation is not relieved from recognition of gain on the distribution of an installment obligation that triggers the built-in gain tax of § 1374 or the tax on passive investment income of § 1375, both discussed later in this Chapter.

Year 6, A's share of X Corp.'s items of income and loss was a capital gain of $200 and an operating loss of $900, and during the year X Corp. distributed $700 to A. A's basis in the X Corp. stock first is increased to $1,200 ($1,000 plus $200 capital gain). The distribution then reduces A's stock basis to $500, with no gain being recognized. Finally, A is able to deduct currently $500 of the $900 loss that passed through, reducing A's basis to zero. The remaining $400 loss is carried forward pursuant to § 1366(d)(2). The net result is that A recognizes currently $200 of capital gain and $500 of ordinary loss.

3.   DISTRIBUTIONS FOLLOWING TERMINATION OF S CORPORATION STATUS

Following termination of an S election, distributions of money may be received by shareholders as a tax-free reduction of basis to the extent of the undistributed taxable income of the S corporation that has been passed through to the shareholders. I.R.C. § 1371(e)(1). The distribution must be made within the "post-termination transition period" as defined in § 1377(b), generally at least a one year period after termination of S corporation status, although the period may differ in certain specified circumstances. See Treas.Reg. § 1.1377–2. If the shareholders fail to withdraw previously taxed income from the corporation within the applicable period, the privilege of tax-free distribution under § 1368 is lost and subsequent corporate distributions are taxable under § 301, i.e., subsequent distributions are taxable dividends if supported by sufficient earnings and profits. (If the corporation has always been an S corporation, earnings and profits will arise only in the period following termination of the election.)

When the corporate tax rate was reduced to 21%, § 1371(f) was enacted to provide additional benefits for a limited period of time to S corporations converting to C corporations. It provides:

> In the case of a distribution of money by an eligible terminated S corporation (as defined in section 481(d)) after the post-termination transition period, the accumulated adjustments account shall be allocated to such distribution, and the distribution shall be chargeable to accumulated earnings and profits, in the same ratio as the amount of such accumulated adjustments account bears to the amount of such accumulated earnings and profits.

This provision allows shareholders to continue to treat at least a portion of any post-termination transition period distributions as though they do not derive from C corporation earnings and profits and instead are in part from the terminated S corporation, thus allowing partial continuation of the privilege of tax-free distributions. An eligible terminated S corporation is a C corporation that was an S corporation on December 21, 2017, the day before enactment of the 2017 Tax Act, and terminates through revocation of its election under § 1362(a) during the following two year period. The owners of the stock when the revocation election is made must be "the same owners (and in identical proportions) as on the date" of the enactment of the legislation. I.R.C. § 481(d)(2)(B).

Section 1371(e)(1) prescribes that only distributions of "money" may be tax-free during the post-termination transition period. Under a requirement of the pre-1983 Subchapter S rules, distributions of money during the first two and one-half months of the taxable year were received tax-free by the shareholders as distributions of previously taxed income of the prior taxable year.[18] Taxpayers attempted various devices to circumvent this "money" distribution requirement, but with a marked lack of success. This case law remains relevant under § 1371(e)(1). See, e.g., DeTreville v. United States, 445 F.2d 1306 (4th Cir.1971) (two transactions treated as one because the shareholders purported to receive cash distributions and immediately purchased property from the corporation; the transactions were in substance a distribution of property); Stein v. Commissioner, 65 T.C. 336 (1975) (fact that shareholders were in constructive receipt of amounts credited to their accounts on the books of the corporation did not satisfy the money requirement); Roesel v. Commissioner, 56 T.C. 14 (1971) (nonacq.) (cash distribution and subsequent loan to corporation by shareholders were disregarded and the transaction was treated as a taxable distribution of the debt obligations).

4.   SHAREHOLDER-EMPLOYEE FRINGE BENEFITS

For purposes of employee fringe benefit provisions, § 1372 treats an S corporation as a partnership and each more than 2% shareholder as a partner. As a result, S corporation shareholders holding more than 2% of the stock are not eligible to receive employee fringe benefits tax-free. Revenue Ruling 91–26, 1991–1 C.B. 184, holds that payments of health and accident insurance premiums with respect to a more than 2% shareholder/employee of an S corporation must be included in income by the shareholder/employee and are not subject to exclusion from gross income under § 106. The corporation may deduct the premiums under § 162 and is required to report the premiums as compensation to the employee/shareholder on a Form W-2.

Section 1372 does not affect the treatment of a qualified pension plan maintained by an S corporation. If an S corporation had a qualified pension plan, a shareholder of the corporation who is also an employee may participate in the corporation's qualified pension plan regardless of the amount of stock that the shareholder-employee owns. But if the shareholder is not also an employee, the shareholder may not participate in the qualified pension plan. Passed-through S corporation income is not self-employment income for purposes of maintaining a Keogh plan.

PROBLEM SET 6

1.   Saffir & Simpson Weathervane Mfg. Corp. has had a valid S election in effect at all times since its incorporation. The Saffir & Simpson stock is owned one-third by Arthur and two-thirds by Bertha. At the beginning of the current year, Arthur's basis in his shares was $6,000, and Bertha's basis in her shares was $2,000. During the current year, Saffir & Simpson earned $36,000 of net income from operations. Arthur's share was $12,000; Bertha's

---

[18]   Otherwise, distributions during the taxable year were taxed as dividends to the extent of the current year's earnings and profits. After current earnings were distributed, distributions of prior years' undistributed taxable income were also received tax-free by shareholders.

share was $24,000. What are the results to Saffir & Simpson Corp., Arthur, and Bertha in the following alternative situations?

(a) On July 1st, Saffir & Simpson distributed $16,000 to Arthur and $32,000 to Bertha.

(b) On December 31st, Saffir & Simpson distributed Blackacre, having a fair market value of $12,000 and a basis of $8,000, to Arthur and Whiteacre, having a fair market value of $24,000 and a basis of $22,000, to Bertha.

(c) On December 31st, Saffir & Simpson distributed $18,000 in cash to Arthur and distributed Greenacre, which had a fair market value of $36,000 and a basis of $42,000, to Bertha.

2. Thunderbird Auto Rentals Corp. has been an S corporation since it was formed. Thelma owns 60% and Louise owns 40% of the stock of Thunderbird Auto Rentals. Thelma's basis for her stock as of December 31st of last year was $280,000; Louise's basis for her stock as of December 31st was $220,000. On January 1st of the current year, Thunderbird Auto Rentals liquidated by distributing Blackacre to Thelma and Whiteacre to Louise. These properties were purchased four years ago. The fair market value of Blackacre was $1,200,000 and Thunderbird Corp.'s basis in Blackacre was $200,000. The fair market value of Whiteacre was $1,100,000 and its basis was $1,400,000; Whiteacre was subject to a $300,000 mortgage, which Louise assumed. What are the tax consequences of the liquidation of Thunderbird Auto Rentals?

3. San Francisco Ice Pick Mfg. Corporation has had an S election in effect since it was formed. Catherine owns 60 shares of the stock of San Francisco Ice Pick Mfg. Corporation, and Rebekah owns 40 shares. Catherine's basis for the 60 shares is $180,000. On December 31st of this year, San Francisco Ice Pick Mfg. Corporation distributes $150,000 in cash to Catherine in redemption of 20 of Catherine's shares. What are the tax consequences to Catherine?

4. Z Corp. has had an S election in effect for all relevant times. G owns one-third of the stock of Z Corp; H owns two-thirds of the stock. Both are employed full time by Z Corp. and each receives a salary of $30,000. Z Corp. pays $3,000 for medical insurance for each of G and H in their capacity as employees. During the current year, Z Corp. earned $90,000 of net profits before taking the salaries and medical insurance premiums with respect to G and H into account. What are the tax consequences to G and H?

SECTION 4. QUALIFIED SUBCHAPTER S SUBSIDIARIES

INTERNAL REVENUE CODE: Section 1361(b)(3).

REGULATIONS: Sections 1.1361–3, –4.

Prior to 1997, an S corporation could not be part of an affiliated group of corporations as defined in § 1504. This meant that an S corporation could not own stock of an 80% or more controlled subsidiary. The limitation was repealed by the 1996 Act, thereby permitting an S corporation to own 80% or more of the stock of a subsidiary that is a C corporation. Such a C corporation subsidiary may elect to join in the filing of a consolidated return with its affiliated C corporations (chains of controlled corporations of which the subsidiary is the common parent), but the S corporation parent is not allowed to join in the consolidated return. See I.R.C. § 1504(b)(8). On the other hand, because a corporation that has another corporation as a shareholder is not eligible to make an S election, a subsidiary of another corporation may not be an S corporation. However, § 1361(b)(3) provides a special rule for "qualified Subchapter S subsidiaries."

A qualified Subchapter S subsidiary (QSub) is any domestic corporation that (1) is not an ineligible corporation, (2) is wholly owned by an S corporation, and (3) for which the parent S corporation elects to treat as a QSub. I.R.C. § 1361(b)(3)(B). Election procedures are described in Treas.Reg. § 1.1361–3(a). A corporation for which a QSub election is made is not treated as a separate corporation. The existence of the stock of a QSub is disregarded for tax purposes. Treas.Reg. § 1.1361–4(a)(4). All assets, liabilities, and items of income, deduction, and credit of the QSub are treated as assets, liabilities, and items of income, deduction, and credit of the parent S corporation. Treas.Reg. § 1.1361–4(a)(1). Transactions between the S corporation parent and the qualified S corporation subsidiary are not taken into account for tax purposes.

DETAILED ANALYSIS

1.   ELECTIONS AND REVOCATIONS

1.1. *Procedures*

Treas.Reg. § 1.1361–3(a)(4) allows the effective date of a QSub election to be any specified date within 2 months and 15 days prior to, or not more than 12 months after, the date the election is made. Unlike an S election, a QSub election does not have to be made within 2 months and 15 days of the beginning of a taxable year to be retroactive, although if the election is made more than 2 months and 15 days after the beginning of a taxable year it cannot be retroactive for the entire year.

A QSub election may be revoked as of any specified date within 2 months and 15 days prior to, or not more than 12 months after, the date of the revocation. Treas.Reg. § 1.1361–3(b)(2). A QSub that ceases to qualify under § 1361(b)(3)(B) or whose election has been revoked is treated as a new corporation that has acquired all of its assets and assumed all of its liabilities from its S corporation parent in exchange for the subsidiary's stock immediately before the cessation of QSub status. I.R.C. § 1361(b)(3)(C); Treas.Reg. § 1.1361–5(b)(1). This hypothetical transaction is governed by general income tax principles, including § 351 and its associated sections. For purposes of determining control under § 351, equity instruments that are not treated as a second class of stock under § 1361(b)(1)(D) are disregarded. The Regulations also provide that the step transaction doctrine is applicable. Thus, a disposition of the stock of the former QSub will affect application of § 351. Treas.Reg. § 1.1361–5(b)(3), Ex. 1.

A QSub whose election has terminated may not have a QSub election made with respect to it (or, if its stock is acquired by eligible shareholders, make an S election itself) before its fifth taxable year that begins after the first taxable year for which the termination is effective without the IRS's consent. I.R.C. § 1361(b)(3)(D); Treas.Reg. § 1.1361–5(c). If a QSub election is terminated by reason of the disposition of the stock of the subsidiary by the parent, the new owners may make an immediate S election, without the consent of the IRS, provided that there has been no intervening period in which the corporation was a C corporation. Treas.Reg. § 1.1361–5(c)(2).

Section 1362(f) permits the IRS to grant relief from inadvertently invalid QSub elections and inadvertent terminations of QSub elections. See Rev.Proc. 2013–30, 2013–36 I.R.B. 173 (providing simplified methods to apply for relief under § 1362(f)).

1.2. *Treatment of Transition*

If a QSub election is made for a newly formed subsidiary, the subsidiary is treated as a QSub from its inception—the parent and subsidiary both are treated as if the subsidiary never had been formed. Treas.Reg. § 1.1361–4(a)(2)(i). In the case of a preexisting C corporation subsidiary, as a result of a QSub election the subsidiary is deemed to have liquidated under § 332 and § 337 immediately before the election is effective. Treas.Reg. § 1.1361–4(a)(2), (b). In Ball v. Commissioner, T.C. Memo. 2013–39, the court rejected the taxpayer's assertion that unrecognized gain on the deemed § 332 liquidation on a QSub election for an existing subsidiary is "exempt" income that permits a basis increase under § 1367(a)(1)(A). The court held that nonrecognition under § 332 does not create an item of tax-exempt income under § 1366(a)(1)(A), but defers recognition through substituted basis rules. The Tax Court's decision in *Ball* was affirmed by the Third Circuit. Ball v. Commissioner, 742 F.3d 552 (3d Cir. 2014). The court reasoned that gains that are not recognized by virtue of a specific Code provision are not items of gross income, citing Treas.Reg. § 1.61–6(b)(1), and § 332 specifically provides nonrecognition on the liquidation of a controlled subsidiary. Thus, making the QSub election did not give rise to an item of gross income.

1.3. *Termination by Stock Sale*

Section 1361(b)(3)(C)(ii) provides that a sale of stock of a QSub that results in termination of the subsidiary's QSub election (which automatically occurs unless the purchaser is another S corporation that elects to continue the QSub election) will be treated as a sale of the QSub's assets in proportion to the percentage of the QSub stock that has been sold. The transaction is then treated as a pro rata transfer of the QSub's assets by the selling S corporation and the purchaser of the stock to a newly formed C corporation in a transaction governed by § 351. The legislative history indicates that § 351 will apply to the deemed contribution regardless of the percentage of stock of the subsidiary held by the Subchapter S former QSub owner, e.g., meeting the 80% control requirement of § 351 is not required. For example, if a Subchapter S corporation sells 21% of the stock of a QSub, the S corporation will be treated as selling 21% of the subsidiary's assets and then contributing the assets to a new corporation in a transaction to which § 351 applies.

PROBLEM SET 7

1.   (a)   X Corp., which is owned by five resident individuals, owns 100% of the voting common stock of Y Corp., which is the only Y Corp. stock outstanding.

        (1)   May X or Y make an S election?

        (2)   May a QSub election be made with respect to Y Corp.? Who makes the election?

    (b)   X Corp., which is owned by five resident individuals, owns 99% of the voting common stock of Y Corp. The other 1% of Y Corp.'s voting common stock is owned by the X Corp. shareholders in the same proportion in which they own the X Corp. stock. May a QSub election be made with respect to Y Corp.?

    (c)   X Corp. owns 100% of the voting common stock of Z Corp. and D, who is unrelated to X Corp. or any of its shareholders, owns 100% of the nonvoting preferred stock of Z Corp. May a QSub election be made with respect to Z Corp.?

2.   Leviathan Recording Corp., which has a valid S election in effect, owns all of the stock of E-Tunes, Inc., which currently is a C Corporation. Leviathan's basis in the stock of E-Tunes is $1,000,000. What are the tax consequences of making a QSub election for E-Tunes under the following alternative fact patterns?

    (a)   E-Tunes's assets have a basis of $900,000 and fair market value of $2,000,000, and E-Tunes is debt free.

    (b)   E-Tunes's assets have a basis of $900,000 and fair market value of $2,000,000, and E-Tunes owes $2,100,000 to the BigOne National Bank.

3.   Fox Book Stores Corp., which has a valid S election in effect, owns all of the stock of The Shop Around the Corner, Inc. (The Shop), for which a valid QSub election is in effect. Fox Book's original basis in the stock of The Shop, before the QSub election was made in a prior year, was $1,000,000. What are the tax consequences of revoking The Shop's QSub election under the following alternative fact patterns?

    (a)   The Shop's assets have a basis of $900,000 and fair market value of $2,000,000, and The Shop is debt free.

    (b)   The Shop's assets have a basis of $900,000 and fair market value of $2,000,000. The Shop owes $1,500,000 to the BigOne National Bank.

SECTION 5. S CORPORATIONS THAT HAVE A C CORPORATION HISTORY

A. DISTRIBUTIONS FROM AN S CORPORATION WITH EARNINGS AND PROFITS ACCUMULATED FROM SUBCHAPTER C YEARS

INTERNAL REVENUE CODE: Section 1368(a), (c)–(e).

REGULATIONS: Sections 1.1368–1(d)–(f), –2, –3.

Conversion of an existing C corporation to S corporation status raises several problems that are related to the double tax regime of Subchapter C. The Subchapter S rules are structured to maintain the possibility of a second layer of tax on income earned or appreciation in assets occurring while the Subchapter S corporation was subject to Subchapter C. Thus, under § 1368(c)(1), distributions by an S corporation that has accumulated earnings and profits from its C corporation years are tax-free to shareholders only to the extent of an "accumulated adjustments account." The accumulated adjustments account, as defined in § 1368(e)(1), reflects the S corporation's taxable income that has been passed through and taxed to shareholders under § 1368 while the corporation has been subject to Subchapter S. Distributions in excess of the accumulated adjustments account are treated as taxable dividends to the shareholders to the extent of the corporation's accumulated earnings and profits. I.R.C. § 1368(c)(2). Distributions in excess of both the accumulated adjustments account and accumulated earnings and profits are treated the same as distributions from a corporation with no earnings and profits; distributions are not included in the shareholder's gross income to the extent of the shareholder's basis in the S corporation's stock, and any excess is capital gain.

DETAILED ANALYSIS

1. SOURCES OF S CORPORATION EARNINGS AND PROFITS

Generally, corporate activities during the period when a Subchapter S election is in effect have no impact on the corporation's earnings and profits. I.R.C. § 1371(c)(1). An S corporation will have earnings and profits only (1) if it has accumulated earnings from a period before its S election during which it was a C corporation, or (2) if it succeeded to the earnings and profits account of a C corporation that was acquired in a merger or other transaction to which § 381 applies (see Chapter 13).

2. ACCUMULATED ADJUSTMENTS ACCOUNT

2.1. *General*

Distributions to shareholders from an S corporation with earnings and profits are excluded from the shareholders' gross incomes only to the extent of the corporation's accumulated adjustments account. I.R.C. § 1368(c)(1). The accumulated adjustments account is basically a running total of the corporation's net taxable income while operating as an S corporation. The account is based on adjustments to the shareholders' bases under § 1367, except that the accumulated adjustments account does not include tax-exempt income, nor is it reduced by deductions not allowed in computing the corporation's taxable income. I.R.C. § 1368(e)(1); Treas.Reg. § 1.1368–2(a)(2) and (3). The exclusion of tax-exempt items from the accumulated adjustments account means that tax-exempt income of the S corporation may not be distributed tax-free to shareholders until after the taxable distributions of accumulated earnings and profits from the Subchapter C period have been made.

Operation of the stacking principle used in § 1368(c) is illustrated as follows: As of January 1, Year 5, the effective date of its Subchapter S election, Y Corporation had $50,000 of Subchapter C accumulated earnings and profits. Y Corporation's sole shareholder, A, had a basis in A's stock of $6,000. For Year 5, Y Corporation had taxable income of $30,000 and made a cash distribution to A of $100,000. Before taking into account the effect of the distribution, the $30,000 of current taxable income generates an increase in the basis of A's stock in Y Corporation from $6,000 to $36,000 and the balance in the accumulated adjustments account is increased from zero to $30,000. The distribution is treated as follows: Pursuant to § 1368(c)(1), the first $30,000, attributable to the accumulated adjustments account, is applied against the basis of the stock, reducing A's basis in the stock to $6,000; and the balance in the accumulated adjustments account is reduced to zero. Under § 1368(c)(2), the next $50,000, attributable to the accumulated earnings and profits, is taxed as a dividend. Once accumulated earnings and profits are exhausted, § 1368(c)(3) brings § 1368(b) into play and the next $6,000 is applied against basis, reducing A's basis in the stock to zero. The final $14,000 is treated as gain from the sale or exchange of the stock.

The accumulated adjustments account is a corporate account that is not apportioned among the shareholders. Treas.Reg. § 1.1368–2(a)(1). If an S corporation makes two or more distributions during the taxable year that in the aggregate exceed the accumulated adjustments account, the accumulated adjustments account determined as of the end of the year without regard to distributions during the year, is allocated among the distributions pro rata. Treas.Reg. § 1.1368–2(b). Application of this rule is illustrated by the following example, derived from Treas.Reg. § 1.1368–3, Ex. 5. Assume that the stock of X Corporation, which as of December 31, Year 3, has earnings and profits of $1,000 and an accumulated adjustments account of $400, is owned 40% by A and 60% by B. For Year 4, X Corp. has taxable income of $120, which increases its accumulated adjustments account to $520. On January 31, Year 4, X Corp. distributes $240 to A and $360 to B. On October 31, Year 4, X Corp. distributes $80 to A and $120 to B. During the year, X Corp. distributed $800, which exceeded its $520 accumulated adjustments account by $280. A's January distribution was 30% of the total distributions ($240/$800), so 30% of the accumulated adjustments account as of December 31, Year 4, or $156 is allocated to A's January distribution. B's January distribution was 45% of the total distributions for the year, so $234 of the accumulated adjustments account is allocated to that distribution. A's October distribution was 10% of the total distributions, so $52 of the accumulated adjustments account is allocated to that distribution; likewise 15% of the accumulated adjustments account, or $78 is allocated to B's October distribution. A has received a total of $208 ($156 + $52) tax-free under § 1368(c)(1) and $112 taxed as a dividend; B has received $312 ($234 + 78) tax-free and a dividend of $168. Earnings and profits are reduced to $720 to reflect the $280 of dividends.

2.2. *Distributions in Loss Years*

Although positive adjustments to a shareholder's stock basis under § 1367(a)(1) to reflect the shareholder's share of corporate income are taken into account before applying the distribution rules of § 1368(c), if the corporation incurs a loss, § 1368(d) directs that distributions be taken into account first. Consonantly, § 1368(e)(1)(C) directs that negative adjustments to the accumulated adjustments account to reflect losses incurred by the corporation be taken into account after distributions. The operation of this rule is illustrated by the following example derived from H.R. Rep. No. 104–586, 104th Cong., 2d Sess. 90–91 (1996):

> B is the sole shareholder of X Corp., an S corporation with $500 of accumulated earnings and profits and an accumulated adjustments account of $200. B's adjusted basis in the X Corp. stock on January 1, 2000, is $1,000. During 2000, X Corp. recognizes a capital gain of $200, incurs an operating loss of $900, and distributes $600 to B. Because there is a net negative adjustment for the year, no adjustment is made to the accumulated adjustments account before determining the effect of the distribution under § 1368(c). First, B's adjusted basis in the X Corp. stock is increased from $1,000 to $1,200 to reflect the capital gain. Second, $200 of the $600 distribution to B is a distribution from X Corp.'s accumulated adjustments account, reducing the accumulated adjustments account to zero. This $200 is applied against B's adjusted basis of $1,200, reducing B's basis in the stock to $1,000. The remaining $400 of the distribution is a distribution of accumulated earnings and profits. It is taxable as a dividend to B and does not reduce B's basis in the X Corp. stock. X Corp.'s earnings and profits account is reduced by $400, to $100. X Corp.'s accumulated adjustments account is then increased by $200 to reflect the recognized capital gain and reduced by $900 to reflect the operating loss, leaving a negative balance in the accumulated adjustments account on January 1, 2001, of $700. Because B's adjusted basis is $1,000, the § 1366(d) loss limitation does not apply, and B may deduct the entire $900 operating loss. As a result, B's basis in the X Corp. stock is decreased by $900, and B's basis in the stock on January 1, 2001, is $100 ($1,000 plus $200 less $200 less $900).

See Staff of the Joint Committee on Taxation, General Explanation of Tax Legislation Enacted in the 104th Congress 122–124 (Comm. Prt. 1996).

3. REDEMPTIONS

Section 1371(c) applies to redemptions by an S corporation with earnings and profits that are treated as a § 301 distribution because none of the tests for redemption treatment in § 302 or § 304 have been met. If a distribution is received by a shareholder as a redemption in exchange for stock under § 302(a) or § 303, a pro rata portion of the distribution is deemed to reduce the accumulated adjustments account. I.R.C. § 1368(e)(1)(B).[19] Rev.Rul. 95–14, 1995–1 C.B. 169, involved a redemption subject to § 1368(c) rather than § 302(a) where both the shareholder's basis in the shareholder's stock and the corporation's accumulated adjustments account exceeded the amount of the distribution. Under § 1368(c), none of the distribution was included in income, and under § 1368(e)(1)(A), the accumulated adjustments account was reduced by an amount equal to the distribution. Section 1368(e)(1)(B) was not applicable because the redemption did not qualify under either § 302(a) or § 303.

4. ELECTIONS

Section 1368(e)(3) provides an election, with the consent of all shareholders, to treat distributions as dividends from accumulated earnings and profits before reducing the accumulated adjustments account. The election may be used to prevent termination for excess passive investment income under § 1362(d)(3), or to avoid the § 1375 tax on passive investment income of an S corporation with accumulated earnings and profits, discussed below. Treas.Reg. § 1.1368–1(f)(3) also provides for an election to reduce Subchapter C earnings and profits by a deemed dividend. The amount deemed to be received as a dividend by shareholders is treated as a cash contribution back to the corporation.

PROBLEM SET 8

1. Ariel Corp. was formed seven years ago by John, who owns one-third of the stock, and Max, who owns two-thirds of the stock. Ariel Corp. did not elect S corporation status until January 1st of the current year. As of December 31st of last year Ariel Corp. had $12,000 of accumulated earnings and profits. On January 1st of the current year, John had a $2,000 basis in his stock, and Max had a $14,000 basis in his stock. For the current year, Ariel Corp. has $36,000 of taxable income from business operations. What are the tax consequences to Ariel Corp., John, and Max in the following alternative situations?

(a) In April of the current year, Ariel Corp. distributes $20,000 to John and in November, Ariel Corp. distributes $40,000 to Max.

(b) During the current year, Ariel Corp. made no distributions. Ariel Corp. validly revoked its election effective January 1, of next year. Next year Ariel Corp. has $10,000 of earnings and profits. On August 1st of next year, X Corp. distributes $12,000 to John and $24,000 to Max.

---

[19] Section 1371(c)(2) requires adjustments to the earnings and profits account in the case of redemptions, liquidations, reorganizations and other transactions to which Subchapter C is applicable. Section 1371(c)(3) provides for an adjustment to earnings and profits in the case of distributions treated as dividends under § 1368(c)(2). See Treas.Reg. § 1.1368–2(d).

B. BUILT-IN GAIN TAX

INTERNAL REVENUE CODE: Section 1374. See also section 1363(d).

REGULATIONS: Sections 1.1374–1, –2, –3, –4(a), (b), (h)(1) and (2), –7, and –9.

Technical and Miscellaneous Revenue Act of 1988, Report of the Committee on Ways and Means, House of Representatives

H.Rep. No. 100–795, 100th Cong., 2d Sess. 62–64 (1988).

A corporate level tax is imposed [by section 1374] on gain that arose prior to the conversion of a C corporation to an S corporation ("built-in gain") that is recognized by the S corporation through sale, distribution, or other disposition within 10 years after the date on which the S election took effect. [Eds: 2015 legislation shortened the recognition period of § 1374(d)(7) to five years.] The total amount of gain that must be recognized by the corporation, however, is limited to the aggregate net built-in gain of the corporation at the time of conversion to S status.

The 1986 Act [section 1374(c)(2)] provided that the amount of recognized built-in gains taken into account for any taxable year shall not exceed the excess (if any) of 1) the net unrealized built-in gain, over 2) the recognized built-in gains for prior years beginning in the 10-year recognition period. Also, recognized built-in gain is not taxed in a year to the extent that it exceeds the taxable income of the corporation for the year computed as if the corporation were a C corporation.

Under [section 1374(b)(2) and (3)], the corporation may take into account certain subchapter C tax attributes in computing the amount of tax on recognized built-in gains. Thus, for example, it may use unexpired net operating losses to offset the gain and may use business credit carryforwards to offset the tax.

Explanation of Provisions

The [1988 Act] modifies the operation of the built-in gains tax. [Section 1374(d)(2)(A)(ii)] retains the net income limitation of the [1986] Act by providing that a net recognized built-in gain for a year will not be taxed to the extent the corporation would not otherwise have taxable income for the year if it were a C corporation (determined in accordance with section 1375(b)(1)(B)). Under [section 1374(d)(2)(A)(ii)], therefore, recognized built-in gain in any post-conversion year is reduced for purposes of the built-in gains tax by any recognized built-in loss for that year, and also by any other post-conversion losses for that year.

Although the committee believes it is appropriate not to impose the built-in gains tax in a year in which the taxpayer experiences losses, the committee also believes it is appropriate to reduce the potential for taxpayers to manipulate the timing of post-conversion losses in a manner that might entirely avoid the built-in gains tax on the net unrealized built-in gain of the former C corporation. Accordingly, [section 1374(d)(2)(B)] provides that any net recognized built-in gain that is not subject to the built-in gains tax due to the net income limitation will be carried forward.

Thus, an amount equal to any net recognized built-in gain that is not subject to the built-in gains tax because of the net income limitation will be carried forward and will be subject to the built-in gains tax to the extent the corporation subsequently has other taxable income (that is not already otherwise subject to the built-in gains tax) for any taxable year within the 10 year recognition period. * * [Eds: 2015 legislation shortened the recognition period of § 1374(d)(7) to five years.]

The provision is illustrated by the following example: Corporation A elects S status on March 31, 1988. The corporation has two assets, one with a value of $200 and an adjusted basis of $0 and the other with a value of $0 and an adjusted basis of $100. It has no other items of built-in gain or loss. The corporation thus has a net unrealized built-in gain of $100. In its first taxable year for which it is an S corporation, the corporation sells both assets for their fair market value and has a net recognized built-in gain of $100. It also has an additional $100 loss from other post-conversion activities. The corporation is not subject to any built-in gains tax in that year because its net recognized built-in gain ($100) exceeds its net income determined in accordance with section 1375(b)(1)(B) ($0). In its next taxable year, the corporation has $200 of taxable income. $100 is subject to the built-in gains tax in that year, because of the carryforward of the $100 of net unrecognized built-in gain that had been untaxed due to the net income limitation.

[Section 1374(d)(8)] clarifies that the built-in gain provision applies not only when a C corporation converts to S status but also in any case in which an S corporation acquires an asset and the basis of such asset in the hands of the S corporation is determined (in whole or in part) by reference to the basis of such asset (or any other property) in the hands of the C corporation. In such cases, each acquisition of assets from a C corporation is subject to a separate determination of the amount of net built-in gain, and is subject to the provision for a separate 10-year recognition period. [Eds: 2015 legislation shortened the recognition period of § 1374(d)(7) to five years.] * * *

[Section 1374(d)(5)(A)] clarifies that, for purposes of this built-in gains tax under section 1374, any item of income which is properly taken into account for any taxable year in the recognition period but which is attributable to periods before the first taxable year for which the corporation was an S corporation is treated as a recognized built-in gain for the taxable year in which it is properly taken into account. Thus, the term "disposition of any asset" includes not only sales or exchanges but other income recognition events that effectively dispose of or relinquish a taxpayer's right to claim or receive income. For example, the term "disposition of any asset" for purposes of this provision also includes the collection of accounts receivable by a cash method taxpayer and the completion of a long-term contract performed by a taxpayer using the completed contract method of accounting.

Similarly, [section 1374(d)(5)(B)] clarifies that amounts that are allowable as a deduction during the recognition period but that are attributable to periods before the first S corporation taxable year are thus treated as recognized built-in losses in the year of the deduction.

As an example of these built-in gain and loss provisions, in the case of a cash method personal service corporation that converts to S status and that has receivables at the time of the conversion, the receivables, when received, are built-in gain items. At the same time, built-in losses would include otherwise deductible compensation paid after the conversion to the persons who performed the services that produced the receivables, to the extent such compensation is attributable to such pre-conversion services. To the extent such built-in loss items offset the built-in gains from the receivables, there would be no amount subject to the built-in gains tax.

[Section 1374(b)(2)] clarifies that capital loss carryforwards may also be used to offset recognized built-in gains.

DETAILED ANALYSIS

1.   SCOPE OF SECTION 1374

Section 1374 is intended to impose double taxation of appreciation that occurred while assets were held by a C corporation that subsequently made an S election if the corporation does not continue to hold the assets for a substantial period of time after making the S election. Double taxation is achieved by imposing a corporate level tax on recognized built-in gain with respect to assets held by the corporation at the time of conversion from C to S corporation status in addition to taxing the shareholders on the gain under § 1366. The tax also applies to built-in gain recognized on the disposition of an asset acquired from a C corporation in a nonrecognition transaction with a transferred basis to the acquiring S corporation. Section 1374 is not applicable to an S corporation that was never a C corporation or to an S corporation that has no assets that it acquired from a C corporation in a nonrecognition transaction. I.R.C. § 1374(c)(1). Nor is § 1374 applicable to assets purchased by the corporation or contributed to it during the period an S election is in effect.

Built-in gain recognized by an S corporation during the five year recognition period is subject to tax at the highest corporate tax rate under § 11, currently 21%. Recognized built-in gain is then subject to a second tax at the shareholder level as the recognized gain is passed through to shareholders under § 1366. Each shareholder's proportionate share of recognized built-in gain is reduced by the shareholder's proportionate share of the § 1374 tax. I.R.C. § 1366(f)(2). For example, if an S Corporation sells a built-in gain asset with a basis of $10 for $110, the corporation's recognized gain of $100 is subject to corporate level tax of 21%. Shareholders are allocated their proportionate share of the $100 of gain, less the $21 corporate level tax, or a net taxable gain of $79. Then, the shareholders pay a tax on the passed-through $79 at the appropriate rate under § 1, which varies depending on the shareholders' marginal tax rates and whether or not the asset was an ordinary income asset, capital asset, or § 1231 asset.

Section 1374(e) grants to the Treasury Department broad authority to promulgate Regulations to ensure that the double tax on assets that were appreciated at the time the corporation converted from C to S corporation status is not circumvented. Treas. Regs. §§ 1.1374–1 through 1.1374–10 provide detailed rules governing the application of § 1374.

2.   AMOUNT OF GAIN SUBJECT TO THE BUILT-IN GAIN TAX

The technical operation of § 1374 is somewhat convoluted. Section 1374(a) imposes the tax on the corporation's "net recognized built-in gain." The term net recognized built-in gain is, in turn, defined in § 1374(d)(2)(A) as the amount that would be the corporation's taxable income for the year if only "recognized built-in gains" and "recognized built-in losses" were taken into account (but not more than the corporation's actual taxable income for the year). "Recognized built-in gain" is defined in § 1374(d)(3) as the amount of the gain recognized with respect to any asset disposed of during the year that was held by the corporation on the first day of its first taxable year as an S corporation to the extent the property's fair market value exceeded its basis on that day. Similarly, recognized built-in loss is defined in § 1374(d)(4) as the loss recognized with respect to any asset disposed of during the year that was held by the corporation on the first day of its first taxable year as an S corporation to the extent the fair market value of the property was less than its basis on that day. Section 1374(c)(2) then limits the net recognized built-in gain taxable under § 1374(a) for the year to the excess of the corporation's "net unrealized built-in gain" over the net recognized built-in gain for previous years. "Net unrealized built-in gain" is defined in § 1374(d)(1) as the excess of the fair market value of the corporation's assets on the first day of its first taxable year as an S corporation over the aggregate basis of those assets on that day.

The purpose of this maze of statutory rules is to assure that the aggregate amount taxed under § 1374, if assets held on the day the S election was made are sold over a number of years, does not exceed the gain that would have been recognized if the corporation had sold all of its assets immediately before making the S election. Furthermore, since the precise wording of § 1374(d)(3) creates rebuttable presumptions that all recognized gain on any asset sold during the five year recognition period is built-in gain and that no loss recognized during the period is built-in loss, it is incumbent on the corporation to appraise all of its assets as of the effective date of an S election.

The limitation in § 1374(c) is illustrated in the following example. Assume that X Corporation made an S election on July 1, Year 10. At that time X Corporation had the following assets:

Asset	Basis	FMV	Built-In Gain/Loss
Blackacre	$150	$225	$ 75
Whiteacre	$300	$550	$250
Greenacre	$450	$350	($100)
			$225

In Year 12, when it has operating profits of $500, X Corporation sells Whiteacre for $650 and Greenacre for $300. The corporation recognizes a gain of $350 on Whiteacre and a loss of $150 on Greenacre. Assuming that X Corporation satisfies its burden of proof as to the properties' fair market values on July 1, Year 10, the recognized built-in gain on Whiteacre is $250 and the recognized built-in loss on Greenacre is $100. The net recognized built-in gain for the year is $150. Since the corporation's net unrealized built-in gain with respect to all of its assets is $225, the entire net recognized built-in gain is taxed under § 1374(a) in Year 12. If Blackacre is sold the following year for $225, the entire gain is net recognized built-in gain, and since the ceiling in § 1374(c)(2) is $75 ($225 net unrealized built-in gain minus $150 net recognized built-in gain from Year 12), the entire $75 gain is taxed at the corporate level under § 1374(a).

Now assume alternatively that in Year 12, X Corporation sells Blackacre for $225 and Greenacre for $300. X Corporation recognizes a gain of $75 on Blackacre and a loss of $150 on Greenacre. Assuming that X Corporation satisfies its burden of proof as to the properties' fair market values on July 1, Year 10, the recognized built-in gain on Blackacre is $75 and the recognized built-in loss on Greenacre is $100. Its net recognized built-in loss for the year is $25, and no tax is due under § 1374(a). If Whiteacre is sold the following year for $650, the corporation recognizes a gain of $350, of which $250 is net recognized built-in gain. But since the corporation's net unrealized built-in gain is only $225, only $225 of that gain is subject to corporate level tax under § 1374(a).

Although § 1371(b) generally proscribes the use by an S corporation of net operating loss carryovers from years when it was a C corporation, there is an exception if built-in gains are required to be recognized and taxed to the S corporation under § 1374. Section 1374(b)(2) permits Subchapter C NOL carryovers to offset net recognized built-in gain for a Subchapter S year solely for the purpose of computing the § 1374 tax.

Treas. Regs. § 1.1374–9 and § 1.1374–10(b)(3) provide anti-abuse rules directed to the acquisition of property for the purpose of avoiding the § 1374 tax.

3.   ACCOUNTING METHOD EFFECT ON APPLICATION OF SECTION 1374 TO PROPERTY GAINS

Treas.Reg. § 1.1374–7 provides that the inventory method maintained by a corporation will be used to determine whether goods required to be included in inventory were on hand with built-in gain at the time of conversion to S corporation status. Reliable Steel Fabricators, Inc. v.

Commissioner, T.C. Memo. 1995–293, held that the valuation of inventory work in progress on the effective date of an S election must include some profit margin for completed work, but not for raw materials.

Treas.Reg. § 1.1374–4(h) imposes the tax under § 1374 on all gains from an installment sale under § 453 recognized during or after the five-year recognition period if the sale occurred prior to or during the five-year recognition period. Tax is imposed under this provision, however, only to the extent that the gain would have been included in net recognized built-in gain if the entire gain had been recognized in the year of sale, taking into account the taxable income limitation. In determining the limitation, if the sale occurred before commencement of the recognition period (generally speaking, while the corporation was still a C Corporation), the sale is deemed to have occurred in the first year of the recognition period.

4. INCOME ITEMS OTHER THAN GAIN FROM THE SALE OF PROPERTY SUBJECT TO SECTION 1374

Section 1374(d)(3)–(4) defines built-in gain and loss as gain or loss "from the disposition of any asset." Treas.Reg. § 1.1374–4(a)(3), Ex. 1, states that income from the sale of oil under a working interest in oil and gas property held by a corporation at the time of its conversion to S corporation status is not recognized built-in gain. The example reasons that at the time of conversion to S status the corporation held a working interest in oil in place, and not the oil itself. By analogy to the example in the Regulations, Rev.Rul. 2001–50, 2001–2 C.B. 343, held that income from the sale of standing timber, or from the sale of coal or iron ore, owned by a corporation at the time of its S corporation election likewise is not recognized built-in gain under § 1374. (The ruling applies both to gains that are treated as capital gains under the special rules of § 631 and to gains that are not subject to § 631.) The ruling indicates that timber cut and sold during the recognition period is sold as inventory that "did not constitute separate assets held by the S corporation on the conversion date." The ruling also states that even though some income from the disposition of timber or coal and iron ore receives capital gains treatment under § 631, "the income received from the sale of the resulting wood product, produced coal, or produced iron ore involves the receipt of normal operating business income in the nature of rent or royalties" that is not subject to tax under § 1374. Both the example in the Regulation and the Revenue Ruling avoid the difficult valuation problem that would exist in attempting to determine built-in gain or loss of natural resources at the time of conversion to S status.

Under Treas.Reg. § 1.1374–4(b)(1) and (2), items of income and deduction attributable to prior periods that are taken into account as built-in gain items under § 1374(d)(5) include items that would have been taken into account before the beginning of the recognition period if the corporation had used the accrual method of accounting. Thus, for example, accounts receivable accrued before conversion to S Corporation status, but collected by a cash method S corporation after conversion, are treated as built-in gain items. See Treas.Reg. § 1.1374–4(b)(3), Ex. 1; Leou, M.D., P.A. v. Commissioner, T.C. Memo. 1994–393 (§ 1374 built-in gains tax applied to collection of cash method accounts receivable of a corporation that elected S status in 1988 and previously had been a C corporation).

Treas.Reg. § 1.1374–4(f) provides that cancellation of debt income or bad debt deductions attributable to debt that exists prior to the beginning of the recognition period will be treated as built-in gain or loss. In addition, built-in gain or loss includes adjustments to income required under § 481 as a result of a change in accounting method effective before the beginning of the second year of the recognition period. Treas.Reg. § 1.1374–4(d).

Under Treas.Reg. § 1.1374–4(i)(1), an S corporation's distributive share of income or loss from a partnership interest owned by the S corporation will be treated as built-in gain or loss to the extent that the item would have been so treated if it had been taken into account directly by the corporation. Among other limitations, the amount of built-in gain or loss recognized by an S corporation as its distributive share of partnership items will be limited to the corporation's built-in gain or loss in the partnership interest itself. Treas.Reg. § 1.1374–4(i)(4). Subject to an anti-abuse rule, these partnership rules do not apply if the fair market value of an S corporation's partnership interest is less than $100,000 and represents less than 10% of the partnership's capital and profits. Treas.Reg. § 1.1374–4(i)(5).

5. LIFO RECAPTURE

Section 1363(d) requires a corporation that makes a Subchapter S election and that has used the last-in-first-out (LIFO) method of inventory accounting to include in gross income for its last year as a C corporation the amount by which its "inventory amount" (i.e., the basis in its inventory) determined as if it had used the first-in-first-out (FIFO) method of inventory accounting exceeds its inventory amount under the LIFO inventory accounting method. Because the FIFO inventory amount often significantly exceeds the LIFO inventory amount, § 1363(d) frequently imposes a significant impediment to an existing corporation that maintains inventory making an S election. Treas.Reg. § 1.1363–2(b) through (d) requires LIFO recapture when a corporation that conducts business through an interest in a partnership makes a Subchapter S election.

6. APPLICATION OF BUILT-IN GAINS TAX TO QUALIFIED SUBCHAPTER S SUBSIDIARY

If an election is made under § 1361(b)(3) to treat an existing wholly owned subsidiary corporation as a qualified Subchapter S subsidiary, the subsidiary is treated as having been liquidated immediately before the election is effective. Section 332 provides nonrecognition to the parent S corporation, and § 337 provides nonrecognition to the subsidiary. The basis of the subsidiary's assets remains the same under § 334(b). Pursuant to § 381, the S corporation parent also inherits any earnings and profits of its subsidiary. If the subsidiary previously was a C corporation, the § 1374 built-in gains tax will apply to the subsidiary's assets as if the subsidiary had made a Subchapter S election. (The LIFO recapture tax under § 1363(d), if applicable, will apply immediately.) H.R. Rep. No. 104–586, 104th Cong., 2d Sess. 89 (1996).

7. BUILT-IN GAINS ATTRIBUTABLE TO A SUBCHAPTER C SUBSIDIARY

If, at the time a corporation elects Subchapter S status, it owns all of the stock of a subsidiary Subchapter C corporation, built-in gain or loss attributable to the stock will be reflected in the S corporation's net unrealized built-in gain or loss. If the subsidiary is subsequently liquidated in a transaction for which § 332 and § 337 provide nonrecognition of gain to the parent and liquidated subsidiary corporations, net unrealized built-in gain or loss attributable to the subsidiary's assets will again be added to the net unrealized built-in gain or loss of the parent, thereby potentially double-counting unrealized appreciation or depreciation attributable to the subsidiary. Treas.Reg. § 1.1374–3(b) provides an adjustment to the net unrealized built-in gain or loss of the parent S corporation to eliminate the effect of any built-in gain or loss attributable to the stock of the subsidiary that is redeemed or cancelled. The adjustment reflects only net unrealized built-in gain or loss attributable to the subsidiary stock at the time the parent corporation first became subject to the tax of § 1374 that has not resulted in recognized built-in gain or loss. The Regulations also disallow an adjustment that is duplicative of an adjustment that has been made to the pool of assets reflected in the subsidiary and its stock. Treas.Reg. § 1.1374–3(b)(2).

PROBLEM SET 9

1. Macadam Corp. was formed seven years ago and did not elect S corporation status until January 1 of this year. It conducts a parking lot business near Enormous State University. Adam is its sole shareholder. Macadam Corp. has neither Subchapter C accumulated earnings and profits nor any NOLs. As of January 1 of this year, Macadam Corp. had the following assets:

Asset	Adj. Basis	FMV
Blackacre	$60,000	$40,000
Whiteacre	$20,000	$50,000
Greenacre	$35,000	$65,000

All three parcels of land are nondepreciable gravel parking lots. What are the shareholder and corporate level tax consequences of the following alternative transactions?

(a) (1) This year, Macadam Corp. sold Whiteacre for $65,000; its taxable income for this year if it were not an S corporation would have been $100,000.

(2) This year, Macadam Corp. sold Whiteacre for $60,000; its taxable income for this year if it were not an S corporation would have been $15,000.

(b)   This year, Macadam Corp. sold Blackacre for $30,000 and sold Greenacre for $60,000; its taxable income for this year if it were not an S corporation would have been $90,000.

(c)   This year, Macadam Corp. sold Blackacre for $50,000 and sold Greenacre for $70,000; its taxable income for this year if it were not an S corporation would have been $90,000.

(d)   (1)   This year, Macadam Corp. sold Whiteacre for $60,000 and sold Greenacre for $70,000; its taxable income for this year if it were not an S corporation would have been $90,000.

(2)   This year, Macadam Corp. sold Whiteacre for $60,000 and sold Greenacre for $70,000; its taxable income for this year if it were not an S corporation would have been $90,000. Macadam Corp. had an unused NOL carryover from a prior C corporation year of $15,000.

(e)   Six years from now, Macadam Corp. sells Whiteacre for $95,000.

C.   PASSIVE INVESTMENT INCOME OF AN S CORPORATION WITH ACCUMULATED EARNINGS AND PROFITS

INTERNAL REVENUE CODE: Sections 1362(d)(3); 1375.

REGULATIONS: Sections 1.1362–2, –3(b).

There are no limitations on the type of income, e.g., passive versus active, that can be earned by an S corporation with no C corporation history. On the other hand, § 1375 imposes a tax on an S corporation with accumulated Subchapter C earnings and profits in any year in which the corporation has passive investment income in excess of 25% of gross receipts. The tax is imposed at the highest rate under § 11(b), currently 21%, on "excess net passive income," which is defined in § 1375(b) as an amount that bears the same ratio to net passive income as the passive investment income in excess of 25% of gross receipts bears to the passive investment income for the taxable year. In other words, the taxable amount is determined from the formula:

$$\text{Net Passive Investment Income} \times \frac{\text{Passive Investment Income Minus 25\% of Gross Receipts}}{\text{Passive Investment Income}}$$

"Net passive investment income" is defined as passive income (defined below) less deductible expenses incurred to produce the passive investment income. By virtue of this definition, the apportionment formula allocates expenses between the passive investment income in excess of 25% of gross receipts, which is subject to the tax, and the passive investment income that is less than 25% of gross receipts, which is not taxed. Finally, the amount subject to tax as net passive investment income is limited to the corporation's regular taxable income for the year. I.R.C. § 1375(b)(1)(B).

Suppose, for example, that an S corporation with earnings and profits from its C corporation history had gross receipts from an active business of $600,000, dividend income of $360,000, and expenses to earn the dividend income of $60,000. The formula in § 1375(b) is as follows:

$$(\$360,000 - \$60,000) \quad \times \quad \frac{\$360,000 - (960,000 \times .25)}{\$360,000} = \$100,000$$

Thus, the § 1375(a) tax is levied on the amount of $100,000, which under the formula is the corporation's "excess net passive investment income." Applying the highest rate under § 11, 21%, the tax is $21,000. Pursuant to § 1366(f)(3), the amount of dividend income passed through to the shareholders will be reduced by the tax imposed on the corporation with respect to that income.

The IRS may waive imposition of the passive investment income tax if the corporation establishes that it determined in good faith that it had no Subchapter C earnings and profits and within a reasonable period of time the corporation distributed its earnings and profits to shareholders. I.R.C. § 1375(d).

In addition, pursuant to § 1362(d)(3), an S election is terminated if the corporation has Subchapter C earnings and profits at the close of each of three consecutive taxable years following the election and during each of the three years more than 25% of the corporation's gross receipts are passive investment income.[20] This provision is intended to prevent an S corporation from utilizing accumulated C corporation earnings and profits for passive investment purposes.

A termination because of excess passive investment income is effective on the first day of the taxable year following the third consecutive year in which the corporation has disqualifying earnings and profits and investment income. Termination may be avoided if the IRS determines that the termination is inadvertent under the standards of § 1362(f).

Both the tax on passive investment income and termination of S status can be avoided either by distributing accumulated earnings and profits to shareholders as a taxable dividend prior to making the S election or by making a deemed dividend and recontribution election under Treas.Reg. § 1.1368–1(f)(3).

---

[20] The termination rule does not apply with respect to earnings and profits accumulated before the effective date of the 1982 Act. Prior to 1983 it was possible for an S corporation to accumulate earnings and profits because earnings and profits could exceed pass-through taxable income.

DETAILED ANALYSIS

1. PASSIVE INVESTMENT INCOME

For purposes of § 1362(d)(3) and § 1375, passive investment income is defined as income from royalties, rents, dividends, interest, and annuities. I.R.C. § 1362(d)(3)(C)(i). The list of passive interest income items in the predecessor to § 1362(d)(3)(C)(i) was held to be exclusive, so that gains from the sale of unimproved real estate did not constitute passive investment income for purposes of the limitation. Howell v. Commissioner, 57 T.C. 546 (1972) (acq.); Rev.Rul. 75–188, 1975–1 C.B. 276.

Passive investment income does not include interest on notes acquired in the ordinary course of business on the sale of inventory, or gross receipts from the regular conduct of a lending or finance business. I.R.C. § 1362(d)(3)(C)(ii), (iii). In addition, § 1362(d)(3)(C)(iv) excludes from passive investment income dividends that are attributable to the active conduct of a trade or business of a C corporation in which the S corporation has an 80% or greater ownership interest (as defined in § 1504(a)(2)). Treas.Reg. § 1.1362–8 provides rules for determining whether the earnings and profits of the subsidiary are "active" or "passive."

If an S corporation receives passive investment income specified in § 1362(d)(3)(C), the fact that it is an active operating company with respect to such income does not prevent application of the disqualification rule. See Zychinski v. Commissioner, 506 F.2d 637 (8th Cir.1974), in which a corporation's Subchapter S status was terminated because too high a percentage of its income was gains on sales of stocks and securities; that the corporation was a dealer did not change the result. This result is mitigated for lending and financing businesses, however, by § 1362(d)(3)(C)(iii), which excludes the interest received in the ordinary course by S corporations engaged in such a business from investment income for purposes of the termination rule. In addition, Treas.Reg. § 1.1362–2(c)(5)(ii)(B)(2) provides that the term "rents" does not include rents derived in an active trade or business of renting property, if the corporation provides significant services or incurs substantial costs in the rental business. Thus, for example the income from hotel and motel operations is not rent. Feingold v. Commissioner, 49 T.C. 461 (1968), held, however, under predecessor Regulations that rental income from summer bungalows did not fall within the "significant services" exception and constituted disqualifying income.

2. GROSS RECEIPTS

Treas.Reg. § 1.1362–2(c)(4)(i) provides that gross receipts are not the same as gross income. A corporation operating at a loss because its cost of goods sold exceeds its receipts will still have gross receipts. In contrast, proceeds from the sale or exchange of capital assets (except for stocks or securities) are taken into account in computing gross receipts only to the extent that gains from the sale or exchange of capital assets exceed losses from the sale or exchange of capital assets. I.R.C. § 1362(d)(3)(B). Gross receipts from the sale of stock or securities are taken into account only to the extent of gains. Losses from the sale of stock or securities do not offset the gains for this purpose. See Treas.Reg. § 1.1362–2(c)(4)(ii)(B). This rule prevents the corporation from acquiring and selling stocks to enhance artificially the amount of its gross receipts. Receipts that are not included in gross income because the corporation is a mere conduit are not included in gross receipts. See Kaiser's Estate v. Commissioner, T.C. Memo. 1997–88 (an insurance agency's gross receipts from its insurance business included only commissions received with respect to policies written by it; gross receipts did not include premiums collected from customers on behalf of the insurance company and remitted to the company).

PROBLEM SET 10

1.   For the current taxable year, Y Corp., which is wholly owned by A, and which has a valid S corporation election, has substantial earnings and profits from its C corporation history. It has gross receipts from an active business of $300,000, deductions attributable to the active business of $100,000, dividend income of $120,000, capital gains on the sale of publicly traded stocks of $60,000, and expenses to earn the dividend income of $30,000. What are the tax consequences to Y Corp. and to A?

D. POLICY ASPECTS OF THE TREATMENT OF SUBCHAPTER S CORPORATIONS WITH A SUBCHAPTER C HISTORY

The policy basis of the various rules dealing with Subchapter S corporations that have previously operated as C corporations is not clearly articulated in the legislative history of the provisions. With respect to the built-in gain rules, the provisions can perhaps best be understood as a variation on the *General Utilities* problem. The conversion from C status to S status and the consequent move to a single tax regime is in many ways like a liquidation of the corporation and a transfer of the assets out of corporate solution. If this change in taxing pattern had been achieved through a liquidation, § 336 would have required recognition of gain at the corporate level, followed by a shareholder level gain. In the Subchapter S situation, rather than impose an immediate tax at the time of conversion, the statute defers the tax until a sale of the assets and in effect turns that deferral into an exemption if the assets are held for five years.

As to the passive income limitations, if the liquidation model is continued, on a liquidation the accumulated but undistributed corporate level earnings would not be subject to dividend taxation when distributed in liquidation, but would incur a shareholder level capital gains tax, the size of which would depend on the stock basis. Since the conversion to S status does not result in any shareholder level tax, Congress apparently felt that it was inappropriate to allow those earnings, unreduced by any second level tax, to be reinvested in assets generating passive income unrelated to the basic business operations of the corporation. Initially, the sanction is an additional level of tax, with the corporation ultimately losing its S status if the situation goes on for too long.

If conversion from C to S status were treated as a liquidation of the old corporation and formation of a new corporation, the rules designed to safeguard the double tax regime with respect to gains accrued during the time the corporation was a C corporation could be eliminated and Subchapter S simplified. The Treasury Department advanced such a proposal in 1995 as part of a broader debate on the extent to which pass-through treatment should be available to small businesses, however organized, in light of the phenomenal growth in the popularity of limited liability companies, which provide limited liability for all members under state law but partnership taxation under federal tax laws. The Treasury Department recommended to Congress that S corporations generally should be permitted to elect to be taxed as a partnership notwithstanding that the corporation was organized as such under state law. Furthermore, the election would not be treated as a liquidation and accrued gains would not be taxed at that time. To offset the revenue loss from this proposal, the Treasury Department further recommended that Congress should consider treating an S election by an existing C corporation as a constructive liquidation. This proposal mirrored a recommendation of the Joint Committee on Taxation in 1990. See Statement of Leslie B. Samuels, Assistant Secretary (Tax Policy), Department of the Treasury, Before the House Committee on Ways and Means (July 28, 1995).

SECTION 6.   SECTION 199A

INTERNAL REVENUE CODE: Section 199A.

REGULATIONS: Sections 1.199A–1, –3, –5, –6.

Section 199A was added by the 2017 Tax Act and applies for taxable years beginning after December 31, 2018, and before December 31, 2025. I.R.C. § 199A(i). The provision allows taxpayers other than C corporations to deduct up to 20% of the "qualified business income" from qualified pass-through businesses, including sole proprietorships, tax partnerships, and "S" corporations. I.R.C. § 199A(b)(2). The § 199A deduction is not an itemized deduction, but it reduces taxable income and does not reduce adjusted gross income. § 63(b)(3), (d)(3).

Section 199A is highly complex and was enacted when the corporate tax rate was reduced to 21% in order to provide a tax cut for pass-through businesses.

DETAILED ANALYSIS

1.   QUALIFIED TRADE OR BUSINESS

A "qualified trade or business" means any trade or business other than those specifically excepted. I.R.C. § 199A(d)(1). The trade or business of being an employee is never a qualified business. Similarly, although located in a different subsection of § 199A, "reasonable compensation paid to the taxpayer by any qualified trade or business of the taxpayer for services rendered with respect to the trade or business" is not qualified business income. I.R.C. § 199A(c)(4)(A). The legislative history indicates that this provision is intended to apply only to S corporation shareholders, and the final Regulations take this approach. The phrase "reasonable compensation" evokes the problem of S corporation shareholders deliberately limiting compensation in order to reduce employment taxes. See Joseph Radtke, S.C. v. United States, 712 F. Supp. 143 (E.D. Wis. 1989), aff'd, 895 F.2d 1196 (7th Cir. 1990); Rev.Rul. 74–44, 1974–1 C.B. 287.

Certain "specified service trade or businesses" (SSTBs) are also not qualifying businesses, but for this category, a threshold tied to taxpayer income applies (described in greater detail below). An SSTB means any trade or business involving the performance of services in the fields of health, law, accounting, actuarial science, performing arts, consulting, athletics, financial services, brokerage services, or any trade or business where the principal asset of such trade or business is the reputation or skill of 1 or more of its employees" and involving "the performance of services that consist of investing and investment management, trading, or dealing in securities, partnership interest, or commodities." I.R.C. § 199A(d)(2). The SSTB list cross-references § 1202(e)(3)(A), but the engineering and architecture fields contained in that section are not included in the § 199A list of SSTBs.

Regulations finalized in 2019 attempt to define the various terms used in the SSTB list. For example, "performance of service in the field of law" means "the provision of services by lawyers, paralegals, legal arbitrators, mediators and similar professionals in their capacity as such . . . [It] does not include the provision of services that do not require skills unique to the field of law, for example, . . . The provision of services by printers, delivery services, or stenography services." Treas.Reg. § 1.199A–5(b)(2)(iii). To prevent taxpayers from attempting to circumvent the SSTB limitation through "cracking" a business into separate components in order to move elements out of the SSTB category,[21] Treas.Reg. § 1.199A–5(c)(2)(i) provides that an SSTB includes "any trade or business that provides 80 percent or more of its property or services to an SSTB if there is 50 percent or more common ownership of the trades or businesses." Further, if a business provides less than 80% of its property or services to an SSTB, but there is 50% or more common ownership with an SSTB, the property or services provided to the SSTB are treated as part of the SSTB. Treas.Reg. § 1.199A–5(c)(2)(ii). A de minimis rule does apply to ensure that a trade or business will not be an SSTB "because it provides a small amount of services in a specified service activity." Preamble to the Prop. § 199A Regs., 83 Fed. Reg. 40884 (Aug. 16, 2018). If the trade or business has gross receipts of $25 million or less, and less than 10% of the gross receipts are attributable to SSTB activities, the trade or business will not be an SSTB; if the trade or business has gross receipts greater than $25 million, it will not be an SSTB if less than 5% of its gross receipts are attributable to SSTB activities. Treas.Reg. § 1.199A–5(c)(1).

---

[21] See Gregg D. Polsky, Taxing Litigation: Federal Tax Concerns of Personal Injury Plaintiffs and Their Lawyers, 22 Fla. Tax Rev. 120 (2018).

2.   QUALIFIED BUSINESS INCOME

Qualified business income (QBI) means the "net amount of qualified items of income, gain, deduction, and loss with respect to any qualified trade or business of the taxpayer." I.R.C. § 199A(c)(1). The amount is determined separately for each trade or business and may be a negative amount for a particular business. See Treas.Reg. § 1.199A–1(d)(2)(iii). Taxpayers have some ability to aggregate trades or businesses, and then treat the aggregate as a single trade or business, but under rules that differ from those used for § 469 or § 465. See Treas.Reg. § 1.199A–4.

QBI items must be effectively connected with a U.S. trade or business and must be "included or allowed in determining taxable income for the taxable year." I.R.C. § 199A(c)(3)(A). When losses previously disallowed under § 1366(d), § 465, § 469 or § 461(*l*) become allowable, they are taken into account for computing QBI on a first-in, first-out basis. Treas.Reg. § 1.199A–3(b)(1)(iv), (v). Disallowed losses that derive from taxable years ending before January 1, 2018, are, however, not taken into account for purposes of computing QBI.

Certain items are not eligible to be included in QBI; these include short- or long-term capital gains and losses; dividends, dividend equivalents and payments in lieu of dividends; interest income, other than business interest income; and gains and losses from certain commodities transactions, foreign currencies, and certain notional principal contracts; amounts received from a non-business annuity; and "[a]ny item of deduction or loss properly allocable" to the preceding list. I.R.C. § 199A(c)(3)(B). Finally, qualified REIT dividends and qualified publicly traded partnership income are not treated as "qualified business income," although such items are eligible for the § 199A deduction via another subsection. I.R.C. § 199A(b)(1)(B), (c)(1).

3.   COMPUTATION FOR TAXPAYERS ABOVE THRESHOLD
     LIMITATIONS

In order for a taxpayer to determine the § 199A deduction, the taxpayer must apply a percentage to the net QBI of each of the taxpayer's qualifying businesses. That percentage is the lesser of (1) 20% or (2) the greater of (a) 50% of the W-2 wages of the qualifying business or (b) 25% of the W-2 wages of the qualifying business, plus 2.5% of the "unadjusted basis immediately after acquisition of all qualified property." I.R.C. § 199A(b)(2). (As discussed below, taxpayers under a certain income threshold use 20% as the percentage without the need to refer to W-2 wages or unadjusted basis.) W-2 wages are essentially the compensation paid to employees of the business and as to which the employee receives an information return. I.R.C. § 199A(b)(4); Treas.Reg. § 1.199A–2(b)(2). "Qualified property" is depreciable tangible property that is "held by, and available for use in" the qualified business, used "at any point during the taxable year in the production of qualified business income," and whose depreciable period has not ended before the close of the taxable year. I.R.C. § 199A(b)(6)(A). "Depreciable period" is defined as the later of 10 years after the property is placed in service or "the last day of the last full year of the applicable recovery period" that applies under § 168 (ignoring the alternative depreciation system).

Section 199A(f)(1)(A) states that the deduction "shall be applied at the partner or shareholder" level, but, for tax items derived from an S corporation, the S corporation determines whether there is a qualifying business as well as the shareholder's allocable amount of QBI. Treas.Reg. § 1.199A–6(b)(2) provides guidance under which the S corporation must determine whether it is engaged in one or more trades or businesses, determine whether any are SSTBs, determine the QBI for each business, and determine the W-2 wages and unadjusted basis of qualified property. Section 199A(f)(1)(A)(ii) states that "each partner or shareholder shall take into account such person's share of each qualified item of income, gain, deduction, and loss." Each shareholder must also be assigned a share of the S corporation's W-2 wages and unadjusted basis in order to complete the § 199A computation. The statute provides that S corporation W-2 wages and unadjusted basis are allocated using "the shareholder's pro rata share of an item." The S corporation must report this information to its shareholders. Treas.Reg. § 1.199A–6(b)(3).

If a business has a net negative QBI, the taxpayer must offset the net negative QBI against the positive QBI of the taxpayer's other qualifying trades or businesses "in proportion to the relative amounts of net QBI in the trades or businesses with positive QBI." Treas.Reg. § 1.199A–1(d)(2)(iii)(A). When a trade or business produces a net negative QBI, its W-2 wages and the unadjusted basis of its qualified property are not taken into account and are not carried over to subsequent years. Treas.Reg. § 1.199A–1(d)(2)(iii)(A). If, considering all of a taxpayer's qualifying businesses, the taxpayer has an overall negative QBI, the loss is carried over and treated as "negative QBI from a separate trade or business in the succeeding taxable year." Treas.Reg. § 1.199A–1(d)(2)(iii)(B). See I.R.C. § 199A(c)(2).

After a taxpayer has computed the potentially deductible amount of QBI for each business, the amounts from each business are then aggregated into the "combined qualified business income amount." I.R.C. § 199A(b)(1). Even after the taxpayer determines the "combined qualified business income," an overall limitation may reduce the taxpayer's ability to deduct the entire amount. I.R.C. § 199A(a). The final deduction is the lesser of (1) the taxpayer's combined qualified business income or (2) 20% of the excess of the taxpayer's taxable income over the taxpayer's net capital gain. I.R.C. § 199A(a).

4.   THRESHOLD LIMITATIONS

Taxpayers below certain income thresholds benefit through the relaxation of two of the rules discussed above. First, such taxpayers are able to treat SSTBs as qualified businesses. Second, such taxpayers are able to take 20% of their net positive QBI without being subject to the W-2 or unadjusted basis limitation. These benefits are lost gradually (and through complicated formulas) for taxpayers within a particular taxable income range. This range begins at $157,500 ($315,000 for joint filers), and the benefits are lost completely at $207,500 ($415,000 for joint filers). I.R.C. § 199A(b)(3), (d)(3), (e)(2). These ranges are indexed for inflation after 2018.

PROBLEM SET 11

1. Zaha is an architect, and her taxable income has for many years placed her in the highest tax rate bracket. She is the sole owner of Elite Designs Co., an S corporation, which has been a valid S corporation since inception. During 2019, Elite Designs has the following items:

Income

Receipts from consulting work	$5,000,000
LTCG from sale of investment asset	$ 10,000

Payments

Wages paid to Zara	$1,500,000
Wages paid to other employees	$ 500,000
Supplies	$ 200,000

In addition, Elite Designs owns the building where the consulting is performed. Elite Designs purchased the building in 2018 for $900,000; assume it properly takes $25,000 of depreciation deductions each year. Determine the amount, if any, of Zaha's § 199A deduction for 2019. How would your answer change if Zaha owned 50% of Elite Designs and a different individual, Hadid, owned the other 50%?

SECTION 7. POLICY ASPECTS OF SUBCHAPTER S

Subchapter S raises significant questions both in theory and in practice. Given the fundamental decision to have a separate corporate income tax, the question is whether there are situations that justify departure from that model. The argument in favor of Subchapter S is that taxes should be as neutral as possible as respects the form of doing business for a closely held enterprise. That argument may justify the special pass-through treatment of S corporations. On the other hand, Subchapter S contains significant differences from the other major form of pass-through enterprise, the partnership, which create significant advantages and disadvantages depending upon particular circumstances. Compared to partnerships, Subchapter S provides a less complex device for pass-through taxation of a joint enterprise. The differences between Subchapters K and S are substantial, however, and require tax motivated choices between the forms of doing business. Does the reduced complexity of Subchapter S justify its variations from the partnership model?

While the partnership rules of Subchapter K adopt an aggregate approach to many issues, with attendant complexity attributable to the aggregate treatment of liabilities and the partners' aggregate shares of the partnership's inside basis if they so elect, the S corporation can be characterized as an entity with a specific pass-through of designated income and loss items. One significant difference for certain types of investments arises from the inclusion of entity level debt in the basis of a partner's partnership interest, while entity level debt is not included in the basis of an S corporation's shareholders stock. The aggregate versus entity distinction also is apparent in the divergent treatment of distributions of appreciated property; distributions by partnerships do not trigger recognition by the partnership and the partners take a carryover basis; and distributions of appreciated property by an S corporation require recognition of gain by all the shareholders and the recipient shareholder receives a step-up in basis to fair market value. Entity level recognition by the S corporation avoids the partnership problems addressed in § 751(b) and the need for adjustments to aggregate basis provided for in § 734, both highly complex provisions. On the other hand, the entity level recognition operates as a disincentive to non-pro rata distributions since the non-recipient shareholders recognize current gain and the tax effect of that recognition may not be reversible until liquidation (by means of a capital loss deduction).

These disparate distribution rules also affect liquidations. Subject to the exceptions of § 751(b), a partnership can be liquidated and assets distributed to the partners without current taxation. The partners substitute their outside basis in their partnership interests for the partnership's basis in the assets distributed to them. The liquidation of an S corporation is subject to the normal rules of Subchapter C (§ 331 and § 336), which require recognition of gain at the corporate level. In tandem, these provisions require recognition of at least corporate level gain on distributed appreciated assets, and perhaps additional gain at the shareholder level depending upon the relationship between the shareholders' stock bases and the value of distributed property. As a result of the taxable nature of the transaction, the shareholders take a fair market value basis in the distributed assets.

Similar disparities exist in comparing the redemption (under § 302) of an S corporation shareholder with the retirement of a partner. A distribution of appreciated property to an S corporation shareholder in a stock redemption will result in recognition of gain by the corporation. The gain is passed through to all shareholders in proportion to stockholdings, while only the redeemed shareholder receives the distributed property. The redeemed shareholder may or may not recognize gain depending on the basis of redeemed stock. A distribution of appreciated property in retirement of a partner's partnership interest will not trigger partnership level recognition of gain or loss, unless § 751 assets (generally ordinary income items) are involved. The distributee partner will recognize gain, loss, or in some cases (if § 736(a) is involved) both ordinary gain and a capital loss.

The entity approach to Subchapter S also affects the potential for shifting income from one shareholder to another as a result of a contribution of appreciated property to the corporation. Section 704(c) operates in Subchapter K to prevent a shift of pre-contribution appreciation or losses to the non-contributing partners by requiring that the difference between basis and fair market value at the time of contribution be reflected in allocations to the partners. There is no provision for equivalent adjustments under Subchapter S where each shareholder is required to report the shareholder's proportionate share of corporate income and loss items.

The restrictions of Subchapter S on the number and types of S corporation shareholders may also be analyzed as a response to perceived problems of complexity. Although Subchapter K demonstrates that pass-through accounting on a large scale is a possible alternative for income tax purposes, the limited number of permissible shareholders of an S corporation and the restrictions on the types of permissible shareholders, excluding other pass-through entities and corporations, substantially reduces the burden of accounting for the pass-through of S corporation income.

The goal of simplicity in Subchapter S creates, however, its own complexity. Differences in the pass-through treatment under Subchapters K and S require careful planning choices regarding the choice of entity. The flexibility permitted by Subchapter K with respect to allocations of income and loss items can be contrasted with the rather rigid requirements of a single class of stock under Subchapter S. Shareholder attempts to create preferential interests in an S corporation through the use of purported debt instruments have been a source of considerable litigation. Additional difficulty is created by the detailed requirements for electing S corporation status. Failure to comply with the statutory requirements regarding timing and form can defeat the attempts of well-intentioned taxpayers to elect S corporation status. No such requirements are imposed on operation as a partnership, an entity also requiring participants to report their share of entity level income and loss, though the question of entity classification represents a somewhat similar problem. Nevertheless, provisions for notifying the IRS of an intent to operate a corporation as a pass-through entity and requiring shareholders to consent to the pass-through of tax significant items are warranted.

Beyond the question of the relationship between Subchapter S and partnership taxation, the Subchapter S provisions raise the more fundamental issue of the extent to which operation in corporate form should be coupled with a double level of tax on distributions. Absent a decision to adopt some general form of integration of corporate and individual taxes, why should closely held corporations with only common stock be subject to a single level of tax while all other corporate entities operate in a two tax world? Do these characteristics have any bearing on whether double tax or single tax is appropriate?

PART VIII

TAXATION OF PARTNERS
AND PARTNERSHIPS

easier to answer than the former, we will first address the issue of whether a business entity, the existence of which has already been established, will be classified as a partnership.

A. PARTNERSHIP VERSUS CORPORATION

INTERNAL REVENUE CODE: Sections 761(a); 7701(a)(2), (3); 7704.

REGULATIONS: Sections 301.7701–1(a) and (b), –2(a), (b)(1)–(7), –3(a), (b)(1), (c)(1)(i)–(iv).

A joint enterprise engaged in a profit seeking activity—a business entity—generally must be classified for federal income tax purposes as either a partnership or a corporation. An entity might so closely resemble a corporation in its structure and operation that it reasonably might be treated as a corporation for tax purposes even though not formally organized as a corporation. Limited liability companies (LLCs) are one such form of business organization that has many of the characteristics of a corporation. Additional classification issues arise because not all partnerships are the same. The substantive rights and liabilities of the partners, as well as the organizational structure of general partnerships and of limited partnerships are quite different. Furthermore, in recent years new forms of partnership, such as the limited liability partnership (LLP), a hybrid between a general partnership and a limited partnership have emerged.

Both limited liability companies and limited partnerships have many characteristics in common with corporations. The resemblance to corporations of these forms of business organization raises the question whether they should be taxable as partnerships or as corporations. Although the Internal Revenue Code provides that the corporate tax applies not only to organizations that are "corporations" under state law but also to any organization that is an "association" as defined in § 7701(a)(3), the statutory definition of "association" is not particularly helpful. The courts and the IRS were forced to grapple with the definition of an "association" through years of litigation and administrative action. The IRS ultimately abandoned the quest by promulgating Regulations that provide business entities that are not formally organized as corporations under governing law with the ability to elect whether to be treated for federal tax purposes as a partnership or as a corporation.

Rules and Regulations, Department of the Treasury, Internal Revenue Service, Simplification of Entity Classification Rules

T.D. 8697, 1997–1 C.B. 215.

Explanation of Provisions

Section 7701(a)(2) of the Code defines a partnership to include a syndicate, group, pool, joint venture, or other unincorporated organization, through or by means of which any business, financial operation, or venture is carried on, and that is not a trust or estate or a corporation. Section 7701(a)(3) defines a corporation to include associations, joint-stock companies, and insurance companies.

The existing regulations for classifying business organizations as associations (which are taxable as corporations under section 7701(a)(3) or as partnerships under section 7701(a)(2) are based on the historical differences under local law between partnerships and corporations. Treasury and the IRS believe that those rules have become increasingly formalistic. This document replaces those rules with a much simpler approach that generally is elective.

As stated in the preamble to the proposed regulations, in light of the increased flexibility under an elective regime for the creation of organizations classified as partnerships, Treasury and the IRS will continue to monitor carefully the uses of partnerships in the international context and will take appropriate action when partnerships are used to achieve results that are inconsistent with the policies and rules of particular Code provisions or of U.S. tax treaties.

A.   Summary of the Regulations

Section 301.7701–1 provides an overview of the rules applicable in determining an organization's classification for federal tax purposes. The first step in the classification process is to determine whether there is a separate entity for federal tax purposes. The regulations explain that certain joint undertakings that are not entities under local law may nonetheless constitute separate entities for federal tax purposes; however, not all entities formed under local law are recognized as separate entities for federal tax purposes. Whether an organization is treated as an entity for federal tax purposes is a matter of federal tax law, and does not affect the rights and obligations of its owners under local law. For example, if a domestic limited liability company with a single individual owner is disregarded as an entity separate from its owner under § 301.7701–3, its individual owner is subject to federal income tax as if the company's business was operated as a sole proprietorship.

An organization that is recognized as a separate entity for federal tax purposes is either a trust or a business entity (unless a provision of the Code expressly provides for special treatment, such as the Qualified Settlement Fund rules (§ 1.468B) or the Real Estate Mortgage Investment Conduit (REMIC) rules, see section 860A(a)). The regulations provide that trusts generally do not have associates or an objective to carry on business for profit. The distinctions between trusts and business entities, although restated, are not changed by these regulations.

Section 301.7701–2 clarifies that business entities that are classified as corporations for federal tax purposes include corporations denominated as such under applicable law, as well as associations, joint-stock companies, insurance companies, organizations that conduct certain banking activities, organizations wholly owned by a state, organizations that are taxable as corporations under a provision of the Code other than section 7701(a)(3), and certain organizations formed under the laws of a foreign jurisdiction (including a U.S. possession, territory, or commonwealth).

* * *

Any business entity that is not required to be treated as a corporation for federal tax purposes (referred to in the regulation as an eligible entity) may choose its classification under the rules of § 301.7701–3. Those rules provide that an eligible entity with at least two members can be classified as either a partnership or an association, and that an eligible entity with a single member can be classified as an association or can be disregarded as an entity separate from its owner. * * *

In order to provide most eligible entities with the classification they would choose without requiring them to file an election, the regulations provide default classification rules that aim to match taxpayers' expectations (and thus reduce the number of elections that will be needed). The regulations adopt a passthrough default for domestic entities, under which a newly formed eligible entity will be classified as a partnership if it has at least two members, or will be disregarded as an entity separate from its owner if it has a single owner. The default for foreign entities is based on whether the members have limited liability. Thus a foreign eligible entity will be classified as an association if all members have limited liability. A foreign eligible entity will be classified as a partnership if it has two or more members and at least one member does not have limited liability; the entity will be disregarded as an entity separate from its owner if it has a single owner and that owner does not have limited liability. * * * An entity's default classification continues until the entity elects to change its classification by means of an affirmative election.

An eligible entity may affirmatively elect its classification on Form 8832, Entity Classification Election. The regulations require that the election be signed by each member of the entity or any officer, manager, or member of the entity who is authorized to make the election and who represents to having such authorization under penalties of perjury. An election will not be accepted unless it includes all of the required information * * *.

Taxpayers are reminded that a change in classification, no matter how achieved, will have certain tax consequences that must be reported. For example, if an organization classified as an association elects to be classified as a partnership, the organization and its owners must recognize gain, if any, under the rules applicable to liquidations of corporations.

B. Discussion of Comments on the General Approach and Scope of the Regulations

Several comments requested clarification with regard to the rules for determining when an owner of an interest in an organization will be respected as a bona fide owner for federal tax purposes. Some commentators * * * relying on Rev.Rul. 93–4, 1993–1 C.B. 225, suggested that if two wholly-owned subsidiaries of a common parent were the owners of an organization, those owners would not be respected as bona fide owners and the organization would be treated as having only one owner (the common parent). Although the determination of whether an organization has more than one owner is based on all the facts and circumstances, the fact that some or all of the owners of an organization are under common control does not require the common parent to be treated as the sole owner. Consistent with this approach, Rev.Rul. 93–4 treated two wholly owned subsidiaries as associates and then classified the foreign entity based on the four corporate characteristics under section 7701. While these four factors will no longer apply with the adoption of the regulations, determining whether the subsidiaries are associates continues to be an issue.

* * *

C. Discussion of Comments Relating to the Elective Regime

Most of the commentators agreed that the default rules included in the proposed regulations generally would match taxpayers' expectations. * * *

Some commentators requested that taxpayers be allowed to make classification elections with their first tax returns. The regulations retain the requirement that elections be made at the beginning of the taxable year. Treasury and the IRS continue to believe that it is appropriate to determine an entity's classification at the time that it begins its operations. Taxpayers can specify the date on which an election will be effective, provided that date is not more than 75 days prior to the date on which the election is filed (irrespective of when the interest was acquired) and not more than 12 months after the date the election was filed. * * *

The regulations limit the ability of an entity to make multiple classification elections by prohibiting more than one election to change an entity's classification during any sixty month period. * * * [T]he regulations permit the Commissioner to waive the application of the sixty month limitation by letter ruling. However, waivers will not be granted unless there has been more than a fifty percent ownership change. The sixty month limitation only applies to a change in classification by election; the limitation does not apply if the organization's business is actually transferred to another entity.

* * *

DETAILED ANALYSIS

1. LIMITED LIABILITY ENTITIES

1.1. *Limited Partnerships*

For many years prior to 1997, under a prior version of Treas.Reg. § 301.7701–2 (the *"Kintner"* Regulations), six characteristics were taken into account as the criteria for distinguishing corporations from other organizations: (1) the presence of associates; (2) an objective to carry on business and divide the gains therefrom; (3) continuity of life, i.e., the death, resignation, etc., of a member does not cause the dissolution of the organization; (4) centralization of management, i.e., fewer than all the members have exclusive authority to make management decisions; (5) limited liability; and (6) free transferability of interests. To be classified as an association taxable as a corporation, the organization was required to have had more corporate than noncorporate characteristics. The corporate characteristics common to the types of organizations being compared were ignored, and since the presence of associates and an objective to carry on a business for profit are common to both corporations and partnerships, the determination whether an organization is an association taxable as a corporation or is a partnership was made with reference only to the other four characteristics.

The test of the prior Regulations virtually always resulted in classification of a limited partnership as a partnership, but the route to that end was somewhat torturous. A limited partner is liable for partnership debts only to the extent of the partner's capital contribution, plus any additional amounts that the partner has agreed to contribute. Thus, there is a strong resemblance to the limited liability of corporate shareholders. On the other hand, all limited partnerships must have at least one general partner who is fully liable for debts of the partnership.

Limited partners have no right to participate in the day-to-day management of the partnership's business; that is the responsibility of the general partner. The limited partners are entitled to examine the partnership's books, receive accountings, and vote on changes in the partnership agreement, which are rights similar to the rights of corporate shareholders. While general partnership interests, because they represent an agency relationship, are not freely transferable—they cannot be sold and bought like corporate stock—limited partnership interests may or may not be transferable, subject to some statutory limitations, depending on the terms of the partnership agreement.

Finally, the death or withdrawal of a limited partner does not terminate the partnership; both the entity and its business continue. The death, bankruptcy, or withdrawal of a general partner, however, generally terminates the formal existence of the legal entity under state law, even if the partnership agreement provides that the business will be continued in a newly constituted successor partnership without interruption.

For many years, all of these attributes of limited partnerships made this form of business organization a popular vehicle for assembling groups of investors who desired limited liability, transferable interests, and professional management of the business, while avoiding treatment as a corporation for tax purposes. In addition, limited partnerships historically enjoyed great popularity as the organization of choice for tax shelters because of the flow through of tax losses. Although amendments to the Internal Revenue Code enacted in the Tax Reform Act of 1986, most particularly the restrictions on deductions from passive activities under § 469, discussed in Chapter 23, generally reduced the availability of tax shelters, these changes did not totally eliminate the desirability of organizing ventures that will produce tax losses in the limited partnership form. After 1986, the limited partnership found a new role, providing a substitute for the corporate form of conducting profitable businesses. The changes in the rate structure introduced by the Tax Reform Act of 1986 increased the relative tax burden on corporate profits by establishing a corporate tax rate higher than the individual rate. In addition, certain technical changes were made in the taxation of gain at the corporate level that increased the tax burden on corporate distributions. This increased taxation of profits realized through the corporate form of business organization made the limited partnership form of investment attractive for potentially profitable operations. However, over a relatively short period beginning in the late 1980s, every state adopted limited liability company statutes, creating a wholly new form of business entity that could be taxed as a partnership rather than a corporation. Because the limited liability company form offers significant state law advantages compared to the limited partnership form, over the last twenty-five years most business organizations that are taxed as partnerships have been formed as limited liability companies.

1.2. *Limited Liability Companies and the Check-the-Box Regulations*

The first modern limited liability company (LLC) statute was enacted in Wyoming in the mid-1980s. The Wyoming statute was carefully crafted to produce partnership classification under the *Kintner* Regulations then in effect. Rev.Rul. 88–76, 1988–2 C.B. 360, dealt with classification under the Wyoming statute. Under state law, the limited liability company could be managed either by the members, in proportion to their capital contributions or by a designated manager. The limited liability company in the Ruling was managed by three designated managers. Under the governing statute, members of the limited liability company could transfer their interests only with the unanimous consent of all other members. If consent was not granted, the assignee could not participate in management, but was entitled to share in profits and a return of contributions. State law provided for the dissolution of the limited liability company upon (1) the expiration of its charter, (2) unanimous consent of the members, or (3) the death, retirement, resignation, expulsion, bankruptcy, or other termination of the membership of a member, unless under a provision in the articles of organization all remaining members consented to continue the business. The IRS ruled that the limited liability company lacked continuity of life because consent to continue the business upon withdrawal of a member was not assured. Free transferability of interests did not exist because the members did not have the right to transfer all of the attributes of their membership interests without the consent of the other members. Accordingly, even though the entity had limited liability and centralized management, it was classified as a partnership.

The rest of the states enacted LLC statutes in the following decade. Some statutes, like the Wyoming statute, were so called "bullet-proof" statutes; that is, partnership classification was inevitable because two of the three remaining determinative factors under the *Kintner* Regulations always would be noncorporate characteristics. Other statutes were flexible. They permitted the organizers to choose to provide centralized management, free transferability of interests, and continuity of life if they so desired, although all of the flexible LLC statutes were constructed to provide default rules regarding these characteristics that were noncorporate. Thus, the typical flexible LLC statute would provide that (1) the LLC was to be managed by all the members, (2) interests were not transferable, and (3) the organization would "dissolve" upon the death, incompetence, or bankruptcy of any member, but the LLC statute would permit the members to vary any of these terms by agreement.

As the states successively enacted limited liability company statutes, the IRS published a string of "cookie cutter" rulings with respect to classification under each state's statute. In every case, the ruling either held that the limited liability company was a partnership under the Regulations because it was formed pursuant to a bullet-proof statute or could be classified as either a corporation or a partnership, depending on how the LLC was organized. See, e.g., Rev.Rul. 93–5, 1993–1 C.B. 227 (Virginia LLC was a partnership because pursuant to statute the LLC dissolved upon the death, resignation, expulsion, bankruptcy or dissolution of any member unless the business was continued by unanimous consent, and an assignee of a member's interest does not become a substituted member with all of the assignee's rights unless the remaining members approved); Rev.Rul. 93–53, 1993–2 C.B. 312 (Florida limited liability company could be either a partnership or a corporation). In addition to the limited partnership and LLC, a number of states have enacted "limited liability partnership" statutes. A limited liability partnership (LLP) is a general partnership in which the traditional joint and several liability of general partners in tort, particularly for professional malpractice, has been eliminated.

The cascade of "cookie-cutter" rulings dealing with the status of LLCs under various state statutes, all of which permitted substantially the same combination of tax and nontax attributes, indicated that no significant policy goal was served by requiring closely held unincorporated organizations to meet formalistic tests to avoid classification as a corporation. Accordingly, in 1997, the IRS and Treasury amended Treas.Reg. §§ 301.7701–1 through 301.7701–4 to simplify the classification of business organizations for federal tax income purposes. These rules, which are colloquially referred to as the "check-the-box" Regulations, apply to all unincorporated business entities, including limited partnerships, LLCs, business trusts, and sole proprietorships.

2. PUBLICLY TRADED PARTNERSHIPS

2.1. *General*

Section 7704 generally treats as a corporation any partnership the interests in which are traded on an established securities market or are readily tradable on a secondary market or a substantial equivalent of a secondary market. The provision, in fact, only applies to limited partnerships and limited liability companies because under state law general partnership interests cannot be traded. The legislative history explains that a secondary market for partnership interests exists if prices are regularly quoted by brokers or dealers who are making a market for such interests. Occasional accommodation trades of partnership interests, a buy-sell agreement between the partners (without more), or the occasional repurchase or redemption by the partnership or acquisition by a general partner of partnership interests will not be treated as a secondary market or the equivalent thereof. However, if the partners have regular and ongoing opportunities to dispose of their interests, the interests are tradable on the equivalent of a secondary market. Meaningful restrictions imposed on the right to transfer partnership interests may preclude classification as a corporation, even if some interests are actually traded. See H.Rep. 100–495, 100th Cong., 1st Sess. 943–950 (1987).

2.2. *Meaning of "Publicly Traded"*

Treas.Reg. § 1.7704–1(b) and (c) provide definitions of the statutory terms "established securities market" and "readily tradable on a secondary market or the substantial equivalent of a secondary market." Established securities markets include not only exchanges but also interdealer quotation systems. A secondary market or a substantial equivalent of a secondary market exists if the partners are readily able to buy, sell, or exchange their interests in a manner that is economically comparable to trading on an established securities market. Interests are readily tradable on a secondary market or its equivalent if (1) firm quote trading exists, even if only one person makes available bid or offer quotes; (2) the holder of an interest has a readily available, regular, and ongoing opportunity to sell or exchange such interest through a public means of obtaining or providing information of offers to buy, sell, or exchange interests; or (3) buyers and sellers have the opportunity to buy, sell, or exchange interests in a time frame and with the regularity and continuity that the existence of a market maker would provide. Interests are not readily tradable, however, unless the partnership participates in establishing the market or recognizes transfers by admission of purchasers to the partnership or recognizes their rights as transferees. Treas.Reg. § 1.7704–1(d). A redemption or repurchase plan can result in partnership interests being publicly traded.

The Regulations provide several "safe harbors." In determining whether there is public trading of the partnership interests, Treas.Reg. § 1.7704–1(e) disregards transfers in which the transferee has a transferred basis, transfers at death, transfers between family members, transfers pursuant to certain redemption agreements, and certain other transfers. The most broadly applicable safe harbor excludes from the definition of publicly traded partnership so-called "private placements"—that is, any partnership whose interests are not required to be registered under the Securities Act of 1933, but only if the partnership does not have more than 100 members. Treas.Reg. § 1.7704–1(h).

In addition, a partnership will not be considered to be traded on the substantial equivalent of a secondary market for any year in which no more than 2% of the total interests in partnership capital or profits are sold or disposed of in transactions other than private transfers, qualifying redemptions, and certain other safe harbors. Treas.Reg. § 1.7704–1(j). It is clear from § 7704(f), dealing with the effect of a partnership becoming a corporation, that § 7704 contemplates the possibility that an entity that is initially taxed as a partnership might in a subsequent year become a corporation under § 7704. The "lack of actual trading" safe harbor, which applies on a year-by-year basis, suggests further that a partnership might be considered to be a corporation in one year and a partnership in the next, when it meets the safe harbor. This result could give rise to a constructive liquidation of the "corporation" with tax consequences to the entity and the investors or, conversely, the constructive formation of a new corporation.

2.3. *Exceptions*

A broad exception to § 7704 allows publicly traded limited partnerships more than 90% of whose gross income is from certain "passive sources" to continue to be treated as partnerships. Qualified income for this purpose, with some narrow exceptions, includes interest, dividends, real property rents, gain from the sale of real property, and income and gains from the exploration, development, extraction, processing, refining, etc., of oil and gas or any other natural resource. While the legislative history is silent as to the reason for this exception, it presumably is based on the historic use of limited partnerships in organizing such ventures and the availability of conduit taxation for other entity forms (e.g., real estate investment trusts) making investments of this type. See I.R.C. § 7704(c)–(d).

An additional exception permits publicly traded partnerships that were in existence on December 31, 1987, to continue to be treated as tax partnerships as long as they do not add a "substantial new line of business." See I.R.C. § 7704(g).

If a publicly traded partnership is not taxed as a corporation, the § 199A deduction is available with respect to the qualifying tax items allocated to its partners. I.R.C. § 199A(e)(4); see Chapter 18.

3.   FOREIGN BUSINESS ENTITIES

Treas.Reg. § 301.7701–2(b)(8) lists certain foreign business entities (including entities organized in U.S. possessions, territories, and commonwealths) that are classified as per se corporations. The listed organizations are limited liability entities, such as the British Public Limited Company, the French Société Anonyme, the German Aktiengesellschaft, and the Sociedad Anónima in South American countries (Sociedade Anônima in Brazil). Other foreign entities can elect under Treas.Reg. § 301.7701–3(a) whether to be treated as a partnership or as a corporation. In contrast to the partnership default classification rules for domestic organizations, under

Treas.Reg. § 301.7701–3(b)(2), the default rule for foreign entities is based on whether the members have limited liability. For a foreign entity that provides limited liability for its members and that is not a per se corporation (listed in Treas.Reg. § 301.7701–2(b)(8)(i)), the default rule is that the entity is a corporation unless it elects to be a partnership (if it has two or more members) or a disregarded entity (if it has only one member). A foreign entity is classified as a partnership if it has two or more members and at least one member does not have limited liability. If a foreign entity has only one owner, who does not have limited liability, the entity is disregarded unless it elects to be regarded as a corporation.

4. BUSINESS TRUSTS

Treas.Reg. § 301.7701–4(a) through (c) distinguish between "ordinary" trusts, the purpose of which are the protection or conservation of trust property, and trusts that are in effect a joint enterprise of the beneficiaries to conduct a business for profit and that will be classified as either a partnership or a corporation under Treas.Reg. § 301.7701–2 and –3. No cases have been decided or rulings issued under the current version of Treas.Reg. § 301.7701–4, but a number of cases were decided under the prior version of the classification Regulations. In most of those cases, the question of whether the trust was an "ordinary trust" or a business association taxable as a corporation turned on whether the trust beneficiaries were in fact business associates. For example, in Outlaw v. United States, 494 F.2d 1376 (Ct.Cl.1974), a trust was formed to own and manage some 10,000 acres of farm land, and it employed 18 to 20 full-time and 60 to 70 temporary workers to engage in a full scale agricultural operation. The trust had 27 original investors, which increased over time to 41 investors; its objective was to carry on a business of owning, developing, and exploiting agricultural lands for income; its existence continued notwithstanding the withdrawal, death, bankruptcy, etc., of an investor; all decisions were made by an operating committee akin to a corporate board of directors; the investor-beneficiaries were liable only to the extent of their proportionate interests in the trust assets; and the investors could freely transfer their interests after giving notice to the trustee. Based on these facts, the trust was classified as a business entity taxable as a corporation. See also Rev.Rul. 80–75, 1980–1 C.B. 314 (trust established by promoter to conduct business activity and to which beneficiaries contributed cash in exchange for income interests and a remainder to person designated by the holder of income interest was classified as a business association).

In contrast, in Estate of Bedell v. Commissioner, 86 T.C. 1207 (1986), a testamentary trust that actively conducted a manufacturing business was held not to be an association because it lacked "associates": the beneficiaries had "not planned a common effort or entered into a combination for the conduct of a business enterprise," only a few of the beneficiaries participated in trust affairs, and their interests were not transferrable.

Under current Treas.Reg. § 301.7701–4, trusts such as those involved in *Outlaw* and *Estate of Bedell* would be classified as business entities rather than as ordinary trusts, and, under Treas.Reg. § 301.7701–2 and –3, they would then be classified as partnerships unless the trusts elected to be taxed as corporations.

Treas.Reg. § 301.7701–4(d) provides, however, a special rule for "liquidating" trusts; under this rule, as long as the primary purpose of the trust is the liquidation and distribution of the assets transferred to it, the trust will not be an association taxable as a corporation. See Rev.Rul. 75–379, 1975–2 C.B. 505, and Rev.Rul. 63–228, 1963–2 C.B. 229, finding certain trusts that engaged in business activities to fall within the "liquidation" exception; Rev.Proc. 82–58, 1982–2 C.B. 847, amplified by Rev.Proc. 91–15, 1991–1 C.B. 484 (guidelines for advance rulings on classification of liquidation trusts), modified and amplified by Rev. Proc. 94–45, 1994–2 C.B. 684 (income reporting requirements and checklist for ruling requests).

PROBLEM SET 1

1.   Anne and Bill plan to form a limited liability company to engage in the business of developing and marketing computer software. They have identified between 35 and 50 potential investors who will contribute varying amounts of cash for membership interests totaling approximately 75%–85% of profits and losses (after Anne and Bill receive handsome salaries). Under the governing state law, the LLC may be member-managed or manager-managed, membership interests may be freely transferable or nontransferable, and the LLC may or may not be dissolved by the death, bankruptcy, retirement, or expulsion of a member, all as provided in the LLC agreement. Anne and Bill want the LLC to be managed by themselves, with the investors having only the minimal rights of members required by state law. Only Anne and Bill will have authority to act on behalf of the LLC. Because of the limited powers that the investor-members will be granted, Anne and Bill think it best that the investors be permitted to sell or assign their membership interests if they so desire, although Anne and Bill think that the actual opportunities for resale will be limited by market forces. Of course, Anne and Bill want the business of the LLC to be uninterrupted by the death, bankruptcy, etc., of an investor-member. Will the LLC be taxed as a partnership or as a corporation if organized in the manner contemplated by Anne and Bill?

2.   X Corporation operates a children's toy business and manufactures automatic weapons. In order to separate potential liabilities, X Corporation forms a Limited Liability company, Guns-R-Us LLC, to which it transfers the weapons manufacturing operation. What is the tax status of the Guns-R-Us LLC?

B. PARTNERSHIP ENTITY VERSUS OTHER BUSINESS ARRANGEMENT

INTERNAL REVENUE CODE: Sections 761(a)–(b); 7701(a)(2).

REGULATIONS: Sections 1.761–1(a), (b), –2(a); 301.7701–1, –2(a), (b)(1)–(7), –3(a), (b)(1).

Sections 761(a) and 7701(a)(2) each define the term "partnership" in virtually identical, sparse language. The Regulations expand upon this sparse statutory language. As discussed in the previous section of this chapter, Treas.Reg. § 301.7701–2 provides that a business entity with two or more members is classified as either a partnership or a corporation. For this purpose, the term "business entity" is broad, as reflected by the provisions of Treas.Reg. § 301.7701–1(a)(2), which includes as activities that may be treated as entities separate from their individual owners "financial operations," "ventures," and "trades and businesses" from which the participants divide the profits. Entities that are listed in Treas.Reg. § 301.7701–2(b), such as an entity incorporated under the laws of one of the United States, are automatically classified as corporations. A "business entity" that is not listed in Treas.Reg. § 301.7701–2(b) is classified as a partnership if it has two or more members. The entity is disregarded if it has only one member.[4] Treas.Reg. § 301.7701–3(a) and (b). An entity that is classified as a partnership may elect to be taxed as a corporation, Treas.Reg. § 301.7701–3(a), but if no election is made, the entity is by default classified as a partnership. Treas.Reg. § 301.7701–3(b). For these classification rules to apply, an entity that is to be classified as a partnership must represent a business or joint enterprise engaged in an endeavor for profit. Treas.Reg. § 301.7701–4 distinguishes businesses, financial operations, and ventures taxed as partnerships from trusts established for the protection and conservation of property (which may include a trade or business operated by the trust as a sole proprietor). The Regulations, however, provide only limited guidance with respect to the types of agreements other than formal partnership agreements, LLC agreements, and articles of incorporation that create an entity separate and distinct from the person or persons conducting a business or owning property in the first place. The classification issue in these cases has been resolved largely by case law and Revenue Rulings.

---

[4] Treas.Reg. § 301.7701–3(b)(1) treats an unincorporated entity with only a single owner (generally an LLC), as a disregarded entity. The single owner is treated as owning directly all of the assets of the entity and is thus taxed directly on the entity's activities. This aspect of the Regulations was upheld in Littriello v. United States, 484 F.3d 372 (6th Cir. 2007), and in McNamee v. Department of the Treasury, 488 F.3d 100 (2d Cir. 2007).

Madison Gas and Electric Co. v. Commissioner

United States Court of Appeals, Seventh Circuit, 1980.
633 F.2d 512.

■ CUMMINGS, CIRCUIT JUDGE.

This is an action under 26 U.S.C. § 7422 for the refund of federal income taxes. The question is whether certain training and related expenses incurred by a public utility in the expansion of its generating capacity through the joint construction and operation of a nuclear plant with two other utilities are deductible as ordinary and necessary expenses in the years of payment or are non-deductible pre-operating capital expenditures of a new partnership venture. The Tax Court in an opinion reported at 72 T.C. 521 held that they are non-deductible capital expenditures. We affirm.

I

All relevant facts have been stipulated by the parties (App. 8–41) and found and set forth at length by the Tax Court. We find it necessary to summarize them only briefly. Taxpayer Madison Gas and Electric Co. (MGE), a Wisconsin corporation, is an operating public utility which has been engaged since 1896 in the production, purchase, transmission and distribution of electricity and the purchase and distribution of natural gas. MGE is subject to the jurisdiction and regulation of the Public Service Commission of Wisconsin (PSC) and the Nuclear Regulatory Commission. The Federal Energy Regulatory Commission (FERC) also has or may have jurisdiction over MGE.

MGE is required to furnish reasonably adequate service and facilities within its service area at rates found reasonable and just by the PSC. During 1969 and 1970, the tax years here in issue, MGE rendered service to some 73,000 residential and commercial customers in a service area of approximately 200 square miles in Dane County, Wisconsin. MGE also sells a small percentage of its electrical power to other utilities in Wisconsin. Its primary responsibility, however, is to its customers in the service area. The number of customers within that area has grown rapidly and continuously during the past 25 years, and the customer demand for electricity has increased with the expansion of commercial and industrial accounts, the substitution of electricity for other forms of energy, and the increasing prevalence of high-energy devices such as air-conditioning units. Thus at the time of trial MGE was servicing almost 90,000 residential, commercial and industrial customers.

MGE has over the years kept pace with the increasing demand for electrical power and provided it at reasonable rates by expanding the generating capacity of its facilities, contracting for the purchase and sale of excess electrical power, interconnecting transmission facilities with those of other Wisconsin utilities, and finally by building and operating additional facilities in conjunction with other utilities. Expenses incurred in connection with one of these joint ventures is the subject of the present suit.

On February 2, 1967, MGE entered into an agreement, entitled "Joint Power Supply Agreement" (Agreement) (App. 42–59), with Wisconsin Public Service Corporation (WPS) and Wisconsin Power and Light Co. (WPL) under which the three utilities agreed, *inter alia,* to construct and own together a nuclear generating plant now known as the Kewaunee Nuclear Power Plant (Plant). Under the Agreement, the Plant is owned by MGE, WPS and WPL as tenants-in-common with undivided ownership interests of 17.8%, 41.2% and 41.0% respectively. Electricity produced by the Plant is distributed to each of the utilities in proportion to their ownership interests. Each utility sells or uses its share of the power as it does power produced by its own individually owned facilities, and the profits thereby earned by MGE contribute only to MGE's individual profits. No portion of the power generated at the Plant is offered for sale by the utilities collectively, and the Plant is not recognized by the relevant regulatory bodies as a separate utility licensed to sell electricity. Each utility also pays a portion of all expenditures for operation, maintenance and repair of the Plant corresponding exactly to its respective share of ownership. Under utility accounting procedures mandated by the PSC and the FERC, these expenses are combined with and treated in the same manner by MGE as expenses from its individually owned facilities. The ownership and operation of the Plant by MGE, WPS and WPL is regarded by the PSC and the FERC as a tenancy-in-common. It was the intention of the utilities to create only a co-tenancy and not a partnership and to be taxed as co-tenants and not as partners.

In its 1969 and 1970 taxable years, MGE incurred certain expenses relating to the nuclear training of WPS employees, the establishment of internal procedures and guidelines for plant operation and maintenance, employee hiring activities, nuclear field management, environmental activities and the purchase of certain spare parts (App. 116–126). MGE had to incur these expenses in order to carry out its Plant activities. Pursuant to order of the PSC, MGE was required to amortize training expenses, net of income taxes, over a 60-month period from the date of commercial operation of the Plant, a date occurring after those in issue here, and the other non-construction expenses associated with the Plant, net of income taxes, over a three-year period beginning January 1, 1978. MGE did not deduct the expenses described above on its tax returns for 1969 and 1970, but in the Tax Court claimed a deduction for them by amendment to its refund petition in the total amounts of $33,418.45 and $114,434.27 for 1969 and 1970 respectively.

MGE's position was, and is, that the claimed expenses were currently deductible under Section 162(a) of the Internal Revenue Code of 1954 (Code) as ordinary and necessary business expenses. The Commissioner's position was, and is, that the claimed expenses were nondeductible capital expenditures. The Tax Court agreed with the Commissioner, holding that the operation of the Plant by MGE, WPS and WPL is a partnership within the meaning of Section 7701(a)(2) of the Code, that the expenses in question were incurred not in the carrying out of an existing business but as part of the start-up costs of the new partnership venture, and that the expenses were therefore not currently deductible but must be capitalized under Section 263(a) of the Code. MGE appeals from this judgment, arguing that its arrangement with WPS and WPL is not a partnership within the meaning of the Code and, alternatively, that even if it is a partnership the expenses are currently deductible.

II

The threshold issue is whether MGE's joint venture with WPS and WPL is a tax partnership. The Commissioner concedes that if it is not, the expenses are currently deductible under Section 162(a). A partnership for federal tax purposes is defined by the Code in Section 7701(a)(2), which provides in pertinent part:

> "The term 'partnership'—includes a syndicate, group, pool, joint venture, or other unincorporated organization, through or by means of which any business, financial operation, or venture is carried on, and which is not, within the meaning of this title, a trust estate or a corporation."

MGE's arrangement with WPS and WPL in connection with the Plant clearly establishes an unincorporated organization carrying on a "business, financial operation, or venture" and therefore falls within the literal statutory definition of a partnership. The arrangement is, of course, not taken out of this classification simply because the three utilities intended to be taxed only as a co-tenancy and not as a partnership. While it is well-settled that mere co-ownership of property does not create a tax partnership, see, e.g., Estate of Appleby v. Commissioner, 41 B.T.A. 18 (1940), co-owners may also be partners if they or their agents carry on the requisite "degree of business activities." Powell v. Commissioner, 26 T.C.M. 161 (1967); Hahn v. Commissioner, 22 T.C. 212 (1954).

MGE's argument is that a co-tenancy does not meet the business activities test of partnership status unless the co-tenants anticipate the earning and sharing of a single joint cash profit from their joint activity. Because its common venture with WPS and WPL does not result in the division of cash profits from joint marketing, MGE contends that the venture constitutes only a co-tenancy coupled with an expense-sharing arrangement and not a tax partnership. The Tax Court held that the Code definition of partnership does not require joint venturers to share in a single joint cash profit and that to the extent that a profit motive is required by the Code it is met here by the distribution of profits in kind. We agree.

The definition of partnership in Section 7701(a)(2) was added to the Code by Section 1111(a) of the Revenue Act of 1932 and first appeared in Section 3797(a)(2) of the 1939 Code. The Congressional Reports accompanying the 1932 Act make clear, in largely identical language, that Congress intended to broaden the definition of partnership for federal tax purposes to include a number of arrangements, such as joint ventures, which were not partnerships under state law. H.P.Rep. No. 708, 72d Cong., 1st Sess., 53 (1932); S.Rep. No. 665, 72d Cong., 1st Sess., 59 (1932). In so doing, they briefly discuss the advantages of requiring a partnership return for joint venturers rather than leaving the sole responsibility for reporting annual gains and losses on the individual members. MGE invites us to infer from these discussions that Congress contemplated inclusion only of those joint ventures that are capable of producing joint cash gains and losses. But even if we were inclined to narrow the statutory language on the basis of such slender evidence, the subsequent legislative history would dissuade us from reaching MGE's suggested construction.

In Bentex Oil Corp. v. Commissioner, 20 T.C. 565 (1953), the Tax Court held that an unincorporated organization formed to extract oil under an operating agreement which called for distribution of oil in kind was a partnership within the meaning of Section 3797(a)(2) of the 1939 Code. The Bentex joint venture is not distinguishable from that presented here in any meaningful way. The co-owners there, as here, shared the expenses of production but sold their shares of the production individually. Following *Bentex,* Congress reenacted the definition of partnership in Section 3797(a)(2) of the 1939 Code without change as Section 7701(a)(2) of the 1954 Code. In addition, it repeated the definition verbatim in Section 761(a), which permits certain qualifying organizations to elect to be excluded from application of some or all of the special Subchapter K partnership provisions. A qualifying [partnership] is one which is used

> "(1) for investment purposes only and not for the active conduct of a business, or

> "(2) for the joint production, extraction, or use of property, but not for the purpose of selling services or property produced or extracted, if the income of the members of the organization may be adequately determined without the computation of partnership taxable income."

In short, Section 761(a) allows unincorporated associations such as the Bentex venture and the one in issue here, which fall within the statutory definition of partnership, to elect out of Subchapter K.[2] The Section has

---

[2]   MGE argues that in enacting Section 761(a) Congress had in mind only oil, gas and mineral ventures acting under operating agreements and that therefore the Section should not be automatically construed to include an operating agreement for the production of electricity. In support of this position, MGE inexplicably cites Taubman, Oil and Gas Partnerships and Section 761(a), 12 Tax L.Rev. 49 (1956), in which the author expressly states:

generally been interpreted, in the absence of any legislative history, as approving the *Bentex* decision while providing relief from certain resulting hardships. * * * This interpretation is surely correct for, as the Tax Court observed:

> "[i]f distribution in kind of jointly produced property was enough to avoid partnership status, we do not see how such distribution could be used as a test for election to be excluded from the partnership provisions of subchapter K" (72 T.C. at 563).

MGE also relies on Treasury Regulation Sections 301.7701–3 and 1.761–1(a) (26 C.F.R.) to support its argument that joint marketing is a *sine qua non* of partnership status. These Sections state in identical language that tenants in common

> "may be partners if they actively carry on a trade, business, financial operations, or venture and divided the profits thereof."

In addition, MGE cites to us case law referring to a joint profit motive as a characteristic of partnerships.[3] See, e.g., Commissioner v. Tower, 327 U.S. 280, 286 * * * ("community of interest in the profits and losses"); Ian Allison v. Commissioner, 35 T.C.M. 1069 (1976) ("an agreement to share profits"). Neither the above-quoted Treasury Regulations Sections nor the case law distinguish between the division of cash profits and the division of in-kind profits, and none of the cited cases involved in-kind profits. Moreover, while distribution of profits in-kind may be an uncommon business arrangement, recognition of such arrangements as tax partnerships is not novel. See, e.g., *Bentex,* supra; Luckey v. Commissioner, 334 F.2d 719 (9th Cir.1964); Bryant v. Commissioner, 46 T.C. 848, affirmed, 399 F.2d 800 (5th Cir.1968).[4]

"Congress thus attempted to establish a workable formula which would be valid not only for oil and gas, but all types of operating agreements, as well as the related and equally difficult field of investment." 12 Tax L.Rev. 49, 67.

The three utilities here in fact did file a partnership return and election-out of Subchapter K (App. 19, 41). The Tax Court held that the filing of a partnership return and election-out under Section 761(a) are not admissions of partnership status (72 T.C. at 558). MGE did not argue below that election-out caused the organization not to be a partnership for non-Subchapter K tax purposes, and the Tax Court declined to decide this possible issue (72 T.C. at 559 n. 9). In its alternative position here, however, MGE contends that the holding below is "inconsistent with the purpose" of Section 761(a) (Br. 41). This argument is indistinguishable from an argument that election-out under Section 761(a) negates partnership status except where the Code explicitly provides to the contrary. Since the issue was not raised and decided below, we do not address it here. We note, however, that Section 7701(a)(2) explicitly states that an organization which is a partnership as defined in that Section is a partnership for the purposes of the entire Code, whereas Section 761(a) provides only for election-out of Subchapter K.

[3] The Commissioner takes the position that the presence of a joint profit motive is merely one factor to be considered in determining partnership status, while MGE argues that it is a necessary element. Because we find a joint profit motive here, albeit for in-kind profits, we need not resolve this dispute.

[4] See generally, McKee, Nelson & Whitmire, *Federal Taxation of Partnerships and Partners,* par. 3.02, pp. 3–8, in which the authors conclude: "A partnership may result from a joint extraction or production agreement among co-owners of mineral property or production facilities, even though the co-owners separately take and sell (or reserve the right to take and

The practical reality of the venture in issue here is that jointly produced electricity is distributed to MGE and the other two utilities in direct proportion to their ownership interest for resale to consumers in their service areas or to other utilities. The difference between the market value of MGE's share of that electricity and MGE's share of the cost of production obviously represents a profit. Just as obviously, the three utilities joined together in the construction and operation of the Plant with the anticipation of realizing these profits. The fact that the profits are not realized in cash until after the electricity has been channeled through the individual facilities of each participant does not negate their joint profit motive nor make the venture a mere expense-sharing arrangement.[5] We hold therefore that MGE's joint venture with WPS and WPL constitutes a partnership within the meaning of Sections 7701(a)(2) and 761(a) of the Code.

III

On the ultimate issue in this case, the Tax Court held that the claimed expenses were incurred as pre-operational costs of the partnership venture and therefore under settled law were non-deductible capital expenditures. See Richmond Television Corp. v. United States, 345 F.2d 901 (4th Cir.1965), vacated on other grounds, 382 U.S. 68.

MGE argues that this holding elevates form over substance in that even if the operating arrangement is technically a tax partnership, the claimed expenses were in actuality simply ordinary and necessary expenses of expanding its existing business. MGE asks us therefore to ignore the partnership entity as lacking economic substance.

* * *

Here MGE, WPS and WPL are engaged in the joint production of electricity for resale, a joint venture for profit. Because they were each already in the business of selling electricity, it can, of course, be argued that the partnership venture itself is an extension or expansion of their existing businesses. It does not follow from this though that we should ignore the partnership as lacking economic substance. Such reasoning would lead to the absurd conclusion that any partnership established to do collectively what its participants formerly did individually or continue to do individually outside the partnership lacks economic substance and should not be treated as a partnership for tax purposes.

At bottom, MGE's position is that it is not sound policy to treat the entity here as a partnership. But we are not free to rewrite the tax laws, whatever the merits of MGE's position. Under the Internal Revenue Code

---

sell) their shares of production. * * * Despite the absence of an objective to earn a joint cash profit, these ventures are generally considered partnerships" (footnotes omitted).

    5   Treasury Regulation Sections 301.7701[-1(a)(2)] and 1.761-1(a) (26 C.F.R.) state that a "joint undertaking merely to share expenses is not a partnership," and go on to give the example of neighboring landowners who jointly construct a ditch "merely to drain surface water from their properties." We agree with the Tax Court that the venture here is "in no way comparable to the joint construction of a drainage ditch" (72 T.C. at 560).

the joint venture here is a partnership and the expenses were non-deductible, pre-operational start-up costs of the partnership venture. Accordingly, the judgment of the Tax Court is affirmed.

DETAILED ANALYSIS

1.   THE NATURE OF THE INQUIRY

1.1. *In General*

A partnership is broadly defined in § 761(a) as any "syndicate, group, pool, joint venture or other unincorporated organization through or by means of which any business, financial operation, or venture is carried on, and which is not * * * a corporation, or a trust or estate." In Commissioner v. Culbertson, 337 U.S. 733 (1949), which interpreted the statutory predecessor of § 761(a), the Supreme Court held that the test for determining the existence of a partnership is whether the parties by their actions intended to join together to conduct a business and share in the profits and losses, regardless of how they characterized the relationship.

Culbertson involved a family ranching partnership composed of a father and four sons, two of whom were minors. The sons had received their interests partly by gift from the father and partly by contribution of funds loaned to them by the father, which were repaid from the proceeds of partnership operations. The Tax Court upheld the IRS determination that all of the ranching income was taxable to the father. In affirming the Second Circuit's decision reversing the Tax Court and remanding the case for a determination of which of the sons were partners, the Supreme Court articulated the relevant test as follows:

> The Tax Court read our decisions in Commissioner v. Tower, (327 U.S. 280), and Lusthaus v. Commissioner, (327 U.S. 293), as setting out two essential tests of partnership for income-tax purposes: that each partner contribute to the partnership either vital services or capital originating with him. Its decision was based upon a finding that none of respondent's sons had satisfied those requirements during the tax years in question. * * *

> The question is not whether the services or capital contributed by a partner are of sufficient importance to meet some objective standard supposedly established by the *Tower* case, but whether, considering all the facts the agreement, the conduct of the parties in execution of its provisions, their statements, the testimony of disinterested persons, the relationship of the parties, their respective abilities and capital contribution, the actual control of income and the purposes for which it is used, and any other facts throwing light on their true intent-the parties in good faith and acting with a business purpose intended to join together in the present conduct of the enterprise. There is nothing new or particularly difficult about such a test. Triers of fact are constantly called upon to determine the intent with which a person acted. * * *

Unquestionably a court's determination that the services contributed by a partner are not "vital" and that he has not participated in "management and control of the business" or contributed "original capital" has the effect of placing a heavy burden on the taxpayer to show the bona fide intent of the parties to join together as partners. But such a determination is not conclusive, * * *.

Two years after the *Culbertson* decision, Congress enacted the predecessors of § 704(e) and § 761(b).

Section 761(b), as amended in 2015, provides: "In the case of a capital interest in a partnership in which capital is a material income-producing factor, whether a person is a partner with respect to such interest shall be determined without regard to whether such interest was derived by gift from any other person." This sentence focuses the inquiry on whether a person is a partner and whether a partnership exists under the totality of the circumstances test of *Culbertson*. Thus, under § 761(b), a person's status as a partner with an interest in a family partnership in which capital is a material income-producing factor acquired by gift should be tested under the same rules as a capital interest acquired by purchase or by a contribution to capital. TIFD III-E, Inc. v. United States, 666 F.3d 836 (2d Cir. 2012), rev'g, 660 F. Supp. 2d 367 (D. Conn. 2009), held, under the predecessor of § 761(b), that holding an interest in a partnership in the form of debt (or an interest overwhelmingly in the nature of debt) did not create a capital interest in a partnership that could qualify as a partnership interest.

1.2. *Multi-Factor Analysis*

In general, the reported cases cite numerous factors that are to be considered in determining whether persons have entered into a partnership. The single most important factual question is whether the parties are acting as co-proprietors. See, e.g., Harlan E. Moore Charitable Trust v. United States, 9 F.3d 623 (7th Cir.1993) (sharecropping arrangement including sharing some expenses was not a partnership because the rent was not a percentage of profits). Nonetheless, no single factor is talismanic. The following passage from Luna v. Commissioner, 42 T.C. 1067, 1077–78 (1964), which involved the question of whether a particular arrangement was a partnership for tax purposes or an employment relationship, discusses some of the relevant factors:

The following factors, none of which is conclusive, bear on the issue * * *: The agreement of the parties and their conduct in executing its terms; the contributions, if any, which each party has made to the venture; the parties' control over income and capital and the right of each to make withdrawals; whether each party was a principal and coproprietor, sharing a mutual proprietary interest in the net profits and having an obligation to share losses, or whether one party was the agent or employee of the other, receiving for his services contingent compensation in the form of a percentage of income; whether business was conducted in the joint names of the parties; whether the parties filed Federal partnership returns or otherwise represented to respondent or to persons with whom they dealt that they were joint venturers; whether separate books of account were maintained for the venture; and whether the parties exercised mutual control over and assumed mutual responsibilities for the enterprise.

Applying these standards, the Tax Court held that the taxpayer in *Luna* was an employee of an insurance company rather than a member of a joint venture with the insurance company. As a result, a payment to him from the insurance company to terminate their relationship was taxable to him as compensation and not as capital gain on the sale of a partnership interest.

In DJB Holding Corp. v. Commissioner, 803 F.3d 1014 (9th Cir. 2015), the court applied the *Luna* factors to hold that a joint venture (NTC Project) between an operating corporation (WCI) and a partnership (WB Partners) owned by related parties who indirectly owned the stock of WCI was not a partnership for tax purposes. All of the work under a large environmental remediation project was performed by WCI under a contract between WCI and a third party. WB Partners was responsible for financial and guarantee services. Profits from the NTC Project environmental remediation work were allocated 30% to WCI and 70% to WB Partners. WB Partners' share of the NTC Project's profits were passed through to tax-exempt retirement plans that benefited the ultimate owners of the entire structure. Relying on the second *Luna* factor, the court held that WB Partners provided nothing of value to the NTC Project venture, adding that the two individual owners of the S corporation partners in the partnership would have been required to provide the financial guarantees claimed to represent contributions by the partnership to the joint venture. Additionally the court observed that the purported partners in the NTC Project joint venture did not in fact respect the terms of the joint venture agreement (the actual income allocation between the partners differed substantially from the terms of the agreement and no partnership tax returns were filed) and that the unilateral control exercised by the WCI belied the existence of a true partnership.

1.3. *Relevance of State Law*

Characterization of an arrangement under state law is not controlling for federal income tax purposes; the Internal Revenue Code controls. Treas.Reg. § 301.7701–1(a)(1), (b); Commissioner v. Culbertson, 337 U.S. 733 (1949); Estate of Kahn v. Commissioner, 499 F.2d 1186 (2d Cir.1974). Thus, Rev.Rul. 77–137, 1977–1 C.B. 178, held that an assignee of a limited partnership interest, who under state law was not admitted to the partnership by virtue of the assignment but who was entitled to distributions of partnership profits, nevertheless was a partner for federal income tax purposes and would be taxed as the owner of the partnership. While local law may distinguish a partnership from a joint venture for some purposes, the latter generally being formed for a single business purpose in contrast to the formation of a partnership to conduct an ongoing business, the distinction is not relevant for tax law; a joint venture is treated the same as a partnership. See Podell v. Commissioner, 55 T.C. 429 (1970). Local law is controlling, however, in determining the rights and responsibilities of the participants that are taken into account in determining whether a partnership exists for tax purposes.

A partnership conducting a professional business may exist for tax purposes between a member of a licensed profession and a person who does not hold a license, even though it could not legally exist under local law. See Nichols v. Commissioner, 32 T.C. 1322 (1959) (finding that a partnership for the practice of medicine existed between a physician and non-physician, an arrangement that would be proscribed under state law); Rev.Rul. 77–332, 1977–2 C.B. 484 (partnership between CPAs and non-CPA "principals" in accounting firm; state law prohibits non-CPA partners).

1.4. *Spousal Partnerships*

Section 761(f) provides that spouses who together operate a qualified joint venture may elect not to treat the joint venture as a partnership. A qualified joint venture is one conducted by spouses, both of whom are material participants, and who file a joint return. The IRS has specified on its website that the venture must not be conducted through a state-law entity, such as an LLC (https://www.irs.gov/businesses/small-businesses-self-employed/election-for-married-couples-unincorporated-businesses).
Each spouse is required to report the spouse's share of income and expense items on a separate schedule C.[5]

Rev.Proc. 2002–69, 2002–2 C.B. 831, deals with the classification of partnerships, including LLCs taxed as partnerships, that are wholly owned by spouses *as community property* in community property law states. If for federal tax purposes the spouses treat the entity as a disregarded entity with a single owner under Treas.Reg. § 301.7701–1(a)(4) and –2(a), the IRS will accept the position that the entity is a disregarded entity for federal tax purposes. On the other hand, if the spouses and the entity treat the entity as a partnership for federal tax purposes and file appropriate partnership returns, the IRS will accept the position that the entity is a partnership for federal tax purposes. (A change in reporting position will be treated for federal tax purposes as a conversion of the entity.) Rev.Proc. 2002–69 provides broader relief than § 761(f), because, among other things, it applies even if one spouse does not materially participate in the venture. Nevertheless, nothing in the Revenue Procedure allows spouses who wholly own an LLC or partnership in a common law property state to avoid entity characterization under Treas.Reg. § 301.7701–2(a) unless § 761(f) applies.

1.5. *State Law Partnership with Wholly Owned LLC*

Suppose a state law partnership, the AL Partnership, has two partners, individual A and L, a limited liability company (LLC) of which A is the sole member. Is the AL Partnership a partnership for federal tax purposes? Rev.Rul. 2004–77, 2004–2 C.B. 119, holds that unless L has elected under Treas.Reg. § 301.7701–3(c) to be taxed as a corporation, under the default rule of Treas.Reg. § 301.7701–3(b)(1), L is disregarded as an entity separate from its owner, A. Because L is disregarded, A is treated as owning all of the interests in AL. Because AL has only one owner for federal tax purposes, AL

---

[5]   Each spouse is individually assessed self-employment tax. I.R.C. § 1402(a)(17).

cannot be classified as a partnership under § 7701(a)(2). It is disregarded as an entity separate from A. The same analysis would apply if AL were an LLC in which A and L were the only members. AL would be disregarded.

2. PARTNERSHIP VERSUS CO-OWNERSHIP OF PROPERTY

2.1. *General*

Determining whether co-owners of property are engaged in business as partners is important for a variety of reasons beyond the requirement in § 6031 that a partnership file a return.[6] For example, if the arrangement is a partnership, all tax accounting elections, including cost recovery methods under § 168, must be made by the partnership, not by the individual co-owners. Other provisions whose proper application cannot be determined without first determining if a partnership exists include § 453, governing installment sales; § 1031, governing like-kind exchanges (undivided interests in real property are eligible for § 1031; partnership interests are not); § 1033, dealing with involuntary conversions; and § 1221, defining capital assets. Also, if ownership is a co-tenancy rather than a partnership, deductions, other than depreciation, attributable to the enterprise do not reduce the individual owners' bases in the property, whereas deductions that flow through to partners reduce their bases in their partnership interests. See I.R.C. § 705(a)(2)(A).

Despite the broad definition of a partnership in § 761(a), the Regulations provide that a joint undertaking to share expenses or the mere co-ownership of property that is maintained, kept in repair, and leased does not constitute a partnership. Co-ownership will, however, be treated as a partnership if active business operations are carried on, such as providing services for a tenant either directly or through an agent. Treas.Reg. § 301.7701–1(a)(2). The principal question in all of the cases described in these sections is, paraphrasing the words of *Culbertson*, whether two or more persons have joined together with a business purpose to conduct an enterprise for profit. And, as indicated by the court in *Culbertson*, the inquiry requires the application of multiple factors to the facts and circumstances of particular arrangements.

2.2. *Cases Finding Partnership*

In Levine v. Commissioner, 72 T.C. 780 (1979), aff'd on other issues, 634 F.2d 12 (2d Cir.1980), the taxpayer and his son owned various commercial real estate properties that they leased to tenants. No partnership returns were filed, and the taxpayers reported the income or loss from the properties pro rata on their individual returns. The issue in the case was whether the gain from the disposition of a particular property was properly reportable by the taxpayer in 1968 or in 1969; if a partnership existed, the gain was properly reportable in 1969, rather than 1968.[7] Even though the parties did

---

[6]   For the importance of filing partnership returns, see Simons v. United States, 89–1 USTC 87,522 (S.D.Fla.1989) (upholding failure to file penalty under § 6698).

[7]   Section 706(a), discussed in Chapter 18, requires partners to report their shares of partnership income in their taxable year during or with which the partnership's taxable year ends. Thus, if the partnership uses a different taxable year than the partner, the proper year for reporting an item can depend on whether or not the item is a partnership item.

not characterize their relationship as a partnership, the Tax Court found that they were partners because they engaged in an active business by leasing the properties to tenants, providing property management services to the tenants, and sharing the gains and losses. These factors were found more indicative of a partnership business than "a mere passive investment." In Rothenberg v. Commissioner, 48 T.C. 369 (1967), co-owners of apartment buildings were found to be partners rather than tenants in common because the operation of the buildings constituted the active conduct of a rental business, and they held themselves out as partners and filed partnership tax returns. As a result, the partnership, and not the individuals, was the proper taxpayer to make the election under § 453 regarding installment method reporting of gains. Alhouse v. Commissioner, T.C. Memo. 1991–652, held that co-owners who leased property under a net lease and for whom property was managed under a management agreement nevertheless were partners; because they did not retain the right separately to convey their interests, they had a joint profit motive. Accordingly, special rules relating to audits of partnerships applied.

In Bergford v. Commissioner, 12 F.3d 166 (9th Cir.1993), the taxpayers purchased an undivided fractional interest in computer equipment that was then leased back to the seller. Whether the Tax Court had jurisdiction to review the deficiency notice turned on whether the taxpayer was a co-owner or a partner. In deciding that the taxpayers had entered into a partnership with the other owners of undivided interests in the equipment as well as with the "manager" of the leasing operation, the court reasoned as follows:

> [T]he Tax Court found that the economic benefits to the individual participants were not derivative of their co-ownership of the computer equipment, but rather came from their joint relationship toward a common goal. It also held that taxpayers' ability to partition out an interest, judicially if needed, was illusory. We cannot say it erred. Taxpayers acted together with AmeriGroup Management in a long-term venture to finance, lease, and remarket the computer equipment. In reality, the participants have an interest in the CSE Program, not just in the equipment. As a practical matter, they must act in concert to buy the equipment and finance it, and none could sell, lease, or encumber the equipment without the consent of other participants. Although any participant has the right voluntarily to withdraw or assign his interest, consent of the manager must be obtained. In addition, the manager has the right to remarket the participants' interests and is to receive a remarketing fee regardless of whether a participant has terminated the management agreement. Termination does not, accordingly, affect the manager's economic interest in the value of the equipment. While taxpayers are correct that they have a right to partition the property, there is no indication that an individual unit interest has any appreciable value. Finally, at least to some extent the manager shares in the risk of gain and loss. Although the management agreement does not require the manager to loan money to participants if rental income fails to meet the anticipated

return, the arrangement is structured to make advances available as needed. As the Tax Court presumed, the manager must have intended to honor that commitment and thus to undertake financial risk if necessary. Because the manager has the right to a remarketing fee regardless of whether a participant exercises the right to terminate the management agreement, the manager, as well as each other participant, has a continuing interest in the residual value of the equipment. These facts suffice to justify the Tax Court's conclusion that taxpayers, other participants, and the manager evidenced an intent to join together in a transaction in order to share profits and losses.

Holdner v. Commissioner, T.C. Memo. 2010–175, aff'd, 483 Fed. Appx. 383 (9th Cir. 2012), found a partnership to exist with respect to a father-son farming venture. The taxpayer invested capital in a family farm for his son to operate, and they agreed to divide the profits. As the farming operation expanded, father and son took title to the property as tenants in common, and the father began to perform services on behalf of the partnership. The taxpayer reported one-half of the income but claimed deductions for significantly more than one-half of the operating expenses. The court rejected the taxpayer's arguments that the father and son operated the farm as separate sole proprietors. It found that the enterprise was a partnership because both father and son contributed labor to the farm operation in the conduct of business activities, divided the net sales proceeds equally, paid the expenses out of farm income, and held themselves out to third parties as partners. The court further held that the taxpayer failed to rebut a presumption that the partners shared all items of income and expense equally and further that the unequal capital contributions to the venture did not justify an allocation of a disproportionate amount of the deductions for expenses to the father.

2.3. *Cases Finding Co-Ownership*

In McShain v. Commissioner, 68 T.C. 154 (1977), no partnership existed where co-owners leased unimproved land to a single tenant, who was required to pay rent, all taxes, assessments, utility bills, and other assessments relating to the land. The only activities of the lessors were collecting rent and signing applications for permits and licenses. Accordingly, when the land was condemned, § 1033 applied to the co-owners individually.

Rev.Rul. 75–374, 1975–2 C.B. 261, provides some examples of maintenance and repair activity that allow co-owners to avoid partnership status. Co-owners of an apartment building hired an unrelated management corporation to manage, operate, and maintain the property. The management company negotiated and executed leases; collected rents and other payments from tenants; paid taxes, assessments, and insurance premiums with respect to the property; and performed all other customary services to maintain and repair the property on behalf of and at the expense of the co-owners. Services provided to the tenants by the co-owners through the management company included heat, air conditioning, hot and cold water, unattended parking, trash removal, and cleaning of public areas. The management company also provided to tenants *on its own behalf* additional services such as attendant parking, cabanas, gas, and other utilities. The Ruling held that the co-owners were not partners between themselves and implies that they were not partners with the management company. Since the Regulations apply the same standard whether services are provided directly or through an agent, the result in the Ruling should not have differed if the co-owners had provided maintenance and repairs directly. Thus, the Ruling appears to be irreconcilable with *Levine* and *Alhouse*, supra. Furthermore, those services provided by the management company on its own behalf appear to have gone beyond maintenance and repair and, if the management company had provided those services on behalf of the co-owners or if the co-owners had provided those services directly, the IRS probably would have concluded that they were partners. The best that can be said about the law in this area is that it is muddled.

2.4. *Internal Revenue Service Ruling Policy*

In Rev.Proc. 2002–22, 2002–1 C.B. 733, the IRS described conditions required for it to issue a private letter ruling that an undivided fractional interest in rental real property is not an interest in a business entity, which is a prerequisite to partnership status. The Revenue Procedure addresses sponsored co-ownership interests in property that is subject to a master lease; the interests are sold to investors primarily as a vehicle to facilitate § 1031 exchanges of real estate. (Section 1031 is not applicable to an exchange of a partnership interest.) The Revenue Procedure identifies the following conditions, among others, for obtaining a ruling that a co-ownership arrangement is not a business entity:

(1) The co-owners must hold title to the property as tenants in common under local law.

(2) There may not be more than 35 co-owners (except that spouses and all persons who acquire an interest by inheritance will be treated as single co-owner).

(3) The co-ownership may neither designate itself nor conduct business as a partnership, corporation, or other business entity. Also the co-owners may not have held title to the property in a corporation or partnership prior to formation of the co-ownership.

(4) In general, each co-owner must have the rights to transfer, partition, and encumber the co-owner's undivided interest in the property without the agreement or approval of any person. However, the co-owners may enter into an agreement that requires any co-owner to offer the co-ownership interest to the other co-owners before exercising rights to partition the co-ownership interest and that certain actions regarding the co-ownership interests require a vote of 50% of the ownership interests.

(5) Certain actions such as a sale, lease, or re-lease of a portion or all of the property, any negotiation or renegotiation of indebtedness secured by a blanket lien, the hiring of any

manager, or the negotiation of any management contract must require unanimous approval of the co-owners. Other actions may be taken by a vote of persons holding 50% of the undivided interests in the property.

(6) If the property is sold, any debt secured by a blanket lien must be satisfied and the remaining sales proceeds must be distributed to the co-owners.

(7) All profits, expenses, losses, and indebtedness must be shared in proportion to co-ownership interests.

(8) A co-owner may issue an option to purchase the co-owner's undivided interest (call option) as long as the purchase price reflects the fair market value of the co-ownership interest. A co-owner is not allowed to hold an option to sell the co-owner's interest (a put option) to the sponsor, the lessee, the lender, or another co-owner (or to any related person).

(9) The co-ownership may not engage in the conduct of an active trade or business. Thus, the co-owners' activities must be limited to those customarily performed in connection with the maintenance and repair of rental real property. See Rev.Rul. 75–374, discussed above.

2.5. *Election Out of Partnership Status*

Section 761(a) authorizes Regulations under which members of "an unincorporated organization" may elect to be excluded from the operation of Subchapter K if the organization is availed of (1) for investment purposes rather than the active conduct of a business; (2) for the joint production, extraction, or use of property, but not for the purpose of selling services or property produced or extracted; or (3) by securities dealers engaged in a short term venture to underwrite, sell, or distribute a particular issue of securities, provided in all cases that the members' incomes can adequately be determined without the computation of partnership taxable income.[8] See Treas.Reg. § 1.761–2 for further details and the manner for making the election. When a valid § 761 election is made, no partnership return need be filed. In addition, the election overrides § 703(b), which requires that all elections (with specified exceptions) be made by the partnership, and thereby permits co-owners to make inconsistent elections with respect to the accounting treatment of items relating to the property. See Rev.Rul. 83–129, 1983–2 C.B. 105 (election to capitalize and amortize mine development expenses under § 616). But where a provision of the Code outside of Subchapter K specifically refers to the treatment of partnerships wholly apart from Subchapter K, a § 761 election has no effect. See Bryant v. Commissioner, 399 F.2d 800 (5th Cir.1968) (investment credit limitation under § 48(c)(2)(d) of 1954 Code applied to partnership that made 761 election); Rev.Rul. 65–118, 1965–1 C.B. 30 (same). Section 1031(a), however, specifically provides that an exchange of an interest in a partnership that has elected out of Subchapter K will be treated as an exchange of the

---

[8] See Martin J. McMahon, Jr., The Availability and Effect of Election Out of Partnership Status Under Section 761(a), 9 Va. Tax Rev. 1 (1989).

underlying assets of the partnership for purposes of determining the extent to which the exchange qualifies as a tax-free like-kind exchange under § 1031. The taxpayers in *Madison Gas and Electric v. Commissioner* had filed an election under § 761(a) to be excluded from Subchapter K, but the court declined to decide whether the election avoided partnership status for purposes of determining whether the taxpayers' startup expenses were to be capitalized because the issue had not been raised in the lower courts. However, the court did point out in footnote 2 "that Section 7701(a)(2) explicitly states that an organization which is a partnership as defined in that Section is a partnership for the purposes of the entire Code, whereas Section 761(a) provides only for election-out of Subchapter K."

3. PARTNERSHIP VERSUS EMPLOYMENT OR AGENCY AGREEMENT

A partnership does not exist if the relationship between the parties is an employment, agency, or independent contractor arrangement. See Rev.Rul. 75–43, 1975–1 C.B. 383 (no partnership where a corporate feedlot owner entered into a service agreement with individual cattle owners to raise cattle for the owners). This issue has arisen most frequently with respect to classifying receipts as ordinary income from compensation or gain from the sale of a capital asset. See Luna v. Commissioner, 42 T.C. 1067 (1964) (taxpayer was found to be an employee of an insurance company rather than a party to a joint venture; hence a lump sum payment to him was taxable as compensation and not as capital gain on the sale of a partnership interest).

In determining whether an arrangement is a partnership or an employment, agency, or contractor arrangement, the same standards used to determine if co-owners are partners apply. But because employees, agents, and independent contractors frequently are compensated on the basis of a percentage of the employer's profits, the sharing of profits aspect of the test may be more difficult to apply; sharing of losses, which is not common in employment or similar relationships may be more significant, but is not always necessary. The essential factual inquiry is whether the persons are "co-proprietors" of the business. In Wheeler v. Commissioner, T.C. Memo. 1978–208, the taxpayer entered into an agreement with Perault to develop specific tracts of land. The taxpayer contributed "know-how" and Perault provided the financing, with the profits to be split 25% to the taxpayer and 75% to Perault. Although title to all properties was held in Perault's name, the parties did business under the name "Perault and Wheeler." The taxpayer had total authority to manage the day-to-day affairs of the business, but he could not borrow on behalf of the venture. Perault, however, was entitled to receive all of the operating income until he received back his entire investment plus 6% interest and was to bear all losses; consistently, he reported all of the operating income and expenses. Upon the sale of properties, however, Perault reported only his share of gains; he did not report the full gain and claim a deduction for compensation paid to the taxpayer. The Tax Court held that Wheeler and Perault were partners. Accordingly, Wheeler's share of the gains was taxable to him as capital gains rather than as compensation for services taxable as ordinary income. See also Rev.Rul. 54–84, 1954–1 C.B. 284 (holding properties in one partner's name and absence of loss sharing did not prevent partnership status).

Dorman v. United States, 296 F.2d 27 (9th Cir.1961), involved an agreement for a ranching venture under which the taxpayer, who contributed no capital, was to be an equal partner, but his interest was not "vested" until he fully paid promissory notes representing his capital contribution to the partnership. The notes, which were for an amount equal to one half of the other venturer's capital contribution, were payable only out of the taxpayer's share of profits from the venture. In the interim, the taxpayer received a salary. The taxpayer was found to be merely an employee with an executory right to become a partner. Therefore, he was not permitted to deduct any portion of the net operating loss incurred by the venture. See also Estate of Smith v. Commissioner, 313 F.2d 724 (8th Cir.1963) (purported partnership between investment advisors and investors in commodities in which investors contributed all of the capital and bore all of the losses, but shared trading profits with investment advisors, was not recognized; investment advisors realized income from compensation).

4.   PARTNERSHIP VERSUS LOAN

Occasionally, a transaction otherwise denominated as a loan may be recharacterized as a partnership. This may occur in the case of an unsecured nonrecourse debt that is to be repaid only out of profits from a venture. See Hartman v. Commissioner, T.C. Memo. 1958–206. Even if there is security for the loan, if it is inadequate, the loan may be recharacterized as an equity investment when the debt is convertible into an equity investment. See Rev.Rul. 72–350, 1972–2 C.B. 394.

Characterization of a transaction as a loan on the one hand or as a partnership on the other hand is significant not only for the purpose of characterizing payments from the "borrower" to the "lender" as interest or as a payment by a partnership to a partner but also for purposes of determining who is entitled to claim losses incurred by the venture, the treatment of the parties if the "loan" is not repaid, and the "lender's" treatment if the "lender" sells the interest.

In 70 Acre Recognition Equipment Partnership v. Commissioner, T.C. Memo. 1996–547, a bank (State Savings) promised to lend approximately $6,500,000 to a corporation (BCI) to provide a cash down payment on a $14,000,000 real estate purchase. The balance of the purchase price was financed by a nonrecourse note back to the seller. The interest on the bank loan was 14% per annum, plus 50% of net profits from resale of the land. On the same day that the purchase was closed, BCI sold a portion of the land for approximately $7,000,000, using the proceeds to pay closing costs and the down payment. State Savings never made the loan, but subsequently lent BCI additional funds, on a nonrecourse basis, to develop the property. BCI and State Savings filed a partnership return allocating the profit on the sale equally, but the Commissioner asserted that no partnership had been formed and that the entire gain was allocable to BCI. Even though the entire transaction had been documented as a loan and BCI had taken and conveyed title in its own name, the court found that an oral partnership had been formed and upheld the taxpayer's treatment of the transaction.

Even though it is well accepted that interest need not be a fixed rate but may be a specified portion of the borrower's profits, see Dorzback v. Collison, 195 F.2d 69 (3d Cir.1952), participating loans and shared appreciation mortgages still raise the question of whether the purported lender and borrower are instead partners. Under certain circumstances, the IRS will treat a shared appreciation mortgage entirely as a loan. Rev.Rul. 83–51, 1983–1 C.B. 48, treats as interest contingent interest equal to a fixed percentage of the appreciation in value of the borrower's personal residence over the term of the loan. Compare Rev.Rul. 76–413, 1976–2 C.B. 213 (certain contingent interest on a mortgage loan made to a real estate developer by a trust was "interest on obligations secured by real property" under § 856(c), relating to real estate investment trusts, rather than profits from active participation in the operation of the property; the result of the Ruling was changed by amendment of § 856, but the analysis appears to continue to be relevant).

5.   PARTNERSHIP VERSUS LEASE

In Form Builders, Inc. v. Commissioner, T.C. Memo. 1990–75, a group of individuals and a corporation controlled by the individuals' parents formed a "partnership" to engage in the business-form printing business, using equipment owned by the individuals with the work to be performed by the corporation. Under the written "partnership agreement" the individuals and the corporation were to share gross receipts in specified percentages. The court held that although the venture was conducted with a profit motive, because the parties shared gross receipts rather than net income there was no "joint profit motive." Accordingly, the arrangement was recharacterized as a lease of the equipment from the individuals to the corporation, and all of the gross income was attributed to the corporation, which was allowed a deduction for a reasonable rental to the individuals.

Rev.Rul. 92–49, 1992–1 C.B. 433, deals with whether an arrangement between the owner of coin operated amusements and the owner of business premises constitutes a partnership when the coin operated amusements are placed on the business premises and the receipts are split between the two owners on a percentage basis. The Ruling provides that whether the arrangement is a lease or a partnership depends on all of the facts and circumstances, but that such an arrangement generally is a lease. Under the Ruling, if the owner of the amusements in good faith treats it as a lease for the information reporting requirements of § 6041 and files the appropriate form with respect to payments to the property owner, the IRS will not challenge the treatment. Conversely, if the parties treat the arrangement as a joint venture and file a partnership tax return, the IRS likewise generally will not challenge the reporting position.

6.   SHAM PARTNERSHIPS

In Duhon v. Commissioner, T.C. Memo. 1991–369, the Tax Court held that the existence of a purported partnership should not be respected. The taxpayer was a partner in a partnership with a corporation, Pernie Bailey

Drilling Company, and other individuals, all of whom (including the taxpayer) were either shareholders or employees of the corporation. The only capital contribution to the partnership was $1,000 provided by the corporation, which sold an oil drilling rig to the partnership on an installment note for the full purchase price of $2,250,000. The corporation then operated the drilling rig on behalf of the partnership, having all management responsibility, and agreed to assume all risks associated with its operation. Disallowing each individual partner's loss deductions attributable to the partnership's depreciation deductions on the drilling rig, the court found the partnership "was merely a paper conduit operated by Pernie Bailey in such manner that it was merely carrying on the corporate business." Accord Merryman v. Commissioner, 873 F.2d 879 (5th Cir.1989) (involving another partner in the same partnership).

Several decisions have disregarded purported partnership arrangements in abusive tax shelter cases. The courts have tended to deny the sought-after tax benefits by finding that there was no valid partnership rather than analyzing the transactions as lacking economic substance. For example, in Superior Trading, LLC v. Commissioner, 137 T.C. 70 (2011), the Tax Court disregarded a purported partnership formed between a U.S. tax shelter promoter and a bankrupt Brazilian retailer, who transferred high basis, low value, uncollectible accounts receivable to the entity. The overall transaction was structured so that the high transferred basis of the receivables could be re-contributed down through a chain of partnerships to create loss deductions for investors. (See the discussion of the § 722 transferred basis rules in Chapter 19.) Shortly after the transfer, the partnership interest of the Brazilian company was liquidated with a cash payment. Among other things, the court treated the transfer of receivables as a sale rather than a contribution to a partnership, on the ground that the Brazilian company lacked a joint profit motive in the transaction and thus was never a partner in a partnership.

A tax shelter arrangement was also disregarded as a partnership in TIFD III-E, Inc. v. United States, 666 F.3d 836 (2d Cir. 2012) (commonly referred to as the *Castle Harbour* case). *Castle Harbour* involved a tax shelter partnership in which 2% of both operating and taxable income was allocated to GECC, a United States partner, and 98% of both book and taxable income was allocated to partners who were Dutch banks—foreign partners who were not liable for United States taxes and thus were indifferent to the U.S. tax consequences of their participation in the partnership. The allocations arguably were technically correct under the allocation rules of § 704(b) and the Regulations thereunder. (See Chapter 20.) The partnership had very large book depreciation deductions and no tax depreciation. As a result, most of the partnership's taxable operating income, which was substantially in excess of book taxable income, was allocated to the tax-indifferent foreign partners, even though a large portion of the cash receipts reflected in that income was devoted to repaying the principal of loans secured by property that GECC had contributed to the partnership. The overall partnership transaction saved GECC approximately $62 million in income taxes. The District Court allowed the claimed deductions, finding nothing in the applicable Regulations to prevent the shifting of taxable income to the tax-indifferent partner. The District Court judge indicated that even though one of the principal motivations for the transaction was to avoid taxes, the transaction was economically real. TIFD III-E, Inc. v. United States, 342 F.Supp.2d 94 (D.Conn. 2004). Reversing the District Court for the first time, the Court of Appeals held, under the facts and circumstances test of *Culbertson*, that the Dutch banks' interests were in the nature of the debt interests of secured lenders, "which would neither be harmed by poor performance of the partnership nor significantly enhanced by extraordinary profits." TIFD III-E, Inc. v. United States, 459 F.3d 220 (2d Cir. 2006). The Second Circuit's analysis followed the approach of other Circuit Courts, which avoided detailed analysis of the transaction under the economic substance doctrine in favor of findings that the Dutch banks in other versions of this transaction were not partners. Boca Investerings Partnership v. United States, 314 F.3d 625 (D.C. Cir. 2003), rev'g 167 F. Supp. 2d 298 (D.D.C. 2001); Saba Partnership v. Commissioner, 273 F.3d 1135 (D.C. Cir. 2001); ASA Investerings Partnership v. Commissioner, 201 F.3d 505 (D.C. Cir. 2000); ACM Partnership v. Commissioner, 157 F.3d 231 (3d Cir. 1998).

Notwithstanding the Second Circuit's strong opinion that the arrangement in the *Castle Harbour* case did not constitute a partnership, on remand the district court nevertheless again held the arrangement was a partnership, this time by applying the predecessor of § 761(b). 660 F. Supp. 2d 367 (D. Conn. 2009), discussed above. Reversing the District Court, a second time, the Court of Appeals held that the banks' interest was debt, which did not constitute a "capital" interest in the partnership within the meaning of the statute. TIFD III-E, Inc. v. United States, 666 F.3d 836 (2d Cir. 2012).

The Third Circuit followed the approach of *Castle Harbour* in Historic Boardwalk Hall LLC v. Commissioner, 694 F.3d 425 (3d Cir. 2012), where a tax-exempt party attempted to transfer § 47 historic rehabilitation tax credits (HRTC) to a taxable corporation using a limited liability company taxed as a partnership. The New Jersey Sports and Exposition Authority (NJSEA) had an ownership interest in the historic East Hall of the Atlantic City Boardwalk Hall under a 35-year lease, and it transferred that interest to Historic Boardwalk Hall, LLC, in which Pitney Bowes (through a subsidiary and an LLC) was the 99.9% member and the NJSEA was the 0.1% member. The transfer included the § 47 federal tax credit of 20% of the qualified rehabilitation expenditures incurred in transforming the run-down East Hall from a flat-floor convention space to a "special events facility" that could host concerts, sporting events, and other civic events. The Tax Court upheld transfer of the HRTC indicating that the purpose of § 47 was to encourage taxpayers to participate in what would otherwise be an unprofitable activity (136 T.C. 1 (2011)). The Third Circuit reversed, holding that Pitney Bowes was not a bona fide partner in Historic Boardwalk Hall LLC. Based on its analysis of the facts, the Third Circuit concluded that Pitney Bowes was not a partner because, as the transaction was structured, (1) Pitney Bowes "had no meaningful downside risk because it was, for all intents and purposes, certain to recoup the contributions it had made to HBH and to receive the primary benefit it sought—the HRTCs or their cash equivalent," and (2) Pitney Bowes's "avoidance of all meaningful downside risk in HBH was accompanied by a dearth of any meaningful upside potential." As for downside risk, the Court of Appeals reversed as clearly erroneous the Tax Court's finding that Pitney Bowes bore a risk because it might not receive an agreed upon 3% preferred return on its contributions to HBH. Referring to Virginia Historic Tax Credit Fund 2001 LP v. Commissioner, 639 F.3d 129 (4th Cir. 2011), the Third Circuit treated Pitney Bowes's 3% preferred return as a "return on investment" that was not a "share in partnership profits," which pointed to the conclusion that Pitney Bowes did not face any true entrepreneurial risk. As for upside potential, applying the substance over form doctrine, the court concluded that "although in form PB had the potential to receive the fair market value of its interest . . . in reality, PB could never expect to share in any upside." The court noted that it was "mindful of Congress's goal of encouraging rehabilitation of historic buildings" and that its holding might "jeopardize the viability of future historic rehabilitation projects," but the court observed that it was not the tax credit provision itself that was under attack but rather the particular transaction transferring the benefits of the credit in the manner that it had.

7. ESTATE PLANNING PARTNERSHIPS

In recent years, the use of partnerships to hold assets solely for estate planning purposes has been significant. The purpose of these partnerships is to facilitate inter vivos gifts of partial interests in property without surrendering control and to reduce the valuation for estate tax purposes of the retained interest. To achieve these objectives, the taxpayer will transfer business or investment assets previously owned solely by the taxpayer to a newly formed partnership in which the objects of the bounty of the taxpayer are the other partners. The other partners receive their partnership interests as gifts (or for nominal consideration). If the taxpayer retains voting control of the partnership and the partnership is respected for tax purposes, the value of the partnership assets that would be received by the other partners in liquidation of the partnership has been eliminated from the taxpayer's estate (although a gift tax usually is payable to achieve this goal). Furthermore, if the partnership is respected, under normal valuation rules the value of the retained partnership interest will be found to be less than the proportionate value of the underlying assets. For example, a 50% partnership interest in a partnership holding a parcel of land worth $1,000,000 will be found to be worth substantially less than $500,000. This planning technique has given rise to a number of cases in which the question of whether a formally organized partnership would be respected for tax purposes.

Shortly before his death, the decedent in Estate of Strangi v. Commissioner, 115 T.C. 478 (2000), formed a family limited partnership for the purpose of reducing the valuation of the decedent's assets for estate tax purposes. He transferred financial assets, real estate, and interests in other partnerships to the family limited partnership in exchange for a 99% interest as a limited partner. A corporation, owned 47% by decedent and 53% by his wife, as trustee, held a 1% general partnership interest. Soon after the decedent limited partner's death, the partnership distributed a substantial portion of its assets. The issue was whether the entity would be respected, which would be the asset to be valued for estate tax purposes, or whether the partnership's assets would be directly included in the decedent's estate (the value of the assets far exceeded the value of the partnership interest due to a substantial discount applicable to the interest). Although the court found as matters of fact that the entity was not a joint investment vehicle, that the entity was not formed for the purpose of managing assets, and that it conducted no active business, the entity was nevertheless recognized as a partnership. The crucial reasoning of the court was as follows.

> SFLP [the partnership] was validly formed under State law. The formalities were followed, and the proverbial "i's were dotted" and "t's were crossed." The partnership, as a legal matter, changed the relationships between decedent and his heirs and decedent and actual and potential creditors. Regardless of subjective intentions, the partnership had sufficient substance to be recognized for tax purposes. Its existence would not be disregarded by potential purchasers of decedent's assets, and we do not disregard it in this case.

A concurring opinion by Judge Laro would have limited the holding to the estate and gift taxes because he believed that the majority opinion's broader reasoning could cause mischief in income tax cases. On appeal, the Fifth Circuit affirmed the Tax Court's conclusions regarding recognition of the partnership but remanded the case to the Tax Court to consider the Commissioner's arguments regarding estate tax provisions. Gulig v. Commissioner, 293 F.3d 279 (5th Cir. 2002). The Commissioner was upheld on remand, T.C. Memo. 2003–145.

Knight v. Commissioner, 115 T.C. 506 (2000), another family limited partnership valuation case, also upheld the validity of the limited partnership's existence solely on the ground that it was a valid partnership under state law.

PROBLEM SET 2

1.   Suphuric Electric Power Co. and the Metropolis Municipal Electric Co. own a coal mine in Kentucky as tenants in common. Each of them pays one-half of the costs of operating the mine and is entitled to take one-half of the output for use in their respective electric generating businesses, which are otherwise unrelated. Are Suphuric Electric Power Co. and the Metropolis Municipal Electric Co. partners with respect to the coal mine operation?

2.   Glenn and Helen are lawyers who share a single office suite and the costs of a receptionist. Glenn is a real estate lawyer, and Helen is a plaintiff's trial lawyer. They share general overhead office expenses (e.g., office rent, utilities, and photocopiers, etc.), but each pays their own share of variable expenses, (e.g., travel, etc.), and they bill their own clients. They do, however, refer clients to each other from time to time for work within the other's area of expertise. Are they partners for tax purposes?

3.   Al, Betty, Carl, and Donna purchased Blackacre, which is 500 acres of undeveloped land on the outskirts of Gotham City, as tenants in common. Each contributed $100,000 toward the purchase price.

(a)   They plan to hold Blackacre as a speculative investment for several years, until Gotham City expands and Blackacre appreciates; they then hope to sell it to an as yet undetermined real estate developer. Have Al, Betty, Carl, and Donna formed a partnership? Would it make any difference if they agreed that none of them would have a right to sell his or her undivided interest in Blackacre independently of the others?

(b)   Al, Betty, Carl, and Donna hire a surveyor to prepare a subdivision plat for Blackacre, which they plan to divide into 200 house lots. Al, Betty, Carl, and Donna sell the lots in differing numbers to 20 different builders and split the profits equally. Have Al, Betty, Carl, and Donna formed a partnership? Would it make any difference if they planned to sell all of the subdivision lots to one builder, but obtained the subdivision approval first in order to increase the value of the entire tract?

4.   (a)   Ed and Fay each contributed $500,000 to the purchase price of a 30-unit apartment building. Is there any way that Ed and Fay can avoid being classified as a partnership if they operate the apartment building?

(b)   What if the property Ed and Fay bought was a warehouse with a single tenant under a 20-year lease?

(c)   What if Ed and Fay are husband and wife who reside in California, a community property state?

5.   Ilene purchased a vacant apartment building and agreed with Jake, who is an architect-contractor, that if Jake would supervise the renovation of the apartment building for sale as condominium units, Jake would be entitled to 30% of the profits from the resale. Are Ilene and Jake partners for federal income tax purposes? Is whether Jake shares losses relevant? Is whether Jake has a voice in determining the nature of the renovation, the costs to be incurred, and the sales price asked for the condominium units relevant?

6.   Kyle started an unincorporated computer software development business. To finance development of a new software program, Kyle borrowed $1,000,000 from the Pari-Mutuel Venture Capital Fund. The loan is evidenced by a nonrecourse promissory note due in 10 years. Interest is set at the prime rate, plus 10% per year, plus 30% of Kyle's net profits from the exploitation of the software. Are Kyle and Pari-Mutuel Venture Capital Fund partners?

7.   A owns the X LLC; A and X LLC formed the AX LLC. Is the AX LLC a partnership for federal income tax purposes?

SECTION 3.   ANTI-ABUSE REGULATIONS

REGULATIONS: Section 1.701–2(a)–(c).

Treas.Reg. § 1.701–2 provides sweeping "anti-abuse" rules with respect to the application of Subchapter K. Under these provisions, a transaction can be recast at the Commissioner's behest "even though the transaction may fall within the literal words of a particular statutory or regulatory provision." Among the possible consequences are: (1) the purported partnership may be disregarded and its assets and activities considered to be owned and conducted by one or more of the purported partners; (2) one or more of the purported partners may not be treated as a partner; (3) accounting methods may be adjusted to reflect clearly the partnership's or the partner's income; (4) the partnership's items of income, gain, loss, deduction, or credit may be reallocated; or (5) the claimed tax treatment may be otherwise adjusted or modified. Treas.Reg. § 1.704–1(b).

The premise of these anti-abuse rules is that "Subchapter K is intended to permit taxpayers to conduct joint business (including investment) activities through a flexible economic arrangement without incurring an entity-level tax." Treas.Reg. § 1.701–2(a). Implicit in this intent are requirements that a partnership be bona fide and that each partnership transaction or series of related transactions have been entered into for a substantial business purpose; the form of partnership transaction should be respected after applying substance over form principles; and the tax consequences to the partnership and to each partner must accurately reflect the partners' economic agreement and clearly reflect each partner's income. The Regulations acknowledge, however, that certain provisions of Subchapter K and the Regulations thereunder have been adopted for administrative convenience and that the proper application of those provisions in some circumstances produce tax results that do not properly reflect income. In such cases, the clear reflection of income requirement is deemed to have been satisfied. See Treas.Reg. § 1.701–2(d), Ex. 11.

Treas.Reg. § 1.701–2(c) provides that whether a partnership was formed or availed of with a purpose to reduce substantially the partners' tax liabilities in a manner inconsistent with the intent of subchapter K is determined with reference to all of the facts and circumstances, including the purported business purpose for the transaction and the claimed tax benefits. The Regulations list seven illustrative factors that may be taken into account, but they disclaim any presumption based on the presence or absence of any of the factors. In addition, thirteen examples illustrate various applications of the factors. The examples include transactions that are consistent with the intent of Subchapter K as well as transactions that are inconsistent with the intent of Subchapter K.

Treas.Reg. § 1.701–2(e)(1) specifically provides that a partnership may be treated as the aggregate of the partners rather than as a separate entity if necessary to carry out the purpose of any provision of the Internal Revenue Code, unless a provision of the Code or Regulations prescribes entity treatment *and* the ultimate tax results are "clearly contemplated" by the provision. This provision is grounded on the Treasury's conclusion that there is significant potential for abuse "in the inappropriate treatment of a partnership as an entity in applying rules outside of subchapter K to transactions involving partnerships." T.D. 8588, 1995–1 C.B. 109. Treas.Reg. § 1.702–2(f) provides some examples of the application of this rule. In an abundance of caution, the Regulations specifically state that the examples "do not delineate the boundaries of either permissible or impermissible types of transactions" and that changing any facts in the examples may change the results.

Because of the generality of the anti-abuse Regulations, the secrecy surrounding the taxpayers and tax practitioners structuring the transactions to which the Regulations presumably are intended to be applied, and the relative dearth of case law laying a groundwork for the Regulations, it is difficult for an observer to suggest hypothetical transactions to which these provisions will be applied. Although the IRS has provided some examples of transactions to which the anti-abuse rules will be applied, as well as transactions to which they will not be applied, it is not possible to extrapolate a broad picture of the ambit of the anti-abuse Regulations from these examples. The best that can be said is that these rules might be intended to serve primarily as an *in terrorem* device to deter taxpayers and their advisors from planning too close to the edge.

payments in the computations of their distributive shares of the partnership's taxable income. The Commissioner assessed deficiencies against each partner-respondent for his distributive share of the amount paid by Kaiser. Respondents, after paying the assessments under protest, filed these consolidated suits for refund.

The Commissioner premised his assessment on the conclusion that Kaiser's payments to the trust constituted a form of compensation to the partnership for the services it rendered and therefore was income to the partnership. And, notwithstanding the deflection of those payments to the retirement trust and their current unavailability to the partners, the partners were still taxable on their distributive shares of that compensation. Both the District Court and the Court of Appeals disagreed. They held that the payments to the fund were not income to the partnership because it did not receive them and never had a "right to receive" them. * * * They reasoned that the partnership, as an entity, should be disregarded and that each partner should be treated simply as a potential beneficiary of his tentative share of the retirement fund.[6] Viewed in this light, no presently taxable income could be attributed to these cash basis[7] taxpayers because of the contingent and forfeitable nature of the fund allocations. * * *

We hold that the courts below erred and that respondents were properly taxable on the partnership's retirement fund income. This conclusion rests on two familiar principles of income taxation, first, that income is taxed to the party who earns it and that liability may not be avoided through an anticipatory assignment of that income, and, second, that partners are taxable on their distributive or proportionate shares of current partnership income irrespective of whether that income is actually distributed to them. * * *

II

Section 703 of the Internal Revenue Code of 1954, insofar as pertinent here, prescribes that "[t]he taxable income of a partnership shall be computed in the same manner as in the case of an individual." 26 U.S.C. § 703(a). Thus, while the partnership itself pays no taxes, 26 U.S.C. § 701, it must report the income it generates and such income must be calculated in largely the same manner as an individual computes his personal income. For this purpose, then, the partnership is regarded as an independently recognizable entity apart from the aggregate of its

---

[6]   The Court of Appeals purported not to decide, as the District Court had, whether the partnership should be viewed as an "entity" or as a "conduit." 450 F.2d 109, 113 n. 5, and 115. Yet, its analysis indicates that it found it proper to disregard the partnership as a separate entity. After explaining its view that Permanente never had a right to receive the payments, the Court of Appeals stated: "When the transaction is viewed in this light, the partnership becomes a mere *agent* contracting on behalf of its members for payments to the trust for their ultimate benefit, rather than a *principal* which itself realizes taxable income." Id., at 115 (emphasis supplied).

[7]   Each respondent reported his income for the years in question on the cash basis. The partnership reported its taxable receipts under the accrual method.

partners. Once its income is ascertained and reported, its existence may be disregarded since each partner must pay a tax on a portion of the total income as if the partnership were merely an agent or conduit through which the income passed.[8]

In determining any partner's income, it is first necessary to compute the gross income of the partnership. One of the major sources of gross income, as defined in § 61(a)(1) of the Code, is "[c]ompensation for services, including fees, commissions, and similar items." 26 U.S.C. § 61(a)(1). There can be no question that Kaiser's payments to the retirement trust were compensation for services rendered by the partnership under the medical service agreement. These payments constituted an integral part of the employment arrangement. The agreement itself called for two forms of "base compensation" to be paid in exchange for services rendered—direct per-member, per-month payments to the partnership and other, similarly computed, payments to the trust. * * * Payments to the trust, much like the direct payments to the partnership, were not forfeitable by the partnership or recoverable by Kaiser upon the happening of any contingency.

Yet the courts below, focusing on the fact that the retirement fund payments were never actually received by the partnership but were contributed directly to the trust, found that the payments were not includable as income in the partnership's returns. The view of tax accountability upon which this conclusion rests is incompatible with a foundational rule, which this Court has described as "the first principle of income taxation: that income must be taxed to him who earns it." Commissioner v. Culbertson, 337 U.S. 733, 739–740 (1949). The entity earning the income—whether a partnership or an individual taxpayer— cannot avoid taxation by entering into a contractual arrangement whereby that income is diverted to some other person or entity. Such arrangements, known to the tax law as "anticipatory assignments of income," have frequently been held ineffective as means of avoiding tax liability. The seminal precedent, written over 40 years ago, is Mr. Justice Holmes' opinion for a unanimous Court in Lucas v. Earl, 281 U.S. 111 (1930). There the taxpayer entered into a contract with his wife whereby she became entitled to one-half of any income he might earn in the future. On the belief that a taxpayer was accountable only for income actually received by him, the husband thereafter reported only half of his income. The Court, unwilling to accept that a reasonable construction of the tax

---

[8] There has been a great deal of discussion in the briefs and in the lower court opinions with respect to whether a partnership is to be viewed as an "entity" or as a "conduit." We find ourselves in agreement with the Solicitor General's remark during oral argument when he suggested that "[i]t seems odd that we should still be discussing such things in 1972." Tr. of Oral Arg. 14. The legislative history indicates, and the commentators agree, that partnerships are entities for purposes of calculating and filing informational returns but that they are conduits through which the taxpaying obligation passes to the individual partners in accord with their distributive shares. See, e.g., H.R.Rep. No. 1337, 83d Cong., 2d Sess., 65–66 (1954); S.Rep. No. 1622, 83d Cong., 2d Sess., 89–90 (1954) * * *.

laws permitted such easy deflection of income tax liability, held that the taxpayer was responsible for the entire amount of his income.

* * *

The principle of *Lucas v. Earl,* that he who earns income may not avoid taxation through anticipatory arrangements no matter how clever or subtle, has been repeatedly invoked by this Court and stands today as a cornerstone of our graduated income tax system. * * * And, of course, that principle applies with equal force in assessing partnership income.

Permanente's agreement with Kaiser, whereby a portion of the partnership compensation was deflected to the retirement fund, is certainly within the ambit of *Lucas v. Earl.* The partnership earned the income and, as a result of arm's-length bargaining with Kaiser, was responsible for its diversion into the trust fund. The Court of Appeals found the *Lucas* principle inapplicable because Permanente "never had the right itself to receive the payments made into the trust as current income." 450 F.2d, at 114. In support of this assertion, the court relied on language in the agreed statement of facts stipulating that "[t]he payments * * * were paid solely to fund the retirement plan, and were not otherwise available to [Permanente] * * *." Ibid. Emphasizing that the fund was created to serve Kaiser's interest in a stable source of qualified, experienced physicians, the court found that Permanente could not have received that income except in the form in which it was received. * * * We think it clear, however, that the tax laws permit no such easy road to tax avoidance or deferment. Despite the novelty and ingenuity of this arrangement, Permanente's "base compensation" in the form of payments to a retirement fund was income to the partnership and should have been reported as such.

III

Since the retirement fund payments should have been reported as income to the partnership, along with other income received from Kaiser, the individual partners should have included their shares of that income in their individual returns. 26 U.S.C. §§ 61(a)(13), 702, 704. For it is axiomatic that each partner must pay taxes on his distributive share of the partnership's income without regard to whether that amount is actually distributed to him. *Heiner v. Mellon,* 304 U.S. 271 (1938), decided under a predecessor to the current partnership provisions of the Code, articulates the salient proposition. After concluding that "distributive" share means the "proportionate" share as determined by the partnership agreement, id., at 280, the Court stated:

"The tax is thus imposed upon the partner's proportionate share of the net income of the partnership, and the fact that it may not be currently distributable, whether by agreement of the parties or by operation of law, is not material." Id., at 281.

Few principles of partnership taxation are more firmly established than that no matter the reason for nondistribution each partner must pay taxes on his distributive share. * * *

The courts below reasoned to the contrary, holding that the partners here were not properly taxable on the amounts contributed to the retirement fund. This view, apparently, was based on the assumption that each partner's distributive share prior to retirement was too contingent and unascertainable to constitute presently recognizable income. It is true that no partner knew with certainty exactly how much he would ultimately receive or whether he would in fact be entitled to receive anything. But the existence of conditions upon the actual receipt by a partner of income fully earned by the partnership is irrelevant in determining the amount of tax due from him. The fact that the courts below placed such emphasis on this factor suggests the basic misapprehension under which they labored in this case. Rather than being viewed as responsible contributors to the partnership's total income, respondent-partners were seen only as contingent beneficiaries of the trust. In some measure, this misplaced focus on the considerations of uncertainty and forfeitability may be a consequence of the erroneous manner in which the Commissioner originally assessed the partners' deficiencies. The Commissioner divided Kaiser's trust fund payments into two categories: (1) payments earmarked for the tentative accounts of *nonpartner* physicians; and (2) those allotted to *partner* physicians. The payments to the trust for the former category of nonpartner physicians were correctly counted as income to the partners in accord with the distributive-share formula as established in the partnership agreement.[16] The latter payments to the tentative accounts of the individual partners, however, were improperly allocated to each partner pursuant to the complex formula in the retirement plan itself, just as if that agreement operated as an amendment to the partnership agreement.

The Solicitor General, alluding to this miscomputation during oral argument, suggested that this error "may be what threw the court below off the track." It should be clear that the contingent and unascertainable nature of each partner's share under the retirement trust is irrelevant to the computation of his distributive share. The partnership had received as income a definite sum which was not subject to diminution or forfeiture. Only its ultimate disposition among the employees and partners remained uncertain. For purposes of income tax computation it made no difference that some partners might have elected not to participate in the retirement program or that, for any number of reasons, they might not ultimately receive any of the trust's benefits. Indeed, as the Government suggests, the result would be quite the same if the

---

[16] These amounts would be divided equally among the partners pursuant to the partnership agreement's stipulation that all income above each partner's drawing account "shall be distributed equally."

"potential beneficiaries included no partners at all, but were children, relatives, or other objects of the partnership's largesse."[18] The sole operative consideration is that the income had been received by the partnership, not what disposition might have been effected once the funds were received.

IV

In summary, we find this case controlled by familiar and long-settled principles of income and partnership taxation. There being no doubt about the character of the payments as compensation, or about their actual receipt, the partnership was obligated to report them as income presently received. Likewise, each partner was responsible for his distributive share of that income. We, therefore, reverse the judgments and remand the case with directions that judgments be entered for the United States.

DETAILED ANALYSIS

1.   PARTNERSHIP TAXABLE INCOME AND SEPARATELY STATED ITEMS

Basye demonstrates the relationship between the determination of partnership taxable income and the treatment of the partnership itself as a mere conduit for purposes of imposing tax liability. While partnership taxable income is computed at the entity level, each partner is then currently taxed on the partner's distributive share of that taxable income, even if it has not been distributed to the partner. This rule is so important to the operation of Subchapter K that it applies, as in *Basye,* even where the partnership agreement or a contractual agreement prevents the current distribution of income. Thus, for example, in Burke v. Commissioner, 485 F.3d 171 (1st Cir. 2007), the taxpayer was required to include in income the taxpayer's distributive share of partnership income even though partnership assets were held in an escrow account established by the partners pending resolution of a dispute between the partners on how to divide the proceeds of the partnership.

Partnership taxable income is computed following the same rules that govern the computation of the taxable income of any individual engaged in business, with a few specific statutory modifications. Section 703(a)(2) disallows deductions for personal exemptions, charitable contributions, net operating losses, foreign taxes, depletion on oil and gas wells, and the special deductions allowed to individuals under §§ 211–223. In addition, the standard deduction provided for individuals by § 63(b) is disallowed for partnerships. I.R.C. § 63(c)(6)(D). Treas.Reg. § 1.703–1(a)(2)(viii) adds to the

---

[18] Brief for United States 21. For this reason, the cases relied on by the Court of Appeals, 450 F.2d, at 113, which have held that payments made into deferred compensation programs having contingent and forfeitable features are not taxable until received, are inapposite. Schaefer v. Bowers, 50 F.2d 689 (C.A.2 1931); Perkins v. Commissioner, 8 T.C. 1051 (1947); Robertson v. Commissioner, 6 T.C. 1060 (1946). Indeed, the Government notes, possibly as a consequence of these cases, that the Commissioner has not sought to tax the nonpartner physicians on their contingent accounts under the retirement plan. Brief for United States 21.

list of disallowed deductions the capital loss carryover deduction under § 1212, because capital gains and losses are separately stated and flow through to the individual partners, who may carry over unused capital losses. In addition, §§ 702(a) and 703(a)(1) require certain items entering into the computation of an individual's income tax liability to be segregated and separately stated on the partnership's return. These items require separate consideration to determine their character as capital gain or loss or ordinary income or loss at the partner's level or the extent to which they are includable in or excludable or deductible from the partner's gross income. In general, under Treas.Regs. §§ 1.703–1(a) and 1.702–1(a)(1)–(8), any item that will differentially affect a partner's taxable income must be separately stated. Expressly listed separately stated items include capital gains and losses, § 1231 gains and losses, charitable contributions, dividends received (if there is a corporate partner), and foreign taxes. I.R.C. § 702(a)(1)–(6). Treas.Reg. § 1.702–1(a)(8)(i)–(ii) adds to the statutory list bad debt recoveries, wagering gains and losses, expenses for the production of nonbusiness income, medical expenses, dependents' care, alimony, taxes and interest paid to housing cooperatives, oil and gas intangible drilling and development costs, solid mineral exploration expenditures, gains and losses recognized under § 751(b) by a partnership possessing substantially appreciated inventory or unrealized receivables upon a disproportionate distribution, and any items of income, gain, loss, deduction, or credit subject to a specific allocation under the partnership agreement that differs from the general profit and loss ratio.

Because under Treas.Reg. § 1.702–2 each partner separately computes the partner's individual net operating loss deduction by taking into account the partner's distributive share of partnership items, any income or deduction item that requires special treatment in computing the partner's § 172 NOL deduction must be separately stated, even if not specifically identified in the Regulations. Thus, for example, the limitations on the deduction of passive losses under § 469, the disallowance of deductions for personal interest under § 163(h), and the limitation on the deduction of investment interest under § 163(d), require that investment interest paid or received be separately stated in many cases. See Rev.Rul. 84–131, 1984–2 C.B. 37 (requiring that interest paid be separately stated by a partnership that has any partner subject to the investment interest deduction limitations of § 163(d)); Rev.Rul. 86–138, 1986–2 C.B. 84 (extending the same rule to lower tier partnerships if any partner in an upper tier partnership is subject to § 163(d)).

Section 108(d)(6) requires that the insolvency exception to discharge of indebtedness income be applied at the individual partner level rather than at the partnership level. Thus, partnership discharge of indebtedness income is a separately stated item under § 702(a). Rev.Rul. 92–97, 1992–2 C.B. 124. In Rev.Proc. 92–92, 1992–2 C.B. 505, the IRS announced that it will not challenge the treatment by an insolvent or bankrupt partnership of a discharge of a purchase money indebtedness as an adjustment to purchase price under § 108(e)(5), rather than as separately stated cancellation of indebtedness income, if the discharge otherwise would have qualified as a purchase price adjustment, as long as all partners report the treatment consistently. In effect, this permits an insolvent partnership to elect whether to treat the discharge as a purchase price reduction or to pass through discharge of indebtedness income that could be excluded only by insolvent partners.

Partnership business income (excluding separately stated items), which in general is the amount described in § 702(a)(8), is computed by including all of the income and deductions attributable to each separate business of the partnership. Because of the passive loss limitations of § 469, however, it may be necessary for a partnership to state separately the net income or loss from each separate business "activity" that it conducts, and this segregation will always be required of limited partnerships. Furthermore, when this segregation is required, it is necessary to attribute separately to each such "activity" any partnership items that are separately stated as required by § 702(a)(1)–(7). Implementation of new § 199A also will require many partnerships to separately state additional items relating to the computation of qualified business income.

A partnership "loss" within the meaning of § 702(a)(8) is any excess of deductions over gross income, as distinguished from a loss within the meaning of § 165, which is a transactionally based concept. In Garcia v. Commissioner, 96 T.C. 792 (1991), the IRS attempted to apply § 165 to limit a general partner's deduction of his distributive share of the partnership's bottom line loss because the taxpayer-partner had filed suit against other partners demanding the return of his original capital investment. The IRS asserted that the taxpayer had not sustained a loss because the taxpayer had the prospect of recovery. In rejecting the IRS's argument, the court distinguished operational losses required to be taken into account by the partner under § 702(a) from a loss of capital investment cognizable under § 165, which is subject to limitation based on the prospect of recovery of the loss.

2.   CHARACTER OF ITEMS AND ACTIVITIES

2.1. *Determination Based on Partnership Activities*

As previously indicated, § 702(a)(1)–(7) and the Regulations thereunder adopt a conduit approach, which requires the partners to report separately their distributive shares of any partnership item of income, credit, or deduction receiving specialized treatment under the Code. These items must be separately stated on the partnership return. I.R.C. § 703(a)(1). Section 702(b) amplifies this conduit concept with respect to the segregated items by treating the partners as if "such item were realized directly from the source from which realized by the partnership, or incurred in the same manner as incurred by the partnership." Section 702(b) has been interpreted to require that the determination of the character of an income or deduction item be made by reference to its characterization at the partnership level. Treas.Reg. § 1.702–1(b); Podell v. Commissioner, 55 T.C. 429 (1970) (real property was not a capital asset in the hands of the partnership, and hence the partner's share of income on the disposition of the asset was ordinary); Rev.Rul. 68–79, 1968–1 C.B. 310 (where the partnership held an asset meeting the long-term capital gain holding period in its hands, the individual partner could treat the partner's distributive share of disposition gain as long-term gain even though he had been a partner for less than the long-term gain holding period). Consistent application of this approach would ignore the activities of the individual partner, as where, for example, the partnership sells investment real estate and one of the partners is a dealer in that type of property in an individual capacity. Rev.Rul. 67–188, 1967–1 C.B. 216, held that a loss on real property determined to be § 1231 property at the partnership level retained that character in the hands of the individual partner, who was a real estate dealer; the ruling, however, did not deal expressly with the effect of the taxpayer's individual activity on the nature of the loss.

As illustrated by *Madison Gas & Electric* (see Chapter 17, Section 2.B), whether a business has commenced or is in the startup period also is determined at the partnership level. The resolution of this issue affects whether expenses may be deducted currently or must be capitalized and amortized over 180 months under § 195.

Although a partner is generally treated as engaged in the trade or business of a partnership in which the partner is a member, Rev.Rul. 2008–12, 2008–1 C.B. 520, concludes that a limited partner in a partnership engaged in the trade or business of trading securities is subject to the investment interest limitation of § 163(d) on the partner's distributive share of the partnership's interest deduction. Section 163(d)(5)(A)(ii) provides that the term "property held for investment" includes any interest held by a taxpayer in an activity involving the conduct of a trade or business that is not a passive activity and with respect to which the taxpayer does not materially participate. Temp.Reg. § 1.469–1T(e)(6) provides that trading personal property for the account of owners of an interest in the activity (without regard to whether or not the activity is a trade or business) is not a passive activity. Thus, the distributive share of interest of a partner who is not a material participant in the partnership is investment interest described in § 163(d)(3). As such it is subject to the § 163(d) limitation on the deduction of investment interest. Rev.Rul. 2008–38, 2008–1 C.B. 129, adds that a partner's distributive share of investment interest that is allocable to the partnership's trade or business of trading securities is, nonetheless, deductible above the line in calculating adjusted gross income. (The effect of § 163(j), enacted in 2017 and discussed in Detailed Analysis 4.2 below, would, however, need to be evaluated.)

2.2. *Determination Based on Contributing Partner's Activities*

Section 724 provides special rules under which certain property contributed to a partnership by a partner retains the character that it had in the partner's hands. Unrealized receivables, such as cash method accounts receivable, retain their ordinary income character. I.R.C. § 724(a). Inventory, however, retains an ordinary income taint for only five years if the partnership holds the property as a capital asset or as § 1231 property (depreciable or real property held for use in the taxpayer's trade or business). I.R.C. § 724(b). After five years the character of gain or loss on the property will be determined with reference to the purpose for which the partnership holds the property at that time. Similarly, capital assets that have built-in loss at the time of their contribution retain their capital character for five years after the date of the contribution, but only to the extent of the built-in loss at the time of the contribution. I.R.C. § 724(c). If the loss is greater because the property loses value while held by the partnership, the character of the excess loss is determined with reference to the purpose for which the partnership held the property. Suppose, for example, that a partner contributes land held as a capital asset, with a basis of $100 and a fair market value of $70, to a partnership that holds the land for sale to customers in the ordinary course of business. Four years later the partnership sells the land for $60. The $40 loss is treated as a $30 capital loss and a $10 ordinary loss. Under § 704(c), the $30 capital loss must be allocated to the partner who contributed the property. The purpose of these rules is to prevent the conversion of ordinary income into capital gain, thereby obtaining a rate preference, or of capital loss into ordinary loss, thereby avoiding the capital loss limitation rules of § 1211 through the contribution of the property to a partnership.

2.3. *Partnership Interests Held in Connection with Performance of Services*

The 2017 Tax Act added a new § 1061, which applies to taxable years beginning after December 31, 2017. It requires that long-term capital gain "with respect to" certain partnership interests held in private equity, hedge fund, or similar structures be treated as short-term capital gain unless the interest has been held for more than three years. This new rule is discussed primarily in Chapter 24.

3.   BASIS OF A PARTNER'S INTEREST

3.1. *General*

In *Basye*, the partnership income taxed to the physician partners is reflected as an upward adjustment to the basis in each partner's partnership interest under § 705(a). This adjustment to basis, coupled with the rule of § 731 that a partner does not recognize any gain on a partnership distribution unless the amount of money distributed exceeds the basis of the partnership interest, is the heart of the mechanism that assures that partners pay one level of tax on partnership profits. As income is earned by the partnership, the partner pays taxes on the income and adjusts the partner's basis upward. When the previously taxed income is distributed, the partner does not recognize income and reduces the partner's basis. Assuming that there have been no other events affecting the partner's basis, the basis after the distribution is identical to what it was before the income was earned. In the absence of a distribution, the partner will recover basis on sale or liquidation of the partner's interest in the partnership.

Section 705(a) prescribes a number of adjustments that must be taken into account in determining the basis of a partner's interest in a partnership. The partner starts with a basis determined under § 722 for contributions to the partnership (see Chapter 19); the basis is then increased by the partner's distributive share of the partnership profits, tax-exempt receipts, and the excess of percentage depletion deductions over the adjusted basis of depletable property; and it is decreased by distributions to the partner and the partner's distributive share of losses as well as nondeductible expenditures not properly chargeable to a capital account. See Treas.Reg. § 1.705–1(a)(2) & (3). A partner's basis is, however, never reduced below zero. If the adjustment that would otherwise reduce basis below zero is a distribution, § 731 directs that the partner recognize gain. A partner's basis in the partnership interest is frequently referred to as "outside basis," while the basis the partnership has in its assets is frequently referred to as "inside basis."

While § 705(a)(1)(B) refers to "income * * * exempt from tax," Treas.Reg. § 1.705–1(a)(2)(ii) properly refers more broadly to "tax-exempt receipts." Suppose the partnership realizes gain on a transaction that it is not required to recognize because of the operation of a section like § 1031 (deferral of gain and loss on real property like-kind exchanges), § 1033 (deferral of gain on replacement of involuntarily converted property), and similar. If the income item is merely deferred (e.g., deferred gain in a like-kind exchange of real property) rather than being completely excluded (e.g., § 103 interest), there should not be an upward adjustment of partnership basis. Rev.Rul. 96–11, 1996–1 C.B. 140, describes the standard for determining whether a basis adjustment is appropriate: "In determining whether a transaction results in exempt income within the meaning of § 705(a)(1)(B), or a nondeductible, noncapital expenditure within the meaning of § 705(a)(2)(B), the proper inquiry is whether the transaction has a permanent effect on the partnership's basis in its assets, without a corresponding current or future effect on its taxable income."[1] If basis were increased when the unrecognized gain is realized, a "double crediting" of the accrued gain would be produced, i.e., once on the exchange and again on disposition of the property received in the exchange.

Similar principles apply with respect to losses and nondeductible expenditures not properly chargeable to a capital account (e.g., a fine that is nondeductible under § 162(f)). Deferred losses do not result in a basis reduction, but disallowed deductions and losses do result in a basis reduction. See Rev.Rul. 96–10, 1996–1 C.B. 138. In both cases the principle is that the partners' bases in their partnership interests should be reduced by the amount by which the partnership's basis in its assets (including cash) was reduced. Thus, Rev.Rul. 96–11, supra, held that when a partnership makes a charitable contribution of appreciated property, the partners reduce their bases in their partnership interests only by their shares of the partnership's basis for the donated property, even if each partner deducts the partner's share of the fair market value of the donated property. See also I.R.C. § 704(d)(3)(B). This treatment preserves the intended benefit of providing a charitable contribution deduction for the fair market value of certain types of property without requiring the recognition of gain with respect to the appreciation. If the partners were required to reduce their bases in their partnership interests by the fair market value of the donated

---

[1]   Similarly, under § 265, which disallows deductions for expenses allocable to tax-exempt income, it has been held that unrecognized gain is not income "wholly exempt" from tax and hence no disallowance of deduction is required. See, e.g., Hawaiian Trust Co. Ltd. v. United States, 291 F.2d 761 (9th Cir.1961); Commissioner v. McDonald, 320 F.2d 109 (5th Cir.1963).

property, then, as a result of the basis reduction, the gain attributable to the appreciation of the donated property would be recognized upon a subsequent sale of the partnership interests.

Outside basis reduction is required whether deductions are disallowed at the partnership or individual partner level. See Rev.Rul. 89–7, 1989–1 C.B. 178 (a partner must reduce basis in the partner's partnership interest by the full amount of § 179 costs expensed by the partnership even though the partner could not fully deduct the partner's distributive share of such costs because of the application of the § 179(b)(1) limitation at the individual partner level).

3.2. *Alternative Basis Rules*

When a partnership is liquidated or a partnership interest sold, § 705(a) read literally would require a partner to go back to the beginning and laboriously determine the partner's outside basis by adjusting each year for the distributive share of each item of the partnership and for each distribution to the partner. The same computation would be necessary to determine whether a distributive share of loss exceeds outside basis. The partnership records may or may not make this possible. Moreover, in a simple partnership, these computations are not really necessary. A partner's outside basis will be the partner's pro rata share of the total adjusted inside basis of the partnership's assets if the following are true: (1) the partners' profit and loss ratios are the same as their capital ratios; (2) the partners' contributions were in cash or in properties whose basis and value were the same at the time of the contributions; (3) any current distributions were pro rata and were either in cash or in property whose basis equaled its value; and (4) there have been no retirements or sales of a partner's interest. Many partnerships will meet these conditions. Using a pro rata share of the partnership's inside basis works under these conditions because the sum of cumulative proportionate adjustments of § 705(a) would yield this result. Hence, § 705(b) authorizes Regulations permitting the use of this simple formula. Treas.Reg. § 1.705–1(b) implements this statutory provision and also authorizes and requires adjustments to the basic formula to reflect any significant discrepancies arising as a result of contributed property, transfers, or distributions.

4.   ELECTIONS AND LIMITATIONS

4.1. *General*

Section 703(b) provides that, in general, elections under the Code are to be made by the partnership, except that the partners individually make separate elections in three cases: (1) elections to reduce the basis of depreciable property instead of other tax attributes when discharge of indebtedness income is not recognized under § 108(b)(5), relating generally to insolvent taxpayers, or § 108(c)(3), relating to cancellation of qualified real property indebtedness; (2) elections under § 617 with respect to mine exploration costs; and (3) elections with respect to the foreign tax credit under § 901. The partnership elects its taxable year and accounting method, including its inventory method, as well as elections with respect to depreciation deductions under § 168, the deduction of intangible drilling and development costs under § 263(c), and election out of installment reporting under § 453(d). Treas.Reg. § 1.703–1(b)(1); see also Rev.Rul. 68–139, 1968–1 C.B. 311.

In Demirjian v. Commissioner, 457 F.2d 1 (3d Cir.1972), a partnership realized a gain on the involuntary conversion of real property. The partners individually replaced the converted partnership property with property similar or related in service or use and attempted to elect nonrecognition of gain under § 1033. The court held that the gain was required to be recognized. Section 703(b) requires that the election under § 1033 be made by the partnership, and to be effective, the partnership, not the partners, must acquire the replacement property. See also McManus v. Commissioner, 583 F.2d 443 (9th Cir.1978) (same).

While Subchapter K is silent as to whether the limitations imposed by the Code on the amount of an item to be taken into account are to be imposed at the partner or partnership level, Treas.Reg. § 1.702–1(a)(8)(iii) generally applies such limitations at the partner level. Thus, the $3,000 limit on deducting capital losses against ordinary income under § 1211(b), the percentage limitations on charitable contributions under § 170, the limitation on the deduction of investment interest under § 163(d), the $25,000 ceiling on the deduction against nonpassive income of losses from active participation real estate activities under § 469(i), and the limitation on percentage depletion of oil and gas under § 613A are applied at the partner level. Section 469, restricting the ability to deduct passive activity losses, and § 461(*l*), limiting the deduction of excess business losses, are also applied at the individual partner level (although partnership decisions will affect how partners' are able to group activities for purposes of § 469, see Chapter 23). Section 179(d)(8) applies the dollar value ceiling on expensing of depreciable property at *both* the partnership and individual partner level. In Hayden v. Commissioner, 204 F.3d 772 (7th Cir. 2000), the court upheld the validity of Treas.Reg. § 1.179–2(c)(2), which limits the amount of the partnership's § 179 deduction passed through to partners to the taxable income of the partnership. This result is dictated by § 179(b)(3)(A) and (d)(8).

4.2. *Limitation on Business Interest*

4.2.1. *General*

Legislation enacted in 2017 imposes a new limitation on the deductibility of interest expense. Under § 163(j), the deduction for business interest shall not exceed the sum of the taxpayer's business interest income plus 30% of the taxpayer's adjusted taxable income, plus the taxpayer's "floor plan financing interest," if any.

Business interest means any interest paid or accrued on indebtedness properly allocable to a trade or business. Business interest income means the amount of interest includible in the gross income of the taxpayer for the taxable year that is properly allocable to a trade or business. Floor plan financing interest is defined as interest paid to finance motor vehicles that are held for sale or lease.

Adjusted taxable income is defined in § 163(j)(8) as the taxpayer's taxable income computed without regard to nonbusiness deductions, any business interest income, any net operating loss deduction, the deduction allowed under § 199A, and any deduction allowable for depreciation. For tax years beginning on or after January 1, 2022, however, depreciation deductions may not be added back.

In scope, the § 163(j) restriction on the deductibility of interest expense applies across-the-board regardless of the form of business entity utilized to conduct the business. However, § 163(j)(3) provides an exception for small businesses, which § 163(j)(3) defines by cross-reference to § 448(c) as a business with average annual gross receipts (computed over 3 years) of $25 million or less. Furthermore, § 163(j)(7) provides additional exceptions by narrowing § 163(j)'s application to trades or businesses other than the following: (i) a trade or business of performing services as an employee; (ii) any electing real property trade or business (cross-referenced to the definition in § 469(c)(7)(C)); (iii) any electing farming business (cross-referenced to § 263A(e)(4) or for cooperatives to § 99A(g)(2)); or (iv) for certain utility trades or businesses (e.g., electrical energy, water, or sewage disposal services).

If a real estate business elects to be exempt from § 163(j), then § 168(i)(8) requires that real estate business to utilize the alternative depreciation system for its real property, thus causing it to have a longer recovery period. Because real estate businesses making the election allowed by § 163(j)(7)(B) must use the alternative depreciation system for so-called qualified improvement property (among other categories), electing out of § 163(j)'s interest expense limitation makes these electing real estate businesses ineligible to claim bonus depreciation with respect to any qualified improvement property even if it might otherwise have been entitled to do so.

Any disallowed interest expense is allowed to be carried forward indefinitely under § 163(j)(2) and utilized in a subsequent year to the extent that the taxpayer has excess limitation when the limitation calculation is made for that later year.

4.2.2.   *Application of § 163(j) to Partnerships*

Section 163(j) contains specific rules for partnerships. The limitation is applied at the partnership level, and "any deduction for business interest shall be taken into account in determining the non-separately stated taxable income or loss of the partnership." I.R.C. § 163(j)(4)(A).

Although an entity-level approach can lead to administrative simplification, in this instance the approach requires an additional set of complex rules. To prevent a partner from using the taxable income distributive share from one partnership to increase the partner's adjusted taxable income for purposes of applying the 30% limitation rule to business interest paid by the partner's other businesses, § 163(j) requires a partner to determine a partner's "adjusted taxable income" for purposes of applying the 30% limitation to any other businesses by disregarding all of the partner's partnership tax items and then adding back in the partner's share, if any, of the "partnership's excess taxable income." I.R.C. § 163(j)(4)(A)(ii). Otherwise, the partner would be able to use a partnership's taxable income twice—once when the partnership determines the limitation for its business and once when the partner determines the limitation as to any of the partner's other businesses. A partner's share of the excess taxable income is determined in the same manner as the partner's distributive share of the nonseparately stated taxable income or loss of the partnership. "Excess taxable income" is determined through a formula. I.R.C. § 163(j)(4)(C). The partnership must create a fraction, the numerator of which is 30% of the partnership's adjusted taxable income minus the amount of business interest it paid that exceeds its business interest income. The denominator is 30% of the partnership's adjusted taxable income. The fraction is then applied to the partnership's adjusted taxable income to obtain the "excess taxable income." For example, if a partnership had $100,000 of adjusted taxable income, $20,000 of business interest paid, and $10,000 of business interest income, the excess taxable income would be $66,667—that is, 2/3 of $100,000 (the numerator would be $20,000, computed as $30,000 (30% of $100,000) minus $10,000 ($20,000 interest paid − $10,000 interest received)); the denominator would be $30,000 (30% of $100,000). A partner receiving a one-third distributive share would increase taxable income for purposes of applying the 30% rule to the partner's other businesses by $22,222 (and change).

Second, a partnership may have business interest income that is less than the maximum amount allowed (i.e., the business interest income is less than 30% of the partnership's adjusted taxable income). In such a situation, a partner should be allowed to use the partner's share of the partnership's excess taxable income for purposes of applying the 30% limitation to the business interest paid by the partner's other businesses.

The statute is silent with respect to another potential problem: a partner's use of the partner's distributive share of a partnership's business interest income to offset business interest paid through other businesses or of the partner's distributive share of a partnership's "floor plan financing" to increase the partner's deduction. The statutory rules described in the preceding paragraphs regarding taxable income are insufficient to address these issues. Notice 2018–28 provides:

> The Treasury Department and the IRS intend to issue regulations providing that, for purposes of calculating a partner's annual deduction for business interest under section 163(j)(1), a partner cannot include the partner's share of the partnership's business interest income for the taxable year except to the extent of the partner's share of the excess of (i) the partnership's business interest income over (ii) the partnership's business interest expense (not including floor plan financing). Additionally, the Treasury Department and the IRS intend to issue regulations providing that a partner cannot include such partner's share of the partnership's floor plan financing interest in determining the partner's annual business interest expense deduction limitation under section 163(j). Such regulations are intended to prevent the double counting of business interest income and floor plan financing interest for purposes of the deduction afforded by section 163(j) and are consistent with general principles of Chapter 1 of the Code.

Proposed Regulations issued in November 2018 incorporate these limitations (REG–106089–18).

As noted above, if the deduction of business interest is limited by § 163(j), the disallowed business interest is carried forward, and partnership specific rules apply. § 163(j)(2), (4). If a partnership has business interest that is limited by § 163(j), it is carried over to the next year. But, instead of the partnership applying the excess business interest payment to its computations for the succeeding year(s), the excess business interest is allocated to the partners, in proportion to their shares of the partnership's nonseparately stated income or loss. This allocation reduces their outside bases (but not below zero). The allocated excess business interest is treated as paid (and thus deductible) only when and to the extent a partner is allocated "excess taxable income." § 163(j)(4)(B). Partners are required to apply "excess taxable income" first to any excess business interest they have been allocated before they may use it for purposes of applying the 30% limitation to business interest paid through other businesses. § 163(j)(4)(B)(ii)(flush language).

If a partner disposes of the partner's partnership interest before all of the excess business interest allocated to the partner has been treated as paid, the partner will increase the partner's basis in the interest immediately before the disposition. The adjustment equals the previous basis reduction(s) over the business interest treated as paid by the partner. § 163(j)(4)(B)(iii)(II). (This adjustment applies even if the basis increase is essentially meaningless—for example, if the disposition occurs by reason of death.) No additional business interest deduction is allowed to either the transferor partner or the transferee.

4.2.3.   *CARES Act Modifications to § 163(j)*

Legislation enacted in response to the COVID-19 pandemic contained temporary amendments to § 163(j). Generally, for tax years beginning in 2019 and 2020, 50% of the taxpayer's adjusted taxable income is used instead of 30%; in addition, taxpayers may elect to use their 2019 taxable income for their 2020 calculation. I.R.C. § 163(j)(10). Partnerships, however, must continue to use 30% of adjusted taxable income for tax years beginning in 2019. Partners, however, are able to treat 50% of excess business interest allocated for tax years beginning in 2019 as deductible business interest during tax years beginning in 2020 without restriction (the remaining 50% of the allocated 2019 excess business interest is governed by the rules described in the preceding section). Elections out of these default rules are available.

5.   PARTNERSHIP TAXABLE YEAR

A partnership has its own taxable year under § 706(b)(1). Section 706(a) provides that a partner includes the partner's distributive share of partnership items in the partner's taxable year in which or with which the partnership year ends. If the partnership's freedom to choose its taxable year were unfettered, this rule would permit significant tax deferral. Individual partners, who almost invariably use a calendar year, could cause the partnership to elect a fiscal year ending on January 31, in which case all of the income of the partnership from February through December would not be reportable by the partners until the next calendar year. To prevent this type of avoidance, § 706(b) restricts the partnership's choice of its taxable year.

In general, a partnership must adopt the same taxable year as any one or more of its partners who have an aggregate interest in partnership profits and capital of more than 50%. Because most individuals use the calendar year, any partnership in which a majority of the partners are individuals usually will use a calendar year. If there is neither a more than 50% partner nor a majority group with the same year, the partnership must adopt the same taxable year as *all* of the "principal partners," who are the partners with a 5% or more interest in profits or capital.[2] To prevent avoidance of the rules restricting the choice of the partnership's taxable year, § 706(b)(2) prohibits a principal partner from changing to a taxable year different from the partnership unless the partner can establish a business purpose for the change.

If neither the majority interest rule nor the principal partner rule can be used to determine a taxable year, Treas.Reg. § 1.706–1 requires the partnership to adopt the taxable year that results in the least aggregate deferral of reporting income by the partners. The aggregate deferral for a year is the sum of the products derived by multiplying the number of months of partnership income that is deferred into a later taxable year of each partner by that partner's interest in partnership income. Treas.Reg. § 1.706–1(b)(3)(i). The partnership must adopt the taxable year that produces the lowest sum when compared to other partnership taxable years. For example, if the ABC partnership has three equal partners A, with a January 31st fiscal year, B, with a July 31st fiscal year, and C, with a calendar year, the partnership must adopt a calendar year under Treas.Reg. § 1.706–1 because the year ending on December 31 is the year of least aggregate deferral.

Year End	Interest in Partnership Profits	1/31 Year Months of Deferral	Interest X Deferral	7/31 Year Months of Deferral	Interest X Deferral	12/31 Year Months of Deferral	Interest X Deferral
1/31	33.3%	0	0	6	2.00	1	0.33
7/31	33.3%	6	2.00	0	0	7	2.33
12/31	33.3%	11	3.66	5	1.67	0	0
			5.66		3.67		2.66

The methodology for computing least aggregate deferral is illustrated in Treas.Reg. § 1.706–1(b)(3).

Under the rules of § 706(b), a partnership may be compelled to change its taxable year if new partners are admitted or, in some cases, if existing partners' percentage interests change. For example, suppose that in the case of the ABC partnership described in the preceding paragraph on February 1,

---

[2] When determining a partnership's permitted year, Treas.Reg. § 1.706–1(b)(6) generally disregards any foreign partners who are not subject to U.S. taxation on a net basis (i.e., foreign partners who are not allocated any effectively connected income or, if claiming treaty benefits, that do not have a permanent establishment). This rule does not apply if as a result the partnership year would be determined with reference to domestic partners no one of which holds at least a 10% interest and which in the aggregate hold less than 20% of the partnership interests.

Year 10, C sells C's interest to A, who becomes a two-thirds partner. Under § 706(b)(1)(B)(i) the partnership must adopt a January 31st fiscal year. Section 706(b)(4)(B) provides, however, that once the partnership's taxable year has been changed under the "majority interest" rule, a subsequent change will not be required during the first two years following the initial change. Thus, continuing the above example, if on February 1, Year 11, D and E, each having a July 31st fiscal year, were admitted to the ABC partnership as one-fifth partners, the partnership would not be required to change to a July 31st fiscal year (the year of B, D, and E, who together hold three-fifths of the partnership interests), until after the fiscal year ending on January 31, Year 13.

These strictures on the adoption of fiscal years by partnerships are relaxed by § 706(b)(1)(C), which allows a partnership to adopt a different taxable year with the permission of the IRS if the partnership can establish a business purpose for the fiscal year. The statute specifically provides that "deferral of income to partners shall not be treated as a business purpose." Rev.Proc. 2002–39, 2002–1 C.B. 1046, provides that a taxpayer "may establish a business purpose for the requested taxable year based on all the relevant facts and circumstances," but "administrative and convenience business reasons . . . will not be sufficient." See also Rev.Proc. 2002–38, 2002–1 C.B. 1037 (procedures for obtaining automatic approval of change). A taxpayer able to demonstrate a "natural business year" and requesting a change to that year will generally be deemed to have satisfied business purpose. Three tests are provided for determining the natural business year. For example, a partnership's natural business year may be established using the 25% gross receipts test, which looks to whether the partnership realizes 25% of its gross receipts (under the method of accounting used to prepare its tax returns) during the last two months of any 12-month period for three consecutive years. If the partnership has more than one natural business year, it may only adopt the one in which the highest percentage of gross receipts are received in the last two months.

The rigid rules of § 706, limiting flexibility in choosing a partnership's taxable year, are somewhat ameliorated by § 444. This provision allows an election, even if there is no business purpose, to a year where the "deferral period" is not longer than the shorter of 3 months or the "deferral period of the taxable year which is being changed." I.R.C. § 444(b)(2). For example, if a newly formed partnership would otherwise be required to use the calendar year, it nevertheless may elect to adopt a fiscal year ending as early as September 30. The § 444 election available to an existing partnership will depend on the length of its current deferral period; if it is shorter than 3 months, the partnership will be limited to that period and will not be able to increase its deferral period to 3 months. If an election is made under § 444, the partnership must make a payment computed under § 7519 to compensate the Treasury for the deferral of taxes. This is a nondeductible, entity-level payment that is not credited against the partners' individual tax liabilities. This payment in effect converts the interest-free loan generated by any tax deferral resulting from the use of a fiscal year into an interest-bearing loan. If a § 444 election is terminated, no subsequent § 444 election may be made the partnership. I.R.C. § 444(d)(2)(B).

The effect of termination of a partnership, the sale of a partnership interest, and the death or retirement of a partner on the partnership's and the partners' taxable years are considered later under those topics.

6.   PARTNERSHIP TAX RETURNS AND AUDIT PROCEDURES

As previously noted, § 6031 requires that a partnership return be filed. Section 6698 imposes additional penalties, over and above the general failure to file penalty of § 7203, on any partnership that fails to file a *complete* partnership tax return. Section 6222 requires a partner to treat a partnership item on the partner's return in a manner that is consistent with the partnership return or to file a statement with the partner's return explaining any inconsistency. If the inconsistency is not explained, any underpayment is "assessed and collected in the same manner as if such underpayment were on account of a mathematical or clerical error." I.R.C. § 6222(b).

The Bipartisan Budget Act of 2015 (BBA) adopted significant revisions to the partnership audit rules that allow the IRS to assess and collect taxes, and impose penalties, at the partnership level. I.R.C. §§ 6221–6223, 6225–6227, 6231–6235, and 6241. These rules are intended to simplify the prior complex procedures for determining who is authorized to settle on behalf of the partnership and to free the IRS from the obligation to send various notices to all of the partners. Deficiencies assessed against the partnership will be payable by the partnership, unless the partnership makes an election to "push out" all or some of adjustments and payments to those who were partners in the tax year at issue. A partnership with 100 or fewer eligible partners may elect out of the partnership audit procedures. I.R.C. § 6221(b). A partnership is not an eligible partner, but an S corporation is eligible. For partnerships that elect out of the new rules, partnership audits will be much more complicated because the IRS will be required to deal separately with each partner. The preamble to the Proposed Regulations noted that these elections will be scrutinized to ensure they are not being made "solely to frustrate IRS compliance efforts." 82 Fed. Reg. 27,334, 27,355 (June 14, 2017). The new rules apply to partnership taxable years beginning after December 31, 2017.[3]

PROBLEM SET 1

1.   Sean and Terry are partners in an investment partnership. Sean's share of partnership profits and losses is two-thirds, and Terry's share is one-third. Sean, Terry, and the partnership are all cash method, calendar year taxpayers. For the current year, the partnership received or incurred the following items.

---

[3]   For a more detailed overview of the BBA audit rules and Final Regulations, see Monica Gianni, Partnership Audit Rules: After the Final Regulations, J. Tax'n, June 2019, at 9.

Receipts and Gains:

Rents	$300,000
Gain from the sale of used computer (§ 1245 gain)	$ 3,000
Gain from sale of apartment building (§ 1231 gain)	$150,000
Short Term Capital Gain on NYSE traded securities	$ 12,000
Long Term Capital Gain on sale of land held for speculative investment	$ 90,000
Interest on City of New York bonds	$ 3,000

Outlays and Losses:

Employee salaries	$ 30,000
Rent	$ 24,000
Depreciation	$ 15,000
Stock broker's fees	$ 3,000
Charitable contributions	$ 9,000
Legal fees incurred to lobby Congress to reduce the tax rate on capital gains	$ 4,500
Long Term Capital Loss on sale of land held for speculative investment	$ 60,000
Short Term Capital Loss on NYSE traded securities	$ 9,000

(a) (1) How should the partnership, Sean, and Terry report these items? Does it matter whether the partnership makes any distributions?

(2) Would your answer change if Terry's primary occupation was as a dealer in real estate and most sales of land owned by him individually resulted in ordinary income characterization?

(b) Assume that the basis of Sean's partnership interest at the beginning of the year was $200,000 and the basis of Terry's partnership interest at the beginning of the year was $100,000. What are their bases in their respective partnership interests at the end of the year?

(c) What would be the tax consequences if the partnership distributed $20,000 to Sean and $10,000 to Terry on the last day of every month during the taxable year?

2. This year the Merrill, Barney & Dean partnership sold a parcel of investment real estate with a basis of $100,000 for $700,000. The partnership received a $150,000 down payment and the purchaser's 10-year promissory note (with interest, compounded semi-annually, at the mid-term federal rate) for $550,000. On the partnership's return, the sale was properly treated as an installment sale under § 453. As a result of transactions unrelated to the partnership, Dean had a significant capital loss carryover to this year and prefers to elect out of § 453 installment sale treatment under § 453(c). May Dean separately elect out of § 453?

3.   Several years ago, Mike and Nora formed a general partnership to purchase, rehabilitate, and rent multifamily residences. Mike contributed $200,000 in cash, and Nora contributed $100,000 in cash. Mike is a two-thirds partner, and Nora is a one-third partner. The partnership has made no distributions. At the end of the year, the partnership held the following assets, at fair market value, book value, and basis:

Asset	F.M.V.	Book Value	Basis
Cash	$120,000	$120,000	$120,000
Blackacre	$150,000	$ 90,000	$ 90,000
Whiteacre	$240,000	$180,000	$180,000
Greenacre	$ 60,000	$ 75,000	$ 75,000

The partnership has no debts. Can you ascertain each of Mike's and Nora's respective bases in their partnership interests?

4.   What taxable year may the partnership adopt in each of the following situations?

     (a)   The partnership is a real estate rental business conducted by 10 individuals, all of whom report on the calendar year.

     (b)   The partnership runs a ski resort in Colorado, which is open from November through April, with most of its business in January and February, and consists of three calendar-year individuals.

     (c)   The partnership operates a coal mine. Two of its partners are electric power utility companies, Carbonic Power Co. and Sulphuric Electric Power Co. What is the taxable year of the partnership if:

         (1)   Both power companies are 30% partners and report on an April 30th fiscal year. All of the remaining partners are individuals.

         (2)   Both power companies are 25% partners and report on an April 30 fiscal year. All of the remaining partners are individuals.

         (3)   Both power companies are 25% partners. Carbonic Power Company reports on an April 30th fiscal year and Sulphuric Electric Power reports on a September 30th fiscal year. All of the remaining partners are individuals.

     (d)   (1)   The partnership operates a coal mine. It has three equal corporate general partners. Two partners report on a May 31st fiscal year and one partner reports on a November 30th fiscal year.

         (2)   What taxable year would be required if the partner on a November 30th fiscal year purchased the entire interest of one of the other two partners?

SECTION 2. LIMITATION ON PARTNERS' DEDUCTIONS OF PARTNERSHIP LOSSES

INTERNAL REVENUE CODE: Sections 704(d); 752.

REGULATIONS: Section 1.704–1(d).

Section 704(d)(1) limits the deductibility of a partner's distributive share of a partnership loss to the partner's basis for the partnership interest. This limitation is related to the reduction of a partner's basis in the partnership interest by an amount equal to the partner's share of partnership losses and separately stated deductions pursuant to § 705; because the partner cannot reduce the basis of the partnership interest below zero, the pass through of deductions that otherwise would reduce the partner's basis for the partnership interest below zero is disallowed. Any disallowed deductions are held in suspense, to be allowed when a basis exists, such as through additional contributions, a future share of partnership earnings left in the partnership, or the incurring of a partnership liability. See Treas.Reg. § 1.704–1(d). Thus, suppose A contributes $100,000 cash and B contributes $50,000 cash, but they agree to share profits and losses equally because B will devote B's full-time effort to the partnership's business but A will work only part time in the partnership's business. The partnership spends $125,000 on deductible research costs. A can deduct $62,500, but B can deduct only $50,000 currently. B may deduct an additional $12,500 when B obtains sufficient basis. Suppose the partnership realizes a loss in Year 12 but an individual partner wishes to postpone the recognition of the loss until Year 13. Can the partner withdraw partnership capital at year end, hold the loss in the suspense account, and then recognize it in Year 13 upon a recontribution of the capital to the partnership, an action which would thereby reestablish basis in the partnership interest? Rev.Rul. 66–94 addresses this issue.

Revenue Ruling 66–94
1966–1 C.B. 166.

Advice has been requested as to the manner in which a partner should compute the basis of his partnership interest under section 705(a) of the Internal Revenue Code of 1954 for purposes of determining the extent to which his distributive share of partnership losses will be allowed as a deduction, and the extent to which gain will be realized by a partner upon the distribution of cash to him by the partnership.

During the taxable year, *A*, a member of the partnership, contributed $50x$ dollars to the partnership as his initial capital contribution, and received $30x$ dollars as a cash distribution from the partnership. *A*'s distributive share of partnership losses at the end of its taxable year was $60x$ dollars.

Section 705(a) of the Code provides, in part, that the adjusted basis of a partner's interest in a partnership shall be the basis of such interest determined under section 722 of the Code (relating to contributions to a partnership)—(1) increased by the sum of his distributive share for the taxable year and prior taxable years of taxable income of the partnership, tax exempt income of the partnership, and the excess of depletion deductions over the basis of depletable property, and (2) decreased, but not below zero, by distributions by the partnership as provided in section 733 and by the sum of his distributive share of partnership losses and nondeductible partnership expenditures not chargeable to capital account.

Section 1.704–1(d)(1) of the Income Tax Regulations provides, in part, that a partner's distributive share of partnership loss will be allowed only to the extent of the adjusted basis (before reduction by current year's losses) of such partner's interest in the partnership at the end of the partnership taxable year in which such loss occurred.

Section 1.704–1(d)(2) of the regulations provides, in part, that in computing the adjusted basis of a partner's interest for the purpose of ascertaining the extent to which a partner's distributive share of partnership loss shall be allowed as a deduction for the taxable year, the basis shall first be increased under section 705(a)(1) of the Code and decreased under section 705(a)(2) of the Code, except for losses of the taxable year and losses previously disallowed.

Section 1.731–1(a) of the regulations provides, in part, that where money is distributed by a partnership to a partner, no gain or loss shall be recognized to the partner except to the extent that the amount of money distributed exceeds the adjusted basis of the partner's interest in the partnership immediately before the distribution. For purposes of sections 731 and 705 of the Code, advances or drawings of money or property against a partner's distributive share of income shall be treated as current distributions made on the last day of the partnership taxable year with respect to such partner.

Based on the foregoing, it is concluded that:

(1) In computing A's adjusted basis for his interest in the partnership under section 705(a) of the Code, A's original basis, which is determined under section 722 relating to contributions to the partnership, should be decreased by first deducting distributions made to A by the partnership and thereafter, by deducting his distributive share of partnership losses. However, A's basis for his interest in the partnership may not be reduced below zero. Thus:

A's contribution to the partnership	50 x dollars
Deduct cash distributions made to A by the partnership	−30 x dollars
	20 x dollars

Deduct *A*'s distributive share of losses (60 × dollars) but only to the extent that *A*'s basis is not reduced below zero	−20 x dollars
A's basis for his interest in the partnership under section 705 of the Code	−0

(2)   In order to determine the extent to which *A*'s distributive share of partnership losses will be allowed as a deduction, *A*'s basis for his interest in the partnership computed in accordance with section 705(a) of the Code, should be determined without taking into account his distributive share of partnership losses for the taxable year. Thus:

A's contribution to the partnership	50 x dollars
Deduct cash distribution made to *A* by the partnership...	−30 x dollars
	20 x dollars
A's distributive share of partnership losses for the taxable year are not taken into account	−0
A's basis for determining the amount of his allowable partnership losses	20 x dollars

(3)   In order to determine the extent to which gain will be realized by *A* upon the distribution of cash to him by the partnership, *A*'s basis for his interest in the partnership computed in accordance with section 705(a) of the Code, should be determined without taking into account cash distributions made to him by the partnership during its current taxable year. Thus:

A's contribution to the partnership	50 x dollars
Cash distributions made by the partnership to *A* during the taxable year are not taken into account	−0
	50 x dollars
Deduct *A*'s distributive share of partnership losses to the extent allowed by section 704(d) of the Code. (See examples (1) and (2).).................	−20 x dollars
A's basis for determining the amount of gain he realized upon the distribution of cash to him by the partnership	30 x dollars

A may deduct his distributive share of the partnership loss to the extent of 20 *x* dollars (see example 2) and he realizes no gain from the cash distribution of 30 *x* dollars because his basis for determining the amount of gain upon such distribution is 30 *x* dollars (example 3).

DETAILED ANALYSIS

1.   TRANSFER OF AN INTEREST WITH SUSPENDED LOSSES

Sennett v. Commissioner, 752 F.2d 428 (9th Cir.1985), upheld the portion of Treas.Reg. § 1.704–1(d) requiring that a partner continue to be a partner to take advantage of the carryover of disallowed losses. In that case the taxpayer's share of partnership losses for 1968, his last year as a partner when his basis was zero, was $109,061. At the close of 1968, he sold his partnership interest back to the partnership in consideration of the partnership's promise to pay him $250,000 in the future, and he agreed to repay the partnership his share of the 1968 losses. In 1969, the partnership's obligation to Sennett was modified to call for a $240,000 payment, and the transaction was completed by the partnership setting off the $109,061 due from Sennett against the $240,000 and paying him only $130,939. Sennett claimed the suspended $109,061 loss in 1969 as an ordinary deduction and reported $240,000 of long-term capital gain. Sennett treated the set off as increasing his basis from zero to $109,061, which enabled him to claim the loss. He reduced his basis to zero and acknowledged the set off amount as included in his amount realized resulting in the $240,000 of long-term capital gain. The Commissioner, however, treated Sennett simply as having received $130,939 in exchange for a partnership interest with a basis of zero. The court held that since Sennett was no longer a partner in 1969 he could not have any basis in a partnership interest. Thus, no carryover of the ordinary loss deduction was allowed. Instead, the repayment was an offset to the amount realized by Sennett on the sale of the partnership interest.

2.   RELATIONSHIP OF SECTION 704(d) TO CHANGES IN SHARES OF PARTNERSHIP INDEBTEDNESS

Suppose that the CD partnership, an equal partnership in which C and D have identical interests, realizes a $5,000 loss, and D, whose distributive share of that loss is $2,500 (50%), has a zero basis. If the partnership were to borrow $5,000, then, under § 752(a) (see Chapter 21), D would be treated as contributing $2,500 in cash and D's basis would be increased by that amount. As a result, § 704(d) would not limit D's loss deduction. See Treas.Reg. § 1.704–1(d)(4), Ex. (2). In some instances, a year-end borrowing for the purpose of increasing basis to permit the deduction of losses might be recognized. In Corum v. United States, 268 F.Supp. 109 (W.D.Ky.1967), the partners of a road building partnership borrowed funds on December 28th and contributed the funds to the partnership; the contribution was returned to the partners and the lender was repaid on the following January 15th. The court agreed with the taxpayers that the business purpose for the transaction was to improve the liquidity on the partnership's year-end balance sheet, which was used by governmental authorities to determine the financial capability of the contractors bidding on jobs. The taxpayers were permitted to include the transitory capital contribution in the basis of their partnership interests for purposes of applying § 704(d) and thereby were allowed to deduct the entire distributive share of the partnership's loss for the year.

Richardson v. Commissioner, 693 F.2d 1189 (5th Cir.1982), held that the end of year basis was controlling for applying § 704(d). Thus, if a new partner is admitted during a year in which a partnership with debts incurs a loss and, as a result of the admission of the new partner, existing partners are treated under § 752(b) as receiving a cash distribution that reduces basis, each partner's basis is determined at the end of the year for purposes of applying § 704(d). Suppose that G is admitted to the EF partnership on December 30. Before G's admission, E and F each had a basis in the partnership interest of $160 and the partnership had debts of $300. As a result of G's admission to the partnership, $50 of debt is shifted from each of E and F to G, and E's and F's basis in their partnership interests is reduced by $50. During the current year prior to December 31, the EF partnership incurred a loss of $300, all of which will be allocated to E and F under § 706(d), discussed in Chapter 20. As a result of G's admission on December 31, before taking into account the loss, E and F each have a basis of $110 ($160 minus the $50 of debt of which each was relieved on C's admission) and a distributive share of the loss of $150. If they can use their December 30 basis, the entire loss is deductible by them. However, under *Richardson*, E and F may each deduct only $110 of the loss as limited by their year end bases. G cannot deduct any of the loss by virtue of § 706(d) (discussed in Chapter 20, Section 5).

3. RELATIONSHIP OF SECTION 704(d) TO CHARITABLE CONTRIBUTIONS AND FOREIGN TAXES

The 2017 Tax Act added § 704(d)(3), which provides that a partner's distributive share of charitable contributions and foreign taxes paid are subject to the basis limitation rule of § 704(d)(1). This provision is aimed at correcting language in the Treasury Regulations suggesting that charitable contributions and foreign taxes paid by the partnership are passed through to partners without limitation, even if those partners have insufficient outside basis. Treas.Reg. § 1.704–2(d); see also Priv.Ltr.Rul. 8405084 (Nov. 3, 1983) (providing that 704(d) was inapplicable to charitable contribution). Because taxpayers are permitted to take a charitable contribution in excess of basis for certain assets (e.g., corporate stock held more than one year), § 704(d)(3)(B) allows the same result for charitable giving by partnerships; it provides that, for "a charitable contribution of property whose fair market value exceeds its adjusted basis," the § 704(d) limitation does not apply "to the extent of the partner's distributive share of such excess." See I.R.C. § 170(e) (describing assets supporting charitable contribution deduction for unrealized asset appreciation).

4. OTHER LIMITATIONS ON PARTNERS' LOSS DEDUCTIONS

Even if a loss is not limited by § 704(d), deductions may be restricted by § 465, the at-risk rules; § 469, dealing with passive losses; or § 461(*l*), imposing limitations on noncorporate taxpayers for "excess business losses." The at-risk rules and passive activity loss limitation are particularly applicable to limited partners but may also affect general partners. These additional limitations are discussed in Chapter 23.

PROBLEM SET 2

1.   Gill and Harriet are general partners who share income and losses equally. Gill's basis in his partnership interest is $7,000, and Harriet's basis in her partnership interest is $12,000.

(a)   During the current year, the partnership incurs an operating loss of $20,000. How much loss can each of Gill and Harriet claim on their individual returns? What are their respective bases in their partnership interests after taking into account their shares of partnership losses?

(b)   In the following year, the partnership realized no operating income but did recognize a $5,000 long-term capital gain. What are the consequences to the partners in that year?

(c)   What are the results if in the current year, in which the partnership incurred a $20,000 loss, between January 1st and December 30th the partnership distributed $4,000 in cash to each of Gill and Harriet?

(d)   Gill died on January 1st of the year following the year in which the loss was incurred, and his wife, Irena, inherited his partnership interest. What would be the tax consequences to Irena if the partnership recognized a $5,000 long-term capital gain in that year?

SECTION 3.   SECTION 199A

INTERNAL REVENUE CODE: Section 199A.

REGULATIONS: Sections 1.199A–1, –3, –5, –6.

Section 199A was added by the 2017 Tax Act and applies for taxable years beginning after December 31, 2018, and before December 31, 2025. I.R.C. § 199A(i). The provision allows taxpayers other than C corporations to deduct up to 20% of the "qualified business income" from qualified pass-through businesses, including sole proprietorships, tax partnerships, and "S" corporations. I.R.C. § 199A(b)(2). The § 199A deduction is not an itemized deduction, but it reduces taxable income and does not reduce adjusted gross income. § 63(b)(3), (d)(3). Section 199A is highly complex and was enacted when the corporate tax rate was reduced to 21% in order to provide a tax cut for pass-through businesses.

DETAILED ANALYSIS

1.   QUALIFIED TRADE OR BUSINESS

A "qualified trade or business" means any trade or business other than those specifically excepted. I.R.C. § 199A(d)(1). The trade or business of being an employee is never a qualified business. Similarly, although located in a different subsection of § 199A, § 707 payments (generally treated as payments to a non-partner, discussed in Chapter 22) made to partners are never qualified business income. I.R.C. § 199A(c)(4)(B)–(C). Section 199A(c)(4) also specifies that "reasonable compensation paid to the taxpayer by any qualified trade or business of the taxpayer for services rendered with respect to the trade or business" is not qualified business income, but the legislative history indicates that this provision is intended to apply only to S corporation shareholders, and the Regulations take this approach.

Certain "specified service trade or businesses" (SSTBs) are also not qualifying businesses, but for this category, a threshold tied to taxpayer income applies (described in greater detail below). An SSTB means "any trade or business involving the performance of services in the fields of health, law, . . . accounting, actuarial science, performing arts, consulting, athletics, financial services, brokerage services, or any trade or business where the principal asset of such trade or business is the reputation or skill of 1 or more of its employees" and involving "the performance of services that consist of investing and investment management, trading, or dealing in securities, partnership interest, or commodities." I.R.C. §§ 199A(d)(2), 1202(e)(3)(A). Section 199A cross-references § 1202(e)(3)(A), but the engineering and architecture fields contained in that section are not included in the § 199A list of SSTBs.

Regulations finalized in 2019 attempt to define the various terms used in the SSTB list. For example, "performance of service in the field of law" means "the provision of services by lawyers, paralegals, legal arbitrators, mediators and similar professionals in their capacity as such . . . [It] does not include the provision of services that do not require skills unique to the field of law, for example, . . . The provision of services by printers, delivery services, or stenography services." Treas.Reg. § 1.199A–5(b)(2)(iii). To prevent taxpayers from attempting to circumvent the SSTB limitation through "cracking" a business into separate components in order to move elements out of the SSTB category,[4] Treas.Reg. § 1.199A–5(c)(2)(i) provides that an SSTB includes "any trade or business that provides 80 percent or more of its property or services to an SSTB if there is 50 percent or more common ownership of the trades or businesses." Further, if a business provides less than 80% of its property or services to an SSTB, but there is 50% or more common ownership with an SSTB, the property or services provided to the SSTB are treated as part of the SSTB. Treas.Reg. § 1.199A–5(c)(2)(ii). A de minimis rule does apply to ensure that a trade or business will not be an SSTB "because it provides a small amount of services in a specified service activity." Preamble to the Prop. § 199A Regs., 83 Fed. Reg. 40884 (Aug. 16, 2018). If the trade or business has gross receipts of $25 million or less, and less than 10% of the gross receipts are attributable to SSTB activities, the trade or business will not be an SSTB; if the trade or business has gross receipts greater than $25 million, it will not be an SSTB if less than 5% of its gross receipts are attributable to SSTB activities. Treas.Reg. § 1.199A–5(c)(1).

2. QUALIFIED BUSINESS INCOME

Qualified business income (QBI) means the "net amount of qualified items of income, gain, deduction, and loss with respect to any qualified trade or business of the taxpayer." I.R.C. § 199A(c)(1). The amount is determined separately for each trade or business and may be a negative amount for a

---

[4] See Gregg D. Polsky, Taxing Litigation: Federal Tax Concerns of Personal Injury Plaintiffs and Their Lawyers, 22 Fla. Tax Rev. 120 (2018).

particular business. See Treas.Reg. § 1.199A–1(d)(2)(iii). Taxpayers have some ability to aggregate trades or businesses, and then treat the aggregate as a single trade or business, but under rules that differ from those used for § 469 or § 465. See Treas.Reg. § 1.199A–4.

QBI items must be effectively connected with a U.S. trade or business and must be "included or allowed in determining taxable income for the taxable year." I.R.C. § 199A(c)(3)(A). When losses previously disallowed under § 1366(d), § 465, § 469, or § 461(*l*) become allowable, they are taken into account for computing QBI on a first-in, first-out basis. Treas.Reg. § 1.199A–3(b)(1)(iv), (v). Disallowed losses that derive from taxable years ending before January 1, 2018, are, however, not taken into account for purposes of computing QBI.

Certain items are not eligible to be included in QBI; these include short- or long-term capital gains and losses; dividends, dividend equivalents and payments in lieu of dividends; interest income, other than business interest income; and gains and losses from certain commodities transactions, foreign currencies, and certain notional principal contracts; amounts received from a non-business annuity; and "[a]ny item of deduction or loss properly allocable" to the preceding list. I.R.C. § 199A(c)(3)(B). Finally, qualified REIT dividends and qualified publicly traded partnership income is not treated as "qualified business income," although such items are eligible for the § 199A deduction via another subsection. I.R.C. § 199A(b)(1)(B), (c)(1).

3. COMPUTATION FOR TAXPAYERS ABOVE THRESHOLD LIMITATIONS

For each qualifying business, a percentage is applied to its net qualifying business income. That percentage is the lesser of (1) 20% or (2) the greater of (a) 50% of the W-2 wages of the qualifying business or (b) 25% of the W-2 wages of the qualifying business, plus 2.5% of the "unadjusted basis immediately after acquisition of all qualified property." I.R.C. § 199A(b)(2). (As discussed below, taxpayers under a certain income threshold use 20% as the percentage without the need to compare it to W-2 wages or unadjusted basis.) W-2 wages are essentially the compensation paid to employees of the business and as to which the employee receives an information return. I.R.C. § 199A(b)(4); Treas.Reg. § 1.199A–2(b)(2). "Qualified property" is depreciable tangible property that is "held by, and available for use in" the qualified business, used "at any point during the taxable year in the production of qualified business income," and whose depreciable period has not ended before the close of the taxable year. I.R.C. § 199A(b)(6)(A). "Depreciable period" is defined as the later of 10 years after the property is placed in service or "the last day of the last full year of the applicable recovery period" that applies under § 168 (ignoring the alternative depreciation system). If a trade or business produces a net negative QBI, the W-2 wages and the unadjusted basis of qualified property are not taken into account and are not carried over to subsequent years. Treas.Reg. § 1.199A–1(d)(2)(iii)(A).

Section 199A states that it "shall be applied at the partner" level, but whether there is a qualifying business and the amount of QBI are determined at the partnership level. Treas.Reg. § 1.199A–6(b)(2) provides guidance under which a partnership must determine whether it is engaged in one or more trades or businesses, determine whether any are SSTBs, determine the QBI for each business, and determine the W-2 wages and unadjusted basis of qualified property. Section 199A(f)(1)(A)(ii) states that "each partner . . . shall take into account such person's share of each qualified item of income, gain, deduction, and loss." Thus, each partner must be assigned a share of the partnership's W-2 wages and unadjusted basis in order to complete the § 199A computation. The statute provides that a partner's share of W-2 wages is determined in the same manner as the partner's share of wage expenses, and a partner's share of unadjusted basis is allocated in the same manner as the partner's share of depreciation. The partnership must report this information to its partners. Treas.Reg. § 1.199A–6(b)(3).

Once a taxpayer has computed the QBI for each business, the amounts from each business are then aggregated into the "combined qualified business income amount." I.R.C. § 199A. If a business has a net negative QBI, the taxpayer must offset the net negative QBI against the positive QBI of the taxpayer's other trades or businesses "in proportion to the relative amounts of net QBI in the trades or businesses with positive QBI." Treas.Reg. § 1.199A–1(d)(2)(iii)(A). If there is, however, an overall negative QBI, the loss is carried over and treated as "negative QBI from a separate trade or business in the succeeding taxable year." Treas.Reg. § 1.199A–1(d)(2)(iii)(B). See I.R.C. § 199A(c)(2).

Even after the taxpayer determines the "combined qualified business income," an overall limitation may limit the taxpayer's ability to deduct the entire amount. I.R.C. § 199A(a). The final deduction is the lesser of (1) the taxpayer's combined qualified business income or (2) 20% of the excess of the taxpayer's taxable income over the taxpayer's net capital gain. I.R.C. § 199A(a).

4.   THRESHOLD LIMITATIONS

Taxpayers below certain income thresholds benefit through the relaxation of two of the rules discussed above. First, such taxpayers are able to treat SSTBs as qualified businesses. Second, such taxpayers are able to take 20% of their net qualifying items from a qualifying business without being subject to the W-2 or unadjusted basis limitation. These benefits are lost gradually (and through complicated formulas) for taxpayers within a particular taxable income range. This range begins at $157,500 ($315,000 for joint filers), and the benefits are lost completely at $207,500 ($415,000 for joint filers). I.R.C. § 199A(b)(3), (d)(3), (e)(2). These ranges are indexed for inflation after 2018.

PROBLEM SET 3

1.   Zaha is an architect, and her taxable income has for many years exceeded $1 million annually. She owns 50% of Elite Designs LLC, which is taxed as a partnership, and her share of all partnership tax items is also 50%. During 2020, Elite Designs has the following items:

Income

Receipts from consulting work	$5,000,000
LTCG from sale of investment asset	$ 10,000

Payments

§ 707(a) payments to Zara	$1,500,000
Wages paid to other employees	$ 500,000
Supplies	$ 200,000

In addition, Elite Designs owns the building where the consulting is performed. Elite Designs purchased the building in 2018 for $900,000; assume it properly takes $25,000 of depreciation deductions each year. Determine the amount, if any, of Zaha's § 199A deduction.

CHAPTER 19

FORMATION OF THE PARTNERSHIP

SECTION 1. CONTRIBUTIONS OF MONEY OR PROPERTY

INTERNAL REVENUE CODE: Sections 721; 722; 723; 704(c)(1)(A); 1223(1) and (2); 1245(b)(3). See also § 168(i)(7).

REGULATIONS: Sections 1.721–1; 1.722–1; 1.723–1; 1.704–1(b)(2)(iv)(*a*) through (iv)(*d*)(*2*), (iv)(*f*)(*1*) through (iv)(*f*)(*4*), (iv)(*f*)(*5*)(*i*), and (iv)(*q*).

When persons form a partnership, the starting point for determining the partners' substantive interests in the partnership's assets upon liquidation is the fair market value of the money or other property contributed by each partner. The fair market value of each partner's contribution should be recorded in the partner's "capital account," and the partnership's "book value" for each asset, the starting point for determining the partnership's accounting profit or loss with respect to the asset, likewise will be its fair market value. As the partnership operates and allocations of partnership items are passed through, adjustments are made to the partners' capital accounts and to the partnership's asset book values. Chapter 18 introduced the pass-through nature of partnerships, and Chapter 20 will discuss the allocation of partnership items in greater detail.

Suppose, for example, that A, B, and C form a partnership to which A contributes $100,000 in cash, B contributes Whiteacre, for which B paid only $40,000 but which is worth $100,000, and C contributes Blackacre, for which C paid $60,000 but which is worth $100,000. Notwithstanding the different original cash outlays by B and C for Whiteacre and Blackacre, each of A, B, and C will be treated as having contributed $100,000 of value to the partnership. For Subchapter K *accounting* purposes, the partnership will track the partners' original contributions through entering the book value of the cash, Blackacre, and Whiteacre each at $100,000. The partners will maintain capital accounts that will similarly track the value of each partner's contribution to the partnership. Note that *tax* Regulations specify the rules governing the maintenance of these accounts; although there are multiple similarities between these rules and generally accepted accounting principles, in order to obtain the benefit of various tax safe harbors (discussed in Chapter 20), the capital account rules specified in the tax Regulations must be followed.

Immediately after the formation of the ABC partnership, its balance sheet is as follows:

	Assets			Partners' Capital	
	Book Value			**Book Value**	
Cash	$100,000		A	$100,000	
Whiteacre	$100,000		B	$100,000	
Blackacre	$100,000		C	$100,000	
Total	$300,000			$300,000	

This method of book accounting gives B and C credit for the appreciation in the properties between the time of purchase and the time of contribution. This treatment reflects the economic bargain between the parties but generally does not directly relate to the income tax consequences of formation of the partnership, although maintenance of these accounts is crucial to evaluating whether pass-through allocations of partnership tax items will be respected under the safe harbor Regulations (see Chapter 20).

In addition to formation requiring the creation of capital accounts, various Code sections apply to determine the tax consequences of formation. Sections 721–723 provide that no gain or loss is recognized by the partnership or partners on a contribution of property to a partnership in exchange for a partnership interest, that a partner's basis for the partnership interest is equal to the sum of the adjusted bases for the contributed property and any cash contributed, and that the partnership's basis for the contributed property is equal to its adjusted basis in the hands of the contributing partner. The nonrecognition rule of § 721 overrides § 1001(c), which generally requires that realized gains and losses be recognized. Section 722 prescribes the partner's basis in the partnership interest, which is a separate and distinct asset from the underlying property owned by the partnership. As noted in Chapter 18, the partner's basis in the partnership interest is commonly referred to in tax jargon as "outside basis." Section 723 prescribes the partnership's basis in the assets contributed by the partners; the partnership will take the partner's basis, except that additional considerations apply with respect to property contributed with built-in loss. See I.R.C. § 704(c)(1)(C), discussed in Chapter 20. The partnership's basis in partnership property, whether contributed by partners or purchased by the partnership is commonly called "inside basis."

Applying these tax rules to the ABC Partnership, the results are that B does not recognize the $60,000 gain realized on the exchange of Whiteacre for B's partnership interest, and C does not recognize the $40,000 gain realized on the exchange of Blackacre for C's partnership interest. Instead, the gains are preserved through the substituted basis rules. B's basis in B's partnership interest is $40,000; C's basis in C's partnership interest is $60,000. ABC Partnership's basis in Whiteacre is $40,000, and its basis in Blackacre is $60,000.

The differences between partnership book accounting and partnership tax accounting can be illustrated by expanding the balance sheet of the ABC Partnership created above to include assets and partners' capital accounts at both book value and tax basis. Notice how partnership asset book value equals partners' capital accounts book value; this is not a coincidence; the Regulations require this balance sheet approach. Treas.Reg. § 1.704–1(b)(2)(iv)(*q*).

	Assets			**Partnership Debts & Partners' Capital Accounts**	
	Book Value	**Tax Basis**		**Book Value**	**Tax Basis**
Cash	$100,000	$100,000	A	$100,000	$100,000
Whiteacre	$100,000	$ 40,000	B	$100,000	$ 40,000
Blackacre	$100,000	$ 60,000	C	$100,000	$ 60,000
	$300,000	$200,000		$300,000	$200,000

As a result of the basis provisions in §§ 722 and 723, the gain that goes unrecognized under § 721 does not permanently escape taxation; it is deferred until a later recognition event occurs. (Unrecognized losses are similarly deferred, but full evaluation requires consideration of additional rules.) If B were to sell the partnership interest for $100,000, its fair market value, B would recognize a gain of $60,000—the amount of gain realized but not recognized on the exchange of Whiteacre for the partnership interest.

The transferred basis rule of § 723 would result in the partnership recognizing a $60,000 gain for tax purposes on the sale of Whiteacre for $100,000, even though it would have no profit for book accounting purposes. As discussed in Chapter 18, the partnership will not be taxed on this $60,000 tax gain; in this fact pattern, B will pay the tax on the gain under § 704(c)(1)(A), an allocation rule that will be discussed in Chapter 20.

The deferral mechanisms do not work perfectly, however, and in some instances, subsequent events may cause nonrecognition of gain or loss to become permanent. Conversely, because these provisions give rise to two bases in two distinct assets, there may be a double recognition of gain in the future (double recognition of loss is generally precluded through the operation of § 704(c)(1)(C)). The various basis adjustment provisions of Subchapter K generally prevent these occurrences as long as partnership interests are not bought and sold or otherwise transferred after the initial formation, but these problems nevertheless frequently do arise when partnership interests have been transferred.

Sections 721–723 apply both to contributions to an existing partnership as well as to contributions to a newly formed partnership. Application of these rules is fairly straightforward where only money and unencumbered property are contributed to the partnership, whether the partnership is already in existence or just being formed. Section 721 does not contain a specific mechanism, commonly known as a "boot" rule, to address the treatment of the partner if the partner has debt assumed by the partnership or receives cash or other property in addition to the partnership interest. Thus, if contributed property is encumbered by liens, the partnership otherwise assumes debts of a contributing partner, or cash or other property is distributed to a contributing partner in connection with the contribution, the tax treatment of the transaction is more complicated. Such transfers and assumptions by the partnership must also be analyzed under the § 707(a) disguised sale rules (discussed in Chapter 22) and the § 731 current distribution rules (discussed primarily in Chapter 25). As with many Subchapter K rules, § 721 can only be fully understood in the context of other provisions of Subchapter K.

Nonrecognition under § 721 is accorded only to contributions of *property* in exchange for a partnership interest. If a partnership interest is received in exchange for services rendered to the partnership or to a partner, § 721 does not apply. Treas.Reg. § 1.721–1(b)(2). Such a transaction generally will be taxable under either § 83 or the general principles of § 61.

DETAILED ANALYSIS

1.   PARTNERS' CAPITAL ACCOUNTS

Treas.Reg. § 1.704–1(b)(2)(iv) provides detailed rules regarding the maintenance of partners' capital accounts, which for practical reasons generally must be followed throughout the life of the partnership. In applying these rules, a partner who has more than one interest in the partnership is treated as having a single capital account that reflects all of the partner's interests, even if one interest is as a general partner and the other is as a limited partner, without regard to the time or manner of acquisition of the interests. Because capital accounts are maintained with reference to the fair market value of property contributed to the partnership, property distributed by the partnership, and allocations of operational items to the partner, a partner's capital account generally is not the same as the partner's basis in the partnership interest. A partner's capital account may be negative whereas the partner's basis may not be taken below zero.

A partner's initial capital account is the sum of the amount of any money contributed to the partnership by the partner, plus the fair market value (not the basis) of any property contributed by the partner. A partner's capital account will be increased in a like manner for any subsequent contributions by the partner to the partnership and by the amount of partnership book income allocated to the partner; the capital account will be decreased by the amount of any money distributed to the partner and by the partner's share of partnership book losses. Treas.Reg. § 1.704–1(b)(2)(iv)(*b*). (These adjustments will seem similar to the adjustments to outside basis required under § 705, discussed in Chapter 18, for the pass-through taxation of partnership income and losses, but because partnership book income and loss allocations may differ in amount from the related partnership tax allocations, it is not correct simply to apply § 705 adjustments to partner capital accounts.) If property is distributed to a partner, the partner's capital account must be reduced by the fair market value of the property. Treas.Reg. § 1.704–1(b)(2)(iv)(*e*).

Upon liquidation of the partnership, all capital accounts must be adjusted to reflect increases and decreases to the value of partnership property. In addition, partners' capital accounts may (but are not required to) be increased or decreased to reflect a revaluation of the partnership's property on the happening of certain events, such as the admission of a new partner, the distribution of property, or the liquidation of a partner's interest. Treas.Reg. § 1.704–1(b)(2)(iv)(*f*). In general, the partners' determination of the fair market value of property will be accepted by the IRS if the value is arrived at in arm's length negotiations in which the partners have sufficiently adverse interests. Treas.Reg. § 1.704–1(b)(2)(iv)(*h*).

2.　THE MEANING OF PROPERTY

2.1. *General*

In addition to tangible property and cash, a variety of intangible property rights, such as patents, may qualify as property, even if those rights were created by the personal efforts of the person who contributed them. Thus, "property" includes business goodwill, Rev.Rul. 70–45, 1970–1 C.B. 17, secret processes and formulae, even if not patented, Rev.Rul. 64–56, 1964–1 (Part 1) C.B. 133, and contracts to acquire property, Ambrose v. Commissioner, T.C. Memo. 1956–125. The line between services and self-created intangible property is not always easy to ascertain.

The problem of identifying "property" that qualifies an exchange for nonrecognition under § 721 also arises in determining whether stock received in exchange for a contribution to a corporation is eligible for nonrecognition under § 351, which governs transfers to a corporation for stock, although § 351 has some additional requirements not imposed by § 721. Accordingly, the precedents may be applied interchangeably, at least insofar as the issue is determining the meaning of "property."

2.2. *Accounts Receivable and Installment Obligations*

Installment obligations are specifically designated as eligible property in Treas.Reg. § 1.721–1(a). Moreover, § 453B does not require recognition of gain upon a transfer of an installment obligation to a partnership. See Treas.Reg. § 1.453–9(c)(2). Accounts receivable from performing services for persons other than the partnership also constitute property for purposes of §§ 721–723. See Hempt Bros., Inc. v. United States, 490 F.2d 1172 (3d Cir.1974) (receivables are property for purposes of § 351). Under § 704(c), discussed in Chapter 20, the remaining deferred tax gain on an installment obligation or the amount realized upon collection of a cash method account receivable must be allocated to the contributing partner when it is recognized.

2.3. *Partners' Own Promissory Notes*

A partner's personal promissory note contributed to the partnership in exchange for a partnership interest meets the definition of property, and the rules of §§ 721 through 723 govern. In this situation, Vision Monitor Software, LLC v. Commissioner, T.C. Memo. 2014–182, upheld the IRS's long-standing position that the contribution of a partner's own note to the partnership is not the equivalent of a contribution of cash, Rev.Rul. 80–235, 1980–2 C.B. 229, and without more, it will not increase the partner's basis in the partnership interest. As payments are made on the note, the partner's outside basis will be increased pro tanto. Treas.Reg. § 1.704–1(b)(2)(iv)(*d*)(*2*) provides that in such a case the partner's capital account is to be increased only as payments are made on the note or upon disposition of the note. Although the contribution of a partner's own promissory note does not directly increase outside basis, as will be discussed in Chapter 21, such a note may operate to increase a partner's share of partnership recourse debt, which will in turn allow for an increase to outside basis. I.R.C. § 752(a); Treas.Reg. § 1.752–2(b)(3).

The partnership's basis in the note would be zero under § 723 if it sells the note before any payments have been made.

2.4. *Contribution of Partnership's Debt to the Partnership*

Section 108(e)(8) provides that when a partnership transfers a partnership interest to a creditor in satisfaction of partnership debt, the partnership is treated as having satisfied the debt for an amount equal to the fair market value of the partnership interest. The partnership must recognize cancellation of indebtedness income to the extent that the amount of the canceled debt exceeds the fair market value of the partnership interest transferred to the creditor. The recognized cancellation of indebtedness income is then passed through to the partners and allocated solely among those who held interests in the partnership immediately prior to the satisfaction of the debt. Thus, under § 108(e)(8), if a debt of $1,000 is contributed to the partnership in exchange for a partnership interest worth $1,000, no cancellation of indebtedness income arises. But if the creditor contributes a debt of $1,000 in exchange for a partnership interest worth only $700, then the partnership must recognize $300 of cancellation of indebtedness income and must allocate it among the partners as constituted immediately before the discharge.

Treas.Reg. § 1.108–8 provides that the fair market value of a partnership interest received by the creditor in exchange for the debt is determined from all of the facts and circumstances. However, Treas.Reg. § 1.108–8(b) provides a safe harbor in which the debtor partnership and the creditor-partner may treat the fair market value of a partnership interest received in satisfaction of the debt as the liquidation value of the interest. The liquidation value of the interest is defined in Treas.Reg. § 1.108–1(b)(2)(iii) as the amount of cash that the creditor-partner would receive immediately after the debt-for-equity exchange if the partnership sold all of its assets (including goodwill and going-concern value) for cash and liquidated. This valuation rule applies only if the debt for equity exchange is an arm's-length transaction and if subsequent to the exchange the creditor's partnership interest is not redeemed by either the partnership or a person related to the partnership in a transaction that is intended to avoid cancellation of indebtedness income by the partnership.

For purposes of determining the creditor-partner's tax consequences, Treas.Reg. § 1.721–1(d) provides that § 721 applies to the creditor's contribution of debt to the partnership in exchange for a partnership interest. Thus, the creditor does not recognize gain or loss on the exchange of partnership debt for a partnership interest. The creditor's basis in the partnership interest is determined under § 722. However, the Regulation provides that the nonrecognition rule of § 721 does not apply to a transfer of a partnership interest in satisfaction of a partnership indebtedness for unpaid rent, royalties, or interest.

In contrast to the treatment of a contributed debt, the payment of a partnership's debt to a third party by a retiring partner is not a contribution to the partnership. Mas One Limited Partnership v. United States, 390 F.3d 427 (6th Cir. 2004), held that the payment of a partnership's debt to a creditor by a withdrawing partner, one day after the partner's withdrawal, for the purpose of obtaining a discharge from the partner's guarantee of certain partnership obligations was gross income to the partnership, rather than a contribution resulting in nonrecognition to the partnership under § 721. The court reasoned that the former partner's payment of the partnership's obligation was governed by Old Colony Trust Co. v. Commissioner, 279 U.S. 716 (1929), holding that the payment of a third party's payment of the taxpayer's debt results in gross income.

3.   BUILT-IN GAINS AND LOSSES

Section 704(c) requires that built-in gains and losses at the time of contribution be allocated for tax purposes to the partner who contributed the property, even though the gains and losses may be allocated otherwise for partnership accounting purposes. See Treas.Reg. § 1.704–1(b)(5), Ex. (13)(i). Section 704(c) is discussed in greater detail in Chapter 20. This provision overrides the general rules of § 704 governing the allocation of items of income and deduction among partners, under which the gain or loss inherent in an asset at the time it is contributed to a partnership would be allocated among the partners according to their general profit sharing ratios. Thus, if A and B formed an equal partnership to which A contributed $10,000 cash and B contributed land with a fair market value of $10,000 and a basis of $3,000, and the land were sold for $10,000, then, under the general rules, the $7,000 gain would be recognized equally by A and B, $3,500 each. Section 704(c) prevents this result, however, by requiring that the $7,000 gain built-in at the time of contribution be allocated to B, the contributing partner. If the property were sold for $11,000, the first $7,000 of tax gain would be allocated to B and the post-contribution gain of $1,000 would be allocated equally between A and B, $500 to each.

4. CHARACTER AND HOLDING PERIOD

4.1. *Treatment of Partner*

A partnership interest is a capital asset in the hands of a partner, even though it may have been acquired in exchange for assets that would produce ordinary income upon sale, such as inventory. I.R.C. § 741. But if a partnership's property consists of inventory or unrealized accounts receivable, § 751(a), discussed in Chapter 24, may require the recognition of ordinary income on a sale of the partnership interest notwithstanding its classification as a capital asset. The 2017 Tax Act added § 1061, which requires a three-year holding period in order to obtain long-term capital gain "with respect to" applicable service interests in certain investment or capital-raising partnerships. Section 1061 is discussed primarily in Chapter 24 (sales of partnership interests).

As a consequence of the exchanged basis rule of § 722, if the contributed property was a § 1231 asset or a capital asset, pursuant to § 1223(1) a partner's holding period for the partnership interest includes the period for which the partner held the contributed property. If the property was an ordinary income asset, however, the holding period commences when the partnership interest is received. For this purpose, potential depreciation recapture with respect to a § 1231 asset is treated as a separate ordinary income asset. Treas.Reg. § 1.1223–3(b)(4). If a mix of assets is contributed, each with a different holding period, or some of which do not result in a tacked holding period, e.g., inventory, Treas.Reg. § 1.1223–3(a) and (b) provide that the partnership interest is divided up for purposes of determining the partner's holding period. The portion of the partnership interest that takes a holding period determined with respect to any particular item of property or amount of cash that was contributed to the partnership generally is the fraction that is equal to the fair market value of the item of property or cash divided by the fair market value of the entire partnership interest. Subsequently, any capital gain or loss realized with respect to the sale of the partnership interest (or with respect to a distribution) is divided between long-term and short-term capital gain or loss in the same proportions as the holding period of the interest in the partnership is divided between the portion of the interest held for more than one year and the portion of the interest held for one year or less.

4.2. *Treatment of Partnership*

Except as provided in § 724, property contributed to a partnership in a transaction subject to §§ 721–723 is characterized as a capital asset, § 1231 asset, or ordinary income asset (e.g., inventory) according to the purpose for which the partnership holds the property. Treas.Reg. § 1.702–1(b). Section 724 provides three special rules designed to prevent the manipulation of the character of gains and losses by contributing property to a partnership that would hold the property for a purpose different than the purpose for which it was held by the contributing partner. Unrealized receivables contributed by a partner, such as a cash method service provider's accounts receivable, retain their ordinary income character permanently. Inventory items contributed by a partner retain their ordinary character for five years, even though not held as inventory by the partnership. Finally, property with a built-in capital loss at the time of the contribution retains its character as a capital asset, to the extent of the built-in loss, for five years even though the partnership holds the asset as an ordinary income asset.

Because § 723 gives the partnership a transferred basis in property contributed to it, § 1223(2) provides that the partnership's holding period for the property includes the period for which the contributing partner held the property. Thus, § 1231 property contributed to a partnership for use in its trade or business retains its character as § 1231 property even though the partnership has not independently met the holding period requirements specified in § 1231.

5.   CONVERSION INTO A PARTNERSHIP OF A SINGLE MEMBER LLC TREATED AS A DISREGARDED ENTITY

Rev.Rul. 99–5, 1999–1 C.B. 434, addresses the sale of an interest in a single-member limited liability company to another person. The ruling treats the transaction as if the selling member sells a partial interest in each of the limited liability company's assets to the purchasing member, followed immediately by a contribution of the assets to a partnership. The selling member recognizes gain or loss on the sale of a partial interest in each asset. No gain or loss is recognized on the contribution of assets to the LLC by the selling and purchasing member under § 721. The selling member's basis in the limited liability company membership interest will be the same as the member's basis in the contributed portion of the limited liability company assets. I.R.C. § 722. The purchasing member's basis in the limited liability company membership interest will be the same as the purchase price of the assets deemed to have been contributed. I.R.C. §§ 722, 1012. If, rather than purchasing an interest in a single member limited liability company, the new member contributes cash to the limited liability company, Rev.Rul. 99–5 treats the transaction as the formation of a new partnership by both the continuing member, who is deemed to contribute the assets of the existing limited liability company, and the new member who contributes cash. The contributions are nonrecognition transactions under § 721, with basis determined under §§ 722 and 723.

6.   "SWAP FUND" PARTNERSHIPS

Section 721(b) withdraws the nonrecognition of gain treatment under § 721(a) for transfers of property to a partnership that involve a diversification of investments. Suppose three investors each own a single block of stock in three different corporations and wish to diversify their investments on a tax-free basis. Without § 721(b), they could each contribute their stock to a newly formed partnership, and each would then have an undivided one-third interest in the stock of the three corporations. They would have thus obtained a diversification of investment with no current tax. This basic technique was used on a larger scale for the establishment of so-called "swap funds" under which a number of investors wishing to diversify their investment portfolios entered into a partnership formed by an investment manager. Typically, the manager and the potential investor both had the right to withdraw from the transaction before it was consummated if the resulting "mix" of investments was not satisfactory to the manager or the investors. The IRS originally issued private rulings that such funds could in fact achieve diversification on a tax free basis, but in 1976 Congress put an end to the practice by enacting § 721(b). Because the contribution of property to a swap fund partnership is a recognition event if gain is realized, § 722 permits the contributing partner to increase the partner's outside basis by the recognized gain.

Section 721(b) is intended to apply the same constraints on diversification transfers to partnerships as apply to transfers to corporations (I.R.C. § 351(e)(1)) or trusts (I.R.C. § 683). However, § 721(b) withdraws nonrecognition only if a gain is realized, and § 722 adjusts a partner's basis only with respect to recognized gains. Thus, if a loss is realized on a contribution to a swap fund, the nonrecognition rules apply and no deduction is allowed currently.

7. PARTNERSHIP ORGANIZATION AND SYNDICATION EXPENSES

Section 709(a) disallows any deduction for partnership organization and syndication expenses. Section 709(b) then allows a deduction for up to $5,000 of organizational expenses, but not syndication expenses. If organizational expenses exceed $50,000, the deduction is reduced dollar for dollar (and is consequently eliminated if organization expenses equal or exceed $55,000). Any organizational expenses that are not deductible must be capitalized and are amortizable over a 180-month period beginning with the month in which the partnership commences business. Although the statutory language of § 709(b) requires an affirmative election in order to obtain the benefits of amortization, Treas.Reg. § 1.709–1(b)(2) deems a partnership to have made the § 709(b) election; a partnership must affirmatively elect out if it does not want § 709(b) to apply. This eliminates the prior harsh consequence that followed from failure to make the statutory election, which was that the partnership was never allowed a loss deduction for organization expenses. Rev.Rul. 87–111, 1987–2 C.B. 160. If the partnership is liquidated before the end of the 180-month period, the partnership is allowed a loss deduction under § 165 for the unamortized deferred deduction. Organizational expenses are defined in § 709(b)(3) and Treas.Reg. § 1.709–2(a) to include items such as legal and accounting fees incident to the negotiation and drafting of the partnership agreement and establishing an accounting system, as well as filing fees. Costs to acquire partnership assets are not organization fees and instead would be analyzed under §§ 162, 195, and 263.

Syndication fees, as defined in Treas.Reg. § 1.709–2(b), are never amortizable or deductible upon liquidation of the partnership. Such fees encompass brokerage fees incurred to sell partnership interests, legal fees in connection with an underwriting, securities laws registration fees, accounting fees connected with offering materials, printing costs of a prospectus, placement memorandum, or promotional material, etc. Rev.Rul. 85–32, 1985–1 C.B. 186. See also Martyr v. Commissioner, T.C. Memo. 1990–558 (expense of tax opinion letter included in private placement memorandum for limited partnership offering is a nondeductible syndication expense); Rev.Rul. 89–11, 1989–1 C.B. 179 (no § 165 loss deduction allowed for syndication expenses incurred in an unsuccessful effort to establish a partnership); Rev.Rul. 88–4, 1988–1 C.B. 264 (attorneys' fees for tax opinion letter included in prospectus of syndicated partnership are syndication fees). For the differences between syndication fees and organizational expenses, see Aboussie v. United States, 779 F.2d 424 (8th Cir.1985); Diamond v. Commissioner, 92 T.C. 423 (1989).

8. NONCOMPENSATORY PARTNERSHIP OPTIONS

Treas.Reg. § 1.721–2 addresses the issuance of noncompensatory partnership options, including convertible debt and convertible equity interests. Under the Regulations, the issuance of an option is not governed by § 721 but instead is governed by general tax principles under which the issuance is an open transaction for the issuer and an investment by the holder. Neither the grant nor the exercise of a noncompensatory option generally results in the recognition of gain or loss to the partnership or the option holder. If, however, the holder uses built-in gain or built-in loss property to acquire the option, the holder will recognize gain or loss.

Upon exercise, the option holder is treated as contributing property to the partnership in exchange for the partnership interest; the contributed property is equal to the sum of the original premium, the exercise price, and the option privilege.[1] Section 721 applies even if the exercise results in a shift of capital from the old partners to the option holder. Section 721 does not apply to the lapse of an option; the lapse of an option results in recognition of income by the partnership and the recognition of loss by the former option holder. To deal with the fact that the option holder generally receives a partnership interest with a value that is greater or less than the sum of the option premium and exercise price, i.e., there is a capital shift, the Regulations under § 704 allocate a disproportionate share of gross income, without a corresponding allocation of book income, to any partner or partners who have benefited from such a capital shift. This aspect of the treatment of partnership options is discussed in Chapter 20.

PROBLEM SET 1

1. Amy, Bill, and Casey are forming a limited liability company (which will be taxed as a partnership) to conduct a bait and tackle shop, fishing guide, and marina business on the Intracoastal Waterway. Each of them will have an equal interest in capital and profits. Each partner will transfer the following assets:

---

[1] The conversion right in convertible debt or convertible equity is taken into account for tax purposes as part of the underlying instrument. (The Regulations do not deal with the consequences of a right to convert partnership debt into an interest in the issuing partnership to the extent of any accrued but unpaid interest on the debt.) Treas.Reg. § 1.1272–1(e) treats partnership interests as stock for purposes of the special OID rules for convertible debt instruments. Treas.Reg. § 1.1272–1(e).

	Adj. Basis	FMV
Amy:		
Marina:		
Land	$10,000	$40,000
Buildings	$30,000	$60,000
Tradename "Shark Bait"	$ 1,000	$10,000
Bill:		
Store Fixtures	$25,000	$45,000
($50,000 = § 1245 recomputed basis)		
Inventory	$34,000	$65,000
Casey: Fishing Boat	$30,000	$20,000
Accounts Receivable	$ 0	$ 5,000
Cash	$85,000	$85,000

Amy and Casey previously conducted their respective sole proprietorships using the cash method of accounting; Bill used the accrual method.

(a) At what values should the contributed property be carried on the partnership's books and what is the amount of each partner's capital account?

(b) What are the tax consequences of the formation of the partnership? What is each partner's basis for his or her partnership interest? What is the partnership's basis in each asset?

(c) If the partnership sells the inventory contributed by Bill for $65,000 and collects $5,000 on the accounts receivable contributed by Casey, how will the partners be taxed?

(d) If the partnership sells the inventory contributed by Bill for $80,000, how will the partners be taxed?

(e) If the partnership sells the fishing boat for $20,000, how will the partners be taxed?

(f) If the partnership sells the fishing boat for $17,000, how will the partners be taxed?

2. Dana and Ed are forming a limited partnership to engage in the real estate development business. Dana, a real estate agent, will be the general partner; Ed, a dentist, will be the limited partner. Dana will contribute an installment promissory note, with a basis of $50,000 and a face amount of $100,000, which she received on the sale of land held for speculative investment, in exchange for a one-quarter interest in partnership profits and capital. Ed will contribute Blackacre, which has a basis of $50,000 and a fair market value of $125,000, and Whiteacre, which has a basis of $200,000 and a fair market value of $175,000, in exchange for a three-quarters interest in

profits and capital. Dana, Ed, and the partnership are cash method taxpayers.

(a) At what values should the contributed property be carried on the partnership's books and what will be the amount of each partner's capital account?

(b) What are the tax consequences of the formation of the partnership? What is each partner's basis for his or her partnership interest? What is the partnership's basis in Blackacre and Whiteacre?

(c) How are the partners taxed when the partnership collects the installment note?

(d) What is the character of the gain when the partnership sells Blackacre and Whiteacre? Does it matter how long Ed held the contributed property?

(e) What would be the amount of loss recognized if Whiteacre had been Ed's residential farm property prior to its contribution to the partnership and the partnership sold it for $165,000?

SECTION 2. CONTRIBUTIONS OF ENCUMBERED PROPERTY

INTERNAL REVENUE CODE: Sections 705(a); 722; 723; 731(a)–(b); 733; 752(a)–(c).

REGULATIONS: Sections 1.704–1(b)(2)(iv)(*d*)(*1*); 1.722–1; 1.752–1(a)–(g) (omit Ex. (2)); 1.752–2(a), (b)(1), (2), (5), (f) Ex. (2); 1.752–3(a); 1.1245–4(c)(4), Exs. (2) and (3).

Subchapter K has no single provision dealing with the tax consequences of a contribution of property subject to liabilities that are assumed by the partnership or to which contributed property remains subject. Instead, the results must be determined by piecing together the rules governing contributions to partnerships in §§ 721–723, treatment of changes in the partners' shares of debts in § 752, partnership distributions in §§ 731 and 733, and partners' bases in their partnership interests in § 705. Gain, but not loss, may be recognized upon the contribution of encumbered property to the partnership or the assumption of a partner's debts by the partnership.

Before examining the application of this matrix of operating rules, the meaning of a "liability" or "debt" for these purposes must be clarified. For purposes of § 752 the term "liability" is defined in Treas.Reg. § 1.752–1(a)(4) as limited to debts that: (1) create or increase basis (including cash balances); (2) give rise to a deduction (e.g., accrual method accounts payable); or (3) give rise to a nondeductible expenditure not chargeable to a capital account (under § 263 or § 263A—e.g., a nondeductible, noncapitalized bribe or fine). Cash method accounts payable are not liabilities for purposes of § 752 and do not increase the partners' bases in their partnership interests.

The starting point of the analysis in any situation in which the partnership assumes a partner's liabilities or takes property subject to a liability in connection with a contribution of property to the partnership is §§ 721–723. Upon contribution of the property, the contributing partner takes a basis in the partner's partnership interest equal to the partner's basis in the contributed property, without regard to the amount of the debt. By virtue of the transfer, however, the contributing partner has been relieved from the debt in an individual capacity, and all of the partners have indirectly assumed the debt in their capacity as partners. Section 752(b) provides that any decrease in a partner's share of liabilities is to be treated as a distribution of money to the partner. Under §§ 731 and 733, distributions of money reduce the partner's basis in the partner's partnership interest and are treated as gain to the extent that the distribution exceeds basis. Section 752(a) provides that an increase in a partner's share of liabilities by reason of a partnership transaction is to be treated as a contribution of cash to the partnership by the partner. The deemed cash contribution by the other partners increases their basis in their partnership interests under § 722. If a partner's share of the liabilities is both increased and decreased in the same transaction, only the net increase or decrease is taken into account. Treas.Reg. § 1.752–1(f). This rule applies whenever a partner contributes encumbered property to a partnership because the partner is simultaneously relieved of all the liabilities in the partner's individual capacity but becomes liable for a share of the liabilities in the partner's capacity as a partner.[2] Thus, the amount of the deemed distribution to the contributing partner is equal to the portion of the debt for which the other partners bear the economic risk of loss.

As a consequence of these provisions, the contribution of encumbered property to a partnership by a partner will reduce the contributing partner's basis in the partnership interest to the extent of the share of the liability assumed by the other partners and will result in recognized gain to the contributing partner to the extent that amount exceeds the contributing partner's basis in the partner's partnership interest. Each noncontributing partner's basis in the partner's partnership interest will be increased to the extent of the noncontributing partner's share of the liability.

Under § 752(c), the same results are achieved even if the partnership merely takes the property subject to the debt and does not assume it. Assuming that either the partnership agreement or controlling state law treats the noncontributing partners as assuming ultimate liability for a share of the debt, the net effect for the contributing partner is the receipt of a deemed cash distribution.

The manner in which partners share the economic risk of loss for partnership debt is determined under Treas.Reg. § 1.752–2 for debt that

---

[2] Partners' shares of partnership indebtedness are determined under Treas.Regs. §§ 1.752–2 and 1.752–3, discussed in Chapter 21.

is with recourse to either the partnership or any partner, and under Treas.Reg. § 1.752–3 for debt that is without recourse to the partnership or any partner.[3] In general, recourse debt is allocated among partners to the extent that a partner is personally responsible for the economic risk of loss with respect to the debt. Nonrecourse debt generally is allocated to the partner who is responsible for recognizing gain with respect to payment or elimination of the debt, including the amount of any gain that would be allocated to the partner under § 704(c) on a transfer of the encumbered property in satisfaction of the debt (the difference between the amount of debt encumbering contributed property and the basis of the property). These rules are discussed in detail in Chapter 21. Treas.Reg. § 1.752–1(g), Ex. (1) provides that there is no deemed distribution if the contributing partner retains ultimate liability to repay an indebtedness encumbering the contributed property.

Pursuant to §§ 731 and 733 (and § 705), the deemed distribution created by § 752 reduces the contributing partner's basis in the partnership interest, and, to the extent that the deemed distribution exceeds the basis in the partnership interest, the excess is treated as gain from the sale or exchange of the partnership interest. Section 741 directs that this gain be treated as capital gain,[4] subject to certain exceptions provided in § 751. The other partners also are treated by § 752(a) as having contributed cash to the partnership in an amount equal to their respective shares of the debt assumed by the partnership, and they increase their bases in their partnership interests accordingly.

The following examples illustrate the above rules:

(1) Partner D contributes to the new DEF Partnership Greenacre, property with a fair market value of $1,100 and a basis of $1,000, subject to a recourse mortgage of $900, which is assumed by the partnership. (Assume that whether the lien is a purchase money mortgage or one that was placed on the property to secure a loan unrelated to its acquisition will not change the analysis; Chapter 22 will discuss the potential for a disguised sale when "nonqualified" debt is assumed.) E and F each contribute $200 in cash, and D, E, and F are equal partners. The book value of D's contribution is the same as the book value of E's and F's contributions because D's contribution is measured by the *net* value of the contributed property, i.e., the property's fair market value minus the mortgage. D's basis for D's partnership interest would be $400, i.e., the original $1,000 basis minus the $600 of the indebtedness that was, in effect, assumed by the other partners. E and F each would increase their

---

[3] A "recourse liability" is any liability "to the extent * * * that any partner or related person bears the economic risk of loss for that liability." Treas.Reg. § 1.752–1(a)(1). Partnership indebtedness is nonrecourse debt only to the extent that no partner (or any person related to a partner under Treas.Reg. § 1.752–4(b)) bears the economic risk of loss on the liability. Treas.Reg. § 1.752–1(a)(2).

[4] However, Treas.Reg. § 1.1245–4(c)(4), Ex. (3) provides that such gain will be ordinary income to the extent that there is any depreciation recapture inherent in the contributed asset. This result conflicts with the statutory mechanics of Subchapter K, which treat the gain as realized on the sale or exchange of the partnership interest.

basis by $300, from $200 to $500. The DEF partnership's balance sheet, at both book value and tax basis would then be as follows:

| | Assets | | Partnership Debts & Partners' Capital Accounts | | |
	Book Value	Tax Basis		Book Value	Tax Basis
Cash	$ 400	$ 400	Mortgage	$ 900	n/a
Greenacre	$1,100	$1,000	D	$ 200	$ 400
			E	$ 200	$ 500
			F	$ 200	$ 500
Total	$1,500	$1,400		$1,500	$1,400

(2) If the mortgage amount in Example (1) were $1,800 (regardless of the fair market value of the property), D would recognize a gain of $200, i.e., the excess of the $1,200 of indebtedness that was in effect assumed by the other partners over D's original $1,000 basis in the contributed property, which is exchanged to become D's starting basis in the partnership. D's basis in D's partnership interest is then reduced to zero as a result of the reduction of D's share of liability that is treated as a cash distribution by § 752(b). E and F each increase their basis again, this time by $600. Realistically, if the mortgage were $1,800 and D, E, and F are to be equal partners, the fair market value of Greenacre in all likelihood would be $2,000, resulting in the net value of each partner's contribution again being $200. In this case, the partnership's balance sheet immediately after formation would be as follows:

| | Assets | | Partnership Debts & Partners' Capital Accounts | | |
	Book Value	Tax Basis		Book Value	Tax Basis
Cash	$ 400	$ 400	Mortgage	$1,800	n/a
Greenacre	$2,000	$1,000	D	$ 200	$ 0
			E	$ 200	$ 800
			F	$ 200	$ 800
Total	$2,400	$1,400		$2,400	$1,600

The partners' aggregate basis for their partnership interests (outside basis) exceeds the partnership's aggregate basis in its assets (inside basis) by an amount equal to the $200 gain recognized by D. Note that if DEF were a pre-existing partnership and D's outside basis were at least

$200 before the contribution, D would not have recognized any gain on the contribution of the encumbered property.

(3) If D were personally liable for the $900 debt in Example (1) and the partnership merely took the property subject to the indebtedness without the partnership, E, or F agreeing to indemnify D for any repayment of the debt, the debt would be a debt that is recourse to D but nonrecourse with respect to the partnership In this case D bears the entire economic risk of loss. Therefore, D would be treated as receiving a distribution of $900 under § 752(b) and making a contribution of $900 under § 752(a). Since only the net contribution or distribution is taken into account, see Treas.Reg. § 1.752–1(f), D's basis for D's partnership interest remains $1,000. See Treas.Reg. § 1.752–1(g), Ex. (1). Applying this rule, D would recognize no gain even if the mortgage were $1,800 as in Example (2).

(4) If the $900 mortgage debt in Example (1) were a nonrecourse debt as to D, upon the contribution of the property to the partnership, the partnership would be treated by § 752(c) and Treas.Reg. § 1.752–1(e) as assuming the debt. Because the debt is a nonrecourse debt, under Treas.Reg. § 1.752–3(a)(2), D will be allocated an amount of the debt equal to the gain that would have been allocated to D under § 704(c) if the property had been conveyed to the lender in satisfaction of the mortgage; the balance of the debt generally will be allocated among the partners according to their profit sharing ratios.[5] Since the basis of the property is $1,000 and the debt is only $900, no gain would be realized if the property were conveyed to the lender in satisfaction of the mortgage, and hence there is no initial allocation to D. Thus, $300 of the $900 debt will be allocated to each of D, E, and F because they share profits equally. As a result, D's basis in D's partnership interest is $400 (the original $1,000 basis minus the $600 of debt in effect assumed by each of E and F), and, as in Example (1), E and F each increase their basis by $300. The partnership's balance sheet would be the same as in Example (1).

(5) If in Example (4) the nonrecourse mortgage amount were $1,800, however, under § 704(c), $800 of gain ($1,800 amount realized minus $1,000 basis) would be allocated to D if the property were transferred to the lender in satisfaction of the mortgage. Accordingly, $800 of the nonrecourse debt initially would be allocated to D. The remaining $1,000 of the debt generally would be allocated among the partners equally, because they share profits equally. Thus, a total of $1,133.33 of the indebtedness is allocated to D, and $333.33 is allocated to each of E and F. D's basis for D's partnership interest is 333.33 (the original $1,000 minus the $666.66 of debt allocated to E and F), and E and F each increase their basis by $333.33. Assuming, as in Example (2), that the fair market value of Greenacre were $2,000 and that E and F

---

[5] In fact, the partners will be allowed some options with respect to both the operation of § 704(c) and in determining exactly how the remaining portion of the debt is allocated. See Treas.Reg. § 1.752–3(a)(3) and the discussion in Chapter 21.

each contributed $200, the partnership's balance sheet immediately after formation would be as follows:

	Assets			Partnership Debts & Partners' Capital Accounts	
	Book Value	Tax Basis		Book Value	Tax Basis
Cash	$ 400	$ 400	Mortgage	$1,800	n/a
Greenacre	$2,000	$1,000	D	$ 200	$ 333.33
			E	$ 200	$ 533.33
			F	$ 200	$ 533.33
Total	$2,400	$1,400		$2,400	$1,400.00

The rule allocating to the contributing partner an amount of nonrecourse debt equal to the excess of the nonrecourse debt over the basis of the property avoids recognition of gain on the deemed distribution when the property is contributed to the partnership. The rationale for permitting the contributing partner to avoid recognizing any gain in this case, in contrast to Example (2) where gain was recognized with respect to property encumbered by a recourse mortgage, is twofold. First, none of the other partners actually has assumed a risk of loss where the mortgage on the contributed property is nonrecourse. Second, under the rules of § 704 governing allocations of partnership income, the contributing partner will be taxed on any partnership income applied to repay the portion of the nonrecourse debt that exceeds the basis of the property. See Chapter 21.

The assumption by a partnership of the accounts payable of a cash method taxpayer who is contributing its business to the partnership presents a special problem. If accounts payable of a cash method partnership were taken into account as liabilities under § 752, a cash method partner who contributed equal amounts of receivables, which have a zero basis, and payables of a previously conducted sole proprietorship, and no other property, would be required to recognize gain. This result generally would adversely affect the formation of personal service partnerships. Section 357(c) specifically addresses this problem in the formation of corporations by providing that cash method accounts payable will not be considered liabilities assumed by the corporation. Subchapter K contains an analogous, albeit somewhat vague, provision in § 704(c)(3). For purposes of § 752, the term "liability," as defined in Treas.Reg. § 1.752–1(a)(4), is limited to debts that: (1) create or increase basis (including cash balances); (2) gave rise to a deduction (e.g., accrual method accounts payable); or (3) gave rise to a nondeductible expenditure not chargeable to a capital account (under § 263 or § 263A—e.g., a nondeductible, noncapitalized bribe or fine).

Thus, the assumption of a cash method partner's accounts payable gives rise to neither a constructive distribution to the contributing partner under § 752(b) nor a constructive contribution by the other partners under § 752(a). See Rev.Rul. 88–77, 1988–2 C.B. 128, which rules that cash method accounts payable, which are not deductible until paid and do not give rise to basis in any asset, should not be treated as liabilities for purposes of § 752. In contrast, accrual method accounts payable are subject to the generally applicable principles of § 752. However, liabilities of an accrual method taxpayer the deduction for which has been deferred under the economic performance rules of § 461(h) and which are assumed by a partnership in connection with the contribution of property to the partnership by the accrual method taxpayer are treated in the same manner as cash method accounts payable for purposes of § 752.

PROBLEM SET 2

1.   Fran, George, and Helen formed the FGH General Partnership. Each of them has a one-third interest in partnership capital, profits, and losses. Fran and George each contributed $20,000 cash to the FGH Partnership, and Helen contributed Greenacre, which is worth $50,000 and subject to a mortgage of $30,000, which was assumed by the partnership.

(a)   Assume that each partner would be responsible for one-third of the debt if the partnership's assets were worthless.

(1)   Ignoring the tax consequences, if the value of Greenacre is unchanged, what happens to the partners if Greenacre is sold, the debt is paid, and all partnership proceeds are distributed to the partners?

(2)   What are the tax consequences if Helen's basis in Greenacre is $35,000?

(3)   What are the tax consequences if Helen's basis in Greenacre is $15,000?

(b)   Assume that the mortgage debt is nonrecourse as to both Helen and the FGH Partnership.

(1)   Ignoring tax consequences, if the value of Greenacre is unchanged, what happens to the partners if Greenacre is sold, the debt is paid, and all partnership proceeds are distributed to the partners?

(2)   What are the tax consequences if Helen's basis in Greenacre is $40,000?

(3)   What are the tax consequences if Helen's basis in Greenacre is $15,000?

2.   Lisa, who previously has conducted a solo medical practice, joined a partnership with two other physicians. Each partner has a one-third interest. Lisa transferred $18,000 of accounts receivable from her solo practice to the partnership, which assumed $12,000 of Lisa's accounts payable.

(a) What are the tax consequences of the transaction if Lisa and the partnership use the cash method of accounting?

(b) What are the tax consequences of the transaction if Lisa and the partnership use the accrual method of accounting?

SECTION 3. CONTRIBUTION OF PROPERTY VERSUS CONTRIBUTION OF SERVICES

A. TREATMENT OF THE PARTNER RECEIVING A PARTNERSHIP INTEREST IN EXCHANGE FOR SERVICES

INTERNAL REVENUE CODE: Sections 83(a)–(d); 721(a).

REGULATIONS: Sections 1.83–1(a), –3(e), –4(b)(2); 1.721–1(b); 1.722–1.

PROPOSED REGULATIONS: Sections 1.83–3(e) and (l) (2005); 1.721–1(b) (2005).

Section 721 does not apply to provide nonrecognition if a partner receives a partnership interest in exchange for services. When a partnership interest received for services includes an interest in partnership capital, i.e., property contributed by other partners, Treas.Reg. § 1.721–1(b)(1) provides that the fair market value of the partnership interest is includable in gross income under §§ 61 and 83 as compensation for services. Treas.Reg. § 1.722–1 provides that any income so recognized increases the partner's basis in the partnership interest. In addition, § 83 provides comprehensive rules regarding the year in which the value of the partnership interest must be included in income if the interest is subject to a risk of forfeiture or other restrictions that prevent the interest from being fully vested. This aspect of § 83 applies, for example, if a partner is required to render services to the partnership for a certain period of time before the interest vests. In such a case, taxation is deferred, but the amount includable is the value of the partnership interest at the time the restrictions lapse rather than on the earlier date when the partnership interest was first received. As a corollary of the receipt of income by the service partner, the partnership either deducts or capitalizes the same amount, depending on the nature of the services, in the year the partner recognizes the income.

Although the basic rules that apply when a service partner receives an interest in partnership capital are clear, receipt of an interest in exchange for services that entitles the service partner only to a share of future profits is more problematic.

Since nonrecognition under § 721 extends only to the receipt of a partnership interest in exchange for "property," a crucial issue in the formation of a partnership is whether a partner's contribution is "property" or services. Neither the Code nor the Regulations define the word "property," and this issue must be resolved on a case-by-case basis.

DETAILED ANALYSIS

1. PROPERTY CREATED BY PERSONAL EFFORTS

The difference between services, which do not qualify under § 721, and self-created intangible property, which does qualify under § 721, sometimes presents problems. The leading cases on this point are United States v. Frazell, 335 F.2d 487 (5th Cir.1964), and United States v. Stafford, 727 F.2d 1043 (11th Cir. 1984). In *Frazell*, the taxpayer was a geologist who entered into a joint venture agreement with the N.H. Wheless Oil Company and W.C. Woolf. Under the agreement, Frazell was to identify potentially productive oil and gas properties, which he would recommend to Wheless and Woolf. With their approval, he would attempt to acquire the properties in the names of Wheless and Woolf, who paid all costs and expenses. In locating properties, Frazell used several oil maps that he had previously acquired. Frazell's ownership of these maps and other geological data and information was an important factor in Wheless and Woolf's decision to enter into the agreement with Frazell. Under the agreement, Frazell was to receive "a monthly salary or drawing account," and, after Wheless and Woolf had recovered their costs and expenses for the properties, a specified interest in the properties. In 1955, after Wheless and Woolf had recovered their costs, an interest worth $91,000 was vested in Frazell. The court held Frazell realized ordinary income to the extent that his interest was received in exchange for his services, but to the extent that the interest in the venture was received in exchange for the oil maps, the nonrecognition rule of § 721 applied. The court remanded the case to the District Court for further proceedings because from the record it was unclear whether Frazell contributed ownership of the maps to the joint venture or retained ownership of the maps as his separate property and merely used them in rendering the services for which the interest was received.

In *Stafford*, the taxpayer obtained from an insurance company a "letter of intent" proposing to lend to the taxpayer or his designee a substantial sum of money on very favorable terms. Although the parties expected that a loan would be made pursuant to the letter of intent, it was not legally enforceable by the taxpayer. After obtaining the letter of intent in his own name, the taxpayer formed a limited partnership of which he was the sole general partner. He contributed $200,000 cash in exchange for two limited partnership shares, and, as required by the partnership agreement, he contributed the letter of intent in exchange for a third limited partnership share. The government asserted that § 721 did not apply to the limited partnership share received in exchange for the letter of intent because the interest was in fact received in consideration of services rendered to the partnership by the taxpayer in negotiating the loan to the partnership. First, the court concluded that the taxpayer owned the letter of intent, since he was working on his own behalf at the time he acquired it. Turning to the question of whether the letter was "property" within the meaning of § 721, the court concluded that the unenforceability of the letter was no bar to property status, citing Rev.Rul. 64–56, Section 1, Detailed Analysis 2.1. Because the taxpayer transferred all of his rights in the letter, the contribution was a transfer of property. However, because the record on appeal contained insufficient evidence to determine whether the third limited partnership interest was received in exchange for the letter or for services to be rendered to the partnership, or for both, the court remanded the case, with directions that if the value of the letter was less than $100,000, the difference between that amount and the value of the letter represented taxable compensation.

2. RECOGNITION OF INCOME UPON RECEIPT OF A CAPITAL INTEREST FOR SERVICES

2.1. *Generally*

When § 721 does not apply because a person exchanges services for a partnership capital interest, the amount includable in income is the fair market value of the partnership interest received. A partnership capital interest is one where the partner has a share in partnership asset value on liquidation. In some cases, the value of the partnership interest may be determined indirectly. In Hensel Phelps Construction Co. v. Commissioner, 74 T.C. 939 (1980), aff'd, 703 F.2d 485 (10th Cir.1983), the Tax Court valued an interest in partnership capital received in exchange for past services with reference to the fair market value of the services provided. Regardless of the valuation method employed, the service partner's basis for the partnership interest is the amount the service partner includes in income, plus any money and the basis of other property contributed to the partnership. Treas.Reg. § 1.722–1.

2.2. *Partnership Interest Subject to Risk of Forfeiture*

If a partnership interest received for services is subject to a substantial risk of forfeiture, pursuant to § 83(a) the service partner's recognition of income is deferred until the interest vests. As a result, the service partner will be taxable on any increase in the value of the partnership interest, whether or not attributable to services performed by the partner for the partnership, at the time the substantial risk of forfeiture lapses. For the meaning of "substantial risk of forfeiture," see I.R.C. § 83(c)(1); Treas.Reg. § 1.83–3(c). Johnston v. Commissioner, T.C. Memo. 1995–140, held that a partnership capital interest received in consideration of a combination of both past and future services must be valued on the date of the transfer where the right to the partnership interest was not legally conditioned on actually performing the future services. In that case, the taxpayer contributed $90 in exchange for a 1% interest in a partnership in which the other partners, holding an aggregate 99% interest, contributed $8,000,000. The documentation of the transaction reflected that the disproportionate interest in capital was received in consideration of services.

Furthermore, under Treas.Reg. § 1.83–1(a), the transferee is not treated as the owner of the property until the risk of forfeiture lapses. Thus, although the recipient of the partnership interest may be a partner under state law, for federal income tax purposes, the recipient is not a partner for tax purposes during this period.

A service provider who receives property, including a partnership interest, subject to a substantial risk of forfeiture may elect under § 83(b) to include the value in income in the year of receipt. If the partner makes a § 83(b) election, any increase in the value of the partnership interest between the date the service partner is admitted to the partnership and the date the restriction lapses will not be taxed as compensation when the restriction lapses but instead will be converted into capital gain that will be recognized at a later time.

In Crescent Holdings, LLC v. Commissioner, 141 T.C. 477 (2013), an individual (Fields) received a 2% capital interest in a partnership (Crescent Holdings) as compensation for entering into a contract to provide services to an LLC owned by the partnership. Fields's membership interest would be forfeited if he terminated his employment within three years. He was entitled to the same distributions as other members of the LLC, and any distributions he received were not subject to forfeiture. Fields did not make a § 83(b) election. Fields did not receive any distributions, but the partnership allocated nearly $4 million to Fields as his distributive share of partnership income. The court held that, although neither § 83 nor Treas.Reg. § 1.83–1(a)(1) specifically addressed the issue, the transferee of a nonvested partnership capital interest does not recognize in income the undistributed partnership profit or loss allocations attributable to that interest. Fields's right to receive the undistributed income allocations attributable to his interest was subject to the same substantial risk of forfeiture as his right to the partnership interest itself; if he forfeited his right to the partnership interest, then he would also forfeit his right to receive any benefit from the undistributed income allocations. The court held that under Treas.Reg. § 1.83–1(a)(1), undistributed partnership allocations attributable to a nonvested partnership capital interest are included in the gross income of the transferor. Based on the contractual provisions regarding the formation of the two LLCs, Crescent Holdings was the transferor. Accordingly, the profits attributable to Fields's forfeitable 2% interest were allocated to the other LLC members (partners) in accordance with their distributive shares. The court noted that if Fields continued his employment until the interest vested, the fair market value of the interest includable in gross income at that time would include the undistributed income.

3. RECEIPT OF A PROFITS-ONLY PARTNERSHIP INTEREST IN EXCHANGE FOR SERVICES

3.1. *The* Diamond *Case*

While the exchange nature of a transfer of an interest in partnership capital for services is relatively clear, and the tax consequences are determinable, the receipt of a partnership profits-only interest for services raises more complex questions that have not been susceptible of easy resolution. Before the decision in Diamond v. Commissioner, 492 F.2d 286 (7th Cir. 1974), it had been generally accepted that the receipt of a partnership *profits* interest for services was not currently taxable. See Rev.Rul. 70–435, 1970–2 C.B. 100, modifying Rev.Rul. 60–31, 1960–1 C.B. 174 (holding that receipt of future income interest in a joint venture is not taxable). The court in *Diamond* questioned this accepted wisdom and held that a receipt of a profits-only interest for services was a taxable event. Subsequent case law and IRS ruling policy generally accepted the position that the receipt of a profits-only interest was taxable, but the authorities found ways to defer immediate taxation. As discussed below, the Treasury

Department has issued Proposed Regulations that deal comprehensively with both the receipt of a partnership capital interest and profits-only interest in exchange for services. Although issued in 2005, these Proposed Regulations have yet to be finalized. In the absence of final regulations or a comprehensive statutory solution, a full account of the history and context is a necessity for navigating this area.

Understanding the tax consequence of receipt of a profits-only interest in a partnership in exchange for services first requires examining the seminal opinion in *Diamond*. The taxpayer in *Diamond* was a mortgage broker. Diamond was approached by Philip Kargman who had acquired buyer's rights in a contract for the sale of an office building. Diamond received a 60% share in the profits of a partnership in exchange for obtaining a mortgage loan for the full $1,100,000 purchase price of the building. Kargman contributed the contract rights to acquire the building, which he had purchased for $25,000, and slightly more than $78,000 of cash required for the purchase beyond the loan proceeds. Under the partnership agreement, proceeds on the sale of the building would first be applied to repay the money contributed by Kargman, then profits would be divided 40% to Kargman and 60% to Diamond. Shortly after the building was acquired by Kargman and Diamond, Diamond sold his partnership interest for $40,000 in a transaction by which a third party became a 50% partner with Kargman. The acquisition of the building and Diamond's transfer of his interest occurred in the same taxable year. Diamond reported the transaction as a sale of a partnership interest resulting in the recognition of $40,000 of capital gain. The Tax Court held that Diamond recognized ordinary income on the receipt of a partnership interest for services. 56 T.C. 530 (1971). The Seventh Circuit affirmed.[6]

Treas.Reg. § 1.721–1(b)(1) provides that, "To the extent that any of the partners gives up any part of his right to be repaid his contributions (as distinguished from a share in partnership profits) in favor of another partner as compensation for services (or in satisfaction of an obligation), section 721 does not apply." The taxpayer in *Diamond* asserted the then widely held view that the first parenthetical phrase in Treas.Reg. § 1.721–1(b)(1) meant that a profits interest for services was not taxable. As quoted in the opinion of the Seventh Circuit, Professor Arthur Willis, who chaired an advisory group in 1956 that reviewed the Regulations under Subchapter K, wrote in his treatise of the time (Willis on Partnership Taxation 84–85 (1971)):

> However obliquely the proposition is stated in the regulations, it is clear that a partner who receives only an interest in future profits of the partnership as compensation for services is not required to report the receipt of his partnership interest as taxable income. The rationale is twofold. In the first place, the present value of a right to participate in future profits is usually too conjectural to be subject to valuation. In the second place, the service partner is

---

[6] The Tax Court analyzed the case treating the venture as a partnership. The Court of Appeals refused to consider suggestions that the relationship may have been an employment or other relationship on the grounds that no such findings had been made by the Tax Court. See Cowan, The Diamond Case, 27 Tax Law Review 161 (1972).

taxable on his distributive share of partnership income as it is realized by the partnership. If he were taxed on the present value of the right to receive his share of future partnership income, either he would be taxed twice, or the value of his right to participate in partnership income must be amortized over some period of time.

The double taxation referred to by Professor Willis occurs because the recipient of a profits interest for services would be taxed (1) on the receipt of the value of the interest and (2) on the partner's share of profits as they are derived. Nonetheless, the Seventh Circuit concluded that, "In the present case, taxpayer's services had all been rendered, and the prospect of earnings from the real estate under Kargman's management was evidently very good. The profit-share had determinable market value." The court addressed the issue of double taxation as follows:

> Each partner determines his income tax by taking into account his distributive share of the taxable income of the partnership. 26 U.S.C.A. § 702. Taxpayer's position here is that he was entitled to defer income taxation on the compensation for his services except as partnership earnings were realized. If a partner is taxed on the determinable market value of a profit-share at the time it is created in his favor, and is also taxed on his full share of earnings as realized, there will arguably be double taxation, avoidable by permitting him to amortize the value which was originally treated as income. Does the absence of a recognized procedure for amortization militate against the treatment of the creation of the profit-share as income?

> Do the disadvantages of treating the creation of the profit-share as income in those instances where it has a determinable market value at that time outweigh the desirability of imposing a tax at the time the taxpayer has received an interest with determinable market value as compensation for services?

> We think, of course, that the resolution of these practical questions makes clearly desirable the promulgation of appropriate regulations, to achieve a degree of certainty. But in the absence of regulation, we think it sound policy to defer to the expertise of the Commissioner and the Judges of the Tax Court, and to sustain their decision that the receipt of a profit-share with determinable market value is income. * * *

The *Diamond* case presented the court with an appealing situation in which to tax the receipt of a profits interest received for services. The profits interest in that case was easily valued, was paid for past services, and was sold shortly after receipt. Nevertheless, even if the court in the *Diamond* case had accepted the taxpayer's argument that the receipt of the interest in future partnership profits was not a taxable event, the subsequent disposition of the partnership interest could nonetheless generate ordinary income. See Hale v. Commissioner, T.C. Memo. 1965–274, so holding, relying on Hort v. Commissioner, 313 U.S. 28 (1941).

3.2. *The* Diamond *Progeny*

The principle, but not the result, of *Diamond*, bolstered by the application of § 83, was reaffirmed in Campbell v. Commissioner, 943 F.2d 815 (8th Cir.1991), rev'g T.C. Memo. 1990–162. In that case, the taxpayer received a profits-only partnership interest in several syndicated tax shelter limited partnerships in consideration for services in organizing the partnerships and selling interests to investors. Both the Tax Court and the Court of Appeals held that the receipt of a profits-only partnership interest in exchange for services was a taxable event. The Tax Court valued the interest in future partnership profits by computing the discounted value of the stream of income and tax benefits expected to be received by the services partner, but the Court of Appeals reversed as clearly erroneous the Tax Court's holding that the partnership interest in question in that case had anything more than speculative value. The Court of Appeals held that because the profits-only partnership interest had no fair market value at the time of receipt, the interest was not includable in gross income. Similarly, in Vestal v. United States, 498 F.2d 487 (8th Cir.1974), the taxpayer contracted with certain limited partners of a partnership, the sole asset of which was oil and gas rights in a then unproductive but proven field, for the transfer of a portion of their partnership interests after they had recovered their original capital investment in exchange for his services in organizing the partnership. The court held that no income was realized in the year the contract rights were received because the value was speculative. On rehearing, this decision was held to be consistent with *Diamond*. The crucial difference between *Diamond* and the opinions in *Campbell* and *Vestal* is that in *Diamond* the Tax Court's finding that the partnership interest had a "determinable market value" was upheld, possibly because of the rather unique fact pattern—the taxpayer's sale of the partnership interest soon after receipt was highly probative direct evidence of its fair market value.

Other cases approached the receipt of a profits-only interest by focusing on the service partner's interest in partnership capital, as measured by the service partner's capital account. In St. John v. United States, 84–1 U.S.T.C. ¶ 9158 (C.D.Ill.1983), the taxpayer received a current partnership interest entitling him only to future profits in exchange for services. The court held that § 83 applied to the receipt of an interest in partnership profits, but that the value of the interest was zero, because if the partnership were liquidated immediately after receipt of the interest, the taxpayer would have received nothing. Applying this analysis to the *Diamond* case suggests that perhaps Diamond in fact received an interest in partnership capital to the extent that the value of the building exceeded the value assigned to it by the partners upon formation of the partnership.[7] Similarly, in Mark IV Pictures, Inc. v. Commissioner, T.C. Memo. 1990–571, aff'd, 969 F.2d 669 (8th Cir.1992), the Tax Court, without any discussion of *Campbell,* found it necessary to determine whether a partnership interest received for services was a profits-only interest or an interest in capital. Presumably, if the court had followed

---

[7] The Court of Appeals in *Diamond* refused to consider the Commissioner's argument that Diamond received more than a future profits interest, because the value of the property may have been greater than its purchase price, as no such findings had been made by the Tax Court.

Campbell, this determination would have been unnecessary and only the value of the interest received for services would have been at issue. Because the partnership agreement provided that the services partner, who received a general partnership interest, had a right to receive 50% of the liquidation proceeds after repayment to the limited partners of their capital contributions, the court found that a capital interest had been received. In affirming the Tax Court's decision in *Mark IV Pictures, Inc.,* the Court of Appeals held that the test to determine whether the interest received is an interest in partnership capital is an examination of the effect of a hypothetical liquidation immediately after the partnership is formed. If the partner would receive a distribution in that hypothetical liquidation, the interest is an interest in capital, not a profits interest

3.3. *Personal Service Partnerships*

The rule of *Diamond* probably cannot be applied to partnership interests in personal services partnerships. The value of an interest as a newly admitted partner in any partnership in which a partner's income is determined largely with reference to income from personal services to be rendered in the future cannot be readily ascertained. Consider the implications of the *Diamond* holding if an associate in a law firm is admitted to the law firm partnership and thus becomes entitled to a certain percentage of future profits. Should the newly admitted partner realize income at that time? While both the associate and Diamond have received a "profits" interest in the sense that they have an interest in a partnership that does not involve a right to be paid out of the capital contributions of the other partners, the two situations intuitively seem quite different. Are the differences substantive or matters of valuation? If the former, are the differences sufficient to support tax distinctions between types of "profits" interests? Should it matter whether the partnership interest is received in exchange for past or future services? If this distinction is to be determinative, are there objective tests that can be used to determine on which side of the line a particular transaction falls? If the value of a partnership interest in future profits received in exchange for future services is taxable in the year of receipt, is the partner also taxable on the income as received in future years? How can double taxation be avoided? The IRS recognized these valuation problems in Rev.Proc. 93–27, 1993–2 C.B. 343, where it indicated that the IRS will not treat the receipt of a profits-only interest in a partnership for services as a taxable event except in circumstances where it is possible to ascertain the value of the profits-only interest.

4.   SECTION 83

Diamond involved tax years before the enactment of § 83. The rules concerning the treatment of a partner who receives a partnership interest as compensation for services must be coordinated with the rules under § 83, which in general are controlling as to the taxability of property transferred in connection with the performance of services. Section 83 requires that the fair market value of the "property" transferred be included in income. However, under § 83 there is a statutory issue whether an interest in partnership profits constitutes "property." Treas.Reg. § 1.83–3(e) defines "property" comprehensively and excludes only "an unfunded and unsecured promise to pay money in the future." The Regulations appear to cover any kind of an interest in a partnership, including a profits interest of the type involved in *Diamond*. There is no significant difference, however, between an unsecured and unfunded promise to pay money in the future, which is not covered by § 83, and a partnership interest in future profits. Applying § 83 to a profits-only partnership interest in exchange for services raises the same valuation problems as in the *Diamond* case. Campbell v. Commissioner, supra, held that a profits-only partnership interest constitutes property for purposes of § 83, although, as discussed above, the Eighth Circuit opinion concluded that the interest could not be valued for purposes of including an amount in gross income.

If § 83 is applied, should it matter whether the services must be performed continuously or only for a specified period of time? If property is received for services and the taxpayer's rights to the property are forfeitable or subject to substantial restrictions on transfer, the value of the property is not includable under § 83 until the property vests or the restrictions lapse. The value of the property is includable at its fair market value at that time. In such a case, the service partner might consider an election under § 83(b) to include the value of the property at the time it is received, particularly if the value at the time of receipt is zero. (The IRS might then, contrary to *Diamond*, seek to take the position that there was no "transfer" of "property" for § 83 purposes.)

5.   INTERNAL REVENUE SERVICE RULING POSITION

In Rev.Proc. 93–27, 1993–2 C.B. 343, the IRS adopted the valuation approach of *Campbell* by announcing that it would treat a partner who performs services "in a partner capacity" in exchange for a profits-only partnership interest as realizing income upon receipt of the partnership interest only in the following three specific situations: (1) the partnership's profits are derived from a substantially certain and predictable stream of income, such as from high quality debt or a net lease; (2) the partner disposes of the partnership interest within two years of its receipt; or (3) the interest is a limited partnership interest in a publicly traded limited partnership as defined in § 7704(b), discussed in Chapter 17. As a practical matter, this position eliminated the issue of whether a partner must recognize income upon receipt of a profits-only interest in most circumstances, but the Revenue Procedure imposed certain other conditions that raised interpretative issues. The safe harbor applied only if the services for which the partnership interest has been received were rendered "to or for the benefit of the partnership" rather than to or for the benefit of another partner. The Revenue Procedure added, however, that services may be rendered "in anticipation of being a partner," as well as in the capacity of being a partner. Nevertheless, it was unclear whether receipt of a future profits interest in consideration of past services to another person, where the receipt creates a two-person partnership, is within the safe harbor. There is no logical reason to distinguish this case from receipt of a future profits interest in a preexisting partnership.

Some of the technical problems raised by Rev.Proc. 93–27 were clarified by Rev. Proc. 2001–43, 2001–2 C.B. 191, which provides that classification of a partnership interest received for services will be determined at the time the interest is granted, even if the interest is not vested. Where the requirements of Rev.Proc. 93–27 are met, the IRS will treat neither the grant of the interest, nor its vesting, as a taxable event to the recipient. Rev.Proc. 2001–43 requires that the service provider be treated as the owner of the partnership interest from the date of its grant. Therefore, the service provider is required to account for the appropriate share of all partnership items. The Revenue Procedure also states that neither the partnership nor any of the partners can claim a deduction for the cost of the services at either the time the interest is granted or at the time the profits-only partnership interest becomes vested. (Note, however, that the allocation of partnership income to the service provider reduces the income of the other partners, which is economically equivalent to allowing a deduction to the other partners.) The treatment of the service provider and the partnership upon vesting presumably is based on the fact that the service provider would have no capital account balance at that time and would, therefore, receive nothing upon liquidation of the partnership.

6.   2005 PROPOSED REGULATIONS

The Court of Appeals in *Diamond* stated: "We think, of course, that the resolution of these practical questions makes clearly desirable the promulgation of appropriate regulations, to achieve a degree of certainty." Over thirty years later, the Treasury Department issued such Proposed Regulations, which if finalized, would comprehensively deal with the treatment of partnership interests received for services. Prop.Regs. § 1.83–3(e) and (*l*) (2005) and § 1.721–1(b) (2005).

The preamble to the Proposed Regulations, Partial Withdrawal of Notice of Proposed Rulemaking Notice of Proposed Rulemaking, and Notice of Public Hearing, Partnership Equity for Services, REG–105346–03, 70 F.R. 29675 (May 24, 2005), explains the proposed rules as follows:

1.   Application of Section 83 to Partnership Interests

[T]he proposed regulations [Prop.Reg. § 1.83–3(e) (2005)] provide that a partnership interest is property within the meaning of section 83, and that the transfer of a partnership interest in connection with the performance of services is subject to section 83.

The proposed regulations apply section 83 to all partnership interests, without distinguishing between partnership capital interests and partnership profits interests. * * * [T]he Treasury Department and the IRS do not believe that there is a substantial basis for distinguishing among partnership interests for purposes of section 83. All partnership interests constitute personal property under state law and give the holder the right to share in future earnings from partnership capital and labor. Moreover, * * * taxpayers may exploit any differences in the tax treatment of partnership profits interests and partnership capital interests. * * * Therefore, all of the rules in these proposed regulations and the accompanying proposed revenue procedure (described below) apply equally to partnership capital interests and partnership profits interests. * * *

Section 83(b) allows a person who receives substantially nonvested property in connection with the performance of services to elect to include in gross income the difference between: (A) the fair market value of the property at the time of transfer (determined without regard to a restriction other than a restriction which by its terms will never lapse); and (B) the amount paid for such property. Under section 83(b)(2), the election under section 83(b) must be made within 30 days of the date of the transfer of the property to the service provider.

Consistent with the principles of section 83, the proposed regulations provide that, if a partnership interest is transferred in connection with the performance of services, and if an election under section 83(b) is not made, then the holder of the partnership interest is not treated as a partner until the interest becomes substantially vested. If a section 83(b) election is made with respect to such an interest, the service provider will be treated as a partner. * * *

These principles differ from Rev.Proc. 2001–43 [2001–2 C.B. 191]. Under that revenue procedure, if a partnership profits interest is transferred in connection with the performance of services, then the holder of the partnership interest may be treated as a partner even if no section 83(b) election is made, provided that certain conditions are met.

Certain changes to the regulations under both subchapter K and section 83 are needed to coordinate the principles of subchapter K with the principles of section 83. Among the changes that are proposed in these regulations are: (1) conforming the subchapter K rules to the section 83 timing rules * * *. In addition, Rev.Procs. 93–27 (1993–2 C.B. 343), and 2001–43 (2001–2 C.B. 191), which generally provide for nonrecognition by both the partnership and the service provider on the transfer of a profits interest in the partnership for services performed for that partnership, must be modified to be consistent with these proposed regulations. Accordingly, in conjunction with these proposed regulations, the IRS is issuing Notice 2005–43 (2005–24 I.R.B.). That Notice contains a proposed revenue procedure that, when finalized, will obsolete Rev.Procs. 93–27 and 2001–43. * * *

5.   Valuation of Compensatory Partnership Interests

* * * Section 83 generally provides that the recipient of property transferred in connection with the performance of services recognizes income equal to the fair market value of the property, disregarding lapse restrictions. * * * However, some authorities have concluded that, under the particular facts and circumstances of the case, a partnership profits interest had only a speculative value or that the fair market value of a partnership interest should

be determined by reference to the liquidation value of that interest. See section 1.704–1(e)(1)(v); Campbell v. Commissioner, 943 F.2d 815 (8th Cir. 1991); St. John v. U.S., 1984–1 USTC 9158 (C.D. Ill. 1983). But see Diamond v. Commissioner, 492 F.2d 286 (7th Cir. 1974) (holding under pre-section 83 law that the receipt of a profits interest with a determinable value at the time of receipt resulted in immediate taxation); Campbell v. Commissioner, T.C. Memo 1990–162, aff'd in part and rev'd in part, 943 F.2d 815 (8th Cir. 1991).

The Treasury Department and the IRS have determined that, provided certain requirements are satisfied, it is appropriate to allow partnerships and service providers to value partnership interests based on liquidation value. [Prop.Reg. § 1.83–3(*l*).] This approach ensures consistency in the treatment of partnership profits interests and partnership capital interests, and accords with other regulations issued under subchapter K, such as the regulations under section 704(b).

In accordance with these proposed regulations, the revenue procedure proposed in Notice 2005–43 (2005–24 I.R.B.) will, when finalized, provide additional rules that partnerships, partners, and persons providing services to the partnership in exchange for interests in that partnership would be required to follow when electing under section 1.83–3(*l*) of these proposed regulations to treat the fair market value of those interests as being equal to the liquidation value of those interests. For this purpose, the liquidation value of a partnership interest is the amount of cash that the holder of that interest would receive with respect to the interest if, immediately after the transfer of the interest, the partnership sold all of its assets (including goodwill, going concern value, and any other intangibles associated with the partnership's operations) for cash equal to the fair market value of those assets, and then liquidated.

For the most part, from the perspective of the partner receiving an interest in a partnership in exchange for services, these Proposed Regulations effect little substantive change.

7.   NEW SECTION 1061

The 2017 Tax Act added a new § 1061, which applies to taxable years beginning after December 31, 2017. It requires that long-term capital gain "with respect to" covered partnership interests be treated as short-term capital gain unless the interest has been held for more than three years. As discussed above, grant of a profits interest is generally not taxable under current (and proposed) authorities. After the service provider is a partner, the partnership can then allocate preferentially taxed long-term capital gains to that partner. The partner may then take distributions of cash tax-free in the same amount as the allocation (because the allocation will increase basis). I.R.C. §§ 705, 731. On the sale of an interest held for more than one year or on distributions in excess of basis, the partner will generally have long-term capital gain (or loss). I.R.C. § 741. (Note: § 751 may apply to alter these general rules. See Chapter 24 (discussing the effect of § 751(a) on sales) and Chapter 25 (discussing the effect of § 751(b) on distributions.)) This ability of a service partner to obtain a profits interest without tax on receipt of the interest followed by long-term capital gain distributive share allocations and long-term capital gain on sale of the interest has become known as the "carried interest" loophole. Section 1061 was enacted in response; however politically helpful its enactment may turn out to be, it is unclear the extent to which it will limit the ability to use partnership profits interests to convert ordinary service income into long-term capital gains. Section 1061 is discussed in greater detail in Chapter 24.

PROBLEM SET 3

1.   Avery and Blair each hold a 50% interest in the AB LLC, a limited liability company taxed as a partnership. The sole asset of the AB LLC is Blackacre, a 1,000 acre farm worth $1,200,000. AB LLC purchased Blackacre several years ago for $900,000, and that amount remains its current adjusted basis. Avery and Blair each have a basis in their interests in the LLC (from cash contributions) of $450,000. Avery and Blair have offered Charlie a one-third interest in the LLC capital and profits (which would reduce Avery's and Blair's interests from one-half each to one-third each). Determine the tax consequences to Charlie under each of the following situations:

(a)   Charlie is a lawyer and receives the one-third interest valued at $400,000 in consideration of legal services previously rendered to the LLC in defending it against an "attractive nuisance" suit by a trespasser injured on the Blackacre premises.

(b)   Charlie is an architect who owns plans for an apartment building drawn for a project that never was undertaken. Charlie will supervise construction of an apartment building on the land using the plans. Avery, Blair, and Charlie value Charlie's contribution at $600,000 and provide him with a capital account in that amount.

(c)   Charlie receives the interest in exchange for agreeing to act for four years as the manager of an apartment complex that will be built on the land. (Assume that Avery and Blair each will contribute one-half of the cash necessary to build the apartment complex.) If, however, Charlie quits working for the LLC during the four-year period, the interest will be forfeited. Are the value and basis of Blackacre (or any of the LLC assets) at the end of Year Four relevant to your answer?

2.   Block & Eggers, C.P.A. is a certified public accounting firm with 50 general partners. Dana, who has been an employee of the firm for 10 years, finally has been admitted to the partnership this year. Dana's opening capital account is fixed at zero, but Dana will share in all profits and losses following admission to the partnership. Is Dana's admission to the partnership a taxable event? What if the partnership is on the cash method of accounting and Dana is entitled to a share of any accounts receivable outstanding on the day of admission to the partnership?

3.   Elliot is the investment manager for Pari-Mutuel Capital Associates, a limited partnership, which has nearly 100 partners (but which is not publicly traded). Elliot received a nonforfeitable, 1% profits-only limited partnership interest in the partnership, whose assets consist of a portfolio of New York Stock Exchange traded securities with a value of $100,000,000, as a bonus for his many years of faithful service to the partnership in managing its portfolio of investments. Income from the portfolio has been averaging $5,000,000 per year for the last five years. What are the tax consequences to Elliot upon receipt of the profits interest? Should *Diamond* apply? Should § 83 apply?

B. TREATMENT OF THE PARTNERSHIP ISSUING A PARTNERSHIP INTEREST IN EXCHANGE FOR SERVICES

INTERNAL REVENUE CODE: Sections 83(h); 721(a).

REGULATIONS: Sections 1.83–6(a)(4), (b); 1.721–1(b); 1.722–1.

PROPOSED REGULATIONS: Sections 1.83–3(e) and (*l*) (2005); 1.721–1(b) (2005).

The treatment of a partnership issuing a partnership capital interest in exchange for services has been more opaque than the treatment of the partner who receives the interest in exchange for services. It is clear that § 83(h) allows the partnership a deduction or capitalized cost of acquiring an asset (tangible or intangible) equal to the amount includable by the partner under § 83(a). See Treas.Reg. § 1.83–6(a). Logically, the service partner should not be entitled to any part of this deduction, and a provision in the partnership agreement pursuant to § 704(b) allocating it to the other partners should be respected. Any deduction allowed would then reduce the outside bases of the other partners under § 705.

A more difficult question, however, has been whether the partnership recognizes any gain or loss—taxable to the other partners— as a result of the transaction. Section 721(a), which provides nonrecognition to a partner who receives a partnership interest in exchange for property, but which does not provide nonrecognition to a partner who receives a partnership interest in exchange for services, is also the section providing that the partnership itself does not recognize gain of loss when it issues a partnership interest in exchange for property. This statutory structure suggests that the partnership that issues a partnership interest in exchange for property also should recognize gain or loss on the admission of a new partner in exchange for services.

McDougal v. Commissioner

Tax Court of the United States, 1974.
62 T.C. 720.

■ FAY, JUDGE:

* * *

FINDINGS OF FACT

* * *

F.C. and Frankie McDougal Maintained Farms at Lamesa, Tex., where they were engaged in the business of breeding and racing horses. Gilbert McClanahan was a licensed public horse trainer who rendered his services to various horse owners for a standard fee. He had numbered the McDougals among his clientele since 1965.

On February 21, 1965, a horse of exceptional pedigree, Iron Card, had been foaled at the Anthony Ranch in Florida. Title to Iron Card was acquired in January of 1967 by one Frank Ratliff, Jr., who in turn transferred title to himself, M. H. Ratliff, and John V. Burnett (Burnett). The Ratliffs and Burnett entered Iron Card in several races as a 2-year-old; and although the horse enjoyed some success in these contests, it soon became evident that he was suffering from a condition diagnosed by a veterinarian as a protein allergy.

When, due to a dispute among themselves, the Ratliffs and Burnett decided to sell Iron Card for whatever price he could attract, McClanahan (who had trained the horse for the Ratliffs and Burnett) advised the McDougals to make the purchase. He made this recommendation because, despite the veterinarian's prognosis to the contrary, McClanahan believed that by the use of home remedy Iron Card could be restored to full racing vigor. * * *

The McDougals purchased Iron Card for $10,000 on January 1, 1968. At the time of the purchase McDougal promised that if McClanahan trained and attended to Iron Card, a half interest in the horse would be his once the McDougals had recovered the costs and expenses of acquisition. This promise was not made in lieu of payment of the standard trainer's fee; for from January 1, 1968, until the date of the transfer, McClanahan was paid $2,910 as compensation for services rendered as Iron Card's trainer.

McClanahan's home remedy proved so effective in relieving Iron Card of his allergy that the horse began to race with success, and his reputation consequently grew to such proportion that he attracted a succession of offers to purchase, one of which reached $60,000. The McDougals decided, however, to keep the horse and by October 4, 1968, had recovered out of their winnings the costs of acquiring him. It was therefore on that date that they transferred a half interest in the horse to McClanahan in accordance with the promise which McDougal had made to the trainer. * * *

Iron Card continued to race well until very late in 1968 when, without warning and for an unascertained cause, he developed a condition called "hot ankle" which effectively terminated his racing career. From 1970 onward he was used exclusively for breeding purposes. That his value as a stud was no less than his value as a racehorse is attested to by the fact that in September of 1970 petitioners were offered $75,000 for him; but after considering the offer, the McDougals and McClanahan decided to refuse it, preferring to exploit Iron Card's earning potential as a stud to their own profit.

On November 1, 1968, petitioners had concluded a partnership agreement by parol to effectuate their design of racing the horse for as long as that proved feasible and of offering him out as a stud thereafter. Profits were to be shared equally by the McDougals and the McClanahans, while losses were to be allocated to the McDougals alone.[4]

Though the partnership initially filed no return for its first brief taxable year ended December 31, 1968, petitioners did make the computations which such a return would show and reported the results in their individual returns. The partnership was considered to have earned $1,314, against which was deducted depreciation in the amount of $278. Other deductions left the partnership with taxable income for the year of $737 * * *.

On their joint return for the year 1968 the McDougals reported, inter alia, gross income of $22,891 from their Lamesa farms. Against this income they deducted $1,390 representing depreciation on Iron Card for the first 10 months of 1968 and $9,213 in training fees.[6] The McDougals appear, however, to have initially claimed no deduction by reason of the transfer to McClanahan of the half interest in Iron Card.

In addition to their distributive share of partnership income referred to above, the McClanahans reported $5,000 of gross income which they identified as [an] interest in a racehorse.

[By an amended return for 1968, filed in 1970, the McDougals claimed] to have transferred the half interest in Iron Card to McClanahan as compensation for services rendered and thus to be entitled to a $30,000 business expense deduction, computed by reference to the last offer to purchase Iron Card received prior to October 4, 1968. Furthermore, the McDougals acknowledged that they had recognized a gain on the aforesaid transfer. By charging the entire depreciation deduction of $1,390 against the portion of their unadjusted cost basis allocable to the half interest in Iron Card which they retained, the McDougals computed this gain to be $25,000 and characterized it as a long-term capital gain under section 1231(a) of the Internal Revenue Code of 1954.

---

4   The oral agreement was reduced to writing in April of 1970. * * *

6   Presumably this included $3,175 paid to McClanahan both before and after the transfer of Oct. 4, 1968, as compensation for the training of Iron Card.

The McClanahans simultaneously increased their income arising out of the transfer from $5,000 to $30,000. They could thus claim to have a tax cost basis of $30,000 in their half interest in the horse. Finally, purporting to have transferred the horse to a partnership in concert on November 1, 1968, petitioner computed the partnership's basis in the horse to be $33,610 under section 723.[8] This increase in basis led the partnership to claim a depreciation deduction of $934 for 1968 instead of $278 and to report only $81 of taxable income for that year. The McDougals thereupon reduced their distributive share of partnership income for 1968 from $405 to $40, while the McClanahans reduced their share from $332 to $41. For the year 1969 the partnership claimed a deduction for depreciation on Iron Card in the amount of $5,602, closing the year with a loss of $8,911. This loss was allocated in its entirety to the McDougals, pursuant to the partnership agreement.

* * *

OPINION

Respondent contends that the McDougals did not recognize a $25,000 gain on the transaction of October 4, 1968, and that they were not entitled to claim a $30,000 business expense deduction by reason thereof. He further contends that were Iron Card to be contributed to a partnership or joint venture under the circumstances obtaining in the instant case, its basis in Iron Card at the time of contribution would have been limited by the McDougals' cost basis in the horse, as adjusted. Respondent justifies these contentions by arguing * * * that at some point in time no later than the transfer of October 4, 1968, McDougal and McClanahan entered into a partnership or joint venture[10] to which the McDougals contributed Iron Card and McClanahan contributed services. Respondent contends that such a finding would require our holding that the McDougals did not recognize a gain on the transfer of October 4, 1968, by reason of section 721, and that under section 723 the joint venture's basis in Iron Card at the time of the contribution was equal to the McDougals' adjusted basis in the horse as of that time.

* * *

A joint venture is deemed to arise when two or more persons agree, expressly or impliedly, to enter actively upon a specific business enterprise, the purpose of which is the pursuit of profit; the ownership of whose productive assets and of the profits generated by them is shared;

---

[8] Having charged the entire amount of the depreciation which they had claimed ($1,390) against their unadjusted cost basis of $5,000 in the half interest in Iron Card which they retained, the McDougals considered themselves to have an adjusted basis of $3,610 in that retained half. The McClanahans claimed a $30,000 tax cost basis in the half interest which they had just received. Under sec. 723 the contribution of the two halves to a partnership would therefore result in the partnership's having a basis of $33,610 in Iron Card.

[10] By reason of sec. 761(a) joint ventures and partnerships have an identical effect on the determination of income tax liability.

the parties to which all bear the burden of any loss; and the management of which is not confined to a single participant [citations omitted].

While in the case at bar the risk of loss was to be borne by the McDougals alone, all the other elements of a joint venture were present once the transfer of October 4, 1968, had been effected. Accordingly, we hold that the aforesaid transfer constituted the formation of a joint venture to which the McDougals contributed capital in the form of the horse, Iron Card, and in which they granted McClanahan an interest equal to their own in capital and profits as compensation for his having trained Iron Card. We further hold that the agreement formally entered into on November 1, 1968, and reduced to writing in April of 1970, constituted a continuation of the original joint venture under section 708(b)(2)(A). Furthermore, that McClanahan continued to receive a fee for serving as Iron Card's trainer after October 4, 1968, in no way militates against the soundness of this holding. See sec. 707(c), and sec. 1.707–1(c), example 1, Income Tax Reg. However, this holding does not result in the tax consequences which respondent has contended would follow from it. See sec. 1.721–1(b)(1), Income Tax Regs.

When on the formation of a joint venture a party contributing appreciated assets satisfies an obligation by granting his obligee a capital interest in the venture, he is deemed first to have transferred to the obligee an undivided interest in the assets contributed, equal in value to the amount of the obligation so satisfied. He and the obligee are deemed thereafter and in concert to have contributed those assets to the joint venture.

The contributing obligor will recognize gain on the transaction to the extent that the value of the undivided interest which he is deemed to have transferred exceeds his basis therein. The obligee is considered to have realized an amount equal to the fair market value of the interest which he receives in the venture and will recognize income depending upon the character of the obligation satisfied.[12] The joint venture's basis in the assets will be determined under section 723 in accordance with the foregoing assumptions. Accordingly, we hold that the transaction under consideration constituted an exchange in which the McDougals realized $30,000, United States v. Davis, 370 U.S. 65 (1962) * * *.

In determining the basis offset to which the McDougals are entitled with respect to the transfer of October 4, 1968, we note the following: that the McDougals had an unadjusted cost basis in Iron Card of $10,000; that they had claimed $1,390 in depreciation on the entire horse for the period January 1 to October 31, 1968; and that after an agreement of

---

[12] For example, if the obligation arose out of a loan, the obligee will recognize no income by reason of the transaction; if the obligation represents the selling price of a capital asset, he will recognize a capital gain to the extent that the amount he is deemed to have realized exceeds his adjusted basis in the asset; if the obligation represents compensation for services, the transaction will result in ordinary income to the obligee in an amount equal to the value of the interest which he received in the joint venture.

partnership was concluded on November 1, 1968, depreciation on Iron Card was deducted by the partnership exclusively.

* * * Consistent with their intent and with our own holding that a joint venture arose on October 4, 1968, we now further hold that the McDougals were entitled to claim depreciation on Iron Card only until the transfer of October 4, 1968. Thereafter depreciation on Iron Card ought to have been deducted by the joint venture in the computation of its taxable income.

In determining their adjusted basis in the portion of Iron Card on whose disposition they are required to recognize gain, the McDougals charged all the depreciation which they had taken on the horse against their basis in the half in which they retained an interest. This procedure was improper. As in accordance with section 1.167(g)–1, Income Tax Regs., we have allowed the McDougals a depreciation deduction with respect to Iron Card for the period January 1 to October 4, 1968, computed on their entire cost basis in the horse of $10,000; so also do we require that the said deduction be charged against that entire cost basis under section 1016(a)(2)(A).[13]

As the McDougals were in the business of racing horses, any gain recognized by them on the exchange of Iron Card in satisfaction of a debt would be characterized under section 1231(a) provided he had been held by them for the period requisite under section 1231(b) * * *. [T]hey had held him for a period sufficiently long to make section 1231(a) applicable to their gain on the transaction. * * *

The joint venture's basis in Iron Card as of October 4, 1968, must be determined under section 723 in accordance with the principles of law set forth earlier in this opinion. In the half interest in the horse which it is deemed to have received from the McDougals, the joint venture had a basis equal to one-half of the McDougals' adjusted cost basis in Iron Card as of October 4, 1968, i.e., the excess of $5,000 over one-half of the depreciation which the McDougals were entitled to claim on Iron Card for the period January 1 to October 4, 1968. In the half interest which the venture is considered to have received from McClanahan, it can claim to have had a basis equal to the amount which McClanahan is considered to have realized on the transaction, $30,000. The joint venture's deductions for depreciation on Iron Card for the years 1968 and 1969 are to be determined on the basis computed in the above-described manner.

When an interest in a joint venture is transferred as compensation for services rendered, any deduction which may be authorized under section 162(a)(1) by reason of that transfer is properly claimed by the party to whose benefit the services accrued, be that party the venture itself or one or more venturers, sec. 1.721–1(b)(2), Income Tax Regs. Prior

---

[13] The depreciation on Iron Card to which the McDougals are entitled, their adjusted basis in the horse as of Oct. 4, 1968, and the gain recognized by them by reason of the transaction on that date remain to be determined in accordance with the decision under Rule 155, Tax Court Rules of Practice and Procedure.

to McClanahan's receipt of his interest, a joint venture did not exist under the facts of the case at bar; the McDougals were the sole owners of Iron Card and recipients of his earnings. Therefore, they alone could have benefited from the services rendered by McClanahan prior to October 4, 1968, for which he was compensated by the transaction of that date. Accordingly, we hold that the McDougals are entitled to a business expense deduction of $30,000, that amount being the value of the interest which McClanahan received. * * *

DETAILED ANALYSIS

1. EFFECT OF ADMISSION OF SERVICE PARTNER WITH A CAPITAL INTEREST

1.1. *Does a Partnership Recognize Gain or Loss on the Admission of a Service Partner?*

If the principles of *McDougal* were applied to an existing partnership rather than only to transfers of an interest in property in consideration of past services where the transfer results in the initial formation of a partnership, the partnership would recognize gain or loss on the admission of the service partner. See Treas.Reg. § 1.83–6(b). Under this model, the partnership would be treated as transferring an undivided portion of each of its assets to the service partner as payment for services, with gain and loss being recognized on the constructive transfer. The service partner then constructively recontributes the property to the partnership, which takes a basis equal to the service partner's "tax cost" basis, i.e., fair market value, in the property under § 723.

An alternative theory—"cash-out-cash-in"—for dealing with an existing partnership's side of the transaction that avoids recognition of gain appears to be favored and the one that has been adopted in practice. Under the cash-out-cash-in theory, the partnership—with the effects passed through to the other partners—is treated as if the partnership paid cash to the service partner equal to the value of the partnership interest, following which the service partner immediately contributed the cash back to the partnership in a transaction subject to § 721. Under this model, the partnership recognizes no gain and the basis of its assets remains unchanged. Although the cash-out-cash-in model is not a wholly implausible alternative theory, it found no support in prior judicial decisions or administrative rulings.

Prop.Reg. §§ 1.721–1(b)(2) (2005) would produce results for the partnership issuing a partnership interest in exchange for services that are identical to the results under the cash-out-cash-in model, although the Proposed Regulations do not explicitly adopt the cash-out-cash-in model as the underlying theory for the result-oriented rules contained therein. The preamble to the Proposed Regulations, Partial Withdrawal of Notice of Proposed Rulemaking Notice of Proposed Rulemaking, and Notice of Public Hearing, Partnership Equity for Services, REG–105346–03, 70 F.R. 29675 (May 24, 2005), explains the proposed rules as follows:

> There is a dispute among commentators as to whether a partnership should recognize gain or loss on the transfer of a

compensatory partnership interest. Some commentators believe that, on the transfer of such an interest, the partnership should be treated as satisfying its compensation obligation with a fractional interest in each asset of the partnership. Under this deemed sale of assets theory, the partnership would recognize gain or loss equal to the excess of the fair market value of each partial asset deemed transferred to the service provider over the partnership's adjusted basis in that partial asset. Other commentators believe that a partnership should not recognize gain or loss on the transfer of a compensatory partnership interest. They argue, among other things, that the transfer of such an interest is not properly treated as a realization event for the partnership because no property owned by the partnership has changed hands. They also argue that taxing a partnership on the transfer of such an interest would result in inappropriate gain acceleration, would be difficult to administer, and would cause economically similar transactions to be taxed differently.

Generally, when appreciated property is used to pay an obligation, gain on the property is recognized. * * * However, the Treasury Department and the IRS believe that partnerships should not be required to recognize gain on the transfer of a compensatory partnership interest. Such a rule is more consistent with the policies underlying section 721—to defer recognition of gain and loss when persons join together to conduct a business—than would be a rule requiring the partnership to recognize gain on the transfer of these types of interests. Therefore, the proposed regulations [Prop. Regs. §§ 1.83–6(b) and 1.721–1(b)(2)] provide that partnerships are not taxed on the transfer or substantial vesting of a compensatory partnership interest. Under section 1.704–1(b)(4)(i) (reverse section 704(c) principles), the historic partners generally will be required to recognize any income or loss attributable to the partnership's assets as those assets are sold, depreciated, or amortized.

The rule providing for nonrecognition of gain or loss does not apply to the transfer or substantial vesting of an interest in an eligible entity, as defined in section 301.7701–3(a) of the Procedure and Administration Regulations, that becomes a partnership under section 301.7701–3(f)(2) as a result of the transfer or substantial vesting of the interest. See McDougal v. Commissioner, 62 T.C. 720 (1974) (holding that the service recipient recognized gain on the transfer of a one-half interest in appreciated property to the service provider, immediately prior to the contribution by the service recipient and the service provider of their respective interests in the property to a newly formed partnership).

As explained in the above excerpt from the preamble, while Prop.Regs. §§ 1.83–6(b) (2005) and 1.721–1(b)(2) (2005) would provide that a partnership does not recognize any gain or loss upon the transfer of a partnership interest to a new partner in exchange for services to the partnership, the Proposed Regulations preserve the recognition result in *McDougal* if the transfer of property in exchange for services creates a partnership out of a relationship that previously was not classified as a partnership. What difference is there between the two situations that justifies different treatment? In both cases, one or more parties transfer an interest in property to another party in exchange for services.

As a practical matter, upon admission of a partner it generally is necessary to revalue the partnership's property for book purposes and adjust the partners' capital account book values to reflect the revaluation. Treas.Reg. § 1.704–1(b)(2)(iv)(*f*) specifically allows the partnership to revalue its property and adjust the existing partners' capital accounts in connection with the grant of an interest in the partnership (other than a *de minimis* interest) in consideration of services to the partnership by an existing partner acting in a partner capacity or by a new partner acting in a partner capacity or in anticipation of being a partner. Thus, for capital account purposes, the exchange of an interest in partnership capital is reflected as a book realization event for the partnership and a transfer of partnership capital from the continuing partners to the service partner. Further, under the Proposed Regulations, the revalued capital account measures the amount of service income the service partner has recognized for tax purposes, and that same amount is allowed either as a deduction to the partnership or capitalized, as is appropriate. The major decision of the Proposed Regulations is to treat the exchange of an interest in partnership property for services as a tax nonrecognition event for the partnership and to defer recognition of tax gain or loss to disposition of partnership property.

Contrary to assertions in the preamble to the Proposed Regulations, the broader pattern of Subchapter K as a whole, which significantly incorporates the aggregate theory of partnership taxation, suggests that the *McDougal* model is a more appropriate principle for determining the tax consequences to the other partners than the legal fiction employed in the cash-out-cash-in model. The position stated in the preamble that a transfer of interests in partnership assets is not a realization event is directly contrary to the result in *McDougal*, which upon careful reading is not really distinguishable on the grounds asserted in the preamble. As a more general tax doctrine, the transfer of any interest in property in exchange for services results in recognition of gain or loss with respect to the transferred property, absent a statutory nonrecognition rule. In the case of the admission of a partner to a partnership, the tax consequences to both the partner and the partnership normally are determined under § 721. That is, the transaction is either a nonrecognition transaction under § 721 for both the partner and the partnership, or it is a recognition transaction for both the partnership and the partner. It should not be a nonrecognition transaction for one and a recognition transaction for the other. And since there has been no prerequisite exchange of property, the admission of a partner with a capital interest in exchange for services should not be a nonrecognition transaction for the partnership.

The tax policy problem is one of tax arbitrage. The Proposed Regulations, in effect, allow a partnership to purchase services in exchange for an interest in appreciated property without recognition of gain while obtaining a deduction (or capitalized amount, which might be depreciable or amortizable) without the concomitant recognition of gain—exactly the result rejected in *McDougal*, and a result clearly unobtainable outside of Subchapter K. There is no policy reason or statutory support for allowing such a result through the use of Subchapter K; because revaluation of asset book value and partner capital accounts typically occurs on the admission of a service partner, administrability concerns are overstated. It is, however, likely that the prevailing practice today is to follow the Proposed Regulations, particularly in the presence of appreciated partnership assets.

1.2. *Application of McDougal Principles to Exchange of Partnership Capital Interest for Services*

As noted above, if the principles of *McDougal* are applied to an existing partnership that admits a partner in exchange for services, the partnership recognizes gain or loss on the admission of the service partner. The partnership is taxed as if it transferred an undivided portion of each of its assets to the service partner as compensation, with gain and loss being recognized on the constructive transfer. This gain should be allocated to the other partners. As a corollary, the partnership constructively receives the property back from the service partner and takes a fair market basis in the recontributed undivided portion of each asset.

The following examples illustrate the application of the *McDougal* principle in a variety of contexts. All of the examples involve the admission of J in exchange for services to the GH Partnership, which holds a single asset, Blackacre. For purposes of simplification, in all of the examples it is assumed that J receives a fully vested partnership interest in exchange for J's promise to perform future services, the services have not yet been performed but are performed in the same year the interest is granted, and the interest is not forfeitable. These conditions rarely, if ever will be encountered in reality, but they vastly simplify the calculations. Note that even after the Proposed Regulations are adopted, if the transactions described in the examples transpired between two co-owners of property—G and H—who were not yet partners, and J performed the assumed services for G and H, with the result that the transfer of an undivided one-third interest in Blackacre gave rise to the GHJ Partnership, the Proposed Regulations would not provide G and H with nonrecognition, and under *McDougal*, their gain would be recognized.

1.2.1. *Example of Admission of Service Partner in Exchange for Services Where Partnership Is Entitled to a Deduction*

Assume that in exchange for services J is admitted to the GH Partnership, in which G and H previously were equal partners, as a full one-third partner, obtaining a present vested capital interest. The partnership owns a single capital asset, Blackacre, having a fair market value of $180,000 and a basis of $60,000. G and H each have a basis in their partnership interest of $30,000. If in connection with J becoming a partner, the GH Partnership adjusts the book value of its assets and partners' capital accounts to fair market value, as permitted (and for practical purposes as required) by Treas.Reg. § 1.704–1(b)(2)(iv)(*f*), immediately before J is admitted as a partner, the GH Partnership balance sheet is as follows:

	Assets			Partnership Debts & Partners' Capital Accounts	
	Book Value	Tax Basis		Book Value	Tax Basis
Blackacre	$180,000	$60,000	G	$ 90,000	$30,000
			H	$ 90,000	$30,000
Totals	$180,000	$60,000		$180,000	$60,000

If J receives a one-third capital interest, G and H each reduce their capital accounts from $90,000 to $60,000, and J will receive a capital account of $60,000. As a result of receiving a capital account worth $60,000, J recognizes $60,000 of ordinary income, and J's basis for the partnership interest is $60,000. As indicated by *McDougal*, however, the treatment of G and H, the original partners, and the determination of the partnership's basis in Blackacre, is a bit more complex. To tax all parties properly, including J, the entire transaction should be recast as follows.

1.   The GH Partnership constructively transfers an undivided one-third of Blackacre to J in exchange for services. Under general tax principles and *McDougal*, the GH Partnership would recognize a gain of $40,000 (the $60,000 amount realized in the form of services, equal to 1/3 of the $180,000 fair market value of the property, minus 1/3 of the $60,000 basis in the property). See Treas.Reg. § 1.83–6(b). (Note that under the Proposed Regulations, however, the GH partnership would not recognize this gain for tax purposes.) G and H would each be allocated and pay tax on a proportionate share of this gain. Pursuant to § 705, G and H would each increase the basis in their partnership interests by $20,000 as a result of the gain allocation. Assuming that the payment to J is for a deductible expense, G and H also account for their distributive share of this expense deduction, and each decreases the basis in their partnership interests by $30,000 as a result of the partnership's $60,000 deduction. This results in a net decrease in the basis of G's and H's partnership interests of $10,000. At this interim point, the balance sheet of the partnership may be conceptualized as follows:

	Assets			Partnership Debts & Partners' Capital Accounts	
	Book Value	Tax Basis		Book Value	Tax Basis
2/3 Blackacre	$120,000	$40,000	G	$ 60,000	$20,000
			H	$ 60,000	$20,000
Totals	$120,000	$40,000		$120,000	$40,000

2. Because J recognizes income of $60,000 on this hypothetical transfer of a one-third interest in Blackacre, J takes a basis in the one-third interest in Blackacre equal to that amount. When J constructively recontributes the one-third of Blackacre to the partnership, under § 721, J recognizes no gain. Under § 722, J's basis in the partnership interest is $60,000; J's basis in the one-third interest in Blackacre is $60,000; and under § 723, the GHJ partnership takes a basis of $60,000 in this one-third interest upon the deemed contribution by J of this portion. GHJ's total basis in Blackacre will be $100,000 when this $60,000 is added to the $40,000 basis in the other two-thirds of Blackacre. After the transaction is completed, the GHI Partnership's balance sheet would be as follows:

	Assets			Partnership Debts & Partners' Capital Accounts	
	Book Value	**Tax Basis**		**Book Value**	**Tax Basis**
Blackacre	$180,000	$100,000	G	$ 60,000	$ 20,000
			H	$ 60,000	$ 20,000
	_____	_____	J	$ 60,000	$ 60,000
Totals	$180,000	$100,000		$180,000	$100,000

If, however, the Proposed Regulations were followed, the tax gain in the one-third interest of Blackacre would not be recognized and passed through to the partners, but the transfer would still be deductible by the partners and reduce their outside basis by $30,000 each. The ending accounts under the Proposed Regulations would instead be as follows:

	Assets			Partnership Debts & Partners' Capital Accounts	
	Book Value	**Tax Basis**		**Book Value**	**Tax Basis**
Blackacre	$180,000	$60,000	G	$ 60,000	$ 0
			H	$ 60,000	$ 0
	_____	_____	J	$ 60,000	$60,000
Total	$180,000	$60,000		$180,000	$60,000

1.2.2. *Example of Admission of Service Partner in Exchange for Services Where Partnership Must Capitalize Compensation for Services*

Assume alternatively that the payment for the services performed by J in the preceding example is not deductible to the partnership but instead is a capital expenditure incurred to improve Blackacre. If this is true, from an economic perspective the total value of the improvements presumably is $90,000; J is contributing the services that produce two-thirds of the improvements, worth $60,000, for a one-third interest in unimproved Blackacre, worth $60,000, and is performing the services that create the remaining one-third of the improvement on J's own account. One way to view the results of the transaction is as follows:

1.   Under general tax principles and *McDougal*, the GH Partnership constructively transfers an undivided one-third of Blackacre to J in exchange for services that produce a two-thirds interest in an improvement to Blackacre with a total value of $90,000, the two-thirds interest being worth $60,000. Again the GH Partnership recognizes a gain of $40,000, and pursuant to § 705, G and H each increase the basis in their partnership interests by $20,000 as a result of the gain recognition. In this case, however, there is no deduction. Instead, the GH partnership capitalizes the $60,000 paid to J. At this interim point, the balance sheet of the partnership may be conceptualized as follows:

	Assets			Partnership Debts & Partners' Capital Accounts	
	Book Value	Tax Basis		Book Value	Tax Basis
2/3 Blackacre	$120,000	$ 40,000	G	$ 90,000	$ 50,000
2/3 Improvement	$ 60,000	$ 60,000	H	$ 90,000	$ 50,000
Totals	$180,000	$100,000		$180,000	$100,000

2.   Once again, J recognizes income of $60,000 and takes a basis in the one-third interest in Blackacre equal to that amount. When J constructively recontributes the one-third of Blackacre to the partnership, along with the remaining one-third interest in the improvements created by J's services, J's basis in the partnership interest under § 722 again is $60,000, J's basis in the one-third interest in Blackacre. The GHJ partnership again takes a basis of $60,000 in this one third-interest in Blackacre under § 723, which is added to the $40,000 basis in the other two-thirds of Blackacre, for a total basis to the partnership of $100,000. Since J had no basis in the one-third interest in the improvements produced by J's services, J does not increase J's basis in the partnership interest with respect to this contribution, and the partnership receives no basis in this portion of the improvements. After the transaction is completed, the GHJ Partnership's balance sheet would be as follows.

	Assets			Partnership Debts & Partners' Capital Accounts	
	Book Value	Tax Basis		Book Value	Tax Basis
Blackacre	$180,000	$100,000	G	$ 90,000	$ 50,000
Improvement	$ 90,000	$ 60,000	H	$ 90,000	$ 50,000
			J	$ 90,000	$ 60,000
Total	$270,000	$160,000		$270,000	$160,000

If the Proposed Regulations applied, then no gain would be recognized by the partnership on a transfer of one-third interest. Instead of yielding a tax deduction, J's services would instead by capitalized into the improvement. The ending accounts would be as follows:

	Assets			Partnership Debts & Partners' Capital Accounts	
	Book Value	Tax Basis		Book Value	Tax Basis
Blackacre	$180,000	$ 60,000	G	$ 90,000	$ 30,000
Improvement	$ 90,000	$ 60,000	H	$ 90,000	$ 30,000
			J	$ 90,000	$ 60,000
Totals	$270,000	$120,000		$270,000	$120,000

PROBLEM SET 4

1.   (a) In problem 1(a) of Problem Set 3, what are the tax consequences under *McDougal* and general tax principles to the AB LLC on the receipt of Charlie's legal services in exchange for admitting Charlie to the partnership as a one-third partner with a $400,000 capital account? How would the answer change if instead the 2005 Proposed Regulations determine the tax consequences?

     (b) Does the answer to (a) change if Avery and Blair hold Blackacre as joint tenants in an arrangement that is not treated as a partnership and then create an LLC with Charlie? Avery and Blair contribute their joint tenancy interest in Blackacre for a one-third interest each. Charlie receives a one-third interest in the LLC in exchange for his legal services.

2.   In problem 1(b) of Problem Set 3, what are the tax consequences under *McDougal* and general tax principles to the AB LLC on the receipt of Charlie's services in exchange for admitting Charlie to the partnership as a one-third partner with a $600,000 capital account? How would the answer change if instead the 2005 Proposed Regulations determine the tax consequences?

CHAPTER 20

DETERMINING PARTNERS' DISTRIBUTIVE SHARES

INTERNAL REVENUE CODE: Sections 702; 704(a)–(e); 761(c).

REGULATIONS: Sections 1.702–1; 1.704–1(a); 1.761–1(c).

Section 702(a) requires each partner to take into account the partner's distributive share of each separately stated item and the residual taxable income or loss entering into the partnership's taxable income. Section 704(a) provides that a partner's distributive share is determined by the partnership agreement, except as otherwise provided in Subchapter K. The partnership agreement is broadly defined as the original agreement plus any modifications agreed to by all the partners or adopted in any other manner provided by the partnership agreement. The modifications may be oral or written and may be made with respect to a particular taxable year subsequent to the close of that year but before the due date for filing the partnership return. Local law governs any matter on which the agreement is silent. I.R.C. § 761(c); Treas.Reg. § 1.761–1(c).

The latitude provided by § 704(a), allowing partners to allocate items of income, expense, or loss in the partnership agreement as they choose, is one of the most important aspects of Subchapter K. Thus, if two partners agree to split partnership net profits or losses in a 75:25 ratio, the partners' distributive shares of each item in § 702(a) will be in that ratio. See Treas.Reg. § 1.704–1(b)(1)(vii). If they agree that profits are to be split 50:50, but net operating losses are to be split 75:25, the profit-sharing ratio would determine distributive shares in a profitable year, and the loss-sharing ratio would control in an unprofitable year.

The freedom to allocate distributive shares of partnership items is not unlimited, however. Allocations in the partnership agreement must satisfy the requirement of § 704(b)(2) that the allocations have "substantial economic effect." Although the Regulations implementing the substantial economic effect test are lengthy and complicated, the test basically requires that allocations of items for tax purposes reflect the economic effect of the allocation to the partners in terms of money. The economic effect of an allocation is demonstrated through properly maintained capital accounts, introduced in Chapter 19, that reflect the amount available to a partner on liquidation of the partnership. In a nutshell, if allocations of tax items in a partnership agreement are consistent with the economic allocation of income and expense or loss as measured by the capital accounts, allocations by the partners will be respected.

If the partnership agreement does not provide for partners' distributive shares or if the distributive share allocation to a partner does not have "substantial economic effect," § 704(b) requires that the partner's distributive share be determined "in accordance with the partner's interest in the partnership (determined by taking into account all facts and circumstances)." As under the substantial economic effect test, application of the facts and circumstances test involves identifying the economic arrangement between the partners. Many partnership agreements are drafted to provide allocations of partnership items that rely on determining the partner's interest in the partnership in lieu of meeting the complicated substantial economic effect test of the Regulations.

A special rule is provided in § 704(c), which allocates items of income, gain, loss, and deduction attributable to property contributed to the partnership to take into account differences between fair market value and basis at the time of the contribution.

As discussed in Chapter 19 and considered in greater detail in Chapter 21, under §§ 722 and 752(a) a partner's share of partnership liabilities is included in the partner's basis for the partnership interest. Allocation of items involving partnership debt complicates the application of the substantial economic effect test. Again, the focus of the Regulations is to provide for allocation of items funded by partnership debt to the partner who is economically affected by the item, generally meaning the partner or partners who are ultimately liable for the debt in the case of recourse debt. In the case of nonrecourse debt, debt for which no partner is personally liable, allocations of items funded by the debt can have no economic effect. As a consequence, Regulations provide special rules to identify partners' shares of deductions attributable to nonrecourse debt.

Section 706(d) provides that if there is a change in a partner's interest in the partnership during the year, each partner's distributive share of income, gain, loss, and deduction shall be determined by a method prescribed by Regulations that takes into account the varying interests of the partners during the taxable year. See Treas.Reg. § 1.706–1(c)(4). In addition, § 706(d)(2) requires that certain deductions be allocated over the year to which they are attributable, thus preventing a newly admitted partner from sharing in any deduction that had economically accrued prior to admission. This rule applies to interest, taxes, and payments for services or for the use of property, and the IRS has the authority to issue Regulations expanding the items covered.

Section 704(e) provides special rules governing allocation of items with respect to certain family partnerships.

Rules outside of Subchapter K may operate to alter the incentives for and consequences of particular distributive share structures. Section 199A, discussed in greater detail in Chapter 18, specifies that long-term capital gains are not taken into account for purposes of computing the

§ 199A deduction. Further, because the § 199A deduction is computed with reference to a qualifying business's "W-2 wages" and "unadjusted basis," a qualifying business conducted through a partnership must allocate these items in order for eligible partners to complete their individual § 199A computations. The statute specifies that W-2 wages are required to be allocated "in the same manner" as the partner's "share of wage expenses," and the partnership's unadjusted basis is required to be allocated "in the same manner" as the partner's "allocable share of depreciation." § 199A(f)(1) (flush language). Section 1061, introduced in Chapter 19 and discussed in greater detail in Chapter 24, will cause certain gains of applicable service partnership interests that would otherwise be long-term capital gains to be re-characterized as short-term capital gains.

SECTION 1. HISTORICAL BACKGROUND

Prior to its amendment by the Tax Reform Act of 1976, § 704(b) provided that special allocations would not be recognized if the "principal purpose" of the allocation was tax avoidance. The Regulations under that version of § 704(b), discussed in Orrisch v. Commissioner, which follows, were issued prior to the 1976 statutory changes, but focused on whether or not the attempted special allocation had "substantial economic effect." The subsequent history of allocations and the substantial economic effect Regulations that ensued owe their origins to the principles described by the court in *Orrisch*.

Orrisch v. Commissioner[*]
Tax Court of the United States, 1970.
55 T.C. 395.

■ FEATHERSTON, JUDGE. Respondent determined deficiencies in petitioners' income tax for 1966 and 1967 in the respective amounts of $2,814.19 and $3,018.11. The only issue for decision is whether an amendment to a partnership agreement allocating to petitioners the entire amount of the depreciation deduction allowable on two buildings owned by the partnership was made for the principal purpose of avoidance of tax within the meaning of section 704(b).

Findings of Fact

* * *

In May of 1963, Domonick J. and Elaine J. Crisafi (hereinafter the Crisafis) and petitioners [Stanley C. and Gerta E. Orrisch] formed a partnership to purchase and operate two apartment houses, one located at 1255 Taylor Street, San Francisco, and the other at 600 Ansel Road, Burlingame, Calif. The cost of the Taylor Street property was $229,011.08, and of the Ansel Road property was $155,974.90. The

---

[*]   The Tax Court decision was affirmed per curiam, 31 A.F.T.R.2d 1069 (9th Cir.1973).

purchase of each property was financed principally by a secured loan. Petitioners and the Crisafis initially contributed to the partnership cash in the amounts of $26,500 and $12,500, respectively. During 1964 and 1965 petitioners and the Crisafis each contributed additional cash in the amounts of $8,800. Under the partnership agreement, which was not in writing, they agreed to share equally the profits and losses from the venture.

During each of the years 1963, 1964, and 1965, the partnership suffered losses, attributable in part to the acceleration of depreciation— the deduction was computed on the basis of 150 percent of straightline depreciation. The amounts of the depreciation deductions, the reported loss for each of the 3 years as reflected in the partnership returns, and the amounts of each partner's share of the losses are as follows:

Year	Depreciation deducted	Total loss	Each partner's share of the losses—50 percent of the total loss
1963	$ 9,886.20	$ 9,716.14	$4,858.07
1964	21,051.95	17,812.33	[1] 8,906.17
1965	19,894.24	18,952.59	[1] 9,476.30

1.   The amounts of the losses allocated to the Crisafis for 1964 and 1965 were actually $8,906.16 and $9,476.29.

Petitioners and the Crisafis respectively reported in their individual income tax returns for these years the partnership losses allocated to them.

Petitioners enjoyed substantial amounts of income from several sources, the principal one being a nautical equipment sales and repair business. In their joint income tax returns for 1963, 1964, and 1965, petitioners reported taxable income in the respective amounts of $10,462.70, $5,898.85, and $50,832, together with taxes thereon in the amounts of $2,320.30, $1,059.80, and $12,834.

The Crisafis were also engaged in other business endeavors, principally an insurance brokerage business. They owned other real property, however, from which they realized losses, attributable largely to substantial depreciation deductions. In their joint income tax returns for 1963, 1964, and 1965, they reported no net taxable income.

Early in 1966, petitioners and the Crisafis orally agreed that, for 1966 and subsequent years, the entire amount of the partnership's depreciation deductions would be specially allocated to petitioners, and that the gain or loss from the partnership's business, computed without regard to any deduction for depreciation, would be divided equally. They further agreed that, in the event the partnership property was sold at a gain, the specially allocated depreciation would be "charged back" to petitioner's capital account and petitioners would pay the tax on the gain attributable thereto.

The operating results of the partnership for 1966 and 1967 as reflected in the partnership returns were as follows:

Year	Depreciation deducted	Loss (including depreciation)	Gain (or loss) without regard to depreciation
1966	$18,412.00	$19,396.00	($984.00)
1967	17,180.75	16,560.78	619.97

The partnership returns for these years show that, taking into account the special arrangement as to depreciation, losses in the amounts of $18,904 and $16,870.76 were allocated to petitioners for 1966 and 1967, respectively, and petitioners claimed these amounts as deductions in their joint income tax returns for those years. The partnership returns reported distributions to the Crisafis in the form of a $492 loss for 1966 and a $309.98 gain for 1967. The Crisafis' joint income tax returns reflected that they had no net taxable income for either 1966 or 1967.

The net capital contributions, allocations of profits, losses and depreciation, and ending balances of the capital accounts, of the Orrisch-Crisafi partnership from May 1963 through December 31, 1967, were as follows:

	Petitioners'	Crisafis'
Excess of capital contributions over withdrawals during 1963	$26,655.55	$12,655.54
Allocation of 1963 loss	(4,858.07)	(4,858.07)
Balance 12/31/63	21,797.48	7,797.47
Excess of capital contributions over withdrawals during 1964	4,537.50	3,537.50
Allocation of 1964 loss	(8,906.17)	(8,906.16)
Balance 12/31/64	17,428.81	2,428.81
Excess of capital contributions over withdrawals during 1965	4,337.50	5,337.50
Allocation of 1965 loss	(9,476.30)	(9,476.29)
Balance 12/31/65	12,290.01	(1,709.98)

Excess of capital contributions over withdrawals during 1966	2,610.00	6,018.00
Allocation of 1966 loss before depreciation	(492.00)	(492.00)
Allocation of depreciation	(18,412.00)	0
Balance 12/31/66	(4,003.99)	3,816.02
Excess of withdrawals over capital contributions during 1967	(4,312.36)	(3,720.35)
Allocation of 1967 profit before depreciation	309.99	309.98
Allocation of depreciation	(17,180.75)	0
Balance 12/31/67	(25,187.11)	405.65

* * *

In the notice of deficiency, respondent determined that the special allocation of the depreciation deduction provided by the amendment to the partnership agreement "was made with the principal purpose of avoidance of income taxes" and should, therefore, be disregarded. Partnership losses for 1966 and 1967, adjusted to reflect a correction of the amount of depreciation allowable, were allocated equally between the partners.

Ultimate Finding of Fact

The principal purpose of the special allocation to petitioners of all of the deductions for depreciation taken by the Orrisch-Crisafi partnership for 1966 and 1967 was the avoidance of income tax.

Opinion

The only issue presented for decision is whether tax effect can be given the agreement between petitioners and the Crisafis that, beginning with 1966, all the partnership's depreciation deductions were to be allocated to petitioners for their use in computing their individual income tax liabilities. In our view, the answer must be in the negative, and the amounts of each of the partners' deductions for the depreciation of partnership property must be determined in accordance with the ratio used generally in computing their distributive shares of the partnership's profits and losses.

Among the important innovations of the 1954 Code are limited provisions for flexibility in arrangements for the sharing of income, losses, and deductions arising from business activities conducted through partnerships. The authority for special allocations of such items appears in section 704(a), which provides that a partner's share of any item of income, gain, loss, deduction, or credit shall be determined by the partnership agreement. That rule is coupled with a limitation in section 704(b), however, which states that a special allocation of an item will be disregarded if its "principal purpose" is the avoidance or evasion of

Federal income tax. See Smith v. Commissioner, 331 F.2d 298 (C.A.7, 1964), affirming a Memorandum Opinion of this Court; Jean V. Kresser, 54 T.C. 1621 (1970). In case a special allocation is disregarded, the partner's share of the item is to be determined in accordance with the ratio by which the partners divide the general profits or losses of the partnership. Sec. 1.704–1(b)(2), Income Tax Regs.

The report of the Senate Committee on Finance accompanying the bill finally enacted as the 1954 Code (S.Rept. No. 1622, to accompany H.R. 8300 (Pub.L. No. 591), 83d Cong., 2d Sess., p. 379 (1954)) explained the tax-avoidance restriction prescribed by section 704(b) as follows:

> Subsection (b) * * * provides that if the principal purpose of any provision in the partnership agreement dealing with a partner's distributive share of a particular item is to avoid or evade the Federal income tax, the partner's distributive share of that item shall be redetermined in accordance with his distributive share of partnership income or loss described in section 702(a)(9) [i.e., the ratio used by the partners for dividing general profits or losses]. * * *

> Where, however, a provision in a partnership agreement for a special allocation of certain items has substantial economic effect and is not merely a device for reducing the taxes of certain partners without actually affecting their shares of partnership income, then such a provision will be recognized for tax purposes. * * *

This reference to "substantial economic effect" did not appear in the House Ways and Means Committee report (H.Rept. No. 1337, to accompany H.R. 8300 (Pub.L. No. 591), 83d Cong., 2d Sess., p. A223 (1954)) discussing section 704(b), and was apparently added in the Senate Finance Committee to allay fears that special allocations of income or deductions would be denied effect in every case where the allocation resulted in a reduction in the income tax liabilities of one or more of the partners. The statement is an affirmation that special allocations are ordinarily to be recognized if they have business validity apart from their tax consequences. * * *

In resolving the question whether the principal purpose of a provision in a partnership agreement is the avoidance or evasion of Federal income tax, all the facts and circumstances in relation to the provision must be taken into account. Section 1.704–1(b)(2), Income Tax Regs., lists the following as relevant circumstances to be considered:

> Whether the partnership or a partner individually has a business purpose for the allocation; whether the allocation has "substantial economic effect", that is, whether the allocation may actually affect the dollar amount of the partners' shares of the total partnership income or loss independently of tax consequences; whether related items of income, gain, loss,

deduction, or credit from the same source are subject to the same allocation; whether the allocation was made without recognition of normal business factors and only after the amount of the specially allocated item could reasonably be estimated; the duration of the allocation; and the overall tax consequences of the allocation. * * *

Applying these standards, we do not think the special allocation of depreciation in the present case can be given effect.

The evidence is persuasive that the special allocation of depreciation was adopted for a tax-avoidance rather than a business purpose. Depreciation was the only item which was adjusted by the parties; both the income from the buildings and the expenses incurred in their operation, maintenance, and repair were allocated to the partners equally. Since the deduction for depreciation does not vary from year to year with the fortunes of the business, the parties obviously knew what the tax effect of the special allocation would be at the time they adopted it. Furthermore, as shown by our findings, petitioners had large amounts of income which would be offset by the additional deduction for depreciation; the Crisafis, in contrast, had no taxable income from which to subtract the partnership depreciation deductions, and due to depreciation deductions which they were obtaining with respect to other housing projects, could expect to have no taxable income in the near future. On the other hand, the insulation of the Crisafis from at least part of a potential capital gains tax was an obvious tax advantage. The inference is unmistakably clear that the agreement did not reflect normal business considerations but was designed primarily to minimize the overall tax liabilities of the partners.

Petitioners urge that the special allocation of the depreciation deduction was adopted in order to equalize the capital accounts of the partners, correcting a disparity ($14,000) in the amounts initially contributed to the partnership by them ($26,500) and the Crisafis ($12,500). But the evidence does not support this contention. Under the special allocation agreement, petitioners were to be entitled, in computing their individual income tax liabilities, to deduct the full amount of the depreciation realized on the partnership property. For 1966, as an example, petitioners were allocated a sum ($18,904) equal to the depreciation on the partnership property ($18,412) plus one-half of the net loss computed without regard to depreciation ($492). The other one-half of the net loss was, of course, allocated to the Crisafis. Petitioners' allocation ($18,904) was then applied to reduce their capital account. The depreciation specially allocated to petitioners ($18,412) in 1966 alone exceeded the amount of the disparity in the contributions. Indeed, at the end of 1967, petitioners' capital account showed a deficit of $25,187.11 compared with a positive balance of $405.65 in the Crisafis' account. By the time the partnership's properties are fully depreciated, the amount of the reduction in petitioners' capital account will approximate the remaining basis for the buildings as of the end of 1967. The Crisafis' capital account will be adjusted only for contributions, withdrawals, gain or loss, without regard to depreciation, and similar adjustments for these factors will also be made in petitioners' capital account. Thus, rather than correcting an imbalance in the capital accounts of the partners, the special allocation of depreciation will create a vastly greater imbalance than existed at the end of 1966. In the light of these facts, we find it incredible that equalization of the capital accounts was the objective of the special allocation.[5]

Petitioners rely primarily on the argument that the allocation has "substantial economic effect" in that it is reflected in the capital accounts of the partners. Referring to the material quoted above from the report of the Senate Committee on Finance, they contend that this alone is sufficient to show that the special allocation served a business rather than a tax-avoidance purpose.

According to the regulations, an allocation has economic effect if it "may actually affect the dollar amount of the partners' shares of the total partnership income or loss independently of tax consequences."[6] The agreement in this case provided not only for the allocation of depreciation to petitioners but also for gain on the sale of the partnership property to be "charged back" to them. The charge back would cause the gain, for tax purposes, to be allocated on the books entirely to petitioners to the extent of the special allocation of depreciation, and their capital account would be correspondingly increased. The remainder of the gain, if any, would be shared equally by the partners. If the gain on the sale were to equal or exceed the depreciation specially allocated to petitioners, the increase in their capital account caused by the charge back would exactly equal the depreciation deductions previously allowed to them and the proceeds of the sale of the property would be divided equally. In such circumstances, the only effect of the allocation would be a trade of tax consequences, i.e., the Crisafis would relinquish a current depreciation deduction in exchange for exoneration from all or part of the capital gains tax when the property is sold, and petitioners would enjoy a larger

---

[5] We recognize that petitioners had more money invested in the partnership than the Crisafis and that it is reasonable for the partners to endeavor to equalize their investments, since each one was to share equally in the profits and losses of the enterprise. However, we do not think that sec. 704(a) permits the partners' prospective tax benefits to be used as the medium for equalizing their investments, and it is apparent that the economic burden of the depreciation (which is reflected by the allowance for depreciation) was not intended to be the medium used.

This case is to be distinguished from situations where one partner contributed property and the other cash. In such cases sec. 704(c) may allow a special allocation of income and expenses in order to reflect the tax consequences inherent in the original contributions.

[6] This language of sec. 1.704–1(b)(2), Income Tax Regs., listing "substantial economic effect" as one of the factors to be considered in determining the principal purpose of a special allocation, is somewhat similar to the material quoted in the text from S.Rept. No. 1622, to accompany H.R. 8300 (Pub.L. No. 591), 83d Cong., 2d Sess., p. 379 (1954). But the latter is broader. It is an explanation of the "principal purpose" test of sec. 704(b), and contemplates that a special allocation will be given effect only if it has business validity apart from its tax consequences. * * *

current depreciation deduction but would assume a larger ultimate capital gains tax liability. Quite clearly, if the property is sold at a gain, the special allocation will affect only the tax liabilities of the partners and will have no other economic effect.

To find any economic effect of the special allocation agreement aside from its tax consequences, we must, therefore, look to see who is to bear the economic burden of the depreciation if the buildings should be sold for a sum less than their original cost. There is not one syllable of evidence bearing directly on this crucial point. We have noted, however, that when the buildings are fully depreciated, petitioners' capital account will have a deficit, or there will be a disparity in the capital accounts, approximately equal to the undepreciated basis of the buildings as of the beginning of 1966.[7] Under normal accounting procedures, if the building were sold at a gain less than the amount of such disparity petitioners would either be required to contribute to the partnership a sum equal to the remaining deficit in their capital account after the gain on the sale had been added back or would be entitled to receive a proportionately smaller share of the partnership assets on liquidation. Based on the record as a whole, we do not think the partners ever agreed to such an arrangement. On dissolution, we think the partners contemplated an equal division of the partnership assets which would be adjusted only for disparities in cash contributions or withdrawals.[8] Certainly there is no evidence to show otherwise. That being true, the special allocation does not "actually affect the dollar amount of the partners' share of the total partnership income or loss independently of tax consequences" within the meaning of the regulation referred to above. * * *

In the light of all the evidence we have found as an ultimate fact that the "principal purpose" of the special allocation agreement was tax avoidance within the meaning of section 701(b). Accordingly, the deduction for depreciation for 1966 and 1967 must be allocated between the parties in the same manner as other deductions.

Decision will be entered for the respondent.

DETAILED ANALYSIS

1.   GAIN CHARGEBACK PROVISIONS

A gain chargeback is a provision in a partnership agreement providing that if depreciable property is sold at a gain, the partner who received a special allocation of depreciation with respect to the property will be specially allocated the gain, up to the amount of depreciation deductions previously allocated to the partner. Any remaining gain will be allocated

---

[7]   This assumes, of course, that all partnership withdrawals and capital contributions will be equal.

[8]   We note that, in the course of Orrisch's testimony, petitioners' counsel made a distinction between entries in the taxpayers' capital accounts which reflect actual cash transactions and those relating to the special allocation which are "paper entries relating to depreciation."

according to the general profit sharing ratio. The operation of a gain chargeback provision can be illustrated by a simple example.

Suppose A and B each contribute $100,000 to the AB Partnership, which buys depreciable property for $200,000. A and B are equal partners except the partnership agreement specially allocates all depreciation to B. The partnership breaks even, apart from depreciation of $20,000 per year, which decreases both partnership asset book value and inside basis. Treas.Reg. § 1.704–1(b)(2)(iv)(g)(1). If at the beginning of the second year, when the property had a basis and book value of $180,000, the property were sold for $200,000, the entire $20,000 book and tax gain would be allocated to B. Likewise, if the property sold for $195,000, the entire $15,000 book and tax gain would be allocated to B. On the other hand, if the property sold for $210,000, B would be allocated $25,000 of book and tax gain, and C would be allocated $5,000. Because these allocations of gain are reflected in the partners' capital accounts, in the final version where the property is sold for $210,000, each partner's capital account immediately prior to liquidation would be $105,000. Accordingly, the net proceeds of the sale would be divided equally since the liquidating distributions would be in accordance with positive capital account balances. Thus, while B initially bore the economic loss of the depreciation (which the Regulations assume to have occurred in fact), that loss was made up by the subsequent allocation of a corresponding amount of income to B.

2.   ANALYSIS OF *ORRISCH*

The gain chargeback was not the flaw in the Orrisch/Crisafi partnership agreement. The partnership maintained capital accounts. Nonetheless, as the court noted, the partners contemplated an equal division of partnership assets, adjusted only for disparities in cash contributions and withdrawals. As the court's rendition of the partnership capital accounts illustrates, with the special allocation of depreciation, the partners' capital accounts did not reflect this 50:50 division of partnership assets. Indeed, Orrisch's capital accounts for the years ending in 1966 and 1967 showed deficits. If the partners intended a 50:50 division of assets, the capital account allocations of depreciation had no economic effect.

The court found that if the property were sold at a gain (presumably meaning a gain over its original cost, not gain computed with reference to adjusted basis), the effect of the special allocation of depreciation coupled with the gain chargeback would be that Orrisch would realize increased deductions in early years at the price of greater capital gains on the sale of the property, and the Crisafis would realize greater income in early years and lesser capital gain on the sale of the property, but over the life of the partnership, neither Orrisch's or the Crisafis's aggregate income would be affected. The effect of the gain chargeback can be illustrated by a simplified example based on *Orrisch*.

Suppose O and C form a partnership by contributing $100 each and buy a depreciable asset for $200. The asset produces no gain or loss apart from depreciation (i.e., gross rental income equals cash flow deductible expenses), and the asset is depreciated by the straight-line method over five years ($40 per year, ignoring conventions). The partnership's opening balance sheet would be as follows:

	Assets			Partners' Capital Accounts	
	Book	Tax Basis		Book	Tax Basis
Asset	$200	$200	C	$100	$100
			O	$100	$100
	$200	$200		$200	$200

If all items were allocated equally, after two years of depreciation, the partnership balance sheet would be as follows:

	Assets			Partners' Capital Accounts	
	Book	Tax Basis		Book	Tax Basis
Asset	$120	$120	C	$ 60	$ 60
			O	$ 60	$ 60
Total	$120	$120		$120	$120

If on the first day of Year 3, the assets were sold for $210 and the $90 book and tax gain were shared equally, the same ratio as the depreciation had been shared, the balance sheet would be as follows:

	Assets			Partners' Capital Accounts	
	Book	Tax Basis		Book	Tax Basis
Cash	$210	$210	C	$105	$105
			O	$105	$105
Total	$210	$210		$210	$210

If, however, the partnership agreement specially allocated all of the depreciation to O with a gain chargeback to O of an amount equal to prior depreciation deductions, and all other items were allocated equally, after two years of depreciation, the balance sheet would be as follows:

Assets			Partners' Capital Accounts		
	Book	Tax Basis		Book	Tax Basis
Asset	$120	$120	C	$100	$100
			O	$ 20	$ 20
Total	$120	$120		$120	$120

If the property were sold for $210 on the first day of Year 3, the gain chargeback would allocate the first $80 of gain to O, an amount equal to O's depreciation deductions, and the remaining $10 of gain would be allocated $5 to each of C and O. The balance sheet would be as follows:

Assets			Partners' Capital Accounts		
	Book	Tax Basis		Book	Tax Basis
Cash	$210	$210	C	$105	$105
			O	$105	$105
Total	$210	$210		$210	$210

Dividing the cash at liquidation 50:50, as was agreed upon in *Orrisch*, would match the balances in the partners' capital accounts.

Consider now the results of a special allocation of depreciation to O, coupled with a gain chargeback, if the asset were sold for only $180 on the first day of Year 3. In this case, the gain would be only $60, all of which would be allocated to O. The partnership balance sheet would be as follows:

Assets			Partners' Capital Accounts		
	Book	Tax Basis		Book	Tax Basis
Cash	$180	$180	C	$100	$100
			O	$ 80	$ 80
Total	$180	$180		$180	$180

In this case, an equal division of the sales proceeds at liquidation, $90, to each of C and O, as was agreed upon in *Orrisch*, does not match the partners' capital accounts. Thus, the allocation of depreciation deductions to O did not reflect economic reality. Over the life of the partnership, the asset actually declined in value by $20. If O really bore the risk of depreciation, O should receive $20 less than C upon liquidation. This analysis indicates that the provision in *Orrisch* for liquidation by a formula that was independent of the allocation of depreciation deductions was the fatal flaw.

3.   1976 REVISION OF SECTION 704(b)

Current § 704(b) was enacted in 1976 to codify the substantial economic effect test of the Regulations applied in *Orrisch*. The following excerpt from S. Rep. No. 94–938, 94th Cong., 2d Sess. 100 (1976), explains the change as follows:

Explanation of provisions

The committee amendment provides generally that an allocation of overall income or loss (described under section [702(a)(8)]), or of any item of income, gain, loss, deduction, or credit (described under section [702(a)(1)–(7)]), shall be controlled by the partnership agreement if the partner receiving the allocation can demonstrate that it has "substantial economic effect", i.e., whether the allocation may actually affect the dollar amount of the partners' shares of the total partnership income or loss independently of tax consequences. (Regs. Sec. 1.704–1(b)(2)). * * * If an allocation made by the partnership is set aside, a partner's share of the income, gain, loss, deduction or credit (or item thereof) will be determined in accordance with his interest in the partnership taking into account all facts and circumstances. * * * Among the relevant factors to be taken into account are the interests of the respective partners in profits and losses (if different from that of taxable income or loss), cash flow; and their rights to distributions of capital upon liquidation. * * *

SECTION 2.   THE SECTION 704(b) REGULATIONS

INTERNAL REVENUE CODE: Section 704(b).

Section 704(a) and (b) provide partners with considerable flexibility in structuring partnership agreements, going so far as to permit the partners, within certain limitations, to agree to individual shares of taxable profits and losses for a particular year that differ from the agreed upon shares of cash flow distributions for the year. Thus, the provisions of the partnership agreement dealing with allocations of items of income, gain, loss, and credits may range from a simple percentage division of all items in the same ratios to complex arrangements with separate allocations of profit and loss, cash flow, distributions from refinancing, liquidation distributions, etc., in different periods and at different levels of income. For example, the partnership agreement of the AB Partnership may provide that profits and losses are shared 50:50 but that current cash flow is distributed 60% to A and 40% to B. Alternatively (or additionally), the partnership agreement might provide that profits (or gross income) is to be allocated 50:50, but that losses (or deductions) are to be allocated 60% to A and 40% to B. The key to allowing such flexibility, of course, is to require an eventual reconciliation in which total taxable income or loss allocated to each partner over the life of the partnership equals the economic gain or loss realized by each partner over that same period. This reconciliation of tax allocations, book profit and loss allocations, and cash flow distributions is the heart of § 704(b), which requires that allocations of the items in the partnership agreement for tax purposes have "substantial economic effect." If the attempted tax allocations in the partnership agreement do not meet the substantial economic effect test, the partner's share of the item in question will be determined in accordance with the partner's overall interest in the partnership, including a consideration of items that are not specially allocated.

The organizing theme of the § 704(b) Regulations is that a tax allocation "must be consistent with the underlying economic arrangement of the partners" in order to have "substantial economic effect." Treas.Reg. § 1.704–1(b). "This means that in the event there is an economic benefit or economic burden that corresponds to an allocation, the partner to whom the tax allocation is made must receive such economic benefit or bear such economic burden." Treas.Reg. § 1.704–1(b)(2)(ii). In general, the Regulations apply the capital account analysis in *Orrisch* but prescribe detailed safe harbor rules that must be followed in making the capital account analysis for assurance that a partnership allocation will be respected, particularly where nonrecourse debt is involved. By requiring that tax allocations be reflected in each partner's capital account and that liquidating distributions be made according to each partner's capital account, the Regulations ensure that (eventually) the tax consequences to each partner accurately reflect the economic gain or loss realized by the partners (at least insofar as the capital account book value rules accurately reflect economic reality).

Treas.Reg. § 1.704–2(b)(1) provides that allocations attributable to nonrecourse debt never can have economic effect and always must be allocated among the partners in accordance with their interests in the partnership. However, Treas.Reg. § 1.704–2 provides a "safe harbor" under which allocations attributable to nonrecourse debt will be deemed to be made in accordance with the partners' interests in the partnership.

Although § 704(b) frequently is said to deal with *special* allocations, the Regulations test *all* allocations for substantial economic effect, including identical fractional allocations of every item. As long as each partner, for both tax and book accounting purposes, is entitled to a fractional share of each and every item that does not vary from item to item for the partner, and the allocations are in the same proportion as the partners' contributions to the partnership, the allocation always will have substantial economic effect under the tests of the Regulations, even though the partners' fractional shares may differ. But if any partner is entitled to a share of any item that differs from the partner's share of any other item, including the partner's liability for partnership debts and contributions to capital, then a detailed analysis under the Regulations is required, regardless of whether the specially allocated item is identified by its tax characteristics or its financial characteristics.

Given the detailed nature of the § 704(b) Regulations, it is important to keep in mind that the tax rules do not determine the economic deal between the partners. Rather, the rules are intended to ensure that the tax results follow the economics, i.e., the partners cannot set up one reality for economic purposes and then try to construct a different reality solely for tax purposes. Nevertheless, since the rules in the § 704(b) Regulations are designed to keep track of each partner's share of the economic profits and losses of the partnership, as a practical matter, most carefully prepared partnership agreements should closely follow the rules of the Regulations. Nonetheless, many partnership agreements are drafted to provide allocations in accord with distributions of cash flow that do not meet the requirements of the substantial economic effect Regulations. These allocations, which are often referred to as "targeted allocations," rely on a facts and circumstances analysis to identify the partner's interest in the partnership. As will be discussed in Section A(1), Detailed Analysis 6, these allocations should be respected because ultimately the allocations of tax items are derived from allocations of economic income and loss and are justified by an analysis of economic effect determined by the use of capital accounts.

As discussed in *Orrisch*, even though the pre-1976 version of § 704(b) provided that special allocations would not be recognized if the "principal purpose" of the allocation was tax avoidance, the Regulations under pre-1976 § 704(b) nevertheless focused on whether or not an attempted special allocation had substantial economic effect. When the substantial economic effect test was specifically incorporated in the statute and the reference to tax avoidance purpose was dropped, the accompanying Committee Reports indicated that there was no intention to change the previously existing law as to what constitutes the requisite economic effect. S.Rep. No. 94–938, 94th Cong., 2d Sess. 100 (1976). Since the promulgation of Regulations under current § 704(b), however, the emphasis has been almost exclusively on the detailed tests in the Regulations. Although the Committee Report also left some room for the argument that a (presumably nontax) business purpose for a special allocation has some significance, the statutory stress is clearly on the substantial economic effect of the allocation, and the Regulations provide no leeway for respecting an allocation that has a purported business purpose but does not meet the substantial economic effect test. Thus, the presence of a colorable "business purpose" should not protect an allocation that does not have the necessary economic effect.

A. ALLOCATIONS OF ITEMS UNRELATED TO NONRECOURSE DEBT

REGULATIONS: Sections 1.704–1(b)(1)(i), (iii), (iv), and (vi), –1(b)(2)(i)–(ii), (iv)(*a*)–(*i*), –1(b)(3), –1(b)(5), Ex. (1), (4), and (15).

Under the Regulations, there are three methods by which an allocation generally can satisfy § 704(b): (1) the allocation has "substantial economic effect" under Treas.Reg. § 1.704–1(b)(2); (2) the allocation is in accordance with the partners' interests in the partnership taking into account all of the facts and circumstances under Treas.Reg. § 1.704–1(b)(3); or (3) the allocation is deemed under Treas.Reg. § 1.704–1(b)(4) to be in accordance with the partners' interests in the partnership under a special rule. The application of the facts and circumstances test of Treas.Reg. § 1.704–1(b)(3) is not clearly delineated, and often allocations written to reflect a partner's interest in the partnership are generally justified in terms of the other tests.

Whether an allocation has "substantial economic effect" is determined under a two-part analysis: "economic effect" and "substantiality." Treas.Reg. § 1.704–1(b)(2)(i) through (iii).

As noted above, "economic effect" means that the partner receiving the allocation of the tax item must also bear the economic benefit or burden, as measured by the capital accounts, that corresponds to the allocation. An allocation generally has economic effect only if three conditions are satisfied: (1) the allocation is reflected by an appropriate increase or decrease in the partner's capital account; (2) liquidation proceeds are, throughout the term of the partnership, to be distributed in accordance with the partners' positive capital account balances; and (3) any partner with a deficit capital account following the distribution of liquidation proceeds is required to restore the amount of that deficit to the partnership for distribution to partners with positive account balances or payment to partnership creditors. Treas.Reg. § 1.704–1(b)(2)(ii)(*b*). A partner's obligation to restore a negative capital account need not be unlimited; an allocation that creates or increases a negative capital account balance will be respected to the extent that the deficit does not exceed the amount that the partner is obligated to restore. The determination whether an allocation has economic effect is made annually. Treas.Reg. § 1.704–1(b)(2)(i). Thus, an allocation may be respected one year, but not the next, or may be respected only in part under Treas.Reg. § 1.704–1(b)(2)(ii)(*e*).

"Substantiality" means that the economic effect of the allocation must have a reasonable possibility of affecting the dollar amounts to be received by the partners independent of the tax consequences of the allocation. Treas.Reg. § 1.704–1(b)(2)(iii)(*a*). Allocations that are transitory (i.e., allocations that offset each other over a relatively brief period of years), or allocations that merely shift the tax character of items allocated among the partners are particularly suspect. Further, any allocation that enhances the after-tax economic consequences to at least one partner, in present value terms, but that does not have a strong likelihood of diminishing the after-tax benefit to at least one other partner, in present value terms, will not be substantial.

(1) ECONOMIC EFFECT

Revenue Ruling 97–38
1997–2 C.B. 69.

ISSUE

If a partner is treated as having a limited deficit restoration obligation under § 1.704–1(b)(2)(ii)(c) of the Income Tax Regulations by reason of the partner's liability to the partnership's creditors, how is the amount of that obligation calculated?

FACTS

In year 1, GP and LP, general partner and limited partner, each contribute $100x to form limited partnership LPRS. In general, GP and LP share LPRS's income and loss 50 percent each. However, LPRS allocates to GP all depreciation deductions and gain from the sale of depreciable assets up to the amount of those deductions. LPRS maintains capital accounts according to the rules set forth in § 1.704–1(b)(2)(iv), and the partners agree to liquidate according to positive capital account balances under the rules of § 1.704–1(b)(2)(ii)(b)(2).

Under applicable state law, GP is liable to creditors for all partnership recourse liabilities, but LP has no personal liability. GP and LP do not agree to unconditional deficit restoration obligations as described in § 1.704–1(b)(2)(ii)(b)(3) (in general, a deficit restoration obligation requires a partner to restore any deficit capital account balance following the liquidation of the partner's interest in the partnership); GP is obligated to restore a deficit capital account only to the extent necessary to pay creditors. Thus, if LPRS were to liquidate after paying all creditors and LP had a positive capital account balance, GP would not be required to restore GP's deficit capital account to permit a liquidating distribution to LP. In addition, GP and LP agree to a qualified income offset, thus satisfying the requirements of the alternate test for economic effect of § 1.704–1(b)(2)(ii)(d). GP and LP also agree that no allocation will be made that causes or increases a deficit balance in any partner's capital account in excess of the partner's obligation to restore the deficit.

LPRS purchases depreciable property for $1,000x from an unrelated seller, paying $200x in cash and borrowing the $800x balance from an unrelated bank that is not the seller of the property. The note is recourse to LPRS. The principal of the loan is due in 6 years; interest is payable semi-annually at the applicable federal rate. GP bears the entire economic risk of loss for LPRS's recourse liability, and GP's basis in LPRS (outside basis) is increased by $800x. See § 1.752–2.

In each of years 1 through 5, the property generates $200x of depreciation. All other partnership deductions and losses exactly equal income, so that in each of years 1 through 5 LPRS has a net loss of $200x.

LAW AND ANALYSIS

Under § 704(b) of the Internal Revenue Code and the regulations thereunder, a partnership's allocations of income, gain, loss, deduction, or credit set forth in the partnership agreement are respected if they have substantial economic effect. If allocations under the partnership agreement would not have substantial economic effect, the partnership's allocations are determined according to the partners' interests in the partnership. The fundamental principles for establishing economic effect require an allocation to be consistent with the partners' underlying economic arrangement. A partner allocated a share of income should enjoy any corresponding economic benefit, and a partner allocated a share of losses or deductions should bear any corresponding economic burden. See § 1.704–1(b)(2)(ii)(*a*).

To come within the safe harbor for establishing economic effect in § 1.704–1(b)(2)(ii), partners must agree to maintain capital accounts under the rules of § 1.704–1(b)(2)(iv), liquidate according to positive capital account balances, and agree to an unconditional deficit restoration obligation for any partner with a deficit in that partner's capital account, as described in § 1.704–1(b)(2)(ii)(*b*)(*3*). Alternatively, the partnership may satisfy the requirements of the alternate test for economic effect provided in § 1.704–1(b)(2)(ii)(*d*). LPRS's partnership agreement complies with the alternate test for economic effect.

The alternate test for economic effect requires the partners to agree to a qualified income offset in lieu of an unconditional deficit restoration obligation. If the partners so agree, allocations will have economic effect to the extent that they do not create a deficit capital account for any partner (in excess of any limited deficit restoration obligation of that partner) as of the end of the partnership taxable year to which the allocation relates. Section 1.704–1(b)(2)(ii)(*d*)(*3*) (flush language).

A partner is treated as having a limited deficit restoration obligation to the extent of: (1) the outstanding principal balance of any promissory note contributed to the partnership by the partner, and (2) the amount of any unconditional obligation of the partner (whether imposed by the partnership agreement or by state or local law) to make subsequent contributions to the partnership. Section 1.704–1(b)(2)(ii)(*c*).

LP has no obligation under the partnership agreement or state or local law to make additional contributions to the partnership and, therefore, has no deficit restoration obligation. Under applicable state law, GP may have to make additional contributions to the partnership to pay creditors. However, GP's obligation only arises to the extent that the amount of LPRS's liabilities exceeds the value of LPRS's assets available to satisfy the liabilities. Thus, the amount of GP's limited deficit restoration obligation each year is equal to the difference between the amount of the partnership's recourse liabilities at the end of the year and the value of the partnership's assets available to satisfy the liabilities at the end of the year.

To ensure consistency with the other requirements of the regulations under § 704(b), where a partner's obligation to make additional contributions to the partnership is dependent on the value of the partnership's assets, the partner's deficit restoration obligation must be computed by reference to the rules for determining the value of partnership property contained in the regulations under § 704(b). Consequently, in computing GP's limited deficit restoration obligation, the value of the partnership's assets is conclusively presumed to equal the book basis of those assets under the capital account maintenance rules of § 1.704–1(b)(2)(iv). See § 1.704–1(b)(2)(ii)(*d*) (value equals basis presumption applies for purposes of determining expected allocations and distributions under the alternate test for economic effect); § 1.704–1(b)(2)(iii) (value equals basis presumption applies for purposes of the substantiality test); § 1.704–1(b)(3)(iii) (value equals basis presumption applies for purposes of the partner's interest in the partnership test); § 1.704–2(d) (value equals basis presumption applies in computing partnership minimum gain).

The LPRS agreement allocates all depreciation deductions and gain on the sale of depreciable property to the extent of those deductions to GP. Because LPRS's partnership agreement satisfies the alternate test for economic effect, the allocations of depreciation deductions to GP will have economic effect to the extent that they do not create a deficit capital account for GP in excess of GP's obligation to restore the deficit balance. At the end of year 1, the basis of the depreciable property has been reduced to $800x. If LPRS liquidated at the beginning of year 2, selling its depreciable property for its basis of $800x, the proceeds would be used to repay the $800 principal on LPRS's recourse liability. All of LPRS's creditors would be satisfied and GP would have no obligation to contribute to pay them. Thus, at the end of year 1, GP has no obligation to restore a deficit in its capital account.

Because GP has no obligation to restore a deficit balance in its capital account at the end of year 1, an allocation that reduces GP's capital account below $0 is not permitted under the partnership agreement and would not satisfy the alternate test for economic effect. An allocation of $200x of depreciation deductions to GP would reduce GP's capital account to negative $100x. Because the allocation would result in a deficit capital account balance in excess of GP's obligation to restore, the allocation is not permitted under the partnership agreement, and would not satisfy the safe harbor under the alternate test for economic effect. Therefore, the deductions for year 1 must be allocated $100x each to GP and LP (which is in accordance with their interests in the partnership).

The allocation of depreciation of $200x to GP in year 2 has economic effect. Although the allocation reduces GP's capital account to negative $200x, while LP's capital account remains $0, the allocation to GP does not create a deficit capital account in excess of GP's limited deficit restoration obligation. If LPRS liquidated at the beginning of year 3, selling the depreciable property for its basis of $600x, the proceeds would be applied toward the $800x LPRS liability. Because GP is obligated to restore a deficit capital account to the extent necessary to pay creditors, GP would be required to contribute $200x to LPRS to satisfy the outstanding liability. Thus, at the end of year 2, GP has a deficit restoration obligation of $200x, and the allocation of depreciation to GP does not reduce GP's capital account below its obligation to restore a deficit capital account.

This analysis also applies to the allocation of $200x of depreciation to GP in years 3 through 5. At the beginning of year 6, when the property is fully depreciated, the $800x principal amount of the partnership liability is due. The partners' capital accounts at the beginning of year 6 will equal negative $800x and $0, respectively, for GP and LP. Because value is conclusive presumed to equal basis, the depreciable property would be worthless and could not be used to satisfy LPRS's $800x liability. As a result, GP is deemed to be required to contribute $800x to LPRS. A contribution by GP to satisfy this limited deficit restoration obligation would increase GP's capital account balance to $0.

HOLDING

When a partner is treated as having a limited deficit restoration obligation by reason of the partner's liability to the partnership's creditors, the amount of that obligation is the amount of money that the partner would be required to contribute to the partnership to satisfy partnership liabilities if all partnership property were sold for the amount of the partnership's book basis in the property.

DETAILED ANALYSIS

1.   PARTNERS' CAPITAL ACCOUNTS

Treas.Reg. § 1.704–1(b)(2)(iv) provides detailed rules regarding the maintenance of partners' capital accounts, which must be followed throughout the life of the partnership, for allocations to be assured of having economic effect. In applying these rules, a partner who has more than one interest in the partnership is treated as having a single capital account that reflects all of the partner's interests, even if one interest is as a general partner and the other is as a limited partner, and without regard to the time or manner of acquisition of the interests. Treas.Reg. § 1.704–1(b)(2)(iv)(*b*). Capital accounts are maintained with reference to the fair market value (not basis) of property contributed to the partnership and property distributed by the partnership. In general, the partners' determination of the fair market value of property will be accepted if it results from arm's length negotiations in which the partners have sufficiently adverse interests. Treas.Reg. § 1.704–1(b)(2)(iv)(*h*). Capital accounts are also increased or reduced by income or gain and deductions or losses as measured for book accounting purposes. Treas.Reg. § 1.704–1(b)(2)(iv)(*f*) and (*g*), and –1(b)(4). Thus, a partner's capital account will frequently not be the same amount as the partner's basis in the partnership interest, and a partner's capital account may be negative.

A partner's capital account must be increased by the amount of any money contributed by the partner and by income (including tax-exempt income) allocated to the partner; and it must be decreased by the amount of any money distributed to the partner and by the partner's share of losses, deductions, and expenditures that are neither deductible nor capitalized, e.g., fines and penalties subject to § 162(f) or interest subject to § 265(a)(2). When the amount of these items differs for partnership book accounting purposes from the amount of such items for tax purposes, for example, because a partner has contributed built-in gain or loss property, special rules apply to allocate tax gain or loss and depreciation. If the disparity between book and tax amounts is attributable to contributed property, § 704(c), discussed later in this Chapter, applies to allocations of tax gain, loss, and depreciation. See Treas.Reg. § 1.704–1(b)(1)(vi), –1(b)(2)(iv)(*d*)(*3*). If the disparity is attributable to a revaluation of partnership assets for book accounting purposes pursuant to Treas.Reg. § 1.704–1(b)(2)(iv)(*f*), then Treas.Reg. § 1.704–1(b)(4)(i) controls the allocation of tax items. In any situation in which book income or loss differs from taxable income or loss, partners' capital accounts always are adjusted by amounts computed for book accounting purposes, Treas.Reg. § 1.704–1(b)(2)(iv)(*g*), and tax items must be allocated among the partners in a manner that properly takes into account the difference between book value and basis.

In addition, a partner's capital account must be increased by the fair market value (not the basis) of any property contributed by the partner to the partnership. A partner's own promissory note contributed to the partnership is not taken into account, however, until the disposition of the note by the partnership or the partner pays the principal. Treas.Reg. § 1.704–1(b)(2)(iv)(*d*)(*2*). If property is distributed to a partner, the partner's capital account must be reduced by the fair market value of the distributed property. Treas.Reg. § 1.704–1(b)(2)(iv)(*e*). If property that is contributed to the partnership or distributed by the partnership is subject to a debt, the effect of the debt must be taken into account so that the amount of the contribution or distribution is the net of the value of the property over the debt. Treas.Reg. § 1.704–1(b)(2)(iv)(*c*). Thus, for example, if a parcel of real estate worth $100, but subject to a $60 mortgage, is distributed to a partner who assumes the mortgage (or who simply takes the property subject to a nonrecourse mortgage), the partner's capital account is reduced by only the $40 net fair market value of the distributed property (total fair market value minus the mortgage). This treatment is parallel to the treatment when encumbered property is contributed to a partnership; in that event, only the net fair market value of the contributed property is added to the contributing partner's capital account.

Upon liquidation of the partnership, all capital accounts must be adjusted to reflect increases and decreases in value of partnership property. In addition, partners' capital accounts may, but technically are not required to, be increased or decreased to reflect a revaluation of the partnership's property on the happening of certain events, such as the admission of a new partner (whether in exchange for a capital contribution or for services), the distribution of property, or the liquidation of a partner's interest. Treas.Reg. § 1.704–1(b)(2)(iv)(*f*). As a practical matter, however, all of the partnership's assets and the partners' capital accounts must be revalued upon the occurrence of any of these events; failure to do so generally would result in allowing a new partner to immediately acquire an interest more valuable than the amount of the new partner's contribution—reflecting a share of the unrealized appreciation of the partnerships assets—a result that would be unacceptable to existing partners (assuming all are acting at arm's length) because the new partner's windfall would be at their expense. If the partnership elects to reflect current values in the capital accounts, the partnership must thereafter adjust capital accounts to reflect certain items, such as depreciation, as computed for revalued book purposes, Treas.Reg. § 1.704–1(b)(2)(iv)(*g*), and tax items must be allocated taking into account the disparity between capital accounts and tax basis created by the revaluation through so-called "reverse" § 704(c) allocations, Treas.Reg. § 1.704–3(a)(6).

2. LIQUIDATION ACCORDING TO CAPITAL ACCOUNTS

As demonstrated by *Orrisch*, the requirements that the partnership agreement provide for liquidation according to capital accounts and that the partners be obligated to restore any deficit in their capital accounts upon liquidation often are the most difficult of the requirements of the economic effect test with which to comply while still meeting the business and economic objectives of the partners. In practice, however, taking partners through a capital account analysis under the Regulations often reveals that the partners have not thoroughly considered the economics of their transaction all the way through to liquidation of the partnership. On the other hand, sometimes the parties understand the economic deal quite well and are trying to engage in the type of avoidance that the Regulations are intended to forestall.

The requirement of restoration of negative capital accounts presents a serious problem for recognition of allocations in tax partnerships that provide limited liability, including LLCs, particularly where deduction items are disproportionately allocated to partners with limited liability. The essence of a partnership interest with limited liability is that under state law there is no obligation to restore a negative capital account balance. Treas.Reg. § 1.704–1(b)(3)(iii) provides some leeway in situations in which a partnership agreement satisfies the capital account maintenance rules except for the unlimited deficit restoration requirement, and all allocations meet the substantiality requirement. In such a case, allocations that do not cause or increase a deficit in the capital account of a partner who does not have a restoration requirement generally will be respected, but allocations of items that would cause or increase a deficit will be reallocated. For example, Elrod v. Commissioner, 87 T.C. 1046 (1986), involved a partnership agreement under which losses were charged to capital accounts and distributions in liquidation of the partnership would be in accordance with capital accounts, but the taxpayer-partner was not required to restore any deficit in his capital account. The loss allocation was recognized only to the extent that it did not create a capital account deficit; for years in which the taxpayer maintained a positive capital account, the allocation was recognized in full. Because *Elrod* involved years before publication of the § 704 Regulations, the court applied the judicially developed capital account analysis rather than the Regulations. See Treas.Reg. § 1.704–1(b)(1)(ii). Although the court stated that it was "unclear" whether the same result would be reached under the Regulations, nothing in the stated facts of the opinion indicates that the Regulations mandate a different result.

As illustrated by Rev.Rul. 97–38, reproduced above, an obligation to make future contributions will be treated as an obligation to restore a negative capital account balance to the extent of the required contribution, as long as the additional contribution is due no later than the close of the taxable year in which the partner's partnership interest is liquidated (or within 90 days of the close of the taxable year, if later). Treas.Reg. § 1.704–1(b)(2)(ii)(c)(2). In addition, if a partner contributes the partner's own promissory note to the partnership, even though the capital account is not increased by the amount of the promissory note, the partner will be treated as having an obligation to restore a negative capital account to the extent of the principal amount of the promissory note, so long as the requirements of the Regulation are met. Treas.Reg. § 1.704–1(b)(2)(ii)(c). Anti-abuse rules, which are generally parallel to those applicable in determining partner economic risk of loss with respect to debt, apply; the economic risk of loss determination and related anti-abuse rules are discussed in Chapter 21.

The operation of the basic rules is illustrated by the following example. Suppose A and B each contribute $15,000 to the AB Partnership, which then borrows $170,000 with full recourse and buys depreciable property for $200,000. A and B each have a capital account of $15,000 since partnership liabilities have no effect on partners' capital accounts. At this point, the partnership's balance sheet, for book accounting and tax purposes, respectively, is as follows:[1]

| | Assets | | | Partnership Liabilities & Partners' Capital Accounts | | |
	Book Value	Tax Basis		Book Value	Tax Basis
Property	$200,000	$200,000	Mortgage	$170,000	n/a
			A	$ 15,000	$100,000
			B	$ 15,000	$100,000
	$200,000	$200,000		$200,000	$200,000

In Year 1, the partnership has no taxable income or loss except for a $20,000 depreciation deduction. If the full $20,000 depreciation deduction is specially allocated to B, the allocation will be recognized only if two conditions are

---

[1] Each partner's basis in the partnership interests depends on the ratio in which the partners share the risk on the debt if the property becomes worthless, see Treas.Reg. § 1.752–2. Computation of basis of partnership interests attributable to partnership indebtedness is discussed in Chapter 21.

met. First, B's capital account must be reduced by $20,000 to negative $5,000 (A's capital account will be unaffected and remain $15,000); the partnership balance sheet then would be as follows:

	Assets			Partnership Liabilities & Partners' Capital Accounts	
	Book Value	Tax Basis		Book Value	Tax Basis
Property	$180,000	$180,000	Mortgage	$170,000	n/a
			A	$ 15,000	$100,000
	_____	_____	B	($ 5,000)	$ 80,000
	$180,000	$180,000		$180,000	$180,000

Second, in Year 2, if the partnership is liquidated, B must be required to contribute $5,000 to the partnership so that A will receive $15,000 on the liquidation. If, however, the agreement of the partners provides that B is not required to restore any negative capital account, for example, because B is a limited partner, the special allocation will be only partly recognized. See Treas.Reg. § 1.704–1(b)(2)(ii)(e), –1(b)(5), Ex. (15)(ii). The partners' interest in the portion of the allocation that does not have economic effect is determined by comparing how distributions (and contributions) would be made if the partnership sold its property for an amount equal to adjusted basis at the end of the prior year with the results of such a sale or liquidation at the end of the current year. Applying this methodology, only $15,000 of depreciation could be specially allocated to B, because A would bear the economic risk of the remaining $5,000 of depreciation. The balance sheet at the end of Year 1 would be as follows:

	Assets			Partnership Liabilities & Partners' Capital Accounts	
	Book Value	Tax Basis		Book Value	Tax Basis
Property	$180,000	$180,000	Mortgage	$170,000	n/a
			A	$ 10,000	$180,000
	_____	_____	B	$ 0	$ 0[2]
Totals	$180,000	$180,000		$180,000	$180,000

In this case, however, because Year 1's special allocation reduced B's capital account to zero and A's capital account to $10,000, in Year 2 the first $10,000 of depreciation must be allocated to A, thereby reducing A's capital account to zero. Furthermore, because B as a limited partner is not required to restore a negative capital account, A bears the entire risk of loss. Thus,

---

[2]   B's basis is zero, because as a limited partner, B bears no risk of loss with respect to recourse liabilities of the partnership, and thus, under Treas.Reg. § 1.752–2, B is not assigned any portion of the partnership's debt to be treated as a deemed contribution to the partnership under § 752(a) (discussed in Chapter 21).

the remaining $10,000 of depreciation cannot be allocated equally; instead, it must be allocated entirely to A, who as the general partner is required to restore a negative capital account, e.g., to repay the loan if the partnership is unprofitable. The partnership's balance sheet at the end of Year 2 would be as follows:

	Assets			Partnership Liabilities & Partners' Capital Accounts	
	Book Value	Tax Basis		Book Value	Tax Basis
Property	$160,000	$160,000	Mortgage	$170,000	n/a
			A	($ 10,000)	$160,000
			B	$ 0	$ 0
Totals	$160,000	$160,000		$160,000	$160,000

If the property were sold at the beginning of Year 3 for $160,000, all of the proceeds would be paid to the mortgage lender; furthermore, A would be required to restore A's $10,000 deficit capital account to satisfy the debt. A thereby bears the economic loss represented by the last $10,000 of depreciation.

Now suppose that B has an obligation to restore a negative capital account, but that the obligation is limited to $20,000. In this case, depreciation deductions could be allocated to B until B's capital account balance is negative $20,000. All of the depreciation in Year 1 could be allocated to B. In Year 2, only the first $15,000 of depreciation deduction could be allocated to B, and the remaining $5,000 of depreciation would have to be allocated to A. The partnership's balance sheet at the end of Year 2 would be as follows:

	Assets			Partnership Liabilities & Partners' Capital Accounts	
	Book Value	Tax Basis		Book Value	Tax Basis
Property	$160,000	$160,000	Mortgage	$170,000	n/a
			A	$ 10,000	$160,000
			B	($ 20,000)	$ 0[3]
Totals	$160,000	$160,000		$160,000	$160,000

Finally, if the agreement of the parties is that notwithstanding the capital account balances (or if the partnership did not maintain capital accounts), the net proceeds from the sale of the building would be divided

---

[3]   B's limited obligation to repay $20,000 will cause B to be assigned $20,000 of debt basis. B's basis is zero at the end of Year 2 because the Year 1 and Year 2 allocations will exhaust B's $35,000 basis ($15,000 contribution plus $20,000 of debt share). A started with $165,000 basis ($15,000 contribution plus $150,000 of debt share) and reduced it by the $5,000 Year 2 allocation. Chapter 21 discusses debt basis assignment.

equally, then the special allocation of depreciation would fail the economic effect test entirely. Instead, the depreciation would be required to be allocated according to the partners' interest in the partnership. In this case, A and B share the economic risk equally, and the depreciation must be allocated equally from the outset. See Treas.Reg. § 1.704–1(b)(3).

3. ALTERNATE TEST FOR ECONOMIC EFFECT

Treas.Reg. § 1.704–1(b)(2)(ii)(*d*) provides a special rule for recognizing allocations that do not create or increase a capital account deficit when the partner does not have an unlimited obligation to restore the negative capital account upon liquidation. This provision is essential for allocations to limited partners or to LLC members, and it may be relevant in general partnerships as well. To qualify under this provision, the partnership must maintain the required capital accounts and liquidate according to capital account balances. Under the alternate test, a limited partner or LLC member (or a general partner without an unlimited obligation to restore a negative capital account) cannot be allocated items of deduction or loss that would create a deficit capital account or increase a deficit in the partner's capital account in excess of any limited amount that the partner is obligated to restore. To prevent manipulations by the partnership, when determining whether an allocation creates a deficit capital account balance under this test, reasonably anticipated distributions to be made in future years that will not be offset by future income allocations must be taken into account. In addition, the partnership agreement must provide for a "qualified income offset." This required provision must allocate to any partner who has a negative capital account as a result of an *unexpected* distribution sufficient income or gain to eliminate the deficit as soon as possible. The required income allocation must be made as soon as the partnership has gross income, even though in that year the partnership may have deductions that result in the partnership realizing no net taxable income.

The alternate test in Treas.Reg. § 1.704–1(b)(2)(ii)(*d*) often is applied when the partnership agreement requires partners to restore negative capital accounts only to the extent necessary to pay partnership creditors, but not to make distributions to partners with positive capital accounts. Assume for example that C and D form an equal partnership to which C and D each contribute $30,000, the CD Partnership borrows $120,000, and it purchases depreciable property for $180,000. The property is depreciated over six years under the straight-line method, and the partnership's gross income equals cash flow deduction items. Thus, the partnership's bottom line loss is $30,000 per year. C and D agree that D is obligated to restore a negative capital account only to the extent necessary to pay creditors while C is unconditionally obligated to restore a negative capital account. The agreement has a qualified income offset provision, and all items are allocated equally. The CD Partnership's initial balance sheet is as follows:

	Assets			Partnership Liabilities & Partners' Capital Accounts	
	Book Value	Tax Basis		Book Value	Tax Basis
Property	$180,000	$180,000	Debt	$120,000	n/a
			C	$ 30,000	$ 90,000
	_____	_____	D	$ 30,000	$ 90,000
Totals	$180,000	$180,000		$180,000	$180,000

In each of the first two years, C and D each may be allocated a $15,000 share of the partnership's loss. At the end of Year 2, the partnership's balance sheet is as follows:

	Assets			Partnership Liabilities & Partners' Capital Accounts	
	Book Value	Tax Basis		Book Value	Tax Basis
Property	$120,000	$120,000	Debt	$120,000	n/a
			C	$ 0	$ 60,000
	_____	_____	D	$ 0	$ 60,000
Totals	$120,000	$120,000		$120,000	$120,000

In Year 3, the partnership again loses $30,000, attributable to the depreciation deduction. Because C's capital account is not positive, D may be allocated a share of the depreciation deductions. Since the partnership holds an asset only worth $90,000 and owes a debt of $120,000, D will be obligated to restore the negative capital account to repay the debt. Thus, both C and D will have capital accounts of negative $15,000 at the end of Year 3. (The § 704(b) Regulations assume that depreciation deductions reflect actual declines in value. Treas.Reg. § 1.704–1(b)(2)(iii)(c)(2).)

If, however, D were a limited partner, with no obligation to restore a negative capital account, no portion of the loss in Year 3 could be allocated to D with economic effect. The entire loss would be allocated to C, who bears the risk of loss because of C's obligation to make contributions to restore creditors (discussed further in Detailed Analysis 5.2). In that case, the partnership balance sheet would be as follows at the end of Year 3:

Assets			Partnership Liabilities & Partners' Capital Accounts		
	Book Value	Tax Basis		Book Value	Tax Basis
Property	$90,000	$90,000	Debt	$120,000	n/a
			C	($ 30,000)	$90,000
	_____	_____	D	$ 0	$ 0
Totals	$90,000	$90,000		$ 90,000	$90,000

The existence of a negative capital account for D and the operation of the qualified income offset can be illustrated by a cash distribution by the CD partnership. Assume that in Year 4 the CD partnership, which again loses $30,000 (all attributable to the depreciation deduction), borrows $20,000 and distributes $10,000 to each of C and D. Again, the entire $30,000 loss is allocated to C; but each partner's capital account also is reduced by the $10,000 distribution, and D now has a negative capital account.[4] The balance sheet at the end of Year 4 is as follows:

Assets			Partnership Liabilities & Partners' Capital Accounts		
	Book Value	Tax Basis		Book Value	Tax Basis
Property	$60,000	$60,000	Debt	$140,000	n/a
			C	($ 70,000)	$70,000
	_____	_____	D	($ 10,000)	$ 0
Totals	$60,000	$60,000		$ 60,000	$70,000[5]

Now assume that in Year 5 the CD partnership again loses $30,000. Because D has a negative capital account due to a distribution, if the partnership has gross income, D must be allocated the first $10,000 of gross income while any remaining gross income and all of the deductions are allocated to C. For example, if the $30,000 loss consisted of gross income of $11,000, § 162 deductible expenses of $11,000, and the $30,000 depreciation deduction, D would be allocated gross income of $10,000, while C would be allocated a loss of $40,000. D's $10,000 of income would consist of a pro rata share (i.e., 10/11th) of each item of gross income. Thus, the partnership's balance sheet at the end of Year 5 would be as follows:

---

    [4] Pursuant to § 731, D recognized gain of $10,000 on the distribution because D had a zero basis prior to the distribution.

    [5] Note that the $10,000 disparity between the partnership's inside basis and the sum of the partners' outside bases is caused by the $10,000 gain recognized by D on the distribution in excess of basis for which there is no basis adjustment. I.R.C. § 731(a)(1).

	Assets			Partnership Liabilities & Partners' Capital Accounts	
	Book Value	Tax Basis		Book Value	Tax Basis
Property	$30,000	$30,000	Debt	$140,000	n/a
			C	($110,000)	$30,000
			D	$ 0	$10,000
Totals	$30,000	$30,000		$ 30,000	$40,000

Rev.Rul. 92–97, 1992–2 C.B. 124, provides another example of the operation of a qualified income offset provision. That ruling dealt with the allocation of discharge of indebtedness income where the partners shared losses in a different ratio than they shared profits. A and B shared profits equally but agreed that A would bear 10% of the losses while B would bear 90% of the losses. A contributed $10 and B contributed $90, and the partnership borrowed $900 with recourse. Accordingly, under Treas.Reg. § 1.752–2, A bore $90 of the economic risk of loss associated with the recourse loan, and B bore $810 of the risk.

In Situation 1 of the Ruling, the partnership maintained capital accounts, but because the partners were obligated to restore negative capital accounts only to the extent necessary to pay creditors, the partnership met the alternate test for economic effect under Treas.Reg. § 1.704–1(b)(2)(ii)(d). At the time the debt was canceled, both partners had negative capital accounts, and their capital accounts both would have remained negative after being increased for discharge of indebtedness income allocated equally, $450 to each, as provided in the partnership agreement. The cancellation of the debt eliminated the partners' obligations to restore their negative capital accounts. Thus, A neither could enjoy any economic benefit from an allocation of discharge of indebtedness income in excess of $90 nor suffer any economic detriment from an allocation of discharge of indebtedness income of less than $90. Similarly, B neither could enjoy any economic benefit from an allocation of discharge of indebtedness income in excess of $810 nor suffer any economic detriment from an allocation of discharge of indebtedness income of less than $810. Accordingly, the equal allocation of discharge of indebtedness income did not have economic effect. Instead, the income must have been allocated $90 to A and $810 to B, which was the same ratio as the decrease in their shares of partnership liability resulting from the cancellation of the debt. Situation 2 of the Ruling was identical to Situation 1 except that A and B had an unlimited deficit capital account restoration obligation as provided in Treas.Reg. § 1.704–1(b)(2)(ii)(b)(3). In this situation, the equal allocation of the discharge of indebtedness income had economic effect because the income allocation could result in one partner's negative capital account restoration obligation being invoked to satisfy the other partner's positive capital account balance.

For additional examples, see Treas.Reg. § 1.704–1(b)(5), Ex. (1)(iii)–(x), (15), (16)(ii).

4.　ECONOMIC EFFECT EQUIVALENCE

Treas.Reg. § 1.704–1(b)(2)(ii)(*i*) provides that an allocation that does not have economic effect under the rules prescribed in Treas.Reg. § 1.704–1(b)(2)(ii) will be deemed to have economic effect if, as of the end of each partnership year, a liquidation of the partnership at that time or at the end of any future year would produce the same economic results to the partners as would occur if the requirements of Treas.Reg. § 1.704–1(b)(2)(ii)(*b*) had been satisfied, regardless of economic performance of the partnership. This provision assures the recognition of any allocation that allocates a consistent fraction of all items to each partner, as long as the partners are fully liable for partnership debts and the partners' capital contributions were in the same ratios as their shares of profits and losses. See Treas.Reg. § 1.704–1(b)(5), Ex. (4)(ii). Thus, for example, if A contributes $40, B contributes $35, and C contributes $25 to form the ABC Partnership, and the partners' respective shares of all items of income and loss are A, 40%; B, 35%; and C, 25%, allocations in those ratios will be respected even if the partnership does not maintain capital accounts. If, however, one of the partner's initial capital contribution differed from the profit and loss sharing ratio (for example, if A had contributed only $38), then the safe harbor would not apply.

5.　PARTNER'S INTEREST IN THE PARTNERSHIP

Treas.Reg. § 1.704–1(b)(3) provides rules governing the determination of a partner's interest in a partnership that must be used if the partnership agreement does not allocate partners' distributive shares or if the allocation in the agreement does not have substantial economic effect. The Regulation provides two tests: a facts-and-circumstances test and an objective test that relies on a comparative liquidation analysis.

5.1. *Facts-and-Circumstances Test*

The facts-and-circumstances approach may be used whether an allocation fails economic effect or substantiality. Under this approach, all of the facts and circumstances are to be taken into account. Treas.Reg. § 1.704–1(b)(3)(i). The Regulation states that except for allocations of deductions attributable to nonrecourse debt, the allocation with respect to any particular item of partnership income, gain, deduction, loss, or credit does not necessarily have to correspond to any other partnership item. Factors to be considered include the partners' relative capital contributions, their interests in economic profits or losses (in contrast to tax profits and losses), their interests in cash flow, and the relative rights of the partners upon liquidation. Treas.Reg. § 1.704–1(b)(3)(ii). No specific guidance regarding the application of these factors is provided, but Treas.Reg. § 1.704–1(b)(5), Ex. (1)(i) and (ii), (4)(i), (5)(i) and (ii), (6), (7), and (8) illustrate reallocation of items according to the partners' interests in a partnership.

In Estate of Ballantyne v. Commissioner, 341 F.3d 802 (8th Cir. 2003), the deceased taxpayer and his brother had operated a partnership for many years. The partnership conducted an oil and gas business, which was managed by the decedent, and a farming business, which was managed by the decedent's brother. The brothers had reported as equal partners, even though the decedent consistently withdrew the profits from the oil and gas business and decedent's brother consistently withdrew the profits from the farming business. After the decedent's death, the estate took the position that all of the income from the farming activity—the more profitable activity—was reportable as the decedent's brother's distributive share. The partnership agreement was not written, and the partnership did not maintain capital accounts; any allocation failed the substantial economic effect test, and the partners' interests in the partnership were determined under the facts and circumstances test of Treas.Reg. § 1.704–1(b)(3). Based on the evidence, the estate could not overcome the presumption, which then was provided in the Regulations but which has since been removed, that the partners were equal partners. There was no record of capital contributions; the amount of profits of each activity varied from year to year, as did withdrawals. The partners' economic interests and interests in cash flow could not be determined because the partnership books and records were inadequate. However, the "facts"—mostly the witnesses' "beliefs" that the brothers were 50:50 partners—indicated that they were to share liquidating distributions equally. That factor, combined with the brothers long-time consistent reporting as equal partners and the absence of any evidence that the brothers' reporting position involved tax avoidance, was sufficient to convince the court that they were equal partners. See also PNRC Limited Partnership v. Commissioner, T.C. Memo. 1993–335 (holding that the allocation of losses in the partnership agreement did not have substantial economic effect because the limited partner was not required to restore a negative capital account; losses were instead allocated in proportion to capital contributions, which was most consistent with the partners' interests in the partnership).

In Renkemeyer, Campbell & Weaver v. Commissioner, 136 T.C. 137 (2011), a law firm partnership attempted to allocate 87.55% of the firm's taxable income to a Subchapter S corporation that was wholly owned by an Employee Stock Ownership Plan under which the firm's three attorneys were the beneficiaries. The court held that the proper allocation was to be determined by looking at (1) the partners' relative capital contributions to the partnership; (2) the partners' respective interests in partnership profits and losses; (3) the partners' relative interests in cash flow and other nonliquidating distributions; and (4) the partners' rights to capital upon liquidation. Because the S corporation made no capital contributions to the partnership, the allocation of economic profits and loss interests of the partnership did not reflect the special allocation to the S corporation partner, and the S corporation received no distributions of cash, unlike the other partners, the allocation of income to the S Corporation did not have economic effect. The court concluded that each of the individual partners should be allocated one-third of the partnership's taxable income.

5.2. *Hypothetical Comparative Liquidation Analysis*

In addition to the facts-and-circumstances test, the Regulations also provide an objective test for determining a partner's interest in the partnership, but this test may not be used for allocations that lack substantiality. In addition, it may only be used if the first two requirements of Treas.Reg. § 1.704–1(b)(2)(ii)(*b*) are present—that is, if capital accounts are maintained in accordance with the Regulations and liquidating distributions will follow those accounts.

If the test is available, a comparison is made between (1) the manner in which distributions/contributions would be made if all partnership property were sold at book value and the partnership liquidated following the end of the taxable year to which the allocation relates and (2) the manner in which distributions/contributions would be made if all partnership property were sold at book value and the partnership were liquidated immediately following the end of the prior taxable year. Treas.Reg. § 1.704–1(b)(3)(iii).

To see how this test operates, consider again the example above in Detailed Analysis 3 involving C and D during Year 3. The partnership agreement provided that $30,000 of depreciation would be allocated 50:50, but D is a limited partner and has no obligation to restore a capital account deficit. At the end of Year 2, the balance sheet was as follows:

	Assets			Partnership Liabilities & Partners' Capital Accounts	
	Book Value	Tax Basis		Book Value	Tax Basis
Property	$120,000	$120,000	Debt	$120,000	n/a
			C	$ 0	$ 60,000
			D	$ 0	$ 60,000
Total	$120,000	$120,000		$120,000	$120,000

If the partnership had liquidated at this point, the property value would have been sufficient to cover the debt, and there would have been no cash for liquidating distributions. An allocation of the Year 3 depreciation to D would, however, lack economic effect because D is a limited partner and has no obligation to restore a deficit. The $15,000 deduction that would have been allocated to D under the agreement must instead be allocated according to each partner's interest in the partnership. If the share allocated to D under the agreement is instead allocated to C, that will correctly reflect each partner's interest in the partnership under the comparative liquidation analysis. The partnership books would be as follows:

	Assets			Partnership Liabilities & Partners' Capital Accounts	
	Book Value	Tax Basis		Book Value	Tax Basis
Property	$90,000	$90,000	Debt	$120,000	n/a
			C	($ 30,000)	$90,000
			D	$ 0	$ 0
Total	$90,000	$90,000		$ 90,000	$90,000

If the partnership were to liquidate at this point, the value of the property is insufficient to pay the debt. C is required to restore a deficit and will pay $30,000 so that the entire debt can be paid. C is allocated all of the depreciation because C bears the economic burden for the Year 3 depreciation, as the two hypothetical liquidations illustrate.

6.   TARGETED ALLOCATIONS UNDER THE ECONOMIC EFFECT EQUIVALENCE AND PARTNER'S INTEREST IN THE PARTNERSHIP TESTS

6.1. *General*

Many, if not most, contemporary investment partnership agreements are drafted with allocation provisions that avoid the complexity of the § 704(b) Regulations substantial economic effect test and instead use allocations of tax items that are based on a waterfall of cash distributions in accord with the partners' expectations of the accrued return on invested capital at the end of each taxable year. Practitioners often prefer these "targeted allocations" to the proper maintenance of capital accounts under the safe-harbor Regulations, asserting that clients are better able to understand the economics of a partnership deal structured around the partners' share of distributable money than they are a deal based on their interests in the partnership determined from capital accounts that follow tax allocations under the safe harbor Regulations.

These targeted allocations are an alternative to another approach, which is termed "layer cake" allocations. Generally speaking, layer cake allocations are designed to follow the safe harbor of the § 704(b) Regulations, but they create different classes of partnership interests. Rather than focus on distributable cash, layer cake allocations apply to partnership items of income and loss that are allocated to partnership units to provide a fixed (or preferred) yield on the invested capital of more senior classes of partnership units. The basic concept of targeted allocations is to allocate profit and loss so that, at the end of every taxable year, each partner's capital account is equal to (1) the amount that would be distributed to that partner in liquidation if all partnership assets were sold at their book value, less (2) the partner's share of minimum gain, which is gain caused by nonrecourse debt exceeding asset book value and is discussed later in this Chapter. Targeted allocation structures also are designed to permit a partnership structure with preferred partnership interests that provide a first call on the return of invested capital (an analog to preferred stock) but that provide a lower yield than interest on a debt with a greater risk of loss. Practitioners thus also assert that the structure of partnership allocation provisions is less complex than compliance with the capital account maintenance rules of the § 704(b) Regulations. Nonetheless, these targeted allocations have their own set of complexities. In order better to understand targeted allocations, it is useful first to explore basic layer cake allocations.

6.2. *Layer Cake Allocations*

A basic layer cake allocation structure begins by providing for liquidation according to capital account balances but provides a preferred return to certain classes of partnership units, usually stated in terms of a specified yield, to more senior partnership interests. A layer cake allocation structure begins with an allocation of income to holders of class A units (the most senior units) to the extent of net losses previously allocated to the class A partners, then to the class B units to the extent of net losses previously allocated to the class B partners, and so on if there are more junior classes of partnership interests. This initial provision assures that income is first allocated to the partners in amounts sufficient to restore the partners' initial capital. The second layer of profits is allocated to the class A partners to the extent of the current and cumulative yield provided to the class A units.[6] This allocation includes income sufficient to offset any losses previously allocated to class A units up to the yield provided for the class A units. The third layer is then allocated to the class B units to the extent of the current and cumulative yield promised to the class B units. The yield to the class B units may be higher to compensate for the greater risk that the yield may not be paid. Once the holders of the class A and B units have been allocated income sufficient to provide the fixed yield on invested capital, the remaining income is divided among the class A and class B units and units held by the partnership managers.

Losses in a layer cake allocation are allocated in reverse order. Losses are first allocated among the class A, class B, and management units to the extent of cumulative profits in excess of the fixed yields of the class A and B units previously allocated to those units. The second layer of losses is then allocated to the higher risk class B units to the extent of the income previously allocated to class B units reflecting the fixed yield previously allocable to the class B capital; then losses are allocated to the class A units to the extent of income previously allocated to the class A units reflecting the fixed yield previously allocable to the class A capital. The third layer of losses is then allocated to the class B partners to the extent of their capital, then to the class A partners to the extent of the class A partners' capital. Finally, any additional losses would be allocated among the class A and class B units in proportion to the aggregate number of class A and class B units.

Distributions in the layer cake are made according to the partners' capital accounts.

For example, suppose that A, B, and C form an investment partnership. A and B each contribute $300, with C contributing nothing but management services. The partnership agreement provides annual profits will be allocated first to A in an amount equal to 10% of A's original invested capital, then to B in an amount equal to 15% of B's original invested capital, then 30% to A, 50% to B, and 20% to C. In Year 1, the partnership has $20 of

---

[6] Note that many partnership agreements provide a preferred return to the more senior classes of partnership interest that can be payable out of the capital of more junior classes of partnership interest. Such an arrangement might provide, for example, that distributions would be made (1) to A to the extent of A's invested capital, amount to yield a 10% annual uncompounded return to A's capital (2) to B to the extent of B's invested capital, plus a 15% annual uncompounded return to B's capital, then (3) 30% to A and 50% to B, and 20% to C. Such an arrangement brings into play § 707(c), which is discussed in Chapter 22 and could result in "guaranteed payments" providing income to A and deductions to B in years in which the partnerships profits were insufficient to meet the required allocations to A. Furthermore, many, if not most, partnership agreements provide for compounded yield (often based on a specified internal rate of return), rather than simple yield.

profit. All of the $20 of Year 1 income would be allocated to A to partially meet A's 10% yield ($30) on A's $300 of capital. At the end of Year 1, the partnership's capital accounts are as follows:

	Partnership Capital	Partners' Capital Accounts		
		A	B	C
Assets	$600	$300	$300	$ 0
Profit	$ 20	$ 20	____	$ 0
	$620	$320	$300	$ 0

Now suppose that in Year 2 the partnership has a $50 loss. Twenty dollars of the loss—an amount equal to A's Year 1 income allocation—would be allocated to A. The remaining $30 of the loss is allocated to B in Year 2. At the end of Year 2, the partnership's capital accounts are as follows:

	Partnership Capital		Partners' Capital Accounts		
			A	B	C
Assets	$620		$320	$300	$ 0
Loss	($ 50)	Year 2	($20)	($ 30)	$ 0
	$570		$300	$270	$ 0

Now suppose that in Year 3 the partnership sells all of its assets for cash and has a $405 gain. The first $30—an amount equal to B's Year 2 loss allocation—would be allocated to B. Second, $90 would be allocated to A to provide A's three-year 10% uncompounded annual return on $300. Third, $135 would be allocated to B to provide B's three-year 15% uncompounded annual return on $300. The remaining $150 would be allocated $45 to A (30% x $150), $75 to B (50% x $150), and $30 to C (20% x $150). At the end of Year 3, the partnership's capital accounts are as follows:

	Partnership Capital		Partners' Capital Accounts		
			A	B	C
Assets	$570		$300	$270	$ 0
Gain	$405	First tier		$ 30	
		Second tier	$ 90		
		Third tier		$135	
	____	Fourth tier	$ 45	$ 75	$30
	$975		$435	$510	$30

The $975 book value of the partnership assets equals the sum of the three partners' capital accounts, which reflect the amount each partner will receive upon liquidation of the partnership.

6.3. *Targeted Allocations*

In a targeted allocation structure, the partner's interest in liquidation of the partnership is based on provisions that allocate partnership cash to the partner, usually representing a return of the partner's invested capital plus a yield provided to the particular class of partnership units held by the partner. The partnership agreement will provide for liquidation of the partnership on the basis of the partners' interests in partnership cash after the partnership has disposed of its assets at book value. As a consequence, the partnership allocations cannot satisfy the requirement of the economic effect test of Treas.Reg. § 1.704–1(b)(2)(ii), which requires that partnership liquidating distributions be based upon properly maintained capital accounts. To avoid this problem, targeted allocations are structured with an expectation that the allocations will be sustained under the economic effect equivalence test of Treas.Reg. § 1.704–1(b)(2)(ii)(*i*), or that the allocations will be sustained as being in accord with the partners' interests in the partnership under the facts and circumstances test. Both of these assertions rely on allocations of tax items in a manner that produces capital accounts that reflect the cash distributable to the partners upon liquidation of the partnership. In other words, tax allocations and capital accounts are derived from the cash liquidation distributions in a manner that reflects the amount of cash distributable to a partner.

In a partnership agreement with targeted allocations, profits and losses are allocated among the partners so that at the end of the partnership year each partner's capital account will reflect the amount that would be distributed to the partner under a distribution waterfall. A typical distribution provision for a partnership that had two classes of investors, as well as non-investor managing partners, might provide: (1) first, distributions to return invested capital to holders of class A partnership units, in proportion to the number of units held by each partner; (2) distributions to return invested capital to holders of class B partnership units, in proportion to the number of units held by each class B partner; (3) distributions to the holders of the class A units to the extent of the agreed yield on invested capital for the class A units; (4) distributions to the class B units to the extent of the agreed upon yield on invested capital for the class B units; and (5) finally, to the holders of the class A units, the class B units, and the management units in specified percentages. On liquidation of the partnership, after payment of debts, the partnership cash is distributed in accord with the waterfall provision.[7]

For example, suppose that A, B, and C form an investment partnership; A and B each contribute $300, with C contributing nothing but management services. The partnership waterfall provides that distributions will be made

---

[7]   The allocation provisions must also be structured to take into account a partner's share of partnership minimum gain and nonrecourse debt under Treas.Reg. § 1.704–2(g), and (i)(3), discussed later in this Chapter.

(1) to A to the extent of A's invested capital, (2) to B to the extent of B's invested capital, (3) to A in an amount to yield a 10% annual uncompounded return to A's capital, (4) to B to yield a 15% annual uncompounded return to B's capital, then (5) 30% to A and 50% to B, and 20% to C. (As with the layer cake allocation example above, the yield to the class B units may be higher to compensate for the greater risk that the yield may not be paid.) In Year 1, the partnership has $20 of profit. Under the waterfall agreement upon liquidation of the partnership, after the return their initial capital of $300 to A and B, only $20 remains to satisfy A's right to a distribution of additional $30 if the partnership liquidated at the end of the year. In order for A's capital account to match this cash distribution, the full $20 of profit is allocated to A for tax purposes.

Partnership Capital		Waterfall Distribution			Partners' Capital Accounts		
		A	B	C	A	B	C
Contributions	$600	$300	$300	$0	$300	$300	$0
Year 1 Profit	$ 20	$ 20	$ 0	$0	$ 20	$ 0	$0
End of Year I:		$320	$300	$0	$320	$300	$0

Now suppose that in Year 2 the partnership has a $50 loss attributable to depreciation. In this case, the book value of the partnership assets is reduced to $570, an amount insufficient to meet the second distribution element of the waterfall. Upon liquidation, the partnership would distribute $300 to A and $270 to B. In order to target allocations to match distributions, the partnership would have to allocate $20 of the loss to A and $30 of the loss to B.

Partnership Capital		Waterfall Distribution			Partners' Capital Accounts		
		A	B	C	A	B	C
Contributions	$600	$300	$300	$0	$300	$300	$0
Year 1 Profit	$ 20	$ 20	$ 0	$0	$ 20	$ 0	$0
Year 2 Loss	($ 50)	($ 20)	($ 30)	$0	($ 20)	($ 30)	$0
End of Year 2:	$570	$300	$270	$0	$300	$270	$0

Now suppose that in Year 3 the partnership sells all of its assets for cash and has a $405 gain. In this case, the book value of the partnership assets is increased to $975. Upon liquidation, the partnership would distribute (1) $300 to A, (2) $300 to B, (3) $90 to A, (4) $135 to B, (5) leaving $150 to be distributed $45 to A, $75 to B, and $30 to C. A's total distribution would be $435, B's total distribution would be $510, and C's total distribution would be $30. In order to target allocations of the $405 gain to match distributions, the partnership would have to allocate $135 to A, $240 to B, and $30 to C.

Partnership Capital		Waterfall Distribution			Partners' Capital Accounts		
		A	B	C	A	B	C
Contributions	$600	$300	$300	$ 0	$300	$300	$ 0
Year 1 Profit	$ 20	$ 20	$ 0	$ 0	$ 20	$ 0	$ 0
Year 2 Loss	($ 50)	($ 20)	($ 30)	$ 0	($ 20)	($ 30)	$ 0
Year 3 Gain	$405	$135	$240	$30	$135	$240	$30
End of Year 3:	$975	$435	$510	$30	$435	$510	$30

In each case, the tax allocations are made in a manner that reflects the economic increase or decrease in the annual amount available for distribution to the partners under the waterfall provision. Because the tax allocations in these examples represent an allocation of the economic changes in the partners' interests, they should be respected as representing each partner's interest in the partnership items. Unlike book and tax allocations in accord with properly maintained capital accounts under the economic effect Regulations, which allocate items to the partners as book and tax items are recognized, targeted allocations first focus on the economic effect of partnership cash, then derive the tax allocations from cash results. Note, however, that if the income or loss in any particular year consisted of items of income or loss that differed in character, allocations of items other than pro rata to net increases or decreases in the waterfall distribution could be subject to challenge by the IRS as lacking substantiality.

In the ABC partnership examples above, the targeted allocations produced the same result as the layer cake allocations produced. This will not always be the case, however, if layer cake allocations are designed to meet the safe harbor in the Regulations. To meet the safe harbor in the Regulations, book depreciation and amortization must be computed using cost recovery periods and methods required for tax depreciation and amortization. However, many investors in partnerships want depreciation and amortization to be determined in accordance with generally accepted accounting principles (GAAP), which differs from the cost recovery periods and methods required for tax depreciation and amortization. This is another reason why, in some instances, targeted allocations are preferred to layer cake allocations.

7. ALLOCATIONS TO SERVICE PARTNERS WITH FORFEITABLE INTERESTS

As discussed in Chapter 19, Section 3, Proposed Regulations under §§ 83 and 721 deal with the transfer of a partnership interest in exchange for services. When a transferred partnership interest is subject to a substantial risk of forfeiture, unless an election is made under § 83(b) to include the value of the forfeitable partnership interest in income when received, the holder of the partnership interest is not treated as a partner until the interest becomes substantially vested. See Treas.Reg. § 1.83–1(a)(1). If a § 83(b) election is made with respect to such an interest, the service provider will be treated as a partner, even though the interest remains forfeitable.

These rules raise special problems regarding the tax treatment of allocations of items of gain or loss to a partner during the period in which the partner's interest remains forfeitable. If the partner who receives a forfeitable partnership interest in exchange for services does not make a § 83(b) election with respect to that interest, the partner cannot be allocated any portion of partnership income or loss, and any distributions made to the service provider with respect to the partnership interest are treated as additional compensation and not partnership distributions. But if a service partner who receives a substantially nonvested partnership interest makes a valid § 83(b) election, the service provider is treated as a partner with respect to such an interest, and the partnership must allocate partnership items to the service provider as if the partnership interest were substantially vested. See Notice 2005–43, 2005–24 C.B. 1221.

Further complications arise if a service provider who has received a forfeitable compensatory partnership interest makes a § 83(b) election, is allocated items of partnership income and loss, and subsequently forfeits the partnership interest. Prop.Reg. § 1.704–1(b)(4)(xii) (2005) would address these issues. The operation of the Proposed Regulations is described in the preamble to Partnership Equity for Services, REG–105346–03, 70 F.R. 29675 (May 23, 2005), as follows:

> If an election under section 83(b) has been made with respect to a substantially nonvested interest, the holder of the nonvested interest may be allocated partnership items that may later be forfeited. For this reason, allocations of partnership items while the interest is substantially nonvested cannot have economic effect. Under the proposed regulations, such allocations will be treated as being in accordance with the partners' interests in the partnership if: (a) the partnership agreement requires that the partnership make forfeiture allocations if the interest for which the section 83(b) election is made is later forfeited; and (b) all material allocations and capital account adjustments under the partnership agreement not pertaining to substantially nonvested partnership interests for which a section 83(b) election has been made are recognized under section 704(b). This safe harbor does not apply if, at the time of the section 83(b) election, there is a plan that a substantially nonvested interest will be forfeited. All of the facts and circumstances (including the tax status of the holder of the substantially nonvested interest) will be considered in determining whether there is a plan that the interest will be forfeited. In such a case, the partners' distributive shares of partnership items shall be determined in accordance with the partners' interests in the partnership under [Treas.Reg. §] 1.704–1(b)(3).

> Generally, forfeiture allocations are allocations to the service provider of partnership gross income and gain or gross deduction and loss (to the extent such items are available) that offset prior distributions and allocations of partnership items with respect to the forfeited partnership interest. These rules are designed to ensure that any partnership income (or loss) that was allocated to

the service provider prior to the forfeiture is offset by allocations on the forfeiture of the interest. Also, to carry out the prohibition under section 83(b)(1) on deductions with respect to amounts included in income under section 83(b), these rules generally cause a forfeiting partner to be allocated partnership income to offset any distributions to the partner that reduced the partner's basis in the partnership below the amount included in income under section 83(b).

Forfeiture allocations may be made out of the partnership's items for the entire taxable year. In determining the gross income of the partnership in the taxable year of the forfeiture, the rules of [Treas.Reg. §] 1.83–6(c) apply. As a result, the partnership generally will have gross income in the taxable year of the forfeiture equal to the amount of the allowable deduction to the service recipient partnership upon the transfer of the interest as a result of the making of the section 83(b) election, regardless of the fair market value of the partnership's assets at the time of forfeiture.

In certain circumstances, the partnership will not have enough income and gain to fully offset prior allocations of loss to the forfeiting service provider. The proposed revenue procedure includes a rule that requires the recapture of losses taken by the service provider prior to the forfeiture of the interest to the extent that those losses are not recaptured through forfeiture allocations of income and gain to the service provider. This rule does not provide the other partners in the partnership with the opportunity to increase their shares of partnership loss (or reduce their shares of partnership income) for the year of the forfeiture by the amount of loss that was previously allocated to the forfeiting service provider.

In other circumstances, the partnership will not have enough deductions and loss to fully offset prior allocations of income to the forfeiting service provider. It appears that, in such a case, section 83(b)(1) may prohibit the service provider from claiming a loss with respect to partnership income that was previously allocated to the service provider. However, a forfeiting partner is entitled to a loss for any basis in a partnership that is attributable to contributions of money or property to the partnership (including amounts paid for the interest) remaining after the forfeiture allocations have been made. See [Treas.Reg. §]1.83–2(a).

PROBLEM SET 1

1.   Al and Brett each contributed $320,000 to form a general partnership, which purchased a parcel of land for $40,000 and constructed an office building for $600,000. Assume that the property has a 30-year cost recovery period under § 168, the depreciation method is straight-line, and conventions are ignored. Thus, the annual depreciation deduction is $20,000. The

partnership's annual rental income exactly equals its deductible cash flow operating expenses, with the result that net partnership taxable income for each year is a loss of $20,000. The partnership agreement allocates all items of income and loss equally, except the depreciation deductions, which are allocated entirely to Brett. Both partners are unconditionally obligated to restore any deficit to their capital accounts upon a liquidation of the partnership.

(a)   What additional provisions must be included in the partnership agreement for the allocation of depreciation to be respected?

(b)   (1)   What should be the amount in each partner's capital account at the end of the third year of partnership operations?

(2)   At the end of 17 years of operations?

(c)   (1)   If the partnership sold the land and building for $660,000 on the first day of the fourth year and then liquidated, how must the proceeds be distributed?

(2)   What if the sales price was $540,000?

(d)   Will the allocations qualify if the partnership agreement contains a "gain chargeback," which allocates first to Brett the portion of any gain on a sale that equals the depreciation deductions specially allocated to her? Assume that the partnership sells the building on January 1 of Year Four for $660,000, and, alternatively, for $540,000.

(e)   Will the allocations qualify if the partnership agreement provides that all nonliquidating distributions are to be made 60% to Al and 40% to Brett?

(f)   Assume that the partnership is a limited partnership, with Al as the general partner and Brett as the limited partner. As a limited partner, Brett is not required to restore a deficit in her capital account, but as the general partner Al is required to restore a deficit capital account.

(1)   May depreciation deductions be specially allocated to Brett? If so, for how many years? How must the depreciation deductions be allocated in the 17th year of partnership operations?

(2)   How would your answer change if at the end of the sixteenth year Brett contributed her promissory note for $160,000 to the partnership?

2.   What would be the result in each of problems 1(a)–(d) if Al and Brett each contributed $30,000 to form the general partnership and the partnership borrowed $580,000 to purchase the land and construct the building?

3.   What would be the result in problem 1(f) if Al and Brett each contributed $30,000 to form the limited partnership and the partnership borrowed $580,000 to purchase the land and construct the building?

4.   Luke, Mona, and Nikita will form the LMN LLC. Luke will contribute $30,000,000 in cash. Mona will contribute $10,000,000 in cash. Nikita will contribute intellectual property with a basis of zero and speculative, if any, market value, but Nikita will agree to work full time running the business

of the LMN LLC. Luke and Mona are simply investors. Nikita will be the managing member; Luke and Mona will be non-managing members. Luke will receive one Class A LLC unit, one Class B LLC unit, and one Class C LLC unit. Mona will receive one Class B LLC unit and one Class C LLC unit. Nikita will receive one Class C LLC unit.

The Class A LLC unit (Luke) will be entitled to the first $30,000,000 upon liquidation of the LMN LLC. Upon liquidation of the LLC, after satisfaction of the $30,000,000 liquidation preference of the Class A LLC unit, the Class B LLC units (Luke and Mona) will share equally the next $20,000,000, with the amount due to each unit to be reduced proportionately if the LMN LLC's assets are insufficient to distribute $10,000,000 with respect to each unit. The Class A LLC unit will be entitled to the first $1,500,000 of annual partnership profits (5%). The two Class B LLC units will share equally the next $1,200,000 of annual partnership profits (6%) after the $1,500,000 allocated to the Class A unit. To the extent the Class A and Class B units' shares of annual income have not been distributed prior to liquidation, after the $20,000,000 attributable to the contributions for Class B units have been satisfied, first, the preferential liquidation distribution due to the Class A unit will be increased by the undistributed amount of profits allocated to it, and, second, the preferential liquidation distribution due to the Class B units will be increased by the undistributed amount of profits allocated to then. After satisfaction of the preferential annual allocations to the Class A and Class B units, the three Class C units share the LMN LLC's residual profits and losses equally. Losses will be allocated first against income allocated to the Class C units, then against income allocated to the Class B units, and then against income allocated to the Class A units. Losses in excess of cumulative profits are allocated first to the Class B units to the extent of the liquidation preference of the Class B units ($20,000,000), then against the liquidation preference of the Class A units. No member of the LLC will be required to make any contribution to the LMN LLC beyond the initial contribution.

Do the Code and Regulations allow a partnership agreement to be written so as to achieve these goals and have the allocations of profits and losses be respected in whole or in part?

(2) SUBSTANTIALITY

REGULATIONS: Section 1.704–1(b)(2)(iii), –1(b)(5), Ex. (2)–(3), (5)–(6), (10).

The substantial economic effect test has two parts. To be respected, an allocation must have economic effect (or its equivalent) and the allocation must be "substantial." To be considered substantial the economic effect of the allocation must have a reasonable possibility of affecting the dollar amounts to be received by the partners independent of the tax consequences of the allocation. Treas.Reg. § 1.704–1(b)(2)(iii)(*a*). An allocation is not substantial if, as a result of the allocation, the after-tax economic consequences to at least one partner may, in present value terms, be enhanced, and there is a strong likelihood that the after-tax consequences of no partner will, in present value terms, be diminished. Determining whether an allocation that has economic effect also is "substantial" often requires an examination of factors extrinsic to the partnership, such as the individual partners' income tax brackets.

Revenue Ruling 99–43
1999–2 C.B. 506.

ISSUE

Do partnership allocations lack substantiality under § 1.704–1(b)(2)(iii) of the Income Tax Regulations when the partners amend the partnership agreement to create offsetting special allocations of particular items after the events giving rise to the items have occurred?

FACTS

A and B, both individuals, formed a general partnership, PRS. A and B each contributed $1,000 and also agreed that each would be allocated a 50-percent share of all partnership items. The partnership agreement provides that, upon the contribution of additional capital by either partner, PRS must revalue the partnership's property and adjust the partners' capital accounts under § 1.704–1(b)(2)(iv)(f).

PRS borrowed $8,000 from a bank and used the borrowed and contributed funds to purchase nondepreciable property for $10,000. The loan was nonrecourse to A and B and was secured only by the property. No principal payments were due for 6 years, and interest was payable semi-annually at a market rate.

After one year, the fair market value of the property fell from $10,000 to $6,000, but the principal amount of the loan remained $8,000. As part of a workout arrangement among the bank, PRS, A, and B, the bank reduced the principal amount of the loan by $2,000, and A contributed an additional $500 to PRS. A's capital account was credited with the $500, which PRS used to pay currently deductible expenses incurred in connection with the workout. All $500 of the currently deductible workout expenses were allocated to A. B made no additional contribution of capital. At the time of the workout, B was insolvent within the meaning of § 108(a) of the Internal Revenue Code. A and B agreed that, after the workout, A would have a 60-percent interest and B would have a 40-percent interest in the profits and losses of PRS.

As a result of the property's decline in value and the workout, PRS had two items to allocate between A and B. First, the agreement to cancel $2,000 of the loan resulted in $2,000 of cancellation of indebtedness income (COD income). Second, A's contribution of $500 to PRS was an event that required PRS, under the partnership agreement, to revalue partnership property and adjust A's and B's capital accounts. Because of the decline in value of the property, the revaluation resulted in a $4,000 economic loss that must be allocated between A's and B's capital accounts.

Under the terms of the original partnership agreement, *PRS* would have allocated these items equally between *A* and *B*. *A* and *B*, however, amend the partnership agreement (in a timely manner) to make two special allocations. First, *PRS* specially allocates the entire $2,000 of COD income to *B*, an insolvent partner. Second, *PRS* specially allocates the book loss from the revaluation $1,000 to *A* and $3,000 to *B*.

While *A* receives a $1,000 allocation of book loss and *B* receives a $3,000 allocation of book loss, neither of these allocations results in a tax loss to either partner. Rather, the allocations result only in adjustments to *A*'s and *B*'s capital accounts. Thus, the cumulative effect of the special allocations is to reduce each partner's capital account to zero immediately following the allocations despite the fact that *B* is allocated $2,000 of income for tax purposes.

LAW

Section 61(a)(12) provides that gross income includes income from the discharge of indebtedness.

Rev. Rul. 91–31, 1991–1 C.B. 19, holds that a taxpayer realizes COD income when a creditor (who was not the seller of the underlying property) reduces the principal amount of an under-secured nonrecourse debt.

Under § 704(b) and the regulations there under, allocations of a partnership's items of income, gain, loss, deduction, or credit provided for in the partnership agreement will be respected if the allocations have substantial economic effect. Allocations that fail to have substantial economic effect will be reallocated according to the partners' interests in the partnership (as defined in § 1.704–1(b)(3)).

Section 1.704–1(b)(2)(iv)(*f*) provides that a partnership may, upon the occurrence of certain events (including the contribution of money to the partnership by a new or existing partner), increase or decrease the partners' capital accounts to reflect a revaluation of the partnership property.

Section 1.704–1(b)(2)(iv)(*g*) provides that, to the extent a partnership's property is reflected on the books of the partnership at a book value that differs from the adjusted tax basis, the substantial economic effect requirements apply to the allocations of book items. Section 704(c) and § 1.704–1(b)(4)(i) govern the partners' distributive shares of tax items.

Section 1.704–1(b)(2)(i) provides that the determination of whether an allocation of income, gain, loss, or deduction (or item thereof) to a partner has substantial economic effect involves a two-part analysis that is made at the end of the partnership year to which the allocation relates. In order for an allocation to have substantial economic effect, the allocation must have both economic effect (within the meaning of § 1.704–1(b)(2)(ii)) and be substantial (within the meaning of § 1.704–1(b)(2)(iii)).

Section 1.704–1(b)(2)(iii)(*a*) provides that the economic effect of an allocation (or allocations) is substantial if there is a reasonable possibility that the allocation (or allocations) will substantially affect the dollar amounts to be received by the partners from the partnership independent of the tax consequences. However, the economic effect of an allocation is not substantial if, at the time the allocation becomes part of the partnership agreement, (1) the after-tax economic consequences of at least one partner may, in present value terms, be enhanced compared to the consequences if the allocation (or allocations) were not contained in the partnership agreement, and (2) there is a strong likelihood that the after-tax economic consequences of no partner will, in present value terms, be substantially diminished compared to the consequences if the allocation (or allocations) were not contained in the partnership agreement. In determining the after-tax economic benefit or detriment to a partner, tax consequences that result from the interaction of the allocation with the partner's tax attributes that are unrelated to the partnership will be taken into account.

Section 1.704–1(b)(2)(iii)(*b*) provides that the economic effect of an allocation (or allocations) in a partnership taxable year is not substantial if the allocations result in shifting tax consequences. Shifting tax consequences result when, at the time the allocation (or allocations) becomes part of the partnership agreement, there is a strong likelihood that (1) the net increases and decreases that will be recorded in the partners' respective capital accounts for the taxable year will not differ substantially from the net increases and decreases that would be recorded in the partners' respective capital accounts for the year if the allocations were not contained in the partnership agreement, and (2) the total tax liability of the partners (for their respective tax years in which the allocations will be taken into account) will be less than if the allocations were not contained in the partnership agreement.

Section 1.704–1(b)(2)(iii)(*c*) provides that the economic effect of an allocation (or allocations) in a partnership taxable year is not substantial if the allocations are transitory. Allocations are considered transitory if a partnership agreement provides for the possibility that one or more allocations (the "original allocation(s)") will be largely offset by other allocations (the "offsetting allocation(s)"), and, at the time the allocations become part of the partnership agreement, there is a strong likelihood that (1) the net increases and decreases that will be recorded in the partners' capital accounts for the taxable years to which the allocations relate will not differ substantially from the net increases and decreases that would be recorded in such partners' respective capital accounts for such years if the original and offsetting allocation(s) were not contained in the partnership agreement, and (2) the total tax liability of the partners (for their respective tax years in which the allocations will be taken into account) will be less than if the allocations were not contained in the partnership agreement.

Section 761(c) provides that a partnership agreement includes any modifications made prior to, or at, the time prescribed for filing a partnership return (not including extensions) which are agreed to by all partners, or which are adopted in such other manner as may be provided by the partnership agreement.

ANALYSIS

PRS is free to allocate partnership items between *A* and *B* in accordance with the provisions of the partnership agreement if the allocations have substantial economic effect under § 1.704–1(b)(2). To the extent that the minimum gain chargeback rules do not apply,[*] COD income may be allocated in accordance with the rules under § 1.704–1(b)(2). This is true notwithstanding that the COD income arises in connection with the cancellation of a nonrecourse debt.

The economic effect of an allocation is not substantial if, at the time that the allocation becomes part of the partnership agreement, the allocation fails each of two tests. The allocation fails the first test if the after-tax consequences of at least one partner may, in present value terms, be enhanced compared to the consequences if the allocation (or allocations) were not contained in the partnership agreement. The allocation fails the second test if there is a strong likelihood that the after-tax economic consequences of no partner will, in present value terms, be substantially diminished compared to such consequences if the allocation (or allocations) were not contained in the partnership agreement.

A and *B* amended the *PRS* partnership agreement to provide for an allocation of the entire $2,000 of the COD income to *B*. *B*, an insolvent taxpayer, is eligible to exclude the income under § 108, so it is unlikely that the $2,000 of COD income would increase *B*'s immediate tax liability. Without the special allocation, *A*, who is not insolvent or otherwise entitled to exclude the COD income under § 108, would pay tax immediately on the $1,000 of COD income allocated under the general ratio for sharing income. *A* and *B* also amended the *PRS* partnership agreement to provide for the special allocation of the book loss resulting from the revaluation. Because the two special allocations offset each other, *B* will not realize any economic benefit from the $2,000 income allocation, even if the property subsequently appreciates in value.

The economics of *PRS* are unaffected by the paired special allocations. After the capital accounts of *A* and *B* are adjusted to reflect the special allocations, *A* and *B* each have a capital account of zero, Economically, the situation of both partners is identical to what it would have been had the special allocations not occurred. In addition, a strong likelihood exists that the total tax liability of *A* and *B* will be less than if

---

* [Ed: Under certain circumstances, the COD income would be allocated between the partners in accordance with their shares of partnership minimum gain, discussed in Section 2.B of this Chapter, because the cancellation of the nonrecourse debt would result in a decrease in partnership minimum gain. See § 1.704–2(d). However, in this situation, there is no minimum gain because the principal amount of the debt never exceeded the property's book value. Therefore, the minimum gain chargeback requirement does not govern the manner in which the COD income is allocated between A and B, and PRS's special allocation of COD income must satisfy the substantial economic effect standard. See Rev.Rul. 92–97, 1992–2 C.B. 124.]

PRS had allocated 50 percent of the $2,000 of COD income and 50 percent of the $4,000 book loss to each partner. Therefore, the special allocations of COD income and book loss are shifting allocations under § 1.704–1(b)(2)(iii)(*b*) and lack substantiality. (Alternatively, the allocations could be transitory allocations under § 1.704–1(b)(2)(iii)(*c*) if the allocations occur during different partnership taxable years.)

This conclusion is not altered by the "value equals basis" rule that applies in determining the substantiality of an allocation. See § 1.704–1(b)(2)(iii)(*c*)(*2*). Under that rule, the adjusted tax basis (or, if different, the book value) of partnership property will be presumed to be the fair market value of the property. This presumption is appropriate in most cases because, under § 1.704–1(b)(2)(iv), property generally will be reflected on the books of the partnership at its fair market value when acquired. Thus, an allocation of gain or loss from the disposition of the property will reflect subsequent changes in the value of the property that generally cannot be predicted.

The substantiality of an allocation, however, is analyzed "at the time the allocation becomes part of the partnership agreement," not the time at which the allocation is first effective. See § 1.704–1(b)(2)(iii)(*a*). In the situation described above, the provisions of the *PRS* partnership agreement governing the allocation of gain or loss from the disposition of property are changed at a time that is after the property has been revalued on the books of the partnership, but are effective for a period that begins prior to the revaluation. See § 1.704–1(b)(2)(iv)(*f*).

Under these facts, the presumption that value equals basis does not apply to validate the allocations. Instead, *PRS*'s allocations of gain or loss must be closely scrutinized in determining the appropriate tax consequences. *Cf.* § 1.704–1(b)(4)(vi). In this situation, the special allocations of the $2,000 of COD income and $4,000 of book loss will not be respected and, instead, must be allocated in accordance with the *A*'s and *B*'s interests in the partnership under § 1.704–1(b)(3).

Close scrutiny also would be required if the changes were made at a time when the events giving rise to the allocations had not yet occurred but were likely to occur or if, under the original allocation provisions of a partnership agreement, there was a strong likelihood that a disproportionate amount of COD income earned in the future would be allocated to any partner who is insolvent at the time of the allocation and would be offset by an increased allocation of loss or a reduced allocation of income to such partner or partners.

HOLDING

Partnership special allocations lack substantiality when the partners amend the partnership agreement to specially allocate COD income and book items from a related revaluation after the events creating such items have occurred if the overall economic effect of the special allocations on the partners' capital accounts does not differ substantially from the economic effect of the original allocations in the partnership agreement.

DETAILED ANALYSIS

1. SUBSTANTIALITY REQUIREMENT

1.1. *General Principles*

The operation of Treas.Reg. § 1.704–1(b)(2)(iii)(*a*) to invalidate an allocation that has "economic effect" but is not "substantial" is illustrated by the following facts. H and J contribute equal amounts to become partners in an investment partnership. The partnership distributes currently all income credited to the partners' capital accounts. H expects consistently to be subject to tax at a 15% bracket, and J expects consistently to be subject to tax at a 28% bracket. There is a strong likelihood that over the next several years the HJ Partnership will realize $500 of tax-exempt interest and $500 of taxable interest and dividends on its investments. If all items were allocated equally between H and J, which would be consistent with their capital interests, each would have $250 of tax-exempt income and $250 of taxable income. As a result, H would realize $462.50 of after-tax income, and J would realize only $430 of after-tax income.

	H Before Tax	H After Tax	J Before Tax	J After Tax
Taxable	$250	$212.50	$250	$180
Tax-Exempt	$250	$250.00	$250	$250
Total	$500	$462.50	$500	$430

If, however, the taxable income were allocated 60% to H and 40% to J, the tax-exempt interest were allocated 42% to H and 58% to J, and each partner's capital account were increased according to those percentages, H would have $300 of taxable income and $210 of tax-exempt income, and J would have $200 of taxable income and $290 of tax-exempt income. On an after-tax basis, however, H would have a total of $465, and J would have a total of $434.

	H Before Tax	H After Tax	J Before Tax	J After Tax
Taxable	$300	$255	$200	$144
Tax-Exempt	$210	$210	$290	$290
Total	$510	$465	$490	$434

Each of the partners would have more after-tax income as a result of the allocation than if the items had been allocated equally, consistent with capital contributions. Therefore, even though it has economic effect, the allocation is not "substantial," and it will not be respected for tax purposes. Because under the allocation, H's capital account is credited with $510 and J's capital account is credited with $490, all items will likely be allocated 51%

to H and 49% to J to reflect each partner's interest in the partnership under the facts-and-circumstances test of Treas.Reg. § 1.701–1(b)(3)(ii). See Treas.Reg. § 1.704–1(b)(5), Ex. (5). The result is as follows:

| | H | | J | |
	Before Tax	After Tax	Before Tax	After Tax
Taxable	$255	$216.75	$245	$176.40
Tax-Exempt	$255	$255.00	$245	$245.00
Total	$510	$471.75	$490	$421.40

As a result of attempting to reduce taxes through a special allocation that is not substantial, J is left worse off than J would have been if all items had been allocated equally, while H is better-off at J's expense.

1.2. *Application of Substantiality Rules to Tiered Entities*

Treas.Reg. § 1.704–1(b)(2)(iii)(*d*) provides that in determining the substantiality of an allocation to a look-through entity that is a partner, the effect of the interaction of the allocation with the tax attributes of the owner of the look-through entity must be taken into account. Look-through entities include a partnership, S corporation, estate, trust, disregarded entity, or controlled foreign corporation that owns at least 10% of the capital or profits of the partnership. In addition, in the case of an allocation to a corporate partner that is a member of a consolidated group, the effect of the allocation on the tax attributes of members of the group is taken into account.

2.   SHIFTING ALLOCATIONS

Treas.Reg. § 1.704–1(b)(2)(iii)(*b*) elaborates the general rule by providing that an allocation that merely shifts tax consequences within a given year and does not affect the economic consequences to the partners will not be substantial. This special rule addresses allocations that, when viewed together with other allocations, result in a net increase or decrease in the partners' capital accounts that does not differ from what would have resulted without the special allocations, but that have the effect of reducing the partners' total tax liability. Assume, for example, that C and D are equal partners. In the year in question, the CD partnership recognizes a $10,000 capital loss and an operating loss of $10,000. In that same taxable year, C individually recognizes capital gains of $10,000, and D individually recognizes no capital gains. If both items were allocated equally between the partners, C and D each would decrease the capital account by $10,000. C would be able personally to deduct $5,000 of the operating loss and $5,000 of the capital loss. D would be able to deduct $5,000 of the operating loss but, due to § 1211(b), only $3,000 of the capital loss. If the partners amended the partnership agreement to allocate the entire capital loss to C and the entire operating loss to D, C and D would still decrease each partner's capital account by $10,000. Thus, such an allocation has economic effect. However, the net decreases in the partners' capital accounts do not differ substantially from the net decreases that would have occurred without the allocation. Due to the ability of C to deduct currently all of the capital losses, the total tax liability of the partners' will be less than it would be without the allocation. Thus, the allocation does not have "substantial" economic effect. The allocation will not be respected, and each item will be allocated in proportion to each partner's interest in the partnership, which will likely be equally, in accordance with the net decreases in the partners' capital accounts.

If, on the other hand, at the time the partnership agreement was amended to provide for the above described allocation there was not a strong likelihood that the partnership would have substantially equal amounts of capital losses and operating losses, then the allocation would have substantial economic effect. Avoiding the shifting allocation rule is difficult, however. The Regulations provide that if, at the end of the year for which a special shifting allocation is in effect, the changes in partners' capital accounts during the year do not differ substantially from the changes that would have occurred if the special allocation had not been in effect, a presumption arises that there was a strong likelihood that the proscribed effect would occur. See Treas.Reg. § 1.704–1(b)(5), Ex. (6), (7), and (10).

3. TRANSITORY ALLOCATIONS

3.1. *In General*

Treas.Reg. § 1.704–1(b)(2)(iii)(*c*) provides another special application of the substantiality rule by treating transitory allocations as insubstantial. An allocation is transitory if: (1) the allocation may be offset by another allocation; (2) at the time the allocations are included in the partnership agreement there is a strong likelihood that the net increases and decreases in the partners' respective capital accounts will not differ substantially from what they would have been absent the initial special allocation and the offsetting allocation; and (3) the total tax liability of the partners will be less than it would have been if the allocations were not in the partnership agreement. If, however, there is a strong likelihood that the offsetting allocations will not be made within five years of the initial allocation, the allocations are presumed to be substantial. As in the case of shifting allocations, occurrence of the proscribed outcome results in the presumption that the allocations were transitory.

The transitory allocation rule applies, for example, in the following circumstances. Assume that the EFGH Partnership owns and operates a rental property, which can be predicted to produce net income of $12,000 per year for each of the next four years. Each partner has a one-quarter capital interest. E has a $9,000 net operating loss carryover under § 172 from an unrelated business that is about to expire. The partnership agreement is amended to allocate to E three-quarters of the partnership net income for the last year in which E can use E's net operating loss carryover, with the other one-quarter being divided equally among F, G, and H, and to allocate one-twelfth of the net income of the partnership to E and the remaining eleven-twelfths equally among F, G, and H for each of the next three years. As a result, E is allocated an additional $6,000 of net income in the first year, while each of the other partners is allocated $2,000 less net income than they otherwise would have been allocated. Over the next three years, E is allocated a total of $6,000 less than E would otherwise have been allocated, and each of the other partners is allocated a total of $2,000 more.

Without Special Allocation

	Year 1	Year 2	Year 3	Year 4	Total
E	$3,000	$3,000	$3,000	$3,000	$12,000
F	$3,000	$3,000	$3,000	$3,000	$12,000
G	$3,000	$3,000	$3,000	$3,000	$12,000
H	$3,000	$3,000	$3,000	$3,000	$12,000

With Special Allocation

	Year 1	Year 2	Year 3	Year 4	Total
E	$9,000	$1,000	$1,000	$1,000	$12,000
F	$1,000	$3,667	$3,667	$3,666	$12,000
G	$1,000	$3,667	$3,667	$3,666	$12,000
H	$1,000	$3,667	$3,667	$3,666	$12,000

On these facts, there was at the time the allocations were made a strong likelihood that over the four-year span each partner would be allocated $12,000 of net income. The allocation to E of more income in the first year was cancelled out by the allocation to E of less of the income in the next three years. Thus, the allocation is transitory and, since it reduced the partners' taxes over the four-year span by allowing E to use E's net operating loss carryover, it will not be respected. The net income of the partnership will be allocated equally in each of the four years. See Treas.Reg. § 1.704–1(b)(5), Ex. (8).

3.2. *Gain Chargebacks*

An important factor in applying the transitory allocation rule is the presumption in Treas.Reg. § 1.704–1(b)(2)(iii)(*c*)(*2*) that the actual fair market value of property decreases by tax depreciation. In some cases, this rule is necessary to prevent a special allocation of depreciation coupled with a gain chargeback on the disposition of property from giving rise to a transitory allocation. As a result of this assumption, any gain that may be realized on the sale of depreciable property is not taken into account in determining whether there was a strong likelihood that an allocation of gain offsetting the depreciation deductions would occur within five years.

Because liquidating distributions must be made in accordance with positive capital account balances, economic considerations of the partners dictate that gain chargebacks be part and parcel of provisions in partnership agreements specially allocating depreciation deductions. As the *Orrisch* opinion points out, if the property is sold for at least its original cost, the special allocation of deductions and the corresponding "chargeback" of gain only affect tax liabilities and do not affect the proceeds received by each partner. The cash proceeds are distributed as if no special allocation had been made. The Regulations, however, take the position that this does not mean that there is no substantial economic effect to the allocations if there is a strong likelihood that the offsetting allocations will not be made within five years. The theory underlying this rule appears to be that an allocation that has effect for such a time interval interposes sufficient risk that the partnership will suffer an actual loss that cannot be eliminated by offsetting a future special allocation, such as a gain chargeback. Furthermore, due to the conclusive presumption in Treas.Reg. § 1.704–1(b)(2)(iii)(c)(2) that the fair market value of the property decreased by tax depreciation, even if a sale of the property within five years at a price equal to its original cost is a virtual certainty, the allocation of depreciation coupled with the gain chargeback is not transitory, since there is no strong likelihood of the gain occurring.

3.3. *Recapture Gain*

An allocation of recapture gain on disposition of property, usually § 1245 depreciation recapture, cannot have substantial economic effect because classifying gain as recapture merely changes the tax characterization of the gain from § 1231 gain to ordinary income. Furthermore, if recapture gain were allocated in the same manner as total gain, a partner might be allocated recapture gain that exceeded the partner's share of prior depreciation attributable to the property while another partner would be allocated recapture gain less than that partner's share of prior depreciation attributable to the property. Because recapture gain is intended to offset the earlier depreciation deductions, recapture should be allocated to the partner who received those depreciation deductions. Treas.Reg. § 1.1245–1(e)(2) addresses this issue by providing that a partner's share of recapture gain equals the lesser of (1) the partner's share of total gain arising from the disposition of the property, or (2) the partner's share of depreciation or amortization from the property. Any recapture gain that is not allocated under the general rule is allocated among those partners whose shares of total gain on the disposition of the property exceed their shares of depreciation or amortization with respect to the property. If after applying these rules, the aggregate amount of recapture income allocated to the partners exceeds the partnership's recapture income, the partnership's recapture income is allocated among the partners in proportion to their shares of prior depreciation (subject to the gain ceiling rule). Treas.Reg. § 1.1245–1(e)(2)(ii)(C)(4). These rules are intended to insure, to the extent possible, that on the disposition of property each partner will recognize recapture income equal to the depreciation or amortization deductions previously allocated to that partner with respect to the property. A mismatch nevertheless may occur if, for example, the gain allocated to a partner on the sale of a property is less than the depreciation previously allocated to that partner. The Regulations provide special rules for determining a partner's share of depreciation or amortization from contributed property subject to § 704(c). See Section 3 of this Chapter.

4. SECTION 1061

Section 1061, added in 2017, applicable to the exchange of services for a profits interest in certain investment-focused partnerships, such as private equity partnerships, requires that the service partner treat as short-term capital gain the excess (if any) of the partner's net long-term capital gain with respect to the interest over the partner's net long-term capital gain computed as though § 1222 said "3 years" instead of "1 year." Regulations have not yet been proposed, and there is uncertainty surrounding the provision. It seems clear (as will be discussed in Chapter 24) that the three-year holding period applies to the partnership interest itself when determining gain on the transfer of the interest. How the provision operates with respect to partnership assets and distributive shares is ambiguous: does it depend on the partnership's capital asset holding period, the partner's holding period in the partner's interest, or both? To the extent § 1061 affects the character of distributive share allocations, special allocations intended to reduce the impact of § 1061 will require careful evaluation under the substantiality requirement.

5.   EFFECT OF BUSINESS PURPOSE

Judicial interpretation of the pre-1976 version of § 704(b), which disallowed allocations if the principal purpose was tax avoidance or evasion, focused primarily on the substantial economic effect test, but sometimes the partners' tax avoidance motives were considered as well. The statutory emphasis of current § 704(b), however, is on the substantial economic effect test for determining the validity of partnership allocations. Estate of Carberry v. Commissioner, 933 F.2d 1124 (2d Cir.1991), specifically rejected the taxpayer's argument that a business purpose could validate an allocation of loss to a partner when the loss did not have substantial economic effect. Even if there is an alleged business purpose for an allocation, the validity of the allocation for tax purposes turns on whether it has substantial economic effect. See also Young v. Commissioner, 923 F.2d 719 (9th Cir.1991). But the Senate Finance Committee Report states that the intent of the 1976 version of § 704(b) is "to prevent the use of special allocations for tax avoidance purposes while allowing their use for bona fide business purposes." Arguably, this language leaves room to consider the partners' purpose for the allocation, including whether an allocation that meets the mechanical tests of the Regulations may be invalidated if it has a tax avoidance purpose. In TIFD III-E, Inc. v. United States, 342 F.Supp.2d 94 (D. Conn. 2004), rev'd 459 F.3d 220 (2d Cir. 2006), the District Court concluded that satisfaction of the mechanical rules of the Regulations under § 704(b) transcends both an intent to avoid tax and the avoidance of significant tax through agreed upon partnership allocations. The Second Circuit reversed, finding that the arrangement did not create a partnership. On remand, notwithstanding the Second Circuit's opinion that the arrangement was not a partnership, the District Court nevertheless again held the arrangement to be a partnership, this time by applying an earlier version of § 704(e), 660 F. Supp. 2d. 367 (D. Conn. 2009), but the District Court was reversed yet again on appeal, with the Second Circuit reaffirming that the arrangement was not a partnership. 666 F.3d 836 (2d Cir. 2012). (This was not the end of the saga: see 604 Fed. Appx. 69 (2d Cir. 2015), reversing 8 F. Supp. 3d 142 (D. Conn.) and upholding a negligence penalty.) See also § 7701(o) (economic substance doctrine);

Treas.Reg. § 1.701–2 (anti-abuse Regulations) and § 1.704–1(b)(1)(iii) (determination under § 704(b) is not conclusive of the tax treatment).

PROBLEM SET 2

1.   Carlos and Diana formed a general partnership to invest in a small commercial office building. Each contributed $100,000 to the partnership, which also borrowed $800,000 from the First State Bank to acquire a building for $1,000,000. Unfortunately, Carlos and Diana purchased their building at the height of a real estate boom. One year after the investment the value of the building declined to $600,000, and the rental income was insufficient to meet payments on the loan. In addition, Carlos, but not Diana, was insolvent. First State Bank agreed to reduce the loan principal to $600,000. Diana contributed $5,000 to the EF partnership to pay the costs of the loan adjustment. Because of Diana's capital contribution, the EF partnership revalued its capital accounts to fair market value pursuant to Treas.Reg. § 1.704–1(b)(2)(iv)(*f*). Carlos and Diana also amended their partnership agreement to allocate the $5,000 expenditure to Diana, allocate the revaluation loss $300,000 to Carlos and $100,000 to Diana, and to allocate discharge of indebtedness income to Carlos. The partnership agreement provides for properly maintained capital accounts and for liquidation distributions to be made in accord with the capital accounts. There is no provision for a deficit make-up. Do these allocations have substantial economic effect?

2.   (a) Eddie and Fran formed a general partnership to operate an adventure vacation tour company, offering hunting, fishing, and whitewater rafting in the Canadian and U.S. Rocky Mountains. Eddie is a Canadian resident; Fran is a U.S. resident. The partnership agreement provides that the partners' capital accounts will be maintained as required by the § 704(b) Regulations, liquidating distributions will be made in accordance with the partners' capital account balances, and any partner must restore a negative capital account upon liquidation. The partnership agreement provides that Eddie will be allocated 80% and Fran 20% of the income or loss from Canadian trips, and Fran will be allocated 80% and Eddie 20% of the income or loss from U.S. trips. The amount of income or loss from each source cannot be predicted with any reasonable certainty. Do these allocations have substantial economic effect?

   (b) Assume the same facts as in (a) except that the partnership agreement provides that all income or loss will be shared equally, but that Eddie will be allocated all income or loss derived from Canadian operations as a part of his equal share of partnership income or loss, up to the amount of that share. As a result of this allocation, the total tax liability of Eddie and Fran for each year to which these allocations relate will be reduced. Do these allocations have substantial economic effect?

3.   Gail and Haley formed a partnership to develop and market computer software. Gail contributed $10,000 in cash, and Haley contributed $200,000. The partnership agreement provides that all § 174 deductions for research and experimental expenditures are to be allocated to Haley. In addition,

Haley will be allocated 90%, and Gail 10%, of all partnership income or loss, excluding allowed § 174 deductions research and experimental expenditures, until Haley has received aggregate allocations of income equal to the sum of such § 174 deductions and his share of such taxable loss. Thereafter, Gail and Haley will share all taxable income and loss equally. Operating cash flow will be distributed equally between Gail and Haley. The partnership agreement also provides that Gail's and Haley's capital accounts will be determined and maintained in accordance with the § 704(b) Regulations, liquidating distributions will be made in accordance with the partners' capital account balances, and that upon liquidation partners must restore deficit capital account balances. Do these allocations have substantial economic effect?

B. ALLOCATIONS ATTRIBUTABLE TO NONRECOURSE DEBT

REGULATIONS: Section 1.704–2 (omitting (h)(3) and (4), (*i*), (j)(1)(ii), (j)(2)(i), (k) through (m)).

It is not uncommon for real estate transactions and other acquisitions to be financed with nonrecourse mortgage debt or other nonrecourse secured debt. Allocations of deductions, e.g., depreciation, attributable to nonrecourse debt present special problems. Treas.Reg. § 1.704–2(b)(1) provides that an allocation of such deductions never can have economic effect because only the creditor bears the burden of economic loss. Accordingly, losses and deductions attributable to nonrecourse debt, which are termed "nonrecourse deductions," must be allocated in accordance with the partners' interests in the partnership. Since allocation of losses under Treas.Reg. § 1.704–1(b)(3), which determines a partner's interest in the partnership if an allocation in the agreement does not have economic effect, turns on risk of loss, it might at first appear that no partner could be allocated any deductions attributable to nonrecourse debt. Pursuant to Treas.Reg. § 1.704–2, however, allocations will be deemed to be made in accordance with the partners' interest in the partnership, and thus given effect, if certain requirements are met.

The rules governing allocations of nonrecourse deductions generally come into play only after previous allocations of losses and deductions have eliminated the partnership's equity in property subject to nonrecourse debt. See Treas.Reg. § 1.704–2(f)(7), Ex. (2). (This rule of thumb is based on the assumption that the fair market value of the property equals the book value of the property.) In addition, deductions attributable to recourse debt are stacked before deductions attributable to nonrecourse debt. Assume, for example, that E and F form a limited partnership in which E is the general partner and F is the limited partner. As equal partners, E and F each contribute $10, the partnership borrows $20 with recourse, borrows $60 nonrecourse, and purchases a depreciable asset for $100. Each year the partnership realizes neither a profit nor a loss apart from depreciation deductions. The opening balance sheet of the EF Partnership is as follows:

	Assets		Partnership Liabilities & Partners' Capital Accounts		
	Book Value	Tax Basis		Book Value	Tax Basis
Property	$100	$100	Recourse Debt	$ 20	n/a
			Nonrecourse Debt	$ 60	n/a
			E	$ 10	$ 60
			F	$ 10	$ 40
Total	$100	$100		$100	$100

The first $40 of depreciation deductions are attributable to E's and F's capital contributions representing an equity investment in the property plus the recourse debt. Thus, Treas.Reg. § 1.704–2 does not apply until the basis of the depreciable asset has been reduced to $60. The first $40 of depreciation deductions, which result in reduction of the partnership's basis for the asset to $60, must be allocated under the substantial economic effect test of Treas.Reg. § 1.704–1(b). Deductions attributable to the recourse debt must be allocated to E, as the general partner, since only E bears the economic risk for repayment of that debt.

A partnership can have nonrecourse deductions generated by a property subject to nonrecourse debt even though the partners still have positive capital accounts attributable to an equity investment in another property. See Treas.Reg. § 1.704–2(f)(7), Ex. (2). Assume, for example, that G and H form the GH Partnership to which they each contribute $50. The GH Partnership purchases undeveloped land, with $80 of the money that G and H contributed. Contemporaneously, the GH Partnership borrows $180 from a third-party lender on a nonrecourse basis and purchases a depreciable asset for $200. Assume further that the basis of the depreciable asset is recovered over 5 years on the straight-line method (ignore conventions). The initial balance sheet of the partnership is as follows:

Assets	Book Value	Tax Basis	Partnership Liabilities & Partners' Capital Accounts	Book Value	Tax Basis
Land	$ 80	$ 80	Nonrecourse Debt	$180	n/a
Depreciable Asset	$200	$200	G	$ 50	$140
			H	$ 50	$140
Total	$280	$280		$280	$280

After one year, the book value and tax basis of the depreciable asset both have been reduced to $160 as a result of $40 of depreciation. Assuming that the partnership had neither net income nor loss apart from the $40 depreciation deduction, the balance sheet of the partnership after Year 1 is as follows:

Assets	Book Value	Tax Basis	Partnership Liabilities & Partners' Capital Accounts	Book Value	Tax Basis
Land	$ 80	$ 80	Nonrecourse Debt	$180	n/a
Depreciable Asset	$160	$160	G	$ 30	$120
			H	$ 30	$120
Total	$240	$240		$240	$240

Because the amount of the nonrecourse debt encumbering the depreciable asset is $180, and its book value/tax basis is only $160, the partnership has $20 of minimum gain with respect to the asset after Year 1; thus, $20 of the $40 Year 1 depreciation was a nonrecourse deduction.

The requirements of Treas.Reg. § 1.704–2 are based on the fact that, under the principles of Commissioner v. Tufts, 461 U.S. 300 (1983), now codified in § 7701(g), the partnership's amount realized on the disposition of property encumbered by nonrecourse debt may not be less than the nonrecourse debt. The adjustments to book value/tax basis caused by depreciation deductions will mean that the partnership will eventually recognize gain equal to the depreciation deductions attributable to nonrecourse debt. The object of these rules is to allocate the gain on the disposition to the partners who enjoyed the benefit of the earlier depreciation deductions. This result is achieved through the interaction of four provisions that must be included in the partnership agreement.

First, Treas.Reg. § 1.704–2(e)(1) requires that capital accounts be maintained under the rules of Treas.Reg. § 1.704–1(b)(4) as required by Treas.Reg. § 1.704–1(b)(2)(ii)(*b*)(*1*), and liquidating distributions must be made in accordance with positive capital account balances under the rules of Treas.Reg. § 1.704–1(b)(2)(ii)(*b*)(*2*). In addition, the partnership agreement is required either (1) to provide a deficit make-up obligation with respect to partners with negative capital account balances or (2) to contain a "qualified income offset." See Treas.Reg. § 1.704–1(b)(2)(ii)(*b*)(*3*) and (*d*)(*3*). Thus, where, as is usually the case in a partnership with nonrecourse deductions, one or more of the partners do not have a deficit make-up obligation, the partnership agreement is required to satisfy the alternate test for economic effect under Treas.Reg. § 1.704–1(b)(2)(ii)(*d*). For purposes of the alternate test, a partner's share of minimum gain is treated as an obligation to restore a negative capital account in that amount. Treas.Reg. § 1.704–2(g)(1). Thus, nonrecourse deductions may be allocated to a partner even though they result in a partner having a negative capital account without violating the requirements of the alternative economic effect test.

Second, beginning in the first year of the partnership in which the partnership has deductions attributable to nonrecourse indebtedness, and for all partnership years thereafter, the partnership agreement must provide for allocations of nonrecourse deductions among the partners in a manner that is reasonably consistent with allocations that have substantial economic effect of some other significant partnership item attributable to the property securing the nonrecourse liability (other than minimum gain realized by the partnership). Treas.Reg. § 1.704–2(e)(2). Although the Regulations do not specify a list of "significant partnership items," Treas.Reg. § 1.704–2(m), Ex. (1)(ii) indicates that gross operating income and cash flow deductions qualify, as does gain or loss on a sale of the property. If the partners' shares of operating income and gain or loss on a sale of the property differ, either ratio, or any ratio in between the two, will meet the "reasonably consistent" requirement.

Third, beginning with the year in which nonrecourse deductions are first claimed or the proceeds of a nonrecourse borrowing are first distributed, the partnership agreement must provide for a "minimum gain chargeback," described below.

Fourth, all other material partnership allocations and capital account adjustments must be recognized under Treas.Reg. § 1.704–1(b). Generally speaking, this final requirement means that allocations of net income or of losses attributable to partners' capital accounts must have substantial economic effect. But the requirement also can be satisfied if allocations are in accordance with the partners' interests in the partnership—for example, the pro rata allocation of all items among members of an LLC or partnership in which the partners shared all gains and losses (and had rights to distributions) in proportion to their capital contributions.

DETAILED ANALYSIS

1. NONRECOURSE DEDUCTIONS

The special rules of Treas.Reg. § 1.704–2 apply only to the allocation of "nonrecourse deductions." The amount of nonrecourse deductions of a partnership equals the increase, if any, in the amount of partnership "minimum gain" during the year. "Minimum gain" is the sum of the amounts, computed separately with respect to each item of partnership property, that would be realized for book purposes if in a taxable transaction the partnership disposed of the property in full satisfaction of the nonrecourse liability secured by it. Treas.Reg. § 1.704–2(d). Thus, a partnership cannot have minimum gain as long as the book value of property secured by a nonrecourse mortgage equals or exceeds the amount of the mortgage debt. (The Regulations specify that if there is a disparity between book value and basis, book value is to be used; thus, using book value will yield the correct result. Treas.Reg. § 1.704–2(d)(3).) For example, assume that the CD partnership purchased an apartment building for $100, paying $20 of the purchase price with partnership capital and $80 with the proceeds of a nonrecourse mortgage. At a time when the book value and adjusted basis of the property are $60 and the balance due on the mortgage is $75, the minimum gain is $15 since that is the amount of book gain that would be recognized if the partnership were to deed the property to the mortgagee in satisfaction of the debt. Nonrecourse deductions are treated as consisting first of cost recovery or depreciation deductions attributable to properties giving rise to the increase in "minimum gain," and then of a pro rata share of other partnership deductions. Treas.Reg. § 1.704–2(c), (j)(1)(ii).

2. "MINIMUM GAIN CHARGEBACK"

2.1. *In General*

A partnership agreement contains a "minimum gain chargeback" only if it provides that if there is a net decrease in partnership minimum gain during a partnership year, each partner must be allocated income or gain in proportion to the greater of the deficit in the partner's capital account (excluding a deficit the partner must restore) or the partner's share of the decrease in minimum gain. Treas.Reg. § 1.704–2(b)(2) and (f). Minimum gain obviously is reduced when there is a sale or other disposition of the mortgaged property, for example, foreclosure of the mortgage. More often, however, minimum gain is reduced and the chargeback triggered as a mortgage loan is amortized. The chargeback also can be triggered by other events, e.g., by a capital contribution by one partner that is invested to increase the basis of partnership assets or by one partner guaranteeing all or part of a previously nonrecourse debt. A minimum gain chargeback must be allocated before any other allocation of any partnership items for the year is made under § 704(b). The Regulations provide rules for determining a partner's share of minimum gain, as well as certain exceptions to the general rules and specific rules to cover a variety of particular transactions. Treas.Reg. § 1.704–2(g), (j)(2)(i). The purpose of the minimum gain chargeback rule is to assure that an offsetting amount of gain is allocated to the partners who received the economic benefit that gave rise to partnership minimum gain. That benefit could have been in the form of either nonrecourse deductions or distributions of proceeds from nonrecourse refinancing of partnership property. Treas.Reg. § 1.704–2(b)(2).

The minimum gain chargeback concept is derived from the more general gain chargeback principle discussed in *Orrisch* (excerpted above in Section 1) and in connection with Treas.Reg. § 1.704–1(b). Minimum gain chargebacks under Treas.Reg. § 1.704–2, however, differ significantly from ordinary gain chargebacks. First, special allocations of deductions attributable to partners' contributions and recourse debt may or may not be subject to a gain chargeback provision, as the partners choose, but all allocations attributable to nonrecourse debt must be subject to a minimum gain chargeback. Second, a routine gain chargeback may relate to whatever portion of prior deductions the partners want, while a minimum gain chargeback must apply to all prior deductions attributable to nonrecourse debt.

2.2. *Waiver of Minimum Gain Chargeback Requirement*

Treas.Reg. § 1.704–2(f)(4) provides that a partnership may request that the IRS waive application of the requirement that a decrease in partnership minimum gain triggers a minimum gain chargeback if application of the minimum gain chargeback would distort the economic relationship among the partners (because of the effect of the chargeback on capital accounts), and it is expected that the partnership will not have sufficient other income to correct the distortion. A waiver of the gain chargeback may be appropriate where there has been additional capital contributed to the partnership to pay down nonrecourse debts or if before the partnership realizes a decrease in partnership minimum gain, the partnership has allocated income to a partner to offset prior nonrecourse deductions allocated to that partner. Treas.Reg. § 1.704–2(f)(7), Ex. (1) illustrates a situation in which such a waiver may be appropriate.

3.   EXAMPLES

3.1. *Depreciation Deductions and Gain on Sale*

Operation of the basic rules governing allocations of nonrecourse deductions is illustrated in the following example. Suppose that C and D respectively contribute $20,000 and $80,000 to the CD Partnership, which then borrows $900,000 from an unrelated lender on a nonrecourse promissory note secured by depreciable property for which the partnership pays $1,000,000. Also suppose that no principal payments are due on the note for the first five years and that $50,000 of depreciation is allowable on the property each year. The partnership agreement requires that capital accounts be maintained in accordance with the Regulations, that liquidation be in accordance with capital accounts, and that C, but not D (who is a limited partner), is required to restore a negative capital account. Because the partnership has $100,000 of equity in the property, the first two years of depreciation deductions (assuming that the partnership does not have any income or loss from other items) are not nonrecourse deductions. At the end of two years, the basis of the property will be $900,000, and the mortgage lien will be the same amount; there is no "minimum gain." Accordingly, D may be allocated up to $80,000 of the first two years' depreciation under the economic effect rules, and C must be allocated at least $20,000 of depreciation. (C may be allocated more than $20,000 of depreciation, and D may be allocated correspondingly less depreciation, and those allocations would still have economic effect.)

At the end of Year 2, the CD Partnership's balance sheet is as follows:

	Assets			Partnership Liabilities & Partners' Capital Accounts	
	Book Value	Tax Basis		Book Value	Tax Basis
Property	$900,000	$900,000	Nonrecourse Debt	$900,000	n/a
			C	$ 0	$180,000
	_____	_____	D	$ 0	$720,000
Total	$900,000	$900,000		$900,000	$900,000

In Year 3, the depreciation deduction reduces the property's basis to $850,000, and $50,000 of minimum gain arises because, if the partnership transferred the property subject to the mortgage (and for no additional consideration), it would recognize this amount of gain for book and tax purposes. See Treas.Reg. § 1.704–2(m), Ex. (1)(i). Neither partner bears the economic risk of loss with respect to this deduction (because the only remedy the creditor has is to foreclose on the property); as a result, no allocation of the deduction can have substantial economic effect. Nevertheless, an allocation will be deemed to be in accordance with the partners' interests in the partnership if the partnership agreement contains a minimum gain chargeback provision and if the deduction is allocated between C and D in any proportion that is reasonably consistent with some other significant allocation relating to the property that has substantial economic effect (as long as a corresponding amount of minimum gain is allocated to each partner).

A special allocation of depreciation alone, with all other items being allocated according to a different consistent fraction, will not meet the regulatory safe harbor.[8] Thus, for example, if C and D agreed to share all income, gain, cash flow deductions, and distributions 60% to C and 40% to D, the only permissible allocation of depreciation attributable to nonrecourse debt (as well as accrued interest if the partnership was an accrual method taxpayer) would be 60% to C and 40% to D. However, partnership agreements often provide for different allocations of items at different times. For example, the agreement may provide that all items of income and deduction, and all distributions will be allocated 80% to D and 20% to C until D has received distributions of $100,000, and thereafter all items and

---

[8] The requirement that allocations of deductions be consistent with allocations of some other item that has substantial economic effect is unique to allocations of deductions attributable to nonrecourse debt. No such requirement attaches to allocations attributable to recourse debt.

distributions will be allocated 50:50 (a so-called "flip-flop"). In this case depreciation may be allocated either equally or 80% to D and 20% to C, or anywhere in the range between those two allocations. In any case, C and D must be allocated the proper amount of minimum gain chargeback. Note that an allocation of minimum gain chargeback alone is not another significant item with substantial economic effect.

Assume then that the agreement validly allocates the depreciation 80% to D and 20% to C. At the end of Year 3, D has a capital account deficit of $40,000, and C has a deficit of $10,000. The balance sheet of the partnership is as follows:

	Assets			Partnership Liabilities & Partners' Capital Accounts	
	Book Value	Tax Basis		Book Value	Tax Basis
Property	$850,000	$850,000	Nonrecourse Debt	$900,000	n/a
			C	($ 10,000)	$170,000
			D	($ 40,000)	$680,000
Total	$850,000	$850,000		$850,000	$850,000

If the property were deeded to the lender in lieu of foreclosure of the mortgage on the first day of Year 4, the partnership would recognize a gain of $50,000—the "minimum gain"—which would be allocated $40,000 to D and $10,000 to C, thereby restoring their respective capital accounts to a zero balance.

3.2. *Depreciation Deductions and Loan Principal Amortization*

A minimum gain chargeback must occur not only when the property is sold but anytime that there is a decrease in partnership minimum gain. Thus, loan principal amortization requires that income be allocated to the partners in the same ratio as the special allocation of depreciation. For example, suppose that the CD Partnership did not sell the property at the beginning of Year 4 but continued to hold the property and paid $100,000 of principal on the first day of Year 6. At that time, the basis of the property would be $750,000. Reduction of the loan principal from $900,000 to $800,000 reduces partnership minimum gain from 150,000 to $50,000, and assuming that the partnership has at least $100,000 of income in Year 6, that amount must be allocated among C and D in the same ratio that nonrecourse depreciation deductions previously had been allocated. (If the partnership has more than $100,000 of income, Treas.Reg. § 1.704–2(j)(2)(i) provides an ordering rule.) Thus, if in Years 3 through 5, D had been allocated $120,000 of depreciation and C had been allocated $30,000 of depreciation, D must be allocated $80,000 of the income, and C must be allocated $20,000. Note that the depreciation allocated in the first two years, which had actual substantial economic effect, is not considered in allocating income pursuant to the minimum gain chargeback.

Despite the fact that nonrecourse depreciation deductions never have substantial economic effect because they cannot affect the actual dollar amounts received by any partner, the Regulations allow them to be allocated among the partners as long as the corresponding income items are allocated in the same manner. Through the minimum gain chargeback provision, the Regulations assure that allocations of nonrecourse depreciation ultimately will be entirely offset by future income allocations. This system is justifiable, given Subchapter K's approach of allowing partners to include basis attributable to debt, because otherwise there would be no way to allocate nonrecourse deductions to *any* partner, even though the deductions must be taken into account in computing partnership taxable income. The requirement that allocations of nonrecourse deductions be reasonably consistent with allocations having substantial economic effect of some other significant partnership item attributable to the secured property is designed to prevent abusive special allocations that specially allocate deductions (but not income) to one or more partners when the minimum gain that will eventually offset those deductions is not expected to be realized until many years in the future.

3.3. *Minimum Gain Attributable to Distributions*

Partnership minimum gain also can arise when the partnership refinances by borrowing money on a nonrecourse basis with the loan being secured by property already owned by the partnership. Suppose, for example, that the ABC Partnership, which owns Blackacre, with a basis of $1,000 and a fair market value of $6,000, borrows $4,000 nonrecourse, pledging Blackacre, which is otherwise unencumbered, as security. As a result of the nonrecourse borrowing secured by Blackacre, the ABC partnership now may have up to $3,000 of partnership minimum gain; the amount will depend on the extent any partner's share of minimum gain increases. Treas.Reg. § 1.704–2(d)(1). (For example, if the borrowed funds are retained as cash balances, no partner's share of minimum gain increases, and thus there is no partnership minimum gain.) If the partnership then distributes the loan proceeds to the partners, each partner's share of minimum gain equals the amount of the distribution to that partner of the proceeds of the nonrecourse loan allocable to an increase in partnership minimum gain. Treas.Reg. § 1.704–2(g)(1). Pursuant to Treas.Reg. § 1.704–2(h)(1), the distribution to the partner is allocable to an increase in partnership minimum gain to the extent the increase results from encumbering partnership property with aggregate nonrecourse liabilities that exceed the property's book value. Thus, for example, if $2,000 were distributed to A and $1,000 were distributed to each of B and C (thereby reducing their capital accounts and bases), the partnership has $3,000 of minimum gain, which is allocated $1,500 to A and $750 to each of B and C. If the partnership were to repay, $1,000 of the loan in the following year, A would be allocated a minimum gain chargeback of $500 and each of B and C would be allocated a minimum gain chargeback of $250 before any other allocations were made under § 704(b).

4.   PARTNERSHIP NONRECOURSE DEBT FOR WHICH A PARTNER BEARS THE RISK OF LOSS

Special rules govern the allocation of deductions attributable to debt that is nonrecourse as to the partnership but as to which a partner bears the economic risk of loss (e.g., a partnership nonrecourse debt that is guaranteed by a partner without any right of indemnification). Treas.Reg. § 1.704–2(*i*) requires that all deductions attributable to such debt be allocated to the partner (or partners) who bear the risk of loss. See also Treas.Reg. § 1.704–2(j)(1)(i), (2)(ii).

5.   JUDICIAL INTERPRETATION OF NONRECOURSE DEBT DEDUCTION REGULATIONS

In Interhotel Co. Ltd. v. Commissioner, T.C. Memo. 2001–151, on remand from 221 F.3d 1348 (9th Cir. 2000), rev'g, T.C. Memo. 1997–44, the Tax Court applied the minimum gain chargeback rules to determine whether special allocations were consistent with the partners' interest in a partnership under the hypothetical comparative liquidation test of Treas.Reg. § 1.704–1(b)(3)(iii), discussed above in Section 2.A(1), Detailed Analysis 5.2. The Interhotel partnership owned interests in two second-tier partnerships that held hotel properties subject to nonrecourse debt and that were depreciated below the amount of the debt, thereby creating minimum gain. The Interhotel partnership agreement provided for liquidation according to positive capital account balances, but it neither required the restoration of negative capital accounts nor provided a qualified income offset as required by Treas.Reg. § 1.704–1(b)(2)(ii)(d). The general partner's partnership interest nominally was 85% and the limited partner's interest nominally was 15%, but as a result of special allocations, the partnership income was allocated 1% to the general partner and 99% to the limited partner, while losses were allocated 85% to the general partner and 15% to the limited partner. As of June 20, 1991, the general partner's capital account was negative $5,920,614, and the limited partner's capital account was positive $14,879,392. In a complex transaction effective on June 21, 1991, the original limited partner's partnership interest was transferred to a new limited partner, who succeeded to the limited partner's positive capital account. In connection with the transfer of the limited partnership interest, the partnership agreement was amended to allocate all partnership income to any partner with a negative capital account, i.e., to the general partner, and, after negative capital accounts had been eliminated, in proportion to the partners' pro rata interests (85% to the general partner and 15% to the new limited partner). Pursuant to this amendment, all of the partnership's income for the remainder of 1991 was allocated to the general partner. The Commissioner asserted that the special allocation of 100% of the income to the general partner was not valid and that 99% of the partnership income— the share of partnership income that reflected the partnership interest of the limited partner's predecessor—was allocable to the limited partner. Because the partnership agreement, as amended, lacked economic effect under the basic test, the alternate economic effect test of Treas.Reg. § 1.704–1(b)(2)(ii)(*d*), or the economic effect equivalence test of Treas.Reg. § 1.704–1(b)(2)(ii)(*i*), the partners' interests in the partnership were determined under the comparative liquidation test of Treas.Reg. § 1.704–1(b)(3)(iii). That test was applied by comparing the liquidation proceeds available to the partners on a hypothetical liquidation of the partnership at the end of 1990, and again at the end of the 1991 tax year. The Commissioner conceded that liquidation of the Interhotel partnership would trigger recognition of its share of the built-in minimum gain of the two second-tier partnerships in which it held interests. Recognition of the minimum gain chargeback would increase the general partner's capital account and thereby eliminate the general partner's capital account deficit. As a consequence, allocation of the partnership income to the general partner was reflected in an increased positive capital account that would be distributable to the general partner in the hypothetical liquidation contemplated under Treas.Reg. § 1.704–1(b)(3)(iii). Allocation of all of the partnership income to the general partner therefore was consistent with the partners' interests in the partnership, even though it technically lacked economic effect.

6. NONRECOURSE DEDUCTIONS IN TARGETED ALLOCATIONS

As discussed in Section 2.A(1), Detailed Analysis 6, partnership agreements with targeted allocations are drafted to provide for liquidation distributions based on a partner's interest in distributable cash rather than on the basis of properly maintained capital accounts. For this reason, targeted allocations cannot have substantial economic effect, and they cannot satisfy the requirements for treating allocations of nonrecourse debt as being in accord with the partner's interest in the partnership under Treas.Reg. § 1.704–2 because they do not satisfy the requirement of Treas.Reg. § 1.704–2(e)(1) that liquidation distributions be in accord with properly maintained capital accounts. Nonetheless, the proponents of targeted allocations believe that allocations of nonrecourse debt in a targeted allocation structure will be sustained, as in *Interhotel,* as reflecting a partner's interest in the partnership.

In order to match the requirements of Treas.Reg. § 1.704–2 as closely as possible without providing for liquidation in accord with capital accounts, targeted allocation provisions are drafted to include provisions for a qualified income offset complying with Treas.Reg. § 1.704–1(b)(2)(ii)(*b*)(3) and a minimum gain chargeback under Treas.Reg. § 1.704–2(b)(2). As discussed earlier in this Chapter, under a targeted allocation structure, a partner's year-end distributable cash is determined as if the partnership sold its assets at book value and distributed the proceeds to the partners in accord with the partnership's cash waterfall provision. Items of book gain and loss are allocated to the partners so that capital accounts will reflect the distributable cash. The amount of distributable cash to each partner at the end of each year is determined by first taking into account allocations of nonrecourse deductions and the partner's share of partnership minimum gain. For this purpose, the book value of assets subject to nonrecourse debt is presumed to be equal to the amount of the debt. Thus, each partner's share of partnership minimum gain will equal the partner's share of nonrecourse deductions and the two items will offset each other in the determination of distributable cash. The net effect of the offsetting provisions is that allocations of nonrecourse debt and minimum gain will have no effect on the cash-based liquidation distributions to the partners.

The New York State Bar Association Tax Section, *Report on Partnership Target Allocations* (2010), illustrates the application of the minimum gain chargeback rules under targeted allocations with the following example. A and B form a partnership with each contributing $10,000. A and B agree that distributions will first go to A to the extent of A's capital contribution, then to B to the extent of B's capital contribution, and then 40% to A and 60% to B. The partnership borrows $80,000 through a nonrecourse loan and purchases a building for $100,000. Each year the building produces $9,000 of gross operating income and cash. None of the cash will be distributed until liquidation. The building also produces a $10,000 depreciation deduction each year, resulting in a $1,000 annual net loss (for simplicity assume no other deductions, including interest). The partners agree that nonrecourse deductions will be allocated 40% to A and 60% to B, matching the provision for distribution of profits, after a return of capital.[9] At the end of Year 1, under the presumption that the book value of the building declines at the rate of depreciation deductions, there is $19,000 of distributable cash in the partnership ($9,000 cash, $90,000 book value of the building, minus $80,000 due to the lender). Under the partnership distribution provisions, $10,000 is distributable to A and the remaining $9,000 is distributable to B. Thus, in order to match capital accounts to the distribution, the $1,000 partnership loss for the year is allocated to B.

	Distribution		Partners' Capital Accounts	
	A	B	A	B
Contribution	$10,000	$10,000	$10,000	$10,000
Year 1 Profit (Loss)		($ 1,000)		($ 1,000)
Distributable Cash	$10,000	$ 9,000	$10,000	$ 9,000

At the end of Year 2, distributable cash is reduced to $18,000, and again the $1,000 loss is allocated to B to account for the reduction in cash distributable to B.

---

[9] As discussed previously, Treas.Reg. § 1.704–2(e)(2) requires that nonrecourse deductions be allocated consistently with an allocation of a significant partnership item that has substantial economic effect. Treas.Reg. § 1.704–2(m), Ex. (1)(ii) indicates that cash flow or operating income are significant items. Thus, the allocation of nonrecourse deductions is consistent. However, since no targeted allocations have economic effect, the requirement of Treas.Reg. § 1.704–2(e)(2) can only be met in spirit.

	Distribution		Partners' Capital Accounts	
	A	B	A	B
Contribution	$10,000	$10,000	$10,000	$10,000
Year 1 Profit (Loss)		($ 1,000)		($ 1,000)
Year 2 Profit (Loss)		($ 1,000)		($ 1,000)
Distributable Cash	$10,000	$ 8,000	$10,000	$ 8,000

In Year 3, the $10,000 depreciation on the building reduces the book value of the building to $70,000, which is less than the nonrecourse debt, thereby creating $10,000 of minimum gain and a $10,000 nonrecourse deduction. Under the partnership agreement, the nonrecourse deduction is allocated $4,000 to A and $6,000 to B. For purposes of determining partnership allocations, each partner's opening "safe harbor capital account" balance is adjusted for both the partner's share of nonrecourse deductions and the partner's share of minimum gain. As a consequence, A's opening balance remains at $10,000, and B's remains at $8,000. The determination of the partner's distributable cash also requires that the book value of the building equal the amount of the outstanding nonrecourse debt, reflecting the fact that on sale of the building the partnership will recognize a $10,000 gain. With this adjustment, at the end of Year 3, the partnership has $27,000 of cash available for distribution ($9,000 of cash from each of three years; the building with an adjusted book value of $80,000 and the liability of $80,000 offset each other). Under the distribution waterfall, the cash is distributable first $10,000 to A, then $10,000 to B, then $2,800 to A (40% of the remaining $7,000), and $4,200 to B (60% of the remaining $7,000). In order to match the distributable amount to capital accounts, the $9,000 of partnership gross income would be allocated $2,800 to A and $6,200 to B.

	Distribution		Partners' Capital Accounts	
	A	B	A	B
Year 2 End Balance	$10,000	$ 8,000	$10,000	$ 8,000
Nonrecourse Deduction	($ 4,000)	($ 6,000)	($ 4,000)	($ 6,000)
Minimum Gain	$ 4,000	$ 6,000		
Partnership Income	$ 2,800	$ 6,200	$ 2,800	$ 6,200
Distributable Cash	$12,800	$14,200	$ 8,800	$ 8,200

Now assume that at the beginning of Year 4, the partnership sells the building for $80,000 and repays the lender. The $10,000 recognized gain, which is also a decrease in partnership minimum gain that is reduced to zero on repayment of the debt, is allocated $4,000 to A and $6,000 to B, reversing their Year 3 nonrecourse deductions. With the charge back of minimum gain to A and B, the cash distributable to each is the same as the partner's capital account.

	Distribution		Partners' Capital Accounts	
	A	B	A	B
Year 2 End Balance	$12,800	$14,200	$ 8,800	$ 8,200
Minimum Gain			$ 4,000	$ 6,000
Distributable Cash	$12,800	$14,200	$12,800	$14,200

In the end, the targeted allocations reflect the partners' economic interests in the partnership. Indeed, the targeted allocations are structured so that the allocation of tax items follows from the partners' economic interests, rather than deriving economic interests from capital accounts structured to follow the tax allocations, as is the case under the substantial economic effect rules of the Regulations.

PROBLEM SET 3

1. Charlie is the general partner, and Denise and Ella are the limited partners of the CDE limited partnership. Charlie contributed $10,000, and Denise and Ella each contributed $45,000 in cash. The initial contribution was used to purchase a parcel of land for $100,000. The partnership then borrowed $1,200,000 from an unrelated commercial lender on a nonrecourse basis to construct an office building to be held for rental. The loan requires only interest payments for 10 years, at the end of which time the full principal balance is due. The partnership agreement allocates all income, gain, loss, and deductions 10% to Charlie and 45% to each of Denise and Ella until the partnership cumulatively has recognized items of income and gain that equal its recognized items of deduction and loss. Thereafter, all partnership items will be allocated 20% to Charlie and 40% to each of Denise and Ella. The partnership agreement requires that capital accounts be properly maintained and that the partnership will be liquidated according to capital account balances. Only Charlie, the general partner, is required to restore a capital account deficit, but the partnership agreement contains a "qualified income offset" and a "minimum gain chargeback" provision. Rental income from the property equals deductible cash flow operating expenses. Assume that the property has a 30-year cost recovery period. Thus, annual taxable income is a net operating loss of $40,000.

(a) What is the significance of the "qualified income offset" and "minimum gain chargeback" provisions?

(b) How will the partnership's depreciation deductions be allocated among the partners for each of the first four years of the partnership?

(c) How would the partnership's depreciation deductions be allocated among the partners for each of the first four years of the partnership if the partnership agreement provided that Charlie would be allocated 2% and Denise and Ella each would be allocated 49% of the partnership's depreciation deductions, but all other items would be allocated as in the basic facts?

2.   Amy, Bill, and Casey are forming a limited liability company (that will be taxed as a partnership) to conduct a restaurant business in a leased building. Each of them will contribute $100,000 in cash to purchase furniture and equipment and to provide start-up working capital. Each of them will have an equal interest in the capital and profits of the LLC. Is it important that the LLC agreement comply with the alternate test for substantial economic effect provided in Treas.Reg. § 1.704–1(b)(2)(i)(*d*)?

SECTION 3.   ALLOCATIONS WITH RESPECT TO CONTRIBUTED PROPERTY

INTERNAL REVENUE CODE: Section 704(c)(1).

REGULATIONS: Section 1.704–3 (omitting (e)(3)); 1.197–2(g)(4).

Section 704(c) requires that allocations of income, deductions, or losses attributable to contributed property take into account the difference between the fair market value and basis of the property at the time of contribution. The purpose of this provision is to ensure that pre-contribution gains and losses are not shifted from the contributing partner to other partners. For example, assume that A and B form a partnership in which they will share profits and losses equally. A contributes property with a basis of $400 and a value of $1,000, and B contributes $1,000 cash. As between the partners, each has contributed property of equal value and each has a capital account of $1,000. But from a tax standpoint, the low basis of A's property presents problems.

Because gain or loss is not recognized on the formation of the partnership, § 723 provides that this basis carries over to the partnership. Hence, if the property is later sold the partnership will have a tax gain of $600 but has no gain for book purposes. The general principles of the § 704(b) Regulations do not apply to the tax allocation of the first $600 of gain because those provisions require tax gain to be allocated in the same manner as book gain, and here there is no book gain. The entire gain accrued while A held the property prior to formation of the partnership. Thus, the entire gain ought to be taxed to A, with B being allocated none of the tax gain because no book gain was allocated to B's capital account. A, on the other hand, received an opening capital account of $1,000, which included the unrealized appreciation. This problem is solved by § 704(c), which requires the first $600 of gain in this case to be taxed to A. If the property were to be sold for $1,200, the first $600 of tax gain is allocated by § 704(c) to A, and the remaining $200 of tax gain, which also represents book gain to the partnership, is allocated equally between A and B in accord with their distributive shares under the partnership agreement.

Similar problems arise if the property is not sold but is held by the partnership as depreciable property. The depreciation on the partnership books will differ from that allowable for tax purposes because, among other things, the depreciable cost will be $1,000 for book purposes, but the depreciable basis for tax purposes will be only $400. Again the § 704(b) Regulations are largely displaced by § 704(c) and the Regulations thereunder.

Section 704(c)(1)(C) provides that built-in losses are personal to the partner who contributed the loss property. If the contributing partner ceases to be a partner before the loss is realized, no partner may realize a loss on the sale of the property. As far as the remaining partners are concerned, the basis of the property is treated as being equal to its fair market value at the time of the contribution. This provision is intended to prevent the transfer of built-in tax losses from one partner (a low tax bracket person, a tax-exempt entity, or a foreign person) to another partner.

A disparity between a partner's capital account and the partner's share of basis can exist when a partner is admitted with a cash contribution to an ongoing partnership that has property with a difference between fair market value and basis. In this situation, built-in gains and losses in the partnership might be attributed to the new partner. Section 704(c) does not apply in this context. Although Congress was aware of the situation in 1986 when § 704(c) was made mandatory rather than elective, Congress was content to rely on a regulatory solution. General Explanation of the Tax Reform Act of 1984, Staff of the Joint Committee on Taxation, 215 (1984). Treas.Reg. §§ 1.704–3(a)(6)(i) and 1.704–1(b)(4)(i) require the application of § 704(c) principles when a partnership revalues partnership assets under Treas.Reg. § 1.704–1(b)(2)(iv)(*f*).

DETAILED ANALYSIS

1.   ALLOCATION OF GAIN AND LOSS

Reconsider the example above, in which A and B form an equal partnership to which A contributes property with a basis of $400 and a value of $1,000 and B contributes $1,000 cash. If the AB Partnership sells the contributed property for $1,000, under § 704(c)(1)(A), the $600 gain recognized by the partnership must be allocated entirely to A, even though that gain is not added to A's capital account. This rule does not conflict with the requirement of § 704(b) that an allocation have substantial economic effect to be recognized because the pre-contribution appreciation is already reflected in capital accounts under Treas.Reg. § 1.704–1(b)(2)(iv)(*d*). See Treas.Reg. § 1.704–1(b)(1)(vi), which subordinates the § 704(b) Regulations to § 704(c). Likewise, where the AB partnership sold the property for $1,200, realizing an $800 gain for tax purposes § 704(c) requires that $600 of gain be allocated to A, while the balance of the $200 gain is allocated under § 704(a), subject to the substantial economic effect rules of § 704(b). Since A and B are equal partners, $100 of the remaining gain is allocated to each of A and B. Thus, A is allocated $700 of gain and B $100. For book purposes, however, the partnership realized a gain of only $200, which is allocated equally between A and B. That these tax results correspond with economic reality is easily illustrated by comparing the partnership's balance sheet at both book account and tax basis amounts, before and after the sale of the asset. Before the sale, the AB partnership's balance sheet is as follows:

| | **Assets** | | | **Partners' Capital Accounts** | |
	Book	**Tax Basis**		**Book**	**Tax Basis**
Cash	$1,000	$1,000	A	$1,000	$ 400
Asset	$1,000	$ 400	B	$1,000	$1,000
Totals	$2,000	$1,400		$2,000	$1,400

As a result of the sale of the asset, all disparities between book and tax basis amounts have been eliminated. The partnership's balance sheet is as follows:

| | **Assets** | | | **Partners' Capital Accounts** | |
	Book	**Tax Basis**		**Book**	**Tax Basis**
Cash	$2,200	$2,200	A	$1,100	$1,100
			B	$1,100	$1,100
Totals	$2,200	$2,200		$2,200	$2,200

Suppose now that the AB partnership sold the property for only $800. For tax purposes, the gain recognized is $400, but for partnership book purposes, there is a $200 loss. Theoretically, A should be allocated $600 of gain attributable to the pre-contribution gain that was realized but not recognized upon formation of the partnership, and A and B should each be allocated $100 of loss realized since the partnership was formed. For many years, however, the Regulations under § 704(c), prior to its amendment in 1984, provided an inviolate "ceiling rule" under which only the amount of gain recognized by the partnership, in this case $400, could be allocated among the partners. Thus, the closest that the partners could get to an appropriate allocation was to allocate the entire $400 gain to A. (Ultimately, of course, B might recognize the $100 loss upon sale of B's partnership interest, which would have a basis $100 higher than it would have had if B had been allowed a current $100 loss.) Congress intended the 1984 amendments to § 704(c) to remedy this distortion. Treas.Reg. § 1.704–3(a)–(d) provides, in addition to what is known as the "traditional method with ceiling rule," two allocation methods to address the distortions caused by the ceiling rule. The operative premise of the Regulations is that the partner who contributed the built-in gain or built-in loss property and the partnership should be allowed to use any reasonable, consistently applied method that allocates to the contributing partner the tax burdens and benefits of any pre-contribution gain or loss. Accordingly, the Regulations specifically permit making allocations under § 704(c) by using either the (1) "traditional method," including the "ceiling rule", (2) the "traditional method" with "curative allocations," or (3) "remedial allocations." The method to be used for each partnership asset subject to § 704(c) should be specified in the partnership agreement. Treas.Reg. § 1.704–3(a)(1) specifies that these allocation methods apply only to contributions to a partnership that "are otherwise respected" as contributions of property to a partnership and that are not recast as a different transaction, such as under the anti-abuse rules of Treas.Reg. § 1.701–2.

1.1. *Traditional Method with the Ceiling Rule*

Under the "traditional method" with the "ceiling rule" provided in Treas.Reg. § 1.704–3(b), upon the disposition of contributed property the partnership must allocate to the contributing partner the built-in gain or loss inherent in the property at the time it was contributed to the partnership. Thus, in the AB Partnership example, if the partnership sold the property for $800, A would be allocated $400 of tax gain and B would be allocated no gain for tax purposes. This option cannot result in the allocation of a net gain of $500 to A and a loss of $100 to B. It does not avoid the distortions.

1.2. *Traditional Method with Curative Allocations*

Under Treas.Reg. § 1.704–3(c), a partnership may eliminate the distortions caused by the ceiling rule by using reasonable curative allocations of other partnership tax items of income, gain, loss, or deduction. These allocations "cure" disparities caused by the ceiling rule by equalizing the overall allocations of book and tax items to noncontributing partners. Assume, for example, that in the year the property contributed by A was sold for $800, the AB Partnership also realized gross income of $400 and deductions of $400, thus breaking even apart from the gain on the property. Under the traditional method with curative allocations, A could be allocated net taxable income of $500 and B could be allocated a net taxable loss of $100 by allocating these items as follows:

	A	B
Gain from Property	$400	$ 0
Other Gross Income	$200	$200
Deductions	($100)	($300)
	$500	($100)

Curative allocations involve only tax items and differ from book allocations of the same items. For book accounting purposes, A and B would have allocated the items as follows:

	A	B
Loss from Property	($100)	($100)
Other Gross Income	$200	$200
Deductions	($200)	($200)
	($100)	($100)

Because the tax allocations of the deductions did not follow the book allocations to capital accounts, in the absence of Treas.Reg. § 1.704–3(c), curative allocations generally would not be valid under Treas.Reg. § 1.704–1(b).

A curative allocation is reasonable only if it is made using items of the same character as the tax items affected by the ceiling rule and only to the extent it offsets the effect of the ceiling rule. Treas.Reg. § 1.704–3(c)(3). (Treas.Reg. § 1.704–3(c)(3)(iii)(B) provides the only narrow exception to this character matching rule.) Thus, if the gain from the sale of the property was capital gain and the deductions were ordinary deductions for business expenses, interest, and depreciation, making a curative allocation would not have been allowed. Only capital losses could have been allocated to B. Curative allocations, however, are flexible. If the gain on the sale of the property contributed by A was capital gain and the other gross income also was capital gain, B could have been allocated a disproportionately low share of the other capital gain, as follows:

	A	B
Gain from Property	$400	$ 0
Other Capital Gain	$300	$100
Deductions	($200)	($200)
	$500	($100)

1.3. *Remedial Allocations*

The final method of ameliorating the ceiling rule is the remedial allocation method provided in Treas.Reg. § 1.704–3(d). This is the most flexible method available to partnerships for dealing with the ceiling rule because remedial allocations are tax allocations of *notional* gain or income *created by the partnership* that are *offset* by tax allocations of *notional* deduction or loss that are *created by the partnership*. Remedial allocations under Treas.Reg. § 1.704–3(d) are the only permissible method of creating notional tax items. Treas.Reg. § 1.704–3(d)(5)(i). Unlike curative allocations, which allocate recognized partnership income and deduction items differently for tax purposes than for book purposes, remedial allocations may be created for tax purposes even though the partnership has no corresponding book items of income or deduction. Remedial allocations must result in each partner recognizing total partnership income, gains, deductions, or loss for the year equal to the partner's share of book gain or loss. These allocations are in addition to the allocations under the traditional method described in Treas.Reg. § 1.704–3(b). Thus, if the ceiling rule results in a tax allocation to a noncontributing partner different than the corresponding book allocation, the partnership makes a remedial allocation of notional income, gain, deduction, or loss (without affecting allocations of actual partnership income, gain, deduction, or loss) to the noncontributing partner equal to the amount of the difference caused by the ceiling limitation and a simultaneous offsetting allocation of income, gain, deduction, or loss to the contributing partner. Unlike the curative allocation approach under

Treas.Reg. § 1.704–3(c), a remedial allocation has no effect on the allocation among the partners of actual partnership items of income, gain, deduction, or loss.

Consider the AB Partnership discussed in the preceding examples, which recognized a $400 tax gain and a $200 book loss on the sale for $800 of property contributed by A. Even if the partnership had no other items of income or deduction for the year, it could make remedial allocations to give each partner aggregate tax items equal to each partner's book items. B would be allocated a $100 notional tax loss, and A would be allocated an additional $100 notional tax gain, as follows:

	A		B	
	Tax	Book	Tax	Book
Gain (Loss) from Property	$400	($100)	$ 0	($100)
Remedial Allocation	$100	n/a	($100)	n/a
	$500	($100)	($100)	($100)

B's remedial deduction and A's corresponding remedial income item must be of the same character as the income item from the property that was sold. Treas.Reg. § 1.704–3(d)(3). If the property is a capital asset, the remedial allocations must be capital gain and loss; if the property is an ordinary income asset, the remedial allocations must be ordinary gain and loss. If, as is often likely, the property is a § 1231 asset, the remedial allocations must be § 1231 gain and loss, even though in some cases a character mismatch may occur after taking into account each partner's other items of § 1231 gain and loss. Finally, for purposes of applying the passive activity loss rules of § 469, discussed in Chapter 23, the offsetting item is deemed to arise from the partnership activity in which the contributed property is used.

Even though remedial allocations involve the creation of notional items, the items are real in terms of the tax consequences to the partners—i.e., in the example above, A must pay taxes on the notional $100 tax gain. As a result, remedial allocations of income, gain, deduction, and loss are taken into account in adjusting partners' bases in their partnership interests under § 705 in the same manner as distributive shares of partnership taxable income. Treas.Reg. § 1.704–3(d)(4)(ii). Remedial allocations, however, do not affect either partnership taxable income under § 703 or the partnership's adjusted basis in any of its property. Treas.Reg. § 1.704–3(d)(4)(i). As will be discussed below, use of the remedial method as to a depreciable asset will, however, affect how the partnership calculates its book depreciation for that asset.

1.4. *Comparison*

When the current effects of the traditional approach with the ceiling rule, on the one hand, and the curative and remedial allocation methods, on the other hand, are balanced with the results upon liquidation, the overall amount of gain or loss recognized by each partner will be identical in nominal terms, although the timing will vary. Under the traditional method, when the ceiling rule applies, the partner contributing low basis property recognizes less current gain, while the other partner is not entitled to a loss on the sale. However, because of the effect of basis adjustments under § 705, the contributing partner recognizes a pro tanto greater gain (or smaller loss) on final liquidation, while the other partner has a smaller gain (or greater loss). Under the curative and remedial allocation methods, the partner who contributed the low basis/high value asset in effect includes the full amount of pre-contribution appreciation when the asset is sold. Consequently, on liquidation, the partner does not have any remaining pre-contribution gain to account for with respect to the asset. Conversely, as a result of either curative and remedial allocation, the other partner has recognized less net taxable income during the life of the partnership than that partner would have realized under the traditional method with the ceiling rule and therefore realizes a relatively larger gain (or smaller loss) on liquidation of the partnership. There are two other differences. First, the character of the gain or loss may be transmuted from ordinary to capital under the traditional approach, while curative and remedial allocations require matching of character. Second, if the partners receive property other than cash in liquidation, recognition of gain or loss may be further postponed. See § 731(a), discussed in Chapter 25.

2.   DEPRECIABLE PROPERTY

2.1. *In General*

Section 704(c) requires that allocations of depreciation and of gain or loss on depreciable property also reflect the difference between the contributing partner's basis in the property and the book value of the property included in the contributing partner's capital account. Section 704(c) principles work to assure that depreciation deductions allocated to the partners for tax purposes reflect the book depreciation allocated to the partners' capital accounts. For example, suppose that C and D form a partnership to which C contributes $1,000 cash and D contributes depreciable property with a basis of $600 and a fair market value of $1,000. Each partner has a 50% interest in partnership capital and profits. Assume, for simplicity, that the property has a 10-year cost recovery period with five years remaining, and its cost is recoverable using the straight-line method (ignore conventions). As a reminder, tax depreciation and book depreciation generally must be computed using the same methods in order to maintain capital accounts in the required manner, see Treas.Reg. § 1.704–1(b)(2)(iv)(*g*)(*3*). Under the traditional method and curative method, book depreciation is computed using the property's remaining tax cost recovery period for the entire book value. See Treas.Reg. § 1.704–3(b)(2), Ex. (2). Tax depreciation would be $120 per year, and book depreciation would be $200 per year. In effect, C purchased a one-half interest in the asset for $500. Since the property has a five-year life, using the straight-line method, C, who contributed the cash, should be entitled to $100 of depreciation per year. The additional $20 of tax depreciation is allocated to D. This approach to allocating depreciation deductions between the partners, which is the traditional method in Treas.Reg. § 1.704–3(b), gives C, the partner contributing cash to the partnership, the tax benefits of acquiring by purchase an interest in the property contributed by D, while preserving for D the nonrecognition treatment accorded by § 721.

Under Treas.Reg. § 1.704–3(b)(1), for tax purposes depreciation deductions are first allocated to noncontributing partners up to their share of the book deductions. Any remaining tax deductions may be allocated by any method consistent with Treas.Reg. § 1.704–1(b). Generally, the remaining deductions are allocated to the contributing partner. The result of this rule is to reduce the disparity, if any, between each partners' book capital account and tax basis in the partnership interest each year over the cost recovery period of the contributed depreciable asset; at the end of the cost recovery period, the disparity has been eliminated.

Assume that the CD partnership breaks even, for both tax and book purposes, apart from depreciation. The partners' capital accounts, at both book and tax basis, change over the years, as follows:

	C		**D**	
	Book	**Tax**	**Book**	**Tax**
Initial Capital Account	$1,000	$1,000	$1,000	$600
Year 1 Depreciation	($ 100)	($ 100)	($ 100)	($ 20)
End of Year 1 Capital Account	$ 900	$ 900	$ 900	$580
Year 2 Depreciation	($ 100)	($ 100)	($ 100)	($ 20)
End of Year 2 Capital Account	$ 800	$ 800	$ 800	$560
Year 3 Depreciation	($ 100)	($ 100)	($ 100)	($ 20)
End of Year 3 Capital Account	$ 700	$ 700	$ 700	$540
Year 4 Depreciation	($ 100)	($ 100)	($ 100)	($ 20)
End of Year 4 Capital Account	$ 600	$ 600	$ 600	$520
Year 5 Depreciation	($ 100)	($ 100)	($ 100)	($ 20)
End of Year 5 Capital Account	$ 500	$ 500	$ 500	$500

Section 704(c) applies to the allocation of depreciation deductions not only when one partner contributes cash and the other property but also when both contribute property. Assume that E and F form a partnership in which each partner has a 50% interest in partnership profits and capital. E contributes depreciable machinery with a fair market value of $1,000 and a basis of $750. The machinery has a remaining cost recovery period of 5 years and is depreciated under the straight-line method (ignore conventions). F contributes depreciable equipment with a fair market value of $1,000 and a basis of $1,500. The equipment has a remaining cost recovery period of 10 years and is depreciated using the straight-line method (ignore conventions). In each of the first 5 years, $200 of book depreciation on the machinery is allocated equally to E and F, and the tax depreciation of $150 is allocated $50 to E and $100 to F. The book depreciation of $100 on the equipment is allocated equally to E and F, and the tax depreciation of $150 is allocated $50 to E and $100 to F.

Cross-Allocations of § 704(c) Depreciation

Asset	Book	Basis	Allocation to E		Allocation to F	
			Book	Tax	Book	Tax
Machinery (contributed by E) 5 years	$1,000	$ 750				
Machinery Depreciation	$ 200	$ 150	$100	$ 50	$100	$100
Equipment (contributed by F) 10 years	$1,000	$1,500				
Equipment Depreciation	$ 100	$ 150	$ 50	$ 50	$ 50	$100
			$150	$100	$150	$200

2.2. *Sales of Depreciable Property*

Section 704(c) further applies to allocate gains and losses on the sale of depreciable property that was contributed to a partnership with a difference between fair market value and basis and that was subject to further depreciation deductions by the partnership. Section 704(c) principles operate to match book gains and losses allocated to the non-contributing partner with tax gains and losses. Suppose that the CD Partnership in the earlier example held the property (contributed by D with a book value of $1,000 and a tax basis of $600) for two years and claimed $240 of tax depreciation deductions, which reduced the tax basis of the property to $360, and $400 of book depreciation, which reduced the book basis to $600. On the first day of Year 3, the partnership sold the property for $900, recognizing a $540 gain for tax purposes and a $300 gain for book purposes. How should this gain be allocated between C and D?

	Amount Realized/ Sales Price	Basis/ Book Value	Gain/ Profit
Tax	$900	$360	$540
Book	$900	$600	$300

Treas.Reg. § 1.704–3(b)(2), Ex. (1)(iii) indicates that taxable gain equal to book gain is allocated to each partner according to the partnership agreement, subject to the § 704(b) Regulations. Taxable gain in excess of book gain is allocated to the contributing partner. Thus, the $240 of the $540 total tax gain in excess of the $300 book gain is allocated to D; the remaining $300 tax gain is allocated equally, $150 to each partner. D recognizes total gain of $390, and C recognizes total gain of $150. Each partner's capital account should be increased by $150. The capital accounts of C and D thus are $950 each, and their respective bases in their partnership interests are also $950.[10]

	C		D	
	Tax	Book	Tax	Book
Initial Capital Account	$1,000	$1,000	$ 600	$1,000
Years 1–2 Depreciation	($ 200)	($ 200)	($ 40)	($ 200)
Gain on Sale of Asset	$ 150	$ 150	$ 390	$ 150
Capital Accounts After Sale	$ 950	$ 950	$ 950	$ 950

Under this allocation method, the amount of potential tax gain allocated to the contributing partner decreases each year as the difference between tax basis and book value of the asset gradually decreases. Note, however, that whenever there is a loss for book purposes but a gain for tax purposes, the entire tax gain is allocated to the contributing partner. Once property is fully depreciated for book and tax purposes, all of the gain on a sale is allocated under the § 704(b) Regulations instead of the § 704(c) rules.

Significant income shifting can occur as a result of the intersection of the rule that book and tax depreciation are computed under the same method—with the cost recovery period of contributed property for both book and tax purposes being the remaining § 168 cost recovery period (or § 167 useful life or § 197 amortization period, if applicable)—and the rule that, once the property is fully depreciated, the gain on property is allocated pursuant to § 704(b), rather than § 704(c). Suppose that G and H form the GH partnership to which G contributes $1,000 in cash, and H contributes a depreciable asset with a basis of $100 and a fair market value of $1,000. If the property were sold immediately after it was contributed, G would recognize all $900 of built-in gain. Assume further that the depreciable asset is 15-year property with only one year of cost recovery remaining. Book depreciation would be $1,000 and tax depreciation would be $100. If the asset were sold for $1,000 on the first day of Year 2, after both book value and tax basis had been reduced to zero, pursuant to the Regulations, the $1,000 gain would be allocated $500 to G and $500 to H. This income shifting might be prevented by the application of Treas.Reg. § 1.704–3(b)(2), Ex. (2), which would allocate $950 of the tax gain to G and only $50 to H.

For purposes of allocating § 1245 recapture gain among the partners on the sale of depreciable or amortizable property, Treas.Reg. § 1.1245–1(e)(2)(ii)(C) provides special rules for determining a partner's share of depreciation or amortization with respect to property subject to § 704(c). In addition to the distributive share of prior depreciation, the contributing partner's share of depreciation includes depreciation allowed prior to the contribution. The Regulation also provides that curative and remedial

---

[10] The partnership has $1,900 in cash to satisfy the partners' capital accounts in the event of liquidation.

allocations reduce the contributing partner's share of depreciation (but not below zero) and increase the noncontributing partners' shares of depreciation.

2.3. *The Ceiling Limitation*

The ceiling rule also presents problems with respect to the allocation of depreciation under § 704(c)(1)(A). Suppose J and K form the JK Partnership as equal partners. J contributes depreciable property with an adjusted basis of $2,000 and a fair market value of $10,000, and K contributes $10,000 in cash. The property is depreciated using the straight-line method with a 10-year cost recovery period, with five years remaining at the time of the transfer to the partnership (ignore conventions). Tax depreciation is $400 per year. Book depreciation (except under the remedial allocation method) is $2,000. K's share of book depreciation, however, is $1,000. K would like the share of tax depreciation to mirror the amount of book depreciation that is allocated to K. Again, the partners may choose to apply one of the three § 704(c) allocation methods—(1) the "traditional method" including the ceiling rule, (2) the "traditional method" with curative allocations, or (3) the "remedial allocation" method.

2.3.1.   *Traditional Method*

Under the traditional method, depreciation deductions are subject to the ceiling rule, limiting total deductions allocated to the partners to the partnership's actual deductions. Treas.Reg. § 1.704–3(b). Applying this method to the JK Partnership, tax depreciation of $400 is allocated to K. K's share of book depreciation is $1,000, which is $600 more than K's share of tax depreciation under the traditional rule. Under the traditional method, the book and tax depreciation for each partner would be as follows:

	J		K	
Year	Book	Tax	Book	Tax
1	($1,000)	$0	($1,000)	($ 400)
2	($1,000)	$0	($1,000)	($ 400)
3	($1,000)	$0	($1,000)	($ 400)
4	($1,000)	$0	($1,000)	($ 400)
5	($1,000)	$0	($1,000)	($ 400)
Total	($5,000)	$0	($5,000)	($2,000)

If the partnership also realized an income item of $2,000 in each year, the allocations would be as follows:

		J		K	
Year		Book	Tax	Book	Tax
1	Depreciation	($1,000)	$ 0	($1,000)	($ 400)
	Income	$1,000	$1,000	$1,000	$1,000
2	Depreciation	($1,000)	$ 0	($1,000)	($ 400)
	Income	$1,000	$1,000	$1,000	$1,000
3	Depreciation	($1,000)	$ 0	($1,000)	($ 400)
	Income	$1,000	$1,000	$1,000	$1,000
4	Depreciation	($1,000)	$ 0	($1,000)	($ 400)
	Income	$1,000	$1,000	$1,000	$1,000
5	Depreciation	($1,000)	$ 0	($1,000)	($ 400)
	Income	$1,000	$1,000	$1,000	$1,000
Total		$ 0	$5,000	$ 0	$3,000

When the ceiling rule applies, under the traditional rule noncontributing partners will be allocated tax deductions in an amount less than their share of book deductions, resulting in a shifting of taxable income. For this reason, in some cases the general anti-abuse rule may apply to limit the use of the traditional method. See Treas.Reg. § 1.704–3(b)(2), Ex. (2)(ii). The anti-abuse rule might apply in the above example, for instance, if K was a tax-exempt entity and J was subject to tax.

2.3.2.   *Curative Allocations*

To apply the curative allocation method provided in Treas.Reg. § 1.704–3(c), the partnership must either have ordinary income that can be allocated to J for tax purposes disproportionately to J's book allocation or other depreciation deductions that can be allocated to K for tax purposes disproportionately to K's book allocation. Under the traditional method, as described above, J and K each would be allocated $1,000 of the income item each year for both book and tax purposes. Under a curative allocation, however, while both J and K would be allocated $1,000 of income for book purposes, J would be allocated $1,600 and K would be allocated only $400 for tax purposes. The effect on J and K would be as follows:

Year		J		K	
		Book	**Tax**	**Book**	**Tax**
1	Depreciation	($1,000)	$ 0	($1,000)	($400)
	Income	$1,000	$1,600	$1,000	$400
2	Depreciation	($1,000)	$ 0	($1,000)	($400)
	Income	$1,000	$1,600	$1,000	$400
3	Depreciation	($1,000)	$ 0	($1,000)	($400)
	Income	$1,000	$1,600	$1,000	$400
4	Depreciation	($1,000)	$ 0	($1,000)	($400)
	Income	$1,000	$1,600	$1,000	$400
5	Depreciation	($1,000)	$ 0	($1,000)	($400)
	Income	$1,000	$1,600	$1,000	$400
Total		$ 0	$8,000	$ 0	$ 0

A curative allocation is reasonable only if it is made using items of the same character as the tax items affected by the ceiling rule and only to the extent it offsets the effect of the ceiling rule. Treas.Reg. § 1.704–3(c)(3). Thus, if the ceiling rule limits an allocation of depreciation to a tax-exempt partner, a curative allocation of dividend income away from the other partners and to the tax-exempt partner would not be valid, but a curative allocation of depreciation deductions from other property would be valid. For other examples of curative allocations, see Treas.Reg. § 1.704–3(c)(4).

2.3.3.   *Remedial Allocations*

Application of the remedial allocation method by the JK Partnership is somewhat more complex. To start with, special rules apply to determine the partners' shares of book items to determine whether tax allocations differ from book allocations. The general rules of Treas.Reg. § 1.704–1(b)(2)(iv)(*g*)(*3*), which provide for computing book depreciation using the applicable tax depreciation method over the portion of the cost recovery period remaining at the time the property was contributed to the partnership, do not apply. Instead, book depreciation is calculated differently, under a two-step process prescribed in Treas.Reg. § 1.704–3(d)(2). First, an amount of the book value of the asset equal to its tax basis is recovered for book purposes over the remaining tax cost recovery period of the contributed asset. In the JK Partnership example, this amount is $400 ($2,000 tax basis divided by 5-year remaining recovery period). Second, the excess of book value over tax basis is recovered for book purposes over the cost recovery period, using the applicable cost recovery method, for new property of the same type if purchased by the partnership. In the JK Partnership, this amount is $800 ($8,000 excess of book value over tax basis, divided by the new 10-year recovery period). Book depreciation for Year 1 is $1,200 ($400 plus $800). K's share of book depreciation is $600, which is $200 more than K's share of tax depreciation under the traditional rule. Accordingly, the partnership would create a remedial allocation of an additional $200 of depreciation to K, offset by an allocation of $200 of income to J. The same allocations would be made in each of Years 2 through 5. In Years 6 through 10, tax depreciation would be zero. K's share of book depreciation would be $400 [($8,000/10) × 50%]. Accordingly, the partnership would create a remedial allocation of an additional $400 of depreciation to K offset by an allocation $400 of income to J.

As a result of the remedial allocation, over the 10-year period that the remedial allocations are in effect, the allocations of the $2,000 annual gross income, $400 tax depreciation, and remedial items would be as follows:

		J		K	
Year		Book	Tax	Book	Tax
1	Depreciation	($ 600)	$ 0	($ 600)	($ 600)
	Income	$1,000	$ 1,200	$1,000	$1,000
2	Depreciation	($ 600)	$ 0	($ 600)	($ 600)
	Income	$1,000	$ 1,200	$1,000	$1,000
3	Depreciation	($ 600)	$ 0	($ 600)	($ 600)
	Income	$1,000	$ 1,200	$1,000	$1,000
4	Depreciation	($ 600)	$ 0	($ 600)	($ 600)
	Income	$1,000	$ 1,200	$1,000	$1,000
5	Depreciation	($ 600)	$ 0	($ 600)	($ 600)
	Income	$1,000	$ 1,200	$1,000	$1,000
6	Depreciation	($ 400)	$ 0	($ 400)	($ 400)
	Income	$1,000	$ 1,400	$1,000	$1,000
7	Depreciation	($ 400)	$ 0	($ 400)	($ 400)
	Income	$1,000	$ 1,400	$1,000	$1,000
8	Depreciation	($ 400)	$ 0	($ 400)	($ 400)
	Income	$1,000	$ 1,400	$1,000	$1,000
9	Depreciation	($ 400)	$ 0	($ 400)	($ 400)
	Income	$1,000	$ 1,400	$1,000	$1,000
10	Depreciation	($ 400)	$ 0	($ 400)	($ 400)
	Income	$1,000	$ 1,400	$1,000	$1,000
Total		$5,000	$13,000	$5,000	$5,000

According to the Regulations, J's income must be "the same type of income that the contributing property produces." Treas.Reg. § 1.704–3(d)(3). Although this arguably may include either the type of income recognized on a sale, e.g., § 1231 or § 1245 gain, or the type of income realized from operations, e.g., rent or gross receipts from sales, the Regulations specify that if the ceiling rule limited item is depreciation, the offsetting item to the contributing partner is ordinary income.

2.3.4.   *Comparison*

A comparison of the total amounts of income or loss realized by the partners in the preceding examples involving the JK partnership reveals that the aggregate income or loss realized by the partners does not differ under the three allocation methods: the traditional method with the ceiling rule, the curative allocation method, and the remedial allocation method. What differs is the amount of income or loss recognized by different partners in different years. One partner's timing advantage is another partner's timing disadvantage. Comparing these alternative allocations reveals that the curative allocation is most beneficial to K, allowing K to receive the additional $3,000 of depreciation deductions more rapidly than either of the other methods, while the traditional method is the least beneficial to K because K must recognize taxable income in excess of book income. Conversely, the traditional method is the most beneficial to J, allowing J to avoid any additional taxable income, while the curative allocation method is the least beneficial to J because it requires recognition of additional taxable income earlier than under the remedial method.

Apart from the tax arbitrage issue that arises because the partners are in different tax rate brackets, including the situation in which one of the partners is a tax-exempt entity, the Treasury, however, is merely a stakeholder. At any given discount rate, the net present value of the aggregate net income or loss of the partners over the cost recovery period of the asset is identical. This is the reason that partners are given the flexibility to choose among the different methods. Because of the tax arbitrage potential, however, the Regulations, provide an anti-abuse rule. An allocation method, or combination of methods if multiple assets are involved, is not reasonable if the allocations are made with a view to shifting tax consequences of built-in gain or built-in loss among the partners in a manner that substantially reduces the present value of the partners' tax liabilities. Treas.Reg. § 1.704–3(a)(10).

Treas.Reg. § 1.704–3(a)(10) requires that in testing for a reduction in the partners' aggregate tax liabilities, the impact on indirect partners must be taken into account. Indirect partners include the owners of interests in a pass-through entity that is a partner, including a partnership, an S corporation, an estate or trust, or a controlled foreign corporation that is a 10% partner. Furthermore, Treas.Reg. § 1.704–3(a)(1) provides that the use of allocation methods with respect to built-in gain or loss property only apply to contributions to a partnership that "are otherwise respected." Even though an allocation may comply with the literal language of Treas.Reg. § 1.704–3(b), (c), or (d) (traditional method, curative allocations, or remedial allocations), "the Commissioner can recast the contribution as appropriate to avoid tax results inconsistent with the intent of subchapter K." Under the Regulation, remedial allocations among related parties are one factor that may be considered.

3.   DE MINIMIS EXCEPTION

To avoid complexity where the disparity between the book value and basis of contributed property is small, Treas.Reg. § 1.704–3(e)(1) permits a partnership to disregard § 704(c) entirely if the aggregate book value of all properties contributed by a partner does not differ from their aggregate adjusted bases by more than 15% of basis *and* the total disparity for all properties contributed by the partner during the year does not exceed $20,000. If the de minimis rule is satisfied, alternatively, the partnership may elect to allocate gain or loss upon disposition, but not depreciation, under § 704(c). In applying the basis-book disparity test, built-in gains and losses are both treated as positive numbers. Thus, for example, if A contributes cash to the AB Partnership, and B contributes Blackacre, with a basis of $100,000 and a fair market value of $110,000, and Whiteacre, with a basis of $29,000 and a fair market value of $20,000, the de minimis rule applies because the aggregate disparity between basis and book value is $19,000 (($110,000 − $100,000) + ($29,000 − 20,000)), and the aggregate book value of the two properties, 130,000 does not differ from aggregate basis, 129,000, by more than 15%. But if Whiteacre were worth only $18,000, the disparity between basis and book value would be $21,000 (($110,000 − $100,000) + ($29,000 − 18,000)), and the de minimis rule would not apply, even though the aggregate fair market value of the two properties, 128,000 does not differ from aggregate basis, 128,000, by more than 15%. Note that the de minimis rule applies partner-by-partner. Thus, for example, if A contributed Blackacre, with a basis of $16,000 and a fair market value of $19,000, and B contributed Whiteacre, with a basis of $5,000 and a fair market value of $4,000, the de minimis rule would not apply to either property because the aggregate disparity between basis and book value with respect to the property contributed by each partner exceeds 15% of the property's basis. Thus, the de minimis test exception rarely applies.

4. APPLICATION OF SECTION 704(c) TO MULTIPLE PARTNERSHIP ASSETS

Generally, § 704(c) is applied property-by-property; aggregation is not allowed in making allocations under § 704(c). However, Treas.Reg. § 1.704–3(e)(2) permits aggregation of three classes of property (other than real property): (1) depreciable property included in the same general asset account of the contributing partner; (2) zero basis property; and (3) inventory.[11]

A partnership may use different allocation methods with respect to different items of § 704(c) property but may not use more than one method with respect to the same item of property. The selected allocation method must be consistently applied to any item of property. In addition, the overall combination of methods must be reasonable under the facts and circumstances. For example, it may be unreasonable to use one method with

---

[11] A management or investment partnership is permitted by Treas.Reg. § 1.704–3(e)(3) to aggregate built-in gains and losses from qualified financial assets, rather than follow the normal property-by-property approach required by the Regulations. For purposes of making reverse allocations of recognized gains and losses under § 704(c) principles, Rev.Proc. 2007–59, 2007–2 C.B. 745, provides automatic permission to aggregate built-in gains and losses to a qualified partnership, which is a partnership that allocates gains and losses in proportion to the partners' capital accounts, which reasonably expects to revalue its assets at least four times a year, which holds publicly traded property of at least 90% of its non-cash assets, has at least 10 unrelated partners, and will make at least 200 trades of financial assets during the year.

respect to gain property and a different method with respect to loss property. Furthermore, it is not reasonable to use an allocation method that creates tax allocations of income, deduction, gain, or loss independent of allocations affecting book capital accounts. Nor is it reasonable to use any method that increases or decreases the basis of property from its basis otherwise properly determined. Treas.Reg. § 1.704–3(a)(1) and (2). Finally, no allocation method is reasonable if the property contribution and tax allocations have been made with a view to reducing substantially the partners' aggregate overall tax liability. Treas.Reg. § 1.704–3(a)(10).

5.　ALLOCATION OF BUILT-IN LOSSES

Section 704(c)(1)(C) requires that built-in losses be allocated only to the partner who contributed the loss property. If the contributing partner ceases to be a partner before the loss is realized, as far as the remaining partners are concerned the basis of the property is treated as being equal to its fair market value at the time of the contribution, and the built-in loss is eliminated. There is no time limit on the application of § 704(c)(1)(C). Assume, for example, that A, B, and C formed the ABC Partnership with A and B each contributing cash of $1,000 and C contributing property with a fair market value of $1,000 and a basis of $7,000. The $6,000 built-in loss with respect to the property contributed by C can be allocated only to C. Assume further that eight years later C withdraws from the partnership, in which A and B continue as equal partners, and the next year the AB partnership sells the property contributed by C. As far as the remaining partners are concerned, the basis of the property is $1,000. If the partnership sells the property for $3,000, the partnership, now consisting of A and B, recognizes a $2,000 gain, not a $4,000 loss. If, alternatively, the partnership sold the property for $700, because as far as A and B are concerned the property has a $1,000 basis, the partnership would recognize a $300 loss, and A and B each would be allocated a $150 loss.

Section 704(c)(1)(C) operates similarly if instead of C withdrawing from the partnership, which was continued by A and B, C sold the partnership interest to D. In the case of a transferred partnership interest, the transferee partner does not "step into the shoes" of the transferor with respect to the § 704(c) built-in loss. The built-in loss is again eliminated.

Proposed Regulations would implement § 704(c)(1)(C) by treating the partnership for all purposes as having an initial basis in contributed built-in loss property equal to its fair market value at the time of contribution and provide the "section 704(c)(1)(C) partner" with a § 704(c)(1)(C) basis adjustment. The § 704(c)(1)(C) basis adjustment to the contributing partner initially is equal to the built-in loss associated with the § 704(c)(1)(C) property at the time of contribution and is subsequently adjusted to account for basis recovery by the contributing partner. The adjustment is similar to the § 743 adjustment, which is discussed in Chapter 24. Under this concept, the partnership's capital recovery and gain or loss with respect to § 704(c)(1)(C) property is determined using the partnership's fair market value basis from the date of contribution. The contributing partner first takes the contributing partner's distributive share of gain, loss, depreciation, or amortization with respect to the property determined with respect to the partnership's common basis. The contributing partner's share of partnership items attributable to the § 704(c)(1)(C) property is then adjusted for tax purposes to account for the contributing partner's basis adjustment, as appropriate. The § 704(c)(1)(C) adjustment does not change the contributing partner's capital account. If § 704(c)(1)(C) property is subject to depreciation, § 197 amortization, or another cost recovery method, the § 704(c)(1)(C) basis adjustment associated with the property is recovered by the contributing partner in accordance with §§ 168(i)(7), 197(f)(2), or any other applicable provision, generally continuing the contributing partner's cost recovery with respect to the basis adjustment under the method used by the partner prior to the contribution. (See Prop.Reg. § 1.704–3(f)(3)(ii)(D)(2), Ex.)

Under the Proposed Regulations, a transferee of a contributing partner's partnership interest does not succeed to the § 704(c)(1)(C) basis adjustment; the share of the § 704(c)(1)(C) basis adjustment attributable to the interest transferred is eliminated. The adjusted partnership basis of § 704(c)(1)(C) property distributed to the contributing partner includes the § 704(c)(1)(C) basis adjustment for purposes of determining any § 734(b) basis adjustment (discussed in Chapter 25), but § 704(c)(1)(C) basis adjustments are not taken into account in making allocations under Treas.Reg. § 1.755–1(c). If § 704(c)(1)(C) property is distributed to another partner, the contributing partner's § 704(c)(1)(C) basis adjustment for the distributed property is reallocated among the remaining items of partnership property under Treas.Reg. § 1.755–1(c). The Proposed Regulations do *not* extend any of these rules to reverse § 704(c) allocations, which are discussed next.

6. REVALUATIONS AND "REVERSE" § 704(c) ALLOCATIONS

The same problem as is dealt with by § 704(c) arises when a new partner contributes cash to enter an existing partnership that holds gain or loss property. Suppose that G contributes $150 cash to the EF Partnership, which owns property having a fair market value of $300 and a basis of $180, to become a one-third partner. Immediately before the contribution, the EF partnership revalues its assets and partners' capital accounts, as provided in Treas.Reg. § 1.704–1(b)(2)(iv)(*f*). The partnership's balance sheet is as follows:

	Asset			Partners' Capital Accounts	
	Book	**Basis**		**Book**	**Basis**
Asset	$180	$180	E	$ 90	$ 90
	——	——	F	$ 90	$ 90
	$180	$180		$180	$180

After the asset and partners' capital accounts are revalued and G is admitted, the partnership's balance sheet is as follows:

	Asset			Partners' Capital Accounts	
	Book	Basis		Book	Basis
Cash	$150	$150	E	$150	$ 90
Asset	$300	$180	F	$150	$ 90
			G	$150	$150
	$450	$330		$450	$330

As a result of the revaluation, a disparity between book value and basis arises that is analogous to the disparity created by contributions of appreciated property, with E and F being analogous to a partner who has contributed appreciated property. Accordingly, E and F should be taxable on that built-in gain. G has in effect paid $100 for a one-third interest in the property and should not recognize any gain if it were sold for $300. All of the first $120 of gain should be recognized by E and F; any gain in excess of $120 should be allocated among the partners according to the principles of § 704(b). Thus, if the property were sold for $390, E and F each should be allocated $90 of tax gain, and G should be allocated $30 of tax gain. Conversely, if the property were sold for $270, E and F each should recognize a tax gain of $50, and G should recognize a tax loss of $10.

Section 704(c) does not expressly apply to this situation, but Treas.Regs. §§ 1.704–1(b)(2)(iv)(*f*), 1.704–3(a)(6)(i), and 1.704–1(b)(4)(i) require the application of § 704(c) principles in allocating tax items whenever the partnership property is revalued and existing partnership capital accounts are adjusted in connection with the admission of a new partner. See Treas.Reg. § 1.704–1(b)(5), Ex. (14)(i)–(ii).[12] Thus, if the asset were sold for $390, E and F each would be allocated $90 of tax gain and $30 of book gain while G would be allocated $30 of tax and book gain. Likewise, because the rules governing alternative allocation methods in Treas.Reg. § 1.704–3 are applicable in the case of tax/book disparities arising from revaluations, if the property were sold for $270, there would be $30 of book loss (which would be allocated one-third each under the partnership agreement) but $90 of tax gain, which would be divided $45 each to E and F as "reverse" § 704(c) allocations. The ceiling rule would, however, prevent G from being allocated a $10 tax loss to match G's share of the book loss, but another method could be used to avoid the impact of the ceiling rule. For example, under the remedial method, G could be allocated a notional tax loss of $10, and E and F could be allocated an offsetting notional tax gain of $5 each ($10 total),

---

[12] A "securities partnership," which can be either a financial assets investment or management partnership, is permitted by Treas.Reg. § 1.704–3(e)(3) to aggregate built-in gains and losses from qualified financial assets, rather than follow the normal property-by-property approach required by Regulations. For purposes of making reverse allocations of recognized gains and losses under § 704(c) principles, Rev.Proc. 2007–59, 2007–2 C.B. 745, provides automatic permission to aggregate built-in gains and losses to a qualified partnership, which is a partnership that (1) allocates gains and losses in proportion to the partners' capital accounts, (2) reasonably expects to revalue its assets at least four times a year, (3) holds publicly traded property of at least 90% of its non-cash assets, (4) has at least 10 unrelated partners, and (5) will make at least 200 trades of financial assets during the year.

thereby bringing the total tax gain recognized by E and F to $50 gain each. (See also Treas.Reg. § 1.704–1(b)(5), Ex. (18), applying § 704(c) principles to book/tax depreciation disparities due to revaluations.)

The same results may be achieved by special allocations without increasing E's and F's capital accounts at the time of G's admission. Treas.Reg. § 1.704–1(b)(5), Ex. (14)(iv). If neither of these alternatives is utilized by the partnership, the result will be that G will be allocated gain of $40 when the property is sold for $300, and G's capital account will be increased by the same amount, even though based on the economics of the transaction G's share of both should have been zero. In this circumstance, Treas.Reg. § 1.704–1(b)(1)(iii) authorizes the recharacterization of the transaction under other provisions of the Code. For example, the amount allocated to G may constitute compensation.

Suppose that C contributes money to the existing AB partnership in exchange for a partnership interest and the partnership revalues its assets under Treas.Reg. § 1.704–1(b)(2)(iv)(*f*). Among the partnership's assets is purchased goodwill, a § 197 intangible that was amortizable by the AB partnership. Rev. Rul. 2004–49, 2004–1 C.B. 939, held that the § 197 anti-churning rules do not apply and that consistent with Treas.Reg. § 1.197–2(h)(12)(vii)(A), the ABC Partnership may make reverse § 704(c) allocations (including curative and remedial allocations) of amortization to take into account the built-in gain or loss from the revaluation of the intangible. Thus, C could be allocated notional § 197 amortization deductions while A and B were allocated notional ordinary income or, alternatively, the partnership could allocate other deduction items to C (or income items to A and B) for tax purposes differently than they were allocated for book purposes. But if the goodwill were self-created goodwill, it would not have been amortizable by the AB partnership. In that case, the ruling held that the anti-churning rules apply and that the ABC Partnership, consistent with Treas.Reg. § 1.197–2(h)(12)(vii)(B), could make remedial, but not traditional or curative, allocations of amortization to take into account the built-in gain or loss from the revaluation of the intangible, provided that C is not related to A or B. Thus, C could be allocated notional § 197 amortization deductions while A and B were allocated notional ordinary income.

7.　DISTRIBUTIONS OF SECTION 704(c) PROPERTY

Section 704(c)(1)(B) requires the contributing partner to recognize gain or loss upon the distribution of property by the partnership to another partner within seven years of the date the property was contributed to the partnership. This provision is discussed in Chapter 25.

PROBLEM SET 4

1.　Sean and Pat formed a general partnership to which Sean contributed $50,000 of cash and Pat contributed depreciable property with a fair market value of $50,000 and a basis of $30,000. The property had a 10-year cost recovery period, of which 5 years were remaining on the contribution date; it is being depreciated under the straight-line method (ignore conventions). The partnership agreement provides that Sean and Pat will share profits and losses equally. Each year the partnership recognized $12,000 of gross income and no deductions other than the depreciation deductions on the contributed property.

(a) How much depreciation will be allocated to Sean and Pat respectively for book and tax purposes?

(b) (1) If the property contributed by Pat is sold for $30,000 after it has been held by the partnership for two years, how will the partnership allocate the gain for book and tax purposes?

(2) If the property contributed by Pat is sold for $60,000 after it has been held by the partnership for two years, how will the partnership allocate the gain for book and tax purposes?

(3) If the property contributed by Pat is sold for $15,000 after it has been held by the partnership for five years and is fully depreciated, how will the partnership allocate the gain for book and tax purposes?

2.   The basic facts of Problem 1 apply but assume that Pat's basis for the depreciable property was only $20,000.

(a) How much depreciation will be allocated to Sean and Pat respectively for book and tax purposes if the partnership applies the "traditional method" with the ceiling rule?

(b) How will the partnership allocate depreciation and partnership gross income, for both book and tax purposes, if the partnership elects to use "curative allocations"?

(c) How will the partnership allocate depreciation and partnership gross income, for both book and tax purposes, if the partnership elects to use "remedial allocations"?

3.   Todd and Ursula are partners in the TU Partnership, which owns Greenacre, a farm that is leased to tenant farmers. The fair market value of Greenacre is $1,200,000, its basis and book value to the partnership is $600,000. Todd and Ursula each have a $300,000 basis in their partnership interests. Veronica joins the partnership by contributing Whiteacre, which has a fair market value of $600,000. Veronica's basis in Whiteacre is $700,000. Todd, Ursula, and Veronica will share all profits and losses one-third each. On Veronica's admission to the partnership, the partnership will revalue its assets to fair market value. What are the tax consequences to the partnership and the partners from the sale of Whiteacre in each of the following circumstances?

(a) One year after Veronica joins the partnership the TUV partnership sells Whiteacre for $540,000.

(b) One year after Veronica joins the partnership, the TUV partnership sells Greenacre for $1,200,000 and distributes $600,000 cash to Veronica, who leaves the partnership. The $600,000 of partnership tax gain on the sale of Greenacre is properly allocated $300,000 each to Todd and Ursula. Veronica recognizes a $100,000 loss on her liquidation distribution. In the next taxable year, the partnership sells Whiteacre for $540,000.

4.   Kim and Lesley each contributed $150,000 to form a limited liability company that is taxed as a partnership. They shared profits and losses equally. Using the initial contribution, the K&L LLC purchased an apartment building and began to renovate it for sale as condominiums. When Kim and Lesley were unable to finish the project, Marion was admitted as a new member of the LLC in consideration of a $250,000 cash contribution to fund completion of the project. At the time Marion was admitted to membership in the LLC, the fair market value of the building project, which was the LLC's sole asset, was $500,000.

(a)   What would be the result if the capital account and allocation provisions of the LLC agreement were not amended to reflect Marion's admission as a member?

(b)   How should the capital account and allocation provisions of the LLC agreement be amended to reflect Marion's admission as a member? Assume that after completion of the project using Marion's contribution, all of the condominium units were sold in the same year for an aggregate price of $1,200,000, resulting in a taxable profit of $650,000.

SECTION 4.   ALLOCATIONS RELATING TO NONCOMPENSATORY PARTNERSHIP OPTIONS

Treas.Reg. § 1.721–2 provides that upon the exercise of a noncompensatory partnership option, the option holder is treated as contributing property to the partnership in exchange for the partnership interest; the contributed property is the sum of the original premium paid by the option holder to the partnership, the exercise price, and the option privilege. Section 721 applies even if the option holder receives a partnership interest with a value greater or less than the sum of the option premium and exercise price, i.e., a capital shift resulting from the exercise. To deal with the fact that the option holder generally receives a partnership interest with a value that is greater or less than the sum of the option premium and exercise price, i.e., there is a capital shift, the Regulations under § 704 allocate a disproportionate share of gross income, without a corresponding allocation of book income, to any partner who has benefited from such a capital shift.

Under Treas.Reg. § 1.704–1(b)(2)(iv)(d)(4), the option holder's initial capital account equals the consideration paid to the partnership for the option plus the fair market value of any property (other than the option itself) contributed to the partnership upon exercise. To meet the substantial economic effect test, Treas.Regs. §§ 1.704–1(b)(2)(iv)(h)(2) and 1.704–1(b)(2)(iv)(s) require the partnership to revalue its property following the exercise of the option and to allocate the unrealized income, gain, loss, and deductions from the revaluation (1) to the option holder to reflect the holder's right to partnership capital, and (2) then, to the historic partners. To the extent that unrealized appreciation or depreciation in the partnership's assets has been allocated to the option holder's capital account, under § 704(c) principles the holder will recognize correlative allocations of any income or loss attributable to that appreciation or depreciation as the underlying assets are sold, depreciated, or amortized.

Suppose the AB Partnership, in which A is a one-third partner and B is a two-thirds partner, had the following assets and partners' capital accounts:

	Assets			Partners' Capital Accounts	
	Book	Tax Basis		Book	Tax Basis
Blackacre	$300	$300	A	$400	$400
Whiteacre	$900	$900	B	$800	$800

In consideration of $100, C is granted an option to acquire a one-quarter partnership interest within two years in exchange for a contribution of $400 at the time C exercises the option. (Upon exercise of the option, A's interest is reduced to one-quarter and B's interest is reduced to one-half.) When C exercises the option, the fair market value of Blackacre is $500, and the fair market value of Whiteacre is $1,500. After revaluation of the partnership's assets and partners' capital accounts as required by Treas.Regs. §§ 1.704–1(b)(2)(iv)(*h*)(*2*) and 1.704–1(b)(2)(iv)(*s*), and taking into account C's contributions, the ABC Partnership's balance sheet is as follows:

	Assets			Partners' Capital Accounts	
	Book	Tax Basis		Book	Tax Basis
Cash	$ 500	$ 500	A	$ 625	$ 400
Blackacre	$ 500	$ 300	B	$1,250	$ 800
Whiteacre	$1,500	$ 900	C	$ 625	$ 500
	$2,500	$1,700		$2,500	$1,700

There has been a reallocation of $125 of capital from A and B to C, as required by Treas.Reg. § 1.704–2(b)(2)(iv)(*s*)(*3*). Pursuant to Treas.Reg. § 1.704–2(b)(2)(iv)(*s*)(*2*)), the first $125 of gross income thereafter realized by the ABC Partnership, whether upon the sale of Blackacre, Whiteacre, from rental receipts, or from any other source, must be allocated to C. For example, if Blackacre were sold for $500, reflecting no book gain, the tax gain of $200 would be allocated $125 to C, $25 to A, and $50 to B. If the partnership had inadequate gross income to eliminate C's book/tax disparity, the partnership would be required to allocate tax deductions differently than book deductions by allocating to A and B tax deductions the correlative book deductions for which were allocated to C. For example, if Blackacre were to be sold for $180 and the $320 book loss allocated $80 to each of A and C and $160 to B, none of the $120 tax loss—being less than the prior $125 capital shift from A and B to C—would be allocated to C; the tax loss would be allocated $40 to A and $80 to B.

If after all of the unrealized gain or loss in the partnership's assets has been allocated to the option holder and the option holder's capital account still does not equal the amount of partnership capital to which the option holder is entitled, then the partnership must adjust the capital accounts of the historic partners by the amounts necessary to provide the option holder with a capital account equal to the holder's rights to partnership capital under the agreement. Starting with the year the option is exercised, the partnership must make corrective allocations of tax items—that differ from the partnership's allocations of book items—of gross income or loss to the partners to reflect any shift in the partners' capital accounts occurring as a result of the exercise of an option.

DETAILED ANALYSIS

1.   REVALUATIONS OF PARTNERS' CAPITAL ACCOUNTS

Treas.Reg. § 1.704–1(b)(2)(iv)(*h*)(*2*) provides rules for revaluing the partners' capital accounts while an option is outstanding. In revaluing partnership property under Treas.Reg. § 1.704–1(b)(2)(iv)(*f*), the aggregate value of partnership property must be reduced by the amount by which the value of the option exceeds its price or is increased by the amount by which the price of the option exceeds its value.

2.   RECHARACTERIZATION OF OPTION HOLDER AS A PARTNER

An option holder will be recharacterized as a partner if (1) under a facts and circumstances test, the option holder's rights are substantially similar to the rights afforded to a partner, and (2) as of the date that the noncompensatory option is issued, transferred, or modified, there is a strong likelihood that the failure to treat the option holder as a partner would result in a substantial reduction in the present value of the partners' and the option holder's aggregate tax liabilities. Treas.Reg. § 1.761–3. If an option is reasonably certain to be exercised, the first half of this test is generally met. If the option holder is treated as a partner under the Regulations, then the holder's distributive share of the partnership's income, gain, loss, deduction, or credit must be determined in accordance with such partner's interest in the partnership under Treas.Reg. § 1.704–1(b)(3). For this purpose, the option holder's share of partnership items should reflect the lesser amount of capital investment if appropriate; the option holder's distributive share of partnership losses and deductions may be limited by § 704(b) and (d) to the amount paid for the option.

SECTION 5. ALLOCATIONS WHERE INTERESTS VARY DURING THE YEAR

INTERNAL REVENUE CODE: Section 706(c)(2)(B), (d).

REGULATIONS: Section 1.706–1(c)(2), (4); 1.706–4.

Section 706(c)(1) provides that a partnership's taxable year does not close on admission of a new partner, the liquidation of a partner's interest, or the sale of a partnership interest.[13] This rule, coupled with the ability of partnerships to provide for special allocations of tax items, raises the question whether an allocation to a partner of items attributable to a portion of a taxable year during which the partner was not a partner will be respected. This problem most frequently arises on the admission of a new partner, either by contribution or by purchase of a partnership interest from a partner, but it may also arise when an existing partner increases the interest through contribution or purchase.

Suppose, for example, that a calendar year, cash-method partnership has incurred a loss of $100,000 prior to December 1, and on that date admits a new partner to whom all of the loss is specially allocated. Section 706(d) will disallow the allocation of this loss to the new partner. This section requires that if there is any change in a partner's interest in the partnership during the year, each partner's distributive share of any partnership item of income, gain, loss, deduction, or credit must be determined using a method prescribed by the Regulations that takes into account the varying interests of the partners in the partnership during the year. The distributive share of "each partner" must be determined taking into account the varying interests of the partners if there is a change in "any partner's interest." See H.Rep. No. 98–432, 98th Cong., 2d Sess. 1213 (1984).

DETAILED ANALYSIS

1. INTERIM CLOSING OF THE BOOKS VERSUS PRORATION

1.1. *General*

Treas.Reg. § 1.706–4 prescribes two methods for taking into account the partners' varying interests during the year: the interim closing of the books method and the proration method. These Regulations mandate the interim closing of the books method whenever a partner's interest is changed, unless the partnership by agreement among the partners elects to use the proration method. Treas.Reg. § 1.706–4(a)(2)(iii). For purposes of determining allocations to partners whose interests vary during the taxable year, the Regulations require the partnership to assign partnership items under its method of accounting for the full taxable year to segments (for interim closing method) and proration periods (for proration method) of the taxable year representing discrete periods during which partners' interests vary.

---

[13] Section 706(c)(2)(A) provides that the taxable year of the partnership closes with respect to a partner who retires or sells or exchanges the partner's *entire* partnership interest.

Treas.Reg. § 1.706–4(a)(2)(vi) through (viii). The partnership is allowed to allocate partnership items under its method of accounting to different segments of the taxable year, using the closing of the books method for some segments and, when the partners agree, using the proration method for other segments. Certain "extraordinary items" may not, however, be prorated. Treas.Reg. § 1.706–4(e)(1).

Although the Regulations apply to a change in a partner's interest attributable to a disposition of a partner's entire interest or a partial interest, the Regulations do not apply to changes in allocations of partnership items among contemporaneous partners that satisfy the allocation rules of § 704(b), provided that a reallocation is not attributable to a capital contribution to the partnership or a distribution of money or property that is a return of capital; these allocations must also satisfy substantial economic effect. Treas.Reg. § 1.706–4(b)(1). The Regulations also do not apply to partnerships in which capital is not a material income producing factor; such partnerships may choose to determine a partner's distributive share of partnership items using any reasonable method to account for the varying interests of the partners in the partnership during the taxable year, provided that the allocations comply with § 704(b). Treas.Reg. § 1.706–4(b)(2).

1.2. *Interim Closing of the Books*

If the interim closing method applies to a variance in ownership, "segments" are created. The first segment begins at the start of the taxable year, and each segment closes according to when the variation is deemed to occur under the applicable convention. Treas.Reg. § 1.706–4(a)(1)(iv). Partnerships may choose from three conventions if using the interim method to determine length of segments. Treas.Reg. § 1.706–4(c)(3)(i).[14] These are the (1) calendar day convention, which is the default unless an agreement is in place for an alternative; (2) semi-monthly; and (3) monthly. A partnership must use the same convention for all its interim closings. Under the calendar day convention, the variation is deemed to occur at the end of the day on which the variation occurs. Treas.Reg. § 1.706–4(c)(1)(i). Under the semi-monthly convention, if the variation occurs on the 1st through 15th day of a calendar month, the variation is deemed to occur at the end of the last day of the preceding calendar month; if the variation occurs on the 16th day through the end of a calendar month, the variation is deemed to occur at the end of the 15th day of the that calendar month. The monthly convention is the same for variations that occur on the 1st through 15th day, but if the variation occurs on the 16th day through the end of the month, the variation is deemed to occur on the last day of that calendar month. These conventions do not, however, apply to "extraordinary items."

Assume that A, B, and C each have both a profits and a capital interest in the ABC partnership of 90%, 5%, and 5%, respectively. The ABC partnership uses the calendar year and uses a calendar day convention for its interim closings. On November 30, B and C contribute additional cash and the partnership agreement is amended to reduce A's profits and capital

---

[14] Partnerships may also agree to perform regular monthly or semi-monthly closings, regardless of whether a variation occurs. Treas.Reg. § 1.706–4(a)(2)(v).

interest to 30% and increase the interest of each of B and C to 35%. During the year, the partnership sustained a loss from business operations of $1,200, of which $1,000 of the loss was incurred before December 1 and $200 was incurred during December.

Under the interim closing of the books method, with the calendar day convention, two segments would be created: January 1 through November 30 and December 1 through December 31. The partnership would determine the exact amount of the operating loss incurred from January 1 through November 30, using its normal method of accounting, and that loss would be allocated 90% to A and 5% to each of B and C. The $200 loss actually incurred in December would be allocated 30% to A and 35% to each of B and C. Thus, the loss would be allocated among the partners as follows:

Partner	Profit/Loss Percentages	Loss Incurred During Months Held	Distributive Shares of Loss
A	90	$1,000	$ 900
	30	200	60
B	5	1,000	50
	35	200	70
C	5	1,000	50
	35	200	70
			$1,200

1.2.1.   Allocable Cash Method Items

When the interim closing of the books method is used by a cash method partnership, certain items are not taken into account on the date of payment. Section 706(d)(2) requires the proration over the taxable year by cash method partnerships of deductions for interest, taxes, rents, and other items which may be specified in the Regulations. This provision reflects the fact that these items may accrue over extended periods either before or after payment; taking them into account on the date of payment may result in a significant misstatement of the partners' taxable incomes. Thus, for example, if the ABC partnership in the preceding example had operated without any gain or loss except for a $1,200 rent payment attributable to the entire year made in arrears on December 31, the interim closing of the books method would result in the same allocation as results under the proration method since $100 of the rent must be attributed to each month. If the rental payment were attributable to only the last six months of the year, however, then $200 of rent would be allocated to each of the last six months of the year. As a result, A's distributive share of the loss would be $960 ((.9 × 5/6 × $1,200) + (.3 × 1/6 × $1,200)), and B's and C's shares would be $120 ((.05 × 5/6 × $1,200) + (.35 × 1/6 × $1,200)).

In addition to the items specified in § 706(d)(2), cash method partnerships are required to apportion depreciation ratably over the year, rather than attributing it entirely to the last day of the year. See Hawkins v. Commissioner, 713 F.2d 347 (8th Cir.1983).

Accrual method partnerships are required to prorate deductions for interest, rent, taxes, depreciation, and similar items over the year without any specific statutory directive. See Williams v. United States, 680 F.2d 382 (5th Cir.1982).

Prop.Reg. § 1.706–2(a)(2) (2015) would provide that the term "allocable cash basis item" generally includes items of deduction, loss, income, or gain specifically listed in the statute: (i) interest, (ii) taxes, and (iii) payments for services or for the use of property. However, Prop.Reg. § 1.706–2(a)(2)(iii) provides an exception for deductions for the transfer of an interest in the partnership in connection with the performance of services; such deductions generally must be allocated under the rules for extraordinary items in Treas.Reg. § 1.706–4(d). Pursuant to the authority granted in § 706(d)(2)(B)(iv), the Proposed Regulations provide that the term "allocable cash basis item" includes (1) any allowable deduction that had been previously deferred under § 267(a)(2), Prop.Reg. § 1.706–2(a)(2)(iv), and (2) any item of income, gain, loss, or deduction that accrues over time and that would, if not allocated as an allocable cash basis item, result in the significant misstatement of a partner's income. Prop.Reg. § 1.706–2(a)(2)(v). Examples of such items include rebate payments, refund payments, insurance premiums, prepayments, and cash advances. Prop.Reg. § 1.706–2(c) provides a de minimis rule that would provide that an allocable cash basis item will not be subject to the rules in § 706(d)(2) if, for the partnership's taxable year (1) the total of the particular class of allocable cash method items (for example, all interest income) is less than 5% of the partnership's (a) gross income, including tax-exempt income described in § 705, in the case of income or gain items, or (b) gross expenses and losses, including § 705(a)(2)(B) expenditures, in the case of losses and expense items; and (2) the total amount of allocable cash basis items from all classes of allocable cash basis items amounting to less than 5% of the partnership's (a) gross income, including tax-exempt income described in § 705(a)(1)(B), in the case of income or gain items, or (b) gross expenses and losses, including § 705(a)(2)(B) expenditures, in the case of losses and expense items, does not exceed $10 million in the taxable year, determined by treating all such allocable cash basis items as positive amounts.

1.2.2.   *Items Attributable to Prior or Future Years*

Suppose that the $1,200 rent paid in December by the ABC partnership in the preceding example was attributable to the year preceding the year in which it was paid and in which there was a change in partnership interests. Since the ABC partnership uses the cash method, the payment must be taken into account in the year in which it was paid, but for purposes of determining the partners' distributive shares, § 706(d)(2)(C) requires that the payment be treated as paid on the first day of the taxable year. Section 706(d)(2)(D) then provides that it is allocated among the partners according to their interests in the prior year to which the payment was attributable. Thus, A's distributive share of the loss would be $1,080 (.9 × $1,200) and B's and C's shares would be $60 (.05 × $1,200). If any person who was a partner in the prior year is no longer a partner in the year in which the item is paid, the distributive share of the item attributable to that partner is not deductible by the partnership. It must be capitalized and allocated to the basis of partnership assets under the rules of § 755. (Section 755 is discussed in Chapter 25.)

Similarly, if in a year in which there is a change in partnership interests, a cash method partnership makes a deductible payment of an item attributable to a future year, the item is attributed to the last day of the year. Assume that the ABC partnership in the preceding examples had neither a profit nor a loss for the taxable year of the change except for a $1,200 payment on July 1 of local real property taxes for the year beginning July 1. The $600 attributable to the current year is allocated ratably over the last six months of the year, and the remaining $600 is attributed to the last day of the year. Accordingly, A's distributive share of the loss is $660 (($600 × 5/6 × .9) + ($600 × 1/6 × .3) + ($600 × .3)), and B's and C's shares each are $270 (($600 × 5/6 × .05) + ($600 × 1/6 × .35) + ($600 × .35)).

1.3. *Proration Method*

Under the proration method, the partnership still first assigns items among segments and then determines its proration periods within each segment. The partnership then prorates all its items in each segment. Treas.Reg. § 1.706–4(a)(2)(ix). Within each proration period, the items are then allocated among the partners based on their respective percentage interests during that period. Only the calendar-day convention is permitted. If no interim closings take place, the entire taxable year would be the relevant segment, and one or more proration periods would occur during that year.

For example, assume the same ABC partnership except that they agree to use the proration method exclusively. Assume that A, B, and C each have both a profits and a capital interest in the ABC partnership of 90%, 5%, and 5%, respectively. The ABC partnership uses the calendar year. On November 30, B and C contribute additional cash and the partnership agreement is amended to reduce A's profits and capital interest to 30% and increase the interest of each of B and C to 35%. During the year, the partnership sustained a loss from business operations of $1,200 and has no "extraordinary items." There would be one segment—the entire taxable year—and two proration periods: January 1 through November 30 (334 days) and December 1 through December 31 (31 days). The partners must compute their distributive shares as follows:

A	B	C
.9 x 334/365 x $1200	.05 x 334/365 x $1200	.05 x 334/365 x $1200
plus	plus	plus
.3 x 31/365 x $1200	.35 x 31/365 x $1200	.35 x 31/365 x $1200
= $1019 (rounded)	=$90.50 (rounded)	=$90.50 (rounded)

1.4. *Extraordinary Items*

Treas.Reg. § 1.706–4(e) requires that "extraordinary items" be allocated to the partners in proportion to their interests at the time of day on which the extraordinary item arose. Extraordinary items include, among others, gain or loss on the disposition or abandonment of capital assets, trade or business property, property excluded from capital gains treatment under § 1221(a)(1), (3), (4), or (5) if substantially all of the assets in a particular category are disposed of in one transaction, discharge of indebtedness (except items subject to § 108(e)(8) or § 108(i)), certain credits, items from the settlement of tort or third-party liability, items that the partners agree are consistently extraordinary for the year (subject to an anti-abuse exception), certain items attributable to accounting method changes, any item identified in published guidance, and any item that in the opinion of the IRS would, if ratably allocated, result in a substantial distortion of income in any return in which the item is included.) Prop.Reg. § 1.706–4(e)(3) (2015) specifies that any deduction for the transfer of a partnership interest for services is also an extraordinary item.

Treas.Reg. § 1.706–4(e)(3) provides an exception for small extraordinary items under which an extraordinary item may be treated as not being an extraordinary item if, for the partnership's taxable year, (1) the total of all items in the particular class of extraordinary items (for example, all tort or similar liabilities) is less than 5% of the partnership's gross income (including tax-exempt income described in § 705) in the case of income or gain items, or gross expenses and losses (including § 705(a)(2)(B) expenditures) in the case of losses and expense items; and (2) the total amount of extraordinary items from all classes of extraordinary items amounting to less than 5% of the partnership's gross income (in the case of income or gain items) or gross expenses and losses (in the case of losses and expense items) does not exceed $10 million in the taxable year, determined by treating all such extraordinary items as positive amounts.

1.5. *Considerations in Choice of Method*

The interim closing of the books is the more accurate method for apportioning income between the period before a change in the partners' interests and the period after the change. The proration method, however, is often more convenient. In deciding whether to agree to use the proration method, each partner must consider the effect of its inaccuracies on tax liability for the year. When a partnership interest is disposed of in its entirety, the selling partner must bear in mind that if the proration method is used, events occurring after the sale can significantly and unexpectedly affect the tax liability for the year of the sale. However, this risk is somewhat mitigated by the extraordinary item rules discussed above.

1.6. *Audit Changes*

Where the IRS asserts a deficiency under § 706(d) it may apply either the proration or closing of the books method. Johnsen v. Commissioner, 84 T.C. 344 (1985), rev'd on other grounds, 794 F.2d 1157 (6th Cir.1986). If the IRS applies the proration method, the taxpayer may prove at trial that the interim closing of the books method is more reasonable. See Sartin v. United

States, 5 Cl.Ct. 172 (1984); Richardson v. Commissioner, 76 T.C. 512 (1981) aff'd, 693 F.2d 1189 (5th Cir.1982). However, if the taxpayer elects to use the interim closing of the books method, the taxpayer must establish the date on which each item was earned, received, accrued, or paid. Sartin v. United States, supra; Moore v. Commissioner, 70 T.C. 1024 (1978).

2.   RELATIONSHIP OF SECTION 706(d) TO SECTION 704(b)

Suppose that C is admitted to the AB partnership on December 30 as a one-third partner with A and B, and the partnership agreement specially allocates all of the depreciation on the partnership's property for the year to C. The ABC partnership maintains capital accounts as required by the § 704(b) Regulations, charges the depreciation to C's capital account, will liquidate according to the partners' capital accounts, and C is required to restore any deficit in his capital account upon liquidation. The allocation has substantial economic effect. Will it be recognized? Ogden v. Commissioner, 84 T.C. 871 (1985), aff'd per curiam, 788 F.2d 252 (5th Cir.1986), held that § 704(b)(2) does not override the requirements of § 706(d). A retroactive allocation is ineffective even if it has substantial economic effect. See also Treas.Reg. § 1.704–1(b)(1)(iii), providing that § 704(b)(2) does not override § 706(d).

Snell v. United States, 680 F.2d 545 (8th Cir.1982), rejected the taxpayer's argument that § 706(d) applies only when the partnership agreement does not expressly provide for allocation of an item for the year. However, § 706(d) does not apply to retroactive reallocations of items among existing partners where the reallocation is not attributable to a capital contribution that results in the reduction of the interest of one or more partners. Lipke v. Commissioner, 81 T.C. 689 (1983). Treas.Reg. § 1.706–4(b) expressly provides that the rules for allocating items to partners whose interest varies will not apply to changes in the allocation of the distributive share of partnership items as long as the variation in partnership interests is not attributable to a contribution of money or property to the partnership and the allocations resulting from a modification satisfy the partnership allocation rules of § 704(b). As previously noted, the Regulations also allow service partnerships to adopt any reasonable method to account for varying interests of the partners during a taxable year in which allocations are valid under § 704(b). Treas.Reg. § 1.761–1(c) permits amendments to a partnership agreement made after the close of the taxable year, but on or before the due date for the partnership's return, to be given retroactive effect. In such a case, however, the reallocation must have substantial economic effect under § 704(b)(2). Thus, for example, if the DEF law partnership, in which each partner had a one-third interest in profits and capital, amended its partnership agreement on April 14, Year 3, effective January 1, Year 2, to give D a one-half interest in partnership profits and E and F each a one-quarter interest, for the purpose of more accurately reflecting the relationship of their services to firm profits for the year, the amended allocation should be effective.

3.   RELATIONSHIP OF SECTION 706(d) TO GENERAL ASSIGNMENT
     OF INCOME DOCTRINE

In Cottle v. Commissioner, 89 T.C. 467 (1987), the taxpayer held a 1% limited partnership interest and a 25% general partnership interest in a partnership organized to acquire an apartment building and convert it to condominiums. Almost all of the effort required to effect the conversion and sale of the units occurred prior to October 21, 1977, but none of the sales of units had been closed. On that day, the taxpayer transferred his 25% general partnership interest to his wholly owned corporation in a transaction subject to § 351. On November 15, 1977, the partnership closed the sale of most of the condominium units. Applying the interim closing of the books method, the taxpayer reported no income for the year attributable to the general partnership interest, which he held until October 21. The Commissioner asserted that the taxpayer and not the corporation was taxable on all of the partnership income attributable to the units sold on November 15 because "due to the assignment of income doctrine, the interim closing of the books was not a reasonable method of determining who should report the income in question." Neither the taxpayer nor the Commissioner urged use of the proration method. Because the taxpayer retained his 1% limited partnership interest, the statutory predecessor of § 706(d) rather than § 706(c)(2)(A) applied. Nevertheless, relying on the legislative history of the statutory predecessor of § 706(d), the court allowed the taxpayer to apply Treas.Reg. § 1.706–1(c)(2), mandating the closing of the books method. The court reasoned that Subchapter K dictates that the timing of the includability of income (and of deductions) is determined at the partnership level under the method of accounting used by the partnership. Because there were contingencies attached to the closing of the sales by the partnership, the court concluded that the income was not earned by the partnership until November 15. Thus, as of October 21, when the partnership closed its books, it had no income and, accordingly, there was no partnership income to be allocated to the taxpayer at that time. The court then turned to the applicability of more general assignment of income principles, which it described as follows:

> Respondent argues that the principles of Commissioner v. Court Holding Co., 324 U.S. 331 (1945), as applied in Murry v. Commissioner, T.C. Memo. 1984–670, should govern the instant case to cause petitioners rather than DRC to be taxable on the profits from the condominium sales.
>
> In *Murry,* the taxpayer owned an apartment complex that was to be converted to a condominium, and the units therein would subsequently be sold. The taxpayer's wholly-owned corporation was to undertake the development of the property as a condominium. Because of certain financial difficulties, the taxpayer had to sell the apartment complex to the lender. However, in order to accommodate the taxpayer's tax considerations, the lender agreed to buy the property from the taxpayer's corporation. The taxpayer thus agreed to make a capital contribution of the property to the

corporation, if the corporation agreed to sell the property immediately thereafter to the lenders.

We held in *Murry* that the taxpayer and not the corporation was taxable on the sale of the property to the lender. In so holding, we applied the *Court Holding* doctrine which provides that "a sale by one person cannot be transformed for tax purposes into a sale by another by using the latter as a conduit through which to pass title." Commissioner v. Court Holding Co., 324 U.S. at 334.

We agree with petitioners that *Murry* is not relevant to this case. Associates in the instant case was the owner and developer of the property. It converted the property to condominium units, sold the units therein, and reported the profits from these sales on its partnership return. There is no question in this case, as was present in *Murry,* as to who earned the income. No conduit was used by Associates to sell the condominium units. The parties agree that Associates earned the income; the only question in the instant case is how that income is to be allocated among the partners. And that question is resolved solely by application of section 706(c)(2)(B), which governs the allocation of partnership items when there are transfers of partial partnership interests during the tax year. The rules thereunder are specifically designed to avoid assignments of income and retroactive allocation of losses between transferor and transferee partners. Moore v. Commissioner, 70 T.C. at 1032–1033. We think they adequately resolve the question in the instant case, and that their use is specifically mandated by Richardson v. Commissioner, 76 T.C. at 526–527.

We hold for petitioners on this issue.

What would have been the result in the *Cottle* case if the partners had agreed to use the proration method?

4. TIERED PARTNERSHIPS

Prior to the enactment of § 706(d)(3) in 1984, it arguably was possible to sidestep the prohibition on retroactive allocations through the use of tiered partnerships. Assume for example that the UT partnership held a 90% interest in the LT partnership, and both partnerships used the calendar year. LT had a $10,000 loss for the year. UT's share of that loss was $9,000. On December 30, A contributed cash to UT in exchange for an 80% interest, and UT used the interim closing of the books method to apply § 706(d). Arguably, UT's $9,000 loss from LT was incurred on December 31, the last day of LT's taxable year, and A's distributive share of the loss would be $7,200. Section 706(d)(3) prevents this avoidance technique by, in effect, ignoring UT, the upper tier partnership, for allocation purposes and flowing through to the partners of UT in accordance with their effective interests in LT on the close of each day UT's distributive share of each LT item. Thus, in the example, if UT's entire $9,000 loss from LT was attributable to depreciation, since A was a partner for two days of LT's taxable year within UT's taxable year, A's share would be $39 (80% × (2/365 × $9,000)). These principles apply whether the upper tier partnership uses the cash or the accrual method. In addition, the rules governing allocable cash method items must be applied in allocating lower tier partnership items to the partners of the upper tier partnership by the flow through method. Section 706(d)(3) generally adopts the position of the IRS set forth in Rev.Rul. 77–311, 1977–2 C.B. 218.

PROBLEM SET 5

1.   Prior to October 1st, Nora and Oliver were equal partners in a general partnership. As of October 1st, Pat made a capital contribution to the partnership, and the partnership agreement was amended to make Nora, Oliver, and Pat equal partners. During the year, the partnership recognized $180,000 of net income from business operations. Net operating income of $90,000 was realized in January through September, and net operating income of $90,000 was realized in October through December. In addition, in November, the partnership sold an item of § 1231 property and recognized a $60,000 loss. The partnership uses the accrual method and is on the calendar year.

(a)   How much income and loss must each partner include under the closing of the books method?

(b)   How much income and loss must each partner include under the proration method?

(c)   When is it likely that the partners will decide whether to elect to use the proration method?

2.   Ursula and Vanessa were equal partners in a partnership that used the cash method of accounting and calendar year. Last year the partnership reported no taxable income or loss; however, it incurred a $90,000 expense item that was not paid but would have been deductible if it had been paid. On June 1st of this year William made a capital contribution to become a one-third partner. This year, the partnership earned net taxable income of $36,000, at the rate of $3,000 per month, and in August it paid the $90,000 expense item.

(a)   What is each partner's distributive share of income or loss for this year using the closing of the books method?

(b)   What is each partner's distributive share of income or loss for this year using the proration method?

SECTION 6.   FAMILY PARTNERSHIPS

INTERNAL REVENUE CODE: Sections 704(e); 761(b).

REGULATIONS: Section 1.704–1(e).

Allocations of partnership items in partnerships in which the partners are family members present problems that are not present when the partnership allocations are bargained at arms' length. In so-called family partnerships, allocations may reflect an attempt to shift income for tax purposes in a manner inconsistent with the principles of Lucas v. Earl, 281 U.S. 111 (1930), and Helvering v. Horst, 311 U.S. 112

(1940). The principal problems involved partnerships where one (or more) partner's capital interest was derived by gift from a family member partner and where partnerships in which personal services were important but one or more partners did not provide any significant services.

As discussed in Chapter 17, the landmark case dealing with family partnerships is Commissioner v. Culbertson, 337 U.S. 733 (1949). That case involved a ranching partnership composed of a father and four sons, two of whom were minors. The sons had received their interests partly by gift from the father and partly by contribution of funds loaned to them by the father, which were repaid from the proceeds of partnership operations. The Court articulated the relevant test as follows:

> The question is not whether the services or capital contributed by a partner are of sufficient importance to meet some objective standard * * * but whether, considering all the facts the agreement, the conduct of the parties in execution of its provisions, their statements, the testimony of disinterested persons, the relationship of the parties, their respective abilities and capital contribution, the actual control of income and the purposes for which it is used, and any other facts throwing light on their true intent-the parties in good faith and acting with a business purpose intended to join together in the present conduct of the enterprise.

Section 761(b), as amended in 2015, focuses on whether a person is a partner and whether a partnership exists under the totality of the circumstances test of *Culbertson*. Thus, as previously noted in Chapter 17, under § 761(b), a person's status as a partner with an interest in a family partnership in which capital is a material income-producing factor acquired by gift should be tested under the same rules as a capital interest acquired by purchase or by a contribution to capital.

If the partnership interest is acquired by gift or through a family transfer, § 704(e) may then apply to change distributive share allocations from those provided in the partnership agreement. Section 704(e) applies only when a partnership interest is acquired by gift or in a transfer between family members. I.R.C. § 704(e). Family is defined to include only an individual's spouse, ancestors, and lineal descendants, and any trusts for the primary benefit of such persons. I.R.C. § 704(e)(2).

Section 704(e)(1) provides that, assuming the recipient of the gift is a bona fide partner, then the donee's distributive share allocation will belong to the donee, "except to the extent that such share is determined without allowance of reasonable compensation for services rendered to the partnership by the donor, and except to the extent that the portion of such share attributable to donated capital is proportionately greater than the share of the donor attributable to the donor's capital." In the case of a family transfer, the seller is treated as the donor, and the fair market value of the purchased interest is treated as the donated capital.

Treas.Reg. § 1.704–1(e)(3) addresses allocations and focuses on reasonableness and facts and circumstances. Distributive shares are to be reallocated by taking into account a "reasonable allowance" for services of the donor and donee, and then attributing the balance to the respective interests in partnership capital of the donor and donee. The statute and Regulation thus are essentially underlining that the assignment of income doctrine applies fully to gifts and transfers among family members of partnership interests. (The Regulations have not been revised to reflect the 2015 amendments to § 704(e) and § 761(b), and they primarily describe factors to consider in determining whether someone is or is not a partner and the extent of their interest. Thus, as a technical matter, many Regulation subsections should be revised and moved to reflect current § 761(b).)

CHAPTER 21

ALLOCATION OF PARTNERSHIP LIABILITIES

INTERNAL REVENUE CODE: Sections 704(d); 705; 733; 752.

Section 752(a) provides that any increase in a partner's share of partnership liabilities is treated as a cash contribution. As a cash contribution, an increase in a partner's share of partnership liabilities increases the partner's outside basis under § 722. A partner's outside basis is crucial to the conduit theory of partnership taxation because that basis is the ceiling on the amount of partnership losses that can be passed through to the partner's individual return. I.R.C. § 704(d). Conversely, a decrease in a partner's share of partnership liabilities, or a decrease in a partner's individual liabilities as a result of the assumption of those liabilities by the partnership, is treated by § 752(b) as a distribution of cash to the partner. This deemed cash distribution reduces the partner's basis in the partner's partnership interest pursuant to § 705(a)(2) and § 733. Gain is recognized to the extent that the deemed distribution exceeds outside basis. I.R.C. § 731(a)(1).

The Code contains no rules for determining a partner's share of partnership liabilities. The guiding principles are found in Treas.Regs. §§ 1.752–1 through 1.752–4 and 1.752–7. These rules are intended to treat as a partner's share of the partnership liabilities only that portion of the partnership liabilities for which the partner bears the ultimate economic risk of loss. In very general terms, debts for which no partner bears a risk of loss, nonrecourse debts, are allocated to the partners in accord with their share of gain attributable to encumbered property or their share of partnership profit.

Section 752 and the Regulations thereunder apply whenever the partnership borrows money or repays a loan. For example, if A and B form a general partnership to which each contributes $20,000 and in which they are equal partners, and the AB general partnership then borrows $100,000, A and B each increase their basis in the partnership by $50,000. If $20,000 of the loan subsequently is repaid, A and B each are treated as receiving a cash distribution of $10,000 that reduces their basis in the partnership by $10,000; and if either or both has a basis of less than $10,000 at that time, the partner recognizes gain: the reduction of liabilities treated as a cash distribution in excess of basis requires recognition of gain under § 731(a). Because § 752 is Subchapter K's way of incorporating the principles that generally govern the treatment of liabilities in computing basis and amount realized with respect to purchases and sales of property, including Crane v. Commissioner, 331 U.S. 1 (1947), and its progeny (dealing with nonrecourse debt), § 752(c) applies these rules to liabilities attached to property when the property is transferred subject to the liabilities.

Whether the liability is recourse or nonrecourse makes a difference under § 752. For example, if a partner transfers property to a partnership subject to a recourse liability that is not assumed by the partnership and for which the contributing partner remains personally liable, the liability remains a recourse liability of the contributing partner. The liability of the contributing partner is not changed; no other partners treat the liability as a cash contribution that increases basis, and the contributing partner does not reduce the partner's basis in the partnership interest. See Treas.Reg. § 1.752–1(g), Ex. (1).

Furthermore, different rules apply to transfers of encumbered property between partners and the partnership, whether by contribution or distribution, and transfers by the partnership to third parties. When the transfer is between the partnership and partners, § 752(c) provides that liabilities to which the property is taken subject, but that are not assumed, are taken into account under § 752(a) and (b) only to the extent of the fair market value of the property, but if the property is sold by the partnership, pursuant to § 752(d), liabilities in excess of the fair market value are taken into account as well. See Commissioner v. Tufts, 461 U.S. 300 (1983).

Allocations of partnership liabilities are closely related to allocations of partnership income and loss. As is explained in the following material, if a partnership agreement specially allocates deductions to a particular partner, the provisions of Treas.Reg. § 1.752–2, governing the allocation of partnership recourse debt generally result in a year-by-year reallocation of partnership debt away from the partners who do not receive the deductions and to the partner who received the special allocation of the deductions. As a result, the partner receiving the special allocation will increase the partner's basis by the amount of the partner's increased share of partnership indebtedness. This basis increase will prevent § 704(d) from coming into play to defer the partner's deductions. (Concomitantly, the other partners will receive deemed distributions that reduce their bases.) Likewise, Treas.Reg. § 1.752–3, which governs the allocation of nonrecourse debt, coordinates allocations of nonrecourse debt with allocations of nonrecourse deductions under Treas.Reg. § 1.704–2, with the result that a partner to whom nonrecourse deductions are allocated will be allocated sufficient debt to prevent § 704(d) from affecting the partner.

SECTION 1.   ALLOCATION OF RECOURSE LIABILITIES

REGULATIONS: Sections 1.752–1, –2(a)–(d), (f)–(h), –4(b), (d).

A "recourse liability" is any liability "to the extent * * * that any partner or related person bears the economic risk of loss for that liability." Treas.Reg. § 1.752–1(a)(1). A partner's share of any recourse liability is the portion of the economic risk of loss for the liability borne by the partner or a person related to that partner. Treas.Reg. § 1.752–2(a).

For purposes of § 752, the term "liability," as defined in Treas.Reg. § 1.752–1(a)(4), is limited to debts that: (1) create or increase basis (including cash balances); (2) give rise to a deduction (e.g., accrual method accounts payable); or (3) give rise to a nondeductible expenditure not chargeable to a capital account (under § 263 or § 263A). Cash method accounts payable are not liabilities for purposes of § 752 and do not increase the partners' bases in their partnership interests. See Rev. Rul. 88–77, 1988–2 C.B. 128, which holds that cash method accounts payable, which are not deductible until paid and do not give rise to basis in any asset, should not be treated as liabilities for purposes of § 752 and should not increase the partners' bases in their partnership interests.

Treas.Reg. § 1.752–2 provides detailed rules for determining the extent to which a partner bears the economic risk of loss associated with partnership liabilities. Generally speaking, a partner's share of partnership recourse liabilities is the amount of the partnership's liabilities for which the partner bears the ultimate burden of payment if the partnership is unable to make the payment. This ultimate burden is determined by taking into account the net effect of: (1) partners' obligations to restore negative capital accounts; (2) partner's obligations to pay notes to the partnership executed by them; (3) partners' obligations to creditors under guarantee agreements; (4) partners' obligations to other partners under any agreement; (5) partners' rights to contribution or indemnification under the partnership agreement or any other agreement; and (6) rights of contribution or indemnification arising by operation of law (e.g., subrogation rights of a guarantor). Contingent obligations, however, are ignored if it appears unlikely that they will be satisfied. See Treas.Reg. § 1.752–2(b)(4). In addition, recently promulgated regulatory anti-abuse rules restrict the use of "bottom dollar" guarantees, indemnities, or obligations, which are payment obligations that are unlikely actually to increase a partner's economic risk of loss. Treas.Reg. § 1.752–2(b)(3)(ii).

DETAILED ANALYSIS

1. DEFINITION OF RECOURSE LIABILITY

Treas.Reg. § 1.752–1(a)(1) defines a "recourse liability" as any liability to the extent any partner or related person bears the risk of loss for the liability. Thus, a nonrecourse mortgage loan to the partnership that is fully guaranteed by a partner is a recourse liability. Treas.Reg. § 1.752–2(f), Ex. (5). If only a portion of the nonrecourse liability has been guaranteed, then the obligation is bifurcated, and the guaranteed amount is treated as a recourse obligation while the remaining portion is treated as a nonrecourse liability. Treas.Regs. §§ 1.752–1(i); 1.752–2(f), Ex. (5). A nonrecourse loan to a partnership by a partner or a person related to a partner (as determined under Treas.Reg. § 1.752–4(b)) also is treated as a recourse liability, the economic risk of which is borne by the creditor-partner or partner related to the lender. Treas.Reg. § 1.752–2(c)(1). Treas.Reg. § 1.752–2(d)(1) excepts from the partner-lender rules certain loans by partners having a partnership interest of 10% or less; in such a case, the debt is allocated under the nonrecourse liability allocation rules of Treas.Reg. § 1.752–3.

Under applicable state law, members of a limited liability company are not personally liable for payment of any of the LLC's debts. Accordingly, the recourse debts owed by an LLC that is taxed as a partnership are not recourse debts as defined by Treas.Reg. § 1.752–1(a)(1) because no member (partner) bears any risk of loss. Such debt is a nonrecourse debt that is allocated under Treas.Reg. § 1.752–3. If, however, a member of an LLC personally guarantees a debt of the LLC, the debt becomes a recourse debt, subject to the allocation rules of Treas.Reg. § 1.752–2 because the guaranteeing partner bears the risk of loss associated with the debt. Likewise, if a member transfers property to an LLC subject to a debt for which the contributing member continues to bear personal liability, the debt remains a recourse liability to the contributing member.

2.   ECONOMIC RISK OF LOSS

2.1. *In General*

Economic risk of loss, which is the key for determining whether a debt is recourse or nonrecourse and for allocating recourse debts among partners, is defined in Treas.Reg. § 1.752–2(b). A partner bears the economic risk of loss with respect to a partnership liability (even if the liability is nonrecourse as to the partnership) if upon a hypothetical liquidation of the partnership in which all of its assets are treated as worthless, the partner (or a related person) "would be obligated to make a payment to any person (or a contribution to the partnership) * * * and the partner or related person would not be entitled to reimbursement from another partner [or person related to that partner]." This means, in general, that a partner is economically at risk if following the liquidation of a partnership with no assets, and after the exercise of all rights to obtain reimbursement from others, the partner is responsible for payment of the debt. An obligation for which a partner is not entitled to reimbursement generally will exist to the extent that a partner would have a negative capital account as a result of the constructive liquidation and the partner is obligated to restore that negative capital account. An unreimbursable payment obligation also may exist if a partner guarantees a loan that is nonrecourse as to the partnership. But if a partner guarantees a loan that is recourse as to the partnership, payment of the loan by the guaranteeing partner would give rise to right of subrogation under state law. Thus, the partner would have a right to reimbursement of a portion of the debt from the other partners and does not bear the risk of loss as to that portion of the debt. See Treas.Reg. § 1.752–2(f), Ex. (3).

A partner bears the economic risk of loss with respect to a debt that is nonrecourse to the partnership if the partner or a related party (as defined in Treas.Reg. § 1.752–4(b)) is the creditor with respect to the nonrecourse liability. Treas.Reg. § 1.752–2(c)(1). Related persons for this purpose are identified in Treas.Reg. § 1.752–4(b) through cross references to § 267(b) and § 707(b), with certain modifications. Thus, for example, the risk on a nonrecourse loan to a partnership from a corporation in which a partner owns more than 80% of the stock is treated as borne entirely by the shareholder-partner.

Although under Treas.Reg. §§ 1.752–1(a)(1) and 1.752–2(c)(2) a liability is recourse if a partner or a related party bears the risk of loss, an exception to this related party provision in Treas.Reg. § 1.752–4(b)(2)(iii) provides that persons owning directly or indirectly interests in the same partnership are not treated as related. In IPO II v. Commissioner, 122 T.C. 295 (2004), an individual was a partner with X Corporation, which he wholly owned, in a partnership that borrowed money to purchase an airplane. The loan was guaranteed by the individual but not by X Corporation. In addition, the loan was guaranteed by Y Corporation, 70% of the stock of which was owned by the individual partner. The parties claimed that X Corporation was at risk for the partnership debt because X Corporation was related to Y Corporation that had guaranteed the debt by virtue of the individual's common ownership of both corporations. The Tax Court held that the relationship between X Corporation and Y Corporation was severed by Treas.Reg. § 1.752–4(b)(2)(iii) because the relationship was traced through the individual who was a partner in the partnership. Thus, none of the liability was allocated to X Corporation.

2.2. *Constructive Liquidation of Partnership*

Treas.Reg. § 1.752–2(b) prescribes the rules governing constructive liquidation analysis for determining partners' economic risk of loss. The following events are considered to happen in the constructive liquidation: (1) all of the partnership's assets (other than property contributed to the partnership solely for the purpose of securing a partnership obligation) become worthless; (2) all of the partnership's liabilities become due and payable in full; (3) the partnership transfers any property contributed to the partnership solely for the purpose of securing a partnership obligation to the creditor in partial or full satisfaction of the debt; (4) the partnership disposes of all its remaining assets for no consideration, except that property subject to nonrecourse mortgage liens is treated as transferred to the creditor in satisfaction of the debt; and (5) the partnership allocates all items of income, gain, deduction, or loss among the partners as provided in the partnership agreement.

In making the required adjustments to the partners' capital accounts, gain is recognized by the partnership to the extent that any property is encumbered by a nonrecourse mortgage in excess of the basis, and loss is recognized to the extent of all remaining basis of the partnership's assets. However, if § 704(c) or Treas.Reg. § 1.704–1(b)(4)(i), governing allocations after capital accounts properly have been revalued (discussed in Chapter 20, Section 3), applies, gain is computed with reference to the excess of nonrecourse mortgages over the book value of the encumbered asset, and loss is computed with respect to the remaining book value of the partnership's assets. The partnership assets that are treated as worthless in the hypothetical liquidation presumably do not include any obligations of partners (or related persons) to make contributions or payments to the partnership. Such obligations are presumed to be satisfied regardless of the obligor's actual net worth or the likelihood of actual performance, unless the facts and circumstances indicate a plan to avoid the obligation or if "there is not a commercially reasonable expectation that the payment obligor will have the ability to make the required payments under the terms of the obligation if the obligation becomes due and payable." Treas.Reg. § 1.752–2(b)(6), (j)(3), and (k).

Operating on the assumption that the partnership is unable to pay its creditors, the constructive liquidation analysis will provide the final capital account balances, both positive and negative, of all partners, prior to any contributions required to wind up the partnership. Partners with a capital account of zero or more following the constructive liquidation generally are not obligated to make any contribution to the partnership. Thus, they will not be allocated any share of partnership recourse liabilities, unless they have an independent obligation to make a payment to a creditor or another party, including a partner. Partners having negative capital accounts following the constructive liquidation will have an economic risk of loss and generally will be allocated an amount of partnership recourse liabilities equal to the negative capital account, unless they are entitled to reimbursement from a partner or other person. In addition, the constructive liquidation triggers deemed satisfaction of all obligations to make payments to creditors and reimbursements to other partners and persons related to other partners. The net result of the constructive settlement of capital accounts and these other payments equals each partner's economic risk of loss.

2.3. *Obligation to Make a Payment*

2.3.1. *General*

Treas.Reg. § 1.752–2(b)(5) provides that a partner's economic risk of loss equals the amount the partner would be required to pay another person or to contribute to the partnership in a constructive liquidation, minus reimbursements that the partner is entitled to receive from other partners or persons as a result of making such payments or contributions. Treas.Reg. § 1.752–2(b)(6) generally deems all partners and related persons capable of making a reimbursement, although recently finalized anti-abuse rules apply and are discussed below. Contingent obligations, however, are not taken into account if it is unlikely that the obligation ever will be discharged. Treas.Reg. § 1.752–2(b)(4).

Payments that a partner would be obligated to make and that are taken into account in determining economic risk of loss include all statutory and contractual obligations relating to partnership liabilities. In addition to any obligation to restore a negative capital account imposed by the partnership agreement or state law, contractual obligations outside the partnership agreement must be taken into account in determining each partner's economic risk of loss. Treas.Reg. § 1.752–2(b)(3)(i). Examples of such contractual obligations include a partner's individual guarantees to creditors of partnership indebtedness, payments to reimburse another partner for paying more than the partner's share of partnership debts (whether by contract or under state law), or payments pursuant to an agreement by one partner to indemnify another partner against loss. If a partner guarantees a partnership obligation but is subrogated to the creditor's rights against the partnership if the partner pays the obligation, the right of reimbursement under the subrogation rights offsets the obligation on the guarantee. See Treas.Reg. § 1.752–2(f), Ex. (3) and Ex. (4).

If an obligation to make a payment, whether by contribution to the partnership or to another partner or a creditor of the partnership, is not required to be satisfied by the end of the taxable year in which the partner's partnership interest is liquidated (if there were to be such a liquidation) or, if later, 90 days after such liquidation, then the obligation will be taken into account only at its discounted present value. Treas.Reg. § 1.752–2(g). If the obligation bears interest at the applicable federal rate (determined under § 1274(d)(1)), its value is its face value. Otherwise, the imputed principal amount is determined under § 1274(b). The Regulations do not explain how to reallocate the portion of the partnership indebtedness that would have been allocated to a particular partner absent this time-value-of-money consideration but that is not allocated to that partner because of this rule. If other partners are the obligees, presumably any such portion of the indebtedness would be allocated among the other partners, but if a creditor is the obligee, allocation among the other partners would not correspond with risk of loss. Perhaps in such a case the "unallocated" recourse debt becomes nonrecourse debt for purposes of the § 752 Regulations.

Treas.Reg. § 1.752–2(g)(3) provides that the transfer of a partner's promissory note is not a satisfaction of the partner's obligation unless the note is readily tradable on an established securities market. Since the context of the operation of this rule is the hypothetical liquidation of the partnership, the rule appears to be directed to situations in which either the partnership agreement or another contractual provision permits a partner to satisfy an obligation by delivery of a promissory note. Actual transfer to the partnership of a partner's promissory note prior to the liquidation should be treated as an obligation to make an additional contribution to the partnership, at the time and on the conditions specified in the promissory note and should be taken into account as such. Treas.Reg. § 1.704–1(b)(2)(ii)(c). Applied literally, Treas.Reg. § 1.752–2(g)(3) would require reallocation of economic risk of loss from the partner who is entitled to satisfy an obligation by delivery of a note to the holder of the note. If the holder would be another partner, then that partner would bear the risk of loss; if the holder would be a creditor, that portion of the debt presumably would be classified as a nonrecourse debt allocable under Treas.Reg. § 1.752–3. However, because this rule is contained in the provisions governing "time-value-of-money considerations," its intended effect may be merely to require that promissory notes used to satisfy obligations bear interest at the applicable federal rate where it has been agreed in advance that an obligation may be satisfied with a note.

Treas.Reg. § 1.752–2(h) provides rules for determining who bears the economic risk of loss where a partner directly or indirectly pledges individual property to secure a partnership debt. Where a partner makes an accommodation pledge of the partner's individual property to secure a partnership debt, without guaranteeing the debt itself, the partner pledging the property bears an economic risk of loss for an amount of the partnership liability equal to the fair market value of the property (but not more than the partnership debt), determined at the time the property is pledged. Treas.Reg. § 1.752–2(h)(1) and (3). Thus, continued revaluation of pledged property is not required. A partner who contributes property to a partnership solely for the purpose of securing a partnership liability bears the economic risk of loss for the partnership liability, subject to the same valuation rules applicable to direct pledges of individual property to secure partnership indebtedness. Treas.Reg. § 1.752–2(h)(2) and (3). Although the Regulations do not expressly so provide, economic risk of loss based on a pledge of property under Treas.Reg. § 1.752–2(h) presumably is subject to being offset by any right of the pledging partner to indemnification from other partners.

2.3.2.   *Anti-Abuse Regulations*

Multiple anti-abuse rules, most finalized in 2019, limit the extent to which partners may use artificial payment obligations to manipulate the economic risk of loss determination in order to assign basis in a particular way. Overall, these anti-abuse rules attempt to ensure that the allocation of debt basis better reflects the reality that, particularly given the increased use of LLCs and other limited liability partnerships, a partnership will satisfy its liabilities with partnership profits, the partnership's assets will not become worthless, and the payment obligations of partners or related persons are not called upon.

First, Regulations finalized in 2019 provide that "bottom dollar" payment obligations will not be recognized as increasing a partner's economic risk of loss. These Regulations address the concern that partners were manipulating economic risk of loss through using guarantees, indemnities, and other payment obligations (including deficit restoration obligations) that were almost certainly never going to be triggered. Treas.Reg. § 1.752–2(f)(10) provides an example of a basic structure. In it, A, B, and C are equal owners of an LLC taxed as a partnership. The LLC borrows $1,000, which in the absence of guarantee agreements would be nonrecourse debt. A, however, guarantees to pay up to $300 if any amount of the full $1,000 is not recovered. In contrast, B guarantees to pay $200 but only if the creditor fails first to collect at least $200. In the example, A and B waive their rights of contribution against each other. B's guarantee is essentially economically meaningless because the likelihood that B's guarantee would be triggered is designed to be vanishingly low. The Regulations confirm that B's guarantee does not increase B's economic risk of loss, while A's guarantee does increase A's economic risk of loss.

Under the Regulations, as long as a partner or related person is or would be liable for the full amount of a payment obligation, the obligation will be recognized. Treas.Reg. § 1.752–2(b)(3)(ii)(C)(1). If a single liability is converted into multiple liabilities through use of intermediaries, tiered partnerships, or similar arrangements, all the facts and circumstances will be considered in determining whether there was a common plan to incur the liabilities and a principal purpose of avoiding the impact of the bottom-dollar rules. A payment obligation is not a bottom-dollar obligation merely because a maximum amount is placed on the partner's or related person's payment obligation, a partner's or related person's payment obligation is stated as a fixed percentage of every dollar of the partnership liability to which such obligation relates, or there is a right of proportionate contribution running between partners or related persons who are co-obligors with respect to a payment obligation for which each of them is jointly and severally liable. Treas.Reg. § 1.752–2(b)(3)(ii)(C)(2). Thus, guarantees of a vertical slice of a partnership liability will be recognized. With respect to capital contribution or deficit restoration obligations, the Regulations provide that, to avoid being a bottom-dollar obligation, the partner is required to meet the full amount of the obligation.

Indemnity and reimbursement agreements are recognized only if the obligation of the person who would benefit from the agreement would have been recognized, not taking into account the indemnity or reimbursement agreement. Treas.Reg. § 1.752–2(b)(3)(iii). A partner who benefits from such an agreement will still have economic risk of loss on the original obligation only if that partner or related person is liable for at least 90% of the initial payment obligation. Treas.Reg. § 1.752–2(b)(3)(ii)(B). To illustrate these two rules, consider again the above example involving A, B, and C. If C were to agree to indemnify A for $100 and B for $200, the agreement as to A would increase C's economic risk of loss because, ignoring the indemnity agreement, A's guarantee was not a bottom-dollar obligation; C's agreement with respect to B would, however, be no more meaningful than B's original guarantee and does not increase C's economic risk of loss. As a result of C's indemnity agreement, A would no longer have any economic risk of loss because A is not liable for at least 90% of the initial $300 obligation. Treas.Reg. § 1.752–2(b)(3)(iii), (f)(11).

Treas.Reg. § 1.752–2(j)(2) provides a related anti-abuse rule providing that if a partner actually bears the economic risk of loss for a partnership liability, partners may not agree among themselves to create a bottom-dollar payment obligation so that the liability will be treated as nonrecourse. The Regulations require partnerships to disclose bottom-dollar payment obligations on the partnership return. Treas.Reg. § 1.752–2(b)(3)(ii)(D).

Even if an obligation is not a bottom-dollar obligation, in order for it to be respected and increase a partner's economic risk of loss, there must be "a commercially reasonable expectation that the payment obligor will have the ability to make the required payments." Treas.Reg. § 1.752–2(b)(6)(ii). Treas.Reg. § 1.752–2(k), after its revision in 2019, provides that the facts and circumstances a third-party creditor would consider are those that are relevant to this determination. The examples focus on undercapitalization and emphasize the Regulation's rule that a payment obligor includes a disregarded entity, such as a single-member LLC, even though its owner is the partner for federal income tax purposes. Thus, the obligation of an undercapitalized, disregarded-entity LLC will generally not be commercially reasonable.

Finally, Treas.Reg. § 1.752–2(b)(6)(i) and (j)(3), also revised in 2019, provide an anti-abuse rule under which a payment obligation (other than an obligation to restore a deficit capital account upon liquidation) would not be respected in determining economic risk of loss if the facts and circumstances evidence a plan to circumvent or avoid the obligation. The Regulations provide a list of non-exclusive factors; the Regulations specify that the weight to be given any one factor also depends on the particular facts. Seven factors are listed: (1) The partner or related person is not subject to commercially reasonable contractual restrictions that protect the likelihood of payment, including, for example, restrictions on transfers for inadequate consideration or distributions by the partner or related person to equity owners in the partner or related person; (2) The partner or related person is not required to provide (either at the time the payment obligation is made or periodically) commercially reasonable documentation regarding the partner's or related person's financial condition to the benefited party; and (3) The term of the payment obligation terminates prior to the term of the partnership liability or the partner or related person has a right to terminate its payment obligation, if the purpose of limiting the duration of the payment obligation is to terminate such payment obligation prior to the occurrence of an event or events that increase the risk of economic loss to the guarantor or benefited party; (4) There exists a plan or arrangement in which the primary obligor or any other obligor (or a person related to the obligor) with respect to the partnership liability directly or indirectly holds money or other liquid assets in an amount that exceeds the reasonable foreseeable needs of such obligor; (5) The payment obligation does not permit the creditor to promptly pursue payment following a payment default on the partnership liability, or other arrangements with respect to the partnership liability or payment obligation otherwise indicate a plan to delay collection; (6) In the case of a guarantee or similar arrangement, the terms of the partnership liability would be substantially the same had the partner or related person not agreed to provide the guarantee; and (7) The creditor or other party benefiting from the obligation did not receive executed documents with respect to the payment obligation from the partner or related person before, or within a commercially reasonable period of time after, the creation of the obligation. Treas.Reg. § 1.752–2(j)(3)(ii).

3. EXAMPLES

Partners' shares of recourse liabilities do not always correspond to the partners' shares of partnership losses. A partners' risk of loss is determined largely by analyzing the amounts that the partners would be required to contribute to the partnership upon a hypothetical liquidation in which the partnership's assets, including cash, are deemed to be worthless, and the required contribution generally is determined with reference to negative balances in partners' capital accounts. Suppose, for example, that C and D each contribute $500 in cash to form the CD partnership, in which profits and losses are to be divided 40% to C and 60% to D. The partnership then borrows $9,000 from an unrelated lender and purchases an asset for $10,000. Initially C and D each had a $500 capital account (following the requirements of Treas.Reg. § 1.704–1(b)(2)(iv), discussed in Chapter 19). The

CD Partnership's opening balance sheet, without the partners' bases in their partnership interests, would be as follows:

	Assets			Indebtedness and Partners' Capital Accounts	
	Book	Tax Basis		Book	Tax Basis
Property	$10,000	$10,000	Debt	$ 9,000	
			C	$ 500	$ 500 + ?
	_____	_____	D	$ 500	$ 500 + ?
	$10,000	$10,000		$10,000	$ 10,000

Assume further that C and D each have an unlimited obligation to restore a capital account deficit. If the building were to become worthless and were sold for $0, then, under the partnership agreement and the § 704(b) Regulations, $4,000 of the $10,000 book loss would be allocated to C, reducing C's capital account to negative $3,500, and $6,000 of the book loss would be allocated to D, reducing D's capital account to negative $5,500. The partnership's capital accounts balance sheet would be as follows:

	Assets		Indebtedness and Partners' Capital Accounts
	Book		Book
Property	$ 0	Debt	$9,000
		C	($3,500)
	_____	D	($5,500)
	$ 0		$ 0

C and D would make contributions equal to the negative amounts, and those contributions would be used by the partnership to pay the debt. Thus, C's economic risk of loss is $3,500 of the $9,000 partnership indebtedness under § 752(a), while D's economic risk of loss is $5,500. See Treas.Reg. § 1.752–2(f), Ex. (2). The results of the hypothetical will then be used to increase actual outside basis. Under § 752(a), basis is increased by each partner's increase in debt share. Thus, C's basis for C's partnership interest immediately after the debt is incurred would be $4,000 ($500 contribution + $3,500 debt share); D's basis in D's partnership interest immediately after the debt is incurred would be $6,000 ($500 contribution + $5,500 debt share).

	Assets			Indebtedness and Partners' Capital Accounts	
	Book	Tax Basis		Book	Tax Basis
Property	$10,000	$10,000	Debt	$ 9,000	
			C	$ 500	$ 4,000
	————	————	D	$ 500	$ 6,000
	$10,000	$10,000		$10,000	$10,000

Note that the effect of allocating the CD Partnership's indebtedness in this manner is to assure that D has sufficient basis to deduct D's disproportionate share of partnership losses without running afoul of the § 704(d) limitation.

Partners will be allocated shares of partnership indebtedness disproportionately to their loss sharing ratios if partners share profits and losses disproportionately to their capital contributions, assuming those disproportionate allocations have substantial economic effect. Assume, for example, that E and F form a partnership in which they share profits and losses equally, but E contributes $4,000 and F contributes $5,000. Assume further that both partners have unlimited deficit restoration obligations that will be respected. The partnership borrows $10,000. The EF Partnership's opening balance sheet, without the partners' bases for their partnership interests, would be as follows:

	Assets			Indebtedness and Partners' Capital Accounts	
	Book	Tax Basis		Book	Tax Basis
Property	$19,000	$19,000	Debt	$10,000	
			E	$ 4,000	$ 4,000 + ?
	————	————	F	$ 5,000	$ 5,000 + ?
	$19,000	$19,000		$19,000	$ 19,000

If the property became worthless and were sold for $0, the partnership would have a $19,000 book loss. Under the agreement, assuming substantial economic effect, this loss would be allocated $9,500 to each partner. E's capital account would be reduced from $4,000 to negative $5,500; F's capital account would be reduced from $5,000 to negative $4,500. The partnership's balance sheet (without the partners' bases for their partnership interests) would be as follows:

Assets		Indebtedness and Partners' Capital Accounts	
	Book		Book
Property	$ 0	Debt	$10,000
		E	($ 5,500)
		F	($ 4,500)
	$ 0		$ 0

E and F would be required to contribute according to these deficits. Thus, $5,500 of the debt would be assigned to E, resulting in E having a basis for E's partnership interest immediately after the debt is incurred of $9,500 ($4,000 contribution + $5,500 debt share) and F having a basis in F's partnership interest immediately after the debt is incurred of $9,500 ($5,000 contribution + $4,500 debt share). E and F have the same basis in their partnership interests, even though their contributions were different because they bear the risk of loss on the debt differently. As a result of each of them having equal partnership interest bases, since E and F share losses equally, neither will run afoul of the § 704(d) limitation of losses to basis rule. Thus:

Assets			Indebtedness and Partners' Capital Accounts		
	Book	Tax Basis		Book	Tax Basis
Property	$19,000	$19,000	Debt	$10,000	
			E	$ 4,000	$ 9,500
			F	$ 5,000	$ 9,500
	$19,000	$19,000		$19,000	$19,000

The principles explained in the preceding paragraphs are the key to an important interrelationship between the § 704(d) limitation on losses, special allocations under Treas.Reg. § 1.704–1(b) of deductions attributable to recourse debt, and § 752(a) and (b). The rules for allocation of partnership recourse indebtedness under Treas.Reg. § 1.752–2 assure that a partner who has an unlimited obligation to restore a negative capital account always will have sufficient basis in the partnership interest to be able to deduct currently any special allocation to the partner of partnership deduction items that are attributable to the debt. Assume, for example, that the GH Partnership is formed by G and H, each of whom contributes $15,000. The partnership borrows $120,000 and purchases an asset, the cost of which is recoverable over 10 years under the straight-line method (ignoring conventions). G and H will share all items equally, except depreciation, all of which is allocable to H. Initially, G and H bear the risk of loss on the debt equally and the GH Partnership's opening balance sheet is as follows:

	Assets			Indebtedness and Partners' Capital Accounts	
	Book	Tax Basis		Book	Tax Basis
Property	$150,000	$150,000	Debt	$120,000	
			G	$ 15,000	$ 75,000
			H	$ 15,000	$ 75,000
	$150,000	$150,000		$150,000	$150,000

Each year for the first five years, the partnership breaks even, apart from depreciation deductions, thus losing $15,000 per year, all of which is allocated to H. As a result of being allocated $75,000 of partnership losses over those five years, H's capital account is reduced to negative $60,000, but H's basis for the partnership interest has not been reduced to zero. At the end of five years, the partnership's balance sheet, apart from partners' bases in their partnership interests, is as follows:

	Assets			Indebtedness and Partners' Capital Accounts	
	Book	Tax Basis		Book	Tax Basis
Property	$75,000	$75,000	Debt	$120,000	
			G	$ 15,000	?
			H	($ 60,000)	?
	$75,000	$75,000		$ 75,000	$75,000

Applying Treas.Reg. § 1.752–2, if all of the partnership assets were worthless, and the $75,000 book loss deduction were allocated equally between G and H, G's capital account would be reduced to negative $22,500, and H's capital account would be reduced to negative $97,500. Thus, at the end of six years, G's share of the debt is $22,500 and H's share is $97,500. H's basis at that time is thus $37,500, computed as follows:

	Cash Contribution	$15,000
+	Original share of debt	$60,000
−	Deductions in Years 1–5	($75,000)
+	Increase in debt share ($97,500 − $60,000)	$37,500
		$37,500

Because the basis of H's partnership interest has been increased by an amount equal to H's increased share of the partnership's indebtedness,[1] the partnership can continue to allocate all depreciation to H without running afoul of § 704(d). Indeed, continued allocations of depreciation to H during years 6–9 will result in a further shift of the risk of loss on the debt from G to H, thus allowing H to deduct the depreciation for the nine years without running afoul of § 704(d). After nine years, however, H will have exhausted H's basis. At the end of eight years, the partnership's balance sheet, apart from partners' bases in their partnership interests, is as follows:

Assets			Indebtedness and Partners' Capital Accounts		
	Book	**Tax Basis**		**Book**	**Tax Basis**
Property	$30,000	$30,000	Debt	$120,000	
			G	$ 15,000	?
	_____	_____	H	($105,000)	?
	$30,000	$30,000		$ 30,000	$30,000

Applying the hypothetical liquidation sequence after eight years, if a $30,000 loss from the worthlessness of the property were split equally, G would have a capital account of zero, and H would have a capital account of negative $120,000. H bears the full risk of loss on the debt because only H would have a negative capital account. Thus, at the end of eight years H has a remaining basis in H's partnership interest of $15,000, computed as follows:

	Cash Contribution	$ 15,000
+	Original share of debt	$ 60,000
−	Deductions in Years 1–8	($120,000)
+	Increase in debt share	
	($120,000 − $60,000)	$ 60,000
		$ 15,000

Accordingly, H has sufficient basis to support deducting $15,000 of partnership losses in Year 9. After nine years, however, H will have exhausted H's basis and continuing to allocate the depreciation deduction to H will result in neither partner being able to claim a current deduction. The deduction will still be allocated to H and have substantial economic effect; it will reduce H's book value and provide H with a suspended loss. That is, use

---

[1] Although the example computes the increase in H's share of partnership indebtedness by comparing the end of Year 6 and the beginning of the partnership, technically under § 705(a) each change should be taken into account separately and all of the changes cumulated. See Treas.Reg. § 1.752–4(d).

of such tax deduction will be deferred until H, the partner to whom they have been allocated, acquires additional basis in a future year.

In contrast to the above examples, when each partner's capital account is proportionate to the partner's share of partnership profits and losses (which also are the same), as a rule of thumb each partner's share of partnership recourse liabilities generally can be determined by multiplying the total liabilities by the partner's profit and loss share percentage. This is a corollary of the shortcut alternative basis rule in § 705(b). However, where any partner's profit sharing ratio differs from the partner's loss sharing ratio, or either ratio differs from the partners' capital contributions ratio, the constructive liquidation analysis must be applied.

4.   CONTINGENT LIABILITIES

Treas.Reg. § 1.752–7 deals with the assumption by a partnership of a partner's fixed or contingent obligation to make a payment that is not one of the three types of liabilities defined in Treas.Reg. § 1.752–1(a)(4)(i) as a liability for purposes of § 752.[2] Accrual method liabilities the deduction for which is deferred under the economic performance rules of § 453(h), such as future environmental remediation expenses, are not a "liability" under this definition. If the partnership satisfies the liability while the originally obligated partner remains in the partnership, the deduction with respect to the built-in loss associated with the § 1.752–7 liability is allocated to the originally obligated partner, thereby reducing that partner's outside basis. Alternatively, if one of three events occurs that separate the originally obligated partner from the liability, then the partner's outside basis is reduced immediately before the occurrence of the event. The events are: (1) a disposition (or partial disposition) of the partnership interest by the partner, (2) a liquidation of the partner's partnership interest, and (3) the assumption (or partial assumption) of the liability by another partner. The basis reduction generally is the lesser of (1) the excess of the partner's basis in the partnership interest over the adjusted value of the interest, or (2) the remaining built-in loss associated with the liability. (In the event of a partial disposition, the reduction is pro-rated.) Thereafter, to the extent of the remaining built-in loss associated with the liability, the partnership (or the assuming partner) is not entitled to any deduction or capital expense upon satisfaction (or economic performance) of the liability, but if the partnership notifies the partner, the partner is entitled to a loss or deduction. If another partner assumed the liability, the partnership must immediately reduce the basis of its assets by the built-in loss, and upon satisfaction, the assuming partner must make certain basis adjustments to the partnership interest. There are exceptions for (1) the transfer of the trade or business with which the liability is associated (not merely the particular assets with which the

---

[2]   As a reminder, under Treas.Reg. § 1.752–1(a)(4)(i), an obligation is a liability for purpose of § 752 to the extent that incurring the obligation: (1) creates or increases the basis of any of the obligor's assets (including cash); (2) gives rise to an immediate deduction; or (3) gives rise to an expense that is not deductible in computing taxable income and is not properly chargeable to capital.

liability is associated) to the partnership, and (2) *de minimis* transactions (liabilities less than 10% of the partnership's assets or $1,000,000).[3]

5. RELATED PARTY RULES

Under Reg. § 1.704–4(b)(1), an individual and a corporation are treated as related persons if the individual is an 80% or greater shareholder. Where the corporation is a lender to a partnership or has a payment obligation with respect to a partnership liability, Prop.Reg. § 1.752–4(b)(1)(iv) (2013), would disregard the application of § 267(c)(1) that provides that stock owned by a partnership is treated as owned proportionately by its partners. As a result, a partner in a partnership that owns 80% of the stock of the corporate lender will not be treated as related to the corporation that bears the economic risk of loss. Prop.Reg. § 1.752–4(b)(2) (2013) would provide that if a person who is a lender or has a payment obligation for a partnership liability is related to more than one partner, the liability will be shared proportionally among the related partners. This rule revises the existing provision that allocates the liability to the partner with the highest percentage of related ownership. In addition, the rule of Treas.Reg. § 1.752–4(b)(2)(iii), which provides that persons owning interests in the same partnership are not treated as related persons for purposes of determining economic risk for partnership liabilities, would be modified to apply only to persons who bear the economic risk for a liability as a lender or have a payment obligation for the partnership liability.

PROBLEM SET 1

1. Sean and Pat formed a general partnership. Sean contributed $50,000 in cash, and Pat contributed $40,000 in cash. Sean and Pat agreed to split profits and losses equally. The partnership borrowed $100,000 from Cottage Savings Bank on a recourse basis. What basis do Sean and Pat have in their partnership interests?

2. David and Ruth formed a general partnership to which they each contributed $50,000 in cash. They agreed to split profits equally, but losses were to be allocated 60% to David and 40% to Ruth. The partnership borrowed $100,000 from Hillsboro National Bank on a recourse basis. What basis do David and Ruth have in their partnership interests?

3. Juan, Kimberly, and Maurice form a partnership to invest in commercial real estate. Kimberly and Maurice each contribute $50,000 in cash to the partnership. Juan forms an LLC, in which he is the sole member. Juan LLC's assets are limited to $90,000 of cash. Juan LLC contributes $50,000 of cash to the JKM partnership. The partnership borrows $1,000,000 with full recourse to the partnership and purchases an office building for $1,500,000. The partners share all partnership items equally, one-third each. The partnership agreement provides for properly maintained capital accounts, liquidation in accord with capital accounts, and that each partner

---

[3]   These Regulations are intended to defeat an abusive tax shelter scheme referred to as "Son of Boss" undertaken through a partnership that attempted to generate tax deductions on disposition of a partnership interest that were not reflected in an economic loss.

is responsible for repayment of the partner's capital account deficit, if any. What is each partner's basis in the partnership interest?

SECTION 2.   ALLOCATION OF NONRECOURSE DEBT

REGULATIONS: Sections 1.752–1, –3.

(1) IN GENERAL

Allocations of partnership nonrecourse debt are based on an entirely different set of principles than are allocations of recourse debt.[4] The rules governing allocation of nonrecourse debt are based on the premise that none of the partners suffers an actual risk of individual loss from nonrecourse debt. The debt will be repaid, if at all, only out of partnership profits. For example, assume a limited partnership, composed of a general partner and two limited partners who share profits equally, acquires property subject to a nonrecourse mortgage of $15,000. Each partner increases the partner's outside basis by $5,000. As the loan is repaid out of partnership profits, each partner increases the partner's basis by the amount of profits (see § 705(a)) and decreases the partner's basis by the reduction in partnership liabilities. Thus, when the loan is fully repaid, each partner's basis is unchanged. However, if the mortgage were with recourse to the partnership, thus making the general partner but not the limited partners liable on the mortgage, the general partner would be treated as solely responsible for the mortgage and would be entitled to the full basis adjustment. This result is justified by the fact that the debt, if not satisfied out of partnership profits, ultimately is the responsibility of the general partner.

Partnership indebtedness is considered to be nonrecourse debt only to the extent that no partner (nor any person related to a partner under Treas.Reg. § 1.752–4(b)) bears the economic risk of loss for the liability. Treas.Reg. § 1.752–1(a)(2). As a result, the hypothetical liquidation test of Treas.Reg. § 1.752–2, discussed in the preceding section, not only determines each partner's share of recourse debt, but also determines whether the debt is recourse for partnership tax purposes in the first place. A debt that is nonrecourse to the partnership, but that is guaranteed by a partner, is subject to the rules governing partners' shares of recourse debt rather than those applicable to nonrecourse debt. See Treas.Reg. § 1.752–2(f), Ex. (5).

---

[4]   Occasionally, limited partners seek to disavow the form of partnership borrowing structures as recourse financing in an attempt to come within the special rules governing allocation of nonrecourse debt. In Kingbay v. Commissioner, 46 T.C. 147 (1966), limited partners were not allowed to include liabilities in the basis for their partnership interests where the general partner was liable on the mortgage obligation. The taxpayers argued that the corporate general partner should be disregarded since it was a corporation with capital of only $1,000 and was wholly owned by one of the partners. But the court held the taxpayers were bound by the form of the transaction; they could not argue that in substance no partner was personally liable on the mortgage obligation, thereby increasing their bases.

Under Treas.Reg. § 1.752–3(a), a partner's share of partnership nonrecourse liabilities is the sum of three amounts: (1) an amount of partnership nonrecourse debt equal to the partner's share of "minimum gain" under Treas.Reg. § 1.704–2(g)(1); (2) an amount equal to the gain that would be recognized to the partner under § 704(c), dealing with contributions of appreciated property (or under Treas.Reg. § 1.704–1(b)(2)(ii)(f) or (b)(4)(i) using § 704(c) principles when partnership capital accounts have been revalued—i.e., "reverse" § 704(c) allocations), if all of the partnership's property subject to nonrecourse mortgages were disposed of in satisfaction of the mortgages and for no additional consideration; and (3) a portion of the remaining partnership nonrecourse indebtedness equal to the partner's share of partnership profits. Under these principles, limited partners are allocated a share of partnership nonrecourse liabilities. These rules also are applicable to allocate among the members of a limited liability company all of its indebtedness, except any debts that have been guaranteed by a member of the LLC. The debts of the LLC that have been guaranteed by one or more members are recourse debts that must be allocated under Treas.Reg. § 1.752–2.

Computation of the first two components of the allocation under Treas.Reg. § 1.752–3 is complex. But, in any case in which each partner's share of each item of income, gain, deduction, loss, and credit is a uniform fraction (or percentage), which may differ from partner to partner, as long as the partnership has no § 704(c) gain or loss and capital accounts never have been revalued, each partner's share of partnership nonrecourse debt will be equal to the total partnership nonrecourse debt multiplied by the partner's fractional profits interest. In such situations, from a practical perspective, it is unnecessary to apply the first and second components of the allocation formula.

(2) ALLOCATION ACCORDING TO PROFIT SHARES

In most cases, the third component of a partner's share of nonrecourse indebtedness, based on the partner's share of profits, actually is the starting point for allocating nonrecourse liabilities among the partners. This ordering occurs because the first component, partnership minimum gain, does not exist until the partnership has been in operation long enough to generate minimum gain through the reduction of the book value of assets encumbered by nonrecourse debt below the principal amount of such nonrecourse debt;[5] and the second component, based on § 704(c) allocations or reverse § 704(c) allocations, does not come into play unless a partner contributes appreciated property subject to a nonrecourse mortgage or the partnership has revalued capital accounts after it has been in existence for some period

---

[5]   Recall from Chapter 20 that the Regulations specify to use basis if there is no disparity between book and basis and to use book value if there is such a disparity. Treas.Reg. § 1.704–2(d)(3). Thus, using book value to measure minimum gain will yield the correct result.

of time. Thus, it is logical to examine the third component first, even though it technically applies only to debt that has not been allocated under either of the first two components of the allocation formula.

Allocation of the partnership's residual nonrecourse debt under Treas.Reg. § 1.752–3(a)(3) generally is dependent upon determining the partners' respective profit shares. However, Treas.Reg. § 1.752–3(a)(3) allows the partnership agreement to specify the partners' respective shares of partnership profits for purposes of allocating residual partnership nonrecourse debt. This provision avoids problems that could arise if the partners' interests in various types of profits differ. The specified shares will be respected as long as they are reasonably consistent with some other significant item of partnership income or gain that has substantial economic effect under the § 704(b) Regulations. Alternatively, Treas.Reg. § 1.752–3(a)(3) permits the partnership agreement to specify that excess nonrecourse indebtedness will be allocated with respect to the proportion in which partners reasonably can be expected to be allocated nonrecourse deductions. It is important, for example, that the partnership agreement take advantage of this latter provision to specify the residual ratio for purposes of allocating nonrecourse debt where depreciation deductions based on nonrecourse debt are not allocated according to profit shares. Otherwise, as the partnership claims depreciation deductions that increase minimum gain, the share of partnership debt allocated to the partners receiving the special allocation will increase. The other partners will have a corresponding decrease in partnership debt, which will give rise to a deemed distribution under § 752(b) and may cause gain recognition.

(3) ALLOCATION ACCORDING TO MINIMUM GAIN

The first component of a partner's share of nonrecourse indebtedness, "minimum gain," is the partner's distributive share of book gain that would be recognized by the partnership if the partnership's property subject to nonrecourse mortgages were disposed of in satisfaction of the mortgages and for no additional consideration. The initial allocation of nonrecourse debt among the partners relative to their shares of minimum gain under the § 704(b) Regulations assures that each partner will have sufficient basis to be able to claim the partner's share of deductions based on nonrecourse debt without running afoul of the § 704(d) limitation. In addition, the allocation attributes nonrecourse debt to the partner who will recognize gain as the partnership's nonrecourse debt is reduced, either through payments out of partnership profits or through relief from the liability, for example, by transfer of the property to a purchaser. The debt allocation rule also assures that partners will not recognize gain if the proceeds of a nonrecourse second mortgage loan are distributed, because Treas.Reg. § 1.704–2(g)(1)(i) provides that a partner's share of minimum gain is increased by any such distribution.

The operation and interaction of the first and third components of the formula for allocating nonrecourse indebtedness, and the relationship of these rules to the rules of Treas.Reg. § 1.704–2, governing allocations of deductions attributable to nonrecourse debt, can be illustrated by the following example. Suppose that C and D respectively contribute $20,000 and $80,000 to the CD Partnership, which then borrows $900,000 from an unrelated lender on a nonrecourse promissory note secured by depreciable property for which the partnership pays $1,000,000. Also suppose that no principal payments are due on the note for 10 years and that $50,000 of depreciation is allowable on the property each year. The partnership agreement complies with Treas.Reg. § 1.704–2 and provides that all items of income and deduction and all distributions will be allocated 20% to C and 80% to D. Assuming that the partnership agreement did not have any provisions specially allocating the nonrecourse debt between C and D, the debt would be allocated according to their 20:80 profit sharing ratio, and C would be allocated $180,000 and D would be allocated $720,000. The CD Partnership's opening balance sheet would be as follows:

Assets			Indebtedness and Partners' Capital Accounts		
	Book	Tax Basis		Book	Tax Basis
Property	$1,000,000	$1,000,000	Debt	$ 900,000	
			C	$ 20,000	$ 200,000
			D	$ 80,000	$ 800,000
	$1,000,000	$1,000,000		$1,000,000	$1,000,000

Because the partnership has $100,000 of equity in the property, the first two years of depreciation deductions (assuming that the partnership does not have any net income or loss from other items) are not nonrecourse deductions and do not give rise to any minimum gain. Thus, allocations of the depreciation deductions must satisfy the substantial economic effect test, or one of its alternatives, under Treas.Reg. § 1.704–1(b)(2). That generally occurs only by allocating the loss against the partners' positive capital account balances. Thus, in each of the first two years, C's distributive share is a $10,000 loss, and D's distributive share is a $40,000 loss. At the end of Year 2, the CD Partnership's balance sheet is as follows:

Assets			Indebtedness and Partners' Capital Accounts		
	Book	Tax Basis		Book	Tax Basis
Property	$900,000	$900,000	Debt	$900,000	
			C	$ 0	$180,000
			D	$ 0	$720,000
	$900,000	$900,000		$900,000	$900,000

Each partner's basis in the partnership interest at this point is entirely attributable to that partners' share of the partnership's nonrecourse indebtedness, allocated under the third component of the formula in Treas.Reg. § 1.752–3(a)(3).[6]

The $50,000 of depreciation in Year 3 will give rise to $50,000 of minimum gain, since the basis of the property will be reduced to $850,000 and the mortgage principal will remain at $900,000. Thus, the first $50,000 of the debt will be allocated between C and D under the first component of the formula in Treas.Reg. § 1.752–3(a)(1), and the remaining $850,000 will be allocated according to the third component of the formula in Treas.Reg. § 1.752–3(a)(3). At the end of three years, the partnership's balance sheet would be as follows:

Assets			Indebtedness and Partners' Capital Accounts		
	Book	Tax Basis		Book	Tax Basis
Property	$850,000	$850,000	Debt	$900,000	
			C	($ 10,000)	$170,000
			D	($ 40,000)	$680,000
	$850,000	$850,000		$850,000	$850,000

C's share of minimum gain is $10,000; D's share of minimum gain is $40,000. Thus, the first $50,000 of the nonrecourse debt is allocated between C and D in those amounts: $10,000 to C and $40,000 to D. The remaining $850,000 of nonrecourse debt is allocated with the partners' 20:80 ratio for sharing profits, $170,000 to C and $680,000 to D. Thus, C's total share of the debt is $180,000, and D's total share of the debt is

---

[6]   The allocation of the indebtedness would be the same if C had contributed $40,000 to the partnership, D had contributed $160,000, and the partnership had used $100,000 as an equity investment in the property and retained $100,000 of cash. The allocation of depreciation to the extent of the $100,000 of equity in the property must satisfy the substantial economic effect test, although the allocation could be made to either partner to the extent of the partner's positive capital account balance. Thereafter, depreciation deductions attributable to the property would create nonrecourse deductions, allocable to the partners to the extent of their respective shares of minimum gain, then profit shares.

$720,000. Since the minimum gain is allocated between C and D in the same ratio as the residual profit shares (20:80), the total debt continues to be allocated in that ratio.

Now assume that instead of all items being allocated 20% to C and 80% to D during the life of the partnership, the partnership agreement provided for a 20:80 split only for the first three years and that, starting in Year 4, profits from the sale of the asset and depreciation would be allocated 40% to C and 60% to D, although all other items would continue to be split in the 20:80 ratio. In Year 4, C would be allocated $20,000 of depreciation, and D would be allocated $30,000 of depreciation; C's distributive share would be a $20,000 loss, and D's distributive share would be a $30,000 loss. Under Treas.Reg. § 1.704–2, the partnership's minimum gain of $100,000 at the end of Year 4 would be allocable $30,000 to C and $70,000 to D. At the end of Year 4, the partnership's balance sheet would be as follows:

	Assets		Indebtedness and Partners' Capital Accounts		
	Book	**Tax Basis**		**Book**	**Tax Basis**
Property	$800,000	$800,000	Debt	$900,000	
			C	($ 30,000)	$160,000
			D	($ 70,000)	$640,000
	$800,000	$800,000		$800,000	$800,000

The first component of the formula, based on minimum gain, allocates $30,000 of the debt to C and $70,000 to D. Absent a special allocation agreement, as permitted by Treas.Reg. § 1.752–3(a)(3), the third component, based on profit shares, allocates $160,000 to C ($800,000 × 20%) and $640,000 to D ($800,000 × 80%). C's total share of the debt is now $190,000 ($10,000 more than at the end of Year 3), and D's total share of the debt is now $710,000 ($10,000 less than at the end of Year 3). As a result, C is treated as contributing $10,000 to the partnership, thereby increasing C's basis by $10,000, and D is treated as receiving a $10,000 distribution, thereby reducing D's basis by a like amount. (C and D also reduced their bases by $20,000 and $30,000, respectively, as a result of their shares of depreciation deductions.)

This shifting of allocations and the concomitant deemed contribution and distribution can be avoided by specifying the partners' respective shares of partnership nonrecourse debt as permitted by Treas.Reg. § 1.704–3(a)(3). In this case, however, such an agreement probably would not be desirable. The change of the ratios in which the partner's shared the debt was caused by the allocation of debt first according to the partner's shares of minimum gain, and the purpose of that allocation is to assure that C will have sufficient basis to claim C's share of the partnership's depreciation deductions without running afoul of the § 704(d) limitation.

(4) ALLOCATION BASED ON SECTION 704(c) GAIN

The second component of the nonrecourse debt allocation formula, as provided in Treas.Reg. § 1.752–3(a)(2), allocates to each partner an amount of partnership nonrecourse debt equal to the gain that would be recognized to the partner under § 704(c), dealing with contributions of appreciated property, if all of the partnership's property subject to nonrecourse mortgages were transferred in satisfaction of the mortgages and for no additional consideration. This allocation is necessary because under Treas.Reg. § 1.704–2(d)(3) partnership minimum gain exists only to the extent that the nonrecourse mortgage exceeds the book value of the encumbered property. Furthermore, this allocation prevents immediate recognition of gain to a partner upon contribution to the partnership of property encumbered by a nonrecourse mortgage because any deemed distribution under § 752(b) will not exceed the contributing partner's basis for the partnership interest.

Assume that D, E, and F form an equal general partnership. D contributes property with a fair market value of $9,000 and a basis of $6,000, subject to a nonrecourse mortgage of $7,500. E and F each contribute $1,500 in cash. Because partnership minimum gain is computed with reference to book value, Treas.Reg. § 1.704–2(d)(3), the partnership has no minimum gain (book value of the property is $9,000 and the mortgage is only $7,500). Thus, none of the debt is allocated under the first component. Under § 704(c), $1,500 of gain ($7,500 amount realized, the mortgage, minus $6,000 basis) would be allocated to D if the property were transferred to the lender in satisfaction of the mortgage. Accordingly, the first $1,500 of the nonrecourse debt would be allocated to D. The remaining $6,000 of the debt initially would be allocated equally among the partners under the third component because they share profits equally. See Rev.Rul. 95–41, 1995–1 C.B. 132. Thus, a total of $3,500 of the indebtedness is allocated to D, and $2,000 is allocated to each of E and F. D's basis for D's partnership interest is $2,000 (the $6,000 basis of the contributed property minus the net relief from indebtedness of $4,000), and E and F each have a basis of $3,500 (the $1,500 contribution plus $2,000 share of indebtedness). Immediately after formation, the DEF Partnership's balance sheet would be as follows:

	Assets		Indebtedness and Partners' Capital Accounts		
	Book	Tax Basis		Book	Tax Basis
Cash	$ 3,000	$ 3,000	Debt	$ 7,500	
Property	$ 9,000	$ 6,000	D	$ 1,500	$ 2,000
			E	$ 1,500	$ 3,500
			F	$ 1,500	$ 3,500
	$12,000	$ 9,000		$12,000	$ 9,000

Now assume that in its first year the partnership breaks even, apart from tax depreciation of $3,000 attributable to the property. Also assume that book depreciation is $4,500 and that under § 704(c) and Treas.Reg. § 1.704–3, the partnership chose to allocate the depreciation under the traditional method with the ceiling rule. Each partner would be allocated $1,500 of book depreciation; D would be allocated no tax depreciation, and E and F each would be allocated $1,500 of tax depreciation. The partners' bases in their partnership interests also must be adjusted to account for the impact of nonrecourse depreciation deductions on the partners' share of the partnership debt. The partners' shares of the nonrecourse debt at the end of the first year depends on how the gain would be allocated among them if the property hypothetically were conveyed to the lender in lieu of foreclosure. In such an event, the partnership would recognize a taxable gain of $4,500 and a book gain of $3,000.

First, pursuant to § 704(c) and Treas.Reg. § 1.704–3, D would be allocated $1,500 of the $4,500 of taxable gain (the excess of tax gain over book gain). Second, because under Treas.Reg. § 1.704–2(d)(3) partnership minimum gain is computed with reference to the excess of the nonrecourse debt over book value, the amount of the partnership's minimum gain is $3,000. That gain would be allocated between E and F in the ratio they claimed the nonrecourse depreciation deductions— $1,500 to each of E and F. Thus, under the first component of the formula in Treas.Reg. § 1.752–3, $1,500 of the nonrecourse debt is allocated to each of E and F; under the second component of the formula, $1,500 is allocated to D; and under the third component of the formula, the remaining $3,000 of the debt is allocated equally among the partners, $1,000 to each. D's total share of the indebtedness is $2,500, and the total share of each of E and F is $2,500. As a result of the shifting shares of partnership indebtedness, E and F each is deemed to have contributed $500 to the partnership, while D is deemed to have received a distribution of $1,000, thereby requiring appropriate basis adjustments for all three partners. At the end of the year, the partnership balance sheet would be as follows:

	Assets			Indebtedness and Partners' Capital Accounts	
	Book	Tax Basis		Book	Tax Basis
Cash	$3,000	$3,000	Debt	$7,500	
Property	$4,500	$3,000	D	$ 0	$1,000
			E	$ 0	$2,500
			F	$ 0	$2,500
	$7,500	$6,000		$7,500	$6,000

Treas.Reg. § 1.752–3(a)(3) also allows the partners to allocate a portion of the liabilities in excess of the liabilities allocated under the first two components of the formula on the basis of the amount of § 704(c) gain that exceeds § 704(c) gain allocated under the second component, which is limited to the excess of the nonrecourse debt over basis. Thus, in the above example, at the time of contribution § 1.752–3(a)(3) would allow an allocation to D of $3,000 of the nonrecourse debt consisting of $1,500 of the debt allocated under Treas.Reg. § 1.752–3(a)(2) (the excess of the $7,500 mortgage over $6,000 basis) and the remaining $1,500 of § 704(c) gain attributable to the property ($9,000 fair market value less the $6,000 basis and less the first $1,500 allocated under § 1.752–3(a)(2)). The remaining $4,500 of the nonrecourse debt would be allocated equally between D, E, and F based on their profit share, $1,500 each. D's share of the debt is $4,500. D's basis is reduced by $3,000, the reduction of D's share of liabilities from $7,500 to $4,500. E's and F's share of the debt is $1,500 each and their bases are increased by $1,500. The partnership balance sheet is as follows:

	Assets			Indebtedness and Partners' Capital Accounts	
	Book	Tax Basis		Book	Tax Basis
Cash	$ 3,000	$3,000	Debt	$ 7,500	
Property	$ 9,000	$6,000	D	$ 1,500	$3,000
			E	$ 1,500	$3,000
			F	$ 1,500	$3,000
	$12,000	$9,000		$12,000	$9,000

(5) Allocation Based on "Reverse Section 704(c) Gain"

When partnership capital accounts are revalued in connection with the admission of a partner or upon a distribution, the revaluation creates book/tax disparities similar to the disparities that trigger allocations under § 704(c). See the discussion in Chapter 20. Thus, in addition to § 704(c) gain, Treas.Reg. § 1.752–3(a)(2) allocates to each partner an amount of partnership nonrecourse debt equal to the gain that would be allocated to the partner if all of the partnership's property subject to nonrecourse mortgages were transferred in satisfaction of the mortgages and for no additional consideration under Treas.Reg. § 1.704–1(b)(2)(ii)(f) or (b)(4)(i), which apply § 704(c) principles when partnership capital accounts have been revalued. This allocation also is required by the definitional limitation of partnership minimum gain to the excess of the mortgage over the book value of the encumbered property. When capital accounts are revalued, book value may exceed the basis of the property and gain attributable to the excess of book value over basis is allocated under Treas.Reg. § 1.704–1(b)(2)(ii)(f) or (b)(4)(i). In this context, when a new partner is admitted, the Regulations allocate nonrecourse debt to the preexisting partners disproportionately to post-admission profit sharing ratios. This allocation reduces the amount of the deemed distribution to the original partners under § 752(b) arising from shifting a portion of the nonrecourse debt to the new partner, and the consequent possibility that gain will be recognized to the original partners under § 731. This rule is important in workout situations for financially troubled real estate partnerships where the original partners' interests are reduced from 100% to a much lower percentage, for example to 20%, without the recognition of any gain.

Assume that J is admitted to the GH Partnership, which owns a single property, with a basis of $90,000 and a fair market value of $120,000, encumbered by a nonrecourse mortgage of $108,000. Immediately before revaluing the partnership's assets and G's and H's capital accounts in connection with the admission of J, the GH Partnership's balance sheet is follows:

Assets			Indebtedness and Partners' Capital Accounts		
	Book	**Tax Basis**		**Book**	**Tax Basis**
Property	$90,000	$90,000	Debt	$108,000	
			G	($ 9,000)	$45,000
			H	($ 9,000)	$45,000
	$90,000	$90,000		$ 90,000	$90,000

At this point, G's and H's share of minimum gain under Treas.Reg. § 1.704–2 is $9,000 each. Each of their shares of the partnership's debt is $54,000.

J contributes $12,000 to become a one-half partner, and G and H each become one-quarter partners. After the partnership's assets and the partners' capital accounts are revalued in connection with J's admission, the GHI Partnership balance sheet is as follows:

	Assets			Indebtedness and Partners' Capital Accounts	
	Book	Tax Basis		Book	Tax Basis
Cash	$ 12,000	$ 12,000	Debt	$108,000	
Property	$120,000	$ 90,000	G	$ 6,000	$ 22,500
			H	$ 6,000	$ 22,500
			J	$ 12,000	$ 57,000
	$132,000	$102,000		$132,000	$102,000

There is no partnership minimum gain because partnership minimum gain under Treas.Reg. § 1.704–2(d)(3) is computed with reference to the excess of the mortgage ($108,000) over book value of the property ($120,000).[7] Thus, none of the nonrecourse mortgage debt is allocated among the partners under the first component of the formula in Treas.Reg. § 1.752–3(a). If the property were deeded to the mortgagee in lieu of foreclosure, under Treas.Reg. § 1.704–2(d)(4)(i), G and H each would be allocated $9,000 of the $18,000 tax gain recognized on the disposition. Thus, pursuant to Treas.Reg. § 1.752–3(a)(2), G and H each are allocated $9,000 of the nonrecourse debt. The remaining $90,000 of the nonrecourse debt is allocated among G, H, and J under the residual rule of Treas.Reg. § 1.752–3(a)(3). As a 50% partner, J will be allocated $45,000. G and H as one-quarter partners each will be allocated $22,500 of the debt under the residual rule, thereby decreasing each of their shares to $31,500.

As a result of their shares of partnership indebtedness being reduced from $54,000 to $31,500, G and E each receive a constructive distribution of $22,500 and reduce their bases from $45,000 to $22,500. J includes J's $45,000 increase in partnership indebtedness in J's basis for a total basis of $57,000 ($12,000 cash contribution + $45,000 debt share).

Detailed Analysis

1. LIABILITIES THAT ARE PART RECOURSE AND PART NONRECOURSE

Treas.Reg. § 1.752–1(i) provides that if one or more partners bear an economic risk of loss for only part of a partnership liability, the liability will

---

[7] The reduction of partnership minimum gain attributable to the revaluation does not trigger a minimum gain chargeback. See Treas.Reg. § 1.704–2(d)(4)(ii), (m), Ex. (3)(ii).

be treated as a recourse liability to the extent that any partner bears an economic risk of loss and the excess will be treated as a nonrecourse liability. This rule applies, for example, when one or more partners personally guarantee part, but less than all, of a partnership nonrecourse debt. See Treas.Reg. § 1.752–2(f), Ex. (5). Suppose, for example, that the ABC limited partnership borrows $1,000 on a nonrecourse basis and A, the sole general partner guarantees $800 of the debt and does so in a way that does not run afoul of the various anti-abuse rules. The Regulations treat $800 of the indebtedness as a recourse loan for which A bears the economic risk of loss. This result follows because if A pays the debt pursuant to the guarantee, A's subrogation rights are limited to the rights of a nonrecourse lender and, under the Regulations, the property secured by the loan is deemed to be worthless for purposes of determining which partners bear the economic risk of loss. Under this test, only A would bear the risk of loss of the $800. Thus, only $200 of the debt would be allocated among the partners according to their profit sharing ratios. The results would be similar if B, a limited partner guaranteed the debt: $800 of the debt would be treated as a recourse debt allocated to B. Treas.Reg. § 1.752–2(c)(2) similarly bifurcates the partnership liability where a partner sells property to the partnership for a nonrecourse obligation that wraps around a primary nonrecourse mortgage. The excess of the debt from the partnership to the partner is a recourse debt, the economic risk of loss of which is borne by the selling partner; the underlying debt is a nonrecourse debt. See Treas.Reg. § 1.752–2(f), Ex. (6).

2. ALLOCATION OF A SINGLE LIABILITY AMONG MULTIPLE PROPERTIES

2.1. *Generally*

Treas.Reg. § 1.752–3(b) permits a partnership that holds multiple properties subject to a single liability to allocate the liability among the properties using any reasonable method. When a partnership holds multiple properties subject to a single nonrecourse liability, the amount of § 704(c) minimum gain or reverse § 704(c) minimum gain cannot be readily determined under the rules of Treas.Reg. § 1.752–3(a)(2). This problem typically occurs when a partnership that holds several properties subject to individual mortgages refinances the individual liabilities with a single nonrecourse mortgage. In order to apply Treas.Reg. § 1.752–3(a)(2), the partnership must determine the amount of the liability that encumbers each asset in order to determine the § 704(c) minimum gain attributable to each asset. A method is not reasonable under Treas.Reg. § 1.752–3(b) if it allocates to any property an amount that exceeds the fair market value of the property. Thus, for example, the liability may be allocated to the properties based on the relative fair market value of each property. The portion of the nonrecourse liability allocated to each item of partnership property is then treated as a separate liability under Treas.Reg. § 1.752–3(a)(2). Once a liability is allocated among the properties, a partnership may not change the method for allocating the liability. If, however, one of the properties ceases to be subject to the liability, the portion of the liability originally allocated to that property must be reallocated to the properties still subject to the liability.

2.2. *Allocation of Limited Liability Company Debts*

Because no member of an LLC bears the risk of loss with respect to an LLC's recourse debts, for purposes of § 752 the debts owed by an LLC are not recourse debts as defined by Treas.Reg. § 1.752–1(a)(1). Except to the extent a member (partner) guarantees any such debt, the debt is a nonrecourse debt that is allocated under Treas.Reg. § 1.752–3. (If, however, a member of an LLC personally guarantees a debt of the LLC, the debt becomes a recourse debt, subject to the allocation rules of Treas.Reg. § 1.752–2 because the guaranteeing partner bears the risk of loss associated with the debt.) This rule applies even with respect to the LLC's unsecured debts. Furthermore, for purposes of allocating the debts among the members, under Treas.Reg. § 1.752–3, all of the LLC's property can be viewed as cross-collateralizing all of the LLC's debts that are recourse as to the LLC but nonrecourse as to the members. (If a debt is nonrecourse to the LLC under applicable debtor/creditor law, it is not cross-collateralized by all LLC property, but it is secured only by the property specifically mortgaged or pledged.) Thus, the rules of Treas.Reg. § 1.752–3(b) should be applicable to virtually every LLC that has more than one asset and any debt that is recourse as to the LLC. There is, however, no specific guidance regarding the method for allocating the LLC's debts among the members beyond the general principles described in the preceding materials.

3. BASIS IN TIERED PARTNERSHIP

Suppose that A contributes $25 to the AB limited partnership in exchange for an interest as a 20% limited partner. The AB limited partnership in turn contributes $100 to become a one-third limited partner in the ABC limited partnership, which acquires a building subject to a nonrecourse liability of $1,200. In the year in question, the ABC limited partnership incurs a loss of $600, of which $200 is allocable to the AB limited partnership. In addition, the AB limited partnership loses an additional $50. A's distributive share of the $250 loss of the AB limited partnership is $50. Rev.Rul. 77–309, 1977–2 C.B. 216, held that the AB limited partnership is entitled to include one-third ($400) of the nonrecourse liability of the ABC partnership in its basis for its interest in that partnership, and that A is, in turn, entitled to include 20% of that amount ($80) in A's basis for A's interest in the AB limited partnership. Thus, A's basis for A's partnership interest is $105, and A can deduct the entire amount of the loss. This approach now is incorporated in Treas.Reg. § 1.752–4(a).

PROBLEM SET 2

1. Art contributed $10,000, and Beverly, Chuck, and Darlene each contributed $30,000 to the ABCD partnership, which then borrowed $900,000 to purchase a building for $1,000,000. The partners share all items of income and deduction in proportion to their respective capital contributions.

(a) The partnership is a general partnership and the loan is a recourse loan. What is each partner's basis in the partner's partnership interest?

(b) The partnership is a limited partnership; Art is the general partner; the others are limited partners; and the loan is a recourse loan. What is each partner's basis in the partner's partnership interest?

(c) The partnership is a general partnership and the loan is a nonrecourse loan secured by the building. What is each partner's basis in the partner's partnership interest?

(d) The partnership is a limited partnership; Art is the general partner; the others are limited partners; and the loan is a nonrecourse loan secured by the building. What is each partner's basis in the partner's partnership interest?

(e) What is the result in (d) if the debt is nonrecourse but Art, the sole general partner, personally guarantees the loan?

(f) What is the result in (d) if the debt is nonrecourse but Art, the sole general partner, personally guarantees up to $500,000 of the nonrecourse debt?

(g) (1) What is the result in (b) if Beverly, a limited partner, personally guarantees the recourse debt?

(2) What is the result in (d) if Beverly, a limited partner, personally guarantees the nonrecourse debt?

(h) What is the result in (d) if each partner personally guarantees a proportionate share of the nonrecourse debt?

2. Elvira and Fred formed a limited partnership in which Elvira is the general partner and Fred is the limited partner. Elvira contributed $10,000 for a 20% interest in partnership income and loss, and Fred contributed $40,000 for an 80% interest in partnership income and loss. The partnership borrowed $850,000 pursuant to a nonrecourse loan and constructed an office building on leased land at a cost of $900,000. Interest on the loan is payable annually, but the principal is not due for 30 years. Assume that the cost recovery period for the building is 30 years; the method is straight-line. The partnership agreement contains all of the provisions necessary for allocations of deductions based on nonrecourse debt to be respected. The partnership's gross income exactly equals its deductible cash flow expenses, so each year the partnership reports a loss of $30,000 attributable to depreciation deductions.

(a) What are Elvira's and Fred's respective shares of the nonrecourse debt, and their respective basis in their partnership interests immediately after the debt was incurred?

(b) What are Elvira's and Fred's respective shares of the nonrecourse debt, and their respective basis in their partnership interests at the end of the second year?

(c) What are Elvira's and Fred's respective shares of the nonrecourse debt, and their respective basis in their partnership interests at the end of the third year?

(d)   What are Elvira's and Fred's respective shares of the nonrecourse debt, and their respective basis in their partnership interests at the end of 30 years?

3.   Gloria and Haben are equal partners in the GH partnership. The partnership owns Whiteacre, which has a basis of $90,000 and a fair market value of $120,000. Whiteacre is subject to a nonrecourse mortgage of $108,000. Ira contributes $12,000 to become a one-half partner, and Gloria's and Haben's interests in profits and losses are reduced to one-quarter. In connection with Ira's admission to the partnership, the partnership revalues its assets and capital accounts for book purposes. What are the respective partner's shares of the nonrecourse debt and their bases in their partnership interests after Ira's admission to the partnership?

CHAPTER 22

TRANSACTIONS BETWEEN PARTNERS AND THE PARTNERSHIP

SECTION 1. TRANSACTIONS INVOLVING SERVICES, RENTS, AND LOANS

INTERNAL REVENUE CODE: Sections 707(a)(1), (a)(2)(A), (c); 267(a)(2), (e)(1)–(4).

REGULATIONS: Sections 1.707–1(a), (c); 1.267(a)–2T(c).

PROPOSED REGULATIONS: Section 1.707–2.

When a partner is acting in a capacity other than as a partner, § 707(a)(1) treats a transaction between the partner and the partnership as a transaction between the partnership and one who is not a partner. Section 707(a)(1) thus requires entity rather than aggregate treatment for various types of transactions, thereby imposing on both the partnership and the partner the same tax consequences that would occur if the partnership had dealt with a person other than a partner in such a transaction. Section 707(a)(1) typically applies to transactions such as (1) a lease of property between a partner and the partnership, regardless of which is the lessor and which is the tenant, (2) a loan from a partner to the partnership or from the partnership to a partner, (3) fees for services rendered to a partner by the partnership or fees for services rendered by a partner to the partnership, if in the provision of the services the partner is not acting as a partner. Payments to a partner in these transactions are generally recognized by the partner as ordinary income. Payments may be deductible by the partnership or subject to the capitalization requirements of §§ 263 and 263A, depending upon the nature of the transaction between the partner and the partnership. Section 707(a)(1) also applies to sales or exchanges of property between a partnership and a partner not acting in a partner capacity; gains and losses recognized by either the partner or the partnership in such transactions generally are characterized under normal characterization rules, except as provided in § 707(b) discussed in Section 2 of this Chapter.[1]

---

[1] Section 707(b) limits tax avoidance possibilities in cases of sales of property between partners and the partnership by denying loss deductions in sale or exchange transactions between a 50% or greater partner and the partnership and sale or exchange transactions between partnerships where the same persons own more than a 50% interest in both partnerships. Section 707(b) also requires ordinary income treatment rather than capital gain treatment on the sale between a partner and the partnership where the transferred property is not a capital asset, i.e., is an ordinary income asset or a § 1231 asset in the hands of the transferee.

The principal issue raised with respect to § 707(a)(1) payments is whether the partner is acting as one who is not a member of the partnership. For example, in Pratt v. Commissioner, 64 T.C. 203 (1975), aff'd, 550 F.2d 1023 (5th Cir. 1977), the court held that a payment of 5% of partnership gross profits to a partner for the performance of management services with respect to partnership properties was an allocation of distributive share to a partner for services within the normal scope of the partner's duties as a general partner, rather than as a payment for non-partner services deductible by an accrual method partnership in the year the payment became due. In contrast, payments to a lawyer who is a partner in a real estate investment partnership for services in connection with performing a title search on property purchased by the partnership would be treated as payment of fees for services performed by the partner other than in the lawyer's capacity as a partner.

Section 707(a)(2) is an anti-abuse rule intended to limit the ability of the partners and partnership to disguise transactions as partnership § 731 distributions that in reality are payments to a partner in exchange for services or in exchange for a transfer of property to the partnership. Section 707(a)(2)(A) provides that if a partner performs services for a partnership or transfers property to a partnership, and there is a related allocation and distribution to the partner, the transaction may be treated as a transaction between the partner and the partnership subject to § 707(a)(1) rather than an allocation of partnership income and a distribution. Similarly, under § 707(a)(2)(B), discussed in Section 2 of this Chapter, a transfer of money or property by a partner to a partnership followed by a related transfer of money or property by the partnership to the partner may be treated as a sale or exchange subject to § 707(a)(1) rather than a contribution or distribution subject to the rules of Subchapter K.

Finally, § 707(c) requires the recognition of gross income by a partner who receives a guaranteed payment from the partnership in exchange for services rendered in a partner capacity or the use of the partner's capital if the partner's right to receive the payment is not dependent on partnership income. The partnership receives a correlative deduction for the payment, provided that the payment would have been deductible if made to a person who is not a partner, i.e., the payment is not a capital expenditure or a noncapital expenditure for which a deduction is expressly disallowed (for example, lobbying expenses under § 162(e)). Section 707(c) is most frequently applied when a partnership pays a "salary" to a partner or makes interest-like payments to a partner as a preferred return on a capital contribution that is not a loan.

Fixed payments to a partner for services thus will be categorized as either § 707(a)(1) or § 707(c) payments, depending on the facts and circumstances. In many, indeed most, instances, the categorization does not affect the tax consequences in terms of absolute value. For example, for purposes of § 199A, qualified business income does not include § 707 payments received by the partner for services, whether categorized under § 707(a)(1) or § 707(c). I.R.C. § 199A(c)(4). There is a difference in timing, however, that in some circumstances may require a determination whether a fixed payment is a payment to a partner not acting in a partner capacity, on the one hand, or a guaranteed payment to a partner in the person's capacity as a partner, on the other hand. The timing of the income and deduction item attributable to payments subject to § 707(a)(1) are governed by normal tax accounting rules, but the timing of the income and deduction item attributable to payments subject to § 707(c) are governed by the timing rule of § 706(a), discussed in Chapter 18.

In summary, application of these rules requires distinguishing payments from a partnership to a partner subject to either § 707(a)(1) or § 707(c) from distributive share allocations and distributions of partnership income. If the distributive share allocation and distribution rules do not govern, the payment must then be categorized as either a § 707(a)(1) or § 707(c) payment. Once a transaction between a partner and the partnership has been properly categorized, the tax treatment under a particular subsection of § 707 is relatively clear.

Revenue Ruling 81–301
1981–2 C.B. 144.

Is an allocation based on a percentage of gross income paid to an advisor general partner subject to section 707(a) of the Internal Revenue Code, under the circumstances described below?

FACTS

ABC is a partnership formed in accordance with the Uniform Limited Partnership Act of a state and is registered with the Securities and Exchange Commission as an open-end diversified management company pursuant to the Investment Company Act of 1940, as amended. Under the partnership agreement, *ABC*'s assets must consist only of municipal bonds, certain readily-marketable temporary investments, and cash. The agreement provides for two classes of general partners: (1) "director general partners" (directors) who are individuals and (2) one "adviser general partner" (adviser) that is a corporate investment adviser registered as such in accordance with the Investment Advisers Act of 1940, 15 U.S.C.A., section 80b–5 (1971).

Under the partnership agreement, the directors are compensated and have complete and exclusive control over the management, conduct, and operation of *ABC*'s activities. The directors are authorized to appoint agents and employees to perform duties on behalf of *ABC* and these agents may be, but need not be, general partners. Under the partnership agreement, the adviser has no rights, powers, or authority as a general partner, except that, subject to the supervision of the directors, the adviser is authorized to manage the investment and reinvestment of *ABC*'s assets. The adviser is responsible for payment of any expenses incurred in the performance of its investment advisory duties, including those for office space and facilities, equipment, and any of its personnel used to service and administer *ABC*'s investments. The adviser is not personally liable to the other partners for any losses incurred in the investment and reinvestment of *ABC*'s assets.

The nature of the adviser's services are substantially the same as those it renders as an independent contractor or agent for persons other than *ABC* and, under the agreement, the adviser is not precluded from engaging in such transactions with others.

Each general partner, including the adviser general partner, is required to contribute sufficient cash to *ABC* to acquire at least a one percent interest in the partnership. The agreement requires an allocation of 10 percent of *ABC*'s daily gross income to the adviser. After reduction by the compensation allocable to the directors and the adviser, *ABC*'s items of income, gain, loss, deduction, and credit are divided according to the percentage interests held by each partner.

The adviser's right to 10 percent of *ABC*'s daily gross income for managing *ABC*'s investment must be approved at least annually by a majority vote of the directors or a majority vote of all the partnership interests. Furthermore, the directors may remove the adviser as investment manager at any time on 60 days written notice to the adviser. The adviser can terminate its investment manager status by giving 60 days written notice to the directors. The agreement provides that the adviser will no longer be a general partner after removal or withdrawal as investment manager, but will continue to participate as a limited partner in the income, gains, losses, deductions, and credits attributable to the percentage interest that it holds.

LAW AND ANALYSIS

Section 61(a)(1) of the Code provides that, except as otherwise provided by law, gross income means all income from whatever source derived, including compensation for services, including fees, commissions, and similar items.

Section 702(a) of the Code provides that in determining the income tax of a partner each partner must take into account separately such partner's distributive share of the partnership's items of income, gain, loss, deduction, or credit.

Section 707(a) of the Code provides that if a partner engages in a transaction with a partnership other than as a member of such partnership, the transaction shall, except as otherwise provided in section 707, be considered as occurring between the partnership and one who is not a partner.

Section 1.707–1(a) of the Income Tax Regulations provides that a partner who engages in a transaction with a partnership other than in the capacity as a partner shall be treated as if not a member of the partnership with respect to such transaction. Such transactions include the rendering of services by the partner to the partnership. In all cases, the substance of the transaction will govern rather than its form.

Section 707(c) of the Code provides that to the extent determined without regard to the income of the partnership, payments to a partner for services shall be considered as made to one who is not a member of the partnership, but only for purposes of section 61(a) and, subject to section 263, for purposes of section 162(a).

Although the adviser is identified in the agreement as an "adviser general partner," the adviser provides similar services to others as part of its regular trade or business, and its management of the investment and reinvestment of *ABC*'s assets is supervised by the directors. Also it can be relieved of its duties and right to compensation at any time (with 60 days notice) by a majority vote of the directors. Further, the adviser pays its own expenses and is not personally liable to the other partners for any losses incurred in the investment and reinvestment of *ABC*'s assets. The services performed by the adviser are, in substance, not performed in the capacity of a general partner, but are performed in the capacity of a person who is not a partner.

The 10 percent daily gross income allocation paid to the adviser is paid to the adviser in its capacity other than as a partner. Therefore, the gross income allocation is not a part of the adviser's distributive share of partnership income under section 702(a) of the Code or a guaranteed payment under section 707(c).

HOLDING

The 10 percent daily gross income allocation paid to the adviser is subject to section 707(a) of the Code and taxable to the adviser under section 61 as compensation for services rendered. The amount paid is deductible by the partnership under section 162, subject to the provisions of section 265.

* * *

DETAILED ANALYSIS

1.   THE ENTITY APPROACH TO PARTNER SERVICES TO A
      PARTNERSHIP

Section 707(a)(1) treats a partner performing services in a non-partner capacity as separate from the partnership, which is treated as an entity separate from its partners. The alternative is to recognize the partnership as an aggregate of its members, which would affect both the timing and character of items of income and deduction related to partner services. Suppose that A, who is a lawyer and who is also a partner in the AB Partnership, in the course of A's law practice, performs services for the AB Partnership and receives a fee of $300. Under the entity approach, A recognizes $300 of compensation income and, assuming that the payment of the fee is deductible by the AB Partnership and is allocated equally, a $150 deduction flows through to A from the partnership. Because of the deduction, A reduces A's basis in A's interest in the AB Partnership by $150. As a result of the transaction, A recognizes net taxable income of $150 in the current year and, because of the basis reduction, A will recognize an additional $150 of capital gain (or $150 less capital loss) in a future year upon sale or liquidation of A's partnership interest. As for B, a $150 deduction flows through to B from the partnership, and B reduces B's basis in the AB Partnership by $150. As a result of the transaction, B receives a $150 deduction in the current year and will recognize an additional $150 of capital gain (or $150 less capital loss) in a future year upon sale or liquidation of B's partnership interest. In this particular fact pattern, the results would not differ under an aggregate approach. Under this approach, $150 would be viewed as a payment by A to A; this would not give rise to compensation income to A or be deductible by the AB partnership; instead it would be a distribution by the partnership to A, reducing A's basis in the partnership interest. The other $150 would represent compensation income to A, and B would have a corresponding $150 deduction that reduces B's basis. Again, as a result of the transaction, A recognizes net taxable income of $150 in the current year and an additional $150 of capital gain (or $150 less capital loss) in a future year upon sale or liquidation of A's partnership interest.

If, however, the payment by the partnership was a nondeductible capital expenditure, the results would differ under the entity and aggregate approaches. Under the entity approach of § 707(a)(1), the only tax consequence in the current year is that A recognizes $300 of compensation income. No current deduction flows through to either A or B. With respect to A, the result under an aggregate approach looks the same as when the payment was for a deductible expense: A would recognize only $150 of current compensation income and the other $150 would be treated as a distribution, reducing A's basis in A's partnership interest. Thus, A recognizes net taxable income of $150 in the current year and an additional $150 of capital gain (or $150 less capital loss) in a future year upon sale of A's interest or liquidation of A's partnership interest (unless the asset to which A's services related was depreciable or amortizable). When A is compensated by the partnership for services that must be capitalized, the aggregate approach results in deferral for A and, possibly, conversion, relative to the entity approach.

The aggregate and entity approaches produce even clearer differences when the partnership performs services for a partner in exchange for a payment by the partner. For example, suppose C, an equal partner in the CD Partnership, which is engaged in the stock brokerage business, pays the partnership a $200 commission for stock purchased for C's individual account. Under the entity approach of § 707(a)(1), the partnership has $200 of income, and C and D are each taxed on their $100 share of the $200 partnership income. C would add the $200 commission to C's cost basis in the purchased stock, and C would also add $100 of basis to C's partnership interest as a result of the distributive share allocation, thereby allowing C to recover the $100 distributive share of partnership income as a tax-free distribution or as a loss at a later date, often on liquidation of the partnership. Under the aggregate theory, C would not be taxed on any part of the $200 paid to the partnership; $100 of the payment is properly allocated to D, and the other $100 is attributable to services C has performed for C. As a result, C would be regarded as having contributed $100 to the partnership, increasing C's basis in the partnership interest, and C would add the $100 paid to D to the cost basis of C's stock. D would be taxed on $100. As compared to the entity approach, C would recognize an additional $100 of income on a future distribution or on liquidation of the partnership as capital gain, thereby deferring the recognition and re-characterizing the income.

Some of the same problems that arise in transactions governed by § 707(a)(1) arise when a partner is entitled to a particular salary or "guaranteed payment" from the partnership that is unrelated to partnership net income. Suppose E and F decide to form the EF Partnership but, as a condition of participating in the venture, E insists on being paid a salary of $5,000 a year whether or not the partnership makes a profit. The partnership has no income for the year, and E is paid $5,000. This payment would thus be governed by § 707(c) as a guaranteed payment for services computed without regard to partnership profits or losses. Under an entity approach, guaranteed payments are treated for purposes of § 61 as gross income to the partner and are deducted by the partnership under § 162 or capitalized under § 263, as appropriate. Thus, under the entity approach, E has $5,000 compensation income, and the partnership has a $5,000 deduction. E and F each have a partnership distributive share of the $2,500 deduction, leaving E with net income of $2,500. While this usually leaves the same dollar result as under the aggregate approach, the tax results may differ when the partnership has special income items. Thus, assume that the partnership had $5,000 of capital gain. Under the aggregate approach, E presumably would merely have a distributive share of $5,000 capital gain. Under the entity approach of § 707(c), E has $5,000 compensation, and E and F each have a distributive share of $2,500 of the capital gain and a distributive share of $2,500 of the partnership $5,000 expense deduction. See Treas.Reg. § 1.707–1(c), Ex. (4). There also is a difference if the payment to E is for services of a nature that require capitalization. In this case, E will have $5,000 of income, and the nondeductible partnership expenditure will be added to the basis of partnership property.

In most cases, the effect of a payment to a partner by the partnership is identical under both § 707(a)(1) and § 707(c). The most important difference between § 707(a)(1) payments to a partner and § 707(c) payments is that § 707(a)(1) payments to a cash method partner are taken into account by both the partnership and the partner in the year paid, while § 707(c) payments are taken into account by both the partnership and the partner in the year to which the item relates under the partnership's method of accounting. Thus, in some cases it is necessary to determine whether a payment is governed by § 707(a)(1) or § 707(c).

Unlike § 707(a)(1), which applies both to payments to a partner by a partnership for services rendered to the partnership and payments by a partner to the partnership for services rendered by the partnership (as well as to rental payments and interest on loans whether paid by a partner to the partnership or by the partnership to the partner), § 707(c) applies only to payments from the partnership to the partner.

The distinction between § 707 payments, in general, and a special distributive share allocation of partnership income to a partner who has rendered services to the partnership is particularly important when a payment to a partner is for an item that must be capitalized by the partnership if § 707 applies. To distinguish § 707 payments from special allocations of distributive shares requires careful analysis of the economic bargain between the partners. Once again, Subchapter K provides significant flexibility. Generally speaking, partners are free to choose whether to compensate a partner through an increased distributive share of partnership income, subject to the rules of § 704(b), or through guaranteed payments, subject to the rules of § 707(c). The economic bargain is different in each case, however, and to obtain the particular tax consequences may require an economic arrangement that differs from that which is acceptable to all of the partners. A special allocation to compensate a partner for services requires an allocation of partnership income to that partner's capital account, which may be coupled with a distribution to that partner. A § 707(a)(1) transaction or a § 707(c) guaranteed payment, in contrast, affects the partnership capital accounts in the same manner as any other partnership outlay. See Treas.Reg. § 1.704–1(b)(2)(iv)(*o*). However, the differing results of characterizing a payment as a § 707 payment versus an increased distributive share can produce abusive transactions that are designed to avoid § 707 in cases in which the entity approach results in capitalization of payments that are made to a partner. To prevent abuse, § 707(a)(2)(A) recharacterizes certain transactions involving the transfer of property or services to a partnership with a related distribution of money or property that purport to be special allocations of a partner's distributive share of partnership income and a partnership distribution as § 707(a)(1) transactions.

2.   WHEN DOES A PARTNER PROVIDE SERVICES UNRELATED TO THE PARTNER'S CAPACITY AS A PARTNER?

The instances where § 707(a)(1) payments have a different impact than payments received as a partner's distributive share have led to litigation over the distinction between the two concepts. In Pratt v. Commissioner, 64 T.C. 203 (1975), aff'd in part, rev'd in part, 550 F.2d 1023 (5th Cir. 1977), cash method general partners of limited partnerships received 5% of the gross profits of the partnership in exchange for the performance of management services with respect to partnership properties. The accrual method partnerships deducted the fees as payment for management services in the year the obligation to make the payments accrued, but the cash method partners accounted for the fees in the later year in which the fees were paid and received (the case pre-dated the application of § 267 to these facts). The Tax Court refused to treat the management fees as § 707(a)(1) payments stating that, "Petitioners in this case were to receive the management fees for performing services within the normal scope of their duties as general partners and pursuant to the partnership agreement.

There is no indication that any one of the petitioners was engaged in a transaction with the partnership other than in his capacity of a partner." The court thus held that the fees were not deductible to the partnership. As a consequence, the fees did not reduce the partners' distributive share of partnership income includable in the partners' income in the year that the obligation to pay the fees accrued.

The court in *Pratt* also indicated that it did not need to decide whether a continuing payment to a partner for services could ever be treated as a § 707(a)(1) payment. This comment in *Pratt* raised a question whether § 707(a)(1) might not have been intended to apply to continuing payments to a partner. In affirming the Tax Court, the Court of Appeals stressed the fact that "in order for the partnership to deal with one of its partners as an 'outsider' the transaction dealt with must be something outside the scope of the partnership." 550 F.2d at 1026. However, Rev.Rul. 81–301 appears to reject this theory, since the services rendered in Rev.Rul. 81–301 were ongoing services just as were the services in *Pratt*. Where § 707(a)(1) is not confined to isolated transactions as suggested in *Pratt*, it is difficult to find a workable distinction between a § 707(a)(1) payment and a § 707(c) payment. Perhaps a key factor is the extent to which the partner provides similar services to other customers, a fact highlighted by Rev.Rul. 81–301 in holding that § 707(a)(1) rather than § 707(c) applied. (The *Pratt* opinion does not discuss the extent to which the taxpayer provided management services other than to the two partnerships involved in the case.) But see Zahler v. Commissioner, T.C. Memo. 1981–112, rev'd on other grounds, 684 F.2d 356 (6th Cir.1982), holding that commissions paid to a partner in a securities brokerage firm, which paid sales commissions to partner and non-partner sales personnel alike, were not subject to § 707(a)(1).

On the other hand, payments from a partner to a partnership for services provided to the partner in the partner's individual capacity clearly should be subject to § 707(a)(1) even though the payments are of a continuing nature. Rev.Rul. 72–504, 1972–2 C.B. 90, allowed a partner whose individual business paid rent to a partnership of which the partner was a member to deduct the full amount of the rent paid.

3.   IDENTIFYING GUARANTEED PAYMENTS SUBJECT TO SECTION 707(c)

3.1. *"Salary" Versus "Draw"*

Section 707(c) most often is applied to amounts received by a partner as "salary" as opposed to "draw." Often the issue arises when a partner receives payments from the partnership in a year in which the partnership has an operating loss. If § 707(c) is not applicable, the payments are distributions, which are charged against the basis of the partner's interest and are recognized as income only after basis has been reduced to zero. In Falconer v. Commissioner, 40 T.C. 1011 (1963), payments to a partner referred to in the partnership agreement as "salary" were classified as § 707(c) payments in a situation in which the partnership had been operating at a loss when the payments were made. The taxpayer unsuccessfully argued that the amounts were advances that he was obligated to repay to the other partners.

Clark v. Commissioner, T.C. Memo. 1982–401, reached the same result on similar facts. At a time when the taxpayer-partner had a negative capital account, the partnership made payments to him by, first, increasing his capital account by an amount that was unrelated to partnership profits and, second, distributing to him an identical amount, which reduced his capital account and left it at its original negative balance.

In Grubb v. Commissioner, T.C. Memo. 1990–425, the taxpayer agreed to perform sales services for a partnership, and the partnership paid him fixed payments of $1,600 per month. Although the checks from the partnership to the taxpayer referred to the payments as "draw," after the taxpayer withdrew as a partner, he continued to perform sales services and to receive $1,600 per month. On these facts, the court concluded that the payments were compensation for services. The court rejected the taxpayer's argument that the partnership's failure to deduct the payments precluded treating them as guaranteed payments: "Includability at the partner level and deductibility at the partnership level of guaranteed payments are two different questions. * * * Accordingly, the fact that a partnership improperly characterizes guaranteed payments or fails to take such payments into account on its information return does not negate the fact that the guaranteed payments were incurred and became fixed at the partnership level, nor does it exonerate the partner receiving such payments from including the payments in gross income."

In Wallis v. Commissioner, T.C. Memo. 2009–243, aff'd, 391 Fed. Appx. 826 (11th Cir. 2010), the taxpayer (a tax lawyer) retired as a partner in his law firm and, among other amounts, received $240,000 in twelve $20,000 payments over four years. The $240,000 represented accumulated amounts that had been awarded to him as an equity partner over many years, but which were neither currently distributable in the years in which they were awarded nor recorded in the partner's capital account. Rather, the amounts, which were determined annually without regard to partnership income, were payable over a period of time after the partner reached age 68 but were forfeitable if the partner left the firm before that date. The Tax Court held that the payments were guaranteed payments under § 707(c) and § 736(a) (discussed in Chapter 25), taxable as ordinary income, and were not received as distributions under § 731.

3.2. *Payments Based on Partnership Gross Income Versus Partnership Net Income*

The Tax Court in Pratt v. Commissioner, supra, also rejected the taxpayers' argument that the payments were § 707(c) payments. The court held that the management fees, based on a fixed percentage of "gross rentals" represented a payment based on "income," which was thereby not to be treated as a § 707(c) payment. Even though the holding of the Tax Court in *Pratt* adopted the Commissioner's argument, the IRS specifically rejected this aspect of *Pratt* in Rev.Rul. 81–300, 1981–2 C.B. 143. That ruling involved payments to the general partners of a limited partnership formed to operate a shopping center. In addition to a specified percentage interest in the partnership's bottom line profit or loss, each general partner was entitled to 5% of the gross rentals received by the partnership in consideration of providing managerial services. The Ruling held that the payments of 5% of gross rents were § 707(c) payments:

> Although a fixed amount is the most obvious form of guaranteed payment, there are situations in which compensation for services is determined by reference to an item of gross income. For example, it is not unusual to compensate a manager of real property by reference to the gross rental income that the property produces. Such compensation arrangements do not give the provider of the service a share in the profits of the enterprise, but are designed to accurately measure the value of the services that are provided.

> Thus, [in] view of the legislative history and the purpose underlying section 707 of the Code, the term "guaranteed payment" should not be limited to fixed amounts. A payment for services determined by reference to an item of gross income will be a guaranteed payment if, on the basis of all of the facts and circumstances, the payment is compensation rather than a share of partnership profits. Relevant facts would include the reasonableness of the payment for the services provided and whether the method used to determine the amount of the payment would have been used to compensate an unrelated party for the services.

> It is the position of the Internal Revenue Service that in *Pratt* the management fees were guaranteed payments under section 707(c) of the Code. On the facts presented, the payments were not disguised distributions of partnership net income, but were compensation for services payable without regard to partnership income.

The legislative history of § 707(a)(2)(A), a provision that has nothing to do with the fact pattern in Rev.Rul. 81–300, endorses the conclusion in Rev.Rul. 81–300 that compensation measured by a percentage of gross income may be a § 707 payment, but states that by virtue of § 707(a)(2)(A), the transaction in the Ruling should be governed by § 707(a)(1) rather than § 707(c). S.Rep. No. 98–169, 98th Cong., 2d Sess. 230 (1984). There is no express explanation of the rationale for this. Nevertheless, the preamble to proposed 2015 amendments to Regulations under § 707(a)(2)(A) states, "Congress revisited the scope of section 707(a) in 1984 * * * and [in legislative history] conclude[ed] that the payment in Rev.Rul. 81–300 should be recharacterized as a section 707(a) payment. Accordingly, the Treasury Department and the IRS are obsoleting Rev.Rul. 81–300 and request comments on whether it should be reissued with modified facts." Disguised Payments for Services, 80 F.R. 43652, 43653 (July 23, 2015) (citation omitted).

3.3. *Distinguishing Section 707(c) Payments from Section 707(a)(1) Payments*

There never has been a clear demarcation of the line between a partner acting in the capacity of a partner, subject to § 707(c), and a partner acting in a capacity other than as a partner, subject to 707(a)(1). Treating payments like those in Rev.Rul. 81–300 as subject to § 707(a)(1) rather than § 707(c), makes the decision even more opaque.

Treas.Reg. § 1.707–1(a) provides that "the substance of the transaction will govern rather than its form," but fails to give any guidance as to what aspects of the "substance" are relevant. Prior to the 1984 Act, which added anti-abuse rules to § 707(a), the inquiry focused on the nature of the services provided. Payments for occasional services always have been considered § 707(a)(1) payments. Payments for ongoing services, however, generally were considered to be subject § 707(c) unless, as in Rev.Rul. 81–301, the partner provided similar services to customers and/or was subject to removal as a general partner. By all standards previously applied, the general partners in Rev.Rul. 81–300 appear to have been acting in their capacity as partners. But the direction in the Senate Finance Committee Report accompanying the 1984 Act that the payment in Rev.Rul. 81–300 is a § 707(a) payment, and the obsoleting of Rev.Rul. 81–300 by the preamble to Proposed Regulations has blurred the distinction.

4.   CAN SECTION 707 PAYMENTS BE EXCLUDABLE FRINGE BENEFITS?

In Armstrong v. Phinney, 394 F.2d 661 (5th Cir.1968), the court held that the entity approach adopted in § 707(a)(1) was also applicable for purposes of the § 119 exclusion for meals and lodging provided to employees. Thus, it would be possible as a matter of law for a partner to qualify as an employee entitled to the exclusion; the case was remanded for findings of fact concerning the partner's employee status. Wilson v. United States, 376 F.2d 280 (Ct.Cl.1967), consistent with prior law, reached the opposite conclusion on the ground that "[a] partnership is not a legal entity separate and apart from the partners, and, accordingly, a partnership cannot be regarded as the employer of a partner for the purposes of section 119," with no discussion of § 707. In Armstrong v. Phinney, the court applied § 707(a)(1), rather than § 707(c), even though the partner in question was providing services as a ranch manager for a ranch owned by the partnership. Under the reasoning of *Pratt*, § 707(c) should have been the relevant statutory provision. Does section § 707(c) help resolve the § 119 issue? Rev. Rul. 91–26, 1991–1 C.B. 184, held that accident and health insurance premiums paid by a partnership for the benefit of partners performing services for the partnership were to be treated as § 707(c) guaranteed payments, includable in the partners' income and deductible by the partnership. The partners were not allowed to exclude the premiums under § 106 but were allowed to claim deductions for the premiums to the extent allowed under § 162(*l*). See also Rev.Rul. 69–184, 1969–1 C.B. 256, holding that members of a partnership are not employees of the partnership for employment tax (FICA) purposes.

Various provisions in the § 132 Regulations treat partners who perform services for the partnership as employees for purposes of the exclusion of miscellaneous fringe benefits under § 132. See, e.g., Treas.Reg. § 1.132–1(b)(1) (partners are treated as employees for purposes of excluding no additional cost fringe benefits and qualified employee discounts); Treas.Reg.

In Cagle v. Commissioner, 63 T.C. 86 (1974), aff'd, 539 F.2d 409 (5th Cir.1976), we held that includability and deductibility of guaranteed payments are two separate questions, and specifically that guaranteed payments are not automatically deductible simply by reason of their being included in the recipient's income. In *Cagle,* we stated * * *:

> We think that all Congress meant was that guaranteed payments should be included in the recipient partner's income in the partnership taxable year ending with or within which the partner's taxable year ends and in which the tax accounting treatment of the transaction is determined at the partnership level. S.Rept. No. 1622, supra at pp. 94, 385, 387.

We believe our statement in *Cagle* is an accurate description of the Congressional intent. We have found nothing in the statutory language, regulations, or legislative history to indicate that includability in the recipient partner's income was intended to be dependent upon deductibility at the partnership level.

Petitioners seem to argue that there is a patent unfairness in taxing them on nonexistent income, namely income that they have neither received nor benefited from (e.g. through a tax deduction at the partnership level). Their argument has a superficial appeal to it, but on closer analysis must fail. Except for certain very limited purposes, guaranteed payments are treated as part of the partner's distributive share of partnership income and loss. Sec. 1.707–1(c), Income Tax Regs. For timing purposes guaranteed payments are treated the same as distributive income and loss. Sec. 706(a); sec. 1.706–1(a) and sec. 1.707–1(c), Income Tax Regs. A partner's distributive share of partnership income is includable in his taxable income for any partnership year ending within or with the partner's taxable year. Sec. 706(a). As is the case with a partner's ordinary distributive share of partnership income and loss, any unfairness in taxing a partner on guaranteed payments that he neither receives nor benefits from results from the conduit theory of partnerships, and is a consequence of the taxpayer's choice to do the business in the partnership form. We find no justification in the statute, regulations, or legislative history to permit these petitioners to recognize their income pro rata as deductions are allowed to the partnership. * * *

Sicard v. Commissioner, T.C.Memo. 1996–173, reached a similar result, holding that unpaid guaranteed payments were includable by the cash method partner to whom they were due in the year in which the partnership accrued the amounts into its cost of goods sold, rather than in the later year in which the payments were actually received.

If a guaranteed payment is not paid to a partner, but nevertheless, as is required, is included in income by the partner, it is not clear whether the claim is a separate asset with a separate "tax cost" basis. There is no definitive answer to this question, but a footnote in *Gaines* suggests that the inclusion of a § 707(c) guaranteed payment increases the partner's basis for the partnership interest and the subsequent payment is governed by § 731. This seems to be the correct solution because it permits the subsequent distribution of the guaranteed payment without further income recognition.

6.   PAYMENTS FOR CAPITAL EXPENDITURES

6.1. *Capitalization of Section 707 Payments*

Payments by a partnership to a partner governed by § 707(a)(1) are not automatically deductible. If the payment is a capital expenditure, the partnership must capitalize it. Even though there is no deduction, the payee partner nevertheless realizes gross income by reason of the payment. See Rev.Rul. 75–214, 1975–1 C.B. 185, holding that payments by a limited partnership to the general partner as compensation for organizing the partnership were subject to § 707 and were required to be capitalized by the partnership pursuant to § 263. (Under current law, with respect to compensation for organizing the partnership the same result is reached under § 709, discussed in Chapter 19.)

Guaranteed payments subject to § 707(c) likewise are subject to the usually applicable requirements of § 263 and cannot be deducted simply because capital expenditures take the form of guaranteed payments. I.R.C. § 707(c). Cagle v. Commissioner, 539 F.2d 409 (5th Cir.1976), reached the same result under a prior version of § 707(c) that did not expressly subject guaranteed payments to § 263. The capitalization rule was applied to guaranteed payments in consideration of services in organizing a partnership and syndicating interests in Tolwinsky v. Commissioner, 86 T.C. 1009 (1986). Rev.Rul. 80–234, 1980–2 C.B. 203, treated a fee paid to a partner for finding acceptable loan applicants as a guaranteed payment. The partner was required currently to include the payment in income, but the partnership was required to capitalize it as a cost of the loan amortizable over the life of the loan.

6.2. *Effect of Section 707: Comparison to Special Allocations*

Assume that A and B each contributed $30,000 to form a partnership that purchased land for $55,000. The partnership balance sheet is as follows:

	Assets			**Capital Accounts**	
	Book	**Tax Basis**		**Book**	**Tax Basis**
Cash	$ 5,000	$ 5,000	A	$30,000	$30,000
Land	$55,000	$55,000	B	$30,000	$30,000
	$60,000	$60,000		$60,000	$60,000

Special Allocation:

Assume the partnership earns $7,000 in Year 1. A and B agree to allocate $5,000 plus 50% of the balance as A's distributive share and 50% of the income in excess of $5,000 as B's share, and to distribute $5,000 to A. This allocation reflects A's performance of services for the partnership that created a new capital asset worth $5,000. Treating this arrangement as an allocation and distribution, A would have income of $6,000 in Year 1 and B would have income of $1,000. Assuming that A and B did not want to change their residual sharing arrangement, the partnership balance sheet at the end of Year 1 would be as follows:

	Assets				Capital Accounts	
	Book	**Tax Basis**			**Book**	**Tax Basis**
Cash	$ 7,000	$ 7,000		A	$31,000	$31,000
Land	$55,000	$55,000		B	$31,000	$31,000
New Asset	$ 0	$ 0				
	$62,000	$62,000			$62,000	$62,000

This arrangement, in effect, ignores the transfer of services by A in exchange for creation of an asset, which is thereby either ignored for balance sheet purposes or reflected in the capital accounts with zero value. Respecting this arrangement permits the AB Partnership to avoid the capitalization requirement of § 263; concomitantly, the new asset has a basis of zero. Assuming a value of $5,000 for the new asset, if the partnership sold its assets and liquidated in Year 2, each of A and B would include $2,500 as distributive share of partnership income and would have no gain on the liquidation of the partnership. They would recognize income as follows:

	A	B
Year 1	$6,000	$1,000
Year 2	$2,500	$2,500
	$8,500	$3,500

Section 707:

Treating the allocation and distribution to A instead as a § 707(a)(1) payment for A's services in creating the new asset recognizes the existence of the asset and its value within the partnership. A would have $5,000 of compensation income as an individual in Year 1 and, because the expense is a nondeductible capital expense, the AB Partnership has $7,000 of income in Year 1, which is taxed equally to the partners. The AB Partnership's balance sheet at the end of Year 1 is as follows:

Assets

	Book	Tax Basis			Book	Tax Basis
Cash	$ 7,000	$ 7,000	A		$33,500	$33,500
Land	$55,000	$55,000	B		$33,500	$33,500
New Asset	$ 5,000	$ 5,000				
	$67,000	$67,000			$67,000	$67,000

When the assets are sold in Year 2, no gain or loss is realized, and neither A nor B realizes gain or loss on the liquidation. Thus, the income recognized by A and B over the life of the partnership is as follows:

	A	B
Year 1	$8,500	$3,500
Year 2	$ 0	$ 0
	$8,500	$3,500

Comparison:

This transaction may be described as a transaction treated as a § 707(a)(1) transaction by virtue of § 707(a)(2)(A) (discussed below in Detailed Analysis 7). As is easily seen, § 707 affects neither the total amount of income realized nor the individual to whom that income is taxed. Rather, § 707 affects the timing of the income recognized by A, the partner who performed the services and, quite possibly, the character of the income recognized by both partners. If the asset created by A's services was a capital asset (or a § 1231 asset) rather than an ordinary income asset, e.g., inventory, the special allocation would have resulted in both A and B recognizing $2,500 of capital gain in Year 2, while A recognized $6,000 of ordinary income in Year 1 and B recognized $1,000 of ordinary income in Year 1. As a result of the application of § 707, neither partner recognizes any capital gain in this example; all of the income is ordinary income.

7.   DISGUISED TRANSACTIONS BETWEEN PARTNERS AND THE PARTNERSHIP: SECTION 707(a)(2)(A)

Suppose A, who is a one-third partner in the ABC partnership, performs services for the partnership related to the acquisition of a new building. If A is paid a fixed sum for performing these services under either § 707(a)(1) or § 707(c), the partnership will be required to capitalize the payment, and A will be required currently to include the payment in income. On the other hand, if the partnership makes a special income allocation to A, which is subsequently distributed, B's and C's distributive shares will be reduced proportionately, in effect allowing the capital expenditure for A's services to be deducted by B and C. Section 707(a)(2)(A) authorizes Regulations, which have not been finalized but which were proposed in 2015, treating as a § 707(a)(1) transaction the performance of services for the partnership by a partner coupled with a related allocation *and* distribution to the partner if, when viewed together, the two events are more properly characterized as a transaction occurring between the partnership and a partner acting in his capacity other than as a partner.

The Senate Finance Committee Report indicates that § 707(a)(2)(A) may apply both to one-time transactions and to continuing arrangements that use allocations and distributions in lieu of direct payments. The provision specifically is intended to apply to partnership organization and syndication fees, which must be capitalized pursuant to § 709. Furthermore, the Regulations may recharacterize a purported partner as not being a partner. The Committee Report lists the following six factors as relevant in determining whether a partner is receiving a putative allocation and distribution in the partner's capacity as a partner: (1) whether the amount of the payment is subject to appreciable risk; (2) whether the partnership status of the recipient is transitory; (3) whether the allocation and distribution are close in time to the performance of services for, or the transfer of property to, the partnership; (4) whether considering all of the facts and circumstances it appears that the recipient became a partner primarily to obtain for himself or the partnership benefits which would not have been available if the partner had rendered services to the partnership in a third party capacity; (5) whether the value of the recipient's interest in general and in continuing partnership profits is small relative to the allocation in question; and (6) whether the requirements for maintaining capital accounts under § 704(b) makes it unlikely that income allocations are disguised payments for capital because it is economically unfeasible. Transitory special allocations are particularly suspect when coupled with the existence of another factor. Furthermore, the mere fact that the amount of an allocation is contingent does not insulate it under § 707(a)(2)(A). Contingent allocations generally will be recharacterized as fees, however, only where the partner in question normally performs, has previously performed or is capable of performing similar services for third parties. S.Rep. No. 98–169, 98th Cong., 2d Sess. 226–229 (1984).

The Senate Finance Committee Report gives the following example of the anticipated application of § 707(a)(2)(A):

> A commercial office building constructed by a partnership is projected to generate gross income of at least $100,000 per year indefinitely. Its architect, whose normal fee for such services is $40,000, contributes cash for a 25-percent interest in the partnership and receives both a 25-percent distributive share of net income for the life of the partnership, and an allocation of $20,000 of partnership gross income for the first two years of partnership operations after leaseup. The partnership is expected to have sufficient cash available to distribute $20,000 to the architect in each of the first two years, and the agreement requires such a distribution. The purported gross income allocation and partnership distribution should be treated as a fee under sec. 707(a), rather than as a distributive share. Factors which contribute to this conclusion are (1) the special allocation to the

architect is fixed in amount and there is a substantial probability that the partnership will have sufficient gross income and cash to satisfy the allocation/distribution; (2) the value of his interest in general and continuing partnership profits is relatively small in relation to the allocation in question; (3) the distribution relating to the allocation is fairly close in time to the rendering of the services; and (4) it is not unreasonable to conclude from all the facts and circumstances that the architect became a partner primarily for tax motivated reasons. If, on the other hand, the agreement allocates to the architect 20 percent of gross income for the first two years following construction of the building a question arises as to how likely it is that the architect will receive substantially more or less than his imputed fee of $40,000. If the building is pre-leased to a high credit tenant under a lease requiring the lessee to pay $100,000 per year of rent, or if there is low vacancy rate in the area for comparable space, it is likely that the architect will receive approximately $20,000 per year for the first two years of operations. Therefore, he assumes limited risk as to the amount or payment of the allocation and, as a consequence, the allocation/distribution should be treated as a disguised fee. If, on the other hand, the project is a "spec building," and the architect assumes significant entrepreneurial risk that the partnership will be unable to lease the building, the special allocation might (even though a gross income allocation), depending on all the facts and circumstances, properly be treated as a distributive share and partnership distribution.

Nonetheless, until Regulations are finalized, this technique might remain available. However, in Tech. Adv. Memo. 9219002 (May 8, 1992), the IRS took the position that § 702(a)(2)(A) is self-executing and its application does not require the promulgation of Regulations.

In 2015, the IRS and Treasury issued Proposed Regulations to address disguised payments for services under § 707(a)(2)(A). Parroting the statutory language, Prop.Reg. § 1.707–2(b)(1) (2015) would treat an arrangement as a disguised payment for services if (1) a person (service provider), either in a partner capacity or in anticipation of being a partner, performs services (directly or through its delegate) to or for the benefit of the partnership; (2) there is a related direct or indirect allocation and distribution to the service provider; and (3) the performance of the services and the allocation and distribution, when viewed together, are properly characterized as a transaction occurring between the partnership and a person acting other than in that person's capacity as a partner. An item that is treated as a disguised payment for services by the Proposed Regulations would be treated as a payment for services for all purposes of the Code. Prop.Reg. § 1.707–2(b)(2)(i) (2015). Such payments would be treated as a payment to a non-partner for purposes of determining the distributive shares of the other partners. Prop.Reg. § 1.707–2(b)(3)(i) (2015) states that the rules of the Proposed Regulations would apply even if it is determined the application of the rules would cause the service provider to be treated as not being a partner or that no partnership exists

The Proposed Regulations would apply a facts and circumstances analysis to identify a disguised payment for services at the time an arrangement is entered into. Prop.Reg. § 1.707–2(b)(2)(i) (2015). The Proposed Regulations generally adopt the factors specified in the Senate Committee Report, but stress significant entrepreneurial risk as the most significant factor. Prop.Reg. § 1.707–2(c) (2015) would provide that a payment that lacks significant entrepreneurial risk relative to the overall entrepreneurial risk of the partnership constitutes a payment for services. Prop.Reg. § 1.707–2(c)(1) (2015) would create a presumption that an arrangement lacks entrepreneurial risk if there is a cap on allocations of partnership income that is reasonably expected to apply in most years; the allocation of the service provider's share of income is reasonably certain for one or more years; the allocation is an allocation of gross income; the allocation is an amount that is fixed or determinable or is designed to assure that significant net profits are available to make the allocation to the service provider; or the arrangement allows the service provide to waive the service provider's right to receive payment for the future performance of services in a manner that is non-binding (this one is designed to prohibit fee waiver arrangements that are popular for equity and hedge fund managers).

The secondary factors included in the Proposed Regulations that indicate that an arrangement is a disguised payment for services include whether the service provider's interest is transitory, the allocation and distribution are in a time frame comparable to the time in which a non-partner service provider would receive payment, the service provider became a partner in order to obtain tax benefits not otherwise available, and the value of the service provider's interest in continuing partnership profits is small relative to the allocation and distribution. Prop.Reg. § 1.707–2(c)(2) through (5) (2015). The Proposed Regulations would add an additional factor, not contained in the Senate Finance Committee Report, that would apply if the arrangement provides for different allocations or distributions with respect to different services provided by one person or related persons and are subject to variable levels of entrepreneurial risk.

8.   GUARANTEED MINIMUM PAYMENTS

Suppose that A and B are partners in the AB Partnership, in which A is a 25% partner, but that the partnership agreement provides that A is entitled to receive not less than $100 per year. If the partnership's income for the year is $400 or more, no portion of A's distributive share is a guaranteed payment. Treas.Reg. § 1.707–1(c), Ex. (2). This is true even if the partnership agreement provides that A's minimum is to be treated as an expense item in computing partnership profits. Rev.Rul. 66–95, 1966–1 C.B. 169. If, however, partnership profits were only $200, under the approach in Treas.Reg. § 1.707–1(c), Ex. (2), $50 (25% of $200) would be A's distributive share, and $50 would be a guaranteed payment. Suppose further that the partnership's taxable income, apart from A's guaranteed payment, consists of $120 of ordinary income and $80 of capital gains. In this case, the $50 guaranteed payment would be deducted from the $120 of ordinary income, leaving $70 of ordinary income and $80 of capital gains to be apportioned between A and B in the ratio that they share partnership profits for the year after deducting the guaranteed payment. Reflecting the partners' economic interests in the partnership, this sharing ratio is one-third to A and two-thirds to B. A's share is $50/$150 and B's share is $100/$150. Thus, in addition to $50 of ordinary income from the guaranteed payment, A has $23.33 of ordinary income and $26.67 of capital gain; B has $46.67 of ordinary income and $53.33 of capital gain. See Rev.Rul. 69–180, 1969–1 C.B. 183.

Amendments proposed in 2015 would, if finalized, modify Treas.Reg. § 1.707–1(c), Ex. (2) to provide that all of the minimum guaranteed amount would be treated as a guaranteed payment. Thus, in the above example, all $100 of A's guaranteed minimum payment would be treated as a guaranteed payment under § 707(c) regardless of the amount and character of partnership income. Only amounts allocated to the partner in excess of the minimum amount would be treated as the partner's distributive share. The preamble to the Proposed Regulations explains that the prior approach of Example (2) is inconsistent with the principle adopted in the Proposed Regulations that an allocation must be subject to significant entrepreneurial risk to be treated as distributive share. 81 F.R. 43,652, 43,655 (July 23, 2015).

9. LOANS AND GUARANTEED PAYMENTS FOR THE USE OF CAPITAL

9.1. *General*

Section 707(c) expressly contemplates guaranteed payments by the partnership for the use of a partner's capital. Guaranteed payments for the use of capital that are subject to § 707(c) are distinguishable from interest on a loan, which is subject to § 707(a)(1), in that § 707(c) governs payments in the nature of a return paid with respect to contributed capital, even if determined under an interest-like computation, while § 707(a)(1) governs interest payments on a bona fide loan. See Treas.Reg. § 1.707–1(a). In Pratt v. Commissioner, supra, the Tax Court applied § 707(c) to tax a partner on accrued but unpaid interest on a loan from the partner to the partnership, 64 T.C. 203, 212–214, but on appeal the Commissioner conceded that because the transaction was a true loan, § 707(a)(1) controlled, and the cash method partner was not taxable until he received the interest payment. 550 F.2d 1023 (5th Cir.1977). A bona fide loan from a partner to the partnership exists only if there is an unconditional obligation to pay a sum certain at a determinable date. Rev.Rul. 73–301, 1973–2 C.B. 215. In contrast, a contribution credited to a partner's capital account, repayable only as a distribution from partnership capital under the terms of the partnership agreement, is not a loan even though it may bear "interest." Thus, strict adherence to the requirements for maintaining partners' capital accounts pursuant to Treas.Reg. § 1.704–1(b)(2)(iv) can be a determining factor in distinguishing true loans from contributions to capital bearing guaranteed payments.

Guaranteed payments for the use of partnership capital are used by partnerships that, for example, desire generally to allocate profits to reflect services provided to the partnership, while providing a proper allowance for disproportionate capital contributions. Assume, for example, that D, E, and F desire to form a partnership in which both capital and services will be a material income producing factor. D, E, and F intend to be "equal" partners, but the partnership requires $300,000 of capital, and E and F each can contribute only $50,000. The solution is for D to contribute $200,000, while E and F each contribute $50,000, and to provide in the partnership agreement that D will receive an annual guaranteed payment equal to a specified percentage of the amount by which D's capital contribution exceeds that of the other partners. Thus, the partnership agreement may provide that D is to receive a guaranteed payment of $15,000 (10% × $150,000) after which the profits of the partnership are to be split equally. Under this arrangement, D's capital account remains at $200,000 after receiving the payments, and E and F have not been taxed on the income used to make the guaranteed payments.

A more flexible formula can be devised to take into account the possibility that the partners desire ultimately to equalize their capital contributions. Thus, the partnership agreement might provide that any partner who has contributed more than any other partner is entitled to an annual guaranteed payment equal to a stated percentage, e.g., 10%, of the partner's excess contribution. As the partnership earns profits, E and F may leave a portion of their distributive shares in the partnership, thereby increasing their capital accounts, while D withdraws not only D's share of profits, but also a portion of D's original capital contribution. Thus, if at the end of a future year the respective capital account balances of the partners are D, $120,000, E, $100,000, and F, $80,000, D would be entitled to a guaranteed payment of $4,000 (10% × ($120,000 − $80,000)), and E would be entitled to a guaranteed payment of $2,000 (10% × ($100,000 − $80,000)). When all partners' capital accounts were equalized, any guaranteed payments would cease. Under this arrangement, E and F must pay tax on amounts they do not currently receive so that all of the partners eventually will have equal capital accounts. The choice between which of the two methods is adopted depends on many factors, only some of which are tax considerations.

9.2. *Characterization of Guaranteed Payments for the Use of Capital*

Guaranteed payments for the use of capital raise characterization questions analogous to some of the characterization questions relating to guaranteed payments for services. In general, guaranteed payments for the use of capital are ordinary income, see Treas.Reg. § 1.707–1(c), but whether they are "interest" is not clear. Characterization of guaranteed payments for the use of capital as interest may be relevant to both the recipient partner and to the partnership. Section 707(c) payments for capital are treated by the partner as interest in applying the passive activity loss rules of § 469. Treas.Reg. § 1.469–2(e)(2)(ii)(A). Characterization as interest also is relevant for purposes of applying other rules, such as the investment interest limitation of § 163(d), but there is no direct precedential authority on this point. However, as far as the recipient is concerned, in private letter rulings the IRS has characterized such payments with reference to the character of the partnership's ordinary income from which they were made. See, e.g., Private Letter Ruling 8728033. From the partnership's perspective, determining whether the deduction is to be treated as an ordinary and necessary business expense under § 162 or as an interest expense under § 163 may be relevant in applying the business interest limitation of § 163(j) or the uniform capitalization rules of § 263A. As far as characterization from the perspective of the partnership is concerned, however, § 707(c) expressly refers to § 162. This raises the possibility that such payments may be characterized differently from the perspective of the recipient and the partnership, since characterization of a deduction as a § 162 deduction is not helpful in characterizing the nature of the receipt.

10.   OTHER ASPECTS OF GUARANTEED PAYMENTS

Section 707(c) applies the entity approach only with respect to § 61 and § 162. For all other purposes, guaranteed payments are considered part of the partner's distributive share of ordinary income. A guaranteed payment is not considered an interest in profits under §§ 706(b)(3), 707(b), and 708(b). Treas. Reg § 1.707–1(c).

A guaranteed payment is not covered by the deferred compensation rules of § 404(a) and (b) or the withholding rules. Treas.Reg. § 1.707–1(c). However, Miller v. Commissioner, 52 T.C. 752 (1969), held that guaranteed payments received by a partner for services performed abroad were excludable under former § 911 as income earned abroad and not, as urged by the Commissioner, simply a distributive share of partnership income. Carey v. United States, 427 F.2d 763 (Ct.Cl.1970), reached the same result.

Rev.Rul. 2007–40, 2007–1 C.B. 1426, held that the transfer of appreciated property by a partnership to a partner in satisfaction of a guaranteed payment owed to the partner is a sale or exchange of the property by the partnership and not a distribution under § 731. Thus, the partnership is required to recognize gain on the transfer. The ruling does not deal with whether the partnership is entitled to deduct the value of the property or whether it must capitalize that amount, as the case may be.

PROBLEM SET 1

1.   Alice and Bob are general partners in a real estate business. Alice is a two-thirds partner, and Bob is a one-third partner. At the beginning of the year, Alice's basis for her partnership interest was $10,000; Bob's basis for his partnership interest was $5,000. This year the AB partnership recognized taxable income of $9,000 from transactions with non-partners. The partnership uses the accrual method of accounting, and the partners use the cash method.

(a) (1) What are the tax consequences to Alice and Bob if Bob is a lawyer and the partnership paid Bob $6,000 to defend a negligence suit against the partnership by a person who was injured in a "slip and fall" in a building owned by the partnership?

(2)   What would be the tax consequences to Alice and Bob if Bob billed the partnership for the services in the current year, but the partnership did not pay Bob until April of next year, in which the partnership again realized $9,000 of taxable income from transactions with unrelated parties?

(b)   Bob is a lawyer and the partnership paid Bob $6,000 to represent it in purchasing an apartment building (e.g., conduct the title search, etc.). What are the tax consequences to Alice and Bob?

(c)   The partnership paid Bob $6,000 to serve as resident manager of one of its apartment buildings; the amount was unconditionally due if he rendered the services. What are the tax consequences to Alice and Bob?

(d)   Bob served as resident manager of one of the partnership's apartment buildings; the partnership agreed to pay Bob $6,000, but the payment was not made until April of the following year, in which the partnership again realized $9,000 of taxable income from transactions with unrelated parties. What are the tax consequences to Alice and Bob?

(e)   What are the tax consequences to Alice and Bob if the partnership paid Bob $6,000 to oversee construction of a new apartment building being constructed for the partnership by an unrelated contracting company? Does it matter whether Bob holds himself out to third parties as engaged in a business providing the services that he provided to the partnership?

2.   (a)   Carla and Don are the members of a limited liability company that is taxed as a partnership and that operates a funeral home. Although they are equal members, because Don has assumed sole responsibility for responding to nighttime calls, the LLC provides Don with an apartment on the second floor of the funeral home. The LLC's expenses allocable to the apartment are $5,000, and the fair rental value of the apartment is $6,000. What are the tax consequences of this arrangement to Carla and Don?

(b)   Don and Carla's LLC paid all of the premiums for group health insurance benefits for its three employees, as well as for Carla and Don. The premium attributable to each person was $2,000. What are the tax results to Carla and Don?

3.   Jackie and Kerry are general partners in an investment partnership. Jackie contributed $450,000, and Kerry contributed $200,000. They agreed that until Jackie had cumulatively withdrawn distributions totaling $250,000 more than Kerry had withdrawn, Jackie would receive annually, before dividing partnership profits, an amount equal to 6% of the excess of Jackie's capital account over Kerry's capital account. For the current year, the partnership has net ordinary income of $12,000 and $8,000 of long-term capital gain. Because Jackie's capital account exceeded Kerry's by $250,000, Jackie was paid $15,000 as a guaranteed return on the excess capital contribution. What are the tax consequences to Jackie and Kerry?

4.   Gorsuch has been admitted as a new partner in the law firm of Thomas, Roberts & Alito. Gorsuch is entitled to 25% of the partnership's profits, but in the first year is guaranteed a minimum cash draw out of profits of $50,000. What are the tax consequences to Gorsuch and the other partners if the partnership's profit in Gorsuch's first year as a partner is $100,000? What if

partnership profits are $200,000? What will happen if the Proposed Regulations discussed in Detailed Analysis 8 are finalized?

5.   Andy is a civil engineer. Yosemite Development Associates, a general partnership, has offered Andy a 10% partnership interest, but with a zero opening capital account, if Andy will become the managing partner of Yosemite for the next four years. The principal activity of Yosemite during that time will be the development and construction of an amusement park, which will be developed in several stages. In Year 1, the expected profits are zero; in Year 2, the expected profits are $1,000,000; in Year 3 the expected profits are $2,000,000; and in Year 4, the expected profits will be $3,000,000. At the end of Year 4, it is expected that Andy will receive a full distribution of the balance in Andy's capital account and Andy will cease to be a partner. How will the allocation of operating profits to Andy be treated under § 704 and § 707? Would your answer change if after Year 4 Andy's capital account balance (if any) were not distributed, but Andy's continuing interest in the partnership profits was reduced to 1%?

SECTION 2.   SALES OF PROPERTY

INTERNAL REVENUE CODE: Sections 707(a)(1), (a)(2)(B), (b); 1239(a)–(c); 267(a)(1), (e)(1)–(3).

REGULATIONS: Sections 1.707–1(b); 1.707–3(a)–(d); 1.707–4(a)(1)–(3); 1.707–5(a); 1.267(b)–1(b); 1.267(a)–2T(c).

Problems similar to those that arise when a partner purchases services from the partnership in an individual capacity or provides services to a partnership of which the partner is a member for a stated salary also arise when a partner sells an asset to the partnership or buys an asset from the partnership. As with transactions in which a partner deals with a partnership as a stranger with respect to the provision of services, § 707(a)(1) applies the entity theory to tax sales of property by a partner to a partnership or by the partnership to a partner. The basic rule of § 707(a)(1) is supplemented by § 707(a)(2), which recharacterizes certain distributions related to the transfer of property by a partner to the partnership as a transaction subject to § 707(a)(1). Because of presumptions contained in this rule, payments received from the partnership by a partner in connection with a § 721 contribution of property in exchange for an interest are generally taxed under § 707(a)(1) rather than as § 731 distributions. (For those who have studied corporate tax, recall from Chapter 19 the absence of a boot rule parallel to § 351(b).)

Section 707(b) disallows loss deductions on sales between a partner and a partnership in which the partner owns more than 50% of either the profits or capital interests (or between two partnerships in which the same partners own more than 50% of the profits or capital interests). In addition, gain on a sale of property other than a capital asset (i.e., § 1231 property) between a partner and a related partnership, i.e., more than 50% owned, is recharacterized as ordinary income.

DETAILED ANALYSIS

1.   LIMITATIONS ON LOSS RECOGNITION

1.1. *Scope of Limitations*

Section 707(b)(1)(A) disallows any loss on a sale or exchange between a person and a partnership in which the person owns, directly or indirectly, more than 50% of either a capital or a profits interest. Section 707(b)(1)(B) applies the same rule to sales or exchanges between two partnerships in which the same persons own more than 50% of either a capital or a profits interest.

Davis v. Commissioner, 866 F.2d 852 (6th Cir.1989), illustrates two aspects of the breadth of § 707(b)(1)(B). A bank foreclosed on real property held by a limited partnership, and one month later the bank sold the property to another partnership in which the profits and capital interests were 100% owned directly or indirectly by the same persons as the first partnership, but in different percentages. First, the court held that § 707(b)(1)(B) applied to the sale even though it was indirect. Second, and more importantly, in applying § 707(b)(1)(B) to deny the first partnership a loss on the foreclosure, the court did not analyze the percentage ownership of each partner in each partnership, even though it appears from the stated facts that the partner in question did not have more than a 50% interest in each partnership. For § 707(b)(1)(B) to apply, however, it is not necessary that the *commonly owned interests* of each partner in each partnership total more than 50%. Thus, § 707(b)(1)(B) applies to deny the loss if the AB partnership in which A holds a 99% interest and B holds a 1% interest sells property at a loss to the BA partnership in which B owns a 99% interest and A holds a 1% interest.

Section 707(b)(3) applies the constructive ownership rules of § 267(c)(1), (2), (4), and (5) to determine who is a partner when applying § 707(b)(1)(A). Thus, a loss on a sale between a partnership and a person who does not actually own any interest in the partnership may be disallowed. For example, if G holds a 51% interest in both profits and capital of the GH partnership and the partnership sells property with a basis of $1,000 to J, who is G's sibling for $500, the loss will be disallowed under § 707(b)(1) because J constructively owns more than a 50% interest in the partnership. However, if G holds only a 50% or less interest in the GH partnership, then § 707(b)(1) does not apply, but the general rule of § 267 still applies to disallow a portion of the loss based on the related partner's percentage interest in the partnership. See Treas.Reg. § 1.267(b)–1(b). For example, if G was a 40% partner, 40% of the loss would be disallowed. When a portion of the loss is disallowed under § 267 on the sale of property by a partnership to a related person, the disallowed loss should be allocated to the partner related to the purchaser. See Casel v. Commissioner, 79 T.C. 424 (1982). In addition, even if § 707(b) does not apply, Treas.Reg. § 1.267(b)–1(b) disallows a portion of the loss realized on the sale of property by one partnership to another partnership to the extent the partnerships have common partners; this loss disallowance rule applies only to the distributive share of the loss allocable to the common partners.

1.2. *Effect of Loss Disallowance on Partners' Bases in Partnership Interests*

If § 707(b)(1) applies to disallow a loss on the sale of partnership property, pursuant to § 705(a)(2) all of the partners nevertheless must reduce the basis of their partnership interests by their distributive shares of the disallowed loss. The basis adjustment applies to all partners, not only the partners directly related to the purchaser. Rev.Rul. 96–10, 1996–1 C.B. 138. Since the partnership's aggregate basis for its assets has been decreased by the amount of the loss, the partners likewise must decrease the basis of their partnership interests by a like amount. This adjustment is necessary in order to prevent the partners from indirectly recognizing the disallowed loss (or reducing gain) upon a subsequent sale of their partnership interests.

Conversely, if § 707(b)(1) applied to disallow a loss on the sale of partnership property by one partnership to a related partnership, and upon the sale of the property by the second partnership § 267(d) applies to limit the amount of gain recognized, the partners of the second partnership nevertheless increase the basis of their partnership interests pursuant to § 705(a)(1) by their distributive shares of the full amount of the gain realized, not only the gain recognized. Rev.Rul. 96–10, supra. Because the nonrecognition accorded by § 267(d) is permanent, this adjustment is necessary to preserve the intended benefit of § 267(d) in cases in which § 707(b)(1) applies.

Suppose, for example, the ABCD partnership, in which A, B, C, and D are equal partners, sold land with a basis of $100 and a fair market value of $60, to the BCDE Partnership, in which B, C, D, and E are equal partners. Subsequently, the BCDE partnership sells the land to an unrelated party for $116. Section 707(b)(1) disallows the $40 loss recognized by the ABCD partnership, but each partner still must reduce the partner's basis in the partnership interest by $10. Upon the sale of the property by the BCDE Partnership, a $56 gain is realized, but pursuant to § 267(d), $40 of that gain is not recognized; only $16 of gain is recognized and each partner reports only a $4 gain. Nevertheless, each partner is entitled to increase the basis of her partnership interest by $14.

2. RECHARACTERIZATION OF CAPITAL GAIN AS ORDINARY INCOME

If gain is recognized on a sale or exchange between a person and a more than 50% controlled partnership, § 707(b)(2) requires that the gain be treated as ordinary gain if the property is *not a capital asset* in the hands of the *transferee*. One object of § 707(b)(2) is § 1231 property. In this respect § 707(b)(2) overlaps § 1239, which requires ordinary gain treatment for property sold between a person and a more than 50% controlled partnership if the property is depreciable in the hands of the purchaser. Both provisions are designed to prevent the transferee from claiming deductible depreciation on a stepped-up basis when the seller is taxed at the preferential capital gains rate. On this rationale, § 707(b)(2) is over-inclusive to the extent that it applies to land, apart from improvements, which will be held for use in the transferee's trade or business.

Section 707(b)(2), but not § 1239, also applies to sales of property that will be inventory in the hands of the purchaser. Thus, for example, if a partnership that holds unimproved real property as a capital asset sells that property to a controlling partner who will hold the land for sale to customers in the ordinary course of business, the gain recognized by the partnership is ordinary, not capital gain.

The same attribution rules that are used to apply § 707(b)(1) are used to apply § 707(b)(2). See Rev.Rul. 67–105, 1967–1 C.B. 167, for the application of the attribution rules. Section 1239 also invokes the attribution rules of § 267(c).

In addition, § 453(g) denies installment sale treatment on any sale between a partner and a partnership in which the partner owns, directly or indirectly, more than 50% of either a capital or a profits interest, unless the transferor establishes that the transaction did not have tax avoidance as one of its principal purposes. Section 453(g) does not apply, however, to sales between related partnerships. There is little administrative or judicial guidance as to what establishes the absence or presence of a tax avoidance purpose in this context. Guenther v. Commissioner, T.C. Memo. 1995–280, suggests that any increase in the amount of depreciation deductions otherwise available as a result of a sale to a related buyer is a factor in determining whether the transfer was motivated by tax avoidance.

3. DISGUISED SALES AND EXCHANGES OF PROPERTY

3.1. *Historical Background*

In Otey v. Commissioner, 70 T.C. 312 (1978), aff'd per curiam, 634 F.2d 1046 (6th Cir.1980), the taxpayer and another individual formed a partnership to construct housing on property owned by the taxpayer. Under the partnership agreement, the taxpayer contributed the property to the partnership with an agreed value of $65,000 and an FHA-insured construction loan was taken out in an amount greater than that needed for the construction. The taxpayer then withdrew $65,000 of the excess mortgage proceeds from the partnership. The Commissioner argued that the taxpayer in effect sold his property to the partnership and recognized gain under § 707(a). The Tax Court, however, held that §§ 721 and 731 controlled with the result that the money distribution merely reduced the taxpayer's basis in his partnership interest: "Were there no partnership at all, a taxpayer could borrow funds on the security of appreciated property and apply them to his personal use without triggering gain. Had the distributed funds come directly from the other partner, [the Commissioner's] case would be stronger. While it may be argued that the funds have come indirectly from [the partner] because his credit facilitated the loan, the fact is that the loan was a partnership loan on which the partnership was primarily liable, and both partners were jointly and separately liable for the full loan if the partnership defaulted. We do not view the factual pattern here as constituting a disguised sale of the land to [the other partner] or the partnership." Similar results were reached in slightly different contexts in Communications Satellite Corp. v. United States, 625 F.2d 997 (Ct.Cl.1980), and Jupiter Corp. v. United States, 2 Cl.Ct. 58 (1983), where the Service unsuccessfully attempted to recharacterize distributions to old partners in connection with contributions by new partners as sales of partnership interests.

3.2. *The Legislative Response*

Congress disagreed with the courts' conclusions that the transactions in *Otey, Communications Satellite Corp.,* and *Jupiter Corp.* did not resemble sales, and in 1984 enacted § 707(a)(2)(A) and (B), which authorize the Treasury to promulgate Regulations treating as a sale subject to § 707(a) any transaction in which there is a direct or indirect distribution of money or property to a partner related to the partner's direct or indirect transfer of money or property to the partnership. The Senate Finance Committee Report indicates that the Regulations should apply this rule only to attempts to disguise sales and not to "nonabusive transactions that reflect the various economic contributions of the partners." S.Rep. No. 98–169, 98th Cong., 2d Sess. 230 (1984). It gives the following example of circumstances in which the rule may be applied:

> For example, when a partner contributes appreciated property to a partnership and receives a distribution of money or property within a reasonable period before or after such contribution, that is approximately equal in value to the portion of contributed property that is in effect given up to the other partner(s) the transaction will be subject to this provision. However, the distribution would not be so subject if there is a corresponding partnership allocation of income or gain, but that arrangement may instead be subject to the new provision [§ 707(a)(2)(A)] relating to partnership payments for property or services * * *. The disguised sale provision also will apply to the extent (1) the transferor partner receives the proceeds of a loan related to the property to the extent responsibility for the repayment of the loan rests, directly or indirectly, with the partnership (or its assets) or the other partners, or (2) the partner has received a loan related to the property in anticipation of the transaction and responsibility for repayment of the loan is transferred, directly or indirectly, to the partnership (or its assets) or the other partners.

> Although the rule applies to sales of property to the partnership, the committee does not intend to prohibit a partner from receiving a partnership interest in return for contributing property which entitles him to priorities or preferences as to distributions, but is not in substance a disguised sale. Similarly, the committee generally does not intend this provision to adversely affect distributions that create deficit capital accounts (maintained in a manner consistent with Treasury regulations under § 704(b)) for which the distributee is liable, regardless of the timing of the distribution, unless such deficit capital account is improperly understated or not expected to be made up until such a distant point in the future that its present value is small. However, if this deficit creating distribution is coupled with an allocation of income or gain, the distribution/allocation arrangement may be subject to

[§ 707(a)(2)(A)] relating to partnership payments for services or property. Similarly, the contribution of encumbered property to a partnership would not suggest a disguised sale to the extent responsibility for the debt is not shifted, directly or indirectly, to the partnership (or its assets) or to the noncontributing partners. The committee anticipates that the Treasury regulations will treat transactions to which the provision applies as a sale of property or partnership interests among the partners or as a partial sale and partial contribution of the property to the partnership, with attendant tax consequences, depending upon the underlying economic substance of the transaction. These regulations may provide for a period, such as three years, during which contributions by and distributions to the same or another partner normally will be presumed related.

Section 707(a)(2)(B) also may recharacterize a contribution by one partner coupled by a distribution to another partner as a transaction between the two partners acting in capacities other than as a partner. This provision may apply if one partner transfers property to the partnership while another transfers cash, followed by the distribution of cash to the partner who contributed property and property to the partner who contributed cash, or in situations such as those presented in *Communications Satellite Corp.* and *Jupiter Corp.*, supra.

To some extent, § 707(a)(2)(B) is redundant. Treas.Reg. § 1.731–1(c)(3) long has provided that a contribution to a partnership followed "within a short period" by a distribution of other property to the contributing partner or a distribution of the contributed property to another partner may be treated as a taxable exchange. This Regulation, which the courts failed to apply, would have been adequate to treat as taxable sales or exchanges the contributions and distributions in *Otey, Communications Satellite Corp.*, and *Jupiter Corp.* Thus, § 707(a)(2)(B) and the detailed Regulations promulgated under its authority have been necessitated by the failure of the courts to look through form to determine the true substance of the transactions in those cases.

3.3. *Section 707(a)(2) Regulations*

3.3.1.   *General*

Treas. Regs. §§ 1.707–3 through –9 implement § 707(a)(2)(B) and so much of § 707(a)(2)(A) as applies to disguised sales. The general theory of these Regulations is that when a partner transfers property to a partnership in a nominal contribution and receives property or money nominally as a distribution, the two transfers should be viewed as related and recharacterized as components of a disguised sale only to the extent that their combined effect allows the transferring partner to withdraw all or a part of the partner's equity in the transferred property. If a partner contributes property to a partnership in exchange for a genuine entrepreneurial interest in partnership capital, any subsequent distributions that liquidate that capital interest will not be treated as related to the contribution. But if the partner's equity in the contributed property is not converted, in substance as well as form, into a genuine interest in partnership capital subject to the entrepreneurial risks of partnership operations, distributions that represent a withdrawal of the partner's equity in the transferred property will be recharacterized as part of a disguised sale of the property under § 707(a)(2). See Notice of Proposed Rulemaking, PS–163–84, 1991–1 C.B. 952.

To implement this approach, Treas.Reg. § 1.707–3(b)(1) provides that the disguised sale rule of § 707(a)(2) applies only if, based on all the facts and circumstances, the transfer of money or other consideration would not have been made but for the transfer of the property and, in cases in which the transfers are not made simultaneously, the subsequent transfer is not dependent on the entrepreneurial risks of partnership operations. Treas.Reg. § 1.707–3(b)(2) sets forth a list of various facts and circumstances to aid in determining whether the transfers are a disguised sale. In addition, Treas.Reg. § 1.707–3(c) provides a rebuttable presumption that transfers within a two year period constitute a disguised sale, unless one of the exceptions under Treas.Reg. § 1.707–4 applicable to guaranteed payments for capital, reasonable preferred returns, or operating cash flow distributions applies. Treas. Regs. §§ 1.707–3(c)(2) and 1.707–8 require disclosure to the IRS of reciprocal transfers by a partner to the partnership and by the partnership to the partner within the presumptive two-year period that the parties do not treat as a sale. Conversely, transfers more than two years apart are presumed not to be components of a disguised sale. Treas.Reg. § 1.707–3(d). For examples of nonsimultaneous transfers, see Treas.Reg. § 1.707–3(f), Ex. (2)–(8).

There are a number of exceptions to the treatment of distributions as a disguised sale, the most important of which is an exception for distributions of operating cash flow. Distributions of money to a partner during a taxable year that do not exceed the partner's interest in net operating cash flow are presumed not to be part of a sale unless the facts and circumstances clearly establish otherwise. Treas.Reg. § 1.707–4(b). A partner's interest in a net operating cash flow distribution generally is the lesser of the partner's percentage interest in overall partnership profits for the year and the partner's percentage interest in overall partnership profits for the life of the partnership. Treas.Reg. § 1.707–4(b)(2).

In addition, Treas.Reg. § 1.707–4(d) treats payments by a partnership to reimburse partners for capital expenditures and costs incurred in anticipation of the formation of a partnership as distributions under § 731, rather than as part of a disguised sale under § 707(a)(2)(B). This exception applies only to expenditures incurred within one year of the transfer of property by the partner to the partnership, and the reimbursed capital expenditures may not exceed 20% of the fair market value of the property. The exception for preformation capital expenditures that do not exceed 20% of fair market value applies property-by-property. Aggregation is permitted, however, to the extent: (i) the total fair market value of the aggregated property (of which no single property's fair market value exceeds 1% of the total fair market value of such aggregated property) is not greater than the lesser of 10% of the total fair market value of all property, excluding money and marketable securities (as defined under § 731(c)), transferred by the partner to the partnership, or $1,000,000; (ii) the partner uses a reasonable aggregation method that is consistently applied; and (iii) the aggregation of property is not part of a plan a principal purpose of which is to avoid Treas.Regs. §§ 1.707–3 through 1.707–5.

Any transfer of property to a partnership that is treated as part of a disguised sale is not reflected in the transferring partner's capital account. If the consideration treated as transferred to a partner pursuant to a sale is less than the fair market value of the property transferred to the partnership, the transfer will be treated as a sale in part and a capital contribution in part, and the transferring partner must prorate the partner's basis in the property between the portion of the property sold and the portion of the property contributed. Suppose, for example, that individuals A, B, and C each contribute $1,000,000 in cash to the ABCD Partnership in exchange for one-quarter partnership interests, while individual D transfers Blackacre to the ABCD Partnership in exchange for a one-quarter interest in the partnership. At the time of the transfer, the fair market value of Blackacre is $4,000,000, and its adjusted basis to D is $1,200,000. Contemporaneously, the ABCD Partnership transfers $3,000,000 in cash to D. Because the cash received by D is less than the fair market value of Blackacre, D is considered to have sold a portion of Blackacre with a value of $3,000,000 to the partnership in exchange for cash; because Blackacre is worth $4,000,000, D is treated as selling an undivided three-quarter interest in Blackacre for $3,000,000. Accordingly, D recognizes $2,100,000 of gain ($3,000,000 amount realized less $900,000 adjusted tax basis ($1,200,000 multiplied by $3,000,000/$4,000,000)). D has contributed to the partnership, in D's capacity as a partner, an undivided one-quarter of the property, with a fair market value of $1,000,000 and an adjusted tax basis of $300,000. See Treas.Reg. § 1.707–3(f), Ex. (1).

If a transfer to a partner that is part of a disguised sale occurs subsequent to the partner's transfer of property to the partnership, the partner will be treated as receiving a partnership obligation as consideration for the property on the date the partnership acquired ownership of the property. If § 453 is otherwise applicable, the partner will be permitted to report gain on the sale under the installment sale rules, but otherwise gain (or loss) will be recognized in the year of the transfer to the partnership. Treas.Reg. § 1.707–3(a)(2).

If the parties structure a disguised sale as a contribution to a partnership, they may not subsequently assert either that the transferor was not a partner or that no partnership existed in order to avoid the application of § 707(a)(2). If no partnership actually exists, the transaction will be considered a sale between the purported partners rather than a sale to a partnership. Treas.Reg. § 1.707–3(a)(3).

In Virginia Historic Tax Credit Fund 2001 LP v. Commissioner, 639 F.3d 129 (4th Cir. 2011), the court applied § 707(a)(2)(B) and Treas.Reg. § 1.707–3 to treat contributions by investors to a partnership formed to transfer State of Virginia historic rehabilitation tax credits to the investing partners as the proceeds of disguised sales by the partnership rather than as contributions to the partnership in exchange for partnership interests subject to § 721. The Virginia Historic Rehabilitation Credit Program allowed a developer partnership to allocate state rehabilitation tax credits to partners in proportion to their ownership interests in the partnership or as the partners mutually agreed. The taxpayer limited partnership, as a state tax credit partner, held a small percentage ownership interest in developer partnerships undertaking Virginia rehabilitation projects, but was allocated most of the rehabilitation tax credits that the developer partnerships otherwise could not use. The taxpayer partnership in turn received capital contributions from 282 investor limited partners. The pooled capital was invested in various developer rehabilitation partnerships. In general, each investor was allocated $1 of Virginia State Rehabilitation credits for each $0.74–$0.80 invested. The investors were "bought out after the partnerships accomplished their purpose." Reversing an opinion of the Tax Court, T.C.Memo 2009–295, the Fourth Circuit described § 707(a)(2) as intended to prevent "the use of the partnership provisions to render nontaxable what would in substance have been a taxable exchange if it had not been 'run through' a partnership." In analyzing whether the Tax Court's findings of fact overcame the two-year presumption of Treas.Reg. § 1.707–3(c), the court applied five of the ten factors of Treas.Reg. § 1.707–3(b)(2) to find sale treatment: (1) the timing and amount of a subsequent transfer were determinable with reasonable certainty at the time of the earlier transfer, (2) the investors had a legally enforceable right to the later transfer of tax credits, (3) the investors' right to receive the promised tax credits was secured by a promise that their contributions would be refunded if the credits were not delivered and a promise not to transfer operating money to developers unless the developers had received certification that the project constituted a qualified rehabilitation and the amount of qualified rehabilitation expenditures, (4) the transfer of money or other consideration was disproportionately large relative to the investors' continuing interest in the partnership, and (5) the investors had no obligation to return to the partnership the money or other property they received. The Fourth Circuit reached the same result in Route 231, LLC v. Commissioner, 810 F.3d 247 (4th Cir. 2016).

3.3.2.   *Assumption of Liabilities as Amount Realized in Disguised Sale*

The legislative history of § 707(a)(2) indicates that a transfer of property by a partner to a partnership should be treated as a disguised sale if the transferor-partner incurs debt in anticipation of the transfer and the partnership assumes or takes the property subject to the debt. See H.R.Rep. No. 98–432, 98th Cong., 2d Sess. 1221 (1984). However, "there will be no disguised sale under [§ 707(a)(2)] to the extent the contributing partner, in substance, retains liability for repayment of the borrowed amounts (i.e., to the extent the other partners have no direct or indirect risk of loss with respect to such amounts) since, in effect, the partner has simply borrowed through the partnership." H.R.Rep. No. 861, 98th Cong., 2d Sess. 862 (1984) (Conf.Rep.). Treas.Reg. § 1.707–5 implements this policy by providing that the assumption of (or taking the property subject to) any liabilities, other than "*qualified liabilities*," by the partnership is treated as a withdrawal of the partner's equity in the transferred property to the extent responsibility for those liabilities is shifted to the other partners. "Qualified liabilities" include all debt incurred more than two years before the transfer, which is never treated as debt incurred in anticipation of the transfer. Treas.Reg. § 1.707–5(a)(6)(i)(A). Purchase money debt, debt to finance improvement of the transferred property, and trade payables related to the transferred property, even if incurred within two years of the transfer, are qualified debt and never are treated as debt incurred in anticipation of the transfer. Treas.Reg. § 1.707–5(a)(6)(i)(C) and (D). For purposes of defining qualified liabilities, the term "capital expenditures" has the same meaning as the term "capital expenditures" generally does, except that it includes capital expenditures taxpayers elect to deduct and does not include deductible expenses taxpayers elect to treat as capital expenditures. Capital expenditures are treated as funded by the proceeds of a qualified liability to the extent the proceeds are either traceable to the capital expenditures under Temp.Reg. § 1.163–8T or are actually used to fund the capital expenditures, irrespective of the tracing requirements under Temp.Reg. § 1.163–8T. Qualified liabilities include those that were not incurred in anticipation of the transfer of the property to a partnership and that were incurred in connection with a trade or business in which property transferred to the partnership was used or held, but only if all the assets related to that trade or business are transferred (other than assets that are not material to a continuation of the trade or business). All other debt incurred within two years of the transfer is presumed to have been incurred in anticipation of the transfer and therefore as consideration for a sale of the property to the extent responsibility for the debt is shifted to other partners. Treas.Reg. § 1.707–5(a)(7). Furthermore, to the extent any qualified liability under Treas.Reg. § 1.707–5(a)(6) is used by a partner to fund capital expenditures and economic responsibility for that borrowing shifts to another partner, the exception for preformation capital expenditures does not apply.

Assumption by the partnership of liabilities that are not "qualified liabilities" is treated as consideration for the transferred property to the extent the amount of the liabilities exceeds the transferring partner's share of the liabilities after the transfer. Treas.Reg. § 1.707–5(a)(1). The assumption of a "qualified liability," however, is treated as part of a sale only to the extent the partner is otherwise treated as having sold a portion of the property. See Treas.Reg. § 1.707–5(a)(5). To the extent the assumption of (or taking subject to) a liability is not treated as part of a sale, the consequences of a shift of the liability are determined under § 752.

For purposes of § 707(a)(2) a partner's share of a recourse liability is the partner's share of the liability under § 752. Treas. Reg. § 1.707–5(a)(2)(i). However, Treas. Reg. § 1.707–5(a)(2)(ii) provides special rules for determining a partner's share of nonrecourse liabilities for purposes of § 707(a)(2). A partner's share of nonrecourse liabilities is determined by multiplying the liability by the partner's percentage interest in partnership profits used generally to determine the partner's share of nonrecourse liability under Treas. Reg. § 1.752–3(a)(3). This formula ignores the allocation of nonrecourse liabilities based on minimum gain and § 704(c) gain. Treas. Reg. § 1.707–5(a)(2)(ii) does not use the rules under Treas. Reg. § 1.752–3 to determine a partner's share of nonrecourse liabilities because to do so would cause the transferring partner's share of a nonrecourse liability to reflect the full amount of built-in gain under § 704(c). If the debt allocation rules of Treas. Reg. § 1.752–3 were used to determine the consideration received by the transferor, the extent to which a disguised sale of the property results from the encumbrance would vary inversely with the gain inherent in the contributed property. The Internal Revenue Service considered such a result to be inappropriate. See Notice of Proposed Rulemaking, PS–163–84, 1991–1 C.B. 951, 955.

Reduction of a partner's share of a liability subsequent to a transfer may be considered to be part of a disguised sale if the reduction was anticipated when the partner transferred the property to the partnership and if the reduction was part of a plan one of the principal purposes of which was minimizing the extent to which the assumption of the liability would be treated as part of a sale. Treas.Reg. § 1.707–5(a)(3). A reduction that is subject to the entrepreneurial risks of partnership operations is not an anticipated reduction.

The application of Treas.Reg. § 1.707–5 to the transfer of property encumbered by a recourse debt is illustrated by the following example, based on Treas.Reg. § 1.707–5(f), Ex. (2). Suppose that individuals C and D form the CD Partnership. C contributes $200,000 for a one-third interest. In exchange for a two-thirds partnership interest, D transfers to the partnership Whiteacre, which has a fair market value of $1,000,000 and is encumbered by a $600,000 mortgage. The partnership assumes the $600,000 liability, which D incurred immediately before transferring Whiteacre to the partnership; D used the proceeds for purposes unrelated to Whiteacre. Under Treas.Reg. § 1.752–3(a)(3), immediately after the partnership's assumption of the liability encumbering Whiteacre, D's share of that liability is $400,000. Because the liability is not a qualified liability, the partnership's assumption of $200,000 of the liability (the excess of the liability assumed by the partnership ($600,000) over D's share of the liability immediately after the assumption ($400,000)) is treated as consideration to D in connection with D's sale of an undivided portion of Whiteacre to the partnership. Since the consideration of $200,000 equals one-fifth of the value of Whiteacre, D is treated as selling an undivided one-fifth of Whiteacre to the CD Partnership and as contributing to the CD Partnership an undivided four-fifths of Whiteacre, having a fair market value of $800,000 and subject to a $400,000 debt. If D's basis for Whiteacre were $250,000, then D's gain recognized on the sale would be $150,000; the $200,000 of debt relief is D's amount realized, and D's basis for the undivided one-fifth is $50,000 (1/5 × $250,000). D contributed the other four-fifths of Whiteacre, having a basis of $200,000.

In Canal Corp. v. Commissioner, 135 T.C. 199 (2010), the court applied the anti-abuse provisions of Treas.Reg. § 1.752–2(j)(1) and (3) in the debt allocation rules to hold that a partner's indemnity agreement in a leveraged partnership acquisition did not create a liability for purposes of avoiding deferred sale treatment under Treas.Reg. § 1.707–5(a). WISCO, a subsidiary in the taxpayer's consolidated corporate group, transferred its operating assets, worth $775 million, to a limited liability company (taxed as a partnership) in exchange for a 5% interest in the LLC, and Georgia Pacific transferred operating assets to the LLC in exchange for the remaining 95% interest in the LLC. Simultaneously, the LLC borrowed $755.2 million from Bank of America and transferred the cash to WISCO, which in turn distributed the money to its parent corporation. After the transaction, WISCO's only assets were a $151 million note from a related corporation and a corporate jet. The Bank of America loan was guaranteed by Georgia Pacific. However, on the advice of the accounting firm that structured the transaction, WISCO provided an indemnity agreement to Georgia Pacific with respect to Georgia Pacific's loan guarantee. Relying on the indemnity agreement, the taxpayer claimed that under Treas.Reg. § 1.752–2 WISCO was liable for the debt to Bank of America and that it thus had retained an obligation to repay the distributed cash under Treas.Reg. § 1.707–5(a).

Treas.Reg. § 1.752–2(j)(1) and (3) provides that a partner's obligation to make a payment may be disregarded if (1) the facts and circumstances indicate that a principal purpose of the arrangement between the parties is to eliminate the partner's risk of loss or to create a facade of the partner's bearing the economic risk of loss with respect to the obligation, or (2) the facts and circumstances of the transaction evidence a plan to circumvent or avoid the obligation. The court held that the transactions had to be viewed together, and they constituted a disguised sale under § 707(a)(2)(B) rather than a tax-free contribution to a partnership under § 721 and a separate distribution under § 731. The indemnity agreement was disregarded by the court based on its conclusion that the indemnity created no more than a remote possibility that WISCO would actually be liable for payment. The court based its conclusion on its findings that the indemnity agreement, which covered principal but not interest, was entered into only to allow tax deferral on the transaction, and that WISCO had insufficient assets to cover the indemnity. The court noted that Georgia Pacific, the guarantor of the debt, did not require the indemnity agreement as part of the transaction. Taken together, these facts resulted in an arrangement that had the appearance of creating an economic risk of loss when the substance of the arrangement actually was otherwise. In addition, the court noted that WISCO's consolidated group treated the transaction as a sale for financial reporting purposes and that it represented to bond rating agencies that the only risk associated with the transaction was the tax risk. Thus, the court held that the distribution of cash to WISCO did not fit within the debt financed transfer provision of Treas.Reg. § 1.707–5(a) and that the taxpayer failed to rebut the two-year presumption of Treas.Reg. § 1.707–3(c). The facts and circumstances indicated a disguised sale.

3.3.3.   Guaranteed Payments and Preferred Returns

A guaranteed payment for capital is not subject to the entrepreneurial risks of partnership operations and, if received with respect to a contribution of property other than cash, would be treated as part of a sale if the payment were tested under the general rules of Treas.Reg. § 1.707–3. Because, however, guaranteed payments for capital are in substance payments for the use of property, Treas.Reg. § 1.707–4(a)(1) provides that "reasonable" guaranteed payments for capital contributions are not treated as amounts paid in exchange for property. The partnership's characterization of a purported guaranteed payment for capital does not determine whether a transfer actually is a guaranteed payment as opposed to a payment to complete a sale. Whether a transfer is part of a sale or a guaranteed payment for capital is determined by examining whether the transfer is designed to liquidate all or part of the partner's interest in property transferred to the partnership or, on the other hand, is designed to provide the partner with a return on an investment in the partnership. Treas.Reg. § 1.707–4(a)(1).

Treas.Reg. § 1.707–4(a)(1)(ii) provides that a payment characterized by the parties as a guaranteed payment will be presumed to be a guaranteed payment for capital if the amount of the guaranteed payment is "reasonable," under standards set forth in Treas.Reg. § 1.707–4(a)(3). A purported guaranteed payment for capital that is not reasonable in amount is presumed not to be a guaranteed payment. Treas.Reg. § 1.707–4(a)(1)(iii). Either presumption can be rebutted by facts and circumstances that clearly establish the contrary. If a purported guaranteed payment for capital is not respected, the payment is treated as any other distribution and, if made within two years of a transfer of property to the partnership, will be presumed to be in exchange for the property. The Regulations do not address the question of whether a guaranteed payment for services is subject to recharacterization as a transfer in consideration of property.

Treas.Reg. § 1.707–4(a) provides that a distribution of money characterized by the parties as a preferred return is presumed not to be part of a sale if the amount is reasonable under Treas.Reg. § 1.707–4(a)(3)(ii) unless the facts and circumstances clearly establish that the transfer is part of a sale.

3.3.4.   *Transactions Involving a Disguised Sale of Property by a Partnership to a Partner*

Treas.Reg. § 1.707–6 provides rules governing disguised sales by a partnership to a partner that are subject to § 707(a)(2)(B). These rules are similar to those provided in Treas. Regs. §§ 1.707–3 and 1.707–5 for disguised sales by a partner to a partnership. For example, if the partnership places a mortgage on property and then distributes the property to a partner in partial or full liquidation of the partnership interest, the transaction will be recharacterized as in part a sale of the property from the partnership to the partner in the partner's individual capacity, and in part a distribution. As a result, the partnership will recognize gain or loss, and the partner's basis in the property will be determined in part under § 1012 (purchase price basis) and in part under § 732. This result follows from the theory of § 707(a)(2)(B) because, under the principles of § 752, the distributee partner's obligation for a share of the debt has been shifted to the other partners.

PROBLEM SET 2

1.   Andy, Bev, Cleo, and Dean are partners in the ABCD Partnership. Andy has a 40% interest in profits and capital; Bev has a 30% interest; Cleo has a

20% interest; and Dean has a 10% interest. Andy sold Blackacre, an office building that had a basis of $120,000, to the partnership for $100,000. Two years later, the partnership sold Blackacre. What are the tax consequences of the two transactions given the following additional facts?

(a) Andy and Dean are siblings; the partners are otherwise unrelated. The partnership sold Blackacre for $80,000 to X Corp., which is equally owned by Andy and Andy's spouse.

(b) Andy and Cleo are siblings; the partners are otherwise unrelated. The partnership sold Blackacre to an unrelated party for $150,000.

(c) Andy and Cleo are siblings; the partners are otherwise unrelated. The partnership sold Blackacre to an unrelated party for $75,000.

(d) The partners of ABCD are unrelated. The ABCD Partnership sold Blackacre for $75,000 to the CA Partnership, in which Cleo's spouse has a 90% interest in profits and capital and Andy's son's wholly owned corporation has a 10% interest.

(e) The partners of ABCD are unrelated. The ABCD Partnership sold Blackacre for $75,000 to Bev's grandchild.

(f) Andy and Cleo are siblings; the partners are otherwise unrelated. The partnership sold Blackacre to Cleo for $150,000.

(2) (a) Ed and Fran are equal partners in the EF LLC, which holds investment assets and cash totaling $4,000,000. Ed's and Fran's bases in their partnership interests are $1,750,000 each. On February 1st, Ed contributed Whiteacre, which had a fair market value of $2,000,000 and an adjusted basis of $600,000, to the LLC, and Ed's capital account was increased by $2,000,000. On July 1st, the EF LLC distributed $1,500,000 in cash to Ed. Ed's capital account was reduced by $1,500,000. How should these transactions be treated for tax purposes?

(b) How should the transactions be treated for tax purposes if the distribution was received by Ed on August 1st three years later and was in the amount of $1,736,438?

3. (a) Gail and Harvey formed the GH Partnership (a general partnership). Gail contributed $400,000 of cash and has a one-third interest in profits and loss. Harvey contributed Greenacre, which had a fair market value of $2,000,000 and was subject to a $1,200,000 mortgage. Harvey's basis in Greenacre was $500,000. Harvey has a two-thirds interest in profits and loss. Harvey incurred the debt secured by the mortgage last year and used the proceeds to purchase publicly traded securities. What are the tax consequences of the transfer of Greenacre to the partnership?

(b) What would be the consequences if Harvey had incurred the loan a year and a half ago to pay for environmental remediation costs (that were deductible under § 162) with respect to Greenacre?

(c) What would be the result if Harvey incurred the loan three years ago to purchase publicly traded securities?

4. Memorial Hospital, a tax-exempt organization, owns a building suitable for use as a medical laboratory. Memorial has formed an LLC with Ben and

Casey, cash method individuals who operate a medical laboratory. Memorial has contributed the building, and Ben and Casey have contributed a going medical laboratory business (previously conducted in leased premises) and cash. Memorial's capital account was credited with $1,000,000, but the fair market value of the building very likely was closer to $2,000,000. The LLC agreement allocates the first $200,000 of annual profits equally between Ben and Casey; all remaining profits are allocated to Memorial until Memorial has been allocated cumulative profits of $1,700,000. At that time, which the parties expect to be in about three years, Memorial will receive a liquidating distribution of the balance in Memorial's capital account, and Memorial's LLC interest will terminate. How should this transaction be treated under §§ 704 and 707?

CHAPTER 23

SPECIAL LIMITATIONS ON LOSS DEDUCTIONS AT THE PARTNER LEVEL

SECTION 1.   TAX SHELTER LOSSES

The combination of the principle of Crane v. Commissioner, 331 U.S. 1 (1947), and its progeny, allowing the taxpayer to include nonrecourse debt in basis, and § 752, which adjusts a partner's basis in a partnership interest to reflect partnership indebtedness, whether recourse or nonrecourse, formed the backbone of the tax shelter phenomenon that reached its zenith in the 1970s and early 1980s. Tax shelter investments provided a significant portion of the investor's return in the form of tax benefits that not only offset any tax liability that might arise from the investment but also "sheltered" other income, usually from the investor's regular business or professional activities. Investors purchased interests in tax shelter investments (usually in the form of an interest in a limited partnership) and received an after-tax return on the purchase price even though the investment was not profitable before taxes.

Virtually all tax shelters had three common elements: deferral, conversion, and leverage. Deferral is obtained by accelerating deductions, that is, claiming deductions in excess of economic costs in the early years of an investment so that income is concentrated in the later years. These accelerated deductions result in taxable income being less than economic income in the years the deductions are claimed. In later years, the investment produces taxable income in excess of economic income. The earlier deductions are offset, but in the interim, the taxpayer has received what was in effect an interest-free loan from the government equal to the amount of the taxes on the deferred income. The value of the deferral increases as the span of time between the year deductions are claimed and the year of disposition of the investment increases.

The second element of many tax shelters was conversion of ordinary income to capital gain. Conversion is achieved when the taxpayer claims a deduction against ordinary income, but the income that later offsets the deduction is taxed at a lower rate, usually due to the capital gains preference. In some cases, conversion is eliminated or limited by "recapture" rules, requiring a portion of the later income realized on a sale of the investment to be recharacterized as ordinary income, but the recapture rules never have been comprehensive.

Leverage, the use of borrowed money to purchase the tax shelter investment, magnifies the effect of the first two elements of the tax-shelter, as well as providing the normal economic benefit of financial leverage. Whenever an investor uses borrowed money to finance an investment that has a yield rate greater than the interest rate on the loan, the investor receives a before-tax rate of return from invested equity greater than what would have been received if the entire investment had been equity financed. In addition, because taxpayers are allowed deductions for costs paid with borrowed funds, the tax shelter benefits of the investment also are increased.[1]

One or more of the basic elements of a tax shelter could be used by tax shelter promoters in a wide variety of activities—real estate, oil and gas, drilling, equipment leasing, master recordings, films and video productions, animal breeding and feeding, mining operations, farm crops, vineyards and many more. Initially, the IRS attacked these tax shelter operations by using generalized statutory or judicially developed approaches. In some cases, the courts applied § 183 (the "hobby loss" rules) to deny deductions, even though that section had been enacted originally to distinguish personal from profit-seeking activities. Compare, e.g., Karr v. Commissioner, 924 F.2d 1018 (11th Cir.1991) and Smith v. Commissioner, 937 F.2d 1089 (6th Cir.1991). In other cases, the courts disallowed deductions associated with tax shelter investments on the basis that the transactions were "shams" or "lacked economic substance." See e.g., Rose v. Commissioner, 868 F.2d 851 (6th Cir.1989). In still other cases, the courts would allow deductions for any actual cash investment but would disallow those related to non-economical debt. See, e.g., Brannen v. Commissioner, 722 F.2d 695 (11th Cir.1984).

While there were a number of weapons at the disposal of the IRS, the result of litigation in any given case was always unpredictable, and taxpayers prevailed in tax shelter litigation in a significant number of cases. As a result, in 1976 and again in 1986, Congress responded with statutory provisions designed to limit tax shelter deductions (which, of course, it had encouraged in the first place by enacting or continuing the preferential tax provisions on which the shelters were built). The initial provision, § 465, was rather limited in scope, and even though its applicability has been expanded a number of times since 1976, it continues to limit only deductions attributable to nonrecourse debt or some other financing arrangement under which the taxpayer-investor is not "at risk." Even then, most commercially financed real estate investment partnerships are beyond its ambit. The second provision, the limitation on "passive activity" loss deductions in § 469, is far more draconian and applies to virtually all limited partners, "silent" general partners, and members of limited liability companies taxed as partnerships who do not actively participate in the activities of the limited liability company.

---

[1] For more detailed discussion, see Borden, Wells, Simmons, McMahon, Federal Income Taxation, 8th ed., ch. 34 § 1 (Foundation Press 2020).

Both § 465 and § 469 are applied at the partner level, after the partners' distributive shares have been determined and the § 704(d) limitation of partnership losses to the individual partner's basis for the partnership interest has been applied. Nevertheless, the terms of the partnership agreement and related collateral agreements often are crucial in determining whether one or both of § 465 and § 469 apply to a particular partner. Congress added § 461(*l*), applicable to tax years beginning after 2020, to further delay the ability to use "excess business loss deductions."

SECTION 2.   THE AT-RISK RULES OF SECTION 465

INTERNAL REVENUE CODE: Sections 465(a)(1) and (2), (b), (d), (e).

PROPOSED REGULATIONS: Sections 1.465–6(b), –22(a), –24(a)(2).

Senate Finance Committee Report, Tax Reform Act of 1976

S.Rep. No. 94–938, 94th Cong., 2D. Sess. 47–51 (1976).

To prevent a situation where the taxpayer may deduct a loss in excess of his economic investment in certain types of activities, [§ 465(a)] provides that the amount of any loss (otherwise allowable for the year under present law) which may be deducted in connection with one of these activities, cannot exceed the aggregate amount with respect to which the taxpayer is at risk in each such activity at the close of the taxable year. * * *

The at risk limitation is to apply on the basis of the facts existing at the end of each taxable year.

In applying the at risk limitation, the amount of any loss which is allowable in a particular year reduces the taxpayer's at risk investment (but not below zero) as of the end of that year and in all succeeding taxable years with respect to that activity. Thus, if a taxpayer has a loss in excess of his at risk amount, the loss disallowed will not be allowed in a subsequent year unless the taxpayer increases his at risk amount.

Losses which are suspended under this provision with respect to a taxpayer because they are greater than the taxpayer's investment which is "at risk" are to be treated as a deduction with respect to the activity in the following year. Consequently, if a taxpayer's amount at risk increases in later years, he will be able to obtain the benefit of previously suspended losses to the extent that such increases in his amount at risk exceed his losses in later years.

The at risk limitation also applies regardless of the method of accounting used by the taxpayer and regardless of the kind of deductible expenses which contributed to the loss.

The at risk limitation is only intended to limit the extent to which certain losses in connection with the covered activities may be deducted in the year claimed by the taxpayer. The rules of this provision do not apply for other purposes, such as the determination of basis. * * *

For purposes of this provision, a taxpayer is generally to be considered "at risk" with respect to an activity to the extent of his cash and the adjusted basis of other property contributed to the activity, as well as any amounts borrowed for use in the activity with respect to which the taxpayer has personal liability for payment from his personal assets. (Also, * * * a taxpayer is at risk to the extent of his net fair market value of personal assets which secure nonrecourse borrowings.)

A taxpayer is not to be considered at risk with respect to the proceeds from his share of any nonrecourse loan used to finance the activity or the acquisition of property used in the activity. In addition, if the taxpayer borrows money to contribute to the activity and the lender's recourse is either the taxpayer's interest in the activity or property used in the activity, the amount of the proceeds of the borrowing are to be considered amounts financed on a nonrecourse basis and do not increase the taxpayer's amount at risk.

Also, under these rules, a taxpayer's capital is not "at risk" in the business, even as to the equity capital which he has contributed to the extent he is protected against economic loss of all or part of such capital by reason of an agreement or arrangement for compensation or reimbursement to him of any loss which he may suffer. Under this concept, an investor is not "at risk" if he arranges to receive * * * compensation for an economic loss after the loss is sustained, or if he is entitled to reimbursement for part or all of any loss by reason of a binding agreement between himself and another person.

* * *

A taxpayer's at risk amount is generally to include amounts borrowed for use in the activity which is secured by property other than property used in the activity. For example, if the taxpayer uses personally-owned real estate to secure nonrecourse indebtedness, the proceeds from which are used in an equipment leasing activity, the proceeds may be considered part of the taxpayer's at risk amount. In such a case, the portion of the proceeds which increases the taxpayer's at risk amount is to be limited by the fair market value of the property used as collateral (determined as of the date the property is pledged as security), less any prior (or superior) claims to which the collateral is subject.

* * *

The rules treating a taxpayer as being "at risk" with respect to the net value of pledged property also do not apply to nonrecourse loans if the lender has an interest, other than as a creditor, in the activity or if the lender is related to the taxpayer (within the meaning of section 267(b)). * * *

Pritchett v. Commissioner

United States Court of Appeals, Ninth Circuit, 1987.
827 F.2d 644.

■ SKOPIL, CIRCUIT JUDGE:

We must decide in this case whether taxpayers, limited partners in five similar partnerships engaged in oil and gas drilling operations, were "at risk" pursuant to 26 U.S.C. § 465 on certain recourse notes and thus entitled to deduct distributive shares of non-cash partnership losses. The Tax Court in a reviewed, split decision held that each taxpayer was at risk only to the extent of actual cash contribution. Pritchett v. Commissioner, 85 T.C. 580 (1985). We reject the Tax Court's rationale in holding that taxpayers were not at risk on the recourse debt. We remand to allow the Tax Court to consider the Commissioner's alternative theory that taxpayers were not at risk because the creditor had an impermissible role in the activity at issue. See 26 U.S.C. § 465(b)(3).

FACTS AND PROCEEDINGS BELOW

Taxpayers are each members in similar limited partnerships formed to conduct oil and gas operations. All five partnerships entered into agreements with Fairfield Drilling Corporation ("Fairfield") whereby Fairfield agreed to drill, develop, and exploit any productive wells. Fairfield provided all necessary equipment and expertise. Pursuant to a "turnkey" agreement, each partnership paid cash and executed a recourse note to Fairfield. Each note was non-interest-bearing and matured in fifteen years. Each was secured by virtually all of the maker-partnership's assets. The principal for each note was to be paid from net income available to each partnership if the drilling operations proved successful. Only the general partners were personally liable under the notes. Nevertheless, each partnership agreement provided that if the notes were not paid off at maturity, the limited partners would be personally obligated to make additional capital contributions to cover the deficiency when called upon to do so by the general partners.

Each partnership elected to use accrual accounting and to deduct intangible drilling costs as an expense. The partnership agreements provided that all losses were to be allocated among limited partners in proportion to their respective capital contributions. Because there was no income in the tax year in question, each limited partner deducted from taxable income a distributive share of partnership loss. The Commissioner disallowed that portion of the deduction based on the note.

The Tax Court affirmed by a 9–7 vote the Commissioner's action. The majority held that under the partnership agreements the limited partners had no personal liability on the notes for the tax year in question and therefore they were at risk under section 465 only for the actual cash contribution made to the partnerships. Pritchett, 85 T.C. at 590. Any potential liability was "merely a contingency" since in the first year of the partnership it was not known whether income would be sufficient to pay off the note or even whether the general partners would in fact exercise their discretion to make a cash call on an unpaid balance fifteen years later. Id. at 588.

Seven judges dissented in three separate opinions. One judge reasoned that for federal tax purposes, "both general and limited partners are personally liable for a pro rata portion of the partnership's recourse obligation to Fairfield." Id. at 594 (Whitaker, J., dissenting). Another found nothing in the agreements to indicate the general partners had unilateral discretion to waive the cash call. Id. at 599 (Cohen, J., dissenting). A majority of the dissenting judges apparently believed, however, that the Commissioner's actions might be affirmed on the alternative ground that section 465(b)(3)(A) provides that amounts borrowed are not at risk if the money is borrowed from someone with an interest in the activity at issue. E.g., id. at 593 (Whitaker, J., dissenting) ("majority may have inadvertently reached the right result, although for the wrong reasons"). The majority notes this alternative ground but expressly does not adopt it. Id. at 590.

These timely appeals followed.

DISCUSSION

In 1976 Congress added section 465 to the Internal Revenue Code to combat abuse of tax shelters caused by nonrecourse financing. * * * Section 465 forbids a taxpayer from taking a loss in excess of amounts at risk in the investment.

The limited partners argue that the notes create at risk debt because each limited partner is personally liable. The contract provisions provide that if the notes are not paid off by the successful drilling operations, "the General Partners will by written notice call for additional capital contributions in an amount sufficient to pay the outstanding balance" and that "[e]ach Limited Partner shall be obligated to pay in cash to the Partnership" the amount called. (Emphasis added). It is clear, however, as the majority opinion notes, that the limited partners are not directly and personally liable to Fairfield. *Pritchett*, 85 T.C. at 587–88. Even assuming a third party beneficiary right, Fairfield had no recourse against the limited partners until the end of the note's fifteen year term.

Whether the Tax Court's decision is correct hinges on its characterization of taxpayers' obligation as indirect and secondary. In a decision rendered shortly after *Pritchett*, the Tax Court sought to distinguish between direct and indirect liability. Abramson v. Commissioner, 86 T.C. 360, 375–76 (1986). In that reviewed decision, the Tax Court, by a 15–1 vote, held that limited partners' pro rata shares of partnership debt that was to be repaid in whole or in part out of partnership revenues was at risk. Id. The limited partners had a direct contractual liability to a third party seller of goods. *Abramson* distinguished *Pritchett* by noting:

In Pritchett the limited partners were not directly liable to the lender on the partnership obligation. Rather, the general partner was personally liable to the lender on the recourse obligation, and the limited partners were, if anything, potential indemnitors of the general partner. The limited partners were not obligated on any debt for purposes of section 465 until the general partner called for contributions to the partnership. Consequently, in *Pritchett*, the limited partners had not borrowed any amount within the meaning of section 465(b)(2). In this case, to the contrary, each partner is personally and directly liable for a pro rata part of the amount owed to the seller * * *. Because each partner's liability for the partnership debt (in the words of the statute, for the "amounts borrowed") ran directly to the seller and each partner's liability was personal, each partner is at risk for his proportionate share of amount owed to the seller.

Id. at 376.

We agree that Congress intended to condition section 465's exclusion of deductions in part on whether the liability for borrowing is primary or secondary. The statute expressly requires that the taxpayer be "personally liable for the repayment." 26 U.S.C. § 465(b)(2)(A). In debate on the Deficit Reduction Act of 1984, a House Report explained that section 465 limits an at-risk loss to, *inter alia*, "amounts borrowed for use in the activity with respect to which the taxpayer has *personal* liability." H.R.Rep. No. 98–432, Part II, 98th Cong., 2d Sess. 1506 * * * (emphasis added). If the limited partnership agreements here create only contingent liability, we will affirm the Tax Court's decision to disallow taxpayers' deductions.

We conclude, however, that the liability of the limited partners was unavoidable and hence not contingent. In Melvin v. Commissioner, 88 T.C. 63 (1987), the Tax Court appeared to answer the question posed here by concluding that

the fact that the partnership or other partners remain in the "chain of liability" should not detract from the at-risk amount of the parties who do have the ultimate liability. The critical inquiry should be who is the obligor of last resort, and in determining who has the ultimate economic responsibility for the loan, the substance of the transaction controls.

Melvin, 88 T.C. at 75 (citing Raphan v. United States, 759 F.2d 879, 885 (Fed.Cir.1985)). Applying that standard we have no reservation in concluding that taxpayers, by virtue of their contractual obligations, have ultimate responsibility for the debt. See Bennion v. Commissioner, 88 T.C. 684, 695 (1987) (applying the *Melvin* standard to taxpayer's "Guarantee Agreement" to determine that taxpayer was ultimately liable on a debt obligation even though the obligation flowed through others). Furthermore, we are not dissuaded by the Tax Court's reasoning that the debt is contingent because the general partners may elect to not make the cash calls. The contracts made the call mandatory and "economic reality" dictates that the partners would do so. See Durkin v. Commissioner, 87 T.C. 1329, 1379 (1986) (concluding that economic reality assured that promissory notes of limited partners to the partnership would be enforced).

The Tax Court also reasoned that the debt was contingent since it was not known in the tax year in question whether sufficient partnership revenues would satisfy the notes prior to or on maturity. We find the Tax Court's reasoning on this point faulty. If the notes required balloon payments upon maturity, the limited partners' obligation to contribute additional funds would be "certain." The acceleration of payments should not be a factor in the taxation analysis. In *Abramson*, like this case, early payment was tied to the success of the operation. No mention was made in *Abramson* that the debt was contingent. Furthermore, the fact that the obligation may not become due for several years in the future is of no significance to the allocation of a pro rata share of the taxpayers' debt in the tax year in question. See Taube v. Commissioner, 88 T.C. 464, 487 (1987) (debt due years in future is nevertheless genuine indebtedness fully includable in basis) * * *.

The Commissioner argued below and on appeal that taxpayers' deductions are alternatively barred by section 465(b)(3). That subsection provides that "amounts borrowed shall not be considered to be at risk with respect to an activity if such amounts are borrowed from any person who * * * has an interest (other than an interest as a creditor) in such activity." 26 U.S.C. § 465(b)(3)(A). The legislative history suggests that *"any type of financial interest* in the activity (other than as a creditor) would constitute a prohibited 'other interest' under section 465." *Bennion*, 88 T.C. at 696 (citing to Staff of Joint Committee on Taxation, General Explanation of Tax Reform Act of 1976 at 39, 1976–3 C.B. (Vol. 2) 51) (emphasis in original). Furthermore, proposed Treasury regulations provide that a lender will be deemed to have a prohibited interest if it has either a capital interest or an interest in the net profits of the activity. See id. (citing Sec. 1.465–8(b), Proposed Income Tax Regs., 44 Fed.Reg. 32239 (June 5, 1979)).

The agreements here provided that Fairfield would receive twenty percent of the gross sales of oil and gas, payable if the partnerships achieved certain profit levels. Judge Simpson concluded that these arrangements gave Fairfield a "substantial interest" in the partnership. *Pritchett*, 85 T.C. at 592 (Simpson, J., concurring). Judge Cohen stated that she shared Judge Simpson's impression that Fairfield appears to be a person having an interest in the activity, but that "[t]his should be explored further by the finder of facts." Id. at 599 (Cohen J., dissenting). We agree with Judge Cohen's suggestion that this possibility should be explored further. Although we may affirm a correct decision on any basis supported by the record, remand is appropriate when a lower court's "application of an incorrect legal standard leaves * * * an inadequate factual record on which to affirm." United States v. Washington, 641 F.2d 1368, 1371 (9th Cir.1981), cert. denied, 454 U.S. 1143 (1982).[*]

* * *

DETAILED ANALYSIS

1.   COVERED ACTIVITIES

Section 465 applies to any activity conducted as a business or for profit by individuals (including trusts and estates), whether as a proprietor, a partner, or as a shareholder in an S corporation. I.R.C. § 465(c). See Peters v. Commissioner, 77 T.C. 1158 (1981). However, because many real estate activities are financed through nonrecourse borrowing that meets the definition of "qualified nonrecourse financing" in § 465(b)(6), discussed below, most real estate investments are effectively excepted.[2]

Identifying the scope of each activity conducted by the taxpayer is an important issue in applying the at-risk rules. Section 465(c)(2) specifically provides that certain activities will be treated as separate, but most business activities are subject to the vague aggregation rules of § 465(c)(3)(B). Suppose that a limited partnership operates a hotel and a shopping center located on the same tract of land. Is it engaged in one activity or two activities? No Regulations governing this issue have been promulgated. Compare Temp.Reg. § 1.465–1T (permitting partnerships and S corporations to aggregate, by type, activities described in § 465(c)(2)(A)(i), and (iii)–(v) during 1984); Ann. 87–26, 1987–15 I.R.B. 39 (extending application of Temp.Reg. § 1.465–1T to certain later taxable years).

2.   AT-RISK AMOUNT

2.1. *General*

2.1.1.   *Contributions and Recourse Borrowing*

Section 465(b) prescribes the rules for determining the amount that a taxpayer has at risk. The taxpayer is at risk for the amount of any money contributed to the activity (e.g., the partnership) and for the basis of any contributed property. Generally, amounts borrowed with respect to the property are at risk to the extent that the taxpayer is personally liable for payment of the debt or has pledged property, other than property used in the activity, to secure the debt. Amounts borrowed from any person with an interest in the activity are not at risk. I.R.C. § 465(b)(3). Thus, if Partner A borrows $50,000 from Partner B, with full recourse, to invest in the ABC Partnership, A is not at risk for the $50,000. Presumably, this result rests on the view that B is the one at risk. But if A has adequate resources to stand behind the liability, as long as the debtor-creditor relationship is not a sham, it is difficult to see how the situation presents the problem to which § 465 is

---

*   On remand, in Pritchett v. Commissioner, T.C. Memo. 1989–21, aff'd by order, 944 F.2d 908 (9th Cir.1991), the Tax Court held that a mineral royalty interest is not a prohibited interest, but that a mineral net profits interest is a prohibited interest.

2   Prior to 1987, § 465 did not apply to the activity of holding real estate, but this exception was repealed in the Tax Reform Act of 1986.

addressed. On the other hand, the bright line rule in § 465(b)(3) eliminates the need to make this inquiry in every case of inter-investor borrowing.

The statutory exclusion of amounts borrowed from lenders with an interest in the activity or from related parties from a taxpayer's "at-risk" amount automatically applies only to activities listed in § 465(c)(1). All other activities, which are subject to § 465 by virtue of § 465(c)(3), are subject to § 465(b)(3) only as provided in Regulations. I.R.C. § 465(c)(3)(D). Treas.Regs. §§ 1.465–8 and 1.465–20 extend to all activities the rule that amounts borrowed from another party with an interest in the activity (other than a creditor) are not at risk, even if the borrowing is with full recourse. This rule does not apply, however, to amounts that are qualified nonrecourse borrowing under § 465(b)(6), or that would have been qualified nonrecourse borrowing if the debt had been nonrecourse.

Suppose that A, B, and C each contribute $10,000 to the ABC Partnership. Thereafter, A loans the partnership $180,000, with full recourse, and the partnership purchases depreciable real property for $210,000. Under § 707(a)(1), discussed in Chapter 22, A's loan generally is treated as if it were made by a person other than a partner. In addition, Treas.Reg. § 1.752–2, discussed in Chapter 21, treats the liability as a recourse liability of the partnership allocable among the partners according to their economic risk of loss. Under those Regulations, A, B, and C each would be entitled to increase their bases in their partnership interests by $60,000 from $10,000 to $70,000 on account of the borrowing. Prop.Reg. § 1.465–7(a) (1979) provides that when a partner lends money to a partnership, the lending partner's at-risk amount is increased only by the lending partner's share of the resulting partnership liability under the § 752 Regulations. Thus, A is at risk for $70,000, the sum of A's contribution of $10,000 plus A's $60,000 share of the debt. B and C, however, each are at risk only with respect to their $10,000 contribution, even though they each have a basis of $70,000 in their partnership interests. Their at-risk amounts will increase as the loan is repaid out of partnership earnings.

Application of § 465(b)(3) in complex arrangements raises numerous interpretative issues regarding exactly what is a prohibited interest and the identity of the true lender. Waddell v. Commissioner, 86 T.C. 848 (1986), held that a creditor had a prohibited interest because payments on the note were contingent on profits. In contrast, Bennion v. Commissioner, 88 T.C. 684 (1987), held that § 465(b)(3) did not apply where a partner was liable to all creditors in a chain and the ultimate lender, who had no interest in the activity, could proceed directly against the taxpayer upon default, even though intermediate creditors had an interest in the activity. In many cases, the question is whether a lender who also has another contractual relationship with the partnership has a prohibited interest through the other contract. See also Brady v. Commissioner, T.C. Memo. 1990–626, holding that a right to rental payments computed with respect to gross receipts was not a prohibited interest.

2.1.2.   *Adjustments for Partnership Income and Distributions*

A partner's at-risk amount is increased by the partner's distributive share of partnership income items and is decreased by distributions to the partner and the partner's distributive share of partnership deductions. See Prop.Reg. § 1.465–22 (1979); Lansburgh v. Commissioner, 92 T.C. 448 (1989). When a partnership earns net income that is applied to make principal payments on a nonrecourse loan, a partner's at-risk amount increases by the partner's share of the income. Thus, depreciation deductions grounded on nonrecourse debt may be claimed to the extent of loan principal amortization. Generally, there will be no net increase in the partner's at-risk amount unless loan principal amortization payments exceed depreciation deductions for the year. To the extent that loan principal payments are out of partnership capital, however, a partner's at-risk amount is unaffected. See generally Prop.Reg. § 1.465–25 (1979); Cooper v. Commissioner, 88 T.C. 84 (1987).

2.2.   *Qualified Nonrecourse Financing*

A partner is not at risk with respect to nonrecourse partnership indebtedness, unless the debt is "qualified nonrecourse financing" as defined in § 465(b)(6). This term generally includes only nonrecourse borrowing related to the holding of real property from an unrelated party (other than the seller of the mortgaged property or the promoter of the partnership) who is regularly engaged in the lending business. Treas.Reg. § 1.465–27(b). Borrowing from related parties regularly engaged in the lending business qualifies only if the terms are commercially reasonable and on substantially the same terms as loans from unrelated persons. In addition, borrowing guaranteed by the federal, state, or local government qualifies. Section 465(b)(6) emphasizes the point that the primary abuse at which § 465 is directed is overvaluation in seller-financed transactions in which the seller is reporting gain under § 453. In the case of third-party lending in real estate transactions, the potential for abuse through artificially inflating basis is not present. Nevertheless, § 465 does apply to third-party nonrecourse financing of activities other than real estate, although third-party nonrecourse financing of such activities never was as common as it was with respect to real estate.

2.3.   *Partner's Guarantee of Partnership Debt*

Generally, a partner's guarantee of a nonrecourse loan made to the partnership avoids the application of § 465. In addition, the entire loan is allocated to the guarantor partner to determine the guarantor partner's basis in the partnership interest under Treas.Reg. § 1.752–2(f), Ex. (5). As illustrated in *Pritchett*, guarantees by limited partners of a portion of a loan to a partnership is a method of limiting each limited partner's liability to the partnership's creditors to the partner's pro rata share of the specific debt while rendering the partner at risk as to that amount.

Partners' guarantees do not always work to avoid § 465, however. In Peters v. Commissioner, 89 T.C. 423 (1987), the taxpayer, along with other limited partners, guaranteed a portion of the partnership's nonrecourse indebtedness. Each partner's guarantee extended only to an amount equal to the aggregate deductions that the partner expected to claim. Relying on Brand v. Commissioner, 81 T.C. 821 (1983), the court concluded that Congress did not intend that a guarantor entitled to reimbursement from the primary obligor would be personally liable under § 465(b)(2)(A). Accordingly, because under the applicable state law the guarantor partners were entitled to reimbursement from the partnership if they made good the partnership debt, they were not at risk under § 465(b)(4).[3] The court distinguished its earlier opinion in *Abramson*, discussed in *Pritchett*, on the ground that under the agreements in *Abramson* "the limited partners were primarily and ultimately liable because neither the partnership nor its general assets (other than the motion picture film in question) was subject to the nonrecourse obligation. Thus, there was no primary obligor against whom the taxpayers would have had a right of subrogation." In contrast, in *Peters* the court concluded that the partnership was the only primary obligor, as evidenced by the manner in which the amounts of the guarantees were computed; the guarantees "having in effect been voluntarily given, were at most lagniappe as far as [the lender] was concerned."

The difference between *Peters* and *Pritchett* might merely be form. Suppose that the partners were called upon to make good on their guarantees. The *Peters* court acknowledged that in such an event it would be unlikely that the partnership would have any assets with which to reimburse the guarantor-partners. Nevertheless, it concluded that since the taxpayers chose the use of guarantees "as their means of making an end run around the rules of § 465," they could not selectively ignore their legal rights as guarantors. The opinion in *Peters* indicates that the court was influenced by the blatancy of the method of computing the guaranteed amounts.

In part, the court in *Pritchett* based its holding on the Tax Court's decision in Melvin v. Commissioner, 88 T.C. 63 (1987), aff'd., 894 F.2d 1072 (9th Cir.1990). In *Melvin*, a limited partner contributed his own $70,000 recourse promissory note to a limited partnership to reflect his obligation to make future capital contributions. The partnership borrowed over $3,000,000 from an unrelated lender on a nonrecourse basis, pledging partnership property, including the taxpayer's promissory note, to secure the loan. The taxpayer stipulated that the mere contribution of the note did not increase the taxpayer's at-risk amount under § 465(b)(1), and the Tax Court approved the stipulation, noting that the contributed promissory note reflected neither a cash contribution nor a borrowing under § 465(b)(1). Nonetheless, the Tax Court held that the taxpayer was at risk with respect to the $70,000 promissory note even though primary responsibility for repayment of the nonrecourse note fell to the partnership: "The relevant question is who, if anyone, will ultimately be obligated to pay the partnership's recourse obligations if the partnership is unable to do so. It is not relevant that the partnership may be able to do so. The scenario that controls is the worst-case scenario, not the best case. Furthermore, the fact

---

[3]   Likewise, if a partner who guarantees a partnership debt is entitled to indemnification or contribution from the partnership or another partner, the guaranteeing partner does not bear the risk of loss with respect to the portion of that debt and concomitantly receives no basis increase. See Treas.Reg. § 1.752–2(f), Ex. (3).

that the partnership or other partners remain in the 'chain of liability' should not detract from the at-risk amount of the parties who do have the ultimate liability. The critical inquiry should be who is the obligor of last resort, and in determining who has the ultimate economic responsibility for the loan, the substance of the transaction controls." 88 T.C. at 75. The court also held, however, that under substantive partnership law, each partner had a right to reimbursement from the other partners for any portion of the partnership debt satisfied from the partner's recourse promissory note in excess of the partner's individual share of partnership liabilities. This right of reimbursement protected the taxpayer from any loss in excess of the taxpayer's pro rata share of partnership debt, and thus constituted a stop loss arrangement under § 465(b)(4). As a consequence, the taxpayer was at risk only to the extent of his $21,000 share of the total partnership debt.

Despite the taxpayer's stipulation in *Melvin*, given the holding in *Pritchett*, it is not clear why the contribution of a partner's promissory note should not increase the partner's at-risk amount. Even if the contributed promissory note is not pledged, the contributing partner does not appear be in a significantly different economic position from the taxpayer in *Pritchett*, who was obligated under the partnership agreement to make additional contributions to pay partnership debts. Perhaps the crucial distinction is one of form in that the contributed promissory note is "property," but its basis to the contributing partner is zero. Hence, the limitation of a partner's at-risk amount to the basis of contributed property in § 465(b)(1)(A) applies. In any event, whether the partner guarantees a partnership nonrecourse debt or contributes a promissory note, the partner's at-risk amount might not be increased if there is no realistic possibility that the partner may be called upon to make a payment on the guarantee or promissory note. See Callahan v. Commissioner, 98 T.C. 276 (1992), in which a limited partner who had the right under the partnership agreement to decline to comply with a cash call by the general partner was held to be at risk only for his capital contributions.

2.4. *Loss Limiting Arrangements*

In American Principals Leasing Corp. v. United States, 904 F.2d 477 (9th Cir.1990), the Ninth Circuit took the application of § 465(b)(4) a step further than *Peters* and *Melvin*, and rejected the "worst case scenario approach" in favor of a test based on whether the taxpayer had a realistic possibility of being called upon to satisfy the indebtedness. The taxpayers in *American Principals Leasing Corp.* were limited partners in June Properties, a partnership engaged in computer equipment leasing. June Properties acquired an interest in computer equipment in a series of sale and leaseback transactions. Southwestern Bell Telephone Company originally acquired the equipment from IBM for approximately $2.6 million. Southwestern sold the equipment to an entity called Finalco for an amount equal to Southwestern's purchase price. Finalco borrowed the purchase price from a third-party lender. Finalco leased the equipment back to Southwestern for a lease payment that was equivalent to Finalco's debt obligations. The indebtedness was secured by Finalco's lease to Southwestern. Finalco sold the equipment, subject to the lease and security agreement, to Softpro for $4.8 million consisting of $20,000 of cash and two recourse notes for the difference. Softpro sold the equipment to June Properties for $4.8 million consisting of $20,000 cash and recourse notes back to Softpro. June Properties leased the equipment to Finalco for rental payments equal to its payment obligation to Softpro. Thus, Finalco's lease payments to June Properties, June Properties' debt obligations on the Softpro note, and Softpro's debt payments to Finalco were identical. In addition, no party had sufficient resources to make its payments without receiving the payments due it. The parties satisfied the three equal obligations each month by offsetting bookkeeping entries. No cash ever changed hands. The taxpayers were personally liable for $120,000 of June Properties recourse debt and claimed that this amount was at risk. Although the taxpayers were ultimately liable for their share of the partnership's recourse obligation, the court held that they were not at risk under section 465(b)(4):

> We believe that although the * * * analysis of whether a taxpayer would legally be responsible for his debt in a worst-case scenario is proper to determine whether under subsection 465(b)(2) a taxpayer is personally liable for amounts he has borrowed for use in an activity, Pritchett v. Commissioner, 827 F.2d 644, 647 (9th Cir.1987) (quoting Melvin v. Commissioner, 88 T.C. 63, 75 (1987), affirmed, 894 F.2d 1072 (9th Cir.1990)), such analysis is improper to determine whether the taxpayer has engaged in a loss-limiting arrangement prohibited by subsection 465(b)(4). * * * [S]ubsection 465(b)(4)'s use of the term 'arrangement'—rather than 'agreement'—indicates that a binding contract is not necessary for this subsection to be applicable. See Melvin at 1075–76, (holding that subsection 465(b)(4) countenances loss protection resulting from California's tort right of contribution among partners); id. at 1074–75 (noting that S.Rep. No. 938's list of examples of 465(b)(4) arrangements, which includes only binding contractual agreements, 'does not constitute an exhaustive list of such arrangements' "); Capek, 86 T.C. at 50–53.

> Rather, the purpose of subsection 465(b)(4) is to suspend at risk treatment where a transaction is structured—by whatever method—to remove any realistic possibility that the taxpayer will suffer an economic loss if the transaction turns out to be unprofitable. See Melvin, at 1074. A theoretical possibility that the taxpayer will suffer economic loss is insufficient to avoid the applicability of this subsection. We must be guided by economic reality. See id. at 1075; Pritchett, 827 F.2d at 647. If at some future date the unexpected occurs and the taxpayer does suffer a loss, or a realistic possibility develops that the taxpayer will suffer a loss, the taxpayer will at that time become at risk and be able to take the deductions for previous years that were suspended under this subsection. I.R.C. § 465(a)(2).

Young v. Commissioner, 926 F.2d 1083 (11th Cir.1991), reached a similar result. Investors in a sale and leaseback transaction with a circular flow of funds effected through bookkeeping entries gave an intermediary a partially recourse note. The investor-partners were not personally liable because the intermediary had purchased the leased equipment on a wholly nonrecourse basis, and "the stated recourse liabilities of the taxpayers were not realistically subject to collection after a discharge of the nonrecourse note." Likewise, in Levien v. Commissioner, 103 T.C. 120 (1994), the Tax Court declined to apply the "worst case scenario" test.

However, in Emershaw v. Commissioner, 949 F.2d 841 (6th Cir.1991), the court reached a contrary result on facts similar to those in *American Principals Leasing Corp.* and *Young.* The court in *Emershaw* held that a circular sale and leaseback was not in itself a loss limiting arrangement, because "[a] loss limiting arrangement within the meaning of § 465(b)(4) is *a collateral agreement* protecting a taxpayer from loss *after the losses have occurred,* either by excusing him from his obligation to make good on losses or by compensating him for losses he has sustained" (emphasis in original). In Martuccio v. Commissioner, 30 F.3d 743 (6th Cir.1994), the Sixth Circuit expressly rejected American Principals Leasing Corp. and Young and continued to adhere to a "worst case scenario" test.

3.   EFFECT OF AT-RISK LIMITATION

3.1. *Deferral of Deductions*

In general, the effect of § 465 is to defer deductions attributable to nonrecourse debt until the debt is repaid. In computing allowable deductions for the year, however, the taxpayer is permitted to treat deductions as being wholly attributable to the taxpayer's at-risk amount—the equity investment or share of recourse debt—until the at-risk amount has been exhausted. Thereafter, deductions in excess of current increases in the partner's at-risk amount are suspended until the taxpayer increases the at-risk amount. A partner's at-risk amount can be increased by an additional contribution. Most often, however, partners' at-risk-amounts are increased when mortgage principal amortization payments in a particular year exceed the depreciation deductions on the property for that year. Upon the sale or other taxable disposition of the activity, deductions that have been deferred under § 465 will be allowable to the extent the sales proceeds are used to repay the debt, thereby increasing the taxpayer's at-risk amount. Likewise, if the property is transferred subject to the nonrecourse debt, the partner's at-risk amount is increased by the partner's distributive share of the gain from the property, thereby allowing suspended deductions to offset some or all of the gain.

Section 465 operates independently of the rules governing a partner's basis in the partnership interest. Even though a partner has sufficient basis to avoid the application of § 704(d), discussed in Chapter 18, deduction of the partner's distributive share of partnership losses will be postponed if the partner's at-risk amount is insufficient. Nevertheless, the partner's basis in the partnership interest is reduced by the full amount of the partner's distributive share of partnership losses. Assume, for example, that A contributes $5,000 cash to acquire a one-third interest in profits and capital of the ABC general partnership. The partnership then borrows $285,000 on a nonrecourse basis to drill an oil well. A's basis in the partnership interest, applying the rules of § 752, is $100,000 ($5,000 + (⅓ × $285,000)). A's at-risk amount, however, is only $5,000. Thus, if for the current year, A's distributive share of partnership items is a $100,000 loss from drilling a dry hole, A may deduct currently only $5,000 of the loss; § 465 defers the remaining $95,000 deduction. But under § 705, A must reduce the basis of A's partnership interest by the full $100,000 loss. Thus, A's basis for the partnership interest is zero. If the oil property is abandoned to the mortgagee the following year, A's distributive share of partnership income will be $95,000, but A will be entitled to claim the $95,000 deduction previously suspended by § 465. The basis of A's partnership interest is unaffected by the allowance of the deduction in the later year under § 465. Basis is increased by A's $95,000 share of partnership income and is reduced by a like amount due to the deemed distribution on the cancellation of the partnership debt, leaving A with a basis of zero.

3.2. *Recapture of Amounts Previously at Risk*

Section 465(e) requires recapture of previous deductions following a reduction in the taxpayer's amount at risk below the amount previously deducted by the taxpayer. Section 465(e) provides that if the taxpayer's amount at risk in an activity is reduced below zero, the taxpayer will recognize gross income to the extent that zero exceeds the amount at risk. For example, if A purchases an investment in an activity for $10,000 cash plus a recourse note for $90,000, then claims $20,000 of deductions from the activity, A's total amount at risk, reduced by the deductions, is $80,000. See I.R.C. § 465(b)(5). If the note is then converted to a nonrecourse note, A's amount at risk becomes a negative $10,000 ($10,000 cash investment minus $20,000 of deductions). A's at-risk amount exceeds zero by $10,000 requiring A to recognize $10,000 of income. Thus, A recaptures $10,000 of deductions as gross income. The amount recaptured into income is treated as a suspended deduction from the activity available in a later year when the taxpayer's amount at risk increases. The amount subject to recapture in any taxable year is limited to the total amount of losses from the activity claimed by the taxpayer in prior years reduced by amounts recaptured in prior years. I.R.C. § 465(e)(2).

4.   APPLICATION TO LIMITED LIABILITY COMPANIES

The limitations imposed by § 465 are of particular importance to members of a limited liability company (LLC) taxed as a partnership. The members are taxed as partners and, thus, pursuant to § 752 increase their bases in their interests in the LLC by their respective shares of the LLC's indebtedness, whether the indebtedness is recourse or nonrecourse to the LLC. For purposes of § 465, however, no member of the LLC is at risk with respect to any portion of the LLC's indebtedness except to the extent that the member has guaranteed the indebtedness without a right of indemnification or contribution.

Assume, for example, that A, B, and C form the ABC LLC, and each contributes $10. The ABC LLC then borrows $330 with full recourse to the entity and pays $360 to purchase depreciable property with a 10-year cost recovery period, using straight line depreciation. The ABC LLC breaks even apart from depreciation; the Year 1 depreciation (ignoring conventions) is $36; and no principal payments are made. Each member's distributive share of the loss is $12. A, B, and C each have a $120 basis in their interest in the LLC but are at risk for only $10. Thus, only $10 of the $12 loss is currently deductible by each member of the LLC. The remaining $2 of each member's share of the loss is deferred. A, B, and C will not be able to deduct losses in any subsequent years until their at-risk amounts increase through either additional contributions or the retention of earnings by the LLC.

In Hubert Enterprises v. Commissioner, T.C. Memo 2008–46, the taxpayer owned 99% of the units of an LLC taxed as a partnership that purchased equipment financed with debt that was recourse to the LLC, but which was not guaranteed by any LLC member. The LLC agreement required members to restore a deficit capital account on liquidation of the LLC in order to pay creditors and to satisfy the positive balance of another member's capital account. Applying the ultimate liability standard of Emershaw v. Commissioner, supra, because the case was appealable to the Sixth Circuit, the Tax Court held that the taxpayer had no personal liability as repayment of any deficit was contingent on liquidation of the LLC and no creditor had a right to force a liquidation under state law. Thus, the taxpayer was not at risk with respect to the LLC's recourse debt, which could not be enforced directly against the partner.

PROBLEM SET 1

1.   (a) Al is a general partner of a limited partnership formed last year to engage in oil and gas drilling and production. Al contributed $5,000 to obtain his interest in January of last year. The partnership borrowed funds on both a recourse basis and a nonrecourse basis to drill an oil well. Al's share of the recourse debt is $20,000, and his share of the nonrecourse debt is $100,000. The oil well produced some oil, but the revenue was less than the deductible expenses to drill and operate the oil well. Last year, Al's distributive share of partnership income or loss was an operating loss of $40,000. The partnership made no distributions. How much of the $40,000 loss is deductible by Al after taking § 465 into account?

(b) This year Al contributed an additional $10,000 to the partnership in connection with the partnership's acquisition of a herd of cattle to be raised on the portion of its ranch land not devoted to oil and gas production. To finance acquisition of the cattle, the partnership borrowed funds from a bank in which a limited partner owns 25% of the stock. Al's share of the recourse debt owed to the bank is $20,000, and his share of the nonrecourse debt owed to the bank is $90,000. Al's share of losses from the cattle ranching was $14,000. Al's share of profits from the oil and gas well, however, was $22,000. The partnership made no distributions. How much must Al include or may Al deduct on his return this year after taking § 465 into account?

2.   Beth invested $50,000 in a limited liability company that is taxed as a partnership, which was formed to develop and market computer software. Beth obtained a one-fifth membership interest. The LLC borrowed $1,000,000 from an unrelated venture capital fund to commence its

operations. Beth's share of the LLC's indebtedness was $200,000. Beth's distributive share of losses, which were largely attributable to § 174 deductions from the LLC for the first year, was $200,000. How much of the $200,000 loss is deductible under the following circumstances?

(a) Each of the five equal members of the LLC guaranteed up to $100,000 of the loan.

(b) Beth personally guaranteed the entire $1,000,000 loan, and none of the other members of the LLC guaranteed the loan.

(c) All five of the equal members of the LLC personally guaranteed the entire $1,000,000 loan.

(d) The LLC agreement provides that each equal member will contribute up to an additional $75,000 to the LLC upon the vote of a majority of the interests in the LLC, which is member managed LLC.

3. (a) Calvin contributed $100,000 to become a limited partner with a one-tenth interest in a limited partnership formed to purchase Blackacre, a high-rise apartment building. The partnership paid $10 million for Blackacre, the portion of the purchase price in excess of the partners' contributions being obtained through a $9,000,000 nonrecourse loan from the Last National Bank. Calvin's share of the debt was $900,000. In each of the first five years of the partnership, Calvin's distributive share of partnership income or loss was a $35,000 loss. To what extent do the at-risk rules limit the amount that Calvin may deduct?

(b) To what extent do the at-risk rules limit the amount that Calvin may deduct if 60% of the stock in the Last National Bank is owned by the spouse of the general partner?

(c) To what extent do the at-risk rules limit the amount that Calvin may deduct if instead of borrowing $9,000,000 from the Last National Bank the partnership gave the seller of Blackacre $1,000,000 in cash and a $9,000,000 nonrecourse promissory note, secured by the property and on commercially reasonable terms?

SECTION 3.   THE PASSIVE ACTIVITY LOSS RULES OF SECTION 469

INTERNAL REVENUE CODE: Sections 469(a), (b), (c)(1)–(4), (7)(A)–(C), (d)(1), (e)(1), (g), (h)(1) and (2), (i)(1)–(3), (6).

REGULATIONS: Section 1.469–4.

TEMPORARY REGULATIONS: Sections 1.469–2T(d)(6)(ii)(A), –5T(a), (b)(2), (c), (e), (f)(2).

Senate Finance Committee Report, Tax Reform Act of 1986

S.Rep. No. 99–313, 99th Cong., 2d Sess. 713–718 (1986).

[Pre-1987] Law

In general, no limitations are placed on the ability of a taxpayer to use deductions from a particular activity to offset income from other activities. Similarly, most tax credits may be used to offset tax attributable to income from any of the taxpayer's activities.

* * *

In the absence of more broadly applicable limitations on the use of deductions and credits from one activity to reduce tax liability attributable to other activities, taxpayers with substantial sources of positive income are able to eliminate or sharply reduce tax liability by using deductions and credits from other activities, frequently by investing in tax shelters. Tax shelters commonly offer the opportunity to reduce or avoid tax liability with respect to salary or other positive income, by making available deductions and credits, possibly exceeding real economic costs or losses currently borne by the taxpayer, in excess or in advance of income from the shelters.

Reasons for Change

* * * Extensive [tax] shelter activity contributes to public concerns that the tax system is unfair, and to the belief that tax is paid only by the naive and the unsophisticated. This, in turn, not only undermines compliance, but encourages further expansion of the tax shelter market, in many cases diverting investment capital from productive activities to those principally or exclusively serving tax avoidance goals.

The committee believes that the most important sources of support for the Federal income tax system are the average citizens who simply report their income (typically consisting predominantly of items such as salaries, wages, pensions, interest, and dividends) and pay tax under the general rules. To the extent that these citizens feel that they are bearing a disproportionate burden with regard to the costs of government because of their unwillingness or inability to engage in tax-oriented investment activity, the tax system itself is threatened.

* * *

The question of how to prevent harmful and excessive tax sheltering is not a simple one. One way to address the problem would be to eliminate substantially all tax preferences in the Internal Revenue Code. For two reasons, however, the committee believes that this course is inappropriate.

First, while the bill reduces or eliminates some tax preference items that the committee believes do not provide social or economic benefits commensurate with their cost, there are many preferences that the committee believes are socially or economically beneficial. This is especially true when such preferences are used primarily to advance the purposes upon which Congress relied in enacting them, rather than to avoid taxation of income from sources unrelated to the preferred activity.

Second, it would be extremely difficult, perhaps impossible, to design a tax system that measures income perfectly. For example, the statutory allowance for depreciation, even under the normative system used under the bill for alternative minimum tax purposes, reflects broad industry averages, as opposed to providing precise item-by-item measurements. Accordingly, taxpayers with assets that depreciate less rapidly than the average, or that appreciate over time (as may be the case with certain real estate), may engage in tax sheltering even under the minimum tax, unless Congress directly addresses the tax shelter problem.

* * *

The question of what constitutes a tax shelter that should be subject to limitations is closely related to the question of who Congress intends to benefit when it enacts tax preferences. For example, in providing preferential depreciation for real estate or favorable accounting rules for farming, it was not Congress's primary intent to permit outside investors to avoid tax liability with respect to their salaries by investing in limited partnership syndications. Rather, Congress intends to benefit and provide incentives to taxpayers active in the businesses to which the preferences were directed.

* * *

The availability of tax benefits to shelter positive sources of income also has harmed the economy generally, by providing a non-economic return on capital for certain investments. This has encouraged a flow of capital away from activities that may provide a higher pre-tax economic return, thus retarding the growth of the sectors of the economy with the greatest potential for expansion.

The committee believes that, in order for tax preferences to function as intended, their benefit must be directed primarily to taxpayers with a substantial and bona fide involvement in the activities to which the preferences relate. The committee also believes that it is appropriate to encourage nonparticipating investors to invest in particular activities, by permitting the use of preferences to reduce the rate of tax on income from those activities; however, such investors should not be permitted to use tax benefits to shelter unrelated income.

There are several reasons why it is appropriate to examine the materiality of a taxpayer's participation in an activity in determining the extent to which such taxpayer should be permitted to use tax benefits from the activity. A taxpayer who materially participates in an activity is more likely than a passive investor to approach the activity with a significant nontax economic profit motive, and to form a sound judgment as to whether the activity has genuine economic significance and value.

A material participation standard identifies an important distinction between different types of taxpayer activities. In general, the more passive investor is seeking a return on capital invested, including returns in the form of reductions in the taxes owed on unrelated income, rather than an ongoing source of livelihood. A material participation standard reduces the importance, for such investors, of the tax-reduction features of an investment, and thus increases the importance of the economic features in an investor's decision about where to invest his funds.

Moreover, the committee believes that restricting the use of losses from business activities in which the taxpayer does not materially participate against other sources of positive income (such as salary and portfolio income) addresses a fundamental aspect of the tax shelter problem. As discussed above, instances in which the tax system applies simple rules at the expense of economic accuracy encourage the structuring of transactions to take advantage of the situations in which such rules give rise to undermeasurement or deferral of income. Such transactions commonly are marketed to investors who do not intend to participate in the transactions, as devices for sheltering unrelated sources of positive income (e.g., salary and portfolio income). Accordingly, by creating a bar against the use of losses from business activities in which the taxpayer does not materially participate to offset positive income sources such as salary and portfolio income, the committee believes that it is possible significantly to reduce the tax shelter problem.

Further, in the case of a nonparticipating investor in a business activity, the committee believes that it is appropriate to treat losses of the activity as not realized by the investor prior to disposition of his interest in the activity. The effort to measure, on an annual basis, real economic losses from passive activities gives rise to distortions, particularly due to the nontaxation of unrealized appreciation and the mismatching of tax deductions and related economic income that may occur, especially where debt financing is used heavily. Only when a taxpayer disposes of his interest in an activity is it possible to determine whether a loss was sustained over the entire time that he held the interest.

The distinction that the committee believes should be drawn between activities on the basis of material participation bears no relationship to the question of whether, and to what extent, the taxpayer is at risk with respect to the activities.[6] In general, the fact that a taxpayer has placed a particular amount at risk in an activity does not establish, prior to a disposition of the taxpayer's interest, that the amount invested, or any amount, has as yet been lost. The fact that a taxpayer is potentially liable with respect to future expenses or losses of the activity likewise has no bearing on the question whether any amount has as yet been lost, or otherwise is an appropriate current deduction or credit.

At-risk standards, although important in determining the maximum amount that is subject to being lost, are not a sufficient basis for determining whether or when net losses from an activity should be deductible against other sources of income, or for determining whether an ultimate economic loss has been realized. Congress' goal of making tax preferences available principally to active participants in substantial businesses, rather than to investors seeking to shelter unrelated income, can best be accomplished by examining material participation, as opposed to the financial stake provided by an investor to purchase tax shelter benefits.

In certain situations, however, the committee believes that financial risk or other factors, rather than material participation, should be the relevant standard. A situation in which financial risk is relevant relates to the oil and gas industry, which at present is suffering severe hardship due to the worldwide collapse of oil prices. The committee believes that relief for this industry requires that tax benefits be provided to attract outside investors. Moreover, the committee believes that such relief should be provided only with respect to investors who are willing to accept an unlimited and unprotected financial risk proportionate to their ownership interests in the oil and gas activities. Granting tax shelter benefits to investors in oil and gas activities who did not accept unlimited risk, proportionate to their ownership investments in the activities, would permit the benefit of this special exception to be diverted unduly to the investors, while providing less benefit to oil and gas activities and threatening the integrity of the entire rule limiting the use of nonparticipatory business losses.

A further area in which the material participation standard is not wholly adequate is that of rental activities. Such activities predominantly involve the production of income from capital. * * *

Rental activities generally require less ongoing management activity, in proportion to capital invested, than business activities

---

[6]   The at-risk rules of present law, while important and useful in preventing overvaluation of assets, and in preventing the transfer of tax benefits to taxpayers with no real equity in an activity, do not address the adverse consequences arising specifically from such transfers to nonparticipating investors.

involving the production or sale of goods and services. Thus, for example, an individual who is employed full-time as a professional could more easily provide all necessary management in his spare time with respect to a rental activity than he could with respect to another type of business activity involving the same capital investment. The extensive use of rental activities for tax shelter purposes under present law, combined with the reduced level of personal involvement necessary to conduct such activities, make clear that the effectiveness of the basic passive loss provision could be seriously compromised if material participation were sufficient to avoid the limitations in the case of rental activities.

A limited measure of relief, however, is believed appropriate in the case of certain moderate-income investors in rental real estate, who otherwise might experience cash flow difficulties with respect to investments that in many cases are designed to provide financial security, rather than to shelter a substantial amount of other income.

Further, additional considerations apply in the case of limited partnerships. In order to maintain limited liability status, a limited partner generally is precluded from materially participating in the business activity of the partnership; in virtually all respects, a limited partner more closely resembles a shareholder in a C corporation than an active business entrepreneur. Moreover, limited partnerships commonly are used as vehicles for marketing tax benefits to investors seeking to shelter unrelated income. In light of the widespread use of limited partnership interests in syndicating tax shelters, the committee believes that losses from limited partnership interests should not be permitted, prior to a taxable disposition, to offset positive income sources such as salary.

* * *

DETAILED ANALYSIS

1.   GENERAL

Section 469 applies to individual partners, not directly to the partnership. Section 469 does not apply to a partner that is a C corporation, however, unless the corporation is "closely held." I.R.C. § 469(a)(2)(B). The rules of § 469 may disallow a partner's deduction of the partner's distributive share of a partnership loss, even though the loss is allowable under both § 704(d) and § 465. For rules governing the coordination of § 469 with § 704(d) and § 465, see Temp.Reg. § 1.469–2T(d)(6). When § 469 disallows a partner's distributive share of a partnership loss, the partner's basis in the partnership interest should be reduced by the full distributive share of partnership losses notwithstanding that § 469 defers the deduction. See S.Rep. No. 993–13, 99th Cong., 2d Sess. 723, n. 9 (1986).

2.   TREATMENT OF PASSIVE ACTIVITY LOSSES

Mechanically, § 469(a) disallows any "passive activity loss." A passive activity loss is defined in § 469(d)(1) as the aggregate losses from all passive activities for the year in excess of the aggregate income from such activities for the year. In this context, the term "losses" means the amount by which all otherwise allowable deductions exceed gross income, and income means the amount by which gross income exceeds deductions. Thus, if Passive Activity A generates $1,000 of income and $1,200 of deductions and Passive Activity B generates $600 of income and $500 of deductions, the taxpayer has a $100 passive activity loss for the year that will be disallowed. Temp.Reg. § 1.469–1T(f) provides rules for allocating the disallowed loss among the various passive activities that contributed to it, and then allocating the loss attributable to each activity among the component deductions. The disallowed loss carries over to the next year, where it enters the computation again; and this carryover continues until the loss is allowed or permanently disallowed. I.R.C. § 469(b). Thus, § 469, like § 465, generally operates to defer, not totally disallow, deductions attributable to passive activities. Furthermore, it allows a full current deduction for passive activity losses to the extent the taxpayer has current passive activity income from other sources.

3. DEFINITION OF PASSIVE ACTIVITY

3.1. *"Passive Activity"*

A "passive activity" generally is any trade or business activity in which the taxpayer does not "materially participate." I.R.C. § 469(c)(1). However, all rental activities are deemed to be passive activities regardless of the level of the taxpayer's participation. I.R.C. § 469(c)(2). For the definition of rental activity, see Temp.Reg. § 1.469–1T(e)(3). Section 469(h) defines material participation as regular, continuous, and substantial involvement in the operations of the activity. In addition, § 469(h)(2) specifically provides that except as provided in Regulations, "no interest in a limited partnership as a limited partner shall be treated as an interest with respect to which a taxpayer materially participates." The Temporary Regulations generally test for material participation by counting the number of hours devoted to the activity each year by the taxpayer and permit limited partners to be treated as materially participating under certain circumstances. Temp.Reg. § 1.469–5T(a). In applying these rules, each partner's individual participation must be tested separately.

Treas.Reg. § 1.469–2(f)(6) contains a special rule providing that rental income from property that is rented for use in a trade or business in which the taxpayer is a material participant is treated as active income. In Beecher v. Commissioner, 481 F.3d 717 (9th Cir. 2007), the taxpayers rented office space to two corporations in which the taxpayers were material participants. The taxpayers also had other rental properties that produced net passive activity losses. Upholding the validity of the self-rental rule in Treas.Reg. § 1.469–2(f)(6), the court held that the taxpayers' rental income from leases to the taxpayers' active businesses was active income and could not be reduced by the taxpayer's passive activity loss from other rental activities. Accord Krukowski v. Commissioner, 279 F.3d 547 (7th Cir. 2002); Sidell v. Commissioner, 225 F.3d 103 (1st Cir. 2000), and Fransen v. United States, 191 F.3d 599 (5th Cir. 1999).

The self-rental recharacterization rule of Treas.Reg. § 1.469–2(f)(6) is applicable to income from "an item of property" and does not apply to net income from an activity renting property to an active business of the taxpayer. This distinction was analyzed in Veriha v. Commissioner, 139 T.C.45 (2013). The taxpayer was the sole owner of JVT, a C corporation that conducted a trucking business in which he actively participated. JVT leased the tractors and trailers used in its business from TRI, an S corporation in which the taxpayer owned 99% of the stock, and JRV, a single-member LLC wholly owned by the taxpayer and thus a disregarded entity. Each lease of a tractor or trailer was governed by a separate contract. During the year in issue, TRI realized net income and JRV realized a net loss. The taxpayer treated the net income from TRI as passive income and treated the net loss from JRV as a passive loss. The court agreed with the IRS that pursuant to Treas.Reg. § 1.469–2(f)(6) each tractor and each trailer should be considered a separate "item of property" and that the income the taxpayer received from TRI should be recharacterized as nonpassive income, while the net loss realized by JRV remained a passive activity loss. The Tax Court rejected the taxpayer's argument that all of the tractors and trailers collectively were one "item of property," and looking to *Webster's Third New International Dictionary* 1203 (2002) for the definition of the term "item" held that for purposes of applying Reg. § 1.469–2(f)(6), each individual tractor or trailer was an "item of property," and the income received from TRI was subject to recharacterization. However, because the IRS had not contested the taxpayer's netting of gains and losses within TRI, only TRI's net income was recharacterized as nonpassive income that could not be offset by losses from JRV.

3.2. *"Material Participation"*

Under Temp.Reg. § 1.469–5T(a), a taxpayer materially participates in an activity if any of the following tests are met: (1) the taxpayer devotes more than 500 hours to the activity in the year; (2) the taxpayer is the only individual who participates in the activity; (3) the taxpayer participates in the activity for more than 100 hours during the year and the taxpayer's participation is not less than that of any other individual; (4) the activity is a trade or business, the taxpayer participates in the activity for more than 100 hours (but not more than 500 hours) during the year, and the taxpayer's total participation in all such trade or business activities during the year exceeds 500 hours; (5) the taxpayer materially participated in the activity for five of the preceding ten taxable years; (6) the activity is a personal service activity in which the taxpayer materially participated for any three preceding years; or (7) based on all the facts and circumstances, the taxpayer participates in the activity on a regular, continuous, and substantial basis. Work not customarily performed by the owner of a business is not taken into account if one of the principal purposes of performing such work is to meet the material participation requirement. Unless an individual also participates in the day-to-day management or operations of the business, work performed in the capacity of an investor is not counted. Temp.Reg. § 1.469–5T(f)(2). A taxpayer who participates in an activity for 100 hours or less during the year cannot qualify as materially participating under the facts and circumstances test. Temp.Reg. § 1.469–5T(b)(2)(iii). Management services are taken into account in determining material participation only to a limited extent in applying the facts and circumstances test. Temp.Reg. § 1.469–5T(b)(2)(ii).

3.3. *"Significant Participation Activities"*

If the taxpayer's gross income from certain passive activities that are "significant participation activities" exceeds the deductions from all significant participation activities for the taxable year, then a portion of the net income from significant participation activities is treated as active income. Temp.Reg. § 1.469–2T(f)(2). The Temporary Regulations define as a "significant participation activity" any activity in which the taxpayer participates for more than 100 hours during the year, but in which the taxpayer does not materially participate.

3.4. *Application to Partners and LLC Members*

It is clear from these rules that a general partner does not qualify as materially participating merely because of the general partner status. The level of participation in each activity in which the partnership is engaged must be tested separately. A partner may be active as to some partnership activities and passive as to others.

Section 469(h)(2) generally requires that a limited partner be treated as not materially participating in any partnership activity. The definition of a limited partner in Treas.Reg. § 1.469–5T(e)(3)(B) as a partner whose liability is limited to a fixed amount (including the partner's capital contribution). Temp.Reg. § 1.469–5T(e) provides two exceptions to § 469(h)(2). First, a limited partner materially participates in a partnership activity if any one of tests (1), (5), or (6) for material participation described above are met. Second, a limited partnership interest held by a general partner is not treated as a limited partnership interest in applying § 469; whether the partner materially participates is determined for both interests together under the above described tests. This final rule may appear to contradict the statutory language of § 469(h)(2) but is within the Treasury's regulatory authority under that provision.

Garnett v. Commissioner, 132 T.C. 368 (2009), held that an interest in an LLC (or a limited liability partnership) is not treated as a limited partnership interest under § 469(h)(2). Thompson v. United States, 87 Fed. Cl. 728 (2009) (acq.), reached the same result. Both courts reasoned that § 469(h)(2) treats limited partners differently because of an assumption that limited partners do not materially participate in their limited partnerships. In an LLC, on the other hand, all members have limited liability, but members may participate in management. Thus, whether or not the taxpayer is a material participant requires a full factual inquiry in which a taxpayer can demonstrate material participation in the activity by using any of the seven tests in Temp.Reg. § 1.469–5T(a). The IRS has acquiesced in *Thompson* (AOD 2010–02, April 5, 2010) and has issued Proposed Regulations that revise the definition of an interest as a limited partner. Rather than rely on limited liability to identify a limited partner interest, Prop.Reg. § 1.469–5(e)(3) (2011) would provide that "an interest in an entity shall be treated as an interest in a limited partnership as a limited partner if . . . [t]he holder of such interest does not have rights to manage the entity at all times during the entity's taxable year under the law of the jurisdiction in which the entity is organized and under the governing agreement." A right to manage includes authority to bind the entity. Furthermore, an individual who holds a limited partnership interest would not be treated as holding a limited partnership interest if the individual also holds an interest in the partnership that is not a limited partnership interest as defined in Prop.Reg. § 1.469–5(e)(3).

4.   APPLICATION ON ACTIVITY-BY-ACTIVITY BASIS

4.1. *General*

Whether a partner's distributive share of any partnership item is treated as active or passive is determined by whether the taxpayer materially participated in the particular activity that gave rise to the item during the partnership's taxable year. Temp.Reg. § 1.469–2T(e)(1). The Code does not provide guidance for determining the scope of an activity, but such a determination is crucial in applying § 469. The Committee Reports indicate that a single activity consists of those "undertakings [that] consist of an integrated and interrelated economic unit, conducted in coordination with or reliance upon each other, and constituting an appropriate unit for the measurement of gain or loss." S.Rep. No. 99–313, 99th Cong., 2d Sess. 739 (1986). Thus, it is clear that a single partnership may be engaged in more than one activity. It is also clear that two related partnerships may be engaged together in a single activity. Under this standard, a partner may materially participate with respect to one partnership activity, but not with respect to a different partnership activity during the same year. In such a case, the partner's distributive share of partnership items attributable to the activity in which the partner did not materially participate would be passive income or loss.

4.2. *Scope of "Activity"*

Treas.Reg. § 1.469–4 adopts a facts and circumstances approach to identifying separate business activities. Two or more business activities are treated as a single activity "if the activities constitute an appropriate economic unit for the measurement of gain or loss for purposes of section 469." Treas.Reg. § 1.469–4(c)(1). In making this determination, five evidentiary factors are given the greatest weight: (1) similarities and differences in the type of business; (2) the extent of common control; (3) the extent of common ownership; (4) geographical location; and (5) business interdependency, such as the extent to which the activities purchase or sell goods between themselves, involve products or services that are normally provided together, have the same customers, have the same employees, or share a single set of books and records. Treas.Reg. § 1.469–4(c)(2).

A taxpayer may use any reasonable method of applying the relevant facts and circumstances in grouping activities, subject to a consistency requirement. Treas.Reg. § 1.469–4(c)(1). Once a taxpayer has grouped activities, they may not be regrouped unless the original grouping was inappropriate. Furthermore, the taxpayer subsequently must regroup the activities if warranted by a material change in facts and circumstances. Treas.Reg. § 1.469–4(e)(2). Finally, a taxpayer generally may elect to treat the disposition of a substantial part of an activity as a complete disposition of a separate activity, thus allowing suspended losses to be used in that year. Treas.Reg. § 1.469–4(g). The IRS may group activities differently than the taxpayer only if the taxpayer's grouping fails to reflect appropriate economic units and a principal purpose of the taxpayer's grouping was to circumvent § 469. Treas.Reg. § 1.469–4(f).

Taxpayers have significant flexibility under these Regulations. For example, if a taxpayer owns a video arcade and a restaurant at a shopping mall in Sacramento and a video arcade and a restaurant in San Francisco, depending on other relevant facts and circumstances, it may be reasonable to (1) group the video arcades and restaurants into a single activity, (2) group the Sacramento video arcade and restaurant into a single activity and the San Francisco video arcade and restaurant into a different activity; or (3) treat each video arcade and restaurant as a separate activity. See Treas.Reg. § 1.469–4(c)(3), Ex. (1).

A rental activity (as defined in Temp.Reg. § 1.469–1T(e)(3)) may not be grouped with a nonrental activity unless one of the activities is insubstantial relative to the other. Treas.Reg. § 1.469–4(d). For example, if the taxpayer owned a six-story office building, occupying three floors to conduct a business and leasing out three floors to tenants, the rental business is a separate activity from the other business. Real property rental activities and personal property rental activities never may be grouped, unless the personal property is provided in connection with the real property, for example, the rental of furnished apartments. Treas.Reg. § 1.469–4(d)(2).

Application of these rules to a taxpayer who is a partner can be a bit more complex. First, the partnership must group its activities under the general rules, and the individual partners must group their interests in activities conducted directly or through different partnerships. A partner may not treat activities that are treated as a group by the partnership as separate activities. Treas.Reg. § 1.469–4(d)(5). Special rules further limit grouping by limited partners of activities conducted through different limited partnerships. Treas.Reg. § 1.469–4(d)(3).

5. SPECIAL RULE FOR RENTAL REAL ESTATE ACTIVITIES OF PERSONS IN REAL PROPERTY BUSINESS

Section 469(c)(7) relaxes the passive activity loss rules for taxpayers who provide more than one-half of their work effort during the year in one or more real estate businesses if (1) the taxpayer materially participates within the meaning of § 469(h), and (2) the taxpayer works more than 750 hours in such activities. If these tests are met, the taxpayer's real estate rental activities are not automatically treated as passive activities under § 469(c)(2). Instead, each activity is evaluated using the material participation rules of § 469(h). Any rental activity in which the taxpayer materially participates under that test is not subject to § 469; any losses from that activity are fully deductible against the taxpayer's income from other sources. Material participation in a rental real estate activity is determined separately with respect to each interest unless the taxpayer elects to aggregate all real estate activities. An election to aggregate real estate activities must be made in a clear statement filed with the tax return. Simply aggregating losses from rental real estate properties is not sufficient notice of an election to aggregate the properties. Treas.Reg. § 1.469–9(g)(3); see also Shiekh v. Commissioner, T.C. Memo. 2010–126. Rev.Proc. 2011–34, 2011–24 I.R.B. 875, provides relief allowing late elections if (i) the taxpayer failed to file the election with an original tax return in the year the election was to take effect as required by Treas.Reg. § 1.469–9(g); (ii) the taxpayer has filed all returns for years subsequent to the year for which an election is made consistent with having made a timely election to aggregate properties; (iii) the taxpayer had timely filed each return affected by the election if it had been made (or filed within six months of the due date excluding extensions); and (iv) the taxpayer had reasonable cause for its failure to file under Treas.Reg. § 1.469–9(g).

This relief provision was intended primarily to benefit real estate developers, allowing them to offset income from development activities with losses from rental operations, but because real estate activities are broadly defined, its application is wider. For example, a real estate broker who is the managing general partner of a limited partnership holding an apartment building for rental may be able to deduct losses from the partnership against commission income from a brokerage business or investment income completely unrelated to real estate activities. Furthermore, if married taxpayers file joint returns and one spouse meets the test for being engaged in a real estate business, losses from that spouse's material participation rental real estate activities may be deducted against all income on the joint return, including the other spouse's income. Rental activity losses of the spouse not in the real estate business, however, remain subject to § 469 and may not be deducted other than as passive activity losses.

6. "ACTIVE PARTICIPATION" RENTAL REAL ESTATE ACTIVITIES

For individuals and some decedent's estates, § 469(i) relaxes the restrictions on deducting losses from passive activities with respect to losses from rental real estate activities in which the taxpayer "actively participates." Section 469(i)(6) defines "active participation." Under this provision, no partner with less than a 10% interest (by value) in the activity (as distinguished from the partnership) may be considered as actively participating. However, no limited partner, regardless of the extent of the limited partner's interest, can be treated as actively participating. If the active participation standard is met, a taxpayer may deduct against income that is not passive income up to $25,000 of rental real estate losses. These losses must first be offset against any passive income, however, and the $25,000 ceiling is reduced by one-half of the amount by which the taxpayer's adjusted gross income (without taking such losses into account) exceeds $100,000. Thus, a partner who fails the material participation standard, but who meets the active participation standard may be able to deduct currently all or a part of his distributive share of partnership losses attributable to rental real estate activities. This provision, however, is directed primarily to individuals who live in one part of a multi-unit residence and rent out the remaining units.

7. PORTFOLIO INCOME

Even if a partner does not materially participate in the activities of a partnership, the partner's distributive share of portfolio income items (defined generally as all income other than income derived in the ordinary course of a trade or business) received by the partnership is not passive income. Temp.Reg. § 1.469–2T(c)(3). Thus, for example, interest on a reserve maintained in connection with a partnership activity with respect to which a partner is passive is not passive activity income for the partner. See Temp.Reg. § 1.469–2T(c)(3)(iv), Ex. (2).

Income from publicly traded limited partnerships that escape classification as associations under § 7704, discussed in Chapter 17, largely resembles portfolio income, such as dividends. To prevent the sheltering of such income by losses from tax shelter limited partnerships, § 469(k) requires that the passive loss rules be applied separately to income and losses from each publicly traded limited partnership. Thus, if a taxpayer has net income from a publicly traded limited partnership and net losses from another limited partnership, whether or not publicly traded, the loss cannot be deducted against the income. In addition, § 469(*l*)(3) authorizes the Treasury to promulgate Regulations "requiring net income or gain from a limited partnership or other passive activity to be treated as not from a passive activity."

8. EFFECT OF DISPOSITION OF ACTIVITY

Because § 469 is intended to disallow only "artificial" losses, § 469(g) allows the taxpayer to deduct previously disallowed losses attributable to any activity in the year in which the taxpayer makes a fully taxable disposition of the taxpayer's entire interest in the activity. Deduction of suspended losses on disposition of an activity is appropriate because artificial losses that were previously suspended will be offset by an equal amount of artificial (phantom) gain on the taxable disposition so that only real losses will remain to offset other income.

Generally, a sale or taxable exchange to an unrelated taxpayer of all of the assets used in the activity is required in order to satisfy the requirements of § 469(g). Abandonment, which is a taxable event, also qualifies. The sale by a partner of all of the partner's interest in a partnership will permit the partner to deduct suspended losses attributable to all partnership activities in which the partner did not materially participate. If the partnership was engaged in two or more activities in which the partner did not materially participate and the partnership sells all of the assets used in one activity, the suspended losses attributable to that activity may be claimed by the partner, but suspended losses attributable to other activities of the partnership remain in suspense. It is important to bear in mind that if the partner sells the partner's entire interest in the partnership, the partner should be allowed to deduct all suspended losses notwithstanding that the partner has no remaining basis. This result is required because a partner's outside basis should be reduced by the partner's full distributive share of partnership losses notwithstanding that § 469 may operate to defer the deduction.

If a partner disposes of less than the partner's entire interest in the partnership (or a partnership disposes of less than its entire interest in a passive activity), disposes of the partner's interest in a nontaxable transaction, or sells the interest to a related party (as defined in either § 267(b) or § 707(b)), any previously disallowed losses continue to be suspended and will be allowed in a future year in which the partner realizes passive activity income from other sources or upon the completion of the disposition. If the initial disposition was a nontaxable transaction, any remaining suspended losses will be allowed upon the fully taxable sale of the property received in the tax-free exchange.

Gain or loss on the sale or other taxable disposition of a partnership interest is characterized as passive or active by looking through the partnership entity to its activities. Temp.Reg. § 1.469–2T(e)(3). However, the gain or loss realized on the sale of the entire partnership interest is a ceiling on the look-through computation. A sale at a gain may be treated as composed of both passive gain and active gain; a sale at a loss may include both passive loss and active loss; but a sale at no gain, for example, will not be treated as composed of equal amounts of active gain and passive loss (or passive gain and active loss). See Temp.Reg. § 1.469–2T(e)(3)(vii) Ex. (1). For the sale of a partnership interest, see Chapter 24.

The deferred deductions are allowable, in order, to the extent of: (1) income from the passive activity, including gain (if any) recognized on the disposition; (2) net income or gain for the year from all other passive activities; (3) other income or gain, including salaries, dividends, etc. If any of the deductions otherwise allowable upon the disposition of the activity are capital losses, either from the disposition or as suspended deductions allowed upon the disposition, § 1211 may limit the amount of the deductions currently allowed. If a disposition is an installment sale and gain recognition is deferred under § 453, suspended losses are allowed in each year payments are received in proportion to the portion of the total gain reportable in each year.

9.   PAYMENTS TO PARTNERS

Payments received by a partner in a transaction subject to § 707(a)(1) are never treated as passive activity income with respect to the partnership activity. Temp.Reg. § 1.469–2T(e)(2)(i). Payments to a partner subject to § 707(c) are treated as compensation or as interest in applying the passive loss rules. Treas.Reg. § 1.469–2(e)(2)(ii). For discussion of § 707(a)(1) and (c), see Chapter 22.

Under the authority of § 469(l)(2), and following the direction of the legislative history of § 469, Treas.Reg. § 1.469–7 provides that interest income and expense on a loan from a member of a passthrough entity to the entity (or from the entity to a member) will be treated as passive activity income and expense with respect to the lender. As a consequence, the member's share of the "self-charged" interest, which would otherwise be treated as portfolio income, can be offset with the member's share of the entity's passive activity interest expense, or vice versa.

Rev.Rul. 95–5, 1995–1 C.B. 100, held that gain recognized under § 731 as a result of a current distribution of cash in excess of the partner's basis in the partnership interest is treated as gain from the sale of a partnership interest under Temp.Reg. § 1.469–2T(e)(3). Thus, if with respect to the partner receiving the distribution the partnership conducts both passive activities and other activities, the gain will be bifurcated into passive activity gain and nonpassive activity gain.

Payments to a retired partner or a deceased partner's successor in interest that are subject to § 736(b) are treated as passive income only if they would have been characterized as passive income if received at the time the liquidation of the partner's interest commenced. Treas.Reg. § 1.469–2(e)(2)(iii)(A). Payments subject to § 736(a) that are attributable to unrealized receivables (as defined in § 751(c)) and goodwill are treated as passive activity income only if the activity to which they are attributable was a passive activity of the partner for the partnership taxable year in which payments commenced. Treas.Reg. § 1.469–2(e)(2)(iii)(B). Section 736 payments are discussed in Chapter 25.

PROBLEM SET 2

1.   Jane is an actor who is a 10% partner in the Macon Mighties, a minor league baseball team. The Macon Mighties partnership had a net loss in the current year. Jane's basis in her partnership interest, prior to taking into account this year's loss, is $150,000.

(a)   Jane is a limited partner. She performed no services for the Macon Mighties. Her distributive share from the Macon Mighties was a $60,000 loss. She earned $2,000,000 from acting this year. May she deduct her distributive share of Macon Mighties' losses against her acting income?

(b)   Jane is a general partner. She performed no services for the Macon Mighties. Her distributive share from the Macon Mighties was a $60,000 loss. She earned $2,000,000 from acting this year. May she deduct her distributive share of Macon Mighties' losses against her acting income?

(c)   Jane is a general partner. She took a hiatus in her acting career and served as the team's general manager, for which she received a guaranteed payment of $40,000. Her distributive share from the Macon Mighties was a $60,000 loss. She received $200,000 of interest and dividends on publicly traded securities this year. May she deduct her distributive share of Macon Mighties' losses against her guaranteed payment and her interest and dividend income?

(d)   Jane is a general partner, but the only service she performed for the partnership was to star in three filmed television commercials, for which she received a guaranteed payment of $10,000. Her distributive share from the Macon Mighties was a $60,000 loss. She received $1,000,000 from acting this year. May she deduct her distributive share of Macon Mighties' losses against her guaranteed payment and acting income?

(e) Jane is a limited partner. She performed no services for the Macon Mighties. Her distributive share from the Macon Mighties was a $60,000 loss; that loss consisted of $5,000 of interest income on the working capital of the Macon Mighties and a $65,000 loss from other items. She earned $2,000,000 from acting this year. What are the tax consequences to Jane?

(f) What would be the result in (a) if Jane also realized $45,000 of net income from a real estate limited partnership interest in which she has invested as a limited partner?

(g) What would be the result in question (b) if the Macon Mighties operated through an LLC classified as a partnership? Does it matter whether the LLC is member managed or manager managed and, if it is manager managed, whether Jane is an LLC manager?

2. Jerry and Kathy formed the JK Partnership for purposes of purchasing and leasing an office building. Each partner contributed $500,000 for a one-half partnership interest. The partnership borrowed $9,000,000 and purchased a building for $10,000,000. For the current year, the partnership realized an operating loss of $200,000; each partner's distributive share of the loss was $100,000. Jerry is engaged primarily in the construction business, from which his annual income is $250,000; Kathy is a physician and earns $300,000 annually.

(a) Jerry serves as managing partner and leasing agent for the building. Kathy performs no services for the partnership. May either Jerry or Kathy deduct his or her share of partnership losses against his or her other income?

(b) Kathy serves as managing partner and leasing agent for the building. Jerry performs no services for the partnership. May either Jerry or Kathy deduct his or her share of partnership losses against his or her other income?

3. Emma is an investment banker, who earns $500,000 per year. She is a limited partner in Derby Associates, a thoroughbred horse breeding partnership in which she does not materially participate. Her basis in the partnership is $100,000, which is attributable to a $25,000 cash contribution, $30,000 of partnership recourse debt, and $45,000 of partnership nonrecourse debt. Her distributive share of partnership losses for the year was $70,000. Emma also is a limited partner in Petro Associates, which produces oil. Her distributive share from Petro Associates is a profit of $8,000. Assuming that Emma has no other relevant items, what is Emma's adjusted gross income for the year?

SECTION 4. THE LIMITATION ON EXCESS BUSINESS LOSSES OF NONCORPORATE TAXPAYERS: SECTION 461(*l*)

For taxable years beginning after December 31, 2020, and before January 1, 2026, the 2017 Tax Act, as amended by the 2020 CARES Act,[4] adds a new limitation on the deduction of business losses for noncorporate taxpayers, including individual partners and S corporation shareholders. Section 461(*l*) disallows the deduction of a taxpayer's "excess business loss." This is defined in § 461(*l*)(3) to mean the taxpayer's aggregate deductions for the year that are "attributable to trades or business of such taxpayer" over the sum of (1) the taxpayer's aggregate gross income or gain for the year attributable to the taxpayer's trades and (2) $250,000 (or $500,000 for joint filers), adjusted for inflation after 2018. Section 461(*l*) specifies that it applies after § 469.

Section 461(*l*) applies at the partner or shareholder level (for S corporations) and provides:

> [E]ach partner's or shareholder's allocable share of the items of income, gain, deduction, or loss of the partnership or S corporation for any taxable year from trades or businesses attributable to the partnership or S corporation shall be taken into account by the partner or shareholder in applying [§ 461(*l*)] to the taxable year of such partner or shareholder with or within which the taxable year of the partnership or S corporation ends.

The statute explains that for S corporation shareholders, "allocable share" means their "pro rata share" of an item. I.R.C. § 461(*l*)(4).

If a taxpayer's deductions are disallowed, the disallowed amount is treated as a § 172 net operating loss in the subsequent year. I.R.C. § 462(*l*)(2).

As is true of many (if not most) of the new rules contained in the 2017 legislation, guidance is needed regarding the definition of key terms and the coordination of § 461(*l*) with other statutory provisions.

---

[4] The CARES Act was enacted in response to the COVID-19 pandemic. Prior to amendment, 461(*l*) was to begin applying for taxable years beginning after December 31, 2017.

CHAPTER 24

SALES OF PARTNERSHIP INTERESTS BY PARTNERS

SECTION 1. THE SELLER'S SIDE OF THE TRANSACTION

A. GENERAL PRINCIPLES

INTERNAL REVENUE CODE: Sections 706(c); 708(a)–(b)(1); 741; 752(d); 1031(e); 1061.

REGULATIONS: Sections 1.704–1(b)(2)(iv)(*l*); 1.741–1; 1.752–1(h); 1.1223–3.

Under the entity approach of § 741, the sale or exchange of a partnership interest is treated as the sale of a unitary asset in its own right, like corporate stock, independent of the assets owned by the partnership. Generally, the sale results in capital gain or loss to the selling partner. In certain circumstances, however, § 751(a) overrides § 741 to impose a modified aggregate approach, under which a partner is treated as having sold the partner's share of certain types of partnership assets that produce ordinary income.

As long as a partnership does not hold "unrealized receivables" or inventory, the primary issues in sales of partnership interests involve the determination of the amount of the selling partner's basis properly taken into account in computing gain or loss and the determination of the effect of partnership indebtedness with respect to both the selling partner's basis and amount realized. The presence of unrealized receivables or inventory invokes § 751, which requires bifurcation of the sale of a partnership interest into an ordinary income component and a capital gain or loss component. Finally, when a partnership interest is sold partway through the partnership's taxable year, the selling partner's taxable income and the basis of the selling partner's partnership interest must be computed to account for the short year.

When a partnership interest is sold, provisions added by legislation in 2017 may be applicable. Section 1061 may affect whether a partner's capital gain on a sale is long-term or short-term. If § 751(a) requires that a partner recognize ordinary income or loss on the sale, that ordinary item is eligible to be included in the § 199A qualified business income computation, assuming the other requirements of § 199A are met (discussed in Chapter 18). Treas.Reg. § 1.199A–3(b)(1)(i). (Capital gains or losses are not included in § 199A qualified business income.)

Revenue Ruling 84–53

1984–1 C.B. 159.

ISSUE.

What are the tax consequences of the sale of a partnership interest in the situations described below?

FACTS.

Situation 1. In 1978, Y was formed as a limited partnership under the Uniform Limited Partnership Act of State N for the purpose of investing and trading in stocks and securities. Y has a calendar taxable year. A contributed $50x to Y in exchange for a general partner interest, entitling A to a 50 percent interest in all partnership distributions and in partnership income, gain, loss, and deduction. B contributed $50x to Y in exchange for a limited partner interest, entitling B to a 50 percent interest in all partnership distributions and in partnership income, gain, loss, and deduction.

On January 1, 1980, when the stock and securities of Y had decreased in value from $100x to $64x, B sold to A one-half of B's limited partner interest for $16x, which interest A holds as a limited partner.

On January 1, 1982, when the stock and securities of Y has risen in value from $64x (its 1980 value) to $120x, A sold to C one-half of A's general partner interest for $30x. Immediately prior to the sale, A's entire partnership interest had a fair market value of $90x and the transferred portion of the interest had a fair market value of $30x. Since formation, the partnership has made cash distributions in an amount equal to its total income (including tax-exempt income). Assume that all partnership allocations (in all situations) are valid, and that A, B, and C are unrelated parties.

Situation 2. The facts are the same as in *Situation 1* except that, in 1981, Y borrowed $80x recourse which was invested in securities that became worthless on December 31, 1981. Furthermore, immediately prior to A's sale to C, A's entire partnership interest had a fair market value of $30x and the transferred portion of A's interest had a fair market value of $10x.

Situation 3. The facts are the same as in *Situation 2* except that, on January 1, 1982, A sold A's entire limited partner interest to C for its fair market value of $10x (rather than one-half of A's general partner interest).

Situation 4. The facts are the same as in Situation 1 except that, in 1981, Y borrowed $96x recourse which is invested in securities that become worthless on December 31, 1981. Furthermore, immediately prior to A's sale to C, A's entire partnership interest had a fair market value of $18x and the transferred portion of A's interest had a fair market value of $6x.

LAW AND ANALYSIS.

Section 705 of the Internal Revenue Code provides rules for determining the adjusted basis of a partner's interest in a partnership.

Section 722 of the Code provides that the basis of an interest in a partnership acquired by a contribution of property equals the transferor partner's adjusted basis in the contributed property.

Section 752(a) of the Code provides that any increase in a partner's share of the partnership's liabilities is considered to be a contribution of money by the partner to the partnership.

Section 752(b) of the Code provides that any decrease in a partner's share of a partnership's liabilities is considered to be a distribution of money by the partnership to the partner.

Section 1.752–[2 and 3] of the Income Tax Regulations provides rules for determining a partner's share of partnership liabilities with respect to both limited partnerships and general partnerships.

Section 752(d) of the Code provides that in the case of a sale or exchange of an interest in a partnership, liabilities shall be treated in the same manner as liabilities in connection with the sale or exchange of property not associated with partnerships.

Section 1.1001–2 of the regulations provides that the amount realized from a sale or other disposition of property includes the amount of liabilities from which the transferor is discharged as a result of the sale or disposition.

Section 1.61–6(a) of the regulations provides that when a part of a larger property is sold, the basis of the entire property shall be equitably apportioned among the several parts for purposes of determining gain or loss on the part sold.

Consistent with the provisions of Subchapter K of the Code, a partner has a single basis in a partnership interest, even if such partner is both a general partner and a limited partner of the same partnership. See Rev.Rul. 84–52, [1984–1 C.B. 157]. Thus, for example, in applying the limitations of section 704(d) of the Code, losses allocated with respect to a partner's limited partner interest will be allowed so long as they do not exceed the partner's basis in the entire partnership interest.

Under section 1.61–6(a) of the regulations, when a partner makes a taxable disposition of a portion of an interest in a partnership, the basis of the transferred portion of the interest generally equals an amount which bears the same relation to the partner's basis in the partner's entire interest as the fair market value of the transferred portion of the interest bears to the fair market value of the entire interest. However, if such partnership has liabilities, special adjustments must be made to take into account the effect of those liabilities on the basis of the partner's interest.

In cases where the partner's share of all partnership liabilities does not exceed the adjusted basis of such partner's entire interest (including basis attributable to liabilities), the transferor partner shall first exclude from the adjusted basis of such partner's entire interest an amount equal to such partner's share of all partnership liabilities, as determined under section 1.752–[2 and 3] of the regulations. A part of the remaining adjusted basis (if any) shall be allocated to the transferred portion of the interest according to the ratio of the fair market value of the transferred portion of the interest to the fair market value of the entire interest. The sum of the amount so allocated plus the amount of the partner's share of liabilities that is considered discharged on the disposition of the transferred portion of the interest (under section 752(d) of the Code and section 1.1001–2 of the regulations) equals the adjusted basis of the transferred portion of the interest.

On the other hand, if the partner's share of all partnership liabilities exceeds the adjusted basis of such partner's entire interest (including basis attributable to liabilities), the adjusted basis of the transferred portion of the interest equals an amount that bears the same relation to the partner's adjusted basis in the entire interest as the partner's share of liabilities that is considered discharged on the disposition of the transferred portion of the interest bears to the partner's share of all partnership liabilities, as determined under section 1.752–[2 and 3].

HOLDINGS.

Situation 1. Prior to the sale of one-half of B's limited partner interest to A, the adjusted basis of B's entire partnership interest was $50x. Because the fair market value of the transferred portion of B's interest ($16x) is one-half of the fair market value of B's entire partnership interest ($32x), $25x (1/2 of $50x) of adjusted basis must be allocated to the interest transferred by B. B sustained a $9 loss ($16x–$25x) on the sale of A. The adjusted basis of the remainder of B's partnership interest is $25x.

Prior to the sale of one-half of A's general partner interest to C, the adjusted basis of A's entire partnership interest was $66x. Because the fair market value of the transferred portion of A's interest ($30x) is one-third of the fair market value of A's entire partnership interest ($90x), $22x (1/3 of $66x) of the adjusted basis must be allocated to the portion of the interest transferred by A. A realizes an $8x gain ($30x–$22x) on the sale of C. The basis of the remainder of A's partnership interest is $44x. The results would be the same to A if A, instead, sold to C the limited partner interest acquired earlier from B.

Situation 2. The tax consequences of B's sale of one-half of B's limited partner interest to A are identical to those described in *Situation 1.*

In 1981, A's basis in A's entire partnership interest was increase[d] from $66x to $146x as a result of the $80x recourse borrowing (which increases only the basis of A, the sole general partner, under * * * sections 752(a) and 722 of the Code) and was decreased to $86x as a result of the $60x loss allocated to A that year when the securities became worthless. Thus, prior to the sale of one-half of A's general partner interest to C, the adjusted basis of A's entire partnership interest was $86x. To take into account the effect of the liability sharing rules of [the section 752 regulations] on A's adjusted basis, $80x (A's share of all partnership liabilities) is subtracted from $86x, leaving $6x. Because the fair market value of the transferred portion of A's interest ($10x) is one-third of the fair market value of the entire interest ($30x), $2x (1/3 of $6x) of the remaining adjusted basis must be allocated to the transferred portion of A's general partner interest. The sum of that amount ($2x) plus the amount of partnership liabilities from which A is discharged on the disposition of the transferred portion of A's general partner interest ($40), or $42x, equals the adjusted basis of the transferred portion of the interest. A realizes an $8x gain ($10x + $40x − $42x) on the sale to C. The basis of the remainder of A's partnership interest is $44x ($86x − $42).

Situation 3. The tax consequences of B's sale of one-half of B's limited partner interest to A are identical to those described in *Situation 1*.

As in *Situation 2*, prior to the sale of A's limited partner interest to C, the adjusted basis of A's entire partnership interest was $86x. To take into account the effect of the liability sharing rules of section 1.752–[2 and 3] of the regulations on A's adjusted basis, $80x (A's share of all partnership liabilities) is subtracted from $86x, leaving $6x. Because the fair market value of the transferred portion of A's limited partner interest ($10x) is one-third of the fair market value of A's entire interest ($30x), $2x (1/3 of $6x) of the remaining adjusted basis must be allocated to the transferred limited partner interest. The sum of that amount ($2x) plus the amount of partnership liabilities from which A is discharged on the disposition of the transferred limited partner interest ($0x), or $2x, equals the adjusted basis of the transferred portion of the interest. A realizes an $8x gain ($10x − $2x) on the sale to C. The basis of the remainder of A's partnership interest is $84x ($86x − $2x).

Situation 4. The tax consequences of B's sale of one-half of B's limited partner interest to A are identical to those described in *Situation 1*.

In 1981, A's basis in A's entire partnership interest was increased from $66x to $162x as a result of the $96x recourse borrowing and was decreased to $90x as a result of the $72x loss allocated to A that year when the securities became worthless. Thus, prior to the sale of one-half of A's general partner interest to C, the adjusted basis of A's entire partnership interest was $90x. In this situation, A's share of all partnership liabilities ($96x) exceeds the adjusted basis of A's entire interest ($90x). Thus, the adjusted basis of the transferred portion of A's general partner interest equals $45x, the amount which bears the same relation to A's adjusted basis in the entire interest ($90x) as the amount of partnership liabilities from which A is discharged on the disposition of the transferred portion of the general partner interest ($48x) bears to A's share of all partnership liabilities ($96x). A realizes a $9x gain ($48x + $6x − $45x) on the sale of C. The basis of the remainder of A's partnership interest is $45x ($90x − $45x).

DETAILED ANALYSIS

1. TREATMENT OF PARTNERSHIP LIABILITIES

As explained in Rev.Rul. 84–53, § 752(d) requires the selling partner to include the partner's share of partnership liabilities, determined under Treas.Regs. §§ 1.752–2 and 1.752–3, in the amount realized on the sale or exchange of a partnership interest. This treatment corresponds to the inclusion of the partner's share of partnership liabilities in the basis of the partnership interest and incorporates the general tax treatment of the transfer of liabilities on a sale or exchange of property into Subchapter K. Furthermore, § 752(d) includes in the amount realized nonrecourse liabilities in excess of the fair market value of the mortgaged property. Commissioner v. Tufts, 461 U.S. 300 (1983). See also I.R.C. § 7701(g)

Exiting a partnership for release of debt may trigger sale treatment. In Slavin v. Commissioner, T.C. Memo. 1989–221, the taxpayer assigned his 50% partnership interest to the other partner for no cash consideration and was discharged by the partnership's creditors from liability on partnership mortgage indebtedness. The taxpayer argued that the transaction gave rise to discharge of indebtedness income under § 61(a)(11), which was excludable under § 108 because the taxpayer was insolvent. The court found a sale because the debt was not extinguished and was instead assumed by the other partner.

In addition, the courts have expanded the scope of liabilities for this purpose to include some contingent liabilities. In Kornman & Associates v. United States, 527 F.3d 443 (5th Cir. 2008), the court held that an obligation to replace property sold in a short sale represented a liability for purposes of § 752. In a notorious abusive tax shelter transaction, taxpayers would enter into a short sale of some commodity (currency or Treasury notes) then contribute the proceeds of the short sale to a partnership, which would assume the obligation to purchase the commodity and repay the lender of the borrowed commodity. In *Kornman*, the taxpayer sold short Treasury notes and contributed the $102.5 million proceeds and the obligation to replace the Treasury notes to a partnership in exchange for a 99% partnership interest. Subsequently the taxpayer sold the partnership interest for a $1.8 million promissory note from the purchaser and claimed a capital loss based on a $102.5 million basis in the partnership interest. The Fifth Circuit held that the taxpayer's obligation to replace the Treasury notes was a liability includable in amount realized on disposition of the interest. See Treas.Reg. § 1.752–1(a)(4)(ii). Cemco Investors, LLC v. United States, 515 F.3d 749 (7th Cir. 2008), reached the same result on substantially the same facts.

2.   TREATMENT OF PARTNERSHIP INCOME FOR PORTION OF YEAR PRIOR TO SALE OF INTEREST

2.1. *General Principles*

Sales of partnership interests do not result in the termination of the partnership or the closing of the partnership's year, unless a sale (or related sales) result in one person owning all the interests.[1] I.R.C. § 708. Nevertheless, under § 706(c)(2)(A), the partnership's taxable year does close as to the partner who sells the partner's entire interest. As a result, the selling partner must include in income the selling partner's distributive share of the partnership profits of the year up to the date of sale and is thus prevented from obtaining capital gain treatment with respect to partnership profits. This distributive share income is characterized under § 702, discussed in Chapter 18. Under Treas.Reg. § 1.705–1(a)(1), when computing gain or loss realized on the sale of the partnership interest, the selling partner adjusts the partner's basis in the partnership interest as of the date of the sale to reflect the partner's distributive share of partnership income (or loss) so taken into account.

If the partner does not sell the partner's entire partnership interest, the partnership year does not close under § 706(c)(2)(A) with respect to the selling partner. See I.R.C. § 706(c)(2)(B). Instead, § 706(d)(1) applies, requiring that the selling partner's distributive share for the year be determined by taking into account the selling partner's varying interests. See Chapter 20, Section 5. In the case of the sale of a partial interest, only a proportional part of the taxpayer's basis for the entire interest in the partnership, computed as in Rev.Rul. 84–53, is taken into account.

2.2. *Modifications of Partners' Distributive Shares in Connection with the Sale of a Partnership Interest*

Section 706(d)(1) generally prevents retroactive allocations of distributive shares of partnership items to periods pre-dating sale of a partnership interest. Lipke v. Commissioner, 81 T.C. 689 (1983), held that § 706(d)(1) (at that time § 706(c)(2)(B)) disallowed retroactive allocations to continuing partners whose interests were increased as a result of making additional capital contributions late in the year. However, *Lipke* allowed retroactive allocations to continuing partners who did not make any additional capital contributions. There is no readily apparent policy reason for permitting retroactive allocations to partners who do not make an additional capital contribution when retroactive allocations to partners who do make an additional capital contribution are statutorily invalid. Nevertheless, Regulations finalized in 2015 adopted the approach in *Lipke*. Treas.Reg. § 1.706–4(b)(1); see also T.D. 9728 (preamble to the Final Regulations, discussing *Lipke*).

---

[1]   Prior to the 2017 tax legislation, a partnership was considered terminated if 50% or more of the partnership interests in capital and profits were sold within a 12-month period.

3. DISPOSITIONS OTHER THAN SALES

3.1. *Abandonment of a Partnership Interest*

Abandonment of a partnership interest may avoid sale or exchange treatment in appropriate cases. In Citron v. Commissioner, 97 T.C. 200 (1991), the taxpayer was a limited partner in a partnership organized to produce a movie. At a time when the partnership had no net assets (other than the partially completed movie) and no liabilities, the general partner called for additional contributions to complete the movie. The taxpayer, along with the other limited partners, decided not to advance further funds to the partnership, and the limited partners voted to cease operations; the limited partners disavowed their interest in the movie negative, which the general partner thereafter attempted to develop into an X-rated movie. The Tax Court allowed the taxpayer-limited partner a loss deduction under § 165 for the abandonment of a partnership interest, finding sufficient manifestation of the taxpayer's intent to abandon the partnership interest from the taxpayer's affirmative refusal to contribute additional funds and the vote of the limited partners to dissolve the partnership and abandon their interest in the film negative. Ordinary loss treatment was allowed because there was no sale or exchange. The absence of liabilities precluded a deemed distribution under § 752(b) and exchange treatment under § 731(a). Rev.Rul. 93–80, 1993–2 C.B. 239, reaches the same result where the partnership has no liabilities but treats the transaction as a liquidating distribution resulting in capital gain or loss if the partnership has liabilities from which the "abandoning" partner is discharged. Echols v. Commissioner, 935 F.2d 703 (5th Cir.1991), rev'g 93 T.C. 553 (1989), allowed a § 165(a) ordinary loss deduction for the abandonment of a partnership interest by a partner who "walked away" from the partnership, even though the partnership had not abandoned its assets and the partnership property was subject to a mortgage that was not foreclosed upon by the mortgagee until the following year. Under the principles that govern liquidating distributions from partnerships, discussed in Chapter 25, Section 3, *Echols* appears to have been wrongly decided by the Court of Appeals.

3.2. *Gifts*

Release of liabilities may transform a gift of a partnership interest into a taxable sale in part. In Madorin v. Commissioner, 84 T.C. 667 (1985), the taxpayer established a grantor trust of which he was treated as the owner under § 674 because of certain retained powers. The trust acquired a partnership interest and during the period that the partnership reported losses, the taxpayer properly included the trust's distributive share of those losses in his return. When the partnership began to show income, the taxpayer renounced his retained powers, thereby completing the transfer. At that time the trust's share of partnership liabilities exceeded its basis in the partnership interest and the partnership had unrealized receivables. The termination of the grantor trust status was treated as a part-gift/part-sale transaction, applying Treas.Reg. § 1.1001–2(c), Ex. (5), and the gain was characterized as ordinary under § 751. See also Rev.Rul. 75–194, 1975–1 C.B. 80 (applying part-gift/part-sale analysis to charitable contribution of partnership interest where partner's share of debt exceeded basis).

3.3. *Exchanges of Partnership Interests*

Section 1031, which provides nonrecognition for certain exchanges of like-kind real property does not apply to exchanges of partnership interests in partnerships holding eligible like-kind property, unless the partnerships have elected out of Subchapter K pursuant to § 761(a). I.R.C. § 1031(e).

4.   SALE VERSUS LIQUIDATION

While § 741 generally allows capital gain treatment to the selling partner on the sale of a partnership interest, amounts paid in liquidation of a partnership interest sometimes result in ordinary income under § 736(b). Thus, the characterization of the transaction as a "sale" or as a "liquidation" is of crucial importance. See Chapter 25, Section 5.

The sale to the other partner of a partnership interest in a two-person partnership terminates the partnership. When a partnership terminates in this manner, Treas.Reg. § 1.741–1(b) provides that the transferor partner is treated as selling the partnership interest, not an undivided share of the partnership assets, even though McCauslen v. Commissioner, 45 T.C. 588 (1966), held that in such a case the purchaser is treated as having acquired by direct purchase the portion of partnership assets attributable to the acquired partnership interest.

5.   HOLDING PERIOD OF PARTNERSHIP INTEREST

Treas.Reg. § 1.1223–3 deals with the holding period of a partnership interest acquired in separate transactions at different times. Although under Rev.Rul. 84–53, supra, a partner has a single basis in a partnership interest, if components of that interest were acquired at different times the components of the partnership interest will have different holding periods under § 1223. Thus, upon the sale of all or a portion of the partnership interest, it might be necessary to apportion the unitary basis between the part of the transaction that results in short-term capital gain, if any, and the part that results in long-term capital gain, if any. Under the Regulations, any capital gain or loss resulting from the sale of a partnership interest is allocated between long-term and short-term capital gain or loss in the same proportion that the holding period of the interest in the partnership is allocated between the portion of the interest held for more than one year and the portion of the interest held for one year or less. The portion of a partnership interest to which a holding period relates is a percentage that equals: (1) the fair market value of the portion of the partnership interest received in the transaction to which the holding period relates (2) divided by the fair market value of the entire partnership interest, (determined immediately after that transaction). Assume, for example, that in Year 1 B purchased a 1/4 interest in a partnership for $1,000, and in January of Year 3, B purchased an additional 1/4 interest for $5,000. Immediately after the second purchase, B holds a 1/2 interest in the partnership with a fair market value of $10,000 and a basis of $6,000. If B then sells the entire 1/2 partnership interest in July of Year 3 for $14,000, B will recognize an $8,000 gain ($14,000 − [$1,000 + $5,000]). Under the Regulations, 1/2 of this gain, $4,000, will be short-term capital gain and the other 1/2 will be long-term capital gain, even though economically B realized a $6,000 gain on the 1/4 interest purchased in Year 1 and only a $2,000 gain on the 1/4 interest purchased and sold in Year 2.

Under the Regulations, a split holding period also can result when a partner's interest in the partnership is increased as a result of cash contributions. But if a partner both makes cash contributions and receives cash distributions within one year prior to the date of sale of the partnership interest, only the net amount of cash contributions are taken into account in determining the portion of the partnership interest with respect to which the partner has a short-term holding period. Treas.Reg. § 1.1223–3(b)(2). In addition, deemed cash contributions and distributions under § 752(a) and (b) are not taken into account at all in determining whether a partner has a split holding period. Treas.Reg. § 1.1223–3(b)(3).

A selling partner may use the actual holding period of the portion of a partnership interest sold if the partnership is a "publicly traded partnership" (see, Chapter 17, Section 2.A), the partnership interest is divided into identifiable units with ascertainable holding periods, and the selling partner can identify the portion of the interest transferred. The IRS has cautioned taxpayers that it may apply judicial doctrines, e.g., substance over form or step transaction, or Treas.Reg. § 1.701–2 (see Chapter 17, Section 3) to attack abusive transactions designed to shift gain from the portion of a partnership interest with a short-term holding period to the portion with a long-term holding period. See Notice of Proposed Rulemaking, Capital Gains, Partnership, Subchapter S, and Trust Provisions, REG–106527–98, 1999–2 C.B. 304.

B. CAPITAL GAIN VERSUS ORDINARY INCOME: SECTION 751

INTERNAL REVENUE CODE: Sections 1(h)(5)(B), (6)(A), (10); 751(a), (c)–(d); 1061.

REGULATIONS: Sections 1.1(h)–1(a), (b)(1)–(3), (c); 1.751–1(a), (c)(1)–(3), (4)(iii) and (vii), (5), (d)(2), (g), Ex. (1).

Section 741, premised on the entity treatment of a partnership, as a general rule treats a partnership interest as a capital asset, so that its sale results in capital gain or loss. Due to the preferential rate for capital gains, however, this approach presents tax avoidance possibilities. When a sole proprietor sells a business, § 1060 requires that each asset be classified separately as to capital gain or loss and ordinary gain or loss; the business is not regarded as a unitary capital asset.[2] The treatment of a partnership interest as a unitary capital asset would avoid the comminution rule of § 1060, even though some of the partnership assets are ordinary assets, such as inventory or cash method accounts receivable. Accordingly, § 751(a) is designed to limit the tax avoidance possibilities of the general rule of § 741.

---

[2] Prior to the enactment of § 1060, this result was dictated by Williams v. McGowan, 152 F.2d 570 (2d Cir.1945).

Where a partnership has "unrealized receivables" or inventory, a sale or taxable exchange by a partner of a partnership interest is treated on an aggregate approach with respect to the unrealized receivables and inventory. The partner is regarded as having sold pro tanto the partner's interest in each of those ordinary assets.[3] Under Treas.Reg. § 1.751–1(a)(2), gain or loss is determined as if the partnership had sold the unrealized receivables and inventory and distributed to the partner the partner's distributive share of the ordinary income. The items selected, unrealized receivables and inventory, represent the significant ordinary income items held by a business or personal service partnership. Section 741 continues to control the character of the gain or loss recognized with respect to the portion of the partner's basis and the amount realized on the sale of the partnership interest that are not allocable to unrealized receivables and inventory. This bifurcated approach may create ordinary income and a related capital loss, even in instances where a partnership interest is sold at no gain or an overall net loss.

Ledoux v. Commissioner
Tax Court of the United States, 1981.
77 T.C. 293.[*]

■ STERRETT, JUDGE:

Pari-mutuel wagering at greyhound dogracing tracks was legalized in the State of Florida in 1935. Prior to July 1955, the Sanford-Orlando Kennel Club, Inc. (hereinafter referred to as the corporation), held a greyhound racing permit issued by the Florida State Racing Commission to operate a racetrack in Seminole County, Fla. The corporation owned certain land in Seminole County, Fla., and improvements thereon including a grandstand, kennels, track, and other facilities and equipment necessary to operate a racetrack and to handle pari-mutuel pools. * * *

Due to problems in managing the dog track, the Sanford-Orlando Kennel Club copartnership entered into a written agreement (dog track agreement) on July 9, 1955, with Jerry Collins, an experienced operator of dogracing tracks, and his son, Jack Collins. Pursuant to the dog track agreement, the Collinses acquired the right "to manage and operate the Greyhound Racing Track, owned by the Sanford-Orlando Kennel Club, Inc.," for a period of 20 years commencing on October 1, 1955. In return,

---

[3] Section 751(a) does not apply if a partnership interest is disposed of by gift even though the partnership holds unrealized receivables. In Rev.Rul. 60–352, 1960–2 C.B. 208, a partner made a charitable contribution of an interest in a partnership holding § 453 installment obligations. The partner was required to recognize the gain attributable to his share of the partnership's installment obligations. If a § 453 installment obligation is viewed as not substantially different than any other unrealized receivable, this Ruling is not consistent with the mechanics of § 741 and § 751(a). It is however, consistent with the policy of § 453B, and presumably reflects the view that § 453B applies aggregate theory to override §§ 741 and 751.

[*] Aff'd per curiam, 695 F.2d 1320 (11th Cir.1983).

the Collinses agreed to pay to the copartnership the first $200,000 of net annual profit from track operations. * * *

On October 1, 1955, petitioner John W. Ledoux, his father-in-law, Jerry Collins, and his brother-in-law, Jack Collins, entered into a partnership agreement creating a partnership (hereinafter the Collins-Ledoux partnership or partnership) for the stated purpose of "carrying on of the business of managing and operating a greyhound dog racing plant in Seminole County, Florida." * * *

* * *

During the period from October 1, 1955, to September 30, 1972, the Collins-Ledoux partnership operated the greyhound racetrack pursuant to and in accordance with the July 9, 1955, agreement, as amended. Petitioner John W. Ledoux was a manager of the operations of the racetrack for the Collins-Ledoux partnership. Petitioner received compensation for his services in the form of salary, which was charged as an expense of the track operation. Along with his salary, petitioner received a share of the net profits of the Collins-Ledoux partnership. Petitioner's duties included, among other things, the directing of promotional, advertising, and development activities on behalf of the Collins-Ledoux partnership.

* * *

The partnership's actions with respect to operation and management of the dog track were eminently successful. During the period from 1955 to 1972, the gross income from track operations increased from $3.6 million to $23.6 million, and the net income to the Collins-Ledoux partnership increased from $72,000 to over $550,000. The increases in gross and net income were attributable to the work of the partnership, including petitioner, and to the general economic growth in the Central Florida area. Accordingly, the fair value of the right to operate the greyhound racetrack in Seminole County, Fla., pursuant to the racing permit held by the corporation and pursuant to the dog track agreement, increased significantly during the period from 1955 to 1972.

* * *

After the 1972 racing season two of the partners, Jerry Collins and Jack Collins, decided to purchase petitioner's 25-percent partnership interest. They agreed to allow Ledoux to propose a fair selling price for his interest. Ledoux set a price based on a price-earnings multiple of 5 times his share of the partnership's 1972 earnings. This resulted in a total value for his 25-percent interest of $800,000. There was no valuation or appraisal of specific assets at the time, and the sales price included his interest in all of the assets of the partnership.

At the request of Jerry Collins, petitioner drafted a "Memorandum Agreement," which reflected the arm's-length agreement of the parties. The memorandum was submitted to Jerry Collins and his attorney, and after slight revision, was executed by the parties to the sale on July 19, 1972. It stated, in part, that the "Seller agrees to sell his complete interest in the partnership of Collins, Collins, and Ledoux and to give up all rights, benefits, and obligations of the various agreements involved." It also stated that "In the determination of the purchase price set forth in this agreement, the parties acknowledge no consideration has been given to any item of goodwill."

* * *

At the closing, there was no discussion about values of, or allocation to, any specific assets. In fact, no part of the sales price was allocated to any specific partnership asset. At the time of the sale, the partnership assets consisted of an escrow deposit; certain prepaid expenses; a stock investment in Sanford-Seminole Development Co.; investment in land, buildings, and equipment; improvements on the corporation's property used in connection with the operation of the dog track; and rights arising out of the dog track agreement. * * *

On his 1972 Federal income tax return, petitioner properly elected to report the gain from the sale of his partnership interest under the installment method as prescribed in section 453. * * * In each of those years, he characterized the reported gain, calculated pursuant to the installment sales method, as capital gain.

* * *

Respondent, in his notice of deficiency, did not disagree with petitioner's calculation of the total gain. However, he determined that $575,392.50 of the gain was related to petitioner's interest in the dog track agreement and should be subject to ordinary income treatment pursuant to section 751.

OPINION

The sole issue presented is whether a portion of the amount received by petitioner on the sale of his 25-percent partnership interest is taxable as ordinary income and not as capital gain. More specifically, we must decide whether any portion of the sales price is attributable to "unrealized receivables" of the partnership.

Generally, gain or loss on the sale or exchange of a partnership interest is treated as capital gain or loss. Sec. 741. Prior to 1954, a partner could escape ordinary income tax treatment on his portion of the partnership's unrealized receivables by selling or exchanging his interest in the partnership and treating the gain or loss therefrom as capital gain or loss. To curb such abuses, section 751 was enacted to deal with the problem of the so-called "collapsible partnership." See S. Rept. 1622, 83d Cong., 2d Sess. 98 (1954). Section 751 provides, in part, as follows:

SEC. 751.   UNREALIZED RECEIVABLES AND INVENTORY ITEMS.

(a) Sale or Exchange of Interest in Partnership.—The amount of any money, or the fair market value of any property, received by a transferor partner in exchange for all or a part of his interest in the partnership attributable to—

     (1)   unrealized receivables of the partnership * * *

* * *

(c) Unrealized Receivables.—For purposes of this subchapter, the term "unrealized receivables" includes, to the extent not previously includible in income under the method of accounting used by the partnership, any rights (contractual or otherwise) to payment for—

* * *

     (2)   services rendered, or to be rendered. * * *

Petitioner contends that the dog track agreement gave the Collins-Ledoux partnership the right to manage and operate the dog track. According to petitioner, the agreement did not give the partnership any contractual rights to receive future payments and did not impose any obligation on the partnership to perform services. Rather, the agreement merely gave the partnership the right to occupy and use all of the corporation's properties (including the racetrack facilities and the racing permit) in operating its dog track business; if the partnership exercised such right, it would be obligated to make annual payments to the corporation based upon specified percentages of the annual mutuel handle. Thus, because the dog track agreement was in the nature of a leasehold agreement rather than an employment contract, it did not create the type of "unrealized receivables" referred to in section 751.

Respondent, on the other hand, contends that the partnership operated the racetrack for the corporation and was paid a portion of the profits for its efforts. As such, the agreement was in the nature of a management employment contract. When petitioner sold his partnership interest to the Collinses in 1972, the main right that he sold was a contract right to receive income in the future for yet-to-be-rendered personal services. This, respondent asserts, is supported by the fact that petitioner determined the sales price for his partnership interest by capitalizing his 1972 annual income (approximately $160,000) by a factor of 5. Therefore, respondent contends that the portion of the gain realized by petitioner that is attributable to the management contract should be characterized as an amount received for unrealized receivables of the partnership. Consequently, such gain should be characterized as ordinary income under section 751.

The legislative history is not wholly clear with respect to the types of assets that Congress intended to place under the umbrella of "unrealized receivables." The House report states:

> The term "unrealized receivables or fees" is used to apply to any rights to income which have not been included in gross income under the method of accounting employed by the partnership. The provision is applicable mainly to cash basis partnerships which have acquired a contractual or other legal right to income for goods or services. * * * [H. Rept. 1337, 83d Cong., 2d Sess. 71 (1954).]

Essentially the same language appears in the report of the Senate committee. S. Rept. 1622, 83d Cong., 2d Sess. 98 (1954). In addition, the Regulations elaborate on the meaning of "unrealized receivables" as used in section 751. Section 1.751–1(c), Income Tax Regs., provides:

> Sec. 1.751–1(c) Unrealized receivables. (1) The term "unrealized receivables", * * * means any rights (contractual or otherwise) to payment for—
>
> (i) Goods delivered or to be delivered (to the extent that such payment would be treated as received for property other than a capital asset), or
>
> (ii) Services rendered or to be rendered, to the extent that income arising from such rights to payment was not previously includible in income under the method of accounting employed by the partnership. Such rights must have arisen under contracts or agreements in existence at the time of sale or distribution, although the partnership may not be able to enforce payment until a later time. For example, the term includes trade accounts receivable of a cash method taxpayer, and rights to payment for work or goods begun but incomplete at the time of the sale or distribution.

* * *

The language of the legislative history and the regulations indicates that the term "unrealized receivables" includes any contractual or other right to payment for goods delivered or to be delivered or services rendered or to be rendered. Therefore, an analysis of the nature of the rights under the dog track agreement, in the context of the aforementioned legal framework, becomes appropriate. A number of cases have dealt with the meaning of "unrealized receivables" and thereby have helped to define the scope of the term. Courts that have considered the term "unrealized receivables" generally have said that it should be given a broad interpretation. * * * For instance, in *Logan v. Commissioner*, 51 T.C. 482, 486 (1968), we held that a partnership's right in quantum meruit to payment for work in progress constituted an unrealized receivable even though there was no express agreement between the partnership and its clients requiring payment.[5]

In *Roth v. Commissioner*, 321 F.2d 607 (9th Cir.1963), affg. 38 T.C. 171 (1962), the Ninth Circuit dealt with the sale of an interest in a partnership which produced a movie and then gave a 10-year distribution right to Paramount Pictures Corp. in return for a percentage of the gross receipts. The selling partner claimed that his right to a portion of the payments expected under the partnership's contract with Paramount did not constitute an unrealized receivable. The court rejected this view, however, reasoning that Congress "meant to exclude from capital gains treatment any receipts which would have been treated as ordinary income to the partner if no transfer of the partnership interest had occurred." 321 F.2d at 611. Therefore, the partnership's right to payments under the distribution contract was in the nature of an unrealized receivable.

A third example of the broad interpretation given to the term "unrealized receivable" is *United States v. Eidson*, 310 F.2d 111 (5th Cir.1962), revg. an unreported opinion (W.D. Tex. 1961). The court there considered the nature of a management contract which was similar to the one at issue in the instant case. The case arose in the context of a sale by a partnership of all of its rights to operate and manage a mutual insurance company. The selling partnership received $170,000 for the rights it held under the management contract, and the Government asserted that the total amount should be treated as ordinary income. The Court of Appeals agreed with the Government's view on the ground that what was being assigned was not a capital asset whose value had accrued over a period of years; rather, the right to operate the company and receive profits therefrom during the remaining life of the contract was the real subject of the assignment. 310 F.2d at 116. The Fifth Circuit found the Supreme Court's holding in *Commissioner v. P. G. Lake, Inc.*, 356 U.S. 260 (1958), to be conclusive:

> The substance of what was assigned was the right to receive future income. The substance of what was received was the present value of income which the recipient would otherwise obtain in the future. In short, consideration was paid for the right to receive future income, not for an increase in the value of the income-producing property. [356 U.S. at 266, cited in 310 F.2d at 115.]

---

[5] In Hale v. Commissioner, T.C. Memo. 1965–274, we went a step further in dealing with the definition of "unrealized receivable." In that case, we dealt with the situation where a withdrawing partner received real property and a promissory note in exchange for his interest in the partnership assets. One such asset was the right to share in future profits of a real estate development company, which right was conditioned upon the partnership's promise to render future services. We held that the right to future income constituted an unrealized receivable because it was based on the obligation to render future services. The fact that the partnership's development rights had not yet become fixed did not affect the status of the development rights as an unrealized receivable, and did not bar the partner's interest therein from being considered an ordinary income asset.

In *United States v. Woolsey*, 326 F.2d 287 (5th Cir.1963), revg. 208 F. Supp. 325 (S.D.Tex.1962), the Fifth Circuit again faced a situation similar to the one that we face herein. The Fifth Circuit considered whether proceeds received by taxpayers on the sale of their partnership interests were to be treated as ordinary income or capital gain. There, the court was faced with the sale of interests in a partnership which held, as one of its assets, a 25-year contract to manage a mutual insurance company. As in the instant case, the contract gave the partners the right to render services for the term of the contract and to earn ordinary income in the future. In holding that the partnership's management contract constituted an unrealized receivable, the court stated:

> When we look at the underlying right assigned in this case, we cannot escape the conclusion that so much of the consideration which relates to the right to earn ordinary income in the future under the "management contract," taxable to the assignee as ordinary income, is likewise taxable to the assignor as ordinary income although such income must be earned. Section 751 has defined "unrealized receivables" to include any rights, contractual or otherwise, to ordinary income from "services rendered, *or to be rendered*," (emphasis added) to the extent that the same were not previously includable in income by the partnership, with the result that capital gains rates cannot be applied to the rights to income under the facts of this case, which would constitute ordinary income had the same been received in due course by the partnership. * * * It is our conclusion that such portion of the consideration received by the taxpayers in this case as properly should be allocated to the present value of their right to earn ordinary income in the future under the "management contract" is subject to taxation as ordinary income. * * * [326 F.2d at 291.]

Petitioner attempts to distinguish *United States v. Woolsey, supra,* and *United States v. Eidson, supra,* from the instant case * * *. After closely scrutinizing the facts in those cases, we conclude that petitioner's position has no merit. * * *

The dog track agreement at issue in the instant case is similar to the management contract considered by the Fifth Circuit in *Woolsey*. Each gives the respective partnership the right to operate a business for a period of years and to earn ordinary income in return for payments of specified amounts to the corporation that holds the State charter. Therefore, based on our analysis of the statutory language, the legislative history, and the regulations and relevant case law, we are compelled to find that the dog track agreement gave the petitioner an interest that amounted to an "unrealized receivable" within the meaning of section 751(c).

Petitioner further contends that the dog track agreement does not represent an unrealized receivable because it does not require or obligate the partnership to perform personal services in the future. The agreement only gives, the argument continues, the Collins-Ledoux partnership the right to engage in a business.

We find this argument to be unpersuasive. The words of section 751(c), providing that the term "unrealized receivable" includes the right to payment for "services rendered, or to be rendered," do not preclude that section's application to a situation where, as here, the performance of services is not required by the agreement. As the Fifth Circuit said in *United States v. Eidson, supra*:

> The fact that * * * income would not be received by the [partnership] unless they performed the services which the contract required of them, that is, actively managed the affairs of the insurance company in a manner that would produce a profit after all of the necessary expenditures, does not, it seems clear, affect the nature of this payment. It affects only the amount. That is, the fact that the taxpayers would have to spend their time and energies in performing services for which the compensation would be received merely affects the price at which they would be willing to assign or transfer the contract. * * * [310 F.2d at 115.]

Consequently, a portion of the consideration received by Ledoux on the sale of his partnership interest is subject to taxation as ordinary income.

Having established that the dog track agreement qualifies as an unrealized receivable, we next consider whether all or only part of petitioner's gain in excess of the amount attributable to his share of tangible partnership assets should be treated as ordinary income. Petitioner argues that this excess gain was attributable to goodwill or the value of a going concern.

With respect to goodwill, we note that petitioner's attorney drafted, and petitioner signed, the agreement for sale of partnership interest, dated October 17, 1972, which contains the following statement in paragraph 7:

> 7.   In the determination of the purchase price set forth in this agreement, the parties acknowledge no consideration has been given to any item of goodwill.

The meaning of the words "no consideration" is not entirely free from doubt. They could mean that no thought was given to an allocation of any of the sales price to goodwill, or they could indicate that the parties agreed that no part of the purchase price was allocated to goodwill. The testimony of the attorney who prepared the document indicates, however, that he did consider the implications of the sale of goodwill and even did research on the subject. He testified that he believed, albeit incorrectly, that, if goodwill were part of the purchase price, his client would not be entitled to capital gains treatment.

Petitioner attempts to justify this misstatement of the tax implications of an allocation to goodwill not by asserting mistake, but by pointing out that his attorney "is not a tax lawyer but is primarily involved with commercial law and real estate." We find as a fact that petitioner agreed at arm's length with the purchasers of his partnership interest that no part of the purchase price should be attributable to goodwill. The Tax Court long has adhered to the view that, absent "strong proof," a taxpayer cannot challenge an express allocation in an arm's-length sales contract to which he had agreed. See, e.g., *Major v. Commissioner*, 76 T.C. 239, 249 (1981), appeal pending (7th Cir., July 7, 1981); *Lucas v. Commissioner*, 58 T.C. 1022, 1032 (1972). In *Spector v. Commissioner*, 641 F.2d 376 (5th Cir.1981), revg. 71 T.C. 1017 (1979), the Fifth Circuit, to which an appeal in this case will lie, appeared to step away from its prior adherence to the "strong proof" standard and move toward the stricter standard enunciated in *Commissioner v. Danielson*, 378 F.2d 771, 775 (3d Cir.1967), remanding 44 T.C. 549 (1965), cert. denied 389 U.S. 858 (1967). However, in this case, we need not measure the length of the step since we hold that petitioner has failed to introduce sufficient evidence to satisfy even the more lenient "strong proof" standard.

We next turn to petitioner's contention that part or all of the purchase price received in excess of the value of tangible assets is attributable to value of a going concern. In *VGS Corp. v. Commissioner*, 68 T.C. 563 (1977), we stated that—

> Going-concern value is, in essence, the additional element of value which attaches to property by reason of its existence as an integral part of a going concern. * * * [The] ability of a business to continue to function and generate income without interruption as a consequence of the change in ownership, is a vital part of the value of a going concern. * * * [68 T.C. at 591–592; citations omitted.]

However, in the instant case, the ability of the dogracing track to continue to function after the sale of Ledoux's partnership interest was due to the remaining partners' retention of rights to operate under the dog track agreement. Without such agreement, there would have been no continuing right to operate a business and no right to continue to earn income. Thus, the amount paid in excess of the value of Ledoux's share of the tangible assets was not for the intangible value of the business as a going concern but rather for Ledoux's rights under the dog track agreement.

Finally, we turn to petitioner's claim that a determination of the value of rights arising from the dog track agreement has never been made and no evidence of the value of such rights was submitted in this case. We note that the $800,000 purchase price was proposed by petitioner and was accepted by Jack Collins and Jerry Collins in an arm's length agreement of sale evidenced in the memorandum of agreement of July

19, 1972, and the agreement for sale of partnership interest of October 17, 1972. In addition, the October 17, 1972, sales agreement, written by petitioner's attorney, provided in paragraph 1 that the "Seller [Ledoux] sells to buyer [Jerry Collins and Jack Collins] all of his interest in [the partnership] * * * including but not limited to, *the seller's right to income* and to acquire the capital stock of The Sanford-Orlando Kennel Club, Inc." (Emphasis added.) * * *

Based on the provision in the agreement that no part of the consideration was attributable to goodwill, it is clear to us that the parties were aware that they could, if they so desired, have provided that no part of the consideration was attributable to the dog track agreement. No such provision was made.[8] Furthermore, the agreement clearly stated that one of the assets purchased was Ledoux's rights to future income. Considering that petitioner calculated the purchase price by capitalizing future earnings expected under the dog track agreement, we conclude that the portion of Ledoux's gain in excess of the amount attributable to tangible assets was attributable to an unrealized receivable as reflected by the dog track agreement.

Decision will be entered for the respondent.

DETAILED ANALYSIS

1.　DEFINITION OF SECTION 751 "HOT" ASSETS

1.1. *Unrealized Receivables*

1.1.1.　*Future Income and Going Concern Value*

Unrealized receivables are broadly defined in § 751(c) to include any rights to payment for goods delivered or to be delivered or for services rendered or to be rendered, to the extent not previously includible in income. Cash method accounts receivable are the most easily recognized unrealized receivable. In contrast, accrual method accounts receivable, having been included in income when they arose, are not "unrealized." The Tax Court's opinion in *Ledoux,* makes it clear that more items than just cash method accounts receivable give rise to ordinary income under § 751(a). Thus, Logan v. Commissioner, 51 T.C. 482 (1968), which is discussed in *Ledoux,* held, in connection with the sale of a partnership interest in a law firm, that unbilled fees for work in progress constituted unrealized receivables. The taxpayer argued that the partnership had no express contractual rights against the clients and that claims in quantum meruit were not covered by § 751(c). The court held to the contrary, finding a congressional intent for a broad interpretation of § 751(c) and stressing the fact that the partner, if he had remained in the partnership, would have realized ordinary income on the collection of the fees.

As result of the broad definition ascribed to "unrealized receivable" in *Ledoux* and similar cases, § 751(a) can be applied to virtually any

---

[8]　We do not mean to imply that an opposite holding would automatically pertain if a provision had been made with respect to the dog track agreement.

partnership holding valuable contracts to provide personal services. There is a fine line, however, between contractual rights, which may be classified as an unrealized receivable invoking § 751(a), and goodwill and going concern value, which is the present value of the ability of a business to earn income in the future. Miller v. United States, 181 Ct.Cl. 331 (1967), held that a partnership had no unrealized receivables because it merely had the expectancy of continuing to represent a client that generated most of its income. The contract with the client was on a day-to-day basis and cancelable at any time. See also Phillips v. Commissioner, 40 T.C. 157 (1963), and Baxter v. Commissioner, 433 F.2d 757 (9th Cir.1970), both finding no § 751 property where the contracts were cancelable at will or with a short notice period. Aliber v. Commissioner, T.C. Memo. 1987–10, held that accounts receivable representing rights to reimbursement for real estate taxes paid by the partnership on behalf of owners of condominium properties managed by the partnership were not unrealized receivables.

1.1.2.   *Recapture Gain*

As defined in § 751(c), "unrealized receivables" also include gain that would have been treated as ordinary income under the various recapture rules (e.g., § 1245(a)) on the sale of an asset by the partnership. For purposes of § 751, the amount of potential recapture income is treated as an unrealized receivable with a basis of zero. Treas.Reg. § 1.751–1(c)(4), (5). Inclusion of recapture income in the definition of unrealized receivables is significant because it results in the potential applicability of § 751(a) to every sale of a partnership interest in a partnership holding depreciable personalty, such as machinery, equipment, and amortizable § 197 intangible assets, even though the partnership uses the accrual method of reporting and thus has no unrealized accounts receivable. See I.R.C. § 197(f)(7).

1.2. *Inventory*

Section 751(a)(2) requires the selling partner to recognize gain or loss from the disposition of the partner's share of inventory as ordinary income. Under § 751(d)(2), "inventory" includes, in addition to stock in trade, all non-capital assets except depreciable property and land governed by § 1231. In determining whether property is to be classified as inventory, the activities of the selling partner are taken into account. For a series of cases dealing with different partners in the same partnership and reaching different results on the § 751 question as to the status of real property held by the partnership, see Morse v. United States, 371 F.2d 474 (Ct.Cl.1967) (capital asset); Estate of Freeland v. Commissioner, 393 F.2d 573 (9th Cir.1968) (inventory); Ginsburg v. United States, 396 F.2d 983 (Ct.Cl.1968) (capital asset).[4]

---

[4]   Treas.Reg. § 1.751–1(d)(2)(ii) includes within the definition of inventory all accounts receivable, including those of both cash and accrual method taxpayers. Inventory does not include other "unrealized receivables," as defined in § 751(c), such as depreciation recapture. The gain attributable to accounts receivable included in inventory is not taxed twice. Rather, including these items in inventory affects the calculation to determine whether the inventory is substantially appreciated, which is important under § 751(b) applicable to distributions, discussed in Chapter 25.

2.   COMPUTATIONS UNDER SECTION 751(a)

2.1. *In General*

Treas.Reg. § 1.751–1(a)(2) provides that the amount of the § 751(a) gain or loss taxed as ordinary income is the net amount of ordinary income or loss that would have been reflected in the partner's distributive share if the partnership had sold all of its items of § 751 property at fair market value for cash (and assumption of liabilities) immediately before the partner sold the partnership interest. This calculation includes the effect of any remedial allocations to the selling partner under Treas.Reg. § 1.704–3(d), discussed in Chapter 20, Section 3. After calculating the § 751(a) gain or loss, the selling partner's gain or loss on the sale of the partnership interest, recognized as capital gain or loss under § 741, is the difference between the partner's overall gain or loss on disposition of the partnership interest and the amount treated as ordinary under § 751(a).

For example, assume that A sells A's one-third interest in the ABC partnership for $100 and that A's basis in that interest is $75. ABC owns inventory having a value of $210 and a basis of $150, and a capital asset having a value of $90 and a basis of $75. If the partnership were to sell the inventory, A would be allocated $20 of the $60 ordinary income recognized by the partnership. Thus, under § 751(a), A recognizes $20 of ordinary income on the sale of A's partnership interest. A's remaining $5 of gain on the sale of A's partnership interest is taxed as capital gain under § 741. This result is illustrated as follows:

Asset Class	Amount Realized	Basis	Gain/ Loss
Total Transaction	$100	$75	$25
§ 751			$20
§ 741			$ 5

Alternatively, if A had sold the partnership interest for only $90, A again would recognize $20 of ordinary income under § 751(a) attributable to the inventory, but this time the difference between A's overall realized gain of $15, and the amount treated as ordinary income under § 751(a), produces a $5 capital loss under § 741.

Asset Class	Amount Realized	Basis	Gain/ Loss
Total Transaction	$90	$75	$15
§ 751			$20
§ 741			($ 5)

This calculation of ordinary gain or loss is satisfactory where the seller's basis for the partnership interest is equivalent to the seller's pro rata share of partnership basis. But where the seller's basis in the partnership interest differs, for example, as the result of the seller's previous purchase of the partnership interest, the allocated gain or loss attributable to § 751 assets may be different than the selling partner's actual economic gain based on the selling partner's purchase cost attributable to the value of the § 751 assets, unless the partnership has elected to adjust basis pursuant to an election under § 754 (discussed below in Section 2). (A transferee partner receiving a distribution within two years of the purchase may elect to treat the partnership basis of the assets as though an inside basis adjustment reflecting the purchase price of the partnership interest had been made. I.R.C. § 732(d).) For example, suppose that the partnership assets consist of inventory with a zero basis but worth $100,000, and that partner B's basis for B's one-fourth partnership interest is $25,000 because of B's previous purchase of the interest at that price. If B sells the interest for $25,000, B will recognize $25,000 ordinary income and $25,000 capital loss in the absence of an inside basis adjustment. This result can be avoided, however, if a § 743(b) election to adjust basis is in effect, in which case B would have a $25,000 basis for B's interest in the inventory and no gain or loss would be recognized as a result of the sale. Basis adjustments are discussed in Section 2.

2.2. *Loss Situations*

Section 751(a) applies to require recognition of ordinary income even though the partnership interest is not sold at an overall gain. For example, assume that C, with a $150 basis for the partnership interest, sells one-half of a one-half interest, i.e., a one-quarter interest, in CD Partnership for $65. The partnership owns inventory having a basis of $100 and a value of $200 and a § 1231 asset with a basis of $200 and a value of $60. Although C has realized an overall loss of $10, C must fragment that overall loss into $25 of ordinary income and $35 of capital loss. Treas.Reg. § 1.751–1(a)(2).

Asset Class	Amount Realized	Basis	Gain/Loss
Total Transaction	$65	$75	($10)
§ 751			$25
§ 741			($35)

In addition, § 751(a) allows recognition of a selling partner's share of ordinary loss attributable to the partner's interest in loss inventory. Treas.Reg. § 1.751–1(a)(2). Assume that D, with a $150 basis for the partnership interest, sells for $100 one-half of a one-half interest, i.e., a one-quarter interest, in DE Partnership, which owns inventory having a basis of $200 and a value of $160 and a § 1231 asset with a basis of $100 and a value of $240. D has recognized an overall gain of $25, but D can fragment that overall gain into $10 of ordinary loss, reflecting D's allocable share of the loss on a hypothetical sale of the § 751 asset, and $35 of capital gain on the remaining partnership interest.

Asset Class	Amount Realized	Basis	Gain/ Loss
Total Transaction	$100	$75	$25
§ 751			($10)
§ 741			$35

3. INSTALLMENT SALES OF PARTNERSHIP INTERESTS

Gain realized on the sale of a partnership interest for deferred payments may be reported on the installment method under § 453. See Rev.Rul. 76–483, 1976–2 C.B. 131. Section 453 is not difficult to apply as long as a partnership does not hold any property that could not be sold on the installment method if the property were owned and sold directly by the partner. The analysis is more complex, and the existing statutory pattern is unclear, if the partnership holds property that may not be sold on the installment method under § 453 (such as inventory, see § 453(b)(2)(A)).

Denying installment reporting entirely if the partnership holds any assets ineligible for installment treatment is inconsistent with the basic entity theory of § 741, as modified by § 751(a). On the other hand, allowing installment reporting on the full gain in such cases may circumvent the restrictions of § 453. Section 453 itself provides a partial answer in § 453(i)(2), which treats as recapture income ineligible for installment reporting any ordinary income realized on the sale of a partnership interest under § 751 that is attributable to depreciation recapture under § 1245 or § 1250. Thus, any gain on the sale of a partnership interest characterized as ordinary income under § 751(a) and (c) because it represents the selling partner's share of depreciation recapture on the partnership's assets is not eligible for installment reporting. This statutory structure might be read to imply that absent a specific statutory directive, the entity approach is to be applied in the case of installment sales of partnership interests, and only depreciation recapture will be denied installment reporting. On the other hand, § 453(i)(2) was a minor technical correction to the depreciation rules, inserted by the Conference Committee. See H.R.Rep. No. 99–841, 99th Cong., 2d Sess. II–845 (1986). The relative obscurity of this amendment supports an argument that it does not preclude a more comprehensive melding of the policies of §§ 453, 741 and 751 to deny installment reporting with respect to gain attributable to inventory as well. Rev.Rul. 89–108, 1989–2 C.B. 100, held that installment reporting is not available for the gain on the sale of a partnership interest to the extent that the gain is attributed to substantially appreciated inventory and taxed as ordinary income under § 751. Although the ruling is silent as to the treatment of § 741 gain that is attributable to partnership inventory that is not substantially appreciated, after the 1997 amendment to § 751(a) requiring ordinary income treatment for all gain recognized on disposition of the selling partner's interest in inventory, the holding of the ruling would seem to encompass all gain attributable to inventory. The facts of the ruling indicate that the partnership held no unrealized receivables and thus provides no guidance on that issue.

In Mingo v. Commissioner, T.C. Memo. 2013–149, aff'd, 773 F.3d 629 (5th Cir. 2014), the taxpayer sold an interest in a partnership holding cash-method accounts receivable, receiving in exchange a promissory note. The value of the taxpayer's partnership interest was $832,090, of which $126,240 was attributable to the partner's interest in partnership unrealized receivables that were uncollected accounts receivable for services. The Tax Court held that § 453 installment reporting is not available for gains attributable to § 751(c) unrealized receivables that represent uncollected cash-method accounts receivable for services. In affirming, the Fifth Circuit relied on Sorensen v. Commissioner, 22 T.C. 321 (1954), and held that "the proceeds from the unrealized receivables, classified as ordinary income, do not qualify for installment method reporting because they do not arise from the sale of property" for purposes of § 453.

The most logical solution, which would be consistent with the basic structure of the sections involved, but which is without any clear statutory basis, would be to require current recognition of the entire portion of the gain attributable to partnership property ineligible for installment method reporting.

4. DETERMINATION OF APPLICABLE CAPITAL GAINS TAX RATE

4.1. *Generally*

Upon the sale of depreciable real property, under § 1(h)(1)(D) "unrecaptured section 1250 gain," is taxed at a maximum rate of 25%, not the more favorable lower rates otherwise available for gains on § 1231 assets held for more than one year. Unrecaptured § 1250 gain is defined by § 1(h)(6) as any § 1231 gain taxed as capital gain that is attributable to prior depreciation deductions claimed with respect to the property. When a partnership holds depreciable real property, § 1(h)(6)(A) requires that a portion of the amount of long-term capital gain recognized on the sale of an interest in the partnership be characterized as "unrecaptured § 1250 gain," subject to tax at the 25% maximum. Treas.Reg. § 1.1(h)–1(b)(3) provides that upon the sale of a partnership interest held for more than one year, the amount of the gain that would have been ordinary income under § 751(a) if the partnership's unrecaptured § 1250 gain had been ordinary income is treated as unrecaptured § 1250 gain by the selling partner. Thus, the amount of the overall gain that is unrecaptured § 1250 gain equals the amount that would have been the partner's share of unrecaptured § 1250 gain if the partnership had sold all of its § 1250 property in a taxable transaction immediately before the transfer of the partnership interest. If the partner recognizes less than all of the gain upon the sale of the interest, a proportionate part of the gain is treated as unrecaptured § 1250 gain.

Section 1(h)(5)(B) provides that any gain from the sale of an interest in a partnership that has been held for more than one year and that is attributable to unrealized appreciation in the value of collectibles held by the partnership is treated as gain from the sale or exchange of a collectible, taxable at rates up to 28% rather than taxable at a maximum rate of 20%. Rules similar to those of § 751(a) are used to determine the amount of the gain on the sale of a partnership interest that is attributable to collectibles held by the partnership. Treas.Reg. § 1.1(h)–1(b)(2) provides that the amount of collectibles gain equals the collectibles gain that would have been allocated to the selling partner with respect to the portion of the transferred interest if the partnership had sold all of its collectibles in a taxable transaction immediately before the transfer of the interest. If the partner recognizes less than all of the gain upon the sale of the interest, a proportionate part of the gain is treated as collectibles gain.

4.2. *"Carried" Partnership Interest*

Section 1061, added by legislation in 2017, requires that capital gain "with respect to" certain partnership interests be treated as short-term capital gain unless the interest has been held for more than three years. As discussed in Chapter 19, Section 3.A, the receipt of a partnership profits interest in exchange for services is generally not taxed to the recipient. In addition to potentially applying to allocations of capital gains and distributions, as briefly discussed in Chapter 20, § 1061 applies to sales of partnership interests

Section 1061 requires that the partner treat as short-term capital gain the excess (if any) of the partner's net long-term capital gain with respect to the interest over the partner's net long-term capital gain computed as though § 1222 said "3 years" instead of "1 year." This would require, for example, that if a partner sells a covered interest held for only two years, any net long term-capital gain on the transaction would be converted to short-term capital gain. (Section 1061 does not contain rules for coordinating with § 751(a).)

Section 1061 applies only to an "applicable partnership interest," which is any interest that is "directly or indirectly" transferred to or held by a partner "in connection with the performance of substantial services by the partner, or any other related person, in any applicable trade or business." I.R.C. § 1061(c).[5] The definition of "applicable trade or business" will likely make the provision principally relevant to private equity funds, which, not coincidentally, have been the main source of concern regarding the "carried interest loophole," in response to which § 1061 was enacted. Trade or business means "any activity conducted on a regular, continuous, and substantial basis" and that consists of (1) "raising or returning capital" and (2) either (a) investing in, disposing of, or identifying for purposes of investing in or disposing of "specified assets," or (b) developing "specified assets." I.R.C. § 1061(c)(2). The assets specified in the section are securities, commodities, rental or investment real estate, cash or cash equivalents, options or derivatives with respect to any of the above, and interests in a partnership to the extent of the partnership's proportionate interest in any of the above.[6] I.R.C. § 1061(c)(3).

The provision does not apply to a capital interest held by the service partner so long as the capital interest's "right to share in partnership capital" is "commensurate" with either (1) the amount of capital contributed at the

---

[5]   The conversion to short-term capital gain applies "notwithstanding section 83 or any election in effect under section 83(b)."

[6]   The Treasury may provide that § 1061 does "not apply to income or gain attributable to any asset not held for portfolio investment on behalf of third party investors." I.R.C. § 1061(b); see also I.R.C. § 1061(c)(5) (defining "third party investor").

time of receipt or (2) the amount included in income under § 83 on receipt or vesting of the capital interest. I.R.C. § 1061(c)(4)(B). The provision also does not apply to partnership interests "held by a corporation." I.R.C. § 1061(c)(4)(A). The IRS has issued a notice stating that the "Treasury Department and the IRS intend that [the] regulations will provide that the term 'corporation' for purposes of section 1061(c)(4)(A) does not include an S corporation." Notice 2018–18, 2018–12 IRB 443.

Section 1061 also requires recognition of short-term capital gain on the direct or indirect transfer of the covered interest to certain related parties. The amount required to be included is the partner's share of long-term capital gains for the taxable year of the transfer "attributable to the sale or exchange of any asset held for not more than 3 years," minus the amount treated as short-term capital gain with respect to the transfer of such interest. A person is related to a partner if either the person is within the taxpayer's family (as defined in § 318(a)(1)) or "the person performed a service within the current calendar year or the preceding three calendar years in any applicable trade or business in which or for which the taxpayer performed a service." I.R.C. § 1061(d)(2).

5. TIERED PARTNERSHIPS

Section 751(f) prevents the use of tiered partnerships to avoid § 751 by holding business assets in a lower-tier partnership. When a partner in an upper-tier partnership sells the partnership interest, § 751(f) requires looking through the upper-tier partnership to the assets of the lower-tier partnership to apply § 751. Thus, the partner selling an interest in an upper-tier partnership must recognize the partner's distributive share of gain attributable to assets held by a lower-tier partnership.

6. CORPORATE DISTRIBUTIONS

Section 761(e) treats any distribution of a partnership interest by a corporation or a trust as an exchange for purposes of § 708 (relating to continuation of a partnership) and § 743 (relating to optional basis adjustments). Section 761(e) also authorizes the Treasury Department to promulgate Regulations treating such a distribution as an exchange for purposes of § 751 but, as of yet, no such Regulations have been promulgated. In the absence of Regulations, the application of § 751 to a corporate dividend distribution of an interest in a partnership with unrealized receivables and/or inventory depends on whether the fair market value of the distributed interest exceeds basis. If the distribution is nonliquidating and the fair market value of the partnership interest exceeds its basis to the corporation, § 751 applies because § 311(b) treats the distribution as a sale or exchange of the property by the corporation. But if the fair market value of the distributed partnership interest is less than its basis, § 311(a) does not treat the distribution as a sale or exchange, and § 751 presumably does not apply even though the partnership holds unrealized receivables or substantially appreciated inventory. Section 336 treats all corporate distributions in liquidation of a corporation as a sale or exchange, so § 751 applies to these distributions.

In Holiday Village Shopping Center v. United States, 773 F.2d 276 (Fed.Cir.1985), a corporation liquidated and distributed its interest in a limited partnership that held § 1250 property. On the facts, § 751 did not apply. The court disregarded the partnership and treated the distribution as a distribution of the underlying partnership property directly by the corporation, reflecting an aggregate approach that cannot be reconciled with the entity approach governing dispositions of partnership interests where § 751 does not apply.

PROBLEM SET 1

1.   Blake is a general partner in the BCD limited partnership; Charlie and Dave are limited partners. Blake's interest is 20%, and Charlie's and Dave's interests are each 40%. The basis of Blake's general partnership interest is $200, and its fair market value is $300. Each of Charlie and Dave has a $400 basis in their partnership interests, which are worth $600. The partnership has no debts and distributes all of its taxable income currently.

    (a)   Blake buys one-half of Charlie's limited partnership interest for $300. What are the tax consequences to Charlie?

    (b)   Blake buys all of Charlie's limited partnership interest for $600, following which Blake sells all of the general partnership interest to Dave for $300. What are the tax consequences to Blake?

    (c)   Blake buys all of Charlie's limited partnership interest for $600, following which Blake sells all of the limited partnership interest to Elvis for $600. What are the tax consequences to Blake?

2.   Ernesto and Fran are general partners in the EF partnership. Ernesto contributed $1,000 for his one-third partnership interest in profits and loss. Fran contributed $2,000 for a two-thirds partnership interest in profits and loss. The partnership borrowed $1,200 to invest in marketable securities, which it purchased for $4,200. When the partnership assets had appreciated to $4,800, Ernesto sold one-half of his general partnership interest to Gary for $600 cash. What is the tax consequence to Ernesto of the sale?

3.   Ken owns a one-third interest in the KLM Partnership, which develops real estate. The partnership both constructs real estate for sale to customers and holds real estate for rental purposes.

    (a)   KLM uses the cash method of accounting. The bases and values of the partnership assets and partners' interests are as follows:

Asset	Adjusted Basis	F.M.V.		Adjusted Basis	F.M.V.
Cash	$ 45,000	$ 45,000	K	$110,000	$180,000
Accounts			L	$110,000	$180,000
Receivable	$ 0	$ 60,000	M	$110,000	$180,000
Store Building					
(for sale)	$150,000	$180,000			
Office Building					
(for rent)	$135,000	$240,000			
Goodwill, etc.	$ 0	$ 15,000			
	$330,000	$540,000		$330,000	$540,000

What are the tax consequences to Ken if, on January 1st, Ken sells his partnership interest to Niki for $180,000 in cash?

(b)　KLM uses the cash method of accounting. The bases and values of the partnership assets and partners' interests are as follows:

Asset	Adjusted Basis	F.M.V.		Adjusted Basis	F.M.V.
Cash	$ 45,000	$ 45,000	K	$190,000	$180,000
Accounts			L	$190,000	$180,000
Receivable	$ 0	$ 60,000	M	$190,000	$180,000
Store Building					
(for sale)	$150,000	$180,000			
Office Building					
(for rent)	$375,000	$240,000			
Goodwill, etc.	$ 0	$ 15,000			
	$570,000	$540,000		$570,000	$540,000

What are the tax consequences to Ken if, on January 1st, Ken sells his partnership interest to Niki for $180,000 in cash?

(c)　KLM use the accrual method of accounting. The assets and partners' capital accounts of the KLM Partnership are as follows:

Asset	Adjusted Basis	Capital F.M.V.	Accounts	Adjusted Basis	F.M.V.
Cash	$ 45,000	$ 45,000	K	$130,000	$180,000
Accounts			L	$130,000	$180,000
Receivable	$ 60,000	$ 60,000	M	$130,000	$180,000
Store					
Building					
(for sale)	$150,000	$180,000			
Office					
Building					
(for rent)	$135,000	$240,000			
Goodwill, etc.	$ 0	$ 15,000			
	$390,000	$540,000		$390,000	$540,000

What are the tax consequences to Ken if on January 1st, Ken sells his partnership interest to Niki for $180,000 in cash?

4.   Oliver and Pam are equal members in the OP LLC. The LLC has a concession to operate a marina on a lake in a national park. The OP LLC uses the accrual method of accounting. The marina is very profitable, and each member earns and withdraws over $100,000 annually. The assets that the LLC carries on its books are as follows:

Asset	Adjusted Basis	F.M.V.
Cash	$ 50,000	$ 50,000
Inventory	$ 40,000	$ 50,000
Marina	$250,000	$500,000
Rental Boats	$ 60,000	$100,000

All of the gain inherent in the rental boats is § 1245 gain; none of the gain inherent in the marina is § 1245 gain. Pam's basis for her interest in the OP LLC is $200,000. Pam sold her interest in the OP LLC to Quinn for $600,000 in cash, which is $250,000 more than the fair market value of one-half of the tangible assets. How much of Pam's gain is ordinary income under § 751? Does it matter how the intangible assets of the OP LLC are characterized, e.g., goodwill versus concession rights?

5.   Ralph and Sandy are equal general partners in a funeral home business. The RS Partnership reports income from sales of caskets on the accrual method and income from services on the cash method. The assets of the RS Partnership, including goodwill, are as follows:

Asset	Adjusted Basis	F.M.V.
Cash	$ 20,000	$ 20,000
Accounts Receivable	$ 20,000	$ 50,000
Inventory	$ 50,000	$ 70,000
Funeral Home	$150,000	$200,000
Equipment	$ 60,000	$100,000
Goodwill	$ 0	$ 60,000

All of the gain inherent in the equipment is § 1245 gain; none of the gain inherent in the funeral home is § 1245 gain. Ralph's basis for his interest in the RS Partnership is $150,000. Ralph sold his interest in the partnership to Sandy for $520,000, of which $130,000 was payable at the closing. The remaining $390,000, with adequate interest, was due two years later. To what extent may Ralph report the sale using the § 453 installment method?

SECTION 2.   THE PURCHASER'S SIDE OF THE TRANSACTION: BASIS ASPECTS

INTERNAL REVENUE CODE: Sections 742; 743(a)–(d); 752(a); 754; 755; 761(e).

REGULATIONS: Sections 1.197–2(g)(3), (h)(12)(v); 1.704–1(b)(2)(iv)(*l*); 1.742–1; 1.743–1(a)–(e), (j)(1)–(3), (4)(i)(A) and (B), (ii)(A) and (B); 1.752–1(d); 1.754–1; 1.755–1(a) and (b)(1)–(3).

Section 742 provides that a person buying an interest in a partnership has a basis for the partnership interest equal to its cost. "Cost" in this context includes not only the amount paid to the selling partner, but, as a result of § 752(d), the purchasing partner's share of partnership liabilities, determined under Treas.Regs. §§ 1.752–2 and 1.752–3. The purchasing partner's concern, however, is not limited to the basis of the partnership interest. The purchasing partner's share of basis in partnership assets is important to determine the amount of gain or loss recognized by the purchasing partner on a subsequent sale of the assets or the amount of depreciation allowable to the purchasing partner with respect to the assets. As a general matter, § 743(a) provides that the basis of partnership assets is not adjusted as a result of a sale or exchange of a partnership interest. However, on an elective basis, § 743(b) provides for adjustments to the basis of partnership assets to reflect the price paid by the purchasing partner. Once again, Subchapter K adopts a dual approach, with the general rule under § 743(a) being the entity approach, but aggregate treatment being permitted under § 743(b) at the election of the partnership.

For example, suppose the ABC partnership has inventory worth $1,500 with a basis of $600, and other assets worth $3,000 with a basis of $3,000. A sells A's one-third interest to D for $1,500. The partnership now sells the inventory for $1,500. The partnership would have a $900 profit and B, C, and D would each be taxed on ordinary income of $300. But economically D has not realized any profit, since D in effect paid $500, the fair market value, for D's share of the inventory. The entity approach of § 743(a) would require D to recognize D's $300 distributive share of the partnership's ordinary gain. Sections 743(b) and 755 avoid this result by allowing the partnership to elect under § 754 to apply an aggregate approach that provides D with a special upward adjustment in the basis of the partnership inventory to reflect D's $500 cost. Although the adjustment applies to "partnership property," the adjustment is applied only with respect to the transferee partner; it does not affect the "inside" basis of the other partners. Thus, the upward adjustment in the basis of partnership inventory to $500 reduces only D's share of the partnership gain. In broad terms, the purpose of § 743(b) is to put the partner who purchases a partnership interest in the same tax position the partner would have occupied if the partner had purchased a proportionate share of the assets directly and contributed the purchased assets to the partnership.

Section 743(b) can be a two-way street. If a purchasing partner's proportionate share of the basis in the partnership assets is greater than the amount paid for the partnership interest, a § 754 election would require a downward adjustment in the basis of partnership property under § 743(b). Furthermore, § 743(d) requires adjustments under § 743(b) to the basis of the partnership's assets whenever (1) the aggregate basis of the partnership's assets exceeds the aggregate fair market value of the partnership's assets by more than $250,000, even if the adjustment with respect to the purchasing partner will not exceed $250,000, or (2) if "the transferee partner would be allocated a loss of more than $250,000 if the partnership assets were sold for cash equal to their fair market value immediately after such transfer."

The desirability of a § 754 election from the point of view of the incoming partner is generally a function of whether the partnership assets have increased or declined in value. Since the election, once made, generally is irrevocable and applies to a number of different situations, it is difficult to generalize as to when it is appropriate for a particular partnership. A § 754 election that was made because it was advantageous at the time may haunt the partnership in the future by resulting in a reduction of basis for partnership assets. In addition, some partnerships that experience frequent changes in partner personnel might find the aggregate approach that the election provides too bothersome a complication. On the other hand, from the point of view of an incoming partner, it may be important that the partner have a commitment from the partnership to make the requisite election or else the basis adjustment that the incoming partner may desire will not be available. Even if the partnership does not make a § 754 election, § 732(d) provides a special basis rule akin to § 743(b) with respect to partnership assets distributed in kind to a buying partner within two years from the date of purchase (see Chapter 25, Section 1.B).

DETAILED ANALYSIS

1. COMPUTATION OF BASIS ADJUSTMENTS UNDER SECTION 743(b)

1.1. *General*

Sections 743(b) and 755 allow the partnership to adjust the basis of the partnership assets upon the transfer of a partnership interest by sale or upon the death of a partner.[7] This basis adjustment is solely for the benefit of the transferee. Treas.Regs. §§ 1.743–1 and 1.755–1(a) and (b) provide detailed rules for computing the amount of the aggregate § 743(b) basis adjustment and allocating the adjustment among the partnership's assets. The goal of

---

[7] In *Mushro v. Commissioner*, 50 T.C. 43 (1968) (nonacq.), the receipt of insurance proceeds by the deceased partner's wife was treated as payment by the remaining partners for the deceased partner's partnership interest and hence a § 743 basis adjustment was allowed.

the Regulations is to provide a transferee partner with a basis in the partnership's assets for purposes of computing that partner's distributive share of future partnership items that reflects the transferee partner's cost of acquisition.

The amount of the aggregate § 743(b) adjustment is the difference between the transferee's basis in the partnership interest and the transferee's "proportionate share of the adjusted basis of the partnership property." Under Treas.Reg. § 1.743–1, the transferee partner's share of the adjusted basis of the partnership property (inside basis) equals the sum of (1) the transferee partner's interest as a partner in the partnership's "previously taxed capital," plus (2) the transferee partner's share of partnership liabilities. The starting point for determining the transferee partner's share of the partnership's previously taxed capital is a hypothetical transaction in which the partnership is assumed to have sold all of its assets for cash (plus assumption of liabilities) equal to the fair market value of the assets immediately after the transfer of the partnership interest, but without taking into account any existing § 743(b) adjustments. The transferee partner's share of the partnership's previously taxed capital is then equal to (1) the amount of cash that the transferee partner would have received on liquidation of the partnership immediately following the hypothetical sale of the partnership's assets, increased by (2) the amount of tax loss that would have been allocated to the transferee from the hypothetical transaction, and decreased by (3) the amount of tax gain that would have been allocated to the transferee from the hypothetical transaction.

For example, suppose that the ABC Partnership has two assets, Blackacre and Whiteacre (both of which are § 1231 assets). Blackacre has a fair market value of $3,000 and a basis of $1,800; Whiteacre has a value of $5,400 and a basis of $3,600. A sells a one-third interest to D for $2,800 and the partnership makes a § 754 election. Before the adjustment, D's share of the partnership's previously taxed capital is $1,800, computed as follows: If the BCD Partnership sold Blackacre and Whiteacre for their fair market values, the partnership would receive $8,400 of cash and, upon an immediate liquidation of the partnership, $2,800 of cash would be distributed to D. The partnership also would recognize gain of $3,000: $1,200 on Blackacre and $1,800 on Whiteacre. One-third of this gain, $1,000, would be allocated to D. D's interest in previously taxed capital is equal to the amount of cash D would receive in the hypothetical liquidation, $2,800, minus D's share of hypothetical gain, $1,000, which equals $1,800. D's special § 743(b) basis adjustment is $1,000—the excess of D's $2,800 basis in the partnership interest over D's $1,800 interest in previously taxed capital.

Under the Regulations, as long as the partnership has neither previously made any special allocations nor holds any property to which § 704(c) applies, if the purchaser pays a price for the partnership interest at least equal to the proportionate fair market value of the partnership's assets, the purchasing partner's share of inside basis will equal the aggregate inside basis of the partnership's assets multiplied by the partner's percentage interest (as is the case in the example above). See Treas.Reg. § 1.743–1(g)(5), Ex. There are situations, however, where application of § 704(c) or differential allocations of partnership items will eliminate this proportional relationship. In determining a partner's "previously taxed capital," the hypothetical allocations of gain and loss are necessary to account for any § 704(c)(1)(A) items that would have been allocated to the transferee partner as a result of stepping into the shoes of the transferor partner under Treas.Reg. § 1.704–3(a)(7), as well as any remedial allocations to the transferor partner. Prior special allocations to the selling partner under § 704(b) also are taken into account because the buyer succeeds to the seller's capital account pursuant to Treas.Reg. § 1.704–1(b)(2)(iv)(*l*).

The following example illustrates the application of § 743(b) where § 704(c) allocations are required. Assume that E contributed nondepreciable property with a fair market value of $100 and an adjusted basis of $10, and F and G each contributed $100 of cash to the EFG partnership, in which each of them received a one-third interest. E's share of the partnership's basis in the partnership property is $10, and F and G's shares are each $100. When the contributed property has appreciated in value to $130, E sells E's partnership interest to H for $110. H's § 743(b) basis adjustment is $100. H's share of inside basis is $10, computed as follows: the $110 that would be distributable to H following a hypothetical sale of the partnership's assets for cash, decreased by the sum of the $90 of § 704(c) gain and the $10 of § 704(b) gain that would have been allocated to H's interest. The $100 adjustment is the difference between H's $110 outside basis and H's $10 share of inside basis.

For further examples of the application of these rules, see Treas.Reg. § 1.743–1(d)(3).

1.2. *Allocation Among Partnership Assets*

1.2.1.   *General Principles*

After the aggregate amount of the partner's basis adjustment is determined under § 743(b), the basis adjustment is allocated among the various assets of the partnership, including goodwill, by the rules of § 755. First, the adjustment is divided into two portions: (1) a portion attributable to § 1231(b) assets and capital assets ("capital gain property") and (2) a portion attributable to other types of property ("ordinary income property"). In general, the amount of the aggregate adjustment allocated to the ordinary income property is the amount of gain or loss that would have been allocated to the purchasing partner on the hypothetical sale by the partnership of the ordinary income property. The amount of the adjustment allocated to the capital gain property is the net § 743(b) adjustment minus the adjustment to the ordinary income property. Treas.Reg. § 1.755–1(b).

Section 1231 properties with § 1245 recapture are treated as two separate assets. Treas.Reg. § 1.755–1. The portion of any gain that is § 1245 recapture is treated as a zero basis ordinary income property. Thus, any adjustment attributable to gain that would be § 1245 recapture is assigned to the ordinary income category. The remaining value of the § 1231 property, to which all of the original basis is attributed, is treated as a capital asset. Most often, all of the excess of the fair market value of equipment over its adjusted basis represents § 1245 recapture, and the adjustment in the basis of the asset will be part of the ordinary income class. To the extent a partnership holds amortizable § 197 intangibles, however, there is a greater likelihood that the asset may be appreciated beyond its recomputed basis and, thus, that its basis will be adjusted in two steps—in part as a constituent of the ordinary income group and in part as a constituent of the capital asset group.

If the assets of the partnership constitute a trade or business, a portion of the basis adjustment often will have to be allocated to partnership goodwill and other § 197 intangibles, (e.g., customer lists, licenses, franchises, trademarks, trade names, advantageous contracts, etc.). In applying the apportionment rules of Treas.Reg. § 1.755–1, the fair market value of the partnership's § 197 intangibles, including goodwill and going concern value, must be determined using the residual method required by § 1060 for applicable asset acquisitions. Pursuant to Treas.Reg. § 1.755–1(a)(5), § 197 intangibles are valued by applying the following procedure. First, the partnership determines the value of all of its assets other than § 197 intangibles. Second, the partnership determines the "partnership gross value." Generally speaking, "partnership gross value" is the amount that, if assigned to all partnership property, would result in a liquidating distribution to the transferee partner equal to that partner's basis (reduced by the amount, if any, of the partner's basis that is attributable to partnership liabilities) in the transferred partnership interest immediately following the acquisition. For most § 743(b) basis adjustments, the benchmark for determining the gross partnership value is the amount paid for a transferred partnership interest. Third, the partnership determines the value of its § 197 intangibles under the residual method, i.e., the value of § 197 intangibles equals the partnership gross value minus the value of partnership assets other than § 197 intangibles. If the aggregate value of partnership property other than § 197 intangibles is equal to or greater than the partnership gross value, all § 197 intangibles are treated as having zero value. If there is any value assigned to the § 197 intangibles, that value is allocated among § 197 intangibles other than goodwill and going concern value before any value is assigned to goodwill and going concern value. In allocating values and basis to § 197 intangibles, value is assigned first to those § 197 intangibles (other than goodwill and going concern value) that would produce § 751(c) flush language unrealized receivables (i.e., those that have been previously amortized or depreciated, to the extent of their basis and the unrealized receivable amount), then among all § 197 intangibles (other than goodwill and going concern value) relative to fair market value, and, finally, to goodwill and going concern.

In simpler terms, if a partner pays more for a partnership interest than the fair market value of all of the tangible and intangible assets other than goodwill and going concern, the excess of the purchase price over the fair market value of the assets other than goodwill and going concern must be allocated to goodwill and going concern.

The operation of the basic rules of § 755 is illustrated in the following example. Suppose that the ABC Partnership has three assets: a capital asset having a fair market value of $3,000 and a basis of $1,800; a depreciable

§ 1231 asset (not subject to § 1245 recapture because it is real estate) having a value of \$5,400 and a basis of \$3,600; and inventory having a value of \$3,000 and an adjusted basis of \$1,500. A sells A's one-third interest to D for \$3,800, and the partnership makes a § 754 election. Under the rules of Treas.Reg. § 1.743–1, D's share of the partnership's basis in its assets is \$2,300, and D's § 743(b) special basis adjustment is \$1,500 (\$3,800—\$2,300). If no § 743(b) adjustment were made and the ordinary income asset (the inventory) was sold by the partnership, D's share of the gain would be \$500. Thus, under Treas.Reg. § 1.755–1(b)(2), \$500 of the overall adjustment is allocated to the inventory. The remaining \$1,000 of the adjustment is allocated to the capital asset class (the capital and the § 1231 asset). The \$1,000 adjustment that is allocated to a particular class of assets is allocated among the assets in the class under Treas.Reg. § 1.755–1(b)(3) according to a formula that generally results in allocating to each asset within the class an adjustment equal to the amount of gain or loss that would be allocated to the transferee partner, D, upon a sale of the assets. Thus, a \$400 positive adjustment is allocated to the capital asset and a \$600 positive adjustment is allocated to the § 1231 asset. These basis adjustments are added to D's proportionate share of the partnership's basis in its assets solely for purposes of computing D's distributive share of partnership gain, loss, and depreciation. D's special basis in the partnership assets is illustrated in the following computation.

Asset	D's share of Partnership Basis Before Adjustment	+ Adjustment =	D's Special § 743(b) Basis
Capital Asset	\$ 600	\$400	\$1,000
§ 1231 Asset	\$1,200	\$600	\$1,800
Inventory	\$ 500	\$500	\$1,000

As far as B and C are concerned, however, the basis of the partnership property remains unchanged.[8]

Even though on its face § 755 allocates either a positive or negative § 743(b) adjustment between the class of assets consisting of capital assets and § 1231 assets and the class consisting of all other assets, the Regulations provide that one class of property may be allocated a negative adjustment while the other class of property is allocated a positive adjustment, with the two opposite signed adjustments netting out to an amount equal to the overall § 743(b) adjustment. See Treas.Reg. § 1.755–1(b)(2)(ii), Ex. (1).

---

[8]   In Rev.Rul. 79–92, 1979–1 C.B. 180, a § 754 election was in effect and, as a result, under § 743(b) one partner had a higher basis in partnership assets than the other partners. The Ruling held that if the partnership sold the assets for deferred payments and the partner with the higher basis realized a loss while the other partners realized a gain, the other partners could report the gain on the installment method under § 453.

Assume for example, that the EFG Partnership, in which E, F, and G are equal partners (and to which each contributed an equal amount of cash), held the following assets.

Asset Class	Basis	F.M.V.
Capital Gain Assets		
§ 1231 Asset	$3,000	$ 9,000
Ordinary Income Assets		
Inventory	$4,500	$ 1,500
	$7,500	$10,500

H purchases G's interest for $3,500. H's § 743(b) basis adjustment is $1,000 ($3,500 − $2,500). If no § 743(b) adjustment were made, on sale of the partnership's assets H would be allocated a $2,000 gain on the sale of the § 1231 asset ([$9,000 − $3,000] ÷ 3) and a $1,000 loss on the sale of inventory ([$1,500 − $4,500] ÷ 3). If a § 754 election is in effect, a negative adjustment of $1,000 is allocated to the class of ordinary income assets and a positive adjustment of $2,000 ($1,000 − ($1,000)) is allocated to the class of capital gain assets. Since there is only one asset in each class in this example, no question arises regarding allocation of the class adjustment among assets within each class.

Basis adjustments also are allowed when, as a result of offsetting increases and decreases in value, the net § 743(b) adjustment is zero. Assume for example, that the AB Partnership, in which A and B are equal partners (and to which each contributed an equal amount of cash), held the following assets.

Asset Class	Basis	F.M.V.
Capital Gain Assets		
§ 1231 Asset	$3,000	$6,000
Ordinary Income Assets		
Inventory	$6,000	$3,000
	$9,000	$9,000

If C buys A's 50% partnership interest for $4,500, the net § 743(b) basis adjustment is zero. Nevertheless, if a § 754 election is in effect, C is allocated a positive basis adjustment of $1,500 with respect to the § 1231 asset, increasing C's special basis from $1,500 to $3,000. Simultaneously, C is allocated a negative basis adjustment of $1,500 with respect to the inventory asset, decreasing C's special basis from $3,000 to $1,500. See Treas.Reg. § 1.755–1(b)(2)(ii), Ex. (2).

1.2.2.   *Situations Involving Section 704(c) Allocations*

Now consider the situation in which the purchasing partner acquires a partnership interest from a selling partner to whom a § 704(c) allocation would have been made with respect to one partnership asset, while a continuing partner would receive a § 704(c)(1)(C) adjustment with respect to a different asset. Assume that the JK Partnership, in which J and K are equal partners, was formed by J's contribution of Blackacre, a capital asset that had a fair market value of $4,000 and a basis of $1,000 at the time of the contribution, and K's contribution of Whiteacre, a § 1231 asset that had a fair market value of $4,000 and a basis of $5,000 at the time of the contribution. L purchased J's partnership interest for $5,500 when the partnership held the following assets.

Asset Class	Basis	F.M.V.
Capital Gain Assets		
Blackacre	$ 1,000	$ 8,000
Whiteacre	$ 4,000[9]	$ 3,000

If no § 743 adjustment were made, on sale of the partnership's assets, after taking into account allocations that would have been required by § 704(c), L would be allocated a $5,000 gain on the sale of Blackacre ($3,000 of § 704(c) gain + [($8,000 − $4,000) ÷ 2]), and a $500 loss on the sale of Whiteacre. L's § 743(b) basis adjustment is thus $4,500. A positive basis adjustment of $5,000 is allocated to Blackacre, giving L a special basis in Blackacre of $6,000, and a negative basis adjustment of $500 is allocated to Whiteacre, effectively giving L a special basis in Whiteacre of $1,500.

Asset	L's share of Partnership Basis Before Adjustment	+ Adjustment =	L's Special § 743(b) Basis
Blackacre	$1,000	$5,000	$6,000
Whiteacre	$2,000	($ 500)	$1,500

Upon the subsequent sale by the partnership of Blackacre for $8,000, L will recognize no gain, while K will recognize a gain of $2,000. Upon the subsequent sale of Whiteacre for $3,000, L will recognize no loss, while K will recognize a $1,500 total tax loss because K would have a $1000 § 704(c)(1)(C) basis adjustment. See Treas.Reg. § 1.755–1(b)(2)(ii), Ex. (1).

When § 704(c) allocations are involved, the purchasing partner's special basis will not be proportionate to the fair market value of the assets; the purchasing partner's basis will be higher than proportionate fair market value if an allocation of § 704(c) gain would have been made to the purchasing partner absent a § 743(b) adjustment, and it will be lower than proportionate fair market value if other partners have § 704(c)(1)(C) basis adjustments.

---

[9]   The partnership's basis is $4,000 following the Proposed Regulations relating to § 704(c)(1)(C). See discussion in Chapter 20. K would have a § 704(c)(1)(C) adjustment (modeled on the § 743 adjustment) to use on the sale of Whiteacre to increase K's tax loss by $1000.

1.2.3. *Technical Aspects of the Apportionment Formula: Allocation to Specific Assets*

In general, the allocation of § 743(b) adjustments between the classes of ordinary income and capital asset properties and among assets within a class of properties depends on the gain or loss that would be allocated to the purchasing partner on a hypothetical sale of the assets for fair market value at the time of the purchase. The general rule for apportioning the § 743(b) basis adjustment between ordinary income assets and capital gain assets is subject to one significant limitation. Treas.Reg. § 1.755–1(b)(2)(i)(B) provides that a negative adjustment to capital gain property may not exceed the partnership's basis in its capital gain property. If a decrease in basis allocated to capital gain property exceeds the partnership's basis in that property, the excess negative adjustment is applied to reduce the basis of ordinary income property.

The formula provided in Treas.Reg. § 1.755–1(b)(3) for the allocation of § 743(b) adjustments to specific assets within a class of property is multi-faceted and varies for ordinary income and capital gains assets in order to account for the limitation on the adjustment to the basis of capital assets under Treas.Reg. § 1.755–1(b)(2)(i). The basis adjustment to each ordinary income asset equals:

> (1) the amount of income, gain, or loss (including remedial allocations under Treas.Reg. § 1.704–3(d)) that would be allocated to the purchasing partner on the hypothetical sale of the item, minus

> (2) any reduction of basis adjustment to ordinary income property required under Treas.Reg. § 1.755–1(b)(2)(i) because the partnership did not have enough basis in capital gain property to reduce, multiplied by a fraction, the numerator of which is the fair market value of the asset whose basis is being adjusted and the denominator of which is the total fair market value of all of the partnership's ordinary income assets.

The amount subtracted under part (2) of this formula will be zero unless the limitation of Treas.Reg. § 1.755–1(b)(2)(i) applies to limit the reduction in the basis of capital gains property. As is discussed below, this limitation can apply only when the purchase price of the partnership interest reflects a discount, and even then, only if the amount of the discount exceeds the purchasing partner's share of the partnership's basis in its assets

This formula applies the general rule for allocating adjustments by the purchasing partner's share of gain or loss on a hypothetical sale plus an apportionment of any decrease required by the limitation on allocations to capital gain property based on relative fair market values. In algebraic form, the formula for the basis adjustment to a particular ordinary income asset is as follows:

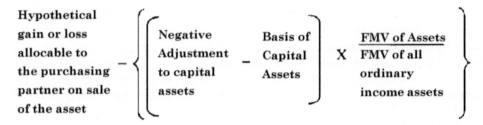

The basis adjustment to each capital gain asset equals:

> (1) the amount of income, gain, or loss (including remedial allocations under Treas.Reg. § 1.704–3(d)) that would be allocated to the purchasing partner on the hypothetical sale of the asset, minus

> (2) the total amount of gain or loss (including remedial allocations) that would be allocated to the purchasing partner on the hypothetical sale of all capital gain assets, minus the positive adjustments to all capital gain assets or plus the negative basis adjustments to all capital gain assets, multiplied by a fraction, the numerator of which is the fair market value of the item of property to the partnership and the denominator of which is the total fair market value of all of the partnership's items of capital gain property.

The second element of this portion of the formula allocates the purchasing partner's share of gain or loss that would be recognized on hypothetical sale of capital gain assets, then reduces the allocation by the reduction of Treas.Reg. § 1.755–1(b)(2)(i) apportioned to each asset by fair market value. This aspect of the computation deals with situations in which the purchase price of a partnership interest differs from the underlying fair market value of a proportionate part of the partnership's assets. In such a case, the overall § 743(b) adjustment will be either greater than or less than the difference between the purchasing partner's share of the aggregate partnership asset basis and the aggregate fair market value of that partner's share of the assets. The formula allocates all of any premium or discount to the basis adjustment of capital gain assets to the extent of the basis of those assets. However, if the partnership's assets include goodwill and going concern value, any premium increases the basis only of goodwill and going concern value. Any discount first reduces the basis of goodwill and going concern value before the basis of any other asset is reduced. Treas.Reg. § 1.755–1(a)(2). After the basis of goodwill and going concern value has been reduced to zero, the basis of other § 197 intangibles is reduced, and when their basis has been reduced to zero, any remaining discount is apportioned among the remaining capital gain assets. If the remaining discount exceeds the basis of the capital gain assets, the limitation of Treas.Reg. § 1.755–1(b)(2)(i) applies, and the discount remaining after the basis of the capital gain assets has been reduced to zero is applied to reduce the basis of ordinary income assets under Treas.Reg. § 1.755–1(b)(3)(i), as discussed above.

In algebraic form, the formula for the basis adjustment to a particular capital asset is as follows:

$$
\begin{array}{c}
\text{Hypothetical} \\
\text{gain or loss} \\
\text{allocable to} \\
\text{the purchasing} \\
\text{partner on sale} \\
\text{of the asset}
\end{array}
-
\left\{
\left[
\begin{array}{c}
\text{Total} \\
\text{hypothetical} \\
\text{gain from} \\
\text{all capital} \\
\text{assets}
\end{array}
-
\begin{array}{c}
\text{Total basis} \\
\text{adjustment} \\
\text{to} \\
\text{capital} \\
\text{assets}
\end{array}
\right]
\times
\begin{array}{c}
\text{FMV of Asset} \\
\overline{\text{FMV of all}} \\
\text{capital assets}
\end{array}
\right\}
$$

If the buying partner would have been allocated gain with respect to an asset (including gain attributable to a § 704(c) allocation that would have been made to the selling partner had the selling partner remained a partner), the asset's basis is increased by that amount. If the buying partner would have been allocated loss with respect to an asset, the asset's basis is decreased by that amount. If some assets in a class have increased in value while other assets within the class have declined in value, the gain assets must be allocated a positive basis adjustment and the loss assets must be allocated a negative basis adjustment.

Assume, for example, that the AB Partnership, in which A and B are equal partners (and to which each contributed an equal amount of cash), held the following assets.

Asset Class	Basis	F.M.V.
Capital Gain Assets		
Capital Asset	$ 2,000	$ 8,000
§ 1231 Asset	$ 6,000	$ 4,000
Ordinary Income Assets		
Inventory	$ 3,000	$ 2,000
Unrealized Receivable	$ 0	$ 4,000
	$11,000	$18,000

C purchases A's interest for $9,000. If no § 743 adjustment were made, on a sale of the partnership's assets C would be allocated a $3,000 gain on the sale of the capital asset ([$8,000 − $2,000] ÷ 2), a $1,000 loss on the sale of the § 1231 asset ([$4,000 − $6,000] ÷ 2), a $500 loss on the sale of inventory ([$3,000 − $4,000] ÷ 2), and a $2,000 gain on the sale of the unrealized receivable ([$4,000 − $0] ÷ 2). These items result in net gain of $3,500, which is C's total § 743(b) adjustment. The net gain allocated to C on the hypothetical sale of the ordinary income assets is $1,500, the net of the $2,000 gain on the sale of the unrealized receivables and the $500 loss on the sale of the inventory allocable to C's interest. Thus, a net adjustment of $1,500 is allocated to the ordinary income assets. The adjustment allocated to the capital gain assets is $2,000, the $3,500 total adjustment minus the $1,500 adjustment allocated to the ordinary income items. Within the ordinary income asset class, the $1,500 net adjustment is allocated by making a $500 negative adjustment to the basis of the inventory, an amount equal to the loss that would have been allocated to C if the inventory had been sold without a § 743(b) adjustment. C's special basis in the inventory is $1,000. A positive adjustment of $2,000 is allocated to the basis of the unrealized receivables, reflecting the gain that would have been allocated to C if the unrealized receivables had been sold without a § 743(b) basis adjustment. C's special basis in the unrealized receivables is $2,000. Within the capital gain class of assets, the $2,000 net adjustment is allocated by making a positive adjustment of $3,000 to the basis of the capital asset, which is an amount equal to the gain that would have been allocated to C if the capital asset had been sold without a § 743(b) basis adjustment. C's special basis in the capital asset is $4,000. A negative adjustment of $1,000 is allocated to the basis of the § 1231 asset, reflecting the loss that would have been allocated to C if the § 1231 asset had been sold without a § 743(b) basis adjustment. C's special basis in the § 1231 asset is $2,000.

Asset	C's share of Partnership Basis Before Adjustment	+ Adjustment =	C's Special § 743(b) Basis
Capital Gains Property			
Capital Asset	$1,000	$3,000	$4,000
§ 1231 Asset	$3,000	($1,000)	$2,000
Ordinary Income Property			
Inventory	$1,500	($ 500)	$1,000
Unrealized Receivables	$ 0	$2,000	$2,000

In this example, C, a 50% partner, ends up with a special basis in each asset equal to 50% of its fair market value on the date C purchased the partnership interest. As long as a partnership interest is purchased for an amount that equals the proportionate fair market value of its assets, including goodwill and going concern, this is the result that generally occurs under the Regulations. See Treas.Reg. § 1.755–1(b)(3)(iv), Ex. (1).

If, however, a partnership interest is purchased for an amount that is less than the proportionate fair market value of its assets, the provisions of Treas.Reg. § 1.755–1(b)(3)(ii)(B) apply and the capital gain assets will be allocated a basis increase that is insufficient to increase the purchasing partner's special basis in those assets to proportionate fair market value. See Treas.Reg. § 1.755–1(b)(3)(iv), Ex. (2).

1.3. *Application of Special Basis Adjustment*

1.3.1.   *Sales and Exchanges of Partnership Property*

Although Treas.Reg. § 1.743–1(j)(1) describes the § 743(b) basis adjustment as an increase or decrease to "the basis of partnership property," Treas.Reg. § 1.743–1(j) provides for the treatment of the § 743(b) basis adjustment as an adjustment to the transferee partner's distributive share of partnership gain or loss computed without regard to the basis adjustment. See Treas.Reg. § 1.743–1(j)(3)(ii), Exs. (1)–(3). Converting the basis adjustment to an adjustment of the purchasing partner's distributive share avoids cumbersome computations that would be required by allocating different bases to each partner.

For example, suppose that the BC Partnership in the immediately preceding example sells the capital asset for $9,000. Under Treas.Reg. § 1.743–1(j), C's gain with respect to the capital asset is computed as one-half of the partnership's gain of $7,000 using the partnership's common basis of $2,000, i.e., $3,500, minus C's special basis adjustment of $3,000, for a gain of $500.

Because the basis of partnership property is adjusted only with respect to the transferee partner, the computations of partnership income and loss would be more complicated if the basis adjustment actually were made directly to the partnership's basis for the property. C has a special basis for C's one-half interest in the capital asset of $4,000 consisting of C's $3,000 basis adjustment plus one-half of the partnership's initial $2,000 basis. The partnership's total basis is $5,000 ($1,000 + $4,000). Although the partnership's gain is $4,000 ($9,000 − [$4,000 + $1,000]), C's distributive share of the gain is only $500. If the partnership's basis were changed by treating the partnership as having a $5,000 basis, C's distributive share of the gain would be computed by adding C's $3,000 basis adjustment to one-half of the $2,000 basis the partnership had before the adjustment ($1,000), resulting in a $4,000 basis that would offset C's one-half share of the amount realized ([$9,000/2] − $4,000), while B's share would be $3,500 ([$9,000/2]−$1,000).

1.3.2.   *Depreciation Deductions with Respect to Property Subject to Section 743(b) Basis Adjustment*

Treas.Reg. § 1.743–1(j)(4) provides detailed rules regarding the effect of § 743(b) basis adjustments on depreciation and amortization deductions with respect to property subject to the basis adjustment. If the basis of a partnership's depreciable property is increased, the increased portion of the basis generally must be depreciated as if it were newly purchased property placed in service on the date the transfer of the partnership interest occurred. The partnership's original basis in the property continues to be depreciated as if there had been no basis increase. This treatment is consistent with the treatment under § 168(i)(7) of increases to basis resulting from the transfers to partnerships subject to § 721.

Assume, for example, that the EF Partnership held two § 1231 assets, Blackacre and Whiteacre, both of which are residential rental buildings on leased land. The basis and fair market values of the properties are as follows:

Asset	Basis	F.M.V.
Blackacre	$18,000	$46,000
Whiteacre	$10,000	$10,000

Blackacre has 12 years remaining in its cost recovery period. (For simplicity, assume a 28 year cost recovery period and ignore the mid-month convention.) G purchases E's partnership interest for $26,000. G's special basis in Blackacre is $23,000. Of that special basis, $9,000 is recovered through annual depreciation deductions of $750 for the remaining 12 years of Blackacre's original class life, and $14,000 is recovered through annual depreciation deductions of $500 over a new 28-year class life. Thus, G is entitled to annual depreciation deductions with respect to Blackacre of $1,250 ($750 + $500) for 12 years, followed by annual depreciation deductions of $500 for another 16 years.

If, however, a § 743(b) basis adjustment has been made with respect to § 704(c) gain that is subject to remedial allocations in effect under Treas.Reg. § 1.704–3(d) (discussed in Chapter 20, Section 3), then the basis increase attributable to § 704(c) built-in gain is depreciated over the partnership's remaining cost recovery period for the property. Treas.Reg. § 1.743–1(j)(4)(i). Any remaining basis increase in the § 704(c) property is depreciated over a new recovery period. The purpose of these bifurcated rules is to attempt to provide a purchasing partner with identical depreciation deductions regardless of whether the purchasing partner purchases an interest from the partner who contributed the § 704(c) property or from a noncontributing partner.

If § 743(b) requires a basis decrease, the decrease in basis must be taken into account over the remaining cost recovery period of the property, beginning with the recovery period in which the basis is decreased. Treas.Reg. § 1.743–1(j)(4)(ii). In general, a negative basis adjustment results in a proportional reduction of the transferee partner's distributive share of depreciation deductions attributable to the property with respect to which the negative basis adjustment is required. Treas.Reg. § 1.743–1(j)(4)(ii)(A) and (B). If the negative basis adjustment attributable to any particular year exceeds the transferee partner's distributive share of depreciation attributable to the property to which the adjustment relates, the negative adjustment is applied to reduce the transferee partner's share of depreciation attributable to other partnership property. If the adjustment does not absorb the entire adjustment attributable to the year, then the distributee partner must recognize ordinary income. Treas.Reg. § 1.743–1(j)(4)(ii)(C), Ex. (3), illustrates the application of the recognition of ordinary income rule, but hypothesizes rather than explains how the circumstances for applying this rule can arise.

Because the basis adjustment under § 743(b) applies only to the transferee partner, the basis adjustment does not affect the common basis of partnership property and thus does not affect the tax consequences of the other partners.

2.   ELECTION PROCEDURES

Pursuant to § 754, a § 743(b) election is made by the partnership—not the incoming partner. The Regulations require the election to be made on the partnership return "for the taxable year during which the distribution or transfer occurs." Treas.Reg. § 1.754–1(b)(1). Jones v. United States, 553 F.2d 667 (Ct.Cl.1977), upheld the validity of the Regulations in a situation in which an election was filed in 1969 with respect to a transfer that had taken place in 1967 on the death of a partner. If such an election is made it applies not only upon all subsequent sales and purchases of partnership interests, but also to require basis adjustments under § 734, attributable to distributions of partnership property (see Chapter 25, Section 4).

3.   MANDATORY NEGATIVE SECTION 743(b) BASIS ADJUSTMENTS

As noted previously, § 743(d) requires a negative § 743(b) adjustment to the basis of the partnership's assets whenever the aggregate basis of the partnership's assets exceeds the aggregate fair market value of the partnership's assets by more than $250,000. This mandatory basis adjustment is required even if the adjustment with respect to the purchasing partner will not exceed $250,000. Further, § 743(d)(1)(B), added in 2017, imposes a mandatory basis adjustment when the purchaser would be allocated a loss of more than $250,000 in a constructive sale of partnership assets at their fair market value after the purchase (for example, through a special distributive share loss allocation). Together, these rules aim to prevent the duplication of losses in a manner that allows a partner to recognize for tax purposes a loss that was not realized economically. See Notice 2005–32, 2005–1 C.B. 895, for procedural details and examples.

4.   EFFECT ON PARTNER'S CAPITAL ACCOUNT

Under Treas.Reg. § 1.704–1(b)(2)(iv)(*l*), the capital account of the transferor carries over to the transferee partner. (Recall from Chapter 20 that a purchase of an interest is not listed as an occasion for revaluation of partnership assets. Treas.Reg. § 1.704–1(b)(2)(iv)(*f*).) A purchaser's § 743(b) basis adjustment does not affect the amount of partnership book gain or loss that will be allocated to the purchasing partner's capital account upon the sale of property with respect to which such an adjustment is in effect. Treas.Reg. § 1.704–1(b)(2)(iv)(*m*)(*2*). Thus, for example, if the BCD Partnership in Detailed Analysis 1.2.1, sold the capital asset for $4,200, the partnership's book gain would be $2,400 ($4,200 sale price − $1,800 book value). D's share of book gain added to D's capital account would be $800 (1/3 × $2,400), even though as a result of the basis adjustment, D's taxable gain was only $400 ((1/3 × $800) − $400).

5.   PURCHASER OF ALL INTERESTS IN A PARTNERSHIP

McCauslen v. Commissioner, 45 T.C. 588 (1966), held that when one partner in a two person partnership purchases the other partner's entire interest, the purchaser is treated as having acquired by direct purchase the portion of partnership assets attributable to the acquired partnership interest (even though Treas.Reg. § 1.741–1(b) provides that the selling partner is treated as selling the partnership interest). Thus, in such a case the purchasing partner obtains a fair market value basis in the newly acquired portion of the former partnership's assets without resort to §§ 754 and 734(b). This same rule would apply whenever all of the interests in a partnership are purchased by one purchaser in an integrated transaction.

6.   APPLICATION TO TIERED PARTNERSHIPS

Suppose that A purchases from B for $50 a one-fourth partnership interest in UTP Partnership, which owns inventory having a basis of $40 and a fair market value of $80 and a one-third interest in LTP Partnership, having a basis of $80 and a fair market value of $120. LTP's sole asset is a capital asset having a basis of $330 and a fair market value of $360. UTP's basis in LTP is less than its pro rata basis in LTP's assets because UTP purchased its interest in LTP at a time when LTP did not have a § 754 election in effect. Assuming that B's pro rata share of UTP's basis in its assets is $30, if UTP has a § 754 election in effect, B is entitled to a § 743(b) basis adjustment of $20, of which $10 is attributable to UTP's interest in LTP.

Rev.Rul. 87–115, 1987–2 C.B. 163, held that a § 743(b) adjustment to the basis of LTP's asset is available if LTP also has a § 754 election in effect. In that case, the sale of A's interest in UTP to B is treated as a deemed sale of an interest in LTP. If LTP does not have a § 754 election in effect, no basis adjustment is allowed. Similarly, if LTP has a § 754 election in effect, but UTP does not, no basis adjustment is allowed.

If a § 743(b) adjustment is available to LTP, it is determined as follows. The deemed price paid by B for an indirect interest in LTP is $30 (¼ of UTP's $80 basis in LTP plus B's $10 special adjustment). B's share of the adjusted basis of LTP's asset is $27.50 (¼ of $110). Thus, B's § 743(b) adjustment in the basis of LTP's asset is only $2.50. What happened to the remaining $7.50 of B's § 743(b) adjustment to UTP's basis in LTP? What would be B's basis adjustment in LTP's basis for its asset if UTP's basis in LTP had been $110, an amount equal to one third of its pro rata basis of LTP's assets?

PROBLEM SET 2

1.   Alex and Berta are equal general partners in a plumbing business. The AB Partnership reports income from sales of inventory on the accrual method and income from services on the cash method. The assets of the AB Partnership, including goodwill, are as follows:

Asset	Adjusted Basis and Book Value	F.M.V.
Cash	$ 10,000	$ 10,000
Accounts Receivable	$ 20,000	$ 50,000
Inventory	$ 50,000	$ 80,000
Equipment	$ 80,000	$130,000
Goodwill	$ 0	$ 60,000
	$160,000	$330,000

The AB Partnership owes a bank $30,000 on a purchase money loan to acquire some of the equipment and $2,000 to trade creditors for bills that it properly accounts for on the cash method. Cliff purchased Alex's partnership interest for a cash payment of $150,000. The "new" BC partnership promised to indemnify Alex on the debts to the bank.

(a) What is Cliff's basis in his partnership interest?

(b) Should Cliff request that a § 754 election be made? Why? Compare the effects on Cliff of subsequent normal partnership operations assuming, alternatively, that an election has been made and that one has not been made.

(c) Are there any reasons why Berta might hesitate to agree to a § 754 election?

2.   Donna purchased Dennis's one-third interest of the DEF LLC (which is taxed as a partnership) for $125,000. In connection with Donna's purchase, the LLC made a § 754 election. The DEF LLC uses the accrual method of accounting with respect to sales of inventory and the cash method with respect to the provision of services. When Donna purchased her one-third interest, the DEF LLC's asset bases and fair market value were as follows:

Assets	Adjusted Basis	F.M.V.		Adjusted Basis	F.M.V.
Cash	$ 9,000	$ 9,000	D	$ 75,000	$125,000
Accounts			E	$ 75,000	$125,000
Receivable	$ 6,000	$ 36,000	F	$ 75,000	$125,000
Inventory	$ 60,000	$120,000			
Land	$ 45,000	$ 30,000			
Building	$105,000	$180,000			
	$225,000	$375,000		$225,000	$375,000

The land and building are § 1231 assets. Determine the § 743(b) special basis for each of the LLC's assets with respect to Donna.

3.   Erin purchased Fritz's one third interest in The Big Short Limited Partnership for $100,000. The partnership, which is a dealer in securities, holds most of its securities as inventory, but some are held as capital assets. Its security holdings at the time Erin purchased her interest were as follows:

Asset	Adjusted Basis	F.M.V.
Inventory	$165,000	$240,000
Capital Assets	$135,000	$ 60,000

Would Erin have benefited from a § 754 election made in connection with her purchase of the partnership interest?

4.   Glenda and Hector are partners in the GH partnership that owns a commercial office building. The fair market value of the building is $600,000; its basis is $1,000,000. The building is subject to a mortgage of $500,000. The basis of each of Glenda's and Hector's partnership interest is $500,000. Hector sells his partnership interest to Inez for $50,000. The partnership does not make a § 754 election. Does the absence of the election make a difference?

CHAPTER 25

PARTNERSHIP DISTRIBUTIONS

SECTION 1. CURRENT DISTRIBUTIONS

A. CASH DISTRIBUTIONS AND REDUCTION OF LIABILITIES

INTERNAL REVENUE CODE: Sections 731; 733; 741; 752(b); 761(d).

REGULATIONS: Sections 1.731–1(a)(1) and (3), (b); 1.733–1; 1.761–1(d).

Under the conduit approach to the taxation of partnership income adopted by Subchapter K, a partner is taxed currently on the partner's share of the partnership income whether the income is distributed or not. Income taxed to a partner is added to the partner's basis in the partnership interest, which thereafter permits a distribution of the income without further tax. I.R.C. § 705(a)(1). The circle is closed by § 731(a)(1), which provides that distributions of money do not result in gain to the partner except to the extent that distributed money exceeds the partner's adjusted basis for the partnership interest. Section § 752(b) treats a reduction in a partner's share of partnership liabilities as a distribution of money. Thus, under §§ 731(a)(1) and 733, a reduction of liabilities also reduces the distributee partner's basis and results in recognized gain if the reduction in liability exceeds the partner's basis in the partnership interest.

Distributions of property likewise, in general, do not result in gain to the partner, even if the fair market value of the distributed property exceeds the partner's basis for the partnership interest. Instead, under § 732(a)(1), the partnership's basis in the distributed property is transferred from the partnership to the partner. The transferred basis is limited by § 732(a)(2) to the partner's basis in the partnership interest. These rules are subject to several limitations and qualifications. Section 751(b), for example, creates a constructive taxable exchange whenever a partner receives a current distribution that alters the partners' respective interests in unrealized receivables or substantially appreciated inventory. Additional rules, discussed in Section 3, apply in the case of a distribution in liquidation of a partner's interest in the partnership.

When a partner receives a current distribution, new provisions added by the 2017 Tax Act may apply. Section 1061 (discussed primarily in Chapter 24) may affect whether a partner's capital gain on a distribution is long-term or short-term. If § 751(b) requires that a partner (or partners) recognize ordinary items on the constructive taxable exchange, those items are eligible to be included in the § 199A qualified business income computation, assuming the other requirements of § 199A are met (discussed in Chapter 18). Treas.Reg. § 1.199A–3(b)(1)(i).

(Capital gains or losses are not included in § 199A qualified business income.)

Revenue Ruling 81–242

1981–2 C.B. 147.

ISSUE

May gain be recognized to each partner when mortgaged property owned by a partnership is involuntarily converted even though the partnership elects to defer the recognition of gain under section 1033 of the Internal Revenue Code?

FACTS

P is a general partnership of five individuals. In 1969, P purchased a building for commercial use. Through depreciation and other adjustments and distributions, the bases of the partners' interests had been reduced below their share of liabilities.

In 1980, City Y, through appropriate proceedings, acquired by condemnation the building owned by P for 20x dollars. At the time of the condemnation, the mortgage debt owed by P was 15x dollars, and P's basis in the property was 10x dollars. The award made by City Y was used to pay off the mortgage debt.

P elected to replace the building within the meaning of section 1033(a)(2) of the Code and within the time prescribed by section 1033(a)(2)(B).

LAW AND ANALYSIS

Section 1033(a)(2) of the Code provides that if property is involuntarily converted into money by condemnation, then any gain shall be recognized. However, section 1033(a)(2)(A) provides that if replacement property is purchased (under circumstances that comply with the pertinent provisions of section 1033), then, at the election of the taxpayer, gain shall be recognized only to the extent that the amount realized on the conversion exceeds the cost of the replacement property.

Section 703(b) of the Code provides that any election affecting the computation of taxable income derived from a partnership must be made by the partnership.

Furthermore, Rev.Rul. 66–191, 1966–2 C.B. 300, holds that the election under section 1033 of the Code not to recognize gain from an involuntary conversion can be made only by the partnership and not by the partners individually.

Section 731(a)(1) of the Code provides that when there is a distribution by a partnership to a partner, gain shall not be recognized to that partner, except to the extent that any money distributed exceeds the adjusted basis of that partner's interest in the partnership immediately before the distribution.

Section 752(b) of the Code provides that any decrease in a partner's share of the liabilities of a partnership, or any decrease in a partner's individual liabilities by reason of the assumption by the partnership of the individual liabilities, shall be considered as a distribution of money to the partner by the partnership.

In this case, P realized 10x dollars of gain from the condemnation of its building. Because P elected to replace the condemned building within the meaning of section 1033(a)(2) of the Code and within the time prescribed by section 1033(a)(2)(B), P is not required to recognize the 10x dollars gain realized from the condemned building.

The award by City Y was used to pay off the 15x dollars of liability on the condemned building, resulting in a decrease in each partner's share of the liability of P. Under section 752(b) of the Code, the decrease is treated as a distribution of money to each partner. Thus, under section 731(a)(1), gain is recognized to each partner to the extent that the deemed distribution to each partner exceeds the adjusted basis of each partner's interest in P immediately before the distribution.

The transaction described above is distinguishable from that considered in Rev.Rul. 79–205, 1979–2 C.B. 255. In that ruling, a partnership made non-liquidating distributions of property to its two equal partners. Because the properties in question were subject to liabilities, the distributions resulted in a decrease in the liabilities of the partnership (a deemed distribution to each partner under section 752(b)), and an increase in each partner's individual liabilities (a deemed contribution by each partner under section 752(a)). The ruling concludes that the distributions were part of a single transaction and that the properties were treated as having been distributed simultaneously to the two partners. Thus, the resulting liability adjustments were treated as having occurred simultaneously.

In this case, the condemnation of the building and the subsequent reinvestment of the proceeds were separate transactions that did not occur simultaneously. When P subsequently acquired replacement property that was subject to a liability, each partner's share of the liability of P increased. Because this increase resulted from a separate transaction, it may not be netted against the decrease in liability on the prior condemnation of the original property. Therefore, the full amount of the decrease in liability was a deemed distribution of money to the partners.

HOLDING

Under section 1033 of the Code, the 10x dollars of gain from the condemnation of P's building is not recognized in 1980. However, under section 731(a)(1), gain is recognized to each partner to the extent that partner's proportionate share of the deemed distribution of the 15x dollars of liability exceeds the adjusted basis of that partner's interest in P immediately before the distribution.

DETAILED ANALYSIS

1.   CURRENT DISTRIBUTIONS OF MONEY

1.1. *Definition of a Current Distribution*

Subchapter K distinguishes between distributions "in liquidation of the partner's interest" and distributions to a partner "other than in liquidation of the partner's interest." The term "liquidation" has reference to the entire interest of the partner and hence applies to the complete dissolution of a partnership or to one of a series of distributions in complete termination of a partner's interest. Treas.Reg. § 1.761–1(d). Any other distribution to a partner falls within the second category, that of distributions other than in liquidation. This latter category is referred to as current distributions. Current distributions include the distribution of a partner's distributive share of profits, distributions from a partner's capital account that reduce the amount that the partner is entitled to receive upon the dissolution of the partnership but that do not otherwise affect the partner's interest in future partnership profits, and distributions in partial liquidations, which reduce a partner's interest but do not end that interest (such as where a partner having a 10% interest in capital becomes one with a 5% interest). Treas.Reg. § 1.761–1(d).

1.2. *Treatment of Distributee Partner*

Current distributions of money reduce the basis of the partner's interest under § 733 and § 705(a)(2) but otherwise have no tax effect, unless the amount of the distribution exceeds the partner's basis in the partnership interest. Since a partner's basis is adjusted upwards under § 705(a)(1) for the partner's distributive share of partnership income that has been taxed to the partner, the distribution of money representing the previously taxed income of necessity gives rise to a downward adjustment. The two adjustments cancel out, leaving the partner's basis the same as it was before the partnership earned and distributed its income. In this simple case, the basis adjustments merely eliminate any possibility of recognition of gain on the distribution of previously taxed partnership income. Money distributions also are tax free to the extent of the distributee partner's basis that is attributable to contributions to the partnership (or to the partner's share of liabilities), representing a return of partnership capital.

Section 731(a)(1) provides for recognition of gain to the extent that a money distribution exceeds the partner's basis in the partnership interest, since otherwise the excess money would go untaxed. The gain recognized under § 731 is treated as gain on the sale of a partnership interest and, under § 741, is capital gain, unless the partnership has unrealized receivables or substantially appreciated inventory so that § 751(b) applies.

A partner's distributive share of income, and hence the basis increase on account of that share, is not computed until the end of the year. As a consequence, interim distributions of earnings during the taxable year might exceed a partner's basis at the time of the distribution. Treas.Reg. § 1.731–1(a)(1)(ii) treats advances or drawings against a partner's distributive share of income as made on the last day of the partnership year for the purposes of §§ 731 and 705. Thus, any basis increase attributable to a partner's distributive share of partnership income for the year is available to offset the distribution.

Section 731(a)(2) prohibits recognition of loss on a current distribution. Because the partner's interest has not been liquidated, there has not been a closed and completed transaction—the prerequisite for a loss deduction—and the partner's remaining basis can attach to the partner's remaining partnership interest.

1.2.1.　*Unitary Basis in Partnership Interest*

In applying § 731, all of a partner's interests in a partnership are considered to be a unitary interest; the bases of general and limited partnership interests are combined into a unitary basis. Thus, for example, Chase v. Commissioner, 92 T.C. 874 (1989), held that a loss could not be recognized by a partner who received a cash distribution of $929,582 in liquidation of an 11.72% limited partnership interest having an adjusted basis of $1,710,344 because the taxpayer continued to hold a general partnership interest. The excess of the basis of the limited partnership over the amount of the distribution is included in the partner's basis in the partner's general partnership interest.

1.3. *Treatment of Other Partners*

When a current distribution of cash results in recognition of gain, the bases of the other partners in their partnership interests do not change, even though the distribution has reduced the partnership's aggregate basis for its assets. In effect, some of the basis of their partnership interests, represented by the amount by which the cash distributed by the partnership exceeded the distributee partner's proportionate share of the partnership's basis for its assets, has been used to acquire an increased interest in the remaining partnership assets. As a general rule, § 734(a) provides that the bases of the remaining partnership property are not affected by the distribution. However, if the partnership has made an election under § 754, then the bases of the partnership assets will be adjusted upwards under § 734(b) by the amount of gain recognized under § 731(a). This adjustment, in effect, reflects the transfer of the basis from the distributed money to the remaining assets. A current distribution of money can only cause an increase in bases of partnership assets; it cannot cause a decrease. Section 734(b) is discussed in more detail in Section 4.

2.　REDUCTION OF PARTNERSHIP LIABILITY AS A CASH DISTRIBUTION: SECTION 752(b)

2.1. *Generally*

As illustrated by Rev.Rul. 81–242, § 752(b) treats a decrease in the partner's share of partnership liabilities as a distribution of money to the partner by the partnership, thus bringing into play the rules of § 731. A reduction in liabilities reduces the partner's basis pro tanto and will result in the recognition of gain if the constructive distribution exceeds the partner's basis in the partnership interest. Section 752(b) is a corollary of § 752(a), which treats any increase in a partner's share of partnership liabilities as a contribution of money by the partner to the partnership, thereby increasing the partner's basis in the partnership interest.

Partnership liabilities can be reduced not only by repayment but by the transfer (or distribution) of encumbered property, the abandonment of encumbered property, or by discharge through compromise. A partner's share of partnership liabilities also will be reduced upon the admission of a new partner to the partnership who assumes a share of partnership liabilities, thereby resulting in a constructive distribution under § 752(b) to the original partners that may require recognition of gain under § 731(a). See Rev.Rul. 84–102, 1984–2 C.B. 119. As discussed in Chapter 19, Section 2, when a partner contributes encumbered property to a partnership, the partner generally is treated as receiving a current distribution to the extent that the liability attached to the property is allocated to other partners. If that portion of the liability exceeds the contributing partner's basis in the partnership interest, the contributing partner recognizes gain under § 731(a), and the partner's basis in the partnership interest is reduced to zero. See Rev.Rul. 84–15, 1984–1 C.B. 158.

Rev.Rul. 94–4, 1994–1 C.B. 195, held that a deemed distribution of money pursuant to § 752(b) is treated as an advance or draw under Treas.Reg. § 1.731–1(a)(1)(ii). Thus, the constructive distribution, like distributions in the nature of a draw, is not taken into account until after the increase in the partner's basis in the partnership interest (under § 705) attributable to the partner's distributive share of partnership income. The ruling is terse, and it is unclear whether it applies to all deemed distributions under § 752(b), including assumptions by a partner of partnership debt in conjunction with a distribution or only those attributable to partnership transactions with third parties.

This timing issue was addressed in Rev.Rul. 2003–56, 2003–1 C.B. 985, in the context of a § 1031 like-kind exchange of encumbered property by a partnership that occurred over two taxable years. In Situation 1 of the Ruling, a partnership in Year 1 transferred property subject to a liability of $100x in a like-kind exchange for property received in Year 2 subject to a liability of $60x. Under Treas.Reg. § 1.1031(b)–1(c), the net decrease in liabilities in a like-kind exchange is treated as the receipt of cash boot thereby requiring recognition of gain to the extent of the boot. The IRS ruled that this gain is recognized by the partnership in Year 1, even though the transaction is not closed until the receipt of property in Year 2.[1] The Ruling also provides, without any statutory or regulatory authority, that the decrease in partnership liabilities in Year 1 is netted with the increase in partnership liabilities in Year 2. Thus, the decrease in partnership liabilities of $100x in Year 1 is netted with the $60x increase of liabilities in Year 2. The overall $40x decrease in partnership liabilities is taken into account by the partners under § 752(b) as a constructive distribution in Year 1. As a consequence, with respect to a partner whose outside basis prior to the transaction is less than the partner's share of the reduction of liabilities, the increase in the partner's basis in Year 1 under § 705(a)(1) because of the

---

[1] Arguably this conclusion is wrong. Since the receipt of consideration is deferred until Year 2, there is no amount realized for the transferred property in Year 1. The transaction is a deferred payment sale and, unless there is an election under § 453(b), recognition of the boot is deferred under § 453(a) and (f)(6) until there is a payment in Year 2 in the form of the receipt of the exchange property.

partnership gain recognized on the exchange permits the § 752(b) distribution without further recognition of gain. Situation 2 of Rev.Rul. 2003–56 addresses the situation where the liability attached to the transferred property is less than the liability attached to the property received in the exchange. Under Treas.Reg. § 1.1031(b)–1(c) the liabilities are netted and because there is a net increase in liabilities on the exchange, there is no boot and thus no gain is recognized by the partnership. The Ruling also concludes that the net increase in partnership liabilities is taken into account under § 752(a) in Year 2 when the exchange property subject to the higher liability is received. Thus, the partners' basis increase under § 722 occurs in Year 2 of the transaction.

2.2. Partnership Cancellation of Indebtedness Income Under Section 61(a)(11) and Related Constructive Distributions

Under § 108(d)(6), cancellation of partnership debt results in income to the partnership that is allocated to the partners in accord with a partner's distributive share. The exceptions to recognition of discharge of indebtedness income provided in § 108 are applied at the individual partner level. Each partner's basis in the partnership interest is increased under § 705 by the amount of discharge of indebtedness income allocable to the partner. In turn, the reduction in partnership indebtedness is treated as a distribution to the partners under § 752, which may result in gain under § 731(a) to the extent that the deemed distribution exceeds a partner's basis in the partnership interest.[2]

Rev.Rul. 92–97, 1992–2 C.B. 124, held that under Treas.Reg. § 1.731–1(a)(1)(ii) a deemed distribution to a partner resulting from the cancellation of a partnership debt that gave rise to cancellation of indebtedness income under § 61(a)(11) is treated as occurring after the increase in the partners' bases in their partnership interests resulting from the cancellation of indebtedness income. Thus, if the partners share income and loss in the same percentages as they share the discharged indebtedness, and no partner is insolvent, each partner will recognize a pro rata share of ordinary cancellation of indebtedness income, and the basis adjustments will exactly offset each other with no gain resulting under § 731. On the other hand, if a particular partner's share of partnership liabilities exceeds the partner's distributive share of partnership income from the cancellation of the debt, the constructive distribution might exceed the partner's basis in the partnership interest, resulting in recognition of gain under § 731.

Pursuant to § 108(a)(1)(B), if a partner is insolvent, cancellation of indebtedness income at the partnership level is not included in gross income by the partner.

---

[2] Section 108(d)(6) was enacted to adopt the Commissioner's position in Stackhouse v. United States, 441 F.2d 465 (5th Cir.1971), contrary to the court's holding that that the reduction in partnership liabilities constituted a distribution to the partners under § 752(b) with the tax results controlled solely by § 731(a).

3.   DISTRIBUTIONS RELATED TO SECTION 707

3.1. *Payments for Partner Transactions*

Section 707(a)(2), as discussed in Chapter 22, Section 1, treats certain distributions related to the performance of services for the partnership or the transfer of property to the partnership as § 707(a)(1) payments, which are treated as payments to a person that is not a partner. Section 707(a)(1) payments received in exchange for services are ordinary income to the payee partner and are deductible by the partnership, subject to the general capitalization rules. When § 707(a)(2) applies, no part of the distribution is treated as a distribution under § 731. If, as suggested in Gaines v. Commissioner, T.C. Memo. 1982–731, the inclusion of accrued, but unpaid, § 707(c) guaranteed payment in a partner's income is treated as an allocation of partnership share that increases the partner's basis for the partnership interest, then distribution in the later year of the guaranteed payment should be governed by § 731.

3.2. *Distribution Versus Loan*

A receipt of money or property by a partner under an obligation to repay such amount or return the property to a partnership is treated as a loan under § 707(a)(1) rather than as a current distribution. A withdrawal will not be treated as a loan, however, unless there is a definite obligation to repay a sum certain at a determinable time. The fact that the distribution creates a deficit in the partner's capital account that must be restored on liquidation or will otherwise be taken into account in making liquidating distributions does not alone establish that the transaction is a loan. Rev.Rul. 73–301, 1973–2 C.B. 215. See Seay v. Commissioner, T.C. Memo. 1992–254 (cash withdrawal from partnership characterized as distribution subject to § 731 rather than a loan subject to § 707(a) because partner never made any attempt to repay and the partnership never made any demand or attempt to enforce repayment). Of course, if the distribution is treated as a loan and the obligation is later canceled, the obligor partner will be considered to have received a distribution of money or property at the time of the cancellation. Treas.Reg. § 1.731–1(c)(2). But where a partner's indebtedness to the partnership is satisfied by the partnership setting off the debt against a distribution otherwise due to the partner, there has been no forgiveness of indebtedness; the transaction is a constructive distribution. See Zager v. Commissioner, T.C. Memo. 1987–107.

B. PROPERTY DISTRIBUTIONS

INTERNAL REVENUE CODE: Sections 731(a), (b) and (d); 732(a), (c)–(d); 733; 734(a)–(b); 735; 741; 752(a)–(c); 761(d).

REGULATIONS: Sections 1.731–1(a)(1); 1.732–1(a), (d)(1)(i)–(v) and (2)–(4); 1.733–1; 1.735–1; 1.752–1(d)–(f); 1.761–1(d).

In general, on a distribution of property that is not in liquidation of a partner's interest in the partnership, the distributee partner recognizes no gain or loss under § 731(a)(1), and the partnership's basis in the distributed property is transferred to the distributee partner under

§ 732(a)(1). The distributee partner reduces the partner's basis in the partnership interest by the amount of the basis assigned to the distributed property. I.R.C. § 733(2).

If a current distribution of property is pro rata among all the partners, the distributee partners simply take a transferred basis in the distributed assets because each partner receives the partner's own undivided share of the distributed assets. If a property distribution is not pro rata, however, in effect there is an exchange among the partners. Nevertheless, unless the distribution alters the partners' interests in substantially appreciated inventory or unrealized receivables, Subchapter K does not treat the distribution as an exchange. Instead, in the case of any distribution of property that is not in complete termination of a partner's interest, Subchapter K applies a simpler rule and merely transfers the basis of the partnership asset, as in a pro rata distribution. See Treas.Reg. § 1.732–1(a), Exs. (1) and (2). As in the case of pro rata distributions, the partner's basis in the partnership interest is reduced by the amount of the transferred basis of the distributed asset. I.R.C. § 733.

Section 732(a)(2) provides that if the distributee partner's basis for the partnership interest (reduced by any money received) is less than the basis of the asset in the partnership's hands, then the basis of the asset in the partner's hands is limited to the partner's basis in the partnership interest (reduced by any money received), i.e., an "exchanged basis." This limitation eliminates the necessity of having to recognize a gain to the distributee partner on a distribution of property.

In the case of a distribution of several properties having an aggregate partnership basis greater than the distributee partner's basis for the partnership interest (less any money received), the partner's exchanged basis is allocated among the properties according to a complex formula contained in § 732(c). The distributee partner's exchanged basis first is allocated to distributed inventory and unrealized receivables, as defined in § 751(c), to the extent of the partnership's basis in these assets. (Unrealized receivables, which include depreciation and other recapture as a separate asset, generally have a zero basis.) If the distributee partner's outside basis is less than the partnership's basis in the distributed inventory and receivables, the basis reduction is allocated among loss inventory and receivables in proportion to the relative unrealized loss in each distributed asset (determined before any basis decrease). I.R.C. § 732(c)(3)(A). Once the unrealized loss in distributed inventory and receivables is eliminated, any further required reduction is allocated in proportion to the adjusted basis of the distributed inventory and receivables. I.R.C. § 732(c)(3)(B).

If the distributee partner's outside basis is sufficient to permit receipt of inventory and receivables with a transferred basis (or there are no distributed inventory and unrealized receivables), then any reduction in basis required by the limitation of § 732(a)(2) is allocated among other distributed property. Again, the reduction is allocated under § 732(c)(3) among loss assets in proportion to the unrealized loss of each distributed asset determined before any basis reduction. Once unrealized loss is eliminated, the basis reduction is allocated in proportion to the adjusted bases of distributed assets.

Under the allocation rules for current distributions of property, the same overall amount of gain is recognized whether the partners sell the property after the distribution or the partnership sells the property before the distribution. But these rules can result in a different allocation of that gain or loss among the partners. Suppose partners A and B each receive property worth $100, but A's property has a transferred basis of $50 while B's has a transferred basis of $150. Upon a later sale of the property by the partners, A would realize a gain of $50 and B a loss of $50. But, because each partner's basis in that partner's partnership interest is reduced by an amount equal to the transferred basis assigned to the distributed property, I.R.C. § 733, B will recognize $100 more gain than A on the sale of their partnership interests or upon the liquidation of the partnership following a cash sale of its assets. On the other hand, if the partnership had first sold the property and distributed $100 of cash to each partner, no net gain or loss would have resulted. The partners should be able to resolve any inequities resulting from the possible shifting of gains and losses by arm's-length negotiations, e.g., an arrangement to compensate the partner currently receiving disproportionately low basis property. Alternatively, the partners might find that a disproportionate allocation of the burdens is desirable, in that the low basis property might be currently distributed to a tax-exempt partner, a low bracket taxpayer, or to one with compensating losses.

The degree of tax avoidance that can be achieved by distributing appreciated inventory or unrealized receivables to low basis partners is considerably reduced by § 751(b), discussed in Section C, which treats an exchange of an interest in unrealized receivables and substantially appreciated inventory as a taxable transaction.

DETAILED ANALYSIS

1. CAPITAL ACCOUNT ADJUSTMENTS

The § 704(b) Regulations, which govern the maintenance of capital accounts, require adjustment of the partnership's capital accounts upon a distribution of property. See Treas.Reg. § 1.704–1(b)(2)(iv)(*e*). Capital account adjustments must be made as if the distribution were a recognition event, even though pursuant to § 731(a) and (b) no taxable gain is recognized by a partner on the distribution of property. Treas.Reg. § 1.704–1(b)(2)(iv)(*e*)(*1*) requires that the partnership capital accounts be adjusted to reflect the gain or loss that would have been recognized if the distributed property had been sold for its fair market value instead of distributed. The capital account of each partner is adjusted to reflect each partner's distributive share of the partnership's book gain or loss. Then the capital account of the distributee partner is decreased by the fair market value of the distributed property.

Some distributions are an appropriate occasion for revaluation of all of the partnership's properties and the partners' book accounts. Treas.Reg. § 1.704–1(b)(2)(iv)(*f*)(*5*)(*ii*) provides that such an adjustment may be made for a substantial non-tax business purpose in connection with a distribution of more than a de minimis amount of money or property. Whenever a current distribution is disproportionate and intended to reduce one or more partner's interest in future profits and losses, a complete revaluation under Treas.Reg. § 1.704–1(b)(2)(iv)(*f*)(*5*)(*ii*) will be necessary (although not required by the Regulations) to achieve the economic objectives of the partners.

2.　BASIS OF PROPERTY RECEIVED IN A DISTRIBUTION

Generally, in a current (non-liquidating) distribution of property, under § 732(a)(1) the partnership's basis in the distributed property is transferred to the distributee partner, with a corresponding reduction of the distributee's basis in the partnership interest pursuant to § 733(2). Section 732(a)(2) limits the basis of distributed assets to the distributee partner's basis in the partnership interest.

In the case of a distribution of multiple assets, when the distributee partner's basis in distributed assets is limited by § 732(a)(2), § 732(c)(1)(A) requires allocation of basis first to distributed unrealized receivables and inventory to the extent of the partnership's basis in these assets, with any remaining basis to be allocated to all other distributed property. If the distributee partner's outside basis is less than the partnership's basis in distributed unrealized receivables and inventory, the decrease in basis required by § 732(a) is allocated among the distributed receivables and inventory, first in proportion to the unrealized loss (if any) built into these assets. For this purpose, unrealized loss is determined by using the partnership's basis in the assets before reducing the basis of the properties because of the distributee partner's lower aggregate basis. Any further reduction required by the § 732(a)(2) limitation is then allocated among distributed assets in proportion to the adjusted basis of the distributed assets, as reduced in the first step.

Assume, for example, that a partner with a $1,500 basis in the partnership interest received three parcels of real estate held as inventory: Blackacre, with a fair market value of $1,200 and a basis of $600; Whiteacre, with a fair market value of $200 and a basis of $500; and Greenacre, with a fair market value of $400 and a basis of $1,000. Absent the limitation of § 732(a)(2), the partner's transferred basis would be $600 in Blackacre, $500 in Whiteacre, and $1,000 in Greenacre. Because the aggregate basis of all three properties to the partnership was $2,100 and the partner is entitled to only a $1,500 aggregate basis for the three properties, the aggregate bases of the properties must be reduced by $600. The first step under § 732(c)(3)(A) is to reduce the basis of the loss properties, Whiteacre and Greenacre, in proportion to their built-in losses. (The basis reduction under § 732(c)(3)(A), however, cannot result in a reduction of basis to less than fair market value.)

	FMV	Basis	Built-In Loss	Decrease	Partner Basis
Blackacre	$1,200	$ 600			$ 600
Whiteacre	$ 200	$ 500	$300	(600) × (300/900) = $200	$ 300
Greenacre	$ 400	$1,000	$600	(600) × (600/900) = $400	$ 600
Total		$2,100	$900	$600	$1,500

Since the total basis reduction of $600 was absorbed by Whiteacre and Greenacre, each of which still has a basis in excess of fair market value, the basis of Blackacre is not adjusted.

If the required basis reduction exceeds the decline in value inherent in the distributed loss assets, a portion of the aggregate basis decrease cannot be allocated in proportion to relative losses under § 732(c)(3)(A). In that case, under § 732(c)(3)(B) the remaining portion of the decrease is allocated among all of the assets received in the distribution relative to their adjusted bases after the adjustments required by § 732(c)(3)(A). Assume that the partner in the above example had a basis in the partnership interest of only $900. Section 732(c) would allow the partner an aggregate basis in the distributed properties of only $900, requiring an aggregate basis reduction of $1,200. Under § 732(c)(3)(A) the basis of distributed property cannot be reduced to less than the unrealized loss built-in to the property. Thus, under § 732(c)(2)(A), the adjusted basis of distributed property cannot be reduced below fair market value. The first part of the $1,200 basis reduction is allocated as follows:

	FMV	Basis	Built-In Loss	Decrease	Basis
Blackacre	$1,200	$ 600			
Whiteacre	$ 200	$ 500	$300	(900) × (300/900) = $300	$200
Greenacre	$ 400	$1,000	$600	(900) × (600/900) = $600	$400
Total		$2,100	$900	$900	

Because only $900 of the total required basis reduction of $1,200 was absorbed by Whiteacre and Greenacre under § 732(c)(3)(A), a further basis adjustment of $300 is required under § 732(c)(3)(B). This adjustment affects the basis of Blackacre as well as the bases of Whiteacre and Greenacre. In this final step, the negative adjustment of $300 is allocated among the properties relative to their adjusted bases to the partner after the application of § 732(c)(3)(A). Thus:

	Partner's Tentative Basis	Decrease	Partner's Basis
Blackacre	$ 600	(300) × (600/1200) = $150	$450
Whiteacre	$ 200	(300) × (200/1200) = $ 50	$150
Greenacre	$ 400	(300) × (400/1200) = $100	$300
Total	$1,200	$300	$900

If any basis remains after allocation among inventory and accounts receivable, the remaining basis is allocated among all other assets. Pursuant to § 732(c)(3), the basis of any other property with a fair market value that is less than its transferred basis to the partner before the limitation of § 732(a) is applied is reduced in proportion to the built-in loss in the same manner as applies to inventory and unrealized receivables. For example, if all of the properties in either of the preceding two examples had been § 1231 assets or capital assets (or any combination of capital assets or § 1231 assets), the calculations would have been the same.

If a partner receives both inventory (and/or unrealized receivables) and other property, and there is any basis remaining after allocating to the inventory and unrealized receivables a basis equal to their basis in the hands of the partnership, the basis decrease rules of § 732(c)(3) are applied solely with respect to the other property. Assume that in the immediately preceding example, Blackacre was held as inventory and Whiteacre and Greenacre were held as capital assets. The transferred basis of Blackacre would be $600. As above, in the first part of the allocation, $900 of the basis decrease is allocated $300 to Whiteacre and $600 to Greenacre. In the second step, the bases of Whiteacre and Greenacre are further reduced by the remaining $300 adjustment as follows:

	Basis	Decrease	Partner Basis
Whiteacre	$200	(300) × (200/600) = $100	$100
Greenacre	$400	(300) × (400/600) = $200	$200
Total	$600	$300	$300

This allocation scheme serves two purposes. First, it is designed to prevent inventory and unrealized receivables from ever receiving a higher basis in the hands of the distributee than they had at the partnership level. Second, it is designed to prevent assets with a relatively low value from taking a higher basis in the partner's hands than assets with a relatively high value, but which had a lower basis in the partnership's hands. See H. Rep. No. 148, 105th Cong, 1st Sess. 148 (1997). The allocation formula clearly is not designed to allocate basis among distributed assets relative to their fair market value. See H. Rep. No. 148, 105th Cong, 1st Sess. 148 (1997).

3.   ANCILLARY EFFECTS OF PROPERTY DISTRIBUTIONS THAT DO
     NOT ALTER INTERESTS IN SUBSTANTIALLY APPRECIATED
     INVENTORY OR UNREALIZED RECEIVABLES

3.1. *Character of Distributed Property*

If the distributed asset is an unrealized receivable, § 735 provides a
perpetual carryover of its non-capital character. The character of
partnership inventory, however, is retained for only five years. See Luckey
v. Commissioner, 334 F.2d 719 (9th Cir.1964), and Sanford Homes, Inc. v.
Commissioner, T.C. Memo. 1986–404, both applying this rule to inventory
sold within the five-year period. Section 735(c)(2) extends these
characterization rules to substituted basis property received by the partner
in a partially or wholly tax-free exchange for the tainted distributed
property. Finally, these carryovers of asset character apparently apply only
to the distributee and not to a donee of the distributee.

3.2. *Effect on Nondistributee Partners*

Where the distributee partner's basis in the distributed property is
limited by § 732(a)(2), the remaining partners, by utilizing property with a
basis higher than the distributee partner's basis, have in effect purchased
part of the distributee partner's interest with that excess amount.
Nevertheless, § 731(b) provides that the partnership (and hence the other
partners) does not recognize gain or loss on the distribution of property.
However, under §§ 754 and 734(b), the effect of this exchange may be
reflected in the bases of the remaining partnership assets. Section 734(b) is
discussed in Section 4.

3.3. *Capital Accounts*

Treas.Reg. § 1.704–1(b)(2)(iv)*(e)(1)* requires that the partnership capital
accounts be adjusted to allocate to each partner the partner's share of gain
or loss that would have been recognized if the property had been sold for its
fair market value instead of distributed. This "book gain" is not recognized
for tax purposes. Then the capital account of the distributee partner is
decreased by the fair market value of the distributed property.

Assume for example that the ABC Partnership has the following
balance sheet:

	Assets			Partners' Capital Accounts	
	Book	**Tax Basis**		**Book**	**Tax Basis**
Cash	$360	$360	A	$198	$198
Whiteacre	$ 75	$ 75	B	$198	$198
Blackacre	$ 60	$ 60	C	$198	$198
Greenacre	$ 99	$ 99			
	$594	$594		$594	$594

Whiteacre, Blackacre, and Greenacre all have a fair market value of $90. The partnership makes a distribution of Whiteacre to A, Blackacre to B, and Greenacre to C. Assume that the partnership does not revalue all its properties and capital accounts pursuant to Treas.Reg. § 1.704–1(b)(2)(iv)(*f*)(*5*)(*ii*) because the distribution is pro rata. Nevertheless, under Treas.Reg. § 1.704–1(b)(2)(iv)(*e*)(*1*) the partnership must adjust the partners' capital accounts as if Whiteacre, Blackacre, and Greenacre each were sold for $90. The deemed sale for $90 results in book gains of $15 with respect to Whiteacre and $30 with respect to Blackacre, and a book loss of $9 with respect to Greenacre. The net deemed book gain is $36. Accordingly, each partner's capital account is increased by $12 and then decreased by $90 for the distribution. Each partner's basis for the partnership interest, however, is decreased by the partnership's basis for the particular property distributed. After the distribution, the ABC Partnership's balance sheet is as follows:

	Assets		Partners' Capital Accounts		
	Book	**Tax Basis**		**Book**	**Tax Basis**
Cash	$360	$360	A	$120	$123
			B	$120	$138
	____	____	C	$120	$ 99
	$360	$360		$360	$360

Thus, upon the subsequent distribution of the $360 cash in liquidation of the partnership, A would recognize a loss of $3, B a loss of $18, and C a gain of $21. If each of A, B, and C sold the real property received in the distribution at its fair market value at the time of the distribution ($90), A would recognize a $15 gain on the sale of Whiteacre ($90 – $75), B a $30 gain on the sale of Blackacre ($90 – $60), and C a $9 loss on the sale of Greenacre ($90 – $99). The combined result of the transactions would be that each partner would recognize $12 of net gain. This is identical to the amount of gain that A, B, and C each would have recognized if the partnership had sold all of its properties and distributed the cash proceeds in a complete liquidation.

The effect of the capital account adjustments in the example is the same as a revaluation of all of the partnership assets to fair market value, an allocation of book gains and losses among the partners in accord with each partner's interest in the item, and then a reduction in each partner's capital account by the fair market value of the distributed property. Distributions often are an appropriate occasion for revaluation of all of the partnership's properties and the partners' book accounts. Treas.Reg. § 1.704–1(b)(2)(iv)(*f*)(*5*)(*ii*) provides that such an adjustment may be made for a substantial non-tax business purpose in connection with a distribution of more than a de minimis amount of money or property. Whenever a current distribution is disproportionate and intended to reduce one or more partner's interest in future profits and losses, a complete revaluation under Treas.Reg. § 1.704–1(b)(2)(iv)(*f*)(*5*)(*ii*) will be necessary (although not required by the Regulations) to achieve the economic objectives of the partners.

4.   DISTRIBUTIONS OF ENCUMBERED PROPERTY

4.1. *Tax Consequences*

If a partnership distributes property subject to a recourse debt, the distributee partner normally can be expected to assume that debt. If the property is subject to a nonrecourse debt, the distributed property is subject to the debt without any express assumption by the distributee partner. In addition, a partnership might distribute unencumbered property to a partner who assumes certain partnership debts in connection with the distribution, even though the distributed property might not be encumbered by the debt. Under the rules of § 752(a) and (b), a distribution of property encumbered by a nonrecourse debt, or in connection with which a partner assumes a recourse debt of the partnership, gives rise to three simultaneous events: (1) a distribution of property; (2) a deemed distribution of cash to a partner whose share of debt is reduced; and (3) a deemed contribution of cash by a partner whose share of debt is increased. The partner who received the encumbered property has received a property distribution. The other partners have received a deemed distribution of cash under § 752(b) because the debt no longer is a partnership debt and their shares of partnership indebtedness therefore have been reduced. Finally, the partner who received the property subject to the nonrecourse debt or assumed the partnership debt has made a deemed cash contribution to the partnership under § 752(a) because the amount of the debt encumbering the property or that the partner has assumed exceeds the partner's share of that debt when it was a partnership indebtedness.

In applying these rules, Treas.Reg. § 1.752–1(d) treats a liability as assumed by the distributee partner only if (1) the partner is personally obligated to pay the liability, (2) the creditor knows of the assumption and can directly enforce the partner's obligation for the liability, and (3) no other partner (or person that is related to another partner) bears the economic risk of loss for the liability. However, Treas.Reg. § 1.752–1(e) provides that if property distributed by a partnership to a partner is subject to a liability, the distributee partner is treated as having assumed the liability to the extent that the amount of the liability does not exceed the fair market value of the property at the time of the contribution or distribution, apparently without any regard to whether the debt is recourse or nonrecourse. Thus, it would appear that the limitation in Treas.Reg. § 1.752–1(d) applies only to debts that do not encumber the distributed property or the amount of debt encumbering the distributed property that exceed the value of the property.

The tax results of the distribution and debt assumption can differ dramatically depending on the order in which the several events described above are deemed to occur. Normally, when cash and property are distributed simultaneously, the cash is deemed to have been distributed first and the property second. See Treas.Reg. § 1.732–1(a), Ex. (1). This ordering minimizes the potential for recognition of gain. Treatment of the deemed cash contribution and deemed cash distribution is also crucial. Treas.Reg. § 1.752–1(f) provides that only the net effect of liabilities is taken into account. Rev.Rul. 79–205, 1972–2 C.B. 255, applied this principle in the case of simultaneous distributions of encumbered property to different partners.

Suppose that the AB Partnership distributes to A property having an adjusted basis to the partnership of $2,000, which is subject to liabilities of $1,600. A's basis for A's partnership interest prior to the distribution is $1,000. The partnership distributes to B property having an adjusted basis of $3,200, subject to liabilities of $2,800. B's adjusted basis for B's partnership interest is $1,500. As a result of these distributions, each partner reduces the partner's share of partnership liabilities by $2,200 ($1,600 plus $2,800, then divided by two). A's individual liabilities treated as a contribution under § 752(a) are increased by $1,600. A is treated as receiving a net cash distribution of $600, which reduces A's basis in the partnership interest from $1,000 to $400; the property then takes a basis of $400; and A has a zero basis in the partnership interest. B's individual liabilities decrease by $2,200 then increase by $2,800, B is treated as having made a net contribution of $600 to the partnership. The basis adjustment attributable to this deemed contribution is treated as occurring before the property distribution, with the result that the basis for B's partnership interest is increased from $1,500 to $2,100. Then under § 732(a)(2) the distributed property takes a $2,100 basis, and B's basis in the partnership interest is reduced to zero.

4.2. *Capital Account Adjustments*

When encumbered property is distributed, as with any distribution of property, the partnership's capital accounts are adjusted to recognize book gain or loss with respect to the distributed property. Under Treas.Reg. § 1.704–1(b)(2)(iv)(*e*)(*1*), each partner's capital account is then adjusted for the partner's distributive share of the book gain or loss. Under Treas.Reg. § 1.704–1(b)(2)(iv)(*b*)(*5*), the distributee partner's capital account is reduced by the fair market value of the property minus the encumbrance.

5. DISTRIBUTIONS OF MARKETABLE SECURITIES

Section 731(c)(1) generally treats distributions of marketable securities as money distributions. The definition of marketable securities in § 731(c)(2) broadly encompasses financial instruments and foreign currencies that are actively traded, including options, futures contracts, derivatives, and precious metals.

Distributed marketable securities are taken into account at their fair market value. As a result, a distribution of marketable securities can result in the recognition of gain to the distributee partner under § 731(a) if the fair market value of the distributed securities exceeds the partner's basis in the partnership interest. However, § 731(c)(3)(B) provides a convoluted rule that reduces the amount of the gain recognized by the partner in certain instances. The gain that otherwise would be recognized under § 731(a) is reduced by the amount by which (1) the distributee partner's share of the net gain that would have been recognized if all of the marketable securities held by the partnership had been sold by the partnership for fair market value immediately before the distribution, exceeds (2) the partner's distributive share of the net gain attributable to the marketable securities held by the partnership immediately after the transaction (using the same fair market value).[3] See Treas.Reg. § 1.731–2(j), Ex. (2). Stated differently, the distribution is not treated as money to the extent the distribution results in shifting built-in gain on all of the partnership's marketable securities, including both the distributed securities and the securities retained by the partnership, from the other partners to the distributee partner. As a result, the reduction rule of § 731(c)(3)(B) completely negates the application of § 731(c)(1) to the extent the distributee partner receives securities in which the appreciation equals that partner's share of the net appreciation inherent in all of the partnership's marketable securities.

Section 731(c)(3)(A) provides a number of exceptions to the rule treating distributions of marketable securities as money. The most important exceptions are for distributions of marketable securities to the partner who contributed them, which restores the status quo ante, and distributions by certain investment partnerships that never have conducted an active business. If the distributed securities are inventory items or unrealized receivables, as defined in § 751(c) and (d), to the partnership, then the gain recognized will be ordinary income rather than capital gain. I.R.C. § 731(c)(6). See generally, Treas.Reg. § 1.731–2.

When § 731(c) applies, the distributee partner's basis in the securities equals the basis the securities would have had under § 732—generally the partnership's basis in the case of a current distribution—plus the amount of any gain recognized by the distributee partner on the distribution. I.R.C. § 731(c)(4). The adjustment is allocated among the securities relative to their appreciation before the distribution. The partner's basis in the partnership interest is reduced under § 733 only by the partnership's basis in the distributed securities, and adjustment to the basis of remaining partnership assets under § 734(b) is permitted. I.R.C. § 731(c)(5).

6. DISTRIBUTION OF PROPERTY TO SATISFY SECTION 707 PAYMENT OBLIGATION

Rev.Rul. 2007–40, 2007–1 C.B. 1426, held that the transfer of appreciated property by a partnership to a partner in satisfaction of a guaranteed payment owed to the partner is a sale or exchange of the property by the partnership and not a distribution under § 731. Thus, the partnership is required to recognize gain on the transfer. The Ruling does not deal with whether the partnership is entitled to deduct the value of the property or whether it must capitalize that amount, as the case may be.

---

[3]   The statutory language applies this rule with respect to "marketable securities of the same class and issuer as the distributed securities," but as permitted by the flush language in § 732(c)(3)(B), Treas.Reg. § 1.732–2(b)(1) provides that all marketable securities held by the partnership are treated as marketable securities of the same class and issuer as the distributed securities.

7. DISTRIBUTIONS OF PROPERTY WHERE BASIS ADJUSTMENTS ARE IN EFFECT

If a § 754 basis adjustment election is in effect, any basis adjustments with respect to distributed property previously made under § 743(b) (upon a transfer of a partnership interest) or under § 734(b) (upon a partnership distribution) are taken into account in determining the partnership's basis for distributed assets. Treas.Reg. § 1.732–2. Assume, for example, that C acquired B's interest in the AB Partnership for $2,000 at a time when the partnership had a nondepreciable capital asset with a basis of $2,000 and value of $3,000 and depreciable property with a basis of $500 and a value of $1,000. If a § 754 election is in effect, under § 743(b) the basis of the capital asset is increased for C's benefit by $500 and the basis of the depreciable property is increased for C's benefit by $250. If the partnership later distributes the depreciable asset to C, the basis carried over to C will be $750, the partnership's initial basis of $500 plus the $250 adjustment attributable to C. If the depreciable asset is distributed to A, however, A's basis in the asset will still be $500, and C's special basis adjustment of $250 will be shifted to the nondepreciable capital asset, so that C's initial $500 basis adjustment with respect to that asset will become $750. Treas.Reg. § 1.732–2(b) and § 1.743–1(g)(2)(ii). This basis shift can only be made to property of the same class as the property having the special basis adjustment. As noted previously, § 755 divides property into two classes: capital assets and depreciable property in one class, and all other property in the other class. Hence, if the partnership had no other capital assets or depreciable property at the time of the distribution to A, C's $250 special basis adjustment would stay in abeyance until the partnership acquired property of the required character. Cf. Treas.Reg. § 1.755–1(c)(4). If no such property is ever acquired, the basis adjustment is permanently lost.

8. DISTRIBUTIONS OF PROPERTY TO TRANSFEREE PARTNER WHERE ELECTION TO ADJUST BASIS IS NOT IN EFFECT

If a distribution is made to a transferee partner within two years from the time the partner acquired the partnership interest and the partnership did not elect under § 754 to adjust the basis of partnership assets under § 743(b), § 732(d) allows the transferee to elect to treat the partnership basis for the distributed property as if the basis adjustment had been in effect. See Treas.Reg. § 1.732–1(d)(1)(iii).

Assume, for example, that the ABC Partnership owned three parcels of land, each of which had an adjusted basis of $5,000 and a fair market value of $55,000, and a depreciable asset with an adjusted basis of $30,000 and a value of $50,000. D purchased A's partnership interest for $105,000 and no § 754 election was in effect. A year later, when D's basis in D's partnership interest was $100,000, the partnership distributed one parcel of land to each of the partners in a current distribution, and D received land that had a basis to the partnership of $5,000. Absent a basis adjustment to the land, D would reduce the basis of the partnership interest from $100,000 to $95,000 and take a $5,000 basis in the land. However, under § 732(d), D can elect to increase the basis of the land by $50,000 to $55,000, and concomitantly as result of the distribution reduce the basis of the partnership interest by

$55,000. However, because no § 754 election was in effect, and § 732(d) applies only to distributed property, D does not receive an inside basis adjustment with respect to the depreciable property.

The transferee-distributee is required to apply the special basis rule of § 732(d) in situations in which not applying it would result in a shift of basis to depreciable property if the transferee partner's interest were liquidated immediately after its acquisition. Treas.Reg. § 1.732–1(d)(4). This rule applies even if the distribution occurs more than two years after the partner acquired the partnership interest. However, application of § 732(d) is required only if the fair market value of the partnership property (other than money) at the time of the transfer exceeds 110% of its adjusted basis to the partnership. Treas.Reg. § 1.732–1(d)(4) was promulgated at a time when such a basis shift was frequently possible under the provisions of § 732(c). Under the current version of § 732(c), such a basis shift rarely, if ever, can occur.

9.   DISTRIBUTIONS BY PARTNERSHIP HOLDING SECTION 704(c) PROPERTY

Section 704(c)(1)(A), discussed in Chapter 20, Section 3, requires the partnership to allocate gain or loss on the sale of contributed property to the contributing partner to the extent of the built-in gain or loss at the time of the contribution of the property. To prevent avoidance of such an allocation through the subsequent distribution of contributed property having a built-in gain or loss to a different partner, § 704(c)(1)(B) treats the distribution of such property within seven years of its contribution to the partnership as a recognition event to the contributing partner.

Section 704(c)(1)(B) does not apply if the contributing partner's interest in the partnership is completely liquidated before the contributed property is distributed to another partner. This situation is governed by § 737, which is designed to prevent avoidance of § 704(c)(1)(B). Sections 704(c)(1)(B) and 737 are discussed in detail in Section 2 of this Chapter.

10. DISTRIBUTIONS OF PARTNER'S INDEBTEDNESS

Rev.Rul. 93–7, 1993–1 C.B. 125, held that a partner receiving a distribution of the partner's own debt instrument recognizes capital gain to the extent that the fair market value of the debt instrument exceeds the partner's basis for its partnership interest and recognizes discharge of indebtedness income to the extent the adjusted issue price, which is the original issue price adjusted for accrued original issue discount and payments, exceeds the fair market value of the debt instrument. For example, suppose that X issues a debt instrument with a $100 issue price and redemption value. Subsequently, the debt instrument is purchased from the original holder by the XYZ Partnership for $100. X is a 50% partner in the XYZ partnership and is otherwise unrelated to Y and Z.[4] Still later, X's interest in the XYZ Partnership is liquidated by a distribution of the indebtedness. At the time of the distribution, X's basis for its partnership interest was $25, and the fair market value of both X's partnership interest

---

[4]   Since X is only a 50% partner, § 108(e)(3) does not apply to treat the acquisition of X's indebtedness by the partnership as cancellation of indebtedness income.

and the indebtedness was $90. Because the indebtedness is extinguished by the distribution, the mechanism by which § 731 and § 732 permit nonrecognition on distributions by preserving gain or loss through basis adjustments does not work. Current recognition of gain or loss is required. X would recognize capital gain of $65 ($90 − $25) and discharge of indebtedness income of $10. (Treas.Reg. § 1.731–1(c)(2) does not apply because that provision applies only to debt incurred directly from a partner to the partnership.) If, however, the partnership has made a § 754 election, for purposes of determining the partnership's basis adjustment under § 734(b), the distribution will be treated as a property distribution. Accordingly, the XYZ partnership would be entitled to a basis adjustment of $75. See Section 4.

PROBLEM SET 1

1.　Amy and Blair are equal partners in a law practice. At the beginning of the year, the basis of Amy's partnership interest was $3,000, and the basis of Blair's partnership interest was $5,000. On the last day of each month during the taxable year, Amy and Blair each withdrew $600 out of current cash flow. At the close of the year, it was determined that each partner's distributive share of partnership profits was $4,000. What are the tax consequences to Amy and Blair?

2.　Connie, Dallas, and Eddie are partners in the CDE partnership. For the current year, the partnership expects to realize no taxable income. The assets and partners' capital accounts of the CDE Partnership are as follows:

Partnership Assets				Partners' Capital		
Asset	Book Value	Basis	FMV		Book Value	Basis	FMV
Cash	$360	$360	$360	Connie	$293	$425	$400
Mauveacre	$110	$110	$190	Dallas	$220	$210	$300
Whiteacre	$ 20	$ 20	$100	Eddie	$147	$ 25	$200
Blackacre	$140	$140	$100				
Greenacre	$ 20	$ 20	$ 80				
Brownacre	$ 10	$ 10	$ 70				
	$660	$660	$900		$660	$660	$900

All of the properties owned by the partnership are § 1231 assets. To reduce Eddie's interest from two-ninths to one-eighth, the partnership plans to distribute $100 worth of property to him on July 1st. What would be the tax consequences of the following alternatives?

    (a)　The partnership distributes Whiteacre to Eddie.

    (b)　The partnership distributes Blackacre to Eddie.

    (c)　The partnership distributes $20 cash and Greenacre to Eddie.

    (d)　The partnership distributes $30 of cash and Brownacre to Eddie.

3.　Regan is a partner in Yosemite Acres Real Estate Development Associates. The basis of Regan's partnership interest is $9,000. The partnership holds various parcels of real estate, some of which are held for sale to customers in the ordinary course of business and some of which are held for rental. To reduce its holdings, the partnership distributed to each partner, in proportion to the partners' capital interests in the partnership, undivided interests in Blackacre and Whiteacre. The fair market value of the interest in Blackacre received by Regan was $7,500, and the portion of the partnership's basis for the interest in Blackacre received by Regan was $12,000. The fair market value of the interest in Whiteacre received by Regan was $15,000, and the portion of the partnership's basis for the interest in Whiteacre received by Regan was $6,000. What is Regan's basis in Whiteacre and Blackacre if:

(a) Whiteacre was held for sale to customers in the ordinary course of business and Blackacre was held for rental?

(b) Blackacre was held for sale to customers in the ordinary course of business and Whiteacre was held for rental?

(c) Both properties were:

(1) held for sale to customers in the ordinary course of business?

(2) held for rental?

4. Gene and Helen, cash method individuals, are equal partners in the AB Partnership. The assets and liabilities of the partnership are as follows:

Assets	Adjusted Basis/Book Value	F.M.V.	Liabilities & Partners' Capital	Basis	Book Value	F.M.V.
Cash	$ 60,000	$ 60,000	Blackacre		$ 90,000	
Blackacre	$ 30,000	$150,000	mortgage			
Whiteacre	$ 80,000	$120,000	Whiteacre		$ 60,000	
			mortgage			
			Gene	$ 85,000	$ 10,000	$ 90,000
			Helen	$ 85,000	$ 10,000	$ 90,000
	$170,000	$330,000		$170,000	$170,000	$180,000

The adjusted basis of the partnership's assets equals their book value. Blackacre and Whiteacre are both § 1231 assets. To reduce Gene's interest in the partnership to a one-quarter interest, the partnership distributed Whiteacre to Gene subject to the mortgage, which Gene assumed. Both Gene and Helen had an $85,000 basis in their respective partnership interests before the distribution. What are the tax consequences to Gene and Helen?

C. DISTRIBUTIONS BY PARTNERSHIPS HOLDING UNREALIZED RECEIVABLES OR SUBSTANTIALLY APPRECIATED INVENTORY

INTERNAL REVENUE CODE: Section 751(b)–(d).

REGULATIONS: Section 1.751–1(b)–(e).

When a distribution of either cash or property changes a partner's interest in the partnership's unrealized receivables or "substantially appreciated inventory," Subchapter K abandons the nonrecognition rule of § 731 and treats the distribution in part as a taxable exchange between the distributee partner and the partnership. This taxable exchange treatment generally applies whenever a partnership has unrealized receivables or substantially appreciated inventory and makes a non-pro rata distribution to one or more partners, regardless of whether the distribution is of unrealized receivables or substantially appreciated inventory, on the one hand, or of other assets (including cash), on the other hand. Under § 751(b), if a partner reduces the partner's interest in unrealized receivables and/or substantially appreciated inventory and increases an interest in other property, the partner is treated as exchanging an interest in the inventory and receivables for the other property in a taxable exchange, and the partner recognizes ordinary income or loss. On the other side of the exchange, the partnership is treated as purchasing an increased interest in the unrealized receivables and inventory in exchange for the partner's increased interest in the other property, and the partnership might recognize capital or § 1231 gain or loss. Similarly, if a partner increases the partner's interest in unrealized receivables and/or substantially appreciated inventory, the partner is treated as selling an interest in other property in a taxable exchange for the inventory and receivables, in which case the partner recognizes capital or § 1231 gain or loss. The partnership is treated as selling the interest in unrealized receivables and inventory in exchange for an increased interest in the other property, in which case the partnership recognizes ordinary income or loss.

In general, unrealized receivables include payments to be received for goods and services. I.R.C. § 751(c), discussed in Chapter 24, Section 1.B. In addition, recapture of depreciation and other capital recovery deductions are treated as an unrealized receivable. In most instances, § 1245 depreciation recapture is a significant, if not the most significant, unrealized receivable in any particular partnership.

Inventory is "substantially appreciated" if the fair market value of inventory held by the partnership exceeds 120% of the partnership's basis in inventory. I.R.C. § 751(b)(3)(A). For purposes of this calculation, inventory includes any item that if sold would produce ordinary income, including unrealized receivables. I.R.C. § 751(d).

Section 751(b) applies if the distribution of one class of property is "in exchange for" the partner's interest in the other class of property. Whether a non-pro rata distribution is to be considered "in exchange for" an interest in other property depends upon the effect of the distribution on the partners' interests in particular partnership assets. Assuming that partnership capital accounts generally are maintained in accordance with the principles of the § 704(b) Regulations, any non-pro rata distribution that is charged to a partner's capital account (which is to say all non-pro rata distributions) will have the effect of a distribution in exchange for an interest in other partnership property. Furthermore, if different partners receive distributions of like amounts, but the distributions are disproportionate as to unrealized receivables and substantially appreciated inventory, § 751(b) will apply.

Section 751(b) generally is intended to prevent partners from allocating among themselves the character of the gain recognized from sales of partnership property. Without this provision, a partnership would be free, for example, to distribute capital gain property to a partner who had capital losses to be offset, while the partnership recognized and allocated to the other partners an offsetting amount of ordinary income. Conversely, the partnership might distribute ordinary income property to a low tax bracket partner, while retaining capital gain property. Given this purpose, § 751(b) does not apply to a distribution of property that the distributee partner contributed to the partnership, presumably on the rationale that the status quo prior to the contribution is being restored. I.R.C. § 751(b)(2)(A).

DETAILED ANALYSIS

1. SECTION 751 PROPERTY: UNREALIZED RECEIVABLES, AND SUBSTANTIALLY APPRECIATED INVENTORY

1.1. *Unrealized Receivables*

As the Tax Court held in Ledoux v. Commissioner, Chapter 24, Section 1.B, unrealized receivables as defined in § 751(c) include any rights to payment for goods and services. Section 751(c) also includes within the definition of unrealized receivables gain that would be treated as ordinary income under any of the various recapture rules, such as § 1245. Under Treas.Reg. § 1.751–1(c)(4) and (5), the amount of potential recapture income of the distributing partnership is treated as an unrealized receivable with zero basis. The remaining value of such property is treated as a § 1231 asset with all of the partnership's basis in the asset. As a consequence, § 751(b) potentially is applicable to any distribution by a partnership holding depreciable personal property such as machinery, equipment, and amortizable § 197 intangibles.

1.2. *Substantially Appreciated Inventory*

A partnership owns inventory that has "appreciated substantially in value" if the fair market value of the inventory is more than 120% of its basis. I.R.C. § 751(b)(3)(A). Even though inventory had not actually appreciated economically, it has been held to be appreciated inventory in a situation in which it had been treated as an expensed item and hence had a zero tax basis. Yourman v. United States, 277 F.Supp. 818 (S.D.Cal.1967).

Under § 751(d), in addition to stock in trade and property held for sale to customers, inventory includes any property that would on sale be treated as property that is not a capital asset or § 1231 property, e.g., any property that would produce ordinary gain on sale. In addition, property that is not a capital or § 1231 asset in the hands of the distributee is included within the definition of inventory. I.R.C. § 751(d)(2).

Treas.Reg. § 1.751–1(d)(2)(ii) includes within the definition of inventory all accounts receivable, including those of both cash and accrual method taxpayers. However, inventory does not include other "unrealized receivables," as defined in § 751(c), such as depreciation recapture. The gain attributable to a change in a partner's interest in accounts receivable included in inventory is not taxed twice. Rather, including these items in inventory affects the determination of whether the inventory is substantially appreciated.

The inclusion in inventory of accounts receivable of an accrual method partnership makes it more difficult to meet the 120% test for substantial appreciation. Assume, for example, that an accrual method partnership holds actual inventory, having a basis of $79 and a fair market value of $100, and accounts receivable having a basis and fair market value of $30. If the accounts receivable were not treated as inventory, the 120% appreciation test would be measured by the $79 basis and $100 fair market value benchmarks, and that test would be met ($100 > [120% × $79 = $94.80]). If the accounts receivable are included in inventory, however, the 120% test is not met because the $130 fair market value of the inventory does not exceed 120% of its $109 basis (120% × $109 = $130.80).

If a partnership's inventory has appreciated in value but not to an extent that results in classification as substantial appreciation under § 751(b)(3), then no part of a distribution that affects a partner's interest in inventory will be subject to exchange treatment under § 751(b). To prevent artificial manipulations of inventories designed to avoid § 751(a) by reducing the amount of appreciation in the partnership's inventory, § 751(b)(3)(B) excludes from the computation of substantial appreciation any inventory property if a principal purpose of the acquisition of the property was avoiding § 751(b). Section 751(b)(3)(B) presumably would apply, for example, if a partnership purchased accrual method accounts receivable at near face value, other than in the ordinary course of business, shortly before a distribution, so as to reduce inventory appreciation below 120%.

2. RULES OF THUMB

Implementation of § 751(b) under current Regulations suggests at least three "rules of thumb." Proposed Regulations, discussed later, would alter the analytical approach if finalized.

2.1. *Distribution of Cash*

A distribution of cash by a partnership holding unrealized receivables or substantially appreciated inventory results in recognition of ordinary income by the distributee partner, but in such a case the other partners will not recognize any gain or loss under § 751(b). The other partners are treated as exchanging an interest in the cash for their interest in unrealized receivables and inventory, but no gain or loss is realized on a cash exchange, which is essentially a purchase for the amount of cash.

2.2. *Disproportionate Distribution of Capital and/or § 1231 Assets*

A disproportionate distribution of capital assets and/or § 1231 assets results in recognition of ordinary income by the distributee partner and recognition of capital gain or loss and/or § 1231 gain or loss by the other partners.

2.3. *Disproportionate Distribution of Unrealized Receivables or Inventory*

A disproportionate distribution of unrealized receivables and/or inventory results in capital gain or loss and/or § 1231 gain or loss by the distributee partner and recognition of ordinary income by the other partners.

3.   EXAMPLES

The following examples illustrates the operation of § 751(b) as interpreted by current Regulations. Proposed Regulations, discussed below in Detailed Analysis 6, would alter the analytical framework if finalized.

3.1. *Example (1)*

Suppose that C and D are equal partners in the CD Partnership, which owns a capital asset having a fair market value of $300 and a basis of $60 and inventory having a fair market value of $900 and a basis of $210. C's basis for C's partnership interest is $135. Suppose further that the partnership distributes the capital asset to C to effect the reduction of C's interest to that of a one-third partner. The inventory is "substantially appreciated" as defined in § 751(d) because $900 is greater than $210 × 120%. Section 751(b) first treats C as having received a § 731 distribution of an undivided interest in a portion of the inventory (none of which was actually distributed). C is then treated as exchanging with the partnership in a taxable transaction the portion of the inventory deemed to have been distributed for an undivided portion of the capital asset (which actually was distributed) of equal value. The remaining portion of the capital asset (which actually was distributed) is received by C as a distribution subject to § 731. The general rules for determining gain or loss under §§ 731 and 741 and basis under § 732 are applied to the preliminary deemed distribution, and this hypothetical exchange is taxed under § 1001, using normal characterization rules, as modified by §§ 724 and 735. See Treas.Reg. § 1.751–1(g), Exs. (2), (3), (4), and (5).

The hypothetical exchange that is at the heart of § 751(b) is best understood by constructing a table to determine the change in the distributee partner's interest in the partnership assets and the partnership's interest in the assets.[5] In the case of the CD Partnership, C's exchange would be as follows:

---

[5]   This analytical method was first advanced in W. McKee, W. Nelson & R. Whitmire, Federal Income Taxation of Partnerships and Partners (Warren, Gorham & Lamont 1977).

<u>C's Exchange</u>

Property	Value of Distributee's Post-distribution Interest as a Partner	+	Value of Distributed Property	-	Value of Distributee's Pre-distribution Interest	=	Increase (Decrease) in Distributee's Interest
§ 751 <u>Property</u>							
Inventory	$300		$ 0		$450		($150)
Other <u>Property</u>							
Capital Asset	$ 0		$300		$150		$150

This table demonstrates that C has exchanged a $150 interest in inventory held by the partnership for an interest in other property (the capital asset) worth the same amount. To reflect this exchange, C is treated as having received $150 worth of the inventory in a § 731 distribution. Under § 732, C's basis for this inventory is $35, which equals the partnership's basis in the distributed portion of the inventory ($150/$900 × $210). C is then treated as having received $150 worth of the capital asset from the partnership in a taxable exchange for the inventory. C's amount realized on the exchange is $150, the fair market value of the capital asset received in exchange for the inventory. C subtracts the $35 basis in the inventory that is treated as distributed, and C recognizes ordinary gain of $115 on the exchange ($150 − $35).

On the other side of the exchange, the partnership is treated as having received the $150 worth of the inventory from C in exchange for $150 worth of the capital asset. The partnership's amount realized on this exchange is $150, the fair market value of the increased interest in inventory received from C. The partnership's basis in the exchanged interest in the capital asset is $30 representing the partnership's basis in portion of the capital asset transferred to C in the exchange ($150/$300 × $60). The partnership recognizes a $120 capital gain on the exchange of the capital asset ($150 − $30). The remaining $150 worth of the capital asset ($300 distributed less $150 treated as sold) is received by C in a § 731 distribution. C's basis in the distributed capital asset is $180, consisting of $150 for the portion acquired in the taxable exchange under § 751(b), plus $30 under § 732 for the portion received in the § 731 distribution. C's basis in the partnership interest is reduced from $135 to $70, reflecting the deemed distribution under § 751(b) of inventory with a basis of $35 and the distribution under § 731 of the capital asset with a basis of $30. The partnership's basis in the inventory is increased from $210 to $325 ($175 for the undistributed five-sixths, plus $150 purchase price for one-sixth).

Treas.Reg. § 1.751–1(b)(2)(ii) and (b)(3)(ii) allocate partnership gain recognized on a constructive § 751(b) exchange to the nondistributee partners, who are the partners whose interest in distributed property is reduced. The distributee partner recognizes gain only on the distributee's own side of the exchange. Thus, in the CD Partnership example, all of the partnership gain on the exchange of the capital asset would be allocated to D.

Section 751(b) also applies if the distributee partner receives more than the distributee's share of the receivables and inventory and, hence, less than the distributee's share of other property or money. In this case, under § 751(b)(1)(A) the partnership is regarded as having sold its interest in the distributed receivables or inventory. The partnership will recognize ordinary income on that imputed sale, and the basis of its remaining assets will be adjusted to reflect the purchase of the distributee partner's share. Likewise, the distributee partner will recognize gain or loss on the imputed sale of other property to the partnership. This gain or loss will be characterized as ordinary or capital with respect to the character of the property.

3.2. *Example (2)*

Application of § 751(b) is more complex when, as is usually the case, the partnership has multiple assets in each class. Consider the EFG Partnership, the assets and partners' capital accounts of which are as follows:

	Assets			Partners' Capital Accounts	
	F.M.V.[6]	Basis		F.M.V.	Basis
Cash	$126,000	$126,000	E	$150,000	$102,000
Accounts Receivable	$ 63,000	$ 0	F	$150,000	$102,000
Inventory	$ 90,000	$ 63,000	G	$150,000	$102,000
Whiteacre	$ 90,000	$ 76,500			
Blackacre	$ 81,000	$ 40,500			
	$450,000	$306,000		$450,000	$306,000

To reduce E's partnership interest from one-third to one-ninth, the partnership distributes $112,500, in the form of Blackacre and $31,500 of cash, to E. Assuming that Whiteacre and Blackacre are capital assets, the constructive exchange under § 751(b) is computed as follows:

---

[6]   It is assumed that in connection with this distribution, pursuant to Treas.Reg. § 1.704–1(b)(2)(iv)(*f*)(5), the partnership will revalue its assets and partners' capital accounts for book purposes so that book value equals fair market value immediately prior to the distribution.

E's Exchange

Property	Value of Distributee's Post-distribution Interest as a Partner	+	Value of Distributed Property	-	Value of Distributee's Pre-distribution Interest	=	Increase (Decrease) in Distributee's Interest
§ 751 Property							
Acc'ts Rec	$ 7,000		$ 0		$21,000		($14,000)
Inventory	$10,000		$ 0		$30,000		($20,000)
Total 751 Property							($34,000)
Other Property							
Cash	$10,500		$31,500		$42,000		$ 0
Whiteacre	$10,000		$ 0		$30,000		($20,000)
Blackacre	$ 0		$81,000		$27,000		$54,000
Total Other Property							$34,000

Although the exchange table reveals that E has exchanged interests in the accounts receivable, inventory, and Whiteacre for an interest in Blackacre, § 751(b) applies only to the exchange of interests in the inventory and accounts receivable for an interest in Blackacre. See Treas.Reg. § 1.751–1(g), Ex. (2). Thus, E is treated as engaging in a taxable exchange of $34,000 of accounts receivable and inventory for a $34,000 interest in Blackacre. E is treated as having received in a hypothetical distribution $14,000 of accounts receivable, in which E takes a zero basis, and $20,000 worth of inventory, in which E takes a $14,000 basis ($63,000 partnership basis × ($20,000/$90,000)). E then exchanges these assets with the partnership for an undivided interest in Blackacre worth $34,000. E's amount realized on this exchange is $14,000 worth of Blackacre for the accounts receivable and $20,000 of Blackacre for the inventory. E recognizes $14,000 of ordinary income attributable to the accounts receivable ($14,000 − 0) and $6,000 of ordinary income attributable to the inventory ($20,000 − $14,000).

The partnership's amount realized for the $34,000 interest in Blackacre transferred in the exchange is a $14,000 interest in accounts receivable and a $20,000 interest in inventory. The partnership allocates $17,000 of the basis of Blackacre ($40,500 × (34,000/81,000)) to this exchange and recognizes a gain of $17,000 on the sale or exchange of Blackacre, all of which is allocated to F and G.

Finally, E is treated as receiving the remaining $47,000 interest in Blackacre ($81,000 − $34,000) and the $31,500 of cash in a § 731 distribution. E's basis in Blackacre is $57,500, consisting of $34,000 for the portion acquired in the taxable exchange under § 751(b) and $23,500 under § 732 for the portion received in the § 731 distribution ($40,500 × $47,000/$81,000). E's basis in the partnership interest is reduced by $69,000 to $33,000, reflecting the deemed distribution under § 751(b) of inventory with a basis of $14,000, the distribution under § 731 of a portion of Blackacre with a basis of $23,500, and cash of $31,500. The partnership's basis in the inventory is increased from $63,000 to $69,000 ($49,000 for the undistributed seven-ninths, plus $20,000 purchase price for one-sixth), and its basis in the accounts receivable is increased to $14,000.

3.3. *Example (3)*

Assume that the partnership in Example (2) distributed to E the $63,000 of accounts receivable and $49,500 of cash. In that case, the exchange table would be as follows:

E's Exchange

Property	Value of Distributee's Post-distribution Interest as a Partner	+	Value of Distributed Property	−	Value of Distributee's Pre-distribution Interest	=	Increase (Decrease) in Distributee's Interest
§ 751 Property							
Acc'ts Rec	$ 0		$63,000		$21,000		$42,000
Inventory	$10,000		$ 0		$30,000		($20,000)
Total 751 Property							$22,000
Other Property							
Cash	$ 8,500		$49,500		$42,000		$16,000
Whiteacre	$10,000		$ 0		$30,000		($20,000)
Blackacre	$ 9,000		$ 0		$27,000		($18,000)
Total Other Property							($22,000)

In this transaction, E has exchanged interests in inventory, Whiteacre, and Blackacre for interests in accounts receivable and cash. Section 751(b), however, is concerned only with the net exchange of interests in § 751 property for other property. Thus, E has received $22,000 of accounts receivable in exchange for other property, i.e., Whiteacre and Blackacre. See Treas.Reg. § 1.751–1(g), Ex. (5). Identifying the precise exchange, however, is more difficult because the Regulations allow some flexibility in this case. Treas.Reg. § 1.751–1(g), Ex. (3) and Ex. (5) appear to sanction an agreement between the partners specifying the "other property" in which the distributee partner has relinquished an interest in situations in which the distributee partner receives § 751 assets in the distribution. Thus, for example, the partners might agree that E surrendered an interest worth $22,000 in Whiteacre and surrendered no interest in Blackacre. Such an agreement would minimize the gain realized by E on the constructive exchange following the hypothetically distributed interest in other assets, i.e., Whiteacre, for an interest in the accounts receivable because Blackacre is more highly appreciated than Whiteacre. If E is treated as hypothetically receiving and exchanging an interest in Whiteacre worth $22,000, E recognizes only $3,300 of gain because a distribution of a 22/90ths undivided interest in Whiteacre would give E a basis of $18,700 in the exchanged property. Conversely, a distribution of a 22/81sts undivided interest in Blackacre would give E a basis of only $11,000 for the property surrendered in the constructive exchange, resulting in a gain to E of $11,000.

In the converse situation, i.e., the distributee relinquishes an interest in § 751 assets, as illustrated in Example (2), the Regulations are silent regarding the ability to designate the property in which the distributee partner surrendered the distributee's interest. Allowing such a designation, either of § 751 assets or of other assets, permits the partners to select assets for the exchange that will minimize the gain realized on the deemed exchange. To permit this with respect to the capital and § 1231 assets retained by the partnership is not inconsistent with the purpose of § 751 and, in light of the flexibility of the other provisions of Subchapter K, is defensible. But to permit such selection if the distributee partner surrenders the distributee's share of ordinary income assets is inconsistent with its purpose.

4. INTERACTION OF SECTIONS 751(b) AND 752(b)

Section 751(b) can require recognition of gain in some unexpected situations due to the deemed distribution rule of § 752(b). Suppose that the HIJ partnership, of which H, I, and J are equal partners, has assets with a value of $175, of which $40 are unrealized receivables (having a basis of zero), and liabilities of $100. Suppose further, that K contributes $25 to the partnership to become a one-quarter partner. Because H, I, and J each have reduced their share of partnership liabilities from $33.33 to $25, each has a deemed distribution of $8.33. Furthermore, because each has reduced the partner's interest in the partnership's unrealized receivables from $13.33 to $10, § 751(b) applies. H, I, and J are each treated as having received $3.33 of receivables in a distribution to which § 731(a) applies. Under § 732 each takes a zero basis in the receivables. Section 751(b) then treats them each as having sold the receivables to the partnership for $3.33, and each must recognize that amount of gain. The remaining $5 deemed distribution to each of H, I, and J is treated as a distribution of cash under § 731. K did not receive a constructive distribution, so § 751(b) does not apply to K. See Rev.Rul. 84–102, 1984–2 C.B. 119. The partnership now has a $10 basis for its unrealized receivables. Although § 743(b) does not apply to give K a $10 basis in K's share of the unrealized receivables, if the partnership's assets and partners' capital accounts were revalued pursuant to Treas.Reg. § 1.704–1(b)(2)(iv)(f), reverse § 704(c) allocations of the remaining $30 of income subsequently realized with respect to the unrealized receivables would be required by Treas.Reg. § 1.704–3(a)(6)(i) and 1.704–1(b)(4)(i). See Chapter 20, Section 3.

Furthermore, if the partnership's assets were not revalued, Treas.Reg. § 1.704–1(b)(5), Ex. (14)(iv) indicates that a special allocation to H, I, and J of all of the income subsequently realized with respect to the receivables will be respected.

5. ANALYSIS

Section 751(b) is theoretically flawed because it measures disproportionality by the value of substantially appreciated inventory and accounts receivable rather than by the excess of value over basis. Thus, it fails to fulfill completely its stated purpose. In Examples (1) through (3), above, each partner's share of ordinary income before the distribution is $30,000. If, however, the partnership distributed $38,250 of accounts receivable and $74,250 of cash to E to reduce E's interest to one-ninth, § 751(b) would be inapplicable because E would have no net change in E's total interest in aggregate § 751 property—accounts receivable and inventory taken together. This result is illustrated in the following computation:

Property	Value of Distributee's Post-distribution Interest as a Partner	+	Value of Distributed Property	–	Value of Distributee's Pre-distribution Interest	=	Increase (Decrease) in Distributee's Interest
§ 751 Property							
Acc'ts Rec	$ 2,750		$38,250		$21,000		$20,000
Inventory	$10,000		$ 0		$30,000		($20,000)
Total 751							$ 0
Other Property							
Cash	$ 5,750		$74,250		$42,000		$38,000
Whiteacre	$10,000		$ 0		$30,000		($20,000)
Blackacre	$ 9,000		$ 0		$27,000		($18,000)
Total Other Property							$ 0

Upon collection of the $63,000 of accounts receivable and sale of the inventory, E recognizes ordinary income of $41,000 attributable to the accounts receivable and $3,000 attributable to the inventory, for a total of $42,000, while F and G each recognize only $24,000 of ordinary income. These results are inconsistent with the objectives of § 751 because the partners have been able to choose among themselves which partners will disproportionately recognize ordinary income and capital gain without affecting the overall amount of gain recognized by each partner.

6. 2014 PROPOSED REGULATIONS

The IRS and Treasury Department proposed amendments to the Regulations under § 751(b) that would completely change the mechanics of the application of § 751(b) in nonliquidating distributions. REG–151416–06, Certain Distributions Treated as Sales or Exchanges, 79 F.R. 65151 (Nov. 11, 2014). As described above, the application of § 751(b) generally requires creation of a constructive taxable exchange whenever a partner receives a current distribution that alters the partners' respective interests in unrealized receivables or substantially appreciated inventory. As noted in Detailed Analysis 5, as implemented by the current Regulations, § 751(b) is flawed because it measures disproportionately by the value of substantially appreciated inventory and accounts receivable rather than by the built-in gain or loss attributable to these assets. Thus, it fails to fulfill completely its stated purpose. The Proposed Regulations would cure that flaw by amending the § 751(b) Regulations to operate similarly to the § 751(a) Regulations, which provide generally that a partner's interest in § 751 property is the amount of income or loss from § 751 property that would be allocated to the partner if the partnership had sold all of its property in a fully taxable transaction for cash in an amount equal to the fair market value of such property. Prop.Reg. § 1.751–1(a)(2). The hypothetical sale approach in the § 751(b) Proposed Regulations shifts the focus away from exchanges of gross value to tax gain and loss and instead requires the application of § 751(b) to the extent the distribution reduces a partner's share of income (or increases a partner's share of loss) related to § 751 assets.

If the distribution reduces the amount of ordinary income (or increases the amount of ordinary loss) from § 751 property that would be allocated to, or recognized by, a partner (thus reducing that partner's interest in the partnership's § 751 property), the distribution triggers § 751(b). To make this method work, Treas.Reg. § 1.704–1(b)(2)(iv)(f) would be amended to require revaluations of partnership property if the partnership distributes money or other property to a partner as consideration for an interest in the partnership and the partnership owns § 751 property immediately after the distribution. Prop.Reg. § 1.751–1(b)(2)(iv). (A partnership that does not own § 751 property immediately after the distribution may revalue its property but is not required to do so.)

Determining whether any partner's share of § 751 gain or loss is reduced in connection with a distribution can be complex because it takes into account (1) § 704(c) and reverse § 704(c) gain and loss with respect to § 751 assets (discussed in the text in Chapter 20, Section 3), (2) § 732 basis adjustments to distributed property discussed above in Section 1.B, (3) § 734(b) basis adjustments (discussed below in Section 4), and (4) shifts of § 743(b) basis adjustments among assets as a result of distributions (discussed above in Section 1.B).

To determine each partner's net § 751 unrealized gain or loss immediately before and after a distribution, the Proposed Regulations use the hypothetical sale approach (as under § 751(a)) to determine a partner's net § 751 unrealized gain or loss. A partner's net § 751 unrealized gain or loss immediately before a distribution equals the amount of net income or loss from § 751 property that would be allocated to the partner if the partnership sold all of its assets for cash equal to their fair market value. Prop.Reg. § 1.751–1(b)(2)(ii). This calculation takes into account (1) any § 743(b) basis adjustments with respect to the partners (as determined under Treas.Reg. § 1.743–1(j)(3)), (2) any remedial allocations under Treas.Reg. § 1.704–3(d), and (3) any carryover basis adjustments described in Treas.Reg. §§ 1.743–1(g)(2)(ii), 1.755–1(b)(5)(iii)(D), or 1.755–1(c)(4) (discussed in Chapter 24) as if those adjustments were applied to the basis of new partnership property with a fair market value of $0.

A partner's net § 751 unrealized gain or loss immediately after a distribution is calculated in the same manner, except that the partnership is deemed to have sold its retained assets and the distributee partner is deemed to have sold the assets received in the distribution. Prop.Reg. § 1.751–1(b)(2)(iii). The partnership's hypothetical sale determines the net § 751 unrealized gain or loss of the non-distributee partners (and of the distributee partner if that partner was not completely redeemed), and the distributee partner's hypothetical sale determines the net § 751 unrealized gain or loss attributable to that partner outside the partnership. (However, any § 734(b) basis adjustments that occur as a result of the distribution are not taken into account in determining a partner's share of net § 751 unrealized gain or loss.)

Although the Proposed Regulations prescribe with specificity the method for determining whether § 751(b) will apply to a distribution, the Proposed Regulations do not require the use of any particular approach for determining the tax consequences of a distribution that triggers § 751(b). Rather, the Proposed Regulations provide that if, under the hypothetical sale approach, a distribution reduces a partner's interest in the partnership's § 751 property, giving rise to a § 751(b) amount, then the partnership must use a reasonable approach that is consistent with the purpose of § 751(b) to determine the tax consequences of the reduction. According to the preamble to the Proposed Regulations, the reason behind this "reasonable approach" rule is that "a deemed gain approach produces an appropriate outcome in the greatest number of circumstances out of the approaches under consideration, and that the hot asset sale approach also produced an appropriate outcome in most circumstances. However, no one approach produced an appropriate outcome in all circumstances."

Generally, a partnership must use one approach consistently. Prop.Reg. § 1.751–1(b)(3)(i). Examples illustrate situations in which the approach adopted in § 1.752–1(b)(2) of the Proposed Regulations for purposes of determining partner's interest in the partnership's property is reasonable and in which it is not reasonable.

The preamble describes the general principle of the purpose of the § 751(b) recognition rules as follows:

> If § 751(b) applies to a distribution, each partner must generally recognize or take into account currently ordinary income equal to the partner's "§ 751(b) amount." If a partner has net § 751 unrealized gain both before and after the distribution, then the partner's § 751(b) amount equals the partner's net § 751 unrealized

gain immediately before the distribution less the partner's net § 751 unrealized gain immediately after the distribution. If a partner has net § 751 unrealized loss both before and after the distribution, then the partner's § 751(b) amount equals the partner's net § 751 unrealized loss immediately after the distribution less the partner's net § 751 unrealized loss immediately before the distribution. If a partner has net § 751 unrealized gain before the distribution and net § 751 unrealized loss after the distribution, then the partner's § 751(b) amount equals the sum of the partner's net § 751 unrealized gain immediately before the distribution and the partner's net § 751 unrealized loss immediately after the distribution.

The examples in the Proposed Regulations illustrate two alternative reasonable approaches—the "deemed gain" approach and the "hot asset" sale approach—for determining the income inclusion for a partner whose net § 751 unrealized gain is reduced (or net § 751 unrealized loss is increased) in connection with a distribution. See Prop.Reg. § 1.751–1(g), Exs. 3–8. Examples also illustrate situations in which the approach adopted is not reasonable.

Under the "deemed gain" approach, the partnership recognizes ordinary income in the aggregate amount of each partner's § 751(b) amount, and the partnership then allocates ordinary income to the partner or partners in proportion to their respective § 751(b) amounts. Thereafter, the partnership makes appropriate basis adjustments to its assets to reflect its ordinary income recognition, and the partners make appropriate adjustments to the bases of their partnership interests.

Under the "hot asset sale" approach, for any partner whose share of § 751 assets is reduced (selling partner), whether or not the selling partner is the distributee, the selling partner would be treated as receiving the relinquished hot assets in a deemed distribution and selling to the partnership the relinquished share of the hot assets immediately before the actual distribution. The hot asset sale approach is straightforward if the distributee partner's share of hot asset appreciation is reduced by the distribution: the partnership would be treated as distributing the relinquished share of § 751 assets to the distributee partner who in turn sells the § 751 assets back to the partnership, recognizing ordinary income, with appropriate adjustments to the distributee partner's basis in the partnership interest and capital account. The asset deemed to have been sold would take a cost basis, and the distribution would be governed by §§ 731 through 736.

Regardless of whether the deemed gain or hot asset sale method is adopted, the Proposed Regulations require a distributee partner to recognize capital gain to the extent necessary to prevent the distribution from triggering a basis adjustment under § 734(b) that would reduce other partners' shares of net unrealized § 751 gain or loss. Prop.Reg. § 1.751–1(b)(3)(ii)(A), –1(g), Exs. 5 & 6. This is required because the § 734(b) basis adjustment is not taken into account in determining the partners' net § 751 unrealized gain or loss immediately after the § 751 distribution. Thus, a nondistributee partner's interest in § 751 property may be reduced without triggering ordinary income under § 751(b). To avoid this result, Prop.Reg. § 1.751–1(b)(3)(ii)(A) requires the distributee partner to recognize capital gain immediately before the distribution in an amount that eliminates the § 734(b) basis adjustment. As a result, the basis of the distributed § 751 property is not reduced under § 732, thereby eliminating any § 734(b) basis adjustment.

In addition, either approach produces problems where the distributee partner has insufficient basis in the partnership interest to absorb the partnership's adjusted basis in the distributed hot assets. In this situation, the results can be inconsistent with the purpose of § 751(b). Thus, the Proposed Regulations allow distributee partners to elect to recognize capital gain in certain circumstances to avoid § 732 decreases to the basis of distributed § 751 property. Prop.Reg. § 1.751–1(b)(3)(ii)(B), –1(g), Ex. 7.

The Proposed Regulations also contain complex anti-abuse rules that apply when a partner engages in a transaction that relies on § 704(c) to eliminate or reduce ordinary income. Prop.Reg. § 1.751–1(b)(4).

The Proposed Regulations would apply to distributions occurring in any taxable period ending on or after the date of publication of Final Regulations. However, a partnership and its partners may rely on Prop.Reg. § 1.751–1(b)(2) for purposes of determining a partner's interest in the partnership's § 751 property on or after November 13, 2014, provided the partnership and its partners apply each of Prop.Regs. §§ 1.751–1(a)(2), 1.751–1(b)(2), and 1.751–1(b)(4) consistently for all partnership distributions and sales or exchanges. Generally speaking (with some exceptions), this means that if the partners' shares of ordinary income remain unchanged after a distribution, either due to reverse § 704(c) allocations or because the distribution carries out to the distributee partner a pro rata share of ordinary income (without regard to whether a pro rata share of the value of hot assets has been distributed), gain recognition under § 751(b) will not be triggered.

PROBLEM SET 2

1.   The LMN Partnership' assets and partner's capital accounts are as follows:

Assets	Adjusted Basis/Book Value	F.M.V.	Partners' Capital	Adjusted Basis/Book Value	F.M.V.
Cash	$120,000	$120,000	L	$105,000	$150,000
Inventory	$ 75,000	$150,000	M	$105,000	$150,000
Blackacre	$ 60,000	$ 75,000	N	$105,000	$150,000
Whiteacre	$ 60,000	$105,000			
	$315,000	$450,000		$315,000	$450,000

Blackacre and Whiteacre are both § 1231 property.

(a)   The partnership distributes $75,000 of cash to L. As a result of the distribution, L's interest is reduced from a one-third to a one-fifth interest in the partnership, worth $75,000, after the distribution. What are the consequences to L and the partnership (including M's and N's distributive share of any income items) as a result of the distribution?

(b) The partnership distributes Blackacre to L to reduce L's interest to one-fifth. What are the consequences to L and the partnership (including M's and N's distributive share of any income items) as a result of the distribution?

(c) The partnership distributes one-half of the inventory to L to reduce L's interest to one-fifth. What are the consequences to L and the partnership (including M's and N's distributive share of any income items) resulting from the distribution?

SECTION 2. "MIXING BOWL" TRANSACTIONS: DISTRIBUTIONS OF CONTRIBUTED PROPERTY

INTERNAL REVENUE CODE: Sections 704(c)(1)(B) and (c)(2); 737.

Section 704(c)(1)(A), discussed in Chapter 20, Section 3, requires the partnership to allocate gain or loss on the sale of contributed property to the contributing partner to the extent of the built-in gain or loss at the time of the contribution of the property. Section 704(c)(1)(C), also discussed in Chapter 20, applies to prevent a partner who contributes built-in loss property from shifting the built-in loss to other partners. Sections 704(c)(1)(A) and (c)(1)(C) will fail to allocate gain or loss to the contributing partner if the property is distributed to another partner before the gain or loss is recognized, or if the contributing partner leaves the partnership before the property is sold. To prevent avoidance of the required allocation of built-in gain or loss through the subsequent distribution of contributed property to a different partner, § 704(c)(1)(B) treats the distribution of such property within seven years of its contribution to the partnership as a recognition event to the contributing partner. Alternatively, under § 737, if other property is distributed to the contributing partner within seven years of a contribution to the partnership of appreciated property, the contributing partner is required to recognize gain to the extent of the lesser of (1) the fair market value of the distributed property over the distributee partner's basis in the partnership interest, or (2) the amount of the gain built in to the contributed property.

In the event of a distribution of contributed property to a non-contributing partner, § 704(c)(1)(B) requires the contributing partner to recognize the amount of the gain or loss that would have been allocated to the contributing partner by reason of § 704(c)(1)(A) if the partnership had sold the property for its fair market value on the date of the distribution. Under Proposed Regulations, if the contributing partner has a § 704(c)(1)(C) basis adjustment in the distributed property, the contributing partner would use that adjustment to determine the loss amount. Prop.Reg. § 1.704–3(f)(3)(v)(B) (2014). (If a distribution of the property in which the contributing partner has a § 704(c)(1)(C) basis adjustment occurs outside of the seven-year window, the Proposed Regulations specify that the section 704(c)(1)(C) basis adjustment is reallocated among the remaining items of partnership property under Treas.Reg. § 1.755–1(c).) Even though the gain or loss is recognized directly by the contributing partner, and not as a distributive share of partnership income, § 704(c)(1)(B)(iii) requires that the contributing partner's basis in the partnership interest be increased or decreased appropriately. Similarly, in applying §§ 732 and 705 to determine the distributee partner's basis for the property and for the partnership interest after the distribution, the partnership's basis in the property immediately before the distribution is increased by the gain recognized by the contributing partner; § 704(c)(1)(C) will have already required the partnership to decrease the basis available to other partners as to any property contributed with built-in loss. Prop.Reg. § 1.704–3(f)(1) (2014).

Assume that A contributes $100 cash and Blackacre, with an adjusted basis of $100 and a fair market value of $400, to the AB Partnership. B contributes $500 cash. Four years later (thereby avoiding a disguised sale under § 707(a)(2)(B)), when Blackacre is worth $450 and the partnership has total assets of $1,100, the partnership distributes Blackacre to B and reduces B's interest in the partnership commensurately. Section 704(c)(1)(B) taxes A in the year of the distribution on the entire $300 gain that was inherent in Blackacre at the time of its contribution. In determining B's basis in Blackacre under § 732(a), the partnership adds the $300 recognized by A to its original basis of $100, so that B takes a $400 basis in Blackacre.

Section 704(c)(1)(B) does not apply if the contributing partner's interest in the partnership is completely liquidated before the contributed property is distributed to another partner. To fill this gap, § 737 prevents avoidance of § 704(c)(1)(B) by requiring recognition of gain on a distribution of other property to the contributing partner within seven years of the contribution of built-in gain property. Section 737 requires that a partner recognize gain on the distribution of property to the partner to the extent of the lesser of (1) the fair market value of distributed property over the partner's adjusted basis in the partnership interest, or (2) the amount of gain the partner would have recognized under § 704(c)(1)(B) on a distribution of contributed property to another partner. For example, suppose that D contributed Capital Asset #1, with a basis of $200 and a fair market value of $1,000, to the ABCD partnership in Year 1; in Year 3, the partnership distributed Capital Asset #2 to D in complete liquidation of D's partnership interest; and in Year 5 the partnership distributed Capital Asset #1 to A. Since D is not a partner in Year 5, § 704(c)(1)(B) does not apply. Apart from § 737, D simply would take Capital Asset #2 with a basis of $200 and would not recognize gain or loss. I.R.C. §§ 731 and 732(b). To prevent such avoidance of § 704(c)(1)(B), § 737 taxes D on the receipt of Capital Asset #2 in Year 3 in an amount equal to the gain that would have been

service partnership to be paid for that partner's share of partnership goodwill, then payments for goodwill remain subject to § 736(b).

As a consequence of § 736(b)(2) and (3), the partners in a service partnership may be able to designate whether some portion of a distribution to a withdrawing partner is subject to either § 736(a) or § 736(b) by providing in the partnership agreement for payment for the withdrawing partner's share of goodwill. A withdrawing partner in a service partnership would generally prefer payments in liquidation of the interest to be classified as § 736(b) payments with basis recovery and capital gain treatment. The continuing partners would, however, generally prefer classification of payments as § 736(a) payments that are taxable in full as ordinary income to the withdrawing partner and that reduce the income of the continuing partners.

Matters are further complicated because Treas.Reg. § 1.736–1(b)(1) and (2) provide that payments attributable to unrealized receivables are governed by § 736(b) to the extent of the withdrawing partner's basis in any unrealized receivables (which will generally be basis resulting from any special basis adjustments under § 743(b)). Unrealized receivables for purposes of § 736(b)(2) and (3) also do not include recapture amounts, which would instead be included in the 736(b) analysis. I.R.C. §§ 751(c) (parenthetical in the flush language) & 736(b)(1).

When a partner receives a liquidating distribution, new provisions (e.g., § 199A, § 1061) added by the 2017 Tax Act may be relevant. Guidance is required, however, regarding the interaction of these new provisions with the specific rules of Subchapter K. For example, § 199A(c)(4)(B) specifies that § 707(c) payments for services do not constitute qualified business income; that may include payments made to a retiring service partner that are treated as § 707(c) payments through application of § 736(a)(2).

DETAILED ANALYSIS

1. EFFECT ON PARTNERS' CAPITAL ACCOUNTS

In the case of a distribution of any property other than money to the withdrawing partner, Treas.Reg. § 1.704–1(b)(2)(iv)(*e*)(*1*) requires that all partners' capital accounts must be adjusted to reflect the gain or loss that would have been recognized if the distributed property had been sold for its fair market value instead of distributed. The withdrawing partner's capital account is then reduced by the fair market value of distributed property, which should reduce the withdrawing partner's capital account to zero as a result of a distribution in complete liquidation of that interest. Only the payments classified as § 736(b) payments, however, will apply to reduce the withdrawing partner's capital account. Alternatively, Treas.Reg. § 1.704–1(b)(2)(iv)(*f*)(*5*)(*ii*) provides that in connection with the liquidation of a partner's interest in the partnership all of the partnership's properties and the partners' book accounts may be adjusted to reflect fair market values if there is a substantial non-tax business purpose for doing so. This book-up often is advisable as the partnership must determine the fair market value of the withdrawing partner's interest in partnership property in any event in order to determine the amount distributable to the partner.

2.   VALUATION OF PARTNERSHIP ASSETS

Determining the amount taxable as ordinary income under § 736(a) or treated as a distribution under § 736(b) requires a valuation of the distributee's interest in all the partnership's assets, including the work in progress (unrealized receivables) held by the partnership at the time of the distribution and, if the partnership agreement provides for payments with respect to goodwill, the partnership's goodwill. Treas.Reg. § 1.736–1(b)(1) states: "Generally, the valuation placed by the partners upon a partner's interest in partnership property in an arm's length agreement will be regarded as correct." Treas.Reg. § 1.736–1(b)(3) similarly allows the valuation placed on goodwill, whether the valuation is specific in amount or based on a formula, to be fixed for purposes of § 736(b) by an arm's length agreement among the partners. However, Treas.Reg. § 1.755–1(a)(2) and (5) provides that for purposes of determining the fair market value of all partnership property when allocating any § 734(b) basis adjustment available to the partnership as a result of a § 736(b) distribution (discussed in Section 4), the fair market value of all partnership property other than goodwill is to be determined taking into account all the facts and circumstances, and the fair market value of goodwill must be determined using the residual method. Whether the broad discretion under that Temporary Regulation to ignore arms' length agreements as to value will be extended to the operation of § 736 is unclear as a matter of statutory interpretation. It would be incongruous, however, to respect a bargained for allocation for purposes of § 736, but not for purposes of §§ 743 and 755.

3.   EFFECT OF RETIREMENT ON PARTNERSHIP TAXABLE YEAR

Where a withdrawing partner has no continuing interest in partnership profits, § 706(c) provides for the closing of the taxable year of the partnership as respects the distributee partner, and the result is similar to the sale of the interest. If, on the other hand, a withdrawing partner is to receive continuing payments, the distributee is treated as a partner so long as the § 736(a) payments continue. Treas.Reg. § 1.736–1(a)(1)(ii) and (6).

The liquidation of a partner's interest does not usually close the taxable year of partnership with respect to the remaining partners. I.R.C. § 706(c)(1). However, a liquidation of an interest in a two-person partnership may result in a termination of the partnership under § 708(b)(1) "because no part of any business * * * continues to be carried on * * * in a partnership." A termination would result in a closing of the partnership taxable year. The Regulations, however, provide that such a termination will not occur so long as payments are being made under § 736, since the recipient is deemed a continuing partner until those payments cease. Treas.Reg. §§ 1.736–1(a)(6); 1.708–1(b)(1)(i) and (ii).

A. SECTION 736(b) PAYMENTS: DISTRIBUTIONS

INTERNAL REVENUE CODE: Sections 731(a), (b), and (d); 732(b)–(c); 734; 735; 736; 741; 751(b); 752(b).

REGULATIONS: Sections 1.731–1; 1.732–1(b)–(c), –2; 1.736–1(b).

As a general rule, assuming that § 751(b) does not apply, liquidating distributions classified as § 736(b) payments do not result in the recognition of gain to the withdrawing distributee partner unless there is a distribution of money in excess of the partner's basis for the partnership interest. I.R.C. § 731(a)(1). Any property distributed generally will take an exchanged basis equal to the distributee's basis for the partnership interest less any money received. I.R.C. § 732(b). The exchanged basis, i.e., partnership interest basis less money received, is then allocated among the distributed assets according to the formula of § 732(c), discussed below. If money received in a liquidating distribution exceeds the withdrawing partner's basis for the partnership interest and the partner recognizes a gain under § 731, any property received in the distribution will take a zero basis. Gain recognized under § 731 is treated as capital gain by § 741.

The general rules governing liquidating distributions to a partner are subject to certain modifications in situations in which inventory or unrealized receivables are distributed and §§ 736(a) and 751(b) are nevertheless not applicable. This situation will occur, for example, if inventory and unrealized receivables, in the aggregate, are distributed in pro rata amounts to the partners in a complete liquidation of the partnership, or if the partnership's inventory is not substantially appreciated. Section 732(c) generally requires a transfer to the distributee partner of the partnership's basis in inventory and unrealized receivables, and § 735 requires the same carryover of asset character as occurs on current distributions. See Wilmot Fleming Engineering Co. v. Commissioner, 65 T.C. 847 (1976), for an application of these rules. Thus, in the allocation of the partner's basis in the partnership interest (less money received) among the various assets, that basis is first allocated to the inventory or unrealized receivables in an amount equal to the partnership's basis, with any remaining basis of the partner allocated to the remaining assets. If a partner's basis for the partnership interest (less any money received) is less than the partnership's basis for distributed inventory or unrealized receivables, the partnership's transferred basis in these assets is decreased as provided in § 732(c)(3), first by allocating the decrease to loss inventory (or receivables with a basis in excess of value), and then among the inventory and receivables in proportion to adjusted basis. Any other distributed assets take a zero basis.

A withdrawing partner may recognize a loss if (1) a distribution consists solely of cash that is less than the distributee's basis in the partnership interest; or (2) the distributee partner receives only cash, unrealized receivables, and inventory, and the sum of the amount of the cash and the distributee partner's basis under § 732(a)(2) for the unrealized receivables and inventory—which cannot exceed the partnership's basis therefor—is less than the partner's basis for the partnership interest. I.R.C. § 731(a)(2). See Pinson v. Commissioner, T.C. Memo. 1990–234 (upon liquidation of a law partnership whose only assets were zero basis accounts receivable, partner was allowed capital loss deduction under § 731(a)(2) equal to the basis of his partnership interest). Unlike in the case of gain recognition under § 731(a)(1), for purposes of the loss recognition rule of § 731(a)(2), "money" means only cash and does not include marketable securities. I.R.C. § 731(c)(1).

Any loss recognized under § 731(a)(2) will be a capital loss under § 741. This recognized loss compensates for the loss of basis resulting from the exchanged basis rule and has no relation to whether any economic loss is sustained. For example, assume that A's basis in the partnership interest is $1,000 and that A received a liquidating distribution of $500 in cash and inventory having a $150 basis to the partnership and a value of $1,000. Although A has realized a $500 gain, A will take the inventory at a $150 basis and recognize a $350 capital loss.

If non-inventory/non-accounts receivable assets are distributed, no loss will be recognized, and the distributed assets will acquire the entire remaining basis of the partner in the partnership interest (the partner's basis less any cash and basis assigned to unrealized receivables and inventory). In extreme situations, assets with a very low value may receive a very high basis. For example, if partner A, above, in addition to receiving cash and the inventory item had received an additional non-inventory/non-accounts receivable asset, A's basis for the asset would be $500. While no loss would be recognized on the distribution, if the asset were then sold for $50, A would recognize a $450 loss. The character of that loss would be determined with respect to the character of the distributed asset in the partner's hands.

As with current distributions, the effect of changes in the partners' shares of partnership liabilities must be taken into account. A distributee partner has a deemed cash distribution under § 752(b) equal in amount to the partner's entire share of partnership liabilities prior to the liquidation of the partner's interest. If a partnership is terminated and the partnership distributes encumbered property to the partners, the increases and decreases in each partner's share of partnership liabilities under §§ 752(a) and (b) are treated as occurring simultaneously. Thus, only the net decrease in liabilities is treated as a cash distribution; and if a partner assumes a greater amount of partnership liabilities than the partner is relieved of, the partner increases the partner's basis in the partnership interest by the net increase prior to determining the basis of distributed property. Treas.Reg. § 1.752–1(f) and (g), Ex.(1); Rev.Rul. 87–120, 1987–2 C.B. 161.

The deemed exchange rules of § 751(b), discussed in Section 1.C, apply to liquidating distributions in which a partner receives either more or less than the partner's pro rata share of partnership unrealized receivables and substantially appreciated inventory, as defined in §§ 751(c) and (d) respectively. As a result, most non-pro rata liquidating distributions are partially taxable at the time of the distribution. Indeed, most distributions to withdrawing partners in general are subject to § 751(b) because in most cases a withdrawing partner receives cash from the continuing partnership, which usually has some § 751 assets. If the distribution is non-pro rata and the withdrawing partner receives less than the partner's share of unrealized receivables and substantially appreciated inventory, and hence more of the partner's share of other property or cash, the withdrawing partner is treated under § 751(b)(1)(B), as having sold to the partnership in a transaction that produces ordinary income the partner's interest in the inventory and unrealized receivables retained by the partnership. The partnership will recognize gain or loss with respect to the sale by it of the other property to the withdrawing partner and will make an adjustment in the basis of its remaining inventory and unrealized receivables reflecting its purchase from the withdrawing partner. These basis adjustments for the partnership occur even though no election had been made under § 754. The gain or loss recognized by the partnership will be characterized with reference to the character of the property in its hands.

Remember that unrealized receivables include recapture income, which significantly expands the sweep of § 751(b). As a result, § 751(b) will apply in virtually all cases in which a partner withdraws from a partnership, including an accrual method partnership, that holds any depreciable property other than real property (which often is not subject to any recapture rule). However, because the § 751(b) exchange computation is based on aggregate substantially appreciated inventory and unrealized receivables, a distribution that is non-pro rata with respect to each category separately, but not with respect to the fair market value of both together, will not be subject to § 751(b). For example, if the ABC partnership held inventory with a basis of $120 and a value of $180 and unrealized receivables of $90 (e.g., an item of depreciable property subject to $90 of § 1245 depreciation recapture), a liquidating distribution to one of the three equal partners of all of the unrealized receivables would not invoke § 751(b) because the distributee partner did not receive a disproportionate share of the partnership's § 751 assets. Similarly, a liquidating distribution of $90 of inventory would not bring § 751(b) into play. See Treas.Reg. § 1.751–1(b)(1)(ii).

DETAILED ANALYSIS

1. EFFECT OF CONTINUING LIABILITY FOR PARTNERSHIP DEBTS

Under state law, a general partner who has withdrawn from a partnership may remain liable to partnership creditors for debts incurred before the withdrawal. Generally, however, the continuing partners agree to indemnify the withdrawing partner if the withdrawing partner is required to pay any debts other than those that the withdrawing partner has agreed to pay. Barker v. Commissioner, T.C. Memo. 1983–643, involved a situation in which such an agreement between the partnership and the withdrawing partner was not entered into until a taxable year following the year in which the withdrawing partner withdrew from the partnership and received an actual liquidating distribution. The court held that the deemed distribution under § 752(b) attributable to the assumption by the continuing partners of the withdrawing partner's share of partnership indebtedness did not occur until the subsequent year in which the agreement became effective.

In Weiss v. Commissioner, 956 F.2d 242 (11th Cir.1992), a partner was expelled from a partnership. The partnership agreement did not contain an express provision in which the continuing partners agreed to indemnify the expelled partner for partnership liabilities, including partnership debts that had been guaranteed by the expelled partner. Nor did any creditor release the partner from liability. Following *Barker*, the court held that the expelled partner's share of partnership liabilities was not treated as a distribution in the year he was expelled from the partnership. The court concluded that whether or not the partner ultimately would be responsible for payment of the debts did not change the fact of his continuing liability to creditors during the year in question. Presumably, the expelled partner would realize subsequent distributions as the partnership's debts were paid, although this treatment gives rise to difficult administrative problems. The issue in *Weiss* arises because under substantive partnership law it is not entirely clear whether a withdrawing partner is entitled to be indemnified for partnership debts by the continuing partners in the absence of an express agreement to that effect.

2. LOSS DEDUCTIONS FOR ABANDONMENT OF A PARTNERSHIP INTEREST

In Neubecker v. Commissioner, 65 T.C. 577 (1975), the Tax Court held that as an independent provision, § 731 precluded any recourse to the general loss provisions of § 165 with respect to a factual situation falling within the ambit of § 731. Thus, no loss was currently recognized by a partner who received assets other than money, receivables, and inventory. The court rejected the taxpayer's argument that the taxpayer was entitled to an ordinary loss under § 165 for the forfeiture or abandonment of the partnership interest. Compare Johnson v. Commissioner, 66 T.C. 897 (1976), which held that where the taxpayer received the proceeds of a life insurance policy on the life of his partner, he was not entitled to a loss deduction under § 731(a)(2) and § 741 on the liquidation of the partnership following the partner's death. The court rested its decision on the ground that under § 165(a) no deduction is allowed for a loss which is "compensated for by insurance or otherwise." Implicit in this reasoning is the premise that § 731 does not provide a statutory ground for claiming losses independently of § 165, but instead establishes further limitations on the availability of a loss deduction on the liquidation of a partnership interest. These two cases might be reconciled on the theory that a loss is allowable to a withdrawing partner with respect to the partner's partnership interest only if the conditions of both § 165 and § 731 have been met; these two sections are not to be viewed as alternative grounds for establishing a loss.

In light of § 731, it is difficult to conceptualize how a partner can "abandon" a partnership interest when the partner is relieved of debt. In O'Brien v. Commissioner, 77 T.C. 113 (1981), the taxpayer "abandoned" an interest in a joint venture that held real estate encumbered by nonrecourse mortgages and claimed an ordinary loss deduction. The court upheld the Commissioner's treatment of the transaction as a liquidating distribution, resulting in capital loss under §§ 731 and 741. Relying on § 752(c), the court rejected the taxpayer's argument that there was no constructive distribution under § 752(b). Nonetheless, Echols v. Commissioner, 935 F.2d 703 (5th Cir.1991), reh. denied, 950 F.2d 209 (5th Cir.1991), rev'g, 93 T.C. 553 (1989), allowed a § 165(a) abandonment loss deduction for a partner who "walked away" from a partnership interest, without considering the significance of existing partnership indebtedness. Alternatively, the court held that a "worthlessness" loss was allowable with respect to the partnership interest because the partnership's only asset was real estate encumbered by a nonrecourse mortgage in excess of the value of the real estate and the partnership had no sources of income. Because the partnership's sole asset in *Echols* was encumbered by a nonrecourse mortgage, upon ceasing to be a partner by virtue of an abandonment the taxpayer-partner would have been relieved of a share of partnership debt, thereby receiving a constructive distribution under § 752(b). Thus, the transaction in *Echols* should have been treated as a sale or exchange of the partnership interest under §§ 731 and 741, with the resulting loss constituting a capital loss rather than an ordinary loss.

The IRS applies the analysis in *O'Brien*, not *Echols*. Rev.Rul. 93–80, 1993–2 C.B. 239, held that a loss from abandoning a partnership interest could qualify for ordinary loss treatment as long as the abandoning partner received neither an actual nor a constructive distribution. Receipt of even a de minimis distribution or any reduction of a share of partnership liabilities results in the entire loss being characterized as a capital loss. Furthermore, ordinary loss treatment will be allowed only if the abandonment is not in substance a sale or exchange.

3. ALLOCATION OF EXCHANGED BASIS AMONG DISTRIBUTED ASSETS

Under § 732(b), the partner whose interest is liquidated obtains an exchanged basis in the property received equal to the partner's basis in the partnership interest less any money received. This exchanged basis is allocated among the distributed assets in a multi-step process prescribed in § 732(c). Generally speaking, each asset first is assigned a transferred basis equal to its basis in the hands of the partnership. The bases of the various assets are then adjusted either upwards or downwards, depending on whether the partner's exchanged basis exceeds the aggregate transferred basis or is less than the transferred basis. If the exchanged basis is less than the aggregate transferred basis, negative basis adjustments are made to the basis of the distributed assets. If a negative basis adjustment is required, the adjustments are made in the same manner as are negative adjustments occasioned by a current distribution of property. See Section 1.B. If the exchanged basis exceeds the aggregate transferred basis, positive basis adjustments are made. In no event, however, may inventory or unrealized receivables take a basis in the hands of the partner that is greater than their basis to the partnership. I.R.C. § 732(c)(1).

If the partner's basis for the partnership interest exceeds the partnership's basis for the property received in the liquidating distribution, the basis increase must be allocated among the assets. First, inventory and accounts receivable are allocated a basis equal to their bases in the hands of the partnership. If any basis remains after the allocation to inventory and accounts receivable, the remaining basis is allocated among all other assets. Each such asset is tentatively allocated a transferred basis in the partner's hands equal to the partnership's basis for the asset. I.R.C. § 732(c)(2)(A). Then the basis of any such property with a fair market value greater than its basis to the partnership is increased in proportion to the relative built-in appreciation. I.R.C. § 732(c)(2)(B). The basis increase in this step cannot increase an asset's basis above its fair market value. Any § 734(b) or § 743(b) basis adjustments previously made with respect to the withdrawing partner's basis for those assets are taken into account in determining the partnership basis for its assets in making the adjustment. Treas.Reg. § 1.732–2.

Assume, for example, that a partner with an $1,800 basis in the partnership interest received three parcels of real estate held as capital assets: Blackacre, with a fair market value of $1,400 and a basis of $600; Whiteacre, with a fair market value of $400 and a basis of $200; and Greenacre, with a fair market value of $200 and a basis of $400. The partner's transferred basis would be $600 in Blackacre, $200 in Whiteacre, and $400 in Greenacre. Because the aggregate basis of all three properties to the partnership was only $1,200 and the partner is entitled to an aggregate basis of $1,800 for the three properties, the bases must be increased by $600. The first step, under § 732(c)(2)(A) is to increase the bases of the appreciated properties, Blackacre and Whiteacre. Blackacre is appreciated by $800 and Whiteacre is appreciated by $200. Thus, the partner increases the basis of Blackacre by $480, from $600 to $1,080, and increases the basis of Whiteacre by $120, from $200 to $320.

	FMV	Basis	Gain/ Loss	Partner's Increase	Basis
Blackacre	$1,400	$ 600	$800	(600)×(800/1000) =$480	$1,080
Whiteacre	$ 400	$ 200	$200	(600)×(200/1000) =$120	$ 320
Greenacre	$ 200	$ 400	($200)		$ 400
Total	$2,000	$1,200	$800		$1,800

Since the basis increase allocated to each property did not exceed the amount of the appreciation in each property, the total basis increase of $600 was absorbed by Blackacre and Whiteacre. Greenacre takes a basis of $400.

If the required basis increase exceeds the appreciation inherent in the distributed appreciated assets, a portion of the aggregate basis increase cannot be allocated in proportion to relative appreciation. In such a case, the remaining portion of the increase is allocated among all of the properties (other than inventory and unrealized receivables) received in the distribution relative to their fair market values. I.R.C. § 732(c)(2)(B). Assume that in the preceding example the partner's basis in the partnership interest was $2,400. Because the aggregate basis of all three properties to the partnership was only $1,200 and the partner is entitled to an aggregate basis of $2,400 for the three properties, the bases must be increased by $1,200. The partner's transferred basis would have been $600 in Blackacre, $200 in Whiteacre, and $400 in Greenacre. If the total basis increase of $1,200 were allocated between Blackacre and Whiteacre relative to appreciation, the partner would increase the basis of Blackacre by $960 to $1,560 and the basis of Whiteacre by $240 to $440. But because the basis increase allocated to each property under § 732(c)(2)(A) cannot exceed the amount of the appreciation in each property, the basis of Blackacre is increased to only $1,400 and the basis of Whiteacre is increased to only $400.

	FMV	Basis	Gain/ Loss	Partner's Increase	Basis
Blackacre	$1,400	$ 600	$800	(1,200)×(800/1000) =$ 96	$1,400
Whiteacre	$ 400	$ 200	$200	(1,200)×(200/1000) =$240	$ 400
Greenacre	$ 200	$ 400	($200)		
Total		$1,200	$800		

Because only $1,000 of the total basis increase of $1,200 was allocated under § 732(c)(2)(A), the remaining $200 of basis increase is allocated among all three properties, including Greenacre, which is a loss property, in proportion to their respective fair market values pursuant to § 732(c)(2)(B). Thus:

	FMV	Increase		Basis
Blackacre	$1,400	(200)×(1400/2000) =	$140	$1,540
Whiteacre	$ 400	(200)×(400/2000) =	$ 40	$ 440
Greenacre	$ 200	(200)×(200/2000) =	$ 20	$ 420
Total	$2,000		$200	$2,400

The allocation formula under § 732 is not designed to reduce all disparities between fair market value and basis because it does not provide for simultaneous increases and decreases in basis if a partner receives some gain assets and some loss assets. Assume for example that a partner with a basis in the partnership interest of $1,000 receives a liquidating distribution of two capital assets, Blackacre, with a fair market value of $300 and a basis of $600, and Whiteacre, with a fair market value of $700 and a basis of $400. Because the partner's basis in the partnership interest equaled the partnership's basis in the distributed assets, there are no § 732(c) adjustments, and the partner takes a $600 basis in Blackacre and a $400 basis in Whiteacre.

4. SPECIAL ALLOCATION OF BASIS UNDER SECTION 732(d)

As in Section 1.B, § 732(d) applies a special basis allocation rule where the withdrawing partner obtained the partnership interest by purchase, death, or other transfer within the preceding two years and the partnership did not have a § 754 election in effect. If a § 754 election had been in effect, the purchase price for the partnership interest would have been reflected in the partner's share of the basis of the partnership's assets under § 743(b), and the allocation rule of § 732(c)(1) would be coordinated with the partner's purchase cost. Treas.Reg. § 1.732–2. But if the partnership did not so elect (the election is made by the partnership, not the partner), then the partnership basis would not reflect the purchasing partner's cost and the allocation limitation under § 732(c)(1) for inventory and unrealized receivables might operate unfairly. Section 732(d) allows the withdrawing partner to elect a hypothetical adjustment to the basis of the assets to reflect the partner's original purchase price for the partnership interest and then applies the allocation rules of § 732(c) discussed above. Treas.Reg. § 1.732–1(d). Where the absence of an election would result in a shift of basis to depreciable property and at the time of the transfer the value of partnership property (other than money) exceeds 110% of its adjusted basis to the partnership, the Regulations require that the distributee partner's basis in the assets must be determined as though the § 732(d) election had been made by the distributee partner. See Treas.Reg. § 1.732–1(d)(4). However, under the basis allocation rules in § 732(c), it is difficult to hypothesize a situation to which Treas.Reg. § 1.732–1(d)(4) applies.

5. CASH DISTRIBUTION VERSUS PROPERTY DISTRIBUTION

In Countryside Limited Partnership v. Commissioner, T.C. Memo. 2008–3, the court rejected the IRS's argument that a distribution of non-tradable, non-marketable corporate notes in liquidation of partners' interests was in effect a distribution of cash resulting in recognized gain in the year of the distribution. The limited partnership held appreciated real property that it intended to sell. Partly through two disregarded LLCs, the partnership borrowed cash, which it used to purchase privately issued notes from AIG Matched Funding Corp. In the same year, the partnership distributed the notes to two partners in complete liquidation of their partnership interests, thereby increasing the interests of the remaining general partner and one limited partner. The withdrawing partners' bases in their partnership interests were sufficient to offset their shares of partnership liabilities, and the partners claimed that no gain was recognized under § 731(a) on the distribution of the notes as property. The following year the partnership sold its appreciated real property.[8] Immediately after the sale, the partnership repaid the debt incurred to purchase the notes.

---

[8]   The partnership also claimed a basis increase under § 732(b), which reduced the gain recognized on sale of its appreciated real estate. The IRS has challenged the basis increase in an action involving a different partnership year.

Thereafter, the AIG notes held by the withdrawing partners were paid. Asserting that the transaction lacked economic substance and violated the anti-abuse rule of Treas.Reg. § 1.702–2(a) (Chapter 17, Section 3), the IRS argued that the distribution of the notes was equivalent to a cash distribution that required recognition of gain. The Tax Court was satisfied that, although the transaction was structured to avoid tax, in economic substance the transaction represented a conversion of the taxpayers' investment in the partnership to an investment in 10-year promissory notes, "two economically distinct forms of investment." The court also rejected the IRS's argument that the notes constituted marketable securities under § 731(c)(2)(B)(ii) (discussed in Section 1.B).

6. DISTINGUISHING A LIQUIDATING DISTRIBUTION FROM A CURRENT DISTRIBUTION

In Brennan v. Commissioner, T.C. Memo. 2012–209, the taxpayer withdrew from his membership in an LLC in 2002 but continued to retain an "economic interest" in payments due the LLC in 2003 and 2004 with respect to sales of institutional accounts for the management of portfolios of high-income individuals. The court rejected the taxpayer's claim that he ceased to be a member of the partnership when his interest was terminated, holding that a retiring partner remains a partner for tax purposes until the partners' interest has been completely liquidated. Thus, the retiring partner was responsible for reporting his share of partnership gain recognized in 2003 and 2004, partnership taxable years after the withdrawal.

PROBLEM SET 4

1. The ABC Partnership conducts a retail lumber and hardware business. It has the following assets and partners' capital accounts restated to reflect fair market values:

Assets	Adjusted Basis/Book Value	F.M.V.	Partners' Capital	Adjusted Basis/Book Value	F.M.V.
Cash	$165,000	$165,000	A	$244,000	$235,000
Lumber			B	$244,000	$235,000
Inventory	$150,000	$120,000	C	$244,000	$235,000
Hardware					
Inventory	$100,000	$114,000			
Blackacre	$120,000	$150,000			
Whiteacre	$197,000	$111,000			
Goodwill	$ 0	$ 45,000			
	$732,000	$705,000		$732,000	$705,000

Blackacre and Whiteacre are § 1231 assets. The partnership is planning to make a liquidating distribution to C and is considering several alternatives. What are the tax consequences of each of the following alternative liquidating distributions?

(a) C receives Blackacre and $85,000 of cash in complete liquidation of C's interest in the partnership.

(b)   C receives the Lumber Inventory and $115,000 of cash in complete liquidation of C's interest in the partnership.

(c)   C receives the Hardware Inventory and $121,000 of cash in complete liquidation of C's interest in the partnership.

2.   The DEF LLC conducts retail men's and women's clothing businesses. It has the following assets, liabilities, and members' capital accounts:

Partnership Capital

Assets	Adjusted Basis	Book Value	F.M.V.
Cash	$255,000	$255,000	$255,000
Men's Inventory	$ 15,000	$ 15,000	$ 90,000
Women's Inventory	$ 90,000	$ 90,000	$180,000
Blackacre	$150,000	$150,000	$180,000
Whiteacre	$135,000	$135,000	$105,000
Goodwill	$ 0	$ 0	$ 45,000
	$645,000	$645,000	$855,000

Partners' Adjusted Basis and Capital

	Adjusted Basis	Book Value	F.M.V.
Loan		$120,000	
D	$215,000	$175,000	$245,000
E	$215,000	$175,000	$245,000
F	$215,000	$175,000	$245,000
	$645,000	$645,000	$735,000

Blackacre and Whiteacre are § 1231 assets. The partnership is planning to make a liquidating distribution to F and is considering several alternatives. The basis of F's partnership interest is $215,000. What are the tax consequences of each of the following alternative liquidating distributions?

(a)   F receives the Men's Clothing Inventory and $155,000 in cash.

(b)   F receives the Men's Clothing Inventory, Whiteacre, and $50,000 in cash.

(c)   F receives $245,000 in cash.

(d)   F receives Blackacre and $65,000 in Cash.

(e)   F receives the Women's Clothing Inventory and $65,000 in cash.

B.   SECTION 736(a) PAYMENTS

INTERNAL REVENUE CODE: Sections 706(c), (d); 734; 736; 751(b); 761(b).

REGULATIONS: Sections 1.706–1(c); 1.736–1(a); 1.761–1(d).

Distributions from a continuing partnership to a withdrawing partner that are not in exchange for the withdrawing partner's interest are governed by § 736(a) and are treated as ordinary income to the distributee. In addition, § 736(b)(2) and (3) together provide that payments to a withdrawing general partner in a service partnership for that general partner's share of the partnership's unrealized receivables and goodwill (unless provided for in the partnership agreement) are not distributions attributable to partnership property subject to § 736(b), and thus are also § 736(a) payments. Distributions treated as § 736(a) payments to the withdrawing partner either are deductible by the partnership or reduce the continuing partners' distributive shares of partnership income. Since § 736(a) reduces the ordinary income realized by the continuing partners, the partnership generally may not adjust its basis for the distributee's share of the receivables which it retained, even if a § 754 election is in effect; § 734 adjustments are not allowable for amounts taxed to a distributee under § 736(a).

The interaction of § 736 and § 751 will ensure that the exiting partner will be taxed on the partner's share of unrealized receivables as ordinary income. If the partner is a general partner in a service partnership, § 736(a) will apply and the payments for unrealized receivables will be ordinary income, treated as either a § 707(c) payment or as the withdrawing partner's distributive share of partnership income. Section 736(a) thus assures that a withdrawing partner is taxed on not less than the partner's share of unrealized receivables, usually cash method accounts receivable, if the partner is paid for them. (For purposes of § 736(a), however, unrealized receivables do not include depreciation and other cost recovery allowance recapture income. I.R.C. § 751(c) (flush language).) If the partner is not a general partner in a service partnership, payments that are for unrealized receivables will be § 736(b) distributions subject to analysis under § 751(b).

DETAILED ANALYSIS

1. CLASSIFICATION OF GOODWILL BETWEEN SECTION 736(a) AND SECTION 736(b)

In the case of liquidation distributions from a partnership in which capital is a material income producing factor as well as in the case of all liquidation distributions to limited partners, payments for the value of the partner's share of goodwill and unrealized receivables always are treated as § 736(b) payments. I.R.C. § 736(b)(3).

With respect to liquidating distributions to a general partner of a service partnership (i.e., where capital is not a material income producing factor), payments for goodwill are classified as § 736(a) payments "except to the extent that the partnership agreement provides for a payment with respect to goodwill." However, Treas.Reg. § 1.736–1(b)(3) treats the withdrawing partner's proportionate share of the partnership's basis, if any, in the goodwill as § 736(b) property. If the partnership agreement specifically provides for payments to a withdrawing partner with respect to partnership goodwill (in excess of any basis), all payments for goodwill are classified as

§ 736(b) payments. I.R.C. § 736(b)(2)(B). In Smith v. Commissioner, 313 F.2d 16 (10th Cir. 1962), the court required the withdrawing taxpayer to treat as an ordinary income payment a "premium" paid in excess of the book value of his interest in the partnership property on the date of withdrawal. The taxpayer argued that the premium was a payment for goodwill entitled to capital gain treatment, but the court held that the failure of the partnership agreement to refer expressly to payments for goodwill required the distribution to be treated under § 736(a): "Paragraph (2)(B) of subsection (b) exempts from ordinary income treatment payments made for goodwill only when the partnership agreement so provides specifically and does not permit an intent to compensate for goodwill to be drawn from the surrounding circumstances as the taxpayer here urges us to do."

In Commissioner v. Jackson Investment Co., 346 F.2d 187 (9th Cir.1965), the original partnership agreement did not make any provision for payment for goodwill on liquidation of a partner's interest. Subsequently, one of the partners withdrew and the partners entered into an agreement referring to a $40,350 payment to the withdrawing partner as "a guaranteed payment or a payment for good will." The Tax Court held, 41 T.C. 675 (1964) (nonacq.), that the subsequent agreement did not constitute a modification of the original partnership agreement; hence the payment was controlled by § 736(a)(2) and was deductible by the partnership. The Court of Appeals reversed, finding that the partners' subsequent agreement was a modification of the original partnership agreement. The language of the agreement was internally inconsistent since "payment for goodwill" and "guaranteed payment" in this context were mutually exclusive, but the court concluded that the parties intended the payments to be governed by § 736(b)(2)(B) and as such were not deductible by the partnership.

2.   ALLOCATION OF PAYMENTS BETWEEN SECTIONS 736(a) AND 736(b)

2.1. *Generally*

Section 736 determines the treatment of money or property distributions received in liquidation of a partner's interest, whether the distribution is a lump sum cash payment, single property distribution, or a series of payments representing a continuing interest in partnership income. See Smith v. Commissioner, 313 F.2d 16 (10th Cir.1962) (§ 736 applied to lump sum payment). When distributions consist of both § 736(a) payments and § 736(b) payments, the portion of each payment subject to the respective rules must be determined. Specific rules for the allocation of payments between § 736(a) and § 736(b) are provided by Treas.Reg. § 1.736–1(b)(5), which, however, allows the parties to provide for any other reasonable method of allocation. When continuing payments are received, the application of § 736 is somewhat more complex than when a partner's interest is liquidated by a lump sum distribution.

2.2. *Fixed Installment Payments*

If the total payments to be made are fixed in amount, each payment is pro-rated between an amount governed by § 736(a) and an amount governed by § 736(b); the portion of each annual payment that the total agreed § 736(b) payments bear to the total payments to be received is taxed as a § 736(b) distribution. Any balance is treated as a § 736(a) income payment. Treas.Reg. § 1.736–1(b)(5)(i). As § 736(b) payments are received, the normal rules of § 731(a) applicable to distributions will govern. Gain is not recognized under § 731(a) until the total amount of § 736(b) cash payments exceeds the partner's basis for the partnership interest, but any gain realized with respect to the § 736(b) payments can be reported ratably as the § 736(b) payments are received if the recipient so elects. Treas.Reg. § 1.736–1(b)(6).

Assume, for example, that A is a general partner who retires from the ABC Partnership, a service partnership in which A was a one-third partner. Assume further that A is entitled to distributions of $30,000 annually for five years and that A's basis in the partnership interest is $76,000. The fair market value of the partnership's assets, other than unrealized receivables, is $300,000, and the amount of the partnership's unrealized receivables is $150,000. The $150,000 aggregate distribution to A consists of $100,000 of § 736(b) payments ($300,000/3) and $50,000 of § 736(a) payments ($150,000/3). Of each $30,000 annual payment, $20,000 is a § 736(b) payment ($30,000 × $100,000/$150,000), and $10,000 is a § 736(a) payment ($30,000 × $50,000/$150,000). The annual $10,000 § 736(a) payment is included in gross income as ordinary income. The annual $20,000 § 736(b) payment is treated as a distribution subject to § 731. All of the $20,000 § 736(b) payments received in each of the first three years are excluded as a recovery of basis under § 731, leaving A with a $16,000 basis in the partnership interest at the beginning of Year 4. The $20,000 § 736(b) distribution in Year 4 exceeds A's $16,000 basis by $4,000, resulting in a $4,000 long-term capital gain. All of the $20,000 § 736(b) payment received in Year 5 is treated as long-term capital gain.

2.3. Contingent Installment Payments

If the total amount to be received is not fixed, e.g., the withdrawing partner is merely to receive a certain percentage of the partnership income for a period of time, then the payments received are treated entirely as distributions subject to § 736(b) until they equal the fair market value of the payments made in exchange for the withdrawing partner's interest in the partnership. Treas.Reg. § 1.736–1(b)(5)(ii). The payments made to a general partner in a service partnership for unrealized receivables and non-partnership agreement goodwill are not, by statutory definition, in exchange for the interest, and the value treated as § 736(b) payments would need to be adjusted accordingly (the Regulations pre-date the addition of § 736(b)(3) to the Code, but this result should follow given the statutory language of § 736(b)(2)). Again, with respect to the § 736(b) payment portion, under § 731(a) gain is not realized until the withdrawing partner's basis has been recouped. Treas.Reg. § 1.736–1(b)(6). Only after all § 736(b) payments have been received does § 736(a) apply to tax the withdrawing partner on ordinary income. Treas.Reg. § 1.736–1(b)(5)(ii).

Assume, for example, that D is a general partner who exits the DEF Partnership, a service partnership in which D was a one-third partner; D is entitled to annual distributions for five years equal to $20,000, plus 10% of the partnership's net income. D's basis in the partnership interest is $76,000. The fair market value of the partnership's assets, other than unrealized receivables, is $300,000 and the amount of partnership's unrealized receivables is $150,000. Assume further that the partnership's net income in each of the next five years is $100,000, which results in total payments of $30,000 annually to D. D's share of § 736(b) property held by the partnership is $100,000 ($300,000/3). Thus, the first $100,000 received by D is subject to § 736(b). All of the $30,000 payment in each of the first three years, and $10,000 of the $30,000 payment in Year 4 is governed by § 736(b) and § 731. The remaining $20,000 payment in Year 4 and all of the $30,000 payment in Year 5 is governed by § 736(a).

3. TREATMENT OF WITHDRAWING PARTNER

Section 736(a) payments that are dependent on partnership income are taxed to the withdrawing partner as a distributive share of partnership income and are excludable by the remaining partners when they compute their distributive shares. In this case, the character of income, determined at the partnership level, flows through to the distributee partner. Fixed payments that are determined without regard to partnership income are ordinary income taxed to the withdrawing partner as guaranteed payments under § 707(c) and are deductible by the partnership. Treas.Reg. § 1.736–1(a)(4). If the withdrawing partner receives only § 736(a) payments and the partner has a basis for the partnership interest, under § 731(a)(2) the partner would recognize a loss equal to that basis. The loss would be considered as loss from the sale of the partnership interest and, accordingly, would be a capital loss under § 741. If a partner receives both § 736(a) payments and § 736(b) payments treated as distributions, the general rules, discussed earlier in the Chapter, for liquidating distributions are applicable to the § 736(b) payments.

Holman v. Commissioner, 564 F.2d 283 (9th Cir.1977), held that the rules of § 736 apply even if the partner has been expelled from the partnership. The partner is still treated as a withdrawing partner for tax purposes despite the involuntary nature of the partner's withdrawal. See also Milliken v. Commissioner, 72 T.C. 256 (1979), aff'd by order, 612 F.2d 570 (1st Cir.1979). In Estate of Quirk v. Commissioner, 928 F.2d 751 (6th Cir.1991), the taxpayer withdrew from a partnership and received payments attributable to unrealized receivables. Because the taxpayer and the continuing partners were unable to agree on the value of his interest, however, the taxpayer brought an action in state court to resolve the valuation issue. In the tax litigation, the taxpayer argued that under state law, the partnership did not terminate until the valuation issue was resolved. Accordingly, the taxpayer further argued that § 736(a) could not apply to treat the distributions as ordinary income, even though they were attributable to his share of partnership unrealized receivables, because under Treas.Reg. § 1.761–1(d) the payments were not in liquidation of his partnership interest. Affirming the Tax Court's decision that § 736(a) was applicable, the Court of Appeals held that under *Holman* and *Milliken*, supra, for purposes of § 736 a partner ceases to be a partner "when that partner ceases to share in the ongoing business of the partnership, rather than in the last year of the liquidation of his interest."

4. TREATMENT OF REMAINING PARTNERS

4.1. *Payments Treated as Distributive Share or Guaranteed Payments*

If the payments to the withdrawing partner are classified under § 736(a) as a distributive share or guaranteed payment, the payments reduce the income of the remaining partners. If the payments are treated as distributive share, the withdrawing partner is taxed directly on the partner's distributive share and, as a consequence, that distributive share is not taxable to the other partners; this produces the same economic result to the continuing partners as a deduction for the payment. If the § 736(a) payment is treated as a guaranteed payment, it is a deductible partnership expense. Treas.Reg. § 1.736–1(a)(4). If the partnership is terminated and the former partners assume the liability to continue the guaranteed payments owing to a partner who exited even earlier, those payments are deductible by them under § 162. Rev.Rul. 75–154, 1975–1 C.B. 186. Similarly, if the business of the partnership is subsequently incorporated and the corporation succeeds to the obligation to make § 736(a) payments to a retired partner, the payments are deductible by the corporation. Rev.Rul. 83–155, 1983–2 C.B. 38.

Section 736(a) payments treated as § 707(c) guaranteed payments in effect often represent the purchase price to the partnership of the withdrawing partner's share of unrealized receivables and/or partnership goodwill and, thus, seemingly should be capitalized as are other § 707(c) payments to acquire an asset. However, the legislative history of the 1976 amendments to § 707(c), expressly imposing the capitalization requirement, indicate that § 736(a) payments treated as § 707(c) payments are to be deductible in all events. See S.Rep. No. 94–938, 94th Cong., 1st Sess. 94, n. 7 (1976). The continued deductibility of these payments obviates the need for any optional basis increase under § 734(b).

4.2. *Payments Treated for Interest in Partnership Property*

If the payments to the withdrawing partner are classified under § 736(b) as in exchange for the withdrawing partner's interest in partnership property, then the remaining partners are taxable on the partnership income unreduced by the payments. To the extent that the payments are made out of partnership capital, these payments appropriately do not increase the continuing partners' bases in their partnership interests. But if the payments are made from partnership income, the partners' bases in their partnership interests are increased by their distributive shares of partnership income paid to the withdrawing partner. This result also is appropriate. The remaining partners, however, may desire that the cost of the additional interests purchased from the withdrawing partner be reflected directly in the bases of the partnership assets as well. While the standard rule in § 734(a) does not permit an adjustment to the bases of partnership property, § 734(b) does provide an elective basis for adjusting the basis of partnership assets.

5. INTERACTION OF SECTION 751(b) AND SECTION 736

Payments to the withdrawing general partner of a service partnership for the partner's interest in unrealized receivables are treated as § 736(a) payments. For purposes of § 736(a), the term "unrealized receivables" is limited to contractual rights to receive payments for goods or services that have not yet been included in income under the taxpayer's method of accounting, most commonly, cash method accounts receivable. As a result, § 736(a) does not apply to potential recapture income that is defined as an unrealized receivable for purposes of § 751. Payments for unrealized receivables treated as ordinary income under § 736(a) are not taken into account under the § 751(b) computation. Section 751(b) applies fully, however, to § 736(b) payments, including § 736(b) payments that are traceable to unrealized receivables not treated as ordinary income under § 736(a). Section 751(b) thus applies to the withdrawing general partner of a service partnership on disposition of the partner's interest in recapture income. Payment for a partner's interest in substantially appreciated inventory will not qualify under § 736(a), even for a general partner in a service partnership, and thus will always be governed by § 751(b).

The interaction of § 736(a) and § 751(b) is illustrated as follows. Assume that D is a general, one-third partner in the DEF partnership, which is a service partnership. Assume further that the DEF partnership holds inventory with a value of $180 and a basis of $120 and unrealized receivables—cash method accounts receivable—of $90. A liquidating distribution to D of $90 of inventory would not bring § 751 into play because D did not receive a disproportionate amount of § 751 assets (because $90 is one-third of $270 total). See Treas.Reg. § 1.751–1(b)(1)(ii). However, D would recognize $30 of income at the time of the distribution under § 736(a). As a result, D would increase D's basis for the inventory received in the distribution from $60 to $90.

A partnership that maintains inventories, however, almost always will use the accrual method of accounting. Also, a partnership that maintains inventories is not likely to be treated as a service partnership from which a distribution for a partner's interest in unrealized receivables is treated as a § 736(a) payment. I.R.C. § 736(b)(3). Thus, it is unlikely for both § 736(a) to apply to accounts receivable and § 751(b) to apply to substantially appreciated inventory. On the other hand, service business partnerships frequently have cash method accounts receivable, subject to § 736(a), and potential depreciation recapture income with respect to equipment, subject to § 751(b), so the interaction is important.

PROBLEM SET 5

1.   Jean owns a one-fourth interest in the profits and capital of the GHIJ Partnership. The GHIJ partnership is a cash method taxpayer and has conducted a travel agency business that the partnership purchased seven years ago. The partnership has the following assets and partners' capital accounts:

Assets	Adjusted Basis/Book Value	F.M.V.	Partners' Capital	Adjusted Basis/Book Value	F.M.V.
Cash	$36,000	$ 36,000	G	$16,000	$ 27,000
Accounts			H	$16,000	$ 27,000
Receivable	$ 0	$ 12,000	I	$16,000	$ 27,000
Office			J	$16,000	$ 27,000
Equipment	$20,000	$ 20,000			
Goodwill	$ 8,000	$ 40,000			
	$64,000	$108,000		$64,000	$108,000

Jean is planning to retire. Her basis for her partnership interest is $16,000. The partnership agreement has no express provisions regarding payments to a retiring partner.

(a) What are the tax consequences to Jean and to the partnership (i.e., the remaining partners) if the partnership distributes $27,000 in cash to Jean in complete liquidation of her partnership interest?

(b) (1) Could the result in (a) be changed by amending the partnership agreement in conjunction with Jean's retirement to provide that a retiring partner would be paid for the partner's share of the partnership's goodwill? If so, is it more likely that Jean or the continuing partners would suggest such an amendment?

(2) What would be the result if the partnership agreement is amended as provided in (b)(1), but Jean is paid $30,000 in cash?

(c) What are the tax consequences to Jean and to the partnership (i.e., the remaining partners) if the partnership agreement has no express provisions regarding payments to a retiring partner and the partnership distributes $10,000 to Jean immediately upon her withdrawal and an additional $10,000 in each of the next two years?

(d) What would be the result in (c) if instead of fixed payments, Jean received $10,000 immediately upon her withdrawal and one-eighth of each year's profits in each of the next two years and partnership profits were $80,000 per year, resulting in two $10,000 payments to Jean?

SECTION 4. BASIS ADJUSTMENTS TO REMAINING PARTNERSHIP ASSETS

INTERNAL REVENUE CODE: Sections 731(b); 734; 754; 755.

REGULATIONS: Sections 1.197–2(g)(3); 1.734–1, –2; 1.754–1; 1.755–1(a) and (c).

The general rule of § 734(a) provides that the basis of remaining partnership assets is not affected by either a current or a liquidating distribution to a partner. (Of course, if § 751(b) applies to the distribution, the basis of the partnership's remaining assets that are involved in the deemed exchange will have been affected.) However, if a § 754 election is in effect, § 734(b) provides for adjustments to the bases of the partnership's remaining assets. Under § 734(b), the partnership's basis for its remaining assets is increased by any gain recognized to the distributee partner under § 731 and by any excess of partnership basis for distributed assets over their basis to the distributee. Conversely, the partnership's basis for its remaining assets is decreased by any loss recognized to the distributee and by any excess of the basis of distributed assets to the distributee over their basis to the partnership. While § 734(b) applies to all distributions, only the increases can apply in the case of a current distribution. A current distribution does not trigger any partnership basis reductions since loss cannot be recognized on a non-liquidating distribution and the distributee's basis in distributed assets cannot exceed that of the partnership. After the aggregate adjustment is computed, it must be spread among the partnership assets under the allocation rules of § 755.

Section 734 requires adjustments under § 734(b) to the basis of the partnership's assets whenever an aggregate basis reduction in excess of $250,000 results even though no § 754 election has been made.[9] I.R.C. § 734(d). See Notice 2005–32, 2005–1 C.B. 895, for procedural details and examples of the application of the rule. The purpose of this rule is to prevent the duplication of losses in a manner that allows a partner to recognize for tax purposes a loss that was not realized economically. Section 734(b) basis adjustments remain elective if the aggregate reduction to the partnership's basis would not exceed $250,000 or if the adjustment would result in a basis increase.

DETAILED ANALYSIS

1.   AGGREGATE THEORY AND THE APPLICATION OF § 734(b)

The general rule of § 734(a), which provides no partnership basis adjustment in the case of distributions, presents no problem to the other partners when a partner receives the partner's pro rata share of each and every partnership asset in the distribution. In that case, the remaining partners simply own the remaining assets to the same extent as they did before. But where the distribution is not pro rata, there is in effect an exchange of properties between the distributee partner and the remaining partners. In a non-pro rata distribution, the remaining partners purchase the distributee's interest in the remaining assets with their interests in the distributed assets. In this case, the remaining partners realize any gain or loss in their share of the distributed assets because, by distributing the assets to the distributee partner, they acquire in exchange the distributee partner's prior share of the remaining partnership assets. This realized gain is reflected in capital account adjustments under Treas.Reg. § 1.704–1(b)(2)(iv)(e), which requires that the distributed property be revalued, that all partners' capital accounts be adjusted to reflect the gain or loss that would have been allocated to each partner if the property had been sold by the partnership, and the distributee partner's capital account be reduced by the

---

[9]   Section 734(e) provides an exception for certain "securitization partnerships" as defined in § 743(f).

fair market value of the distributed property. Section 731(b), however, avoids recognition of this gain or loss for tax purposes.

The § 734(b) adjustment is a device for incorporating the aggregate view of a non-pro rata distribution or a retirement as an exchange of interests between the distributee partner and the remaining partners without, however, requiring the immediate recognition of gain or loss that a fully taxable exchange would entail. The basis adjustment reflects the cost to the other partners of purchasing the distributee partner's interest in the remaining partnership assets. Thus, the partnership increases the basis of its remaining assets when a cash distribution results in gain because the other partners have in effect paid cash for the distributee partner's share of undistributed assets. The cash distribution in excess of the distributee partner's share of basis (the partner's outside basis) represents a purchase of unrealized value in remaining partnership assets. The adjustments under § 734(b) also are intended to reflect any realized gain or loss to the partnership that goes unrecognized by virtue of § 731(b). This aspect of the basis adjustment is the reason that the partnership must decrease the basis of its remaining assets if the distributee partner takes a basis in the assets that is higher than the partnership's basis in those assets. In this case, the remaining partners have in effect exchanged an interest in low basis assets for high basis assets.

Example (1)

Assume that the ABC Partnership holds Blackacre with a value of $90 and a basis of $0; Whiteacre with a value and a basis of $90; and $90 of cash. Each partner has a $60 basis for the partnership interest. (Both Blackacre and Whiteacre are § 1231 assets that would not give rise to depreciation recapture, and § 751(b) is thus inapplicable; assume further that, prior to the distribution, there are no § 704(c) or reverse § 704(c) allocations with respect to these properties.) Blackacre is distributed to partner A on A's withdrawal from the partnership. In connection with the distribution, the partnership revalued its assets and capital accounts pursuant to Treas.Reg. § 1.704–1(b)(2)(iv)(*f*). Immediately before the distribution, the ABC Partnership's balance sheet, with book accounts reflecting fair market value, is as follows:

	Assets			Partners' Capital Accounts	
	Book	Tax Basis		Book	Tax Basis
Cash	$ 90	$ 90	A	$ 90	$ 60
Whiteacre	$ 90	$ 90	B	$ 90	$ 60
Blackacre	$ 90	$ 0	C	$ 90	$ 60
	$270	$180		$270	$180

On the distribution of Blackacre to A, Blackacre's zero tax basis to the partnership is increased to $60—its exchanged basis in A's hands under § 732(b). In the absence of a § 754 election, the application of § 734(a) creates a mismatch between the partnership's basis in its assets and B and C's basis in their partnership interests.

	Assets			Partners' Capital Accounts	
	Book	Tax Basis		Book	Tax Basis
Cash	$ 90	$ 90	B	$ 90	$ 60
Whiteacre	$ 90	$ 90	C	$ 90	$ 60
	$180	$180		$180	$120

The inside/outside basis disparity exists because A exchanged A's one-third interest in each of the cash and Whiteacre, which had a total basis to the partnership of $60, for B's and C's two-thirds interest in Blackacre, in which the partnership had a zero basis. The exchanged basis rule of § 732(a) substitutes A's $60 basis in the interests that A surrendered for the partnership basis in the distributed property, but without adjustment to the bases of partnership assets to account for the $60 exchange of basis. On the other side of the transaction, B and C received A's one-third interest in cash and Whiteacre in exchange for their two-thirds interest in Blackacre, which had a zero basis. The $60 of gain realized by B and C on this exchange is not recognized. The $60 of realized but unrecognized gain is reflected in the $60 difference between the partnership's basis in cash and Whiteacre, and the partners' outside basis.

With a § 754 election in place, under § 734(b)(2)(B) the partnership's basis in its other property would be decreased by the excess of A's $60 basis in Blackacre over the partnership's former zero basis. As a consequence, the gain that was realized but not recognized by B and C on the exchange of their interests in Blackacre for A's interest in cash and Whiteacre is transmuted into unrecognized built-in tax gain in Whiteacre and is thereby preserved at the partnership level for allocation to B and C on the disposition of Whiteacre. The BC Partnership's balance sheet will be as follows:

	Assets			Partners' Capital Accounts	
	Book	Tax Basis		Book	Tax Basis
Cash	$ 90	$ 90	B	$ 90	$ 60
Whiteacre	$ 90	$ 30	C	$ 90	$ 60
	$180	$120		$180	$120

Example (2)

Suppose, instead, that Whiteacre had been distributed to partner A. A's exchanged basis in Whiteacre is $60 under § 732(b). This exchanged basis in Whiteacre is $30 less than the partnership's $90 basis. Section 734(b)(1)(B) provides for a $30 increase in the bases of the partnership's remaining assets to reflect the excess of the partnership's basis in Whiteacre over A's basis. Here the remaining partners transferred $60 worth of property (their two-thirds interest in Whiteacre having a basis to them of $60) in exchange for $30 cash (the distributee partner's interest in the $90 partnership cash) and A's interest in Blackacre, worth $30. Hence, they paid $30 value for the distributee partner's one-third interest in Blackacre. The zero basis of Blackacre, therefore, should be increased by the $30 cost of that one-third interest. It need not then be reduced since the remaining partners' original basis for their two-thirds interest in Whiteacre, $60, was exactly equal to the amount they realized on the exchange and they therefore had no gain on the exchange. Here again, § 734(b) produces the correct result since the $90 partnership basis for Whiteacre exceeds by $30 the $60 basis that A takes in Whiteacre under § 732(b).[10] The BC Partnership's balance sheet would be as follows:

	Assets			Partners' Capital Accounts	
	Book	Tax Basis		Book	Tax Basis
Cash	$ 90	$ 90	B	$ 90	$ 60
Blackacre	$ 90	$ 30	C	$ 90	$ 60
	$180	$120		$180	$120

Example (3)

Finally, suppose the $90 cash had been distributed to partner A. A recognizes $30 of gain under § 731(a)(1), and § 734(b)(1)(A) provides for a $30 increase in the basis of the remaining partnership assets. Here the remaining partners have transferred $60 (their two-thirds interest in the cash) in exchange for the distributee partner's one-third interest in each of Blackacre and Whiteacre. Since the partnership's basis in the one-third interest in Whiteacre acquired from A already was $30, no adjustment is necessary. The cost of Whiteacre is $60, the remaining partners' original basis, plus the $30 paid for A's interest, or $90. But the partnership's basis in the one-third interest in Blackacre purchased from A was zero. Thus, the basis of Blackacre should be increased by $30. The BC Partnership's balance sheet is as follows:

---

[10] In determining whether the basis of Blackacre is increased to reflect its acquisition cost, the character of the distributed asset theoretically should be immaterial. Under Treas.Reg. § 1.755–1(c), however, if Whiteacre were inventory and Blackacre were a § 1231 asset, no adjustment would be made at the time of the distribution, but one could be made when the partnership later acquired an asset other than a capital or § 1231 asset. Treas.Reg. § 1.755–1(c)(4). (If the adjustment is triggered instead by the partner recognizing gain or loss under § 731, then the adjustment must be made only to a capital or § 1231 asset. Treas.Reg. § 1.755–1(c)(1)(ii).)

	Assets			Partners' Capital Accounts	
	Book	Tax Basis		Book	Tax Basis
Whiteacre	$ 90	$ 90	B	$ 90	$ 60
Blackacre	$ 90	$ 30	C	$ 90	$ 60
	$180	$120		$180	$120

After A's retirement, B's and C's aggregate basis for their partnership interests will be $120, and by virtue of the foregoing basis adjustments, the aggregate basis for all of the partnership's assets also will be $120. Thus, the partners could still apply the alternative rule of § 705(b) and compute the basis for their partnership interests with reference to their pro rata share of the partnership's basis for its assets. If the partners' aggregate outside basis equals the aggregate basis for partnership assets prior to the distribution, the § 734(b) adjustment works to maintain that equality after the distribution. But if outside basis and inside basis are not equal prior to the distribution (e.g., due to distributions at a time when there was not a § 754 election in effect), the § 734(b) adjustment cannot restore that equality.

In the long run, the difference between the general rule of § 734(a), under which the basis of partnership assets is not adjusted, and the optional rule of § 734(b), under which the basis of partnership assets is adjusted, is primarily one of timing, although some character differences may result if depreciable assets are involved. If an upward adjustment is appropriate but is not made, the partners will recognize greater current income (greater gains and smaller depreciation deductions) during the life of the partnership than they would have recognized if a basis adjustment had been made. On liquidation of their interests, however, due to a higher basis in their partnership interests resulting from the relatively larger basis adjustments under § 705, the partners will recognize relatively less capital gain or greater capital loss if no basis adjustments were made than if basis adjustments had been made. (Or, if liquidating distributions were in kind, the partners would have a greater basis in the distributed assets.) In other words, an upwards basis adjustment reduces gain in early years and increases gain (or reduces loss) in later years. If a downward adjustment is appropriate but is not made, the partners will recognize less current income (smaller gains and greater depreciation deductions) during the life of the partnership than they would have recognized if a basis adjustment had been made. On liquidation of their interests, however, the partners correspondingly will have a lower basis in their partnership interests and will recognize relatively more gain or smaller losses than if no basis adjustments were made than if basis adjustments had been made (or, if liquidating distributions were in kind, lower basis in the distributed assets).

These tradeoffs—less current income for more future income or more current income for less future income—obviously can be important if the future is many years down the line. If a partner dies while still holding the partnership interest, § 1014, which provides the partner's successor in interest with a basis for the partnership interest equal to its fair market value at the date of the partner's death (except for any portion that represents § 691 income in respect of a decedent, Treas.Reg. § 1.742–1), will eliminate the future gain or loss, leaving the distortions permanent. In addition, setting to one side § 751, because gain or loss on liquidation of a partnership interest always is capital gain or loss but the affected current income could be ordinary, rate arbitrage (whether to the taxpayer's advantage or disadvantage) may occur. Finally, even apart from time value of money and rate arbitrage considerations, a partner who receives lower depreciation deductions, thereby recognizing greater current income, is not made whole by an offsetting future capital loss due to the limitations of § 1211.

The § 734(b) basis adjustment is one of the few instances in the Code providing a current basis step-up without current recognition of gain. It is premised on the idea that both the distributing partnership and the distributee partner will recognize gains and losses on the distributed and undistributed property contemporaneously and, in this situation, produces the correct result. Because these events may be widely separated in time, however, § 734 presents the potential for abusive transactions.

2.   ALLOCATION OF BASIS ADJUSTMENT UNDER SECTION 755

2.1. *General Rules*

As is the case with § 743(b) adjustments, discussed in Chapter 24, Section 2, under § 755(b) any overall § 734(b) adjustment first is divided into an adjustment attributable to § 1231 assets and capital assets and an adjustment attributable to all other assets. The Regulations interpret this provision to require adjustments to remaining partnership property having the same character as that of the distributed assets that have a basis in the hands of the distributee different from the basis the partnership had in those assets. Treas.Reg. § 1.755–1(c)(1)(i). If the distributee partner recognizes gain or loss under § 731, the Regulations require, however, that the related adjustment be made only to § 1231 and capital assets. Treas.Reg. § 1.755–1(c)(1)(ii). Whether the adjustment is positive or negative, the allocation process involves two steps. Treas.Reg. § 1.755–1(c)(2).

A positive § 734(b) basis adjustment is first allocated among appreciated partnership assets (in the class of assets subject to a basis adjustment) in proportion to their respective unrealized appreciation, but only to the extent of each property's unrealized appreciation. Second, any remaining positive adjustment is then allocated among the assets within the class in proportion to their respective fair market values. Treas.Reg. § 1.755–1(c)(2)(i).

If the assets of the partnership constitute a trade or business, a portion of the basis adjustment usually will have to be allocated to partnership goodwill and other § 197 intangibles (e.g., customer lists, licenses, franchises, trademarks, trade names, advantageous contracts, etc.). In applying the apportionment rules of Treas.Reg. § 1.755–1, the fair market value of the partnership's § 197 intangibles, including goodwill and going concern value, must be determined using the residual method required by § 1060 for applicable asset acquisitions. Treas.Reg. § 1.755–1(a)(2). Pursuant to Treas.Reg. § 1.755–1(a)(5), § 197 intangibles are valued by applying the following procedure. First, the partnership determines the value of all of its assets other than § 197 intangibles. Second, the partnership determines the "partnership gross value." Treas.Reg. § 1.755–1(a)(4)(iii). The Regulations define partnership gross value for purposes of § 734(b) as "the value of the entire partnership as a going concern immediately following the distribution causing the adjustment, increased by the amount of partnership liabilities immediately following the distribution." Third, the partnership determines the value of its § 197 intangibles under the residual method, i.e., the value of § 197 intangibles equals the partnership gross value minus the value of partnership assets other than § 197 intangibles. If the aggregate value of partnership property other than § 197 intangibles is equal to or greater than the partnership gross value, all § 197 intangibles are treated as having zero value. If there is any value assigned to the § 197 intangibles, that value is allocated among § 197 intangibles other than goodwill and going concern value before any value is assigned to goodwill and going concern value. In allocating values and basis to § 197 intangibles, value is assigned first to those § 197 intangibles (other than goodwill and going concern value) that would produce § 751(c) flush language unrealized receivables—i.e., those that have been previously amortized or depreciated—to the extent of their basis and the unrealized receivable amount, then among all § 197 intangibles (other than goodwill and going concern value) relative to fair market value, and finally to goodwill and going concern. Treas.Reg. § 1.755–1(c)(5)(ii) and (iii).

Suppose the ABC Partnership (in which capital is a material income producing factor) has the following assets and partners' capital accounts, the book value of which has been adjusted to fair market value as allowed by Treas.Reg. § 1.704–1(b)(2)(iv)(*f*) in connection with a liquidating distribution to C.

Assets				Partners' Capital Accounts		
	Book	Tax Basis			Book	Tax Basis
Cash	$ 90	$ 90		A	$150	$ 60
Accounts				B	$150	$ 60
Receivable	$ 90	$ 0		C	$150	$ 60
Inventory	$ 90	$ 10				
§ 1231 Asset	$ 60	$ 50				
Capital Asset	$120	$ 30				
	$450	$180			$450	$180

The partnership distributes $60 worth of accounts receivable and $90 of cash to C in complete liquidation of C's interest. Neither § 736(a) nor § 751(b) applies on the facts. C recognizes a $30 gain on the distribution and takes a zero basis in the receivables. The § 734(b) adjustment, which is allocable to the class consisting of the capital asset and the § 1231 asset, is $30. The capital asset is appreciated by $90 and the § 1231 asset is appreciated by $10. Thus, 90% ($90/($90 + $10)) of the $30 § 734(b) adjustment, or $27, is allocated to the capital asset, giving it a basis of $57, and 10% ($10/($90 + $10)) of the $30 § 734(b) adjustment, or $3, is allocated to the § 1231 asset, giving it a basis of $53.

Now suppose that the partnership had distributed $60 worth of accounts receivable and $100 of cash to C, reflecting that the partnership had going concern value and goodwill worth $30, but with a zero basis. In this case, A would recognize a $40 gain on the distribution. The partnership's § 734(b) basis adjustment would be $40. The basis adjustments to the capital asset and the § 1231 asset remain the same, but the partnership increases its basis in goodwill to $10.

A negative § 734(b) basis adjustment is first allocated among loss partnership assets within the appropriate class in proportion to their respective amounts of unrealized loss, but only to the extent of each property's unrealized loss. Any excess negative adjustment is then allocated among the properties within the class in proportion to their remaining adjusted bases after taking into account the basis reduction in the first step. Treas.Reg. § 1.755–1(c)(2)(ii). Negative basis adjustments cannot reduce the basis of any partnership asset below zero. Treas.Reg. § 1.755–1(c)(3).

If the adjustment is attributable to the distributee partner recognizing either a gain or a loss, then the adjustment is allocated solely to capital and § 1231 assets. Treas.Reg. § 1.755–1(c)(1)(ii). Within that class of assets, the overall adjustment again is allocated among the assets in proportion to the difference between basis and fair market value, with all adjustments being required to decrease the difference. Treas.Reg. § 1.755–1(c)(2). Suppose the GHI Partnership, in which capital is a material income producing factor, has the following assets and partners' capital accounts, the book value of which has been adjusted to fair market value.

Assets	Book	Tax Basis		Partners' Capital Accounts	Book	Tax Basis
Cash	$ 90	$ 90	G		$120	$ 50
Accounts Receivable	$ 90	$ 0	H		$120	$ 50
Inventory	$ 90	$ 30	I		$120	$ 50
Capital Asset	$ 90	$ 30			____	____
	$360	$150			$360	$150

The partnership distributes $60 worth of accounts receivable and $60 of cash to G in complete liquidation of G's interest. Neither § 736(a) nor § 751(b) applies on the facts, and G recognizes a $10 gain on the distribution, taking a zero basis in the receivables. Section 734(b) calls for a $10 basis increase. In theory, $5 should be added to the basis of each of the inventory and capital asset, but under Treas.Reg. § 1.755–1(c)(1)(ii), only the basis of the capital asset can be adjusted.

If the partnership owns "no property of the character required to be adjusted," or a downward adjustment has been limited by the zero basis floor of Treas.Reg. § 1.755–1(c)(3), the remaining adjustment is held in suspense and applied when the partnership acquires property to which the adjustment can be applied. Treas.Reg. § 1.755–1(c)(4). For example, if a partner recognizes gain as a result of a cash distribution in liquidation of the partnership interest from a partnership that holds only inventory that was not substantially appreciated (as defined in § 751(b)(3)), the partnership's § 734(b) basis adjustment will be held in suspense until the partnership acquires a capital or § 1231 asset. Immediately upon the acquisition of such an asset, its basis will be increased by the suspended adjustment, even if the adjustment results in a basis in excess of its fair market value.

These rules present a problem because, as is illustrated in the examples involving the DEF and GHI Partnerships, the adjustment, in fact, may have been attributable to an increase or decrease in the value of a remaining asset having a character different from that of the distributed assets, or to a cash distribution that triggered gain or loss to the distributee partner that was attributable to ordinary income assets of the partnership (although in most cases a cash distribution attributable to ordinary inventory will trigger the application of § 751(b), thereby obviating the need for a § 734(b) adjustment). In theory, in the example involving the DEF Partnership, the basis of both the inventory and Whiteacre should have been reduced. Under the Regulations, however, no adjustment would be made at the time of the distribution, but one could be made when the partnership later acquired a capital or § 1231 asset, but only when the asset's basis exceeded its fair market value. These defects in the § 755 rules for allocating basis adjustments could be cured by providing that the adjustments be made to property of the same character as that to which the adjustment is attributable and not as that of the distributed property. See H. Rep. No. 86–1231, 86th Cong., 2d Sess. 98 (1960).

2.2. Post-Adjustment Depreciation

Treas.Reg. § 1.734–1(e) provides rules regarding the method for computing depreciation deductions with respect to increases and decreases in the basis of depreciable assets pursuant to § 734(b). If the basis of the partnership's depreciable property is increased under § 734(b), the increased portion of the basis must be depreciated as if it were newly purchased property placed in service on the date the distribution occurred. The partnership's original basis in the property continues to be depreciated as before the distribution, as if there had been no basis increase. If § 734(b) requires a decrease in the basis of the partnership's depreciable property, the decrease in basis must be taken into account over the remaining recovery period of the property beginning with the recovery period in which the basis is decreased.

3. PROBLEMS IN THE SECTION 734(b) FORMULA

The formula in § 734(b) will provide the correct overall adjustment in most cases. But it appears inadequate in some instances because it is based on the distributee's basis in the partnership interest—which governs gain or loss to the distributee. The formula will not produce the correct result if the basis for the distributee partner's interest differs from the distributee partner's share of the partnership's basis for its assets. Thus, if in the ABC Partnership example, Detailed Analysis 2.1, A had purchased the interest from a previous partner, paying $90, or if A were an estate succeeding to a decedent partner's interest and having a $90 basis, there would be no adjustment under the formula.

This defect is most glaring in cases in which an estate's interest in a partnership is terminated by a distribution of cash and no gain is recognized to the estate to the extent § 1014 applies to give it a stepped-up basis for its partnership interest. No adjustment is allowed even though the partnership is paying for the estate's interest in assets that have increased in value. If the formula in § 734(b) related to the distributee's pro rata share of the partnership's aggregate basis for its assets (as is done in § 743(b)), the formula would work correctly. The obvious solution to this problem is for the partnership to make the § 754 election with respect to the transfer from the decedent partner to the successor partner. Under § 743(b), the bases of the partnership's assets are increased by an amount equal to the step-up in the basis of the partnership interest resulting from § 1014. Then, if the withdrawing partner who inherited the partnership interest receives a liquidating distribution of property in which it did not have a special basis adjustment in exchange for property in which it did have a special basis adjustment, under Treas.Reg. § 1.734–2(b) the basis adjustment is reallocated to the partnership's remaining property for the benefit of the continuing partners.

If a cash distribution to a withdrawing general partner in a service partnership is attributable to unrealized receivables and is taxed under § 736(a), § 734(b) does not permit any increase in the basis of the retained unrealized receivables. In this case, however, a basis adjustment is unnecessary because the remaining partners have, in effect, received a deduction for the amount paid for the unrealized receivables. See Treas.Reg. § 1.736–1(a)(4). Therefore, it is appropriate not to increase the partnership's basis in the receivables.

4. APPLICATION OF SECTION 734(b) TO CURRENT DISTRIBUTIONS

Although all of the preceding examples involved liquidating distributions to a withdrawing partner, if a § 754 election is in effect, a current distribution to a partner may also result in basis adjustments under § 734(b). Unlike the case under § 743(b), where the Regulations provide that the basis adjustment under that section is special to the transferee partner, neither § 734(b) nor the Regulations allocate the basis adjustment solely to the nondistributee partners. Thus, a § 734(b) basis adjustment presumably applies for all partners.

Suppose the JKL Partnership has the following assets and partners' capital accounts, the book value of which has been adjusted to fair market value.

	Assets			Partners' Capital Accounts	
	Book	Tax Basis		Book	Tax Basis
Whiteacre	$ 600	$ 900	J	$ 800	$ 700
Blackacre	$1,800	$1,200	K	$ 800	$ 700
			L	$ 800	$ 700
	$2,400	$2,100		$2,400	$2,100

To reduce J from a one-third partner to a one-ninth partner, the partnership distributes Whiteacre to J. Although the partnership's basis in Whiteacre is $900, because J's basis for the partnership interest is only $700, § 732(a)(2) limits J's basis for Blackacre to $700. (After the distribution, J has no remaining basis in the partnership interest.) Since J's basis for Whiteacre is $200 less than the partnership's basis, the partnership is entitled to increase the basis of Blackacre by $200, from $1,200 to $1,400 under § 734(b)(1)(B). Upon a subsequent sale of Blackacre for $1,800, the partnership recognizes a gain of $400, of which $44.44 is allocated to J and $177.78 is allocated to each of K and L. If J sold Whiteacre for $600, J would recognize a $100 loss. Thus, the income realized by each of the partners on the sale of the partnership's assets is as follows:

Partner	Whiteacre	Blackacre	Total
J	($100)	$ 44.44	($ 55.56)
K	$ 0	$177.78	$177.78
L	$ 0	$177.78	$177.78
			$300.00

Upon liquidation of the partnership following the sale of Blackacre, J receives $200, and K and L each receive $800 in liquidation of their partnership interests. J's gain under § 731 is $155.56, since J's basis in the partnership interest was increased from zero to $44.44 as a result of inclusion of that amount of gain on the sale of Blackacre. K and L each recognize a loss of $77.78 since their bases for their partnership interests were increased from $700 to $877.78 as a result of including the gain on the sale of Blackacre. The net result is that each partner recognizes the same $100 of net income that the partner would have recognized if the partnership had sold both properties and liquidated. The timing of the recognition, however, may be dramatically different.

This shifting of the timing of gains and losses recognized to the various partners as a result of the distribution of Whiteacre to J theoretically could be eliminated by special allocations of gain on the sale of Blackacre. The partners might agree that upon a sale of Blackacre, the first $400 of taxable gain would be allocated $200 to J and $100 to each of K and L, even though capital account adjustments would be $66.67 to J and $266.67 to each of K and L. However, there appears to be no authority in the § 704(b) Regulations sanctioning such an allocation.

5.   TIMING OF BASIS ADJUSTMENTS

Rev.Rul. 93–13, 1993–1 C.B. 126, held that if a partnership completely liquidates the interest of a withdrawing partner by making a series of cash payments treated as distributions under § 736(b)(1), the § 734(b) basis adjustments to the partnership property correspond in timing and amount with the recognition of gain or loss by the withdrawing partner under § 731. Assume that the GHI partnership has cash of $75,000 and a capital asset with a basis of $15,000 and a fair market value of $150,000. Withdrawing partner G has a $30,000 basis in the partnership interest and receives fixed-sum cash distributions of $25,000 per year for three years in liquidation of the partnership interest. In Year 1, G recognizes no gain, and the partnership has no basis adjustment; in Year 2, G recognizes $20,000 of gain, and the partnership increases its basis in the capital asset from $15,000 to $35,000; in Year 3, G recognizes $25,000 of gain, and the partnership increases its basis in the asset to $60,000.

If a § 734(b) basis adjustment increases the basis of depreciable property, the basis increase is treated as newly acquired property placed in service at the time of the adjustment. It has a class life and recovery method the same as the class life of the asset to which it relates. See Treas.Reg. § 1.734–1(e).

6.   SPECIAL RULE FOR PARTNERSHIP HOLDING CORPORATE PARTNER'S STOCK

Section 755(c) provides that in applying the rules of § 755 for allocating a decrease in basis of the partnership's assets under § 734(b), the basis of stock of a partner that is a corporation (or a person related to the corporation under § 267(b) or § 707(b)(1)) will not be reduced. Any decrease in basis that otherwise would have been allocated to the stock must be allocated to other partnership assets. If the decrease in basis exceeds the basis of those other partnership assets, the partnership must recognize gain equal to the amount of the excess.

7.   SPECIAL PROBLEM OF TIERED PARTNERSHIPS

Rev.Rul. 92–15, 1992–1 C.B. 215, holds that if an upper tier partnership and a lower tier partnership both have § 754 elections in effect, and the upper tier partnership distributes to a partner property other than an interest in the lower tier partnership and as a consequence adjusts its basis in the interest in the lower tier partnership, then the lower tier partnership also adjusts its basis in its own assets pursuant to § 734(b). Assume, for example, that A and B are each 50% partners in UTP, which owns a capital asset with a basis of $140 and a fair market value of $240 and a 10% interest in LTP, which has a basis of $30 and a fair market value of $80. LTP has a capital asset with a basis of $200 and a fair market value of $700 and a noncapital asset with a basis of $0 and a fair market value of $100. UTP's share of the basis of LTP's assets is $20. Partner A has a basis of $0 in A's 50% interest in UTP, which has a fair market value of $160. To reduce A's interest in UTP to 20%, UTP distributes to A one-half interest in the capital asset, worth $120, having a basis to the partnership of $70. Since A takes a $0 basis in one-half of the capital asset, under § 734(b), UTP increases the basis of its assets by $70. The remaining one-half of the capital asset and UTP's interest in LTP each reflect unrealized gain in the amount of $50; thus under § 755(b), UTP's basis in each asset is increased by $35. UTP's basis increase for its interest in LTP is an event triggering a basis increase in UTP's share of the basis of LTP's property of a similar character to the distributed property. Accordingly, UTP increases the amount of its share of the basis of LTP's capital asset from $20 to $55.

Suppose that the AB Partnership holds two assets: Blackacre with a basis of zero and a fair market value of $100, and Whiteacre with a basis of $100 and a fair market value of $100. If Whiteacre is distributed to A, who has a zero basis for the partnership interest, A would take a zero basis for Whiteacre, and, if a § 754 election is in effect, the partnership would increase its basis for Blackacre to $100. As a result, the $100 basis of Whiteacre is transferred to Blackacre, and $100 of total gain will be recognized if they are both sold. Now suppose that instead the AB Partnership contributes Whiteacre to another partnership (LT) in which it has a 99% interest, following which it distributes its interest in the LT Partnership to A. A will take a zero basis for A's interest in LT, but the basis of Whiteacre remains $100. If the AB Partnership can make a § 734(b) adjustment to the basis of Blackacre, then both assets can be sold without the recognition of any gain, although A would recognize gain if the proceeds were distributed to A by LT. Congress perceived this result as abusive, and in 1984 added the last sentence of § 734(b), disallowing an upward § 734 adjustment for the upper tier partnership, in this case AB, if the distributed property is an interest in another partnership, in this case LT, unless the other partnership also has a § 754 election in effect. Because § 761(e), also added in 1984, treats the distribution of a partnership interest as an exchange, Congress intended that § 734(b) require that the distributed partnership (LT) reduce the basis of its assets. See Staff of the Joint Committee on Taxation, 98th Cong., 2d Sess., General Explanation of the Tax Reform Act of 1984, at p. 249 (1984). See also Rev.Rul. 92–15, 1992–1 C.B. 215 (holding that § 734(b) required the distributed lower tier partnership to decrease the basis of its assets in such a case but, under the predecessor of Treas.Reg. § 1.755–1(c)(4), could defer the date the required basis decrease was implemented).

PROBLEM SET 6

1.   The ABC Partnership had three equal partners, Al, Bette, and Claude. It had the following assets and partners' capital accounts:

Assets	Adjusted Basis/Book Value	F.M.V.	Partners' Capital	Adjusted Basis/Book Value	F.M.V.
Cash	$ 40,000	$ 40,000	Al	$ 60,000	$ 90,000
Blackacre	$ 90,000	$ 45,000	Bette	$ 60,000	$ 90,000
Whiteacre	$ 10,000	$ 55,000	Claude	$ 60,000	$ 90,000
Greenacre	$ 40,000	$130,000			
	$180,000	$270,000		$180,000	$270,000

All of the assets are § 1231 assets. In the current year, Claude received Blackacre in a disproportionate nonliquidating distribution. As a result of the distribution, Claude thereafter had a one-fifth interest in partnership capital and profits worth $50,000. Assuming that the partnership has not already made a § 754 election, should it make a § 754 election in connection with the distribution to Claude?

2.   Don, Eve, and Fay are partners in the DEF Partnership, which is engaged in real estate investment and development. The partnership holds some subdivision lots for sale and two properties, Blackacre and Whiteacre, for rental purposes. The DEF Partnership had the following assets and partners' capital accounts:

Assets	Adjusted Basis/Book Value	F.M.V.	Partners' Capital	Adjusted Basis/Book Value	F.M.V.
Cash	$ 30,000	$ 30,000	Don	$ 40,000	$ 60,000
Lots held for sale	$ 50,000	$ 60,000	Eve	$ 40,000	$ 60,000
			Fay	$ 40,000	$ 60,000
Blackacre	$ 10,000	$ 60,000			
Whiteacre	$ 30,000	$ 30,000			
	$120,000	$180,000		$120,000	$180,000

The partnership distributed Blackacre to Don in complete liquidation of his interest in the partnership. Should the partnership make a § 754 election in connection with the distribution?

3.   Gina, Hank, and Ike are partners in the GHI Partnership, which is engaged in real estate investment and development. The partnership holds some subdivision lots for sale and three properties, Blackacre, Greenacre, and Whiteacre, for rental purposes. The GHI Partnership had the following assets and partners' capital accounts:

Assets	Adjusted Basis/Book Value	F.M.V.	Partners' Capital	Adjusted Basis/Book Value	F.M.V.
Lots	$ 50,000	$ 60,000	Gina	$ 40,000	$ 60,000
Blackacre	$ 5,000	$ 60,000	Hank	$ 40,000	$ 60,000
Greenacre	$ 20,000	$ 30,000	Ike	$ 40,000	$ 60,000
Whiteacre	$ 45,000	$ 30,000			
	$120,000	$180,000		$120,000	$180,000

The three parcels of land are capital assets to the partnership. Gina receives Blackacre as a distribution in liquidation of her interest in the partnership.

(a)   Disregarding § 736(a) and § 751, which are inapplicable under the facts, what are the tax consequences to Gina and to the partnership if there is no § 754 election in effect.

(b)   What would be the result in (a) if the partnership made a § 754 election?

SECTION 5.   SALE OF INTEREST TO OTHER PARTNERS VERSUS DISTRIBUTION

INTERNAL REVENUE CODE: Sections 731(a); 736(a) and (b); 741; 752(b) and (d).

REGULATIONS: Sections 1.736–1(b)(1); 1.741–1(a) and (b).

By its nature, a non-pro rata distribution to a partner that reduces the distributee's interest in the distributing partnership increases the partnership interests of the other partners. As discussed in Section 4 relating to basis adjustments, a non-pro rata distribution that does not trigger application of § 751(b) and that changes a partner's interest may be viewed as an exchange in which the distributee partner may realize gain or loss (but the gain or loss is not recognized under the distribution rules of § 731(a) except to the extent that cash distributions exceed basis). In contrast to the nonrecognition rule of § 731 applicable to non-pro rata distributions that have the effect of exchanging partnership interests, § 741 requires recognition of gain or loss on the sale or exchange of a partnership interest, including a sale to other partners. See Treas.Reg. § 1.741–1(b). The distinction between a distribution that restructures interests in a partnership, and a sale or exchange of partnership interests between partners is not always clear.

Colonnade Condominium, Inc. v. Commissioner

Tax Court of the United States, 1988.
91 T.C. 793.

■ WRIGHT, JUDGE: [Colonnade Condominium, Inc. ("Colonnade") was a general partner in Georgia King Associates ("Georgia King"), holding a 50.98 percent interest. There were three other unrelated partners. The shares of Colonnade were held equally by Bernstein, Feldman, and Mason. Prior to April 1978, Colonnade was obligated to make capital contributions to Georgia King in a series of installments in the total amount of $1,330,300. At that time, it had actually contributed less than $400,000. Colonnade's basis in its partnership interest was $8,262,710. Its share of partnership liabilities was $10,074,456. Colonnade had a negative capital account balance. In April, 1978 the partnership agreement of Georgia King was amended to admit each of Bernstein, Feldman, and Mason as a 13.66 percent general partner. Colonnade's interest was reduced from 50.98 percent to 10 percent. Bernstein, Feldman, and Mason each assumed responsibility for contributing $272,000 of the future capital contribution previously required from Colonnade. * * * Colonnade did not treat the April 1, 1978 transfer of its 40.98 percent partnership interest to Bernstein, Feldman, and Mason as a taxable event. The Commissioner asserted that the transaction was a sale of a portion of Colonnade's partnership interest.]

OPINION

Respondent contends that Colonnade's transfer of a portion of its partnership interest in Georgia King Associates to its three shareholders pursuant to the April 1, 1978, amendment to the partnership agreement resulted in the sale of a 40.98-percent general partnership interest by Colonnade in return for the discharge of recourse and nonrecourse partnership liabilities. Accordingly, respondent argues that such disposition should be governed by sections 741 and 1001. * * * Petitioner, on the other hand, asserts that the April 1, 1978, amendment merely provided for the admission of new partners in an existing partnership and is a nontaxable event.

We agree with respondent.

* * *

The statutory scheme under subchapter K gives partners great latitude in selecting the form the partnership takes and in allocating economic benefits and tax burdens of partnership transactions among themselves. See, e.g., * * * Foxman v. Commissioner, 41 T.C. 535, 551 (1964), affd. 352 F.2d 466 (3d Cir.1965) * * *. Under the partnership provisions of the Code, this flexibility is achieved by, inter alia, allowing a partner to choose either to sell his partnership interest to a third person or to reorganize the partnership to allow the admission of the third person as a new partner.

This flexibility, however, is not unlimited. The form of the transaction must be in keeping with its true substance and the intent of the parties. See Commissioner v. Court Holding Co., 324 U.S. 331 (1945); Gregory v. Helvering, 293 U.S. 465 (1935) (the substance, rather than the form, of the transaction is controlling). In this regard, the provisions of written documents are not necessarily conclusive for tax purposes. * * * Nor will a "label" attached by a tax-conscious litigant control the proper characterization of a transaction involving the disposition of a partnership interest. * * * In short, "the legislative policy of flexibility does not permit a taxpayer to avoid the tax ramifications of a sale of a partnership interest simply by recasting the intended or constructive sale in the form of a reorganization to a partnership. Jupiter Corp. v. United States," 2 Cl.Ct. 58, 79 (1983).

Section 741 provides that in the case of the sale or exchange of a partnership interest, gain or loss shall be recognized to the transferor partner. The gain or loss, except to the extent that section 751 applies, is capital. Section 741 shall apply whether the partnership interest is sold to a member or nonmember of the partnership. Sec. 1.741–1(b), Income Tax Regs.

Section 721(a) states the general rule that gain or loss is not recognized through contributions of property to a partnership in exchange for partnership interests. Correspondingly, in a distribution by a partnership to a partner under section 731(a)(1), gain shall not be recognized except to the extent the distribution exceeds adjusted basis. Decreases in a partner's liabilities or share of the partnership's liabilities are considered distributions under section 752(b). Section 705(a)(2) provides that a partner's adjusted basis is decreased by his distributions from the partnership as well as the partner's distributive share of partnership losses. Petitioner argues that, as of April 1, 1978, three new partners were admitted to the partnership and, as a result, petitioner received a distribution as a result of being relieved of its share of partnership liabilities. Petitioner's basis in the partnership was reduced pursuant to section 705(a)(2).

The Code and regulations do not offer any guidance for distinguishing between an admission of new partners (pursuant to a contribution of property which is nontaxable under section 721), as petitioner contends is the correct characterization of the transaction before us, and a sale of a partnership interest under section 741, taxable as respondent urges. In one of the few cases addressing this issue, this Court in Richardson v. Commissioner, 76 T.C. 512 (1981), aff'd. 693 F.2d 1189 (5th Cir.1982), commented on the difference between the admission of a new partner into a partnership and the sale or exchange of a partnership interest:

> Admission of new partners is not in all respects identical to a sale or exchange of a partnership interest. In the former situation, the transaction is between the new partners and the partnership. The latter situation involves a transaction between a new partner and an existing partner. * * * [76 T.C. at 528.]

In *Richardson*, the taxpayers unsuccessfully maintained that they had sold their interest in three partnerships on December 30, 1974. 76 T.C. at 527–528. The admission of the new partners in *Richardson* corresponded with the infusion of large amounts of new capital into the partnership, although capital was not reduced with respect to the old partners. The transaction was essentially between the new partners and the partnership. Upon the admission of the new partners, the interests of all the original partners were reduced substantially. This Court viewed the transaction as an admission rather than a sale.

Unlike *Richardson*, the form and substance of the transaction at issue herein reflects transfers between an existing partner, Colonnade, and new partners, Bernstein, Feldman, and Mason and, therefore, was a sale of a partnership interest. The partnership as a whole was essentially unaffected. Prior to the April 1, 1978, amendment, Colonnade held a

50.98-percent partnership interest. As a result of the amendment, Colonnade divested itself of a 40.98-percent interest, which was acquired collectively by Bernstein, Feldman, and Mason at 13.66 percent each. Colonnade was left with a 10-percent interest, but together with its three shareholders, Colonnade still controlled the partnership as the majority general partner. The interests of the other partners in Georgia King were unchanged by the amendment.

Similarly, Colonnade divested itself of its rights under sections 10.03(c) and 10.05(a)(vi) of the partnership agreement (allocations of certain gains and losses) to the extent of 30 percent which were acquired collectively by Bernstein, Feldman, and Mason at 10 percent each. Again, the allocations under these two sections remained unchanged with respect to [the other partners]. Most notably, the aggregate capital contributions of Georgia King, $2,226,800, remained the same before and after the April 1, 1978, amendment. No additional contributions were required under the April 1, 1978, amendment to the partnership agreement. Colonnade, however, was discharged of its recourse obligation to contribute $816,060 in the future, an obligation which was acquired equally between Bernstein, Feldman, and Mason at $272,020 each. The total payment schedule for the contributions (in yearly installments) remained unchanged and continued to mirror the total equity payments required of the partnership. Colonnade was also discharged of 40.98 percent of its partnership nonrecourse liabilities, which were acquired by the three individual shareholders.

The fact that the three shareholders of Colonnade expressly assumed Colonnade's liabilities, in return for partnership interests which are capital assets under section 741, is especially significant. In determining whether an actual or constructive sale or exchange took place, we note that the touchstone for sale or exchange treatment is consideration. In LaRue v. Commissioner, 90 T.C. 465, 483–484 (1988), we noted that where liabilities are assumed as consideration for a partnership interest, a sale or exchange exists:

> If, in return for assets, any consideration is received, even if nominal in amount, the transaction will be classified as a sale or exchange. Blum v. Commissioner, 133 F.2d 447 (2d Cir.1943). * * * When the transferee of property assumes liabilities of the transferor encumbering the property, the liability is an amount realized by the transferor. Crane v. Commissioner, [331 U.S. 1 (1947)]; Commissioner v. Tufts, [461 U.S. 300 (1983)]. Assumption of liabilities by the transferee constitutes consideration making the transaction a sale or exchange. * * *

> * * * Where assets are transferred to third parties, assumption of liabilities constitutes consideration. * * *

> * * * [T]he assumption of liabilities by a third party transferee constitutes an amount realized, and this is consideration to the transferor. * * *

In arguing that the form of the arrangement reflects the substance, petitioner points out that the documents show that Bernstein, Feldman, and Mason were admitted to the partnership upon obtaining the required approval of [the New Jersey Housing Finance Agency], as well as * * * the managing general partner. Petitioner contends that the documents demonstrate an agreement between the partnership and the partners for the admission of new partners and do not reflect a transaction between petitioner and the new general partners. However, as we noted earlier, labels, semantics, technicalities, and formal documents do not necessarily control the tax consequences of a given transaction. * * * To look solely to the documents in this case and ignore the substance and reality of the transaction would exalt form over substance.

Aside from the transfer of a portion of Colonnade's partnership interest to the three new partners in return for a discharge of liabilities, there were no other changes in the structure or the operation of the Georgia King partnership as a result of the April 1, 1978, amendment. The substance of the transaction did not transpire between the partnership and the new partners, but rather, between Colonnade, an existing partner, and three new partners. Because there was no new or additional capital transferred to the partnership, there were no modifications of the partnership assets and liabilities. The only change was the transfers from the transferor partner's capital account to the transferees' capital accounts. As such, the transaction warrants sale and exchange treatment under section 741.

DETAILED ANALYSIS

1.   PURCHASE AND SALE VERSUS LIQUIDATION

Structuring a transaction as purchase and sale of a partnership interest rather than as a distribution to a withdrawing partner may avoid the tension created by § 736 between the withdrawing general partner and the continuing partners in a service partnership. See the discussion in Section 3.B above. Structuring the transaction as a sale of the withdrawing partner's interest to the other partners allows the selling partner to claim capital gain or capital loss treatment under § 741 for realized gain or loss on the disposition of the partnership interest. The purchasing partners increase their bases in their partnership interests, which may be reflected in an adjustment to the basis of partnership assets if an election under § 754 is in effect. Treas.Reg. § 1.741–1(b) expressly sanctions sales treatment with respect to the sale of a partnership interest to continuing partners. As indicated by the opinion in *Colonnade Condominium*, the substance of the transaction controls over its form. Distribution treatment requires a change in the partnership's internal capital accounts.

In Foxman v. Commissioner, 41 T.C. 535 (1964), referring to committee reports, the Tax Court recognized that the legislative scheme is intended to permit partners flexibility to arrange the tax consequence of partnership transactions. The court indicated that "one of the underlying philosophic objectives of the 1954 Code was to permit the partners themselves to determine their tax burdens *inter sese* to a certain extent, and this is what the committee reports meant when they referred to 'flexibility.' The theory was that the partners would take their prospective tax liabilities into account in bargaining with one another. * * * "(551). See H.Rep. No. 1337, 83d Cong., 2d Sess., 65; S.Rep. No. 1622, 83d Cong., 2d Sess., 89.

Foxman is a good example of the conflict that can arise between the departing and continuing partners. Foxman, Grenell, and Jacobowitz were one-third partners in a business that manufactured phonograph records. Because of conflicts among the partners, Foxman and Grenell agreed to continue the partnership business without Jacobowitz. The partners individually entered into an agreement for the purchase of Jacobowitz's interest for $242,550 plus an automobile that was in the name of the partnership and the stock of a related corporation, called Sound Plastics, owned individually by Foxman, Grenell, and Jacobowitz. The cash was payable in installments over a period of approximately two years. The installment obligation was represented by a series of promissory notes on which the partnership appeared as the maker with the signatures of Foxman and Grenell on behalf of the partnership. The agreement described the transaction as a purchase of Jacobowitz's partnership interest but also provided that Jacobowitz "hereby retires from the partnership." Foxman and Grenell agreed to continue the partnership business in substantially the same form. Foxman and Grenell also agreed to indemnify Jacobowitz from any liabilities arising out of the partnership business. On the advice of an attorney, the partnership was made a party to the agreement, but the court noted that there was no specific undertaking on the part of the partnership any place in the instrument. The first $67,500 payment to Jacobowitz was made by cashier's check. Foxman and Grenell decided to prepay the remaining installment notes due to Jacobowitz. The partnership borrowed the cash and distributed the money to Jacobowitz. On its tax return, the partnership treated the payment as a distribution of partnership earnings to Jacobowitz in the nature of a guaranteed payment. On his tax return, Jacobowitz treated the transaction as a sale and reported a long-term capital gain. The Commissioner, taking inconsistent positions, assessed a deficiency against Jacobowitz claiming that the transaction was a liquidation distribution resulting in ordinary income in part under § 736(a), and against Foxman and Grenell treating the transaction as a purchase of Jacobowitz's partnership interest, thereby disallowing deductions for the distribution as a guaranteed payment. The cases were consolidated before the Tax Court to allow the former partners to fight it out. The Tax Court sided with Jacobowitz finding that the partners intended to structure the transaction as a sale:

> The agreement of May 21, 1957, indicates a clear intention on the part of Jacobowitz to sell, and Foxman and Grenell to purchase, Jacobowitz's partnership interest. The * * * "whereas" clause refers to Jacobowitz as "selling" his interest and part "First" of the agreement explicitly states not only that the "second parties [Foxman and Grenell] hereby purchase * * * the * * * interest of

* * * [Jacobowitz] * * * in [the partnership]," but also that "the first party [Jacobowitz] does hereby sell" his interest in [the partnership]. Thus, Foxman and Grenell obligated themselves individually to purchase Jacobowitz's interest. Nowhere in the agreement was there any obligation on the part of [the partnership] to compensate Jacobowitz for withdrawing from the partnership. Indeed, a portion of the consideration received by him was the Sound Plastics stock, not a partnership asset at all. That stock was owned by Foxman and Grenell as individuals and their undertaking to turn it over to Jacobowitz as part of the consideration for Jacobowitz's partnership interest reinforces the conclusion that they as individuals were buying his interest, and that the transaction represented a "sale" of his interest to them rather than a "liquidation" of that interest by the partnership. Moreover, the chattel mortgage referred to in part "First" of the agreement of May 21, 1957, states that Jacobowitz "has sold * * * his * * * interest as a partner."

In addition to the foregoing, we are satisfied from the evidence before us that Foxman and Grenell knew that Jacobowitz was interested only in a sale of his partnership interest. The record convincingly establishes that the bargaining between them was consistently upon the basis of a proposed sale. And the agreement of May 21, 1957, which represents the culmination of that bargaining, reflects that understanding with unambiguous precision. The subsequent position of Foxman and Grenell, disavowing a "sale," indicates nothing more than an attempt at hindsight tax planning to the disadvantage of Jacobowitz.

Foxman and Grenell argue that Jacobowitz looked only to [the partnership] for payment, that he was in fact paid by [the partnership], that there was "in substance" a liquidation of his interest, and that these considerations should be controlling in determining whether section 736 or section 741 applies. But their contention is not well taken.

Jacobowitz distrusted Foxman and Grenell and wanted all the security he could get; he asked for, but did not receive, guarantees from their wives and mortgages on their homes. Obviously, the assets of [the partnership] and its future earnings were of the highest importance to Jacobowitz as security that Foxman and Grenell would carry out their part of the bargain. But the fact remains that the payments received by Jacobowitz were in discharge of their obligation under the agreement, and not that of [the partnership]. It was they who procured those payments in their own behalf from the assets of the partnership which they controlled. The use of [the partnership] to make payment was wholly within their discretion and of no concern to Jacobowitz; his only interest was payment. The terms of the May 21, 1957, agreement did not obligate [the partnership] to pay Jacobowitz.

Nor is their position measurably stronger by reason of the fact that Jacobowitz was given promissory notes signed in behalf of [the partnership]. These notes were endorsed by Foxman and Grenell individually, and the liability of [the partnership] thereon was merely in the nature of security for their primary obligation under the agreement of May 21, 1957. The fact that they utilized partnership resources to discharge their own individual liability in such manner can hardly convert into a section 736 "liquidation" what would otherwise qualify as a section 741 "sale." It is important to bear in mind the object of "flexibility" which Congress attempted to attain, and we should be slow to give a different meaning to the arrangement which the partners entered into among themselves than that which the words of their agreement fairly spell out. Otherwise, the reasonable expectations of the partners in arranging their tax burdens *inter sese* would come to naught, and the purpose of the statute would be defeated. While we do not suggest that it is never possible to look behind the words of an agreement in dealing with problems like the one before us, the considerations which Foxman and Grenell urge us to take into account here are at best of an ambiguous character and are in any event consistent with the words used. We hold that the Commissioner's determination in respect of this issue was in error in Jacobowitz's case but was correct in the cases involving Foxman and Grenell. * * * (552–553)

As the opinion in *Foxman* demonstrates, historically the real controversy in this area has been between the withdrawing partner, who preferred a sale classification with the resulting capital gain treatment, and the remaining partners, who preferred a "liquidation" classification since the payments would then reduce their distributive shares of partnership income. Section 736(b)(3) eliminated the ability of partnerships in which capital is a material income producing factor to classify payments to a withdrawing partner as § 736(a) payments that reduce the remaining partners' distributive shares of income. Thus, this tension under § 736 between the withdrawing partner and the continuing partnership is confined primarily to partnerships in which capital is not a material income producing factor. However, there remains the possibility, as in *Foxman*, to classify the transaction as a sale under § 741.

The IRS is, of course, concerned that, however characterized, the transaction be treated the same by both parties. It was able to obtain this result in *Foxman* by joining all of the parties in the same suit. The IRS was not so fortunate, however, in another situation in which the same transaction was treated by the Tax Court as a capital gain-generating sale under § 741 for the withdrawing partner, Phillips v. Commissioner, 40 T.C. 157 (1963) (nonacq.), while the remaining partners were allowed deductions under a § 736 liquidation theory by the Court of Claims, Miller v. United States, 181 Ct.Cl. 331 (1967). The *Phillips-Miller* situation involved a two-person partnership and the Court of Claims, following Treas.Reg. § 1.736–1(b)(6), had no difficulty in treating the payments by the remaining partner as liquidation distributions by the partnership despite the fact that no partnership was actually in existence after the withdrawal. To the same effect is Stilwell v. Commissioner, 46 T.C. 247 (1966).

The taxpayer in Spector v. Commissioner, 71 T.C. 1017 (1979), rev'd and remanded, 641 F.2d 376 (5th Cir.1981), was a partner in an accounting partnership with Wilson.[11] To effect Spector's withdrawal from the partnership, the Spector-Wilson partnership was merged with another accounting partnership, following which Spector withdrew from the merged partnership in consideration of four equal annual payments. The withdrawal agreement specifically stated that one-half of each payment was a payment subject to § 736, none of which was for partnership property, and the other one-half of the payment was for a covenant not to compete. Finding that the taxpayer had adduced "strong proof" that the form of the transaction did not reflect its substance, the Tax Court held that the payments were not controlled by § 736. Instead, the court concluded that, in essence, the partnership into which the Spector-Wilson partnership had merged had purchased the taxpayer's share of the goodwill of the Spector-Wilson partnership, and it allowed the taxpayer capital gains treatment. The Court of Appeals reversed the Tax Court, on the ground that it had applied an erroneous standard. Economic reality does not provide a ground to set aside the structure chosen to effect a partner's withdrawal. The court explained that the fundamental theory underlying Subchapter K is that given the substantial, if not total, identity in terms of economic net result between a sale and a liquidation, the withdrawing and continuing partners should be allowed to allocate the tax benefits and burdens as they see fit. It then remanded the case for a determination of whether the taxpayer had adduced proof of mistake, fraud, undue influence, or any other ground that in an action between the parties to the agreement would be sufficient to set it aside or alter its construction. On remand, the Tax Court concluded that this burden had not been met. Accordingly, § 736 controlled treatment of the payments. T.C. Memo. 1982–433.

In Crenshaw v. United States, 450 F.2d 472 (5th Cir.1971), the taxpayer desired to sell her interest in a partnership. A transaction was arranged whereby she received a distribution of real property from the partnership, which she then transferred to the estate of her deceased husband in exchange for another parcel of real estate. The estate subsequently sold the property back to the original partners for cash, after which it was recontributed to the old partnership. The taxpayer argued that the transaction should be treated as a liquidating distribution under § 736 followed by a tax-free like-kind exchange under § 1031. The Court of Appeals, reversing the District Court, applied the step transaction doctrine and held that the net result of the various exchanges was in effect a sale of her partnership interest for cash, which was taxable under § 741.

---

[11] Before 1993, all partnerships were allowed under § 736(b)(2)(B) to designate a portion of liquidation distributions as in exchange for the withdrawing partner's interest in partnership goodwill, regardless of whether capital was a material income producing factor in the partnership.

In contrast, Harris v. Commissioner, 61 T.C. 770 (1974), declined to recharacterize as a sale a transaction carefully structured to produce a § 1231 loss rather than a capital loss on the disposition of a partnership interest. To effect the taxpayer's withdrawal from a partnership in which he held a 40% interest, the partnership first sold to a trust for the benefit of children of another partner an undivided 10% interest in the real estate that was its principal asset. The trust immediately leased its undivided interest back to the partnership. The loss on the sale was specially allocated to the taxpayer, and the sales proceeds were distributed to him; the taxpayer's capital account was reduced by the loss and the distribution, and his partnership interest was reduced to 33%. The following year, the partnership distributed to the taxpayer in full liquidation of the partnership interest an undivided 30% interest in the real estate, which the taxpayer immediately leased back to the partnership. About two months later, the taxpayer sold the undivided 30% interest to the trust, which had purchased the 10% interest the prior year. Because the trust did not become a partner and the taxpayer's partnership interest did not survive the transaction, the court distinguished *Crenshaw* and allowed the taxpayer a § 1231 loss on the sale of the real estate.

The problem of the withdrawing partner and the partnership taking inconsistent positions regarding characterization of a transaction as a sale versus the liquidation of a partnership interest is not easily discoverable by the IRS.

PROBLEM SET 7

1.   Arnie is a one-third limited partner in a real estate partnership. Each of the three partners contributed $450,000 in cash, although each partner is liable for an additional contribution of $450,000 if called for by the general partner. The partnership borrowed $9,000,000 from the Roulette Savings & Loan Association on a nonrecourse mortgage and purchased a shopping mall for $10,350,000. Cumulatively, Arnie's distributive share of profit and loss during the life of the partnership has been $1.8 million of losses. The partnership has conducted no other business, made no distributions, made no principal payments on its loan, and has no other assets. Arnie's basis in the partnership interest is $1,650,000; Arnie's capital account is negative $1,350,000. The general partner has called for each limited partner to contribute an additional $450,000 to be used for improvements to the property. Arnie does not want to contribute more than an additional $150,000 and is willing to reduce his interest in partnership profits and losses to one-ninth if the partnership will accept this lesser contribution. To accommodate Arnie's desires, Dale, who is not yet a partner, will contribute $300,000 to the partnership and become a two-ninths partner. Is this transaction a sale of two-thirds of Arnie's partnership interest to Dale or is it a distribution to Arnie coupled with the admission of Dale as a new partner? What difference does it make?

SECTION 6.   COMPLETE LIQUIDATION OF THE PARTNERSHIP

INTERNAL REVENUE CODE: Sections 708; 731(a), (b); 732(b)–(e); 735; 741; 751(b); 752(a)–(c).

REGULATIONS: Sections 1.708–1(b)(1); 1.736–1(a)(1)(ii); 301.7701–3(g)(1)(i).

Complete liquidation of a partnership is governed by the same provisions that govern liquidation of a partner's interest, except that § 736 usually is inapplicable because, other than in very narrow circumstances, there is no continuing partnership. Generally speaking, the tax consequences of the complete liquidation of a partnership are the sum of the consequences to the individual partners. A partner does not recognize any gain unless the partner receives a cash distribution (including net debt relief under §§ 752(a) and (b) if the other partners assume a disproportionate share of the partnership's liabilities) in excess of the partner's basis for the partnership interest. I.R.C. § 731(a)(1). Any gain that is recognized is a capital gain under § 741. Property received in the liquidation generally will take an exchanged basis equal to the partner's basis for the partnership interest less any cash received. I.R.C. § 732(b). The exchanged basis, i.e., partnership interest basis less cash received, is then allocated among the distributed assets according to the formula of § 732(c), discussed in Section 3. A partner may recognize a loss upon liquidation of the partnership if (1) a distribution consists solely of cash that is less than the partner's basis for the partnership interest, or (2) the partner receives only cash, unrealized receivables, and inventory, *and* the sum of the amount of the cash and the partner's basis under § 732(a)(2) for the unrealized receivables and inventory—which cannot exceed the partnership's basis therefor—is less than the partner's basis for the partnership interest. I.R.C. § 731(a)(2). Any loss recognized under § 731(a) is a capital loss under § 741.

In the simple case of a complete dissolution in which the distribution is pro rata and the partners' bases do not differ from their pro rata share of the aggregate partnership basis for its assets (e.g., there were no contributions of assets having differing bases and credited value, and no transfers of partnership interests or non-pro rata distributions without basis adjustments being made), the dissolution results in no alteration of the bases of the properties involved and no gain or loss consequences. In more complex cases, however, the basis limitation rules in § 732(b) and (c) may affect the result. If the distribution does not involve a pro rata interest in each partnership asset, the deemed exchange rules of § 751(b) also may be applicable.

Revenue Ruling 84–111

1984–2 C.B. 88.

* * *

FACTS

The three situations described in Rev. Rul. 70–239 involve partnerships X, Y, and Z, respectively. Each partnership used the accrual method of accounting and had assets and liabilities consisting of cash, equipment, and accounts payable. The liabilities of each partnership did not exceed the adjusted basis of its assets. The three situations are as follows:

Situation 1

X transferred all of its assets to newly-formed corporation R in exchange for all the outstanding stock of R and the assumption by R of X's liabilities. X then terminated by distributing all the stock of R to X's partners in proportion to their partnership interests.

Situation 2

Y distributed all of its assets and liabilities to its partners in proportion to their partnership interests in a transaction that constituted a termination of Y under section [708(b)(1)] of the Code. The partners then transferred all the assets received from Y to newly-formed corporation S in exchange for all the outstanding stock of S and the assumption by S of Y's liabilities that had been assumed by the partners.

Situation 3

The partners of Z transferred their partnership interests in Z to newly-formed corporation T in exchange for all the outstanding stock of T. This exchange terminated Z and all of its assets and liabilities became assets and liabilities of T.

In each situation, the steps taken by X, Y, and Z, and the partners of X, Y, and Z, were parts of a plan to transfer the partnership operations to a corporation organized for valid business reasons in exchange for its stock and were not devices to avoid or evade recognition of gain. Rev. Rul. 70–239 holds that because the federal income tax consequences of the three situations are the same, each partnership is considered to have transferred its assets and liabilities to a corporation in exchange for its stock under section 351 of the Internal Revenue Code, followed by a distribution of the stock to the partners in liquidation of the partnership.

LAW AND ANALYSIS

* * *

Section 351(a) of the Code provides that no gain or loss will be recognized if property is transferred to a corporation by one or more persons solely in exchange for stock or securities in such corporation and immediately after the exchange such person or persons are in control (as defined in section 368(c)) of the corporation.

Section 1.351–1(a)(1) of the Income Tax Regulations provides that, as used in section 351 of the Code, the phrase "one or more persons" includes individuals, trusts, estates, partnerships, associations, companies, or corporations. To be in control of the transferee corporation, such person or persons must own immediately after the transfer stock possessing at least 80 percent of the total combined voting power of all classes of stock entitled to vote and at least 80 percent of the total number of shares of all other classes of stock of such corporation.

Section 358(a) of the Code provides that in the case of an exchange to which section 351 applies, the basis of the property permitted to be received under such section without the recognition of gain or loss will be the same as that of the property exchanged, decreased by the amount of any money received by the taxpayer.

Section 358(d) of the Code provides that where, as part of the consideration to the taxpayer, another party to the exchange assumed a liability of the taxpayer or acquired from the taxpayer property subject to a liability, such assumption or acquisition (in the amount of the liability) will, for purposes of section 358, be treated as money received by the taxpayer on the exchange.

Section 362(a) of the Code provides that a corporation's basis in property acquired in a transaction to which section 351 applies will be the same as it would be in the hands of the transferor.

Under section [708(b)(1)] of the Code, a partnership is terminated if no part of any business, financial operation, or venture of the partnership continues to be carried on by any of its partners in a partnership. * * *

Section 732(b) of the Code provides that the basis of property other than money distributed by a partnership in a liquidation of a partner's interest shall be an amount equal to the adjusted basis of the partner's interest in the partnership reduced by any money distributed. Section 732(c) of the Code provides rules for the allocation of a partner's basis in a partnership interest among the assets received in a liquidating distribution.

Section 735(b) of the Code provides that a partner's holding period for property received in a distribution from a partnership (other than with respect to certain inventory items defined in section 751(d)(2)) includes the partnership's holding period, as determined under section 1223, with respect to such property.

Section 1223(1) of the Code provides that where property received in an exchange acquires the same basis, in whole or in part, as the property surrendered in the exchange, the holding period of the property received includes the holding period of the property surrendered to the extent such surrendered property was a capital asset or property described in section 1231. Under section 1223(2), the holding period of a taxpayer's property, however acquired, includes the period during which the property was held by any other person if that property has the same basis, in whole or in part, in the taxpayer's hands as it would have in the hands of such other person.

Section 741 of the Code provides that in the case of a sale or exchange of an interest in a partnership, gain or loss shall be recognized to the transferor partner. Such gain or loss shall be considered as a gain or loss from the sale or exchange of a capital asset, except as otherwise provided in section 751.

Section 751(a) of the Code provides that the amount of money or the fair value of property received by a transferor partner in exchange for all or part of such partner's interest in the partnership attributable to unrealized receivables of the partnership, or to inventory items of the partnership that have appreciated substantially in value, shall be considered as an amount realized from the sale or exchange of property other than a capital asset.

Section 752(a) of the Code provides that any increase in a partner's share of the liabilities of a partnership, or any increase in a partner's individual liabilities by reason of the assumption by the partner of partnership liabilities, will be considered as a contribution of money by such partner to the partnership.

Section 752(b) of the Code provides that any decrease in a partner's share of the liabilities of a partnership, or any decrease in a partner's individual liabilities by reason of the assumption by the partnership of such individual liabilities, will be considered as a distribution of money to the partner by the partnership. Under section 733(1) of the Code, the basis of a partner's interest in the partnership is reduced by the amount of money received in a distribution that is not in liquidation of the partnership.

Section 752(d) of the Code provides that in the case of a sale or exchange of an interest in a partnership, liabilities shall be treated in the same manner as liabilities in connection with the sale or exchange of property not associated with partnerships.

The premise in Rev. Rul. 70–239 that the federal income tax consequences of the three situations described therein would be the same, without regard to which of the three transactions was entered into, is incorrect. As described below, depending on the format chosen for the transfer to a controlled corporation, the basis and holding periods of the various assets received by the corporation and the basis and holding periods of the stock received by the former partners can vary.

* * * Recognition of the three possible methods to incorporate a partnership will enable taxpayers to avoid the above potential pitfalls and will facilitate flexibility with respect to the basis and holding periods of the assets received in the exchange.

HOLDING

Rev. Rul. 70–239 no longer represents the Service's position. The Service's current position is set forth below, and for each situation, the methods described and the underlying assumptions and purposes must be satisfied for the conclusions of this revenue ruling to be applicable.

Situation 1

Under section 351 of the Code, gain or loss is not recognized by X on the transfer by X of all of its assets to R in exchange for R's stock and the assumption by R of X's liabilities.

Under section 362(a) of the Code, R's basis in the assets received from X equals their basis to X immediately before their transfer to R. Under section 358(a), the basis to X of the stock received from R is the same as the basis to X of the assets transferred to R, reduced by the liabilities assumed by R, which assumption is treated as a payment of money to X under section 358(d). In addition, the assumption by R of X's liabilities decreased each partner's share of the partnership liabilities, thus, decreasing the basis of each partner's partnership interest pursuant to sections 752 and 733.

On distribution of the stock to X's partners, X terminated under section [708(b)(1)] of the Code. Pursuant to section 732(b), the basis of the stock distributed to the partners in liquidation of their partnership interests is, with respect to each partner, equal to the adjusted basis of the partner's interest in the partnership.

Under section 1223(1) of the Code, X's holding period for the stock received in the exchange includes its holding period in the capital assets and section 1231 assets transferred (to the extent that the stock was received in exchange for such assets). To the extent the stock was received in exchange for neither capital nor section 1231 assets, X's holding period for such stock begins on the day following the date of the exchange. See Rev. Rul. 70–598, 1970–2 C.B. 168. Under section 1223(2), R's holding period in the assets transferred to it includes X's holding period. When X distributed the R stock to its partners, under sections 735(b) and 1223, the partners' holding periods included X's holding period of the stock. Furthermore, such distribution will not violate the control requirement of section 368(c) of the Code.

Situation 2

On the transfer of all of Y's assets to its partners, Y terminated under section [708(b)(1)] of the Code, and, pursuant to section 732(b), the basis of the assets (other than money) distributed to the partners in liquidation of their partnership interests in Y was, with respect to each partner, equal to the adjusted basis of the partner's interest in Y, reduced by the money distributed. Under section 752, the decrease in Y's liabilities resulting from the transfer to Y's partners was offset by the partners' corresponding assumption of such liabilities so that the net effect on the basis of each partner's interest in Y, with respect to the liabilities transferred, was zero.

Under section 351 of the Code, gain or loss is not recognized by Y's former partners on the transfer to S in exchange for its stock and the assumption of Y's liabilities, of the assets of Y received by Y's partners in liquidation of Y.

Under section 358(a) of the Code, the basis to the former partners of Y in the stock received from S is the same as the section 732(b) basis to the former partners of Y in the assets received in liquidation of Y and transferred to S, reduced by the liabilities assumed by S, which assumption is treated as a payment of money to the partners under section 358(d).

Under section 362(a) of the Code, S's basis in the assets received from Y's former partners equals their basis to the former partners as determined under section 732(c) immediately before the transfer to S.

Under section 735(b) of the Code, the partners' holding periods for the assets distributed to them by Y includes Y's holding period. Under section 1223(1), the partners' holding periods for the stock received in the exchange includes the partners' holding periods in the capital assets and section 1231 assets transferred to S (to the extent that the stock was received in exchange for such assets). However, to the extent that the stock received was in exchange for neither capital nor section 1231 assets, the holding period of the stock began on the day following the date of the exchange. Under section 1223(2), S's holding period of the Y assets received in the exchange includes the partner's holding periods.

Situation 3

Under section 351 of the Code, gain or loss is not recognized by Z's partners on the transfer of the partnership interests to T in exchange for T's stock.

On the transfer of the partnership interests to the corporation, Z terminated under section [708(b)(1)] of the Code.

Under section 358(a) of the Code, the basis to the partners of Z of the stock received from T in exchange for their partnership interests equals the basis of their partnership interests transferred to T, reduced by Z's liabilities assumed by T, the release from which is treated as a payment of money to Z's partners under sections 752(d) and 358(d).

T's basis for the assets received in the exchange equals the basis of the partners in their partnership interests allocated in accordance with section 732(c). T's holding period includes Z's holding period in the assets.

Under section 1223(1) of the Code, the holding period of the T stock received by the former partners of Z includes each respective partner's holding period for the partnership interest transferred, except that the holding period of the T stock that was received by the partners of Z in exchange for their interests in section 751 assets of Z that are neither capital assets nor section 1231 assets begins on the day following the date of the exchange.

* * *

DETAILED ANALYSIS

1. PURCHASE OF PARTNERSHIP INTEREST VERSUS PURCHASE OF PARTNERSHIP ASSETS

Suppose that A and B are partners and that A purchases B's entire partnership interest. Since the purchase results in the termination of the partnership, A could either take a cost basis in an undivided one-half of the partnership assets, as if A purchased them directly from B, and a basis in the other half determined under § 732, or A could take a basis in the assets determined by treating the transaction first as the purchase of a partnership interest to which § 742 and § 743 apply, followed by the liquidation of the partnership, in which A's basis in all of the assets is determined under § 732. McCauslen v. Commissioner, 45 T.C. 588 (1966), held that for purposes of determining the purchaser's tax consequences, the partnership is deemed to have liquidated and distributed its assets to the two partners, following which the purchasing partner is treated as having acquired by direct purchase from the seller the portion of partnership assets attributable to the acquired partnership interest. Rev.Rul. 67–65, 1967–1 C.B. 168, followed *McCauslen.* For the seller, however, Treas.Reg. § 1.741–1(b) provides that the transferor partner is treated as selling the partner's partnership interest, not an undivided share of the partnership assets. This same rule would apply whenever all of the interests in a partnership are sold to one or more purchasers in an integrated transaction.

Although Rev.Rul. 67–65 has not been revoked, Rev.Rul. 84–111, indicates that the IRS might not follow *McCauslen* if the issue were raised currently. Rev.Rul. 84–111 respected the form of each alternative transaction by which the same end result was reached. In the third situation the partners were treated as exchanging their partnership interests for stock in a transaction governed by § 351. Although the partnership was terminated under the predecessor of § 708(b)(1) upon the transfer of the partnership interests, the corporation was held to have acquired the partnership assets by virtue of liquidation of the partnership. If *McCauslen* were followed, the assets would have been acquired in exchange for stock.

Rev.Rul. 2004–59, 2004–1 C.B. 1050, held that when a partnership converts into a state law corporation under a state law formless conversion statute, the partnership contributes all its assets and liabilities to the corporation in exchange for stock in such corporation and, immediately thereafter, the partnership liquidates, distributing the stock of the corporation to its partners. Rev.Rul. 84–111 does not apply.

2. LIQUIDATION OF A LIMITED LIABILITY COMPANY

The form of the transaction also is important when a limited liability company with two or more members becomes a single member limited liability company, as is permitted under the laws of many states. A single member limited liability company that has not elected to be taxed as a corporation is a disregarded entity—i.e., not recognized as a separate business entity from its owner for tax purposes. See Treas.Reg. § 301.7701–2(c)(1) and (2), discussed in Chapter 17, Section 2.A. In Rev.Rul. 99–6, 1999–1 C.B. 432, the IRS applied the *McCauslen* analysis to hold that termination of the partnership on sale of a membership interest by one member of a two-member limited liability company to the other member will be treated by the selling member as the sale of a partnership interest under § 741. With respect to the purchasing member, the transaction is treated as a liquidation distribution to the selling member followed by the purchase of the selling member's interest in the former partnership assets with respect to the purchasing member. The purchasing member may recognize gain under § 731(a) with respect to the liquidation distribution of the purchasing member's interest in the pre-sale partnership interest if there is a distribution of cash in excess of the purchasing member's basis in the membership interest. As in *McCauslen,* the purchasing member acquires a cost basis in the purchased portion of the acquired assets.

Rev.Rul. 99–6 also holds that the sale of membership interests by both of the members of a two-member limited liability company to a single purchaser will be treated as the sale of their partnership interests that is governed by § 741 with respect to each of the selling members. The purchaser, however, is treated as acquiring an undivided interest in each of the limited liability company's assets. Rev.Rul. 99–6 takes note, without comment, of the contrary result in the third situation of Rev.Rul. 84–111.

3.   APPLICABILITY OF SECTION 751(b)

It is not clear on the face of § 751 and the Regulations thereunder whether § 751 applies to disproportionate distributions on dissolution of the partnership. This ambiguity arises because § 751(b) requires distributions representing an exchange of a distributee's interest in § 751 assets for other partnership property (or vice versa) "to be considered as a sale or exchange of such property between the distributee and the partnership (as constituted after the distribution)." In a complete liquidation, no partnership would exist after the distribution and the exchange would have to be between the distributee and the other partners. Yourman v. United States, 277 F.Supp. 818 (S.D.Cal.1967), held that § 751(b) was applicable to a non-pro rata distribution of assets on the dissolution of a partnership. Rev.Rul. 77–412, 1977–2 C.B. 223, is to the same effect, holding that each partner can be treated as a distributee partner in determining gain or loss recognized under § 751(b), and in the case of a two person partnership, the other partner can be treated as the continuing partnership. See also Wolcott v. Commissioner, 39 T.C. 538 (1962).

Assume, for example, that the AB Partnership has two assets, Blackacre, a § 1231 asset (that is not subject to any depreciation recapture), with a basis of $500 and a fair market value of $1,000, and inventory, with a basis of $600 and a fair market value of $1,000. A and B each have a basis of $550 in their respective partnership interests. The partnership liquidates by distributing the inventory to A and Blackacre to B. A and B are each treated as receiving a pro rata share of Blackacre and the inventory, taking a $300 basis in the inventory and a $250 basis in the undivided one-half interest in Blackacre, following which A exchanges one-half of the inventory to B for an undivided one half interest in Blackacre. On the exchange, A recognizes ordinary income of $200, and B recognizes $250 of § 1231 gain. A's basis in Blackacre is $750, a $500 cost basis in the undivided one-half received in the deemed § 751(b) exchange plus $250 for the other one-half under § 732(b). B's basis in the inventory is $800, a $500 cost basis in the inventory received in the deemed § 751(b) exchange plus $300 for the remaining portion.

4.   WHEN IS A PARTNERSHIP "LIQUIDATED"?

The exact time and method of liquidation of a partnership may be ambiguous. A partnership is not necessarily terminated for federal income tax purposes merely because it has dissolved under state law. For example, Sirrine Building No. 1 v. Commissioner, T.C. Memo. 1995–185, held that a partnership that under state law dissolved more than six years earlier did not terminate prior to the year it was required to report gain from the sale of land on the installment method.

Tapper v. Commissioner, T.C. Memo. 1986–597, held that a partnership organized to construct and sell a particular building was liquidated upon the sale of the building even though no actual distribution of cash or property was received by the partners; the taxpayer received a distribution equal to his share of the mortgage assumed by the buyer. This result presumably occurs whenever a partnership sells all of its assets and receives no net cash because encumbrances equal or exceed the fair market value of its assets.

In Goulder v. United States, 64 F.3d 663 (6th Cir.1995) (unpublished disposition; opinion text at 1995 WL 478595), a partnership that owned a single apartment building defaulted on the mortgage loan. The loan was foreclosed in 1980 and the property sold, without any distribution of proceeds to the partnership. The partnership ceased rental activities but still held some tenant security deposits. In 1981, the partnership determined that the lender was not claiming the security deposits and distributed them to the partners. The court allowed the taxpayer-partner to claim a loss on the liquidation of his partnership interest in 1980, even though all assets were not distributed until 1981. The decision may be based more on the government's stipulation that the partnership ceased all activities in 1980 rather than on the actual facts.

7050 Ltd. v. Commissioner, T.C. Memo. 2008–112, suggests that a partnership liquidation cannot occur in steps that straddle two taxable years. One of the issues in the case was whether a distribution of property (foreign currency) from the partnership (which was an LLC) was a liquidating distribution, resulting in an exchanged basis for the property determined with reference to the partnership interest pursuant to § 732(b), or a current distribution, resulting in a transferred basis from the partnership pursuant to § 732(a). In 2001, the partnership distributed almost all of its assets (Canadian currency) to its two partners and filed a Cancellation of Domestic Certificate of Limited Partnership with the secretary of state's office in which it had been formed. However, the partnership retained a balance of Can $6,892.16 in its bank account, which was not completely closed until 2003. The partnership also filed a 2001 tax return that it labeled "final return." The Tax Court held that the partnership had not liquidated in 2001 and that the distribution was not a liquidating distribution, but rather was a current distribution, with the resulting transferred basis to the partners. For a partnership to terminate "section [708(b)(1)] * * * require[s] complete cessation of all partnership activity, including the distribution to the partners of all the partnership's assets. * * * Holding Canadian currency in a bank account is quite similar to the kinds of minimal activity that we've already found were enough to keep a partnership unterminated." Accordingly, the partners took a transferred basis in the Canadian currency under § 732(a), not an exchanged basis under § 732(b).

5.　APPLICATION OF SECTION 736(a)

In most partnership liquidations, § 736 is not relevant because there is no continuing partnership. The exception is the termination of a two-person partnership in which one partner retires and the other partner agrees to make payments to the retired partner over a period of years. If any of these payments are classified as § 736(a) payments under the standards discussed in Section 3.B, the partnership continues in existence as long as such payments are due. Treas.Reg. §§ 1.736–1(a)(1)(ii) and (6); 1.708–1(b)(1)(i)(b). This situation most frequently will occur where a member of a two-person professional practice retires and the partner who continues the practice as a sole proprietor makes continuing payments of either a fixed amount or a share of profits from the practice to the retired partner.

6.　SPECIAL ALLOCATION OF BASIS UNDER SECTION 732(d)

Section 732(d) applies a special basis allocation rule where the withdrawing partner obtained the partnership interest by purchase, death, or other transfer within the two years preceding the partnership liquidation. In Rudd v. Commissioner, 79 T.C. 225 (1982) (acq.), § 732(d) was applied to give a partner a substantial basis in partnership goodwill, which was found to have been distributed to the partners in liquidation of a professional accounting partnership. Upon abandonment of the use of the partnership name following the liquidation of the partnership, the individual partner who had succeeded to the right to use the name was allowed an ordinary loss under § 165 for the portion of the basis of the goodwill allocated to the partnership name. Because the business of the partnership was continued by a new partnership, no loss was allowed with respect to the remaining partnership goodwill.

PROBLEM SET 8

1.　Alex and Bev are partners in the AB Partnership. Alex is a two-thirds partner; Bev is a one-third partner. The assets and partners' capital accounts of the AB Partnership are as follows:

Partnership Capital

Assets	Adjusted Basis	Book	F.M.V.
Cash	$ 45,000	$ 45,000	$ 45,000
Accounts Receivable	$ 0	$ 0	$ 60,000
Store Building (for sale)	$150,000	$150,000	$180,000
Office Building (for rent)	$135,000	$135,000	$240,000
Goodwill, etc.	$ 0	$ 0	$ 15,000
	$330,000	$330,000	$540,000

Partners' Capital and Liabilities

	Adjusted Basis	Book	F.M.V.
Bank Loan		$ 30,000	
Alex	$220,000	$200,000	$340,000
Bev	$110,000	$100,000	$170,000
	$330,000	$330,000	$510,000

Alex paid Bev $170,000 in cash to purchase Bev's partnership interest. What are the tax consequences to the parties? How much income will Alex recognize on collection of the accounts receivable? How much gain would Alex recognize if she sold the Store Building for $190,000 one month later? How will Alex compute depreciation on the office building? Does it matter whether the AB Partnership had a § 754 election in effect?

2.   Charlie, Dean, and Evan are one-third partners in the CDE partnership, which is engaged in real estate investment and development. The partnership holds some subdivision lots for sale and two properties, Blackacre and Whiteacre, for rental purposes. The CDE Partnership had the following assets and partners' capital accounts:

Assets	Adjusted Basis/Book Value	F.M.V.	Partners' Capital	Adjusted Basis/Book Value	F.M.V.
Cash	$60,000	$ 60,000	Charlie	$30,000	$ 60,000
Lots held			Dean	$30,000	$ 60,000
for sale	$21,000	$ 60,000	Evan	$30,000	$ 60,000
Blackacre	$ 9,000	$ 60,000			
	$90,000	$180,000		$90,000	$180,000

Blackacre is a § 1231 asset that is not subject to § 1245 recapture. The partnership liquidated by distributing the cash to Charlie, the lots to Dean, and Blackacre to Evan. What are the tax consequences to the partners? How would your answer differ if the partnership did not own and distribute Blackacre to Evan but instead owned and distributed to Evan a bulldozer (which originally cost the partnership $75,000) with an adjusted basis of $9,000 and a fair market value of $60,000?

3. Fran, Gene, and Hector were partners in the FGH partnership. The assets and partners' capital accounts of the FGH Partnership were as follows:

Assets	Adjusted Basis & Book Value	F.M.V.	Liabilities & Partners' Capital	Adjusted Basis & Book Value	F.M.V.
Greenacre	$460	$ 360	Fran	$450	$ 400
Whiteacre	$120	$ 190	Gene	$150	$ 400
Blackacre	$ 70	$ 450	Hector	$ 50	$ 200
	$650	$1,000		$650	$1,000

All of the properties are § 1231 assets. The FGH partnership was a cash method, calendar year taxpayer. On July 1st of last year, Fran sold her partnership interest to Ike. On June 30th of this year, Hector sold his partnership interest to Jane. What are the tax consequences to Gene and Ike resulting from Hector's sale of his partnership interest to Jane?

SECTION 7.   PARTNERSHIP MERGERS AND DIVISIONS

REGULATIONS: Sections 1.708–1(c), (d); 1.752–1(g), Ex. (2).

In 2001, the Treasury Department promulgated Regulations dealing specifically with mergers and divisions of partnerships. T.D. 8925, Partnership Mergers and Divisions, 2001–1 C.B. 496. These Regulations were issued in proposed form in 2000. The preamble to the Proposed Regulations, which follows, generally describes the purpose and operation of the Final Regulations.

Notice of Proposed Rulemaking, Partnership Mergers and Divisions

2000–1 C.B. 455.

Partnership Mergers

Background

Section 708(b)(2)(A) provides that in the case of a merger or consolidation of two or more partnerships, the resulting partnership is, for purposes of section 708, considered the continuation of any merging or consolidating partnership whose members own an interest of more than 50 percent in the capital and profits of the resulting partnership. Section 1.708–1(b)(2)(i) of the Income Tax Regulations provides that if the resulting partnership can be considered a continuation of more than one of the merging partnerships, the resulting partnership is the continuation of the partnership that is credited with the contribution of the greatest dollar value of assets to the resulting partnership. If none of the members of the merging partnerships own more than a 50 percent interest in the capital and profits of the resulting partnership, all of the merged partnerships are considered terminated, and a new partnership results. The taxable years of the merging partnerships that are considered terminated are closed under section 706(c).

Although section 708 and the applicable regulations provide which partnership continues when two or more partnerships merge, the statute and regulations do not prescribe a form for the partnership merger. (Often, state merger statutes do not provide a particular form for a partnership merger.) In revenue rulings, however, the IRS has prescribed the form of a partnership merger for Federal income tax purposes.

In Rev.Rul. 68–289 (1968–1 C.B. 314), three existing partnerships (P1, P2, and P3) merged into one partnership with P3 continuing under section 708(b)(2)(A). The revenue ruling holds that P1 and P2, the two terminating partnerships, are treated as having contributed all of their respective assets and liabilities to P3, the resulting partnership, in exchange for a partnership interest in P3. P1 and P2 are considered terminated and the partners of P1 and P2 receive interests in P3 with a basis under section 732(b) in liquidation of P1 and P2 (Assets-Over Form). Rev.Rul. 77–458 (1977–2 C.B. 220), and Rev.Rul. 90–17 (1990–1 C.B. 119), also follow the Assets-Over Form for a partnership merger.

Explanation of Provisions

A.   Form of a Partnership Merger

The IRS and Treasury are aware that taxpayers may accomplish a partnership merger by undertaking transactions in accordance with jurisdictional laws that follow a form other than the Assets-Over Form. For example, the terminating partnership could liquidate by distributing its assets and liabilities to its partners who then contribute the assets and liabilities to the resulting partnership (Assets-Up Form). In addition, the partners in the terminating partnership could transfer their terminating partnership interests to the resulting partnership in exchange for resulting partnership interests, and the terminating partnership could liquidate into the resulting partnership (Interest-Over Form).

In the partnership incorporation area, a taxpayer's form generally is respected if the taxpayer actually undertakes, under the relevant jurisdictional law, all the steps of a form that is set forth in one of three situations provided in Rev.Rul. 84–111 (1984–2 C.B. 88). The three situations that Rev.Rul. 84–111 sets forth are the Assets-Over Form, Assets-Up Form, and Interest-Over Form. Rev. Rul. 84–111 explains that, depending on the form chosen to incorporate the partnership, the adjusted basis and holding periods of the various assets received by the corporation and the adjusted basis and holding periods of the stock received by the former partners can vary. Like partnership incorporations, each form of a partnership merger has potentially different tax consequences.

Under the Assets-Up Form, partners could recognize gain under sections 704(c)(1)(B) and 737 (and incur state or local transfer taxes) when the terminating partnership distributes the assets to the partners. However, under the Assets-Over Form, gain under sections 704(c)(1)(B) and 737 is not triggered. See §§ 1.704–4(c)(4) and 1.737–2(b). Additionally, under the Assets-Up Form, because the adjusted basis of the assets contributed to the resulting partnership is determined first by reference to section 732 (as a result of the liquidation) and then section 723 (by virtue of the contribution), in certain circumstances, the adjusted basis of the assets contributed may not be the same as the adjusted basis of the assets in the terminating partnership. These circumstances occur if the partners' aggregate adjusted basis of their interests in the terminating partnership does not equal the terminating partnership's adjusted basis in its assets.

Under the Assets-Over Form, because the resulting partnership's adjusted basis in the assets it receives is determined solely under section 723, the adjusted basis of the assets in the resulting partnership is the same as the adjusted basis of the assets in the terminating partnership.

The regulations propose to respect the form of a partnership merger for Federal income tax purposes if the partnerships undertake, pursuant to the laws of the applicable jurisdiction, the steps of either the Assets-Over Form or the Assets-Up Form. (This rule applies even if none of the merged partnerships are treated as continuing for Federal income tax purposes.) Generally, when partnerships merge, the assets move from one partnership to another at the entity level, or in other words, like the Assets-Over Form. However, if as part of the merger, the partnership titles the assets in the partners' names, the proposed regulations treat the transaction under the Assets-Up Form. If partnerships use the Interest-Over Form to accomplish the result of a merger, the partnerships will be treated as following the Assets-Over Form for Federal income tax purposes.

In the context of partnership incorporations, Rev.Rul. 84–111 distinguishes among all three forms of incorporation. However, with respect to the Interest-Over Form, the revenue ruling respects only the transferors' conveyances of partnership interests, while treating the receipt of the partnership interests by the transferee corporation as the receipt of the partnership's assets (i.e., the Assets-Up Form). The theory for this result, based largely on McCauslen v. Commissioner, 45 T.C. 588 (1966), is that the transferee corporation can only receive assets since it is not possible, as a sole member, for it to receive and hold interests in a partnership (i.e., a partnership cannot have only one member; so, the entity is never a partnership in the hands of the transferee corporation).

Adherence to the approach followed in Rev.Rul. 84–111 creates problems in the context of partnership mergers that are not present with respect to partnership incorporations. Unlike the corporate rules, the partnership rules impose certain tax results on partners based upon a concept that matches a contributed asset to the partner that contributed the asset. Sections 704(c) and 737 are examples of such rules. The operation of these rules breaks down if the partner is treated as contributing an asset that is different from the asset that the partnership is treated as receiving.

Given that the hybrid treatment of the Interest-Over Form transactions utilized in Rev.Rul. 84–111 is difficult to apply in the context of partnership mergers, another characterization will be applied to such transactions. The Assets-Over Form generally will be preferable for both the IRS and taxpayers. For example, when partnerships merge under the Assets-Over Form, gain under sections 704(c)(1)(B) and 737 is not triggered. Moreover, the basis of the assets in the resulting partnership is the same as the basis of the assets in the terminating partnership, even if the partners' aggregate adjusted basis of their interests in the terminating partnership does not equal the terminating partnership's adjusted basis in its assets.

If partnerships merge under applicable law without implementing a form, the proposed regulations treat the partnerships as following the Assets-Over Form. This approach is consistent with the treatment of partnership to corporation elective conversions under the check-the-box regulations and technical terminations under section 708(b)(1)(B), other formless movements of a partnership's assets.

B.   Adverse Tax Consequences of the Assets-Over Form

The IRS and Treasury are aware that certain adverse tax consequences may occur for partnerships that merge in a transaction that will be taxed in accordance with the Assets-Over Form. These proposed regulations address some of the adverse tax consequences regarding section 752 liability shifts and buyouts of exiting partners.

1.   Section 752 Revisions

If a highly leveraged partnership (the terminating partnership) merges with another partnership (the resulting partnership), all of the partners in the terminating partnership could recognize gain because of section 752 liability shifts. Under the Assets-Over Form, the terminating partnership becomes a momentary partner in the resulting partnership when the terminating partnership contributes its assets and liabilities to the resulting partnership in exchange for interests in the resulting partnership. If the terminating partnership (as a momentary partner in the resulting partnership) is considered to receive a deemed distribution under section 752 (after netting increases and decreases in liabilities under § 1.752–1(f) that exceeds the terminating partnership's adjusted basis of its interests in the resulting partnership, the terminating partnership would recognize gain under section 731. The terminating partnership's gain then would be allocated to each partner in the terminating partnership under section 704(b). In this situation, a partner in the terminating partnership could recognize gain even though the partner's adjusted basis in its resulting partnership interest or its share of partnership liabilities in the resulting partnership is large enough to avoid the recognition of gain, provided that the decreases in liabilities in the terminating partnership are netted against the increases in liabilities in the resulting partnership.

The proposed regulations clarify that when two or more partnerships merge under the Assets-Over Form, increases or decreases in partnership liabilities associated with the merger are netted by the partners in the terminating partnership and the resulting partnership to determine the effect of the merger under section 752. The IRS and Treasury consider it appropriate to treat the merger as a single transaction for determining the net liability shifts under section 752. Therefore, a partner in the terminating partnership will recognize gain on the contribution under section 731 only if the net section 752 deemed distribution exceeds that partner's adjusted basis of its interest in the resulting partnership.

2.   Buyout of a Partner

Another adverse tax consequence may occur when a partner in the terminating partnership does not want to become a partner in the resulting partnership and would like to receive money or property instead of an interest in the resulting partnership. Under the Assets-Over Form, the terminating partnership will not recognize gain or loss under section 721 when it contributes its property to the resulting partnership in exchange for interests in the resulting partnership. However, if, in order to facilitate the buyout of the exiting partner, the resulting partnership transfers money or other consideration to the terminating partnership in addition to the resulting partnership interests, the terminating partnership may be treated as selling part of its property to the resulting partnership under section 707(a)(2)(B). Any gain or loss recognized by the terminating partnership generally would be allocated to all the partners in the terminating partnership even though only the exiting partner would receive the consideration.

The IRS and Treasury believe that, under certain circumstances, when partnerships merge and one partner does not become a partner in the resulting partnership, the receipt of cash or property by that partner should be treated as a sale of that partner's interest in the terminating partnership to the resulting partnership, not a disguised sale of the terminating partnership's assets. Accordingly, the proposed regulations provide that if the merger agreement (or similar document) specifies that the resulting partnership is purchasing the exiting partner's interest in the terminating partnership and the amount paid for the interest, the transaction will be treated as a sale of the exiting partner's interest to the resulting partnership. This treatment will apply even if the resulting partnership sends the consideration to the terminating partnership on behalf of the exiting partner, so long as the designated language is used in the relevant document. [Ed.: The Final Regulations provide that sale treatment will be accorded to the transaction under this special rule only if the exiting partner consents to sale treatment prior to or contemporaneously with the transfer.]

In this situation, the exiting partner is treated as selling a partnership interest in the terminating partnership to the resulting partnership (and the resulting partnership is treated as purchasing the partner's interest in the terminating partnership) immediately prior to the merger. Immediately after the sale, the resulting partnership becomes a momentary partner in the terminating partnership. Consequently, the resulting partnership and ultimately its partners (determined prior to the merger) inherit the exiting partner's capital account in the terminating partnership and any section 704(c) liability of the exiting partner. If the terminating partnership has an election in effect under section 754 (or makes an election under section 754), the resulting partnership will have a special basis adjustment regarding the terminating partnership's property under section 743. * * * [Ed.: Where the resulting partnership, as part of the merger, has acquired an interest in the terminating partnership in accordance with the special buy-out rule, the terminating partnership is treated as distributing its assets to the resulting partnership in liquidation of the resulting partnership's interest in the terminating partnership. Accordingly, the resulting partnership takes an exchanged basis in the distributed assets under section 732(b).]

C. Merger as Part of a Larger Transaction

The proposed regulations provide that if the merger is part of a larger series of transactions, and the substance of the larger series of transactions is inconsistent with following the form prescribed for the merger, the form may not be respected, and the larger series of transactions may be recast in accordance with their substance. An example illustrating the application of this rule is included in the proposed regulations.

D. Measurement of Dollar Value of Assets

As discussed above, the regulations currently provide that in a merger of partnerships, if the resulting partnership can be considered a continuation of more than one of the merging partnerships, the resulting partnership is the continuation of the partnership that is credited with the contribution of the greatest dollar value of assets to the resulting partnership. Commentators have questioned whether this rule refers to the gross or net value of the assets of a partnership. The proposed regulations provide that the value of assets of a partnership is determined net of the partnership's liabilities.

* * *

Partnership Divisions

Background

Section 708(b)(2)(B) provides that, in the case of a division of a partnership into two or more partnerships, the resulting partnerships (other than any resulting partnership the members of which had an interest of 50 percent or less in the capital and profits of the prior partnership) are considered a continuation of the prior partnership. Section 1.708–1(b)(2)(ii) provides that any other resulting partnership is not considered a continuation of the prior partnership but is considered a new partnership. If the members of none of the resulting partnerships owned an interest of more than 50 percent in the capital and profits of the prior partnership, the prior partnership is terminated. Where members of a partnership that has been divided do not become members of a resulting partnership that is considered a continuation of the prior partnership, such partner's interest is considered liquidated as of the date of the division.

Section 708(b)(2)(B) and the applicable regulations do not prescribe a particular form for the division involving continuing partnerships. The IRS has not addressed in published guidance how the assets and liabilities of the prior partnership move into the resulting partnerships. Taxpayers generally have followed either the Assets-Over Form or the Assets-Up Form for partnership divisions.

Under the Assets-Over Form, the prior partnership transfers certain assets to a resulting partnership in exchange for interests in the resulting partnership. The prior partnership then immediately distributes the resulting partnership interests to partners who are designated to receive interests in the resulting partnership.

Under the Assets-Up Form, the prior partnership distributes certain assets to some or all of its partners who then contribute the assets to a resulting partnership in exchange for interests in the resulting partnership.

Explanation of Provisions

A.　*Form of a Partnership Division*

As with partnership mergers, the IRS and Treasury recognize that different tax consequences can arise depending on the form of the partnership division. Because of the potential different tax results that could occur depending on the form followed by the partnership, the regulations propose to respect for Federal income tax purposes the form of a partnership division accomplished under laws of the applicable jurisdiction if the partnership undertakes the steps of either the Assets-Over Form or the Assets-Up Form. Thus, the same forms allowed for partnership mergers will be allowed for partnership divisions.

Generally, an entity cannot be classified as a partnership if it has only one member. This universally has been held to be the case in classifying transactions where interests in a partnership are transferred to a single person, so that the partnership goes out of existence. McCauslen v. Commissioner, 45 T.C. 588 (1966); Rev.Rul. 99–6, 1999–1 C.B. 432; Rev.Rul. 67–65, 1967–1 C.B. 168; Rev.Rul. 55–68, 1955–1 C.B. 372. However, in at least one instance involving the contribution of assets by an existing partnership to a newly-formed partnership, regulations have provided that the momentary existence of the new partnership will be respected for Federal income tax purposes. See § 1.708–1(b)(1)(iv). Pursuant to the proposed regulations, under the Assets-Over Form of a partnership division, the prior partnership's momentary ownership of all the interests in a resulting partnership will not prevent the resulting partnership from being classified as a partnership on formation.

The example in current § 1.708–1(b)(2)(ii) indicates that when a partnership is not considered a continuation of the prior partnership under section 708(b)(2)(B) (partnership considered a new partnership under current § 1.708–1(b)(2)(ii)), the new partnership is created under the Assets-Up Form. The regulations propose to modify this result and provide examples illustrating that partnerships can divide and create a new partnership under either the Assets-Over Form or the Assets-Up Form.

Consistent with partnership mergers, if a partnership divides using a form other than the two prescribed, it will be treated as undertaking the Assets-Over Form.

These proposed regulations use four terms to describe the form of a partnership division. Two of these terms, prior partnership and resulting partnership, describe partnerships that exist under the applicable jurisdictional law. The prior partnership is the partnership that exists under the applicable jurisdictional law before the division, and the resulting partnerships are the partnerships that exist under the applicable jurisdictional law after the division. The other two terms, divided partnership and recipient partnership, are Federal tax concepts. A divided partnership is a partnership that is treated, for Federal income tax purposes, as transferring assets in connection with a division, and a recipient partnership is a partnership that is treated, for Federal income tax purposes, as receiving assets in connection with a division. The divided partnership must be a continuation of the prior partnership. Although the divided partnership is considered one continuing partnership for Federal income tax purposes, it may actually be two different partnerships under the applicable jurisdictional law (i.e., the prior partnership and a different resulting partnership that is considered a continuation of the prior partnership for Federal income tax purposes).

Finally, because in a formless division it generally will be unclear which partnership should be treated, for Federal income tax purposes, as transferring assets (i.e., the divided partnership) to another partnership (i.e., the recipient partnership) where more than one partnership is a continuation of the prior partnership, the proposed regulations provide that the continuing resulting partnership with the assets having the greatest fair market value (net of liabilities) will be treated as the divided partnership. This issue also is present where the partnership that, in form, transfers assets is not a continuation of the prior partnership, but more than one of the other resulting partnerships are continuations of the prior partnership. The same rule applies to these situations.

B. Consequences under Sections 704(c)(1)(B) and 737

Gain under sections 704(c)(1)(B) and 737 may be triggered when section 704(c) property or substituted section 704(c) property is distributed to certain partners. These rules often will be implicated in the context of partnership divisions.

Where a division is accomplished in a transaction that is taxed in accordance with the Assets-Over Form, the partnership interest in the recipient partnership will be treated as a section 704(c) asset to the extent that the interest is received by the divided partnership in exchange for section 704(c) property. Section 1.704–4(d)(1). Accordingly, the distribution of the partnership interests in the recipient partnership by the divided partnership generally will trigger section 704(c)(1)(B) where the interests in the recipient partnership are received by a partner of the divided partnership other than the partner who contributed the section 704(c) property to the divided partnership. In addition, section 737 may be triggered if a partner who contributed section 704(c) property to the divided partnership receives an interest in the recipient partnership that is not attributable to the section 704(c) property.

Where a division is accomplished under the Assets-Up Form, assets are distributed directly to the partners who will hold interests in the recipient partnership. The distribution could trigger section 704(c)(1)(B) or 737 depending on the identity of the distributed asset and the distributee partner.

The regulations under section 737 provide an exception for certain partnership divisions. Section 737 does not apply when a transferor partnership transfers all the section 704(c) property contributed by a partner to a second partnership in a section 721 exchange, followed by a distribution of an interest in the transferee partnership in complete liquidation of the interest of the partner that originally contributed the section 704(c) property to the transferor partnership. Section 1.737–2(b)(2). This rule, however, may not apply to many partnership divisions because the original contributing partner often remains a partner in the divided partnership. No similar rule is provided under section 704(c)(1)(B).

In many instances, the application of sections 704(c)(1)(B) and 737 will be appropriate when a partnership divides under either the Assets-Over Form or the Assets-Up Form. Consider the following example: A, B, C, and D form a partnership. A contributes appreciated property X ($0 basis and $200 value), B contributes property Y ($200 basis and $200 value), and C and D each contribute $200 cash. The partnership subsequently divides into two partnerships using the Assets-Over Form, distributing interests in the recipient partnership in accordance with each partner's pro rata interest in the prior partnership. Property X remains in the prior partnership, and property Y is contributed to the recipient partnership. Under these facts, section 737 could be avoided if an exception were created for the distribution of the recipient partnership interests. If, subsequent to the division, half of property Y is distributed to A, section 737 would not be triggered because property X (the section 704(c) property) is no longer in the same partnership as property Y.

* * *

C. Division as Part of a Larger Transaction

The proposed regulations provide the same rule for partnership divisions that applies to partnership mergers.

DETAILED ANALYSIS

1.   PARTNERSHIP MERGERS

Generally, the Regulations require that the partnership actually convey ownership of its assets to the partners under the law of the applicable jurisdiction for the "assets-up form" to be respected. The preamble to the Final Regulations notes that it should not be necessary for the partners actually to assume the liabilities of the partnership in order to follow that form. T.D. 8925, Partnership Mergers and Divisions, 2001–1 C.B. 496, 497. The preamble also explains that an actual transfer and recording of the deed or certificate of title will not be required if local law allows ownership to be conveyed without the actual transfer and recording of a deed or certificate of title. Thus, it might be said that *"form lite"* controls in this regard.

Under the Regulations, a partnership cannot pick and choose among its assets and treat some as having been conveyed under the "assets-over form" and others as having been conveyed under the "assets-up form." If a partnership wants to adopt the assets-up form, that form must be followed with respect to all of its assets and all of its partners. If the partnership attempts to bifurcate the merger between the assets-over form and the assets-up form, the entire merger will be treated as an assets-over form of merger.

Treas.Reg. § 1.704–4(c)(4) and Prop.Reg. § 1.737–2(b) (2007) deal with the application of §§ 704(c)(1)(B) and 737(b) in partnership mergers. The partnership merger itself does not trigger recognition of gain under §§ 704(c)(1)(B) or 737(b). Following an assets-over partnership merger, the seven-year holding period of §§ 704(c)(1)(B) and 737(b) with respect to built-in gain property contributed to the merged partnership would begin on the date of the original contribution of the built-in gain property to the merged partnership. However, the seven-year period would re-commence with respect to built-in gain present in property transferred from the merged partnership to the continuing partnership at the time of the merger, reduced by the amount of original built-in gain at the time of contribution to the merged partnership. Thus, a distribution within seven years after the merger of property previously held by the disappearing partnership will trigger gain recognition. The IRS reserved consideration of the treatment of built-in losses. Neither § 704(c)(1)(B) nor § 737(b) would apply to newly created reverse § 704(c) gain or loss resulting from a revaluation of property in the continuing partnership.

2. PARTNERSHIP DIVISIONS

When a partnership divides into two or more partnerships, a resulting partnership will be a continuation of the original partnership if the partners of the continuing partnership owned more than 50% of the capital and profits of the original partnership. Other partnerships are new partnerships, and their partners are treated as having had their original partnership interests liquidated in the division. Treas.Reg. § 1.708–1(d)(1).

To constitute a partnership division, at least two members of the prior partnership must be members of each resulting partnership that exists after the transaction. Treas.Reg. § 1.708–1(d)(4)(iv). For example, suppose the ABC Partnership owns an apartment building and an office building. A and B each own a 15% interest, and C owns a 70% interest in the Partnership. C does not want to continue in the partnership with A and B and would like to operate the office building with D. To this end, the ABC Partnership distributes the office building to C in liquidation of C's interest in partnership ABC. Immediately thereafter, C forms a partnership with D and contributes the office building to the CD Partnership. After the distribution and contribution of the office building, the AB Partnership owns the apartment building and the CD Partnership owns the office building. Despite appearances, this transaction is not a partnership division under the Regulations because C is the only member of the ABC Partnership in the CD Partnership. This transaction would be treated as a liquidation distribution from the ABC partnership to C, followed by a contribution of the office building to the new CD Partnership, with the ABC Partnership continuing as the AB Partnership.

In the case of partnership divisions, the treatment of the transfer of assets to any particular resulting partnership must consistently follow the assets-over form or the asset-up form, as with partnership mergers. But where the transfer to each of two or more successor partnerships is considered separately, the transfer to one may follow the assets-over form while the transfer to another follows the assets up-form. See Treas.Reg. § 1.708–1(d)(5), Ex. (7).

PROBLEM SET 9

1. Ann and Bob were the members of the AB LLC, which had assets with a value of $600,000. Each had a one-half interest. Carla, Donnie, and Erin were the members of the CDE LLC, which had assets with a fair market value of $900,000. Each had a one-third interest.

(a) The AB LLC transferred all of its assets to the CDE LLC. Ann and Bob each received a one-fifth interest in the CDE LLC and the interests of

Carla, Donnie, and Erin were reduced to one-fifth each. The CDE LLC was renamed the ABCDE LLC

(1) Is the ABCDE LLC a new partnership, with each of the AB LLC and the CDE liquidating or is the ABCDE LLC a continuation of either the AB or CDE LLC?

(2) Would your answer differ if the AB LLC had assets worth $1,800,000 and Ann and Bob each acquired a one-third interest in the CDE LLC, which was renamed the ABCDE LLC, and Carla, Donnie, and Erin's interests were each reduced to one-ninth?

(3) Would your answer differ if the AB LLC had assets worth $900,000 and Ann and Bob each acquired a one-fourth interest in the CDE LLC, which was renamed the ABCDE LLC, and Carla, Donnie, and Erin's interests were each reduced to one-sixth?

(b) Would your answers to Part (a) differ if the combination of the two LLCs had been effected under a state statute providing for the merger of the two LLCs by operation of law?

(c) Would your answers to Part (a) differ if the combination of the two LLCs had been effected by Ann and Bob transferring their interests in the AB LLC to the CDE LLC, in exchange for interests in the CDE LLC (renamed the ABCDE LLC, with the AB LLC continuing to exist under state law as wholly owned by the ABCDE LLC?

2. The members of the FGHIJ LLC were Fran, George, Helen, Ike, and Jean. The assets of the FGHIJ LLC were worth $1,000,000 and each member held a one-fifth interest.

(a) The FGHIJ LLC divided by transferring $400,000 of assets to the newly formed FG LLC, which momentarily was wholly owned by the FGHIJ LLC, and immediately distributing a one-half interest in the FG LLC to each of Fran and George in complete liquidation of their interests in the FGHIJ LLC, immediately after which the FGHIJ LLC was renamed the HIJ LLC. Which, if any of the FG LLC and the HIJ LLC is a continuing partnership and which, if any, is a newly formed partnership?

(b) Would your answer differ if, as part of the transaction described in Part (a), the interest of H was liquidated for $200,000 of cash and only IJ remained as members of the original LLC, which was renamed the IJ LLC?

SECTION 8.   SPECIAL PROBLEMS OF THE LIQUIDATION OF A PARTNERSHIP INTEREST FOLLOWING THE DEATH OF A PARTNER

INTERNAL REVENUE CODE: Sections 706(c); 731(a)–(c); 732(a)–(e); 734; 735; 736(a); 741; 742; 743(a)–(d); 751(c), (d)(2); 753; 754; 755(a) and (b); 761(d).

REGULATIONS: Sections 1.708–1(b)(1)(i); 1.732–1(d); 1.734–2; 1.736–1; 1.742–1; 1.743–1(b); 1.753–1; 1.754–1; 1.755–1.

Under state law, a general partnership technically is dissolved on the death of a general partner. However, under § 708 the partnership continues for federal tax purposes as long as the business of the partnership is continued, unless the partnership had only two partners. The deceased partner's interest in the partnership typically is disposed of in one of three ways: the deceased partner's estate (or other designated successor in interest) may receive a liquidating distribution; the deceased partner's interest may be purchased by the surviving partners, frequently pursuant to a prearranged agreement; or the deceased partner's designated successor may be substituted as a partner. Limited partnership interests are generally subject to the same treatment, but a limited partnership ordinarily is not automatically dissolved under state law by the death of a limited partner. Limited liability companies taxed as partnerships also ordinarily do not dissolve on the death of a member, and the tax treatment of the interest of a deceased member of a limited liability company taxed as a partnership raises the same issues.

When a deceased partner's interest is liquidated, the rules regarding distributions in liquidation generally govern the taxation of the liquidating distributions and their effect on the partnership. Similarly, if the interest is sold to the remaining partners, the rules governing sales of partnership interests, discussed in Chapter 24, generally govern. In both cases, however, either § 1014, providing that the basis of property acquired by bequest or inheritance is the fair market value at the decedent's date of death, or § 691, which denies a date of death basis to "income in respect of a decedent," must be taken into account. Where the deceased partner's successor in interest is substituted as a partner, there is no distribution or taxable transfer, but the transfer nevertheless has important effects. For example, if a § 754 election is in effect, a § 743(b) adjustment to the basis of partnership property is required.

In all three cases, consideration must be given to the effect of the partner's death on the taxable year of the partner and of the partnership. Section 443(a)(2) closes the deceased partner's taxable year on the date of death. Section 706, however, not only provides the rules governing the partnership's taxable year but modifies the application of § 443(a)(2) with respect to the deceased partner's distributive share of partnership items. Most controversy in this area involves the allocation of partnership income or loss between the decedent's final return and the income tax return of the decedent's estate.

DETAILED ANALYSIS

1. ALLOCATION OF PARTNERSHIP INCOME BETWEEN THE DECEASED PARTNER AND THE ESTATE

Under § 706(c)(2)(A), the death of the partner is a disposition of the partner's entire interest in the partnership, which requires that the partnership year be closed with respect the deceased partner. Section 443(a)(2) requires the deceased partner's executor to file an income tax return for the deceased partner for the period ending on the date of death, including therein income of the decedent allocable to that period under the decedent's method of accounting. A difference in the taxable year of a deceased partner and the partnership can result in a bunching of partnership income on the deceased partner's final return. For example, suppose that a partnership is on a February 1–January 31 fiscal year, and a partner who is on a calendar year dies on November 30 of Year 2. The deceased partner's return for the decedent's short taxable year ending on November 30, Year 2, includes the decedent's distributive share of partnership income for the partnership year ending on January 31, Year 1. In addition, the decedent's return for the short Year 2 taxable year also must include the decedent's share of the partnership income for the period February 1, Year 2–November 30, Year 2. As a consequence, 22 months of income will be bunched in the decedent's final return.

2. TWO-PERSON PARTNERSHIPS

If a partner of a two-person partnership dies, and the deceased partner's interest is purchased by the surviving partner who continues the business as a sole proprietor, the partnership is terminated because no part of its operations continues to be carried on "in a partnership." However, the partnership continues for tax purposes so long as the estate or other successor in interest continues to share in the profits or losses of the partnership business or receives payments under § 736. Treas.Regs. §§ 1.708–1(b)(1)(i), 1.736–1(a)(6); see also Rev.Rul. 66–325, 1966–2 C.B. 249; Estate of Skaggs v. Commissioner, 672 F.2d 756 (9th Cir.1982).

3. TREATMENT OF DECEASED PARTNER'S SUCCESSOR IN INTEREST

3.1. *Basis of Partnership Assets*

The basis problems and the Subchapter K solutions to those problems on the death of a partner are essentially the same as in the case of the sale of a partnership interest, see Chapter 24, Section 2. In the case of the death of a partner, § 742 refers to the general basis rules of § 1011 et seq. for determining the basis of a partnership interest acquired at death. Thus, under § 1014 the successor's basis for the partnership interest is the fair market value of the partnership interest at the deceased partner's date of death. Under § 743(a), the basis of partnership assets is not affected. However, if the estate or successor continues as a partner and a § 754 election has been made, then the basis of the partnership assets will be adjusted under § 743(b) to eliminate any difference between the basis in the partnership interest and the new partner's share of the basis in the partnership assets.

3.2. *Transferees Eligible for Basis Adjustments*

Under § 761(e) the distribution of a partnership interest from an estate to the beneficiary may be an exchange for purposes of § 743(b), and if a § 754 election is in effect, a basis adjustment may be required. However, since the distribution is a nonrecognition event to the estate and under § 643(e)(1) the distributee takes a transferred basis, unless the estate elects under § 643(e)(3) to treat the distribution as a recognition event, a second adjustment will not be made.

Rev.Rul. 79–124, 1979–1 C.B. 224, held that an adjustment to the basis of partnership assets under § 743(b) is to be made with respect to the partnership property attributable to the entire interest of a deceased partner which was held as community property if pursuant to § 1014(b)(6) the entire interest is treated as received by the surviving spouse from the decedent.

3.3. *Income in Respect of a Decedent: Partnerships Holding Unrealized Receivables*

The basis rules of § 1014 and § 743(b) present problems if the assets of the partnership include accounts receivable with a zero basis. If the basis for such a partnership interest were the estate tax value determined under § 1014(a), it would be attributable in part to a value represented by the accounts receivable. Ordinarily, however, accounts receivable of a decedent take a carryover basis under § 691 as income in respect of a decedent, thereby preserving their inherent ordinary income. In the case of a partnership holding accounts receivable, if a basis adjustment under § 743(b) were allowed to the decedent's successor, then realization of the potential ordinary income in the accounts receivable could be permanently avoided. The Regulations attempt to close this obvious loophole by providing that the basis of the partnership interest acquired from a decedent is the fair market value of the interest reduced to the extent that such value is attributable to items constituting income in respect of a decedent under § 691. Treas.Reg. § 1.742–1. Assuming that this is a fair interpretation of the reference in § 742 to the general basis provisions, the question remains whether accounts receivable held by the partnership would constitute income in respect of a decedent. Clearly, if the accounts receivable had been held by the partner individually, they would have represented income in respect of a decedent in the hands of the estate or heirs. Here, however, the receivables are technically property of the partnership, and not of the individual partner. Section 691(e) refers to § 753 for the application of § 691 to income in respect of a deceased partner and that section merely provides that § 736(a) payments in liquidation of the deceased partner's interest are to be treated as income in respect of a decedent.

The obvious inadequacy of the statutory treatment of the problem has not prevented the courts from achieving the correct result. In Quick Trust v. Commissioner, 54 T.C. 1336 (1970), aff'd per curiam, 444 F.2d 90 (8th

Cir.1971), the court held that the right of a successor partner to share in the collection of accounts receivable could be separated from the general "bundle of rights" represented by the partnership interest and such right was covered by § 691. The reference in § 753 to § 736(a) payments was not to be treated as exclusive. As a result, the new basis of the partnership interest was reduced by the fair market value of the accounts receivable and the increase in the basis of the accounts receivable under § 743(b) was eliminated. A similar analysis was applied in Woodhall v. Commissioner, 454 F.2d 226 (9th Cir.1972), involving the sale of a partnership interest received from a decedent partner in a situation in which the partnership held unrealized receivables at the time of the partner's death.

4. PAYMENTS OR DISTRIBUTIONS

When a general partner dies, under state law the partnership is dissolved, and the partner's estate is entitled to distribution of the deceased general partner's capital account, unless the partnership agreement provides otherwise. Limited liability company agreements may call for a liquidation distribution to the successor in interest of a deceased limited liability company member. If such a liquidating distribution is made, the general rules governing liquidating distributions under §§ 731–736 and 751(b) control. See Section 3. Of course, due to the change in basis to fair market value under § 1014, gain or loss generally will not be recognized under § 731(a), even if the entire distribution is in cash. Nevertheless, §§ 736(a) and 751(b) may result in ordinary income treatment.

4.1. *Cash Payments*

4.1.1. *Initial Classification of Payments*

Partnership agreements often provide that the estate of a deceased partner will receive a percentage of the profits for several years or a fixed annual amount, or some combination of the various alternatives. These payments are in liquidation of the decedent's interest in the partnership assets and goodwill, or in the nature of mutual insurance. These classification problems are identical with those considered earlier on the retirement of a partner, and the Subchapter K solution is the same. Section 736(a), discussed in Section 3, classifies these payments between those considered as in exchange for the estate's interest in partnership property and those considered to be the estate's distributive share of partnership income or a guaranteed payment to the estate. See Treas.Regs. §§ 1.736–1(a)(2) and 1.736–1(b). While a payment made for a decedent's share of substantially appreciated inventory is treated as a § 736(b) distribution, § 751(b) applies and results in ordinary income unless basis adjustments under §§ 754 and 743(b) have been made.

4.1.2. *Income in Respect of a Decedent*

Section 753 provides that the amounts classified under § 736(a) are considered income in respect of a decedent under § 691. The Regulations also include as § 691 income any amounts paid by a third party in exchange for rights to future partnership § 736(a) payments. Treas.Reg. § 1.753–1(a). *Quick's Trust* and *Woodhall*, supra, indicate that the statutory reference to § 736(a) in § 753 is not exclusive.

If the estate receives § 736(a) payments that are treated as income in respect of a decedent, Treas.Reg. § 1.742–1 requires any § 1014 basis of the partnership interest to be reduced by the amount of the payments, thus preventing the estate from realizing a loss equal to the amount of the § 736(a) payments, i.e., the difference between any § 1014 basis and the § 736(b) payments.

The income in respect of a decedent treatment provided by § 753 implies that the value of the § 736(a) payments, e.g., for unrealized receivables and goodwill in the absence of an agreement in the case of a general partner in a partnership in which capital is not a material income producing factor, will be subject to estate tax and, consequently, will qualify for the deduction under § 691 for estate tax paid. See Rev.Rul. 71–507, 1971–2 C.B. 331.

Only the value of the decedent's distributive share as of the date of death is an asset of the estate for estate tax purposes. The Regulations provide that the amount of the estate's distributive share included in its income will be treated as income in respect of a decedent. Treas.Reg. § 1.753–1(b).

4.2. *Property Distributions*

Property distributions to an estate in liquidation of the interest of a deceased partner are subject to the general rules governing recognition of gain or loss by the distributee, the basis of property distributed, and the disposition of the property by the distributee discussed in Section 3. The § 1014 date of death value basis of the partnership interest is used in assigning basis to the distributed property under § 732(b) and (c).

5. TREATMENT OF REMAINING PARTNERS

The rules applicable to the treatment of the remaining partners on the retirement of a partner are equally applicable to the liquidation of a deceased partner's interest. These rules are discussed in Section 3.

If as a result of an election under § 754, the partnership must adjust the bases of the partnership assets, the formula of § 734(b) does not provide the correct result. The gain or loss to the estate is affected by the application of § 1014(a). To the extent that § 1014 produces a step-up in basis for the estate, gain that would otherwise be recognized on a liquidating distribution of cash is reduced pro tanto and hence the premise of the formula of § 734(b) is not satisfied. Conversely, if basis is stepped down, loss that otherwise would be recognized is eliminated. This problem is corrected to some extent by the Regulations in allowing any unused special basis adjustment the estate may have by virtue of § 743(b) or § 732(d) to shift to the remaining assets for the benefit of the remaining partners. Treas.Reg. § 1.734–2(b)(1). But this is not a principled compensation and the results are not theoretically correct.

In Estate of Skaggs v. Commissioner, 672 F.2d 756 (9th Cir.1982), the surviving partner of a husband-wife partnership, who inherited the deceased partner's interest, unsuccessfully asserted that the partnership automatically terminated upon the death of the deceased partner and that under § 1014 the basis of an undivided one-half of the partnership's assets should be increased to the fair market value on the date of death. The court found that the partnership continued for purposes of paying its debts and winding up its affairs, and that absent a valid § 754 election, no basis adjustment was allowable with respect to the partnership assets. For the possibility of filing a § 754 election on an amended partnership return for the year of the partner's death on facts similar to *Estate of Skaggs*, see Rev.Rul. 86–139, 1986–2 C.B. 95.

PROBLEM SET 10

1.   Art was a 20% partner in the AX Partnership. X Corporation was the only other partner. Because X Corporation reported on a fiscal year ending January 31st, the AX Partnership reported on a January 31st fiscal year. For the fiscal year that ended in January of this year, Art's distributive share of partnership income was $50,000. Art died on December 31st of this year, and his estate succeeded to his interest as a partner. For the fiscal year ending on January 31st of next year, the AX Partnership recognized $300,000 of income, of which $60,000 was allocable to Art and/or Art's estate. How much partnership income is reportable on the joint return filed by Art's surviving spouse for this year, and how much partnership income is reportable by Art's estate?

2.   Juan, Karen, and Leo were members of the JKL LLC, which is taxed as a partnership. Each of them has a one-third interest. The LLC uses the cash method of accounting. Karen died last year, and her estate succeeded to her interest as a member. At the time of Karen's death, the assets and capital accounts of the JKL LLC were as follows:

Assets	Adjusted Basis	F.M.V.	Capital Accounts	Adjusted Basis	F.M.V.
Cash	$ 45,000	$ 45,000	J	$190,000	$180,000
Accounts			K	$190,000	$180,000
Receivable	$ 0	$ 60,000	L	$190,000	$180,000
Store Building					
(for sale)	$150,000	$180,000			
Office Building					
(for rent)	$375,000	$240,000			
Goodwill, etc.	$ 0	$ 15,000			
	$570,000	$540,000		$570,000	$540,000

(a)   This year the LLC collected the accounts receivable and sold the store building for $210,000. What are the tax consequences to Karen's estate?

(b)   Can the LLC make a § 754 election as a result of Karen's death? If so, what are the tax consequences to Karen's estate upon the collection of the accounts receivable and sale of the store building for $210,000? Taking into account all of the facts, would a § 754 election be beneficial?

INDEX

References are to Pages